Recommended Dietary Allowances (RDA) and Adequate Intakes (AI) for Vitamins

Age (yr)	Thiamin RDA (mg/day)	Riboflavin RDA (mg/day)	Niacin RDA (mg/day)[a]	Biotin AI (µg/day)	Pantothenic Acid AI (mg/day)	Vitamin B6 RDA (mg/day)	Folate RDA (µg/day)[b]							
Infants														
0–0.5	0.2	0.3	2	5	1.7	0.1	65	0.4	125	40	400	5	4	2.0
0.5–1	0.3	0.4	4	6	1.8	0.3	80	0.5	150	50	500	5	5	2.5
Children														
1–3	0.5	0.5	6	8	2	0.5	150	0.9	200	15	300	5	6	30
4–8	0.6	0.6	8	12	3	0.6	200	1.2	250	25	400	5	7	55
Males														
9–13	0.9	0.9	12	20	4	1.0	300	1.8	375	45	600	5	11	60
14–18	1.2	1.3	16	25	5	1.3	400	2.4	550	75	900	5	15	75
19–30	1.2	1.3	16	30	5	1.3	400	2.4	550	90	900	5	15	120
31–50	1.2	1.3	16	30	5	1.3	400	2.4	550	90	900	5	15	120
51–70	1.2	1.3	16	30	5	1.7	400	2.4	550	90	900	10	15	120
>70	1.2	1.3	16	30	5	1.7	400	2.4	550	90	900	15	15	120
Females														
9–13	0.9	0.9	12	20	4	1.0	300	1.8	375	45	600	5	11	60
14–18	1.0	1.0	14	25	5	1.2	400	2.4	400	65	700	5	15	75
19–30	1.1	1.1	14	30	5	1.3	400	2.4	425	75	700	5	15	90
31–50	1.1	1.1	14	30	5	1.3	400	2.4	425	75	700	5	15	90
51–70	1.1	1.1	14	30	5	1.5	400	2.4	425	75	700	10	15	90
>70	1.1	1.1	14	30	5	1.5	400	2.4	425	75	700	15	15	90
Pregnancy														
≤18	1.4	1.4	18	30	6	1.9	600	2.6	450	80	750	5	15	75
19–30	1.4	1.4	18	30	6	1.9	600	2.6	450	85	770	5	15	90
31–50	1.4	1.4	18	30	6	1.9	600	2.6	450	85	770	5	15	90
Lactation														
≤18	1.4	1.6	17	35	7	2.0	500	2.8	550	115	1200	5	19	75
19–30	1.4	1.6	17	35	7	2.0	500	2.8	550	120	1300	5	19	90
31–50	1.4	1.6	17	35	7	2.0	500	2.8	550	120	1300	5	19	90

NOTE: For all nutrients, values for infants are AI. The table on page Y defines units of nutrient measure.

[a]Niacin recommendations are expressed as niacin equivalents (NE), except for recommendations for infants younger than 6 months, which are expressed as preformed niacin.

[b]Folate recommendations are expressed as dietary folate equivalents (DFE).

[c]Vitamin A recommendations are expressed as retinol activity equivalents (RAE).

[d]Vitamin D recommendations are expressed as cholecalciferol and assume an absence of adequate exposure to sunlight.

[e]Vitamin E recommendations are expressed as α-tocopherol.

Recommended Dietary Allowances (RDA) and Adequate Intakes (AI) for Minerals

Age (yr)	Sodium AI (mg/day)	Chloride AI (mg/day)	Potassium AI (mg/day)	Calcium AI (mg/day)	Phosphorus RDA (mg/day)	Magnesium RDA (mg/day)	Iron RDA (mg/day)	Zinc RDA (mg/day)	Iodine RDA (µg/day)	Selenium RDA (µg/day)	Copper RDA (µg/day)	Manganese AI (mg/day)	Fluoride AI (mg/day)	Chromium AI (µg/day)	Molybdenum RDA (µg/day)
Infants															
0–0.5	120	180	400	210	100	30	0.27	2	110	15	200	0.003	0.01	0.2	2
0.5–1	370	570	700	270	275	75	11	3	130	20	220	0.6	0.5	5.5	3
Children															
1–3	1000	1500	3000	500	460	80	7	3	90	20	340	1.2	0.7	11	17
4–8	1200	1900	3800	800	500	130	10	5	90	30	440	1.5	1.0	15	22
Males															
9–13	1500	2300	4500	1300	1250	240	8	8	120	40	700	1.9	2	25	34
14–18	1500	2300	4700	1300	1250	410	11	11	150	55	890	2.2	3	35	43
19–30	1500	2300	4700	1000	700	400	8	11	150	55	900	2.3	4	35	45
31–50	1500	2300	4700	1000	700	420	8	11	150	55	900	2.3	4	35	45
51–70	1300	2000	4700	1200	700	420	8	11	150	55	900	2.3	4	30	45
>70	1200	1800	4700	1200	700	420	8	11	150	55	900	2.3	4	30	45
Females															
9–13	1500	2300	4500	1300	1250	240	8	8	120	40	700	1.6	2	21	34
14–18	1500	2300	4700	1300	1250	360	15	9	150	55	890	1.6	3	24	43
19–30	1500	2300	4700	1000	700	310	18	8	150	55	900	1.8	3	25	45
31–50	1500	2300	4700	1000	700	320	18	8	150	55	900	1.8	3	25	45
51–70	1300	2000	4700	1200	700	320	8	8	150	55	900	1.8	3	20	45
>70	1200	1800	4700	1200	700	320	8	8	150	55	900	1.8	3	20	45
Pregnancy															
≤18	1500	2300	4700	1300	1250	400	27	12	220	60	1000	2.0	3	29	50
19–30	1500	2300	4700	1000	700	350	27	11	220	60	1000	2.0	3	30	50
31–50	1500	2300	4700	1000	700	360	27	11	220	60	1000	2.0	3	30	50
Lactation															
≤18	1500	2300	5100	1300	1250	360	10	13	290	70	1300	2.6	3	44	50
19–30	1500	2300	5100	1000	700	310	9	12	290	70	1300	2.6	3	45	50
31–50	1500	2300	5100	1000	700	320	9	12	290	70	1300	2.6	3	45	50

NOTE: For all nutrients, values for infants are AI. The table on page Y defines units of nutrient measure.

Tolerable Upper Intake Levels (UL) for Vitamins

Age (yr)	Niacin (mg/day)[a]	Vitamin B_6 (mg/day)	Folate (μg/day)[a]	Choline (mg/day)	Vitamin C (mg/day)	Vitamin A (μg/day)[b]	Vitamin D (μg/day)	Vitamin E (mg/day)[c]
Infants								
0–0.5	—	—	—	—	—	600	25	—
0.5–1	—	—	—	—	—	600	25	—
Children								
1–3	10	30	300	1000	400	600	50	200
4–8	15	40	400	1000	650	900	50	300
9–13	20	60	600	2000	1200	1700	50	600
Adolescents								
14–18	30	80	800	3000	1800	2800	50	800
Adults								
19–70	35	100	1000	3500	2000	3000	50	1000
>70	35	100	1000	3500	2000	3000	50	1000
Pregnancy								
≤18	30	80	800	3000	1800	2800	50	800
19–50	35	100	1000	3500	2000	3000	50	1000
Lactation								
≤18	30	80	800	3000	1800	2800	50	800
19–50	35	100	1000	3500	2000	3000	50	1000

[a]*The UL for niacin and folate apply to synthetic forms obtained from supplements, fortified foods, or a combination of the two.*

[b]*The UL for vitamin A applies to the preformed vitamin only.*

[c]*The UL for vitamin E applies to any form of supplemental α-tocopherol, fortified foods, or a combination of the two.*

Tolerable Upper Intake Levels (UL) for Minerals

Age (yr)	Sodium (mg/day)	Chloride (mg/day)	Calcium (mg/day)	Phosphorus (mg/day)	Magnesium (mg/day)[d]	Iron (mg/day)	Zinc (mg/day)	Iodine (μg/day)	Selenium (μg/day)	Copper (μg/day)	Manganese (mg/day)	Fluoride (mg/day)	Molybdenum (μg/day)	Boron (mg/day)	Nickel (mg/day)	Vanadium (mg/day)
Infants																
0–0.5	—	—	—	—	—	40	4	—	45	—	—	0.7	—	—	—	—
0.5–1	—	—	—	—	—	40	5	—	60	—	—	0.9	—	—	—	—
Children																
1–3	1500	2300	2500	3000	65	40	7	200	90	1000	2	1.3	300	3	0.2	—
4–8	1900	2900	2500	3000	110	40	12	300	150	3000	3	2.2	600	6	0.3	—
9–13	2200	3400	2500	4000	350	40	23	600	280	5000	6	10	1100	11	0.6	—
Adolescents																
14–18	2300	3600	2500	4000	350	45	34	900	400	8000	9	10	1700	17	1.0	—
Adults																
19–70	2300	3600	2500	4000	350	45	40	1100	400	10,000	11	10	2000	20	1.0	1.8
>70	2300	3600	2500	3000	350	45	40	1100	400	10,000	11	10	2000	20	1.0	1.8
Pregnancy																
≤18	2300	3600	2500	3500	350	45	34	900	400	8000	9	10	1700	17	1.0	—
19–50	2300	3600	2500	3500	350	45	40	1100	400	10,000	11	10	2000	20	1.0	—
Lactation																
≤18	2300	3600	2500	4000	350	45	34	900	400	8000	9	10	1700	17	1.0	—
19–50	2300	3600	2500	4000	350	45	40	1100	400	10,000	11	10	2000	20	1.0	—

[d]*The UL for magnesium applies to synthetic forms obtained from supplements or drugs only.*

NOTE: An Upper Limit was not established for vitamins and minerals not listed and for those age groups listed with a dash (—) because of a lack of data, not because these nutrients are safe to consume at any level of intake. All nutrients can have adverse effects when intakes are excessive.

NUTRITION

Concepts & Controversies

With Diet Analysis Plus Student Guide

Frances Sizer | Ellie Whitney

CENGAGE Learning™

Australia • Brazil • Japan • Korea • Mexico • Singapore • Spain • United Kingdom • United States

CENGAGE Learning™

NUTRITION: Concepts & Controversies With Diet Analysis Plus Student Guide

Executive Editors:
Maureen Staudt
Michael Stranz

Senior Project Development Manager:
Linda deStefano

Marketing Specialist:
Courtney Sheldon

Senior Production/Manufacturing Manager:
Donna M. Brown

PreMedia Manager:
Joel Brennecke

Sr. Rights Acquisition Account Manager:
Todd Osborne

Cover Image:
Getty Images*

*Unless otherwise noted, all cover images used by Custom Solutions, a part of Cengage Learning, have been supplied courtesy of Getty Images with the exception of the Earthview cover image, which has been supplied by the National Aeronautics and Space Administration (NASA).

Nutrition: Concepts and Controversies, 12th Edition
Frances Sizer | Ellie Whitney

ISBN-13: 978-1-111-52095-3

ISBN-10: 1-111-52095-X

Cengage Learning
5191 Natorp Boulevard
Mason, Ohio 45040
USA

Cengage Learning is a leading provider of customized learning solutions with office locations around the globe, including Singapore, the United Kingdom, Australia, Mexico, Brazil, and Japan. Locate your local office at:
international.cengage.com/region.
Cengage Learning products are represented in Canada by Nelson Education, Ltd.
For your lifelong learning solutions, visit **www.cengage.com/custom.**
Visit our corporate website at **www.cengage.com.**

Printed in the United States of America

ABOUT THE AUTHORS

Frances Sienkiewicz Sizer

M.S., R.D., F.A.D.A., attended Florida State University where, in 1980, she received her B.S. and, in 1982, her M.S. in nutrition. She is certified as a charter Fellow of the American Dietetic Association. She is a founding member and vice president of Nutrition and Health Associates, an information and resource center in Tallahassee, Florida, that maintains an ongoing bibliographic database tracking research in more than 1,000 topic areas of nutrition. Her textbooks include *Life Choices: Health Concepts and Strategies; Making Life Choices; The Fitness Triad: Motivation, Training, and Nutrition;* and others. She was a primary author of *Nutrition Interactive,* an instructional college-level nutrition CD-ROM that pioneered the animation of nutrition concepts for use in college classrooms. She has lectured at universities and at national and regional conferences, and actively supports ECHO, a local hunger and homelessness relief organization in her community.

To all who seek nutrition knowledge and to all who teach and nourish others.

–*Fran*

Eleanor Noss Whitney

Ph.D., received her B.A. in Biology from Radcliffe College in 1960 and her Ph.D. in Biology from Washington University, St. Louis, in 1970. Formerly on the faculty at Florida State University, and a dietitian registered with the American Dietetic Association, she now devotes full time to research, writing, and consulting in nutrition, health, and environmental issues. Her earlier publications include articles in *Science, Genetics,* and other journals. Her textbooks include *Understanding Nutrition, Understanding Normal and Clinical Nutrition, Nutrition and Diet Therapy,* and *Essential Life Choices* for college students and *Making Life Choices* for high-school students. Her most intense interests presently include energy conservation, solar energy uses, alternatively fueled vehicles, and ecosystem restoration.

To Max, Zoey, Emily, Rebecca, Kalijah, and Duchess with love.

–*Ellie*

BRIEF CONTENTS

CONTENTS

PREFACE

A billboard in Louisiana reads, "Come as you are. Leave different," meaning that once you've seen, smelled, tasted, and listened to Louisiana, you'll never be the same. This book extends the same invitation to its readers: Come to nutrition science as you are, with all of the knowledge and enthusiasm you possess, with all of your unanswered questions and misconceptions, and with the habits and preferences that now dictate what you eat.

But leave different. Take with you from this study a more complete understanding of nutrition science. Take a greater ability to discern between nutrition truth and fiction, to ask sophisticated questions, and to find the answers. Finally, take with you a better sense of how to feed yourself in ways that not only please you and soothe your spirit, but that nourish your body as well.

For over a quarter of a century, *Nutrition: Concepts and Controversies* has been a cornerstone in nutrition classes across North America, serving the needs of students and professors in building a healthier future. In keeping with our tradition, in this, our 12th edition, we continue exploring the ever-changing frontier of nutrition science, confronting its mysteries through its scientific roots. We maintain our sense of personal connection with instructors and learners alike, writing for them in the clear, informal style that has become our trademark.

Pedagogical Features

Throughout these chapters, features tickle the reader's interest and inform. For both verbal and visual learners, our logical presentation and our lively figures keep interest high and understanding at a peak. Our many figures throughout the chapters reinforce important basic concepts. The photos that adorn many of our pages add pleasure to reading.

New in this edition, *Concept Links* in margins direct students to earlier foundation discussions relating to topics at hand. Page numbers ease the finding of critical subject matter in earlier chapters.

Many tried-and-true features return in this edition: Each chapter begins with "Do You Ever . . ." questions to pique interest and set a personal tone for the information that follows. *My Turn* features follow, inviting the reader to hear stories from students in nutrition classes around the nation and to offer evidence-based solutions to real-life situations. *Think Fitness* reminders appear from time to time to alert readers to ways in which physical activity links with nutrition to support health. The *Food Feature* sections that appear in most chapters act as bridges between theory and practice; they are practical applications of the chapter concepts that help readers to choose foods according to sound nutrition principles. **New** in this edition are *Concepts in Action* activities that integrate chapter concepts with the Diet Analysis Plus program. *Consumer Corners* present information on whole-grain foods, mercury in seafood, amino acid supplements, vitamin C and the common cold, bottled water, organic foods, and other nutrition-related marketplace issues.

By popular demand, we have retained our *Snapshots* of vitamins and minerals. These concentrated capsules of information depict food sources of vitamins and minerals, present the DRI recommended intakes and Tolerable Upper Intake Levels, and offer the chief functions of each nutrient along with deficiency and toxicity symptoms.

New or major terms are defined in the margins of chapter pages where they are introduced and also in the Glossary at the end of the book. Definitions in Controversy sections are grouped together in tables and also appear in the Glossary. The reader who wishes to locate any term can quickly do so by consulting the index, which lists the page numbers of definitions in boldface type.

Two useful features close each chapter. First, the *Media Menu* offers important and useful Internet web sites, The second is the popular *Self Check* that provides study questions, with answers in Appendix G to provide immediate feedback to the learner.

Controversies

The *Controversies* of this book's title invite you to explore beyond the safe boundaries of established nutrition knowledge. These optional readings, which appear at the end of each chapter, delve into current scientific topics and emerging controversies. All are up to date; those that are new to this edition are listed next.

Chapter Contents

Chapter 1 begins the text with a personal challenge to students. It asks the question so many people ask of nutrition educators—"Why should people care about nutrition?" We answer with a lesson in the ways in which nutritious foods affect diseases, and present a continuum of diseases from purely genetic in origin to those almost totally preventable by nutrition. After presenting some beginning facts about the genes, nutrients, bioactive food components, and nature of foods, the chapter goes on to present the *Healthy People* goals for the nation. It concludes with a discussion of scientific research in nutrition to lend a perspective on the context in which study results may be rightly viewed.

Chapter 2 brings together the concepts of nutrient allowances, such as the *Dietary Reference Intakes,* and diet planning using the *Dietary Guidelines for Americans* and the USDA *MyPyramid* Food Guide. **Chapter 3** presents a thorough, but brief, introduction to the workings of the human body from the genes to the organs, with major emphasis on the digestive system. New in

this edition is an introduction to the topic of inflammation as part of the immune response. **Chapters 4–6** are devoted to the energy-yielding nutrients—carbohydrates, lipids, and protein. The inflammation concept introduced in Chapter 3 is expanded in discussions of diabetes, colon health, and heart disease. Gene regulation takes its place among major functions of body proteins. Controversy 4 is entirely new, addressing the theories and fables surrounding the health effects of dietary carbohydrates. In Controversy 6 a new emphasis on diet planning for vegetarians will assist in sound vegetarian meal planning.

Chapters 7 and 8 present the vitamins, minerals, and water. **Chapter 9** relates energy balance to body composition, obesity, and underweight and provides guidance to life-long weight maintenance. **Chapter 10** presents the relationships between physical activity, athletic performance, and nutrition, with some guidance about products marketed to athletes. **Chapter 11** applies the essence of the first ten chapters to two broad and rapidly changing areas within nutrition: immunity and disease prevention. Readers will revisit the relationships among oxidation, inflammation, and diseases that were introduced in earlier chapters. The new Controversy 11 provides a general overview of the emerging science of nutritional genomics.

Chapter 12 delivers urgently important concepts of food safety. It also addresses the usefulness and safety of food additives, including artificial sweeteners and artificial fats, formerly topics found in Chapters 4 and 5. **Chapters 13 and 14** emphasize the importance of nutrition through the life span and issues surrounding childhood obesity in Controversy 13. **Chapter 14** includes nutrition advice for feeding preschoolers, schoolchildren, teens, and the elderly, where readers will find the concluding discussion of inflammation, immunity, and chronic diseases.

Chapter 15 touches on the vast problems of the global food supply and world and U.S. hunger, and links each reader to the meaningful whole through sustainable daily choices available to them. The Controversy introduces some challenges in providing the world's food.

New to This Edition

Every section of each chapter of this text reflects the changes in nutrition science occurring since the last edition. The changes range from subtle shifts of emphasis to entirely new sections that demand our attention. Here, we mention just a few of the most salient changes from the last edition. Readers will discover many, many others.

Chapter 1

As of this edition, the term *nonnutrient* has been replaced with "phytochemical," "nutrient," or "bioactive food component," as appropriate.

Condensed several sections and figures.

Defined double-blind controlled human study.

Clarified cost of nutritious food: price per calorie versus cost per serving.

Controversy 1

Added definition of certified diabetes educator.

Chapter 2

New greater emphasis on discretionary calories.

New table of discretionary calories.

New photos illustrating food components that provide discretionary calories.

Changed vegetable and fruit reference sizes to 1 cup for consistency with MyPyramid.

Revamped ethnic food figure.

New Healthy Eating Index defined.

New figure, "How Does the U.S. Diet Stack Up?"

Controversy 2

Updated with new phytochemical information and reorganized table of phytochemicals, sources, and actions.

Chapter 3

New section explains and defines inflammation as part of the immune response.

New table introduces digestive enzyme terms and names general categories.

Expanded coverage of ulcer, GERD.

Controversy 3

Improved organization.

New figure (simple) and expanded text conveys new emphasis on free-radical generation and damage from oxidative stress from alcohol metabolism.

New statistics from CDC on binge drinking.

New figure correlating likelihood of traffic accidents with BAC.

Much new information on alcohol intake and increased cancer risks.

Chapter 4

New organization.

New material on inflammation, particularly with colon health and diabetes.

New paragraphs on sugar alcohols, with reference to artificial sweetener coverage in Chapter 12 and to dental caries in Chapter 14.

Updated diabetes maps.

Controversy 4

New Controversy on health effects of carbohydrates.

Chapter 5

Reorganized several topics.

Expanded coverage of omega-3 fatty acids, with new Consumer Corner on choosing safe varieties of seafood, including risks from mercury in both saltwater and freshwater fish.

New emphasis that saturated fat guidelines apply to women (dispelling myth that heart disease is a man's disease).

Controversy 5

Introduces importance of dietary pattern.

Chapter 6

Updated. Moved most epigenetic information to new Controversy 11.

Included gene regulation among major functions.

Controversy 6

New emphasis on vegetarian meal planning, with new tables and figures to assist.

New health correlations for red and processed vs white meats.
Information correlated to 2009 ADA position paper.

Chapter 7
New organization, with more subheadings.
Updated information throughout the chapter.
New content on vitamin D; new figure of declining U.S. serum vitamin D values.
New figure depicting B vitamin deficiency symptoms of the tongue and mouth.
New photo depiction of niacin deficiency dermatitis.
All graphs updated.

Controversy 7
Updated; new research on contamination of today's supplements.

Chapter 8
New organization with more subheadings.
Updated information throughout the chapter.
New figure on U.S. beverage consumption.
New CDC guidelines for sodium.
New theory: lifetime sodium exposure and irreversible hypertension.
New figure: calcium economy example, which demonstrates the arithmetic behind calcium recommendations.

Controversy 8
Addresses inflammatory processes and osteoporosis.

Chapter 9
Updated information throughout the chapter.
Reorganized much of the information with new subheadings.
New figure of obesity rates vs Healthy People target.
New section explaining the adipokine/inflammation/central obesity links. Defined adipokine.
New information on brown adipose tissue.
New *2008 Physical Activity Guidelines for Americans* information.
New Consumer Corner on Fad Diets with new figure comparing popular diets.
New figure for gastric surgeries.
New emphasis on society's role in eating disorders.

Chapter 10
New, contemporary approach updates this chapter with many new figures and tables, new terminology, and ACSM guidelines.
Included *2008 Physical Activity Guidelines for Americans* and ACSM guidelines for conditioning.
Greater emphasis on resistance training for physical activity and sports.
Added new tables and figures.

Chapter 11
Revised figure showing interrelationships among chronic diseases.
Expanded information on oxidized LDL cholesterol, inflammation, and plaque.
New Food Feature: the DASH diet.
New table: risk factors for chronic diseases.
New table: lifestyle modifications to reduce blood pressure.
Revised the AHA table of strategies to reduce heart disease risk; moved it into heart disease section.
Updated, reorganized table: selected herbs, claims, risks, and evidence.
Moved into cancer discussion and updated the table: recommendations to reduce cancer risk.
Revised the table of cancer at specific sites and factors that increase or decrease risk.

Controversy 11
This new Controversy presents a simple introduction to nutritional genomics. It places the emerging science in the context of today's applications and marketplace.

Chapter 12
Updated information throughout.
Added artificial sweeteners and artificial fats.
New explanation of the process of extrusion and its effects on nutrients.

Controversy 12
Updated information throughout; introduces the *Svalbard Global Crop Diversity Trust* seed vault.

Chapter 13
New discussion of vitamin D during pregnancy.
Enhanced discussion of weight gain during pregnancy.
Updated table of weight gain guidelines during pregnancy.
New section on weight loss after pregnancy.
Added a list of the harms of smoking during pregnancy.
Enhanced discussion of diabetes during pregnancy.
New discussion of hypertension during pregnancy.
Revised spina bifida figure.
New figure comparing breast milk, formula, and cow's milk.
New table of supplements for full-term infants.

Controversy 13
New obesity diet recommendations and activity guidelines.

Chapter 14
New information on lead's lingering effects through life.
New MyPyramid for preschoolers and kids figure.
Expanded discussion of dental caries and added caries figure formerly in Controversy 4.
New food skills table adapted from MyPyramid website.
New table: *2008 Physical Activity for Americans*—Key Guidelines for Older Adults.
New discussion of inflammation and aging effects on immunity and chronic disease.

Controversy 14
New table on high-tyramine foods.

Chapter 15
All hunger data updated.
New emphasis on the obesity-poverty paradox, with new figure.
New name: Feed America, formerly America's Second Harvest
New name: Supplemental Nutrition Assistance Program (SNAP), formerly the Food Stamp Program.

New table: tips for thrifty food shopping.
New discussion of aquaculture.

Controversy 15
Extensively revised to emphasize sustainability.

Ancillary Materials

Students and instructors alike will appreciate the innovative teaching and learning materials that accompany this text. The popular "Do It!" exercises appear in **CengageNow**, an online resource center of study tools for students that includes outcomes assessment through student self-testing and automatic grading features; "Do It!" exercises that provide an opportunity for students to practice chapter concepts interactively; a behavior-change planner for healthy eating, weight control, and physical activity; **new Pop-up Tutors** that reinforce key concepts and provide students with further instruction and practice on particularly difficult topics, such as metabolism, digestion, and absorption; and MyTurn case study videos that give students the opportunity to problem-solve with relevant, contemporary nutrition stories of their peers. Students also can access these videos via WebTutor for Blackboard and WebCT, and through links embedded in the Cengage Learning eBook.

The **Instructor's Manual** features ready-to-use assignment materials including food label and diet planning worksheets, ideas for in-class activities, and class preparation tools such as learning objectives, chapter summaries, lecture presentation outlines, and text-specific handouts. The **Test Bank** offers a rich assortment of multiple-choice and essay questions to test for both fact recall and deeper comprehension. Both of these publications, along with PowerPoint lectures and images, videos, JoinIn quizzes, and **ExamView** testing software preloaded with the test bank questions will be available on the **PowerLecture DVD-ROM**.

Transparency acetates from the 10th edition are also available; instructors can request the handy correlation guide to assist in reorganizing their transparencies for the 12th edition.

Diet Analysis Plus 9.0

Diet Analysis Plus allows students to track their diet and physical activity and to analyze the nutritional value of the food they eat so that they can adjust their diets to reach personal health goals—all while gaining a better understanding of how nutrition relates to, and impacts, their lives.

It includes a 20,000+ food database; 11 customizable reports for analysis; 10 new assignable labs; custom food and recipe features; the latest Dietary Reference Intakes; and goals and actual percentages of essential nutrients, vitamins, and minerals. Use the Concepts in Action activities in ***Nutrition: Concepts and Controversies*** to show students how the concepts they learn in the text relate to their personal nutrition goals.

Message to You

Our purpose in writing this text, as always, is to enhance our readers' understanding of nutrition science and motivation to apply it. We hope the information on this book's pages will reach beyond the classroom into our readers' lives. Take the information you find inside this book home with you. Use it in your life: nourish yourself, educate your loved ones, and nurture others to be healthy. Stay up with the news, too. For despite all the conflicting messages, inflated claims, and even quackery that abound in the marketplace, true nutrition knowledge progresses with a genuine scientific spirit, and important new truths are constantly unfolding.

Acknowledgments

To Philip, most heartfelt thanks. Our sincere thanks also to Linda Kelly DeBruyne for her work with Chapter 11, Chapter 13, and beyond. Thanks also to Spencer Webb for his valuable assistance and contemporary perspectives in Chapter 10, and thanks to Wende Webb for taking the lead in development of our new Concepts in Action feature. Rebbecca Skinner, thank you for your early mornings and creative input into Chapter and Controversy 15. Thanks also to Alex Rodriguez and Kathy Guilday for their cheerful and competent attention to details.

Our special thanks to our publishing team: Yolanda Cossio, Peggy Williams, Nedah Rose, Miriam Myers, Elesha Feldman, Alexis Glubka, Carol Samet, and Melanie Field for their dedication to excellence. Thank you, Laura McGinn, for your creative and energetic marketing ideas and approach.

We would also like to thank the authors of the student and instructor ancillaries for the 12th edition: Alana Cline, who revised and expanded the test bank; Mary Ellen Clark, who contributed materials to the instructor's manual; Jana R. Kicklighter, who authored the study guide; and Michelle Grodner and Daniel Santibanez, who provided content for the student website.

Reviewers of the 12th Edition

As always, we are grateful for the instructors who took the time to comment on this revision. Your suggestions were invaluable in strengthening the book and suggesting new lines of thought. We hope you will continue to provide your comments and suggestions.

Alex Kojo Anderson, *University of Georgia, Athens*
Sharon Antonelli, *San Jose City College*
L. Rao Ayyagari, *Lindenwood University*
James W. Bailey, *University of Tennessee*
Karen Basinger, *Montgomery College*
Leah Carter, *Bakersfield College*
Melissa Chabot, *SUNY @ Buffalo*
Priscilla Connors, *University of North Texas*
Monica L. Easterling, *Wayne County Community College District*
Jena Nelson Hall, *Butte Community College*
Eimear M. Mullen, *Northern Kentucky University*
Steven Nizielski, *Grand Valley State University*
David J. Pavlat, *Central College*
Begoña Cirera Perez, *Chabot College*
Liz Quintana, *West Virginia University*
Janice M. Rueda, *Wayne State University*
Donal Scheidel, *University of South Dakota*
Carole A. Sloan, *Henry Ford Community College*
Leslie S. Spencer, *Rowan University*
Ilene Sutter, *California State University, Northridge*
Barbara P. Zabitz, *Wayne County Community College District*

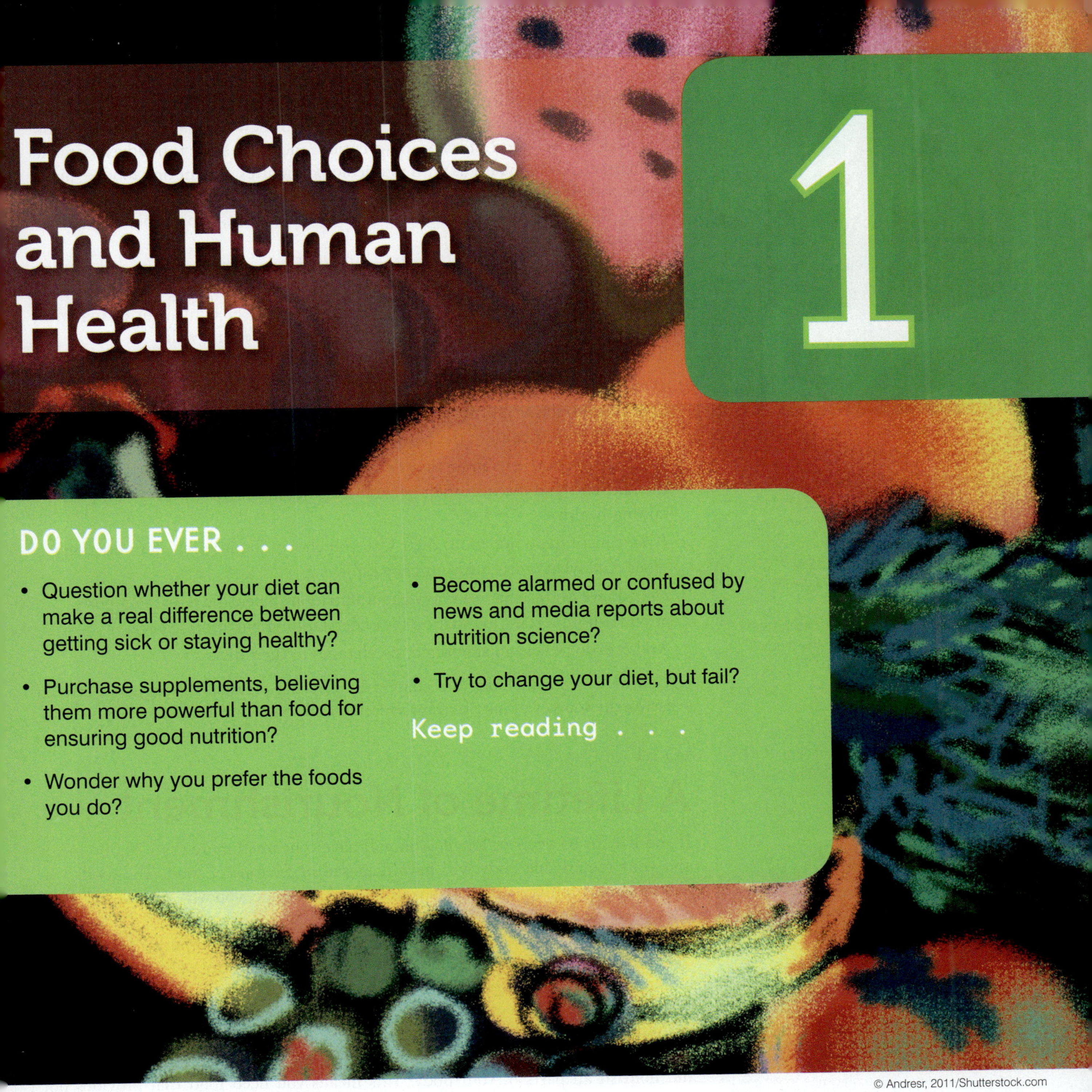

Food Choices and Human Health

1

DO YOU EVER . . .

- Question whether your diet can make a real difference between getting sick or staying healthy?
- Purchase supplements, believing them more powerful than food for ensuring good nutrition?
- Wonder why you prefer the foods you do?
- Become alarmed or confused by news and media reports about nutrition science?
- Try to change your diet, but fail?

Keep reading . . .

Learning Objectives

To find learning objective topics in this chapter, look for text headings with a corresponding "LO" number above the heading. After reading this chapter, you should be able to accomplish the following:

LO 1.1 Discuss how particular lifestyle choice can either positively impact or harm overall health.

LO 1.2 Define the term *nutrient* and be able to list the six major nutrients.

LO 1.3 Recognize the five characteristics of a healthy diet and give suggestions for using them.

LO 1.4 Summarize how a particular culture or circumstance can impact a person's food choices.

LO 1.5 Describe and give an example of the major types of research studies.

LO 1.6 Discuss why national nutrition survey data are important for the health of the population.

LO 1.7 List the major steps in behavior change and devise a plan for making successful long-term changes in the diet.

LO 1.8 Recognize misleading nutrition claims in advertisements for dietary supplements and in the popular media.

Andresr, 2011/Shutterstock.com

When you choose foods with nutrition in mind, you can enhance your own well-being.

food medically, any substance that the body can take in and assimilate that will enable it to stay alive and to grow; the carrier of nourishment; socially, a more limited number of such substances defined as acceptable by each culture.

nutrition the study of the nutrients in foods and in the body; sometimes also the study of human behaviors related to food.

diet the foods (including beverages) a person usually eats and drinks.

nutrients components of food that are indispensable to the body's functioning. They provide energy, serve as building material, help maintain or repair body parts, and support growth. The nutrients include water, carbohydrate, fat, protein, vitamins, and minerals.

malnutrition any condition caused by excess or deficient food energy or nutrient intake or by an imbalance of nutrients. Nutrient or energy deficiencies are forms of undernutrition; nutrient or energy excesses are forms of overnutrition.

chronic diseases long-duration degenerative diseases characterized by deterioration of the body organs. Examples include heart disease, cancer, and diabetes.

genome (GEE-nome) the full complement of genetic information in the chromosomes of a cell. In human beings, the genome consists of about 35,000 genes and supporting materials. The study of genomes is *genomics*. Also defined in Controversy 11.

genes units of a cell's inheritance; sections of the larger genetic molecule DNA (deoxyribonucleic acid). Each gene directs the making of one or more of the body's proteins.

DNA an abbreviation for deoxyribonucleic (dee-OX-ee-RYE-bow-nu-CLAY-ick) acid, the threadlike molecule that encodes genetic information in its structure; DNA strands coil up densely to form the chromosomes (Chapter 3 provides more details).

If you care about your body, and if you have strong feelings about **food,** then you have much to gain from learning about **nutrition**—the science of how food nourishes the body. Nutrition is a fascinating, much talked about subject. Each day, newspapers, radio, and television present stories of new findings on nutrition and heart health or nutrition and cancer prevention, and at the same time advertisements and commercials bombard us with multicolored pictures of tempting foods—pizza, burgers, cakes, and chips. If you are like most people, when you eat you sometimes wonder, "Is this food good for me?" or you berate yourself, "I probably shouldn't be eating this."

When you study nutrition, you learn which foods serve you best, and you can work out ways of choosing foods, planning meals, and designing your **diet** wisely. Knowing the facts can enhance your health and your enjoyment of eating while relieving your feelings of guilt or worry that you aren't eating well.

This chapter addresses these "why, what, and how" questions about nutrition:

- *Why* care about nutrition? The **nutrients** interact with body tissues, adding a little or subtracting a little, day by day, and thus change the very foundations upon which the health of the body is built.
- *What* are the nutrients in foods, and what roles do they play in the body? Meet the nutrients and discover their general roles in building body tissues and maintaining health.
- *What* constitutes a nutritious diet? Can you choose foods wisely, for nutrition's sake? And what motivates your choices?
- *How* do we know what we know about nutrition? Scientific research reports provide an important foundation for understanding nutrition science.
- And *how* do people go about making changes to their diets?

Controversy 1 concludes the chapter by offering ways to distinguish between trustworthy sources of nutrition information and those that are less reliable.

LO 1.1

A Lifetime of Nourishment

If you live for 65 years or longer, you will have consumed more than 70,000 meals and your remarkable body will have disposed of 50 tons of food. The foods you choose have cumulative effects on your body. As you age, you will see and feel those effects—if you know what to look for.

Your body renews its structures continuously, and each day it builds a little muscle, bone, skin, and blood, replacing old tissues with new. It may also add a little fat if you consume excess food energy (calories) or subtract a little if you consume less than you require. Some of the food you eat today becomes part of "you" tomorrow.

The best food for you, then, is the kind that supports the growth and maintenance of strong muscles, sound bones, healthy skin, and sufficient blood to cleanse and nourish all parts of your body. This means you need food that provides not only the right amount of energy but also sufficient nutrients, that is, enough water, carbohydrates, fats, protein, vitamins, and minerals. If the foods you eat provide too little or too much of any nutrient today, your health may suffer just a little today. If the foods you eat provide too little or too much of one or more nutrients every day for years, then in later life you may suffer severe disease effects.

A well-chosen array of foods supplies enough energy and enough of each nutrient to prevent **malnutrition.** Malnutrition includes deficiencies, imbalances, and excesses of nutrients, alone or in combination, any of which can take a toll on health over time.

KEY POINT The nutrients in food support growth, maintenance, and repair of the body. Deficiencies, excesses, and imbalances of energy and nutrients bring on the diseases of malnutrition.

The Diet and Health Connection

Your choice of diet profoundly affects your health, both today and in the future. Only two common lifestyle habits are more influential: smoking and other tobacco use, and excessive drinking of alcohol. Of the leading causes of death listed in Table 1-1, four are directly related to nutrition, and another—motor vehicle and other accidents—is related to drinking alcohol.

Many older people suffer from debilitating conditions that could have been largely prevented had they known and applied the nutrition principles known today. The **chronic diseases**—heart disease, diabetes, some kinds of cancer, dental disease, and adult bone loss—all have a connection to poor diet.[1*] These diseases cannot be prevented by a good diet alone; they are to some extent determined by a person's genetic constitution, activities, and lifestyle. Within the range set by your genetic inheritance, however, the likelihood of developing these diseases is strongly influenced by your food choices.

KEY POINT Nutrition profoundly affects health.

Genetics and Individuality

Consider the role of genetics. Genetics and nutrition affect different diseases to varying degrees (see Figure 1-1). The anemia caused by sickle-cell disease, for example, is purely hereditary and thus appears at the left of Figure 1-1 as a genetic condition largely unrelated to nutrition. Nothing a person eats affects the person's chances of contracting this anemia, although nutrition therapy may help ease its course. At the other end of the spectrum, iron-deficiency anemia most often results from undernutrition. Diseases and conditions of poor health appear all along this continuum, from almost entirely genetically based to purely nutritional in origin; the more nutrition-related a disease or health condition is, the more successfully sound nutrition can prevent it.

Furthermore, some diseases, such as heart disease and cancer, are not one disease but many. Two people may both have heart disease, but not the same form; one person's cancer may be nutrition-related but another's may not be. Individual people differ genetically from each other in thousands of subtle ways, so no simple statement can be made about the extent to which diet can help any one person avoid such diseases or slow their progress.

The recent identification of the human **genome** establishes the entire sequence of the **genes** in human **DNA.** This work has, in essence, revealed the body's instructions for making all of the working parts of a human being. A new wealth of information has emerged to explain the workings of the body, and nutrition scientists are working quickly to apply this knowledge to benefit human health.[2] Later chapters expand on the emerging story of nutrition and the genes.

*Reference notes are found in Appendix F.

TABLE 1-1 Leading Causes of Death, U.S.

Blue shading indicates that a cause of death is related to nutrition; the light yellow indicates that it is related to alcohol.[a]

	Percentage of Total Deaths
1. Heart disease	26.5%
2. Cancers	22.8%
3. Strokes	5.9%
4. Chronic lung disease	5.3%
5. Accidents	4.7%
6. Alzheimer's disease	3.1%
7. Diabetes mellitus	2.9%
8. Pneumonia and influenza	2.6%
9. Kidney disease	1.8%
10. Blood infections	1.4%

[a]Hypertension (high blood pressure), a nutrition-related cause of death, ranks at number 13.

Source: National Center for Health Statistics.

Did You Know?

Anemia is a blood condition in which red blood cells, the body's oxygen carriers, are inadequate or impaired and so cannot meet the oxygen demands of the body. (More about the anemia of sickle-cell disease in Chapter 6; iron-deficiency anemia is described in Chapter 8.)

FIGURE 1-1 Nutrition and Disease

Not all diseases are equally influenced by diet. Some are almost purely genetic, like the anemia of sickle-cell disease. Some may be inherited (or the tendency to develop them may be inherited in the genes) but may be influenced by diet, like some forms of diabetes. Some are purely dietary, like the vitamin and mineral deficiency diseases.

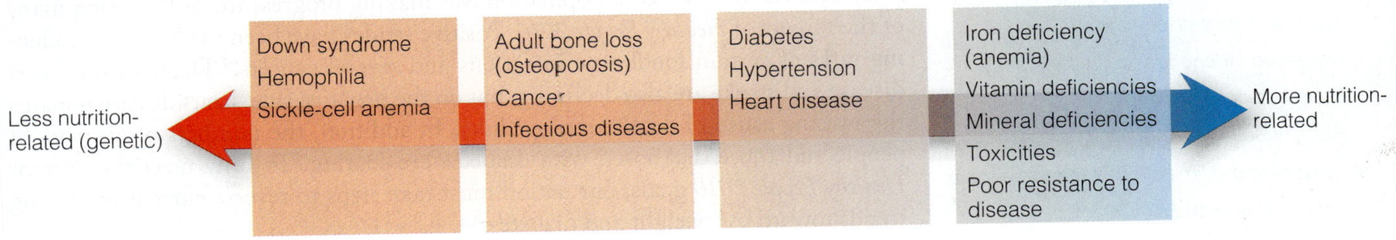

THINK FITNESS

Why Be Physically Active?

Why should people bother to be physically active? While a person's daily food choices can powerfully affect health, the combination of nutrition and physical activity is more powerful still. People who are physically active can expect to receive at least some of the benefits listed in the margin. If even half of these benefits were yours for the asking, wouldn't you step up to claim them? In truth, they are yours to claim, at the price of including physical activity in your day. Chapter 10 explores the topics of fitness and physical activity.

START NOW CENGAGENOW Ready to make a change? Consult the online behavior-change planner to explore a method for changing your current behaviors at **www.cengage.com/sso.**

Did You Know?

The human genome is 99.9% the same in all people; all of the normal variations such as differences in hair color, as well as variations that result in diseases such as sickle-cell anemia, lie in the 0.1% of the genome that varies.

Only about 2% of the human genome contains genes. Scientists are asking, "What does the rest do?"

KEY POINT Choice of diet influences long-term health within the range set by genetic inheritance. Nutrition has little influence on some diseases but strongly affects others.

Other Lifestyle Choices

Besides food choices, other lifestyle choices also affect people's health. Tobacco use and alcohol and other substance abuse can destroy health. Physical activity, sleep, stress, and other environmental factors can also help prevent or reduce the severity of some diseases. Physical activity is so closely linked with nutrition in supporting health that most chapters of this book offer features called Think Fitness, such as the one above.

- Potential benefits of physical activity include:
  - *Reduced risk of cardiovascular diseases.*
  - *Increased cardiovascular endurance.*
  - *Increased muscle strength and endurance.*
  - *Increased flexibility.*
  - *Reduced risk of some types of cancer (especially colon and breast).*
  - *Improved mental outlook and lessened likelihood of depression.*
  - *Improved mental functioning.*
  - *Feeling of vigor.*
  - *Feeling of belonging—the companionship of sports.*
  - *Strong self-image and belief in one's abilities.*
  - *Reduced body fat, increased lean tissue.*
  - *A more youthful appearance, healthy skin, and improved muscle tone.*
  - *Greater bone density and lessened risk of adult bone loss in later life.*
  - *Increased independence in the elderly.*
  - *Sound, beneficial sleep.*
  - *Faster wound healing.*
  - *Lessening or elimination of menstrual pain.*
  - *Improved resistance to infection.*

KEY POINT Personal life choices, such as staying physically active or using tobacco or alcohol, also affect health for the better or worse.

Healthy People 2010: Nutrition Objectives for the Nation

The U.S. Department of Health and Human Services sets 10-year health objectives to reduce disease risks for the nation in its publication *Healthy People*.[3] The nutrition-related objectives for the year 2010, listed in Table 1-2, provide a quick scan of the nutrition-related objectives set for this decade. The inclusion of nutrition and food-safety objectives shows that public health officials consider these areas to be top national priorities.

By mid-decade, the U.S. population was making progress toward meeting many of the targets of *Healthy People 2010*. Positive strides have been made toward reducing rates of certain foodborne infections and several cancers.[4] Deaths from heart disease and stroke are also declining, but on the negative side, heart disease remains the leading cause of death among adults. In addition, the numbers of overweight people and those diagnosed with diabetes are soaring. To fully meet the current *Healthy People 2010* goals, our nation must take steps to reverse current increasing trends toward overweight and diabetes.[5]

TABLE 1-2 *Healthy People 2010* Nutrition-Related Objectives

• Increase *nutrition education* among consumers and in educational settings at all levels.
• Increase the proportion of children, adolescents, and adults who are at a *healthy weight.*
• Reduce *growth retardation* among low-income children under age 5 years.
• Increase the proportion of persons aged 2 years and older who consume at least two daily servings of *fruit.*
• Increase the proportion of persons aged 2 years and older who consume at least three daily servings of *vegetables,* with at least one-third being dark green or orange vegetables.
• Increase the proportion of persons aged 2 years and older who consume at least six daily servings of *grain products,* with at least three being whole grains.
• Increase the proportion of persons aged 2 years and older who consume less than 10% of calories from *saturated fat.*
• Increase the proportion of persons aged 2 years and older who consume no more than 30% of calories from *total fat.*
• Increase the proportion of persons aged 2 years and older who consume 2,400 milligrams or less of *sodium.*
• Increase the proportion of adults with *high blood pressure* who are taking action to control their blood pressure.
• Increase the proportion of persons aged 2 years and older who meet dietary recommendations for *calcium.*
• Reduce *iron deficiency* among young children, females of childbearing age, and pregnant females.
• Reduce *anemia* among low-income pregnant females in their third trimester.
• Reduce *key vitamin and mineral deficiencies* in pregnant women.
• Increase the proportion of children and adolescents aged 6 to 19 years whose intake of *meals and snacks at school* contributes to good overall dietary quality.
• Increase the proportion of worksites that offer *nutrition or weight management classes or counseling.*
• Increase the proportion of physician office visits made by patients with a diagnosis of cardiovascular disease, diabetes, or hyperlipidemia that include *counseling or education related to diet and nutrition.*
• Reduce deaths from anaphylaxis caused by *food allergies.*
• Increase the number of consumers and retail establishments who follow key *food-safety* practices and reduce key foodborne illnesses.
• Increase *food security* among U.S. households and in so doing reduce hunger.

Source: Details about these and hundreds of other objectives are available from the U.S. Department of Health and Human Services, Healthy People 2010: Cornerstone to Prevention *(Washington, D.C.: Government Printing Office, 2000), online at www.health.gov/healthypeople or call (800) 367-4725.*

The next section shifts our focus to the nutrients at the core of nutrition science. As your course of study progresses, the individual nutrients may become like old friends, revealing more and more about themselves as you move through the chapters.

KEY POINT The U.S. Department of Health and Human Services sets nutrition objectives for the nation each decade.

LO 1.2

The Human Body and Its Food

As your body moves and works each day, it must use **energy.** The energy that fuels the body's work comes indirectly from the sun by way of plants. Plants capture and store the sun's energy in their tissues as they grow. When you eat plant-derived foods such as fruits, grains, or vegetables, you obtain and use the solar energy they have stored. Plant-eating animals obtain their energy in the same way, so when you eat animal tissues, you are eating compounds containing energy that came originally from the sun.

The body requires six kinds of nutrients—families of molecules indispensable to its functioning—and foods deliver these. Table 1-3 lists the six classes of nutrients.

energy the capacity to do work. The energy in food is chemical energy; it can be converted to mechanical, electrical, thermal, or other forms of energy in the body. Food energy is measured in calories, defined on page 7.

TABLE 1-3 Elements in the Six Classes of Nutrients

The nutrients that contain carbon are organic.

	Carbon	Oxygen	Hydrogen	Nitrogen	Minerals
Water		✓	✓		
Carbohydrate	✓	✓	✓		
Fat	✓	✓	✓		
Protein	✓	✓	✓	✓	b
Vitamins	✓	✓	✓	✓a	b
Minerals					✓

[a]*All of the B vitamins contain nitrogen; amine means nitrogen.*

[b]*Protein and some vitamins contain the mineral sulfur; vitamin B_{12} contains the mineral cobalt.*

Four of these six are **organic;** that is, the nutrients contain the element carbon derived from living things.

Meet the Nutrients

The human body and foods are made of the same materials, arranged in different ways (see Figure 1-2). When considering quantities of foods and nutrients, scientists often measure them in **grams,** units of weight.

- Energy-yielding nutrients are also called *macronutrients* because they are needed in relatively large amounts in the diet.
- Vitamins and minerals are known as *micronutrients* because they are needed in only tiny amounts.

The Energy-Yielding Nutrients

Foremost among the six classes of nutrients in foods is water, which is constantly lost from the body and must constantly be replaced. Of the four organic nutrients, three are **energy-yielding nutrients,** meaning that the body can use the energy they contain. The carbohydrates and fats (fats are also called lipids) are especially important energy-yielding nutrients. As for pro-

FIGURE 1-2 Components of Food and the Human Body

Foods and the human body are made of the same materials.

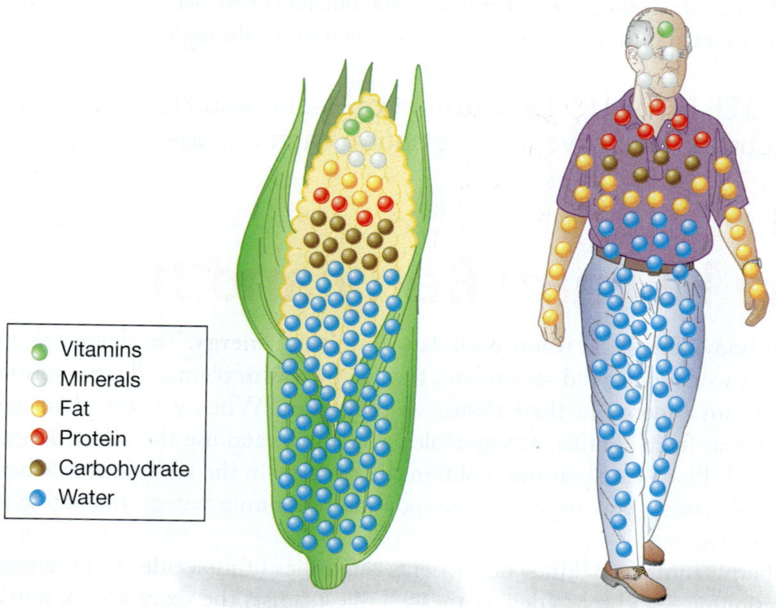

organic carbon containing. Four of the six classes of nutrients are organic: carbohydrate, fat, protein, and vitamins. Strictly speaking, organic compounds include only those made by living things and do not include compounds such as carbon dioxide, diamonds, and a few carbon salts.

grams units of weight. A gram (g) is the weight of a cubic centimeter (cc) or milliliter (ml) of water under defined conditions of temperature and pressure. About 28 grams equal an ounce.

energy-yielding nutrients the nutrients the body can use for energy—carbohydrate, fat, and protein. These also may supply building blocks for body structures.

tein, it does double duty: it can yield energy, but it also provides materials that form structures and working parts of body tissues. (Alcohol yields energy, too, but it is a toxin, not a nutrient—see the note to Table 1-4.)

Vitamins and Minerals The fifth and sixth classes of nutrients are the vitamins and the minerals. These provide no energy to the body. A few minerals serve as parts of body structures (calcium and phosphorus, for example, are major constituents of bone), but all vitamins and minerals act as regulators. As regulators, the vitamins and minerals assist in all body processes: digesting food; moving muscles; disposing of wastes; growing new tissues; healing wounds; obtaining energy from carbohydrate, fat, and protein; and participating in every other process necessary to maintain life. Later chapters are devoted to these six classes of nutrients.

The Concept of Essential Nutrients When you eat food, then, you are providing your body with energy and nutrients. Furthermore, some of the nutrients are **essential nutrients,** meaning that if you do not ingest them, you will develop deficiencies; the body cannot make these nutrients for itself. Essential nutrients are found in all six classes of nutrients. Water is an essential nutrient; so is a form of carbohydrate; so are some lipids, some parts of protein, all of the vitamins, and the minerals important in human nutrition.

Calorie Values Food scientists measure food energy in kilocalories, units of heat. This book uses the common word **calories** to mean the same thing. It behooves the person who wishes to control food energy intake and body fatness to learn the calorie values of the energy nutrients, listed in Table 1-4. The most energy-rich of the nutrients is fat, which contains 9 calories in each gram. Carbohydrate and protein each contain only 4 calories in a gram (see Table 1-4).

Scientists have worked out ways to measure the energy and nutrient contents of foods. They have also calculated the amounts of energy and nutrients various types of people need—by gender, age, life stage, and activity. Thus, after studying human nutrient requirements (in Chapter 2), you will be able to state with some accuracy just what your own body needs—this much water, that much carbohydrate, so much vitamin C, and so forth. So why not simply take pills or **dietary supplements** in place of food? Because, as it turns out, food offers more than just the six basic nutrients.[6]

KEY POINT Food supplies energy and nutrients. Foremost among the nutrients is water. The energy-yielding nutrients are carbohydrates, fats (lipids), and protein. The regulator nutrients are vitamins and minerals. Food energy is measured in calories; food and nutrient quantities are often measured in grams.

TABLE 1-4 Calorie Values of Energy Nutrients

The energy a person consumes in a day's meals comes from these three energy-yielding nutrients; alcohol, if consumed, also contributes energy.

Energy Nutrient	Energy
Carbohydrate	4 cal/g
Fat (lipid)	9 cal/g
Protein	4 cal/g

Note: Alcohol contributes 7 calories/gram that the human body can use for energy. Alcohol is not classed as a nutrient, however, because it interferes with growth, maintenance, and repair of body tissues.

CONCEPT LINK 1-1

Throughout this text, Concept Links like this one point the reader to previous concepts that underlie current discussions.

- Weight, measure, and other conversion factors needed for the study of nutrition are found in Appendix C.

Can I Live on Just Supplements?

Nutrition science can state what nutrients human beings need to survive—at least for a time. Scientists are becoming skilled at making **elemental diets**—liquid diets with a precise chemical composition that are lifesaving for people in the hospital who cannot eat ordinary food. These formulas, administered to severely ill people for days or weeks, support not only continued life but also recovery from nutrient deficiencies, infections, and wounds.

Lately, marketers have taken these liquid supplement formulas out of the medical setting and have advertised them heavily to healthy people of all ages as "meal replacers" or "insurance" against malnutrition. The truth is that a diet of real food is superior to supplements.[7] Nutrients and other food components interact with each other in the body and operate best in harmony with one another.[8] Formula diets are essential to help sick people to survive, but they do not enable people to thrive over long periods. Even in hospitals, elemental diet formulas do not support optimal growth and health, and they often lead to medical complications.[9] Although serious problems are rare and can be detected and corrected, they show that the composition of these diets is not yet perfect for all people in all settings. Healthy people

essential nutrients the nutrients the body cannot make for itself (or cannot make fast enough) from other raw materials; nutrients that must be obtained from food to prevent deficiencies.

calories units of energy. In nutrition science, the unit used to measure the energy in foods is a kilocalorie (kcalorie or *Calorie*): it is the amount of heat energy necessary to raise the temperature of a kilogram (a liter) of water 1 degree Celsius. This book follows the common practice of using the lowercase term *calorie* (abbreviated *cal*) to mean the same thing.

dietary supplements pills, liquids, or powders that contain purified nutrients or other ingredients (see Controversy in Chapter 7).

elemental diets diets composed of purified ingredients of known chemical composition; intended to supply all essential nutrients to people who cannot eat foods.

© LWA-Stephen Welstead/Corbis

When you eat foods, you are receiving more than just nutrients.

© Richard Fukuhara/Corbis

Some foods offer phytochemcials in addition to the six classes of nutrients.

who eat a healthful diet do not need such formulas and, with a nutritious diet, most need no dietary supplements at all. Even if a person's basic nutrient needs are perfectly understood and met, concoctions of nutrients still lack something that foods provide. Hospitalized clients who are fed nutrient mixtures through a vein often improve dramatically when they can finally eat food. Something in real food is important to health—but what is it? What does food offer that cannot be provided through a needle or a tube? Science has some partial explanations, some physical and some psychological.

In the digestive tract, the stomach and intestine are dynamic, living organs, changing constantly in response to the foods they receive—even to just the sight, aroma, and taste of food. When a person is fed through a vein, the digestive organs, like unused muscles, weaken and grow smaller. Lack of digestive tract stimulation may even weaken the body's defenses against certain infections, such as infections of the respiratory tract. Medical wisdom now dictates that a person should be fed through a vein for as short a time as possible and that real food taken by mouth should be reintroduced as early as possible. The digestive organs also release hormones in response to food, and these send messages to the brain that bring the eater a feeling of satisfaction: "There, that was good. Now I'm full." Eating offers both physical and emotional comfort.

Food does still more than maintain the intestine and convey messages of comfort to the brain. Foods are chemically complex. In addition to their nutrients, foods contain **phytochemicals,** compounds that confer color, taste, and other characteristics to foods. Some may be **bioactive** food components that interact with metabolic processes in the body and may affect disease risks. Even an ordinary baked potato contains hundreds of different compounds. In view of all this, it is not surprising that food gives us more than just nutrients. If it were otherwise, *that* would be surprising.

KEY POINT In addition to nutrients, food conveys emotional satisfaction and hormonal stimuli that contribute to health. Foods also contain phytochemicals that give them their tastes, aromas, colors, and other characteristics. Some phytochemicals may play roles in reducing disease risks.

LO 1.3, 1.4

The Challenge of Choosing Foods

Well-planned meals convey pleasure and are nutritious, too, fitting your tastes, personality, family and cultural traditions, lifestyle, and budget. Given the astounding numbers and varieties available, consumers can lose track of what individual foods contain and how to put them together into health-promoting diets. A few guidelines can help.

The Abundance of Foods to Choose From

A list of the foods available 100 years ago would be relatively short. It would consist of **whole foods**—foods that have been around for a long time, such as vegetables, fruits, meats, milk, and grains (Table 1-5). These foods have been called basic, unprocessed, natural, or farm foods. By whatever name, choosing a sufficient variety of these foods each day is an easy way to obtain a nutritious diet. On a given day, however, almost three-quarters of our population consume too few vegetables, and two-thirds of us fail to consume enough fruit.[10] Also, although people generally consume a few servings of vegetables, the vegetable they most often choose is potatoes, usually prepared as French fries. Such dietary patterns make development of chronic diseases more likely.

phytochemicals compounds in plant-derived foods (*phyto* means "plant").

bioactive having biological activity in the body. See also the Controversy in Chapter 2.

TABLE 1-5 Glossary of Food Types

The purpose of this little glossary is to show that good-sounding food names don't necessarily signify that foods are nutritious. Read the comment at the end of each definition.

- **whole foods** milk and milk products; meats and similar foods such as fish and poultry; vegetables, including dried beans and peas; fruits; and grains. These foods are generally considered to form the basis of a nutritious diet Also called *basic foods.*
- **enriched foods** and **fortified foods** foods to which nutrients have been added. If the starting material is a whole, basic food such as milk or whole grain, the result may be highly nutritious. If the starting material is a concentrated form of sugar or fat, the result may be less nutritious.
- **fast foods** restaurant foods that are available within minutes after customers order them—traditionally, hamburgers, French fries, and milkshakes; more recently, salads and other vegetable dishes as well. These foods may or may not meet people's nutrient needs, depending on the selections made and on the energy allowances and nutrient needs of the eaters.
- **functional foods** whole or modified foods that contain bioactive food components believed to provide health benefits, such as reduced disease risks, beyond the benefits that their nutrients confer. However, all nutritious foods can support health in some ways; Controversy 2 provides details.
- **medical foods** foods specially manufactured for use by people with medical disorders and prescribed by a physician.
- **natural foods** a term that has no legal definition but is often used to imply wholesomeness.
- **nutraceutical** a term that has no legal or scientific meaning but is sometimes used to refer to foods, nutrients, or dietary supplements believed to have medicinal effects. Often used to sell unnecessary or unproven supplements.
- **organic foods** understood to mean foods grown without synthetic pesticides or fertilizers. In chemistry, however, all foods are made mostly of organic (carbon-containing) compounds. (See Chapter 12 for details.)
- **processed foods** foods subjected to any process, such as milling, alteration of texture, addition of additives, cooking, or others. Depending on the starting material and the process, a processed food may or may not be nutritious.
- **staple foods** foods used frequently or daily, for example, rice (in East and Southeast Asia) or potatoes (in Ireland). If well chosen, these foods are nutritious.

The number of foods supplied by the food industry today is astounding. Thousands of foods now line the market shelves—many are processed mixtures of the basic ones, and some are even constructed mostly from artificial ingredients. Ironically, this abundance often makes it more difficult, rather than easier, to plan a nutritious diet.

The food-related terms defined in Table 1-5 reveal that all types of food—including **fast foods** and **processed foods**—offer various constituents to the eater. You may also hear about **functional foods,** a marketing term coined to identify those foods containing substances, natural or added, that might lend protection against chronic diseases. The trouble is, scientists trying to single out the most health-promoting foods find that almost every naturally occurring food—even chocolate—

Did You Know?

In 1900, Americans chose from among 500 or so different foods; today, they choose from more than 50,000.

Izzy Schwartz/Photodisc/Getty Images

All foods once looked like this . . .

© Polara Studios, Inc.

. . . but now many foods look like this.

is functional in some way with regard to human health.[11] Controversy 2 in Chapter 2 provides more information about functional foods.

The extent to which foods support good health depends on the calories, nutrients, and phytochemicals they contain. In short, to select well among foods, you need to know more than their names; you need to know the foods' inner qualities. Even more important, you need to know how to combine foods into nutritious diets. Foods are not nutritious by themselves; each is of value only insofar as it contributes to a nutritious diet. A key to wise diet planning is to make sure that the foods you eat daily, your **staple foods,** are especially nutritious.

KEY POINT Foods come in a bewildering variety in the marketplace, but the foods that form the basis of a nutritious diet are whole foods, such as ordinary milk and milk products; meats, fish, and poultry; vegetables and dried peas and beans; fruits; and grains.

How, Exactly, Can I Recognize a Nutritious Diet?

A nutritious diet has five characteristics. First is **adequacy:** the foods provide enough of each essential nutrient, fiber, and energy. Second is **balance:** the choices do not overemphasize one nutrient or food type at the expense of another. Third is **calorie control:** the foods provide the amount of energy you need to maintain appropriate weight—not more, not less. Fourth is **moderation:** the foods do not provide excess fat, salt, sugar, or other unwanted constituents. Fifth is **variety:** the foods chosen differ from one day to the next. In addition, to maintain a steady supply of nutrients, meals should occur with regular timing throughout the day.

Adequacy

Any nutrient could be used to demonstrate the importance of dietary adequacy. Iron provides a familiar example. It is an essential nutrient: you lose some every day, so you have to keep replacing it; and you can get it into your body only by eating foods that contain it.† If you eat too few of the iron-containing foods, you can develop iron-deficiency anemia: with anemia you may feel weak, tired, cold, sad, and unenthusiastic; you may have frequent headaches; and you can do very little muscular work without disabling fatigue. Some foods are rich in iron; others are notoriously poor. If you add iron-rich foods to your diet, you soon feel more energetic. Meat, fish, poultry, and **legumes** are in the iron-rich category, and an easy way to obtain the needed iron is to include these foods in your diet regularly.

Balance

To appreciate the importance of dietary balance, consider a second essential nutrient, calcium. A diet lacking calcium causes poor bone development during the growing years and increases a person's susceptibility to disabling bone loss in adult life. Most foods that are rich in iron are poor in calcium. Calcium's richest food sources are milk and milk products, which happen to be extraordinarily poor iron sources. Clearly, to obtain enough of both iron and calcium, people have to balance their food choices among the types of foods that provide specific nutrients. Balancing the whole diet to provide enough but not too much of every one of the 40-odd nutrients the body needs for health requires considerable juggling, however. As you will see in Chapter 2, food group plans that cluster rich sources of nutrients into food groups can help you to achieve dietary adequacy and balance because they recommend specific amounts of foods from each group. Balance among the food groups then becomes the goal.

Calorie Control

Energy intakes should not exceed energy needs. Nicknamed calorie control, this diet characteristic ensures that energy intakes from food balance energy expenditures required for body functions and physical activity. Eating such a diet helps to control body fat content and weight. The many strategies that promote this goal appear in Chapter 9.

adequacy the dietary characteristic of providing all of the essential nutrients, fiber, and energy in amounts sufficient to maintain health and body weight.

balance the dietary characteristic of providing foods of a number of types in proportion to each other, such that foods rich in some nutrients do not crowd out the diet foods that are rich in other nutrients. Also called *proportionality.*

calorie control control of energy intake; a feature of a sound diet plan.

moderation the dietary characteristic of providing constituents within set limits, not to excess.

variety the dietary characteristic of providing a wide selection of foods—the opposite of monotony.

legumes (leg-GOOMS, LEG-yooms) beans, peas, and lentils, valued as inexpensive sources of protein, vitamins, minerals, and fiber that contribute little fat to the diet. Also defined in Chapter 6.

† A person can also take supplements of iron, but as later discussions demonstrate, eating iron-rich foods is preferable.

Moderation Intakes of certain food constituents such as fat, cholesterol, sugar, and salt should be limited for health's sake. A major guideline for healthy people is to keep fat intake below 35 percent of total calories.[12] Some people take this to mean that they must never indulge in a delicious beefsteak or hot-fudge sundae, but they are misinformed: moderation, not total abstinence, is the key. A steady diet of steak and ice cream might be harmful, but once a week as part of an otherwise moderate diet plan, these foods may have little impact; as once-a-month treats, these foods would have practically no effect at all. Moderation also means that limits are necessary, even for desirable food constituents. For example, a certain amount of fiber in foods contributes to the health of the digestive system, but too much fiber leads to nutrient losses.

- A nutritious diet follows the A, B, C, M, V principles:
  - *Adequacy.*
  - *Balance.*
  - *Calorie control.*
  - *Moderation.*
  - *Variety.*

Variety As for variety, nutrition scientists agree that people should not eat the same foods, even highly nutritious ones, day after day. One reason is that a varied diet is more likely to be adequate in nutrients.[13] In addition, some less-well-known nutrients and phytochemicals could be important to health and some foods may be better sources of these than others. Another reason is that a monotonous diet may deliver large amounts of toxins or contaminants. Such undesirable compounds in one food are diluted by all the other foods eaten with it and are diluted still further if the food is not eaten again for several days. Last, variety adds interest—trying new foods can be a source of pleasure.

A caution is in order. Any one of these dietary principles alone cannot ensure a healthful diet. For example, the most likely outcome of relying solely on variety could easily be a low-nutrient, high-calorie diet consisting of a variety of snack foods and nutrient-poor sweets.[14] If you establish the habit of using all of the principles just described, you will find that choosing a healthful diet becomes as automatic as brushing your teeth or falling asleep. Establishing the A, B, C, M, V habit may take some effort, but the payoff in terms of improved health is overwhelming. Table 1-6 takes an honest look at some common excuses for not eating well.

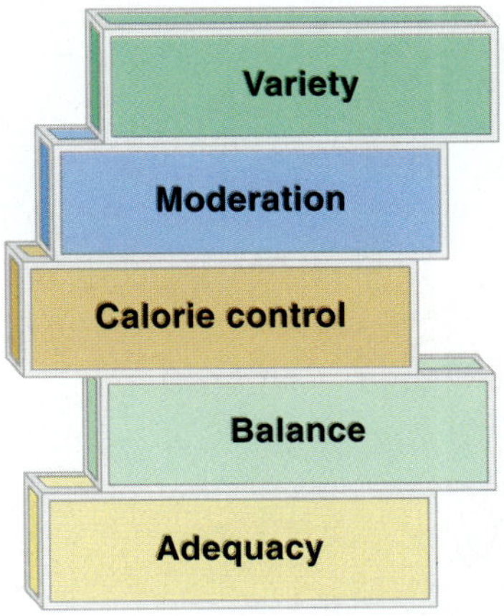

All of these factors help to build a nutritious diet.

KEY POINT A well-planned diet is adequate in nutrients, is balanced with regard to food types, offers food energy that matches energy expended in activity, is moderate in unwanted constituents, and offers a variety of nutritious foods.

Why People Choose Foods

Eating is an intentional act. Each day, people choose from the available foods, prepare the foods, decide where to eat, which customs to follow, and with whom to dine. Many factors influence food-related choices.

TABLE 1-6 What's Today's Excuse for Not Eating Well?

If you find yourself saying, "I know I should eat well, but I'm too busy" (or too fond of fast food, or have too little money, or a dozen other excuses), take note:

- *No time to cook.* Everyone is busy. Convenience packages of frozen vegetables, jars of pasta sauce, and prepared meats and salads make nutritious meals in little time.
- *Not a high priority.* Priorities change drastically and instantly when illness strikes—better to spend a little effort now nourishing your body's defenses than to spend enormous resources later fighting illnesses.
- *Crave fast food and sweets.* Occasional fast-food meals and sweets in moderation are acceptable in a nutritious diet.
- *Too little money.* Eating right costs no more than eating poorly. Chips, colas, fast food, and premium ice cream cost as much or more per serving as nutritious foods.[a]
- *Take vitamins instead.* Vitamin pills cannot make up for consistently poor food choices.

[a]For a discussion of this topic, see L. M. Lipsky, Are energy-dense foods really cheaper? Reexamining the relation between food price and energy density, American Journal of Clinical Nutrition *90* (2009): 1397–1401.

Sharing ethnic food is a way of sharing culture.

Cultural and Social Meanings Attached to Food Like wearing traditional clothing or speaking a native language, enjoying traditional **cuisines** and **foodways** can be a celebration of your own or a friend's heritage. Sharing **ethnic food** can be symbolic: people offering foods are expressing a willingness to share cherished values with others. People accepting those foods are symbolically accepting not only the person doing the offering but the person's culture. Developing **cultural competence** is particularly important for professionals who help others to achieve a nutritious diet.[15]

Cultural traditions regarding food are not inflexible; they keep evolving as people move about, learn about new foods, and teach each other. Today some people are ceasing to be **omnivores** and are becoming **vegetarians.** Vegetarians often choose this lifestyle because they honor the lives of animals or because they have discovered the health and other advantages associated with diets rich in beans, whole grains, fruits, nuts, and vegetables.[16] The Chapter 6 Controversy explores the pros and the cons of both the vegetarian's and the meat-eater's diets.

- Figure 2-10 in Chapter 2 depicts some ethnic foods that have become an integral part of the "American diet."

Factors That Drive Food Choices Consumers today value convenience so highly that they are willing to spend over half of their food budget on meals that require little or no preparation. They frequently eat out, bring home ready-to-eat meals, cook meals ahead in commercial kitchens, or have food delivered.[17] In their own kitchens, they want to prepare a meal in 15 to 20 minutes, using only four to six ingredients. Such convenience doesn't have to mean that nutrition is out the window. This chapter's Food Feature addresses the time, money, and nutrition trade-offs that many busy people face today.

Convenience is only one consideration. Physical, psychological, social, and philosophical factors all influence how you choose the foods you generally eat. These include:

- *Advertising.* The media have persuaded you to consume these foods.[18]
- *Availability.* They are present in the environment and accessible to you.[19]
- *Cost.* They are within your financial means.
- *Emotional comfort.* They can make you feel better for a while.
- *Habit.* They are familiar; you always eat them.
- *Personal preference and genetic inheritance.* You like the way these foods taste, with some preferences possibly determined by the genes.[20]
- *Positive or negative associations. Positive:* They are eaten by people you admire, or they indicate status, or they remind you of fun. *Negative*: They were forced on you or you became ill while eating them.
- *Region of the country.* They are foods favored in your area.
- *Social pressure.* They are offered; you feel you can't refuse them.
- *Values or beliefs.* They fit your religious tradition, square with your political views, or honor the environmental ethic.
- *Weight.* You think they will help to control body weight.
- *Nutrition and health benefits.* You think they are good for you.

Just the last two of these reasons for choosing foods assign a high priority to nutritional health. Similarly, the choice of where, as well as what, to eat is often based more on social considerations than on nutrition judgments. College students often choose to eat at fast-food and other restaurants to socialize, to get out, to save time, or to date; they are not always conscious of the need to obtain nutritious food.

Nutrition understanding depends upon a firm base of scientific knowledge. The next section describes the nature of such knowledge and addresses one of the "how" questions posed earlier in this chapter: How do we know what we know about nutrition?

KEY POINT Cultural traditions and social values revolve around food and often find expression through foodways. Many factors other than nutrition drive food choices.

cuisines styles of cooking.

foodways the sum of a culture's habits, customs, beliefs, and preferences concerning food.

ethnic foods foods associated with particular cultural subgroups within a population.

cultural competence having an awareness and acceptance of one's own and other cultures and the ability to interact effectively with people of those cultures.

omnivores people who eat foods of both plant and animal origin, including animal flesh.

vegetarians people who exclude from their diets animal flesh and possibly other animal products such as milk, cheese, and eggs.

LO 1.5, 1.6

The Science of Nutrition

Nutrition is a science—a field of knowledge composed of organized facts. Unlike sciences such as astronomy and physics, nutrition is a relatively young science. Most nutrition research has been conducted since 1900. The first vitamin was identified in 1897, and the first protein structure was not fully described until the mid-1940s. Because nutrition science is an active, changing, growing body of knowledge, scientific findings often seem to contradict one another or are subject to conflicting interpretations. Bewildered consumers complain in frustration, "Those scientists don't know anything. If they don't know what's true, how am I supposed to know?"

Yet, many facts in nutrition are known with great certainty. To understand why apparent contradictions sometimes arise in nutrition science, we need to look first at what scientists do.

The Scientific Approach

In truth, though, it is a scientist's business not to know. Scientists obtain facts by systematically asking honest objective questions—that's their job.[21] Following the scientific method (outlined in Figure 1-3), they attempt to answer scientific questions. They design and conduct various experiments to test for possible answers (see Figure 1-4 and Table 1-7). When they have ruled out some possibilities and found evidence for others, they submit their findings, not to the news media, but to boards of reviewers composed of other scientists who try to pick the findings apart. Finally, the work is published in scientific journals where still more scientists can read it. Then the news reporters read it and write about it and you can read it, too. Table 1-8 explains what you can expect to find in a journal article.

KEY POINT Scientists ask questions and then design research experiments to test possible answers.

Scientific Challenge

An important truth in science is that one experiment does not "prove" or "disprove" anything. Even after publication, other scientists try to duplicate the work of the first researchers to support or refute the original finding.

Only when a finding has stood up to rigorous, repeated testing in several kinds of experiments performed by several different researchers is it finally considered confirmed. Even then, strictly speaking, science consists not of facts that are set in stone, but of *theories* that can always be challenged and revised. Some findings, though, like the theory that the earth revolves about the sun, are so well supported by observations and experimental findings that they are generally accepted as facts. What we "know" in nutrition is confirmed in the same way—through years of replicating

FIGURE 1-3 ANIMATED! **The Scientific Method**

Research scientists follow the scientific method. Note that most research projects result in new questions, not final answers. Thus, research continues in a somewhat cyclical manner.

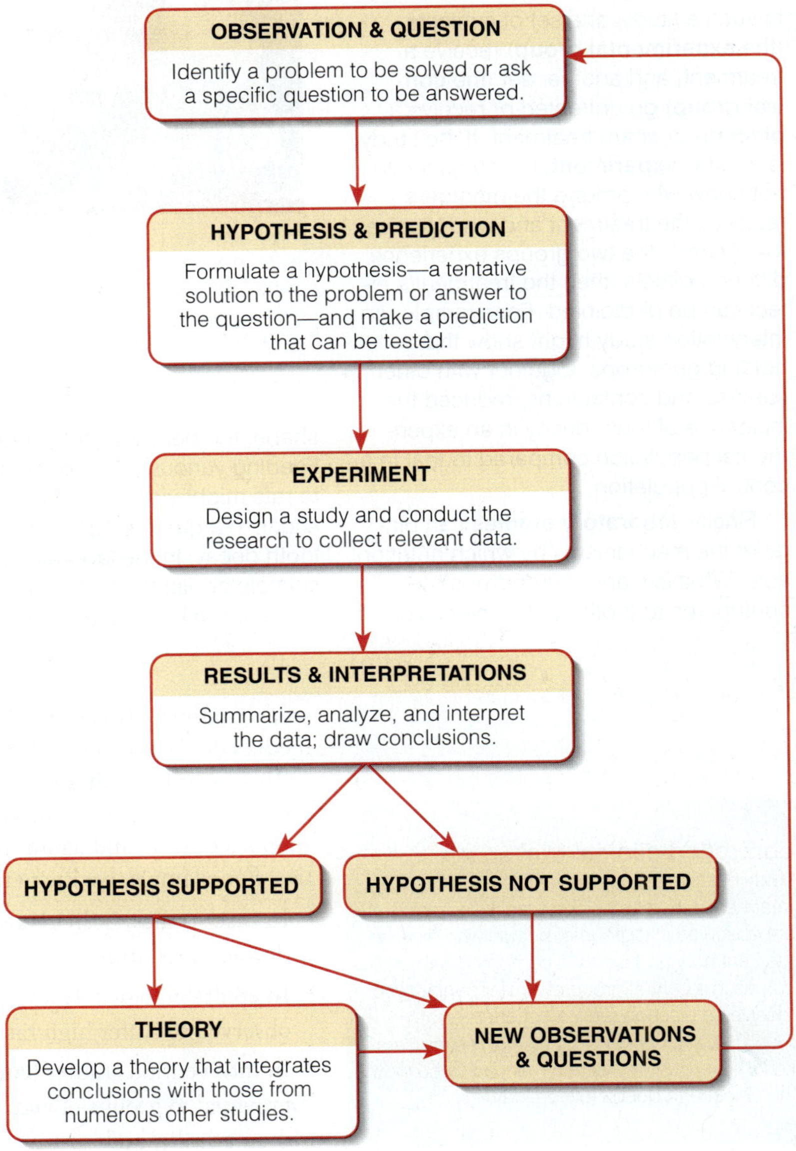

FIGURE 1-4 Examples of Research Design

The type of study chosen for research depends upon what sort of information the researchers require. Studies of individuals (**case studies**) yield observations that may lead to possible avenues of research. A study of a man who ate gumdrops and became a famous dancer might suggest that an experiment be done to see if gumdrops contain dance-enhancing power.

Studies of whole populations (**epidemiological studies**) provide another sort of information. Such a study can reveal a **correlation.** For example, an epidemiological study might find no worldwide correlation of gumdrop eating with fancy footwork but, unexpectedly, might reveal a correlation with tooth decay.

Studies in which researchers actively intervene to alter people's eating habits (**intervention studies**) go a step further. In such a study, one set of subjects (the **experimental group**) receive a treatment, and another set (the **control group**) go untreated or receive a **placebo** or sham treatment. If the study is a **blind experiment,** the subjects do not know who among the members receives the treatment and who receives the sham. If the two groups experience different effects, then the treatment's effect can be pinpointed. For example, an intervention study might show that withholding gumdrops, together with other candies and confections, reduced the incidence of tooth decay in an experimental population compared to that in a control population.

Finally, **laboratory studies** can pinpoint the mechanisms by which nutrition acts. What is it about gumdrops that contributes to tooth decay: their size, shape, temperature, color, ingredients? Feeding various forms of gumdrops to rats might yield the information that sugar, in a gummy carrier, promotes tooth decay. In the laboratory, using animals or plants or cells, scientists can inoculate with diseases, induce deficiencies, and experiment with variations on treatments to obtain in-depth knowledge of the process under study. Intervention studies and laboratory experiments are among the most powerful tools in nutrition research because they show the effects of treatments.

Case Study

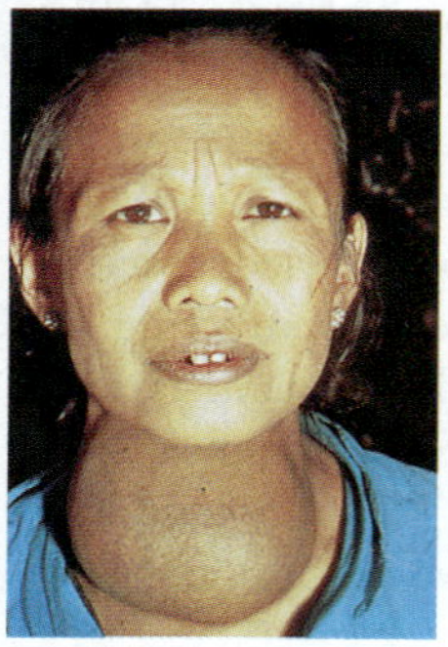

© Lester V. Bergman/Corbis

"This person eats too little of nutrient X and has illness Y."

Epidemiological Study

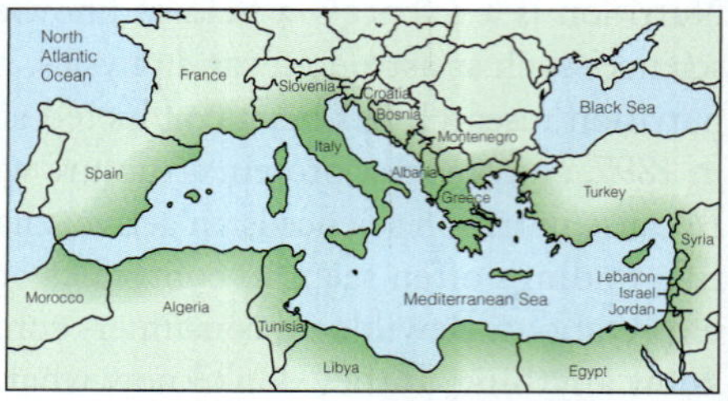

"This country's food supply contains more nutrient X, and these people suffer less illness Y."

Intervention Study

David Buffington/Photodisc/Getty Images

"Let's add foods containing nutrient X to some people's food supply and compare their rates of illness Y with the rates of others who don't receive the nutrient."

Laboratory Study

Leslie Newman & Andrew Flowers/Photo Researchers, Inc.

"Now let's prove that a nutrient X deficiency causes illness Y by inducing a deficiency in these rats."

study findings. This slow path of repeated studies stands in sharp contrast to the media's desire for today's latest news.

To repeat: the only source of valid nutrition information is slow, painstaking, authentic scientific research. We believe a nutrition fact to be true because it has been supported, time and again, in experiments designed to rule out all other possibilities. For example, we know that eyesight depends partly on vitamin A because

- In case studies, individuals with blindness report having consumed a steady diet devoid of vitamin A, and
- In epidemiological studies, populations with diets lacking in vitamin A are observed to suffer high rates of blindness, and
- In intervention studies (**controlled clinical trials**), vitamin A–rich foods provided to groups of vitamin A–deficient people reduce their blindness rates dramatically, and

controlled clinical trial a research study design that often reveals the effects of a treatment in human beings. Health outcomes are observed in a group of people who receive the treatment and are then compared with outcomes in a control group of similar people who received a placebo (an inert or sham treatment). Ideally, neither subjects nor researchers know who receives the treatment and who gets the placebo (a double-blind study).

TABLE 1-7 Research Design Terms

- **blind experiment** an experiment in which the subjects do not know whether they are members of the experimental group or the control group. In a *double-blind experiment,* neither the subjects nor the researchers know to which group the members belong until the end of the experiment.
- **case studies** studies of individuals. In clinical settings, researchers can observe treatments and their apparent effects. To prove that a treatment has produced an effect requires simultaneous observation of an untreated similar subject (a *case control*).
- **control group** a group of individuals who are similar in all possible respects to the group being treated in an experiment but who receive a sham treatment instead of the real one. Also called *control subjects.* See also *experimental group* and *intervention studies.*
- **correlation** the simultaneous change of two factors, such as the increase of weight with increasing height (a *direct* or *positive* correlation) or the decrease of cancer incidence with increasing fiber intake (an *inverse* or *negative* correlation). A correlation between two factors suggests that one may cause the other but does not rule out the possibility that both may be caused by chance or by a third factor.
- **epidemiological studies** studies of populations; often used in nutrition to search for correlations between dietary habits and disease incidence; a first step in seeking nutrition-related causes of diseases.
- **experimental group** the people or animals participating in an experiment who receive the treatment under investigation. Also called *experimental subjects.* See also *control group* and *intervention studies.*
- **intervention studies** studies of populations in which observation is accompanied by experimental manipulation of some population members—for example, a study in which half of the subjects (the *experimental subjects*) follow diet advice to reduce fat intakes while the other half (the *control subjects*) do not, and both groups' heart health is monitored.
- **laboratory studies** studies that are performed under tightly controlled conditions and are designed to pinpoint causes and effects. Such studies often use animals as subjects.
- **placebo** a sham treatment often used in scientific studies; an inert harmless medication. The *placebo effect* is the healing effect that the act of treatment, rather than the treatment itself, often has.

- In laboratory studies, animals deprived of vitamin A and only that vitamin begin to go blind; when it is restored soon enough in the diet, their eyesight returns, and
- Further laboratory studies elucidated the molecular mechanisms for vitamin A activity in eye tissues, and
- Replication of these studies provides the same results.

Now we can say with certainty, "eyesight depends upon sufficient vitamin A."

KEY POINT Nutrition knowledge builds slowly through years of research. Single studies must be replicated before their findings can be considered valid.

Can I Trust the Media to Deliver Nutrition News?

The news media are hungry for new findings, and reporters often latch onto ideas from the scientific laboratories before they have been fully tested. Also, a reporter who lacks a strong understanding of science may misunderstand complex scientific principles. To tell the truth, sometimes scientists get excited about their findings,

TABLE 1-8 The Anatomy of a Research Article

Here's what you can expect to find inside a research article:

- *Abstract.* The abstract provides a brief overview of the article.
- *Introduction.* The introduction clearly states the purpose of the current study.
- *Review of literature.* A review of the literature reveals all that science has uncovered on the subject to date.
- *Methodology.* The methodology section defines key terms and describes the procedures used in the study.
- *Results.* The results report the findings and may include summary tables and figures.
- *Conclusions.* The conclusions drawn are those supported by the data and reflect the original purpose as stated in the introduction. Usually, they answer a few questions and raise several more.
- *References.* The references list relevant studies (including key studies several years old as well as current ones).

MY TURN

© Cengage Learning

Gabriel

Lose Weight While You Sleep!

See two students talking about how they learned the truth about nutrition claims made in advertising.

CENGAGENOW To hear their stories, log on to www.cengage.com/sso

Did You Know?

Some newspapers, magazines, talk shows, Internet websites, and other media strive for accuracy in reporting, but others specialize in sensationalism that borders on quackery—see this chapter's Controversy for details.

too, and leak them to the press before they have been through a rigorous review by the scientists' peers. As a result, the public is often exposed to late-breaking nutrition news stories before the findings are fully confirmed. Then, when the hypothesis being tested fails to hold up to a later challenge, consumers feel betrayed by what is simply the normal course of science at work.

It also follows that people who take action based on single studies are almost always acting impulsively, not scientifically. The real scientists are trend watchers. They evaluate the methods used in each study, assess each study in light of the evidence gleaned from other studies, and modify little by little their picture of what is true. As evidence accumulates, the scientists become more and more confident about their ability to make recommendations that apply to people's health and lives. The Consumer Corner in this chapter offers some tips for evaluating news stories about nutrition.

Sometimes media sensationalism overrates the importance of even true, replicated findings. For example, a few years ago the media eagerly reported that oat bran lowers blood cholesterol, a lipid indicative of heart disease risk. Although the reports were true, oat bran is only one of several hundred factors that affect blood cholesterol. News reports on oat bran often failed to mention that cutting intakes of certain fats is still the major step to take to lower blood cholesterol.

- The links between lipids and heart disease are discussed in Chapters 5 and 11.

Also, new findings need refinements. Oat bran and oatmeal truly are cholesterol reducers, but how much must a person eat to produce the desired effects? Do little oat bran pills or powders meet the need? Do oat bran cookies? If so, how many cookies? For oatmeal, it takes a bowl-and-a-half daily to affect blood lipids. A few cookies cannot provide nearly so much and certainly cannot undo all the damage from a high-fat meal.

Today, oat bran's cholesterol-lowering effect is established, and labels on food packages can proclaim that a diet high in oats may reduce the risk of heart disease. The whole process of discovery, challenge, and vindication took almost 10 years of research. Some other lines of research have taken many years longer. In science, a single finding almost never makes a crucial difference to our knowledge as a whole, but like each individual frame in a movie, it contributes a little to the big picture. Many such frames are needed to tell the whole story.

KEY POINT News media often sensationalize single study findings, and are not always trustworthy sources of nutrition information.

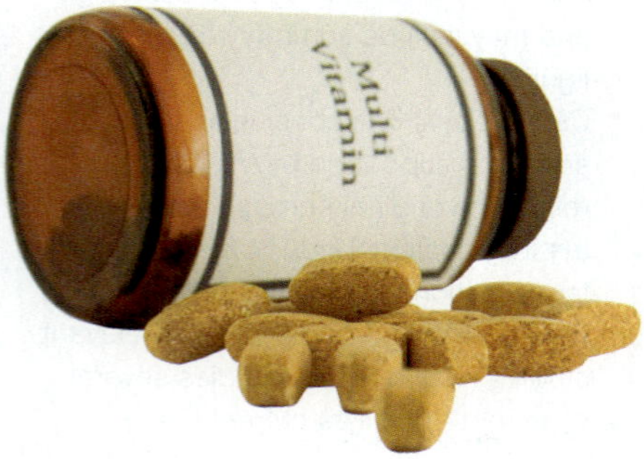

© Mona Makela, 2011/Shutterstock.com

National Nutrition Research

As you study nutrition, you are likely to hear of findings based on two ongoing national scientific research projects. The first, the National Health and Nutrition

CONSUMER CORNER

Reading Nutrition News with an Educated Eye

A newspaper reader, who had sworn off butter years ago for his heart's sake, bemoaned this headline: *"Margarine as Bad as Butter for Heart Health."* "Do you mean to say that I could have been eating butter all these years? That's it. I quit. No more diet changes for me." His response is understandable—diet changes, after all, take effort to make and commitment to sustain. He, like many others, feels betrayed when, years later, science appears to have turned its advice upside down.

It bears repeating: a single study never proves or disproves anything. Study results may support one view or another, but they rarely merit the sort of finality implied by journalistic phrases such as "Now we know" or "The answer has been found." Misinformed readers looking for simple answers to complex nutrition problems often take such phrases literally.

To read news stories with an educated eye, keep these points in mind:

- A scientific study under discussion should be published in a peer-reviewed journal, such as the *American Journal of Clinical Nutrition.* An unpublished study or one from a less credible source may or may not be valid; the reader has no way of knowing because the study lacks scrutiny by other experts.
- The news report should describe the researchers' methods; in truth, few provide these details. For example, it matters whether the study participants numbered 8 or 8,000, and whether researchers personally observed participants' behaviors or relied on self-reports given over the telephone.
- The report should define the study subjects—single cells, animals, or human beings. If they were human beings, the more you have in common with them (age and gender, for example), the more applicable the findings may be for you.
- Valid reports also present new findings in the context of previous research. Some reporters regularly follow developments in a research area and thus acquire the background knowledge needed to write meaningfully.
- Review articles provide a broad perspective on a single topic; they appear in journals such as *Nutrition Reviews.* Review articles describe findings of many studies on the same topic.

A person wanting the whole story on a nutrition topic is wise to seek articles from peer-reviewed journals such as these. A review journal examines all available evidence on major topics. Other journals report details of the methods, results, and conclusions of single studies.

Finally, ask yourself if the study makes sense for you. Even if it turns out that the fat of margarine is damaging to the heart, do you eat enough margarine to worry about its effects? Is butter even worse? When a headline touts a shocking new "answer" to a nutrition question, read the story with a critical eye. It may indeed be a carefully researched report, but often it is a sensational story intended to catch the attention of newspaper and magazine buyers, not to offer useful nutrition information.

Examination Surveys (NHANES), is a nationwide project that gathers information from about 50,000 people using diet histories, physical examinations and measurements, and laboratory tests. Boiled down to its essence, NHANES involves

- asking people what they have eaten;
- recording measures of their health status.

The second project is the Continuing Survey of Food Intakes by Individuals (CSFII), which involves

- recording what people have actually eaten for two days;
- comparing the foods they have chosen with recommended food selections.

Nutrition monitoring makes it possible for research scientists to assess the nutrient status, health indicators, and dietary intakes of the U.S. population. The agencies involved with these efforts are listed in the margin.

KEY POINT Ongoing national nutrition research provides data on food consumption and nutrient status of the U.S. population.

- Agencies active in nutrition policy, research, and monitoring:
  - *Department of Health and Human Services (DHHS).*
  - *United States Department of Agriculture (USDA).*
  - *Centers for Disease Control and Prevention (CDC).*
- Ongoing national nutrition research projects:
  - *National Health and Nutrition Examination Surveys (NHANES).*
  - *Continuing Survey of Food Intakes by Individuals (CSFII).*

LO 1.7

A Guide to Behavior Change

Nutrition knowledge is of little value if it only helps people to make As on tests. The value comes when people use it to improve their diets. To act on knowledge, people must change their behaviors, and while this may sound simple enough, behavior change often takes substantial effort.

Otto Greule Jr./Time Life Pictures/Getty Images

Many people need to change their daily routines to include physical activity.

The Process of Change

Psychologists describe six stages of behavior change, offered in Table 1-9. Knowing these stages can help you to recognize where you stand in relation to your own goals. Table 1-9 also demonstrates how to use this information to move forward in achieving your behavior change goals.

Assessments and Goals

To make a change, you must first be aware of a problem. Some problems, such as *never* consuming a vegetable, can be easy to spot. More subtle dietary problems, such as failing to meet your need for a particular vitamin or mineral, can have serious repercussions but often must be revealed by a study of the diet. Tracking food intakes over several days' time and then comparing intakes to standards (see Chapter 2) is a revealing exercise. Then, setting small, achievable goals in areas that need changing is the next step to making improvements. Realistic goals for body weight are discussed in Chapter 9.

- A dietary analysis computer program is available on the CengageNow website (**www.cengage.com/sso**) to help you through the process of examining your diet and comparing it to standards.

Obstacles to Change

It is a rare person who, upon setting out to change a behavior, encounters only smooth progress toward the final goal. Obstacles that derail plans or cause **lapses** often arise in these general areas:

- Competence—the person lacks needed knowledge or skill to make the change.
- Confidence—the person possesses the needed knowledge and skills but *believes* that the needed change is beyond the scope of his or her ability or that the problem lies outside the realm of personal control.
- **Motivation**—the person possesses both competence and confidence but lacks sufficient reason to change.

lapses times of falling back into former habits, a normal and expected part of behavior change.

motivation the force that moves people to act. Motivation may be either instinctive (inborn drives such as hunger and thirst) or learned (such as the drive to acquire possessions or to improve health).

TABLE 1-9 Stages of Behavior Change

Stage	Characteristics	Actions
Precontemplation	Not considering a change, have no intention of changing; see no problems with current behavior.	Collect information about health effects of current behavior and potential benefits of change.
Contemplation	Admit that change may be needed; weigh pros and cons of changing and not changing.	Commit to making a change and set a date to start.
Preparation	Preparing to change a specific behavior, taking initial steps, and setting some goals.	Write an action plan, spelling out specific parts of the change. Set small-step goals; tell others about the plan.
Action	Committing time and energy to making a change; following a plan set for a specific behavior change.	Perform the new behavior. Manage emotional and physical reactions to the change.
Maintenance	Striving to integrate the new behavior into daily life and striving to make it permanent.	Persevere through lapses. Teach others and help them achieve their own goals. (This stage can last for years.)
Adoption/Moving On	The former behavior is gone and the new behavior is routine.	After months or a year of maintenance without lapses, move on to other goals.

Competence The first obstacle, competence, is by far the most easily corrected. For example, a student who recognizes a lack of vegetables in her diet and wishes to increase her intake may not know how to prepare vegetables. Seeking information from a family cook can supply the missing knowledge, and trying out some recipes can bolster her skills. To deal with a serious threat, such as an eating disorder or excessive alcohol intake, outside help from reputable agencies may be needed to accomplish a change.

Confidence When a task seems insurmountable, confidence flags. Our vegetable-deprived student who sets the broad goal "I will eat all of the vegetables I need every day" might grumble, "I'll never be able to eat all those vegetables—I give up." If, instead, she sets a small, specific goal, such as "I will purchase carrot sticks tomorrow and eat them for my snacks this week," she may feel empowered to attempt it. Jotting down records of her snacks allows her to measure her success and identify obstacles to vegetable consumption.

People who take action and often succeed tend to be those with the quality of **self-efficacy,** that is, they believe in their own abilities. To boost self-efficacy, it helps to develop a strong internal **locus of control**—the belief that the individual has control over life's events. The opposite, an *external* locus of control, leaves one feeling helpless against outside forces, such as luck or fate. In other words, the more you believe in yourself and your ability to change your life for the better, the more likely that you will succeed in doing so.

Motivation The toughest obstacle to changing, however, may be a lack of motivation. Even if our student possesses both competence and confidence, she will not make a change unless she has sufficient motivation to do so: "I'm healthy now—why should I bother to eat more vegetables?" Motivation arises when the expected benefit or reward of the behavior change outweighs its perceived costs.

The Concept of Rewards Motivation is often based on the concept of rewards—the person making a change must expect that important rewards will follow the altered behaviors. Rewards are affected by four factors:

1. The value of the reward. (How big is the reward?)
2. Its timing. (How soon will the reward come, or how soon will the price have to be paid?)
3. The costs. (What will be the risks or consequences of seeking the reward?)
4. Its probability. (How likely is the reward to occur, and how certain the price?)

If motivation to make dietary changes eludes people, the reason is often because of timing, cost, and probability factors. They have to wait too long to receive the reward, or they perceive too high a cost, or they aren't sure they'll ever receive it. Here's an example:

- If you enjoy ice cream now (reward now), you won't notice your weight gain until next month (pay later).
- If you forgo the pleasure of eating ice cream now (pay now), you can't expect to see any weight loss until next month (reward later).

No wonder so many people fail to change their poor food habits!

Start Now

It is natural, as you progress through this text, to contemplate changing some of your own food habits. If you are ready to move beyond contemplation to preparation and action, the CengageNow Internet website offers some help. Little reminders entitled *Start Now* that appear at the end of each of this book's chapters invite you to visit the website to take inventory of your current behaviors, to set goals for a needed change, and to follow through until the new behavior becomes as comfortable and familiar as the old one once was.

Did You Know?

Outside help for making a change may be available from the professionals at a campus health center, counseling center, or community helping agency.

- If you wish to make a change during your study of nutrition, you can find help at the website **www.cengage.com/sso.** There, a series of exercises can help you to:
  - *Assess your current diet and exercise habits.*
  - *Identify behaviors to improve.*
  - *Determine your readiness to change.*
  - *Create a plan for change.*
  - *Track your efforts toward making the change.*

self-efficacy the belief in one's ability to take action and successfully perform a specific behavior.

locus of control the assigned source of responsibility for one's life events; an internal locus of control identifies the individual's behaviors as the driving force; an external locus of control blames chance, fate, or some other external factor. Most people's attitude falls somewhere in between.

FOOD FEATURE

How Can I Get Enough Nutrients Without Consuming Too Many Calories?

According to the experts, people in the United States are not very successful at selecting diets that meet their nutrition needs. In particular, only a tiny percentage of adults manage to achieve both adequacy and moderation. In trying to control calories while balancing the diet and making it adequate, certain foods are especially useful. These foods are rich in nutrients relative to their energy contents; that is, they are foods with high **nutrient density.**[22] Figure 1-5 is a simple depiction of this concept. Consider calcium sources, for example. Ice cream and fat-free milk both supply calcium, but the milk is denser in calcium per calorie. A cup of rich ice cream contributes more than 350 calories, a cup of fat-free milk only 85—and with almost double the calcium. Most people cannot, for their health's sake, afford to choose foods without regard to their energy contents. Those who do very often exceed calorie allowances while leaving nutrient needs unmet.

Nutrient density is such a useful concept in diet planning that this book encourages you to think in those terms. Right away, the next chapter asks you to apply your knowledge of nutrient density while developing skills in meal planning. Watch for tables and figures in later chapters that show the best buys among foods, not necessarily in nutrients per dollar, but in nutrients per calorie. Among foods that often rank high in nutrient density are the vegetables, particularly the nonstarchy vegetables such as broccoli, carrots, mushrooms, peppers, and tomatoes. These inexpensive foods take time to prepare, but time invested in this way pays off in nutritional health. Twenty minutes spent peeling and slicing vegetables for a salad is a better investment in nutrition than 20 minutes spent fixing a fancy, high-fat, high-sugar dessert. Besides, the dessert ingredients often cost more money and strain the calorie budget, too.[23]

nutrient density a measure of nutrients provided per calorie of food.

FIGURE 1-5 A Way to Judge Which Foods Are Most Nutritious

Some foods deliver more nutrients for the same number of calories than others do. These two breakfasts provide about 500 calories each, but they differ greatly in the nutrients they provide per calorie. Note that the sausage in the larger breakfast is lower-calorie turkey sausage, not the high-calorie pork variety. Making small choices like this at each meal can add up to large calorie savings, making room in the diet for more servings of nutritious foods and even some treats.

Time, however, is another concern. Today's working families, college students, and active people of all ages may have little time to devote to food preparation. Busy chefs should seek out convenience foods that are nutrient-dense, such as bags of ready-to-serve salads, refrigerated prepared low-fat meats and poultry, canned beans, and frozen vegetables. Dried fruit and dry-roasted nuts require only that they be kept on hand and make a tasty, nutritious topper for salads and other foods. To round out the meal, fat-free milk is both nutritious and convenient. Other convenient selections, such as most pot pies, many frozen pizzas, ramen noodles, and "pocket"-style sandwiches, are less nutritious overall because they contain too few vegetables and too many calories, making them low in nutrient density. The Food Features of later chapters offer many more tips for choosing convenient and nutritious foods.

All of this discussion leads to a principle that is central to achieving nutritional health: It is not the individual foods you choose, but the way you combine them into meals and the way you arrange meals to follow one another over days and weeks that determine how well you are nourishing yourself. Nutrition is a science, not an art, but it can be used artfully to create a pleasing, nourishing diet. The remainder of this book is dedicated to helping you make informed choices and combine them artfully to meet all the body's needs.

Diet Analysis

PLUS + Concepts in Action

Track Your Diet

After each Food Feature section in this text, exercises like this one provide an ongoing diet analysis activity that asks you to apply what you've learned in the chapter to your own diet. To do so, use the Diet Analysis Plus (DA+) program that accompanies this book. To get started, do the following:

1. From the Home page of the DA+ program (after your personal data has been entered), select the Reports tab from the red navigation bar then Profile DRI Goals. Click Create PDF button. You will now have DRI values for calories, carbohydrates, and fat appropriate for your Profile.
2. For the next three days, with pencil and paper, keep track of everything you eat and drink. Be honest and careful in your record-keeping. Measure or estimate amounts of foods and beverages you consume, as well as margarine or butter, salt, cream sauces, gravies, pasta sauce, ketchup, relish, jams, jellies, and other add-ons. Even a slice of tomato and a lettuce leaf on a sandwich count toward the day's intake. Distribute your data among four meals for each day: breakfast, lunch, dinner, and snacks.
3. Keep track of your physical activity for all three of those days. Record all the minutes spent walking or biking to class, working out, vacuuming rugs, washing cars, playing sports, dancing with friends, or any other nonsedentary behavior. Hold on to this data: you'll need it in chapters to come.
4. From the Home page of DA+, select the Track Diet tab and enter each food item that you recorded for Day One, Day Two, and Day Three into the Find Foods area. When finished, select the Reports tab and go to Intake vs. Goals. Click the Generate Report button and choose all meals. What information on the report most surprised you?
5. From the Reports tab, go to Energy Balance. Using Day Two (from the three-day diet intake), choose all meals and generate a report. Was your calorie intake over or under the recommended calories (kcals) for your profile? Was it higher or lower than expected? You will analyze your energy balance in more detail later, in Chapter 9.

MEDIA MENU

CENGAGENOW Throughout this chapter, the CengageNOW logo indicates an opportunity for online self-study, linking you to interactive tutorials and videos based on your level of understanding. Go to **www.cengage.com/sso.**

Search for "nutrition" at the U.S. Government health and nutrition sites: **www.healthfinder.gov** or **www.nutrition.gov.**

Learn more about basic science research from the National Science Foundation and Research!America: **www.nsf.gov** and **researchamerica.org.**

View *Healthy People Objectives for the Nation:* **www.healthypeople.gov.**

Visit the food and nutrition center of the Mayo Clinic: **www.mayohealth.org.**

Create a chart of your family health history at the U.S. Surgeon General's site: **familyhistory.hhs.gov.**

SELF CHECK

Answers to these Self Check questions are in Appendix G.

1. Energy-yielding nutrients include all of the following except:
   A. vitamins
   B. carbohydrates
   C. fat
   D. protein
2. Organic nutrients include all of the following except:
   A. minerals
   B. fat

C. carbohydrates

D. protein

3. One of the characteristics of a nutritious diet is that the diet provides no constituent in excess. This principle of diet planning is called:

A. adequacy

B. balance

C. moderation

D. variety

4. A slice of peach pie supplies 357 calories with 48 units of vitamin A; one large peach provides 42 calories and 53 units of vitamin A. This is an example of:

A. calorie control

B. nutrient density

C. variety

D. essential nutrients

5. Which of the following is an example of a processed food?

A. carrots

B. bread

C. nuts

D. watermelon

6. Studies of populations in which observation is accompanied by experimental manipulation of some population members are referred to as:

A. case studies

B. intervention studies

C. laboratory studies

D. epidemiological studies

7. Both heart disease and cancer are due to genetic causes, and diet cannot influence whether they occur.

T F

8. Both carbohydrates and protein have 4 calories per gram.

T F

9. People most often choose foods for the nutrients they provide.

T F

10. The belief in one's own abilities is the quality of self-efficacy.

T F

CONTROVERSY 1

Sorting the Imposters from the Real Nutrition Experts

LO 1.8

From the time of salesmen selling snake oil from horse-drawn wagons to the Internet sales schemes of today, nutrition **quackery** has plagued the nation. Government attempts at quackery regulation and enforcement over the past decades have largely failed. To protect themselves, consumers must learn to distinguish authentic and useful nutrition products and services from the vast array of well-meaning but misinformed advice and outright scams used to steal people's money.

INFORMATION SOURCES AND COSTS OF WRONG CHOICES

Most people say that television is their source for nutrition information, with magazines a close second, and the Internet quickly gaining in popularity.[1]* Sometimes, these sources provide sound and scientific, and therefore trustworthy, information. More often, though, **infomercials, advertorials,** and **urban legends** (defined in Table C1-1) pretend to inform, but in fact aim to sell products by making fantastic promises for health or weight loss with minimal effort and at bargain prices.

When scam products are garden tools or stain removers, hoodwinked consumers may lose a few dollars and some pride. When the products are ineffective, untested, or even hazardous "dietary supplements" or "medical devices," consumers stand to lose the very thing they are seeking: good health. When a sick person wastes time with quack treatments, serious problems can easily advance while proper treatment is delayed.[2] And dietary supplements have inflicted liver failure and other dire outcomes on previously well people who took them in hopes of *improving* their health.

Each year, consumers spend a deluge of dollars on nutrition-related services and products from both legitimate and fraudulent businesses. Each year, nutrition and other health

*Reference notes are found in Appendix F.

© PictureNet/Corbis

Who is speaking on nutrition?

TABLE C1-1 Quackery and Internet Terms

- **advertorials** lengthy advertisements in newspapers and magazines that read like feature articles but are written for the purpose of touting the virtues of products and may or may not be accurate.
- **anecdotal evidence** information based on interesting and entertaining, but not scientific, personal accounts of events.
- **fraud** or **quackery** the promotion, for financial gain, of devices, treatments, services, plans, or products (including diets and supplements) claimed to improve health, well-being, or appearance without proof of safety or effectiveness. (The word *quackery* comes from the term *quacksalver,* meaning a person who quacks loudly about a miracle product—a lotion or a salve.)
- **infomercials** feature-length television commercials that follow the format of regular programs but are intended to convince viewers to buy products and not to educate or entertain them. The statements made may or may not be accurate.
- **Internet (the Net)** a worldwide network of millions of computers linked together to share information.
- **urban legends** stories, usually false, that may travel rapidly throughout the world via the Internet gaining strength of conviction solely on the basis of repetition.
- **websites** Internet resources composed of text and graphic files, each with a unique URL (Uniform Resource Locator) that names the site (for example, www .usda.gov).
- **World Wide Web** (the Web, commonly abbreviated **www**) a graphical subset of the Internet.

fraud diverts tens of *billions* of consumer dollars from legitimate health care.[3] Consumers with questions or suspicions about fraud can contact the FDA on the Internet at www.FDA.gov or by telephone at (888) INFO-FDA.

How can people learn to distinguish valid nutrition information from misinformation? Some quackery is easy to identify—like the claims of the salesman in Figure C1-1. Other fraudulent nutrition claims are subtle and so more difficult to detect.

Between the extremes of accurate scientific data and intentional quackery lies an abundance of less easily recognized nutrition misinformation.[4†] An instructor at a gym, a physician, a health-store clerk, an author of books, or an advocate for juice machines or weight-loss gadgets may all sincerely believe that the nutrition regimens they recommend are beneficial. But what qualifies them to give advice? Would following their advice be helpful or harmful? To sift the meaningful nutrition information from the rubble, you must first learn to recognize quackery wherever it presents itself.

†*Quackery-related definitions are available from the National Counsel Against Health Fraud, www.ncahf.org/pp/definitions.html.*

IDENTIFYING VALID NUTRITION INFORMATION

Nutrition derives information from scientific research, which has these characteristics:

- Scientists test their ideas by conducting properly designed scientific experiments. They report their methods and procedures in detail so that other scientists can verify the findings through replication.
- Scientists recognize the inadequacy of **anecdotal evidence** or testimonials.
- Scientists who use animals in their research do not apply their findings directly to human beings.
- Scientists may use specific segments of the population in their research. When they do, they are careful not to generalize the findings to all people.
- Scientists report their findings in respected scientific journals. Their work must survive a screening review

FIGURE C1-1 **Earmarks of Nutrition Quackery**

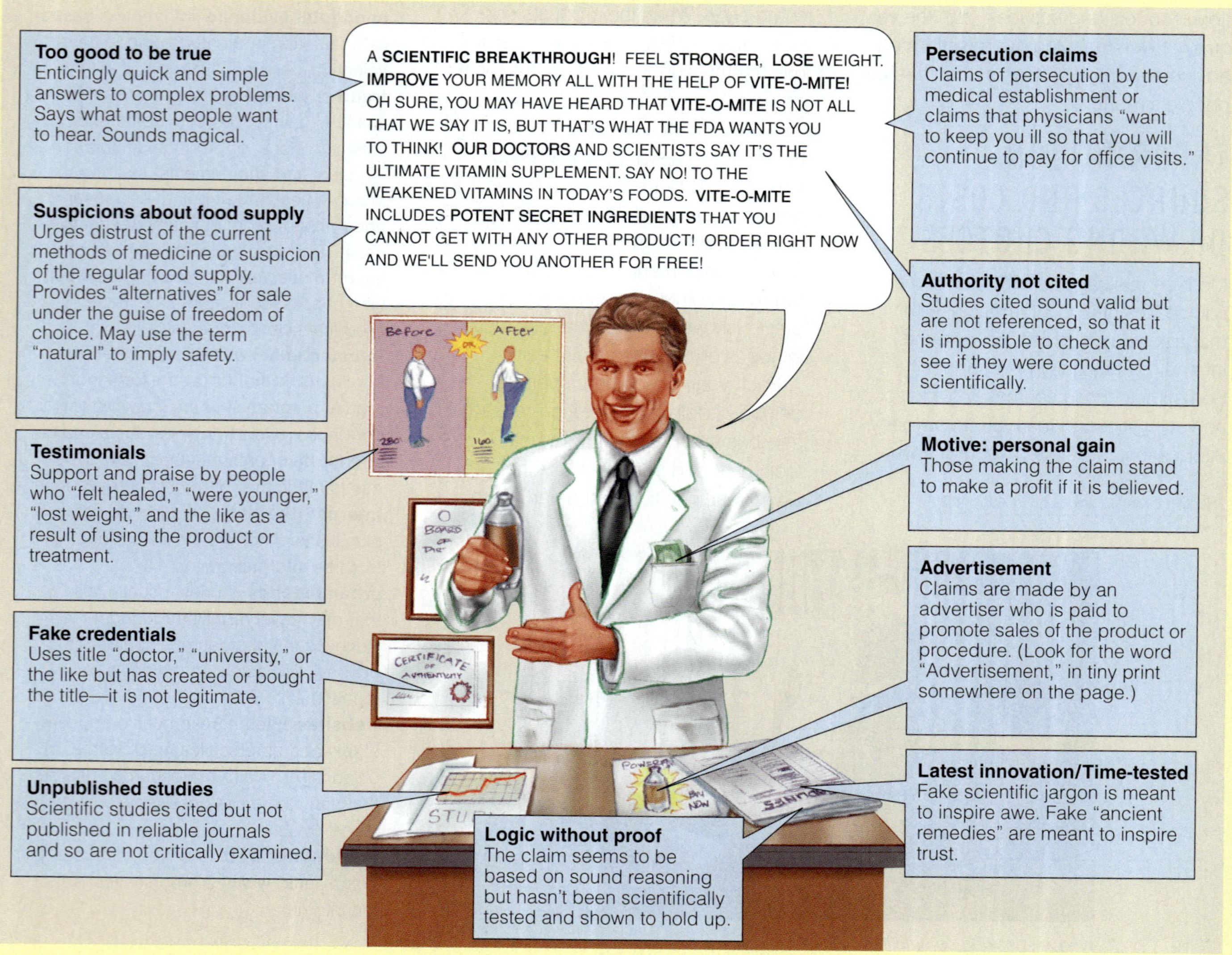

TABLE C1-2

Credible Sources of Nutrition Information

Professional health organizations, government health agencies, volunteer health agencies, and consumer groups provide consumers with reliable health and nutrition information. Credible sources of nutrition information include:

- Professional health organizations, especially the American Dietetic Association's National Center for Nutrition and Dietetics (NCND), www.eatright.org/ncnd.html, also the Society for Nutrition Education, www.sne.org and the American Diabetes Association, www.diabetes.org
- Government health agencies such as the Federal Trade Commission (FTC), www.ftc.gov and the National Institutes of Health Office of Dietary Supplements, www.dietary-supplements.info.nih.gov
- Certain consumer watchdog agencies such as the National Council Against Health Fraud, www.ncahf.org, Stephen Barrett's Quackwatch, www.quackwatch.com, and Snopes.com—Rumor Has It, www.snopes.com
- Reputable consumer groups such as the Better Business Bureau, www.bbb.org, the Consumers Union, www.consumersunion.org and the American Council on Science and Health, www.acsh.org

TABLE C1-3

Is This Site Reliable?

To judge whether an Internet site offers reliable nutrition information, answer the following questions.

- **Who is responsible for the site?** Clues can be found in the three-letter "tag" that follows the dot in the site's name. For example, "gov" and "edu" indicate government and university sites, usually reliable sources of information.
- **Do the names and credentials of information providers appear? Is an editorial board identified?** Many legitimate sources provide e-mail addresses or other ways to obtain more information about the site and the information providers behind it.
- **Are links with other reliable information sites provided?** Reputable organizations almost always provide links with other similar sites because they want you to know of other experts in their area of knowledge. Caution is needed when you evaluate a site by its links, however. Anyone, even a quack, can link a webpage to a reputable site without the organization's permission. Doing so may give the quack's site the appearance of legitimacy, just the effect the quack is hoping for.
- **Is the site updated regularly?** Nutrition information changes rapidly, and sites should be updated often.
- **Is the site selling a product or service?** Commercial sites may provide accurate information, but they also may not, and their profit motive increases the risk of bias.
- **Does the site charge a fee to gain access to it?** Many academic and government sites offer the best information, usually for free. Some legitimate sites do charge fees, but before paying up, check the free sites. Chances are good you'll find what you are looking for without paying.
- **Some other credible websites include:**
  - Government agencies
    Department of Agriculture (USDA)
    www.usda.gov
    Department of Health and Human Services (DHHS)
    www.os.dhhs.gov
    Food and Drug Administration (FDA)
    www.fda.gov
    Health Canada
    www.hc-sc.gc.ca/index-eng.php
  - Volunteer health agencies
    American Cancer Society
    www.cancer.org
    American Diabetes Association
    www.diabetes.org
    American Heart Association
    www.americanheart.org
  - Reputable consumer and professional groups:
    American Council on Science and Health
    www.acsh.org
    American Dietetic Association
    www.eatright.org
    American Medical Association
    www.ama-assn.org
    Dietitians of Canada
    www.dietitians.ca
    Federal Citizen Information Center
    www.pueblo.gsa.gov
    International Food Information Council
    www.ific.org
  - Journals
    American Journal of Clinical Nutrition
    www.ajcn.org
    Journal of the American Dietetic Association
    www.adajournal.org
    New England Journal of Medicine
    www.nejm.org
    Nutrition Reviews
    www.ilsi.org

by their peers before it is accepted for publication.

With each report from scientists, the field of nutrition changes a little—each finding contributes another piece to the whole body of knowledge. Table C1-2 lists some sources of credible nutrition information.

NUTRITION ON THE NET

Got a question? The **World Wide Web** on the **Internet** has an answer. The Internet offers endless opportunities to obtain high-quality information, but it also delivers an abundance of incomplete, misleading, or inaccurate information.[5] Simply put: anyone can publish anything on the Internet. For example, popular self-governed Internet "encyclopedia" **websites** allow anyone to post information or change others' postings on topics.‡ Information on the sites may be correct, but it may not be—readers must evaluate it for themselves. Table C1-3 provides some clues to judging the reliability of nutrition information websites.

‡*An example is Wikipedia.*

Hoaxes and scare stories abound on websites and in e-mails. Be suspicious when:

- The contents were written by someone other than the sender or some authority you know.
- A phrase like "Forward this to everyone you know" appears anywhere in the piece.

- The piece states "This is not a hoax"; chances are, it is.
- The information seems shocking or something that you've never heard from legitimate sources.
- The language is overly emphatic or sprinkled with capitalized words or exclamation marks.
- No references are offered or, if present, are of questionable validity when examined.
- The message has been debunked on websites such as www.quackwatch.com or www.urbanlegends.com.

Of course, these hints alone are insufficient to judge nutrition information from any source. The user must also scrutinize "nutrition experts" who make statements, even when they possess legitimate degrees, as described in the next section.

In contrast, one of the most trustworthy sites for scientific investigation is the National Library of Medicine's PubMed website, which provides free access to over 10 million abstracts (short descriptions) of research papers published in scientific journals around the world. Many abstracts provide links to full articles posted on other sites. The site is easy to use and offers instructions for beginners. Figure C1-2 introduces this resource.

WHO ARE THE TRUE NUTRITION EXPERTS?

Most people turn to their physicians for dietary advice. Physicians are expected to know all about health-related matters. Only about 30 percent of all medical schools in the United States require students to take a comprehensive nutrition course; less than half require the minimum 25 hours of nutrition instruction recommended by the National Academy of Sciences.[6] By comparison, most students reading this text are taking a nutrition class that provides an average of 45 hours of instruction.

The American Dietetic Association

The **American Dietetic Association (ADA),** the professional association of dietitians, asserts that nutrition education should be part of the curriculum for health-care professionals: physicians' assistants, dental hygienists, physical and occupational therapists, social workers, and all others who provide services directly to clients. This plan would bring access to reliable nutrition information to more people.

Physicians who specialized in clinical nutrition in medical school are highly qualified to advise on nutrition. Membership in the American Society for Clinical Nutrition, whose journal is cited many times throughout this text, is another sign of nutrition knowledge. Still, few physicians have the knowledge, time, or experience to develop diet plans and provide detailed diet instruction for clients, and they often refer their clients to nutrition specialists. Table C1-4 lists the best specialists to choose.

Registered Dietitians: The Nutrition Specialists

Fortunately, the credential that indicates a qualified nutrition expert is easy to spot—you can confidently call on a **registered dietitian (RD).** Additionally, some states require that **nutritionists** and **dietitians** obtain a **license to practice.** Meeting state-established criteria in addition to **registration** with the American Dietetic Association certifies that an expert is the genuine article.

RDs are easy to find in most communities because they perform a multitude of duties in a variety of settings. They work in foodservice operations, pharmaceutical companies, sports nutrition programs, corporate wellness programs, the food industry, home health agencies, long-term care institutions, private practice, community and public health settings, cooperative extension offices,[§] research centers, universities and other educational settings, and hospitals, health maintenance organizations (HMOs), and other health-care facilities.

FIGURE C1-2 **PubMed (www.ncbi.nlm.nih.gov/pubmed): Internet Resource for Scientific Nutrition References**

The U.S. National Library of Medicine's PubMed website offers tutorials to help teach the beginner to use the search system effectively. Often, simply visiting the site, typing a query in the "Search for" box, and clicking "Search" will yield satisfactory results.

For example, to find research concerning calcium and bone health, typing in "calcium bone" nets almost 3,000 results. To refine the search, try setting limits on dates, types of articles, languages, and other criteria to obtain a more manageable number of abstracts to peruse.

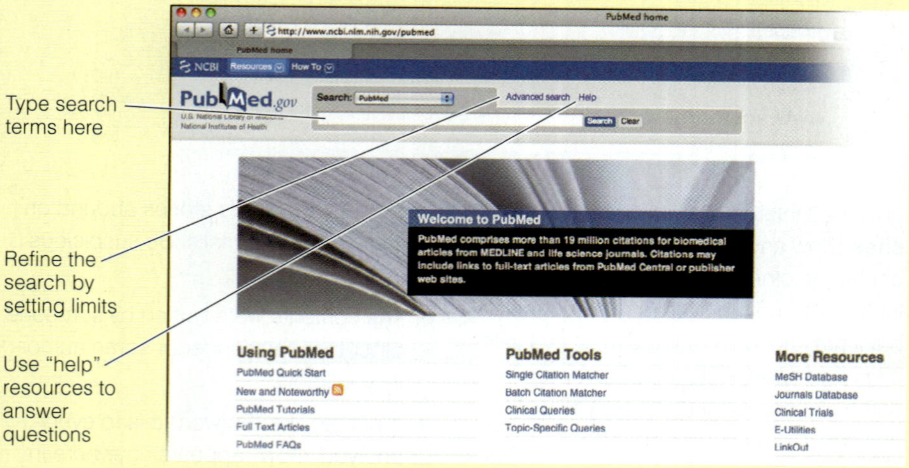

[§]Cooperative extension agencies are associated with land grant colleges and universities and may be found in the phone book's government listings.

TABLE C1-4 Terms Associated with Nutrition Advice

- **American Dietetic Association (ADA)** the professional organization of dietitians in the United States. The Canadian equivalent is the Dietitians of Canada (DC), which operates similarly.
- **certified diabetes educator (CDE)** a health-care professional who specializes in educating people with diabetes to help them manage their disease through medical and lifestyle means. Extensive training, work experience, and an examination are required to achieve CDE status.
- **dietetic technician** a person who has completed a two-year academic degree from an accredited college or university and an approved dietetic technician program. A **dietetic technician, registered** (DTR) has also passed a national examination and maintains registration through continuing professional education.
- **dietitian** a person trained in nutrition, food science, and diet planning. See also *registered dietitian.*
- **license to practice** permission under state or federal law, granted on meeting specified criteria, to use a certain title (such as *dietitian*) and to offer certain services. Licensed dietitians may use the initials LD after their names.
- **medical nutrition therapy** nutrition services used in the treatment of injury, illness, or other conditions; includes assessment of nutrition status and dietary intake and corrective applications of diet, counseling, and other nutrition services.
- **nutritionist** someone who studies nutrition. Some nutritionists are RDs, whereas others are self-described experts whose training is questionable and who are not qualified to give advice. In states with responsible legislation, the term applies only to people who have master of science (MS) or doctor of philosophy (PhD) degrees from properly accredited institutions.
- **public health nutritionist** a dietitian or other person with an advanced degree in nutrition who specializes in public health nutrition.
- **registered dietitian (RD)** a dietitian who has graduated from a university or college after completing a program of dietetics. The program must be approved or accredited by the American Dietetic Association (or Dietitians of Canada). The dietitian must serve in an approved internship, coordinated program, or preprofessional practice program to practice the necessary skills; pass the five parts of the association's registration examination; and maintain competency through continuing education.[a] Many states also require licensing for practicing dietitians.
- **registration** listing with a professional organization that requires specific course work, experience, and passing of an examination.

[a]*The five content areas of the registration examination for dietitians are food and nutrition; clinical and community nutrition; education and research; food and nutrition systems; and management. New emphasis is placed on genetics, cultural competency, complementary care, and reimbursement.*

RDs in hospitals have many subspecialties. Administrative dietitians manage the foodservice system; clinical dietitians provide client care and are leaders in disease prevention services (see Table C1-5); and nutrition support team dietitians coordinate nutrition care, such as **medical nutrition therapy,** with the efforts of other health-care professionals.[7] A registered dietitian can become a **certified diabetes educator (CDE),** a specialist who educates people with diabetes about the management of their disease.

In the food industry, dietitians conduct research, develop products, and market services. In government, **public health nutritionists** play key roles in delivering nutrition services to people in the community. A public health nutritionist may plan, coordinate, administer, and evaluate food assistance programs; act as a consultant to other agencies; manage finances; and much more.

In some facilities, a **dietetic technician** assists registered dietitians in both administrative and clinical responsibilities. A dietetic technician has been educated and trained to work under the guidance of a registered dietitian; upon passing a national examination, the technician earns the title **dietetic technician, registered (DTR).**

TABLE C1-5 Selected Responsibilities of a Clinical Dietition

The first six items in this list play essential roles in medical nutrition therapy as part of a medical treatment plan. Dietitians also play leading roles in health promotion and disease prevention.

- Assesses clients' nutrition status.
- Determines clients' nutrient requirements.
- Monitors clients' nutrient intakes.
- Develops, implements, and evaluates clients' medical nutrition therapy.
- Counsels clients to cope with unique diet plans.
- Teaches clients and their families about nutrition and diet plans.
- Provides training for other dietitians, nurses, interns, and dietetics students.
- Serves as liaison between clients and the foodservice department.
- Communicates with physicians, nurses, pharmacists, and other health-care professionals about clients' progress, needs, and treatments.
- Participates in professional activities to enhance knowledge and skill.

DETECTING FAKE CREDENTIALS

In contrast to RDs and other credentialed nutrition professionals, thousands of people possess fake nutrition degrees and claim to be nutrition counselors, nutritionists, or "dietists." These and other such titles may sound meaningful, but most of these people lack the established credentials of the ADA-sanctioned dietitian. If you look closely, you can see signs that their expertise is fake.

Educational Background

Take, for example, a nutrition expert's educational background. The minimum standards of education for a dietitian specify a bachelor of science (BS) degree in food science and human nutrition (or related fields) from an **accredited**

TABLE C1-6

Terms Describing Institutions of Higher Learning, Legitimate and Fradulent

- **accredited** approved; in the case of medical centers or universities, certified by an agency recognized by the U.S. Department of Education.
- **diploma mill** an organization that awards meaningless degrees without requiring its students to meet educational standards.

college or university (Table C1-6 defines this term). Such a degree generally requires four to five years of study.

In contrast, a fake nutrition expert may display a degree from a six-month course of study; such a degree is simply not the same. In some cases, schools posing as legitimate institutions are actually **diploma mills**—fraudulent businesses that sell certificates of competency to anyone who pays the fees, from under a thousand dollars for a bachelor's degree to several thousand for a doctorate. To obtain these "degrees," a candidate need not read any books or pass any examinations, and the only written work is a signature on a check.

Accreditation and Licensure

Lack of proper accreditation is the identifying sign of a fake educational institution. To guard educational quality, an accrediting agency recognized by the U.S. Department of Education certifies that certain schools meet the criteria defining a complete and accurate schooling, but in the case of nutrition, quack accrediting agencies cloud the picture. Fake nutrition degrees are available from schools "accredited" by more than 30 phony accrediting agencies.**

State laws do not necessarily help consumers distinguish experts from fakes; some states allow anyone to use the title *dietitian* or *nutritionist.* But other states have responded to the need by allowing only RDs or people with certain graduate degrees and state licenses to call themselves dietitians. Licensing provides a way to identify people who have met minimum standards of education and experience.

A Failed Attempt to Fail

To dramatize the ease with which anyone can obtain a fake nutrition degree, for $82 one writer enrolled in a nutrition diploma mill that billed itself as a correspondence school. She made every attempt to fail, intentionally answering all the examination questions incorrectly. Even so, she received a "nutritionist" certificate at the end of the course, together with a letter from the "school" officials explaining that they were sure she must have misread the test.

Would You Trust a Nutritionist Who Eats Dog Food?

In a similar stunt, Mr. Eddie Diekman was named a "professional member" of an association of nutrition "experts." For his efforts, Eddie received a diploma suitable for framing and displaying. Eddie is a cocker spaniel. His owner, Connie B. Diekman, then president of the American Dietetic Association, paid Eddie's tuition to prove that he could be awarded the title "nutritionist" merely by sending in his name.††

Staying Ahead of the Scammers

In summary, to stay one step ahead of the nutrition quacks, check a provider's qualifications. First look for the degrees and credentials listed after the person's name (such as MD, RD, MS, PhD, or LD). Next find out what you can about the reputations of the institutions that awarded the degrees. Then call your state's health-licensing agency and ask if dietitians are licensed in your state. If they are, find out whether the person giving you dietary advice has a license—and if not, find someone better qualified. Your health is your most precious asset, and protecting it is well worth the time and effort it takes to do so.

††The stunt described was patterned after that of the late Victor Herbert, whose cat Charlie and poodle Sassafras were also awarded nutritionist credentials by mail.

***To find out whether an online school is accredited, write the Distance Education and Training Council, Accrediting Commission, 1601 Eighteenth Street, NW, Washington, D.C. 20009; call (202) 234-5100; or visit their website (www.detc.org).*

To find out whether a school is properly accredited for a dietetics degree, write the American Dietetic Association, Division of Education and Research, 120 South Riverside Plaza, Suite 2000, Chicago, Illinois 60606-6995, phone: 800/877-1600; or visit their website (www.eatright.org/caade).

The American Council on Education publishes a directory of accredited institutions, professionally accredited programs, and candidates for accreditation in Accredited Institutions of Postsecondary Education Programs *(available at many libraries). For additional information, write the American Council on Education, One Dupont Circle NW, Suite 800, Washington, D.C. 20036; call (202) 939-9382; or visit their website (www.acenet.edu).*

© Courtesy of eatright.org

Eddie displays his professional credentials.

Nutrition Tools—Standards and Guidelines

2

DO YOU EVER . . .

- Wonder how scientists decide how much of each nutrient you need to consume each day?
- Dismiss government dietary recommendations as too simplistic to help you plan your diet?
- Consume the portions offered in restaurants and fast-food places, believing them to be in keeping with nutrition recommendations?
- Wish that your foods could boost your health by providing substances beyond the nutrients they contain?

Keep reading . . .

Learning Objectives

To find learning objective topics in this chapter, look for text headings with a corresponding "LO" number above the heading. After completing this chapter, you should be able to accomplish the following:

LO 2.1 Explain how RDA, AI, DV, and EAR serve different functions in describing nutrient values and discuss how each is used.

LO 2.2 List the major categories of the *Dietary Guidelines for Americans* and explain their importance to the population.

LO 2.3 Describe how foods are grouped in the USDA Food Guide and MyPyramid.

LO 2.4 Describe the concept of the discretionary calorie allowance, and explain how it can be used in diet planning.

LO 2.5 Plan a day's meals that follow the pattern of the USDA Food Guide within a given calorie budget.

LO 2.6 Define the term *functional foods,* and discuss some potential effects of such foods on human health.

© Norman Chan, 2011/Shutterstock.com

Eating well is easy in theory—just choose foods that supply appropriate amounts of the essential nutrients, fiber, phytochemicals, and energy without excess intakes of fat, sugar, and salt and be sure to get enough exercise to balance the foods you eat. In practice, eating well proves harder than it appears. Many people are overweight, or undernourished, or suffer from nutrient excesses or deficiencies that impair their health—that is, they are malnourished. You may not think that this statement applies to you, but you may already have less than optimal nutrient intakes and activity without knowing it. Accumulated over years, the effects of your habits can seriously impair the quality of your life.

Putting it positively, you can enjoy the best possible vim, vigor, and vitality throughout your life if you learn now to nourish yourself optimally. To learn how, you first need some general guidelines and the answers to several basic questions. How much energy and how much of each nutrient should you consume? How much physical activity do you need to balance your energy intake from food? Which types of foods supply which nutrients? How much of each type of food do you have to eat to get enough? And how can you eat all these foods without gaining weight? This chapter begins by identifying some ideals for nutrient intakes and ends by showing how to achieve them.

LO 2.1

Nutrient Recommendations

Nutrient recommendations are sets of "yardsticks," or standards, for measuring healthy people's energy and nutrient intakes. Nutrition experts use the recommendations to assess intakes and to offer advice on amounts to consume. Individuals may use them to decide how much of a nutrient they need to consume and how much is too much.

- A directory of recommendations:
  - *DRI lists—inside front cover pages A, B, and C.*
  - *Daily Values—see inside back cover, page Y.*

Dietary Reference Intakes

The standards in use in the United States and Canada are the **Dietary Reference Intakes (DRI).** A committee of nutrition experts from the United States and Canada develops and publishes the DRI.* The DRI committee has set values for all of the vitamins and minerals, as well as for carbohydrates, fiber, lipids, protein, water, and energy. Values for other food constituents that may play roles in health maintenance are forthcoming.

Another set of nutrient standards is useful for the person trying to make wise choices among packaged foods. These are the **Daily Values,** familiar to anyone who has read a food label. These standards—the DRI and Daily Values—are used and referred to so often that they are printed on the inside front and back cover pages of this book.

Dietary Reference Intakes (DRI) a set of four lists of values for measuring the nutrient intakes of healthy people in the United States and Canada. The four lists are Estimated Average Requirements (EAR), Recommended Dietary Allowances (RDA), Adequate Intakes (AI), and Tolerable Upper Intake Levels (UL).

Daily Values nutrient standards that are printed on food labels and on grocery store and restaurant signs. Based on nutrient and energy recommendations for a general 2,000-calorie diet, they allow consumers to compare foods with regard to nutrients and calorie contents.

Estimated Average Requirements (EAR) the average daily nutrient intake estimated to meet the requirement of half of the healthy individuals in a particular life stage and gender group; used in nutrition research and policymaking and is the basis upon which RDA values are set (see below).

Recommended Dietary Allowances (RDA) nutrient intake goals for individuals; the average daily nutrient intake level that meets the needs of nearly all (97 to 98 percent) healthy people in a particular life stage and gender group. Derived from the Estimated Average Requirements (see above).

KEY POINT The Dietary Reference Intakes are nutrient intake standards set for people living in the United States and Canada. The Daily Values are U.S. standards used on food labels.

Goals of the DRI Committee

For each nutrient, the DRI establish a number of values, each serving a different purpose. Most people need to focus on only two kinds of DRI values: those that set nutrient intake goals for individuals (RDA and AI, described next) and those that define an upper limit of safety for nutrient intakes (UL, addressed later). In total, the DRI include:

- **Estimated Average Requirements (EAR)**
- **Recommended Dietary Allowances (RDA)**

*This is a committee of the Food and Nutrition Board of the National Academy of Sciences' Institute of Medicine, working in association with Health Canada.

- **Adequate Intakes (AI)**
- **Tolerable Upper Intake Levels (UL)**

The following sections address the different DRI values, arranged by the goals of the DRI committee.

Goal #1. Setting Recommended Intake Values—RDA and AI One of the great advantages of the DRI values lies in their applicability to the diets of individuals.[1†] The committee offers two sets of values that individuals may use for their own nutrient intake goals: Recommended Dietary Allowances (RDA) and Adequate Intakes (AI).‡

The RDA form the indisputable bedrock of the DRI recommended intakes because they derive from solid experimental evidence and reliable observations—they are expected to meet the needs of almost all healthy people. AI values, in contrast, are based as far as possible on the available scientific evidence but also on some educated guesswork. Whenever the DRI committee finds insufficient evidence to generate an RDA, they establish an AI value instead. This book refers to the RDA and AI values collectively as the DRI recommended intakes.

Did You Know?

The DRI table on the inside front cover, page B distinguishes the RDA from AI values, but both kinds of values are intended as nutrient intake goals for individuals.

Goal #2. Facilitating Nutrition Research and Policy—EAR Another set of values established by the DRI committee, the Estimated Average Requirements (EAR), establishes nutrient requirements for given life stages and gender groups that researchers and nutrition policymakers use in their work. Public health officials may also use them to assess nutrient intakes of populations and make recommendations.

To set the EAR, the DRI committee decides on criteria for each nutrient based on its roles in the body and in reducing disease risks.[2] The EAR values form the scientific basis upon which the RDA values are set (a later section explains how).

- Tolerable Upper Intake Levels (UL) are listed on page C, inside the front cover.

Goal #3. Establishing Safety Guidelines—UL Beyond a certain point, it is unwise to consume large amounts of any nutrient, so the DRI committee sets the Tolerable Upper Intake Levels (UL) to identify potentially toxic levels of nutrient intake.[3] The UL are indispensable to consumers who take supplements or consume foods and beverages to which vitamins or minerals have been added—a group that includes almost everyone. Public health officials also rely on UL values to set safe upper limits for nutrients added to our food and water supplies.

Nutrient needs fall within a range, and a danger zone exists both below and above that range. Figure 2-1 on page 32 illustrates this point. People's tolerances for high doses of nutrients vary, so caution is in order when nutrient intakes approach the UL values.

Some nutrients do not have UL values. The absence of a UL for a nutrient does not imply that it is safe to consume it in any amount, however. It means only that insufficient data exist to establish a value.

Goal #4. Preventing Chronic Diseases The DRI committee also takes into account chronic disease prevention, wherever appropriate. For example, the committee set lifelong intake goals for the mineral calcium at the levels believed to lessen the likelihood of osteoporosis-related fractures in the later years.

In addition to the four basic DRI lists just named, the DRI committee also set healthy ranges of intake for carbohydrate, fat, and protein known as **Acceptable Macronutrient Distribution Ranges (AMDR).** Each of these three energy-yielding nutrients contributes to the day's total calorie intake, and their contributions can be expressed as a percentage of the total. According to the committee, a diet that provides adequate energy in the following proportions can provide adequate nutrients while reducing the risk of chronic diseases:

- 45 to 65 percent of calories from carbohydrate.

Adequate Intakes (AI) nutrient intake goals for individuals; the recommended average daily nutrient intake level based on intakes of healthy people (observed or experimentally derived) in a particular life stage and gender group and assumed to be adequate. Set whenever scientific data are insufficient to allow establishment of an RDA value.

Tolerable Upper Intake Levels (UL) the highest average daily nutrient intake level that is likely to pose no risk of toxicity to almost all healthy individuals of a particular life stage and gender group. Usual intake above this level may place an individual at risk of illness from nutrient toxicity.

Acceptable Macronutrient Distribution Ranges (AMDR) values for carbohydrate, fat, and protein expressed as percentages of total daily calorie intake; ranges of intakes set for the energy-yielding nutrients that are sufficient to provide adequate total energy and nutrients while reducing the risk of chronic diseases.

†Reference notes are found in Appendix F.
‡For simplicity, this book refers to two sets of nutrient goals (AI and RDA) collectively as the *DRI recommended intakes*. The AI values are not the scientific equivalent of the RDA, however.

FIGURE 2-1 The Naïve View Versus the Accurate View of Optimal Nutrient Intakes

Consuming too much of a nutrient endangers health, just as consuming too little does. The DRI recommended intake values fall within a safety range with the UL marking tolerable upper levels.

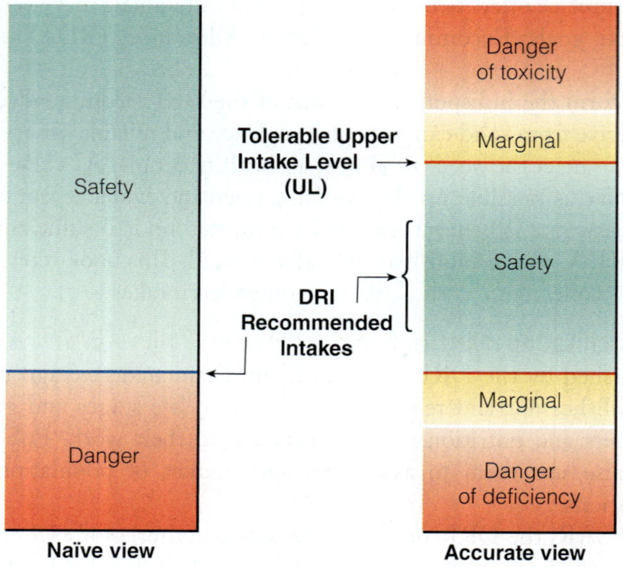

- 20 to 35 percent of calories from fat.
- 10 to 35 percent of calories from protein.

The chapters on the energy-yielding nutrients come back to these ranges.

KEY POINT The DRI provide nutrient intake goals for individuals, supply a set of standards for researchers and public policymakers, establish tolerable upper limits for nutrients that can be toxic in excess, and take into account evidence from research on disease prevention. The DRI are composed of the RDA, AI, UL, and EAR lists of values, along with the AMDR ranges for energy-yielding nutrients.

Photodisc/Getty Images

Don't let the "alphabet soup" of nutrient intake standards confuse you. Their names make sense when you learn their purposes.

Understanding the DRI Intake Recommendations

Nutrient recommendations have been much misunderstood. One young woman posed this question: "Do you mean that some bureaucrat says that I need exactly the same amount of vitamin D as every other young woman in my group? Do they really think that 'one size fits all'?"

DRI for Groups The DRI committee acknowledges differences between individuals. It has made separate recommendations for specific groups of people—men, women, pregnant women, lactating women, infants, and children—and for specific age ranges. Children aged 4 to 8 years, for example, have their own DRI recommended intakes. Each individual can look up the recommendations for his or her own age and gender group. Within your own age and gender group, the committee advises adjusting nutrient intakes in special circumstances that may increase or decrease nutrient needs, such as illness, smoking, or vegetarianism. Later chapters provide details about which nutrients may need adjustment.

For almost all healthy people, a diet that consistently provides the RDA or AI amount for a specific nutrient is very likely to be adequate in that nutrient. On average, you should try to get 100 percent of the DRI recommended intake for every nutrient to ensure an adequate intake over time.

Other Characteristics of the DRI The following facts will help put the DRI recommended intakes into perspective:

- The values are based on available scientific research to the greatest extent possible and are updated periodically in light of new knowledge.
- The values are based on the concepts of probability and risk. The DRI recommended intakes are associated with a low probability of deficiency for people of a given life stage and gender group, and they pose almost no risk of toxicity for that group.
- The values are recommendations for optimal intakes, not minimum requirements. They include a generous safety margin and meet the needs of virtually all healthy people in a specific age and gender group.
- The values are set in reference to certain indicators of nutrient adequacy, such as blood nutrient concentrations, normal growth, and reduction of certain chronic diseases or other disorders when appropriate, rather than prevention of deficiency symptoms alone.
- The values reflect daily intakes to be achieved, on average, over time. They assume that intakes will vary from day to day and are set high enough to ensure that the body's nutrient stores will meet nutrient needs during periods of inadequate intakes lasting several days to several months, depending on the nutrient.

The DRI Apply to Healthy People Only The DRI are designed for health maintenance and disease prevention in healthy people, not for the restoration of health or repletion of nutrients in those with deficiencies. Under the stress of serious illness or malnutrition, a person may require a much higher intake of certain nutrients or may not be able to handle even the DRI amount. Therapeutic diets take into account the increased nutrient needs imposed by certain medical conditions, such as recovery from surgery, burns, fractures, illnesses, malnutrition, or addictions.

KEY POINT The DRI represent up-to-date, optimal, and safe nutrient intakes for healthy people in the United States and Canada.

How the Committee Establishes DRI Values—An RDA Example

A theoretical discussion will help to explain how the DRI committee goes about setting DRI values. Suppose we are the DRI committee members with the task of setting an RDA for nutrient X (an essential nutrient).[§] Ideally, our first step will be to find out how much of that nutrient various healthy individuals need. To do so, we review studies of deficiency states, nutrient stores and their depletion, and the factors influencing them. We then select the most valid data for use in our work. Of the DRI family of nutrient standards, the setting of an RDA value demands the most rigorous science and tolerates the least guesswork.

Determining Individual Requirements One experiment we would review or conduct is a **balance study.** In this type of study, scientists measure the body's intake and excretion of a nutrient to find out how much intake is required to balance excretion. For each individual subject, we can determine a **requirement** to achieve balance for nutrient X. With an intake below the requirement, a person will slip into negative balance or experience declining stores that could, over time, lead to deficiency of the nutrient.

We find that different individuals, even of the same age and gender, have different requirements. Mr. A needs 40 units of the nutrient each day to maintain balance; Mr. B needs 35; Mr. C, 57. If we look at enough individuals, we find that their

[§]This discussion describes how an RDA value is set; to set an AI value, the committee would use some educated guesswork as well as scientific research results to determine an approximate amount of the nutrient most likely to support health.

balance study a laboratory study in which a person is fed a controlled diet and the intake and excretion of a nutrient are measured. Balance studies are valid only for nutrients like calcium (chemical elements) that do not change while they are in the body.

requirement the amount of a nutrient that will just prevent the development of specific deficiency signs; distinguished from the DRI recommended intake value, which is a generous allowance with a margin of safety.

FIGURE 2-2 **Individuality of Nutrient Requirements**

Each square represents a person. A, B, and C are Mr. A, Mr. B, and Mr. C. Each has a different requirement.

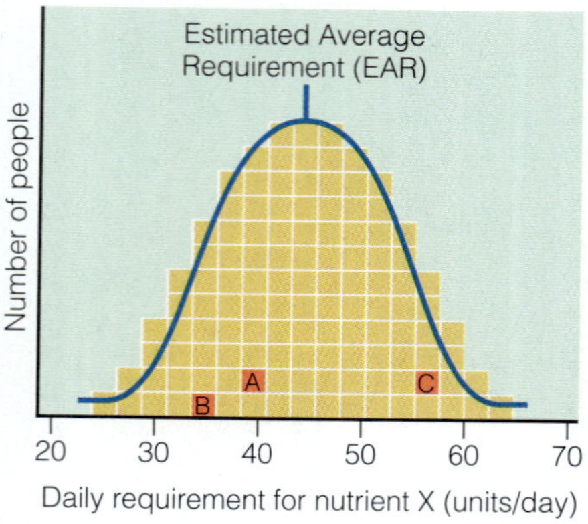

FIGURE 2-3 **Nutrient Recommended Intake: RDA Example**

Intake recommendations for most vitamins and minerals are set so that they will meet the requirements of nearly all people (boxes represent people).

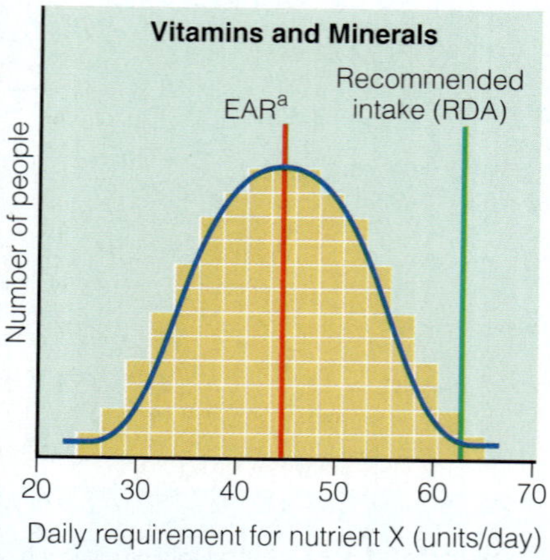

[a]Estimated Average Requirement

- The DRI Estimated Energy Requirements (EER) are found on the inside front cover, page A.

requirements are distributed as shown in Figure 2-2—with most requirements near the midpoint (here, 45) and only a few at the extremes.

Accounting for the Needs of the Population To set the value, we have to decide what intake to recommend for everybody. Should we set it at the mean (45 units in Figure 2-2)? This is the Estimated Average Requirement (EAR) for nutrient X, mentioned earlier as valuable to scientists but not appropriate as an individual's nutrient goal. The EAR value is probably close to everyone's minimum need, assuming the distribution shown in Figure 2-2. (Actually, the data for most nutrients indicate a distribution that is much less symmetrical.) But if people took us literally and consumed exactly this amount of nutrient X each day, half the population would begin to develop internal deficiencies and possibly even observable symptoms of deficiency diseases. Mr. C (at 57) would be one of those people.

Perhaps we should set the recommendation for nutrient X at or above the extreme, say, at 70 units a day, so that everyone will be covered. (Actually, we didn't study everyone, and some individual we didn't happen to test might have an even higher requirement.) This might be a good idea in theory, but what about a person like Mr. B who requires only 35 units a day? The recommendation would be twice his requirement and to follow it he might spend money needlessly on foods containing nutrient X to the exclusion of foods containing other vital nutrients.

The Decision The decision we finally make is to set the value high enough so that 97 to 98 percent of the population will be covered but not so high as to be excessive (Figure 2-3 illustrates such a value). In this example, a reasonable choice might be 63 units a day. Moving the DRI further toward the extreme would pick up a few additional people, but it would inflate the recommendation for most people, including Mr. A and Mr. B. The committee makes judgments of this kind when setting the DRI recommended intakes for many nutrients. Relatively few healthy people have requirements that are not covered by the DRI recommended intakes.

KEY POINT The DRI are based on scientific data and are designed to cover the needs of virtually all healthy people in the United States and Canada.

Setting Energy Requirements

In contrast to the recommendations for nutrients, the value set for energy, the **Estimated Energy Requirement (EER),** is not generous; instead, it is set at a level predicted to maintain body weight for an individual of a particular age, gender, height, weight, and physical activity level consistent with good health. The energy DRI values reflect a balancing act: enough food energy is critical to support health and life, but too much energy causes unhealthy weight gain. Because even small amounts of excess energy consumed day after day cause weight gain and associated diseases, the DRI committee did not set a Tolerable Upper Intake Level for energy.

People don't eat energy directly. They derive energy from foods containing carbohydrate, fat, and protein, each in proportion to the others. The Acceptable Macronutrient Distribution Ranges, listed earlier, are designed to provide a healthy balance among these nutrients and minimize a person's risk of chronic diseases. These ranges resurface in later chapters of this book wherever intakes of the energy-yielding nutrients are discussed with regard to chronic disease risks.

KEY POINT Estimated Energy Requirements are energy-intake recommendations predicted to maintain body weight and to discourage unhealthy weight gain.

Why Are Daily Values Used on Labels?

Most careful diet planners are already familiar with the Daily Values because they appear on U.S. food labels. After learning about the DRI, you may wonder why yet another set of nutrient standards is needed for food labels. One answer is that while DRI values vary from group to group, values appearing on food labels must apply to the "average" person—someone eating 2,000 to 2,500 calories a day.

While the Daily Values are ideal for allowing comparisons among *foods*, they cannot serve as nutrient intake goals for individuals. The Daily Values are set at the highest nutrient needs among all people, from children of age 4 through aging adults; for example, the Daily Value for iron, 18 mg, an amount that far exceeds a man's RDA of 8 mg (but that meets a young woman's high need precisely). Also, DRI values have changed over the years as new data emerged; the Daily Values have remained static. Using the Daily Values appropriately is a topic of this chapter's Consumer Corner.

- The Daily Values are found on the inside back cover, page Y.

KEY POINT The Daily Values are standards used only on food labels to enable consumers to compare the nutrient values among foods.

- Agencies that put forth nutrient recommendations for the world's people include the World Health Organization (WHO) and the Food and Agriculture Organization (FAO) of the United Nations.

LO 2.2

Dietary Guidelines for Americans

Many countries set forth dietary guidelines, striving to answer the question asked by their citizens, "What should I eat to stay healthy?" The guidelines and nutrient standards are related: if everyone followed the guidelines for individuals, most people's nutrient needs would fall into place.

The Guidelines Promote Health The U.S. Department of Agriculture's Dietary Guidelines for Americans (listed in Figure 2-4) offer science-based advice to promote health and to reduce risk of major chronic diseases through diet and physical activity.[4] People who balance their energy (calorie) intakes with expenditures, consume diets that meet nutrient recommendations, and engage in regular physical activity most often enjoy optimum health. The Dietary Guidelines apply to most healthy people age 2 years or older.

Choose Nutritious Foods and Limit Some Food Components A major recommendation of the Dietary Guidelines for Americans is to choose a healthy diet based on the diet-planning guide, the USDA Food Guide, explained next. To meet its recommendations, most U.S. consumers need to limit calorie intakes and obtain more and varied selections among fruits, vegetables, whole grains, and nonfat or low-fat milk or milk products (for reasons that will become clear as you move through this book). A basic premise of both the Dietary Guidelines and of this book is that foods, not supplements, should provide the needed nutrients whenever possible.

Another focus of the *Dietary Guidelines* is on limiting potentially harmful dietary constituents. A healthful diet is carefully chosen to supply the kinds of carbohydrates that the body needs, but little sugar, and to offer the needed fats and oils while limiting saturated fat, *trans* fat, and cholesterol (Chapters 4 and 5 explain these distinctions). People are also asked to consume less salt and to choose sensibly if they use alcohol. Finally, foods should be kept safe from spoilage or contamination (see Chapter 12).

Notice that the *Dietary Guidelines* do not require that you give up your favorite foods or eat strange, unappealing foods. With a little planning and a few adjustments, almost anyone's diet can approach these recommendations. As for physical activity, this chapter's Think Fitness box spells out some guidelines.

Canada's Guidelines Canadian Guidelines also recommend many of the same ideals. Canadian readers can find Canada's 2007 food group plan, Eating Well with Canada's Food Guide, in Appendix B.

Getty Images

The Dietary Guidelines recommend that physical activity balance food intake.

Estimated Energy Requirement (EER) the average dietary energy intake predicted to maintain energy balance in a healthy adult of a certain age, gender, weight, height, and level of physical activity consistent with good health.

FIGURE 2-4 *Dietary Guidelines for Americans*—Key Recommendations

These *Guidelines* apply to all healthy people over 2 years of age.

ADEQUATE NUTRIENTS WITHIN ENERGY NEEDS

- Consume a variety of nutrient-dense foods and beverages within and among the basic food groups; limit intakes of saturated and *trans* fats, cholesterol, added sugars, salt, and alcohol.
- Meet recommended intakes within energy needs by adopting a balanced eating pattern, such as the USDA Food Guide (explained in a later section).

WEIGHT MANAGEMENT

- To maintain body weight in a healthy range, balance calories from foods and beverages with calories expended (Chapter 9).
- To prevent gradual weight gain over time, make small decreases in food and beverage calories and increase physical activity.

PHYSICAL ACTIVITY

- Engage in regular physical activity and reduce sedentary activities to promote health, psychological well-being, and a healthy body weight (Chapter 10).
- Achieve physical fitness by including cardiovascular conditioning, stretching exercises for flexibility, and resistance exercises or calisthenics for muscle strength and endurance.

FOOD GROUPS TO ENCOURAGE

- Consume a sufficient amount of fruits, vegetables, milk and milk products, and whole grains while staying within energy needs.
- Select a variety of fruits each day. Include vegetables from all five subgroups (dark green, orange, legumes, starchy vegetables, and other vegetables) several times a week. Make at least half of the grain selections whole grains. Select fat-free or low-fat milk products.

FATS

- Keep saturated fat, *trans* fat, and cholesterol consumption low—less than 10 percent of calories from saturated and *trans* fats and less than 300 milligrams of cholesterol per day (Chapter 5).
- Keep total fat intake between 20 to 35 percent of calories, mostly from foods that provide unsaturated fats, such as fish, nuts, olives, and vegetable oils.
- Select and prepare foods that are lean, low-fat, or fat-free.

CARBOHYDRATES

- Choose fiber-rich fruits, vegetables, and whole grains often (Chapter 4).
- Choose and prepare foods and beverages with little added sugars.
- Reduce the incidence of dental caries by practicing good oral hygiene and consuming sugar- and starch-containing foods and beverages less frequently.

SODIUM AND POTASSIUM

- Choose and prepare foods with little salt (less than 2,300 milligrams sodium, or approximately 1 tsp salt). At the same time, consume potassium-rich foods, such as fruits and vegetables (Chapter 8).

ALCOHOLIC BEVERAGES

- Those who choose to drink alcoholic beverages should do so sensibly and in moderation.
- Some individuals should not consume alcoholic beverages (Controversy 3).

FOOD SAFETY

- To avoid microbial foodborne illness, keep foods safe: clean hands, food contact surfaces, and fruits and vegetables; separate raw, cooked, and ready-to-eat foods; cook foods to a safe internal temperature; chill perishable food promptly; and defrost food properly (Chapter 12).

The U.S. Diet and Dietary Guidelines Compared To assess how well a diet meets the Dietary Guidelines and the USDA Food Guide (described next), researchers use the **Healthy Eating Index (HEI).**[5] The HEI allows comparison between the recommendations and various aspects of a diet and yields a score. For example, a diet that provides enough grain foods with at least half from whole grains scores 10 out of 10 possible points for the category. A diet with no grains scores a 0 for grains. For diet components that must be limited, such as saturated fat, lower intakes earn higher HEI scores. The current American diet scores only 58 out of 100 possible points, and most people's diets show room for improvement.[6]

As a nation, Americans eat too few of the foods that supply certain key nutrients (listed in the margin on the next page) and too many that are rich in calories and fats. For most people, then, meeting the diet ideals of the *Dietary Guidelines* requires choosing *more* of these foods:

- Vegetables (especially dark green vegetables, orange vegetables, and legumes).
- Fruits.
- Whole grains.
- Fat-free or low-fat milk and milk products.

And choosing *less* of these:

Healthy Eating Index (HEI) a measure that assesses how well a diet meets the recommendations of the *Dietary Guidelines for Americans* and MyPyramid.

- Refined grains.
- Total fats (especially saturated fat, *trans* fat, and cholesterol).
- Added sugars.
- Salt.

In addition, many people should reduce total calorie intakes. The diet planner can achieve these ideals with the help of the USDA Food Guide.

Our Two Cents' Worth If the experts who develop the Dietary Guidelines were to ask us, we would add one more recommendation to their lists: take time to enjoy and savor your food. The joys of eating are physically beneficial to the body because they trigger health-promoting changes in the nervous, hormonal, and immune systems. When the food is nutritious as well as enjoyable, then the eater obtains all the nutrients needed for healthy body systems, as well as for the healthy skin, glossy hair, and natural attractiveness that accompany robust health. Remember to enjoy your food.

KEY POINT The Dietary Guidelines for Americans, Nutrition Recommendations for Canadians, and other such standards address the problems of undernutrition and overnutrition. To implement them requires exercising regularly, following the USDA Food Guide, seeking out vegetables, fruits, whole grains, and low-fat milk while limiting intakes of saturated and *trans* fats, sugar, and salt, and moderating alcohol intake.

Did You Know?

The key nutrients most often lacking in the U.S. diet are:

- Fiber.
- Vitamin A.
- Vitamin C.
- Vitamin E.
- Calcium.
- Magnesium.
- Potassium.

LO 2.3, 2.4

Diet Planning with the USDA Food Guide

Diet planning connects nutrition theory with the food on the table, and a few minutes invested in meal planning can pay off in better nutrition. To help people achieve the goals set forth by the *Dietary Guidelines for Americans 2005*, the USDA provides a **food group plan**—the USDA Food Guide.[9] Figure 2-5 displays this plan. By

food group plan a diet-planning tool that sorts foods into groups based on their nutrient content and then specifies that people should eat certain minimum numbers of servings of foods from each group.

THINK FITNESS

Recommendations for Daily Physical Activity

The *2008 Physical Activity Guidelines for Americans* set by the USDA and the Department of Health and Human Services suggest that to maintain good health, adults should engage in about 2½ hours of moderate physical activity each week.[7] A brisk walk at a pace of about 100 steps per minute (1,000 steps over 10 minutes) constitutes "moderate" activity.[8] In addition:

- Physical activity can be intermittent, 10 minutes here and there, throughout the week.
- Resistance activity (such as weight-lifting) can be included as part of the exercise total for the week.

For weight control and additional health benefit, more than the minimum amount of physical activity is required. Details are found in Chapter 10.

START NOW

CENGAGENOW

Ready to make a change? Consult the online behavior-change planner to plan how you might obtain the recommended 30 minutes of daily physical activity at **www.cengage.com/sso.**

FIGURE 2-5 **USDA MyPyramid Food Guide**

Key:
- ● Foods generally high in nutrient density (choose most often)
- ▲ Foods lower in nutrient density (limit selections)

GRAINS

© Polara Studios, Inc.

Make at least half of the grain selections whole grains.

These foods contribute folate, niacin, riboflavin, thiamin, iron, magnesium, selenium, and fiber.

1 oz grains is equivalent to 1 slice bread; ½ c cooked rice, pasta, or cereal; 1 oz dry pasta or rice; 1 c ready-to-eat cereal; 3 c popped popcorn.

- ● Whole grains (amaranth, barley, brown rice, buckwheat, bulgur, millet, oats, quinoa, rye, wheat) and whole-grain, low-fat breads, cereals, crackers, and pastas; popcorn.
- ● Enriched bagels, breads, cereals, pastas (couscous, macaroni, spaghetti), pretzels, rice, rolls, tortillas.
- ▲ Biscuits, cakes, cookies, cornbread, crackers, croissants, doughnuts, french toast, fried rice, granola, muffins, pancakes, pastries, pies, presweetened cereals, taco shells, waffles.

VEGETABLES

© Polara Studios, Inc.

Choose a variety of vegetables each day, and choose from all five subgroups several times a week.

These foods contribute folate, vitamin A, vitamin C, vitamin K, vitamin E, magnesium, potassium, and fiber.

1 c vegetables is equivalent to 1 c cut-up raw or cooked vegetables; 1 c cooked legumes; 1 c vegetable juice; 2 c raw, leafy greens.

Vegetable subgroups

- ● 1. Dark green vegetables: Broccoli and leafy greens such as arugula, beet greens, bok choy, collard greens, kale, mustard greens, romaine lettuce, spinach, and turnip greens.
- ● 2. Orange and deep yellow vegetables: Carrots, carrot juice, pumpkin, sweet potatoes, and winter squash (acorn, butternut).
- ● 3. Legumes: Black beans, black-eyed peas, garbanzo beans (chickpeas), kidney beans, lentils, navy beans, pinto beans, soybeans and soy products such as tofu, and split peas.
- ● 4. Starchy vegetables: Cassava, corn, green peas, hominy, lima beans, and potatoes.
- ● 5. Other vegetables: Artichokes, asparagus, bamboo shoots, bean sprouts, beets, brussels sprouts, cabbages, cactus, cauliflower, celery, cucumbers, eggplant, green beans, iceberg lettuce, mushrooms, okra, onions, peppers, seaweed, snow peas, tomatoes, vegetable juices, zucchini.
- ▲ Baked beans, candied sweet potatoes, coleslaw, french fries, potato salad, refried beans, scalloped potatoes, tempura vegetables.

FRUITS

© Polara Studios, Inc.

Consume a variety of fruits and no more than one-half of the recommended intake as fruit juice.

These foods contribute folate, vitamin A, vitamin C, potassium, and fiber.

1 c fruit is equivalent to 1 c fresh, frozen, or canned fruit; ½ c dried fruit; 1 c fruit juice.

- ● Apples, apricots, avocados, bananas, blueberries, cantaloupe, cherries, grapefruit, grapes, guava, kiwi, mango, nectarines, oranges, papaya, peaches, pears, pineapples, plums, raspberries, strawberries, tangerines, watermelon; dried fruit (dates, figs, raisins); unsweetened juices.
- ▲ Canned or frozen fruit in syrup; juices, punches, and fruit drinks with added sugars; fried plantains.

FIGURE 2-5 **USDA MyPyramid Food Guide (continued)**

MILK, YOGURT, AND CHEESE

© Polara Studios, Inc.

Make fat-free or low-fat choices. Choose lactose-free products or other calcium-rich foods if you don't consume milk.

These foods contribute protein, riboflavin, vitamin B_{12}, calcium, magnesium, potassium, and, when fortified, vitamin A and vitamin D.

1 c milk is equivalent to 1 c fat-free milk or yogurt; $1\frac{1}{2}$ oz fat-free natural cheese; 2 oz fat-free processed cheese.

● Fat-free milk and fat-free milk products such as buttermilk, cheeses, cottage cheese, yogurt; fat-free fortified soy milk.

▲ 1% low-fat milk, 2% reduced-fat milk, and whole milk; low-fat, reduced-fat, and whole-milk products such as cheeses, cottage cheese, and yogurt; milk products with added sugars such as chocolate milk, custard, ice cream, ice milk, milk shakes, pudding, sherbet; fortified soy milk.

MEAT, POULTRY, FISH, LEGUMES, EGGS, AND NUTS

© Polara Studios, Inc.

Make lean or low-fat choices. Prepare them with little, or no, added fat.

Meat, poultry, fish, and eggs contribute protein, niacin, thiamin, vitamin B_6, vitamin B_{12}, iron, magnesium, potassium, and zinc; legumes and nuts are notable for their protein, folate, thiamin, vitamin E, iron, magnesium, potassium, zinc, and fiber.

1 oz meat is equivalent to 1 oz cooked lean meat, poultry, or fish; 1 egg; $\frac{1}{4}$ c cooked legumes or tofu; 1 tbs peanut butter; $\frac{1}{2}$ oz nuts or seeds.

● Poultry (no skin), fish, shellfish, legumes, eggs, lean meat (fat-trimmed beef, game, ham, lamb, pork); low-fat tofu, tempeh, peanut butter, nuts (almonds, filberts, peanuts, pistachios, walnuts) or seeds (flaxseeds, pumpkin seeds, sunflower seeds).

▲ Bacon; baked beans; fried meat, fish, poultry, eggs, or tofu; refried beans; ground beef; hot dogs; luncheon meats; marbled steaks; poultry with skin; sausages; spare ribs.

OILS

Matthew Farruggio

Select the recommended amounts of oils from among these sources.

These foods contribute vitamin E and essential fatty acids (see Chapter 5), along with abundant calories.

1 tsp oil is equivalent to 1 tbs low-fat mayonnaise; 2 tbs light salad dressing; 1 tsp vegetable oil; 1 tsp soft margarine.

● Liquid vegetable oils such as canola, corn, flaxseed, nut, olive, peanut, safflower, sesame, soybean, and sunflower oils; mayonnaise, oil-based salad dressing, soft *trans*-free margarine.

● Unsaturated oils that occur naturally in foods such as avocados, fatty fish, nuts, olives, seeds (flaxseeds, sesame seeds), and shellfish.

SOLID FATS AND ADDED SUGARS

Matthew Farruggio

Limit intakes of food and beverages with solid fats and added sugars.

Solid fats deliver saturated fat and *trans* fat, and intake should be kept low. Solid fats and added sugars contribute abundant calories but few nutrients, and intakes should not exceed the discretionary calorie allowance—calories to meet energy needs after all nutrient needs have been met with nutrient-dense foods. Alcohol also contributes abundant calories but few nutrients, and its calories are counted among discretionary calories. See Table 2-2 on page 44 for some discretionary calorie allowances.

▲ Solid fats that occur in foods naturally such as milk fat and meat fat (see ▲ in previous lists).

▲ Solid fats that are often added to foods such as butter, cream cheese, hard margarine, lard, sour cream, and shortening.

▲ Added sugars such as brown sugar, candy, honey, jelly, molasses, soft drinks, sugar, and syrup.

▲ Alcoholic beverages include beer, wine, and liquor.

CONCEPT LINK 2-1

The A, B, C, M, V principles were explained in Chapter 1, pages 10–11.

- Another eating plan, the DASH eating plan of Chapter 11, also meets the goals of the *Dietary Guidelines for Americans 2005.*

CONCEPT LINK 2-2

Phytochemicals and their potential biological actions are explained in Controversy 2.

using it wisely and by learning about the energy-yielding nutrients, vitamins, and minerals in various foods (as you will in coming chapters), you can achieve the goals of a nutritious diet first mentioned in Chapter 1: adequacy, balance, calorie control, moderation, and variety.

If you design your diet around this plan, it is assumed that you will obtain adequate and balanced amounts not only of the nutrients of greatest concern but also of the two dozen or so other essential nutrients as well as beneficial phytochemicals because all of these are distributed among the same food groups. It can also help you to limit potentially harmful dietary constituents and calories.

A different kind of planning tool, the **exchange system** (see Appendix D), was developed for use by those with diabetes. The exchange system focuses on controlling the carbohydrate, fat, protein, and energy (calories) in the diet. Canada's *Beyond the Basics,* a similar planning system, is presented in Appendix B.

The Food Groups and Subgroups

Figure 2-5 defines the major food groups and their subgroups and specifies portions of various foods that are considered equivalents in each group. It also lists the key nutrients provided by foods within each group, information worth noting and remembering. Note also that the figure sorts foods within each group by nutrient density (as the key to Figure 2-5 explains).

Key Nutrients in Vegetable Subgroups The foods in each group are well-known contributors of the key nutrients listed (but you can count on these foods to supply many other nutrients as well). Vegetables, for example, are sorted into subgroups according to their nutrient contents. All vegetables provide valuable fiber and the mineral potassium, but the vegetables of each subgroup reliably provide a key nutrient as well, such as vitamin A from the "orange and deep yellow vegetables," the vitamin folate from the "dark green vegetables," abundant carbohydrate energy from the "starchy vegetables," and iron and protein from "legumes." Many of the same nutrients but few calories come from "other vegetables."

- Legumes were defined in Chapter 1 as dried beans, peas, and lentils.

Grains and Others Among the grains, whole grains supply nutrients and fiber lacking from refined grains. The Food Guide suggests that at least half of the grains in a day's meals be whole grains, or at least three 1-ounce equivalents of whole grains each day.[10]

Spices, herbs, coffee, tea, and diet soft drinks, excluded from the USDA Food Guide, provide few if any nutrients but can add flavor and pleasure to meals. They can also provide some potentially beneficial phytochemicals, such as those in tea or certain spices—see this chapter's Controversy section.

Variety Among and Within the Food Groups Varying your food choices, both among the food groups and within each group, helps to ensure adequate nutrients and also protects against large amounts of toxins or contaminants from any one source, as Chapter 1 made clear. [11] Achieving variety may require some effort but knowing the food groups eases the task. Figure 2-6 demonstrates that people in the United States choose too few servings of vegetables, fruits, and milk, and too many of refined grains and meats. For health's sake, U.S. citizens are urged to more closely follow the Food Guide recommendations.

KEY POINT The USDA Food Guide divides foods into food groups based on key nutrient contents. People who consume the specified amounts of foods from each group achieve dietary adequacy, balance, and variety. Most U.S. diets fail to achieve these amounts.

exchange system a diet-planning tool that organizes foods with respect to their nutrient content and calories. Foods on any single exchange list can be used interchangeably. See the U.S. Exchange System, Appendix D (or Appendix B for Canada), for details.

discretionary calorie allowance the balance of calories remaining in a person's energy allowance after accounting for the number of calories needed to meet recommended nutrient intakes through consumption of nutrient-dense foods.

The Discretionary Calorie Concept

To help people control calories to prevent excess weight gain, the USDA developed the concept of the **discretionary calorie allowance.** The concept can also help people to moderate intakes of certain fats and added sugars.

Discretionary Calorie Demonstration As Figure 2-7 demonstrates, a person needing 2,000 calories of energy in a day to maintain weight may need only 1,700 calories or so of the most nutrient-dense foods to supply the nutrients required for

FIGURE 2-6 **How Does the U.S. Diet Stack Up?**

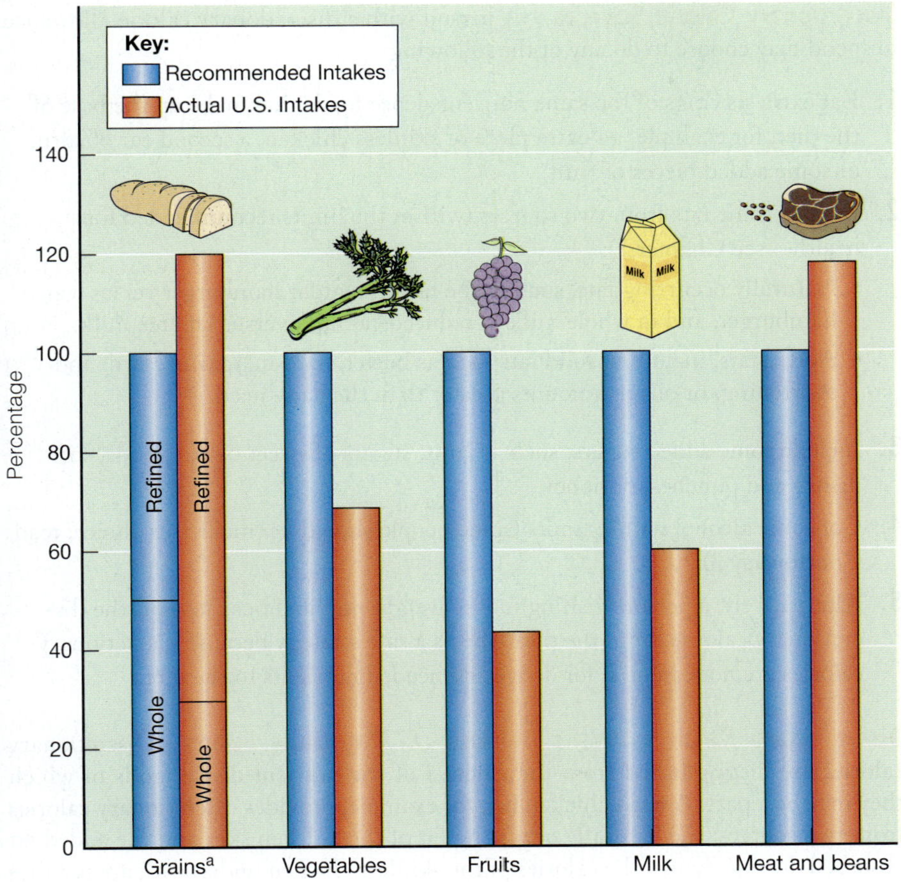

[a]*At least half of the grain selections should be whole grains.*

FIGURE 2-7 **Discretionary Calorie Allowance in a 2,000-Calorie Diet**

A well-chosen diet may leave room in the calorie budget for some discretionary calories. Additional servings of nutritious foods, some fats, or added sugars may be chosen to supply them.

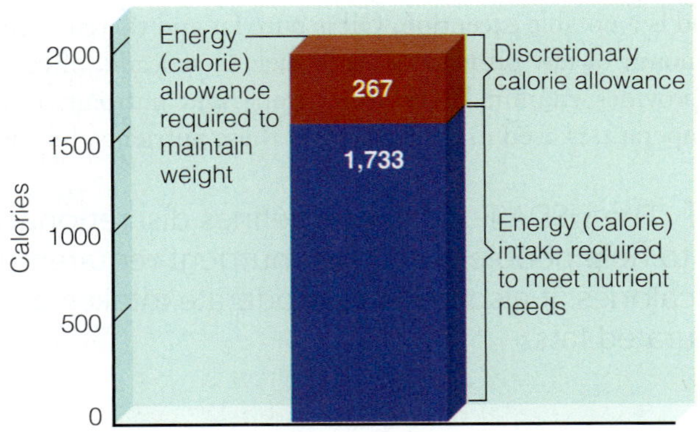

the day. The difference between the calories needed to maintain weight and those needed to supply nutrients from the most nutrient-dense foods is the person's discretionary calorie allowance (in this case, 267 calories).

Physically active people use greater numbers of calories each day than do sedentary people, a fact reflected in their greater discretionary calorie allowances. People who need fewer calories to maintain their weight have fewer discretionary calories to spend.

- Within calorie limits, small amounts of added sugars can be enjoyed as part of the discretionary calories in a nutrient-dense diet:
  - *3 tsp for 1,600 cal*
  - *5 tsp for 1,800 cal*
  - *8 tsp for 2,000 cal*
  - *9 tsp for 2,200 cal*
  - *12 tsp for 2,400 cal*

Discretionary Calorie Sources A person with a discretionary calorie allowance to spend may choose to do any of the following:

1. Eat extra servings of the same nutrient-dense foods that make up the base of the diet, for example, an extra piece of skinless chicken, a second ear of corn, or some added pieces of fruit.
2. Include some fats from two sources (within the limits recommended for health—see Chapter 5):
   - Naturally occurring fats, such as the fats in regular hamburger versus lean hamburger, and in whole milk or reduced-fat milk versus fat-free milk.
   - Added fats, including solid fats such as butter, hard margarine, lard, and shortening; or oils in amounts greater than the daily need.
3. Include some added sugars, such as jams, sugars of sweet baked goods, soft drinks and punches, or honey.
4. Consume alcohol within limits (some people should *not* make this choice; read Controversy 3).
5. Alternatively, a person wishing to lose weight might choose to omit the discretionary calories from the diet. This is a safe strategy because discretionary calories are not essential for delivering needed nutrients to the diet.

Discretionary Calories Versus Calories of Nutritious Foods Discretionary calories are distinguished from the calories of the nutrient-dense foods of which they may be a part. A fried chicken leg, for example, provides discretionary calories from two sources: the naturally occurring fat of the chicken skin and the added fat absorbed during frying. The calories of the skinless chicken underneath are not discretionary (unless consumed in excess of need)—they are necessary to provide the nutrients of chicken. Likewise, an oatmeal cookie provides discretionary calories of sugar and shortening, but its oatmeal contributes to the day's intake of whole grains. Table 2-1 provides additional examples.

Nutrient-Dense Foods To control calories and prevent overweight or obesity, the USDA Food Guide instructs diet planners to choose the most nutrient-dense foods from each group. Unprocessed or lightly processed foods are generally best because some processes strip foods of beneficial nutrients and fiber, while others add many calories in the form of sugar or fat. Figure 2-5 identified a few of the most nutrient-dense food selections in each food group and some foods of lower nutrient density to give you an idea of which are which.

Uncooked oil is a notable exception. Oil is pure fat and therefore rich in calories, but a small amount of raw oil from sources such as avocado, olives, nuts, fish, or vegetable oil provides vitamin E and other important nutrients that other foods lack. High temperatures used in frying destroy these nutrients, however.

CONCEPT LINK 2-3

Nutrient density was explained in Chapter 1, page 20.

- Chapter 9 will help you determine your energy needs. For a quick approximation, find your EER on the inside front cover, page A.

KEY POINT The USDA Food Guide defines discretionary calorie allowances to help people meet their nutrient requirements while controlling calories. It also helps to moderate intakes of potentially harmful saturated fats.

TABLE 2-1

Examples of Discretionary Calorie Sources

Notice that foods providing zero discretionary calories are naturally low in fat and have no added fats or sugars. These form the base of the diet in the USDA Food Guide. When choosing foods, pay close attention to portion size. More food means more calories from all sources.

Food	Amount	Total Calories[a]	Discretionary Calories[a]	Discretionary Calorie Sources
Milk and Milk Products				
Fat-free milk	1 cup	85	0	—
Whole milk	1 cup	145	65	Fat
Low-fat chocolate milk	1 cup	160	75	Fat, sugar
Cheddar cheese	1½ oz	170	90	Fat
Ice cream, vanilla	1 cup	290	205	Fat, sugar
Meat				
Extra lean ground beef (95% lean)	3 oz, cooked	165	0	—
Regular ground beef (80% lean)	3 oz, cooked	230	65	Fat
Roast chicken breast (skinless)	3 oz	140	0	—
Fried chicken breast with skin & batter	3 oz	245	105	Fat
Beef bologna	3 slices (1 oz each)	265	100	Fat
Grains				
Bread	1 slice (1 oz)	70	0	—
Blueberry muffin	1 small (2 oz)	185	45	Fat, sugar
Biscuit, plain	1 (2.5″ diameter)	130	60	Fat
Chocolate chip cookies	2 large	135	70	Fat, sugar
Glazed doughnut, yeast type	1 medium	240	165	Fat, sugar
Vegetables				
Potato, boiled or baked	1 (2.5″ diam)	120	0	—
French fries	1 medium order	460	325	Fat
Onion rings	8 to 9 rings	275	160	Fat
Fruit				
Peach slices, fresh	1 cup	60	0	—
Canned peaches, heavy syrup	1 cup	195	135	Sugar
Extras				
Diet soda	12 oz	0	0	—
Regular soda	12 oz	155	155	Sugar
Fruit punch	1 cup	115	115	Sugar
Table wine	5 oz	115	115	Alcohol
Beer (regular)	12 oz	145	145	Alcohol
Butter or stick margarine	1 teaspoon	35	35	Fat
Cream cheese	1 tablespoon	50	50	Fat

[a]*Estimated calories*

Source: Data from USDA

The fat in this chicken skin and the oil that soaked into the coating during frying provide over 100 discretionary calories.

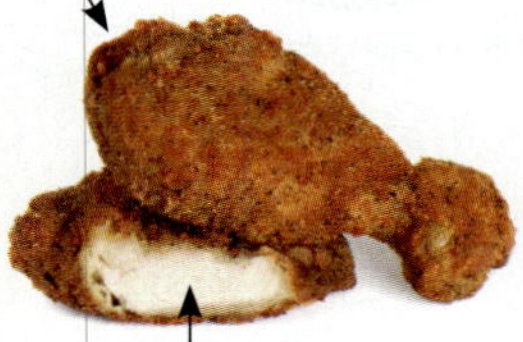

This skinless chicken meat, a nutrient-dense food, provides 140 calories.

The added sugars in the heavy canning syrup of these peaches provide 135 discretionary calories.

A cup of plain peaches provides 60 calories of a nutritious food.

LO 2.5

Diet Planning Application

© iStockphoto.com

The USDA Food Guide specifies the amounts needed from each food group to create a healthful diet for a given number of calories. Look at the top line of Table 2-2 and find yourself among the people described there (for other calorie levels, see Table E-1 of Appendix E). Then look at the column of numbers below for amounts from each food group that meet your calorie need. Table 2-2 also specifies the discretionary calorie allowance for each calorie level. Note that the more energy spent in physical activity in a day, the higher the calorie need and the greater the discretionary calorie allowance.

For vegetables, intakes should be divided among all the vegetable subgroups over a week's time, as shown in Table 2-3. Look across the top row for your calorie level (obtained from Table 2-2)—a healthful diet includes the listed amounts of each type of vegetable each *week*. It is *not* necessary to eat vegetables from each subgroup every day.

With judicious selections, the diet can supply all the necessary nutrients and provide some luxury items, as well. A sample diet plan demonstrates how the theory of the USDA Food Guide translates to food on the plate. The USDA Food Guide ensures that a certain amount from each of the five food groups is represented in the diet. The diet planner begins by assigning each of the food groups to meals and snacks, as shown in Table 2-4. Then the plan can be filled out with real foods to create a menu. For example, the breakfast calls for 1 ounce grains, 1 cup milk, and ½ cup fruit. Here's one possibility for this meal:

1 cup ready-to-eat cereal = 1 ounce grains.

1 cup fat-free milk = 1 cup milk.

1 medium banana = ½ cup fruit.

TABLE 2-2 **MyPyramid Recommended Daily Intakes from Each Food Group**

	Sedentary Women: 51+ Yr	Sedentary Women: 31–50 Yr	Sedentary Women: 19–30 Yr Active Women: 51+ Yr Sedentary Men: 51+ Yr	Active Women: 31–50 Yr Sedentary Men: 31–50 Yr	Active Women: 19–30 Yr Active Men: 51+ Yr Sedentary Men: 19–30 Yr	Active Men: 31–50 Yr	Active Men: 19–30 Yr
Calories[a]	1,600	1,800	2,000	2,200	2,400	2,800	3,000
Fruits	1½ c	1½ c	2 c	2 c	2 c	2½ c	2½ c
Vegetables[b]	2 c	2½ c	2½ c	3 c	3 c	3½ c	4 c
Grains	5 oz	6 oz	6 oz	7 oz	8 oz	10 oz	10 oz
Meats and legumes	5 oz	5 oz	5½ oz	6 oz	6½ oz	7 oz	7 oz
Milk	3 c	3 c	3 c	3 c	3 c	3 c	3 c
Oils[c]	5 tsp	5 tsp	6 tsp	6 tsp	7 tsp	8 tsp	10 tsp
Discretionary calorie allowance	132 cal	195 cal	267 cal	290 cal	362 cal	426 cal	512 cal

Note: In addition to gender, age, and activity levels, energy needs vary with height and weight (see Chapter 9 and Appendix H).

[a] *Assumes high nutrient density choices—lean, low-fat, and fat-free with no added sugars.*

[b] *Divide these amounts among the vegetable subgroups as specified in Table 2-3.*

[c] *Approximate measures; the gram values are 22, 24, 27, 29, 31, 34, and 36, respectively.*

TABLE 2-3 Weekly Amounts from Vegetable Subgroups

Table 2-2 specifies the recommended amounts (in cups) of total vegetables per *day.* This table shows those amounts dispersed among five vegetable subgroups per *week.*

Vegetable Subgroups	1,600 cal	1,800 cal	2,000 cal	2,200 cal	2,400 cal	2,600 cal	2,800 cal	3,000 cal
Dark green	2 c	3 c	3 c	3 c	3 c	3 c	3 c	3 c
Orange and deep yellow	1½ c	2 c	2 c	2 c	2 c	2½ c	2½ c	2½ c
Legumes	2½ c	3 c	3 c	3 c	3 c	3½ c	3½ c	3½ c
Starchy	2½ c	3 c	3 c	6 c	6 c	7 c	7 c	9 c
Other	5½ c	6½ c	6½ c	7 c	7 c	8½ c	8½ c	10 c

TABLE 2-4 Sample Diet Plan

This diet plan is one of many possibilities for a day's meals. It follows the amounts suggested for a 2,000-calorie diet (with an extra ½ cup of vegetables).

Food Group	Recommended MyPyramid Amounts	Breakfast	Lunch	Snack	Dinner	Snack
Fruits	2 c	½ c		½ c	1 c	
Vegetables	2½ c		1 c		2 c	
Grains	6 oz	1 oz	2 oz	½ oz	2 oz	½ oz
Meat and legumes	5½ oz		2 oz		3½ oz	
Milk	3 c	1 c		1 c		1 c
Oils	5½ tsp		1½ tsp		4 tsp	
Discretionary calorie allowance	267 cal					

Then the planner moves on to complete the menu for lunch, supper, and snacks, as shown in Figure 2-8. This day's choices are explored further as "Monday's Meals" in the Food Feature at the end of the chapter.

KEY POINT Food patterns for calorie levels can guide food choices in diet planning. Some discretionary calories often fit into the diet.

MyPyramid: Steps to a Healthier You

For consumers with Internet access, the USDA's MyPyramid online educational tool makes applying the Food Guide easier. Figure 2-9 explains its graphic image. MyPyramid guides users through diet planning to create a diet that more closely meets the ideals of the USDA Food Guide and the recommendations of the *Dietary Guidelines for Americans.*

FIGURE 2-8 A Sample Menu

This sample menu provides about 1,850 calories of the 2,000-calorie plan. About 150 discretionary calories remain available to spend on more nutrient-dense foods or luxuries such as added sugars and fats.

Amounts	Sample Menu	Energy (Cal)
	BREAKFAST	
1 oz whole grains	1 c whole-grain cereal	108
1 c milk	1 c fat-free milk	100
1/2 c fruit	1 medium banana (sliced)	105
	LUNCH	
2 oz meats, 2 oz whole grains	1 turkey sandwich on whole-wheat roll	272
1 1/2 tsp oils	1 1/2 tbs low-fat mayonnaise	71
1 c vegetables	1 c vegetable juice	50
	SNACK	
1/2 oz whole grains	4 whole-wheat reduced-fat crackers	86
1 c milk	1 1/2 oz low-fat cheddar cheese	74
1/2 c fruit	1 medium apple	72
	DINNER	
1/2 c vegetables	1 c raw spinach leaves	8
1/4 c vegetables	1/4 c shredded carrots	11
1 oz meats	1/4 c garbanzo beans	71
2 tsp oils	2 tbs oil-based salad dressing and olives	76
3/4 c vegetables, 2 1/2 oz meat, 2 oz enriched grains	Spaghetti with meat and tomato sauce	425
1/2 c vegetables	1/2 c green beans	22
2 tsp oils	2 tsp soft margarine	67
1 c fruit	1 c strawberries	49
	SNACK	
1/2 oz whole grains	3 graham crackers	90
1 c milk	1 c fat-free milk	100

Note: This plan meets the recommendations to provide 45 to 65 percent of calories from carbohydrate, 20 to 35 percent from fat, and 10 to 35 percent from protein.

- To make a start at changing your own diet, use the *Diet Analysis Plus* program on this textbook's website to work through the questions at the end of the Food Feature section on page 59.

For many, the dietary changes required to do so may seem daunting or even insurmountable, and taken all at once they may be. However, small steps taken each day can add up to substantial dietary changes over time. If everyone would begin, today, to take such steps, the rewards in terms of less heart disease, less cancer, greater quality of life, and better overall health would prove well worth their effort.

Computer-savvy consumers will also find an abundance of MyPyramid support material and diet assessment tools on the Internet (**www.MyPyramid.gov**). Those without computer access can achieve the MyPyramid goals by following the USDA Food Guide principles and working with pencil and paper, as illustrated later.

KEY POINT The concepts of the USDA Food Guide are conveyed to consumers through the MyPyramid educational tool.

Flexibility of the USDA Food Guide

Although it may appear rigid, the USDA Food Guide can actually be very flexible once its intent is understood. For example, the user can substitute fat-free yogurt for fat-free milk because both supply the key nutrients for the milk, yogurt, and cheese group. Legumes provide many of the nutrients of the meat group, but they also constitute a vegetable subgroup, so legumes in a meal can count as a serving of meat or of vegetables. Consumers can adapt the plan to mixed dishes such as casseroles and to national and cultural foods as well, as Figure 2-10 demonstrates.

FIGURE 2-9 **MyPyramid: Steps to a Healthier You**

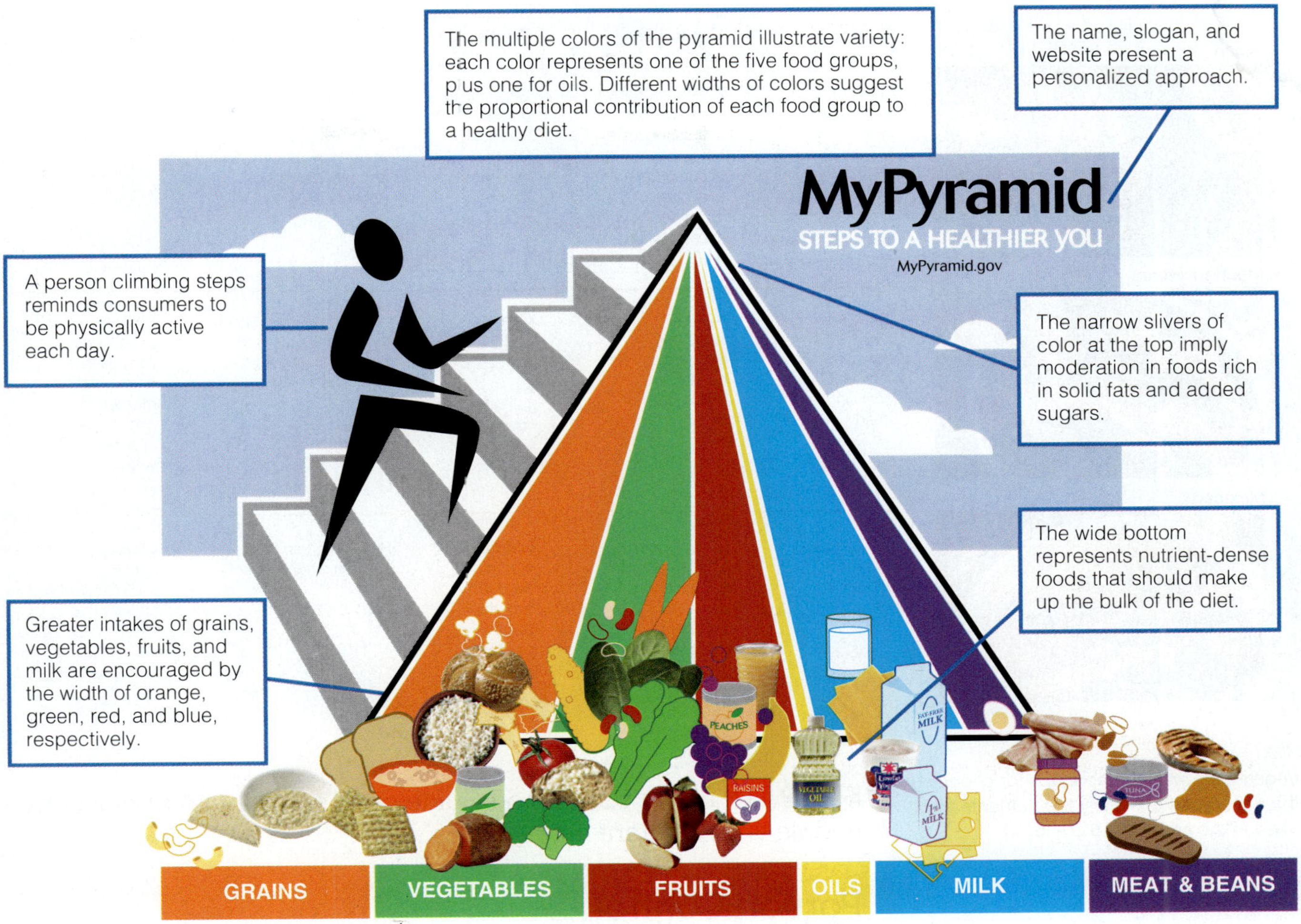

The USDA Food Guide can help vegetarians in making their food choices, too. The food group that includes the meats also includes legumes, nuts, seeds, and products made from soybeans. In the food group that includes milk, soy drinks and soy milk (beverages made from soybeans) can fill the same nutrient needs, provided that they are fortified with calcium, riboflavin, vitamin A, vitamin D, and vitamin B_{12}. Thus, for all sorts of careful diet planners, the USDA Food Guide provides a general road map for designing a healthful diet.

MY TURN

Stephanie

Right Size—Supersize?

Do you often overeat when you eat out? Listen to two students talk about making healthy choices in restaurants.

CENGAGENOW To hear their stories, log on to www.cengage.com/sso.

FIGURE 2-10 **Ethnic Food Choices**

Asian

© Becky Luigart-Stayner/Corbis

Mediterranean

Photodisc/Getty Images

Mexican

Mitch Hrdlicka/Photodisc/Getty Images

	Grains	Vegetables	Fruits	Meats and Legumes	Milk
Asian	Rice, white or rice noodles, millet, wheat or rice wrappers and crepes	Amaranth, baby corn, bamboo shoots, chayote, bok choy, mung bean sprouts, snow peas, mushrooms, water chestnuts, kelp	Carambola, guava, kumquat, lychee, persimmon, melons, mandarin orange	Soybeans and soy products such as miso and tofu, squid, duck eggs, pork, poultry, fish and other seafood, peanuts, cashews	Soy milk
Mediterranean	Pita pocket bread, pastas, rice, couscous, polenta, bulgur, focaccia, Italian bread	Eggplant, tomatoes, peppers, cucumbers, grape leaves	Olives, grapes, figs	Fish and other seafood, gyros, lamb, chicken, beef, pork, sausage, lentils, fava beans	Ricotta, provolone, parmesan, feta, mozzarella, and goat cheeses; yogurt
Mexican	Tortillas (corn or flour), taco shells, rice	Chayote, corn, jicama, tomato salsa, cactus, cassava, tomatoes, yams, chilies	Guava, mango, papaya, avocado, plantain, bananas, oranges	Refried beans, fish, chicken, chorizo, beef, eggs	Cheese, custard

- Vegetarians will find more tips for choosing the right foods to supply the nutrients they need in the chapters to come.

KEY POINT The USDA Food Guide can be used with flexibility by people with different eating styles.

Portion Control

To control calories, the diet planner must learn to control food portions. It's often hard to judge portion sizes, though. Restaurants may deliver colossal helpings to ensure repeat business; a server on a cafeteria line may be instructed to deliver "about a spoonful"; fast-food burgers range from a 1-ounce mini-sized burger to a ¾-pound triple deluxe. What amount is right to choose?

- To estimate the size of food portions, remember these common objects:
  - *3 ounces of meat = the size of the palm of a woman's hand or a deck of cards.*
  - *1 medium piece of fruit or potato = the size of a regular (60-watt) lightbulb.*
  - *1½ ounces cheese = the size of a 9-volt battery.*
  - *1 ounce lunch meat or cheese = 1 slice.*
  - *1 pat (1 tsp) butter or margarine = a slice from a quarter-pound stick of butter about as thick as 280 pages of this book (pressed together).*

Colossal Cuisine In the United States, the trend has been toward consuming larger and larger food portions, especially of foods rich in fat and sugar (see Figure 2-11). At the same time, body weights have been creeping upward, suggesting an increasing need for portion control. Consumers need more helpful guidance about portion sizes, and the margin note offers some notable comparisons among portion sizes and everyday objects.

Tips on Weights and Measures Among volumetric measures, 1 "cup" refers to an 8-ounce measuring cup (not a teacup or drinking glass) filled to level (not heaped up, or shaken, or pressed down). Tablespoons and teaspoons refer to measuring spoons (not flatware), filled to level (not rounded or heaping). Ounces signify weight, not volume. Two ounces of meat, for example, refers to ⅛ of a pound of cooked meat. One ounce (weight) of crispy rice cereal measures a full cup (volume), but take care: 1 ounce of granola cereal measures only ¼ cup.

Also, some foods are specified as "medium," as in "one medium apple," but the word *medium* means different things to different people. When college students are asked to bring medium-sized foods to class, they reliably bring bagels weighing from 2 to 5 ounces, muffins from about 2 to 8 ounces, baked potatoes from 4 to 9 ounces, and so forth. The Table of Food Composition, Appendix A, can help in determining serving sizes because it lists both weights and volumes of a wide variety of foods.

Did You Know?

You can use an ice cream scoop to serve mashed potatoes, pasta, vegetables, rice, cereals, or other foods. Most scoops hold ¼ cup. Test the size of your scoop—fill it with water and pour the water into a measuring cup.

FIGURE 2-11 **U.S. Trend Toward Colossal Cuisine**

Chapter 9 discusses the consequences of increasing portion sizes in terms of body fatness.

Food	Typical 1970s	Today's colossal
Cola	10 oz bottle, 120 cal	40–60 oz fountain, 580 cal
French fries	about 30, 475 cal	about 50, 790 cal
Hamburger	3–4 oz meat, 330 cal	6–12 oz meat, 1,000 cal
Bagel	2–3 oz, 230 cal	5–7 oz, 550 cal
Steak	8–12 oz, 690 cal	16–22 oz, 1,260 cal
Pasta	1 c, 200 cal	2–3 c, 600 cal
Baked potato	5–7 oz, 180 cal	1 lb, 420 cal
Candy bar	1½ oz, 220 cal	3–4 oz, 580 cal
Popcorn	1½ c, 80 cal	8–16 c tub, 880 cal

Note: Calories are rounded values for the largest portions in a given range.

© Tony Freeman/PhotoEdit

1970s Today

1970s Today

© Matthew Farruggio (both)

1970s Today

KEY POINT People wishing to avoid overconsuming calories must pay attention to the size of their food portions.

A Note About Exchange Systems

Exchange systems, defined earlier, can be useful to careful diet planners, especially those wishing to control calories (weight watchers), those who must control carbohydrate intakes (people with diabetes), and those who should control their intakes of fat and saturated fat (almost everyone). An exchange system, presented in Appendix D (Appendix B for Canada), lists the estimated carbohydrate, fat, saturated fat, and protein contents of food portions, as well as their calorie values. The values in the exchange lists differ from the exacting values given for individual foods in Appendix A because exchange lists estimate values for whole groups of foods. With these estimates, exchange system users can make an informed approximation of the nutrients and calories in almost any food they might encounter.

The exchange system also highlights a fact pointed out by the USDA Food Guide: most foods provide more than just one energy nutrient. Meat, for example, is famous for protein, but meats like bacon and sausage deliver many more calories from fat than from protein. A slice of bread provides most of its calories as carbohydrate, but biscuits provide many of their calories as fat, and so on. This focus on energy-yielding nutrients leads to some unexpected food groupings in the exchange lists. The high-fat meats mentioned here and also many cheeses are listed together as "high-fat meats" because fat constitutes the predominant form of energy in these foods, followed by protein. Potatoes and other vegetables high in starch are listed with the breads because one serving of bread and one serving of a starchy vegetable contain about the same amount of carbohydrate. To explore the usefulness of this powerful aid to diet planning, spend some time studying Appendix D (or B).

KEY POINT Exchange lists facilitate calorie control by providing an understanding of how much carbohydrate, fat, and protein are in each food group.

© Matthew Farruggio

How much does your bagel weigh?

CONSUMER CORNER

Checking Out Food Labels

A potato is a potato and needs no label to tell you so. But what can a package of potato chips tell you about its contents? By law, its label must list the chips' ingredients—potatoes, fat, and salt—and its **Nutrition Facts** panel must also reveal details about their nutrient composition (see Table 2-5). If the oil is high in saturated fat, the label will tell you so (more about fats in Chapter 5). A label may also warn consumers of a food's potential for causing an allergic reaction (Chapter 14 provides details). In addition to required information, labels may make optional statements about the food being delicious, or good for you in some way, or a great value. Some of these comments, especially some that are regulated by the Food and Drug Administration (FDA), are reliable. Many others are based on less convincing evidence.

This Consumer Corner introduces food labels and points out the accurate, tested, regulated, and therefore helpful information that consumers need to make wise food choices. It then turns the spotlight on claims whose purpose is to attract consumer dollars by treading beyond established nutrition science into the realm of pure marketing. Consumers must acquire some tools for digging out the truth from among the rubble and then hone their skills by comparing actual labels. This Consumer Corner provides the tools; Chapter 5 presents an opportunity to compare some labels, and for those with Internet access, more practice can be gained at the USDA's *Make Your Calories Count* website.*

TABLE 2-5 Food Label Terms

- **health claims** claims linking food constituents with disease states; allowable on labels within the criteria established by the Food and Drug Administration.
- **nutrient claims** claims using approved wording to describe the nutrient values of foods, such as a claim that a food is "high" in a desirable constituent or "low" in an undesirable one.
- **Nutrition Facts** on a food label, the panel of nutrition information required to appear on almost every packaged food. Grocers may also provide the information for fresh produce, meats, poultry, and seafoods.
- **structure-function claim** a legal but largely unregulated claim permitted on labels of dietary supplements and conventional foods.

WHAT FOOD LABELS *MUST* INCLUDE

The Nutrition Education and Labeling Act of 1990 set the requirements for certain label information to ensure that food labels truthfully inform consumers about the nutrients and ingredients in the package. This information remains reliable and true today. According to the law, every packaged food must state the following:

- The common or usual name of the product.
- The name and address of the manufacturer, packer, or distributor.
- The net contents in terms of weight, measure, or count.
- The nutrient contents of the product (Nutrition Facts panel).

*USDA's *Make Your Calories Count* website is available at www.cfsan.fda.gov/~ear/hwm/hwmintro.html.

© David Young-Wolff/PhotoEdit

Food labels provide clues for nutrition sleuths.

Then the label must list the following in ordinary language:

- The ingredients in descending order of predominance by weight.

Not every package need display information about every vitamin and mineral. A large package, such as the box of cereal in Figure 2-12, must provide all of the information just listed. A smaller label, such as the label on a can of tuna, provides some of the information in abbreviated form. A label on a roll of candy rings provides only a phone number, which is allowed for the tiniest labels. The Canadian version of a food label can be found in Appendix B.

The Nutrition Facts Panel

Most food packages are required to display a Nutrition Facts panel, like the one shown in Figure 2-12. Grocers also voluntarily post placards or offer handouts in fresh-food departments to provide consumers with similar sorts of nutrition information for the most popular types of fresh fruits, vegetables, meats, poultry, and seafoods.

When you read a Nutrition Facts panel, be aware that only the top portion of the panel conveys information specific to the food inside the package. The bottom portion is identical on every label—it stands as a reminder of the Daily Values.

The highlighted items in this section correspond with those of Figure 2-12, which shows the location of the items that follow.

- Serving size. Common household and metric measures to allow comparison of foods within a food category. This amount of food constitutes a single serving and that portion containing the nutrient amounts listed. A serving of chips may be 10 chips, so if you eat 50 chips, you will have consumed five times the nutrient amounts listed on the label. When you compare nutrients or calories in two or more brands of the same food, check the serving size—it may differ.
- Servings per container. Number of servings per box, can, package, or other unit.

FIGURE 2-12 ANIMATED! What's on a Food Label?

This cereal label maps out the locations of information needed to make wise purchases. The text provides details about each label section. Labels may also warn consumers of potential allergy risks (see Chapter 14 for details).

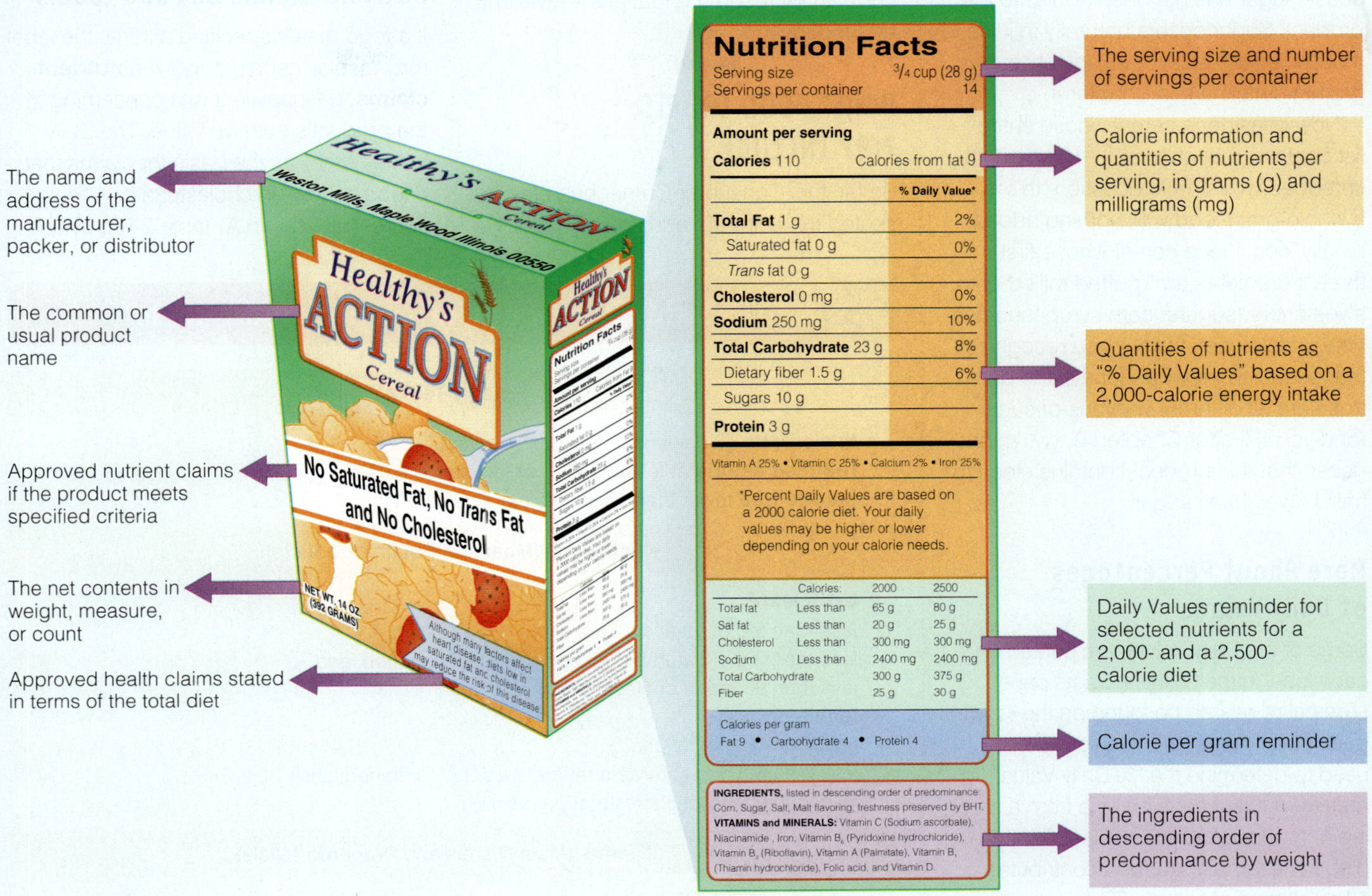

- Calories/calories from fat. Total food energy per serving and energy from fat per serving.
- Nutrient amounts and percentages of Daily Values. This section provides the core information concerning these nutrients:
  - *Total fat.* Grams of fat per serving with a breakdown showing grams of *saturated fat* and *trans* fat per serving.
  - *Cholesterol.* Milligrams of cholesterol per serving.
  - *Sodium.* Milligrams of sodium per serving.
  - *Total carbohydrate.* Grams of carbohydrate per serving, including starch, fiber, and sugars, with a breakdown showing grams of dietary *fiber* and *sugars*. The sugars include those that occur naturally in the food plus any added during processing.
  - *Protein.* Grams of protein per serving.

In addition, the label must state the contents of these nutrients expressed as percentages of the Daily Values:

- *Vitamin A.*
- *Vitamin C.*
- *Calcium.*
- *Iron.*

Other nutrients present in significant amounts in the food may also be listed on the label. The percentages of the Daily Values (see the inside front cover, page Y) are given in terms of a 2,000-calorie diet.

- Daily Values and calories-per-gram reminder. This portion lists the Daily Values for a person needing 2,000 or 2,500 calories a day and provides a calories-per-gram reminder as a handy reference for label readers.

Ingredients List

An often neglected but highly valuable body of information is the list of:

- Ingredients. The product's ingredients must be listed in descending order of predominance by weight.

Knowing how to read an ingredients list puts you many steps ahead of the naïve buyer. Consider the ingredients list on an orange drink powder whose first three entries are "sugar, citric acid, orange flavor." You can tell that sugar is the chief ingredient. Now consider a canned juice whose ingredients list begins with "water, orange juice concentrate, pineapple juice concentrate." This product is clearly made of *reconstituted* juice. Water is first on the label because it is the main constituent of juice. Sugar is nowhere to be found among the ingredients because sugar has not been added to the product. Sugar occurs naturally in juice, though, so the label does specify sugar grams; details are in Chapter 4.

Now consider a cereal whose entire list contains just one item: "100 percent shredded wheat." No question, this is a whole-grain food with nothing added. Finally, consider a cereal whose first three ingredients are "puffed milled corn, sweeteners (sugars: corn syrup, sucrose, honey, dextrose), salt." If you recognize that sugar, corn syrup, honey, and dextrose are all different versions of sugar (and you will after Chapter 4), you might guess that this product contains close to half its weight as sugar.

More About Percentages of Daily Values

Some of the Daily Values are printed on each label in the Nutrition Facts panel. (The entire list can be found on the inside back cover, page Y.) The calculations used to determine the "% Daily Value" figures for nutrient contributions from a serving of food are based on a 2,000-calorie diet. For example, if a food contributes 13 milligrams of vitamin C per serving and the Daily Value is 60 milligrams, then a serving of that food provides about 22 percent of the Daily Value for vitamin C.

The Daily Values are of two types. Some, such as those for fiber, protein, vitamins, and most minerals, are akin to other nutrient intake recommendations. They suggest an intake goal to strive for; below that level, some people's needs may go unmet. Other Daily Values, such as those for cholesterol, total fat, saturated fat, and sodium, constitute healthy daily maximums.

Of course, though the Daily Values are based on a 2,000-calorie diet, people's actual calorie intakes vary widely; some people need fewer calories and some need many more. This makes the Daily Values most useful for comparing one food with another and less useful as nutrient intake targets for individuals. Still, by examining a food's general nutrient profile, you can determine whether the food contributes "a little" or "a lot" of a nutrient, whether it contributes "more" or "less" than another food, and how well it fits into your overall diet. Consumers may soon see updated Daily Values based on current DRI recommendations—revisions are underway.[1]

WHAT FOOD LABELS *MAY* INCLUDE

So far, this Consumer Corner has presented the accurate and reliable facts on nutrition labels. This section looks at reliable claims and also describes the unreliable but legal claims that can be made on food labels.

Nutrient Claims on Food Labels

If a food meets specified criteria, the label may display certain approved **nutrient claims,** descriptive terms concerning the product's nutritive value. The Daily Values serve as the basis for claims that a food is "low" in cholesterol or a "good source" of vitamin A. Table 2-6 provides

TABLE 2-6 Reliable Nutrient Claims on Food Labels

Energy Terms

- **low calorie** 40 calories or fewer per serving.
- **reduced calorie** at least 25% lower in calories than a "regular," or reference, food.
- **calorie free** fewer than 5 calories per serving.

Fat Terms (Meat and Poultry Products)

- **extra lean**[a]
  less than 5 g of fat *and*
  less than 2 g of saturated fat and *trans* fat combined, *and*
  less than 95 mg of cholesterol per serving.
- **lean**[a]
  less than 10 g of fat *and*
  less than 4.5 g of saturated fat and *trans* fat combined, *and*
  less than 95 mg of cholesterol per serving.

Fat Terms (Main Dishes and Prepared Meals)

- **extra lean**[a]
  less than 5 g total fat *and*
  less than 2 g saturated fat *and*
  less than 95 mg cholesterol per serving.
- **lean**[a]
  less than 8 g total fat *and*
  3.5 g or less saturated fat *and*
  less than 80 mg cholesterol per serving.

Fat and Cholesterol Terms (All Products)

- **cholesterol free**[b]
  less than 2 mg of cholesterol *and*
  2 g or less saturated fat and *trans* fat combined per serving.
- **fat free** less than 0.5 g of fat per serving.
- **less saturated fat** 25% or less saturated fat and *trans* fat combined than the comparison food.
- **low cholesterol**[b]
  20 mg or less of cholesterol *and*
  2 g or less saturated fat per serving.
- **low fat** 3 g or less fat per serving.[a]

(continued)

[a]*The word lean as part of the brand name (as in "Lean Supreme") indicates that the product contains fewer than 10 grams of fat per serving.*

[b]*Foods containing more than 13 grams total fat per serving or per 50 grams of food must indicate those contents immediately after a cholesterol claim.*

TABLE 2-6

Reliable Nutrient Claims on Food Labels (continued)

Fat and Cholesterol Terms (continued)

- **low saturated fat** 1 g or less saturated fat and less than 0.5 g of *trans* fat per serving.
- **percent fat free** may be used only if the product meets the definition of low fat or fat free. Requires disclosure of grams of fat per 100 g food.
- **reduced** or **less cholesterol**[b]
  at least 25% less cholesterol than a reference food *and*
  2 g or less saturated fat per serving.
- **reduced saturated fat**
  at least 25% less saturated fat *and*
  reduced by more than 1 g saturated fat per serving compared with a reference food.
- **saturated fat free**
  less than 0.5 g of saturated fat *and*
  less than 0.5 g of *trans* fat.
- ***trans* fat free**
  less than 0.5 g of *trans* fat *and*
  less than 0.5 g of saturated fat per serving.

Fiber Terms

- **high fiber** 5 g or more per serving. (Foods making high-fiber claims must fit the definition of low fat, or the level of total fat must appear next to the high-fiber claim.)
- **good source of fiber** 2.5 g to 4.9 g per serving.
- **more** or **added fiber** at least 2.5 g more per serving than a reference food.

Sodium Terms

- **low sodium** 140 mg or less sodium per serving.
- **reduced sodium** at least 25% lower in sodium than the regular product.
- **sodium free** less than 5 mg per serving.
- **very low sodium** 35 mg or less sodium per serving.

Other Terms

- **free, without, no, zero** none or a trivial amount. **Calorie free** means containing fewer than 5 calories per serving; **sugar free** or **fat free** means containing less than half a gram per serving.
- **fresh** raw, unprocessed, or minimally processed with no added preservatives.
- **good source** 10 to 19% of the Daily Value per serving.
- **healthy** low in fat, saturated fat, *trans* fat, cholesterol, and sodium and containing at least 10% of the Daily Value for vitamin A, vitamin C, iron, calcium, protein, or fiber.
- **high in** 20% or more of the Daily Value for a given nutrient per serving; synonyms include "rich in" or "excellent source."
- **less, fewer, reduced** containing at least 25% less of a nutrient or calories than a reference food. This may occur naturally or as a result of altering the food. For example, pretzels, which are usually low in fat, can claim to provide less fat than potato chips, a comparable food.
- **light** this descriptor has three meanings on labels:
  1. A serving provides one-third fewer calories or half the fat of the regular product.
  2. A serving of a low-calorie, low-fat food provides half the sodium normally present.
  3. The product is light in color and texture, so long as the label makes this intent clear, as in "light brown sugar."
- **more, extra** at least 10% more of the Daily Value than in a reference food. The nutrient may be added or may occur naturally.

[a]*The word lean as part of the brand name (as in "Lean Supreme") indicates that the product contains fewer than 10 grams of fat per serving.*

[b]*Foods containing more than 13 grams total fat per serving or per 50 grams of food must indicate those contents immediately after a cholesterol claim.*

a list of these regulated, reliable label terms along with their definitions. By remembering the meanings of these terms, consumers can make informed choices among foods. For example, any food providing 10 percent or more of the Daily Value for a nutrient can boast that it is "a good source" of the nutrient; a food providing 20 percent is considered "high" in the nutrient.

For nutrients that can be harmful if consumed excessively, such as saturated fat or sodium, foods providing less than 5 percent are desirable. For hard-to-get nutrients such as iron or calcium, a reasonable goal might be to choose foods that are "good sources" of or "high" in those nutrients several times a day. (See the Snapshot features of Chapters 7 and 8 for foods qualifying as "good sources" or better for the vitamins and minerals.)

Health Claims: The Reliable and Less Reliable

In the past, the FDA held manufacturers to the highest standards of scientific evidence before allowing them to place **health claims** (defined on page 50) on food labels. When a label stated "Diets low in sodium may reduce the risk of high blood pressure," for example, consumers could be sure that the FDA had substantial scientific support for the claim. Such reliable health claims still appear on food labels and they have a high degree of scientific validity (see Table 2-7).

Today, however, the FDA also allows other claims backed by weaker evidence to be made on labels. These are "qualified" claims in the sense that labels bearing them must also state the strength of the scientific evidence backing them up. Unfortunately, most people cannot distinguish between scientifically reliable claims and those that are best ignored.[2]

Structure/Function Claims

A label-reading consumer is much more likely to encounter a **structure-function claim** on either a food or supplement label than the more heavily regulated health claims just described. For the food manufacturer, printing a health claim stating that a product prevents or cures a disease involves acquiring

TABLE 2-7

Reliable Health Claims on Labels

These claims of potential health benefits are well-supported by research, but other similar-sounding claims may not be.

- Calcium and reduced risk of osteoporosis
- Sodium and reduced risk of hypertension
- Dietary saturated fat and cholesterol and reduced risk of coronary heart disease
- Dietary fat and reduced risk of cancer
- Fiber-containing grain products, fruits, and vegetables and reduced risk of cancer
- Fruits, vegetables, and grain products that contain fiber, particularly soluble fiber, and reduced risk of coronary heart disease
- Fruits and vegetables and reduced risk of cancer
- Folate and reduced risk of neural tube defects
- Sugar alcohols and reduced risk of tooth decay
- Soluble fiber from whole oats and from psyllium seed husk and reduced risk of coronary heart disease
- Soy protein and reduced risk of coronary heart disease
- Whole grains and reduced risk of coronary heart disease and certain cancers
- Plant sterol and plant stanol esters and reduced risk of coronary heart disease
- Potassium and reduced risk of hypertension and stroke

FIGURE 2-13

A Supplement Label

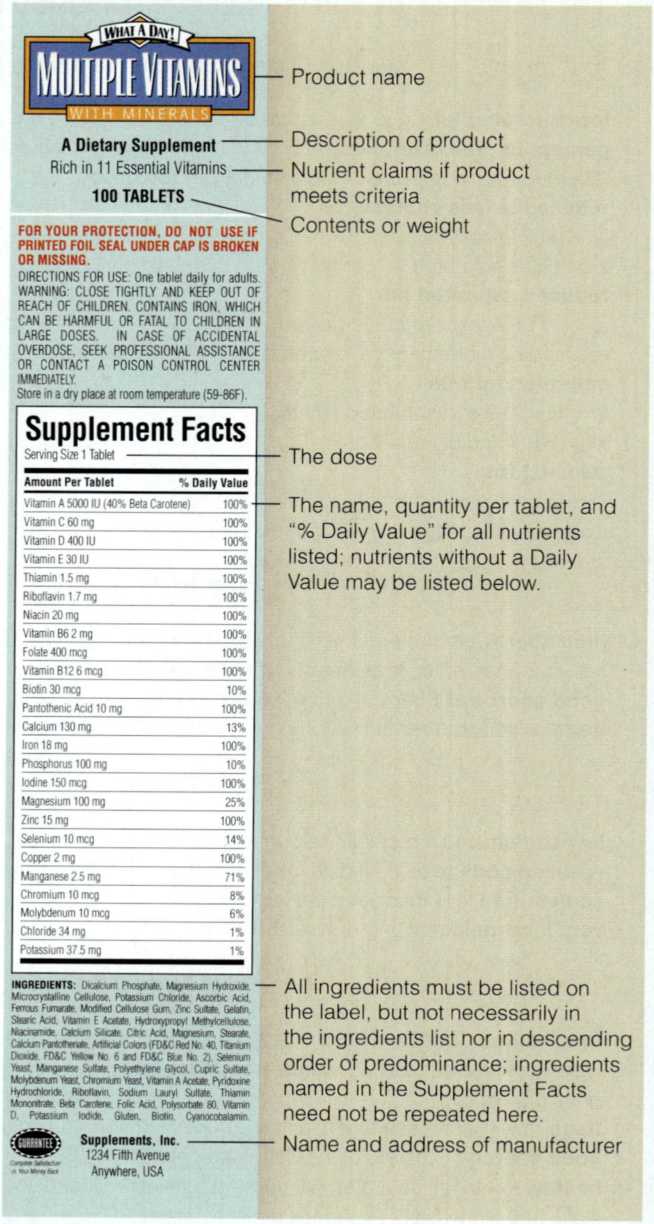

scientific evidence and submitting it in advance to petition the FDA for permission, a process costing much effort and expense. Instead, the manufacturer can use a similar-looking structure/function claim requiring no prior approval. Notification of the FDA is sufficient.

A problem is that, to a reasonable consumer, the two kinds of claims may seem to be identical:

- "Lowers cholesterol."
- "Helps maintain normal cholesterol levels."

The first, because it claims to reverse a disease-related condition (high cholesterol), requires FDA evaluation and approval before printing. The second structure/function claim refers only to a healthy body state, and so can be printed without prior approval.

A required label disclaimer (often found in tiny print) states that the FDA has not evaluated the claim and that the product is not intended to diagnose, treat, cure, or prevent any disease.[3] Often, however, structure/function claims stretch the truth.

Unfortunately, the presence of valid-appearing but unreliable label claims diminishes the usefulness of all health-related claims. Until laws require solid scientific backing for all claims on labels, consumers should ignore health-related claims and rely on the Nutrient Facts and Supplement Facts panels for nutrient information, directions, and warnings. Figure 2-13 provides a demonstration of a supplement label.

CONSUMER EDUCATION

Because labels are valuable only if people know how to use them, the FDA has designed several programs to educate consumers. Consumers who understand how to read labels are best able to apply the information to achieve and maintain healthful dietary practices.

By design, the nutrition messages from the *Dietary Guidelines for Americans,* the USDA Food Guide/MyPyramid, and food labels coordinate with each other, as Table 2-8 demonstrates. For example, a person striving to improve "Weight Management" (one of the *Dietary Guidelines*) can "select nutrient-dense foods" (USDA Food Guide advice) by searching for the words "low-calorie" or "calorie-reduced" on food labels. Label information about fats and sugars can provide more insight into the nutrient density of foods that bear labels. Our informed consumer can then make meaningful comparisons among the Nutrition Facts panels of selected foods. By making good use of food labels, our consumer can be confident that the foods going home in grocery sacks will help to meet the chosen Dietary Guideline, in this case, weight management.

TABLE 2-8 From Guidelines to Groceries

Dietary Guidelines for Americans set goals for nutritional health. The USDA Food Guide/MyPyramid offers a meal pattern to meet them. Food labels can then assist consumers in choosing among packaged foods with these goals and patterns in mind. (Don't forget that *unlabeled* fresh fruits, vegetables, and meats often excel in meeting nutrient needs and goals.)

Dietary Guidelines	USDA Food Guide/MyPyramid	Food Labels
Obtain adequate nutrients within energy needs	Select the recommended amounts from each food group at the energy level appropriate for your energy needs.	Look for foods that describe their vitamin, mineral, or fiber contents as a *good source* or *high*.
Weight management	Select nutrient-dense foods and beverages within and among the food groups. Limit high-fat foods and foods and beverages with added fats and sugars. Use appropriate portion sizes.	Look for foods that describe their calorie contents as *free, low, reduced, light,* or *less*.
Food groups to encourage	Select a variety of fruits each day. Include vegetables from all five subgroups (dark green, orange, legumes, starchy vegetables, and other vegetables) several times a week. Make at least half of the grain selections whole grains. Select fat-free or low-fat milk products.	Look for foods that describe their fiber contents as *good source* or *high*. Look for foods that provide at least 10% of the Daily Value for fiber, vitamin A, vitamin C, iron, and calcium from a variety of sources.
Fats	Choose foods within each group that are lean, low-fat, or fat-free. Choose foods within each group that have little added fat.	Look for foods that describe their fat, saturated fat, *trans* fat, and cholesterol contents as *free, less, low, light, reduced, lean,* or *extra lean*. Look for foods that provide no more than 5% of the Daily Value for fat, saturated fat, and cholesterol.
Carbohydrates	Choose fiber-rich fruits, vegetables, and whole grains often. Choose foods and beverages within each group that have little added sugars.	Look for foods that describe their sugar contents as *free* or *reduced*. A food may be high in sugar if its ingredients list begins with or contains several of the following: *sugar, sucrose, fructose, maltose, lactose, honey, syrup, corn syrup, high-fructose corn syrup, molasses, evaporated cane juice,* or *fruit juice concentrate*.
Sodium and potassium	Choose foods within each group that are low in salt or sodium. Choose potassium-rich foods such as fruits and vegetables.	Look for foods that describe their salt and sodium contents as *free, low,* or *reduced*. Look for foods that provide no more than 5% of the Daily Value for sodium. Look for foods that provide at least 10% of the Daily Value for potassium.
Alcoholic Beverages	Use sensibly and in moderation (no more than one drink a day for women and two drinks a day for men).	*Light* beverages contain fewer calories and less alcohol than regular versions.
Food Safety		Follow the *safe handling instructions* on packages of meat and other safety instructions, such as *keep refrigerated,* on packages of perishable foods.

CONCLUSION

The Nutrition Facts panels and ingredients lists on labels provide reliable information on which consumers can base their food choices. Regrettably, more and more of the health-related claims printed on labels are based on less-than-convincing scientific evidence. In the world of food and supplement marketing, label rulings put the consumer on notice: "Let the buyer beware."

FOOD FEATURE

Getting a Feel for the Nutrients in Foods

Figures 2-14 and 2-15 illustrate a playful contrast between two days' meals. "Monday's Meals" were selected according to the recommendations of this chapter and follow the sample menu of Figure 2-8, shown earlier (page 46). "Tuesday's Meals" were chosen more for convenience and familiarity than out of concern for nutrition.

COMPARING THE NUTRIENTS

How can a person compare the nutrients that these sets of meals provide? One way is to look up each food in a table of food composition, write down the food's nutrient values, and compare each one to a standard such as the DRI recommended intakes for nutrients, as we've done in Figures 2-14 and 2-15. By this measure, Monday's meals are the clear winners in terms of meeting nutrient needs within a calorie budget. Tuesday's meals oversupply calories and saturated fat while undersupplying fiber and critical vitamins and minerals.

Another useful exercise is to compare the total amounts of foods provided by a day's meals with the recommended amounts from each food group. A tally of the cups and ounces of foods consumed is provided in both Figures 2-14 and 2-15. The totals are then compared with MyPyramid recommendations in the tabular portion of the figures. The tables also identify whole grains and vegetable subgroups and tally discretionary calories from solid fats and sugars to complete the assessment.

MONDAY'S MEALS IN DETAIL

Monday's meals provide the necessary servings from each food group along with a small amount of oil needed for health, while the energy provided falls well within the 2,000-calorie allowance. A closer look at Monday's foods reveals that the whole-grain cereal at breakfast, whole-grain sandwich roll at lunch, and whole-grain crackers at snack time meet the recommendation to obtain at least half of the day's grain servings from whole grains.

For the vegetable subgroups, dark green vegetables, orange vegetables, and legumes are represented in the dinner salad, and "other vegetables" are prominent throughout. To repeat: it isn't necessary to choose vegetables from each subgroup every day, and the person eating this day's meals will need to include vegetables from other subgroups throughout the week. In addition, Monday's eating plan has room to spare in the discretionary calorie allowance for additional servings of favorite foods or for some sweets or fats.

TUESDAY'S MEALS IN DETAIL

Tuesday's meals, though abundant in oils, meats, and enriched grains, completely lack fruit and whole grains and are too low in vegetables and milk to provide adequate nutrients. Tuesday's meals supply too much saturated fat and sugar, as well as excessive meats and refined grains, pushing the calorie total well above the day's allowance. A single day of such fare poses little threat to the eater, but a steady diet of "Tuesday meals" presents a high probability of nutrient deficiencies and weight gain and greatly increases the risk of chronic diseases in later life.

COMPUTER—OR NOT?

If you have access to a computer, it can be a time saver—diet analysis programs perform all of these calculations at lightning speed. This convenience may make working it out yourself, using paper and a sharp pencil with a big eraser, seem a bit old-fashioned. But there are times when using a laptop or PDA (personal digital assistant) may not be practical—such as standing in line at the cafeteria or at a fast-food counter—where real-life food decisions must be made quickly.

People who work out diet analyses for themselves on paper and those who put extra time into studying, changing, and reviewing their computer results often learn to "see" the nutrients in foods (a skill you can develop by the time you reach Chapter 10). They can quickly assess their food options and make informed choices at mealtimes. People who fail to develop such skills must wait until they can access their computer programs to find out how well they did after the fact.

FIGURE 2-14

Monday's Meals—Nutrient-Dense Choices

Breakfast

© Polara Studios, Inc.

Lunch

© Polara Studios, Inc.

Afternoon snack

© Polara Studios, Inc.

Dinner

© Matthew Farruggio

Bedtime snack

© Quest Photographic, Inc.

Foods	MyPyramid Amounts	Energy (cal)	Saturated Fat (g)	Fiber (g)	Vitamin C (mg)	Calcium (mg)
Before heading off to class, a student eats breakfast:						
1 c whole-grain cold cereal	1 oz grains	108	—	3	14	95
1 c fat-free milk	1 c milk	100	—	—	2	306
1 medium banana (sliced)	½ c fruit	105	—	3	10	6
Then goes home for a quick lunch:						
1 roasted turkey sandwich	2 oz meat	50	—	1	60	27
on 2-oz whole-grain roll with	2 oz grains	343	4	2	—	89
1½ tsp low-fat mayonnaise	1½ tsp oils					
1 c low-salt vegetable juice	1 c vegetables					
While studying in the afternoon, the student eats a snack:						
4 whole-wheat reduced-fat crackers	½ oz grains	86	1	2	—	—
1½ oz low-fat cheddar cheese	1 c milk	74	2	—	—	176
1 apple	½ c fruit	72	—	3	6	8
That night, the student makes dinner:						
A salad:						
1 c raw spinach leaves, shredded carrots	1 c vegetables	19	—	2	18	61
¼ c garbanzo beans	1 oz legumes	71	—	3	2	19
5 lg olives and 2 tbs oil-based salad dressing	2 tsp oils	76	1	1	—	2
A main course:						
1 c spaghetti	2 oz grains	425	3	5	15	56
with meat sauce	2½ oz meat	22	—	2	6	29
½ c green beans	1 c vegetables	67	1	—	—	—
2 tsp soft margarine	2 tsp oils					
And for dessert:						
1 c strawberries	1 c fruit	49	—	3	89	24
Later that evening, the student enjoys a bedtime snack:						
3 graham crackers	½ oz grains	90	—	—	—	—
1 c fat-free milk	1 c milk	100	—	—	2	306
Totals:		1,857	12	30	224	1,204
DRI recommended intakes:[a]		2,000	<20[b]	25	75	1,000
Percentage of DRI recommended intakes:		93%	60%	120%	299%	120%

Intakes Compared with MyPyramid Amounts

Food Group	Breakfast	Lunch	Snack	Dinner	Snack	Monday's Totals	Recommended MyPyramid Amounts
Fruits	½ c		½ c	1 c		2 c	2 c
Vegetables		1 c		2 c		3 c	2½ c
Grains	1 oz	2 oz	½ oz	2 oz	½ oz	6 oz	6 oz
Meat and legumes		2 oz		3½ oz		5½ oz	5½ oz
Milk	1 c		1 c		1 c	3 c	3 c
Oils		1½ tsp		4 tsp		5½ tsp	5½ tsp
Calorie allowance						1,857 cal	2,000 cal

[a]*DRI values for a sedentary woman, age 19–30. Other DRI values are listed on the inside front cover, page B.*

[b]*The 20-gram value listed is the maximum allowable saturated fat for a 2,000-calorie diet. The DRI recommends consuming less than 10 percent of calories from saturated fat.*

FIGURE 2-15

Tuesday's Meals—Less Nutrient-Dense Choices

Breakfast

© Quest Photographic, Inc.

Lunch

© Quest Photographic, Inc.

Afternoon snack

© Polara Studios, Inc.

Dinner

© Quest Photographic, Inc.

Bedtime snack

© Michael Newman/PhotoEdit

Foods	MyPyramid Amounts	Energy (cal)	Saturated Fat (g)	Fiber (g)	Vitamin C (mg)	Calcium (mg)
Today, the student starts the day with a fast-food breakfast:						
1 c coffee	2 oz grains	5	—	—	—	—
1 English muffin with egg, cheese, and bacon	2 oz meat 1 c milk	436	9	2	—	266
Between classes, the student returns home for a quick lunch:						
1 peanut butter and jelly sandwich on white bread	2 oz grains 1 oz legumes	426	4	3	—	93
1 c whole milk	1 c milk	156	6	—	4	290
While studying, the student has:						
12 oz diet cola		—	—	—	—	—
Bag of chips (14 chips)[a]		105	2	—	4	—
That night for dinner, the student eats:						
A salad:						
1c lettuce						
1 tbs blue cheese dressing	1/2 c vegetables	84	2	1	2	23
A main course:						
6 oz steak	6 oz meat	349	6	—	—	27
1/2 baked potato	1/2 c vegetables	161	—	4	17	26
1 tbs butter		102	7	—	—	3
1 tbs sour cream[b]		31	2	—	—	17
12 oz diet cola		—	—	—	—	—
And for dessert:						
4 sandwich-type cookies	1 oz grains	158	2	1	—	—
Later on, a bedtime snack:						
2 cream-filled snack cakes	2 oz grains	250	2	2	—	20
1 c herbal tea		—	—	—	—	—
Totals:		2,263	42	13	27	765
DRI recommended intakes:[c]		2,000	<20[d]	25	75	1,000
Percentage of DRI recommended intakes:		113%	210%	52%	36%	77%

Intakes Compared with MyPyramid Amounts

Food Group	Breakfast	Lunch	Snack	Dinner	Snack	Tuesday's Totals	Recommended MyPyramid Amounts
Fruits						0 c	2 c
Vegetables			[a]	1 c		1 c	2 1/2 c
Grains	2 oz	2 oz		1 oz	2 oz	7 oz	6 oz
Meat and legumes	2 oz	2 oz		6 oz		9 oz	5 1/2 oz
Milk	1 c	1 c				2 c	3 c
Oils						7 1/2 tsp[b]	5 1/2 tsp
Calorie allowance						2,263 cal	2,000 cal

[a] *The potato in 14 potato chips provides less than 1/2 cup vegetables.*

[b] *The saturated fats of steak, butter, and sour cream are among the solid fats and do not qualify as oils.*

[c] *DRI values for a sedentary woman, age 19–30. Other DRI values are listed on the inside front cover, page B.*

[d] *The 20-gram value listed is the maximum allowable saturated fat for a 2,000-calorie diet. The DRI recommends consuming less than 10 percent of calories from saturated fat.*

Diet Analysis PLUS Concepts in Action

Compare Your Intakes with MyPyramid

The purpose of this chapter's exercise is to give you a feel for how your diet compares with MyPyramid and help you consider your discretionary calorie sources.

1. From the Home page of DA+, select the Reports tab and select MyPyramid Analysis. Choose Day Two of your three-day diet intake (from Chapter 1). Choose all meals for that day. Generate a report. Did your intake for that day conform to the MyPyramid pattern? Did you consume too few foods from any particular food group(s)? Which, if any, were lacking? Using Table 2-2 (page 44) and Figure 2-5 (pages 38–39) to guide you, suggest ways that you might realistically change your intake to better conform to the MyPyramid diet pattern.
2. What about fat? Select the Reports tab then Macronutrient Ranges. Generate a report. Did your fat intake fall between 20–35 percent of your total energy? Did you take in enough raw oils to meet your need (see Table 2-2, page 44)? Which ones? Change your date to include all three days of your record and generate a report to see a fat intake average. How does your single day's fat intake compare with your three-day average?
3. Find your discretionary calorie allowance on the bottom line of Table 2-2. Select the Track Diet tab and look over your day's food list. Which foods provided discretionary calories? (Use Table 2-1 on page 43 as a guide.)
4. Breaking this information down further, consider that the USDA generally recommends that no more than half of the day's discretionary calories come from added sugars. Which foods on your food list contribute added sugars? If you consumed substantial amounts of added sugars, suggest realistic ways to reduce your intake.
5. A great feature of the Diet Analysis program is its Source Analysis Report that allows you to list food sources of calories (kcal) or specific nutrients in order of predominance. From the Reports tab, select Source Analysis, Day Three, and choose all meals. Generate a report. Which foods provided most to your calorie intake on that day? If you consumed vegetables, where did they fall on the list? In later chapters you'll use this report again to analyze various nutrients in your diet.

MEDIA MENU

CENGAGENOW Throughout this chapter, the Cengage NOW logo indicates an opportunity for online self-study, linking you to interactive tutorials and videos based on your level of understanding. Go to **www.cengage.com/sso.**

Search for "diet" and "food labels" at the U.S. Government health information site: **www.healthfinder.gov.**

Learn more about the Dietary Guidelines for Americans: **www.healthierus.gov/dietaryguidelines.**

Learn more about the USDA Food Guide and MyPyramid: **www.mypyramid.gov.**

Get healthy eating tips and ideas of ways of eating more fruits and vegetables: **www.fruitsandveggiesmatter.gov.**

Find Canadian information on nutrition guidelines and food labels at: **www.hc-sc.gc.ca.**

SELF CHECK

Answers to these Self Check questions are in Appendix G.

1. The nutrient standards in use today include all of the following *except:*

   A. Adequate Intakes (AI)

   B. Daily Minimum Requirements (DMR)

   C. Daily Values (DV)

   D. (a) and (c)

2. The Dietary Reference Intakes were devised for which of the following purposes?
   A. to set nutrient goals for individuals
   B. to suggest upper limits of intakes, above which toxicity is likely
   C. to set average nutrient requirements for use in research
   D. all of the above
3. According to the USDA Food Guide, which of the following may be counted among either the meats or the vegetables?
   A. chicken
   B. avocados
   C. black beans
   D. potatoes
4. The USDA Food Guide recommends a small amount of daily oil from which of these sources?
   A. olives
   B. nuts
   C. vegetable oil
   D. all of the above
5. Which of the following values is found on food labels?
   A. Daily Values
   B. Dietary Reference Intakes
   C. Recommended Dietary Allowances
   D. Estimated Average Requirements
6. The energy intake recommendation is set at a level predicted to maintain body weight.
   T F
7. The Dietary Reference Intakes (DRI) are for all people, regardless of their medical history.
   T F
8. People who choose not to eat meat or animal products need to find an alternative to the USDA Food Guide when planning their diets.
   T F
9. By law, food labels must state as a percentage of the Daily Values the amounts of vitamin C, vitamin A, niacin, and thiamin present in food.
   T F
10. To be labeled "low fat," a food must contain 3 grams of fat or less per serving.
   T F

CONTROVERSY 2

Are Some Foods "Superfoods" for Health?

LO 2.6

Headlines these days often focus on the latest "superfoods" for health: "Forgetful? Blueberries sharpen brain function!" "Too many colds? Try immune-boosting soybeans!" "Worried about cancer? Eat tomatoes!" Can simply eating certain foods accomplish these wondrous things? Although headlines tend to overstate their talents, what these foods and many others have in common is a rich supply of **phytochemicals**—nonnutrient components of plants, introduced in Chapter 1. Phytochemicals often act as bioactive food components, food constituents with the ability to alter body processes (terms are defined in Table C2-1).

Just a few of today's "superfoods" appear here; later chapters address others, such as olive oil and nuts (Controversy 5) and broccoli and its relatives (Chapter 11). These are **functional foods** of the simplest kind—they naturally contain substances having biological activity in the body beyond those of the nutrients. Other functional foods arise when manufacturers dose candy bars, juices, margarine, snack chips, and the like with nutrients, phytochemicals, herbs, or other bioactive food components.[1]* Which kind might be most beneficial to health and why are topics of the last section of this Controversy.

A SCIENTIST'S VIEW OF PHYTOCHEMICALS

At one time, phytochemicals were known only for their sensory properties in foods, such as taste, aroma, texture, and color. Thank phytochemicals for the burning sensation of hot peppers, the pungent flavor of onions and garlic, the bitter tang of chocolate, the aromatic qualities of herbs, and the beautiful colors of tomatoes, spinach, pink grapefruit, and watermelon.

Today, phytochemicals are emerging as potential regulators of health: many act as antioxidants that protect DNA and other cellular compounds from oxidative damage; some interact with genes to regulate protein synthesis; some mimic hormones; while others alter the blood chemistry in other ways.[2]

Of the tens of thousands of phytochemicals known to exist, just a few have been researched at all, and only a sampling of those are mentioned in this Controversy—enough to illustrate their potential roles in human health and the wide array of foods that supply them. So far, the most promising results have come from studies of cells or animals; studies of human beings are less encouraging.[3]

Many phytochemicals belong to the large chemical group known as **flavonoids.** Many plant foods, including many fruits, vegetables, whole grains, nuts, red wine, spices, and even dark chocolate (see Table C2-2), contain them. Such phytochemicals may act at the level of the genes to reduce inflammatory processes related to many disease processes.[4]

Blueberries

C Squared Studios/Photodisc/Getty Images

When researchers feed rats on chow rich in blueberry extracts, they exhibit fewer age-related mental declines than rats on plain chow.[5] The **antioxidant** phytochemicals of blueberries are credited with the effect because they reduce oxidative stress.[6] Oxidative stress is a chemical imbalance that promotes inflammation and damages molecular structures of cells. Chronic oxidative stress worsens the brain's loss of mental powers as it ages. The brain cannot readily replace its damaged cells, so when oxidative damage builds over time, memory and reasoning, loss of muscle control, and other brain function diminish.[7]

Are blueberries a brain superfood, then? Although blueberries currently lead the way in antioxidant and brain research, it is unknown whether or not they can prevent aging effects in the human brain. Furthermore, antioxidants in other berries, artichokes, coffee, pomegranates, spinach, or even seaweed could turn out to play similar or better roles.[8] In addition, the brain needs carbohydrate, certain lipids, and vitamins and minerals for peak performance. Rather than gambling on one particular food's phytochemical, the wisest course is to choose a variety of phytochemical-rich fruits and vegetables in the context of an adequate, balanced diet needed to sustain brain functioning.

Chocolate

© Matthew Farruggio

Imagine the delight of young research subjects who were paid to eat 3 ounces of dark (bittersweet) chocolate for an experiment. Less appealingly, researchers then drew blood from the subjects to test whether an antioxidant flavonoid in chocolate was absorbed into

*Reference notes are found in Appendix F.

TABLE C2-1 **Phytochemical and Functional Food Terms**

- **antioxidants** (anti-OX-ih-dants) compounds that protect other compounds from damaging reactions involving oxygen by themselves reacting with oxygen (*anti* means "against"; *oxy* means "oxygen"). *Oxidation* is a potentially damaging effect of normal cell chemistry involving oxygen (more in Chapters 5 and 7).
- **bioactive food components** compounds in foods, either nutrients or phytochemicals, that alter physiological processes.
- **broccoli sprouts** the sprouted seed of *Brassica italica,* or the common broccoli plant; believed to be a functional food by virtue of its high phytochemical content.
- **drug** any substance that when taken into a living organism may modify one or more of its functions.
- **edamame** fresh green soybeans, a source of phytoestrogens.
- **flavonoids** (FLAY-von-oyds) members of a chemical family of yellow pigments in foods; phytochemicals that may exert physiological effects on the body. *Flavus* means "yellow."
- **flaxseed** small brown seed of the flax plant; used in baking, cereals, or other foods. Valued in nutrition as a source of fatty acids, lignans, and fiber.
- **functional foods** whole or modified foods that contain bioactive food components believed to provide health benefits, such as reduced disease risks, beyond the benefits that their nutrients confer. All whole foods are functional in some ways because they provide at least some needed substances, but certain foods stand out as rich sources of bioactive food components. Also defined in Chapter 1.
- **genistein** (GEN-ih-steen) a phytoestrogen found primarily in soybeans that both mimics and blocks the action of estrogen in the body.
- **kefir** (KEE-fur) a liquid form of yogurt, based on milk, probiotic microorganisms, and flavorings.
- **lignans** phytochemicals present in flaxseed, but not in flax oil, that are converted to phytoestrogens by intestinal bacteria and are under study as possible anticancer agents.
- **lutein** (LOO-teen) a plant pigment of yellow hue; a phytochemical believed to play roles in eye functioning and health.
- **lycopene** (LYE-koh-peen) a pigment responsible for the red color of tomatoes and other red-hued vegetables; a phytochemical that may act as an antioxidant in the body.
- **miso** fermented soybean paste used in Japanese cooking. Soy products are considered to be functional foods.
- **organosulfur compounds** a large group of phytochemicals containing the mineral sulfur. Organosulfur phytochemicals are responsible for the pungent flavors and aromas of foods belonging to the onion, leek, chive, shallot, and garlic family and are thought to stimulate cancer defenses in the body.
- **phytochemicals** (FIGH-toe-CHEM-ih-cals) compounds in plants that confer color, taste, and other characteristics. Often, the bioactive food components of functional foods. Also defined in Chapter 1. *Phyto* means "plant."
- **phytoestrogens** (FIGH-toe-ESS-troh-gens) phytochemicals structurally similar to the female sex hormone estrogen. Phytoestrogens weakly mimic estrogen or modulate hormone activity in the human body.
- **phytosterols** phytochemicals that resemble cholesterol in structure, but that lower blood cholesterol by interfering with cholesterol absorption in the intestine. Phytosterols include sterol esters and stanol esters.
- **prebiotic** a substance that may not be digestible by the host, such as fiber, but that serves as food for probiotic bacteria and thus promotes their growth.
- **probiotic** a live microorganism which, when administered in adequate amounts, alters the bacterial colonies of the body in ways believed to confer a health benefit on the host.
- **resveratrol** (rez-VER-ah-trol) a flavonoid of grapes under study for potential health benefits.
- **soy milk** a milklike beverage made from soybeans, claimed to be a functional food. Soy drinks should be fortified with vitamin A, vitamin D, riboflavin, and calcium to approach the nutritional equivalency of milk.
- **tofu** a white curd made of soybeans, popular in Asian cuisines, and considered to be a functional food.

the bloodstream. The tests were positive: the flavonoid had indeed accumulated in their blood. At the same time, the level of potentially harmful oxidizing compounds had dropped by 40 percent.

The heart, vulnerable to damage by oxidation, could benefit from such flavonoids and other antioxidants (Table C2-3 lists some contributors).[†9] In addition, dark chocolate may reduce the likelihood of blood clots, promote normal blood pressure, help to relax blood vessels, improve blood lipids, and reduce inflammation, factors associated with heart disease prevention.[10] A recent study, however, detected no benefits of chocolate in terms of heart risk factors or as an indicator of inflammation.[11] No one yet knows whether chocolate fans actually suffer less heart disease.

If eating chocolate daily sounds appealing, consider another centuries-old medicinal use of chocolate: promoting weight gain. Three ounces of sweetened chocolate candy contain over 400 calories, a significant portion of most people's daily calorie allowance. At the same time, chocolate contributes few nutrients, save two—fat and sugar. For most people, antioxidant phytochemicals are best obtained from nutrient-dense, low-calorie fruits and vegetables—with chocolate savored as an occasional treat.

Flaxseed

Flaxseed is valued for relieving constipation and digestive distress, but other potential health benefits are

†*Dark chocolate is rich in flavonoids; milk chocolate or "Dutch" processed chocolate have reduced flavonoid content.*

TABLE C2-2 **Phytochemicals—Their Food Sources and Potential Actions**

Chemical Name	Possible Effects	Food Sources
Alkylresorcinols (phenolic lipids)	May contribute to the protective effect of grains in reducing the risks of diabetes, heart disease, and some cancers.	Whole-grain wheat and rye
Allicin (organosulfur compound)	Antimicrobial that may reduce ulcers; may lower blood cholesterol.	Chives, garlic, leeks, onions
Capsaicin	Modulates blood clotting, possibly reducing the risk of fatal clots in heart and artery disease.	Hot peppers
Carotenoids (include beta-carotene, lycopene, lutein, and hundreds of related compounds)	Act as antioxidants, possibly reducing risks of cancer and other diseases.	Deeply pigmented fruits and vegetables (apricots, broccoli, cantaloupe, carrots, pumpkin, spinach, sweet potatoes, tomatoes)
Curcumin	Acts as an antioxidant and anti-inflammatory agent; may reduce blood clot formation; may inhibit enzymes that activate carcinogens.	Turmeric, a yellow-colored spice
Flavonoids (include flavones, flavonols, isoflavones, catechins, and others)	Act as antioxidants; scavenge carcinogens; bind to nitrates in the stomach, preventing conversion to nitrosamines; inhibit cell proliferation.	Berries, black tea, celery, citrus fruits, green tea, olives, onions, oregano, purple grapes, purple grape juice, soybeans and soy products, vegetables, whole wheat, wine
Genistein and daidzein (isoflavones)	Phytoestrogens that inhibit cell replication in GI tract; may reduce or elevate risk of breast, colon, ovarian, prostate, and other estrogen-sensitive cancers; may reduce cancer cell survival; may reduce risk of osteoporosis.	Soybeans, soy flour, soy milk, tofu, textured vegetable protein, other legume products
Indoles (organosulfur compound)	May trigger production of enzymes that block DNA damage from carcinogens; may inhibit estrogen action.	Cruciferous vegetables such as broccoli, brussels sprouts, cabbage, cauliflower, horseradish, mustard greens, kale
Isothiocyanates (organosulfur compounds that include sulforaphane)	Act as antioxidants; inhibit enzymes that activate carcinogens; activate enzymes that detoxify carcinogens; may reduce risk of breast cancer, prostate cancer.	Cruciferous vegetables such as broccoli, brussels sprouts, cabbage, cauliflower, horseradish, mustard greens, kale
Lignans	Phytoestrogens that block estrogen activity in cells possibly reducing the risk of cancer of the breast, colon, ovaries, and prostate.	Flaxseed and its oil, whole grains
Monoterpenes (including limonene)	May trigger enzyme production to detoxify carcinogens; inhibit cancer promotion and cell proliferation.	Citrus fruit peels and oils
Phenolic acids	May trigger enzyme production to make carcinogens water-soluble, facilitating excretion.	Coffee beans, fruits (apples, blueberries, cherries, grapes, oranges, pears, prunes), oats, potatoes, soybeans
Phytic acid	Binds to minerals, preventing free-radical formation, possibly reducing cancer risk.	Whole grains
Resveratrol	Acts as antioxidant; may inhibit cancer growth; reduce inflammation, LDL oxidation, and blood clot formation.	Red wine, peanuts, grapes, raspberries
Saponins (glucosides)	May interfere with DNA replication, preventing cancer cells from multiplying; stimulate immune response.	Alfalfa sprouts, other sprouts, green vegetables, potatoes, tomatoes
Tannins	Act as antioxidants; may inhibit carcinogen activation and cancer promotion.	Black-eyed peas, grapes, lentils, red and white wine, tea

TABLE C2-3

Common Foods Ranked by Antioxidant Content

1.	Blackberries
2.	Walnuts
3.	Strawberries
4.	Spinach
5.	Artichokes, prepared
6.	Cranberries
7.	Coffee
8.	Raspberries
9.	Pecans
10.	Blueberries
11.	Cloves, ground
12.	Grape juice, cranberry juice, pomegranate juice
13.	Chocolate, dark, unsweetened
14.	Cherries, sour
15.	Wine, red

emerging from research. Flaxseed contains **lignans,** compounds converted into biologically active **phytoestrogens** by bacteria that normally reside in the human intestine. Some evidence about their effects follows:

- Flaxseed intake, but not flaxseed oil, appears to improve blood lipids in ways supportive of heart health, particularly among older women.[12]
- Rats fed chow high in flaxseed develop fewer cancerous changes and reduced tumor growth in mammary tissue under experimental conditions.[13]
- In one study, men with prostate cancer given flaxseed had less cancer cell proliferation than controls.[14]

Some evidence also suggests that flaxseed may lower blood pressure.[15] Some risks are associated with flaxseed overuse, however. Flaxseed contains compounds that interfere with vitamin or mineral absorption, and thus high daily flaxseed intakes could cause nutrient deficiencies. Large quantities of flaxseed also cause digestive distress. Including a spoonful or two of flaxseed in the diet may not be a bad idea, however. Flaxseed richly supplies linolenic acid, an essential fatty acid often lacking in the U.S. diet (see Chapter 5).

Garlic

EyeWire, Inc.

For thousands of years, people have credited garlic with medicinal properties. Descriptions of its uses for headaches, heart disease, and tumors are recorded in early Egyptian medical writings. Scientific study of garlic's properties are ongoing.

Among garlic's most promising constituents are antioxidant **organosulfur compounds,** reported to inhibit cancer development.[16] Oxidizing compounds damage DNA in animal cells and trigger cancerous changes.[17] Antioxidants of garlic quench these oxidizing compounds, at least in test tubes. Whether garlic prevents cancers in people is unknown.[18] Other potential roles for garlic include opposing allergies, heart disease, infections, and ulcers, but these effects remain uncertain.[19] However, if you like garlicky foods, you can consume them with confidence; history and at least some research are on your side.

Often, studies of garlic *supplements,* such as powders and oil, have been disappointing. No one can say with certainty whether large doses of concentrated chemicals from garlic may improve a person's health, but for those who like garlic, fresh garlic may offer the best hope of obtaining benefits.[20]

Soybeans and Soy Products

Mitch Hrdlicka/ Photodisc/Getty Images

Compared with people in the West, Asians living in Asia suffer less frequently from heart disease; cancers, especially of the breast, colon, and prostate; and osteoporosis (adult bone loss). Women in Asia also suffer less from symptoms related to menopause, the midlife decline in women's estrogen secretion when menstruation ceases. When Asians immigrate to the United States and adopt Western diets and habits, however, they experience these diseases and problems at the same rates as native Westerners.

Asians consume far more soybeans and soy products, such as **edamame, miso, soy milk, tofu,** and other soy foods than do Westerners. Soybeans are rich sources of **phytoestrogens.** However, soy is just one among many diet and lifestyle differences between East and West—and even the forms of soy foods consumed in these areas differ.[21] To determine whether soy foods account for differences in disease rates requires clinical evidence, not just correlation.

Soy and Chronic Diseases A small drop in blood cholesterol occurs when subjects, particularly men with elevated cholesterol, replace meat and dairy foods in their diets with soy protein sources.[22] It takes a lot of soy to achieve this effect—more than half the daily protein intake must come from soy.[23] Also, the effect comes from food; benefits are diminished if the phytoestrogen is removed from the soybean matrix.[24] As is true for flaxseed, soy foods contain compounds that intestinal bacteria convert to biologically active forms.[25]

With regard to cancer, concerns about breast cancer, colon cancer, and prostate cancer involve estrogen-sensitive varieties—cancers that grow when exposed to estrogen. Soy phytoestrogens are chemical relatives of the human hormone estrogen and may weakly mimic or oppose the hormone's effects. Age of the eater affects the results: a high soy intake during childhood and adolescence seems to reduce breast cancer risk in women before menopause; soy intake by adults may or may not reduce this risk, but more research is needed to clarify these relationships.[26]

Soy's Downsides Low doses of one soy phytoestrogen, genistein, appear to speed up division of breast cancer cells in laboratory cultures and in mice, and high doses seemed to do the opposite.[27] Still under study is whether consuming soy phytoestrogens may do the same in living people, but it seems unlikely that moderate intakes of soy foods would do so.[28] If they did, soy-eating cultures would have higher, not lower, incidences of these cancers. In concentrated supplement form, soy phytoestrogens may interfere with the actions of a **drug** used in breast cancer treatment, however.[29] Also, high doses of genistein given to pregnant mice produced female offspring with a high risk of cancer of the uterus.[‡] Pregnant women should never take chances with unproven supplements of any kind (Chapter 13 explains why).With regard to the biological activity of soy, scientific understanding is incomplete.[30]

As for menopause, no consistent findings indicate that soy phytoestrogens can eliminate the common sensations of elevated body temperature known as "hot flashes."[31] Some evidence does suggest that soy phytoestrogens may help to preserve women's bone density after menopause but more research is required to confirm or refute this finding.[32] Hormone replacement therapy, once routinely used in menopause to prevent symptoms and bone loss, involves serious health risks, so alternatives are needed. Phytoestrogen supplements sold as "natural" hormone therapy are unproven, however, and may pose health risks.

The opposing actions of phytoestrogens should raise a red flag against taking supplements, especially by people who have had cancer or whose close relatives have developed cancer. The American Cancer Society recommends that breast cancer survivors and those under treatment for breast cancer should consume only moderate amounts of soy foods as part of a healthy plant-based diet and should not intentionally ingest very high levels of soy products.

Tomatoes

PhotoDisc/Getty Images

People around the world who eat the most tomatoes, about five tomato-containing meals per week, are less likely to suffer from cancers of the esophagus, prostate, or stomach than those who avoid tomatoes. Among phytochemical candidates for promoting this effect is **lycopene,** a red pigment with antioxidant activity found in guava, papaya, pink grapefruit, tomatoes (especially cooked tomatoes and tomato products), and watermelon.

Lycopene and some of its chemical relatives filter high-energy wavelengths of visible light. In the skin, they may act as a sort of internal sunscreen, protecting skin from damaging sun rays that cause skin cancer.[§33] Lycopene and some products of its metabolism also act as antioxidants and, theoretically, could inhibit the growth of cancer cells, but so far, research does not support the idea.[34] Something else about tomato-eating peoples may be reducing their risks.

An evidence-based review by the FDA concluded that no or very little credible evidence exists to support an association between lycopene or tomato consumption and reduced cancer rates.[35] It does appear that lycopene supplements are not as hazardous as those of its chemical cousins, beta-carotene and lutein, which clearly raise the risk of lung cancer in smokers.[36]

Tea, Wine, Pomegranate, and Whole Grain

Photodisc/Getty Images

Diets containing flavonoid-rich foods are frequently credited with health-promoting qualities. For example, a recent study suggests that young women who drink three or more cups of tea each day suffer less breast cancer than others.[37] When researchers reviewed the results of 51 studies, the evidence for green tea and cancer was mixed—sometimes drinking the tea seemed protective but other times it did not, so no conclusion can be drawn.[38]

People in Japan who drink five cups of green tea each day die less often from a form of stroke than people who drink less than a cup.[39] Green tea consumption has also been associated with reduced oxidative stress and inflammation among smokers, lower blood lipids, and even reduced body fatness.[40] Whether such associations will hold up under further scrutiny is unknown. High-dose supplements of green tea extract have caused liver toxicity and should be avoided.[41]

A flavonoid in purple grape juice and red wine, **resveratrol,** seems to hold promise as a disease fighter, but the amount present in wine or a serving of grape juice may be too small to benefit human health.[**] The flavonoid has been credited with extending the life of yeast cells, worms, flies, and fish but no one knows if such an effect is plausible for human beings.[42] In population studies, people who regularly consume red wine, grapes and their products, and other flavonoid-rich fruits and vegetables often have a lower incidence of cardiovascular disease than others.[43] Scientists have suggested biological mechanisms by which these foods might reduce disease risks but controlled clinical human trials to show that people's hearts actually benefit from grape consumption are still lacking.[44]

In high doses, resveratrol has also demonstrated some anticancer activities, but such doses are larger than those attainable by diet, even with daily red wine intake.[45] As for drinking red wine for health, Controversy 3 concludes that the immediate risks from alcoholic beverages for young adults may outweigh potential benefits.

The juice of the pomegranate fruit ranks high among juices in antioxidants. Antioxidants reduce the oxidative stress and tissue inflammation, conditions associated with many chronic diseases.[46] Much is yet to be learned about the bioavailability, metabolism, and health effects of the principal phytochemicals of pomegranates.

Flavonoids in whole grains may confer health benefits on the eater but also impart a bitter taste. To please consumers who tend to prefer mild or sweet flavors, food producers refine away flavonoid-rich plant parts, such as bran or fruit skins. Thus, white bread, white grape juice, and white wine lack the flavonoid contents of their darker counterparts.

Yogurt

Yogurt is a special case among "superfoods." Although yogurt lacks

‡The drug is DES, or diethylstilbestrol, once given to pregnant women before discovery of the greatly increased risk of uterine and breast cancer among their daughters.

§The other carotenoid relatives of lycopene are lutein and zeaxanthin—more about them in Chapter 7.

***The flavonoid is resveratrol.*

phytochemicals from plants, it contains living *Lactobacillus* or other bacteria that ferment milk into yogurt or a liquid yogurt beverage called **kefir.** Such microorganisms, or **probiotics,** can set up residence in the digestive tract and alter its functioning in ways that are claimed to reduce diseases such as colon cancer, ulcers, and other digestive problems; reduce allergies; or improve immunity and resistance to infections.[47] *Lactobacillus* organisms may indeed be useful for improving the diarrhea that often occurs from the use of antibiotic drugs or from other causes.[48] Reports of increased mortality among patients with diseases of the pancreas and serious infections in those with compromised immunity raise concerns about the safety of probiotic microorganism supplements for some groups of people.[49]

© Sue Wilson/Alamy

Certain foods provide **prebiotics,** nutrients such as certain carbohydrates, that probiotic organisms need to grow. Certain by-products of such bacterial growth appear to decrease inflammation of the colon, a condition related to disease.[50] More research is needed to clarify whether probiotics and prebiotics may benefit or harm human health.[51]

PHYTOCHEMICAL SUPPLEMENTS

No doubt exists that diets rich in whole grains, legumes, vegetables, fruits, and other whole foods reduce the risks of heart disease and cancer, but isolating the responsible food, nutrient, or phytochemical has proved difficult. Foods deliver thousands of bioactive food components, all within a food matrix that maximizes their availability and effectiveness.[52] Broccoli, and particularly **broccoli sprouts,** may contain as many as 10,000 different phytochemicals—each with the potential to influence some action in the body. These foods are under study for their potential to defend against cancers at the DNA level, and Chapter 11 comes back to them.[53]

Even if it were known with certainty which foods protect against which diseases, no one can yet predict what diseases any given person may suffer, much less whether an isolated supplement might be of use. Individual phytochemicals, like actors in a play, are part of a larger story with intertwining and complementary roles—a fact that reinforces the principle of variety in diet planning.

Supporters of Phytochemical Supplements

Users and sellers of phytochemical supplements argue that existing evidence is good enough to recommend that people take supplements of purified phytochemicals. Users, eager for potential benefits, and sellers, hoping for profits, tend to discount the potential for harm from "natural" substances. People have been consuming foods containing phytochemicals for tens of thousands of years, they say, and because the body can handle phytochemicals in foods, it stands to reason that supplements of those phytochemicals are safe as well.

Detractors of Phytochemical Supplements

Such thinking raises concerns among scientists. They point out that although the body is equipped to handle phytochemicals when diluted in the other constituents of whole foods, it is not adapted to concentrated supplement doses. Further, the body absorbs only small amounts of these compounds into the bloodstream and quickly destroys most types with its detoxifying equipment.[54] No one knows why the body thus defends itself against these substances, but supplements of them overwhelm the body's defenses.

Consider these facts about phytochemical supplements and health:

1. Phytochemicals alter body functions, sometimes powerfully, in ways that are only partly understood.
2. Evidence for the safety of isolated phytochemicals in human beings is lacking.
3. No regulatory body oversees the safety of phytochemicals sold to consumers. No studies proving their safety or effectiveness are required before they are marketed.
4. Phytochemical labels may make structure-function claims but existing research to support such claims is generally weak or nonexistent.

Phytochemical researchers conclude that the best-known, most effective, and safest sources for bioactive food components are foods, not supplements. Even those in foods, however, can interfere with the activities of certain drugs and undermine the medical treatment of serious diseases.[55] Such food and drug interactions are of critical importance, and the Controversy section of Chapter 14 is devoted to them.

THE CONCEPT OF FUNCTIONAL FOODS

Virtually all whole foods have some special value in supporting health and are therefore functional foods. Cranberries may help prevent urinary tract infections; garlic may lower blood cholesterol; and green tea may inhibit ulcer infections, just to name a few examples.[56] Manufactured functional foods, however, often consist of processed foods that are fortified with nutrients or enhanced with bioactive food components (calcium-fortified orange juice, for example). The creation of these functional foods is a fast-growing trend in the global food supply.[57]

An example of a popular manufactured food is a margarine blended with a **phytosterol** intended to lower blood cholesterol.[58] Such novel functional foods raise questions:

- Does the margarine constitute a food or a drug?[59]
- Which is the better choice for the health-conscious diet planner: to eat a food with additives that affect body function or to adjust the diet?
- Does it make more sense to add cholesterol-lowering margarine to the diet or to replace butter with unsaturated oils and eat more plant foods to supply phytosterols?[60]
- Is it more beneficial to eat fried snack foods sprinkled with phytochemicals and candy bars laced with vitamins than to obtain these substances from ordinary foods?
- What about smoothies packed with medicinal herbs—are these foods safe to consume regularly? Are they safe for children?

Critics suggest that the designation "functional foods" may be nothing more than a marketing tool. After all, even the most experienced researchers cannot yet identify the perfect combination of bioactive food components to support optimal health. Yet manufacturers freely generate and distribute such concoctions as if they possessed that knowledge.

© Craig M. Moore

Functional foods currently on the market promise to "enhance mood," "promote relaxation and good karma," "increase alertness," and "improve memory," among other claims.

THE FINAL WORD

In light of all of the evidence for and against phytochemicals and functional foods, it seems clear that a moderate approach is warranted. People who eat the recommended amounts of a variety of fruits and vegetables each day may cut their risk for many diseases by as much as half. Replacing some meat with soy foods and other legumes may also lower heart disease and cancer risks. Choosing green tea or vegetable juice, or fruit juice within bounds, instead of daily soft drinks may also cut risks. In the context of a healthy diet, ordinary foods are time-tested for safety, posing virtually no risk of toxic levels of nutrients or phytochemicals (although some contain natural toxins; see Chapter 12). Table C2-4 offers some tips for consuming the foods known to provide phytochemicals.

Various beneficial constituents are widespread among foods, and research indicates that a diverse selection of fruits and vegetables in the diet is more beneficial than an equal number of servings from just a few types.[61] In other words, don't try to single out a few "superfoods" or phytochemicals for their magical health effects. Instead, take a no-nonsense approach where your health is concerned: choose a wide variety of whole grains, legumes, nuts, fruits, and vegetables in the context of an adequate, balanced, and varied diet to receive all of the health benefits these foods can offer.

TABLE C2-4 Tips for Consuming Phytochemicals

- Eat more fruit. The average U.S. diet provides little more than ½ cup fruit a day. Remember to choose juices and raw, dried, or cooked fruits and vegetables at mealtimes as well as for snacks. Choose dried fruit in place of candy.
- Increase vegetable portions. Double the normal portion of cooked plain, nonstarchy vegetables to 1 cup.
- Use herbs and spices. Cookbooks offer ways to include parsley, basil, garlic, hot peppers, oregano, and other beneficial seasonings.
- Replace some meat. Replace some of the meat in the diet with grains, legumes, and vegetables. Oatmeal, soy meat replacer, or grated carrots mixed with ground meat and seasonings make a luscious, nutritious meat loaf, for example.
- Add grated vegetables. Carrots in chili or meatballs, celery and squash in spaghetti sauce, etc. add phytochemicals without greatly changing the taste of the food.
- Try new foods. Try a new fruit, vegetable, or whole grain each week. Walk through vegetable aisles and visit farmers' markets. Read recipes. Try tofu, fortified soy drink, or soybeans in cooking.

3 The Remarkable Body

DO YOU EVER . . .

- Feel your heart beat and wonder where the blood goes?
- Hear people say "You are what you eat" and think it is just an old saying?
- Wonder how food on the plate becomes nourishment for your body?
- Take antacids to relieve heartburn?

Keep reading . . .

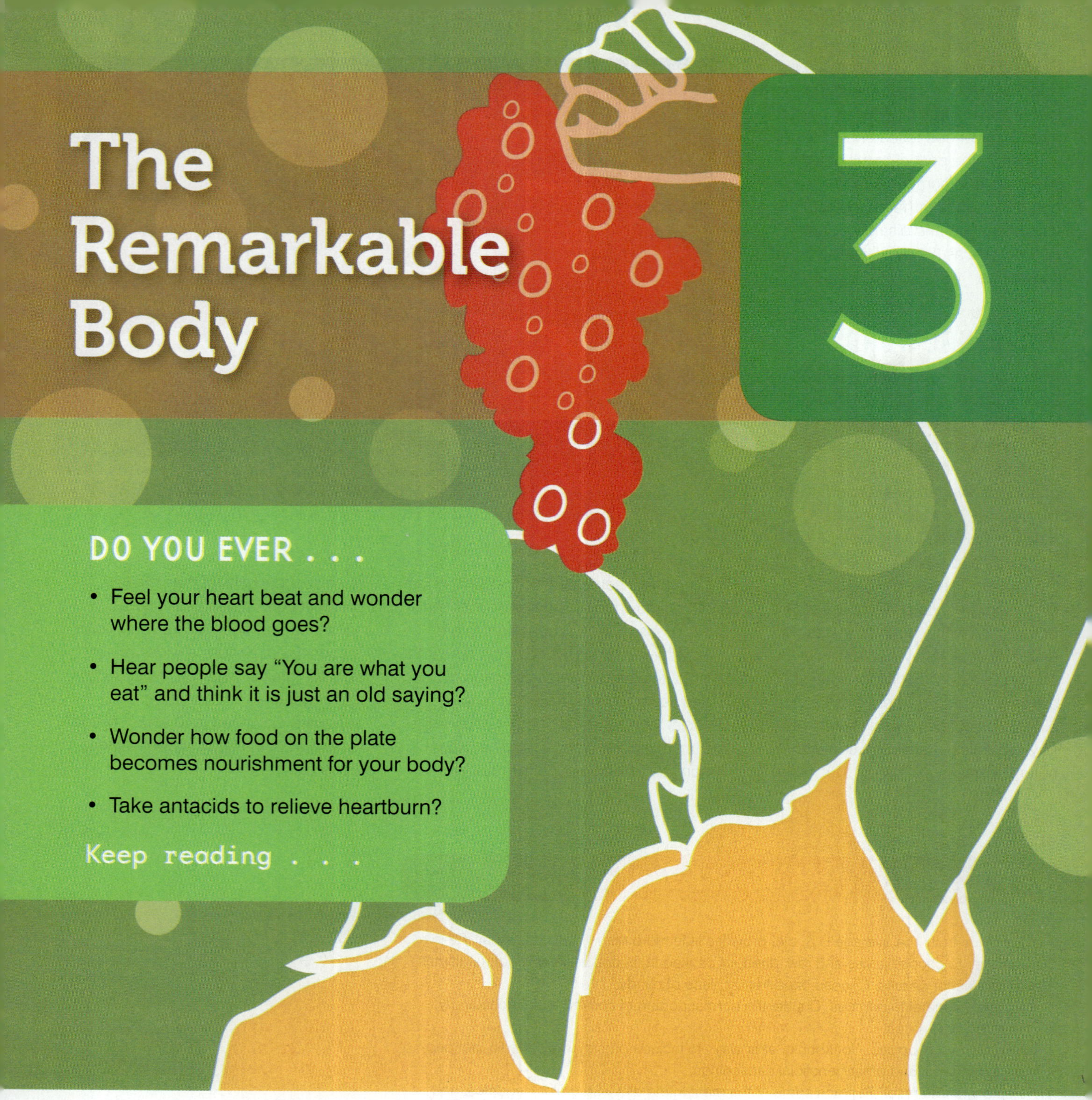

Art Box Images/Getty Images

Learning Objectives

To find learning objective topics in this chapter, look for the text headings with a corresponding "LO" number above the heading. After reading this chapter, you should be able to accomplish the following:

LO 3.1 Describe the levels of organization in the body, and identify some basic ways in which nutrition supports them.

LO 3.2 Compare the terms *mechanical digestion* and *chemical digestion,* and point out where these processes occur along the digestive tract.

LO 3.3 Trace the breakdown and absorption of carbohydrate, fat, and protein from the mouth to the colon.

LO 3.4 Explain how nutrients are transported and stored in the body.

LO 3.5 Define the term *moderate alcohol consumption,* and discuss the potential health effects, both negative and positive, associated with this level of drinking.

At the moment of conception, you received genes in the form of DNA from your mother and father, who, in turn, had inherited them from their parents, and so on into history. Since that moment, your genes have been working behind the scenes, directing your body's development and functioning. Many of your genes are ancient in origin and are little changed from genes of thousands of centuries ago, but here you are—living with the food, the luxuries, the smog, the contaminants, and all the other pleasures and problems of the 21st century. There is no guarantee that a diet haphazardly chosen from today's foods will meet the needs of your "ancient" body. Unlike your ancestors, who nourished themselves from the wild plants and animals surrounding them, you must learn how your body works, what it needs, and how to select foods to meet its needs.

CONCEPT LINK 3-1

DNA was defined in Chapter 1 (page 2) as the molecule that encodes genetic information in its structure; *genes* were defined as units of a cell's inheritance situated along the DNA strands.

LO 3.1

The Body's Cells

The human body is composed of trillions of **cells,** and none of them knows anything about food. *You* may get hungry for fruit, milk, or bread but each cell of your body needs nutrients—the vital components of foods. The ways in which the body's cells cooperate to obtain and use nutrients are the subjects of this chapter.

Each of the body's cells is a self-contained, living entity (see Figure 3-1), but at the same time it depends on the rest of the body's cells to supply its needs. Among the cells' most basic needs are energy and the oxygen with which to burn it. Cells also need water to maintain the environment in which they live. They need building blocks and control systems. They especially need the nutrients they cannot make for themselves—the essential nutrients first described in Chapter 1—which must be supplied from food. The first principle of diet planning is that the foods we choose must provide energy and the essential nutrients, including water.

FIGURE 3-1 **A Cell (Simplified Diagram)**

This cell has been greatly enlarged; real cells are so tiny that 10,000 can fit on the head of a pin.

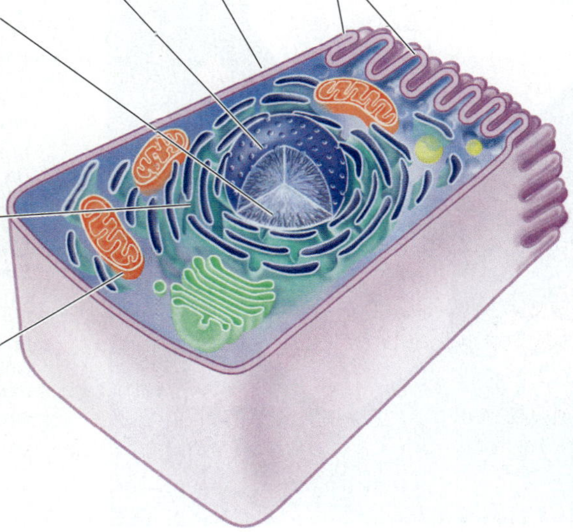

cells the smallest units in which independent life can exist. All living things are single cells or organisms made of cells.

As living things, cells also die off, although at varying rates. Some skin cells and red blood cells must replenish themselves every 10 to 120 days. Cells lining the digestive tract replace themselves every three days. Under ordinary conditions, many muscle cells reproduce themselves only once every few years. Liver cells have the ability to reproduce quickly and do so whenever repairs to the organ are needed. Certain brain cells do not reproduce at all; if damaged by injury or disease, they are lost forever.

The cells work in cooperation with each other to support the whole body. Gene activity within each cell determines the nature of that work.

enzyme any of a great number of working proteins that speed up a specific chemical reaction, such as breaking the bonds of a nutrient, without undergoing change themselves. Enzymes and their actions are described in Chapter 6.

fat cells cells that specialize in the storage of fat and form the fat tissue. Fat cells also produce fat-metabolizing enzymes; they also produce hormones involved in appetite and energy balance (see Chapter 9).

Genes Control Functions

Each gene is a blueprint that directs the production of one or more proteins, such as an **enzyme** that performs cellular work. Genes also provide the instructions for all of the structural components cells need to survive (see Figure 3-2). Each cell contains a complete set of genes, but different ones are active in different types of cells. For example, in some intestinal cells, the genes for making digestive enzymes are active; in some of the body's **fat cells,** the genes for making enzymes that metabolize fat are active.

Genes affect the way the body handles its nutrients. Certain variations in some of the genes alter the way the body absorbs, metabolizes, or excretes nutrients from

FIGURE 3-2 **From DNA to Living Cells**

If the human genome were a book of instructions on how to make a human being, then the 23 chromosomes of DNA would be chapters. Each gene would be a word, and the individual molecules that form the DNA would be letters of the alphabet.

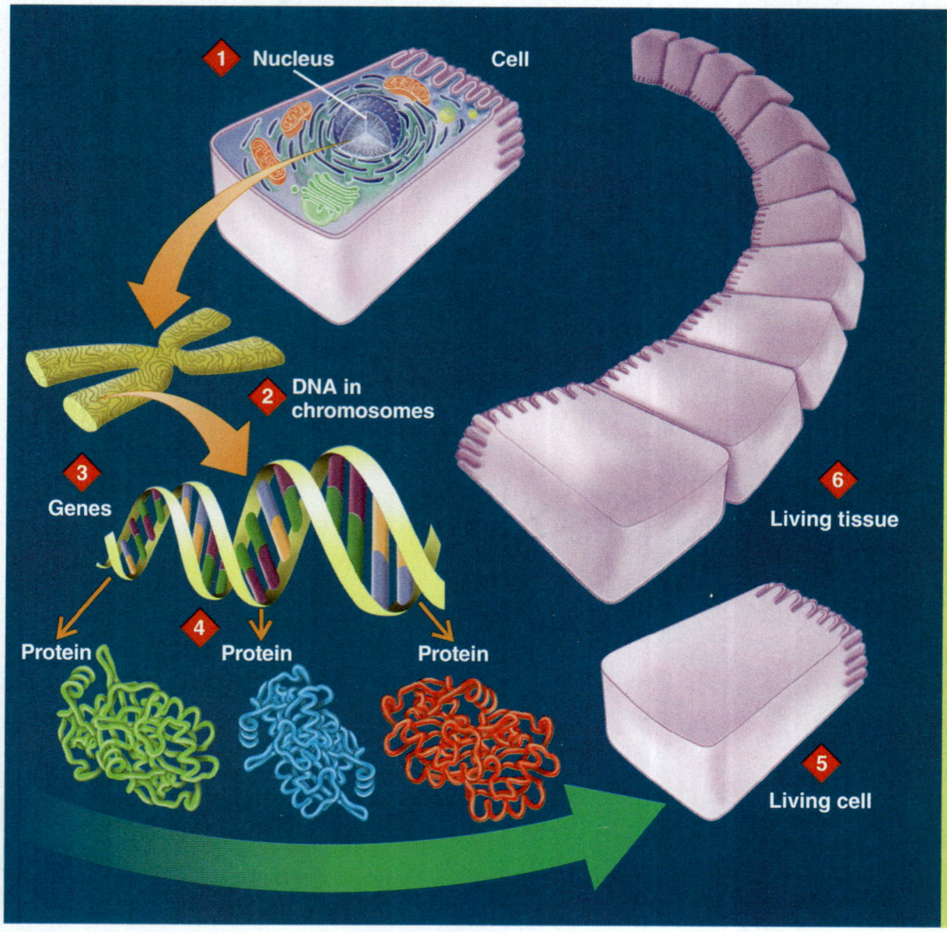

1. Each cell's nucleus contains DNA — the material of heredity in all living things.
2. Long strands of human DNA coil into 23 pairs of chromosomes. If the strands of DNA in all the body's cells were uncoiled and laid end to end, they would stretch to the sun and back four hundred times. Yet DNA strands are so tiny that about 5 million of them could be threaded at once through the eye of a needle.
3. Genes contain instructions for making proteins. Genes are sections along the strands of DNA that serve as templates for the building of proteins. Some genes are involved in building just one protein; others are involved in building more than one.
4. Many other steps are required to make a protein. See Figure 6-6 of Chapter 6.
5. Proteins do the work of living cells. Cells employ proteins to perform essential functions and provide structures.
6. Communities of functioning cells make up the living tissue.

the body. Occasionally, a gene variation can cause a lifelong malady—that is, an **inborn error of metabolism**—that may require a special diet to minimize its potential to harm the body. An example is the inborn error **phenylketonuria (PKU),** in which a genetic variation compromises the body's ability to handle the amino acid phenylalanine. People with this condition must carefully limit their intakes of phenylalanine, so food manufacturers are required to print warning labels on foods, such as certain artificial sweeteners, that contain it.

- Interactions between vitamins and minerals and the genes are addressed in Chapters 7 and 8; other nutrient and gene interactions are addressed in the chapters on pregnancy and disease prevention.

Nutrients also affect the genes. For example, the concentrations of certain nutrients and phytochemicals in the body fluids and tissues influence the genes to make more or less of certain proteins. These changes, in turn, alter body functions and ultimately hold meaning for health and disease. Controversy 11 presents details.

Cells, Tissues, Organs, Systems

Cells are organized into **tissues** that perform specialized tasks. For example, individual muscle cells are joined together to form muscle tissue, which can contract. Tissues, in turn, are grouped together to form whole **organs.** In the organ we call the heart, for example, muscle tissues, nerve tissues, connective tissues, and others all work together to pump blood. Some body functions are performed by several related organs working together as part of a **body system.** For example, the heart, lungs, and blood vessels cooperate as parts of the cardiovascular system to deliver oxygen to all the body's cells. The next few sections present the body systems with special significance to nutrition.

KEY POINT The body's cells need energy, oxygen, and nutrients, including water, to remain healthy and do their work. Genes direct the making of each cell's protein machinery, including enzymes. Genes and nutrients interact in ways that affect health. Specialized cells are grouped together to form tissues and organs; organs work together in body systems.

The Body Fluids and the Cardiovascular System

Body fluids supply the tissues continuously with energy, oxygen, and nutrients, including water. The fluids constantly circulate to pick up fresh supplies and deliver wastes to points of disposal. Every cell continuously draws oxygen and nutrients from those fluids and releases carbon dioxide and other waste products into them.

The body's circulating fluids are the **blood** and the **lymph.** Blood travels within the **arteries, veins,** and **capillaries,** as well as within the heart's chambers (see Figure 3-3). Lymph travels in separate vessels of its own.

Circulating around the cells are other fluids such as the **plasma** of the blood, which surrounds the white and red blood cells, and the fluid surrounding muscle cells (see Figure 3-4). The fluid surrounding cells (**extracellular fluid**) is derived from the blood in the capillaries; it squeezes out through the capillary walls and flows around the outsides of cells, permitting exchange of materials.

Some of the extracellular fluid returns directly to the bloodstream by reentering the capillaries. The fluid remaining outside the capillaries forms lymph, which travels around the body by way of lymph vessels. The lymph eventually returns to the bloodstream near the heart where a large lymph vessel empties into a large vein. In this way, all cells are served by the cardiovascular system.

The fluid inside cells (**intracellular fluid**) provides a medium in which all cell reactions take place. Its pressure also helps the cells to hold their shape. The intracellular fluid is drawn from the extracellular fluid that bathes the cells on the outside.

inborn error of metabolism a genetic variation present from birth that may result in disease.

phenylketonuria (PKU) an inborn error of metabolism that interferes with the body's handling of the amino acid phenylalanine, with potentially serious consequences to the brain and nervous system in infancy and childhood. Often referred to by its abbreviation, PKU.

tissues systems of cells working together to perform specialized tasks. Examples are muscles, nerves, blood, and bone.

organs discrete structural units made of tissues that perform specific jobs. Examples are the heart, liver, and brain.

body system a group of related organs that work together to perform a function. Examples are the circulatory system, respiratory system, and nervous system.

blood the fluid of the cardiovascular system; composed of water, red and white blood cells, other formed particles, nutrients, oxygen, and other constituents.

lymph (LIMF) the fluid that moves from the bloodstream into tissue spaces and then travels in its own vessels, which eventually drain back into the bloodstream (see Figure 3-6).

arteries blood vessels that carry blood containing fresh oxygen supplies from the heart to the tissues (see Figure 3-3).

veins blood vessels that carry blood, with the carbon dioxide it has collected, from the tissues back to the heart (see Figure 3-3).

capillaries minute, weblike blood vessels that connect arteries to veins and permit transfer of materials between blood and tissues (see Figures 3-3 and 3-4).

plasma the cell-free fluid part of blood and lymph.

extracellular fluid fluid residing outside the cells that transports materials to and from the cells.

intracellular fluid fluid residing inside the cells that provides the medium for cellular reactions.

FIGURE 3-3 ANIMATED! **Blood Flow in the Cardiovascular System**

The blood is routed through the body as follows:
- Heart to tissues to heart to lungs to heart (repeat).

The portion of the blood that flows through the blood vessels of the intestine travels from:
- Heart to intestine to liver to heart.

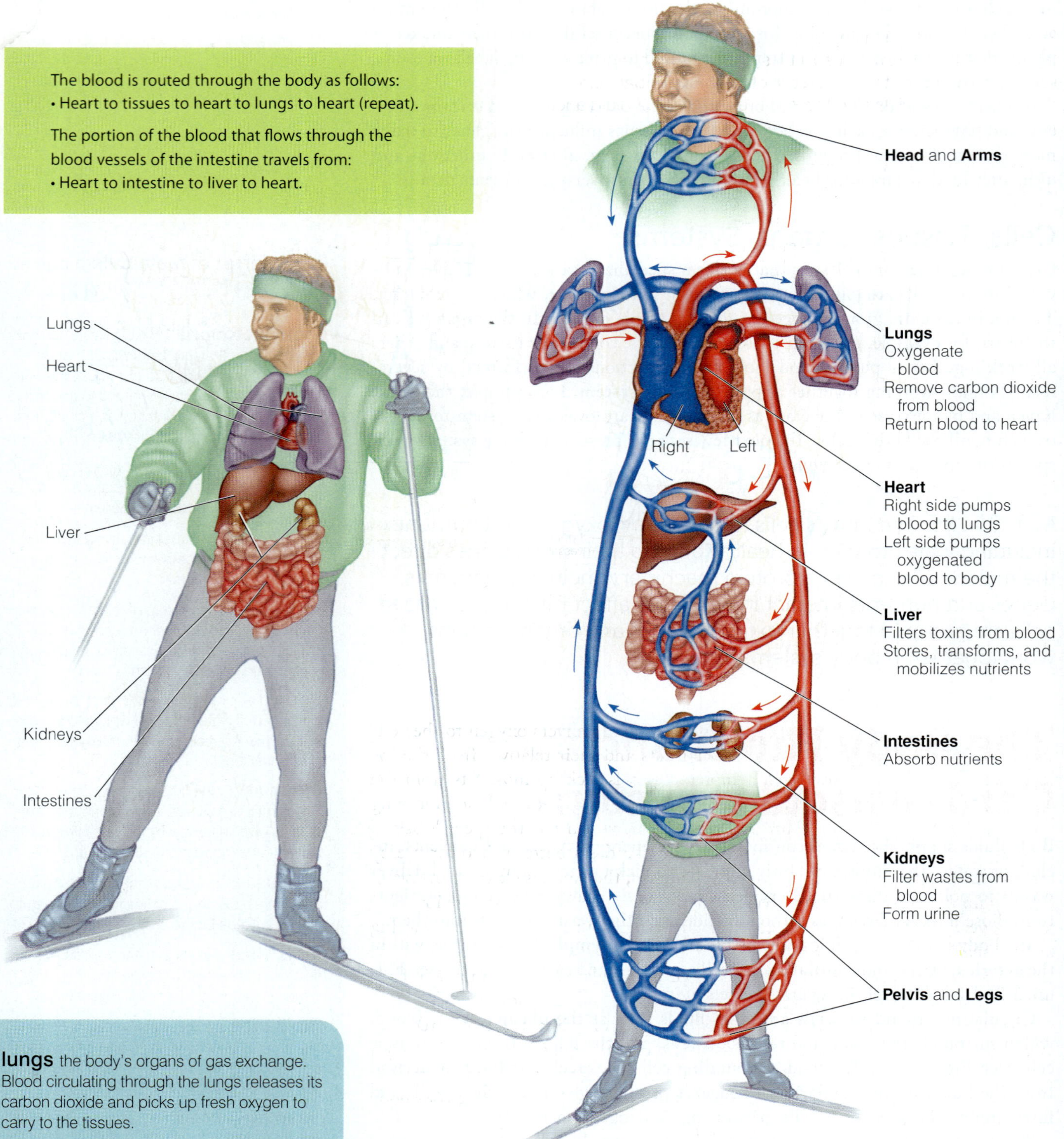

lungs the body's organs of gas exchange. Blood circulating through the lungs releases its carbon dioxide and picks up fresh oxygen to carry to the tissues.

intestine the body's long, tubular organ of digestion and the site of nutrient absorption.

liver a large, lobed organ that lies just under the ribs. It filters the blood, removes and processes nutrients, manufactures materials for export to other parts of the body, and destroys toxins or stores them to keep them out of the circulatory system.

All the blood circulates to the **lungs,** where it picks up oxygen and releases carbon dioxide wastes from the cells, as Figure 3-5 shows. Then the blood returns to the heart, where the pumping heartbeats push this fresh oxygenated blood from the lungs out to all body tissues. As the blood travels through the rest of the cardiovascular system, it delivers materials cells need and picks up their wastes.

FIGURE 3-4 ANIMATED! How the Body Fluids Circulate Around Cells

The upper box shows a tiny portion of tissue with blood flowing through its network of capillaries (greatly enlarged). The lower box illustrates the movement of the extracellular fluid. Exchange of materials also takes place between cell fluid and extracellular fluid.

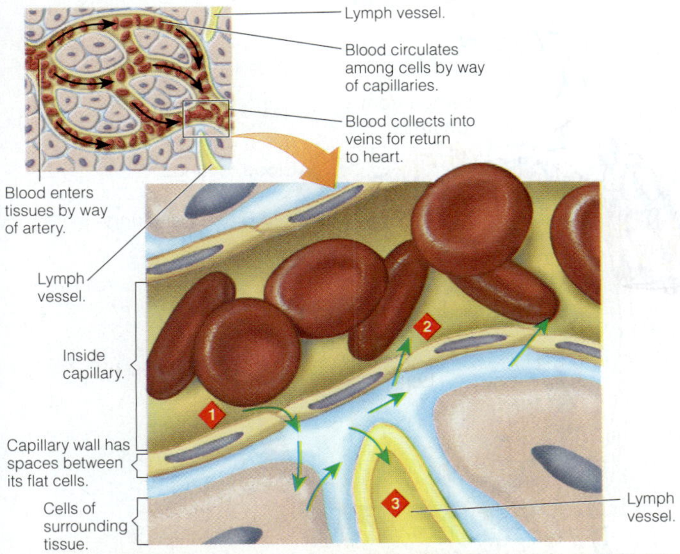

1 Fluid filters out of blood through the capillary whose walls are made of cells with small spaces between them.

Fluid may flow back into 2 the capillary or into 3 a lymph vessel. Lymph enters the bloodstream later through a large lymphatic vessel that empties into a large vein.

FIGURE 3-5 Oxygen–Carbon Dioxide Exchange in the Lungs

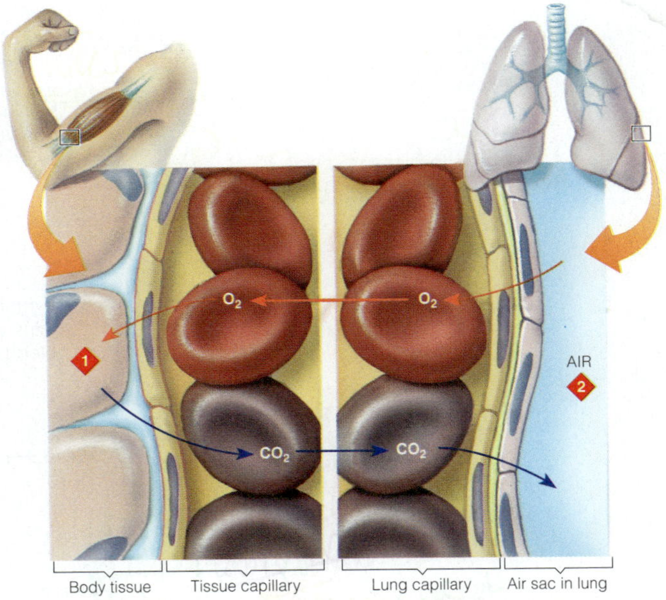

1 In body tissues, red blood cells give up their oxygen (O_2) and absorb carbon dioxide (CO_2).

2 In the air sacs of the lungs, the red blood cells give up their load of carbon dioxide (CO_2) and absorb oxygen (O_2) from air to supply to body tissues.

As it passes through the digestive system, the blood delivers oxygen to the cells there and picks up most nutrients other than fats and their relatives from the **intestine** for distribution elsewhere. Lymphatic vessels pick up most fats from the intestine and then transport them to the blood (see Figure 3-6). All blood leaving the digestive system is routed directly to the **liver,** which has the special task of chemically altering the absorbed materials to make them better suited for use by other tissues. Later, in passing through the **kidneys,** the blood is cleansed of wastes (look again at Figure 3-3). Note that the blood carries nutrients from the intestine to the liver, which releases them to the heart, which pumps them to the waiting body tissues.

To ensure efficient circulation of fluid to all your cells, you need an ample fluid intake. This means drinking sufficient water to replace the water lost each day. Cardiovascular fitness is essential, too, and constitutes an ongoing project that requires attention to both nutrition and physical activity. Healthy red blood cells also play a role, for they carry oxygen to all the other cells, enabling them to use fuels for energy. Since red blood cells arise, live, and die within about four months, your body replaces them constantly, a manufacturing process that requires many essential nutrients from food. Consequently, the blood is very sensitive to malnutrition and often serves as an indicator of disorders caused by dietary deficiencies or imbalances of vitamins or minerals.

All the body's cells live in water.

• Chapter 8 offers guidelines for water intake.

KEY POINT Blood and lymph deliver nutrients to all the body's cells and carry waste materials away from them. Blood also delivers oxygen to cells. The cardiovascular system ensures that these fluids circulate properly among all organs.

kidneys a pair of organs that filter wastes from the blood, make urine, and release it to the bladder for excretion from the body.

FIGURE 3-6 **Lymph Vessels and the Bloodstream**

1 Nutrients are absorbed via two kinds of vessels in the intestines: blood capillaries and small lymph vessels. The capillaries lead to larger blood vessels that lead to the liver.

2 The lymph in the lymph vessels carries most of the absorbed dietary fat to the large vein near the heart. Some lymph vessels are depicted in Figure 3-13 (lower right), later on.

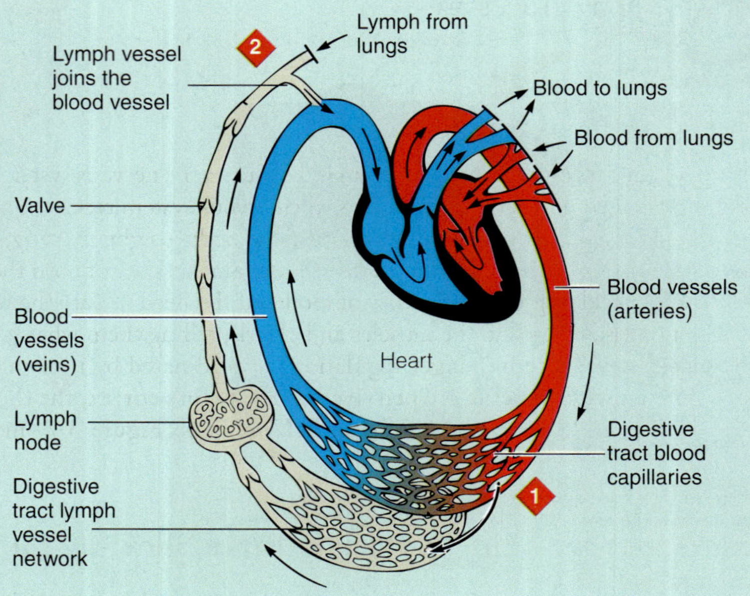

The Hormonal and Nervous Systems

In addition to nutrients, oxygen, and wastes, the blood carries chemical messengers, **hormones,** from one system of cells to another. Hormones communicate changing conditions that demand responses from the body organs.

What Do Hormones Have to Do with Nutrition?

Hormones are secreted and released directly into the blood by organs known as glands. Glands and hormones abound in the body. Each gland monitors a condition and produces one or more hormones to regulate it. Each hormone acts as a messenger that stimulates various organs to take appropriate actions.

For example, when the **pancreas** (a gland) detects a high concentration of the blood's sugar, glucose, it releases **insulin,** a hormone. Insulin stimulates muscle and other cells to remove glucose from the blood and to store it. The liver also stores glucose. When the blood glucose level falls, the pancreas secretes another hormone, **glucagon,** to which the liver responds by releasing into the blood some of the glucose it stored earlier. Thus, a normal blood glucose level is maintained.

Nutrition affects the hormonal system. Fasting, feeding, and exercise alter hormonal balances. In people who become very thin, for example, altered hormonal balance causes their bones to lose minerals and weaken. Hormones also affect nutrition. Along with the nervous system, hormones regulate hunger and affect appetite. They

hormones chemicals that are secreted by glands into the blood in response to conditions in the body that require regulation. These chemicals serve as messengers, acting on other organs to maintain constant conditions.

pancreas an organ with two main functions. One is an endocrine function—the making of hormones such as insulin, which it releases directly into the blood (*endo* means "into" the blood). The other is an exocrine function—the making of digestive enzymes, which it releases through a duct into the small intestine to assist in digestion (*exo* means "out" into a body cavity or onto the skin surface).

insulin a hormone from the pancreas that helps glucose enter cells from the blood (details in Chapter 4).

glucagon a hormone from the pancreas that stimulates the liver to release glucose into the bloodstream.

carry messages to regulate the digestive system, telling the digestive organs what kinds of foods have been eaten and how much of each digestive juice to secrete in response. A hormone produced by the fat tissue informs the brain about the degree of body fatness and helps to regulate appetite. Hormones also regulate the menstrual cycle in women, and they affect the appetite changes many women experience during the cycle and in pregnancy. An altered hormonal state is thought to be at least partially responsible, too, for the loss of appetite that sick people experience. Hormones also regulate the body's reaction to stress, suppressing hunger and the digestion and absorption of nutrients. When there are questions about a person's nutrition or health, the state of that person's hormonal system is often part of the answer.

• Details about hormones, menstruation, and the bones appear in Controversy 8 and Controversy 9.

KEY POINT Glands secrete hormones that act as messengers to help regulate body processes.

How Does the Nervous System Interact with Nutrition?

The body's other major communication system is, of course, the nervous system. With the brain and spinal cord as central controllers, the nervous system receives and integrates information from sensory receptors all over the body—sight, hearing, touch, smell, taste, and others—which communicate to the brain the state of both the outer and inner worlds, including the availability of food and the need to eat. The nervous system also sends instructions to the muscles and glands, telling them what to do.

The nervous system's role in hunger regulation is coordinated by the brain. The sensations of hunger and appetite are perceived by the brain's **cortex,** the thinking, outer layer. Deep inside the brain, the **hypothalamus** (see Figure 3-7) monitors

cortex the outermost layer of something. The brain's cortex is the part of the brain where conscious thought takes place.

hypothalamus (high-poh-THAL-uh-mus) a part of the brain that senses a variety of conditions in the blood, such as temperature, glucose content, salt content, and others. It signals other parts of the brain or body to adjust those conditions when necessary.

FIGURE 3-7 **Cutaway Side View of the Brain Showing the Hypothalamus and Cortex**

The hypothalamus monitors the body's conditions and sends signals to the brain's thinking portion, the cortex, which decides on actions. The pituitary gland is called the body's master gland, referring to its roles in regulating the activities of other glands and organs of the body.

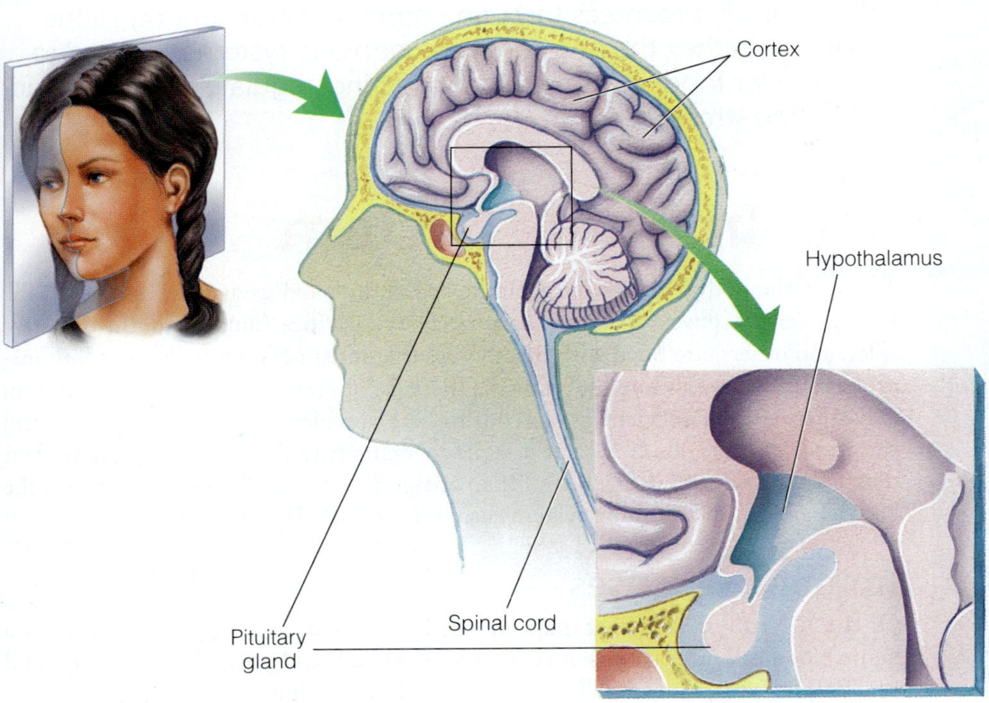

many body conditions, including the availability of nutrients and water. To signal hunger, the physiological need for food, the digestive tract sends messages to the hypothalamus by way of hormones and nerves. The signals also stimulate the stomach to intensify its contractions and secretions, causing hunger pangs (and gurgling sounds). When your brain's cortex perceives these hunger sensations, you want to eat. The conscious mind of the cortex, however, can override such signals, and a person can choose to delay eating despite hunger or to eat when hunger is absent.

In a marvelous adaptation of the human body, the hormonal and nervous systems work together to enable a person to respond to physical danger. Known as the **fight-or-flight reaction,** or the *stress response,* this adaptation is present with only minor variations in all animals, showing how universally important it is to survival. When danger is detected, nerves release **neurotransmitters,** and glands supply the compounds **epinephrine** and **norepinephrine.** Every organ of the body responds and **metabolism** speeds up. The pupils of the eyes widen so that you can see better; the muscles tense up so that you can jump, run, or struggle with maximum strength; breathing quickens and deepens to provide more oxygen. The heart races to rush the oxygen to the muscles, and the blood pressure rises so that the fuel the muscles need for energy can be delivered efficiently. The liver pours forth glucose from its stores, and the fat cells release fat. The digestive system shuts down to permit all the body's systems to serve the muscles and nerves. With all action systems at peak efficiency, the body can respond with amazing speed and strength to whatever threatens it.

In ancient times, stress usually involved physical danger, and the response to it was violent physical exertion. In the modern world, stress is seldom physical, but the body reacts the same way. What stresses you today may be a checkbook out of control or a teacher who suddenly announces a pop quiz. Under these stresses, you are not supposed to fight or run as your ancient ancestor did. You smile at the "enemy" and suppress your fear. But your heart races, you feel it pounding, and hormones still flood your bloodstream with glucose and fat.

Your number-one enemy today is not a saber-toothed tiger prowling outside your cave, but a disease of modern civilization: heart disease. Years of fat and other constituents accumulating in the arteries and stresses that strain the heart often lead to heart attacks, especially when a body accustomed to chronic underexertion experiences sudden high blood pressure. Daily exercise as part of a healthy lifestyle releases pent-up stress and helps to protect the heart.

KEY POINT The nervous system joins the hormonal system to regulate body processes through communication among all the organs. Together, the hormonal and nervous systems respond to the need for food, govern the act of eating, regulate digestion, and call for the stress response.

fight-or-flight reaction the body's instinctive hormone- and nerve-mediated reaction to danger. Also known as the *stress response*.

neurotransmitters chemicals that are released at the end of a nerve cell when a nerve impulse arrives there. They diffuse across the gap to the next cell and alter the membrane of that second cell to either inhibit or excite it.

epinephrine (EP-ih-NEFF-rin) the major hormone that elicits the stress response.

norepinephrine (NOR-EP-ih-NEFF-rin) a compound related to epinephrine that helps to elicit the stress response.

metabolism the sum of all physical and chemical changes taking place in living cells; includes all reactions by which the body obtains and spends the energy from food.

microbes bacteria, viruses, or other organisms invisible to the naked eye, some of which cause diseases. Also called *microorganisms*.

antigen a microbe or substance that is foreign to the body.

immune system a system of tissues and organs that defend the body against antigens, foreign materials that have penetrated the skin or body linings.

lymphocytes (LIM-foh-sites) white blood cells that participate in the immune response; B-cells and T-cells.

The Immune System

Many of the body's tissues cooperate to maintain defenses against infection. The skin presents a physical barrier, and the body's cavities (lungs, mouth, digestive tract, and others) are lined with membranes that resist penetration by invading **microbes** and other unwanted substances. These linings are highly sensitive to vitamin and other nutrient deficiencies, and health-care providers inspect both the skin and the inside of the mouth to detect signs of malnutrition. (Later chapters present details of the signs of deficiencies.) If an **antigen,** or foreign invader, penetrates the body's barriers, the **immune system** rushes in to defend the body against harm.

Immune Defenses

Of the 100 trillion cells that make up the human body, one in every hundred is a white blood cell. The actions of two types of white blood cells, the phagocytes and the **lymphocytes,** known as T-cells and B-cells, are of interest:

- **Phagocytes.** These scavenger cells travel throughout the body and are the first to defend body tissues against invaders. When a phagocyte recognizes a foreign particle, such as a bacterium, the phagocyte forms a pocket in its own outer membrane, engulfing the invader. The phagocytes may then attack the invader with oxidizing chemicals in an "oxidative burst" or may otherwise digest or destroy them. Phagocytes also leave a chemical trail that helps other immune cells to find the infection and join the defense.

• More about oxidation in Chapters 5 and 7.

- **T-cells.** Killer T-cells are lymphocytes that "read" and "remember" the chemical messages put forth by phagocytes to identify invaders. The killer T-cells then seek out and destroy all foreign particles having the same identity. T-cells defend against fungi, viruses, parasites, some bacteria, and some cancer cells (see the photo). They also pose a formidable obstacle to a successful organ transplant—the physician must prescribe immunosuppressive drugs following surgery to hold down the T-cells' attack against the "foreign" organ. Another group, helper T-cells, does not attack invaders directly but helps other immune cells to do so. People suffering from the disease AIDS (acquired immunodeficiency syndrome) are rendered defenseless against other diseases because the virus that causes AIDS selectively attacks and destroys their helper T-cells.*

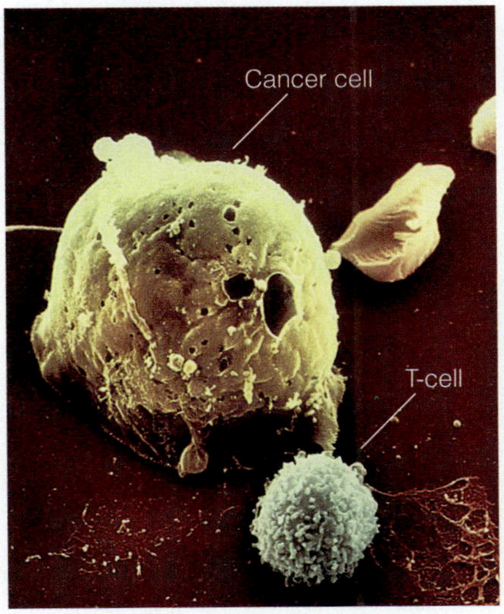

A killer T-cell (the smaller cell on the bottom) has recognized a cancer cell and is attacking it with toxic chemicals that punch holes in the cancer cell's surface.

- **B-cells.** B-cells respond rapidly to infection by dividing and releasing invader-fighting proteins, **antibodies,** into the bloodstream. Antibodies travel to the site of the infection and stick to the surface of the foreign particles, killing or inactivating them. Like T-cells, B-cells also retain a chemical memory of each invader, and if the encounter recurs, the response is swift. Immunizations work this way: a disabled or harmless form of a disease-causing organism is injected into the body so that the B-cells can learn to recognize it. Later, if the live infectious organism invades, the B-cells quickly release antibodies to destroy it.

In addition to the phagocytes and lymphocytes, the immune system includes many other categories of white blood cells and many organs and tissues. To function properly, all of these cells and organs depend on a steady flow of nutrients, delivered to the bloodstream from the digestive system.

• Chapter 11 explores the roles of nutrition in supporting the immune system.

KEY POINT A properly functioning immune system enables the body to resist diseases.

Inflammation

When tissues become injured or irritated they undergo **inflammation,** a condition of increased white blood cells, redness, heat, pain, swelling, and sometimes loss of function of the affected body part. Inflammation is the immune system's normal, healthy response to cell injury.

Many diseases, particularly chronic diseases of later life, such as heart disease, diabetes, and a severe type of arthritis, involve chronic inflammation.[1†] When chronic, low-grade, unrelieved inflammation exists in chronic diseases, it often foretells of an increase in both the severity of the disease and the risk of death from the disease.[2] Inflammation is a sign that a disease process is underway and worsening. Dietary factors, such as lipids and phytochemicals, may promote or inhibit inflammation, but an important predictor is being overweight.[3] The links among diet, inflammatory processes, and diseases are topics of intense current research and they are discussed in later chapters.

KEY POINT Inflammation is the normal, healthy response of the immune system to cell injury. Chronic inflammation may play roles in disease development.

phagocytes (FAG-oh-sites) white blood cells that can ingest and destroy antigens. The process by which phagocytes engulf materials is called *phagocytosis*. The Greek word *phagein* means "to eat."

T-cells lymphocytes that attack antigens. *T* stands for the thymus gland of the neck, where the T-cells are stored and matured.

B-cells lymphocytes that produce antibodies. *B* stands for bursa, an organ in the chicken where B-cells were first identified.

antibodies proteins, made by cells of the immune system, that are expressly designed to combine with and inactivate specific antigens.

inflammation the immune system's response to cellular injury characterized by an increase in white blood cells, redness, heat, pain, and swelling. Inflammation plays a role in many chronic diseases.

*The AIDS virus is the human immunodeficiency virus (HIV).
† Reference notes are found in Appendix F.

LO 3.2, 3.3

The Digestive System

When your body needs food, your brain and hormones alert your conscious mind to the sensation of hunger. Then, when you eat, your taste buds guide you in judging whether foods are acceptable.

Taste buds contain surface structures that detect four basic chemical tastes: sweet, sour, bitter, and salty.[4] A fifth taste is sometimes included on this list: the taste of monosodium glutamate, sometimes called *savory* or *umami* (ooh-MOM-ee), its Asian name.[5] These basic tastes, along with aroma, texture, temperature, and other flavor elements, affect a person's experience of a food's flavor. In fact, the human ability to detect a food's aroma is thousands of times more sensitive than the sense of taste. The nose can detect just a few molecules responsible for the aroma of frying bacon, for example, even when they are diluted in several rooms full of air.

Why Do People Like Sugar, Salt, and Fat?

Sweet, salty, and fatty foods are almost universally desired, but most people have aversions to bitter and sour tastes (see Figure 3-8).[6] The enjoyment of sugars encourages people to consume ample energy, especially in the form of foods containing carbohydrates, which provide the energy fuel for the brain. The pleasure of a salty taste prompts eaters to consume sufficient amounts of two very important minerals—sodium and chloride. Likewise, foods containing fats provide concentrated energy and essential nutrients needed by all body tissues. The aversion to bitterness discourages consumption of foods containing bitter toxins and also affects people's food preferences.[7] People born with great sensitivity to bitter tastes are apt to avoid foods with slightly bitter flavors, such as turnips and broccoli.

The instinctive liking for sugar, salt, and fat can lead to drastic overeating of these substances. Sugar has become widely available in pure form only in the last hundred

FIGURE 3-8 **The Innate Preference for Sweet Taste**

This newborn baby is (a) resting, (b) tasting distilled water, (c) tasting sugar, (d) tasting something sour, and (e) tasting something bitter.

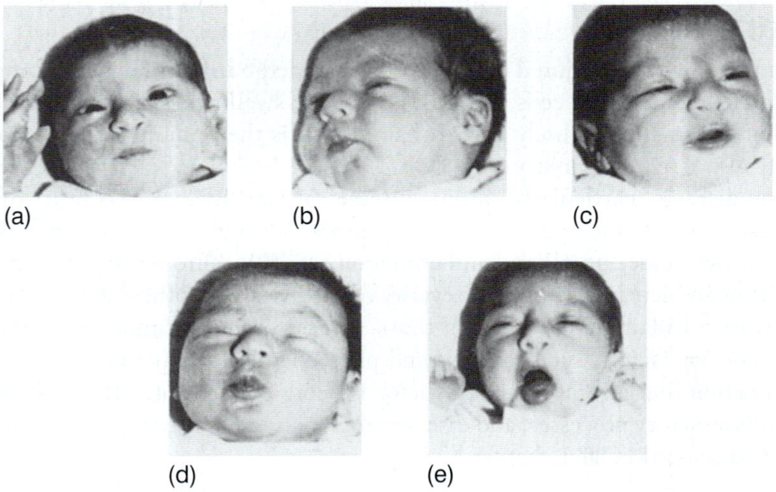

Source: Taste-induced facial expressions of neonate infants from the classic studies of J. E. Steiner, in Taste and Development: The Genesis of Sweet Preference, *ed. J. M. Weiffenbach, HHS publication no. NIH 77–1068 (Bethesda, MD: U.S. Department of Health and Human Services, 1977), pp. 173–189, with permission of the author.*

years, so it is relatively new to the human diet. Although salt and fat are much older, today all three substances are added liberally to foods by manufacturers to tempt us to eat their products.

© Stephen Orsillo, 2011/Shutterstock.com

KEY POINT The preference for sweet, salty, and fatty tastes seems to be inborn and can lead to overconsumption of foods that offer them.

The Digestive Tract

Once you have eaten, your brain and hormones direct the many organs of the **digestive system** to **digest** and **absorb** the complex mixture of chewed and swallowed food. A diagram showing the digestive tract and its associated organs appears in Figure 3-9. The tract itself is a flexible, muscular tube extending from the mouth through the throat, esophagus, stomach, small intestine, large intestine, and rectum to the anus, for a total length of about 26 feet. The human body surrounds this digestive canal. When you swallow something, it still is not inside your body—it is only inside the inner bore of this tube. Only when a nutrient or other substance passes through the wall of the digestive tract does it actually enter the body's tissues. Many things pass into the digestive tract and out again, unabsorbed. A baby playing with beads may swallow one, but the bead will not really enter the body. It will emerge from the digestive tract within a day or two.

The digestive system's job is to digest food to its components and then to absorb the nutrients and some nonnutrients, leaving behind the substances, such as fiber, that are appropriate to excrete. To do this, the system works at two levels: one, mechanical; the other, chemical.

KEY POINT The digestive tract is a flexible, muscular tube that digests food and absorbs its nutrients and some nonnutrients. Ancillary digestive organs aid digestion.

The Mechanical Aspect of Digestion

The job of mechanical digestion begins in the mouth, where large, solid food pieces such as bites of meat are torn into shreds that can be swallowed without choking. Chewing also adds water in the form of saliva to soften rough or sharp foods, such as fried tortilla chips, to prevent them from tearing the esophagus. Saliva also moistens and coats each bite of food, making it slippery so that it can pass easily down the esophagus.

Nutrients trapped inside indigestible skins, such as the hulls of seeds, must be liberated by breaking these skins before they can be digested. Chewing bursts open kernels of corn, for example, which would otherwise traverse the tract and exit undigested. Once food has been mashed and moistened for comfortable swallowing, longer chewing times provide no additional advantages to digestion. In fact, for digestion's sake, a relaxed, peaceful attitude during a meal aids digestion much more than chewing for an extended time.

The stomach and intestines then take up the task of liquefying foods through various mashing and squeezing actions. The best known of these actions is **peristalsis,** a series of squeezing waves that start with the tongue's movement during a swallow and pass all the way down the esophagus (see Figure 3-10). The stomach and the intestines also push food through the tract by waves of peristalsis. Besides these actions, the **stomach** holds swallowed food for a while and mashes it into a fine paste; the stomach and intestines also add water so that the paste becomes more fluid as it moves along.

digestive system the body system composed of organs that break down complex food particles into smaller, absorbable products. The *digestive tract* and *alimentary canal* are names for the tubular organs that extend from the mouth to the anus. The whole system, including the pancreas, liver, and gallbladder, is sometimes called the *gastrointestinal,* or *GI,* system.

digest to break molecules into smaller molecules; a main function of the digestive tract with respect to food.

absorb to take in, as nutrients are taken into the intestinal cells after digestion; the main function of the digestive tract with respect to nutrients.

peristalsis (per-ri-STALL-sis) the wavelike muscular squeezing of the esophagus, stomach, and small intestine that pushes their contents along.

stomach a muscular, elastic, pouchlike organ of the digestive tract that grinds and churns swallowed food and mixes it with acid and enzymes, forming chyme.

FIGURE 3-9 **ANIMATED! The Digestive System**

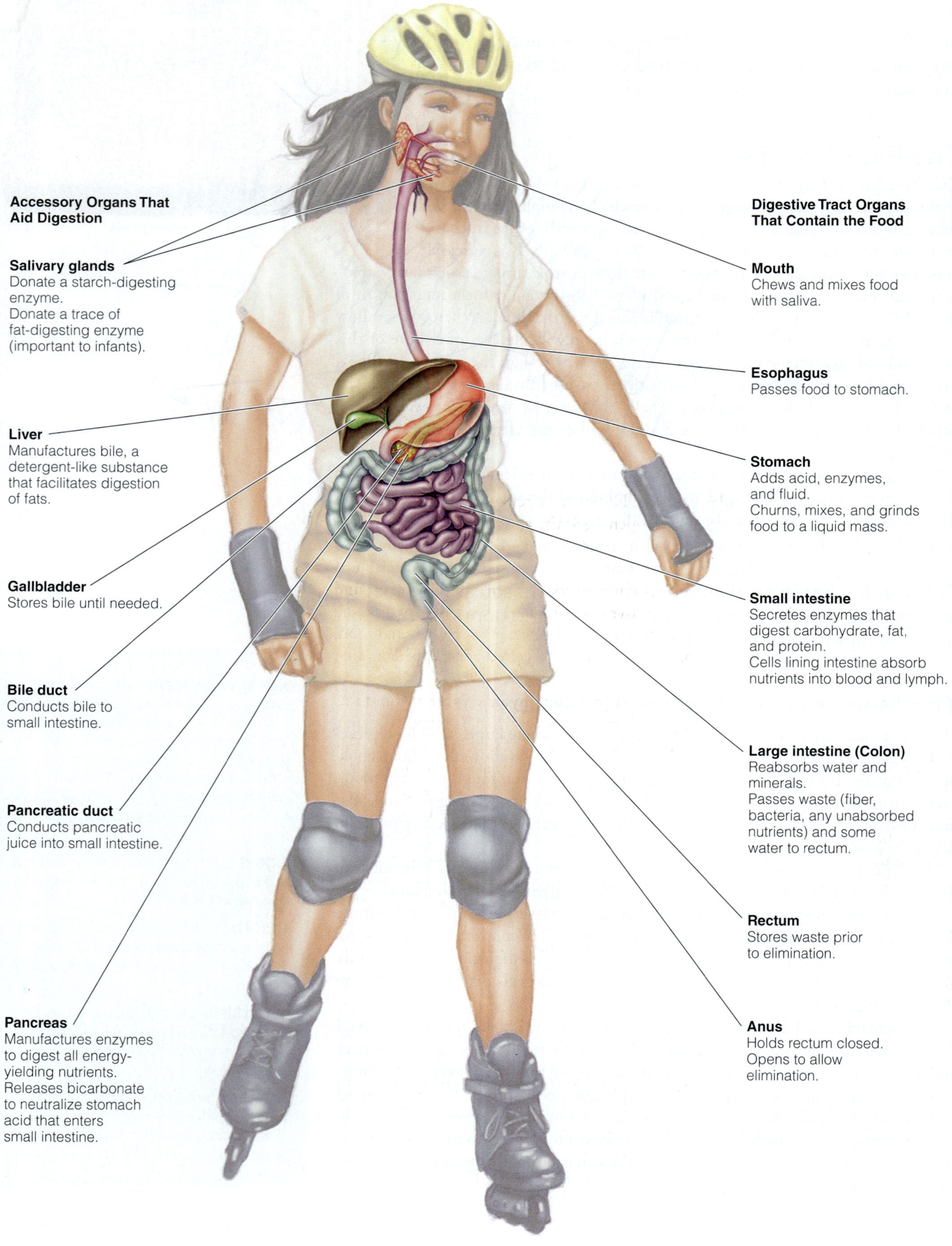

FIGURE 3-10 **Peristaltic Wave Passing Down the Esophagus and Beyond**

Peristalsis moves the digestive tract contents.

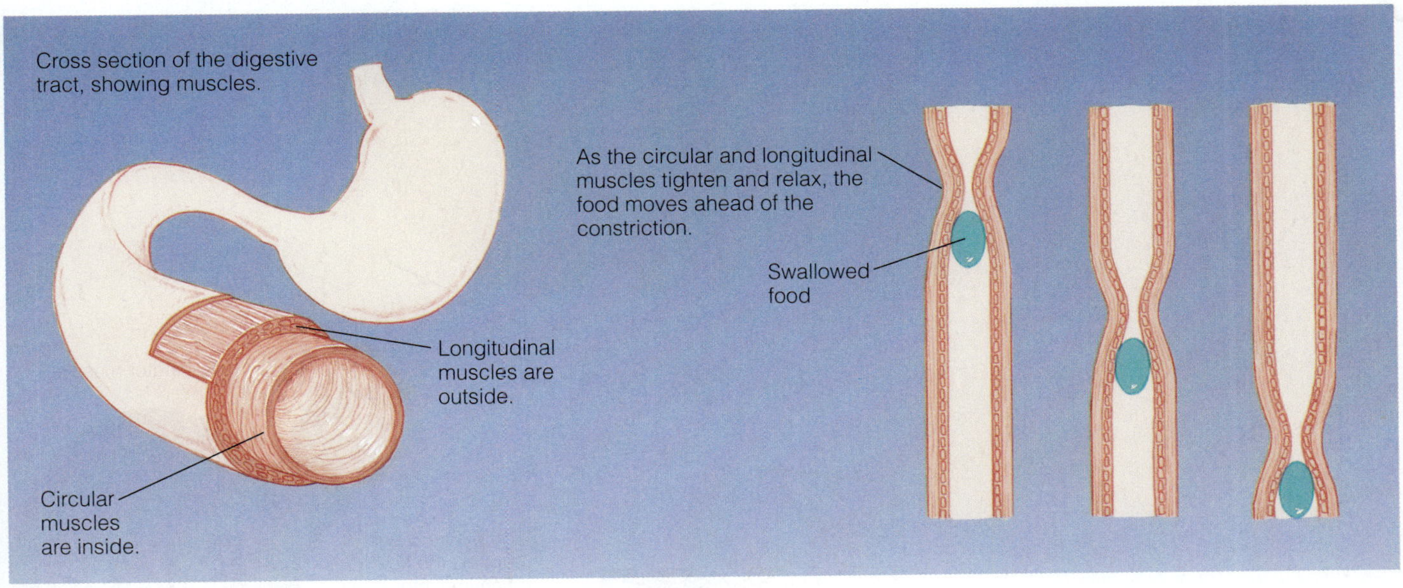

Figure 3-11 shows the muscular stomach. Notice the circular **sphincter** muscle at the base of the esophagus. It squeezes the opening at the entrance to the stomach to narrow it and prevent the stomach's contents from creeping back up the esophagus as the stomach contracts. Swallowed food remains in a lump in the stomach's upper portion, squeezed little by little to its lower portion. There the food is ground and mixed thoroughly, ensuring that digestive chemicals mix with the entire thick liquid mass, now called **chyme.** Chyme bears no resemblance to the original food. The starches have been partly split, proteins have been uncoiled and clipped, and fat has separated from the mass.

The stomach also acts as a holding tank. The muscular **pyloric valve** at the stomach's lower end (look again at Figure 3-11) controls the exit of the chyme, allowing only a little at a time to be squirted forcefully into the **small intestine.** Within a few hours after a meal, the stomach empties itself by means of these powerful squirts. The small intestine contracts rhythmically to move the contents along its length.

By the time the intestinal contents have arrived in the **large intestine** (also called the **colon**), digestion and absorption are nearly complete. The colon's task is mostly to reabsorb the water donated earlier by digestive organs and to absorb minerals, leaving a paste of fiber and other undigested materials, the **feces,** suitable for excretion. The fiber provides bulk against which the muscles of the colon can work. The rectum stores this fecal material to be excreted at intervals. From mouth to rectum, the transit of a meal is accomplished in as short a time as a single day or as long as three days.

Some people wonder whether the digestive tract works best at certain hours in the day and whether the timing of meals can affect how a person feels. Timing of meals is important to feeling well, not because the digestive tract is unable to digest food at certain times, but because the body requires nutrients to be replenished every few hours. Digestion is virtually continuous, being limited only during sleep and exercise. For some people, eating late may interfere with normal sleep. As for exercise, it is best pursued a few hours after eating because digestion can inhibit physical work (see Chapter 10 for details).

KEY POINT The digestive tract moves food through its various processing chambers by mechanical means. The mechanical actions include chewing, mixing by the stomach, adding fluid,

sphincter (SFINK-ter) a circular muscle surrounding, and able to close, a body opening.

chyme (KIME) the fluid resulting from the actions of the stomach upon a meal.

pyloric (pye-LORE-ick) **valve** the circular muscle of the lower stomach that regulates the flow of partly digested food into the small intestine. Also called *pyloric sphincter.*

small intestine the 20-foot length of small-diameter intestine, below the stomach and above the large intestine, that is the major site of digestion of food and absorption of nutrients.

large intestine the portion of the intestine that completes the absorption process.

colon the large intestine.

feces waste material remaining after digestion and absorption are complete; eventually discharged from the body.

FIGURE 3-11 The Muscular Stomach

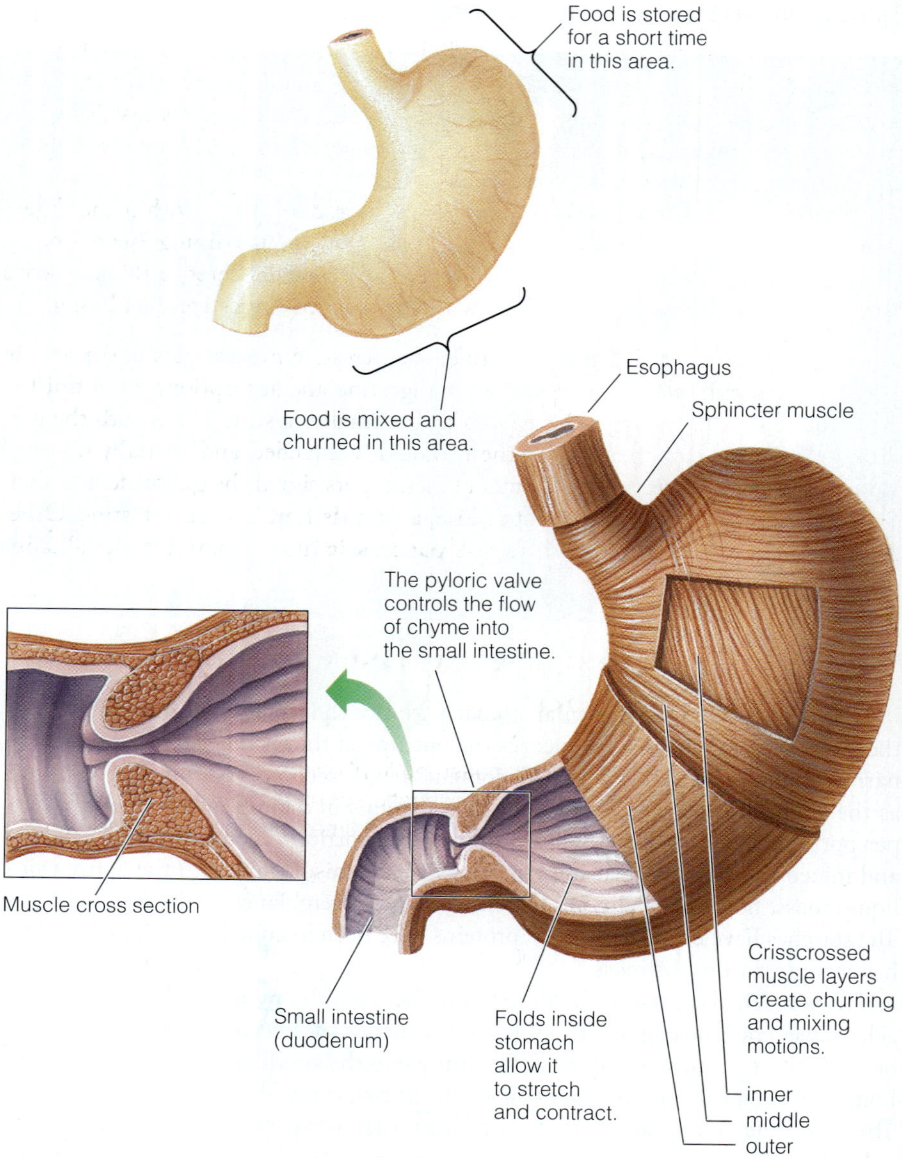

TABLE 3-1 **Digestive Enzyme Terms**

Over 30 digestive enzymes reduce food in the human digestive tract into nutrients that can be absorbed. Naming them all is beyond the scope of this book, but some general enzyme terms may prove useful.

-ase (ACE) a suffix meaning *enzyme.* Categories of digestive and other enzymes and individual enzyme names often contain this suffix.
carbohydrase (car-boh-HIGH-drace) any of a number of enzymes that break the chemical bonds of carbohydrates.
lipase (LYE-pace) any of a number of enzymes that break the chemical bonds of fats (lipids).
protease (PRO-tee-ace) any of a number of enzymes that break the chemical bonds of proteins.

and moving the tract's contents by peristalsis. After digestion and absorption, wastes are excreted.

The Chemical Aspect of Digestion

Several organs of the digestive system secrete special digestive juices that perform the complex chemical processes of digestion. Digestive juices contain enzymes that break down nutrients into their component parts (Table 3-1 presents some enzyme terms). The digestive organs that release digestive juices are the salivary glands, the stomach, the pancreas, the liver, and the small intestine. Their secretions were listed previously in Figure 3-9 (on page 80).

In the Mouth Digestion begins in the mouth. An enzyme in saliva starts rapidly breaking down starch, and another enzyme initiates a little digestion of fat, especially the digestion of milk fat (important in infants). Saliva also helps maintain the health of the teeth in two ways: by washing away food particles that would otherwise foster decay and by neutralizing decay-promoting acids produced by bacteria in the mouth.

In the Stomach In the stomach, protein digestion begins. Cells in the stomach release gastric juice, a mixture of water, enzymes, and **hydrochloric acid.** This strong acid mixture is needed to activate a protein-digesting enzyme and to initiate digestion of protein—protein digestion is the stomach's main function. The strength of an acid solution is expressed as its **pH.** The lower the pH number, the more acidic the solution; solutions with higher pH numbers are more basic. As Figure 3-12 demonstrates, saliva is only weakly acidic; the stomach's gastric juice is much more strongly acidic. Notice on the right side of Figure 3-12 that the range of tolerance for the blood's pH is exceedingly small.

Upon learning of the powerful digestive juices and enzymes within the digestive tract, students often wonder how the tract's own cellular lining escapes being digested along with the food. The answer: specialized cells secrete a thick, viscous substance known as **mucus,** which coats and protects the digestive tract lining.

In the Intestine In the small intestine, the digestive process gets under way in earnest. The small intestine is the organ of digestion and absorption, and it finishes what the mouth and stomach have started. The small intestine works with the precision of a laboratory chemist. As the thoroughly liquefied and partially digested nutrient mixture arrives there, hormonal messengers signal the gallbladder to contract and to squirt the right amount of **bile,** an **emulsifier,** into the intestine. Other hormones notify the pancreas to release **pancreatic juice** containing the alkaline

Did You Know?

Alcohol needs no assistance from digestive juices to ready it for absorption; its handling by the body is described in this chapter's Controversy section.

FIGURE 3-12 **pH Values of Digestive Juice and Other Common Fluids**

A substance's acidity or alkalinity is measured in pH units. Each step down the scale indicates a tenfold increase in concentration of hydrogen particles, which determine acidity. For example, a pH of 2 is 1,000 times stronger than a pH of 5.

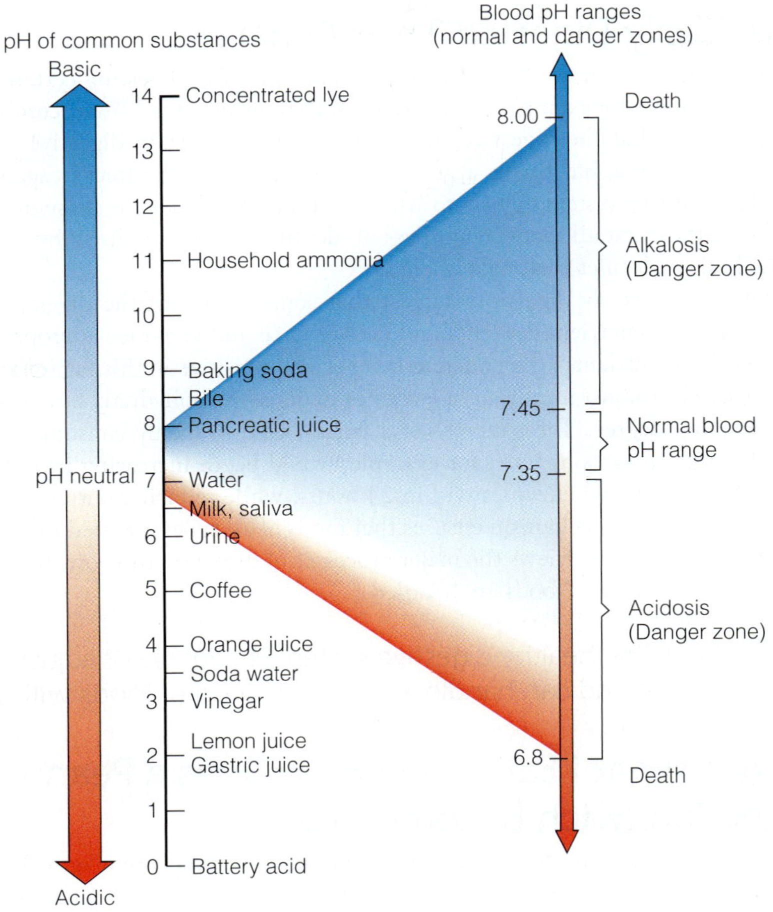

hydrochloric acid a strong corrosive acid of hydrogen and chloride atoms, produced by the stomach to assist in digestion.

pH a measure of acidity on a point scale. A solution with a pH of 1 is a strong acid; a solution with a pH of 7 is neutral; a solution with a pH of 14 is a strong base.

mucus (MYOO-cus) a slippery coating of the digestive tract lining (and other body linings) that protects the cells from exposure to digestive juices (and other destructive agents). The adjective form is *mucous* (same pronunciation). The digestive tract lining is a *mucous membrane.*

bile a cholesterol-containing digestive fluid made by the liver, stored in the gallbladder, and released into the small intestine when needed. It emulsifies fats and oils to ready them for enzymatic digestion (described in Chapter 5).

emulsifier (ee-MULL-sih-fire) a compound with both water-soluble and fat-soluble portions that can attract fats and oils into water, combining them.

pancreatic juice fluid secreted by the pancreas that contains both enzymes to digest carbohydrates, fats, and proteins and sodium bicarbonate, a neutralizing agent.

compound **bicarbonate** in amounts precisely adjusted to neutralize the stomach acid that has reached the small intestine. All these actions alter the intestinal environment to perfectly support the work of the digestive enzymes.

Meanwhile, as the pancreatic and intestinal enzymes act on the chemical bonds that hold the large nutrients together, smaller and smaller pieces are released into the intestinal fluids. The cells of the intestinal wall also hold some digestive enzymes on their surfaces; these enzymes perform last-minute breakdown reactions required before nutrients can be absorbed. Finally, the digestive process releases pieces small enough for the cells to absorb and use. Digestion by human enzymes and absorption of carbohydrate, fat, and protein are essentially complete by the time the intestinal contents enter the colon. Water, fiber, and some minerals, however, remain in the tract.

Certain kinds of fiber, which cannot be digested by human enzymes, can often be broken down by the billions of living inhabitants of the human digestive tract, the resident bacteria.[8] So active are these inhabitants in breaking down substances from food that they have been likened to an organ of the body specializing in nutrient salvage. They also affect health in other ways that are just beginning to be understood.[9] The intestinal cells then absorb the small fat fragments released from the fiber to provide a tiny bit of energy. Table 3-2 provides a summary of all the processes involved.

KEY POINT Chemical digestion begins in the mouth, where food is mixed with an enzyme in saliva that acts on carbohydrates. Digestion continues in the stomach, where stomach enzymes and acid break down protein. Digestion progresses in the small intestine; there the liver and gallbladder contribute bile that emulsifies fat, and the pancreas and small intestine donate enzymes that continue digestion so that absorption can occur. Bacteria in the colon break down certain fibers.

Are Some Food Combinations More Easily Digested Than Others?

© iStockphoto.com/Lisa Thornberg

People sometimes wonder if the digestive tract has trouble digesting certain foods in combination—for example, fruit and meat. Proponents of fad "food-combining" diets claim that the digestive tract cannot perform certain digestive tasks at the same time, but this is a gross underestimation of the tract's capabilities. The digestive system adjusts to whatever mixture of foods is presented to it. The truth is that all foods, regardless of identity, are broken down by enzymes into the basic molecules that make them up.

Scientists who study digestion suggest that some organs of the digestive tract analyze the diet's nutrient contents and deliver juice and enzymes appropriate for digesting those nutrients. The pancreas is especially sensitive in this regard and has been observed to adjust its output of enzymes to digest carbohydrate, fat, or protein to an amazing degree. The pancreas of a person who suddenly consumes a meal unusually high in carbohydrate, for example, would begin increasing its output of carbohydrate-digesting enzymes within 24 hours, while reducing outputs of other types. This sensitive mechanism ensures that foods of all types are used fully by the body. The next section reviews the major processes of digestion by showing how the nutrients in a mixture of foods are handled.

KEY POINT The healthy digestive system is capable of adjusting to almost any diet and can handle any combination of foods with ease.

bicarbonate a common alkaline chemical; a secretion of the pancreas; also the active ingredient of baking soda.

If "I Am What I Eat," Then How Does a Peanut Butter Sandwich Become "Me"?

The process of rendering foods into nutrients and absorbing them into the body fluids is remarkably efficient. Within about 24 to 48 hours of eating, a healthy body

TABLE 3-2 Summary of Chemical Digestion

	Mouth	Stomach	Small Intestine, Pancreas, Liver, and Gallbladder	Large Intestine (Colon)
SUGAR AND STARCH	The salivary glands secrete saliva to moisten and lubricate food; chewing crushes and mixes it with a salivary enzyme that initiates starch digestion.	Digestion of starch continues while food remains in the upper storage area of the stomach. In the lower digesting area of the stomach, hydrochloric acid and an enzyme in the stomach's juices halt starch digestion.	The pancreas produces a starch-digesting enzyme and releases it into the small intestine. Cells in the intestinal lining possess enzymes on their surfaces that break sugars and starch fragments into simple sugars, which then are absorbed.	Undigested carbohydrates reach the large intestine and are partly broken down by intestinal bacteria.
FIBER	The teeth crush fiber and mix it with saliva to moisten it for swallowing.	No action.	Fiber binds cholesterol and some minerals.	Most fiber is excreted with the feces; some fiber is digested by bacteria in the large intestine.
FAT	Fat-rich foods are mixed with saliva. The tongue produces traces of a fat-digesting enzyme that accomplishes some breakdown, especially of milk fats. The enzyme is stable at low pH and is important to digestion in nursing infants.	Fat tends to rise from the watery stomach fluid and foods and float on top of the mixture. Only a small amount of fat is digested. Fat is last to leave the stomach.	The liver secretes bile; the gallbladder stores it and releases it into the small intestine. Bile emulsifies the fat and readies it for enzyme action. The pancreas produces fat-digesting enzymes and releases them into the small intestine to split fats into their component parts (primarily fatty acids), which then are absorbed.	Some fatty materials escape absorption and are carried out of the body with other wastes.
PROTEIN	Chewing crushes and softens protein-rich foods and mixes them with saliva.	Stomach acid (hydrochloric acid) works to uncoil protein strands and to activate the stomach's protein-digesting enzyme. Then the enzyme breaks the protein strands into smaller fragments.	Enzymes of the small intestine and pancreas split protein fragments into smaller fragments or free amino acids. Enzymes on the cells of the intestinal lining break some protein fragments into free amino acids, which then are absorbed. Some protein fragments are also absorbed.	The large intestine carries undigested protein residue out of the body. Normally, almost all food protein is digested and absorbed.
WATER	The mouth donates watery, enzyme-containing saliva.	The stomach donates acidic, watery, enzyme-containing gastric juice.	The liver donates a watery juice containing bile. The pancreas and small intestine add watery, enzyme-containing juices; pancreatic juice is also alkaline.	The large intestine reabsorbs water and some minerals.

digests and absorbs about 90 percent of the carbohydrate, fat, and protein in a meal. Here we follow a peanut butter and banana sandwich on whole-wheat, sesame seed bread through the tract.

In the Mouth In each bite, food components are crushed, mashed, and mixed with saliva by the teeth and the tongue. The sesame seeds are crushed and torn open by the teeth, which break through the indigestible fiber coating so that digestive

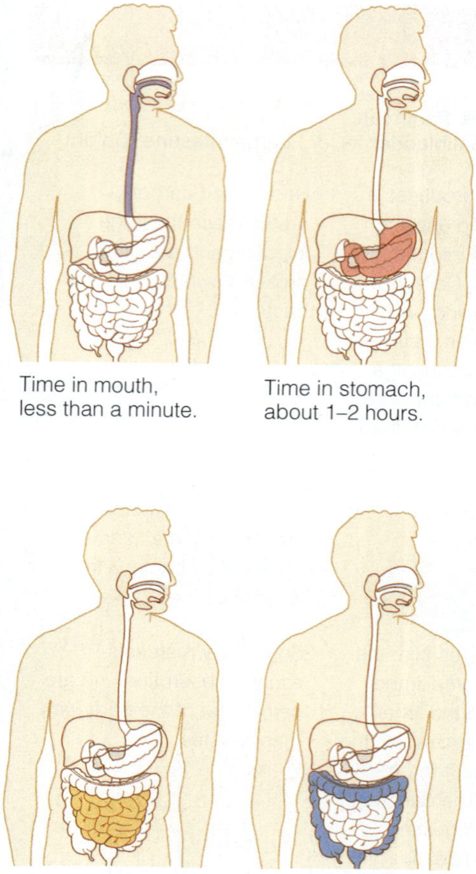

Time in mouth, less than a minute.

Time in stomach, about 1–2 hours.

Time in small intestine, about 7–8 hours.*

Time in colon, about 12–14 hours.*

*Based on a 24-hour transit time. Actual times vary widely.

enzymes can reach the nutrients inside the seeds. The peanut butter is the "extra crunchy" type, but the teeth grind the chunks to a paste before the bite is swallowed. The carbohydrate-digesting enzyme of saliva begins to break down the starch of the bread, banana, and peanut butter to sugars. Each swallow triggers a peristaltic wave that travels the length of the esophagus and carries one chewed bite of sandwich to the stomach.

In the Stomach The stomach collects bite after swallowed bite in its upper storage area, where starch continues to be digested until the gastric juice mixes with the salivary enzymes and halts their action. Small portions of the mashed sandwich are pushed into the digesting area of the stomach, where gastric juice mixes with the mass. Acid in **gastric juice** unwinds proteins from the bread, seeds, and peanut butter; then an enzyme clips the protein strands into pieces. The sandwich has now become chyme. The watery carbohydrate- and protein-rich part of the chyme enters the small intestine first; a layer of fat follows closely behind.

In the Small Intestine Some of the sweet sugars in the banana require so little digesting that they begin to cross the linings of the small intestine immediately on contact. Nearby, the liver donates bile through a duct into the small intestine. The bile blends the fat from the peanut butter and seeds with the watery, enzyme-containing digestive fluids. The nearby pancreas squirts enzymes into the small intestine to break down the fat, protein, and starch in the chemical soup that just an hour ago was a sandwich. The cells of the small intestine itself produce enzymes to complete these processes. As the enzymes do their work, smaller and smaller chemical fragments are liberated from the chemical soup and are absorbed into the blood and lymph through the cells of the small intestine's wall. Vitamins and minerals are absorbed here, too. They all eventually enter the bloodstream to nourish the tissues.

In the Large Intestine (Colon) Only fiber fragments, fluid, and some minerals are absorbed in the large intestine. The fibers from the seeds, whole-wheat bread, peanut butter, and banana are partly digested by the bacteria living in the colon, and some of the products are absorbed. Most fiber is not absorbed, however, and it passes out of the colon along with some other components, excreted as feces.

KEY POINT The mechanical and chemical actions of the digestive tract break down foods to nutrients, and large nutrients to their smaller building blocks, with remarkable efficiency.

Absorption and Transportation of Nutrients

Once the digestive system has broken down food to its nutrient components, the rest of the body awaits their delivery. First, though, every molecule of nutrient must traverse one of the cells of the intestinal lining. These cells absorb nutrients from the mixture within the intestine and deposit the water-soluble compounds in the blood and the fat-soluble ones in the lymph. The cells are selective: they recognize that some nutrients may be in short supply in the diet. Take the mineral calcium, for example. The less calcium in the diet, the greater the percentage of calcium the intestinal cells absorb from the intestinal contents. The cells are also extraordinarily efficient: they absorb enough nutrients to nourish all the body's other cells.

The Intestine's Absorbing Surface The cells of the intestinal tract lining are arranged in sheets that poke out into millions of finger-shaped projections (**villi**). Every cell on every villus has a brushlike covering of tiny hairlike projections (**microvilli**) that can trap the nutrient particles. Each villus (projection) has its own capillary network and a lymph vessel so that, as nutrients move across the cells, they can immediately mingle with the body fluids. Figure 3-13 provides a close look at these details.

gastric juice the digestive secretion of the stomach.

villi (VILL-ee, VILL-eye) fingerlike projections of the sheets of cells lining the intestinal tract. The villi make the surface area much greater than it would otherwise be (*singular:* villus).

microvilli (MY-croh-VILL-ee, MY-croh-VILL-eye) tiny, hairlike projections on each cell of every villus that greatly expand the surface area available to trap nutrient particles and absorb them into the cells (*singular:* microvillus).

FIGURE 3-13 Details of the Small Intestine Lining

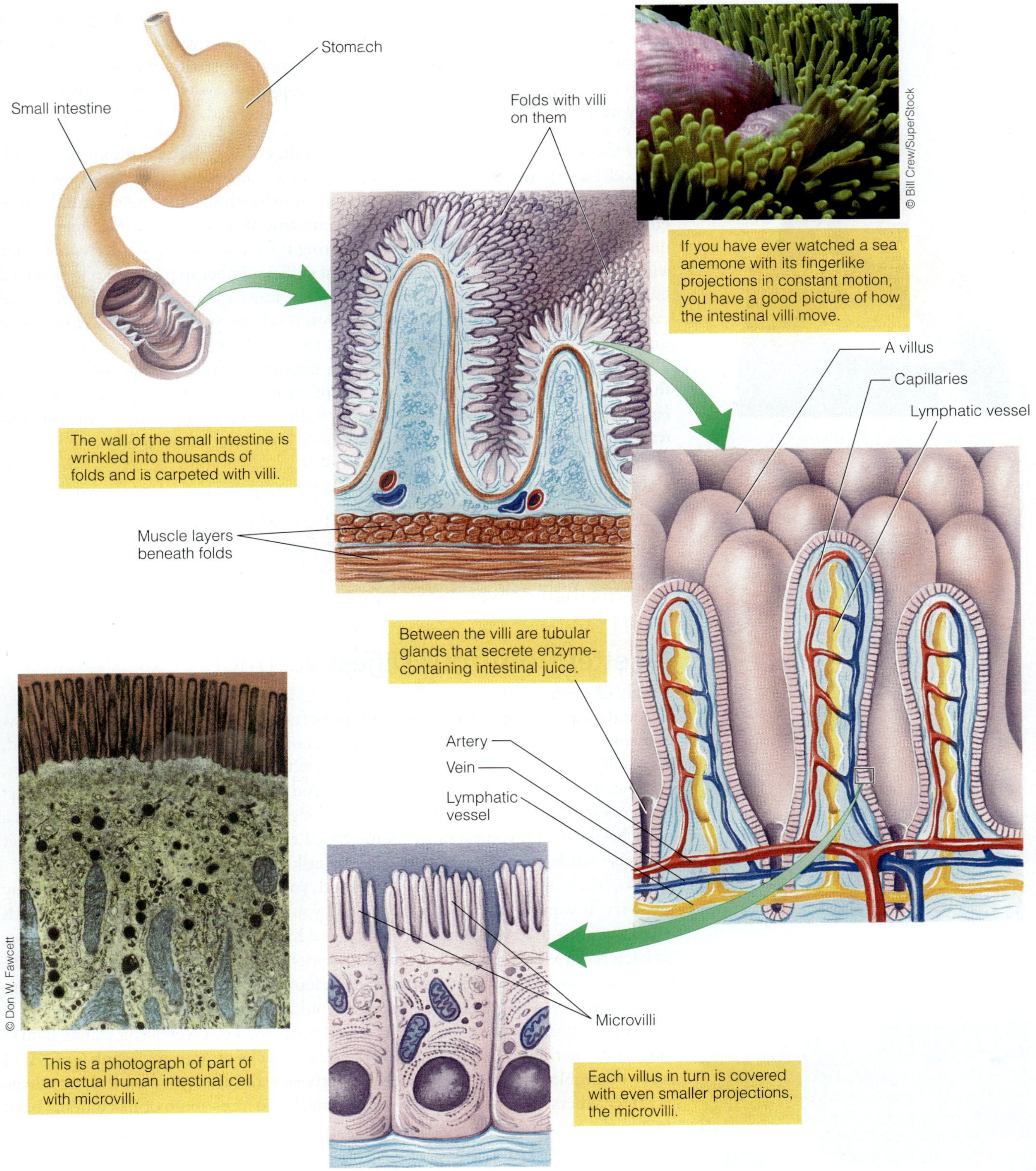

The small intestine's lining, villi and all, is wrinkled into thousands of folds, so its absorbing surface is enormous. If the folds, and the villi that poke out from them, were spread out flat, they would cover a third of a football field. The billions of cells of that surface weigh only 4 to 5 pounds, yet they absorb enough nutrients to nourish the other 150 or so pounds of body tissues.

What is your digestive tract trying to tell you?

Nutrient Transport in the Blood and Lymph Vessels After the nutrients pass through the cells of the villi, the blood and lymph vessels transport the nutrients to their ultimate consumers, the body's cells. The lymph vessels initially transport most of the products of fat digestion and the fat-soluble vitamins, ultimately conveying them into a large blood vessel near the heart. The blood vessels directly transport the products of carbohydrate and protein digestion, most vitamins, and the minerals from the digestive tract to the liver. Thanks to these two transportation systems, every nutrient soon arrives at the place where it is needed.

Nourishment of the Digestive Tract The digestive system's millions of specialized cells are themselves exquisitely sensitive to an undersupply of energy, nutrients, or dietary fiber. In cases of severe undernutrition with too little energy and nutrients, the absorptive surface of the small intestine shrinks. The surface may be reduced to a tenth of its normal area, preventing it from absorbing what few nutrients a limited food supply may provide. Without sufficient fiber to provide an undigested bulk for the tract's muscles to push against, the muscles become weak from lack of exercise. Malnutrition that impairs digestion is self-perpetuating because impaired digestion makes malnutrition worse.

The digestive system's needs are few, but important. The body has much to say to the attentive listener, stated in a language of symptoms and feelings that you would be wise to study. The next section takes a lighthearted look at what your digestive tract might be trying to tell you.

KEY POINT The digestive system feeds the rest of the body and is itself sensitive to malnutrition. The folds and villi of the small intestine enlarge its surface area to facilitate nutrient absorption through countless cells to the blood and lymph. These transport systems then deliver the nutrients to all the body's cells.

A Letter from Your Digestive Tract

To My Owner,

You and I are so close; I hope that I can speak frankly without offending you. I know that sometimes I *do* offend with my gurgling noises and belching at quiet times and, oh yes, the gas. But, as you can read for yourself in Table 3-3, when you chew gum, drink carbonated beverages, or eat hastily, you gulp air with each swallow. I can't help making some noise as I move the air along my length or release it upward in a noisy belch. And if you eat or drink too fast, I can't help getting **hiccups.** Please sit and relax while you dine. You will ease my task, and we'll both be happier.

Also, when someone offers you a new food, you gobble away, trusting me to do my job. I try. It would make my life easier, and yours less gassy, if you would start with small amounts of new foods, especially those high in fiber. The breakdown of fiber by bacteria produces gas, so introduce fiber-rich foods slowly. But please, if you do notice more gas than normal from a specific food, avoid it. If the gas becomes excessive, check with a physician. The problem could be something simple—or serious.

When you eat or drink too much, it just burns me up. Overeating causes **heartburn** because the acidic juice from my stomach backs up into my esophagus. Acid poses no problem to my healthy stomach, whose walls are coated with thick mucus to protect them. But when my too-full stomach squeezes some of its contents back up into the esophagus, the acid burns its unprotected surface. Also, those tight jeans you wear constrict my stomach, squeezing the contents upward into the esophagus. Just leaning over or lying down after a meal may allow the acid to escape up the esophagus because the muscular sphincter separating the two spaces is much looser than other sphincters. And if we need to lose a few pounds, let's get at it—excess body fat can also squeeze my stomach, causing acid to back up. When heartburn is a problem, do me a favor: try to eat smaller meals; drink liquids an hour before or after, but not during, meals; wear reasonably loose clothing; and relax after eating, but sit up (don't lie down).

hiccups spasms of both the vocal cords and the diaphragm, causing periodic, audible, short, inhaled coughs. Can be caused by irritation of the diaphragm, indigestion, or other causes. Hiccups usually resolve in a few minutes, but can have serious effects if prolonged. Breathing into a paper bag (inhaling carbon dioxide) or dissolving a teaspoon of sugar in the mouth may stop them.

heartburn a burning sensation in the chest (in the area of the heart) caused by backflow of stomach acid into the esophagus.

TABLE 3-3 Foods and Intestinal Gas

Recent experiments have shed light on the causes and prevention of intestinal gas. Here are some recent findings.

- Milk intake causes gas in those who cannot digest the milk sugar lactose. Most people, however, can consume up to a cup of milk without producing excessive gas.
  Solution: Drink up to 4 ounces of fluid milk at a sitting, or substitute reduced-fat cheeses or yogurt without added milk solids. Use lactose-reduced products, or treat regular products with lactose-reducing enzyme products.
- Beans cause gas because some of their carbohydrates are indigestible by human enzymes, but are broken down by intestinal bacteria. The amount of gas may not be as much as most people fear, however.
  Solution: Use rinsed canned beans or dried beans that are well cooked, because cooked carbohydrates are more readily digestible. Try enzyme drops or pills that can help break down the carbohydrate before it reaches the intestine.
- Air swallowed during eating or drinking can cause gas, as can the gas of carbonated beverages. Each swallow of a beverage can carry three times as much gas as fluid, which some people belch up.
  Solution: Slow down during eating and drinking, and don't chew gum or suck on hard candies that may cause you to swallow air. Limit carbonated beverages.
- Vegetables may or may not cause gas in some people, but research is lacking.
  Solution: If you feel certain vegetables cause gas, try eating small portions of the cooked products. Do try the vegetable again: the gas you experienced may have been a coincidence and had nothing to do with eating the vegetable.

Sometimes your food choices irritate me. Specifically, chemical irritants in foods, such as the "hot" component of chili peppers, chemicals in coffee, fat, chocolate, carbonated soft drinks, and alcohol, may worsen heartburn in some people. Avoid the ones that cause trouble. Above all, do not smoke. Smoking makes my heartburn worse—and you should hear your lungs bellyache about it.

By the way, I can tell you've been taking heartburn medicines again. You must have been watching those misleading TV commercials. You need to know that **antacids** are designed only to temporarily relieve pain caused by heartburn by neutralizing stomach acid for a while. But when the antacids reduce my normal stomach acidity, I respond by producing *more* acid to restore the normal acid condition. Also, the ingredients in antacids can interfere with my ability to absorb nutrients. Please check with our doctor if heartburn occurs more than just occasionally and certainly before you decide that we need to take the heavily advertised **acid reducers;** these restrict my normal ability to produce acid so much that my job of digesting food becomes harder. They may also reduce our defense against serious infections, even pneumonia.[10]

Given a chance, my powerful stomach acid helps to fight off many bacterial infections—most disease-causing bacteria won't survive a bath in my caustic juices.[11] Acid-reducing drugs reduce acid (I'll bet you knew that), and so allow more bacteria to pass through. And, even worse, self-prescribed heartburn medicine can mask the symptoms of **ulcer, hernia,** or the severe destructive form of chronic heartburn known as **gastroesophageal reflux disease (GERD).**[12] This can be serious because, although the bacterium *H. pylori* that causes most ulcers responds to antibiotic drugs, some ulcers have other causes, such as frequent use of certain painkillers—the *cause* of the ulcer must be treated as well as its symptoms.[‡13] Left untreated, *H. pylori* raises the risk of stomach cancer.[14] A hernia can cause food to back up into the esophagus, so it can feel like heartburn, but many times hernias require corrective treatment by a physician. GERD can feel like heartburn, too, but requires the correct drug therapy to prevent respiratory problems, severe damage to tissues, or even cancer of the throat or esophagus.[15] So please don't wait too long to get medical help for chronic or severe heartburn—it may not be simple indigestion.

‡ Anti-inflammatory drugs such as aspirin, ibuprofen, and napron sodium.

antacids medications that react directly and immediately with the acid of the stomach, neutralizing it. Antacids are most suitable for treating occasional heartburn.

acid reducers prescription and over-the-counter drugs that reduce the acid output of the stomach; effective for treating severe, persistent forms of heartburn but not for neutralizing acid already present. Side effects are frequent and include diarrhea, other gastrointestinal complaints, and reduction of the stomach's capacity to destroy alcohol, thereby producing higher-than-expected blood alcohol levels from each drink (see this chapter's Controversy section). Also called *acid controllers.*

ulcer an erosion in the topmost, and sometimes underlying, layers of cells that form a lining. Ulcers of the digestive tract commonly form in the esophagus, stomach, or upper small intestine.

hernia a protrusion of an organ or part of an organ through the wall of the body chamber that normally contains the organ. An example is a *hiatal* (high-AY-tal) *hernia,* in which part of the stomach protrudes up through the diaphragm into the chest cavity, which contains the esophagus, heart, and lungs.

gastroesophageal (GAS-tro-eh-SOFF-ah-jeel) **reflux disease (GERD)** a severe and chronic splashing of stomach acid and enzymes into the esophagus, throat, mouth, or airway that causes injury to those organs. Untreated GERD may increase the risk of esophageal cancer; treatment may require surgery or management with medication.

- For more information about ulcers and medication, call the Centers for Disease Control and Prevention at 1-888-MY-ULCER, toll free.

When you eat too quickly, I worry about choking (see Figure 3-14). Please take time to cut your food into small pieces, and chew it until it is crushed and moistened with saliva. Also, refrain from talking or laughing before swallowing, and never attempt to eat when you are breathing hard. Also, for our sake and the sake of others, learn first aid for choking as shown in Figure 3-15.

When I'm suffering, you suffer, too. When **constipation** or **diarrhea** strikes, neither of us is having fun. Slow, hard, dry bowel movements can be painful, and failing to have a movement for too long brings on headaches, backaches, stomachaches, and other ills; if chronic, constipation may cause **hemorrhoids** or other ills.[16] Most people suffer occasional harmless constipation, and laxatives may help, but too frequent use of laxatives and enemas can lead to dependency; upset our fluid, salt, and mineral balances; and, with mineral-oil laxatives, can interfere with the absorption of fat-soluble vitamins. (Mineral oil, which is not absorbed, dissolves the vitamins and carries them out of the body with it.)

Instead of relying on laxatives, listen carefully for my signal that it is time to defecate, and make time for it even if you are busy. The longer you ignore my signal, the more time the colon has to extract water from the feces, hardening them. Also, please choose foods that provide enough fiber (some high-fiber foods are listed in Chapter 4, pages 114–115).[§] Fiber attracts water, creating softer, bulkier stools that stimulate my muscles to contract, pushing the contents along. Fiber helps my muscles to stay fit, too, making elimination easier. Be sure to drink enough water because dehydration causes the colon to absorb all the water it can get from the feces. And please make time to be physically active; exercise strengthens not just the muscles of your arms, legs, and torso, but those of the colon, too.[17]

When I have the opposite problem, diarrhea, my system will rob you of water and salts. In diarrhea my intestinal contents have moved too quickly, drawing water and minerals from your tissues into the contents. When this happens, please rest a while and drink fluids (I prefer clear juices and broths). However, if diarrhea is bloody, or if it worsens or persists, call our doctor—severe diarrhea can be life-threatening.

To avoid diarrhea, try not to change my diet too drastically or quickly. I'm willing to work with you and learn to digest new foods, but if you suddenly change your

§ Rarely, a spastic, constricted bowel causes constipation; this condition requires medical attention, not fiber.

FIGURE 3-14 **Normal Swallowing and Choking**

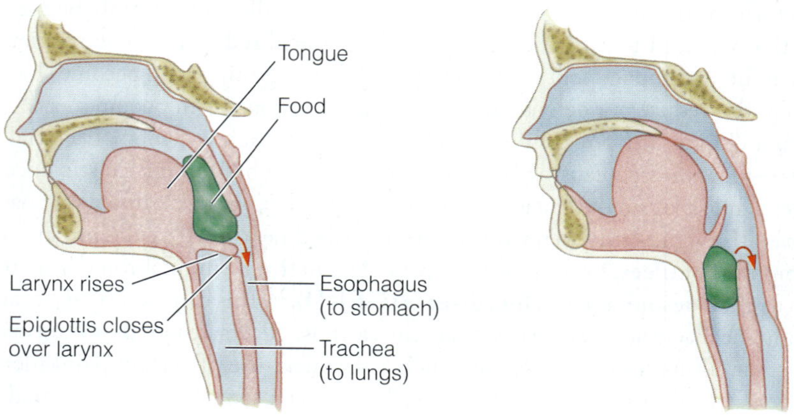

A normal swallow. The epiglottis acts as a flap to seal the entrance to the lungs (trachea) and direct food to the stomach via the esophagus.

Choking. A choking person cannot speak or gasp because food lodged in the trachea blocks the passage of air. The red arrow points to where the food should have gone to prevent choking.

constipation infrequent, difficult bowel movements often caused by diet, inactivity, dehydration, or medication. Also defined in Chapter 4.

diarrhea frequent, watery bowel movements usually caused by diet, stress, or irritation of the colon. Severe, prolonged diarrhea robs the body of fluid and certain minerals, causing dehydration and imbalances that can be dangerous if left untreated.

hemorrhoids (HEM-or-oids) swollen, hardened (varicose) veins in the rectum, usually caused by the pressure resulting from constipation.

FIGURE 3-15 First Aid for Choking

The first-aid strategy most likely to succeed is abdominal thrusts, sometimes called the Heimlich maneuver.[a] Grabbing the throat is the universal sign for choking.

To lend assistance to a choking person:

1. Stand behind the person.
2. Wrap your arms around him.
3. Place the thumb side of one fist snugly against his body, slightly above the navel and below the rib cage.
4. Grasp your fist with your other hand and give him a sudden strong hug inward and upward.
5. Repeat thrusts as necessary.

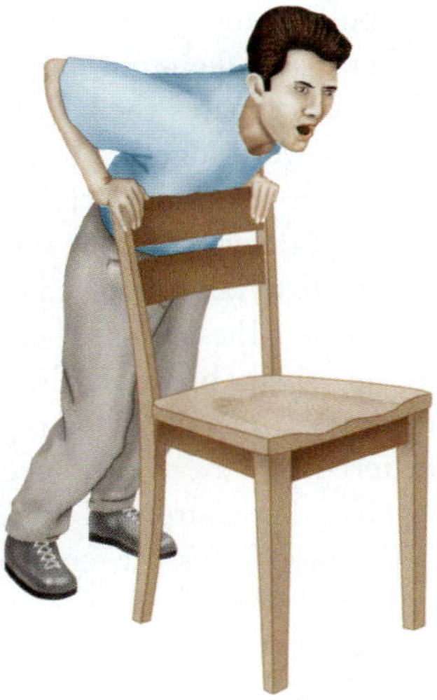

If *you* are choking and alone, you can help yourself:

1. Place the thumb side of one fist slightly above your navel and below your rib cage.
2. Grasp the fist with your other hand.
3. Press inward and upward with a quick motion.
4. If this fails, forcefully press your upper abdomen over any firm surface such as the back of a chair, a countertop, or a railing.
5. Repeat as necessary.

[a]*The Heimlich maneuver may not be an effective first-aid measure for unconscious drowning victims.*

diet, we're both in for it. I hate even to think of it, but one likely cause of diarrhea is dangerous food poisoning. (*Please* read, and use, the tips in Chapter 12 to keep us safe.) Also, if diarrhea lasts longer than a day or two, or if it alternates with constipation, the cause could be **irritable bowel syndrome (IBS),** and you should go see a physician.[18] In IBS, strong contractions speed intestinal contents through quickly, causing gas, bloating, diarrhea, and frequent or severe abdominal discomfort.[19] Weakened and slowed contractions may then follow, causing constipation. You might try eating smaller meals and avoiding onions or other irritating foods, but if that doesn't work, by all means, call our doctor—IBS often responds to antispasmodic drugs or even peppermint oil taken under medical supervision.[20]

By the way, I trust you not to believe false claims that health troubles can be solved by washing the colon with a powerful enema machine—in fact, this "colonic irrigation" is unnecessary and has caused illness and even death from equipment contamination, electrolyte depletion, and intestinal perforation.

Thank you for listening. I know we'll both benefit from communicating like this because you and I are in this together for the long haul.

Affectionately,
Your Digestive Tract

KEY POINT The digestive tract has many ways to communicate its needs. Maintenance of a healthy digestive tract requires preventing or responding to symptoms with a carefully chosen diet and sound medical care.

irritable bowel syndrome (IBS) intermittent disturbance of bowel function, especially diarrhea or alternating diarrhea and constipation, often with abdominal cramping or bloating; managed with diet, physical activity, or relief from psychological stress. The cause is uncertain, but IBS does not permanently harm the intestines nor lead to serious diseases.

Did You Know?

The lungs also excrete some small percentage of ingested alcohol—the basis for the "breathalyzer" test given to drivers to determine if they've been drinking.

The Excretory System

Cells generate a number of wastes, and all of them must be eliminated. Many of the body's organs play roles in removing wastes. Carbon dioxide waste from the cells travels in the blood to the lungs, where it is exchanged for oxygen. Other wastes are pulled out of the bloodstream by the liver. The liver processes these wastes and either tosses them out into the digestive tract with bile, to leave the body with the feces, or prepares them to be sent to the kidneys for disposal in the urine. Organ systems work together to dispose of the body's wastes, but the kidneys are waste- and water-removal specialists.

The kidneys straddle the cardiovascular system and filter the passing blood. Waste materials, dissolved in water, are collected by the kidneys' working units, the **nephrons.** These wastes become concentrated as urine, which travels through tubes to the urinary **bladder.** The bladder empties periodically, removing the wastes from the body. Thus, the blood is purified continuously throughout the day, and dissolved materials are excreted as necessary. One dissolved mineral, sodium, helps to regulate blood pressure, and its excretion or retention by the kidneys is a vital part of the body's blood pressure–controlling mechanism.

Though they account for just 0.5 percent of the body's total weight, the kidneys use up 10 percent of the body's oxygen supply, indicating intense metabolic activity. The kidney's waste-excreting function rivals breathing in importance to life, but the kidneys act in other ways as well. By sorting among dissolved substances, retaining some while excreting others, the kidneys regulate the fluid volume and concentrations of substances in the blood and extracellular fluid with great precision. Through these mechanisms, the kidneys help to regulate blood pressure (see Chapter 11 for details). As you might expect, the kidneys' work is regulated by hormones secreted by glands that respond to conditions in the blood (such as the sodium concentration). The kidneys also release certain hormones.

• Extracellular fluid is defined on page 71 and depicted in Figure 3-4.

Because the kidneys remove toxins that could otherwise damage body tissues, whatever supports the health of the kidneys supports the health of the whole body. A strong cardiovascular system and an abundant supply of water are important to keep blood flushing swiftly through the kidneys. In addition, the kidneys need sufficient energy to do their complex sifting and sorting job, and many vitamins and minerals serve as the cogs of their machinery. Exercise and nutrition are vital to healthy kidney function.

KEY POINT The kidneys adjust the blood's composition in response to the body's needs, disposing of everyday wastes and helping remove toxins. Nutrients, including water, and exercise help keep the kidneys healthy.

nephrons (NEFF-rons) the working units in the kidneys, consisting of intermeshed blood vessels and tubules.

bladder the sac that holds urine until time for elimination.

MY TURN

© Cengage Learning
Ashley

© Cengage Learning
Christopher

I Am What I Drink

What do college students think about drinkin alcohol? Two students talk about their drinkin habits—how much, how often, and where.

CENGAGENOW To hear their stories, log on to www.cengage.com/sso.

LO 3.4

Storage Systems

The human body is designed to eat at intervals of about four to six hours, but cells need nutrients around the clock. Providing the cells with a constant flow of the needed nutrients requires the cooperation of many body systems. These systems store and release nutrients to meet the cells' needs between meals. Among the major storage sites are the liver and muscles, which store carbohydrate, and the fat cells, which store fat and other fat-related substances.

When I Eat More Than My Body Needs, What Happens to the Extra Nutrients?

Nutrients collected from the digestive system sooner or later all move through a vast network of capillaries that weave among the liver cells. This arrangement ensures that liver cells have access to the newly arriving nutrients for processing. Body tissues store excess energy-containing nutrients in two forms (details will follow in later chapters). The liver makes some of the excess into **glycogen** (a carbohydrate), and some is stored as body fat. Liver glycogen can sustain cell activities when the intervals between meals become long. Should no food be available, the liver's glycogen supply dwindles; it can be effectively depleted within as few as three to six hours. Muscle cells make and store glycogen, too, but selfishly reserve it for their own use.

Whereas the liver stores glycogen, it ships out fat in packages (see Chapter 5) to be picked up by cells that need it. All body cells may withdraw the fat they need from these packages, and the fat cells of the **adipose tissue** pick up the remainder and store it to meet long-term energy needs. Unlike the liver, fat tissue has virtually infinite storage capacity. It can continue to supply the body's cells with fat for days, weeks, or possibly even months when no food is eaten.

These storage systems for glucose and fat ensure that the body's cells will not go without energy even if the body is hungry for food. Body stores also exist for many other nutrients, each with a characteristic capacity. For example, liver and fat cells store many vitamins, and bones provide reserves of calcium and other minerals. Stores of nutrients are available to keep the blood levels constant and to meet cellular demands.

Variations in Nutrient Stores

Some nutrients are stored in the body in much larger quantities than others. For example, certain vitamins are stored without limit, even if they reach toxic levels within the body. Other nutrients are stored in only small amounts, regardless of the amount taken in, and these can readily be depleted. As you learn how the body handles various nutrients, pay particular attention to their storage so that you can know your tolerance limits. For example, you needn't eat fat at every meal, because fat is stored abundantly. On the other hand, you normally do need to have a source of carbohydrate at intervals throughout the day because the liver stores less than one day's supply of glycogen.

KEY POINT The body's energy stores are of two principal kinds: glycogen in muscle and liver cells (in limited quantities) and fat in fat cells (in potentially large quantities). Other tissues store other nutrients.

- Later chapters provide details about storage of energy nutrients.

Conclusion

In addition to the systems just described, the body has many more: bones, muscles, reproductive organs, and others. All of these cooperate, enabling each cell to carry on its own life. For example, the skin and body linings defend other tissues against microbial invaders, while being nourished and cleansed by tissues specializing in these tasks. Each system needs a continuous supply of many specific nutrients to

glycogen a storage form of carbohydrate energy (glucose); described more fully in Chapter 4.

adipose tissue the body's fat tissue, consisting of masses of fat-storing cells and blood vessels to nourish them.

maintain itself and carry out its work. Calcium is particularly important for bones, for example; iron for muscles; glucose for the brain. But all systems need all nutrients, and every system is impaired by an undersupply or oversupply of them.

While external events clamor and vie for attention, the body quietly continues its life-sustaining work. Most of the body's work is directed automatically by the unconscious portions of the brain and nervous system, and this work is finely regulated to achieve a state of well-being. But you need to involve your brain's cortex, your conscious thinking brain, to cultivate an understanding and appreciation of your body's needs. In doing so, attend to nutrition first. The rewards are liberating—ample energy to tackle life's tasks, a robust attitude, and the glowing appearance that comes from the best of health. Read on, and learn to let nutrition principles guide your food choices.

KEY POINT To achieve optimal function, the body's systems require nutrients from outside. These have to be supplied through a human being's conscious food choices.

MEDIA MENU

Throughout this chapter, the CengageNOW logo indicates an opportunity for online self-study, linking you to interactive tutorials and videos based on your level of understanding. Go to **www.cengage.com/sso.**

Learn more about digestive disorders by searching "digestion" or specific diseases by name at **www.healthfinder.gov.**

Find out more about digestion, absorption, organs of the gastrointestinal tract, and digestive diseases at **www.nlm.nih.gov/medlineplus.**

Learn more about digestive diseases at **www.nal.usda.gov/fnic** (under Browse by Subject, select Diet and Disease, and click on Digestive Diseases and Disorders).

SELF CHECK

Answers to these Self Check questions are in Appendix G.

1. All of the following are correct concerning ulcers *except:*
   - A. they usually occur in the large intestine
   - B. some are caused by a bacterium
   - C. if not treated correctly, they can lead to stomach cancer
   - D. their symptoms can be masked by using antacids regularly
2. Which of the following increases the production of intestinal gas?
   - A. chewing gum
   - B. drinking carbonated beverages
   - C. eating certain vegetables
   - D. all of the above
3. Chemical digestion of all nutrients mainly occurs in which organ?
   - A. mouth
   - B. stomach
   - C. small intestine
   - D. large intestine
4. Which chemical substance released by the pancreas neutralizes stomach acid that has reached the small intestine?
   - A. mucus
   - B. enzymes
   - C. bicarbonate
   - D. bile
5. Which of the following passes through the large intestine mostly unabsorbed?
   - A. starch
   - B. vitamins
   - C. minerals
   - D. fiber
6. T-cells are immune cells that ingest and destroy antigens in a process known as phagocytosis.
   T F
7. Bile starts the process of protein digestion in the stomach.
   T F
8. To digest food efficiently, people should not combine certain foods, such as meat and fruit, at the same meal.
   T F
9. The gallbladder stores bile until it is needed to emulsify fat.
   T F
10. Absorption of the majority of nutrients takes place across the mucus-coated lining of the stomach.
   T F

CONTROVERSY 3

Alcohol and Nutrition: Do the Benefits Outweigh the Risks?

LO 3.5

On average, people in the United States consume from 6 to 10 percent of their total daily energy intake as alcohol. Their drinking habits span a wide spectrum: many drink no alcohol whatsoever, some take a glass of wine only with meals, others drink lightly on social occasions, whereas some are heavy social drinkers, and still others take in large quantities of alcohol daily because of a life-shattering addiction. A third of U.S. college students drink alcohol in a pattern that identifies them as **binge drinkers,** though when asked, more than 90 percent reject this description. Thirty percent of all binge drinking in the United States involves people aged 18 to 25 years, and white men in particular.[1*]

Heavy drinkers often pay a high price in terms of their health and safety. **Moderate drinkers,** in contrast, consume less alcohol and so suffer fewer of its effects. Some may even benefit from small amounts of alcohol but, because alcoholic beverages present many discretionary calories, they may also gain weight.

Alcohol is not just an energy source, however; it is also a psychoactive drug and a toxin to the body. Despite its toxicity, many people want to know if there is an amount of alcohol they can drink safely or whether they may derive benefits, particularly for the health of the heart, by drinking. This Controversy starts by defining some terms in Table C3-1. Then, it examines alcohol's immediate actions within the body and its effects on the brain and other organs. It summarizes the long-term effects of alcohol on the body and nutrition and concludes with research on moderate drinking. In the end, after learning all of alcohol's effects, you must choose for yourself how, and if, alcohol fits into your own life and health.

*Reference notes are found in Appendix F.

WHAT IS ALCOHOL?

In chemistry, the term *alcohol* refers to a class of chemical compounds whose names end in *-ol.* The glycerol molecule of a triglyceride is an example. Alcohols affect living things profoundly, partly because they act as lipid solvents. Alcohols can easily penetrate a cell's outer lipid membrane, and once inside, they denature the cell's protein structures and kill the cell. Because some alcohols kill microbial cells, they make useful disinfectants and antiseptics.

The alcohol of alcoholic beverages, **ethanol,** is somewhat less toxic than others. Sufficiently diluted and taken in small enough doses, its action in the brain produces euphoria. Used in this way, alcohol is a drug, and like many drugs, alcohol presents both benefits and hazards to the taker. Its effects depend on the quantity of alcohol consumed.

WHAT IS A "DRINK"?

Alcoholic beverages contain a great deal of water and some other substances, as well as the alcohol ethanol. In beer, wine, and wine coolers, alcohol contributes a relatively low percentage of the beverage's volume—about 5 percent in most beers to about 13 to 15 percent in many wines.[†] Malt beverages, even those with sugar and fruity flavors or caffeine added, range from 5 to 10 percent ethanol. In contrast, about 50 percent of the volume of whiskey, vodka, rum, and brandy may be ethanol. The percentage of alcohol is stated as **proof.** Proof equals twice the percentage of alcohol; for example, 100 proof liquor is 50 percent alcohol.

[†] *Nonalcoholic beers and wine may contain a small amount of alcohol, up to 0.5 percent.*

A serving of an alcoholic beverage, commonly called a **drink,** delivers ½ ounce of pure ethanol. Figure C3-1 depicts servings of alcoholic beverages that are considered to be one drink. These standard measures may have little in common with the drinks served by enthusiastic bartenders, however. Many wine glasses easily hold 6 to 8 ounces of wine; wine coolers may come packaged 12 ounces to a bottle; a large beer stein can hold 16, 20, or even more ounces; a strong liquor drink may contain 2 or 3 ounces of various liquors.

DEFINING DRINKING

When people congregate to enjoy conversation and companionship, beverages are usually a part of the scene. How alcohol affects the picture depends on how (and whether) it is consumed.

Social Drinkers

Many people are **social drinkers**—they often choose wine, beer, or mixed drinks over cola, juice, milk, tea, or coffee to accompany a meal, to celebrate occasions, or to relax with friends. In moderation, alcohol reduces inhibitions, eases social interactions, and produces feelings of **euphoria,** a pleasant sensation that people seek. The term *moderation* is important in this regard because more alcohol *impedes* social interactions. Euphoria

TABLE C3-1 Alcohol and Drinking Terms

- **acetaldehyde** (ass-et-AL-deh-hide) a substance to which ethanol is metabolized on its way to becoming harmless waste products that can be excreted.
- **alcohol dehydrogenase** (dee-high-DRAH-gen-ace) **(ADH)** an enzyme system that breaks down alcohol. The antidiuretic hormone listed below is also abbreviated ADH.
- **alcoholism** a dependency on alcohol marked by compulsive uncontrollable drinking with negative effects on physical health, family relationships, and social health.
- **antidiuretic** (AN-tee-dye-you-RET-ick) **hormone (ADH)** a hormone produced by the pituitary gland in response to dehydration (or a high sodium concentration in the blood). It stimulates the kidneys to reabsorb more water and so to excrete less. (This hormone should not be confused with the enzyme alcohol dehydrogenase, which is also abbreviated ADH.)
- **beer belly** central-body fatness associated with alcohol consumption.
- **binge drinkers** people who drink four or more drinks in a short period.
- **cirrhosis** (seer-OH-sis) advanced liver disease, often associated with alcoholism, in which liver cells have died, hardened, turned an orange color, and permanently lost their function.
- **congeners** (CON-jen-ers) chemical substances other than alcohol that account for some of the physiological effects of alcoholic beverages, such as appetite, taste, and aftereffects.
- **drink** a dose of any alcoholic beverage that delivers half an ounce of pure ethanol.
- **ethanol** the alcohol of alcoholic beverages, produced by the action of microorganisms on the carbohydrates of grape juice or other carbohydrate-containing fluids.
- **euphoria** (you-FOR-ee-uh) an inflated sense of well-being and pleasure brought on by a moderate dose of alcohol and by some other drugs.
- **fatty liver** an early stage of liver deterioration seen in several diseases, including kwashiorkor and alcoholic liver disease, in which fat accumulates in the liver cells.
- **fibrosis** (fye-BROH-sis) an intermediate stage of alcoholic liver deterioration. Liver cells lose their function and assume the characteristics of connective tissue cells (become fibrous).
- **formaldehyde** a substance to which methanol is metabolized on the way to being converted to harmless waste products that can be excreted.
- **gout** (GOWT) a painful form of arthritis caused by the abnormal buildup of the waste product uric acid in the blood, with uric acid salt deposited as crystals in the joints.
- **methanol** an alcohol produced in the body continually by all cells.
- **moderate drinkers** people who do not drink excessively and do not behave inappropriately because of alcohol. A moderate drinker's health may or may not be harmed by alcohol over the long term.
- **nonalcoholic** a term used on beverage labels, such as wine or beer, indicating that the product contains less than 0.5% alcohol. The terms *dealcoholized* and *alcohol removed* mean the same thing. *Alcohol free* means that the product contains no detectable alcohol.
- **problem drinkers** or **alcohol abusers** people who suffer social, emotional, family, job-related, or other problems because of alcohol. A problem drinker is on the way to alcoholism.
- **proof** a statement of the percentage of alcohol in an alcoholic beverage. Liquor that is 100 proof is 50% alcohol, 90 proof is 45%, and so forth.
- **social drinkers** people who drink only on social occasions. Depending on how alcohol affects a social drinker's life, the person may be a moderate drinker or a problem drinker.
- **urethane** a carcinogenic compound that commonly forms in alcoholic beverages.
- **Wernicke-Korsakoff** (VER-nik-ee KOR-sah-koff) **syndrome** a cluster of symptoms involving nerve damage arising from a deficiency of the vitamin thiamin in alcoholism. Characterized by mental confusion, disorientation, memory loss, jerky eye movements, and staggering gait.

FIGURE C3-1 Servings of Alcoholic Beverages That Equal One Drink

occurs only with the first few drinks and not with higher alcohol intakes.[2]

All beverages seem to ease conversation, whether they contain alcohol or not. For example, **nonalcoholic** beers and wines on the market also elevate mood and encourage social interaction, as do tea, coffee, or sodas. To mimic the look and taste of cocktails (and to minimize social pressure to drink alcohol), sparkling ciders or ginger ale, tomato juice with a stalk of celery, or cola with a slice of lime can do the trick.

Problem Drinkers and Alcoholism

In contrast to moderate social drinking, the effect of alcohol on **problem drinkers** or people with **alcoholism** is overwhelmingly negative. For these people, drinking alcohol brings irrational and often dangerous behavior, such as driving a car while intoxicated and regrettable human interactions, such as arguments, violence, or unplanned and risky sexual activity.[3] With continued drinking, such people face psychological depression, physical illness, severe malnutrition, and demoralizing erosion of self-esteem. A tool for self-analysis for alcohol use disorder is found in Table C3-2.

Defining Moderation

Moderation is not easily defined because tolerance to alcohol differs among individuals, partly because of inherited genetic makeup. In general, women

TABLE C3-2 Symptoms of Problem Drinking and Alcohol Addiction

A health professional can diagnose and evaluate problem drinking or alcohol addiction with the answers to these questions.

In the past year, have you:

1. Ever ended up drinking more or for longer than you intended?
2. Wanted to cut down or stop drinking, or tried to, but couldn't on more than one occasion?
3. Endangered yourself more than once while or after drinking (such as driving, swimming, using machinery, walking in a dangerous area, or having unsafe sex) on more than one occasion?
4. Found that your usual number of drinks no longer produced the desired effect?
5. Continued to drink even though it made you feel depressed or anxious? Or after having had a memory blackout?
6. Spent a lot of time drinking, or being sick, or getting over other aftereffects?
7. Continued to drink even though it was causing trouble with your family or friends?
8. Found that drinking—or being sick from drinking—often interfered with taking care of your home or family? Or caused job troubles? Or school problems?
9. Given up or cut back on activities that were important or interesting to you, or gave pleasure, in order to drink?
10. Been arrested, been held at a police station, or had other legal problems because of your drinking?
11. Found that when the effects of alcohol were wearing off, you had withdrawal symptoms, such as trouble sleeping, shakiness, restlessness, nausea, sweating, racing heartbeat, or seizure? Or sensed things that were not there?

If you have any of these symptoms, or if people close to you are concerned about your drinking, then alcohol may be a cause for concern. The more symptoms you have and the more often you have them, the more urgent the need for change. See a health professional.

Note: These questions are based on symptoms for alcohol use disorders in the American Psychiatric Association's Diagnostic and Statistical Manual (DSM) of Mental Disorders, *Fourth Edition. The DSM is the most commonly used system in the United States for diagnosing mental health disorders.*

Source: Adapted from Rethinking Drinking: Alcohol and Your Health, *NIH pub. no. 09-3770, February 2009.*

TABLE C3-3 Who Should Not Drink Alcohol?

The *Dietary Guidelines for Americans 2005* suggest that these people not drink alcoholic beverages at all:

- *Children and adolescents.* The earlier in life drinking begins, the greater the risk of alcoholism later on.
- *People of any age who cannot restrict their drinking to moderate levels.* Especially, people recovering from alcoholism, problem drinkers, and people whose family members have alcohol problems.
- *Women who may become pregnant or who are pregnant or breastfeeding.* No safe level of alcohol intake has been established for women during pregnancy (see Chapter 13), and alcohol may be especially hazardous during the first few weeks, before a woman knows she is pregnant.
- *People who plan to drive, operate machinery, or take part in other activities that require attention, skill, or coordination to remain safe.* Alcohol remains in the blood for several hours after taking even a single drink.
- *People taking medications that can interact with alcohol.* Alcohol alters the effectiveness or toxicity of many medications, and some drugs may increase blood alcohol levels.
- *People with medical conditions* worsened by alcohol, such as liver disease.

Source: U.S. Department of Agriculture and U.S. Department of Health and Human Services, 2005 Dietary Guidelines for Americans, *6th ed. (Washington, D.C.: 2005), available at www.usda.gov/cnpp or call (888) 878-3256.*

cannot handle as much alcohol as men and should never try to match drinks with male companions. People of Asian or Native American descent may have lower-than-average tolerance to alcohol, too.

Health authorities define moderation as:

- no more than two drinks a day for the average-sized, healthy man.
- no more than one drink a day for the average-sized, healthy woman.

These amounts are supposed to be enough to elevate mood without incurring long-term harm to health—note that these are not average amounts, but 24-hour maximums. In other words, a person who drinks no alcohol during the week but has seven drinks on Saturday night is not a moderate drinker—instead, that alcohol intake pattern characterizes binge drinking.

Who Should Never Drink Alcohol?

Doubtless some people can safely consume slightly more than the alcohol dose called moderate; others, especially those prone to alcohol addiction, cannot handle nearly so much without significant risk. The *Dietary Guidelines for Americans* advises these and some others not to drink at all (listed in Table C3-3).

If you suspect that your own drinking may not be moderate or if alcohol has caused problems in your life, you may want to seek a professional evaluation.‡ Table C3-4 contrasts some behaviors of moderate drinkers with those of problem drinkers.

Binge Drinking

Young adults enjoy parties, sports events, and other social occasions, but these settings often encourage binge drinking (defined as at least four drinks in a row for women and five drinks in

‡ *The U.S. Center for Facts on Alcohol is the National Clearinghouse for Alcohol and Drug Information: (800) 729-6686.*

TABLE C3-4 **Behaviors Typical of Moderate Drinkers and Problem Drinkers**

Moderate Drinkers Typically	Problem Drinkers Typically
• Drink slowly, casually. • Eat food while drinking or beforehand. • Don't binge drink; know when to stop. • Respect nondrinkers. • Avoid drinking when solving problems or making decisions. • Do not admire or encourage drunkenness. • Remain peaceful, calm, and unchanged by drinking. • Cause no problems to others or themselves by drinking.	• Gulp or "chug" drinks. • Drink on an empty stomach. • Binge drink; drink to get drunk. • Pressure others to drink. • Turn to alcohol when facing problems or decisions. • Consider drunks to be funny or admirable. • Become loud, angry, violent, or silent when drinking. • Physically or emotionally harm themselves, family members, or others when drinking.

a row for men).§[4] Alcoholic beverages with caffeine added, either premixed or homemade, appeal to binge drinkers because of a "pep up" effect.[5] The FDA is investigating whether such beverages may mask feelings of drunkenness, allow continued drinking, and increase the likelihood of reckless behavior.[6]

Binge drinkers skew the statistics on alcohol use on college campuses. The median number of drinks consumed by all college students is 1.5 per week, but for binge drinkers, it is 14.5 per week. Some of the heaviest binge drinkers consume 8 to 10 drinks on a single drinking occasion.[7] Among drinkers under age 21, binge drinking accounts for 90 percent of the total alcohol consumed and accounts for most of their alcohol-related problems.[8]

Harms from Binge Drinking

Binge drinking poses serious health and social consequences to drinkers and nondrinkers alike. Compared with nondrinkers or moderate drinkers, binge drinkers are more likely to damage property, to assault other people, to cause fatal automobile accidents, and to engage in risky, unprotected sexual intercourse, resulting in sexually transmitted diseases and unplanned pregnancies.[9] Female binge drinkers are more likely to be victims of rape.

Binge drinkers on and off campus may find it difficult to recognize themselves as problem drinkers (refer again to Table C3-4) until their drinking behavior causes a crisis, such as a car crash, or until they've binged long enough to cause substantial damage to their health.

IMMEDIATE EFFECTS OF ALCOHOL

From the moment an alcoholic beverage is swallowed, the body gives it special attention. As alcohol passes through body tissues, it affects their functioning.

Alcohol Enters the Body

Unlike food, which requires digestion before it can be absorbed, tiny alcohol molecules start diffusing right through the stomach walls and they reach the brain within a minute. As a toxin, a too-high dose of ethanol in the stomach triggers one of the body's primary defenses against poison—vomiting. Many times, though, alcohol arrives gradually, diluted in enough fluid or food that the vomiting reflex is delayed and the alcohol passes into the small intestine, which readily absorbs it.[10]

A drinker can soon become intoxicated, especially when drinking on an empty stomach. When the stomach is full of food, molecules of alcohol have less chance of touching the stomach walls and diffusing through, so alcohol reaches the brain more gradually. Also, a full stomach delays alcohol's flow into the small intestine, allowing time for a stomach enzyme to destroy some of it.[11] Once in the small intestine, however, alcohol is rapidly absorbed whether food is present or not. A person who wants to drink socially and not become intoxicated should eat the snacks provided by the host (avoid the salty ones, they increase thirst).

Alcohol Dehydrates the Tissues Anyone who has had an alcoholic drink has experienced one of alcohol's physical effects: alcohol increases urine output (because alcohol depresses the brain's production of antidiuretic hormone). Loss of body water leads to thirst. The only fluid that relieves dehydration is water, so adding ice to alcoholic drinks to dilute them and alternating alcoholic beverages with nonalcoholic ones will quench thirst. Otherwise, each alcoholic drink may worsen the thirst, leading to more drinking.

The water lost due to hormone depression takes with it important minerals, such as magnesium, potassium, calcium, and zinc, depleting the body's reserves. These minerals are vital to fluid balance and to nerve and muscle coordination. When drinking results in mineral loss, minerals must be made up in subsequent meals to avoid deficiencies.

If a person drinks slowly enough, the alcohol will be collected by the liver after absorption and processed without much effect on other parts of the body. If a person drinks more rapidly, however, some of the alcohol bypasses the liver and flows for a while through the rest of the body and the brain.

ALCOHOL ARRIVES IN THE BRAIN

Some people use alcohol as a kind of social anesthetic to help them relax or to relieve anxiety. One drink relieves inhibitions, which gives people the impression that alcohol is a stimulant. It gives this impression by sedating the *inhibitory* nerves, allowing excitatory nerves to take over. This effect is temporary, and ulti-

§ *This definition of binge drinking, without specification of time elapsed, is consistent with standard practice in alcohol research.*

mately alcohol acts as a depressant that sedates the nerve cells (see Figure C3-2).

A Lethal Dose of Alcohol

It is lucky that the brain centers respond to rising blood alcohol in the order shown in Figure C3-2, because a person usually passes out before drinking a lethal dose. If a person drinks fast enough, though, the alcohol continues to be absorbed, and its effects continue to accelerate after the person has gone to sleep. Every year, deaths attributed to this effect take place during drinking contests. Before passing out, the drinker drinks fast enough to receive a lethal dose. Figure C3-3 shows blood alcohol levels that correspond with progressively greater

FIGURE C3-2 Alcohol's Effects on the Brain

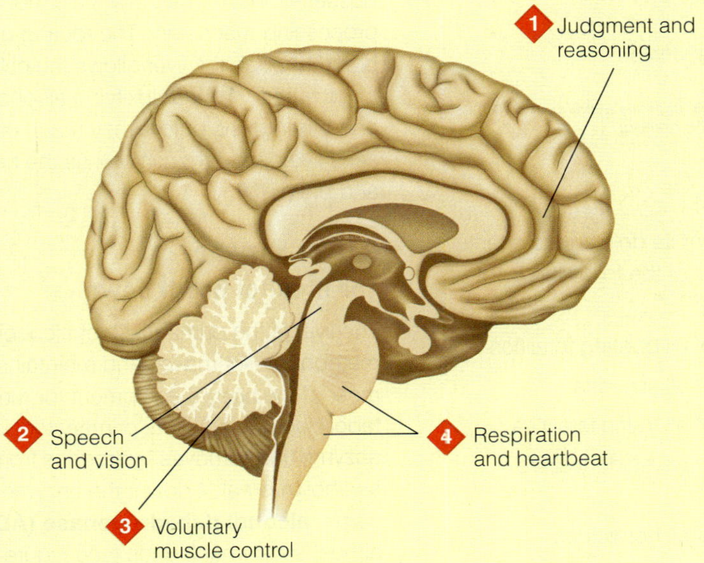

1. Judgment and reasoning centers are most sensitive to alcohol. When alcohol flows to the brain, it first sedates the brain center responsible for all conscious activity. As the alcohol molecules diffuse into the cells of these areas, they interfere with judgment and reasoning.

2. Speech and vision centers in the midbrain are affected next. If the drinker drinks faster than the rate at which the liver can oxidize the alcohol, blood alcohol concentrations rise: the speech and vision centers of the brain become sedated.

3. Voluntary muscular control is then affected. At still higher concentrations, the cells in the brain area responsible for coordination of voluntary muscles are affected, including those used in speech, eye-hand coordination, and limb movements. At this point, people under the influence stagger or weave when they try to walk, or they may slur their speech.

4. Respiration and heart action are the last to be affected. Finally, the conscious brain is completely subdued, and the person passes out. Now the person can drink no more; this is fortunate because higher doses would anesthetize the deepest brain centers that control breathing and heartbeat, causing death.

FIGURE C3-3 Alcohol Doses and Average Blood Level Percentages for Men and Women

Drinks[a]	Body Weight in Pounds—Men								
	100	120	140	160	180	200	220	240	
	00	00	00	00	00	00	00	00	ONLY SAFE DRIVING LIMIT
1	.04	.03	.03	.02	.02	.02	.02	.02	IMPAIRMENT BEGINS
2	.08	.06	.05	.05	.04	.04	.03	.03	
3	.11	.09	.08	.07	.06	.06	.05	.05	DRIVING SKILLS SIGNIFICANTLY AFFECTED
4	.15	.12	.11	.09	.08	.08	.07	.06	
5	.19	.16	.13	.12	.11	.09	.09	.08	
6	.23	.19	.16	.14	.13	.11	.10	.09	
7	.26	.22	.19	.16	.15	.13	.12	.11	LEGALLY INTOXICATED
8	.30	.25	.21	.19	.17	.15	.14	.13	
9	.34	.28	.24	.21	.19	.17	.15	.14	
10	.38	.31	.27	.23	.21	.19	.17	.16	

Drinks[a]	Body Weight in Pounds—Women									
	90	100	120	140	160	180	200	220	240	
	00	00	00	00	00	00	00	00	00	ONLY SAFE DRIVING LIMIT
1	.05	.05	.04	.03	.03	.03	.02	.02	.02	IMPAIRMENT BEGINS
2	.10	.09	.08	.07	.06	.05	.05	.04	.04	DRIVING SKILLS SIGNIFICANTLY AFFECTED
3	.15	.14	.11	.10	.09	.08	.07	.06	.06	
4	.20	.18	.15	.13	.11	.10	.09	.08	.08	
5	.25	.23	.19	.16	.14	.13	.11	.10	.09	
6	.30	.27	.23	.19	.17	.15	.14	.12	.11	LEGALLY INTOXICATED
7	.35	.32	.27	.23	.20	.18	.16	.14	.13	
8	.40	.36	.30	.26	.23	.20	.18	.17	.15	
9	.45	.41	.34	.29	.26	.23	.20	.19	.17	
10	.51	.45	.38	.32	.28	.25	.23	.21	.19	

NOTE: In some states, driving under the influence is proved when an adult's blood contains 0.08 percent alcohol, and in others, 0.10. Many states have adopted a "zero-tolerance" policy for drivers under age 21, using 0.02 percent as the limit.

[a]Taken within an hour or so: each drink equivalent to ½ ounce pure ethanol.

Source: National Clearinghouse for Alcohol and Drug Information

TABLE C3-5 Blood Alcohol Levels and Brain Responses

Blood Alcohol Level (%)	Brain Response
0.05[a]	Judgment impaired
0.10	Emotional control impaired
0.15	Muscle coordination and reflexes impaired
0.20	Vision impaired
0.30	Drunk, lacking control
0.35	In a stupor
0.50–0.60	Loss of consciousness, death

[a] *A 0.08 percent level is the legal limit for intoxication according to most states' highway safety ordinances; however, driving ability may be impaired at blood alcohol levels lower than 0.08 percent.*

intoxication, and Table C3-5 shows brain and nervous system responses that occur at these levels.

Alcohol Toxicity, Oxidative Stress, and the Brain

Brain cells are particularly sensitive to exposure to alcohol. The working brain tissue shrinks, even in people who drink only moderately. The extent of the shrinkage is proportional to the amount drunk. Alcohol addicts are prone to brain hemorrhages and strokes; postmortem examinations reveal brain cell loss, brain swelling, and diminished functioning of the barrier that protects the brain from toxins. All of these conditions are related to the oxidative stress that accompanies ethanol metabolism.[12] Free radicals that arise during ethanol metabolism attack brain cell lipids and cause inflammation. Then, the working brain cells become injured, die off, and disintegrate.

Abstinence from alcohol, together with good nutrition, reverses some of the brain damage, if heavy drinking has not continued for more than a few years. Prolonged drinking beyond an individual's capacity to recover, however, can do severe and irreversible harm to vision, memory, learning and reasoning, speech, and other brain functions.

Alcohol and Accidents

Accidents constitute an immediate and often severe consequence of alcohol use, arising from its deleterious effects on the brain. All of the following involve alcohol use:

- 20 percent of all boating fatalities
- 23 percent of all suicides
- 39 percent of all traffic fatalities
- 40 percent of all residential fire fatalities
- 47 percent of all homicides
- 65 percent of all domestic violence incidents

Figure C3-4 shows that the risk of having an auto accident rises precipitously with greater amounts of alcohol in the blood. The data were derived from police accident reports about people who were driving after drinking alcohol.

ALCOHOL ARRIVES IN THE LIVER

The capillaries that surround the digestive tract merge into veins that carry the alcohol-laden blood to the liver. Here the veins branch and rebranch into capillaries that touch every liver cell, which possess most of the body's alcohol-processing machinery. The routing of blood through the liver allows the cells to go right to work detoxifying alcohol and other toxins before they reach other sensitive body organs such as the heart and brain.

A Liver Enzyme for Alcohol Breakdown

The liver is the primary site of alcohol metabolism—it makes and maintains most of the body's equipment for metabolizing alcohol.[13] Its primary tool is an enzyme that removes hydrogens from alcohol to break it down; the enzyme's name, **alcohol dehydrogenase (ADH),** almost says what it does (see Figure C3-5).** This enzyme converts about 80 percent of the alcohol in the body to

***ADH exists in several variants.*

FIGURE C3-4 The Probability of Causing an Accident Rises with Blood Alcohol Content (BAC)

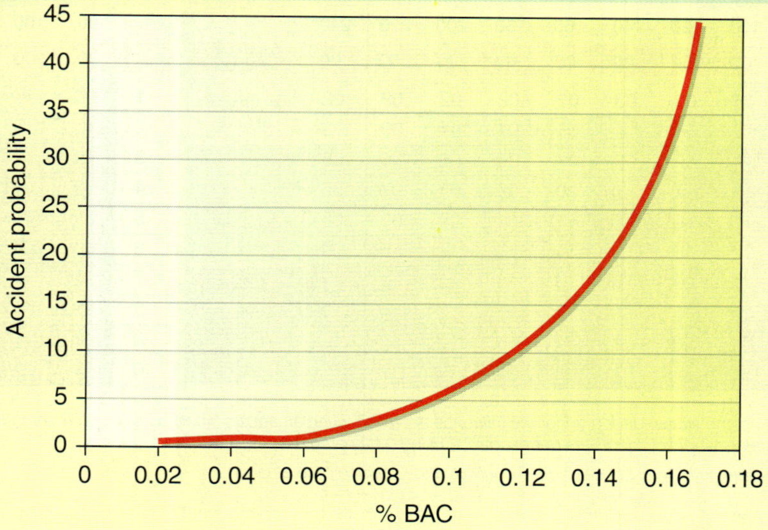

FIGURE C3-5 Alcohol Breakdown

The major route of alcohol breakdown produces acetaldehyde, creates free radicals, and increases oxidative stress in the tissues.

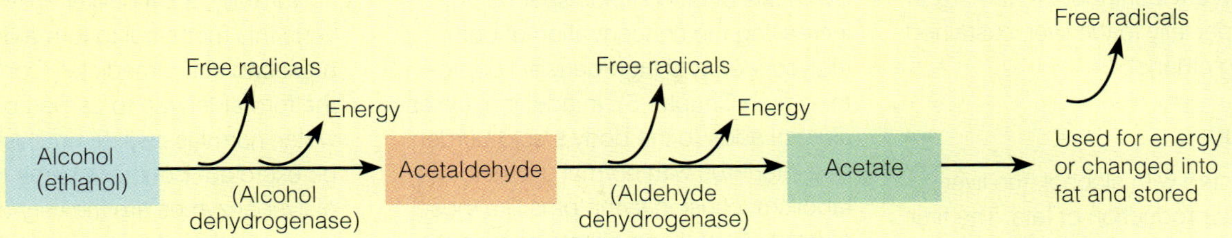

acetaldehyde, the major breakdown product of alcohol. Other alcohol-metabolizing enzymes help out too, especially when alcohol levels exceed ADH capacity.

The maximum amount of blood alcohol a person's body can process in a given time is limited by the amount of ADH residing in the liver. If more alcohol arrives at the liver than the enzymes can handle, the extra alcohol circulates again and again through the brain, liver, and other organs until enzymes are available to degrade it.

Alcohol Breakdown in the Stomach

The stomach wall also produces ADH that breaks down some alcohol before it reaches the bloodstream. Research shows that people with alcoholism make less stomach ADH than others and that women make less than men.

Earlier, this Controversy warned that women should not try to keep up with male drinkers, and here are the reasons why: pound for pound of body weight, men have more lean tissue and therefore a greater volume in which to dilute a given amount of alcohol. In women, the same amount of alcohol becomes more concentrated. Also, with her lower stomach ADH levels, a woman absorbs more alcohol from each drink than a man of equal body weight does.

Excretion in Breath and Urine

About 10 percent of blood alcohol is not metabolized at all, but is excreted as is, about half exhaled by the lungs in the breath and the other half excreted by the kidneys in urine. The alcohol in the breath is directly proportional to the alcohol in the blood, so the breathalyzer test that law enforcement officers administer to someone suspected of driving while intoxicated accurately reveals the person's degree of intoxication.

Rate of Alcohol Clearance

The liver can process about ½ ounce of blood ethanol (one drink's worth) per hour, depending on the person's body size, previous drinking experience, food intake, gender, and general health. Fasting for as little as one day causes degradation of body proteins, including ADH levels, and cuts the rate of alcohol metabolism by half.

The liver's maximum rate of alcohol clearance cannot be accelerated. This explains why only time restores sobriety. Walking doesn't help, because muscles cannot metabolize alcohol. Nor will drinking a cup of coffee be effective. Caffeine is a stimulant, but it won't speed up the metabolism of alcohol. The police say that a cup of coffee only makes a sleepy drunk into a wide-awake drunk. Table C3-6 presents other alcohol myths.

ALCOHOL AFFECTS THE LIVER AND OTHER ORGANS

Among energy sources, ethanol receives the body's highest priority for breakdown. Toxic ethanol cannot be stored in body tissues without first being converted to something safer. Along the way, however, *other* harmful chemicals arise. For example, alcohol's first breakdown product, acetaldehyde, can bind to enzymes and other structures, disrupting their functions.[14] Also, as Figure C3-5 showed, alcohol metabolism generates damaging free radicals.[15] Free radicals increase oxidative stress (introduced

TABLE C3-6 Myths and Truths Concerning Alcohol

Myth:	A shot of alcohol warms you up.
Truth:	Alcohol diverts blood flow to the skin making you feel warmer, but it actually cools the body.
Myth:	Wine and beer are mild; they do not lead to addiction.
Truth:	Wine and beer drinkers worldwide have high rates of death from alcohol-related illnesses. It's not what you drink but how much that makes the difference.
Myth:	Mixing drinks is what gives you a hangover.
Truth:	Too much alcohol in any form produces a hangover.
Myth:	Alcohol is a stimulant.
Truth:	Alcohol depresses the brain's activity.
Myth:	Alcohol is legal; therefore, it is not a drug.
Truth:	Alcohol is legal, but it alters body functions and is medically defined as a depressant drug.

in Controversy 2), a condition linked with inflammation and the development of diabetes, cancer, and other serious diseases. Together, these factors are thought to greatly contribute to the organ damage, especially to the liver, sustained from drinking ethanol.[16]

Fatty Liver

When presented with alcohol, the liver speeds up its production of fats. The first stage of liver deterioration seen in heavy drinkers is therefore known as **fatty liver;** it interferes with the distribution of nutrients and oxygen to the liver cells. Fat is known to accumulate in the livers of young men after a single night of heavy drinking and to remain there for more than a day.

Liver Fibrosis

If heavy drinking continues for long enough, fibrous scar tissue invades the liver. This is the second stage of liver deterioration, called **fibrosis.** Fibrosis is reversible with good nutrition and abstinence from alcohol, but the next (last) stage, **cirrhosis,** is not. In cirrhosis, the liver cells harden, turn orange, and die, losing function forever.

Reproductive and Other Organs

The reproductive system is vulnerable to alcohol's effects. Heavy drinking in women may lead to infertility or spontaneous abortion. Alcohol may also suppress the male reproductive hormone testosterone, leading to decreases in muscle and bone tissue, altered immunity, abnormal prostate gland, and decreased reproductive ability.[17]

Alcohol also affects other systems and organs. It slows the synthesis of some immune system proteins, weakening the body's defenses against infection. Synthesis of blood lipids speeds up, increasing the concentration of both triglycerides and high-density lipoproteins (see Chapter 5). In addition, excess alcohol adds to the body's acid burden and interferes with normal uric acid metabolism, causing symptoms like those of **gout.** All of these effects point to the wisdom of strictly moderating alcohol intakes.

THE HANGOVER

The hangover—the awful feeling of headache, pain, unpleasant sensations in the mouth, and nausea the morning after drinking too much—is a mild form of drug withdrawal. (The worst form is a delirium with severe tremors that presents a danger of death and demands medical management.) Hangovers depress mood, disrupt sleep, increase anxiety, cause fatigue, reduce cognitive ability, and reduce the ability to cope with stress.[18]

Congeners and Dehydration

Hangovers are caused by several factors. One is the toxic effects of **congeners** that accompany the alcohol in alcoholic beverages. Mixing or switching drinks will not prevent hangover, because congeners are only one factor. Dehydration of the brain is a second factor: alcohol reduces the water content of the brain cells. When they rehydrate the morning after and swell back to their normal size, nerve pain results.

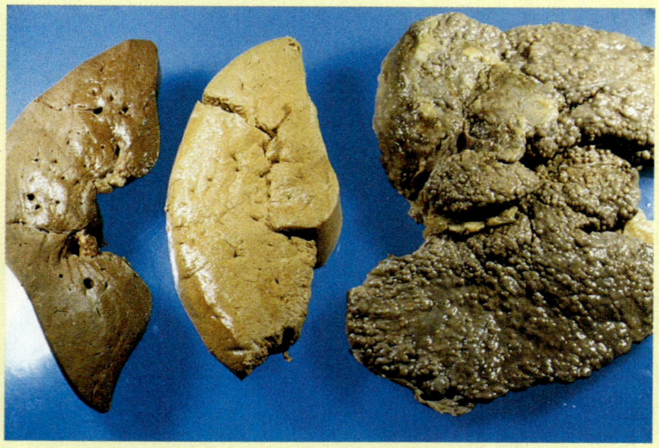

Arthur Glauberman/Photo Researchers, Inc.

Left, normal liver; center, fatty liver; right, cirrhosis.

Formaldehyde and Methanol

Another contributor to the hangover is **formaldehyde,** the smelly chemical laboratories use to preserve dead animals. Formaldehyde arises from **methanol,** another alcohol produced in tiny amounts by cellular metabolic processes. Occupational exposure to formaldehyde is known to raise the risk for certain cancers; no one knows whether formaldehyde generated from alcohol does the same.[19]

Normally, a set of liver enzymes converts this methanol to formaldehyde, with a second set immediately converting the formaldehyde to carbon dioxide and water, harmless waste products that can be excreted. But these same two sets of liver enzymes are the very ones that process ethanol to its own intermediate (and highly toxic) waste product, acetaldehyde, and finally to carbon dioxide and water. The enzymes prefer ethanol 20 times over methanol. Both alcohols are metabolized without delay until the excess acetaldehyde monopolizes the second set of enzymes, leaving formaldehyde to wait for later detoxification. At that point, formaldehyde starts accumulating and the hangover begins.

Time alone is the cure for a hangover. Vitamins, tranquilizers, aspirin, drinking more alcohol, breathing pure oxygen, exercising, eating, and drinking something awful are all useless. Fluid replacement can help to normalize the body's chemistry. The headache, bad mood, nausea, and other effects of a hangover come simply from drinking too much.

ALCOHOL'S LONG-TERM EFFECTS

A couple of drinks set in motion many destructive processes in the body. The next day's abstinence can reverse them only if the doses taken are moderate, the time between them is ample, and nutrition is adequate. If the doses of alcohol are heavy, however, and the time between them is short, complete recovery cannot take place, and repeated onslaughts of alcohol take a toll on the body.

Effects in Pregnancy

By far the longest-term effects of alcohol are those felt by the child of a woman who drinks during pregnancy. When a pregnant woman takes a drink, her fetus takes the same drink within minutes and its body is defenseless against the effects. Pregnant women should not drink alcohol—this topic is so important that Chapter 13 devotes a section to it. The rest of this section concerns effects on drinkers themselves.

Effects on Heart and Brain

Alcohol is directly toxic to skeletal and cardiac muscle, causing weakness and deterioration that is greater, the larger the dose. Alcoholism makes heart disease likely, probably because chronic alcohol use raises blood pressure. At autopsy, the heart of a person with alcoholism appears bloated and weighs twice as much as a normal heart.

Alcohol attacks brain cells directly and heavy drinking can result in dementia. Alcohol's metabolic product acetaldehyde and the free radicals arising from alcohol metabolism can adversely affect brain tissues. In people with alcoholism, mental functioning remains impaired even between drinking bouts. Women may be particularly vulnerable to such impairment despite drinking less alcohol for fewer years than men, but the reasons why are not yet known.[20] In the liver, cirrhosis also develops after 10 to 20 years from the cumulative effects of frequent episodes of heavy drinking.

Cancer

Experts include daily ethanol exposure among cancer-causing substances for human beings. Even moderate drinking increases the chances of developing cancers of the breast, colon and rectum, esophagus, liver, mouth, pancreas, prostate gland, stomach, and throat.[††21] In smokers, alcohol greatly increases the risk of developing lung cancer. And once cancer is established, alcohol seems to speed up its development. Alcohol's by-products, acetaldehyde and free radicals, may contribute to cancer risk, as well as ethanol itself.

A convincing body of evidence implicates alcohol in the causation of breast cancer in women—even those who drink less than one drink per day elevate their risk slightly and, with greater consumption, the risk rises accordingly. In men, moderate drinking increases the risks of cancers at many sites, risks that increase substantially with increasing daily alcohol consumption.[22] A popular myth holds that red wine is safer for women than other types—in reality, all colors of wine present identical breast cancer risks.[23] In the case of beer, alcohol may be acting together with other compounds formed during brewing to promote the cancer. For example, the compound **urethane,** often found in alcoholic beverages, is known to cause cancer in animals, but the risk to human beings remains unknown.

†† In 2002, 389,100 cases (3.6 percent) of cancer worldwide were attributable to drinking alcohol.

Long-Term Effects of Alcohol Abuse

While many of the effects just mentioned may also affect people who drink socially, the long-term effects of alcohol abuse and alcoholism can be devastating. They include the following:

- Bladder, kidney, pancreas, and prostate damage.
- Bone deterioration and osteoporosis.
- Brain disease, central nervous system damage, and stroke.
- Deterioration of the testicles and adrenal glands.
- Diabetes (type 2 diabetes).
- Disease of the muscles of the heart.
- Feminization and sexual impotence in men.
- Impaired immune response.
- Impaired memory and balance.
- Increased risks of death from all causes.
- Major psychological depression, possibly caused by alcohol.[24]
- Malnutrition.
- Nonviral hepatitis.[25]
- Skin rashes and sores.
- Ulcers and inflammation of the stomach and intestines.

This list is by no means all-inclusive. Alcohol abuse exerts direct toxic effects on all body organs. Monetarily, alcoholism costs our society an estimated $186 *billion* every year in medical services, lost wages, criminal offenses, auto crashes, and other losses.[26]

ALCOHOL'S EFFECT ON NUTRITION

Alcohol causes disturbances in nutrition. Its calories are all discretionary calories, often overlooked by drinkers. Alcohol also causes direct negative effects on nutrients that the body needs to function.

The Fattening Power of Alcohol

Metabolic interactions occur between fat and alcohol in the body. Presented with both fat and alcohol, the body stores the comparatively harmless fat and rids itself of the toxic alcohol by using it preferentially for energy.[27] Thus alcohol promotes fat storage, and particularly in the central abdominal area—the **"beer belly"** effect seen in moderate drinkers.[28] Excess abdominal fat poses risks, as described in Chapter 9.

Alcoholic drinks can be much more fattening than their nonalcoholic counterparts. Ethanol yields 7 calories of energy per gram and drink mixers often present many additional calories. Table C3-7 shows the calorie amounts of typical alcoholic beverages and mixers. A general guideline states that each ounce of ethanol represents the same number of calories as about half an ounce of fat. An observant reader, knowing that in the laboratory, a gram of fat and a gram of alcohol yield 9 and 7 calories, respectively, may wonder why alcohol in a drink is worth only half the calorie value of fat. The answer lies in the small amount of alcohol excreted in the breath and urine.

Alcohol's Effects on Vitamins

In addition to alcohol's direct toxic effects, its abuse damages the body indirectly via malnutrition. The more alcohol a person drinks, the less likely he or she will eat enough food to obtain adequate nutrients. Like pure sugar and pure fat, alcohol provides discretionary calories without nutrients; in fact, it displaces other nutritious foods and beverages from the diet.

Alcohol abuse also disrupts every tissue's metabolism of nutrients. Stomach cells oversecrete both acid and histamine, the latter, an agent of the immune system that produces inflammation. Intestinal cells fail to absorb thiamin, folate, vitamin B_{12}, and other vitamins. Liver cells lose efficiency in activating vitamin D. Cells of the eye's retina, which normally process the alcohol form of vitamin A (retinol) to the form needed in vision (retinal), must process ethanol instead. Liver cells, too, suffer a reduced

TABLE C3-7 Calories in Alcoholic Beverages and Mixers

Beverage	Amount (oz)	Energy (cal)
Malt beverage (sweetened)	16[a]	350
Wine cooler	12	170
Pina colada mix (no alcohol)	4	160
Malt beverage (unsweetened)	16	175
Beer	12	150
Dessert wine	3½	140
Fruit-flavored soda, Tom Collins mix	8	115
Gin, rum, vodka, whiskey (86 proof)	1½	105
Cola, root beer, tonic, ginger ale	8	100
Margarita mix (no alcohol)	4	100
Light beer	12	100
Table wine	3½	85
Tomato juice, Bloody Mary mix (no alcohol)	8	45
Club soda, plain seltzer, diet drinks	8	1

[a]*Typical container size, but up to 32-oz containers are common.*

capacity to process and use vitamin A. The kidneys excrete needed minerals: magnesium, calcium, potassium, and zinc.

The inadequate food intake and impaired nutrient absorption that accompany chronic alcohol abuse frequently lead to a deficiency of the B vitamin thiamin. In fact, the cluster of thiamin-deficiency symptoms commonly seen in chronic alcoholism has its own name—the **Wernicke-Korsakoff syndrome.** This syndrome is characterized by paralysis of the eye muscles, poor muscle coordination, impaired memory, and damaged nerves; the syndrome and other alcohol-related memory problems may respond somewhat to treatment with thiamin supplements.

Most dramatic is alcohol's effect on folate. When an excess of alcohol is present, the body actively expels folate from all of its sites of action and storage. The liver, which normally contains enough folate to meet all needs, leaks its folate into the blood. As blood folate rises, the kidneys excrete it, as if it were in excess. The intestine normally releases and retrieves folate continuously, but it becomes so damaged by folate deficiency and alcohol toxicity that it fails to absorb folate. Alcohol also interferes with the action of what little folate is left, causing a buildup in the blood of a compound suspected of involvement with many diseases, including heart disease, stroke, and birth defects.‡‡ This interference inhibits the production of new cells, especially the rapidly dividing cells of the intestine and the blood.

Nutrient deficiencies are thus an inevitable consequence of alcohol abuse, not only because alcohol displaces food but also because alcohol interferes directly with the body's use of nutrients. People treated for alcohol addiction also need nutrition therapy to reverse deficiencies and even deficiency diseases rarely seen in others: night blindness, beriberi, pellagra, scurvy, and protein-energy malnutrition.

‡‡ *The compound is homocysteine; see Chapter 6.*

DOES MODERATE ALCOHOL USE BENEFIT HEALTH?

Among middle-aged people, consuming alcohol in moderation often correlates with certain health benefits, including reduced risks of heart attacks, strokes, dementia, diabetes, and osteoporosis.[29] In fact, moderate alcohol intake correlates with lower mortality from all causes, but only in middle-aged adults over age 35.[30] Among younger light drinkers, the risk of dying is greater than among nondrinkers of the same age.[31] Then, after middle age, the correlation with health benefits disappears again as aging body organs become more sensitive to toxic substances.[32]

Research Problems

Such epidemiological findings of disease prevention would normally trigger the kind of studies that could verify or refute them—that is, controlled clinical human trials. In the case of alcohol, however, the potential for addiction, traffic and other fatalities, and other harms makes it unethical for researchers to administer alcohol to people over long periods to study its effects.[33] Additionally, because alcohol's effects on the brain are almost immediately detectible, administering it without the knowledge of study subjects (a blind study) is impossible.

Benefits Versus Risks

As mentioned, young people do not benefit from any amount of alcohol; rather, they increase their risk of dying from all causes and particularly car crashes, homicides, and other violence that account for the great majority of deaths among young people each year.[34] In fact, for all U.S. populations, the sum of alcohol-related deaths tops 79,000 annually, making alcohol a substantial contributor to mortality.[35]

Young women in particular should not drink alcohol for the sake of their heart. Prior to menopause, the risk of heart disease for women is low, but the risk of breast cancer is substantial and daily alcohol contributes to that risk. As mentioned, even the single drink per day that might provide heart benefits to older people also raises breast cancer risk in young women by up to 10 percent.[36] More alcohol poses greater risks.

In middle-aged populations, taking one to two drinks (moderate drinking) a day may benefit the heart, but more than this amount substantially *increases* the risk of cardiovascular diseases.[37] Experts conclude that the theoretical benefits from alcohol consumption to the population as a whole are many times outweighed by the known risks, and a population-wide recommendation to consume alcohol would do more harm than good.[38]

The Health Effects of Wine

Red wine has been credited with special health-supporting properties and, recently, white wine has won attention for an antioxidant effect, too. The following two statements concerning wine and health have been approved to appear on U.S. wine labels: "The proud people who made this wine encourage you to consult your family doctor about the health effects of wine consumption." Or, "To learn the health effects of wine consumption, send for the Federal Government's Dietary Guidelines for Americans, Center for Nutrition Policy and Promotion, USDA, 1120 20th Street, NW, Washington, DC 20036 or visit its website."

These statements seem to promise that good news about wine and health awaits the information seeker, but the science on wine and health is mixed:

- The good news: the high potassium content of grape juice, a heart-healthy constituent, persists when the grape juice is made into wine.
- The bad news: alcohol in large amounts raises blood pressure, so grape juice may be more suitable for those with hypertension and heart disease.
- More good news: wine contains phytochemicals that, when metabolized by the body, may help reduce the risk of heart disease or cancers of the colon or rectum.[39]
- More bad news: compared with a diet rich in foods such as onions, berries, or leafy vegetables, wine delivers only a small amount of such phytochemicals. Dealcoholized wine, purple grape juice, and whole grapes also provide phytochemicals and do so more safely.
- Good news about alcohol and the brain: some studies report that moderate drinkers may suffer less age-related decline of mental function than abstainers or heavy drinkers.
- Bad news: improved cognition among older people probably results from social, economic, and educational advantages of moderate drinkers, and not from alcohol itself.[40]

And so it goes.

Alcohol and Appetite

Alcoholic beverages affect the appetite. Usually, they reduce it, making people unaware that they are hungry. But in people who are tense and unable to eat or in the elderly who have lost interest in food, a small dose of wine taken 20 minutes before meals may improve appetite. For undernourished people and for people with severely depressed appetites, wine may facilitate eating even when psychotherapy fails to do so.

Another example of the beneficial use of alcohol comes from research showing that moderate use of wine in later life improves morale, stimulates social interaction, and promotes restful sleep. In nursing homes, improved patient and staff relations have been attributed to greater self-esteem among elderly patients who drink moderate amounts of wine. Researchers hypothesize that chronic fatigue may be responsible for some behaviors associated with old age. The positive effects of wine on sleep may alleviate fatigue.

THE FINAL WORD

This discussion has explored some of the ways alcohol affects health and nutrition. In the end, each person must decide individually whether or not to consume alcohol and can change the decision at any time. The surest way to escape the harmful effects of alcohol is, of course, to refuse alcohol altogether. If you do choose to drink, do so with care and strictly in moderation.

Tess Stone/Getty Images

Carbohydrates: Sugar, Starch, Glycogen, and Fiber

4

DO YOU EVER . . .

- Think of carbohydrates as providing nothing but calories to the body?
- Wonder why nutrition authorities unanimously recommend foods high in fiber?
- Have trouble distinguishing whole-grain foods from others at the grocery store?
- Blame carbohydrates in the diet for obesity or diseases?

Keep reading . . .

Learning Objectives

To find learning objective topics in this chapter, look for the text headings with a corresponding "LO" number above the heading. After completing this chapter, you should be able to accomplish the following:

- LO 4.1 Describe the major types of carbohydrates, and identify their food sources.
- LO 4.2 Describe the various roles of carbohydrates in the body, and explain why avoiding dietary carbohydrates may be ill-advised.
- LO 4.3 Summarize how fiber differs from other carbohydrates and how fiber may contribute to health.
- LO 4.4 Explain how complex carbohydrates are broken down in the digestive tract and absorbed into the body.
- LO 4.5 Describe how hormones control blood glucose concentrations during fasting and feasting.
- LO 4.6 Explain the term *glycemic index* and how it may relate to diet planning.
- LO 4.7 Describe the scope of the U.S. diabetes problem and educate someone about the long- and short-term effects of untreated diabetes and prediabetes.
- LO 4.8 Name components of a lifestyle plan to effectively control blood glucose and describe the characteristics of a diet that can assist in managing type 2 diabetes.
- LO 4.9 Compare the symptoms of postprandial hypoglycemia with those of fasting hypoglycemia, and name some diseases associated with the latter type.
- LO 4.10 Discuss current research regarding the relationships among dietary carbohydrates, obesity, diabetes, and other ills.

Carbohydrates are ideal nutrients to meet your body's energy needs, to feed your brain and nervous system, to keep your digestive system fit, and within calorie limits, to help keep your body lean. Digestible carbohydrates, together with fats and protein, add bulk to foods and provide energy and other benefits for the body. Indigestible carbohydrates, which include most of the fibers in foods, yield little or no energy but provide other important benefits.

All carbohydrates are not equal in terms of nutrition. This chapter invites you to learn the differences between foods containing **complex carbohydrates** (starch and fiber) and those made of **simple carbohydrates** (the sugars) and to consider the effects of both on the body. Controversy 4 goes on to explore current theories about how consumption of certain carbohydrates may affect human health.

This chapter on the carbohydrates is the first of three on the energy-yielding nutrients. Chapter 5 deals with the fats and Chapter 6 with protein. Controversy 3 in Chapter 3 already addressed one other contributor of energy to the human diet, alcohol.

LO 4.1

A Close Look at Carbohydrates

Carbohydrates contain the sun's radiant energy, captured in a form that living things can use to drive the processes of life. Green plants make carbohydrate through **photosynthesis** in the presence of **chlorophyll** and sunlight. In this process, water (H_2O) absorbed by the plant's roots donates hydrogen and oxygen. Carbon dioxide gas (CO_2) absorbed into its leaves donates carbon and oxygen. Water and carbon dioxide combine to yield the most common of the **sugars,** the single sugar **glucose.** Scientists know the reaction in the minutest detail but have yet to reproduce it—green plants are required to make it happen (see Figure 4-1).[1*]

Light energy from the sun drives the photosynthesis reaction. The light energy becomes the chemical energy of the bonds that hold six atoms of carbon together in the sugar glucose. Glucose provides energy for the work of all the cells of the stem, roots, flowers, and fruits of the plant. For example, in the roots, far from the energy-giving rays of the sun, each cell draws upon some of the glucose made in the leaves, breaks it down (to carbon dioxide and water), and uses the energy thus released to fuel its own growth and water-gathering activities.

Plants do not use all of the energy stored in their sugars, so it remains available for use by the animal or human being that consumes the plant. Thus, carbohydrates form the first link in the food chain that supports all life on earth. Carbohydrate-rich foods come almost exclusively from plants; milk is the only animal-derived food that contains significant amounts of carbohydrate. The next few sections describe the forms assumed by carbohydrates: sugars, starch, glycogen, and fiber.

KEY POINT Through photosynthesis, plants combine carbon dioxide, water, and the sun's energy to form glucose. Carbohydrates are made of carbon, hydrogen, and oxygen held together by energy-containing bonds: *carbo* means "carbon"; *hydrate* means "water."

Sugars

Six sugar molecules are important in nutrition. Three of these are single sugars, or **monosaccharides.** The other three are double sugars, or **disaccharides.** All of their chemical names end in *ose,* which means "sugar." Although they all sound alike at first, they exhibit distinct characteristics once you get to know them as individuals. Figure 4-2 shows the relationships among the sugars.

*Reference notes are found in Appendix F.

carbohydrates compounds composed of single or multiple sugars. The name means "carbon and water," and a chemical shorthand for carbohydrate is CHO, signifying carbon (C), hydrogen (H), and oxygen (O).

complex carbohydrates long chains of sugar units arranged to form starch or fiber; also called *polysaccharides.*

simple carbohydrates sugars, including both single sugar units and linked pairs of sugar units. The basic sugar unit is a molecule containing six carbon atoms, together with oxygen and hydrogen atoms.

photosynthesis the process by which green plants make carbohydrates from carbon dioxide and water using the green pigment chlorophyll to capture the sun's energy (*photo* means "light"; *synthesis* means "making").

chlorophyll the green pigment of plants that captures energy from sunlight for use in photosynthesis.

sugars simple carbohydrates; that is, molecules of either single sugar units or pairs of those sugar units bonded together. By common usage, *sugar* most often refers to sucrose.

glucose (GLOO-cose) a single sugar used in both plant and animal tissues for energy; sometimes known as blood sugar or *dextrose.*

monosaccharides (mon-oh-SACK-ah-rides) single sugar units (*mono* means "one"; *saccharide* means "sugar unit").

disaccharides pairs of single sugars linked together (*di* means "two").

FIGURE 4-1

ANIMATED!

Carbohydrate—Mainly Glucose—Is Made by Photosynthesis

The sun's energy becomes part of the glucose molecule—its calories, in a sense. In the molecule of glucose on the leaf here, black dots represent the carbon atoms; bars represent the chemical bonds that contain energy.

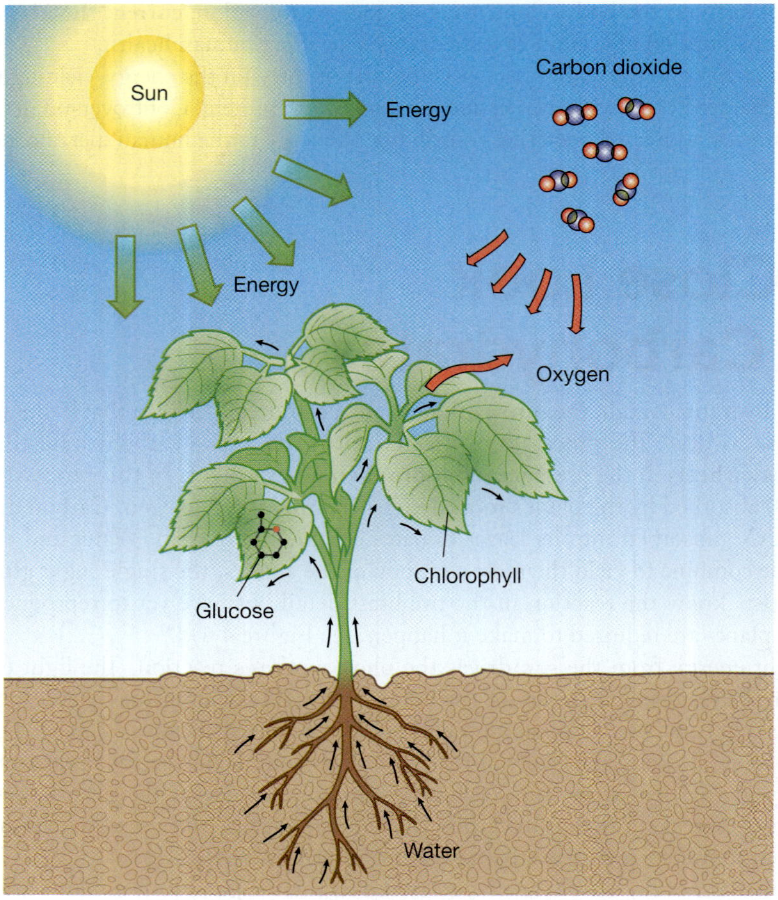

- Single sugars are monosaccharides.
- Pairs of sugars are disaccharides.

fructose (FROOK-tose) a monosaccharide; sometimes known as fruit sugar (*fruct* means "fruit"; *ose* means "sugar").

galactose (ga-LACK-tose) a monosaccharide; part of the disaccharide lactose (milk sugar).

lactose a disaccharide composed of glucose and galactose; sometimes known as milk sugar (*lact* means "milk"; *ose* means "sugar").

maltose a disaccharide composed of two glucose units; sometimes known as malt sugar.

sucrose (SOO-crose) a disaccharide composed of glucose and fructose; sometimes known as table, beet, or cane sugar and, often, as simply *sugar.*

Monosaccharides The three monosaccharides are glucose, fructose, and galactose. **Fructose** or fruit sugar, the intensely sweet sugar of fruit, is made by rearranging the atoms in glucose molecules. Fructose occurs mostly in fruits, in honey, and as part of table sugar. Other sources include soft drinks, ready-to-eat cereals, and other products sweetened with high-fructose corn syrup (defined later on). Glucose and fructose are the most common monosaccharides in nature.

The other monosaccharide, galactose, has the same number and kind of atoms as glucose and fructose but in another arrangement. **Galactose** is one of two single sugars that are bound together to make up the sugar of milk. Galactose rarely occurs free in nature but is tied up in milk sugar until it is freed during digestion.

Disaccharides The three other sugars important in nutrition are disaccharides, which are linked pairs of single sugars, or disaccharides. They are lactose, maltose, and sucrose. All three contain glucose. In **lactose,** the milk sugar just mentioned, glucose is linked to galactose. Malt sugar, or **maltose,** has two glucose units. Maltose appears wherever starch is being broken down. It occurs in germinating seeds and arises during the digestion of starch in the human body.

The last of the six sugars, **sucrose,** is familiar table sugar, the product most people think of when they refer to *sugar.* In sucrose, fructose and glucose are bonded to-

FIGURE 4-2 **How Monosaccharides Join to Form Disaccharides**

Single sugars are monosaccharides while pairs of sugars are disaccharides.

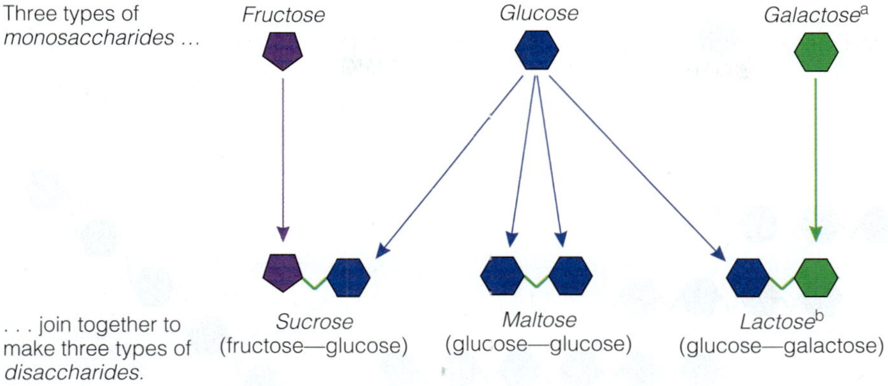

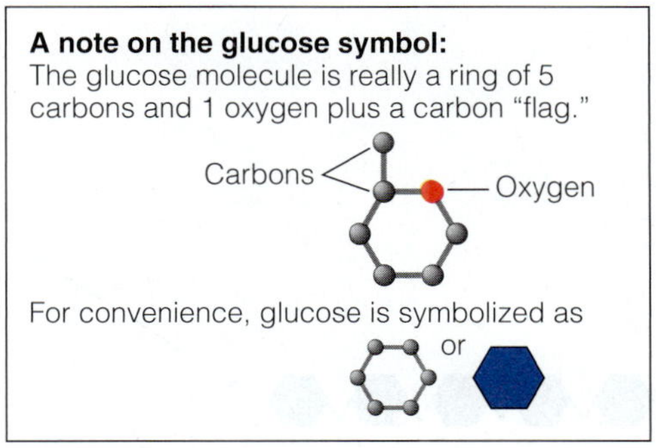

[a]Galactose does not occur in foods singly but only as part of lactose.
[b]The chemical bond that joins the monosaccharides of lactose differs from those of other sugars and makes lactose hard for some people to digest—lactose intolerance (see later section).

gether. Table sugar is obtained by refining the juice from sugar beets or sugarcane, but sucrose also occurs naturally in many vegetables and fruits. It tastes sweet because it contains the sweetest of the monosaccharides, fructose.

When you eat a food containing monosaccharides, you can absorb them directly into your blood. When you eat disaccharides, though, you must digest them first. Enzymes in your intestinal cells must split the disaccharides into separate monosaccharides so that they can enter the bloodstream. The blood delivers all products of digestion first to the liver, which possesses enzymes to modify nutrients, making them useful to the body. Glucose is the most used monosaccharide inside the body, so the liver quickly converts fructose or galactose to glucose or to smaller compounds that can serve as building blocks for glucose, fat, or other needed molecules.

CONCEPT LINK 4-1
The digestive system was introduced in Chapter 3 (page 78).

Although it is true that the energy of fruits and many vegetables comes from sugars, this doesn't mean that eating them is the same as eating concentrated sweets such as candy or drinking cola beverages. From the body's point of view, fruits are vastly different from purified sugars (as a later section makes clear) except that both provide glucose in abundance.

KEY POINT Glucose is the most important monosaccharide in the human body. Most other monosaccharides and disaccharides become glucose in the body.

• Strands of many monosaccharides are polysaccharides.

Starch

In addition to occurring in sugars, the glucose in food also occurs in long strands of thousands of glucose units. These are the **polysaccharides** (see Figure 4-3). **Starch** is a polysaccharide, as are glycogen and most of the fibers.

Starch is a plant's storage form of glucose. As a plant matures, it not only provides energy for its own needs but also stores energy in its seeds for the next generation. For example, after a corn plant reaches its full growth and has many leaves manufacturing glucose, it links glucose together to form starch, stores packed clusters of starch molecules in **granules,** and packs the granules into its seeds. These giant starch clusters are packed side by side in the kernels of corn. For the plant, starch is useful because it is an insoluble substance that will stay with the seed in the ground and nourish it until it forms shoots with leaves that can catch the sun's rays. Glucose, in contrast, is soluble in water and would be washed away by the rains while the seed lay in the soil. The starch of corn and other plant foods is nutritive for people,

polysaccharides another term for complex carbohydrates; compounds composed of long strands of glucose units linked together (*poly* means "many"). Also called *complex carbohydrates.*

starch a plant polysaccharide composed of glucose. After cooking, starch is highly digestible by human beings; raw starch often resists digestion.

granules small grains. Starch granules are packages of starch molecules. Various plant species make starch granules of varying shapes.

FIGURE 4-3

ANIMATED!

How Glucose Molecules Join to Form Polysaccharides

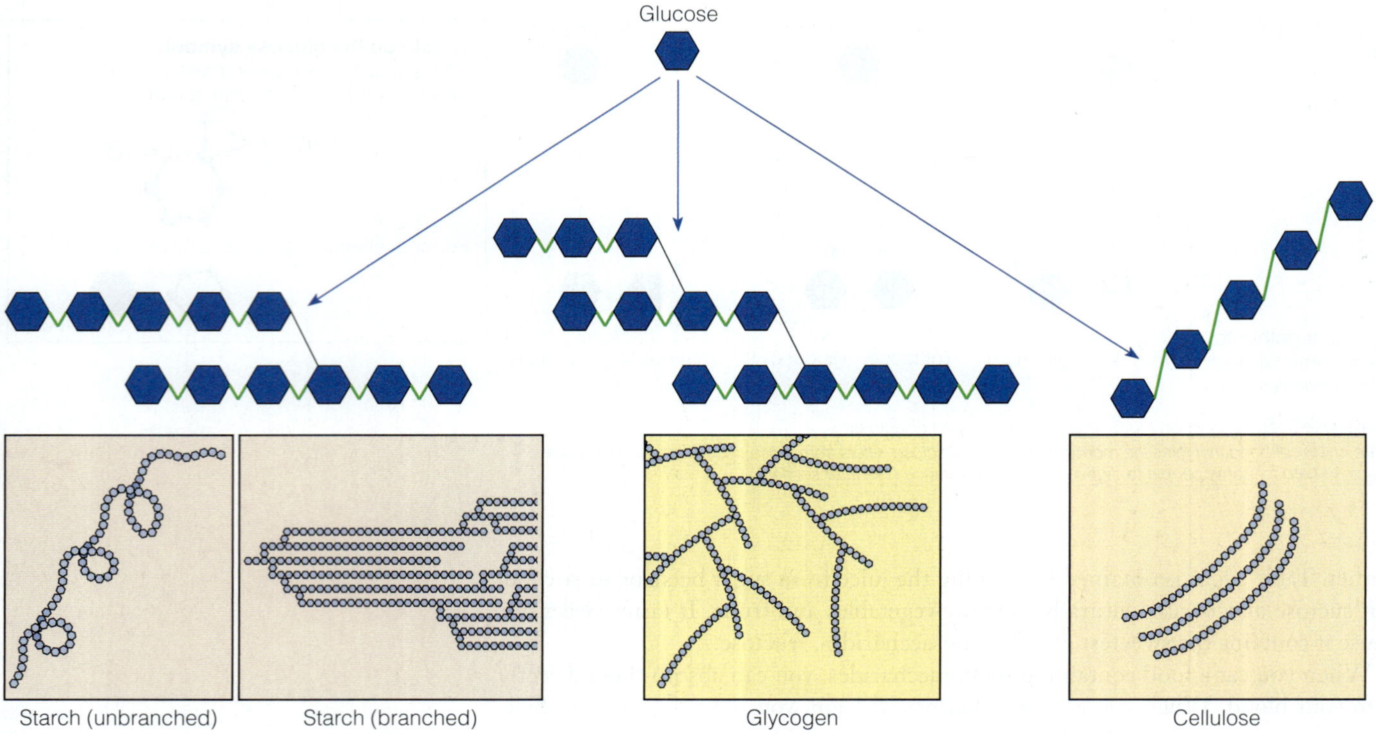

Starch Glucose units are linked in long, occasionally branched chains to make starch. Human digestive enzymes can digest these bonds, retrieving glucose. Real glucose units are so tiny that you can't see them, even with the highest-power light microscope.

Glycogen Glycogen resembles starch in that the bonds between its glucose units can be broken by human enzymes, but the chains of glycogen are more highly branched.

Cellulose (fiber) The bonds that link glucose units together in cellulose are different from the bonds in starch or glycogen. Human enzymes cannot digest them.

too, because they can digest the starch to glucose and extract the sun's energy stored in its chemical bonds. A later section describes starch digestion in detail.

KEY POINT Starch is the storage form of glucose in plants and is also nutritive for human beings.

© Gala/SuperStock

The sugars in fruit are diluted with water and naturally packaged with vitamins, minerals, phytochemicals, and fiber.

Glycogen

Just as plant tissues store glucose in long chains of starch, animal bodies store glucose in long chains of **glycogen.** Glycogen resembles starch in that it consists of glucose molecules linked together to form chains, but its chains are longer and more highly branched (see Figure 4-3). Unlike starch, which is abundant in grains, potatoes, and other foods from plants, glycogen is nearly undetectable in meats because glycogen breaks down rapidly when the animal is slaughtered. A later section describes how the human body handles its own packages of stored glucose.

KEY POINT Glycogen is the storage form of glucose in animals and human beings.

Fiber

Some of the **fibers** of a plant form the supporting structures of its leaves, stems, and seeds. Other fibers play other roles, for example, to retain water and thus protect seeds from drying out. Like starch, most fibers are polysaccharides—chains of sugars—but they differ from starch in that the sugar units are held together by bonds that human digestive enzymes cannot break. Most fibers therefore pass through the human body without providing energy for its use. Billions of bacteria residing within the human large intestine, however, do possess enzymes that can digest fibers to varying degrees by fermenting them.[2] Through this process, the fibers are broken down to waste products, mainly tiny fat fragments that the large intestine (colon) absorbs. Many animals, such as cattle, depend heavily on their digestive system's bacteria to make the energy of glucose available from the abundant cellulose, a form of fiber, in their fodder. Thus, when we eat beef, we indirectly receive some of the sun's energy that was originally stored in the fiber of the plants. Beef itself contains no fiber, nor do other meats and dairy products.

Researchers often divide fibers into two general groups by their chemical, physical, and functional properties.[†3] In the first group are fibers that dissolve in water (**soluble fibers**). These form gels (are **viscous**) and are easily digested by bacteria in the human colon (are easily fermented). Commonly found in oats, barley, legumes, and citrus fruits, soluble fibers often lower blood cholesterol and can help to control blood glucose, thus protecting against heart disease and diabetes.[4] In foods, soluble fibers add pleasing consistency, such as the pectin that puts the gel in jelly and the gums added to salad dressings to thicken them.

- Fiber characteristics in foods:
  - *Soluble, viscous, fermentable fibers are often gummy or add thickness to foods.*
  - *Insoluble, nonviscous, less fermentable fibers are often tough, stringy, or gritty in foods.*

Other fibers (**insoluble fibers**) do not dissolve in water, do not form gels (are not viscous), and are less readily fermented. Insoluble fibers, such as cellulose, are found in the outer layers of whole grains (bran), the strings of celery, the hulls of seeds, and the skins of corn kernels. These fibers retain their structure and rough texture even after hours of cooking. In the body, they aid the digestive system by easing elimination.

In summary, plants combine carbon dioxide, water, and the sun's energy to form glucose, which can be stored as the polysaccharide starch. Then animals or people eat the plants and retrieve the glucose. In the body, the liver and muscles may store the glucose as the polysaccharide glycogen, but ultimately it becomes glucose again. The glucose delivers the sun's energy to fuel the body's activities. In the process, glucose breaks down to the waste products carbon dioxide and water, which are excreted. Later, these compounds are used again by plants as raw materials to make carbohydrate. Fibers are plant constituents that are not digested directly by human enzymes, but their presence in the diet contributes to the health of the body.

- Chapter 15 revisits humankind's relationship with the earth's food chain.

KEY POINT Human digestive enzymes cannot break the bonds in fiber, so most of it passes through the digestive tract unchanged. Some fiber, however, is susceptible to fermentation by bacteria in the colon.

LO 4.2, 4.3

The Need for Carbohydrates

Glucose from carbohydrate is an important fuel for most body functions. Only two other nutrients provide energy to the body: protein and fats. Protein-rich foods are usually expensive and, when used to make fuel for the body, they provide no advantage over carbohydrates. Moreover, overuse of dietary protein has disadvantages, as explained in Chapter 6. Fats normally are not used as fuel by the brain and central nervous system. Thus, glucose is a critical energy source, particularly for nerve cells, including those of the brain. And starchy whole foods that supply complex carbohydrates—and especially the fiber-rich ones—are the preferred source of glucose in the diet.

glycogen (GLY-co-gen) a highly branched polysaccharide that is made and stored by liver and muscle tissues of human beings and animals as a storage form of glucose. Glycogen is not a significant food source of carbohydrate and is not counted as one of the complex carbohydrates in foods.

fibers the indigestible parts of plant foods, largely nonstarch polysaccharides that are not digested by human digestive enzymes, although some are digested by resident bacteria of the colon. Fibers include cellulose, hemicelluloses, pectins, gums, mucilages, and the nonpolysaccharide lignin.

soluble fibers food components that readily dissolve in water and often impart gummy or gel-like characteristics to foods. An example is pectin from fruit, which is used to thicken jellies. Soluble fibers are indigestible by human enzymes but may be broken down to absorbable products by bacteria in the digestive tract.

viscous (VISS-cuss) having a sticky, gummy, or gel-like consistency that flows relatively slowly.

insoluble fibers the tough, fibrous structures of fruits, vegetables, and grains; indigestible food components that do not dissolve in water.

†The committee on Dietary Reference Intakes (DRI) proposed other fiber definitions to accommodate products that may contain new fiber sources, but consumers may find these too confusing to be used on food labels.

Sugars also play vital roles in the functioning of body tissues. For example, sugars that dangle from protein molecules, once thought to be mere hitchhikers, are now known to dramatically alter the shape and function of certain proteins. Such a sugar-protein complex is responsible for the slipperiness of mucus, the watery lubricant that coats and protects the body's internal linings and membranes. Sugars also bind to the outside of cell membranes, affecting cell-to-cell communication, nerve and brain cell function, and certain disease processes. Clearly, the body needs carbohydrates for more than just energy.

Did You Know?

Alcohol provides energy but it is a toxin, not a nutrient.

If I Want to Lose Weight and Stay Healthy, Should I Avoid Carbohydrates?

Many popular books and magazines wrongly accuse carbohydrates of being the "fattening" ingredient of foods, thereby misleading millions of weight-conscious people into eliminating nutritious carbohydrate-rich foods from their diets.[5] In truth, people who wish to lose fat, maintain lean tissue, and stay healthy can do no better than to attend closely to portion sizes and calorie intakes and to design their diets around carbohydrate-rich whole foods that supply fiber, other needed nutrients, and beneficial phytochemicals.[6]

Lower in Calories Gram for gram, carbohydrates donate fewer calories than do dietary fats, and converting glucose into fat for storage is metabolically costly. Still, it is possible to consume enough calories of carbohydrate to exceed the need for energy, which reliably leads to weight gain. To lose weight, the dieter must plan a diet to provide fewer calories from all sources that are needed by the body each day; Chapter 9 describes the roles energy nutrients play in management of body weight.

- 1 gram carbohydrates = 4 calories
- 1 gram fat = 9 calories

CONCEPT LINK 4-2

Chapter 1 defined a gram (g) as a unit of weight used in nutrition (page 6).

An Exception: Refined Sugars Recommendations to choose carbohydrate-rich foods do not extend to refined added sugars. Purified, refined sugars (mostly sucrose or fructose) contain no other nutrients—no protein, vitamins, minerals, or fiber—and thus are low in nutrient density.[7] A person choosing 400 calories of sugar in place of 400 calories of whole-grain bread loses the protein, vitamins, minerals, phytochemicals, and fiber of the bread. You can afford to do this only if you have already met all of your nutrient needs for the day and still have discretionary calories to spend.

CONCEPT LINK 4-3

Chapter 2 describes discretionary calories as the balance of calories remaining in a person's energy allowance after consuming the nutrient-dense foods sufficient to meet the day's nutrient needs (page 41).

Overuse of sugars may have other effects as well. Some evidence suggests that, for many obese people, a diet too high in added sugars and other refined carbohydrates may alter blood lipids in ways that may worsen their heart disease risk (Controversy 4 comes back to this topic).[8] For these people, weight loss on a calorie-controlled diet that provides the recommended amounts of whole grains, legumes, fruits, and vegetables reduces the blood lipid response to sugars and lowers their heart disease risk. In fact, consumption of whole grains consistently lowers the risk of cardiovascular diseases, including heart disease, in research studies.[9]

- Details about controlling body fatness are in Chapter 9.

Guidelines For health's sake, then, most people should increase their intakes of fiber-rich whole food sources of carbohydrates and reduce intakes of foods high in refined white flour, added sugars, and the kinds of fats associated with heart disease (see Chapter 5).[10] Table 4-1 presents carbohydrate recommendations and guidelines from several authorities. This chapter's Consumer Corner describes various whole-grain foods, and the Food Feature comes back to the sugars in foods. As for weight loss, authorities do not recommend omitting carbohydrates. In fact, many recommend the opposite.

- The DRI committee recommends that 45 to 65 percent of daily calories come from carbohydrate. An example of how to convert this recommendation into grams of carbohydrate in the diet is found in the Food Feature on page 136.

KEY POINT The body tissues use carbohydrates for energy and other functions; the brain and nerve tissues prefer carbohydrate as fuel. Nutrition authorities recommend a diet based on foods rich in complex carbohydrates and fiber.

TABLE 4-1 Recommendations Concerning Intakes of Carbohydrates

1. Recommendations for total carbohydrates

   Dietary Guidelines for Americans

   - Consume between 45% and 65% of calories from carbohydrate.

   Dietary Reference Intakes (DRI)

   - At a minimum, 130 grams per day for adults and children to provide glucose to the brain.
   - For health, most people should consume between 45% and 65% of total calories from carbohydrate.

   USDA Food Guide, MyPyramid

   - Grains, fruit, starchy vegetables, and milk contribute to the day's total carbohydrate intake.

2. Recommendations for added sugars

   Dietary Guidelines for Americans

   - Choose and prepare foods and beverages with little added sugars.

   Dietary Reference Intakes (DRI)

   - Insufficient evidence exists to set an upper limit for added sugars; however, the DRI committee suggests a high maximum of 25% or less of total calories for people who otherwise meet their nutrient needs, maintain a healthy body weight, and need additional energy.[a]

   USDA Food Guide, MyPyramid

   - Added sugars may provide discretionary calories within the energy recommendation after meeting all nutrient recommendations with nutritious foods.

   The American Heart Association

   - A prudent upper limit of not more than one-half the discretionary calorie allowance (no more than 100 calories of added sugars for most women or 150 calories for most men).

3. Recommendations for fiber

   USDA Food Guide, MyPyramid

   - Increase intakes of whole fruits and vegetables, make at least half the grain choices whole grains, and choose legumes several times per week.

   Dietary Reference Intakes (DRI)

   - 38 grams of total fiber per day for men through age 50; 30 grams for men 51 and older.
   - 25 grams of total fiber per day for women through age 50; 21 grams for women 51 and older.

[a]An example might be an athlete in training whose high energy need allows greater amounts of added sugars from sports drinks without compromising nutrient intakes; for most sedentary people, maximums of 3 to 12 teaspoons per day are suggested.

Why Do Nutrition Experts Recommend Fiber-Rich Foods?

As mentioned, carbohydrate-rich foods offer additional benefits if they are also rich in fiber. Foods such as whole grains, vegetables, legumes, and fruits supply valuable vitamins, minerals, and phytochemicals, along with a healthy dose of fiber and little or no fat. Fiber's best-known health benefits include:

1. Promotion of normal blood cholesterol concentrations and reduced risk of heart disease.
2. Control of blood pressure (reduced risk of hypertension).[11]
3. Modulation of blood glucose concentrations (reduced risk of diabetes).
4. Maintenance of healthy bowel function (reduced risk of bowel diseases).
5. Promotion of a healthy body weight.

The obvious choice for anyone placing a value on health is to obtain fibers from a variety of sources each day.

Figure 4-4 shows the diverse effects of different fibers, and Figure 4-5 provides a brief guide to finding these fibers in foods. Most unrefined plant foods contain a mix of fiber types. The following paragraphs describe health benefits associated with daily intakes of these foods.

• Appendix A lists the fiber contents of over 2,000 foods.

KEY POINT Fiber-rich diets benefit the body by helping to normalize blood cholesterol and blood glucose and by maintaining healthy bowel function. They are also associated with healthy body weight.

Lower Cholesterol and Heart Disease Risk Diets rich in legumes, vegetables, and whole grains—and therefore rich in complex carbohydrates—may protect against heart disease and stroke. Such diets are generally low in saturated fat, *trans* fat, and cholesterol and high in fibers, vegetable proteins, and phytochemicals—all factors associated with a lower risk of heart disease.[12] Oatmeal was first to be identified among cholesterol-lowering foods; apples, barley, carrots, and legumes are

• The roles of saturated fat, *trans* fat, cholesterol, and other lipids in heart disease are discussed in Chapters 5 and 11. The role of vegetable proteins in heart disease is presented in Chapter 6.

FIGURE 4-4 **Characteristics, Sources, and Health Effects of Fibers**

People who eat these foods . . .		obtain these types of fibers . . .	with these actions in the body . . .	and these probable health benefits . . .
		Viscous, soluble, more fermentable		
 Stockbyte/Getty Images	• Barley, oats, oat bran, rye, fruits (apples, citrus), legumes (especially young green peas and black-eyed peas), seaweeds, seeds and husks, many vegetables, fibers used as food additives	• Gums • Pectins • Psyllium[a] • Some hemicellulose	• Lower blood cholesterol by binding bile • Slow glucose absorption • Slow transit of food through upper GI tract • Hold moisture in stools, softening them • Yield small fat molecules after fermentation that the colon can use for energy • Increase satiety	• Lower risk of heart disease • Lower risk of diabetes • Lower risk of colon and rectal cancer • Increased satiety, and may help with weight management
		Nonviscous, insoluble, less fermentable		
 Brian Leatart/Getty Images	• Brown rice, fruits, legumes, seeds, vegetables (cabbage, carrots, brussels sprouts), wheat bran, whole grains, extracted fibers used as food additives	• Cellulose • Lignins • Resistant starch • Hemicellulose	• Increase fecal weight and speed fecal passage through colon • Provide bulk and feelings of fullness	• Alleviate constipation • Lower risk of diverticulosis, hemorrhoids, and appendicitis • Lower risk of colon and rectal cancer

[a]*Psyllium, a soluble fiber derived from seeds, is used as a laxative and food additive.*

FIGURE 4-5 **Fiber Composition of Common Foods**

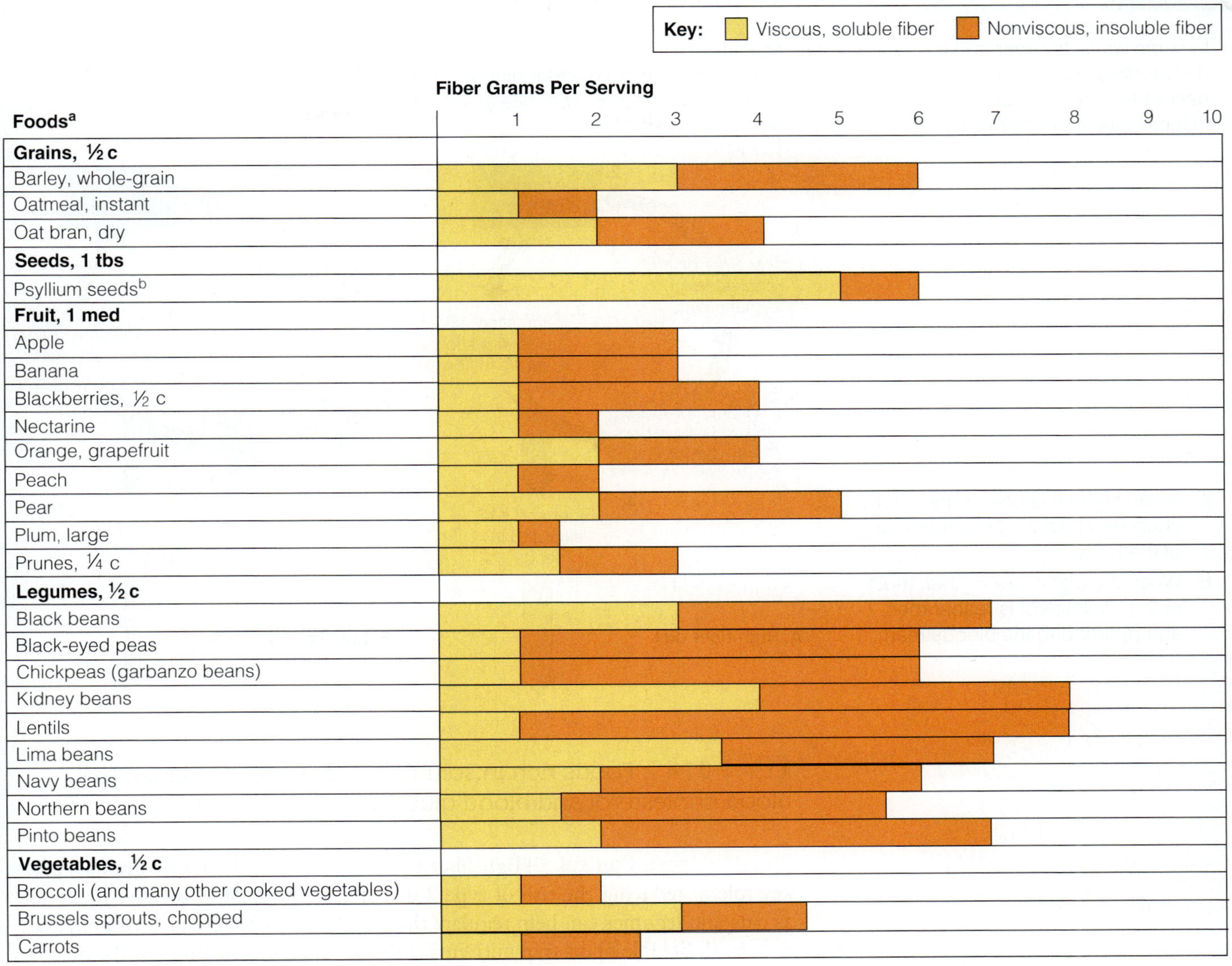

[a]*Values are for cooked or ready-to-serve foods unless specified.*

[b]*Psyllium is used as a fiber laxative and fiber-rich food additive.*

Source: Data from the National Heart, Lung and Blood Institute. Third Report of the National Cholesterol Education Program (NCEP) Expert Panel on Detection, Evaluation and Treatment of High Blood Cholesterol in Adults (Adult Treatment Panel 10, NIH publication no. 02-5215, 2002); V-6; ESHA Research, 2004.

also rich in the viscous fibers having a significant cholesterol-lowering effect.[13] In contrast, diets high in refined grains and added sugars may push blood lipids toward elevated heart disease risk; Controversy 4 explores these concerns.

Foods rich in viscous fibers may lower blood cholesterol by binding with cholesterol-containing compounds in bile. Normally, much of this cholesterol would be reabsorbed from the intestine for reuse, but viscous fiber carries some of it out with the feces (see Figure 4-6).[14] These bile compounds are needed in digestion, so the liver responds to their loss by drawing on the body's cholesterol stocks to synthesize more. Another way in which fiber in the diet may reduce cholesterol in the blood is through the actions of one of the small fatty acids released during bacterial fermentation of fiber. This fatty acid is absorbed and travels to the liver, where it may help to reduce cholesterol synthesis. The net result of either mechanism is lowered blood cholesterol.

CONCEPT LINK 4-4

The benefits of phytochemicals in disease prevention are featured in Controversy 2, page 61.

FIGURE 4-6

ANIMATED!

One Way Fiber in Food May Lower Cholesterol in the Blood

In some ways, the liver is like a vacuum cleaner, sucking up cholesterol from the blood, using the cholesterol to make bile, and discharging the bile into its storage bag, the gallbladder. The gallbladder empties its bile into the intestine, where bile performs necessary digestive tasks. In the intestine, some of the cholesterol from bile associates with fiber and is carried out of the body in feces instead of being reabsorbed into the blood.

A. When the diet is rich in fiber, more cholesterol (as bile) is carried out of the body.

B. When the diet is low in fiber, most of the cholesterol is reabsorbed and returned to the bloodstream.

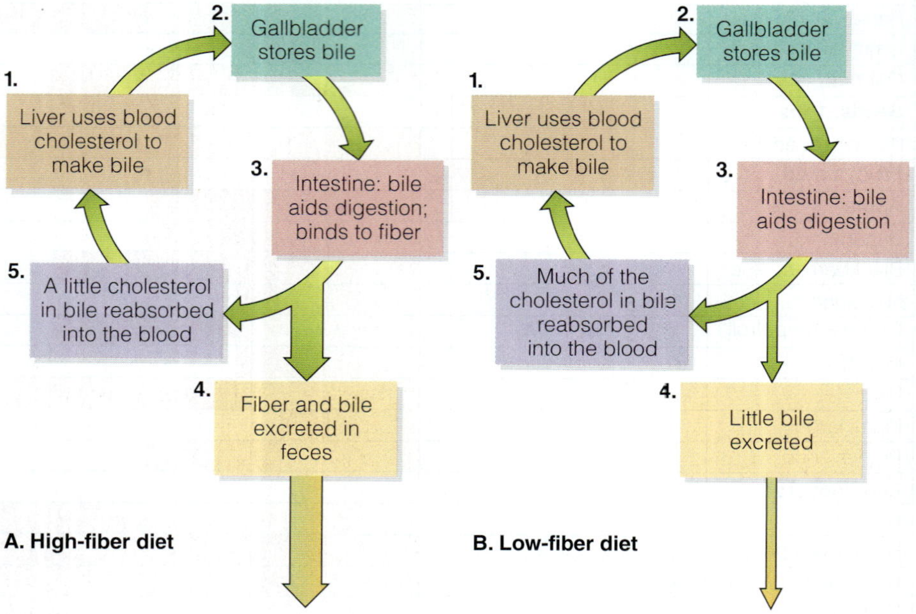

KEY POINT Foods rich in soluble viscous fibers help control blood cholesterol and blood glucose.

Blood Glucose Control High-fiber foods—and especially whole grains—play a key role in reducing the risk of type 2 diabetes.[15] The soluble fibers of foods such as oats and legumes can help regulate the blood glucose following a carbohydrate-rich meal. Soluble fibers trap nutrients and delay their transit through the digestive tract, slowing glucose absorption and preventing the glucose surge and rebound often associated with diabetes onset. In people with established diabetes, high-fiber foods can modulate blood glucose and insulin levels, thus helping to prevent medical complications. A later section comes back to diabetes and its control.

KEY POINT Foods rich in viscous fibers help to modulate blood glucose concentrations.

constipation difficult, incomplete, or infrequent bowel movements associated with discomfort in passing dry, hardened feces from the body.

hemorrhoids (HEM-or-oids) swollen, hardened (varicose) veins in the rectum, usually caused by the pressure resulting from constipation.

appendicitis inflammation and/or infection of the appendix, a sac protruding from the intestine.

Maintenance of Digestive Tract Health All kinds of fibers, along with an ample fluid intake, probably play roles in maintaining proper colon function. Fibers such as cellulose (as in wheat bran and other cereal brans, fruits, and vegetables) enlarge and soften the stools, easing their passage out of the body and speeding up their transit time through the intestine. Thus, foods rich in these fibers help to alleviate or prevent **constipation.**

Large, soft stools ease the task of elimination for the rectal muscles. Pressure is then reduced in the lower bowel (colon), making it less likely that rectal veins will swell (**hemorrhoids**). Fiber prevents compaction of the intestinal contents, which could obstruct the appendix and permit bacteria to invade and infect it (**appendicitis**). In addition, fiber stimulates the GI tract muscles so that they retain their strength and resist bulging out into pouches known as **diverticula** (illustrated in Figure 4-7 in the margin).[16]

Evidence Concerning Digestive Tract Cancer and Inflammation Many studies support a role for fiber in defending against cancers of the colon and rectum. In a study of over a half-million Europeans, for example, people who ate the most dietary fiber (35 grams per day) reduced their risk of colon cancer by 40 percent compared with those who ate the least fiber (15 grams per day).[17] In the United States, data from over 3,000 people suggest that men (but not women) who were given a diet high in fiber had significantly less risk of developing colon or rectal cancers.[18] In contrast, a study of almost a half-million older U.S. adults suggests that consumption of whole grains, but not fiber itself, may offer moderate protection against these cancers.[19] When researchers examine other lifestyle factors, fiber shows some effect but alcohol intake, physical activity, red and processed meat intakes, and other factors emerge as associated with colon and rectal cancers, too.[20] More investigation into this important area of research is needed.

Fiber-rich foods may work against colon cancer in a number of ways. Fiber attracts water, thereby diluting potential cancer-causing agents and speeding their removal from the colon.[21] Also, many fiber-rich foods supply the vitamin folate, and diets rich in folate correlate with low rates of colon cancer (folate *supplements* have proved ineffective in this regard, however).[22] Another possibility involves the intestine's resident bacteria. In fiber-rich intestinal contents, feasting bacteria reproduce rapidly, and in doing so, they bind nitrogen and carry it out of the body in the feces. Nitrogen is a suspected contributor to cancer causation.

Additionally, the colon's bacteria ferment soluble fibers, forming the small fat molecules mentioned earlier, which activate cancer-killing enzymes and reduce inflammation in the colon.[23] Also, the cells of the colon prefer one of these little fats, **butyrate,** as a source of energy.[24] A colon well supplied with butyrate from a diet high in soluble fibers may resist chemical injury that could otherwise lead to cancer formation. A well-fed colon frequently replaces its own lining, sloughing damaged cells before they can initiate the cancer process.

As research progresses, cancer experts recommend that fiber in the diet come from five to nine ½-cup servings of vegetables and fruit, along with generous portions of whole grains and legumes. Note that fiber supplements or additives are not substitutes for whole, fiber-rich foods—the foods provide valuable nutrients and phytochemicals in a structure that benefits the body, while the supplements provide only fiber.

KEY POINT Fibers in foods help to maintain digestive tract health.

Healthy Weight Management Foods rich in fibers tend to be low in fat and added sugars and can therefore prevent weight gain and promote weight loss by delivering less energy per bite.[25] In addition, fibers absorb water from the digestive juices; as they swell, they create feelings of fullness, delay hunger, and reduce food intake.[26] Soluble fibers may be especially useful for appetite control. In a recent study, soluble fiber from barley modified the mix of appetite-stimulating hormones in the blood in ways that may reduce food intake.[27] By whatever mechanism, as populations choose foods lower in fiber, body fat stores creep up.[28]

Weight-loss products may contain bulky fibers such as methylcellulose, but pure fiber compounds are not advised. Instead, consumers should select whole grains, legumes, fruits, and vegetables. High-fiber foods not only add bulk to the diet but are economical, nutritious, and supply health-promoting phytochemicals—benefits that no purified fiber preparation can match.

KEY POINT Diets that are adequate in fiber assist the eater in maintaining a healthy body weight.

FIGURE 4-7 Diverticula

Diverticula are abnormally bulging pockets in the colon wall. These pockets can entrap feces and become painfully infected and inflamed, requiring hospitalization, antibiotic therapy, or surgery.

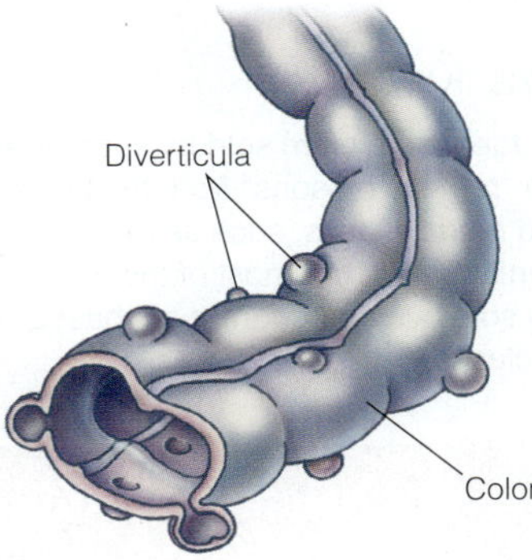

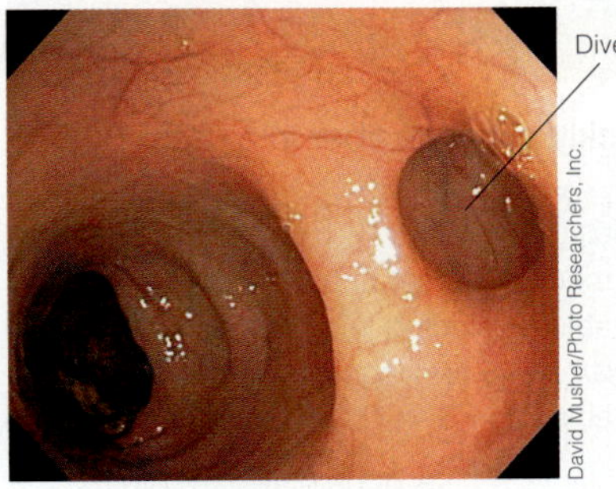

- Carbohydrate: 4 cal/g
- Fat: 9 cal/g

diverticula (dye-ver-TIC-you-la) sacs or pouches that balloon out of the intestinal wall, caused by weakening of the muscle layers that encase the intestine. The painful inflammation of one or more of the diverticula is known as *diverticulitis.*

butyrate (BYOO-tier-ate) a small fat fragment produced by the fermenting action of bacteria on viscous, soluble fibers; the preferred energy source for the colon cells.

Fiber DRI:

- Men, age 19–50: 38 g/day.
- Men, age 51 and up: 30 g/day.
- Women, age 19–50: 25 g/day.
- Women, age 51 and up: 21 g/day.

- No Tolerable Upper Intake Level for fiber has been established.

Did You Know?

Chelating agents are often sold by supplement vendors to "remove poisons" from the body. Some valid medical uses, such as treatment of lead poisoning, exist, but most of the chelating agents sold over the counter are based on unproven claims.

Recommendations and Intakes

Few people in the United States or Canada eat a diet providing all of their needed fiber. To see how fiber stacks up in two day's meals, turn back to Figures 2-14 and 2-15 on pages 57–58. Tuesday's meals, typical of many college students' intakes, provide abundant calories but only half the needed fiber. In contrast, the more nutritious Monday's meals provide more than enough fiber to meet recommendations with calories to spare. The American Dietetic Association suggests 20 to 35 grams of fiber daily, or about two times higher than the average intake of about 14 to 15 grams.[29] The DRI committee's fiber recommendations are based on energy needs and so vary widely among age and gender groups (see the margin).

Fiber recommendations are given in terms of total fiber without distinction between fiber types. This makes sense because most fiber-rich foods supply a mixture of fibers (recall Figure 4-5, page 115). This chapter's Consumer Corner provides detailed information about choosing wisely among grain foods. You can make a quick approximation of a day's fiber intake by following the instructions in Table 4-2.

An effective way to add fiber while lowering fat is to substitute plant sources of protein (legumes) for some of the animal sources of protein (meats and cheeses) in the diet. Another way is to focus on consuming the recommended amounts of fruits, vegetables, and whole grains each day. People choosing high-fiber foods are wise to seek out a variety of fiber sources and to drink extra fluids to help the fiber do its job.

TABLE 4-2 A Quick Method for Estimating Fiber Intake

To quickly estimate fiber in a day's meals:

1. Multiply servings (½ c cut up or 1 medium piece) of any fruit or vegetable (excluding juice) by 1.5 g.[a]
   Example: 5 servings of fruits and vegetables × 1.5 = 7.5 g fiber
2. Multiply ½ c servings of refined grains by 1.0 g.
   Example: 4 servings of refined grains × 1.0 = 4.0 g fiber
3. Multiply ½ c servings of whole grains by 2.5 g.
   Example: 3 servings of whole grains × 2.5 = 7.5 g fiber
4. Add fiber values for servings of legumes, nuts, seeds, and high-fiber cereals and breads; look these up in Appendix A.
   Example: ½ c navy beans = 6.0 g fiber
5. Add up the grams of fiber from the previous lines.
   Example: 7.5 + 4.0 + 7.5 + 6.0 = 25 g fiber

Day's total fiber = 25 g fiber

[a]*Most cooked and canned fruits and vegetables contain about this amount, while whole raw fruits and some vegetables contain more.*

Can My Diet Have Too Much Fiber? Adding purified fibers, such as oat or wheat bran, to foods can be taken to extremes. One enthusiastic eater of purified oat bran in muffins required emergency surgery for a blocked intestine; too much oat bran and too little fluid overwhelmed his digestive system. This doesn't mean that you should avoid bran-containing foods, of course, but that you should approach bran and other purified fibers with an attitude of moderation and be sure to drink an extra beverage with it.

Purified fibers are like refined sugars in one way: the nutrients that originally accompanied the fibers have been lost. Too much purified fiber can displace nutrients from the diet by taking up space ordinarily dedicated to nutritious foods. Fiber can also cause nutrient loss by binding with nutrients in the digestive tract or speeding up their transit out of the body, both effects that prevent nutrient absorption. For health's sake, purified fibers may not affect the body in the same way as fiber-rich foods in the diet. Some of the health benefits attributed to a fiber may in fact come from other constituents of fiber-containing foods.

The Binders in Fiber Binders in some fibers act as **chelating agents.** This means that they link chemically with important nutrient minerals (iron, zinc, calcium, and others) and then carry them out of the body. The mineral iron is mostly absorbed at the beginning of the intestinal tract, and excess insoluble fibers may limit its absorption by speeding foods through the upper part of the digestive tract. Too much bulk in the diet can also limit the total amount of food consumed and cause deficiencies of both nutrients and energy. People with marginal intakes, such as the malnourished, the elderly, and children who consume no animal products, are particularly vulnerable to this chain of events. Fibers also carry water out of the body and can cause dehydration. Add an extra glass or two of water to go along with the fiber added to your diet.

The next section focuses on the handling of carbohydrates by the digestive system. Table 4-3 sums up the points made so far concerning the functions of carbohydrates in the body and in foods.

chelating (KEE-late-ing) **agents** molecules that attract or bind with other molecules and are therefore useful in either preventing or promoting movement of substances from place to place.

KEY POINT Most adults need between 24 and 38 grams of total fiber each day, but few consume this amount. Fiber needs are best met with whole foods. Purified fiber in large doses can have undesirable effects. Fluid intake should increase with fiber intake.

TABLE 4-3 Usefulness of Carbohydrates

Carbohydrates in the Body	Carbohydrates in Foods
• *Energy source.* Sugars and starch from the diet provide energy for many body functions; they provide glucose, the preferred fuel for the brain and nerves. • *Glucose storage.* Muscle and liver glycogen store glucose. • *Raw material.* Sugars are converted into other compounds, such as amino acids (the building blocks of proteins), as needed. • *Structures and functions.* Sugars interact with protein molecules, affecting their structures and functions. • *Digestive tract health.* Fibers help to maintain healthy bowel function (reduce risk of bowel diseases). • *Blood cholesterol.* Fibers promote normal blood cholesterol concentrations (reduce risk of heart disease). • *Blood glucose.* Fibers modulate blood glucose concentrations (help control diabetes). • *Satiety.* Fibers and sugars contribute to feelings of fullness. • *Body weight.* A fiber-rich diet may promote a healthy body weight.	• *Flavor.* Sugars provide sweetness. • *Browning.* When exposed to heat, sugars undergo browning reactions, lending appealing color, aroma, and taste. • *Texture.* Sugars help make foods tender. Cooked starch lends a smooth, pleasing texture. • *Gel formation.* Starch molecules expand when heated and trap water molecules, forming gels. The fiber pectin forms the gel of jellies when cooked with sugar and acid from fruit. • *Bulk and viscosity (thickness).* Carbohydrates lend bulk and increased viscosity to foods. Soluble, viscous fibers lend thickness to foods such as salad dressings. • *Moisture.* Sugars attract water and keep foods moist. • *Preservative.* Sugar in high concentrations dehydrates bacteria and preserves the food. • *Fermentation.* Carbohydrates are fermented by yeast, a process that causes bread dough to rise and beer to brew, among other uses.

LO 4.4

From Carbohydrates to Glucose

You may eat bread or a baked potato, but the body's cells cannot use foods or even whole molecules of lactose, sucrose, or starch for energy. They need the glucose in those molecules. The various body systems must make glucose available to the cells, not all at once when it is eaten, but at a steady rate all day.

Digestion and Absorption of Carbohydrate

To obtain glucose from newly eaten food, the digestive system must first render the starch and disaccharides from the food into monosaccharides that can be absorbed through the cells lining the small intestine. The largest of the digestible carbohydrate molecules, starch, requires the most extensive breakdown. Disaccharides, in contrast, need be split only once before they can be absorbed.

Starch Digestion of most starch begins in the mouth, where an enzyme in saliva mixes with food and begins to split starch into maltose. While chewing a bite of bread, you may notice that a slightly sweet taste develops—maltose is being liberated from starch by the enzyme. The salivary enzyme continues to act on the starch in the bite of bread while it remains tucked in the stomach's upper storage area. As each chewed lump is pushed downward and mixed with the stomach's acid and other juices, the salivary enzyme (made of protein) is deactivated by the stomach's protein-digesting acid. Not all digestive enzymes are susceptible to digestion in the stomach—one enzyme that digests protein works best in the stomach. Its structure protects it from the stomach's acid.

With the breakdown of the salivary enzyme in the stomach, starch digestion ceases, but it resumes at full speed in the small intestine, where another starch-splitting enzyme is delivered by the pancreas. This enzyme breaks starch down into disaccharides and small polysaccharides. Other enzymes liberate monosaccharides for absorption.

© iStockphoto.com

Some forms of starch are easily digested. The starch in bread made of refined white flour, for example, breaks down rapidly to glucose that is absorbed high up in

CONSUMER CORNER

Refined, Enriched, and Whole-Grain Foods

The USDA Food Guide, illustrated in Chapter 2, urges everyone to make at least half of their daily grain choices *whole* grains, an amount equal to at least three 1-ounce equivalents of whole grains a day.[1] To do this, you must distinguish among grain foods that are **refined, enriched, fortified,** and **whole grain** (see Table 4-4). For many people, bread supplies much of the carbohydrate, or at least most of the starch, in a day's meals. Bread provides a convenient example, but the principles demonstrated in this section hold true for cereals, rice, pasta, and, in fact, all grain foods.

FLOUR TYPES

The part of a typical grain plant, such as the wheat, that is made into flour and then into bread, other baked goods, cereals, and pasta noodles is the seed or kernel. The kernel (a whole grain) has four main parts: the **germ,** the **endosperm,** the **bran,** and the **husk,** as shown in Figure 4-8. The germ is the part that grows into a new plant, in this case wheat, and therefore contains concentrated food to support the new life—it is especially rich in oils, vitamins, and minerals. The endosperm is the soft, white inside portion of the kernel, containing starch and proteins that help nourish the seed as it sprouts. The kernel is encased in the bran, a protective coating that is similar in function to the shell of a nut; the bran is also rich in nutrients and fiber. The husk, commonly called chaff, is the dry outermost layer and is inedible by human beings but can be used in animal feed.

In earlier times, people milled wheat by grinding it between two stones, blowing or sifting out the chaff, and retaining the

FIGURE 4-8 A Wheat Plant and a Single Kernel of Wheat

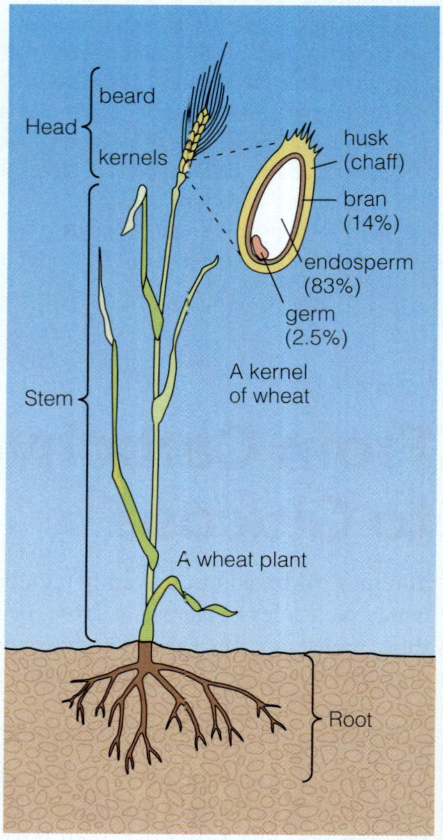

TABLE 4-4 Terms That Describe Grain Foods

- **bran** the protective fibrous coating around a grain; the chief fiber donator of a grain.
- **brown bread** bread containing ingredients such as molasses that lend a brown color; may be made with any kind of flour, including white flour.
- **endosperm** the bulk of the edible part of a grain, the starchy part.
- **enriched, fortified** refers to the addition of nutrients to a refined food product. As defined by U.S. law, these terms mean that specified levels of thiamin, riboflavin, niacin, folate, and iron have been added to refined grains and grain products. The terms *enriched* and *fortified* can refer to the addition of more nutrients than just these five; read the label.[a]
- **germ** the nutrient-rich inner part of a grain.
- **husk** the outer, inedible part of a grain.
- **refined** refers to the process by which the coarse parts of food products are removed. For example, the refining of wheat into flour involves removing three of the four parts of the kernel—the chaff, the bran, and the germ—leaving only the endosperm, composed mainly of starch and a little protein.
- **stone ground** refers to a milling process using limestone to grind any grain, including refined grains, into flour.
- **unbleached flour** a beige-colored refined endosperm flour with texture and nutritive qualities that approximate those of regular white flour.
- **wheat bread** bread made with any wheat flour, including refined enriched white flour.
- **wheat flour** any flour made from wheat, including refined white flour.
- **white flour** an endosperm flour that has been refined and bleached for maximum softness and whiteness.
- **white wheat** a wheat variety developed to be paler in color than common red wheat (most familiar flours are made from red wheat). White wheat is similar to red wheat in carbohydrate, protein, and other nutrients, but it lacks the dark and bitter, but potentially beneficial, phytochemicals of red wheat.
- **100% whole grain** a label term for food in which the grain is entirely whole grain, with no added refined grains.
- **whole grain** grains, or foods made from them, that contain all the essential parts and naturally occurring nutrients of the entire grain seed (except the husk); not refined.
- **whole-wheat flour** flour made from whole-wheat kernels; a whole-grain flour. Also called *graham flour.*

[a]*Formerly,* enriched *and* fortified *carried distinct meanings with regard to the nutrient amounts added to foods, but a change in the law has made these terms virtually synonymous.*

nutrient-rich bran and germ as well as the endosperm. Then milling machinery was "improved," and it became possible to remove the dark, heavy germ and bran, leaving a whiter, smoother-textured flour with a higher starch content and far less fiber. People favored this refined soft white flour more than the crunchy, dark brown, "old-fashioned" flour.

FIGURE 4-9 **Nutrients in Whole-Grain, Enriched White, and Unenriched White Breads**

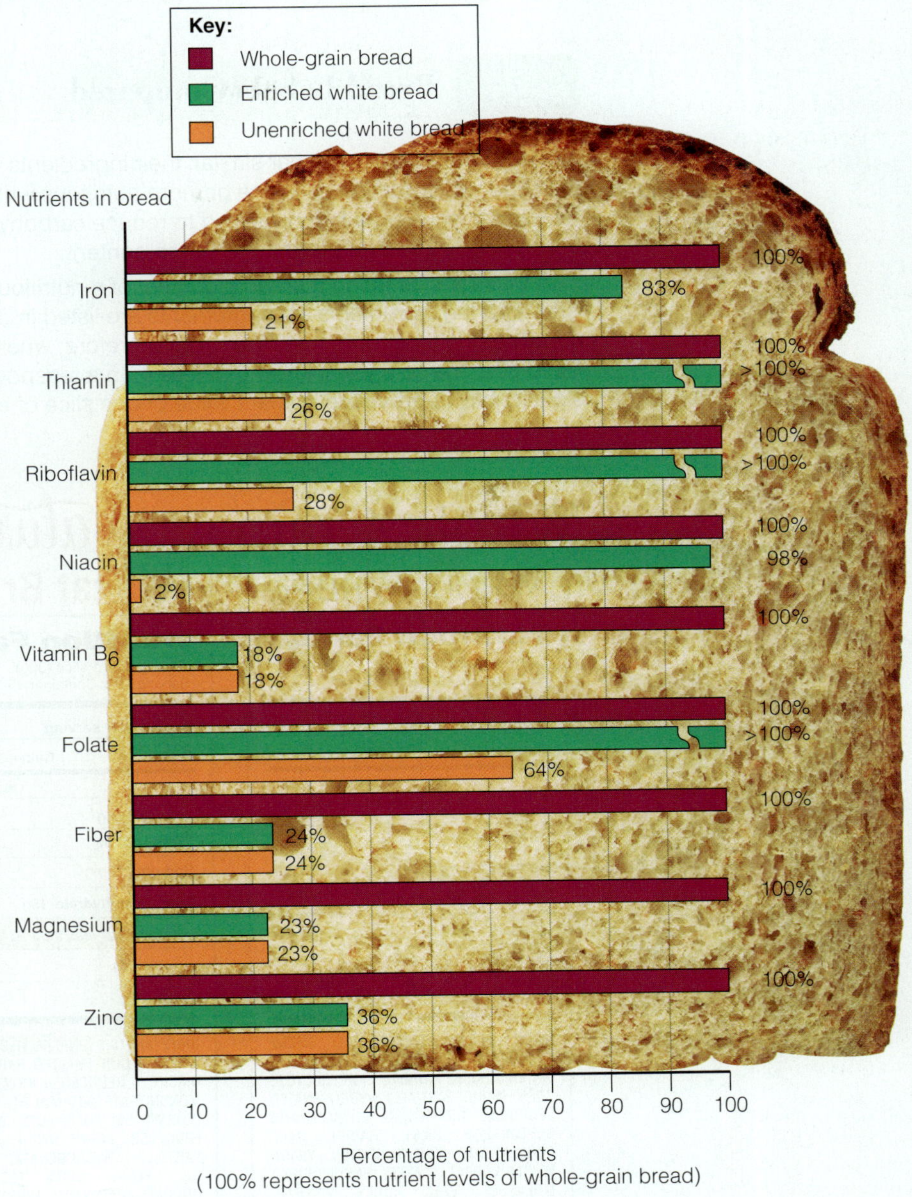

ENRICHMENT OF REFINED GRAINS

In turning to highly refined grains, many people suffered deficiencies of iron, thiamin, riboflavin, and niacin—nutrients formerly obtained from whole grains. To reverse this tragedy, Congress passed the U.S. Enrichment Act of 1942 requiring that iron, niacin, thiamin, and riboflavin be added to all refined grain products before they were sold. In 1996, the vitamin folate (often called *folic acid* on labels) was added to the list. Today, all refined grain products are enriched with at least the nutrients mandated by the Act.

A single serving of enriched grain food is not "rich" in the enrichment nutrients, but people who eat several servings a day obtain significantly more of these nutrients than they would from unenriched refined products, as the bread example of Figure 4-9 shows.

Enriched grain foods are comparable to whole grain only with respect to the added nutrients; whole grains provide more beneficial magnesium, zinc, vitamin B_6, vitamin E, and chromium. Whole grains also provide more fiber (see Table 4-5), along with potentially beneficial phytochemicals and essential oils associated with the bran and germ.

FINDING THE WHOLE GRAINS IN FOODS

Notice the distinctions between **wheat flour, whole-wheat flour, refined flour** (often called *white flour*), and **unbleached flour** among the terms that describe grain foods; also notice that the terms **wheat bread, brown bread,** and **stone ground** on a label do not guarantee that the bread has been made entirely of whole-grain flour (see Figure 4-10). Gaining in popularity is a light-colored bread made from a specially bred **white wheat.**

Whole-grain rice, commonly called brown rice, cannot be judged by color alone. Whole-grain rice comes in red and other colors, too. Also, many rice dishes appear brown because of brown-colored ingredients such as soy sauce, beef broth, or seasonings.

Whole-grain pasta noodles are delicious—but be sure that the ingredients list on the label agrees with any

TABLE 4-5 **Grams of Fiber in One Cup of Flour**

Dark rye, 18 g
Whole wheat, 15 g
Light rye, 14 g
Buckwheat, 12 g
Whole-grain cornmeal, 9 g
Enriched white, 3 g

claims being made for the product.[2] For cereals, too, look for whole grains listed as the first ingredients. Food names and marketing claims on labels can be deceiving, so rely on the ingredients list as your guide.

If you are just now making a change to whole grains in your diet, blends of whole and refined grains can make a good starting point. However you go about it, you are well advised to learn to like the hearty flavor of whole-grain foods.

FIGURE 4-10 Bread Labels Compared

Although breads may appear similar, their ingredients vary widely. "High-fiber" breads may derive their fiber from purified cellulose or more nutritious whole grains. "Low carbohydrate" breads may be regular white bread, thinly sliced to reduce carbohydrates per serving, or may contain soy flour, barley flour, or flaxseed to reduce starch content.

A trick for estimating a bread's content of a nutritious ingredient, such as whole-grain flour, is to read the ingredients list (ingredients are listed in order of predominance). Bread generally contains one teaspoon of salt per loaf. Therefore, when a bulky ingredient, such as whole grain, is listed after the salt, you'll know that less than a teaspoonful was added to the loaf—not enough to significantly improve the nutrient value of one slice of bread.

Whole Grain
WHOLE WHEAT

Nutrition Facts
Serving size 1 slice (30g)
Servings Per Container 18

Amount per serving	
Calories 90	Calories from Fat 14
	% Daily Value*
Total Fat 1.5g	2%
Trans Fat 0g	
Sodium 135mg	6%
Total Carbohydrate 15g	5%
Dietary fiber 2g	8%
Sugars 2g	
Protein 4g	

MADE FROM: UNBROMATED STONE GROUND 100% WHOLE WHEAT FLOUR, WATER, CRUSHED WHEAT, HIGH FRUCTOSE CORN SYRUP, PARTIALLY HYDROGENATED VEGETABLE SHORTENING (SOYBEAN AND COTTONSEED OILS), RAISIN JUICE CONCENTRATE, WHEAT GLUTEN, YEAST, WHOLE WHEAT FLAKES, UNSULPHURED MOLASSES, SALT, HONEY, VINEGAR, ENZYME MODIFIED SOY LECITHIN, CULTURED WHEY, UNBLEACHED WHEAT FLOUR AND SOY LECITHIN.

Natural
Wheat Bread

Nutrition Facts
Serving size 1 slice (30g)
Servings Per Container 15

Amount per serving	
Calories 90	Calories from Fat 14
	% Daily Value*
Total Fat 1.5g	2%
Trans Fat 0g	
Sodium 220mg	9%
Total Carbohydrate 15g	5%
Dietary fiber less than 1g	2%
Sugars 2g	
Protein 4g	

INGREDIENTS: UNBLEACHED ENRICHED WHEAT FLOUR [MALTED BARLEY FLOUR, NIACIN, REDUCED IRON, THIAMIN MONONITRATE (VITAMIN B1), RIBOFLAVIN (VITAMIN B2), FOLIC ACID], WATER, HIGH FRUCTOSE CORN SYRUP, MOLASSES, PARTIALLY HYDROGENATED SOYBEAN OIL, YEAST, CORN FLOUR, SALT, GROUND CARAWAY, WHEAT GLUTEN, CALCIUM PROPIONATE (PRESERVATIVE), MONOGLYCERIDES, SOY LECITHIN.

Multi-fiber
Low carb

Nutrition Facts
Serving size 1 slice (30g)
Servings Per Container 21

Amount per serving	
Calories 60	Calories from Fat 15
	% Daily Value*
Total Fat 1.5g	2%
Trans Fat 0g	
Sodium 135mg	6%
Total Carbohydrate 9g	3%
Dietary fiber 3g	12%
Sugars 0g	
Protein 5g	

INGREDIENTS: UNBLEACHED ENRICHED WHEAT FLOUR, WATER, WHEAT GLUTEN, CELLULOSE, YEAST, SOYBEAN OIL, CRACKED WHEAT, SALT, BARLEY, NATURAL FLAVOR PRESERVATIVES, MONOCALCIUM PHOSPHATE, MILLET, CORN, OATS, SOYBEAN FLOUR, BROWN RICE, FLAXSEED, SUCRALOSE.

the small intestine. Some starch, such as that of cooked beans, digests more slowly and releases its glucose later in the digestion process. Less digestible starch, called **resistant starch,** is technically a kind of fiber because it passes through the small intestine undigested into the colon, and can contribute to the daily fiber need.[30] The starch of raw potatoes, for example, resists digestion. So does the resistant starch that forms when foods are overheated as well as the starch tucked inside the unbroken hulls of swallowed seeds.[31] Barley, chilled cooked potatoes and pasta, cooked dried beans and lentils, oatmeal, and underripe bananas are all sources. Some resistant starch may be digested, but slowly, and most remains intact until the bacteria of the colon eventually break it down. Similar to insoluble fibers, resistant starch may support a healthy colon.[32]

resistant starch the fraction of starch in a food that is digested slowly, or not at all, by human enzymes.

Sugars Sucrose and lactose from food, along with maltose and small polysaccharides freed from starch, undergo one more split to yield free monosaccharides before they are absorbed. This split is accomplished by enzymes attached to the cells of the lining of the small intestine. The conversion of a bite of bread to nutrients for the body is completed when monosaccharides cross these cells and are washed away in a rush of circulating blood that carries them to the waiting liver. Figure 4-11 presents a quick review of carbohydrate digestion.

The absorbed carbohydrates (glucose, galactose, and fructose) travel in the bloodstream to the liver, which can convert fructose and galactose to glucose. The circulatory system transports the glucose and other products to the cells. Liver and muscle cells may store circulating glucose as glycogen; all cells may split glucose for energy.

Fiber As mentioned, although molecules of most fibers are not changed by human digestive enzymes, many of them can be digested (fermented) by the bacterial inhabitants of the human colon. A by-product of this fermentation can be any of several odorous gases. Don't give up on high-fiber foods if they cause gas. Instead, start with small servings and gradually increase the serving size over several weeks; chew foods thoroughly to break up hard-to-digest lumps that can ferment in the intestine; and try a variety of fiber-rich foods until you find some that do not cause the problem. Some people also find relief from excessive gas by using commercial enzyme preparations sold for use with beans. Such products contain enzymes that help to break down some of the indigestible fibers in foods before they reach the colon. In other people, persistent painful gas may indicate that the digestive tract has undergone a change in its ability to digest the sugar in milk, a condition known as **lactose intolerance.**

KEY POINT With respect to starch and sugars, the main task of the various body systems is to convert them to glucose to fuel the cells' work. Fermentable fibers may release gas as they are broken down by bacteria in the intestine.

Why Do Some People Have Trouble Digesting Milk?

Among adults, the ability to digest the carbohydrate of milk varies widely. As they age, upward of 75 percent of the world's people lose much of their ability to produce the enzyme **lactase** to digest the milk sugar lactose.[33] In the United States, the incidence is estimated to be much lower: about 12 percent.[34] Lactase, which is made by the small intestine, splits the disaccharide lactose into its component monosaccharides glucose and galactose, which are then absorbed. Almost all mammals lose some of their ability to produce lactase as they age.

Symptoms of Lactose Intolerance People with lactose intolerance experience some degree of nausea, pain, diarrhea, and excessive gas on drinking milk or eating lactose-containing products. The undigested lactose remaining in the intestine demands dilution with fluid from surrounding tissue and the bloodstream. Intestinal bacteria use the undigested lactose for their own energy, a process that produces gas and intestinal irritants.

Sometimes sensitivity to milk is due not to lactose intolerance but to an allergic reaction to the protein in milk. Milk allergy arises the same way other allergies do—from sensitization of the immune system to a substance. In this case, the immune system overreacts when it encounters the protein of milk. Food allergies can be serious and should be diagnosed by a specialist (see Chapter 14 for more on food allergies).

Consequences to Nutrition Infants produce abundant lactase, which helps them absorb the sugar of breast milk and milk-based formulas; a very few suffer inborn lactose intolerance and must be fed solely on lactose-free formulas. Because milk is

- Whole grains include:
  - *Amaranth,* a grain of the ancient Aztec people.*
  - *Barley*
  - *Buckwheat**
  - *Corn, including whole cornmeal and popcorn.*
  - *Millet*
  - *Oats, including oatmeal*
  - *Quinoa (KEEN-wah),* a grain of the ancient Inca people.*
  - *Rice, including brown, red, and others.*
  - *Rye*
  - *Sorghum (also called milo), a drought-resistant grain.*
  - *Teff, popular in Ethiopia, India, and Australia.*
  - *Triticale, a cross of durum wheat and rye.*
  - *Wheat, in many varieties such as spelt, emmer, farro, einkorn, Kamut®, durum; and forms such as bulgur, cracked wheat and wheatberries.*
  - *Wild rice*

If some of these sound unfamiliar, why not try them? They could be your new favorites.

**While not botanical grains, these foods are similar to grains in nutrient contents, preparation, and use.*

CONCEPT LINK 4-5

The names of the digestive enzymes were explained in Chapter 3, Table 3-1 (page 82).

Approximate percentages of adults with lactose intolerance by ethnicity:

• 85–100%	Asians
• 80–100%	Native Americans
• 70–95%	Black Africans
• 60–80%	African Americans
• 20–30%	Indians (Northern)
• 60–70%	Indians (Southern)
• 60–80%	Ashkenazi Jews
• 50–80%	Hispanics
• 6–22%	U.S. Whites
• 2–7%	Northern Europeans

Source: Data from S. R. Hertzler and coauthors, Intestinal disaccharidase depletions, Modern Nutrition in Health and Disease *(Philadelphia: Lippincott Williams & Wilkins, 2006), p. 1191.*

lactose intolerance impaired ability to digest lactose due to reduced amounts of the enzyme lactase.

lactase the intestinal enzyme that splits the disaccharide lactose to monosaccharides during digestion.

FIGURE 4-11

ANIMATED!

How Carbohydrate in Food Becomes Glucose in the Body

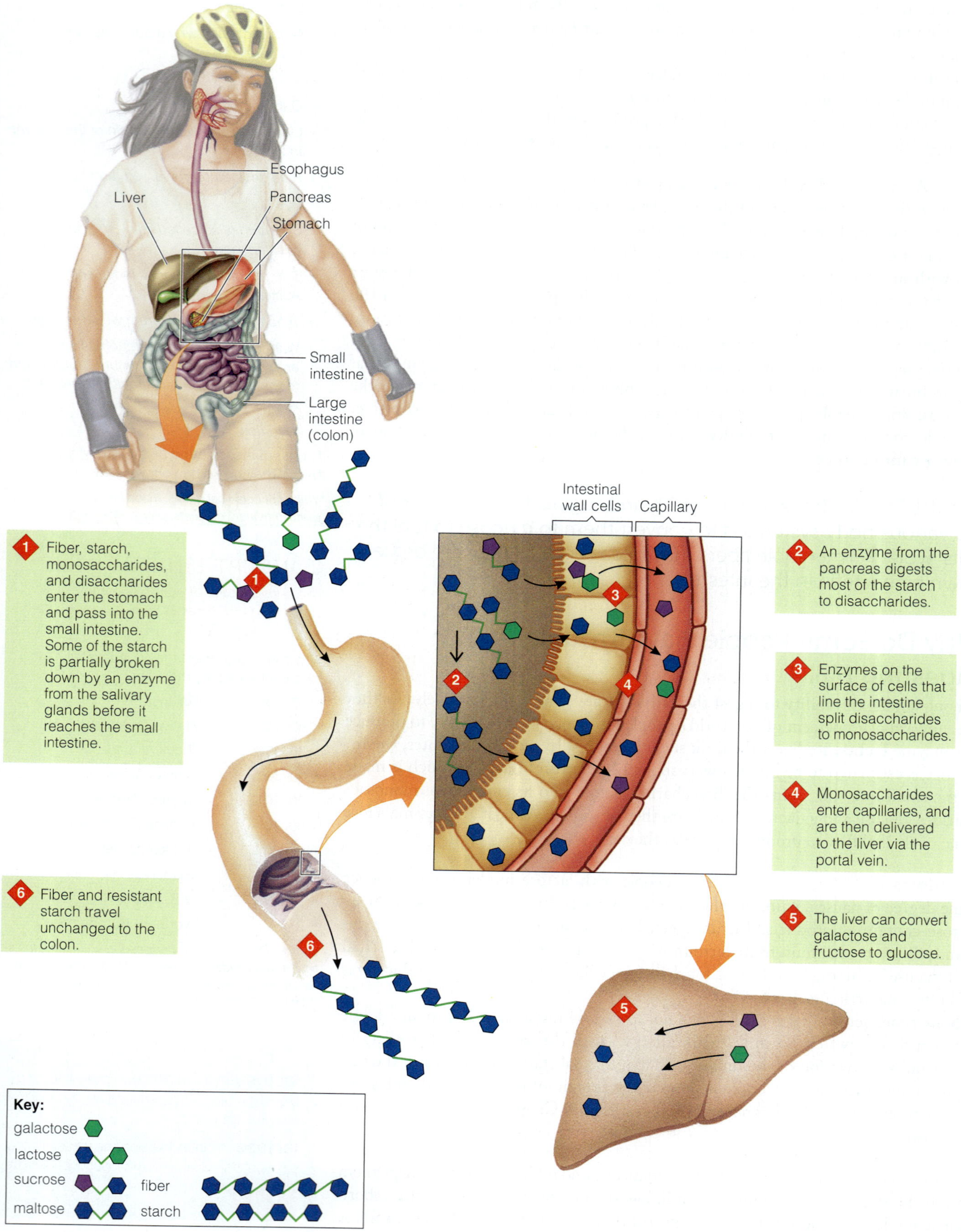

an almost indispensable source of the calcium every child needs for growth, a milk substitute must be found for any child who becomes lactose intolerant. Disadvantaged young children of the developing world sustain the most severe consequences of lactose intolerance when it combines with disease, malnutrition, or parasites to produce a loss of nutrients that greatly reduces the children's chances of survival. And girls everywhere who fail to consume enough calcium may later develop weak bones, so young women must find substitutes if they become unable to tolerate milk.

Milk Tolerance and Strategies The failure to digest lactose affects people to differing degrees. Only a few people cannot tolerate lactose in any amount. Many affected people can consume up to 6 grams of lactose (½ cup milk) without symptoms. The most successful strategies seem to be increasing intakes of milk products gradually, consuming them with meals, and spreading them out through the day. Often, people overestimate the severity of their lactose intolerance, blaming it for symptoms most probably caused by something else—a mistake that could cost them the health of their bones.

Aged cheese often causes little trouble for lactose-intolerant people—the bacteria or molds that help create cheese digest lactose as they convert milk to a fermented product. Some kinds of yogurt contain live bacterial cultures that may take up residence in the intestinal tract, where they seem to reduce symptoms of lactose intolerance. This bacterial shift allows some lactose-intolerant people to adapt to consuming some milk products.[35] Yogurts that contain added milk solids also contain extra lactose that can overwhelm the system; such yogurts list milk solids and live cultures among the ingredients on their labels.

Lactose-free milk products that have undergone treatment with lactase are available at most grocery stores. Alternatively, people can treat milk products themselves with over-the-counter enzyme pills and drops. The pills are taken with milk-containing meals, and the drops are added to milk-based foods; both products help to digest lactose by replacing the missing natural enzyme. The trick is to find ways of splitting lactose to glucose and galactose so that the body can absorb the products, rather than leaving the lactose undigested to feed the bacteria of the colon. Other choices to replace the calcium of milk are calcium-fortified orange juice, calcium- and vitamin-fortified soy drink, and canned sardines or salmon with the bones.

- Chapter 8 and its Controversy examine the topic of milk in adult diets in relation to the adult bone disease osteoporosis.

Lactose in selected foods:

• Whole-wheat bread, 1 slice	0.5 g
• Dinner roll, 1	0.5 g
• Cheese, 1 oz	
• *Cheddar or American*	*0.5 g*
• *Parmesan or cream*	*0.8 g*
• Doughnut (cake type), 1	1.2 g
• Chocolate candy, 1 oz	2.3 g
• Sherbet, 1 c	4.0 g
• Cottage cheese (low-fat), 1 c	7.5 g
• Ice cream, 1 c	9.0 g
• Milk, 1 c	12.0 g
• Yogurt (low-fat, 1 c with added milk solids)	15.0 g

KEY POINT In lactose intolerance, the body fails to produce sufficient amounts of the enzyme needed to digest the sugar of milk. Uncomfortable symptoms result and can lead to milk avoidance. Lactose-intolerant people and those allergic to milk need milk alternatives that contain the calcium and vitamins of milk.

LO 4.5, 4.6

The Body's Use of Glucose

Glucose is the basic carbohydrate unit used for energy by each of the body's cells. The body handles its glucose judiciously—maintaining an internal supply to be used when needed and tightly controlling its blood glucose concentration to ensure a steady supply. Recall that carbohydrates serve functional roles, too, such as forming part of mucus, but they are best known for providing energy.

Splitting Glucose for Energy

Glucose fuels the work of every cell in the body to some extent, but the cells of the brain and nervous system depend almost exclusively on glucose, and the red blood cells use glucose alone. When a cell splits glucose for energy, it performs an intricate sequence of maneuvers that are of great interest to the biochemist—and of no interest whatever to most people who eat bread and potatoes. What everybody needs to

FIGURE 4-12

ANIMATED!

The Breakdown of Glucose Yields Energy and Carbon Dioxide

Cell enzymes split the bonds between the carbon atoms in glucose, liberating the energy stored there for the cell's use. 1 The first split yields two 3-carbon fragments. The two-way arrows mean that these fragments can also be rejoined to make glucose again. 2 Once they are broken down further into 2-carbon fragments, however, they cannot rejoin to make glucose. 3 The carbon atoms liberated when the bonds split are combined with oxygen and released into the air, via the lungs, as carbon dioxide. Although not shown here, water is also produced at each split.

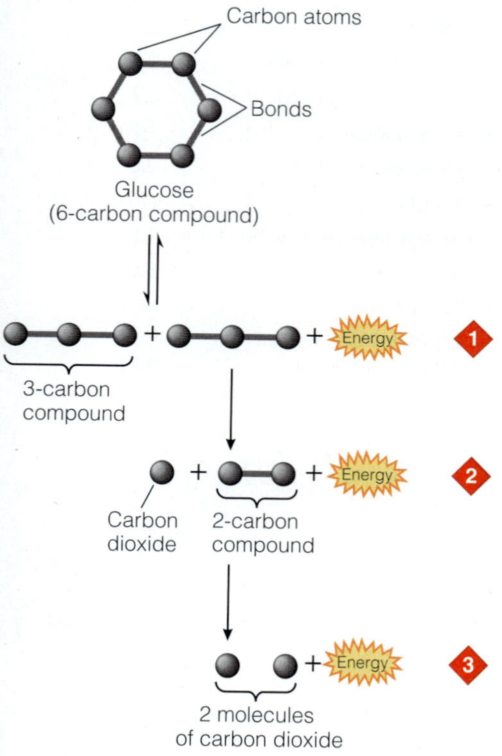

protein-sparing action the action of carbohydrate and fat in providing energy that allows protein to be used for purposes it alone can serve.

ketone (kee-tone) **bodies** acidic, fat-related compounds that can arise from the incomplete breakdown of fat when carbohydrate is not available.

ketosis (kee-TOE-sis) an undesirable high concentration of ketone bodies, such as acetone, in the blood or urine.

understand, though, is that there is no good substitute for carbohydrate. Carbohydrate is *essential,* as the following details illustrate.

The Point of No Return At a certain point in the process of splitting glucose energy, glucose itself is forever lost to the body. First, glucose is broken in half, releasing some energy. Then, two pathways open to these glucose halves. They can be put back together to make glucose again, or they can be broken into smaller molecules. If they are broken further, they cannot be reassembled to form glucose.

The smaller molecules can also take different pathways. They can continue along the breakdown pathway to yield still more energy and eventually break down completely to just carbon dioxide and water. Or, they can be formed into building blocks of protein or be hitched together into units of body fat. Figure 4-12 shows how glucose is broken down to yield energy and carbon dioxide.

Below a Healthy Minimum Although glucose can be converted into body fat, body fat cannot be converted into glucose to feed the brain adequately. When the body faces a severe carbohydrate deficit, it has two problems. Having no glucose, it must turn to protein to make some (the body has this ability), diverting protein from its own critical functions, such as maintaining the body's immune defenses. When body protein is used, it is taken from blood, organ, or muscle proteins; no surplus of protein is stored specifically for such emergencies. Protein is indispensable to body functions and carbohydrate should be kept available precisely to prevent the use of protein for energy. This is called the **protein-sparing action** of carbohydrate. As for fat, it cannot regenerate enough glucose to feed the brain and prevent ketosis.

Ketosis The second problem with an inadequate supply of carbohydrate concerns a precarious shift in the body's energy metabolism. Instead of producing energy by following its main metabolic pathway, fat takes another route in which fat fragments combine with each other. This shift causes an accumulation of the normally scarce acidic products, **ketone bodies.**[36]

Ketone bodies can accumulate in the blood (**ketosis**) to reach levels high enough to disturb the normal acid-base balance. Diets that produce ketosis may also promote deficiencies of vitamins and minerals, increase loss of bone minerals, elevate blood cholesterol, set the stage for kidney stones, and impair mood.[37] Glycogen stores become too scanty to meet a metabolic emergency or to support vigorous muscular work.

Ketosis isn't all bad, however. Ketone bodies provide fuel for brain and nerve cells when glucose is lacking, such as in starvation or very-low-carbohydrate diets.[38] Not all brain areas use ketones—some rely exclusively on glucose, so the body must still sacrifice protein to provide it, but at a slower rate. Some children and adults with epilepsy may benefit from a therapeutic ketosis-inducing diet, used along with medication, although many find the diet difficult to follow for long periods.[39]

The DRI Minimum Recommendation for Carbohydrate The minimum amount of digestible carbohydrate determined by the DRI committee to adequately feed the brain and reduce ketosis has been set at 130 grams a day for an average-sized person.[40] Several times this minimum is recommended to maintain health and glycogen stores (explained in the next section). The amounts of vegetables, fruits, legumes, grains, and milk recommended in the USDA Food Guide (see Chapter 2) deliver abundant carbohydrates.

KEY POINT Without glucose, the body is forced to alter its uses of protein and fats. To help supply the brain with glucose, the body breaks down protein to make glucose and converts its fats into ketone bodies, incurring ketosis.

How Is Glucose Regulated in the Body?

Should your blood glucose ever climb abnormally high, you might become confused or have difficulty breathing. Should your glucose supplies ever fall too low, you would feel dizzy and weak. The healthy body guards against both conditions with two safeguard activities:

- siphoning off excess blood glucose into the liver and into the muscles for storage as glycogen and to the adipose tissue for storage as body fat.
- replenishing diminished blood glucose from liver glycogen stores.

Two hormones prove critical to these processes. The hormone **insulin** stimulates glucose storage as glycogen while the hormone **glucagon** helps to release glucose from its glycogen nest.

The Role of Insulin After a meal, as blood glucose rises, the pancreas is the first organ to respond. It releases insulin, which signals the body's tissues to take up surplus glucose. Muscle and adipose tissue respond by taking up some of this excess glucose to build the polysaccharide glycogen (in muscles) or convert it into fat (in fat cells). The liver takes up excess glucose and makes glycogen, too, but it needs no help from insulin to do so.[41]

Tissue Glycogen Stores The muscles hoard two-thirds of the body's total glycogen to use for physical activity. The brain stores a tiny fraction of the total as an emergency reserve to fuel the brain for an hour or two in severe glucose deprivation.[42] The liver stores the remainder and is generous with its glycogen, releasing glucose into the bloodstream for the brain or other tissues when the supply runs low. Without carbohydrate from food to replenish it, the liver glycogen stores can be depleted in less than one waking day.

The Release of Glucose from Glycogen The glycogen molecule is highly branched with hundreds of ends bristling from each molecule's surface (review this structure in Figure 4-3 on page 110). When blood glucose starts to fall too low, the hormone glucagon floods the bloodstream and triggers the breakdown of liver glycogen to free glucose. Enzymes within the liver cells respond to glucagon by attacking a multitude of glycogen ends simultaneously to release a surge of glucose into the blood for use by all the body's cells. Thus, the highly branched structure of glycogen uniquely suits the purpose of releasing glucose on demand.

Be Prepared: Eat Carbohydrate Another hormone, epinephrine, also breaks down liver glycogen as part of the body's defense mechanism in times of danger.‡ To store glucose for emergencies, we are advised to eat carbohydrate at each meal.

You may be asking, "What kind of carbohydrate?" Candy, "energy bars," and sugary beverages are quick sources of abundant sugar energy, but they are not the best choices. Balanced meals and snacks, eaten on a regular schedule, help the body to maintain its blood glucose. Meals with starch and fiber combined with some protein and a little fat slow digestion so that glucose enters the blood gradually in an ongoing, steady rate.

KEY POINT Glucose stored as liver glycogen is released and used by the whole body. Muscles store their own glycogen for their own use. Insulin promotes glycogen storage, whereas glucagon acts to liberate glucose from liver glycogen. Healthy people have no problem regulating their blood glucose when they consume mixed meals at regular intervals.

Handling Excess Glucose

Suppose you have eaten dinner and are now sitting on the couch, munching pretzels and drinking cola as you watch a ball game on television. Your digestive tract is delivering molecules of glucose to your bloodstream, and your blood is carrying these

‡Epinephrine is also called adrenaline.

CONCEPT LINK 4-6
The acid-base balance of the blood was described in Chapter 3 on page 83.

© Gene Lee, 2011/Shutterstock.com

CONCEPT LINK 4-7
Epinephrine and the body's stress response were described in Chapter 3, page 76.

insulin a hormone secreted by the pancreas in response to a high blood glucose concentration. It assists cells in drawing glucose from the blood.

glucagon (GLOO-cah-gon) a hormone secreted by the pancreas that stimulates the liver to release glucose into the blood when blood glucose concentration dips.

THINK FITNESS

What Can I Eat to Make Workouts Easier?

A working body needs carbohydrate fuel to replenish glycogen, and when it runs low, physical activity can seem more difficult. If your workouts seem to drag and never get easier, take a look at your diet. Are your meals regularly timed? Do they provide abundant carbohydrate from nutritious whole foods to fill up glycogen stores so they last through a workout and provide nutrients to use that fuel?

Here's a trick: at least an hour before your workout, eat a small snack of about 300 calories of foods rich in complex carbohydrates and drink some extra fluid (see Chapter 10 for ideas). Remember to cut back your intake at other meals by an equivalent amount. The snack provides glucose at a steady rate to spare glycogen, and the fluid helps to maintain hydration.

START NOW CENGAGENOW Ready to make a change? Consult the online behavior-change planner to explore a method for changing your current behaviors at **www.cengage.com/sso.**

molecules to your liver and other body cells. The body cells use as much glucose as they can for their energy needs of the moment. Excess glucose is linked together and stored as glycogen until the muscle and liver stores are full to overflowing with glycogen. Still, the glucose keeps coming.

To handle the excess, body tissues shift to burning more glucose for energy in place of fat. As a result, more fat is left to circulate in the bloodstream until it is picked up by the fatty tissues and stored there. If these measures still do not accommodate all of the incoming glucose, the liver has no choice but to handle the excess. Excess glucose left circulating in the blood can harm the tissues.

Ryan McVay/Photodisc/Getty Images

You had better play the game if you are going to eat the food.

Carbohydrate Stored as Fat The liver breaks the extra glucose into smaller molecules and assembles these into its durable energy-storage compounds—fats. These newly made fats are then released into the blood, carried to the adipose tissues, and deposited. Fat cells also take up some glucose directly and convert it to fat. Unlike the liver cells, which store only about 2,000 calories of glycogen, the fat cells of an average-size person store over 70,000 calories of fats, and their capacity to store fat is almost limitless.

Human beings possess enzymes to convert excess glucose to fat, but the process requires many enzymatic steps costing a great deal of energy. The body is thrifty by nature, so when presented with both glucose and fat from a mixed meal, it prefers to store the fat and use the glucose to meet immediate energy needs. In this way, the maximum available food energy is retained because the dietary fat slips easily into storage with few conversions—its energy is conserved. Moral: You had better play the game if you are going to eat the food. (The Think Fitness feature offers tips to help you play.)

glycemic index (GI) a ranking of foods according to their potential for raising blood glucose relative to a standard such as glucose or white bread.

glycemic load (GL) a mathematical expression of both the glycemic index and the carbohydrate content of a food, meal, or diet (glycemic index × carbohydrate).

Carbohydrate and Weight Maintenance A balanced diet that is high in complex carbohydrates helps control body weight and maintain lean tissue. Bite for bite, carbohydrate-rich foods contribute less to the body's available energy than do fat-rich foods, and they best support physical activity to promote a lean body. Thus, if you want to stay healthy and remain lean, you should make every effort to choose a calorie-appropriate diet providing 45 to 65 percent of its calories from mostly unrefined sources of complex carbohydrates and 20 to 35 percent from the right kind of fats.

This chapter's Food Feature provides the first set of tools required for the job of designing such a diet. Once you have learned to identify the carbohydrates in foods, you must then set about learning which fats are which (Chapter 5) and how to obtain adequate protein without overdoing it (Chapter 6). By Chapter 9, you can put it all together with the goal of achieving and maintaining a healthy body weight.

KEY POINT The liver has the ability to convert glucose into fat; under normal conditions, most excess glucose is stored as glycogen or used to meet the body's immediate needs for fuel.

The Glycemic Index of Food

Carbohydrate-rich foods vary in the degree to which they elevate both blood glucose and insulin concentrations. When this effect is measured, a food's average score can be ranked on a scale known as the **glycemic index (GI).** It can then be compared with the score of a standard food, usually white bread or glucose, taken by the same person.[43] A food's ranking may surprise you. For example, baked potatoes rank higher than ice cream, partly because ice cream contains sucrose. Fructose makes up half of each sucrose molecule, and fructose only slightly elevates blood glucose. The starch of the potatoes is all glucose. Figure 4-13 shows where some foods fall on the glycemic index scale on average, but test results vary widely.

Diabetes and the Glycemic Index The glycemic index, and its mathematical offshoot, **glycemic load (GL),** may be of interest to people with diabetes who must regulate their blood glucose to protect their health.[44] The lower the GL of the diet, the less glucose builds up in the blood and the less insulin is needed to maintain normal blood glucose concentrations. Study subjects given carefully controlled diets of low-glycemic foods may indeed lower their blood glucose levels, and some may improve their blood lipids, too.[45]

Interpreting studies on the GI and GL proves to be complex because other dietary factors affect the results.[46] For example, although popular books claim that consumers can lose weight on a low-GL diet, research is mixed on whether the GL of the diet can truly assist in weight loss.[47] Low-GI foods often provide abundant soluble fiber, which slows glucose absorption, sustains feelings of fullness, and improves blood lipids; soluble fiber may in fact be responsible for some effects attributed to the GI.[48] In any case, the glycemic index is not of primary concern for diabetes control, but modest benefit may come from choosing foods low on the scale in addition to using primary strategies for controlling blood glucose.[49]

Limitations of the Glycemic Index Some researchers cast doubt on whether the glycemic index is practical or beneficial.[50] An individual's blood glucose may rise predictably after eating a particular food, but for groups of people, many problems exist in applying the glycemic index.[51] Among them:

- the glycemic response to any one food varies widely among individuals.
- a person's body size and weight, blood volume, and metabolic rate affect glycemic response.[52]
- glycemic responses tend to differ more between individuals for the same food than within one person for different foods.
- within the same person, results for a particular food vary with the time of day.
- many *food* factors also change glycemic index results, including plant variety, food ripeness, processing, preparation, and *other* foods eaten at the same time.[53]
- very few foods have been tested and for those that have, different laboratories often yield different results.[54]

Given these limitations, it becomes clear why researchers dismiss the notion of "good" and "bad" foods based on the glycemic response (see this chapter's Controversy section).

FIGURE 4-13 Glycemic Index of Selected Foods

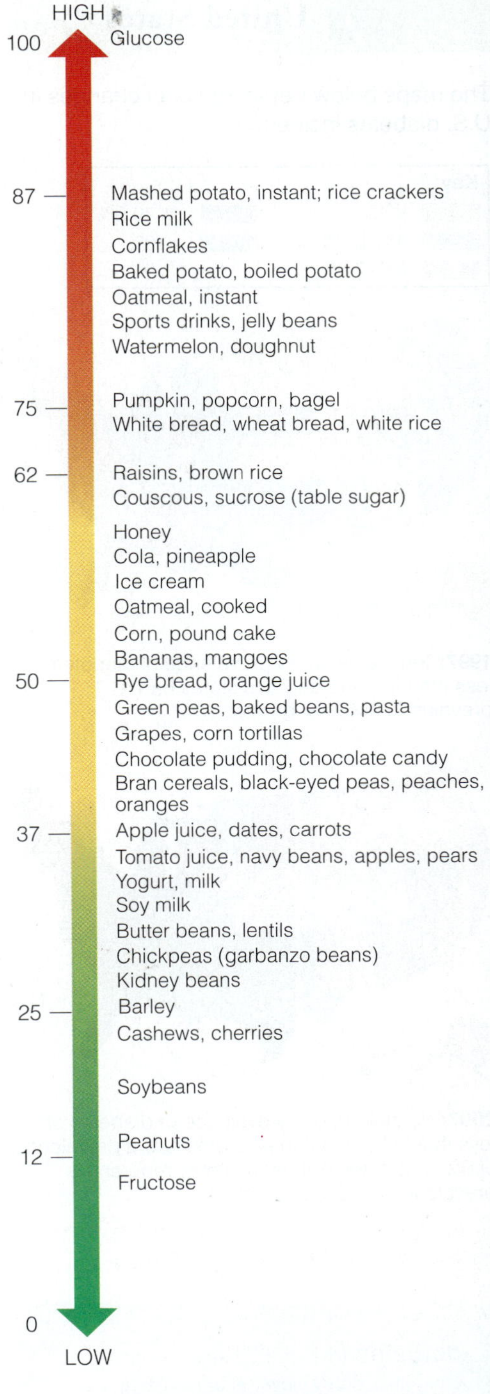

Source: F. S. Atkinson, K. Foster-Powell, and J. C. Brand-Miller, International tables of glycemic index and glycemic load values: 2008, Diabetes Care *31 (2008): 2281–2283.*

FIGURE 4-14 **Prevalence of Diabetes Among Adults in the United States**

The maps below depict regional changes in U.S. diabetes incidence.

Key:
- <4%
- 4%–5.9%
- 6%–7.9%
- 8%–9.9%
- ≥10%

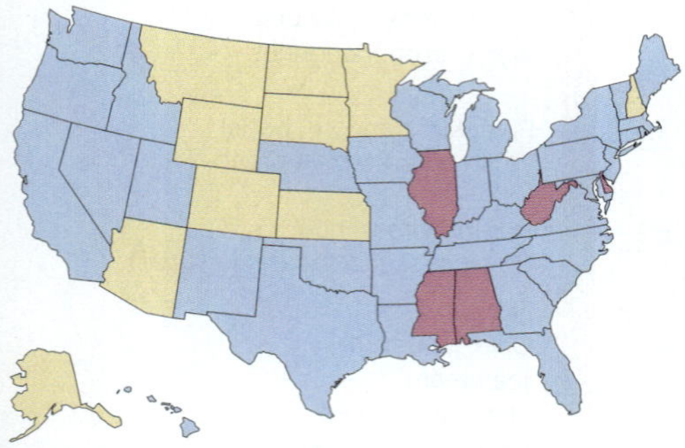

1997: Ten states had a prevalence of diabetes of less than 4% and only five states had a prevalence of 6% or greater.

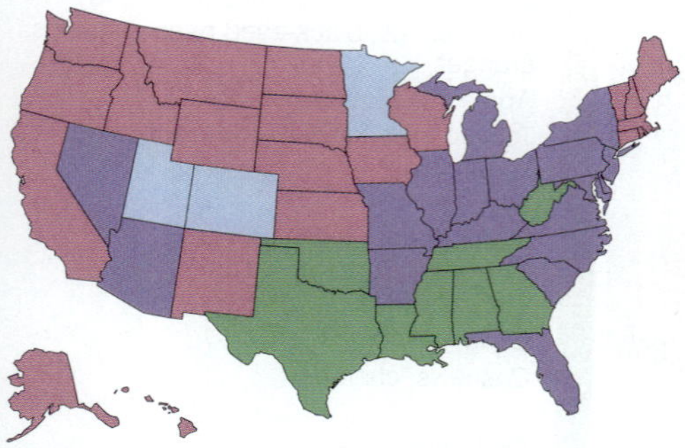

2007: No state had a prevalence of diabetes of less than 4%; all but three states had a prevalence of 6% or greater, with eight states reporting a prevalence of 10% or greater.

Source: Centers for Disease Control and Prevention, www.cdc.gov/needphp/aag/aag_ddt.htm.

diabetes (dye-uh-BEET-eez) a disease characterized by elevated blood glucose and inadequate or ineffective insulin, which impairs a person's ability to regulate blood glucose normally. The technical name is *diabetes mellitus* (*mellitus* means "honey-sweet" in Latin, referring to sugar in the urine).

prediabetes condition in which blood glucose levels are higher than normal but not high enough to be diagnosed as diabetes; considered a major risk factor for future diabetes and cardiovascular diseases.

KEY POINT The glycemic index is a measure of blood glucose response to foods relative to the response to a standard food. The glycemic load is the product of the glycemic index multiplied by the carbohydrate content of a food. The concept of good and bad foods based on the glycemic response is an oversimplification.

LO 4.7

Diabetes

What happens if the body cannot handle carbohydrates normally? One result is **diabetes,** which is common in developed nations and can be detected by a blood test. Diabetes afflicts a rapidly growing number of U.S. adults (see Figure 4-14), and diabetes has reached record numbers in children. Almost 24 million people in the United States have been diagnosed with diabetes.[55] As many as 57 million U.S. adults 20 years of age and older have **prediabetes**—their blood glucose is elevated but not to such an extent as to be classified as diabetes.[56] Of these, over 6 million are unaware of it and so go untreated.

The Perils of Diabetes

Diabetes ranks seventh among all causes of death in the United States.[57] For people with diabetes, the risk of heart disease and stroke is doubled, and in the United States diabetes is the leading cause of permanent blindness and of fatal kidney failure.[58] Each year, diabetes costs nearly $132 billion in U.S. health-care services.[59] The common forms of diabetes are type 1 and type 2, both disorders of blood glucose regulation; their characteristics are summarized in Table 4-6.[60]

The Toxic Effects of Excess Glucose Chronically elevated blood glucose associated with diabetes alters metabolism in virtually every cell of the body. Some cells convert excess glucose to toxic alcohols, causing the cells to swell—in the lenses of the eyes, for example, the distended cells distort vision. Other cells respond by at-

TABLE 4-6 **Types 1 and 2 Diabetes Compared**

	Type 1	Type 2
Percentage of cases	5–10%	90–95%
Age of onset	<30 years	>40 years[a]
Associated characteristics	Autoimmune diseases, viral infections, inherited factors	Obesity, aging, inherited factors
Primary problems	Destruction of pancreatic beta cells; insulin deficiency	Insulin resistance, insulin deficiency (relative to needs)
Insulin secretion	Little or none	Varies; may be normal, increased, or decreased
Requires insulin	Always	Sometimes
Older names	Juvenile-onset diabetes Insulin-dependent diabetes mellitus (IDDM)	Adult onset-diabetes Noninsulin-dependent diabetes mellitus (NIDDM)

[a]*Incidence of type 2 diabetes is increasing in children and adolescence; in more than 90 percent of these cases, it is associated with overweight or obesity and a family history of type 2 diabetes.*

taching excess glucose to protein molecules in abnormal ways; these altered proteins cannot function, causing many problems. The structures of the blood vessels and nerves become damaged, leading to loss of circulation and nerve function. Loss of blood flow to the kidneys damages them, often resulting in the need to cleanse the blood by means of kidney **dialysis,** or, in later stages, to undergo kidney transplant.

Inflammation Chronic inflammation of body tissues accompanies diabetes and may contribute to **insulin resistance,** a condition related to diabetes, discussed later.[61] Inflammation also occurs in obesity, heart disease, and cancer, as other chapters point out, and may contribute to disease progression.[62]

Circulation Problems Poor circulation also increases the likelihood of infections. With loss of both circulation and nerve function, undetected injury and infection may lead to death of tissue (gangrene), necessitating amputation of the limbs (most often the legs or feet).

KEY POINT Diabetes is an example of the body's abnormal handling of glucose. It is a major threat to health and life, and its prevalence is rapidly increasing.

TABLE 4-7 Warning Signs of Diabetes

These signs appear reliably in type 1 diabetes and, often, in the later stages of type 2 diabetes.

- Excessive urination and thirst
- Glucose in the urine
- Weight loss with nausea, easy tiring, weakness, or irritability
- Cravings for food, especially for sweets
- Frequent infections of the skin, gums, vagina, or urinary tract
- Vision disturbances; blurred vision
- Pain in the legs, feet, or fingers
- Slow healing of cuts and bruises
- Itching
- Drowsiness
- Abnormally high glucose in the blood

Prediabetes and the Importance of Testing

Prediabetes, a fasting blood glucose level just slightly higher than normal, presents few or no warning signs (see Table 4-7), but tissue damage may silently progress.[63] According to one estimate, 54 million people in the United States have prediabetes, but few are aware of it.[64] Yet, treatment can delay or prevent the progression to diabetes, sparing much misery and pain. Therefore, the American and Canadian diabetes associations call for everyone over 45 years of age (40 in Canada), and younger people with risk factors such as overweight, to be tested regularly.

Diagnosis is made when two or more fasting blood glucose tests register positive. In this test, a clinician draws blood after a night of fasting and measures an indicator of blood glucose to determine whether it falls within the normal range (values are listed in the margin). A registered dietitian, a Certified Diabetes Educator, or a physician can help those with prediabetes or diabetes learn to manage their condition.

- Fasting blood glucose (milligrams per deciliter)
  - *Normal:* *70–99 mg/dL*
  - *Prediabetes:* *100–125 mg/dL*
  - *Diabetes:* *≥126 mg/dL*

KEY POINT Prediabetes silently threatens the health of tens of millions of people in the United States.

Type 1 Diabetes

Type 1 diabetes is responsible for 5 to 10 percent of diabetes cases. It commonly occurs in childhood and adolescence but can occur at any age, even late in life.[65] Its incidence seems to be on the rise and it currently ranks as the leading chronic disease among children and adolescents.[66] An **autoimmune disorder** influenced by genetic inheritance, type 1 diabetes arises when the person's own immune system misidentifies the protein insulin as an enemy and attacks the cells of the pancreas that produce it.[67] Soon the pancreas can no longer produce insulin. Then, after each meal, glucose concentration builds up in the blood while body tissues are simultaneously starving for glucose, a life-threatening situation. The person must receive insulin from an external source to assist the cells in taking up the fuels they need from the bloodstream that is carrying too much.

Insulin is a protein and if it were taken orally, the digestive system would digest it. Insulin must therefore be taken as daily shots or pumped from an insulin pump that delivers it through a tiny tube implanted under the skin. Fast-acting and long-lasting forms of insulin allow more flexibility in managing meals and treatments, but users must still plan ahead to balance blood insulin and glucose concentrations.[68] Doing so can make a difference to health—those who control their blood glucose suffer less cardiovascular and other diseases than those who do not.[69] Experimental

dialysis (die-AL-ih-sis) in kidney disease, treatment of the blood to remove toxic substances or metabolic wastes; more properly, *hemodialysis,* meaning "dialysis of the blood."

insulin resistance a condition in which a normal or high level of circulating insulin produces a less-than-normal response in muscle, liver, and adipose tissues; thought to be a metabolic consequence of obesity.

type 1 diabetes the type of diabetes in which the pancreas produces no or very little insulin; often diagnosed in childhood, although some cases arise in adulthood. Formerly called *juvenile-onset* or *insulin-dependent diabetes.*

autoimmune disorder a disease in which the body develops antibodies to its own proteins and then proceeds to destroy cells containing these proteins. Examples are type 1 diabetes and lupus.

Did You Know?

The first use of genetic engineering was to alter the DNA of a bacterium to produce insulin for treatment of diabetes.

treatments such as surgical transplants of insulin-producing pancreatic cells and a vaccine to prevent type 1 diabetes are under development.[70]

KEY POINT Type 1 diabetes is an autoimmune disease that attacks the pancreas. Inadequate insulin leaves blood glucose high and cells undersupplied with glucose energy. People with type 1 diabetes depend on external sources of insulin.

Type 2 Diabetes

The past few decades have seen a sharp rise in the rate of the predominant type of diabetes mellitus, **type 2 diabetes** (responsible for 90 to 95 percent of cases).[71] In type 2 diabetes, body tissues lose their sensitivity to insulin. The insulin-resistant muscle and adipose tissues no longer respond to insulin by increasing their uptake of glucose from the blood. As blood glucose climbs higher, the pancreas compensates by producing larger and larger amounts of insulin. Blood insulin may rise abnormally high, but to no avail. Eventually, the overtaxed cells of the pancreas begin to fail and reduce their insulin output while blood glucose spins further out of control.

Type 2 Diabetes and Obesity Obesity underlies many cases of type 2 diabetes.[72] Middle age and physical inactivity also foreshadow its development. The greater the accumulation of body fat, particularly around the waistline, the more insulin-resistant the cells become, and the higher the blood glucose rises.[73] Even moderate weight gain in adults increases the risk. Among children and adolescents, both obesity and type 2 diabetes have increased dramatically during the past two decades.[74]

- Controversy 13 describes the trends in childhood obesity and chronic diseases.

One theory of how obesity and type 2 diabetes may worsen each other is depicted in Figure 4-15. Many factors may contribute to obesity but according to the theory, once obesity sets in, inflammation and other metabolic changes trigger the tissues to resist insulin.[75] As insulin resistance develops, glucose builds up in the blood while the tissues are deprived of glucose (type 2 diabetes). Meanwhile, blood lipid levels also rise, resulting in an overabundance of circulating fuels available to be stored as fat in the adipose tissue. Fat mass increases, insulin resistance worsens, and obesity is perpetuated. Given this series of events, is it any wonder that obese people with type 2 diabetes have trouble losing weight?

A person's genetic inheritance also strongly influences the risk of developing type 2 diabetes, and genetic researchers are working steadily toward pinpointing genetic risk factors.[76] A goal of this research, to develop genetic tests to identify susceptible people, holds the potential to avert much disease and suffering.

Preventing Type 2 Diabetes In the great majority of cases today, however, prevention is not only possible but is also likely when individuals take action to control their lifestyle choices. Men and women who maintain a healthy body weight; choose a diet high in vegetables, fruit, fish, poultry, and whole grains; and exercise regularly, restrict alcohol, and abstain from smoking have a greatly reduced inci-

FIGURE 4-15 **An Obesity-Diabetes Cycle**

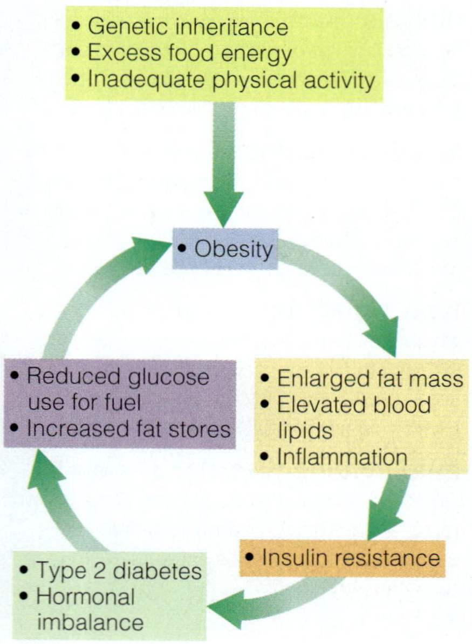

MY TURN

Liz *Ariela*

21st Century Epidemic?

Two young people talk about living with diabetes.

CENGAGENOW To hear their stories, log on to www.cengage.com/sso.

dence of type 2 diabetes compared to those with less healthy lifestyles. It's never too late—even older adults can lower their diabetes risk by changing their lifestyles.[77]

KEY POINT Type 2 diabetes is a growing problem. The risk of developing it rises with weight gain, aging, and physical inactivity and falls with a nutritious diet as part of a healthy lifestyle.

- Lifestyle factors that lower diabetes risk:
  - *Physical activity.*
  - *Never smoking.*
  - *Diet follows the* Dietary Guidelines for Americans.
  - *Limited alcohol intake.*
  - *Healthy body weight.*

Source: D. Mozaffarian and coauthors, Lifestyle risk factors and new-onset diabetes mellitus in older adults: The Cardiovascular Health Study, Archives of Internal Medicine *169 (2009): 798–807.*

LO 4.8

Management of Diabetes

The effects of diabetes can be severe, but controlling blood glucose can reduce the likelihood of harm.[78] Monitoring blood glucose and taking medication often become part of the daily routine. A person with diabetes is especially advised to control body fatness because overweight worsens diabetes and its associated conditions. All lifestyle factors that affect heart and blood vessel diseases (discussed in Chapter 11) demand special attention from those with diabetes because diabetes greatly elevates the risks for developing those diseases. A person diagnosed with diabetes must establish patterns of eating, exercise, and medication to control blood glucose.

© Tony Freeman/PhotoEdit

Monitoring blood glucose is a critical step in learning to manage diabetes.

Nutrition

A major goal of medical nutrition therapy for diabetes and prediabetes is to keep blood glucose levels in the normal range or as close to normal as is safely and practically possible.[79] Controlling carbohydrate intake, in turn, plays a central role in controlling the blood glucose. A common misconception is that people with diabetes need to avoid sugar and sugar-containing foods. As far as blood glucose is concerned, the *amount* of carbohydrate often matters more than its *source*.

How Much Carbohydrate Is Best? The amount of carbohydrate recommended for a person with diabetes varies with glucose tolerance. A low-carbohydrate diet (less than 130 grams of carbohydrate per day) is not recommended.[80] A dietary pattern that includes carbohydrate from fruits, vegetables, whole grains, legumes, and low-fat milk promotes good health, so long as the carbohydrate in the diet is monitored. Several approaches can be used to plan such diets, but many people with diabetes learn to count carbohydrates using the exchange system that is presented in Appendix D (Appendix B for Canadians). As is true for everyone, people with diabetes should choose at least half of their grains as whole grains.

© Polara Studios, Inc.

Like others, people with diabetes benefit from fruits, vegetables, whole grains, legumes, and low-fat milk products.

type 2 diabetes the type of diabetes in which the pancreas makes plenty of insulin but the body's cells resist insulin's action; often diagnosed in adulthood. Formerly called *adult-onset* or *noninsulin-dependent diabetes*.

CONCEPT LINK 4-8

Exchange systems, introduced in Chapter 2, provide a valuable tool for estimating the carbohydrate and other energy nutrients in foods. They are presented in full in Appendix D.

- For more on low-carbohydrate, high-protein diets, see Chapter 9.

- Sweeteners, calories per gram:
  - *Sugars 4*
  - *Artificial sweeteners 0*
  - *Sugar alcohols:*
    - *Erythritol 0*
    - *Isomalt, lactitol, maltitol 2*
    - *Mannitol 1.6*
    - *Sorbitol 2.6*
    - *Xylitol 2.4*

- Chapter 13 discusses a form of diabetes seen only in pregnancy—gestational diabetes.

Why Is Timing of Carbohydrate Important? To maintain near-normal blood glucose levels, food should deliver the same amount of carbohydrate each day, spaced evenly throughout the day. Eating too much carbohydrate at one time can raise blood glucose too high, stressing the already compromised insulin-producing cells. Eating too little carbohydrate can lead to abnormally low blood sugar (**hypoglycemia**). The glycemic index of foods is not of primary importance for diabetes control.[81]

Sugar Alcohols and Artificial Sweeteners Products sweetened with **sugar alcohols,** such as cookies, sugarless gum, hard candies, and jams and jellies, are safe in moderation.[82] They provide fewer calories and a lower glycemic response compared with sugars (see margin list). Most sugar alcohols provide about half the calories of sugars. The exception, erythritol, cannot be metabolized by human beings and so is calorie-free.

Sugar alcohols are safer for teeth than sugars, making them useful in chewing gums, breath mints, toothpaste, and other products that people keep in their mouths for a while. Mouth bacteria rapidly metabolize regular sugars into acids that cause **dental caries;** sugar alcohols resist such metabolism. Side effects such as gas, abdominal discomfort, and diarrhea arise from ingesting large quantities of sugar alcohols.

In the same vein, **artificial sweeteners** can sweeten foods without calories but people have concerns about their use. Their nature and safety is discussed in Chapter 12.

Diet Recommendations in Summary Constructed of a balanced pattern of foods, the same diet that best controls diabetes can also help to control body weight and support physical activity. This diet is:

- Controlled in total carbohydrate (to regulate glucose concentration).
- Low in saturated and *trans* fat (these worsen cardiovascular disease risks) and should provide some raw unsaturated oils (to provide essential nutrients).[83]
- Adequate in nutrients from food, not supplements (to avoid deficiencies).
- Adequate in fiber (from whole grains, fruits, legumes, and vegetables).
- Moderate in added sugars (must be counted among the day's carbohydrates).
- Adequate but not too high in protein (too much may damage kidneys weakened by diabetes).[84]

Such a diet also has all the characteristics important to prevention of chronic diseases and meets most of the recommendations of the United States and Canada. A person at risk for diabetes can do no better than to adopt such a diet long before symptoms appear.

KEY POINT Diet plays a central role in controlling diabetes and the illnesses that accompany it. The balanced diet recommended for diabetes also supports a healthy body weight and physical activity.

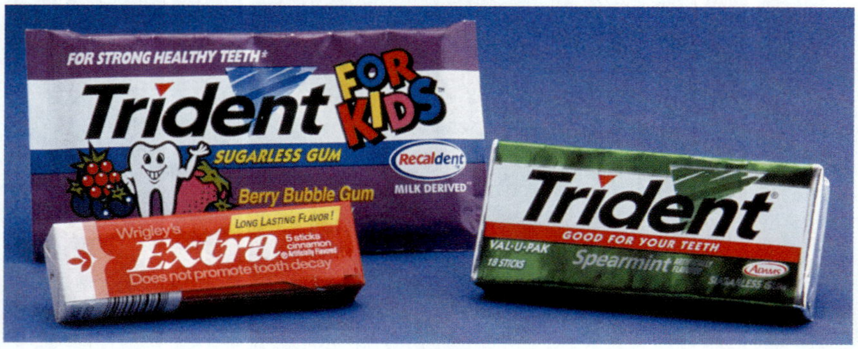

© Craig M. Moore

Sugar alcohols can protect the teeth against decay.

hypoglycemia (HIGH-poh-gly-SEE-mee-uh) a blood glucose concentration below normal, a symptom that may indicate any of several diseases, including impending diabetes.

sugar alcohols sugarlike compounds in the chemical family *alcohol* derived from fruits or the sugar dextrose that are absorbed more slowly than other sugars, are metabolized differently, and do not elevate the risk of dental caries. Examples are maltitol, mannitol, sorbitol, xylitol, isomalt, and lactitol.

dental caries decay of the teeth (*caries* means "rottenness"). Dental caries are a topic of Chapter 14.

artificial sweeteners sugar substitutes that provide negligible, if any, energy; also called *nonnutritive sweeteners.*

Physical Activity

The role of regular physical activity in preventing and controlling diabetes, particularly type 2 diabetes, cannot be overstated.[85] Exercise helps reduce the body's fatness and also heightens tissue sensitivity to insulin. Even with modest weight loss, increasing physical activity in overweight people seems to delay type 2 diabetes onset; in those with the disease, increased activity, even without weight loss, often helps to control it, sometimes to the degree that medication can be reduced or eliminated.

People with type 1 diabetes should check with a physician before increasing their physical activity. Hypoglycemia can occur during or after physical activity.[86] Scrupulous monitoring of blood glucose before and after activity can identify needed changes in insulin or food intake, and both carbohydrate-rich foods and insulin should be kept at the ready. Like a juggler who keeps three balls in motion, the person with diabetes must constantly balance three factors—diet, exercise, and medication—to control the blood glucose level.

KEY POINT Regular physical activity, in addition to diet and medication, contributes to controlling blood glucose in diabetes.

Purestock/Getty Images

Physical activity: a key player in controlling diabetes.

LO 4.9

If I Feel Dizzy Between Meals, Do I Have Hypoglycemia?

The disease *hypoglycemia* is rare as a true disease, but many people believe they experience its symptoms at times. The term *hypoglycemia* refers to abnormally low blood glucose.

Postprandial Hypoglycemia People with the condition **postprandial hypoglycemia**—literally, "low blood glucose after a meal"—may experience fatigue, weakness, dizziness, irritability, a rapid heartbeat, anxiety, sweating, trembling, hunger, or headaches. They may feel confused or find mental work difficult. These symptoms are so general and common, however, that people can easily misdiagnose themselves as having postprandial hypoglycemia. A true diagnosis requires a test to detect low blood or tissue glucose while the symptoms are present to confirm that both occur simultaneously. Most often, however, no correlation is found.[87]

Fasting Hypoglycemia A person who has symptoms while fasting (overnight, for example) has a different kind of hypoglycemia—**fasting hypoglycemia**—heralded by headache, mental dullness, fatigue, confusion, amnesia, and even seizures and unconsciousness. It can arise from serious conditions, such as cancer, pancreatic damage, uncontrolled diabetes, liver infection (hepatitis), and advanced liver damage from alcohol overuse. Fasting hypoglycemia requires immediate medical evaluation.

For Most People To bring on even mild hypoglycemia with symptoms in normal, healthy people requires extreme measures—administering drugs that overwhelm the body's glucose-controlling hormones, insulin and glucagon. Without such intervention, these hormones hardly ever fail to keep blood glucose within normal limits in healthy people. Still, those who believe their symptoms arise from hypoglycemia may benefit from eating regularly timed, balanced meals. Minimizing alcohol intake and eliminating smoking can be important because alcohol can injure an otherwise healthy pancreas and smoking makes hypoglycemia likely.[88]

KEY POINT Postprandial hypoglycemia is an uncommon medical condition in which blood glucose falls too low. It can be a warning of organ damage or disease.

postprandial hypoglycemia an unusual drop in blood glucose that follows a meal and is accompanied by symptoms such as anxiety, rapid heartbeat, and sweating; also called *reactive hypoglycemia*.

fasting hypoglycemia hypoglycemia that occurs after 8 to 14 hours of fasting.

Part of eating right is choosing wisely among the many foods available. As we have discussed, largely without your awareness, the body responds to the carbohydrates supplied by your diet. Now you take the controls by learning how to integrate carbohydrate-rich foods into a diet that meets your body's needs for nutrients and phytochemicals.

FOOD FEATURE

Finding the Carbohydrates in Foods

- Example for 45% of calories in a 2,700-calorie diet:
  - *2,700 cal × 0.45 = 1,215 cal*
  - *1,215 cal ÷ 4 cal/g = 304 g*
- Example for 65% of calories in a 2,700-calorie diet:
  - *2,700 cal × 0.65 = 1,755 cal*
  - *1,775 cal ÷ 4 cal/g = 439 g*
- The range of carbohydrate intake recommended in a 2,700-calorie diet ranges between about 300 and 440 grams per day.

- Fiber recommendations are listed in the margin on page 118.

- The U.S. Food Exchange System (Appendix D) lists carbohydrate values for a variety of foods. Gram values listed in this section are from the Exchange System.

To support optimal health, a diet must supply enough of the right kinds of carbohydrate-rich foods. Dietary recommendations for a *health-promoting,* 2,000-calorie diet suggest that carbohydrates provide in the range of 45 percent and 65 percent of calories, or 225 and 325 grams, respectively, each day. This amount more than meets the minimum DRI amount of 130 grams needed to feed the brain and ward off ketosis.[89] People needing more or less energy need proportionately more or less carbohydrate.

If you are curious about your own carbohydrate need, find your DRI estimated energy requirement (see the inside front cover, page A) and multiply by 45 percent to obtain the bottom of your carbohydrate intake range and then by 65 percent for the top; then divide both answers by 4 calories per gram (see the example in the margin).

Breads and cereals, starchy vegetables, fruits, and milk are all good contributors of starch and dilute sugars. Many foods also provide fiber in varying amounts, as Figure 4-16 demonstrates. Concentrated sweets provide sugars but little else, as the last section demonstrates.

FRUITS

© Polara Studios, Inc.

A fruit portion of ½ cup of juice, a small banana, apple, or orange, ½ cup of most canned or fresh fruit, or ¼ cup of dried fruit supplies an average of about 15 grams of carbohydrate, mostly as sugars, including the fruit sugar fructose. Fruits vary greatly in their water and fiber contents and in their sugar concentrations. Juices should contribute no more than one-half of a day's intake of fruit. Except for avocado and olives, which are high in fat, fruits contain insignificant amounts of fat and protein.

VEGETABLES

© Polara Studios, Inc.

Starchy vegetables are major contributors of starch in the diet. Just one small white or sweet potato or ½ cup of cooked dry beans, corn, peas, plantain, or winter squash provides 15 grams of carbohydrate, as much as in a slice of bread, though as a mixture of sugars and starch. One-half cup of carrots, okra, onions, tomatoes, cooked greens, or most other nonstarchy vegetables or a cup of salad greens provides about 5 grams as a mixture of starch and sugars.

BREADS, GRAINS, CEREALS, RICE, AND PASTA

© Polara Studios, Inc.

Breads and other starchy foods are famous for their carbohydrate. Nutrition authorities encourage people to eat grains often and recommend that half of the grain choices should be whole grains. A slice of bread, half an English muffin, a 6-inch tortilla, ⅓ cup of rice or pasta, or ½ cup of cooked cereal provides about 15 grams of carbohydrate, mostly as starch.

Not all high-fiber foods are whole grains. One hundred percent bran cereal and bran muffins may be high-fiber foods, but added bran doesn't qualify as whole grain. Bran is just one part of the grain, and it may be added to mostly refined, enriched white flour and sugar in cereals and muffins. Conversely, puffed

FIGURE 4-16 Fiber in the Food Groups

Fruits

Food[a]	Fiber (g)	Food	Fiber (g)
Pear, raw, 1 medium	5	Other berries, raw, 1/2 c	2
Blackberries/raspberries, raw, 1/2 c	4	Peach, raw, 1 medium	2
Prunes, cooked, 1/4 c	4	Strawberries, sliced, 1/2 c	2
Figs, dried, 3	3	Cantaloupe, raw, 1/2 c	1
Apple, 1 medium	3	Cherries, raw, 1/2 c	1
Apricots, raw, 4 each	3	Fruit cocktail, canned, 1/2 c	1
Banana, raw, 1	3	Peach half, canned	1
Orange, 1 medium	3	Raisins, dry, 1/4 c	1
		Orange juice, 3/4 c	<1

Vegetables

Food	Fiber (g)	Food	Fiber (g)
Baked potato with skin, 1	4	Mashed potatoes, home recipe, 1/2 c	2
Broccoli, chopped, 1/2 c	3	Bell peppers, 1/2 c	1
Brussels sprouts, 1/2 c	3	Broccoli, raw, chopped, 1/2 c	1
Spinach, 1/2 c	3	Carrot juice, 1/2 c	1
Asparagus, 1/2 c	2	Celery, 1/2 c	1
Baked potato, no skin, 1	2	Dill pickle, 1 whole	1
Cabbage, red, 1/2 c	2	Eggplant, 1/2 c	1
Carrots, 1/2 c	2	Lettuce, romaine, 1 c	1
Cauliflower, 1/2 c	2	Onions, 1/2 c	1
Corn, 1/2 c	2	Tomato, raw, 1 medium	1
Green beans, 1/2 c	2	Tomato juice, canned, 3/4 c	1

Grains

Food	Fiber[a] (g)	Food	Fiber (g)
100% bran cereal, 1 oz	10	Pumpernickel bread, 1 slice	2
Barley, pearled, 1/2 c	3	Shredded wheat, 1 large biscuit	2
Cheerios, 1 oz	3	Cornflakes, 1 oz	1
Whole-wheat bread, 1 slice	3	Muffin, blueberry, 1	1
Whole-wheat pasta,[b] 1/2 c	3	Puffed wheat, 1 1/2 c	1
Wheat flakes, 1 oz	3	White pasta,[b] 1/2 c	1
Brown rice, 1/2 c	2	Cream of wheat, 1/2 c	<1
Light rye bread, 1 slice	2	White bread, 1 slice	<1
Muffin, bran, 1 small	2	White rice, 1/2 c	<1
Oatmeal, 1/2 c	2		
Popcorn, 2 c	2		

Meat, Poultry, Fish, Dry Peas and Beans, Eggs, and Nuts

Food	Fiber (g)	Food	Fiber (g)
Lentils, 1/2 c	8	Soybeans, 1/2 c	5
Kidney beans, 1/2 c	8	Almonds or mixed nuts, 1/4 c	4
Pinto beans, 1/2 c	8	Peanuts, 1/4 c	3
Black beans, 1/2 c	7	Peanut butter, 2 tbs	2
Black-eyed peas, 1/2 c	6	Cashew nuts, 1/4 c	1
Lima beans, 1/2 c	5	Meat, poultry, fish, and eggs	0

[a] *All values are for ready-to-eat or cooked foods unless otherwise noted. Fruit values include edible skins. All values are rounded values.*

[b] *Pasta includes spaghetti noodles, lasagna, and other noodles.*

wheat cereal, a whole-grain food, registers low in fiber per cup because the air that puffs up the grains takes up space in the measuring cup.

Also, do not assume that a brown-colored grain food is a whole grain; rather, rely on ingredient lists organized in descending order of prominence as your guide. Brown-colored baked goods may be made from white flour with brown coloring and flecks of bran added. Also, product names like "multigrain," "seven-grain," and the like mean only that the product contains some portion of grains other than wheat, but they say nothing about their degree of refinement or the amounts added—ingredients lists tell the truth.

Most grain choices should be low in fat and sugar. When extra calories are required to meet energy needs, some selections higher in fat (specifically, unsaturated fat; see Chapter 5) and sugar can supply discretionary calories and pleasure in eating. These choices might include biscuits, cookies, croissants, muffins, and snack crackers.

MEAT, POULTRY, FISH, DRY BEANS, EGGS, AND NUTS

© Polara Studios, Inc.

With two exceptions, foods of this group provide almost no carbohydrate to the diet. The exceptions are nuts, which provide a little starch and fiber along with their abundant fat, and legumes (dried beans), revered by diet-watchers as low-fat sources of both starch and fiber. Just ½ cup of cooked beans, peas, or lentils provides 15 grams of carbohydrate, an amount equaling the richest carbohydrate sources. Among sources of fiber, legumes are peerless, providing as much as 8 grams in ½ cup.

MILK, CHEESE, AND YOGURT

© Polara Studios, Inc.

A cup of milk or plain yogurt is a generous contributor of carbohydrate, donating about 12 grams. Cottage cheese provides about 6 grams of carbohydrate per cup, but most other cheeses contain little if any carbohydrate. These foods also contribute high-quality protein (a point in their favor), as well as several important vitamins and minerals. Calcium-fortified soy beverages (soy milk) and soy yogurts approximate the nutrients of milk, providing some amount of added calcium and 14 grams of carbohydrate. Milk and soy milk products vary in fat content, an important consideration in choosing among them; Chapter 5 provides the details. Sweetened milk and soy products contain added sugars.

Butter and cream cheese, though dairy products, are not equivalent to milk because they contain little or no carbohydrate and insignificant amounts of the other nutrients important in milk. They are appropriately associated with the solid fats.

OILS, SOLID FATS, AND ADDED SUGARS

© Matthew Farruggio, © Matthew Farruggio

Oils and solid fats are devoid of carbohydrate, but sweets provide almost pure carbohydrate. Most people enjoy sweets, so it is important to learn something of their nature and to account for them in the diet. First, the definitions of "sugar" come into play (Table 4-8 defines sugar terms).

All sugars originally develop by way of photosynthesis in a plant. A sugar molecule inside a grape (one of the **naturally occurring sugars**) is chemically indistinguishable from one taken from sugar cane or corn and added at the factory (**added sugars**) to sweeten grape jam. The term *added sugars* refers to all sugars that have been extracted from their original source and added to other foods. Honey added to food is also an added sugar. The combined total of naturally occurring and added sugars appears on food labels in the line reading "sugars." The body handles all the sugars in the same way, whatever their source.

The committee on the *Dietary Guidelines for Americans 2005* offers clear advice on added sugars: treat them as discretionary calories.[90] That is, added sugars bring only calories, with no other significant nutrients, to the diet; conversely, the naturally occurring sugars of, say, an orange provide calories but also the vitamins, minerals, fiber, and phytochemicals of oranges. Because current law requires manufacturers to list only total sugars on food labels, consumers remain largely in the dark about how much added sugar, and therefore how many discretionary calories, their foods contain. Added sugars can contribute to nutrient deficiencies by displacing nutritious food from the diet.[91] Most people can afford only a little added sugar in their diets if they are to meet nutrient needs within calorie limits. The USDA Food Guide suggests about 9 teaspoons of sugar, or one soft drink's worth, in a nutrient-dense 2,200-calorie diet (the margin on page 139 lists other amounts).

Whether they come from beets, corn, grapes, honey, or sugar cane, the added sugars in foods are all alike. All arise naturally and, through processing, are purified of most or all of the original plant material—bees process honey and machines process the other types. The health effects of refined sugars are discussed in Controversy 4. A strawberry spread sweetened with grape juice concentrate, for example, may claim to be "100% fruit" but can contain more sugars than regular sucrose-sweetened jam.

THE NATURE OF SUGAR

Each teaspoonful of any sweet can be assumed to supply about 16 calories and 4 grams of carbohydrate. You may not think of candy or molasses in terms of *teaspoons,* but this helps to emphasize that all sugary items are like white sugar—in spite of many people's belief that some are different or "better." If you use ketchup liberally, remember that a tablespoon of it contains a teaspoon of sugar. And for the soft-drink user, a 12-ounce can of sugar-sweetened cola contains about 8 or more teaspoons of added sugar, usually in the form of **high-fructose corn syrup.** Figure 4-17 shows that processed foods contain surprisingly large amounts of sugar.

TABLE 4-8 Terms That Describe Sugar

Note: The term *sugars* here refers to all of the monosaccharides and disaccharides. On a label's ingredients list, the term *sugar* means sucrose. See Chapter 12 for terms related to noncaloric artificial sweeteners.

- **added sugars** sugars and syrups added to a food for any purpose, such as to add sweetness or bulk or to aid in browning (baked goods). Also called *carbohydrate sweeteners,* they include glucose, fructose, corn syrup, concentrated fruit juice, and other sweet carbohydrates.
- **agave syrup** a carbohydrate-rich sweetener made from a Mexican plant; a higher fructose content gives some agave syrups a greater sweetening power per calorie than sucrose.
- **brown sugar** white sugar with molasses added, 95% pure sucrose.
- **concentrated fruit juice sweetener** a concentrated sugar syrup made from dehydrated, deflavored fruit juice, commonly grape juice; used to sweeten products that can then claim to be "all fruit."
- **confectioner's sugar** finely powdered sucrose, 99.9% pure.
- **corn sweeteners** corn syrup and sugar solutions derived from corn.
- **corn syrup** a syrup, mostly glucose, partly maltose, produced by the action of enzymes on cornstarch.
- **dextrose** an older name for glucose.
- **evaporated cane juice** raw sugar from which impurities have been removed.
- **fructose, galactose, glucose** the monosaccharides.
- **granulated sugar** common table sugar, crystalline sucrose, 99.9% pure.
- **high-fructose corn syrup** a commercial sweetener used in many foods, including soft drinks. Composed almost entirely of the monosaccharides fructose and glucose, its sweetness and caloric value are similar to sucrose.
- **honey** a concentrated solution primarily composed of glucose and fructose, produced by enzymatic digestion of the sucrose in nectar by bees.
- **invert sugar** a mixture of glucose and fructose formed by the splitting of sucrose in an industrial process. Sold only in liquid form and sweeter than sucrose, invert sugar forms during certain cooking procedures and works to prevent crystallization of sucrose in soft candies and sweets.
- **lactose, maltose, sucrose** the disaccharides.
- **levulose** an older name for fructose.
- **maple sugar** a concentrated solution of sucrose derived from the sap of the sugar maple tree, mostly sucrose. This sugar was once common but is now usually replaced by sucrose and artificial maple flavoring.
- **molasses** a syrup left over from the refining of sucrose from sugar cane; a thick, brown syrup. The major nutrient in molasses is iron, a contaminant from the machinery used in processing it.
- **naturally occurring sugars** sugars that are not added to a food but are present as its original constituents, such as the sugars of fruit or milk.
- **raw sugar** the first crop of crystals harvested during sugar processing. Raw sugar cannot be sold in the United States because it contains too much filth (dirt, insect fragments, and the like). Sugar sold as "raw sugar" is actually evaporated cane juice.
- **turbinado** (ter-bih-NOD-oh) **sugar** raw sugar from which the filth has been washed; legal to sell in the United States.
- **white sugar** pure sucrose, produced by dissolving, concentrating, and recrystallizing raw sugar.

What about the nutritional value of a product such as molasses, honey, or concentrated fruit juice sweetener compared to white sugar? Molasses contains 1 milligram of iron per tablespoon so, if used frequently, it can contribute some of this important nutrient. Molasses is less sweet than the other sweeteners, however, so more molasses is needed to provide the same sweetness as sugar. Also, the iron comes from the iron machinery in which the molasses is

- The USDA Food Guide suggests that, within calorie limits, small amounts of added sugars can be enjoyed as part of the discretionary calories in a nutrient-dense diet:
  - *3 tsp for 1,600 cal*
  - *5 tsp for 1,800 cal*
  - *8 tsp for 2,000 cal*
  - *9 tsp for 2,200 cal*
  - *12 tsp for 2,400 cal*

FIGURE 4-17 Sugar in Processed Foods

½ c canned corn = 1 tsp sugar[a]

12 oz cola = 10 tsp sugar

1 tbs ketchup = 1 tsp sugar

1 tbs creamer = 2 tsp sugar

8 oz sweetened yogurt = 8 tsp sugar

2 oz chocolate = 8 tsp sugar

© Polara Studios, Inc.

[a]*Values based on 1 tsp = 4g.*

Did You Know?

Sugars on the Nutrition Facts panel of a food label reflect both added and naturally occurring sugars in foods. Sugars listed among the ingredients are all added.

Did You Know?

Sugar alcohols protect against tooth decay.

TABLE 4-9 The Empty Calories of Sugar

At first glance, honey, jelly, and brown sugar look more nutritious than plain sugar, but when compared with a person's nutrient needs, none contributes anything to speak of. The cola beverage is clearly an empty-calorie item, too.

Food	Energy (cal)	Protein (g)	Fiber (g)	Calcium (mg)	Iron (mg)	Magnesium (mg)	Potassium (mg)	Zinc (mg)	Vitamin A (µg)	Thiamin (mg)	Riboflavin (mg)	Niacin (mg)	Vitamin B_6 (mg)	Folate (µg)	Vitamin C (mg)
Sugar (1 tbs)	46	0	0	0	0	0	0	0	0	0	0	0	0	0	0
Honey (1 tbs)	64	0	0	1	0.1	0	11	0	0	0	0	0	0	<1	0
Molasses (1 tbs)	55	0	0	42	1.0	50	300	0.1	0	0	0	0.2	0.1	0	0
Concentrated grape or fruit juice sweetener (1 tbs)	30	0	0	0	0	0	0	0	0	0	0	0	0	0	
Jelly (1 tbs)	49	0	0	1	0	1	12	0	0	0	0	0	0	0	<1
Brown sugar (1 tbs)	54	0	0	8	0.2	3	31	0	0	0	0	0	0	0	0
Cola beverage (12 fl oz)	153	0	0	11	0.1	4	4	0	0	0	0	0	0	0	0
Daily Values	2,000	56	25	1,000	18	400	3,500	15	1,000	1.5	1.7	20	2	400	60

made and is in the form of an iron salt not easily absorbed by the body.

Honey is no better for health than sugars by virtue of being "natural"—honey is chemically almost indistinguishable from sucrose. Honey contains the two monosaccharides, glucose and fructose, in approximately equal amounts. Sucrose contains the same monosaccharides but joined together in the disaccharide form. Spoon for spoon, however, sugar contains fewer calories than honey because the dry crystals of sugar take up more space than the sugars of honey dissolved in its water.

As for concentrated juice sweeteners, these are highly refined and have lost virtually all of the beneficial nutrients and phytochemicals of the original fruit. No form of sugar is any "more healthy" than white sugar, as Table 4-9 shows.

It would be absurd to rely on any sugar for nutrient contributions. A tablespoon of honey (64 calories) does offer 0.1 milligram of iron, but it would take 180 tablespoons of honey—11,500 calories—to provide 100 percent of a young woman's recommended intake of 18 milligrams of iron. The nutrients of honey just don't add up as fast as its calories. Thus, if you choose molasses, brown sugar, or honey, choose them not for their nutrient contributions, but for the pleasure they give.

These tricks can help magnify the sweetness of foods without boosting their calories:

- Serve sweet food warm (heat enhances sweet tastes).
- Add sweet spices such as cinnamon, nutmeg, allspice, or clove.
- Add a tiny pinch of salt; it will make food taste sweeter.
- Try reducing the sugar added to recipes by one-third.
- Select fresh fruits or fruit juice, or those prepared without added sugar.
- Use small amounts of sugar substitutes in place of sucrose.
- Read food labels for clues on sugar content.

Finally, enjoy whatever sugar you do eat. Sweetness is one of life's great sensations, so enjoy it in moderation.

Diet Analysis

PLUS Concepts in Action

Analyze Your Carbohydrate Intake

The purpose of this chapter's exercise is to help you examine the carbohydrate-rich foods in your diet, compare your intakes with recommendations, and help you to obtain the recommended amounts of soluble and insoluble fiber.

1. In the DA+ program, select the Reports tab then select Macronutrient Ranges. Using your three-day diet records, choose Day Two and choose all meals. Generate a report. Did your intake meet the recommendation to consume between 45 percent and 65 percent of total energy calories as carbohydrate?
2. Determine the distribution of carbohydrate among the day's foods. Select Reports, then Source Analysis, and then Carbohydrate from the drop-down box. Generate a separate report for each meal: breakfast, lunch, and dinner. At which meal did you consume the most carbohydrate? Which foods were the greatest contributors?
3. Did your fiber intake fall within the recommended range of intake (25–35 grams)? From the Reports tab select Intake vs. Goals. Choose Day One, all meals, and generate a report. Did you meet your fiber needs?
4. From Reports, select Source Analysis. Using Day Three, choose all meals and generate a report. Which foods provided the greatest amounts of fiber for the day's intake? If you are short on fiber, look at Figure 4-4 (page 114), Figure 4-5 (page 115), and Figure 4-16 (page 137) which suggests fiber-rich foods to increase your intake of both soluble and insoluble fibers.
5. Whole grains provide more than just fiber. From the Track Diet tab, create a new day (do not alter your three-day record). Enter two food items as a snack: 2.5 cups of Fruit Loops cereal and .5 cup granola (these are equal in calories). Select Reports, Source Analysis, and mineral magnesium from the drop-down box. Generate a report for the new snack. Which was the better magnesium source?

MEDIA MENU

CENGAGENOW Throughout this chapter, the CengageNOW logo indicates an opportunity for online self-study, linking you to interactive tutorials and videos based on your level of understanding. Go to **www.cengage.com/sso.**

Learn more about topics like lactose intolerance, tooth decay, diabetes, and artificial sweeteners at **www.healthfinder.gov.**

Search for "sugars" and "fiber" at the International Food Information Council site: **www.foodinsight.org.**

Search the American Diabetes Association website for information about diabetes, including research, prevention, and living with diabetes: **www.diabetes.org.**

Learn more about dental health by searching A-Z Public Topics at **www.ada.org.**

SELF CHECK

Answers to these Self Check questions are in Appendix G.

1. The dietary monosaccharides include:
   A. sucrose, glucose, and lactose
   B. fructose, glucose, and galactose
   C. galactose, maltose, and glucose
   D. glycogen, starch, and fiber
2. The polysaccharide that helps form the supporting structures of plants is:
   A. cellulose
   B. maltose
   C. glycogen
   D. sucrose

3. Digestible carbohydrates are absorbed as ________ through the small intestinal wall and are delivered to the liver, where they are converted to ________.

A. disaccharides; sucrose

B. glucose; glycogen

C. monosaccharides; glucose

D. galactose; cellulose

4. When blood glucose concentration rises, the pancreas secretes _______, and when blood glucose levels fall, the pancreas secretes _______.

A. glycogen; insulin

B. insulin; glucagon

C. glucagon; glycogen

D. insulin; fructose

5. When the body uses fat for fuel without the help of carbohydrate, this results in the production of _______ .

A. ketone bodies

B. glucose

C. starch

D. galactose

6. Foods rich in soluble fiber lower blood cholesterol.

T F

7. Type 1 diabetes is most often controlled by successful weight-loss management.

T F

8. Around the world, most people are lactose intolerant.

T F

9. By law, enriched white bread must equal whole-grain bread in nutrient content.

T F

10. The fiber-rich portion of the wheat kernel is the bran layer.

T F

CONTROVERSY 4

Are Carbohydrates "Bad" for Health?

LO 4.10

Lately, dietary carbohydrates have been the target of some serious accusations. Popular writers proclaim, sometimes persuasively, that juicy apples, baked potatoes, warm muffins, blueberry pancakes, freshly baked bread, tasty rice or pasta dishes, and other carbohydrate-rich foods are "bad" for health.[1]* In the scientific realm, researchers have been investigating carbohydrates for potential roles in obesity and heart disease.[2] Meanwhile, the current *Dietary Guidelines for Americans* urge people to consume a variety of carbohydrate-rich whole grains, legumes, fruits, vegetables, and milk to support good health. Who's right?

This Controversy investigates some of the accusations launched against carbohydrate-rich foods by the popular media. It also demonstrates how authentic nutrition researchers pursue answers to questions, step-by-step, via scientific inquiry.

ACCUSATION 1: CARBOHYDRATES ARE MAKING US FAT

Over the past several decades, people in the United States have grown dramatically fatter (Figure C4-1).[3] At the same time, their carbohydrate intakes have increased. Does that mean, as some popular writers claim, that carbohydrate-rich foods *cause* obesity? To examine this conclusion, investigators may begin by looking at national nutrient and energy intake data.

*Reference notes are found in Appendix F.

FIGURE C4-1 **Increases in Adult Body Weight over Time**

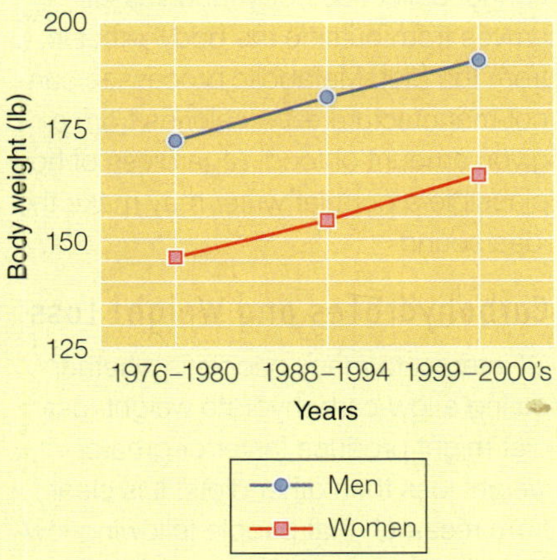

Carbohydrate Intake and Calorie Trends

Figure C4-2 presents a summary of energy nutrient intake data over the past three decades. It demonstrates that the percentage of calories from carbohydrates in the U.S. diet increased from 42 percent in the 1970s to 49 percent today.[4] During the same period, the percentage of calories from fat dropped from 41 percent to 34 percent. The percentage of protein intake stayed about the same.

While percentages among energy nutrients in the U.S. diet shifted somewhat, a more significant trend was also taking place: People were consuming many more total calories each day.[5] Figure C4-2 shows that since the 1970s, the average food energy intake has

FIGURE C4-2 **Percentages of Calories from Energy Nutrients, United States, 1977–2006**

The total daily calories in the U.S. diet are divided into three columns for each time period to reveal the relative contributions of carbohydrate, fat, and protein.

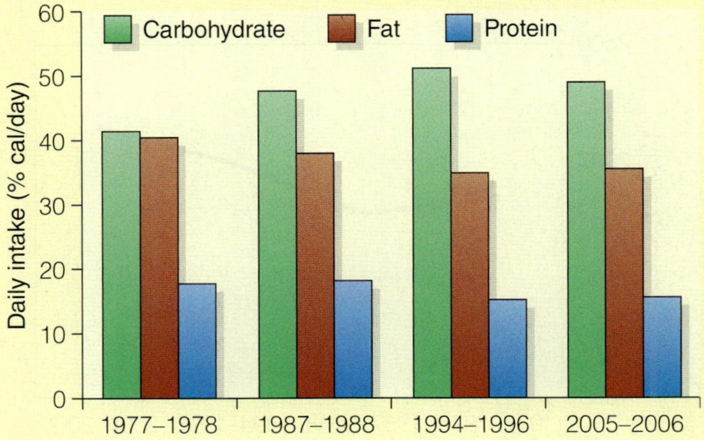

increased by at least 300 calories per day, with other estimates as high as 500 calories per day.[6] Another factor was also in play: most people were not active enough to use up those extra calories—physical activity levels declined.[7] Not surprisingly, the average body weight for adults over these decades increased by about 20 pounds (see Figure C4-3).

Carbohydrates or Calories?

Intriguingly, carbohydrates provided almost all of the national calorie increase in recent decades. This fact has led to speculation that something about dietary carbohydrate itself, and not the calories it provides, may be to blame for people's weight gain. Plausible-sounding metabolic explanations for a special "fattening power" of carbohydrates have been offered by the popular media.

In the realm of science, epidemiological studies report an *inverse* relationship between carbohydrate intake and body weight.[8] That is, people with higher carbohydrate intakes may have lower body weights. Some of this association, but not all, may be explained by dietary fiber intake, which follows whole food sources of carbohydrate into the diet. Whole food diets favor a healthy body weight.

If carbohydrate itself caused overweight, then people around the world consuming traditional high-carbohydrate rice- or root-based diets, such as the Japanese, Chinese, or many Africans, should have high rates of obesity, diabetes, and heart disease. The reverse is generally true: the world's grain- and root-consuming peoples eating traditional diets most often stay lean even though most of their daily calories derive from carbohydrate. Also, as people in such societies abandon their traditional diets in favor of "Western" style high-fat, high-protein, and high-calorie foods, obesity and chronic disease rates soar. Obesity rates in China, for example, are quickly approaching those of the West.[9] In 1985, less than 2 percent of China's schoolchildren were overweight; by the year 2002, the number was about 17 percent for boys and 10 percent for girls. During the same period, intakes of animal protein jumped from 8 to 25 percent of total calories and fat intakes soared as well.

Finally, the first law of thermodynamics comes into play.[†] Energy (calories) cannot collect as body fat unless it arrives from outside the body—that is, from the diet. Metabolic processes cannot manufacture extra calories from a given amount of food, regardless of how plausible a popular writer may make the idea sound.

Carbohydrates and Weight Loss

Of interest to many people is whether eating a low-carbohydrate weight-loss diet might produce faster or greater weight loss than other diets. It is clear from research that people following low-carbohydrate diets do lose weight, and may even lose a little extra during the first few months of dieting, but the difference disappears over time.[10] Chapter 9 provides details, but the punch line seems to be that, over time, people lose about the same amount of weight on any kind of low-calorie diet.[11] Weight-loss success reflects the degree of adherence to a calorie-restricted diet, and not the proportion of energy nutrients in that diet.

[†]The first law of thermodynamics states that energy cannot be created or destroyed.

FIGURE C4-3 **Daily Energy Intake over Time**

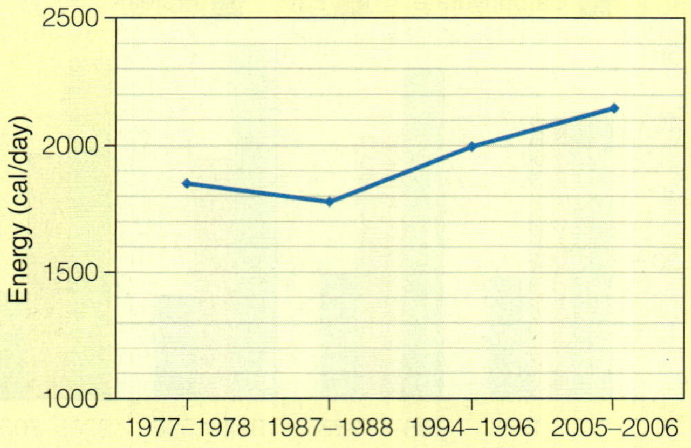

ACCUSATION 2: CARBOHYDRATES CAUSE DIABETES

Diabetes impairs blood glucose regulation following a carbohydrate-containing meal. At one time, people thought that eating carbohydrate *caused* diabetes by "overstraining the pancreas," but now we know that this is not the case. Body fatness is more closely related to diabetes than diet composition is; high rates of diabetes have not been reported in societies where obesity is rare.

Refined Carbohydrates and Diabetes

In some people, however, intakes of certain forms of carbohydrates accompany diabetes development. Particularly among certain Native Americans, a profound increase in the prevalence of diabetes is observed when refined flour and sugars replace whole foods of traditional diets. In addition, evidence from two studies of over 160,000 U.S. women reports an increased diabetes risk in those who drink one or more sugar-sweetened soft drinks each day compared with women consuming less than one per month.[12] Other studies report no link between sugar intake and metabolic markers of diabetes when calorie intakes do not exceed calorie needs, however.

Glycemic Load and Diabetes

Over a decade ago, a study tracking the dietary habits of over 100,000 men and women revealed a positive correlation between diabetes and eating a diet with a high glycemic load based on mashed potatoes, white rice, highly refined cold breakfast cereals, and white bread. However, a subsequent study of this nature did not support this finding. No effect on diabetes risk from such a diet was detected in almost 36,000 women. What this study *did* uncover was a lower incidence of type 2 diabetes and cardiovascular disease in those consuming greater amounts of whole grains and other whole foods, a finding that has been repeated many times.[13]

In summary, whenever whole foods provide most of the carbohydrate in a diet of moderate calories, diabetes is rare. Such evidence does not prove that refined carbohydrates cause diabetes or that whole foods prevent it, however. The apparent protective effect of whole foods might be due to factors other than carbohydrates, such as fiber, other nutrients, or the phytochemicals of whole grains, fruits, and vegetables. In addition, people who tend to their diets by choosing whole grains probably make other healthy choices, such as being physically active, too. Still, refined carbohydrates easily provide excess calories that contribute to body fat stores, and type 2 diabetes risk rises in direct proportion to body fatness.

ACCUSATION 3: ADDED SUGARS CAUSE OBESITY AND ILLNESS

Many vocal carbohydrate opponents point out, rightly, that added sugars (and refined grains) are relatively new in the diet of humankind. Then they conclude that these foods must therefore be responsible for the current high rates of obesity and chronic illnesses. Indeed, many carbohydrate-rich foods that people eat today bear little resemblance to the seeds, grains, fruits, and roots that provided almost all of the carbohydrate in the early human diet. Today, softer, whiter, and sweeter carbohydrate sources predominate.

Trends in Added Sugars

In past centuries, the only concentrated sweetener was honey, a rare addition to the diet. Today, each person in the United States uses up almost three-quarters of a cup (31 teaspoons) of refined sugars added to their foods and beverages each day.‡ This amount is enough, on average, to provide every man, woman, and child with more than 140 pounds of added sugars per year.[14] Figure C4-4 depicts the dramatic upward trend in available added sugars in the U.S. diet and offers the USDA suggested upper intake limits for added sugars for comparison.[15] Note that the columns in the figure represent sugars in the food supply and do not account for waste, such as the syrup drained from sweet pickles or jam that molds and is tossed out. They also do not account for sweetened imported food products, a fast-growing source of added sugars in the United States.[16] The great majority of these sugars in U.S. foods and beverages are added by manufacturers before consumers purchase them. Most people add little sugar from the sugar bowl at home, so they remain unaware of how much sugar they take in each year.

‡This estimate from the USDA Economic Research Service includes all caloric sweeteners in the U.S. human food supply, including cane and beet sugars, corn sweeteners, honey, and syrups.

Added Sugars and Diseases

Data from the world's developing nations seem to clinch the case against added sugars: as a population's income rises, consumption of added sugars increases, and the rates of obesity, diabetes, and related diseases rise, too. Before concluding that sugars must cause health problems, however, scientists also look exhaustively for *other* potential causes occurring simultaneously. For example, newly wealthy peoples do buy and eat more sweets but, as in the China example described earlier, they also choose more fats (particularly oils for frying), animal proteins, fast foods, and refined processed

© Polara Studios, Inc.

Most people remain unaware of how much added sugar they take in each year.

FIGURE C4-4 **Added Sugars: Average U.S. Supply per Person Compared with USDA Prudent Upper Intake Limits**

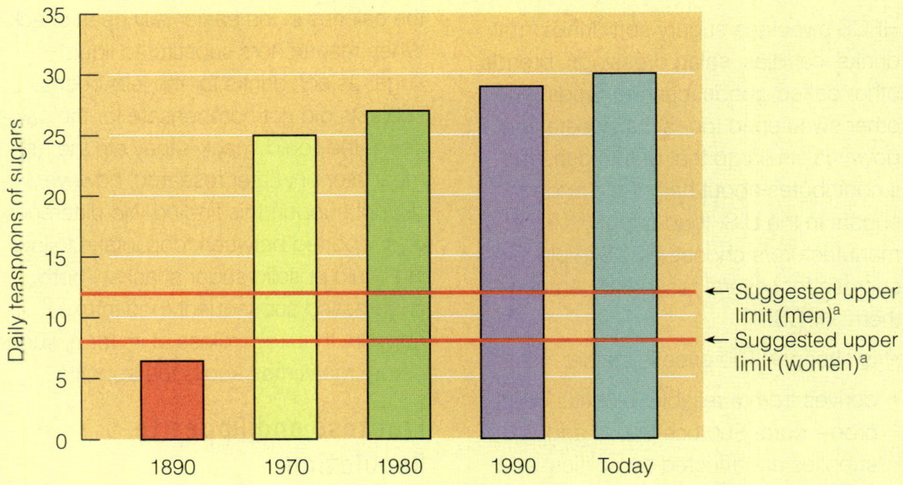

aThese USDA suggested upper limits for added sugars reflect one-half of the average discretionary calorie allowance for sedentary men aged 19–30 consuming 2,400 cal/day and sedentary women aged 19–30 consuming 2,000 cal/day. For other people, see Appendix E. The American Heart Association sets a prudent upper limit of 6 tsp of sugar for most women, and 9 tsp for most men.

Sources: USDA Food Guide; R. K. Johnson and coauthors, Dietary sugars intake and cardiovascular health: A Scientific Statement from the American Heart Association, Circulation 120 (2009): 1011–1020.

foods, all at newly affordable prices.[17] And as they increase their calorie intake, they decrease their physical activity. To say that one of these factors alone—in this case, sugar intake—is causing the world's problems would be naïve. Still, added sugars provide more and more energy to the human diet, so their relationships with health are worth exploring.

ACCUSATION 4: HIGH-FRUCTOSE CORN SYRUP HARMS HEALTH

In 2004, scientists noted that as high-fructose corn syrup (HFCS) replaced sucrose in many foods and beverages, unprecedented U.S. gains in body fatness were burdening the nation's health.[18] Since then, investigators have been testing theories concerning potential roles for HFCS in obesity and disease causation.[19] Their results quickly made the news and became popular topics for writers and speakers. With repetition, the villainy of fructose was exaggerated to the point that consumers adopted unproven hypotheses as common knowledge. Today, some food manufacturers are replacing HFCS with the more familiar sucrose to boost consumer acceptance of their products. Meanwhile, scientists continue to methodically test their ideas, one-by-one, to reveal the effects of HFCS on the body.

The Nature of High-Fructose Corn Syrup

HFCS sweetens sugary soft drinks, fruit drinks, candies, salad dressings, breads, other baked goods, canned foods, and other sweetened foods. Its sweetening power is similar to that of sucrose, and it contributes about half of the added sugars in the U.S. food supply.[20] Food manufacturers choose HFCS in place of sucrose for several reasons.[21] Among them, HFCS:

- is cheaper. The price is stable.
- derives from a reliable, plentiful U.S. crop—corn. Sucrose prices and supplies are affected by political and weather conditions in other cane-growing countries.
- is a ready-to-use liquid. Dry sucrose often must be dissolved in liquid before use.
- remains stable in acidic foods and beverages. Sucrose breaks down in acid.

The decision to sweeten foods with HFCS makes good business sense.

HFCS and Obesity

One question of concern is whether individuals who consume large amounts of HFCS, usually in the form of sugary beverages, weigh more than people who consume less. Overall, findings indicate that people in the United States who consume the most HFCS from sugary sodas, fruit punches, and other sugary beverages do weigh more than people who consume less, and they take in more total calories, too.[22] When results of many such studies are compiled, the data confirm these findings—HFCS consumption and obesity often occur together.[23] This correlation does not prove that HFCS causes obesity, however. Scientists must also find plausible biological mechanisms through which HFCS might have an effect.

Liquid Sugar and Calorie Control

Several such mechanisms involve the body's appetite control system. The first suggests that the body cannot detect calories of liquid sugars and so does not compensate for them with reduced calorie intakes at later meals.[24] To test this idea, some subjects were given jelly beans (solid sugar) before a meal. Later, at mealtime, they ate fewer calories of food—they seemed to compensate for the calories in the earlier jelly bean snack. When researchers substituted liquid sugar as soft drinks for the jelly beans, subjects did not compensate for the calories in the liquid snack—they ate the full meal later on. Later research, however, did not support this finding. No difference was reported between food intake following liquid or solid sugar snacks—both suppressed subsequent food intake.[25] It appears that, regardless of its form, sugar before mealtimes spoils the appetite.

Fructose and Appetite Regulation

A second idea suggests that fructose may impair appetite regulation, possibly by way of insulin or other appetite-regulating signals.[26] Release of insulin causes a shift in the body's appetite-regulating hormones toward appetite suppression.[27] Recall from Chapter 4 that glucose from food stimulates the release of insulin from the pancreas. Fructose, in contrast, does not trigger the release of insulin.[28] (Appetite regulation is described in Chapter 9.) Because fructose ingestion fails to stimulate insulin release, fructose does not suppress the appetite through this mechanism as glucose does.[29] Rats given a solution of glucose, fructose, or sucrose all gain body fatness, but the rats receiving fructose gain the most.[30] Theoretically, then, chronic fructose consumption could lead to greater food intakes, which could contribute to the nation's obesity problem. Although this idea seems plausible, one flaw exists: hardly anyone eats pure fructose. They eat sucrose or HFCS and both of these sugars contain sufficient glucose to stimulate the release of insulin and reduce the appetite accordingly.

Researchers tested the fructose-weight gain theory on monkeys.[31] They fed one group large amounts of pure fructose, while another group received glucose. Some changes in energy balance were observed at several points over the course of the study, but at the end of one year body weights of fructose- and glucose-fed monkeys did not differ. Fructose did not cause excess weight gain, even when monkeys consumed almost half of their daily calories from fructose.

Finally, when overweight or obese human subjects consumed large, equally caloric amounts of fructose or glucose with their regular diets, both sugars caused about the same degree of weight gain.[32] An important difference in the nature of these gains was evident, however. The fructose group gained more of their fat in the abdominal area, and abdominal body fatness elevates the risks of diabetes and heart disease to a greater degree than fat stored elsewhere in the body. While scientifically interesting, these results cannot be applied to the entire U.S. population, many of whom are not obese.

Delicious, Economical, Easily Consumed Calories

All kinds of sugary foods and beverages taste delicious, cost little money, and are constantly available. These factors make overconsumption likely. Also the liquid HFCS of fruit punches and soft drinks is easy to consume quickly—no chewing required. Few people realize that a typical 16-ounce carbonated soft drink can easily deliver 200 calories, and soda drinkers often drink several at a sitting.

It may be tempting, then, to close the book on HFCS as just another calorie source. One other link between HFCS and obesity has held researchers' attention, however. It concerns subtle shifts in lipid metabolism when body tissues encounter fructose.

Effects of Fructose on Lipid Metabolism

When laboratory animals are fed purified fructose, their metabolism shifts toward fat-making and fat-conserving pathways.[33] The same effect is observed in people who consume large amounts (about a third of daily calories) of purified fructose.[34] Fructose intake causes fats to accumulate in the blood and liver. Instead of being used immediately for energy, the fructose is readily converted into triglycerides by the liver, the form of fat stored by adipose tissue. High fructose intakes may not be necessary to bring on this effect, however: adding a single HFCS-sweetened soft drink at each meal for 10 weeks significantly increases blood triglycerides.[35]

Nutrition scientists conclude that a diet high in fructose could set into motion metabolic activities leading to excess body fatness and a buildup of blood lipids associated with heart disease.[36] In addition, study subjects given fructose had higher concentrations of blood insulin but lower tissue insulin sensitivity, two conditions associated with prediabetes.

Fructose in Foods and HFCS

On hearing these results about fructose and lipid metabolism, diet book writers and others often conclude that the obvious way to avoid and cure obesity, diabetes, or heart disease is to eliminate fructose from the diet. They single out HFCS (after all, its name even *says* "fructose") as an obesity-causing sugar. They urge their readers to avoid the fructose of sucrose and even the natural fructose of fruits and vegetables to avoid the effects of fructose seen in laboratories.

Consumers often believe these ideas because they don't know that foods such as fruits, vegetables, honey, sucrose, and even HFCS provide fructose in about a 50:50 mixture with glucose. The metabolic effects of such mixtures differ substantially from those of the 100 percent fructose compound reported in research (see Figure C4-5). When researchers test HFCS and sucrose against each other, they report virtually identical metabolic effects from these two sweeteners.[37] This is expected, given their similar chemical makeup.

In a notable exception, however, human subjects were fed one of the following: a solution of 100 percent fructose, a 50:50 glucose-to-fructose mixture, HFCS (also about an equal mixture of glucose and fructose), and 100 percent glucose solution. Based on previous results, the researchers expected that fructose would elicit the greatest blood lipid response and glucose the smallest, with other mixtures falling in between. Curiously, blood lipids rose similarly for all subjects except those receiving 100 percent glucose.[38] This evidence warrants further study to clarify the health implications of consuming sugars with a similar makeup.

Conclusions of Experts

In the end, not even fructose can make a person fat when food energy intake does not exceed the body's energy need.[39] The studies in which sugars produce weight gain invariably add sugars to an already calorie-rich diet. Added prudent amounts of sugars may be enjoyed as part of the discretionary calories in a nutritious diet with virtually no risk to health.

ACCUSATION 5: BLOOD INSULIN IS TO BLAME

If HFCS cannot be blamed for obesity and disease, perhaps other carbohydrates are the villains. Starch, for example, comprised almost entirely of glucose, has been blamed for obesity and illness because it causes the release of insulin into the bloodstream. Among its many roles, insulin facilitates the transport of glucose into the cells, the storage of fatty acids as body fat, and the synthesis of cholesterol. When insulin is present, the body tends to store energy nutrients rather than using them up.[40] Overweight people commonly suffer from insulin resistance—they release excess insulin. Does insulin therefore *cause* their obesity and can a low-glycemic diet reverse it, as some diet books claim?

Claims Made About Insulin

Because insulin promotes storage of body fat, popular writers often assume

FIGURE C4-5 **Glucose and Fructose in Common Added Sugars**

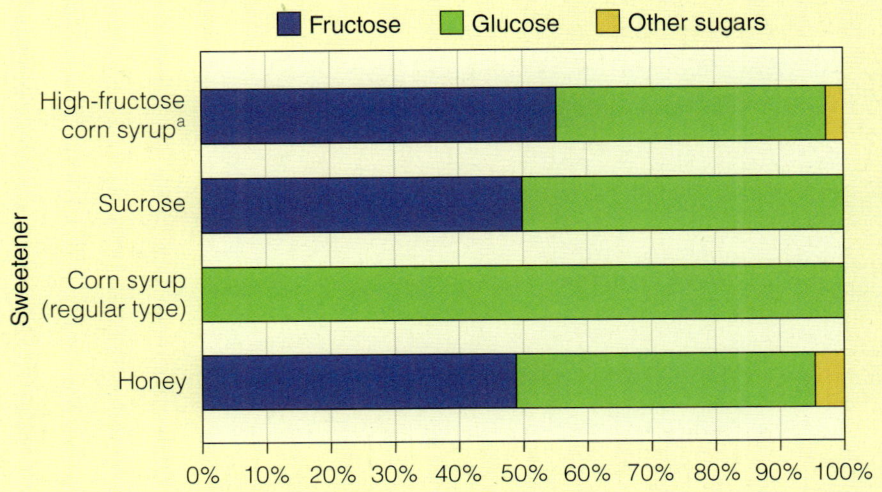

[a]*A typical mixture. Corn syrup purchased for use at home, for example in a pecan pie recipe, is not high-fructose corn syrup; it consists almost entirely of glucose.*

Source: Data from J. S. White, Straight talk about high-fructose corn syrup: What it is and what it ain't, American Journal of Clinical Nutrition 88 (2008): 1716S–1721S.

that insulin must therefore cause excess body fatness and obesity. They argue that to avoid gains of body fat, people needn't bother controlling discretionary calories or exercising but should simply eat meats, eggs, cheese, salads, and other nonstarchy vegetables and avoid carbohydrates to avoid stimulating the release of insulin. Alternatively, they recommend choosing foods that trigger a reduced insulin response—foods low on the glycemic index scale. Logically, then, less insulin should lead to less storage of body fat, and less body fatness means less type 2 diabetes and a lower risk of heart disease. Keep in mind, however, that logic is not science.

What Nutrition Experts Say About Insulin

When scientists speak on these issues, they agree on this point: insulin regulates carbohydrate and fat storage in the body. However, they disagree that insulin, and not excess calories, causes accumulation of excess body fat.[41]

Do scientists rule insulin to be innocent in causing weight gain, then? Perhaps not entirely. Individual differences in insulin's metabolism may affect how efficiently a person stores food energy. In a 6-year study, people who released normal amounts of insulin following either a high-carbohydrate diet or a low-carbohydrate diet gained about the same amount of weight.[42] But those with insulin resistance gained more weight, especially when they ate a high-carbohydrate diet.

Although insulin disturbances may trigger weight gain, this scientific truth remains: insulin can only assist in the storage of body fat when calories taken in are in excess of need. In all people, weight gain can occur only when the food energy they take in exceeds the energy they use up each day.[43]

CONCLUSION

Investigation into the potential health effects of carbohydrates is ongoing. The idea that the nation's obesity problem might be easily solved by removing an ingredient, HFCS, from the food supply is inviting, but research shows this to be a false hope.[44] Today's larger calorie intakes alone are more than sufficient to explain why people are fatter today than in the past.[45] From the nutritionist's point of view, fad diets that advise people to avoid sugars provided by fruits and vegetables should be ignored. As you will see in later chapters, research overwhelmingly supports consuming 5 to 9 servings of these health-promoting foods.

Enjoying the pleasure of sweets within the discretionary calorie limit is possible in the context of a nutritious diet.[46] However, people who consume many empty calories of daily sugary soft drinks, punches, and other sources of added sugars would do well to replace some of them with water, nonfat milk, vegetable juices, or artificially sweetened beverages and whole foods that are naturally sweet. (Controversies often arise around the use of artificial sweeteners, and Chapter 12 presents the facts.)

The Lipids: Fats, Oils, Phospholipids, and Sterols

5

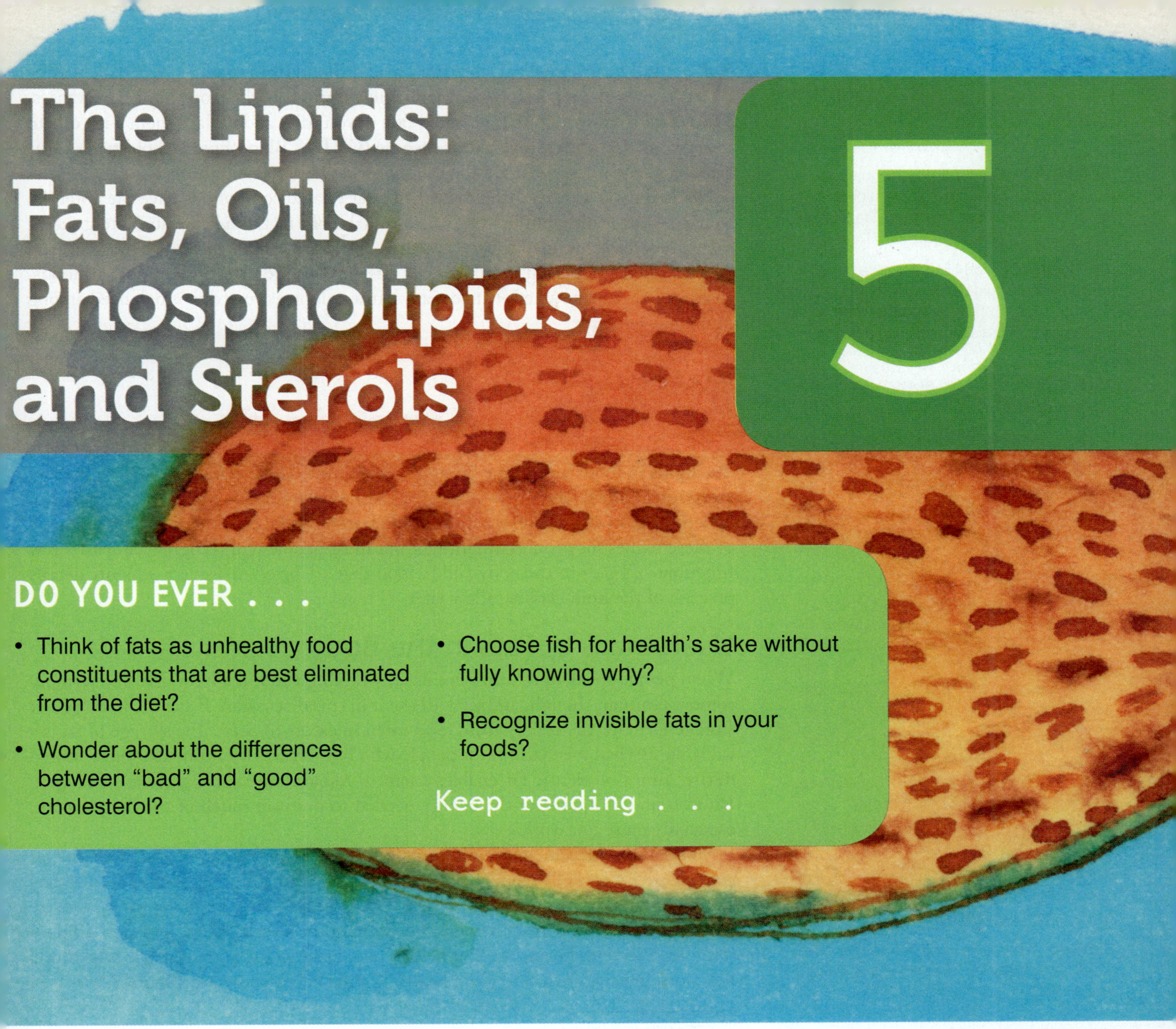

Rebecca Bradley/Getty Images

DO YOU EVER . . .

- Think of fats as unhealthy food constituents that are best eliminated from the diet?
- Wonder about the differences between "bad" and "good" cholesterol?
- Choose fish for health's sake without fully knowing why?
- Recognize invisible fats in your foods?

Keep reading . . .

Learning Objectives

To find learning objective topics in this chapter, look for the text headings with a corresponding "LO" number above the heading. After completing this chapter, you should be able to accomplish the following:

LO 5.1 Discuss the reasons why a moderate intake of lipids is an essential part of a healthy diet.

LO 5.2 Compare and contrast the physical properties and the sources of saturated, polyunsaturated, and monounsaturated fats.

LO 5.3 Describe how and where dietary lipids are broken down and absorbed during digestion and how they are transported throughout the body.

LO 5.4 Describe the significance of the blood tests for HDL and LDL cholesterol.

LO 5.5 Describe the roles of omega-3 and omega-6 fatty acids in the body, and discuss which may be too low in some people's diets and how they can increase their intakes.

LO 5.6 Justify the recommendation to eat fatty fish instead of relying on fish oil supplements, and discuss safety issues surrounding both choices.

LO 5.7 Describe the formation and structure of a *trans*-fatty acid, and state ways in which consumers may reduce their intakes.

LO 5.8 Develop a diet plan that provides enough of the right kinds of fats within calorie limits.

LO 5.9 Discuss evidence for the benefits and drawbacks of specific dietary fats in terms of their potential effects on human health.

Your bill from a medical laboratory reads "Blood **lipid** profile—$250." A health-care provider reports, "Your blood **cholesterol** is high." Your physician advises, "You must cut down on the saturated **fats** in your diet and replace them with **oils** to lower your risk of **cardiovascular disease (CVD).**" Blood lipids, cholesterol, saturated fats, and oils—what are they, and how do they relate to health?

No doubt you are expecting to hear that fat-related compounds have the potential to harm your health, but lipids are also valuable. In fact, lipids are absolutely necessary. The diet recommended for health is moderate in fats, but it is by no means a "no-fat" diet. Luckily, at least traces of fats and oils are present in almost all foods, so you needn't make an effort to eat any extra so long as your diet is balanced among nutritious foods.

lipid (LIP-id) a family of organic (carbon-containing) compounds soluble in organic solvents but not in water. Lipids include triglycerides (fats and oils), phospholipids, and sterols.

cholesterol (koh-LESS-ter-all) a member of the group of lipids known as sterols; a soft, waxy substance made in the body for a variety of purposes and also found in animal-derived foods.

fats lipids that are solid at room temperature (70°F or 21°C).

oils lipids that are liquid at room temperature (70°F or 21°C).

cardiovascular disease (CVD) disease of the heart and blood vessels; disease of the arteries of the heart is called *coronary heart disease (CHD)*. Also defined in Chapter 11.

triglycerides (try-GLISS-er-ides) one of the three main classes of dietary lipids and the chief form of fat in foods and in the human body. A triglyceride is made up of three units of fatty acids and one unit of glycerol (fatty acids and glycerol are defined later). Triglycerides are also called *triacylglycerols.*

phospholipids (FOSS-foh-LIP-ids) one of the three main classes of dietary lipids. These lipids are similar to triglycerides, but each has a phosphorus-containing acid in place of one of the fatty acids. Phospholipids are present in all cell membranes.

lecithin (LESS-ih-thin) a phospholipid manufactured by the liver and also found in many foods; a major constituent of cell membranes.

sterols (STEER-alls) one of the three main classes of dietary lipids. Sterols have a structure similar to that of cholesterol.

LO 5.1

Introducing the Lipids

The lipids in foods and in the human body fall into three classes. About 95 percent are **triglycerides.** The other classes of the lipid family are the **phospholipids** (of which **lecithin** is one) and the **sterols** (cholesterol is the best known of these). Some of these names may sound unfamiliar, but most people will recognize at least a few functions of lipids in the body and in food that are listed in Table 5-1. More details on each of the lipid classes follow later.

Usefulness of Fats in the Body

When people speak of fat, they are usually talking about triglycerides. The term *fat* is more familiar, though, and we will use it in this discussion. Fat is the body's chief storage form for the energy from food eaten in excess of need. The storage of fat is a valuable survival mechanism for people who live a feast-or-famine existence: stored during times of plenty, fat enables them to remain alive during times of famine. Fat also provides most of the energy needed to perform much of the body's work, especially muscular work.

Most body cells can store only limited fat, but some cells are specialized for fat storage. These fat cells seem able to expand almost indefinitely—the more fat they store, the larger they grow. An obese person's fat cells may be many times the size of a thin person's. Far from being a collection of inert sacks of fat, however, adipose (fat) tissue secretes hormones that help to regulate appetite and influence other body functions in ways critical to good health.[1*] A fat cell is shown in Figure 5-1.

*Reference notes are found in Appendix F.

TABLE 5-1 The Usefulness of Fats

Fats in the Body	Fats in Food
• *Energy stores* Fats are the body's chief form of stored energy. • *Muscle fuel* Fats provide most of the energy to fuel muscular work. • *Emergency reserve* Fats serve as an emergency fuel supply in times of illness and diminished food intake. • *Padding* Fats protect the internal organs from shock through fat pads inside the body cavity. • *Insulation* Fats insulate against temperature extremes through a fat layer under the skin. • *Cell membranes* Fats form the major material of cell membranes. • *Raw materials* Fats are converted to other compounds, such as hormones, bile, and vitamin D, as needed.	• *Nutrient* Fats provide essential fatty acids. • *Energy* Fats provide a concentrated energy source in foods. • *Transport* Fats carry fat-soluble vitamins A, D, E, and K along with some phytochemicals and assist in their absorption. • *Raw materials* Fats provide raw material for making needed products. • *Sensory appeal* Fats contribute to the taste and smell of foods. • *Appetite* Fats stimulate the appetite. • *Satiety* Fats contribute to feelings of fullness. • *Texture* Fats help make foods tender.

FIGURE 5-1 A Fat Cell

Within the fat cell, lipid is stored in a droplet. This droplet can greatly enlarge, and the fat cell membrane will expand to accommodate its swollen contents. More about fat tissue (also called *adipose tissue*) and body functions in Chapter 9.

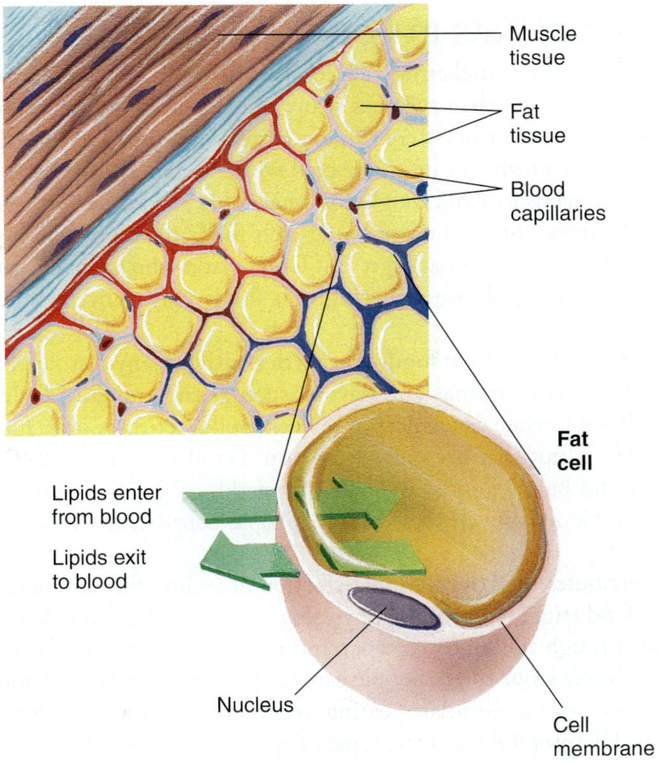

• Chapter 9 comes back to the hormones of adipose tissue.

You may be wondering why the carbohydrate glucose is not the body's major form of stored energy. As mentioned in Chapter 4, glucose is stored in the form of glycogen. Because glycogen holds a great deal of water, it is quite bulky and heavy, and the body cannot store enough to provide energy for very long. Fats, however, pack tightly together without water and can store much more energy in a small space. Gram for gram, fats provide more than twice the energy of carbohydrate, making fat an efficient storage form of energy. The body fat found on a normal-weight person contains more than enough energy to fuel an entire marathon run or to battle disease should the person become ill and stop eating for a while.

Fat serves many other purposes in the body, too. Pads of fat surrounding the vital internal organs serve as shock absorbers. Thanks to these fat pads, you can ride a horse or a motorcycle for many hours with no serious internal injuries. A fat blanket under the skin also insulates the body from extremes of temperature, thus assisting with internal climate control. Lipids also play critical roles in all of the body's cells as part of their surrounding envelopes, the cell membranes.

Matthew Leete/Getty Images

Thanks to internal fat pads, vital organs are cushioned from shock.

Some essential nutrients are soluble in fat. They are therefore found mainly in foods that contain fat and are absorbed most efficiently from them. These nutrients are the fat-soluble vitamins: A, D, E, and K. Other essential nutrients, the **essential fatty acids,** constitute parts of the fats themselves. As a later section explains, the essential fatty acids serve as raw materials from which the body makes molecules it requires. Fat also aids in the absorption of some phytochemicals, plant constituents believed to benefit health.

essential fatty acids fatty acids that the body needs but cannot make in amounts sufficient to meet physiological needs.

CONCEPT LINK 5-1

Controversy 2 describes the current research on phytochemicals (page 61).

FIGURE 5-2 Two Lunches

Both lunches contain the same number of calories, but the fat-rich lunch takes up less space and weighs less.

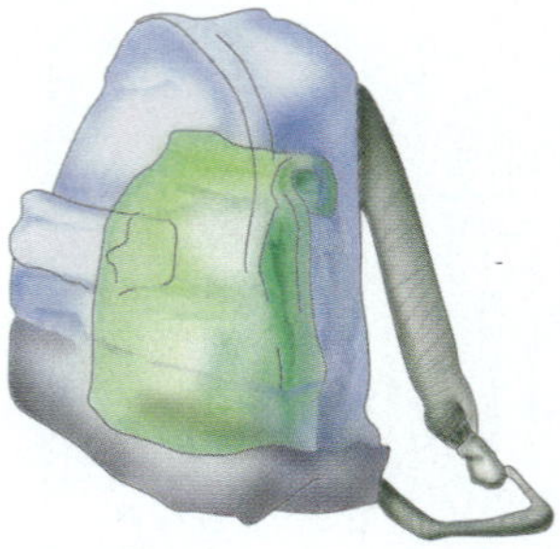

Carbohydrate-rich lunch
1 low-fat muffin
1 banana
2 oz carrot sticks
8 oz fruit yogurt

calories = 550
weight (g) = 500

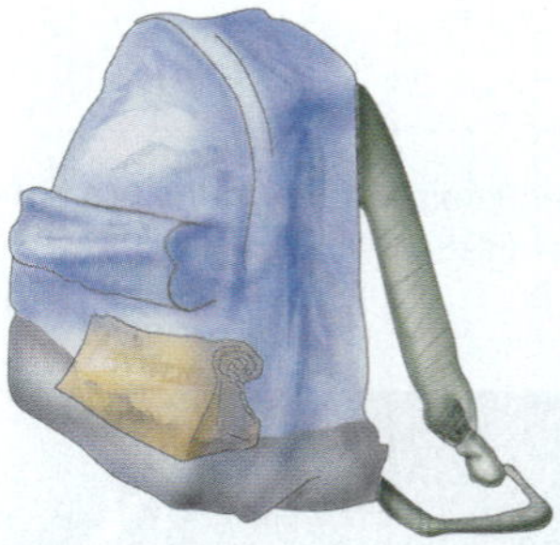

Fat-rich lunch
6 butter-style crackers
1 1/2 oz American cheese
2 oz trail mix with candy

calories = 550
weight (g) = 115

CONCEPT LINK 5-2

A reminder from Chapter 1:

- 1 g carbohydrate = 4 calories
- 1 g fat = 9 calories
- 1 g protein = 4 calories

KEY POINT Lipids not only serve as energy reserves but also cushion the vital organs, protect the body from temperature extremes, carry the fat-soluble nutrients and phytochemicals, serve as raw materials, and provide the major component of which cell membranes are made.

Usefulness of Fats in Food

The energy density of fats makes fat-rich foods valuable in many situations. A gram of fat or oil delivers more than twice as many calories as a gram of carbohydrate or protein. A hunter or hiker must consume a large amount of food energy to travel long distances or to survive in intensely cold weather. An athlete must meet often enormous energy needs to avoid weight loss that could impair performance. As Figure 5-2 demonstrates, for such a person fat-rich foods most efficiently provide the needed energy in the smallest package. But for a person who is not expending much energy in physical work, those same high-fat foods may deliver many unneeded calories in only a few bites.

People naturally like high-fat foods. Fat carries with it many dissolved compounds that give foods enticing aromas and flavors, such as the aroma of frying bacon or French fries. In fact, when a sick person refuses food, dietitians offer foods flavored with some fat to tempt that person to eat again. Fat also lends tenderness to foods such as meats and baked goods. Around the world, as fats become less expensive and more available in a given food supply, people consistently choose fatty foods more often.

Fat also contributes to **satiety,** the satisfaction of feeling full after a meal. The fat of swallowed food triggers a series of physiological events that slow down the movement of food through the digestive tract and promote satiety.[2] Even so, before the sensation of fullness stops them, people can easily overeat on fat-rich foods because the delicious taste of fat stimulates eating and each bite of a fat-rich food delivers many calories. Chapter 9 revisits the topic of appetite and its control.

KEY POINT Lipids provide more energy per gram than carbohydrate and protein, enhance the aromas and flavors of foods, and contribute to satiety, or a feeling of fullness, after a meal.

LO 5.2

A Close Look at Lipids

Each class of lipids—triglycerides, phospholipids, and sterols—possesses unique characteristics. As mentioned, the term *fat* refers to triglycerides, the major form of lipid found in the body and in foods. Triglycerides, in turn, are made of fatty acids and glycerol.

Triglycerides: Fatty Acids and Glycerol

Very few **fatty acids** are found free in the body or in foods; most are incorporated into large, complex compounds: triglycerides. The name almost explains itself: three fatty acids (*tri*) are attached to a molecule of **glycerol** to form a triglyceride molecule (Figure 5-3). Tissues all over the body can easily assemble triglycerides or disassemble them as needed.

Fatty acids can differ from one another in two ways: in chain length and in degree of saturation (explained next). Triglycerides usually include mixtures of various fatty acids. Depending on which fatty acids are incorporated into a triglyceride, the resulting fat will be soft or hard. Triglycerides containing mostly the shorter-chain

FIGURE 5-3 Triglyceride Formation

Glycerol, a small, water-soluble carbohydrate derivative, plus three fatty acids equals a triglyceride.

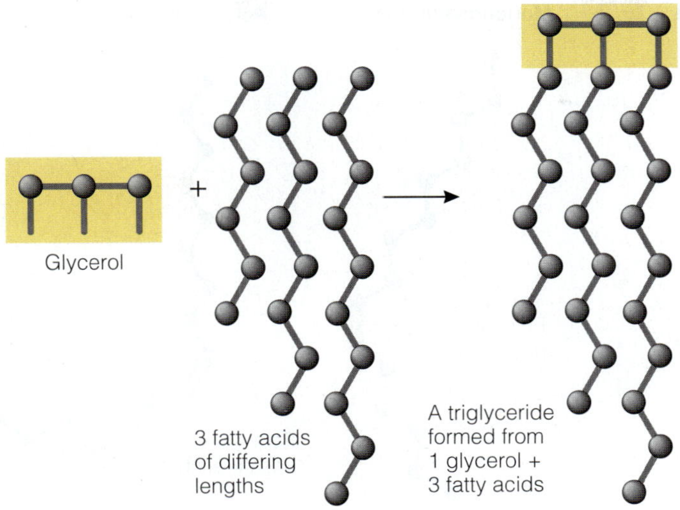

Small amounts of fat offer eaters both pleasure and needed nutrients.

fatty acids or the more unsaturated ones are softer and melt more readily at lower temperatures.

Each species of animal (including people) makes its own characteristic kinds of triglycerides, a function governed by genetics. Fats in the diet, though, can affect the types of triglycerides made because dietary fatty acids are often incorporated into triglycerides in the body. For example, many animals raised for food can be fed diets containing specific triglycerides to give the meat the types of fats that consumers demand.

KEY POINT The body combines three fatty acids with one glycerol to make a triglyceride, its storage form of fat. Fatty acids in food influence the composition of fats in the body.

Saturated Versus Unsaturated Fatty Acids

Saturation refers to whether or not a fatty acid chain is holding all of the hydrogen atoms it can hold. If every available bond from the carbons is holding a hydrogen, the chain forms a **saturated fatty acid;** it is filled to capacity with hydrogen. The zigzag structure on the left in Figure 5-4 represents a saturated fatty acid.

Saturation of Fatty Acids Sometimes, especially in the fatty acids of plants and fish, the chain has a place where hydrogens are missing: an "empty spot," or **point of unsaturation.**† A fatty acid carbon chain that possesses one or more points of unsaturation is an **unsaturated fatty acid.** With one point of unsaturation, the fatty acid is a **monounsaturated fatty acid** (see the second structure in Figure 5-4). With two or more points of unsaturation, it is a **polyunsaturated fatty acid,** sometimes abbreviated PUFA (see the third structure in Figure 5-4; other examples are given later in the chapter).

Melting Point and Fat Hardness The degree of saturation of the fatty acids in a fat affects the temperature at which the fat melts. Generally, the more unsaturated the fatty acids, the more liquid the fat is at room temperature. In contrast, the more saturated the fatty acids, the firmer the fat. Thus, looking at three fats—beef tallow

†These points of unsaturation can also be referred to as double bonds.

satiety (sat-EYE-uh-tee) the feeling of fullness or satisfaction that people experience after meals.

fatty acids organic acids composed of carbon chains of various lengths. Each fatty acid has an acid end and hydrogens attached to all of the carbon atoms of the chain.

glycerol (GLISS-er-all) an organic compound, three carbons long, of interest here because it serves as the backbone for triglycerides.

saturated fatty acid a fatty acid carrying the maximum possible number of hydrogen atoms (having no points of unsaturation). A saturated fat is a triglyceride that contains three saturated fatty acids.

point of unsaturation a site in a molecule where the bonding is such that additional hydrogen atoms can easily be attached.

unsaturated fatty acid a fatty acid that lacks some hydrogen atoms and has one or more points of unsaturation. An unsaturated fat is a triglyceride that contains one or more unsaturated fatty acids.

monounsaturated fatty acid a fatty acid containing one point of unsaturation.

polyunsaturated fatty acid (PUFA) a fatty acid with two or more points of unsaturation.

© Quest Photographic, Inc.

Fats melt at different temperatures: The more unsaturated a fat, the more liquid it is at room temperature. The more saturated a fat, the higher the temperature at which it melts.

FIGURE 5-4 Three Types of Fatty Acids

The more carbon atoms in a fatty acid, the longer it is. The more hydrogen atoms attached to those carbons, the more saturated the fatty acid is.

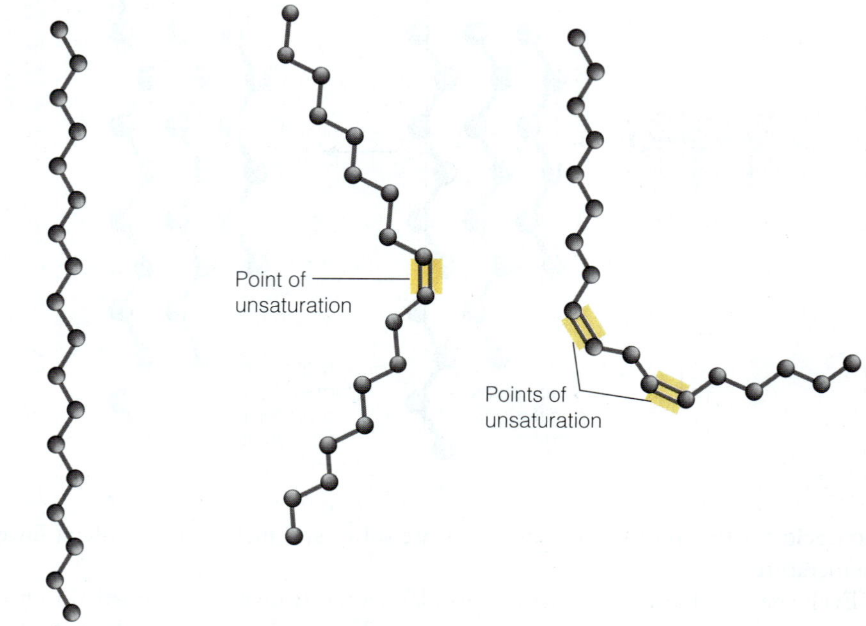

Did You Know?

There are three types of fatty acids: saturated, monounsaturated, and polyunsaturated.

Did You Know?

Health-care providers recommend replacing saturated fats with the "*UN*" fats—poly*UN*saturated and mono*UN*saturated—to benefit the heart.

- *Trans* fats are the topic of a later section.

saturated fats triglycerides in which most of the fatty acids are saturated.

***trans* fats** fats that contain any number of unusual fatty acids—*trans*-fatty acids—formed during processing.

monounsaturated fats triglycerides in which most of the fatty acids have one point of unsaturation (are monounsaturated).

polyunsaturated fats triglycerides in which most of the fatty acids have two or more points of unsaturation (are polyunsaturated).

(a type of beef fat), chicken fat, and safflower oil—beef tallow is the most saturated and the hardest; chicken fat is less saturated and somewhat soft; and safflower oil, which is the most unsaturated, is a liquid at room temperature.

If a health-care provider recommends limiting **saturated fats** or ***trans* fats** and using **monounsaturated fats** or **polyunsaturated fats** instead to protect your health, you can generally judge by the hardness of the fats which ones to choose. Figure 5-5 compares the percentages of saturated, monounsaturated, and polyunsaturated fatty acids in various fats and oils. To determine the degree of saturation of the fats in the oil you use, place it in a clear container in the refrigerator and watch for cloudiness. The least saturated oils remain clear. Olive oil, mostly monounsaturated fat, turns cloudy in the refrigerator while polyunsaturated vegetable oil stays clear. Olive oil is still excellent oil, however, from the standpoint of the health of the heart, as this chapter's Controversy reveals.

Where the Fatty Acids Are Found Most vegetable and fish oils are rich in polyunsaturated fatty acids; some vegetable oils, olive oil and canola oil in particular, are also rich in monounsaturated fatty acids; animal fats are generally the most saturated. But you have to know your oils—it is not enough to choose foods with labels claiming plant oils over those containing animal fats. Some nondairy whipped dessert toppings use coconut oil in place of cream (butterfat). Coconut oil does come from a plant, but it disobeys the rule that plant oils are less saturated than animal fats; the fatty acids of coconut oil are more saturated than those of cream and may add to heart disease risk. Palm oil, a vegetable oil used in food processing, is also highly saturated and has been shown to elevate blood cholesterol. Likewise, shortenings, stick margarine, and commercially fried or baked products may claim to be "all vegetable fat," but much of their fat may be of the harmful saturated or *trans* kind, as a later section makes clear.

When polyunsaturated fat replaces saturated fat and *trans* fat in the diet, the heart and blood lipids benefit.[3] Olive oil, rich in monounsaturated fatty acids and antioxidant phytochemicals, also benefits the heart when it replaces butter and other satu-

FIGURE 5-5 **Fatty Acid Composition of Common Food Fats**

Most fats are a mixture of saturated, monounsaturated, and polyunsaturated fatty acids.

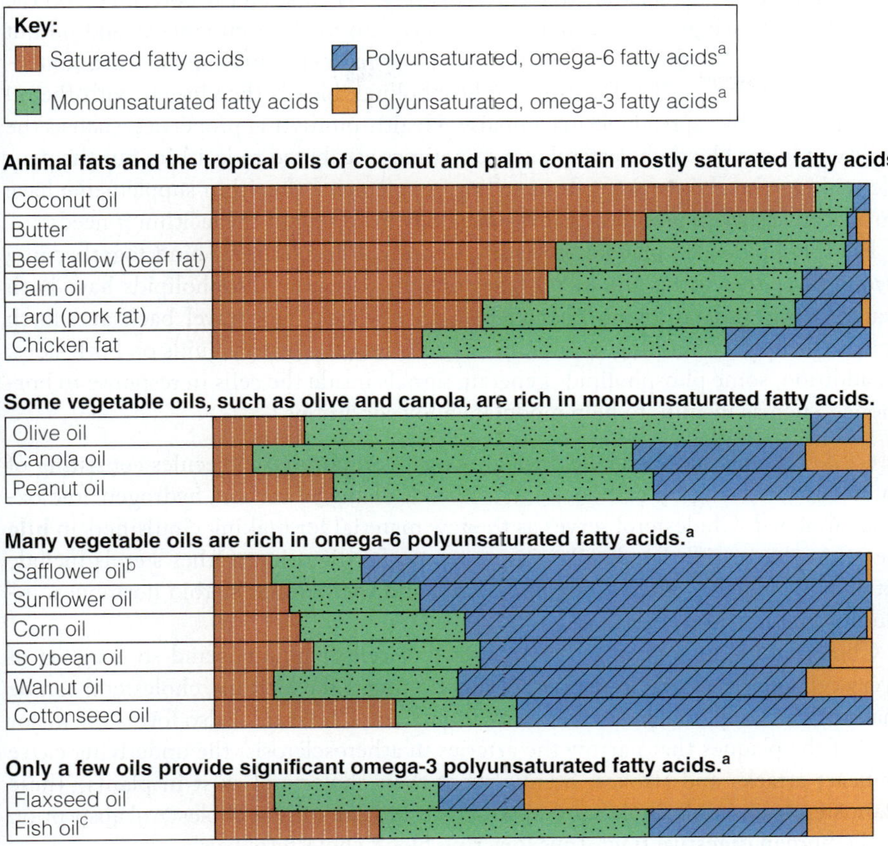

[a]*These families of polyunsaturated fatty acids are explained in a later section.*
[b]*Salad or cooking type over 70% linoleic acid.*
[c]*Fish oil average values derived from USDA data for salmon, sardine, and herring oils.*

Study this chart ASAP

rated fats in the diet, as it does in many traditional Mediterranean diets (see the Controversy section).[4] If you are a woman, take note: these observations apply to you as well as to men. By far, more women suffer from heart disease than from breast cancer, and the old myth that heart disease is a "man's disease" should be put to rest forever. In truth, heart disease kills more women in the United States than any other cause.

KEY POINT Fatty acids are energy-rich carbon chains that can be saturated (filled with hydrogens) or monounsaturated (with one point of unsaturation) or polyunsaturated (with more than one point of unsaturation). The degree of saturation of the fatty acids in a fat determines the fat's softness or hardness. Health-care providers recommend that both women and men consume unsaturated fats instead of saturated fats for heart health.

Phospholipids and Sterols

Thus far we have dealt with the largest of the three classes of lipids—the triglycerides and their component fatty acids. The other two classes—phospholipids and sterols—play important structural and regulatory roles in the body.

Phospholipids A phospholipid, like a triglyceride, consists of a molecule of glycerol with fatty acids attached, but it contains two, rather than three, fatty acids. In place of the third is a molecule containing phosphorus, which makes the phospholipid

Without help from emulsifiers, fats and water separate into layers.

soluble in water, while its fatty acids make it soluble in fat. This versatility permits any phospholipid to play a role in keeping fats dispersed in water—it can serve as an **emulsifier.**

Food manufacturers blend fat with watery ingredients by way of **emulsification.** Some salad dressings separate to form two layers—vinegar on the bottom, oil on the top. Other dressings, such as mayonnaise, are also made from vinegar and oil but never separate. The difference lies in a special ingredient of mayonnaise, the emulsifier lecithin in egg yolks. Lecithin, a phospholipid, blends the vinegar with the oil to form the stable, spreadable mayonnaise. Health-promoting properties, such as the ability to lower blood cholesterol, are sometimes attributed to lecithin, but the people making the claims profit from selling supplements. Lecithin supplements have no special ability to promote health—the body makes all of the lecithin it needs.

Phospholipids also play key roles in the body. Phospholipids bind together in a strong layer that forms the membranes of cells. Because phospholipids have both water-loving and fat-loving characteristics, they help fats travel back and forth across the lipid-containing membranes of cells into the watery fluids on both sides. In addition, some phospholipids generate signals inside the cells in response to hormones, such as insulin, to help modulate body conditions.

Sterols Sterols such as cholesterol are large, complicated molecules consisting of interconnected rings of carbon atoms with side chains of carbon, hydrogen, and oxygen attached. Cholesterol serves as the raw material for making emulsifiers in **bile** (see the next section for details), important to fat digestion. Other sterols include vitamin D, which is made from cholesterol, and the familiar steroid hormones, including the sex hormones.

Cholesterol is important in the structure of cell membranes and so is a part of every cell and necessary to the body's functioning. Like lecithin, cholesterol can be made by the body, so it is not an essential nutrient. Cholesterol also forms the major part of the plaques that narrow the arteries in atherosclerosis, the underlying cause of heart attacks and strokes. Sterols other than cholesterol exist in plants. These plant sterols resemble cholesterol in structure and can inhibit cholesterol absorption in the human digestive tract, thus lowering blood cholesterol levels.

KEY POINT Phospholipids, including lecithin, play key roles in cell membranes; sterols play roles as part of bile, vitamin D, the sex hormones, and other important compounds. Plant sterols inhibit cholesterol absorption.

LO 5.3

Lipids in the Body

From the moment they enter the body, lipids affect the body's functioning and condition. They also demand special handling, because fat separates from water and body fluids consist largely of water.

Digestion and Absorption of Fats

A bite of food in the mouth first encounters the enzymes of saliva. An enzyme produced by the tongue plays a major role in digesting milk fat in infants but is of little importance to digestion in adults.

Fat in the Stomach After being chewed and swallowed, the food travels to the stomach, where droplets of fat separate from the watery components and tend to float as a layer on top. Even the stomach's powerful churning cannot completely disperse the fat in the watery parts, so little fat digestion takes place in the stomach.

Fat in the Small Intestine As the stomach contents empty into the small intestine, the digestive system faces a problem: how to thoroughly mix fats, which are

emulsifier a substance that mixes with both fat and water and permanently disperses the fat in the water, forming an emulsion.

emulsification the process of mixing lipid with water by adding an emulsifier.

bile an emulsifier made by the liver from cholesterol and stored in the gallbladder. Bile does not digest fat as enzymes do but emulsifies it so that enzymes in the watery fluids may contact it and split the fatty acids from their glycerol for absorption.

now separated, with its own watery fluids. The solution is an emulsifier: bile. Bile contains compounds made from cholesterol that work as emulsifiers; one end of each molecule attracts and holds fat, while the other end is attracted to and held by water.

By the time fat enters the small intestine, the gallbladder, which stores the liver's output of bile, has contracted and squirted its bile into the intestine. Bile mixes fat droplets with watery fluid by emulsifying them (see Figure 5-6) and suspending them in the fluid until the fat-digesting enzymes contributed by the pancreas can split them into smaller molecules for absorption. To review: first, the digestive system mixes fats with bile-containing digestive juices to emulsify the fats; then, fat-digesting enzymes can break the fats down.

People sometimes wonder how a person without a gallbladder can digest food. The gallbladder is just a storage organ. Without it, the liver still produces bile but delivers it into a duct which conducts it into the small intestine instead of into the gallbladder.

Fat Absorption Once the intestine's contents are emulsified, fat-splitting enzymes act on triglycerides to split fatty acids from their glycerol backbones. Free fatty acids, phospholipids, and **monoglycerides** cling together in balls surrounded by bile emulsifiers. At this point, the fats face another watery barrier, the watery layer of mucus that coats the absorptive lining of the digestive tract. Fats must traverse this layer to enter the cells of the digestive tract lining. The solution again depends on bile, this time in the balls of digested lipids. The bile shuttles the lipids across the watery mucus layer to the waiting absorptive cells of the intestinal villi. The cells then extract the lipids. The bile may be absorbed and reused by the body, or it may exit with the feces, as was shown in Figure 4-6 of Chapter 4.

The digestive tract absorbs triglycerides from a meal with remarkable efficiency: up to 98 percent of fats consumed are absorbed. Very little fat is excreted by a healthy system. The process of fat digestion takes time, though, so the more fat taken in at a meal, the slower the digestive system action becomes. The efficient series of events just described is depicted in Figure 5-7.

KEY POINT In the stomach, fats separate from other food components. In the small intestine, bile emulsifies the fats, enzymes digest them, and the intestinal cells absorb them.

CONCEPT LINK 5-3

Chapter 3 defined *bile* as a cholesterol-containing digestive fluid made by the liver, stored in the gallbladder, and released into the small intestine when needed (page 83).

FIGURE 5-6 The Action of Bile in Fat Digestion

Detergents are emulsifiers and work the same way, which is why they are effective in removing grease spots from clothes. Molecule by molecule, the grease is dissolved out of the spot and suspended in the water, where it can be rinsed away.

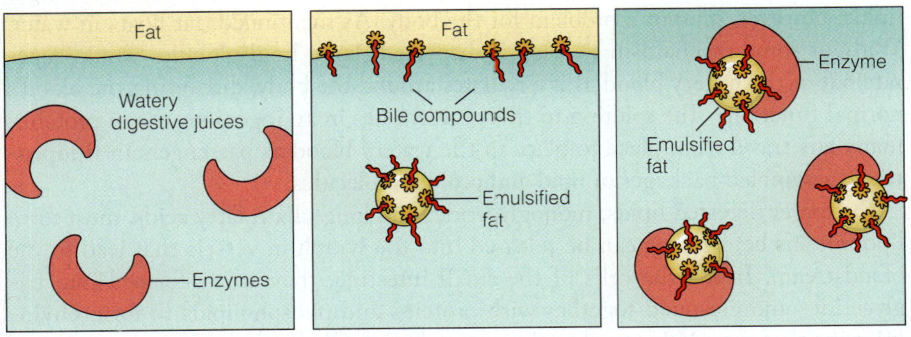

In the stomach, the fat and watery digestive juices tend to separate. Enzymes are in the water and can't get at the fat.

When fat enters the small intestine, the gallbladder secretes bile. Bile compounds have an affinity for both fat and water, so bile can mix the fat into the water.

After emulsification, more fat is exposed to the enzymes, and fat digestion proceeds efficiently.

monoglycerides (mon-oh-GLISS-er-ides) products of the digestion of lipids; consist of glycerol molecules with one fatty acid attached (*mono* means "one"; *glyceride* means "a compound of glycerol").

FIGURE 5-7

ANIMATED!

The Process of Lipid Digestion and Absorption

1. In the mouth and stomach:
   Little fat digestion takes place.

2. In the small intestine:
   Digestive enzymes accomplish most fat digestion in the small intestine. There, bile emulsifies fat, making it available for enzyme action. The enzymes cleave triglycerides into free fatty acids, glycerol, and monoglycerides.

3. At the intestinal lining:
   The parts are absorbed by intestinal villi. Glycerol and short-chain fatty acids enter directly into the bloodstream.

4. The cells of the intestinal lining convert large lipid fragments, such as monoglycerides and long-chain fatty acids, back into triglycerides and combine them with protein, forming chylomicrons (a type of lipoprotein) that travel in the lymph vessels to the bloodstream.

5. In the large intestine:
   A small amount of cholesterol trapped in fiber exits with the feces

Note: In this diagram, molecules of fatty acids are shown as large objects, but, in reality, molecules of fatty acids are too small to see even with a powerful microscope, while villi are visible to the naked eye.

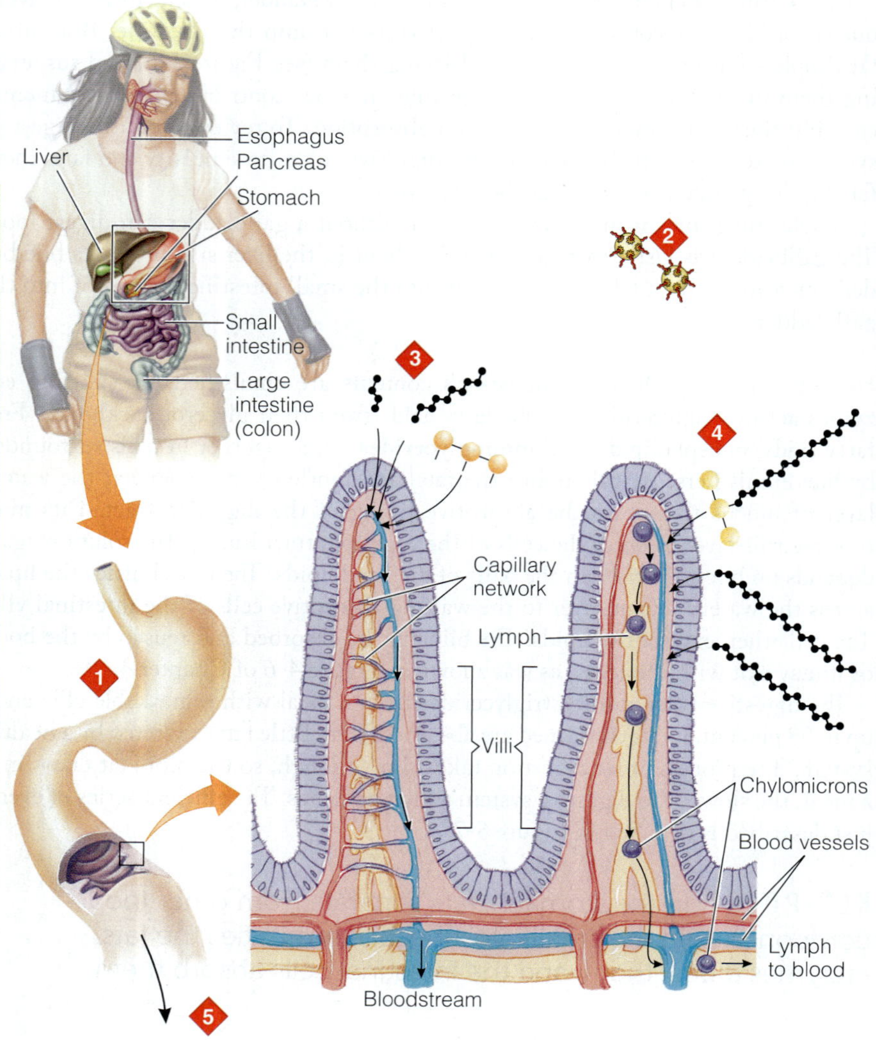

lipoproteins (LYE-poh-PRO-teens, LIH-poh-PRO-teens) clusters of lipids associated with protein, which serve as transport vehicles for lipids in blood and lymph.

chylomicrons (KYE-low-MY-krons), lipoproteins formed when lipids from a meal are combined with carrier proteins in the cells of the intestinal lining. Chylomicrons transport food fats through the watery body fluids to the liver and other tissues.

Transport of Fats

Glycerol and shorter-chain fatty acids pass directly through the cells of the intestinal lining into the bloodstream where they travel unassisted to the liver. The larger lipids, however, present a problem for the body. As mentioned, fat floats in water. Without some mechanism to keep it dispersed, large lipid globules would separate out of the watery blood as it circulates around the body, disrupting the blood's normal functions. The solution to this problem lies in an ingenious use of proteins: many fats travel from place to place in the watery blood as passengers in **lipoproteins,** assembled packages of lipid and protein molecules.

The larger digested lipids, monoglycerides and long-chain fatty acids, must form lipoproteins before they can be released into the lymph in vessels that lead to the bloodstream. Inside the cells of the small intestine, they are re-formed into triglycerides and clustered together with proteins and phospholipids to form **chylomicrons** that can safely travel in the watery blood. Chylomicrons form one type of lipoproteins (shown in Figure 5-7); other types are discussed later with regard to their profound effects on health.

KEY POINT Glycerol and short-chain fatty acids travel in the bloodstream unassisted. Other lipids are incorporated into chylomicrons for transport in the lymph and blood. Fats need special transport vehicles—the lipoproteins—to carry them in watery body fluids.

CONCEPT LINK 5-4
The body's circulatory system and lymphatic system are described and depicted in Chapter 3, pages 71–74.

Storing and Using the Body's Fat

Methodically, the body conserves fat molecules not immediately required for energy. Stored fat serves as a sort of "rainy day" fund to fuel the body's activities at times when food is unavailable, when illness impairs the appetite, or when energy expenditures increase.

The Body's Fat Stores Many triglycerides eaten in foods are transported by the chylomicrons to the fat depots—muscles, breasts, the external fat layer under the skin, the internal fat pads of the abdomen, and others—where they are stored by the body's fat cells for later use. When a person's body starts to run out of available fuel from food, it begins to retrieve this stored fat to use for energy. (It also draws on its stored glycogen, as the last chapter described.)

- Chapter 9 discusses health risks of too much abdominal fat.

The body can also store excess carbohydrate as fat, but this conversion is not energy-efficient. Figure 5-8 illustrates a simplified series of conversion steps from carbohydrate to fat. Before excess glucose can be stored as fat, it must first be broken into tiny fragments and then reassembled into fatty acids, steps that require energy to perform. Fat requires fewer chemical steps before storage.

What Happens When the Tissues Need Energy? Fat cells respond to the call for energy by dismantling stored fat molecules (triglycerides) and releasing fatty acids into the blood. Upon receiving these fatty acids, the energy-hungry cells break them down further into small fragments. Finally, each fat fragment is combined with a fragment derived from glucose, and the energy-releasing process continues, liberating energy, carbon dioxide, and water. The way to use more of the energy stored as body fat, then, is to create a greater demand for it in the tissues by decreasing intake of food energy, by increasing the body's expenditure of energy, or both.

Carbohydrate in Fat Breakdown When fat is broken down to provide cellular energy, carbohydrate helps the process run most efficiently. Without carbohydrate, products of incomplete fat breakdown (ketones) build up in the tissues and blood, and they spill out into the urine.

© Image Source/Jupiter Images

Body fat supplies much of the fuel these muscles need to do their work.

FIGURE 5-8 Glucose to Fat

Glucose can be used for energy, or it can be changed into fat and stored.

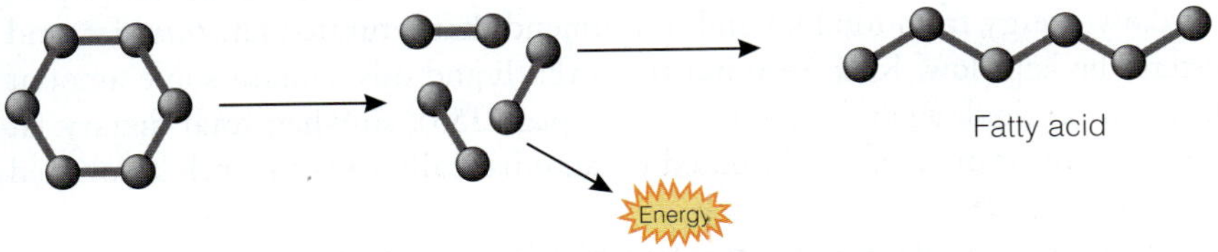

Glucose is broken down into fragments.

The fragments can provide immediate energy for the tissues.

Or, if the tissues need no more energy, the fragments can be reassembled, not back to glucose but into fatty acid chains.

CONCEPT LINK 5-5

Chapter 4 described the need for carbohydrate in fat breakdown on page 126.

For weight-loss dieters who want to use their body fat for energy, knowing these details of energy metabolism is less important than remembering what research and common sense tell us: successful weight loss depends on taking in less energy than the body needs—not on the proportion of energy nutrients in the diet.[5] For the body's health, however, the proportions of certain lipids in the diet matter greatly, as the next section makes clear.

- Metabolic interactions among energy nutrients are of interest to people wanting to manage body weight; Chapter 9 describes them in more detail.

KEY POINT When low on fuel, the body draws on its stored fat for energy. Carbohydrate is necessary for the complete breakdown of fat.

LO 5.4

Dietary Fat, Cholesterol, and Health

High intakes of certain dietary fats are associated with serious diseases. So much research has focused on the links between diet and diseases that an entire chapter, Chapter 11, is devoted to presenting the details of these connections.

Heart and Artery Disease The person who chooses a diet too high in saturated fats or *trans* fats and too low in healthy oil from fish invites heart and artery disease (CVD), the number-one killer of adults in the United States and Canada.[6] Saturated fatty acids and *trans*-fatty acids both worsen the blood lipid profile; saturated fatty acids also contribute to blood clotting associated with heart attacks, while oils from fish oppose this action.[7] Some have questioned whether *trans* fat made by ruminant animals might be less harmful to consumers than the manufactured kind, but this idea has not gained support from research.[8]

© Colour, 2011/Shutterstock.com

Cancer As for cancer, a few studies link a diet high in saturated fats with greater-than-average risk of developing certain cancers.[9] However, authorities conclude that saturated fats pose the greatest public health hazard in terms of heart disease, not cancers.[10]

Obesity Obesity carries serious risks to health. A diet high in energy-rich fatty foods makes overconsumption of calories likely and encourages unneeded weight gain. Chapter 9 provides many details.

Recommendations for Lipid Intakes

Some fat in the diet is essential for good health, but too much fat, especially saturated fat, increases the risks for chronic diseases. Guidelines aim to keep fat intakes within healthy limits.

A Healthy Range of Fat Intakes Defining an exact gram amount of fat, saturated fat, or cholesterol that begins to harm people's health is not possible, so the DRI committee did not set Tolerable Upper Intake Levels for the lipids (see Table 5-2). Instead, the DRI and 2005 Dietary Guidelines set a range of 20 to 35 percent of daily energy from total fat and recommend that saturated fat, *trans* fat, and cholesterol be kept low. Keep in mind that even liquid oils contain some amount of saturated fat (look again at Figure 5-5 on page 155), so when total dietary fat exceeds 35 percent of calories, saturated fat automatically rises to levels associated with chronic diseases.

Today's average fat intake as a percentage of calories is lower than it was 40 years ago: 34 percent of total daily calories now versus 45 percent then.[11] At first glance this appears to be a healthy trend—until grams of fat are inspected. Today, people eat more grams of fat, not less, but they also take in far more grams of carbohydrate than before. The shift in the energy nutrient balance toward carbohydrate produced

TABLE 5-2 **Lipid Intake Recommendations for Healthy People**

1. Total fat[a]

Dietary Guidelines for Americans

- Keep total fat intake between 20 and 35% of calories from mostly polyunsaturated and monounsaturated fat sources such as fish, nuts, and vegetable oils.
- Select and prepare foods that are lean, low-fat, or fat-free.

Dietary Reference Intakes

- An acceptable range of fat intake is estimated at 20 to 35% of total calories.

2. Saturated fat

American Heart Association

- Limit saturated fat to less than 7% of total energy.

Dietary Guidelines for Americans;[b] Dietary Reference Intakes[c]

- Keep saturated fat intake low, less than 10% of calories, within the context of an adequate diet.

3. *Trans* fat

Dietary Guidelines for Americans

- Keep *trans* fat intake as low as possible.

American Heart Association

- Limit *trans* fat to less than 1% of total energy.

4. Polyunsaturated fatty acids

Dietary Reference Intakes[c]

- Linoleic acid (5 to 10% of total calories):
  17 grams per day for young men.
  12 grams per day for young women.
- Linolenic acid (0.6 to 1.2% of total calories):
  1.6 grams per day for men.
  1.1 grams per day for women.

5. Cholesterol

American Heart Association, Dietary Guidelines for Americans, and World Health Organization

- Limit cholesterol to less than 300 milligrams per day.[d]

Dietary Reference Intakes[c]

- Minimize cholesterol intake within the context of a healthy diet.

[a]*Includes monounsaturated fatty acids.*

[b]The Dietary Guidelines for Americans, *2005 use the term solid fats to describe sources of saturated fatty acids. Solid fats include milk fat, fats of high-fat meats and cheeses, hard margarines, butter, lard, and shortening.*

[c]*For DRI values set for various life stages, see the inside front cover. Linoleic and linolenic acids are defined later in this chapter.*

[d]*People with heart disease should aim for less than 200 mg/day.*

a misleading mathematical drop in the percentage of fat calories. Bottom line: before fat recommendations in terms of percentages can be of benefit, total calorie intakes must be brought under control.

In practical terms, for a 2000-calorie diet, 20 to 35 percent represents 400 to 700 calories from fat (roughly 45 to 75 grams, or about 9 to 19 teaspoons). Part of this fat allowance should provide the essential fatty acids linoleic acid and linolenic acid (these are described in a later section). DRI recommended intakes have been set for these two fatty acids, listed in Table 5-2. To supply these fatty acids, the USDA Food Guide of Chapter 2 recommends that people consume a small amount of raw vegetable oils daily. For saturated and *trans* fat, in contrast, the lower the better.

U.S. Fat and Saturated Fat Intakes According to surveys, people in the United States consume about 34 percent of their total energy from fat, a percentage within bounds. Saturated fat, however, contributes about 12 percent of calories, thus exceeding the Dietary Guidelines limit of 10 percent.[12]

Some points about fats and heart health are presented next because they form the foundation of lipid intake recommendations. The lipoproteins take center stage, because they play important roles concerning the heart.

KEY POINT Energy from fat should provide 20 to 35 percent of the total energy in the diet; intakes of saturated fat, *trans* fat, and cholesterol should be kept low.

Lipoproteins and Heart Disease Risk

Recall that monoglycerides and long-chain fatty acids from digested food fat depend on chylomicrons, a type of lipoprotein, to transport them around the body.

CONCEPT LINK 5-6

The USDA MyPyramid suggests calorie intakes for groups of people. They can be found in Table 2-2 on page 44.

- The *Dietary Guidelines for Americans 2005* urge people to consume less than 10 percent of calories from saturated fatty acids within a healthy diet. Some examples:
  - *1,600-calorie diet: 18 grams*
  - *2,000-calorie diet: 20 grams*
  - *2,200-calorie diet: 24 grams*
  - *2,500-calorie diet: 25 grams*
  - *2,800-calorie diet: 31 grams*

- The American Heart Association Diet and Lifestyle Recommendations are found in Chapter 11.

Chylomicrons and other lipoproteins are clusters of protein and phospholipids that act as emulsifiers—they attract both water and fat to enable their large lipid passengers to travel dispersed in the watery body fluids. The tissues of the body can extract whatever fat they need from chylomicrons passing by in the bloodstream. The remnants are then picked up by the liver, which dismantles them and reuses their parts.

very-low-density lipoproteins (VLDL) lipoproteins that transport triglycerides and other lipids from the liver to various tissues in the body.

low-density lipoproteins (LDL) lipoproteins that transport lipids from the liver to other tissues such as muscle and fat; contain a large proportion of cholesterol.

high-density lipoproteins (HDL) lipoproteins that return cholesterol from the tissues to the liver for dismantling and disposal; contain a large proportion of protein.

inflammation (in-flam-MAY-shun) an immune defense against injury, infection, or allergens and marked by heat, fever, and pain. Also defined in Chapter 3.

oxidation interaction of a compound with oxygen; in this case, a damaging effect by a chemically reactive form of oxygen. Chapter 7 provides details.

dietary antioxidant (anti-OX-ih-dant) a substance in food that significantly decreases the damaging effects of reactive compounds, such as reactive forms of oxygen and nitrogen, on tissue functioning (*anti* means "against"; *oxy* means "oxygen").

Major Lipoproteins: VLDL, LDL, HDL

In addition to the chylomicrons, the body uses three other types of lipoproteins to carry fats:

- **Very-low-density lipoproteins (VLDL),** which carry triglycerides and other lipids made in the liver to the body cells for their use.
- **Low-density lipoproteins (LDL),** which transport cholesterol and other lipids to the tissues. LDL are made from VLDL after they have donated many of their triglycerides to body cells.
- **High-density lipoproteins (HDL),** which are critical in carrying cholesterol away from body cells to the liver for disposal.

The last two of these lipoproteins, LDL and HDL, play major roles in heart health and are the focus of most lipid recommendations aimed at reducing the risk of heart disease. Figure 5-9 depicts typical lipoproteins and demonstrates how a lipoprotein's density changes with its lipid and protein contents.

The LDL and HDL Difference

The separate functions and effects of LDL and HDL are worth a moment's attention because they carry important implications for the health of the heart and blood vessels.

- Both LDL and HDL carry lipids in the blood, but LDL are larger, lighter, and richer in cholesterol; HDL are smaller, denser, and packaged with more protein.
- LDL deliver triglycerides and cholesterol to the tissues; HDL scavenge excess cholesterol and other lipids from the tissues to the liver for disposal.
- LDL carry lipids that trigger **inflammation** that may contribute to heart disease; HDL oppose inflammatory processes and protect against heart attacks.[13]

FIGURE 5-9 **Lipoproteins**

As the graph shows, the density of a lipoprotein is determined by its lipid-to-protein ratio. All lipoproteins contain protein, cholesterol, phospholipids, and triglycerides in varying amounts. An LDL has a high ratio of lipid to protein (about 80 percent lipid to 20 percent protein) and is especially high in cholesterol. An HDL has more protein relative to its lipid content (about equal parts lipid and protein).

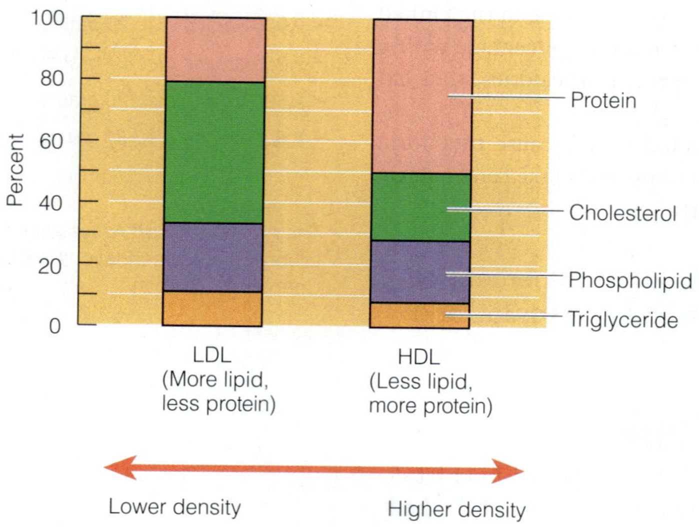

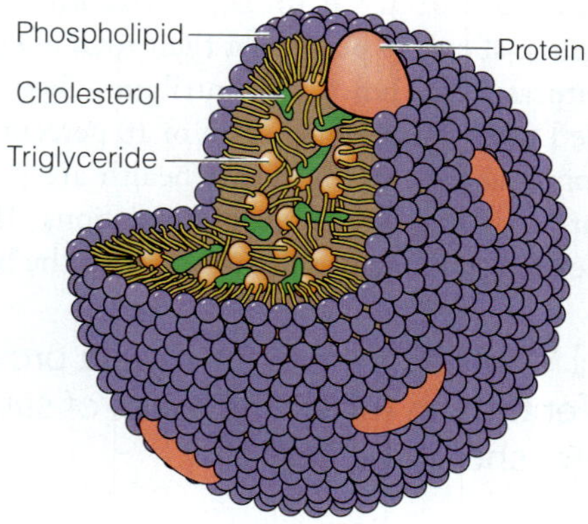

A typical lipoprotein

Both LDL and HDL carry cholesterol, but elevated blood LDL concentrations warn of an increased risk of heart attack, whereas elevated HDL concentrations point to a reduced risk. Thus, some people refer to LDL as "bad" cholesterol and HDL as "good" cholesterol—yet they carry the same kind of cholesterol. The difference to health between LDL and HDL lies in the proportions of lipids they contain and the tasks they perform, not in the *type* of cholesterol they carry.

The Importance of LDL and HDL Cholesterol The importance of blood cholesterol to heart health cannot be overstated.‡ The blood lipid profile, a medical test mentioned at the beginning of this chapter, tells much about a person's blood concentrations of cholesterol and the lipoproteins that carry it. High blood LDL cholesterol and low HDL cholesterol account for two major risk factors for CVD (see Table 5-3). And for LDL cholesterol, the lower the better for heart health.[14]

LDL Oxidation An important detail about LDL concerns its susceptibility to damage by **oxidation.** Oxidation of the lipid part of LDL may trigger inflammation, thus contributing to the damage to the arteries of the heart. Adequate intakes of **dietary antioxidants,** such as vitamin C, vitamin E, the mineral selenium, and antioxidant phytochemicals consumed in foods oppose LDL oxidation and correlate with low heart disease risk; supplements of these compounds generally provide no heart benefits and they carry some risks of their own, as Chapter 7 points out.[15]

KEY POINT The chief lipoproteins are chylomicrons, VLDL, LDL, and HDL. Blood LDL and HDL concentrations are among the major risk factors for heart disease. LDL are susceptible to oxidation and cause inflammation.

What Does *Food* Cholesterol Have to Do with *Blood* Cholesterol?

The answer may be "Not as much as most people think." Most saturated food fats (and *trans* fats) raise harmful blood cholesterol more than food *cholesterol* does.

Does Cholesterol Matter? When told that dietary cholesterol doesn't matter as much as saturated fat, people may then jump to the wrong conclusion—that blood cholesterol doesn't matter. It does matter. High blood LDL cholesterol and low blood HDL cholesterol are major indicators of CVD risk. The main dietary factors associated with such harmful blood cholesterol levels are high saturated fat and *trans* fat intakes.

Cholesterol Sources and Body Response Dietary cholesterol makes a smaller but still significant contribution to elevated blood cholesterol.[16] Cholesterol intakes in the United States average 237 milligrams a day for women and 358 for men. The margin note lists the top contributors of cholesterol to the U.S. diet. The Dietary Guidelines 2005 recommend a cholesterol intake of below 300 milligrams per day for healthy people.

Genetic inheritance modifies everyone's ability to handle dietary cholesterol.[17] Most healthy people exhibit little increase in their blood cholesterol when they consume limited amounts of eggs, shellfish, liver, and other cholesterol-containing foods because the body slows its cholesterol synthesis when the diet provides cholesterol. Cholesterol differs from salt and solid fats and added sugar in this respect: it cannot be omitted from the diet without omitting foods that are nutritious and sometimes low in fat. Moderation, not elimination, is key for most people as far as cholesterol-containing foods are concerned. People with high blood cholesterol, however, may benefit from limiting their cholesterol intake to less than 200 milligrams per day.

‡*Blood, plasma,* and *serum* all refer to about the same thing; this book uses the term *blood* cholesterol. Plasma is blood with the cells removed; in serum, the clotting factors are also removed. The concentration of cholesterol is not much altered by these treatments.

• Chapter 11 provides details about the effects of dietary factors on heart disease.

Did You Know?

Here's a trick:
Remember **H**DL is **H**ealthy.
LDL is **L**ess healthy.

• Standards for blood lipids are found in Chapter 11.

CONCEPT LINK 5-7

Phytochemicals are discussed in Controversy 2 (page 61).

Did You Know?

The best diet to oppose heart disease is low in saturated fats, including *trans* fats, and high in fruit, vegetables, whole grains, and legumes, with enough polyunsaturated oils to meet nutrient needs within energy needs.

• These five foods contribute about 70% of the food cholesterol in the U.S. diet:

- *eggs*
- *beef*
- *poultry*
- *cheese*
- *milk*

TABLE 5-3 Modifiable Lifestyle Factors in Heart Disease Risk

The more of these factors present in a person's life, the more urgent the need for changes in diet and lifestyle to reduce heart disease risk:

- High blood LDL cholesterol.
- Low blood HDL cholesterol.
- High blood pressure (hypertension).
- Diabetes (insulin resistance).
- Obesity.
- Physical inactivity.
- Cigarette smoking.
- A diet high in saturated fats, including *trans* fats, and low in fish, vegetables, legumes, fruit, and whole grains.

Family history, older age, and male gender are risk factors that cannot be changed.

- Sources of monounsaturated fats:
  - *Olive oil, canola oil, peanut oil*
  - *Avocados*
- Sources of polyunsaturated fats:
  - *Vegetable oils (safflower, sesame, soy, corn, sunflower)*
  - *Nuts and seeds*
  - *Fatty fish*

KEY POINT Elevated blood cholesterol is a risk factor for cardiovascular disease. Among major dietary factors that raise blood cholesterol, saturated fat and *trans* fat intakes are most influential. Dietary cholesterol raises blood cholesterol to a lesser degree. Low-fat cholesterol-containing foods are nutritious and most people can eat them in moderation.

Recommendations Applied

In a welcome trend, the number of U.S. citizens with high total and LDL cholesterol is dropping.[18] Even so, heart disease still tops the charts of killer diseases in the United States and most people are wise to choose a diet that provides 20 to 35 per-

FIGURE 5-10 **Food Fat, Saturated Fat, and Calories**

You can find much of the saturated fat and calories in food by looking for the fat. The fats of meat, milk, and added fats are the main contributors of saturated fat to the U.S. diet. When you trim fat, you trim calories and often saturated fat.

Nutrition Facts

Amount Per Serving

Pork chop (5 ounces) with 1/2 inch of fat

Calories 450	Calories from Fat 315
	% Daily Value
Total Fat 35g	**54%**
Saturated Fat 13g	**65%**
Cholesterol 130mg	**43%**

Potato (5 ounces) with 1 tablespoon butter and 1 tablespoon sour cream

Calories 400	Calories from Fat 250
	% Daily Value
Total Fat 28g	**43%**
Saturated Fat 18g	**90%**
Cholesterol 37mg	**12%**

Whole milk (1 cup)

Calories 150	Calories from Fat 70
	% Daily Value
Total Fat 8g	**12%**
Saturated Fat 5g	**25%**
Cholesterol 24mg	**8%**

Pork chop (4 ounces) with fat trimmed off

Calories 230	Calories from Fat 100
	% Daily Value
Total Fat 11g	**17%**
Saturated Fat 4g	**20%**
Cholesterol 107mg	**36%**

Plain potato (5 ounces)

Calories 150	Calories from Fat 0
	% Daily Value
Total Fat 0g	**0%**
Saturated Fat 0g	**0%**
Cholesterol 0mg	**0%**

Fat-free milk (1 cup)

Calories 90	Calories from Fat 0
	% Daily Value
Total Fat 0g	**0%**
Saturated Fat 0g	**0%**
Cholesterol 5mg	**2%**

© Polara Studios Inc. (all)

cent of its calories from mostly unsaturated fats and that keeps saturated fat and *trans* fat as low as possible (less than 10 percent and 1 percent of calories, respectively).[19]

Trimming Saturated Fat to Lower LDL To repeat, dietary saturated fat and *trans* fat are potent in triggering a rise in LDL cholesterol in the blood. A dietary tactic often effective against high blood cholesterol is to trim the saturated fat and *trans* fat from foods and replace them with monounsaturated and polyunsaturated fats, within a reasonable calorie intake.[20] The Controversy section provides evidence about both monounsaturated and polyunsaturated fats in relation to disease risk.

The photos of Figure 5-10 show that food trimmed of fat is also trimmed of saturated fat and energy.[21] A pork chop trimmed of its border of fat loses almost 70 percent of its saturated fat, 23 milligrams of cholesterol, and 220 calories. A plain baked potato has no saturated fat or cholesterol and about 40 percent of the calories of one with butter and sour cream. Choosing fat-free milk over whole milk provides large savings of saturated fat, calories, and cholesterol. Note that much of the cholesterol of the pork chop remained after trimming because cholesterol forms part of the cell membranes of muscle tissue. Figure 5-11 identifies top sources of saturated fat in the U.S. diet. Fats from animal sources (meat fats and butterfat) contribute about 60 percent of the saturated fats in most people's diets.[22] *Trans* fat sources are identified later on.

Raising HDL As for HDL cholesterol, dietary measures are generally ineffective at significantly raising its concentrations. Instead, regular physical activity defends against heart disease partly because it effectively raises HDL, as the Think Fitness feature on page 166 points out.

KEY POINT Trimming fat from food trims calories and, often, saturated fat as well. Dietary measures to lower LDL in the blood involve reducing saturated fat and *trans* fat and substituting monounsaturated and polyunsaturated fats.

FIGURE 5-11

Top Contributors of Saturated Fats to the U.S. Diet

These foods supply about 80% of the saturated fat in the U.S. diet. The remainder comes from foods supplying less than 2% each, such as cold cuts, pork, cream, bacon, ham, nuts and seeds, pies and cobblers, and nondairy creamers and toppings. Note that fruits, grains, and vegetables are insignificant sources, unless saturated fats are added during processing or preparation.

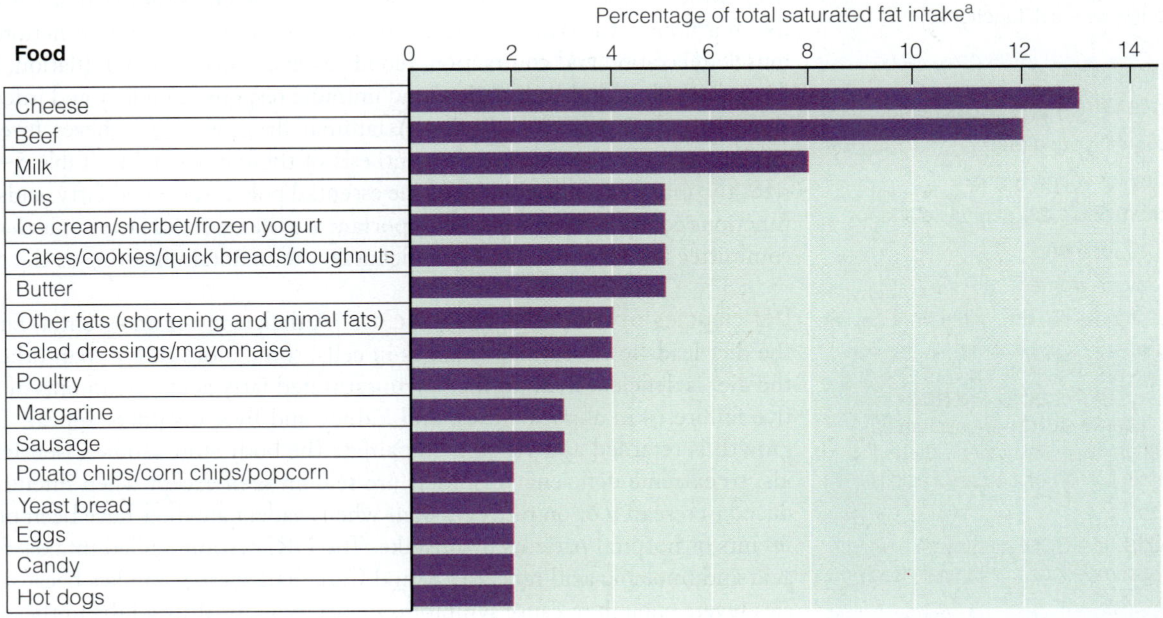

[a]Rounded values

THINK FITNESS

Why Exercise the Body for the Health of the Heart?

Every leading authority recommends physical activity to promote and maintain the health of the heart. The blood, arteries, heart, and other body tissues respond to exercise in these ways:

- Blood HDL concentration increases, shifting blood lipids in a healthy direction.
- The muscles of the heart and arteries strengthen and circulation improves, easing delivery of blood to the lungs and tissues.
- A larger volume of blood is pumped with each heartbeat, reducing the heart's workload.
- The body grows leaner, reducing overall risk of cardiovascular disease.

START NOW — CENGAGENOW Ready to make a change? Consult the online behavior-change planner to help plan for enough physical activity each day to strengthen the health of your heart at **www.cengage.com/sso.**

TABLE 5-4 Functions of the Essential Fatty Acids

These roles for the essential fatty acids are known, but others are under investigation.

- Provide raw material for eicosanoids.
- Serve as structural and functional parts of cell membranes.
- Contribute lipids to the brain and nerves.
- Promote normal growth and vision.
- Assist in gene regulation.
- Maintain outer structures of the skin, thus protecting against water loss.
- Help regulate genetic activities affecting metabolism.
- Support immune cell functions.

Dietary Reference Intakes

Linoleic acid (5 to 10% of total calories):

- 17 g per day for young men.
- 12 g per day for young women.

Linolenic acid (0.6 to 1.2% of total calories):

- 1.6 g per day for men.
- 1.1 g per day for women.

For other life stages, see the inside front cover.

linoleic (lin-oh-LAY-ic) **acid** and **linolenic** (lin-oh-LEN-ic) **acid** polyunsaturated fatty acids that are essential nutrients for human beings. The full name of linolenic acid is *alpha-linolenic acid.*

eicosanoids (eye-COSS-ah-noyds) biologically active compounds that regulate body functions.

LO 5.5, 5.6

Essential Polyunsaturated Fatty Acids

The human body needs fatty acids, and it can use carbohydrate, fat, or protein to synthesize nearly all of them. Two are well-known exceptions: **linoleic acid** and **linolenic acid.** Body cells cannot make these two polyunsaturated fatty acids from scratch nor can the cells convert one to the other.

The Need for Essential Fatty Acids

Linoleic and linolenic acids must be supplied by the diet and are therefore essential nutrients. These two essential fatty acids are indispensible to health.

Functions of Essential Fatty Acids Essential fatty acids serve as raw materials from which the body makes substances known as **eicosanoids** that act somewhat like hormones. Eicosanoids affect a wide range of diverse body functions, such as muscle relaxation and contraction, blood vessel constriction and dilation, blood clot formation, blood lipid regulation, and immune response to injury and infection such as fever, inflammation, and pain. A familiar drug, aspirin, relieves fever, inflammation, and pain by slowing the synthesis of these eicosanoids. Table 5-4 summarizes the many established roles of the essential polyunsaturated fatty acids, and new functions continue to emerge. So important are the essential fatty acids that the DRI committee has recommended specific intakes to maintain health (see the margin).

Deficiencies of Essential Fatty Acids A deficiency of an essential fatty acid in the diet leads to observable changes in cells, some more subtle than others. When the diet is deficient in all of the polyunsaturated fatty acids, symptoms of reproductive failure, skin abnormalities, and kidney and liver disorders appear. In infants, growth is retarded and vision is impaired. The body stores some essential fatty acids, so extreme deficiency disorders are seldom seen except when intentionally induced in research or on rare occasions when inadequate diets have been provided to infants or hospital patients by mistake. The DRI recommended intakes for linoleic acid and linolenic acid reflect U.S. and Canadian average intakes because deficiencies severe enough to cause symptoms in otherwise healthy adults in these countries are unknown. The story doesn't end there, however.

KEY POINT Two polyunsaturated fatty acids, linoleic acid and linolenic acid, are essential nutrients used to make substances that perform many important functions.

Omega-6 and Omega-3 Fatty Acid Families

Linoleic acid is the "parent" member of the **omega-6 fatty acid** family, so named for the chemical structure of these compounds. Given dietary linoleic acid, the body can produce other needed members of the omega-6 family. One of these is **arachidonic acid,** notable for its role as a starting material from which a number of eicosanoids are made. Omega-6 fatty acids are supplied abundantly in vegetable oils.

Linolenic acid is the parent member of the **omega-3 fatty acid** family. Given dietary linolenic acid, the body can make other members of the omega-3 series. Two family members of greatest interest to researchers in the fields of heart health and human development are **EPA** and **DHA.** The body makes only limited amounts of these omega-3 fatty acids, but they are found abundantly in the oils of certain fish. Because evidence indicates that health benefits may result from consuming these two fatty acids, scientists have proposed setting DRI intake values for them and listing them on Nutrition Facts panels of food labels.[23]

Omega-3 Fatty Acids and Heart Health

Years ago, someone thought to ask why the native peoples of Greenland, northern Canada, and Alaska, who eat a diet very high in fat, have such low rates of death from heart disease.[24] The trail led to the abundant fish and other marine life in their diets, then to the oils in fish, and finally to EPA and DHA in fish oils. Since that time, researchers have identified a potential mechanism underlying the heart benefits from eating fatty fish: dietary EPA and DHA appear to lower blood pressure, prevent blood clot formation, and protect against irregular heartbeats.[25] Evidence in animals suggests that they may also reduce the inflammation associated with heart disease.[26]

EPA and DHA tend to collect in cell membranes. Unlike saturated fatty acids, which physically stack closely together, unsaturated fatty acids need more elbow room (refer back to Figure 5-4, p. 154). When the highly unsaturated EPA and DHA amass in cell membranes, they profoundly change cellular structures and activities thought to benefit the heart.[27]

Today, as younger generations of native peoples of the north abandon traditional marine-based diets for more modern foodways, the incidence of high blood pressure, elevated blood lipids, and obesity has soared. Figure 5-12 demonstrates that seafood-consuming populations generally have lower rates of death from cardiovascular diseases than those that omit it. Based on available evidence, scientists conclude that a lack of marine oils in diet probably contributes to heart disease development.[28] For healthy people who want to stay that way, many population studies and controlled clinical trials support the recommendation to eat fatty fish.[29] Even some hospitalized patients who have suffered heart failure or heart attack may benefit from fish oil.[30] Fish, low in saturated fat while high in protein, contributes many nutrients other than fatty acids to the diet, including selenium, a mineral of concern for heart health (see Chapter 8).[31]

Brain Function and Vision

Human breast milk provides abundant DHA, thought to be essential for normal brain development and for visual acuity in infants and possibly young children.[32] The brain is a fatty organ, with a quarter of its dry weight as lipid. EPA and DHA readily join other lipids in the brain's cell membranes.[33] Evidence so far suggests that these fatty acids may benefit the production of the brain's communication molecules, improve signaling processes, and reduce inflammation.[34]

Early studies raised hopes that ample DHA may delay the loss of brain functions in aging, but recent population studies report no association.[35] In several reports on psychological depression, low fish intake seemed to correlate with depression; one study reported improvements in depressive symptoms when subjects received

FIGURE 5-12 Fish Oil Intakes and Cardiovascular Death Rates

Cardiovascular deaths occur less often in countries with higher EPA and DHA intakes from seafood. The percentage of total energy supplied by fish oils is listed for each country.

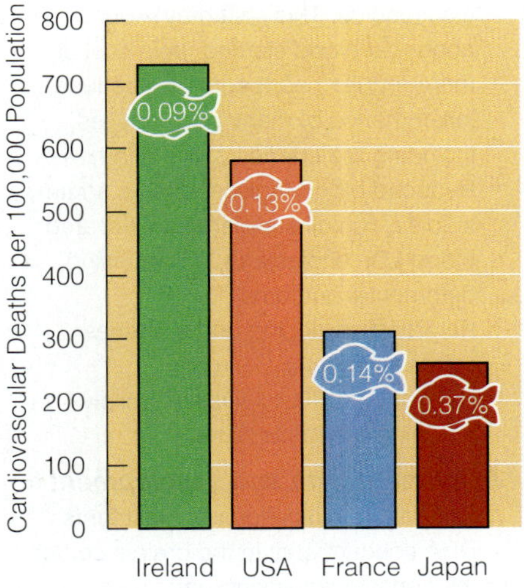

Fish is a good source of omega-3 fatty acids.

omega-6 fatty acid a polyunsaturated fatty acid with its endmost double bond six carbons from the end of the carbon chain. Linoleic acid is an example.

arachidonic (ah-RACK-ih-DON-ik) **acid** an omega-6 fatty acid derived from linoleic acid.

omega-3 fatty acid a polyunsaturated fatty acid with its endmost double bond three carbons from the end of the carbon chain. Linolenic acid is an example.

EPA, DHA eicosapentaenoic (EYE-cossa-PENTA-ee-NO-ick) acid, docosahexaenoic (DOE-cossa-HEXA-ee-NO-ick) acid; omega-3 fatty acids made from linolenic acid in the tissues of fish.

TABLE 5-5 **Potential Health Benefits of Fish Oils**

These benefits from fish or fish oil are well-established but researchers are investigating many others.

Against heart disease

- A shift toward omega-3 eicosanoids by reducing production of omega-6 eicosanoids. This shift may reduce abnormal blood clotting, help sustain more regular heartbeats, and reduce inflammation of many body tissues, including the arteries of the heart.
- Reduced blood triglycerides (in some studies, fish oil supplements elevated blood LDL cholesterol, an opposing, detrimental outcome).
- Retarded hardening of the arteries (atherosclerosis).
- Relaxation of blood vessels, mildly reducing blood pressure.

In infant growth and development

- Normal brain development in infants. DHA concentrates in the brain's cortex, the conscious thinking part.
- Normal vision development in infants. DHA helps to form the eye's retina, the seat of normal vision.

supplements of EPA and DHA.[36] In contrast, other studies report no effect of fish oil on mental well-being.[37] Further research will reveal the meaning, if any, of such findings for people's mental health.

Inflammation Chronic inflammation occurs with many diseases and may contribute to their progression. Omega-3 fatty acids have been reported to reduce indicators of inflammation in some experiments but not in others.[38] Whether an anti-inflammatory effect of fish oil bears a relation to disease risks is unknown. Other potential beneficial effects of these remarkable lipids are listed in Table 5-5.

KEY POINT The omega-6 family of polyunsaturated fatty acids includes linoleic acid and arachidonic acid. The omega-3 family includes linolenic acid, EPA, and DHA. DHA from human breast milk plays special roles in early development, and EPA and DHA from marine oils play roles in disease prevention.

Recommendations for Omega-3 Fatty Acid Intake

Obtaining the health benefits from the essential fatty acids requires consuming enough of both fatty acid families.[39] In the body's cells, both types compete for the same metabolic enzymes, so a flood of omega-6 fatty acids prevents the omega-3s from interacting with the enzymes that convert them to needed compounds.[40] On average in this country, people take in plenty of omega-6 fatty acids from vegetable oils, margarine, and salad dressings. What they lack is omega-3 fatty acids from fatty fish.

A previous theory suggested that a ratio between omega-3 and omega-6 fatty acids best serves the body's health, but research does not support this idea.[41] Most people need simply to increase the omega-3 fatty acids in their diets.[42] The American Heart Association recommends doing so by including two fatty fish servings totaling 8 ounces a week in a heart-healthy diet.[43] For pregnant women, two 3-ounce servings of fatty fish per week are compatible with good health.[44]

CONCEPT LINK 5-8

Table 2-2 of Chapter 2 (page 44) provides the USDA recommendations for oil intakes.

KEY POINT Most people consume plenty of the omega-6 fatty acids but need more omega-3 fatty acids from fish.

What About Fish Oil Supplements? Fish, not fish oil supplements, is the preferred source of omega-3 fatty acids, except for persons with cardiovascular disease who cannot obtain enough EPA and DHA from fish and must use supplements, and then only under a physician's supervision.[45] Supplements of 2 grams a day of EPA or more than 3 grams of fish oil interfere with blood clotting and cause prolonged bleeding times.[46] In mice, fish oil supplements impair immune resistance to flu viruses.[47] Supplements also lack the other beneficial nutrients that fish provides. Some fish oil supplements also taste fishy and people often complain of a lingering or repeating taste for hours after taking them.

Finally, fish oil supplements are made from fish skins and livers, which can accumulate toxic concentrations of dioxins and other industrial contaminants from polluted waters.[§48] Mercury contamination is also a problem in the flesh of both freshwater and saltwater species; the Consumer Corner section discusses the risks of fish consumption. For supplements, newer processing methods can rid fish oil of most contaminants but not all supplements are refined in this way. In addition to contamination, fish liver oil naturally contains high levels of the two most potentially toxic vitamins, A and D. Lastly, supplements of fish oil are expensive—they must be purchased in addition to food, whereas fatty fish replaces other protein foods that would have been purchased instead.

- Chapters 12 and 15 provide more information about the contaminants from human activities that end up in the earth's oceans and lakes, and ultimately, in our food and water.

§Contaminants include organically bound arsenic, organochlorines, polychlorinated biphenyls (PCBs), and others.

Omega-3 Enriched Foods and Flaxseed Food products that have been enriched with omega-3 fatty acids can help meet the needs of those people who do not eat fish. For example, when laying chickens are fed grains enriched with fish oil or algae oil, some of the EPA and DHA from the oils ends up in the eggs. Likewise, flaxseed in chicken feed produces eggs enriched with mostly linolenic acid.[49] Omega-3 fatty acids and fish oil cannot simply be added to foods such as milk, juice, and bread because they change the taste of the food and because they are rapidly oxidized to rancidity products. Food chemists are working on a way to encapsulate microscopic droplets of fish oil in digestible coatings to create a more stable additive, but most omega-3 enriched foods today contain only linolenic acid unless the label specifies "EPA or DHA added."[50] Eating flaxseed or its oil directly adds linolenic acid to the diet, but its conversion to EPA and DHA in the human body is limited. Some conversion does take place, however, but whether the amount is sufficient to approach the benefits of eating fish is unknown.[51]

People who consume wild game meat or beef from pasture-fed cattle also obtain more omega-3 fatty acids and less saturated fat from these sources than from traditional meats. In addition, several forms of marine algae and their oils provide DHA.[52] Today's infant formulas also contain DHA for brain and vision development, and no law says that adults cannot use the formulas in cooking or in beverages.[53] No exotic, expensive food choices are necessary, however—common foods chosen wisely can provide a healthy, balanced fatty acid intake (see Table 5-6).[54]

KEY POINT Supplements are not recommended and enriched foods are expensive. Ordinary foods can provide the needed essential fatty acids.

TABLE 5-6 Food Sources of Omega-6 and Omega-3 Fatty Acids

Omega-6	
Linoleic acid	Seeds, nuts, vegetable oils (corn, cottonseed, safflower, sesame, soybean, sunflower), poultry fat
Omega-3	
Linolenic acid[a]	Oils (canola, flaxseed, soybean, walnut, wheat germ; liquid or soft margarine made from canola or soybean oil) Nuts and seeds (flaxseeds, walnuts, soybeans) Vegetables (soybeans)
EPA and DHA	Human milk Fish and seafood: *>500 mg per 3.5 oz serving:* European seabass (bronzini), herring (Atlantic and Pacific), mackerel, oyster (Pacific wild), salmon (wild and farmed), sardines, toothfish (includes Chilian seabass), trout (wild and farmed) *150–500 mg per 3.5 oz serving:* black bass, catfish (wild and farmed), clam, cod (Atlantic), crab (Alaskan king), croakers, flounder, haddock, hake, halibut, oyster (eastern and farmed), perch, scallop, shrimp (mixed varieties), sole, swordfish, tilapia (farmed) *<150 mg per 3.5 oz serving:* cod (Pacific), grouper, lobster, mahi-mahi, monkfish, red snapper, skate, triggerfish, tuna, wahoo

[a]*Alpha-linolenic acid. Also found in the seed oil of the herb* evening primrose.

Source for fish data: K. L. Weaver and coauthors, The content of favorable and unfavorable polyunsaturated fatty acids found in commonly eaten fish, Journal of the American Dietetic Association *108 (2008): 1178–1185; P. M. Kris-Etherton, W. S. Harris, and L. J. Appel, Fish consumption, fish oil, omega-3 fatty acids, and cardiovascular disease,* Circulation *106 (2002): 2747–2757.*

CONSUMER CORNER

Seafood Safety—Balancing Risks and Benefits

On learning of its contamination with industrial pollutants, consumers may question the safety of eating fish.[1] Most healthy people, however, can safely consume two 4-ounce servings per week of most cooked ocean fish; intakes of freshwater fish should be limited to local guidelines. Consuming raw fish and shellfish is never recommended—it causes many cases of serious or fatal bacterial, viral, and other illness each year (read Chapter 12 for details).

Varying fish choices is a good idea to minimize exposure to any single contaminant that may accumulate in a favored species. Of particular concern is the toxic metal mercury. When industrial mercury escapes into natural waterways, bacteria in the water convert the mercury into a more toxic form, **methylmercury,** which often concentrates in large predatory species of both saltwater and freshwater fish.[2] A recent study reports increasing mercury levels in U.S. women, revealing that once in the body, mercury settles in the liver, immune tissue, brain, and other organs where it accumulates over time.[3] Another study linked high intakes of fish oils and fish to an increased risk of type 2 diabetes; contaminants typically found in fish may raise diabetes risks.[4]

Children and pregnant or lactating women, especially, should avoid consuming methylmercury and other contaminants. At the same time, these groups benefit from consuming safer fish varieties—the risks from not eating fish may outweigh the risks from doing so. For these groups, experts recommend two servings of EPA- and DHA-rich fish from safer fish species each week.[5] People with existing heart disease also

FIGURE 5-13 **Mercury in Fish Species**

Many seafood species that provide beneficial EPA and DHA (see Table 5-6) are contaminated with mercury from polluted water.

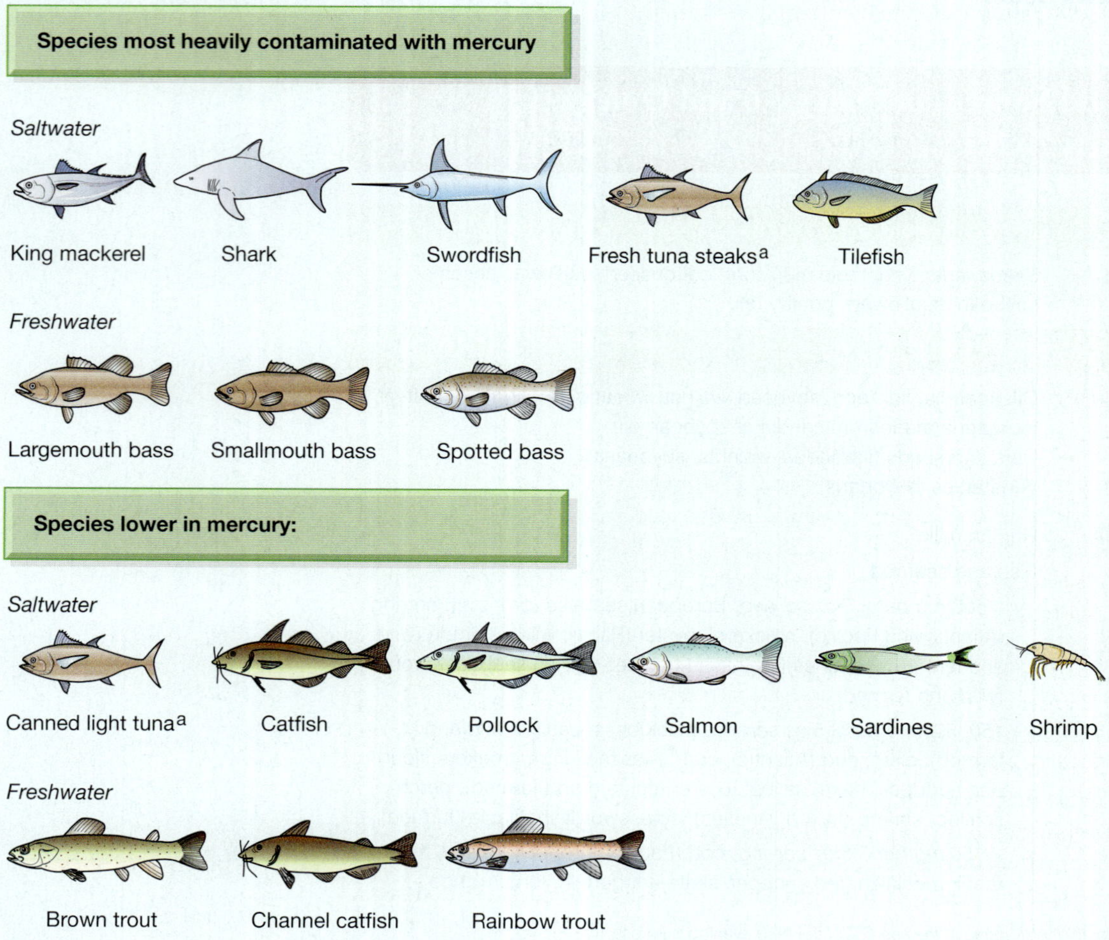

[a]*Canned albacore ("white") tuna generally contains more mercury than light tuna varieties.*

Source for tuna: S. L. Gerstenberger, A. Martinson, and J. L. Kramer, An evaluation of mercury concentrations in three brands of canned tuna, Environmental Chemistry *29 (2010): 237–242.*

pose a concern because mercury may worsen heart disease, while EPA and DHA of fish may benefit the heart. Figure 5-13 lists fish species known to be lower in mercury.

Farm-raised fish offer an alternative to wild fish but the "farms" are often giant ocean cages, exposed to whatever contaminants float by in the water. Compared with wild fish, farm-raised fish do tend to collect less methylmercury in their flesh, and the levels of other harmful industrial pollutants generally test below the maximums set by the U.S. Food and Drug Administration. Pollutants in fish demonstrate that monitoring is essential. They also serve as a reminder that our health is inextricably linked with the health of our planet (see Chapter 15).

After weighing the available evidence, experts conclude that the heart benefits from consuming moderate amounts of safer fatty fish outweigh the potential risks.[6] The greatest health benefits can be expected from grilled, baked, or broiled fish partly because the species of fish prepared this way often contain more EPA and DHA than species used for deep frying in fast-food restaurants or available as frozen fish products.[7] Also, commercial frying fats are often laden with saturated fat and *trans* fat, so avoiding commercially fried fish reduces heart disease risks in this way, too. Further benefits arise when fish displaces high-fat meats or other saturated fat-rich foods in the diet.

In the end, the arguments for eating the recommended fatty fish each week outweigh those against it. However, the dietary principles of adequacy and moderation come into play: choose enough of the safer varieties of fish to meet your needs—but don't go overboard.

LO 5.7

The Effects of Processing on Unsaturated Fats

Vegetable oils make up most of the added fat in the U.S. diet because fast-food chains use them for frying, food manufacturers add them to processed foods, and consumers tend to choose margarine over butter. Consumers of vegetable oils may feel safe in choosing them because they are generally less saturated than animal fats. If consumers choose a liquid oil, they may be justified in feeling secure. If the choice is a processed food, however, their security may be questionable, especially if the words *partially hydrogenated* appear on the label's ingredients list.

What Is "Hydrogenated Vegetable Oil," and What's It Doing in My Chocolate Chip Cookies?

When manufacturers process foods, they often alter the fatty acids in the fat (triglycerides) the foods contain through a process called **hydrogenation.** Hydrogenation of fats makes them stay fresher longer and also changes their physical properties.

Oxidation of Unsaturated Oils Points of unsaturation in fatty acids are weak spots that are vulnerable to attack by oxygen. Oxidative damage is not confined to fats within body tissues but occurs anywhere oxygen mixes with fats. When the unsaturated points in the oils of food are oxidized, the oils become rancid and the food tastes "off." This is why cooking oils should be stored in tightly covered containers that exclude air. If stored for long periods, they need refrigeration to retard oxidation.

Hydrogenation of Oils One way to prevent spoilage of unsaturated fats and also to make them harder and more stable when heated to high temperatures is to change their fatty acids chemically by hydrogenation, as shown on the left side of Figure 5-14. When food producers want to use a polyunsaturated oil such as soybean oil to make a spreadable margarine, for example, they hydrogenate it by forcing hydrogen into the liquid oil. Some of the unsaturated fatty acids become more saturated as they accept the hydrogen, and the oil hardens. The resulting product is more saturated and more spreadable than the original oil. It is also more resistant to damage from oxidation or breakdown from high cooking temperatures. Hydrogenated oil has a high **smoking point,** so it is suitable for purposes such as frying.

Hydrogenated oils are thus easy to handle, easy to spread, and store well. Makers of peanut butter often replace a small quantity of the liquid oil from the ground peanuts with hydrogenated vegetable oils to create a creamy paste that does not

methylmercury any toxic compound of mercury to which a characteristic chemical structure, a methyl group, has been added, usually by bacteria in aquatic sediments. Methylmercury is readily absorbed from the intestine and causes nerve damage in people.

hydrogenation (high-dro-gen-AY-shun) the process of adding hydrogen to unsaturated fatty acids to make fat more solid and resistant to the chemical change of oxidation.

smoking point the temperature at which fat gives off an acrid blue gas.

FIGURE 5-14 ANIMATED!

Hydrogenation Yields Both Saturated and *Trans*-Fatty Acids

Unsaturated fatty acid
Points of unsaturation are places on fatty acid chains where hydrogen is missing. The bonds that would normally be occupied by hydrogen in a saturated fatty acid are shared, reluctantly, as a double bond between two carbons that both carry a slightly negative charge.

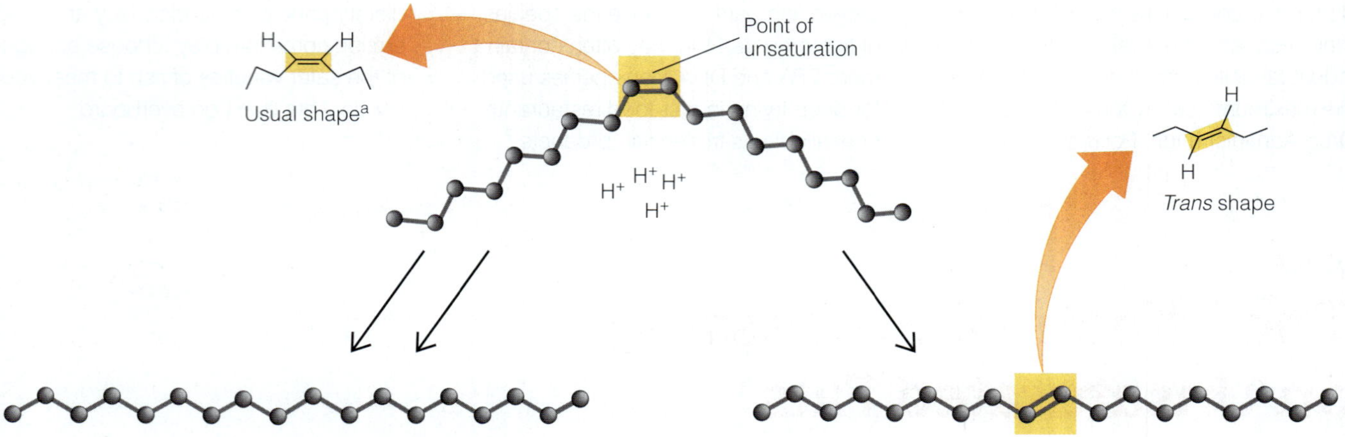

Hydrogenated fatty acid (now fully saturated)
When a positively charged hydrogen is made available to an unsaturated bond, it readily accepts the hydrogen and, in the process, becomes saturated. The fatty acid no longer has a point of unsaturation.

***Trans*-fatty acid**
The hydrogenation process also produces some *trans*-fatty acids. The *trans*-fatty acid retains its double bond but takes a twist instead of becoming fully saturated. It resembles a saturated fatty acid both in shape and in its effects on health.

[a]*The usual shape of the double bond structure is known as a cis (pronounced sis) formation.*

C Squared Studios/Photodisc/Getty Images

Baked goods often contain hydrogenated fats.

separate into layers of oil and peanuts as the "old-fashioned" types do. Neither type of peanut butter is high in saturated fat, however.

Nutrient Losses Once fully hydrogenated, oils lose their unsaturated character and the health benefits that go with it. Hydrogenation may affect not only the essential fatty acids in oils but also vitamins, such as vitamin K, decreasing their activity in the body. If you, the consumer, are looking for health benefits from polyunsaturated oils, hydrogenated oils such as those in shortening or stick margarine will not meet your need.

An alternative to hydrogenation is to add a chemical preservative that will compete for oxygen and thus protect the oil. The additives are antioxidants, and they work by reacting with oxygen before it can do damage. Examples are the additives BHA and BHT** listed on snack food labels. Another alternative, already mentioned, is to keep the product refrigerated.

KEY POINT Vegetable oils become more saturated when they are hydrogenated. Hydrogenated fats resist rancidity better, are firmer textured, and have a higher smoking point than unsaturated oils, but they also lose the health benefits of unsaturated oils.

***trans*-fatty acids** fatty acids with unusual shapes that can arise when hydrogens are added to the unsaturated fatty acids of polyunsaturated oils (a process known as *hydrogenation*).

What Are *Trans*-Fatty Acids, and Are They Harmful?

Many consumers now identify *trans* fats—that is, fats that contain ***trans*-fatty acids**—as health risks. Some cities have even set limits on the amount of *trans* fats

**BHA and BHT are butylated hydroxyanisole and butylated hydroxytoluene.

allowed in restaurant meals within city borders.[55] Does the villainy of *trans* fats warrant their bad reputation?

Formation of *Trans*-Fatty Acids *Trans*-fatty acids occur only in small amounts in nature, mostly in dairy products, but form generously during hydrogenation. When polyunsaturated oils are hardened by hydrogenation, some of the unsaturated fatty acids end up changing their shapes instead of becoming saturated (look at the right side of Figure 5-14). This change in chemical structure creates *trans* unsaturated fatty acids that are similar in shape to saturated fatty acids. The change in shape changes their effects on the health of the body.

Health Effects of *Trans*-Fatty Acids Consuming manufactured *trans* fat poses a risk to the heart and arteries by raising blood LDL cholesterol and, at higher intakes, lowering beneficial HDL cholesterol.[56] *Trans*-fatty acids may also increase tissue inflammation, a key player in heart disease development. In addition, when hydrogenation changes essential fatty acids into their saturated or *trans* counterparts, the consumer loses the health benefits of the original raw oil.[57] Compared with the risk to heart health posed by saturated fat, the risk from *trans* fat is similar or slightly greater.[58] The Dietary Guidelines 2005 therefore suggest that people keep *trans* fat intake as low as possible.

Trans Fat in Foods The largest contributors of *trans* fat to the U.S. diet have been commercially fried foods, from doughnuts to chicken, along with baked goods and other commercial foods (see the margin). Food makers have recently responded to the clamor surrounding *trans* fats by reducing their use, however.[59] Newly formulated commercial oils and fats can now perform the same jobs as the old hydrogenated fats, but with fewer *trans*-fatty acids.[60]

Are the New Fats Better for Health? Whether the new fats are better for heart health is a valid question. Some new fats merely substitute saturated fat for *trans* fat—and the risk to the heart and arteries from saturated fats is well established.[61] Others use hydrogenated fat made from monounsaturated fatty acids instead of polyunsaturated; monounsaturated fats create far fewer *trans*-fatty acids during hydrogenation. Other options are under investigation.[62]

Intense media coverage has led some consumers to believe that if a food lacks *trans* fats, it is safe for the heart. But saturated fat matters, too, and it is far more prevalent in foods. On the label shown in Figure 5-15, note that 1 ounce of *trans* fat–free crackers contains 6 grams of saturated fat, or about a third of the entire day's allowance. A glance back at Figure 5-5 (page 155) reveals that saturated fats are present even in the vegetable and fish oils required to provide essential nutrients to the diet—and saturated fat grams add up quickly in a day's meals.

MY TURN

sica

© Cengage Learning

Katy

Heart to Heart

How often do you think about the consequences of your food choices now on your heart health later in life? Two people talk about planning heart-healthy meals.

CENGAGENOW To hear their stories, log on to www.cengage.com/sso.

- Foods most likely to supply *trans*-fatty acids:
  - *Fast foods.*
  - *Chips, cookies, crackers.*
  - *Cake products and frostings.*
  - *Breads.*
  - *Stick margarines.*
  - *Commercial fried chicken and fish products.*
  - *Other commercially prepared foods.*

- Guidelines suggest keeping *trans*-fatty acid consumption as low as possible.

Did You Know?

The Nutrition Facts section of food labels lists the grams of *trans*-fatty acids in foods.

FIGURE 5-15 **Saturated Fat in a *Trans* Fat–Free Food**

Consumers must look beyond the *trans* fat line to judge a food. One serving of these crackers presents no *trans* fat, but it contains almost a third of the saturated fat allowable for the day, with only small contributions of essential nutrients.

Nutrition Facts

Serving Size 8 Crackers (28g)
Servings Per Container about 9

Amount per serving	
Calories 165	Calories from Fat 77
	% Daily Value*
Total Fat 8g	**13%**
Saturated Fat 6g	**30%**
Trans Fat 0g	
Cholesterol 0mg	**0%**
Sodium 290mg	**12%**
Total Carbohydrate 19g	**6%**
Dietary fiber less than 1g	**3%**
Sugars 3g	
Protein 3g	

Vitamin A	0%	Vitamin C	0%
Calcium	2%	Iron	8%
Thiamin	15%	Riboflavin	8%
Niacin	6%	Folate	8%

INGREDIENTS: ENRICHED FLOUR (WHEAT FLOUR, NIACIN, REDUCED IRON, THIAMIN MONONITRATE, RIBOFLAVIN, FOLIC ACID), VEGETABLE OIL (CONTAINS ONE OR MORE OF THE FOLLOWING OILS: SAFFLOWER, CANOLA, SOYBEAN, PALM, COTTONSEED, COCONUT), WHEAT GERM, SUGAR, SALT, HIGH FRUCTOSE CORN SYRUP, EXTRACT OF MALTED CORN AND BARLEY, MOLASSES, LEAVENING (BAKING SODA, MONOCALCIUM PHOSPHATE), EXTRACTIVES OF ANNATTO AND TURMERIC FOR COLOR), MALTED BARLEY FLOUR, SODIUM METABISULFITE.

KEY POINT The process of hydrogenation also creates *trans*-fatty acids. *Trans* fats act like saturated fats in the body. Consumers should not lose sight of saturated fats as the main dietary risk factor for heart and artery disease.

LO 5.8

Fat in the Diet

The remainder of this chapter and its Controversy show you how to choose fats wisely with the goals of providing optimal health and pleasure in eating. As you read, notice which foods offer unsaturated fat and which offer saturated fat and *trans* fat. Your choices can make a difference in the unseen condition of your arteries.

Essential Fat in the Diet Remember that some fat is necessary for essential nutrients. People who take fat recommendations to an extreme and try to eliminate all traces of fat from food do so at their peril. Most people need about 20 percent of their daily energy in the form of unsaturated fat. The needed fats of fatty fish, nuts, and vegetable oils provide beneficial EPA and DHA, linoleic acid and linolenic acid, and vitamin E and provide necessary calories, not discretionary, when consumed within calorie limits. The needed amounts of these fats are small, however, and most people take in many more calories of fats than they need each day.

Visible vs. Invisible Fats Keep in mind that the fat of some foods, such as the rim of fat on a steak, is visible (and therefore removable). Other fats are invisible, such as the fats in the marbling of meat, the fat ground into lunchmeats and hamburger, the fats blended into sauces of mixed dishes, and the fats in avocados, biscuits, cheese, coconuts, other nuts, olives, and fried foods. Invisible fats contribute much of the fat in the U.S. diet.

CONCEPT LINK 5-9

The concept of discretionary calories was first addressed in Chapter 2 (page 42).

CONCEPT LINK 5-10

The Canadian Food Guide is found in Appendix B.

A serving of ten small olives or a sixth of an avocado each provides about 5 grams of mostly monounsaturated fat.

Added Fats

A dollop of dessert topping, a spread of butter on bread, oil or shortening in a recipe, dressing on a salad—all of these are examples of *added* fats. All sorts of fats can be added to foods during commercial or home preparation or at the table. The following amounts of these fats contain about 5 grams of pure fat, providing 45 calories and negligible protein and carbohydrate:

- 1 teaspoon oil or shortening.
- 1½ teaspoon mayonnaise, butter, or margarine.
- 1 tablespoon regular salad dressing, cream cheese, or heavy cream.
- 1½ tablespoon sour cream.

The majority of added fats in the diet are invisible. They are the hidden fats of fried foods and baked goods, sauces and mixed dishes, and dips and spreads.

KEY POINT Fats added to foods during preparation or at the table are a major source of fat in the diet.

Meat, Poultry, Fish, Dried Peas and Beans, Eggs, and Nuts

Meats conceal a good deal of the fat—and much of the saturated fat—that people consume. To help "see" the fat in meats, it is useful to think of them in four categories according to their fat contents—very lean, lean, medium-fat, and high-fat meats—as the exchange lists do in Appendix D. Meats in all four categories contain about equal amounts of protein, but their fat contents differ and their saturated fat

FIGURE 5-16 **Calories, Fat, and Saturated Fat in Cooked Ground Meat Patties**

Only the ground round, at 10 percent fat by raw weight, qualifies to bear the word *lean* on its label. To be called "lean," products must contain fewer than 10 grams of fat, 4 grams of saturated fat, and 95 milligrams of cholesterol per 100 grams of food. The red labels on these packages list rules for safe meat handling, explained in Chapter 12.

Higher in fat ← → Lower in fat

Regular ground beef 23% fat	Ground chuck 16% fat	Commercial ground turkey[a] (with skin ground in) 13% fat	Ground round 10% fat

Regular ground beef	Ground chuck	Commercial ground turkey	Ground round
260 cal/3 oz[b]	220 cal/3 oz[b]	200 cal/3 oz[b]	180 cal/3 oz[b]
4½ tsp fat 8 g saturated fat	3 tsp fat 6 g saturated fat	2¼ tsp fat 3 g saturated fat	1½ tsp fat 4 g saturated fat

[a]*Values for 3 ounces of cooked turkey breast ground without skin are 108 calories, ½ teaspoon fat, and 1 gram saturated fat.*

[b]*Larger servings will, of course, provide more fat, saturated fat, and calories than the values listed here.*

and calorie amounts vary significantly. Figure 5-16 shows fat and calorie data for some ground meats. Table 2-6 in Chapter 2 provided some definitions concerning the fat contents of meats. The 2005 USDA Food Guide suggests that most adults limit a day's intake of meats or its equivalents to about 5 or 7 ounces. For comparison, the smallest fast-food hamburger weighs about 3 ounces. Steaks served in restaurants often run 8, 12, or 16 ounces, more than a whole day's meat allowance. You may have to weigh a serving or two of meat to see how much you are eating.

The Hidden Fat of Meats People think of meat as protein food, but calculation of its nutrient contents reveals a surprising fact. A big (4-ounce), fast-food hamburger sandwich contains 23 grams of protein and 20 grams of fat. Because protein offers 4 calories per gram and fat offers 9, the sandwich provides 92 calories from protein but 180 calories from fat. Hot dogs, fried chicken sandwiches, and fried fish sandwiches also provide hundreds of fat calories, mostly hidden in the food. Because so much meat fat is hidden from view, meat eaters can easily and unknowingly overeat on high-fat, high-calorie food.

Clues to Lower-Fat Meats When choosing beef or pork, look for lean cuts named loin or round from which the fat can be trimmed, and eat small portions. Chicken and turkey flesh are naturally lean, but commercial processing and frying add fats, especially in "patties," "nuggets," "fingers," and "wings." Watch out for ground turkey or chicken products. The skin is often ground in to add moistness when cooked, and these products end up with a higher fat content than lean beef. Also, some people (even famous chefs) misinterpret Figure 5-5, earlier, believing the fats of poultry and pork to be harmless to the heart because they are less saturated than beef fat. Nutrition authorities emphatically state, however, that all sources of saturated fat pose a risk to the heart and even the skin of poultry should be removed for heart health.

KEY POINT Meats account for a large proportion of the hidden fat and saturated fat in many people's diets. Most people consume meat in larger amounts than recommended and types that present a great deal of fat.

Milk, Yogurt, and Cheese

Some milk products contain fat and saturated fat, as Figure 5-17 shows. In homogenizing whole milk, milk processors blend in the cream, which otherwise would float and could be removed by skimming. A cup of whole milk contains the protein and carbohydrate of fat-free milk, but in addition it contains about 60 extra calories from fat. A cup of reduced-fat (2 percent fat) milk falls between whole and fat-free, with 45 calories of fat. The fat of whole milk occupies only a teaspoon or two of the volume but nearly doubles the calories in the milk. Depending on its fat content, milk bears one of the names listed in the margin.

- Milk's names:
  - *Milk, whole milk.*
  - *Reduced-fat, less-fat, or 2% milk.*
  - *Low-fat, or 1% milk.*
  - *Fat-free, zero-fat, no-fat, skim, or nonfat milk.*

Milk and yogurt appear in the milk group, but cream and butter do not. Milk and yogurt are rich in calcium and protein, but cream and butter are not. Cream and butter are fats, as are whipped cream, sour cream, and cream cheese, so they are

FIGURE 5-17 **Lipids in Milk, Yogurt, and Cheese**

Red boxes below indicate foods with higher lipid contents that warrant moderation in their use. Green indicates lower-fat choices.

Nutrition Facts
Amount Per Serving

© Polara Studios, Inc.

Fat-free, skim, zero-fat, no-fat, or nonfat milk, 8 oz (<0.5% fat by weight)

Calories 80	Calories from Fat 0
	% Daily Value*
Total Fat 0g	**0%**
Saturated Fat 0g	**0%**
Cholesterol 5mg	**2%**

Whole milk, 8 oz (3.3% fat by weight)

Calories 150	Calories from Fat 70
	% Daily Value*
Total Fat 8g	**12%**
Saturated Fat 5g	**25%**
Cholesterol 24mg	**8%**

Low-fat milk, 8 oz (1% fat by weight)

Calories 105	Calories from Fat 20
	% Daily Value*
Total Fat 2g	**3%**
Saturated Fat 1.5g	**8%**
Cholesterol 10mg	**3%**

Reduced-fat, less-fat milk, 8 oz (2% fat by weight)

Calories 120	Calories from Fat 45
	% Daily Value*
Total Fat 5g	**8%**
Saturated Fat 2g	**10%**
Cholesterol 20mg	**7%**

Low-fat cheddar cheese, 1.5 oz

Calories 70	Calories from Fat 30
	% Daily Value*
Total Fat 3g	**5%**
Saturated Fat 2g	**10%**
Cholesterol 10mg	**3%**

Strawberry yogurt, 8 oz

Calories 250	Calories from Fat 45
	% Daily Value*
Total Fat 5g	**8%**
Saturated Fat 3g	**15%**
Cholesterol 15mg	**5%**

Cheddar cheese, 1.5 oz

Calories 165	Calories from Fat 130
	% Daily Value*
Total Fat 14g	**22%**
Saturated Fat 9g	**45%**
Cholesterol 40mg	**13%**

Low-fat strawberry yogurt, 8 oz

Calories 240	Calories from Fat 20
	% Daily Value*
Total Fat 2.5g	**4%**
Saturated Fat 2g	**10%**
Cholesterol 15mg	**5%**

grouped together with the solid fats. Cheeses are the single greatest contributor of saturated fat in the diet. Among food fats, only the lipids of palm oil and coconut oil rank higher for saturation than the butterfat in fatty dairy products.

KEY POINT The choice between whole and fat-free milk products can make a large difference to the fat and saturated fat content of a diet. Cheeses are a major contributor of saturated fat.

Grains

Grain foods in their natural state are very low in fat, but fat, including saturated and *trans* fats, may be added during manufacturing, processing, or cooking (see Figure 5-18). The fats in these foods can be particularly hard to detect, so diners must

FIGURE 5-18 **Lipids in Bread, Cereal, Rice, and Pasta**

Red boxes below indicate foods with higher lipid contents that warrant moderation in their use. Green indicates lower-fat choices.

Nutrition Facts

Amount Per Serving

Low-fat granola, 1/2 c	
Calories 195	Calories from Fat 35
	% Daily Value*
Total Fat 3g	5%
Saturated Fat 1g	5%
Cholesterol 0mg	0%

Crispy oat bran, 1/2 c	
Calories 150	Calories from Fat 45
	% Daily Value*
Total Fat 5g	8%
Saturated Fat 1.5g	8%
Cholesterol 0mg	0%

Buttery crackers, 5 crackers	
Calories 80	Calories from Fat 35
	% Daily Value*
Total Fat 4g	6%
Saturated Fat 1g	5%
Cholesterol 0mg	0%

Fried rice, 1/2 c[a]	
Calories 140	Calories from Fat 65
	% Daily Value*
Total Fat 7g	11%
Saturated Fat 1g	5%
Cholesterol 20mg	7%

A homemade waffle	
Calories 220	Calories from Fat 100
	% Daily Value*
Total Fat 11g	17%
Saturated Fat 2g	10%
Cholesterol 50mg	17%

© Polara Studios, Inc.

A dinner roll	
Calories 80	Calories from Fat 20
	% Daily Value*
Total Fat 2g	3%
Saturated Fat 0g	0%
Cholesterol 0mg	0%

Fettuccine alfredo, 1/2 c	
Calories 250	Calories from Fat 130
	% Daily Value*
Total Fat 14g	22%
Saturated Fat 8g	40%
Cholesterol 60mg	20%

A breakfast bar	
Calories 150	Calories from Fat 55
	% Daily Value*
Total Fat 6g	9%
Saturated Fat 2.5g	13%
Cholesterol 0mg	0%

A muffin	
Calories 160	Calories from Fat 54
	% Daily Value*
Total Fat 6g	9%
Saturated Fat 1g	5%
Cholesterol 20mg	7%

A large biscuit	
Calories 260	Calories from Fat 80
	% Daily Value*
Total Fat 11g	17%
Saturated Fat 2.5g	13%
Cholesterol 0mg	0%

A large croissant	
Calories 270	Calories from Fat 130
	% Daily Value*
Total Fat 14g	22%
Saturated Fat 8g	40%
Cholesterol 45mg	15%

[a]*The calorie and fat contents of fried rice vary by preparation method.*

remember which foods stand out as being high in fat. Notable are granola and certain other ready-to-eat cereals, croissants, biscuits, cornbread, fried rice, pasta with creamy or oily sauces, quick breads, snack and party crackers, muffins, pancakes, and homemade waffles. Packaged breakfast bars often resemble vitamin-fortified candy bars in their fat and sugar contents.

KEY POINT Fat in breads and cereals can be well hidden. Consumers must learn which foods of this group contain fats.

Now that you know where the fats in foods are found, how can you reduce or eliminate the harmful ones from your diet? The Food Feature provides some pointers.

FOOD FEATURE Defensive Dining

Meeting today's guidelines for reducing solid fats and including raw liquid oils in the diet while controlling their contributions of discretionary calories can be tricky. These feats require not only identifying fatty foods but also recognizing sources of saturated fats and *trans* fats, and then doing something about them. This can be accomplished by:

1. Reducing saturated and *trans* fats in the diet, thereby reducing calorie intakes.
2. Replacing saturated and *trans* fats with unsaturated fats, holding calories steady.
3. Replacing saturated and *trans* fats with lower-calorie carbohydrate, protein, or other fat replacers, reducing calorie intakes, as well as saturated fats.[63]

The recommendation to limit daily intakes of saturated and *trans* fats for the health of the heart applies to all people. To repeat: No amount of these fats is needed for health and to stay healthy. For healthy people, consuming diets that supply over 35 percent of calories as fat presents health and nutrition risks. For people with heart disease or obesity, total dietary fat must be kept even lower to prevent worsening their illnesses.

Although such advice is easily dispensed, it is not easily followed. The first step in doing so is to learn which foods contain heavy doses of saturated and *trans* fats and then keep these foods to a minimum.

PORTION SIZES

Perhaps most important for many people is learning to control portion sizes, particularly of fatty foods that can pack hundreds of calories and many grams of saturated fats into just a few bites. Higher-fat foods may be included in the diet, but the calories they provide must fit within a person's discretionary calorie allowance and saturated fat limit.

IN THE GROCERY STORE

The right choices in the grocery store can save you many grams of fat, saturated fat, and *trans* fats, while the wrong ones can undermine your efforts. Food labels can reveal much about a processed food's fat contents. With that knowledge, you can decide whether to use the food as a staple item in your diet or as an occasional treat. Choose foods lowest in harmful fats for everyday use; limit others to occasional use only. For example, choose frozen vegetables (a staple food) without butter or other high-fat sauces, which are often highly saturated and inevitably drive up the calories, as well as the price; add your own flavorings such as a touch of olive oil or liquid margarine with some herbs, garlic, or lemon pepper at home. If you choose precooked meats, avoid those that are coated and fried or prepared in fatty sauces. Try rotisserie chicken from the deli section—rotisserie cooking lets much of the fat and saturated fat drain away.

FAT REPLACERS AND ARTIFICIAL FATS

Look for new innovations aimed at reducing saturated and *trans* fats.[64] Some foods contain **fat replacers**—ingredients made from carbohydrate or protein that provide some of the taste and texture of fats, but with fewer calories. Others contain **artificial fats,** synthetic compounds offering the sensory properties of fat but none of the calories. For example, "lite" potato chips and other snack foods contain **olestra,** an artificial fat. Formerly, questions about olestra's safety limited its popularity but manufacturers have reformulated their products to remedy the problems. Chapter 12 provides details about artificial fats and other food additives.

Keep in mind that "fat-free" versions of normally high-fat foods do not necessarily provide fewer calories than the original product, particularly when carbohydrates such as added sugars replace the fats. They may be very low in saturated fats, however; read their labels to evaluate whether they are useful in your diet.

COOKING AT HOME

Once at home, minimize solid saturated fats used as seasonings. This means eating cooked vegetables without butter, bacon, or stick margarine; replacing shortening with oils such as olive or canola oil; omitting high-fat meat gravies and cheese or cream sauces; and leaving off most other last-minute fatty additions. As for calories, butter and regular margarine contain the same number of calories (about 35 per teaspoon); diet margarine contains fewer calories because water, air, or fillers have been added. Imitation butter-flavored sprinkles contain no fat and few calories.

For snacks, make it a habit to choose lower-fat microwave popcorn, and then sprinkle on butter or cheese flavoring, if you like it. Keep that flavoring on hand together with other substitutes such as diet, soft, or liquid margarine (generally low in saturated and *trans* fats), reduced-fat sauce mixes or recipes, and nonstick spray or olive oil for frying. Table 5-7 provides a list of other possible substitutes in recipes. These replacements will not change the taste or appearance of the finished product very much, but they will dramatically lower the calories and the saturated fat.

USE FLAVORFUL FATS

When you add fats to foods, be sure that they are detectable and that you enjoy them. For example, if you use strongly flavored fat, a little goes a long way. Sesame oil, peanut butter, nut oils, and the fats of strong cheeses are equal in calories to others, but they are so strongly flavored that you can use much less. Try small amounts of grated Asiago, Romano, or other hard, intensely flavored cheeses to replace larger amounts of less flavorful cheeses. Some cheeses undergo processing to remove saturated butterfat and cholesterol, which are then replaced by unsaturated vegetable oils to maintain a taste and texture close to the original cheese. These cheeses provide the same calories as regular cheese but help to reduce saturated fat intakes.

CHOOSE UNSATURATED OILS

When choosing oils, trade off among different types to obtain the benefits different oils offer. Peanut and safflower oils are especially rich in vitamin E. Olive oil presents the heart with health benefits (see the Controversy section for details), and canola oil is rich with monounsaturates and the essential fatty acids. High temperatures, such as those used in frying, destroy some omega-3 acids and other beneficial constituents, so treat your oils gently. Especially important: take care to *substitute* oils for saturated fats in the diet; do not add oils to an

- Artificial fats and other food additives are topics of Chapter 12.

TABLE 5-7 Substitute Ingredients to Lower Saturated Fat Intakes

In addition to reducing foods high in saturated fat, use these substitutions.

Use	Instead of
Fat-free milk products	Whole-milk products
Evaporated fat-free ("skim") milk (canned)	Cream
Yogurt[a] or fat-free sour cream replacer	Sour cream
Soft or liquid margarine, olive oil, butter replacers	Butter
Wine, lemon juice, or broth	Butter
Fruit butters, nut butters	Butter
Part-skim or fat-free ricotta, low-fat or fat-free cottage cheese[a]	Whole-milk ricotta
Part-skim or reduced-fat cheeses, "filled" cheeses in which vegetable oil has replaced saturated fat, avocado for cold dishes	Regular cheeses
Toasted nuts or seeds (in small amounts)	Fried onion or potato chip toppings
Lean ground beef and grain mixture	Ground beef
Low-fat frozen yogurt or sherbet	Ice cream
Herbs, lemons, spices, fruits, liquid smoke flavoring, olive oil, liquid margarine, or ham-flavored bouillon cubes	Butter, bacon, bacon fat
Baked tortilla or potato chips, pretzels	Regular chips

[a]*If the recipe calls for the food to be boiled, the yogurt or cottage cheese must be stabilized with a small amount of cornstarch or flour.*

fat replacers ingredients that replace some or all of the functions of fat and may or may not provide energy.

artificial fats zero-energy fat replacers that are chemically synthesized to mimic the sensory and cooking qualities of naturally occurring fats but are totally or partially resistant to digestion.

olestra a noncaloric artificial fat made from sucrose and fatty acids; formerly called *sucrose polyester.* A trade name is *Olean.*

Did You Know?

USDA facts:

- 70% of teenage males eat meals away from home each day.
- 57% of all Americans and 40% of those over 60 years old eat out daily.
- The foods chosen away from home are higher in fat, saturated fat, *trans* fat, and cholesterol and lower in vitamins and minerals than meals typically eaten at home.

already fat-rich diet. No benefits are expected unless oils replace other, more saturated fats.

REVAMP RECIPES

Here are some other tips to revise high-fat recipes that contribute excess fat calories and saturated fats:

- Grill, roast, broil, boil, bake, stir-fry, microwave, or poach foods. Don't fry in solid fats, such as shortening or butter. If you must fry, use a little liquid oil for pan frying.
- Choose large portions of salad greens and other vegetables, and dress lightly. Reduce or eliminate "add-ons" such as batter, creamy sauces, cheese, sour cream, and bacon that drive up the calories and saturated fat. Add a small amount of olives, nuts, or avocado for rich flavor.
- Cut recipe amounts of meat in half; use only lean meats. Fill in the lost bulk with soy meat replacers, shredded vegetables, legumes, pasta, grains, or other low-fat items.[65]
- Replace a thick slice of ham with two or three wafer-thin slices. The serving will be smaller and thus provide less fat, but the taste will be as satisfying because the ham surface area that imparts flavor to the taste buds is greater.
- Refrigerate meat pan drippings and broth, and lift off the fat when it solidifies. Then add the defatted broth to a recipe.
- Make prepared mixes, such as rice or potato mixtures, without the fats called for on the label, or substitute liquid oils for solid fats in preparing them.

FIND LOWER-FAT FAST FOODS

All of these suggestions work well when a person plans and prepares each meal at home. But in the real world, people fall behind schedule and don't have time to cook, so they eat fast food. Figure 5-19 compares some fast-food choices and offers tips to reduce the calories and saturated fat to make fast-food meals healthier.

Keep these facts about fast food in mind:

- Salads are a good choice, but beware of toppings such as fried noodles, bacon bits, greasy croutons, sour cream, or shredded cheese that can drive up the calories, saturated fat, and *trans* fat contents. To reduce calories, avoid mixed salad-bar items, such as macaroni salad. Use only about a quarter of the dressing provided with fast-food salads or use low-fat dressing.
- If you are really hungry, order a small hamburger or "veggie burger" and a side salad. Hold the cheese; use mustard or ketchup as condiments.
- A small bowl of chili (hold the cheese and sour cream) poured over a plain baked potato can also satisfy a bigger appetite. Top with chopped raw onions or hot sauce for spice.
- Tacos and other Mexican treats are delicious topped with salsa instead of cheese and sour cream.
- Fast-food fried fish or chicken sandwiches provide at least as much fat as hamburgers and more *trans* fat. Broiled sandwiches are far less fatty if you order them made without spreads, dressings, cheese, bacon, or mayonnaise.
- Chicken wings are mostly fatty skin, and the tastiest wing snacks are fried in cooking fat (often a saturated hydrogenated type with *trans*-fatty acids), smothered with a buttery, spicy sauce, and then dipped in blue cheese dressing, making wings an extraordinarily high-fat food. If you snack on wings, plan on eating low-fat foods at several other meals to balance them out.

Because fast foods are short on variety, let them be part of a lifestyle in which they complement the other parts. Eat differently, often, elsewhere.

CHANGE YOUR HABITS

By this time you may be wondering if you can realistically make all the changes recommended for your diet. In truth, even small changes yield big dividends

FIGURE 5-19

Compare the Calories and Saturated Fat in Fast-Food Choices

Key:
- Calories
- Grams saturated fat
- % Daily Value (DV=20 g saturated fat)

Higher in saturated fat | **Lower in saturated fat**

When ordering Mexican-style fast food, you can reduce both calories and saturated fat by limiting cheese, meat, and sour cream.

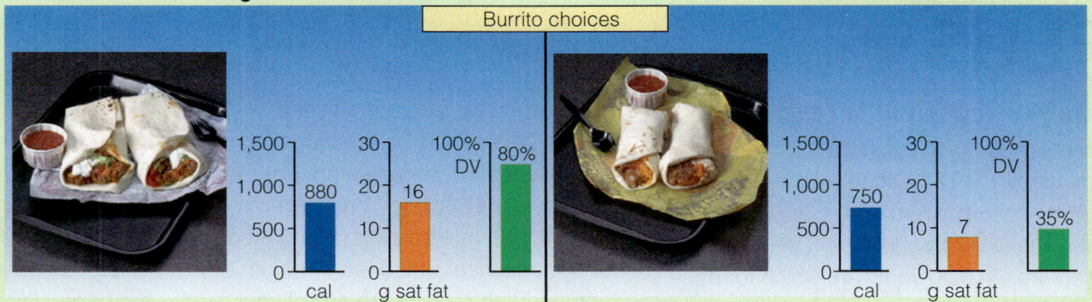

2 "grande" burritos with beef, beans, cheese, and sour cream; salsa

2 bean burritos; salsa

A broiled chicken breast sandwich with spicy mustard is just as tasty as a burger but delivers far less saturated fat and fewer calories. Beware of fried chicken sandwiches or "patties"—these can be as fatty as the hamburger choice.

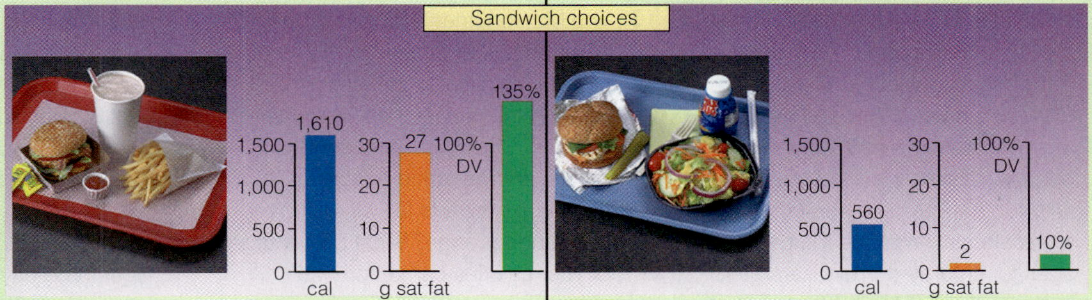

Big double bacon cheeseburger, large fries, regular milkshake

Big broiled chicken breast sandwich, pickle, side salad with low-calorie dressing, fat-free milk

Don't let add-ons, such as greasy croutons, chips, bacon bits, full-fat cheese, and sour cream pile the calories and saturated fat onto your otherwise healthy fast-food salad. To cut fats and calories, leave off most of the toppings and use just half the dressing.

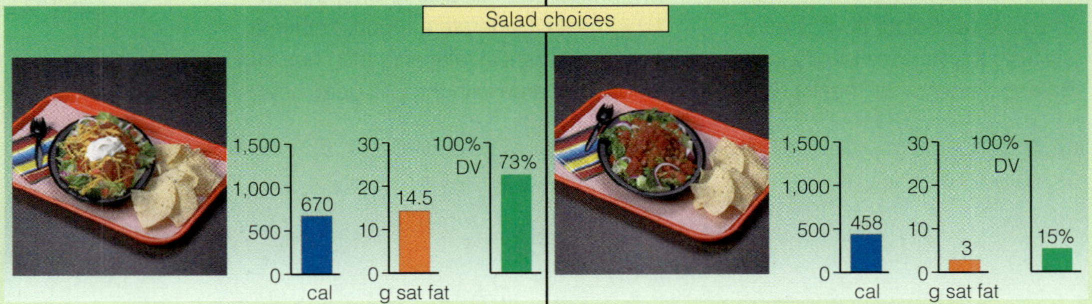

Taco salad with chili, cheese, sour cream, salsa, and taco chips

Taco salad with chili, salsa, and taco chips

Reduce calories and saturated fat even further: try ordering your veggie pizza with half the regular melted cheese and sprinkle it with parmesan cheese, herbs, or hot peppers for flavor.

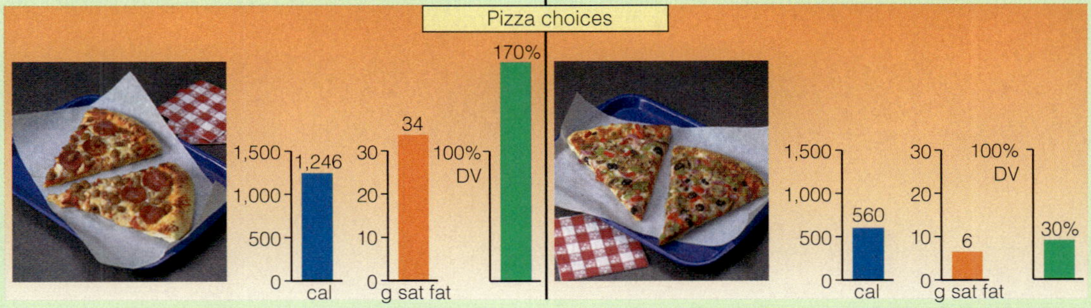

Two slices extra cheese pizza with sausage and pepperoni

Two slices cheese pizza with mushrooms, olives, onions, and peppers in terms of reducing harmful fats in the diet. Be assured that most such changes can become habits after a few repetitions. You do not have to give up all high-fat treats, nor should you strive to eliminate all fats. You need only learn to exercise moderation. You decide what the treats should be and then choose them judiciously, just for pure pleasure. Meanwhile, make sure that your everyday, ordinary choices are those whole, nutrient-dense foods suggested throughout this book. That way you'll meet all your body's needs for nutrients and never feel deprived.

Diet Analysis PLUS Concepts in Action

Analyze Your Lipid Intake

The purpose of this exercise is to help you identify fatty foods in your diet, as well as sources of saturated and *trans* fats. The Diet Analysis Plus (DA+) program will help you learn which foods contain which fats and help you to choose unsaturated fats.

1. No amount of dietary saturated or *trans* fat is required for health. Open the DA+ Home page. From the Reports tab, select Fat Breakdown. Choose a date, choose all meals, then generate a report. Your report will show a breakdown of your fat intake for that day as a percentage of total calories. What are the percentages for saturated, monosaturated, polyunsaturated, and *trans* fats in your day's intake?
2. Which foods contribute the most fat to your diet? Select Source Analysis from the Reports tab. Select a date and choose all meals. Generate a report for saturated fat and select Create PDF. Do the same for monosaturated, polyunsaturated, and *trans* fatty acids. What three foods contributed the most saturated and monounsaturated fats? Polyunsaturated and *trans*? Are any of your foods listed as top saturated fat contributors in Figure 5-11 (page 165)?
3. The Macronutrient Ranges report compares your intakes to the recommended intake ranges. From the Reports tab, select the Macronutrient Ranges. Choose a date, choose all meals, and generate a report. Did your intake for fats fall within the recommended range? What percentage of your calories came from fat?
4. To study your intake of essential fatty acids, select Reports, Intake vs. Goals, select Day One, and all meals. Generate a report. Look for the essential fatty acid (*efa*) heading. Compared with the DRI goal, how did your intake stack up? Use the Source Analysis Report to find the sources of omega-3 and omega-6 essential fatty acids in your meals. What foods might you change to improve your intake (see Figure 5-5 on page 155).
5. Toppings and dressings added to nutritious foods drive up calories and fats. The Food Feature (page 178) gives suggestions for reducing these add-ons. From the Track Diet tab, select the Recipes button, then Create New Recipe to create an appealing heart-healthy salad with little saturated and *trans* fats. Save, and close your recipe. Select a new day (not from your three-day record) and select only your salad. Click on View: Favorites and then click the "i" icon next to the recipe name to display the nutrients in the salad. How did you do?

MEDIA MENU

Throughout this chapter, the CengageNOW logo indicates an opportunity for online self-study, linking you to interactive tutorials and videos based on your level of understanding. Go to **www.cengage.com/sso.**

Search for information on atherosclerosis, heart disease, and stroke at **www.healthfinder.gov.**

Learn more about specific cardiovascular diseases or explore tools under the Health Tools tab that allow you to assess your disease risk at **www.mayoclinic.com.**

Read practical information about diet, exercise, and cardiovascular risk reduction under the Healthy Lifestyle tab at **www.americanheart.org.**

SELF CHECK

Answers to these Self Check questions are in Appendix G.

1. Which of the following is *not* one of the ways fats are useful in foods?
   A. Fats contribute to the taste and smell of foods.
   B. Fats carry fat-soluble vitamins.
   C. Fats provide a low-calorie source of energy compared to carbohydrates.
   D. Fats provide essential fatty acids.
2. Generally speaking, vegetable and fish oils are rich in which of these?
   A. polyunsaturated fat
   B. saturated fat
   C. cholesterol
   D. *trans*-fatty acids
3. A benefit to health is seen when _______ is used in place of _______ in the diet.
   A. a. saturated fat/monounsaturated fat
   B. saturated fat/polyunsaturated fat
   C. monounsaturated fat/saturated fat
   D. polyunsaturated fat/cholesterol
4. Chylomicrons, a class of lipoproteins, are produced in the:
   A. gallbladder
   B. small intestinal cells
   C. large intestinal cells
   D. liver
5. The roles of the essential fatty acids include:
   A. forming parts of cell membranes.
   B. supporting infant growth and vision development.
   C. supporting immune function.
   D. all of the above.
6. LDL deliver triglycerides and cholesterol from the liver to the body's tissues.
   T F
7. Taking supplements of fish oil is recommended for those who don't like fish.
   T F
8. Consuming large amounts of *trans*-fatty acids lowers LDL cholesterol and thus lowers the risk of heart disease and heart attack.
   T F
9. *Trans* fatty acids form in foods primarily when saturated fats are heated, as in frying.
   T F
10. Fried fish from fast-food restaurants and frozen fried fish products are often low in omega-3 and high in saturated fatty acids.
    T F

CONTROVERSY 5

Good Fats and Bad Fats—Which Are Which?

LO 5.9

To consumers, advice about dietary fats appears to change almost daily. "Eat less fat—choose more fatty fish." "Give up butter and margarine—use soft margarine." "Forget soft margarine—replace it with olive oil." To researchers, however, the evolution of advice about fats reflects decades of study to reveal the truth about dietary fats. As scientific understanding has grown, dietary guidelines have become more specific and therefore more meaningful.

This Controversy begins with a closer look at today's guidelines for lipid intakes. It also singles out the Mediterranean diet as an eating style famous for supporting the health of the heart despite its inclusion of high-fat foods.[1*] It concludes with strategies for choosing the right amounts of the right kinds of fats within the context of a heart-healthy diet and lifestyle.

THE OBJECTIONS TO "LOW-FAT" GUIDELINES

For years, consumers were urged to cut their fat intakes in everything from hot dogs to salad dressings to preserve their good health. This advice was straightforward: cut the fat and improve your health. Dietary saturated fat is a well-established culprit behind elevated blood cholesterol, but the guidelines focused on limiting *total* fat to 30 percent or less of calories. Did this strategy work to cut saturated fat intake? Yes, but only for those few who consistently applied the advice. Most who tried failed, finding the low-fat diet impossible to maintain over months or years.

In addition to poor compliance, low-fat diets present several other problems. For one, a low-fat diet is not necessarily low in calories, and many overweight people with heart disease need to reduce calorie consumption. For another, diets high in refined carbohydrates, even if low in fat, can cause blood triglycerides to rise and HDL to fall, a deleterious combination for heart health.[2] Finally, taken to the extreme, a low-fat diet may exclude nutritious foods, such as fatty fish, nuts, seeds, and vegetable oils, that provide the essential fatty acids along with many phytochemicals, vitamins, and minerals.

Are Low-Fat Diets Helpful for Anyone?

It should be said that low-fat diets remain a critical centerpiece of treatment plans for people with elevated blood lipids or heart disease and therefore are important in nutrition.[3] But what about healthy people? Evidence from around the world has led researchers to change population-wide recommendations from a "low-fat" to a "wise-fat" approach to help healthy people to stay healthy.

A classic study of the effects of diet on the world's people, the Seven Countries Study, first revealed the strong association between death rates from heart disease and diets high in saturated fats.[4] Even early on, evidence for harm from total fat was weak. In fact, the two countries with the highest fat intakes were Finland and the Greek island of Crete; yet Finland had the highest rate of death from heart disease while Crete had the lowest.

In both countries, fat provided 40 percent or more of total calories. Total fat was clearly not to blame for a high rate of heart disease—something else had to be responsible. When researchers more closely examined the diets of these fat-loving peoples, they found that the Cretes ate diets high in olive oil but low in saturated fat (less than 10 percent of calories), a pattern they linked with relatively low disease risks.

Many studies that followed yielded similar results—people who eat traditional "Mediterranean-type" diets typical of the region in the mid-1900s have low rates of heart disease, some cancers, and other chronic diseases and their life expectancy is high. Unfortunately, many busy Mediterranean people today, and especially the young, are trading labor-intensive traditional diets for convenient and fast Western-style foods. At the same time, their health advantages are rapidly disappearing.[5]

The New Guidelines

On reviewing the evidence, the DRI committee concluded that a diet containing a slightly greater percentage of fat—up to 35 percent of total calories—but reduced in saturated fat and *trans* fat and controlled in energy (calories) is compatible with low rates of heart disease, diabetes, obesity, and cancer. The *Dietary Guidelines for Americans 2005* and the American Heart Association therefore suggest replacing the "bad" saturated and *trans* fats with "good" unsaturated fats and enjoying these fats within calorie limits.[6] These authorities make clear, however, that the human body requires a diet adequate in nutrients, including the es-

*Reference notes are found in Appendix F.

sential fatty acids, and that no saturated or *trans* fats are essential for health.

HIGH-FAT FOODS AND HEART HEALTH

Avocados, salami, cheese, walnuts, potato chips, and mackerel are all high-fat foods, yet the fats of these foods differ markedly in their health effects. The following evidence can help to clarify why some high-fat foods rightly belong in a heart-healthy diet and why others are best left on the shelf.

Olive Oil: The Mediterranean Connection

The traditional health-promoting diets of Greece and the Mediterranean region are exemplary in their use of "good" fats, especially olives and their oil. In population and laboratory studies, use of dark green (virgin) olive oil instead of other cooking fats, especially butter, stick margarine, and meat fats, has been linked with numerous potential health benefits. When olive oil replaces saturated fats in the diet, such as those of butter, coconut or palm oil, hydrogenated stick margarine, lard, or shortening, it may help protect against heart disease by some of these mechanisms:

- Lowering total and LDL cholesterol and not lowering or raising HDL cholesterol.[7]
- Reducing LDL cholesterol's vulnerability to oxidation.[8]
- Reducing blood-clotting factors.
- Providing phytochemicals that act as antioxidants (see Controversy 2).[9]
- Lowering blood pressure.[10]
- Interfering with the inflammatory response.[11]

When choosing olive oil, go for the darker, "extra virgin" kind because it contains the highest levels of potentially beneficial phytochemicals. When researchers studied the effects of olive oils on 200 healthy men, they found that extra virgin oil elevated blood HDL levels to a greater extent than lighter, more refined olive oils. When processors lighten the oils, they strip away the intensely flavored phytochemicals of the olives, thus diminishing not only the bitter flavor of the oils

© Matthew Farruggio

Olives and their oil may benefit heart health.

but also their potential for protecting the health of the heart. Treat olive oils gently when cooking—olive oil burns easily.

Other liquid unhydrogenated vegetable oils, such as avocado oil, canola oil, grapeseed oil, walnut oil, and other nut oils, provide little saturated fat with their abundant unsaturated fats. Such oils, when they replace solid, saturated fats in the diet, preserve heart health. In fact, canola oil qualifies to claim heart benefits on its label by virtue of its low saturated fat content.

People who treat olive or nut oil like a magic potion against heart disease are bound to be disappointed. Drizzling olive oil on a high-saturated-fat food, such as a cheese and sausage pizza, does not make the food healthier. Also, like other fats, olive oil delivers 9 calories per gram. Adding oils to foods can easily add hundreds of calories to a day's intake, making weight gain inevitable in those who fail to balance energy intake with energy output (see Chapter 9).

The Mediterranean Diet Beyond Olive Oil

Olive oil alone cannot account for the heart benefits associated with the traditional Mediterranean diet. Such features as low intakes of red meats, and higher intakes of nuts, vegetables, and seasonal fruits probably also deserve some credit.[12] The traditional Mediterranean diet features fresh, whole foods and few processed foods.[13] Though each of the countries bordering the Mediterranean Sea has its own culture and dietary traditions, researchers have identified some common characteristics.

Traditional Mediterranean people focus their diets on crusty breads, whole grains, nuts, potatoes, and pastas; a variety of vegetables (including wild greens) and legumes; feta and mozzarella cheeses and yogurt; and fruits (especially lemons, grapes, and figs). They eat some fish, other seafood, poultry, a few eggs, and a little meat. Along with olives and olive oil, their principal sources of fat are nuts and fish; they rarely use butter or encounter hydrogenated fats. Consequently, traditional Mediterranean diets are:

- Low in saturated fat.
- Very low or absent in *trans* fat.
- Rich in unsaturated fats, including monounsaturated fats and EPA and DHA.
- Rich in carbohydrates from whole foods, including fiber.
- Rich in nutrients and phytochemicals.

As a result, lipid profiles improve, inflammation diminishes, and the risks of heart disease, stomach cancer, and many other conditions decline.[14] Early research even reveals a correlation with preserved mental faculties in old age—and the more stringently the diet is followed, the better.[15]

In traditional Mediterranean diets, omega-3 fatty acids derive from some atypical foods, such as wild plants and snails unavailable to U.S. consumers. In addition, because food animals graze in fields, their meat, dairy products, and eggs are richer in omega-3 fatty acids than those from animals fed grain, as done elsewhere. Apparently, each of the foods in a traditional Mediterranean diet contributes some small benefit that harmonizes with others to produce a substantial cumulative or synergistic benefit.

Fish: A Key Mediterranean Food

The Mediterranean regions are surrounded by the sea, and seafood provides a great deal of the protein in a traditional diet. The preceding chapter made clear that fish oils hold the potential to improve health, and particularly the health of the heart. Research studies cited in the preceding chapter lend strong support for increasing omega-3 fatty acids in the diet to lower the risk of heart disease.[16] People who eat some

© www.comstock.com

Fish and other seafood contributes key nutrients to the traditional Mediterranean diet.

fish each week lower their risks of heart attack and stroke. Table 5-6 on page 169 of the chapter identified fish varieties that supply at least 1 gram of omega-3 fatty acids per serving.

Nuts: More Than a High-Calorie Snack Food

Nuts are extraordinarily popular in traditional Mediterranean cuisines and show up in everything from savory sauces to desserts. In fact, nuts are popular with most people around the world. Not only do nuts taste good, they seem to have favorable effects on heart health, too.[17]

Nuts for the Heart People who eat an ounce of nuts on five or more days a week appear to have lower heart disease risks than those consuming no nuts.[18] Even in women with diabetes, whose risks are high, nuts (5 oz per week) or peanut butter (5 tbs per week) were associated with reduced heart disease risk.[19] As little as 2 ounces of nuts a week may provide a detectable benefit.

The nuts under study are the common varieties: almonds, Brazil nuts, cashews, hazelnuts, macadamia nuts, pecans, pistachios, walnuts, even peanuts with skins, and, as mentioned, peanut butter.[20] On average, such nut varieties contain mostly monounsaturated fat (59 percent), some polyunsaturated fat (27 percent), and just a small amount of saturated fat (14 percent). Walnuts are well-studied. Time and again, walnuts, when substituted for other fats in the diet, produce favorable effects on blood lipids—even in people whose total and LDL cholesterol were elevated at the outset. In animals, walnuts improve other markers of heart health as well.[21]

Evidence on Almonds Some observations suggest a reduction of heart disease in people who consume almonds, but the results can be difficult to interpret. In one study, subjects with high blood LDL cholesterol added about an ounce of almonds to a low-fat, low-cholesterol diet and also consumed margarine enriched with plant sterols, along with foods rich in soluble fibers and soy foods each day.[22] Most subjects had no problem consuming almonds and margarine but failed to include the fiber and soy. While the average blood LDL concentration had dropped by 13 percent, no one can say with certainty whether almonds were responsible for the drop. In a recent meta-analysis of studies on almonds and blood lipids, researchers concluded that almonds themselves have a neutral effect on blood lipids.[23] If eating almonds lowers heart disease risk, then, another mechanism may be in play.

Potential for Benefits from Nuts Nuts may lower heart disease risk because they are:

- Low in saturated fats.
- High in fibers, vegetable protein, and other valuable nutrients, including the antioxidant vitamin E.
- A source of antioxidant phytochemicals that oppose inflammation related to chronic diseases; antioxidants are concentrated in the brown papery skins that surround the nutmeats.[24]
- A source of plant sterols that block cholesterol absorption.

Walnuts also supply linolenic acid, a little of which the tissues can convert to mostly EPA and less of DHA. Linolenic acid is currently under study for heart protective effects, anti-inflammatory roles, and benefits to the brain and nerves.[25]

High-Calorie Foods Nuts and peanuts once had no place in a low-fat or low-calorie diet, with good reason—up to 80 percent of their calories come from fat, and an ounce (¼ c) of nuts provides over 200 calories. Research does not report greater weight gain in those who consume nuts, so even dieters may choose to include a few nuts each day for their potential health benefits.[26]

Stay mindful of calories when snacking on nuts.

Researchers studying nut effects must carefully adjust the calories of test diets to make room for the nuts—that is, they use carefully measured amounts of nuts instead of, not in addition to, other fat sources (such as meats, potato chips, oils, margarine, and butter) to keep calories constant. If you decide to snack on nuts, you should do the same thing. Remember that nuts provide substantially more calories per bite than, say, whole-grain pretzels or crunchy raw vegetables. People struggling to maintain enough body weight can welcome the extra calories of added nuts; all others must adjust for them to avoid unneeded weight gain.

Butter or Margarine: Which to Choose?

When news of the possible effects of *trans*-fatty acids on heart health first emerged, oversimplified reports implied that margarine provides no heart-health advantage over butter. Admittedly, hard margarines and virtually all shortenings are made largely from hydrogenated fats and therefore contain substantial saturated fatty acids. Since the 2006 requirement that *trans* fat be listed on the Nutrition Facts panel of food labels, margarine makers have reformulated their products to contain much less *trans* fat.[27] Soft or liquid varieties are made from unhydrogenated oils, which are mostly unsaturated and so are less likely to elevate blood cholesterol than the saturated fats of butter. Some contain olive oil or omega-3 fatty acids, making these margarines preferable to butter and other margarines for the heart.

Read the Labels With over 57 types of margarines and spreads on the market in sticks, tubs, sprays, and liquids containing from 0 percent to 80 percent fat, consumers must educate themselves, read labels, and select margarines that provide the preferred flavor with the least saturated and *trans* fat.[28] When oils (but not hydrogenated oils) are the first ingredient listed on a margarine label, the margarine is, in all probability, low in saturated and *trans* fats and therefore a good choice for a healthy heart.

Instead of, Not in Addition to

Simply adding margarine that contains plant sterols, olive oil, or fish oils to a diet high in saturated fat is unlikely to bring health benefits. These substances cannot undo the damage from a diet consistently high in saturated fats. Plant-enriched margarines have drawbacks. They cost much more than regular margarine, they equal regular margarine in calories, and they are not proven safe for use by certain populations, such as growing children. Recently, plant sterols have been added to juices and candies, foods that appeal to children.

Food manufacturers may soon come to the assistance of consumers wishing to choose unsaturated fats instead of saturated and *trans* fats. Most major snack manufacturers are reducing the saturated and *trans* fats in some of their products and offering snack foods in smaller packages to reduce serving sizes.

Fats to Avoid: Saturated Fats and *Trans* Fats

The number-one dietary determinant of LDL cholesterol is saturated fat. Figure C5-1 shows that each 1 percent increase in energy from saturated fatty acids in the diet produces an estimated 2 percent jump in heart disease risk by way of elevating blood LDL cholesterol. Conversely, reducing saturated fat intake by 1 percent is estimated to produce a 2 percent drop in heart disease risk by the same mechanism. Even a 2 percent drop in LDL represents a significant improvement for the health of the heart.[29] Similarly, *trans* fats also raise heart disease risk by elevating LDL cholesterol. A heart-healthy diet limits foods rich in these two types of fat.

To limit saturated fat intake, consumers must choose carefully among high-fat foods. Over a third of the fat in most meats is saturated. Over half of the fat in whole milk and other high-fat dairy products, such as cheese, butter, cream, half-and-half, cream cheese, sour cream, and ice cream, is saturated (review Figure 5-5 of the chapter). The saturated fats of palm and coconut oils are rarely used by consumers in the kitchen but their stability and other properties make them useful to food manufacturers, so commercially prepared foods provide these fats in abundance.

To choose among meats, milk products, and commercially prepared foods, rely on the Nutrition Facts panels of labels to point to those lowest in saturated fat and *trans* fat. Appendix A lists the saturated fat in thousands of foods that bear no labels.

Designing a diet with zero saturated fat is not possible, even for experts.[30] A nutritionally adequate diet will always provide some saturated fat because foods that provide the essential polyunsaturated fatty acids also supply some amount of saturated fatty acids as well. Diets based on fruits, greens, legumes, nuts, soy products, vegetables, and whole grains can, and often do, deliver less saturated fat than diets based on animal-derived foods, however. Table C5-1 summarizes which foods provide which fats.

CONCLUSION

Are some fats "good" and others "bad" from the body's point of view? Certainly, saturated and *trans* fats seem mostly bad for the health of the heart. Aside from providing energy, which unsaturated fats can do equally well, saturated and *trans* fats bring no indispensable benefits to the body. Furthermore, no harm can come from consuming diets low in saturated fats and *trans* fats.

In contrast, unsaturated fats are mostly good for the health of the heart when consumed in moderation and within a sensible calorie limit. To date, their one proven fault seems to be that they, like all fats, provide abundant energy and so may promote obesity if they drive calorie intakes higher than energy needs.[31] Obesity, in turn, often begets many body ills (see Chapter 9).

Fatty Acids Occur in Mixtures When judging foods by their fatty acids, keep in mind that food fats present the body with a mixture of both saturated and unsaturated fatty acids. As the preceding chapter showed, even olive oil and other vegetable oils deliver some saturated fat. Consequently, even when a person chooses foods with mostly unsaturated fats, saturated fat can still add up if total fat is high.

FIGURE C5-1 **Impact of Change in Saturated Fatty Acid Intake on Blood LDL Cholesterol and Heart Disease Risk**

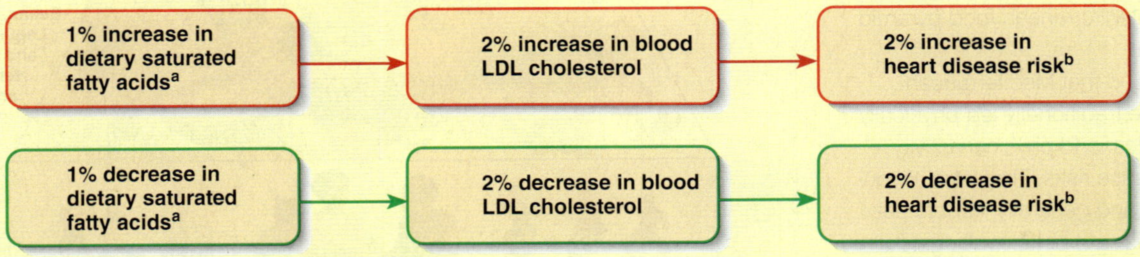

[a]Percentage of change in total energy intake from saturated fatty acids.

[b]The change in an individual's risk may compound when blood lipid changes are sustained over time.

TABLE C5-1 **Food Sources of Fatty Acids**

HEALTHFUL FATTY ACIDS		
Monounsaturated	**Omega-6 Polyunsaturated**	**Omega-3 Polyunsaturated**
Avocado Nuts (almonds, cashews, filberts, hazelnuts, macadamia nuts, peanuts, pecans, pistachios) Oils (canola, olive, peanut, safflower, sesame) Olives Peanut butter (old-fashioned) Seeds (sesame)	Margarine (nonhydrogenated) Mayonnaise Nuts (walnuts) Oils (corn, cottonseed, soybean) Salad dressing Seeds (pumpkin, sunflower)	Fatty fish (listed in Table 5-6 of the preceding chapter) Flaxseed Nuts

HARMFUL FATTY ACIDS		
Saturated		***Trans***
Bacon Butter Cheese Chocolate Coconut Cream, half-and-half Cream cheese	Lard Meat Milk fat (whole milk products) Oils (coconut, palm, palm kernel) Shortening Sour cream	Commercial baked goods, including cookies, cakes, pies, or other goodies made with margarine or vegetable shortening Fried foods, particularly restaurant and fast foods Many fried or processed snack foods, including microwave popcorn, chips, and crackers Margarine (hydrogenated or partially hydrogenated) Nondairy creamer Shortening

Note: Keep in mind that foods contain a mixture of fatty acids; see Figure 5-5, p. 155.

The Synergy of a Whole Foods Diet Pattern and Lifestyle While some traditional Mediterranean foods stand out as sources of beneficial or benign fats, it may not be possible to tease apart the pieces that make up the whole. The health benefits results observed in research arise most often from a diet pattern, chosen in various forms, day after day, rather than from a single food's presence or absence.[32] To achieve similar results for yourself, try designing your own diet on traditional Mediterranean principles. That is, dine on vegetables, fruits, whole grains, seafood, and legumes most often, and replace saturated fats with unsaturated sources such as oils from nuts and olives. In addition, reduce intakes of convenience foods and fast foods; choose small portions of meats, fish, and poultry; and select portion sizes that do not exceed your energy requirement. Figure C5-2 presents a Mediterranean food pyramid for guidance.

Keep in mind that Mediterranean peoples have traditionally led physically active lifestyles, and physical activity reduces disease risks. Therefore, if you love olive oil and generally want to eat like a Greek, you'd better walk, garden, bicycle, and swim like one, too.

FIGURE C5-2 **A Mediterranean Diet Pyramid**

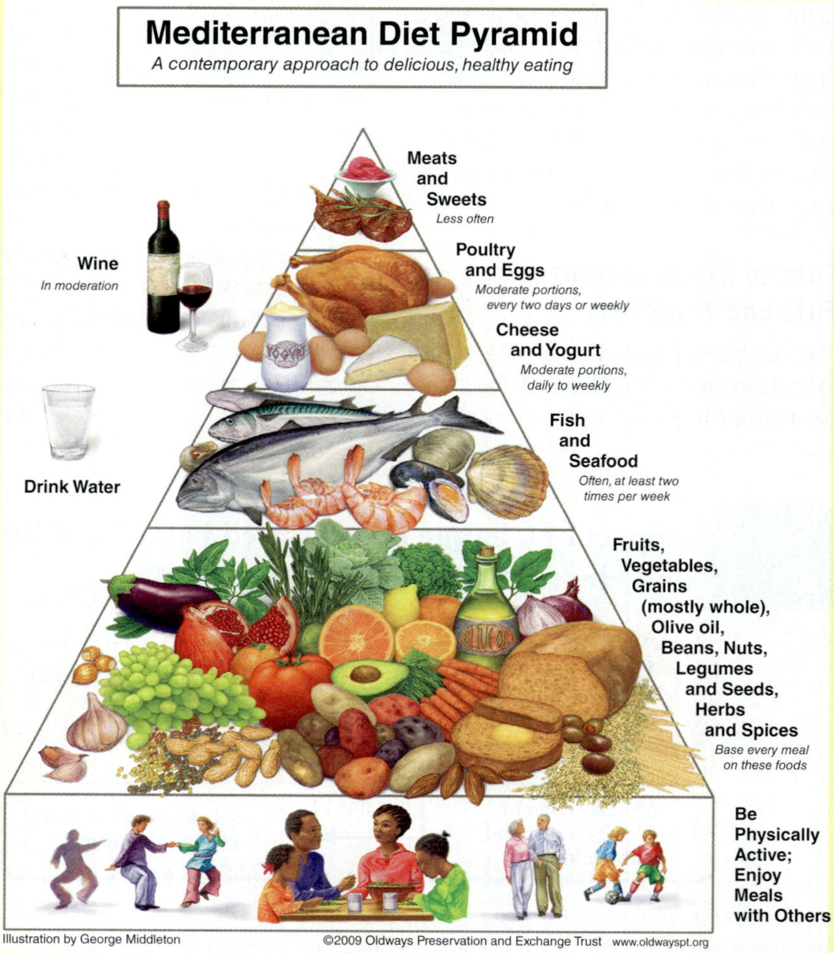

6 The Proteins and Amino Acids

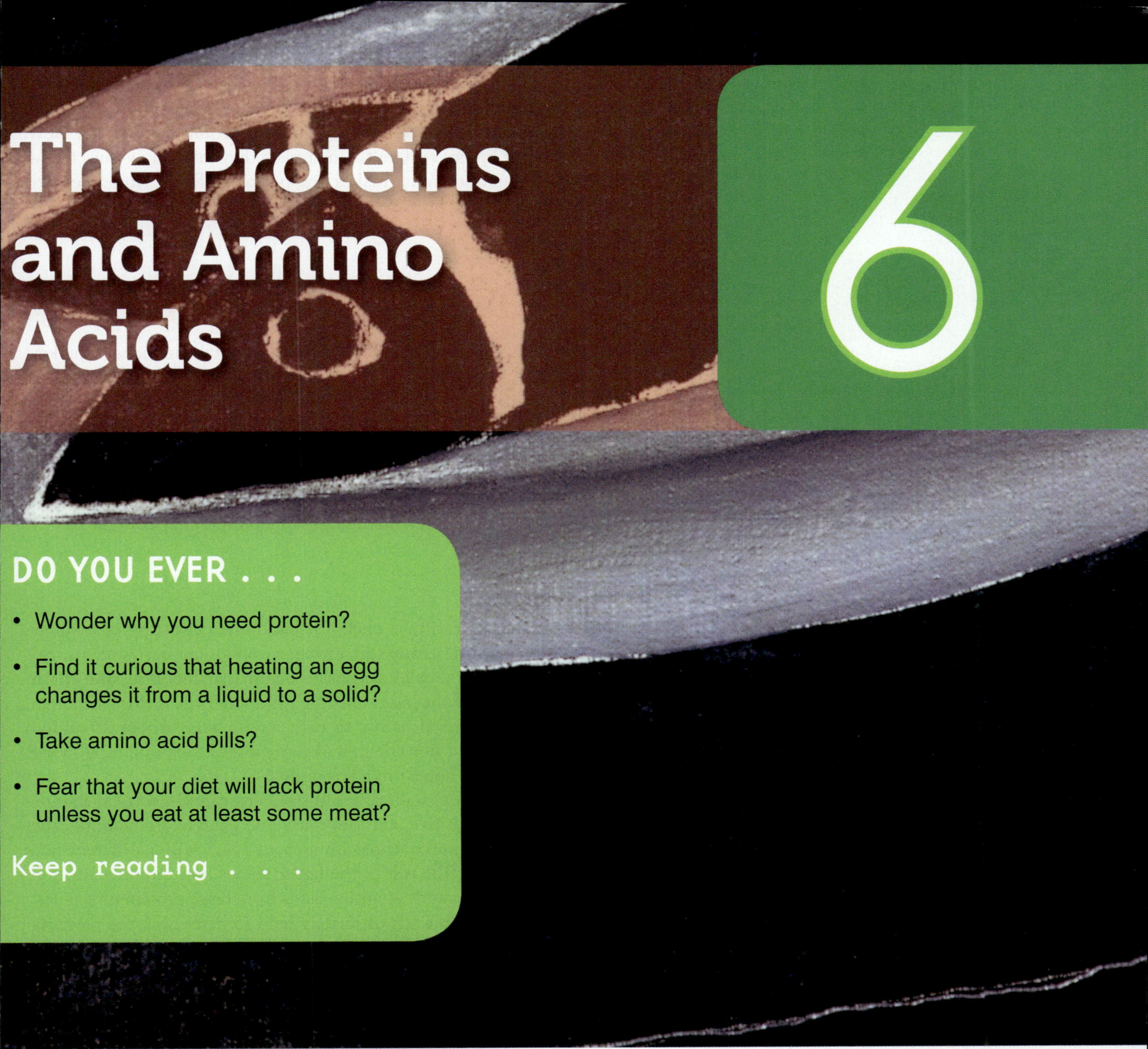

© Peter Willi/SuperStock

DO YOU EVER . . .

- Wonder why you need protein?
- Find it curious that heating an egg changes it from a liquid to a solid?
- Take amino acid pills?
- Fear that your diet will lack protein unless you eat at least some meat?

Keep reading . . .

Learning Objectives

To find learning objective topics in this chapter, look for the text headings with a corresponding "LO" number above the heading. After completing this chapter, you should be able to accomplish the following:

- LO 6.1 Describe why some amino acids are essential, nonessential, or conditionally essential to the human body, and state the outcome should any one of them be lacking from the diet.
- LO 6.2 Compare the digestion of protein and transport of amino acids with digestion and transport of lipids in the body.
- LO 6.3 Discuss the roles that various proteins and amino acids can play in the body.
- LO 6.4 Describe the fate of amino acids consumed with a balanced diet versus a carbohydrate-poor diet.
- LO 6.5 Discuss the concept of nitrogen balance and compute the amount of protein needed for a healthy college student.
- LO 6.6 Identify the major forms of protein malnutrition, and discuss reasons why consuming too much protein is not recommended.
- LO 6.7 Summarize the health advantages and nutritional risks of a vegan diet.
- LO 6.8 Develop a lacto-ovo vegetarian diet plan that meets all nutrient requirements for a given individual.

The proteins are amazing, versatile, and vital cellular working molecules. Without them, life would not exist. First named 150 years ago after the Greek word *proteios* (meaning "of prime importance"), **proteins** have revealed countless secrets of the processes of life and have helped to answer many questions in nutrition: How do we grow? How do our bodies replace the materials they lose? How does blood clot? What gives us immunity? What makes one person different from another? Understanding the nature of the proteins helps to solve these mysteries.

LO 6.1

The Structure of Proteins

The structure of proteins enables them to perform many vital functions. One key difference from carbohydrates and fats is that proteins contain nitrogen atoms in addition to the carbon, hydrogen, and oxygen atoms that all three energy-yielding nutrients contain. These nitrogen atoms give the name *amino* (which means "nitrogen containing") to the **amino acids,** the building blocks of proteins. Another key difference is that in contrast to the carbohydrates—whose repeating units, glucose molecules, are identical—the amino acids in a strand of protein are different from one another. A strand of amino acids that makes up a protein may contain 20 *different* kinds of amino acids.

Amino Acids

All amino acids have the same simple chemical backbone consisting of a single carbon atom with both an **amine group** (the nitrogen-containing part) and an acid group attached to it. Each amino acid also has a distinctive chemical **side chain** attached to the center carbon of the backbone (see Figure 6-1). It is this side chain that gives identity and its chemical nature to each amino acid. About 20 amino acids, each with its own different side chain, make up most of the proteins of living tissue.[1*] Other rare amino acids appear in a few proteins.

The side chains make the amino acids differ in size, shape, and electrical charge. Some are negative, some are positive, and some have no charge (are neutral). The first part of Figure 6-2 is a diagram of three amino acids, each with a different side chain attached to its backbone. The rest of the figure shows how amino acids link to form protein strands. Long strands of amino acids form large protein molecules, and the side chains of the amino acids ultimately help to determine the protein's molecular shape and behavior.

Essential Amino Acids

The body can make about half of the 20 amino acids for itself, given the needed parts: fragments derived from carbohydrate or fat to form the backbones and nitrogen from other sources to form the amine groups. The healthy adult body cannot make some amino acids or makes them too slowly to meet its needs. These are the **essential amino acids** (listed in the margin on page 193). Without these essential nutrients, the body cannot make the proteins it needs to do its work. Because the essential amino acids can only be replenished from foods, a person must frequently eat the foods that provide them.

Under special circumstances, a nonessential amino acid can become essential. For example, the body normally makes tyrosine (a nonessential amino acid) from the essential amino acid phenylalanine. If the diet fails to supply enough phenylalanine or if the body cannot make the conversion for some reason (as happens in the inherited disease phenylketonuria; see Chapter 3, page 71), then tyrosine becomes a **conditionally essential amino acid.**

Recycling Amino Acids

The body not only makes some amino acids but also breaks protein molecules apart and reuses those amino acids. Both food proteins after digestion and body proteins when they have finished their cellular work are dismantled to liberate their component amino acids.[2] Amino acids from both sources

*Reference notes are found in Appendix F.

FIGURE 6-1 An Amino Acid

The "backbone" is the same for all amino acids. The side chain differs from one amino acid to the next. The nitrogen is in the amine group.

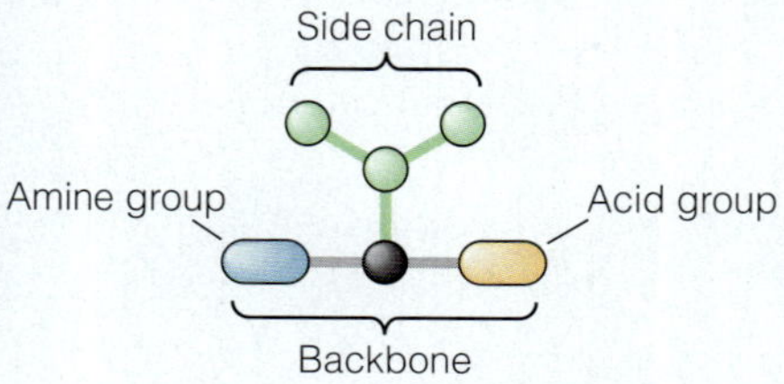

proteins compounds composed of carbon, hydrogen, oxygen, and nitrogen and arranged as strands of amino acids. Some amino acids also contain the element sulfur.

amino (a-MEEN-o) **acids** the building blocks of protein. Each has an amine group at one end, an acid group at the other, and a distinctive side chain.

amine (a-MEEN) **group** the nitrogen-containing portion of an amino acid.

side chain the unique chemical structure attached to the backbone of each amino acid that differentiates one amino acid from another.

essential amino acids amino acids that either cannot be synthesized at all by the body or cannot be synthesized in amounts sufficient to meet physiological need. Also called *indispensable amino acids.*

conditionally essential amino acid an amino acid that is normally nonessential but must be supplied by the diet in special circumstances when the need for it exceeds the body's ability to produce it.

FIGURE 6-2

Different Amino Acids Join Together

This is the basic process by which proteins are assembled.

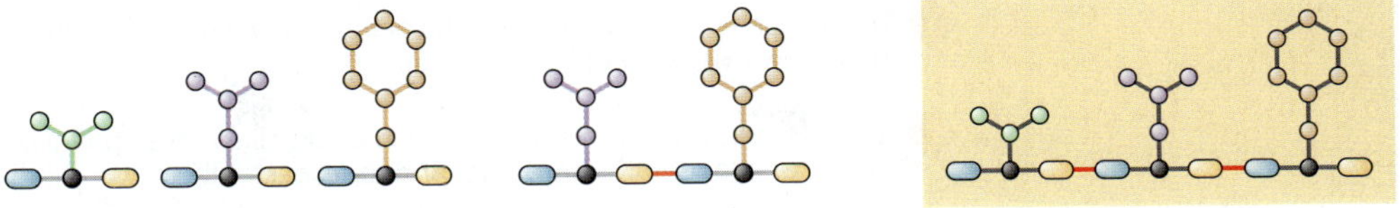

Single amino acids with different side chains . . .

can bond to form . . .

a strand of amino acids, part of a protein.

provide the cells with raw materials from which they can build the protein molecules they need. Cells can also use the amino acids for energy and discard the nitrogen atoms as wastes. By reusing intact amino acids to build proteins, however, the body recycles and conserves a valuable commodity while easing its nitrogen disposal burden.

This recycling system also provides access to an emergency fund of amino acids in times of fuel, glucose, or protein deprivation. At such times, tissues can break down their own proteins, sacrificing working molecules before the ends of their normal lifetimes, to supply energy and amino acids to the body's cells. The body employs a priority system in selecting the tissue proteins to dismantle—it uses the most dispensable ones first, such as the small proteins of the blood and muscles.[3] It guards the structural proteins of the heart and other organs until forced, by dire need, to relinquish them.

© iStockphoto.com/Boris Katsman

Hair, skin, eyesight, and the health of the whole body depend on protein from food.

KEY POINT Proteins are unique among the energy nutrients in that they possess nitrogen-containing amine groups and are composed of 20 different amino acid units. Of the 20 amino acids, some are essential and some are essential only in special circumstances.

How Do Amino Acids Build Proteins?

In the first step of making a protein, each amino acid is hooked to the next (as shown in Figure 6-2). A chemical bond, called a **peptide bond,** is formed between the amine group end of one amino acid and the acid group end of the next. The side chains bristle out from the backbone of the structure, giving the protein molecule its unique character.

The strand of protein does not remain a straight chain. Figure 6-2 shows only the first step in making proteins—the linking of amino acid units with peptide bonds until the strand contains from several dozen to as many as 300 amino acids. Amino acids at different places along the strand are chemically attracted to each other, and this attraction causes some segments of the strand to coil, somewhat like a metal spring. Also, each spot along the coiled strand is attracted to, or repelled from, other spots along its length (demonstrated in Figure 6-3). These interactions cause the entire coil to fold this way and that, forming either a globular structure, as shown in Figure 6-4, or a fibrous structure (not shown).

The amino acids whose side chains are electrically charged are attracted to water. Therefore, in the body's watery fluids, they orient themselves on the outside of the protein structure. The amino acids whose side chains are neutral are repelled by water and are attracted to one another; these tuck themselves into the center away from the body fluids. All these interactions among the amino acids and the surrounding fluids fold each protein into a unique architecture, a form to suit its function.

One final detail may be needed for the protein to become functional. Several strands may cluster together into a functioning unit, or a metal ion (mineral), a vitamin, or a carbohydrate molecule may join to the unit and activate it.

peptide bond a bond that connects one amino acid with another, forming a link in a protein chain.

FIGURE 6-3 ANIMATED! The Coiling and Folding of a Protein Molecule

1. The first shape of a strand of amino acids is a chain, which can be very long. This shows just a portion of the strand.
2. Coiling the strand. The strand of amino acids takes on a springlike shape as their side chains variously attract and repel each other.
3. Folding the coil. The coil then folds and flops over on itself to take a functional shape.
4. Once coiled and folded, the protein may be functional as is, or it may need to join with other proteins, or add a carbohydrate molecule or a vitamin or mineral, as the iron of the protein hemoglobin demonstrates in Figure 6-4 (page 193).

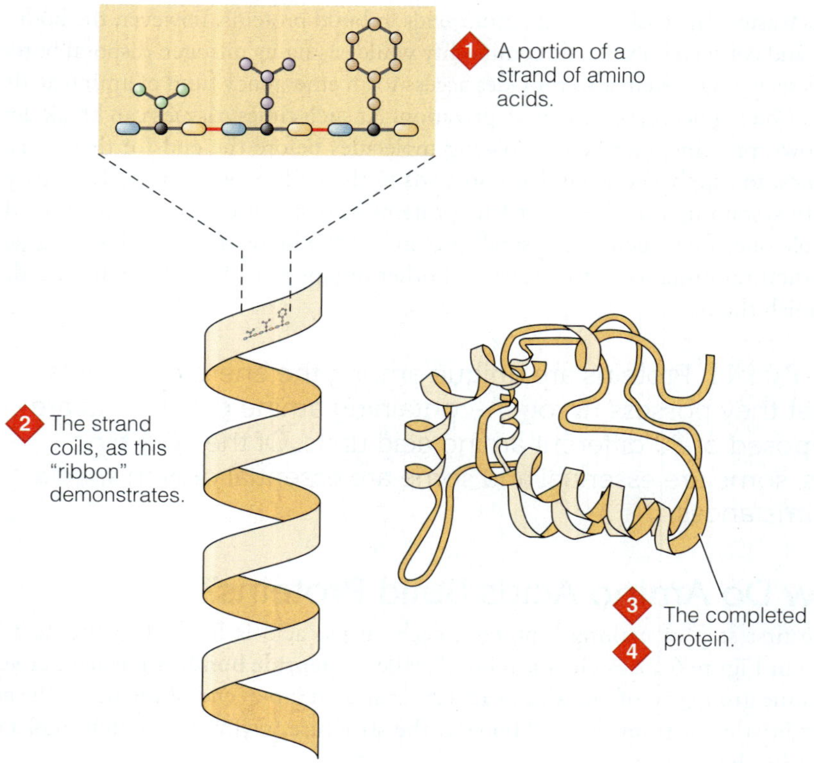

KEY POINT Amino acids link into long strands that coil and fold to make a wide variety of different proteins.

The Variety of Proteins

The particular shapes of proteins enable them to perform different tasks in the body. Those of globular shape, such as some proteins of blood, are water-soluble. Some form hollow balls, which can carry and store materials in their interiors. Some proteins, such as those of tendons, are more than 10 times as long as they are wide, forming stiff, rodlike structures that are somewhat insoluble in water and very strong. A form of the protein **collagen** acts somewhat like glue between cells. The hormone insulin, a protein, helps to regulate blood glucose. Among the most fascinating proteins are the **enzymes,** which act on other substances to change them chemically. More of the body's proteins are discussed in a later section.

collagen (KAHL-ah-jen) a type of body protein from which connective tissues such as scars, tendons, ligaments, and the foundations of bones and teeth are made.

enzymes (EN-zimes) proteins that facilitate chemical reactions without being changed in the process; protein catalysts.

hemoglobin the globular protein of red blood cells, whose iron atoms carry oxygen around the body via the bloodstream (more about hemoglobin in Chapter 8).

FIGURE 6-4 **The Structure of Hemoglobin**

Four highly folded protein strands form the globular hemoglobin protein.

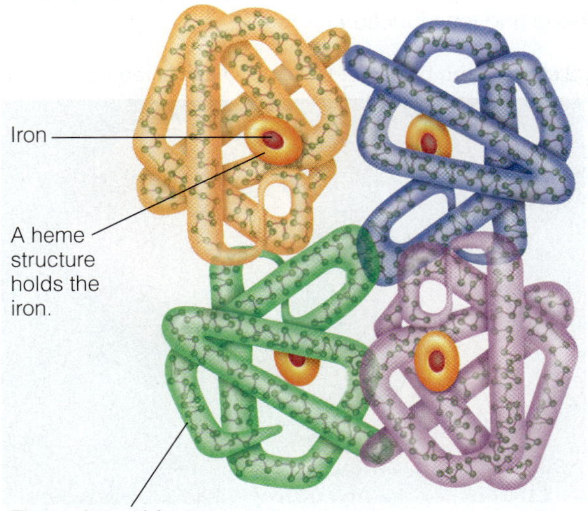

Some protein strands work alone, while others must associate in groups of strands to become functional. One molecule of **hemoglobin**—the large, globular protein molecule that is packed into the red blood cells by the billions and carries oxygen—is made of four associated protein strands, each holding the mineral iron (see Figure 6-4).

The great variety of proteins in the world is possible because an essentially infinite number of sequences of amino acids can be formed. To understand how so many different proteins can be designed from only 20 or so amino acids, think of how many words are in an unabridged dictionary—all of them constructed from just 26 letters. If you had only the letter "G," all you could write would be a string of Gs: G–G–G–G–G–G–G. But with 26 different letters available, you can create poems, songs, or novels. Similarly, the 20 amino acids can be linked together in a huge variety of sequences—many more than are possible for letters in a word, which must alternate consonant and vowel sounds. Thus, the variety of possible sequences for amino acid strands is tremendous. A single human cell may contain as many as 10,000 different proteins, each one present in thousands of copies.

Inherited Amino Acid Sequences For each protein there exists a standard amino acid sequence, and that sequence is specified by heredity. Often, if a wrong amino acid is inserted, the result can be disastrous to health.

Sickle-cell disease—in which hemoglobin, the oxygen-carrying protein of the red blood cells, is abnormal—is an example of an inherited variation in the amino acid sequence. Normal hemoglobin contains two kinds of protein strands. In sickle-cell disease, one of the strands is an exact copy of that in normal hemoglobin, but in the other strand, the sixth amino acid is valine rather than glutamic acid. This replacement of one amino acid so alters the protein that it is unable to carry and release oxygen. The red blood cells collapse from the normal disk shape into crescent shapes (see Figure 6-5). If too many crescent-shaped cells appear in the blood, the result is abnormal blood clotting, strokes, bouts of severe pain, susceptibility to infection, and early death.[4]

You are unique among human beings because of minute differences in your body proteins that establish everything from eye color and shoe size to susceptibility to

- The essential amino acids:
  - *Histidine (HISS-tuh-deen).*
  - *Isoleucine (eye-so-LOO-seen).*
  - *Leucine (LOO-seen).*
  - *Lysine (LYE-seen).*
  - *Methionine (meh-THIGH-oh-neen).*
  - *Phenylalanine (fen-il-AL-ah-neen).*
  - *Threonine (THREE-oh-neen).*
  - *Tryptophan (TRIP-toe-fan, TRIP-toe-fane).*
  - *Valine (VAY-leen).*
- Other amino acids important in nutrition:
  - *Alanine (AL-ah-neen).*
  - *Arginine (ARJ-ih-neen).*
  - *Asparagine (ah-SPAR-ah-geen).*
  - *Aspartic acid (ah-SPAR-tic acid).*
  - *Cysteine (SIS-the-een).*
  - *Glutamic acid (GLU-tam-ic acid).*
  - *Glutamine (GLU-tah-meen).*
  - *Glycine (GLY-seen).*
  - *Proline (PRO-leen).*
  - *Serine (SEER-een).*
  - *Tyrosine (TIE-roe-seen).*

NOTE: In special cases, some nonessential amino acids may become conditionally essential (see the text).

FIGURE 6-5

Normal Red Blood Cells and Sickle Cells

Normal red blood cells are disk shaped. In sickle-cell disease, one amino acid in the protein strands of hemoglobin takes the place of another, causing the red blood cell to change shape and lose function.

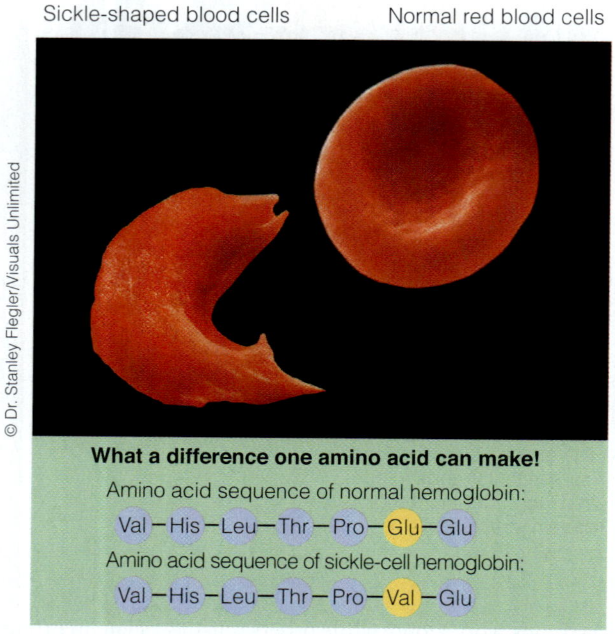

certain diseases.[5] These differences are determined by the amino acid sequences of your proteins, which are written into the genetic code you inherited from your parents and they from theirs. Ultimately, the genes determine the sequence of amino acids in each finished protein, and some genes are involved in making more than one protein (how DNA directs protein synthesis is described in Figure 6-6). As scientists completed the identification of the human genome, they recognized a still greater task that lies ahead: the identification of every protein made by the human body.[†]

Nutrients and Gene Expression When a cell makes a protein, as shown in Figure 6-6, scientists say that the gene for that protein has been "expressed." Every cell nucleus contains the DNA for making every human protein, but cells do not make them all. Some cells specialize in making certain proteins; for example, cells of the pancreas express the gene for the protein hormone insulin. The gene for making insulin exists in all other cells of the body, but it is idle, or silenced.

Nutrients, including amino acids and proteins, do not change DNA structure, but they greatly influence genetic expression.[6] As research advances, researchers hope to one day use nutrients to influence a person's genes in ways that reduce disease risks but, for now, that day is firmly in the future.[7] The Controversy section of Chapter 11 comes back to this fascinating area of nutrient and gene interactions. The Think Fitness feature on page 196 addresses a related concern of exercisers and athletes about whether extra dietary protein or amino acids can trigger the synthesis of muscle tissue and increase strength.

CONCEPT LINK 6-1

Chapters 1 and 3 provided background on DNA, cells, and their fluids (pages 2–3 and 70–71).

KEY POINT Each type of protein has a distinctive sequence of amino acids and so has great specificity. Often, cells specialize in synthesizing particular types of proteins in addition to the proteins necessary to all cells. Nutrients can greatly affect genetic expression.

[†]The identification of the entire collection of human proteins, the *human proteome* (PRO-tee-ohme), is a work in progress.

FIGURE 6-6 ANIMATED!

Protein Synthesis

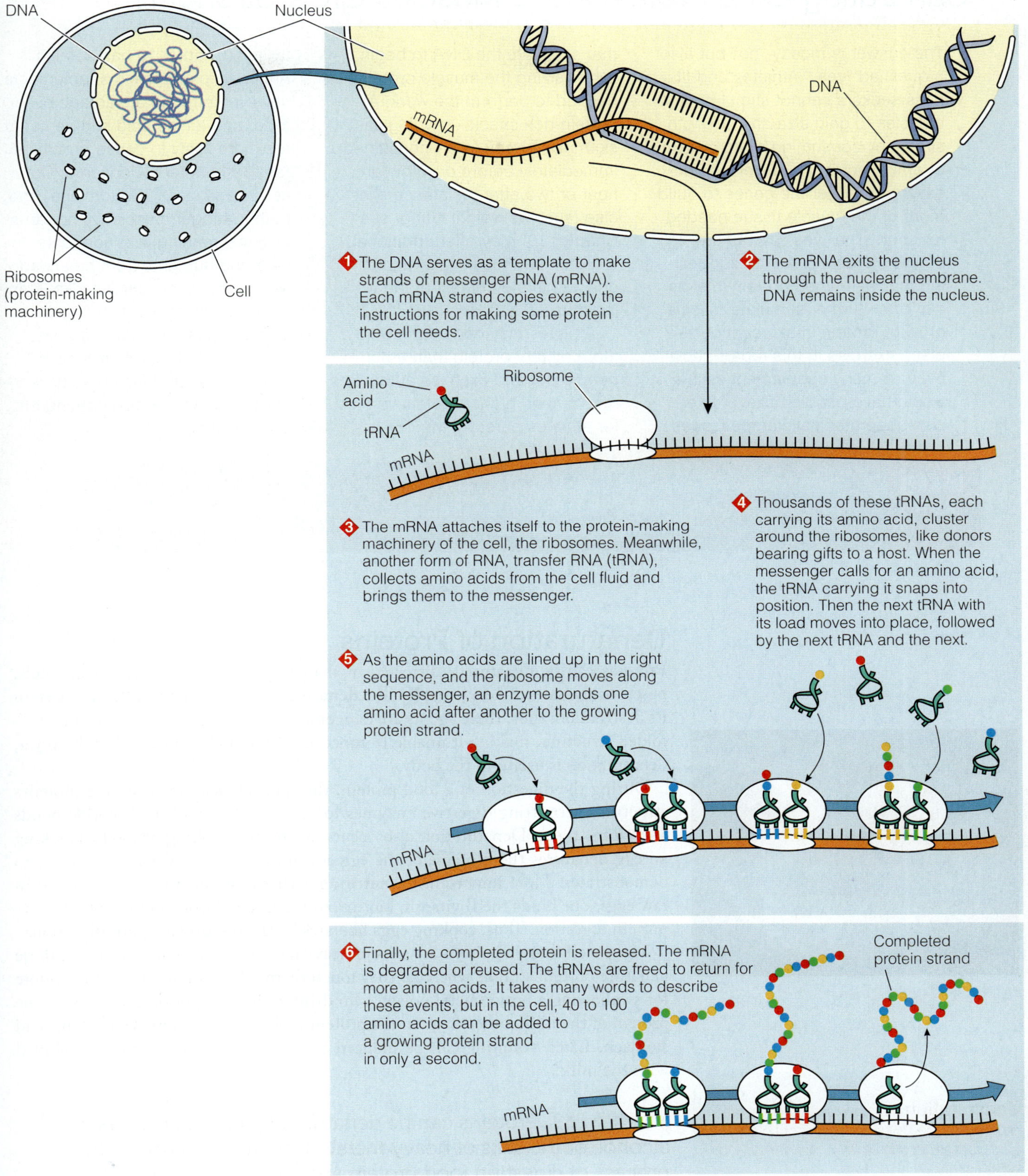

THINK FITNESS

Can Eating Extra Protein Make Muscles Grow Stronger?

The answer is mostly "no" but also a qualified "yes." Athletes and fitness seekers cannot stimulate their muscles to gain size and strength simply by consuming more protein or amino acids. Hard work is necessary to trigger the genes to build more of the muscle tissue needed for sport. The "yes" part of the answer reflects research suggesting that well-timed protein intakes can often further stimulate muscle growth. Protein intake cannot replace exercise in this regard, however, as many supplement sellers would have people believe. Exercise generates cellular messages that stimulate the DNA to begin synthesizing the muscle proteins needed to perform the work. A protein-rich snack—say, a glass of skim milk or soy milk—consumed immediately before or within an hour or two after resistance exercise (such as weight lifting; see Chapter 10) may offer additional stimulus for muscle growth, but only within the context of the working muscle.

Athletes may need somewhat more dietary protein than other people do, and exercise authorities recommend higher protein intakes for athletes pursuing various activities (Chapter 10 has details).[8] Amino acid or protein supplements, however, offer no advantage over food, and amino acid supplements are more likely to cause problems (as this chapter's Consumer Corner makes clear). Bottom line: The path to bigger muscles is rigorous physical training with adequate energy and nutrients from balanced, well-timed meals and snacks. Many more details about dietary protein and muscles are interesting and important, but this truth remains: extra protein and amino acids without physical work add nothing but excess calories.

START NOW CENGAGENOW Ready to make a change? Consult the online behavior-change planner to help you plan to provide your muscles with the physical work and nutrients they need to grow stronger at **www.cengage.com/sso.**

© iStockphoto.com/Vladimir Glazkov

Heat denatures protein, making it firm.

denaturation the irreversible change in a protein's folded shape brought about by heat, acids, bases, alcohol, salts of heavy metals, or other agents.

Denaturation of Proteins

Proteins can be denatured (distorted in shape) by heat, radiation, alcohol, acids, bases, or the salts of heavy metals. The **denaturation** of a protein is the first step in its destruction; thus, these agents are dangerous because they can disrupt a protein's folded structure, making it unable to function in the body. In digestion, however, denaturation is useful to the body.

During the digestion of a food protein, the stomach acid opens up the protein's structure, permitting digestive enzymes to make contact with the peptide bonds and cleave them. Denaturation also occurs during the cooking of foods. Cooking an egg denatures the proteins of the egg and makes it firm, as the margin photo demonstrates. More important for nutrition is that heat denatures two proteins in raw eggs: one binds the B vitamin biotin and the mineral iron, and the other slows protein digestion. Thus, cooking eggs liberates biotin and iron and aids digestion.

Many well-known poisons are salts of heavy metals like mercury and silver; these denature protein strands wherever they touch them. The common first-aid antidote for swallowing a heavy-metal poison is to drink milk. The poison then acts on the protein of the milk rather than on the protein tissues of the mouth, esophagus, and stomach. Later, vomiting can be induced to expel the poison that has combined with the milk.

KEY POINT Proteins can be denatured by heat, acids, bases, alcohol, or the salts of heavy metals. Denaturation begins the process of digesting food protein and can also destroy body proteins.

LO 6.2

Digestion and Absorption of Dietary Protein

Each protein performs a special task in a particular tissue of a specific kind of animal or plant. When a person eats food proteins, whether from cereals, vegetables, beef, fish, or cheese, the body must first alter them by breaking them down into amino acids; only then can it rearrange them into specific human body proteins.

The whole process of digestion is an ingenious solution to a complex problem. Proteins (enzymes), activated by acid, digest proteins from food, denatured by acid. The coating of mucus secreted by the stomach wall protects its own proteins from attack by either acid or enzymes. The normal acid in the stomach is so strong (pH 1.5) that no food is acidic enough to make it stronger; for comparison, the pH of vinegar is about 3.

CONCEPT LINK 6-2

pH, stomach acidity, and the medicines that control it are topics of Chapter 3, pages 83 and 89.

Protein Digestion

Other than being crushed and torn by chewing and moistened with saliva in the mouth, nothing happens to protein until it reaches the stomach. Then, the action begins.

In the Stomach Strong acid produced by the stomach denatures proteins in food. This acid helps to uncoil the protein's tangled strands so that molecules of the stomach's protein-digesting enzyme can attack the peptide bonds. You might expect that the stomach enzyme, being a protein itself, would be denatured by the stomach's acid. Unlike most enzymes, though, the stomach enzyme functions best in an acid environment. Its job is to break other protein strands into smaller pieces. The stomach lining, which is also made partly of protein, is protected against attack by acid and enzymes by its coat of mucus, secreted by its cells.

FIGURE 6-7 A Dipeptide and Tripeptide

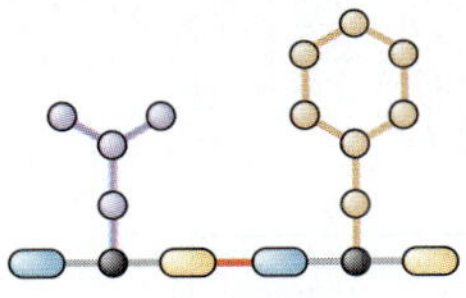

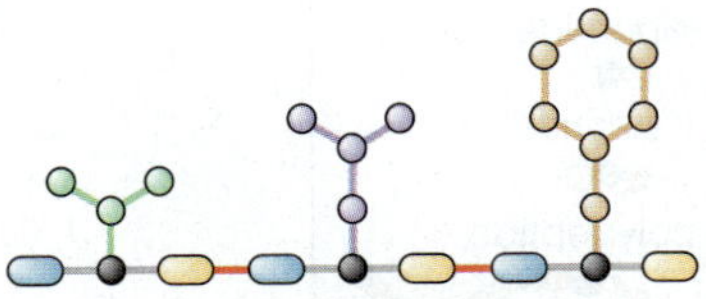

In the Small Intestine By the time most proteins slip from the stomach into the small intestine, they are denatured and cleaved into smaller pieces. A few are single amino acids, but the majority remain in large strands called **polypeptides.** In the small intestine, alkaline juice from the pancreas neutralizes the acid delivered by the stomach. The pH rises to about 7 (neutral), enabling the next enzyme team to accomplish the final breakdown of the strands. Protein-digesting enzymes from the pancreas and intestine continue working until almost all pieces of protein are broken into single amino acids or into strands of two or three amino acids, **dipeptides** and **tripeptides,** respectively (see Figure 6-7). Figure 6-8 summarizes the whole process of protein digestion.

Common Misconceptions Consumers who fail to understand the basic mechanism of protein digestion are easily misled by advertisers of books and other products who urge, "Take enzyme A to help digest your food" or "Don't eat foods containing enzyme C, which will digest cells in your body." The writers of such statements fail to realize that enzymes (proteins) are digested before they are absorbed, just as all proteins are. Even the stomach's digestive enzymes are denatured and digested when their jobs are through. Similar false claims are made that predigested proteins (amino acid supplements) are "easy to digest" and can therefore protect the digestive system from "overworking." Of course, the healthy digestive system is superbly designed to digest whole proteins with ease. In fact, it handles whole proteins better than predigested ones because it dismantles and absorbs the amino acids at rates that are optimal for the body's use.

KEY POINT Digestion of protein involves denaturation by stomach acid, then enzymatic digestion in the stomach and small intestine to amino acids, dipeptides, and tripeptides.

polypeptides (POL-ee-PEP-tides) protein fragments of many (more than 10) amino acids bonded together (*poly* means "many"). A peptide is a strand of amino acids. A strand of between 4 and 10 amino acids is called an *oligopeptide*.

dipeptides (dye-PEP-tides) protein fragments that are 2 amino acids long (*di* means "two").

tripeptides (try-PEP-tides) protein fragments that are 3 amino acids long (*tri* means "three").

FIGURE 6-8 **ANIMATED!**

How Protein in Food Becomes Amino Acids in the Body

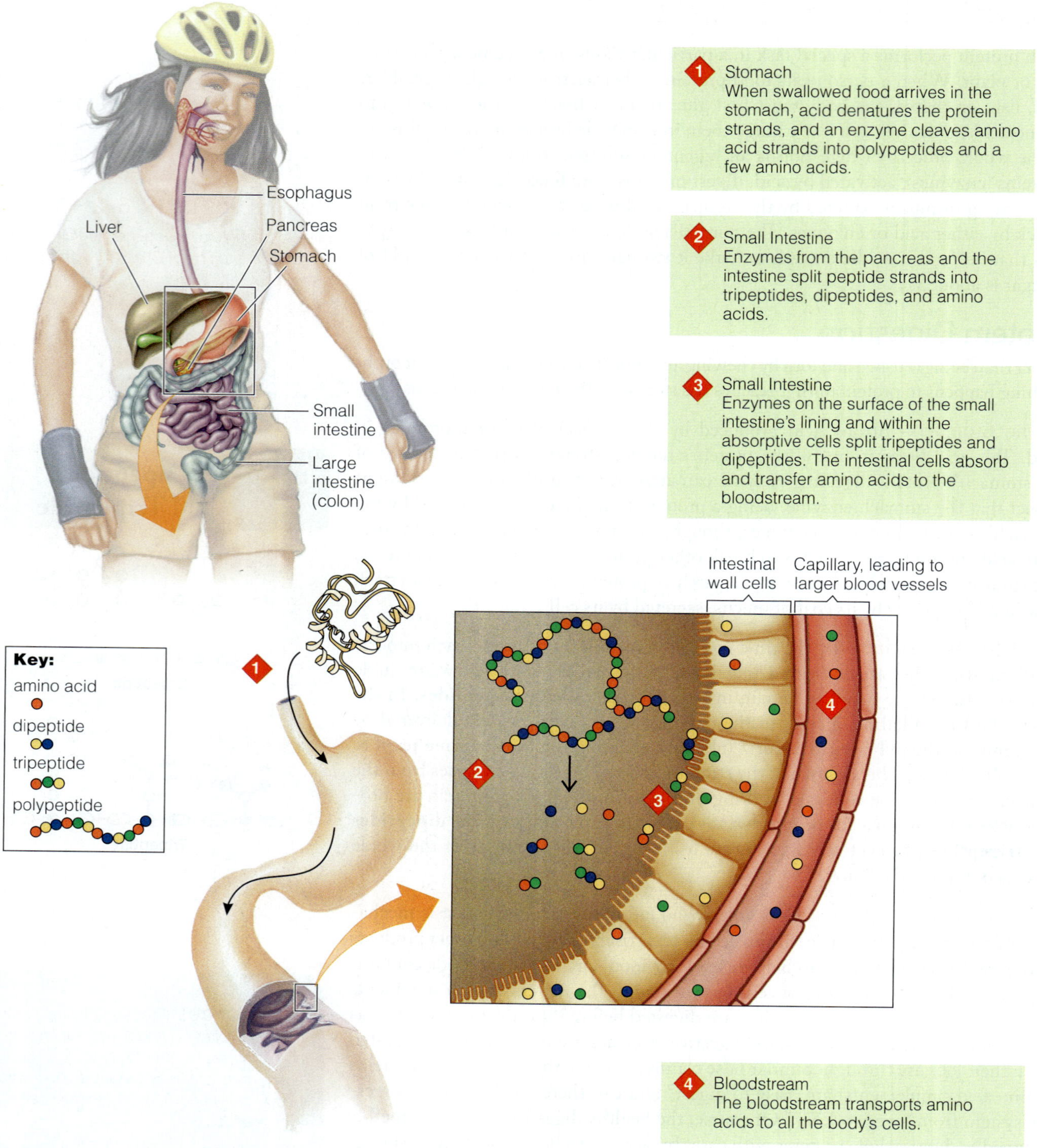

What Happens to Amino Acids After Protein Is Digested?

The cells all along the small intestine absorb single amino acids. As for dipeptides and tripeptides, enzymes on the cells' surfaces split most of them into single amino acids, and the cells absorb them, too. Dipetides and tripeptides are also absorbed as is into the cells, where they are split into amino acids and join with the others to be released into the bloodstream. A few larger peptide molecules can escape the digestive process altogether and enter the bloodstream intact. Scientists believe these larger particles may act as hormones to regulate body functions and provide the body with information about the external environment. The larger molecules may also stimulate an immune response and thus play a role in food allergy.

The cells of the small intestine possess separate sites for absorbing different types of amino acids. Amino acids of the same type compete for the same absorption sites. Consequently, when a person ingests a large dose of any single amino acid, that amino acid may limit absorption of others of its general type. The Consumer Corner (page 205) cautions against taking single amino acids as supplements partly for this reason.

Once amino acids are circulating in the bloodstream, they are carried to the liver where they may be used or released into the blood to be taken up by other cells of the body. The cells can then link the amino acids together to make proteins that they keep for their own use or liberate into lymph or blood for other uses. When necessary, the body's cells can also use amino acids for energy.

© Stockphoto.com/Oner

KEY POINT The cells of the small intestine complete digestion, absorb amino acids and some larger peptides, and release them into the bloodstream for use by the body's cells.

LO 6.3, 6.4

The Importance of Protein

Amino acids must be continuously available to build the proteins of new tissue. The new tissue may be in an embryo; in the muscles of an athlete in training; in a growing child; in new blood cells needed to replace blood lost in menstruation, hemorrhage, or surgery; in the scar tissue that heals wounds; or in new hair and nails.

Less obvious is the protein that helps to replace worn-out cells and internal cell structures. Each of your millions of red blood cells lives for only three or four months. Then it must be replaced by a new cell produced by the bone marrow. The millions of cells lining your intestinal tract live for only three days; they are constantly being shed and replaced. The cells of your skin die and rub off, and new ones grow from underneath. Nearly all cells arise, live, and die in this way, and while they are living, they constantly make and break down their proteins. In addition, cells must continuously replace their own internal working proteins as old ones wear out. Amino acids conserved from these processes provide a great deal of the required raw material from which new structures are built. The entire process of breakdown, recovery, and synthesis is called **protein turnover.**

Each day, about a quarter of the body's available amino acids are irretrievably diverted to other uses, such as being used for fuel. For this reason, amino acids from food are needed each day to support the new growth and maintenance of cells and to make the working parts within them. The following sections spell out some of the critical roles that proteins play in the body.

KEY POINT The body needs dietary amino acids to grow new cells and to replace worn-out ones.

The Roles of Body Proteins

Only a sampling of the many roles proteins play can be described here, but these illustrate their versatility, uniqueness, and importance in the body. One important role was already mentioned: regulation of gene expression. Others range from digestive enzymes and antibodies to tendons and ligaments, scars, filaments of hair, the materials of nails, and more. No wonder their discoverers called proteins the primary material of life.

Providing Structure and Movement A great deal of the body's protein (about 40 percent) exists in muscle tissue. Specialized muscle protein structures allow the body

protein turnover the continuous breakdown and synthesis of body proteins involving the recycling of amino acids.

to move. In addition, muscle proteins can release some of their amino acids should the need for energy become dire, as in starvation. These amino acids are integral parts of the muscle structure and their loss exacts a cost of functional protein. Other structural proteins confer shape and strength on bones, teeth, skin, tendons, cartilage, blood vessels, and other tissues. All are important to the workings of a healthy body.

Building Enzymes, Hormones, and Other Compounds Among proteins formed by living cells, enzymes are metabolic workhorses. An enzyme acts as a **catalyst:** it speeds up a reaction that would happen anyway, but much more slowly. Thousands of enzymes reside inside a single cell, and each one facilitates a specific chemical reaction. Figure 6-9 shows how a hypothetical enzyme works—this one synthesizes a compound from two chemical components. Other enzymes break compounds apart into two or more products or rearrange the atoms in one kind of compound to make another. A single enzyme can facilitate several hundred reactions in a second.

The body's **hormones** are messenger molecules, and many of them are made from amino acids. Various body glands release hormones when changes occur in the internal environment; the hormones then elicit tissue responses necessary to restore normal conditions. For example, the familiar pair of hormones, insulin and glucagon, oppose each other to maintain blood glucose levels. Both are built of amino acids. For interest, Figure 6-10 shows how many amino acids are linked in sequence to form human insulin. It also shows how certain side groups attract one another to complete the insulin molecule and make it functional.

CONCEPT LINK 6-3

Insulin and glucagon were topics of Chapter 4, page 127.

- Recall from Chapter 5 that other hormones are made from lipids.

In addition to serving as building blocks for proteins, amino acids also perform other tasks in the body. For example, the amino acid tyrosine forms parts of the neurotransmitters epinephrine and norepinephrine, which relay messages throughout the nervous system. The body also uses tyrosine to make the brown pigment melanin, which is responsible for skin, hair, and eye color. Tyrosine is also converted into the thyroid hormone **thyroxine,** which regulates the body's metabolism. Another amino acid, tryptophan, serves as starting material for the neurotransmitter **serotonin** and the vitamin niacin.

CONCEPT LINK 6-4

Neurotransmitters were introduced in Chapter 3, page 76.

- The vitamin niacin is discussed in Chapter 7.

Building Antibodies Of all the proteins in living organisms, the **antibodies** best demonstrate that proteins are specific to one organism. Antibodies distinguish foreign particles (usually proteins) from all the proteins that belong in "their" body. When they recognize an intruder, they mark it as a target for attack. The foreign protein may be part of a bacterium, a virus, or a toxin, or it may be present in a food that causes an allergic reaction.

Each antibody is designed to help destroy one specific invader. An antibody active against one strain of influenza is of no help to a person ill with another strain. Once the body has learned how to make a particular antibody, it remembers. The next time the body encounters that same invader, it destroys the invader even more rapidly. In

catalyst a substance that speeds the rate of a chemical reaction without itself being permanently altered in the process. All enzymes are catalysts.

hormones chemical messengers secreted by a number of body organs in response to conditions that require regulation. Each hormone affects a specific organ or tissue and elicits a specific response. Also defined in Chapter 3.

thyroxine (thigh-ROX-in) a principle peptide hormone of the thyroid gland that regulates the body's rate of energy use.

serotonin (SARE-oh-TONE-in) a compound related in structure to (and made from) the amino acid tryptophan. It serves as one of the brain's principal neurotransmitters.

antibodies (AN-te-bod-ees) large proteins of the blood, produced by the immune system in response to an invasion of the body by foreign substances (antigens). Antibodies combine with and inactivate the antigens. Also defined in Chapter 3.

FIGURE 6-9 **Enzyme Action**

Compounds A and B are attracted to the enzyme's active site and park there for a moment in the exact position that makes the reaction between them most likely to occur. They react by bonding together and leave the enzyme as the new compound, AB.

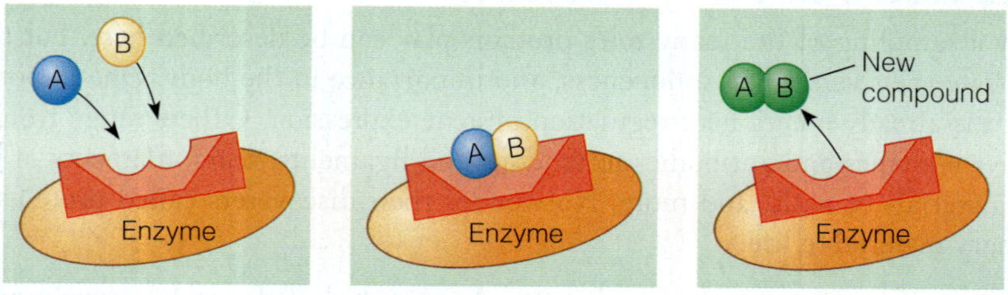

Enzyme plus two compounds A and B

Enzyme complex with A and B

Enzyme plus new compound AB

FIGURE 6-10 **Amino Acid Sequence of Human Insulin**

This picture shows a refinement of protein structure not mentioned in the text. The amino acid cysteine (cys) has a sulfur-containing side group. The sulfur groups on two cysteine molecules can bond together, creating a bridge between two protein strands or two parts of the same strand. Insulin contains three such bridges.

other words, the body develops **immunity** to the invader. This molecular memory underlies the principle of immunizations, injections of drugs made from destroyed and inactivated microbes or their products that activate the body's immune defenses. Some immunities are lifelong; others, such as that to tetanus, must be "boosted" at intervals.

CONCEPT LINK 6-5

A discussion of the immune system is found in Chapter 3, pages 76–77.

Transporting Substances A large group of proteins specialize in transporting other substances, such as lipids, vitamins, minerals, and oxygen around the body. To do their jobs, such substances must travel within the bloodstream, into and out of cells, or around the cellular interiors. Two familiar examples are the protein hemoglobin that carries oxygen from the lungs to the cells and the lipoproteins that transport lipids in the watery blood.

Maintaining Fluid and Electrolyte Balance Proteins help to maintain the **fluid and electrolyte balance** by regulating the quantity of fluids in the compartments of the body. To remain alive, cells must contain a constant amount of fluid. Too much can cause them to rupture; too little makes them unable to function. Although water can diffuse freely into and out of cells, proteins cannot; and proteins attract water.

By maintaining stores of internal proteins and also of some minerals, cells retain the fluid they need. By the same mechanism, fluid is kept inside the blood vessels by proteins too large to move freely across the capillary walls. The proteins attract water and hold it within the vessels, preventing it from freely flowing into the spaces between the cells. Should any part of this system begin to fail, too much fluid will soon collect in the spaces between the cells of tissues, causing **edema.**

- The control of water's location by electrolytes is discussed further in Chapter 8.

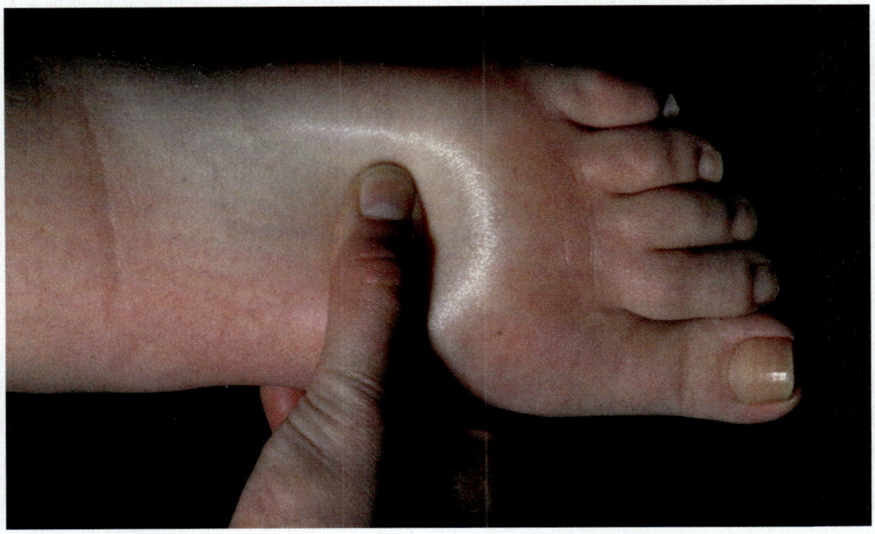

SPL/Photo Researchers, Inc.

Edema results when body tissues fail to control the movement of water.

immunity protection from or resistance to a disease or infection by development of antibodies and by the actions of cells and tissues in response to a threat.

fluid and electrolyte balance the distribution of fluid and dissolved particles among body compartments (see also Chapter 8).

edema (eh-DEEM-uh) swelling of body tissue caused by leakage of fluid from the blood vessels; seen in protein deficiency (among other conditions).

FIGURE 6-11 ANIMATED! **Proteins Transport Substances Into and Out of Cells**

A transport protein within the cell membrane acts as a sort of two-door passageway—substances enter on one side and are released on the other, but the protein never leaves the membrane. The protein differs from a simple passageway in that it actively escorts the substances in and out of cells; therefore, this form of transport is often called active transport.

Molecule enters protein from inside cell. | Protein changes shape; molecule exits protein outside the cell. | Molecule enters protein from outside cell. | Molecule exits protein; proper balance restored.

Not only is the quantity of the body fluids vital to life but so also is their composition. Transport proteins in the membranes of cells also help maintain this composition by continuously transferring substances into and out of cells (see Figure 6-11). For example, sodium is concentrated outside the cells, and potassium is concentrated inside. A disturbance of this balance can impair the action of the heart, lungs, and brain, triggering a major medical emergency. Cell proteins avert such a disaster by holding fluids and electrolytes in their proper chambers.

Maintaining Acid-Base Balance Normal processes of the body continually produce **acids** and their opposite, **bases,** that must be carried by the blood to the organs of excretion. The blood must do this without allowing its own **acid-base balance** to be affected. This feat is another trick of the blood proteins, which act as **buffers** to maintain the blood's normal pH. The protein buffers pick up hydrogens (acid) when there are too many in the bloodstream and release them again when there are too few. The secret is that negatively charged side chains of amino acids can accommodate additional hydrogens, which are positively charged.

Blood pH is one of the most rigidly controlled conditions in the body. If blood pH changes too much, **acidosis** or the opposite basic condition, **alkalosis,** can cause coma or death. These conditions constitute medical emergencies because of their effect on proteins. When the proteins' buffering capacity is filled—that is, when they have taken on all the acid hydrogens they can accommodate—additional acid pulls them out of shape, denaturing them and disrupting many body processes.

Blood Clotting To prevent dangerous blood loss, special blood proteins respond to an injury by clotting the blood. In an amazing series of chemical events, these proteins form a stringy net that traps blood cells to form a clot. The clot acts as a plug to stem blood flow from the wound. Later, as the wound heals, the protein collagen finishes the job by replacing the clot with scar tissue.

The final function of protein, providing energy, depends upon some metabolic adjustments, as described in the next section. Table 6-1 provides a summary of the functions of proteins in the body.

Providing Energy and Glucose Only protein can perform all the functions just described, but protein will be surrendered to provide energy if need be. Under conditions of inadequate energy or carbohydrate, protein breakdown speeds up, as the next section explains.[9]

KEY POINT Proteins provide structure and movement; serve as enzymes, hormones, and antibodies; provide molecular transport,

acids compounds that release hydrogens in a watery solution.

bases compounds that accept hydrogens from solutions.

acid-base balance equilibrium between acid and base concentrations in the body fluids.

buffers compounds that help keep a solution's acidity or alkalinity constant.

acidosis (acid-DOH-sis) the condition of excess acid in the blood, indicated by a below-normal pH (*osis* means "too much in the blood").

alkalosis (al-kah-LOH-sis) the condition of excess base in the blood, indicated by an above-normal blood pH (*alka* means "base"; *osis* means "too much in the blood").

fluid and electrolyte regulation, buffers for blood; contribute to blood clotting, energy supplies, and glucose for the body.

Amino Acids to Glucose

The body must have energy to live from moment to moment, so obtaining that energy is a top priority. Not only can amino acids supply energy but many of them can be converted to glucose, as fatty acids can never be. Thus, if the need arises, protein can help to maintain a steady blood glucose level and serve the glucose need of the brain.

When amino acids are degraded for energy or converted into glucose, their nitrogen-containing amine groups are stripped off and used elsewhere or are incorporated by the liver into **urea** and sent to the kidneys for excretion in the urine. The fragments that remain are composed of carbon, hydrogen, and oxygen, as are carbohydrate and fat, and can be used to build glucose or fatty acids or can be metabolized like them.

Protein Lack and Abundance Glucose is stored as glycogen and fat as triglycerides, but no specialized storage compound exists for protein. Body protein is present only as the active working molecular and structural components of body tissues. When protein-sparing energy from carbohydrate and fat is lacking and the need becomes urgent, as in starvation, prolonged fasting, or severe calorie restriction, the body must dismantle its tissue proteins to obtain amino acids for building the most essential proteins and for energy. Each protein is taken in its own time: first, small proteins from the blood; then, proteins from the muscles, liver, and other organs. Thus, energy deficiency (starvation) always incurs wasting of lean body tissue as well as loss of fat.

When amino acids are oversupplied, the body cannot store them. It has no choice but to remove and excrete their amine groups and then use the residues in one of three ways: to meet immediate energy needs, to make glucose for storage as glycogen, or to make fat for energy storage.[10] The body readily converts amino acids to glucose. The body also possesses enzymes to convert amino acids into fat and can produce fatty acids for storage as triglycerides in the fat tissue. An indirect contribution of amino acids to fat stores also exists—the body speeds up its use of amino acids for fuel, burning them instead of fat, which is then abundantly available for storage in the fat tissue.

The similarities and differences of the three energy-yielding nutrients should now be clear. Carbohydrate offers energy; fat offers concentrated energy; and protein can offer energy plus nitrogen (see Figure 6-12).

TABLE 6-1 **Summary of Protein Functions**

- *Acid-base balance.* Proteins help maintain the acid-base balance of various body fluids by acting as buffers.
- *Antibodies.* Proteins form the immune system molecules that fight diseases.
- *Blood clotting.* Proteins provide the netting on which blood clots are built.
- *Energy and glucose.* Proteins provide some fuel for the body's energy needs.
- *Enzymes.* Proteins facilitate needed chemical reactions.
- *Fluid and electrolyte balance.* Proteins help to maintain the water and mineral composition of various body fluids.
- *Gene expression.* Proteins associate and interact with DNA, regulating gene expression.
- *Hormones.* Proteins regulate body processes. Some hormones are proteins or are made from amino acids.
- *Structure.* Proteins form integral parts of most body tissues and confer shape and strength on bones, skin, tendons, and other tissues. Structural proteins of muscles allow body movement.
- *Transportation.* Proteins help transport needed substances, such as lipids, minerals, and oxygen, around the body.

• More about the effects of fasting in Chapter 9.

FIGURE 6-12 **Three Different Energy Sources**

Carbohydrate offers energy; fat offers concentrated energy; and protein, if necessary, can offer energy plus nitrogen. The compounds at the left yield the 2-carbon fragments shown at the right. These fragments oxidize quickly in the presence of oxygen to yield carbon dioxide, water, and energy.

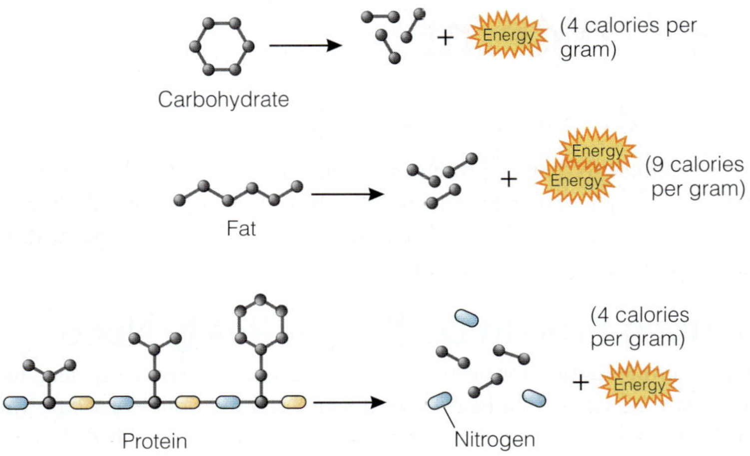

urea (yoo-REE-uh) the principal nitrogen-excretion product of protein metabolism; generated mostly by removal of amine groups from unneeded amino acids or from amino acids being sacrificed to a need for energy.

The Fate of an Amino Acid To review the body's handling of amino acids, let us follow the fate of an amino acid that was originally part of a protein-containing food. When the amino acid arrives in a cell, it can be used in one of several ways, depending on the cell's needs at the time:

- The amino acid can be used as is to build part of a growing protein.
- The amino acid can be altered somewhat to make another needed compound, such as the vitamin niacin.
- The cell can dismantle the amino acid in order to use its amine group to build a different amino acid. The remainder can be used for fuel or, if fuel is abundant, converted to glucose or fat.

- Amino acids in a cell can be:
  - *Used to build protein.*
  - *Converted to other amino acids or small nitrogen-containing compounds.*

In a cell that is starved for energy and has no glucose or fatty acids, the cell strips the amino acid of its amine group (the nitrogen part) and uses the remainder of its structure for energy. The amine group is excreted from the cell and then from the body in the urine. In a cell that has a surplus of energy and amino acids, the cell takes the amino acid apart, excretes the amine group, and uses the rest to meet immediate energy needs or converts it to glucose or fat for storage.

- Stripped of their nitrogen, amino acids can be:
  - *Burned as fuel.*
  - *Converted to glucose or fat.*

When not used to build protein or make other nitrogen-containing compounds, amino acids are "wasted" in a sense. This wasting occurs under any of four conditions:

1. When the body lacks energy from other sources.
2. When the diet supplies more protein than the body needs.
3. When the body has too much of any single amino acid, such as from a supplement.
4. When the diet supplies protein of low quality, with too few essential amino acids, as described in the next section.

- Amino acids are wasted when:
  - *Energy is lacking.*
  - *Protein is overabundant.*
  - *An amino acid is oversupplied in supplement form.*
  - *The protein is of low quality (too few essential amino acids).*

To prevent the wasting of dietary protein and permit the synthesis of needed body protein, the dietary protein must be of adequate quality; it must supply all essential amino acids in the proper amounts; it must be accompanied by enough energy-yielding carbohydrate; and fat must be present to permit the dietary protein to be used as such.

KEY POINT Amino acids can be metabolized to protein, nitrogen plus energy, glucose, or fat. They will be metabolized to protein only if sufficient energy is present from other sources. The nitrogen part is removed from each amino acid, and the resulting fragment is oxidized for energy. No storage form of amino acids exists in the body.

LO 6.5

Food Protein: Need and Quality

A person's response to dietary protein depends on many factors. To know whether, say, 60 grams of a particular protein is enough to meet a person's daily needs, one must consider the effects of factors discussed in this section, some pertaining to the body and some to the nature of the protein.

How Much Protein Do People Really Need?

The DRI recommendation for protein intake is designed to cover the need to replace protein-containing tissue that healthy adults lose and wear out every day. Therefore, it depends on body size: larger people have a higher protein need. For adults of

CONSUMER CORNER

Protein and Amino Acid Supplements

Why do people take protein supplements? Athletes often take them when trying to build muscle. Dieters may take them in hopes of speeding the process of weight loss or preserving lean tissue. Some women take them to strengthen their fingernails. People take individual amino acids, too—to cure herpes, to make themselves sleep better, to lose weight, and to relieve pain and depression. Do protein and amino acid supplements really do these things? Probably not. Are they safe? Not always.

In the skilled hands of clinical registered dietitians, formulas with supplemental protein or amino acids may help to reverse malnutrition in some critically ill patients. Not every patient is a candidate for such therapy, however, because supplemental amino acids may also stimulate inflammation and so worsen some illnesses.

PROTEIN SUPPLEMENTS

Protein supplements are popular with athletes but well-fed athletes do not need them (see Controversy 10 for details). True, dietary protein is necessary for building muscle tissue and, true, consuming protein in conjunction with resistance exercise helps muscles build new proteins.[1] But protein supplements do not improve athletic performance beyond the gains from well-timed meals of ordinary foods. And, if supplements create a surplus of protein or certain amino acids, the excess must be metabolized, placing a burden on the kidneys to excrete excess nitrogen.

Weight-loss dieters may benefit from making a habit of consuming the needed protein-rich foods because protein often satisfies the appetite, while insufficient protein may increase it.[2] However, extra protein from powders, pills, or beverages is unlikely to dampen the appetite further, although it contributes unneeded calories—the wrong effect for weight loss. Evidence does not support taking protein supplements for weight loss, and common sense opposes it.

AMINO ACID SUPPLEMENTS

Enthusiastic popular reports have led to widespread use of individual amino acids. One such amino acid is lysine, touted to prevent or relieve the infections that cause herpes sores on the mouth or genital organs. Lysine does not cure herpes infections. Whether it reduces outbreaks or even whether it is safe is unknown because scientific studies are lacking.

Tryptophan supplements are advertised to relieve pain, depression, and insomnia. Tryptophan plays a role as a precursor for the brain neurotransmitter serotonin, an important regulator of sleep, appetite, mood, and sensory perception. The DRI committee concludes that high doses of tryptophan may induce sleepiness, but they may also cause side effects, such as nausea and skin disorders. A serious blood disorder, EMS, probably caused by contaminants, once threatened takers of tryptophan supplements, but improved regulations have reduced this risk.*[3]

The body is designed to handle whole proteins best. It breaks them into manageable pieces (dipeptides and tripeptides), then splits these a few at a time, simultaneously releasing them into the blood. This slow, bit-by-bit assimilation is ideal because groups of chemically similar amino acids compete for the carriers that absorb them into the blood. An excess of one amino acid can tie up a carrier and disturb amino acid absorption, creating a temporary imbalance.[4] Amino acids are key players in complex mechanisms for gene regulation, and excesses may affect these processes in unpredictable ways.[5] In mice, for example, excess methionine causes the blood buildup of an amino acid associated with heart disease (homocysteine) and increases inflammation in the liver. No one knows if the same is true in people.[6] Many supplement takers experience digestive disturbances. Amino acids in concentrated supplements cause excess water to flow into the digestive tract, causing diarrhea.[7]

A lack of research prevents the DRI committee from setting Tolerable Upper Intake Levels for amino acids.[8] Therefore, no level of amino acid supplementation can be assumed safe; Table 6-2 lists people most likely to be harmed. In fact, Canada bans sales of single amino acids to consumers.† The warning is

*EMS is short for eosinophilia-myalgia syndrome.

†*Canada only allows single amino acid supplements to be sold as drugs or used as food additives.*

TABLE 6-2 People Most Likely to Be Harmed by Amino Acid Supplements

Growth or altered metabolism makes these people especially likely to be harmed by self-prescribed amino acid supplements:

- All women of childbearing age.
- Pregnant or lactating women.
- Infants, children, and adolescents.
- Elderly people.
- People with inborn errors of metabolism that affect their bodies' handling of amino acids.
- Smokers.
- People on low-protein diets.
- People with chronic or acute mental or physical illnesses.

this: much is still unknown, and the taker of amino acid supplements cannot be certain of their safety or effectiveness.[9]

CONCLUSION

Many chapters of this book present evidence that whole foods are superior sources for nutrients and phytochemicals for human health.[10] The Consumer Corner in Chapter 4 showed that a nutritionally inferior food (refined bread) enriched with a few added nutrients is still inadequate in many others compared with whole grains. The Controversy section in Chapter 7 points out potential dangers of vitamin and mineral supplements and their lack of efficacy for preventing any disease except nutrient deficiencies. The same is true of amino acids—whole food proteins, in balance with other needed foods, best support human health. Even with all that we know about science, it is hard to improve on nature.

- The DRI recommended intake for protein (adult) = 0.8 g/kg.
- To figure out your protein need:
  1. Find your body weight in pounds.
  2. Convert pounds to kilograms (by dividing pounds by 2.2).
  3. Multiply kilograms by 0.8 to find total grams of protein recommended.

For example:

- *Weight = 130 lb.*
- *130 lb ÷ 2.2 = 59 kg.*
- *59 kg × 0.8 = 47 g.*

healthy body weight, the DRI recommended intake is set at 0.8 gram for each kilogram (or 2.2 pounds) of body weight (see inside front cover). The minimum amount is set at 10 percent of total calories. As mentioned in the Think Fitness feature earlier, athletes may need slightly more protein but the increased need is well covered by most people's diets.[11]

For infants and growing children, the protein recommendation, like all nutrient recommendations, is higher per unit of body weight. The DRI committee set an upper limit for protein intake of no more than 35 percent of total calories, an amount significantly higher than average intakes. Table 6-3 reviews recommendations for protein intake, and the margin provides a method for determining your own protein need. The DRI committee suggests that vegetarians need more iron than the general population. The following factors also modify protein needs.

The Body's Health Malnutrition or infection may greatly increase the need for protein while making it hard to eat even normal amounts of food. In malnutrition, secretion of digestive enzymes slows as the tract's lining degenerates, impairing protein digestion and absorption. When infection is present, extra protein is needed for enhanced immune functions.

Other Nutrients and Energy The need for ample energy, carbohydrate, and fat has already been emphasized. To be used efficiently by the cells, protein must also be accompanied by the full array of vitamins and minerals.

Protein Quality The remaining factor, protein quality, helps determine how well a diet supports the growth of children and the health of adults. Two factors influence protein quality: a protein's digestibility and its amino acid composition, discussed later.

Recommendations for protein intake assume a normal mixed diet, that is, a diet that includes sufficient nutrients and a combination of animal and plant protein. Because not all proteins are used with 100 percent efficiency, the recommendation is generous. Many healthy people can consume less than the recommended amount and still meet their bodies' protein needs. What this means in terms of food selections is presented in this chapter's Food Feature.

TABLE 6-3 Protein Intake Recommendations for Healthy Adults

DRI Recommended Intake[a]
• 0.8 gram protein per kilogram of body weight per day. • Women: 46 grams per day; men: 56 grams per day. • Acceptable intake range: 10 to 30 percent of calories from protein.
USDA Food Guide, MyPyramid
• Every day most adults should eat 5- to 6½-ounce equivalents of lean meat, poultry without skin, fish, legumes, eggs, nuts, or seeds. • Every day most adults need 3 cups of fat-free or low-fat milk or yogurt, or the equivalent of fat-free cheese or vitamin- and mineral-fortified soy beverage. • Eat a variety of foods to provide small amounts of protein from other sources.

[a]*Protein recommendations for infants, children, and pregnant and lactating women are higher; see inside front cover, page B.*

MY TURN

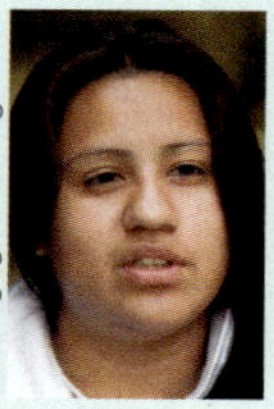
© Cengage Learning

Aira

© Cengage Learning

Joshua

Veggin' Out

Have you ever considered not eating meat? Listen to two students discuss how becoming vegetarian affected their social life.

CENGAGENOW To hear their stories, log on to www.cengage.com/sso.

KEY POINT The protein intake recommendation depends on size and stage of growth. The DRI recommended intake for adults is 0.8 gram of protein per kilogram of body weight. Factors concerning both the body and food sources modify an individual's protein need.

Growing children end each day with more bone, blood, muscle, and skin cells than they had at the beginning of the day.

Nitrogen Balance

Underlying the protein recommendation are **nitrogen balance** studies, which compare nitrogen lost by excretion with nitrogen eaten in food. In healthy adults, nitrogen-in (consumed) must equal nitrogen-out (excreted). Scientists measure the body's daily nitrogen losses in urine, feces, sweat, and skin under controlled conditions and then estimate the amount of protein needed to replace these losses.[‡12]

How Nitrogen Balance Varies Under normal circumstances, healthy adults are in nitrogen equilibrium, or zero balance; that is, they have the same amount of total protein in their bodies at all times. When nitrogen-in exceeds nitrogen-out, people are said to be in positive nitrogen balance; somewhere in their bodies more proteins are being built than are being broken down and lost. When nitrogen-in is less than nitrogen-out, people are said to be in negative nitrogen balance; they are losing protein. Figure 6-13 illustrates these different states.

Positive Nitrogen Balance Growing children add new blood, bone, and muscle cells to their bodies every day, so children must have more protein, and therefore more nitrogen, in their bodies at the end of each day than they had at the beginning. A growing child is therefore in positive nitrogen balance. Similarly, when a woman is pregnant, she must be in positive nitrogen balance until after the birth, when she once again reaches equilibrium.

Negative Nitrogen Balance Negative nitrogen balance occurs when muscle or other protein tissue is broken down and lost. Illness or injury triggers the release of powerful messengers that signal the body to break down some of the less vital proteins, such as those of the skin and even muscle.[§] This action floods the blood with

nitrogen balance the amount of nitrogen consumed compared with the amount excreted in a given time period.

‡The average protein is 16 percent nitrogen by weight; that is, each 100 grams of protein contain 16 grams of nitrogen. As a general rule, multiply the nitrogen's weight by 6.25 to estimate the protein's weight.

§The messengers are cytokines.

FIGURE 6-13 **Nitrogen Balance**

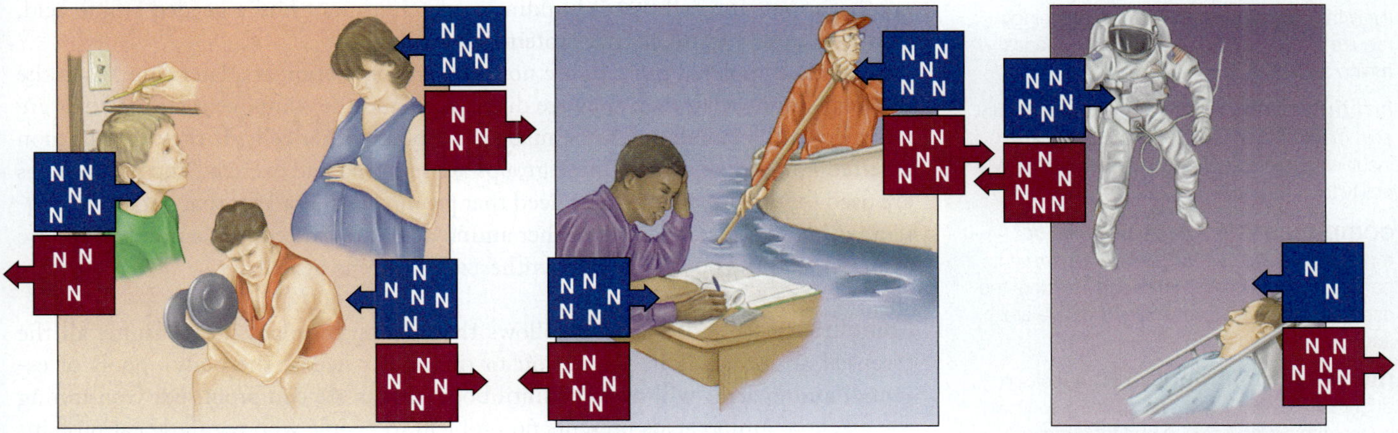

Positive Nitrogen Balance
These people—a growing child, a person building muscle, and a pregnant woman—are all retaining more nitrogen than they are excreting.

Nitrogen Equilibrium
These people—a healthy college student and a young retiree—are in nitrogen equilibrium.

Negative Nitrogen Balance
These people—an astronaut and a surgery patient—are losing more nitrogen than they are taking in.

amino acids and energy needed to fuel the body's defenses and fight the illness. The result is negative nitrogen balance. Astronauts, too, experience negative nitrogen balance. In the stress of space flight, and with no need to support the body's weight against gravity, the astronauts' muscles waste and weaken. To minimize the inevitable loss of muscle tissue, the astronauts must do special exercises in space.

KEY POINT Protein recommendations are based on nitrogen balance studies, which compare nitrogen excreted from the body with nitrogen ingested in food.

Which Foods Provide High-Quality Protein?

Put simply, **high-quality proteins** provide enough of all the essential amino acids needed by the body to create its own working proteins, whereas low-quality proteins don't. In making their required proteins, the cells need a full array of amino acids. If a nonessential amino acid (that is, one the cell can make) is unavailable from food, the cell synthesizes it and continues attaching amino acids to the protein strands being manufactured. If the diet fails to provide enough of an essential amino acid (one the cell cannot make), the cells begin to adjust their activities. The cells:

- Break down more internal proteins to liberate the needed essential amino acid.
- Conserve the essential amino acid by limiting their synthesis of proteins.[13]

As the deprivation continues, tissues make one adjustment after another in the struggle to survive.

Just as each letter of the alphabet is important in forming whole words, each amino acid must be available to build finished proteins.

high-quality proteins dietary proteins containing all the essential amino acids in relatively the same amounts that human beings require. They may also contain nonessential amino acids.

limiting amino acid an essential amino acid that is present in dietary protein in an insufficient amount, thereby limiting the body's ability to build protein.

complementary proteins two or more proteins whose amino acid assortments complement each other in such a way that the essential amino acids missing from one are supplied by the other.

mutual supplementation the strategy of combining two incomplete protein sources so that the amino acids in one food make up for those lacking in the other food. Such protein combinations are sometimes called *complementary proteins*.

Limiting Amino Acids

The measures just described help the cells to channel the available **limiting amino acid** to its wisest use: making new proteins. Even so, the normally fast rate of protein synthesis slows to a crawl as the cells make do with the proteins on hand. When the limiting amino acid once again becomes available in abundance, the cells resume their normal protein-related activities. If the shortage becomes chronic, however, the cells begin to break down their protein-making machinery. Consequently, when protein intakes become adequate again, protein synthesis lags behind until the needed machinery can be rebuilt. Meanwhile, the cells function less and less effectively as their proteins wear out and are only partially replaced.

Thus, a diet that is short in any of the essential amino acids limits protein synthesis. An earlier analogy likened amino acids to letters of the alphabet. To be meaningful, words must contain all the right letters. For example, a print shop that has no letter "N" cannot make personalized stationery for Jana Johnson. No matter how many Js, As, Os, Hs, and Ss are in the printer's possession, they cannot replace the missing Ns. Likewise, in building a protein molecule, no amino acid can fill another's spot. If a cell that is building a protein cannot find a needed amino acid, synthesis stops and the partial protein is released.

Partially completed proteins are not held for completion at a later time when the diet may improve. Rather, they are dismantled and the component amino acids are returned to the circulation to be made available to other cells. If they are not soon inserted into protein, their amine groups are removed and excreted and the residues are used for other purposes. The need that prompted the call for that particular protein will not be met. Since the other amino acids are wasted, the amine groups are excreted, and the body cannot resynthesize the amino acids later.

Complementary Proteins

It follows that if a person does not consume all the essential amino acids in proportion to the body's needs, the body's pools of essential amino acids will dwindle until body organs are compromised. Consuming the essential amino acids presents no problem to people who regularly eat proteins containing ample amounts of all of the essential amino acids, such as those of meat, fish, poultry, cheese, eggs, milk, and most soybean products.

An equally sound choice is to eat a combination of foods from plants so that amino acids that are low in some foods will be supplied by the others. The protein-

FIGURE 6-14 Complementary Protein Combinations

Healthful foods like these contribute substantial protein (42 grams total) to this day's meals without meat. Additional servings of nutritious foods, such as milk, bread, and eggs, can easily supply the remainder of the day's need for protein (14 additional grams for men and 4 for women).

John A. Rizzo/Photodisc/Getty Images

3/4 c oatmeal =	5 g
Protein total	5 g

© Polara Studios, Inc.

1 c rice =	4 g
1 c beans =	16 g
Protein total	20 g

© Michael Newman/PhotoEdit

1 1/2 c pasta =	11 g
1 c vegetables =	2 g
2 tbs Parmesan cheese =	4 g
Protein total	17 g

FIGURE 6-15 How Complementary Proteins Work Together

Legumes provide plenty of the amino acids isoleucine (Ile) and lysine (Lys), but fall short in methionine (Met) and tryptophan (Trp). Grains have the opposite strengths and weaknesses, making them a perfect match for legumes.

	Ile	Lys	Met	Trp
Legumes	✓	✓		
Grains			✓	✓
Together	✓	✓	✓	✓

rich foods are combined to yield **complementary proteins** (see Figure 6-14), or proteins containing all the essential amino acids in amounts sufficient to support health.[14] This concept, called **mutual supplementation,** is illustrated in Figure 6-15. The figure demonstrates that the amino acids of **legumes** and grains balance each other to provide all of the needed amino acids. The complementary proteins need not be eaten together, so long as the day's meals supply them all and the diet provides enough energy and total protein from a variety of sources.

Protein Digestibility In measuring a protein's quality, digestibility is important. Simple measures of the total protein in foods are not useful by themselves—even animal hair and hooves would receive a top score by those measures alone. They are made of protein, but not in a form that people can use.

The digestibility of protein varies from food to food and bears profoundly on protein quality. The protein of oats, for example, is less digestible than that of eggs. In general, amino acids from animal proteins, such as chicken, beef, and pork, are most easily digested and absorbed (over 90 percent). Those from legumes are next (about 80 to 90 percent). Those from grains and other plant foods vary (from 70 to 90 percent). Cooking with moist heat improves protein digestibility, whereas dry heat methods can impair it.

© Amana Images Inc./Alamy

Cooking with moist heat improves protein digestibility, whereas frying makes protein harder to digest.

KEY POINT Digestibility of protein varies from food to food, and cooking can improve or impair it.

Perspective on Protein Quality Concern about the quality of individual food proteins is of only theoretical interest in settings where food is abundant. Most people in the United States and Canada eat a variety of nutritious foods to meet their energy needs. Healthy adults in these places would find it next to impossible not to meet their protein needs, even if they were to eat no meat, fish, poultry, eggs, or cheese products at all. They need not pay attention to mutual supplementation, so long as the diet is varied, nutritious, and adequate in energy and other nutrients—not made up just of, say, cookies, potato chips, or alcoholic beverages. Protein sufficiency follows effortlessly behind a balanced, nutritious diet.

For people in areas where food sources are less reliable, protein quality can make the difference between health and disease. When food energy intake is limited (where malnutrition is widespread) or when the selection of foods available is severely limited (where a single low-protein food, such as **fufu** made from cassava root,** provides

legumes (leg-GOOMS, LEG-yooms) plants of the bean, pea, and lentil family that have roots with nodules containing special bacteria. These bacteria can trap nitrogen from the air in the soil and make it into compounds that become part of the plant's seeds. The seeds are rich in protein compared with those of most other plant foods. Also defined in Chapter 1.

fufu a low-protein staple food that provides abundant starch energy to many of the world's people; fufu is made by pounding or grinding root vegetables or refined grains and cooking them to a smooth semisolid consistency.

**Cassava is also called *manioc* or *yucca*.

90 percent of the calories), the primary food source of protein must be checked because its quality is crucial.

KEY POINT A protein's amino acid assortment greatly influences its usefulness to the body. Proteins lacking essential amino acids can be used only if those amino acids are present from other sources.

LO 6.6

Protein Deficiency and Excess

Protein deficiencies are well known because, together with energy deficiencies, they are the world's leading form of malnutrition. The health effects of too much protein are far less well known. Both deficiency and excess are of concern.

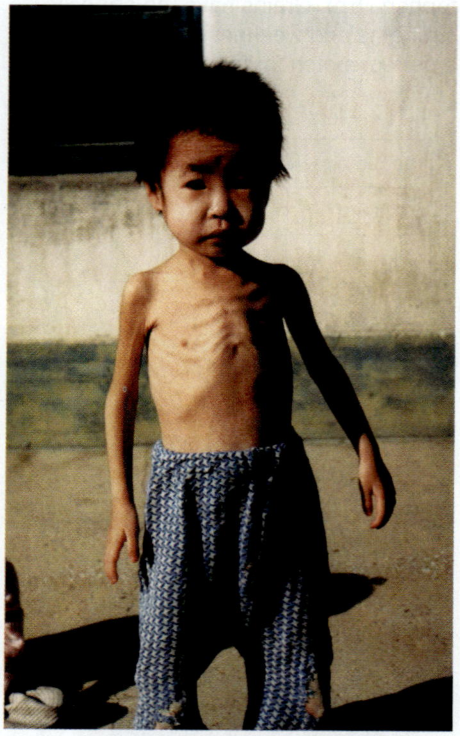

© AP/Wide World Photos

The extreme loss of muscle and fat characteristic of marasmus is apparent in this child's "matchstick" arms.

What Happens When People Consume Too Little Protein?

Protein deficiency and energy deficiency go hand in hand. This combination—**protein-energy malnutrition (PEM)**—is the most widespread form of malnutrition in the world today. Over 500 million children face imminent starvation and suffer the effects of severe malnutrition and **hunger.** Most of the 33,000 children who die each day are malnourished. PEM is prevalent in Africa, Central America, South America, the Middle East, and East and Southeast Asia, but developed countries, including those in North America, are not immune to it.

PEM strikes early in childhood, but it endangers many adults as well. Inadequate food intake leads to poor growth in children and to weight loss and wasting in adults. Stunted growth due to PEM is easy to overlook because a small child can look normal. The small stature of children in impoverished nations was once thought to be a normal adaptation to the limited availability of food; now it is known to be an avoidable failure of growth due to a lack of food during the growing years.

PEM takes two different forms, with some cases exhibiting a combination of the two. In one form, the person is shriveled and lean all over—this disease is called **marasmus.** In the second, a swollen belly and skin rash are present, and the disease is named **kwashiorkor.**[††] In the combination, some features of each type are present. Marasmus reflects a chronic inadequate food intake and therefore inadequate energy, vitamins, and minerals as well as too little protein. Kwashiorkor may result from severe acute malnutrition, with too little protein to support body functions.

KEY POINT Protein-deficiency symptoms are always observed when either protein or energy is deficient. Extreme food-energy deficiency is marasmus; extreme protein deficiency is kwashiorkor. The two diseases most often overlap and together are called PEM.

protein-energy malnutrition (PEM) the world's most widespread malnutrition problem, including both marasmus and kwashiorkor and states in which they overlap; also called *protein-calorie malnutrition (PCM)*.

hunger the physiological craving for food; the progressive discomfort, illness, and pain resulting from the lack of food. See also Chapters 9 and 15.

marasmus (ma-RAZ-mus) a form of PEM related to protein malnutrition and infections, with a set of recognizable symptoms, such as edema.

kwashiorkor (kwash-ee-OR-core, kwashee-or-CORE) a form of PEM related to protein malnutrition and infections, with a set of recognizable symptoms, such as edema.

Marasmus

Marasmus occurs most commonly in children from 6 to 18 months of age in overpopulated city slums. Children in impoverished nations subsist on a weak cereal drink with scant energy and protein of low quality; such food can barely sustain life, much less support growth. A starving child often looks like a wizened little old person—just skin and bones.

Muscle Wasting and Other Impairments Without adequate nutrition, muscles, including heart muscle, waste and weaken. Brain development is stunted and learning is impaired. Metabolism is so slow that body temperature is subnormal. There is

[††]A term gaining acceptance for use in place of kwashiorkor is *hypoalbuminemic-type PEM.*

little or no fat under the skin to insulate against cold, and hospital workers find that children with marasmus need to be wrapped up and kept warm. They also need love because they have often been deprived of parental attention as well as food.

The starving child faces this threat to life by engaging in as little activity as possible—not even crying for food. The body collects all its forces to meet the crisis and so cuts down on any expenditure of energy not needed for the heart, lungs, and brain to function. Growth ceases; the child is no larger at age four than at age two. The skin loses its elasticity and moisture, so it tends to crack; when sores develop, they fail to heal. Digestive enzymes are in short supply, the digestive tract lining deteriorates, and absorption fails. The child can't assimilate what little food is eaten.

Disease Conditions Blood proteins, including hemoglobin, are no longer produced, so the child becomes anemic and weak. If a bone breaks, healing is delayed because the protein needed to heal it is lacking. Antibodies to fight off invading bacteria are degraded to provide amino acids for other uses, leaving the child an easy target for infection. Then **dysentery,** an infection of the digestive tract, causes diarrhea, further depleting the body of nutrients, especially minerals. Measles, which might make a healthy child sick for a week or two, kills a child with PEM within two or three days. In the marasmic child, once infection sets in, kwashiorkor often follows and the immune response weakens further. Infections that occur with malnutrition are responsible for two-thirds of the deaths of young children in developing countries.

Preventing Death Ultimately, marasmus progresses to the point of no return when the body's machinery for protein synthesis, itself made of protein, has been degraded. At this point, attempts to correct the situation by giving food or protein fail to prevent death. If caught before this time, however, the starvation of a child can be reversed by careful nutrition therapy. The fluid balances are most critical. Diarrhea will have depleted the body's potassium and upset other electrolyte balances. The combination of electrolyte imbalances, anemia, fever, and infections often leads to heart failure and sudden death. Careful correction of fluid and electrolyte balances usually raises the blood pressure and strengthens the heartbeat within a few days. Later, fat-free milk, providing protein and carbohydrate, can safely be given; fat is introduced still later, when body protein is sufficient to provide carriers. Years after PEM is corrected, a child may experience deficits in thinking and school achievement compared with well-nourished peers.

KEY POINT PEM is starvation, in which muscles waste away, growth ceases, brain development is stunted, body temperature falls, diseases set in, and nutrient absorption fails. Without proper and timely nutrition therapy, death ensues.

Did You Know?

The term *electrolyte balance,* defined earlier, refers to the proper concentrations of salts (dissolved particles) within the body fluids (see Chapter 8 for details).

Kwashiorkor

Kwashiorkor is a Ghanaian name for "the evil spirit that infects the first child when the second child is born." In countries where kwashiorkor is prevalent, each baby is weaned from breast milk as soon as the next one comes along. The older baby no longer receives breast milk, which contains high-quality protein designed perfectly to support growth, but is instead given a watery cereal with scant protein of low quality. Small wonder the just-weaned child sickens when the new baby arrives. Though rare in the United States and Canada, kwashiorkor is not entirely unknown, usually occurring when fad diets replace sound nutrition in children.

Some kwashiorkor symptoms resemble those of marasmus (see Table 6-4) but often without severe wasting of body fat. Proteins and hormones that previously maintained fluid balance are now diminished, so fluid leaks out of the blood and accumulates in the belly and legs, causing edema, a distinguishing feature of kwashiorkor. The kwashiorkor victim's belly often bulges with a fatty liver, caused by lack of the protein carriers that transport fat out of the liver. The fatty liver loses some of

The edema and enlarged liver characteristic of kwashiorkor are apparent in this child's swollen belly.

dysentery (DISS-en-terry) an infection of the digestive tract that causes diarrhea.

TABLE 6-4 **Features of Marasmus and Kwashiorkor in Children**

Separating PEM into two classifications oversimplifies the condition, but at the extremes, marasmus and kwashiorkor exhibit marked differences. Marasmus-kwashiorkor mix presents symptoms common to both marasmus and kwashiorkor. In all cases, children are likely to develop diarrhea, infections, and multiple nutrient deficiencies.

Marasmus	Kwashiorkor
Infants and toddlers (less than 2 yr)	Older infants and young children (1 to 3 yr)
Severe deprivation or impaired absorption of protein, energy, vitamins, and minerals	Inadequate protein intake or, more commonly, infections
Develops slowly; chronic PEM	Rapid onset; acute PEM
Severe weight loss	Some weight loss
Severe muscle wasting with fat loss	Some muscle wasting, with retention of some body fat
Growth: <60% weight-for-age	Growth: 60 to 80% weight-for-age
No detectable edema	Edema
No fatty liver	Enlarged, fatty liver
Anxiety, apathy	Apathy, misery, irritability, sadness
Appetite may be normal or impaired	Loss of appetite
Hair is sparse, thin, and dry; easily pulled out	Hair is dry and brittle; easily pulled out; changes color; becomes straight
Skin is dry, thin, and wrinkled	Skin develops lesions

Did You Know?

Melanin, a brown pigment of hair, skin, and eyes, was mentioned earlier as a product made from tyrosine.

its ability to clear poisons from the body, prolonging their toxic effects. Thus, toxins can worsen the condition. Without sufficient tyrosine to make melanin, the child's hair loses its normal color; inadequate protein synthesis leaves the skin patchy and scaly; sores fail to heal. Measles or other infections easily penetrate the weakened immune defenses of the protein-deficient child and often precipitate kwashiorkor.

KEY POINT Kwashiorkor sets in when too little protein is provided to a growing child. Symptoms include edema, fatty liver, changes in hair color, scaly skin, reduced disease resistance, and sores that fail to heal.

PEM at Home

PEM occurs among some groups in the United States and Canada: the poor living on U.S. Indian reservations, in inner cities, and in rural areas; some elderly people; hungry and homeless children; and those suffering from the eating disorder anorexia nervosa. Occasionally, well-meaning but misinformed parents inflict PEM and other serious deficiency diseases on their infants and toddlers by replacing their formula or milk with unenriched, protein-poor "health-food" soy or rice drinks.[15] Also at risk for PEM are those with wasting diseases such as cancer or AIDS and those addicted to drugs and alcohol. In a downward spiral, PEM and serious illness worsen each other, so treating the PEM often reduces medical complications and suffering even when the underlying disease is untreatable.

Today, in the United States, tens of millions of people who work to support their children earn so little that they cannot afford a steady supply of nutritious food. Almost 14 million U.S. children live in households where hunger threatens or is painfully experienced. Hunger, especially in children, harms everyone's future. Hungry children do not learn as well as fed children, nor are they as competitive. They are ill more often, they have higher absentee rates from school, and when they attend, they cannot concentrate for long. The forces driving poverty and hunger will require many great minds working together to find solutions.

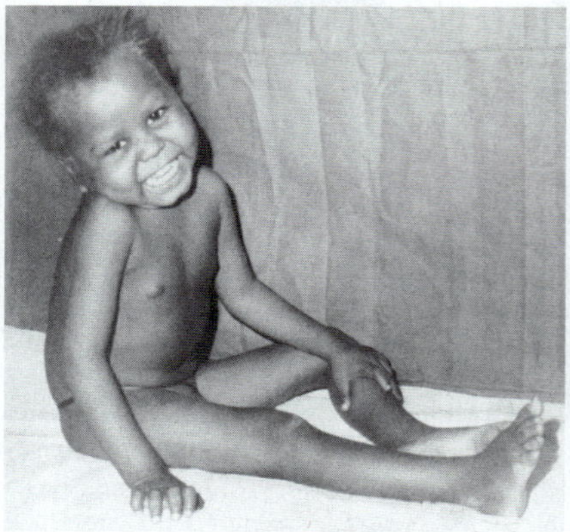

Given appropriate nutrition care, this child has successfully recovered from kwashiorkor.

• Turn to Chapter 15 for details concerning the causes of hunger at home and abroad.

KEY POINT PEM is not unknown in the United States, where millions live on the edge of hunger.

Is It Possible to Consume Too Much Protein?

Overconsumption of protein-rich foods offers no benefits and may pose health risks, particularly for weakened kidneys.[16] Selecting too many protein-rich foods, such as red meats and fat-containing milk products, adds saturated fat and crowds out fruits, vegetables, and whole grains, a problem from the standpoint of chronic disease risks, too.

© Stockphoto.com

U.S. Protein Intakes Most people assume that Americans eat too much protein. Research demonstrates that a median protein intake for U.S. adult males is about 16 percent of total calories, an amount well within the DRI suggested range of between 10 and 35 percent of calories.[17] Women, children, and some elderly people may typically take in less protein—13 to 15 percent. A small percentage of adolescent girls and elderly women consume insufficient protein or barely enough to meet their needs.[18]

In contrast to the average, some people follow popular diet advice to load up on up to 65 percent or more of calories from protein as a way to lose weight. Obtaining enough protein to meet the DRI recommended intake is important for appetite control and retention of lean body tissue during weight loss.[19] However, as Chapter 9 explains, it is calorie reduction, not the proportion of energy nutrients, that produces long-term weight loss.[20] Let it suffice here to say that the best weight-loss diet is one that provides a health-promoting balance of energy nutrients from a variety of whole foods.

Heart Disease Foods rich in animal protein can also be rich in saturated fats. Consequently, it is not surprising that people who take in a great deal of animal protein (red meats and dairy products) have a greater risk of heart disease.[21] In the United States, meat consumption often accompanies higher energy (calorie) intakes and increased abdominal body fatness, and excess abdominal fat raises the risk for heart disease.[22] As the Controversy points out, people who substitute vegetable protein for animal protein lower their risk of dying from heart disease.[23]

Currently, researchers are debating about the meaning of an observed link between an amino acid, **homocysteine,** and heart disease.[24] A high blood level of homocysteine often accompanies heart disease and stroke.[25] In addition, people with elevated blood homocysteine less often survive a heart attack than those with lower levels.[26] Many suspected factors—including a high-protein diet—can raise homocysteine in the blood, but it is unknown whether elevated homocysteine might be a cause of heart disease or an effect of it.[27] Research is focused on clarifying these relationships.[28]

Kidney Disease Animals fed experimentally on high-protein diets often develop enlarged kidneys or livers. In human beings, a high-protein diet increases the kidneys' workload, but this alone does not appear to damage healthy kidneys or cause kidney disease.[29] In people with kidney stones or other kidney diseases, however, a high-protein diet may speed the kidneys' decline. One of the most effective treatments for people with established kidney problems is to limit protein intakes to improve the symptoms of their disease.[30] Taken to an extreme, very low protein diets, even when supplemented with essential amino acids, do not delay kidney deterioration further and may increase fatality.[31]

Adult Bone Loss When human subjects are given increasing doses of purified protein, they spill larger and larger amounts of calcium from the body into the urine. This fact raises concerns that a high-protein diet may cause or worsen adult bone loss and the crippling effects of **osteoporosis**. In a recent study, however, researchers concluded that, unlike the effect of purified protein, high protein intakes from whole food sources, such as meat or milk products, do not appear to increase calcium losses.[32] Other factors, such as low intakes of vitamin D and bone minerals, ultimately harm bone health to a greater degree than high intakes of protein.[33]

Conversely, too little dietary protein almost certainly weakens the bones, both during young years of bone development and in malnourished elderly individuals.

homocysteine (hoe-moe-SIS-teen) an amino acid produced as an intermediate compound during amino acid metabolism. A buildup of homocysteine in the blood is associated with deficiencies of B vitamins and may increase the risk of diseases. See also Chapter 7.

osteoporosis (OSS-tee-oh-pore-OH-sis) a disease of older persons characterized by porous and fragile bones that easily break, leading to pain, infirmity, and death. Also defined in Chapter 8.

- Chapter 8 and Controversy 8 provide details about calcium and the bones.

Protein deficiency and hip fractures often occur together, while restoring dietary protein along with calcium and vitamin D supplements improves bone status.[‡‡34] In establishing protein recommendations, the DRI committee considered the effect of excess protein on the bones but found the evidence insufficient to set a Tolerable Upper Intake Level.[35]

Did You Know?

Red meats include beef, pork, mutton, lamb, veal, goat, venison, and others. White meats include poultry, fish, and other seafood. (Claims that pork is a "white" meat are scientifically inaccurate.)

Cancer The effects of protein on cancer causation cannot be easily separated from the various foods that provide protein to the diet. When researchers consider all sources of animal protein in the diet, for example, no association with cancers of the colon and rectum are evident.[36] However, when researchers limit their focus to well-cooked red meats and processed meats (typical protein sources for those on high-protein diets), they often report moderately increased risk for cancers, particularly of the colon and rectum.[37] Intakes of frankfurters, sausages, ham, luncheon meats, bacon, and other processed meats may best be limited for two other reasons, as well: these foods contain large amounts of saturated fat and salt, factors associated with heart disease and hypertension. Chapter 11 delves deeper into apparent links between diet and cancer.

KEY POINT Most U.S. protein intakes fall within the DRI recommended protein intake range of 10 and 35 percent of calories. No Tolerable Upper Intake Level exists for protein. Health risks may follow the overconsumption of protein-rich foods.

‡‡The calcium supplement was citrate malate.

FOOD FEATURE

Getting Enough but Not Too Much Protein

People in developed nations usually eat more than ample protein. The DRI recommendation for protein is generous and more than adequately covers the estimated needs of most people, even those with unusually high requirements. Most foods contribute at least some protein to the diet.

PROTEIN-RICH FOODS

Foods in the meat, poultry, fish, dry peas and beans, eggs, and nuts group and in the milk, yogurt, and cheese group contribute an abundance of high-quality protein. Two others, the vegetable group and the grains group, contribute smaller amounts of protein, but they can add up to significant quantities. What about the fruit group? Don't rely on fruit for protein—fruit contains only small amounts. Figure 6-16 demonstrates that a wide variety of foods contribute protein to the diet. Figure 6-17 lists the top protein contributors in the U.S. diet.

Protein is critical in nutrition, but too many protein-rich foods can displace other important foods from the diet. Foods richest in protein carry with them a characteristic array of vitamins and minerals, including vitamin B_{12} and iron, but they lack others—vitamin C and folate, for example. In addition, many protein-rich foods such as meat are high in caloriés, and to overconsume them is to invite obesity.

In Chapter 2, Figures 2-14 and 2-15 (pages 57–58) demonstrated this effect in two diets. What the figure did *not* show was that Monday's meals provided 87 grams of protein from a small amount of meat in harmony with all the other foods needed for the day *and* fell within the calorie budget. The more typical Tuesday's meals provided 106 grams of protein but fell short of meeting many other needs and exceeded the calorie allowance. Protein recommendations for adults generally fall between 46 and 56 grams per day, so both these day's meals provided much more than enough protein. Moral: Protein-rich meats are not always the best, or even the most desirable, sources of protein in a balanced nutritious diet.

Because American consumption of protein is ample, you can plan meatless or reduced-meat meals with confidence. Of the many interesting, protein-rich meat equivalents available, one has already been mentioned: the legumes.

THE ADVANTAGES OF LEGUMES

The protein of some legumes is of a quality almost comparable to that of meat, an unusual trait in a fiber-rich vegetable. For practical purposes, the quality of soy protein can be considered equivalent to that of meat. Figure 6-18 shows

FIGURE 6-16

Finding the Protein in Foods[a]

Fruits

Food		Protein g	%DV[b]
Avocado	1/2 c	2	4
Cantaloupe	1/2 c	1	2
Orange sections	1/2 c	1	2
Strawberries	1/2 c	1	2

Vegetables

Food		Protein g	%DV[b]
Corn	1/2 c	3	6
Broccoli	1/2 c	2	4
Collard greens	1/2 c	2	4
Sweet potato	1/2 c	2	4
Baked potato	1/2 c	1	2
Bean sprouts	1/2 c	1	2
Winter squash	1/2 c	1	2

Grains

Food		Protein g	%DV[b]
Pancakes	2 sm	6	12
Bagel	1/2	4	8
Brown rice	1/2 c	3	6
Grain bread	1 sl	3	6
Noodles, pasta	1/2 c	3	6
Oatmeal	1/2 c	3	6
Barley	1/2 c	2	4
Cereal flakes	1 oz	2	4

Meat, Poultry, Fish, Dry Peas and Beans, Eggs, and Nuts

Food		Protein g	%DV[b]
Roast beef	2 oz	19	33
Turkey leg	2 oz	16	32
Chicken breast	2 oz	15	30
Pork meat	2 oz	15	30
Tuna	2 oz	14	28
Lentils, beans, peas	1/2 c	9	18
Peanut butter	2 tbs	8	16
Almonds	1/4 c	8	16
Hot dog	1 reg	7	14
Lunch meat	2 oz	6	12
Egg	1 lg	6	12
Cashew nuts	1/4 c	5	10

Milk, Yogurt, and Cheese

Food		Protein g	%DV[b]
Cheese, processed	2 oz	13	26
Milk, yogurt	1 c	10	20
Pudding	1 c	5	10

Oils, Solid Fats, and Added Sugars

Not a significant source

[a]All foods are prepared and ready to eat.

[b]The Daily Value (DV) for protein is 50 g, based on an energy intake of 2,000 calories per day.

FIGURE
6-17
Top Contributors of Protein to the U.S. Diet

These foods supply about 70 percent of the protein in the U.S. diet. The remainder comes from foods contributing less than 2 percent of the total, such as cold cuts; ready-to-eat cereal; white potatoes; sausage; flour and baking ingredients; ice cream, sherbet, and frozen yogurt; nuts and seeds; cooked rice and other grains; and canned tuna.

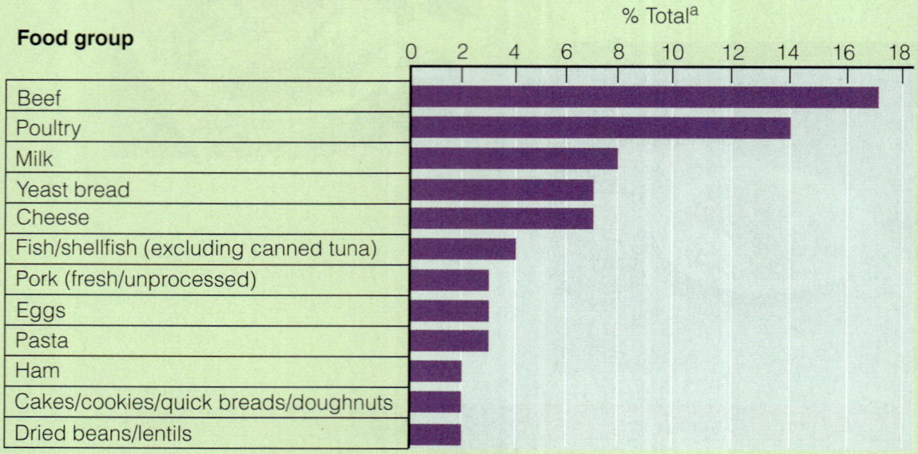

[a]*Rounded values*

Source: Data from P. A. Cotton and coauthors, Dietary sources of nutrients among U.S. adults, 1994–1996, Journal of the American Dietetic Association *104 (2004): 921–930.*

a legume plant's special root system that enables it to make abundant protein by obtaining nitrogen from the soil.[38] Legumes are also excellent sources of many B vitamins, iron, calcium, and other minerals, making them exceptionally nutritious. On average, a cup of cooked legumes contains about 30 percent of the Daily Values for both protein and iron.[§§] Like meats, though, legumes do not offer every nutrient, and they do not make a complete meal by themselves. They contain no vitamin A, vitamin C, or vitamin B_{12}, and their balance of amino acids can be much improved by using grains and other vegetables with them.

Soybeans are versatile legumes and many nutritious products are made from them. Heavy use of soy products in place of meat, however, inhibits iron absorption. The effect can be alleviated by using small amounts of meat and/or foods rich in vitamin C in the same meal with soy products. Vegetarians and others sometimes use convenience foods made from **textured vegetable protein** (soy protein) formulated to look and taste like hamburgers or breakfast sausages. Many of these are intended to match the known nutrient contents of animal protein foods, but they often fall short.[***] A wise vegetarian uses such foods sparingly and learns to use combinations of whole foods to supply the needed nutrients. The nutrients of soybeans are also available as bean curd, or **tofu,** a staple used in many Asian dishes. Thanks to the use of calcium salts when some tofu is

[§§]*Data from the* Food Processor Plus, *ESHA research, version 7.11.*

[***]*In Canada, regulations govern the nutrient contents of such products.*

textured vegetable protein processed soybean protein used in products formulated to look and taste like meat, fish, or poultry.

tofu (TOE-foo) a curd made from soybeans that is rich in protein, often rich in calcium, and variable in fat content; used in many Asian and vegetarian dishes in place of meat. (Also defined in Controversy 2.)

Legumes: protein-rich and exceptionally nutritious.

FIGURE
6-18
A Legume

The legumes include such plants as the kidney bean, soybean, green pea, lentil, black-eyed pea, and lima bean. Bacteria in the root nodules can "fix" nitrogen from the air, contributing it to the beans. Ultimately, thanks to these bacteria, the plant accumulates more nitrogen than it can get from the soil and also contributes more nitrogen to the soil than it takes out. The legumes are so efficient at trapping nitrogen that farmers often grow them in rotation with other crops to fertilize fields. Legumes are included with the meat group in Figure 6-16.

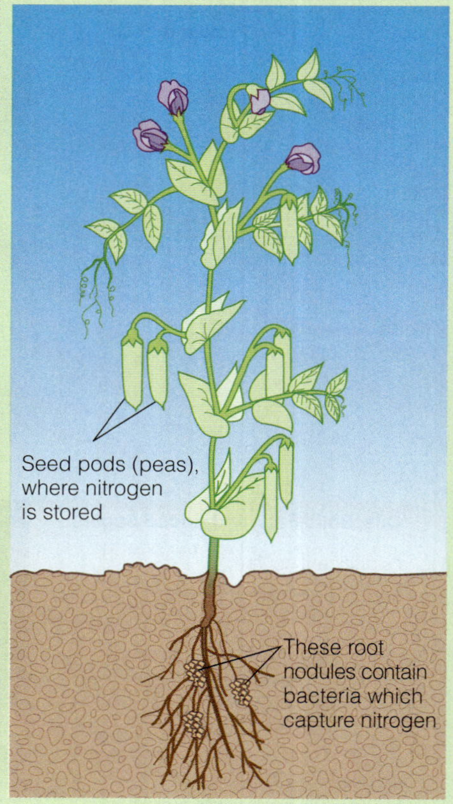

made, it can be high in calcium. Check the Nutrition Facts panel on the label.

The Food Features presented so far show that the recommendations for the three energy-yielding nutrients occur in balance with each other. The diets of most people, however, supply too little fiber, too much fat, too many calories, and abundant protein. To bring their diets into line with recommendations, then, requires changing the bulk of intake from calorie-rich fried foods, fatty meats, and sweet treats to lower-calorie complex carbohydrates and fiber-rich choices, such as whole grains, legumes, and vegetables. With these changes, protein totals automatically come into line with the requirements.

Diet Analysis PLUS Concepts in Action

Analyze Your Protein Intake

The purpose of this exercise is to make you aware of the effects of choosing protein-rich foods in balancing the three energy-yielding nutrients while planning a nutritious diet.

1. Most people in the United States and Canada eat a variety of foods that provide high-quality protein, making it almost impossible not to meet their protein needs. Do you think that your diet contains adequate protein? From the DA+ Home page, select Reports, then Macronutrient Ranges. Choose Day Three, include the entire day's meals, and generate a report. Is your intake within the recommended 10–35 percent of total energy intake range, as recommended by the DRI? What percent of your calorie intake consists of protein? If your protein intake is higher than 35 percent, what foods could you choose less of to bring you within range? If your intake is lower, what foods would you add to your diet?
2. From the Reports tab, select Intake vs. Goals report, choose Day Two, all meals. Generate a report. Table 6-3 provides protein intake recommendations (page 206) against which to compare your intake. Did your protein gram values fall into line with your DRI recommended intake (multiply your weight in kilograms by 0.8 gram)?
3. Which foods in your meals provide the greatest amounts of protein? From the Reports tab, select Source Analysis, choose Day Two, all meals. Select protein in the drop-down box, then generate a report. This report will help you determine your protein sources.
4. Using the same report and date from the previous question, break it down further to see how many grams of protein you eat for each meal: breakfast, lunch, and dinner.
5. Using Figure 6-14 (page 209), Figure 6-16 (page 215), and the Controversy section, create a vegan vegetarian meal that provides one-third of daily requirement for protein for a 19-year-old female vegan. Pick a new date, select Track Diet, and input the foods in the meal; then generate a report on the Intake Spreadsheet. Compare with DRI values on the inside front cover. If the meal fell short of one-third the protein DRI goal, what vegan foods can you change or add to provide the needed protein?

MEDIA MENU

CENGAGENOW To find additional quiz questions, view videos and animations, and explore interactive exercises, go to **www.cengage.com/sso.**

Search for information on vegetarianism and food allergies at **www.healthfinder.gov.**

Also search for information on food allergens and vegetarian diets at **www.fda.gov.**

Search for more information about protein-energy malnutrition worldwide at **www.who.int/nut.**

Learn more about sickle-cell anemia from the National Heart, Lung, and Blood Institute or the Sickle Cell Disease Association of America: **www.nhlbi.nih.gov** or **www.sicklecelldisease.org.**

SELF CHECK

Answers to these Self Check questions are in Appendix G.

1. The basic building blocks for protein are:
   - A. glucose units
   - B. amino acids
   - C. side chains
   - D. saturated bonds
2. Protein digestion begins in the:
   - A. mouth
   - B. stomach
   - C. small intestine
   - D. large intestine
3. To prevent wasting of dietary protein, which of the following conditions must be met?
   - A. Dietary protein must be adequate in quantity.
   - B. Dietary protein must supply all essential amino acids in the proper amounts.
   - C. The diet must supply enough calories from carbohydrate and fat.
   - D. All of the above.
4. For healthy adults, the DRI recommended intake for protein has been set at:
   - A. 0.8 gram per kilogram of body weight
   - B. 2.2 pounds per kilogram of body weight
   - C. 12 to 15 percent of total calories
   - D. 100 grams per day
5. Which of the following statements is correct regarding protein and amino acid supplements?
   - A. They help athletes build muscle without exercise.
   - B. They help dieters lose weight quicker.
   - C. They can assist in relieving depression.
   - D. None of the above.
6. Under certain circumstances, protein can be converted to glucose and so serve the energy needs of the brain.
   T F
7. Too little protein in the diet can have severe consequences, but excess protein has not been proven to have adverse effects.
   T F
8. Although protein energy malnutrition (PEM) is prevalent in underdeveloped nations, it is not seen in the United States.
   T F
9. Partially completed proteins are not held for completion at a later time when the diet may improve.
   T F
10. An example of a person in positive nitrogen balance is a pregnant woman.
   T F

CONTROVERSY 6

Vegetarian and Meat-Containing Diets: What Are the Benefits and Pitfalls?

LO 6.7, 6.8

In affluent countries around the world, people who eat well-planned **vegetarian** diets suffer less often from major chronic diseases than people whose diets center on meat.[1*] Should everyone consider eating a vegetarian diet, then? If so, should people simply omit meat, or is more demanded of the vegetarian diet planner? What positive contributions do animal products make to the diet? This Controversy looks first at the positive health aspects of vegetarian diets, then at the positive aspects of meat eaters' diets. It ends with some practical advice for the vegetarian diet planner.

A vegetarian lifestyle may mistakenly be associated with a particular culture, religion, or belief system, but there are many reasons why individuals might choose it:

- Health concerns: omitting meats is a way to reduce saturated fat intakes and increase whole-grain, fruit, vegetable, and legume intakes—changes associated with good health.
- Moral objections: some believe that we should not kill animals and so do not consume animal products, such as milk, cheese, eggs, or honey, or use items made from leather, wool, feathers, or silk.
- Other animal concerns: many people object to inhumane treatment of livestock. Some fear diseases, such as food poisoning or "mad cow disease," associated with meats.
- Religious beliefs: some religions prohibit eating meat.
- Environmental concerns: producing meat protein requires a much greater input of resources than does an equal amount of vegetable protein.[2] (See Chapter 15 for more on these topics.)

In any case, vegetarians are not categorized by their motivations but by the foods they choose to eat (see Table C6-1).

Why do meat eaters choose to eat meat and other animal products? Some reasons include:

- Convenience: some people find that a hamburger or chicken sandwich makes a convenient lunch.

*Reference notes are found in Appendix F.

© Polara Studios, Inc.

Can a diet without animal products supply the needed nutrients?

TABLE C6-1 Terms Used to Describe Vegetarians and Their Diets

Some of the terms below are in common usage, but others are useful only to researchers.

- **fruitarian** includes only raw or dried fruits, seeds, and nuts in the diet.
- **lacto-ovo vegetarian** includes dairy products, eggs, vegetables, grains, legumes, fruits, and nuts; excludes flesh and seafood.
- **lacto-vegetarian** includes dairy products, vegetables, grains, legumes, fruits, and nuts; excludes flesh, seafood, and eggs.
- **macrobiotic diet** a vegan diet composed mostly of whole grains, beans, and certain vegetables; taken to extremes, macrobiotic diets can compromise nutrient status.
- **ovo-vegetarian** includes eggs, vegetables, grains, legumes, fruits, and nuts; excludes flesh, seafood, and milk products.
- **partial vegetarian** a term sometimes used to mean an eating style that includes seafood, poultry, eggs, dairy products, vegetables, grains, legumes, fruits, and nuts; excludes or strictly limits certain meats, such as red meats.
- **pesco-vegetarian** same as partial vegetarian, but eliminates poultry.
- **vegan** includes only food from plant sources: vegetables, grains, legumes, fruits, seeds, and nuts; also called *strict vegetarian*.
- **vegetarian** includes plant-based foods and eliminates some or all animal-derived foods.

- Nutrients: some people rely on animal products for the energy and key nutrients they supply.
- Taste: others enjoy the taste of roasted chicken, barbecued ribs, or a grilled steak.
- Habit: some people wouldn't know what to eat without meat; they are accustomed to seeing it on the plate.
- Misguided weight-control efforts: people may mistakenly think that eating meats instead of grains, potatoes, and breads speeds weight loss (it doesn't). Conversely, teens may hide an eating disorder under the guise of being "vegetarian" (Chapter 9 takes up the issues of weight-loss dieting and eating disorders).[3]

Whatever your eating style or reasons for choosing it, choose carefully: the foods that you eat regularly make an impact on your health.

POSITIVE HEALTH ASPECTS OF VEGETARIAN DIETS

Today, nutrition authorities state with confidence that a well-chosen vegetarian diet can meet nutrient needs while supporting health superbly.[4] Although much evidence links vegetarian diets with reduced incidence of chronic diseases, particularly heart and artery diseases, such evidence is not easily obtained. It would be easy if vegetarians differed from others only in the absence of meat, but they often have *increased* intakes of whole grains, legumes, nuts, fruits, and vegetables as well.[5] Such diets are rich contributors of carbohydrates, fiber, vitamins, minerals, and phytochemicals that also correlate with low disease risks.

Also, many vegetarians avoid tobacco, use alcohol in moderation if at all, and are more physically active than other adults. When researchers take into account all of the effects of a total health-conscious lifestyle on disease development, the evidence weighs in favor of vegetarian diets, as the next sections make clear.

Defense Against Obesity

Among both men and women and across many ethnic groups, vegetarians more often maintain a healthier body weight than nonvegetarians.[6] The converse is also true: meat consumption correlates with increased energy intake and increased obesity.[7] The reason for this is not clear, but may reflect a lifestyle adopted by many vegetarians that makes health a high priority. Obesity impairs health in a number of ways (see Chapter 9), and vegetarians who maintain a healthy weight enjoy a health advantage.

Defense Against Heart Disease

Vegetarians die less often from heart disease and related illnesses than do meat-eating people.[8] Plant-based diets can be low in saturated fat, and saturated fat intake correlates directly with heart disease risk. The unsaturated fats of soybeans, seeds, avocados, nuts, olives, and other unsaturated vegetable oils reduce the risk of heart disease when they replace saturated fat sources in the diet.[9] Furthermore, diets that contain such foods generally provide more dietary fiber, a bonus to blood lipids and to the heart.

The lowest blood lipids are found in **vegans;** the blood lipids of **lacto-ovo vegetarians** are higher; and the blood lipids of people eating typical, meat-rich Western diets are the highest.[10] Vegetarians who eat cheese, sour cream, and butter take in more saturated fat than those who limit or eliminate these foods, and their blood lipids reflect it.

Courtesy of the United Soybean Board

When consumed in sufficient quantity, soy foods, such as this roasted tofu, may improve the health of the heart.

Decades of experimentation have revealed that when soy protein *replaces* animal protein in the diet, a slight but significant decline in LDL cholesterol occurs.[11] However, to achieve this benefit requires consuming large amounts of daily soy protein—50 grams, the amount in about five average soy "burgers" or two and a half cups of tofu.[12] Half this amount has proved ineffective.[13] In contrast, supplements of soy phytochemicals do not seem to benefit the heart.[14] Any protective effect of soy, therefore, may arise from the abundant soy protein, polyunsaturated fatty acids, fibers, vitamins, and minerals in these foods; they also often displace foods high in saturated fat from the diet.[15]

Defense Against High Blood Pressure

Vegetarians tend to have lower blood pressure and lower rates of hypertension than nonvegetarians. Often, vegetarians maintain a healthy body weight, and appropriate body weight helps to maintain healthy blood pressure; so does a diet low in total and saturated fat and high in fiber, fruits, vegetables, the mineral potassium, and soy protein.[16] A low sodium intake also promotes normal blood pressure, as do lifestyle factors such as not smoking, keeping alcohol intake moderate, and being physically active.

Defense Against Cancer

In a 2007 report, cancer authorities made this statement: "Red meat is a convincing cause of colorectal cancer."[17] Stated another way, colon and rectal cancer are reported to occur less frequently among people who eat mostly plant-based diets than among those who regularly consume red meat and processed meat.[18] The amount of red or processed meat reported to have this effect is surprisingly small—only 120 grams, or a little over 4 ounces per day.

Is the case closed on meat's culpability in colon and rectal cancers, then? "Not so fast," is the answer from a surprising study of over 60,000 people in the United Kingdom.[19] In this study, people who ate fish but not red meats had the lowest overall cancer rates—so far, so good. Vegetarians also had lower rates than meat eaters for total cancers—also not surprising. However, vegetarians had the *highest* number of colon and rectal cancers of any group, while fish eaters again had the lowest. No one yet knows the meaning of these results, but the findings may reflect the unusually small meat intakes (2 to 3 ounces per day) or the high vegetable and fruit intakes (just 20 percent lower than in the vegetarians) reported among these particular meat eaters.

The finding about fish in the study just described brings up questions about the so-called white meats: poultry and fish. Did the fish eaters in the British study gain some protection from fish? A hint comes from a study tracking cancer deaths among a half-million educated, non-Hispanic white men and women over age 50.[20] In support of many other findings, those who consumed the least red and processed meat had modestly lower cancer death rates, mostly colon and rectal cancers, than those who ate more meat. Unexpectedly, however, people who ate the *most* poultry and fish suffered the *least* cancer, making it clear that researchers must take into account types, not just totals, of meats consumed when studying links with cancer. Critics of the study also point out that people who eat less red meat (and choose poultry and fish most often) may also adopt other healthy habits, such as exercising regularly, which may reduce their cancer risks.[21] In that case, red meat intake may correlate with, but perhaps not be the cause of, an increased cancer risk.

Colon cancer risk also appears to increase with:

- Alcohol (moderate-to-high intakes).[22]
- Body and abdominal fatness.[23]

Other Health Benefits

In addition to obesity, heart disease, high blood pressure, and cancer, vegetarian diets may help prevent diabetes, osteoporosis, diverticular disease, and gallstones.[24] However, these effects may arise more from what vegetarians include in the diet—abundant fruit, legumes, vegetables, and whole grains—than from omission of meat. Lean meats, poultry, and seafood, while not essential to a healthy diet, can be used wisely to provide beneficial nutrients, as the next sections point out.

POSITIVE HEALTH ASPECTS OF THE MEAT EATER'S DIET

Unlike vegetarians, for whom suitable replacements exist for meat and milk in a healthy diet, meat eaters find no adequate substitutes for whole grains, fruits, and vegetables (not even antioxidant supplement pills, as the next chapter points out). A meat eater who excludes or minimizes intakes of these foods imperils health. The following sections consider a *balanced, adequate* diet, in which lean meat, poultry, seafood, eggs, and milk play a part.

Both meat eaters and lacto-ovo vegetarians can generally rely on their diets during critical times of life. In contrast, a vegan diet poses challenges. Protein is critical for building new tissues during growth, for fighting illnesses, and for building bone during youth and maintaining bone and muscle tissue integrity in old age.[25] While protein from plant sources can meet most people's needs, very young children and very elderly people with small appetites may not consume enough legumes, whole grains, or nuts to supply the protein they need.

The chapter made clear that animal protein from meat, fish, milk, and eggs is the clear winner in tests of digestibility and availability to the body, with soy protein a close second. Also, animal-derived foods provide abundant iron, zinc, vitamin D, and vitamin B_{12} needed by everyone, but particularly by pregnant women, infants, children, adolescents, and the elderly (details about these needs appear in later chapters).

© Polara Studios, Inc.

This 5-ounce steak provides almost all of the meat recommended for an entire day's intake in a 2,000-calorie diet.

In Pregnancy and Infancy

Women who eat meat, eggs, or milk products can be sure of receiving enough energy, vitamin B_{12}, vitamin D, calcium, iron, and zinc, as well as protein, to support pregnancy and breastfeeding. A woman following a well-planned lacto-ovo vegetarian diet can also relax in the knowledge that she is superbly supplied with energy and all necessary nutrients. And if she also habitually eats abundant vegetables and fruits, she can relax further, knowing that diet supplies the vitamin folate in amounts needed to protect her developing fetus from certain birth defects. A vegan woman who doesn't meet her nutrient needs, however, may enter pregnancy too thin and with scant nutrient stores to draw on as the nutrient demands of the fetus grow.

Of particular interest is vitamin B_{12}, a vitamin abundant in foods of animal origin but absent from vegetables. In fact, obtaining enough vitamin B_{12} poses a challenge to vegans of all ages. For pregnant and lactating women, obtaining vitamin B_{12} is critical. A severe and sometimes fatal disorder is occasionally reported among breastfed infants of vegan mothers who fail to obtain sufficient vitamin B_{12}.[26] The infant may die or suffer permanent damage if the condition goes untreated.[27] If caught in time, death and disability can be averted by administering the missing vitamin.

In Childhood

Children who eat meat, poultry, and fish receive abundant protein, iron, zinc, and vitamin B_{12}; such foods are reliable, convenient sources of nutrients needed for growth. Likewise, children eating well-planned lacto-ovo vegetarian diets also receive adequate nutrients and grow as well as their meat-eating peers.[28] Child-sized servings of vegan foods, however, can fail to provide sufficient energy or several key nutrients needed for normal growth. A child's small stomach can hold only so much food, and the vegan child may feel full before eating enough to meet his or her nutrient needs. Compared with meat-eating children, well-fed vegan children tend to be shorter and lighter in weight but not excessively so.

Small, frequent meals of fortified breads, cereals, or pastas with legumes, nuts, nut butters, and sources of unsaturated fats can help to meet protein and energy needs in a smaller volume at each sitting.[29] Because vegan children derive protein only from plant foods, their daily protein requirement may be somewhat higher than the DRI indicates for the general meat-eating population.[30] Other nutrients of concern for vegan children include vitamin B_{12}, vitamin D, calcium, iron, and zinc. A later section provides tips to help meet these nutrient needs within the context of a vegan diet.

In Adolescence

The healthiest vegetarian adolescents choose balanced diets that are heavy in fruits and vegetables but light on the sweets, fast foods, and salty snacks that tempt the teenage palate. These healthy vegetarian teens often meet national dietary objectives, such as those of *Healthy People 2010* (listed in Chapter 1)—a rare accomplishment in the United States.

Other teens, however, adopt poorly planned vegetarian diets lacking in energy, protein, vitamin B_{12}, calcium, zinc, and vitamin D. Omissions of calcium and vitamin D lead to weak bone development at precisely the time when bones must develop strength to protect them through later life. Also, teens must plan a source of vitamin B_{12} to avoid serious nerve damage from a deficiency. If a vegetarian child or teen refuses sound dietary advice, a registered dietitian can help identify problems, dispense appropriate guidance, and put unwarranted parental worries to rest.

In Aging and in Illness

For elderly people with diminished appetites or impaired digestion or for people recovering from illnesses, soft or ground meats can provide a well-liked, well-tolerated concentrated source of nutrients. People battling life-threatening diseases may encounter testimonial stories of cures attributed to restrictive eating plans, such as **macrobiotic diets,** but these diets often severely limit food selections and can fail to deliver the energy and nutrients needed for recovery.

PLANNING A VEGETARIAN DIET

Most vegetarians easily obtain large quantities of the nutrients that are abundant in plant foods: carbohydrate, fiber, thiamin, folate, and vitamins B_6, C, A, and E. Vegetarian food guides help to ensure adequate intakes of the main nutrients vegetarian diets might otherwise lack: protein, iron, zinc, calcium, vitamin B_{12}, vitamin D, and omega-3 fatty acids. Table C6-2 presents good vegetarian sources of these key nutrients.

If not properly balanced, any diet—vegetarian or otherwise—can lack nutrients. Poorly planned vegetarian diets typically lack iron, zinc, calcium, vitamin B_{12}, and vitamin D; poorly planned meat-eater's diets may lack vitamin A, vitamin C, folate, and fiber. Simply put, a diet that omits key foods omits essential nutrients.

Vegetarian Food Guide

The MyPyramid resources, introduced in Chapter 2, include tips for planning vegetarian diets using the USDA Food Guide. In addition, several vegetarian food guides have been developed to address the diet-planning needs of vegetarians.[31] Figure C6-1 presents one version.

When selecting from the vegetable and fruit groups, vegetarians should emphasize sources of calcium and iron. Green leafy vegetables provide both calcium and iron. Similarly, dried fruits deserve special notice in the fruit group because they can deliver more iron than other fruits. Note that the milk group features fortified soy milk for those who do not use milk, cheese, or yogurt. Their similarities are demonstrated in Figure C6-2 on page 225. The meat group, called "proteins," emphasizes legumes, soy products, nuts, and seeds. The oils group encourages the use of vegetable oils, nuts, and seeds rich in unsaturated fats and omega-3 fatty acids.

To ensure adequate intakes of vitamin B_{12}, vitamin D, and calcium, vegetarians need to select fortified foods or use supplements daily. Like MyPyramid, this vegetarian food pyramid also encourages physical activity. In planning a vegetarian diet, scrutinize the labels of convenience and prepared vegetarian foods just as you would those of ordinary foods. Some prepared foods constitute a nutritional bargain, such as vegetarian "hot dogs." Made of soy, these hot dogs look and taste like the original meat product but contain much less fat and saturated fat and no cholesterol. Conversely, banana chips, often sold as "healthy" alternative snack food, are no bargain: a quarter cup of banana chips fried in saturated coconut oil provides 150 calories with 7 grams of saturated fat (a big hamburger has 8 grams). A plain banana has 100 calories and practically no fat.

Protein

Vegetarians who consume eggs and low-fat milk products receive high-quality complete protein that provides all the essential amino acids required for health. Even vegans are likely to meet protein needs provided that they meet their energy needs with nutritious whole foods and that their protein sources are varied.[32]

Foods made from textured vegetable protein, usually soybean products, are formulated to look and taste like meat. They may fall short of the nutrients in meats, however, and they may be high in salt, sugar, or other additives. Labels list all of the ingredients in such foods. Vegetarians may also use soybeans in other forms, such as plain tofu (bean curd), edamame (cooked green soybeans, pronounced *ed-eh-MAH-may*), or soy flour, to bolster protein intake without consuming unwanted salt, sugar, or other additives.

Iron

Getting enough iron can be a problem even for meat eaters; vegetarians must be vigilant about obtaining iron. The iron in plant foods such as legumes, dark green leafy vegetables, iron-fortified cereals, and whole-grain breads and cereals may not be as well absorbed (see Chapter 8 for more details). Such foods also contain inhibitors of iron absorp-

TABLE C6-2 **Vegetarian Sources of Key Nutrients**

	FOOD GROUPS					
NUTRIENTS	Grains	Vegetables	Fruits	Legumes and Other Protein-Rich Foods	Milk or Soy Milk	Oils
PROTEIN	Whole grains[a]			Legumes, seeds, nuts, soy products (tempeh, tofu, veggie burgers)[a] Eggs (for ovo-vegetarians)	Milk, cheese, yogurt (for lacto-vegetarians); soy milk, soy yogurt, soy cheeses	
IRON	Fortified cereals, enriched and whole grains	Dark green leafy vegetables (spinach, turnip greens)	Dried fruits (apricots, prunes, raisins)	Legumes (black-eyed peas, kidney beans, lentils), soy products		
ZINC	Fortified cereals, whole grains			Legumes (garbanzo beans, kidney beans, navy beans), nuts, seeds (pumpkin seeds)	Milk, cheese, yogurt (for lacto-vegetarians); soy milk, soy yogurt, soy cheeses	
CALCIUM	Fortified cereals	Dark green leafy vegetables (bok choy, broccoli, collard greens, kale, mustard greens, turnip greens, watercress)	Fortified juices, figs	Fortified soy products, nuts (almonds), seeds (sesame seeds)	Milk, cheese, yogurt (for lacto-vegetarians); fortified soy milk, fortified soy yogurt, fortified soy cheese	
VITAMIN B_{12}	Fortified cereals			Eggs (for ovo-vegetarians); fortified soy products	Milk, cheese, yogurt (for lacto-vegetarians); fortified soy milk, fortified soy yogurt, fortified soy cheese	
VITAMIN D	Fortified cereals				Milk, cheese, yogurt (for lacto-vegetarians); fortified soy milk, fortified soy yogurt, fortified soy cheese	
OMEGA-3 FATTY ACIDS		Marine algae and its oils		Flaxseed, walnuts, soybeans, fortified margarine,[b] fortified eggs (for ovo-vegetarians)[b]		Flaxseed oil, walnut oil, soybean oil

[a]*Many plant proteins lack certain essential amino acids or contain them in insufficient amounts for human health. A variety of daily plant protein sources, such as grains and legumes, can meet protein needs when energy intake is sufficient.*

[b]*Fortification sources of EPA and DHA may be fish oil or marine algae oil; read the ingredients list on the label.*

tion, so the DRI committee suggests that vegetarians need 1.8 times the amount of iron recommended for meat eaters.[33] At some point, the body begins to adapt to a vegetarian diet by absorbing iron more efficiently. Also, iron absorption is enhanced by vitamin C consumed with iron-rich foods, and vegetarians typically eat many vitamin C–rich fruits and vegetables. Consequently, vegetarians suffer no more iron deficiency than other people do.

FIGURE C6-1 My Vegetarian Food Pyramid

Review Figure 2-5 on page 38 and Table 2-2 on page 44 of Chapter 2 to find the recommended daily amounts from each food group, serving size equivalents, and examples of foods within each group. Tips for planning a vegetarian diet can be found at MyPyramid.gov.

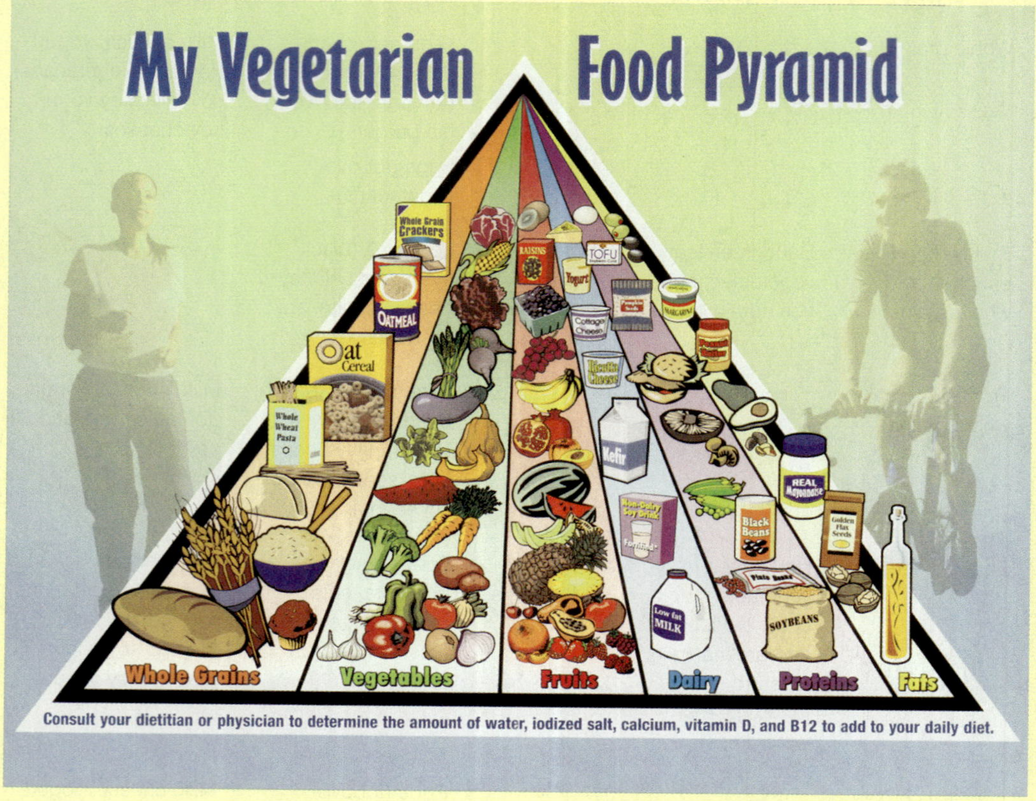

Source: © GC Nutrition Council, 2006, adapted from USDA 2005 Dietary Guidelines and www.mypyramid.gov

Zinc

Zinc is similar to iron in that meat is its richest food source, and zinc from plant sources is not as well absorbed. Zinc can be a problem for growing children, but few vegetarian adults eating nutrient-dense diets are zinc deficient.

Calcium

The calcium intakes of vegetarians who use milk and milk products are similar to those of the general population. For vegans, ample quantities of calcium-fortified foods, such as juices, soy milk, and breakfast cereals, are required regularly. Not all such products are well endowed with calcium, however, so label reading must become a passion. This is especially important when feeding children and adolescents whose developing bones demand ample calcium.

Some absorbable calcium is also present in figs, calcium-set tofu, some legumes, some green vegetables (broccoli, kale, and turnip greens, but not spinach—see Chapter 8), some nuts such as almonds, and certain seeds such as sesame seeds.† One cup of cooked kale, for example, provides about 90 milligrams of calcium and 1.2 milligrams of iron, or about 7 percent of both the daily calcium and iron needs of an adolescent girl.[34] The choices should be varied because calcium absorption from some plant foods is limited and the amounts present may be insufficient to meet many people's calcium requirements.

Vitamin B_{12}

The requirement for vitamin B_{12} is small, but this vitamin is critical, as already mentioned. Found naturally only in animal-derived foods, such as meats, milk, and eggs, these foods are reliable sources. For vegans, fermented soy products may contain some vitamin B_{12} from the bacteria that did the fermenting, but much of it may be an inactive form. Seaweeds such as nori and chlorella supply just a trace of vitamin B_{12}, and excessive intakes of these foods can lead to iodine toxicity. For a reliable supply of vitamin B_{12}, vegans can use vitamin B_{12}–fortified foods (such as soy milk or breakfast cereals) or take a supplement that contains it.

Vitamin D

Overall, vegetarians are similar to nonvegetarians in their vitamin D status; factors such as taking supplements, skin color, and sun exposure have a greater influence on vitamin D than diet.[35] People who do not use vitamin D–fortified foods and do not receive enough exposure to sunlight to synthesize adequate vitamin D may need supplements to

†Calcium salts are often added to tofu during processing to coagulate it.

FIGURE C6-2 Nutrients in Nonfat Milk and Light Soy Milk

Manufacturers of soy milk often fortify it with many of the nutrients that milk provides.

Nonfat milk

Nutrition Facts
Serving Size 1 cup (240mL)
Servings Per Container About 8

Amount Per Serving	
Calories 80 Calories from Fat 0	
	% Daily Value*
Total Fat 0g	0%
Saturated Fat 0g	0%
Trans Fat 0g	
Polyunsaturated Fat 0g	
Monounsaturated Fat 0g	
Cholesterol 5mg	2%
Sodium 100mg	4%
Potassium 380mg	11%
Total Carbohydrate 13g	4%
Dietary Fiber 0g	0%
Sugars 12g	
Protein 8g	
Vitamin A 10% • Vitamin C	0%
Calcium 30% • Iron	0%
Vitamin D 25% • Riboflavin	30%
Vitamin B_{12} 20%	

Light soy milk

Nutrition Facts
Serving Size 1 cup (240mL)
Servings Per Container About 8

Amount Per Serving	
Calories 70 Calories from Fat 0	
	% Daily Value*
Total Fat 0g	0%
Saturated Fat 0g	0%
Trans Fat 0g	
Polyunsaturated Fat 0g	
Monounsaturated Fat 0g	
Cholesterol 0mg	0%
Sodium 120mg	5%
Potassium 300mg	8%
Total Carbohydrate 8g	3%
Dietary Fiber 1g	4%
Sugars 6g	
Protein 6g	
Vitamin A 10% • Vitamin C	0%
Calcium 30% • Iron	6%
Vitamin D 30% • Riboflavin	30%
Vitamin B_{12} 50%	

fend off bone loss. Of particular concern are infants, children, and older adults in northern climates during winter months.

Omega-3 Fatty Acids

Vegetarian diets typically provide enough of the essential fatty acids linoleic acid and linolenic acid, but they lack a dietary source of EPA and DHA.[36] Fatty fish and DHA-fortified eggs and other fortified products can provide EPA and DHA, but all of these sources ultimately derive from fish, an unacceptable food for vegans.[37] Alternatively, certain marine algae and their oils provide DHA and more foods are being fortified with such oils, which are listed among the ingredients on a food's label.[‡38] A vegetarian's daily diet should include small amounts of flaxseed, walnuts, and their oils, as well as soybeans and canola oil to provide essential fatty acids.

‡*The algae are* Cryptherodinium cohnii *and* Schizochytrium *spp.*

CONCLUSION

This comparison has shown that both a meat-eater's diet and a vegetarian's diet are best approached scientifically. Some people make much of the distinctions among types of vegetarians; and although these distinctions are useful academically, they do not represent uncrossable lines. Some people use meat as a condiment or seasoning for vegetable or grain dishes. Some people eat meat only once a week and use plant protein foods the rest of the time. Many people rely mostly on milk products to meet their protein needs but eat fish twice weekly, and so forth. To force people into the categories of "vegetarians" and "meat eaters" leaves out all these in-between styles of eating that have much to recommend them.

If you are just beginning to study nutrition, consider adopting the attitude that the choice to make is not whether to be a meat eater or a vegetarian, but where along the spectrum to locate yourself. Your preferences should be honored with only these caveats: that you plan your own diet and the diets of those in your care to be adequate, balanced, and varied and that you use moderation when choosing foods high in saturated fat or calories.

7

The Vitamins

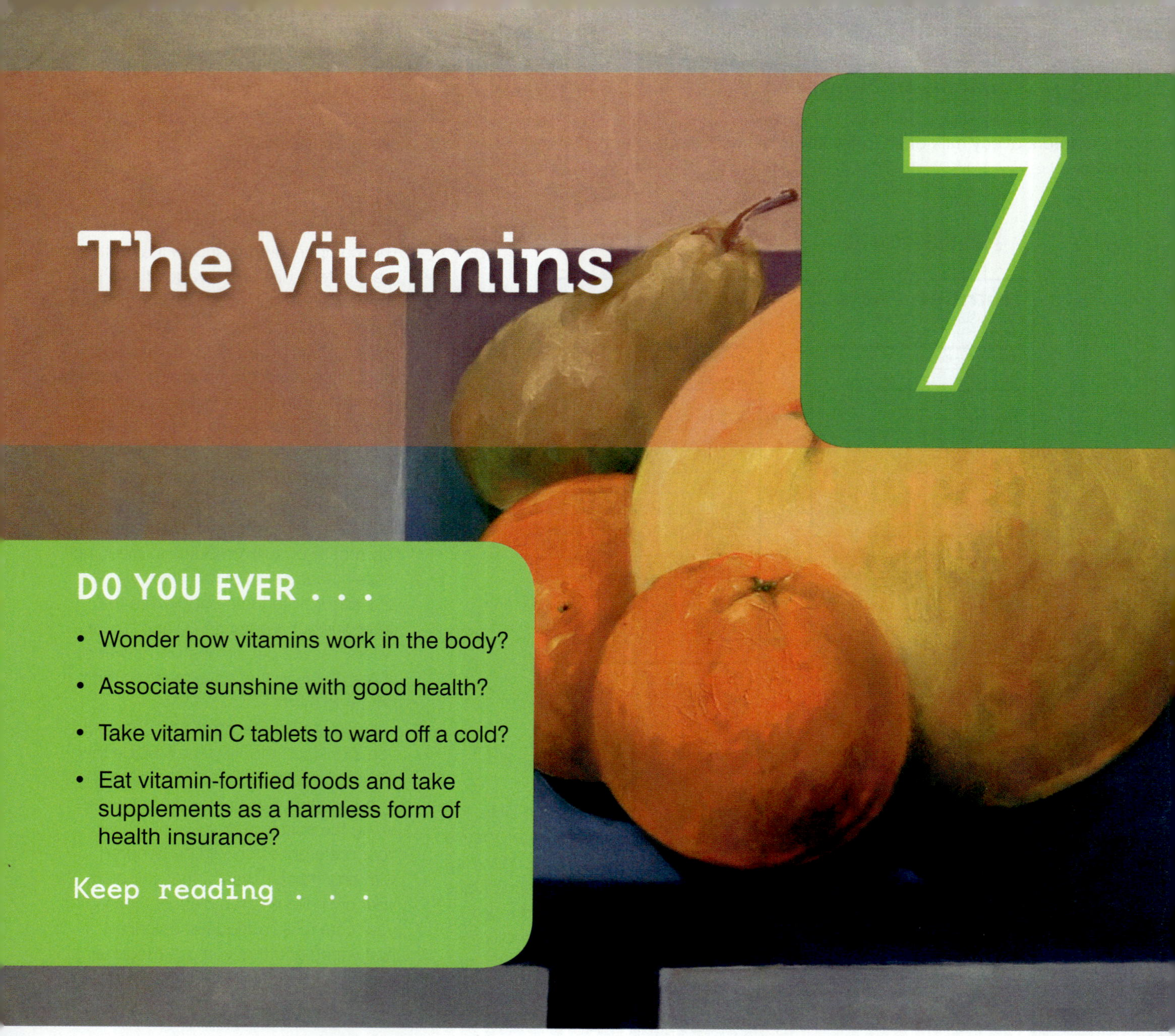

© Norman Baugher

DO YOU EVER . . .

- Wonder how vitamins work in the body?
- Associate sunshine with good health?
- Take vitamin C tablets to ward off a cold?
- Eat vitamin-fortified foods and take supplements as a harmless form of health insurance?

Keep reading . . .

Learning Objectives

To find learning objective topics in this chapter, look for the text headings with a corresponding "LO" number above the heading. After completing this chapter, you should be able to accomplish the following:

LO 7.1 List the fat-soluble and water-soluble vitamins, and describe how solubility affects the absorption, transport, storage, and excretion of each type.

LO 7.2 Explain how vitamins and minerals work in combination to maintain the health of the bones.

LO 7.3 Name some functions of vitamin D not associated with the bones.

LO 7.4 Define the term *antioxidant,* and name the vitamins that act as antioxidants in the body.

LO 7.5 Discuss the roles of B vitamins in body tissues, and explain in a general way how B vitamins assist with energy metabolism.

LO 7.6 Present arguments both for and against vitamin fortification of foods.

LO 7.7 Suggest foods that can help to ensure adequate vitamin intakes without providing too many calories.

LO 7.8 Justify this statement: "It is better to get vitamins from food than from supplements."

LO 7.9 List some valid reasons why supplements may be required by some people.

Early in the 20th century, the thrill of the discovery of the first **vitamins** captured the world's imagination. Seemingly miraculous cures took place—a whole group of people were unable to walk (or were going blind or bleeding profusely) until an alert scientist stumbled onto the substance missing from their diets. The scientist confirmed the discovery by feeding vitamin-deficient feed to laboratory animals, which responded by becoming unable to walk (or going blind or bleeding profusely). When the missing vitamin was restored to their diets, both people and animals soon recovered.

In the decades that followed, advances in chemistry, biology, and genetics allowed scientists to isolate the vitamins, define their chemical structures, and reveal their functions in maintaining health and preventing deficiency diseases. Today, research hints that certain vitamins may be linked with the development of two major scourges of humankind: cardiovascular disease (CVD) and cancer. Deficiencies of some vitamins may mimic radiation in their disruption of cellular genetic functioning.[1*] Many other conditions, from infections to cracked skin, bear relation to vitamin nutrition, details that unscrupulous sellers of vitamins often use to market their wares (see the Controversy section).

Can foods rich in vitamins protect us from life-threatening diseases? What about vitamin pills? For now, we can say this with certainty: the only disease a vitamin will *cure* is the one caused by a deficiency of that vitamin. As for chronic disease *prevention,* research is ongoing but evidence so far supports the conclusion that vitamin-rich *foods,* but not vitamin supplements, are protective.[2]

If we could give every individual the right amount of nourishment and exercise, not too little and not too much, we would have found the safest way to health.

—Hippocrates

LO 7.1

Definition and Classification of Vitamins

A child once defined a vitamin as "what, if you don't eat, you get sick." Although the grammar left something to be desired, the definition was accurate. Less imaginatively, a vitamin is defined as an essential, noncaloric, organic nutrient needed in tiny amounts in the diet. The role of many vitamins is to help make possible the processes by which other nutrients are digested, absorbed, and metabolized or built into body structures. Although small in size and quantity, the vitamins accomplish mighty tasks.

As each vitamin was discovered, it was given a name and some were given letters and numbers—vitamin A came before B vitamins, then came vitamin C, and so forth. This led to the confusing variety of vitamin names that still exists today. This chapter uses the names in Table 7-1; alternative names are given in Tables 7-6 and 7-7 at the end of the chapter.

Did You Know?

The only disease a vitamin can cure is the one caused by a deficiency of that vitamin.

- Vitamin intake recommendations are found on the inside front cover, page B.

TABLE 7-1 Vitamin Names[a]

Fat-Soluble Vitamins
Vitamin A
Vitamin D
Vitamin E
Vitamin K
Water-Soluble Vitamins
B vitamins
Thiamin (B_1)
Riboflavin (B_2)
Niacin (B_3)
Folate
Vitamin B_{12}
Vitamin B_6
Biotin
Pantothenic acid
Vitamin C

[a]*Vitamin names established by the International Union of Nutritional Sciences Committee on Nomenclature. Other names are listed in Tables 7-6 and 7-7 (pp. 260, 261).*

The Concept of Vitamin Precursors Some of the vitamins occur in foods in a form known as **precursors,** or **provitamins.** Once inside the body, these are transformed chemically to one or more active vitamin forms. Thus, to measure the amount of a vitamin found in food, we often must count not only the amount of the true vitamin but also the vitamin activity potentially available from its precursors. Tables 7-6 and 7-7 specify which vitamins have precursors.

Two Classes of Vitamins: Fat-Soluble and Water-Soluble The vitamins fall naturally into two classes: fat-soluble and water-soluble (listed in Table 7-1). Solubility confers on vitamins many of their characteristics. It determines how they are absorbed into and transported around by the bloodstream, whether they can be stored in the body, and how easily they are lost from the body.

In general, like other lipids, fat-soluble vitamins are absorbed into the lymph, and they travel in the blood in association with protein carriers. Fat-soluble vitamins can be stored in the liver or with other lipids in fatty tissues, and some can build up

vitamins organic compounds that are vital to life and indispensable to body functions but are needed only in minute amounts; noncaloric essential nutrients.

precursors, provitamins compounds that can be converted into active vitamins.

*Reference notes are found in Appendix F.

Vitamins fall into two classes—fat-soluble and water-soluble.

to toxic concentrations. The water-soluble vitamins are absorbed directly into the bloodstream, where they travel freely. Most are not stored in tissues to any great extent; rather, excesses are excreted in the urine. Thus, the risks of immediate toxicities are not as great as for fat-soluble vitamins.

Table 7-2 sums up the general features of the fat-soluble and water-soluble vitamins. This chapter examines the fat-soluble vitamins first and then the water-soluble ones. The tables at the end of the chapter present basic facts about all of them.

KEY POINT Vitamins are essential, noncaloric nutrients that are needed in tiny amounts in the diet and help to drive cell processes in the body. Vitamin precursors in foods are transformed into active vitamins by the body. The fat-soluble vitamins are vitamins A, D, E, and K; the water-soluble vitamins are vitamin C and the B vitamins.

LO 7.2, 7.3, 7.4

The Fat-Soluble Vitamins

The fat-soluble vitamins—A, D, E, and K—are found in the fats and oils of foods and require bile for absorption. Once absorbed, these vitamins are stored in the liver and fatty tissues until the body needs them. Because they are stored, you need not eat foods containing these vitamins every day. If the diet provides sufficient amounts of the fat-soluble vitamins on average over time, the body can survive for weeks without consuming them. This capacity to be stored also sets the stage for toxic buildup if you take in too much. Excesses of vitamins A and D from supplements and highly fortified foods are especially likely to reach toxic levels.

CONCEPT LINK 7-1

Look back at Figure 5-6, page 157, to see how bile acts in lipid absorption.

Deficiencies of the fat-soluble vitamins occur when the diet is consistently low in them. We also know that any disease that produces fat malabsorption (such as

TABLE 7-2 **Characteristics of the Fat-Soluble and Water-Soluble Vitamins**

While each of the vitamins have unique functions and features, a few generalizations about the fat-soluble and water-soluble vitamins can aid understanding.

	Fat-Soluble Vitamins: Vitamins A, D, E, and K	Water-Soluble Vitamins: B Vitamins and Vitamin C
ABSORPTION	Absorbed like fats, first into the lymph, then the blood.	Absorbed directly into the blood.
TRANSPORT AND STORAGE	Must travel with protein carriers in watery body fluids; stored in the liver or fatty tissues.	Travel freely in watery fluids; most are not stored in the body.
EXCRETION	Not readily excreted; tend to build up in the tissues.	Readily excreted in the urine.
TOXICITY	Toxicities are likely from supplements, but occur rarely from food.	Toxicities are unlikely but possible with high doses from supplements.
REQUIREMENTS	Needed in periodic doses (perhaps weeks or even months) because the body can draw on its stores.	Needed in frequent doses (perhaps 1 to 3 days) because the body does not store most of them to any extent.

liver disease that prevents bile production) can cause the loss of vitamins dissolved in undigested fat and so bring on deficiencies. In the same way, a person who uses mineral oil (which the body cannot absorb) as a laxative risks losing fat-soluble vitamins because they readily dissolve into the oil and are excreted. Deficiencies are also likely when people eat diets that are extraordinarily low in fat because such diets interfere with absorption of these vitamins.

Fat-soluble vitamins play diverse roles in the body. Vitamins A and D act somewhat like hormones, directing cells to convert one substance to another, to store this, or to release that. They also directly influence the genes, thereby regulating protein production. Vitamin E flows throughout the body, guarding the tissues against harm from destructive oxidative reactions. Vitamin K is necessary for blood to clot and is thought to affect bone health. Each is worth a book in itself.

Vitamin A

Vitamin A has the distinction of being the first fat-soluble vitamin to be recognized. Today, after a century of scientific investigation, vitamin A and its plant-derived precursor, **beta-carotene,** are still very much a focus of research.

Three forms of vitamin A are active in the body; one of the active forms, **retinol,** is stored in specialized cells of the liver. The liver makes retinol available to the bloodstream and thereby to the body's cells. The cells convert retinol to its other two active forms, retinal and retinoic acid, as needed.

Foods derived from animals provide forms of vitamin A that are readily absorbed and put to use by the body. Foods derived from plants provide beta-carotene, which must be converted to active vitamin A before it can be used as such.

CONCEPT LINK 7-2

Gene expression, protein synthesis, and the work of proteins in the body were topics of Chapter 6 (pages 194–195).

Roles of Vitamin A and Consequences of Deficiency

Vitamin A is a versatile vitamin, with roles in gene expression, vision, maintenance of body linings and skin, immune defenses, growth of bones and of the body, and normal development of cells. It is of critical importance for reproduction. In short, vitamin A is needed everywhere (its chief functions in the body are listed in the Snapshot on page 233 and in Table 7-6 on page 260).

Gene Regulation Vitamin A exerts considerable influence on body functions through its regulation of genes.[3] Genes direct the synthesis of proteins, including enzymes, and enzymes perform the metabolic work of the tissues. Hence, factors that influence gene expression also affect the metabolic activities of the tissues, and, in turn, the health of the body. Hundreds of genes are regulated by the retinoic acid form of vitamin A.[4]

Researchers have long known that the presence of genetic equipment needed to make a particular protein does not guarantee that the protein will be made, any more than owning a car guarantees you a ride across town. To get the car rolling, you must also use the right key to trigger the events that start up its engine and, to prevent its racing out of control, to turn it off at the appropriate times. Some dietary components, including the retinoic acid form of vitamin A, are now known to act like such keys—they help activate or deactivate genes and thus affect the production of proteins essential to body functions and health.[5]

Eyesight The most familiar function of vitamin A is to sustain normal eyesight. Vitamin A plays two indispensable roles: in the process of light perception at the **retina** and in the maintenance of a healthy, crystal-clear outer window, the **cornea** (see Figure 7-1).

When light falls on the eye, it passes through the clear cornea and strikes the cells of the retina, bleaching many molecules of the pigment **rhodopsin** that lie within those cells.[6] Vitamin A is a part of the rhodopsin molecule. When bleaching occurs, the vitamin is broken off, initiating the signal that conveys the sensation of

FIGURE 7-1 **An Eye**

This eye is sectioned to reveal its inner structures.

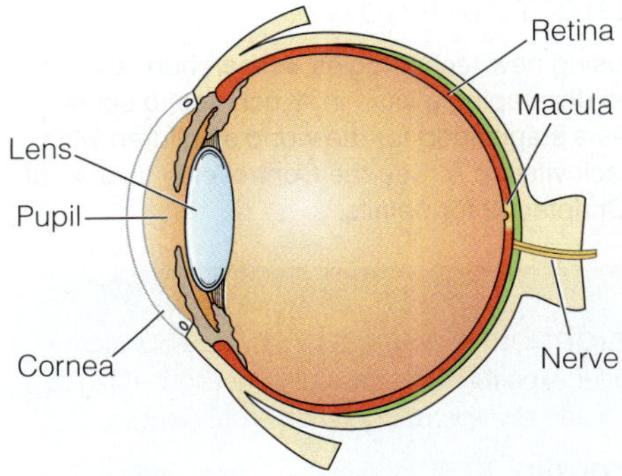

beta-carotene an orange pigment with antioxidant activity; a vitamin A precursor made by plants and stored in human fat tissue.

retinol one of the active forms of vitamin A made from beta-carotene in animal and human bodies; an antioxidant nutrient. Other active forms are *retinal* and *retinoic acid.*

retina (RET-in-uh) the layer of light-sensitive nerve cells lining the back of the inside of the eye.

cornea (KOR-nee-uh) the hard, transparent membrane covering the outside of the eye.

rhodopsin (roh-DOP-sin) the light-sensitive pigment of the cells in the retina; it contains vitamin A (*opsin* means "visual protein").

FIGURE 7-2 Night Blindness

This is one of the earliest signs of vitamin A deficiency.

© David Farr/Imagesmythe

In dim light, you can make out the details in this room.

A flash of bright light momentarily blinds you as the pigment in the retina is bleached.

You quickly recover and can see the details again in a few seconds.

With inadequate vitamin A, you do not recover but remain blind for many seconds; this is night blindness.

sight to the optic center in the brain. The vitamin then reunites with the pigment, but a little vitamin A is destroyed each time this reaction takes place, and fresh vitamin A must replenish the supply.

Night Blindness If the vitamin A supply begins to run low, a lag occurs before the eye can see again after a flash of bright light at night (see Figure 7-2). This lag in the recovery of night vision, termed **night blindness,** often indicates a vitamin A deficiency.[7] A bright flash of light can temporarily blind even normal, well-nourished eyes, but if you experience a long recovery period before vision returns, your health-care provider may want to check your vitamin A intake.

Xerophthalmia and Blindness A more profound deficiency of vitamin A is exhibited when the protein **keratin** accumulates and clouds the eye's outer vitamin A–dependent part, the cornea. The condition is known as **keratinization,** and if the deficiency of vitamin A is not corrected, it can worsen to **xerosis** (drying) and then progress to thickening and permanent blindness, **xerophthalmia.** Tragically, a half million of the world's vitamin A–deprived children become blind each year from this often preventable condition; about half die within a year after losing their sight. Vitamin A supplements given early to children developing vitamin A deficiency can reverse the process and save lives.[8] Better still, a child fed a variety of fruits and vegetables regularly is virtually assured protection.

Cell Differentiation Vitamin A is needed by all **epithelial tissue** (external skin and internal linings), not just by the cornea. The skin and all of the protective linings of the lungs, intestines, vagina, urinary tract, and bladder serve as barriers to infection and other threats.

An example of vitamin A's health-supporting work is the process of **cell differentiation,** in which each type of cell develops to perform a specific function. For example, when goblet cells (cells populating the linings of internal organs) mature, they specialize in synthesizing and releasing mucus to protect delicate tissues from toxins or bacteria and other microbial invaders. In the body's outer layers, vitamin A helps to protect against skin damage from sunlight.

If vitamin A is deficient, the cell differentiation is impaired and goblet cells fail to mature, then fail to make protective mucus, and eventually die off. Goblet cells are then displaced by cells that secrete keratin, mentioned earlier with regard to the eye. Keratin is the same protein that provides toughness in hair and fingernails, but in the wrong place, such as skin and body linings, keratin makes the tissue surfaces dry, hard, and cracked. As dead cells accumulate on the surface, the tissue becomes vulnerable to infection (see Figure 7-3). In the cornea, keratinization leads

Did You Know?

Using new technologies, researchers are close to developing a vitamin A–rich rice to serve as a staple food for the world's children who lack vitamin A. See the Controversy section of Chapter 12 for details.

night blindness slow recovery of vision after exposure to flashes of bright light at night; an early symptom of vitamin A deficiency.

keratin (KERR-uh-tin) the normal protein of hair and nails.

keratinization accumulation of keratin in a tissue; a sign of vitamin A deficiency.

xerosis (zeer-OH-sis) drying of the cornea; a symptom of vitamin A deficiency.

xerophthalmia (ZEER-ahf-THALL-me-uh) progressive hardening of the cornea of the eye in advanced vitamin A deficiency that can lead to blindness (*xero* means "dry"; *ophthalm* means "eye").

epithelial (ep-ith-THEE-lee-ull) **tissue** the layers of the body that serve as selective barriers to environmental factors. Examples are the cornea, the skin, the respiratory tract lining, and the lining of the digestive tract.

cell differentiation (dih-fer-en-she-AY-shun) the process by which immature cells are stimulated to mature and gain the ability to perform functions characteristic of their cell type.

to xerophthalmia; in the lungs, the displacement of mucus-producing cells makes respiratory infections likely; in the urinary tract, the same process leads to urinary tract infections.[9]

Immune Function Vitamin A has gained a reputation as an "anti-infective" vitamin because so many of the body's defenses against infection depend on an adequate supply.[10] Much research supports the need for vitamin A in the regulation of the genes involved in immunity. Without sufficient vitamin A, these genetic interactions produce an altered response to infection that weakens the body's defenses.

When the defenses are weak, especially in vitamin A–deficient children, an illness such as measles can become severe. A downward spiral of malnutrition and infection can set in. The child's body must devote its scanty store of vitamin A to the immune system's fight against the measles virus, but this destroys the vitamin. As vitamin A dwindles further, the infection worsens. Measles takes the lives of more than 500 of the world's children every day.[11] Even if the child survives the infection, blindness is likely to occur. The corneas, already damaged by the chronic vitamin A shortage, degenerate rapidly as their meager supply of vitamin A is diverted to the immune system.

Growth Vitamin A is essential for normal growth of bone (and teeth). Normal children's bones grow longer, and the children grow taller, by remodeling each old bone into a new, bigger version. To do so, the body dismantles the old bone structures and replaces them with new, larger bone parts. Growth cannot take place just by adding on to the original small bone; vitamin A must be present for critical dismantling steps. Failure to grow is one of the first signs of poor vitamin A status in a child. Restoring vitamin A to such children is imperative, but correcting dietary deficiencies may be more effective than giving vitamin A supplements alone because many other nutrients from nutritious foods are also needed for children to gain weight and grow taller.

FIGURE 7-3 **The Skin in Vitamin A Deficiency**

The hard lumps on the skin of this person's arm reflect accumulations of keratin in the epithelial cells.

© H. Sanstead, U. of Texas/Galveston

Vitamin A Deficiency Around the World

Vitamin A deficiency presents a vast problem worldwide, placing a heavy burden on society. Between 3 and 10 million of the world's children suffer from signs of severe vitamin A deficiency—not only xerophthalmia and blindness but diarrhea, appetite loss, and reduced food intake that rapidly worsen their condition.[12] A staggering 275 million more children suffer from milder deficiency that impairs immunity, leaving them open to infections.

In countries where children receive vitamin A supplements, childhood rates of blindness and death have declined dramatically.[13] Even in the United States, vitamin A supplements are recommended for certain groups of infants and for children with measles. Vitamin A supplementation may also offer some protection against the complications of other life-threatening infections, including malaria, lung diseases, and HIV. The World Health Organization (WHO) and UNICEF (United Nations International Children's Emergency Fund) are working to eliminate vitamin A deficiency; achieving this goal would improve child survival throughout the developing world.

• World hunger is a topic of Chapter 15.

Vitamin A Toxicity

For people who take excess active vitamin A in supplements or fortified foods, toxicity is a real possibility.[14] Figure 7-4 shows that toxicity compromises the tissues just as deficiency does and is equally dangerous. The many symptoms of vitamin A toxicity include nausea, vomiting, diarrhea; joint pain; loss of coordination; rashes; hair loss; stunted growth; possibly irreversible damage to the liver; and enlargement of the spleen. The earliest symptoms of overdoses include appetite loss, dizziness, blurred vision, headache, itching of the skin, and irritability. Over the years, even relatively small vitamin A excesses may silently weaken the bones and contribute to hip fractures later in life.[15]

FIGURE 7-4 **Vitamin A Deficiency and Toxicity**

Danger lies both above and below a normal range of intake of vitamin A.

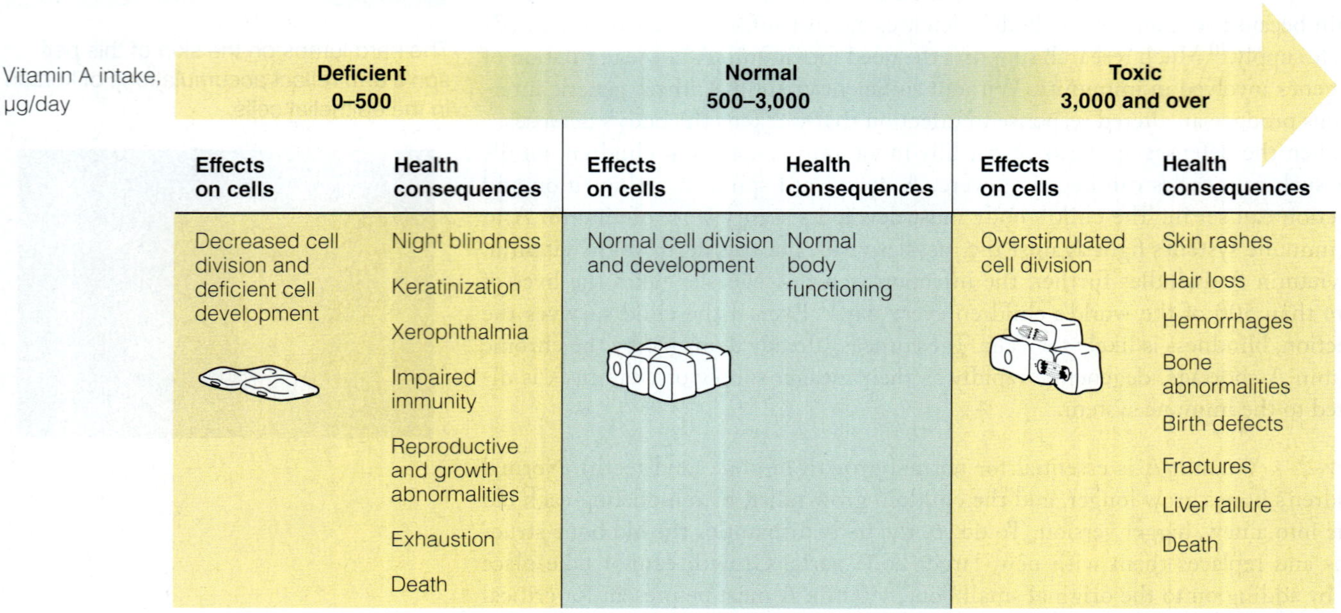

TABLE 7-3 **Sources of Active Vitamin A**

Vitamin A from highly fortified foods and other rich sources can add up. The UL for vitamin A is 3,000 µg per day.

High-potency vitamin pill	3,000 µg
Calf's liver, 1 oz cooked	2,300 µg
Regular multivitamin pill	1,500 µg
Vitamin gumball, 1	1,500 µg
Chicken liver, 1 oz cooked	1,400 µg
"Complete" liquid supplement drink, 1 serving	350–1,500 µg
Instant breakfast drink, 1 serving	600–700 µg
Cereal breakfast bar, 1	350–400 µg
"Energy" candy bar, 1	350 µg
Milk, 1 c	150 µg
Vitamin-fortified cereal, 1 serving	150 µg
Margarine, 1 tsp	55 µg

- The effects of excessive vitamin A intakes during pregnancy are discussed in Chapter 13.

- The U.S. and Canadian standard for vitamin A intake is the DRI, listed on the inside front cover, page B.

Ordinary vitamin supplements taken in the context of today's heavily fortified food supply can easily add up to small daily excesses of vitamin A. Even fortified candy bars and bubble gum supply substantial amounts (see Table 7-3). Some experts are asking whether this level of fortification is doing more harm than good in the population.

Pregnant women, especially, should be wary—excessive vitamin A during pregnancy can injure the spinal cord of the developing fetus, causing birth defects.[16] Even a single massive vitamin A dose (100 times the need) can do so. Children, too, can be easily hurt by vitamin A excesses; they often mistake chewable vitamin pills and vitamin bubble gum for treats.[17] Even misinformed adolescents put themselves at risk when they take high doses of vitamin A in misguided attempts to cure acne. An effective acne medicine, *Accutane,* and topical prescription acne creams are *derived* from vitamin A but are chemically altered—vitamin A itself has no effect on acne.[18]

Vitamin A Recommendations

The ability of vitamin A to be stored in the tissues means that, although the DRI recommendation is stated as a daily amount, you need not consume vitamin A every day. An intake that meets the daily need when averaged over several months is sufficient. The vitamin A recommendation is based on body weight. According to the DRI committee, a man needs a daily average of about 900 micrograms of active vitamin A; a woman, who typically weighs less, needs about 700 micrograms. During lactation, her need is higher. Children need less. A regular balanced diet that includes the recommended fruits and vegetables each day supplies more than adequate amounts.

As for vitamin A supplements, the DRI committee recommends against exceeding the Tolerable Upper Intake Level of 3,000 micrograms (for adults over age 18). The best way to ensure a safe intake of vitamin A is to steer clear of supplements that contain it and rely on food sources instead.

Food Sources of Vitamin A

Active vitamin A is present in foods of animal origin. The richest sources are liver and fish oil but milk and milk products and other fortified foods such as cereals, to which active vitamin A is added, can also be good sources. Even butter and eggs provide some vitamin A.

Can Fast Foods Provide Vitamin A? The definitive fast-food meal—a hamburger, fries, and cola—lacks vitamin A. Many fast-food restaurants, however, now offer salads with cheese and carrots, fortified milk, and other vitamin A–rich foods. These selections greatly improve the nutritional quality of fast food.

Liver: A Lesson in Moderation Foods naturally rich in vitamin A pose little risk of toxicity, with the possible exception of liver. When young laboratory pigs eat daily chow made from salmon parts, including the livers, their growth halts and they fall ill from vitamin A toxicity. Inuit people and Arctic explorers know that polar bear livers are a dangerous food source because the bears eat whole fish (with the livers) and in turn concentrate large amounts of vitamin A in their own livers.

An *ounce* of ordinary beef or pork liver delivers 3 times the Dietary Reference Intake (DRI) recommendation for vitamin A, and a common portion is 4 to 6 ounces. An occasional serving of liver can provide abundant nutrients and boost nutrient status. Daily use invites vitamin A toxicity, however, especially in young children and pregnant women who eat other fortified foods or take supplements.[19] Snapshot 7-1 is the first of a series of figures that show a sampling of foods that provide more than 10 percent of the Daily Value for a vitamin in a standard-size portion and therefore qualify as "good" or "rich" sources.

© Marc Vaughn/Masterfile

Colorful foods are often rich in vitamins.

KEY POINT Vitamin A is essential to vision, integrity of epithelial tissue, bone growth, reproduction, and more. Vitamin A deficiency causes blindness, sickness, and death and is a major problem worldwide. Overdoses are possible and cause many serious symptoms. Foods are preferable to supplements for supplying vitamin A.

SNAPSHOT 7-1

Vitamin A and Beta-Carotene

DRI Recommended Intakes

Men: 900 μg/day[a]

Women: 700 μg/day[a]

Tolerable Upper Intake Level

Adults: 3,000 μg vitamin A/day

Chief Functions

Vision; maintenance of cornea, epithelial cells, mucous membranes, skin; bone and tooth growth; regulation of gene expression; reproduction; immunity

Deficiency

Night blindness, corneal drying (xerosis), and blindness (xerophthalmia); impaired bone growth and easily decayed teeth; keratin lumps on the skin; impaired immunity

Toxicity

Vitamin A: Increased activity of bone-dismantling cells causing reduced bone density and pain; liver abnormalities; birth defects

Beta-carotene: Harmless yellowing of skin

GOOD SOURCES*

*These foods provide 10 percent or more of the vitamin A Daily Value in a serving. For a 2,000-calorie diet, the DV is 900 μg/day.

[a]Vitamin A recommendations are expressed in retinol activity equivalents (RAE).

[b]This food contains preformed vitamin A.

[c]This food contains the vitamin A precursor, beta-carotene.

MY TURN

Claudio Steve

Take Your Vitamins?

Two students talk about vitamins and minerals in campus foods and in supplements.

CENGAGENOW To hear their stories, log on to www.cengage.com/sso.

Functional Group

Key antioxidant vitamins:

- *Beta-carotene, vitamin E, and vitamin C.*

A key antioxidant mineral:

- *Selenium.*

Beta-Carotene

In plants, vitamin A exists only in its precursor forms. Beta-carotene, the most abundant of these **carotenoid** precursors, has the highest vitamin A activity. While not vitamins, other carotenoids may play other roles in human health.[20] Diets that lack dark green, leafy vegetables, rich sources of carotenoids, are associated with the most common form of age-related blindness, **macular degeneration.**[†21] The macula, a yellow spot of pigment at the focal center of the retina (identified in Figure 7-1 on page 229), loses integrity, impairing the most important field of vision, the central focus. Several other nutrients are under study for roles in preventing this cause of blindness, as well.[22]

- 1 IU = 0.3 μg retinol
- The Aids to Calculations appendix (Appendix C) provides factors for converting many kinds of units used in nutrition.

Does Eating Carrots Really Promote Good Vision? Bright orange fruits and vegetables derive their color from beta-carotene and are so colorful that they decorate the plate. Carrots, sweet potatoes, pumpkins, mango, cantaloupe, and apricots are all rich sources of beta-carotene—and therefore contribute vitamin A to the eyes and to the rest of the body—so, yes, eating carrots does promote good vision. Another colorful group, *dark* green vegetables, such as spinach, other greens, and broccoli, owe their deep dark green color to the blending of orange beta-carotene with the green leaf pigment chlorophyll. As mentioned, they provide the other carotenoids needed for eye health, as well.

Beta-Carotene, an Antioxidant Beta-carotene is one of many **dietary antioxidants** present in foods—others include vitamin E, vitamin C, the mineral selenium, and many phytochemicals. Dietary antioxidants are just one class of a complex array of constituents in whole foods that seem to benefit health synergistically.[23] Foods supply all of these factors and more in ideal amounts and combinations that supplements cannot duplicate.

Measuring Beta-Carotene The conversion of beta-carotene to retinol in the body entails losses, however, so vitamin A activity for precursors is measured in **retinol activity equivalents (RAE).** It takes about 12 micrograms of beta-carotene from food to supply the equivalent of 1 microgram of retinol to the body. Some food tables and supplement labels express beta-carotene and vitamin A contents using **IU (international units).** When comparing vitamin A in foods, be careful to notice whether a food table or supplement label uses micrograms or IU. To convert one to the other, use the factor in the margin.

Toxicity Beta-carotene from food is not converted to retinol efficiently enough to cause vitamin A toxicity. A steady diet of abundant pumpkin, carrots, carrot juice, and the like, however, has been known to turn light-skinned people bright yellow because beta-carotene builds up in the fat just beneath the skin and imparts a harm-

carotenoid (CARE-oh-ten-oyd) a member of a group of pigments in foods that range in color from light yellow to reddish orange and are chemical relatives of beta-carotene. Many have a degree of vitamin A activity in the body. Also defined in Controversy 2.

macular degeneration a common, progressive loss of function of the part of the retina that is most crucial to focused vision (the macula is shown on page 229). This degeneration often leads to blindness.

dietary antioxidants compounds typically found in plant foods that significantly decrease the adverse effects of oxidation on living tissues. The major antioxidant vitamins are vitamin E, vitamin C, and beta-carotene.

retinol activity equivalents (RAE) a new measure of the vitamin A activity of beta-carotene and other vitamin A precursors that reflects the amount of retinol that the body will derive from a food containing vitamin A precursor compounds.

IU (international units) a measure of fat-soluble vitamin activity sometimes used in food composition tables and on supplement labels.

†The carotenoids associated with protection from macular degeneration are lutein (LOO-tee-in) and its close chemical relative zeaxanthin (zee-ZAN-thin).

less yellow cast; see Figure 7-5. Concentrated beta-carotene supplements, however, may have adverse effects of their own, as a later section points out.

Food Sources of Beta-Carotene Plants contain no active vitamin A, but many vegetables and fruits provide the vitamin A precursor, beta-carotene. Snapshot 7-1 shows good sources of beta-carotene. Other colorful vegetables, such as red beets, red cabbage, and yellow corn, can fool you into thinking they contain beta-carotene, but these foods derive their colors from other pigments and are poor sources of beta-carotene. As for "white" plant foods such as grains and potatoes, they have none. Concerning the term *yam*: a white-fleshed Mexican root vegetable called "yam" is devoid of beta-carotene, but the orange-fleshed sweet potato called "yam" in the United States is one of the richest beta-carotene sources known. In choosing fruits and vegetables, follow the guidance of the USDA Food Guide of Chapter 2.

KEY POINT The vitamin A precursor in plants, beta-carotene, is an effective antioxidant in the body. Brightly colored plant foods are richest in beta-carotene, and diets containing these foods are associated with good health.

CONCEPT LINK 7-3

Potential roles for carotenoids and other phytochemicals in human health were topics of Controversy 2 on page 61.

FIGURE 7-5 **Excess Beta-Carotene Symptom: Discoloration of the Skin**

The hand on the right shows skin discoloration from excess beta-carotene. Another person's normal hand (left) is shown for comparison.

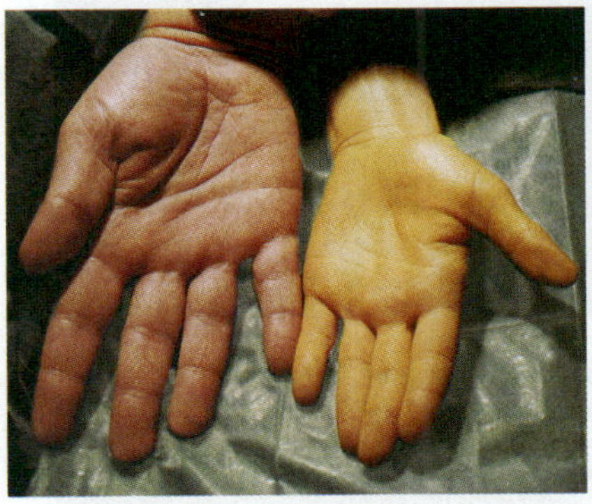

Vitamin D

Vitamin D is unique among nutrients in that the body can synthesize all it needs with the help of sunlight. Therefore, in a sense, vitamin D is not an essential nutrient. Given enough sun each day, most people need consume no vitamin D at all from foods. Whether made from sunlight or obtained from food, vitamin D undergoes chemical transformations in the liver and kidneys to activate it.[24]

As simple as it may sound to obtain vitamin D, recent surveys indicate that many people, particularly African Americans and Mexican Americans, border on insufficiency of this critical nutrient.[25] By one estimate, two-thirds of U.S. residents over 1 year of age take in too little vitamin D.[26]

Roles of Vitamin D

Vitamin D is the best-known member of a large cast of nutrients and hormones that interact to regulate blood calcium and phosphorus levels, and thereby maintain bone integrity.[27] Calcium is indispensable to the proper functioning of cells in all body tissues, including muscles, nerves, and glands, which draw calcium from the blood as they need it. To replenish blood calcium, vitamin D acts at three body sites to raise the calcium level.[28] First, the skeleton serves as a vast warehouse of stored calcium that can be tapped when blood calcium begins to fall. Only two other organs can increase blood calcium: the digestive tract, where food brings calcium in, and the kidneys, which recycle calcium that would otherwise be lost in urine.

Vitamin D functions as a hormone, that is, a compound manufactured by one organ of the body that acts on other organs or tissues.[29] Beyond bone regulation, vitamin D acts at the genetic level, affecting how cells grow, multiply, and specialize. Vitamin D influences over 30 body tissues, from hair follicles, to reproductive system cells, to cells of the immune system.[30]

Research is hinting (sometimes strongly) that to incur a deficit of vitamin D is to invite problems of many kinds, including high blood pressure, cardiovascular diseases, some common cancers, infections such as tuberculosis or flu, high blood pressure, inflammatory conditions, and autoimmune diseases such as type 1 diabetes, rheumatoid arthritis, the skin disease psoriasis (so-RYE-ah-sis), multiple sclerosis, and even a higher risk of dying.[31]* The well-established vitamin D roles, however, concern calcium balance and the bones during growth and throughout life.

Functional Group

Key bone vitamins:

- *Vitamin A, vitamin D, vitamin K, vitamin C, other vitamins*

Key bone minerals:

- *Calcium, phosphorus, magnesium, fluoride, other minerals*

Key bone protein:

- *Collagen*

The sunshine vitamin: vitamin D.

*Read more about these preliminary findings in the articles cited in note 31, Appendix F.

FIGURE 7-6 **Rickets**

This child has the bowed legs of the vitamin D–deficiency disease rickets.

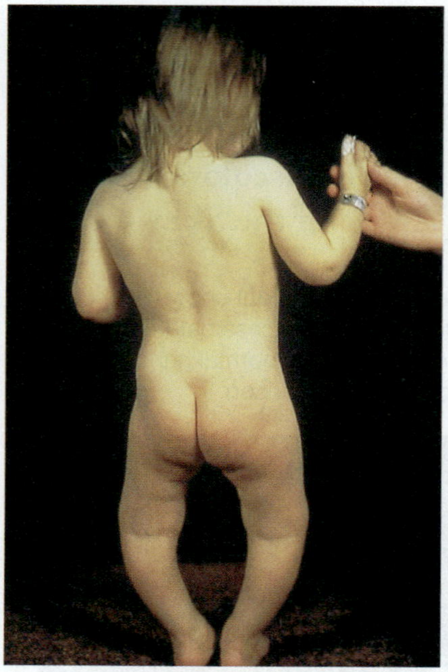

Biophoto Associates/Science Source/Photo Researchers, Inc.

This child displays the beaded ribs common in rickets.

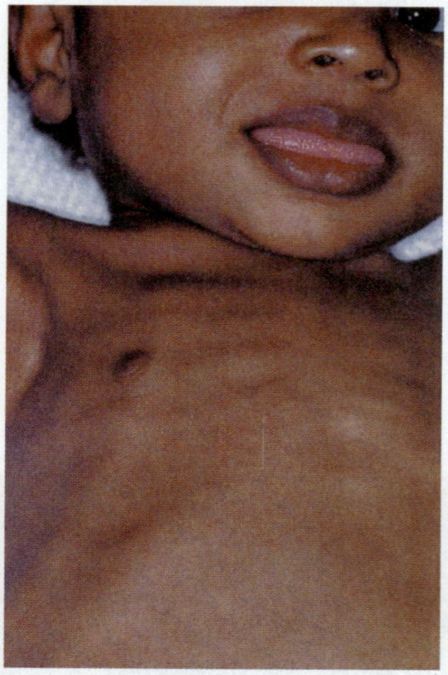

Photo Courtesy of Dr. Norman Carvalho at Children's Healthcare of Atlanta

Too Little Vitamin D—A Danger to Bones

The most obvious sign of vitamin D deficiency occurs in early life—the abnormality of the bones in the disease **rickets** is shown in Figure 7-6. Children with rickets develop bowed legs because they are unable to mineralize newly forming bone material, a rubbery protein matrix. As gravity pulls their body weight against these weak bones, the legs bow. Many such children also have a protruding belly because of lax abdominal muscles.

As early as the 1700s, rickets was known to be curable with cod-liver oil, which is rich in vitamin D. More than a hundred years later, a Polish physician linked sunlight exposure to prevention and cure of rickets. Today, in some areas of the world, such as Mongolia, Tibet, and the Netherlands, more than half of the children suffer the bowed legs, knock-knees, beaded ribs, and protruding (pigeon) chests of rickets.[32] In the United States, over 58 million children are reported to be vitamin D–deficient or insufficient, but rickets itself is uncommon.[33] When it occurs, black children and adolescents—especially females and overweight teens—are most likely to be affected.[34] To prevent rickets, the American Academy of Pediatrics recommends a minimum daily intake of 400 IU vitamin D for all infants, children, and adolescents.[35] Adolescents, who often abandon vitamin D–fortified milk in favor of soft drinks and punches, may also prefer indoor pastimes such as video games to outdoor activities during daylight hours. Such teens often lack vitamin D and so fail to develop the bone density needed to prevent bone loss in later life.[36]

In adults, the poor mineralization of bone results in the painful bone disease **osteomalacia.**[37] The bones become increasingly soft, flexible, brittle, and deformed. Older people can suffer painful joints and muscles if their vitamin D levels are low, although the condition is easily missed during examinations and may be mistaken for arthritis or other painful conditions. Inadequate vitamin D also sets the stage for a loss of calcium from the bones, which can result in fractures from **osteoporosis.** The simple act of taking a combined vitamin D and calcium supplement could easily save the life of an elderly person who might otherwise suffer dangerous bone fractures and falls.[38] Vitamin D alone seems ineffective in this regard, however.[39]

Too Much Vitamin D—A Danger to Soft Tissues

Vitamin D is the most potentially toxic vitamin. In excess, vitamin D raises the concentration of blood calcium, which can then collect in the soft tissues, forming stones.[40] The kidneys, which must concentrate calcium in order to excrete it, are particularly vulnerable to forming stones.[41] Calcification may also harden the blood vessels, a condition that may be fatal when it affects major arteries of the brain, heart, and lungs. Early symptoms of toxicity include pain, chills, appetite loss, nausea, vomiting, and increased urination and thirst. Among people taking vitamin D supplements, infants and older people are most often reported to develop toxicities.[42]

Vitamin D from Sunlight

Most of the world's people rely on exposure to sunlight for vitamin D. When ultraviolet (UV) B light rays from the sun shine on a cholesterol compound in human skin, the compound is transformed into a vitamin D precursor and is absorbed directly into the blood. Slowly, over the next day and a half, the liver and kidneys finish converting the precursor to the active form of vitamin D. Diseases that affect either the liver or the kidneys can impair the conversion of the inactive precursor to the active vitamin and therefore produce symptoms of vitamin D deficiency. People who wear concealing clothing for religious reasons, particularly girls and women, may also lack vitamin D. The factors listed in Table 7-4 can all interfere with vitamin D synthesis, as well.

- Chapter 8 and Controversy 8 present more about bone minerals and their regulation and about osteoporosis, the bone-weakening disease of aging.

Did You Know?

Too much vitamin D causes high blood calcium, but a high calcium intake does not (see the next chapter).

Is Sunlight Exposure a Safe Source of Vitamin D?

Sunlight presents no risk of vitamin D toxicity; the sun itself begins breaking down excess vitamin D made in the skin. Sunbathers run *other* risks, however, such as

TABLE 7-4 Factors Affecting Vitamin D Synthesis

The more of these factors present in a person's life, the more critical it becomes to obtain vitamin D from food or supplements.

Factor	Effect on Vitamin D Synthesis
Advanced age	With age, the skin loses some of its capacity to synthesize vitamin D.
Air pollution	Particles in the air screen out the sun's rays.
City living	Tall buildings block sunlight.
Clothing	Most clothing blocks sunlight.
Geography	Sunlight exposure is limited: • September through March at latitudes above 50 degrees (most of Canada) • November through February at latitudes between 35 and 50 degrees (most U.S. locations) In locations south of 35 degrees (much of the southern United States), direct sun exposure is sufficient for vitamin D synthesis year-round.
Homebound	Living indoors prevents sun exposure.
Season	Warmer seasons of the year bring more direct sun rays.
Skin pigment	Darker-skinned people synthesize less vitamin D per minute than lighter-skinned people.
Sunscreen	Use reduces or prevents skin exposure to sun's rays.
Time of day	Midday hours bring maximum direct sun exposure.

premature skin wrinkling and skin cancers. UV radiation from the sun, including UVB that promotes vitamin D synthesis, is carcinogenic, contributing to about a million skin cancers per year in the United States alone.[43] Successful public health campaigns to promote sunscreen use (sun protection factor, or SPF, of 15 and above) and to avoid sun exposure, along with an increasingly indoor, sedentary lifestyle may be responsible for a recent downturn in serum vitamin D among people in the United States (Figure 7-7).[44]

The pigments of dark skin protect against UV radiation, but dark-skinned people require up to 3 hours of direct sun (depending on the climate) for several days' worth of vitamin D. Light-skinned people need much less time (an estimated 5 minutes without sunscreen or 10 to 30 minutes with sunscreen).[45] Tanning booths may or may not promote vitamin D synthesis but they, like the sun, deliver UV radiation that promotes skin cancer. Given that any amount of UV exposure increases the risk of skin cancer, some experts conclude that dietary vitamin D may be the safer source.[46]

Intake Recommendations

Advancing age increases the risk of vitamin D deficiency, so intake recommendations increase with age: 5 micrograms per day for adults 19 to 50 years, 10 micrograms for those 51 to 70 years, and 15 micrograms for those over 70. The DRI committee has set a Tolerable Upper Intake Level for vitamin D at 50 micrograms per day (2,000 IU on supplement labels). Some experts are calling for significant increases in both the target vitamin D intakes (up to 125 micrograms per day) and in the Tolerable Upper Intakes.[47]

Food Sources

Snapshot 7-2 shows the few significant naturally occurring food sources of vitamin D. Butter, cream, and fortified margarine also contribute small amounts. In the United States and Canada, milk, whether fluid, dried, or evaporated, is fortified with vitamin D. Yogurt and cheese products are often not fortified, so read the labels.

FIGURE 7-7 Downturn in Vitamin D Blood Levels Among Population Groups, 1988–2004

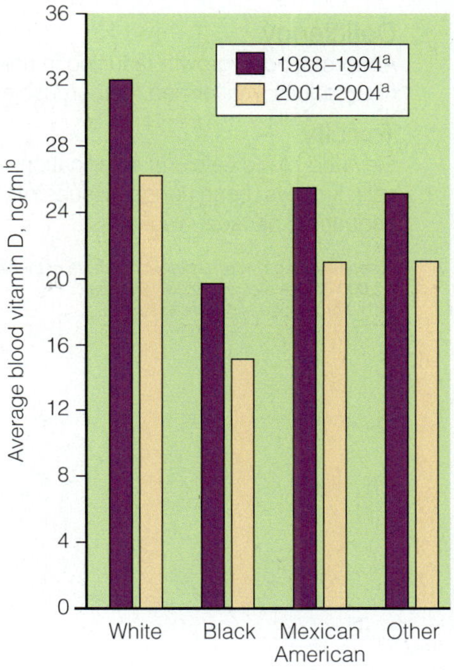

[a]NHANES data.

[b]Nanograms per milliliter of blood serum.

Source: Adapted from A. A. Ginde and coauthors, Demographic differences and trends of vitamin D insufficiency in the US population, 1988–2004, Archives of Internal Medicine *169 (2009): 626–632.*

rickets the vitamin D–deficiency disease in children; characterized by abnormal growth of bone and manifested in bowed legs or knock-knees, outward-bowed chest, and knobs on the ribs.

osteomalacia (OS-tee-o-mal-AY-shuh) the adult expression of vitamin D–deficiency disease, characterized by an overabundance of unmineralized bone protein (*osteo* means "bone"; *mal* means "bad"). Symptoms include bending of the spine and bowing of the legs.

osteoporosis a weakening of bone mineral structures that occurs commonly with advancing age. Also defined in Chapter 8.

SNAPSHOT 7-2

Vitamin D

DRI Recommended Intakes

Adults: 5 μg/day (19–50 yr)
10 μg/day (51–70 yr)
15 μg/day (>70 yr)

Tolerable Upper Intake Level

Adults: 50 μg/day

Chief Functions

Mineralization of bones and teeth (raises blood calcium and phosphorus by increasing absorption from digestive tract, withdrawing calcium from bones, stimulating retention by kidneys)

Deficiency

Abnormal bone growth resulting in rickets in children, osteomalacia in adults; malformed teeth; muscle spasms

Toxicity

Elevated blood calcium; calcification of soft tissues (blood vessels, kidneys, heart, lungs, tissues of joints), excessive thirst, headache, nausea, weakness

*These foods provide 10 percent or more of the vitamin D Daily Value in a serving. For a 2,000-calorie diet, the DV is 10 μg/day.
[a]Avoid prolonged exposure to sun.

GOOD SOURCES*

Young adults who drink 3 cups of milk a day receive half of their daily requirement; the other half comes from exposure to sunlight and other food sources. Without adequate sunshine, fortification, or supplementation, strict vegetarians cannot meet vitamin D needs. Vegan sources include vitamin D–fortified soy milk and cereals. Importantly, feeding infants and young children unfortified "health beverages" instead of milk or infant formula can create severe nutrient deficiencies, including rickets.

KEY POINT Vitamin D raises mineral levels in the blood, notably calcium and phosphorus, permitting bone formation and maintenance. A deficiency can cause rickets in childhood or osteomalacia in later life. Vitamin D is the most toxic of all the vitamins, and excesses cause health problems. People exposed to the sun make vitamin D from a cholesterol-like compound in their skin, but skin cancer arises from sun exposure; fortified milk is an important source.

Vitamin E

Almost a century ago, researchers discovered a compound in vegetable oils essential for reproduction in rats.[48] This compound was named **tocopherol** from *tokos,* a Greek word meaning "offspring." A few years later, the compound was named vitamin E.

Four tocopherol compounds have been identified, and each is designated by one of the first four letters of the Greek alphabet: alpha, beta, gamma, and delta. Of these, alpha-tocopherol is the gold standard for vitamin E activity. For this reason, DRI intake recommendations are expressed as alpha-tocopherol. Although not readily

tocopherol (tuh-KOFF-er-all) a kind of alcohol. The active form of vitamin E is alpha-tocopherol.

converted to alpha-tocopherol, the other tocopherols are of interest to researchers for potentially beneficial roles in the body.‡[49]

Roles of Vitamin E

Vitamin E is an antioxidant and thus acts as a bodyguard against oxidative damage.[50] Such damage occurs when highly unstable molecules known as **free radicals,** formed during normal cell metabolism, run amok and disrupt the structures of lipids in cell membranes, of lipoproteins (LDL), of DNA in genetic material, and of proteins that perform cellular work. Free radicals, left unchecked, cause inflammation that may contribute to some cancers, heart disease, or other diseases.[51] Vitamin E, by being oxidized itself, quenches free radicals and reduces inflammation.[52] Figure 7-8 provides an overview of the activity of vitamin E and its potential role in disease prevention.

The protection of vitamin E is especially crucial in the lungs, where high oxygen concentrations would otherwise disrupt vulnerable membranes. Red blood cells also need protection as they transport oxygen from the lungs to other tissues, and vitamin E defends their cell membranes, too. White blood cells that fight diseases also depend on vitamin E, and sensitive brain tissues rely on its antioxidant nature, as well.[53]

Vitamin E Deficiency

A deficiency of vitamin E produces a wide variety of symptoms in laboratory animals, but these are almost never seen in healthy human beings. Deficiency of vitamin E, which dissolves in fat, may occur in people with diseases that cause fat malabsorption or in infants born prematurely. Disease or injury of the liver (which makes bile, necessary for digestion of fat), the gallbladder (which delivers bile into the intestine), or the pancreas (which makes fat-digesting enzymes) make vitamin E deficiency likely. In people without diseases, low blood levels of vitamin E are most likely when diets extremely low in fat are consumed for years.

A classic vitamin E deficiency occurs in premature babies born before the transfer of the vitamin from the mother to the infant, which takes place late in pregnancy. Without sufficient vitamin E, the infant's red blood cells rupture (**erythrocyte hemolysis**), and the infant becomes anemic. The few symptoms of vitamin E

‡Other tocopherols may also function as antioxidants.

free radicals atoms or molecules with one or more unpaired electrons that make the atom or molecule unstable and highly reactive

erythrocyte (eh-REETH-ro-sight) **hemolysis** (HEE-moh-LIE-sis, hee-MOLL-ih-sis) rupture of the red blood cells, caused by vitamin E deficiency (*erythro* means "red"; *cyte* means "cell"; *hemo* means "blood"; *lysis* means "breaking"). The anemia produced by the condition is *hemolytic* (HEE-moh-LIT-ick) *anemia.*

FIGURE 7-8 **Free-Radical Damage and Antioxidant Protection**

Free-radical formation occurs during metabolic processes, and it accelerates when diseases or other stresses strike.

Free radicals cause chain reactions that damage cellular structures.

Antioxidants quench free radicals and protect cellular structures.

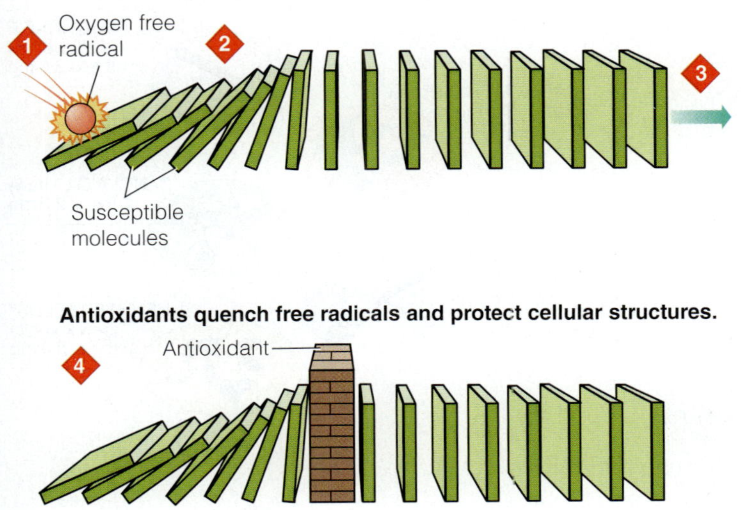

1. A chemically reactive oxygen free radical attacks fatty acid, DNA, protein, or cholesterol molecules, which form other free radicals in turn.
2. This initiates a rapid, destructive chain reaction.
3. The result is:
   - cell membrane lipid damage.
   - cellular protein damage.
   - DNA damage.
   - oxidation of LDL cholesterol.
   - inflammation.

   These changes may initiate steps leading to diseases such as heart disease, cancer, macular degeneration, and others.
4. Antioxidants, such as vitamin E, stop the chain reaction by changing the nature of the free radical.

Did You Know?

Cooking methods using high heat, such as frying, destroy vitamin E. Uncooked oils supply vitamin E to the diet.

deficiency observed in adults include loss of muscle coordination and reflexes and impaired vision and speech. Vitamin E corrects all of these symptoms.

People with low blood vitamin E concentrations but without overt symptoms die more often from chronic diseases and other causes than do people with higher blood levels.[54] The Controversy section provides details, but you should know right away that experts do not recommend taking vitamin E to ward off chronic diseases.[55]

Toxicity of Vitamin E

Vitamin E in foods is safe to consume. Reports of vitamin E toxicity symptoms are rare across a broad range of intakes.[56] However, vitamin E in supplements augments the effects of anticoagulant medication used to oppose unwanted blood clotting, so people taking such drugs risk uncontrollable bleeding if they also take vitamin E. Vitamin E prolongs blood clotting times by interfering with the activity of vitamin K by a mechanism yet to be defined.[57]An increase in brain hemorrhages, a form of stroke, has also been noted among smokers taking just 50 milligrams of vitamin E per day.

Recently, the pooled results from 67 experiments involving almost a quarter-million people suggested that taking vitamin E supplements may slightly increase mortality in both healthy and sick people.[58] Other studies find no effect or a slight decrease in mortality among certain groups.[59] To err on the safe side, people who use vitamin E supplements should probably keep their dosages low, and they should not exceed the Tolerable Upper Intake Level of 1,000 milligrams alpha-tocopherol per day.

FIGURE 7-9 **Vitamin E Recommendations and U.S. Intakes Compared**

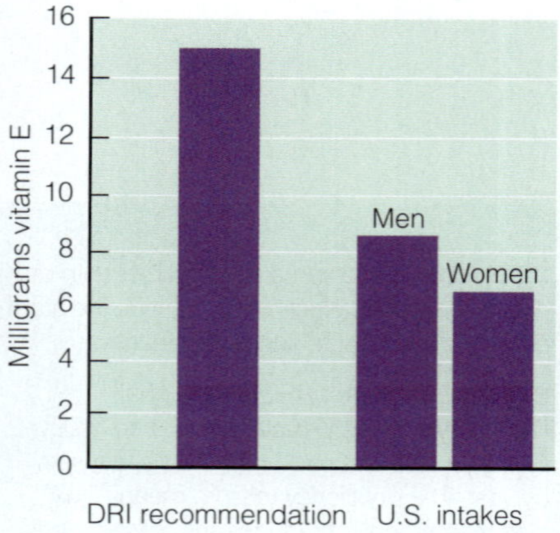

Source: USDA Agricultural Research Service, Table 1, Nutrient Intakes from Food: Mean Amounts Consumed per Individual, One Day, 2005–2006, What We Eat in America: NHANES, *available at www.ars.usda.gov.*

Vitamin E Recommendations and U.S. Intakes

The DRI recommended intake (inside front cover, page B) for vitamin E is 15 milligrams a day for adults. This amount seems sufficient to maintain healthy, normal blood values for vitamin E for most people. Smokers may have higher needs. On average, U.S. intakes of vitamin E fall substantially below the recommendation (see Figure 7-9).[60] The need for vitamin E rises as people consume more polyunsaturated oil because the oil requires antioxidant protection by the vitamin. Luckily, most raw oils also contain vitamin E, so people who eat raw oils also receive the vitamin.

Food Sources of Vitamin E

Vitamin E is widespread in foods (see Snapshot 7-3). Much of the vitamin E in the diet comes from vegetable oils and products made from them, such as margarine

SNAPSHOT 7-3

Vitamin E

DRI Recommended Intake
Adults: 15 mg/day

Tolerable Upper Intake Level
Adults: 1,000 mg/day

Chief Functions
Antioxidant (protects cell membranes, regulates oxidation reactions, protects polyunsaturated fatty acids)

Deficiency
Red blood cell breakage, nerve damage

Toxicity
Augments the effects of anticlotting medication

GOOD SOURCES*

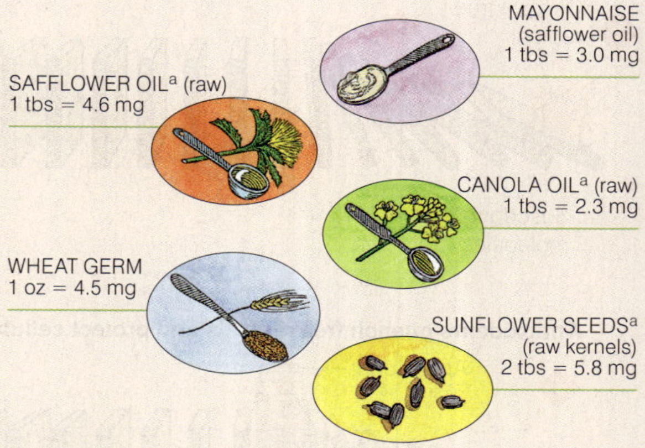

*These foods provide 10 percent or more of the vitamin E Daily Value in a serving. For a 2,000-calorie diet, the DV is 30 IU or 20 mg/day.
[a]Cooking destroys vitamin E.

and salad dressings. Wheat germ oil is especially rich in vitamin E. Animal fats have almost none.

Vitamin E is readily destroyed by heat and oxidation, so fresh, raw oils or lightly processed foods are the best sources. As people choose more highly processed foods, fried fast foods, or "convenience" foods, they lose vitamin E because little vitamin E survives the heating and other processes used to make these foods.

© Gary Houlder/Corbis

Raw vegetable oils contain substantial vitamin E but high temperatures destroy it.

KEY POINT Vitamin E acts as an antioxidant in cell membranes and is especially important for the integrity of cells that are constantly exposed to high oxygen concentrations. Vitamin E deficiency is rare in human beings, but it does occur in newborn premature infants. The vitamin is widely distributed in plant foods; it is destroyed by high heat. Toxicity is rare but supplements may carry risks.

Vitamin K

Have you ever thought about how remarkable it is that blood can clot? The liquid turns solid in a life-saving series of reactions—if blood did not clot, wounds would just keep bleeding, draining the blood from the body.

Roles of Vitamin K

The main function of vitamin K is to help activate proteins that help clot the blood. Hospitals measure the clotting time of a person's blood before surgery and, if needed, administer vitamin K to reduce bleeding during the operation. Vitamin K is of value only if a vitamin K deficiency exists. Vitamin K does not improve clotting in those with other bleeding disorders, such as the inherited disease hemophilia.

Some people with heart problems need to *prevent* the formation of clots within their circulatory system—this is popularly referred to as "thinning" the blood. One of the best-known medicines for this purpose is warfarin, which interferes with vitamin K's clot-promoting action. Vitamin K therapy may be needed for people on warfarin if uncontrolled bleeding should occur. People taking warfarin who self-prescribe vitamin K supplements risk interfering with the action of the drug.[61]

Vitamin K is also necessary for the synthesis of key bone proteins. Without vitamin K, the bones produce an abnormal protein that cannot bind the minerals that normally form bones, causing low bone mineral density.[62] People who consume abundant vitamin K in the form of green leafy vegetables suffer fewer hip fractures than those with lower intakes. Vitamin K supplements seem ineffective against bone loss, however.[63] Vitamin K is also under investigation for roles in heart disease prevention.[64]

Did You Know?

K stands for the Danish word *koagulation* (clotting).

CONCEPT LINK 7-4

The roles of protein in blood clotting were described in Chapter 6 on page 202.

- Warfarin is pronounced WAR-fuh-rin.

Deficiency of Vitamin K

Few U.S. adults are likely to experience vitamin K deficiency, even if they seldom eat vitamin K–rich foods. This is because, like vitamin D, vitamin K can be obtained from a nonfood source—in this case, the intestinal bacteria. Billions of bacteria normally reside in the intestines, and some of them synthesize vitamin K.

Newborn infants present a unique case with regard to vitamin K because they are born with a sterile intestinal tract, and the vitamin K–producing bacteria take weeks to establish themselves. To prevent hemorrhage, the newborn is given a single dose of vitamin K at birth. People who have taken antibiotics that have killed the bacteria in their intestinal tracts also may develop vitamin K deficiency. In certain other medical conditions, bile production falters, making lipids, including all of the fat-soluble vitamins, unabsorbable. Supplements of the vitamin are needed in these cases because a vitamin K deficiency can be fatal.

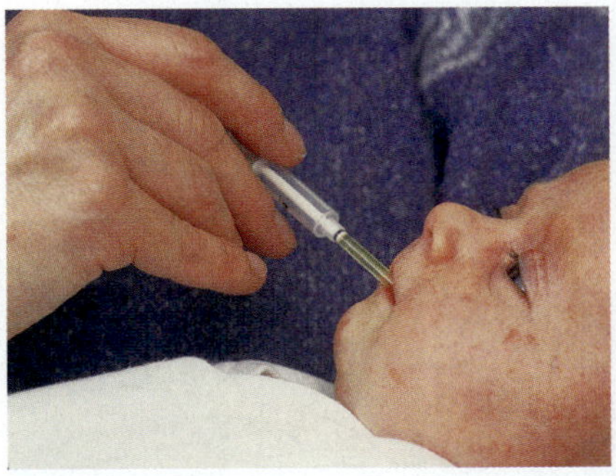
Simon Fraser/Photo Researchers, Inc.

Soon after birth, newborn infants receive a dose of vitamin K.

SNAPSHOT 7-4

Vitamin K

DRI Recommended Intakes
Men: 120 µg/day
Women: 90 µg/day

Chief Functions
Synthesis of blood-clotting proteins and bone proteins

Deficiency
Hemorrhage; abnormal bone formation

Toxicity
Opposes the effects of anti-clotting medication

These foods provide 10 percent or more of the vitamin K Daily Value in a serving. For a 2,000-calorie diet, the DV is 80 µg/day.
Data from USDA.

GOOD SOURCES*

Vitamin K Toxicity

Reports of vitamin K toxicity among healthy adults are rare, and the DRI committee has not set a Tolerable Upper Intake Level. For infants and pregnant women, however, vitamin K toxicity can result when supplements of a synthetic version of vitamin K are given too enthusiastically.§ Toxicity induces breakage of the red blood cells and release of their pigment, which colors the skin yellow. A toxic dose of synthetic vitamin K causes the liver to release the blood cell pigment (bilirubin) into the blood (instead of excreting it into the bile) and leads to **jaundice.**

Requirements and Sources of Vitamin K

The vitamin K requirement for men is 120 micrograms a day; women require 90 micrograms. As Snapshot 7-4 shows, vitamin K's richest plant food sources include dark green, leafy vegetables such as cooked spinach and other greens, which provide an average of 300 micrograms per half-cup serving. Lettuces, broccoli, brussels sprouts, and other members of the cabbage family are also good sources.

Only one rich animal food source of vitamin K exists: liver. Canola and soybean oils (unhydrogenated liquid oils) provide smaller but still significant amounts, while fortified cereals can be rich sources of added vitamin K. One egg and a cup of milk contain about equal amounts, or 25 micrograms each. Tables of food composition do not include the vitamin K contents of foods because they are not well enough known.

KEY POINT Vitamin K is necessary for blood to clot; deficiency causes uncontrolled bleeding. The bacterial inhabitants of the digestive tract produce vitamin K. Toxicity causes jaundice.

LO 7.5, 7.6

The Water-Soluble Vitamins

Vitamin C and the B vitamins dissolve in water, which has implications for their handling in food and by the body. In food, water-soluble vitamins easily dissolve and drain away with cooking water, and some are destroyed on exposure to light,

jaundice (JAWN-dis) yellowing of the skin due to spillover of the bile pigment bilirubin (bill-ee-ROO-bin) from the liver into the general circulation.

§The version of vitamin K responsible for this effect is menadione.

THINK FITNESS

Vitamins for Athletes

Do athletes who strive for top performance need more vitamins than foods can supply? Competitive athletes who choose their diets with reasonable care almost never need nutrient supplements. The reason is elegantly simple. The need for energy to fuel exercise requires that people eat extra calories of food, and if that extra food is of the kind shown in this chapter's Snapshots—fruits, vegetables, milk, eggs, whole or enriched grains, lean meats, and some oils—then the extra vitamins needed to support the activity follow naturally into the body. Chapter 10 comes back to the roles of vitamins in physical activity.

START NOW CENGAGENOW Ready to make a change? Consult the online behavior-change planner to plan how you might change your food selections to better meet the needs of your active body at **www.cengage.com/sso.**

heat, or oxygen during processing.[65] Later sections examine vitamin vulnerability and provide tips for retaining vitamins in foods.

In the body, water-soluble vitamins are easily absorbed and just as easily excreted in the urine. A few of the water-soluble vitamins can remain in the lean tissues for a month or more, but these tissues actively exchange materials with the body fluids all the time. At any time, the vitamins may be picked up by the extracellular fluids, washed away by the blood, and excreted in the urine.

Advice for meeting the need for these nutrients is straightforward: choose foods rich in water-soluble vitamins to achieve an average intake that meets the recommendation over a few days' time. The Snapshots in this section can help to guide your choices. Foods never deliver toxic doses of the water-soluble vitamins, but the large doses concentrated in some vitamin supplements can reach toxic levels. Normally, though, the most likely hazard to the supplement taker is to the wallet: "If you take supplements of the water-soluble vitamins, you may have the most expensive urine in town." The Think Fitness feature asks whether athletes need vitamin supplements.

- The Food Feature section of Chapter 12 provides details about the effects of processing on vitamins and other nutrients in foods.

- Recall characteristics of water-soluble vitamins from Table 7-2:
  - *Dissolve in water.*
  - *Are easily absorbed and excreted.*
  - *Are not stored extensively in tissues.*
  - *Seldom reach toxic levels.*

KEY POINT Water-soluble vitamins are easily absorbed and excreted from the body and must be consumed frequently in the diet. They are easily lost or destroyed during food preparation and processing.

Vitamin C

More than 200 years ago, any man who joined the crew of a seagoing ship knew he had only half a chance of returning alive—not because he might be slain by pirates or die in a storm, but because he might contract **scurvy,** a disease that often killed as many as two-thirds of a ship's crew on a long voyage. Ships that sailed on short voyages, especially around the Mediterranean Sea, were safe from this disease. The special hazard of long ocean voyages was that the ship's cook used up the fresh fruits and vegetables early and relied on cereals and live animals for the duration of the voyage.

Long voyages without fresh fruits and vegetables spelled death by scurvy for the crew.

The first nutrition experiment to be conducted on human beings was devised 250 years ago to find a cure for scurvy. A physician divided some British sailors with scurvy into groups.** Each group received a different test substance: vinegar, sulfuric acid, seawater, oranges, or lemons. Those receiving the citrus fruits were

scurvy the vitamin C–deficiency disease.

**The physician was James Lind.

cured within a short time. Sadly, it took 50 years for the British navy to make use of the information and require all its vessels to provide lime juice to every sailor daily. British sailors were mocked with the term *limey* because of this requirement. The name later given to the vitamin that the fruit provided, **ascorbic acid,** literally means "no-scurvy acid." It is more commonly known today as vitamin C.

The Roles of Vitamin C

Vitamin C performs a variety of functions in the body. It is best known for two of them: its work in maintaining the connective tissues and as an antioxidant.

A Cofactor for Enzymes Vitamin C assists several enzymes in performing their jobs. In particular, the enzymes involved in the formation and maintenance of the protein **collagen** depend on vitamin C for their activity. Collagen forms the base for all of the connective tissues: bones, teeth, skin, and tendons. Collagen forms the scar tissue that heals wounds, the reinforcing structure that mends fractures, and the supporting material of capillaries that prevents bruises. Vitamin C also acts as a cofactor in other synthetic reactions, such as in the production of carnitine, an important compound for transporting fatty acids within the cells and in the creation of certain hormones.[66]

An Antioxidant In addition to assisting enzymes, vitamin C also acts in a more general way as an antioxidant. Vitamin C protects substances found in foods and in the body from oxidation by being oxidized itself. For example, cells of the immune system maintain high levels of vitamin C to protect themselves from free radicals generated during assaults on bacteria and other invaders. Some oxidized vitamin C is degraded irretrievably and must be replaced by the diet, but much more is not lost but recycled back to the active form for reuse. This recycling plays a key role in maintaining sufficient vitamin C in the cells to allow it to perform its critical work.

In the intestines, vitamin C protects iron from oxidation and so promotes its absorption. In the blood, vitamin C protects sensitive blood constituents from oxidation, reduces inflammation, and helps to protect vitamin E and recycle it to its active form. The antioxidant roles of vitamin C are the focus of extensive study, especially in relation to disease prevention.[67] Unfortunately, research has yielded only disappointing results: vitamin C supplements seem useless against heart disease, cancer, and other diseases, unless they are prescribed to treat a deficiency.[68]

In test tubes, a high concentration of vitamin C has the opposite effect from antioxidants; that is, it acts as a **prooxidant** by activating oxidizing elements, such as iron and copper. A few studies suggest that this may happen in people, too, under some conditions. The question of what, if anything, such findings may mean for human health remains unanswered.

Functional Group

Key antioxidant vitamins:

- *Vitamin C, vitamin E, beta-carotene*

Key antioxidant mineral:

- *Selenium*

Deficiency Symptoms

Most of the symptoms of scurvy can be attributed to the breakdown of collagen in the absence of vitamin C: loss of appetite, growth cessation, tenderness to touch, weakness, bleeding gums (shown in Figure 7-10), loose teeth, swollen ankles and wrists, and tiny red spots in the skin where blood has leaked out of capillaries (also shown in the figure).[69] One symptom, anemia, reflects an important role worth repeating—vitamin C helps the body to absorb and use iron. Table 7-7 at the end of the chapter summarizes deficiency symptoms and other information about vitamin C.

In the United States, vitamin C status has been improving but people who smoke or have low incomes continue to be at risk for deficiency.[70] The disease scurvy is seldom seen today except in a few elderly people, people addicted to alcohol or other drugs, and a few infants who are fed only cow's milk.[71] Breast milk and infant formula supply enough vitamin C, but infants who are fed cow's milk and receive no vitamin C in formula, fruit juice, or other outside sources are at risk. Low intakes of fruits and vegetables and a poor appetite overall lead to low vitamin C intakes and are not uncommon among people aged 65 and older. Vitamin C also supports immune system

ascorbic acid one of the active forms of vitamin C (the other is *dehydroascorbic* acid); an antioxidant nutrient.

collagen (COLL-a-jen) the chief protein of most connective tissues, including scars, ligaments, and tendons, and the underlying matrix on which bones and teeth are built.

prooxidant (pro-OX-ih-dant) a compound that triggers reactions involving oxygen.

FIGURE 7-10 **Scurvy Symptoms—Gums and Skin**

Vitamin C deficiency causes the breakdown of collagen, which supports the teeth.

Small pinpoint hemorrhages (red spots) appear in the skin indicating that invisible internal bleeding may also be occurring.

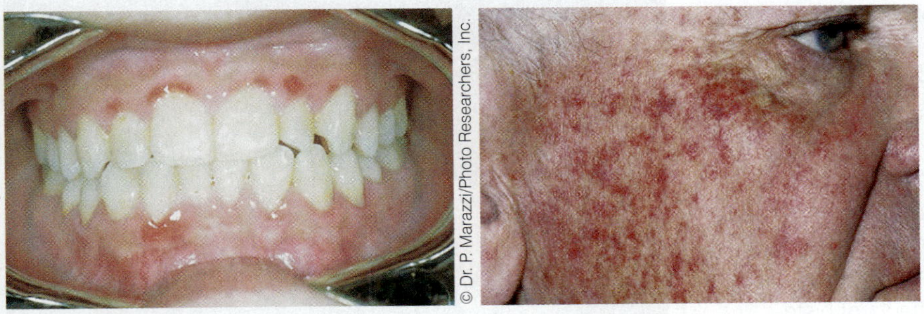

functions and so protects against infection. A long-claimed relationship between vitamin C and the common cold is the topic of this chapter's Consumer Corner.

- The DRI Tolerable Upper Intake Level for vitamin C is set at 2,000 mg (2 g) a day.

Vitamin C Toxicity

The easy availability of vitamin C in pill form and the publication of books recommending vitamin C to prevent and cure colds and cancer have led thousands of people to take huge doses of vitamin C (see the margin drawing). These "volunteer" subjects enabled researchers to study potential adverse effects of large vitamin C doses. One effect observed with a 2-gram dose is alteration of the insulin response to carbohydrate in people with otherwise normal glucose tolerances. People taking anticlotting medications may unwittingly counteract the effect if they also take massive doses of vitamin C. Those with kidney disease, a tendency toward gout, or a genetic abnormality that alters vitamin C's breakdown to its excretion products are prone to forming kidney stones if they take large doses of vitamin C.[††] Vitamin C supplements in any dosage may be dangerous for people with an overload of iron in the body because vitamin C increases iron absorption from the intestine and releases iron from storage. Other adverse effects are mild, including digestive upsets, such as nausea, abdominal cramps, excessive gas, and diarrhea.

The safe range of vitamin C intakes seems to be broad, from the absolute minimum of 10 milligrams a day to the Tolerable Upper Intake Level of 2,000 milligrams (2 grams). Doses approaching 10 grams can be expected to be unsafe. Vitamin C from food is always safe.

Vitamin C Recommendations

The adult DRI intake recommendation for vitamin C is 90 milligrams for men and 75 milligrams for women. These amounts are far higher than the 10 or so milligrams per day needed to prevent the symptoms of scurvy. In fact, they are close to the amount at which the body's pool of vitamin C is full to overflowing: about 100 milligrams per day.

Tobacco use introduces oxidants that deplete the body's vitamin C. Thus, smokers generally have lower blood vitamin C levels than nonsmokers.[72] Even "passive smokers" who live and work with smokers and those who regularly chew tobacco need more vitamin C than others. Intake recommendations for smokers are set high, at 125 milligrams for men and 110 milligrams for women, in order to maintain blood levels comparable to those of nonsmokers. Importantly, vitamin C cannot reverse other damage caused by tobacco use. Physical stressors including infections,

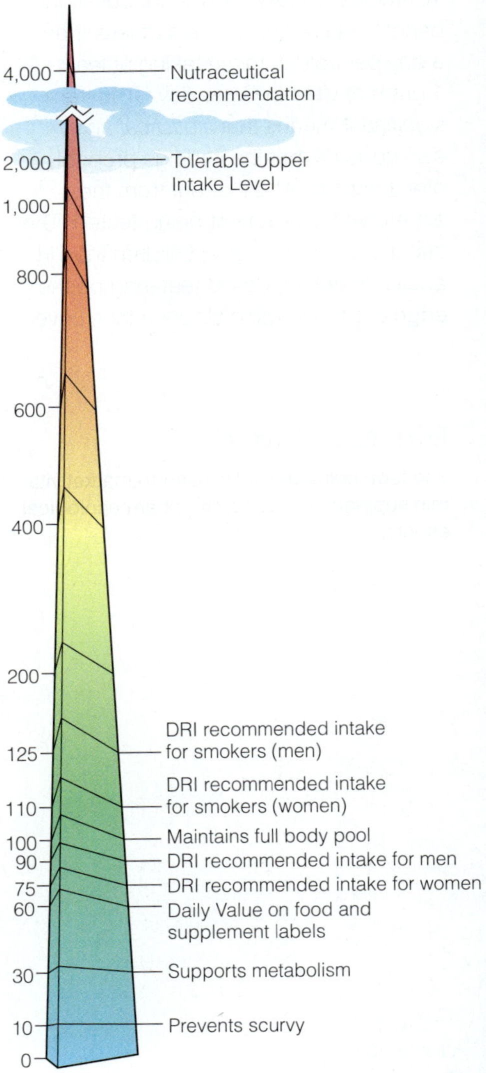

Vitamin C Tower of Recommendations

[††]Vitamin C is inactivated and degraded by several routes, and oxalate, which can form kidney stones, is sometimes produced along the way. People may also develop oxalate crystals in their kidneys regardless of vitamin C status.

CONSUMER CORNER

Vitamin C and the Common Cold

Why do so many people take vitamin C supplements to relieve colds? Does any research support this practice? While the term "common cold" does not precisely define any one condition, researchers generally define it as a group of viral upper respiratory infections untreatable by antibiotics.[1]

In a recent review, 30 trials of over 11,350 people reported no relationship between routine vitamin C supplementation and prevention of the common cold.[2] A few others report modest benefits—fewer colds, fewer days, and shorter duration of severe symptoms, especially for those exposed to physical and environmental stresses.[3]

For treatment of colds once they set in, studies reveal a significant but slight benefit—a shorter duration of less than a day per cold in those taking at least 1 gram of vitamin C per day.[4] The term *significant* means that *statistical* analysis suggests that the findings probably didn't arise by chance, but from the experimental treatment being tested. The effect may be greater in children than in adults; in adults, doses teetering on the edge of the Tolerable Upper Intake Level (2 grams a day) may be required to produce an effect.

© Lester V. Bergman/Corbis

Can vitamin C ease the suffering of a person with a cold?

Vitamin C (2 grams taken daily for two weeks) seems to reduce blood histamine. Anyone who has ever had a cold knows the effects of histamine: sneezing, a runny or stuffy nose, and swollen sinuses. In druglike doses, vitamin C may work like a weak antihistamine drug, familiar to those who have taken them to treat a cold, by reducing histamine levels. Vitamin C supplements are not recommended as a cold remedy, but, for people who choose to take them, they may slightly reduce the duration and severity of some colds.[5]

One other effect of vitamin C supplements might also provide relief—the placebo effect. Half of the experimental subjects in one study received a placebo but were told they were receiving vitamin C. These subjects reported having fewer colds than the group who had in fact received vitamin C but thought they were receiving the placebo. At work was the powerful healing effect of faith in treatment. One thing is certain—no drug is risk-free, and vitamin C in large doses may have side effects.[6]

Did You Know?

The term *nutraceutical* is used to market vitamin supplements as having pharmacological effects.

burns, fever, toxic heavy metals such as lead, and certain medications also increase the body's use of vitamin C.

Food Sources of Vitamin C

Fruits and vegetables are the foods to remember for vitamin C, as Snapshot 7-5 shows. A cup of orange juice at breakfast, a salad for lunch, a stalk of broccoli and a potato for dinner easily provide 300 milligrams, making pills unnecessary. People commonly identify citrus fruits and juices as sources of vitamin C, but they often overlook other rich sources that may be lower in calories.

Vitamin C is vulnerable to heat and destroyed by oxygen, so for maximum vitamin C, consumers should treat their fruits and vegetables gently. Losses occurring when a food is cut, processed, and stored may be large enough to reduce vitamin C's activity in the body. Fresh, raw, and quickly cooked fruits, vegetables, and juices retain the most vitamin C, and they should be stored properly and consumed within a week after purchase. Table 7-5 gives tips for maximizing vitamin retention in foods.

Because of their enormous popularity, white potatoes contribute significantly to vitamin C intakes, despite providing less than 10 milligrams per half-cup serving. The sweet potato, often ignored in favor of its paler cousin, is a gold mine of nutrients: a single half-cup serving provides about a third of many people's recommended intake for vitamin C, in addition to its lavish contribution of vitamin A.

SNAPSHOT 7-5

Vitamin C

DRI Recommended Intakes
Men: 90 mg/day
Women: 75 mg/day
Smokers: add 35 mg/day

Tolerable Upper Intake Level
Adults: 2,000 mg/day

Chief Functions
Collagen synthesis (strengthens blood vessel walls, forms scar tissue, provides matrix for bone growth), antioxidant, restores vitamin E to active form, supports immune system, boosts iron absorption

Deficiency
Scurvy, with pinpoint hemorrhages, fatigue, bleeding gums, bruises; bone fragility, joint pain; poor wound healing, frequent infections

Toxicity
Nausea, abdominal cramps, diarrhea; rashes; interference with medical tests and drug therapies; in susceptible people, aggravation of gout or kidney stones

**These foods provide 10 percent or more of the vitamin C Daily Value in a serving. For a 2,000-calorie diet, the DV is 60 mg/day.*

GOOD SOURCES*

KEY POINT Vitamin C helps to maintain collagen, the protein of the connective tissue; it protects against infection; it acts as an antioxidant; and it helps in iron absorption. Taking high vitamin C doses may be unwise. Ample vitamin C can be easily obtained from foods.

TABLE 7-5 Minimizing Nutrient Losses

Each of these tactics saves a small percentage of the vitamins in foods, but repeated each day this can add up to significant amounts in a year's time.

Prevent enzymatic destruction:
- Refrigerate most fruits, vegetables, and juices to slow breakdown of vitamins.

Protect from light and air:
- Store milk and enriched grain products in opaque containers to protect riboflavin.
- Store cut fruits and vegetables in the refrigerator in airtight wrappers; reseal opened juice containers before refrigerating.

Prevent heat destruction or losses in water:
- Wash intact fruits and vegetables before cutting or peeling to prevent vitamin losses during washing.
- Cook fruits and vegetables in a microwave oven, or quickly stir fry, or steam them over a small amount of water to preserve heat-sensitive vitamins and to prevent vitamin loss in cooking water. Recapture dissolved vitamins by using cooking water for soups, stews, or gravies.
- Avoid high temperatures and long cooking times.

FIGURE 7-11 ANIMATED! **Coenzyme Action**

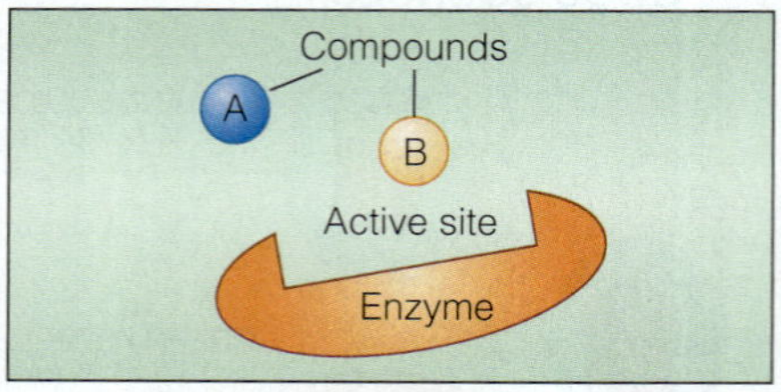

Without the coenzyme, compounds A and B don't respond to the enzyme.

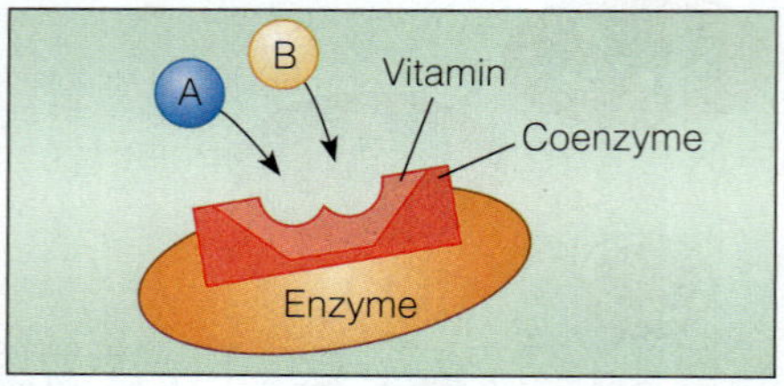

With the coenzyme in place, compounds A and B are attracted to the active site on the enzyme, and they react.

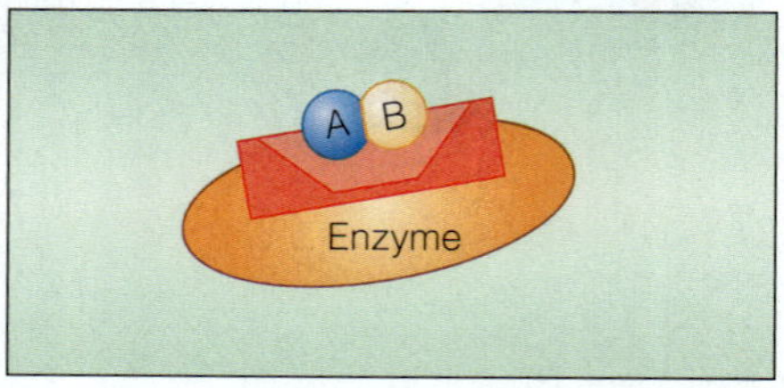

The reaction is completed with the formation of a new product. In this case the product is AB.

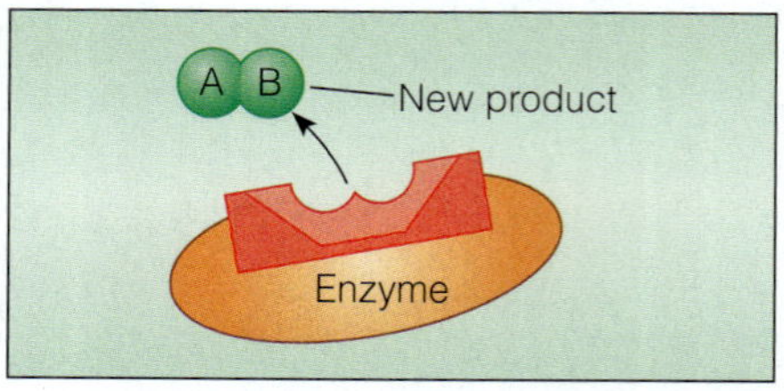

The product AB is released.

CONCEPT LINK 7-5

Recall from Chapter 6, page 200, that enzymes are large proteins that do the body's building, dismantling, and other work.

- To memorize the names of the eight B vitamins, try remembering this silly sentence or make up one of your own:

Tender	*(thiamin)*
romance	*(riboflavin)*
never	*(niacin)*
fails	*(folate)*
with 6 or 12	*(B_6 and B_{12})*
beautiful	*(biotin)*
pearls.	*(pantothenic acid)*

The B Vitamins in Unison

The B vitamins function as part of coenzymes. A **coenzyme** is a small molecule that combines with an enzyme and activates it. Figure 7-11 shows how a coenzyme enables an enzyme to do its job. Sometimes the vitamin part of the enzyme is the active site, where the chemical reaction takes place. The substance to be worked on is attracted to the active site and snaps into place; the reaction proceeds instantaneously. The shape of each enzyme predestines it to accomplish just one kind of job. Without its coenzyme, however, the enzyme is as useless as a car without wheels.

Each of the B vitamins has its own special nature, and the amount of detail known about each one is overwhelming. To simplify things, this introduction describes the teamwork of the B vitamins and emphasizes the consequences of deficiencies. Many of these nutrients are so interdependent that it is sometimes difficult to tell which vitamin deficiency is the cause of which symptom; the presence or absence of one affects the absorption, metabolism, and excretion of others. Later sections present a few details about the vitamins as individuals.

B Vitamin Roles in Metabolism

Figure 7-12 shows some body organs and tissues in which the B vitamins help the body metabolize carbohydrates, lipids, and amino acids. The purpose of the figure is not to present a detailed account of metabolism, but to give you an impression of where the B vitamins work together with enzymes in the metabolism of energy nutrients and in the making of new cells.

Many people mistakenly believe that B vitamins supply the body with energy. They do not, at least not directly. The B vitamins are "helpers." The energy-yielding nutrients—carbohydrate, fat, and protein—give the body fuel for energy; the B vitamins *help* the body use that fuel. More specifically, active forms of five of the B vitamins—thiamin, riboflavin, niacin, pantothenic acid, and biotin—participate in the release of energy from carbohydrate, fat, and protein. Vitamin B_6 helps the body use amino acids to synthesize proteins; the body then puts the protein to work in many ways—to build new tissues, to make hormones, to fight infections, or to serve as fuel for energy, to name only a few.

Folate and vitamin B_{12} help cells to multiply, which is especially important to cells with short life spans that must replace themselves rapidly. Such cells include both the red blood cells (which live for about 120 days) and the cells that line the digestive tract (which replace themselves every 3 days). These cells absorb and deliver energy to all the others. In short, each and every B vitamin is involved, directly or indirectly, in energy metabolism.

B Vitamin Deficiencies

As long as B vitamins are present, their presence is not felt. Only when they are missing does their absence manifest itself in a lack of energy and a multitude of other symptoms, as you can imagine after looking at Figure 7-13. The reactions by which B vitamins facilitate energy release take place in every cell, and no cell can do its work without energy. Thus, in a B vitamin deficiency, every cell is affected. Among the symptoms of B vitamin deficiencies are nausea, severe exhaustion, irritability, depression, forgetfulness, loss of appetite and weight, pain in muscles, impairment of the immune response, loss of control of the limbs, abnormal heart action, severe skin problems, swollen red tongue, cracked skin at the corners of the mouth, and teary or bloodshot eyes. Figure 7-13 shows some of these signs. Because cell renewal depends on energy and protein, which in turn depend on the B vitamins, the digestive tract and the blood are invariably damaged. In children, full recovery may be impossible. In the case of a thiamin deficiency during growth, permanent brain damage can result.

In academic discussions of the B vitamins, different sets of deficiency symptoms are given for each one. Such clear-cut sets of symptoms are found only in laboratory animals that have been fed fabricated diets that lack just one vitamin. In real life, a

FIGURE 7-12 Some Roles of the B Vitamins in Metabolism: Examples

This figure does not attempt to teach intricate biochemical pathways or names of B vitamin–containing enzymes. Its sole purpose is to show a few of the many tissue functions that depend on a host of B vitamin–containing enzymes working together in harmony. The B vitamins work in every cell, and this figure displays less than a thousandth of what they actually do.

Every B vitamin is part of one or more coenzymes that make possible the body's chemical work. For example, the niacin, thiamin, and riboflavin coenzymes are important in the energy pathways. The folate and vitamin B_{12} coenzymes are necessary for making RNA and DNA and thus new cells. The vitamin B_6 coenzyme is necessary for processing amino acids and, therefore, protein. Many other relationships are also critical to metabolism.

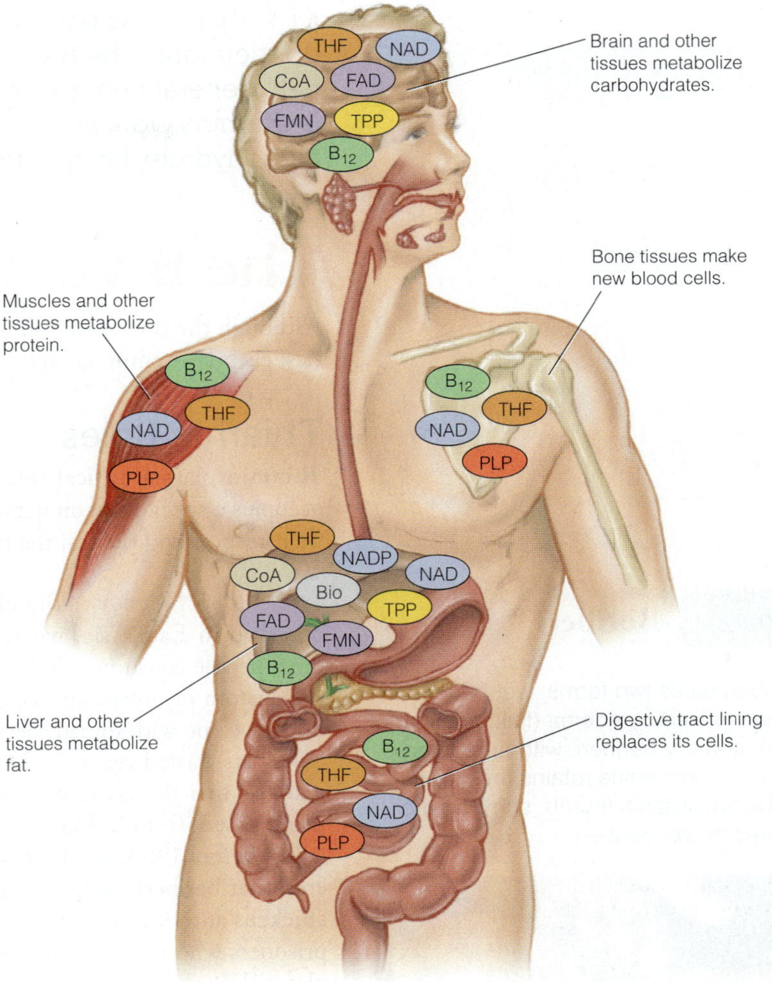

Key:

Coenzyme		Vitamin
TPP	=	thiamin
FAD FMN	=	riboflavin
NAD NADP	=	niacin
PLP	=	vitamin B_6
THF	=	folate
CoA	=	pantothenic acid
Bio	=	biotin
B_{12}	=	vitamin B_{12}

FIGURE 7-13 B Vitamin Deficiency Symptoms of the Tongue and Mouth

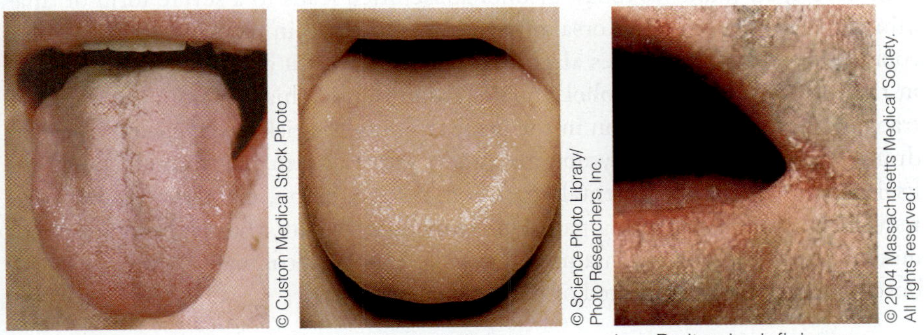

A healthy tongue has a rough and somewhat bumpy surface.

In a B vitamin deficiency, the tongue becomes smooth and swollen.

In a B vitamin deficiency, the corners of the mouth become inflamed and cracked.

deficiency of any one B vitamin seldom shows up by itself because people don't eat nutrients singly; they eat foods that contain mixtures of nutrients. A diet low in one B vitamin is likely low in other nutrients, too. If treatment involves giving wholesome food rather than a single supplement, subtler deficiencies and impairments

coenzyme (co-EN-zime) a small molecule that works with an enzyme to promote the enzyme's activity. Many coenzymes have B vitamins as part of their structure (*co* means "with").

will be corrected along with the major one. The symptoms of B vitamin deficiencies and toxicities are listed in Table 7-7 at the end of the chapter.

KEY POINT As part of coenzymes, the B vitamins help enzymes do their jobs. The B vitamins facilitate the work of every cell. Some help generate energy; others help make protein and new cells. B vitamins work everywhere in body tissues to help metabolize carbohydrate, fat, and protein.

The B Vitamins as Individuals

Although the B vitamins all work as part of coenzymes and share other characteristics, each B vitamin has special qualities. The next sections provide a few details.

Thiamin Roles

Thiamin plays a critical role in the energy metabolism of all cells. Thiamin also occupies a special site on nerve cell membranes. Consequently, nerve processes and their responding tissues, the muscles, depend heavily on thiamin.

FIGURE 7-14 Beriberi

Beriberi takes two forms: wet beriberi, characterized by edema (fluid accumulation), and dry beriberi, without edema. This person's ankle retains the imprint of the physician's thumb, showing the edema of wet beriberi.

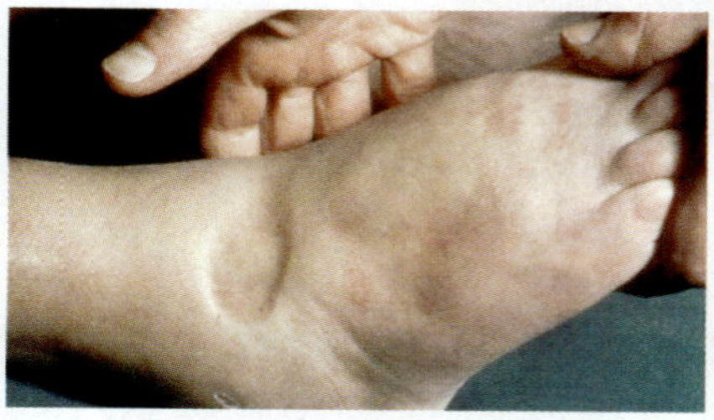

Thiamin Deficiency

The classic thiamin-deficiency disease, **beriberi,** was first observed in East Asia, where rice provided 80 to 90 percent of the total calories most people consumed and was therefore their principal source of thiamin. When the custom of polishing rice (removing its brown coat, which contained the thiamin) became widespread, beriberi swept through the population like an epidemic. Scientists wasted years of effort hunting for a microbial cause of beriberi before they realized that the cause was not something present in the environment, but something absent from it. Figure 7-14 depicts beriberi and describes its two forms.

Just before 1900, an observant physician working in a prison in East Asia discovered that beriberi could be cured with proper diet. The physician noticed that the chickens at the prison had developed a stiffness and weakness similar to that of the prisoners who had beriberi. The chickens were being fed the rice left on prisoners' plates. When the rice bran, which had been discarded in the kitchen, was given to the chickens, their paralysis was cured. The physician met resistance when he tried to feed the rice bran, the "garbage," to the prisoners, but it worked—it produced a miracle cure like those described at the beginning of the chapter. Later, extracts of rice bran were used to prevent infantile beriberi; still later, thiamin was synthesized.

In developed countries today, alcohol abuse often leads to a severe form of thiamin deficiency, Wernicke-Korsakoff syndrome, defined in Controversy 3. Alcohol contributes energy but carries almost no nutrients with it and often displaces food in the diet. In addition, alcohol impairs absorption of thiamin from the digestive tract and hastens its excretion in the urine, tripling the risk of deficiency. The syndrome is characterized by symptoms almost indistinguishable from alcohol abuse itself: apathy, irritability, mental confusion, disorientation, memory loss, jerky eye movements, and a staggering gait. Unlike alcohol toxicity, the syndrome responds quickly to an injection of thiamin, and some experts recommend a precautionary dose for any patients suspected of having it.[73]

Recommended Intakes and Food Sources

The DRI committee set the thiamin intake recommendation at 1.2 milligrams per day for men and at 1.1 milligrams per day for women. Pregnancy and lactation demand somewhat more thiamin (see the DRI, inside front cover, page B). Thiamin occurs in small amounts in many nutritious foods. Ham and other pork products, sunflower seeds, enriched and whole-grain cereals, and legumes are especially rich in thiamin (see Snapshot 7-6). If you

thiamin (THIGH-uh-min) a B vitamin involved in the body's use of fuels.

beriberi (berry-berry) the thiamin-deficiency disease; characterized by loss of sensation in the hands and feet, muscular weakness, advancing paralysis, and abnormal heart action.

SNAPSHOT 7-6

Thiamin

DRI Recommended Intakes

Men: 1.2 mg/day
Women: 1.1 mg/day

Chief Functions

Part of coenzyme active in energy metabolism

Deficiency[a]

Beriberi with possible edema or muscle wasting; enlarged heart, heart failure, muscular weakness, pain, apathy, poor short-term memory, confusion, irritability, difficulty walking, paralysis, anorexia, weight loss

Toxicity

None reported

*These foods provide 10 percent or more of the thiamin Daily Value in a serving. For a 2,000-calorie diet, the DV is 1.5 mg/day.
[a]Severe thiamin deficiency is often related to heavy alcohol consumption.

GOOD SOURCES*

keep empty-calorie foods to a minimum and focus your meals on nutritious foods each day, you will easily meet your thiamin needs.

KEY POINT Thiamin works in energy metabolism and in nerve cells. Its deficiency disease is beriberi. Many foods supply small amounts of thiamin.

Riboflavin Roles and Sources

Like thiamin, **riboflavin** plays a role in the energy metabolism of all cells. When thiamin is deficient, riboflavin may be lacking, too, but its deficiency symptoms, such as cracks at the corners of the mouth, sore throat, or hypersensitivity to light, may go undetected because those of thiamin deficiency are more severe. Worldwide, riboflavin deficiency has been documented among children whose diets lack milk products and meats, and researchers suspect that it occurs among some U.S. elderly as well.[74] A diet that remedies riboflavin deficiency invariably contains some thiamin and so clears up both deficiencies.

Riboflavin recommendations are listed in Snapshot 7-7. People in this country obtain over a quarter of their riboflavin from enriched breads, cereals, pasta, and other grain products, while milk and milk products supply another 20 percent. Certain vegetables, eggs, and meats contribute most of the rest (see Snapshot 7-7).[75] Ultraviolet light and irradiation destroy riboflavin. For these reasons, milk is sold in cardboard or opaque plastic containers, and precautions are taken if milk is processed by irradiation. Riboflavin is stable to heat, so cooking does not destroy it.

KEY POINT Riboflavin works in energy metabolism. It is destroyed by ordinary light.

• Table 7-7 on page 262 lists the symptoms of riboflavin deficiency.

riboflavin (RIBE-o-flay-vin) a B vitamin active in the body's energy-releasing mechanisms.

SNAPSHOT 7-7

Riboflavin

DRI Recommended Intakes

Men: 1.2 mg/day
Women: 1.1 mg/day

Chief Functions

Part of coenzyme active in energy metabolism

Deficiency

Cracks and redness at corners of mouth; painful, smooth, purplish red tongue; sore throat; inflamed eyes and eyelids, sensitivity to light; skin rashes

Toxicity

None reported

**These foods provide 10 percent or more of the riboflavin Daily Value in a serving. For a 2,000-calorie diet, the DV is 1.7 mg/day.*

GOOD SOURCES*

FIGURE 7-15 Pellagra

The typical "flaky paint" dermatitis of pellagra develops on skin that is exposed to light. The skin darkens and flakes away.

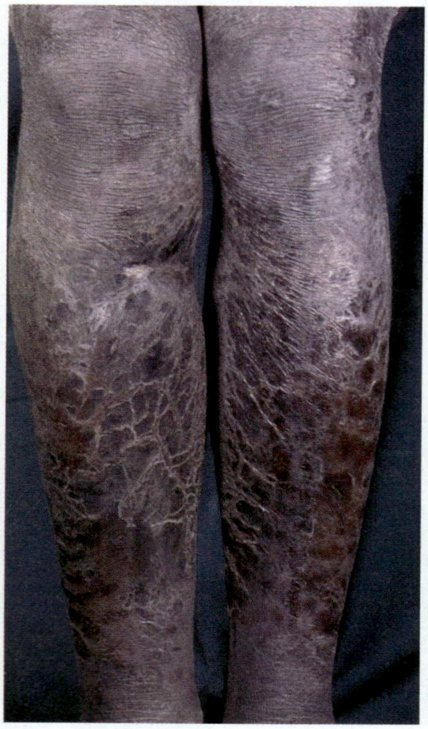

Dr. M.A. Ansary/Photo Researchers, Inc.

Niacin Functions

The vitamin **niacin,** like thiamin and riboflavin, participates in the energy metabolism of every cell. Its absence causes serious illness.

Niacin Deficiency The niacin-deficiency disease **pellagra** appeared in Europe in the 1700s when corn from the New World became a staple food. In the early 1900s in the United States, pellagra was devastating lives throughout the South and Midwest. Hundreds of thousands of pellagra victims were thought to be suffering from a contagious disease until this dietary deficiency was identified. The disease still occurs among poorly nourished people living in urban slums and particularly in those with alcohol addiction. Pellagra is also still common in parts of Africa and Asia. Its symptoms are known as the four "Ds": diarrhea, dermatitis, dementia, and, ultimately, death.

Figure 7-15 shows the skin disorder (dermatitis) associated with pellagra. For comparison, Figure 7-3 (page 231) and Figure 7-18 (page 257) show skin disorders associated with vitamin A and vitamin B_6 deficiency, respectively, a reminder that any nutrient deficiency affects the skin and all other cells. The skin just happens to be the organ you can see. Table 7-7 at the end of the chapter lists the symptoms of niacin deficiency.

Niacin Toxicity Physicians may administer large doses of a form of niacin as part of a treatment regimen to improve blood lipids associated with cardiovascular disease.[‡‡][76] When used this way, niacin leaves the realm of nutrition to become a pharmacological agent—a drug. Ordinary niacin supplements do not improve blood lipids, and large doses can cause low blood pressure, liver injury, peptic ulcers, or vision loss.[77] Some niacin supplements taken in large amounts create a "niacin flush," a dilation of the capillaries of the skin with perceptible tingling that, if intense, can be painful. For safety's sake, anyone considering taking large doses of niacin should consult a physician, who may prescribe safe, effective alternatives.[78]

‡‡The form of niacin is nicotinic acid.

Niacin Recommendations and Food Sources Niacin recommendations are listed in Snapshot 7-8. The key nutrient that prevents pellagra is niacin, but any protein containing sufficient amounts of the amino acid tryptophan will serve in its place. Tryptophan, which is abundant in almost all proteins (but is limited in the protein of corn), is converted to niacin in the body, and it is possible to cure pellagra by administering tryptophan alone. Thus, a person eating adequate protein (as most people in developed nations do) will not be deficient in niacin. The amount of niacin in a diet is stated in terms of **niacin equivalents (NE),** a measure that takes available tryptophan into account.

Early workers seeking the cause of pellagra observed that well-fed people never got it. From there the researchers defined a diet that reliably produced the disease—one of cornmeal, salted pork fat, and molasses. Corn not only is low in protein but also lacks tryptophan. Salt pork is almost pure fat and contains too little protein to compensate; and molasses is virtually protein-free. Snapshot 7-8 shows some good food sources of niacin. Research into optimal intakes and sources of niacin are ongoing.[79]

KEY POINT The infamous niacin deficiency disease pellagra can be prevented by adequate dietary protein because the amino acid tryptophan can be converted to niacin in the body.

Folate Roles

To make new cells, tissues must have the vitamin **folate.** Each new cell must be equipped with new genetic material—copies of the parent cell's DNA—and folate helps to synthesize DNA. Folate also plays critical roles in the normal metabolism of several amino acids.

Folate Deficiency Folate deficiencies may result from consuming a diet too low in folate or from illnesses that impair its absorption, increase its excretion, require

niacin a B vitamin needed in energy metabolism. Niacin can be eaten preformed or can be made in the body from tryptophan, one of the amino acids. Other forms of niacin are *nicotinic acid, niacinamide,* and *nicotinamide.*

pellagra (pell-AY-gra) the niacin-deficiency disease (*pellis* means "skin"; *agra* means "rough"). Symptoms include the "4 Ds": diarrhea, dermatitis, dementia, and, ultimately, death.

niacin equivalents (NE) the amount of niacin present in food, including the niacin that can theoretically be made from its precursor tryptophan that is present in the food.

folate (FOH-late) a B vitamin that acts as part of a coenzyme important in the manufacture of new cells. The form added to foods and supplements is *folic acid.*

SNAPSHOT 7-8

Niacin

DRI Recommended Intakes
Men: 16 mg/day[a]
Women: 14 mg/day

Tolerable Upper Intake Level
Adults: 35 mg/day

Chief Functions
Part of coenzymes needed in energy metabolism

Deficiency
Pellagra, characterized by flaky skin rash (dermatitis) where exposed to sunlight; mental depression, apathy, fatigue, loss of memory, headache; diarrhea, abdominal pain, vomiting; swollen, smooth, bright red or black tongue

Toxicity
Painful flush, hives, and rash ("niacin flush"); excessive sweating; blurred vision; liver damage, impaired glucose tolerance

GOOD SOURCES*

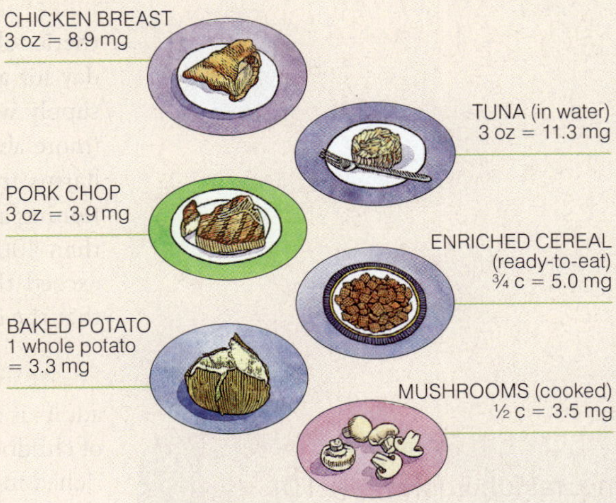

*These foods provide 10 percent or more of the niacin Daily Value in a serving. For a 2,000-calorie diet, the DV is 20 mg/day. The DV values are for preformed niacin, not niacin equivalents.
[a]Niacin DRI Recommended Intakes are expressed in niacin equivalents (NE); the Tolerable Upper Intake Level refers to preformed niacin.

medication that interacts with folate, or otherwise increase the body's folate need. However it occurs, folate deficiency has wide-reaching effects.

Immature red and white blood cells and the cells of the digestive tract divide most rapidly and therefore are most vulnerable to folate deficiency. Deficiencies of folate cause anemia, diminished immunity, and abnormal digestive function. The anemia of folate deficiency is related to the anemia of vitamin B_{12} malabsorption because the two vitamins work as teammates in producing red blood cells—see Figure 7-17 later in the chapter. Research suggests that a diet deficient in folate also elevates the risk of cancer of the cervix (in women infected with a sexually transmitted virus, HPV[§§]), breast cancer (in women who drink alcohol), and pancreatic cancer.[80] In a strange twist, however, folate may *enhance* the progression of some cancers once they have begun.[81]

Of all the vitamins, folate is most likely to interact with medications. Many drugs, including antacids and aspirin and its relatives, have been shown to interfere with the body's use of folate. Occasional use of these drugs to relieve headache or upset stomach presents no concern, but frequent users may need to pay attention to their folate intakes. These include people with chronic pain or ulcers who rely heavily on aspirin or antacids as well as those who smoke or take oral contraceptives or anticonvulsant medications.

- Drug and nutrient interactions are the topic of the Controversy that follows Chapter 14.

Birth Defects and Folate Enrichment By consuming enough folate during pregnancy, a woman can reduce her child's risk of having one of the devastating birth defects known as **neural tube defects (NTD).**[82] NTD range from slight problems in the spine to mental retardation, severely diminished brain size, and death shortly after birth. NTD arise in the first days or weeks of pregnancy, long before most women suspect that they are pregnant.

Most young women eat too few fruits and vegetables from day to day to supply even half the folate needed to prevent NTD. In the late 1990s, the FDA ordered all enriched grain products such as bread, cereal, rice, and pasta sold in the United States to be fortified with an absorbable synthetic form of folate, *folic acid.* Since this fortification began, typical folate intakes from fortified foods have increased dramatically, along with average blood folate values.[83] Among women of childbearing age, for example, prevalence of low serum folate concentrations dropped from 21 percent before fortification to less than 1 percent after fortification was introduced.[84] During the same period, the U.S. incidence of NTD dropped by 25 percent, even among women receiving late or no prenatal care (see Figure 7-16).[85] Miscarriages and certain other birth defects, such as cleft lip, have diminished as well.[86]

Did You Know?

The B vitamins thiamin, riboflavin, niacin, and folate (as folic acid) are among the enrichment nutrients added to grain foods such as breads and cereals sold in the United States.

CONCEPT LINK 7-6

More details on enrichment of grain foods were in Chapter 4, page 120.

Folate Toxicity As for folate toxicity, a Tolerable Upper Intake Level for synthetic folic acid from supplements and enriched foods is set at 1,000 micrograms a day for adults. A question raised about the wisdom of fortifying the nation's food supply with folic acid concerns folate's ability to mask deficiencies of vitamin B_{12} (more about this effect later).[87] Among other suspected but unconfirmed potential harms from high blood folic acid levels are suppression of normal immune functioning and increased cancer risks.[88] Except for people taking supplements of more than 400 micrograms of folic acid, few (less than 3 percent of the U.S. population) exceed the Tolerable Upper Intake Level for folate.[89] Thus, researchers conclude that the current level of fortification of the food supply appears to be safe.

Folate Recommendations The DRI recommended intake for folate for healthy adults is set at 400 micrograms per day. The DRI committee also advises all women of childbearing age to consume 400 micrograms of *folic acid* from supplements or enriched foods each day in addition to the folate that occurs naturally in their foods.

neural tube defects (NTD) abnormalities of the brain and spinal cord apparent at birth and believed to be related to a woman's folate intake before and during pregnancy. Also defined in Chapter 13.

Food Sources of Folate The name *folate* is derived from the word *foliage,* and sure enough, leafy green vegetables such as spinach and turnip greens provide

§§Human papilloma virus.

FIGURE 7-16 **Incidence of a Common Neural Tube Defect, Spina Bifida, Over Time**

Neural tube defects have declined since folate fortification began in 1996.

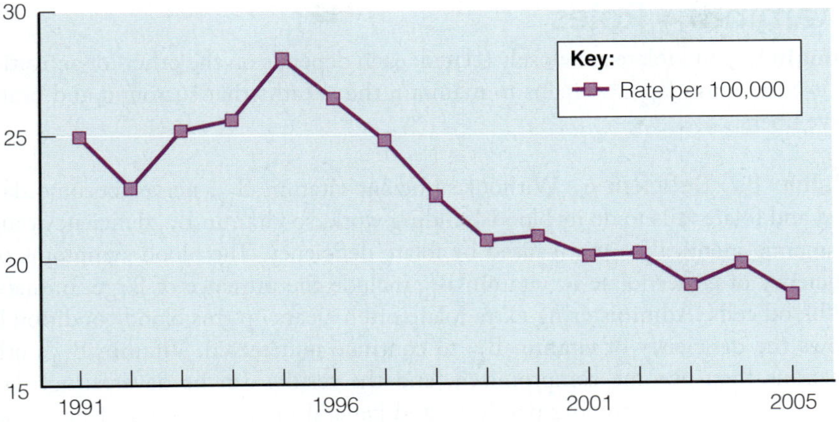

Source: National Vital Statistics System, National Center for Health Statistics, Centers for Disease Control, December 2007.

abundant folate (see Snapshot 7-9). Fresh, uncooked vegetables and fruits are often superior sources because the heat of cooking and the oxidation that occurs during storage destroy much of the folate in foods. Eggs also provide some folate.

A difference in absorption between naturally occurring food folate and the synthetic folic acid necessitates compensation when measuring folate. The unit of measure, **dietary folate equivalent,** or **DFE,** converts all forms of folate into micrograms that are equivalent to the folate in foods. Some food and supplement labels still express folate values in micrograms, not DFE; Appendix C offers a conversion factor.

dietary folate equivalent (DFE) a unit of measure expressing the amount of folate available to the body from naturally occurring sources. The measure mathematically equalizes the difference in absorption between less absorbable food folate and highly absorbable synthetic folate added to enriched foods and found in supplements.

SNAPSHOT 7-9

Folate

DRI Recommended Intake
Adults: 400 µg/day[a]

Tolerable Upper Intake Level
Adults: 1,000 µg/day

Chief Functions
Part of a coenzyme needed for new cell synthesis

Deficiency
Anemia, smooth, red tongue; depression, mental confusion, weakness, fatigue, irritability, headache; a low intake increases the risk of neural tube birth defects

Toxicity
Masks vitamin B_{12}–deficiency symptoms

These foods provide 10 percent or more of the folate Daily Value in a serving. For a 2,000-calorie diet, the DV is 400 µg/day.
[a]*Folate recommendations are expressed in dietary folate equivalents (DFE). Note that for natural folate sources, 1 µg = 1 DFE; for enrichment sources, 1 µg = 1.7 DFE.*
[b]*Some highly enriched cereals may provide 400 or more micrograms in a serving.*

GOOD SOURCES*

FIGURE 7-17 **Anemic and Normal Blood Cells**

The anemia of folate deficiency is indistinguishable from that of vitamin B_{12} deficiency.

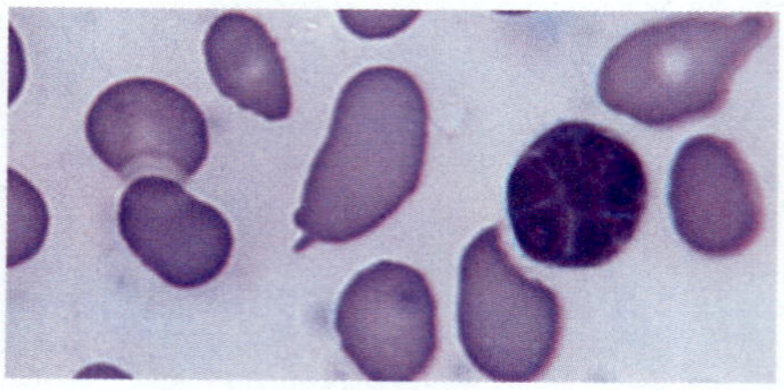

Carolina Biological/Visuals Unlimited

Blood cells of pericious anemia. The cells are larger than normal and irregular in shape.

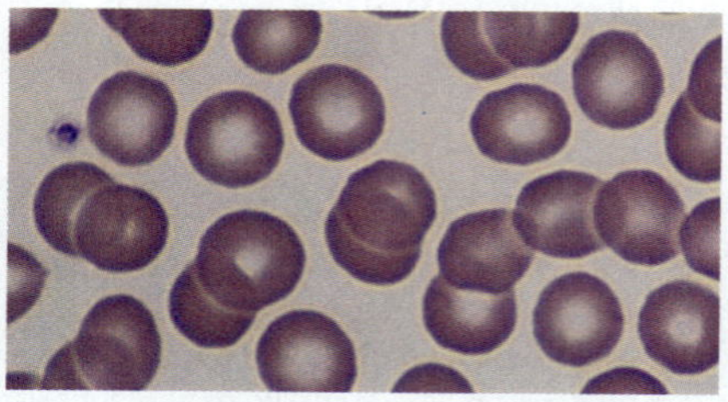

Ed Reschke/Peter Arnold

Normal blood cells. The size, shape, and color of these red blood cells show that they are normal.

- Controversy 6 describes vitamin B_{12} deficiency in infants born to women who lacked the vitamin during pregnancy and lactation.

vitamin B_{12} a B vitamin that helps to convert folate to its active form and also helps maintain the sheath around nerve cells. Vitamin B_{12}'s scientific name, not often used, is *cyanocobalamin.*

intrinsic factor a factor found inside a system. The intrinsic factor necessary to prevent pernicious anemia is now known to be a compound that helps in the absorption of vitamin B_{12}.

pernicious (per-NISH-us) **anemia** a vitamin B_{12}–deficiency disease, caused by lack of intrinsic factor and characterized by large, immature red blood cells and damage to the nervous system (*pernicious* means "highly injurious or destructive").

KEY POINT Folate is added to enriched foods as folic acid and occurs naturally in leafy green vegetables and fruits. Low intakes of folate cause birth defects. High intakes can mask the blood symptom of vitamin B_{12} deficiency.

Vitamin B_{12} Roles

Vitamin B_{12} and folate are closely related: each depends on the other for activation. By itself vitamin B_{12} also helps to maintain the sheaths that surround and protect nerve fibers.

Vitamin B_{12} Deficiency Without sufficient vitamin B_{12}, nerves become damaged and folate fails to do its blood-building work, so vitamin B_{12} deficiency causes an anemia identical to that caused by folate deficiency. The blood symptoms of a deficiency of either folate or vitamin B_{12} include the presence of large, immature red blood cells. Administering extra folate often clears up this blood condition but allows the deficiency of vitamin B_{12} to continue undetected. Vitamin B_{12}'s other functions then become compromised, and the results can be devastating: damaged nerve sheaths, creeping paralysis, and general malfunctioning of nerves and muscles.

Diagnosing a vitamin B_{12} problem is difficult, and often the damage will proceed unchecked. In an effort to prevent excessive folate intakes that could mask symptoms of a vitamin B_{12} deficiency, the FDA specifies the exact amounts of folic acid that can be added to enriched foods.

A Special Case: Vitamin B_{12} Absorption Absorption of vitamin B_{12} requires an **intrinsic factor,** a compound made by the stomach with instructions from the genes. With the help of the stomach's acid to liberate vitamin B_{12} from the food proteins that bind it, intrinsic factor attaches to the vitamin and the complex is absorbed into the bloodstream.

A few people have an inherited defect in the gene for intrinsic factor, which makes vitamin B_{12} absorption abnormal, beginning in mid-adulthood. In later years, many others lose the ability to produce enough stomach acid and intrinsic factor to allow efficient absorption of vitamin B_{12}.***[90] In these cases, vitamin B_{12} must be supplied by injection to bypass the defective absorptive system. The anemia of the vitamin B_{12} deficiency caused by lack of intrinsic factor is known as **pernicious anemia** (see Figure 7-17).

Food Sources of Vitamin B_{12} As Snapshot 7-10 shows, vitamin B_{12} is present only in foods of animal origin, so vitamin B_{12} deficiency poses a threat to strict vegetarians. Controversy 6 discussed vitamin B_{12} sources for vegetarians.

Perspective The way folate masks the anemia of vitamin B_{12} deficiency underscores a point about supplements. It takes a skilled professional to correctly diagnose and treat a nutrient deficiency, and self-diagnosis or acting on advice from self-proclaimed experts poses serious risks. A second point: Since vitamin B_{12} deficiency in the body may be caused by either a lack of the vitamin in the diet or a lack of the intrinsic factor necessary to absorb the vitamin, a change in diet alone may not correct the deficiency; a professional diagnosis can identify such problems.

KEY POINT Vitamin B_{12} occurs in animal products. A deficiency anemia that mimics folate deficiency arises with low intakes or poor absorption. This deficiency also causes nerve damage.

***The condition is atrophic gastritis (a-TROH-fik gas-TRY-tis), a chronic inflammation of the stomach accompanied by a diminished size and functioning of the stomach's mucous membrane and glands.

SNAPSHOT 7-10

Vitamin B_{12}

DRI Recommended Intake

Adults: 2.4 μg/day

Chief Functions

Part of coenzymes needed in new cell synthesis; helps to maintain nerve cells

Deficiency

Pernicious anemia;[a] anemia (large-cell type);[b] smooth tongue; tingling or numbness; fatigue, memory loss disorientation, degeneration of nerves progressing to paralysis

Toxicity

None reported

*These foods provide 10 percent or more of the vitamin B_{12} Daily Value in a serving. For a 2,000-calorie diet, the DV is 6 μg/day.

[a]The name pernicious anemia refers to the vitamin B_{12} deficiency caused by a lack of stomach intrinsic factor, but not to anemia from inadequate dietary intake.

[b]Large cell–type anemia is known as either macrocytic or megaloblastic anemia.

GOOD SOURCES*

Vitamin B_6 Roles

Vitamin B_6 participates in over 100 reactions in body tissues and is needed to help convert one kind of amino acid, which cells have in abundance, to other nonessential amino acids that the cells lack. In addition, vitamin B_6 functions in these ways:

- Aids in the conversion of tryptophan to niacin.
- Plays important roles in the synthesis of hemoglobin and neurotransmitters, the communication molecules of the brain. For example, vitamin B_6 assists the conversion of the amino acid tryptophan to the neurotransmitter **serotonin.**
- Assists in releasing stored glucose from glycogen and thus contributes to the regulation of blood glucose.
- Has roles in immune function and steroid hormone activity.
- Is critical to the developing brain and nervous system of a fetus; deficiency during this stage causes behavioral problems later.
- Is under investigation for roles in maintaining DNA integrity and thus reducing cancer risk.[91]

FIGURE 7-18 **Vitamin B_6 Deficiency**

In this dermatitis, the skin is greasy and flaky, unlike the skin affected by the dermatitis of pellagra.

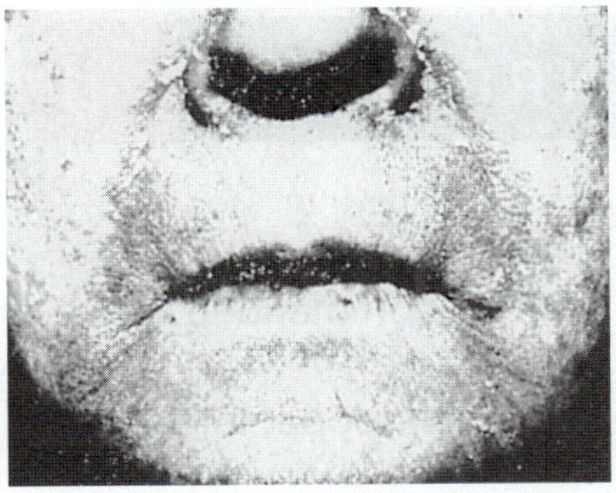

© George L. Blackburn, M.D., Ph.D., Harvard Medical School

Vitamin B_6 Deficiency Because of these diverse functions, vitamin B_6 deficiency is expressed in general symptoms, such as weakness, psychological depression, confusion, irritability, and insomnia. Other symptoms include anemia, the greasy dermatitis depicted in Figure 7-18, and, in advanced cases of deficiency, convulsions. A shortage of vitamin B_6 may also weaken the immune response. Some evidence suggests that low vitamin B_6 intakes may also be related to increased incidence of heart disease. Some people have taken vitamin B_6 supplements to relieve **carpal tunnel syndrome** and sleep disorders even though such treatment seems to be ineffective.

Vitamin B_6 Toxicity Large doses of vitamin B_6 from supplements can be dangerous. Years ago it was generally believed that, like most of the other water-soluble vitamins, vitamin B_6 could not reach toxic concentrations in the body. Then a report told of women who took more than 2 grams of vitamin B_6 daily (the Tolerable Upper Intake Level is set at 100 *milligrams,* or 0.1 gram) for two months or more, attempting to cure premenstrual syndrome (science doesn't support this use). The women developed numb feet, then lost sensation in their hands, and eventually

vitamin B_6 a B vitamin needed in protein metabolism. Its three active forms are *pyridoxine, pyridoxal,* and *pyridoxamine.*

serotonin (SER-oh-TONE-in) a neurotransmitter important in sleep regulation, appetite control, and mood regulation, among other roles. Serotonin is synthesized in the body from the amino acid tryptophan with the help of vitamin B_6.

carpal tunnel syndrome a pinched nerve at the wrist, causing pain or numbness in the hand. It is often caused by repetitive motion of the wrist.

became unable to walk or work. Since the first report of vitamin B_6 toxicity, researchers have seen toxicity symptoms in more than 100 women who took vitamin B_6 supplements for more than five years. The women recovered after they stopped taking the supplements.

The potential for a toxic dose from supplements seems clear, but food sources are safe. Consider that one small capsule can easily deliver 2 grams of vitamin B_6, but it would take almost 3,000 bananas, more than 1,600 servings of liver, or more than 3,800 chicken breasts to supply an equivalent amount. Moral: Stick with food. Table 7-7 on page 263 lists common deficiency and toxicity symptoms of vitamin B_6 and other water-soluble vitamins.

People may take supplements of vitamin B_6 and other B vitamins in hopes of preventing heart disease by lowering an amino acid, homocysteine, in the blood. People who suffer a rare disorder of high blood homocysteine almost invariably develop cardiovascular disease (CVD).††† Also, CVD sufferers without the inherited disorder sometimes accumulate homocysteine in the blood. When healthy men with elevated homocysteine take supplements of vitamin B_6, vitamin B_{12}, and folate, their homocysteine values drop significantly. However, the real prize, a drop in CVD occurrence by lowering homocysteine in healthy people, has yet to be demonstrated.[92]

Intake Recommendations and Food Sources Vitamin B_6 plays so many roles in protein metabolism that the body's requirement for vitamin B_6 is roughly proportional to protein intakes. The DRI committee set the vitamin B_6 intake recommendation high enough to cover most people's needs, regardless of differences in protein intakes (see the inside front cover, page B). Meats, fish, and poultry (protein-rich foods), potatoes, leafy green vegetables, and some fruits are good sources of vitamin B_6 (see Snapshot 7-11). Other foods such as legumes and peanut butter provide smaller amounts.

KEY POINT Vitamin B_6 works in amino acid metabolism.

†††Although chemically an amino acid, homocysteine is not incorporated into body proteins, but is metabolized to other compounds.

SNAPSHOT 7-11

Vitamin B_6

DRI Recommended Intake
Adults (19–50 yr): 1.3 mg/day

Tolerable Upper Intake Level
Adults: 100 mg/day

Chief Functions
Part of a coenzyme needed in amino acid and fatty acid metabolism; helps to convert tryptophan to niacin and to serotonin; helps to make hemoglobin for red blood cells

Deficiency
Anemia, depression, confusion, abnormal brain wave pattern, convulsions; greasy, scaly dermatitis

Toxicity
Depression, fatigue, impaired memory, irritability, headaches, nerve damage causing numbness and muscle weakness progressing to an inability to walk and convulsions; skin lesions

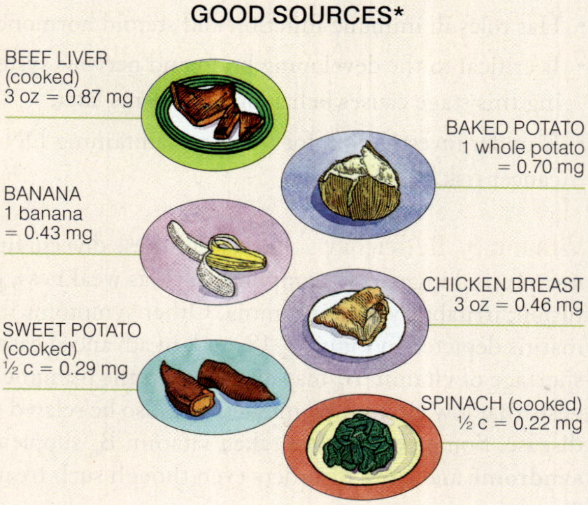

These foods provide 10 percent or more of the vitamin B_6 Daily Value in a serving. For a 2,000-calorie diet, the DV is 2 mg/day.

Biotin and Pantothenic Acid

Two other B vitamins, **biotin** and **pantothenic acid,** are, like thiamin, riboflavin, and niacin, important in energy metabolism. Biotin is a cofactor for several enzymes in the metabolism of carbohydrate, fat, and protein. Recently, scientists have revealed roles for biotin in gene expression. No adverse effects from high biotin intakes have been reported, but some research indicates that high-dose biotin supplementation may damage DNA. No Tolerable Upper Intake Level has yet been set for biotin. Pantothenic acid is a component of a key coenzyme that makes possible the release of energy from the energy nutrients. It also participates in more than 100 steps in the synthesis of lipids, neurotransmitters, steroid hormones, and hemoglobin.

Although rare diseases may precipitate deficiencies of biotin and pantothenic acid, both vitamins are readily available in foods. A steady diet of raw egg whites, which contain a protein that binds biotin, can produce biotin deficiency, but you would have to consume more than two dozen raw egg whites daily to produce the effect. Cooking eggs denatures the protein. Healthy people eating ordinary diets are not at risk for deficiencies.

• The DRI recommended intakes for biotin and pantothenic acid are listed on the inside front cover, page B.

KEY POINT Biotin and pantothenic acid are important to the body and are abundant in food.

© Alex Staroseltsev, 2011/Shutterstock.com

Non-B Vitamins

In addition to the B vitamins just discussed, a few compounds that are topics of debate among researchers deserve mention. **Choline** might be called a conditionally essential nutrient because when the diet is devoid of choline, the body cannot make enough of the compound to meet its needs, and it plays important roles in fetal development.[93] Choline is common in foods, though, and deficiencies are practically unheard of outside the laboratory. DRI intake recommendations have been set for choline (see inside front cover, page B).

The compounds **carnitine, inositol,** and **lipoic acid** might appropriately be called *nonvitamins* because they are not essential nutrients for human beings. Carnitine, sometimes called "vitamin BT," is an important piece of cell machinery, but it is not a vitamin. Although deficiencies can be induced in laboratory animals for experimental purposes, these substances are abundant in ordinary foods. Even if these compounds were essential in human nutrition, supplements would be unnecessary for healthy people eating a balanced diet. Vitamin companies often include these substances to make their formulas appear more "complete," but there is no physiological reason to do so.

Other substances have been mistakenly thought to be essential in human nutrition because they are needed for growth by bacteria or other life-forms. These substances include PABA (para-aminobenzoic acid), bioflavonoids ("vitamin P" or hesperidin), and ubiquinone (coenzyme Q). Other names you may hear are "vitamin B_{15}" and pangamic acid (hoaxes) or "vitamin B_{17}" (laetrile or amygdalin, not a cancer cure as claimed and not a vitamin by any stretch of the imagination).‡‡‡

KEY POINT Choline is needed in the diet, but it is not a vitamin and deficiencies are unheard of outside the laboratory. Many other substances that people claim are B vitamins are not. Among these substances are carnitine, inositol, and lipoic acid.

This chapter has addressed all 13 of the vitamins. The basic facts about each one are summed up in Tables 7-6 and 7-7.

biotin (BY-o-tin) a B vitamin; a coenzyme necessary for fat synthesis and other metabolic reactions.

pantothenic (PAN-to-THEN-ic) **acid** a B vitamin.

choline (KOH-leen) a nonessential nutrient used to make the phospholipid lecithin and other molecules.

carnitine a nonessential nutrient that functions in cellular activities.

inositol (in-OSS-ih-tall) a nonessential nutrient found in cell membranes.

lipoic (lip-OH-ic) **acid** a nonessential nutrient.

‡‡‡Read about these and many other claims at the website of the National Council Against Health Fraud, www.ncahf.org.

TABLE 7-6 **The Fat-Soluble Vitamins—Functions, Deficiencies, and Toxicities**

VITAMIN A

Other Names
Retinol, retinal, retinoic acid; main precursor is beta-carotene

Chief Functions in the Body
Vision; health of cornea, epithelial cells, mucous membranes, skin; bone and tooth growth; regulation of gene expression; reproduction; immunity

Beta-carotene: antioxidant

Deficiency Disease Name
Hypovitaminosis A

Significant Sources
Retinol: fortified milk, cheese, cream, butter, fortified margarine, eggs, liver

Beta-carotene: spinach and other dark, leafy greens; broccoli; deep orange fruits (apricots, cantaloupe) and vegetables (winter squash, carrots, sweet potatoes, pumpkin)

	Deficiency Symptoms	Toxicity Symptoms
Blood	Anemia (small-cell type)[a]	Red blood cell breakage, cessation of menstruation, nosebleeds
Bones/Teeth	Cessation of bone growth, painful joints; impaired enamel formation, cracks in teeth, tendency toward tooth decay	Bone pain; growth retardation; increased pressure inside skull; headaches; possible bone mineral loss
Digestive System	Diarrhea, changes in intestinal and other body linings	Abdominal pain, nausea, vomiting, diarrhea, weight loss
Immune System	Frequent infections	Overreactivity
Nervous/Muscular System	Night blindness (retinal) Mental depression	Blurred vision, muscle weakness, fatigue, irritability, loss of appetite
Skin and Cornea	Keratinization, corneal degeneration leading to blindness,[b] rashes	Dry skin, rashes, loss of hair; cracking and bleeding lips, brittle nails; hair loss
Other	Kidney stones, impaired growth	Liver enlargement and liver damage; birth defects

VITAMIN D

Other Names
Calciferol, cholecalciferol, dihydroxy vitamin D; precursor is cholesterol

Chief Functions in the Body
Mineralization of bones (raises blood calcium and phosphorus via absorption from digestive tract and by withdrawing calcium from bones and stimulating retention by kidneys)

Deficiency Disease Name
Rickets, osteomalacia

Significant Sources
Self-synthesis with sunlight; fortified milk or margarine, liver, sardines, salmon, shrimp

	Deficiency Symptoms	Toxicity Symptoms
Blood/Circulatory System		Raised blood calcium; calcification of blood vessels and heart tissues
Bones/Teeth	Abnormal growth, misshapen bones (bowing of legs), soft bones, joint pain, malformed teeth	Calcification of tooth soft tissues; thinning of tooth enamel
Nervous System	Muscle spasms	Excessive thirst, headaches, irritability, loss of appetite, weakness, nausea
Other		Kidney stones; calcification of soft tissues (kidneys, lungs, joints); mental and physical retardation of offspring

[a]*Small-cell anemia is termed* microcytic anemia*; large-cell type is* macrocytic *or* megaloblastic anemia.

[b]*Corneal degeneration progresses from* keratinization *(hardening) to* xerosis *(drying) to* xerophthalmia *(thickening, opacity, and irreversible blindness).*

TABLE 7-6 The Fat-Soluble Vitamins—Functions, Deficiencies, and Toxicities (continued)

VITAMIN E

Other Names
Alpha-tocopherol, tocopherol

Chief Functions in the Body
Antioxidant (quenching of free radicals), stabilization of cell membranes, support of immune function, protection of polyunsaturated fatty acids; normal nerve development

Deficiency Disease Name
(No name)

Significant Sources
Polyunsaturated plant oils (margarine, salad dressings, shortenings), green and leafy vegetables, wheat germ, whole-grain products, nuts, seeds

	Deficiency Symptoms	Toxicity Symptoms
Blood/Circulatory System	Red blood cell breakage, anemia	Augments the effects of anti-clotting medication
Digestive System	Nerve degeneration, weakness, difficulty walking, leg cramps	General discomfort, nausea
Eyes		Blurred vision
Nervous/Muscular System		Fatigue

VITAMIN K

Other Names
Phylloquinone, naphthoquinone

Chief Functions in the Body
Synthesis of blood-clotting proteins and proteins important in bone mineralization

Deficiency Disease Name
(No name)

Significant Sources
Bacterial synthesis in the digestive tract; green leafy vegetables, cabbage-type vegetables, soybeans, vegetable oils

	Deficiency Symptoms	Toxicity Symptoms
Blood/Circulatory System	Hemorrhage	Interference with anticlotting medication
Bones	Poor skeletal mineralization	

TABLE 7-7 The Water-Soluble Vitamins—Functions, Deficiencies, and Toxicities

VITAMIN C

Other Names
Ascorbic acid

Chief Functions in the Body
Collagen synthesis (strengthens blood vessel walls, forms scar tissue, matrix for bone growth), antioxidant, restores vitamin E to active form, hormone synthesis, supports immune cell functions, helps in absorption of iron

Deficiency Disease Name
Scurvy

Significant Sources
Citrus fruits, cabbage-type vegetables, dark green vegetables, cantaloupe, strawberries, peppers, lettuce, tomatoes, potatoes, papayas, mangoes

	Deficiency Symptoms	Toxicity Symptoms
Digestive System		Nausea, abdominal cramps, diarrhea, excessive urination
Immune System	Immune suppression, frequent infections	
Mouth, Gums, Tongue	Bleeding gums, loosened teeth	
Nervous/Muscular System	Muscle degeneration and pain, depression, disorientation	Headache, fatigue, insomnia
Skeletal System	Bone fragility, joint pain	Aggravation of gout
Skin	Pinpoint hemorrhages, rough skin, blotchy bruises	Rashes
Other	Failure of wounds to heal	Interference with medical tests; kidney stones in susceptible people

TABLE 7-7 The Water-Soluble Vitamins—Functions, Deficiencies, and Toxicities (continued)

THIAMIN

Other Names
Vitamin B_1

Chief Functions in the Body
Part of a coenzyme needed in energy metabolism, supports normal appetite and nervous system function

Deficiency Disease Name
Beriberi (wet and dry)

Significant Sources
Occurs in all nutritious foods in moderate amounts; pork, ham, bacon, liver, whole and enriched grains, legumes, seeds

	Deficiency Symptoms	Toxicity Symptoms
Blood/Circulatory System	Edema, enlarged heart, abnormal heart rhythms, heart failure	(No symptoms reported)
Nervous/Muscular System	Degeneration, wasting, weakness, pain, apathy, irritability, difficulty walking, loss of reflexes, mental confusion, paralysis	
Other	Anorexia; weight loss	

RIBOFLAVIN

Other Names
Vitamin B_2

Chief Functions in the Body
Part of a coenzyme needed in energy metabolism, supports normal vision and skin health

Deficiency Disease Name
Ariboflavinosis

Significant Sources
Milk, yogurt, cottage cheese, meat, liver, leafy green vegetables, whole-grain or enriched breads and cereals

	Deficiency Symptoms	Toxicity Symptoms
Mouth, Gums, Tongue	Cracks at corners of mouth,[a] smooth magenta tongue[b]; sore throat	(No symptoms reported)
Nervous System and Eyes	Hypersensitivity to light, reddening of cornea	
Skin	Skin rash	

NIACIN

Other Names
Nicotinic acid, nicotinamide, niacinamide, vitamin B_3; precursor is dietary tryptophan

Chief Functions in the Body
Part of coenzymes needed in energy metabolism

Deficiency Disease Name
Pellagra

Significant Sources
Synthesized from the amino acid tryptophan; milk, eggs, meat, poultry, fish, whole-grain and enriched breads and cereals, nuts, and all protein-containing foods

	Deficiency Symptoms	Toxicity Symptoms
Digestive System	Diarrhea; vomiting; abdominal pain	Nausea, vomiting
Mouth, Gums, Tongue	Black or bright red swollen smooth tongue[b]	
Nervous System	Irritability, loss of appetite, weakness, headache, dizziness, mental confusion progressing to psychosis or delirium	
Skin	Flaky skin rash on areas exposed to sun	Painful flush and rash, sweating
Other		Liver damage; impaired glucose tolerance

[a] *Cracks at the corners of the mouth are termed* cheilosis *(kee-LOH-sis).*
[b] *Smoothness of the tongue is caused by loss of its surface structures and is termed* glossitis *(gloss-EYE-tis).*

TABLE 7-7 The Water-Soluble Vitamins—Functions, Deficiencies, and Toxicities (continued)

FOLATE

Other Names
Folic acid, folacin, pteroylglutamic acid

Chief Functions in the Body
Part of a coenzyme needed for new cell synthesis

Deficiency Disease Name
(No name)

Significant Sources
Asparagus, avocado, leafy green vegetables, beets, legumes, seeds, liver, enriched breads, cereal, pasta, and grains

	Deficiency Symptoms	Toxicity Symptoms
Blood/Circulatory System	Anemia (large-cell type),[a] elevated homocysteine	Masks vitamin B_{12} deficiency
Digestive System	Heartburn, diarrhea, constipation	
Immune System	Suppression, frequent infections	
Mouth, Gums, Tongue	Smooth red tongue[b]	
	Increased risk of neural tube birth defects	
Nervous System	Depression, mental confusion, fatigue, irritability, headache	

VITAMIN B_{12}

Other Names
Cyanocobalamin

Chief Functions in the Body
Part of coenzymes needed in new cell synthesis, helps maintain nerve cells

Deficiency Disease Name
(No name)[c]

Significant Sources
Animal products (meat, fish, poultry, milk, cheese, eggs)

	Deficiency Symptoms	Toxicity Symptoms
Blood/Circulatory System	Anemia (large-cell type)[a]	(No toxicity symptoms known)
Mouth, Gums, Tongue	Smooth tongue[b]	
Nervous System	Fatigue, nerve degeneration progressing to paralysis	
Skin	Tingling or numbness	

VITAMIN B_6

Other Names
Pyridoxine, pyridoxal, pyridoxamine

Chief Functions in the Body
Part of a coenzyme needed in amino acid and fatty acid metabolism, helps convert tryptophan to niacin and to serotonin, helps make red blood cells

Deficiency Disease Name
(No name)

Significant Sources
Meats, fish, poultry, liver, legumes, fruits, potatoes, whole grains, soy products

	Deficiency Symptoms	Toxicity Symptoms
Blood/Circulatory System	Anemia (small-cell type)[a]	Bloating
Nervous/Muscular System	Depression, confusion, abnormal brain wave pattern, convulsions	Depression, fatigue, impaired memory, irritability, headaches, numbness, damage to nerves, difficulty walking, loss of reflexes, restlessness, convulsions
Skin	Rashes; greasy, scaly dermatitis	Skin lesions

[a] *Small-cell anemia is termed* microcytic anemia; *large-cell type is* macrocytic *or* megaloblastic anemia.

[b] *Smoothness of the tongue is caused by loss of its surface structures and is termed* glossitis *(gloss-EYE-tis).*

[c] *The name* pernicious anemia *refers to the vitamin B_{12} deficiency caused by lack of intrinsic factor, but not to that caused by inadequate dietary intake.*

TABLE 7-7 The Water-Soluble Vitamins—Functions, Deficiencies, and Toxicities (continued)

PANTOTHENIC ACID

		Deficiency Symptoms	Toxicity Symptoms
Other Names (None) ***Chief Functions in the Body*** Part of a coenzyme needed in energy metabolism ***Deficiency Disease Name*** (No name) ***Significant Sources*** Widespread in foods	**Digestive System**	Vomiting, intestinal distress	Water retention (infrequent)
	Nervous/Muscular System	Insomnia, fatigue	
	Other	Hypoglycemia, increased sensitivity to insulin	

BIOTIN

		Deficiency Symptoms	Toxicity Symptoms
Other Names (None) ***Chief Functions in the Body*** A cofactor for several enzymes needed in energy metabolism, fat synthesis, amino acid metabolism, and glycogen synthesis ***Deficiency Disease Name*** (No name) ***Significant Sources*** Widespread in foods	**Blood/Circulatory System**	Abnormal heart action	(No toxicity symptoms reported)
	Digestive System	Loss of appetite, nausea	
	Nervous/Muscular System	Depression, muscle pain, weakness, fatigue, numbness of extremities	
	Skin	Dry around eyes, nose, and mouth	

FOOD FEATURE Choosing Foods Rich in Vitamins LO 7.7

On learning how important the vitamins are to their health, most people want to choose foods that are vitamin-rich. How can they tell which are which? Not by food labels—these are required to list only two of the vitamins—vitamin C and vitamin A—of a food's contents. A way to find out more about the vitamin contents of foods is to look down the columns of vitamins and calories in a table of food composition, such as Appendix A at the end of this book, to identify some of the vitamin-rich foods in your diet. If you are interested in folate, for instance, you can see that cornflakes are an especially good source (folic acid is added to cornflakes), as is orange juice (folate occurs naturally in this food).

Another way of looking at such data appears in Figure 7-19—the long bars show some foods that are rich sources of a particular vitamin and the short or nonexistent bars indicate poor sources. The colors of the bars represent the various food groups.

WHICH FOODS SHOULD I CHOOSE?

After looking at Figure 7-19, don't think that you must memorize the richest sources of each vitamin and eat those foods daily. That false notion would lead you to limit your variety of foods while overemphasizing the components of a few foods. Although it is reassuring to know that your carrot-raisin salad at lunch provided more than your entire day's need for vitamin A, it is a mistake to think that you must then select equally rich sources of all the other vitamins. Such rich sources do not exist for many vitamins—rather, foods work in harmony to provide most nutrients. For example, a baked potato, not a star performer among vitamin C providers, contributes substantially to a day's need for this nutrient and contributes some thiamin, too. By the end of the day, assuming that your food choices were made with reasonable care, the bits of thiamin, vitamin B_6, and vitamin C from each serving of food have accumulated to make a more-than-adequate total diet.

A VARIETY OF FOODS WORKS BEST

With a few exceptions, nutritious foods provide small quantities of thiamin, as shown in Figure 7-19. Members of the

FIGURE 7-19 Food Sources of Vitamins Selected to Show a Range of Values

Food	Amount (Energy)	µg
VITAMIN A		
Beef liver	3 oz fried (184 cal)	9,092
Sweet potato	1 whole boiled (159 cal)	1,287
Carrots	1/2 c boiled (35 cal)	957
Cantaloupe	1/2 melon (97 cal)	860
Spinach	1/2 c boiled (21 cal)	369
Butternut squash	1/2 c baked (41 cal)	361
Milk, fat-free	1 c (85 cal)	161
Tomatoes	1/2 c boiled (33 cal)	89
Peach	1 fresh medium (42 cal)	26
Orange juice	1 c (fresh)	25
Summer squash	1/2 c boiled (18 cal)	13
Apple	1 fresh medium (81 cal)	5
Sirloin steak	3 oz lean (171 cal)	0
Whole-wheat bread	1 slice (70 cal)	0
Baked potato	1 whole (220 cal)	0

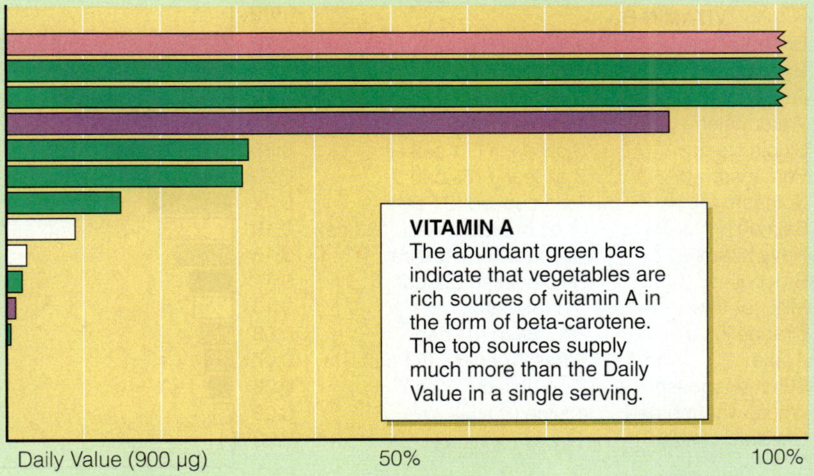

Food	Amount (Energy)	mg
VITAMIN E		
Sunflower seeds	2 tbs dry (103 cal)	9.6
Sunflower seed oil	1 tbs (124 cal)	6.5
Wheat germ	1 oz (117 cal)	6.0
Safflower oil	1 tbs (124 cal)	6.0
Cottonseed oil	1 tbs (124 cal)	5.0
Peanuts	1 oz dry roasted (166 cal)	3.0
Corn oil	1 tbs (124 cal)	3.0
Peanut butter	2 tbs (190 cal)	3.0
Canola oil	1 tbs (124 cal)	2.9
Shrimp	3 oz boiled (84 cal)	1.0
Parsley	1/2 c fresh chopped (11 cal)	1.0
Apple	1 fresh medium (81 cal)	0.4
Sweet potato	1 baked (117 cal)	0.3
Cheddar cheese	1 1/2 oz (170 cal)	0.2
Whole-wheat bread	1 slice (70 cal)	0.0

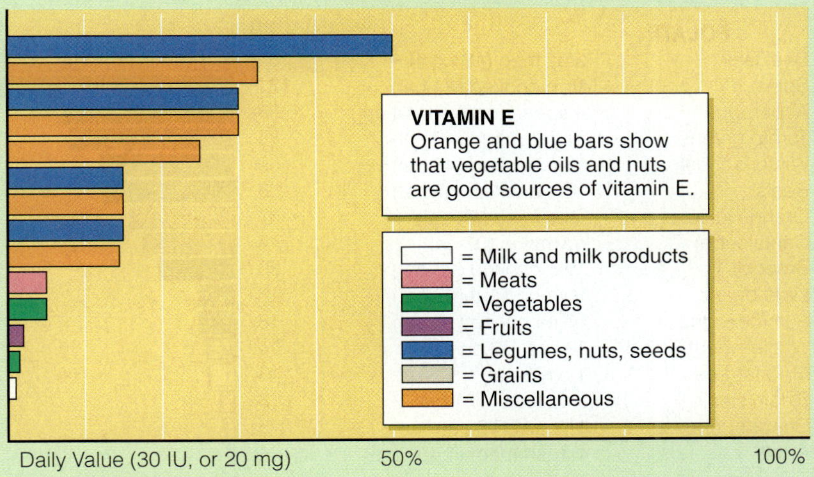

Food	Amount (Energy)	mg
THIAMIN		
Pork chop	3 oz broiled (275 cal)	0.98
Black beans	1 c cooked (228 cal)	0.42
Sunflower seeds	2 tbs dry (103 cal)	0.41
Watermelon	1 slice (91 cal)	0.23
Green peas	1/2 c cooked (67 cal)	0.23
Orange juice	3/4 c fresh (84 cal)	0.17
Oysters	5 oysters simmered (125 cal)	0.16
Oatmeal	1/2 c cooked (73 cal)	0.13
Sirloin steak	3 oz lean (171 cal)	0.11
Whole-wheat bread	1 slice (70 cal)	0.10
Milk, fat-free	1 c (85 cal)	0.09
Cabbage	1/2 c cooked (33 cal)	0.09
Summer squash	1/2 c cooked (18 cal)	0.04
Apple	1 fresh medium (81 cal)	0.02
Cheddar cheese	1 1/2 oz (170 cal)	0.02

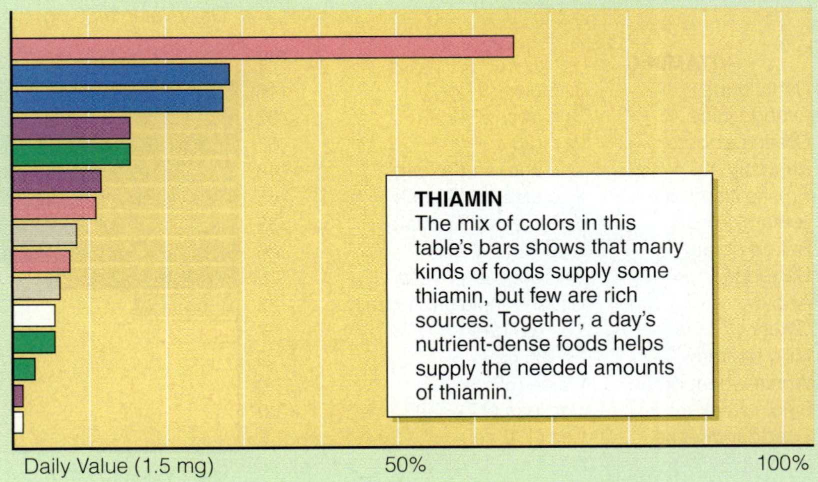

pork family are an exceptionally good thiamin source with one small pork chop (275 calories) providing over half of the Daily Value for thiamin—but again, this does not suggest that you eat pork every day. Legumes and grains are also good, low-fat sources, and they provide beneficial fiber and nutrients lacking from meats. Beans lack the vitamin B_{12} provided by meats, however. Peanut butter is a good source of thiamin, and of most other B vitamins (except vitamin B_{12}) as well, but its high fat and calorie contents call for moderation in its use.

The vitamin B_6 data provide another insight to support the argument for variety. From just the few foods listed here, you can see that no one source can provide

FIGURE 7-19

Food Sources of Vitamins Selected to Show a Range of Values (continued)

Food	Amount (Energy)	mg
VITAMIN B_6		
Baked potato	1 whole (220 cal)	0.70
Banana	1 peeled (109 cal)	0.68
Turkey breast	3 oz (133 cal)	0.46
Watermelon	1 slice (91 cal)	0.41
Sirloin steak	3 oz lean (171 cal)	0.38
Pork roast	3 oz lean (175 cal)	0.29
Spinach	1/2 c cooked (21 cal)	0.22
Salmon	3 oz broiled/baked (183 cal)	0.19
Navy beans	1/2 c cooked (129 cal)	0.15
Broccoli	1/2 c cooked (22 cal)	0.11
Milk, fat-free	1 c (85 cal)	0.10
Orange juice	3/4 c fresh (84 cal)	0.08
Apple	1 fresh medium (81 cal)	0.07
Summer squash	1/2 c boiled (18 cal)	0.06
Whole-wheat bread	1 slice (69 cal)	0.05
Cheddar cheese	1 1/2 oz (170 cal)	0.03

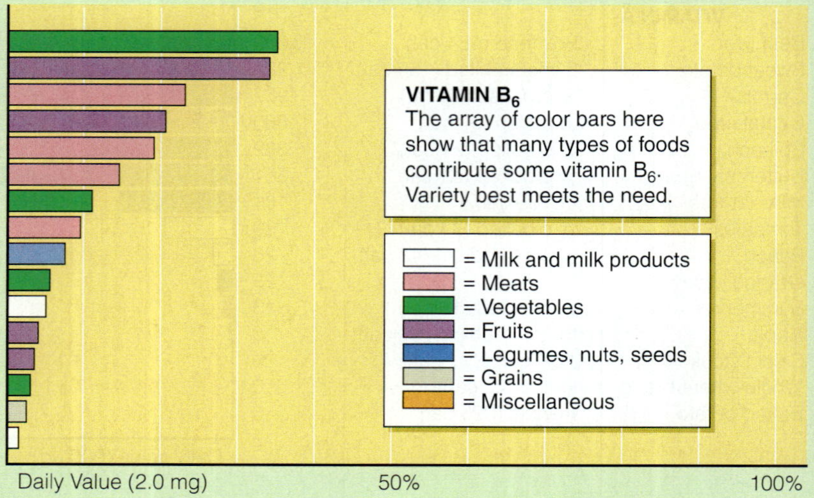

Food	Amount (Energy)	µg
FOLATE		
Beef liver	3 oz fried (184 cal)	185
Spinach	1/2 c cooked (21 cal)	131
Asparagus	4 spears cooked (14 cal)	88
Turnip greens	1/2 c cooked (15 cal)	85
Winter squash	1/2 c cooked (48 cal)	69
Beets	1/2 c cooked (37 cal)	68
Orange juice	3/4 c fresh (84 cal)	57
Cantaloupe	1/2 melon (97 cal)	47
Broccoli	1/2 c cooked (22 cal)	39
Lima beans	1/2 c cooked (85 cal)	18
Summer squash	1/2 c cooked (18 cal)	18
Whole-wheat bread[a]	1 slice (70 cal)	14
Milk, fat-free	1 c (85 cal)	13
Sirloin steak	3 oz lean (171 cal)	8
Cheddar cheese	1 1/2 oz (170 cal)	5
Apple	1 fresh medium (81 cal)	4

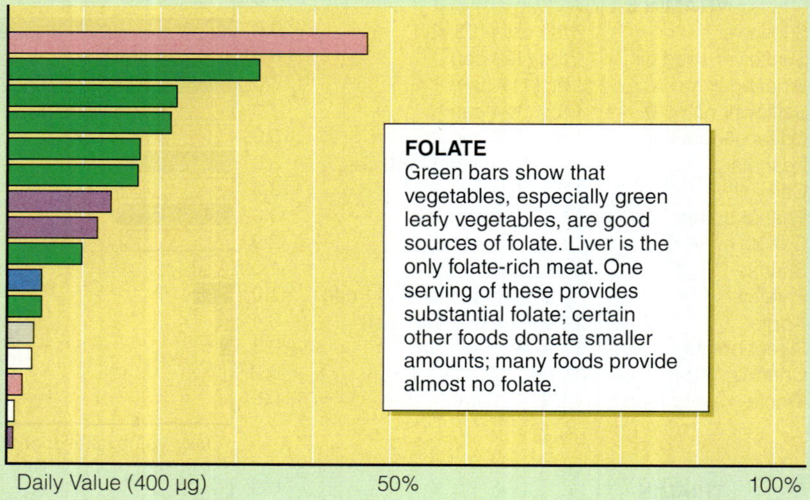

Food	Amount (Energy)	mg
VITAMIN C		
Cantaloupe	1/2 melon (97 cal)	116
Orange juice	3/4 c fresh (84 cal)	93
Green peppers	1/2 c (20 cal)	67
Broccoli	1/2 c cooked (26 cal)	48
Brussels sprouts	1/2 c cooked (30 cal)	48
Tomato juice	3/4 c canned (31 cal)	33
Baked potato	1 whole (220 cal)	26
Cabbage	1/2 c cooked (17 cal)	15
Apple	1 fresh medium (81 cal)	8
Oysters	3 oz (69 cal)	7
Milk, fat-free	1 c (85 cal)	2
Whole-wheat bread	1 slice (69 cal)	0
Sirloin steak	3 oz lean (171 cal)	0
Cheddar cheese	1 oz (170 cal)	0

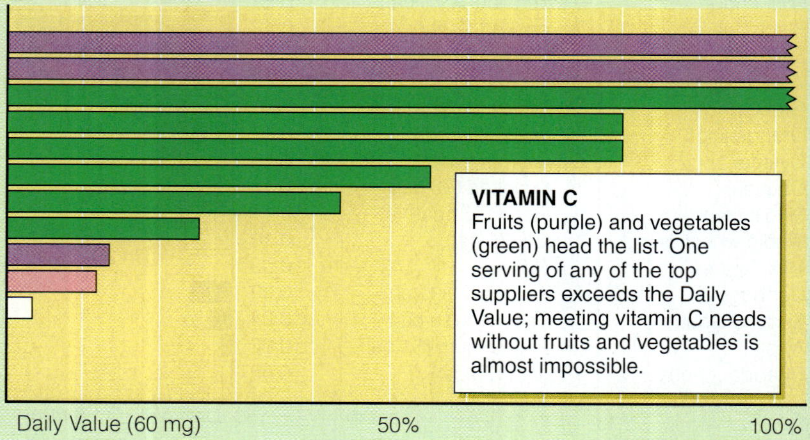

[a]Unenriched.

the whole day's requirement for vitamin B_6, but that many small servings of a variety of meats, fish, and poultry along with potatoes and a few other vegetables and fruits consumed throughout the day work together to supply it.

The last two graphs of Figure 7-19 show sources of folate and vitamin C. These nutrients are both richly supplied by fruits and vegetables. The richest source of either may be only a moderate source of the other, but the recommended amounts of fruits and vegetables in the USDA Food Guide of Chapter 2 cover both needs amply. As for vitamin E, vegetable oils and some seeds and nuts are the richest sources, and vegetables and fruits contribute a little, too.

By now, you should recognize a pattern in nutrition. The diet best for providing nutrients includes a wide variety of whole foods and it provides more than just isolated nutrients.[94] Phytochemicals are widespread among fruits and vegetables, and may play roles in human health, as does fiber and other constituents of whole foods. When aiming for adequate intakes of vitamins, therefore, aim for a diet that meets the recommendations of Chapter 2. Even supplements cannot duplicate the benefits of such a diet, a point made in this chapter's Controversy section.

Diet Analysis PLUS Concepts in Action

Analyze Your Vitamin Intake

The purpose of this exercise is to help you identify your food sources of water-soluble and fat-soluble vitamins. Many foods rich in vitamins work in harmony to provide a full complement of nutrients, which ultimately contributes to a health-promoting diet.

1. Determine whether your food provides enough vitamins. From the Reports tab, select Intake vs. Goals. Choose Day Two, all meals. Generate a report. Did your actual intakes on that day meet your DRI recommended intake values for vitamins? If not, list the vitamins which have not met the DRI goals. Did your intakes exceed any DRI values? If so, list them.
2. Some fruits and vegetables are good sources of fat-soluble vitamins (see the Snapshots on pages 233, 238, 240, and 242). From the Reports tab, select MyPyramid Analysis and include all meals. Generate a report. Have you met your minimum recommended fruit and vegetable intake? What percentage of your goal have you met for fruits and vegetables? Did you consume any fruits and vegetables listed in the Snapshots for the fat-soluble vitamins? Which ones?
3. From the Reports tab, select Source Analysis, choose any day, and include all meals. From the drop-down box, select vitamin C, then folate, and generate a report for each vitamin. What is your best food source for vitamin C? And for folate? Were your best sources shown in the Snapshots on pages 247 and 255?
4. After viewing the Intake vs. Goals report in question 1, if you fell short on any vitamin, what foods could you add to your diet that would bring you up to the DRI recommended intake value? If you exceeded the DRI values, which foods were responsible?
5. The MyPyramid patterns suggest that a person who requires 2,000 calories per day should aim to consume 3 cups of a variety of dark green, 2 cups of orange, 3 cups of starchy, and 6.5 cups of other vegetables each week. Create a dish from vegetables or fruits that you enjoy. Get some ideas by using Figure 7-19 (pages 265–266). From the Track Diet tab, select Source Analysis, and select one water-soluble, then one fat-soluble vitamin from the drop-down menu. Generate a report for each. Identify the vitamin-rich foods from the report. What does the bar graph show?

MEDIA MENU

CENGAGENOW To find additional quiz questions, view videos and animations, and explore interactive exercises, go to **www.cengage.com/sso.**

Search for information on individual vitamins at **www.healthfinder.gov.**

Visit the World Health Organization to learn more about "vitamin deficiencies" around the world: **www.who.int.**

Learn more about dietary supplements as well as individual vitamins and minerals at **www.fda.gov.**

Under Browse by Subject, select Dietary Supplements at **www.nutrition.gov.**

Search for information about herbal dietary supplements, vitamins, and minerals at **www.nlm.nih.gov/medlineplus.**

SELF CHECK

Answers to these Self Check questions are in Appendix G.

1. Which of the following vitamins are classified as fat-soluble?
   A. vitamins B, D
   B. vitamins A, D, E, and K
   C. vitamins B, E, D, and C
   D. vitamins B and C
2. Night blindness and xerophthalmia are the result of a deficiency of which vitamin?
   A. niacin
   B. vitamin C
   C. vitamin A
   D. vitamin K
3. Which of the following foods is (are) rich in beta-carotene?
   A. sweet potatoes
   B. pumpkin
   C. spinach
   D. all of the above
4. A deficiency of niacin may result in which disease?
   A. pellagra
   B. beriberi
   C. scurvy
   D. rickets
5. Which of the following describes the fat-soluble vitamins?
   A. vitamins B and C
   B. easily absorbed and excreted
   C. stored extensively in tissues
   D. (a) and (c)
6. Which vitamin(s) is (are) present only in foods of animal origin?
   A. the active form of vitamin A
   B. vitamin B_{12}
   C. riboflavin
   D. (a) and (b)
7. The theory that vitamin C prevents or cures colds is well supported by research.
   T F
8. Xerophthalmia results from advanced vitamin A deficiency and can lead to permanent blindness.
   T F
9. Vitamin D functions as a hormone to help maintain bone integrity.
   T F
10. Vitamin A supplements can help treat acne.
   T F

CONTROVERSY 7

Vitamin Supplements: Do the Benefits Outweigh the Risks?

LO 7.8, 7.9

At least half of the U.S. population dose themselves with dietary supplements, spending tens of *billions* of dollars a year to do so.[1*] Most take a daily multivitamin and mineral pill to make up for dietary shortfalls. Some take single nutrient supplements to ward off diseases.[2] Do people need these supplements? Which ones prevent diseases? Is someone ensuring their safety? Finally, if people do need supplements, which ones are best? This Controversy examines evidence surrounding these questions and concludes with some advice for those choosing to take a supplement.

Reference notes are found in Appendix F.

Which is the best source of vitamins to support good health: supplements or food?

ARGUMENTS IN FAVOR OF TAKING SUPPLEMENTS

Indisputably, the people listed in Table C7-1 need supplements. For them, nutrient supplements can prevent or reverse illnesses. Because supplements are not risk-free, these people should consult a health-care provider who is alert to potential adverse effects and nutrient–drug interactions.[3]

People with Deficiencies

In the United States and Canada, few adults suffer nutrient deficiency diseases such as scurvy, pellagra, and beriberi but the conditions still occasionally occur, as the preceding chapter made clear. When they do, prescribed supplements of the missing nutrients quickly stop or reverse most deficiency diseases (exceptions include vitamin A–deficiency blindness, some vitamin B_{12}–deficiency nerve damage, and birth defects caused by folate deficiency in pregnant women).

People with Increased Nutrient Needs

Nutrient needs increase during certain stages of life, and many people find it difficult or impossible to meet some of those needs without supplements. For example, women who lose a lot of blood and therefore a lot of iron during

TABLE C7-1 Some Valid Reasons for Taking Supplements

These People May Need Supplements:
• People with nutrient deficiencies.
• Women in their childbearing years (supplemental or enrichment sources of folic acid are recommended to reduce risk of neural tube defects in infants).
• Pregnant or lactating women (they may need iron and folate).
• Newborns (they are routinely given a vitamin K dose).
• Infants (they may need various supplements, see Chapter 13).
• Those who are lactose intolerant (they need calcium to forestall osteoporosis).
• Habitual dieters (they may eat insufficient food).
• Elderly people often benefit from some of the vitamins and minerals in a balanced supplement (they may choose poor diets, have trouble chewing, or absorb or metabolize nutrients less efficiently; see Chapter 14).
• Victims of AIDS or other wasting illnesses (they lose nutrients faster than foods can supply them).
• Those addicted to drugs or alcohol (they absorb fewer and excrete more nutrients; nutrients cannot undo damage from drugs or alcohol).
• Those recovering from surgery, burns, injury, or illness (they need extra nutrients to help regenerate tissues).
• Strict vegetarians (they may need vitamin B_{12}, vitamin D, iron, and zinc).
• People taking medications that interfere with the body's use of nutrients.

menstruation each month may need an iron supplement. In women of childbearing age, supplements of folic acid reduce the risks of neural tube defects.[4] Similarly, pregnant and breastfeeding women have exceptionally high nutrient needs and often must rely on special supplements to meet them. Even newborns require a dose of vitamin K at birth, as the preceding chapter pointed out. (Details about nutrient needs through life are found in Chapters 13 and 14.)

People with Low Nutrient Status

Subtle borderline deficiencies that do not cause classic symptoms are easily overlooked or misdiagnosed—and they often occur. People who diet habitually or elderly people with diminished appetite may eat so little nutritious food that they teeter on the edge of deficiency, with no reserve to handle any increase in demand.[5] Similarly, people who omit entire food groups without planning to replace the missing nutrients will fail to meet nutrient needs; people who are too busy, lack knowledge, lack money, or for any reason fail to obtain the nutritious foods they need also fail to meet their needs.[6] If correcting nutrient shortfalls with nutritious food is not feasible, then vitamin-mineral supplements can help prevent the worst of the deficiency diseases they might otherwise face.

People Coping with Physical Stress

Any interference with a person's appetite, ability to eat, or ability to absorb or use nutrients will impair nutrient status. Prolonged illnesses, extensive injuries, surgery, and addictions to alcohol or other drugs all have these effects, and such stressors increase nutrient requirements of the tissues, too. In addition, medications used to treat such conditions often increase nutrient needs further or impair their absorption or use by the body. In all these cases, supplements are appropriate.

ARGUMENTS AGAINST TAKING SUPPLEMENTS

Foods rarely cause nutrient imbalances or toxicities, but supplements easily can. The higher the dose, the greater the risk. People's tolerances for high doses of nutrients vary, just as their risks of deficiencies do, and amounts tolerable for some may be harmful for others. No one knows who falls where along the spectrum, so determining just how much of a nutrient is enough—or too much—for a particular person is difficult. The Tolerable Upper Intake Levels of the DRI define the highest amount that appears safe for *most* healthy people. A few sensitive people may experience toxicities at lower doses, however. Table C7-2 presents these suggested Upper Levels for selected vitamins and minerals and also lists nutrient doses in typical supplements.

Toxicity

Supplement users are more likely to have excessive intakes of certain nutrients—notably iron, zinc, vitamin A, and niacin.[7] The true extent of supplement toxicity in this country is unknown, but many adverse events are reported each year from vitamins, minerals, essential oils, herbs, and other supplements.[8] Reported toxicities may greatly underestimate the true occurrence because only an alert health-care professional knowledgeable in nutrition can reliably recognize nutrient toxicity and report it to the Food and Drug Administration (FDA). A chronic, subtle toxicity that progresses slowly often goes unrecognized and unreported.

Toxic overdoses of vitamins and minerals in children are more readily recognized and, unfortunately, fairly common.[9] Fruit-flavored, chewable vitamins shaped like cartoon characters entice youngsters to eat them like candy, thus poisoning themselves.[10] High-potency iron supplements have been known to cause accidental poisoning deaths among children, and even mild iron overdoses cause nausea and black diarrhea that reflects internal bleeding. Some authorities suggest that supplements should bear labels to warn consumers of their potential for harm.

Supplement Contamination

The U.S. Food and Drug Administration recently identified over 140 dietary supplements sold on the U.S. market that were contaminated with pharmaceutical drugs, such as steroid hormones and stimulants. Toxic plant material, toxic heavy metals, bacteria, and other substances have also shown up in a wide variety of dietary supplements. Even some children's chewable vitamins have contained appreciable lead, a destructive heavy metal that harms young children.[11] While hazardous products are quickly removed from the market upon discovery, many others remain on store shelves because current regulations make the supplement market difficult to monitor and control.[12] Plain multivitamin and mineral supplements from reputable sources, without herbs or add-ons, often test free from contamination.

Life-Threatening Misinformation

Another problem arises when people who are ill come to believe that self-prescribed high doses of vitamins or minerals can be therapeutic. For example, a man who suffered from mental illness arrived at an emergency room with dangerously low blood pressure.[13] He had ingested 11 grams of niacin on the advice of an Internet website that falsely touted niacin as an effective therapy for schizophrenia. The DRI sets a Tolerable Upper Intake Level for niacin at 35 *milligrams*.

Supplements are rarely effective for purposes other than those already listed in Table C7-1. This doesn't stop marketers from making enticing claims in materials of all kinds—in print, on labels, and on television or the Internet. These claims often fall far short of the FDA standard that claims should be "truthful and not misleading."

Unknown Needs

Another argument against the use of supplements is that no one knows exactly how to formulate the "ideal" supplement. What nutrients should be included? Which, if any, of the phytochemicals should be included? How much of each? On whose needs should the choices be based? Surveys have repeatedly shown that the nutrients in the supplements people take are ones that they do not actually need. Most people taking vitamins or minerals in supplements already receive those nutrients from food, while people with low nutrient intakes rarely take supplements at all.

TABLE C7-2 **Intake Guidelines (Adults) and Nutrient Supplement Values**

Nutrient	Tolerable Upper Intake Levels[a]	Daily Values	Typical Multivitamin-Mineral Supplement	Average Single-Nutrient Supplement
Vitamins				
Vitamin A	3,000 µg (10,000 IU)	5,000 IU	5,000 IU	8,000 to 10,000 IU
Vitamin D	50 µg (2,000 IU)	400 IU	400 IU	400 IU
Vitamin E	1,000 mg (1,500 to 2,200 IU)[b]	30 IU	30 IU	100 to 1,000 IU
Vitamin K	—[c]	80 µg	40 µg	—[e]
Thiamin	—[c]	1.5 mg	1.5 mg	50 mg
Riboflavin	—[c]	1.7 mg	1.7 mg	25 mg
Niacin (as niacinamide)	35 mg[b]	20 mg	20 mg	100 to 500 mg
Vitamin B_6	100 mg	2 mg	2 mg	100 to 200 mg
Folate	1,000 µg[b]	400 µg	400 µg	400 µg
Vitamin B_{12}	—[c]	6 µg	6 µg	100 to 1,000 µg
Pantothenic acid	—[c]	10 mg	10 mg	100 to 500 mg
Biotin	—[c]	300 µg	30 µg	300 to 600 µg
Vitamin C	2,000 mg	60 mg	10 mg	500 to 2,000 mg
Choline	3,500 mg	—	10 mg	250 mg
Minerals				
Calcium	2,500 mg	1,000 mg	160 mg	250 to 600 mg
Phosphorus	4,000 mg	1,000 mg	110 mg	—[e]
Magnesium	350 mg[d]	400 mg	100 mg	250 mg
Iron	45 mg	18 mg	18 mg	18 to 30 mg
Zinc	40 mg	15 mg	15 mg	10 to 100 mg
Iodine	1,100 µg	150 µg	150 µg	—[e]
Selenium	400 µg	70 µg	10 µg	50 to 200 µg
Fluoride	10 mg	—	—	—[e]
Copper	10 mg	2 mg	0.5 mg	—[e]
Manganese	11 mg	2 mg	5 mg	—[e]
Chromium	—[c]	120 µg	25 µg	200 to 400 µg
Molybdenum	2,000 µg	75 µg	25 µg	—[e]

[a] *Unless otherwise noted, Upper Levels represent total intakes from food, water, and supplements.*

[b] *Upper Levels represent intakes from supplements, fortified foods, or both.*

[c] *These nutrients have been evaluated by the DRI Committee for Tolerable Upper Intake Levels, but none were established because of insufficient data. No adverse effects have been reported with intakes of these nutrients at levels typical of supplements, but caution is still advised, given the potential for harm that accompanies excessive intakes.*

[d] *Upper Levels represent intakes from supplements only.*

[e] *Available as a single supplement by prescription.*

False Sense of Security

Another argument against supplement use is that it may lull people into a false sense of security. A person might eat irresponsibly, thinking, "My supplement will cover my needs." Or, experiencing a warning symptom of a disease, a person might postpone seeking a diagnosis, thinking, "I probably just need a supplement to make this go away." Such self-diagnosis can postpone effective medical treatment and give their disease a chance to worsen.

Whole Foods Are Best for Nutrients

In general, the body absorbs nutrients best from foods that dilute and disperse them among other substances to facilitate their absorption and use by the body.[14] Taken in pure, concentrated form, nutrients are likely to interfere with one another's absorption or with the absorption of other nutrients from foods eaten at the same time. Such effects are particularly well known among the minerals. For example, zinc hinders copper and calcium absorption, iron hinders zinc absorption, and calcium hinders magnesium and iron absorption. Among vitamins, vitamin C supplements *enhance* iron absorption, making iron overload likely in susceptible people. High doses of vitamin E interfere with vitamin K functions, delaying blood clotting and possibly raising the risk of brain hemorrhage (a form of stroke).[15] The vitamin A precursor beta-carotene interferes with vitamin E metabolism. These and other interactions present drawbacks to supplement use.

CAN SUPPLEMENTS PREVENT HEART DISEASE OR CANCER?

Many people take supplements, and antioxidant supplements in particular, in the belief that **antioxidant nutrients** can prevent heart disease and cancer. Can taking a supplement prevent these killers?

Oxidative Stress, Marginal Deficiencies, and Chronic Diseases

Central to the idea that antioxidant nutrients might fight diseases is the theory of **oxidative stress** (terms are defined in Table C7-3). Body cells use oxygen to produce energy, and in this and other processes, they produce free radicals (highly unstable molecules of oxygen). Oxidative stress results when free-radical activity in the body exceeds its antioxidant defenses. Then, a destructive chain reaction of oxidation damages cellular lipids, DNA, LDL cholesterol, and other structures. When such damage accumulates, this triggers inflammation, which may lead to heart disease and cancer, among other conditions. Antioxidant nutrients help to quench these free radicals, rendering them harmless to cellular structures and stopping the chain of events.

Vitamin C: Population, Animal, and Cell Studies

According to the theory, even subclinical deficiencies with no observable deficiency symptoms can allow free-radical damage to accumulate in the tissues. For example, people consuming a diet low in vitamin C can silently incur an increase in oxidative stress in the tissues long before the symptoms of scurvy appear.[16]

Convincing evidence exists linking high intakes of antioxidant-rich fruits and vegetables with good health and disease prevention (see Chapter 11).[17] Results from epidemiological studies draw the link to human health, while cell and animal studies demonstrate that reduced oxidative stress is a plausible mechanism. In our vitamin C example, at normal doses from foods, vitamin C clearly acts as an antioxidant in the tissues.

Logically, it might seem that higher vitamin C doses might offer even greater protection.[18] However, such a benefit is not observed when mice receive supplemental vitamin C throughout their lives. The presence of *surplus* vitamin C causes the animals' tissues to compensate by reducing their production of their own native antioxidant enzymes.[19] In human research, lower levels of native antioxidant enzymes correlate with elevated risk of heart disease.[20] In the end, no net reduction in oxidative damage is gained by regular supplementation with vitamin C, and supplements may lower native antioxidant protection.

The preceding chapter mentioned that acute, high doses of vitamin C act as a prooxidant, generating free radicals. This action sounds destructive, but it may not be entirely detrimental: research suggests that free radicals from pharmaceutical doses of vitamin C, administered under controlled conditions, may help to destroy cancer cells in mice.[21] No evidence exists to suggest that the same is true in people.

Vitamin C: Intervention Studies

Population studies, animal studies, and cell studies of the type just discussed lack the power to state conclusively whether a nutrient may affect the health of human beings. To follow up these forms of evidence, researchers must give supplements to a group of people and then compare their rates of chronic diseases with those of others who received a placebo. Such studies indicate no effect of vitamin C and other antioxidant nutrients on chronic diseases.[22]

The results are different for one group, however. People who test *low* for blood levels of antioxidant nutrients and who then consume foods that supply the missing nutrients often resist chronic diseases better than people whose deficiencies go untreated. People eating diets low in fruits and vegetables that supply the antioxidant nutrients are clearly more likely to suffer chronic diseases, but whether this effect is caused by a lack of antioxidant nutrients, a lack of phytochemicals, or a combination of other lifestyle choices that may accompany such diets is unknown.[23]

Vitamin E Supplements and Heart Disease

In the past decade, much scientific research has focused on vitamin E supplements in the hope of finding an accessible, safe agent to reduce heart disease risks. Early studies seemed promising: people who reported taking vitamin E supplements were observed to have lower rates of death from heart disease than others.[24] In laboratory studies, vitamin E opposes oxidation of blood lipids (LDL), tissue inflammation, injury to arteries, and blood clotting. In principle, it makes sense that vitamin E might reduce disease risks.

With these clues in hand, researchers undertook the final studies needed to establish or refute the idea that vitamin E supplements prevent heart disease: controlled clinical human trials involving thousands of people, some of whom agreed to take a supplement, and some to take a placebo. After years of recording health data, scientists found no protective effect from vitamin E supplements

TABLE C7-3 Antioxidant Terms

- **antioxidant nutrients** vitamins and minerals that oppose the effects of oxidants on human physical functions. The antioxidant vitamins are vitamin E, vitamin C, and beta-carotene. The mineral selenium also participates in antioxidant activities.
- **electrons** parts of an atom; negatively charged particles. Stable atoms (and molecules, which are made of atoms) have even numbers of electrons in pairs. An atom or molecule with an unpaired electron is an unstable free radical.
- **oxidants** compounds (such as oxygen itself) that oxidize other compounds. Compounds that prevent oxidation are called antioxidants, whereas those that promote it are called prooxidants (*anti* means "against"; *pro* means "for").
- **oxidative stress** damage inflicted on living systems by free radicals.
- **subclinical,** or **marginal, deficiency** a nutrient deficiency that has no outward clinical symptoms. The term is often used to market unneeded nutrient supplements to consumers.

against heart attack incidence, hospitalization, or death from heart failure.[25] In fact, when results from high-quality studies were pooled, a slight but alarming *increased* risk for death emerged for people taking vitamin E supplements.[26]

Such studies have been criticized for testing too low a dose or failing to account for differences such as illness, radiation exposure, or smoking—conditions that create excess free radicals.[27] Some people's genetic makeup causes their tissues to produce more free radicals, and this reduces vitamin E in their tissues; such people may benefit from vitamin E supplements.[28] Also, the fact that most people in the United States fail to obtain enough vitamin E in the diet causes some to conclude that supplements may be beneficial.[29] New investigations in the field of nutritional genomics may soon provide more clarity about whether some individuals may benefit from extra vitamin E.

The Story of Beta-Carotene

It is well known that people whose diets are rich in fruits and vegetables have low rates of many cancers, and this is particularly true for beta-carotene. Based on such evidence, the popular media hailed beta-carotene as a powerful anticancer substance and consumers eagerly bought and took beta-carotene supplements.

A sudden reversal crumbled the beta-carotene theory overnight. Not only did the early results from controlled clinical human trials reveal no benefit from beta-carotene, but major clinical trials around the world were abruptly stopped upon finding a 28 percent *increase* in lung cancer among smokers taking beta-carotene compared with placebos. Supplements of another common carotenoid, lutein, may also raise lung cancer risk, along with supplements of vitamin A itself.[30] Evidence is mixed on whether smokers may be at particular risk in this regard.

Three mechanisms have been proposed to explain these connections. Carotenoid supplements may increase DNA damage by free radicals, they may interfere with other micronutrients, or they may interfere with the beneficial production of reactive oxygen species needed by the healthy immune defenses that kill cancer cells.[31]

The unscientific-minded may find such research reversals frustrating or shocking, but scientists expect them as research unfolds. In this case, scientists have rediscovered a long-known basic nutrition principle: lower disease risks follow a *diet* of nutritious whole foods that presents a balance of nutrients to the body.

SUPPLEMENTS MUST BE SAFE, OR THE GOVERNMENT WOULD NOT ALLOW THEIR SALE, RIGHT?

The spectacular fall from favor of antioxidant supplements reinforces the principle that consumers who take needless supplements are at best wasting money, or at worst risking their health. Many consumers wrongly believe that government scientists, in particular those of the Food and Drug Administration (FDA), test each new **dietary supplement** (see Table C7-4) to ensure their safety and effectiveness before allowing it on the market.

Under current law, the FDA is responsible only for taking action against unsafe dietary supplements already on the market. No advance registration or approval by the FDA is needed before a manufacturer can put a supplement on store shelves.[32] To act against unsafe supplements, the FDA must receive manufacturers' reports concerning serious adverse health effects reported to them by consumers.[33] Manufacturers do list contact information on supplement labels for this purpose, but many symptoms of adverse reactions are easily mistaken for something else—stomach flu or headache or fatigue. Consumers can also report adverse reactions directly to the FDA via its hotline or website, but few people know how to do so.†

WHAT ARE THE RISKS OF TAKING NUTRIENT SUPPLEMENTS?

Supplements of single nutrients may endanger the taker's health in these ways:

- Ordinary doses (400 IU) of vitamin E taken daily may slightly increase the risk of death from all causes.[34]
- Supplements of vitamin A, vitamin E, beta-carotene, or combinations produce no benefit and may increase mortality.[35]
- Vitamin C supplements may *increase* markers of oxidation in the blood or the risk of cataracts in the eyes.[36]
- High doses of vitamin C taken by women with diabetes may increase their likelihood of dying of cardiovascular disease.[37]
- Biotin-supplemented cell cultures suffer DNA damage of a type related to cancer formation.[38]
- Daily supplements of beta-carotene may increase lung cancer in smokers or in people exposed to asbestos.
- Vitamin A supplements reliably and quickly produce liver injury at doses greater than 10,000 micrograms, but liver problems can appear with much lower doses taken regularly over many years.
- Vitamin A intakes of only about twice the DRI taken over years are associated with osteoporosis and hip fractures.[39]
- Supplements of vitamin D and many minerals can be toxic in large doses.

For most people, foods, not supplements, are the best sources of nutrients. While an orange and a pill may both contain vitamin C, the orange presents a balanced array of nutrients, phytochemicals, and fiber that modulate vitamin C's effects. The pill provides only vitamin C, a lone chemical. However, most people can safely consume an ordinary daily multiple vitamin and mineral supplement, when they follow the directions.[40] And for those who need them, nutrient supplements constitute a modern-day miracle.

SELECTION OF A MULTINUTRIENT SUPPLEMENT

If you fall into one of the categories listed earlier in Table C7-1 and if you absolutely cannot meet your nutrient needs from foods, a supplement containing *nutrients*

†Consumers should report suspected harm from dietary supplements to their health providers or to the FDA's MedWatch program at (800) FDA-1088 or on the Internet at www.fda.gov/medwatch/.

TABLE C7-4 Dietary Supplement Terms

- **aristolochic acid** a Chinese herb ingredient known to attack the kidneys and to cause cancer; U.S. consumers have required kidney transplants and must take lifelong antirejection medication after use. Banned by the FDA but available in supplements sold on the Internet.
- **coenzyme Q-10** an enzyme made by cells and important for its role in energy metabolism. With diminished coenzyme Q-10 function, oxidative stress increases, as may occur in aging. Preliminary research suggests that it may be of value for treating certain conditions; toxicity in animals appears to be low. No safe intake levels for human beings have been established.
- **DHEA**[a] a hormone secretion of the adrenal gland whose level falls with advancing age. DHEA may protect antioxidant nutrients. Real DHEA is available only by prescription; the herbal DHEA imitator for sale in health-food stores is not active in the body. No safety information exists for either.
- **dietary supplement** a product, other than tobacco, that is added to the diet and contains one of the following ingredients: a vitamin, mineral, herb, botanical (plant extract), amino acid, metabolite, constituent, or extract, or a combination of any of these ingredients.
- **ephedrine** one of a group of compounds with dangerous amphetamine-like stimulant effects; extracted from the herb ma huang and recently banned by the FDA but still available from Internet sources. The most severe reported side effects of ephedrine include heart attack, stroke, and sudden death.
- **garlic oil** an extract of garlic; may or may not contain the chemicals associated with garlic; claims for health benefits unproved.
- **green pills, fruit pills** pills containing dehydrated, crushed vegetable or fruit matter. An advertisement may claim that each pill equals a pound of fresh produce, but in reality a pill may equal one small forkful—minus nutrient losses incurred in processing.
- **kelp tablets** tablets made from dehydrated kelp, a kind of seaweed used by the Japanese as a foodstuff.
- **ma huang** an evergreen plant that supposedly boosts energy and helps with weight control. Ma huang, also called ephedra, contains ephedrine (see above) and is especially dangerous in combination with kola nut or other caffeine-containing substances.
- **melatonin** a hormone of the pineal gland believed to help regulate the body's daily rhythms, to reverse the effects of jet lag, and to promote sleep. Claims for life extension or enhancement of sexual prowess are without merit.
- **nutritional yeast** a preparation of yeast cells, often praised for its high nutrient content. Yeast is a source of B vitamins as are many other foods. Also called brewer's yeast; not the yeast used in baking.
- **organ and glandular extracts** dried or extracted material from brain, adrenal, pituitary, or other glands or tissues providing few nutrients but posing a theoretical risk of "mad cow disease." See Chapter 12.
- **SAM-e** an amino acid derivative that may have an antidepressant effect on the brain in some people, but it is not recommended as a substitute for standard antidepressant therapy.
- thousands of others.

[a]*Dehydroepiandrosterone.*

Note: According to legal definitions, all of the substances listed qualify as dietary supplements, even though some appear to have the effects of drugs, not nutrients. Table 11-9 in Chapter 11 describes many more medicinal herbs, including their effects and their hazards.

only, with no added extras such as herbs, can prevent serious problems. In these cases, the benefits probably outweigh the risks.

Choosing a Type

Which supplement to choose? The first step is to remain aware that sales of vitamin supplements often approach the realm of quackery because the profits are high and the industry is largely free of oversight. To escape the clutches of the health hustlers, use your imagination and delete the picture on the label of sexy people on the beach and the meaningless, glittering generalities stating "Advanced formula," "Maximum power," and the like. Avoid "extras" such as herbs (see Chapter 11). And don't be misled into buying and taking unneeded supplements, because none are risk-free (Table C7-5 provides some *invalid* reasons for taking supplements in which the risks clearly outweigh the benefits).

Reading the Label

Now all you have left is the Supplement Facts panel that lists the nutrients, a list of ingredients, the form of the supplement, and the price—the plain facts. You have two basic questions to answer. The first question: What form do you want—chewable, liquid, or pills? If you'd rather drink your vitamins and minerals than chew them, fine. If you choose a fortified liquid meal replacer or "energy bar" (a candy bar to which vitamins and other nutrients are added), you must then proportionately reduce the calories you consume as food, or you may gain unwanted weight. If you choose chewable pills, be aware that vitamin C can erode tooth enamel. Swallow promptly and flush the teeth with a drink of water. Avoid vitamin-fortified bubble gum to protect both the teeth and gum-loving children who may chew a whole boxful and receive too large a dose for their small bodies.

Targeting Your Needs

The second question: Who are you? What vitamins and minerals do you actually need? Compare the DRI nutrient intake recommendations listed for your age and gender (the tables are on the inside front cover, page B) with the supple-

This symbol means that a supplement contains the nutrients stated and that it will dissolve in the digestive system—the symbol does not guarantee safety, or health advantages.

TABLE C7-5 Some Invalid Reasons for Taking Supplements

Watch out for plausible-sounding, but false, reasons given by marketers trying to convince you, the consumer, that you need supplements. The invalid reasons listed below have gained strength by repetition among friends, on the Internet, and by the media:

- You fear that foods grown on today's soils lack nutrients (a common false statement made by sellers of supplements).
- You feel tired and falsely believe that supplements can provide energy.
- You hope that supplements can help you cope with stress.
- You wish to build up your muscles faster or without physical exercise.
- You want to prevent or cure self-diagnosed illnesses.
- You hope excess nutrients will produce unnamed mysterious beneficial reactions in your body.

People who should never take supplements without a physician's approval include those with kidney or liver ailments (they are susceptible to toxicities), those taking medications (nutrients can interfere with their actions), and smokers (who should avoid products with beta-carotene).

ment choices. The DRI values meet the needs of all reasonably healthy people.

Choosing Doses

As for doses of nutrients, for most people, an appropriate supplement provides all the vitamins and minerals in amounts smaller than, equal to, or very close to the intake recommendations. For those who require a higher dose, such as young women who need supplemental folate in the childbearing years, choose a supplement with just the needed nutrient or in combination with a reasonable dose of others.

Avoid any preparation that in a daily dose provides more than the DRI recommended intake of vitamin A, vitamin D, or any mineral or more than the Tolerable Upper Intake Level for any nutrient. In addition, avoid high doses of iron (more than 10 milligrams per day) except for menstruating women. People who menstruate need more iron, but people who don't, don't. Warning: Expect to reject about 80 percent of available preparations when you choose according to these criteria; be choosy where your health is concerned.

Going for Quality

If you see a USP symbol on the label, it means that a manufacturer has voluntarily paid an independent laboratory to test the product and affirm that it contains the ingredients listed and that it will dissolve or disintegrate in the digestive tract to make the ingredients available for absorption. The symbol does not imply that the supplement has been tested for safety or effectiveness with regard to health, however.

A high price also does not ensure the highest quality; generic brands are often as good as or better than expensive name-brand supplements. If they are less expensive, it may mean that their price doesn't have to cover the cost of national advertising. In any case, buy from a well-known retailer who keeps stocks fresh and stores them properly.

Avoiding Marketing Traps

In addition, avoid these:

- "For low-carb diets." Preparations containing extra biotin are claimed to better metabolize the excessive protein these diets present, but no evidence supports these claims and, as mentioned, high doses of biotin may damage DNA.
- "Organic" or "natural" preparations with added substances. They are no better than standard types, but they cost much more and the substances added may also hold risks.
- "High-potency" or "therapeutic dose" supplements. More is not better.
- Items not needed in human nutrition, such as carnitine and inositol. These particular items won't harm you, but they reveal a marketing strategy that makes the whole mix suspect. The manufacturer wants you to believe that its pills contain the latest "new" nutrient that other brands omit, but, in fact, for every valid discovery of this kind, there are 999,999 frauds.
- "Time release." Medications such as some antibiotics or pain relievers often must be sustained at a steady concentration in the blood to be effective, but nutrients are incorporated into the tissues where they are needed whenever they arrive.
- "Stress formulas." Although the stress response depends on certain B vitamins and vitamin C, the recommended amount provides all that is needed of these nutrients. If you are under stress (and who isn't?), generous servings of fruits and vegetables will more than cover your need.
- Pills containing extracts of alfalfa, berries, parsley, or other vegetable or fruit components (these are generally safe but a serving of the original food brings benefits that pills can't match).
- Geriatric "tonics." They are generally poor in vitamins and minerals and yet may be so high in alcohol as to threaten inebriation.
- Any supplement sold with claims that today's foods lack sufficient nutrients to support health. Plants make vitamins for their own needs, not ours. Nutrient levels may vary from season to season and among varieties, but a plant lacking a mineral or failing to make a needed vitamin dies before it can bear food for our consumption.

To get the most from a supplement of vitamins and minerals, take it with food. A full stomach retains and dissolves the pill with its churning action.

CONCLUSION

People in developed nations are far more likely to suffer from *overnutrition* and poor lifestyle choices than from nutrient deficiencies. People wish that swallowing vitamin pills would boost their health. The truth—that they need to improve their eating and exercise habits—is harder to swallow.

Don't waste time and money trying to single out a few nutrients to take as supplements. Invest energy in eating a wide variety of fruits and vegetables in generous quantities, along with the recommended daily amounts of whole grains, lean meats, and milk products every day, and take supplements only when they are truly needed.

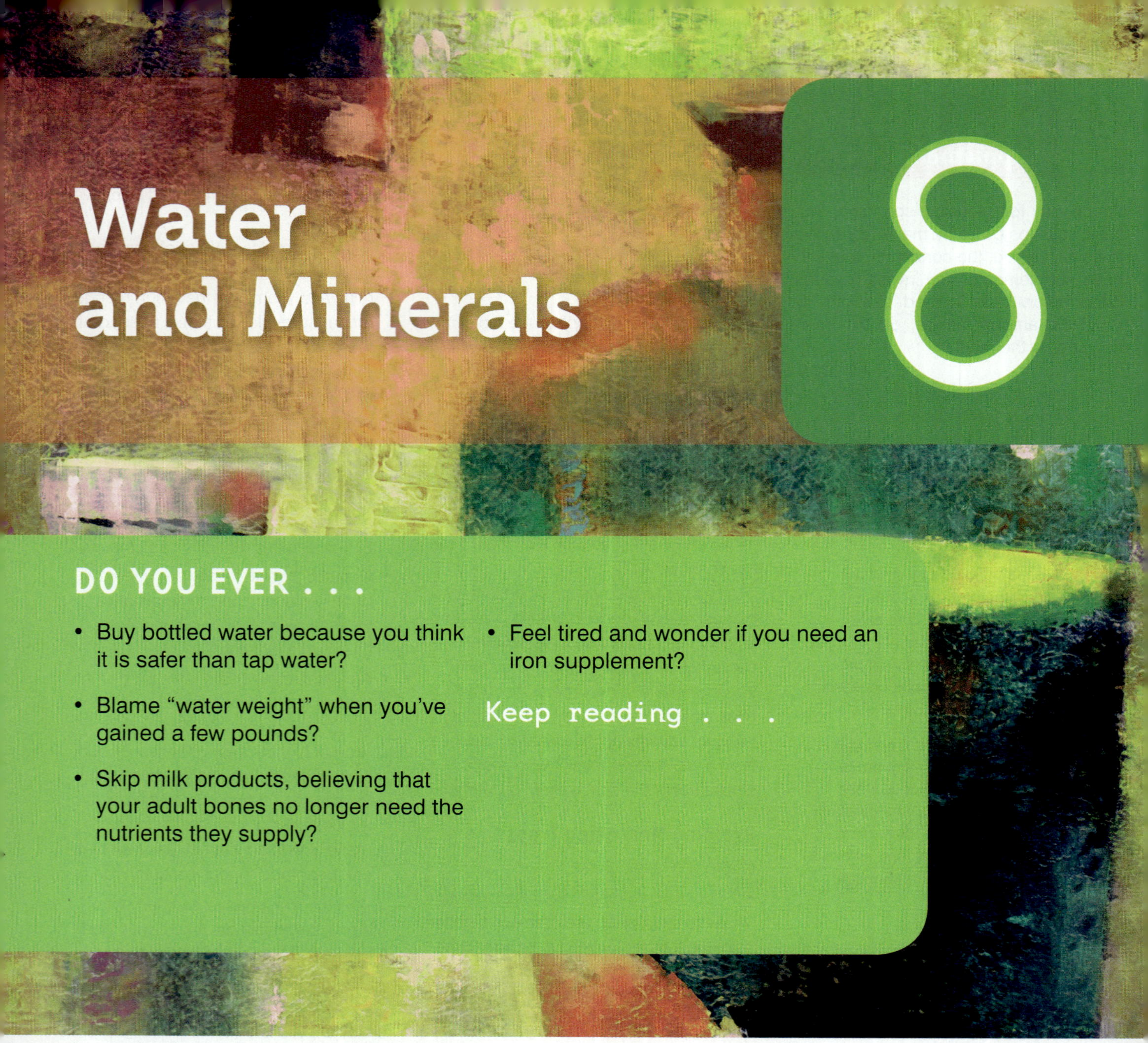

8

Water and Minerals

DO YOU EVER . . .

- Buy bottled water because you think it is safer than tap water?
- Blame "water weight" when you've gained a few pounds?
- Skip milk products, believing that your adult bones no longer need the nutrients they supply?
- Feel tired and wonder if you need an iron supplement?

Keep reading . . .

Learning Objectives

To find learning objective topics in this chapter, look for text headings with a corresponding "LO" number above the heading. After completing this chapter, you should be able to accomplish the following:

LO 8.1 Identify the best beverage choices to obtain enough water for the body's needs.

LO 8.2 Describe the body's water sources and routes of water loss, and name factors that influence the need for water.

LO 8.3 Compare and contrast various sources of drinking water for safety.

LO 8.4 Discuss why electrolyte balance is critical for the health of the body.

LO 8.5 Describe the nutrients needed to maintain blood calcium levels, and explain why this is important.

LO 8.6 Describe a diet that follows the DASH principles, and specify who might benefit from such a diet and in what ways.

LO 8.7 Compare the availability of iron from plant and animal sources.

LO 8.8 Discuss the function and importance of copper, zinc, chromium, fluoride, and selenium in the body.

LO 8.9 Describe a diet that a young woman can follow to help prevent osteoporosis later in life.

"Ashes to ashes and dust to dust"—it is true that when the life force leaves the body, what is left behind becomes nothing but a small pile of ashes. Carbohydrates, proteins, fats, vitamins, and water are present at first, but they soon disappear. The carbon atoms in all the carbohydrates, fats, proteins, and vitamins combine with oxygen to produce carbon dioxide, which vanishes into the air; the hydrogens and oxygens of those compounds unite to form water; and this water, along with the water that made up a large part of the body weight, evaporates. The ashes left behind are the **minerals,** a small pile that weighs only about 5 pounds. The pile may not be impressive in size, but the work of those minerals is critical to living tissue.

Consider calcium and phosphorus. If you could separate these two minerals from the rest of the pile, you would take away about three-fourths of the total. Crystals made of these two minerals, plus a few others, form the structure of bones and so provide the architecture of the skeleton.

Run a magnet through the pile that remains and you pick up the iron. It doesn't fill a teaspoon, but it consists of billions and billions of iron atoms. As part of hemoglobin, these iron atoms are able to attach to oxygen and make it available at the sites inside the cells where metabolic work is taking place.

If you then extract all the other minerals from the pile of ashes, leaving only copper and iodine, close the windows first. A slight breeze would blow these remaining bits of dust away. Yet the copper in the dust enables iron to hold and to release oxygen, and iodine is the critical mineral in the thyroid hormones. Figure 8-1 shows the amounts of the seven **major minerals** and a few of the **trace minerals** in the human body. Other minerals such as gold and aluminum are present in the body but are not known to have nutrient functions.

The distinction between major and trace minerals doesn't mean that one group is more important in the body than the other. A daily deficiency of a few micrograms of iodine is just as serious as a deficiency of several hundred milligrams of calcium. The major minerals are simply present in larger quantities in the body and are needed in greater amounts in the diet.[1*]

This chapter begins with a discussion of water. Water is unique among the nutrients—standing alone as the most indispensable of all. The body needs more water

- The DRI Recommended Intakes and Tolerable Upper Intake Levels for minerals appear on the inside front cover, pages B and C.

*Reference notes are found in Appendix F.

FIGURE 8-1 **Minerals in a 60-Kilogram (132-Pound) Person (Grams)**

The major minerals are needed by the body in larger amounts than the trace minerals and, as shown in the graph, they are present in larger amounts, too.

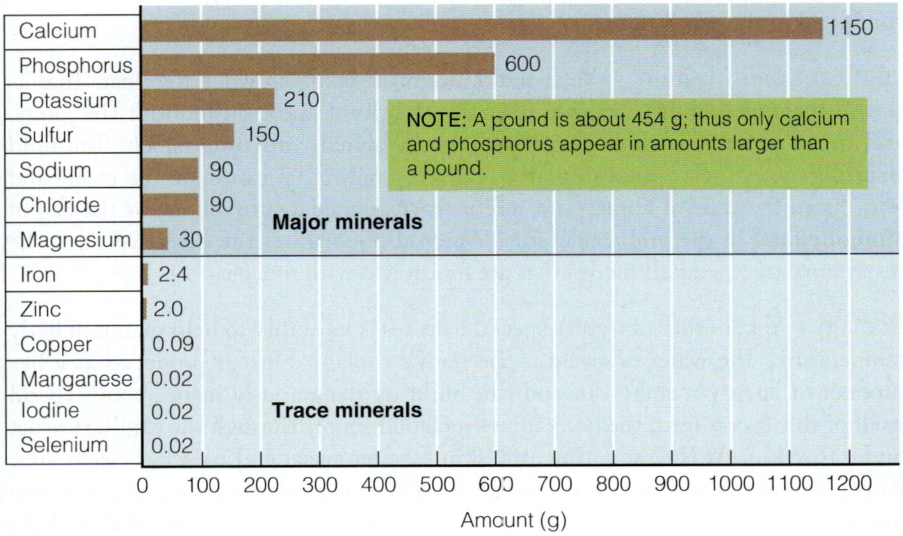

minerals naturally occurring, inorganic, homogeneous substances; chemical elements.

major minerals essential mineral nutrients required in the adult diet in amounts greater than 100 milligrams per day. Also called *macrominerals*.

trace minerals essential mineral nutrients required in the adult diet in amounts less than 100 milligrams per day. Also called *microminerals*.

each day than any other nutrient—50 times more water than protein and 5,000 times more water than vitamin C. You can survive a deficiency of any of the other nutrients for a long time, in some cases for months or years, but you can survive only a few days without water. In less than a day, a lack of water alters the body's chemistry and metabolism.

Our discussion begins with water's many functions. Next we examine how water and the major minerals mingle to form the body's fluids and how cells regulate the distribution of those fluids. Then we take up the specialized roles of each of the minerals.

© David Young-Wolff/PhotoEdit

Water is the most indispensable nutrient.

LO 8.1, 8.2

Water

You began as a single cell bathed in a nourishing fluid. As you became a beautifully organized, air-breathing body of trillions of cells, each of your cells had to remain next to water to stay alive.

Water makes up about 60 percent of an adult person's weight—that's almost 80 pounds of water in a 130-pound person. All this water in the body is not simply a river coursing through the arteries, capillaries, and veins. Some of the water is incorporated into the chemical structures of compounds that form the cells, tissues, and organs of the body. For example, proteins hold water molecules within them, water that is locked in and not readily available for any other use. Water also participates actively in many chemical reactions.

Did You Know?

The brain is composed of approximately 80% water.

Why Is Water the Most Indispensable Nutrient?

Water brings to each cell the exact ingredients the cell requires and carries away the end products of the cell's life-sustaining reactions. The water of the body fluids is thus the transport vehicle for all the nutrients and wastes. Without water, cells quickly die.

- Boasting scientist: "I'm working on discovering the universal solvent."
- Skeptic: "Is that so? Well, when you've got it, what are you going to keep it in?"

Solvent Water is a nearly universal **solvent:** it dissolves amino acids, glucose, minerals, and many other substances needed by the cells. Fatty substances, too, can travel freely in the watery blood and lymph because they are specially packaged in water-soluble proteins.

Cleansing Agent Water is also the body's cleansing agent. Small molecules, such as the nitrogen wastes generated during protein metabolism, dissolve in the watery blood and must be removed before they build up to toxic concentrations. The kidneys filter these wastes from the blood and excrete them, mixed with water, as urine. When the kidneys become diseased, as can happen in diabetes and other disorders, toxins can build to life-threatening levels. A kidney **dialysis** machine must then take over the task of cleansing the blood by filtering wastes into water contained in the machine.

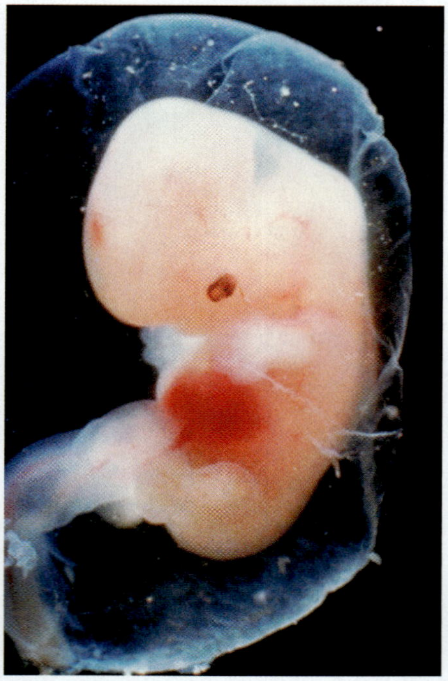
Claude Edelmann/Photo Researchers, Inc.

Human life begins in water.

Lubricant and Cushion Water molecules resist being crowded together. Thanks to this incompressibility, water can act as a lubricant and a cushion for the joints, and it can protect sensitive tissue such as the spinal cord from shock. The fluid that fills the eye serves in a similar way to keep optimal pressure on the retina and lens. From the start of human life, a fetus is cushioned against shock by the bag of amniotic fluid in the mother's uterus. Water also lubricates the digestive tract, the respiratory tract, and all tissues that are moistened with mucus.

Coolant Yet another of water's special features is its ability to help maintain body temperature. The water of sweat is the body's coolant. Heat is produced as a byproduct of energy metabolism and can build up dangerously in the body. To rid itself of this excess heat, the body routes its blood supply through the capillaries just under the skin. At the same time, the skin secretes sweat and its water evaporates. Converting water to vapor takes energy; therefore, as sweat evaporates, heat energy dissipates, cooling the skin and the underlying blood. The cooled blood then flows back to cool the body's core. Sweat evaporates continuously from the skin, usually in slight amounts that go unnoticed; thus, the skin is a major organ through which water is lost from the body. Lesser amounts are lost by way of exhaled breath and the feces.[2]

To sum up, water:

- carries nutrients throughout the body.
- serves as the solvent for minerals, vitamins, amino acids, glucose, and other small molecules.
- cleanses the tissues and blood of wastes.
- actively participates in many chemical reactions.
- acts as a lubricant around joints.
- serves as a shock absorber inside the eyes, spinal cord, joints, and amniotic sac surrounding a fetus in the womb.
- aids in maintaining the body's temperature.

KEY POINT Water makes up about 60 percent of the body's weight. Water provides the medium for transportation, acts as a solvent, participates in chemical reactions, provides lubrication and shock protection, and aids in temperature regulation in the human body.

solvent a substance that dissolves another and holds it in solution.

dialysis (dye-AL-ih-sis) a medical treatment for failing kidneys in which a person's blood is circulated through a machine that filters out toxins and wastes and returns cleansed blood to the body. Also called *hemodialysis*.

water balance the balance between water intake and water excretion, which keeps the body's water content constant.

dehydration loss of water. The symptoms progress rapidly, from thirst to weakness to exhaustion and delirium, and end in death.

water intoxication a dangerous dilution of the body's fluids resulting from excessive ingestion of plain water. Symptoms are headache, muscular weakness, lack of concentration, poor memory, and loss of appetite.

The Body's Water Balance

Water is such an integral part of us that people seldom are conscious of water's importance, unless they are deprived of it. Since the body loses some water every day, a person must consume at least the same amount to avoid life-threatening losses, that is, to maintain **water balance.** The total amount of fluid in the body is kept balanced by delicate mechanisms. Imbalances such as **dehydration** and **water intoxication** can occur, but the balance is restored as promptly as the body can manage it. The body controls both intake and excretion to maintain water equilibrium.

The amount of the body's water varies by pounds at a time, especially in women who retain water during menstruation. Eating a meal high in salt can temporarily increase the body's water content; the body sheds the excess over the next day or so as the sodium is excreted. These temporary fluctuations in body water show up

An extra drink of water benefits both young and old.

FIGURE 8-2 Water Balance—A Typical Example

Each day, water enters the body in liquids and foods, and some water is created in the body as a by-product of metabolic processes. Water leaves the body through the evaporation of sweat, in the moisture of exhaled breath, in the urine, and in the feces.

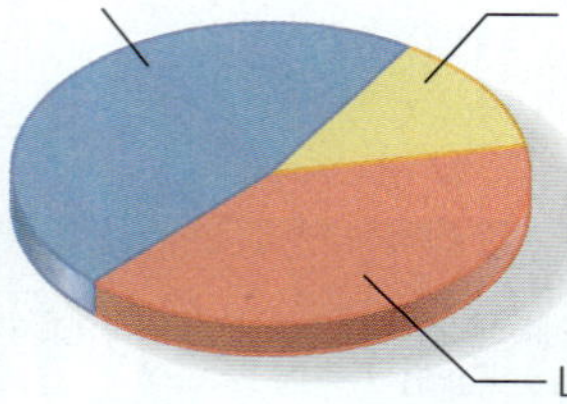

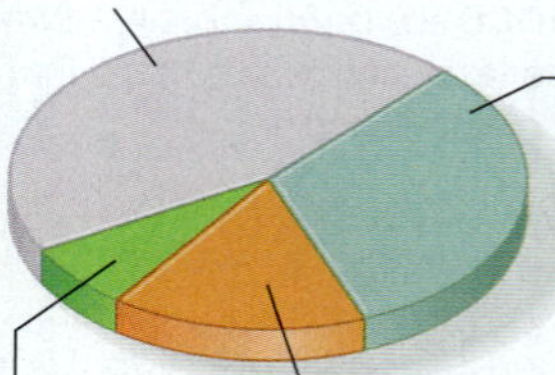

on the scale, but gaining or losing water weight does not reflect a change in body fat. Fat weight takes days or weeks to change noticeably, whereas water weight can change overnight.

KEY POINT A change in the body's water content can bring about a temporary change in body weight.

Quenching Thirst and Balancing Losses

Thirst and satiety govern water intake.[3] When the blood is too concentrated (having lost water but not salt and other dissolved substances), the molecules and particles in the blood attract water out of the salivary glands, and the mouth becomes dry. The brain center known as the hypothalamus senses the concentrated blood particles, low blood volume, or low blood pressure and initiates nerve impulses to the brain that register as "thirst." The hypothalamus also signals the pituitary gland to release a hormone that directs the kidneys to shift water back into the bloodstream from the fluid destined to become urine. The kidneys themselves respond to the sodium concentration in the blood passing through them and secrete regulatory substances of their own. The net result is that the more water the body needs, the less it excretes. Figure 8-2 shows how intake and excretion naturally balance out.

CONCEPT LINK 8-1

The hypothalamus was described in Chapter 3, page 75.

Dehydration Thirst lags behind a lack of water. When too much water is lost from the body and is not replaced, dehydration can threaten survival. A first sign of dehydration is thirst, the signal that the body has already lost up to 2 cups of its total fluid and that the need to obtain fluid is urgent. But suppose a thirsty person is unable to obtain fluid or, as in many elderly people, fails to perceive the thirst message. Instead of "wasting" precious water in sweat, the dehydrated body diverts most of its water into the blood vessels to maintain the life-supporting blood pressure. Meanwhile, body heat builds up because sweating has ceased, creating the possibility of serious consequences (see Table 8-1). A water deficiency that develops slowly can switch on drinking behavior in time to prevent serious dehydration, but one that develops quickly may not.

To ignore the thirst signal is to invite dehydration. With a loss of just 1 percent of body weight as fluid, perceptible symptoms appear: headache, fatigue, confusion or forgetfulness, and an elevated heart rate. A loss of 2 percent impairs physical functioning and impedes a wide range of physical activities.[4] People should stay attuned to thirst and drink whenever they feel thirsty to replace fluids lost throughout the day.[5] Older adults in whom thirst is blunted should drink regularly throughout the day, regardless of thirst.

Did You Know?

A 150-lb person contains 90 lb of water; a 5% loss of body fluid for this person amounts to about 4½ lb of water.

Water Intoxication At the other extreme from dehydration, water intoxication occurs when too much plain water floods the body's fluids and disturbs their normal composition. Most adult victims have consumed several gallons of plain water in a few hours' time. Water intoxication is rare, but when it occurs, immediate action is needed to reverse dangerously diluted blood before death ensues.

- For more about water intoxication, see Chapter 10.

KEY POINT Water losses from the body necessitate intake equal to output to maintain balance. The brain regulates water intake; the brain and kidneys regulate water excretion. Dehydration and water intoxication can have serious consequences.

How Much Water Do I Need to Drink in a Day?

Water needs vary greatly depending on the foods a person eats, the air temperature and humidity, the altitude, the person's activity level, and other factors (see Table 8-2). Fluid needs vary widely among individuals and also within the same person

- The DRI Recommended Intakes for water are listed on the inside front cover, page A.

TABLE 8-1 Effects of Mild Dehydration, Severe Dehydration, and Chronic Lack of Fluid

Mild Dehydration (Loss of <5% Body Weight)	Severe Dehydration (Loss of >5% Body Weight)	Chronic Low Fluid Intake May Increase the Likelihood of:[a]
Thirst	Pale skin	Cardiac arrest (heart attack) and other heart problems
Sudden weight loss	Bluish lips and fingertips	Constipation
Rough, dry skin	Confusion; disorientation	Dental disease
Dry mouth, throat, body linings	Rapid, shallow breathing	Gallstones
Rapid pulse	Weak, rapid, irregular pulse	Glaucoma (elevated pressure in the eye)
Low blood pressure	Thickening of blood	Hypertension
Lack of energy; weakness	Shock; seizures	Kidney stones
Impaired kidney function	Coma; death	Pregnancy/childbirth problems
Reduced quantity of urine; concentrated urine		Stroke
Decreased mental functioning		Urinary tract infections
Decreased muscular work and athletic performance		
Fever or increased internal temperature		
Fainting		

[a]*Evidence for bladder and colon cancer is inconsistent.*

Source: K. M. Kolasa, C. J. Lacky, and A. C. Grandjean, Hydration and health promotion, Nutrition Today *44 (2009): 190–201; F. Manz, Hydration and disease,* Journal of the American College of Nutrition *26 (2007): 535S–541S, Standing Committee on the Scientific Evaluation of Dietary Reference Intakes, Food and Nutrition Board, Institute of Medicine,* Dietary Reference Intakes: Water, Potassium, Sodium, Chloride, and Sulfate *(Washington, D.C.: National Academies Press, 2004): 4-31–4-48.*

in various environmental conditions, so a specific water recommendation is hard to pin down.

Water from Fluids and Foods A wide range of fluid intakes can maintain adequate hydration. As a general guideline, however, the DRI committee recommends that, given a normal diet and moderate environment, the reference man needs about 13 cups of fluid from beverages including drinking water, and the reference woman needs about 9 cups.[6] This amount of fluid provides about 80 percent of the body's daily water need. On average, most people in the United States consume close to these amounts.[7]

Most of the rest of the body's daily water comes from the water in foods. Nearly all foods contain some water: water constitutes up to 95 percent of the volume of most fruits and vegetables and at least 50 percent of many meats and cheeses (see the margin on the next page and Appendix A). A small percentage of the day's fluid is generated in the tissues themselves as energy-yielding nutrients release **metabolic water** as a product of chemical breakdown.

The Effect of Sweating on Fluid Needs Sweating increases water needs. Especially when performing physical work outdoors in hot weather, people can lose 2 to 4 gallons of fluid in a day. An athlete training in the heat can sweat out more than a half-gallon of fluid each hour. The importance of maintaining hydration for athletes exercising in the heat cannot be overemphasized, and Chapter 10 provides detailed instructions on exactly how to hydrate the exercising body.

Which Fluids to Choose? Which beverages are best? Any beverage can readily meet the body's fluid needs, but those with few or no calories do so without contributing to weight gain. Beverages contribute more than 20 percent of the total energy intake in the United States, so for controlling body weight, water may be the superior choice.[8] Other choices include tea, coffee, nonfat and low-fat milk and soy milk, artificially sweetened beverages, and fruit and vegetable juices. By far, carbonated soft drinks are chosen most often (see Figure 8-3) but this choice often crowds

TABLE 8-2 Factors That Increase Fluid Needs

These conditions increase a person's need for fluids:

- Alcohol consumption
- Cold weather
- Dietary fiber
- Diseases that disturb water balance, such as diabetes and kidney diseases
- Forced-air environments, such as airplanes and sealed buildings
- Heated environments
- High altitude
- Hot weather, high humidity
- Increased protein, salt, or sugar intakes
- Ketosis
- Medications (diuretics)
- Physical activity
- Pregnancy and breastfeeding (see Chapter 13)
- Prolonged diarrhea, vomiting, or fever
- Surgery, blood loss, or burns
- Very young or old age

metabolic water water generated in the tissues during the chemical breakdown of the energy-yielding nutrients in foods.

FIGURE 8-3 U.S. Fluid Sources

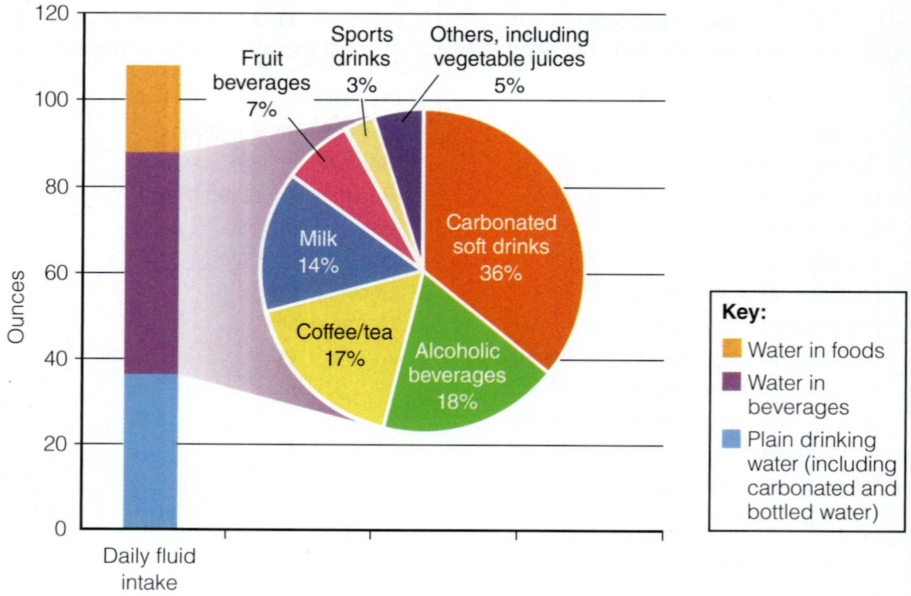

Source: Data from A. K. Kant, B. I. Graubard, and E. A. Atchison, Intakes of plain water, moisture in foods and beverages, and total water in the adult US population—nutritional, meal pattern, and body weight correlates: National Health and Nutrition Examination Surveys 1999–2006, American Journal of Clinical Nutrition *90 (2009): 655-663; American Beverage Association, What America Drinks, available at www.ameribev.org.*

- Water content of various foods and beverages:
  - *100% = water, diet soft drinks, seltzer (unflavored), plain tea.*
  - *95–99% = sugar-free gelatin dessert, clear broth, Chinese cabbage, celery, cucumber, lettuce, summer squash, black coffee.*
  - *90–94% = Gatorade, grapefruit, fresh strawberries, broccoli, tomato.*
  - *80–89% = sugar-sweetened soft drinks, milk, yogurt, egg white, fruit juices, low-fat cottage cheese, cooked oatmeal, fresh apple, carrot.*
  - *60–79% = low-calorie mayonnaise, instant pudding, banana, shrimp, lean steak, pork chop, baked potato, cooked rice.*
  - *40–59% = diet margarine, sausage, chicken, macaroni and cheese.*
  - *20–39% = bread, cake, cheddar cheese, bagel.*
  - *10–19% = butter, margarine, regular mayonnaise.*
  - *5–9% = peanut butter, popcorn.*
  - *1–4% = ready-to-eat cereals, pretzels.*
  - *0% = cooking oils, meat fats, shortening, white sugar.*

more nutritious beverages out of the diet, and the regular sugar-sweetened varieties provide a great deal of added sugar to the day's discretionary calorie intake.[9]

A word about caffeine: People who drink caffeinated beverages lose a little more fluid than when they drink water because caffeine acts as a **diuretic.** The DRI Committee considered such findings in their recommendations for water intake and concluded: "Caffeinated beverages contribute to the daily total water intake similar to that contributed by non-caffeinated beverages."[10] In other words, the mild diuretic effect of moderate caffeine intake doesn't seem to prevent people from meeting their fluid needs. The Controversy section of Chapter 14 comes back to the effects of caffeine.

KEY POINT Many factors influence a person's need for water. The water of beverages and foods meets nearly all of the need for water, and a little more is supplied by the water formed during cellular breakdown of energy nutrients.

CONCEPT LINK 8-2

Discretionary calories were a topic of Chapter 2; the health effects of added sugars were discussed in Controversy 4, page 145.

Are Some Kinds of Water Better for My Health Than Others?

Water occurs as **hard water** or **soft water,** a distinction that affects your health with regard to three minerals. Hard water has high concentrations of calcium and magnesium. Soft water's principal mineral is sodium. In practical terms, soft water makes more bubbles with less soap; hard water leaves a ring on the tub, a jumble of rocklike crystals in the teakettle, and a gray residue in the wash.

Soft water may seem more desirable, and some homeowners purchase water softeners that remove magnesium and calcium and replace them with sodium. The sodium of soft water, even when it bubbles naturally from the ground, may aggravate hypertension, however. Soft water also more easily dissolves certain contaminant metals, such as cadmium and lead, from pipes. Cadmium can harm the body, affecting enzymes by displacing zinc from its normal sites of action. Lead, another

diuretic (dye-you-RET-ic) a compound, usually a medication, causing increased urinary water excretion; a "water pill."

hard water water with high calcium and magnesium concentrations.

soft water water with a high sodium concentration.

toxic metal, is absorbed more readily from soft water than from hard water, possibly because the calcium in hard water protects against its absorption. Old plumbing may contain cadmium or lead, so people living in old buildings should run the cold water tap a minute to flush out harmful minerals before drawing water for the first use in the morning and whenever no water has been drawn for more than six hours.[11]

KEY POINT Hard water is high in calcium and magnesium. Soft water is high in sodium, and it dissolves cadmium and lead from pipes.

LO 8.3

Safety and Sources of Drinking Water

Remember that water is practically a universal solvent: it dissolves almost anything it encounters to some degree. Hundreds of contaminants—including disease-causing bacteria and viruses from human wastes, toxic pollutants from highway fuel runoff, spills and heavy metals from industry, organic chemicals such as pesticides from agriculture, and manure bacteria from farm animals—have been detected in public drinking water.

Safety of Public Water

Public water systems remove many hazards. They add disinfectant (usually chlorine) to kill most microorganisms and may expose the water to other treatments to purify it. Private well water is usually not chlorinated, so the 40 million Americans who drink water from private wells should have them tested regularly for harmful microorganisms.

Testing and Reporting All public drinking water must be tested regularly for contamination. The Environmental Protection Agency (EPA) ensures that public water systems meet minimum standards for health. Public utility customers receive a yearly statement, written in plain language, listing the chemicals and bacteria found in local water. This document makes fascinating reading for those interested in the purity of their tap water.

Chlorination and Cancer By-products of water chlorination have been found to cause cancer-related changes in human cells and cancer in laboratory animals.[12] Investigators acknowledge the possibility of a connection between chlorinated drinking water and cancer incidence.[13] Even so, they also passionately defend chlorination as a benefit to public health. In areas of the world without chlorination, an estimated 25,000 people die each day from diseases caused by organisms carried by water and easily killed by chlorine. Substitutes for chlorine exist but they are too expensive or too slow to be practical for treating a city's water, and some may create by-products of their own.[14]

Water Sources

Meanwhile, what is a consumer to drink? The first option is to drink tap water because municipal water is held to minimum standards for purity, as described. It comes from any of several sources.

Surface Water **Surface water** flowing from lakes, rivers, and reservoirs fills about half of the nation's need for drinking water, mostly in major cities. Surface water is exposed to contamination by acid rain, petroleum products, pesticides, fertilizer, human and animal wastes, and industrial wastes that run directly from pavements, septic tanks, farmlands, and industrial areas into streams that feed surface

Did You Know?

Lead is exceptionally harmful to children (details in Chapter 14).

© A. Kozyreva, 2011/Shutterstock.com

surface water water that comes from lakes, rivers, and reservoirs.

water bodies. Surface water generally moves faster than groundwater and stays above ground where aeration and exposure to sunlight can cleanse it. The plants and microorganisms that live in surface water also filter it. These processes can remove some contaminants, but others stay in the water.

Groundwater **Groundwater** comes from protected **aquifers,** deep underground rock formations saturated with water. People in rural areas rely mostly on groundwater pumped from private wells, and some cities tap this resource, too. Groundwater can become contaminated from hazardous waste sites, dumps, oil and gas pipelines, and landfills, as well as downward seepage from surface water bodies. Groundwater moves slowly and is not aerated or exposed to sunlight, so contaminants break down more slowly than in surface water. To mingle with water in the aquifer, surface water must first "percolate," or seep, through soil, sand, or rock, which filters out some contaminants.

Did You Know?

If electric service fails in your community, the water supply may become contaminated; use bottled water during emergencies. Alternatively, follow these directions:

- Boil the available water for 1 to 3 minutes.
- If you cannot boil it, add 8 drops of clean household bleach (regular strength) per gallon of water; stir it well, and let it sit for 30 minutes before using it.
- More information is available at the EPA website: www.epa.gov.

Home Water Purification A second option is to further purify tap water with home purifying equipment, which ranges in price from about $20 to $5,000. Some home systems do an adequate job of removing lead, chlorine, and other contaminants, but others only improve the water's taste. Many are not designed to remove microorganisms that are not affected by chlorine. Each system has advantages and drawbacks, and all require periodic maintenance or filter replacements that vary in price. Not all companies or representatives are legitimate—some perform water tests that yield dramatic-appearing but meaningless results to sell unneeded systems. Verify all claims of contamination by checking reports from local municipal water agencies or by independently testing well water before buying any purifying system.

Bottled Water A third option is to use **bottled water.** Many people turn to bottled water as an alternative to tap water. Read the Consumer Corner for more about bottled water. Whether water comes from the tap or is poured from a bottle, all water comes from the same sources—surface water and groundwater.

Given water's importance in the body, the world's supply of clean, wholesome water is a precious resource to be guarded. The remainder of this chapter addresses other important nutrients—the minerals.

KEY POINT Public drinking water is tested and treated for safety. All drinking water originates from surface water or groundwater, which are vulnerable to contamination from human activities.

LO 8.4

Body Fluids and Minerals

Most of the body's water weight is contained inside the cells, and some water bathes the outsides of the cells. The remainder fills the blood vessels. How do cells keep themselves from collapsing when water leaves them and from swelling up when too much water enters them?

Water Follows Salt

The cells cannot regulate the amount of water directly by pumping it in and out because water slips across membranes freely. The cells can, however, pump minerals across their membranes. The major minerals form **salts** that dissolve in the body fluids; the cells direct where the salts go, and this determines where the fluids flow because water follows salt.

When mineral (or other) salts dissolve in water, they separate into single, electrically charged particles known as **ions.** Unlike pure water, which conducts electricity poorly, ions dissolved in water carry electrical current; for this reason, these electrically charged ions are called **electrolytes.**

groundwater water that comes from underground aquifers.

aquifers underground rock formations containing water that can be drawn to the surface for use.

bottled water drinking water sold in bottles.

salts compounds composed of charged particles (ions). An example is potassium chloride (K^+Cl^-).

ions (EYE-ons) electrically charged particles, such as sodium (positively charged) or chloride (negatively charged).

electrolytes compounds that partly dissociate in water to form ions, such as the potassium ion (K^+) and the chloride ion (Cl^-).

CONSUMER CORNER Bottled Water

About 1 in 15 households uses bottled water as its main drinking water source, believing it to taste better and be safer than tap water and therefore worth its substantial cost—typically 250 to 10,000 times the price of tap water. As for taste, most water-bottling plants disinfect their products with ozone, which, unlike chlorine, leaves no flavor or odor in the water.

With regard to safety, when a consumer group tested bottled water, it disproved the notion of superiority: of 1,000 bottles and 103 brands tested, about a third were contaminated with bacteria, arsenic, or synthetic organic chemicals.*[1] In another analysis, lead exceeded accepted limits in about half of the bottles tested.[2]

BOTTLED WATER REGULATION AND SAFETY

Only bottled water that is sold across state lines is regulated by the Food and Drug Administration (FDA). This regulated water must pass yearly tests for purity and adherence to sanitation standards, but the standards are less rigorous than those applied to U.S. tap water. For example, bottled water need not be tested for the presence of asbestos contamination as tap water sources must be. Water sold within state lines escapes FDA oversight. In response to research findings, the FDA has strengthened its regulation of bottled water to include yearly tests for fecal bacteria, arsenic, uranium, disinfectants, and certain other contaminants. If contamination is found, it must be eliminated at its source before the water is bottled and sold.[3]

In addition to the water itself, some people question the safety of BPA, a chemical used to make refillable hard clear-plastic water bottles and baby bottles (but not thinner flexible disposable water bottles).† Such chemicals migrate into the bottle's contents and are consumed along with the water. Some manufacturers have stopped using BPA.

© Polara Studios, Inc.

The label on a water bottle may imply purity, but what counts is the purity of the product inside.

The FDA is currently studying U.S. BPA intake levels, but estimated previously that the highest intakes were 100 times lower than potentially harmful levels.[4]

CHOOSING AMONG BOTTLED WATERS

Gaining in popularity is water spiked with colors, flavors, sweeteners, caffeine, herbal extracts, vitamins, minerals, protein, or oxygen, often sold in swanky-looking bottles. These "fitness" waters are really just liquid supplements, and those with caffeine and herbs may present some risks (explained in Chapter 11 and the Controversy section of Chapter 14).

As a consumer who wants pure bottled water, what should you look for? Look for the trademark of the International Bottled Water Association (IBWA), a trade organization supporting the FDA's regulations and enforcement efforts. Next, look for the water's place of origin. Water bottled in another state might be the safest choice because only water sold across state lines must meet the FDA's sanitation and safety requirements.

Then try to determine the water's source. At least a quarter of bottled water is drawn directly from the tap and has met the stricter standards of public water supplies. If the water you buy is from a spring or a stream in your state, is the area agricultural, residential, industrial, or undeveloped? Agricultural, industrial, and residential activities can expose water sources to contamination. Finally, ask whether your state strictly enforces standards for purity and sanitation of bottled water—many states have unenforced rules on the books.

Table 8-3 defines some terms that appear on labels. What you are unlikely to find on the label is the water's mineral content. Some bottling companies will provide mineral information if a consumer requests it. For nutrition's sake, the best choice is water rich in calcium and magnesium but low in sodium. Most bottled waters lack needed minerals, however, unless they are identified as "mineral water" on the label.[5] As for fluoride, an important mineral for children's teeth and bones, bottled water is an unpredictable source.

SMALL BOTTLES, BIG BOTTLES

Consumers may be shifting away from individual water bottles as they learn more about them. Considerable fossil

© Rungroj Yongrit/epa/Corbis

Billions of expensive, empty water bottles end up in landfills around the nation.

Dougal Waters/Iconica/Getty Images

Using refillable bottles saves money and cuts waste.

*The group was the National Resources Defense Council. Read its report, Bottled Water: Pure Drink or Pure Hype?, available at www.nrdc.org/water/drinking/nbw.asp.
†BPA is bisphenol A.

TABLE 8-3 Water Terms That May Appear on Labels

- **artesian water** water drawn from a well that taps a confined aquifer in which the water is under pressure.
- **baby water** ordinary bottled water treated with ozone to make it safe but not sterile.
- **caffeine water** bottled water with caffeine added.
- **carbonated water** water that contains carbon dioxide gas, either naturally occurring or added, that causes bubbles to form in it; also called *bubbling* or *sparkling water*. Seltzer, soda, and tonic waters are legally soft drinks and are not regulated as water.
- **distilled water** water that has been vaporized and recondensed, leaving it free of dissolved minerals.
- **filtered water** water treated by filtration, usually through activated carbon filters that reduce the lead in tap water, or by reverse osmosis units that force pressurized water across a membrane, removing lead, arsenic, and some microorganisms from tap water.
- **fitness water** lightly flavored bottled water enhanced with vitamins, supposedly to enhance athletic performance.
- **mineral water** water from a spring or well that typically contains 250 to 500 parts per million (ppm) of minerals. Minerals give water a distinctive flavor. Many mineral waters are high in sodium.
- **natural water** water obtained from a spring or well that is certified to be safe and sanitary. The mineral content may not be changed, but the water may be treated in other ways such as with ozone or by filtration.
- **public water** water from a municipal or county water system that has been treated and disinfected.
- **purified water** water that has been treated by distillation or other physical or chemical processes that remove dissolved solids. Because purified water contains no minerals or contaminants, it is useful for medical and research purposes.
- **spring water** water originating from an underground spring or well. It may be bubbly (carbonated) or "flat" or "still," meaning not carbonated. Brand names such as "Spring Pure" do not necessarily mean that the water comes from a spring.
- **vitamin water** bottled water with a few vitamins added; does not replace vitamins from a balanced diet and may worsen overload in people receiving vitamins from enriched food, supplements, and other enriched products such as "energy" bars.
- **well water** water drawn from groundwater by tapping into an aquifer.

fuels and many gallons of water are required to create and transport plastic water bottles. Billions of empties now pose a serious disposal problem for communities and the environment.

Water delivered in large refillable bottles must be kept safe from bacteria to avert illness. If your water is dispensed from a water cooler, cleanse the cooler once a month by running half a gallon of white vinegar through it. Remove the vinegar residue by rinsing the cooler with 4 or 5 gallons of tap water. For individual bottles of water, be aware that bacteria from the mouth enter the water with the first sip from the bottle. Thereafter, keep the unfinished remainder of water in the refrigerator to minimize bacterial growth.[6]

CONCLUSION

In the end, the choice to drink water from any source instead of sugary soft drinks can help to meet fluid needs with fewer calories, a step in the right direction for many people. The choice of where to obtain that water—public water supplies, disposable bottles, or refillable bulk water bottles—is also important. It can affect the environment for better or worse long after your thirst is satisfied (see Chapter 15).

© Craig M. Moore

The slices of eggplant on the right were sprinkled with salt. Notice their beads of "sweat," formed as cellular water moves across each cell's membrane (water-permeable divider) toward the higher concentration of salt (dissolved particles) on the surface.

As Figure 8-4 shows, when dissolved particles, such as electrolytes, are present in unequal concentrations on either side of a water-permeable membrane, water flows toward the more concentrated side to equalize the concentrations. Cells and their surrounding fluids work in the same way. Think of a cell as a sack made of a water-permeable membrane. The sack is filled with watery fluid and suspended in a dilute solution of salts and other dissolved particles. Water flows freely between the fluids inside and outside the cell but generally moves from the more dilute solution toward the more concentrated one (the photo of salted eggplant slices shows this effect).

KEY POINT Cells regulate water movement by pumping minerals across their membranes. Water follows.

Fluid and Electrolyte Balance

To control the flow of water, the body must spend energy moving its electrolytes from one compartment to another (Figure 8-5). Transport proteins form the pumps that move mineral ions across cell membranes. The result is **fluid and electrolyte balance,** the proper amount and kind of fluid in every body compartment.

If the fluid balance is disturbed, severe illness can develop quickly because fluid can shift rapidly from one compartment to another. For example, in vomiting or diarrhea, the loss of water from the digestive tract pulls fluid from between the

FIGURE 8-4

ANIMATED!

How Electrolytes Govern Water Flow

Water flows in the direction of the more highly concentrated solution.

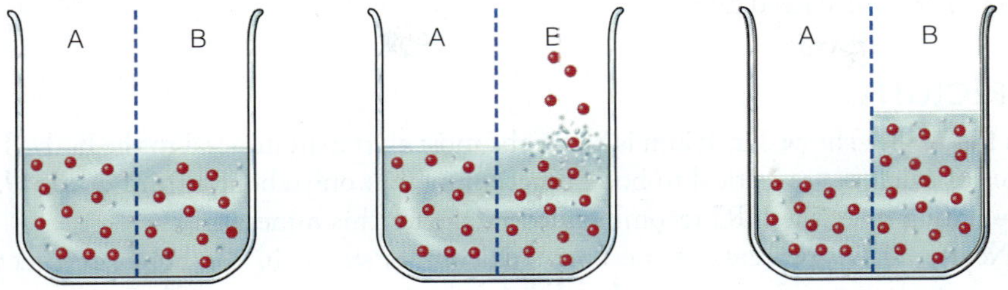

1. With equal numbers of dissolved particles on both sides of a water-permeable divider, water levels remain equal.
2. Now additional particles are added to increase the concentration on side B. Particles cannot flow across the divider. In the case of a cell, the divider (cell membrane) partitions fluids inside and outside the cell.
3. Water can flow both ways across the divider but tends to move from side A to side B, where the concentration of dissolved particles is greater. The *volume* of water increases on side B, and the particle *concentrations* on sides A and B become equal.

FIGURE 8-5

Electrolyte Balance

Transport proteins in cell membranes maintain the proper balance of sodium (mostly outside the cells) and potassium (mostly inside the cells).

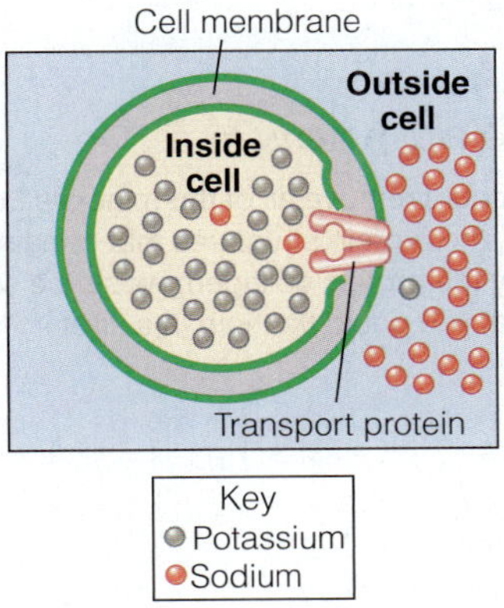

cells in every part of the body. Fluid then leaves the cell interiors to restore balance. Meanwhile, the kidneys detect the water loss and attempt to retrieve water from the pool destined for excretion. To do this, they raise the sodium concentration outside the cells, and this pulls still more water out of them. The result is **fluid and electrolyte imbalance,** a medical emergency. Water and minerals lost in vomiting or diarrhea ultimately come from all the body's cells. This loss disrupts the heartbeat and threatens life. It is a cause of death among those with eating disorders.

KEY POINT Mineral salts form electrolytes that help keep fluids in their proper compartments and buffer these fluids, permitting all life processes to take place.

CONCEPT LINK 8-3

Chapter 6 explained how transport proteins work, moving substances into and out of cells (page 202).

CONCEPT LINK 8-4

Figure 3-12 showed the pH of common substances (page 83); Figure 3-4 depicted fluid movement in and around cells (page 73).

Acid-Base Balance

The minerals help manage still another balancing act, the **acid-base balance,** or pH of the body's fluids. In pure water, a small percentage of water molecules (H_2O) exist as positive (H) and negative (OH) ions, but they exist in equilibrium—the positive charges exactly equal the negatives. When dissolved in watery body fluids, some of the major minerals give rise to acids (H, or hydrogen, ions), and others to bases (OH). Excess H ions in a solution make it an acid; they lower the pH. Excess OH ions in a solution make it a base; they raise the pH.

Maintenance of body fluids at a nearly constant pH is critical to life. Even slight changes in pH drastically change the structure and chemical functions of most biologically important molecules. The body's proteins and some of its mineral salts help prevent changes in the acid-base balance of its fluids by serving as **buffers**—molecules that gather up or release H ions as needed to maintain the correct pH. The kidneys help to control the pH balance by excreting more or less acid (H ions). The lungs also help by excreting more or less carbon dioxide. (Dissolved in the blood, carbon dioxide forms an acid, carbonic acid.) This tight control of the acid-base balance permits all other life processes to continue.

KEY POINT Minerals act as buffers to help maintain body fluids at the correct pH.

fluid and electrolyte balance maintenance of the proper amounts and kinds of fluids and minerals in each compartment of the body.

fluid and electrolyte imbalance failure to maintain the proper amounts and kinds of fluids and minerals in every body compartment; a medical emergency.

acid-base balance maintenance of the proper degree of acidity in each of the body's fluids.

buffers molecules that can help to keep the pH of a solution from changing by gathering or releasing H ions.

- Major minerals:
  - Calcium
  - Chloride
  - Magnesium
  - Phosphorus
  - Potassium
  - Sodium
  - Sulfate

The major minerals are also called *macro-minerals.* The need for each of these is greater than 100 milligrams per day, often far greater.

LO 8.5, 8.6

The Major Minerals

All the major minerals help to maintain the fluid balance, but each one also has some special duties of its own. Table 8-8 on pages 310–311 summarizes the roles of the minerals discussed below.

Calcium

As Figure 8-1 showed, calcium is by far the most abundant mineral in the body. The roles of calcium are critical to body functioning, but only about a third of the U.S. population meet the DRI recommended intake for this mineral.[15]

Nearly all (99 percent) of the body's calcium is stored in the bones and teeth, where it plays two important roles. First, it is an integral part of bone structure. Second, bone calcium serves as a bank that can release calcium to the body fluids if even the slightest drop in blood calcium concentration occurs. Many people think that once deposited in bone, calcium (together with the other minerals of bone) stays there forever—that once a bone is built, it is inert, like a rock. Not so. The minerals of bones are in constant flux, with formation and dissolution taking place every minute of the day and night (see Figure 8-6).

Did You Know?

If you could remove all of the minerals from bones, the protein structures that remained (mostly the protein collagen) would be so flexible that you could tie them in a knot.

Calcium in Bone and Tooth Formation Calcium and phosphorus are both essential to bone formation: calcium phosphate salts crystallize on a foundation material composed of the protein collagen. The resulting **hydroxyapatite** crystals invade the collagen and gradually lend more and more rigidity to a youngster's maturing bones until they are able to support the weight they will have to carry. During and after

FIGURE 8-6 **A Bone**

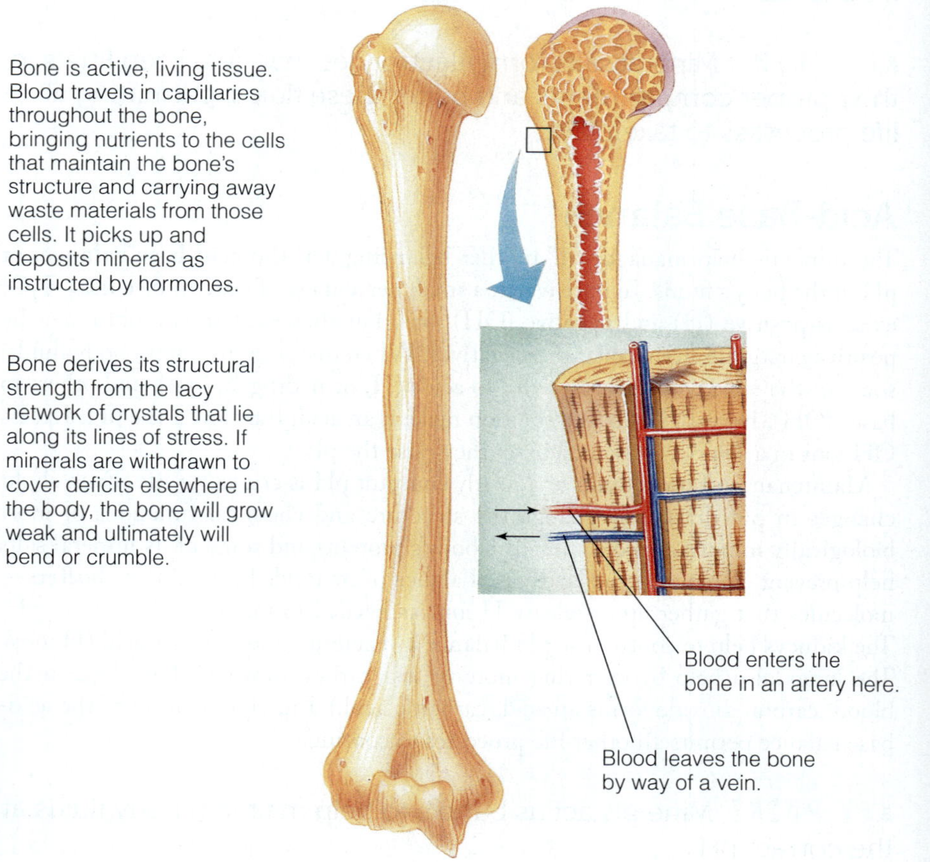

hydroxyapatite (hi-DROX-ee-APP-uh-tight) the chief crystal of bone, formed from calcium and phosphorus.

the bone-strengthening processes, fluoride may displace the "hydroxy" parts of these crystals, making **fluorapatite,** a compound that resists bone-dismantling forces.[16]

Teeth are formed in a similar way: hydroxyapatite crystals form on a collagen matrix to create the dentin that gives strength to the teeth (see Figure 8-7). The turnover of minerals in teeth is not as rapid as in bone, but some withdrawal and redepositing do take place throughout life. As a later section makes clear, fluoride hardens and stabilizes the crystals of teeth.

Calcium in Body Fluids The fluids that bathe and fill the cells contain 1 percent of the body's calcium, but this tiny amount is vital to life. It plays these major roles:

- regulates the transport of ions across cell membranes and is particularly important in nerve transmission.
- helps maintain normal blood pressure.[17]
- plays an essential role in the clotting of blood.
- is essential for muscle contraction and therefore for the heartbeat.
- allows secretion of hormones, digestive enzymes, and neurotransmitters.
- activates cellular enzymes that regulate many processes.

Because of its importance, blood calcium is tightly controlled.

Other roles for calcium are emerging as well. Calcium may protect against hypertension. Some research also suggests protective relationships between calcium and blood cholesterol, diabetes, and colon and rectal cancers.[18] Calcium from low-fat milk and milk products (but not from supplements) has been linked with having a healthy body weight in some, but not all, studies.[19] Large, well-designed clinical studies are needed to clarify any effects of dietary calcium on body weight.[20]

Calcium Balance The key to bone health lies in the body's calcium balance, a system of hormones and vitamin D.[21] Cells need continuous access to calcium, so the body maintains a constant calcium concentration in the blood. The skeleton serves as a bank from which the blood can borrow and return calcium as needed. Thus, a person whose calcium intake is inadequate maintains normal blood calcium but at the expense of **bone density.** The body is sensitive to an increased need for calcium but sends no signals to the conscious brain indicating calcium need. Instead, three organ systems quietly respond:

1. The intestines increase absorption of calcium from the intestine.
2. The bones release more calcium into the blood.
3. The kidneys prevent its loss in the urine.

Bone Loss Despite the body's adjustments, some bone loss is an inevitable consequence of aging. Sometime around age 30, or 10 years after adult height is achieved, the skeleton no longer adds significantly to bone density.[22] After about age 40, regardless of calcium intake bones begin to lose density but the loss can be slowed somewhat by a diet that provides adequate calcium along with regular physical activity.

A person whose calcium savings account is not sufficient is more likely to develop the fragile bones of **osteoporosis,** or **adult bone loss.** Osteoporosis constitutes a major health problem for many older people—its possible causes and prevention are the topics of this chapter's Controversy. To protect against bone loss, attention to calcium intakes during early life is crucial. A diet too low in calcium-rich foods during the growing years may prevent a person from achieving **peak bone mass** (Figure 8-8 illustrates the timing).[23] Supplements of calcium seem to be less successful than foods for building strong bones.[24] Vitamin D, vitamin A, other vitamins, magnesium, phosphorus, other minerals, and protein all play metabolic roles necessary for building the bones.[25]

Calcium Absorption On average, adults absorb about 30 percent of the calcium they ingest. The stomach's acidity helps to keep calcium soluble, and vitamin D

FIGURE 8-7 A Tooth

The inner layer of dentin is bonelike material that forms on a protein (collagen) matrix. The outer layer of enamel is harder than bone. Both dentin and enamel contain hydroxyapatite crystals (made of calcium and phosphorus). The crystals of enamel may become even harder when exposed to the trace mineral fluoride.

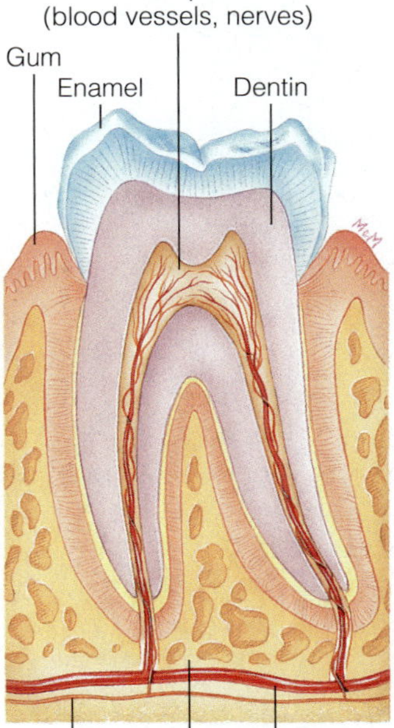

Functional Group

Key bone vitamins:

- *Vitamin A, vitamin D, vitamin K, vitamin C, other vitamins.*

Key bone minerals:

- *Calcium, phosphorus, magnesium, fluoride, other minerals.*

fluorapatite (floor-APP-uh-tight) a crystal of bones and teeth, formed when fluoride displaces the "hydroxy" portion of hydroxyapatite. Fluorapatite resists being dissolved back into body fluid.

bone density a measure of bone strength, the degree of mineralization of the bone matrix.

osteoporosis (OSS-tee-oh-pore-OH-sis) a reduction of the bone mass of older persons in which the bones become porous and fragile (osteo means "bones"; poros means "porous"); also known as **adult bone loss.** (Also defined in Chapter 6).

peak bone mass the highest attainable bone density for an individual; developed during the first three decades of life.

FIGURE 8-8

Bone Throughout Life

From birth to about age 20, the bones are actively growing. Between the ages of 12 and 30 years, the bones achieve their maximum mineral density for life—the peak bone mass. Beyond those years, bone resorption exceeds bone formation, and bones lose density.

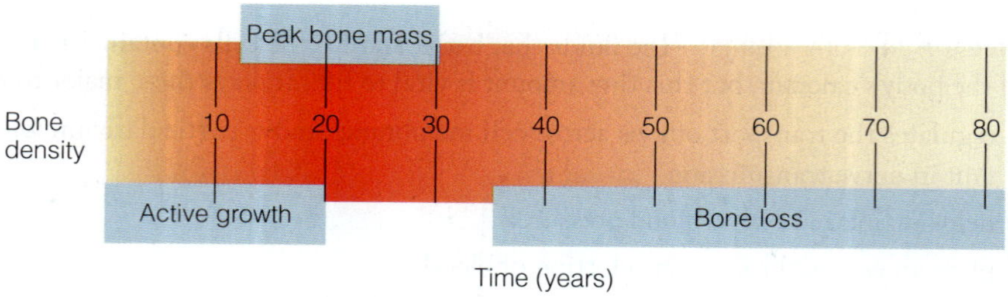

helps calcium absorption. When the body needs more calcium, proteins in the intestinal lining increase its absorption.[26] The result is obvious in the case of a pregnant woman, who absorbs 50 percent of the calcium from the milk she drinks. Similarly, growing children and teens absorb 50 to 60 percent of the calcium they consume.[27]

The body also absorbs a higher percentage of the available calcium when the routine daily diet provides less calcium.[28] Deprived of the mineral for months or years, an adult may double the calcium absorbed; conversely, when supplied for years with abundant calcium, the same person may absorb only about one-third the normal amount. Despite these adjustments, increased calcium absorption cannot fully compensate for a reduced intake. A person who cuts back on calcium is likely to lose calcium from the bones.

CONCEPT LINK 8-5

The importance of vitamin D in calcium absorption was described in Chapter 7, page 235.

Did You Know?

In osteoporosis, bones of older adults become brittle and fragile.

How Much Calcium Do I Need? Setting recommended intakes for calcium is difficult because absorption varies (the Food Feature comes back to calcium absorption). The DRI committee took such variations into account and set recommendations for calcium at levels that produce maximum calcium retention (see the inside front cover, page B). At lower intakes, the body does not store calcium to capacity; at greater intakes, the excess calcium is excreted and thus is wasted.

Snapshot 8-1 provides a look at some foods that are good or excellent sources of calcium, and the Food Feature at the end of the chapter focuses on foods that can help to meet calcium needs. Fiber and the binders phytate (in whole grains) and oxalate (in vegetables) interfere with calcium absorption, but their effects are only minor in a typical U.S. diet.

High intakes of calcium from supplements may have adverse effects, such as kidney stone formation, and supplements may not provide all of the beneficial effects of calcium-rich foods on the bones.[29] Because adverse effects are possible, an Upper Level has been established (see inside front cover, page C).

MY TURN

© Cengage Learning

Kathryn

© Cengage Learning

Cynthia

Drink Your Milk!

Listen to two students talk about how they learned about the importance of calcium.

CENGAGENOW To hear their stories, log on to www.cengage.com/sso.

SNAPSHOT 8-1

Calcium

DRI Recommended Intakes
Adults: 1,000 mg/day (19–50 yr)
1,200 mg/day (>51 yr)

Tolerable Upper Intake Level
Adults: 2,500 mg/day

Chief Functions
Mineralization of bones and teeth; muscle contraction and relaxation, nerve functioning, blood clotting

Deficiency
Stunted growth and weak bones in children; bone loss (osteoporosis) in adults

Toxicity
Constipation; interference with absorption of other minerals; increased risk of kidney stone formation

**These foods provide 10 percent or more of the calcium Daily Value in a serving. For a 2,000-calorie diet, the DV is 1,000 mg/day.*
[a]Broccoli, kale, and some other cooked green leafy vegetables are also important sources of bioavailable calcium. Almonds also supply calcium. Spinach and chard contain calcium in an unabsorbable form. Some calcium-rich mineral waters may also be good sources.

GOOD SOURCES*

KEY POINT Calcium makes up bone and tooth structure and plays roles in nerve transmission, muscle contraction, and blood clotting. Calcium absorption rises when there is a dietary deficiency or an increased need such as during growth.

Phosphorus

Phosphorus is the second most abundant mineral in the body, next to calcium. About 85 percent of the body's phosphorus is found combined with calcium in the crystals of the bones and teeth. The rest is everywhere else.

Roles in the Body All body cells rely on phosphorus for these functions:

- Phosphorous salts are critical buffers, helping to maintain the acid-base balance of cellular fluids.
- Phosphorus is part of the DNA and RNA of every cell and thus is essential for growth and renewal of tissues.
- Phosphorous compounds carry, store, and release energy in the metabolism of energy nutrients.
- Phosphorous compounds assist many enzymes and vitamins in extracting the energy from nutrients.
- Phosphorus forms part of the molecules of the phospholipids that are principal components of cell membranes (discussed in Chapter 5).
- Phosphorus is present in some proteins.

Recommendations and Food Sources Luckily, the body's need for phosphorus is easily met by almost any diet, deficiencies are unlikely, and most people in the United States meet their need.[30] As Snapshot 8-2 shows, animal protein is the best source of phosphorus (because phosphorus is abundant in the cells of animals). Milk

SNAPSHOT 8-2

Phosphorus

DRI Recommended Intake
Adults: 700 mg/day

Tolerable Upper Intake Level
Adults (19–70 yr): 4,000 mg/day

Chief Functions
Mineralization of bones and teeth; part of phospholipids, important in genetic material, energy metabolism, and buffering systems

Deficiency
Muscular weakness, bone pain[a]

Toxicity
Calcification of soft tissues, particularly the kidneys

**These foods provide 10 percent or more of the phosphorus Daily Value in a serving. For a 2,000-calorie diet, the DV is 1,000 mg/day.*
[a]Dietary deficiency rarely occurs, but some drugs can bind with phosphorus, making it unavailable.

GOOD SOURCES*

Did You Know?

The mineral is *phosphorus*. The adjective form is spelled with an *-ous* (as in *phosphorous salts*).

and cheese are also rich sources. Food additives, such as modified starches used in gravies, prepared meals, creamy desserts, and other processed foods and phosphates added to colas also contribute phosphorus to the diet.

KEY POINT Phosphorus is abundant in bones and teeth. Phosphorus helps maintain acid-base balance, is part of the genetic material in cells, assists in energy metabolism, and forms part of cell membranes. Under normal circumstances, deficiencies of phosphorus are unlikely.

Magnesium

Magnesium qualifies as a major mineral by virtue of its dietary requirement, but only about 1 ounce is present in the body of a 130-pound person, over half of it in the bones. Most of the rest is in the muscles, heart, liver, and other soft tissues, with only 1 percent in the body fluids. The supply of magnesium in the bones can be tapped to maintain a constant blood level whenever dietary intake falls too low. The kidneys can also act to conserve magnesium.

Roles in the Body Like phosphorus, magnesium is critical to many cell functions. Magnesium:

- assists in the operation of more than 300 enzymes.
- is needed for the release and use of energy from the energy-yielding nutrients.
- directly affects the metabolism of potassium, calcium, and vitamin D.
- is critical to normal heart functioning.

Magnesium and calcium work together for proper functioning of the muscles: calcium promotes contraction, and magnesium helps the muscles relax afterward. In the teeth, magnesium promotes resistance to tooth decay by holding calcium in tooth enamel.

Magnesium Deficiency A magnesium deficiency may occur as a result of inadequate intake, vomiting, diarrhea, alcoholism, or protein malnutrition. It may also occur in hospital clients who have been fed magnesium-poor fluids through a vein for too long or in people who are using diuretics. People whose drinking water provides adequate magnesium experience a lower incidence of sudden death from heart failure than other people, probably because magnesium deficiency makes the heart unable to stop spasms once they start. Magnesium solution given in a vein can often correct an abnormal heartbeat.[31] A deficiency also causes hallucinations that can be mistaken for mental illness or drunkenness. Although almost half the U.S. population has intakes below those recommended, deficiency symptoms are rare in healthy people.[32]

Magnesium Toxicity Magnesium toxicity is rare, but it can be fatal. Toxicity occurs only with high intakes from nonfood sources such as supplements or magnesium salts. Accidental poisonings may occur in children with access to medicine chests and in older people who abuse magnesium-containing laxatives, antacids, and other medications. The consequences can be severe diarrhea, acid-base imbalance, and dehydration. For safety, be mindful of the UL for magnesium when using magnesium-containing medications.

Recommendations and Food Sources Magnesium DRI recommendations vary slightly among adult age groups (see the inside front cover, page B).[33] Snapshot 8-3 shows magnesium-rich foods. Magnesium is easily washed and peeled away from foods during processing, so slightly processed or unprocessed foods are the best sources. In some parts of the country, water contributes significantly to magnesium intakes, so people living in those regions need less from food.

KEY POINT Most of the body's magnesium is in the bones and can be drawn out for all the cells to use in building protein and using energy. Many people in the United States choose diets that lack sufficient magnesium.

SNAPSHOT 8-3

Magnesium

DRI Recommended Intakes

Men (19–30 yr): 400 mg/day
Women (19–30 yr): 310 mg/day

Tolerable Upper Intake Level

Adults: 350 mg/day[a]

Chief Functions

Bone mineralization, protein synthesis, enzyme action, muscle contraction, nerve function, tooth maintenance, and immune function

Deficiency

Weakness, confusion; if extreme, convulsions, uncontrollable muscle contractions, hallucinations, and difficulty in swallowing; in children, growth failure

Toxicity

From nonfood sources only; diarrhea, pH imbalance, dehydration

GOOD SOURCES*

*These foods provide 10 percent or more of the magnesium Daily Value in a serving. For a 2,000-calorie diet, the DV is 400 mg/day.
[a]From nonfood sources, in addition to the magnesium provided by food.
[b]Wheat bran provides magnesium, but refined grain products are low in magnesium.
[c]Magnesium in oysters varies.

Did You Know?

To the chemist, a salt results from the reaction between a base and an acid. Sodium chloride, table salt, arises when the base sodium hydroxide reacts with hydrochloric acid.

Base + acid = salt + water.

Sodium hydroxide + hydrochloric acid = sodium chloride + water.

Sodium

Salt has been known and valued throughout recorded history. "You are the salt of the earth" means that you are valuable. If "you are not worth your salt," you are worthless. Even our word *salary* comes from the Latin word for *salt.* Chemically, sodium is the positive ion in the compound sodium chloride (table salt) and makes up 40 percent of its weight: a gram of salt contains 400 milligrams of sodium.

Roles of Sodium Sodium is a major part of the body's fluid and electrolyte balance system because it is the chief ion used to maintain the volume of fluid outside cells. Sodium also helps maintain acid-base balance and is essential to muscle contraction and nerve transmission. Scientists think that 30 to 40 percent of the body's sodium is stored on the surface of the bone crystals, where the body can easily draw on it to replenish the blood concentration.

Sodium Deficiency A deficiency of sodium would be harmful, but no known human diets lack sodium.[34] Most foods include more salt than is needed, and the body absorbs it freely. The kidneys filter the surplus out of the blood into the urine. They can also sensitively conserve sodium. In the rare event of a deficiency, they can return to the bloodstream the exact amount needed. Small sodium losses occur in sweat, but the amount of sodium excreted in a day equals the amount ingested that day. But, if sodium is so well controlled by the body, why do authorities urge people to limit their intakes? To understand why, you must first understand how sodium interacts with body fluids.

Did You Know?

Too little sodium can pose a danger to endurance athletes performing in hot, humid conditions (see Chapter 10).

How Are Salt and "Water Weight" Related? Blood sodium levels are well controlled.[35] If blood sodium begins to rise, as it will after a person eats salted foods, a series of events trigger thirst and ensure that the person will drink water until the sodium-to-water ratio is restored. Then the kidneys excrete the extra water along with the extra sodium.

Dieters sometimes think that eating too much salt or drinking too much water will make them gain weight, but they do not gain fat, of course. They gain water, but a healthy body excretes this excess water immediately. Excess salt is excreted as soon as enough water is drunk to carry the salt out of the body. From this perspective, then, the way to keep body salt (and "water weight") under control is to control salt intake and drink more, not less, water.

If blood sodium drops, body water is lost, and both water and sodium must be replenished to avert an emergency. Overly strict use of low-sodium diets in the treatment of hypertension, kidney disease, or heart disease can deplete the body of needed sodium; so can vomiting, diarrhea, or extremely heavy sweating.

FIGURE 8-9 **Sodium Intakes of U.S. Adults**

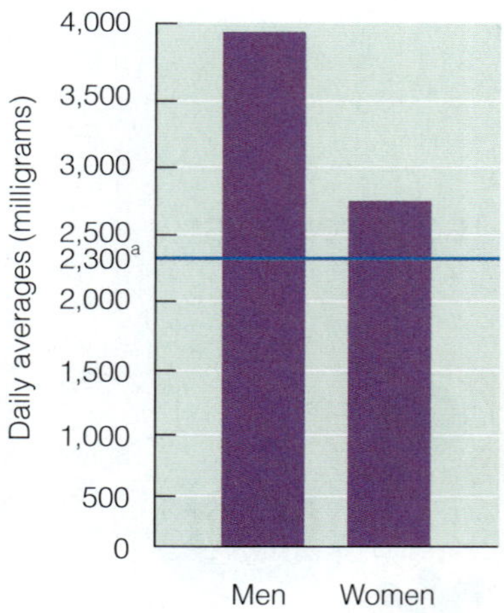

[a]*DRI Tolerable Upper Intake Level (UL).*

Sodium Recommendations and Intakes The DRI intake recommendation for sodium has been set at 1,500 milligrams for healthy, active young adults; at 1,300 for people ages 51 through 70; and at 1,200 for the elderly.[36] These amounts are sufficient to ensure an overall diet that provides adequate amounts of other needed nutrients.

Figure 8-9 shows that the average U.S. sodium intake tops 3,400 mg per day, an amount that far exceeds the DRI UL of 2,300 mg per day (equal to approximately 1 tsp of salt).[37] Three groups of people encompassing about 70 percent of U.S. adults—persons with hypertension, all middle-aged and older adults, and all African Americans—are urged to limit their sodium intakes for the sake of their blood pressure and heart health (see Table 8-4).[38]

- Chapter 11 presents more details about blood pressure and lists standard ranges for blood pressure readings.

Sodium and Blood Pressure High intakes of salt among the world's people correlates with high rates of **hypertension,** heart disease, and cerebral hemorrhage, a hypertension-related stroke.[39] An estimated 29 percent of U.S. adults have hypertension (that is, high blood pressure), and another 28 percent have **prehypertension.**[40]

In many people, the relationship between salt intake and blood pressure is immediate and direct—as sodium intakes increase, blood pressure rises with them in a stepwise fashion in just days or weeks of exposure.[41] And with high blood pressure, the heart becomes damaged and risk of death from stroke and heart disease climbs

hypertension high blood pressure; also defined in Chapter 11.

prehypertension blood pressure values that predict hypertension. See Chapter 11.

steeply.[42] In a large 15-year intervention study, when people with prehypertension reduced their sodium intakes, they reduced their risk of developing heart disease or dying from it by 25 to 30 percent.[43]

A different form of hypertension, so far observed in rats, baboons, and chimpanzees, occurs slowly over a lifetime of high sodium intakes. This progressive form of hypertension is particularly sinister because it proves irreversible when sodium is reduced.[44] If the same holds true for human beings, as population evidence suggests that it does, some people in apparent good health may be on the road to developing an irreversible form of hypertension, making it all the more urgent to cut sodium intakes early on before disease sets in. More human research is needed in this area.

Variations among people's blood pressure responses to sodium can be partly explained by their genetic inheritance.[45] The relationships are complex but researchers suspect that the genes that affect blood pressure do so by altering the kidneys' handling of sodium.

Can Diet Lower Blood Pressure? Luckily, most people can modify their salt response by consuming more potassium-rich foods, especially fruits and vegetables, in the context of a nutritious diet. One proven eating pattern can help people to reduce their sodium and increase potassium intakes, thereby reducing their disease risks.[46] This dietary approach can lower blood pressure in salt-sensitive and non–salt-sensitive people alike. The DASH (Dietary Approaches to Stop Hypertension) diet often achieves a lower blood pressure than restriction of sodium intake alone. It calls for greatly increased intakes of potassium-rich fruits and vegetables, with adequate amounts of nuts, fish, whole grains, and low-fat dairy products. At the same time, red meat, butter, and other high-fat foods and sweets are held to occasional small portions. The diet not only often lowers elevated blood pressure but may prevent it from occurring in the first place.[47]

Other Reasons to Cut Salt Intakes Many Americans have much to gain in terms of cardiovascular health and nothing to lose from cutting back on salt as part of an overall lifestyle strategy to reduce blood pressure. Physical activity should also be part of that lifestyle because regular moderate exercise reliably lowers blood pressure.

Other valid reasons exist for most people to hold their salt intakes at or below the recommended maximum. For example, older people without clinical hypertension often die of stroke, and reducing dietary sodium may lower their blood pressure enough to reduce their stroke risk. Excess salt in the diet also increases calcium excretion, an effect that could potentially compromise the integrity of the bones.[48] Excessive salt may also directly stress a weakened heart or aggravate kidney problems, and high salt intakes among many Asian peoples have been linked with their high rates of stomach cancer.[49]

Controlling Salt Intake Cutting down on salt and sodium may be easier than people believe, and Table 8-5 demonstrates how, with a few thoughtful food choices, a meal's sodium can be drastically reduced. Notice that in the meal in the left-hand column, sauces, dressings, and the salt added to corn, chips, pickles, and piecrust and sprinkled on foods are the major modifiable sources of sodium. Notice, too, that even without added sauces and salt, most foods contain enough sodium to easily meet most people's needs. Foods eaten without salt may seem less tasty at first, but with repetition, tastes adjust and the natural flavor becomes the preferred taste. Also, remember that the recommendation is to consume little sodium, not eliminate it altogether. Many experts today are calling for legislation to reduce the sodium in the food supply.[50]

While an obvious step is to control the saltshaker, this source may contribute as little as 15 percent of the total salt consumed. As Figure 8-10 indicates, a more productive step is to cut down on processed and fast foods, the source of almost 75 percent of salt in the U.S. diet. Often, the least processed foods in each food group are not only lowest in sodium but also highest in potassium. Low potassium may equal high sodium in its effects on blood pressure, so processed foods have two strikes against them.[51] The margin list on page 296 provides the FDA's guidelines for judging sodium in processed foods.[52]

TABLE 8-4 Sodium and Salt Intake Guidelines

DRI Recommendations

- Recommended intakes for sodium:
  - *Adults: (19–50 years): 1,500 mg per day.*
  - *Adults: (51–70 years): 1,300 mg per day.*
  - *Adults: (71 years and older): 1,200 mg per day.*
- Tolerable Upper Intake Level for sodium and salt:
  - *Adults (19 years and older): 2,300 mg sodium, or 5.6 g salt (sodium chloride) per day.*

The Centers for Disease Control and Prevention urge these groups of people to consume no more than 1,500 mg of sodium per day:

- People 40 years of age or older
- African Americans
- People with high blood pressure

• The DASH diet is presented in full in the Food Feature of Chapter 11.

Herbs add delicious flavors to foods without adding salt.

TABLE 8-5 How to Cut Sodium from a Barbecue Lunch

Lunch #1 exceeds the whole day's Tolerable Upper Intake Level of 2,300 milligrams sodium. With careful substitutions, the sodium drops dramatically in the second lunch, but it still provides over 40 percent of the suggested maximum intake. In lunch #3, just three small changes—omitting the sauce, coleslaw dressing, and salt—cut the sodium by half again.

Lunch #1: Highest	Sodium (mg)	Lunch #2: Lower	Sodium (mg)	Lunch #3: Lowest	Sodium (mg)
• Chopped pork sandwich, sauce and meat mixture	950	• Sliced pork sandwich, with 1 tbs sauce	400	• Sliced pork sandwich (no sauce)	210
• Creamed corn, ½ c	460	• Corn, 1 cob, soft margarine, salt	190	• Corn, 1 cob, soft margarine	50
• Potato chips, 2.5 oz	340	• Coleslaw, ½ c	180	• Green salad, oil and vinegar	10
• Dill pickle, ½ medium	420	• Watermelon, slice	10	• Watermelon, slice	10
• Milk, low-fat, 1 c	120	• Milk, low-fat, 1 c	120	• Milk, low-fat, 1 c	120
• Pecan pie, slice	480	• Ice cream, low-fat, ½ c	80	• Ice cream, low-fat, ½ cup	80
	Total 2,770		**Total 980**		**Total 480**

- Food labels help consumers evaluate sodium in foods:
  - *Low-sodium foods provide 5% or less of the Daily Value.*
  - *Moderate-sodium foods provide 6% to 20% of the Daily Value.*
  - *High-sodium foods provide above 20% of the Daily Value.*

In addition to salt, sodium-containing additives are listed among the ingredients: sodium benzoate, monosodium glutamate, sodium nitrite, or sodium ascorbate, to name a few.

Many people are unaware that foods high in sodium do not always taste salty. Who could guess by taste alone that half a cup of instant chocolate pudding provides almost one-fifth of the daily upper limit for sodium? Moral: Read the Nutrition Facts labels.

KEY POINT Sodium is the main positively charged ion outside the body's cells. Sodium attracts water. Sodium chloride is table salt. Too much dietary salt raises blood pressure and aggravates hypertension. Diets rarely lack sodium.

Potassium

Outside the body's cells, sodium is the principal positively charged ion. *Inside* the cells, potassium takes the role of the principal positively charged ion.

Roles in the Body Potassium plays a major role in maintaining fluid and electrolyte balance and cell integrity, and it is critical to maintaining the heartbeat. During nerve impulse transmission and muscle contraction, potassium and sodium briefly trade places across the cell membrane. The cell then quickly pumps them back into place. Controlling potassium distribution is a high priority for the body because it affects many aspects of homeostasis, including a steady heartbeat.

Low potassium intakes, especially when combined with high sodium intakes, raise blood pressure and increase the risk of death from heart disease.[53] Diets providing ample potassium, especially those also low in sodium, appear to both prevent and correct hypertension.

Potassium Deficiency In healthy people, almost any reasonable diet provides enough potassium to prevent the dangerously low blood potassium that indicates a severe deficiency. However, dehydration leads to a loss of potassium from inside cells. This condition is dangerous because when the cells of the brain lose potassium, the person loses the ability to notice the need for water. The sudden deaths that occur during fasting, with severe diarrhea, in children with kwashiorkor, or in people with eating disorders may be due to heart failure caused by potassium loss. Adults are warned not to take diuretics (water pills) that cause potassium loss or to give them to children, except under a physician's supervision. Physicians prescribing diuretics will tell clients to eat potassium-rich foods to compensate for the losses.

CONCEPT LINK 8-6

Kwashiorkor was described in Chapter 6 (page 211).

FIGURE 8-10 **Sources of Sodium in the U.S. Diet**

Unprocessed Foods

Those that are low in sodium contribute less than 10 percent of the total sodium in the U.S. diet.

Fresh foods higher in sodium
- *Milk,* 120 mg per 1 c
- *Scallops,* 260 mg per 3 oz

Fresh meats, about 30 to 70 mg per 3 oz
- *Chicken, beef, fish, lamb, pork*

Fresh vegetables, about 30 to 50 mg per 1/2 c
- *Celery, Chinese cabbage, sweet potatoes*

Fresh vegetables, about 10 to 20 mg per 1/2 c
- *Broccoli, brussels sprouts, carrots, corn, green beans, legumes, potatoes, salad greens*

Grains (cooked without salt), about 0 to 10 mg per 1/2 c
- *Barley, oatmeal, pasta, rice*

Salt

Salt added at home, in cooking or at the table, contributes 15 percent of the total sodium in the U.S. diet. Many seasonings and sauces also contribute salt and sodium.

Salts, about 2,000 mg per teaspoon
- *Salt, sea salt, seasoned salt, onion salt, garlic salt*[a]

Soy sauce, about 300 mg per teaspoon

Condiments and sauces, about 100 to 200 mg per tablespoon
- *Barbecue sauce, ketchup, mustard, salad dressings, sweet pickle relish, taco sauce, Worcestershire sauce*

[a]Note that herb seasoning blends may or may not contain substantial sodium; read the labels.

Processed Foods

These contribute 75 percent of the sodium in the U.S. diet.

© Matthew Farruggio (all)

Dry soup mixes (prepared), about 1,000 to 2,000 mg per 1 c
- *Bouillon cube, noodle soups, onion soup, ramen*

Smoked and cured meats, about 700 to 2,000 mg per 2 oz
- *Canned ham products, corned or chipped beef, ham, lunchmeats*

Fast foods and TV dinners, about 700 to 1,500 mg per serving
- *Breakfast biscuit (cheese, egg, and ham), cheeseburger, chicken wings (10 spicy wings), frozen TV dinners, pizza (2 slices), taco, vegetarian soy burger (on bun)*

Canned soups (prepared), about 700 to 1,500 mg per 1 c
- *Bean soup, beef or chicken soups, broths, "hearty" soups, tomato soup, vegetable soup*

Canned pasta, about 800 to 1,000 mg per serving
- *Beefaroni, macaroni and cheese, ravioli*

Hot dogs, about 500 to 700 mg per 2 oz
- *Hot dogs, smoked sausages*

Foods prepared in brine, about 300 to 800 mg per serving
- *Anchovies (2 fillets), dill pickles (1), olives (5), sauerkraut 1/2 c*

Cheeses, processed, about 550 mg per 1 1/2 oz
- *American, cheddar, Swiss*

Pudding, instant, about 420 mg per 1/2 c
- *All flavors*

Canned vegetables, about 200 to 450 mg per 1/2 c
- *Carrots, corn, green beans, legumes, peas, potatoes*

Cereals, dry ready-to-eat, about 180 to 260 mg per 1 oz
- *Cheerios, cornflakes, corn bran, Cocoa Puffs, Total, others*

Potassium Toxicity Potassium from foods is safe, but potassium injected into a vein can stop the heart. Potassium chloride pills are available over the counter and are sold in health-food stores without a warning label, but they should not be used except on a physician's advice. Potassium overdoses normally are not life-threatening as long as they are taken by mouth because the presence of excess potassium in the stomach triggers a vomiting reflex that expels the unwanted substance. A person with a weak heart, however, should not go through this trauma, and a baby may not be able to withstand it. Several infants have died when well-meaning parents overdosed them with potassium supplements.

Potassium Recommendations and Food Sources A typical U.S. diet, with its low intakes of fruits and vegetables, provides only about half of the daily 4,700 milligrams of potassium recommended by the DRI committee.[54] Although blood potassium may remain normal on such a diet, chronic diseases are more likely to occur. Low potassium intakes raise blood pressure, whereas high potassium intakes, especially when combined with low sodium intakes, appear to both prevent and correct hypertension.[55] In addition, low potassium intakes may worsen glucose intolerance, increase metabolic acidity, accelerate calcium losses from bones, and make kidney stone formation more likely.

Potassium is found inside all living cells and cells remain intact unless foods are processed; therefore, the richest sources of potassium are fresh, whole foods (see Snapshot 8-4). Most vegetables and fruits are outstanding. Bananas, despite their fame as the richest potassium source, are only one of many rich sources, which also include spinach, cantaloupe, and almonds. Nevertheless, bananas are readily available, are easy to chew, and have a sweet taste that almost everyone likes, so health-care professionals often recommend them.

The amount of fruits and vegetables recommended in both the USDA Food Guide and the DASH diet provide all the needed potassium. Potassium chloride, a salt substitute for people with hypertension who must strictly limit salt, provides potassium but does not reverse many of the conditions associated with diets that lack potassium-rich foods.[56]

Did You Know?

Unlike sodium, potassium may exert a positive effect against hypertension and related ills.

KEY POINT Potassium, the major positive ion inside cells, is important in many metabolic functions. Fresh, whole foods are the best sources of potassium. Diuretics can deplete the body's potassium and so can be dangerous; potassium excess can also be dangerous.

Chloride

In its elemental form, chlorine forms a deadly green gas. In the body, the chloride ion plays important roles as the major negative ion. In the fluids outside the cells, it

SNAPSHOT 8-4

Potassium

DRI Recommended Intake
Adults: 4,700 mg/day

Chief Functions
Maintains normal fluid and electrolyte balance; facilitates chemical reactions; supports cell integrity; assists in nerve functioning and muscle contractions

Deficiency[a]
Muscle weakness, paralysis, confusion

Toxicity
Muscle weakness; vomiting; for an infant given supplements, or when injected into a vein in an adult, potassium can stop the heart

*These foods provide 10 percent or more of the potassium Daily Value in a serving. For a 2,000-calorie diet, the DV is 3,500 mg/day.
[a]Deficiency accompanies dehydration.

GOOD SOURCES*

accompanies sodium and so helps to maintain the crucial fluid balances (acid-base and electrolyte balances). The chloride ion also plays a special role as part of hydrochloric acid, which maintains the strong acidity of the stomach necessary to digest protein. The principal food source of chloride is salt, both added and naturally occurring in foods, and no known diet lacks chloride.

KEY POINT Chloride is the body's major negative ion; it is responsible for stomach acidity and assists in maintaining proper body chemistry. No known diet lacks chloride.

- The DRI committee set recommended intake values for chloride; see the inside front cover, page B.

Sulfate

Sulfate is the oxidized form of sulfur as it exists in food and water. The body requires sulfate for synthesis of many important sulfur-containing compounds. Sulfur-containing amino acids play an important role in helping strands of protein assume their functional shapes. Skin, hair, and nails contain some of the body's more rigid proteins, which have high sulfur contents.

There is no recommended intake for sulfate, and deficiencies are unknown. Too much sulfate in drinking water, either naturally occurring or from contamination, causes diarrhea and may damage the colon. The summary table at the end of this chapter presents the main facts about sulfate and the other major minerals.

KEY POINT Sulfate is a necessary nutrient used to synthesize sulfur-containing body compounds.

LO 8.7, 8.8

The Trace Minerals

People require only miniscule amounts of the trace minerals but these quantities are vital for health and life. Intake recommendations have been established for nine trace minerals—see Table 8-6. Others are recognized as essential nutrients for some animals but have not been proved to be required for human beings.

Iodine

The body needs only traces of iodine, but this amount is indispensable to life. Once absorbed, the form of iodine that does the body's work is the ionic form, iodide.

TABLE 8-6 Trace Minerals

Human Intake Recommendations Established	Known Essential for Animals; Human Requirements Under Study	Known Essential for Some Animals; No Evidence That Intake by Humans Is Ever Limiting
Iodine	Arsenic	Cobalt
Iron	Boron	
Zinc	Nickel	
Selenium	Silicon	
Fluoride	Vanadium	
Chromium		
Copper		
Manganese		
Molybdenum		

Note: The evidence for requirements and essentiality is weak for the trace minerals cadmium, lead, lithium, and tin.

Iodide Roles Iodide is a part of the hormone thyroxine, made by the thyroid gland. Thyroxine regulates the body's metabolic rate, temperature, reproduction, growth, heart functioning, and more.[57] Iodine must be available for thyroxine to be synthesized.

Iodine Deficiency The ocean is the world's major source of iodine. In coastal areas, kelp, seafood, water, and even iodine-containing sea mist are dependable iodine sources. In many inland areas of the world, however, misery caused by iodine deficiency is all too common. In iodine deficiency, the cells of the thyroid gland enlarge in an attempt to trap as many particles of iodine as possible. Sometimes the gland enlarges making a visible lump in the neck, a **goiter.** People with iodine deficiency this severe become sluggish and may gain weight. Goiter afflicts about 200 million people the world over, many of them in South America, Asia, and Africa, almost all due to iodine deficiency.

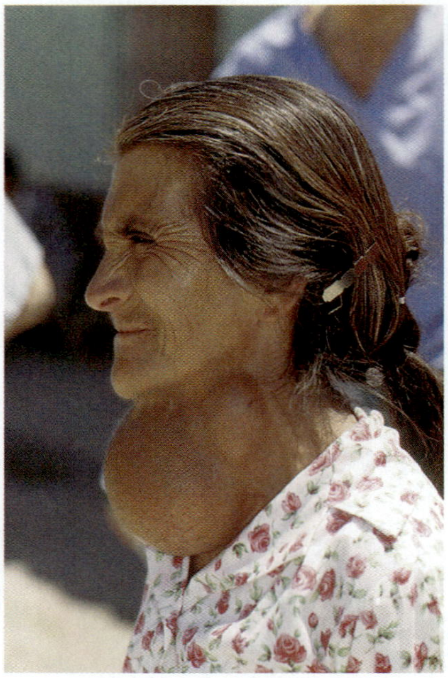
© Bob Daemmrich/The Image Works

In iodine deficiency, the thyroid gland enlarges—a condition known as simple goiter.

Iodine deficiency during pregnancy causes fetal death and reduced infant survival; extreme and irreversible mental and physical retardation in the infant, known as **cretinism;** and it constitutes one of the world's most common and preventable causes of mental retardation.† In iodine-poor areas of the world, families that fail to use iodized foods are often those who suffer child malnutrition and mortality.[58] Much of the mental retardation can be averted if the woman's deficiency is detected and treated within the first six months of pregnancy, but if treatment comes too late or not at all, the child may have an IQ as low as 20 (100 is average).[59] Children with even a mild iodine deficiency typically have goiters and may perform poorly in school; many times, treatment with iodine relieves the deficiency.[60]

Iodine Toxicity Excessive intakes of iodine can enlarge the thyroid gland just as a deficiency can.[61] Although U.S. intakes are above the recommended intake of 150 micrograms, they are still below the Tolerable Upper Intake Level of 1,100 micrograms per day for an adult.[62] Like chlorine and fluorine, iodine is a deadly poison in large amounts.

Food Sources of Iodine The iodine in food varies with the amount in the soil in which plants are grown or on which animals graze. Because iodine is plentiful in the ocean, seafood is a dependable source. In the central parts of the United States that were never beneath an ocean, the soil is poor in iodine. In those areas, once widespread iodine deficiencies have been wiped out by the use of iodized salt and the consumption of foods shipped in from iodine-rich areas. Surprisingly, sea salt delivers little iodine because iodine becomes a gas and flies off into the air during the salt-drying process. In the United States, salt labels state whether the salt is iodized; in Canada, all table salt is iodized. Less than a half-teaspoon of iodized salt meets the entire recommendation, but U.S. consumers rarely need extra iodine; most people exceed the DRI recommended intake but fall short of the UL.

- The iodine UL for adults is 1,100 mcg; the UL for pregnant women is 900 mcg; the UL for young children is 300 mcg.

Much of the iodine in U.S. diets comes from iodized salt added liberally to fast food and prepared foods and from bakery products and milk. Commercial bakeries often use iodine-rich dough conditioners, and most dairies feed iodized grain to dairy cows, which passes iodine into the milk.[63] When researchers in Massachusetts measured the iodine in bread, they were astonished to find from 10 micrograms (mcg) to 587 mcg *per slice.* Just two slices of the highest-iodine bread exceeds the iodine UL for both adults and pregnant women and presents almost 4 times the UL for children. In the same study, a single cup of milk contained nearly the entire adult DRI intake value for iodine; thus, people drinking the required three cups of milk from this source each day obtained 3 times their iodine requirement from milk alone. The meaning of these results goes beyond a few bakeries and dairies near Boston. Currently, U.S. consumers cannot gauge their iodine intakes against the DRI standards because food labels list neither iodine quantities nor specify ingredients that contain iodine in plain language.[64]

goiter (GOY-ter) enlargement of the thyroid gland due to iodine deficiency is *simple goiter;* enlargement due to an iodine excess is *toxic goiter.*

cretinism (CREE-tin-ism) severe mental and physical retardation of an infant caused by the mother's iodine deficiency during pregnancy.

†Collectively, the problems caused by iodine deficiency are sometimes referred to as *iodine deficiency disorder.*

KEY POINT Iodine is part of the hormone thyroxine, which influences energy metabolism. The deficiency diseases are goiter and cretinism. Iodine occurs naturally in seafood and in foods grown on land that was once covered by oceans; it is an additive in milk and bakery products. Large amounts are poisonous. Label information needs improvement.

Iron

Every living cell, whether plant or animal, contains iron. Most of the iron in the body is a component of two proteins: **hemoglobin** in red blood cells and **myoglobin** in muscle cells.

Roles of Iron Iron-containing hemoglobin in the red blood cells carries oxygen from the lungs to tissues throughout the body. Iron in myoglobin holds and stores oxygen in the muscles for their use.

All the body's cells need oxygen to combine with the carbon and hydrogen atoms released from energy nutrients during their metabolism. This generates carbon dioxide and water waste products that are then removed from the cells; thus, body tissues constantly need fresh oxygen to keep the cells cleansed and functioning. As cells use up their oxygen, iron (in hemoglobin) shuttles fresh oxygen into the tissues from the lungs. In addition to this major task, iron is part of dozens of enzymes, particularly those involved in energy metabolism. Iron is also needed to make new cells, amino acids, hormones, and neurotransmitters.

Iron Stores Iron is clearly the body's gold, a precious mineral to be hoarded. The liver packs iron sent from the bone marrow into new red blood cells, and ships them out to the bloodstream. Red blood cells live for about three to four months. When they die, the spleen and liver break them down, salvage their iron for recycling, and send it back to the bone marrow to be kept until it is reused. The body does lose iron from the digestive tract, in nail and hair trimmings, and in shed skin cells but only in tiny amounts.[65] Bleeding, however, can cause significant iron loss from the body.

Special measures are needed to contain iron in the body. Left free, iron is a powerful oxidant that generates free-radical reactions.[66] Free radicals increase oxidative stress and inflammation and damage cell structures in ways that may underlie diseases such as diabetes, heart disease, and cancer.[67] Consequently, the body guards against iron's renegade nature. Special proteins transport and store the body's iron, keeping it away from vulnerable body compounds and preventing damaging reactions. Iron's actions are thus tightly controlled.

Absorbing Iron The body also has special provisions for absorbing iron. Only about 10 to 15 percent of dietary iron is absorbed, but if the body's supply of iron is diminished or if the need increases (say, during pregnancy), absorption can increase several-fold.[68] The reverse is also true: absorption declines when iron is abundant.

Iron occurs in two forms in foods. Some is bound into **heme,** the iron-containing part of hemoglobin and myoglobin in meat, poultry, and fish. Some is **nonheme iron,** in plants and also in meats. The form affects absorption. Healthy people with adequate iron stores absorb heme iron at a rate of about 23 percent over a wide range of meat intakes. People absorb nonheme iron at rates of 2 to 20 percent, depending on dietary factors and iron stores.

Meat, fish, and poultry also contain a factor (**MFP factor**) that promotes the absorption of nonheme iron from other foods eaten at the same time.[69] Vitamin C also improves absorption of nonheme iron, tripling iron absorption from foods eaten in the same meal. The bit of vitamin C in dried fruit, strawberries, or watermelon helps absorb the nonheme iron in these foods. Overall, the body absorbs an average of about 18 percent of the iron in a mixed meal.

Some substances impair iron absorption. They include the **tannins** of tea and coffee, the calcium and phosphorus in milk, and the **phytates** that accompany fiber in lightly processed legumes and whole-grain cereals. Ordinary black tea excels

CONCEPT LINK 8-7
To read about the damage caused by free radicals and oxidation, see Chapter 7 (page 239).

CONCEPT LINK 8-8
Figure 6-4 in Chapter 6 (page 193) depicted the iron-containing heme molecule of hemoglobin.

- Forms of iron affect absorption:
  - *Heme iron is easily absorbed.*
  - *Nonheme iron is less easily absorbed.*

Benjamin F. Fink/Brand X Pictures/Getty Images

The chili dinner provides iron and MFP factor from meat, iron from legumes, and vitamin C from tomatoes. The combination of heme iron, nonheme iron, MFP factor, and vitamin C helps to achieve maximum iron absorption.

hemoglobin (HEEM-oh-globe-in) the oxygen-carrying protein of the blood; found in the red blood cells (*hemo* means "blood"; *globin* means "spherical protein").

myoglobin (MYE-oh-globe-in) the oxygen-holding protein of the muscles (*myo* means "muscle").

heme (HEEM) the iron-containing portion of the hemoglobin and myoglobin molecules.

nonheme iron dietary iron not associated with hemoglobin; the iron of plants and other sources.

MFP factor a factor present in meat, fish, and poultry that enhances the absorption of nonheme iron present in the same foods or in other foods eaten at the same time.

tannins compounds in tea (especially black tea) and coffee that bind iron. Tannins also denature proteins.

phytates (FYE-tates) compounds present in plant foods (particularly whole grains) that bind iron and may prevent its absorption.

- Dietary factors that increase iron absorption:
  - *Vitamin C.*
  - *MFP factor.*
- Factors that hinder iron absorption:
  - *Tea.*
  - *Coffee.*
  - *Calcium and phosphorus.*
  - *Phytates, tannins, and fiber.*

Courtesy of Ray Stanyard

The old-fashioned iron skillet adds supplemental iron to foods.

at reducing iron absorption—clinical dietitians advise people with iron overload to drink it with their meals. For those who need more iron, the opposite advice applies—drink tea between meals, not with food.

Thus, the amount of iron absorbed from a regular meal depends partly on the interaction between promoters and inhibitors. When you eat meat with legumes (for example, a ham sandwich and baked beans or chili with beans and meat), the iron from the meat is well absorbed and MFP factor enhances iron absorption from the beans. If the sandwich and chili also contain some tomato, the vitamin C will enhance iron absorption from the bread or beans. Cooking in an old-fashioned iron pan also adds iron salts, somewhat like the iron found in supplements. The iron content of 100 grams of spaghetti sauce simmered in a glass pan is 3 milligrams, but it increases to 87 milligrams when the sauce is cooked in a black iron pan. This iron salt is not as well absorbed as iron from meat, but some does get into the body, especially if the meal also contains MFP factor or vitamin C.

What Happens in Iron Deficiency? If absorption cannot compensate for losses or low dietary intakes, then iron stores are used up and iron deficiency sets in. **Iron deficiency** and **iron-deficiency anemia** are not one and the same, though they often occur together. Iron deficiency develops in stages, and the distinction between iron deficiency and its anemia is a matter of degree. People may be iron deficient, meaning that they have depleted iron stores, without being anemic; with worsening iron deficiency, they may become anemic.

A body severely deprived of iron becomes unable to make enough hemoglobin to fill new blood cells, and **anemia** results. A sample of iron-deficient blood examined under the microscope shows cells that are smaller and lighter red than normal (see Figure 8-11). These cells contain too little hemoglobin to deliver sufficient oxygen to the tissues. As iron deficiency limits the cells' oxygen and energy metabolism, the person develops fatigue, apathy, and a tendency to feel cold. The blood's lower concentration of its red pigment hemoglobin also explains the pale appearance of fair-skinned iron-deficient people and the paleness of the normally pink tongue and eye linings of those with darker skin.

Mental Symptoms of Iron Deficiency Long before the red blood cells are affected and anemia is diagnosed, a developing iron deficiency affects behavior.[70] Even slightly lowered iron levels cause fatigue, mental impairments, and impaired physical work capacity and productivity.[71] Symptoms associated with iron deficiency are easily mistaken for behavioral or motivational problems (see Table 8-7). With reduced energy, people work less, play less, and think or learn less eagerly. Lack of energy does not always indicate a need for iron, however—see the Think Fitness feature. Taking supplements for fatigue without a deficiency will not increase energy levels.

TABLE 8-7 The Mental Symptoms of Anemia

Apathy, listlessness
Behavior disturbances
Clumsiness
Hyperactivity
Irritability
Lack of appetite
Learning disorders (vocabulary, perception)
Low scores on latency and associative reactions
Lowered IQ
Reduced physical work capacity
Repetitive hand and foot movements
Shortened attention span

Note: These symptoms are not caused by anemia itself but by iron deficiency in the brain. Children with much more severe anemias from other causes, such as sickle-cell anemia and thalassemia, show no reduction in IQ when compared with children without anemia.

FIGURE 8-11 Normal and Anemic Blood Cells

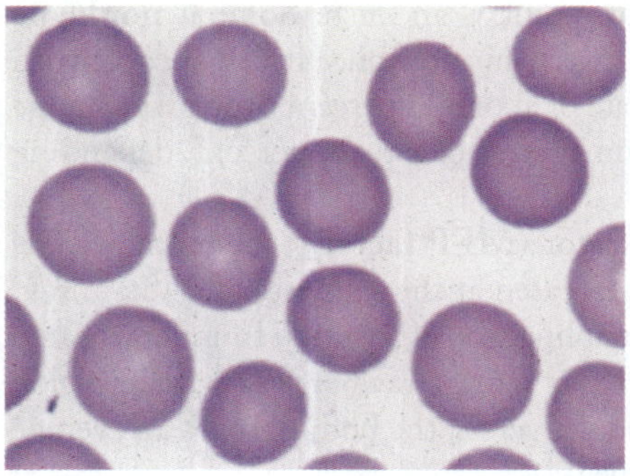
© Steven Vidler/Eurasia Press/Corbis

Normal red blood cells. Both size and color are normal.

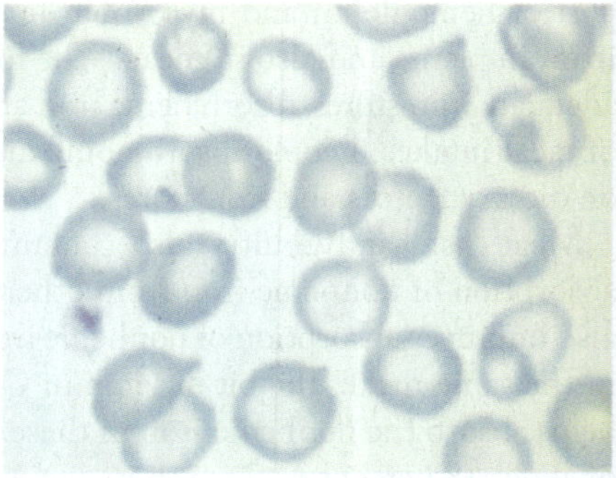
© Steven Vidler/Eurasia Press/Corbis

Blood cells in iron-deficiency anemia. These cells are small and pale because they contain less hemoglobin.

THINK FITNESS

Exercise-Deficiency Fatigue

On hearing about symptoms of iron deficiency, tired people may jump to the conclusion that they need to take iron supplements to restore their pep. More likely, they can obtain help by simply getting to bed on time and getting enough exercise. Few realize that too little exercise over weeks and months is as exhausting as too much—the less you do, the less you're able to do, and the more fatigued you feel. The condition even has a name: "sedentary inertia."

START NOW CENGAGENOW Ready to make a change? Consult the online behavior-change planner to set goals to obtain sufficient physical activity to energize your days at **www.cengage.com/sso.**

Children deprived of iron become restless, irritable, unwilling to work or play, and unable to pay attention, and they may fall behind their peers academically. Some symptoms in children, such as irritability, disappear when iron intake improves. Others, such as academic failure, may linger after iron repletion, although more studies are needed to clarify this association.[72] In iron-deficient adults, mental symptoms clear up reliably when iron is restored.[73]

A poorly understood behavior seen among some iron-deficient people, particularly low-income women and children, is **pica**—the craving and consumption of ice, chalk, starch, clay, soil, and other nonfood substances. These substances cannot remedy a deficiency; in fact, ingested clay inhibits iron absorption, and may cause or worsen iron deficiency. Researchers hypothesize that pica may result from hunger, nutrient deficiencies, or attempts at self-treatment of medical conditions.[74]

Causes of Iron Deficiency and Anemia Iron deficiency is usually caused by inadequate iron intake, either from sheer lack of food or from a steady diet of iron-poor foods. In developed nations, high-calorie foods that are rich in refined carbohydrates and fats and poor in nutrients often displace nutritious iron-rich foods from the diet. This may explain why obesity and iron deficiency often occur together in the United States—a steady diet of such foods presents too many calories with too few nutrients.[75] In contrast, Snapshot 8-5 shows some foods that are good or excellent sources of iron.

The number-one nonnutritional factor that can cause anemia is blood loss. Because the majority of the body's iron is in the blood, losing blood means losing iron. Menstrual losses increase women's iron needs to more than double that of men. Digestive tract problems such as ulcers and inflammation can also cause blood loss severe enough to cause anemia.

Who Is Most Susceptible to Iron Deficiency? Women of childbearing age can easily develop iron deficiency because they not only need more iron but they also eat less food than men, on average. In addition to menstruation, pregnancy demands additional iron to support the added blood volume, growth of the fetus, and blood loss during childbirth. Infants and toddlers receive little iron from their high-milk diets, yet need extra iron to support their rapid growth. The rapid growth of adolescence, especially for males, and the menstrual losses of females also demand extra iron that a typical teen diet may not provide. An adequate iron intake is especially important during these stages of life.

In the United States, 2.4 million young children suffer from iron deficiency while almost a half-million are diagnosed with iron-deficiency anemia. Most often, the children are from urban, low-income, and Hispanic families, but children from all groups can develop these conditions.[76] As for women in childbearing years, the percentage of iron deficiency remains 3 times higher than the goal of *Healthy People Objectives for the Nation*. To combat iron deficiency, the Special Supplemental

- Feeling fatigued, weak, and apathetic does not necessarily mean that you need iron supplements. Three actions are called for:
  1. Get your diet in order.
  2. Get some exercise.
  3. If symptoms persist for more than a week or two, consult a physician for a diagnosis.

Did You Know?

Iron deficiency makes children more susceptible to lead poisoning.

iron deficiency the condition of having depleted iron stores, which, at the extreme, causes iron-deficiency anemia.

iron-deficiency anemia a form of anemia caused by a lack of iron and characterized by red blood cell shrinkage and color loss. Accompanying symptoms are weakness, apathy, headaches, pallor, intolerance to cold, and inability to pay attention. (For other anemias, see the index.)

anemia the condition of inadequate or impaired red blood cells; a reduced number or volume of red blood cells along with too little hemoglobin in the blood. The red blood cells may be immature and, therefore, too large or too small to function properly. Anemia can result from blood loss, excessive red blood cell destruction, defective red blood cell formation, and many nutrient deficiencies. Anemia is not a disease, but a symptom of another problem; its name literally means "too little blood."

pica (PIE-ka) a craving for nonfood substances. Also known as *geophagia* (gee-oh-FAY-gee-uh) when referring to clay eating and *pagophagia* (pag-oh-FAY-gee-uh) when referring to ice craving (*geo* means "earth"; *pago* means "frost"; *phagia* means "to eat").

SNAPSHOT 8-5

Iron

DRI Recommended Intakes
Men: 8 mg/day
Women (19–50 yr): 18 mg/day
Women (51+): 8 mg/day

Tolerable Upper Intake Level
Adults: 45 mg/day

Chief Functions
Carries oxygen as part of hemoglobin in blood or myoglobin in muscles; required for cellular energy metabolism

Deficiency
Anemia: weakness, fatigue, headaches; impaired mental and physical work performance; impaired immunity; pale skin, nailbeds, and mucous membranes; concave nails; chills; pica

Toxicity
GI distress; with chronic iron overload, infections, fatigue, joint pain, skin pigmentation, organ damage

These foods provide 10 percent or more of the iron Daily Value in a serving. For a 2,000-calorie diet, the DV is 18 mg/day.
Note: Dried figs contain 0.6 mg per ¼ cup; raisins contain 0.8 mg per ¼ cup.
[a]Some clams may contain less, but most types are iron-rich foods.
[b]Legumes contain phytates that reduce iron absorption.
[c]Enriched cereals vary widely in iron content.

GOOD SOURCES*

- These people are at higher risk for iron deficiency:
  - *Women in their reproductive years.*
  - *Pregnant women.*
  - *Infants and toddlers.*
  - *Teenagers.*

- Chapter 14 offers guidance for preventing iron deficiency in young children.

Feeding Program for Women, Infants, and Children (WIC) provides low-income families with credits redeemable for high-iron foods.

Worldwide, iron deficiency is the most common nutrient deficiency, affecting more than 1.6 billion people.[77] In developing countries, parasitic infections of the digestive tract cause people to lose blood daily. For their entire lives, they may feel fatigued and listless but never know why. Almost half of the preschool children and pregnant women in these countries suffer from iron-deficiency anemia.[78] Iron supplements can reverse iron-deficiency anemia from dietary causes in short order.[79] They may, however, create digestive upsets, oxidative damage in the digestive tracts of some people, and worse problems in others.

Can a Person Take in Too Much Iron? Iron is toxic in large amounts, largely due to increased oxidative stress in body tissues.[80] Once absorbed inside the body, iron is difficult to excrete. The healthy body defends against iron overload by controlling its entry: the intestinal cells trap some of the iron and hold it within their boundaries. When they are shed, these cells carry out of the intestinal tract the excess iron that they collected during their brief lives.

In healthy people, when iron stores fill up, less iron is absorbed, protecting them against **iron overload.** In people with a tendency to absorb too much iron, mostly Caucasian men, excess iron builds up in the tissues.[81] Early symptoms include fatigue, mental depression, or abdominal pain; untreated, the condition can cause liver failure, bone damage, diabetes, and heart failure.[82] Infections are also likely because bacteria thrive on iron-rich blood.[83] Alcohol abusers often suffer severe effects because the alcohol-damaged intestine can no longer defend against absorbing too much iron. Anyone with the condition must monitor and limit their iron intakes and avoid supplemental iron.

Iron-containing supplements can easily cause accidental poisonings in young children.[84] As few as five ordinary iron tablets have proved fatal in young children. Keep iron-containing supplements out of children's reach.

- Table 8-8 on pages 310–311 summarizes the effects of iron toxicity.

iron overload the state of having more iron in the body than it needs or can handle, usually arising from a hereditary defect. Also called *hemochromatosis.*

Iron Recommendations and Sources The usual diet in the United States provides about 6 to 7 milligrams of iron for every 1,000 calories. Men need 8 milligrams of iron each day, and so do women past age 51, so these people have little trouble meeting their iron needs. For women of childbearing age, the recommendation is higher—18 milligrams—to replace menstrual losses. During pregnancy, a woman needs even more—27 milligrams a day; pregnant women need a supplement. If a man has a low hemoglobin concentration, his health-care provider should examine him for a blood-loss site. Vegetarians, because vegetable sources of iron are poorly absorbed, should aim for 1.8 times the normal requirement (see the margin).

Iron fortification of foods helps some to fend off iron deficiency but it can be a problem for people who tend toward iron overload. A single ounce of fortified cereal for breakfast, an ordinary ham sandwich at lunch, and a cup of chili with meat for dinner present almost twice the iron a man needs in a day but only about 800 calories. Most men need about 3,000 calories, and more food means still more iron. The U.S. love affair with vitamin C supplements makes matters worse because vitamin C enhances iron absorption. For healthy people, however, fortified foods pose virtually no risk for iron toxicity.

Did You Know?

The iron Daily Value used on food labels, 18 milligrams, is more than double the DRI recommended intake for men.

- To calculate the amount of daily iron needed by vegetarians, multiply the DRI intake recommendation for the age and gender group (listed on the inside front cover, page B) by a factor of 1.8:

Vegetarian men:
8 mg × 1.8 = 14 mg/day.

Vegetarian women (19 to 50 yr):
18 mg × 1.8 = 32 mg/day.

KEY POINT Most iron in the body is contained in hemoglobin and myoglobin or occurs as part of enzymes in the energy-yielding pathways. Iron-deficiency anemia is a problem worldwide; too much iron is toxic. Iron is lost through menstruation and other bleeding; reduced absorption and the shedding of intestinal cells protect against overload. Meat and vitamin C enhance iron.

Zinc

Zinc occurs in a very small quantity in the human body, but it works with proteins in every organ, helping nearly 100 enzymes to:

- make parts of the cells' genetic material.
- protect cell structures against damage from oxidation.[85]
- make heme in hemoglobin.
- assist the pancreas with its digestive and insulin functions.
- help metabolize carbohydrate, protein, and fat.
- liberate vitamin A from storage in the liver.

Besides helping enzymes to function, several hundred zinc-containing proteins associate with DNA, where it is indispensible for synthesis of proteins and cell division critical to normal growth before and after birth.[86] Zinc is also needed to produce the active form of vitamin A in visual pigments. Even a mild zinc deficiency can impair immunity, taste perception, and night vision. Zinc also:

- affects behavior, learning, and mood.
- assists in proper immune functioning.[87]
- is essential to wound healing, sperm production, taste perception, normal metabolic rate, nerve and brain functioning, bone growth, normal development in children, and others.[88]

When zinc deficiency—even a slight deficiency—occurs, it packs a wallop to the body, impairing all these functions.

Problem: Too Little Zinc Zinc deficiency in human beings was first observed a half-century ago in children and adolescent boys in the Middle East who failed to grow and develop normally. Their native diets were typically low in animal protein and high in whole grains and beans; consequently, the diets were high in fiber and phytates, which bind zinc as well as iron. Furthermore, the bread was not **leavened;** in leavened bread, yeast breaks down phytates as the bread rises. Since that time, zinc deficiency has been identified as a substantial contributor to illness throughout the developing

leavened (LEV-end) literally, "lightened" by yeast cells, which digest some carbohydrate components of the dough and leave behind bubbles of gas that make the bread rise.

© H. Sanstead, University of Texas-Galveston

How old does the boy in the picture appear to be? He is 17 years old but is only 4 feet tall, the height of a 7-year-old in the United States. His reproductive organs are like those of a 6-year-old. The retardation is rightly ascribed to zinc deficiency because it is partially reversible when zinc is restored to the diet. The photo was taken in Egypt.

world and responsible for almost a half-million deaths each year.[89] Marginal zinc status also causes widespread problems in pregnancy, infancy, and early childhood.[90] Zinc deficiency alters digestive function profoundly and causes diarrhea, which worsens the malnutrition already present, not only of zinc but of all nutrients. It drastically impairs the immune response, making infections likely.[91] Infections of the intestinal tract then worsen the malnutrition and further increase susceptibility to infections—a classic cycle of malnutrition and disease. Zinc therapy often reduces diarrhea and death in malnourished children but often fails to restore normal weight and height.[92]

Although zinc deficiencies are not common in developed countries, they do occur among some groups, including pregnant women, young children, the elderly, and the poor. When pediatricians or other health workers note poor growth accompanied by poor appetite in children, they should think zinc.

Problem: Too Much Zinc Zinc is toxic in large quantities. High doses (over 50 milligrams) of zinc may cause vomiting, diarrhea, headaches, exhaustion, and other symptoms. A UL for adults was set at 40 milligrams—an amount based on degeneration of the heart muscle in animals.

High doses of zinc inhibit iron absorption from the digestive tract. A blood protein that carries iron from the digestive tract to tissues also carries some zinc. If this protein is burdened with excess zinc, little or no room is left for iron to be picked up from the intestine. The opposite is also true: too much iron also inhibits zinc absorption. Zinc and iron are often found together in foods but, unlike supplements, food sources never cause imbalances in the body. Zinc from cold-relief lozenges, nasal gels, and throat spray products may or may not relieve a cold, but they contribute zinc to the body and the FDA has reported permanent loss of the sense of smell in people who used nasal zinc products.[93]

Food Sources of Zinc Meats, shellfish, poultry, and milk and milk products are among the top providers of zinc in the U.S. diet (see Snapshot 8-6).[94] Among plant sources, some legumes and whole grains are rich in zinc, but the zinc is not as well absorbed as it is from meat.[95] Most people meet the recommended 11 milligrams

SNAPSHOT 8-6

Zinc

DRI Recommended Intakes
Men: 11 mg/day
Women: 8 mg/day

Tolerable Upper Intake Level
Adults: 40 mg/day

Chief Functions
Activates many enzymes; associated with hormones; synthesis of genetic material and proteins, transport of vitamin A, taste perception, wound healing, reproduction

Deficiency[a]
Growth retardation, delayed sexual maturation, impaired immune function, hair loss, eye and skin lesions, loss of appetite

Toxicity
Loss of appetite, impaired immunity, reduced copper and iron absorption, low HDL cholesterol (a risk factor for heart disease)

GOOD SOURCES*

These foods provide 10 percent or more of the zinc Daily Value in a serving. For a 2,000-calorie diet, the DV is 15 mg/day.
[a]*A rare inherited form of zinc malabsorption causes additional and more severe symptoms.*
[b]*Some oysters contain more or less than this amount, but all types are zinc-rich foods.*
[c]*Enriched cereals vary widely in zinc content.*

per day for men and 8 milligrams per day for women. Vegetarians are advised to eat varied diets that include zinc-enriched cereals or whole-grain breads well leavened with yeast, which helps make zinc available for absorption.[96]

KEY POINT Zinc assists enzymes in all cells. Deficiencies in children cause growth retardation with sexual immaturity. Zinc supplements can reach toxic doses, but zinc in foods is nontoxic. Foods from animals are the best sources.

© Barbro Bergfeldt, 2011/Shutterstock.com

Selenium

Selenium is a nutrient in the news. Hints of its relationships with chronic diseases, as described below, make fascinating reading.

Roles in the Body Selenium-containing enzymes are necessary for the proper functioning of the iodine-containing thyroid hormones that regulate metabolism.[97] Selenium has also attracted the attention of the world's scientists for its role in protecting vulnerable body chemicals against oxidative destruction.[98] Selenium is an essential constituent of a group of enzymes that, in concert with vitamin E, work to limit the formation of free radicals and oxidative harm to cells and tissues.[99]

Relationship with Chronic Diseases Evidence is mixed on whether selenium plays a role in common forms of heart disease.[100] Low blood selenium does seem to correlate with the development of cardiovascular diseases, but this evidence is insufficient to conclude that low selenium contributes to heart disease.[101] In fact, elevated blood selenium also correlates with high blood cholesterol and diabetes, two factors that raise the risk for heart disease.[102] As for cancer, men with adequate selenium in their bloodstreams contract prostate cancer less often than men whose blood measures are low.[103] Should all men, then, take selenium supplements to ward off prostate cancer? No. Research has yet to establish whether extra selenium may benefit or harm healthy, well-fed people.[104]

Deficiency Without an adequate supply of selenium, the body's ability to make the needed selenium-containing molecules is compromised. Severe deficiencies cause muscle disorders with weakness and pain in people and animals. A specific type of heart disease is brought on by selenium deficiency. This condition, identified in selenium-deficient regions of China, prompted researchers to place selenium among the essential nutrients.

More subtle deficiencies may also adversely affect body tissues. For example, a shortage of selenium in cells of the immune system may unleash harmful levels of free radicals, increasing inflammation and weakening immune defenses against infections.[105]

- Find the DRI intake recommendation for selenium on the inside front cover, page B.

Toxicity Toxicity is possible when people take selenium supplements over a long period. Selenium toxicity brings on symptoms such as hair loss, diarrhea, and nerve abnormalities. The Tolerable Upper Intake Level for selenium is set at 400 micrograms per day.

Sources Clearly, adequate selenium is important, but research does not support taking selenium supplements. If you eat a normal diet composed of mostly unprocessed foods, you need not worry about selenium. It is widely distributed in foods such as meats and shellfish and in vegetables, nuts, and grains grown on selenium-rich soil.[106] As few as two Brazil nuts a day can improve selenium status.[107] Soils in the United States and Canada vary in selenium, but foods from many regions mingle on supermarket shelves, ensuring that consumers are well supplied with selenium.

KEY POINT Selenium works with an enzyme system to protect body compounds from oxidation. A deficiency induces disease of muscles and other tissues. Deficiencies are rare in developed countries, but toxicities can occur from overuse of supplements. Selenium in foods varies by region.

Fluoride

Fluoride is not essential to life. It is beneficial in the diet, however, because of its ability to inhibit the development of dental caries in both children and adults.

Roles in the Body Only a trace of fluoride occurs in the human body, but the crystalline deposits in bones and teeth are larger and more perfectly formed because this fluoride replaces the hydroxy portion of hydroxyapatite, forming the more decay-resistant fluorapatite in developing teeth. Once teeth have erupted through the gums, fluoride helps prevent dental caries by promoting the remineralization of early lesions of the enamel that might otherwise progress to form caries. Fluoride also acts directly on the bacteria of plaque, suppressing their metabolism and reducing the amount of acid they produce.

Deficiency Where fluoride is lacking, dental decay is common, and fluoridation of water is recommended for public dental health. Based on evidence of its benefits, fluoridation has been endorsed by the National Institute of Dental Health, the American Dietetic Association, the American Medical Association, the National Cancer Institute, and the Centers for Disease Control and Prevention as beneficial and presenting virtually no risk.

Toxicity In communities where the water contains too much fluoride—2 to 8 milligrams per million—discoloration of the teeth, or **fluorosis,** may occur.[108] Fluorosis occurs only during tooth development, never after the teeth have formed—and it is irreversible. Widespread availability of fluoridated toothpaste and mouthwash, foods made with fluoridated water, and fluoride-containing supplements has led to an increase in the mildest form of fluorosis. In this condition, characteristic white spots form in the tooth enamel; a more severe form is shown in Figure 8-12.

To prevent fluorosis, people in areas with fluoridated water should limit other sources, such as fluoride-enriched formula for infants and fluoride supplements for infants or children, unless prescribed by a physician. Children younger than six years should use only a pea-sized squeeze of toothpaste and should be told not to swallow their toothpaste when brushing their teeth. The Tolerable Upper Intake Level for fluoride for all people older than eight years is 10 mg per day.

Sources of Fluoride Drinking water is the usual source of fluoride. Almost 70 percent of the U.S. population has access to water with an optimal fluoride concentration, which typically delivers about 1 milligram per person per day, or about 1 part per million.[109] Figure 8-13 shows the percentage of the population in each state with access to fluoridated water. Fluoride is rarely present in bottled waters unless it was added at the source, as in bottled municipal tap water.

KEY POINT Fluoride stabilizes bones and makes teeth resistant to decay. Excess fluoride discolors teeth; large doses are toxic.

Chromium

Chromium is an essential mineral that participates in carbohydrate and lipid metabolism. Chromium in foods is safe and essential to health. Industrial chromium is toxic, a known carcinogen that damages the DNA.[110]

Roles in the Body Chromium helps maintain glucose homeostasis by enhancing the activity of the hormone insulin. When chromium is lacking, a diabetes-like condition may develop with elevated blood glucose and impaired glucose tolerance, insulin response, and glucagon response. Some research findings suggest that chromium supplements improve glucose or insulin responses in diabetes, but these relationships are uncertain.[111]

Chromium Recommendations and Sources Chromium is present in a variety of foods. The best sources are unrefined foods, particularly liver, brewer's yeast, and whole grains. The more refined foods people eat, the less chromium they receive.

- Fluoride helps prevent caries in three ways:
  - *In developing teeth:*
    1. Forms decay-resistant crystals.
  - *In erupted teeth:*
    2. Promotes remineralization.
    3. Reduces acidity of plaque.

© Caroline Fleischer

To prevent fluorosis, young children should not swallow toothpaste.

FIGURE 8-12 Fluorosis

The brown mottled stains on these teeth indicate exposure to high concentrations of fluoride during development.

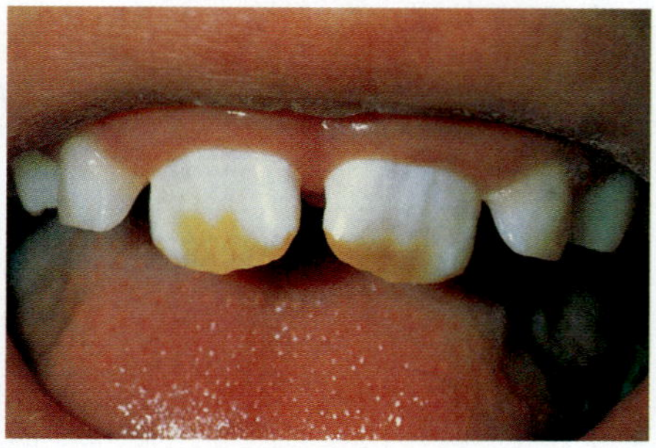

Dr. P. Marazzi/Science Photo Library/ Photo Researchers, Inc.

fluorosis (floor-OH-sis) discoloration of the teeth due to ingestion of too much fluoride during tooth development.

Chromium Supplements Supplement advertisements may convince consumers that they can lose fat and build muscle by taking chromium picolinate. Chromium supplements probably do not reduce body fat or improve muscle strength more than diet and exercise alone, however.

KEY POINT Chromium works with the hormone insulin to control blood glucose concentrations. Chromium is present in a variety of unrefined foods.

Copper

One of copper's most vital roles is helping to form hemoglobin and collagen. In addition, many enzymes depend on copper for its oxygen-handling ability. Copper plays roles in the body's handling of iron and, like iron, assists in reactions leading to the release of energy. One copper-dependent enzyme helps to control damage from free-radical activity in the tissues.‡ Researchers are investigating the possibility that a low-copper diet may contribute to heart disease by suppressing the activity of this enzyme.

Copper deficiency is rare but not unknown: it has been seen in severely malnourished infants fed a copper-poor milk formula. Deficiency can severely disturb growth and metabolism, and in adults, it can impair immunity and blood flow through the arteries. Excess zinc interferes with copper absorption and can cause deficiency.

Copper toxicity from foods is unlikely, but supplements can cause it. The Tolerable Upper Intake Level for adults is set at 10,000 micrograms (10 milligrams) per day. The best food sources of copper include organ meats, seafood, nuts, and seeds. Water may also supply copper, especially where copper plumbing pipes are used. In the United States, copper intakes are thought to be adequate.[112]

KEY POINT Copper is needed to form hemoglobin and collagen and assists in many other body processes. Copper deficiency is rare.

Other Trace Minerals and Some Candidates

DRI intake recommendations have been established for two other trace minerals, molybdenum and manganese. Molybdenum functions as part of several metal-containing enzymes, some of which are giant proteins. Manganese works with dozens of different enzymes that facilitate body processes and is widespread among whole grains, vegetables, fruits, legumes, and nuts.

Several other trace minerals are now recognized as important to health. Boron influences the activity of many enzymes and may play a key role in bone health, brain activities, and immune response.[113] The richest food sources of boron are noncitrus fruits, leafy vegetables, nuts, and legumes. Cobalt is the mineral in the vitamin B_{12} molecule; the alternative name for vitamin B_{12}, *cobalamin,* reflects cobalt's presence. Nickel is important for the health of many body tissues; deficiencies harm the liver and other organs. Silicon is known to be involved in bone calcification in animals. Future research may reveal key roles played by other trace minerals, including barium, cadmium, lead, lithium, mercury, silver, tin, and vanadium. Even arsenic, a known poison and carcinogen, may turn out to be essential in tiny quantities.

All trace minerals are toxic in excess, and Tolerable Upper Intake Levels exist for boron, nickel, and vanadium (see the inside front cover, page C). Overdoses are most likely to occur in people who take multiple nutrient supplements. The way to obtain the trace minerals is from food, which is not hard to do—just eat a variety of whole foods in the amounts recommended in Chapter 2.

Research on the trace minerals is uncovering many interactions among them: an excess of one may cause a deficiency of another. A slight manganese overload, for example, may aggravate an iron deficiency. A deficiency of one mineral may open

‡The enzyme is superoxide dismutase.

FIGURE 8-13 **U.S. Population with Access to Fluoridated Water Through Public Water Systems**

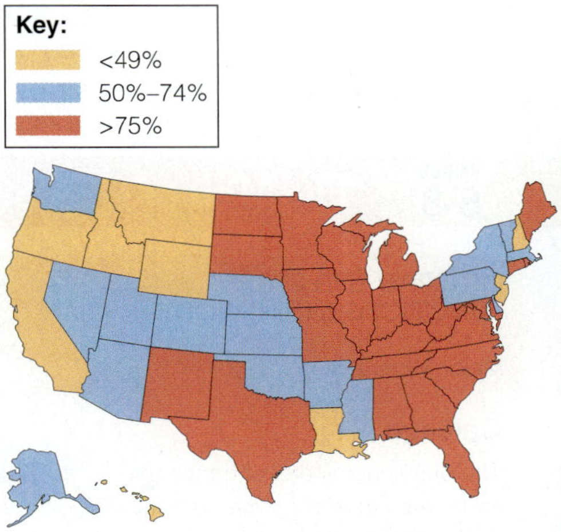

the way for another to cause a toxic reaction. Iron deficiency, for example, makes the body much more susceptible to lead poisoning. Good food sources of one are poor food sources of another, and factors that cooperate with some trace elements oppose others. The continuous outpouring of new information about the trace minerals is a sign that we have much more to learn, but the basics of diet planning remain valid. Table 8-8 sums up what this chapter has said about the minerals and fills in some additional information.

KEY POINT Many different trace elements play important roles in the body. All of the trace minerals are toxic in excess.

TABLE 8-8 The Minerals—A Summary

MINERAL AND CHIEF FUNCTIONS IN THE BODY Major Minerals	Deficiency Symptoms	Toxicity Symptoms	Significant Sources
Calcium The principal mineral of bones and teeth. Also acts in normal muscle contraction and relaxation, nerve functioning, regulation of cell activities, blood clotting, blood pressure, and immune defenses.	Stunted growth in children; adult bone loss (osteoporosis).	Constipation; urinary tract stone formation; kidney dysfunction; interference with absorption of other minerals.	Milk and milk products, oysters, small fish (with bones), calcium-set tofu (bean curd), certain leafy greens, broccoli, legumes.
Phosphorus Mineralization of bones and teeth; important in cells' genetic material, in cell membranes as phospholipids, in energy transfer, and in buffering systems.	Appetite loss, bone pain, muscle weakness, impaired growth, and rickets in infants.[a]	Calcification of nonskeletal tissues, particularly the kidney.	Foods from animal sources, some legumes.
Magnesium A factor involved in bone mineralization, the building of protein, enzyme action, normal muscular function, transmission of nerve impulses, proper immune function and maintenance of teeth.	Weakness; muscle twitches; appetite loss; confusion; if extreme, convulsions, bizarre movements (especially of eyes and face), hallucinations, and difficulty in swallowing. In children, growth failure.[b]	Excess magnesium from abuse of laxatives (Epsom salts) causes diarrhea with fluid and electrolyte and pH imbalances.	Nuts, legumes, whole grains, dark green vegetables, seafoods, chocolate, cocoa.
Sodium Sodium, chloride, and potassium (electrolytes) maintain normal fluid balance and acid-base balance in the body. Sodium is critical to nerve impulse transmission.	Muscle cramps, mental apathy, loss of appetite.	Hypertension.	Salt, soy sauce, seasoning mixes, processed foods, condiments, fast foods.
Potassium Potassium facilitates reactions, including the making of protein; the maintenance of fluid and electrolyte balance; the support of cell integrity; the transmission of nerve impulses; and the contraction of muscles, including the heart.	Deficiency accompanies dehydration; causes muscular weakness, paralysis, and confusion; can cause death.	Causes muscular weakness; triggers vomiting; if given into a vein, can stop the heart.	All whole foods: meats, milk, fruits, vegetables, grains, legumes.

[a] *Seen only rarely in infants fed phosphorus-free formula or in adults taking medications that interact with phosphorus.*

[b] *A still more severe deficiency causes tetany, an extreme, prolonged contraction of the muscles similar to that caused by low blood calcium.*

TABLE 8-8 **The Minerals—A Summary (continued)**

Major Minerals	Deficiency Symptoms	Toxicity Symptoms	Significant Sources
Chloride Chloride is part of the hydrochloric acid found in the stomach, necessary for proper digestion. Helps maintain normal fluid and electrolyte balance.	Growth failure in children; muscle cramps, mental apathy, loss of appetite; can cause death (uncommon).	Normally harmless (the gas chlorine is a poison but evaporates from water); can cause vomiting.	Salt, soy sauce; moderate quantities in whole, unprocessed foods, large amounts in processed foods.
Sulfate A contributor of sulfur to many important compounds, such as certain amino acids, antioxidants, and the vitamins biotin and thiamin; stabilizes protein shape by forming sulfur-sulfur bridges (see Figure 6-10 in Chapter 6, p. 201).	None known; protein deficiency would occur first.	Would occur only if sulfur amino acids were eaten in excess; this (in animals) depresses growth.	All protein-containing foods.
Iodine A component of the thyroid hormone thyroxine, which helps to regulate growth, development, and metabolic rate.	Goiter, cretinism.	Depressed thyroid activity; goiter-like thyroid enlargement.	Iodized salt, seafood, bread, plants grown in most parts of the country and animals fed those plants.
Iron Part of the protein hemoglobin, which carries oxygen in the blood; part of the protein myoglobin in muscles, which makes oxygen available for muscle contraction; necessary for the use of energy.	Anemia: weakness, fatigue, pale skin and mucous membranes, pale concave nails, headaches, inability to concentrate, impaired cognitive function (children), lowered cold tolerance.	Iron overload: fatigue, abdominal pain, infections, liver injury, joint pain, skin pigmentation, growth retardation in children, bloody stools, shock.	Red meats, fish, poultry, shellfish, eggs, legumes, green leafy vegetables, dried fruits.
Zinc Associated with hormones; needed for many enzymes; involved in making genetic material and proteins, immune cell activation, transport of vitamin A, taste perception, wound healing, the making of sperm, and normal fetal development.	Growth failure in children, dermatitis, sexual retardation, loss of taste, poor wound healing.	Nausea, vomiting, diarrhea, loss of appetite, headache, immune suppression, decreased HDL, reduced iron and copper status.	Protein-containing foods: meats, fish, shellfish, poultry, grains, yogurt.
Selenium Assists a group of enzymes that defend against oxidation.	Predisposition to a form of heart disease characterized by fibrous cardiac tissue (uncommon).	Nausea; abdominal pain; nail and hair changes; nerve, liver, and muscle damage.	Seafoods, organ meats, other meats, whole grains, and vegetables depending on soil content.
Fluoride Helps form bones and teeth; confers decay resistance on teeth.	Susceptibility to tooth decay.	Fluorosis (discoloration) of teeth, nausea, vomiting, diarrhea, chest pain, itching.	Drinking water if fluoride-containing or fluoridated, tea, seafood.
Chromium Associated with insulin; needed for energy release from glucose.	Abnormal glucose metabolism.	Possibly skin eruptions.	Meat, unrefined grains, vegetable oils.
Copper Helps form hemoglobin; part of several enzymes.	Anemia; bone abnormalities.	Vomiting, diarrhea; liver damage.	Organ meats, seafood, nuts, seeds, whole grains, drinking water.

FOOD FEATURE

Meeting the Need for Calcium

Many people act as though calcium nutrition is of little consequence to their health and neglect to meet their need.[114] Yet, a low calcium intake is associated with all sorts of major illnesses, including adult bone loss (see the Controversy that follows this chapter), high blood pressure and colon cancer (see Chapter 11), kidney stones, and even lead poisoning (Chapter 14).

Consumption of one of the best sources of calcium—milk—has declined in recent years while consumption of other beverages, such as sweet soft drinks and fruit drinks, has increased dramatically.[115] This Food Feature focuses on food and beverage sources of calcium and provides guidance about how to include them in the diet to meet the need for calcium.

MILK, YOGURT, AND CHEESE GROUP

Milk and milk products are traditional sources of calcium for people who can tolerate them (see Figure 8-14). Table 8-9 shows the current milk recommendations that help to meet the calcium needs of various age groups. People who shun milk products because of lactose intolerance, allergy, or other aversions can obtain calcium from other sources, but care is needed—*wise* substitutes must be chosen.[116] This is especially true for children. Children who don't drink milk often have lower calcium intakes and poorer bone health than those who drink milk regularly, and they may also be smaller in stature. Most of milk's many relatives are recommended choices: yogurt, **kefir,** buttermilk, cheese (especially the low-fat or fat-free varieties), and, for people who can afford the calories, ice milk. Cottage cheese and frozen yogurt desserts contain about half the calcium of milk; 2 cups are needed to provide the amount of calcium in 1 cup of milk. Butter, cream, and cream cheese are almost pure fat and contain negligible calcium.

Tinker with milk products to make them more appealing. Add cocoa to milk and fruit to yogurt, make your own fruit smoothies from milk or yogurt, or add fat-free milk powder to any dish. The cocoa powder added to make chocolate milk does contain a small amount of oxalic acid, which binds with some of milk's calcium and inhibits its absorption, but the effect is insignificant. Sugar lends both sweetness and calories to chocolate milk, so mix your chocolate milk at home where you control the amount of sugary chocolate added to the milk.

FIGURE 8-14 Food Sources of Calcium in the U.S. Diet

Milk and milk products contribute over half of the calcium in a typical U.S. diet.

[a]Other sources include foods contributing at least 1% in descending order: yogurt, ready-to-eat cereal, soft drinks, tortillas, eggs, dried beans and lentils, canned tomatoes, meal replacements and protein supplements, corn bread and corn muffins, hot breakfast cereal, and coffee.

Source: Data from P. A. Cotton and coauthors, Dietary sources of nutrients among US adults, 1994–1996, Journal of the American Dietetic Association 104 (2004): 921–930, supplemental Table 21 from www.eatright.org.

TABLE 8-9 Suggested Minimum Daily Fluid Milk Intakes

Young Children (2–8 years)	2 cups
Older children (9 years +)	3 cups
Adults	3 cups
Pregnant or lactating women	3 cups
Women past menopause	3 cups

Chocolate milk is an excellent source of calcium for those who can afford the extra calories.

VEGETABLES

Absorption of calcium varies among foods, and it affects the body's calcium economy (see Figure 8-15). Among vegetables, rutabaga, broccoli, beet greens, turnip greens, mustard greens, bok choy (a Chinese cabbage), and kale are good sources of available calcium. So are collard greens, green cabbage, kohlrabi, watercress, parsley, and probably some seaweeds, such as the **nori** popular in Japanese cookery. Certain other foods, including spinach, Swiss chard, and rhubarb, appear equal to milk in calcium content but provide very little or no calcium to the body because they contain binders that prevent calcium's absorption (see Figure 8-16). The presence of calcium binders does not make spinach an inferior food. Spinach is also rich in iron, beta-carotene, and dozens of other essential nutrients and potentially helpful phytochemicals. Just don't rely on it for calcium. Dark greens of all kinds are superb sources of riboflavin and indispensable for the vegan or anyone else who does not drink milk.

FIGURE 8-15
Calcium Economy

The lefthand box shows typical daily calcium losses. The right-hand box shows that calcium intakes must be higher when calcium is not well absorbed to offset losses.

Typical Daily Calcium Losses	
Urine, feces	180 mg
Skin, hair	60 mg
Sweat	30 mg
Menopause (women)	30 mg
Total loss	**300 mg**

Calcium Intake to Offset Losses

1,200 mg/day (at 25% absorption)

-or-

1,000 mg per day (at 30% absorption)

Source: Data from K. Rafferty and R. P. Heaney, Nutrient effects on the calcium economy: Emphasizing the potassium controversy, Journal of Nutrition *138 (2008): 166S–171S.*

FIGURE 8-16
Calcium Absorption from Food Sources

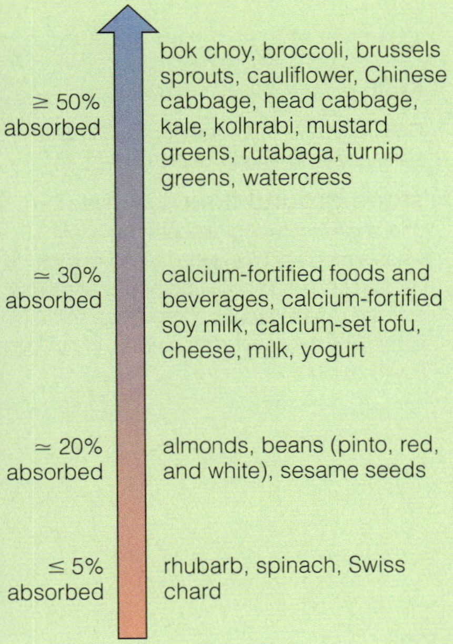

CALCIUM IN OTHER FOODS

For the many people who cannot use milk and milk products, small fish such as canned sardines and other canned fishes prepared with their bones are rich sources of calcium. One-third cup of almonds supplies about 100 milligrams of calcium along with almost 300 calories—a high-energy calcium source. Calcium-rich mineral water may also be a useful calcium source.[117] Recent evidence seems to indicate that the calcium from mineral water, including hard tap water, may be as absorbable as the calcium from milk. Many other foods contribute smaller, but still significant, amounts of calcium to the diet.

CALCIUM-FORTIFIED FOODS

Next in order of preference among nonmilk sources of calcium are foods that contain large amounts of calcium salts by an accident of processing or by intentional fortification. In the processed category are soybean curd, or tofu (calcium salt is often used to coagulate it, so check the label); canned tomatoes (firming agents donate 63 milligrams per cup of tomatoes); **stone-ground flour** and self-rising flour; stone-ground cornmeal and self-rising cornmeal; and blackstrap molasses.

Milk with extra calcium added can be an excellent source; it provides more calcium per cup than any natural milk, 500 milligrams per 8 ounces. Then comes calcium-fortified orange juice, with 300 milligrams per 8 ounces, a good choice because the bioavailability of its calcium is comparable to that of milk. Calcium-fortified soy milk can also be prepared so that it contains more calcium than whole cow's milk.

Finally, calcium supplements are available, sold mostly to people hoping to ward off osteoporosis. The Controversy following this chapter points out, however, that, while often useful, supplements are not magic bullets against bone loss.

MAKING MEALS RICH IN CALCIUM

For those who tolerate milk, many cooks slip extra calcium into meals by sprinkling a tablespoon or two of fat-free dry milk into almost everything. The added calorie value is small, changes to the taste and texture of the dish are practically nil, but each 2 tablespoons adds about 100 extra milligrams of calcium (see Figure 8-17). Dried buttermilk powder can also add flavor and calcium to baked goods and other dishes. Here are some more tips for including calcium-rich foods in your meals:

At Breakfast

- Choose calcium-fortified orange or vegetable juice.
- Lighten tea or coffee, hot or iced, with milk or calcium-rich replacement such as soy milk.
- Eat cereals, hot or cold, with milk.

FIGURE 8-17
Milk, Yogurt, and Cheese Group Average Intakes[a]

On average, people in the United States fall far short of the recommended intake of milk, yogurt, or cheese (or replacements) each day. The picture is worse for the dark green vegetables that supply calcium—only 3% of the vegetables consumed each day meet this description.

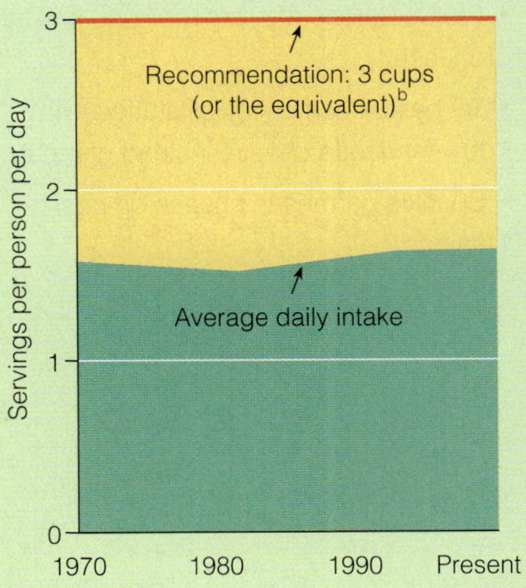

[a]*Includes all forms of milk, yogurt, cheese, and frozen dairy desserts.*

[b]*Recommended amount for adults from the 2005 USDA Food Guide. Details in Figure 2-5 of Chapter 2.*

Source: Intake data from U.S. Department of Agriculture, Economic Research Service.

- Cook hot cereals with milk instead of water, then mix in 2 tablespoons of fat-free dry milk.
- Make muffins or quick breads with milk and extra fat-free powdered milk or dried buttermilk powder.
- Add milk to scrambled eggs.
- Moisten cereals with flavored yogurt.

At Lunch

- Add low-fat cheeses to sandwiches, burgers, or salads.
- Use a variety of green vegetables, such as watercress or kale, in salads and on sandwiches.
- Drink fat-free milk or calcium-fortified soy milk as a beverage or in a smoothie. For tartness and extra calcium, add 2 tbs dried buttermilk powder.
- Drink calcium-rich mineral water as a beverage.
- Marinate cabbage shreds or broccoli spears in low-fat Italian dressing for an interesting salad that provides calcium.
- Choose coleslaw over potato and macaroni salads.
- Mix the mashed bones of canned salmon into salmon salad or patties.
- Eat sardines with their bones.
- Stuff potatoes with broccoli and low-fat cheese.
- Try pasta such as ravioli stuffed with low-fat ricotta cheese instead of meat.
- Sprinkle parmesan cheese on pasta salads.

At Supper

- Toss a handful of thinly sliced green vegetables, such as kale or young turnip greens, with hot pasta; the greens wilt pleasingly in the steam of the freshly cooked pasta.
- Serve a green vegetable every night and try new ones—how about kohlrabi? It tastes delicious when cooked like broccoli.
- Learn to stir-fry Chinese cabbage and other Asian foods.
- Try tofu (the calcium-set kind); this versatile food has inspired whole cookbooks devoted to creative uses.
- Add fat-free powdered milk to almost anything—meat loaf, sauces, gravies, soups, stuffings, casseroles, blended beverages, puddings, quick breads, cookies, brownies. Be creative.
- Choose frozen yogurt, ice milk, or custards for dessert.

Here is a shortcut for tracking the amount of calcium in a day's meals. To start, memorize these two facts:

1. A cup of milk provides about 300 milligrams of calcium.
2. Adults need 1,000 to 1,200 milligrams each day. Broken down in terms of "cups of milk," the need is 3⅓ to 4 cups each day.

To estimate calcium from an entire day's foods, not just milk, assign "cups of milk" points to various calcium sources. The goal is to achieve 3½ to 4 points per day:

- 1 point = 1 cup milk, yogurt, calcium-fortified beverage, or 1½ ounces cheese.
- 1 point = 4 ounces canned fish with bones.
- ½ point = 1 cup ice cream, cottage cheese, or calcium-rich vegetables (see the text).

Also, because bits of calcium are present in many foods, (a bagel has about 50 milligrams, for example):

- 1 point = a well-balanced, adequate, and varied diet.

Example: Say a day's calcium-rich foods include cereal and a cup of milk, a ham and cheese sandwich, and a broccoli and pasta salad.

1 point (cup of milk) + 1 point (cheese) + ½ point (broccoli) = 2½ points

Add 1 point for the other foods eaten that day.

1 point + 2½ points = 3½ points

This day's foods provided a calcium intake approximately equal to the lower of the DRI committee's recommendation. The tips in this section offer many ways to aim higher.

kefir a yogurt-based beverage.

nori a type of seaweed popular in Asian, particularly Japanese, cooking.

stone-ground flour flour made by grinding kernels of grain between heavy wheels made of limestone, a kind of rock derived from the shells and bones of marine animals. As the stones scrape together, bits of the limestone mix with the flour, enriching it with calcium.

Diet Analysis

PLUS Concepts in Action

Analyze Your Calcium Intakes

Many people do not meet their daily requirement for calcium. The purpose of this exercise is to make you aware of your calcium intake and to give you ideas about how you might meet your DRI recommended intake. Using the Diet Analysis program that accompanies this book, complete the following.

1. From the Reports tab, select Profile DRI Goals. Find your calcium information. What is the DRI Adequate Intake for calcium for your profile?
2. From the Reports tab, select Intake vs. Goals. Choose Day One (from your three-day diet intake record) and include all meals. What percentage of your calcium DRI did you meet on that day? Was this intake typical?
3. From the Reports tab, select Source Analysis. Choose Day One, include all meals, select calcium from the drop-down box, and generate a report. What were the top three food sources of calcium that day? What were your three lowest sources? Which of your top sources matched those of the calcium Snapshot on page 291?
4. From the Reports tab, select Intake Spreadsheet, choose Day Three, choose breakfast, and then generate a report. Look at the Calcium column. Did the calcium values of any of the foods surprise you? If so, which ones? How many milligrams of calcium did you consume for breakfast?
5. Using the same Intake Spreadsheet, choose Day Three, and choose lunch, then dinner. At which meal did you consume the most calcium? Which meal had the least calcium: breakfast, lunch, or dinner?
6. Many nondairy foods can provide calcium. Using the Food Feature, create a calcium-rich side dish without milk or milk products. Select the Track Diet tab and enter the ingredients for your side dish. From the Reports tab, select Source Analysis, select calcium from the drop-down menu, and generate a report. Did you raise your intake of calcium by choosing nondairy calcium sources? How absorbable was the calcium in these foods? (Check Figure 8-16, page 313.)

MEDIA MENU

CENGAGENOW To find additional quiz questions, view videos and animations, and explore interactive exercises, go to **www.cengage.com/sso.**

Search for information on individual minerals at **www.healthfinder.gov.**

Read the latest calcium and nutrition research at **www.nationaldairycouncil.org.**

Search the National Women's Health Information Center for information about bone health: **www.4women.gov.**

Learn more about the DASH Eating Plan by clicking on the brochure "Lowering Your Blood Pressure with DASH" from this government website: **www.nhlbi.nih.gov/health/public/heart/hbp/dash.**

Find tips and recipes for including more milk in your diet at **www.whymilk.com.**

SELF CHECK

Answers to these Self Check questions are in Appendix G.

1. Water balance is governed by the:
   - A. liver
   - B. kidneys
   - C. brain
   - D. (b) and (c)
2. Which two minerals are the major constituents of bone?
   - A. calcium and zinc
   - B. phosphorus and calcium
   - C. sodium and magnesium
   - D. magnesium and calcium
3. All of the following are correct concerning zinc except:
   - A. it is needed for vitamin A activity in the eye
   - B. in high doses it may inhibit iron absorption from the digestive tract
   - C. fruits and vegetables are the best sources for zinc
   - D. deficiencies in children retard growth
4. A deficiency of which mineral is a leading cause of mental retardation worldwide?
   - A. iron
   - B. iodine
   - C. zinc
   - D. chromium
5. Which mineral supplement is a likely cause of accidental poisonings of U.S. children under 6 years old?
   - A. iron
   - B. sodium
   - C. chloride
   - D. potassium
6. After about 50 years of age, bones begin to lose density.
   T F
7. The best way to control salt intake is to cut down on processed and fast foods.
   T F
8. The most abundant mineral in the body is iron.
   T F
9. Dairy foods such as butter, cream, and cream cheese are good sources of calcium, whereas vegetables such as broccoli are poor sources.
   T F
10. Bottled water must meet higher standards for purity and sanitation than U.S. tap water.
    T F

CONTROVERSY 8

Osteoporosis: Can Lifestyle Choices Reduce the Risks?

LO 8.9

An estimated 52 million people in the United States, the majority of them women over 50, have or are developing osteoporosis.[1*] Each year, a million and a half people, 30 percent of them men, break a hip, leg, arm, hand, ankle, or other bone as a result of having osteoporosis. Of these, hip fractures prove most serious. The break is rarely clean—the bone explodes into fragments that cannot be reassembled. Just removing the pieces is a struggle, and replacing them with an artificial joint requires major surgery. Many elderly people with hip fracture never walk or live independently again. About a fifth die from related complications within a year. By the year 2020, the number of hip fractures could double or even triple in the United States.[2] Both men and women are urged to do whatever they can to prevent fractures related to osteoporosis.

Fractures from osteoporosis occur during the later years, but osteoporosis itself develops silently much earlier. Younger adults are rarely aware of the strength sapping out of their bones but then suddenly, 40 years later, a hip gives way. People say, "She fell and broke her hip," but in fact the hip may have been so fragile that it broke *before* she fell.

The causes of osteoporosis are tangled, and most are beyond a person's control. Insufficient dietary calcium and vitamin D certainly play roles, but age, gender, physical activity, genetics, and other factors are also major players. Certain actions people can take undoubtedly reduce the risk of developing it. No controversy exists as to the nature and victims of osteoporosis; more controversial, however, are its causes and what people should do about it.

*Reference notes are found in Appendix F.

DEVELOPMENT OF OSTEOPOROSIS

To understand how the skeleton loses minerals in later years, you must first know a few things about bones. Table C8-1 offers definitions of relevant terms. The photograph on this page shows a human leg bone sliced lengthwise, exposing the lattice of calcium-containing crystals (the **trabecular bone**) inside that are part of the body's calcium bank. Invested as savings during the milk-drinking years of youth, these deposits provide a nearly inexhaustible fund of calcium. **Cortical bone** is the dense, ivorylike bone that forms the exterior shell of a bone and the shaft of a long bone (look closely at the photograph). Both types of bone are crucial to overall bone strength. Cortical bone forms a sturdy outer wall, and trabecular bone provides strength along the lines of stress.

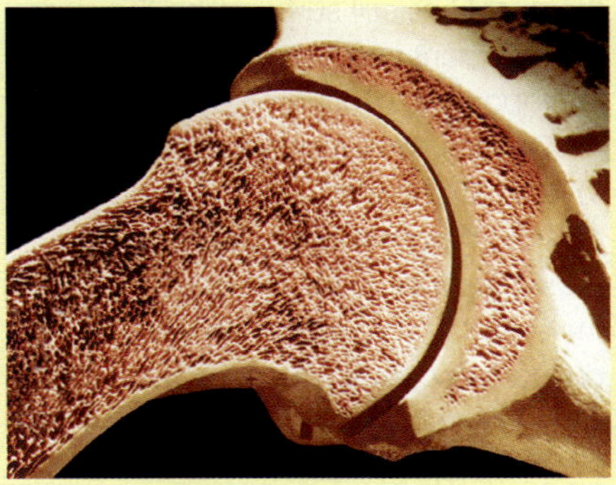

© Donald Fawcett/Visuals Unlimited

A sectioned bone.

TABLE C8-1 Osteoporosis Terms

- **cortical bone** the ivorylike outer bone layer that forms a shell surrounding trabecular bone and that comprises the shaft of a long bone.
- **trabecular** (tra-BECK-you-lar) **bone** the weblike structure composed of calcium-containing crystals inside a bone's solid outer shell. It provides strength and acts as a calcium storage bank.

The two types of bone handle calcium in different ways. The lacy crystals of the trabecular bone are tapped to raise blood calcium when the supply from the day's diet runs short; the calcium crystals are redeposited in bone when dietary calcium is plentiful.

Trabecular bone, generously supplied with blood vessels, readily gives up its minerals at the necessary rate whenever blood calcium needs replenishing. Loss of trabecular bone begins to be significant for men and women around age 30. Calcium in cortical bone can also be withdrawn, but more slowly, beginning around age 40.

As bone loss continues (Figure C8-1), bone density declines. Soon, osteoporosis sets in, and bones become so fragile that the body's weight can overburden the spine. Vertebrae may suddenly disintegrate and crush down, painfully pinching major nerves.[3] Or they may compress into wedges, forming what is insensitively called "dowager's

FIGURE C8-1 Losses of Trabecular Bone

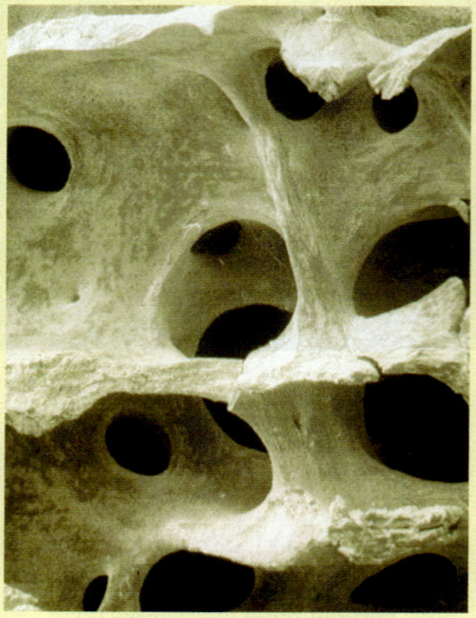

© Fred Hossler/Visuals Unlimited

Electron micrograph of healthy trabecular bone.

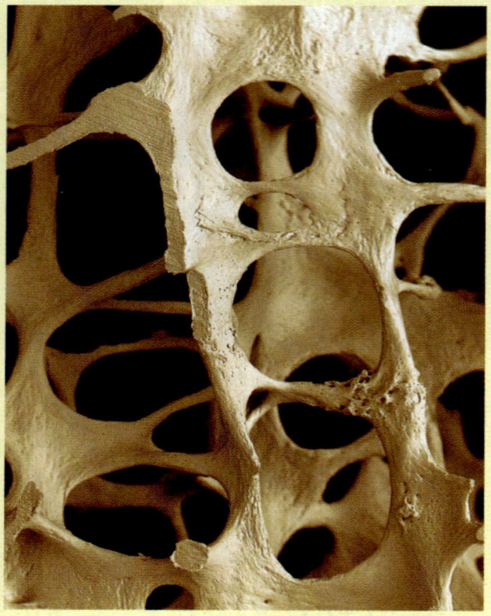

© Ana Boyde/Visuals Unlimited

Electron micrograph of trabecular bone affected by osteoporosis.

hump," the bent posture of many older men and women as they "grow shorter" (see Figure C8-2). Wrists may break as trabecula-rich bone ends weaken, and teeth may loosen or fall out as the trabecular bone of the jaw recedes. As the cortical bone shell weakens as well, breaks often occur in the hip.

TOWARD PREVENTION—UNDERSTANDING THE CAUSES OF OSTEOPOROSIS

Scientists are searching for ways to prevent osteoporosis, but they must first establish its causes. Gender and advanced age are clearly associated, but genetic inheritance and factors in the environment are also in play. Some of these may include:

- Poor calcium and vitamin D nutrition.
- Estrogen deficiency in women.
- Lack of physical activity.
- Body thinness.
- Smoking and alcohol abuse.
- Others.

Bone Density and the Genes

A strong genetic component contributes to osteoporosis, bone density, and increased risk of fractures.[4] The human genome is under investigation in this regard, and a number of genes may interact with vitamin D and calcium nutrition, or may otherwise affect bone density.[5] Genes exert influence over:

- the activities of bone-forming cells and bone-dismantling cells.
- the cellular mechanisms that make collagen (the major structural protein of bones).
- the mechanisms for absorbing and employing vitamin D.
- and many other contributors to bone metabolism.[6]

Researchers hope that, once unsnarled, this tangle of genetic leads will help to answer some of the questions still surrounding the development and prevention of osteoporosis.

Genetic inheritance appears to most strongly influence the maximum bone mass attainable during growth. It also influences the extent of a woman's bone loss during menopause, the time when women's estrogen production declines and menstruation ceases.[7]

Risks of osteoporosis differ by race and ethnicity.[8] African Americans, for example, use and conserve calcium more efficiently than do Caucasians.[9] African American women may lose bone at just half the rate of white women as they age, and an 80-year-old white woman is 3 times more likely to fracture her hip than is a black woman of the same age.

Some ethnic groups have even lower bone densities than do Caucasians. Asian people from China and Japan, Hispanic people from Central and South America, and Inuit people from St. Lawrence Island all have lower bone density. Do lower bone densities forecast a higher rate of hip fractures in these groups? Not always. Chinese people living in Singapore have low bone density, but their hip fracture rates are among the lowest in the world. No one really knows why.

Your genes set a tendency for strong or weak bones. Your environment, includ-

FIGURE C8-2 Loss of Height in a Woman Caused by Osteoporosis

The woman on the left is about 50 years old. On the right, she is 80 years old. Her legs have not grown shorter; only her back has lost length, due to collapse of her spinal bones (vertebrae). When collapsed vertebrae cannot protect the spinal nerves, the pressure of bones pinching the nerves causes excruciating pain.

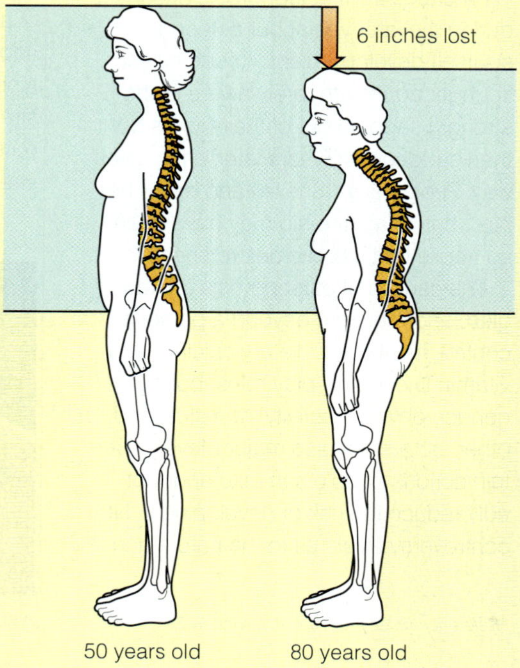

ing diet and other life choices, influences the final outcome.

Calcium and Vitamin D

In the later years, an adequate calcium intake alone cannot protect against bone fractures.[10] Bone strength later in life depends most on how well the bones were built during childhood and adolescence. Preteen children who consume enough calcium and vitamin D lay more calcium into the structure of their bones than children with less adequate intakes. Unfortunately, most girls in their bone-building years fail to meet their calcium needs.[11]

When people reach the bone-losing years of middle age, those who formed dense bones during youth have more bone tissue to lose before suffering ill effects—see Figure C8-3. Building strong bones in youth helps prevent or delay osteoporosis later on.[12]

Milk is not the only food rich in calcium, but milk and milk products supply most of the calcium to the U.S. diet and they are fortified with vitamin D. Children who do not consume milk do not meet their calcium needs unless they use calcium-fortified foods or supplements.[13]

Dietary calcium and vitamin D in later life cannot make up for earlier deficiencies, but they may help to slow the rate of bone loss. Additionally, calcium absorption declines with age, and older bodies become less efficient at making and activating vitamin D. Unfortunately, older people take in less calcium and vitamin D than do others, and they may fail to go outdoors for the sunlight necessary to form vitamin D and their skin becomes less efficient in synthesizing it. For these people, supplements may be of benefit.

Gender and Hormones

Gender is a powerful predictor of osteoporosis: men have greater bone density than women at maturity, and women often lose a great deal of bone in the years surrounding menopause. On hearing this, some men believe that osteoporosis is a "woman's disease." However, each year, millions of men suffer fractures from osteoporosis. Their fractures are treated, but their underlying disease often goes unrecognized.[14]

In women, bone dwindles rapidly when the hormone estrogen diminishes in menopause. Accelerated losses continue for six to eight years following menopause and then taper off, so women again lose bone at the same rate as their male counterparts. Losses of bone minerals continue throughout the remainder of a woman's lifetime but not at the free-fall pace of the menopause years (refer again to Figure C8-3).

Should *young* women fail to produce enough estrogen, they lose bone rapidly, too. Diseased ovaries are often to blame, but estrogen may be low because the woman suffers from an eating disorder with a dangerously low body weight (see Controversy 9). Even with treatment, the bone loss remains long after the eating disorder has been resolved.

If estrogen deficiency is a major cause of osteoporosis in women, what is the cause of bone loss in men? Men produce only a little estrogen, yet they resist osteoporosis better than women. Does the male sex hormone testosterone play a role? Probably, because elderly men in whom testosterone production has fallen off suffer more fractures than others.[†15]

†The condition is known as hypogonadism.

FIGURE C8-3 Two Women's Bone Mass History Compared

Woman A entered adulthood with enough calcium in her bones to last a lifetime. Woman B had less bone mass starting out and so suffered ill effects from bone loss later on.

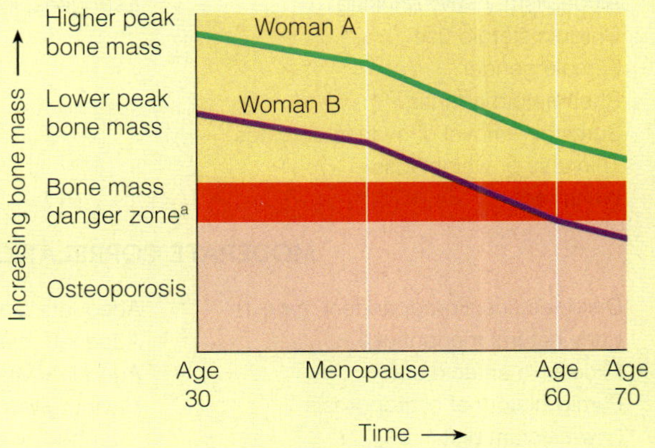

[a]People with a moderate degree of bone mass reduction are said to have osteopenia and are at increased risk of fractures.

Source: Data from Standing Committee on the Scientific Evaluation of Dietary Reference Intakes, Food and Nutrition Board, Institute of Medicine, Dietary Reference Intakes for Calcium, Phosphorus, Magnesium, Vitamin D, and Fluoride *(Washington, D.C.: National Academies Press, 1997), pp. 71–145.*

Body Weight

After age and gender, the next risk factor for osteoporosis is being underweight or losing weight (see Table C8-2). Weight loss reduces bone density and increases the risk of fractures—in part because energy restriction diminishes calcium absorption, tipping the scale toward bone loss.

Women who are thin throughout life, and especially those who lose 10 percent or more of their body weight after the age of menopause, face a hip fracture rate twice as high as that of most other women. Heavier body weight may lead to stronger bones, even when dietary calcium is low.[16] An appetite-regulating hormone, leptin, may be a link between body weight and bone mass (more about leptin in Chapter 9).[17] Also, fat tissue serves as a storage depot for hormones, and the more abundant the body fat stores, the greater amount of hormones.

Physical Activity

Physical activity supports bone growth during adolescence and may protect the bones later on.[18] When combined with adequate calcium intake, the effect is greater still.

When people lie idle—for example, when they are confined to bed—the bones lose strength just as the muscles do. Astronauts who live without gravity for days or weeks experience rapid and extensive bone loss. The harm to the bones from a sedentary lifestyle equals that of nutrient deficiencies and cigarette smoking (Table C8-2). The best exercises to keep bones healthy and prevent falls seem to be the weight-bearing kinds, such as calisthenics, dancing, jogging, vigorous walking, or weight training on most days throughout life. Preventing falls is becoming a new focus for fracture prevention in the elderly.[19]

TABLE C8-2 Risk and Protective Factors That Correlate with Osteoporosis

Risk Factors	Protective Factors
HIGH CORRELATION	
Advanced age	Black race
Alcoholism, heavy drinking	Estrogens, long-term use
Chronic steroid use	
Female gender	
Rheumatoid arthritis	
Surgical removal of ovaries or testes	
Thinness or weight loss	
White race	
MODERATE CORRELATION	
Diabetes (insulin-dependent, type 1)	Adequate dietary calcium
Early natural menopause	Adequate dietary protein (in later years)
Excessive antacid use	Adequate vitamin D
Family history of osteoporosis	Having given birth
Low-calcium diet	High body weight
Low-milk diet (in children)	High-calcium diet
Low-protein diet (in elderly)	Regular physical activity
Low-vitamin D status	
Sedentary lifestyle	
Smoking	
Hypogonadism (in men)	
MAY BE IMPORTANT BUT NOT YET PROVED	
Caffeine intake	Adequate vitamin K intake
High-fiber diet	Low-sodium diet (later years)
High blood homocysteine	Other dietary factors, including bicarbonate, omega-3 fatty acids, potassium, vitamin C
High-protein diet	
Lactose intolerance	

DigitalVision/PictureQuest

These young people are putting bone in the bank.

Tobacco Smoke and Alcohol

Smoking is hard on the bones. The bones of smokers are less dense than those of nonsmokers of similar body weight, age, and physical activity levels.[20] Fortunately, quitting can reverse much of the damage. With time, the bone density of former smokers approaches that of nonsmokers.

People who are addicted to alcohol also experience more frequent fractures.[21] Alcohol may induce calcium losses in urine through its diuretic effect. It may also upset the hormonal balance that maintains healthy bones: it is also directly toxic to the bone-building cells. Finally, drinking contributes to accidents and falls.

Protein

When elderly people take in too little protein, their bones suffer.[22] Recall that the mineral crystals of bone form on a protein matrix—collagen. Restoring protein sources to the diet can often improve bone status and reduce the incidence of hip fractures even in the elderly. However, a diet lacking protein no doubt also lacks other critical bone nutrients, such as vitamin D, vitamin K, and calcium, so restoring protein to the diet brings other needed nutrients into play, as well.

An opposite possibility, that a *high*-protein diet causes bone loss, has also received attention.[23] Excess dietary protein causes urinary calcium losses. Previously, researchers suspected that this extra urinary calcium might have come from the bones, but it appears that a high-protein diet may also stimulate calcium absorption, offsetting urinary calcium losses.[24]

Animal Versus Vegetable Protein Sources

Soy foods may help stem the rapid bone losses of the menopause years by virtue of their protein content—as mentioned, a negative correlation is evident between dietary protein intake and bone loss reported.[25] Soy phytochemicals may or may not affect bone loss—research is mixed.[26]

Some protein-rich foods from animals may benefit calcium balance. Milk is a good example. A milk-rich diet provides high-quality protein, vitamin D, and calcium, and also potassium and phosphorus, minerals that may help to *oppose* withdrawal of calcium from the skeleton.[27] It follows, then, that vegan vegetarians, who do not consume milk products, would have lower bone mineral density than people who consume milk and milk products—and they generally do.[28]

Sodium, Caffeine, Soft Drinks

A high sodium intake is also associated with urinary calcium excretion, and lowering sodium intakes seems to lessen calcium losses.[29] In study subjects eating the DASH diet, a controlled sodium diet that provides all of the foods in the USDA MyPyramid plan, urinary calcium losses are reduced.[30] In addition, the DASH diet is higher in calcium than most diets, a critical feature that stands against bone loss.

Long-term evidence is lacking to show that a reduced sodium intake prevents osteoporosis, however. Still, no harm can come from recommending that people reduce their sodium intakes.[31] Also, increasing potassium may help—some research shows that potassium may counteract the effects of sodium on calcium excretion. The person who wishes to lower sodium and increase potassium should choose a diet rich in unprocessed or lightly processed foods such as fruits and vegetables while restricting heavily processed, convenience, or fast foods.

Heavy users of caffeinated beverages, such as coffee, tea, and colas, should be aware that some evidence links caffeine use and osteoporosis, although other findings tend to absolve caffeine use from posing a risk. It may be that ordinary caffeine intakes, say the amount in two cups of coffee, increase calcium losses only when calcium intakes are low. Such losses may be so small that the calcium in just one or two *tablespoons* of milk is enough to replace them.

About cola beverages—they may also have adverse effects on calcium and bone density, although the reasons why are unclear.[32] For one thing, they contain phosphoric acid (many other soft drinks do not), and high dietary phosphorus and cola beverages both seem to speed bone dismantling.[33] For another, all soft drinks displace milk from the diet, especially in children and adolescents. More research is needed to determine whether cola beverages might pose a unique risk to the bones.

Other Nutrients Important to Bones

Vitamin K, because it plays roles in the production of at least one bone protein important in bone maintenance, has been investigated for links with osteoporosis. In fact, people with hip fractures often have low intakes of vitamin K–rich vegetables. However, giving people vitamin K does not appear to prevent bone loss.[34] It may be that increased vegetable intakes may improve both vitamin K status and skeletal health, but by unrelated mechanisms.[35]

Vitamin A is needed in the bone-remodeling process, and vitamin C may slow bone losses.[36] Magnesium may help to maintain bone mineral density.[37] Sufficient omega-3 fatty acids in the diet may also help preserve bone integrity.[38] Fluoride may oppose bone fractures, although some debate exists on this point.[39]

Clearly, a well-balanced diet that supplies abundant fruits and vegetables and a full array of nutrients is central to bone health. In contrast, diets containing too much salt, candy, or colas and possibly caffeine are associated with bone losses. Additional research points to the bone benefits not of a specific nutrient, but of a diet rich in fruits and vegetables.

Review Table C8-2 and the risk factors covered here. The more risk factors that apply to you, the greater your chances of developing osteoporosis in the future and the more seriously you should take the advice offered in this Controversy.

DIAGNOSIS AND MEDICAL TREATMENT

Diagnosis of osteoporosis includes measuring bone density using an advanced form of X ray (DEXA, see the photo below) or ultrasound.‡ Men with osteoporosis risk factors and all women should have a bone density test after age 50. A thorough examination also includes factors such as race, family history, and physical activity level.

Several drug therapies can reverse bone loss. Some inhibit the activities of the bone-dismantling cells, thus allowing the bone-building cells to slowly shore up bone tissue with new calcium deposits. Others stimulate the bone-building cells, resulting in greater bone formation. Such drugs, alone or in combination, have worked minor miracles in reversing even severe bone loss in some people, but for others they are ineffective or their side effects prove intolerable.

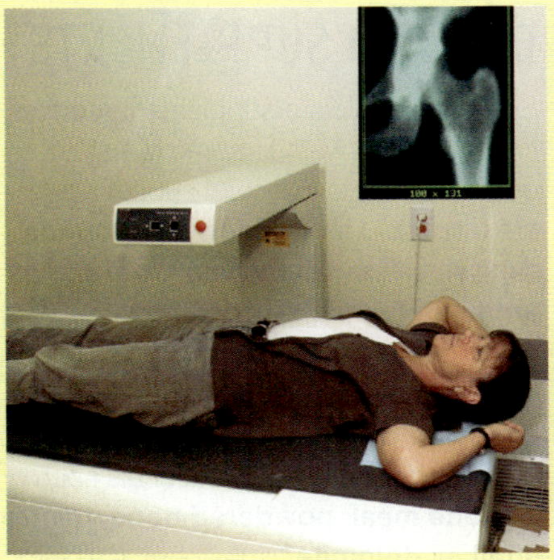

© David Young-Wolff/PhotoEdit

A DEXA scan measures bone density to help detect the early stages of bone loss, assess fracture risks, and measure the responses to bone-building treatments. (DEXA stands for dual-energy X-ray absorptiometry.)

Estrogen replacement therapy can help nonmenstruating women prevent further bone loss. However, the National Institutes of Health concludes that hormone therapy should not be used to prevent disease in healthy postmenopausal women because of increased risks for heart disease and cancers.[40]

CALCIUM RECOMMENDATIONS

Adequate calcium nutrition during the growing years is essential to achieving optimal peak bone mass. Yet only 10 percent of girls and 25 percent of boys meet the recommendation for calcium during their bone-forming years. The DRI committee recommends 1,300 milligrams of calcium, the amount in about 4 cups of milk, each day for everyone 9 through 18 years of age, 1,000 milligrams through age 50, and 1,200 milligrams thereafter.

How should you obtain this calcium? Nutritionists strongly recommend foods and beverages as your source of calcium and that you take supplements only when advised to do so by a physician.[41] Healthy children, especially, should receive a carefully planned diet that provides the calcium they need from foods—calcium supplements only marginally increase children's bone density, at best.[42] People can best support the health of their bones by following the lifetime recommendations for healthy bones in Table C8-3. Calcium supplements cannot equal any of the actions listed in the table.

Bone loss is not a calcium-deficiency disease comparable to iron-deficiency anemia, in which iron intake reliably reverses the condition. Calcium alone cannot reverse bone loss. For those who are unable to consume enough calcium-rich foods, however, taking calcium supplements—especially in combination with vitamin D—may help to enhance bone density and protect against bone

TABLE C8-3 **A Lifetime Plan for Healthy Bones**

Ages	Goal	Guidelines
CHILDHOOD		
2 through 12 or 13 years (sexual maturity)	Grow strong bones.	• Use milk as the primary beverage to meet the need for calcium within a balanced diet that provides all nutrients. • Play actively in sports or other activities. • Limit television and other sedentary entertainment. • Do not start smoking or drinking alcohol. • Drink fluoridated water.
ADOLESCENCE THROUGH YOUNG ADULTHOOD		
13 or 14 through 30 years	Achieve peak bone mass.	• Choose milk as the primary beverage, or if milk causes distress, include other calcium sources. • Commit to a lifelong program of physical activity. • Do not smoke or drink alcohol—if you have started, quit. • Drink fluoridated water.
MATURE ADULT		
31 through 50 years	Maximize bone retention.	• Continue as for 13- to 30-year-olds. • Adopt bone-strengthening exercises. • Obtain the recommended amount of calcium from food. • Take calcium supplements only if calcium needs cannot be met through foods.
MATURE ADULT		
51 years and above	Minimize bone loss.	• Continue as for 13- to 30-year-olds. • Continue striving to meet the calcium need from diet. • Continue bone-strengthening exercises. • Obtain a bone density test; follow physician's advice concerning bone-restoring medications and supplements.

Note: The exact ages of cessation of bone accretion and onset of loss vary among people, but in general, data indicate that the skeleton continues to accrete mass for approximately 10 years after adult height is achieved and begins to lose bone around age 35.

loss and fractures.[43] In a recent trial of over 36,000 postmenopausal women, supplements improved hip bone density, but, unfortunately, did *not* reduce hip fractures and increased the women's risk of developing kidney stones.[44]

Taking self-prescribed calcium supplements entails a few risks (see Table C8-4) and cannot take the place of sound food choices and other healthy habits.[45] One study's finding that calcium supplements may increase the risk of heart attacks is a matter of controversy among researchers.[46] Much more research is needed to support or refute this idea before its meaning can be known. The next section provides some details about the variety of calcium supplements.

CALCIUM SUPPLEMENTS

Selecting a calcium supplement requires finding the answers to some questions about each type. Calcium supplements are often sold as **calcium compounds,** such as calcium carbonate (as in some **antacids**), citrate, gluconate, lactate, malate, or phosphate, and compounds of calcium with amino acids (called **amino acid chelates**). Others are powdered, calcium-rich materials such as **bone meal, powdered bone, oyster shell,** or **dolomite** (limestone). Calcium from calcium-rich mineral waters also provides some amount of calcium that appears to be highly absorbable.[47] See Table C8-5 for supplement terms.

Question 1: How much calcium does the supplement provide? Most provide between 250 and 1,000 milligrams of calcium, as stated on the label. To be safe, calcium from foods and supplements should provide less than the Tolerable Upper Level for calcium of 2,500 milligrams.

Question 2: How digestible is the supplement? No matter how much calcium a supplement contains, the body cannot use it unless the tablet disintegrates in the digestive tract. Manufacturers compress large quantities of calcium into small pills, which must be penetrated by the stomach acid. To test a supplement's ability to dissolve, drop a pill into 6 ounces of vinegar and stir occasionally. A digestible pill will dissolve within half an hour.

TABLE C8-4

Calcium Supplement Risks

People who take calcium supplements risk:

- *GI distress.* Constipation, intestinal bloating, and excess gas are common.
- *Impaired iron status.* Calcium inhibits iron absorption.
- *Urinary tract stones or kidney damage in susceptible individuals.* People who have a history of kidney stones should be monitored by a physician and choose calcium citrate if they must take supplements.
- *Exposure to contaminants.* Some preparations of bone meal and dolomites are contaminated with hazardous amounts of arsenic, cadmium, mercury, and lead.
- *Vitamin D toxicity.* Vitamin D, which is present in many calcium supplements, can be toxic. Users must eliminate other concentrated vitamin D sources.
- *Excess blood calcium.* This complication is seen only with doses of calcium fourfold or more greater than customarily prescribed.
- *Other nutrient interactions.* Calcium inhibits absorption of magnesium, phosphorus, and zinc.
- *Drug interactions.* Calcium and tetracycline form an insoluble complex that impairs both mineral and drug absorption.

Question 3: How absorbable is the form of calcium in the supplement? Most healthy people absorb calcium equally well (and as well as from milk) from any of these forms: calcium carbonate, citrate, or phosphate. To improve absorption, take smaller doses (less than 500 milligrams) twice a day instead of 1,000 milligrams all at once. Table C8-6 lists some sources of supplemental calcium, the amount of calcium delivered, and the form of the calcium along with the number of calories in a dose or serving.

One last pitch: Think one more time before you decide to take supplements instead of including calcium-rich foods in your diet. The Consensus Conference on Osteoporosis recommends milk. The American Society for Bone and Mineral Research recommends calcium-rich foods in preference to supplements. The National Institutes of Health concludes that foods are best and recommends supplements only when intake from food is insufficient. The authors of this book are so impressed with the importance of using abundant, calcium-rich foods that we have worked out ways to do so at every meal. Seldom do nutritionists agree so unanimously.

TABLE C8-5

Calcium Supplement Terms

- **amino acid chelates** (KEY-lates) compounds of minerals (such as calcium) combined with amino acids in a form that favors their absorption. A chelating agent is a molecule that surrounds another molecule and can then either promote or prevent its movement from place to place (*chele* means "claw").
- **antacids** acid-buffering agents used to counter excess acidity in the stomach. Calcium-containing preparations (such as Tums) contain available calcium. Antacids with aluminum or magnesium hydroxides (such as Rolaids) can accelerate calcium losses.
- **bone meal** or **powdered bone** crushed or ground bone preparations intended to supply calcium to the diet. Calcium from bone is not well absorbed and is often contaminated with toxic materials such as arsenic, mercury, lead, and cadmium.
- **calcium compounds** the simplest forms of purified calcium. They include calcium carbonate, citrate, gluconate, hydroxide, lactate, malate, and phosphate. These supplements vary in the amount of calcium they contain, so read the labels carefully. A 500-milligram tablet of calcium gluconate may provide only 45 milligrams of calcium, for example.
- **dolomite** a compound of minerals (calcium magnesium carbonate) found in limestone and marble. Dolomite is powdered and is sold as a calcium-magnesium supplement but may be contaminated with toxic minerals, is not well absorbed, and interacts adversely with absorption of other essential minerals.
- **oyster shell** a product made from the powdered shells of oysters that is sold as a calcium supplement but is not well absorbed by the digestive system.

TABLE C8-6

A Sampling of Supplemental Calcium Sources

Calcium Source	Typical Amount per Serving	Calories
Antacid medication, regular strength ("Tums" type)	500 mg per 2 tablets	10
Breads with "more" calcium[a]	80 mg per slice	70
Calcium-fortified candies or chewable candy supplements	500 mg per dose	20
Calcium-fortified or "100% nutrient" cereals	1,000 mg per serving	110
Calcium-fortified fat-free milk and milk products	500 mg per 8-oz serving	100
Calcium-fortified orange juice or other fruit beverages	350 mg per 8-oz serving	110
Calcium pills	A wide variety of pills provide varying doses. Read the label.	Negligible
Meal replacer: cereal bars "with milk"	250 mg	160
Meal replacer: "complete nutrition" drinks	200–350 mg per 8-oz drink	360
Meal replacer: "energy" bars	300 per one bar	230

[a]*Bread, though not rich in calcium, is heavily consumed and may contribute significantly to many people's intakes.*

Energy Balance and Healthy Body Weight

9

DO YOU EVER . . .

- Wish you could control your body weight, once and for all?
- Feel tempted by a favorite treat when you don't feel hungry?
- Wonder how extra calories from food become fat in your body?
- Try popular diets to lose weight?

Keep reading . . .

Farida Zaman/Stock Illustration Source/Getty Images

Learning Objectives

To find learning objective topics in this chapter, look for text headings with a corresponding "LO" number above the heading. After completing this chapter, you should be able to accomplish the following:

LO 9.1 Delineate the health risks of too little and too much body fatness, with emphasis on *central obesity* and its associated health risks.

LO 9.2 Describe the roles of BMR and several other factors in determining an individual's daily energy needs.

LO 9.3 Calculate the BMI when given height and weight information for various people, and describe the health implications of any given BMI value.

LO 9.4 Compare and contrast the roles of the hormones ghrelin and leptin in appetite regulation, and name several other influences on both hunger and satiety.

LO 9.5 Discuss the potential impact of "outside the body" factors on weight-control efforts.

LO 9.6 Develop a weight-loss plan that includes controlled portions of nutrient-dense foods to produce gradual weight loss while meeting nutrient needs.

LO 9.7 Discuss the role of physical activity in maintaining a healthy body composition.

LO 9.8 Defend the importance of behavior modification in weight loss and weight maintenance over the long term.

LO 9.9 Compare and contrast the characteristics of anorexia nervosa and bulimia nervosa, and provide strategies for combating eating disorders.

Are you pleased with your body weight? If you answered yes, you are a rare individual. Nearly all people in our society think they should weigh more or less (mostly less) than they do. Their primary concern is usually appearance but they often perceive, correctly, that physical health is somehow related to weight. Both **overweight** and **underweight** present risks to health and life.[1*]

People also think of their weight as something they should control, once and for all. Three misconceptions in their thinking frustrate their efforts, however—the focus on weight, the focus on *controlling* weight, and the focus on a short-term endeavor. Simply put, it isn't your weight you need to control; it's the fat, or **adipose tissue,** in your body in proportion to the lean—your **body composition.** And controlling body composition directly isn't possible—you can only control your *behaviors.* Sporadic bursts of activity, such as "dieting," are not effective; the behaviors that achieve and maintain a healthy body weight take a lifetime of commitment. Luckily, with time, these behaviors become second nature.

This chapter starts by presenting problems associated with deficient and excessive body fatness and then examines how the body manages its energy budget. The following sections show how to judge body weight on the sound basis of health. The chapter then explores some theories about causes of obesity and reveals how the body gains and loses weight. It goes on to present science-based lifestyle strategies for achieving and maintaining a healthy body weight, and it closes with a Controversy section on eating disorders.

FIGURE 9-1 ANIMATED! **Increasing Prevalence of Obesity**

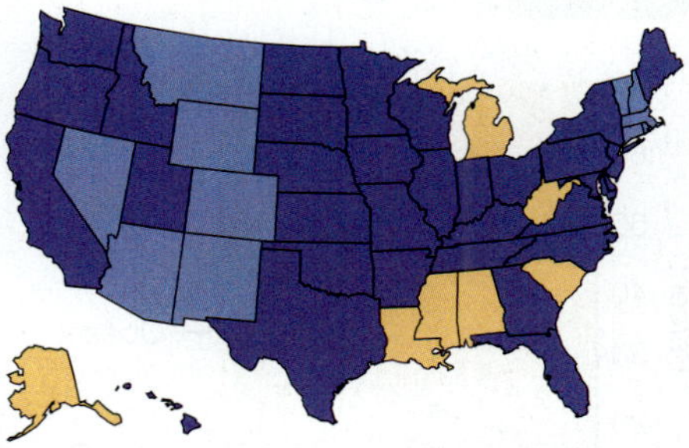

1998: Most states had obesity prevalence rates of less than 20 percent.

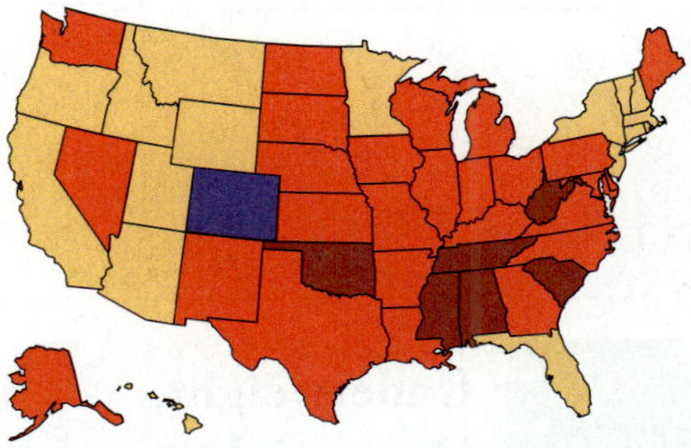

2008: Most states had prevalence rates of greater than 25 percent, with six states reporting prevalence rates greater than or equal to 30 percent.

Key:
- 10%–14%
- 15%–19%
- 20%–24%
- 25%–29%
- ≥ 30%

Source: www.cdc.nccdphp/dnpa/obesity/trend/maps/index.htm

LO 9.1

The Problems of Too Little or Too Much Body Fat

Both deficient and excessive body fat present risks to health, but in the United States, too little body fat is not a widespread problem. **Obesity,** in contrast, is an epidemic—see Figure 9-1.[2] In 1960, about 13 percent of U.S. adults were obese. Today, 66 percent are overweight while about a third of the population is obese. Even severe obesity increased alarmingly, although some welcomed recent news reports a slowdown in the rate of increase.[†3] Among children and adolescents, 33 percent are overweight or are on their way to becoming overweight.[4] Figure 9-2 shows that overweight and obesity stand far above the Healthy People target of 15 percent of the population. The problem reaches around the globe, in urban and rural areas alike.[5]

The problem of *underweight,* while affecting fewer than 2 percent of adults in the United States, also poses health threats to those who drop below a healthy minimum.[6] People at either extreme of body weight face increased risks (see Figure 9-3).[7]

What Are the Risks from Underweight?

Thin people die first during a siege or in a famine. Overly thin people are also at a disadvantage in the hospital, where their nutrient status can easily deteriorate if they have to go without food for days at a time while undergoing tests or surgery.[8] Underweight also increases the risk for any person fighting a **wasting** disease. People with cancer often die not from the cancer itself, but from starvation. Thinner people may also have worse outcomes when they develop heart disease (but heavier people develop it far more often).[9] Thus, excessively underweight people are urged to gain body fat as an energy reserve and to acquire protective amounts of all the nutrients that can be stored.

KEY POINT Deficient body fatness threatens survival during a famine or when a person has a disease.

overweight body weight above a healthy weight; BMI 25 to 29.9 (BMI is defined later).

underweight body weight below a healthy weight; BMI below 18.5.

adipose tissue the body's fat tissue. Adipose tissue performs several functions, including the synthesis and secretion of the hormone leptin involved in appetite regulation.

body composition the proportions of muscle, bone, fat, and other tissue that make up a person's total body weight.

obesity overfatness with adverse health effects, as determined by reliable measures and interpreted with good medical judgment. Obesity is officially defined as a body mass index of 30 or higher.

wasting the progressive, relentless loss of the body's tissues that accompanies certain diseases and shortens survival time.

*Reference notes are found in Appendix F.
†Defined as more than 100 pounds overweight.

FIGURE 9-2 **Adult Obesity and Overweight Compared with *Healthy People* Target**

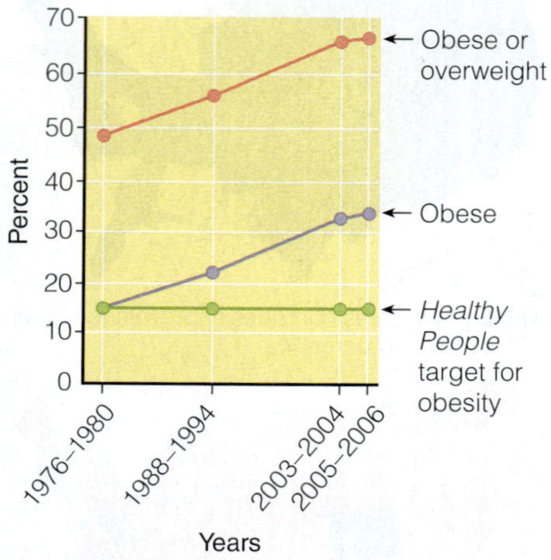

Source: National Center for Health Statistics

FIGURE 9-3 **Underweight, Overweight, and Mortality**

This J-shaped curve describes the relationship between body mass index (BMI) and mortality. It shows that both underweight and overweight present risks of a premature death.

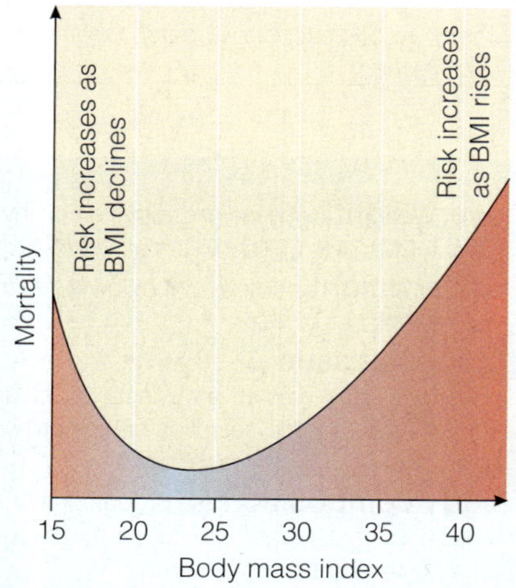

- Obesity elevates the risk of these major conditions:
  - *Hypertension*
  - *Heart disease*
  - *Stroke*
  - *Diabetes*
  - *Certain cancers*

What Are the Risks from Too Much Body Fat?

If tomorrow's headlines read, "Obesity gone! U.S. Population Loses Excess Fat!" tens of millions of people would be freed from obesity-related illnesses—heart disease, diabetes, arthritis, cancer, and others.[10] In just one year, an estimated 300,000 lives could be saved, along with the estimated $147 billion spent on obesity-related health care.[11]

Chronic Diseases To underestimate the threat from obesity is to invite calamity. The risk of dying young increases proportionally with increasing body weight.[12] With extreme obesity, the risk of dying equals that from smoking.[13]

Over 70 percent of obese people suffer from at least one other major health problem. Excess body fatness causes up to half of all cases of hypertension, increasing the risk of heart attack and stroke.[14] Obesity triples a person's risk of developing diabetes, and even modest weight gain raises the risk. Chapter 4 presented maps (page 130) depicting increasing U.S. rates of diabetes over the last decade, which bear a striking resemblance to the obesity maps of Figure 9-1. Central obesity, discussed in a moment, particularly elevates these risks.

Other Risks Obese adults also face these threats: abdominal hernias, arthritis, complications in pregnancy and surgery, flat feet, gallbladder disease, gout, high blood lipids, kidney stones, nonalcoholic fatty liver disease, reproductive disorders, respiratory problems, skin problems, sleep disturbances, sleep apnea (dangerous abnormal breathing during sleep), varicose veins, and even a high accident rate.[15] Some of these maladies start to improve with the loss of just 5 percent of body weight, and risks improve markedly after a 10 percent loss. So great are the harms from obesity that obesity itself is classified as a chronic disease.[16]

KEY POINT Most obese people suffer illnesses. Obesity is considered a chronic disease.

What Are the Risks from Central Obesity?

Fat that collects deep within the central abdominal area of the body, called **visceral fat,** poses the greatest risks with regard to:

- diabetes.
- heart disease.[17]
- hypertension.
- gallbladder stones.
- stroke.[18]
- some types of cancer.[19]

In fact, this **central obesity** elevates the risk of death from *all* causes to a greater extent than does excess fat lying just beneath the skin (**subcutaneous fat**) of the abdomen, thighs, hips, and legs (Figure 9-4).[20]

Central Obesity and Inflammation Why should fat in the abdomen bring extra risk to the heart? Part of the answer may involve **adipokines,** hormones released by visceral adipose tissue. Adipokines help to regulate inflammatory processes and energy metabolism in the tissues.[21]

In central obesity, a shift occurs in the balance of adipokines favoring those that increase both inflammation and insulin resistance of tissues.[22] The resulting chronic inflammation and insulin resistance contribute to diabetes, atherosclerosis (a cause of heart disease), and other chronic diseases.[23] With weight loss, the adipokine balance is restored, and inflammation and insulin resistance are relieved.[24] Chronic disease risks drop in response.

In addition to inflammation, visceral adipose tissue produces more free fatty acids than other types of fat tissue, contributing to a blood lipid profile associated with metabolic syndrome that predicts heart disease (see Chapter 11).[25] Also, when fat is deposited in the abdomen, it collects in the liver and around the heart, as well.[26] Both these fat depots are under investigation for increasing disease risks.

Who Develops Central Obesity? Men of all ages and women who are past menopause are more prone to develop the "apple" profile that characterizes central obesity, whereas women in their reproductive years typically develop more of a "pear" profile (fat around the hips and thighs). Some women change profiles at menopause, and life-long "pears" may suddenly face the increased disease risks associated with central obesity.

Two other factors also affect body fat distribution. Moderate-to-high intakes of alcohol associate directly with central obesity, while higher levels of physical activity correlate with leanness.[27] A later section explains how to judge whether a person carries too much fat around the middle.

KEY POINT Central obesity is more hazardous to health than other forms of obesity. Adipokines are hormones produced by visceral adipose tissue that contribute to inflammation and diseases. Certain factors affect body fat distribution.

How Fat Is Too Fat?

People want to know exactly how much body fat is too much. The answer is not the same for everyone, but scientists have developed guidelines.

Evaluating Risks from Body Fatness Obesity experts commonly evaluate the health risks of obesity by way of three indicators (each is described more fully later on). The first is a person's BMI, or **body mass index.** The BMI, which defines average relative weight for height in people older than 20 years, generally (but not always) correlates with body fatness and disease risks.[28]

The second indicator is waist circumference, reflecting the degree of visceral fatness, or central obesity, in proportion to total body fat (see Table 9-1).[29] The third indicator is the person's disease risk profile, which takes into account other personal factors, such as a diagnosis of hypertension, type 2 diabetes, or elevated blood

TABLE 9-1 Chronic Disease Risks According to BMI Values and Waist Circumference[a]

The degree of risk is heightened by the presence of specific diseases, other risk factors (such as elevated blood LDL cholesterol, as described in Chapter 11), or smoking.

BMI		Waist ≤ 40 in. (Men) or ≤ 35 in. (Women)	Waist ≥ 40 in. (Men) or ≥ 35 in. (Women)
18.5 or less	Underweight	Low	—
18.5–24.9	Normal	Low	—
25.0–29.9	Overweight	Increased	High
30.0–34.9	Obese, class I	High	Very high
35.0–39.9	Obese, class II	Very high	Very high
40 or greater	Extremely obese, class III	Extremely high	Extremely high

[a]*Risk for type 2 diabetes, hypertension, and cardiovascular disease.*

Source: National Heart, Lung, and Blood Institute, National Institutes of Health, The Practical Guide: Identification, Evaluation, and Treatment of Overweight and Obesity in Adults, *NIH publication no. 00-4084.*

FIGURE 9-4 Visceral Fat and Subcutaneous Fat

The fat deep within the body's abdominal cavity may pose an especially high risk to health.

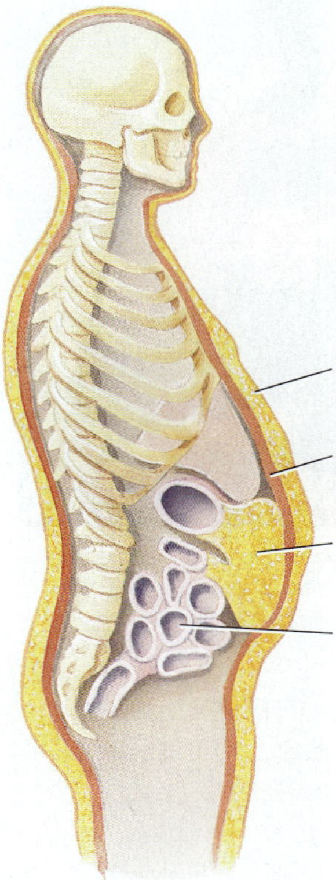

CONCEPT LINK 9-1

Diabetes and its damaging effects on the body were discussed in Chapter 4, pages 130–131.

- Leptin, an appetite-controlling hormone discussed in a later section, is another adipokine.

visceral fat fat stored within the abdominal cavity in association with the internal abdominal organs; also called *intra-abdominal fat.*

central obesity excess fat in the abdomen and around the trunk.

subcutaneous fat fat stored directly under the skin (*sub* means "beneath"; *cutaneous* refers to the skin).

adipokines (AD-ih-poh-kynz) protein hormones made and released by adipose tissue (fat) cells.

body mass index (BMI) an indicator of obesity or underweight, calculated by dividing the weight of a person by the square of the person's height.

© Joe Sampson, Courtesy of Jennifer Portnick

Being active—even if overweight—is healthier than being sedentary. Weight loss itself, however, best reduces disease risks.

TABLE 9-2 Indicators of an Urgent Need for Weight Loss

The National Heart, Lung, and Blood Institute states that aggressive treatment may be needed for extremely obese people who also have any of the following:

- Established cardiovascular disease (CVD).
- Established type 2 diabetes or impaired glucose tolerance.
- Sleep apnea, a disturbance of breathing in sleep, including temporary stopping of breathing.

The same urgency for treatment exists for an obese person with any three of the following:

- Hypertension.
- High LDL.
- Smoking.
- Low HDL cholesterol.
- Sedentary lifestyle.
- Age older than 45 years (men) or 55 years (women).
- Heart disease of an immediate family member before age 55 (male) or 65 (female).

Source: National Heart, Lung, and Blood Institute, National Institutes of Health, The Practical Guide: Identification, Evaluation, and Treatment of Overweight and Obesity in Adults, *NIH publication no. 00-4084.*

cholesterol; whether the person smokes; and so forth (see Table 9-2). The more of these factors a person has and the greater the degree of obesity, the greater the urgency to control body fatness.

Why, then, do some obese people remain healthy and live long lives and some average-weight people die young of diseases? Genetic inheritance, smoking habits, and level of physical activity may help to explain why some such individuals stay well while others fall ill.[30] These factors are discussed in later sections.

CONCEPT LINK 9-2

Inflammation was discussed in Chapter 3 (page 77) and Chapter 5 (page 162).

Factors affecting body fat distribution:

- Gender.
- Menopause in women.
- Smoking.
- Alcohol intake.
- Physical activity.

- If you are wondering about your own BMI, find it on the inside back cover, page Z.

Three indicators used to evaluate risks from obesity:

- Body mass index.
- Waist circumference.
- Disease risk profile and family medical history.

Social and Economic Costs of Body Fatness Although a few overfat people escape health problems, no one who is fat in our society quite escapes the social and economic handicaps. Our society places enormous value on thinness, especially for women, and fat people are less sought after for romance, less often hired, and less often admitted to college.[31] They pay higher insurance premiums, and they pay more for clothing. An estimated 30 to 40 percent of all U.S. women (and 20 to 25 percent of U.S. men) are trying to lose weight at any given time, spending $50 billion each year, with little long-term success.

Prejudice defines people by their appearance rather than by their abilities and characters. Obese people suffer emotional pain when others treat them with insensitivity, hostility, and contempt, and they may internalize a sense of guilt and self-deprecation. Health-care professionals, even dietitians, can be among the offenders without realizing it.[32] To free our society of its obsession with body fatness and prejudice against obese people, activists are promoting respect for individuals of all body weights.

KEY POINT Health risks from obesity are reflected in BMI, waist circumference, and a disease risk profile. Fit people are healthier than unfit people of the same body fatness. Overweight people face social and economic handicaps and prejudice.

LO 9.2

The Body's Energy Balance

What happens inside the body when you eat too much or too little food? The body ends up with an unbalanced energy budget—you have taken in more or less food energy than you spent. The body's energy budget works somewhat like a cash budget that grows and dwindles in proportion to the flow of currency. When more food energy is consumed than is needed, excess fat accumulates in the fat cells in the body's adipose tissue where it is stored. When energy supplies run low, stored fat is withdrawn. The daily energy balance can therefore be stated like this:

Change in energy stores equals food energy taken in minus energy spent on metabolism and muscle activities.

More simply:

Change in energy stores = energy in − energy out.

Too much or too little fat on the body today does not necessarily reflect today's energy budget. Small imbalances in the energy budget compound over time.

Energy In and Energy Out

The energy in foods and beverages is the only contributor to the "energy in" side of the energy balance equation. Before you can decide how much food will supply the energy you need in a day, you must first become familiar with the amounts of energy in foods and beverages. One way to do so is to look up calorie amounts associated with foods and beverages in the Table of Food Composition (Appendix A). Alternatively, computer programs can provide this information at a touch of a key. Such numbers are always fascinating to people concerned with managing body fatness. For example, an apple gives you 70 calories from carbohydrate; a regular-size candy bar gives you about 250 calories mostly from fat and carbohydrate. You may already know that for each 3,500 calories you eat in excess of expenditures, you store approximately 1 pound of body fat.‡

On the "energy out" side of the equation, no easy method exists for determining the energy an individual spends and therefore needs. Energy expenditures vary so widely among individuals that estimating an individual person's need requires knowing something about the person's lifestyle and metabolism.

KEY POINT The "energy in" side of the body's energy budget is measured in calories taken in each day in the form of foods and beverages. No easy method exists for determining the "energy out" side of a person's energy balance equation.

Did You Know?

1 lb body fat = 3,500 cal.

Ariel Skelley/Jupiter Images

Balancing food energy intake with physical activity can add to life's enjoyment.

How Many Calories Do I Need Each Day?

Simply put, you need to take in enough calories to cover your energy expenditure each day—your energy budget must balance. One way to estimate your energy need is to monitor your food intake and body weight over a period of time in which your activities are typical and are sufficient to maintain your health. If you keep an accurate record of all the foods and beverages you consume and if your weight is in a healthy range and has not changed during the past few months, you can conclude that your energy budget is balanced. Your average daily calorie intake is sufficient to meet your daily output—your need, therefore, is the same as your current intake.[33] At least three, and preferably seven, days, including a weekend day, of honest record keeping are necessary because intakes and activities fluctuate from day to day.

An alternative method of determining energy need is based on energy output. The two major ways in which the body spends energy are (1) to fuel its **basal metabolism** and (2) to fuel its **voluntary activities.** Basal metabolism requires energy to support the body's work that goes on all the time without our conscious awareness. A third energy component, the body's metabolic response to food, or the **thermic effect of food,** uses up about 10 percent of a meal's energy value in stepped-up metabolism in the five or so hours after finishing a meal.[34]

Basal metabolism consumes a surprisingly large amount of fuel, and the **basal metabolic rate (BMR)** varies from person to person (Figure 9-5). Depending on activity level, a person whose total energy need is 2,000 calories a day may spend as

basal metabolism the sum total of all the involuntary activities that are necessary to sustain life, including circulation, respiration, temperature maintenance, hormone secretion, nerve activity, and new tissue synthesis, but excluding digestion and voluntary activities. Basal metabolism is the largest component of the average person's daily energy expenditure.

voluntary activities intentional activities (such as walking, sitting, or running) conducted by voluntary muscles.

thermic effect of food (TEF) the body's speeded-up metabolism in response to having eaten a meal; also called *diet-induced thermogenesis.*

basal metabolic rate (BMR) the rate at which the body uses energy to support its basal metabolism.

‡Pure fat is worth 9 calories per gram. A pound of it (450 g), then, would store 4,050 calories. A pound of *body* fat is not pure fat, though; it contains water, protein, and other materials of living tissue—hence the lower calorie value.

FIGURE 9-5

Components of Energy Expenditure

Typically, basal metabolism represents a person's largest expenditure of energy, followed by physical activity and the thermic effect of food.

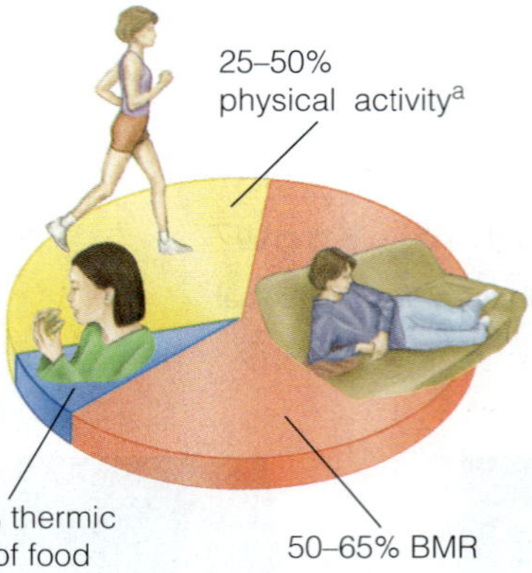

[a]*For a sedentary person, physical activities may account for less than half as much energy as basal metabolism, whereas a very active person's activities may equal the energy cost of basal metabolism.*

TABLE 9-3

Factors That Affect the BMR

Factor	Effect on BMR
Age	The BMR is higher in youth; as lean body mass declines with age, the BMR slows. Physical activity may prevent some of this decline.
Height	Tall people have a larger surface area, so their BMRs are higher.
Growth	Children and pregnant women have higher BMRs.
Body composition	The more lean tissue, the higher the BMR. A typical man has greater lean body mass than a typical woman, making his BMR higher.
Fever	Fever raises the BMR.
Stress	Stress hormones raise the BMR.
Environmental temperature	Adjusting to either heat or cold raises the BMR.
Fasting/starvation	Fasting/starvation hormones lower the BMR.
Malnutrition	Malnutrition lowers the BMR.
Thyroxine	The thyroid hormone thyroxine is a key BMR regulator; the more thyroxine produced, the higher the BMR.

many as 1,000 to 1,600 of them to support basal metabolism. The iodine-dependent hormone thyroxine directly controls basal metabolism—the less secreted, the lower the energy requirements for basal functions. The rate is lowest during sleep.[§] Many other factors also affect the BMR (see Table 9-3).

CONCEPT LINK 9-3

Thyroxine contains the mineral iodine, as explained in Chapter 8, page 300.

People often wonder whether they can speed up their metabolism to spend more daily energy. You cannot increase your BMR very much *today*. You can, however, amplify the second component of your energy expenditure—your voluntary activities. If you do, you will spend more calories today, and if you keep doing so day after day, your BMR will also increase as you build lean tissue. Lean tissue is more metabolically active than fat tissue, so a way to speed up your BMR is to make muscle-building physical activities a daily habit to nudge your body composition toward the lean. Energy spent on voluntary activities depends largely on two factors. In general, the heavier the weight of the body parts you move and the longer the time you invest in moving them, the more calories you expend.

- To estimate basal energy output:
  - *Men: kg body weight × 24 = cal/day.*
  - *Women: kg body weight × 23 = cal/day.*

(To convert pounds to kilograms [kg], divide pounds by 2.2.)

Be aware that some ads for weight-loss diets claim that certain substances, such as grapefruit or herbs, can elevate the BMR and thus promote weight loss. This claim is false. Any meal temporarily steps up energy expenditure due to the thermic effect of food, and grapefruit or herbs are not known to accelerate it further.

KEY POINT Two major components of the "energy out" side of the body's energy budget are basal metabolism and voluntary activities. A third component of energy expenditure is the thermic effect of food. Many factors influence the basal metabolic rate.

Estimated Energy Requirements (EER)

A person wishing to know how much energy he or she needs in a day to maintain weight might look up his or her **Estimated Energy Requirement (EER)** value listed on the inside front cover of this book. The numbers listed there seem to imply that for each age and gender group, the number of calories needed to meet the daily requirement is known as precisely as, say, the recommended intake for vitamin A. The printed EER values, however, reflect the needs of only those people who ex-

Estimated Energy Requirement (EER) the DRI recommendation for energy intake, accounting for age, gender, weight, height, and physical activity. Also defined in Chapter 2.

[§]A measure of energy output taken while the person is awake but relaxed yields a slightly higher number called the *resting metabolic rate*, sometimes used in research.

actly match the characteristics of the "reference man and woman" (see the margin). People who deviate in any way from these characteristics must use other methods for determining their energy needs, and almost everyone deviates.

Taller people need proportionately more energy than shorter people to balance their energy budgets because their greater surface area allows more energy to escape as heat. Older people generally need less than younger people due to slowed metabolism and reduced muscle mass, which occur in part because of reduced physical activity. (As Chapter 14 points out, these losses may not be inevitable for people who stay active.) On average, energy need diminishes by 5 percent per decade beyond the age of 30 years.

In reality, no one is average. In any group of 20 similar people with similar activity levels, one may expend twice as much energy per day as another. A 60-year-old person who bikes, swims, or walks briskly each day may need as many calories as a sedentary person of 30. Clearly, with such a wide range of variation, a necessary step in determining any person's energy need is to study that person.

- The DRI committee sets EER for a reference man and woman:
  - Reference man: *"Active" physical activity level, 22.5 BMI, 5 ft 10 in. tall, weighing 154 lb.*
  - Reference woman: *"Active" physical activity level, 21.5 BMI, 5 ft 4 in. tall, weighing 126 lb.*
- Instructions for determining whether you are sedentary, lightly active, active, or very active are provided in Appendix H.

Did You Know?

About 80% of people in the United States and Canada fall into the sedentary or lightly active categories.

KEY POINT The DRI committee sets Estimated Energy Requirements for a reference man and woman. People's energy needs vary greatly.

The DRI Method of Estimating Energy Requirements

The DRI committee provides a way of estimating EER values for individuals. These calculations take into account the ways in which energy is spent, and by whom. The equation includes:

- *Gender.* Women generally have less lean body mass than men; in addition, women's menstrual hormones influence the BMR, raising it just prior to menstruation.
- *Age.* The BMR declines by an average of 5 percent per decade, as mentioned, so age is a determining factor when calculating EER values.
- *Physical activity.* To help in estimating the energy spent on physical activity each day, activities are grouped according to their typical intensity.
- *Body size and weight.* The higher BMR of taller and heavier people calls for height and weight to be factored in when estimating a person's EER.
- *Growth.* The BMR is high in people who are growing, so pregnant women and children have their own sets of energy equations.

Full instructions for determining your own EER are presented in Appendix H. Alternatively, the margin note offers a quick-and-easy but more approximate way to determine your energy need and suggests a range of energy intakes that covers most people's needs based on the EER.

- A quick-and-easy estimate of energy need:
  - *First, look up the EER listed for your age and gender group (inside front cover).*
  - *Then, calculate a range of energy needs. For most people, the energy requirement falls within these ranges: (Men) EER ± 200 cal. (Women) EER ± 160 cal.*
  - *Virtually everyone's energy requirement falls within these larger ranges: (Men) EER ± 400 cal. (Women) EER ± 320 cal.*

KEY POINT The DRI committee has established a method for determining an individual's approximate energy requirement.

LO 9.3

Body Weight Versus Body Fatness

For most people, weighing themselves on a scale provides a convenient and accessible way to monitor body fatness, but researchers and health-care providers must rely on more accurate assessments. This section describes some of the preferred methods to assess overweight and underweight.

- To determine your BMI:

  (In pounds and inches)

  $$\text{BMI} = \frac{\text{weight (lb)} \times 703}{\text{height (in}^2\text{)}}$$

  (In kilograms and meters)

  $$\text{BMI} = \frac{\text{weight (kg)}}{\text{height (in}^2\text{)}}$$

- A table of BMI values is provided on the inside back cover, page Z.

© Rick Schaff

At 6 feet 3 inches tall and 245 pounds, Mike O'Hearn would be judged to be obese by BMI standards alone. Further measures reveal that his body contains only 8% of its weight as fat, less than the average fat percentage for men, and that his waist circumference is within a healthy range.

Body Mass Index (BMI)

BMI values correlate significantly with body fatness, and experts use them to help evaluate a person's health risks associated with underweight or overweight. The inside back cover of this book provides tables in which to find and evaluate BMI values for adults and adolescents. A formula for determining your BMI is given in the margin.

No one can tell you exactly how much you should weigh; but with health as a value, you have a starting framework in the BMI table. Your weight should fall within the range that best supports your health. As a general guideline, underweight for adults is defined as BMI of less than 18.5, overweight as BMI of 25.0 through 29.9, and obesity as BMI of 30 or more.

Health risks associated with BMI values often follow racial lines—the risks associated with a high BMI appear to be greater for white people than for black people, perhaps because, pound for pound, blacks often have a greater bone density and more lean tissue than whites.[35] Likewise, health risks appear to be greater for Asians than for Caucasians at the same BMI.

The BMI values have two major drawbacks: they fail to indicate how much of a person's weight is fat and where that fat is located. These drawbacks limit the value of the BMI for use with:

- Athletes (because their highly developed musculature falsely increases their BMI values).
- Pregnant and lactating women (because their increased weight is normal during childbearing).
- Adults over age 65 (because BMI values are based on data collected from younger people and because people "grow shorter" with age).

In addition, BMI values may overestimate the rates of overweight and obesity among some racial groups.[36]

The athletic man in the margin proves this point: with a BMI over 30, he would be classified as obese by BMI standards alone. However, a clinician would find that his percentage of body fat is well below average and his waist circumference is within a healthy range. A diagnosis of obesity or overweight requires a BMI value *plus* some measure of body composition and fat distribution. There is no easy way to look inside a living person to measure bones and muscles, but several indirect measures can provide an approximation.

Waist circumference measurements indicate visceral fatness (Figure 9-6); above a certain girth, disease risks rise.[37] Health professionals often use both BMI and waist circumference to assess a person's health risks and monitor changes over time.[38]

KEY POINT The BMI values mathematically correlate heights and weights with risks to health. They are especially useful for evaluating health risks of obesity but fail to measure body composition or fat distribution. They are not equally useful in all populations. Central adiposity can be assessed by measuring waist circumference.

Measures of Body Composition and Fat Distribution

A person who stands about 5 feet 10 inches tall and weighs 150 pounds carries about 30 of those pounds as fat. The rest is mostly water and lean tissues: muscles; organs such as the heart, brain, and liver; and the bones of the skeleton (see Figure 9-7). This lean tissue is vital to health. The person who seeks to lose weight wants to lose fat, not this precious lean tissue. And for someone who wants to gain weight, it is desirable to gain lean and fat in proportion, not just fat.

Researchers needing precise measures of body composition may choose any of several techniques to estimate body fat, including the **skinfold test, underwater**

weighing, or **bioelectrical impedance;** body fat distribution can be determined by radiographic techniques, such as **dual-energy X-ray absorptiometry** (see Figure 9-8). Mastering these and other sophisticated techniques requires proper instruction and practice to ensure reliability. Each method has advantages and disadvantages with respect to cost, technical difficulty, and precision of estimating body fat.

KEY POINT A clinician can determine the percentage of fat in a person's body by measuring skinfolds, underwater weight, or other parameters. Distribution of fat can be estimated by radiographic techniques.

How Much Body Fat Is Ideal?

After you have a body fatness estimate, the question arises: What is the "ideal" amount of fat for a body to have? This prompts another question: Ideal for what? If the answer is "society's perfect body shape," be aware that fashion is fickle and today's popular body shapes are not achievable by most people.

If the answer is "health," then the ideal depends partly on your gender and your age. For people in the healthy BMI range:

- A man should have between 12 and 20 percent of his body weight as fat.
- A woman should have between 20 and 30 percent of her body weight as fat.

Researchers draw the line and declare a person overly fat when body fat exceeds these values:

- 22 percent in men age 40 and younger.
- 25 percent in men over age 40.
- 32 percent in women age 40 and younger.
- 35 percent in women over age 40.

Besides gender and age, standards differ because of lifestyle and stage of life. For example, competitive endurance athletes need just enough body fat to provide fuel,

FIGURE 9-7 Average Body Composition of Men and Women

The substantially greater fat tissue of women is normal and necessary for reproduction

Andersen Ross/Blend Images/Getty Images

© 2010/Jupiterimages Corporation

FIGURE 9-6 Measuring Waist Circumference

Using a nonstretching tape measure, measure around the body near the belly button. (The skeleton shows the tape position relative to the hip bone.) Exhale normally while taking the measurement. Then compare your measurement with these cutoff points:

- Men: 102 cm (40 in.).
- Women: 88 cm (35 in.).

Anyone with a waist measurement larger than these standards may have an increased risk of disease.

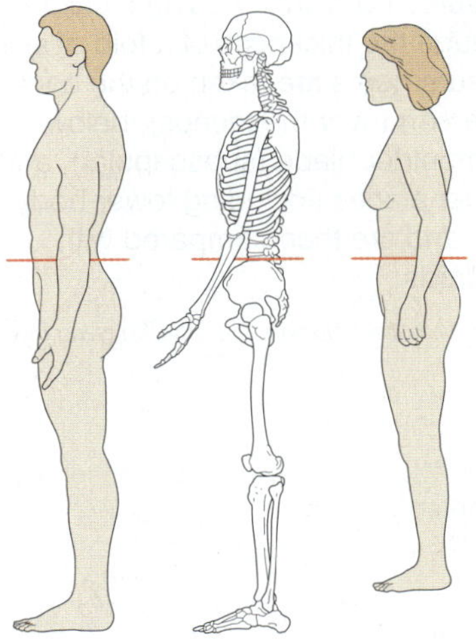

skinfold test measurement of the thickness of a fold of skin on the back of the arm (over the triceps muscle), below the shoulder blade (subscapular), or in other places, using a caliper (depicted in Figure 9-8); also called *fatfold test.*

underwater weighing a measure of density and volume used to determine body fat content.

bioelectrical impedance (im-PEE-dense) a technique for measuring body fatness by measuring the body's electrical conductivity.

dual-energy X-ray absorptiometry (ab-sorp-tee-OM-eh-tree) a noninvasive method of determining total body fat, fat distribution, and bone density by passing two low-dose X-ray beams through the body. Also used in evaluation of osteoporosis. Abbreviated DEXA.

FIGURE 9-8 **Three Methods of Assessing Body Fatness[a]**

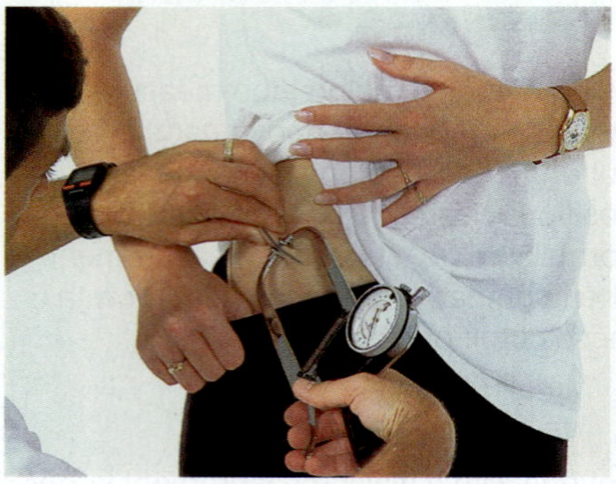

© Fitness & Wellness, Boise, Idaho

Skinfold measures can yield accurate results when a trained technician measures body fat by using a caliper to gauge the thickness of a fold of skin. Measurements are taken on the back of the arm (over the triceps), below the shoulder blade (subscapular), and in other places (including lower body sites) and are then compared with standards.

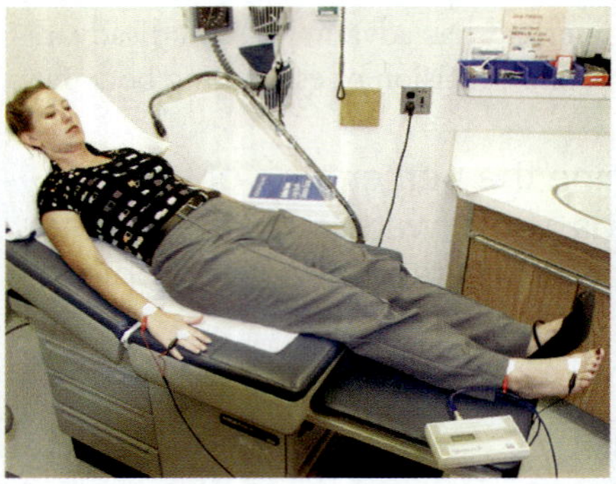

© Geri Engberg

Bioelectrical impedance is accurate when properly administered; the method determines body fatness by measuring conductivity. Lean tissue conducts a mild, painless electric current; fat tissue does not.

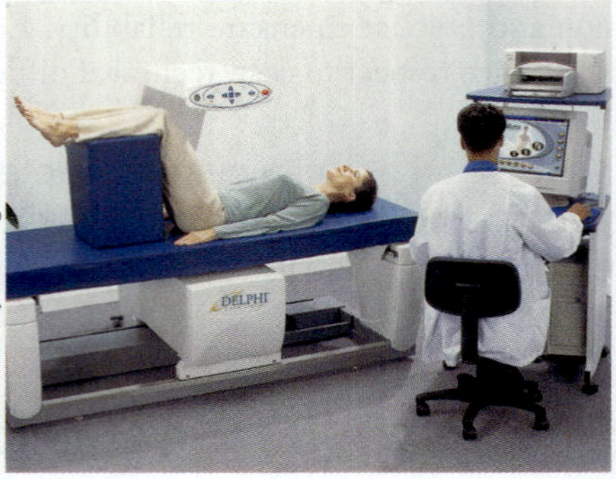

© Photo Courtesy of Hologic, Inc.

Dual-energy X-ray absorptiometry (DEXA) employs two low-dose X rays that differentiate among fat-free soft tissue (lean body mass), fat tissue, and bone tissue, providing a precise measurement of total fat and its distribution in all but extremely obese subjects.

[a] *Other methods include underwater weighing (hydrodensitometry), computed tomography, and magnetic resonance imaging.*

- More about optimal weight for pregnancy in Chapter 13.

insulate the body, and permit normal hormone activity, but not so much as to weigh them down. An Alaskan fisherman, in contrast, needs a blanket of extra fat to insulate against the cold. For a woman starting pregnancy, the outcome may be compromised if she begins with too much or too little body fat. Below a threshold for body fat content set by heredity, some individuals become infertile, develop depression or abnormal hunger regulation, or become unable to keep warm. These thresholds are not the same for each function or in all individuals, and much remains to be learned about them.

KEY POINT No single body composition or weight suits everyone; needs vary by gender, lifestyle, and stage of life.

- Research links obesity with:
  - *Birth order, number of brothers.*
  - *Divorced/single parents, nonprofessional or unemployed parents.*
  - *Early menstruation.*
  - *Ethnicity (being black or Mexican American elevates risk).*
  - *Exposure to a variety of foods; fast-food and soft-drink consumption.*
  - *Fat intake, protein intake, sugar intake.*
  - *Increased wealth (in developing nations).*
  - *Lower economic status (in developed nations).*
  - *Less frequent alcohol intake; high alcohol intake.*
  - *Less leisure time, international travel, geographic location.*
  - *Maternal starvation or obesity during gestation.*
  - *Meal skipping (particularly breakfast), meals eaten away from home.*
  - *Napping habits, sleep deprivation.*
  - *Sedentary behavior, television viewing.*
  - *Substandard housing.*
  - *Many more.*

LO 9.4, 9.5

The Mystery of Obesity

Why do some people get fat while others stay thin? Does fatness depend more on inherited metabolic factors or on environmental influences? Is it a matter of eating habits? If so, what directs eating behaviors—internal controls or a person's free will? Many factors, some of them conflicting, *correlate* with obesity (for interest, the margin lists some of them), but obesity's *cause* remains elusive. One component under intense scientific study is the appetite and its controls.

Hunger and Appetite—"Go" Signals

Food is critical to the body, so the brain and digestive tract communicate about the need for food and food sufficiency. Their means of communication, hormones and sensory nerve signals, fall roughly into two broad functional categories: "go" mechanisms that stimulate eating and "stop" mechanisms that suppress it. One view of the whole process of food intake regulation is summarized in Figure 9-9.

FIGURE 9-9 **Hunger, Appetite, Satiation, and Satiety**

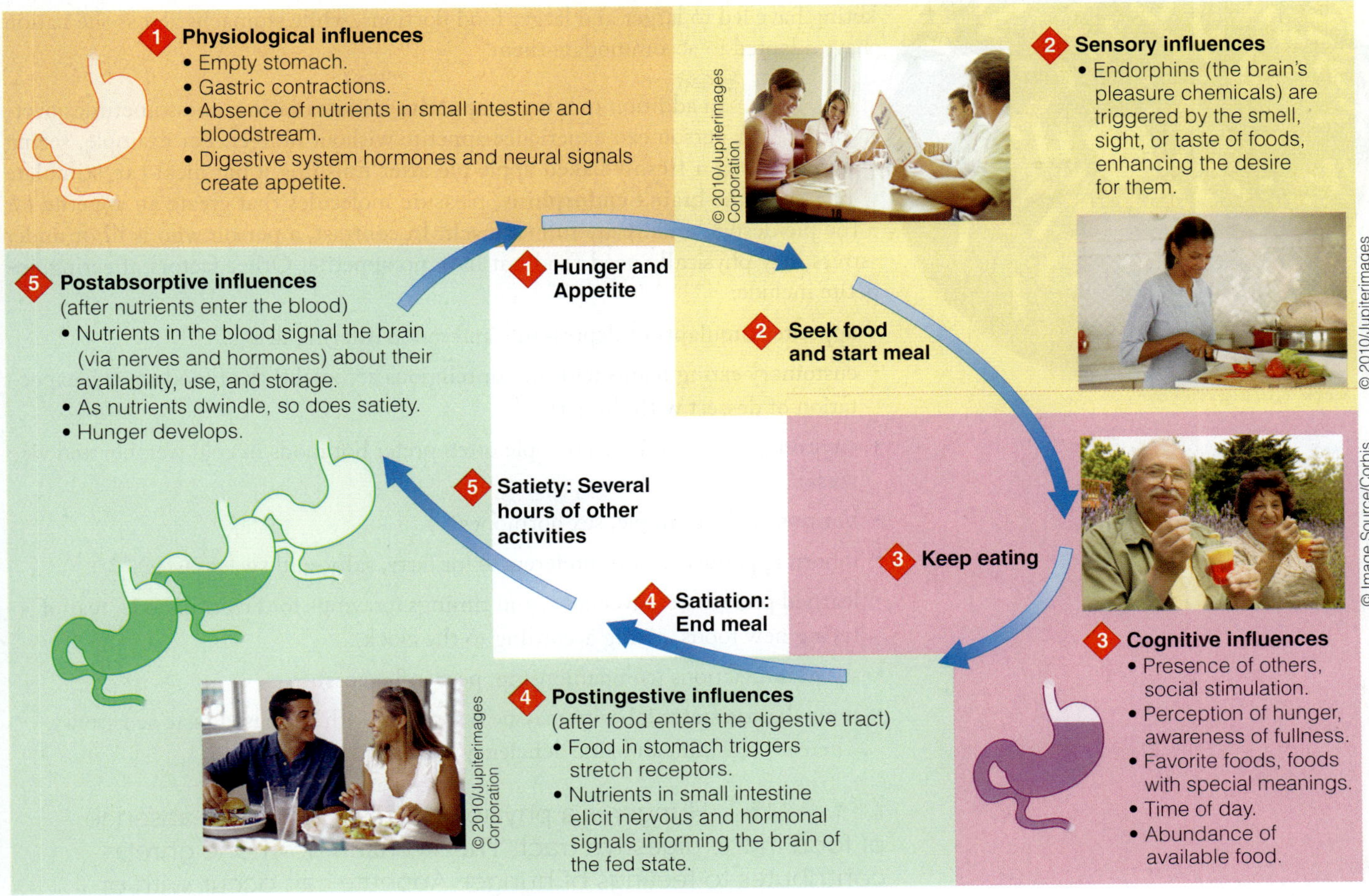

Hunger Beats Satiety The regulation of the human appetite is unbalanced, tipping in favor of food consumption.[39] **Hunger** commands food seeking and eating behaviors in a life-or-death drive for survival. In comparison, **satiation** and **satiety** are weaker suggestions to curb eating-related behaviors that are easily overruled.

Hunger Most people recognize hunger as a strong, unpleasant sensation that signals the need to seek and eat food. Hunger, the response to a physiological need for food, makes itself known roughly four to six hours after eating, after the food has left the stomach and much of the nutrient mixture has been absorbed by the intestine.

Hunger arises in part from chemical messengers acting on or originating in the brain's hypothalamus.[40] The physical contractions of an empty stomach trigger hunger signals, as does the stomach hormone **ghrelin,** a powerful appetite-stimulating hormone. Ghrelin is just one of many appetite-regulating messengers that inform the brain of the need for food. The brain itself produces a neurotransmitter that potently stimulates hunger sensations.**

The body's hunger response adapts quickly to changes in food intake. A person who suddenly eats smaller meals may feel extra hungry for a few days, but then hunger may diminish for a time. During this period, a large meal may make the person feel uncomfortably full, partly because the stomach's capacity has adapted to a smaller quantity of food. At this time a dieter may report "My stomach has shrunk," but the stomach has simply adjusted to smaller meals. At some point in food deprivation, hunger returns with a vengeance and can lead to bouts of extensive overeating.

Concept Link 9-4

Chapter 3 described the brain's hypothalamus (page 75).

hunger the physiological need to eat, experienced as a drive for obtaining food; an unpleasant sensation that demands relief.

satiation (SAY-she-AY-shun) the perception of fullness that builds throughout a meal, eventually reaching the degree of fullness and satisfaction that halts eating. Satiation generally determines how much food is consumed at one sitting.

satiety (sah-TIE-eh-tee) the perception of fullness that lingers in the hours after a meal and inhibits eating until the next mealtime. Satiety generally determines the length of time between meals.

ghrelin (GREL-in) a hormone released by the stomach that signals the hypothalamus of the brain to stimulate eating.

**The neurotransmitter is neuropeptide Y.

Just as the stomach's capacity can adapt to small meals, it quickly adapts to larger ones until a meal of normal size no longer satisfies. This observation may partly explain the increasing U.S. calorie intakes: popular demand and food industry marketing have led to larger and larger food portions, while stomachs across the nation have adapted to accommodate them.

Appetite In addition to hunger, **appetite** initiates eating, and sometimes overeating.[41] A person can experience appetite without hunger. For example, seeing and smelling a freshly baked apple pie after finishing a big meal can stimulate release of the brain's **endorphins,** pleasure molecules that create an appetite for the pie despite an already full stomach. In contrast, a person who is ill or under stress may physically need food but have no appetite. Other factors affecting appetite include:

- appetite stimulants or depressants and mood-altering drugs.
- customary eating habits (cultural or religious acceptability of foods or the expectation of dessert with dinner).
- environmental conditions (people often prefer hot foods in cold weather and vice versa).
- hormones (for example, sex hormones).
- inborn appetites (inborn preferences for fatty, salty, and sweet tastes).[42]
- learned preferences, aversions, and timings (cravings for favorite foods, fear of trying new foods, eating according to the clock).
- social interactions (companionship, peer influences).[43]
- some disease states (obesity may be associated with increased taste sensitivity, whereas colds, flu, and zinc deficiency reduce taste sensitivity).

KEY POINT Hunger is a physiologic response to an absence of food in the digestive tract. The stomach hormone ghrelin contributes to feelings of hunger. Appetite can occur with or without hunger, and many factors affect it. Hunger outweighs satiety in the appetite control system.

Satiation and Satiety—"Stop" Signals

To balance energy in with energy out, eating behaviors must be counterbalanced with ending meals and fasts between meals. As with the "go" signals for food intake, a series of hormones and sensory nerve messages influence these processes.[44]

Satiation At some point during a meal, the brain receives signals that enough food has been eaten. The resulting satiation limits the size of the meal (consult Figure 9-9 again). Food in the digestive tract triggers satiation, starting in the mouth. Greater exposure of the mouth to food triggers increased satiation.[45] When the stomach stretches to accommodate a meal, nerve receptors in the stomach fire, sending a signal to the brain that the stomach is full.[46] As nutrients from the meal enter the small intestine, they stimulate receptor nerves and trigger the release of hormones, signaling the hypothalamus about the size and nature of the meal.[47] The brain also detects absorbed nutrients delivered by the bloodstream, and it responds by releasing neurotransmitters that suppress food intake.

Together, stomach distention and the presence of nutrients trigger nervous and hormonal signals to inform the brain's hypothalamus that a meal has been consumed. Satiation occurs; the eater feels full and stops eating.[48]

Satiety After a meal, the feeling of satiety continues to suppress hunger over a period of hours, regulating the frequency of meals. Hormones, nervous signals, and the brain work in harmony to sustain feelings of fullness. At some later point, signals from the digestive tract once again sound the alert that more food is needed.

Did You Know?

Satiation regulates meal size; satiety regulates meal frequency.

appetite the psychological desire to eat; a learned motivation and a positive sensation that accompanies the sight, smell, or thought of appealing foods.

endorphins brain compounds that reduce pain and produce pleasure in ways similar to opiate drugs. In appetite control, endorphins are released on seeing, smelling, or tasting delicious food and may enhance the drive to eat or continue eating.

Leptin: An Adiposity Regulating Hormone **Leptin,** one of the adipokine hormones, is produced primarily by the adipose tissue in direct proportion to body fat.[††49] Leptin travels via the bloodstream to the brain, where it acts as part of the brain's appetite-regulating chemistry to suppress the appetite. Leptin operates on a feedback mechanism—a gain in body fatness stimulates leptin production, which in turn reduces food consumption, resulting in fat loss.[50] Fat loss brings the opposite effect—suppression of leptin production and an increase in appetite. Thus, the fat tissue that produces leptin is ultimately controlled by it.

A rare form of severe obesity arises from an inherited inability to produce leptin.[51] In those cases, restoring the missing hormone quickly produces weight and fat loss and reversal of the insulin resistance that follows obesity.[52] More commonly, obese people produce plenty of leptin but they fail to respond to it, a condition called *leptin resistance*.[53] Providing more leptin is therefore useless against most people's obesity.

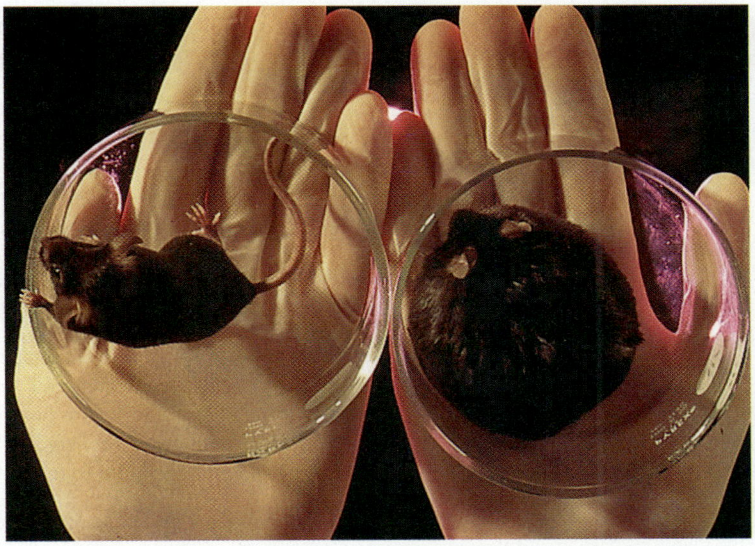
R. Benali/Getty Images

The mouse on the right is genetically obese—it lacks the gene for producing leptin. The mouse on the left is also genetically obese but remains lean because it receives leptin injections.

Energy Nutrients and Satiety The composition of a meal also affects satiation and satiety. Of the three energy-yielding nutrients, protein seems to be the most satiating, an effect that may be due to elevated blood concentrations of certain amino acids in the bloodstream.[54] Carbohydrates in food also contribute to satiation and satiety, however, while fat triggers a hormone that contributes longer-term satiety.[55]

Among carbohydrates, those ranking low on the glycemic index may lend greater satiety to the diet than those ranking higher.[56] Low-glycemic foods, such as legumes or barley, are often high in soluble fibers, and soluble fibers appear to increase satiation.[57] Can a low-glycemic diet produce a lower body weight, then? Not unless the diet also presents a calorie deficit; the glycemic load alone is not correlated with body weight in research.[58]

Researchers have also reported increased satiety from foods high in water and even from foods that have been puffed up with air. As dieters await news of foods that might be useful against hunger, researchers have not yet identified any one food, nutrient, or attribute that is especially effective for weight loss and its maintenance.

CONCEPT LINK 9-5

Chapter 4 described the glycemic index and glycemic load, and Controversy 4 discussed the relationships among various carbohydrate sources and body fatness (pages 128–129 and 145).

KEY POINT Satiation ends a meal when the nervous and hormonal signals inform the brain that enough food has been eaten. Satiety postpones eating until the next meal. The adipokine leptin suppresses the appetite and regulates body fatness.

Inside-the-Body Causes of Obesity

Findings about appetite regulation, the "energy in" side of the energy budget, do not fully explain why some people gain too much body fatness while others stay lean. On the opposite "energy out" side of the energy budget, many theories have emerged to explain obesity in terms of metabolic function. And whenever discussions turn to metabolism, topics in genetics follow closely behind.

Selected Metabolic Theories of Obesity Metabolic theories attempt to explain variations in the ease with which individuals gain or lose body fat. When given a constant number of excess calories over a period of weeks, some people gain many pounds of body fat while other people gain far fewer. The former use calories efficiently: they seem to have a "thrifty" metabolism.

Table 9-4 provides some theories about how metabolic variations may affect weight gain. For example, during metabolism, enzymes "waste" a small percentage

leptin an appetite-suppressing hormone produced in the fat cells that conveys information about body fatness to the brain; believed to be involved in the maintenance of body composition (*leptos* means "slender").

[††]Leptin is also produced in the stomach, where it helps to regulate digestion and contributes to satiation.

TABLE 9-4 Selected Theories of Metabolic Causes of Obesity

Theory	Mechanism of Action
Enzyme theory	Excess fat storage may stem from elevated concentrations of an enzyme, lipoprotein lipase (LPL), that enables fat cells to store triglycerides. The more LPL, the more easily fat cells store lipid. The fat cells of obese people contain more LPL than the fat cells of lean people.
Fat cell number theory	Body fatness is determined by both the number and the size of fat cells. Fat cells increase in number during the growing years, tapering off in adulthood.
Fetal programming theory	The children of mothers who either starved or were obese during their pregnancies more often grow to be overweight or obese themselves. An energy-lean or an energy-rich prenatal environment may influence fetal genetic expression for enzymes involved in energy metabolism: the underfed fetus adapts by producing more energy-conserving metabolic systems; the richly supplied fetus may adapt by producing more fat-storing enzymes and cells.
Thermogenesis I: Energy-wasting proteins and brown fat theory	Proteins control the body's heat production, or thermogenesis. A type of adipose tissue, brown fat, has abundant energy-wasting proteins that specialize in converting chemical energy to heat. Brown fat is more abundant in lean animals than in fat ones. Human infants have abundant brown fat. In 2009, functional brown fat was identified in human adults.
Thermogenesis II: Adaptive thermogenesis theory	Many tissues, such as muscle, spleen, and bone marrow, convert stored energy into heat in response to cold temperature, physical conditioning, overfeeding, starvation, trauma, and other stress. Genetic inheritance is thought to determine the efficiency of this system.
Thermogenesis III: Diet-induced thermogenesis theory	The thermic effect of food varies between obese and nonobese people. In lean people who have just eaten a meal, energy use speeds up for a while, but in many obese people, no change in energy use occurs after eating. In theory, this small difference in energy expenditure may account for an accumulation of body fat, but overweight people often spend more energy each day than lean people do because their heavier bodies require more energy to move and maintain.

of energy. The energy is radiated away as heat in a process called **thermogenesis.** Some enzymes, however, expend copious energy in thermogenesis, producing abundant heat but performing no other useful work. In radiating more energy away as heat, the body spends more, rather than storing more, excess energy.

One tissue extraordinarily gifted in performing thermogenesis is **brown adipose tissue (BAT).** Formerly detected only in animals and human infants, functional BAT has recently been identified in many young adult human subjects, too.[59] Intriguingly, subjects with the greatest body fatness in these studies had the least BAT.[60]

Is it wise, then, to strive to stimulate metabolic enzymes to step up thermogenesis? Probably not. In rats, upping the rate of thermogenesis has no effect on overall energy expenditure or body fatness.[61] Also, at a level of activity not far beyond that of normal functioning, energy-wasting activity causes cell death. Sham "metabolic" diet products may claim to increase energy expenditures, but no tricks of metabolism can produce effortless fat loss.

thermogenesis the generation and release of body heat associated with the breakdown of body fuels. *Adaptive thermogenesis* describes adjustments in energy expenditure related to changes in environment such as cold and to physiological events such as underfeeding or trauma.

brown adipose tissue (BAT) a type of adipose tissue abundant in hibernating animals and human infants and recently identified in human adults. Abundant pigmented enzymes of energy metabolism give BAT a dark appearance under a microscope; the enzymes release heat from fuels without accomplishing other work. Also called *brown fat.*

Genetics and Obesity If genes carry the instructions for making enzymes, and enzymes are involved in energy metabolism, then genetic variations might reasonably be expected to explain why some people get fat and some stay lean. Indeed, genomic researchers have identified hundreds of genes likely to play roles in obesity development but have not so far identified genetic causes of common obesity.[62] Inherited genes clearly do influence a person's tendency to gain weight or stay lean. For someone with at least one obese parent, the chance of becoming obese is estimated to fall between 30 and 70 percent.[63]

Exceptionally complex relationships exist among the many genes related to energy metabolism and obesity, and they each interact with environmental factors, too.[64] Although an individual's genetic inheritance may make obesity likely, the disease of obesity cannot develop unless the environment—factors that lie outside the body—provides the means of doing so.[65]

MY TURN

© Cengage Learning

ie   Lauren

How Many Calories?

Two students talk about portion control, physical activity, and dessert.

CENGAGENOW To hear their stories, log on to www.cengage.com/sso.

KEY POINT Metabolic theories attempt to explain obesity on the basis of molecular functioning. A person's genetic inheritance greatly influences, but does not ensure, the development of obesity.

Outside-the-Body Causes of Obesity

Food is a source of pleasure. Being creatures of free will, people can easily override satiety signals and eat whenever they wish, especially when tempted with delicious treats and large servings. People also value physical ease and seek out labor-savers, such as automobiles and elevators. Over past decades, the abundance of food has increased enormously while the daily demand for physical activity for survival has all but disappeared.[66] By some counts, today's food energy intakes alone account for the rise in U.S. obesity rates.[67]

External Cues to Overeating Almost everyone has had the experience of walking into a food store, feeling not particularly hungry, and, after viewing an array of goodies, walking out snacking on a favorite treat. A classic experiment showed that rats, known to precisely maintain body weight when fed standard chow, overeat and rapidly become obese when fed "cafeteria style" on a variety of rich, palatable foods. People may also overconsume foods when offered a delicious smorgasbord, often without realizing they are doing so.[68] Like the rats, they respond to external cues.

Overeating behavior also occurs in response to complex human sensations such as loneliness, yearning, craving, addiction, or compulsion.[69] Any kind of stress can also cause overeating and weight gain.[70] ("What do I do when I'm worried? Eat. What do I do when I'm concentrating? Eat!").

People also overeat when given large portions of food. In a classic study, moviegoers given large buckets of popcorn consumed proportionately more than when given small bags of popcorn.[71] In an amusing twist, researchers dispensed large and small containers of stale 14-day-old popcorn; moviegoers still ate more from the larger size, despite complaining about the taste. This phenomenon seems unaffected by prior knowledge of it. Graduate students in nutrition who had been taught about the "big bowl" effect on portion size, were invited to a party and offered snack mix from big and small bowls. Despite superior education, they ate bigger portions of snack mix from big bowls than from small ones.[72]

Physical Inactivity Some people may be obese not because they eat too much, but because they move too little. In as little as one month of inactivity, muscles shrink measurably and collect small deposits of fat.[73] Conversely, sustained exercise is known to stimulate muscle cells to develop more fat-metabolizing equipment that uses up fat and other fuels during and after activity.[74]

In addition to intentional physical activity, a spontaneous kind of activity produces **nonexercise activity thermogenesis (NEAT).** Lean people tend to be more spontaneously active, both at work and at leisure, and so expend more NEAT energy.[75]

Did You Know?

Quacks often sell "genetic tests" and diets that promise to "reset your genetic code to be thin. Beware.

- Controversy 11 provides a look into the science of nutritional genomics.

CONCEPT LINK 9-6

The rise in U.S. calorie intakes was depicted in Figure C4-3, page 144.

CONCEPT LINK 9-7

Figure 2-11 in Chapter 2 (page 49) demonstrated how portion sizes have increased over recent decades.

The war on muscular work has been a remarkable success.

—C. Bouchard, *Physical Activity and Obesity* (Champaign, Ill: Human Kinetics Publishers, Inc., 2000).

nonexercise activity thermogenesis (NEAT) energy expenditure associated with everyday spontaneous activities, as opposed to consciously undertaken physical activities.

THINK FITNESS

Activity for a Healthy Body Weight

Some people believe that physical activity must be long and arduous to obtain benefits, such as improved body composition. Not so. A brisk, 30-minute walk at a pace of about 100 steps per minute each day can help significantly (a pedometer can help count steps).[76] To achieve an "active lifestyle" requires walking for an hour a day. Even in increments of 10 minutes throughout the day, exercising can measurably improve fitness.[77] In one study, as little as 72 minutes of physical activity a *week* measurably reduced waist circumference in overweight and obese women, even in the absence of weight loss.[78] Weight loss brought greater reductions in waist circumference, however.

According to the American College of Sports Medicine's 2009 position paper:

- A negative energy balance incurred through physical activity will result in weight loss, and the larger the negative energy balance, the greater the weight loss.
- Preventing weight gain and augmenting loss occurs with at least 2 hours and 30 minutes (150 minutes) a week of at least moderate intensity physical activity.
- Episodes of physical activity of at least 10 minutes duration count toward exercise goals.
- Both aerobic (endurance) and muscle-strengthening (resistance) physical activities are beneficial, but calorie restriction must accompany resistance training to achieve weight loss.[79]

A useful strategy is to incorporate bits of physical activity into your daily schedule in many simple, small-scale ways. Work in the garden; work your abdominal muscles while you stand in line; stand up straight; walk up stairs; fidget while sitting down; tighten your buttocks each time you get up from your chair. Small energy expenditures can add up to significant contributions. Chapter 10 provides many more details.

START NOW

CENGAGENOW Ready to make a change? Consult the online behavior-change planner to commit to obtaining enough physical activity to help build lean tissue and improve fitness while managing body fatness at **www.cengage.com/sso**.

- Physical activity for weight loss or maintenance:
  1. Choose moderate or vigorous activities.
  2. Move large muscle groups.
  3. Invest longer times in physical activity.
  4. Adopt informal strategies to be more active.
- Physical activity for building lean body mass:
  1. Choose strength-building exercises.
  2. Use a balanced exercise routine.
  3. Perform exercises with increasing intensity.
  4. Adopt informal strategies to be more active.

Their brains somehow signal them to stand up more, walk around, and fidget.[80] Collectively, NEAT expenditures may contribute to energy balance to some degree.[81]

The United States seems locked in an epidemic of inactivity. Television and sedentary video and computer entertainment have all but replaced outdoor play for many people.[82] In addition, most people work at sedentary jobs. A hundred years ago, 30 percent of the energy used in farm and factory work came from human muscle power; today, only 1 percent does. The same trend follows at home, at work, at school, and in transportation. The more hours spent sitting still, the higher the risk of dying from heart disease and other causes.[83] The Think Fitness feature offers perspective on the contribution of physical activity to weight management, and Table 9-5 lists the energy costs of some activities.

The Built Environment Experts urge people to "take the stairs instead of the elevator" or "walk or bike to work." These are good suggestions: climbing stairs provides an impromptu workout, and people who walk or ride a bicycle for transportation most often meet their needs for physical activity.[84] For many, though, such healthy lifestyle choices are challenging.

Some aspects of the **built environment,** including buildings, sidewalks, and transportation opportunities, can discourage physical activity. For example, most stairwells of modern buildings are inconvenient, stuffy, isolated, and unsafe. Roadways often lack sidewalks, crosswalks, or lanes marked for bicycles. The air on roadways can be dangerously high in carbon monoxide gas and other pollutants from gasoline engine emissions.‡‡ Hot and cold weather also pose hazards for outdoor

built environment the buildings, roads, utilities, homes, fixtures, parks, and all other man-made entities that form the physical characteristics of a community.

food deserts urban and rural low-income areas with limited access to affordable and nutritious foods. Also defined in Chapter 15.

‡‡Carbon monoxide (CO) avidly binds to hemoglobin in the blood, reducing blood oxygen content: CO in air surrounding roadways can reach levels sufficient to impair driving ability.

commuters. In contrast, those with access to health-promoting built environments more easily make healthy choices. Safe, attractive, affordable biking and walking areas and public exercise facilities help maintain health and body leanness and so does access to nutritious foods.[85]

Food Access The kinds of foods recommended for weight management—fresh fruits, vegetables, lean meats, and other lower-calorie foods—are not equally available across the United States. Residents of low-income urban and rural areas called **food deserts** may lack access to even a single supermarket but find convenience stores and fast-food restaurants in abundance.[86] Often overweight and without transportation, such people lack access to distant supermarkets that offer nutritious fresh foods.[87] They base their diets on refined packaged sweets and starches and fatty canned meats, or they eat mostly fast food, inviting malnutrition.[88] A correlation exists between eating fast food and being obese, but this does not prove that eating fast food causes obesity.[89] It may, but fast foods may simply coexist with a number of other factors that make obesity likely. After all, many lean people also eat fast food in moderation.

End of Story? Anyone involved in a good mystery wants to know how it ends. In the case of the causes of obesity, no one yet knows which of the suspects are the real culprits, and until evidence proves otherwise, any or all may be guilty as charged. In real life, the best way for most people to attain a healthy body composition boils down to control in three areas: diet, physical activity, and behavior change. Later sections focus on these areas, while the next section delves into the details of how, exactly, the body loses and gains weight.

KEY POINT Studies of human behavior identify stimuli that lead to overeating. Too little physical activity, the built environment, and a lack of access to fresh foods are also linked with overfatness.

How the Body Loses and Gains Weight

The causes of obesity may be complex, but the body's energy balance is straightforward. The balance between the energy you take in and the energy you spend determines whether you will gain, lose, or maintain body *fat*. A change in body *weight* of a pound or two may not indicate a change in body fat—it can reflect shifts in body fluid content, in bone minerals, in lean tissues such as muscles, or in the contents of the bladder or digestive tract. A change often correlates with the time of day: people generally weigh the least before breakfast. One of the most important things for people concerned with weight control to realize is that quick, large changes in weight may not indicate fat loss.

The type of tissue lost or gained depends on how you go about losing or gaining it. To lose fluid, for example, you can take a "water pill" (diuretic), causing the kidneys to siphon extra water from the blood into the urine; intense exercise while wearing heavy clothing in hot weather also causes abundant fluid loss in sweat. (Both practices are dangerous and are not being recommended here.) To gain water weight, you can overconsume salt and water; for a few hours, your body will retain water until it manages to excrete the salt. (This, too, is not recommended.) Most quick weight-change schemes promote large changes in body fluids that register dramatic, but temporary, changes on the scale and accomplish little weight change in the long run.

One other practice is hazardous and not recommended: smoking. Each year, many adolescents, particularly girls, take up smoking as a means to control weight.[90] Nicotine blunts feelings of hunger and smokers do tend to weigh less than nonsmokers.

TABLE 9-5 Energy Spent in Activities

To determine the calorie cost of an activity, multiply the number listed by your weight in pounds. Then multiply by the number of minutes spent performing the activity.

Example: Jessica (125 pounds) rode a bike at 17 mph for 25 minutes:

$$.057 \times 125 = 7.125$$
$$7.125 \times 25 = 178.125$$

(about 180 calories)

Activity	Cal/lb Body Weight/min
Aerobic dance (vigorous)	.062
Basketball (vigorous, full court)	.097
Bicycling	
13 mph	.045
15 mph	.049
17 mph	.057
19 mph	.076
21 mph	.090
23 mph	.109
25 mph	.139
Canoeing (flat water, moderate pace)	.045
Computer sports games[a]	
bowling	.021
boxing	.021
tennis	.022
Cross-country skiing	
8 mph	.104
Golf (carrying clubs)	.045
Handball	.078
Horseback riding (trot)	.052
Rowing (vigorous)	.097
Running	
5 mph	.061
6 mph	.074
7.5 mph	.094
9 mph	.103
10 mph	.114
11 mph	.131
Soccer (vigorous)	.097
Studying	.011
Swimming	
20 yd/min	.032
45 yd/min	.058
50 yd/min	.070
Table tennis (skilled)	.045
Tennis (beginner)	.032
Walking (brisk pace)	
3.5 mph	.035
4.5 mph	.048
Weight lifting	
light-to-moderate effort	.024
vigorous effort	.048
Wheelchair basketball	.084
Wheeling self in wheelchair	.030

[a]*Such as Wii™, by Nintendo.*

CONCEPT LINK 9-8

Chapter 8 discussed the body's water and electrolyte balancing systems, pages 286–287.

- Smoking may keep some people's weight down, but at what cost?
  - *Cancer.*
  - *Chronic lung diseases.*
  - *Heart disease.*
  - *Low-birthweight babies.*
  - *Miscarriage.*
  - *Osteoporosis.*
  - *Shortened life span.*
  - *Sudden infant death.*
  - *Many others.*

Fear of weight gain prevents many people from quitting smoking, too. The best advice to those hoping to quit is to adjust eating and exercise habits to maintain weight during and after cessation. To the person flirting with the idea of taking up smoking for weight control, don't do it—many thousands of people who became addicted as teenagers die from tobacco-related illnesses each year.

Moderate Weight Loss Versus Rapid Weight Loss

Being able to eat periodically, store fuel, and then use up that fuel between meals is a great advantage. Relieved of the need to constantly seek food, human beings are free to dance, study, converse, wonder, fall in love, and concentrate on endeavors other than eating. The between-meal interval is normally about 4 to 6 waking hours—about the length of time the body takes to use up most of the readily available fuel—or 12 to 18 hours at night, when body systems slow down and the need is less.

When you eat less food energy than you need, your body draws on its stored fuel to keep going. If a person exercises appropriately, moderately restricts calories, and consumes an otherwise balanced diet that meets protein and carbohydrate needs, the body is forced to use up its stored fat for energy. Gradual weight loss will occur. This is preferred to rapid weight loss because lean body mass is spared and fat is lost.

- In early food deprivation:
  - *The nervous system cannot use fat as fuel; it can only use glucose.*
  - *Body fat cannot be converted to glucose.*
  - *Body protein can be converted to glucose.*
- In later food deprivation:
  - *Ketone bodies help feed the nervous system and so help spare tissue protein.*

The Body's Response to Fasting If a person doesn't eat for, say, three whole days, then the body makes one adjustment after another. Less than a day into the fast, the liver's glycogen is essentially exhausted. Where, then, can the body obtain glucose to keep its nervous system going? Not from the muscles' glycogen because that is reserved for the muscles' own use. Not from the abundant fat stores most people carry because these are of no use to the nervous system. Fat cannot be converted to glucose—the body lacks enzymes for this conversion.[§§] The muscles, heart, and other organs use fat as fuel, but at this stage the nervous system needs glucose. The body does, however, possess enzymes that can convert protein to glucose. Therefore, the underfed body sacrifices the proteins in its lean tissue to supply raw materials from which to make glucose.

If the body were to continue to consume its lean tissue unchecked, death would ensue within about ten days. After all, in addition to skeletal muscle, the blood proteins, liver, digestive tract linings, heart muscle, and lung tissue—all vital tissues—are being burned as fuel. (Fasting or starving people remain alive only until their stores of fat are gone or until half their lean tissue is gone, whichever comes first.) To prevent this, the body plays its last ace: it converts fat into compounds that the nervous system can adapt for use and so forestalls the end. This process is ketosis, an adaptation to prolonged fasting or carbohydrate deprivation.

Ketosis In ketosis, instead of breaking down fat molecules all the way to carbon dioxide and water, the body takes partially broken-down fat fragments and combines them to make **ketone bodies,** compounds that are normally kept to low levels in the blood. It converts some amino acids—those that cannot be used to make glucose—to ketone bodies, too. These ketone bodies circulate in the bloodstream and help to feed the brain; about half of the brain's cells can make the enzymes needed to use ketone bodies for energy. Under normal conditions, the brain and nervous system devour glucose—about 400 to 600 calories' worth each day. After about ten days of fasting, the brain and nervous system can meet most of their energy needs using ketone bodies.

CONCEPT LINK 9-9

Chapter 4 discussed ketosis and some of its drawbacks (page 126).

Thus, indirectly, the nervous system begins to feed on the body's fat stores. Ketosis reduces the nervous system's need for glucose, spares the muscle and other lean tissue from being quickly devoured, and prolongs the starving person's life. Thanks to ketosis, a healthy person starting with average body fat content can live totally deprived of food for as long as six to eight weeks. Figure 9-10 reviews how energy is used during both feasting and fasting.

ketone bodies acidic compounds derived from fat and certain amino acids. Normally rare in the blood, they help to feed the brain during times when too little carbohydrate is available. Also defined in Chapter 4.

Fasting Respected, wise people in many cultures have practiced fasting as a periodic discipline. The body tolerates short-term fasting, and at least in animal studies,

[§§]Glycerol, which makes up 5 percent of fat, can yield glucose but is a negligible source.

FIGURE 9-10 **Feasting and Fasting**

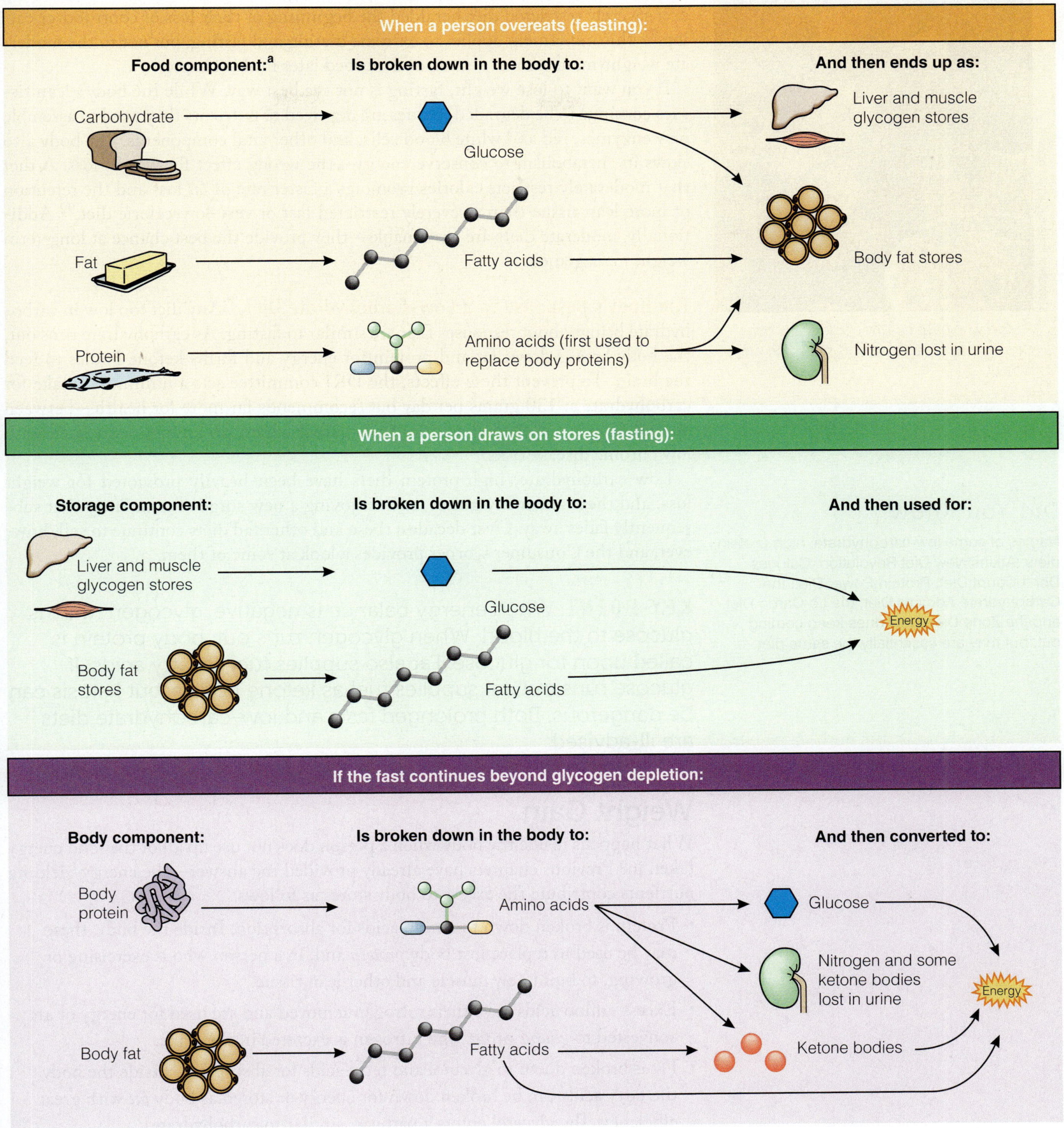

[a]*Alcohol is not included because it is a toxin and not a nutrient, but it does contribute energy to the body. After detoxifying the alcohol, the body uses the remaining two-carbon fragments to build fatty acids and stores them as fat.*

short-term fasting seems to benefit the body in some ways, although there is no evidence that the body becomes internally "cleansed," as some believe. Fasting may harm the body, however, when ketosis upsets the acid-base balance of the blood or when fasting promotes excessive mineral losses in the urine. In as little as 24 hours of fasting, the intestinal lining begins to lose its integrity.

Comstock Images/Getty Images

People who have healthy body weight consume more, not less, carbohydrate-rich whole foods.

Food deprivation also leads to a tendency to overeat or even binge when food becomes available. The effect seems to last beyond the point when weight is restored to normal, sometimes for years; people with eating disorders often report that fasting or a severely restricted diet heralded the beginning of their loss of control over eating.[91] This indictment applies to extreme dieting and fasting, but not to the moderate weight-management strategies described later in this chapter.

If you want to lose weight, fasting is not the best way. While the body's lean tissues continue to be degraded, tissues are deprived of nutrients they need to assemble new enzymes, red and white blood cells, and other vital components. The body also slows its metabolism to conserve energy—the wrong effect for weight loss. A diet that moderately restricts calories promotes a faster rate of *fat* loss and the retention of more lean tissue than a severely restricted fast or very-low-calorie diet.[92] Additionally, moderate diets are sustainable—they provide the best chance at long-term weight management.

The Body's Response to a Low-Carbohydrate Diet Any diet too low in carbohydrate brings about responses that are similar to fasting. As carbohydrate runs out, the body breaks down fat and protein for energy and forms ketone bodies to feed the brain. To prevent these effects, the DRI committee sets a minimum intake for carbohydrate at 130 grams per day but recommends far more for health—between 45 and 65 percent of total calories from carbohydrate, an amount associated with low chronic disease risks.

Low-carbohydrate, high-protein diets have been heavily promoted for weight loss, and they take many guises, each enjoying a new surge of popularity that subsequently fades away. Over decades, these and other fad diets continue to sell, however, and the Consumer Corner provides a look at some of them.

Did You Know?

Names of some low-carbohydrate, high-protein diets: Atkins New Diet Revolution, Calories Don't Count Diet, Protein-Power Diet, the Carbohydrate Addict's Diet, the Lo-Carbo Diet, and the Zone Diet. New ones keep coming out, but they are essentially the same diet.

KEY POINT When energy balance is negative, glycogen returns glucose to the blood. When glycogen runs out, body protein is called upon for glucose. Fat also supplies fuel as fatty acids. If glucose runs out, fat supplies fuel as ketone bodies, but ketosis can be dangerous. Both prolonged fasts and low-carbohydrate diets are ill-advised.

Weight Gain

What happens inside the body when a person does not use up all of the food energy taken in? Previous chapters have already provided the answer—the energy-yielding nutrients contribute the excess to body stores as follows:

- Protein is broken down to amino acids for absorption. Inside the body, these may be used to replace lost body *protein* and, in a person who is exercising or growing, to build new muscle and other lean tissue.
- Excess amino acids have their nitrogen removed and are used for energy or are converted to *glucose* or *fat*. The nitrogen is excreted in the urine.
- Fat is broken down to glycerol and fatty acids for absorption. Inside the body, the fatty acids can be broken down for energy or stored as body *fat* with great efficiency. The glycerol enters a pathway similar to carbohydrate.
- Carbohydrate (other than fiber) is broken down to sugars for absorption. In the body tissues, excesses of these may be built up to *glycogen* and stored, used for energy, or converted to *fat* and stored.
- Alcohol is absorbed and, once detoxified, used for fuel or converted into body fat for storage.

Four sources of energy—the three energy-yielding nutrients and alcohol—may enter the body, but they become only two kinds of energy stores: glycogen and fat. Glycogen stores amount to about three-fourths of a pound; fat stores can amount to

CONSUMER CORNER Popular Fad Diets

Weight-loss books and products are a $33 billion-a-year business—so many fad diets exist that they could fill a bookstore. Some restrict fats or carbohydrates, some disallow certain foods, some advocate certain food combinations, some claim that a person's genetic type or blood type determines the best diet, and so forth.

Unfortunately, many of these diets are more fiction than science. The writers may skillfully weave in bits of authentic nutrition knowledge and include impressive-sounding terms, such as *eicosanoids* or *adipokines,* to make their ideas sound credible. Table 9-6 presents some fad diet fantasies along with the scientific truths. What is it about these diets that consumers find so irresistible?

TABLE 9-6 Fantasies and Truths About Weight-Loss Fads

Fantasy: *You'll lose weight fast without counting calories or exercising because the diet or product alters metabolism.* Truth: No known trick of metabolism produces significant weight loss without diet or exercise.
Fantasy: *On this diet, you can eat all you want and still lose weight.* Truth: Unless the diet is composed entirely of celery or lettuce, basic laws governing energy disprove this claim—energy consumed must be used to fuel the body or stored as fat.
Fantasy: *You'll never regain the weight, even after you stop using the diet or product.* Truth: Maintenance of a new lower weight requires life-long changes in diet and exercise.
Fantasy: *Lose more than 3 pounds per week without medical supervision.* Truth: Weight loss in this range carries substantial risks to health and even to life, making medical supervision prudent.
Fantasy: *This product is 100% successful in producing weight loss.* Truth: The causes of obesity are multiple, and even prescription medications and stomach-shrinking surgeries are not 100% effective.
Fantasy: *You'll lose weight just by wearing the product or rubbing it on the skin.* Truth: No over-the-counter patch, cream, wrap, ring, bracelet, other jewelry, shoe inserts, or other gimmick is known to cause loss of weight or fat.
Fantasy: *Reset your genetic code to be thin.* Truth: You inherited your genes and no diet can alter them.
Fantasy: *Stress hormones make you fat.* Truth: Supplements sold to block stress hormones and produce weight loss do neither.
Fantasy: *High-protein diets are so popular because they are the best way to lose weight.* Truth: See this chapter's Consumer Corner.
Fantasy: *High-protein diets energize the brain.* Truth: The brain depends on carbohydrate for energy.
Fantasy: *Dietitians know nothing about "modern" nutrition.* Truth: Dietitians are, by training and experience, nutrition experts who rely on scientific approaches and cannot be swayed by the claims of quacks.

ARE THE DIETS EFFECTIVE?

If fad diets were entirely ineffective, consumers would eventually stop buying into them. If they were especially effective, the obesity problem would have been solved. In reality, most fad diets succeed in limiting calorie intakes and so produce weight loss (at least in the short term). Plain old calorie deficit, as it turns out, is the key to weight loss; an emphasis on protein, carbohydrate, or fat or any other gimmick does not improve weight loss.[1]

ARE THEY ADEQUATE?

Diets vary in their nutrient contents, but those that severely limit or eliminate one or more food groups are inadequate[2] Recognizing this fact, fad diet plans often recommend taking nutrient and other supplements (often conveniently sold by the diet authors at a greatly inflated price). True weight-loss experts correct nutrient deficits by improving the diet, not by adding supplements, because even the most costly pills cannot match the health benefits of whole foods.

High-protein diets may provide more satiety than other diets and they may even produce somewhat greater weight loss over the first few months of dieting. After that, however, most people cannot maintain a restrictive diet and relapse to their original or higher weights. Over a year's time, calorie deficits produce weight loss while physical activity helps to maintain it. Singling out protein, carbohydrate, or fat for elimination from the diet does not enhance long-term weight loss or help to maintain it.[3]

ARE THEY SAFE?

Although many diets are tolerated by most people, exceptions exist. For example, a rare but life-threatening form of severe blood acid imbalance has been associated with a low-carbohdrate diet.[4] In addition, recent evidence suggests that such a diet may produce unfavorable effects on both blood lipids and artery linings associated with heart disease.[5] More evidence comes from a documented case of heart disease and other health problems in a previously healthy man who had begun following the Atkins low-carbohydrate diet; his problems resolved after he gave up the diet, suggesting that such diets may pose a danger to some people.[6] No one knows the extent to which dietary extremes might affect, say, people with established diabetes or heart disease—the very people who diet to regain their health.[7]

PERSONAL RESPONSIBILITY

A major failing of most fad weight-loss schemes is that they fail to create lifestyle changes needed to support long-term weight maintenance.[8] For that, people must do the hard work of learning about nutrition, setting their own realistic goals, and then devising a lifestyle plan to achieve them. A balanced, calorie-restricted diet with sufficient physical activity to support it may not be the shortcut that most people wish for, but it ensures nutrient adequacy and provides the best chance of long-term success.[9]

Each gram of alcohol presents 7 calories of energy to the body—energy that is easily stored as body fat.

CONCEPT LINK 9-10

The fat produced from alcohol metabolism also infiltrates and damages the drinker's liver; see Controversy 3, pages 102–103.

many pounds. Thus, if you eat enough of any food, whether it's steak, brownies, or baked beans, any excess will be turned to fat within hours. Weight gain comes from spending less food energy than is taken in. Weight can be gained as body fat or as lean tissue, depending mostly upon whether the eater is also exercising.

Ethanol, the alcohol of alcoholic beverages, slows down the body's use of fat for fuel by as much as a third, causing more fat to be stored. This storage is primarily in the abdominal fat tissue of the "beer drinker's belly" and on the thighs, legs, or anywhere the person tends to store surplus fat.[93] Alcohol therefore is fattening, both through the calories it provides and through its effects on fat metabolism.*** The obvious conclusion is that weight control and abundant alcohol intake cannot easily coexist.

These points are worth repeating:

- Any food can make you fat if you eat enough of it. A net excess of energy is almost all stored in the body as fat in fat tissue.
- Fat from food is particularly easy for the body to store as fat tissue.
- Protein is not stored in the body except in response to exercise; it is present only as working tissue. Protein is converted to glucose to help feed the brain when carbohydrate is lacking; excess protein can be converted to fat.
- Alcohol both delivers calories and facilitates storage of body fat.
- Too little physical activity encourages body fat accumulation.

KEY POINT When energy balance is positive, carbohydrate is converted to glycogen or fat, protein is converted to fat, and food fat is stored as fat. Alcohol delivers calories and encourages fat storage.

LO 9.6, 9.7

Achieving and Maintaining a Healthy Body Weight

Before setting out to change your body weight, think about your motivation for doing so. Many people strive to change their weight not because of potential health risks, but because their weight fails to meet society's ideals of attractiveness. Unfortunately, this kind of thinking sets people up for disappointment—they aim for unrealistic goals.[94] The human body is not infinitely malleable—few overweight people will ever become rail-thin, even with the right diet, exercise habits, and behaviors. Likewise, most underweight people will remain on the slim side even after much effort spent in putting on some heft.

Modest weight loss, even for the person who is still overweight, can lead to rapid improvements in control over diabetes, blood pressure, and blood lipids. With gains in fitness, stair climbing, walking, and other tasks of daily living become noticeably easier. Adopting health or fitness as the ideal rather than some ill-conceived image of beauty can avert much misery; Table 9-7 offers some tips to that end. The rest of this chapter stresses health and fitness as goals and uses weight only as a convenient gauge for progress.

To repeat, control in three realms produces results:

- Diet.
- Physical activity.
- Behavior modification.

The first two, diet and physical activity, are explained next. Behavior modification therapy is the topic of this chapter's Food Feature section.

CONCEPT LINK 9-11

For an introduction to behavior-change concepts, see Chapter 1, page 18.

***People addicted to alcohol are often overly thin beceause of diseased organs, depressed appetite, and subsequent malnutrition.

TABLE 9-7 Tips for Accepting a Healthy Body Weight

- Value yourself and others for traits other than body weight; focus on your whole self including your intelligence, social grace, and professional and scholastic accomplishments.
- Realize that prejudging people by weight is as harmful as prejudging them by race, religion, or gender.
- Use only positive, nonjudgmental descriptions of your body; never use degrading, negative descriptions.
- Accept positive comments from others.
- Accept that no magic diet exists.
- Stop dieting to lose weight. Adopt a healthy eating and exercise lifestyle permanently.
- Follow the USDA Food Guide (Chapter 2, pages 38–39). Never restrict food intake below the minimum levels that meet nutrient needs.
- Become physically active, not because it will help you get thin, but because it will enhance your health.
- Seek support from loved ones. Tell them of your plan for a healthy life in the body you have been given.
- Seek professional counseling, *not* from a weight-loss counselor, but from someone who supports your self-esteem.
- Join with others to fight weight discrimination and stereotypes.

KEY POINT Setting realistic weight goals provides an important starting point for weight loss. Many benefits follow even modest reductions in body fatness among overweight people.

What Diet Strategies Are Best for Weight Loss?

Overweight takes years to accumulate. Achieving a healthy weight is possible, but it takes time, patience, and perseverance. People willing to take one step at a time, even if it feels like just a baby step, are on the right path. An excellent first step is to set realistic goals.

Aim for a Realistic Target A lesson can be learned from a study on obese women.[95] At the start of a one-year weight-loss program, the women set their "dream," "happy," "acceptable," and "disappointing" weights (see Figure 9-11) as goals. All of their goal weights, even the "disappointing" weights, were set far lower than the reasonable loss of 5 to 10 percent of body weight. By the end of the year, most women had lost a remarkable 35 pounds on average, or 16 percent of their starting weight. The women reported physical, social, and psychological benefits from their weight loss, but they still felt discouraged because they had not met even their "disappointing" weight. Their unrealistic expectations brought them feelings of defeat despite spectacular success.

A reasonable first goal for an overweight person might be to stop gaining weight. A next goal might be to reduce body weight by about 5 to 10 percent over a year's time. Put another way, shoot for a weight that falls two BMI categories lower than a present unhealthy one. For example, a 5-foot-5-inch woman with hypertension weighing 180 pounds (BMI of 30—see the BMI table on the inside back cover) may aim for a BMI of 28, or about 168 pounds. If her health indicators fall into line, she may decide to maintain this weight. If her blood pressure is still high or she has other risks, she may repeat the process to achieve a healthier weight.

Set Small-Step Goals Once you have identified your overall target, set specific, achievable, small-step goals for diet, activity, and behavior changes. Dramatic weight loss overnight is not possible or even desirable; a pound or two of body fat lost each week will safely and effectively bring you to your goal. Losses greater or faster than these are not recommended because they are almost invariably followed by rapid regain. Also, rapid weight loss through excessive restriction can cause gallbladder stones or dangerous electrolyte imbalances.

It's better to take your time and achieve a lasting change. New goals can be built on prior achievements, and a lifetime goal may be to maintain the new, healthier body weight. Weight maintenance often proves the most difficult.

Keep Records Keeping records is critical. Recording your food intake and exercise can help you to spot trends and identify areas needing improvement. The Food

- *Dietary Guidelines for Americans 2005, Key Recommendations for weight management:*
  - *To maintain body weight in a healthy range, balance calories from foods and beverages with calories expended.*
  - *To prevent gradual weight gain over time, make small decreases in food and beverage calories and increase physical activity.*

Did You Know?

Children in particular suffer when they learn to dislike their healthy bodies because of unrealistic ideals.

FIGURE 9-11 Reasonable Goals Vs. Unreasonable Expectations

Obese women achieved remarkable success during a year's weight-loss program, but they were disappointed because they had set unrealistic expectations at the outset.

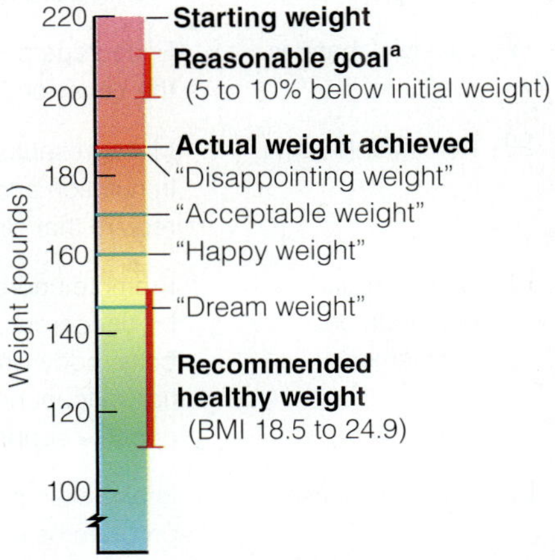

[a]Reasonable goal weights reflect pounds lost over one year's time. Given more time, reasonable goals may eventually fall within the recommended weight range.

Did You Know?

For a person whose BMI is too high for health, a reasonable and achievable goal might be to aim for 2 BMI levels below the current one.

- The CengageNow website (www.cengage.com/sso) can help lead you through the steps for setting goals and changing behaviors.

Feature at the end of the chapter demonstrates how to maintain a food and exercise diary. Changes in body weight can provide a rough estimate of changes in body fatness. In addition to weight, measure your waist circumference to track changes in central adiposity.

It's Your Diet, So You'd Better Plan It Contrary to the claims of faddists, no particular food plan is magical, and no particular food must be either included or excluded. You are the one who will have to live with the plan, so you had better be the one to design it. Remember, you are adopting a healthy eating plan for the long run, so it must consist of satisfying foods that you like, that are readily available, and that you can afford.

As for fad diets, only those that reduce calorie intake produce weight loss, and only those providing all the needed nutrients can support health. Table 9-8 provides a way to judge weight-loss plans according to sound nutrition principles.

TABLE 9-8 Rating Sound and Unsound Weight-Loss Schemes

Each diet or program starts with 160 points and is rated on 12 factors. Whenever a plan falls short of ideals, subtract points in the third column as instructed. A plan that loses more than 20 points might still be of value but deserves careful scrutiny.

Factor	Does the Diet or Program:	Start: 160 Points
1. Calories	Provide a reasonable number of calories (not fewer than 1,200 calories for an average-size man or 1,000 for an average-size woman)?	If NO, minus 10
2. Protein	Provide enough, but not too much, protein (at least the DRI recommended intake, but not more than twice that much)?	If NO, minus 10
3. Fat	Provide enough fat for balance but not so much fat as to go against current recommendations (between 20% and 35% calories from fat)?	If NO, minus 10
4. Carbohydrate	Provide enough carbohydrate to spare protein and prevent ketosis (at least 100 grams of carbohydrate)? Does it provide 20–30 grams fiber from whole foods?	If NO to either or both, minus 10
5. Vitamins and minerals	Offer a balanced assortment of vitamins and minerals by including foods from all food groups and subgroups? If it omits a food group (for example, meats), does it provide a suitable food (not supplement) substitute?	For EACH food group omitted, minus 10
6. Variety	Offer variety, in the sense that different foods can be selected each day? Would you classify it as boring or monotonous?	If YES, minus 10
7. Ordinary foods	Consist of ordinary foods that are available locally (for example, in the main grocery stores) at the prices people normally pay? Or does the dieter have to buy special, expensive, or unusual foods to adhere to the diet? Would class it as "bizarre" or "requiring special foods"?	If YES, minus 10
8. False promises	Promise dramatic, rapid weight loss (more than 2 pounds per week)?	If YES, minus 10
9. Lifestyle changes	Encourage permanent, realistic lifestyle changes, including regular exercise and the behavioral changes needed for weight maintenance?	If NO, minus 10
10. Reasonable costs	Misrepresent salespeople as "counselors" supposedly qualified to give guidance in nutrition and/or general health, or collect large sums of money at the start, or require that clients sign contracts for expensive, long-term programs?	If YES, minus 10
11. No gimmicks or mandatory supplements	Promote unproven or spurious weight-loss aids such as hormones (hormones can be dangerous; reject such a plan immediately), starch blockers, diuretics, sauna belts, body wraps, passive exercise, dieters' "tea," herbal cures, any type of injections, acupuncture, electric muscle-stimulating devices, amino acid supplements, appetite suppressants, "unique" ingredients, and so forth?	If YES, minus 10
12. Warnings of risks	Inform clients about the risks associated with weight loss in general or the specific program being promoted?	If NO, minus 10
	If a plan loses more than 20 points, carefully consider whether it may benefit or harm your health.	*Total points lost:* ________

Plan for Realistic Calorie Intakes Recommendations for cutting calories are based on a person's BMI. Dieters with a BMI of 35 or greater are encouraged to reduce their daily calories by about 500 to 750 calories from their usual intakes. People with a BMI between 27 and 35 should reduce energy intake by 300 to 500 calories a day.

Most dieters can lose weight safely on a diet providing 1,000 to 1,200 calories per day for women and 1,200 to 1,600 calories per day for men, while still meeting nutrient needs (as demonstrated in Table 9-9). Diets providing fewer than about 800 calories per day are notoriously unsuccessful at achieving lasting weight loss, lack necessary nutrients, and may set in motion the unhealthy behaviors of eating disorders (see the Controversy) and so are not recommended.

- USDA's "*Make Your Calories Count*" website provides practice in reading calorie information on food labels: http://www.cfsan.fda.gov/~ear/hwm/hwmintro.html.

Make the Diet Adequate Healthy weight-loss diets should provide all of the needed nutrients in the form of fresh fruits and vegetables, low-fat milk products or substitutes, legumes, lean meats, fish, poultry, nuts, and whole grains. Such diets are adequate in protein, carbohydrate, fiber, vitamins, and minerals and low in the kinds of fats associated with diseases.

- The DRI recommends:
  - *45 to 65% calories from carbohydrate.*
  - *20 to 35% calories from fat.*
  - *10 to 35% calories from protein.*

Choose fats sensibly by avoiding saturated and *trans* fats and including enough of the health-supporting fats (details in Controversy 5) but not so much as to oversupply calories. Nuts provide fat and protein, and including a moderate amount in the diet may assist in controlling body weight.[96] Lean meats or other low-fat protein sources also play an important role: an ounce of lean ham contains about the same number of calories as an ounce of bread, but the ham produces greater satiety. Also, sufficient dietary protein is needed to preserve lean tissue, including muscle tissue. Use restraint, though—people with high meat intakes are often overweight or obese.[97] Do strictly limit alcohol, which provides abundant calories but no nutrients. Furthermore, alcohol reduces inhibitions and can sabotage even the most committed dieter's plans.

Consider a Supplement A supplement providing vitamins and minerals at or below 100 percent of the Daily Values (see inside back cover, page Y) may help to meet nutrient needs. Calcium is of particular interest (see later section) and most supplements are low in calcium—the diet must therefore include enough calcium-rich foods each day to meet the body's need. If you plan resolutely to include all of the foods from each food group that you need each day, you will find that you will be satisfied and have little appetite left for high-calorie treats.

- Controversy 7 discussed the pros and cons of vitamin and mineral supplements.

TABLE 9-9 Recommended Daily Food Intakes for Low-Calorie Diets

These intakes allow most people to lose weight and still meet their nutrient needs with careful, nutrient-dense food selections. Note that the discretionary calorie allowance for these patterns is about 100 calories (see Chapter 2 for diet-planning details).

Food Group	1,000 Calories	1,200 Calories	1,400 Calories	1,600 Calories
Fruit	1 c	1 c	1½ c	1½ c
Vegetables	1 c	1½ c	1½ c	2 c
Grains	3 oz	4 oz	5 oz	5 oz
Meat and Legumes	2 oz	3 oz	4 oz	5 oz
Milk	3 c	3 c	3 c	3 c
Oils	3 tsp	3 tsp	3 tsp	4 tsp

Note: The USDA Food Guide patterns for 1,000, 1,200, and 1,400 calories were designed for children and provided 2 cups milk. They were modified here to include an additional cup of milk, as 3 cups per day is recommended for all adults.

- To avoid overeating without your awareness:
  - *Choose smaller plates, glasses, and utensils.*
  - *Decide how much you will eat in advance of sitting down to a meal.*
  - *Slow down: pace yourself with the slowest person at the table.*

Manage Portion Sizes Pay careful attention to portion sizes—large portions increase energy intakes, and the monstrous helpings served by restaurants and sold in packages are the enemy of the person striving to control weight.[98] Popular 100-calorie single-serving packages may be useful but only if the food in the package fits into your calorie budget—100 calories of cookies or fried snacks are still 100 discretionary calories that can be safely eliminated. Reduced-calorie foods are not calorie-free. Eating a reduced-calorie cookie instead of an ordinary cookie saves calories—eating half the bag defeats the purpose.

People eat more from large portions than from standard-sized portions. Yet, after they've finished, they report about the same level of fullness and satisfaction as those who ate less. The trick seems to be to eat just until satisfied and then to stop; more eating provides less satisfaction while unneeded calories mount up. And, as mentioned, big bowls, plates, utensils, and drinking glasses encourage people to take and consume bigger portions. Small plates and bowls, tall and thin drinking glasses, and luncheon-sized plates have the opposite effect.[99]

Almost every dieter needs to retrain, using measuring cups for a while to learn to judge portion sizes. Stay focused on calories and portions—don't be distracted by product reductions in a particular nutrient, be it fat or carbohydrate. Read labels and compare *calories* per serving.

Calorie Calculation If you doubt that small daily decisions can make a difference to your body weight, try this: turn back to page 49 in Chapter 2 and look at the foods depicted in Figure 2-11. Add up the calories in a 1970s hamburger, cola, and French fries (similar to today's "small" sizes). Do the same for the calories in the "colossal" size hamburger, cola, and French fries typical of today's meals. Now find the calorie difference between the two meals (subtract the smaller sum from the larger) and multiply the difference by 52 (for weeks in a year):

$$\begin{array}{l} \text{Today's calorie total} = 2020 \\ -\ \text{1970s calorie total} = 925 \\ \hline \text{Calorie difference} = 1095 \times 52 = 56{,}940 \end{array}$$

If a pound of body fat can be gained with each excess 3,500 calories, then a person who chooses the largest-sized fast-food meal instead of the smallest *just once per week* will consume enough additional energy (56,940 calories) to gain over 16 pounds in one year's time. Many little daily decisions such as this add up over time.

- The energy density of a food can be calculated mathematically. Find the energy density of carrot sticks and French fries by dividing their calories by their weight in grams.

  A serving of carrot sticks providing 31 calories and weighing 72 grams:

  $$\frac{31 \text{ cal}}{72 \text{ g}} = 0.43 \text{ cal/g}$$

  Now do the same for French fries, contributing 167 calories and weighing 50 grams:

  $$\frac{167 \text{ cal}}{50 \text{ g}} = 3.34 \text{ cal/g}$$

  The higher calories per gram (cal/g), the greater the energy density.

Using the Concept of Energy Density People who consume diets of foods high in **energy density** are more often overweight.[100] Turning this around, people who wish to be leaner and to improve their nutrient intakes would be well advised to select foods low in energy density.[101] Such foods often contain substantial water or fiber and are low in fat; they provide more food and greater satiety for the same number of calories. For example, a snack of grapes with their high water content is lower in energy density than the same weight or volume of their dehydrated counterparts (raisins). Likewise, a half-cup serving of fiber-rich, water-rich broccoli delivers about a quarter the calories of the same-sized serving of starch-rich potatoes. Figure 9-12 demonstrates this principle.

When people eat diets of lower energy density, they consume more health-promoting nutrients such as vitamins and minerals and less sodium and saturated fat.[102] Importantly, however, the *energy* density of foods does not always reflect their *nutrient density* (nutrients per calorie). Beverages provide an example. The energy density of low-fat milk almost equals that of sugary soft drinks (they weigh about the same), but these beverages rank far apart in measures of nutrient density and therefore in their contributions toward a nutritious diet.

CONCEPT LINK 9-12

The Food Feature of Chapter 1 discussed the concept of nutrient density (page 20).

energy density a measure of the energy provided by a food relative to its weight (calories per gram).

Artificial Sweeteners Research suggests links among sugary soft drink consumption, higher calorie intakes, and heavier body weight.[103] Whether choosing artificially sweetened beverages reduces the total calories in a person's diet, however, is not known with certainty.[104] Some people who successfully maintain previous weight loss report liberal use of artificially sweetened beverages and fat-modified products.[105] In

FIGURE 9-12 Examples of Energy Density

The larger meals on the right weigh more, provide more fiber, and take far more time to enjoy than the meals on the left, yet the meals in both columns provide equal calories. Much of the additional weight of the meals on the right is made up of water. Note that the hamburger is a modest serving of very lean beef, not the huge fatty burger typical of fast-food restaurants. Keep in mind that even foods of lower energy density can be overconsumed, so watch total calories as well as energy density of foods.

HIGHER ENERGY DENSITY | **LOWER ENERGY DENSITY**

Caesar salad; croutons (fast-food size).

500 calories / 280 g total weight = 1.78 energy density

OR

Mixed salad with 3 oz chicken breast, mixed vegetables, almonds, cranberries, and 3 tbs low-calorie dressing; whole-wheat dinner roll with 1.5 oz lean ham.

500 calories / 570 g total weight = 0.88 energy density

Large hot dog on bun; 1/2 c potato salad.

650 calories / 265 g total weight = 2.45 energy density

OR

© Matthew Farruggio (all)

Homemade, very lean (8% fat), 3-oz hamburger on whole-wheat bun; grilled vegetables with 1 tsp margarine; 1/2 c pork and beans; slice watermelon.

650 calories / 810 g total weight = 0.8 energy density

any case, people who choose soft drinks of any kind often consume less milk—and a diet that contains low-fat milk products may help to control body fatness.[106]

Did You Know?

In general, foods high in fat or low in water, such as cookies or chips, rank high in energy density; foods high in water and fiber, such as fruits and vegetables, rank lower.

Demonstration Diet The meals shown in Figure 9-13 demonstrate how a day's meals look before and after trimming 1,100 calories. Full-calorie meals (left side of the figure) were modified in both portions and energy density to produce lower-calorie meals (on the right). Some 350 calories were trimmed by reducing added sugars: less syrup at breakfast and sugar-free gelatin instead of apple pie at lunch. (The diet planner kept the brownie at supper, however—pleasure matters, too.) These calorie reductions alone, repeated each day for one month, are more than sufficient for a 3-pound weight loss. Try your hand at reducing calories further—the challenge is to keep the diet adequate while doing so.

Meal Spacing Three meals a day is standard in our society, but no law says you can't have four or five—just be sure they are smaller, of course. People who eat small, frequent meals can be as successful at weight loss and maintenance as those who eat three.[107] Also, make sure that mild hunger, not appetite, is prompting you to eat—and eat regularly, before you become extremely hungry. When you do decide to eat, eat the entire meal you have planned for yourself. Then don't eat again until the next meal or snack. Save calorie-free or favorite foods or beverages for a planned snack at the end of the day if you need insurance against late-evening hunger.

FIGURE 9-13 **Meal Makeover—Reducing the Calories in Meals**

Day's meals = about 3,400 cal | **Day's meals = about 2,300 cal**

2% milk, 1 c, 121 cal
Orange juice, 1 c, 112 cal
Whole-grain waffles, 2 each, 402 cal
Soft margarine, 2 tsp, 68 cal
Syrup, 4 tbs, 210 cal
Banana slices, ½ c, 69 cal
Breakfast total: 982

© Matthew Bridwell/PhotoEdit (both)

Fat-free milk, 1 c, 83 cal
Orange juice, 1 c, 112 cal
Whole-grain waffle, 1 each, 201 cal
Soft margarine, 1 tsp, 34 cal
Syrup, 2 tbs, 105 cal
Banana slices, ½ c, 69 cal
Breakfast total: 604

2% milk, 1 c, 121 cal
Hamburger, quarter-pound, 430 cal
French fries, large (about 50), 540 cal
Ketchup, 2 tbs, 32 cal
Apple pie, 1 each, 225 cal
Lunch total: 1,348

© Polara Studios, Inc. (both)

Fat-free milk, 1 c, 83 cal
Cheeseburger, small, 330 cal
Green salad, 1 c, with light dressing, 1 tbs, 67 cal; croutons, ½ c, 50 cal
French fries, regular (about 30), 210 cal
Ketchup, 1 tbs, 16 cal
Gelatin dessert, sugar-free, 20 cal
Lunch total: 776

Italian bread, 2 slices, 162 cal
Soft margarine, 2 tsp, 68 cal
Stewed skinless chicken breast, 4 oz, 202 cal
Tomato sauce, ½ c, 40 cal
Brown rice, 1 c, 216 cal
Mixed vegetables, ½ c, 59 cal
Regular cheese sauce, ¼ c, 121 cal
Brownie, 1 each, 224 cal
Supper total: 1,092
Day's total: 3,422

© Polara Studios, Inc. (both)

Day's calorie reduction = 1,100 calories

Italian bread, 1 slice, 81 cal
Soft margarine, 1 tsp, 34 cal
Stewed skinless chicken breast, 4 oz, 202 cal
Tomato sauce, ½ c, 40 cal
Brown rice, 1 c, 216 cal
Mixed vegetables, ½ c, 59 cal
Low-fat cheese sauce, ¼ c, 85 cal
Brownie, 1 each, 224 cal
Supper total: 941
Day's total: 2,321

One meal you should strive to include is breakfast. People who skip breakfast are more often overweight than breakfast eaters.[108] Much evidence supports the health effects of breakfast, and eating breakfast may reduce food intake all day long. Another meal timing issue shared by many obese people is frequent awakening at night to eat, **night eating syndrome.**[109]

KEY POINT To achieve and maintain a healthy body weight, set realistic goals, keep records, and expect to progress slowly. Watch energy density, make the diet adequate and balanced, limit calories, reduce alcohol, and eat regularly, especially at breakfast. Night eating can be a problem.

night eating syndrome a disturbance in the daily eating rhythm associated with obesity, characterized by no breakfast, more than half of the daily calories consumed after 7 p.m., frequent nighttime awakenings to eat, and often a greater total calorie intake than others.

Physical Activity in Weight Loss and Maintenance

Physical activity guidelines were offered in the Think Fitness feature, earlier. The effect of aerobic physical activity on weight loss depends somewhat on individual differences. For most people, however, physical activity augments a calorie-restricted diet to produce weight loss, but weight loss through physical activity alone is not easily achieved.[110]

Weight Maintenance Physical activity seems to play a key role in weight maintenance. People who successfully maintain a reduced body weight often report high levels of physical activity.[111] This idea is borne out in the laboratory: when obesity-prone rats are first made to lose weight and subsequently given unrestricted access to food, the rats that stay leanest are those that run regularly on a treadmill.[112] Researchers note that the running rats spontaneously reduced their daily food intakes while sedentary control rats did not. This could mean that aerobic physical activity helps to normalize the appetite in obesity-prone rats.

Appetite Effects Many people fear that exercising will increase their hunger, and it may, but there's more to the story. Active people do have healthy appetites, but the appetite is suppressed following a workout and satiation during meals is heightened.[113] The reasons are unclear but, as noted, exercise helps to normalize the appetite, possibly by altering levels of the appetite-regulating hormones.[114]

Other Benefits and a Warning Muscle-strengthening exercise performed on at least two days per week adds and maintains healthful muscle tissue and provides a trim, attractive appearance.[115] In addition, over the long term, lean muscle tissue burns more calories pound for pound than fat does. Physical activity reduces waist circumference, and reducing central obesity reduces health risks.[116] Physical activity has also been praised for raising the BMR in the hours following exercise, but few weight-loss seekers work out at a high-enough intensity for long enough to achieve significant energy loss in this way.[117]

Physically active dieters may also avoid some of the bone mineral loss that often accompanies weight-loss dieting, and those who also attend to calcium needs offer their bones even more protection.[118] Finally, physical activity of all kinds helps to reduce stress, and stress can lead to increased eating.[119] A word of warning: nonathletes spend little energy during physical activity. Exercisers who reward themselves with high-calorie treats for "good behavior" can easily negate any calorie deficits incurred.[120]

- Current physical activity guidelines are provided in Chapter 10.

Choosing Activities What exercise routine is best? For health, a combination of moderate-to-vigorous aerobic exercise along with strength exercises at a safe level provides benefits. However, any physical activity is better than being sedentary.[121] Most important: perform at a comfortable pace within your current abilities. Rushing to improve is practically a guarantee for injury.

A new twist on physical activity comes from interactive sports computer games that get players up and moving. Playing these games burns more calories than sedentary pursuits (but not nearly as much as actually playing the sport itself).[†††122] Physically active games played while seated, such as boxing, could help provide needed physical activity for people of limited mobility, too.[123]

People exercising at low-to-moderate intensity are more likely to stick with their activity for longer times and are less likely to injure themselves. For those at higher fitness levels, higher-intensity activities may be performed for shorter periods to gain similar benefits. A 175-pound person who replaces a 30-minute television program with a 2-mile daily walk can spend enough energy to lose (or at least not gain) 18 pounds in a year.

Fitness also benefits from hundreds of energy-spending activities required for daily living: parking farther away, washing your car, raking leaves, and many, many others. However you do it, be active. Walk. Swim. Skate. Dance. Cycle. Skip. Above all, enjoy moving—and move often.

Tim Robberts/The Image Bank/Getty Images

Playing a computer sports game burns calories but not as many as playing the actual sport.

KEY POINT Physical activity greatly augments diet in weight-loss efforts. Improvements in health and body composition follow an active lifestyle.

Did You Know?

The estimated energy expended when walking at a moderate pace = 1 calorie per mile per kilogram of body weight. (kg = lb ÷ 2.2)

[†††]An example is Wii, by Nintendo.

What Strategies Are Best for Weight Gain?

Should a thin person try to gain weight? Not necessarily. If you are healthy at your present weight, stay there. If your physician has advised you to gain, if you are excessively tired, if you are unable to keep warm, if you fall into the "underweight" category of the BMI table (see inside back cover), or if, for women, you have missed at least three consecutive menstrual periods, you may be in danger from a too low body weight.

Physical Activity to Gain Muscle and Fat A healthful weight gain is best achieved through physical activity, particularly resistance training (see Chapter 10 for details), combined with a high-calorie diet. Diet alone can bring about weight gain, but the gain will be mostly fat. Overly thin people need both muscle and fat, so physical activity is an essential component of a sound weight-gain plan. Many an underweight person has simply been too busy (for months) to eat or to exercise enough to gain or to maintain weight.

Exercise training demands extra calories from food—otherwise, you will lose weight. If you eat just enough to fuel the activity, you can build muscle initially but at the expense of body fat, which is also needed to fuel the exercise. Soon, as muscles adapt to the work, muscle gains cease, and a steady state ensues. Hence, gains of both muscle and fat are possible only when the body receives the extra fuel it needs from food. To gain a pound of muscle and fat requires taking in about 3,000 extra calories.[‡‡‡] Conventional advice on diet to the person building muscle is to eat about 500 to 700 calories a day above normal energy needs; this range often supports both the added activity and the formation of new muscle.

Choose Foods with High Energy Density The weight gainer needs nutritious energy-dense foods. No matter how many sticks of celery you consume, you won't gain weight because celery simply doesn't offer enough calories per bite. Energy-dense foods (the very ones the weight-loss dieter is trying to avoid) are often high in fat, but fat energy is spent in building new tissue; if the fat is mostly unsaturated, such foods will not contribute to heart disease. Be sure your choices are nutritious.

Choose an ounce of peanut butter instead of an ounce of lean meat on a sandwich, avocado instead of cucumber on a salad, olives instead of pickles, whole-wheat muffins instead of whole-wheat bread, and flavored milk and milkshakes instead of milk. When you do eat celery, stuff it with tuna salad (use oil-packed tuna); choose flavored coffee drinks over plain coffee; use olive oil or mayonnaise-based dressings on salads, whipped toppings on fruit, and soft or liquid margarine on potatoes. Because fat contains more than twice as many calories per teaspoon as sugar, its calories add up quickly without adding much bulk, and its energy is in a form that is easy for the body to store.

Portion Sizes and Meal Spacing Increasing portion sizes increases calorie intakes. Choose extra slices of meats and cheeses on sandwiches; use larger plates, bowls, and glasses to disguise the appearance of the larger portions. Expect to feel full. Most underweight individuals are accustomed to small quantities of food. When they begin eating significantly more food, they complain of uncomfortable fullness. This feeling is normal, and it passes as the stomach gradually adapts to the extra food.

Eat frequently and keep easy-to-eat foods on hand for quick meals. Make three sandwiches in the morning and eat them between classes in addition to the day's three regular meals. Include favorite foods or ethnic dishes often—the more varied and palatable, the better. If you fill up fast during a meal, start with the main course or a meat- or cheese-filled appetizer, not carrot sticks or clear soup. Drink between meals, not with them, to save space for higher-calorie foods. Make milkshakes of milk, a frozen banana, a tablespoon of vegetable oil, and flavorings for between-meal treats. Always finish with dessert. Other tips for weight gain are listed in the margin.

- Other tips for increasing food intakes:
  - *Cook and bake often—delicious cooking aromas whet the appetite.*
  - *Invite others to the table—companionship often boosts eating.*
  - *Make meals interesting—try new vegetables and fruit, add crunchy nuts or creamy avocado, and explore the flavors of herbs and spices.*
  - *Keep a supply of favorite snacks, such as trail mix or granola bars, handy for grabbing.*
  - *Control stress and relax. Enjoy your food.*

[‡‡‡]Theoretically, it takes an excess of 2,000 to 2,500 calories to gain a pound of only lean tissue and about 3,500 calories to gain a pound of fat.

Avoid Tobacco Smoking tobacco depresses the appetite and makes taste buds and olfactory (smelling) organs less sensitive. A person who smokes should quit before trying to gain weight. Quitters find that appetite picks up, food tastes and smells better, and the body reaps numerous benefits.

KEY POINT Weight gain requires a diet of calorie-dense foods, eaten frequently throughout the day. Physical activity builds lean tissue, and no special supplements can speed the process.

Medical Treatment of Obesity

To someone fatigued from years of battling overweight, the idea of curing obesity by taking pills or undergoing surgery may be attractive. These approaches can cause dramatic weight loss and save the lives of obese people at critical risk, but they also present serious risks.[124]

Obesity Medications Each year, a million-and-a-half U.S. citizens take prescription weight-loss medications, and many millions more take over-the-counter (OTC) preparations, including many "dietary supplements." Of these people, a fourth are not overweight, but they take the products believing them to be safe.[125]

In an investigation of OTC weight-loss pills, powders, and herbal and other "dietary supplements," the FDA found an alarming number to illegally contain prescription medications. Strong diuretics, unproven experimental drugs, psychotropic drugs used to treat mental illnesses, and even drugs deemed unsafe and so banned from U.S. markets were among those discovered, and all pose serious health risks.[126] At this time, the FDA is taking steps to remove the unsafe products from the market but warns that others exist and new ones keep coming because current regulations are insufficient to keep them out.

Prescription weight-loss drugs are carefully regulated and are used under a physician's care. For people with a BMI of 30 or above and those with elevated disease risks, the benefits of weight loss achieved with the help of prescription medication often exceed the risks. Still, weight-loss drugs can help only temporarily while they are being taken; lifestyle changes, in comparison, can help manage weight for a lifetime. Table 9-10 presents some of the known side effects and other details about selected weight-loss medications.

Obesity Surgery A person with **extreme obesity,** that is, someone whose BMI is 40 or above (35 with coexisting disease), urgently needs to reduce body fatness, and surgery may be an option for those healthy enough to withstand it. Surgical procedures effectively limit food intake by reducing the size of the stomach and delaying the passage of food into the intestine (see Figure 9-14). The results can be dramatic: greater than 90 percent of surgical patients achieve a lasting weight loss of more than 50 percent of their excess body weight. Weight loss, in turn, often brings rapid relief from such threats as diabetes, high blood cholesterol, hypertension, and sleep apnea and can lower the long-term risks from heart disease.[127] Even surgery is not a sure cure for obesity, however. A few people do not lose the expected pounds, and some who lose initially regain all the lost weight in a few years' time.

Complications after surgery often include infections, nausea, vomiting, and dehydration; vitamin and mineral deficiencies; and psychological problems. Deficiency diseases of thiamin, vitamin B_{12}, folate, iron, calcium, and vitamin D, mostly rare in the general population, commonly occur after obesity surgery.[128] These deficiencies often occur despite the use of multivitamin and mineral supplements.[129] Calcium metabolism may be disturbed—in one study, all surgical patients had elevated indicators of bone loss.[130] The safety and effectiveness of gastric surgery depend, in large part, on compliance with dietary instructions. Life-long nutrition and medical supervision is necessary following the surgery. For many suitable candidates, the health benefits of sustained weight loss, such as reduced blood pressure, improved blood lipids, and improved glucose metabolism, may prove worth the risk.[131]

Did You Know?

People's hormone status also affects their ability to gain and lose weight, but taking steroids and other drugs to enhance weight gain is a bad idea—see the Controversy section of Chapter 10.

- Gastric surgery patients are advised to:
  - *Choose small portions.*
  - *Chew food slowly and completely.*
  - *Drink beverages separately and not with meals.*
  - *Avoid foods that cause symptoms.*

extreme obesity clinically severe overweight, presenting very high risks to health; the condition of having a BMI of 40 or above; also called *morbid obesity.*

TABLE 9-10 Pharmaceutical Treatments of Obesity[a]

Names	Actions	Known Side Effects	Comments
PRESCRIPTION DRUGS			
Sibutramine Trade name: Meridia	Suppresses appetite.	Dry mouth, headache, constipation, insomnia, and high blood pressure[b]	The FDA advises those with high blood pressure or CVD against its use; others should monitor their blood pressure.
Orlistat (see below)			
Phentermine	Suppresses appetite	Dry mouth, constipation, insomnia	Most widely prescribed for short term (≤ 3 months) weight loss
OVER-THE-COUNTER DRUGS			
Benzocaine Trade names: Diet Ayds (candy) or Slim Mint (gum)	Anesthetizes the tongue, reducing taste sensations	None known	Few over-the-counter weight-loss medications have FDA approval.
Orlistat[c] Trade name: alli[c] (prescription name: Xenical)	Inhibits pancreatic lipase activity, thus blocking dietary fat absorption by about 30%.	Gas, frequent loose bowel movements, and reduced absorption of fat-soluble vitamins	Most effective with a nutritionally balanced, reduced-calorie, low-fat diet
Phenylpropanolamine (PPA) (also called norephedrine)	Appetite suppressant; nasal and sinus decongestant	Dry mouth, rapid pulse, nervousness, sleeplessness, hypertension, irregular heartbeat, kidney failure, liver damage, liver failure, seizures, and hemorrhagic strokes (bleeding in the brain)	The FDA has removed PPA from drug products and has warned consumers not to consume products containing it (check labels).
OTHER PRODUCTS			
Ephedrine, ephedra, or ma huang	Enhances effects of the stress hormone norepinephrine, including reduced appetite.	Nervousness, headache, insomnia, dizziness, palpitations, skin flush, serious heart problems; almost 1,400 reported adverse events, including 81 deaths	Prohibited in the United States and Canada, but available via the Internet. Consumers owning products should stop taking them (check labels).
Bitter orange extract Trade names: Xenadrine EFX, Metabolife Ultra, NOW Diet Support	Often a replacement for ephedrine, this stimulant mimics ephedra in chemical composition and function.	High blood pressure; increased risk of heart arrhythmias, heart attack, stroke	The FDA has currently taken no action against bitter orange extract.
"Carb blockers," "fat blockers" or "binders," chromium picolinate, chitosan, many others	None known	Not studied	The FDA prohibits weight-loss and fat-loss claims for such products.

[a]*For answers to drug-related questions, call FDA Information toll free: (888) 463-6332 or visit www.fda.gov.*

[b]*Sibutramine may also be associated with memory impairment.*

[c]*The trade name is alli (pronounced AL-eye). In 2009, the FDA was reviewing reports of liver damage and liver failure in people taking orlistat.*

Lipectomy Plastic surgeons can extract some subcutaneous fat deposits by lipectomy, or "liposuction." Promises of cosmetic improvement often motivate people to seek lipectomy but the outcome may not always be as expected. If fat is gained back after liposuction, as often happens, it can appear lumpy and worse than the original fat. Lipectomy is popular in part because it seems safe, but any surgery carries risks and lipectomy does not bring the health benefits that follow weight loss.

FIGURE 9-14 **Surgical Obesity Treatments**

Both of these surgical procedures limit the amount of food that can be comfortably eaten.

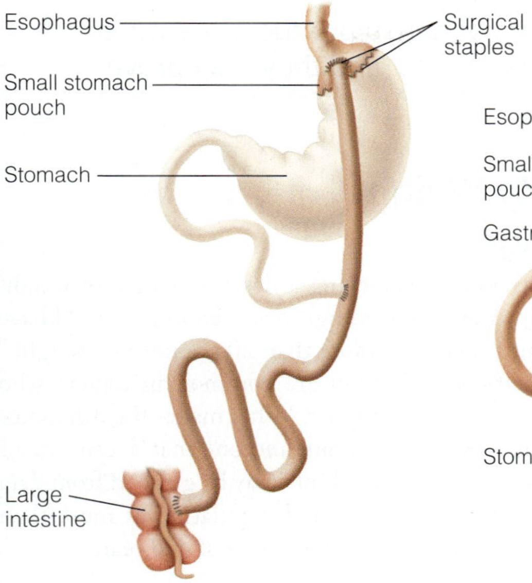

In gastric bypass, the surgeon constructs a small stomach pouch and creates an outlet directly to the lower small intestine. (Dark areas highlight the redirected flow of food.)

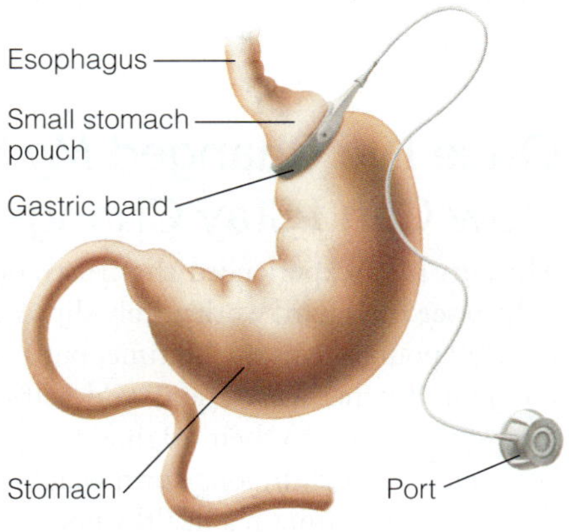

In gastric banding, the surgeon uses a gastric band to reduce the opening from the esophagus to the stomach. The size of the opening can be adjusted by inflating or deflating the band by way of a port placed in the abdomen just beneath the skin.

KEY POINT For people whose obesity threatens their health, medical science offers drugs and surgery.

Herbal Products and Gimmicks

Some herbs or **botanical** products may be useful for some purposes, but wise consumers avoid products containing substances not proved safe in laboratory studies. The risks are too high.

Herbals and Botanicals Herbal and botanical weight-loss products are wildly popular, but their effectiveness and safety are largely unknown. Many are among the dangerous adulterated products already mentioned. People may falsely believe that "natural" plant products are safe to use, but many plants make poisonous toxins in their tissues. Belladonna and hemlock are infamous examples, but many lesser-known herbs, such as sassafras, also contain toxins. Herbs and botanicals are sold as "dietary supplements," so manufacturers need not present scientific evidence of their safety or effectiveness to the FDA before marketing them. Evidence about safety is gathered largely through reports of consumers who sicken or die after using them.

An example is ephedra (also called *ma huang*), sold as a diet aid in many preparations. Ephedra and its active constituent, ephedrine, showed promise as a weight-loss drug, but after numerous reports of cardiac arrest, abnormal heartbeats, hypertension, strokes, seizures and deaths, the FDA finally banned the sale of supplements that contain it. Many other "herbal" weight-loss supplements have caused kidney or liver failure or proved to be cancer-causing agents. The FDA also bans claims that hoodia (an herb) suppresses appetite.[132] Hundreds of other examples could fill many pages.

Other Gimmicks The FDA also prohibits claims that products block starch, fat, or sugar absorption or promote weight loss with no effort. Steam baths and saunas do not melt the fat off the body as claimed, although they may dehydrate you so that

botanical pertaining to or made from plants; any drug, medicinal preparation, dietary supplement, or similar substance obtained from a plant.

you lose water weight. Brushes, sponges, wraps, creams, and massages intended to move, burn, or break up "**cellulite**" are useless for fat loss. Cellulite—the rumpled, dimpled fat tissue on the thighs and buttocks—is simply fat, awaiting the body's call for energy. Such nonsense distracts people from the serious business of planning effective weight-management strategies.

KEY POINT The effectiveness of herbal products and other gimmicks has not been demonstrated, and they may prove hazardous.

Once I've Changed My Weight, How Can I Stay Changed?

Millions have experienced the frustration of achieving a desired change in weight only to see their hard work visibly slip away in a seemingly never-ending cycle: "I have lost 200 pounds over my lifetime, but I was never more than 20 pounds overweight." Disappointment, frustration, and self-condemnation are common in dieters who have slipped back to their original weight or even higher. What makes the difference between a successful, long-term weight-control program and one that doesn't stick? How can you maintain a healthy body weight? Some hints may be gleaned from data of the National Weight Control Registry, a self-selected population of more than 4,000 people who lost at least 30 pounds and kept it off for at least one year.

© marcstock, 2011/Shutterstock.com

Don't forget to consume enough water—it can produce feelings of fullness and it's calorie-free.

A Lifelong Commitment Without a doubt, a key to weight maintenance is accepting it as a life-long endeavor and not a goal to be achieved and then forgotten. People who maintain their weight loss continue to employ the behaviors that reduced their weight in the first place. They cultivate the habits of people who maintain a healthy weight, such as eating low-calorie meals (averaging 1,800 cal/day) and being physically active. They must also control susceptibility to overeating regardless of the initial weight-loss method.[133]

Self-Efficacy and Other Success Keys Those who maintain weight losses over time also generally:

- believe they have the ability to control their weight, an attribute known as **self-efficacy.**
- eat breakfast every day.[134]
- average about 1 hour of physical activity a day.
- monitor body weight about once a week.[135]
- maintain consistent lower-calorie eating patterns.
- quickly address small **lapses** to prevent small gains from turning into major ones.
- watch less than 10 hours of television per week.[136]
- eat high-fiber foods, particularly whole grains, vegetables, and fruit, and consume sufficient water each day.[137]
- cultivate and honor realistic expectations regarding body size and shape.

Physical Activity The importance of physical activity cannot be overstated. Those who endeavor to lose weight without physical activity may become trapped in endless repeating rounds of weight loss and regain—"yo-yo" dieting. A history of such **weight cycling** can predict a person's future success (or lack thereof) in maintaining weight. The Food Feature, next, explores how a person who is ready to change can modify daily diet and exercise behaviors into healthy, life-long habits.

KEY POINT People who succeed at maintaining lost weight keep to their eating routines, keep exercising, and keep track of calorie intakes and body weight.

cellulite a term popularly used to describe dimpled fat tissue on the thighs and buttocks; not recognized in science.

self-efficacy a person's belief in his or her ability to succeed in an undertaking.

lapses periods of returning to old habits; also defined in Chapter 1.

weight cycling repeated rounds of weight loss and subsequent regain, with reduced ability to lose weight with each attempt; also called *yo-yo dieting.*

FOOD FEATURE

Behavior Modification for Weight Control

LO 9.8

Supporting both diet and exercise is **behavior modification.** This form of therapy can help the dieter to cement into place all the behaviors that lead to and perpetuate the desired body composition.[138]

FIGURE 9-15 A Sample Food and Activity Diary

Record the times and places of meals and snacks, the types and amounts of foods consumed, surroundings and people present, and mood while eating. Describe physical activities, their intensity and duration, and your feelings about them, too. Use this information to structure eating and exercise in ways that serve your physical and emotional needs.

Time	Place	Activity or food eaten	People present	Mood
10:30–10:40	School vending machine	6 peanut butter crackers and 12 oz. cola	by myself	starved
12:15–12:30	Restaurant	Sub sandwich and 12 oz. cola	friends	relaxed & friendly
3:00–3:45	Gym	Weight training	work out partner	tired
4:00–4:10	Snack bar	Small frozen yogurt	by myself	OK

HOW DOES BEHAVIOR MODIFICATION WORK?

Behavior modification involves changing both behaviors and thought processes. It is based on the knowledge that habits drive behaviors. Suppose a friend tells you about a shortcut to class. To take it, you must make a left-hand turn at a corner where you now turn right. You decide to try the shortcut the next day, but when you arrive at the familiar corner, you turn right as always. Not until you arrive at class do you realize that you failed to turn left, as you had planned. You can learn to turn left, of course, but at first you will have to make an effort to remember to do so. After a while, the new behavior will become as automatic as the old one was.

A food and activity diary is a powerful ally to help you learn what particular eating stimuli, or cues, affect you and to track your progress. Such self-monitoring is indispensable for learning to control eating and exercising cues, both positive and negative. Figure 9-15 provides a sample of an informal food and activity diary for self-monitoring.

Once you identify the behaviors you need to change, do not attempt to modify all of them at once. No one who attempts too many changes at one time is successful. Set your priorities and begin with behaviors you can handle—then practice until they become habitual and automatic. Then select one or two more.[139] For those striving to lose weight, learning to say "No, thank you" might be among the first habits to establish. Learning not to "clean your plate" might follow.

MODIFYING BEHAVIORS

Behavior researchers have identified six elements useful in replacing old eating and activity habits with new ones:

1. Eliminate inappropriate eating and activity cues.
2. Suppress the cues you cannot eliminate.
3. Strengthen cues to appropriate eating and activities.
4. Repeat the desired eating and physical activity.
5. Arrange or emphasize negative consequences of inappropriate eating or sedentary behaviors.
6. Arrange or emphasize positive consequences of appropriate eating and exercise behaviors.

Table 9-11 provides specific examples of putting these six elements into action. Before doing so, however, you must establish a baseline, a record of your present eating behaviors against which to measure future progress.

To begin, set about eliminating or suppressing the cues that prompt you to eat inappropriately. An overeater's life may include many such cues: watching television, talking on the telephone, entering a convenience store, studying late at night. Resolve that you will no longer respond to such cues by eating. Respond only to one set of cues designed by you, in one particular place in one particular room. If some cues to inappropriate eating behavior cannot be eliminated, suppress them, as described in Table 9-11; then strengthen the appropriate cues and reward yourself for doing so. The list in the margin on page 360 suggests some activities and rewards to substitute for eating.

In addition, be aware that the food marketing industry spends huge sums each year developing cues to modify

behavior modification alteration of behavior using methods based on the theory that actions can be controlled by manipulating the environmental factors that cue, or trigger, the actions.

- Activities and rewards to substitute for eating:
  - *Attending sporting events.*
  - *Enjoying leisure activities.*
  - *Exercising or playing sports.*
  - *Gardening.*
  - *Getting praise from others.*
  - *Going to a movie or play.*
  - *Listening to music.*
  - *Napping.*
  - *Praising yourself.*
  - *Reading.*
  - *Receiving token rewards (stickers, stars).*
  - *Redecorating.*
  - *Relaxing.*
  - *Saving money for future treats.*
  - *Shopping.*
  - *Taking a bubble bath.*
  - *Telephoning.*
  - *Tidying your room or house.*
  - *Vacationing.*
  - *Working on hobbies or crafts.*

cognitive skills as taught in behavior therapy, changes to conscious thoughts with the goal of improving adherence to lifestyle modifications; examples are problem-solving skills or the correction of false negative thoughts, termed *cognitive restructuring.*

TABLE 9-11 Applying Behavior Modification to Control Body Fatness

1. Eliminate inappropriate eating cues:
   - Don't buy problem foods.
   - Eat only in one room at the designated time.
   - Shop when not hungry.
   - Avoid vending machines, fast-food restaurants, and convenience stores.
   - Turn off the television, video games, and computer.
2. Suppress the cues you cannot eliminate:
   - Serve individual plates; don't serve "family style."
   - Measure your portions; avoid large servings or packages of food.
   - Make small portions look large by spreading them over the plate.
   - Create obstacles to consuming problem foods—wrap them and freeze them, making them less quickly accessible.
   - Control deprivation; plan and eat regular meals.
   - Likewise, plan to spend only one hour in sedentary activities, such as watching television or using a computer.
3. Strengthen cues to appropriate eating and exercise:
   - Share appropriate foods with others.
   - Store appropriate foods in convenient spots in the refrigerator.
   - Learn appropriate portion sizes.
   - Plan appropriate snacks.
   - Keep sports and play equipment by the door.
4. Repeat the desired eating and exercise behaviors:
   - Slow down eating—put down utensils between bites.
   - Always use utensils.
   - Leave some food on your plate.
   - Move more—shake a leg, pace, stretch often.
   - Join groups of active people and participate.
5. Arrange or emphasize negative consequences for inappropriate eating:
   - Ask that others respond neutrally to your deviations (make no comments—even negative attention is a reward).
   - If you slip, don't punish yourself.
6. Arrange or emphasize positive consequences for appropriate eating and exercise behaviors:
   - Buy tickets to sports events, movies, concerts, or other nonfood amusement.
   - Indulge in a new small purchase.
   - Get a massage; buy some flowers.
   - Take a hot bath; read a good book.
   - Treat yourself to a lesson in a new active pursuit such as horseback riding, handball, or tennis.
   - Praise yourself; visit friends.
   - Nap; relax.

consumers' behaviors in the opposite direction—toward buying more foods, soft drinks, and other products. These cues work on a subconscious level; they leverage the human tendency to eat (and buy) more from oversized food containers.

COGNITIVE SKILLS

Behavior therapists often teach **cognitive skills,** or new ways of thinking, to help dieters solve problems and correct false thinking that can short-circuit healthy eating behaviors.[140] Thinking habits turn out to be as important as eating habits to achieving a healthy body weight, and thinking habits can be changed.[§§§] A paradox of making a change is that it takes belief in oneself and honoring of oneself to lay the foundation for changing that self. That is, self-acceptance predicts success, while self-loathing predicts failure. "Positive self-talk" is a concept worth cultivating—many people succeed because their mental dialogue supports, rather than degrades, their efforts. Negative thoughts ("I'm not getting thin anyway, so what's the use of continuing?") should be viewed in the light of empirical evidence ("my starting weight: 174 pounds; today's weight: 163 pounds").

Give yourself credit for your new behaviors; take honest stock of any physical improvements, too, such as lower blood pressure or less painful knees, even without a noticeable change in pant size. Finally, remember to enjoy your emerging fit and healthy self.

§§§*Psychologists have a term for changing thinking habits:* cognitive restructuring.

Diet Analysis PLUS Concepts in Action

Analyze Your Energy Balance

The purpose of this exercise is to help you to use critical thinking to evaluate correlations between nutrition, physical activity, and body weight.

1. Energy balance is the balance between the energy (calories) you take in and the energy you expend. From the Reports tab, select the Energy Balance Analysis report, choose Day One of your three-day diet intake, include the entire day's meals, and generate a report to determine your calorie (kCal) intake for the day. How does it compare to the DRI energy recommendation for the reference man or woman of your age, as listed on the inside front cover of the text?

2. Energy balance is affected not just by food eaten but also by energy expended. Compare the effects of two levels of activity on your energy balance. You've already generated an Energy Balance report for Day One. Select the Track Activity tab, add a new 30-minute activity for Day One. Look at the list of activities in Table 9-5 (page 341) for suggestions. Generate a new report. Compare the Energy Balance report with and without the added activity. What changes do you see?

3. If you want to lose body fat, you must expend more energy than you take in. To lose 1 pound of body weight requires a deficit of about 3,500 calories. Look over your food diaries. Is there a day that you were in positive energy balance (took in more energy than you used)? If so, input a revised food record for that day with the goal of reducing calories but still maintaining a wholesome and satisfying diet. Now, select the Track Diet tab to evaluate the revised meal plan. Did you succeed in trimming calories but still consume the recommended nutrients? How many calories did you trim? Do you think the revised meal plan would be more or less satisfying than the original?

4. A food and an activity diary are essential in helping you recognize appropriate and inappropriate cues that affect your eating habits (some cues are listed in Table 9-11, page 360). Parties, late-night study sessions, and boredom often lead to unplanned, low-nutrient, high-fat and/or high-calorie snack consumption. Although all three energy-yielding nutrients can contribute excess calories, fat is the least satiating, contains the most calories per gram, and can easily lead to overconsumption of calories, often without our awareness. Hidden fats abound in our food supply, and it's worth a moment to identify them and expose any mindless patterns in their consumption. From the Reports tab, select Source Analysis, then select Fat Total from the drop-down menu. Evaluate your daily food records for total fat. Then, choose the day that contained the most fat in grams or the highest percentage of calories from fat. Find the foods that contributed the most fat to your intake. What would you say led to higher intake of fat on that day as compared to another? Which part of the day did you consume the most fat? Were you aware that you were doing so? Try to identify some of your own cues to overconsuming calories from fat.

MEDIA MENU

To find additional quiz questions, view videos and animations, and explore interactive exercises, go to **www.cengage.com/sso.**

Search for information on overweight, obesity, underweight, and eating disorders at **www.healthfinder.gov.**

Search under Subjects and select Steps to a Healthier Weight at **www.mypyramid.gov.**

Learn more about portion control and improving one's health at **www.smallstep.gov.**

Get answers to commonly asked questions and additional information, including an interactive BMI calculator, menu planner, information on portion sizes, and more at **www.nhlbi.nih.gov/guidelines/obesity/bmi_tbl.htm.**

Learn more about eating disorders at **www.nationaleatingdisorders.org.**

SELF CHECK

Answers to these Self Check questions are in Appendix G.

1. All of the following are health risks associated with excessive body fat except:
   A. respiratory problems
   B. sleep apnea
   C. gallbladder disease
   D. low blood lipids
2. Which of the following statements about basal metabolic rate (BMR) is correct?
   A. The greater a person's age, the higher the BMR.
   B. The more thyroxine produced, the higher the BMR.
   C. Fever lowers the BMR.
   D. Pregnancy lowers the BMR.
3. Percent body fat can be measured by which of the following techniques?
   A. skinfold test
   B. bioelectrical impedance
   C. underwater weighing
   D. all of the above
4. The appetite-stimulating hormone ghrelin is made by the:
   A. brain
   B. fat tissue
   C. pancreas
   D. stomach
5. Which of the following is *not* true of popular fad diets?
   A. skillful writing
   B. profit motive
   C. superior weight loss
   D. limited calorie intakes
6. Which of the following is a possible physical consequence of fasting?
   A. loss of lean body tissues
   B. lasting weight loss
   C. body cleansing
   D. all of the above
7. The thermic effect of food plays a major role in energy expenditure.
   T F
8. The nervous system cannot use fat as fuel.
   T F
9. The BMI standard is an excellent tool for evaluating obesity in athletes and the elderly.
   T F
10. A diet too low in carbohydrate brings about responses that are similar to fasting.
   T F

CONTROVERSY 9

The Perils of Eating Disorders

LO 9.9

Almost 5 million people in the United States, many of them girls and women, suffer from the **eating disorders** of **anorexia nervosa** and **bulimia nervosa.**[1*] Over 8 million more, almost 3 million of them men, suffer from **binge eating disorder** or related conditions that imperil physical and mental health. Young adult women ages 18 to 30 years comprise the greatest percentage of those with eating disorders, but other people are by no means immune.[2] Table C9-1 defines eating disorder terms.

An estimated 85 percent of eating disorders start during adolescence. Children of this age often exhibit warnings of disordered eating such as restrained eating, binge eating, purging, fear of fatness, and distorted body image. In U.S. surveys of adolescents in grades 5 through 12, about half of girls and up to a third of boys report having dieted to lose weight.[3] Many adolescent dieters choose unhealthy dieting behaviors associated with disordered eating, and by college age the behaviors can be entrenched, producing less, not more, control of body weight.[4] Importantly, healthful dieting and physical activity to reduce body fatness do not appear to trigger eating disorders in overweight adolescents.[5]

*Reference notes are found in Appendix F.

TABLE C9-1 Eating Disorder Terms

- **anorexia nervosa** an eating disorder characterized by a refusal to maintain a minimally normal body weight, self-starvation to the extreme, and a disturbed perception of body weight and shape; seen (usually) in teenage girls and young women (*anorexia* means "without appetite"; *nervos* means "of nervous origin").
- **binge eating disorder** an eating disorder whose criteria are similar to those of bulimia nervosa, excluding purging or other compensatory behaviors.
- **bulimia** (byoo-LEEM-ee-uh) **nervosa** recurring episodes of binge eating combined with a morbid fear of becoming fat; usually followed by self-induced vomiting or purging.
- **cathartic** a strong laxative.
- **cognitive therapy** psychological therapy aimed at changing undesirable behaviors by changing underlying thought processes contributing to these behaviors; in anorexia, a goal is to replace false beliefs about body weight, eating, and self-worth with health-promoting beliefs.
- **eating disorder** a disturbance in eating behavior that jeopardizes a person's physical or psychological health.
- **emetic** (em-ETT-ic) an agent that causes vomiting.
- **female athlete triad** a potentially fatal triad of medical problems seen in female athletes: disordered eating, amenorrhea, and osteoporosis.

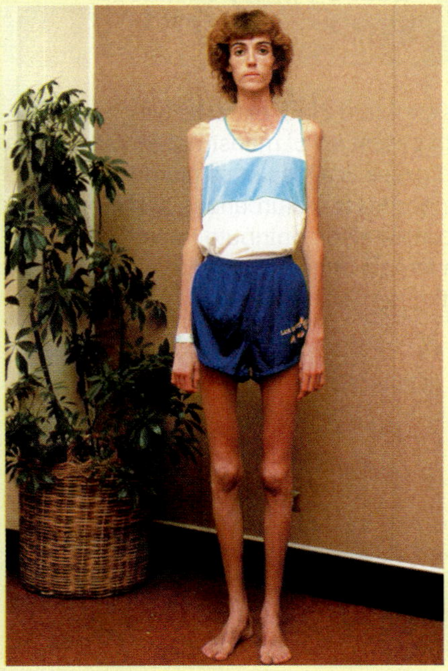
William Thompson/PhotoLibrary

Anorexia nervosa.

SOCIETY'S INFLUENCE

Why do so many people in our society suffer from eating disorders? Most experts agree that eating disorders have many causes: sociocultural, psychological, hereditary, and probably also neurochemical.[6] However, excessive pressure to be thin in our society is at least partly to blame. Normal-weight girls as young as 5 years old are placed "on diets" for fear that they are too fat.

When thinness takes on heightened importance, people begin to view the normal, healthy body as too fat—their body images become distorted. People of all shapes, sizes, and ages—including emaciated fashion models with anorexia nervosa—have learned to be unhappy with their "overweight" bodies. Many take serious risks to lose weight. These behaviors and attitudes are much less prevalent among people of other societies and are almost nonexistent where body leanness is not valued as central to self-worth.

Media Messages

No doubt our society sets unrealistic ideals and devalues those who do not conform to them. The Miss America beauty pageant, for example, puts forth a standard of female desirability—thinner and thinner women over the years have won the crown. Magazines and other media convey a message that to be happy, beautiful, and desirable, one must first be thin. In their quest for identity, adolescent girls are particularly vulnerable to such messages.[7]

Dieting as Risk

Severe food restriction often precedes an eating disorder.[8] Ill-advised "dieting" can create intense stress and extreme hunger that lead to binges. Painful emotions such as anger, jealousy, or disappointment may be turned inward by youngsters who express dissatisfaction with body weight or say they "feel fat." As weight loss and severe food restraint become more and more a focus, psychological problems worsen, and the likelihood of developing full-blown eating disorders intensifies.

EATING DISORDERS IN ATHLETES

Athletes and dancers are at special risk for eating disorders.[9] They may severely restrict energy intakes in an attempt to enhance performance or appearance, or meet weight guidelines of a sport. They fail to realize that severe energy restriction causes a loss of lean tissue that impairs physical performance and carries a risk of eating disorders. Risk factors for eating disorders among athletes include:

- young age (adolescence).
- pressure to excel in a sport.
- focus on achieving or maintaining an "ideal" body weight or body fat percentage.
- participation in sports or competitions that emphasize a lean appearance or judge performance on aesthetic appeal, such as gymnastics, wrestling, figure skating, or dance.[10]
- unhealthy, unsupervised weight-loss dieting at an early age.

Female athletes are most vulnerable, but males—especially dancers, wrestlers, skaters, jockeys, and gymnasts—suffer from eating disorders, too, and their numbers may be increasing.[11]

The Female Athlete Triad

In female athletes, three associated medical problems form the **female athlete triad:** disordered eating, amenorrhea (cessation of menstruation), and osteoporosis.[12] For example, at age 14, Suzanne was a top contender for a spot on the state gymnastics team. Each day her coach reminded team members that they would not qualify to compete if they weighed more than a few ounces above the assigned weights.

Suzanne weighed herself several times a day to ensure that she did not top her 80-pound limit. She dieted and exercised to extreme; unlike many of her friends, she never began to menstruate. A few months before her 15th birthday, Suzanne's coach dropped her back to the second-level team because of a slow-healing stress fracture. Mentally and physically exhausted, she quit gymnastics and began overeating between periods of self-starvation. Suzanne exhibited all the signs of female athlete triad—disordered eating, amenorrhea, and weakened bones.

An athlete's body must be heavier for a given height than a nonathlete's body because it contains more muscle and dense bone tissue with less fat. However, coaches often use weight standards, such as BMI, that cannot properly assess an athletes' body. For athletes, body composition measures such as skinfold tests yield more useful information.

The prevalence of amenorrhea among premenopausal women in the United States is about 2 to 5 percent overall, but it may be as high as 66 percent among female athletes. Amenorrhea is *not* a normal adaptation to strenuous physical training, but a symptom of something going wrong and is hazardous to the bones.[13]

For most people, weight-bearing exercise helps to protect bones against the calcium losses of aging.[14] For young women with disordered eating and amenorrhea, strenuous activity can imperil bone health.[15] Bone loss can lead to stress fractures today and osteoporosis in later life (see Figure C9-1).[16]

Male Athletes and Eating Disorders

Male athletes and dancers with eating disorders often deny having them because they mistakenly believe that such disorders strike only women.[17] Under the same pressures as female athletes, males develop eating disorders, too. On average, teenage males carry about 15 percent of body weight as fat; many male high school wrestlers, gymnasts, and figure skaters strive for 5 percent body fat. Wrestlers, especially, must "make weight" to compete in the lowest possible weight class to face smaller opponents.

Male athletes may also suffer weight-*gain* problems, in which young men with well-muscled bodies falsely see themselves as underweight and weak—a condition sometimes termed *muscle dysmorphia* (dis-MORF-ee-uh).[18] When

FIGURE C9-1 **The Female Athlete Triad**

In the female athlete triad, extreme weight loss causes both cessation of menstruation (amenorrhea) and excessive loss of calcium from the bones. The hormone disturbances associated with amenorrhea also contribute to osteoporosis, making the female athlete triad extraordinarily harmful to the bones.

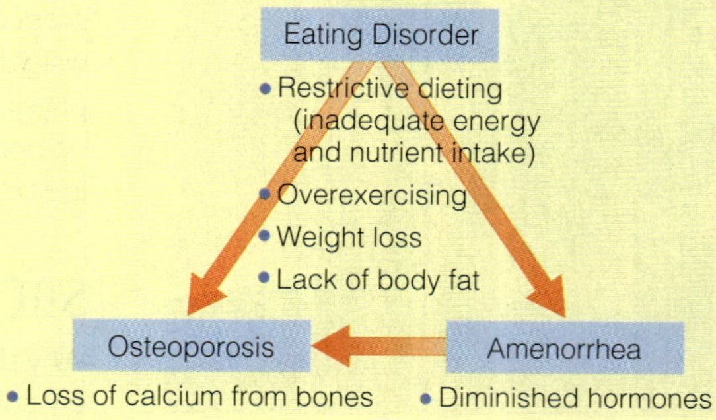

young men with low self-esteem internalize unrealistic male body images, they can become dissatisfied with their own healthy bodies.[19] Perfectionism then leads to obsessive weighing, excessive exercise, overuse of diets or supplements, or even steroid abuse in the attempt to bulk up their muscles.

For young people, unrealistic standards based on slim appearance, low weight, or overly muscled bodies should be replaced with performance-based standards. Table C9-2 provides some suggestions to help athletes and dancers protect themselves against eating disorders.

TABLE C9-2 **Tips for Combating Eating Disorders**

General Guidelines

- Never restrict food intakes to below the amounts suggested for adequacy by the USDA Food Guide (Chapter 2).
- Eat frequently. The person who eats frequently never gets so hungry as to allow hunger to dictate food choices.
- If not at a healthy weight, establish a reasonable weight goal based on a healthy body composition.
- Allow a reasonable time to achieve the goal. A reasonable rate for losing excess fat is about 1% of body weight per week.
- Learn to recognize media image biases, and reject ultrathin standards for beauty. Shift focus to health, competencies, and human interactions; bring behaviors in line with those beliefs.

Specific Guidelines for Athletes and Dancers

- Replace weight-based or appearance-based goals with performance-based goals.
- Remember that eating disorders impair physical performance. Seek confidential help in obtaining treatment if needed.
- Restrict weight-loss activities to the off-season.
- Focus on proper nutrition as an important facet of your training, as important as proper technique.

ANOREXIA NERVOSA

Julie is 17 years old and a straight-A superachiever in school. She also watches her diet with great care, and she exercises daily, maintaining a heroic schedule of self-discipline. She stands 5 feet 6 inches tall and weighs only 85 pounds but she is determined to lose weight. She has anorexia nervosa.

Characteristics of Anorexia Nervosa

Julie is unaware that she is undernourished, and she sees no need to obtain treatment. She insists that she is too fat, although her eyes are sunk in deep hollows in her face. She visits pro-anorexia Internet websites (or *pro-ana* websites) for support of her distorted body image and to learn more starvation tips.[20] When Julie looks at herself in the mirror, she sees her 85-pound body as fat. The more Julie overestimates her body size, the more resistant she is to treatment and the more unwilling to examine misperceptions.

© Tony Freeman/PhotoEdit

Women with anorexia nervosa see themselves as fat, even when they are dangerously underweight.

She stopped menstruating and is moody and chronically depressed but blames external circumstances. She is close to physical exhaustion, but she no longer sleeps easily. Her family is concerned, and although reluctant to push her, they have finally insisted that she see a psychiatrist. Julie's psychiatrist has prescribed group therapy as a start but warns that if Julie does not begin to gain weight soon, she will need to be hospitalized.

No one knows for certain what causes anorexia nervosa. Central to its diagnosis is a distorted body image that overestimates body fatness. Most anorexia nervosa victims come from middle- or upper-class families. Most are female. Malnutrition is known to affect brain functioning and judgment. People with anorexia nervosa cannot recognize it in themselves; only professionals can diagnose it. Table C9-3 shows the criteria that experts use.

The Role of the Family

Certain family attitudes, and especially parental attitudes, stand accused of contributing to or maintaining eating disorders.[21] Families of persons with anorexia nervosa are likely to be critical and to overvalue outward appearances. When symptoms appear, unhelpful emotional reactions, such as making excuses or becoming angry, may inadvertently enable and maintain the eating disorder.[22]

Julie is a perfectionist, just as her parents are—she identifies so strongly with her parents' ideals and goals that she cannot get in touch with her own identity. She is respectful of authority: polite but controlled, rigid, and unspontaneous.[23] For Julie, rejecting food is a way of gaining control.

Self-Starvation

How can a person as thin as Julie continue to starve herself? Julie uses tremendous discipline to strictly limit her portions of low-calorie foods. She will deny her hunger, and having become accustomed to so little food, she feels full after eating only a few bites. She can recite the calorie contents of dozens of foods and the calorie costs of as many

TABLE C9-3 Criteria for Diagnosis of Anorexia Nervosa

A person with anorexia nervosa demonstrates the following:

A. Refusal to maintain a minimal normal weight for age and height.

B. Intense fear of gaining weight or becoming fat, even though underweight.

C. Disturbance in the way in which one's body weight or shape is experienced; undue influence of body weight or shape on self-evaluation, or denial of the seriousness of the current low body weight.

D. In females past puberty, amenorrhea.

Two types of anorexia nervosa include:

- Restricting type: the person does not regularly engage in binge eating or purging behavior.
- Binge eating/purging type: the person regularly engages in binge eating or purging behavior (i.e., self-induced vomiting or the misuse of laxatives, diuretics, or enemas).

Source: Adapted from the Diagnostic and Statistical Manual of Mental Disorders, *Fourth Edition, Text Revision. Copyright 2000 American Psychiatric Association.*

physical activities. If she feels that she has gained an ounce of weight, she runs or jumps rope until she thinks it's gone. She drinks water incessantly to fill her stomach, risking dangerous mineral imbalances and water intoxication. She takes laxatives to hasten the passage of food from her system; her other methods of staying thin are so effective that she is unaware that laxatives have no effect on body fat. She is desperately hungry. In fact, she is starving, but she doesn't eat because her need for self-control outweighs her need for food.

Physical Perils

From the body's point of view, anorexia nervosa is starvation and thus brings the same damage as classic protein-energy malnutrition. The person with anorexia depletes the body tissues of needed fat and protein. In young people, growth ceases and normal development falters, and they lose so much lean tissue that basal metabolic rate slows. In athletes, physical performance suffers. Bones weaken, too.[24]

Internal organs suffer as nutrient status declines. The heart pumps inefficiently and irregularly, the heart muscle becomes weak and thin, the heart chambers diminish in size, and the blood pressure falls. As iron diminishes, anemia ensues, and the heart struggles to pump oxygen to the tissues.[25] Electrolytes that help to regulate the heartbeat go out of balance. Many deaths in people with anorexia nervosa are due to heart failure. Kidneys often fail as well.[26]

Starvation also brings neurological and digestive consequences. The brain loses significant amounts of tissue, nerves function abnormally, the electrical activity of the brain becomes abnormal, and insomnia is common. Digestive functioning becomes sluggish, the stomach empties slowly, and the lining of the intestinal tract shrinks. The ailing digestive tract fails to adequately digest the small amount of food consumed. The pancreas slows its production of digestive enzymes. Diarrhea sets in, further worsening malnutrition.

In addition to anemia, blood changes include impaired immune response, altered blood lipids, high concentrations of vitamin A and vitamin E, and low blood proteins. Dry skin, low body temperature, and the development of fine body hair (the body's attempt to keep warm) also occur. In adulthood, both women and men lose their sex drives. Mothers with anorexia nervosa may severely underfeed their children, who then fail to thrive and suffer the other harms typical of starvation.

About 1,000 women die of anorexia nervosa each year, mostly from heart abnormalities brought on by malnutrition or from suicide. Anorexia nervosa has one of the highest mortality rates among psychiatric disorders.[27]

Treatment of Anorexia Nervosa

Treatment of anorexia nervosa requires a multidisciplinary approach that addresses two areas of concern: those relating to food and weight and those involving psychological processes. Teams of physicians, nurses, psychiatrists, family therapists, and dietitians work together to treat people with anorexia nervosa. The expertise of a registered dietitian is essential because an appropriate, individually crafted diet is crucial for normalizing body weight, and nutrition counseling is indispensable.[28]

Professionals classify clients based on the risks posed by the degree of malnutrition present.† Clients with low risks may benefit from family counseling, **cognitive therapy,** behavior modification, and nutrition guidance; those with greater risks may also need other forms of psychotherapy and supplemental formulas to provide extra nutrients and energy.

Clients in later stages are seldom willing to eat, but if they are, chances are they can recover without other interventions. Sometimes, intensive behavior management treatment in a live-in facility can help to normalize food intake and exercise.[29] When starvation leads to severe underweight (less than 75 percent of ideal body weight), high medical risks ensue and patients require hospitalization. They must be stabilized and carefully fed to forestall death.[30] However, involuntary feeding through a tube can cause psychological trauma and may not be necessary in all cases.[31] Antidepressant and other drugs are commonly prescribed but are often ineffective in anorexia nervosa.[32]

Stopping weight loss is a first goal; establishing regular eating patterns is next. Because body weight is low and fear of weight gain is high, initial food intake may be small—1,200 calories per day can be an achievement.[33] A variety of high-energy foods and beverages can help deliver needed calories and nutrients.[34] Even after recovery, however, energy intakes and eating behaviors may not fully return to normal.

Almost half of women who are treated can successfully maintain their body weight at just below a healthy weight; at

† Indicators of malnutrition include a low percentage of body fat, low blood proteins, and impaired immune response.

that weight, many of them begin menstruating again. The other half have poor or fair outcomes of treatment. Many, fearing the growing pads of fat on hips and abdomen, relapse into abnormal eating behaviors.

Before drawing conclusions about someone who is extremely thin, be aware that a diagnosis requires professional assessment.[35] People seeking help for anorexia nervosa for themselves or for others should not delay, but visit the National Eating Disorders Association website or call them.‡

BULIMIA NERVOSA

Sophia is a 20-year-old flight attendant, and although her body weight is healthy, she thinks constantly about food. She alternately starves herself and then secretly binges; when she has eaten too much, she vomits. Few people would fail to recognize that these symptoms signify bulimia nervosa. Official diagnostic criteria are found in Table C9-4.

Characteristics of Bulimia Nervosa

Bulimia nervosa is distinct from anorexia nervosa and is much more prevalent, although the true incidence is difficult to establish. People with bulimia nervosa often suffer in secret and, when asked, may deny the existence of a problem. More men suffer from bulimia nervosa than from anorexia nervosa, but bulimia nervosa is still more common in women.

As is typical, Sophia is single, female, and white. She is well educated and close to her ideal body weight, although her weight fluctuates over a range of 10 pounds or so every few weeks. She has always been a high achiever but emotionally insecure. As a young teen, Sophia cycled on and off crash diets.

Sophia seldom lets her bulimia nervosa interfere with her work or other activities. However, she has low self-esteem, feels anxious at social events, and cannot easily establish close relationships. She is usually depressed and often impulsive. When crisis hits, Sophia responds by binge eating.[36]

‡ *The National Eating Disorders website address is www.nationaleatingdisorders.org; the toll-free referral line is (800) 931-2237.*

TABLE C9-4 Criteria for Diagnosis of Bulimia Nervosa

A person with bulimia nervosa demonstrates the following:

A. Recurrent episodes of binge eating characterized by both of the following:
  1. Eating, in a discrete period of time (e.g., within any two-hour period), an amount of food that is larger than most people would eat during a similar period of time and under similar circumstances, and,
  2. A sense of lack of control over eating during the episode.

B. Recurrent inappropriate compensatory behavior in order to prevent weight gain, such as self-induced vomiting; misuse of laxatives, diuretics, enemas, or other medications; fasting; or excessive exercise.

C. Binge eating and inappropriate compensatory behaviors that both occur, on average, at least twice a week for three months.

D. Self-evaluation unduly influenced by body shape and weight.

E. The disturbance does not occur exclusively during episodes of anorexia nervosa.

Two types:

- Purging type: the person regularly engages in self-induced vomiting or the misuse of laxatives, diuretics, or enemas.
- Nonpurging type: the person uses other inappropriate compensatory behaviors, such as fasting or excessive exercise, without purging.

Source: Adapted from the Diagnostic and Statistical Manual of Mental Disorders, *Fourth Edition, Text Revision. Copyright 2000 American Psychiatric Association.*

The Role of the Family

Parents and other family members may foster bulimia by example or by direct interactions.[37] Children, particularly daughters, often adopt the dieting behaviors or body dissatisfaction displayed by parents, particularly mothers.[38]

Families may also be controlling but emotionally unsupportive, resulting in a stifling negative self-image believed to perpetuate bulimia (see Figure C9-2). Dieting, arguments, and criticism of body shape or weight commonly arise in families of people with bulimia and a sensitive child may react with anxiety and self-doubt.[39] The family may also rarely eat meals together, a factor common to those with bulimia nervosa.[40] In the extreme, bulimic women who report having been abused by family members or friends may become emotionally inhibited and continually suffer a sense of being unable to gain control.[41]

Binge Eating and Purging

A bulimic binge is unlike normal eating, and the food is not consumed for its nutritional value. During a binge, Sophia's eating is accelerated by her hunger from previous calorie restriction.

FIGURE C9-2 The Cycle of Bingeing, Purging, and Negative Self-Perception

Each of these factors helps to perpetuate disordered eating.

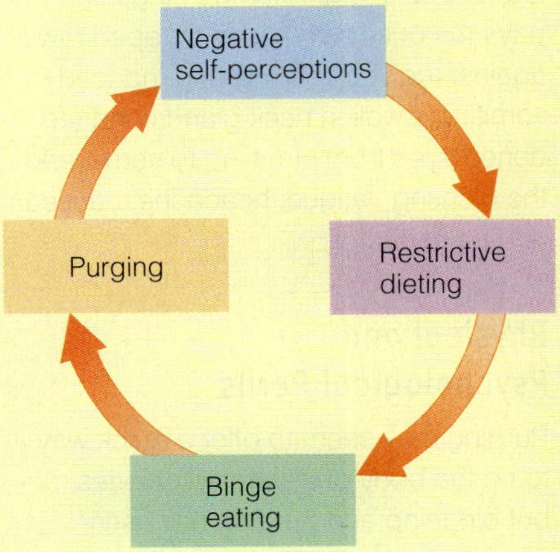

She regularly takes in extra food approaching 1,000 calories at each binge, and she may have several binges in a day. Typical binge foods are easy-to-eat, low-fiber, smooth-textured, high-fat,

© Felicia Martinez/PhotoEdit

A typical binge consists of easy-to-eat, low-fiber, smooth-textured, high-calorie foods.

and high-carbohydrate foods, such as cookies, cakes, and ice cream; and she eats the entire bag of cookies, the whole cake, and every spoonful in a carton of ice cream. By the end of the binge, she has vastly overcorrected for her earlier attempts at calorie restriction.

The binge is a compulsion and usually occurs in several stages: anticipation and planning, anxiety, urgency to begin, rapid and uncontrollable consumption of food, relief and relaxation, disappointment, and finally shame or disgust. Then, to purge the food from her body, she may use a **cathartic**—a strong laxative that can injure the lower intestinal tract. Or she may induce vomiting, sometimes with an **emetic**—a drug intended as first aid for poisoning. After the binge she pays the price with hands scraped raw against the teeth during gag-induced vomiting, swollen neck glands and reddened eyes from straining to vomit, and the bloating, fatigue, headache, nausea, and pain that follow.

Physical and Psychological Perils

Purging may seem to offer a quick way to rid the body of unwanted calories, but bingeing and purging have serious physical consequences. Fluid and electrolyte imbalances caused by vomiting or diarrhea can lead to abnormal heart rhythms; one common emetic causes heart muscle damage, and its overuse can cause death from heart failure.[§42] Urinary tract infections can lead to kidney failure. Vomiting causes irritation and infection of the pharynx, esophagus, and salivary glands; erosion of the teeth; and dental caries. The esophagus or stomach may rupture or tear.

Purging behaviors are often followed by feelings of shame or guilt. Hence a vicious cycle ensues: negative self-perceptions trigger restrictive dieting; dieting leads to bingeing; a binge is followed by purging to compensate, which leads to further self-deprecation. Unlike Julie, Sophia is aware that her behavior is abnormal, and she is deeply ashamed of it. She wants to recover, and this makes recovery more likely for her than for Julie, who clings to denial.

Treatment of Bulimia Nervosa

To gain control over food and establish regular eating patterns requires adherence to a structured eating and exercise plan. Restrictive dieting is forbidden, for it almost always precedes binges. Steady maintenance of weight and prevention of cyclic gains and losses are the goals. Many a former bulimia nervosa sufferer has taken a major step toward recovery by learning to consistently eat enough food to satisfy hunger (at least 1,600 calories a day).

Table C9-5 offers some ways to begin correcting the eating problems of bulimia nervosa. About half of women receiving a diagnosis of bulimia nervosa may recover completely after five to ten years, with or without treatment. Treatment, and even self-help programs, probably speed the recovery process.[43] If Sophia's depression deepens, however, she may need antidepressant medication.

Family cooperation is important for the member recovering from bulimia nervosa because making changes requires effort from everyone. Such effort is well spent, however.

§ The heart-damaging emetic is ipecac (IP-eh-kak). In a nationally known "right-to-die" case, a lawsuit blamed Terri Schiavo's 15-year coma on heart stoppage from ipecac abuse in bulimia.

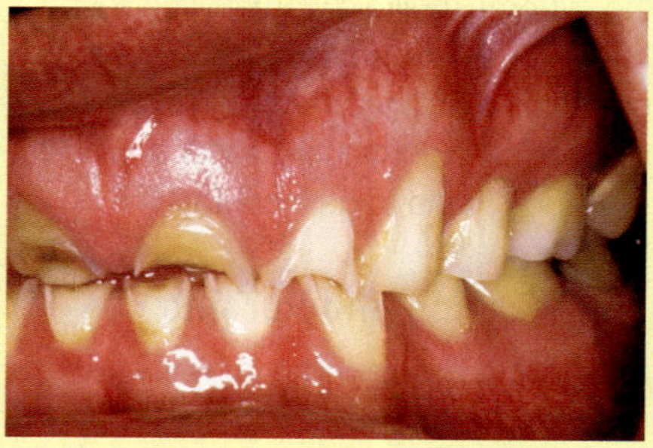

© 2009 Edward H. Gill/Custom Medical Stock Photo

Tooth damage from stomach acid in bulimia nervosa.

BINGE EATING DISORDER

Charlie is a 40-year-old former baseball outfielder who, after becoming a spectator instead of a player, has gained excess body fat. He believes that he has the willpower to diet until he loses the fat. Periodically he restricts his food intake for several days, only to eventually succumb to cravings for his favorite high-calorie treats. Like Charlie, many overweight people end up bingeing after dieting.

People with binge eating disorder are not bulimic. They consume less during a binge, rarely purge, and exert less restraint during times of dieting. Similarities also exist, including feeling out of control, disgusted, depressed, embarrassed, guilty, or distressed because of their self-perceived gluttony. Table C9-6 lists the official diagnostic criteria for binge eating disorder.

Binge eating behavior responds more readily to treatment than other eating disorders. Intervention, even obtained on a reliable Internet website, improves physical and mental health and may permanently break the cycle of rapid weight losses and gains.[44]

TOWARD PREVENTION

Treatments for existing eating disorders have evolved, but prevention of these conditions would be far preferable.[45] One approach may be to provide children and adolescents with defenses

TABLE C9-5 Diet Strategies for Combating Bulimia Nervosa

Planning Principles

- Plan meals and snacks; record plans in a food diary prior to eating.
- Plan meals and snacks that require eating at the table and using utensils.
- Refrain from eating "finger foods."
- Refrain from "dieting" or skipping meals.

Nutrition Principles

- Eat a well-balanced diet and regularly timed meals consisting of a variety of foods.
- Include raw vegetables, salad, or raw fruit at meals to prolong eating times.
- Choose whole-grain, high-fiber breads, pasta, rice, and cereals to increase bulk.
- Consume adequate fluid, particularly water.

Other Tips

- Choose meals that provide protein and fat for satiety and bulky, fiber-rich carbohydrates for immediate feelings of fullness.
- Try including soups and other water-rich foods for satiety (water contents of foods are listed in Appendix A).
- Consume the amounts of food specified in the USDA Food Guide (Chapter 2).
- Select foods that naturally divide into portions. Select one potato, rather than rice or pasta that can be overloaded onto the plate; purchase yogurt and cottage cheese in individual containers; look for small packages of precut steak or chicken; choose frozen dinners with metered portions.
- Include 30 minutes or more of physical activity on most days—exercise may be an important tool in controlling bulimia.

TABLE C9-6 Criteria for Diagnosis of Binge Eating Disorder

A person with a binge eating disorder demonstrates the following:

A. Recurrent episodes of binge eating. An episode of binge eating is characterized by both of the following:
   1. Eating, in a discrete period of time (e.g., within any two-hour period), an amount of food that is larger than most people would eat in a similar period of time under similar circumstances.
   2. A sense of lack of control over eating during the episode.

B. Binge eating episodes are associated with at least three of the following:
   1. Eating much more rapidly than normal.
   2. Eating until feeling uncomfortably full.
   3. Eating large amounts of food when not feeling physically hungry.
   4. Eating alone because of being embarrassed by how much one is eating.
   5. Feeling disgusted with oneself, depressed, or guilty after overeating.

C. The binge eating causes marked distress.

D. The binge eating occurs, on average, at least twice a week for six months.

E. The binge eating is not associated with the regular use of inappropriate compensatory behaviors (e.g., purging, fasting, excessive exercise) and does not occur exclusively during the course of anorexia nervosa or bulimia nervosa.

Source: Adapted from the Diagnostic and Statistical Manual of Mental Disorders, *Fourth Edition, Text Revision. Copyright 2000 American Psychiatric Association.*

against influences that promote eating disorders. A set of suggestions intended to help pediatricians avert eating disorders in their patients might also apply to teachers, coaches, and others who deal with children:[46]

1. Encourage positive eating and physical behaviors that can be maintained over a lifetime; discourage unhealthy dieting.
2. Promote a positive body image; do not use body dissatisfaction as a motivator for behavior change.
3. Encourage frequent and enjoyable family meals consumed at home; discourage hasty meals eaten alone.
4. Help children and teens to nurture their bodies through healthy eating, physical activity, and self-talk; divert focus from weight and body shape.
5. Talk to children and teens and their families about mistreatment because of body weight or size; assume it has occurred in overweight children.

On college campuses, the programs that help students to bring their health beliefs into line with their behaviors, based on the so-called *cognitive-dissonance theory,* may be most effective.[47] Media literacy programs that debunk the overthin body ideal can also open college-age people's eyes.

Protection against eating disorders in the next generation largely depends upon the actions of adults in authority today. Perhaps a young person's best defense against eating disorders is to learn about normal, expected growth patterns, especially the characteristic weight gain of adolescence (see Chapter 14), and to learn respect for the inherent wisdom of the body. When people discover and honor the body's real needs for nutrition and exercise, they often will not sacrifice health for conformity.

10 Nutrients, Physical Activity, and the Body's Responses

DO YOU EVER . . .

- Wonder if physical activity can help you live longer?
- Wish that your diet would help you compete?
- Take vitamins to help your game?
- Use sports drinks but wonder why?

Keep reading . . .

Learning Objectives

To find learning objective topics in this chapter, look for text headings with a corresponding "LO" number above the heading. After completing this chapter, you should be able to accomplish the following:

LO 10.1 Discuss the short-term and long-term benefits of achieving cardiorespiratory fitness.

LO 10.2 Explain how the *2008 Physical Activity Guidelines for Americans* can be incorporated into anyone's lifestyle. Suggest simple ways to increase activity level throughout the day.

LO 10.3 Explain why it is important for an athlete to maintain blood glucose levels before, during, and after vigorous exercise.

LO 10.4 Describe how an athlete's body uses dietary protein during and after strenuous exercise.

LO 10.5 Discuss some reasons why female endurance athletes may be vulnerable to iron deficiency.

LO 10.6 Evaluate whether conjugated linoleic acid (CLA) and other ergogenic aids are useful for obtaining an ideal body composition for sports.

In the body, nutrition and physical activity work together and influence each other. The working body demands energy-yielding nutrients—carbohydrate, lipid, and protein—to fuel **physical activity.** It also needs protein for a balance of amino acids from which it builds new muscle tissues. Vitamins and minerals play critical roles in the use of fuels and in building muscles and other structures necessary for **exercise.**

The body's nutrition, in turn, also benefits from physical activity. Physical activity helps to regulate the use of energy-yielding nutrients, improves body composition, and increases the daily calorie allowance. Then, if the extra calories come from nutritious whole foods, more beneficial nutrients and phytochemicals enter the body tissues for their use. When combined, a nutritious diet and regular physical activity become a powerful force for human health.

This chapter addresses many of the concerns of physically active people, starting with some basic concepts about health and physical activity. Later, you will see how foods, fluids, and nutrients fuel physical activities and learn how to choose them for yourself in the Food Feature section. The Controversy that follows discusses just a few of the many supplements sold with promises of enhanced athletic performance.

LO 10.1, 10.2

Fitness

Physical **fitness** depends on a certain minimum amount of physical activity or exercise. Both physical activity and exercise involve movement, muscle contraction, and enhanced energy expenditure. A distinction is sometimes made between these terms, but this chapter uses them interchangeably because muscles use their fuels in identical ways, whether an individual is running around a track or to catch a bus. People's fitness goals vary from the competitive **athlete** in **training** to the casual exerciser working toward improved health and appearance. Both need the right foods and fluids at the right times to support their efforts.

Benefits of Fitness

For those just beginning a program of physical fitness, be assured that improvement is not only possible but inevitable as you become more active. Soon, a beneficial cycle of more physical activity and higher levels of fitness ensues. The risk factors for developing chronic diseases soon improve, too.[1*] The mechanism also runs in reverse: a sedentary lifestyle robs people of their fitness and fosters the development of several chronic diseases.[2]

The Nature of Fitness If you are physically fit, the following describes you: You move with ease and balance. You have endurance that lasts for hours. You are strong and meet daily physical challenges without strain. You are prepared for mental and emotional challenges, too, because physical activity can help to relieve stress, depression, or anxiety. So effective is physical activity that mental health clinicians are encouraged to recommend it as part of their treatment plans.[3] As your fitness improves, you not only begin to feel better and stronger but you look better, too. As you strengthen your muscles, your posture and self-image often improve.

Longevity and Disease Resistance People who regularly engage in moderate physical activity live longer on average than those who are physically inactive.[4] A sedentary lifestyle ranks with smoking and obesity as a powerful predictor of the major killer diseases of our time—cardiovascular disease, some forms of cancer, stroke, diabetes, and hypertension.[5] Sedentary people may even be more likely to catch a cold.[6] Despite the well-known health benefits of physical activity, only about half of adults in the United States are regularly active, and about 20 percent are completely inactive.[7]

*Reference notes are found in Appendix F.

physical activity bodily movement produced by muscle contractions that substantially increase energy expenditure.

exercise planned, structured, and repetitive bodily movement that promotes or maintains physical fitness.

fitness the characteristics that enable the body to perform physical activity; more broadly, the ability to meet routine physical demands with enough reserve energy to rise to a physical challenge; or the body's ability to withstand stress of all kinds.

athlete a competitor in any sport, exercise, or game requiring physical skill; for the purpose of this book, anyone who trains at a high level of physical exertion, with or without competition. From the Greek *athlein,* meaning "to contend for a prize."

training regular practice of an activity, which leads to physical adaptations of the body with improvement in flexibility, strength, or endurance.

- Similar differences in risks for chronic disease and death exist between:
  - *Vigorous exercise versus minimal exercise.*
  - *Healthy weight versus 20% overweight.*
  - *Nonsmoking versus smoking (one pack a day).*

Other Benefits of Fitness As a person becomes physically active, the health of the entire body improves. Compared with unfit people, physically fit people may enjoy:

- *More restful, beneficial sleep.* Rest and sleep occur naturally after periods of physical activity. During rest, the body repairs injuries, disposes of wastes generated during activity, and builds new physical structures.[8]
- *Improved nutritional health.* Active people expend more energy than sedentary people; those wishing to maintain their weight can meet their increased energy needs with nutrient-rich whole foods.
- *Improved body composition.* A balanced program of physical activity helps limit body fat, particularly abdominal fat, and increases or maintains lean tissue.[9] Thus, physically active people are often leaner than sedentary people at the same weight.[10]
- *Improved bone density.* Weight-bearing physical activity builds bone strength and protects against the bone loss of osteoporosis.[11]
- *Enhanced resistance to colds and other infectious diseases.* Fitness enhances immunity.[†]
- *Lower risks of some types of cancers.* Life-long physical activity may help to protect against colon cancer, breast cancer, and some other cancers.[12]
- *Stronger circulation and lung function.* Physical activity that challenges the heart and lungs strengthens both the circulatory and the respiratory system.
- *Lower risks of cardiovascular disease.* Physical activity lowers blood pressure, slows resting pulse rate, lowers total blood cholesterol, and raises HDL cholesterol, thus reducing the risks of heart attacks and strokes.[13] Reduction of abdominal fat through physical activity further reduces disease risks.[14]
- *Lower risk of developing type 2 diabetes.* Regular physical activity reduces the risk of developing type 2 diabetes.
- *Improved control of existing type 2 diabetes.* Physical activity helps to normalize blood glucose concentrations and trim excess body fat.[15] With regular physical activity, many people with diabetes find their blood glucose easier to control and may even need less insulin or other medication.
- *Reduced risk of gallbladder disease.* Regular physical activity reduces risk of gallbladder disease.[16]
- *Lower incidence and severity of anxiety and depression.* Physical activity may improve mood and enhance the quality of life by reducing depression and anxiety.[17]
- *Stronger self-image.* The sense of achievement that comes from meeting physical challenges promotes self-confidence.
- *Longer life and higher quality of life in the later years.* Active people live longer, healthier lives than sedentary people do.[18] Even a two-mile walk daily can add years to a person's life. In addition to extending longevity, physical activity supports independence and mobility in later life by reducing falls and, if a fall should occur, by minimizing injuries.[19]
- **Resistance exercise** has also been found to reduce an individual's use of the health-care system.[20]

KEY POINT Physical activity and fitness benefit people's physical and psychological well-being and improve their resistance to disease.

Physical Activity Guidelines

You don't have to run marathons to reap rewards from physical activity. You need only meet the *2008 Physical Activity Guidelines for Americans* set forth by the USDA and the Department of Health and Human Services, described next.[21]

aerobic physical activity activity in which the body's large muscles move in a rhythmic manner for a sustained period of time. Aerobic activity, also called *endurance activity,* improves cardiorespiratory fitness. Brisk walking, running, swimming, and bicycling are examples.

resistance exercise physical activity that develops muscle strength, power, endurance, and mass. Resistance can be provided by free weights, weight machines, other objects, or the person's own body weight. Also called *weight training* or *muscular strength exercises.*

moderate intensity physical activity physical activity that requires some increase in breathing and/or heart rate and expends 3.5 to 7 calories per minute. Walking at a speed of 3 to 4.5 miles per hour (about 15 to 20 minutes to walk one mile) is an example.

vigorous intensity physical activity physical activity that requires a large increase in breathing and/or heart rate and expends more than 7 calories per minute. Race walking (+4.5 miles per hour) or running at a pace of at least 5 miles per hour are examples.

[†]Moderate physical activity can stimulate immune function. Intense, vigorous, prolonged activity such as marathon running, however, may compromise immune function.

FIGURE 10-1 Physical Activity Guidelines for Americans[1]

Meeting these guidelines requires physical activity beyond the usual light or sedentary activities required in daily living, such as cooking, cleaning, and walking from an automobile to a store. Table 10-3 provides a sample plan that meets these goals.

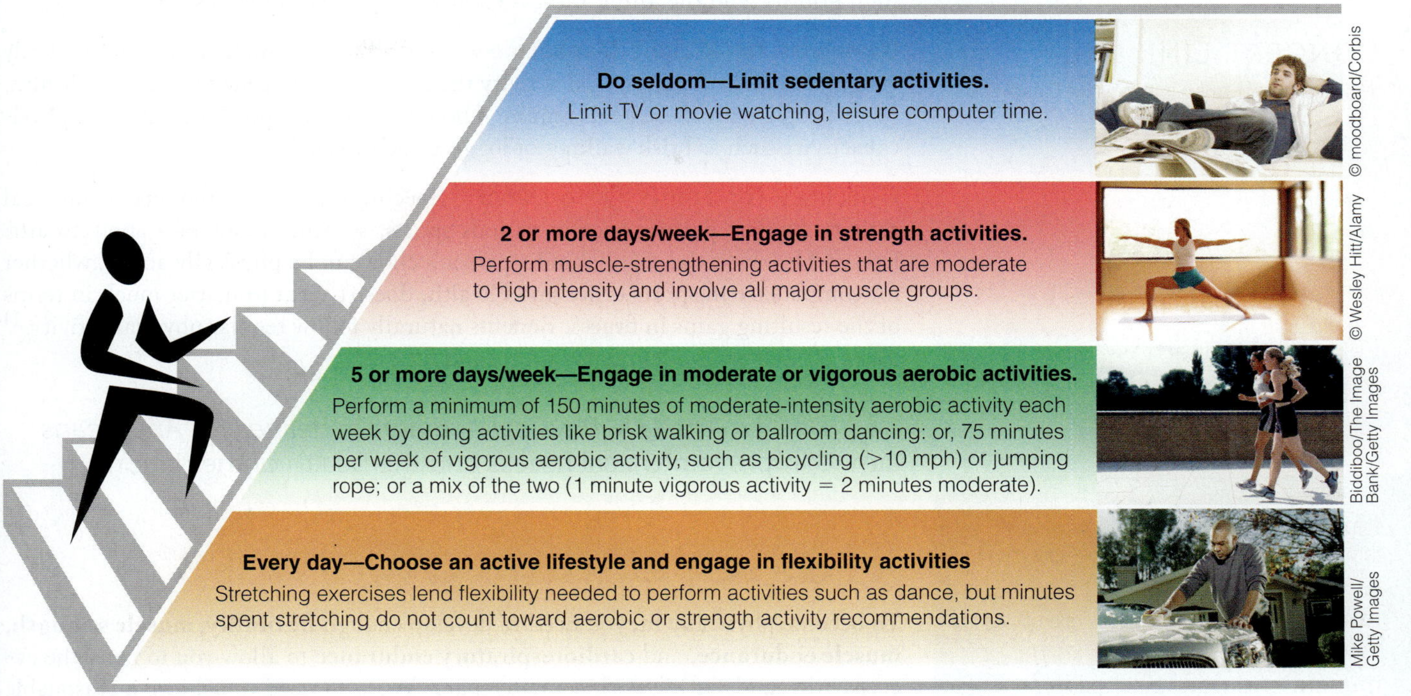

[1]*For most men and women, aged 18 to 64 years.*

Source: U.S. Department of Agriculture and U.S. Department of Health and Human Services, 2008 Physical Activity Guidelines for Americans, *available at www.health.gov/paguidelines/default.aspx.*

Physical Activity Guidelines for Americans The *2008 Physical Activity Guidelines for Americans* specify an amount of **aerobic physical activity** needed to improve the health of adults aged 18 to 64 years (see Figure 10-1). The *Guidelines* also state that resistance training is beneficial and counts toward meeting activity goals. The length of time (or exercise duration) required to meet these guidelines varies by intensity of the activity—longer periods for **moderate intensity physical activity,** shorter times for **vigorous intensity physical activity** (Table 10-1 describes activity levels).

Most health benefits occur with the recommendations listed in Figure 10-1, but additional benefits can result from higher intensity, greater frequency, or longer duration of activity. Older people and the disabled who cannot meet the *Guidelines* should

TABLE 10-1 Intensity of Physical Activity

Level of Intensity	Breathing and/or Heart Rate	Perceived Exertion (on a Scale of 0 to 10)	Talk Test	Energy Expenditure	Walking Pace
Light	Little to no increase	<5	Able to sing	<3.5 kcal/min	<3 mph
Moderate	Some increase	5 or 6	Able to have a conversation	3.5 to 7 kcal/min	3 to 4.5 mph (100 steps per minute)
Vigorous	Large increase	7 or 8	Conversation is difficult or "broken"	>7 kcal/min	>4.5 mph

Source: Centers for Disease Control and Prevention, www.cdc.gov/physicalactivity/everyone; site updated October 7, 2005; S. J. Marshall and coauthors, Translating physical activity recommendations into a pedometer-based step goal, American Journal of Preventive Medicine *36 (2009): 410–415.*

be as active as their conditions allow: those with chronic illnesses should seek advice from a health-care provider. For everyone, some physical activity is better than none.

The guidelines are stated in accumulated weekly totals. This allows individuals to split up their activity into sessions of at least 10 minutes each, performed throughout the days of the week in any combination that suits their lifestyles. Safety is a high priority, and the Think Fitness feature on page 377 provides some tips.

CONCEPT LINK 10-1

Weight management is a topic of Chapter 9.

Guidelines for Weight Management To achieve or maintain a healthy body weight demands more physical activity than the amount needed to improve health. Most people with these goals require 4 hours or more of moderate-intensity physical activity such as brisk walking or jogging each week.[22]

Guidelines for Sports Performance Specific types and amounts of physical activity support performance in various sports, so other guidelines apply to athletes.[23] However, the *why* behind a person's choice to be physically active, whether for competence in sports or for good health, doesn't seem to matter much in terms of the resulting gains in fitness. Benefits naturally follow regular physical activity.[24] Table 10-2 offers guidelines for sports and fitness.

KEY POINT The U.S. *Physical Activity Guidelines for Americans* aim to improve physical fitness and the health of the nation.

flexibility the capacity of the joints to move through a full range of motion; the ability to bend and recover without injury.

muscle strength the ability of muscles to work against resistance.

muscle endurance the ability of a muscle to contract repeatedly within a given time without becoming exhausted.

cardiorespiratory endurance the ability to perform large-muscle dynamic exercise of moderate-to-high intensity for prolonged periods.

muscle power the efficiency of a muscle contraction, measured by force and time.

reaction time the interval between stimulation and response.

agility nimbleness; the ability to quickly change directions.

fatigue temporarily diminished capacity, due to exertion. Muscle fatigue may result from depleted glucose or oxygen supplies or other causes.

overload an extra physical demand placed on the body; an increase in the frequency, duration, or intensity of an activity. A principle of training is that for a body system to improve, it must be worked at frequencies, durations, or intensities that increase by increments.

hypertrophy (high-PURR-tro-fee) an increase in size (for example, of a muscle) in response to use.

atrophy (AT-tro-fee) a decrease in size (for example, of a muscle) because of disuse.

aerobic (air-ROH-bic) requiring oxygen. Aerobic activity strengthens the heart and lungs by requiring them to work harder than normal to deliver oxygen to the tissues.

The Essentials of Fitness

To become physically fit, you need to develop enough **flexibility, muscle strength, muscle endurance,** and **cardiorespiratory endurance** to allow you to meet the everyday demands of life with some to spare. You also need to achieve a reasonable body composition. A person who engages in physical activity *adapts* by becoming better able to perform it after each session—with more flexibility, more strength, and more endurance.

So far, the description of fitness applies to anyone interested in improving health. For athletes, however, excellent sports performance often becomes the primary motivator for working out. To achieve this goal, athletes must strive to develop strength

TABLE 10-2 American College of Sports Medicine's Guidelines for Physical Fitness

Cardiorespiratory: Perform aerobic activities using large muscle groups maintained continuously at moderate intensity (equivalent to walking at a pace of 3 to 4 miles per hour)[a]

- At least 30 minutes/day on 5 to 7 days/week
- *Examples:* running, cycling, swimming, rowing, fast walking, jumping rope; sports such as basketball, soccer, racquetball, tennis, volleyball

Strength: Perform resistance activities at a controlled speed through a full range of motion at an intensity sufficient to enhance muscle strength and improve body composition

- 8 to 12 repetitions of 8 to 10 difference exercises (minimum) on ≥2 nonconsecutive days/week
  Example: Pull-ups, push-ups, weight lifting

Flexibility: Perform stretching activities that use the major muscle groups, enough to develop and maintain a full range of motion

- 2 to 4 repetitions of 15 to 30 seconds per muscle group on 2 to 7 days/week
  Examples: Various muscle stretches; yoga

[a] *For those who prefer vigorous-intensity aerobic activity such as walking at a very brisk pace (>4.5 mph) or running (≥5 mph), a minimum of 20 minutes per day, 3 days per week is recommended.*

Source: Adapted from W. L. Haskell and coauthors, Physical activity and public health: Updated recommendation for adults from the American College of Sports Medicine and the American Heart Association, Medicine & Science in Sports & Exercise *39 (2007): 1423–1434.*

and endurance, of course, but they also need **muscle power** to drive their movements, quick **reaction times** to respond with speed, **agility** to instantly change direction, increased resistance to **fatigue,** and mental toughness to carry on when fatigue sets in.

How Do Muscles Gain in Size and Strength?

People shape their bodies by what they choose to do and not do. Muscle cells and tissues respond to an **overload** of physical activity by gaining strength and size, a response called **hypertrophy.** The opposite is also true: if not used, muscles diminish in size and weaken, a response called **atrophy.** Thus, cyclists often have well-developed legs but less relative size in the arms or chest; a tennis player may have one superbly strong arm while the other is just average.

The Functions of Balanced Activity and Rest

Balanced fitness arises from performing a variety of physical activities that work different muscle groups from day to day. Stretching enhances flexibility, **aerobic** activity improves cardiorespiratory and muscle endurance, and resistance training develops strength, size, and endurance of the worked muscles. Table 10-3 presents one balanced workout program but other variations can be effective, so long as they supply the body with the required amounts of the needed activities.

Muscles need rest, too, because it takes a day or two to replenish muscle fuel supplies and to repair wear and tear. With greater work comes more damage, and muscles require longer rest periods for a full recovery. (A muscle or joint that remains sore after about a week of rest may be injured and in need of medical attention.) Periodic rest also gives muscles time to adapt to an activity. During sleep, muscles build more of the cellular structures required to perform the activity that preceded the rest.

Specific Training for Specific Development

The muscle cells of a superbly trained weight lifter store extra granules of glycogen, build up strong connective tissues, and add bulk to the special proteins that contract the muscles, thereby increasing their ability to perform.[‡] In the same way, the muscle cells of a distance swimmer adapt to burn fat and to sustain prolonged exertion. Therefore, if you wish to become a better jogger, swimmer, or biker, you should train mostly by jogging, swimming, or biking. Your performance will improve as your muscles adapt to a particular activity.

© 2010/Jupiterimages Corporation

Bodies are shaped . . .

Courtesy of the Author

. . . by the activities they perform.

[‡]All muscles contain a variety of muscle fibers, but there are two main types—slow-twitch (also called *red fibers*) and fast-twitch (also called *white fibers*). Slow-twitch fibers contain extra metabolic equipment to perform fat-burning aerobic work, which gives them a reddish appearance under a microscope; the fast-twitch type store extra glycogen for anaerobic work, giving them a lighter appearance.

TABLE 10-3 A Sample Balanced Fitness Program

To achieve the minimum recommended amount of physical activity in a week, use the lower numbers in each range. Individuals seeking greater than 300 minutes per week should use the higher minute values.

Monday	Tuesday	Wednesday	Thursday	Friday	Saturday and/or Sunday
5 minutes warm-up[a] 15–45 minutes resistance training: chest & back 15–20 minutes moderate aerobic activity 5 minutes stretching	5 minutes warm-up 30–45 minutes moderate aerobic activity 5 minutes stretching	5 minutes warm-up 15–45 minutes resistance training: legs & abdomen (core) 15–20 minutes moderate aerobic activity 5 minutes stretching	5 minutes warm-up 30–45 minutes moderate aerobic activity 5 minutes stretching	5 minutes warm-up 15–45 minutes resistance training: shoulders, arms, & abdomen (core) 15–20 minutes moderate aerobic activity 5 minutes stretching	Sports, walking, hiking, biking, or swimming

[a] *The warm-up can be a slower or less-intense version of the activity ahead, and may count toward the week's activity requirement if it is at least moderate in intensity.*

© ericlefrancais, 2011/Shutterstock.com

Hormones and Muscle Growth To understand the growth of muscles, you must learn a few things about hormones. Particularly, the body's **growth hormone** in both men and women and **testosterone** mostly in men affect muscle protein synthesis and increase the body's working muscles. Growth hormone also stimulates increased use of fatty acids for fuel, producing a double benefit for those who hope to increase muscle and decrease body fatness. Physical activity, particularly resistance exercise, elicits the release of the hormones that stimulate accretion of muscle tissue. No additional hormones are needed (and they are *not* recommended—see this chapter's Controversy). Much more is known about how to train to achieve muscle size and performance.

KEY POINT The components of fitness are flexibility, muscle strength, muscle endurance, and cardiorespiratory endurance. Physical activity builds muscles, which adapt to activities they are called upon to perform repeatedly. Growth hormone and testosterone play key roles in muscle tissue accretion.

What Are the Benefits of Resistance Training?

Most people know that resistance training builds lean body mass and develops and maintains muscle strength and endurance. Less well known is that **progressive weight training** can help to prevent and manage several chronic diseases, including cardiovascular disease, and can enhance psychological well-being, too.[25]

Resistance Exercise for Muscle Strength and Size, Power, or Endurance Resistance exercise can help an athlete to achieve specific goals in sports. To build strength, an athlete combines high resistance (heavy weight) with few (3 to 6) repetitions.[26] For muscle power, a combination of moderate resistance (light to medium weight) with high velocity (the lift performed as fast as safely possible) is best. To emphasize muscle endurance, an athlete uses less resistance—lighter weights—with more (15 to 20) repetitions. Resistance training enhances performance in other sports, too. Swimmers can develop a more efficient stroke and tennis players a more powerful serve when they engage in resistance training.[27]

Some people, and particularly women, needlessly avoid resistance training for fear that their muscles will become bulky, like those of body builders. In truth, body builders of both genders work to achieve their look by training intensely with heavy weights and by consuming hundreds or even thousands of calories beyond a normal person's intake.[28] Some body builders even resort to using illegal drugs or other substances to aid in hypertrophy, at their great peril (the Controversy comes back to this topic). In truth, ordinary people who regularly lift lighter weights even 2 days a week develop a pleasing appearance as muscles strengthen and firm without excessive bulk.[29] They may also increase their daily energy expenditure by a little—evidence suggests that resistance training for as little as 11 minutes on 3 days per week may produce a small but significant rise in 24-hour energy expenditure.[30]

Mobility in Aging and Prevention of Bone Loss As people age, resistance training slows the gradual loss of physical mobility that often impairs quality of life in the elderly.[31] People in their seventies and eighties who regularly train with weights can gain strength and improve endurance, enabling them to walk longer distances before tiring and to hold their balance to prevent falls. Preventing muscle loss in the elderly is an ongoing battle—leg strength and walking endurance are powerful indicators of an older adult's physical abilities and general health. In fact, among previously sedentary old people, taking up physical activity may help delay the loss of independent daily living and may even help to improve survival.[32]

Resistance training also helps to maximize and maintain bone mass, particularly in combination with adequate calcium and vitamin D intakes. Research shows that even in women past menopause (when most women are losing bone), a one-year program of resistance training improves bone density; the more weight lifted,

growth hormone a hormone produced by the brain's pituitary gland, necessary for growth of body tissues.

testosterone (tess-TAH-ster-own) a hormone produced primarily by the male testes; also produced to a lesser extent by the male and female adrenal gland and by the female ovaries; testosterone produces sexual maturity and functioning in males, and contributes to muscle growth in both sexes.

progressive weight training the gradual increase of stress placed upon the body with the use of resistance.

the greater the improvement. By strengthening muscles in the back and abdomen, weight training also improves posture and reduces the risk of back injury.

KEY POINT Resistance training can benefit physical and mental health. People can improve sports performance through resistance training, but bulky muscles are the intentional result of body building regimens. Weight training improves physical mobility and helps maintain bone mass in older adults.

CONCEPT LINK 10-2

Athletes need ample vitamin D for bone health, as do others (see Chapter 7, pages 236–237).

How Does Cardiorespiratory Training Benefit the Heart?

Weight training provides some cardiovascular benefits but the best kind of physical activity for heart health is cardiorespiratory endurance training. Cardiorespiratory endurance training enhances the capacity of the heart, lungs, and blood to deliver oxygen to, and remove wastes from, the body's cells.[33] It also encourages leanness and confers a fit, healthy appearance to limbs and torso.

CONCEPT LINK 10-3

Legitimate and fake nutrition credentials were described in Controversy 1. The same kinds of skullduggery occur in the field of physical training, too.

Improvements to Blood, Heart, and Lungs Exercisers who feel the heartbeat pick up its pace during work can appreciate cardiorespiratory endurance. It allows the body to remain active with an elevated heart rate during aerobic activity. As cardiorespiratory endurance improves, the body delivers oxygen to the tissues more efficiently. In fact, the accepted measure of a person's cardiorespiratory fitness is a measure of the rate at which the tissues consume oxygen—the maximal oxygen uptake (**$VO_{2\,max}$**).[34] This measure reflects many facets of oxygen delivery, many that improve with regular aerobic exercise.

$VO_{2\,max}$ the maximum rate of oxygen consumption by an individual (measured at sea level).

The blood's volume and the number of red blood cells partly determine $VO_{2\,max}$; the greater the volume and number, the more oxygen the blood can carry. The size

THINK FITNESS

Exercise Safety

Keeping safe during physical activity involves both common sense and education. The USDA suggests following these guidelines:

- Choose activities appropriate for your current fitness level.
- Gradually increase the amount of physical activity you perform.
- Wear appropriate safety gear, including correct shoes, helmet, pads, and other protection.
- Make sensible choices about when and where to exercise; for example, avoid the hottest hours of the day in southern locales, choose safe bike paths away from heavy traffic, and run with a buddy on isolated trails.
- People with medical problems should consult a physician before beginning any program of physical activity.

In addition, people can easily injure themselves by failing to use proper technique during exercise, particularly when it involves equipment. To work out safely and effectively, many people can benefit from the professional advice of a Certified Personal Trainer (CPT). A CPT can help develop effective individualized exercise programs using safe exercise techniques to avoid injury. Personal trainers are not all alike, however. The best ones have completed college-level training that includes human anatomy and exercise physiology and have passed a nationally recognized examination, as is true for professionals bearing the more advanced credential, Certified Strength and Conditioning Specialist (CSCS). Also, unless a trainer also possesses a legitimate nutrition credential (as described in Controversy 1), he or she is not qualified to dispense diet advice.

START NOW CENGAGENOW Ready to make a change? Consult the online behavior-change planner to develop your plan to increase your physical activity and fitness by safe increments at **www.cengage.com/sso**.

and strength of the heart also play roles—as the heart muscle grows stronger and larger, the heart's **cardiac output** increases. Each beat empties the heart's chambers more completely, so the heart pumps more blood per beat—its **stroke volume** increases. The resting heart rate slows because a greater volume of blood is moved with fewer beats. Working muscles also push blood more efficiently through the veins on their return trip to the heart and lungs.

Muscles that inflate and deflate the lungs gain strength and endurance, too, so breathing becomes more efficient. Circulation through the arteries and veins improves, blood moves easily, and blood pressure falls.[35] Figure 10-2 shows the major

FIGURE 10-2

ANIMATED!

Delivery of Oxygen by the Heart and Lungs to the Muscles

The cardiorespiratory system responds to increased demand for oxygen by building up its capacity to deliver oxygen. Researchers can measure cardiovascular fitness by measuring the amount of oxygen a person consumes per minute while working out. This measure of fitness, which indicates the person's maximum rate of oxygen consumption, is called $VO_{2\ max}$.

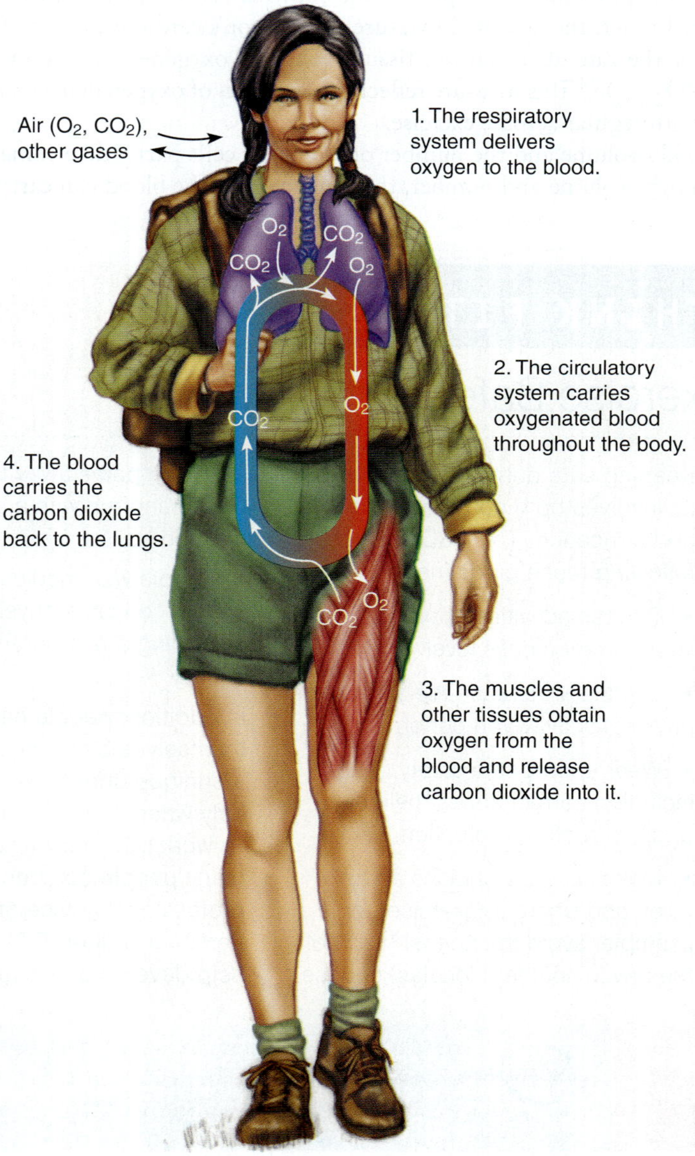

cardiac output the volume of blood discharged by the heart each minute.

stroke volume the volume of oxygenated blood ejected from the heart toward body tissues at each beat.

relationships among the heart, lungs, and muscles. Lastly, cardiorespiratory endurance raises blood HDL, the lipoprotein associated with lower heart disease risk (discussed in Chapter 11).

To summarize, cardiorespiratory endurance is characterized by:

- increased cardiac output and oxygen delivery.
- increased heart strength and stroke volume.
- slowed resting pulse.
- increased breathing efficiency.
- improved circulation.
- reduced blood pressure.
- increased blood HDL cholesterol.

Anyone who possesses cardiorespiratory endurance can celebrate a lowered risk for cardiovascular diseases.

Cardiorespiratory Training Activities Which activities produce these beneficial changes? Effective activities have three characteristics:

- They elevate the heart rate.
- They are sustained for longer than 20 minutes.
- They use most of the large-muscle groups of the body (legs, buttocks, and abdomen).

In other words, they are the aerobic activities recommended for heart health. Examples are swimming, cross-country skiing, rowing, fast walking, jogging, running, fast bicycling, soccer, hockey, basketball, in-line skating, lacrosse, and rugby.

An informal pulse check can give you some indication of how conditioned your heart is. The average resting pulse rate for adults is around 70 beats per minute. Active people can have resting pulse rates of 50 or even lower. To take your pulse, follow the directions in the margin.

The rest of this chapter describes the interactions between nutrients and physical activity. Nutrition alone cannot endow you with fitness or athletic ability, but along with the right mental attitude, it complements your effort to obtain them. Conversely, unwise food selections can stand in your way.

- To take your resting pulse:
  1. Sit down and relax for 5 minutes before you begin. Using a watch or clock with a second hand, place your hand over your heart or your finger firmly over an artery at the underside of the wrist or side of the throat under the jawbone.
  2. Start counting your pulse at a convenient second, and continue counting for 30 seconds. If a heartbeat occurs exactly on the tenth second, count it as one-half beat. Multiply by 2 to obtain the beats per minute.
  3. To ensure a true count, use only fingers, not your thumb, on the pulse point (the thumb has a pulse of its own).
  4. Press just firmly enough to feel the pulse. Too much pressure can interfere with the pulse rhythm.

KEY POINT Cardiorespiratory endurance training enhances the ability of the heart and lungs to deliver oxygen to body tissues. With cardiorespiratory endurance training, the heart becomes stronger, breathing becomes more efficient, and the health of the entire body improves.

LO 10.3, 10.4

The Active Body's Use of Fuels

The fuels that support physical activity are glucose (from carbohydrate), fatty acids (from fat), and, to a small extent, amino acids (from protein). The body uses different mixtures of fuels depending largely on the intensity and duration of its activities and prior training.

Athletes in training can expend huge numbers of calories each day to fuel their physical activity, calories that must be replaced by food to avoid unwanted weight loss. Even during rest, an athlete's metabolism may remain elevated, continuing to expend extra fuels for some minutes or hours following activity, a phenomenon known as **excess postexercise oxygen consumption (EPOC).**[36] Measurable EPOC occurs mainly with activities of high intensity (greater than 70 percent of

excess postexercise oxygen consumption (EPOC) a measure of increased metabolism (energy expenditure) that continues for minutes to hours after cessation of exercise.

VO_{2max}) and lasts longest after intense resistance exercise. Weight-loss seekers and casual athletes may wish for a workout that will "burn fat while they sleep," but they almost never attain the exercise intensity required to produce significant EPOC.[37] Physical activity contributes to weight management in many *other* ways, however, as the previous chapter made clear.[38]

Fuel Usage During rest, the body derives a little more than half of its energy from fatty acids, most of the rest from glucose, and a little from amino acids. During physical activity, the body adjusts its fuel mix to use the stored glucose of muscle glycogen. In the early minutes of an activity, muscle glycogen provides the majority of energy the muscles use to go into action. As activity continues, messenger molecules, including the hormones epinephrine and norepinephrine, flow into the bloodstream to signal the liver and fat cells to liberate their stored energy nutrients, primarily glucose and fatty acids.

CONCEPT LINK 10-4

Epinephrine and norepinephrine, defined in Chapter 3 (page 76), are major hormones that elicit the body's stress response, mobilize fuels, and ready the body for action.

Glucose Use and Storage

Both the liver and skeletal muscles store glucose as glycogen. Glucose comes from dietary sources, but the liver can also make glucose from fragments of other nutrients.

Muscle Glucose Conservation and Sources Muscles retain their glycogen stores for their own use—they lack an enzyme needed to release their glucose into the bloodstream as the liver does. This is fortunate because a muscle that conserves its glycogen is prepared to act quickly in emergencies, say, when running from danger. As activity continues, glucose liberated from liver glycogen and glucose absorbed from food in the digestive tract also become important sources of fuel for muscle activity. The body constantly uses and replenishes its glycogen. The more carbohydrate a person eats, the more glycogen muscles store (up to a limit), and the longer the stores will last to support physical activity.

Glycogen and Endurance A classic study compared fuel use during physical activity by three groups of runners, each on a different diet.[39] For several days before testing, one of the groups ate a normal mixed diet (55 percent of calories from carbohydrate); a second group ate a high-carbohydrate diet (83 percent of calories from carbohydrate); and the third group ate a high-fat diet (94 percent of calories from fat). As Figure 10-3 shows, the high-carbohydrate diet enabled the athletes to work longer before exhaustion. These results, many times confirmed, established that dietary carbohydrate sustains an athlete's endurance by ensuring ample glycogen stores.[40]

KEY POINT Glucose is supplied by dietary carbohydrate or made by the liver. It is stored in both liver and muscle tissue as glycogen. Total glycogen stores affect an athlete's endurance.

Activity Intensity, Glucose Use, and Glycogen Stores

The body stores far less glycogen than fat. Glycogen amounts to less than 2,000 calories of stored energy, sufficient to support everyday activities. Fat stores, in comparison, can total 70,000 calories or more and can fuel many hours of activity. During exercise, a person's glycogen can dwindle quickly; how long it will last depends on diet, as mentioned, and also on the intensity of the activity.

Anaerobic Use of Glucose Intense physical activity—the kind that makes it difficult "to catch your breath," such as a quarter-mile race—uses glycogen quickly. Muscles must begin to rely more heavily on glucose, which (unlike fat) can be partially broken down by **anaerobic** metabolism. Thus, the muscles draw on their limited glycogen supply to fuel their work. As the upper portion of Figure 10-4 shows, glucose can yield energy quickly in anaerobic metabolism. Anaerobic breakdown

anaerobic (AN-air-ROH-bic) not requiring oxygen. Anaerobic activity may require strength but does not work the heart and lungs very hard for a sustained period.

FIGURE 10-3 ANIMATED!

The Effect of Diet on Physical Endurance

A high-carbohydrate diet best supports an athlete's endurance. In this classic study, the high-fat diet provided 94 percent of calories from fat and 6 percent from protein; the normal mixed diet provided 55 percent of calories from carbohydrate; and the high-carbohydrate diet provided 83 percent of calories from carbohydrate.

Source: J. Bergstrom and coauthors, Diet, muscle glycogen, and physical performance, Acta Physiologica Scandinavica *71 (1967): 140–150.*

of glucose yields energy to muscle tissue when energy demands exceed the ability to provide energy aerobically. Anaerobic energy metabolism draws on the muscles' glycogen reserves.

Aerobic Use of Glucose In contrast, moderate physical activity, such as easy jogging, uses glycogen more slowly. The individual breathes easily, and the heart beats at a faster pace than at rest but steadily—the activity is aerobic. The bottom half of Figure 10-4 shows that during aerobic metabolism muscles extract their energy from both glucose and fatty acids. By depending partly on fatty acids, moderate aerobic activity conserves glycogen stores.

Lactate for Fuel and Muscle Growth During intense activity, anaerobic breakdown of glucose yields **lactate.** Most people recognize the burning sensation of lactate accumulating in a working muscle. Muscles release this lactate into the blood and it travels to the liver where enzymes convert it back into glucose. The liver sends the revived glucose back to the working muscles via the bloodstream.

At low exercise intensities, the small amounts of lactate produced are readily cleared from the blood by the liver. At higher intensities, however, blood lactate can exceed the liver's capacity to clear it and lactate can build up. When this happens, intense activity can be sustained for only up to about 3 minutes (as in a 400- or 800-meter race or a round of boxing). Accumulation of lactate was long blamed for muscle fatigue, but recent thought disputes this idea. True, muscles produce lactate as they become fatigued but the lactate does not cause the fatigue.[41] In fact, lactate may even trigger certain muscle adaptations to exercise, improving the ability to perform muscular work.

Lactate also plays a key role in an elegant feedback system that helps to regulate muscle size and strength. Blood lactate slightly lowers blood pH, producing a broadcast signal that the muscles have been overworked. The message is picked up by the glands that produce testosterone (mostly in males) and growth hormone (in everyone) and they release more muscle-building hormones. The end result: muscles

lactate a compound produced during the breakdown of glucose in anaerobic metabolism.

FIGURE 10-4

ANIMATED!

Glucose and Fatty Acids in Their Energy-Releasing Pathways in Muscle Cells

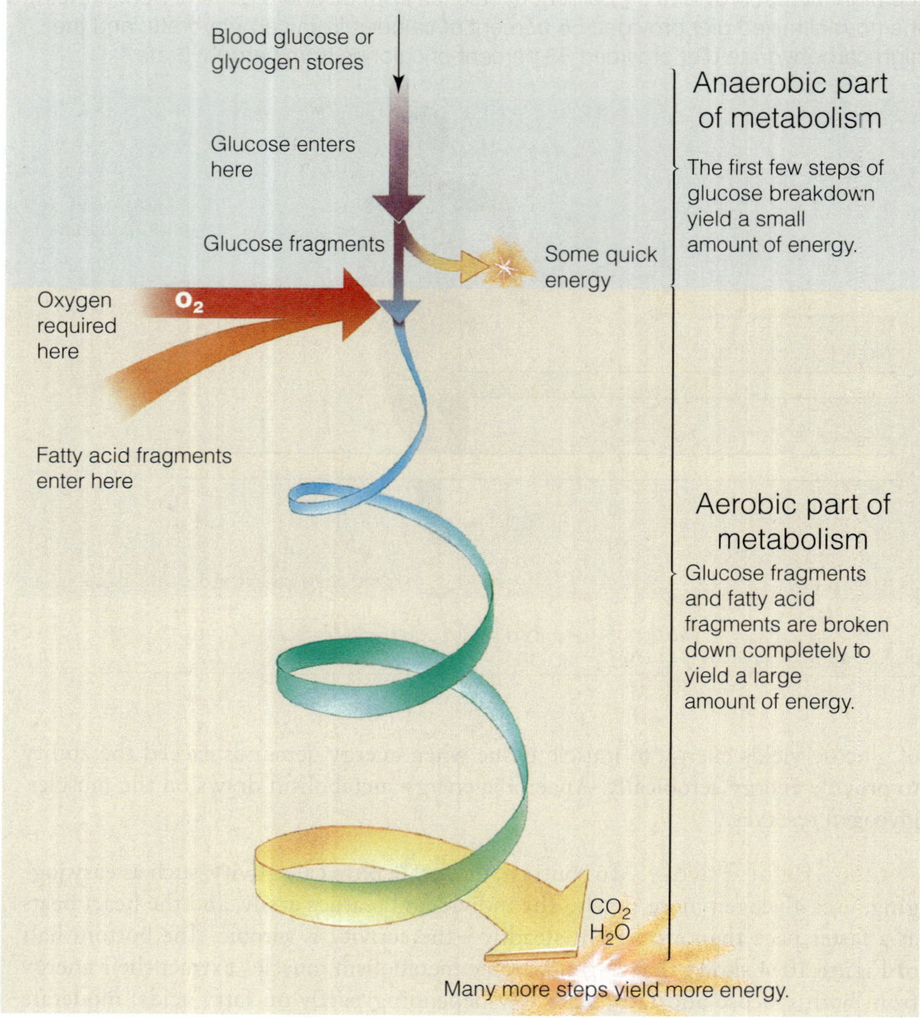

- To use lactate buildup to enhance muscle gains:
  - *Work large muscle groups at moderately high intensity using exercises that include several joints (squats, for example; not biceps curls) and taking short rest periods of about a minute.*
  - *After 5 or 6 weeks, switch to lighter workouts for a week or two.*
  - *To continue progressive gains in muscle strength, resume the original workout.*

build new tissues to better meet the exercise challenge.[42] A trick used to stimulate muscle growth is to perform resistance exercise in ways that cause a buildup of lactate (see the margin).

KEY POINT The more intense an activity, the more glucose it demands. During anaerobic metabolism, the body spends glucose rapidly and accumulates lactate. Lactate slightly lowers blood pH, triggering hormone release that stimulates muscle growth.

Activity Duration, Glucose Use, and Glycogen Stores

The *duration* of a physical activity as well as its *intensity* affect glucose use. In the first 10 minutes or so of an activity, the active muscles rely almost entirely on their own stores of glycogen for glucose. Within the first 20 minutes of moderate activity, a person uses up about one-fifth of the available glycogen. As the muscles devour their own glycogen, they become ravenous for more glucose and increase their uptake of blood glucose dramatically. When measured during moderate activity, blood glucose declines slightly, reflecting its use by the muscles.

A person who exercises moderately for longer than 20 minutes begins to use less glucose and more fat for fuel. Still, glucose use continues, and if the activity goes on long enough and at a high enough intensity, muscle and liver glycogen stores will run out almost completely. Performance suffers as glycogen reaches depletion, generally after about 2 hours of vigorous exercise.§ Vigorous physical activity can continue beyond this time only because the liver produces some glucose from lactate and certain amino acids. This minimum amount of glucose may briefly forestall fatigue, but when hypoglycemia accompanies glycogen depletion it brings nervous system function almost to a halt, making continued activity at the same intensity impossible. Marathon runners call this "hitting the wall."

Maintaining Blood Glucose for Activity To postpone fatigue, athletes must maintain their blood glucose concentrations for as long as they can. Three proven dietary strategies can help to delay glucose depletion. The first is to eat a high-carbohydrate diet on a daily basis (see Table 10-4). The second is to take in some glucose during the activity, usually in fluid (see the next section). The third prepares for future bouts of exercise: the athlete consumes carbohydrate-rich foods within a couple of hours after exercise. About 0.5 to 0.7 gram of carbohydrate per pound of body weight (~75–100 grams for a 150-pound athlete) enhances the storage of glycogen.[43] Body tissues absorb glucose (and amino acids) at an increased rate during this time.[44]

Another strategy, **carbohydrate loading,** involves training the muscles to store as much glycogen as they can, while supplying the dietary glucose to enable them to do so. This strategy benefits only endurance athletes who exercise at high intensity for longer than 90 minutes and who cannot meet their carbohydrate needs during competition. Although studies show that individuals can increase their glycogen stores, performance may or may not improve.[45] Those who exercise for shorter times or at a slower pace are better served by a regular high-carbohydrate diet, as demonstrated in this chapter's Food Feature.

Consuming Glucose During Activity Glucose ingested before and during endurance activities of longer than about an hour's duration makes its way from the digestive tract to the working muscles.[46] This augments the glucose from dwindling

§Here "vigorous exercise" means exercise at 75 percent of $VO_{2\ max}$.

CONCEPT LINK 10-5

For a discussion of hypoglycemia, see Chapter 4, page 135.

- Four strategies can help to maintain blood glucose to support endurance sport performance:
  1. Eat a high-carbohydrate diet regularly (see Table 10-4).
  2. Take glucose (usually in sports drinks) periodically during endurance activities.
  3. Eat carbohydrate-rich foods after performance.
  4. Train the muscles to maximize glycogen stores.

- For perspective, snack ideas providing 60 grams of carbohydrate:
  - *16 oz sports drink and a small bagel.*
  - *16 oz milk and four oatmeal-raisin cookies.*
  - *8 oz milk and three slices of bread.*
  - *8 oz pineapple juice and a granola bar.*

TABLE 10-4 Carbohydrate Needs of Athletes

To calculate daily grams (g) of carbohydrate appropriate for an athlete, first divide pounds of body weight by 2.2 to find kilograms (kg). Then identify the number of carbohydrate grams best suited to the athlete's performance: multiply kg by g.

Athletes	Carbohydrate g/kg/day	Reference Male (70 kg)	Reference Female (55 kg)
Most athletes in training	5–7	350–490	275–385
Endurance athletes	7–10	490–700	385–550
Ultraendurance athletes (such as "Ironman" triathletes)	10–11	700–770	550–605
Typical U.S. intake	4–5	280–350	220–275

Source: Data from Position of the American Dietetic Association, Dietitians of Canada, and the American College of Sports Medicine, Journal of the American Dietetic Association *109 (2009): 509–527; M. Dunford, ed.,* Sports Nutrition: A Practice Manual for Professionals *(Chicago: The American Dietetic Association, 2006), p. 16.*

Endurance activities demand fluid and carbohydrate fuel. Don't forget to hydrate.

carbohydrate loading consumption of a high-carbohydrate diet in a way that enables muscles to temporarily store glycogen beyond their normal capacity; also called *glycogen loading* or *glycogen supercompensation.*

MY TURN

© Cengage Learning
Julian

© Cengage Learning
Adam

How Much Is Enough?

Listen to two athletes talk about carbohyc intakes and other eating strategies.

CENGAGENOW To hear their stories, log on to www.cengage.com/sso.

muscle and liver glycogen stores.[47] Athletes can benefit from drinks containing 30 to 60 grams of carbohydrate taken each hour during games such as soccer or hockey or even sports training regimens that last for hours and demand repeated bursts of intense activity.[48]

Before concluding that glucose might be good for your own performance, consider first whether you engage in *endurance* activity. Do you run, swim, bike, or ski nonstop at a rapid pace for more than an hour at a time or compete in games lasting for hours? If not, the glucose picture changes. For an everyday jog or swim lasting less than an hour, ingesting glucose during activity probably won't help (or harm) performance—but it will add calories to the day's intake. Even in athletes, extra carbohydrate is of no help when their fatigue is unrelated to blood glucose, such as in 100-meter sprinting, 100-meter swimming, or power lifting.

Glucose Consumed After Activity For most exercisers, normal carbohydrate intakes from meals supply all the carbohydrate they need to replenish glycogen stores. For athletes, though, eating high-carbohydrate foods within two hours after physical activity can help speed up the rate of glycogen storage.[49] This benefits athletes who train at maximum intensity more than once a day. The faster rate of glycogen storage ensures sufficient glycogen will be available for the next bout of high-intensity training or competition. An athlete without sufficient glycogen may feel tired or sluggish—feelings that impair performance. Some examples of athletes who might benefit from carbohydrate after activity include those who:

- train more than once a day.
- train intensely on consecutive days with less than a 24-hour recovery period.
- play in sports tournaments, such as basketball, track, or wrestling, that last multiple consecutive days.

To optimize glycogen stores, athletes should train normally; then, within two hours after physical activity, consume a high-carbohydrate meal, such as a glass of orange juice and some graham crackers, toast, or cereal. Timing is important—after two hours the effect diminishes by half.[50]

For athletes who cannot eat so soon after exercise, **high-carbohydrate energy drinks** are sold commercially. Such drinks are higher in calories and carbohydrate than the fluid-replacement sports drinks discussed in the Consumer Corner, later. However, the carbohydrate of sports drinks is sufficient to restore glycogen; even regular low-fat chocolate milk works well in this regard.[51]

high-carbohydrate energy drinks flavored commercial beverages used to restore muscle glycogen after exercise or as a pregame beverage.

Are High-Glycemic Foods of Particular Value? Chapter 4 made clear that low-glycemic index foods may benefit people with problems of glucose metabolism. For the athlete who needs fast glycogen replacement, however, some judiciously applied high-glycemic index foods may be of benefit (see the margin on page 129) because they elicit a greater rate of glycogen storage than do low-glycemic foods.[52]

Popular magazines and Internet sites often toot a horn about "high-impact carbs" (high on the glycemic index) while disparaging "low-impact carbs" for athletes, but research is mixed on whether high-glycemic foods affect performance.[53] All kinds of carbohydrate-rich foods can support the work of the athlete in training, and whole foods provide extra benefits to health.

KEY POINT Physical activity of long duration demands glycogen. Carbohydrate ingested before and during such activity may delay hypoglycemia and fatigue. Within two hours after strenuous training, eating carbohydrate-rich foods rapidly restores glycogen.

Degree of Training Affects Glycogen Use

Training affects glycogen use during activity in two major ways. First, muscles adapt to their work by storing greater amounts of glycogen needed to support that work. Second, trained muscles burn more fat, and at higher intensities, than untrained muscles, so they require less glucose to perform the same amount of work. A person first attempting an activity uses up much more glucose per minute than an athlete trained to perform it.

KEY POINT Highly trained muscles use less glucose and more fat than do untrained muscles to perform the same work, so their glycogen lasts longer.

Fat and Physical Activity

Unlike the body's limited glycogen stores, fat stores can fuel hours of activity without running out; body fat is (theoretically) an unlimited source of energy. Even the lean bodies of elite runners carry enough fat to fuel several marathon runs.

Body Fat as Fuel for Activity Early in activity, muscles begin to draw on fatty acids from two sources—fats stored within the working muscles and fats from fat deposits such as the adipose tissue under the skin. Areas with the most fat to spare donate the greatest amounts. This is why "spot reducing" doesn't work: muscles do not own the fat that surrounds them. Fat cells release fatty acids into the blood for all the muscles to share. Proof is found in a tennis player's arms: the fatfolds measure the same in both arms, even though the muscles of one arm are more developed than the other. A balanced fitness program that includes strength training will tighten muscles beneath the fat, improving appearance, while preserving the amount of body fat essential to good health.

Fat in the Athlete's Diet For endurance athletes, eating a high-fat, low-carbohydrate diet for even a day or two reduces precious glycogen stores and impairs performance. Eventually, muscles do adapt to such a diet and use more fat to fuel activity, but no performance benefits come from doing so.[54] In fact, athletes on high-fat diets report greater fatigue and perceive physical work as more strenuous than those on high-carbohydrate diets.

Essential fatty acids and fat-soluble nutrients are as important for athletes as they are for everyone else, so experts recommend a diet with 20 to 35 percent of calories from fat.[55] Athletes should make it a point to include the needed raw vegetable oil, nuts, olives, fatty fish, and other sources of health-promoting fats in their diets.

Omega-3 fatty acids, such as those found in fish oil, have not only been linked to decreased risk of heart disease, hypertension, type 2 diabetes, as well as decreased depression, they also have anti-inflammatory properties, of importance to anyone with joint pain associated with exercise. Some research suggests that decreasing omega-6 fatty acid intakes and consuming 1–2 grams per day of fish oil may decrease inflammation, but these findings are preliminary.[56]

Did You Know?

For people with diabetes, a registered dietitian, a physician, or a Certified Diabetes Educator can provide safe food and exercise strategies.

CONCEPT LINK 10-6

The glycemic index was described in Chapter 4, pages 128–129.

- Factors that affect glucose use during physical activity:
  - *Carbohydrate intake.*
  - *Intensity and duration of the activity.*
  - *Degree of training.*

CONCEPT LINK 10-7

Lipid intake guidelines are found in Chapter 5, page 161.

Saturated fats carry risks to the heart. Physical activity offers some protection against cardiovascular disease but athletes still suffer heart attacks and strokes. These risks make controlling saturated fat intake a must for athletes.

Intensity and Duration Affect Fat Use Fat can be broken down for energy only by aerobic metabolism. When the *intensity* of activity becomes so great that energy demands surpass the ability to provide energy aerobically, the body cannot burn more fat. It burns more glucose instead.

The *duration* of activity also affects fat use. At the start of activity, the blood fatty acid concentration falls, but a few minutes into an activity, the hormone epinephrine signals the fat cells to break apart their stored triglycerides and to liberate fatty acids into the blood. After about 20 minutes of activity, the blood fatty acid concentration rises above the normal resting concentration. During this phase of sustained, moderate activity, the fat cells begin to shrink in size as they empty out their lipid stores.

- Factors that affect fat use during physical activity:
  - *Fat intake.*
  - *Intensity and duration of the activity.*
  - *Degree of training.*

Now you can understand the whole picture of the body's use of fuel during physical activity. At rest and during activities of daily living, fatty acids provide 80 to 90 percent of the body's energy and glucose provides only 5 to 18 percent (amino acids provide a small amount—2 to 5 percent). At the point of exercise intensity (above about 65 percent $VO_{2\ max}$) when fat cannot be metabolized fast enough to provide the needed energy, the muscles shift to using a great deal more glucose to provide the required energy.[57] The degree of a person's training greatly influences the energy use picture, however.

Degree of Training Affects Fat Use Training—repeated aerobic activity—stimulates the muscles to develop more fat-burning enzymes, so aerobically trained muscles burn fat more readily than untrained muscles do. With aerobic training, the heart and lungs also become stronger and better able to deliver oxygen to the muscles during high-intensity activities. This improved oxygen supply, in turn, enables the muscles to burn more fat.

KEY POINT A high-fat diet raises an athlete's risk of heart disease. The intensity and duration of activity, as well as the degree of training, affect fat use.

Protein for Building Muscles and for Fuel

The human body uses amino acids from protein to build and maintain muscle and other lean tissue and, to a small extent, to fuel activity. Not only do athletes retain more protein in their muscles and other lean tissues but they also use a little more protein as fuel.

Courtesy of the Author

Physical activity itself triggers the building of muscle proteins.

Physical Activity Triggers Muscle Protein Synthesis Repeated activity signals the muscle cells to begin producing more of the proteins needed to perform the specific kind of physical work at hand. For up to two days following physical activity, muscles speed up their rate of protein synthesis—they build more of the proteins they need to perform the activity.[58] And whenever the body rebuilds a part of itself, it must tear down the old structures to make way for the new ones.

Physical activity, with just a slight overload, calls into action both the protein-dismantling and the protein-synthesizing equipment of muscle cells. The genetic protein-making equipment inside the nuclei of muscle cells receives signals indicating which proteins are needed to support each type of physical activity.

The intensity and pattern of muscle contractions create unique signals. For example, a weight lifter's workout sends notice that muscle fibers need additional contractile proteins for strength and more enzymes for making and using glycogen. A jogger's workout stimulates production of proteins to strengthen heart tissues and build red blood cells, along with additional enzymes for aerobic oxidation of fat and glucose. Muscle cells are exquisitely responsive to the need for specific proteins, and they build them conservatively, only as needed.

Dietary Protein and Muscle Protein Synthesis Finally, after muscle cells have established exactly which proteins they need to build, sufficient protein nutrition becomes a prerequisite for building and maintaining muscle tissues. During active muscle-building phases of training, a weight lifter might add between ¼ ounce and 1 ounce (between 7 and 28 grams) of protein to existing muscle mass each day. This extra protein comes from ordinary protein-rich food. Protein supplements are unnecessary for building muscles. (See this chapter's Controversy.)

In addition, a small amount of high-quality protein, such as in a cup-and-a-half of milk, consumed immediately following physical activity, may speed up muscle protein synthesis for a while.[59] "High-quality" means protein with the complete array of essential amino acids needed for protein synthesis, as explained in Chapter 6.

CONCEPT LINK 10-8

Discussions of dietary protein quality are found in Chapter 6, pages 206–207.

Protein Fuel Use in Physical Activity Studies of nitrogen balance show that the body speeds up its use of amino acids for energy during physical activity, just as it speeds up its use of glucose and fatty acids. The factors that regulate protein use during activity seem to be the same three that regulate the use of glucose and fat: diet, exercise intensity and duration, and degree of training. As for diet, carbohydrates spare protein from being used as fuel. The liver can convert some amino acids into glucose when needed, while others, the **branched-chain amino acids (BCAA),** can be used by muscles directly. A diet too low in carbohydrate forces the use of amino acids in place of glucose.

CONCEPT LINK 10-9

The protein-sparing effect of carbohydrate was explained in Chapter 6, page 203.

Athletes who take BCAA pills in hopes of increasing protein synthesis and inhibiting muscle breakdown should know that the BCAAs they seek are delivered in the protein-rich foods that they eat every day, such as milk products or turkey. Such foods present the BCAAs in just the right mix to support protein synthesis.[60] Not only are the pills a waste of money but they present risks from amino acid imbalances. This often-repeated story of unneeded products sold to athletes is the topic of this chapter's Controversy.

Exercise intensity and duration also affect protein use. When endurance athletes train for over an hour a day and deplete their glycogen stores, they become more dependent on protein fuel. In contrast, anaerobic strength training does not use as much protein fuel, but does demand protein for building muscle tissue. Thus, for both endurance and strength, athletes need more protein than do sedentary people. On learning of their higher protein needs, many athletes go to extremes consuming double or triple their protein need, to the exclusion of other foods that they need for health. Finally, the extent of training also affects the use of protein. Particularly in strength athletes such as body builders, the higher the degree of training, the less protein a person uses during activity at a given intensity.

- Factors that affect protein use during physical activity:
  - *Carbohydrate intake.*
  - *Intensity and duration of the activity.*
  - *Degree of training.*

KEY POINT Physical activity stimulates muscle cells to both break down and synthesize proteins, resulting in muscle adaptation to activity. Athletes use amino acids for building muscle tissue and for energy. Dietary carbohydrate spares amino acids, and foods are better than pills for amino acids. Diet, intensity and duration of activity, and degree of training affect protein use during activity.

How Much Protein Should an Athlete Consume?

The DRI does not recommend greater-than-normal protein intakes for athletes, but other authorities do.[61] These recommendations vary for athletes by the nature of their chosen activities (see Table 10-5).[62]

You may be wondering whether your diet provides the protein you need. Athletes who eat a balanced, high-carbohydrate diet that provides enough total energy usually consume enough protein—they do not need huge meat servings, special foods, or protein supplements. Athletes need protein but they must back up the protein with ample carbohydrate. Otherwise, they will burn off as fuel the very protein they wish to retain in muscle. This chapter's Food Feature answers other questions about choosing a performance diet.

branched-chain amino acids (BCAA) leucine, isoleucine, and valine; amino acids present in skeletal muscle tissue and theorized to enhance protein synthesis and diminish muscle protein breakdown; supplements of BCAA are not needed by athletes who eat sufficient dietary protein.

TABLE 10-5 **Recommended Protein Intakes for Athletes**

	RECOMMENDATIONS (g/kg/day)	PROTEIN INTAKES (g/day)	
		Reference[a] Male (70 kg)	Reference[a] Female (55 kg)
DRI recommended intake	0.8	56	44
Recommended intake for power (strength or speed) athletes	1.2–1.7	84–119	66–94
Recommended intake for endurance athletes	1.2–1.4	84–98	66–77
U.S. average intake		102	70

[a] *Daily protein intakes are based on a 70-kilogram (154-pound) reference man and a 55-kilogram (121-pound) reference woman. Other individuals must calculate their recommended intakes using the numbers of column 1. (For kg, divide lbs by 2.2.)*

Sources: Position of the American Dietetic Association, Dietitians of Canada, and the American College of Sports Medicine: Nutrition and athletic performance, Journal of the American Dietetic Association *109 (2009): 509–527; U.S. Department of Agriculture, Agricultural Research Service, 2008. Nutrient Intakes from Food: Mean Amounts Consumed per Individual, One Day, 2005–2006. Available: www.ars.usda.gov/ba/bhnrc/fsrg; Committee on Dietary Reference Intakes,* Dietary Reference Intakes for Energy, Carbohydrate, Fiber, Fat, Fatty Acids, Cholesterol, Protein, and Amino Acids *(Washington, D.C.: National Academies Press, 2005), pp. 660–661.*

CONCEPT LINK 10-10

For diet planning guidance, see Chapter 2.

KEY POINT Although athletes need more protein than sedentary people, a balanced, high-carbohydrate diet provides sufficient protein to cover an athlete's needs.

LO 10.5

Vitamins and Minerals—Keys to Performance

Vitamins and minerals are crucial for the working body. Many B vitamins participate in releasing energy from fuels. Vitamin C is needed for the formation of the protein collagen, the foundation material of bones, cartilage, and other connective tissues. Folate and vitamin B_{12} help build the red blood cells to carry oxygen to working muscles. Calcium and magnesium allow muscles to contract, and so on. Do active people need more of these vitamins and minerals to support their work? Do they need supplements?

Do Nutrient Supplements Benefit Athletic Performance?

Many athletes take vitamin and mineral supplements.[63] Elite athletes use them to a greater extent than college athletes, who, in turn, use more supplements than high school athletes. One of the most common reasons athletes at all levels give for supplement use is "to improve performance."

More Food Means More Nutrients For the well-nourished athlete, nutrient supplements do not enhance performance. Strenuous physical activity requires abundant energy but athletes and active people who eat enough nutrient-dense foods to meet their greater energy needs also consume more of the vitamins and minerals needed to process that energy. Active people eat more food; it stands to reason that with the right choices, they'll get more nutrients.

Supplement Timing Contrary to some athletes' beliefs, taking vitamins or minerals just before competition will not help performance. Most vitamins and minerals function as small parts of larger working units. After entering the blood from the digestive tract, they must wait for the cells to combine them with their other parts before they can function. This takes time—hours or days. Nutrients taken right before an event cannot help performance, even if the person is deficient in those nutrients.

Preventing Deficiencies Deficiencies of vitamins and minerals do impede performance, however. Athletes who starve themselves to meet a sport's weight requirement can easily fail to obtain needed nutrients.[64] Most authorities oppose rigid weight requirements because athletes often risk their health to meet them. For athletes forced to "make weight," or for those who simply cannot eat enough food to maintain body weight during intense periods of training and competition, a balanced multivitamin-mineral tablet providing no more than the DRI recommended intakes may prevent deficiencies.

CONCEPT LINK 10-11

Stringent weight standards impose a risk of developing an eating disorder (Controversy 9).

KEY POINT Vitamins are essential for releasing the energy trapped in energy-yielding nutrients and for other functions that support physical activity. Active people can meet their vitamin needs if they eat enough nutrient-dense foods to meet their energy needs.

Nutrients of Concern

While it is true that active people who eat well-balanced meals do not need supplements, two nutrients, vitamin E and iron, merit attention. The first, vitamin E, ranks high among supplements taken by athletes, and the second, iron, is of special concern to certain athletes.

Vitamin E During physical activity, muscle oxygen consumption increases up to tenfold or more, creating extra free radicals in the tissues.[65] Fearing oxidative damage to their muscles, some athletes take huge doses of vitamin E, a potent fat-soluble antioxidant. Studies conflict on whether vitamin E might protect against oxidative stress or enhance it by suppressing the body's own antioxidant enzyme systems.[66] It turns out that the free radicals generated during physical activity trigger the genes to synthesize more antioxidant enzymes.[67] It is possible that vitamin E pills short-circuit this response. In addition, 10 or more times the recommended intake of vitamin E and vitamin C seems to prevent the beneficial increase in insulin sensitivity that normally follows physical activity.[68]

Vitamin E supplements cannot improve performance, and high doses can interfere with the absorption of other fat-soluble antioxidants, such as lycopene and beta-carotene. It also carries the other risks outlined in Controversy 7.[69] To be safe, physically active people should obtain vitamin E and other antioxidants from their food sources: raw vegetable oils, nuts, whole grains, fruits, and vegetables. If you do take a supplement, be sure that it does not exceed the Tolerable Upper Intake Level (UL) for vitamin E.

Did You Know?

The UL for vitamin E is 1,000 mg per day.

Rocky Widner/NBAE/Getty Images

Female athletes may be at special risk of iron deficiency.

Iron and Performance Iron deficiency impairs performance because iron must be present to deliver oxygen to the working muscles. Iron-containing molecules of aerobic metabolism and the iron-containing muscle protein myoglobin are essential to physical performance. With insufficient iron, aerobic work capacity is compromised and the person tires easily. Whether marginal deficiency without clinical signs of anemia hinders physical performance is less clear.[70]

Varying Iron Needs Physically active young women, especially those who engage in endurance activities such as distance running, may develop true iron deficiency.[71] Habitually low intakes of iron-rich foods, high iron losses through menstruation,

CONCEPT LINK 10-12

Vegetarian diet planning was a topic of Controversy 6, page 219; iron absorption was discussed in Chapter 8 on pages 301–302.

© Polara Studios, Inc.

Foods like these are packed with the nutrients that active people need.

and the high demands of physical performance contribute to iron deficiency in young female athletes. Active teens of both genders have high iron needs, as well, because they are growing.

Vegetarian athletes also may lack iron.[72] Fiber and phytic acid in plant-based diets inhibit iron absorption and plant foods provide iron in its less well-absorbed nonheme form. To protect against iron deficiency, vegetarian athletes should consume fortified cereals, legumes, nuts, and seeds and include some vitamin C–rich foods with each meal—vitamin C enhances iron absorption. A well-chosen vegetarian diet of nutrient-dense foods can meet nutrient needs for health and athletic performance. For anyone found to be iron-deficient through medical testing, prescribed supplements can reverse the condition in short order.

Sports Anemia Early in training, athletes may develop low blood hemoglobin. This condition, sometimes called "sports anemia," is not a true iron-deficiency condition. Strenuous training promotes destruction of older, more fragile red blood cells. At the same time, the blood's fluid increases; with fewer red cells distributed in more fluid, the red blood cell count per unit of blood drops. Most researchers view sports anemia as an *adaptive,* temporary response to endurance training that goes away by itself and that does not require treatment with iron supplements.

KEY POINT Iron-deficiency anemia impairs physical performance because iron is the blood's oxygen handler. Sports anemia is a harmless temporary adaptation to physical activity.

Fluids and Temperature Regulation in Physical Activity

The body's need for water, while always greater than the need for any other nutrient, takes on particular urgency during physical activity (see the margin). If the body loses too much water, even its life-supporting chemistry is compromised.

- Performance-hindering effects of inadequate hydration:
  - *Impaired body temperature control.*
  - *Reduced blood volume.*
  - *Increased heart rate.*
  - *Reduced exercise performance.*
  - *Headache, nausea, insomnia.*
  - *Impaired mental function.*
  - *Increased risk of heat stroke.*

Source: R. J. Maughan, S. M. Shirreffs, and P. Watson, Exercise, heat, hydration and the brain, Journal of the American College of Nutrition *26 (2007): 604S–621S.*

Water Losses During Physical Activity

The exercising body loses water primarily via sweat; second to that, breathing uses water, exhaled as vapor. Endurance athletes can lose 1.5 quarts or more of fluid during *each hour* of activity.

Dehydration During physical activity, both routes can be significant, and dehydration is a real threat. The first symptom of dehydration is fatigue. A water loss of greater than 2 percent of body weight can reduce a person's capacity for muscular work.[73] A person with a water loss of about 7 percent is likely to collapse. The athlete who arrives at an event even slightly dehydrated starts out at a competitive disadvantage.

Sweat and Temperature Regulation Sweat is the body's coolant. The conversion of water to vapor uses up a great deal of heat, so as sweat evaporates, it cools the skin's surface and the blood flowing beneath it. During exercise, blood flow must divert to the skin to radiate heat away from the body's core. Sufficient water in the bloodstream is therefore crucial to provide sweat, accommodate blood flow to the skin, and still supply muscles with the blood flow they need to perform.[74]

CONCEPT LINK 10-13

Chapter 8 explained the importance of water in the body (pages 278–279).

Heat Stroke In hot, humid weather, sweat may fail to evaporate because the surrounding air is already laden with water. Little cooling takes place and body heat builds up. In such conditions, athletes must take precautions to avoid **heat stroke**—a potentially fatal medical emergency. To reduce the risk of heat stroke:

heat stroke an acute and life-threatening reaction to heat buildup in the body.

1. Drink enough fluid before and during the activity.
2. Rest in the shade when tired.
3. Wear lightweight clothing that allows sweat to evaporate.

Never wear rubber or heavy suits sold with promises of weight loss during physical activity. They promote profuse sweating, prevent sweat evaporation, and invite heat stroke. If you experience any of the symptoms in the margin, stop your activity, sip cold fluids, seek shade, and ask for help—heat stroke demands immediate medical attention.

- Symptoms of heat stroke:
  - *Clumsiness.*
  - *Confusion, other mental changes, loss of consciousness.*
  - *Dizziness.*
  - *Headache.*
  - *Internal (rectal) temperature above 104° Fahrenheit.*
  - *Nausea.*
  - *Stumbling.*
  - *Sudden cessation of sweating (hot, dry skin).*

Hypothermia Even in cold weather, the body still sweats and needs fluids. However, the fluids should be warm or at room temperature to help prevent **hypothermia.** Inexperienced runners in long races on cold or wet chilly days may produce too little body heat to keep warm, especially if their clothing is inadequate. Early symptoms of hypothermia include shivers, apathy, and social withdrawal.[75] As body temperature continues to fall, shivering stops; disorientation or slurred speech ensues. People with these symptoms soon become helpless to protect themselves from further body heat losses and need immediate medical attention.

KEY POINT Evaporation of sweat cools the body. Heat stroke can be a threat to physically active people in hot, humid weather. Hypothermia threatens those who exercise in the cold.

Thinkstock/Getty Images

Active people need extra fluid, even in cold weather.

Fluid and Electrolyte Needs During Physical Activity

To prepare for fluid losses, the athlete must hydrate before activity. To replace fluid losses, the person must rehydrate during and after activity. (Table 10-6 presents one schedule of hydration for physical activity.) Even then, in hot weather, the digestive tract may not be able to absorb enough water fast enough to keep up with an athlete's sweat losses, and some degree of dehydration may be inevitable.

Athletes who are preparing for competition are often advised to drink extra fluids in the last few days of training before the event. The extra fluid is not stored in the body, but drinking extra ensures maximum tissue hydration at the start of the event. Full hydration is imperative for every athlete both in training and in competition. Any coach or athlete who withholds fluids during practice for any reason takes a great risk.

TABLE 10-6 Hydration Schedule for Physical Activity

Each cup equals 8 ounces of fluid.

When to Drink	Amount of Fluid
2 to 3 hr before activity	2 to 3 c
15 min before activity	1 to 2 c
Every 15 min during activity	½ to 1 c (Drink enough to minimize loss of body weight, but don't overdrink.)
After activity	2 c for each pound of body weight lost[a]

[a] *Drinking 2 cups of fluid every 20 to 30 minutes after exercise until the total amount required is consumed is more effective for rehydration than drinking the needed amount all at once. Rapid fluid replacement after exercise stimulates urine production and results in less body water retention.*

Sources: Adapted from American College of Sports Medicine. Position stand: Exercise and fluid replacement, Medicine and Science in Sports and Exercise *39 (2007): 377–390; C. K. Seto, D. Way, and N. O'Connor, Environmental illness in athletes,* Clinics in Sports Medicine *24 (2005): 695–718; R. Murray, Fluid, electrolytes, and exercise in* Sports Nutrition: A Practice Manual for Professionals. *4th ed., ed. M. Dunford (Chicago: The American Dietetic Association, 2006), pp. 94–115; D. J. Casa, P. M. Clarkson, and W. O. Roberts, American College of Sports Medicine Roundtable on Hydration and Physical Activity: Consensus statements,* Current Sports Medicine Reports *4 (2005): 115–127.*

hypothermia a below-normal body temperature.

Athletes who rely on thirst to govern fluid intake can easily become dehydrated. During activity, thirst becomes detectable only *after* fluid stores are depleted. Don't wait to feel thirsty before drinking. A fluid replacement plan for an individual athlete, the **hourly sweat rate,** can be determined by weighing before and after exercise and factoring in the duration of activity. The weight difference is all water.

Water What is the best fluid to support physical activity? Just plain cool water, for two reasons: (1) water rapidly leaves the digestive tract to enter the tissues, and (2) it cools the body from the inside out. Endurance athletes are an exception: they need more from their fluids than water alone. The first priority for endurance athletes should always be replacement of fluids to prevent life-threatening heat stroke. But endurance athletes also need carbohydrate to supplement their limited glycogen stores, so glucose is important, too. This chapter's Consumer Corner compares water and sports drinks as fluid sources for endurance athletes.

Electrolyte Losses and Replacement During physical activity, the body loses electrolytes—the minerals sodium, potassium, and chloride—in sweat. Beginners lose these electrolytes to a much greater extent than do trained athletes. The body's adaptation to physical activity includes better conservation of these electrolytes. To replenish lost electrolytes, a person ordinarily needs only to eat a regular diet that meets energy and nutrient needs. During intense activity lasting more than 45 minutes in hot weather, sports drinks provide a convenient way to replace fluids and electrolytes. Most friendly sporting games never reach the intensity that requires electrolyte replacement, and a pregame meal well covers electrolyte needs. Even participants in casual events require fluid replacement, particularly in hot weather, and water is the best fluid source under these conditions. Salt tablets can worsen dehydration and impair performance; they increase potassium losses, irritate the stomach, and cause vomiting. Athletes should avoid them.

© Food and Drink/SuperStock

KEY POINT Water is the best drink for most physically active people, but endurance athletes may need glucose as well as fluids. The body adapts to compensate for sweat losses of electrolytes. Athletes are advised to use foods, not supplements, to make up for these losses.

Sodium Depletion and Water Intoxication

Replenishing electrolytes becomes crucial after 4 hours of competition in endurance sports.[76] Athletes who sweat profusely over a long period of time and do not replace lost sodium risk developing dangerous **hyponatremia.** The symptoms of hyponatremia differ somewhat from those of dehydration (see the margin). Depending on individual variation, exercise intensity, and changes in ambient temperature and humidity, athletes can sweat at rates exceeding 2 quarts per hour.[77]

In studies, about 10 percent of endurance athletes exercising for longer than 4 hours, such as triathletes, consume too much plain water and overhydrate, diluting the body's fluids to the extent that sodium concentration drops too low.[78] Such water intoxication, introduced in Chapter 8, can result in life-threatening hyponatremia. Research shows that some athletes who sweat profusely may also lose more sodium in their sweat than others—and are prone to debilitating **heat cramps.**[79] These athletes lose twice as much sodium in sweat as athletes who don't cramp.

Some athletes may even be vulnerable to hyponatremia when they drink sports drinks during an event.[80] Sports drinks contain some sodium, but as the Consumer Corner points out, it may be too little to replace extreme sodium losses in sweat. Still, sports drinks offer more sodium than plain water. To prevent hyponatremia, endurance athletes who compete for hours need to replace sodium during the events. Sports drinks, salty pretzels, and other sodium sources can provide sodium during a long event. In the days before the event, especially an event in the heat, athletes should not restrict salt in their diets.

- Symptoms of hyponatremia:
  - *Severe headache.*
  - *Vomiting.*
  - *Bloating, puffiness from water retention (shoes tight, rings tight).*
  - *Confusion.*
  - *Seizure.*

hourly sweat rate the amount of weight lost plus fluid consumed during exercise per hour.

hyponatremia (HIGH-poh-na-TREE-mee-ah) a decreased concentration of sodium in the blood (*hypo* means "below"; *natrium* means "sodium"; *emia* means "blood").

heat cramps painful cramps of the abdomen, arms, or legs, often occurring hours after exercise; associated with inadequate intake of fluid or electrolytes or heavy sweating.

CONSUMER CORNER

What Do Sports Drinks Have to Offer?

Dozens of **sports drinks, flavored waters, nutritionally enhanced beverages,** and **recovery drinks** (see Table 10-7 for terms) compete for their share of a $1 billion market. Plain, freely available water meets the fluid needs of most exercising people, but some commercial beverages, particularly sports drinks, can offer some advantages to certain athletes.

TABLE 10-7 Sports Drinks and Related Terms

- **sports drinks** flavored beverages designed to help athletes replace fluids and electrolytes and to provide carbohydrate before, during, and after physical activity, particularly endurance activities.
- **flavored waters** lightly flavored beverages with few or no calories, but often containing vitamins, minerals, herbs, or other unneeded substances. Not superior to plain water for athletic competition or training.
- **nutritionally enhanced beverages** flavored beverages that contain any of a number of nutrients, including some carbohydrate, along with protein, vitamins, minerals, herbs, or other unneeded substances. Such "vitamin waters" may not contain useful amounts of carbohydrate or electrolytes to support athletic competition or training.
- **recovery drinks** flavored beverages that contain protein, carbohydrate, and often other nutrients; intended to support postexercise recovery of energy fuels and muscle tissue. These can be convenient, but are not superior to ordinary foods and beverages, such as chocolate milk or a sandwich, to supply carbohydrate and protein after exercise. Not intended for hydration during athletic competition or training because their high carbohydrate and protein contents may slow water absorption.

FLUID

First, sports drinks offer fluids to help offset losses during physical activity, but plain water can do this, too. Many people find sports drinks tasty, and if a drink tastes good, they may drink more of it, ensuring adequate hydration. (A squirt of lemon or other fruit juice added to plain water may do the same thing.)

GLUCOSE

Second, unlike water, sports drinks offer monosaccharides or glucose polymers that help maintain hydration, contribute to blood glucose, and enhance performance in some circumstances. Sports drinks may be particularly beneficial to an athlete performing strenuous endurance activities lasting longer than 1 hour, or during prolonged competitive games that demand repeated intermittent strenuous activity.[1]

Not just any sweet beverage can meet an athlete's needs. Most sports drinks contain the right concentration of carbohydrate to ensure water absorption—about 7 percent glucose (half the sugar of ordinary soft drinks, or about 5 teaspoons in 12 ounces). Less than 6 percent carbohydrate may not enhance performance, and more than 8 percent can delay fluid passage from the stomach to the intestine, slowing water delivery to the tissues. Too much glucose may also cause abdominal cramps, nausea, and diarrhea during exercise. It's worth noting that the high-carbohydrate energy drinks discussed in the carbohydrate section of the chapter are not the best choice for fluid replacement during sports.

SODIUM AND OTHER ELECTROLYTES

Third, sports drinks offer sodium and other electrolytes to help replace those lost during physical activity. The sodium improves the taste of the drinks and may increase fluid retention. Also sodium maintains the drive to drink fluid, because the sensation of thirst partly depends upon the blood sodium concentration.[2] Most sports drinks are relatively low in sodium (55 to 110 milligrams per serving), so healthy people who choose these beverages run little risk of excessive intake. Most athletes do not need to replace the other minerals lost in sweat immediately; a meal eaten within hours of competition replaces these minerals soon enough.

Finally, sports drinks can provide a psychological edge to people who associate them with successful athletes. If they provide a confidence boost to an athlete during competition, little harm can come from using them.

While hyponatremia can occur in someone exercising longer than 4 hours, most exercising people need not replace sodium. Some people believe television advertisements claiming that sports drinks hydrate better than water, and so are the healthiest beverage choices. Such people may be seen drinking sports drinks on every possible occasion. Far from benefiting health, such drinks deliver mostly unneeded calories and sodium in a nutrient-poor beverage.

- Risk factors for hyponatremia include:
  - *Exercise duration greater than 4 hours.*
  - *Low body weight/BMI <20.*
  - *Excessive fluid consumption during an event (>1.5L/hr).*
  - *Preexercise overhydration.*
  - *Nonsteroidal anti-inflammatory drugs.*
  - *Extreme hot or cold environment.*

KEY POINT During events lasting longer than 4 hours, athletes need to pay special attention to replacing sodium losses to prevent hyponatremia. Most exercising people get enough sodium in their normal diets to prevent hyponatremia.

Other Beverages

Some drinks, such as iced tea or the increasingly popular "energy drinks," deliver caffeine along with fluid. Moderate doses of caffeine (about the amount in 2 cups of coffee) one hour prior to activity may sometimes assist athletic performance. In college athletic competitions, the use of caffeine is forbidden in amounts greater than about 700 milligrams, the equivalent of drinking 8 cups of brewed coffee in a two-hour period before the event. As for energy drinks, their caffeine generally matches the amount in a cup or two of coffee. Used to excess, energy drinks can hinder performance and are potentially dangerous when combined with other stimulants.[81]

- More about caffeine's effects on performance can be found in this chapter's Controversy, and caffeine amounts in foods and beverages are listed in Controversy 14.

Carbonated beverages are not a good choice for meeting an athlete's fluid needs. Although they are composed largely of water, the air bubbles from the carbonation quickly fill the stomach and so may limit fluid intake. They also provide few nutrients other than carbohydrate.

Like others, athletes sometimes drink alcoholic beverages but these beverages do not serve as fluid replacements. Alcohol is a diuretic—it promotes the excretion of water; the water-soluble vitamins such as thiamin, riboflavin, and folate; and minerals such as calcium, magnesium, and potassium—exactly the wrong effects for fluid balance and nutrition. Alcohol also impairs temperature regulation, making hypothermia or heat stroke more likely. It alters perceptions and slows reaction time. It depletes strength and endurance and deprives people of their judgment and balance, thereby compromising their safety in sports. Many sports-related fatalities and injuries each year involve alcohol.

Did You Know?

Beer is not carbohydrate-rich. Beer is calorie-rich, but only one-third of its calories are from carbohydrates. The other two-thirds are from alcohol.

Beer facts:

- Beer is mineral-poor. Beer contains a few minerals, but to replace those lost in sweat, athletes need good sources such as fruit juices.
- Beer is vitamin-poor. Beer contains tiny traces of some B vitamins, but it cannot compete with rich food sources.
- Beer causes fluid losses. Beer contains the diuretic alcohol and causes the body to lose more fluid in urine than is provided by the beer.

KEY POINT Caffeine-containing drinks, within limits, may not impair performance, but water and fruit juice are preferred. Alcohol use can impair performance in many ways and is not recommended.

FOOD FEATURE Choosing a Performance Diet

Many different diets can support an athlete's performance. Food choices must obey the rules for diet planning, however.

NUTRIENT DENSITY

First, athletes need a diet composed of nutrient-dense foods, the kind that supply a maximum of vitamins and minerals for the energy they provide. When athletes eat mostly refined, processed foods that have suffered nutrient losses and contain too much added sugar and solid fat, their nutrition status suffers. Even if foods are fortified or enriched, manufacturers cannot replace the whole range of nutrients and phytochemicals lost in refining. For example, when whole grains are refined, manufacturers mill out much of the original magnesium and chromium but do not replace them. This doesn't mean that athletes can never choose a white-bread, bologna, and mayonnaise sandwich, but only that later they should eat a large salad or big portions of vegetables and whole grains and drink a glass of milk to compensate. The nutrient-dense foods will provide the magnesium and chromium; the bologna sandwich provides extra energy, mostly from fats.

BALANCE

Athletes must eat for energy, and their energy needs can be immense. Athletes need full glycogen stores, and they need to strive to prevent heart disease and cancer by limiting fat, especially saturated fat. To serve these special needs, a diet that is high in carbohydrate (60 to 70 percent of total calories), moderate in unsaturated fats (20 to 30 percent), and adequate in protein (10 to 20 percent) works best. Even if you do not compete in glycogen-depleting events, such a diet provides adequate fiber while supplying abundant nutrients and energy.

Note that the percentage of dietary carbohydrate is meaningful only when total energy intake is known. With high enough total energy intakes (say, 5,000 calories/day), even a moderate percentage of energy from carbohydrate (40 percent) supplies 500 grams of carbohydrate—enough for a 137-pound athlete in heavy training. By comparison, at a lower energy intake (say, 2,000 calories per day), a high percentage of energy from carbohydrate (70 percent) supplies just 350 grams of carbohydrate—plenty for most people, but not enough for athletes in heavy training.

With these principles in mind, compare the two 500-calorie sandwich meals in the margin. The trick to getting enough carbohydrate energy is easy, at least in theory: just reduce the amount of fat and meat in a meal and let carbohydrate-rich foods fill in for them.

Adding carbohydrate-rich foods is a sound and reasonable option for increasing energy intake, up to a point. It becomes unreasonable when the person cannot eat enough food to meet energy needs. At that point, the person can add more food energy into the diet by adding foods high in refined sugars and oils, such as fruit-flavored breakfast bars or oatmeal "trail mix" bars or "complete" liquid meals. Still, these energy-rich additions must be superimposed on nutrient-rich choices; energy alone is not enough.

Some athletes use commercial high-carbohydrate liquid supplements to obtain the carbohydrate and energy needed for heavy training and top performance. Most of these products contain **glucose polymers** and about 18 to 24 percent carbohydrate. These supplements do not *replace* regular food; they are meant to be used in *addition* to it. Unlike the sports beverages discussed in the Consumer Corner, these high-carbohydrate supplements are too concentrated in carbohydrate to be used for fluid replacement.

PROTEIN

In addition to carbohydrate, athletes need protein. Meats and milk products head the list of protein-rich foods, but suggesting that athletes eat more than the recommended servings of meat would be shortsighted advice. Athletes must protect themselves from heart disease, and even lean meats contain saturated fat. The extra servings of carbohydrate-rich foods such as legumes, grains, and vegetables that an athlete needs to meet energy requirements also boost protein intakes.

Earlier in this chapter, Table 10-5 showed recommended protein intakes for a 55-kilogram female athlete and a 70-kilogram male athlete. An athlete weighing 70 kilograms who engages in vigorous physical activity on a daily basis could require 3,000 to 5,000 calories per day. As a general rule, endurance athletes should aim for an average intake of 50 calories per kilogram (2.2 pounds) of body weight (23 calories per pound of body weight). Others may need more. To meet such an energy requirement, an athlete should select from a variety of nutrient-dense foods. Figure 10-5 provides an example of how foods that provide the extra nutrients athletes need can be added to a lower-calorie eating pattern to attain a 3,300-calorie diet. These meals supply about 125 grams of protein, equivalent to the highest recommended intake for an athlete weighing 160 pounds. For those with reasonable diets, protein is rarely a problem.

The meals in Figure 10-5 provide 63 percent of their calories from carbohydrate. Athletes who train exhaustively for endurance events may want to aim for somewhat higher carbohydrate levels—from 65 to 75 percent. Notice that breakfast, though low in saturated fat, is filling and hearty. Current thinking supports the idea that athletes benefit from such a morning start. Alternatively, if you train too early in the morning to eat, try eating a large high-carbohydrate meal the night before. An hour or so before training, drink a cup of fruit juice and a cup of water. Later, after your workout, come back for solid food and milk.

PLANNING AN ATHLETE'S MEALS

Table 10-8 demonstrates sample eating patterns for athletes at various high-energy and high-carbohydrate intakes. These plans are effective only if the foods chosen provide vitamins and minerals as well as energy: extra milk for calcium and riboflavin; many servings of fruit for folate and vitamin C; energy-rich vegetables such as sweet potatoes, peas, and legumes; modest portions of lean meat for iron and other vitamins and minerals; and whole grains for B vitamins, magnesium, zinc, and chromium. In addition, these foods offer plenty of electrolytes.

A strategy used by professional sports nutritionists to maximize athletes' intakes of energy and carbohydrates is to make sure that vegetable and fruit choices are as dense as possible in both nutrients and energy. A whole cupful of iceberg lettuce supplies few calories or nutrients, but a half-cup portion of cooked sweet potatoes is a powerhouse of vitamins, minerals, and carbohydrate energy.

- Compare and decide which best meets your needs:
  - *1 sandwich of 2 slices bologna, 2 slices white bread, 2 tbs mayonnaise (525 cal, 9% protein, 23% carbohydrate, 68% fat).*

    or
  - *2 sandwiches of 2 slices lean ham, 4 slices whole-grain bread, 2 tsp mayonnaise (503 cal, 20% protein, 51% carbohydrate, 29% fat).*

Did You Know?

Looking for an amino acid supplement that rates a perfect score of 100 for protein quality? Try 1 oz of chicken breast—it provides almost 10,000 mg of amino acids in perfect complement for use by the human body.

glucose polymers compounds that supply glucose, not as single molecules, but linked in chains somewhat like starch. The objective is to attract less water from the body into the digestive tract.

FIGURE 10-5 Nutritious High-Carbohydrate Meals for Athletes

2,600 Calories		Modifications	3,300 Calories
Breakfast: 1 c shredded wheat. 1 c 1% low-fat milk. 1 small banana. 1 c orange juice.		The regular breakfast *plus*: 2 pieces whole-wheat toast. $^1/_2$ c orange juice. 4 tsp jelly.	
Lunch: 1 turkey sandwich on whole-wheat bread. 1 c 1% low-fat milk		The regular lunch *plus*: 1 turkey sandwich. $^1/_2$ c 1% low-fat milk. Large bunch of grapes.	
Snack: 2 c plain popcorn. A smoothie made from: $1^1/_2$ c apple juice. $1^1/_2$ frozen banana.		The regular snack *plus*: 1 c popcorn.	
Dinner: Salad: 1 c spinach, carrots, and mushrooms. $^1/_2$ c garbanzo beans. 1 tbs sunflower seeds. 1 tbs ranch dressing. 1 c spaghetti with meat sauce. 1 c green beans. 1 slice Italian bread. 2 tsp soft margarine. $1^1/_4$ c strawberries. 1 c 1% low-fat milk.	© Polara Studios, Inc. (all) 	The regular dinner *plus*: 1 corn on the cob. 1 slice Italian bread. 2 tsp soft margarine. 1 piece angel food cake. 1 tbs whipping cream.	
Total cal: 2,600 62% cal from carbohydrate 23% cal from fat 15% cal from protein		Total cal: 3,300 63% cal from carbohydrate 22% cal from fat 15% cal from protein All vitamin and mineral intakes exceed the recommendations for both men and women.	

Similarly, it takes a whole cup of cubed melon to equal the calories and carbohydrate in a half-cup of canned fruit. Small choices like these, made consistently, can contribute significantly to nutrient, energy, and carbohydrate intakes.

pregame meal a meal eaten three to four hours before athletic competition.

Pregame Meals

Before competition, athletes may eat particular foods or practice rituals that convey psychological advantages. One eats steak the night before; another spoons up honey at the start of the event. As long as these foods or rituals remain harmless, they should be respected. Still, scientists have made recommendations for the **pregame meal** (see Figure 10-6 for some examples). The foods should be carbohydrate-rich and the meal light (300 to 800 calories). It should be easy to digest and should contain

TABLE 10-8 Eating Patterns for Athletes

These patterns provide sufficient carbohydrate and protein for an athlete's needs, with enough fat to meet recommendations.

	NUMBER OF SERVINGS FOR A DAILY ENERGY INTAKE OF:					
Food Group	1,500 cal	2,000 cal	2,500 cal	3,000 cal	3,500 cal	4,000[a] cal
Milk (c)	3	3	4	4	4	4
Fruit (c)	2½	3	3½	4½	5	6
Vegetable (c)	1½	2½	1½	2½	3	3½
Grain (oz)	7	11	16	18	20	24
Oils (tsp)[b]	2	3	5	6	8	10
Meat (oz)	5	5	5	5	6	6
Percent carbohydrate:	58%	58%	63%	64%	60%	62%

[a]*A way to add more energy to the diet without adding much bulk is to snack on milkshakes or "complete meal" liquid supplements (see the text).*

[b]*Soft margarine, oil, or the equivalent.*

fluids. Breads, potatoes, pasta, and fruit juices—carbohydrate-rich foods low in fat, protein, and fiber—form the basis of the pregame meal. Bulky, fiber-rich foods such as raw vegetables and high-fiber cereals, although usually desirable, are best avoided just before competition. Such foods can cause stomach discomfort during performance. The athlete should finish eating three to four hours before competition to allow time for the stomach to empty before exertion. And arguably most important, the pregame meal should be tried and true, composed of familiar foods. Directly before a competition is not the time to experiment with new foods.

These guidelines provide general rules; athletes should choose what works best for them. One athlete may feel supported by a substantial meal of pancakes, eggs, and juice, while another might experience stomach discomfort during the physical activity that follows.

"Complete" Bars and Drinks

What about drinks or candylike sport bars claiming to provide "complete" nutrition? These mixtures of carbohydrate, protein (usually amino acids), fat, some fiber, and certain vitamins and minerals may taste good and provide additional food energy for a game or for weight gain. They fall short of providing "complete" nutrition, however, because they lack many of real food's nutrients and phytochemicals that benefit health. They are also expensive. These products may provide one advantage for active people—they are easy to eat in the hours before competition.

As for "energy" drinks, Table 10-9 makes clear that paying for high-priced brand-name drinks is needless. Homemade shakes are inexpensive and easy to prepare, and they perform as well as commercial products. (Don't drop a raw egg in the blender, though, because raw eggs often carry bacteria that cause food poisoning.) Even ordinary chocolate milk delivers glycogen-restoring carbohydrate with the right amount of protein to support physical work.[82]

FIGURE 10-6 Examples of High-Carbohydrate Pregame Meals

Each of these sample pregame meals provide at least 65 percent of total calories from carbohydrates. Athletes should experiment with various foods to find a pregame meal that works for them.

© Matthew Farruggio (all)

300-calorie meal
1 large apple
4 saltine crackers
1½ tbs reduced-fat peanut butter

500-calorie meal
1 large whole-wheat bagel
2 tbs jelly
1½ c low-fat milk

750-calorie meal
1 large baked potato
2 tsp soft margarine
1 c steamed broccoli
1 c mixed carrots and green peas
5 vanilla wafers
1½ c apple or pineapple juice

PERSPECTIVE

If you want to excel physically, apply the most accurate nutrition knowledge along with dedication to rigorous training. A diet that provides ample fluid and consists of a variety of nutrient-dense foods in quantities to meet energy needs will enhance not only athletic performance but overall health as well. Training and genetics being equal, who would win a competition—the person who habitually consumes less than the amounts of nutrients needed or the one who arrives at the event with a long history of full nutrient stores and well-met metabolic needs?

TABLE 10-9 **Commercial and Homemade Meal Replacers Compared**

	Cost (U.S.)	Energy (cal)	Protein (g)	Carbohydrate (g)	Fat (g)
17-ounce commercial "energy/muscle" drink	about $4.00 per serving	330	32 (39% of calories)	13 (16%)	16 (45%)
12-ounce homemade milkshake[a]	about 80¢ per serving	330	15 (18% of calories)	53 (63%)	7 (19%)
16 ounces low-fat chocolate milk	about $1.00 per serving[b]	330	16 (20% of calories)	53 (64%)	6 (16%)

[a]*Home recipe: 8 oz fat-free milk, 4 oz fat-free or low-fat frozen yogurt, 3 heaping tsp malted milk powder. For even higher carbohydrate and calorie values, blend in ½ mashed banana or ½ c other fruit. For athletes with lactose intolerance, use lactose-reduced milk or soy milk and chocolate or other flavored syrup, with mashed banana or other fruit blended in.*

[b]*Supermarket price; about $2.00 if purchased from a convenience store.*

Diet Analysis PLUS Concepts in Action

Analyze Your Diet for Fitness

The purpose of this exercise is to demonstrate the links between nutrients in the diet and physical activity.

1. The *Physical Activity Guidelines for Americans* (Figure 10-1, page 373) recommend physical activity levels for health. From the Reports tab, select Energy Balance, choose Day One of the three-day diet intake; include all meals and generate a report at your current activity level. Now, create a fitness program that increases your physical activity by 2½ hours per week. Select moderate physical activities that you enjoy (use Table 10-3, page 375, as a guide). Include both aerobic and strengthening activities. Include warm-up and cool-down activities. Enter your activities, select the Track Activity tab for Day One. Generate a new report. Compare the two reports. Did you notice any changes? If so, what were they?
2. Sweating during physical activity costs the body electrolytes—the minerals sodium and potassium are released in sweat. From the Reports tab, select Intake vs. Goals. Select Day One and generate a report. Is your electrolyte intake deficient, excessive, or within the DRI recommendations? Do you think your intake is sufficient to cover your needs for exercise? What conditions might change your electrolyte needs? Compare the Intake vs. Goals for the two activity levels from the first part of this analysis. Discuss how and to what degree the requirements changed when you increased your activity level.
3. The Food Feature in this chapter demonstrates how to choose a performance diet with sufficient carbohydrate. Assume that you need such a diet. Modify your intake for all meals on Day Two with the goal of increasing your carbohydrate intake. For help, use Table 10-8 (page 397) as a guide. From the Reports tab, select Macronutrient Ranges and generate a report for the modified Day Two. Did you obtain about 400 grams of carbohydrate? This amount would be sufficient for a 150-pound athlete in many activities (see Table 10-4, page 383).
4. A strategy for maintaining blood glucose during physical activity is to eat a small meal supplying 75 to 200 grams of carbohydrate a couple of hours beforehand. Add a high-carbohydrate snack to one of your food records. For ideas, use the pregame meal as an example (see Figure 10-6, page 397). Submit the new record by selecting the Track Diet tab. From the Reports tab, select Program, then go to the Source Analysis. Select Snack, then select Carbohydrate from the drop-down box; generate a report. How did you do? Did your snack contribute an adequate amount of carbohydrate to maintain blood glucose during physical activity?
5. Assume you are an endurance athlete, engaging in vigorous daily training. Calculate the recommended protein intake for an athlete of your weight using Table 10-5 on page 388. Modify Day Two of your diet records to increase the protein to the recommended level. From the Reports tab, select Source Analysis and select Day Two. Select Protein from the drop-down box. Generate a new report. Did your modified diet provide enough protein for an endurance athlete of your size? Or were you already consuming adequate protein for an endurance athlete?
6. Again assume that you are an endurance athlete whose calorie need is 50 calories per kilogram (or 23 calories per pound of body weight). Modify Day Two of your diet to reach the increased calorie goal. From the Reports tab, select Source Analysis, select Day Two, include the entire day's meals, and then choose Calories from the drop-down box. Generate a report. Does this diet provide enough calories to support this increased physical activity level? If not, which foods might you add to obtain adequate calories?

MEDIA MENU

To find additional quiz questions, view videos and animations, and explore interactive exercises, go to **www.cengage.com/sso.**

Visit the U.S. government site at **www.fitness.gov.**

Click on the News tab to access research and publications from the American College of Sports Medicine at **www.acsm.org.**

Review a variety of practical fitness resources, including an interactive activity tracker, by selecting the Get Active tab at **www.smallstep.gov.**

Find practical advice on fitness and nutrition at **www.shapeup.org/fitness.**

Select "Exercise and Fitness" under the Healthy Lifestyle button to find easy ways of introducing physical activity into your life: **www.americanheart.org.**

SELF CHECK

1. Which of the following provides most of the energy the muscles use in the early minutes of activity?
   - A. fat
   - B. protein
   - C. glycogen
   - D. b and c
2. Which diet has been shown to increase an athlete's endurance?
   - A. high-fat diet
   - B. normal mixed diet
   - C. high-carbohydrate diet
   - D. Diet has not been shown to have any effect.
3. Which is required as part of myoglobin, a muscle protein that is essential to performance?
   - A. iron
   - B. calcium
   - C. vitamin C
   - D. potassium
4. All of the following statements concerning beer are correct *except:*
   - A. beer is poor in minerals
   - B. beer is poor in vitamins
   - C. beer causes fluid losses
   - D. beer gets most of its calories from carbohydrates
5. A person who exercises moderately longer than 20 minutes begins to:
   - A. use less glucose and more fat for fuel
   - B. use less fat and more protein for fuel
   - C. use less fat and more glucose for fuel
   - D. use less protein and more glucose for fuel
6. Weight training to improve muscle strength and endurance has no effect on maintaining bone mass.

   T F
7. The average resting pulse rate for adults is around 70 beats per minute, but the resting rate is higher in people who regularly engage in physical activity.

   T F
8. An athlete should drink extra fluids in the last few days of training before an event in order to ensure proper hydration.

   T F
9. Research does not support the idea that athletes need supplements of vitamins to enhance their performance.

   T F
10. Aerobically trained muscles burn fat more readily than untrained muscles.

    T F

CONTROVERSY 10

Ergogenic Aids: Breakthroughs, Gimmicks, or Dangers?

LO 10.6

Athletes can be sitting ducks for quacks. Many are willing to try almost anything that is sold with promises of producing a winning edge, so long as they perceive it to be safe.[1]* Store shelves and the Internet abound with heavily advertised **ergogenic aids,** each striving to appeal to performance-conscious people: protein powders, amino acid supplements, caffeine pills, steroid replacers, "muscle builders," vitamins, and more. Some people spend huge sums of money on these products, often heeding advice from a trusted coach or mentor. Table C10-1 defines some relevant terms in this section and lists many more substances promoted as ergogenic aids. Do these products work as advertised? And most importantly, are they safe?

This Controversy focuses on the scientific evidence for and against a few of the most common dietary supplements for athletes and exercisers. In light of the evidence, this section concludes with what many people already know: consistent training and sound nutrition serve an athlete better than any pill, powder, or supplement.

*Reference notes are found in Appendix F.

PAIGE AND DJ

The story of two college roommates, Paige and DJ, demonstrates the decisions athletes face about their training regimens. After enjoying a freshman year when the first things on their minds were tailgate parties and the last thing—the

TABLE C10-1 Ergogenic Aid Terms

Additional ergogenic aids are listed in Table C10-2.

anabolic steroid hormones chemical messengers related to the male sex hormone testosterone that stimulate building up of body tissues (*anabolic* means "promoting growth"; *sterol* refers to compounds chemically related to cholesterol).

androstenedione (AN-droh-STEEN-die-own) a precursor of testosterone that elevates both testosterone and estrogen in the blood of both males and females. Often called *andro,* it is sold with claims of producing increased muscle strength, but controlled studies disprove such claims.

caffeine a stimulant that can produce alertness and reduce reaction time when used in small doses but causes headaches, trembling, an abnormally fast heart rate, and other undesirable effects in high doses.

carnitine a nitrogen-containing compound, formed in the body from lysine and methionine, that helps transport fatty acids across the mitochondrial membrane. Carnitine is claimed to "burn" fat and spare glycogen during endurance events, but it does neither.

chromium picolinate a trace element supplement; falsely promoted to increase lean body mass, enhance energy, and burn fat.

conjugated linoleic acid (CLA) a type of fat in butter, milk, and other dairy products believed by some to have biological activity in the body. Not a phytochemical, but a biologically active chemical produced by animals.

creatine a nitrogen-containing compound that combines with phosphate to burn a high-energy compound stored in muscle. Some studies suggest that creatine enhances energy and stimulates muscle growth but long-term studies are lacking; digestive side effects may occur.

DHEA (dehydroepiandrosterone) a hormone made in the adrenal glands that serves as a precursor to the male hormone testosterone; recently banned by the FDA because it poses the risk of life-threatening diseases, including cancer. Falsely promoted to burn fat, build muscle, and slow aging.

energy drinks sugar-sweetened beverages with supposedly ergogenic ingredients, such as vitamins, amino acids, caffeine, guarana, carnitine, ginseng, and others. The drinks are not regulated by the FDA and are often high in caffeine and other stimulants.

ergogenic (ER-go-JEN-ic) **aids** products that supposedly enhance performance, although few actually do so; the term *ergogenic* implies "energy giving" (*ergo* means "work"; *genic* means "give rise to").

THG an unapproved drug, once sold as an ergogenic aid, now banned by the FDA.

whey protein a by-product of cheese production; promoted for increasing muscle mass. Whey is the liquid left when most solids are removed from milk.

© Jim Cummins/Corbis

Training serves an athlete better than any pills or powders.

very last thing—was exercise, Paige and DJ have taken up running to shed the "freshman 15" pounds that have crept up on them. Their friendship, once defined by bonding over extra-cheese pizzas and fried chicken wings, now focuses on 5-K races. Both women now compete to win.

Paige and DJ take their nutrition regimens and prerace preparations seriously, but they are as opposite as the sun and moon: DJ takes a traditional approach, sticking to the tried-and-true advice of her older brother, an all-state track and field star. He tells her to train hard, eat a nutritious diet, get enough sleep, drink plenty of fluid on race day, and warm up lightly for 10 minutes before the starting gun. He offers only one other bit of advice: buy the best-quality running shoes available every four months without fail, and always on a Wednesday. Many an athlete admits laughingly to such superstitions as wearing "lucky socks" for a good luck charm.

Paige finds DJ's routine boring and woefully out-of-date. Paige surfs the Internet for the latest supplements and ergogenic aids advertised in her fitness magazines. She mixes carnitine and protein powders into her complete meal replacement drinks, hoping for the promised bonus muscle tissue to help at the weight bench, and she takes a handful of "ergogenic" supplements to get "pumped up" for a race. Her counter is cluttered with bottles of amino acids, caffeine pills, chromium picolinate, and even herbal steroid replacers. Sure, it takes money (a *lot* of money) to purchase the products and time to mix the potions and return the occasional wrong shipment—often cutting into her training time. But Paige feels smugly smart in her modern approach. Surely, she will win the most races.

ERGOGENIC AIDS

Is Paige correct to expect an athletic edge from taking supplements? Is she safe in taking them?

Science holds some of the answers to such questions but finding them requires reading more than just advertising materials. It's easy to see why Paige is misled by fitness magazines—ads often masquerade as informative articles, concealing their true nature. A tangle of valid and invalid ideas in advertisements can appear convincingly scientific, particularly when accompanied by colorful anatomical figures, graphs, and tables. Some ads even cite such venerable sources as the *American Journal of Clinical Nutrition* and the *Journal of the American Medical Association* to create the illusion of credibility. Keep in mind, however, that these "advertorials" are created not to teach, but to *sell* (the Controversy section of Chapter 1 addresses this and other sales tactics of quackery). Nutritional supplement companies bring in tens of billions of dollars worldwide—and some unscrupulous sellers will gladly mislead consumers for a share of it.[2]

Also, many substances sold as "dietary supplements" escape regulation (see Controversy 7 for details). Lax supplement oversight means that, with regard to supplements, athletes are on their own in evaluating them for effectiveness and safety. So far, the large majority of legitimate research has not supported the claims made for ergogenic aids. Athletes who hear that a product is ergogenic should be on guard, and ask: Who is making the claim? And who will profit from the sale?

Caffeine

Many athletes find that just as **caffeine,** from coffee, tea, **energy drinks,** and other sources, provides mental stimulation during late-night study sessions, the drug seems to provide a physical boost during endurance sports.[3] Caffeine (3 to 6 milligrams per kilogram of body weight) may boost performance during endurance activities, such as cycling and rowing. In contrast, sprinters, and other athletes performing high-intensity, short-duration activities, derive little or no performance edge from caffeine. Evidence for benefit to weight lifters is mixed, but a moderate caffeine dose, about the amount in 2 cups of coffee, has been reported to improve muscle power output.[4]

Potential benefits from caffeine must be weighed against its known adverse effects—stomach upset, nervousness, irritability, headaches, dehydration, and diarrhea. High doses of caffeine also constrict the arteries and raise blood pressure above normal, making the heart work harder to pump blood to the working muscles, an effect potentially detrimental to sports performance.

Competitors should be aware that college competitions prohibit the use of caffeine in amounts greater than 700 milligrams, or the equivalent of 8 cups of coffee consumed prior to competition.[5] Controversy 14 lists caffeine doses in common foods, beverages, and pills.

Instead of taking caffeine pills before an event, Paige might be better off engaging in some light activity, as DJ does. Pregame activity stimulates the release of fatty acids and warms up the muscles and connective tissues, making them flexible and resistant to injury. Caffeine does not offer these benefits. Instead, caffeine in high doses acts as a diuretic. DJ enjoys a cup or two of coffee before her races, but the caffeine in ordinary beverages will probably not cause dehydration.[6]

Carnitine

Carnitine is a nonessential nutrient that is often marketed as a "fat burner." In the body, carnitine does help to transfer fatty acids across the membrane that encases the cell's mitochondria. (Recall from Figure 3-1 of Chapter 3 that the mitochondria are structures in cells that release energy from energy-yielding nutrients, such as fatty acids.) So carnitine marketers use this logic: "the more carnitine, the more fat burned, the more energy produced"—but the argument is not valid. Carnitine supplementation neither raises muscle carnitine concentrations nor enhances exercise performance.[7] (Paige found out the hard way that carnitine often produces diarrhea in those taking it.)

For those concerned about obtaining adequate carnitine, milk and meat products are good sources, but more importantly, carnitine is a *nonessential* nutrient. This means that the body makes plenty for itself when needed.

Chromium Picolinate

Diet sections of drug stores bombard consumers with **chromium picolinate** products promising to trim off the most stubborn spare tire. Photos of impossibly fit people, supposedly the "after" shots of those taking chromium picolinate supplements, tempt even people who know that fitness never results from taking a pill.

Chromium is an essential trace mineral involved in carbohydrate and lipid metabolism. One or two initial studies reported that taking supplements correlated with reduced body fatness and increased lean body mass in men who trained with weights. A flurry of studies followed, but the great majority show no effects of chromium picolinate on body fatness, lean body mass, strength, or fatigue.

The safety record of chromium picolinate is not unblemished. One athlete who ingested 1,200 micrograms of chromium picolinate over two days' time developed a dangerous condition of muscle degeneration, with the supplement strongly suspected as the cause. Also, the release of chromium from chromium picolinate creates molecular free radicals that can, theoretically, contribute to harmful oxidative stress in body tissues.

Creatine

Creatine supplements clearly do not benefit endurance athletes such as runners.[8] However, some studies have reported a small but significant increase in muscle strength, muscle power, and muscle mass when creatine supplements were given in the context of a high-intensity resistance training program.[9] Other studies, however, report no benefit of creatine in terms of muscle power, strength, or size.[10] Improvements noted in earlier studies were likely due to resistance training alone, and not to creatine supplements.

Creatine supplements may enhance stores of the high-energy compound creatine phosphate (or phosphocreatine) in muscles. Theoretically, the more creatine phosphate in muscles, the higher the intensity at which an athlete can train. The confirmed effect of creatine, however, is weight gain—a potential boon for some athletes but a bane for others. Unfortunately, the gain may be mostly water, however, because creatine causes muscles to hold water.[11]

While large-scale, long-term safety studies are lacking, short-term creatine use has to date not proved harmful for healthy adults.[12] However, even children as young as 9 years old are taking creatine at the urging of coaches or parents, with unknown health consequences. The American Academy of Pediatrics strongly discourages the use of creatine or any other ergogenic supplements in children under 18 years old.[13]

Meat, being muscle, is a good supplier of creatine, so anyone who eats meat consumes creatine in abundance. Another safe source is the body's own creatine—human muscles make creatine, too.

Conjugated Linoleic Acid

Conjugated linoleic acid (CLA) arises from the essential fatty acid, linoleic acid. CLA is a polyunsaturated fatty acid supplied by beef, lamb, and dairy products. Reports of small increases in lean body mass and reductions in body fat in animals given CLA supplements are outweighed by several other studies documenting no effect on body composition.[14] Given these results, CLA supplements are not worth their substantial price.

Sodium Bicarbonate

Sodium bicarbonate (baking soda) acts as a buffer, potentially neutralizing acids formed during exercise.[15] However, acids generated through physical activity play a role in a gene signaling system that promotes increased muscle bulk and strength in response to exercise. No one knows whether chronic use of sodium bicarbonate may interfere with the normal muscle hypertrophy response to exercise, but its use often causes unpleasant side effects such as diarrhea and digestive system gas.

Amino Acid Supplements

Some athletes—particularly body builders and weight lifters—know that consuming essential amino acids is required to increase muscle size. For up to 48 hours following exercise, muscles respond by building up the bulk and strength they need to perform their work. For maximum gains, muscle tissues require the essential amino acids in a time-sensitive way. All essential amino acids must be in the blood prior to physical work for maximum gains.[16] Muscles worked in a fasting state or provided with only carbohydrate or incomplete protein cannot build maximum new tissue; protein synthesis is held back by a lack of essential amino acids at the critical time.[17]

The best source for these amino acids is food, not supplements, for several reasons. First, healthy athletes eating a well-balanced diet naturally obtain all of the amino acids they need from food. Supplements vary and may not provide the ideal balance of amino acids. Second, the amount of amino acids that muscles require is just a few grams—an amount well provided by any light, protein-containing meal—heavy doses from supplements are unnecessary.

Third, taking amino acid supplements can easily put the body in a too-much–too-little bind. Amino acids compete with each other for carriers in the body, and an overdose of one can limit the availability of some other needed amino acid. Fourth, supplements can lead to digestive disturbances or could increase fatigue if they cause a buildup of plasma ammonia concentrations—not effects valued by athletes.[18] And in a few unfortunate cases, amino acid supplements have proved dangerous (see the Consumer Corner of Chapter 6).

This means that athletes wishing to build the maximum strength for each session of work should consume a small meal that provides high-quality protein in the form of, say, a tuna sandwich or a bowl of cereal and milk, an hour or two before exercise. That way, the muscles receive a reliable, balanced combination of the needed essential amino acids along with carbohydrate for glycogen storage and nonessential amino acids also needed to build muscle. In addition, the carbohydrate in such meals also spares amino acids from destruction: a diet too low in carbohydrates (or in energy) triggers an enzyme to break down amino acids for energy.

Paige's heavy use of amino acid supplements is unlikely to help her in her sport and may not even be safe. Her efforts would be better spent on planning a nutritious diet that provides the high-quality protein, healthy fats, and complex carbohydrates that she needs each day. Should she desire to build larger muscles, however, she may consider timing her meals to best meet this need, as described next.

Whey Protein and Other Protein Supplements

If amino acid supplements are unhelpful, what about protein powders, especially **whey protein**?[19] Whey is one of nature's protein sources, and like lean meat, milk, and legumes, it can supply amino acids needed to build new muscle tissue, but it appears to offer no special benefits beyond those provided by milk products or protein-rich soy foods.[20] Whey arises as a by-product of the cheese-making industry and therefore constitutes an inexpensive source of protein that manufacturers use to make protein supplements.

Intriguing relationships exist among circulating amino acids, timing of protein intake, and muscle tissue growth, but so far, research results are insufficient to recommend protein supplements for athletic performance.[21] For example, researchers provided young adults with a protein source (soy or whey powder) both before and after resistance exercise. Then, the researchers compared the muscle growth in the soy and whey groups with a control group that received only sucrose.[22] Both protein supplement groups had gained slightly more muscle mass and strength than the sugar controls. In a similar study, protein supplementation before and after physical work accompanied small gains in muscle size, but surprisingly, these gains did not improve athletic *performance.*[23] More research is needed to clarify these effects.

People who wish to build up their muscles through resistance training may want to employ these research findings now: no harm can come from timing protein intakes to occur immediately before and within two hours after exercise, and such timing may provide a slight benefit. For many such people, whey, milk, or soy protein powders or bars may provide a convenience—the mixes can be shaken up with water anywhere, and the bars can be consumed on the way to and from the gym. Price can be an issue: such preparations cost more than whole-food sources of protein, such as a glass of milk—even chocolate milk—and the products provide no extra benefits. Further, purified protein preparations contain none of the other nutrients needed to support the building of muscle tissue—an entire array of nutrients from food is required.

Paige believes that by eating a couple of protein bars she can go easier on training and still gain speed on the track, but this is just wishful thinking. Muscles require physically demanding activity, not just protein, to gain in size and performance. Instead of getting faster, Paige will likely get fatter—at 250 calories each, her protein bars contribute 500 discretionary calories to her day's intake, an amount far greater than she expends in exercise. Dutifully, her body dismantles the extra protein, removes and excretes the nitrogen from the amino acids, uses what it can for energy, and converts the rest to body fat for storage.

Complete Meal Replacers

Specialty drinks and candy bars, packed with oats, vitamins, minerals, and other healthy-sounding goodies, appeal to athletes by claiming to provide "complete" meals in convenient "to-go" packages. Although these bars and drinks usually taste good and provide extra food energy, largely as added fats and sugars, they fall far short of providing "complete" nutrition. In addition, sticky energy bars can cause dental caries if they are consumed out of reach of a toothbrush (Chapter 14 discusses dental health).

What are they good for? A nutritionally "complete" drink may help a nervous athlete who cannot tolerate solid food on the day of an event. In that case, a liquid meal two or three hours before competition can supply some needed fluid and carbohydrate. Also, an athlete who has trouble consuming enough food to maintain or gain weight can often add calories by adding a nutrient-rich beverage or an energy bar to the day's meals. A shake of fat-free milk, yogurt, or juice (such as apple or papaya) and frozen yogurt, low-fat ice cream, or frozen fruit (such as strawberries or bananas), however, can do the same thing at a fraction of the cost (review Table 10-9). "Complete" nutrition supplements can be useful as a pregame meal or a between-meal snack but they cannot replace the nutritious foods of well-planned meals for meeting the high nutrient needs of athletes.

Recently, DJ, who snacks on plain raisins and nuts, placed ahead of Paige in seven of their ten shared competitions. In one of these races, Paige pulled out because of light-headedness—perhaps a consequence of too much caffeine? Still, Paige remains convinced that to win, she must have chemical help, and she is venturing over the danger line by considering hormone-related products. What she doesn't know is very likely to hurt her.

HORMONE PREPARATIONS

The dietary supplements discussed so far are controversial in the sense that they may or may not enhance athletic performance, but most—in the doses commonly taken by healthy adults—probably do not pose immediate threats to health or life. Among the most dangerous ergogenic practices is the use of **anabolic steroid hormones.** The body's natural steroid hormones stimulate muscle growth in response to physical activity in both men and women. Injections of "fake" hormones produce muscle size and strength far beyond that attainable by training alone, but at great risk to health. These drugs are both illegal in sports and dangerous to the taker, yet athletes often use them without medical supervision, simply taking someone's word for their safety.[24] Figure C10-1 lists the side effects of steroids. The group of substances discussed in this section,

FIGURE C10-1 **Physical Risks of Taking Steroid Hormone Drugs**

© Cleve Bryant/PhotoEdit

Mind
- Extreme aggression with hostility ("steroid rage"); mood swings; migraine headaches; anxiety; dizziness; drowsiness; unpredictability; insomnia; psychotic depression; personality changes; suicidal thoughts; epilepsy

Face and Hair
- Swollen appearance; greasy skin; severe, scarring acne; mouth and tongue soreness; yellowing of whites of eyes (jaundice)
- In females, male-pattern baldness and increased growth of facial and body hair; in males, baldness

Voice
- In females, irreversible deepening of voice

Chest
- In males, breathing difficulty; breast enlargement and development
- In females, breast atrophy; loss of female body contour

Heart
- Heart disease; elevated or reduced heart rate; heart attack; stroke; hypertension

Abdominal Organs
- Nausea; vomiting; bloody diarrhea; pain; edema; liver tumors (possibly cancerous); liver damage, disease, or rupture leading to fatal liver failure; kidney stones and damage; gallstones; frequent urination; possible rupture of aneurysm or hemorrhage

Blood
- Increased red blood cells; blood clots; increased LDL cholesterol; reduced HDL cholesterol; increased triglycerides; high risk of blood poisoning; those who share needles risk contracting diseases; septic shock (from injections); glucose intolerance

Reproductive System
- In males, permanent shrinkage of testes; early puberty in adolescents; prostate enlargement with increased risk of cancer; sexual dysfunction; loss of fertility; excessive and painful erections
- In females, loss of menstruation and fertility; increased libido; early puberty in adolescents; permanent enlargement of external genitalia; thickening of uterine lining; fetal damage, if pregnant

Muscles, Bones, and Connective Tissues
- Weight gain; altered body composition; increased susceptibility to injury with delayed recovery times; cramps; tremors; seizurelike movements; injury at injection site
- In adolescents, failure to grow to normal height

Other
- Fatigue; edema; increased risk of liver and uterine cancer; sleep, breathing disorders

Thinkstock Images/Getty Images

however, is clearly damaging to the body. Don't consider using these products—just steer clear.

Steroid Alternative Supplements

Because of the clear danger and illegality of steroid hormones, many athletes, and particularly school-age athletes, have tried herbal or insect sterols hawked as "natural" alternatives to steroid drugs. The body cannot convert these products into human steroids, and they do not stimulate the body's own steroid production. These products may contain toxins, however. Remember: "natural" doesn't mean "harmless."

Prohormones

Steroid alternatives, such as the officially banned "andro" (**androstenedione**) and **DHEA,** produce unpredictable results. In males, steroid alternatives may have little or no effect. Any small contribution to the male body's testosterone would be slight, compared with the large amount produced by the testes.[25] For those seeking to increase testosterone, the chapter made clear that resistance exercise alone can do so. Females using steroid alternatives may experience a greater proportional blood level of testosterone along with increased estrogens. The effects can be problematic, however, because any gains in muscle strength are temporary but the ill effects from excess steroid hormones last a lifetime. Prohormone products may carry similar risks to those of steroid drugs (listed in Figure C10-1).

Recently, the Food and Drug Administration (FDA) sent letters to producers of dietary supplements warning that products containing androstenedione are considered to be adulterated and therefore are illegal to sell and that criminal penalties could result from continued sales. The National Collegiate Athletic Association, the National Football League, and the International Olympic Committee have banned the use of androstenedione and DHEA in competition. The American Academy of Pediatrics and many other medical professional groups have spoken out against the use of these and other "hormone replacement" substances.

Drugs Posing as Supplements

Some ergogenic aids sold as dietary supplements turn out to contain powerful drugs. A potent thyroid hormone known as TRIAC was recalled by the FDA for interfering with normal thyroid functioning, and causing heart attack and stroke.† Another is **THG,** a potentially harmful synthetic steroid. The FDA has reclassified both TRIAC and THG as drugs, but products containing them are still making their way into the hands of athletes. Such synthetic steroid derivatives, or "designer steroids," are designed to sneak steroid use past detection tests in athletic events. Although the FDA has banned these two, others are likely to crop up to take their place because the demand is strong and profits high.

†Two of the products containing TRIAC (triiodothyroacetic acid, or tiratricol) have the trade names BioPharm T-Cuts *and* Triax Metabolic Accelerator.

Also, a dietary supplement is not always what the label says it is. The product names in both Table C10-1, earlier, and in Table C10-2 may appear on labels, but the contents of the bottle may be something else entirely. It is not uncommon for an ergogenic supplement to be contaminated with steroid drugs or prescription stimulants. In one recent study, almost 19 percent of supplements sold to athletes worldwide were found to contain a steroid drug.[26] Anyone taking such a supplement faces serious health consequences, but an athlete risks being forever banned from competition. A recent study demonstrated that taking a creatine supplement contaminated with just 0.00005 percent of a steroid drug can produce a positive drug test.[27]

TABLE C10-2 Additional Substances Promoted as Ergogenic Aids

Dietary Supplement	Claims	Evidence	Risks
Arginine (an amino acid)	Increased muscle mass	Ineffective	Generally well tolerated; may be harmful to people with heart disease
Boron (trace mineral)	Increased muscle mass	Ineffective	No adverse effects reported with doses up to 10 mg/day; should be avoided by those with kidney disease or women with hormone-sensitive conditions
Casein (milk protein)	Increased muscle mass	As with all dietary protein, contributes to positive nitrogen balance	Well tolerated by many people; triggers allergic reaction in people with milk allergy
Ephedra (ephedrine, ma huang)	Weight loss; muscle enhancement; improved athletic performance	May increase feelings of nervous energy and alertness	Dry mouth, insomnia, nervousness, palpitation, and headache; blood pressure spikes; cardiac arrest; banned by FDA as an unreasonable risk to health
Coenzyme Q10 (carrier in the electron transport chain)	Enhanced exercise performance	Ineffective	Mild indigestion
Gamma-oryzanol (plant sterol)	Increased muscle mass; said to mimic anabolic steroids without side effects	Ineffective	No adverse effects reported with short-term use; no long-term safety studies
Ginseng (plant)	Enhanced exercise performance	Ineffective	No adverse effects reported with moderate doses; large doses may cause hypertension, nervousness, sleeplessness, acne, edema, headache, and diarrhea; those with diabetes should be aware of hypoglycemic effects; should be avoided by those at risk for estrogen-related cancers, those with blood-clotting issues, and pregnant or lactating women

TABLE C10-2 Additional Substances Promoted as Ergogenic Aids (continued)

Dietary Supplement	Claims	Evidence	Risks
Glycerol (a 3-carbon molecule that is part of triglycerides and phospholipids)	Improved hydration during exercise; regulation of body temperature during exercise; enhanced exercise performance	Inconsistent findings for improving hydration and regulating body temperature; ineffective for enhancing exercise performance	May cause nausea, headaches, and blurred vision; should be avoided by those with edema, congestive heart failure, kidney disease, hypertension, and other conditions that may be aggravated by fluid retention
Glycine (an amino acid)	Precursor of creatine	Ineffective	Potential amino acid imbalances
Guarana	Enhanced speed and endurance, mental, and sexual functions	Ineffective	High doses may stress the heart and cause panic attacks
HMB (beta-hydroxy-beta-methylbutyrate) (a metabolite of the branched-chain amino acid leucine)	Increased muscle mass and strength	Inconsistent findings	No adverse effects with short-term use and doses up to 76 mg/kg of body weight
Pyruvate (a 3-carbon sugar)	Enhanced endurance	Ineffective	No long-term safety studies; digestive problems with short-term use (< 6 weeks)
Ribose (a 5-carbon sugar)	Increased ATP production and enhanced high-intensity exercise performance	Ineffective	Naturally generated in body; submitted to USDA to become a Generally Recognized As Safe food additive (pending)
Royal jelly (produced by bees)	Enhanced stamina and reduced fatigue	No studies on human beings to date	No adverse effects with doses up to 12 mg/day; should be avoided by those with a history of asthma or allergic reactions
Sodium bicarbonate (baking soda)	Buffers muscle acid; delayed fatigue; enhanced power and strength	May buffer acid and delay muscle fatigue; more research is needed for definitive conclusions	Gastrointestinal distress including diarrhea, cramps, gas, and bloating; should be avoided by those on sodium-restricted diets
Yohimbe	Weight loss; stimulant effects	No evidence available	Kidney failure; seizures

Source: Data from A. S. Fragakis and C. Thomson, The Health Professional's Guide to Popular Dietary Supplements, *3rd ed. (Chicago: American Dietetic Association, 2007); M. Dunford and M. Smith, Dietary supplements and ergogenic aids, in* Sports Nutrition: A Practice Manual for Professionals, *4th ed., M. Dunford, ed. (Chicago: American Dietetic Association, 2006), pp. 116–141.*

CONCLUSION

The general scientific response to ergogenic claims is "let the buyer beware." In a survey of advertisements in a dozen popular health and body-building magazines, researchers identified over 300 products containing 235 different ingredients advertised as beneficial, mostly for muscle growth. None had been scientifically shown to be effective.

Athletes like Paige who fall for the promises of better performance through supplements are taking a gamble with their money, their health, or both. They abandon one product after another when the placebo effect wears thin and the promised miracles fail to materialize. DJ, who takes the scientific approach reflected in this Controversy, faces a problem: how does she tell Paige about the hoaxes and still preserve their friendship?

Explaining to someone that a long-held belief is not true involves a risk: the person often becomes angry with the one telling the truth, rather than with the source of the misinformation. To avoid this painful outcome, DJ decides to mention only the supplements in Paige's routine that are most likely to cause harm—the chromium picolinate, the overdoses of caffeine, and the hormone replacers. As for the meal replacers, protein powders, and other supplements, they are probably just a waste of money, and DJ decides to keep quiet. Perhaps they may serve as harmless superstitions.

As for those occasions when Paige believes her performance was boosted by a new concoction, DJ understands that the effect probably came from the power of the mind over the body—the placebo effect. Don't discount that power, by the way, for it is formidable.[28] You don't have to rely on unproven supplements for an extra edge because you already have a real one—your mind. And you can use the extra money you save to buy a great pair of running shoes—perhaps on a Wednesday?

11

Diet and Health

© Zurbaran Galeria/SuperStock

DO YOU EVER . . .

- Wish that your diet could strengthen your immune system?
- Wonder whether your food choices may be damaging your heart?
- Use herbs or alternative medicine to improve your health?
- Choose "natural" foods without additives to avoid developing cancer?

Keep reading . . .

Learning Objectives

To find learning objective topics in this chapter, look for text headings with a corresponding "LO" number above the heading. After completing this chapter, you should be able to accomplish the following:

LO 11.1 Describe relationships between immunity and nutrition, and explain how malnutrition and infection worsen each other.

LO 11.2 Compare and contrast the progression and the symptoms of heart disease in men and in women.

LO 11.3 Describe what dietary and genetic factors may affect CVD risks and why higher LDL levels are a health concern.

LO 11.4 Develop a general eating plan for a person with prehypertension.

LO 11.5 Speculate about possible mechanisms by which a diet high in red meat might increase the risk of breast cancer or colorectal cancer.

LO 11.6 Develop a healthy eating plan that reduces the intake of *trans* fats and saturated fats but maintains sufficient intakes of essential nutrients.

LO 11.7 Describe some recent advances in nutritional genomics with regard to the health of the body through life.

Can your diet affect your risk of developing a disease? The answer to this question depends on the disease. Two main kinds of diseases afflict people around the world: **infectious diseases** and **chronic diseases.*** Infectious diseases such as tuberculosis, smallpox, influenza, and polio have been major killers of humankind since before the dawn of history. In any society not well defended against them, infectious diseases can cut life so short that the average person dies at 20, 30, or 40 years of age.

With the advent of vaccines and antibiotics, people in developed countries had become complacent about infectious diseases—until recently. Scientists now warn of growing infectious threats: the possibility of the rapid global spread of new and emerging human diseases, such as the current H1N1 virus, originally called "swine flu," and a rising death toll from once-conquered diseases, such as tuberculosis and foodborne infections that have become resistant to antibiotic drugs.[1†] While scientists work to develop new controls for these perils, government health agencies hasten to strengthen emergency response systems and to protect our food and water supplies.

Individuals can take steps to protect themselves, too. Each of us encounters millions of microbes each day, and some of these can cause diseases. Although nutrition cannot directly prevent or cure infectious diseases, it can strengthen or weaken your body's defenses against them.[2] One warning: many "immune-strengthening" foods, dietary supplements, and herbs are hoaxes. For healthy, well-fed people, supplements cannot trigger extra immune power to fend off dangerous infections.

In the United States and Canada, chronic diseases far outrank infections as the leading causes of death and illness.[3] Examples are heart disease, cancer, and diabetes, as Figure 11-1 shows. The longer a person dodges life's other perils, the more likely that these diseases will take their toll.

Chronic diseases do not arise from a straightforward cause such as infection, but from a mixture of factors in three areas: genetic inheritance, prior or current diseases such as obesity or hypertension, and lifestyle choices. The first two, inherited susceptibility and disease states, people cannot control. People control daily life choices directly, however, and these can often prevent or delay the onset of certain diseases. Young people choose whether to nourish their bodies well, to smoke, to exercise, or to abuse alcohol, and these choices are potent determinants of disease risks later on.

infectious diseases diseases that are caused by bacteria, viruses, parasites, and other microbes and can be transmitted from one person to another through air, water, or food; by contact; or through vector organisms such as mosquitoes and fleas.

chronic diseases diseases characterized by slow progression, long duration, and degeneration of body organs due in part to such personal lifestyle elements as poor food choices, smoking, alcohol use, and lack of physical activity. Also called *lifestyle diseases*, *degenerative diseases*, or the *diseases of old age*.

*The term *disease* is also used to refer to conditions such as birth defects, alcoholism, obesity, and mental disorders.
†Reference notes are found in Appendix F.

FIGURE 11-1 **The Ten Leading Causes of Death in the United States**[a]

The causes identified with the red bars are related to nutrition; those with green bars are alcohol related.

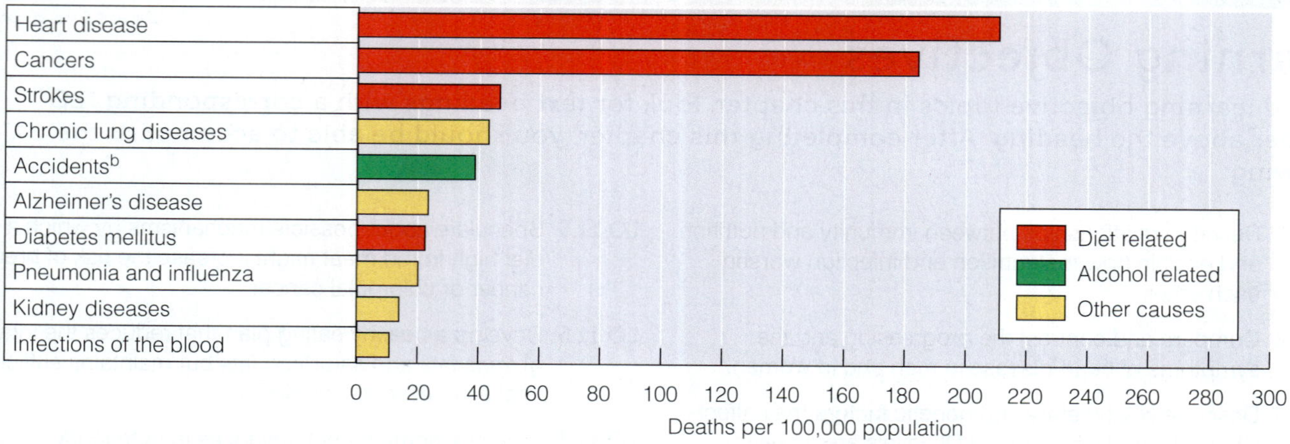

[a]*Rates are age adjusted to allow relative comparisons of mortality among groups and over time.*

[b]*Motor vehicle and other accidents are the leading cause of death among people aged 15–24, followed by homicide, suicide, cancer, and heart disease. Alcohol contributes to about half of all accident fatalities.*

Source: Data from National Center for Health Statistics, 2009.

As people age, their bodies accumulate the effects of a lifetime of choices, and in the later years these impacts can make the difference between a life of health or one of chronic disability. This chapter begins with a discussion of nutrition's impact on the immune system, with the remainder devoted to the diet-related factors that can advance or inhibit the development of chronic diseases.

If there is any deficiency in food or exercise the body will fall sick.
—Hippocrates, a Greek physician, c. 400 B.C.

LO 11.1

Nutrition and Immunity

Without your awareness, your immune system continuously stands guard against thousands of attacks mounted against you by microorganisms and cancer cells. If your immune system falters, you become vulnerable to disease-causing agents, and disease invariably follows.

A well-nourished immune system provides the best protection for these reasons:

- Deficient intakes of many vitamins and minerals are associated with impaired disease resistance, as are some excessive intakes.[4]
- Immune tissues are among the first to be impaired in the course of a nutrient deficiency or toxicity.
- Some deficiencies are more immediately harmful to immunity than others; the speed of the impact is affected by whether another nutrient can perform some of the metabolic tasks of the missing nutrient, how severe the deficiency is, whether an infection has already taken hold, and the person's age.
- Once a person becomes malnourished, malnutrition often worsens disease, which, in turn, worsens malnutrition. A destructive cycle often begins when impaired immunity opens the way for disease; then disease impairs food assimilation, and nutrition status suffers further. Drugs become necessary, and many of them impair nutrition status (see Chapter 14's Controversy). Other treatments, such as surgery or radiation, take a further toll. Thus, disease and poor nutrition together form a downward spiral that must be broken for recovery to occur (see Figure 11-2).

FIGURE 11-2 Malnutrition and Disease

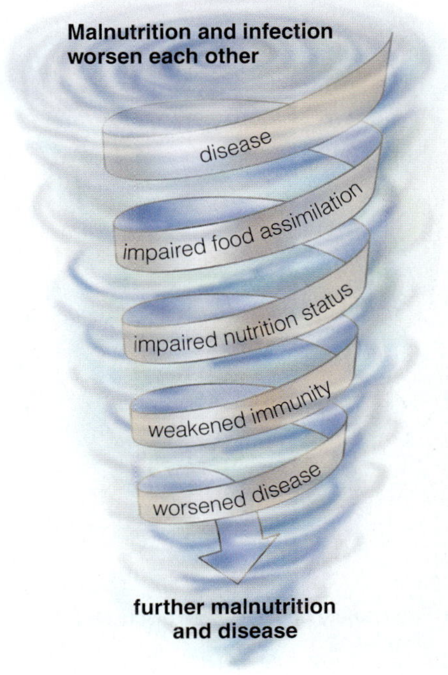

- Drug–nutrient interactions are discussed in Controversy 14.

People who restrict their food intakes, whether because of lack of appetite, eating disorders, or desire for weight loss, are more likely than others to be caught in this downward spiral of malnutrition and weakened immunity. Also susceptible are those who are one or more of the following: very young or old, poor, hospitalized, or malnourished. Rates of sickness and death increase dramatically when medical tests of a malnourished person indicate weakened immunity.

In protein-energy malnutrition (PEM), indispensable tissues and cells of the immune system dwindle in size and number, leaving the whole body vulnerable to infection. Table 11-1 shows PEM's effects on body defenses. The skin and body linings, the first line of defense against infections, become thinner because their connective tissue is broken down, allowing agents of disease easy access to body tissues. For example, a healthy digestive system normally musters a formidable defense—its linings act as a barrier and are heavily laced with immune tissues, cells, and antibodies that intercept intruders. When PEM sets in, the linings, immune cells, and antibodies of the digestive tract diminish, leaving easy passage for infectious agents.

A deficiency or a toxicity of just a single nutrient can seriously weaken immune defenses. For example, vitamin A deficiency weakens the body's skin and membranous linings. Vitamin C deficiency robs white blood cells of their killing power. Too little vitamin E may impair immunity in several ways, especially among the aged. Both deficient and excessive zinc intakes impair immunity by reducing the number of effective white blood cells in the first case and impairing the immune response in the second.[5] Clearly, a well-balanced diet is the cornerstone that supports immune system defenses.

Did You Know?

The term *immunonutrition* is used to describe the influence of nutrients on the functioning of the immune system, especially regarding medical nutrition therapies.

- Deficiencies (↓) and toxicities (↑) known to impair immunity:
  - *Protein* (↓).
  - *Energy* (↓).
  - *Vitamin A* (↓).
  - *Vitamin E* (↓).
  - *Vitamin D* (↓).
  - *Vitamin C* (↓).
  - *B vitamins* (↓).
  - *Folate* (↓).
  - *Iron* (↓↑).
  - *Zinc* (↓↑).
  - *Copper* (↓).
  - *Magnesium* (↓).
  - *Selenium* (↓).

TABLE 11-1 Effects of Protein-Energy Malnutrition (PEM) on the Body's Defense Systems

System Component	Effects of PEM
Skin	Skin becomes thinner, with less connective tissue to serve as a barrier for protection of underlying tissues; skin sensitivity reaction to antigens is delayed.
Digestive tract membrane and other body linings	Antibody secretions and immune cell numbers are reduced.
Lymph tissues	Immune system organs[a] are reduced in size; cells of immune defense are depleted.
General response	Invader kill time is prolonged; circulating immune cells are reduced; immune response is impaired.

[a] *Thymus gland, lymph nodes, and spleen.*

Malnutrition can result not only from a lack of available food but also from diseases, such as **AIDS** and cancer, and their treatments. These depress the appetite and speed up metabolism, causing a wasting away of the body's tissues similar to that seen in the last stages of starvation—the body uses its fat and protein reserves for survival. In people with AIDS, wasting or nutrient deficiencies can shorten survival, making medical nutrition therapy a critical need.[6] Nutrients cannot cure AIDS or cancer, of course, but an adequate diet may improve responses to drugs, shorten hospital stays, promote independence, and improve the quality of life. Physical activity that strengthens muscles may also help hold wasting to a minimum. In addition, food safety is paramount because common food bacteria and viruses can easily overwhelm a compromised immune system.

• Food-safety principles are discussed in Chapter 12.

To repeat: a *diet* of foods that supplies adequate nutrients ensures the proper functioning of the immune system, but extra daily doses of nutrients, herbs, or other substances do not enhance it. Furthermore, toxic doses clearly diminish it.

KEY POINT Adequate nutrition is a key component in maintaining a healthy immune system to defend against infectious diseases. Both deficient and excessive nutrients can harm the immune system.

The Concept of Risk Factors

In contrast to the infectious diseases, each of which has a distinct microbial cause such as a bacterium or virus, the chronic diseases have suspected contributors known as **risk factors.** Risk factors show a correlation with a disease—that is, they often occur together with the disease—and although they are candidates for causes, they have not yet been voted in or out. We can say with certainty that a virus causes influenza, but we cannot name the cause of heart disease with such confidence.

An analogy may help clarify the concept of risk factors. A risk factor is like a person who is often seen lurking around the scene of a particular type of crime, say, arson. The police may suspect that person of setting fires, but it may very well be that another, sneakier individual who goes unnoticed is actually pouring the fuel and lighting the match. The evidence against the known suspect is only circumstantial. The police can be sure of guilt only when they observe the criminal in the act. Risk factors have not yet been caught in the act of causing diseases.

AIDS acquired immune deficiency syndrome; caused by infection with human immunodeficiency virus (HIV), which is transmitted primarily by sexual contact, contact with infected blood, needles shared among drug users, or fluids transferred from an infected mother to her fetus or infant.

risk factors factors known to be related to (or correlated with) diseases but not proved to be causal.

hypertension higher than normal blood pressure.

TABLE 11-2 Risk Factors and Chronic Diseases

	Cancers	Hypertension	Diabetes (type 2)	Atherosclerosis	Obesity	Stroke
Dietary Risk Factors						
Diets high in added sugars					✓	
Diets high in salty or pickled foods	✓	✓				
Diets high in saturated and/or *trans* fat	✓		✓	✓	✓	✓
Diets low in fruits, vegetables, and other foods rich in fiber and phytochemicals	✓		✓	✓	✓	✓
Diets low in vitamins and/or minerals	✓	✓		✓		
Excessive alcohol intake	✓	✓		✓	✓	✓
Other Risk Factors						
Age	✓	✓	✓	✓		✓
Environmental contaminants	✓					
Genetics	✓	✓	✓	✓	✓	✓
Sedentary lifestyle	✓	✓	✓	✓	✓	✓
Smoking and tobacco use	✓	✓		✓		✓
Stress		✓		✓		✓

Cause Versus Increased Risk You may notice a philosophical shift in this chapter from previous chapters. There, we could say "a deficiency of nutrient X causes disease Y." Here, we only cite theories and discuss research that illuminates current thinking. We can say with certainty, for example, that "a diet lacking vitamin C causes scurvy," but to say that a low-fiber diet that lacks vegetables causes cancer would be inaccurate.

Among disease risk factors are genetic, environmental, behavioral, and social factors that tend to occur in clusters and interact with each other. Food behaviors often underlie many risk factors. Choosing to eat a diet too high in saturated fat, salt, and calories, for example, is choosing to risk becoming obese and contracting atherosclerosis, type 2 diabetes, cancer, **hypertension,** or other diseases.[7] Table 11-2 identifies diet-related behaviors and other risk factors associated with chronic diseases. Figure 11-3 demonstrates that in many cases, one disease or condition intensifies the risk of another.

The exact contribution diet makes to each disease is hard to estimate. Many experts believe that diet accounts for about a third of all cases of coronary heart disease. The links between diet and cancer incidence are harder to pin down because each of cancer's many forms associates with different dietary factors.

Estimating Your Risks Some choices, such as avoiding tobacco, are important to everyone's health. Other choices, such as some relating to diet, are more important for people who are genetically predisposed to certain diseases. To pinpoint your own areas of concern, you can search your family's medical history for diseases common to your forebears. Any condition that shows up in several close blood relatives may be a special concern for you (Table 11-3 lists some of these).‡ Also, after your next physical examination, find out which test results are out of line. The combination of family medical history and laboratory test results is a powerful predictor of disease.

FIGURE 11-3 Interrelationships Among Chronic Diseases

The arrows indicate which chronic diseases can lead to others. The diseases highlighted in blue define the metabolic syndrome. Note that obesity can lead to diabetes, atherosclerosis, and hypertension, its coconspirators in metabolic syndrome; it also increases the risk of some types of cancer.

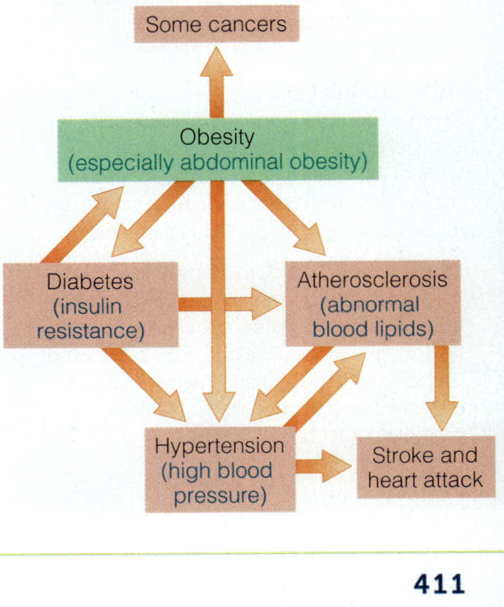

‡The U.S. Surgeon General offers a free online tool, "My Family Health Portrait," to help organize family health information. It is available over the Internet at www.hhs.gov/family history/order.html.

TABLE 11-3 **Family Medical History**

These conditions in parents, grandparents, or siblings, especially occurring early in life, may raise a warning flag for you:

Alcoholism
Cancer
Diabetes
Heart and artery diseases
Hypertension
Liver disease (cirrhosis)
Osteoporosis

Accepting that everyone has certain unchangeable "givens," an effective strategy is to look to the risk factors that can be changed and choose the most influential among them. For example, a person whose parents, grandparents, or other close blood relatives suffered from diabetes and heart disease is urgently advised to avoid becoming obese and not to smoke. Even people without a family history of diseases can develop them; the guidelines presented in this chapter can benefit most people.

KEY POINT The same diet and lifestyle risk factors may contribute to several chronic diseases. A person's family history and laboratory test results can reveal strategies for disease prevention.

LO 11.2, 11.3

Cardiovascular Diseases

In the United States today, 80 million men and women suffer some form of disease of the heart and blood vessels, collectively known as **cardiovascular disease (CVD).** Cardiovascular disease claims the lives of nearly 1 million people each year in the United States (see Figure 11-4).[§8] These numbers, while unacceptably high, represent a substantial improvement over the numbers of a half-century ago.[9] The margin on page 413 lists the symptoms of the major CVD killers, heart attack and stroke. One reason heart disease is so deadly is that the heart is one of the least regenerative organs in the body. When cardiac muscle is lost—for example, by way of a heart attack—the heart heals mainly by forming scar tissue. As a result, the contractile function of the heart declines, and heart failure often follows.[10]

A treacherous myth is that heart disease is a man's disease. In fact, over 41 million U.S. women have CVD, and the number is increasing.[11] Men still suffer heart attacks more often and earlier in life than women do, but the gap is narrowing. In

[§]Deaths from CVD in the United States include 52 percent from coronary heart disease, 17 percent from stroke, 6 percent from hypertension, 4 percent from congestive heart failure, 4 percent from other artery diseases, and the remainder from rheumatic fever/heart disease, congenital cardiovascular defects, and other causes.

Did You Know?

A bystander can recognize a stroke by asking three simple questions that begin with the letters **S T R** (the first three letters of the word *stroke*):

- **S** Ask the person to **SMILE**.
- **T** Ask the person to **TALK** and speak a simple sentence such as "It is sunny out today."
- **R** Ask the person to **RAISE BOTH ARMS.**

If the person has trouble with *ANY ONE* of these tasks, call 911 immediately and describe the symptoms to the dispatcher.

- Another sign of a stroke: Ask the individual to stick out his or her tongue. If the tongue is "crooked," if it goes to one side or the other, this is also an indicator of stroke.

FIGURE 11-4 **U.S. Heart Disease Death Rates[a]**

This map depicts the distribution of heart disease risk, adjusted for population density.

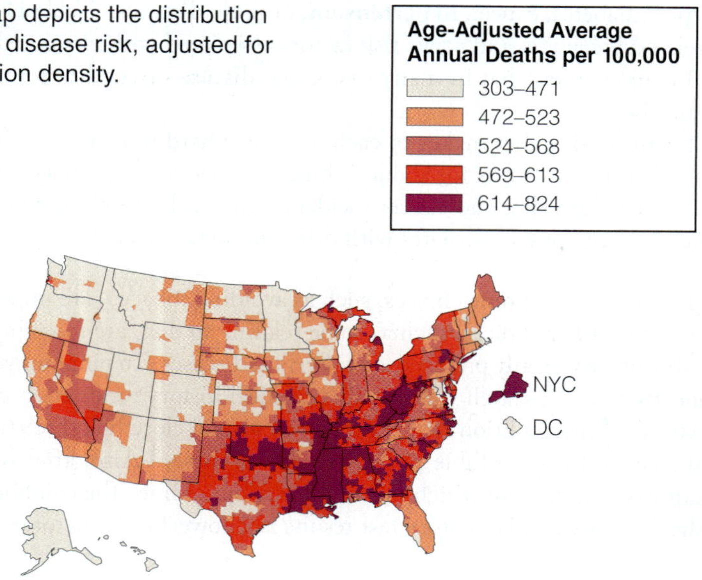

[a]*Adults ages 35 years and older.*

Source: Centers for Disease Control and Prevention, www.cdc.gov

cardiovascular disease (CVD) a general term for all diseases of the heart and blood vessels. Atherosclerosis is the main cause of CVD. When the arteries that carry blood to the heart muscle become blocked, the heart suffers damage known as *coronary heart disease (CHD)*. Also defined in Chapter 5.

atherosclerosis (ath-er-oh-scler-OH-sis) the most common form of cardiovascular disease; characterized by plaques along the inner walls of the arteries (*scleros* means "hard"; *osis* means "too much"). The term *arteriosclerosis* is often used to mean the same thing.

plaques (PLACKS) mounds of lipid material mixed with smooth muscle cells and calcium that develop in the artery walls in atherosclerosis (*placken* means "patch"). The same word is also used to describe the accumulation of a different kind of deposits on teeth, which promote dental caries.

fact, in all its forms CVD kills more U.S. women, especially those who are past menopause, than any other cause.[12] Importantly, women may or may not experience classic symptoms such as chest discomfort (see the margin). Learning to recognize the symptoms can be lifesaving because the sooner medical help arrives, the more likely is the person's recovery.

How can you minimize your risks of heart attack and stroke? Or, more positively, what steps can you take to help maintain your heart health and vigor throughout life? Many people have done so by quitting smoking or not starting. They have also changed their diets, consuming less saturated fat, less *trans* fat, less cholesterol, more vegetables, more fruits, and more whole grains.[13] In contrast, many people are consuming too many calories, too much sodium, and too few fruits and vegetables; obtaining regular exercise presents a difficult stumbling block for most people.

- Minutes and seconds count when heart attack strikes. Should any of these signs occur, call for emergency medical help; in most areas, dial 911.

In men and women:

- *Chest discomfort. An uncomfortable pressure, squeezing, fullness, or pain in the center of the chest that lasts more than a few minutes or that goes away and comes back.*
- *Upper body discomfort. Pain or discomfort in one or both arms, the back, neck, jaw, or stomach.*
- *Shortness of breath, accompanying or preceding chest discomfort.*
- *Other signs: Cold sweat, nausea, or lightheadedness.*

Women may instead experience:

- *Breathlessness.*
- *Cold sweat.*
- *Dizziness.*
- *Nausea.*
- *Neck, shoulder, or abdominal pain.*
- *Unusual fatigue.*
- *Vomiting.*
- *Weakness.*

Atherosclerosis

At the root of most forms of CVD is **atherosclerosis.** Atherosclerosis is the common form of hardening of the arteries. No one is free of all signs of atherosclerosis. The question is not whether you are developing it, but how far advanced it is and what you can do to retard or reverse it. Atherosclerosis usually begins with the accumulation of soft, fatty streaks along the inner walls of the arteries, especially at branch points. These gradually enlarge and become hardened fibrous **plaques** that damage artery walls and make them inelastic, narrowing the passageway for blood to travel through them (see Figure 11-5). Most people have well-developed plaques by the time they reach age 30.[14]

How Plaques Form What causes the plaques to form? A diet high in saturated fat is a major contributor to the development of plaques and the progression of atherosclerosis.[15] But atherosclerosis is much more than the simple accumulation of lipids within

FIGURE 11-5 ANIMATED!
The Formation of Plaques in Atherosclerosis

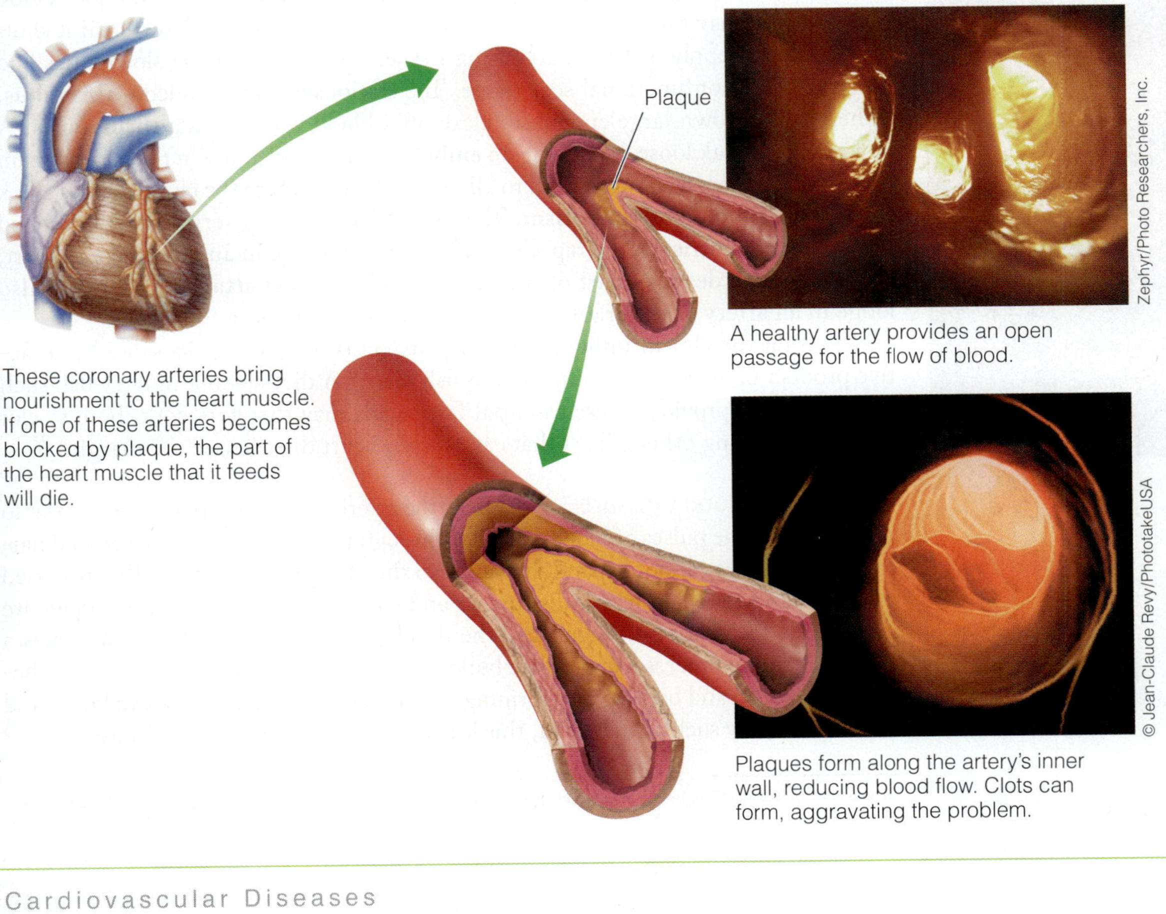

These coronary arteries bring nourishment to the heart muscle. If one of these arteries becomes blocked by plaque, the part of the heart muscle that it feeds will die.

A healthy artery provides an open passage for the flow of blood.

Plaques form along the artery's inner wall, reducing blood flow. Clots can form, aggravating the problem.

the artery wall—it is a complex response of the artery to tissue damage and **inflammation.**[16] Inflammation plays a central role in all stages of atherosclerosis, and a blood test for compounds released during inflammation can help identify people at high or very high risk of cardiovascular disease before a life-threatening event occurs.[17]**

The damage may begin from a number of factors interacting with cells that line the arteries: high LDL cholesterol, hypertension, diabetes, toxins from cigarette smoking, elevated blood concentrations of the amino acid homocysteine, or certain viral or bacterial infections.[18] Such damage produces inflammation that triggers the immune system to send white blood cells to the site to try to repair the damage. Soon, particles of LDL cholesterol become trapped in the blood vessel walls, and these become oxidized by the abundant free radicals produced during inflammation. The white blood cells—**macrophages**—flood the scene to scavenge and remove the oxidized LDL, but to no avail. As the macrophages become engorged with oxidized LDL, they become known as foam cells, which themselves become triggers of oxidation and inflammation that attract more immune scavengers to the scene. Muscle cells of the arterial wall proliferate in an attempt to heal the damage, but they mix with the foam cells to form hardened areas of plaque. Mineralization increases hardening of the plaques. The process is repeated until many inner artery walls become virtually covered with disfiguring plaques.

Plaque Rupture Once plaques have formed, a sudden spasm of the artery wall or surge in blood pressure can tear away part of the fibrous coat covering a plaque, causing it to rupture. Unstable plaques with a thin fibrous layer over a large lipid core are most vulnerable to rupture.[19] When a plaque ruptures, the body responds to the damage as an injury—by clotting the blood.

CONCEPT LINK 11-1

The process of blood clotting was described in Chapter 6 (page 202).

Plaques and Blood Clots Small, cell-like bodies in the blood, known as **platelets,** normally cause clots to form when they encounter injuries in blood vessels. Clots form and dissolve in the blood all the time, and when these processes are balanced, the clots do no harm. That balance is disturbed in atherosclerosis, however. Arterial damage, plaques in the arteries, and inflammation all favor the formation of blood clots.

Abnormal blood clotting can trigger life-threatening events. For example, a clot, once formed, may remain attached to a plaque in an artery and grow until it shuts off the blood supply to the surrounding tissue. The starved tissue slowly dies and is replaced by nonfunctional scar tissue. The stationary clot is called a **thrombus.** When it has grown large enough to close off a blood vessel, it is a **thrombosis.** A clot can also break loose, becoming an **embolus,** and travel along in the bloodstream until it reaches an artery too small to allow its passage. There the clot becomes stuck and is referred to as an **embolism.** The tissues fed by this artery, suddenly robbed of oxygen and nutrients, die rapidly. Such a clot can lodge in an artery of the heart, causing sudden death of part of the heart muscle, a **heart attack.** A clot may also lodge in an artery of the brain, killing a portion of brain tissue, a **stroke.**

Opposing the clot-forming actions of platelets is one of the eicosanoids, an active product of an omega-3 fatty acid in fish oils.[20] A diet lacking in fatty fish such as salmon that provides these essential fatty acids may therefore contribute to clot formation, among other effects that can worsen heart disease (see the margin).[21]

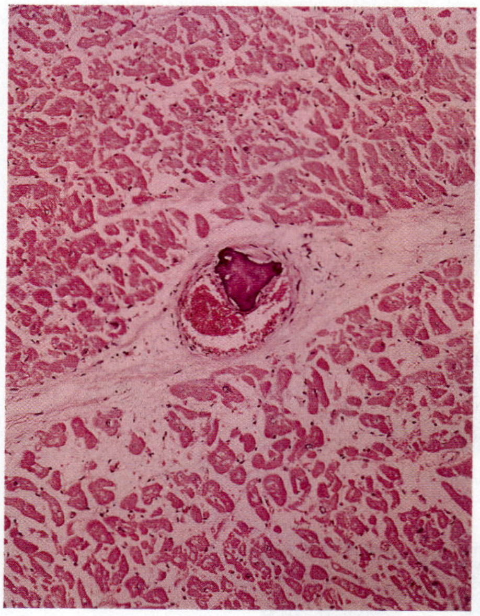

SPL/Photo Researchers, Inc.

A blood clot in an artery, such as this fatal heart embolism, blocks the blood flow to tissues fed by that artery.

Plaques and Blood Pressure Normally, the arteries expand with each heartbeat to accommodate the pulses of blood that flow through them. Arteries hardened and narrowed by plaques cannot expand, however, so the blood pressure rises. The increased pressure damages the artery walls further and strains the heart. Because plaques are more likely to form at damage sites, the development of atherosclerosis becomes a self-accelerating process. As pressure builds up in an artery, the arterial wall may become weakened and balloon out, forming an **aneurysm.** An aneurysm can burst, and in a major artery such as the **aorta,** this leads to massive bleeding and death.

- Eicosanoids help to regulate these functions important in heart disease:
  - *Blood pressure.*
  - *Blood clot formation.*
  - *Blood vessel contractions.*

**Compounds released during inflammation include c-reactive protein, lipoprotein-associated phospholipase A(2), adiponectin, and interleukin-6.

On many occasions, heart attacks and strokes occur with no apparent blockage. An artery may go into spasms, restricting or cutting off the blood supply to a portion of the heart muscle or brain. Much research today is devoted to finding out what causes plaques to form, what causes arteries to go into spasms, what governs the activities of platelets, and why the body allows clots to form unopposed by clot-dissolving cleanup activity.

CONCEPT LINK 11-2

Eicosanoids and omega-3 fatty acids were topics of Chapter 5, pages 166–168.

KEY POINT Plaques of atherosclerosis trigger hypertension and abnormal blood clotting, leading to heart attacks or strokes.

Risk Factors for CVD

Efforts to fight atherosclerosis and resulting diseases have led to discoveries about their prevention. An expert panel of the National Cholesterol Education Program defined major heart disease risk factors already listed briefly in Chapter 5; they are presented in full in Table 11-4. Many of the same factors also predict the occurrence of stroke. All people reaching middle age exhibit at least one of these factors (middle age is a risk factor), and many people have several factors, silently increasing their risk.[22]

It befits a nutrition book to focus on dietary strategies, but Table 11-4 shows that diet is not the only, and perhaps not even the most important, factor in the development of heart disease or stroke. Age, gender, genetic inheritance, cigarette smoking, certain diseases, and physical inactivity predict their development as well. The next few sections address these factors; discussions of diet and physical activity for CVD prevention follow.

Age, Gender, and Genetic Inheritance Three of the major risk factors for CVD cannot be modified by lifestyle choices: age, gender, and genes. The increasing risk associated with growing older reflects the steady progression of atherosclerosis in most people as they age.[23]

Gender alters risks at many life stages. In men, aging becomes a significant risk factor for heart disease at age 45 years or older; in women, the risk increases after age 55. Up to age 45, a woman's risk of developing heart disease is lower than a man's of the same age. Women in the menopause years suddenly face heart disease risks of 2 or 3 times their previous rates. Young women can easily become complacent

TABLE 11-4 Major Risk Factors for Heart Disease

See Figure 11-7 for standards by which to judge blood lipids, obesity, and blood pressure.

Risk factors that cannot be modified:
- Increasing age
- Male gender
- Genetic inheritance

Risk factors that can be modified:
- High blood LDL cholesterol
- Low blood HDL cholesterol
- High blood pressure (hypertension)
- Diabetes
- Obesity (especially central obesity)
- Physical inactivity
- Cigarette smoking
- An "atherogenic" diet (high in saturated fats including *trans* fats and low in vegetables, fruits, and whole grains)

Note: Risk factors highlighted in color have relationships with diet.

Source: Expert Panel on Detection, Evaluation, and Treatment of High Blood Cholesterol in Adults (Adult Treatment Panel III), Third Report of the National Cholesterol Education Program (NCEP), *NIH publication no. 02-5215 (Bethesda, Md.: National Heart, Lung, and Blood Institute, 2002), pp. II-15–II-20.*

inflammation (in-flam-MAY-shun) part of the body's immune defense against injury, infection, or allergens, marked by increased blood flow, release of chemical toxins, and attraction of white blood cells to the affected area (from the Latin *inflammare,* meaning "to flame within"). Also defined in Chapter 5.

macrophages (MACK-roh-fah-jez) large scavenger cells of the immune system that engulf debris and remove it (*macro* means "large"; *phagein* means "to eat"). Also defined in Chapter 3.

platelets tiny cell-like fragments in the blood, important in blood clot formation (*platelet* means "little plate").

thrombus a stationary blood clot.

thrombosis a thrombus that has grown enough to close off a blood vessel. A *coronary thrombosis* closes off a vessel that feeds the heart muscle. A *cerebral thrombosis* closes off a vessel that feeds the brain (*coronary* means "crowning" [the heart]; *thrombo* means "clot"; the cerebrum is part of the brain).

embolus (EM-boh-luss) a thrombus that breaks loose and travels through the blood vessels (*embol* means "to insert").

embolism an embolus that causes sudden closure of a blood vessel.

heart attack the event in which the vessels that feed the heart muscle become closed off by an embolism, thrombus, or other cause with resulting sudden tissue death. A heart attack is also called a *myocardial infarction* (*myo* means "muscle"; *cardial* means "tissue death").

stroke the sudden shutting off of the blood flow to the brain by a thrombus, embolism, or the bursting of a vessel (hemorrhage).

aneurysm (AN-you-rism) the ballooning out of an artery wall at a point that is weakened by deterioration.

aorta (ay-OR-tuh) the large, primary artery that conducts blood from the heart to the body's smaller arteries.

Did You Know?

The Centers for Disease Control and Prevention has developed WISEWOMAN projects nationwide to provide low-income women with resources needed to reduce their risks of CVD.

about heart disease because men die earlier of heart attacks than do women. It bears repeating that CVD kills more U.S. women than any other cause.[24]

As for genetic inheritance, early heart disease in immediate family members (siblings or parents) is a major risk factor for developing it. The more family members affected and the earlier the age at which they became ill, the greater the risk to the individual.[25]

These relationships suggest a genetic influence on CVD risk, but specific genetic links are still under investigation. In the realm of nutritional genomics and CVD risk, scientists are uncovering a vast interrelated network of influences, but the relationships among them are complex and likely to become more knotty before being untangled.[26] Many of these relationships center on blood lipids.

High LDL and Low HDL Cholesterol Low-density lipoprotein (LDL) cholesterol and high-density lipoprotein (HDL) cholesterol in the blood are strongly linked to a person's risk of developing atherosclerosis and heart disease. The higher the LDL, the greater the risk (see Figure 11-6). Conversely, higher HDL is protective. The first four columns of Figure 11-7 list blood lipid values considered normal and those that exceed a healthy level; the last two columns present values for body mass index (BMI) and blood pressure. For stroke risk, blood lipids may not be as influential as blood pressure and other factors.[27]

LDL cholesterol is made up of the most atherogenic lipoproteins. LDL carries cholesterol to the cells, including the cells that line the arteries, where it can build up as part of the plaques of atherosclerosis described earlier. The lower the LDL cholesterol and blood pressure, the slower the progression of atherosclerosis.[28] In clinical trials, lowering LDL greatly reduces the incidence of heart disease. By one estimate, for every percentage point drop in LDL cholesterol, the risk of heart disease falls proportionately. For this reason, the National Heart, Lung, and Blood Institute urges those at high risk for heart disease to lower blood LDL cholesterol and to use medication if need be to lower it.

High-density lipoproteins (HDL) also carry cholesterol, but they carry it away from the cells to the liver for recycling to other uses or for disposal. Elevated HDL indicates a *reduced* risk of atherosclerosis and heart attack. For this reason, heart disease risk assessment inventories, such as the one in Figure 11-8, give extra credit for having a high HDL value.

FIGURE 11-6 **LDL, HDL, and Risk of Heart Disease**

A blood lipid profile with low HDL (<40 mg/dL) and high LDL (≥160 mg/dL) elevates risk.

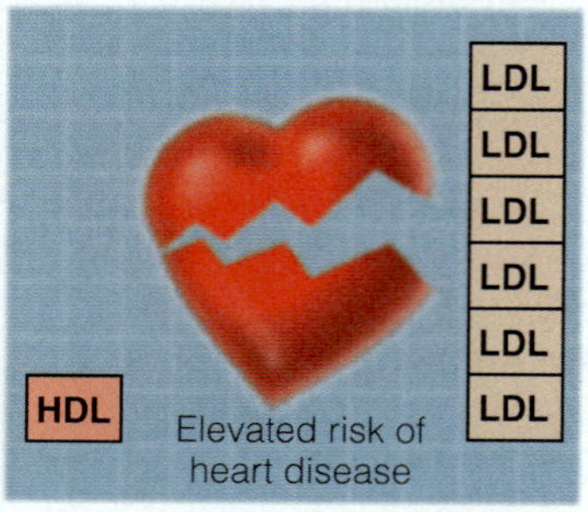

The opposite, high HDL (≥60 mg/dL) and low LDL (<100 mg/dL) lowers risk.

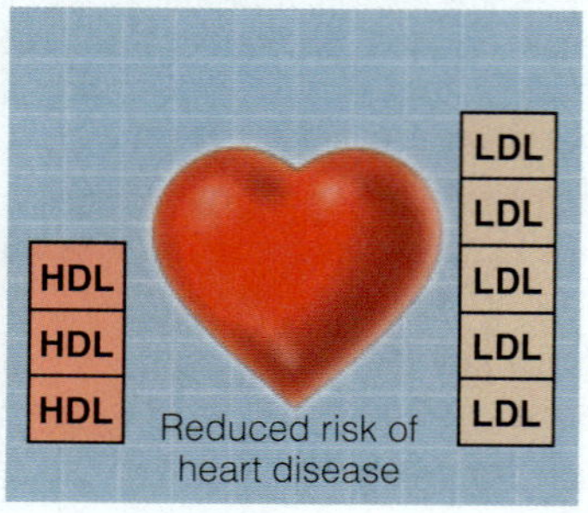

FIGURE 11-7 **Adult Standards for Blood Lipids, Body Mass Index (BMI), and Blood Pressure**

	Total blood cholesterol (mg/dL)	LDL cholesterol (mg/dL)	HDL cholesterol (mg/dL)	Triglycerides, fasting (mg/dL)	Body mass index (BMI)[a]	Blood pressure systolic / diastolic (mm Hg)
Unhealthy	≥240	160–189[b]	<40	200–499[c]	≥30	≥140 / ≥90
Borderline	200–239	130–159[d]	59–40	150–199	25–29.9	120/80–139/89[e]
Healthy	<200	<100[f]	≥60	<150	18.5–24.9	<120 / <80

[a] *Body Mass Index (BMI) was defined in Chapter 9; BMI standards are found on the inside back cover.*
[b] *>190 mg/dL LDL indicates a very high risk.*
[c] *>500 mg/dL triglycerides indicates a very high risk.*
[d] *LDL cholesterol-lowering medication may be needed at 130 mg/dL, depending on other risks.*
[e] *These values indicate prehypertension.*
[f] *100–129 mg/dL LDL indicates a near or above optimal level.*

FIGURE 11-8 How to Assess Your Heart Disease Risk

Do you know your heart disease risk score? This assessment estimates your 10-year risk for heart disease using charts from the Framingham Heart Study.* Be aware that a high score does not mean that you *will* develop heart disease, but it should warn you of the possibility and prompt you to consult a physician about your health. You will need to know your blood cholesterol (ideally, the average of at least two recent measurements) and blood pressure (ideally, the average of several recent measurements). With this information in hand, find yourself in the charts below and add the points for each risk factor.

Age (years)	Points: Men	Points: Women
20–34	−9	−7
35–39	−4	−3
40–44	0	0
45–49	3	3
50–54	6	6
55–59	8	8
60–64	10	10
65–69	11	12
70–74	12	14
75–79	13	16

HDL (mg/dL)	Points: Men	Points: Women
≥60	−1	−1
50–59	0	0
40–49	1	1
<40	2	2

Systolic Blood Pressure (mm Hg)	Points: Untreated Men	Untreated Women	Treated Men	Treated Women
<120	0	0	0	0
120–129	0	1	1	3
130–139	1	2	2	4
140–159	1	3	2	5
≥160	2	4	3	6

Total Cholesterol (mg/dL)	Points									
	Age 20–39		Age 40–49		Age 50–59		Age 60–69		Age 70–79	
	Men	Women	Men	Women	Men	Women	Men	Women	Men	Women
<160	0	0	0	0	0	0	0	0	0	0
160–199	4	4	3	3	2	2	1	1	0	1
200–239	7	8	5	6	3	4	1	2	0	1
240–279	9	11	6	8	4	5	2	3	1	2
≥280	11	13	8	10	5	7	3	4	1	2
Smoking (any cigarette smoking in the past month)										
Smoker	8	9	5	7	3	4	1	2	1	1
Nonsmoker	0	0	0	0	0	0	0	0	0	0

Scoring Your Heart Disease Risk

Add up your total points: _______ . Now find your total in the first column for your gender in the chart at the right and then look to the next column for your approximate risk of developing heart disease within the next 10 years. Depending on your risk category, the following strategies can help reduce your risk:

- *>20% = High risk.* Try to lower LDL using all lifestyle changes and, most likely, lipid-lowering medications as well.
- *10–20% = Moderate risk.* Try to lower LDL using all lifestyle changes and, possibly, lipid-lowering medications.
- *<10% = Low risk.* Maintain or initiate lifestyle choices that help prevent elevation of LDL to prevent future heart disease.

Men: Total Points	Men: Risk	Women: Total Points	Women: Risk
<0	<1%	<9	<1%
0–4	1%	9–12	1%
5–6	2%	13–14	2%
7	3%	15	3%
8	4%	16	4%
9	5%	17	5%
10	6%	18	6%
11	8%	19	8%
12	10%	20	11%
13	12%	21	14%
14	16%	22	17%
15	20%	23	22%
16	25%	24	27%
≥17	≥30%	≥25	≥30%

An electronic version of this assessment is available on the ATP III page of the National Heart, Lung, and Blood Institute's website (www.nhlbi.nih.gov/guidelines/cholesterol). Another risk inventory is available from the American Heart Association (www.americanheart.org).

Source: Adapted from Expert Panel on Detection, Evaluation, and Treatment of High Blood Cholesterol in Adults (Adult Treatment Panel III), Third Report of the National Cholesterol Education Program (NCEP), *NIH publication no. 02-5215 (Bethesda, Md.: National Heart, Lung, and Blood Institute, 2002), section III.*

- Reminder: Cholesterol is carried in several lipoproteins, chief among them LDL and HDL (see Chapter 5 for details). Remember them this way:
  - *LDL = Low-density lipoproteins = Less healthy.*
  - *HDL = High-density lipoproteins = Healthy.*

Any LDL cholesterol that remains in the blood after the body's cells take up the amount they need becomes vulnerable to oxidation. High blood levels of LDL cholesterol, especially oxidized LDL, can trigger a series of events that promote plaque development and contribute to plaque instability.[29] Oxidized LDL cholesterol stimulates production of atherogenic signaling molecules. These signaling molecules attract immune cells and allow them to adhere to, and penetrate, the innermost layer of the arterial wall. Within the arterial wall, these immune cells undergo transformation and replication into macrophages that form the lipid-rich foam cells characteristic of fatty streaks. Macrophages within the arterial wall perpetuate chronic inflammation by releasing proinflammatory particles that contribute to plaque rupture.[30] When plaque ruptures, it can cause a heart attack or stroke. In advanced atherosclerosis, a goal of treatment is to lower LDL cholesterol to stabilize existing plaques while slowing the development of new ones.

Twin Demons—Hypertension and Atherosclerosis Hypertension and atherosclerosis are twin demons that worsen CVD, and each worsens the other. Hypertension worsens atherosclerosis because a stiffened artery, already strained by each pulse of blood surging through it, is stressed further by high internal pressure. Injuries multiply, more plaques grow, and more weakened vessels become likely to burst and bleed.

Atherosclerosis also worsens hypertension. Since hardened arteries cannot expand, the heart's beats raise the blood pressure. Hardened arteries also fail to let blood flow freely through the kidneys, which control blood pressure. The kidneys sense the reduced flow of blood and respond as if the blood pressure were too low; they take steps to raise it further. The higher the blood pressure above normal, the greater the risk of heart attack or stroke. The relationship between hypertension and disease risk holds for men and women, young and old. A later section gives details about hypertension because it constitutes a major threat to health on its own.

Diabetes Diabetes, a major independent risk factor for all forms of CVD, substantially increases the risk of death from these causes.[31] In diabetes, atherosclerosis progresses rapidly, blocking blood vessels and diminishing circulation. For many people with diabetes, the risk of a future heart attack is roughly equal to that of a person with a confirmed diagnosis of heart disease—2 to 4 times as high as that of a person without diabetes.[32] When heart disease occurs in conjunction with diabetes, the condition is likely to be severe. In fact, any loss of control of blood glucose, even a transitory one, can be costly in terms of the condition of the arteries.[33] Few people with diabetes recognize that, left uncontrolled, diabetes holds a grave threat of all forms of CVD.

CONCEPT LINK 11-3

Diabetes and insulin resistance were explained in detail in Chapter 4 (page 127).

Physical Inactivity Without routine physical activity, muscles, including the muscles of the heart and arteries, weaken and reduce the heart's ability to meet everyday demands. Regular physical activity expands the heart's capacity to pump blood to the tissues with each beat, thereby reducing the number of heartbeats required and the heart's workload. The slower pulse of fit people reflects the heart's greater pumping capacity.

Walking is man's best medicine.

—Hippocrates

Physical activity also stimulates development of new arteries to nourish the heart muscle, which may be a factor in the excellent recovery seen in some heart attack victims who exercise. In addition, physical activity favors lean over fat tissue for a healthy body composition. If pursued on at least 5 days each week, 30 minutes or more of brisk walking can improve the odds against heart disease considerably. If you are pressed for time, 15 minutes of more vigorous physical activity, such as jogging, on at least 5 days a week can provide the same benefits. The Think Fitness feature offers suggestions for incorporating physical activity into your daily routine.

- Chapter 10 provided the *2008 Physical Activity Guidelines for Americans*.

Smoking Cigarette smoking powerfully increases the risk for CVD. The more a person smokes, the higher the CVD risk—a relationship that holds for both men and women. Smoking tobacco in all its forms damages the heart directly with toxins and

THINK FITNESS

Ways to Include Physical Activity in a Day

The benefits of physical activity are compelling, so why not tie up your athletic shoes, head out the door, and get going? Here are some ideas to get you started:

- Coach a sport.
- Garden.
- Hike, bike, or walk to nearby stores or to classes.
- Mow, trim, and rake by hand.
- Park a block from your destination and walk.
- Play a sport.
- Play with children.
- Take classes for credit in dancing, sports, conditioning, or swimming.
- Take the stairs, not the elevator.
- Walk a dog.
- Walk 10,000 steps per day. This amounts to about 5 miles, enough to meet the "active" daily activity level. Use an inexpensive pedometer to count your steps.
- Wash your car with extra vigor or bend and stretch to wash your toes in the bath.
- Work out at a fitness club.
- Work out with friends to help one another stay fit.

Also, try these:

- Give two labor-saving devices to someone who needs them.
- Lift small hand weights while talking on the phone, reading e-mail, or watching TV.
- Stretch often during the day.
- If you have access to the Internet, try the President's Challenge for improving fitness: www.presidentschallenge.org.

START NOW CENGAGENOW Ready to make a change? Consult the online behavior-change planner to help integrate physical activity into your day at **www.cengage.com/sso**.

burdens it by raising the blood pressure. Body tissues starved for oxygen by smoke demand more heartbeats to deliver oxygenated blood, thereby increasing the heart's workload. At the same time, smoking deprives the heart muscle itself of the oxygen it needs to maintain a steady beat. Smoking also damages platelets, making blood clots likely. Damage to the linings of the blood vessels from tobacco smoke toxins makes atherosclerosis likely. When people quit smoking, their risk of heart disease begins to drop within a few months; a year later, their risk has dropped by half, and after 15 years of staying smoke-free, their risks equal those of lifetime nonsmokers.[34]

Atherogenic Diet Diet influences the risk of CVD. An "atherogenic diet"—high in saturated fats, *trans* fats, and cholesterol—increases LDL cholesterol. Fortunately, a well-chosen diet such as the DASH eating plan detailed in the Food Feature at the end of this chapter often lowers the risk of CVD and does so to a greater degree than might be expected from its effects on blood lipids alone.[35] Any of a number of beneficial factors in such diets may take the credit, among them the vitamins, minerals, antioxidant phytochemicals, and omega-3 fatty acids.[36]

Obesity and Metabolic Syndrome A distinct array of risk factors often occurs with CVD.[37] This deadly cluster, commonly called **metabolic syndrome,** consists of central obesity combined with any two or more of the following: high fasting blood glucose (insulin resistance) or type 2 diabetes, hypertension, low blood HDL cholesterol, and elevated blood triglycerides.[38]

Metabolic syndrome, like the chronic diseases associated with it, involves inflammation and elevates the risk for thrombosis (the process that underlies heart attack and stroke).[39] By one estimate, 25 percent of the U.S. adult population has three or more risk factors for metabolic syndrome, but many are unaware of it and so do not seek treatment.[40] Even obesity alone, especially central obesity, raises LDL cholesterol, lowers HDL cholesterol, raises blood pressure, and promotes insulin resistance.[41] The opposite also holds true: weight loss and physical activity lower LDL, raise HDL, improve insulin sensitivity, and lower blood pressure.[42]

CONCEPT LINK 11-4

Links among central obesity, hormones (adipokines), and chronic diseases were discussed in Chapter 9 (pages 326–327).

metabolic syndrome a combination of characteristic factors—high fasting blood glucose or insulin resistance, central obesity, hypertension, low blood HDL cholesterol, and elevated blood triglycerides—that greatly increase a person's risk of developing CVD. Also called *insulin resistance syndrome* or *syndrome X*.

- Metabolic syndrome includes central obesity and at least two of the following:
  - *Type 2 diabetes or high fasting blood glucose.*
  - *Hypertension.*
  - *Low blood HDL.*
  - *High blood triglycerides.*

Other Risk Factors Factors other than the major ones listed earlier in Table 11-4 are under investigation. These emerging risk factors may one day prove influential in CVD development. For example, research suggests links among the B vitamins, elevated homocysteine, and atherosclerosis, but authorities have not yet declared homocysteine a risk factor for CVD, and B vitamins to lower homocysteine have proved useless in heart disease prevention.[43]

Some people with heart disease, especially those with diabetes and those who are overweight, have elevated triglycerides. Researchers debate whether having elevated blood triglycerides alone poses a risk for heart disease.[44] When triglycerides are moderately high, remnants of very-low-density lipoproteins (VLDL) collect in the blood and are highly atherogenic.[45] However, the role of triglycerides in heart disease is unclear due to a flaw in the current technique for measuring triglycerides; more definitive answers may emerge with new testing techniques in place.[46] Today, experts designate elevated blood triglycerides as a marker for other risk factors, but not as a major risk factor for heart disease.

KEY POINT Major risk factors for CVD put forth by the National Cholesterol Education Program include age, gender, family history, high LDL cholesterol and low HDL cholesterol, hypertension, diabetes, obesity, physical inactivity, smoking, and an atherogenic diet. Other potential risk factors are under investigation.

Recommendations for Reducing CVD Risk

Recommendations to reduce the risk of CVD focus first on lifestyle changes. To that end, people are encouraged to increase physical activity, lose weight (if necessary), implement dietary changes, and reduce exposure to tobacco smoke either by quitting smoking or by avoiding secondhand smoke.[47] If such lifestyle changes fail to lower LDL or blood pressure to acceptable levels, then medications are prescribed. Table 11-5 summarizes strategies to reduce the risk of heart disease.[48] The Food Feature on page 435 offers one example of a heart-healthy diet, the DASH eating plan.

TABLE 11-5 Strategies to Reduce Risk of CVD

Dietary Strategies
• *Energy:* Balance energy intake and physical activity to prevent weight gain and to achieve or maintain a healthy body weight. • *Saturated fat,* trans *fat, and cholesterol:* Choose lean meats, vegetables, and low-fat milk products; minimize intake of hydrogenated fats. Limit saturated fats to less than 7 percent of total kcalories, *trans* fat to less than 1 percent of total kcalories, and cholesterol to less than 300 milligrams a day. • *Soluble fibers:* Choose a diet rich in vegetables, fruits, whole grains, and other foods high in soluble fibers. • *Potassium and sodium:* Choose a diet high in potassium-rich fruits and vegetables, low-fat milk products, nuts, and whole grains. Choose and prepare foods with little or no salt (limit sodium intake to 2,300 milligrams per day). • *Added sugars:* Minimize intake of beverages and foods with added sugars. • *Fish and omega-3 fatty acids:* Consume fatty fish rich in omega-3 fatty acids (salmon, tuna, sardines) at least twice a week. • *Plant sterols and stanols:* Consume food products that contain added phytosterols (defined in Controversy 2, page 62). • *Soy:* Consume soy foods to replace animal and dairy products that contain saturated fat and cholesterol. • *Alcohol:* If alcohol is consumed, limit it to one drink daily for women and two drinks daily for men.
Lifestyle Choices
• *Physical activity:* Participate in at least 30 minutes of moderate-intensity endurance activity on most days of the week. Chapter 10 specifies types and amounts of physical activity required to develop and maintain a healthy body. • *Smoking cessation:* Minimize exposure to any form of tobacco or tobacco smoke.

Sources: AHA Scientific Statement: Diet and Lifestyle recommendations revision 2006, Circulation *114 (2006) 82–96; F. M. Sacks and coauthors for the American Heart Association Nutrition Committee, Soy protein, isoflavones, and cardiovascular health,* Circulation *113 (2006): 1034–1044; Expert Panel on Detection, Evaluation, and Treatment of High Blood Cholesterol in Adults (Adult Treatment Panel III)* Third Report of the National Cholesterol Education Program (NCEP), *NIH publication no. 02-5215 (Bethesda, Md.: National Heart, Lung, and Blood Institute, 2002), pp. V1–V28.*

TABLE 11-6 How Much Does Changing the Diet Change LDL Cholesterol?

Diet-Related Component	Modification	Possible LDL Reduction
Saturated fat	<7% of calories	8–10%
Dietary cholesterol	<200 mg/day	3–5%
Weight reduction (if overweight)	Lose 10 lb	5–8%
Soluble, viscous fiber	5–10 g/day	3–5%

Source: Expert Panel on Detection, Evaluation, and Treatment of High Blood Cholesterol in Adults (Adult Treatment Panel III), Third Report of the National Cholesterol Education Program (NCEP), *NIH publication no. 02-5215 (Bethesda, Md.: National Heart, Lung, and Blood Institute, 2002), p. V-21.*

Diet to Reduce CVD Risk What role can diet play in minimizing the risk of developing CVD? The answer focuses primarily on how diet relates to high blood cholesterol. The effects of diet are two sides of the same coin: side one, a diet high in saturated fat and *trans* fatty acids contributes to high blood LDL cholesterol; side two, reducing those fats in the diet lowers blood LDL cholesterol and may reduce the risk of CVD. Table 11-6 demonstrates the power of diet-related factors to reduce LDL cholesterol.

Wherever in the world populations consume diets high in saturated fat and low in fish, fruits, vegetables, and whole grains, blood cholesterol is high and heart disease takes a great toll on health and life. Conversely, wherever dietary fats are mostly unsaturated and where fish, fruits, vegetables, and whole grains are abundant, blood cholesterol and rates of heart disease are low.

It matters, too, what people choose to eat instead of saturated fats. Relationships between carbohydrate intakes and heart disease are not fully defined, but a diet too high in refined starches and added sugars has the potential to worsen heart disease risk by elevating blood triglycerides and reducing HDL cholesterol.[49] People with elevated triglycerides would do well to limit their intakes of highly refined carbohydrate foods; replacing refined starches and sugars with whole grains, legumes, or vegetables may help to improve blood lipids.[50]

Fish oils, rich in omega-3 polyunsaturated fatty acids, reduce inflammation, lower triglycerides, prevent blood clots, improve insulin response, and produce other effects that may reduce the risk of sudden death associated with both heart disease and stroke.[51] For these reasons, the American Heart Association recommends two meals of fish per week. People diagnosed with heart disease may require more than this amount, preferably from additional servings of fatty fish, but a physician may prescribe fish oil supplements in some cases.[52] These supplements may carry their own risks, however, and should be taken under the supervision of a physician.

Other Dietary Factors Earlier chapters addressed other dietary factors that may reduce heart disease risks, and many of these are listed in Table 11-5. A potentially helpful innovation is the sterol esters that have been added to certain kinds of margarine, orange juice, and other foods; authorities recommend their use when other lifestyle changes fail to adequately bring blood cholesterol down.

Sterol esters block absorption of cholesterol from the intestine, an effect that can be as powerful as some medications in lowering blood LDL cholesterol. The cost of sterol-ester enriched foods is high, however, and a caution is in order: sterol esters also reduce absorption of *other* potentially beneficial phytochemicals in the diet.

A small reduction in blood LDL cholesterol may also be realized when soy foods provide the majority of protein in a diet, but the amount of daily soy foods needed to produce the effect is larger than an amount most people may choose.[53] Still, additional benefits may come with soybeans, soy protein products such as imitation meats, and soy milk consumed as part of a heart-healthy diet.[54]

CONCEPT LINK 11-5
Food sources of saturated fats and *trans* fatty acids were listed in Chapter 5 (pages 165, 173).

CONCEPT LINK 11-6
Fats that pose a danger to the heart and those thought to be safer were described in Controversy 5.

Michael Rosenfeld/Getty Images

When diets are rich in whole grains, vegetables, and fruits, life expectancies are long.

CONCEPT LINK 11-7
The Consumer Corner in Chapter 5 provides some guidance for choosing safer varieties of fish (pages 170–171).

CONCEPT LINK 11-8
Sterol esters were defined in Controversy 2 (page 62). The potential benefits of soybeans and soy products to heart health were discussed in Controversy 6 (page 219).

Low-carbohydrate diet books often claim that lowering carbohydrate intake lowers blood LDL cholesterol and lowers blood pressure and thus lowers the risk of chronic diseases. Research is mixed on whether such diets may elevate LDL cholesterol, lower it, or have no effect.[55]

Although diet and physical activity are not the easy route to heart health that everyone hopes for, they form a powerful and safe combination for improving health. The pattern of protection from the recommended diet and physical activity regimen becomes clear—the effects of each small choice add to the beneficial whole. While you are at it, don't smoke. Relax. Meditate or pray. Control stress. Play. Relaxed, happy people who make time to enjoy life have lower blood pressure and fewer heart attacks.[56]

KEY POINT Diet and exercise are key factors in supporting heart health. Dietary measures to lower LDL cholesterol include reducing intakes of saturated fat, *trans* fat, and cholesterol, along with obtaining the fiber, nutrients, and phytochemicals of fruits, vegetables, legumes, fish, and whole grains.

LO 11.4

Nutrition and Hypertension

People with healthy blood pressure generally enjoy a long life and suffer less often from heart disease.[57] Chronic high blood pressure, or hypertension, remains one of the most prevalent forms of CVD, affecting 65 million U.S. adults, and its rate has been rising steadily.[58] Hypertension contributes to half a million strokes and over a million heart attacks each year. The higher above normal the blood pressure goes, the greater the risk.

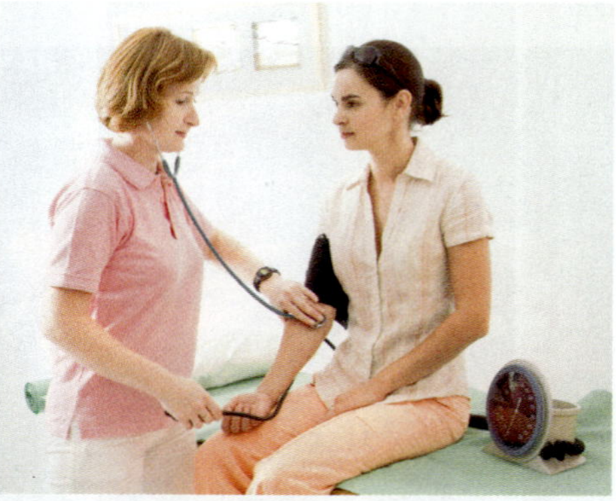
© iStockphoto.com/Zsolt Nyulaszi

The most effective single step you can take against hypertension is to learn your own blood pressure.

You cannot tell if you have high blood pressure—it presents no symptoms you can feel. The most effective single step you can take to protect yourself from hypertension is to find out whether you have it. During a checkup, a health-care professional can take an accurate resting blood pressure reading. Self-test machines in drugstores and other public places are often inaccurate. If your resting blood pressure is above normal, the reading should be repeated before confirming the diagnosis of hypertension. Thereafter, blood pressure should be checked at regular intervals.

When blood pressure is measured, two numbers are important: the pressure during contraction of the heart's ventricles (large pumping chambers) and the pressure during their relaxation. The numbers are given as a fraction, with the first number representing the **systolic pressure** (ventricular contraction) and the second number the **diastolic pressure** (relaxation). Return to Figure 11-7 (page 416) to see how to interpret your resting blood pressure.

Ideal resting blood pressure is lower than 120 over 80. Just above this value lies **prehypertension**—blood pressure values in the borderline range of 120 over 80 to 139 over 89. Blood pressure in this range means that high blood pressure is likely to develop in the future and that taking steps to keep blood pressure low may avert illness later on.[59] Above this borderline level, though, the risks of heart attacks and strokes rise in direct proportion to increasing blood pressure.

systolic (sis-TOL-ik) **pressure** the first figure in a blood pressure reading (the "dupp" sound of the heartbeat's "lubb-dupp" beat is heard), which reflects arterial pressure caused by the contraction of the heart's left ventricle.

diastolic (dye-as-TOL-ik) **pressure** the second figure in a blood pressure reading (the "lubb" of the heartbeat is heard), which reflects the arterial pressure when the heart is between beats.

prehypertension borderline blood pressure between 120 over 80 and 139 over 89 millimeters of mercury, an indication that hypertension is likely to develop in the future.

KEY POINT Hypertension is silent, progressively worsens atherosclerosis, and makes heart attacks and strokes likely. All adults should know their blood pressure.

How Does Blood Pressure Work in the Body?

Blood pressure is vital to life. It pushes the blood through the major arteries into smaller arteries and finally into tiny capillaries whose thin walls permit exchange of fluids between the blood and the tissues (see Figure 11-9). Blood pressure arises

FIGURE 11-9 The Blood Pressure

Three major factors contribute to the pressure inside an artery. First, the heart pushes blood into the artery. Second, the small-diameter arteries and capillaries at the other end resist the blood's flow (peripheral resistance). Third, the volume of fluid in the circulatory system, which depends on the number of dissolved particles in that fluid, adds to the blood pressure.

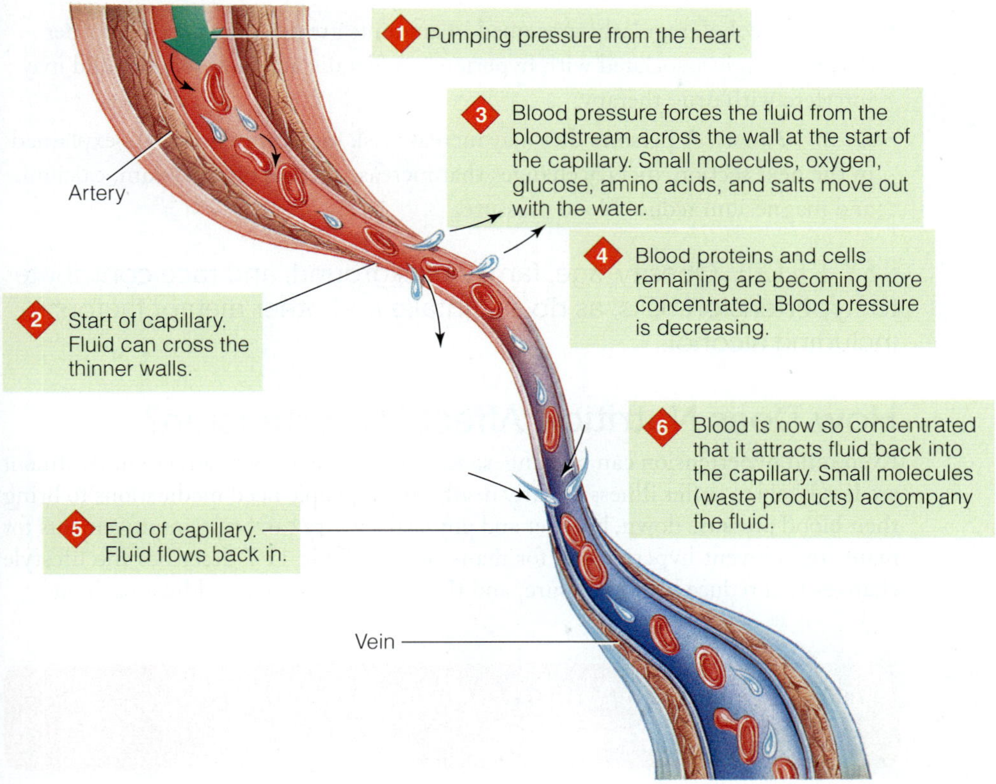

from contractions in the heart muscle that pump blood away from the heart (**cardiac output**) and the resistance blood encounters in the small arteries (**peripheral resistance**).

When either cardiac output or peripheral resistance increases, blood pressure rises. Cardiac output is raised when heart rate or blood volume increases; peripheral resistance is affected mostly by the diameters of the arteries. Blood pressure is therefore influenced by the nervous system, which regulates heart muscle contractions and the arteries' diameters, and hormonal signals, which may cause fluid retention or blood vessel constriction. The kidneys also play a role in regulating blood pressure. If the blood pressure is too low, the kidneys act to increase it—they send hormones to constrict blood vessels and to retain water and salt in the body.[60] When the pressure is right, the cells receive a constant supply of nutrients and oxygen and can release their wastes.

Risk Factors for Hypertension

Several major risk factors predict the development of hypertension:[61]

- *Age.* Hypertension risk increases with age. For people age 55 or older, the lifetime risk of developing it approaches 90 percent.[62]
- *Genetics.* Hypertension often runs in families and along racial lines: a family history of hypertension raises the risk of developing it, and among African Americans, prevalence of high blood pressure is among the highest in the world.[63] Compared with others, African Americans typically develop high blood pressure earlier in life and their average blood pressure is much higher.

cardiac output the volume of blood discharged by the heart each minute. Also defined in Chapter 10.

peripheral resistance the resistance to pumped blood in the small arterial branches (arterioles) that carry blood to tissues.

- *Obesity.* More than half of people with hypertension—an estimated 60 percent—are obese.[64] Obesity raises blood pressure in part by altering kidney function and partly by way of promoting blood vessel damage through insulin resistance.[65] Excess fat also means miles of extra capillaries through which the blood must be pumped.
- *Salt Intake.* As salt intake increases, so does blood pressure.[66] Most people with hypertension can benefit from reducing salt in their diets.
- *Alcohol.* Alcohol, regularly consumed in amounts greater than two drinks per day, is strongly associated with hypertension (details in a later section) and may interfere with drug therapy.
- *Dietary Factors.* A person's diet may increase risk for hypertension. As explained in the next section, dietary changes that increase intakes of potassium, calcium, and magnesium reduce blood pressure.

KEY POINT Obesity, age, family background, and race contribute to hypertension risks, as do salt intake and other dietary factors, including alcohol.

How Does Nutrition Affect Hypertension?

Even mild hypertension can be dangerous, but individuals who adhere to treatment are less likely to suffer illness or early death. Some people need medications to bring their blood pressure down, but diet and physical activity can bring improvements for many and prevent hypertension for many others. Table 11-7 describes the lifestyle changes that reduce blood pressure, and the following sections address each one.

TABLE 11-7 Lifestyle Modifications to Reduce Blood Pressure

Modification	Recommendation	Expected Reduction in Systolic Blood Pressure
Weight reduction	Maintain healthy body weight (BMI below 25).	5–20 mm Hg/10 kg lost
DASH eating plan	Adopt a diet rich in fruits, vegetables, and low-fat milk products with reduced saturated fat intake.	8–14 mm Hg
Sodium restriction	Reduce dietary sodium intake to less than 2,400 milligrams sodium (less than 6 grams salt) per day.[a]	2–8 mm Hg
Physical activity	Perform aerobic physical activity for at least 30 minutes per day, most days of the week.	4–9 mm Hg
Moderate alcohol consumption	Men: Limit to 2 drinks per day. Women and lighter-weight men: Limit to 1 drink per day.	2–4 mm Hg

[a]*According to the Dietary Guidelines and DRI recommendations, sodium intake should be limited to 2,300 milligrams daily.*

Source: Adapted from Reference Card from the Seventh Report of the Joint National Committee on Prevention, Detection, Evaluation, and Treatment of High Blood Pressure (JNC 7), *NIH publication no. 03-5231 (Bethesda, Md.: National Institutes of Health, National Heart, Lung, and Blood Institute, and National High Blood Pressure Education Program, May 2003).*

The DASH Diet The results of the Dietary Approaches to Stop Hypertension (DASH) trial show that a diet rich in fruits, vegetables, nuts, whole grains, and low-fat milk products and low in total fat and saturated fat can significantly lower blood pressure.[67] In addition to lowering blood pressure, the DASH diet improves vascular function and lowers total cholesterol and LDL cholesterol.[68] Compared to the typical American diet, the DASH diet provides more fiber, potassium, magnesium, and calcium, emphasizes legumes and fish over red meat, limits added sugars and sugar-containing beverages, and meets other recommendations of the *Dietary Guidelines for Americans.* Diets like DASH consistently improve blood pressure, both in study subjects whose diets are provided by researchers and those freely choosing and preparing their own foods according to guidelines.[69] The Food Feature at the end of this chapter describes the DASH diet in detail.

CONCEPT LINK 11-9

The DASH diet was introduced in Chapter 8 (page 295).

Weight Control and Physical Activity For people who have hypertension and are overweight, a weight loss of as little as 10 pounds can significantly lower blood pressure. Those who are taking medication to control their blood pressure can often cut down their doses or eliminate their medication if they lose weight.

Physical activity can lower almost everyone's blood pressure, even people without hypertension. Physical activity helps with weight control, of course, but moderate- or vigorous-intensity aerobic activity, such as 30 to 60 minutes of brisk walking or running on most days, also helps to lower blood pressure directly.[70] Even activity performed in manageable 10-minute segments throughout the day that add up to the recommended total provides benefits. Those who engage in regular aerobic activity may not need medication for mild hypertension.[71]

Physical activity also alters the body's hormones in beneficial ways. Physical activity decreases the secretion of stress hormones, reducing stress and lowering blood pressure. Physical activity also redistributes body water and eases transit of the blood through the small arteries that feed the tissues, including those of the heart.

CONCEPT LINK 11-10

Aerobic activity for cardiorespiratory fitness was described in Chapter 10 (pages 372–374).

Salt, Sodium, and Blood Pressure As mentioned, high intakes of salt and sodium are associated with hypertension.[72] Lowering sodium intake reduces blood pressure regardless of gender or race, presence or absence of hypertension, or whether people follow the DASH diet or a typical American diet. The combination of the DASH diet with a limited intake of sodium, however, improves blood pressure better than either strategy alone.[73] As salt intakes decrease, blood pressure drops in a stepwise fashion.[74] This direct relationship is reported at all levels of intake, from very low to much higher than average. Research also suggests that reducing salt intake may provide additional protection against heart disease, beyond lowering blood pressure.[75]

MY TURN

© Cengage Learning

i Alicia

Fast-Food Generation?

How many fast-food meals do you eat each week? Listen to two students tell you about their weekly fast-food fare.

CENGAGENOW To hear their stories, log on to www.cengage.com/sso.

The World Health Organization estimates that a significant reduction in sodium intake could reduce by half the number of people requiring medication for hypertension and greatly reduce deaths from CVD. Certain people respond more sensitively than others to sodium intakes, including African Americans, people with a family history of hypertension, people with kidney problems or diabetes, and older people. The recommendation of many professionals and agencies is that everyone (even those with normal blood pressure) should moderately restrict salt and sodium intake. No one should consume more than the DRI committee's Tolerable Upper Intake Level—that is, no more than 2,300 milligrams of sodium per day.[76] African Americans, people over the age of 40, and those who have been diagnosed with hypertension should limit their sodium intakes to no more than 1,500 milligrams of sodium per day.[77]

CONCEPT LINK 11-11

Processed foods contribute the majority of sodium in the U.S. diet, as Figure 8-10 (page 297) indicated.

Alcohol In moderate doses, alcohol initially relaxes the arteries and so reduces blood pressure, but higher doses raise blood pressure.[78] Hypertension is common among people with alcoholism and is apparently caused directly by the alcohol. Hypertension caused by alcohol leads to CVD, the same as hypertension caused by any other factor. Furthermore, alcohol may cause strokes—even *without* hypertension. The *Dietary Guidelines for Americans* urge a sensible, moderate approach for those who drink alcohol. *Moderation* means no more than one drink a day for women or two drinks a day for men, an amount that seems safe relative to blood pressure. The same amount, however, raises women's risk of breast cancer, so other routes to relaxation may prove safer.[79]

Calcium, Potassium, Magnesium, and Vitamin C Other dietary factors may help to regulate blood pressure. A diet providing enough calcium may be one such factor—in both healthy people and those with hypertension, increasing calcium often reduces blood pressure.[80]

Adequate potassium and magnesium may also help in this regard. Hypertension occurs more frequently in areas where diets lack potassium-rich fruits and vegetables. Conversely, diets rich in potassium and low in sodium appear to both prevent and correct hypertension.[81] As for magnesium, deficiency causes the walls of the arteries and capillaries to constrict and so may raise the blood pressure. Similarly, consuming a diet adequate in vitamin C seems to help normalize blood pressure, while vitamin C deficiency may tend to raise it.[82] Other dietary factors may also affect blood pressure; caffeine raises blood pressure temporarily, and the roles of cadmium, selenium, lead, protein, and fat are currently under study.[83]

How can people be sure of getting all of the nutrients needed to keep blood pressure low? Vitamin and mineral supplements have been disappointing in this regard, showing no promise for lowering blood pressure. Therefore, the best answer is to consume a low-fat diet with abundant fruits, vegetables, and low-fat dairy products that provide the needed nutrients while holding sodium intake within bounds. Should diet and physical activity fail to reduce blood pressure, though, antihypertensive drugs such as diuretics can be lifesaving. Some of these work by increasing fluid loss in the urine, so they may also cause potassium losses. People taking these drugs should make it a point to consume potassium-rich foods daily.

CONCEPT LINK 11-12

Potassium-rich foods were shown in Snapshot 8-4 of Chapter 8 (page 298).

Some people doubt the power of ordinary food to improve health, despite libraries full of evidence in its favor. In the search for something extra, such people often combine nutrient supplements with herbs and other alternatives to mainstream nutrition and medicine. The Consumer Corner provides a look at some of these practices.

KEY POINT For most people, maintaining a healthy body weight, engaging in regular physical activity, minimizing salt and sodium intakes, limiting alcohol intake, and eating a diet high in fruits, vegetables, fish, and low-fat dairy products work together to keep blood pressure normal.

CONSUMER CORNER

Complementary and Alternative Medicine

Where do you turn for help when illness strikes? Do you see a physician who offers **conventional medicine**—treatment methods sanctioned by the established medical community? Or do you seek out an herbalist, an acupuncturist, or another practitioner of **complementary** and **alternative medicine (CAM)**? As more people turn to alternative medicine, U.S. consumers are spending more than 34 billion dollars each year on such treatments.[1] Terms are defined in Table 11-8.

CAM includes a variety of approaches, philosophies, and treatments. When these therapies are used instead of conventional medicine, they are called *alternative;* when used together with conventional medicine, they are called *complementary.* **Integrative medicine** combines conventional medicine and CAM treatments for which there is some high-quality scientific evidence of safety and effectiveness.[2] More than ever before, health-care professionals are incorporating certain helpful CAM therapies into their practices.[3] This open-minded approach often combines some humane elements of alternative therapies along with the best of scientific medicine, delivered by skilled physicians. It is difficult to estimate how many patients of more traditional doctors also use CAM because, fearing disapproval, they may keep it a secret.[4]

Unlike relatively new conventional therapies, some CAM therapies have been used for centuries but have not been scientifically evaluated for safety or effectiveness.[5] A growing number of health-care professionals are learning about alternative therapies; more than half of U.S. medical schools now offer elective courses in alternative medicine, and even more include discussions of these therapies in their required courses. Unfortunately, anyone can claim to be an expert in a "new" or "natural" therapy, and many practitioners act knowledgeable but either are misinformed or are frauds (see Controversy 1).

On the Internet and in the media, testimonials for mysterious "cures" by alternative therapies abound. Consumers may think that, unless the speaker is lying, the therapies really do cure diseases. But a third option also exists: an ill person's belief in a treatment, even a placebo or sham treatment, often leads to physical healing (*placebo* was defined in Table 1-7 of Chapter 1).

Not all alternative therapies are ineffective; several examples of effective therapies are described in this section. However, a common contention of CAM practitioners—that many of today's alternative therapies will become tomorrow's mainstream medical treatments—is unfounded. Most, on testing, have proved ineffective, or harmful. The toxic drug laetrile, for example, was popularized in the 1970s but no research to date supports its use, and its high cyanide (poison) content speaks against it.[6] Along with a thousand other sham treatments, laetrile is still sold to unsuspecting cancer sufferers by way of Internet websites, however. Intelligent, clear-minded people can fall for such hoaxes when standard medical therapies fail; loving life and desperate, they fall prey to the worst kind of quackery on the feeblest promise of a cure.

The prestigious National Institutes of Health established its National Center for Complementary and Alternative Medicine (NCCAM) to help tease apart potentially useful and safe alternative therapies from the worthless or harmful. So far, NCCAM has found **acupuncture** useful for quelling nausea from surgery, cancer chemotherapy, and pregnancy, treating chronic low-back pain, and for relieving pain following dental surgeries, although underlying mechanisms for these effects are not known.[7] Other potential uses include treating chronic headaches and migraines. The attraction of acupuncture, when performed by skilled practitioners using sterile instruments, lies in its greatly reduced risks to the user compared with the risks from drugs prescribed for these conditions.

Dozens of **herbal medicines** contain effective natural drugs. For example, the resin called myrrh contains an analgesic (pain-killing) compound; willow bark contains aspirin; the herb valerian contains a tranquilizing oil; senna leaves produce a powerful laxative. The World Health Organization currently recommends the use of an herbal Chinese drug in tropical developing nations as a tool for combating malaria.*

*The herb is artemisinin (ar-TEM-is-in-in), derived from sweet wormwood.

TABLE 11-8 Alternative Therapy Terms

- **acupuncture** (ak-you-punk-chur) a technique that involves piercing the skin with long, thin needles at specific anatomical points to relieve pain or illness. Acupuncture sometimes uses heat, pressure, friction, suction, or electromagnetic energy to stimulate the points.
- **complementary** and **alternative medicine (CAM)** a group of diverse medical and health-care systems, practices, and products that are not considered to be a part of conventional medicine. Examples include acupuncture, biofeedback, chiropractic, faith healing, and many others.
- **conventional medicine** diagnosis and treatment of diseases as practiced by medical doctors (M.D.) and doctors of osteopathy (D.O.) and allied health professionals such as physical therapists and registered dieticians.
- **herbal medicine** use of herbs and other natural substances with the intention of preventing or curing diseases or relieving symptoms.
- **integrative medicine** care that combines conventional and complementary therapies for which there is some high-quality scientific evidence of safety and effectiveness. Integrative medicine emphasizes the importance of the relationship between the practitioner and the patient and focuses on wellness, healing, and the whole person.

Many herbal medicines have several serious drawbacks, however. When analyzed, a majority of herb pills and supplements on today's market shelves do not contain the species or the active ingredients stated on their labels.[8] In several cases, supplements did not even contain herbs, but drugs that can interact with prescription medicines and lower blood pressure to dangerous levels.[9] Such discrepancies in the contents of supplements can be dangerous to the consumer, interfere with scientific research, and make it difficult to interpret the findings. Consumers may want to shop for supplements bearing a logo from either the U.S. Pharmacopeia or Consumer Lab indicating the contents have been analyzed and found to contain the ingredients and quantities listed on the label.

Contamination can also be a problem. An analysis of one popular herbal remedy purchased via the Internet revealed that more than 20 percent of the products contained detectable levels of lead, mercury, or arsenic.[10]

Interactions of herbs with medications are also common (see Chapter 14's Controversy). Like drugs, herbs may interfere with, or potentiate, the effects of medication.[11] For example, because *Ginkgo biloba* impairs blood clotting, it can cause bleeding problems for people taking aspirin or other blood-thinning medicines regularly.[12]

Consumers who self-diagnose illnesses, and then choose herbs for treatment, are inviting problems. Few herbalists selling the pills possess the necessary knowledge of botany, pharmacology, or human physiology but instead rely on hearsay, folklore, and manufacturers' claims to plan treatments. By delaying effective medical help, consumers choosing herbs while postponing standard medical therapy may allow serious conditions time to worsen. Also, perilous mistakes with herbs are extraordinarily likely. For example, most mint is safe when brewed as tea, but some may contain highly toxic pennyroyal oil. Folk medicine urges parents to soothe a colicky baby with mint tea, but one concoction laden with pennyroyal was blamed for liver and neurological injuries to at least two infants, one of whom died. Table 11-9 lists some additional herbs and their potential actions.[†] Bottom line: Complementary and alternative medicines warrant a cautious approach.

[†] *A reliable source of information about herbs is V. Tyler,* The Honest Herbal *(New York: Pharmaceutical Products Press). Look for the latest edition.*

TABLE 11-9 Selected Herbs: Claims, Evidence, and Risks

Common Name	Claims	Evidence	Risks[a]
Aloe (gel)	Promote wound healing	May help heal minor burns and abrasions; may cause infections in severe wounds	Generally considered safe
Black cohosh (stems and roots)	Ease menopause symptoms	Conflicting evidence	May cause headaches, stomach discomfort, liver damage
Chamomile (flowers)	Relieve indigestion	Little evidence available	Generally considered safe
Chaparral (leaves and twigs)	Slow aging, "cleanse" blood, heal wounds, cure cancer, treat acne	No evidence available	Acute, toxic hepatitis; liver damage
Cinnamon (bark)	Relieve indigestion, lower blood glucose and blood lipids	May lower blood glucose in type 2 diabetes	May have a "blood-thinning" effect; not safe for pregnant women or those taking diabetes medication
Comfrey (leafy plant)	Soothe nerves	No evidence available	Liver damage
Echinacea (roots)	Alleviate symptoms of colds, flus, and infections; promote wound healing; boost immunity	Ineffective in preventing colds or other infections	Generally considered safe; may cause headache, dizziness, nausea
Ephedra (stems)	Promote weight loss	Little evidence available	Rapid heart rate, tremors, seizures, insomnia, headaches, hypertension; FDA has banned the sale of ephedra-containing supplements
Feverfew (leaves)	Prevent migraine headaches	May prevent migraine headaches	Generally considered safe; may cause mouth irritation, swelling, ulcers, and GI distress; not safe for pregnant women
Garlic (bulbs)	Lower blood lipids and blood pressure	May lower blood cholesterol slightly; conflicting evidence on blood pressure	Generally considered safe; may cause garlic breath, body odor, gas, and GI distress; inhibits blood clotting

TABLE 11-9 Selected Herbs: Claims, Evidence, and Risks (continued)

Common Name	Claims	Evidence	Risks[a]
Ginger (roots)	Prevent motion sickness, nausea	May relieve pregnancy-induced nausea; conflicting evidence on nausea caused by motion, chemotherapy, or surgery	Generally considered safe
Ginkgo (tree leaves)	Improve memory, relieve vertigo	Little evidence available	Generally considered safe; may cause headache, GI distress, dizziness; may inhibit blood clotting
Ginseng (roots)	Boost immunity, increase endurance	Little evidence available	Generally considered safe; may cause insomnia, headaches, increased oxidative stress, and high blood pressure
Goldenseal (roots)	Relieve indigestion, treat urinary infections	Little evidence available	Generally considered safe; not safe for people with hypertension or heart disease; not safe for pregnant women
Kava (roots)	Relieves anxiety, promotes relaxation	Little evidence available	Liver failure
Kombucha tea (fermentation product of yeast and bacteria)	Boosts immunity; prevents cancer; improves digestion	No evidence available	Stomach upset; allergic reactions; toxic reactions; metabolic acidosis
Saw palmetto (ripe fruits)	Relieve symptoms of enlarged prostate; diuretic; enhance sexual vigor	Little evidence available	Generally considered safe; may cause nausea, vomiting, diarrhea
St. John's wort (leaves and tops)	Relieve depression and anxiety	May relieve mild depression	Generally considered safe; may cause fatigue, increased sensitivity to sunlight, and GI distress
Tumeric (roots)	Reduces inflammation; relieves heartburn; prevents or treats cancer	No evidence available	Generally considered safe; may cause indigestion; not safe for people with gallbladder disease
Valerian (roots)	Calm nerves, improve sleep	Little evidence available	Long-term use associated with liver damage
Yohimbe (tree bark)	Enhance "male performance"	No evidence available	Kidney failure, seizures

[a]*Allergies are always a possible risk; see Controversy 14 for drug interactions. Pregnant women should not use herbal supplements.*

LO 11.5

Nutrition and Cancer

Cancer ranks second only to heart disease as a leading cause of death and disability in the United States. For some groups, such as women aged 40 to 79 years and men aged 60 to 79 years, cancer is the leading cause of death.[84] Still, over the past decade, a small but steady trend toward declining cancer deaths has occurred in the United States.[85] Contributors may include early detection and treatment that have transformed several common cancers into curable diseases or treatable chronic illnesses. Although the potential for cure is exciting, *prevention* of cancer remains far and away preferable.

Can an individual's chosen behaviors affect the risk of contracting cancer? They can, sometimes powerfully so.[86] Just a few rare cancers are known to be caused primarily by genetic influences and will appear in members of an affected family regardless of lifestyle choices. A few more are linked with microbial infections.[††‡‡]

[††]Examples include viral hepatitis and liver cancer, human papilloma virus and cervical cancer, and *H. pylori* bacterium (the ulcer bacterium) and stomach cancer.
[‡‡]A free scientific database summarizes evidence concerning breast cancer and environmental exposure to chemical compounds; see the Internet website www.komen.org/environment.

cancer a disease in which cells multiply out of control and disrupt normal functioning of one or more organs.

For the great majority of cancers, lifestyle factors and environmental exposures become the major risk factors.[87] For example, if everyone in the United States quit smoking right now, future total cancers would likely drop by almost a third. A lack of physical activity almost certainly plays a role in the development of colon and breast cancer and probably contributes to others.[88] Alcohol intakes contribute to cancer of the mouth, pharynx, and larynx, cancer of the esophagus, breast cancer, and probably others.[89] Further, incidence of hormone-related breast cancer has dropped significantly at a time when millions of women have ceased taking hormone replacement therapy for symptoms of menopause.[90]

An estimated 30 to 40 percent of cancers are influenced by diet, and these relationships are the focus of this section.[91] Diet patterns that emphasize fat, meat, alcohol, and excess calories and that minimize fruits and vegetables have been the targets of much cancer research. Such constituents of the diet relate to cancer in several ways:

- Foods or their components may cause cancer.
- Foods or their components may promote cancer.
- Foods or their components may protect against cancer.

Also, for the person who has cancer, diet can make a crucial difference in recovery. Some dietary and environmental factors currently believed to be important in cancer causation are listed in Table 11-10.

Did You Know?

Environmental tobacco smoke (passive or secondhand smoke), overexposure to sun, and possibly exposure to water and air pollution or other toxic compounds are responsible for a percentage of cancers.

How Does Cancer Develop?

Cancer arises in the genes.[92] It often begins when a cell's genetic material (DNA) sustains damage from a **carcinogen,** such as a free-radical compound, radiation, and other factors. Such damage occurs every day, but most is quickly repaired. Sometimes DNA collects bits of damage here and there over time. Usually, if the damage cannot be repaired and the cell becomes unable to faithfully replicate its genome, the cell self-destructs, committing a sort of cellular suicide to prevent its progeny from inheriting faulty genes. Occasionally, a damaged cell loses its ability to self-destruct and also loses its ability to stop reproducing. It replicates uncontrollably, and the result is a mass of abnormal tissue—a tumor. Life-threatening cancer results when the tumor tissue, which cannot perform the critical functions of healthy tissues, overtakes the healthy organ in which it developed or disseminates its cells through the bloodstream to other parts of the body.

Simplified, cancer develops through the following steps (illustrated in Figure 11-10):

1. Exposure to a carcinogen.
2. Entry of the carcinogen into a cell.
3. **Initiation** of cancer as the carcinogen damages or changes the cell's genetic material (**carcinogenesis**).
4. Acceleration by other carcinogens, called **promoters,** so that the cell begins to multiply out of control—tumor formation.
5. Often, spreading of cancer cells via blood and lymph (**metastasis**).
6. Disruption of normal body functions.

Researchers think that the first four steps, which culminate with tumor formation, are key to cancer prevention. On hearing this, many people mistakenly believe that they should avoid eating all foods that contain carcinogens. Doing so proves impossible, however, because most carcinogens occur naturally in foods amidst thousands of other chemicals and nutrients needed by the body. The body is well equipped to deal with the minute amounts of carcinogens that occur naturally in foods, such as those listed in the margin.

For those who suspect food additives of being carcinogenic, be assured that additives are held to strict standards, and no additive approved for use in the United

- Here are some selected chemicals and carcinogens occurring naturally in breakfast foods:
  - *Coffee: acetaldehyde, acetic acid, acetone, atractylosides, butanol, cafestol palmitate, chlorogenic acid, dimethyl sulfide, ethanol, furan, furfural, guaiacol, hydrogen sulfide, isoprene, methanol, methyl butanol, methyl formate, methyl glyoxal, propionaldehyde, pyridine, 1,3,7,-trimethylxanthine.*
  - *Toast and coffee cake: acetic acid, acetone, butyric acid, caprionic acid, ethyl acetate, ethyl ketone, ethyl lactate, methyl ethyl ketone, propionic acid, valeric acid.*

Of course, consuming coffee, toast, and coffee cake does not elevate a person's risk of developing cancer because the body detoxifies small doses of carcinogens found in foods.

carcinogen (car-SIN-oh-jen) a cancer-causing substance (*carcin* means "cancer"; *gen* means "gives rise to").

initiation an event, probably occurring in a cell's genetic material, caused by radiation or by a chemical carcinogen that can give rise to cancer.

carcinogenesis the origination or beginning of cancer.

promoters factors that do not initiate cancer but speed up its development once initiation has taken place.

metastasis (meh-TASS-ta-sis) movement of cancer cells from one body part to another, usually by way of the body fluids.

TABLE 11-10 Diet-Related Factors and Cancer at Specific Sites

Cancer Sites	Risk Factors	Protective Factors
Breast (postmenopause)	Alcoholic drinks, body fatness, adult attained height,[a] abdominal fatness, adult weight gain	Lactation, physical activity
Breast (premenopause)	Alcoholic drinks, adult attained height,[a] greater birth weight	Lactation, body fatness[b]
Colon and rectum	Red meat, processed meat, alcoholic drinks, body fatness, abdominal fatness, adult attained height[a]	Physical activity, foods containing dietary fiber, garlic, milk, calcium
Endometrium	Body fatness, abdominal fatness	Physical activity
Esophagus	Alcoholic drinks, body fatness	Nonstarchy vegetables, fruits, foods containing beta-carotene, foods containing vitamin C
Gallbladder	Body fatness	
Kidney	Body fatness	
Liver	Aflatoxins,[c] alcoholic drinks	
Lung	Arsenic in drinking water, beta-carotene supplements[d]	Fruits, foods containing carotenoids
Mouth, pharynx, and larynx	Alcoholic drinks	Nonstarchy vegetables, fruits, foods containing carotenoids
Nasopharynx	Cantonese-style salted fish	
Ovary	Adult attained height[a]	
Pancreas	Body fatness, abdominal fatness, adult attained height[a]	Foods containing folate
Prostate	Diets high in calcium	Foods containing lycopene, foods containing selenium, selenium[e]
Skin	Arsenic in drinking water	
Stomach	Salt, salty and salted foods	Nonstarchy vegetables, allium vegetables,[f] fruits

Note: Strength of evidence for all these factors is either "convincing" or "probable."

[a]*Adult attained height is unlikely to directly modify the risk of cancer. It is a marker for genetic, environmental, hormonal, and also nutritional factors affecting growth during the period from preconception to completion of linear growth.*

[b]*Most studies show an increased risk of postmenopausal breast cancer with increased body fatness, but a decreased risk of premenopausal breast cancer with increased body fatness.*

[c]*Aflatoxins are toxins produced by molds or fungi. The main foods that may be contaminated are all types of grains (wheat, rye, rice, corn, barley, oats) and legumes, notably peanuts.*

[d]*The evidence is derived from studies using high-dose supplements (20 mg/day for beta-carotene; 25,000 international units/day for retinol) in smokers.*

[e]*The evidence is derived from studies using supplements at a dose of 200 μg/day. Selenium is toxic at higher doses.*

[f]*This includes vegetables such as garlic, onions, leeks, and shallots.*

Source: World Cancer Research Fund/American Institute for Cancer Research, Food, Nutrition, Physical Activity and the Prevention of Cancer: A Global Perspective (Washington, D.C.: AICR, 2007).

States causes cancer when used appropriately in food. Food *contaminants*, however, that enter foods by accident or toxins that arise through natural processes, for example when a food becomes moldy, may indeed be powerful carcinogens, or they may be converted to carcinogens during the body's attempts to break them down. Most such constituents are monitored in the U.S. food supply and are generally present, if at all, in amounts well below those that could pose risks to consumers.

FIGURE 11-10 **Cancer Development**

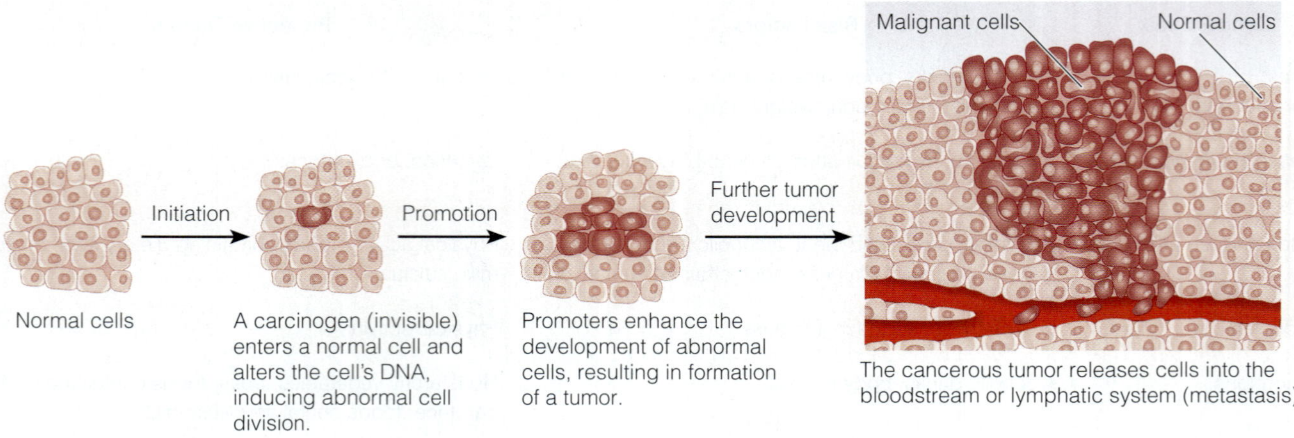

The cancerous tumor releases cells into the bloodstream or lymphatic system (metastasis).

KEY POINT Cancer arises from genetic damage and develops in steps, including initiation and promotion, which are thought to be sometimes influenced by diet. The body is equipped to handle tiny doses of carcinogens that occur in foods. Contaminants and naturally occurring toxins can be carcinogenic, but they are monitored in the U.S. food supply.

Which Diet Factors Affect Cancer Risk?

Certain dietary factors substantially influence cancer development.[93] The degree of risk imposed by food depends partly on the eater's genetic inheritance, but knowledge of these relationships is still unfolding. The following sections explore some of the suspected links between food constituents and prevention or development of certain cancers. The Controversy section delves into areas of scientific advancement that promise to clarify at least some of the relationships between diet and cancer.

Energy Intake When calorie intakes are reduced, cancer rates fall. In animal experiments, this **caloric effect** proves to be one of the most effective dietary interventions to prevent cancer. When researchers establish a cancer-causing condition in laboratory animals and then restrict the energy in their feed, the onset of cancer in the restricted animals is delayed beyond the time when unrestricted animals have died of the disease. Population observations seem to imply that calorie restriction, voluntary or involuntary, may delay cancer in people, too, and clinical experiments to resolve the issue are currently underway.[94] An important note: this effect occurs only in cancer prevention; once started, cancer continues advancing even in a person who is starving. It is also true that when a population's calorie intake rises, cancer rates rise in response; excess calories from carbohydrate, fat, and protein all raise cancer rates. This raises concerns about future U.S. cancer rates among an increasingly overweight population.

Obesity Obesity itself is clearly a risk factor for certain cancers (such as colon, breast in postmenopausal women, endometrial, pancreas, kidney, and esophageal) and possibly for other types (such as gallbladder) as well.[95] Obesity's influence on cancer development depends on the site as well as other factors. In the case of breast cancer in postmenopausal women, for example, the hormone estrogen is implicated. Obese women have higher levels of circulating estrogen than lean women do because adipose tissue converts other hormones into estrogen and releases it into the blood. In normal weight women, blood estrogen drops dramatically with the onset of menopause. In obese women, extended exposure to estrogen increases their breast cancer risk.[96] A lifestyle that embraces physical activity, no or little alcohol consumption, a healthy body weight, and avoidance of hormone replacement therapy (when medically possible) may substantially reduce a woman's breast cancer risk.

caloric effect the drop in cancer incidence seen whenever intake of food energy (calories) is restricted.

Physical Activity An energy budget that balances calorie intake with physical activity may lower the risk of developing some cancers. People whose lifestyles include regular, vigorous physical activity often have lower risks of colon and breast cancer.[97] Physical activity may protect against cancer by reducing body weight and by other mechanisms not related to body weight.[98]

Alcohol Cancers of the head and neck correlate strongly with the combination of alcohol and tobacco use and with low intakes of green and yellow fruits and vegetables. Alcohol intake alone raises the risk of breast cancer and is associated with cancers of the mouth, throat, and esophagus, while alcoholism often damages the liver in ways that promote liver cancer.[99]

CONCEPT LINK 11-13

Alcoholic beverages and cancer risks were addressed in Controversy 3 (page 103).

Fat and Fatty Acids Laboratory studies using animals often reveal that high dietary fat intakes correlate with development of cancer. Simply feeding fat to experimental animals is not enough to get tumors started, however; an experimenter must also expose the animals to a known carcinogen. After that exposure, animals fed the high-fat diet develop more cancers faster than animals fed low-fat diets. Thus, fat appears to be a cancer promoter in animals.

Studies of people, however, have not proved that the effects of fat are independent of the effects of energy intake and physical activity.[100] Recent studies have weakened the overall evidence associating fats and oils with cancer risk.[101] The type of fat in the diet, however, may influence cancer promotion or prevention. Studies of colon cancer implicate animal fats but not vegetable fat, and a number of studies suggest that omega-3 fatty acids from fish may protect against some cancers.[102] Thus the same dietary fat advice applies to cancer protection as to heart health: reduce saturated fat intake and increase omega-3 fatty acids.

Red Meats Population studies spanning the globe for over 30 years consistently report that diets high in red meat and processed meat (meat preserved by smoking, curing, or salting, or by the addition of preservatives) increase the risk of colon cancer.[103] Processed meats may be of special concern. Processed meats contain additives, nitrites or nitrates, that contribute a pink color and deter bacterial growth in meats. In the digestive tract, nitrites and nitrates form other nitrogen-containing compounds that may be carcinogenic.[104]

Cooking meats at high temperatures (frying, broiling) causes amino acids and creatine in the meats to react together and form carcinogens.[105] Grilling meat, fish, or other foods—even vegetables—over a direct flame causes fat and added oils to splash on the fire and then vaporize, creating other carcinogens that rise and stick to the food. Smoking foods has the same effect. Eating these foods, or even well-browned meats cooked to the crispy well-done stage, introduces carcinogens into the digestive system. These chemicals may or may not cause problems in the digestive tract, but once absorbed, they are detoxified by the liver's competent detoxifying system. A steady diet of foods containing significant amounts of these toxins, however, can overwhelm the system and may increase cancer risk.[106] If you eat broiled, fried, grilled, or smoked foods, choose them in moderation, and dilute their effects by varying your choices among foods prepared differently, such as boiled soups, stews, or pastas or baked, steamed, microwaved, or sautéed dishes.

- To minimize carcinogen formation during cooking:
  - *Roast or bake meats in the oven.*
  - *When grilling, line the grill with foil, or wrap the food in the foil.*
  - *Take care not to burn foods.*
  - *Marinate meats before cooking.*

Health-savvy diners vary their protein sources among poultry, fish, low-fat milk products, eggs, and vegetable proteins such as soy foods and other legumes. In addition, they limit red meats to a few servings per week.

Fiber-Rich Foods Many studies show that as people increase their dietary fiber intakes, their risk for colon cancer declines.[107] Fiber may protect against cancer by binding, diluting, and rapidly removing potential carcinogens from the GI tract; alternatively, other constituents of fiber-rich foods, such as the phytochemicals of whole grains or the nutrients of fruits and vegetables, may be at work.[108] The mechanisms for a protective role for fiber are not yet known.

As research takes its course, much evidence now weighs in favor of eating a diet rich in high-fiber, low-fat foods. Such a diet helps to regulate blood glucose and blood insulin and is linked with low rates of heart disease as well as some forms

© iStockphoto.com

Often, whole foods like these, not individual chemicals, lower people's cancer risks.

of cancer. If a meat-rich, calorie-dense diet is implicated in causation of certain cancers and if a vegetable-rich, whole-grain-rich diet is associated with prevention, then shouldn't vegetarians have a lower incidence of those cancers? They do, as the many studies cited in Controversy 6 have shown.

CONCEPT LINK 11-14
Other compelling reasons to attend to folate needs were presented in Chapter 7 (pages 253–254).

Folate and Antioxidant Vitamins Folate may protect against cancer of the esophagus and the colon, although evidence at this time is limited.[109] Folate plays roles in DNA synthesis and repair; thus, inadequate folate intakes may allow DNA damage to accumulate. This reason alone is enough to warrant everyone attending to their folate intake.

Vitamin E, vitamin C, and beta-carotene received attention in Controversy 7. Suffice it to say here that taking supplements has not been proved to prevent or cure cancer. In fact, once cancer is established, antioxidants may do more harm than good.

Calcium and Vitamin D Sufficient dietary calcium or foods that contain it may be protective against colon cancer.[110] Calcium intakes of about 600 to 1,000 milligrams per day—an amount easily provided by daily calcium-rich foods—appear to trigger the effect.[111] For example, Swedish men who consumed one-and-a-half servings a day of milk or milk products had a 33 percent lower risk of colorectal cancer than men consuming less than two servings a week.[112]

Another possibility is that the vitamin D added to milk in many areas might also be at work. Some intriguing evidence makes vitamin D a candidate for anticancer effects.[113] Although no iron-clad case exists for cancer prevention, with all the other points in their favor, prudence dictates that everyone should arrange to meet their calcium and vitamin D needs every day.

Iron Iron, both in the diet and in body stores, is under study for links with colon cancer. How iron may promote cancer is not known, but iron is a powerful oxidizing agent that can damage DNA in ways that initiate cancer. A high-meat diet generously supplies iron and it also correlates with greater risk of colon cancer.[114]

Erika Craddock/Photo Researchers, Inc.

Cruciferous vegetables belong to the cabbage family: arugula, bok choy, broccoli, broccoli sprouts, brussels sprouts, cabbages (all sorts), cauliflower, greens (collard, mustard, turnip), kale, kohlrabi, rutabaga, and turnip root.

Foods and Phytochemicals In the end, whole foods and whole diets composed of them, not single nutrients, may be most influential on cancer development. Almost without exception, epidemiological studies find a link between eating plenty of fruits and vegetables and a low incidence of cancers.[115] Fruits and vegetables contain a wide spectrum of nutrients and phytochemicals that may prevent or reduce oxidative damage to cell structures, including DNA. Some phytochemicals in fruits and vegetables are thought to act as **anticarcinogens** that stimulate the buildup of the body's arsenal of carcinogen-destroying enzymes. For example, the **cruciferous vegetables**—broccoli, brussels sprouts, cabbage, cauliflower, turnips, and the like—contain a variety of phytochemicals that defend against cancers of the esophagus and endometrium.[116] In addition, fruits and vegetables are rich in fiber. If you are considering making just one change to your diet, here is a place to begin—consume the recommended servings of fruits and vegetables each day. Table 11-11 summarizes dietary and lifestyle recommendations for reducing cancer risk.

KEY POINT Obesity, physical inactivity, alcohol consumption, and diets high in red meats are associated with cancer development. Foods containing ample fiber, folate, calcium, many other vitamins and minerals, and phytochemicals are thought to be protective.

anticarcinogens compounds in foods that act in any of several ways to oppose the formation of cancer.

cruciferous vegetables vegetables with cross-shaped blossoms—the cabbage family. Their intake is associated with low cancer rates in human populations. Examples are broccoli, brussels sprouts, cabbage, cauliflower, rutabagas, and turnips.

Conclusion

Nutrition is often associated with promoting health, and medicine with fighting disease, but no clear line separates nutrition and medicine. Every major agency involved with health promotion or medicine recommends a varied diet of whole foods as part of a lifestyle that provides the best possible chance for a long and healthy life. The Food Feature that follows presents an example of such a diet, the DASH diet.

TABLE 11-11 Recommendations for Reducing Cancer Risk

Body fatness: Be as lean as possible within the normal range of body weight.

- Ensure that body weight throughout childhood and adolescence projects toward the lower end of the normal adult BMI range by age 21.
- Maintain body weight within the normal range from age 21.
- Avoid weight gains and increases in waist circumference throughout adulthood.

Physical activity: Be physically active as part of everyday life.

- Be moderately physically active, equivalent to brisk walking, for at least 30 minutes every day.
- As fitness improves, aim for at least 60 minutes of moderate, or at least 30 minutes of vigorous, physical activity every day.
- Limit sedentary habits such as watching television.

Foods and drinks that promote weight gain: Limit consumption of energy-dense foods and avoid sugary drinks.

- Consume energy-dense foods (225 kcal/100 g food), sparingly.
- Avoid drinks with added sugar and limit fruit juices.
- Consume "fast foods" sparingly, if at all.

Plant foods: Eat mostly foods of plant origin.

- Eat at least five servings of a variety of nonstarchy vegetables and fruits every day.
- Eat relatively unprocessed grains and/or legumes with every meal.
- Limit refined starchy foods.

Animal foods: Limit intake of red meat and avoid processed meat.

- Eat no more than 18 oz of red meat a week, very little if any of which is processed.

Alcoholic drinks: Limit alcoholic drinks.

- If alcoholic drinks are consumed, limit consumption to no more than two drinks a day for men and one drink a day for women.

Preservation, processing, preparation: Limit consumption of salt and avoid moldy grains or legumes.

- Avoid salt-preserved, salted, or salty foods.
- Limit consumption of processed foods with added salt to ensure an intake of less than 6 g of salt (2.4 g of sodium) a day.
- Throw away moldy grains or legumes.

Dietary supplements: Aim to meet nutritional needs through diet.

- Dietary supplements are not recommended for cancer prevention.

Source: World Cancer Research Fund/American Institute for Cancer Research, Food, Nutrition, Physical Activity and the Prevention of Cancer: A Global Perspective *(Washington, D.C.: AICR, 2007), pp. 373–390.*

FOOD FEATURE The DASH Diet: Preventive Medicine

LO 11.6

"*If* you do not smoke or drink excessively, your choice of diet can influence your long-term health prospects more than any other action you might take," states a former surgeon general. Indeed, healthy young adults today are privileged to be among the first generations with enough nutrition knowledge to lay a foundation of health for today and tomorrow. Figure 11-11 illustrates this point.

DIETARY GUIDELINES AND THE DASH DIET

The more detailed our knowledge about nutrition science, it seems, the simpler the truth becomes: people who consume the adequate, balanced, calorie-controlled, moderate, and varied diet recommended by the *Dietary Guidelines for Americans* enjoy a longer, healthier life than those who do not. The DASH eating plan, presented in Table 11-12, can help people to meet these goals. People who require fewer or more than the 2,000 calories listed in the table should add or subtract food servings proportionally.

People who eat the DASH diet often see their blood pressure drop, along with total and LDL blood cholesterol—heart-healthy changes. To lower saturated fat and cholesterol intakes, the DASH diet emphasizes fruits, vegetables, whole grains, and fat-free or low-fat milk and milk products. It also features fish, poultry, and nuts instead of some of the red meat so common in U.S. diets. The foods of the DASH diet provide greater intakes of potassium, calcium, and magnesium, minerals shown to lower blood pressure. More protein and fiber bring added benefits.

Because the DASH diet centers on fresh, unprocessed, or lightly processed foods, it can present less sodium, too. It seems, with regard to sodium, "the lower the better" for reducing blood pressure, with most people benefiting from holding sodium intake to about 1,500 mg per day. Even at higher levels of intake, the DASH diet can still produce a drop in blood pressure, although not as great as with sodium restriction.[117]

Changes in diet are often best attempted a few at a time. A good place to start is by increasing the intake of fruits and vegetables.

FRUITS AND VEGETABLES: MORE MATTERS

The National Fruit & Vegetable Program is a confederation composed of the Centers for Disease Control and Prevention, the American Heart Association, the American Diabetes Association, the American Cancer Society, and many other national organizations. These agencies work together to urge people to increase their intakes of a variety of fruits, vegetables, and legumes, not just for nutrients they provide but also for the phytochemicals that combine synergistically to promote health. Although the amount depends upon energy intake and activity level, as

- Tricks to choosing enough fruits, vegetables, and legumes:
  - *Vow to try a new fruit or vegetable once each month. Read some cookbooks for ideas.*
  - *Eat a rainbow of fruits and vegetables: the more reds, oranges, yellows, greens, blues, and purples the better.*
  - *Use the salad bar to buy ready-to-eat vegetables and legumes if you are in a hurry.*
  - *Keep a fruit bowl in plain view, filled with fresh fruit, small raisin or dried cranberry packs, and shelf-stable fruit cups.*
  - *Add dried fruit bits to salads, cereal, or yogurt.*
  - *Place carrot and celery sticks in a glass of water like a bouquet, and keep them in the refrigerator for crisp, healthy snacks.*
  - *Try a grilled mushroom sandwich or a soy "veggie burger" instead of a beef hamburger sandwich.*
  - *Try using soy products in many ways. Soy milk drinks, ground and patty meat replacers, tofu, and soy snacks count as a vegetable and may offer unique benefits from soy protein, fiber, and phytochemicals.*
  - *Drink 100 percent fruit or vegetable juices. Choose 100 percent juice bars for a frozen treat.*
  - *Vegetable sauces count: ½ cup tomato spaghetti sauce or salsa counts as ½ cup "other vegetables" (see Chapter 2).*
  - *Blend smoothies from bananas, fruit juice, and berries with ice or yogurt.*
  - *Choose larger portions of lower-calorie vegetables, such as cooked leafy greens or carrots.*
  - *Add beans and peas to salads, stews, and meat dishes. Beans and peas soak up the flavor of meat and stretch the servings per pound.*

fruits & veggies more matters™

Courtesy of Produce for Better Health Foundation

FIGURE 11-11 **Proper Nutrition Shields Against Diseases**

A well-chosen diet can protect your health.

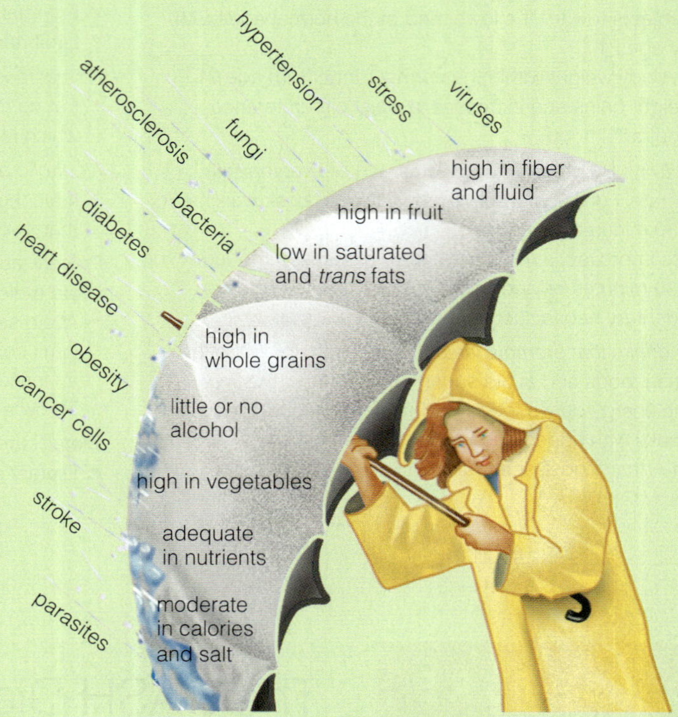

a general rule, nine servings seems to be supportive of men's health; seven to be appropriate for most women and children older than 6 years; and five servings to be about right for children under age 6.[118] You can find out how many servings are right for you by visiting the Internet website: www.fruitsandveggiesmatter.org. Some tips for increasing your intakes appear in the margin.

Who knows? Foods destined to become your favorites may still await you on the produce shelves. An adventurous spirit is a plus in this regard.

CONCLUSION

In the end, people's choices are their own. Whoever you are, we encourage you to take the time to work out ways of making your diet meet the guidelines you know will support your health. If you are healthy and of normal weight, if you are physically active, and if your diet on most days follows the *Dietary Guidelines*, then you can indulge occasionally in a cheesy pizza, marbled steak, banana split, or even a greasy fast-food burger and fries without inflicting much damage on your health. (Once a week may be harmless, but the less frequently the better.) Especially, take time to enjoy your meals: the sights, smells, and tastes of good foods are among life's greatest pleasures. Joy, even the simple joy of eating, contributes to a healthy life.

David Madison/Photographer's Choice/Getty Images

Don't forget: Be physically active all your life.

TABLE 11-12 **The DASH Eating Plan at a 2,000-Calorie Level**

Food Group	Daily Servings	Serving Sizes	Examples and Notes	Significance of Each Food Group to the DASH Eating Pattern
Grains*	6–8	1 slice bread 1 oz dry cereal† ½ cup cooked rice, pasta, or cereal	Whole-wheat bread and rolls, whole-wheat pasta, English muffin, pita bread, bagel, cereals, grits, oatmeal, brown rice, unsalted pretzels and popcorn	Major sources of energy and fiber
Vegetables	4–5	1 cup raw leafy vegetable ½ cup cut-up raw or cooked vegetable ½ cup vegetable juice	Broccoli, carrots, collards, green beans, green peas, kale, lima beans, potatoes, spinach, squash, sweet potatoes, tomatoes	Rich sources of potassium, magnesium, and fiber
Fruits	4–5	1 medium fruit ¼ cup dried fruit ½ cup fresh, frozen, or canned fruit ½ cup fruit juice	Apples, apricots, bananas, dates, grapes, oranges, grapefruit, grapefruit juice, mangoes, melons, peaches, pineapples, raisins, strawberries, tangerines	Important sources of potassium, magnesium, and fiber
Fat-free or low-fat milk and milk products	2–3	1 cup milk or yogurt 1½ oz cheese	Fat-free (skim) or low-fat (1%) milk or buttermilk; fat-free, low-fat, or reduced-fat cheese; fat-free or low-fat regular or frozen yogurt	Major sources of calcium and protein
Lean meats, poultry, and fish	6 or less	1 oz cooked meats, poultry, or fish 1 egg‡	Select only lean; trim away visible fats; broil, roast, or poach; remove skin from poultry	Rich sources of protein and magnesium
Nuts, seeds, and legumes	4–5 per week	⅓ cup or 1½ oz nuts 2 tbs peanut butter 2 tbs or ½ oz seeds ½ cup cooked legumes (dry beans and peas)	Almonds, hazelnuts, mixed nuts, peanuts, walnuts, sunflower seeds, peanut butter, kidney beans, lentils, split peas	Rich sources of energy, magnesium, protein, and fiber
Fats and oils§	2–3	1 tsp soft margarine 1 tsp vegetable oil 1 tbs mayonnaise 2 tbs salad dressing	Soft margarine, vegetable oil (such as canola, corn, olive, or safflower), low-fat mayonnaise, light salad dressing	The DASH study had 27 percent of calories as fat, including fat in or added to foods
Sweets and added sugars	5 or less per week	1 tbs sugar 1 tbs jelly or jam ½ cup sorbet, gelatin 1 cup lemonade	Fruit-flavored gelatin, fruit punch, hard candy, jelly, maple syrup, sorbet and ices, sugar	Sweets should be low in fat

**Whole grains are recommended for most grain servings as a good source of fiber and nutrients.*

†Serving sizes vary between ½ cup and 1¼ cups, depending on cereal type. Check the product's Nutrition Facts label.

‡Since eggs are high in cholesterol, limit egg yolk intake to no more than four per week; two egg whites have the same protein content as 1 oz of meat.

§Fat content changes serving amount for fats and oils. For example, 1 tbs of regular salad dressing equals one serving; 1 tbs of a low-fat dressing equals one-half serving; 1 tbs of a fat-free dressing equals zero servings.

Diet Analysis PLUS Concepts in Action

Analyze Your Diet for Health Promotion

The purpose of this exercise is to increase your awareness of the well-balanced diet recommended for disease prevention.

1. One way to lower your risk of heart attack is to keep your blood pressure in a normal range. Study Table 11-12 (page 437), which provides an eating plan that supports normal blood pressure. Create a meal that follows the principles of the DASH diet. Select the Track Diet tab from the red navigation bar. Select a date and find the foods that you wish to include in this lunch. From the Reports tab, go to Source Analysis Report for that meal, and select Sodium from the drop-down box. Generate a report. How much sodium did your meal contain? Which foods contributed the most sodium to the meal? Again from the Reports tab, go to the Intake vs. Goals Report. Generate a report. Locate sodium and find the percentage of the DRI intake recommendation provided by your DRI for sodium. If the sodium was higher than 33 percent (one-third) of your allowance, what can you change to bring it into compliance?
2. When the immune system falters, nutrition status often suffers. For people with weak immune systems where protein-energy malnutrition (PEM) occurs (see Table 11-1, page 410), medical nutrition therapy is critical. Select the Track Diet tab from the red navigation bar. Select a new day and find foods to create one meal that provides one-third of the day's requirement of high-quality, easily digestible protein for an immune-compromised adult with PEM. Take into account a diminished appetite, and make the food appealing and easy to eat. From the Reports tab, select the Source Analysis Report and select Protein. Generate a report. How many grams of protein did the meal provide? Now select the Intake vs. Goals Report to see what percentage of the day's protein the meal supplied. Did it supply about a third of the day's need? If not, what adjustments can you make to better meet this person's need?
3. Chronic diseases interact as risk factors for each other (Figure 11-3, page 411). One diet characteristic recommended to reduce chronic disease risk is reduced saturated fat intake. Create a meal low in saturated fat following the instructions in item number 2. Generate a Fat Breakdown Report and an Intake vs. Goals Report for that meal. How much saturated fat did your meal supply? Was it less than 10 percent of total calories for the meal? If not, what can you change to lower it?
4. Although diet and exercise are not easy or quick, they are a powerful and safe combination for improving heart health. Select the Track Diet tab and select the day you used in item number 3. Take a look at Table 11-5, page 420, then create a full day's menu by adding foods for breakfast, lunch, and snack that achieve the diet modifications listed for saturated fat, cholesterol, and soluble fiber (ignore the others). Select the Reports tab and the MyPyramid Report for that date and generate a report. Did your day's meals meet your goals?
5. Research reports that vegetarians have a lower incidence of certain cancers as well as a lower rate of heart disease. A well-chosen vegetarian diet is high in fiber, phytochemicals, whole grains, and vitamins, and it is ideally low in saturated fat. Using Table 11-10 and Table 11-11, pages 431 and 435, to guide you, create a vegetarian meal that includes foods associated with low cancer risks. Enter the data from the Track Diet tab. Select the Intake vs. Goals Report for that date and meal and generate a report. What nutrients would be of interest when evaluating your vegetarian meal for adequacy (consult Table C6-2 on page 223)? Did the meal contain enough protein, vitamins, and minerals? How about fiber? Was it low enough in saturated fat?

MEDIA MENU

CENGAGENOW To find additional quiz questions, view videos and animations, and explore interactive exercises, go to **www.cengage.com/sso.**

Search for "chronic diseases," "disease prevention," "men's health," "women's health," "heart disease," "cancer," and "stroke" at **www.healthfinder.gov.**

Assess your heart disease risk at the American Heart Association site: **www.americanheart.org.**

Find current information and papers on heart disease and stroke at **www.nhlbi.nih.gov.**

Search for information on health at the NIH Consumer Health Information site at **www.health.nih.gov.**

Examine your family's health history at the U.S. Surgeon General's site: **www.familyhistory.hhs.gov.**

SELF CHECK

Answers to these Self Check questions are in Appendix G.

1. By what age do most people have well-developed plaques in their arteries?
   - A. 20 years
   - B. 30 years
   - C. 40 years
   - D. 50 years
2. Which of the following is a risk factor for cardiovascular disease?
   - A. high blood HDL cholesterol
   - B. low blood pressure
   - C. low LDL cholesterol
   - D. diabetes
3. An "atherogenic diet" is high in all of the following *except:*
   - A. fiber
   - B. cholesterol
   - C. saturated fats
   - D. *trans* fats
4. Which of the following dietary factors may help to regulate blood pressure?
   - A. calcium
   - B. magnesium
   - C. potassium
   - D. all of the above
5. Which of the following have been associated with an increase in cancer risk?
   - A. alcohol
   - B. high intakes of red meat
   - C. high intakes of processed meats
   - D. all of the above
6. When calorie intakes rise, cancer rates also increase.
   T F
7. Laboratory evidence suggests that a high-calcium diet may increase the risk of colon cancer.
   T F
8. The DASH diet is designed for athletes who compete in sprinting events.
   T F
9. Hypertension is more severe and occurs earlier in life among people of European or Asian descent than among African Americans.
   T F
10. Most alternative therapies, such as herbal medicine, have not been well established by scientific experimentation to be safe and effective.
   T F

CONTROVERSY 11

Nutritional Genomics: Can It Deliver on Its Promises?

LO 11.7

Health care appears to be standing at the edge of a **genomics** revolution.[1]* Today's health-care system emphasizes treatment only after disease symptoms arise. This may soon give way to a system aimed at identifying in healthy people—even children—traits in the **genome** that raise the odds of developing diseases in the future. Once identified, people with those tendencies may be helped to prevent or minimize disease through customized care based on each individual's genetic profile.[2] A registered dietitian, for example, may use the information to individualize medical nutrition therapy for those who already suffer illness or to provide diets with just the right nutrients and other **bioactive food components** that precisely meet the client's needs.[3]

This Controversy offers just a taste of the exciting research in these areas—there is much more to learn and the science advances daily. To help get started, Table C11-1 distinguishes among the terms genomics, ***nutritional genomics, epigenetics,*** and others.[4] Then it tells about some evidence that suggests explanations for links between chronic diseases, including cancer, and diet. The closing section brings up some ethical concerns surrounding genetic tests of all kinds and unveils fraud already occurring in the genetic testing marketplace.

*Reference notes are found in Appendix F.

TABLE C11-1 Nutritional Genomic Terms

- **bioactive food components** nutrients and phytochemicals of foods that alter physiological processes often by interacting, directly or indirectly, with the genes.
- **DNA microarray technology** research tools that analyze the expression of thousands of genes simultaneously and search for particular genes associated with a disease. DNA microarrays are also called *DNA chips*.
- **epigenetics** the science of heritable changes in gene function that occur without a change in the DNA sequence.
- **epigenome** the proteins and other molecules associated with chromosomes that affect gene expression. The epigenome is modulated by bioactive food components and other factors in ways that can be inherited. *Epi* is a Greek prefix, meaning "above" or "on."
- **genome** (GEE-nohm) the full complement of genetic material in the chromosomes of a cell. Also defined in Chapter 1.
- **genomics** the study of all the genes in an organism and their interactions with environmental factors.
- **histones** proteins that lend structural support to the chromosome structure and that activate or silence gene expression.
- **methyl groups** small carbon-containing molecules that, among their activities, silence genes when applied to DNA strands by enzymes.
- **mutation** a permanent, heritable change in an organism's DNA.
- **nucleotide** (NU-klee-oh-tied) one of the subunits from which DNA and RNA are composed.
- **nutritional genomics** the science of how food (and its components) interacts with the genome.
- **SNP** a single misplaced nucleotide in a gene that causes formation of an altered protein. The letters SNP stand for *single nucleotide polymorphism.*

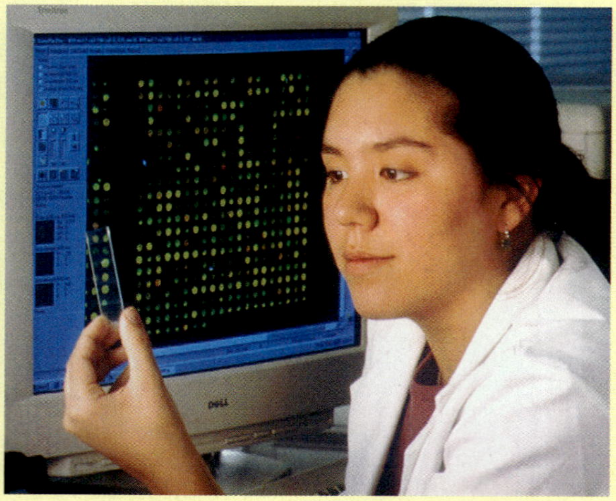

NUTRITIONAL GENOMICS RESEARCH

With unprecedented speed, new revelations are emerging from laboratories worldwide.[5] Until recently, no one knew *how* identical twins, with their identical DNA, could develop different diseases; or how a pregnant woman's diet might forever affect the health of her grandchildren and her great-grandchildren; or how phytochemicals might alter the course of certain cancers. At least partial answers to these and other mysteries lie in the realm of nutritional genomics.[6]

In general, today's nutritional genomics researchers strive to:

- identify the genes: which genes can be regulated by diet, and which of these participate in the onset, progression, or severity of chronic disease?
- explain the mechanisms: how exactly do bioactive food components modify the activities of disease-related genes?
- develop practical applications: which nutrient intake levels best maintain health, and which foods or whole diets might prevent or relieve chronic diseases or other conditions by modifying genetic activity?

With a new research tool, **DNA microarray technology,** scientists now have the power to uncover and integrate such information.[7] In DNA microarray technology, robotic arms precisely fasten a DNA strand of a known sequence onto a slide. Then, a computer compares the pattern of gene expression of the known sequence with that of an unknown DNA sample taken from an individual's cells. This comparison reveals which of the sample genes are expressed (actively making proteins—details in Chapter 6) and which are silenced (inactive), and how they respond under certain conditions. The results allow identification of inherited disease tendencies, unusual nutrient needs, and many other medical concerns.[8] The technique promises major advancements in health care for people worldwide.[9]

DNA VARIATIONS, NUTRITION, AND DISEASE

Small variations in DNA sequences, called **mutations,** dictate many of the differences among human beings. The most common are **SNPs** (pronounced "snips"), involving the variation of a single tiny molecule (a **nucleotide**) in a strand of DNA. About 10 million such SNPs are known to exist among people.

SNPs and Diseases

Most individuals carry tens of thousands of SNPs, and most have no effect at all.[10] Rarely, however, a single SNP in a high-powered gene can produce a severe disease immediately from birth, such as PKU, described in Chapter 3. More commonly, SNPs do not cause a disease directly but may subtly work with other gene variants and with environmental factors such as diet to increase the risk of developing a chronic disease, such as heart disease, later in life. SNPs set the stage for a chronic disease to occur, but the person's own choices are among the actors that bring on the disease.

As an example, a common SNP in a fat metabolism gene changes the body's response to dietary fats. People with this SNP maintain lower blood LDL cholesterol when they eat a diet rich in polyunsaturated fatty acids (PUFA) and they develop higher LDL when they consume less PUFA.[11] A gene (in this case, a fat metabolism gene with a SNP) interacts with a nutrient from the diet (in this case, PUFA) to influence a risk factor for a disease (LDL cholesterol implicated in heart disease).

Complexity of SNP-Disease Relationships

Genetic risks for chronic diseases may appear to be straightforward—just identify the SNPs to identify an increased disease risk—but these associations are proving difficult to pin down. They often involve SNPs in multiple genes, each of which may interact with many dietary constituents or other environmental factors. Furthermore, another realm of influence on gene behavior exists—the **epigenome.**

EPIGENETICS

People often think of chromosomes as simple strands of DNA, but chromosomes exist as complex combinations of DNA, proteins, and other molecules. DNA strands are the primary carrier of inherited information, but the epigenome constitutes another parallel bank of inheritable information.[12] The epigenome consists of proteins and other molecules that act to regulate the expression of genes on the strands of DNA, turning the genes on or off. Like DNA, the epigenome can be inherited from generation to generation, but it can also be altered by environmental influences.[13]

The genome and the epigenome have been likened to nature's pen and pencil set.[14] The genome, made of DNA, is written in indelible ink, so to speak, making its sequence more permanent and difficult to change. The epigenome is written in pencil in the margins, allowing for erasures and changes.

A Cell Differentiation Specialist

The epigenome specializes in differentiating one type of cell from another. It does not change the DNA sequence itself, but instead controls which genes are turned on or off—that is, which are expressed or silenced. For example, a cone cell of a person's eye and a blood-producing cell of that person's bone marrow contain identical DNA strands. Luckily for the person, the epigenome activates and silences genes on the DNA strands so that each cell type reliably makes only the correct proteins to allow its own specialized functions.[15]

How Epigenetic Regulation Works

Mechanisms for epigenetic regulation include, among others, proteins known as **histones** and small organic molecules called **methyl groups.**† Both of these mechanisms can be modified by way of diet and other environmental influences.

Chromosome Structural Proteins in Gene Expression Millions of globular proteins, the histones, reside within the chromosomes (shown in Figure C11-1). Like thread wound around a spool, sections of DNA "thread" are tightly wrapped around protein histones. Thus, the huge DNA molecules are condensed to fit inside the tiny cell nucleus.

Once believed to confer only structural support to the chromosomes, histones are now known to regulate gene expression, too. Genes on DNA segments wrapped around a histone are silent—they physically lack the room to perform the tasks of protein synthesis. Histones, though, can change this situation in response to changing environmental conditions. Histones sport little protein "tails" that stick out from their DNA wrappings. These tails serve as landing sites

†Other mechanisms include acetylation of DNA (and histones), other chromatin remodeling factors, and noncoding regulatory RNA molecules.

FIGURE C11-1 Two Epigenetic Factors and Gene Activity

This figure shows methyl groups attached to a DNA strand and histones, globular protein "spools" wrapped with lengths of DNA. Other epigenetic factors also exist.

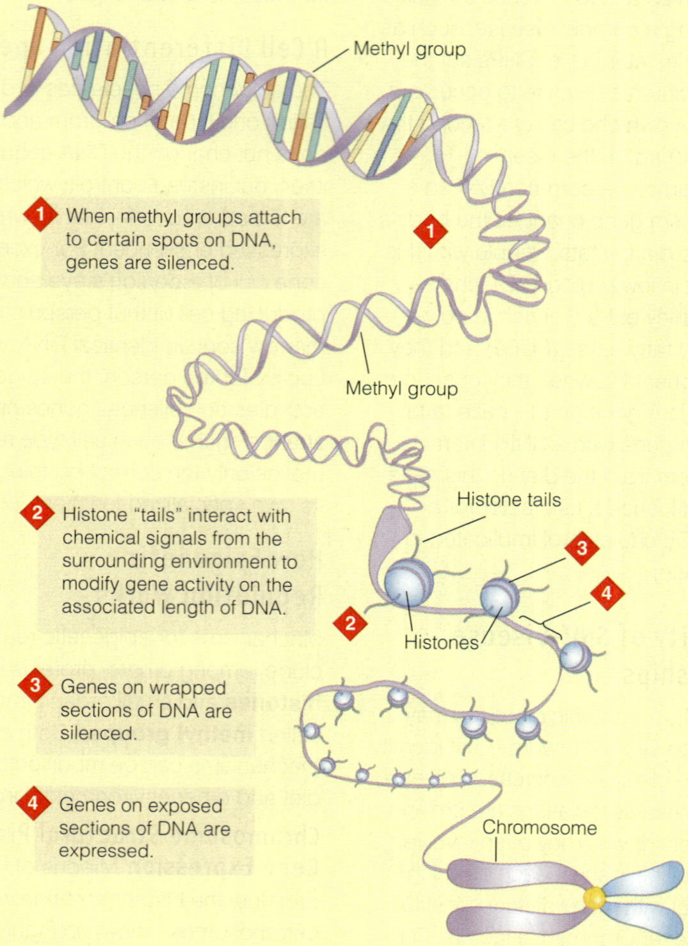

for many molecules that signify cellular conditions.

With the right chemical signals, a histone loosens its grip on its wraps of DNA, allowing a bit of the strand to stretch out. Genes on these stretched out segments can then express their encoded proteins—they are activated. Here's where nutrition comes in: many of the molecular signals to which histones respond arise from the diet—they consist of nutrients and phytochemicals themselves or of compounds generated during their metabolism (Figure C11-2).

A Broccoli Phytochemical Example A phytochemical, sulforaphane (see Controversy 2), found in broccoli, broccoli sprouts, and other cabbage-family vegetables, may affect cancer processes by way of histone changes in cancer cells.[16] One characteristic of cancerous tissue is uncontrolled cell division. In cancer cells, histones inappropriately silence genes that ordinarily prevent cells from multiplying out of control.

In test tubes, sulforaphane reverses those cancer-promoting histone changes and reinstates control of cell division. In mice, sulforaphane inhibits certain cancers. In people, ingestion of one cup of broccoli sprouts alters histone activities in blood cells. Does consumption of broccoli or other cabbage-family food actually prevent cancer in people? People who consume these foods regularly do seem to suffer fewer of some cancers.[17] No one knows whether the foods themselves are protective, however; researchers are still investigating that question.

DNA Methyl Groups and Gene Regulation Genes are also regulated by molecules that adhere to the DNA strand itself. Methyl groups, tiny organic compounds, arise from the diet. Methyl groups attach directly onto DNA (look again at Figure C11-1), altering gene expression.[18] Attachment of a methyl group to a beginning of a gene on the DNA strand silences gene expression; removal of the methyl groups allows gene expression and protein replication to occur.[19]

B Vitamins and Methyl Groups A powerful example of the effect of diet on gene expression involves the influence of the B vitamin folate on DNA methylation. Folate (along with other B vitamins) is essential for transferring methyl groups to other molecules, including to DNA. With too little folate, genes may be insufficiently methylated to allow normal suppression of unneeded proteins. The flip side is also true: too much folate can inappropriately silence genes whose proteins are necessary for health.[20]

This effect is illustrated in the accompanying photo of two mice. Despite their strikingly different appearance, both of these mice have identical DNA. Both possess a gene that tends to produce fat, yellow pups, but their gene expression was altered when their mothers were fed different diets during pregnancy. The mother of the lean, brown mouse received doses of the B vitamins folate and vitamin B_{12}. By way of the methyl group transfer activity of these vitamins, the gene for "yellow and fat" was silenced, resulting in brown, lean pups.[21]

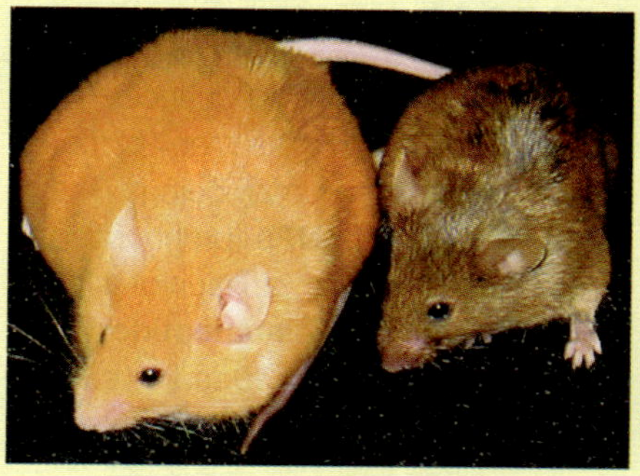

© Jirtle and Waterland

These two mice share an identical gene that tends to produce fat, yellow mice. The mother of the lean, brown mouse received supplemental B vitamins that silenced the gene.

FIGURE C11-2 **Bioactive Food Components and Gene Expression**

Nutrients and phytochemicals (bioactive food components) in the diet can affect gene expression directly or indirectly.

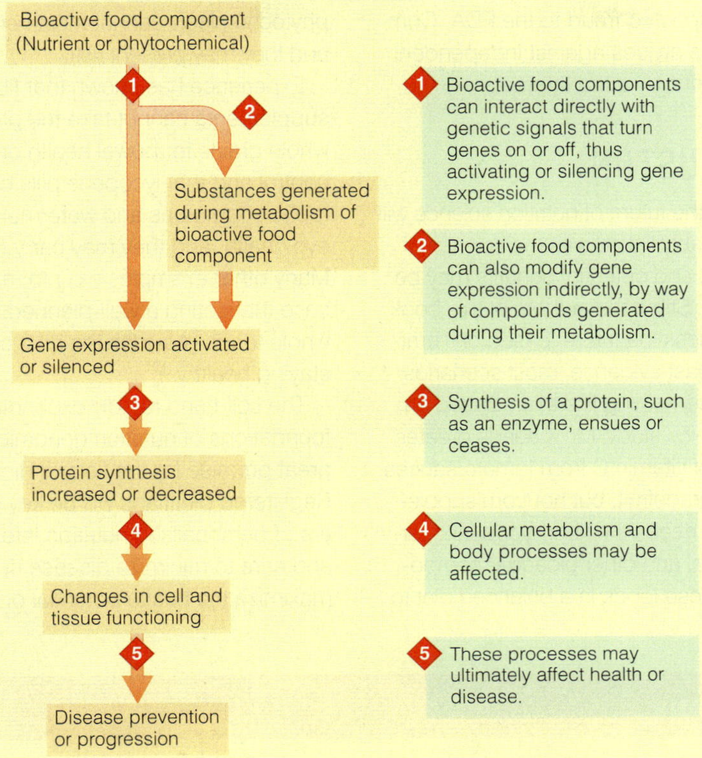

Note that the extra vitamins did not change the DNA sequence. Still, such epigenomic changes established during pregnancy can persist through several generations.

Future Generation Effects

Exactly how epigenomic changes can survive from generation to generation involves some details of embryonic development. In a developing embryo, primitive egg and sperm cells form in the budding ovaries and testes, and these primitive reproductive cells undergo epigenomic changes along with all of the embryo's other cells.[22] Later, when this first generation reaches breeding maturity, their stored up primitive reproductive cells ripen and transmit the epigenomic changes acquired during gestation to their offspring and to future generations.[23] While not conclusive, evidence suggests that similar mechanisms involving different genes may be at work in people, too.[24]

Importantly, pregnant women should not attempt to alter their children's and grandchildren's risks of obesity or other diseases by loading up on B vitamins or other substances. The effects of imbalances are unpredictable and can be severe (see the next chapter for details).

Can Adults Modify Their Epigenome?

Researchers believe that the greatest epigenomic changes from environmental influences occur early during embryonic development.[25] Some changes can still occur into adolescence and even adulthood, however, and they can affect health outcomes.[26] The findings on sulforaphane of broccoli, described earlier, provide evidence that certain epigenome factors in adult cells can indeed be changed, at least temporarily, by bioactive constituents of foods.

Now a theory emerges to suggest at least a partial solution to the mystery of how identical twins can develop different diseases. Although the twins have identical DNA, they acquire differences in their epigenomes.[27] Each encounters different environmental influences at various times of life that change their genetic expression.

Health Implications

When genes are activated or silenced, human health hangs in the balance. Silencing a gene that promotes tumor growth, for example, would be beneficial if it slowed or stopped a person's cancer. Conversely, silencing a gene that *suppresses* cancer growth could increase the likelihood of cancer or worsen an existing condition.

Although research is ongoing, it has established that bioactive constituents of whole foods affect genetic processes in both known and unknown ways. Therefore, the advice of Chapter 2 to eat a nutritious diet based on a variety of whole foods takes on a greater meaning.

ARGUMENTS SURROUNDING GENETIC TESTING

For nutritional genomics to be of practical value requires that people undergo genetic testing. Researchers and others debate the merits and demerits of all kinds of genetic testing for currently healthy people. Supporters point out that genetic testing holds enormous promise for improving human health and that application of the technology should keep pace with advances in research.

Critics of this position raise some important points, however.[28] They question whether identifying a genetic marker for disease by way of expensive testing would translate into better health for the nation or waste limited health-care dollars. They also voice fears that certain DNA results, once known, could be misused. Table C11-2 provides the scope of the arguments.

NUTRITIONAL GENOMICS FRAUD

Fraud is a problem in the genetic testing marketplace today, particularly as it relates to nutrition. Investigators with the U.S. Government Accountability Office reported clear evidence of widespread fraud among Internet-based nutritional genomics testing laboratories.[29] To assess the validity of such testing, the investigators submitted one individual's cells under many names to a variety of laboratories. Authentic tests would have revealed the identical nature of the DNA but the samples came back with widely varied analyses, recommendations, and sales pitches. The investigators suggested that in many cases their sample DNA may not have been analyzed at all and that results and recommendations were likely to have been based on investigators' answers to simple medical history questions posed by the test providers.

Unethical companies may also try to frighten customers into ordering expensive supplements.[30] The companies claim that the supplements they sell are tailored to meet "personal nutrient requirements" or to "strengthen the body against disease risks" (needs supposedly determined by their fake DNA tests). The supplements can cost up to 30 times the price of comparable products sold in stores.

Certainly, much genetic testing, conducted through legitimate medical providers, is useful and important to proper medical care. As Controversy 1 of this book established, however, consumers must be on guard against all kinds of health and nutrition quackery and should report suspected fraud to the FDA. Common sense argues against independent genetic testing via the Internet.

CONCLUSION

No doubt the future of nutrition science will be inextricably linked with the science of genomics, and potential benefits may be enormous. Still, if the authors of this book were to guess the future, based on libraries full of past evidence, most scenarios might go something like this: "Based on our genomics study, Mr. X needs greater amounts of vitamin C from tomato sauces and pink grapefruit, but not from supplements. He needs the fiber, lycopene, carbohydrates, and other bioactive components of these foods in a balanced diet to ensure their efficient use by the body, and to ward off additional problems." Or, for a woman with an increased risk of cancer: "In addition to a nutritious plant-based diet, the phytochemicals from legumes, citrus, broccoli, and berries may help Ms. Y to delay cancer onset. Pills of isolated phytochemicals cannot meet her needs, and they may present risks."

Experience has shown that fiber supplements cannot take the place of whole grains for bowel health or diabetes control and that lycopene pills cannot replace tomatoes and watermelon for eye health, and they may carry risks.[31] Many other examples exist to make the case that eating a well-planned diet of whole foods provides the best chance of staying healthy.[32]

The solid and rapidly expanding foundations of nutrition genomics hold great promise for the field of dietetics.[33] Registered dietitians will be key providers of personalized nutrition information and care to minimize disease risks and maximize the health potential of clients.

TABLE C11-2 Genetic Testing: Pros and Cons

Arguments for Genetic Testing	Arguments Against Genetic Testing
1. Genetic tests provide additional information for improved understanding of a patient's medical profile.	1. More information may not be better. Genetic testing has so far yielded minimally more useful information than less expensive clinical tests.
2. With forewarning, genetically susceptible people could make lifestyle changes to reduce their risks.	2. Most people who test positive for risk factors such as diabetes and high LDL cholesterol do not make needed lifestyle changes to reduce their risks. More detailed warnings will probably not help them to do so.
3. Nutritional genomic testing in particular holds the promise of some urgently needed help in fighting today's major killers—heart disease and cancer—despite details in application yet to be worked out. Supporters ask, "should we let perfectionism stand in the way of progress?	3. Current knowledge does not support application. • Lifestyle changes to match gene profiles have not yet been defined. • Links between specific genetic variations and chronic disease are often not fully defined. • Astronomical numbers of potential interactions between environmental factors with genome and epigenome variations must be pinned down before effective application is possible.
4. Regulations concerning use and ownership of genetic information are under development, and some, such as the Genetic Information Nondiscrimination Act of 2008, are currently in force.	4. Regulation loopholes exist, and information may be accessible to other parties. Genetic discrimination can be disguised making it difficult to prove.
5. Ethical concerns are minor and protections and protocol will be established as genetic testing grows more common. Some controls already exist.	5. Today's safeguards are incomplete and not universally enforced. Ethical concerns include: • Unintentional disclosure of family relationships (such as adoptions or other parentage issues). • Insurance discrimination or limitations against those with certain genetic traits. • Employer discrimination against certain traits to reduce potential sick time expenses.

Sources: S. Vakili and M. A. Caudill, Personalized nutrition: Nutritional genomics as a potential tool for targeted medical nutrition therapy, Nutrition Reviews *65 (2009): 301–315; M. M. Bergmann, U. Görman, and J. C. Mathers, Bioethical considerations for human nutrigenomics,* Annual Review of Nutrition *28 (2008): 447–467; J. M. Ordovas, Nutrigenetics, plasma lipids, and cardiovascular risk,* Journal of the American Dietetic Association *106 (2006): 1074–1081.*

Food Safety and Food Technology

12

DO YOU EVER . . .

- Blame digestive tract symptoms on "stomach flu"?
- Think that foods from grocery stores are germ-free?
- Refrigerate uneaten party foods *after* the guests have gone home?
- Eat raw sushi but avoid additives to stay well?

Keep reading . . .

© Images.com/Corbis

Learning Objectives

To find learning objective topics in this chapter, look for text headings with a corresponding "LO" number above the heading. After completing this chapter, you should be able to accomplish the following:

LO 12.1 Describe two ways in which foodborne microorganisms can cause illness in the body, and give examples of each.

LO 12.2 Develop a plan, from purchase to table, by which consumers can reduce their risks of foodborne illnesses from seafood, eggs, meats, and produce.

LO 12.3 Name some recent advances aimed at reducing microbial food contamination, and describe their potential contribution to the safety of the U.S. food supply.

LO 12.4 Describe how pesticides enter the food supply, and suggest possible actions to reduce consumption of residues.

LO 12.5 Discuss potential advantages and disadvantages associated with organic foods.

LO 12.6 Provide evidence to justify this statement: "Food additives used in the United States serve some important functions and are safe to consume."

LO 12.7 Compare and contrast the advantages and disadvantages of food production by way of genetic modification and conventional farming.

Consumers in the United States and Canada enjoy food supplies ranking among the safest, most pleasing, and most abundant in the world. Along with these benefits comes the consumer's responsibility to distinguish between choices leading to food **safety** and those that pose a **hazard.**

As human populations grow and food supplies become more global, new food-safety challenges arise that require new processes, new technologies, and greater cooperation to solve.[1*] Food safety is, therefore, a moving target. The Food and Drug Administration (FDA), the major agency charged with maintaining the safety of the U.S. food supply, focuses its ongoing efforts in these main areas of concern:

1. *Microbial foodborne illness.* Each year in the United States, an estimated 76 million people become ill from foodborne diseases, and about 5,000 of them die.[2]
2. *Natural toxins in foods.* These constitute a hazard mostly when people consume large quantities of single foods either by choice (fad diets) or by necessity (poverty).
3. *Residues in food.*
   a. *Environmental and other contaminants* (other than pesticides). Household and industrial chemicals are increasing yearly in number and concentration, and their impacts are hard to foresee and to forestall.
   b. *Pesticides.* A subclass of environmental contaminants, they are listed separately because they are applied intentionally to foods and, in theory, can be controlled.
   c. *Animal drugs.* These include hormones and antibiotics that increase growth or milk production and combat diseases in food animals.
4. *Nutrients in foods.* These require close attention as more and more highly processed and artificially constituted foods appear on the market.
5. *Intentional approved food additives.* These are of little concern because so much is known about them that they pose virtually no hazard to consumers and because their use is well regulated.
6. *Genetically modified foods.* Listed last because such foods undergo rigorous scrutiny before going to market.

*Reference notes are found in Appendix F.

TABLE 12-1 Agencies that Monitor the U.S. Food Supply

- **CDC (Centers for Disease Control and Prevention)** a branch of the Department of Health and Human Services that is responsible for monitoring foodborne diseases.
  - Together with the USDA and FDA, CDC operates *FoodNet,* an organization that tracks the prevalence, trends, causes, and interventions of U.S. foodborne illnesses.
  - These groups also conduct molecular DNA tracking of foodborne illness-causing microorganisms through *PulseNet,* a network of scientists in every state who react quickly to identify illness outbreaks.
- **EPA (Environmental Protection Agency)** the federal agency that is responsible for regulating pesticides and establishing water quality standards.
- **FDA (Food and Drug Administration)** the part of the Department of Health and Human Services' Public Health Service that is responsible for ensuring the safety and wholesomeness of all foods sold in interstate commerce except meat, poultry, and eggs (which are under the jurisdiction of the USDA); inspecting food plants and imported foods; and setting standards for food consumption. The FDA also regulates food additives.
- **USDA (U.S. Department of Agriculture)** the federal agency that is responsible for enforcing standards for the wholesomeness and quality of meat, poultry, and eggs produced in the United States; conducting nutrition research; and educating the public about nutrition.
- **WHO (World Health Organization)** an international agency that develops standards to regulate pesticide use. A related organization is the FAO (Food and Agricultural Organization).

safety the practical certainty that injury will not result from the use of a substance.

hazard a state of danger; used to refer to any circumstance in which harm is possible under normal conditions of use.

Other government and world agencies involved in food safety are listed in Table 12-1. In addition, industry groups cooperate with government organizations to develop their own voluntary food-safety guidelines.

Microbial **foodborne illness,** commonly called *food poisoning,* is first on the list because illnesses and deaths from food poisoning far outnumber other kinds of food-related threats. The last, genetic modification of foods, is of least concern. The others fall somewhere in between.

A related concern beyond the scope of this text is **food bioterrorism**—the possibility of deliberate microbial or chemical contamination of the U.S. food supply. The FDA employs broad strategies to counter food bioterrorism; food producers and importers can use a computerized risk-assessment system to help identify and correct vulnerable points in their own facilities.[3]

With the privilege of abundance comes the responsibility to choose and handle foods wisely.

This chapter focuses first on the most immediate food-related threat: foodborne illness. It also addresses concerns about food contamination by naturally occurring toxicants, pesticide residues, and industrial compounds. Food additive questions then take the stage, and the Consumer Corner aims a spotlight on organically grown foods. The Controversy addresses foods that arise through genetic modifications.

Did You Know?

On average, *each day,* over 200,000 people in the United States fall ill with foodborne illnesses. Of those, 14 die.

- Especially vulnerable to foodborne illnesses are:
  - *Pregnant women.*
  - *Newborns, infants, and toddlers.*
  - *Older adults.*
  - *People with immune systems weakened by cancer treatments, AIDS, and other causes.*
- Get medical help for these symptoms:
  - *Bloody stools.*
  - *Headache with muscle stiffness and fever.*
  - *Rapid heart rate, fainting, dizziness.*
  - *Fever of longer than 24 hours' duration.*
  - *Diarrhea of more than 3 days' duration.*
  - *Numbness, muscle weakness, tingling sensations in the skin.*
  - *Dehydration.*
  - *Severe intestinal cramps.*

LO 12.1, 12.2

Microbes and Food Safety

Some people brush off the threat from foodborne illnesses caused by **microbes** as less likely and less serious than the threat of flu, but they are misinformed—foodborne illnesses can be life-threatening and some kinds increasingly do not respond to standard antibiotic drug therapy. Even normally mild foodborne illnesses can be lethal for a person who is ill or malnourished; has a compromised immune system; lives in an institution; has liver or stomach illnesses; or is pregnant, very old, or very young. Within these facts lies some good news—because of improved safety procedures in the U.S. food system, diseases from a number of problem organisms have declined.[4] However, as if to take their place, illnesses from other organisms became more frequent. Progress toward meeting U.S. objectives for reducing foodborne illnesses has currently stalled, and greater efforts will be required to regain momentum.[5]

If digestive tract disturbances are the major or only symptoms of your next bout of what some people erroneously call "stomach flu," chances are that what you really have is a foodborne illness. By learning something about these illnesses and taking a few preventive steps, you can maximize your chances of staying well.

How Do Microbes in Food Cause Illness in the Body?

Microorganisms can cause foodborne illness either by infection or by intoxication. Infectious agents such as *Salmonella* bacteria or viruses that cause forms of the liver disease hepatitis infect the tissues of the human body and multiply there.

Other microorganisms in foods produce **enterotoxins** or **neurotoxins,** poisonous chemicals released as the bacteria multiply; once absorbed into the tissues, the poisons cause various kinds of harm, ranging from mild stomach pain and headache to paralysis and death (see the margin). The toxins may arise in food during improper preparation or storage or within the digestive tract after a person eats contaminated food. The sources and symptoms of foodborne illnesses are listed in Table 12-2.

Although the most common cause of food intoxication is the *Staphylococcus aureus* bacterium, the most infamous is undoubtedly *Clostridium botulinum,* an organism that produces a toxin so deadly that an amount as tiny as a single grain of salt can kill several people within an hour. To reproduce and release the toxin, *Clostridium botulinum* requires anaerobic conditions such as those found in improperly canned

foodborne illness illness transmitted to human beings through food and water; caused by an infectious agent (*foodborne infection*) or a poisonous substance arising from microbial toxins, poisonous chemicals, or other harmful substances (*food intoxication*). Also called *food poisoning.*

food bioterrorism the intentional adulteration or depletion of the food supply through the use of biological agents, such as pathogenic organisms or agricultural pests, to cause fear and destruction in a population.

microbes a shortened name for *microorganisms;* minute organisms too small to observe without a microscope, including bacteria, viruses, and others.

enterotoxins poisons that act upon mucous membranes, such as those of the digestive tract.

neurotoxins poisons that act upon the cells of the nervous system.

TABLE 12-2 **Foodborne Illnesses**

Disease and Organism That Causes It	Most Frequent Food Sources	Onset and General Symptoms	Prevention Methods
FOODBORNE INFECTIONS			
CAMPYLOBACTERIOSIS (KAM-pee-loh-BAK-ter-ee-OH-sis) *Campylobacter jejuni* bacterium	Raw and undercooked poultry, unpasteurized milk, contaminated water.	Onset: 2 to 5 days; diarrhea, vomiting, abdominal cramps, fever; sometimes bloody stools; lasts 2 to 10 days.	Cook foods thoroughly; use pasteurized milk; use sanitary food-handling methods.
CRYPTOSPORIDIOSIS (KRIP-toe-spo-rid-ee-OH-sis) *Crytosporidium parvum* parasite	Commonly contaminated swimming or drinking water, even from treated sources. Highly chlorine-resistant. Contaminated raw produce and unpasteurized juices and ciders.	Onset: 2 to 10 days; diarrhea, stomach cramps, upset stomach, slight fever; symptoms may come and go for weeks or months.	Wash all raw vegetables and fruits before peeling. Use pasteurized milk and juice. Do not swallow drops of water while using pools, hot tubs, ponds, lakes, rivers, or streams for recreation.
CYCLOSPORIASIS (sigh-clo-spore-EYE-uh-sis) *Cyclospora caetanensis* parasite	Contaminated water; contaminated fresh produce.	Onset: 1 to 14 days; watery diarrhea, loss of appetite, weight loss, stomach cramps, nausea, vomiting, fatigue; symptoms may come and go for weeks or months.	Use treated, boiled, or bottled water; cook foods thoroughly; peel fruits.
***E. COLI* INFECTION** *Escherichia coli*[a] bacterium	Undercooked ground beef, unpasteurized milk and juices, raw fruits and vegetables, contaminated water, and person-to-person contact.	Onset: 1 to 8 days; severe bloody diarrhea, abdominal cramps, vomiting; lasts 5 to 10 days. Can be fatal.	Cook ground beef thoroughly; use pasteurized milk; use sanitary food-handling methods; use treated, boiled, or bottled water.
GASTROENTERITIS[b] *Norovirus*	Person-to-person contact; raw foods, salads, sandwiches.	Onset: 1 to 2 days; vomiting; lasts 1 to 2 days.	Use sanitary food-handling methods.
GIARDIASIS (JYE-are-DYE-ah-sis) *Giardia lamblia* parasite	Contaminated water; uncooked foods.	Onset: 7 to 14 days; diarrhea (but occasionally constipation), abdominal pain, gas.	Use sanitary food-handling methods; avoid raw fruits and vegetables where protozoa are endemic; dispose of sewage properly.
HEPATITIS (HEP-ah-TIE-tis) Hepatitis A virus	Undercooked or raw shellfish.	Onset: 15 to 50 days (28 to 30 days average); diarrhea, dark urine, fever, headache, nausea, abdominal pain, jaundice (yellowed skin and eyes from buildup of wastes); muscle pain; lasts 2 to 12 weeks.	Cook foods thoroughly.
LISTERIOSIS (lis-TER-ee-OH-sis) *Listeria monocytogenes* bacterium	Unpasteurized milk; fresh soft cheeses; luncheon meats, hot dogs.	Onset: 1 to 21 days; fever, muscle aches; nausea, vomiting, blood poisoning, complications in pregnancy, and meningitis (stiff neck, severe headache, and fever).	Use sanitary food-handling methods; cook foods thoroughly; use pasteurized milk.
PERFRINGENS (per-FRINGE-enz) **FOOD POISONING** *Clostridium perfringens* bacterium	Meats and meat products stored at between 120° and 130°F.	Onset: 8 to 16 hr; abdominal pain, diarrhea, nausea; lasts 1 to 2 days.	Use sanitary food-handling methods; cook foods thoroughly; refrigerate foods promptly and properly.

TABLE 12-2 Foodborne Illnesses (continued)

Disease and Organism That Causes It	Most Frequent Food Sources	Onset and General Symptoms	Prevention Methods
FOODBORNE INFECTIONS			
SALMONELLOSIS (sal-moh-neh-LOH-sis) *Salmonella* bacteria (>2,300 types)	Raw or undercooked eggs, meats, poultry, raw milk and other dairy products, shrimp, frog legs, yeast, coconut, pasta, and chocolate.	Onset: 1 to 3 days; fever, vomiting, abdominal cramps, diarrhea; lasts 4 to 7 days; can be fatal.	Use sanitary food-handling methods; use pasteurized milk; cook foods thoroughly; refrigerate foods promptly and properly.
SHIGELLOSIS (shi-gel-LOH-sis) *Shigella* bacteria (>30 types)	Person-to-person contact, raw foods, salads, sandwiches, and contaminated water.	Onset: 1 to 2 days; bloody diarrhea, cramps, fever; lasts 4 to 7 days.	Use sanitary food-handling methods; cook foods thoroughly; proper refrigeration.
VIBRIO (VIB-ree-oh) *Vibrio vulnificus*[c] bacterium	Raw or undercooked seafood and contaminated water.	Onset: 1 to 7 days; diarrhea, abdominal cramps, nausea, vomiting; lasts 2 to 5 days; can be fatal.	Use sanitary food-handling methods; cook foods thoroughly.
YERSINIOSIS (yer-SIN-ee-OH-sis) *Yersinia enterocolitica* bacterium	Raw or undercooked foods (especially pork); unpasteurized milk; unsanitary water.	Onset: 1 to 2 days; fever, stomach pain, diarrhea; lasts 1 to 3 weeks.	Cook foods thoroughly; use pasteurized milk; use treated, boiled, or bottled water.
FOOD INTOXICATIONS			
BOTULISM (BOT-you-lizm) Botulinum toxin [produced by *Clostridium botulinum* bacterium, which grows without oxygen, in low-acid foods and at temperatures between 40° and 120°F; the botulinum (BOT-you-line-um) toxin responsible for botulism is called botulin (BOT-you-lin)]	Anaerobic environment of low acidity (canned corn, peppers, green beans, soups, beets, asparagus, mushrooms, ripe olives, spinach, tuna, chicken, chicken liver, liver pâté, luncheon meats, ham, sausage, stuffed eggplant, lobster, and smoked and salted fish).	Onset: 4 to 36 hr; nervous system symptoms, including double vision, inability to swallow, speech difficulty, and progressive paralysis of the respiratory system; often fatal; leaves prolonged symptoms in survivors.	Use proper canning methods for low-acid foods; refrigerate homemade garlic and herb oils; avoid commercially prepared foods with leaky seals or with bent, bulging, or broken cans.
STAPHYLOCOCCAL (STAF-il-oh-KOK-al) **FOOD POISONING** Staphylococcal toxin (produced by *Staphylococcus aureus* bacterium)	Toxin produced in improperly refrigerated meats; egg, tuna, potato, macaroni, and other chopped salads; cream-filled pastries.	Onset: 1 to 6 hr; diarrhea, nausea, vomiting, abdominal cramps, fever; lasts 1 to 2 days.	Use sanitary food-handling methods; cook food thoroughly; refrigerate foods promptly and properly; use proper home-canning methods.

Note: Travelers' diarrhea is most commonly caused by E. coli, Campylobacter jejuni, Shigella, *and* Salmonella.

[a]*The most virulent strain is* E. coli *STEC O157, which causes hemolytic-uremic syndrome and acute kidney failure, often in children.*

[b]*Gastroenteritis refers to an inflammation of the stomach and intestines but is the most common name used for illnesses caused by* Norovirus *infection (formerly called* Norwalk *virus).*

[c]*Most cases of* Vibrio vulnificus *occur in persons with underlying illness, particularly those with liver disorders, diabetes, cancer, and AIDS and those who require long-term steroid use. The fatality rate is 50 percent for this population.*

(especially home-canned) foods, home-fermented foods such as tofu, and homemade garlic or herb-flavored oils stored at room temperature.‡[6] **Botulism** quickly paralyzes muscles, making seeing, speaking, swallowing, and breathing difficult. Because death can occur as soon as 24 hours later, botulism demands immediate medical attention (see the margin on the next page for warning signs). Even then, survivors may suffer the effects for months or years.

botulism an often fatal food poisoning caused by botulinum toxin, a toxin produced by the *Clostridium botulinum* bacterium that grows without oxygen in nonacidic canned foods.

‡Complete, up-to-date, home canning instructions are available in the USDA's *Complete Guide to Home Canning*, available from the Superintendent of Documents, Government Printing Office, Washington, DC 20402.

- Warning signs of botulism—a medical emergency:
  1. Difficulty breathing.
  2. Difficulty swallowing.
  3. Double vision.
  4. Weak muscles.

Did You Know?

Anaerobic means "without oxygen."

For safety, when making flavored oils, wash and dry the herbs before use and keep the oil refrigerated. Discard it after a week to 10 days.

The botulinum toxin is heat sensitive and can be easily destroyed by boiling contaminated canned foods for 10 minutes. Not all bacterial toxins succumb to heat, however. The *Staphylococcus aureus* toxin survives cooking.

KEY POINT Each year in the United States, many millions of people suffer mild to life-threatening symptoms caused by foodborne illness, and some die from these illnesses.

Food Safety from Farm to Table

A safe food supply depends upon safe food practices by both domestic and international food industries—on the farm or at sea, in processing plants, during transportation, and at supermarkets, institutions, and restaurants (see Figure 12-1). Experts from the Institutes of Medicine describe these characteristics of an effective national food-safety system. It should:

- systematically apply effective food-safety measures from farm to table in predictable, verifiable ways.
- clearly establish priorities and practices based on known risks.
- involve participants at all levels of food production and delivery.
- be cost-effective and minimally disruptive of trade.[7]

Equally critical in the chain of food safety, however, is the final handling of food by people who purchase it and consume it at home. Tens of millions of people needlessly suffer preventable foodborne illnesses each year because they make mistakes in purchasing and handling their food.

Commercially prepared food is usually safe, but an **outbreak** of illness from this source often makes the headlines because outbreaks can affect many people at once.[8] Dairy farmers, for example, rely on **pasteurization,** a process that heats milk to kill most disease-causing organisms thereby making the milk safe to consume. Because a few bacteria may survive the pasteurization process, the milk must be refrigerated to hold bacterial growth to a minimum. (Shelf-stable milk sold in boxes from grocery store shelves undergoes an **ultra-high temperature** treatment that sterilizes it and so needs no refrigeration.) When a major dairy develops flaws in its pasteurization systems, many thousands of cases of illness can result.

FIGURE 12-1 Flow of Food Safety: From Farm to Table

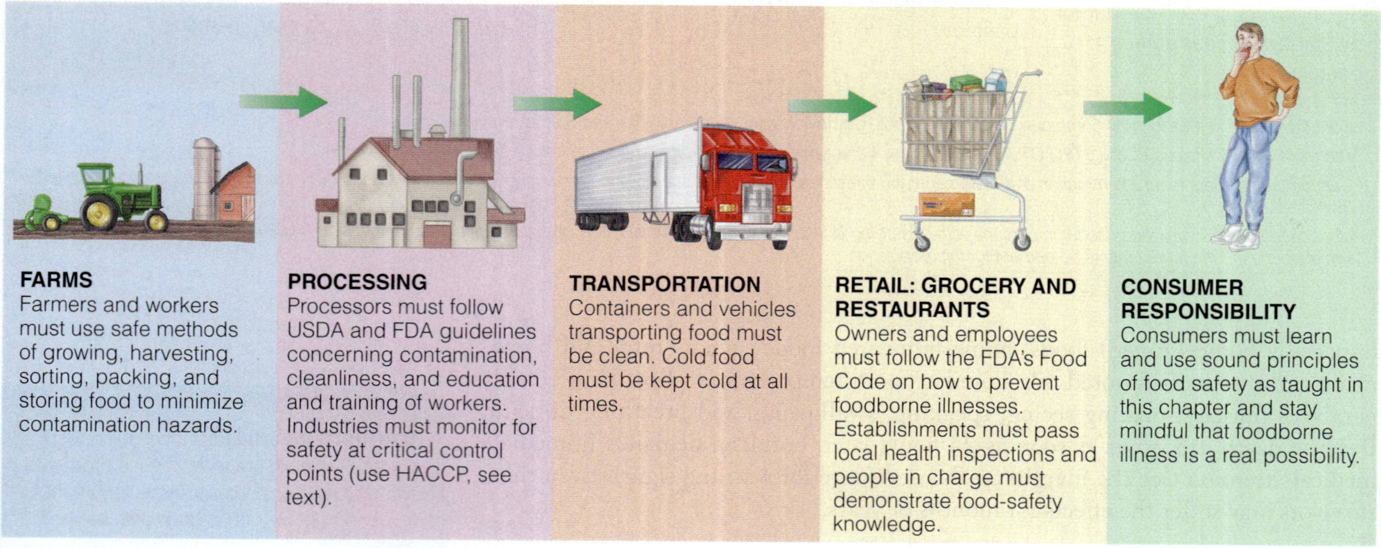

Other types of farming require other safeguards. Growing food usually involves soil, and soil contains abundant bacterial colonies that can contaminate food. Animal waste deposited onto soil may contain disease-causing microbes. Additionally, farm workers and other food handlers who are ill can easily pass disease-causing organisms to consumers through routine handling of foods during and after harvest, a particular concern with regard to foods consumed raw, such as produce.

Attention on *E. coli* In 2006, a fast-food taco restaurant chain in the Northeast served shredded lettuce that had been contaminated with the dangerous bacterium *E. coli* O157:H7.[9] A total of 71 people fell ill, 53 were hospitalized, and 8 developed the most dangerous malady associated with the bacterium—**hemolytic-uremic syndrome.** News coverage focused the national spotlight on two important food-safety issues: raw foods routinely contain live, disease-causing organisms of many types, and strict, effective industry controls are essential to make foods safe.

In most cases, *E. coli* O157:H7 infection causes bloody diarrhea, severe intestinal cramps, and dehydration, starting a few days after eating tainted meat, raw milk, or contaminated fresh raw produce, such as lettuce, green onions, berries, or even organically grown spinach. In the worst cases, *hemolytic-uremic syndrome* causes a dangerous failure of organ systems that very young, very old, or otherwise vulnerable people may not survive. Antibiotics and self-prescribed antidiarrheal medicines worsen the condition by increasing absorption and retention of the toxin. Severe cases require hospitalization.

Food Industry Controls Inspections of U.S. meat-processing plants, performed every day by USDA inspectors, help to ensure that these facilities meet government standards. Seafood, egg, produce, and processed food facilities are inspected less often, but all food producers must employ a **Hazard Analysis Critical Control Point (HACCP)** plan to help prevent foodborne illnesses at their source.[10] Each slaughterhouse, producer, packer, distributor, and transporter of susceptible foods must identify "critical control points" in its procedures that pose a risk of food contamination and then devise and implement verifiable ways to eliminate or minimize the risk.

The HACCP system has proved a remarkable success. *Salmonella* contamination of U.S. poultry, eggs, ground beef, and pork has been greatly reduced, and *E. coli* O157:H7 infection from meats has dropped dramatically.

Grocery Safety for Consumers The safety of canned and packaged foods sold in grocery stores is achieved through universal food-safety practices, but accidents do happen and foods can become contaminated. When they do, FDA scientists trace both likely production sources and distribution paths to prevent or minimize consumer exposure. Batch numbering enables the recall of contaminated foods through public announcements in the media.

You can help protect yourself, too. Check the freshness dates printed on many food packages and avoid those with expired dates (see Table 12-3). Carefully inspect the seals and wrappers: reject open, torn, leaking, or bulging cans, jars, and packages. Many jars have safety "buttons" on the lid, designed to pop up once the jar is opened; make sure that they have not "popped." If a package on the shelf looks ragged, soiled, or punctured, do not buy the product; turn it in to the store manager. A badly dented can or a mangled package is useless in protecting food from microorganisms, insects, or other spoilage. Frozen foods should be solidly frozen, and those in a chest-type freezer case should be stored below the frost line. The margin lists some tips for preventing foodborne illness by smart grocery shopping.

KEY POINT Industry employs sound practices to safeguard the commercial food supply from microbial threats. Still, outbreaks of commercial foodborne illnesses have caused widespread harm to health. Consumers should carefully inspect foods before purchasing them.

- Smart shoppers:
  - *Shop at stores that appear to be clean.*
  - *Carefully inspect jars, cans, and frozen food packages.*
  - *Reject cracked fresh eggs and those past the freshness date.*
  - *Select frozen foods and fresh meats and produce last, just before leaving the store.*

outbreak two or more cases of a disease arising from an identical organism acquired from a common food source within a limited time frame. Government agencies track and investigate outbreaks of foodborne illnesses, but tens of millions of individual cases go unreported each year.

pasteurization the treatment of milk, juices, or eggs with heat sufficient to kill certain pathogens (disease-causing microbes) commonly transmitted through these foods; not a sterilization process. Pasteurized products retain bacteria that cause spoilage.

ultra-high temperature (UHT) a process of sterilizing food by exposing it for a short time to temperatures above those normally used in processing.

hemolytic-uremic (HE-moh-LIT-ic you-REE-mick) **syndrome** a severe result of infection with *E. coli* O157:H7, characterized by abnormal blood clotting with kidney failure, damage to the central nervous system and other organs, and death, especially among children.

Hazard Analysis Critical Control Point (HACCP) a systematic plan to identify and correct potential microbial hazards in the manufacturing, distribution, and commercial use of food products. *HACCP* may be pronounced "HASS-ip."

TABLE 12-3 Food Freshness Dates

Food manufacturers voluntarily print the following kinds of dates on labels to inform both sellers and consumers of the products' freshness.[a]

- *Sell by:* Specifies the shelf life of the food. After this date, the food may still be safe for consumption if it has been handled and stored properly (check Table 12-6, page 456, for safe storage times). Also called *pull date.*
- *Best if used by:* Specifies the last date the food will be of the highest quality. After this date, quality is expected to diminish, although the food may still be safe for consumption if it has been handled and stored properly. Also called *freshness date* or *quality assurance date.*
- *Expiration date:* The last day the food should be consumed. All foods except eggs should be discarded after this date. For eggs, the expiration date refers to the last day the eggs may be sold as "fresh eggs." For safety, purchase eggs before the expiration date, keep them in their original carton in the refrigerator, and use them within 30 days.[b]
- *Open dating:* A general term referring to label dates that are stated in ordinary language that consumers can understand, as opposed to *closed dating,* which refers to dates printed in codes decipherable only by manufacturers. Open dating is used primarily on perishable foods, and closed dating on shelf-stable products such as some canned goods.
- *Pack date:* The day the food was packaged or processed. When used on packages of fresh meats, pack dates can provide a general guide to freshness.

[a]*Dating of infant formula and some baby foods is mandatory.*

[b]*For best quality, use eggs within 3 weeks of purchase.*

Did You Know?

The three requirements of disease-causing bacteria are warmth, moisture, and nutrients.

- The Fight Bac "Core Four" Practices:
  1. *CLEAN:* Wash hands and surfaces often.
  2. *SEPARATE:* Don't cross-contaminate.
  3. *COOK:* Cook to proper temperature.
  4. *CHILL:* Refrigerate promptly.

Safe Food Practices for Individuals

Some people have come to accept a yearly bout or two of intestinal illness as inevitable, but these illnesses can and should be prevented. Take the safety quiz in Table 12-4 to see how well you follow food-safety rules.

Food can provide ideal conditions for bacteria to multiply and to produce toxins. Disease-causing bacteria require these three conditions to thrive: nutrients, moisture, and warmth (40°F to 140°F; 4°C to 60°C).[§][11] To defeat bacteria, you must prevent them from contaminating food or deprive them of one of these conditions. Four core practices help to achieve these purposes: keep your hands and surfaces clean; keep raw foods separated; keep hot food hot; and keep cold food cold (see Figure 12-2).

Any food with an "off" appearance or odor should be thrown away, of course, and not even tasted. However, you cannot rely on your senses of smell, taste, and sight to warn you because most hazards are not detectable by odor, taste, or appearance. As the old saying goes, "when in doubt, throw it out."

Core Practice #1: Clean Keeping your hands and surfaces clean requires using freshly washed utensils and laundered towels and washing your hands properly, not just rinsing them, before and after handling raw food (see Figure 12-3). Normal, healthy skin is covered with bacteria, some of which may cause foodborne illness when deposited on moist, nutrient-rich food and allowed to multiply. Remember to use a nailbrush to clean under fingernails when washing hands and tend to routine nail care—artificial nails, long nails, chipped polish, and even a hangnail harbor more bacteria than do natural, clean, short, healthy nails.

For routine cleansing, washing hands with ordinary soap and warm water is effective; using an alcohol-based hand sanitizing gel can also provide killing power against many bacteria and most viruses.[12] Following up a good washing with a sanitizer may provide an extra measure of protection useful when someone in the house is ill or when preparing food for an infant, an elderly person, or someone with a compromised immune system.** If you are ill or have open cuts or sores, stay away from food preparation.

Microbes love to nestle down in small, damp spaces such as the inner cells of sponges or the pores between the fibers of wooden cutting boards. Antibacterial

FIGURE 12-2 Fight Bac!

Four ways to keep food safe. The Fight Bac! website is at www.fightbac.org.

[§]The FDA suggests these temperatures to consumers at the FDA/CFSAN website; see www.fda.gov. For food industry professionals, the FDA makes other recommendations; see U.S. Public Health Service, *Food Code 2009*, available at www.cfsan.fda.gov.

**Effective hand sanitizers contain between 60 and 70 percent alcohol.

TABLE 12-4 Can You Pass the Kitchen Food-Safety Quiz?

How food-safety savvy are you? Give yourself 2 points for each correct answer.

1. The temperature of the refrigerator in my home is:
   A. 50°F (10°Celsius).
   B. 40°F (4°C).
   C. I don't know; I don't own a refrigerator thermometer.
2. The last time we had leftover cooked stew or other meaty food, the food was:
   A. cooled to room temperature, then put in the refrigerator.
   B. put in the refrigerator immediately after the food was served.
   C. left at room temperature overnight or longer.
3. If I use a cutting board to cut raw meat, poultry, or fish and it will be used to chop another food, the board is:
   A. reused as is.
   B. wiped with a damp cloth or sponge.
   C. washed with soap and water.
   D. washed with soap and hot water and then sanitized.
4. The last time I had a hamburger, I ate it:
   A. rare.
   B. medium.
   C. well-done.
5. The last time there was cookie dough where I live, the dough was:
   A. made with raw eggs, and I sampled some of it.
   B. store-bought, and I sampled some of it.
   C. not sampled until baked.
6. I clean my kitchen counters and food preparation areas with:
   A. a damp sponge that I rinse and reuse.
   B. a clean sponge or cloth and water.
   C. a clean cloth with hot water and soap.
   D. the same as above, then a bleach solution or other sanitizer.
7. When dishes are washed in my home, they are:
   A. cleaned by an automatic dishwasher and then air-dried.
   B. left to soak in the sink for several hours and then washed with soap in the same water.
   C. washed right away with hot water and soap in the sink and then air-dried.
   D. washed right away with hot water and soap in the sink and immediately towel-dried.
8. The last time I handled raw meat, poultry, or fish, I cleaned my hands afterward by:
   A. wiping them on a towel.
   B. rinsing them under warm tap water.
   C. washing with soap and water.
9. Meat, poultry, and fish products are defrosted in my home by:
   A. setting them on the counter.
   B. placing them in the refrigerator.
   C. microwaving and cooking promptly when thawed.
   D. soaking them in warm water.
10. I realize that eating raw seafood poses special problems for people with:
   A. diabetes.
   B. HIV infection.
   C. cancer.
   D. liver disease.

ANSWERS

1. Refrigerators should stay at 40°F or less, so if you chose answer B, give yourself 2 points; 0 for other answers.
2. Answer B is the best practice. Give yourself 2 points if you picked it; 0 for other answers.
3. If answer D best describes your household's practice, give yourself 2 points; if C, 1 point.
4. Give yourself 2 points if you picked answer C; 0 for other answers.
5. If you answered A, you may be putting yourself at risk for infection from bacteria in raw shell eggs. Answer C—eating the baked product—will earn you 2 points; answer B, 1 point. Commercial dough is made with pasteurized eggs, but some bacteria may remain.
6. Answer C or D will earn you 2 points each; answer B, 1 point; answer A, 0.
7. Answers A and C are worth 2 points each; other answers, 0.
8. The only correct practice is answer C. Give yourself 2 points if you picked it; 0 for others.
9. Give yourself 2 points if you picked B or C; 0 for others.
10. This is a trick question: all of the answers apply. Give yourself 2 points for knowing one or more of the risky conditions.

RATING YOUR HOME'S FOOD-SAFETY PRACTICES

20 points: Feel confident about the safety of foods served in your home.

12 to 19 points: Reexamine food-safety practices in your home. Some key rules are being violated.

11 points or below: Take steps immediately to correct food-handling, storage, and cooking techniques used in your home. Current practices are putting you and other members of your household in danger of foodborne illness.

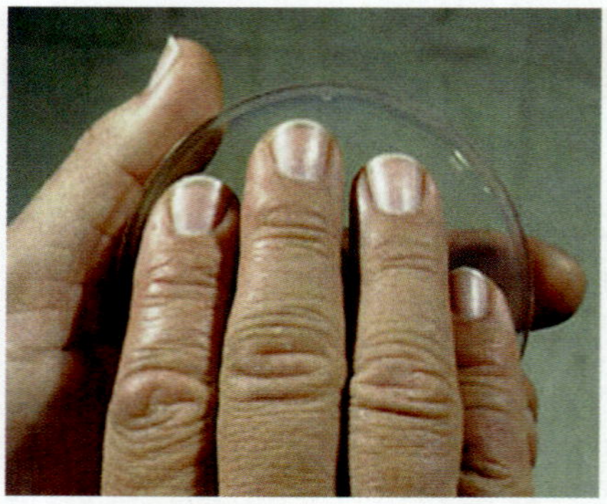

Courtesy of A. Estes Reynolds, George A. Schuler, James A. Christian, and William C. Hurst.

This person's clean-looking but unwashed hand is touching a sterile nutrient-rich gel.

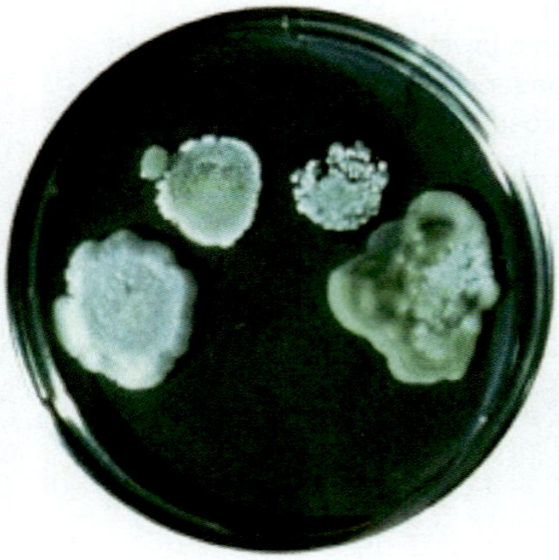

Courtesy of A. Estes Reynolds, George A. Schuler, James A. Christian, and William C. Hurst.

After 24 hours, these large colonies provide visible evidence of the microorganisms that were transferred from the hand to the gel.

FIGURE 12-3 Proper Hand Washing Prevents Illness

Many people do not wash their hands at critical times or wash them without soap or for too short a time. You can avoid many illnesses by following these hand washing procedures before, during, and after food preparation; before eating; after using the bathroom, blowing your nose, or touching your hair; after handling animals or their waste; or when hands are dirty. Wash hands more frequently when someone in the house is sick.

Suza Scalora/Photodisc/Getty Images

soaps, detergents, sponges, cloths, boards, and utensils possess a chemical additive intended to deter bacterial growth, but they have not proved superior to regular products in tests. You can ensure the safety of regular cutting boards and reduce the microbes in sponges by washing them in a dishwasher or by treating them as suggested below. Alternatively, save the sponges for car washing and other heavy cleaning chores and clean the kitchen with washable dishcloths and towels, and launder them often.

To eliminate microbes on surfaces, utensils, and cleaning items, you have four choices, each with benefits and drawbacks:

1. Poison the microbes with highly toxic chemicals such as bleach (one teaspoon per quart of water). Chlorine kills most organisms. However, chlorine is toxic to handle, can ruin clothing, and when washed down household drains into the water supply, it forms chemicals harmful to people and wildlife.
2. Kill the microbes with heat. Soapy water heated to 140°F kills most harmful organisms and washes most others away. This method takes effort, though, since the water must be truly scalding hot, well beyond the temperature of the tap.
3. Use an automatic dishwasher to combine both methods: it washes in water hotter than hands can tolerate and most dishwasher detergents contain chlorine.
4. Use a microwave to kill microbes on sponges. Place the *wet* sponge in a microwave oven and heat it until steaming hot (times vary). Caution: heat only wet sponges in the microwave oven and watch them carefully; dry sponges or those that contain metal can catch on fire.[13] Also, to prevent scalding your hands, use tongs to remove the steaming-hot sponge.

The third and fourth options turned out to be most effective for sanitizing sponges in an experiment by USDA microbiologists.[14] Washing in a dishwasher and microwaving killed virtually all bacteria trapped in sponges, while soaking in a bleach solution missed over 10 percent. The dishwasher may be preferable, however, for overall safety.

Core Practice #2: Separate Keeping raw food separated means preventing **cross-contamination** of foods. Raw foods, especially meats, eggs, and seafood, are likely to contain illness-causing bacteria. To prevent bacteria from spreading, keep the raw foods and their juices away from ready-to-eat foods. For example, if you take burgers out to the grill on a plate, wash that plate in hot, soapy water before using it to retrieve the cooked burgers. If you use a cutting board to cut raw meat, wash the board, the knife, and your hands thoroughly with soap before handling other foods, and especially before making a salad or other foods that are eaten raw. Many cooks keep a separate cutting board just for raw meats.

Core Practice #3: Cook Cooking foods long enough to reach a high enough internal temperature is necessary to kill microbes. The USDA urges consumers to use a food thermometer to test the temperatures of cooked foods and not to rely on appearance. Figure 12-4 specifies the safe internal temperatures of cooked foods

FIGURE 12-4 Food-Safety Temperatures (Fahrenheit) and Household Thermometers

Different thermometers do different jobs. To choose the right one, pay attention to its temperature range: some have high temperature ranges intended to test the doneness of meats and other hot foods. Others have lower ranges for testing temperatures of refrigerators and freezers. (Table 12-5 defines thermometer types.)

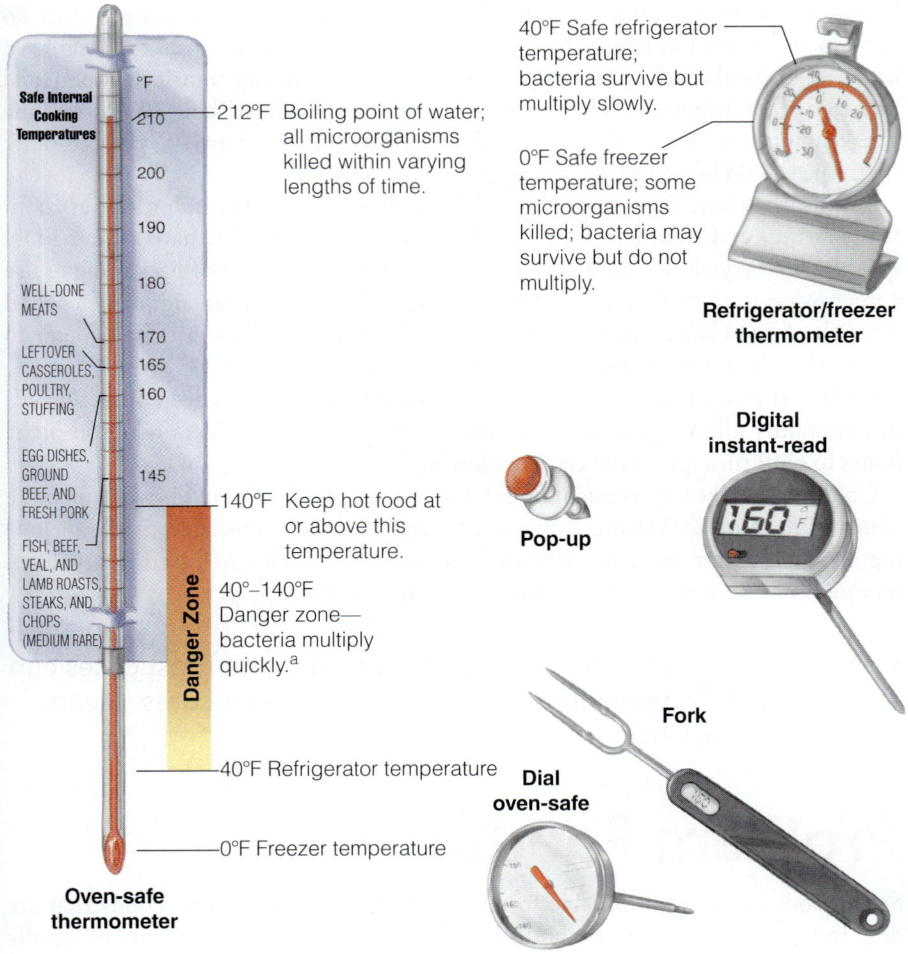

[a]FDA's food storage danger zone for use by consumers. Food professionals adhere to more specific guidelines as put forth in the FDA's Food Code 2009, available at www.cfsan.fda.gov.

cross-contamination the contamination of a food through exposure to utensils, hands, or other surfaces that were previously in contact with a contaminated food.

TABLE 12-5 Glossary of Thermometer Terms

- **appliance thermometer** a thermometer that verifies the temperature of an appliance. An *oven thermometer* verifies that the oven is heating properly; a *refrigerator/freezer thermometer* tests for proper refrigerator (<40°F, or <4°C) or freezer temperature (0°F, or −17°C).
- **fork thermometer** a utensil combining a meat fork and an instant-read food thermometer.
- **instant-read thermometer** a thermometer that, when inserted into food, measures its temperature within seconds; designed to test temperature of food at intervals, and not to be left in food during cooking.
- **oven-safe thermometer** a thermometer designed to remain in the food to give constant readings during cooking.
- **pop-up thermometer** a disposable timing device commonly used in turkeys. The center of the device contains a stainless steel spring that "pops up" when food reaches the right temperature.
- **single-use temperature indicator** a type of instant-read thermometer that changes color to indicate that the food has reached the desired temperature. Discarded after one use, they are often used in commercial food establishments to eliminate cross-contamination.

TABLE 12-6 Safe Food Storage Times: Refrigerator (≤40°F)

1 to 2 Days
Raw ground meats, breakfast or other raw sausages, variety meats; raw fish or poultry; gravies
3 to 5 Days
Raw steaks, roasts, or chops; cooked meats, vegetables, and mixed dishes; ham slices; mayonnaise salads (chicken, egg, pasta, tuna)
1 Week
Hard-cooked eggs, bacon or hot dogs (opened packages); whole or half hams; smoked sausages
2 to 4 Weeks
Raw eggs (in shells); bacon or hot dogs (packages unopened); dry sausages (pepperoni, hard salami); most aged and processed cheeses (Swiss, brick)
2 Months
Mayonnaise (opened jar); most dry cheeses (Parmesan, Romano)

and illustrates various types of thermometers. Table 12-5 provides a glossary of thermometer terms.

After cooking, keeping hot foods hot requires that they be held at 140°F or higher until served.[15] A temperature of 140°F on a thermometer feels hot, not just warm. Even well-cooked foods, if handled improperly prior to serving, can cause illness. Delicious-looking meatballs on a buffet may harbor bacteria unless they have been kept steaming hot. After the meal, cooked foods should be refrigerated immediately or within two hours at the maximum (one hour if room temperature approaches 90°F, or 32°C). If food has been left out longer than this, toss it out.

Core Practice #4: Chill Chilling and keeping cold food cold starts when you leave the grocery store. If you are running errands, shop last so that the groceries do not stay in the car too long. (If ice cream begins to melt, it has been too long.) An ice chest or insulated bag can help to keep foods cold during transit. Upon arrival home, load foods into the refrigerator or freezer immediately. Table 12-6 lists some safe keeping times for foods stored in the refrigerator at or below 40°F. Foods older than this should be discarded, not ingested.

To ensure safety, thaw frozen meats or poultry in the refrigerator, not at room temperature, and marinate meats in the refrigerator, too. To thaw a food more quickly, submerge it in cold (not hot or warm) water in waterproof packaging or use a microwave to thaw food just before cooking it. Most foods can simply be cooked from the frozen state—just increase the cooking time and use a thermometer to ensure that the food reaches a safe internal temperature.

Chill prepared or cooked foods in shallow containers, not in deep ones. A shallow container allows quick chilling throughout; deeper containers take too many hours to chill through to the center, allowing bacteria time to grow.

Cold foods make a convenient buffet, but to keep perishable cold foods safe, place plates of food on ice during serving. This applies to all perishable foods, including custards, cream pies, and whipped-cream or cream-cheese–based treats. Even pumpkin pie, because it contains milk and eggs, should be kept cold.

KEY POINT Foodborne illnesses are common but most cases can be prevented. To prevent them, remember the four cores: Clean, Separate, Cook, Chill.

bovine spongiform encephalopathy (BOW-vine SPON-jih-form en-SEH-fell-AH-path-ee) **(BSE)** an often fatal illness of the nerves and brain observed in cattle and wild game and in people who consume affected meats. Also called *mad cow disease*.

prion (PREE-on) an infective agent consisting of an unusually folded protein that disrupts normal cell functioning, causing disease. Prions cannot be controlled or killed by cooking or disinfecting, nor can the disease they cause be treated; prevention is the only form of control.

Problem Foods

Some foods are more hospitable to microbial growth than others. Foods that are high in moisture and nutrients and those that are chopped or ground are especially favorable hosts. Bacteria in these foods are likely to grow quickly without proper refrigeration.

Meats and Poultry

Raw meats and poultry require special handling, and packages bear labels to instruct consumers on meat safety (see Figure 12-5).[††] Meats in the grocery cooler very often contain bacteria and provide a moist, nutritious environment that is just right for microbial growth. Therefore, controlling temperature becomes the critical factor in keeping meats safe to eat.

Ground Meats Ground meat or poultry is handled more than meats left whole, and grinding exposes much more surface area for bacteria to land on, so experts advise cooking these foods to the well-done stage. Use a thermometer to test the internal temperature of poultry and meats, even hamburgers, before declaring them done. Don't trust appearance alone: burgers often turn brown and appear cooked before their internal temperature is high enough to kill harmful bacteria. New U.S. beef sanitation systems are helping to reduce contamination of ground beef. The measures target the dangerous *E. coli* O157:H7 bacteria in particular and the number of infections acquired from beef has dropped dramatically.[16]

Unrelated to sanitation, a disease of cattle and wild game such as deer and elk, **bovine spongiform encephalopathy (BSE),** has been linked with a rare but fatal human brain disorder.[‡‡17] An oddly shaped self-replicating infectious protein, known as a **prion,** is a suspected cause.[18] U.S. beef industry regulations minimize the risk of BSE to almost zero.[19]

Did You Know?

Meats provide moisture and nutrients that bacteria require to grow; to thwart them, control temperature.

Eric O'Connell/Taxi/Getty Images

A safe hamburger is cooked well-done (internal temperature of 160°F) and has juices that run clear. Place it on a clean plate when it's done.

[††]The USDA's meat and poultry hotline answers questions about meat and poultry safety: 1-888-674-6854.

[‡‡]The human disease is variant Creutzfeldt-Jakob disease (vCJD).

FIGURE 12-5 Safe Handling Instructions for Meat and Poultry

The USDA "Safe Handling" label on meats and poultry outlines how to keep these foods safe to eat. Other USDA labels, such as grading descriptions or inspection stickers, do not guarantee that meats are free of potentially harmful bacteria.

Never allow frozen meat to defrost at room temperature or in a bath of warm water. In both cases, meat thaws from outside in, and the outside meat layer can easily warm up to temperatures that permit bacterial growth before the core defrosts.

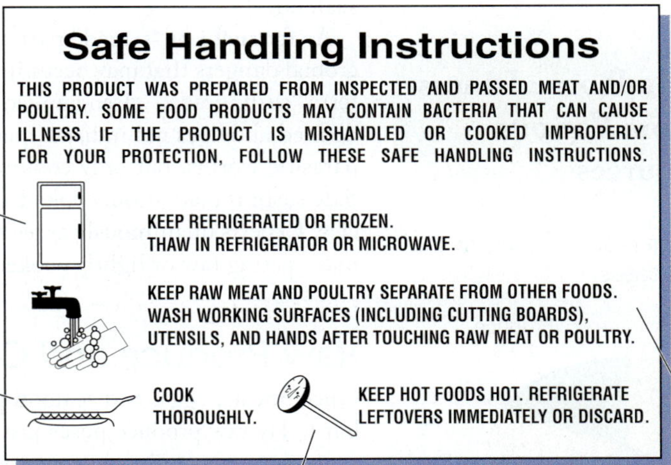

Microwave cooking of meats requires special care. Large, thick, dense foods such as roasts or meat loaves may register "cooked" on an internal meat thermometer but may harbor cool spots in which dangerous microorganisms can survive. Such foods are best cooked by another method or divided into thin individual portions to be microwaved.

Properly cooked food hot from the oven or stove is relatively free of bacteria, but as soon as it is taken out to serve, kitchen utensils recontaminate the food or airborne microbes land on its surface. Promptly after serving, even while the food is still hot, refrigerate leftovers in shallow containers for quick, even chilling. Large amounts of food refrigerated in deep containers may take more than 4 hours to cool through, allowing bacteria time to multiply in the warm internal portions.

Take care when preparing meats along with foods intended to be served raw, such as chopped salads or lettuce and tomato toppers for hamburgers. A grave error is to prepare foods that will be consumed raw on the same board or with the same utensils as were used to prepare raw meats. Wash hands after handling raw meats.

- These common myths about raw seafood can lead to dangerous foodborne illnesses:
  - *Myth: If a seafood was consumed raw in the past with no ill effect, it is safe to do so today.*
  - *Myth: Drinking alcohol or consuming hot sauce with raw seafood will "kill the germs."*

Did You Know?

In many states, containers of raw oysters must bear this warning: "There is a risk associated with consuming raw oysters or any raw animal protein. If you have chronic illness of the liver, stomach or blood or have immune disorders, you are at greater risk of serious illness from raw oysters and should eat oysters fully cooked. If unsure of your risk, consult a physician."

FIGURE 12-6 Foodborne Illness from Various Sources

Note that produce is second only to seafood in reported cases.

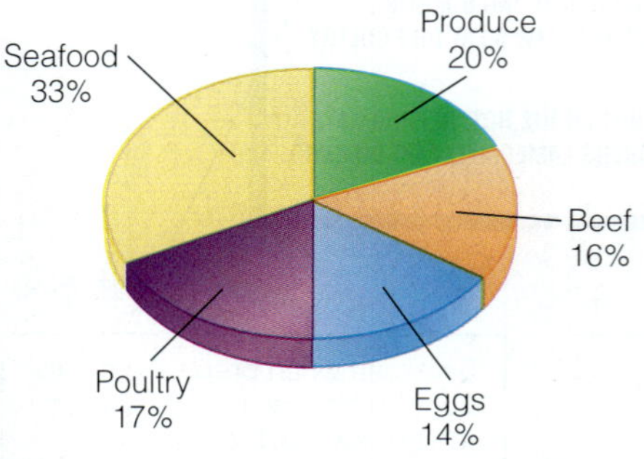

sushi a Japanese dish that consists of vinegar-flavored rice, seafood, and colorful vegetables, typically wrapped in seaweed. Some sushi is wrapped in raw fish; other sushi contains only cooked ingredients.

Eggs Raw, unpasteurized eggs may be contaminated by *Salmonella* or other bacteria. Measures to counter this threat have reduced the percentage of *Salmonella* outbreaks from eggs in recent years.[20] During the same period, however, total *Salmonella* illness remained largely unchanged, meaning that problems with *other* foods, such as fresh juices, salsas, meats, sprouts, fruit, and salads, increased.[21]

Bacteria from the intestinal tract of hens contaminate eggs as they are laid, and some bacteria may enter the egg itself if the hen is infected. All commercially available eggs are washed and sanitized before packing, and a few are pasteurized in the shell to make them safer. To further reduce illnesses from *Salmonella,* the FDA requires measures to control bacteria on major egg-producing poultry farms, too.[22] For consumers, egg cartons bear reminders to keep eggs refrigerated, cook eggs until their yolks are firm, and cook egg-containing foods thoroughly before eating them.

What about favorite foods that call for raw or undercooked eggs, such as homemade ice cream, hollandaise sauce, or raw cookie dough? Healthy people can enjoy them if they are made safer by choosing pasteurized liquid egg products. Even these products, because they are made from raw eggs, may contain a few live bacteria that survived pasteurization, making them unsafe for pregnant women, the elderly, young children, or those suffering from immune dysfunction.

Seafood Properly cooked fish and other seafood sold in the United States and Canada is safe from microbial threats. However, even the freshest, most appealing, raw or partly cooked seafood can harbor a variety of microbial dangers from seawater, such as disease-causing viruses; worms, flukes, and other parasites; and bacteria that cause illnesses ranging from self-limiting digestive disturbances to severe, life-threatening illnesses.[23]

The dangers posed by seafood are increasing.[24] As burgeoning human populations along the world's shorelines release more contaminants into lakes, rivers, and oceans, the seafood living there becomes less safe to consume. Government agencies monitor commercial fishing areas and close unsafe waters to harvesters, but illegal harvesting is common, and shoppers may unknowingly buy infected fresh seafood.

As for **sushi** or "seared" partially raw fish, even a master chef cannot detect microbial dangers that may occur in even the best-quality, freshest fish. The marketing term "sushi grade," often applied to seafood to imply wholesomeness, is not legally defined and does not indicate quality, purity, or freshness. Also, freezing kills adult parasitic worms, but only cooking kills all worm eggs and other microorganisms. Safe sushi is made from cooked seafood, seaweed, vegetables, and other safe delicacies. Experts unanimously agree that today's high levels of microbial contamination make eating raw or lightly cooked seafood too risky, even for healthy adults.

Raw Produce and Other Foods

Once, meats, eggs, and seafood posed the greatest foodborne illness threat by far, but today raw produce poses just as great a threat (see Figure 12-6).[25] Foods such as lettuce, salad spinach, tomatoes, sprouts, herbs, and scallions grow close to the ground, making bacterial contamination from the soil, animal waste runoff, and organic fertilizers likely.[26]

In 2007, more than 200 consumers fell seriously ill and 3 died from dangerous *E. coli* O157:H7 infection from eating raw bagged spinach; soon after, another 180 people developed *Salmonella* infections from raw tomatoes; just weeks later, the *E. coli* O157:H7 outbreak, mentioned earlier, was caused by produce served at popular taco restaurants.[27] The year 2009 brought a recall of *Salmonella*-tainted peanut butter. These problems and others that followed sprang from sanitation mistakes made by growers and producers.[28]

Imported Produce Produce may be imported from developing countries where farmers do not adhere to safe growing and harvesting practices and where contagious diseases are widespread. Fields may be irrigated with contaminated water, crops may be fertilized with untreated animal or even human manure, or produce may be picked by infected farm workers in areas with poor sanitation. Cooked, frozen, or canned produce is generally safe, however.

Washing produce at home is important but a quick rinse does not eliminate all microbial contamination because certain microbes—*E. coli* O157:H7, among others—exude a **biofilm** that survives the washing process. Somewhat more effective is vigorous scrubbing with a vegetable brush, rinsing with vinegar, and removing and discarding the outer leaves from heads of leafy vegetables, such as cabbage and lettuce, before washing.[29] Vinegar doesn't sterilize foods, but it can reduce certain bacterial populations and it's safe for consumption.[30]

Precut Salads and Vegetables Ready-to-eat packaged produce, such as salad greens and cut vegetables, has been triple washed (the label states this) and often rinsed in chlorinated water or treated with oxygen disinfectant (ozone), before packaging. Keep prewashed produce at refrigerator temperatures at all times to reduce bacterial hazards.[31] Buy salads well before their "sell by" date.

Melons and Berries Rough skins of melons such as cantaloupes provide crevices where bacteria hide and so should be scrubbed with a stiff brush under running water before peeling or cutting. Otherwise, a knife blade or fingers can transfer contaminants from the skin to a food's interior. Raspberries, other berries, and, in fact, all produce should be rinsed thoroughly under running water for at least 10 seconds (see Table 12-7). Unpasteurized or raw juices and ciders pose a special problem because microbes on the original fruit may multiply in the juice during storage. Labels of unpasteurized juices must carry the warning shown in the margin. Refrigerated pasteurized juices are generally safe.

Sprouts Sprouts (including alfalfa, clover, and radish) are often eaten raw, but the only sure way to make sprouts safe is to cook them. Sprout seeds may harbor *E. coli* O157:H7 or *Salmonella* bacteria that cannot be washed away, so even homegrown, well-rinsed raw sprouts may pose a risk. The elderly, young children, and those with weakened immunity are particularly vulnerable.[32]

- Unpasteurized or untreated juice must bear the following warning on its label:

> **WARNING:** This product has not been pasteurized and therefore may contain harmful bacteria that can cause serious illness in children, the elderly, and persons with weakened immune systems.

TABLE 12-7 Produce Safety

Cleaning Fresh Fruits and Vegetables
1. Remove and discard the outer leaves from vegetables such as lettuce and cabbage before washing.
2. Wash all fruits and vegetables (including organically grown and homegrown, regardless of place of purchase) just before cooking or eating.
3. Wash fruits and vegetables under clean running water and scrub with clean scrub brush, or with your hands. Commercial vegetable washing products are safe to use; do not use soap, detergents, or bleach solutions.
4. Dry fruits and vegetables before cutting or eating.
5. Cut away damaged or bruised areas that may contain microbes. Toss out moldy fruit or vegetables.
6. Refrigerate prewashed cut fruits, vegetables, and salads.
Juice Safety
1. Choose chilled pasteurized juices or shelf-stable juices (canned or boxed) that have been treated with high temperature to kill microbes and check their seals to be sure no microbes have entered after processing.
2. Especially infants, children, the elderly, and people with weakened immune systems should never be given raw or unpasteurized juice products.

biofilm a protective coating of proteins and carbohydrates exuded by certain bacteria; biofilm adheres bacteria to surfaces and can survive rinsing.

Honey Honey can contain dormant spores of *Clostridium botulinum* that, when eaten, can germinate and begin to grow and produce their deadly botulinum toxin in the human body. Mature, healthy adults are usually protected against this threat, but infants under 1 year of age should never be fed honey.

Picnics and Lunch Bags Picnics can be fun and packed lunches a convenience, but to keep them safe, do the following:

- Choose foods that are safe without refrigeration, such as whole fruits and vegetables, breads and crackers, shelf-stable foods, and canned spreads and cheeses to open and use on the spot.
- Choose aged cheeses, such as cheddar and Swiss, over soft cheeses. Aged cheese does well without chilling for an hour or two, but carry them in a cooler or thermal lunch bag for longer periods.
- Keep meat, egg, cheese, or seafood sandwiches cold until eaten.
- Chill lunch bag foods and use a thermal lunch bag.
- Freeze beverages to pack in with the foods. As the beverages thaw in the hours before lunch, they keep the foods cold.
- Prepackaged single servings of cheese, cold cuts, and crackers promoted as lunch foods keep well, but they are high in saturated fat and sodium, cost triple the price of the foods purchased separately, and their excessive packaging adds to the nation's waste disposal burden.

Mayonnaise, despite its reputation for easy spoilage, is itself somewhat spoilage-resistant because of its acid content. Mayonnaise mixed with chopped ingredients in pasta, meat, or vegetable salads, however, spoils readily. The chopped ingredients have extensive surface areas for bacteria to invade, and cutting boards, hands, and kitchen utensils used in preparation often harbor bacteria. For safe chopped raw foods, start with clean chilled ingredients then chill the finished product in shallow containers; keep it chilled before and during serving; and promptly refrigerate any remainder.

Take-Out Foods and Leftovers Many people rely on take-out foods—rotisserie chicken, pizza, Chinese dishes, and the like—for parties, picnics, or weeknight suppers. When buying these foods, food-safety rules apply: hot foods should be steaming hot and cold foods should be thoroughly chilled.

Leftovers of all kinds make a convenient later lunch or dinner. For safety, store these foods properly and reheat them to steaming hot (165°F) before eating. Discard any portion held at room temperature for longer than 2 hours from the time it was served at table until you place it in your refrigerator. Follow the 2, 2, and 4 rules of leftover safety: within 2 hours of cooking, refrigerate the food in shallow containers about 2 inches deep, and use it up within 4 days or toss it out. Exceptions: stuffing and gravy must be used within 2 days, and if room temperature reaches 90°F, all cooked foods must be chilled after 1 hour of exposure.[33]

Consumers bear a responsibility for food safety, and an essential first step is to cultivate an awareness that foodborne illness is likely. Consumers must discard old notions that put them at risk (see the margin for some food-safety myths that often make consumers sick) and adopt an attitude of self-defense to prevent illness.

Did You Know?

Myths that often make consumers sick:

- "If it tastes and smells okay, it's safe to eat."
- "We have always handled our food this way, so it must be safe."
- "I sampled it a couple of hours ago and didn't get sick, so it is safe to eat."

KEY POINT Some foods pose special microbial threats and so require special handling. Almost all types of food poisoning can be prevented by safe food preparation, storage, and cleanliness.

How Can I Avoid Illness When Traveling?

People who travel to places where cleanliness standards are lacking have a 50-50 chance of contracting a foodborne illness, commonly known as traveler's diarrhea (listed earlier in Table 12-2). A bout of illness can ruin a trip, or worse. To avoid foodborne illness while traveling:

- Before you travel, ask your physician which medicines to take with you in case you get sick.
- Wash your hands often with soap and water, especially before handling food or eating.
- Eat only cooked and canned foods. Eat raw fruits or vegetables only if you have washed them with your own clean hands in boiled water and peeled them yourself. Skip salads.
- Be aware that water, ice, and beverages made from water may be unsafe. Take along disinfecting tablets or an element that boils water in a cup. Drink only treated, boiled, canned, or bottled beverages and drink them without ice, even if they are not chilled to your liking.
- Avoid using the local water, even if you are just brushing your teeth, unless you boil or disinfect it first.

In general, remember these rules: boil it, cook it, peel it, or forget it. If you follow these recommendations along with frequent hand washing, chances are excellent that you will remain well.

© Stephen VanHorn, 2011/Shutterstock.com

KEY POINT Some special food-safety concerns arise when traveling. To avoid foodborne illnesses, remember to boil it, cook it, peel it, or forget it.

LO 12.3

Advances in Microbial Food Safety

Advances in technology, such as pasteurization, have dramatically improved the quality and safety of foods over the past century. Today, other technologies promise similar benefits, but some raise concerns among consumers.

Irradiation

Food **irradiation** has been extensively evaluated over the past 50 years. Approved in more than 40 countries, its use is endorsed by numerous health agencies, including the World Health Organization (WHO) and the American Medical Association. Food irradiation protects consumers from foodborne illnesses by:

- controlling mold in grains.
- sterilizing spices and teas.
- controlling insects.
- extending shelf life in fresh fruits and vegetables (inhibits the growth of sprouts on potatoes and onions and delays ripening in some fruits, such as strawberries and mangoes).
- destroying disease-causing bacteria in fresh and frozen beef, poultry, lamb, and pork.

Supporters of irradiation say that if more everyday foods were irradiated, the nation's rates of foodborne illnesses would drop dramatically.

How Irradiation Works Irradiation exposes foods to controlled doses of gamma rays from the radioactive compound cobalt 60. As the rays pass through living cells, they disrupt living internal DNA, protein, and other structures, killing or deactivating the cells. For example, low radiation doses can kill the growing cells in the "eyes" of potatoes, preventing them from sprouting. Low doses also delay ripening

irradiation the application of ionizing radiation to foods to reduce insect infestation or microbial contamination or to slow the ripening or sprouting process. Also called *cold pasteurization*.

- Foods approved for irradiation by the FDA:
  - *Citrus fruits.*
  - *Eggs.*
  - *Flour.*
  - *Fresh and frozen red meats, such as lamb, beef, and pork.*
  - *Mushrooms.*
  - *Onions.*
  - *Potatoes.*
  - *Poultry.*
  - *Spices.*
  - *Strawberries.*
  - *Tomatoes.*
  - *Tropical fruits.*
  - *Wheat.*

of bananas, avocados, and other fruits.[34] Higher doses easily penetrate tough insect exoskeletons and mold or bacterial cell walls to destroy them. Irradiation works even while food is frozen, making it uniquely useful in protecting foods such as whole frozen turkeys.

Irradiation Effects on Foods Irradiation does not sterilize most foods because doses high enough to kill all microorganisms would also destroy the food. Dried herbs and spices are notable exceptions—they can withstand sterilizing doses. Irradiation does not noticeably change the taste, texture, or appearance of FDA-approved foods (see the margin list), nor does it make foods radioactive. Some vitamins are destroyed by irradiation, but the losses are comparable to those from other food-processing methods such as canning. Some food cannot be irradiated. High-fat meats develop off-odors, egg whites turn milky, grapefruits become mushy, and milk products change flavor, for example.

Consumer Concerns About Irradiation Many consumers, associating radiation with cancer, birth defects, and mutations, respond negatively to the idea of irradiating their foods. Some erroneously fear that food will become contaminated with radioactive particles. More founded fears concern transport of radioactive materials, training of workers to handle them safely, and then safe disposal of spent wastes, which remain radioactive for many years. The food industry echoes these concerns and strives to safeguard both workers and consumers through strict operating standards and compliance with regulations.

Finally, a concern exists that unscrupulous manufacturers could potentially irradiate old or bacterially tainted foods, thereby escaping detection by USDA testers. Instead of being seized or destroyed, the food could be passed off as wholesome to unsuspecting consumers. This objection raises an important point: irradiation is intended to complement, not replace, other traditional food-safety methods. Irradiation cannot entirely protect people from poor sanitation on the farm, in industry, or at home.

This "radura" logo is the international symbol for foods treated with irradiation.

Labeling of Irradiated Foods Each food that has been treated with irradiation must say so on its label. Foods that include irradiated ingredients, such as spices, need not provide this information.

KEY POINT Food irradiation kills bacteria, insects, molds, and parasites on foods. Consumers have concerns about its safety

Other Technologies

Several technologies warrant mentioning. They have potential to help resolve some of the threat from contamination.

Improved Testing and Surveillance Testing foods before they reach consumers is a critical step toward preventing foodborne illness. Microbial testing has improved in accuracy through automated contamination detection systems, from farms to markets. Recent outbreaks of disease caused by the pathogen *E. coli* O157:H7 have taught scientists to keep potential sources under surveillance. For example, using a mobile laboratory, FDA scientists can now test fresh produce at the growing field and analyze it for bacterial contamination.[35] Other developments include better detection methods for *E. coli* in water, sediment, and other environmental harbors to allow intervention before it can contaminate food crops.[36]

modified atmosphere packaging (MAP) a preservation technique in which a perishable food is packaged in a gas-impermeable container from which air has been removed or to which another gas mixture has been added.

Modified Atmospheric Packaging Certain packaging methods improve the safety and shelf life of many fresh and prepared foods. Vacuum packaging or **modified atmosphere packaging (MAP)** make it possible for soft pasta noodles, baked goods, prepared foods, fresh and cured meats, seafood, dry beans and other dry products, ground and whole-bean coffee, left unopened, to stay fresh and safe much longer than they would in conventional packaging.

Food manufacturers package foods in plastic film or other wraps that oxygen cannot penetrate. Then, they remove the air inside the package, creating a vacuum, or they replace the air with a mixture of oxygen-free gases, such as carbon dioxide and nitrogen. By excluding oxygen, the method:

- reduces growth of oxygen-dependent microbes.
- prevents discoloration of cut vegetables and fruits.
- prevents spoilage of fats by rancidity and development of "off" flavors.
- slows ripening of fruits and vegetables and enzyme-induced breakdown of vitamins.

Perishable foods packaged with MAP must still be chilled properly, however, to keep them safe from microbes that flourish in anaerobic environments, such as the *Clostridium botulinum* bacterium. Chilling of precut salad greens is also a must: temperatures above 50°F cause a dangerous change in *E. coli* bacteria strains present in MAP-bagged lettuces that help them to survive the eater's stomach acid, increasing their ability to cause infection.[37]

© Feng Yu, 2011/Shutterstock.com

Bacteria-Killing Wraps and Films Bacteria-killing food wraps and films hold promise. One biodegradable wrap made from the milk protein may soon protect perishable foods from oxidation spoilage and may also receive a dose of antimicrobial materials to prevent bacterial growth.[38] Other films under testing are intended for consumption along with the food they protect. These are made from fruit or vegetable purees with a dose of oregano oil, a natural antibacterial agent. Such films not only kill dangerous *E. coli* organisms but they can add pleasing flavors to foods.[39]

Microbial foodborne illnesses undoubtedly pose the most immediate threat to consumers, but other factors also affect food safety. The next sections address some of these concerns.

KEY POINT Advances in many areas are aimed at improving food safety.

LO 12.4

Toxins, Residues, and Contaminants in Foods

Nutrition-conscious consumers often wonder if our nation's foods are made unsafe by chemical contamination. The FDA, along with the Environmental Protection Agency (EPA), regulates many chemicals in foods that occur as a result of human activities. A later section describes these substances. First, some toxins produced naturally by the foods themselves are worthy of attention.

Natural Toxins in Foods

Some people think they can eliminate all poisons from their diets by eating only "natural" foods. On the contrary, nature has provided many plants with natural poisons to fend off diseases, insects, and other predators. Humans rarely suffer actual harm from such poisons, but the *potential* for harm does exist.

Herbs and Cabbages The herbs belladonna and hemlock are infamous poisons, but few people know that the herb sassafras contains a carcinogen and liver toxin so potent that it is banned from use in commercially produced foods and beverages.*** Cabbage, turnips, mustard greens, and radishes all contain small quantities of harmful goitrogens, compounds that can enlarge the thyroid gland and aggravate

***The carcinogen is safrole.

CONCEPT LINK 12-1

Table 11-9 provided more information on potentially harmful herbs (page 428).

thyroid problems. Ordinarily, cabbages and their relatives are celebrated for their nutrients and phytochemicals associated with low cancer rates. However, in extreme conditions when people have little to eat but cabbages, the goitrogens in these foods can become a problem.

Foods with Cyanogens Other natural poisons are members of a group called cyanogens, which are precursors to the deadly poison cyanide. Many countries restrict lima bean production to varieties with low cyanogen contents. Most cassava, a root vegetable eaten by many of the world's people, contains just traces of cyanogens; the amount in bitter varieties, however, can be exceedingly high, posing a threat to starving people with nothing else to eat. Certain fruit seeds and pits also contain cyanogens, but these items are seldom deliberately eaten; an occasional swallowed seed or two presents no danger, but a few dozen seeds could be fatal to a small child. One infamous cyanogen extracted from apricot pits is laetrile, a fake cancer cure often passed off as a vitamin.[†††] True, the poison laetrile kills cancer cells, but only at doses that can kill the person, too.

Potatoes Potatoes contain many natural poisons, including solanine, a powerful, bitter, narcotic-like substance. The small amounts of solanine normally found in potatoes are harmless, but solanine can build up to toxic levels when potatoes are exposed to light during storage. Cooking does not destroy solanine, but because most of a potato's solanine develops in a thin green layer just beneath the skin, it can be peeled off, making the potato safe to eat. If a potato tastes bitter, however, throw it out.

Seafood Red Tide Toxin At certain times of the year, seafood may become contaminated with the so-called red tide toxin that occurs during algae blooms. Eating seafood contaminated with red tide causes a form of food poisoning that paralyzes the eater. The FDA monitors fishing waters and closes them to fishing when red tide algae appear.

These examples of naturally occurring toxins serve as a reminder of three principles. First, poisons are poisons, whether made by people or by nature. It is not the source of a compound that makes it hazardous, but its chemical structure. Second, because any substance—even water—can be toxic when consumed in excess, practice moderation when choosing food portions. Third, by choosing a variety of foods, toxins present in one food are diluted by the volume of the other foods in the diet.

KEY POINT Natural foods contain natural toxins that can be hazardous under some conditions. To avoid poisoning by toxins, eat all foods in moderation, treat chemicals from all sources with respect, choose a variety of foods, and respect bans on seafood.

- Agricultural pesticides:
  - *Protect crops from insect damage.*
  - *Potentially increase yields per acre.*

  But they also:
  - *Accumulate in the food chain.*
  - *Kill pests' natural predators.*
  - *Pollute the water, soil, and air.*

Pesticides

The use of **pesticides** helps to ensure the survival of food crops, but the damage pesticides do to the environment is considerable and increasing. Moreover, there is some question about whether the widespread use of pesticides has truly increased overall yields of food. Even with extensive pesticide use, the world's farmers lose large quantities of their crops to pests every year.

Do Pesticides on Foods Pose a Hazard to Consumers? Many pesticides are broad-spectrum poisons that damage all living cells, not just those of pests. Their use poses hazards to the plants and animals in natural systems and involve special risks to workers in pesticide production, transport, and application. High doses of pesticides applied to laboratory animals cause birth defects, sterility, tumors, organ damage, and central nervous system impairment. Equivalent doses are extremely unlikely to occur in human beings, however, except through accidental spills. As Figure 12-7 demonstrates, pesticide **residues** on agricultural products can survive processing and traces are often present in foods served to people.[40]

pesticides chemicals used to control insects, diseases, weeds, fungi, and other pests on crops and around animals. Used broadly, the term includes *herbicides* (to kill weeds), *insecticides* (to kill insects), and *fungicides* (to kill fungi).

residues whatever remains; in the case of pesticides, those amounts that remain on or in foods when people buy and use them.

[†††]Also called *amygdalin* and, erroneously, *vitamin* B_{17}.

FIGURE 12-7 How Processing Affects Pesticide Residues

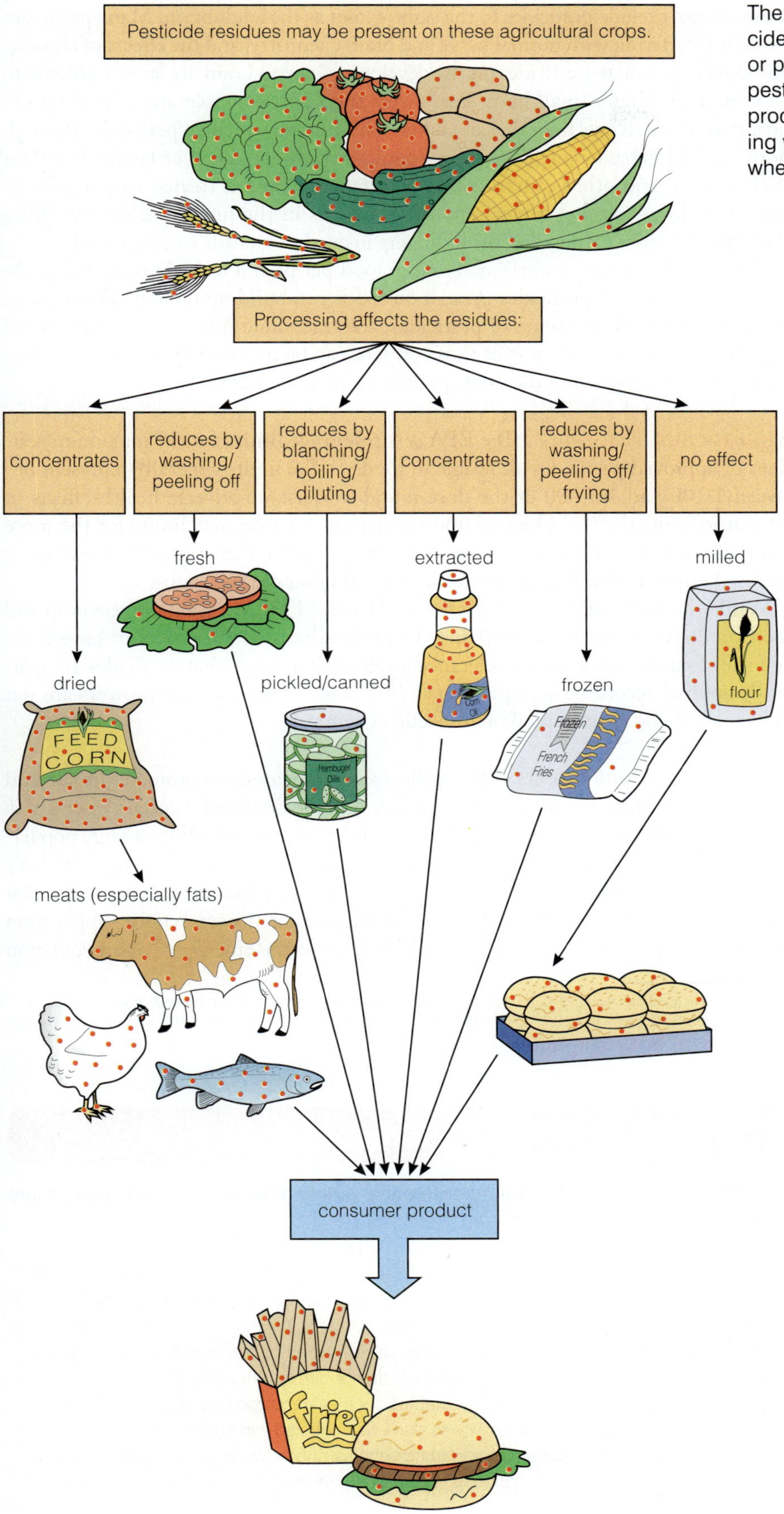

The red dots in the figure represent pesticide residue left on foods from field spraying or postharvest application. Notice that most pesticides follow fats in foods and that some processing methods, such as washing and peeling vegetables, reduce pesticide concentrations, whereas others tend to concentrate them.

Wash fresh fruits and vegetables to remove pesticide residues.

Especially Vulnerable: Infants and Children Infants and children are more susceptible than adults to ill effects of pesticides, for three reasons. First, the immature human detoxifying system cannot effectively cope with poisons, and the developing brain cannot exclude pesticides to the same extent as the adult brain. Many pesticides work by interfering with normal nerve and brain chemistry, and the effects of chronic, low-dose exposure to pesticides on the developing human brain are largely unknown.

Second, children's small body size lowers their pesticide tolerance, yet their exposure is often greater than that of adults. Children may pick up pesticides through normal child behavior such as playing outdoors on treated soil or lawns; handling sticks, rocks, and other contaminated objects; crawling on treated carpets, furniture, and floors; placing fingers and other objects in the mouth; seldom washing their hands before eating; and using fingers instead of utensils to grasp foods.

Third, children eat proportionally more food per pound of body weight than do adults, and traces of pesticides present on foods can build up quickly. Fortunately, compared with other sources of pesticides, the traces found on foods rarely exceed set allowable limits, and most of those present can be removed by washing produce thoroughly and following the other guidelines in Table 12-8.[‡‡‡]

Did You Know?

Each year, the United States applies 4.5 billion pounds of pesticides.

Regulation of Pesticides The EPA sets **tolerance limits** for the maximum residues of approved pesticides allowable in foods.[41] The limits generally represent between 1/100 and 1/1,000 of the dose found to cause no adverse health effects in laboratory animals.[§§§42] Over 10,000 regulations set tolerance limits for the more than 300 pesticide chemicals allowed for use on specific U.S. crops. If a pesticide is misused, growers risk fines, lawsuits, and destruction of their crops.

While the EPA sets limits, both the USDA and FDA occasionally test crop and food product samples for compliance. Over decades of testing, seldom have these agencies found residues above tolerance levels, so it appears that pesticides are generally applied according to regulations. This makes sense because growers are not anxious to spend extra capital on unneeded chemicals.

- Pesticides are used to:
  - *kill pests in and around homes.*
  - *control pests in flower and vegetable gardens.*
  - *reduce loss of farm crops to insects.*
  - *preserve wood products.*
  - *cure lice, scabies, worms, and other parasites in people and their pets.*
  - *repel mosquitoes, fleas, and other biting insects from people and pets.*
  - *many other uses.*

Pesticide-Resistant Insects Ironically, some pesticides also promote the survival of the very pests they are intended to wipe out. A pesticide aimed at certain insects may kill almost 100 percent of them, but because of the genetic variability of large populations, a few hardy individuals survive exposure. These resistant insects then multiply free of competition and soon produce offspring with inherited pesticide resistance that attack the crop with enhanced vigor. Controlling resistant insects requires application of new and more powerful pesticides, which leads to the emergence of a population

‡‡‡For answers to questions about pesticides, call the national pesticide information center: 1-800-858-PEST.
§§§Read more about the effects of pesticides at the EPA website: www.epa.gov/pesticides/health/human.htm.

tolerance limit the maximum amount of a residue permitted in a food when a pesticide is used according to label directions.

TABLE 12-8 Ways to Reduce Pesticide Residue Intakes

In addition to these steps, remember to eat a variety of foods to minimize exposure to any one pesticide.

- Trim the fat from meat, and remove the skin from poultry and fish; discard fats and oils in broths and pan drippings. (Pesticide residues concentrate in the animal's fat.)
- Select fruits and vegetables with intact skins.
- Wash fresh produce in warm running water. Use a scrub brush, and rinse thoroughly.
- Use a knife to peel an orange or grapefruit; do not bite into the peel.
- Discard the outer leaves of leafy vegetables such as cabbage and lettuce.
- Peel waxed fruits and vegetables; waxes don't wash off and can seal in pesticide residues.
- Peel vegetables such as carrots and fruits such as apples when appropriate. (Peeling removes pesticides that remain in or on the peel, but also removes fibers, vitamins, and minerals.)
- Consider buying certified organic foods.

MY TURN

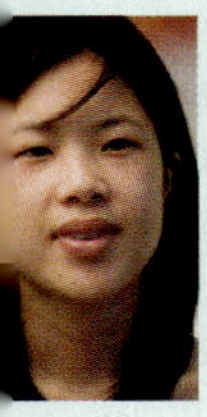

nifer *Lisa*

Organic: Does It Matter?

Two students talk about the pros and cons of choosing organic foods.

CENGAGENOW To hear their stories, log on to www.cengage.com/sso.

of still more resistant insects. The same effects arise from use of herbicides and fungicides. One alternative to this destructive series of events is to manage pests using a combination of natural and biological controls, as discussed in Controversy 15.

Natural Pesticides Pesticides are not produced only in laboratories; they also occur in nature. The nicotine in tobacco and phytochemicals of celery are examples.**** A bacterium from soil yields a biodegradable peptide pesticide approved for use in **organic gardens.** Natural pesticides are less damaging to other living things and leave less **persistent** residues in the environment than most human-made ones. An ideal pesticide would destroy pests in the field but vanish long before consumers ate the food.

While chemical companies are working to develop such safer pesticides, advances in **biotechnology** have reduced the need for pesticide sprays on many crops (see the Controversy section). Another possibility for consumers who want fewer pesticides in their produce and meat is to choose **organic foods;** they are discussed in the Consumer Corner near here.

****The celery plant produces psoralens that repel insects.

CONCEPT LINK 12-2

Peptide refers to the bond that joins amino acids, described in Chapter 6, page 191.

Foods imported from other countries may contain residues of pesticides that are banned from use here.

organic gardens gardens grown with techniques of *sustainable agriculture,* such as using fertilizers made from composts and introducing predatory insects to control pests, in ways that have minimal impact on soil, water, and air quality.

persistent of a stubborn or enduring nature; with respect to food contaminants, the quality of remaining unaltered and unexcreted in plant foods or in the bodies of animals and human beings.

biotechnology the science of manipulating biological systems or organisms to modify their products or components or create new products; also called *genetic engineering* or *recombinant DNA (rDNA) technology* (see the Controversy).

organic foods foods meeting strict USDA production regulations for *organic,* including prohibition of synthetic pesticides, herbicides, fertilizers, drugs, and preservatives and produced without genetic engineering or irradiation.

CONSUMER CORNER Organic Foods LO 12.5

Sales of certified organic foods skyrocketed from under $4 billion in 1997 to $21 billion in 2008.[1] No longer produced solely by a few elite "hobby" farms and sold only to wealthy consumers in farmer's markets or specialty shops, organic foods are now produced under alternative names by giant U.S. cereal makers and other well-known food companies. They are snapped up by shoppers in national grocery stores and even in bulk sales "clubs" across the nation.*

Consumers willing to pay the 10 to 40 percent higher prices for organic foods say they want more freshness or nutrients, or they want to avoid pesticides or genetically modified foods.[2] Many people are also willing to pay more for foods produced in ways benevolent to the environment and with respect for animals.[3] Do organic foods deliver what consumers are paying for?

To receive an organic certification, a U.S. farmer or producer must pass USDA inspections at every step of production, from the seed sown in the ground, through the methods of making compost for fertilizer, to the manufacturing of the final product. To be labeled as *certified organic,* or to bear the USDA organic seal (see Figure 12-8), a food must be produced according to strict standards.

For example, Kellogg owns Kashi and Bear Naked organic food lines; Dean Foods, General Mills, and Cargill own others.

In contrast, foods bearing "natural," "free-range," or other wholesome-sounding labels are not required to meet the organic standards. Freshness and nutrient contents of organic foods are not ensured, however.

PESTICIDE RESIDUES

When tested, organic foods mostly contain no pesticides or lower levels of pesticides than similar, conventionally grown products.[4] About 25 percent of organic foods test positive for pesticides, however, probably from residues in fields that were once sprayed with persistent chemicals that do not break down in soil (now banned from use) or from spray drift from nearby conventional fields.

Still, consuming a diet of organic foods measurably reduces pesticide exposure. Scientists provided 23 elementary school-age children a five-day diet composed entirely of organic foods and tested their urine for markers of pesticide ingestion.[5] The results were immediate and dramatic: the concentration of chemicals fell and remained low during the organic diet period and rose once again when the children resumed their regular conventional diet.

A question *not* answered by the study is whether pesticide exposure from conventional foods poses health risks. As mentioned, the tolerance limit set for a pesticide typically reflects a value 100 times lower than the highest level of exposure known to have no adverse effect on the most sensitive test species. In people, a pesticide exposure of 1 percent of the tolerance limit (a typical exposure for most pesticides in use today) represents an amount 10,000 times lower than a level that does not cause toxicity.[6] Children are more sensitive than adults to pesticides, however, so parents may wish to reduce their children's exposure from all sources, including foods.

These 12 foods have tested positive for pesticides most often: apples, bell peppers, celery, cherries, grapes (imported), lettuce, nectarines, peaches, pears, potatoes, spinach, and strawberries.[7] Choosing organic versions of these foods can probably reduce consumers' pesticide exposure but, if the high price causes them to eat fewer of these foods, the trade-off may not be a good one—consuming more fruits and vegetables of all kinds is associated with lower risks of many diseases.

NUTRIENT COMPOSITION

In tests of nutrient composition, differences reported between conventional and organic foods generally fall within expected variations among food crops.[8] Reported differences may be due to soil type, soil nutrients, rainfall, or other environmental conditions.[9] Limited research does suggest that organic foods

FIGURE 12-8 **USDA Seal and Organic Food Label Claims**

A Food Meeting This Description...	Can Bear This On Its Label.
Made with exclusively 100% organic ingredients	[USDA ORGANIC seal] "100% Organic"
Made with at least 95% organic ingredients	[USDA ORGANIC seal] "Organic"
Made with at least 70% organic ingredients	"Made with organic ingredients" (May not use seal; may list up to three organic ingredients on front of package)
Made with less than 70% organic ingredients	(May not use seal and must make no claims on the front of the package; may list organic ingredients on side panel.)

may develop greater amounts of certain phytochemicals, which makes sense: the plants must muster their own defenses to survive.[10] Importantly, however, from a nutritionists' view, organic candy bars, frozen soy desserts, and fried organic snack chips are not more nutritious (or less fattening) than ordinary treats.

ENVIRONMENTAL BENEFITS

Organic foods are grown using techniques of *sustainable* agriculture (see Chapter 15 and its Controversy), methods that minimize harm to the environment. Properly composted animal manure or vegetable matter replaces synthetic fertilizers that often run off into waterways and pollute them. Pests and diseases are battled by rotating crops each season, by introducing predatory insects to kill off pests, or by picking off large insects or diseased plant parts by hand. Only pesticides derived from natural sources, such as the bacterial peptide toxin mentioned in the text, are allowed for use on organic fruits and vegetables.

To produce organic eggs, dairy products, and meats, farmers and ranchers raise food-producing animals in surroundings natural to their species with access to the outdoors.[11] Animals raised this way can grow large and stay healthy without growth hormones, daily antibiotics, and other drugs that are required in stressed animals raised in overcrowded pens. Without overcrowding, the threat to the nation's waterways from waste runoff is also greatly reduced.

As large industries take over organic foods businesses, less costly imported ingredients are creeping into organic foods. Some overseas farms adhere to strict standards—even in the "breadbasket" region of India, with millions of people to feed, some farmers find organic methods economical and sustainable.[12] Others, however, are lax, and monitoring overseas farms is problematic. Also, shipping even organic ingredients over long distances violates principles of sustainability, making a case for seeking out local organic products.

POTENTIAL HEALTH RISKS

Certified organic foods present no greater or lesser risk of microbial contamination than ordinary foods.[13] Untreated animal manure, whether from use as fertilizer, from farm or ranch runoff, or from wild or stray animal feces, may expose consumers to dangerous microorganisms, such as *E. coli* 0157:H7. Certified organic food producers must adhere to national standards for composting that ensure elimination of disease-causing microbes. To help protect themselves, consumers buying perishable foods of any kind should buy amounts that can be consumed within a few days, store and cook the food properly, wash raw produce vigorously, and buy only pasteurized dairy products and juices.

TASTE

Growers of organic fruits and vegetables may grow "heirloom" varieties that emphasize delicious flavor or tender texture over "perfect" appearance and sturdiness. And if improved flavor, or the perception of it, encourages people to eat more fruits and vegetables, then nutrition may benefit. Table C12-4 of this chapter's Controversy compares the characteristics of organic foods with those of conventionally grown foods and the products of biotechnology.

KEY POINT Pesticides can be part of a safe food production process but can also be hazardous if mishandled. The FDA tests domestic and imported foods for pesticide residues. Consumers can take steps to minimize their ingestion of pesticide residues in foods.

Animal Drugs

Consumer groups express concern about drugs administered to livestock that produce food. Of particular concern to some consumers are hormones, antibiotics, and drugs that contain arsenic compounds.

Growth Hormone in Meat and Milk Cattle producers in the United States commonly inject their herds with a form of **growth hormone—bovine somatotropin (bST)**—to increase lean tissue growth, increase milk production, and reduce feed requirements. The hormone, produced by genetically altered bacteria, is identical to growth hormone made in the pituitary gland of the animal's brain. The FDA deems the drug safe and does not require testing of food products for traces of it.[43]

Ranchers advocate the use of bST because more meat and milk on less feed means higher profits. The environment may profit as well. Smaller herds that eat sparingly require less cleared land and fewer resources used to produce and transport feed.

Consumer groups counter that while ranchers may benefit from the use of bST, consumers do not and so its use is not justified. Their concerns center on the safety of another bovine hormone stimulated by bST, insulin-like growth factor I (IGF-I).[44] However, when tested, IGF-I levels in milk from bST-treated cows fall within the

growth hormone a hormone (somatotropin) that promotes growth and that is produced naturally in the pituitary gland of the brain.

bovine somatotropin (bST) (so-mat-oh-TROPE-in) growth hormone of cattle, which can be produced for agricultural use by genetic engineering. Also called *bovine growth hormone (bGH)*.

normal range, so both the FDA and WHO conclude that milk from treated cows presents no additional risk to milk consumers.[45] In tests of over 300 samples of conventional milk, hormone-free milk, and organic milk, no differences were found in terms of antibiotic, bacteria, hormone, or nutrient contents.[46]

Antibiotics in Livestock For a half-century, ranchers and farmers have dosed livestock with antibiotic drugs as part of a daily feeding regimen to ward off infections that commonly afflict animals living in crowded conditions and to help promote rapid growth. As this book is written, a federal proposal under consideration would restrict such routine farm use of antibiotics important in the treatment of human diseases.[47]

A substantial threat to human health and life arises from antibiotic-resistant bacteria. A limited number of antibiotic drugs exist—the same or related drugs used in livestock also treat illnesses in people. When bacteria in any intestinal tract, human or animal, too frequently encounter antibiotics, the bacteria adapt, losing their sensitivity to the drugs over time. The resulting bacteria cause severe infections that do not yield to standard antibiotic therapy, often ending in fatality. Yearly, over 60,000 people die from such infections.[48] So long as antibiotics are overused, new resistant strains can be expected to arise; previous attempts at controlling them after emergence have proved ineffective.

Trends toward increasing numbers of infection and increasing drug resistance show no sign of abating.

—Joshua Sharfstein, principal deputy commissioner of the FDA, 2009.

Arsenic in Food Animals The USDA regulates administration of **arsenic,** a naturally occurring element and a poison of murder mystery fame, to food animals. Trace amounts of arsenic are thought to be essential for normal growth in several animal species. Too much arsenic leads to swelling of the brain, damage to the liver, and other deadly effects. Chronic human exposure to small amounts is associated with cancers, heart disease, diabetes, birth defects, and miscarriages.[49]

Conventionally raised young poultry flocks receive arsenic in tiny amounts to control parasites that would otherwise inhibit their growth. The USDA concludes that this use poses little or no risk to healthy consumers who eat ordinary portions (2 to 3 ounces) of chicken in the context of a varied diet. Arsenic is also present in foods such as fish, eggs, milk products, and red meats to a lesser extent; drinking water and environmental exposure may be the chief sources in some areas.[50]

KEY POINT Bovine somatotropin causes cattle to produce more meat and milk on less feed than untreated cattle, and the FDA has deemed products from treated cattle to be safe. Antibiotic overuse fosters antibiotic resistance in bacteria, threatening human health. Arsenic drugs are used to promote growth in chickens and other livestock.

Environmental Contaminants

As world populations increase and become more industrialized, concerns grow about contamination of foods. A food **contaminant** is anything that does not belong there.

Chemical contaminants of concern in foods:

- Heavy metals:
  - *Arsenic.*
  - *Cadmium.*
  - *Lead.*
  - *Mercury.*
  - *Selenium.*
- Halogens and organic halogens:
  - *Chlorine.*
  - *Ethylene dichloride.*
  - *Iodine.*
  - *Polybrominated biphenyl (PBB).*
  - *Polychlorinated biphenyls (PCBs).*
  - *Trichloroethylene (TCE).*
  - *Vinyl chloride.*
- Others:
  - *Acrylamide.*
  - *Antibiotics (in animal feed).*
  - *Asbestos.*
  - *Diethylstilbestrol (DES).*
  - *Dioxins.*
  - *Heat-induced mutagens.*
  - *Lysinoalanine.*

Harmfulness of Contaminants The potential for harm from a contaminant depends partly on how long it lingers in the environment or in the human body—that is, on how *persistent* it is. Some contaminants are short-lived because microorganisms, sunlight, or oxygen break them down. Some contaminants stay in the body for only a short time because the body rapidly excretes or destroys them. Such contaminants present little cause for concern.

Other contaminants linger and resist environmental breakdown, and they interact with the body's systems without being metabolized or excreted. These contaminants can pass from one species to the next and accumulate at higher concentrations in each level of the food chain, a process called **bioaccumulation**—see Figure 12-9.

When an environmental contaminant is detected in a person's blood or urine, this does not automatically mean that the chemical will cause disease. The toxicity of a chemical depends largely upon an interplay of two factors: the potency of its toxic-

arsenic a poisonous metallic element. In trace amounts, arsenic is believed to be an essential nutrient in some animal species. Arsenic is often added to insecticides and weed killers and, in tiny amounts, to certain animal drugs.

contaminant any substance occurring in food by accident; any food constituent that is not normally present.

bioaccumulation the accumulation of a contaminant in the tissues of living things at higher and higher concentrations along the food chain.

FIGURE 12-9 **Bioaccumulation of Toxins in the Food Chain**

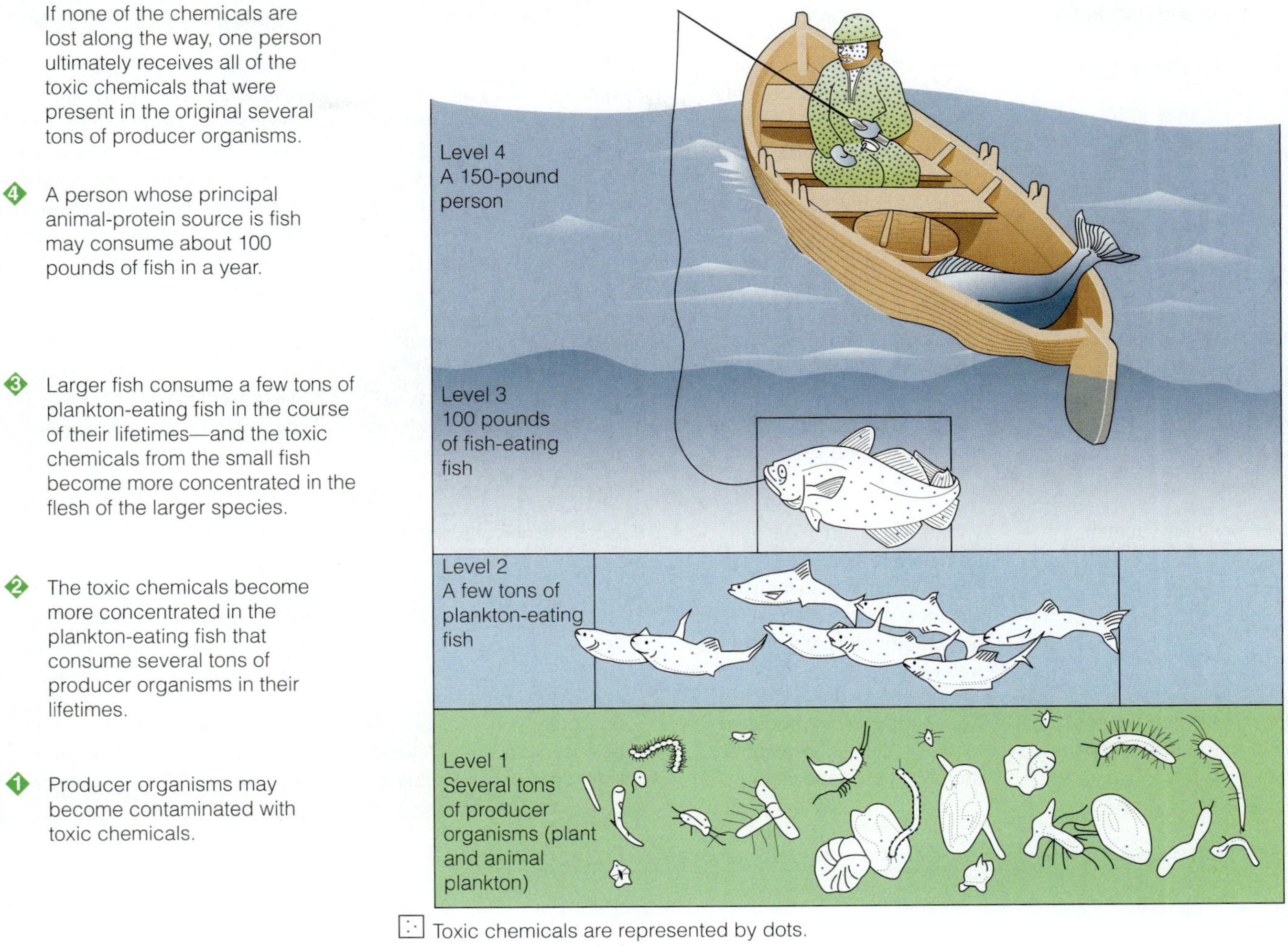

ity and the degree of human exposure.[51] In small enough amounts, even poisonous substances may be tolerable and of no consequence to health; in larger amounts, even innocuous substances may be dangerous. Normally benign substances, even sand, can kill if a person consumes enough of them.

How much of a threat do environmental contaminants pose to the food supply? It depends on the contaminant. In general, the threat remains small because the FDA monitors contaminants in foods and issues warnings when food contamination is evident. In the event of an industrial spill or a natural occurrence, such as a volcanic eruption, however, the hazard can suddenly become great. Contaminants may also build up in the food supply more insidiously. For example, increasing levels of the **heavy metal** mercury expelled from industrial sites have been detected in U.S. lakes, rivers, and ocean fisheries. Virtually all fish have at least trace amounts of mercury. Mercury, **PCBs,** chlordane, dioxins, and DDT are the toxins responsible for most fish contamination, but mercury leads the list by threefold. Table 12-9 describes a few contaminants of great concern in foods.

Mercury in Seafood Scientists learned of mercury's potential for harm through tragedy. In 1953, a number of people in Minamata, Japan, became ill with a strange disease. By 1960, 121 cases had been reported, including 23 infants. Mortality was high; 46 died, and the survivors suffered progressive, irreversible blindness, deafness, loss of coordination, and severely impaired mental function. *Minamata disease* was named for the location of the disaster.

Did You Know?

An old saying, "The dose makes the poison," means that with a large enough dosage, even normally benign substances can be toxic. The reverse is also true: even poisons can be benign in miniscule doses.

heavy metal any of a number of mineral ions such as mercury and lead, so called because they are of relatively high atomic weight; many heavy metals are poisonous.

PCBs stable oily synthetic chemicals used in hundreds of industrial and commercial operations that persist as pollution in the environment. PCBs cause cancer in animals and a number of other serious health effects. The Environmental Protection Agency monitors their levels.

TABLE 12-9 Examples of Contaminants in Foods

Name and Description	Sources	Toxic Effects	Typical Route to Food Chain
Cadmium (heavy metal)	Used in industrial processes including electroplating, plastics, batteries, alloys, pigments, smelters, and burning fuels. Present in cigarette smoke and in smoke and ash from volcanic eruptions.	No immediately detectable symptoms; slowly and irreversibly damages kidneys and liver.	Enters air in smokestack emissions, settles on ground, absorbed into food plants, consumed by farm animals, and eaten in vegetables and meat by people. Sewage sludge and fertilizers leave large amounts in soil; runoff contaminates shellfish.
Lead[a] (heavy metal)	Lead crystal decanters and glassware, painted china, old house paint, batteries, pesticides, old plumbing, and some food-processing chemicals.	Displaces calcium, iron, zinc, and other minerals from their sites of action in the nervous system, bone marrow, kidneys, and liver, causing failure of function.	Originates from industrial plants and pollutes air, water, and soil. Still present in soil from many years of leaded gasoline use.
Mercury (heavy metal)	Widely dispersed in gases from earth's crust; local high concentrations from industry, electrical equipment, paints, and agriculture; present in most U.S. waterways.	Poisons the nervous system, especially in fetuses.	Inorganic mercury released into waterways by industry and acid rain is converted to methylmercury by bacteria and ingested by food species of fish (tuna, swordfish, and others).
Polychlorinated biphenyls (PCBs) (organic compounds)	No natural source; produced for use in electrical equipment (transformers, capacitors).	Long-lasting skin eruptions, eye irritations, growth retardation in children of exposed mothers, anorexia, fatigue, others.	Discarded electrical equipment; accidental industrial leakage or reuse of PCB containers for food.

[a]*For answers to questions concerning lead, call the National Lead Information Center at (800) 424-LEAD.*

Finally, the cause of this misery was discovered: manufacturing plants in the region were discharging mercury into the waters of the bay, where it became the nerve poison methylmercury. The fish in the bay were accumulating the poison in their bodies, and townspeople who regularly ate fish from the bay fell ill. The infants had not eaten any fish but their mothers had during their pregnancies; the mothers were spared because the poison concentrates in the tissues of the fetus.

CONCEPT LINK 12-3

Guidelines for choosing fish were offered in Chapter 5's Consumer Corner, page 170.

Today, in the United States, the FDA and the Environmental Protection Agency (EPA) warn of unacceptably high methylmercury levels in our nation's oceans, freshwater lakes, and streams; they issue advisories urging consumers to limit consumption of many food fish, particularly large fish that live in the most contaminated waters.[52] Over time, mercury has been building up in people, too, with potential risks to the brain, nerves, and other tissues.[53] The FDA advises all pregnant women, women who may become pregnant, nursing mothers, and young children against eating fish species known to be high in methylmercury (Chapter 13 provides details of this warning). Freshwater fish also often contain PCBs and other industrial contaminants; check local advisories.

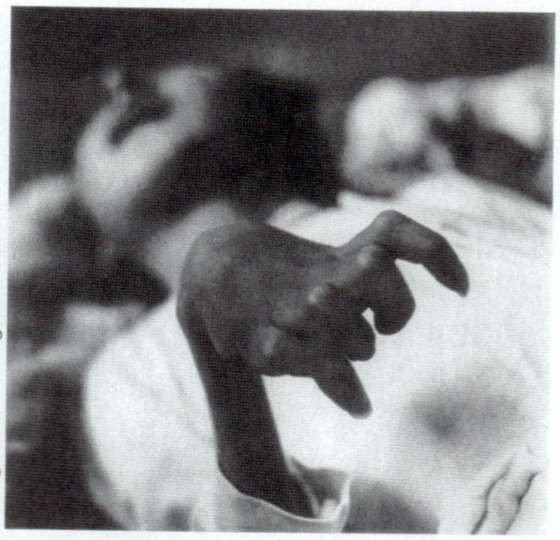
W. Eugene Smith/Magnum Photos

Minamata disease. The effects of mercury contamination can be severe.

No one expects the tragic results of 1953 to occur again, but lower doses of methylmercury cause headaches, fatigue, memory loss, impaired ability to concentrate, and muscle or joint pain in adults. In children, the threats may be greater and long-lasting. Methylmercury is persistent in the environment, so efforts begun today to clean up U.S. waters will take years to diminish this threat.

Country of Origin Labeling U.S. consumers have become increasingly aware that imported foods from certain developing countries may be produced with less than stringent food purity standards. To help consumers distinguish between imported and domestic foods, regulators now require certain foods, including fish, shellfish, meats, other perishable items, and some nuts, to bear a **Country of Origin Label (COOL)** specifying where they were produced.[54]

KEY POINT Persistent environmental contaminants present in food pose a significant, but generally small, threat to U.S. consumers. An accidental spill can create an extreme hazard. Mercury and other contaminants are of greatest concern during pregnancy, lactation, and childhood.

Did You Know?

The fish highest in mercury include:

- Saltwater: king mackerel, swordfish, shark, fresh tuna steaks, and tilefish.
- Freshwater: largemouth bass, smallmouth bass, and spotted bass.

LO 12.6

Are Food Additives Safe?

Many foods contain **additives,** and consumers rightly want to know why they are there and if they are safe to consume. On the FDA's list of food worries, food additives rank low. The 3,000 or so food additives approved for use in the United States are strictly controlled and well studied for safety. In fact, many food additives foil mold and bacterial growth, thereby improving food safety. Often, food additives give foods desirable characteristics: color, flavor, texture, stability, enhanced nutrient composition, or resistance to spoilage and enhanced safety. Some common classes of additives and their functions in foods are listed in Table 12-10.

© Polara Studios, Inc.

Without additives, bread would quickly mold and salad dressing would go rancid.

Regulations Governing Additives

Before using a new additive in food products, a manufacturer must test the additive and satisfy the FDA that:

- it is effective (it does what it is supposed to do).
- it can be detected and measured in the final food product.

Then the manufacturer must provide proof that it is safe (causes no birth defects or other injuries) when fed in large doses to experimental animals. Finally, the manufacturer must submit all test results to the FDA for approval. The whole process may take several years.

Country of Origin Label (COOL) the required label stating the country of origination of many imported meats, chicken, fish and shellfish, other perishable foods, certain nuts, peanuts, and ginseng.

additives substances that are added to foods but are not normally consumed by themselves as foods.

TABLE 12-10 Selected Food Additives and Their Functions

Agent Type	Function in Foods	Examples
Antimicrobial agents (preservatives)	Prevent food spoilage by mold or bacterial growth.	Acetic acid (vinegar), benzoic acid, nitrates and nitrites, proprionic acid, salt, sugar, sorbic acid.
Antioxidants (preservatives)	Prevent or delay rancidity of fats; prevent browning of fruit and vegetable products.	BHA, BHT, propyl gallate, sulfites, vitamin C, vitamin E.
Artificial colors	Add color to foods.	Certified food colors such as dyes from vegetables (beet juice or beta-carotene) or synthetic dyes (tartrazine and others).
Artificial flavors, flavor enhancers	Add flavors; boost natural flavors of foods.	Amyl acetate (artificial banana flavor), artificial sweeteners, MSG (monosodium glutamate), salt, spices, sugars.
Bleaching agents	Whiten foods such as flour or cheese.	Peroxides.
Chelating (KEE-late-ing) agents (preservatives)	Prevent discoloration, off flavors, and rancidity.	Citric acid, malic acid, tartaric acid (cream of tartar).
Nutrient additives	Improve nutritional value.	Vitamins and minerals.
Stabilizing and thickening agents	Maintain emulsion, foams, or suspensions or lend a desirable thick consistency to foods.	Dextrins (short glucose chains), pectin, starch, or gums such as agar, carrageenan, guar, locust bean, and other gums.

Manufacturers must comply with other regulations as well. Additives must not be used:

- in quantities larger than those necessary to achieve the needed effects.
- to disguise faulty or inferior products.
- to deceive the consumer.
- where they significantly destroy nutrients.
- where their effects can be achieved by economical, sound manufacturing processes.

The FDA holds a public hearing and invites consumer comments; at the hearing, experts present testimony for and against granting permission to use the additive. Upon approval, the FDA specifies the amounts, purposes, and foods for which the additive may be used.

The GRAS List Many additives were exempted from complying with this procedure when it was first instituted because they had been used for a long time and their use entailed no known hazards. Some 700 substances were put on the **generally recognized as safe (GRAS)** list. No additives are permanently approved; all are periodically reviewed.

The Margin of Safety An important distinction between **toxicity** and hazard arises during evaluation of an additive's safety. Toxicity is a general property of all substances; hazard is the capacity of a substance to produce injury *under conditions of its use.*[††††] As mentioned, all substances can be toxic at some level of consumption, but they are called hazardous only if they are toxic in the amounts ordinarily consumed. To determine risk, experimenters feed test animals the substance at different concentrations throughout their lifetimes.

An approved food additive has a wide **margin of safety.** Most additives that involve risk are allowed in foods only at levels 100 times below those at which the risk is still known to be zero (1/100). Some *natural* toxins produced in food by plants occur at levels that bring their margins of safety close to 1/10. The margin of safety for vitamins A and D is 1/25 to 1/40; it may be less than 1/10 in infants. For some trace elements, it is about 1/5. People consume common table salt daily in amounts only 3 to 5 times less than those that cause serious toxicity.

Risks and Benefits Most additives used in foods offer benefits that may outweigh their risks or that make the risks worth taking. In the case of color additives that only enhance the appearance of foods without improving their health value or safety, no amount of risk may be deemed worth taking. Only 10 of an original 80 synthetic color additives are still approved by the FDA for use in foods, and screening of these substances continues. A few food additives receive the most publicity and consumers have questions about them. The following sections address these additives.

KEY POINT The FDA regulates the use of intentional additives. Additives must be safe, effective, and measurable in the final product. Additives on the GRAS list are assumed to be safe because they have long been used. Approved additives have wide margins of safety.

generally recognized as safe (GRAS) list a list, established by the FDA, of food additives long in use and believed to be safe.

toxicity the ability of a substance to harm living organisms. All substances, even pure water or oxygen, can be toxic in high enough doses.

margin of safety in reference to food additives, a zone between the concentration normally used and that at which a hazard exists. For common table salt, for example, the margin of safety is 1/5 (five times the concentration normally used would be hazardous).

Additives to Improve Safety and Quality

Some additives improve food safety. They restrict bacterial growth or otherwise affect food quality.

Salt and Sugar Since before the dawn of history, salt has been used to preserve meat and fish; sugar, a relative newcomer to the food supply, serves the same pur-

[††††]The Delaney Clause, a legal requirement of zero cancer risk for additives, is no longer universally applied.

pose in jams, jellies, and canned and frozen fruits. Both salt and sugar work by withdrawing water from the food; microbes cannot grow without sufficient moisture. Safety questions surrounding these two preservatives center on their overuse as flavoring agents—salt and sugar make foods taste delicious and are often added with a liberal hand. Chapters 4 and 8 provided detailed discussions of these issues.

© Polara Studios, Inc.

Two long-used preservatives.

Nitrites The *nitrites* added to meats and meat products help to preserve their color (especially the pink color of hot dogs and other cured meats) and to inhibit rancidity and thwart bacterial growth. In particular, nitrites prevent the growth of the deadly botulinum bacterium. While useful, nitrites also raise safety issues. Once in the stomach, nitrites can be converted to nitrosamines, chemicals linked with colon cancer in animals. Other nitrite sources may make greater contributions to a person's overall exposure to nitrosamine-related compounds, however. For example, an average cigarette smoker inhales 100 times the nitrosamines that the average bacon eater ingests. Likewise, a beer drinker imbibes up to roughly 5 times the amount that the bacon eater receives. Still, processed meats are associated with an elevated risk of colon cancer, and cautious consumers limit their intake.[55]

Did You Know?

Salt and sugar are antimicrobial additives that work by depriving microorganisms of moisture.

Sulfites Sulfites prevent oxidation in many processed foods, in alcoholic beverages (especially wine), and in drugs. Some people experience dangerous allergic reactions to the sulfites, and so their use is strictly controlled. The FDA prohibits sulfite use on food meant to be eaten raw (fresh grapes are an exception), and it requires foods and drugs to list on their labels any sulfites that are present. For most people, sulfites do not pose a hazard in the amounts used in products, but they have one other drawback: because sulfites can destroy a lot of thiamin in foods, you can't count on a food that contains sulfites to contribute to your daily thiamin intake.

CONCEPT LINK 12-4

Chapter 11 explained the cancer risk associated with nitrites and processed meats on page 433.

KEY POINT Food spoilage can be prevented by certain additives. Of these, sugar and salt have the longest history of use. Nitrites and sulfites have advantages and drawbacks.

Flavoring Agents

Many additives add desirable flavors to foods. Among them, the **noncaloric sweeteners,** including both artificial sweeteners and herbal sweeteners may be added by manufacturers or by consumers at home.

Noncaloric Sweeteners Noncaloric sweeteners make foods taste sweet without promoting dental decay or providing the empty calories of sugar. The human taste buds perceive them as supersweet, so just tiny amounts are added to foods to achieve the desired sweet taste. The Food and Drug Administration (FDA) endorses the use of noncaloric sweeteners as safe over a lifetime when used within **acceptable daily intake (ADI)** levels.[56] Table 12-11 provides some details about the noncaloric sweeteners, including ADI levels for each one.

Through the years, questions have emerged about the safety of some artificial sweeteners. For example, early research indicated that large quantities of saccharin caused bladder tumors in laboratory animals, but these issues have since been resolved.[57] Overloading on huge saccharin doses is probably not safe, but consuming moderate amounts poses no hazard.

Aspartame, a sweetener made from two amino acids (phenylalanine and aspartic acid) is one of the most thoroughly studied food additives ever approved. In the digestive tract, the two amino acids are split apart, absorbed, and metabolized just as they would be if they had come from protein in food. Aspartame also breaks down when heated and so cannot replace sugar in cooking or baking.

Aspartame's phenylalanine base poses a threat to people with the inherited disease phenylketonuria (PKU), which, without a therapeutic diet, can cause brain damage in children. PKU children need protein-rich foods to grow but intakes must be limited because food proteins contain phenylalanine. Such children cannot afford to squander their small phenylalanine allowance on purified phenylalanine

noncaloric sweeteners sugar substitutes that provide negligible or no energy. Also called *nonnutritive sweeteners.*

acceptable daily intake (ADI) the estimated amount of a sweetener that can be consumed daily over a person's lifetime without any adverse effects.

TABLE 12-11 Noncaloric Sweeteners

Sweetener	Chemical Composition	Body's Response	Sweetness Relative to Sucrose[a]	Energy (cal/g)	Acceptable Daily Intake (ADI) and (Estimated Equivalent[b])
ARTIFICIAL SWEETENERS					
Acesulfame potassium or Acesulfame K[c] (AY-sul-fame)	Potassium salt	Not digested or absorbed	200	0	15 mg/kg body weight[d] (30 cans diet soda)
Aspartame[e] (ah-SPAR-tame or ASS-par-tame)	Amino acids (phenylalanine and aspartic acid) and a methyl group	Digested and absorbed	200	4[f]	50 mg/kg body weight[g] (18 cans diet soda)
Cyclamate[h] (SIGH-kla-mate)	Sodium or calcium salt of cyclamic acid	Incompletely absorbed; absorbed cyclamate is excreted unchanged; unabsorbed cyclamate may be metabolized by bacteria in the GI tract	30	0	11 mg/kg body weight (8 cans of diet soda)
Neotame (NEE-oh-tame)	Aspartame with an additional side group attached	Not digested or absorbed	8000	0	18 mg/day
Saccharin[i] (SAK-ah-ren)	Benzoic sulfimide	Rapidly absorbed and excreted	450	0	5 mg/kg body weight (10 packets of sweetener)
Sucralose[j] (SUE-kra-lose)	Sucrose with Cl atoms instead of OH groups	Not digested or absorbed	600	0	5 mg/kg body weight (6 cans diet soda)
Tagatose[k] (TAG-ah-tose)	Monosaccharide similar in structure to fructose; naturally occurring or derived from lactose	Not well absorbed	0.8	1.5	7.5 g/day
HERBAL SWEETENERS					
Stevia[l] (STEE-vee-ah)	Glycosides found in the leaves of the *Stevia rebaudiana* herb	Digested and absorbed	200–300	0	4 mg/kg body weight

[a]*Relative sweetness is determined by comparing the approximate sweetness of a sugar substitute with the sweetness of pure sucrose, which has been defined as 1.0. Chemical structure, temperature, acidity, and other flavors of the foods in which the substance occurs all influence relative sweetness.*

[b]*Based on a person weighing 70 kg (154 lbs).*

[c]*Marketed under the trade name Sunett, Sweet One.*

[d]*Recommendations from the World Health Organization: limit acesulfame-K intake to 9 mg per kilogram of body weight per day.*

[e]*Marketed under the trade names NutraSweeet, Equal, NatraTaste, Canderel.*

[f]*Aspartame provides 4 cal per gram, as does protein, but because so little is used, its energy contribution is negligible. In powdered form, it is sometimes mixed with lactose, however, so a 1-g packet may provide 4 cal.*

[g]*Recommendations from the World Health Organization and in Europe and Canada limit aspartame intake to 40 mg per kilogram of body weight per day.*

[h]*Cyclamate is approved for use in Canada; U.S. approval is pending.*

[i]*Marketed under the trade names Sweet'N Low, Necta Sweet.*

[j]*Marketed under the trade names Splenda, SucraPlus.*

[k]*Marketed under the trade names Nutralose, Nutrilatose, Tagatesse.*

[l]*Marketed under the trade names Sweetleaf, Purevia, Truvia, Honey Leaf.*

CONCEPT LINK 12-5

PKU was a topic of Chapter 3 (page 71).

from aspartame. Food labels warn people with PKU of the presence of phenylalanine in aspartame-sweetened foods (see Figure 12-10). Artificially sweetened foods and drinks have no place in the diets of even healthy infants or toddlers.

Urban legends circulated on the Internet have accused aspartame of causing everything from Alzheimer's disease and brain cancer to skin warts, but scientific

FIGURE 12-10 **Artificial Sweeteners on Food Labels**

© Scott Goodwin Photography

INGREDIENTS: ARTIFICIAL AND NATURAL FLAVORING, TITANIUM DIOXIDE (COLOR), ASPARTAME, ACESULFAME POTASSIUM, STEVIA.
PHENYLKETONURICS: CONTAINS PHENYLALANINE.

This partial ingredient list is for a sugar-free food.

Products containing aspartame must carry a warning for people with phenylketonuria.

Nutrition Facts

Serving Size 8 oz
Servings 6
Calories 0

Amount per serving	% DV*
Total Fat 0g	0%
Sodium 0mg	0%
Total Carb. 0g	0%
Sugars 0g	
Protein 0g	

*Percent Daily Values (DV) are based on a 2,000 calorie diet.

Not a significant source of other nutrients.

Products containing less than 0.5 g of sugar per serving can claim to be "sugarless" or "sugar-free."

evidence shows that they are unfounded. People who believe aspartame gives them symptoms should use a different sweetener.

Monosodium Glutamate (MSG) Another well-known flavor additive is the flavor enhancer monosodium glutamate, or MSG (trade name Accent), the sodium salt of the amino acid glutamic acid. MSG is used widely in restaurants, especially Asian restaurants. In addition to enhancing other flavors, MSG itself possesses a basic taste (termed *umami*) independent of the well-known sweet, salty, bitter, and sour tastes.[58]

In a few sensitive individuals, MSG produces adverse reactions known as the **MSG symptom complex.** Plain broth with MSG seems most likely to bring on symptoms in sensitive people, while carbohydrate-rich meals seem to protect against them. When dining on Asian-style foods, sensitive people should order food without MSG or try ordering soups that contain noodles and eat plenty of plain rice, as do Asians themselves. MSG, deemed safe for adults, is prohibited in baby foods because very large doses destroy brain cells in developing mice, and the brains of human infants cannot fully exclude such substances.[59] Consumers can easily identify foods that contain MSG because, with the exception of additives used in fresh meats, the FDA requires that food labels disclose each additive by its full name.

KEY POINTS Among flavor additives, noncaloric sweeteners are widely used by industry and consumers. People with PKU should avoid aspartame. The flavor enhancer MSG causes reactions in people with sensitivities to it.

Fat Replacers and Artificial Fats

Fat replacers and artificial fats, introduced in Chapter 5, are ingredients that provide some of the taste, texture, and cooking qualities of fats, but with fewer or no calories (see Table 12-12). Some fat replacers are derived from carbohydrate, protein, or fat, and these provide a few calories (but fewer than the fats they replace).

MSG symptom complex the acute, temporary, and self-limiting reactions, including burning sensations or flushing of the skin with pain and headache, experienced by sensitive people upon ingesting a large dose of MSG. Formerly called *Chinese restaurant syndrome*.

TABLE 12-12 A Sampling of Fat Replacers

For comparison, remember that fat has 9 calories per gram.

Fat Replacers	Energy (cal/g)
Carbohydrate-Based Fat Replacers	
• *Fruit* purees and pastes; add bulk and tenderness to baked goods.	1–4
• *Maltodextrins* made from corn; powdered and flavored to resemble butter.	1–4
Fiber-Based Fat Replacers	
• *Gels* derived from cellulose or starch to mimic the texture of fats in fat-free margarine and other products.	0–4[a]
• *Gums* extracted from beans, sea vegetables, or other sources. Used to thicken salad dressings and desserts.	0–4
• *Oatrim* derived from oat fiber; has the added advantage of providing satiety; lends creaminess to many foods.	4
• *Z-trim* a modified form of insoluble fiber; is powdered and feels like fat in the mouth; lends creaminess to many foods.	0
Fat-Based Replacers	
• *Olestra*[b] a noncaloric artificial fat made from sucrose and fatty acids; formerly called *sucrose polyester*; used for frying and cooking snacks and crackers.	0
• *Salatrim*[c] derived from fat and contains short- and long-chain fatty acids; can be used in baking but not frying.	5
Protein-Based Fat Replacers	
• *Microparticulated protein*[d] proteins of milk or egg white processed into mistlike particles that feel and taste like fat. Not suitable for frying.	4

[a] *Energy made available by action of colonic bacteria.*
[b] *Trade name: Olean. Not available in Canada.*
[c] *Trade name: Benefat.*
[d] *Trade names: Simplesse and K-Blazer.*

Carbohydrate-based fat replacers are used primarily as thickeners or stabilizers in foods such as soups and salad dressings. Protein-based fat replacers provide a creamy feeling in the mouth and are often used in foods such as ice creams and yogurts. Fat-based replacers act as emulsifiers and are heat stable, making them most versatile in shortenings used in cake mixes and cookies.

An artificial fat used to make low-fat snack foods such as potato chips, crackers, and tortilla chips is **olestra.** Olestra's chemical composition is similar to that of a regular fat, but enzymes in the digestive tract cannot break its chemical bonds, so olestra cannot be absorbed. As it passes through the digestive tract, olestra binds some fat-soluble vitamins and phytochemicals and carries them out of the body, robbing the person of these valuable food constituents. To partly compensate for these losses, the FDA requires the manufacturer to fortify olestra with vitamins A, D, E, and K. Saturating olestra with these vitamins does not make the product a good vitamin source, but it does block olestra's ability to bind with the vitamins from other foods. No reports of cancer, birth defects, or other serious problems have been reported with years of use of olestra.

KEY POINTS Fat replacers and artificial fats reduce the calories in processed foods, and the FDA deems them safe to use.

olestra a noncaloric artificial fat made from sucrose and fatty acids; formerly called *sucrose polyester.*

Incidental Food Additives

Consumers are often unaware that many substances can migrate into food during production, processing, storage, packaging, or consumer preparation. These substances, although called indirect or **incidental additives,** are really contaminants because no one intentionally adds them to foods. Examples of incidental additives include compounds released from plastics; tiny bits of glass, paper, metal, and the like from packages; or chemicals from processing, such as the solvent used to decaffeinate some coffees. Incidental additives find their way into many foods, but adverse effects are rare. These additives are well regulated and, once discovered in food, their safety must be confirmed by strict procedures like those governing intentional additives. For example, the incidental additive BPA, mentioned in Chapter 8's Consumer Corner with regard to bottled water, migrates into foods from plastic-lined food and baby formula containers.[‡‡‡‡] The FDA is evaluating the safety of BPA and taking steps to reduce consumer exposure.[60]

Microwave Packages Some microwave products are sold in "active packaging" that participates in cooking the food. Pizza, for example, may rest on a cardboard pan coated with a thin film of metal that absorbs microwave energy and may heat up to 500°F (260°C). During the intense heat, some particles of the packaging components migrate into the food. This is expected, and the particles have been tested for safety.

In contrast, plastic packages and containers heat up less while microwaving, but particles still migrate from them into foods and some plastic substances may not be entirely safe for consumption. To avoid them, avoid reusing disposable containers for microwaving, such as margarine tubs or single-use trays from frozen microwavable meals, and wrap foods in microwave-safe plastic wraps, waxed paper, cooking bags, parchment paper, and white microwave-safe paper towels before cooking. Glass or ceramic containers or plastic ones labeled as safe for microwaving do not generate particles that enter foods during microwave cooking.

Bleached Paper Coffee filters, paper milk cartons, paper plates, and frozen food boxes can all be made of bleached paper and so can contaminate foods with trace amounts of dioxins. Dioxins are carcinogenic by-products of a chlorination step in making bleached paper. Dioxins can migrate into foods that come in contact with bleached paper, but these amounts are infinitesimally small—1 part per trillion, or the equivalent of 1 second in 32,000 years. Such amounts do not appear to present a health risk to people. Dioxins are persistent, however, and can build up to hazardous levels in land, water, and animals.

Decaffeinated Coffee As for chemicals left behind from decaffeinating, methylene chloride can be detected at a concentration of 0.1 part per million in prepared coffee. An average decaffeinated coffee drinker consuming 100 times as much every day for a lifetime has a one-in-a-million chance of developing cancer from it. Other sources, such as hair sprays and paint-stripping products, contribute much greater amounts of methylene chloride than daily coffee. Consumers may avoid the small exposure from daily coffee by choosing coffees that are decaffeinated with steam or water.

Conclusion

To sum up the messages of this chapter, the U.S. food supply is largely safe and hazards are rare. Foodborne microbial illnesses pose the greatest threat by far, and an urgent need exists for new preventive technologies and procedures. Consumers must also develop an awareness of foodborne illnesses and take the needed measures to avoid becoming ill. The Food Feature that follows explores how food processing affects the nutrients in foods and offers pointers on the selection, storage, and cooking of foods to preserve their nutrients.

KEY POINT Incidental additives are substances that get into food during processing. They are well regulated, and most do not constitute a hazard.

incidental additives substances that can get into food not through intentional introduction, but as a result of contact with the food during growing, processing, packaging, storing, or some other stage before the food is consumed. Also called *accidental* or *indirect additives*.

‡‡‡‡BPA is an abbreviation of bisphenol A, a plastic hardener and component of epoxy resin.

FOOD FEATURE

Processing and the Nutrients in Foods

In general, the more heavily processed foods are, the less nutritious they become. Does that mean that you should avoid all processed food? The answer is not simple: in each case, it depends on the food and on the process (Table 12-13 provides examples). Some effects of process on nutrients were mentioned in Chapters 7 and 8. As an example, consider the case of orange juice and vitamin C.

THE CHOICE OF ORANGE JUICE

Orange juice is available in several forms, each processed a different way. Fresh juice is squeezed from the orange, a process that extracts the fluid juice from the fibrous structures that contain it. Each 100 calories of the fresh-squeezed juice contain 98 milligrams of vitamin C. When this juice is condensed by heat, frozen, and then reconstituted, as is the juice from the freezer case of the grocery store, 100 calories of the reconstituted juice contain just 85 milligrams of vitamin C because vitamin C is destroyed in the condensing process. Canning is even harder on vitamin C: 100 calories of canned orange juice have 82 milligrams of vitamin C.

These figures seem to indicate that fresh juice is the superior food, but consider this: most people's recommended intake of vitamin C (75 milligrams for women or 90 milligrams for men) is fully or nearly met by a 100-calorie serving of any of the above choices. Thus, for vitamin C, the losses due to processing are not a problem. Besides, processing confers enormous convenience in distribution and consumer price advantages. Fresh orange juice spoils. Shipping fresh juice to distant places in refrigerated trucks costs much more than shipping frozen juice (which takes up less space) or canned juice (which requires no refrigeration). The fresh product still contains active enzymes that continue to degrade its compounds (including vitamin C) and so cannot be stored indefinitely without compromising nutrient quality. Without canned or frozen juice, people with limited incomes or those with no access to fresh juice would be deprived of this excellent food. Vitamin C is readily destroyed by oxygen, so whatever the processing methods, orange juice and other vitamin C–rich foods and juices should be stored properly and consumed within a week of opening.

extrusion processing techniques that transform whole or refined grains, legumes, and other foods into shaped, colored, and flavored snacks, breakfast cereals, and other products.

PROCESSING MISCHIEF

Some processing stories are not so rosy. Chapter 8, for instance, explained how processed foods often gain sodium, which people must limit, while needed potassium is leached away. Another misdeed of processors is the addition of sugar and fat—palatable, high-calorie additives that reduce nutrient density. For example, nuts and raisins covered with "natural yogurt" may sound like one healthy food being added to another, but about 75 percent of the weight of the "yogurt" topping is sugar and fat; only 8 percent is yogurt. These sugar- and fat-coated foods taste so good that wishful thinking can take hold, but they are, in reality, candy.

A particularly severe food process is **extrusion.**[61] Extrusion involves grinding and cooking grains, legumes, or other foods, often at high heat and under pressure. The food may then undergo mixing with salt, sugar, flavors, colors, conditioners, and other ingredients; shaping by being pushed through a die; expansion by puffing; and frying. The finished product may be attractive with bright colors, tasty flavors, and pretty shapes, but it has sustained oxidation and heat losses of about 30 percent of its vitamin A, 50 percent of vitamin K, 90 percent of vitamin C, with similar losses for almost every other vitamin.[62] Losses of phytochemicals are likely to be similar. Beware of processed foods that appear puffy, cute, or colorful—they may lack many of the beneficial constituents that you seek, even if they were made from whole grains and other once-nutritious foods.

BEST NUTRIENT BUYS

Here are two good general rules for making food choices:

- Choose whole foods to the greatest extent possible.
- Among processed foods, use those that processing has improved nutritionally or left intact. For example, processing that removes saturated fat, as in fat-free milk, is nutritionally beneficial; the washing and cutting of fresh vegetables is benign.

Commercially prepared whole-grain breads, frozen cuts of meats, bags of frozen vegetables, and canned or frozen fruit juices do little disservice to nutrition

Purchase mostly whole foods or those that processing has benefited nutritionally.

TABLE 12-13 **Effects of Food Processing on Nutrients**

Process	Method and Purpose	Typical Foods	Effects on Nutrients
Canning	Boil food to sterilize it and seal it in an impervious can or jar to preserve it.	Fruit, fruit preserves, prepared foods such as soups or pasta dishes, vegetables, and meats.	Causes substantial losses of water-soluble vitamins, particularly thiamin and riboflavin; other water-soluble vitamins are dissolved in cooking liquid.
Drying	Dehydrate foods to eliminate the water that microbes require for growth.	Fruit, vegetables, meats.	Commercial drying (especially freeze-drying performed at low temperatures) leaves most nutrients intact; home drying may destroy substantial vitamin content, particularly thiamin in foods treated with sulfur dioxide.
Extruding	Grind, heat, and blend foods with certified colors and flavors and push the resulting paste through screens to form various shapes.	Grains or soybeans, particularly as cereals, baconlike salad toppings, or snack foods in the form of puffs, crisps, or bits.	Considerable nutrient losses occur, notably all vitamins, fiber, and magnesium.
Freezing	Cool a food to its frozen state to stop bacterial reproduction and slow enzymatic reactions.	Fruit, vegetables, ready-to-bake doughs, prepared grain products, meats, soy meat replacers, and mixed dishes.	Negligible effects on nutrients.
Modified atmospheric packaging	Package food in a gas-impermeable container from which air is removed or replaced with other gases to preserve food freshness.	Ready-to-eat salads, cut fruits, soft fresh pasta noodles, baked goods, prepared foods, fresh and preserved meats.	Preserves vitamins by slowing enzymatic breakdown.
Pasteurizing	Expose food to elevated temperature for long enough to reduce bacterial contamination.	Refrigerated foods such as milk, fruit juice, and eggs.	Causes trivial losses of some vitamins.
Ultra-high-temperature processing	Expose food to high temperatures for a short time to eliminate microbial contamination.	Shelf-stable foods such as boxed milk, boxed fruit juice, shelf-stable entrée dishes for microwaving.	Causes trivial losses of some vitamins.

and enable the consumer to eat a wide variety of foods at great savings in time and human energy. The nutrient density of processed foods exists on a continuum:

Whole-grain bread > refined white bread > sugared doughnuts.

Milk > fruit-flavored yogurt > canned chocolate pudding.

Corn on the cob > canned creamed corn > caramel popcorn.

Oranges > canned orange juice > orange-flavored drink.

Baked pork loin > ham lunch meat > fried bacon.

The nutrient continuum is paralleled by another continuum—the nutrition status of the consumer. The closer to the farm the foods you eat, the better nourished you are likely to be, but that doesn't mean you have to live in the fields. Making wise food choices is half the story of smart nutrition self-care; skillful food preparation is the other half. In modern commercial processing, losses of vitamins seldom exceed 25 percent. In contrast, losses in the 60 to 75 percent range during food preparation at home are not unusual, and they can be close to 100 percent. In general, short cooking times with little water, such as those of microwaving or stir frying, best preserves the nutrients of vegetables, while long boiling in copious water that is discarded increases nutrient losses. With reasonable care, if you start with fresh whole foods containing ample amounts of vitamins, you will receive a bounty of the nutrients that they contain.

MEDIA MENU

CENGAGENOW To find additional quiz questions, view videos and animations, and explore interactive exercises, go to **www.cengage.com/sso.**

Get food safety tips from the Government Food Safety Information site or from the Fight BAC! Campaign of the Partnership for Food Safety Education: **http://www.foodsafety.gov** or **www.fightbac.org.**

Research foodborne illnesses, food safety, or international travel at **www.cdc.gov.**

Get fish advisories from the Environmental Protection Agency at **http://www.epa.gov/waterscience/fish.**

Review tips from the Environmental Protection Agency on methods of food buying and preparation that will help minimize pesticide exposure: **www.epa.gov/pesticides/food.**

Get information and tips on food preparation and storage at **www.nutrition.gov.** Under Browse by Subject, select Shopping, Cooking and Meal Planning; then scroll down and click on Food Storage and Preservation.

SELF CHECK

Answers to these Self Check questions are in Appendix G.

1. Which of the following food hazards has the FDA identified as its number-one concern?
   A. pesticides in food
   B. microbial foodborne illnesses
   C. intentional food additives
   D. genetically modified food
2. To prevent foodborne illnesses, the refrigerator's temperature should be less than:
   A. 70°F
   B. 65°F
   C. 40°F
   D. 30°F
3. Which of the following may be contracted from fresh raw or undercooked seafood?
   A. hepatitis
   B. worms and flukes
   C. viral intestinal disorders
   D. all of the above
4. Which of the following is correct concerning fruits that have been irradiated?
   A. They decay and ripen more slowly.
   B. They lose substantial nutrients.
   C. They lose their sweetness.
   D. They emit gamma radiation.
5. Which of the following organisms can cause *hemolytic-uremic syndrome*?
   A. *Listeria monocytogenes*
   B. *Campylobacter jejuni*
   C. *Escherichia coli* O157:H7
   D. *Salmonella*
6. It is possible to eliminate all toxins from your diet by eating only "natural" foods.
   T F
7. Pregnant women are advised not to eat certain species of fish because the FDA and the EPA have detected unacceptably high lead levels in them.
   T F
8. The threat of foodborne illness from meats or seafood is far greater than that from produce.
   T F
9. Packaging can contribute to food safety.
   T F
10. Infants under 1 year of age should never be fed honey because it can contain spores of *Clostridium botulinum.*
   T F

CONTROVERSY 12

Genetically Modified Foods: What Are the Pros and Cons?

LO 12.7

With or without their awareness, most people in this country consume foods that contain products of genetic engineering (GE). Ubiquitous food additives, such as soy lecithin, high-fructose corn syrup, and other common ingredients arise from GE plant materials. Some consumers recoil from the idea of eating food with altered genes; whole countries have banned such foods outright.[1*] While some objections are based on credible ideas, many others arise from unfounded fears and misinformation. This Controversy sorts out the scientific knowledge from the fiction.

Advances in **genetic modification** techniques, particularly **recombinant DNA (rDNA) technology,** hold promise for solving some age-old agricultural problems while boosting profits for food producers. Worldwide, farmers in developing nations who planted crops altered by genetic engineering saw an increase in income of $2.7 billion over a 10-year period.[2] Although GE technologies are relatively new, their roots lie in naturally occurring genetic events and in centuries-old farming techniques. Table C12-1 provides definitions.

TABLE C12-1 Genetic Engineering Terms

- **clone** an individual created asexually from a single ancestor, such as a plant grown from a single stem cell; a group of genetically identical individuals descended from a single common ancestor, such as a colony of bacteria arising from a single bacterial cell; in genetics, a replica of a segment of DNA, such as a gene, produced by genetic engineering.
- **GE foods** genetically engineered foods; food plants and animals altered by way of rDNA technology.
- **genetic engineering (GE)** the direct, intentional manipulation of the genetic material of living things in order to obtain some desirable trait not present in the original organism. Also called *recombinant DNA technology* and *biotechnology*.
- **genetic modification** intentional changes to the genetic material of living things brought about through a range of methods, including rDNA technology, natural cross-breeding, and agricultural selective breeding.
- **outcrossing** the unintended breeding of a domestic crop with a related wild species.
- **plant pesticides** substances produced within plant tissues that kill or repel attacking organisms.
- **recombinant DNA (rDNA) technology** a technique of genetic modification whereby scientists directly manipulate the genes of living things; includes methods of removing genes, doubling genes, introducing foreign genes, and changing gene positions to influence the growth and development of organisms.
- **selective breeding** a technique of genetic modification whereby organisms are chosen for reproduction based on their desirability for human purposes, such as high growth rate, high food yield, or disease resistance, with the intention of retaining or enhancing these characteristics in their offspring.
- **stem cell** an undifferentiated cell that can mature into any of a number of specialized cell types. A stem cell of bone marrow may mature into one of many kinds of blood cells, for example.
- **transgenic organism** an organism resulting from the growth of an embryonic, stem, or germ cell into which a new gene has been inserted.

NATURAL CROSS-POLLINATING AND SELECTIVE BREEDING

Genomes of species have been evolving and changing since long before human beings emerged to domesticate animals and plants. Wild plants cross-pollinated and animals bred randomly, introducing new genetic combinations into the world. In plants, most such crosses failed to thrive but occasionally a new plant, such as today's wheat, formed with a genetic biological advantage for survival. In animals, too, new traits that conferred survival advantages were passed on to new generations. New DNA segments from wild bacteria and viruses that implanted into the cells of other species also blended with host genomes to be replicated over generations.

With the advent of human agriculture, season after season, farmers selected the best farm animals and plants for breeding, thereby influencing genetic makeup of the food supply. Today's lush, hefty, healthy agricultural crops and

*Reference notes are found in Appendix F.

Smithsonian Photo by Antonio Mortaner

This wild corn, with its sparse kernels, bears little resemblance to today's large, full, sweet ears.

animals, from cabbage and squash to pigs and cattle, are the result of this **selective breeding.** A consumer of today's sweet large cobs of corn, for example, may not recognize the original wild native corn with its sparse four or five kernels to a stalk (shown in the photo).

Today, accelerated selective breeding techniques involve hundreds of thousands of cross-bred seeds planted on vast acreage. To develop crops with desired traits, DNA data from successful seedlings are analyzed by computer. Seedlings with the right genes are grown to maturity and reproduced to yield new breeds in a relatively short time. The unusually colorful carrots in the photo below, for example, are products of this kind of selective breeding. Selective breeding must stay within the boundaries of a species—a carrot, for example, cannot be crossed with a mosquito. Genetic engineering, however, knows no such limits.

© Stephen Ausmus/USDA

These colorful carrots resulted from intensive selective breeding, not rDNA technology. Researchers bred carrots with high levels of colorful phytochemicals at each generation.

GENETIC ENGINEERING BASICS

With economy, speed, and precision, rDNA technology can change one or more characteristics of a living thing. The genes for a desirable trait in one organism are transferred directly into another organism's DNA. Figure C12-1 compares the genetic results of selective breeding and rDNA technology. Table C12-2 presents examples of food-related biotechnology research.

Obtaining Desired Traits

Using rDNA technology, scientists can confer useful traits, such as disease resistance, on food crops. To make a disease-resistant potato plant, for example, the process begins with the DNA of an immature cell, known as a **stem cell,** from the "eye" of a potato. Into that stem cell scientists insert a gene snipped from the DNA of a virus that attacks potato plants (enzymes do the snipping). This gene codes for a harmless viral protein, not the infective part.

The newly created stem cell is then stimulated to replicate itself, creating **clone** cells—exact genetic replicas of the altered original GE cell. With time, what was once a single cell grows into a **transgenic organism,** in this case, a potato plant that makes a piece of viral protein in each of its cells. The presence of the viral protein stimulates the potato plant to develop resistance against an attack from the real wild virus in the potato field.

FIGURE C12-1 ANIMATED! **Comparing Selective Breeding and rDNA Technology**

Selective Breeding—DNA is a strand of genes, depicted as a strand of pearls. Traditional selective breeding combines many genes from two individuals of the same species.

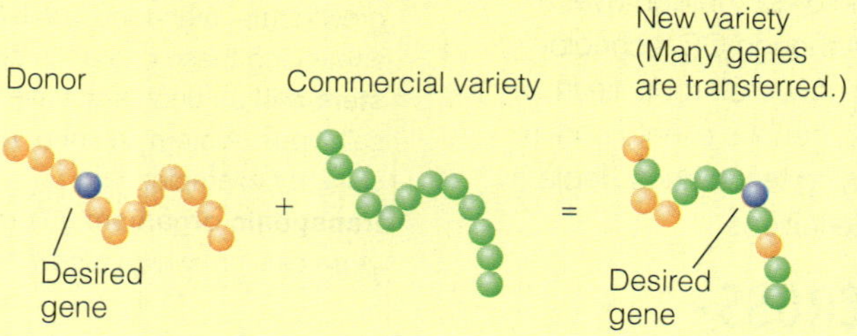

rDNA Technology—Through rDNA technology, a single gene or several may be transferred to the receiving DNA from the same species or others.

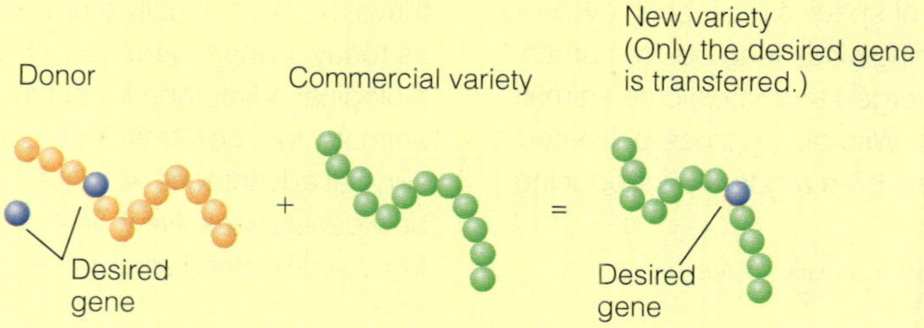

TABLE C12-2 **Some Examples of Biotechnology Research Directions**

Research in genetic engineering is currently directed at creating:

- GE crops and animals with added desired traits, such as altered nutrient composition, extended shelf life, freedom from allergy-causing constituents, or resistance to diseases or insect pests.
- GE crops that survive harsh conditions, such as applications of herbicides, heavily polluted or salty soils, or drought conditions.
- GE microorganisms that produce needed substances, such as pharmaceuticals or other products that do not occur in nature or occur only in small amounts.

Suppressing Unwanted Traits

rDNA technology can also remove an unwanted protein from a plant by silencing the genes responsible for its creation. For example, scientists are striving to make peanuts safer by silencing the genes for proteins that commonly cause allergic reactions.

Plants make likely candidates for genetic engineering because a single plant cell can often be coaxed into producing an entire new plant. Animals can also be modified by rDNA technology, however. Under development is a line of goats that, thanks to a spider's gene, express spider silk protein in their milk. Once processed, the stronger-than-steel silk fiber can be used to make artificial ligaments and bulletproof vests.[3]

THE PROMISES OF BIOTECHNOLOGY

Supporters hail genetic engineering as nothing short of a revolutionary means of overcoming many of the planet's pressing problems, such as food shortages, nutrient deficiencies, medicine shortages, dwindling farmland, and environmental degradation. The American Dietetic Association takes the position that agricultural and food biotechnology can enhance the quality, safety, nutritional value, and variety of the food supply, while helping to solve problems of production, processing, distribution, and environmental and waste management.[4] A few examples follow.

Human Nutrition

Rice leads the way in a genomic revolution of the world's food supply.[5] A GE rice (called *Golden Rice*) provides up to 35 micrograms of beta-carotene per gram of rice (for comparison, carrots have about 80 micrograms), sufficient to fight vitamin A deficiency and childhood blindness worldwide.[6] Other rice varieties, some offering 80 percent more iron and zinc than ordinary rice, could relieve much iron-deficiency anemia and zinc deficiency around the world. Other rice varieties may resist drought or insects and thus provide more food for hungry populations. In addition, favorite foods such as potatoes may be "biofortified" with minerals, fatty acids, or disease-fighting phytochemicals.[7]

In addition, pigs that develop high levels of omega-3 fatty acids of fish are under development. Livestock can also be engineered to develop less fat or to produce more milk. Animals themselves also stand to benefit: increased resistance to crippling diseases, such as "mad cow" and udder infections, is on the horizon.

Molecules from Microbes and Other Products

Through rDNA technology, the genes of microorganisms have been altered to make pharmaceutical and industrial products. For example, a transgenic bacterial factory now mass-produces the hormone insulin used by people with diabetes. Other hormones and enzymes are produced the same way. One GE bacterium received a bovine gene to make the enzyme rennin, necessary in cheese production. Historically, rennin was harvested from the stomachs of calves, an expensive process.

Plants and animals may also play similar roles. Researchers have induced bananas and potatoes to produce a hepatitis vaccine. Animals can be engineered to secrete vaccines in their milk and herds could provide both nourishment and immunization to villages now lacking both food and medicine. Pigs are being engineered for genetic compatibility with human beings to reduce the risk of immune rejection of surgically transplanted pig tissues.[8]

Greater Crop Yields

Most of today's GE crops fall within two main categories: herbicide-resistant and insect-resistant, both designed to increase food yield per acre of farmed land. Herbicide-resistant crops ease weed control by allowing farmers to spray whole fields, not just weeds, with potent herbicides. The weeds die but altered food crops in the sprayed fields remain healthy.

Insect-resistant crops make what the Environmental Protection Agency (EPA) calls **plant pesticides**—pesticides made by the plant tissues themselves. For example, a type of GE corn used for animal feed produces a pesticide that kills a common corn-destroying worm, thereby greatly increasing yields.

In areas where people cannot afford to lose a single morsel of food, and where plant diseases and insects can claim up to 80 percent of a season's food, GE plants can save the crop. Such innovations promise some relief for the world's chronically hungry people.

Food from Cloned Animals

According to the FDA, milk and meat from cloned adult cattle, pigs, and goats and their offspring are as safe as similar conventional foods, so food labels are not required to distinguish between these sources.[9] However, many consumers have reservations about consuming food from cloned animals.[10] The high cost of producing animal clones limits their practicality.

ISSUES SURROUNDING GE FOODS

Consumers want to know about any potential risks from rDNA technology. The FDA, in exploring the same issues, asks whether **GE foods** differ substantially from other foods in their nutrient contents or safety.

Nutrient Composition

In most cases, except for intentional variation created through rDNA technology, the nutrient composition of GE foods is identical to that of comparable traditional foods. From the body's point of view, therefore, eating Golden Rice, mentioned earlier, would be the same as eating plain rice and taking a beta-carotene supplement—and beta-carotene supplements carry risks (see Controversy 7). Thus, while GE foods may contribute to *overdoses* of nutrients or phytochemicals, they pose no unusual threat of deficiencies.

Accidental Ingestion of Drugs from Foods

The arrival of GE corn, soybeans, rice, and other food crops that make human and animal drugs, hormones, and proteins used in industry have set off warning bells. Although these crops must be grown indoors in selected locations, the containment areas often border farms where conventional food crops are grown. Critics fear that DNA from drug-producing GE crops might contaminate the regular food supply, despite USDA oversight.[11] Disasters such as tornadoes, floods, or other events could liberate the sequestered plants, and high winds or water could transport their pollen long distances to mingle undetected with food crops.

Pesticide Residues

Industry scientists contend that rDNA technology could virtually end problems associated with pesticide use on foods. When genes determine both the nature and the amount of pesticide produced, the chance of human error is eliminated. Critics counter that while GE crops may be protected from one or two common pests that may or may not be present on a particular field, farmers must still spray for other pests devouring their crops. In addition, from constant exposure to plant pesticides in GE plants, some target insects are becoming resistant to their effects.[12]

The plant pesticide produced by GE corn, a worm-killing peptide, is the same compound in the "natural pesticide" that organic farmers spray onto their corn to control the same worm. Originally discovered in a common soil bacterium, this peptide is harvested directly from industrial bacterial colonies.

Pesticide sprays can be largely removed by washing or peeling produce, but consumers cannot remove GE pesticides that form within the tissues of the food. Still, plant pesticides are highly unlikely to pose a health hazard because they are made of peptide chains (small protein strands) that human digestive enzymes readily denature. Plant pesticides, like other pesticide residues, are regulated as food additives by the FDA (see Chapter 12).

Unintended Health Effects

The possibility that genetic engineering of food plants or animals may have unintended and therefore unpredictable effects on human consumers is a concern.[13] A lesson comes from an unexpected negative effect of selective breeding. Over many years, celery growers had crossed their most attractive celery plants because consumers paid a premium for good-looking celery. Unbeknownst to the growers, however, the most beautiful celery stayed that way because it was especially high in a natural plant pesticide in celery. With each breeding cycle, the pesticide concentration increased. Farm and grocery workers who handled the celery began suffering from serious skin rashes until the problem was finally traced to high levels of natural pesticide in the beautiful plants.

Another example, this time an unintended *positive* effect of genetic engineering, involved a cancer-causing fungus that sometimes grows on corn.† After several growing seasons, scientists confirmed that GE corn with plant pesticide suffered reduced worm damage. Surprisingly, the crops also had far less than the expected growth of the dangerous fungus. It turns out that the worms spread the fungus as they burrowed into cobs of ordinary corn, but the plant pesticide in the GE corn killed the worms and stopped the spread of fungal infection. Whether negative or positive, unintended effects are by nature unpredictable.

Environmental Effects

Some striking benefits to the environment have emerged over the past 10 years from the use of GE crops. However, some detrimental environmental issues remain.

From 1996 to 2006, the planting of GE crops reduced pesticide use by almost 500 million pounds of active ingredients worldwide.[14] Also, GE herbicide-resistant crops require far less plowing to kill weeds and so minimize soil erosion. Traditional farmers must turn over the soil before each planting to reduce weed growth, and exposed soil can easily blow or wash away (more about soil conservation in Controversy 15).[15]

A remaining environmental concern is the likelihood of **outcrossing,** the accidental cross-pollination of plant pesticide crops with related wild weeds.[16] If a weed inherits a pest-resistant trait from a neighboring field of GE crops, it could gain an enormous survival advantage over other important wild species and crowd them out.

Loss of species is a serious threat. Crops on which humankind depends are vulnerable in a changing environment, and valuable genetic traits that could help food crops recover may exist in species teetering on the brink of extinction. One effort to preserve genetic diversity is depicted in the photo on page 487. A global seed bank buried in a frozen mountain in Norway stores vast numbers of diverse food crop seeds to use in the restoration of global food supplies, should they fail due to pests, diseases, or climate change.

GE crops may also directly damage wildlife. In the laboratory, monarch butterfly larvae die when fed pollen from the pesticide-producing corn already described. In real life, wild butterflies do not seem to consume enough toxic corn pollen for populations to be harmed. The new technology may even protect mon-

†*The fungus* (Aspergillus flavus) *produces the carcinogenic toxin* aflatoxin.

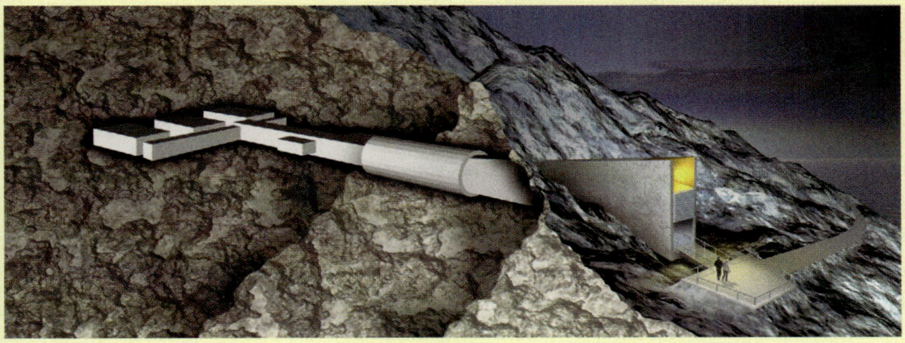

Global Crop Diversity Trust

This giant frozen mountain vault is the work of the Svalbard Global Crop Diversity Trust, founded in part by the United Nations Food and Agriculture Organization. Safely inside, diverse food crop seeds are stored and preserved for future human need.
Source: www.croptrust.org

archs and other harmless or beneficial insects that now die when they feed on conventionally sprayed fields.

Ethical Arguments About Genetic Engineering

Some fear that by tampering with the basic blueprint of life, GE technology will sooner or later unleash mayhem on an unsuspecting world. Any degree of risk is unjustified, they say, because while rDNA technology raises profits for biotechnology companies and farmers, it has produced no real benefits for consumers. Others object to rDNA technology on religious grounds, holding that genetic decisions are best left to nature or a higher power. Table C12-3 summarizes some of these issues.

Proponents of genetic engineering respond that most of the world's people cannot afford the luxury of rejecting the potential benefits of biotechnology—they lack the abundant foods and fertile lands that protesters take for granted. Delays hurt the poorest of the poor, they say. GE opponents counter that the scope of world hunger far exceeds simple solutions such as increasing food supplies—it involves war, politics, and education. (Chapter 15 explores the tragedy of world hunger.)

The FDA's Position on GE Foods

The FDA can evaluate only the safety of today's GE fruits, vegetables, and grains for human consumption and takes the position that they are safe, unless they differ substantially from similar foods already in use.[17] Foods from GE animals cannot be marketed without FDA approval.[18] Many scientific organizations agree that rDNA technology can deliver on the promise to improve the food supply if we give it a chance to do so.

THE FINAL WORD

For those who would worry themselves into a diet of crackers and water, overwhelming evidence supports eating abundant fruits and vegetables regardless of their source. Theoretical future risks from GE foods pale next to the real and immediate perils of increased cancer and heart disease associated with diets that lack sufficient fruits and vegetables. Table C12-4 sums up the pros and cons of three methods of food production to help choose among them.

TABLE C12-3 GE Foods: Point, Counterpoint

Arguments in Opposition to Genetic Engineering	Arguments in Support of Genetic Engineering
1. *Ethical and moral issues.* It's immoral to "play God" by mixing genes from organisms unable to do so naturally. Religious and vegetarian groups object to genes from prohibited species occurring in their allowable foods.	1. *Ethical and moral issues.* Scientists throughout history have been persecuted and even put to death by fearful people who accuse them of playing God. Yet today, many of the world's citizens enjoy a long and healthy life of comfort and convenience due to once-feared scientific advances put to practical use.
2. *Imperfect technology.* The technology is young and imperfect; genes rarely function in just one way, their placement is often imprecise, and potential effects are impossible to predict. Toxins are as likely to be produced as the desired trait.	2. *Advanced technology.* Recombinant DNA technology is precise and reliable. Many of the most exciting recent advances in medicine, agriculture, and technology were made possible by the application of this technology.
3. *Environmental concerns.* Environmental side effects are unknown. The power of a genetically modified organism to change the world's environments is unknown until such changes actually occur—then the "genie is out of the bottle." Once out, the genie cannot be put back in the bottle because insects, birds, and the wind distribute genetically altered seed and pollen to points unknown.	3. *Environmental protection.* Genetic engineering may be the only hope of saving rain forest and other habitats from destruction by impoverished people desperate for arable land. Through genetic engineering, farmers can make use of previously unproductive lands such as salt-rich soils and arid areas.
4. "*Genetic pollution.*" Other kinds of pollution can often be cleaned up with money, time, and effort. Once genes are spliced into living things, those genes forever bear the imprint of human tampering.	4. *Genetic improvements.* Genetic side effects are more likely to benefit the environment than to harm it.

(continued)

TABLE C12-3 **GE Foods: Point, Counterpoint (continued)**

Arguments in Opposition to Genetic Engineering	Arguments in Support of Genetic Engineering
5. *Crop vulnerability.* Pests and disease can quickly adapt to overtake genetically identical plants or animals around the world. Diversity is key to defense.	5. *Improved crop resistance.* Pests and diseases can be specifically fought on a case-by-case basis. Biotechnology is the key to defense.
6. *Loss of gene pool.* Loss of genetic diversity threatens to deplete valuable gene banks from which scientists can develop new agricultural crops.	6. *Gene pool preserved.* Thanks to advances in genetics, laboratories around the world are able to stockpile the genetic material of millions of species that, without such advances, would have been lost forever.
7. *Profit motive.* Genetic engineering will profit industry more than the world's poor and hungry.	7. *Everyone profits.* Industries benefit from genetic engineering, and a thriving food industry benefits the nation and its people, as witnessed by countries lacking such industries. Genetic engineering promises to provide adequate nutritious food for millions who lack such food today. Developed nations gain cheaper, more attractive, more delicious foods with greater variety and availability year-round.
8. *Unproven safety for people.* Human safety testing of genetically altered products is generally lacking. The population is an unwitting experimental group in a nationwide laboratory study for the benefit of industry.	8. *Safe for people.* Human safety testing of genetically altered products is unnecessary because the products are essentially the same as the original foodstuffs.
9. *Increased allergens.* Allergens can unwittingly be transferred into foods.	9. *Control of allergens.* Allergens can be transferred into foods, but these are known, and thus can be avoided. Allergen-free peanuts and other foods are under development.
10. *Decreased nutrients.* A fresh-looking tomato or other produce held for several weeks may have lost substantial nutrients.	10. *Increased nutrients.* Genetic modifications can easily enhance the nutrients in foods.
11. *No product tracking.* Without labeling, the food industry cannot track problems to the source.	11. *Excellent product tracking.* The identity and location of genetically altered foodstuffs are known, and they can be tracked should problems arise.
12. *Overuse of herbicides.* Farmers, knowing that their crops resist herbicide effects, will use them liberally.	12. *Conservative use of herbicides.* Farmers will not waste expensive herbicides in second or third applications when the prescribed amount gets the job done the first time.
13. *Increased consumption of pesticides.* When a pesticide is produced by the flesh of produce, consumers cannot wash it off the skin of the produce with running water as they can with most ordinary sprays.	13. *Reduced pesticides on foods.* Pesticides produced by plants in tiny amounts known to be safe for consumption are more predictable than applications by agricultural workers who make mistakes. Because other genetic manipulations will eliminate the need for postharvest spraying, fewer pesticides will reach the dinner table.
14. *Lack of oversight.* Government oversight is run by industry people for the benefit of industry—no one is watching out for the consumer.	14. *Sufficient regulation, oversight, and rapid response.* The National Academy of Sciences has established protocol for safety testing of GE foods. Government agencies are efficient in identifying and correcting problems as they occur in the industry.

TABLE C12-4 **Food Production Methods Compared: Organic, Conventional, and rDNA Technology**

Soil Condition and Environment

- *Organic:* Improves soil condition through crop rotation and the addition of complex fertilizers such as manure; controls erosion; highly protective of waterways and wildlife. Uses sustainable agriculture techniques.
- *Conventional:* Depletes soil; adds synthetic chemical fertilizers containing only a few key elements; can create soil erosion problems. Runoff pollutes waterways, and sprays poison wildlife such as birds and beneficial insect predators.
- *Genetic engineering:* No direct effect on soil or erosion; may require fewer pesticide sprays, thus protecting waterways and wildlife, but may harm wildlife by exposing wild species to altered genes or plant pesticides; may soon make use of salty, dry, or other currently unusable lands. May produce "genetic pollution."

Nutrients in Foods

- *Organic:* Suggestive evidence of slightly increased content of trace minerals, vitamin C, and improved amino acid balance in produce over conventionally farmed produce.
- *Conventional:* Standards for nutrient composition of foods are set by analysis of conventionally produced foods.
- *Genetic engineering:* Potential for increasing nutrient and phytochemical content, at the will of the producer.

Benefits to Consumers

- *Organic:* Reduced exposure to pesticides and other sprays and animal medications and hormones. New standards define organic techniques, with regulatory oversight. Long history of safety for human consumption of food varieties. Ethical comfort of knowing that food-producing animals are well treated.
- *Conventional:* General safety and pesticide residues monitored regularly; many varieties of foods available at low cost.
- *Genetic engineering:* Greater food production at low cost, keeping consumer prices low and availability high. Particular products may meet particular consumer demands, such as better flavor, increased vitamin or phytochemical content, or improved freshness of foods. Potential exists for helping to ease world hunger. Crops may produce medicines needed in impoverished areas of the world.

Consumer Safety Issues

- *Organic:* Consumer must wash produce well to remove possible dangerous microbial contamination and pesticides that may have "drifted" onto produce.
- *Conventional:* Consumer must wash produce well to remove possible dangerous microbial contamination and pesticides that are applied to produce.
- *Genetic engineering:* Consumer must wash produce well to remove possible dangerous microbial contamination and pesticides (especially herbicides) that are applied to produce. Internally produced plant pesticides do not wash off. Other dangers include introduction of allergens from other species and unproven safety of consuming rDNA products over a lifetime. Unknown dangers may also exist.

Life Cycle Nutrition: Mother and Infant

13

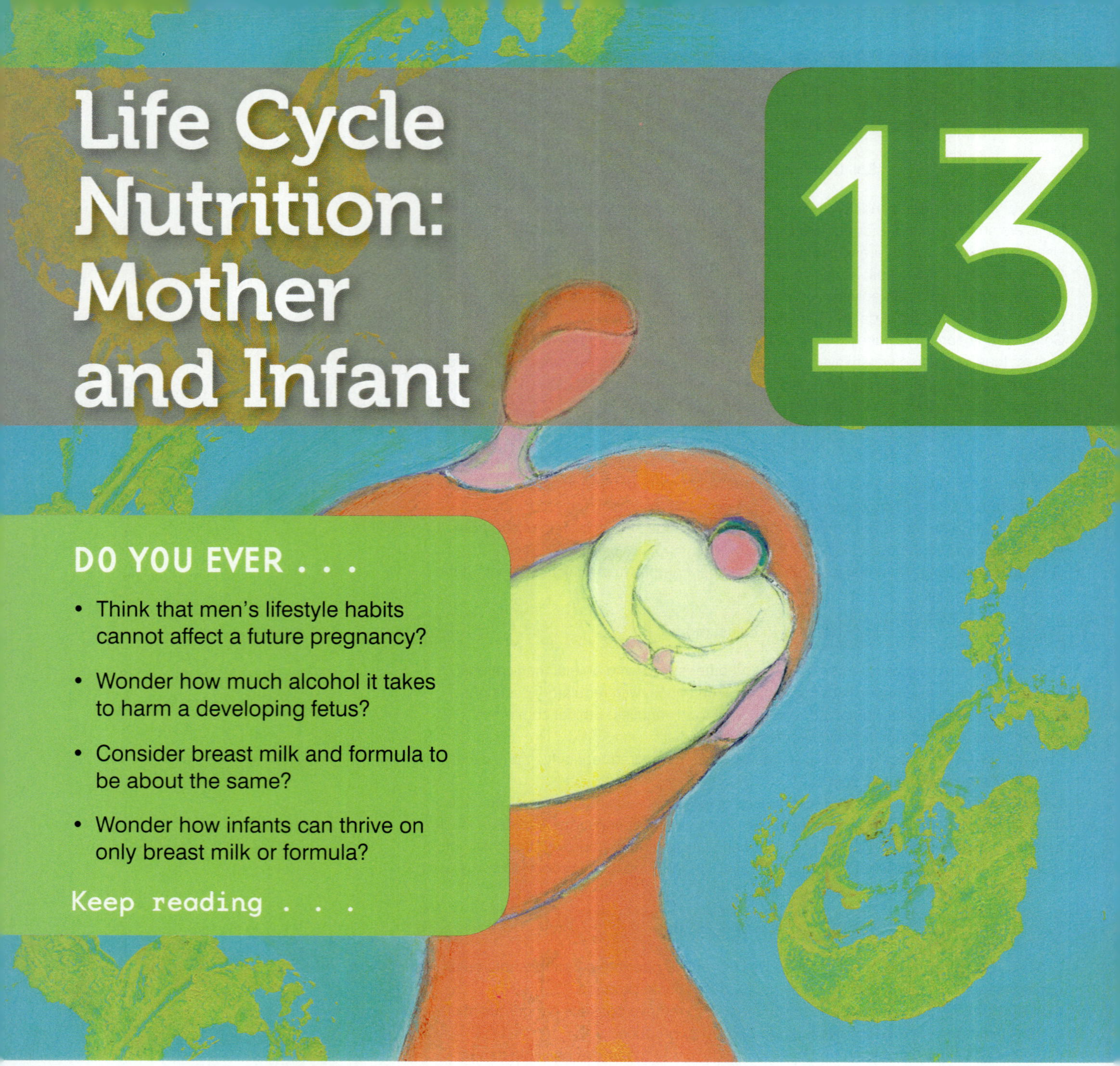

© Marie Bertrand/Corbis

DO YOU EVER . . .

- Think that men's lifestyle habits cannot affect a future pregnancy?
- Wonder how much alcohol it takes to harm a developing fetus?
- Consider breast milk and formula to be about the same?
- Wonder how infants can thrive on only breast milk or formula?

Keep reading . . .

Learning Objectives

To find learning objective topics in this chapter, look for text headings with a corresponding "LO" number above the heading. After completing this chapter, you should be able to accomplish the following:

LO 13.1 Explain why a nutritionally adequate diet is important long before a pregnancy is established.

LO 13.2 Identify the special nutritional needs of a pregnant teenager as compared to a pregnant adult.

LO 13.3 Evaluate the statement that "no level of alcoholic beverage intake is safe or advisable during pregnancy."

LO 13.4 Describe the impacts of gestational diabetes and preeclampsia on the health of a mother and her unborn child.

LO 13.5 Discuss the nutrition and health benefits of breastfeeding to both the mother and the child.

LO 13.6 Discuss some relationships between childhood obesity and chronic diseases.

LO 13.7 Develop a healthy eating and activity plan to help an obese child improve his or her short-term and long-term health overall.

All people need the same nutrients, but in differing amounts throughout life. This chapter is the first of two on life's changing nutrient needs. It focuses on the two life stages that might be the most important to an individual's life-long health—pregnancy and infancy.

LO 13.1, 13.2

Pregnancy: The Impact of Nutrition on the Future

People normally think of nutrition as personal, affecting them alone. For the woman who is pregnant, or who soon will be, however, nutrition choices today profoundly affect the health of her future child and the adult that the child will one day become. The nutrient demands of pregnancy are extraordinary.

Preparing for Pregnancy

Before she becomes pregnant, a woman must establish eating habits that will optimally nourish both the growing **fetus** and herself. She must be well nourished at the outset because early in pregnancy the **embryo** undergoes rapid and significant developmental changes that depend on good nutrition.

Fathers-to-be are also wise to examine their eating and drinking habits. For example, a sedentary lifestyle and consuming too few fruits and vegetables may affect men's **fertility** (and the fertility of their children), and men who drink too much alcohol or encounter other toxins in the weeks before conception can sustain damage to their sperm's genetic material.[1*] When both partners adopt healthy habits, they will be better prepared to meet the demands of parenting that lie ahead.

© Jose Luis Pelaez, Inc./Corbis

Both parents can prepare in advance for a healthy pregnancy.

Prepregnancy Weight Before pregnancy, all women, but underweight women in particular, should strive for an appropriate body weight. A woman who starts out underweight and who fails to gain sufficiently during pregnancy is very likely to bear a baby with a dangerously **low birthweight.**[2] (A later section comes back to the needed gains in pregnancy.) Infant birthweight is the most potent single indicator of an infant's future health. A low-birthweight baby, defined as one who weighs less than 5½ pounds (2,500 grams), is nearly 40 times more likely to die in the first year of life than a normal-weight baby. To prevent low birthweight, underweight women are advised to gain weight before becoming pregnant and to strive to gain adequately thereafter.

When nutrient supplies during pregnancy fail to meet demands, the fetus may adapt to the sparse conditions in ways that may make obesity or chronic diseases more likely in later life.[3] Low birthweight is also associated with lower adult IQ and other brain impairments, short stature, and educational disadvantages.[4] Nutrient deficiency coupled with low birthweight is the underlying cause of more than half of all the deaths worldwide of children under 5 years of age. In the United States, the infant mortality rate in 2006 was just under 7.0 deaths per 1,000 live births.[5] This rate, though higher than that of some other developed countries, represents a significant decline over the last two decades and is a tribute to public health efforts aimed at reducing infant deaths (see Figure 13-1).

Low birthweight may also reflect heredity, disease conditions, smoking, and drug (including alcohol) use during pregnancy.[6] Even with optimal nutrition and health during pregnancy, some women give birth to small infants for unknown reasons. But poor nutrition is the major factor in low birthweight—and an avoidable one, as later sections make clear.[7]

Obese women are also urged to strive for healthy weights before pregnancy. The infant of an obese mother may be larger than normal and may be large even if born prematurely. The large early baby may not be recognized as premature and thus may

Did You Know?

Underweight is defined as BMI <18.5. Obese is defined as BMI ≥30.0 (see Table 13-4 on page 500).

fetus (FEET-us) the stage of human gestation from eight weeks after conception until the birth of an infant.

embryo (EM-bree-oh) the stage of human gestation from the third to the eighth week after conception.

fertility the capacity of a woman to produce a normal ovum periodically and of a man to produce normal sperm; the ability to reproduce.

low birthweight a birthweight of less than 5½ pounds (2,500 grams); used as a predictor of probable health problems in the newborn and as a probable indicator of poor nutrition status of the mother before and/or during pregnancy. Low-birthweight infants are of two different types. Some are *premature infants;* they are born early and are the right size for their gestational age. Other low-birthweight infants have suffered growth failure in the uterus; they are small for gestational age (small for date) and may or may not be premature.

*Reference notes are found in Appendix F.

FIGURE 13-1

Infant Mortality Decline Over Time

The graph shows infant deaths per 1,000 live births.

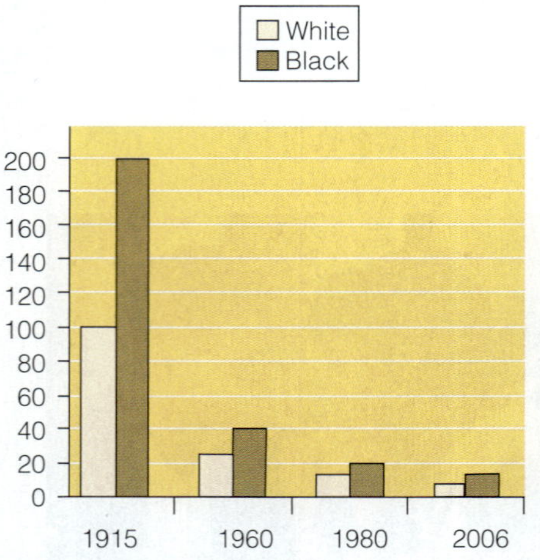

Source: Data from M. Heron and coauthors, Deaths: Final data for 2006, National Vital Statistics Reports 57 (2009): 1–135.

not receive the special medical care required. The baby of an obese mother may be twice as likely to be born with a neural tube defect, too.[8] The vitamin folate may play a role, but a more likely explanation seems to be poor blood glucose control.[9] Obese women themselves are likely to suffer gestational diabetes, hypertension, and complications during and infections after the birth.[10] In addition, both overweight and obese women have a greater risk of giving birth to infants with heart defects and other abnormalities.[11] The obese woman who strives for a healthier prepregnancy body weight helps protect both herself and her future child.

A Healthy Placenta and Other Organs A woman's nutrition before pregnancy is crucial because it determines whether her **uterus** will be able to support the growth of a healthy **placenta** during the first month of **gestation.** The placenta is both a supply depot and a waste-removal system for the fetus. If the placenta works perfectly, the fetus wants for nothing; if it doesn't, no alternative source of sustenance is available, and the fetus will fail to thrive. Figure 13-2 shows the placenta, a mass of tissue in which maternal and fetal blood vessels intertwine and exchange materials. The two bloods never mix, but the barrier between them is notably thin. Nutrients and oxygen move across this thin barrier from the mother's blood into the fetus's blood, and wastes move out of the fetal blood to be excreted by the mother. Thus, by way of the placenta, the mother's digestive tract, respiratory system, and kidneys serve the needs of the fetus as well as her own. The fetus has these organ systems, but they do not yet function. The **umbilical cord** is like a pipeline that conducts fetal blood to and from the placenta. The **amniotic sac** surrounds and cradles the fetus, which floats inside its cushioning fluids.

The placenta is a highly metabolic organ that actively gathers up hormones, nutrients, and protein molecules such as antibodies and transfers them into the fetal bloodstream. The placenta also produces a broad range of hormones that act in

FIGURE 13-2

ANIMATED!

The Placenta

The placenta is composed of spongy tissue in which fetal blood and maternal blood flow side by side, each in its own vessels. The maternal blood transfers oxygen and nutrients to the fetus's blood and picks up fetal wastes to be excreted by the mother. The placenta performs the nutritive, respiratory, and excretory functions that the fetus's digestive system, lungs, and kidneys will provide after birth.

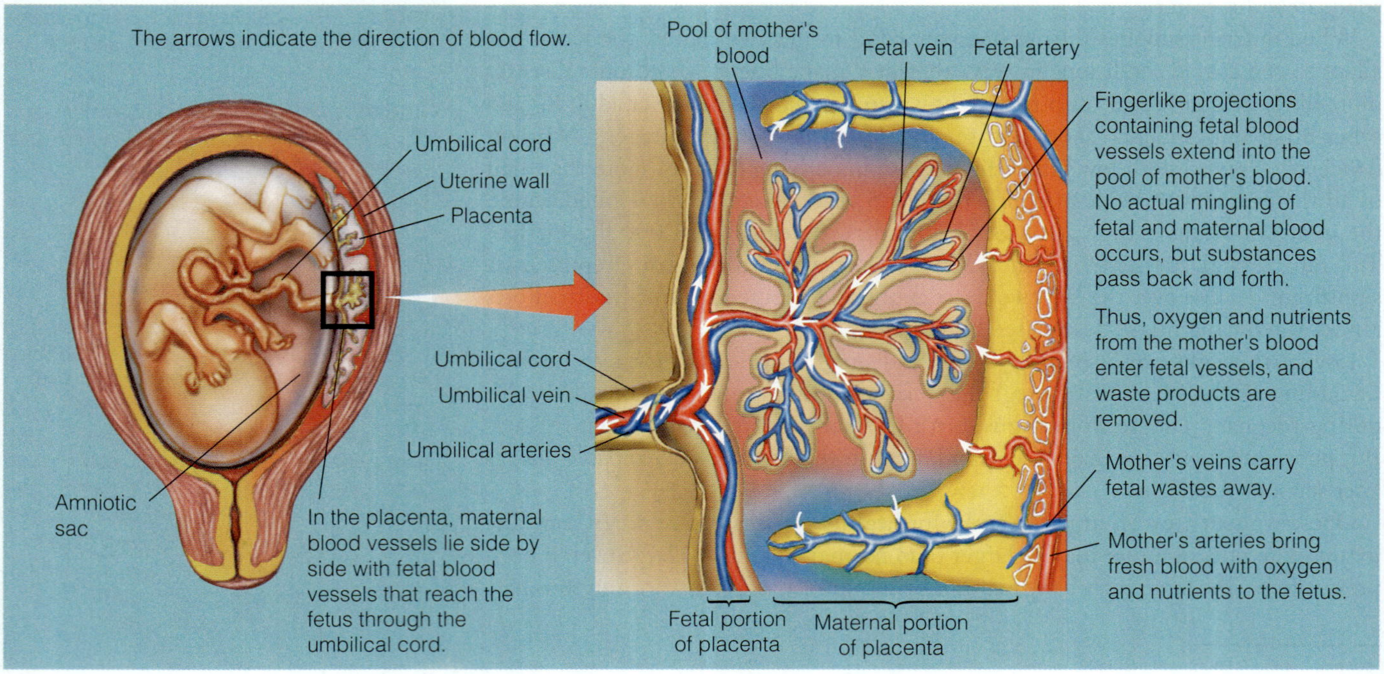

many ways to maintain pregnancy and prepare the mother's breasts for **lactation.**[12] Is it any wonder that a healthy placenta is essential for the developing fetus?

If the mother's nutrient stores are inadequate during placental development, no amount of nutrients later on in pregnancy can make up for the lack. If the placenta fails to form or function properly, the fetus will not receive optimal nourishment. After getting such a poor start on life, the child may be ill equipped, even as an adult, to store sufficient nutrients, and a girl may later be unable to grow an adequate placenta or bear healthy full-term infants. For this and other reasons, a woman's poor nutrition during her early pregnancy could affect her grandchild as well as her child.[13]

CONCEPT LINK 13-1

The interactions between the maternal nutrition and the genes may also affect a future grandchild's health; see Controversy 11, page 440.

uterus (YOO-ter-us) the womb, the muscular organ within which the infant develops before birth.

placenta (pla-SEN-tuh) the organ of pregnancy in which maternal and fetal blood circulate in close proximity and exchange nutrients and oxygen (flowing into the fetus) and wastes (picked up by the mother's blood).

gestation the period of about 40 weeks (three trimesters) from conception to birth; the term of a pregnancy.

umbilical (um-BIL-ih-cul) **cord** the rope-like structure through which the fetus's veins and arteries reach the placenta; the route of nourishment and oxygen into the fetus and the route of waste disposal from the fetus.

amniotic (AM-nee-OTT-ic) **sac** the "bag of waters" in the uterus in which the fetus floats.

lactation production and secretion of breast milk for the purpose of nourishing an infant.

ovum the egg, produced by the mother, that unites with a sperm from the father to produce a new individual.

zygote (ZYE-goat) the product of the union of ovum and sperm; a fertilized ovum.

implantation the stage of development, during the first two weeks after conception, in which the fertilized egg (fertilized ovum, or zygote) embeds itself in the wall of the uterus and begins to develop.

KEY POINT Adequate nutrition before pregnancy establishes physical readiness and nutrient stores to support fetal growth. Both underweight and overweight women should strive for appropriate body weights before pregnancy. Newborns who weigh less than 5½ pounds face greater health risks than normal-weight babies. The healthy development of the placenta depends on adequate nutrition before pregnancy.

The Events of Pregnancy

The newly fertilized **ovum** is called a **zygote.** It begins as a single cell and rapidly divides into many cells during the days after fertilization. Within two weeks, the cluster of cells embeds itself in the uterine wall in a process known as **implantation,** and the placenta begins to grow inside the uterus. Minimal growth in size takes place at this time, but it is a crucial period in development. Adverse influences such as smoking, drug abuse, and malnutrition at this time lead to failure to implant or to abnormalities such as neural tube defects that can cause loss of the developing embryo, often before the woman knows she is pregnant.

The Embryo and Fetus

During the next six weeks, the embryo registers astonishing physical changes (see Figure 13-3). At eight weeks, the fetus has a complete

FIGURE 13-3 **Stages of Embryonic and Fetal Development**

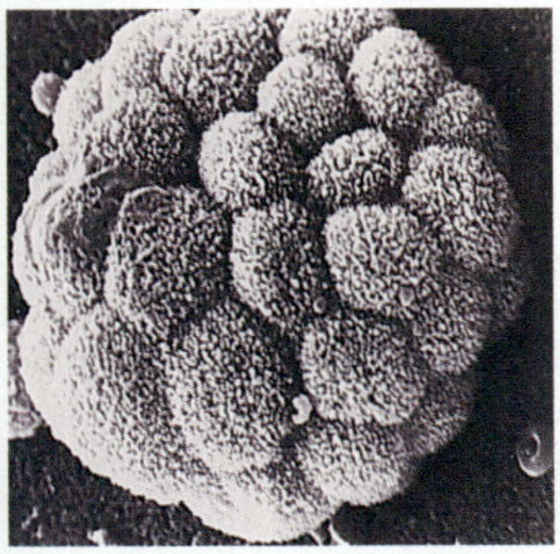

Petit Format/Nestle/Photo Researchers, Inc.

(1) A newly fertilized ovum, called a zygote, is about the size of the period at the end of this sentence. Less than 1 week after fertilization, the zygote has rapidly divided many times and becomes ready for implantation.

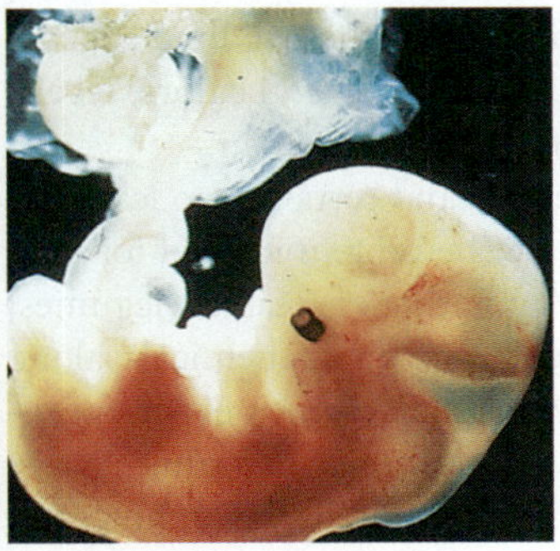

Petit Format/Nestle/Photo Researchers, Inc.

(2) After implantation, the placenta develops and begins to provide nourishment to the developing embryo. An embryo 5 weeks after fertilization is about ½ inch long.

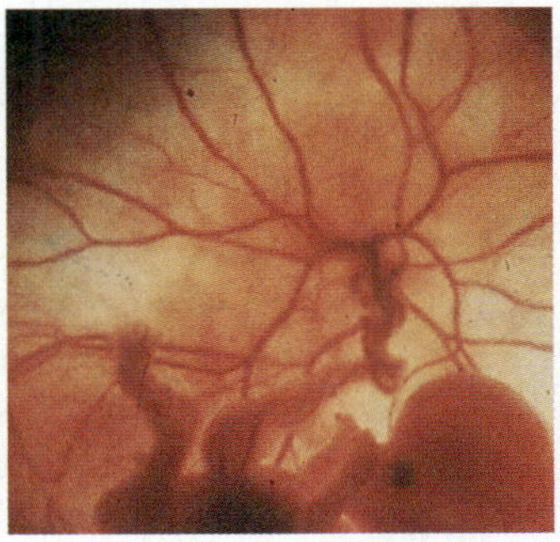

Petit Format/Nestle/Photo Researchers, Inc.

(3) A fetus after 11 weeks of development is just over an inch long. Notice the umbilical cord and blood vessels connecting the fetus with the placenta.

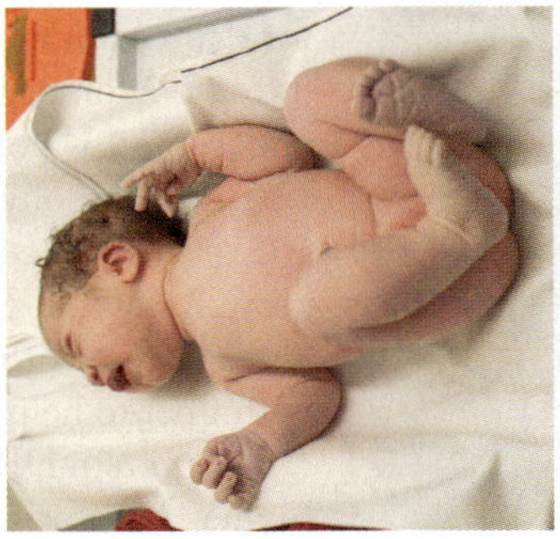

© Masterfile

(4) A newborn infant after 9 months of development measures close to 20 inches in length. The average birthweight is about 7½ pounds. From 8 weeks to term, this infant grew 20 times longer and 50 times heavier.

central nervous system, a beating heart, a fully formed digestive system, well-defined fingers and toes, and the beginnings of facial features.

In the last seven months of pregnancy, the fetal period, the fetus grows 50 times heavier and 20 times longer. Critical periods of cell division and development occur in organ after organ. The amniotic sac fills with fluid, and the mother's body changes. The uterus and its supporting muscles increase in size, the breasts may become tender and full, the nipples may darken in preparation for lactation, and the mother's blood volume increases by half to accommodate the added load of materials it must carry. Gestation lasts approximately 40 weeks and ends with the birth of the infant. The 40 or so weeks of pregnancy are divided into thirds, each of which is called a **trimester.**

A Note About Critical Periods Each organ and tissue type grows with its own characteristic pattern and timing. The development of each takes place only at a certain time—the **critical period.** Whatever nutrients and other environmental conditions are necessary during this period must be supplied on time if the organ is to reach its full potential. If the development of an organ is limited during a critical period, recovery is impossible. For example, the fetus's heart and brain are well developed at 14 weeks; the lungs, 10 weeks later. Therefore, early malnutrition impairs the heart and brain; later malnutrition impairs the lungs.

The effects of malnutrition during critical periods of pregnancy are seen in defects of the nervous system of the embryo (explained later), in the child's poor dental health, and in the adolescent's and adult's vulnerability to infections and possibly higher risks of diabetes, hypertension, stroke, or heart disease.[14] The effects of malnutrition during critical periods are irreversible: abundant and nourishing food, fed after the critical time, cannot remedy harm already done.

Table 13-1 identifies characteristics of a **high-risk pregnancy.** The more factors that apply, the higher the risk. All pregnant women, especially those in high-risk categories, need **prenatal** medical care, including dietary advice.

TABLE 13-1 High-Risk Pregnancy Factors

- Prepregnancy BMI either <18.5 or ≥25
- Insufficient or excessive pregnancy weight gain
- Nutrient deficiencies or toxicities; eating disorders
- Poverty, lack of family support, low level of education, limited food available
- Smoking, alcohol, or other drug use
- Age, especially 15 years or younger or 35 years or older
- Many previous pregnancies (3 or more to mothers under age 20; 4 or more to mothers age 20 or older)
- Short or long intervals between pregnancies (<18 months or >59 months)
- Previous history of problems such as low- or high-birthweight infants
- Twins or triplets
- Pregnancy-related hypertension or gestational diabetes
- Diabetes; heart, respiratory, and kidney disease; certain genetic disorders; special diets and medications

KEY POINT Implantation, fetal development, and critical periods depend on maternal nutrition before and during pregnancy.

Increased Need for Nutrients

During pregnancy a woman's nutrient needs increase more for certain nutrients than for others. Figure 13-4 shows the percentage increase in nutrient intakes recommended for pregnant women compared to nonpregnant women. To meet the high nutrient demands of pregnancy, a woman must make careful food choices, but her body will also do its part by maximizing nutrient absorption and minimizing losses.

- DRI nutrient and energy intake recommendations for pregnant women are listed on the inside front cover.

Energy, Carbohydrate, Protein, and Fat Energy needs vary with the progression of pregnancy. In the first trimester, the pregnant woman needs no additional energy, but her energy needs rise as pregnancy progresses. She requires an additional 340 daily calories during the second trimester and an extra 450 calories each day during the third trimester.[15] Well-nourished pregnant women meet these demands for more energy in several ways: some eat more food, some reduce their activity, and some store less of their food energy as fat. A woman can easily meet the need for extra calories by selecting more nutrient-dense foods from the five food groups. Table 2-2 (on page 44) provided suggested eating patterns for several calorie levels, and Table 13-2 offers a sample menu for pregnant and lactating women.

Ample carbohydrate (ideally, 175 grams or more per day and certainly no less than 135 grams) is necessary to fuel the fetal brain and spare the protein needed for fetal growth. Whole-grain breads and cereals, dark green and other vegetables, legumes, and citrus and other fruit provide carbohydrates, nutrients, and phytochemicals, along with fiber to help alleviate the constipation that many pregnant women experience.

The protein DRI recommendation for pregnancy is an additional 25 grams per day higher than for nonpregnant women. Most women in the United States, however,

trimester a period representing gestation. A trimester is about 13 to 14 weeks.

critical period a finite period during development in which certain events may occur that will have irreversible effects on later developmental stages. A critical period is usually a period of cell division in a body organ.

high-risk pregnancy a pregnancy characterized by risk factors that make it likely the birth will be surrounded by problems such as premature delivery, difficult birth, retarded growth, birth defects, and early infant death. A *low-risk pregnancy* has none of these factors.

prenatal (pree-NAY-tal) before birth.

FIGURE 13-4 Comparison of Selected Nutrient Recommendations for Nonpregnant, Pregnant, and Lactating Women[a]

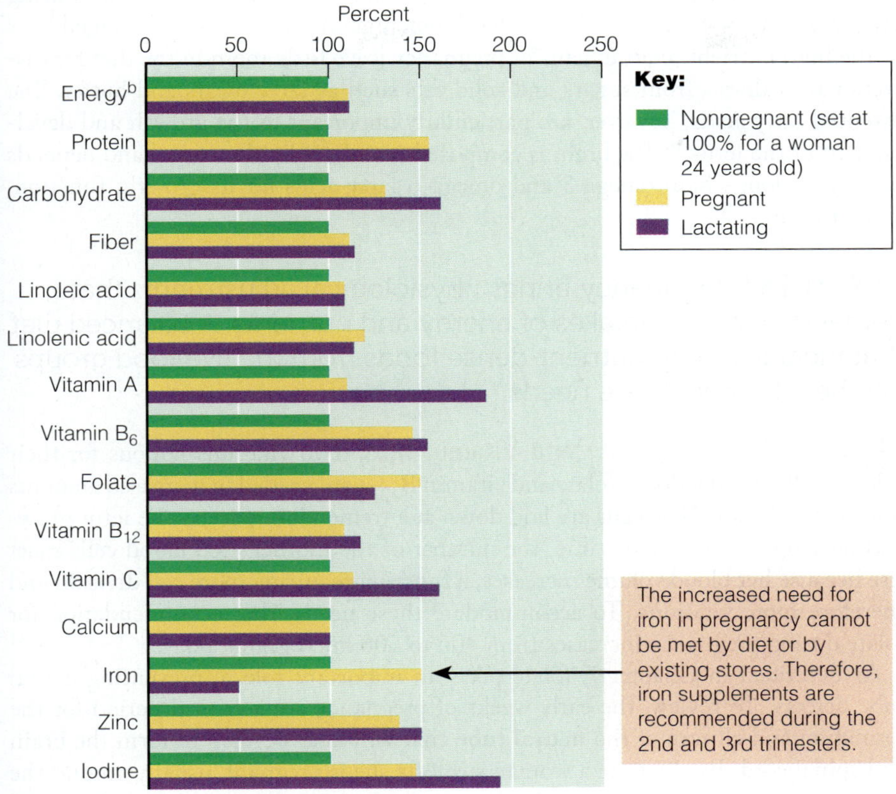

[a]Values for other nutrients are listed on the inside front cover, pages A and B.

[b]Energy allowance during pregnancy is for 2nd trimester; energy allowance during the 3rd trimester is slightly higher; no additional allowance is provided during the 1st trimester. Energy allowance during lactation is for the first 6 months; energy allowance during the second 6 months is slightly higher.

TABLE 13-2 Daily Food Choices for Pregnancy (2nd and 3rd Trimesters) and Lactation

Food Group	Amounts
Fruits	2 c
Vegetables	3 c
Grains	8 oz
Meats and Legumes	6½ oz
Milk	3 c

SAMPLE MENU

Breakfast
1 whole-wheat English muffin
2 tbs peanut butter
1 c low-fat vanilla yogurt
½ c fresh strawberries
1 c orange juice

Midmorning snack
½ c cranberry juice
1 oz pretzels

Lunch
Sandwich (tuna salad on whole-wheat bread)
½ carrot (sticks)
1 c low-fat milk

Dinner
Chicken cacciatore
  3 oz chicken
  ½ c stewed tomatoes
1 c rice
½ c summer squash
1½ c salad (spinach, mushrooms, carrots)
1 tbs salad dressing
1 slice Italian bread
2 tsp soft margarine
1 c low-fat milk

Note: This sample meal plan provides about 2,500 calories (55% from carbohydrate, 20% from protein, and 25% from fat) and meets most of the vitamin and mineral needs of pregnant and lactating women.

CONCEPT LINK 13-2

To read about vegetarian diets during pregnancy, see Controversy 6 (page 219).

CONCEPT LINK 13-3

Good food sources of the essential fatty acids were listed in Table 5-6 (page 169).

need not add protein-rich foods to their diets because they already consume plenty of meats, fish, poultry, and eggs. Low-fat milk and milk products provide protein, calcium, and other nutrients. Some vegetarian women limit or omit protein-rich meats, eggs, and dairy products from their diets. For them, meeting the recommendation for food energy each day and including plant-protein foods such as legumes, tofu, whole grains, nuts, and seeds are imperative. Protein supplements during pregnancy can be harmful to infant development, and their use is discouraged.

The high nutrient requirements of pregnancy leave little room in the diet for discretionary calories from sugars and solid fats such as fatty meats and butter. The essential fatty acids, however, are particularly important to the growth and development of the fetus.[16] The brain is composed mainly of lipid material and depends heavily on long-chain omega-3 and omega-6 fatty acids for its growth, function, and structure.

KEY POINT Pregnancy brings physiological adjustments that demand increased intakes of energy and nutrients. A balanced diet that includes more nutrient-dense foods from the five food groups can help to meet these needs.

Of Special Interest: Folate and Vitamin B_{12} Two vitamins famous for their roles in cell reproduction—folate and vitamin B_{12}—are needed in increased amounts during pregnancy. New cells are laid down at a tremendous pace as the fetus grows and develops. At the same time, the number of the mother's red blood cells must rise because her blood volume increases, a function requiring more cell division and therefore more vitamins. To accommodate these needs, the recommendation for folate during pregnancy increases from 400 to 600 micrograms a day.

As described in Chapter 7, folate plays an important role in preventing neural tube defects. To review, the early weeks of pregnancy are a critical period for the formation and closure of the **neural tube** that will later develop to form the brain and spinal cord. By the time a woman suspects she is pregnant, usually around the sixth week of pregnancy, the embryo's neural tube normally has closed. A **neural tube defect (NTD)** occurs when the tube fails to close properly. In the United States, an estimated 2,500 infants with NTDs are born each year.[17] In the worst cases, when the neural tube fails to close properly and brain development fails, an invariably fatal defect known as **anencephaly** occurs.

- A pregnancy affected by a neural tube defect can occur in any woman, but these factors make it more likely:[18]
  - *A previous pregnancy affected by a neural tube defect.*
  - *Maternal diabetes.*
  - *Maternal use of certain antiseizure medications.*
  - *Maternal obesity.*

In a more common NTD, **spina bifida,** the spinal cord and backbone do not develop normally (see Figure 13-5). The membranes covering the spinal cord, and sometimes the cord itself, may protrude from the spine as a sac. Spina bifida often produces paralysis in varying degrees, depending on the extent of spinal cord damage. Mild cases may not be noticed. Moderate cases may involve curvature of the spine, muscle weakness, mental handicaps, and other ills; severe cases can result in death.

To reduce the risk of neural tube defects, women who are capable of becoming pregnant should obtain 400 micrograms of folic acid daily from supplements, fortified foods, or both, *in addition* to eating folate-rich foods (see Table 13-3). The DRI committee recommends intake of synthetic folate, folic acid, in supplements and fortified foods because it is better absorbed than the folate naturally present in foods. Foods that naturally contain folate are still important, however, because they contribute to folate intakes while providing other needed vitamins, minerals, fiber, and phytochemicals.

The enrichment of grain products (cereal, grits, pasta, rice, bread, and the like) sold commercially in the United States with folic acid has improved folate status in women of childbearing age and lowered the number of neural tube defects that occur each year.[19] Researchers expect to see declines in some other birth defects (cleft lip and cleft palate) and miscarriages as well.[20] A safety concern arises, however. The pregnant woman also needs a greater amount of vitamin B_{12} to assist folate in the manufacture of new cells. Because high intakes of folate complicate the diagnosis of a vitamin B_{12} deficiency, quantities of 1 milligram of folate or more

neural tube the embryonic tissue that later forms the brain and spinal cord.

neural tube defect (NTD) a group of nervous system abnormalities caused by interruption of the normal early development of the neural tube.

anencephaly (an-en-SEFF-ah-lee) an uncommon and always fatal neural tube defect in which the brain fails to form.

spina bifida (SPY-na BIFF-ih-duh) one of the most common types of neural tube defects in which gaps occur in the bones of the spine. Often the spinal cord bulges and protrudes through the gaps, resulting in a number of motor and other impairments.

FIGURE 13-5 Spina Bifida

Spina bifida, a common neural tube defect, occurs when the vertebrae of the spine fail to close around the spinal cord, leaving it unprotected. The B vitamin folate helps prevent spina bifida and other neural tube defects.

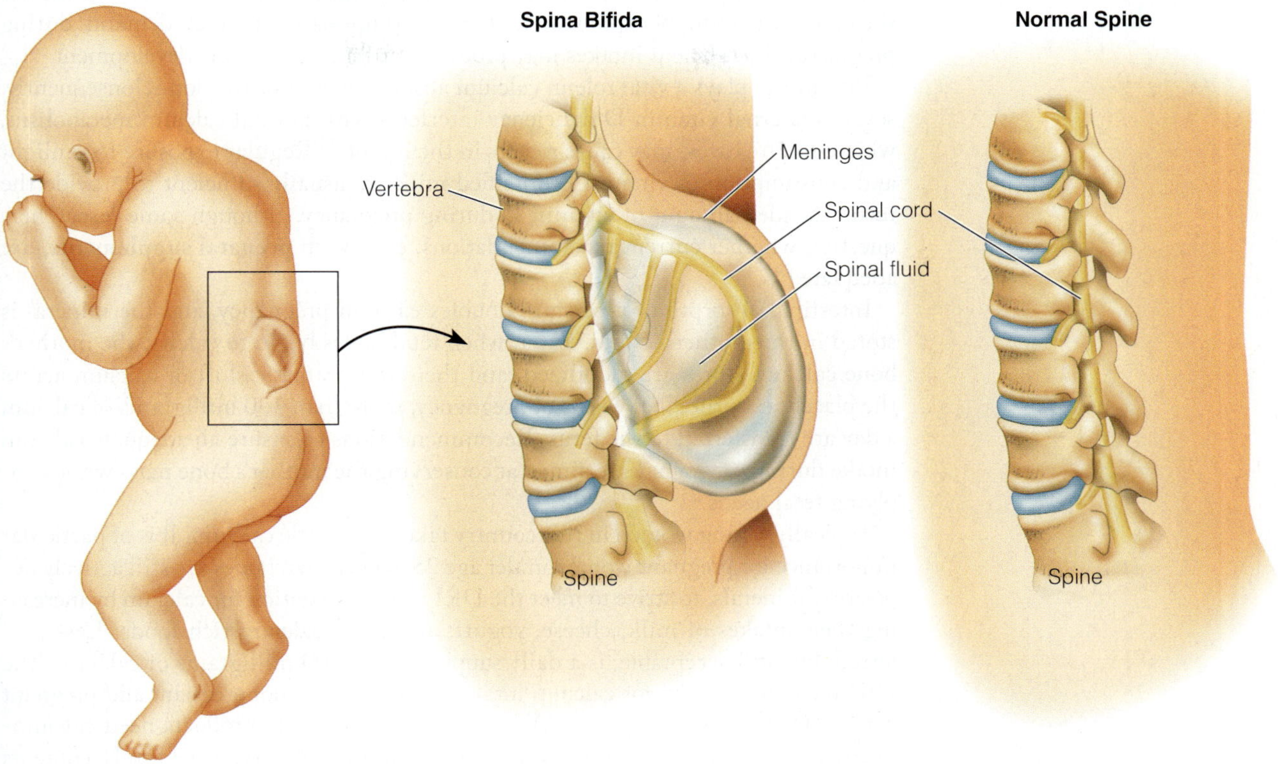

Source: From the Journal of the American Medical Association, *June 20, 2001, Vol. 285, No. 23, p. 3050. Reprinted with permission of the* American Medical Association.

TABLE 13-3 Rich Folate Sources[a]

Natural Folate Sources	Fortified Folate Sources
Liver (3 oz) 221 μg	Multi-Grain Cheerios Plus cereal (1 c) 400 μg[b]
Lentils (½ c) 179 μg	Product 19 cereal (1 c) 400 μg[b]
Chickpeas or pinto beans (½ c) 145 μg	Total cereal (1 c) 400 μg[b]
Asparagus (½ c) 134 μg	Pasta, cooked (1 c) 110 μg
Spinach (1 c raw) 58 μg	Rice, cooked (1 c) 134 μg
Avocado (½ c) 105 μg	Bagel (1 small whole) 75 μg
Orange juice (1 c) 74 μg	Waffles, frozen (2) 36 μg
Beets (½ c) 68 μg	Bread, white (1 slice) 28 μg

[a]*Folate amounts for these and thousands of other foods are listed in the Table of Food Composition in Appendix A.*

[b]*Folate in cereals varies; read the Nutrition Facts panel of the label.*

require a prescription. Most over-the-counter multivitamin supplements contain 400 micrograms of folate; supplements for pregnant women usually contain at least 800 micrograms.

People who exclude all animal products from the diet need vitamin B_{12}–fortified foods or supplements.[21] Limited research suggests that low vitamin B_{12} during pregnancy may act synergistically with low folate status to increase the risk of NTD.[22]

CONCEPT LINK 13-4

Chapter 7 described how excessive folate intakes can mask symptoms of vitamin B_{12} deficiency (page 254).

KEY POINT Due to their key roles in cell reproduction, folate and vitamin B_{12} are needed in large amounts during pregnancy. Folate plays an important role in preventing neural tube defects.

Vitamin D and Calcium Vitamin D and the minerals involved in building the skeleton—calcium, phosphorus, and magnesium—are in great demand during pregnancy. Insufficient intakes may produce abnormal fetal bone development.

Vitamin D plays a vital role in calcium absorption and utilization. Consequently, severe maternal vitamin D deficiency interferes with normal calcium metabolism, which, in rare cases, may cause rickets in the infant.[23] Regular exposure to sunlight and consumption of vitamin D-fortified milk are usually sufficient to provide the recommended amount of vitamin D during pregnancy, although some researchers question whether current recommendations, even with **prenatal supplements,** are adequate.[24]

Intestinal absorption of calcium doubles early in pregnancy, and the mineral is stored in the mother's bones. Later, when fetal bones begin to calcify, the mother's bone calcium stores are mobilized, and there is a dramatic shift of calcium across the placenta. In the final weeks of pregnancy, more than 300 milligrams of calcium a day are transferred to the fetus. Recommendations to ensure an adequate calcium intake during pregnancy are aimed at conserving the mother's bone mass while supplying fetal needs.[25]

Typically, young women in this country take in too little calcium. It is of particular importance for pregnant women under age 25, whose own bones are still actively depositing minerals, to strive to meet the DRI recommendation for calcium by increasing their intakes of milk, cheese, yogurt, and other calcium-rich foods. Less preferred, but still acceptable, is a daily supplement of 600 milligrams of calcium. The DRI recommendation for calcium intake is the same for nonpregnant and pregnant women in the same age group. Women who exclude milk products need calcium-fortified foods such as soy milk, orange juice, and cereals. Read the labels: contents vary and products fortified with both calcium and vitamin D are recommended.

Iron A pregnant woman needs iron to help increase her blood volume and to provide for placental and fetal needs. The developing fetus draws heavily on the mother's iron stores to accumulate a sufficient supply to carry it through the first four to six months of life.[26] Even a woman with inadequate iron stores transfers a significant amount of iron to the fetus, suggesting that the iron needs of the fetus take priority over those of the mother. In addition, blood losses are inevitable at birth, especially during a delivery by **cesarean section,** further draining the mother's iron supply.

During pregnancy, the body makes several adaptations to help meet the exceptionally high need for iron. Menstruation, the major route of iron loss in women, ceases, and absorption of iron increases up to threefold. Without sufficient intake, though, iron stores quickly dwindle.

Few women enter pregnancy with adequate iron stores. Women who enter pregnancy with iron-deficiency anemia have a greater-than-normal risk of delivering low-birthweight or preterm infants.[27] All women not taking supplemental iron are urged to do so, particularly during the second and third trimesters of pregnancy. When a low hemoglobin or hematocrit is confirmed by a repeat test, more than the standard iron dose of 30 milligrams may be prescribed. To enhance iron absorption, the supplement should be taken between meals and with liquids other than milk, coffee, or tea, which inhibit iron absorption.

Zinc Zinc is vital for protein synthesis and cell development during pregnancy. Typical zinc intakes of pregnant women are lower than recommendations, but fortunately, zinc absorption increases when intakes are low.[28] Large doses of iron can interfere with zinc absorption and metabolism, but most prenatal supplements supply the right balance of these minerals for pregnancy. Zinc is abundant in protein-rich foods such as shellfish, meat, and nuts, and routine zinc supplementation during pregnancy is not advised.[29]

prenatal supplements nutrient supplements specifically designed to provide the nutrients needed during pregnancy, particularly folate, iron, and calcium, without excesses or unneeded constituents.

cesarean (see-ZAIR-ee-un) **section** surgical childbirth, in which the infant is taken through an incision in the woman's abdomen.

KEY POINT Severe maternal vitamin D deficiency interferes with normal calcium metabolism in the fetus. All pregnant women, but especially those who are under 25 years of age, need to pay special attention to ensure adequate calcium intakes. A daily iron supplement is recommended for all pregnant women during the second and third trimesters. Iron interferes with zinc absorption, so women need a balanced intake.

Prenatal Supplements Physicians often recommend daily prenatal multivitamin-mineral supplements for pregnant women that typically provide more folate, iron, and calcium than regular supplements (see Figure 13-6). Women who do not eat adequately need them urgently, as do women in high-risk groups: women carrying twins or triplets, and those who smoke cigarettes, drink alcohol, or abuse drugs.[30] For multiple births, prenatal supplements may be of some help in reducing the risks of preterm delivery, low birthweights, and birth defects. Supplements cannot prevent the vast majority of fetal harm from tobacco, alcohol, and drugs, however, as later sections explain.

KEY POINT Women most likely to benefit from multivitamin-mineral supplements during pregnancy include those who do not eat adequately, those carrying twins or triplets, and those who smoke cigarettes, drink alcohol, or abuse drugs.

FIGURE 13-6 Example of a Prenatal Supplement Label

Notice that vitamin A is reduced to guard against birth defects, while extra amounts of folate, iron, and other nutrients are provided to meet the specific needs of pregnant women.

Prenatal Vitamins

Supplement Facts
Serving Size 1 Tablet

Amount Per Tablet	% Daily Value for Pregnant/ Lactating Women
Vitamin A 4000 IU	50%
Vitamin C 100 mg	167%
Vitamin D 400 IU	100%
Vitamin E 11 IU	37%
Thiamin 1.84 mg	108%
Riboflavin 1.7 mg	85%
Niacin 18 mg	90%
Vitamin B6 2.6 mg	104%
Folate 800 mcg	100%
Vitamin B12 4 mcg	50%
Calcium 200 mg	15%
Iron 27 mg	150%
Zinc 25 mg	167%

INGREDIENTS: calcium carbonate, microcrystalline cellulose, dicalcium phosphate, ascorbic acid, ferrous fumarate, zinc oxide, acacia, sucrose ester, niacinamide, modified cellulose gum, di-alpha tocopheryl acetate, hydroxypropyl methylcellulose, hydroxypropyl cellulose, artificial colors (FD&C blue no. 1 lake, FD&C red no. 40 lake, FD&C yellow no. 6 lake, titanium dioxide), polyethylene glycol, starch, pyridoxine hydrochloride, vitamin A acetate, riboflavin, thiamin mononitrate, folic acid, beta carotene, cholecalciferol, maltodextrin, gluten, cyanocobalamin, sodium bisulfite.

Food Assistance Programs

Women of limited financial means may eat diets too low in calcium, iron, vitamins A and C, and protein. Often, they and their children need help in obtaining food and benefit from nutrition counseling. At the federal level, the **Special Supplemental Nutrition Program for Women, Infants, and Children (WIC)** provides vouchers redeemable for nutritious foods, along with nutrition education and referrals to health and social services to low-income pregnant and lactating women and their children.[31] For infants given infant formula, WIC also provides iron-fortified formula. WIC encourages mothers to breastfeed their infants, however, and offers incentives to those who do.[32]

More than 9 million people—most of them infants and young children—receive WIC benefits each month. Participation in the WIC program benefits both the nutrient status and the growth and development of infants and children. WIC participation during pregnancy can effectively reduce infant mortality, low birthweight, and maternal and newborn medical costs. The Supplemental Nutrition Assistance Program (formerly, the Food Stamp Program) can also help to stretch the low-income pregnant woman's grocery dollars. In addition, any communities and organizations such as the American Dietetic Association and local hospitals provide educational services and materials, including nutrition, food budgeting, and shopping information.

- To provide certain key nutrients for pregnancy, lactation, and growth, WIC offers vouchers for:
  - *baby foods*
  - *eggs, dried beans, tuna fish, peanut butter*
  - *fruit, vegetables, and their juices*
  - *iron-fortified cereals*
  - *milk and cheese*
  - *soy-based beverages and tofu*
  - *whole-wheat bread, and other whole-grain products*
  - *iron-fortified formula for infants who are not breastfed.*

KEY POINT Food assistance programs such as WIC can provide nutritious food for pregnant women of limited financial means.

Special Supplemental Nutrition Program for Women, Infants, and Children (WIC) a USDA program offering low-income pregnant and lactating women and those with infants or preschool children coupons redeemable for specific foods that supply the nutrients deemed most necessary for growth and development. For more information, visit www.usda.gov/FoodandNutrition.

How Much Weight Should a Woman Gain During Pregnancy?

Women must gain weight during pregnancy—fetal and maternal well-being depends on it. Ideally, a woman will have begun her pregnancy at a healthy weight, but even more importantly, she will gain within the recommended weight range for her prepregnancy body mass index (BMI), as shown in Table 13-4. Even obese women are urged to gain during pregnancy.[33] Pregnancy weight gains within the

TABLE 13-4 **Recommended Weight Gains Based on Prepregnancy Weight**

	RECOMMENDED WEIGHT GAIN	
Prepregnancy Weight	*For single birth*	*For twin birth*
Underweight (BMI <18.5)	28 to 40 lb (12.5 to 18.0 kg)	Insufficient data to make recommendation
Healthy weight (BMI 18.5 to 24.9)	25 to 35 lb (11.5 to 16.0 kg)	37 to 54 lb (17.0 to 25.0 kg)
Overweight (BMI 25.0 to 29.9)	15 to 25 lb (7.0 to 11.5 kg)	31 to 50 lb (14.0 to 23.0 kg)
Obese (BMI ≥30)	11 to 20 lb (5.0 to 9.0 kg)	25 to 42 lb (11.0 to 19.0 kg)

Source: Institute of Medicine, Weight Gain during Pregnancy: Reexamining the Guidelines *(Washington, D.C.: National Academies Press, 2009).*

recommended ranges are associated with fewer surgical births, a greater number of healthy birthweights, and other positive outcomes for both mothers and infants, but many U.S. women exceed the recommended ranges—only a few fall short.[34] To improve pregnancy outcomes, researchers and health-care providers are placing greater emphasis on preventing excessive weight gains during pregnancy than in the past.[35]

Weight loss during pregnancy is not recommended.[36] Ideally, overweight women will achieve a healthy body weight before becoming pregnant, avoid excessive weight gain during pregnancy, and postpone weight loss until after childbirth.[37]

The ideal weight-gain pattern for a woman who begins pregnancy at a healthy weight is 3½ pounds during the first trimester and 1 pound per week thereafter. If a woman gains more than is recommended early in pregnancy, she should not restrict her energy intake later on in order to lose weight. Also, any sudden, large weight gain is a danger signal, however, because it may indicate the onset of preeclampsia (see the section titled "Troubleshooting").

The weight the pregnant woman puts on is nearly all lean tissue: placenta, uterus, blood, milk-producing glands, and the fetus itself (see Figure 13-7). The fat she gains is needed later for lactation. Physical activity can help a pregnant woman cope with the extra weight, as a later section explains.

Weight Loss After Pregnancy

The pregnant woman loses some weight at delivery. In the following weeks she loses more as her blood volume returns to normal and she gets rid of accumulated fluids. The typical woman does not, however, return to her prepregnancy weight. In general, the more weight a woman gains beyond the needs of pregnancy, the more she retains—mostly as body fat.[38] Even without excessive gain, most women tend to retain a few pounds with each pregnancy. When those few pounds become 7 or more and BMI increases by a unit or more, complications such as diabetes and hypertension in future pregnancies as well as chronic diseases later in life can increase—even for women who are not overweight.[39] Women who achieve a healthy weight prior to the first pregnancy and maintain it between pregnancies best avoid the cumulative weight gain that threatens health later on.[40]

KEY POINT Weight gain is essential for a healthy pregnancy. A woman's prepregnancy BMI, her own nutrient needs, and the number of fetuses she is carrying help to determine appropriate weight gain.

FIGURE 13-7 Components of Weight Gain During Pregnancy

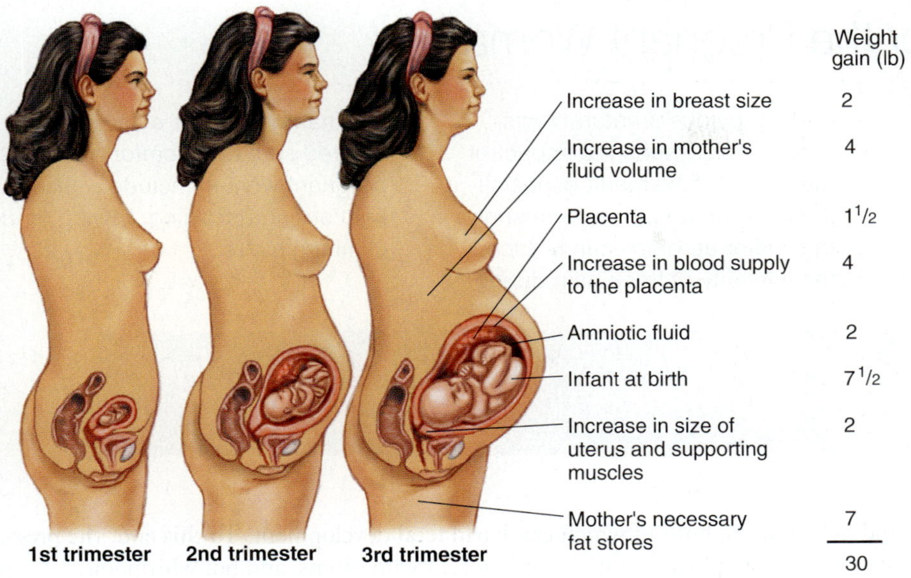

Should Pregnant Women Be Physically Active?

An active, physically fit woman experiencing a normal pregnancy can and should continue to exercise throughout pregnancy, adjusting the intensity and duration as the pregnancy progresses. Staying active during the course of a normal, healthy pregnancy improves the fitness of the mother-to-be, facilitates labor, helps to prevent or manage gestational diabetes, and reduces psychological stress.[41] Women who remain active during pregnancy report fewer discomforts throughout their pregnancies and retain habits that help in losing excess weight and regaining fitness after the birth.

Pregnant women should choose "low-impact" activities and avoid sports in which they might fall or be hit by other people or objects (for some suggestions, see the Think Fitness feature). Pregnant women with medical conditions or pregnancy complications should undergo a thorough evaluation by their health-care professional before engaging in physical activity. A few more guidelines are offered in Figure 13-8. Several of the guidelines are aimed at preventing excessively high internal body temperature

FIGURE 13-8 Guidelines for Physical Activity During Pregnancy

DO

- Do exercise regularly (most, if not all, days of the week).
- Do warm up with 5 to 10 minutes of light activity.
- Do 30 minutes or more of moderate physical activity.
- Do cool down with 5 to 10 minutes of slow activity and gentle stretching.
- Do drink water before, after, and during exercise.
- Do eat enough to support the additional needs of pregnancy plus exercise.
- Do rest adequately.

Tracy Frankel/The Image Bank/Getty Images

Pregnant women can enjoy the benefits of physical activity.

DON'T

- Don't exercise vigorously after long periods of inactivity.
- Don't exercise in hot, humid weather.
- Don't exercise when sick with fever.
- Don't exercise while lying on your back after the first trimester of pregnancy or stand motionless for prolonged periods.
- Don't exercise if you experience any pain or discomfort.
- Don't participate in activities that may harm the abdomen or involve jerky, bouncy movements.
- Don't scuba dive.

THINK FITNESS

Physical Activities for the Pregnant Woman

Is there an ideal physical activity for the pregnant woman? There might be. Swimming and water aerobics offer advantages over other activities during pregnancy. Water cools and supports the body, provides a natural resistance, and lessens the impact of the body's movement, especially in the later months. Research shows that water aerobics can reduce the intensity of back pain during pregnancy.[42] Other activities considered safe and comfortable for pregnant women include walking, light strength training, rowing, and climbing stairs.

START NOW

CENGAGENOW Ready to make a change? If you are expecting, consult the online behavior-change planner to plan to obtain enough physical activity for a healthy pregnancy at **www.cengage.com/sso.**

and dehydration, both of which can harm fetal development. To this end, the pregnant woman should also stay out of saunas, steam rooms, and hot whirlpools.

KEY POINT Physically fit women can continue to be physically active throughout pregnancy. Pregnant women should be cautious in their choice of activities.

Teen Pregnancy

Each year in the United States, more than 400,000 infants are born to teenage mothers.[43] A pregnant adolescent presents a special case of intense nutrient needs. Young teenage girls have a hard enough time meeting nutrient needs for their own rapid growth and development, let alone those of pregnancy. Many teens enter pregnancy with deficiencies of vitamins B_{12} and D, folate, and iron that can impair fetal growth.[44] Pregnant adolescents are less likely to receive early prenatal care and are more likely to smoke during pregnancy—two factors that predict low birthweight and infant death.[45] The rates of stillbirths, preterm births, and low-birthweight infants are high when either parent is a teen.[46] Adequate nutrition and appropriate weight gain during pregnancy are indispensable components of prenatal care for teenagers and can substantially improve the outlook for both mother and infant.[47]

To support the needs of both mother and fetus, a pregnant teenager with a normal BMI is encouraged to gain about 35 pounds. However, concerns about obesity have focused attention on proper weight gain advice for pregnant adolescents.[48] Grown women who gave birth during their adolescent years often have higher body weights, BMIs, and body fat than women who bore their children later in life.[49]

Meanwhile, pregnant and lactating teenagers can follow the eating pattern presented in Table 2-2 (page 44), making sure to choose a calorie level high enough to support adequate, but not excessive, weight gain.

KEY POINT Of all the population groups, pregnant teenage girls have the highest nutrient needs and an increased likelihood of having problem pregnancies.

Why Do Some Women Crave Pickles and Ice Cream While Others Can't Keep Anything Down?

Does pregnancy give a woman the right to demand pickles and ice cream at 2 a.m.? Perhaps so, but not for nutrition's sake. Food cravings and aversions during pregnancy are common but do not seem to reflect real physiological needs. In other words, a woman who craves pickles is not in need of salt. Food cravings and aversions that arise during pregnancy are probably due to homone-induced changes in taste and sensitivities to smells, and they quickly disappear after the birth.

Some pregnant women develop cravings for nonfood items such as laundry starch, clay, soil, or ice—a practice known as pica.[50] Pica may be practiced for cultural reasons that reflect a society's folklore; it is especially common among African American women. Pica is often associated with iron deficiency, but whether iron deficiency leads to pica or pica leads to iron deficiency is unclear.[51] Eating clay or soil may interfere with iron absorption and displace iron-rich foods from the diet. Furthermore, if the soil or clay contains environmental contaminants such as lead or parasites, health and nutrition suffer.

CONCEPT LINK 13-5

Pica was described in Chapter 8 (page 303).

The nausea of "morning" (actually, anytime) sickness seems unavoidable and may even be a welcome sign of a healthy pregnancy because it arises from the hormonal changes of early pregnancy. Many women complain that odors, especially cooking smells, make them sick. Thus, minimizing odors can alleviate morning sickness. Sipping carbonated drinks and nibbling plain crackers or other salty snack foods before getting out of bed can sometimes prevent nausea. Some women do best by simply eating what they desire whenever they feel hungry. Table 13-5 offers some other suggestions, but morning sickness can be persistent. If morning sickness interferes with normal eating for more than a week or two, the woman should seek medical advice to prevent nutrient deficiencies.

As the hormones of pregnancy alter her muscle tone and the thriving fetus crowds her intestinal organs, an expectant mother may complain of heartburn or constipation. Raising the head of the bed with two or three pillows can help to relieve nighttime heartburn. A high-fiber diet, physical activity, and a plentiful water intake will help relieve constipation. The pregnant woman should use laxatives or heartburn medications only if her physician prescribes them.

TABLE 13-5 **Tips for Relieving Common Discomforts of Pregnancy**

To alleviate the nausea of pregnancy:
- On waking, get up slowly.
- Eat dry toast or crackers.
- Chew gum or suck hard candies.
- Eat small, frequent meals whenever hunger strikes.
- Avoid foods with offensive odors.
- When nauseated, do not drink citrus juice, water, milk, coffee, or tea.

To prevent or alleviate constipation:
- Eat foods high in fiber.
- Exercise daily.
- Drink at least 8 glasses of liquids a day.
- Respond promptly to the urge to defecate.
- Use laxatives only as prescribed by a physician; avoid mineral oil—it carries needed fat-soluble vitamins out of the body.

To prevent or relieve heartburn:
- Relax and eat slowly.
- Chew food thoroughly.
- Eat small, frequent meals.
- Drink liquids between meals.
- Avoid spicy or greasy foods.
- Sit up while eating.
- Wait an hour after eating before lying down.
- Wait 2 hours after eating before exercising.

KEY POINT Food cravings usually do not reflect physiological needs, and some may interfere with nutrition. Nausea arises from normal hormonal changes of pregnancy.

Some Cautions for the Pregnant Woman

Some choices that pregnant women make or substances they encounter can harm the fetus, sometimes severely. Among these threats, smoking, medications, herbal supplements, illegal drugs, environmental contaminants, foodborne illness, vitamin-mineral megadoses, dieting, sugar substitutes, and caffeine deserve consideration. Alcohol constitutes a major threat to fetal health and is given a section of its own.

Cigarette Smoking A surgeon general's warning states that parental smoking can kill an otherwise healthy fetus or newborn. Unfortunately, an estimated 10 percent of pregnant women in the United States smoke, and rates are even higher for unmarried women and those who have not graduated from high school.[52] Constituents of cigarette smoke, such as nicotine, carbon monoxide, arsenic, and cyanide, are toxic to a fetus.[53] Smoking during pregnancy can damage fetal DNA, which could lead to developmental defects or diseases such as cancer.[54] Smoking restricts the blood supply to the growing fetus and so limits the delivery of oxygen and nutrients and the removal of wastes. It slows fetal growth, can reduce brain size, and may impair the intellectual and behavioral development of the child later in life.[55]

A mother who smokes is more likely to have a complicated birth and a low-birthweight infant.[56] The more a mother smokes, the smaller her baby will be. Of all preventable causes of low birthweight in the United States, smoking has the greatest impact. Smokers tend to have lower intakes of dietary fiber, vitamin A, beta-carotene, folate, and vitamin C—nutrients necessary for a healthy pregnancy. The margin on page 504 lists complications of smoking during pregnancy.

- Complications associated with smoking during pregnancy:
  - *Slowed fetal growth.*
  - *Low birthweight.*
  - *Complications in labor.*
  - *Spontaneous abortion.*
  - *Fetal death.*
  - *Sudden infant death syndrome (SIDS).*
  - *Childhood middle ear infections; cardiac and respiratory diseases.*

CONCEPT LINK 13-6

The Consumer Corner in Chapter 11 offered more information about herbal supplements and other alternative therapies (page 427).

CONCEPT LINK 13-7

Chapter 12 offers details on mercury, other contaminants in foods, and many foodborne illnesses.

- To protect their fetuses and newborns from listeriosis, pregnant women should:
  - *Avoid the following Mexican soft cheeses: queso blanco, queso fresco, queso de hoja, queso de crema, and asadero. Also avoid feta cheese, brie, Camembert, and blue-veined cheeses like Roquefort.*
  - *Use only pasteurized juices and dairy products.*
  - *Eat only thoroughly cooked meat, poultry, eggs, and seafood.*
  - *Before eating hot dogs and luncheon or deli meats, including cured meats like salami, thoroughly reheat them until steaming hot.*
  - *Wash all fruits and vegetables.*
  - *Do not eat refrigerated smoked seafood, such as salmon or trout, or any fish labeled "nova-style," "lox," or "kippered," unless it is an ingredient in a cooked dish.*
  - *Do not eat refrigerated pâté or meat spreads. Canned or shelf-stable pâté and meat spreads are safer.*

environmental tobacco smoke the combination of exhaled smoke (mainstream smoke) and smoke from lighted cigarettes, pipes, or cigars (sidestream smoke) that enters the air and may be inhaled by other people.

listeriosis a serious foodborne infection that can cause severe brain infection or death in a fetus or a newborn; caused by the bacterium *Listeria monocytogenes*, which is found in soil and water.

Smoking during pregnancy interferes with fetal lung development and increases the risks of respiratory infections and childhood asthma.[57] Sudden infant death syndrome (SIDS), the unexplained deaths that sometimes occur in otherwise healthy infants, has been linked to the mother's cigarette smoking during pregnancy.[58] Research suggests that even in nonsmokers, regular exposure to **environmental tobacco smoke** (or secondhand smoke) during pregnancy increases the risk of low birthweight and the likelihood of SIDS.[59]

Medicinal Drugs and Herbal Supplements Medicinal drugs taken during pregnancy can cause serious birth defects. Pregnant women should not take over-the-counter drugs or any medications not prescribed by a physician; then, they should read the labels and take warnings seriously.

Some pregnant women mistakenly consider herbal supplements to be safe alternatives to medicinal drugs and take them to relieve nausea, promote water loss, alleviate depression, aid sleep, or for other reasons. Some herbal products may be safe, but almost none have been tested for safety or effectiveness during pregnancy. Pregnant women should stay away from herbal supplements, teas, or other products unless their safety during pregnancy has been ascertained.[60]

Drugs of Abuse Drugs of abuse such as cocaine easily cross the placenta and impair fetal growth and development. Furthermore, such drugs are responsible for preterm births, low-birthweight infants, and sudden infant deaths. If these newborns survive, central nervous system damage is evident: their cries, sleep, and behaviors early in life are abnormal, and their cognitive development later in life is impaired.[61] They may be hypersensitive or underaroused; infants who test positive for drugs suffer the greatest effects of toxicity and withdrawal. Their childhood growth continues, but at a slow rate.[62]

Environmental Contaminants Pregnant women who are exposed to contaminants such as lead often bear low-birthweight infants with delayed mental and psychomotor development who struggle to survive. During pregnancy, lead readily moves across the placenta, inflicting severe damage on the developing fetal nervous system. For pregnant women, a diet free of contamination takes on extra urgency. Dietary calcium can help to defend against lead toxicity by reducing its absorption.

Mercury is a contaminant of concern as well. As discussed in Chapter 5, fatty fish are a good source of omega-3 fatty acids, but some fish contain large amounts of the pollutant mercury, which can harm the developing fetal brain and nervous system.[63] Because the benefits of moderate fish consumption outweigh the risks, women who may become pregnant, pregnant women, lactating women, and children up to the age of 12 are advised to do the following:[64]

- Avoid eating shark, swordfish, king mackerel, and tilefish (also called golden snapper or golden bass).
- Limit average weekly consumption to 12 ounces (cooked or canned) of seafood *or* to 6 ounces (cooked or canned) of white (albacore) tuna.

Foodborne Illness The vomiting and diarrhea caused by many foodborne illnesses can leave a pregnant woman exhausted and dangerously dehydrated. Particularly threatening, however, is **listeriosis,** which can cause miscarriage, stillbirth, or severe brain or other infections in fetuses and newborns. Pregnant women are about 20 times more likely than other healthy adults to get listeriosis. A woman with listeriosis may develop symptoms such as fever, vomiting, and diarrhea in about 12 hours after eating a contaminated food; serious symptoms may develop a week to six weeks later. A blood test can reliably detect listeriosis, and antibiotics given promptly to the pregnant sufferer can often prevent infection of the fetus or newborn. The margin lists preventive measures pregnant women can take to avoid contracting listeriosis.

Vitamin-Mineral Megadoses Many vitamins and minerals are toxic when taken in excess. Excessive vitamin A is widely known for its role in fetal malformations of the cranial nervous system. Intakes before the seventh week of pregnancy appear to be the most damaging. For this reason, vitamin A supplements are not given during pregnancy, unless there is specific evidence of deficiency, which is rare.

Dieting As mentioned, weight loss is not recommended during pregnancy and dieting, even for short periods, can be hazardous. In particular, low-carbohydrate diets or fasts that cause ketosis deprive the growing fetal brain of needed glucose and may impair its development. Many popular diets are deficient in many nutrients vital to fetal growth. Energy restriction during pregnancy is not recommended, regardless of the woman's prepregnancy weight or the amount of weight gained in the previous month.

Sugar Substitutes Artificial sweeteners have been studied extensively and found to be acceptable during pregnancy if used within the FDA's guidelines.[65] Women with the inborn error of metabolism known as phenylketonuria should not use the artificial sweetener aspartame.

CONCEPT LINK 13-8

The safety of artificial sweeteners was discussed in Chapter 12 (pages 475–478).

Caffeine Caffeine crosses the placenta, and the fetus has only a limited ability to metabolize it. Research studies do not indicate that caffeine (even in high doses) causes birth defects in human infants (as it does in animals), but limited evidence suggests that heavy use—intake equaling three or more cups of coffee a day—may increase the risk of miscarriage and fetal death.[66] Depending on the quantities consumed and the mother's metabolism, caffeine may also interfere with fetal growth.[67] The most sensible course, therefore, is to limit caffeine consumption to the equivalent of about one cup of coffee or two 12-ounce cola beverages a day. Caffeine amounts in food and beverages are listed in Controversy 14 on page 571.

KEY POINT Abstaining from smoking and other drugs, limiting intake of foods known to contain unsafe levels of contaminants such as mercury, taking precautions against foodborne illness, avoiding large doses of nutrients, refraining from dieting, using artificial sweeteners in moderation, and limiting caffeine use are recommended during pregnancy.

LO 13.3

Drinking During Pregnancy

Alcohol is arguably the most hazardous drug to future generations because it is legally available, heavily promoted, and widely abused. Society sends mixed messages concerning alcohol. Beverage companies promote an image of drinkers as healthy and active. Opposing this image, health authorities warn that alcohol can injure health, especially during pregnancy (see Figure 13-9). Every container of beer, wine, liquor, or mixed drinks for sale in the United States is required to warn pregnant women of the dangers of drinking during pregnancy.

FIGURE 13-9 **Mixed Messages in Alcohol Advertisements**

Labels on alcoholic beverages often display "healthy" images, but their warnings tell the truth.

Alcohol's Effects

Women of childbearing age need to know about alcohol's harmful effects on a fetus. Alcohol crosses the placenta freely and is directly toxic:[68]

- A sudden dose of alcohol can halt the delivery of oxygen through the umbilical cord. The fetal brain and nervous system are extremely vulnerable to a glucose or oxygen deficit, and alcohol causes both by disrupting placental functioning. Alcohol slows cell division, reducing the number of cells produced and inflicting abnormalities on those that are produced and all of their progeny.
- During the first month of pregnancy, the fetal brain is growing at the rate of 100,000 new brain cells a minute. Even a few minutes of alcohol exposure during this critical period can exert a major detrimental effect.

Did You Know?

One "drink" is the equivalent of:

- 5 oz wine (12% alcohol).
- 10 oz wine cooler.
- 12 oz beer.
- 1½ oz hard liquor (80 proof).

- Alcohol interferes with placental transport of nutrients to the fetus and can cause malnutrition in the mother; then, all of malnutrition's harmful effects compound the effects of the alcohol.
- Before fertilization, alcohol can damage the ovum or sperm in the mother- or father-to-be, leading to abnormalities in the child.

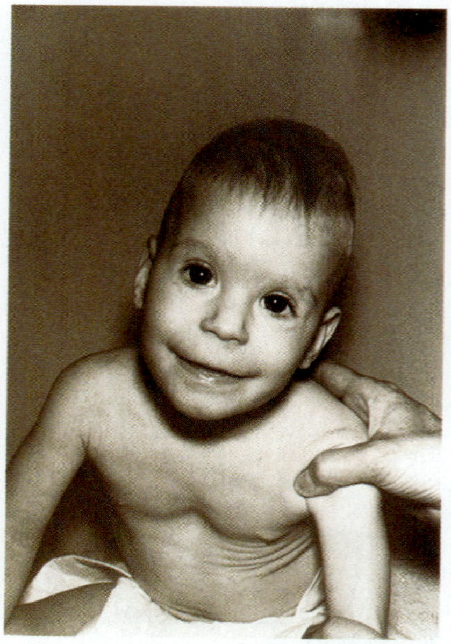

© James W. Hanson, M.D./NICHD

A child with FAS.

KEY POINT Alcohol limits oxygen delivery to the fetus, slows cell division, and reduces the number of cells organs produce. Alcoholic beverages must bear warnings to pregnant women.

Fetal Alcohol Syndrome

Drinking alcohol during pregnancy threatens the fetus with irreversible brain damage, growth retardation, mental retardation, facial abnormalities, vision abnormalities, and many more health problems—a spectrum of symptoms known as **fetal alcohol spectrum disorders,** or **FASD.** Children at the most severe end of the spectrum (those with all of the symptoms) are defined as having **fetal alcohol syndrome,** or **FAS.**[69] The life-long mental retardation and other tragedies of FAS can be prevented by abstaining from drinking alcohol during pregnancy. Once the damage is done, however, the child remains impaired. Figure 13-10 shows the facial abnormalities of FAS, which are easy to depict. A visual picture of the internal

fetal alcohol spectrum disorders (FASD) a spectrum of physical, behavioral, and cognitive disabilities caused by prenatal alcohol exposure.

fetal alcohol syndrome (FAS) the cluster of symptoms including brain damage, growth retardation, mental retardation, and facial abnormalities seen in an infant or child whose mother consumed alcohol during her pregnancy.

FIGURE 13-10 Typical Facial Characteristics of FAS

The severe facial abnormalities shown here are just outward signs of severe mental impairments and internal organ damage. These defects, though hidden, may create major health problems later.

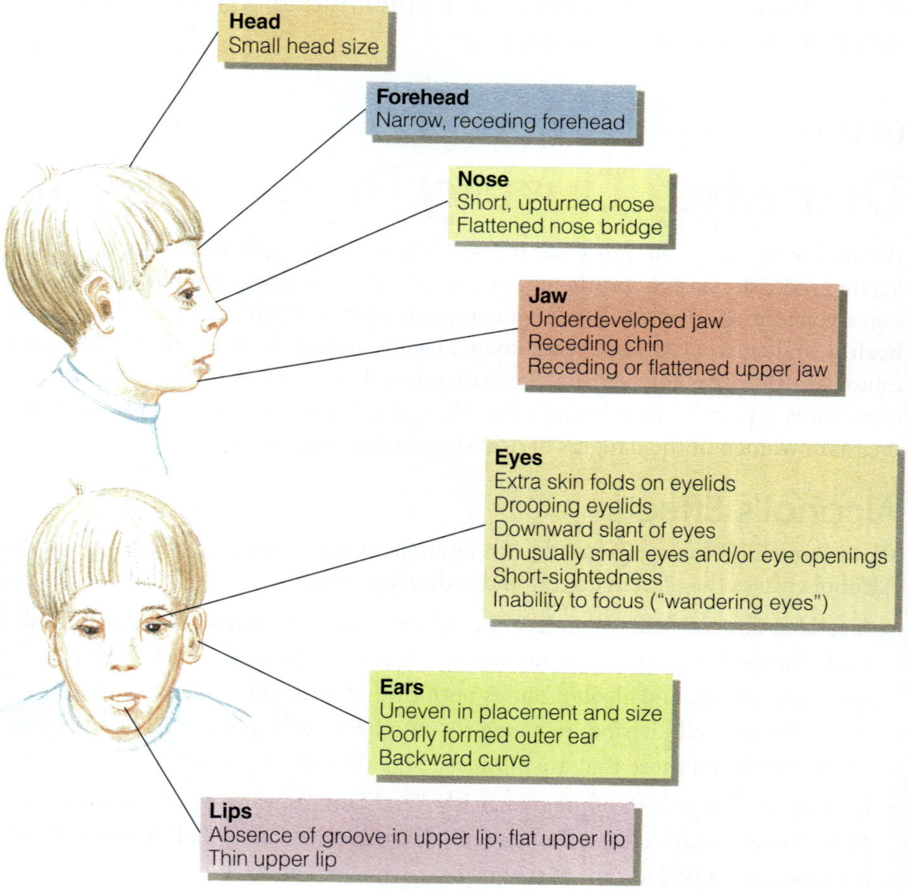

harm is impossible, but that damage seals the fate of the child. An estimated 5 to 20 of every 10,000 children are victims of FAS, making it one of the leading known preventable causes of mental retardation in the world.[70]

Even when a child does not develop full FAS, prenatal exposure to alcohol can lead to less severe, but nonetheless serious, mental and physical problems. The cluster of mental problems is known as **alcohol-related neurodevelopmental disorder (ARND),** and the physical malformations are referred to as **alcohol-related birth defects (ARBD).**† Some of these children show no outward sign of impairment, but others are short in stature or display subtle facial abnormalities. Many perform poorly in school and in social interactions and suffer a subtle form of brain damage. Mood disorders and problem behaviors, such as aggression, are common.[71]

Many children with ARND or ARBD go undiagnosed until problems develop in the preschool years. Upon reaching adulthood, such children are ill equipped for employment, relationships, and the other facets of life most adults take for granted. Anyone exposed to alcohol before birth may always respond differently to it, and also to certain drugs, than if no exposure had occurred, making addictions likely.

KEY POINT The birth defects of fetal alcohol syndrome arise from severe damage to the fetus caused by alcohol. Lesser conditions, ARND and ARBD, may be harder to diagnose but also rob the child of a normal life.

Experts' Advice

Despite alcohol's potential for harm, 1 out of 8 pregnant women drinks alcohol sometime during pregnancy; 1 out of 50 report "binge" drinking (five or more drinks on one occasion).[72] For women who know they are pregnant and choose to drink alcohol, the question is how much alcohol is too much. Even one drink a day threatens neurological development and behaviors. Low birthweight is reported among infants born to women who drink 1 ounce (two drinks) per day during pregnancy, and FAS is also known to occur with as few as two drinks a day. Birth defects have been reliably observed among the children of women who drink 2 ounces (four drinks) of alcohol daily during pregnancy. Compared to women who do not drink, a sizable and significant increase in stillbirths occurs in women who drink five or more drinks per week.[73] The most severe impact is likely to occur in the first two months, when the woman may not even be aware that she is pregnant.

Given such evidence, the American Academy of Pediatrics takes the position that women should stop drinking as soon as they *plan* to become pregnant. This step is important for fathers-to-be as well. Researchers have looked for a "safe" alcohol intake limit during pregnancy and have found none. Their conclusion: abstinence from alcohol is the best policy for pregnant women. The authors of this book recommend this choice, too. After the birth of a healthy baby, celebrate, with one glass of champagne. For a pregnant woman who has already been drinking alcohol, the best advice is "stop now." A woman who has drunk heavily during the first two-thirds of her pregnancy can still prevent some organ damage by stopping during the third trimester.

KEY POINT Abstinence from alcohol is critical to preventing irreversible damage to the fetus.

Did You Know?

The *Dietary Guidelines for Americans* lists pregnant women and women who may become pregnant among those who should not drink alcohol at all.

CONCEPT LINK 13-9

Controversy 3 provided details about alcohol's potential to harm living cells and tissues (page 95).

LO 13.4

Troubleshooting

Disease during pregnancy can endanger the health of the mother and the health and growth of the fetus. If discovered early, many diseases can be controlled—another reason early prenatal care is recommended.

alcohol-related neurodevelopmental disorder (ARND) behavioral, cognitive, or central nervous system abnormalities associated with prenatal alcohol exposure.

alcohol-related birth defects (ARBD) malformations in the skeletal and organ systems (heart, kidneys, eyes, ears) associated with prenatal alcohol exposure.

†Formerly, ARND and ARBD were grouped together and called fetal alcohol effects (FAE).

Diabetes

Pregnancy presents special challenges for the management of diabetes.[74] Without proper management, pregnant women with type 1 or type 2 diabetes may experience episodes of severe hypoglycemia or hyperglycemia, preterm labor, and pregnancy-related hypertension. Infants may be large, suffer physical and mental abnormalities, or experience other complications such as respiratory distress. Signs of fetal health problems are apparent even when maternal glucose is above normal but still below the diagnosis for diabetes.[75]

Excellent glycemic control in the first trimester and throughout the pregnancy is associated with the lowest frequency of maternal, fetal, and newborn complications.[76] Ideally, a woman will receive the prenatal care needed to achieve glucose control before conception and continued glucose control throughout pregnancy. For optimal long-term outcomes, continuation of intensified diabetes management after pregnancy is in the best interest of the mother's health.[77]

Some women are prone to develop a pregnancy-related form of diabetes, **gestational diabetes.** Gestational diabetes usually resolves after the infant is born, but some women go on to develop diabetes (usually type 2) later in life, especially if they are overweight.[78] About half of women who have had gestational diabetes go on to develop other forms of diabetes within a few years.[79] When gestational diabetes is identified early and managed properly, the most serious risks, fetal or infant illness or mortality, fall dramatically.[80] More commonly, gestational diabetes leads to surgical birth and high infant birthweight.[81] Physicians screen for the risk factors listed in the margin and test glucose tolerance in all pregnant women.[82]

- Risk factors for gestational diabetes:
  - *Age 25 or older.*
  - *BMI ≥25 or excessive weight gain.*
  - *Complications in previous pregnancies, including gestational diabetes or high birthweight.*
  - *Prediabetes or symptoms of diabetes.*
  - *Family history of diabetes.*
  - *African American, Asian American, Hispanic American, Native American, Pacific Islander.*

Hypertension

Hypertension during pregnancy may be **chronic hypertension** or **gestational hypertension.**[83] In chronic hypertension, the condition is generally present before and remains after pregnancy.[84] In women with gestational hypertension, blood pressure usually returns to normal during the first few weeks after childbirth.

Both types of hypertension pose risks to the mother and fetus; the higher the blood pressure, the worse the risk. In addition to heart attack and stroke, high blood pressure may increase the likelihood of a low-birthweight infant or spontaneous abortion.

Did You Know?

Hypertension is defined as blood pressure ≥140/90 millimeters of mercury.

Preeclampsia

Preeclampsia involves not only high blood pressure but also protein in the urine.[85] Preeclampsia usually appears in first pregnancies and starts to disappear within a few days after delivery.[86]

Preeclampsia affects almost all of the mother's organs—the circulatory system, liver, kidneys, and brain. If the condition progresses, she may experience seizures; when this occurs, the condition is called **eclampsia.** Maternal mortality during

- Warning signs of preeclampsia:
  - *Hypertension.*
  - *Protein in the urine.*
  - *Upper abdominal pain.*
  - *Severe and constant headaches.*
  - *Swelling, especially of the face.*
  - *Dizziness.*
  - *Blurred vision.*
  - *Sudden weight gain (1 lb/day).*

gestational diabetes abnormal glucose tolerance appearing during pregnancy.

chronic hypertension in pregnant women, hypertension that is present and documented before pregnancy; in women whose prepregnancy blood pressure is unknown, the presence of sustained hypertension before 20 weeks of gestation.

gestational hypertension high blood pressure that develops in the second half of pregnancy and usually resolves after childbirth.

preeclampsia (PRE-ee-CLAMP-see-ah) a potentially dangerous condition during pregnancy characterized by edema, hypertension, and protein in the urine.

eclampsia (eh-CLAMP-see-ah) a severe complication during pregnancy in which seizures occur.

MY TURN

© Cengage Learning
Cari

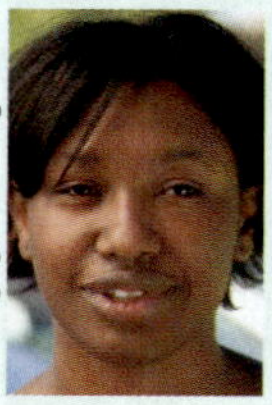
© Cengage Learning
Natasha

Bringing Up Baby

Two students talk about some of the choices they make about the care and feeding of their babies.

CENGAGENOW To hear their stories, log on to www.cengage.com/sso.

pregnancy is rare in developed countries, but eclampsia is one of the most common causes. Preeclampsia and eclampsia demands prompt medical attention.

KEY POINT Gestational diabetes, hypertension, and preeclampsia are problems of some pregnancies that must be managed to minimize associated risks.

Lactation

As the time of childbirth nears, a woman must decide whether she will feed her baby breast milk, infant formula, or both. These options are the only foods recommended for an infant during the first four to six months of life. A woman who plans to breastfeed her baby should begin to prepare toward the end of her pregnancy. No elaborate or expensive preparations are needed, but the expectant mother can read one of the many handbooks available on breastfeeding or consult a **certified lactation consultant,** employed at many hospitals.[‡] Part of the preparation involves learning what dietary changes are needed, because adequate nutrition is essential to successful lactation.

In rare cases, women produce too little milk to nourish their infants adequately. Severe consequences, including infant dehydration, malnutrition, and brain damage, can occur should the condition go undetected for long. Early warning signs of insufficient milk are dry diapers (a well-fed infant wets about six diapers a day) and infrequent bowel movements.

Nutrition During Lactation

A nursing mother produces about 25 ounces of milk a day, with considerable variation from woman to woman and in the same woman from time to time. The volume produced depends primarily on the infant's demand for milk.

Energy Cost of Lactation Producing milk costs a woman almost 500 calories per day above her regular need during the first six months of lactation. To meet this energy need, the woman is advised to eat an extra 330 calories of food each day. The other 170 calories can be drawn from the fat stores she accumulated during pregnancy. The food energy consumed by the nursing mother should carry with it abundant nutrients. A lactating woman's nutrient recommendations are listed on the inside front cover; see Table 13-2 on page 495 for a sample menu to meet them.

Fluid Need Breast milk contains a lot of water, so the nursing mother is advised to drink plenty of fluid each day (about 13 cups) to protect herself from dehydration. To help themselves remember, many women make a habit of drinking a glass of milk, juice, or water each time the baby nurses as well as at mealtimes.

- The DRI recommendation for *total* water intake during lactation is 3.8 L/day. This includes 3.1 L, or about 13 cups, as total beverages, including water.

Variations in Breast Milk A common question is whether a mother's milk may lack a nutrient if she fails to get enough in her diet. The answer differs from one nutrient to the next, but in general, the effect of nutritional deprivation of the mother is to reduce the *quantity,* not the *quality,* of her milk. Women can produce milk with adequate protein, carbohydrate, fat, folate, and most minerals, even when their own supplies are limited. For these nutrients, milk quality is maintained at the expense of maternal stores. This is most evident in the case of calcium: dietary calcium has no effect on the calcium concentration of breast milk, but maternal bones lose some of their density during lactation if calcium intakes are inadequate.[87] Such losses are generally made up quickly when lactation ends, and breastfeeding has no long-term harmful effects on women's bones. Nutrients in breast milk most likely to decline in response to prolonged inadequate intakes are the vitamins—especially vitamins B_6, B_{12}, A, and D. Vitamin supplementation of undernourished women appears to help normalize the vitamin concentrations in their milk and may be beneficial.

certified lactation consultant a health-care provider, often a registered nurse or a registered dietitian, with specialized training and certification in breast and infant anatomy and physiology who teaches the mechanics of breastfeeding to new mothers.

[‡]La Leche League is an international organization that helps women with breastfeeding concerns: www.lalecheleague.org.

Some infants may be sensitive to foods such as onions or garlic in the mother's diet and become uncomfortable when she eats them. A mother who is breastfeeding her infant is advised to eat whatever nutritious foods she chooses. If a particular food seems to cause an infant discomfort, the mother can eliminate that food from her diet for a few days and see if the problem goes away.

Current evidence does not support a major role for maternal dietary restrictions during lactation to prevent or delay the onset of food allergy in infants.[88] Infants who develop symptoms of food allergy, however, may be more comfortable if the mother's diet excludes the most common offenders—cow's milk, eggs, fish, peanuts, and tree nuts. Generally, infants with a strong family history of food allergies benefit from breastfeeding.[89]

© s.lyudmila, 2011/Shutterstock.com

Lactation and Weight Loss Another common question is whether breastfeeding promotes a more rapid loss of the extra body fat accumulated during pregnancy. Studies on this question have not provided a definitive answer. How much weight a woman retains after pregnancy depends on her gestational weight gain and the duration and intensity of breastfeeding. Many women who follow recommendations for gestational weight gain and breastfeeding can readily return to prepregnancy weight by six months.[90] Neither the quality nor the quantity of breast milk is adversely affected by moderate weight loss, and infants grow normally. Women often choose to be physically active to lose weight and improve fitness, and this is compatible with breastfeeding and infant growth.[91] A gradual weight loss (1 pound per week) is safe and does not reduce milk output.[92] Too large an energy deficit, especially soon after birth, will inhibit lactation.

KEY POINT The lactating woman needs extra fluid and enough energy and nutrients to make sufficient milk each day. Malnutrition most often diminishes the quantity of the milk produced without altering quality. Physical activity to lose excess weight is compatible with breastfeeding and infant growth.

When Should a Woman Not Breastfeed?

Some substances impair maternal milk production or enter breast milk and interfere with infant development, making breastfeeding an unwise choice. Some medical conditions also prohibit breastfeeding.

Alcohol and Illicit Drugs Alcohol enters breast milk and can adversely affect production, volume, composition, and ejection of breast milk as well as overwhelm an infant's immature alcohol-degrading system.[93] Alcohol concentration peaks within one hour after ingestion of even moderate amounts (equivalent to a can of beer). This amount may alter the taste of the milk to the disapproval of the nursing infant, who may, in protest, drink less milk than normal. Mothers who use illicit drugs should not breastfeed. Breast milk can deliver such high doses of drugs as to cause irritability, tremors, hallucinations, and even death in infants.

Tobacco and Caffeine Lactating women who smoke tobacco produce less milk, and milk with a lower fat content, than mothers who do not smoke. Consequently, their infants gain less weight than infants of nonsmokers. A lactating woman who smokes not only transfers nicotine and other chemicals to her infant via her breast milk but also exposes the infant to sidestream smoke. Babies who are "smoked over" experience a wide array of health problems—poor growth, hearing impairment, vomiting, breathing difficulties, and even unexplained death. Excess caffeine can make breastfed infants jittery and wakeful. As during pregnancy, caffeine consumption should be moderate when breastfeeding.

Medicines Many medicines pose no danger during breastfeeding, but others cannot be used because they suppress lactation or are secreted into breast milk and can harm the infant.[94] If a nursing mother must take medication that is secreted in breast milk and is known to affect the infant, then breastfeeding must be put off for the duration of treatment. Meanwhile, the flow of milk can be sustained by pumping the breasts and discarding the milk. A nursing mother should consult with her physician before taking medicines or herbal supplements.

Many women wonder about using oral contraceptives during lactation. One type that combines the hormones estrogen and progestin seems to suppress milk output, lower the nitrogen content of the milk, and shorten the duration of breastfeeding. In contrast, progestin-only pills have no effect on breast milk or breastfeeding and are considered appropriate for lactating women.[95]

Environmental Contaminants A woman sometimes hesitates to breastfeed because she has heard warnings that contaminants in fish, water, and other foods may enter breast milk and harm her infant. Although some contaminants do enter breast milk, others may be filtered out. Because formula is made with water, formula-fed infants consume any contaminants that may be in the water supply. Any woman who is concerned about breastfeeding on this basis can consult with a physician or dietitian familiar with the local circumstances. With the exception of rare, massive exposure to a contaminant, the many benefits of breastfeeding far outweigh the risk associated with environmental hazards in the United States.

Maternal Illness If a woman has an ordinary cold, she can continue nursing without worry. The infant will probably catch it from her anyway, and thanks to immunological protection, a breastfed baby may be less susceptible than a formula-fed baby. With appropriate treatment, a woman who has an infectious disease such as hepatitis or tuberculosis can breastfeed; transmission is rare.[96] If a woman has active, untreated tuberculosis, however, breastfeeding is contraindicated.[97]

The human immunodeficiency virus (HIV), responsible for causing AIDS, can be passed from an infected mother to her infant during pregnancy, at birth, or through breast milk, especially during the early months of breastfeeding. In developed countries such as the United States, where safe alternatives are available, HIV-positive women should not breastfeed their infants.[98] In developing countries, where feeding inappropriate or contaminated formulas causes 1.5 million infant deaths each year, breastfeeding can be critical to infant survival. The World Health Organization (WHO) recommends exclusive breastfeeding for infants of HIV-infected women for the first six months of life unless replacement feeding is acceptable, feasible, affordable, sustainable, and safe for mothers and their infants.[99]

KEY POINT Breastfeeding is not advised if the mother's milk is contaminated with alcohol, drugs, or environmental pollutants. Most ordinary infections such as colds have no effect on breastfeeding. Where safe alternatives are available, HIV-infected women should not breastfeed their infants.

FIGURE 13-11 **Weight Gain of Human Infants and Children in the First Five Years of Life**

The colored vertical bars show how the yearly increase in weight gain slows its pace over the years.

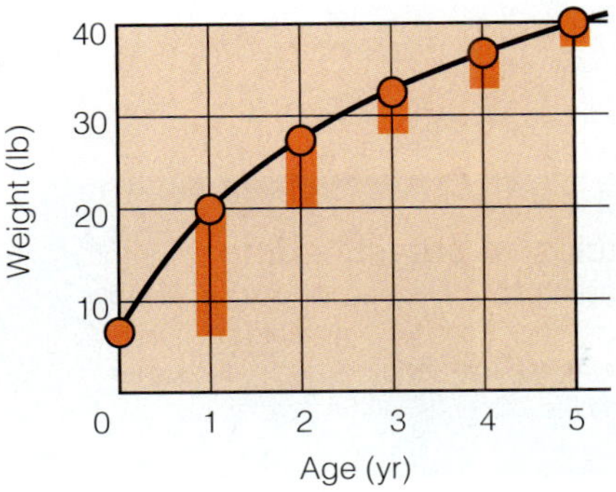

LO 13.5

Feeding the Infant

Early nutrition affects later development, and early feedings establish eating habits that influence nutrition throughout life. Trends change and experts may argue the fine points, but nourishing a baby is relatively simple. Common sense and a nurturing, relaxed environment go far to promote the infant's well-being.

Nutrient Needs

A baby grows faster during the first year of life than ever again, as Figure 13-11 shows. Pediatricians carefully monitor the growth of infants and children because growth directly reflects their nutrition status. An infant's birthweight doubles by about 5 months of age and triples by the age of 1 year. (If a 150-pound adult were to grow like this, the person would weigh 450 pounds after a single year.) The infant's length changes more slowly than weight, increasing about 10 inches from birth to 1 year. By the end of the first year, the growth rate slows considerably; an infant typically gains less than 10 pounds during the second year and grows about 5 inches in height.

Not only do infants grow rapidly but their basal metabolic rate is remarkably high—about twice that of an adult's, based on body weight. The rapid growth and metabolism of the infant demand an ample supply of all the nutrients. Of special importance during infancy are the energy nutrients and the vitamins and minerals critical to the growth process, such as vitamin A, vitamin D, and calcium.

Because they are small, babies need smaller *total* amounts of these nutrients than adults do, but as a percentage of body weight, babies need more than twice as much of most nutrients. Infants require about 100 calories per kilogram of body weight per day; most adults require fewer than 40 (see Table 13-6). Figure 13-12 compares a 5-month-old baby's needs (per unit of body weight) with those of an adult man. You can see that differences in vitamin D and iodine, for instance, are extraordinary. Around 6 months of age, energy needs begin to increase less rapidly as the growth rate begins to slow down, but some of the energy saved by slower growth is spent in increased activity. When their growth slows, infants spontaneously reduce their energy intakes. Parents should expect their babies to adjust their food intakes downward when appropriate and should not force or coax them to eat more.

Andersen Ross/Photodisc/Getty Images

After 6 months of age, the energy saved by slower growth is spent on increased activity.

One of the most important nutrients for infants, as for everyone, is water. The younger a child is, the more of its body weight is water. Breast milk or infant formula normally provides enough water to replace fluid losses in a healthy infant. If the environmental temperature is extremely high, however, infants need supplemental water.[100] Because proportionately more of an infant's body water compared to an adult's is between the cells and in the vascular space, this water is easy to lose. Conditions that cause rapid fluid loss, such as vomiting or diarrhea, require an electrolyte solution designed for infants.

KEY POINT Infants' rapid growth and development depend on adequate nutrient supplies, including water from breast milk or formula.

Why Is Breast Milk So Good for Babies?

Both the AAP (American Academy of Pediatrics) and the Canadian Pediatric Society stand behind this statement: "Breastfeeding is strongly recommended for full term infants, except in the few instances where specific contraindications exist." The American Dietetic Association (ADA) advocates breastfeeding for the nutritional health it confers on the infant as well as for the many other benefits it provides both infant and mother (see Table 13-7).[101] The AAP and the ADA recognize **exclusive breastfeeding** for 6 months, and breastfeeding with complementary foods for at least 12 months, as an optimal feeding pattern for infants.[102] All legitimate nutrition authorities share this view, but some makers of baby formula try to convince women otherwise—see the Consumer Corner on page 517.

exclusive breastfeeding an infant's consumption of human milk with no supplementation of any type (no water, no juice, no nonhuman milk, and no foods) except for vitamins, minerals, and medications.

TABLE 13-6 Infant and Adult Heart Rate, Respiration Rate, and Energy Needs Compared

	Infants	Adults
Heart rate (beats/minutes)	120 to 140	70 to 80
Respiration rate (breaths/minute)	20 to 40	15 to 20
Energy needs (cal/body weight)	45/lb (100/kg)	<18/lb (<40/kg)

FIGURE 13-12

Nutrient Recommendations for a 5-Month-Old Infant and an Adult Male Compared on the Basis of Body Weight

Infants may be relatively small and inactive, but they use a large amount of energy and nutrients in proportion to their body size to keep all their metabolic processes going.

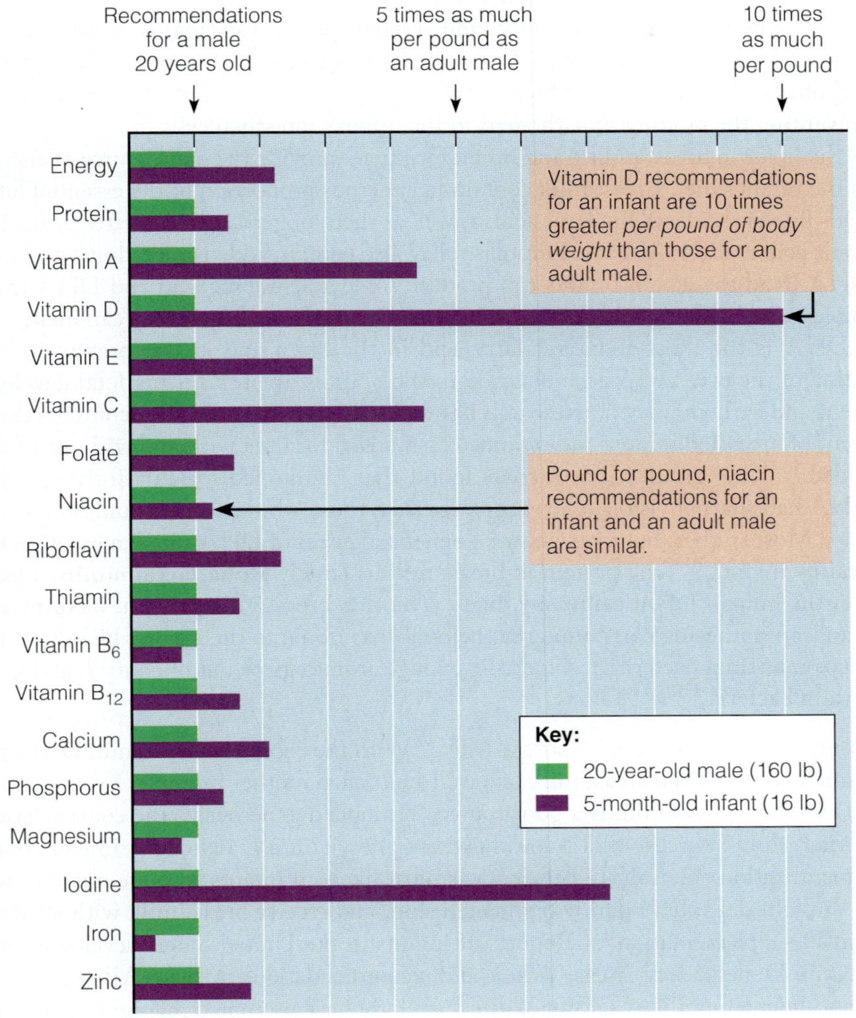

TABLE 13-7

Benefits of Breastfeeding

For Infants:

- Provides the appropriate composition and balance of nutrients with high bioavailability.
- Provides hormones that promote physiological development.
- Improves cognitive development.
- Protects against a variety of infections.
- May protect against some chronic diseases, such as diabetes and hypertension, later in life.
- Protects against food allergies.

For Mothers:

- Contracts the uterus.
- Delays the return of regular ovulation, thus lengthening birth intervals. (It is not, however, a dependable method of contraception.)
- Conserves iron stores (by prolonging amenorrhea).
- May protect against breast and ovarian cancer.

Other:

- Provides cost savings from not needing medical treatment for childhood illnesses or time off work to care for sick children.
- Provides cost savings from not needing to purchase formula (even after adjusting for added foods in the diet of a lactating mother).
- Provides environmental savings to society from not needing to manufacture, package, and ship formula or dispose of packaging.

Breast milk excels as a source of nutrients for the young infant. With the exception of vitamin D (discussed later), breast milk provides all the nutrients a healthy infant needs for the first six months of life.[103] Breast milk also conveys immune factors, which both protect an infant against infection and inform its body about the outside environment.

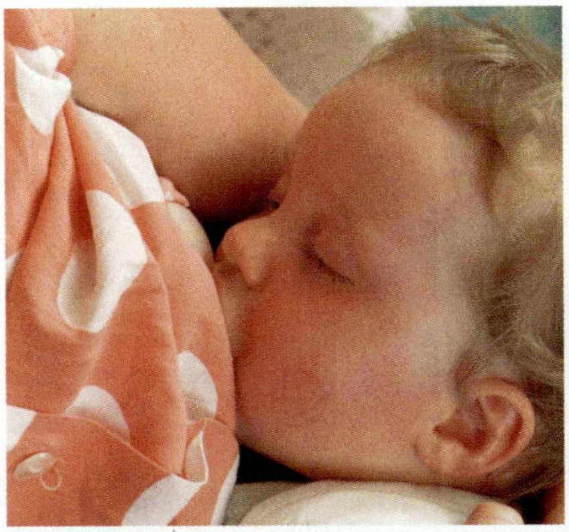

© Jennie Woodcock; Reflections Photolibrary/Corbis

Breastfeeding is a natural extension of pregnancy—the mother's body continues to nourish the infant.

Breastfeeding Tips Breast milk is more easily and completely digested than infant formula, so breastfed infants usually need to eat more frequently than formula-fed infants do. During the first few weeks, approximately 8 to 12 feedings a day, on demand, as soon as the infant shows early signs of hunger such as increased alertness, activity, or suckling motions, promote optimal milk production and infant growth.[104] Crying is a late indicator of hunger. An infant who nurses every two to three hours and sleeps contentedly between feedings is adequately nourished. As the infant gets older, stomach capacity enlarges and the mother's milk production increases, allowing for longer intervals between feedings.

FIGURE 13-13

Percentages of Energy-Yielding Nutrients in Breast Milk and Recommended Adult Diets

The proportions of energy-yielding nutrients in human breast milk differ from those recommended for adults.[a]

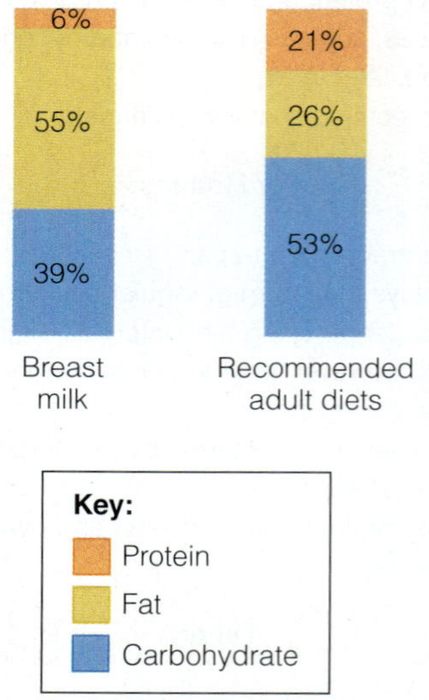

[a]The values listed for adults represent approximate midpoints of the acceptable ranges for protein (10 to 35 percent), fat (20 to 35 percent), and carbohydrate (45 to 65 percent).

CONCEPT LINK 13-10

Chapter 5 discussed the need for the essential fatty acids (page 166).

CONCEPT LINK 13-11

To review the role of vitamin K in blood clotting, see Chapter 7 (page 241).

alpha-lactalbumin (lact-AL-byoo-min) the chief protein in human breast milk. The chief protein in cow's milk is *casein* (CAY-seen).

lactoferrin (lack-toe-FERR-in) a factor in breast milk that binds iron and keeps it from supporting the growth of the infant's intestinal bacteria.

Even though the baby obtains about half the milk from the breast during the first 2 or 3 minutes of suckling, the infant should be encouraged to breastfeed on the first breast for as long as he or she wishes, before being offered the second breast. Begin each feeding on the breast offered last. The infant's suckling, as well as the complete removal of milk from the breast, stimulates lactation.

Energy Nutrients in Breast Milk The energy-nutrient balance of breast milk differs dramatically from that recommended for adults (see Figure 13-13). Yet, for infants, breast milk is the most nearly perfect food, affirming that people at different stages of life have different nutrient needs.

The carbohydrate in breast milk (and standard infant formula) is lactose. In addition to being easily digested, lactose enhances calcium absorption. One of the carbohydrate components of breast milk helps protect the infant from infection by preventing the binding of pathogens to the infant's intestinal cells.[105]

The lipids in breast milk—and infant formula—provide the main source of energy in the infant's diet. Breast milk contains a generous proportion of the essential fatty acids linoleic acid and linolenic acid, as well as their longer-chain derivatives, arachidonic acid and DHA. Most formulas today also contain added arachidonic acid and DHA (read the label). Infants can produce some arachidonic acid and DHA from linoleic and linolenic acid, but some infants may need more than they can make.

DHA is the most abundant fatty acid in the brain and is also present in the retina of the eye. DHA accumulation in the brain is greatest during fetal development and early infancy.[106] Research has focused on the visual and mental development of breastfed infants and infants fed standard formula with and without DHA added.[107] One group of researchers found that infants fed formula fortified with DHA had sharper vision at 4 years of age than those who were fed standard formula.[108] Most studies, however, show no beneficial effect of DHA supplementation for healthy infants.[109] The protein in breast milk is largely **alpha-lactalbumin,** a protein the human infant can easily digest. Another breast milk protein, **lactoferrin,** is an iron-gathering compound that helps absorb iron into the infant's bloodstream, keeps intestinal bacteria from getting enough iron to grow out of control, and kills certain bacteria.[110]

Vitamins and Minerals in Breast Milk With the exception of vitamin D, the vitamin content of the breast milk of a well-nourished mother is ample. Even vitamin C, for which cow's milk is a poor source, is supplied generously. The concentration of vitamin D in breast milk is low, however, and vitamin D deficiency impairs bone mineralization. Vitamin D deficiency is most likely in infants who are not exposed to sunlight daily, have darkly pigmented skin, and receive breast milk without vitamin D supplementation.[111] Reports of infants in the United States developing the vitamin D–deficiency disease rickets and recommendations by the AAP to keep infants under 6 months of age out of direct sunlight have prompted revisions in vitamin D guidelines. The AAP currently recommends a vitamin D supplement for all infants who are breastfed exclusively, and for any infants who do not receive at least 1 liter (1,000 milliliters) or 1 quart (32 ounces) of vitamin D–fortified formula daily.[112]

As for minerals, the calcium content of breast milk is ideal for infant bone growth, and the calcium is well absorbed. Breast milk is also low in sodium. The limited amount of iron in breast milk is highly absorbable, and its zinc, too, is absorbed better than from cow's milk, thanks to the presence of a zinc-binding protein.

Supplements for Infants Pediatricians may prescribe supplements containing vitamin D, iron, and fluoride (after 6 months of age). Table 13-8 offers a schedule of supplements during infancy. Vitamin K nutrition for newborns presents a unique case. A newborn's digestive tract is sterile, and vitamin K–producing bacteria take weeks to establish themselves in the baby's intestines. To prevent bleeding in the newborn, the AAP recommends that a single dose of vitamin K be given at birth.

Immune Factors in Breast Milk Breast milk offers the infant unsurpassed protection against infection.[113] Protective factors include antiviral agents, antibacterial agents, and infection inhibitors.

TABLE 13-8 Supplements for Full-Term Infants

	Vitamin D[a]	Iron[b]	Fluoride[c]
Breastfed infants:			
Birth to 6 months of age	✓		
6 months to 1 year	✓	✓	✓
Formula-fed infants:			
Birth to 6 months of age			
6 months to 1 year		✓	✓

[a]*Vitamin D supplements are recommended for all infants who are exclusively breastfed and for any infants who do not receive at least 1 liter (1,000 milliliters) or 1 quart (32 ounces) of vitamin D–fortified formula per day.*

[b]*All infants 6 months of age need additional iron, preferably in the form of iron-fortified infant cereal and/or infant meats. Formula-fed infants need iron-fortified infant formula.*

[c]*At 6 months of age, breastfed infants and formula-fed infants who receive ready-to-use formulas (these are prepared with water low in fluoride) or formula mixed with water that contains little or no fluoride (less than 0.3 ppm) need supplements.*

Source: Adapted from Committee on Nutrition, American Academy of Pediatrics, Pediatric Nutrition Handbook, *6th ed., ed. R. E. Kleinman (Elk Grove Village, Ill.: American Academy of Pediatrics, 2009).*

During the first two or three days of lactation, the breasts produce **colostrum,** a premilk substance containing antibodies and white cells from the mother's blood. Colostrum (like breast milk) helps protect the newborn infant from infections against which the mother has developed immunity—precisely those in the environment likely to infect the infant. The maternal antibodies in colostrum and breast milk inactivate harmful bacteria within the infant's digestive tract before they can start infections.[114]

Immune factors in breast milk interfere with the growth of bacteria that could otherwise attack the infant's vulnerable digestive tract linings. Breastfed babies are less prone to develop stomach and intestinal disorders during the first few months of life and so experience less vomiting and diarrhea than formula-fed babies. Breast milk contains antibodies and other factors against the most common cause of diarrhea in infants and young children (rotavirus).[115] Breastfeeding reduces the severity and duration of symptoms associated with this infection.

Breastfeeding also protects against other common illnesses of infancy, such as middle ear infection and respiratory illness.[116] Breast milk may offer protection against the development of allergies as well.[117] Compared with formula-fed infants, breastfed infants have a lower incidence of allergic reactions such as asthma, wheezing, and skin rash.[118] This protection is especially noticeable among infants with a family history of allergies.[119] Breast milk may also offer protection against the development of cardiovascular disease. Compared with formula-fed infants, breastfed infants have lower blood pressure and lower blood cholesterol as adults.[120]

In addition to their protective features, colostrum and breast milk contain hormones and other factors that stimulate the development of the infant's digestive tract. Clearly, breast milk is a very special substance.

Other Potential Benefits Breastfeeding may offer some protection against excessive weight gain later, although findings are inconsistent.[121] One extensive review suggests that initial breastfeeding protects against obesity in later life.[122] Another study confirms this finding and adds that the longer the duration of breastfeeding, the lower the risk of overweight in childhood.[123] Still another review reports that various studies have shown a protective effect, a protective effect only in certain groups, or no effect.[124] Researchers note that many other factors—socioeconomic status, other infant and child feeding practices, and especially the mother's weight—strongly predict a child's body weight.

Many studies suggest a beneficial effect of breastfeeding on later intelligence, but when subjected to strict standards of methodology (for example, large sample

colostrum (co-LAHS-trum) a milklike secretion from the breasts during the first day or so after delivery before milk appears; rich in protective factors.

size and appropriate intelligence testing), the evidence is less convincing.[125] Nevertheless, the possibility that breastfeeding may positively affect later intelligence is intriguing. It may be that some specific component of breast milk, such as DHA, contributes to brain development or that certain factors associated with the feeding process itself promote the intellect.[126] Most likely, a combination of factors is involved. More large, well-controlled studies are needed to confirm the effects, if any, of breastfeeding on later intelligence.

KEY POINT Breast milk is the ideal food for infants because it provides the needed nutrients in the right proportions and protective factors as well.

- Formula options:
  - *Liquid concentrate (moderately expensive, relatively easy)—mix with equal part water.*
  - *Powdered formula (least expensive, lightest for travel)—follow label directions.*
  - *Ready-to-feed (most expensive, easiest)—pour directly into clean bottles.*

Never an option—whole cow's milk before 12 months of age.

Formula Feeding

Formula feeding offers an acceptable alternative to breastfeeding. Nourishment for an infant from formula is adequate, and parents can choose this course with confidence. One advantage is that parents can see how much milk the infant drinks during feedings. Another is that other family members can participate in feeding sessions, giving them a chance to develop the special closeness that feeding fosters. Mothers who return to work early after giving birth may choose formula for their infants, but they have another option. Breast milk can be pumped into bottles and given to the baby in day care. At home, mothers may breastfeed as usual. Many mothers use both methods—they breastfeed at first but **wean** their children within 1 to 12 months. If infants are less than a year of age, mothers must wean them onto *infant formula,* not onto plain cow's milk of any kind—whole, reduced fat, low fat, or fat-free.

FIGURE 13-14 Percentages of Energy-Yielding Nutrients in Breast Milk, Infant Formula, and Cow's Milk

The average proportions of energy-yielding nutrients in human breast milk and formula differ slightly. In contrast, cow's milk provides too much protein and too little carbohydrate.

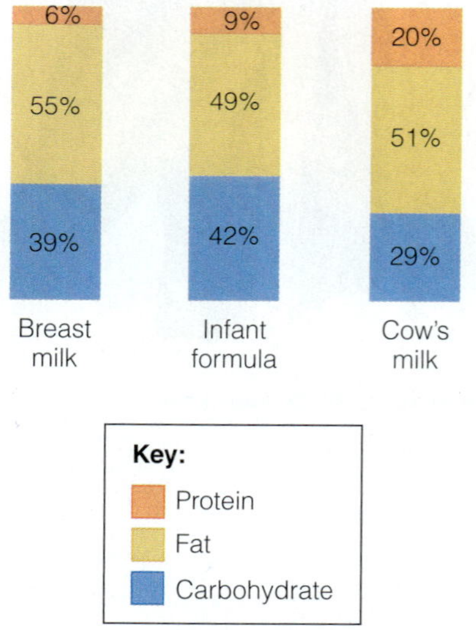

Infant formula Composition The substitution of formula feeding for breastfeeding involves striving to copy nature as closely as possible. Human milk and cow's milk differ; cow's milk is significantly higher in protein, calcium, and phosphorus, for example, to support the calf's faster growth rate. Thus, to prepare a formula from cow's milk, the formula makers must first dilute the milk and then add carbohydrate and nutrients to make the proportions comparable to those of human milk. Figure 13-14 compares the energy-nutrient balance of breast milk, standard infant formula, and cow's milk. Notice the higher protein concentration of cow's milk, which can stress the infant's kidneys. The AAP recommends that all formula-fed infants receive iron-fortified infant formulas.[127] Low-iron formulas have no role in infant feeding. Use of iron-fortified formulas has risen in recent decades and is credited with the decline of iron-deficiency anemia in U.S. infants.

Special Formulas Standard cow's milk–based formulas are inappropriate for some infants. Special formulas have been designed to meet the dietary needs of infants with specific conditions such as prematurity or inherited diseases. Most infants allergic to milk protein can drink formulas based on soy protein.[128] Soy formulas also use cornstarch and sucrose instead of lactose and so are recommended for infants with lactose intolerance as well. They are also useful as an alternative to milk-based formulas for vegan families. Some infants who are allergic to cow's milk protein may also be allergic to soy protein.[129] For these infants, special formulas based on hydrolyzed protein are available.

wean to gradually replace breast milk with infant formula or other foods appropriate to an infant's diet.

The Transition to Cow's Milk For good reasons, the AAP advises that whole cow's milk is not appropriate for infants younger than 1 year old.[130] In some infants, particularly those younger than 6 months of age, whole cow's milk causes intestinal bleeding, which can lead to iron deficiency. Cow's milk is also a poor source of iron. Consequently, plain cow's milk both causes iron loss and fails to replace iron. Furthermore, the bioavailability of iron from infant cereal and other foods is reduced when cow's milk replaces breast milk or iron-fortified formula during the first year.

CONSUMER CORNER

Formula's Advertising Advantage

Most women are free to choose whatever feeding method best suits their needs. For a few, however, breastfeeding may be prohibited because of physical conditions or for medical reasons or if medically indicated for special needs of the infant. With the strong scientific consensus that breastfeeding is preferable for most infants, why do women who could breastfeed their infants choose formula? Some women find the time and logistics of breastfeeding burdensome. For many women, though, the decision to forgo breastfeeding is influenced by aggressive advertising of formulas.

Advertisers of infant formulas often strive to create the illusion that formula is identical to human milk. No formula can match the nutrients, agents of immunity, and environmental information conveyed to infants through human milk, but the ads are convincing: "Like mother's milk, our formula provides complete nutrition" or "Our brand is scientifically formulated to meet your baby's needs." Such advertising efforts seem to be working. According to a recent survey, one out of four people of various ages, races, and socioeconomic backgrounds agree with the statement "infant formula is as good as breast milk."[1] Infant formula is an appropriate substitute for breast milk when breastfeeding is specifically contraindicated, but for most infants, the benefits of breast milk outweigh those of formula.

To increase market share, formula manufacturers give coupons and samples of free formula to pregnant women. After childbirth, women in the hospital may receive "goody bags" with more coupons to tempt them to receive their "formula gifts." More coupons arrive by mail a couple of months later, at a time when many women give up breastfeeding, even though nutrition authorities urge continued breastfeeding for several more months. Aggressive marketing tactics can undermine a woman's confidence concerning her breastfeeding choice, and lack of confidence has a significant influence on early discontinuation of breastfeeding.[2]

National efforts to promote breastfeeding seem to be working, at least to some extent: the percentage of infants who were ever breastfed rose from 60 percent among those born in 1994 to 77 percent among infants born in 2006.[3] Despite this encouraging trend, the rate of breastfeeding at 6 months of age did not change for infants born between 1993 and 2004.[4] Only about one in three infants is still being breastfed at 6 months of age. The AAP and many other health organizations recommend exclusive breastfeeding for the first six months of life.[5] Once complementary foods are offered, the AAP recommends that breastfeeding continue for at least a year and thereafter for as long as mutually desired. In the United States, only about one in five infants is still breastfeeding at 1 year of age. Increasing the rates of breastfeeding initiation and duration is one of the goals of *Healthy People 2010*. The percentage of mothers choosing to breastfeed their infants and continuing to do so still falls short of goals.

Many hospitals employ certified lactation consultants who specialize in helping new mothers establish a healthy breastfeeding relationship with their newborns. Table 13-9 lists 10 steps hospitals and birth centers can take to promote successful long-term breastfeeding.

Formula-fed infants in developed nations are healthy and grow normally, but they miss out on the breastfeeding advantages described in the text. In developing nations, however, the consequence of choosing not to breastfeed can be tragic. Feeding formula is often fatal to the infant in nations where poverty limits access to formula mixes, clean water is unavailable for safe formula preparation, and medical help is limited. The WHO strongly supports breastfeeding for the world's infants in its "babyfriendly" initiative and opposes the marketing of infant formulas to new mothers.

Women are free to choose between breast and bottle, but the decision should be made by weighing valid factual information and not be influenced by sophisticated advertising ploys.

TABLE 13-9 Ten Steps to Successful Breastfeeding

To promote breastfeeding, every maternity facility should:

- Develop a written breastfeeding policy that is routinely communicated to all health-care staff.
- Train all health-care staff in the skills necessary to implement the breastfeeding policy.
- Inform all pregnant women about the benefits and management of breastfeeding.
- Help mothers initiate breastfeeding within ½ hour of birth.
- Show mothers how to breastfeed and how to maintain lactation, even if they need to be separated from their infants.
- Give newborn infants no food or drink other than breast milk, unless medically indicated.
- Practice rooming-in, allowing mothers and infants to remain together 24 hours a day.
- Encourage breastfeeding on demand.
- Give no artificial nipples or pacifiers to breastfeeding infants.[a]
- Foster the establishment of breastfeeding support groups and refer mothers to them at discharge from the facility.

[a] *Compared with nonusers, infants who use pacifiers breastfeed less frequently and stop breastfeeding at a younger age.*

Source: United Nations Children's Fund, the World Health Organization, the Breastfeeding Hospital Initiative Feasibility Study Expert Work Group, and Baby Friendly U.S.A.

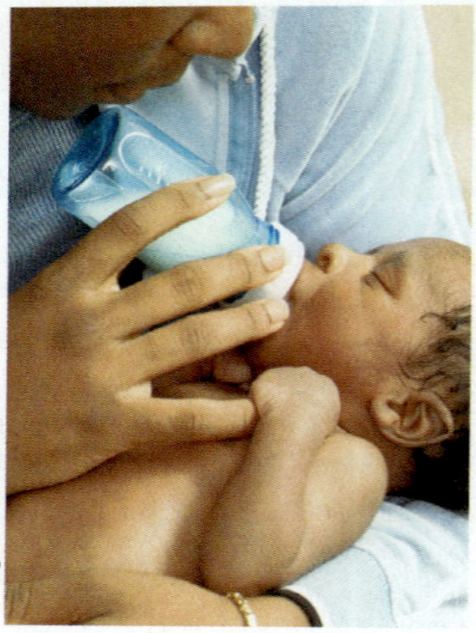

© Artiga Photo/Masterfile

The infant thrives on formula offered with affection.

Compared with breast milk or iron-fortified formula, cow's milk is higher in calcium and lower in vitamin C, characteristics that reduce iron absorption. In short, cow's milk is a poor choice during the first year of life; infants need breast milk or iron-fortified formula.

Once the baby is obtaining at least two-thirds of total daily food energy from a balanced mixture of cereals, vegetables, fruits, and other foods (after 12 months of age), whole cow's milk, fortified with vitamins A and D, is an acceptable accompanying beverage. Children 1 to 2 years of age should not be given reduced-fat, low-fat, or fat-free milk routinely. Between the ages of 2 and 5 years, a gradual transition from whole milk to the lower-fat milks can take place, but care should be taken to avoid excessive restriction of dietary fat.

KEY POINT Infant formulas are designed to resemble breast milk and must meet an AAP standard for nutrient composition. Special formulas are available for premature infants, allergic infants, and others. Formula should be replaced with milk only after the baby's first birthday.

- Dietary Guidelines:
  - *Children 2 to 8 years should consume 2 cups of fat-free or low-fat milk or equivalent milk products.*

An Infant's First Foods

Foods can be introduced into the diet as the infant becomes physically ready to handle them. This readiness develops in stages. A newborn can swallow only liquids that are well back in the throat. Later (at 4 months or so), the tongue can move against the palate to swallow semisolid food such as cooked cereal. The stomach and intestines are immature at first; they can digest milk sugar (lactose) but not starch. At about 4 months, most infants can begin to digest starchy foods. Still later, the first teeth erupt, but not until sometime during the second year can a baby begin to handle chewy food.

Stockbyte/Getty Images

With the first birthday comes the possibility of tasting whole, unmodified cow's milk for the first time.

When to Introduce Solid Food

The AAP recognizes that infants between 4 and 6 months of age are often developmentally ready to accept some foods other than breast milk.[131] Solid foods can provide needed nutrients that are no longer supplied adequately by breast milk or formula alone. The foods chosen must be those that the infant is developmentally capable of handling both physically and metabolically. The exact timing depends on the individual infant's needs, developmental readiness (see Table 13-10), and tolerance of the food.

In short, the addition of foods to an infant's diet should be governed by three considerations: the infant's nutrient needs, the infant's physical readiness to handle different forms of foods, and the need to detect and control allergic reactions, as described next. With respect to increased nutrient needs, the nutrient needed first is iron, then vitamin C.

© Polara Studios, Inc.

Foods such as iron-fortified cereals and formulas, mashed legumes, and strained meats provide iron.

Foods to Provide Iron and Vitamin C

Rapid growth demands iron. At about 4 to 6 months, the infant begins to need more iron than body stores plus breast milk or iron-fortified formula can provide. In addition to breast milk or iron-fortified formula, infants can receive iron from iron-fortified cereals and, once they readily accept solid foods, from meat or meat alternates such as legumes. Iron-fortified cereals contribute a significant amount of iron to an infant's diet, but the iron's bioavailability is poor.[132] Caregivers can enhance iron absorption from iron-fortified cereals by serving vitamin C–rich foods with meals.

The best sources of vitamin C are fruits and vegetables. It has been suggested that infants who are introduced to fruits before vegetables may develop a preference for sweets and find the vegetables less palatable, but there is no evidence to support offering these foods in a particular order.[133] Fruit juice is a source of vitamin C, but excessive juice intake can lead to diarrhea in infants and young children.[134] AAP recommendations limit juice consumption for infants and young children (1 to 6 years of age) to between 4 and 6 ounces per day.[135] Fruit juices should be diluted and served in a cup, not a bottle, once the infant is 6 months of age or older.

TABLE 13-10 Infant Development and Recommended Foods

Note: Because each stage of development builds on the previous stage, the foods from an earlier stage continue to be included in all later stages.

Age (mo)	Feeding Skill	Foods Introduced into the Diet
0–4	Turns head toward any object that brushes cheek. Initially swallows using back of tongue; gradually begins to swallow using front of tongue as well. Strong reflex (extrusion) to push food out during first 2 to 3 months.	Feed breast milk or infant formula.
4–6	Extrusion reflex diminishes, and the ability to swallow nonliquid foods develops. Indicates desire for food by opening mouth and leaning forward. Indicates satiety or disinterest by turning away and leaning back. Sits erect with support at 6 months. Begins chewing action. Brings hand to mouth. Grasps objects with palm of hand.	Begin iron-fortified cereal mixed with breast milk, formula, or water. Begin pureed meats, legumes, vegetables, and fruits.
6–8	Able to feed self with fingers. Develops pincher (finger to thumb) grasp. Begins to drink from cup.	Begin mashed vegetables and fruits. Begin plain baby food meats. Begin plain, unsweetened fruit juices from cup.
8–10	Begins to hold own bottle. Reaches for and grabs food and spoon. Sits unsupported.	Begin breads and cereals from table. Begin yogurt. Begin pieces of soft, cooked vegetables and fruit from table. Gradually begin finely cut meats, fish, casseroles, cheese, eggs, and legumes.
10–12	Begins to master spoon, but still spills some.	Add variety. Gradually increase portion sizes.[a]

[a]*Portions of foods for infants and young children are smaller than those for an adult. For example, a grain serving might be ½ slice of bread instead of 1 slice, or ¼ cup rice instead of ½ cup.*

Source: Adapted in part from Committee on Nutrition, American Academy of Pediatrics, Pediatric Nutrition Handbook, *6th ed., ed. R. E. Kleinman (Elk Grove Village, Ill.: American Academy of Pediatrics, 2009), pp. 113–142.*

Physical Readiness for Solid Foods Foods introduced at the right times contribute to an infant's physical development. The ability to swallow food develops at around 4 to 6 months, and food offered by spoon helps to develop swallowing ability. At 8 months to a year, a baby can sit up, can handle finger foods, and begins to teethe. At that time, hard crackers and other finger foods may be introduced to promote the development of manual dexterity and control of the jaw muscles. These feedings must occur under the watchful eye of an adult because the baby can also choke on such foods. Babies and young children cannot safely chew and swallow any of the foods listed in the margin; they can easily choke on these foods, a risk not worth taking. Nonfood items of small size should always be kept out of the infant's reach to prevent choking.

Some parents want to feed solids as early as possible on the theory that "stuffing the baby" at bedtime will promote sleeping through the night. There is no proof for this theory. Babies start to sleep through the night when they are ready, no matter when solid foods are introduced.

Preventing Food Allergies To prevent allergy or identify one promptly, experts recommend introducing single-ingredient foods, one at a time, in small portions, and waiting three to five days before introducing the next new food.[136] For example, on introducing cereals, try fortified rice cereal first for several days; it causes allergy least often. Try wheat-containing cereal last; it is a common offender. If a food causes an allergic reaction (irritability due to skin rash, digestive upset, or respiratory

CONCEPT LINK 13-12

Vitamin C–rich foods were shown in Snapshot 7-5 (page 247).

- To prevent choking, do not give infants or young children:
  - *Gum.*
  - *Popcorn.*
  - *Whole grapes.*
  - *Cherries.*
  - *Raw celery.*
  - *Carrots.*
  - *Whole beans.*
  - *Hot dog slices.*
  - *Hard or gel-type candies.*
  - *Marshmallows.*
  - *Nuts.*
  - *Peanut butter.*
- Keep these nonfood items out of their reach:
  - *Coins.*
  - *Balloons.*
  - *Small balls.*
  - *Pen tops.*
  - *Other items of similar size.*

• Chapter 14 offers more information on allergies.

discomfort), discontinue its use before going on to the next food. If allergies run in your family, use extra caution in introducing new foods. Parents or caregivers who detect allergies early in an infant's life can spare the whole family much grief.

Choice of Infant Foods Infant foods should be selected to provide variety, balance, and moderation. Commercial baby foods in the United States and Canada offer a wide variety of palatable, nutritious foods in a safe and convenient form. Brands vary in their use of starch fillers and sugar—check the ingredients lists. Parents or caregivers should not feed directly from the jar—remove portions to a dish for feeding in order not to contaminate the leftovers that will be stored in the jar.

• Appendix A includes the nutrient composition of many commercial baby foods.

An alternative to commercial baby food is to process a small portion of the family's table food in a blender, food processor, or baby food grinder. This necessitates cooking without salt or sugar, though, as the best baby food manufacturers do. Adults can season their own food after taking out the baby's portion. Pureed food can be frozen in an ice cube tray to yield a dozen or so servings that can be quickly thawed, heated, and served on a busy day.

Because recommendations to restrict fat do not apply to children under age 2, labels on foods for children under 2 (such as infant meats and cereals) cannot carry information about fat. Fat information is omitted from infant food labels to prevent parents from restricting fat in infants' diets. Fearing that their infant will become overweight, parents may unintentionally malnourish the infant by limiting fat. In fact, infants and young children, because of their rapid growth, need more fat than older children and adults.

Did You Know?

Infants and young children are particularly sensitive to foodborne illnesses and should not receive unpasteurized milk, milk products, or juices; raw or undercooked eggs, meat, poultry, fish, or shellfish; or raw sprouts. Infants also should not have honey.

Foods to Omit Sweets of any kind (including baby food "desserts") have no place in a baby's diet. The added food energy can promote obesity, and they convey few or no nutrients to support growth. Products containing sugar alcohols such as sorbitol should also be limited, as these may cause diarrhea. Canned vegetables are inappropriate for babies because they often contain too much salt. Awareness of foodborne illness and precautions against it are imperative. Honey and corn syrup should never be fed to infants because of the risk of botulism. Infants and young children are vulnerable to foodborne illnesses, and the *Dietary Guidelines* address this risk.

Foods at 1 Year For the infant weaned to whole milk after 1 year of age, whole milk can supply most of the needed nutrients: 2 to 3 cups a day meet those needs. More milk than this displaces iron-rich foods and can lead to the iron-deficiency anemia known as **milk anemia.** A variety of other foods—meat and meat alternates, iron-fortified cereal, enriched or whole-grain bread, fruits, and vegetables—should be supplied in amounts sufficient to round out total energy needs. Ideally, the 1-year-old sits at the table, eats many of the same foods everyone else eats, and drinks liquids from a cup, not a bottle. Table 13-11 shows a sample menu that meets the requirements for a 1-year-old.

Courtesy of the Author

Older babies love to eat what their families eat. Let them enjoy their food.

KEY POINT Solid food additions to an infant's diet should begin at about 6 months and should be governed by the infant's nutrient needs and readiness to eat. By 1 year, the baby should be receiving foods from all food groups.

Looking Ahead

The first year of life is the time to lay the foundation for future health. From the nutrition standpoint, the problems most common in later years are obesity and dental disease. Prevention of obesity may also help prevent the obesity-related diseases: atherosclerosis, diabetes, and cancer.

The most important single measure to undertake during the first year is to encourage eating habits that will support continued normal weight as the child grows. This means introducing a variety of nutritious foods in an inviting way (not forcing the baby to finish the bottle or baby food jar) and avoiding concentrated sweets and empty-calorie foods while encouraging physical activity. Parents should not teach

milk anemia iron-deficiency anemia caused by drinking so much milk that iron-rich foods are displaced from the diet.

babies to seek food as a reward, to expect food as comfort for unhappiness, or to associate food deprivation with punishment. If they cry for companionship, pick them up—don't feed them. If they are hungry, by all means, feed them appropriately. More pointers are offered in this chapter's Food Feature.

An irrational fear of obesity leads some parents to underfeed their infants, depriving them of the energy and nutrients they need to grow. Others wonder if they should feed their infants a low-fat diet to reduce heart disease risk, but the AAP recommends fat intakes of 40 to 50 percent of total calories for infants. A diet too low in fat hinders growth and development even when energy from carbohydrate and protein is ample. With rare exceptions, to be identified by physicians, babies from age 1 to 2 years need the food energy and fat of whole milk. They also need frequent servings of food containing the essential fatty acids.

Dentists strongly discourage the practice of giving a baby a bottle as a pacifier and recommend limiting treats. Sucking for long periods of time pushes the normal jaw line out of shape and causes a bucktoothed profile: protruding upper and receding lower teeth. Prolonged sucking on a bottle of milk or juice also bathes the upper teeth in a carbohydrate-rich fluid that favors the growth of acid-producing bacteria, which dissolves tooth material. Babies regularly put to bed with a bottle sometimes have teeth decayed all the way to the gum line, a condition known as nursing bottle syndrome, shown in the photos below.

KEY POINT The early feeding of the infant lays the foundation for lifelong eating habits. It is desirable to foster preferences that will support normal development and health throughout life.

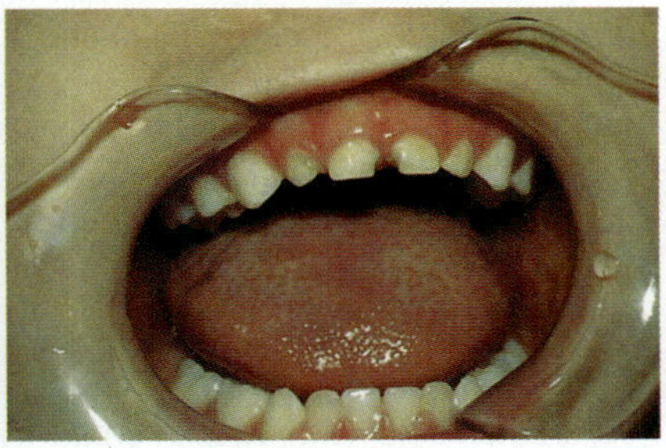
Courtesy of Pamela R. Erickson

Nursing bottle syndrome in an early stage.

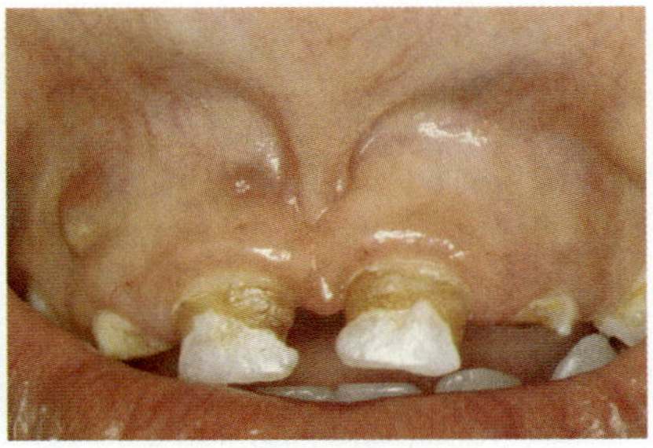
© 2009 Edward H. Gill/Custom Medical Stock Photo

Nursing bottle syndrome, an extreme example. The upper teeth have decayed all the way to the gum line.

TABLE 13-11 Sample Meal Plan for a 1-Year-Old

SAMPLE MENU	
BREAKFAST	1 scrambled egg 1 slice whole-wheat toast ½ c whole milk
MORNING SNACK	½ c yogurt ¼ c fruit[a]
LUNCH	½ grilled cheese sandwich: 1 slice whole-wheat bread with 1 slice cheese ½ c vegetables[b] (steamed carrots) ¼ c 100% fruit juice
AFTERNOON SNACK	½ c fruit[a] ½ c toasted oat cereal
DINNER	1 oz chopped meat or ¼ c well-cooked mashed legumes ½ c rice or pasta ½ c vegetables[b] (chopped broccoli) ½ c whole milk

Note: This sample menu provides about 1,000 calories.

[a]*Include citrus fruits, melons, and berries.*

[b]*Include dark green, leafy and deep yellow vegetables.*

FOOD FEATURE Mealtimes with Infants

The nurturing of a young child involves more than nutrition. Those who care for young children are responsible not only for providing nutritious foods, milk, and water but also a safe, loving, secure environment in which the children may grow and develop.

FOSTER A SENSE OF AUTONOMY

The person feeding a 1-year-old has to be aware that the child's exploring and experimenting are normal and desirable behaviors. The child is developing a sense of autonomy that, if allowed to develop, will provide the foundation for later assertiveness in choosing when and how much to eat and when to stop eating.

SOME FEEDING GUIDELINES

In light of the developmental and nutrient needs of 1-year-olds and in the face of their often contrary and willful behavior, a few feeding guidelines may be helpful:

- *Discourage unacceptable behavior (such as standing at the table or throwing food) by removing the child from the table to wait until later to eat.* Be consistent and firm, not punitive. For example, instead of saying "You make me mad when you don't sit down," say "The fruit salad tastes good—please sit down and eat some with me." The child will soon learn to sit and eat.
- *Let young children explore and enjoy food.* This may mean eating with fingers for a while. Learning to use a spoon will come in time. Children who

are allowed to touch, mash, and smell their food while exploring it are more likely to accept it.

- *Don't force food on children.* Rejecting new foods is normal and acceptance is more likely as children become familiar with new foods through repeated opportunities to taste them. Instead of saying "You cannot go outside to play until you taste your carrots," say "You can try the carrots again another time."
- *Provide nutritious foods, and let children choose which ones, and how much, they will eat.* Gradually, they will acquire a taste for different foods.
- *Limit sweets.* Infants and young children have little room for empty-calorie foods in their daily energy allowance. Do not use sweets as a reward for eating meals.

These recommendations reflect a spirit of tolerance that best serves the emotional and physical interests of the infant. This attitude, carried throughout childhood, helps the child to develop a healthy relationship with food. The next chapter finishes the story of growth and nutrition.

Diet Analysis PLUS Concepts in Action

Analyze the Adequacy of a Diet for Pregnancy

The purpose of this exercise is to reinforce the importance of good nutrition during pregnancy and infancy.

1. To reduce the risk for neural tube defects in infants, women who are capable of pregnancy are urged to obtain 400 micrograms (mcg) of folic acid, the most absorbable form of folate, daily in addition to a varied diet. To help meet a woman's need, find folic acid among enriched grains and other fortified foods. Select the Track Diet tab from the red navigation bar. Select a new date and enter the foods to create a meal that provides folic acid from enriched sources (see Table 13-3, page 497). (*Hint:* A good meal to choose is breakfast.) Select the Reports tab, then Source Analysis. Select Folate from the drop-down box, and generate a report. How close did you come to providing one-third of the needed 400 mcg?
2. A pregnant teenager's need for calcium soars to 1,300 mg a day to meet her need and that of the developing fetus. Many teenagers fail to meet their calcium needs, even before pregnancy. Select the Track Diet tab and select a new day. Add foods to create a high-calcium meal for a pregnant teen. (For tips, see Snapshot 8-3, page 293.) Select the Reports tab, then Source Analysis. Select Calcium from the drop-down box and generate a report. How much calcium was provided by the foods you selected for this meal? What did you take into consideration when choosing the foods high in calcium? How can you increase the likelihood that the teenager will consume this meal?
3. During lactation, a woman needs an additional 330 calories per day above her regular need. Create a new profile from the Profile drop down box; make it for a woman, and select "pregnant and lactating." To meet this woman's need, choose among nutrient-dense foods (refer to Table 13-2, page 495) and create a one-day diet to meet her increased energy need. Select the Reports tab, then Energy Balance, and generate a report for the day's meals. Did your food choices help this woman to meet her increased energy need? Was "330" listed in the "net kcal" column?
4. Zinc is required for protein synthesis and cell development. Snapshot 8-6 on page 306 demonstrated that animal products contain abundant zinc, posing a challenge to vegetarians. Create a vegetarian meal that includes zinc-rich foods. Select the Track Diet tab and select the profile for the pregnant woman. Select a new date. Choose some zinc-rich foods to create a meal. Select Reports, and then Source Analysis. Select Zinc from the drop-down box and generate a report. What foods would you advise for a pregnant vegetarian to increase her intake of zinc?
5. The fetal brain needs carbohydrate fuel each day and the pregnant woman needs carbohydrate, too. Select the Track Diet tab and select the profile for the pregnant woman. Select a new date. Choose nutrient and carbohydrate-rich foods for a dinner. Select the Reports tab, then Source Analysis. Select Carbohydrate from the drop-down menu and generate a report. What other reports would be helpful as you analyze this meal? Does it meet one-third of most of the woman's nutrient requirements? What is lacking and how might you correct deficiencies?
6. When an infant begins eating solid foods, the nutrients needed first in increased amounts are iron and vitamin C. From the Profile drop-down box, create a profile for a 30-inch, 24-pound, 1-year-old child. Select the Track Diet tab and create a breakfast and snack that includes foods high in iron and vitamin C. Select the Reports tab, then Source Analysis and select Iron from the drop-down box. Generate a report. What were the top sources of iron? Do the same for vitamin C and name the top sources. Did your food choices supply more than a third of the child's iron and vitamin C requirement? If not, what other foods might you select?

MEDIA MENU

CENGAGENOW To find additional quiz questions, view videos and animations, and explore interactive exercises, go to **www.cengage.com/sso.**

Search for "birth defects," "pregnancy," "adolescent pregnancy," "maternal and infant health," and "breastfeeding" at **www.healthfinder.gov.**

Learn more about breastfeeding from LaLeche League International at **http://www.llli.org.**

Get prenatal nutrition guidelines from Health Canada at **www.hc-sc.gc.ca.**

Learn more about birth defects from the March of Dimes at **www.marchofdimes.org.**

Visit the American College of Obstetricians and Gynecologists at **www.acog.org.**

SELF CHECK

Answers to these Self Check questions are in Appendix G.

1. A pregnant woman needs an extra 450 calories above the allowance for nonpregnant women during which trimester(s)?
   A. first
   B. second
   C. third
   D. first, second, and third
2. A deficiency of which nutrient appears to be related to an increased risk of neural tube defects in newborns?
   A. vitamin B_6
   B. folate
   C. calcium
   D. niacin
3. Which of the following preventive measures should a pregnant woman take to avoid contracting listeriosis?
   A. avoid feta cheese
   B. avoid pasteurized milk
   C. thoroughly heat hot dogs
   D. (a) and (c)
4. Breastfed infants may need supplements of:
   A. fluoride, iron, and vitamin D
   B. zinc, iron, and vitamin C
   C. vitamin E, calcium, and fluoride
   D. vitamin K, magnesium, and potassium
5. Which of the following foods poses a choking hazard to infants and small children?
   A. pudding
   B. marshmallows
   C. hot dog slices
   D. (b) and (c)
6. Sweets of any kind (including baby food "desserts") have no place in a baby's diet .
   T F
7. A major reason why a woman's nutrition before pregnancy is crucial is that it determines whether her uterus will support the growth of a normal placenta.
   T F
8. Fetal alcohol syndrome (FAS) is the leading known preventable cause of mental retardation in the world.
   T F
9. In general, the effect of nutritional deprivation on a breastfeeding mother is to reduce the quality of her milk.
   T F
10. A sure way to get a baby to sleep through the night is to feed solid foods as soon as the baby can swallow them.
    T F

CONTROVERSY 13

Childhood Obesity and Early Chronic Diseases

LO 13.6, 13.7

When most people think of health problems in children and adolescents, they most often think of measles and acne, not type 2 diabetes and hypertension. Today, however, 32 percent of U.S. children and adolescents 2 to 19 years of age are overweight and many of these are obese (shown in Figure C13-1).[1]* Serious risk factors and "adult diseases," such as type 2 diabetes, often accompany obesity, even in a child.[2] U.S. children are not alone in these problems—childhood obesity rates are soaring around the globe.[3]

*Reference notes are found in Appendix F.

FIGURE C13-1 Trends in Childhood Obesity

Today, almost 17% of children and adolescents have BMI values at or above the 95th percentile (are obese)[a] as measured on BMI-for-age growth charts (see inside back cover), while almost 12% have BMI values at or above the 97th percentile.

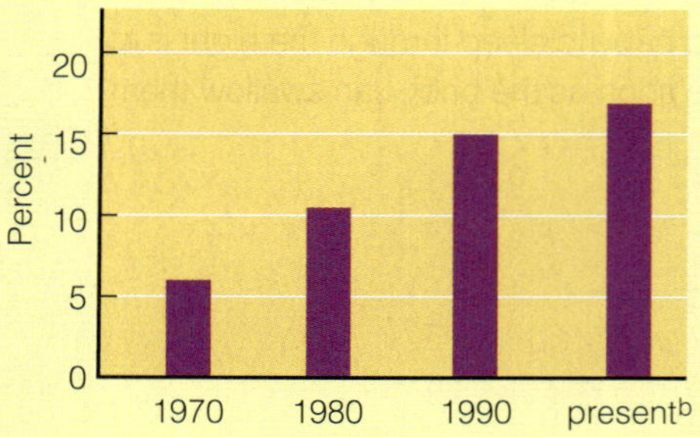

[a]*Obesity defined by U.S. Preventive Services Task Force, Screening for obesity in children and adolescents: U.S. Preventive Services Task Force Recommendation Statement,* Pediatrics *(2010), published online January 18, 2010, doi: 10.1542/peds.2009-2037.*

[b]*Childhood obesity rates remained largely unchanged between 1999 and 2008.*

Source: Data for 1999–today from C. L. Ogden and coauthors, Prevalence of high body mass index in U.S. children and adolescents, Journal of the American Medical Association *303 (2010): 242–249.*

Although no group has fully escaped the national gain in body weight, obese children tend to have these characteristics:

- Are male.[4]
- Are older.
- Are of African American, Hispanic, or Native American descent.[5]
- Are sedentary.[6]
- Have parents who are obese.

Additionally, low family income predicts obesity among non-Hispanic white children.[7]

Medical wonders of today prevent or cure many of even the most serious childhood diseases. Obesity, however, remains an unanswered challenge.[8]

THE CHALLENGE OF CHILDHOOD OBESITY

Obesity takes a heavy toll on the well-being of a child. Education is urgently needed—most overweight children and their parents all but discount the health threats, focusing instead on appearance and the social costs of obesity.

Physical and Emotional Perils

Obese adolescent children often display a risky blood lipid profile that foreshadows development of atherosclerosis—43 percent of obese children test high for total cholesterol, triglycerides, or LDL cholesterol.[9] Overweight children also tend to have high blood pressure; obesity is a

Children with obesity may develop type 2 diabetes among other ills.

leading cause of pediatric hypertension.[10] Without intervention, millions of U.S. children may be destined to develop type 2 diabetes and hypertension in childhood and heart disease in early adulthood.[11] Actions to prevent or treat childhood obesity are of critical importance.

One-third of U.S. children have poor cardiorespiratory fitness, reflective of sedentary lifestyles and body fatness.[12] Asthma is also much more prevalent among obese children than among their thinner peers.[13] A disease of the liver, nonalcoholic liver disease, also occurs more often, and obese children have a greater risk of complications from anesthesia.[14]

Obesity, high blood cholesterol, and hypertension stand with diabetes at the top of the list of factors associated with development of cardiovascular disease (CVD). When these conditions appear in childhood, CVD may set in soon afterward, and much sooner than most people expect.

Obese children may also suffer psychologically.[15] Adults may discriminate against them, and peers may make thoughtless comments or reject them. An obese child may develop a poor self-image, a sense of failure, and a passive approach to life. Television shows and movies, two major influences on children's thought processes, often denigrate and stigmatize the fat person as a social misfit.[16] Children have few defenses against these unfair portrayals and quickly internalize negative attitudes toward bulky body sizes.

Overweight or Chubby and Healthy: How Can You Tell?

An accurate assessment of a child's body mass index (BMI) for age is essential—guesswork can lead to unneeded lifestyle changes for a healthy-weight child, or to a missed opportunity to help a truly overweight child. Physicians, registered dietitians, and other health-care providers can accurately assess a child's BMI and interpret it using a growth chart (see the inside back cover).[17] Although cutoffs for children generate controversy, children and adolescents are generally considered *overweight* from the 85th to the 94th percentile on the charts and *obese* at the 95th percentile and above.[18]

Unrealistic expectations can undermine good intentions. Most overweight children tend to remain "stocky" long after losing some of their fatness, even into adulthood, and no amount of diet or exercise will make them willowy.[19] Early maturation and the greater bone and muscle mass needed to carry their extra weight contribute to the bulk retained by obese children.[20] In young children, genetic inheritance also plays an important determining role in body size and shape, perhaps even more so than in adults. Still, the child's environment remains a major player in obesity development.[21]

Darla and Gabby

Eight-year-old Gabby and her worried mother Darla tell a typical story of childhood obesity, and they model some appropriate responses. Recently, a note from the school nurse explained that, during a routine screening, Gabby's BMI was found to be too high. "The kids next door look skinny to me," says Darla, "Like if they got sick they couldn't fight it off." Because Gabby's BMI exceeds the 95th percentile, however, her health may be in peril and the nurse has suggested further testing for risk factors of chronic diseases.[22] With Gabby's health in danger, Darla's concern grows, "Both my father and his father died of diabetes-related disease, and I'm worried."

DEVELOPMENT OF TYPE 2 DIABETES

An estimated 85 percent of the children with type 2 diabetes are obese. Diabetes is most often diagnosed around the age of puberty, but diabetes is quickly encroaching on younger and younger age groups as children become more overweight. Ethnicity (being Native American, or of African, Asian, or Hispanic descent) increases the risk, as does having a family history of type 2 diabetes. Chapter 4 described the risks associated with type 2 diabetes and Chapter 11 revealed its connection with CVD.

Determining exactly how many children suffer from type 2 diabetes is tricky. The symptoms of type 2 and type 1 diabetes differ only subtly in children. The child with type 2 diabetes may lack classic telltale symptoms, such as glucose in the urine, ketones in the blood, weight loss, or excessive thirst and urination, so the condition often advances undetected. Undiagnosed diabetes means that children suffering with the condition are left undefended against its ravages.

DEVELOPMENT OF HEART DISEASE

Atherosclerosis, first apparent as heart disease in adulthood, begins in youth. By adolescence, most children have formed fatty streaks in their coronary arteries. By early adulthood, the arterial lesions that make heart attacks and strokes likely have formed.

Research is ongoing, but results often indicate that children with the highest risks of developing heart disease in adulthood are sedentary and have central obesity; they may have diabetes, high blood pressure, and high blood LDL cholesterol.[23] Adolescents who take up smoking greatly compound their risk.

High childhood BMI alone may not always predict increased adulthood heart disease risk, however. Many overweight youngsters appear to grow into adults with average weight and disease risks.[24] Still, authorities recommend that all children aged 6 years and older be screened for obesity, and obese children be treated with intensive counseling that includes diet, physical activity, and behavior changes.[25]

The note from Gabby's school nurse prompted medical testing, including a family history, a fasting blood glucose test, a blood lipid profile, and a blood pressure test. Luckily, the results for both glucose and blood pressure were normal.

High Blood Cholesterol

Gabby's blood lipid results, however, confirmed her mother's fears: her LDL cholesterol is 135—too high for health. Cholesterol standards for children and adolescents (ages 2 to 18 years) are in Table C13-1.

Obesity, especially central obesity, and high blood cholesterol often occur together. As children mature into adolescents, they often choose more foods rich in saturated fats, and their blood cholesterol levels tend to rise. Further, sedentary children and adolescents have lower HDL, higher LDL, and higher blood pressure than those who are physically active.

Family history sometimes predicts high blood cholesterol. If the parents or grandparents suffered from early heart

TABLE C13-1 Cholesterol Values for Children and Adolescents

Disease Risk	Total Cholesterol (mg/dL)	LDL Cholesterol (mg/dL)
Acceptable	<170	<110
Borderline	170–199	110–129
High	≥200	≥130

Note: Adult values appeared in Chapter 11.

disease, chances are that a child's blood cholesterol will be higher than average and will remain so through life. For this reason, some experts recommend universal cholesterol screening for all children and adolescents and particularly for those who are overweight, are sedentary, who smoke, or who consume diets high in saturated fat.

High Blood Pressure

High blood pressure in a child or adolescent is a concern—it can signal the early onset of hypertension. Childhood hypertension, left untreated, tends to worsen with time and can accelerate atherosclerosis.[26] Diagnosing hypertension in children must account for age, gender, and height; simple tables like the ones for adults are useless for children.

Dramatic improvements often occur when children with hypertension take up regular aerobic activity and hold their weight down as they grow taller ("grow into their weight"). Restricting sodium intake also causes an immediate drop in most children's and adolescents' blood pressure.[27]

EARLY CHILDHOOD INFLUENCES ON OBESITY

Young children learn food behaviors largely from their families. Whole families may be eating too much, dieting inappropriately, and exercising too little.[28]

Calories—and Cautions

Gabby, who loves sweets, budgets her pocket money (she's saving for a bicycle) to join her friends for a chocolate granola bar (160 calories) every day after school.[29] In addition, she knows how to bake a few peanut butter cookies from a roll of dough kept in the refrigerator to enjoy at bedtime (another 180 calories). Gabby knows that oats and peanut butter are better than candy for health, but she doesn't know that calories from granola bars and cookies cause her to greatly exceed her discretionary calorie limit of 130 calories each day.

Intuitively, Darla would like to eliminate these treats. However, pediatricians warn parents and caregivers to avoid overly restricting a child's eating; while intentions may be good, excessive restriction of sweets or calories can intensify cravings, create nutrient deficiencies, impair growth, and spark unnecessary battles about food. Worse, children who feel deprived or hungry may begin to sneak banned foods or hide them and binge on them in secret—behaviors that often predict eating disorders.

Figure C13-2 lists frequent high-calorie snacking as a potential contributing factor in a child's weight gain, but good-tasting snacks and meals are important to all children. A balanced approach may be to include favorite high-calorie treats occasionally in the context of structured, nutritious, and appealing meals and snacks. The next chapter presents more details about designing eating plans for children.

Physical Activity

Children have grown more sedentary, and sedentary children are more often overweight.[30] A child who spends more than an hour or two in "screen time," that is, sitting in front of a television, computer monitor, or other media, often eats fewer family meals and may become obese (Figure C13-3).[31] Children who watch more TV not only move less but they may also snack more, both during television viewing and afterward because of the influence of food advertising.[32]

Darla recalls, "My sisters and I hit the door on Saturday mornings with sandwiches in a bag. We explored, climbed trees, played softball with our friends, jumped in puddles, and played 'tag.' But Gabby and her friends have 252 television channels to choose from, not to mention computer games and the Internet—we had only 4 channels when I was little!" The American Academy of Pediatrics (AAP) supports Darla's view and recommends no television time before 2 years of age and a limit of two hours per day of television, computer, and other "screen time" for older children to help prevent obesity.[33]

Food Advertising to Children

Children and youth influence a huge portion of the nation's food spending—up

FIGURE C13-2 **Factors Affecting Childhood Weight Gain**

The more of these factors in a child's life, the greater the likelihood of unhealthy weight gain.

Food Factors
- Frequent snacks consisting of high-energy foods, such as candies, cookies, crackers, fried foods, and ice cream.
- Irregular or sporadic mealtimes; missed meals.
- Eating when not hungry; eating while watching TV or doing homework.
- Fast-food meals more than once per week.
- Frequent meals of fried or sugary foods and beverages.
- Exposure to advertising that promotes high-calorie foods.

Activity Factors
- More than an hour of sedentary activity, such as television, each day.
- Less than 20 minutes of physical activity, such as outdoor play, each day.
- No access to recreational facilities.

Family and Other Factors
- Overweight family members, particularly parents.
- Low-income family.
- Tall for age.

FIGURE C13-3 **Prevalence of Obesity by Hours of TV per Day, Children Ages 10–15 Years**

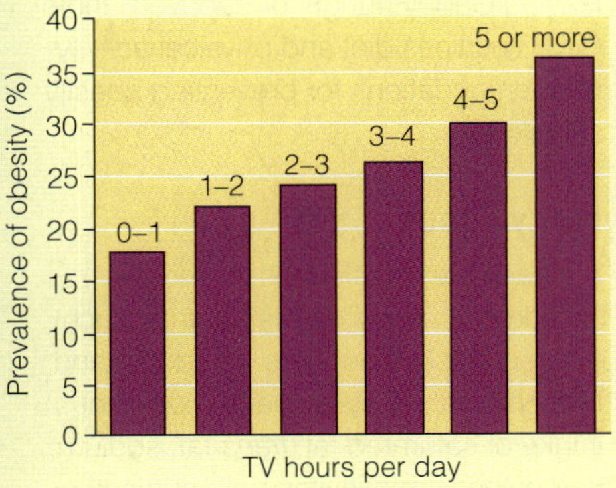

Source: Centers for Disease Control and Prevention, Youth Risk Behavior Survey, available at www.cdc.gov.

to $200 billion of their own pocket money each year—and influence hundreds of billions more in annual family purchases of foods, beverages, and restaurant meals.[34] As a result, the average child sees an estimated 40,000 TV commercials a year and uncounted Internet commercials—many peddling foods high in sugar, saturated fat, and salt, such as sugar-coated breakfast cereals, candy and "energy" bars, chips, fast foods, and carbonated beverages.[35] The advertisers use developmental psychology to tap children's needs for peer acceptance, fun, love, safety, security, independence, maturity, and identity.[36] Not surprisingly, the more time children spend watching television, the more they request the foods and beverages in advertisements—and they get their requests about half of the time.[37]

On the Internet, food marketing agencies develop free, child-attracting "advergames," that is, games built around a manufacturer's foods and beverages, intended to spark brand loyalty in young children. Appealing animated "spokes-characters" speak directly to children, bypassing parents and teachers, to increase children's desire for mostly highly processed, high-fat, high-sugar, low-nutrient treats and fast foods.[38] Do the ads work? Yes, they do. Otherwise, the billions of dollars spent annually on advertising to children would be spent elsewhere.

A few major food companies have stopped advertising directly to children, while others have agreed to voluntarily promote physical activity and health-promoting products, while reducing the use of beloved animated characters to sell sweets and fats to children.[39] A consumer advocacy group has questioned whether these steps are sufficient to counterbalance the effective abundant marketing of less-than-nutritious foods still aimed at children.[40]

PREVENTING AND REVERSING OVERWEIGHT IN CHILDREN: A FAMILY AFFAIR

Prevention and treatment of childhood obesity are national priorities.[41] Parents are a starting point: they are encouraged to make major efforts to prevent childhood obesity or to begin treatment early—before adolescence.[42]

For a child who is overweight or obese, an initial goal might be to slow the child's rate of gain while the child grows taller. Weight loss ordinarily is not recommended because diet restriction can easily interfere with normal growth, but may depend on the severity of the condition.[43] By including the whole family in an effort to consume balanced meals of appropriate portion sizes and nutritious satisfying snacks and boost physical activity, the goal is often accomplished, and the child does not feel singled out.[44]

Gabby's pediatrician has recommended lifestyle changes to improve both her BMI and blood lipids. Darla is motivated, "I need to take some action!" A warning to Darla: the lifestyle changes may sound easy, but implementing them may prove more difficult than she expects—people's behaviors are notoriously resistant to change. Further, the person, in this case Gabby, must be involved at the planning stage for the changes to be successful.

Parents Set an Example

Parents are among the most influential forces shaping the self-concept, weight concerns, and eating habits of children.[45] Successful plans for stabilizing a child's weight center on whole-family lifestyle changes (see Table C13-2) because when parents set patterns for family behaviors, the children will most often follow their lead.[46]

Lifestyle Changes First, Medications Later

A general rule for treating overweight children is "lifestyle changes first; medications later, if at all." Children with elevated disease risk factors, such as high blood cholesterol or a family history of early heart disease, should still first be treated with diet and physical activity, but should blood cholesterol remain high after 6 to 12 months, then certain drugs may safely be used to lower blood cholesterol without interfering with normal growth or development. Two obesity drugs, orlistat and sibutramine, have been approved for limited use in children and adolescents.[47]

Obesity Surgery

Limited research shows that, after surgery, extremely obese adolescents lose significant weight and reduce their risk factors for type 2 diabetes and cardiovascular disease.[48] Surgery may be an option for physically mature adolescents with a BMI of 50 or above or a BMI of 40 or above with significant weight-related health problems who have failed at previous lifestyle modifications and will adhere to the long-term lifestyle changes required after surgery.

Positive, Loving Support

To preserve the child's healthy sense of self, setting realistic, achievable goals is a first priority. Keeping a positive, upbeat attitude is another. The reverse—impossible goals and a critical, blaming adult—may damage the child's developing self-image and may set the stage for eating disorders later on.

Most of all, Darla must let Gabby know that she is loved, regardless of weight. Blame is a useless concept and can trigger emotional withdrawal of the child

TABLE C13-2 Family Lifestyle Changes to Help the Overweight Child

Everyone can benefit when the whole family adopts health-promoting habits such as these:

- Learn and use appropriate food portions.
- Involve children in shopping for and preparing family meals.
- Set regular mealtimes and dine together frequently.
- For other days, plan and provide a wide variety of nutritious snacks that are low in fat and sugar.
- Provide an appropriate nutritious breakfast every day.
- Provide recommended amounts of fruit juices but no more than this amount.
- Limit high-sugar, high-fat foods, including sugar-sweetened soft drinks and fruit-flavored punches.
- Set a good example and demonstrate positive behaviors for children to imitate.
- Slow down eating and pause to enjoy table companions; stop eating when full.
- Do not use foods to reward or punish behaviors.
- Involve children in daily active outdoor play or structured physical activities, as a family or with friends.
- Limit television time; set a rule to eliminate television-watching during meals.
- Celebrate family special events and holidays with outdoor activities, such as a softball game, a hike, or a summer swim.
- Keep a calendar of scheduled family meals and activity events where everyone can read it.
- Obtain parent and child nutrition and physical activity education and training or family counseling to guide family-based behavioral and other interventions as needed.
- Work with schools to institute school-wide food and activity policies to support a healthy body weight and prevent obesity (see Chapter 14).

Sources: American Medical Association Working Group on Managing Childhood Obesity, Expert Committee recommendations on the assessment, prevention, and treatment of child and adolescent overweight and obesity, June 2007, available at www.ama-assn.org/ama1/pub/upload/mm/433/ped_obesity_recs.pdf; H. Fiore and coauthors, Potentially protective factors associated with healthful body mass index in adolescents with obese and nonobese parents: A secondary data analysis of the Third National Health and Nutrition Examination Survey, 1988–1994, Journal of the American Dietetic Association *106 (2006): 55–64; Position of the American Dietetic Association: Individual-, family-, school-, and community-based interventions for pediatric overweight,* Journal of the American Dietetic Association *106 (2006): 925–945.*

just when the opposite—active engagement—is needed most. By being supportive, Darla can help Gabriella grow into a healthy young woman with positive attitudes about food and herself. Meanwhile, she must make some changes to diet and physical activity—but exactly which ones? And how?

DIET MODERATION, NOT DEPRIVATION

All children should eat an appropriate amount and variety of foods, regardless of body weight (Chapter 14 provides many details). For the health of the heart, children older than 2 years of age benefit from the same diet recommended for older individuals, that is, a diet limited in fats, especially saturated fat, *trans* fat, and cholesterol; rich in nutrients; and age-appropriate in calories. Such a diet benefits blood lipids without compromising nutrient adequacy, physical growth, or neurological development.

Fruits and vegetables, whole grains, low-fat and nonfat dairy products, beans, fish, and lean meats appropriately make up the bulk of the child's diet. Ice cream, doughnuts, and other high-calorie foods can supply 100–200 calories a day of discretionary calories, depending upon the child's age and activity level. For perspective, a large (5-inch diameter) glazed doughnut provides 480 calories. Gabby's daily treats add up to over 350 calories a day.

Gabby loves her daily granola bar. Recognizing that pleasure is important, too, Darla decides to set some goals for providing nutritious, good-tasting lower-calorie foods at regular mealtimes and other snacks to make room for Gabby's favorite treat. Together, they decide to replace the evening cookies with whole-grain crackers or apple slices spread with a little peanut butter, which cuts the evening snack calories in half without leaving Gabby hungry or deprived. Table C13-3 outlines diet and physical activity recommendations for preventing obesity in children.

Fatty Foods

A steady diet of offerings on most "children's menus" in restaurants, such as fried chicken nuggets, hot dogs, and French fries, easily exceeds a prudent intake of saturated fat, *trans* fat, sodium, and calories and invites both nutrient shortages and gains of body fat. Often, better choices can be found among appetizers, soups, salads, and side sections, and the best establishments offer steamed vegetables, fresh fruit, and broiled or grilled poultry on menus for both children and adults.[49]

Other fatty foods, such as nuts, avocado, vegetable oils, and safer varieties of fish, are important to include for their essential fatty acids. Fatty foods can be calorie-rich, however, making portion sizes of critical importance. Low-fat and nonfat milk products or equivalent substitutes deserve a special place in a child's diet for the calcium and other nutrients they supply.

Soft Drinks

Most, but not all, research links sugar-sweetened soft drinks and punches, but not milk or fruit juice, with excess body fatness in children.[50] Soft drinks amounting to just over two cans—the daily consumption of many adolescents—provide an extra 300 calories each day. Children everywhere seem to adore sugary soft drinks and punches, but these treats are best enjoyed in moderation and not as everyday replacements for milk, juice, or water.

PHYSICAL ACTIVITY

Active children have a better lipid profile and lower blood pressure than

TABLE C13-3 Recommended Diet and Physical Activity to Prevent Childhood Obesity

The Expert Committee of the American Medical Association recommends these dietary habits for children 2 to 18 years of age:

- Limit consumption of sugar-sweetened beverages, such as soft drinks and fruit-flavored punches.
- Eat recommended amounts of fruits and vegetables every day (2 to 4.5 cups per day based on age).
- Learn to eat age-appropriate portions of food.
- Eat foods low in energy density such as those high in fiber and/or water and modest in fat.
- Eat a nutritious breakfast every day.
- Eat a diet rich in calcium.
- Eat a diet balanced in recommended proportions for carbohydrate, fat, and protein.
- Eat a diet high in fiber.
- Eat together as a family as often as possible.
- Limit the frequency of restaurant meals.
- Limit television and other screen time to no more than 2 hours a day.

***2008 Physical Activity Guidelines for Americans* for Children:**

- Children and adolescents should do 60 minutes (1 hour) or more physical activity daily.
- Aerobic: Most of the 60 or more minutes a day should be either moderate- or vigorous-intensity aerobic physical activity and should include vigorous-intensity physical activity at least 3 days a week.[a]
- Muscle-strengthening: As part of their 60 minutes of daily physical activity, children and adolescents should include muscle-strengthening physical activity on at least 3 days of the week.
- Bone-strengthening: As part of their 60 or more minutes of daily physical activity, children and adolescents should include bone-strengthening physical activity on at least 3 days of the week.

[a]*Chapter 10 specified activities that characterize various intensity levels.*

Sources: U.S. Department of Agriculture and U.S. Department of Health and Human Services, 2008 Physical Activity Guidelines for Americans, *available at www.health.gov/paguidelines/default.asps; S. E. Barlow, Expert Committee recommendations regarding the prevention, assessment, and treatment of child and adolescent overweight and obesity: Summary report,* Pediatrics *120 (2007): S164–S192.*

more sedentary children. Additionally, the effects of combining a nutritious calorie-controlled diet with exercise can be seen in observable improvements in children's outer measures of health, such as reduced waist circumference and increased muscle strength, along with the inner benefits of greatly improved condition of the heart and arteries.[51] Opportunities to be physically active can include team, individual, and recreational activities (see Figure C13-4).

A new generation of computer games offers some amount of physical activity—they simulate sports games and participants must move their bodies to play them. These games are better than sedentary screen time, but better still is getting outside and playing the actual sport.[†52] Table C13-3 lists the *2008 Physical Activity Guidelines for Americans* that apply to children.

Finally, if efforts to stabilize the weight of the youngster fail, the family may benefit from the expertise of an experienced professional. Overweight in children must be sensitively addressed, however. Children are impressionable and can easily come to believe that their worth or lovability is somehow tied to their weight. A registered dietitian or a credentialed childhood weight-loss program may provide assistance.

[†]*For example, Wii by Nintendo.*

FIGURE C13-4 Physical Activity Pyramid for Kids

Preschoolers (2 to 5 years)

Games in the yard or park
Family walks after dinner
Playing with the dog
Dancing freestyle
Tumbling and gymnastics
T-ball
Playing catch
Family bike rides
Building a snowman
Family swimming at the pool or beach
Playing hide-and-seek

Older children (6 to 12 years)

Throwing a Frisbee
Jumping rope
Bicycling
Playing games and sports such as soccer, softball, baseball, and basketball
Rollerblading
Running
Weight training with light weights
Dancing
Competitive swimming
Snowboarding or skiing
Family kayaking, canoeing, or surfing

DARLA'S EFFORTS AND GABBY'S FUTURE

"I'm achieving three of our goals now," says Darla, "and others are planned. First, I'm packing Gabby a healthy, tasty, lower-calorie lunch for school. It's easy to make ahead whole-grain sandwiches for the week and freeze them and then toss one into a lunch bag with a low-fat yogurt, or low-fat cheese sticks, and water (not soda!). I'm also including some snacks of good-for-her foods that she loves, like baby carrots and raisins, to tempt her away from the granola bar machine on some days.

"Second, because we both have a sweet tooth, I keep ready-to-eat snacks of fresh fruit, like grapes and strawberries, in clear plastic containers on a refrigerator shelf at eye level. Third, although I work days and go to school four nights a week, we have started a new tradition: family meal night each Friday at 6:00 sharp. Gabby and I choose the menu during the week and look forward to making dinner together. We find it easier to talk about healthy eating as we cook, and she doesn't feel threatened. We also switched from full-sized dinnerware to pretty new luncheon-sized plates and small dessert-sized bowls. Gabby was charmed with the bright colors, and we both find the smaller portions just as satisfying.

"Although my daughter's idea of a good vegetable has always been a fried potato, she's gradually opening up to trying new foods, which is goal number four. During Friday meal preparation, she's tried bites of broccoli, green beans—even squash! French fries are now just an occasional treat when we eat out.

"Goal number five has proved harder: we must start walking together, but when? I need to let her see that I am serious about my personal fitness, but I'm tired after work and my studies gobble my time. To get Gabby moving after school, I've offered her credits toward her bike in exchange for physical chores, such as raking, planting flowers, and washing the car—and when she gets her bike, she'll be active while riding it, too. Today though, rain or shine, tired or not, I'm going to pull on my running shoes and walk around our neighborhood. And I hope Gabby will join me.

"I love my smart, stubborn, sturdy girl—chubby or lean! But I know her future will be shaped by what we are doing right now. She will grow into her weight if we can hold the line with our new healthy habits. I see her potential to do great things, and what she is learning today about taking care of herself she can pass on to others—to her own children maybe." Darla smiles, "I am so happy we are in this together, and taking charge of our health."

Child, Teen, and Older Adult

14

DO YOU EVER . . .

- Or will you in the future provide nourishment to children?
- Suspect that symptoms you feel may be from a food allergy?
- Think that teenagers are old enough to decide for themselves what to eat?
- Wonder whether good nutrition can help you live longer?

Keep reading . . .

Macara, Andrew (Contemporary Artist)/Private Collection/The Bridgeman Art Library International.

Learning Objectives

To find learning objective topics in this chapter, look for text headings with a corresponding "LO" number above the heading. After completing this chapter, you should be able to accomplish the following:

LO 14.1 Discuss how a toddler's nutritional needs differ from an adult's needs.

LO 14.2 Distinguish among a food allergy, food intolerance, and food aversion, and describe how they can impact the diet.

LO 14.3 Explain ways in which a teenager's choice of soda over milk or soy milk may jeopardize nutritional health.

LO 14.4 Discuss the importance of physical activity in the later years.

LO 14.5 Outline food-related factors that can predict malnutrition in older adults.

LO 14.6 Design a healthy meal plan for an elderly widower with a fixed income.

LO 14.7 Describe several specific drug-nutrient interactions, and name some herbs that may interfere with medication.

To grow and to function well in the adult world, children need a firm background of sound eating habits, which begin during babyhood with the introduction of solid foods. At that point, the person's nutrition story has just begun; the plot thickens. Nutrient needs change in childhood and throughout life, depending on the rate of growth, gender, activities, and many other factors. Nutrient needs also vary from individual to individual, but generalizations are possible and useful.

In a national assessment of children's diets in the United States, the great majority (81 percent) ranked "poor" or "needing improvement."* The consequences of such diets may not be evident to the casual observer, but nutritionists know that nutrient deficiencies during growth often have far-reaching effects on physical and mental development. Likewise, dietary excesses during childhood often set up a life-long struggle against obesity and chronic diseases. Anyone who cares about children in their lives, now or in the future, would profit from knowing how to provide the nutrients that children require to reach their potential, while setting patterns that support health through life.

LO 14.1, 14.2

Early and Middle Childhood

Imagine growing 10 inches taller in just one year, as the average healthy infant does during the first dramatic year of life. At age 1, infants have just learned to stand and toddle, and growth has slowed by half; by 2 years, they can take long strides with solid confidence and are learning to run, jump, and climb. These accomplishments reflect the accumulation of a larger mass, greater density of bone and muscle tissue, and refinement of nervous system coordination. These same growth trends, a lengthening of the long bones and an increase in musculature, continue until adolescence but more slowly.

Mentally, too, the child is making rapid advances, and proper nutrition is critical to normal brain development. The child malnourished at age 3 often demonstrates diminished mental capacities compared with peers at age 11.

Feeding a Healthy Young Child

At no time in life does the human diet change faster than during the second year. From 12 to 24 months, a child's diet changes from infant foods consisting of mostly formula or breast milk to mostly modified adult foods. This doesn't mean, of course, that milk loses its importance in the toddler's diet—it remains a central source of calcium, protein, and other nutrients. Nevertheless, the rapid growth and changing body composition (see Figure 14-1) during this remarkable period demand more nutrients than can be provided by milk alone. Further, the toddling years are marked by bustling activity made possible by new muscle tissue and refined neuromuscular coordination. To support both their activity and growth, toddlers need nutrients and plenty of them.

Appetite Regulation An infant's appetite decreases markedly near the first birthday and fluctuates thereafter. At times children seem insatiable, and at other times they seem to live on air and water. Parents and other caregivers need not worry: given an ample selection of nutritious foods at regular intervals, internal appetite regulation in healthy, normal-weight children guarantees that their overall energy intakes remain remarkably constant and will be right for each stage of growth.[1†]

This ideal situation depends upon the relegation of low-nutrient, high-calorie foods to the status of treats, however. Today's children too often consume a constant stream of tempting foods high in added sugars, saturated fat, refined grains, and calories throughout the day, short-circuiting normal hunger and satiety cues. Children who receive regularly timed snacks and meals of a variety of nutritious

CONCEPT LINK 14-1

The *Dietary Guidelines for Americans* appeared in Chapter 2, page 35.

*As measured by the Healthy Eating Index, a diet assessment tool that measures compliance with the *Dietary Guidelines for Americans* (Chapter 2).

†Reference notes are found in Appendix F.

FIGURE 14-1 Composition of Weight Gain, Infants and Toddlers

These graphs demonstrate that a young infant deposits much more fat than lean tissue, but a toddler deposits more lean than fat. Water follows lean tissue, demonstrated by the water gains in the toddler. You can see that the body shape of a 1-year-old (left photo) changes dramatically by age 2 (right photo). The 2-year-old has lost much baby fat; the muscles (especially in the back, buttocks, and legs) have firmed and strengthened; and the leg bones have lengthened.

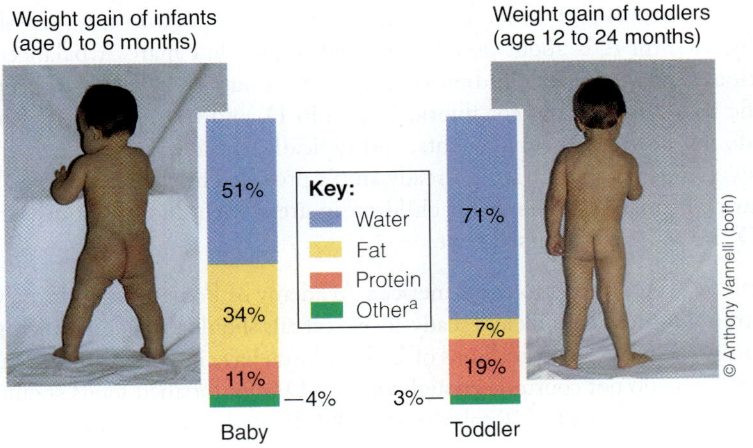

[a]"Other" consists of carbohydrate and minerals.

Source: Data from K. L. McCohany and M. F. Picciano, How to grow a healthy toddler—12 to 24 months, Nutrition Today *38 (2003): 156–163.*

foods, with only occasional special treats, often are those who gain weight appropriately and grow normally.[2] The *Dietary Guidelines for Americans* are safe and appropriate goals for the diets of healthy children 2 years of age and older to provide nutrients and energy needed for growth without excesses.

Energy Individual children's energy needs vary widely, depending on their growth and physical activity. On average, though, a 1-year-old child needs about 800 calories a day; at age 6, the child needs about 800 calories more. By age 10, about 1,800 calories a day support normal growth and activity without causing excess storage of body fat. As children age, the total number of calories needed increases, but per pound of body weight, the need declines from the extraordinarily high demand of infancy. Table 14-1 shows that both age and activity levels help to determine calorie needs in children.

Some children, notably those fed a vegan diet, may have difficulty meeting their energy needs. Whole grains, many kinds of vegetables, and fruits provide plenty of fiber and other goodies, but their bulk may make them too low in calories to support growth. Soy products, other legumes, and nut or seed butters offer more concentrated sources of energy and nutrients to support optimal growth and development.[3]

Protein The total amount of protein needed increases somewhat as a child grows larger. On a pound-for-pound basis, however, the older child's need for protein *decreases* slightly relative to the younger child's need (see the DRI values, inside front cover). Protein needs of children are well covered by typical U.S. diets and well-planned vegetarian diets.

Carbohydrate and Fiber Glucose use by the brain sets the carbohydrate intake recommendations. A 1-year-old's brain is large relative to the size of the body, so the glucose demanded by the 1-year-old falls in the adult range (see inside front cover).[4] Fiber recommendations derive from adult intakes and should be adjusted downward for children who are picky eaters and take in little energy (see the margin).

TABLE 14-1 Estimated Daily Calorie Needs for Children

Children	Sedentary[a]	Active[b]
2 to 3 yr	1,000	1,400
Females		
4 to 8 yr	1,200	1,800
9 to 13 yr	1,600	2,200
Males		
4 to 8 yr	1,400	2,000
9 to 13 yr	1,800	2,600

[a]*Sedentary describes a lifestyle that includes only the activities typical of day-to-day life.*

[b]*Active describes a lifestyle that includes at least 60 minutes per day of moderate physical activity (equivalent to walking more than 3 miles per day at 3 to 4 miles per hour) in addition to the activities of day-to-day life.*

- DRI estimated energy requirements for infants and children derive from values for weight, age, physical activity, and other parameters (see Appendix H).

CONCEPT LINK 14-2

For more on vegetarian diets during growth and development, see Controversy 6, page 219.

- Fiber recommendations for children:

Age (yr)	*fiber (g)*
1–3	*19*
4–8	*25*
9–13	
Boys	*31*
Girls	*26*
14–18	
Boys	*38*
Girls	*26*

Source: Position of the American Dietetic Association: Nutrition guidance for healthy children ages 2 to 11 years, Journal of the American Dietetic Association 108 (2008): 1038–1047.

- The DRI range for total fat intakes:
  - *30 to 40% of energy for children 1 to 3 years of age.*
  - *25 to 35% of energy for children 4 to 18 years of age.*

Fat and Fatty Acids Keeping fat intake within bounds helps to control saturated fat and so may help protect children from developing early signs of adult diseases. Taken to extremes, however, a low-fat diet can lack essential nutrients and energy needed for growth. The essential fatty acids are critical to proper development of nerve, eye, and other tissues.

Children's small stomachs can hold only so much food, and fat provides a concentrated source of food energy needed for growth. The DRI recommended range for fat in a child's diet (see the margin) assumes that energy is sufficient.[5] Specific DRI recommendations are on the inside front cover.

The Need for Vitamins and Minerals As a child grows larger, so does the demand for vitamins and minerals. On a pound-for-pound basis, a 5-year-old's need for, say, vitamin A is about double the need of an adult man. A balanced diet of nutritious foods can meet children's needs for most nutrients, with the exceptions of specific recommendations for fluoride, vitamin D, and iron. Well-nourished children do not need other supplements, and typically, those who receive them end up with extra amounts of nutrients already amply provided by their diets.[6] For fluoride, pediatricians may prescribe it for children in areas with fluoride-poor water; vitamin D and iron are discussed next.

Vitamin D According to the American Academy of Pediatrics, children's intakes of vitamin D–fortified milk and ready-to-eat cereals should provide 10 micrograms of vitamin D each day. Many millions of U.S. children have intakes below this amount.[7] Children who do not consume enough vitamin D from fortified foods should receive a vitamin D supplement of 10 micrograms (400 IU on labels) per day.[8]

Iron As for iron, iron deficiency is a major problem worldwide and is prevalent in U.S. and Canadian toddlers 1 to 3 years of age.[9] During the second year of life, toddlers progress from a diet of iron-rich infant foods such as breast milk, iron-fortified formula, and iron-fortified infant cereal to a diet of adult foods and iron-poor cow's milk. Their stores of iron from birth are exhausted, but their rapid growth demands new red blood cells to fill a larger volume of blood. Compounding the problem is the variability in toddlers' appetites: sometimes 2-year-olds are finicky, sometimes they eat voraciously, and they may go through periods of preferring milk and juice while rejecting solid foods for a time. All of these factors—switching to whole milk and unfortified foods, diminished iron stores, and unreliable food consumption—make iron deficiency likely at a time when iron is critically needed for normal brain growth and development. A later section comes back to iron deficiency and its consequences.

To prevent iron deficiency, children's foods must deliver 7 to 10 milligrams of iron per day. To achieve this goal, snacks and meals should include iron-rich foods. Milk intake, though critical for the calcium needed for dense, healthy bones, should not exceed daily recommendations to avoid the displacing of lean meats, fish, poultry, eggs, legumes, and whole-grain or enriched grain products from the diet. Table 14-2 lists some iron-rich foods that many children like to eat.

TABLE 14-2 Iron-Rich Foods Kids Like[a]

Breads, Cereals, and Grains
Canned macaroni (½ c)
Canned spaghetti (½ c)
Cream of wheat (½ c)
Fortified dry cereals (1 oz)[b]
Noodles, rice, or barley (½ c)
Tortillas (1 flour or whole wheat, 2 corn)
Whole-wheat, enriched, or fortified bread (1 slice)
Vegetables
Cooked mung bean sprouts or snow peas (½ c)[c]
Cooked mushrooms (½ c)
Green peas (½ c)
Mixed vegetable juice (1 c)
Fruits
Canned plums (3 plums)
Cooked dried apricots (¼ c)
Dried peaches (4 halves)
Raisins (1 tbs)
Meats and Legumes
Bean dip (¼ c)
Canned pork and beans (⅓ c)
Lean chopped roast beef or cooked ground beef (1 oz)
Liverwurst on crackers (½ oz)
Meat casseroles (½ c)
Mild chili or other bean/meat dishes (¼ c)
Peanut butter and jelly sandwich (½ sandwich)
Sloppy joes (½ sandwich)

[a]*Each serving provides at least 1 milligram iron, or one-tenth of a child's iron recommendation. Vitamin C–rich foods included with these snacks increase iron absorption.*

[b]*Some fortified breakfast cereals contain more than 10 milligrams iron per half-cup serving (read the labels).*

[c]*Raw sprouts may pose a bacterial hazard to young children.*

Planning Children's Meals To provide all the needed nutrients, children's meals should include a variety of foods from each food group in amounts suited to their appetites and needs. MyPyramid for Preschoolers (2 to 5 years) and MyPyramid for Kids (6 to 11 years), shown in Figure 14-2 (see page 536), demonstrate patterns for planning nutritious meals for children who need 1,200 and 1,800 calories per day.‡ Table 14-3 translates other calorie levels into daily food intakes from each food group.

KEY POINT Other than specific recommendations for fluoride, vitamin D, and iron, well-fed children do not need supplements. The DRI recommended intakes, the *Dietary Guidelines for Americans,* and *MyPyramid* establish food patterns that provide adequate nourishment for growth without obesity.

‡MyPyramid for Preschoolers (2 to 5 years) and MyPyramid for Kids (6 to 11 years) are available online at www.mypyramid.gov.

TABLE 14-3 Recommended Daily Amounts from Each Food Group (1,000 to 1,800 Calories)

Food Group	1,000 cal	1,200 cal	1,400 cal	1,600 cal	1,800 cal
Fruits	1 c	1 c	1½ c	1½ c	1½ c
Vegetables	1 c	1½ c	1½ c	2 c	2½ c
Grains	3 oz	4 oz	5 oz	5 oz	6 oz
Meat and legumes	2 oz	3 oz	4 oz	5 oz	5 oz
Milk	2 c	2 c	2 c	3 c	3 c
Oils	3 tsp	3 tsp	3 tsp	4 tsp	5 tsp

Note: The discretionary calorie allowance for these patterns is about 100 calories.

Mealtimes and Snacking

The childhood years are the parents' last chance to influence their child's food choices.[10] Appropriate eating habits and attitudes toward food, developed in childhood, can help future adults emerge with healthy habits that reduce risks of chronic diseases in later life. The challenge is to deliver nutrients in the form of meals and snacks that are both nutritious and appealing so that children will learn to enjoy a variety of foods that best support health.

Current U.S. Children's Food Intakes A comprehensive survey, called the Feeding Infants and Toddlers Study, assessed the food and nutrient intakes of more than 3,000 infants and toddlers.[11] The survey found most infants take in too few fruits and vegetables, and in fact, on a typical day, about 25 percent of those older than 9 months take in none at all.[12] By age 15 months, one vegetable and one fruit stand out as predominant: French fries and bananas, neither a particularly rich source of many needed nutrients. Most children take in too little vitamin E, calcium, magnesium, potassium, and fiber and too much sodium and saturated fat for health.[13] Children's tastes and preferences often lean toward nutrient-poor selections, and providing the nutritious foods they need can prove challenging.

Dealing with Children's Preferences Many children prefer sweet fruits and mild-flavored vegetables served raw or undercooked and crunchy and easy to eat. Cooked foods should be served warm, not hot, because a child's mouth is much more sensitive than an adult's. The flavors should be mild because a child has more taste buds. Smooth, bland, familiar foods such as cooked cereals, mashed potatoes, and soft pasta are often well received.[14]

Little children prefer small portions of food served at little tables. If offered large portions, children may fill up on favorite foods, ignoring others. Toddlers often go on food jags—consecutive days of eating only one or two favored foods. For food jags lasting a week or so, make no response, because 2-year-olds regard any form of attention as a reward. After two weeks of serving the favored foods, try serving small portions of many foods, including the favored items. Invite the child's friends to occasional meals and make other foods as attractive as possible.

Bribing a child to eat certain foods by, for example, allowing extra television time as a reward for eating vegetables often fails to produce the desired effect: the child will likely *not* develop a preference for those foods. Likewise, when children are forbidden to eat favorite foods, they yearn for them more—the reverse of the well-meaning caregiver's goal. Include favorites as occasional treats.

Treats Versus Dinner This is not to say that children cannot enjoy occasional treats of high-calorie foods, but such treats should also be nutritious. From the milk

FIGURE 14-2 MyPyramid for Preschoolers and for Kids

Grains	Vegetables	Fruits	Milk	Meat & Beans
Make half your grains whole	Vary your veggies	Focus on fruits	Get your calcium-rich foods	Go lean with protein
Start smart with breakfast. Look for whole-grain cereals. Just because bread is brown doesn't mean it's whole grain. Search the ingredients list to make sure the first word is "whole" (like "whole wheat").	Color your plate with all kinds of great-tasting veggies. What's green and orange and tastes good? Veggies! Go dark green with broccoli and spinach, or try orange ones like carrots and sweet potatoes.	Fruits are nature's treats—sweet and delicious. Go easy on juice and make sure it's 100%.	Move to the milk group to get your calcium. Calcium builds strong bones. Look at the carton or container to make sure your milk, yogurt, or cheese is low fat or fat-free.	Eat lean or low-fat meat, chicken, turkey, and fish. Ask for it baked, broiled, or grilled—not fried. It's nutty, but true. Nuts, seeds, peas, and beans are all great sources of protein, too.
For a 1,200-calorie diet (suitable for many preschoolers ages 2 to 5), include the amounts below from each food group.				
Eat 4 oz. every day; at least half should be whole	Eat 1 1/2 cups every day	Eat 1 cup every day	Get 2 cups every day	Eat 3 oz. every day
For an 1,800-calorie diet (suitable for many children ages 6 to 11), include the amounts below from each food group.				
Eat 6 oz. every day; at least half should be whole	Eat 2 1/2 cups every day	Eat 1 1/2 cups every day	Get 3 cups every day; for kids ages 6 to 8, it's 2 cups	Eat 5 oz. every day

Oils Oils are not a food group, but you need some for good health. Get your oils from fish, nuts, and liquid oils such as corn oil, soybean oil, and canola oil.

Find your balance between food and fun

- Move more. Aim for at least 60 minutes every day, or most days.
- Walk, dance, bike, rollerblade—it all counts. How great is that!

Fats and sugars—know your limits

- Get your facts and sugar smarts from the Nutrition Facts label.
- Limit solid fats as well as foods that contain them.
- Choose food and beverages low in added sugars and other caloric sweeteners.

group, ice cream or pudding is good now and then; from the grains group, whole-grain or enriched cakes, oatmeal cookies, snack crackers, or even small doughnuts are an acceptable *occasional* addition to a nutritious diet. These foods encourage a child to learn that pleasure in eating is important. A steady diet of these treats, however, leads only to nutrient deficiencies, obesity, or both.

Fear of New Foods A fear of new foods, **food neophobia,** is almost universal among toddlers and preschoolers.[15] Without so much as a taste, the child rejects the new food on sight, but the reason why this occurs isn't fully known. The child may remember tasting and disliking foods with a similar appearance or aroma. Or, food neophobia may be a protective mechanism that prevented curious toddlers of ages past from tasting toxic plants in their environment. Regardless of its causes, food neophobia causes much distress among parents striving to nourish their children. Thankfully, the fear diminishes as a child matures, often disappearing completely by adolescence.[16]

In the meanwhile, some practical tips can help. First, keep an upbeat but persistent attitude: a child may ignore or reject a food the first 14 times it is offered, but on the 15th may suddenly recognize it as a familiar, accepted food in the diet. Parents' negative attention or attempts to force "just a taste" before the child is ready interrupts this learning process. Offering new foods at the beginning of a meal when the child is hungry often works best, as does serving the child samples of the same foods that adults are enjoying; children follow the examples of adults.

Child Preferences Versus Parental Authority Just as parents are entitled to their likes and dislikes, a child who genuinely and consistently rejects a food should be allowed the same privilege. Also, children should be believed when they say they are full: the "clean-your-plate" dictum should be stamped out for all time.[17] Children who are forced to override their own satiety signals are in training for obesity.

A bright, unhurried atmosphere free of conflict is conducive to good appetite and provides a climate in which a child can learn to enjoy eating. Parents who beg, cajole, and demand that their children eat make power struggles inevitable. A child may find mealtimes unbearable if they are accompanied by a barrage of accusations—"Susie, your hands are filthy . . . your report card . . . and clean your plate!" The child's stomach recoils as both body and mind react to stress of this kind.

Honoring children's preferences does not mean allowing them to dictate the diet, however, because children naturally prefer fatty, sugary, and salty foods, such as heavily advertised snack chips, cookies, crackers, fast foods, and sugary cereals and drinks. When children's tastes are allowed to rule the family's pantry, everyone's nutrition suffers: parents of young children consume much more fat and saturated fat than do adults without children.[18] The responsibility for *what* the child is offered to eat lies squarely with the adult caregiver, but the child should be allowed to decide *how much* and even *whether* to eat.

Many parents overlook perhaps the single most important influence on their child's food habits—their own habits.[19] Parents who don't prepare, serve, and eat carrots shouldn't be surprised when their child refuses to eat carrots.

Snacking As mentioned, parents often find that their children snack so much that they are not hungry at mealtimes. This is not a problem if children are taught how to snack—nutritious snacks are just as health promoting as small meals. Keep snack foods simple and available: milk, cheese, crackers, fruit, vegetable sticks, yogurt, peanut butter sandwiches, and whole-grain cereal.

Restaurant Choices It takes some artful maneuvering to choose nutritious restaurant meals that children can enjoy. Children's menus reliably offer fatty, salty sandwiches, "nuggets," and French fries. For better choices:

- ask to split a regular meal among several children.
- choose from appetizers, soups, salads, and side dishes.
- order vegetable toppings and lean meats on pizza (skip the sausages and hamburger); reduce the saturated fat by requesting half the cheese.
- request water, fat-free milk, or fruit juice (not punch) for beverages.

Parents who make nutritious restaurant choices for themselves also set good examples for children.

© Myrleen Ferguson Cate/PhotoEdit

Little children like to eat small portions of food at little tables.

- How to be a role model:
  - *Set a good example: Eat fruits, vegetables, whole grains, and other nutritious foods when dining with children.*
  - *Shop and cook together: Let the child help pick out and prepare nutritious foods.*
  - *Reward yourself and children with attention, not food: Save treats for dessert.*
  - *Turn off the television: Sit down and eat together.*
  - *Share conversation at mealtimes: Listen to the child.*
  - *Play together: Encourage physical activity.*

food neophobia (NEE-oh-FOE-bee-ah) the fear of trying new foods, common among toddlers.

CONCEPT LINK 14-3

Actions to prevent choking and to save a life should choking occur were discussed in Chapter 3, page 91. Foods that often cause choking are listed on page 519.

Choking A child who is choking may make no sound, so an adult should keep an eye on children when they are eating. A child who is coughing most often dislodges the food and recovers without help. To prevent choking, encourage the child to sit when eating—choking is more likely when children are running or reclining. Round foods such as grapes, nuts, hard candies, and pieces of hot dog can become lodged in a child's small windpipe. Other potentially dangerous foods include tough meat chunks, popcorn, chips, and peanut butter eaten by the spoonful.

Food Skills Children love to be included in meal preparation, and they like to eat foods they helped to prepare (see Table 14-4). A positive experience is most likely when tasks match developmental abilities and are undertaken in a spirit of enthusiasm and enjoyment, not criticism or drudgery. Praise for a job well done (or at least well attempted) expands a child's sense of pride and helps to develop skills and positive feelings toward healthy foods.

TABLE 14-4 Food Skills of Preschool Children[a]

Age 1 to 2 years, when large muscles develop:

- Uses a spoon
- Helps feed self
- Lifts and drinks from a cup
- Helps scrub fruits and vegetables, tear lettuce or greens, snap green beans, or dip foods
- Wipes tables
- Places empty paper and plastic containers in recycle bins

Age 3 years, when medium hand muscles develop:

- Spears food with a fork
- Feeds self independently
- Adds ingredients to pancake batters, cookie recipes, salads, or other mixed dishes
- Helps wrap, pour, mix, shake, stir, or spread foods
- Helps crack nuts with supervision

Age 4 years, when small finger muscles develop:

- Uses all utensils and napkin
- Helps roll, juice, or mash foods
- Helps measure dry ingredients
- Cracks egg shells
- Helps make sandwiches and toss salads
- Peels foods such as hard-boiled eggs and bananas

Age 5 years, when fine coordination of fingers and hands develops:

- Measures liquids
- Helps grind, grate, and cut (soft foods with dull knife)
- Uses hand mixer with supervision

[a]These ages are approximate. Healthy, normal children develop at their own pace.

Source: Adapted from MyPyramid for Preschoolers, Kitchen Activities, available at www.mypyramid.gov.

KEY POINT Healthy eating habits and positive relationships with food are learned in childhood. Parents teach children best by example. Choking can often be avoided by supervision during meals and avoiding hazardous foods.

How Do Nutrient Deficiencies Impair a Child's Brain?

A child who suffers from nutrient deficiencies exhibits physical and behavioral symptoms: the child feels sick and out of sorts. Such children may be irritable, aggressive, and disagreeable or sad and withdrawn. They may be labeled "hyperactive," "depressed," or "unlikable." Diet-behavior connections are of keen interest to caregivers who both feed children and live with them.

Iron plays key roles in many molecules of the brain and nervous system. An iron deficit in the brain, even before anemia shows up in the blood, has well-known and widespread effects on children's behavior and intellectual performance.[20] The motivation to persist at intellectually challenging tasks is dampened, attention span shortened, and overall intellectual performance reduced. Administering iron resolves some of the problems, but others may persist for ten years after treatment.[21] Both iron deficit and the poverty and poor health often associated with it may contribute to these effects.[22] Despite public health efforts to prevent iron deficiency, such as food fortification, iron deficiency remains a key problem among U.S. children and adolescents.

Only a health-care provider, such as a registered dietitian, should make the decision to give a child a single-nutrient iron supplement. Iron is toxic and overdoses can easily injure or even kill a toddler or child who accidentally ingests iron pills. All supplements should be kept out of children's reach.

KEY POINT Iron deficiency causes abnormalities in physical and mental health and behavior. Iron toxicity poses a threat to children.

The Problem of Lead

More than 300,000 children in the United States, most under the age of 6, have blood lead concentrations high enough to cause mental, behavioral, and other health problems.[23] Lead is an indestructible metal element; once inside, the body cannot alter it or easily excrete it.

Sources of Lead Babies love to explore and put everything into their mouths, including chips of old lead paint, pieces of metal that contain lead, and other unlikely substances. Lead may also leach into a home's drinking water supply from old lead pipes and end up in a baby's formula and the family's beverages. In older children, lead dust mixed into outdoor soil can stick to clothing and hands and eventually be consumed. Appreciable amounts of lead have shown up in some chewable vitamins and other children's medications.[24] Once exposed to lead, infants and young children absorb 5 to 10 times as much of the toxin as adults do.

© Tony Freeman/PhotoEdit

Old paint is the main source of lead in most children's lives.

Harm from Lead Lead can build up so silently in a child's body that caregivers may not notice its symptoms until much later, after toxicity has damaged organs. Tragically, once symptoms set in, medical treatments may not reverse all of the functional damage, some of which may linger long beyond childhood.[25]

Impaired thinking, reasoning, perception, and other academic skills, as well as hearing impairment, kidney malfunction, and decreased growth, are associated with even very low blood lead levels in children.[26] Higher levels are associated with scholastic failures, antisocial or hyperactive behavior, and possibly a smaller brain size attained by adulthood.[27] Among adolescents, early lead exposure is linked with lower scores on IQ tests and more arrests for violent crimes.[28] In older women, even low levels of lead in the bones, a measure of lifetime lead exposure, correlates with worsened mental performance.[29]

As lead toxicity slowly injures the kidneys, nerves, brain, bone marrow, and other organs, the child may slip into coma, have convulsions, and may even die if an accurate diagnosis is not made in time. Older children with high blood lead may be suffering physical consequences but be mislabeled as delinquent, aggressive, or learning disabled.

Lead and Nutrient Interactions Malnutrition makes lead poisoning especially likely to occur because children absorb more lead from empty stomachs or if they lack calcium, zinc, vitamin C, vitamin D, or iron. A child with iron-deficiency anemia is 3 times as likely to have elevated blood lead as a child with normal iron status. The chemical properties of lead are similar to those of nutrient minerals like iron, calcium, and zinc, and lead displaces these minerals from their sites of action in body cells but cannot perform their biological functions. Even slight iron and zinc deficiencies may open the door to lead toxicity severe enough to lower a child's scores on tests of verbal ability while increasing feelings of anxiety.[30]

Bans on leaded gasoline, leaded house paint, and lead-soldered food cans have dramatically reduced the amount of lead in the U.S. environment in past decades and have produced a steady decline in children's average blood lead concentrations. However, lead still remains a threat in older communities of homes with lead pipes and layers of old lead paint. Some tips for avoiding lead toxicity are offered in Table 14-5.

Did You Know?

The Environmental Protection Agency (EPA) provides a toll-free hotline for lead information: 1-800-LEAD-FYI (1-800-532-3394).

TABLE 14-5 Steps to Prevent Lead Poisoning

To protect children:

- If your home was built before 1978, wash floors, windowsills, and other surfaces weekly with warm water and detergent to remove dust released by old lead paint; clean up flaking paint chips immediately.
- Feed children balanced, timely meals with ample iron and calcium.
- Prevent children from chewing on old painted surfaces.
- Wash children's hands, bottles, and toys often.
- Wipe soil off shoes before entering the home.
- Ask a pediatrician whether your child should be tested for lead.

To safeguard yourself:

- Avoid daily use of handmade, imported, or old ceramic mugs or pitchers for hot or acidic beverages, such as juices, coffee, or tea. Commercially made U.S. ceramic, porcelain, and glass dishes or cups are safe. If ceramic dishes or cups become chalky, use them for decorative purposes only.
- Do not use lead crystal decanters for storing alcoholic or other beverages.
- If your home is old and may have lead pipes, run the water for a minute before using, especially before the first use in the morning.
- Remove lead foil from wine bottles, and wipe the mouth of the bottle before pouring.

KEY POINT Blood lead levels have declined dramatically over past decades but even low lead levels can inflict serious damage on growing children. Awareness of the remaining sources of lead can further reduce lead poisoning.

Food Allergy, Intolerance, and Aversion

Parents, when asked, frequently blame food **allergy** for physical and behavioral abnormalities in children, but when children are tested, just 6 to 8 percent are diagnosed with true food allergies.[31] Food allergies affect only about 1 or 2 percent of the adult population.[32] The prevalence of food allergy, especially peanut allergy, is on the rise, but no one knows exactly why.[33] About 20 percent of children with peanut allergies "grow out" of them.

© William Berry, 2011/Shutterstock.com

Food Allergy A true food allergy occurs when a food protein or other large molecule enters body tissues and triggers an immune response. Most food proteins are dismantled to smaller fragments in the digestive tract before absorption, but some larger fragments enter the bloodstream before being fully digested. The immune system of an allergic person reacts to the foreign molecules as it does to any other **antigen:** it releases **antibodies, histamine,** or other defensive agents to attack the invaders. In some people, the result is the life-threatening food allergy reaction of **anaphylactic shock.** Peanuts, tree nuts, milk, eggs, wheat, soybeans, fish, and shellfish are the foods most likely to trigger this extreme reaction, with peanuts, milk, eggs, and soy the most prevalent in children.[34]

If a child reacts to allergens with a life-threatening response, two courses of action are required: first, the child's family and school must guard against any ingestion of the allergen. Second, easy-to-administer doses of the life-saving drug **epinephrine** must be kept close at hand.

Allergen Ingestion Parents must teach the child which foods to avoid, but avoiding allergens can be tricky because they often sneak into foods in unexpected ways. For example, a pork chop (an innocent food) may be dipped in egg (egg allergy) and breaded (wheat allergy) before being fried in peanut oil (peanut allergy); marshmallow candies may contain egg whites; lunchmeats may contain milk protein binders; and so forth.

Invisible traces of allergen from, say, peanut butter left on tables, chairs, or other surfaces can easily contaminate the hands of a severely allergic child who may then unknowingly ingest them.[35] Even a trace can cause a life-threatening reaction. Scrupulous cleaning of surfaces with soaps and cleansers and regular hand washing by the allergic child can often prevent such an occurrence. By the way, the protein allergens of peanuts are not volatile—that is, they do not fly off the food into the air under normal conditions, such as when they are being eaten. The distinctive aroma of peanuts can alert people to their presence, but the aroma itself does not cause allergy—only ingestion of peanut protein can do so.[36]

Caregivers of allergic children must pack safe lunches and snacks at home and ask school officials to strictly enforce a "no-swapping" policy in the lunchroom. To prevent nutrient deficiencies, caregivers must also provide adequate substitutes that supply the essential nutrients in the omitted foods.[37] For example, a child allergic to milk must be supplied with calcium from fortified foods, such as calcium-rich orange juice.

A rumor has it that severe food allergy can be improved by ingestion of small amounts of the offending food. In truth, strictly controlled oral therapy under medical supervision has worked in research settings, but it often brings on significant allergic symptoms.[38] Those attempting such therapy on their own put themselves at risk.

Food Labels Food labels must announce the presence of common allergens in plain language, using common names of the eight foods most likely to cause allergic reactions.[39] For example, a food containing "textured vegetable protein" must say "soy" on its label. Similarly, "casein," a protein in milk, must be identified as "milk." Food producers must also prevent cross-contamination during production

allergy an immune reaction to a foreign substance, such as a component of food. Also called *hypersensitivity* by researchers.

antigen a substance foreign to the body that elicits the formation of antibodies or an inflammation reaction from immune system cells. Food antigens are usually large proteins. Inflammation consists of local swelling and irritation and attracts white blood cells to the site. Also defined in Chapter 3.

antibodies large protein molecules that are produced in response to the presence of antigens to inactivate them. Also defined in Chapters 3 and 6.

histamine a substance that participates in causing inflammation; produced by cells of the immune system as part of a local immune reaction to an antigen.

anaphylactic (an-ah-feh-LACK-tick) **shock** a life-threatening whole-body allergic reaction to an offending substance.

epinephrine (epp-ih-NEFF-rin) a hormone of the adrenal gland that counteracts anaphylactic shock by opening the airways and maintaining heartbeat and blood pressure.

and clearly label the foods in which it is likely to occur, as Figure 14-3 demonstrates. Equipment used for making peanut butter must be scrupulously clean before being used to pulverize cashew nuts for cashew butter to protect unsuspecting consumers from peanut allergens.

Epinephrine The allergic child must learn to recognize the symptoms of impending anaphylactic shock, such as a tingling of the tongue, throat, or skin or difficulty breathing (see the margin). The responsible child and the school staff should be prepared to promptly (the sooner, the better) administer injections of epinephrine, which prevents anaphylaxis after exposure to the allergen.[40] Too many preventable deaths occur each year among people with food allergies who accidentally ingest the allergen but have no access to epinephrine or receive their dose too late.[41]

Detection of Food Allergy Allergies have one or two components. They *always* involve antibodies; they *sometimes* involve symptoms. Therefore, allergies cannot be diagnosed from symptoms alone. Anyone who has suffered anaphylaxis or other severe symptoms should not reintroduce suspected foods, but should undergo immediate medical testing.

An immediate allergic reaction is easy to identify because symptoms correlate with the time of eating the food. A delayed reaction, taking 24 hours or more, is more difficult to pinpoint. For mild suspected allergy symptoms, a good starting point is to keep a record of food intakes and symptoms. Then, eliminating suspected foods from the diet for a week or two and reintroducing them one at a time may help spot the allergen; an oral challenge test in which the foods are ground up and mixed with other foods or placed in capsules can prevent expectations from skewing the results. If the symptoms correlate with a food, then a blood test for elevated levels of food-specific antibodies and a skin prick test in which a clinician applies

© Polara Studios, Inc.

These eight normally wholesome foods—milk, shellfish, fish, peanuts, tree nuts, eggs, wheat, and soy—may cause life-threatening symptoms in people with allergies.

- Any of these symptoms can occur in minutes or hours after ingesting an allergen:
  - Airway: *difficulty breathing, wheezing, asthma.*
  - Digestive tract: *vomiting, abdominal cramps, diarrhea.*
  - Eyes: *irritated, reddened eyes.*
  - Mouth and throat: *tingling sensation, swelling of the tongue and throat.*
  - Skin: *hives, swelling, rashes.*
  - Other: *drop in blood pressure, loss of consciousness; in extreme reactions, death.*

FIGURE 14-3 A Food Allergy Warning Label

A food that contains, or could contain, even a trace amount of any of the most common food allergens must clearly say so on its label. For instance, if a product contains the milk protein casein, the label must say "contains milk," or the ingredients list must include "milk." The sunflower seeds below carry a warning about peanut allergy—traces of peanuts may have contaminated the seeds during processing.

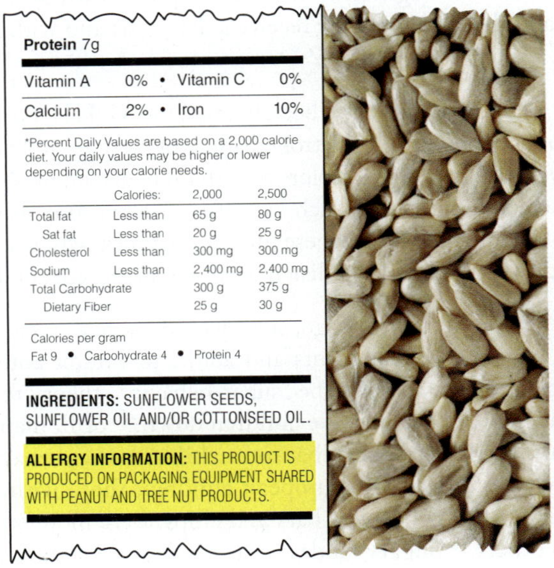

Glow Images/Getty Images

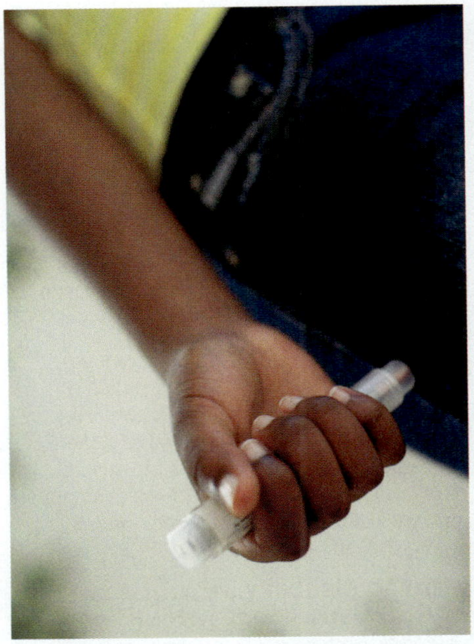

© Ian Hooton/Science Photo Library/Corbis

An epinephrine "pen" can deliver prompt life-saving treatment to a person suffering from anaphylactic shock.

droplets of food extracts to the skin and then lightly pricks or scratches the skin or other tests can confirm the allergy. False positive results can occur, but despite this failing, such tests can support or refute other evidence in making a diagnosis.[42]

Quick, easy, but scientific-sounding allergy quackery may deceive people into believing that everything from itchy skin to mental depression is caused by food allergies. Beware of "food sensitivity testing" offered by charlatans on the Internet or elsewhere. It involves fake blood or other tests that supposedly determine which foods to eat and which supplements the "patient" should buy from the quack to relieve the "allergy."

Technology may soon offer new solutions for those with food allergy. Drugs under development may interfere with the immune response that causes allergic reactions, but so far, they remain unavailable.[43] Through genetic engineering, scientists may one day banish allergens from peanuts, soybeans, and other foods to make them safer.[44]

CONCEPT LINK 14-4

Lactose intolerance was a topic of Chapter 4, pages 123 and 125.

Food Aversion and Intolerance A **food intolerance** is characterized by unpleasant symptoms that reliably occur after consumption of certain foods—lactose intolerance is an example. Unlike allergy, a food intolerance does not involve an immune response. A **food aversion** is an intense dislike of a food that may be a biological response to a food that once caused trouble. Parents are advised to watch for signs of food aversion and to take them seriously. Such a dislike may turn out to be a whim or fancy, but it may turn out to be an allergy or other valid reason to avoid a certain food. Don't prejudge. Test. Then, if an important staple food must be excluded from the diet, find other foods to provide the omitted nutrients.

Foods are often unjustly blamed when behavior problems arise, but children who are sick from any cause are likely to be cranky. The next section singles out one such type of misbehavior.

KEY POINT Food allergies can cause serious illness. Diagnosis is based on the presence of antibodies, and tests are imperative to determine whether allergy exists. Food aversions can be related to food allergies or to adverse reactions to food.

Can Diet Make a Child Hyperactive?

Attention-deficit/hyperactivity disorder (ADHD), or **hyperactivity,** is a **learning disability** that occurs in 5 to 10 percent of young, school-aged children—or in 1 to 3 in every classroom of 30 children.[45] ADHD is characterized by the chronic inability to pay attention, along with overly active behavior and poor impulse control (see the margin). It can delay growth, lead to academic failure, and cause major behavioral problems. Although some children improve with age, many reach the college years or adulthood before they receive a diagnosis and with it the possibility of treatment.

- A child with attention-deficit/hyperactivity disorder (ADHD) often:
  - *Has a short attention span, even while playing.*
  - *Has trouble with tasks that require sustained mental effort.*
  - *Has trouble learning and earns failing grades in school.*
  - *Has poor impulse control and acts physically or verbally before thinking.*
  - *Angers friends by not taking turns or playing by the rules.*
  - *Runs instead of walks, climbs instead of sitting still, talks excessively.*

These symptoms are clues to ADHD, but diagnosis depends on assessment by a knowledgeable clinician.

food intolerance an adverse reaction to a food or food additive not involving an immune response.

food aversion an intense dislike of a food, biological or psychological in nature, resulting from an illness or other negative experience associated with that food.

hyperactivity (in children) a syndrome characterized by inattention, impulsiveness, and excess motor activity; usually diagnosed before age 7, lasts six months or more, and usually does not entail mental illness or mental retardation. Properly called *attention-deficit/hyperactivity disorder (ADHD)*.

learning disability a condition resulting in an altered ability to learn basic cognitive skills such as reading, writing, and mathematics.

Food Allergies Food allergies have been blamed for ADHD, but research to date has shown no connection. A well-controlled study of close to 300 children suggests that food additives such as artificial colors or sodium benzoate preservative (or both) may worsen hyperactive symptoms such as inattention and impulsivity.[46] More research is needed to confirm or refute these findings but meanwhile, parents who wish to avoid such additives can find them listed with the ingredients on food labels.

Sugar and Behavior Many years ago, sugary foods were accused of causing children to become unruly and adolescents and adults to exhibit antisocial and even criminal behaviors. Science has put the "sugar-behavior" theory to rest; according to research, sugar may even calm some children down.[47] Still, many teachers, parents, grandparents, and others assert that some children react behaviorally to sugar. In a recent study of almost 8,000 European children, those with high intakes of sugary, fatty treats, such as chocolate bars and chips, were more often described as hyperactive than others.[48] Sugary foods clearly displace vegetables and other nutritious choices from the diet, and nutrient deficiencies are known causes of behavioral problems. Sugar itself, however, is unlikely to do so.

Inconsistent Care and Poverty Common sense says that all children get unruly and "hyper" at times. A child who often fills up on caffeinated colas and chocolate, misses lunch, becomes too cranky to nap, misses out on outdoor play, and spends hours in front of a television suffers stresses that can trigger chronic patterns of crankiness. This detrimental cycle resolves itself when the caregivers begin insisting on regular hours of sleep, regular mealtimes, a nutritious diet, and regular outdoor physical activity.

Hunger and poverty can cause a child's misbehavior and poor achievement; simply lifting the child from poverty often significantly improves behavior.[49] An estimated 12 million U.S. children are hungry at least some of the time. Such children often lack iron, magnesium, zinc, or omega-3 polyunsaturated fatty acids, and a link between these nutrient deficiencies and ADHD may be emerging.[50] Once the obvious causes of misbehavior are eliminated, a physician can recommend other strategies such as special educational programs or psychological counseling and, in many cases, prescription medication.[51]

- Cranky or rambunctious children may:
  - *Be chronically hungry.*
  - *Be overstimulated.*
  - *Consume too much caffeine from colas or chocolate.*
  - *Desire attention.*
  - *Lack exercise.*
  - *Lack sleep.*
- The Controversy section of this chapter lists caffeine amounts in common foods and beverages.
- Hunger issues are many; see Chapter 15.

KEY POINT Hyperactivity, properly named attention-deficit/hyperactivity disorder (ADHD), is not caused by food allergies or additives. Research disproves the sugar-hyperactivity idea, but temporary "hyper" behavior may reflect excess caffeine consumption or inconsistent care. Hunger and poverty may cause behavior problems.

Physical Activity, Television, and Children's Nutrition Problems

Physical activity and outdoor play contribute to health and vigor, yet the activity of U.S. children has declined over recent decades.[52] Children have become more sedentary, and sedentary children are more often overweight.[53] Almost half of the children in the United States exceed the recommended maximum television and other "screen time" of two hours a day, often without their parents' awareness.[54] Longer television time is linked with overweight in children, so parents would do well to monitor the television habits of their children.[55] Healthy children should never have television sets in their bedrooms.[56] The topic of childhood obesity is so pressing that Controversy 13 was devoted to it.

The Impact of Television on Nutrition Television viewing exerts four major adverse impacts on children's nutrition. First, it requires no energy above the resting level of expenditure. Second, it consumes time that could be spent in energetic play. Third, more television watching correlates with more between-meal snacking and with eating the high-calorie fatty and sugary foods most heavily advertised on children's programs.[57] Fourth, children who watch more than four hours of television a day, or watch during meals, are least likely to eat fruits and vegetables and most likely to be obese.[58]

CONCEPT LINK 14-5

The relationships between childhood obesity and chronic diseases along with the influence of food marketing to children were addressed in Controversy 13, page 524.

KEY POINT The nation's children are growing fatter and face increasing risks of diseases. Television viewing can contribute to obesity through lack of exercise and by promoting overconsumption of calorie-dense snacks.

Dental Caries

Dental caries are a serious public health problem afflicting the majority of people in the country, half by the age of 2, with a prevalence rate of 90 percent in some

dental caries decay of the teeth (*caries* means "rottenness").

FIGURE 14-4 Dental Caries

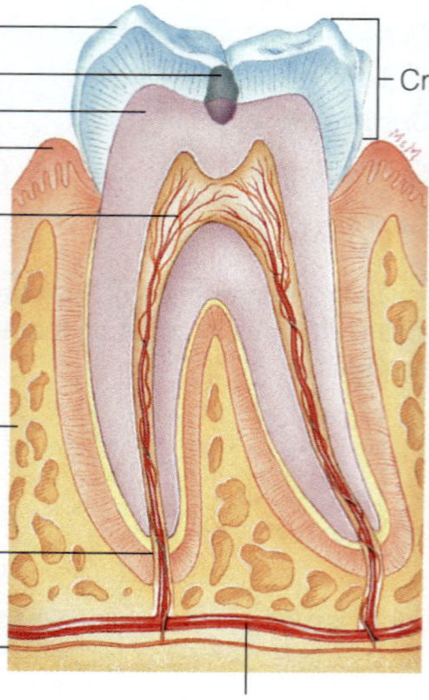

Caries begin when acid dissolves the enamel that covers the tooth. If not repaired, the decay may penetrate the dentin and spread into the pulp of the tooth, causing inflammation and an abscess.

groups.[59] A very lucky few *never* get dental caries because they have an inherited resistance; others have a sealant applied to their teeth during childhood to stop caries before they can begin. Another successful measure taken to reduce the incidence of dental decay is fluoridation of community water. Perhaps the greatest weapon against caries is simple oral hygiene. But diet has something to do with dental caries, too.

How Caries Develop Caries develop as acids produced by bacterial growth in the mouth eat into tooth enamel (see Figure 14-4). Bacteria form colonies in **plaque,** which sticks more and more firmly to tooth surfaces unless they are brushed, flossed, or scraped away. Eventually, the acid of plaque creates pits that deepen into cavities. The cavities can be treated by a dentist—the decay is removed and replaced with filling material. Scare stories that mercury-containing fillings can harm health are unfounded; the mercury in fillings is present in very small amounts and in a different form from the toxic methylmercury that contaminates many seafoods.[60]

Advanced Dental Disease Left alone, plaque works its way below the gum line until the acid erodes the roots of teeth and the jawbone in which they are embedded, loosening the teeth and leading to infections of the gums. Bacteria from inflamed, infected gums can then migrate by way of the bloodstream to other tissues such as the heart; researchers now suspect a link between these bacteria and heart disease.[61] Gum disease severe enough to threaten tooth loss afflicts the majority of our population by their later years.

Food and Caries Bacteria thrive on carbohydrate, producing acid for 20 to 30 minutes after carbohydrate exposure. Of prime importance is the length of time the teeth are exposed to carbohydrate, and this depends on the food's composition, how sticky it is, how long it lasts in the mouth, frequency of consumption, and especially on whether the teeth are brushed soon afterward. Table 14-6 lists foods of both high and low caries potential. Beverages such as soft drinks, orange juice, and sports drinks not only contain sugar but also have a low pH, and their acidic nature can erode the tooth enamel, weakening it. A growing preference for sugary soft

plaque (PLACK) a mass of microorganisms and their deposits on the surfaces of the teeth, a forerunner of dental caries and gum disease. The term *plaque* is also used in another connection—arterial plaque in atherosclerosis (see Chapter 11).

TABLE 14-6 The Caries Potential of Foods

Low Caries Potential	
These foods are less damaging to teeth:	
• Eggs, legumes	• Pizza
• Fresh fruit, fruits packed in water	• Popcorn, pretzels
• Lean meats, fish, poultry	• Sugarless gum and candy,[a] diet soft drinks
• Milk, cheese, plain yogurt	• Toast, hard rolls, bagels
• Most cooked and raw vegetables	
High Caries Potential	
Brush teeth after eating these foods:	
• Cakes, muffins, doughnuts, pies	• Jams, jellies, preserves
• Candied sweet potatoes	• Lunchmeats with added sugar
• Chocolate milk	• Meats or vegetables with sugary glazes
• Cookies, granola or "energy" bars, crackers	• Oatmeal, oat cereals, oatmeal baked goods[b]
• Dried fruits (raisins, figs, dates)	• Peanut butter with added sugar
• Frozen or flavored yogurt	• Potato and other snack chips
• Fruit juices or drinks	• Ready-to-eat sugared cereals
• Fruits in syrup	• Sugared gum, soft drinks, candies, honey, sugar, molasses, syrups
• Ice cream or ice milk	• Toaster pastries

[a]*Cariogenic bacteria cannot efficiently metabolize the sugar alcohols in these products, so they do not contribute to dental caries.*

[b]*The soluble fiber in oats makes this grain particularly sticky and therefore cariogenic.*

drinks or sports drinks instead of water to quench thirst throughout the day may explain why dental erosion is becoming more common.[62]

KEY POINT Carbohydrate-rich foods contribute to dental caries, a major U.S. health problem.

Is Breakfast Really the Most Important Meal of the Day for Children?

A nutritious breakfast is a central feature of a child's diet that supports healthy growth and development.[63] When a child consistently skips breakfast or is allowed to choose sugary foods (candy or marshmallows) in place of nourishing ones (whole-grain cereals), the child will fail to get enough of several nutrients. Nutrients missed from a skipped breakfast won't be "made up" at lunch and dinner, but will be left out completely that day.

Children who eat no breakfast are more likely to be overweight, snack on sweet and fatty foods, perform poorly in tasks requiring concentration, have shorter attention spans, achieve lower test scores, and be tardy or absent more often than their well-fed peers.[64] Common sense tells us that it is unreasonable to expect anyone to study and learn when no fuel has been provided. Even children who have eaten breakfast suffer from distracting hunger by late morning. Chronically underfed children suffer more intensely.

The U.S. government funds several programs for the purpose of providing nutritious, high-quality meals, including breakfast, to U.S. schoolchildren.[65] Children who eat school breakfast consume less fat and more magnesium during the day and are more replete with vitamin C and folate. When schools participate in federal school meal programs, students often improve not only in terms of nutrition but also in their academic, behavioral, emotional, and social performance. Attendance goes up, while tardiness declines.

KEY POINT Breakfast is critical to school performance. Not all children start the day with an adequate breakfast, but school breakfast programs help to fill the need.

- Breakfast ideas for rushed mornings:
  - *Make ahead and freeze sandwiches to thaw and serve with juice. Fillings may include peanut butter, low-fat cream cheese, other cheeses, jams, fruit slices, or meats. Or use flour tortillas with cheese; roll up, wrap, and freeze for later heating in a toaster oven or microwave oven.*
  - *Teach school-aged children to help themselves to dry cereals, milk, and juice. Keep unbreakable bowls and cups in low cabinets, and keep milk and juice in small unbreakable pitchers on a low refrigerator shelf.*
  - *Keep a bowl of fresh fruit and small containers of shelled nuts, trail mix (the kind without candy), or roasted peanuts for grabbing. Granola or other grain cereal poured into an 8-ounce yogurt tub is easy to eat on the run. So are plain, toasted, whole-grain frozen waffles—no syrup needed.*
  - *Nontraditional choices are often acceptable. Purchase or make ahead enough carrot sticks to divide among several containers; serve with yogurt or bean dip. Leftover casseroles, stews, or pasta dishes are nutritious choices that children can eat hot or cold.*

How Nourishing Are the Meals Served at School?

In the United States today, 50 million children ages 5 to 19 years spend a large portion of each day in school for about nine months of each year. More than 30 million children receive lunches through the National School Lunch Program—more than half of them free or at a reduced price.[66] Ten million children eat breakfast at school through the School Breakfast Program. For many children, school food programs constitute their major source of nutrients each day.[67]

The National School Lunch and Breakfast Programs The USDA-regulated school meals provide age-appropriate servings of low-fat or nonfat milk, protein-rich foods (meat, poultry, fish, cheese, eggs, legumes, or peanut butter), generous amounts of vegetables and fruits, and whole-grain breads or other grain foods each day (see Table 14-7). The lunches are designed to meet on average at least a third of the recommended intake for certain nutrients (see the margin) and are often more nutritious than typical lunches brought from home. Students who regularly eat school lunches have higher intakes of many nutrients and fiber than students who do not.[68] To help reduce cardiovascular risk, all government-funded meals served at schools should meet the goals set forth by the *Dietary Guidelines for Americans* (listed in Chapter 2).[69]

Federal legislation mandates that all school districts that participate in the USDA's National School Lunch Program develop and put in place a local wellness policy that:

- A school breakfast must contain at least:
  - *One serving of fluid milk.*
  - *One serving of fruit or vegetable, or full-strength juice.*
  - *Two servings of bread or bread alternates; or two servings of meat or meat alternates; or one of each.*

- As of 2009, USDA school lunches must meet standards set for the following:
  - *Energy (calories)*
  - *Total fat*
  - *Saturated fat*
  - *Protein*
  - *Calcium*
  - *Iron*
  - *Vitamin A*
  - *Vitamin C*
- Standards for added sugars and sodium may soon join this list.

TABLE 14-7 School Lunch Patterns for Different Ages

Food Group	Preschool (Age in Years)		Grade School Through High School[a]		
	Age 1 to 2	Age 3 to 4	Grade K to 3	Grade 4 to 6	Grade 7 to 12
Milk					
1 serving of fluid milk[b]	¾ c	¾ c	1 c	1 c	1 c
Meat or Meat Alternate					
1 serving:					
Lean meat, poultry, or fish	1 oz	1½ oz	1½ oz	2 oz	3 oz
Cheese	1 oz	1½ oz	1½ oz	2 oz	3 oz
Large egg(s)	½	¾	¾	1	1½
Cooked dry beans or peas	¼ c	⅜ c	⅜ c	½ c	¾ c
Peanut butter	2 tbs	3 tbs	3 tbs	4 tbs	6 tbs
Peanuts, soynuts, tree nuts, or seeds[c]	½ oz	¾ oz	¾ oz	1 oz	1½ oz
Vegetable and/or Fruit					
2 or more servings	½ c	½ c	½ c	¾ c (plus ½ c extra over a week)	¾ c
Bread or Bread Alternate					
Servings[d]	5 per week (minimum ½ per day)	8 per week (minimum 1 per day)	8 per week (minimum 1 per day)	8 per week (minimum 1 per day)	10 per week (minimum 1 per day)

[a]*These patterns may be used so long as the meals served meet the* Dietary Guidelines for Americans *and provide one-third of the child's recommendations for nutrients.*

[b]*Whole milk and unflavored low-fat milk must be offered; flavored milks or fat-free milk may also be offered.*

[c]*These foods may meet no more than one-half serving of meat and must be accompanied by other meat or alternate in the meal.*

[d]*A serving is 1 slice of whole-grain or enriched bread; a whole-grain or enriched biscuit, roll, muffin, or the like; or ½ cup cooked rice, pasta, or other grain.*

Source: U.S. Department of Agriculture.

- sets goals for nutrition education, physical activity, and other school-based activities.
- establishes nutrition guidelines for all foods available on school campuses during the school day.
- develops a plan to measure policy implementation.[70]

School districts across the nation have made progress toward meeting these goals, but implementation is inconsistent. Because wellness policies are established locally, some are well-defined while others are vague and difficult to follow.[71]

Competitive Foods at School Recent concern about childhood obesity has focused attention on private vendors in school lunchrooms who offer **competitive foods.**[72] U.S. children develop a taste for these energy-dense, low-nutrient foods early in life and may reject more nutritious meals at school and elsewhere. Policies concerning competitive foods vary widely from state to state.[73] In places that restrict the sale of competitive foods, more students participate in USDA school meal programs. More schools today recognize that promoting fatty foods and sugary beverages to students leads to less nutritious diets and higher body mass index rankings, and more schools now limit these choices.[74]

With one voice, nutrition and medical experts are calling for a national mandate to limit competitive foods in public schools and to require them to consist of nutritious fruits, vegetables, whole grains, and nonfat or low-fat milk and dairy products.[75] The Institute of Medicine has spelled out standards for competitive foods and beverages served in schools regarding upper limits for fat, saturated fat, energy, sugar, and sodium contents.[76]

competitive foods unregulated meals, including fast foods, that compete side-by-side with USDA-regulated school lunches.

KEY POINT School meals are designed to provide at least a third of certain nutrients needed daily by growing children and to stay within limits set by the *Dietary Guidelines for Americans*. Today's competitive foods are often high in fat, salt, and sugar and low in key nutrients.

LO 14.3

Nutrition in Adolescence

Teenagers are not fed; they eat. Food choices made during the teen years profoundly affect health, both now and in the future. In the face of new demands on their time, including after-school jobs, social activities, sports, and home responsibilities, these older children easily fall into irregular eating habits, relying on quick snacks or fast foods for meals. Within this setting, **adolescence** brings a transforming physical maturation and a psychological search for identity, acquired largely through trial and error.

Parents, peers, and the media act as primary influences in shaping the adolescent's behaviors and beliefs. Adolescents who frequently eat meals with their families eat more fruits, vegetables, grains, and calcium-rich foods and drink fewer soft drinks than those who seldom eat with their families.[77] They may even smoke, drink alcohol, or abuse drugs less often.[78]

- The tragedy of drug or alcohol abuse often begins in adolescence and causes multiple nutrition problems:
  - *A drug- or alcohol-focused lifestyle does not include nutrition.*
  - *Medical treatment for drug abuse may alter nutrition needs.*
  - *Money is spent on drugs or alcohol instead of food.*
  - *Substance-induced euphoria depresses the appetite.*
  - *See Controversy 3 for details concerning alcohol and nutrition.*

The Adolescent Growth Spurt

The adolescent growth spurt brings rapid growth and hormonal changes that affect every organ of the body, including the brain. An average girl's growth spurt begins at 10 or 11 years of age and peaks at about 12 years. Boys' growth spurts begin at 12 or 13 years and peak at about 14 years, slowing down at about 19. Two boys of the same age may vary in height by a foot, but if growing steadily, each is fulfilling his genetic destiny according to an inborn schedule of events. A negative assessment of the two may injure the developing identity and open the door to taking such risks as using alcohol, tobacco, and drugs of abuse such as marijuana.

Energy Needs and Physical Activity

The energy needs of adolescents vary tremendously depending on growth rate, gender, body composition, and physical activity. Energy balance is often difficult to regulate in this society—an estimated 15 percent of U.S. children and adolescents 6 to 19 years of age are overweight. On the output side, the spontaneous physical activity of childhood diminishes significantly around the age of adolescence and, by age 15, slumps far below the recommended levels.[79]

An active, growing boy of 15 may need 3,500 calories or more a day just to maintain his weight, but an inactive girl of the same age whose growth has slowed may need fewer than 1,800 calories to avoid unneeded weight gain. She may benefit from choosing more lower-calorie fruit, vegetables, fat-free milk, whole grains, and other nutritious foods with limited cookies, cakes, soft drinks, fried snacks, and other treats. Extra physical activity throughout the day can help to balance the energy budget, as well.

CONCEPT LINK 14-6

Controversy 13, page 529, included activity guidelines for adolescents.

Weight Standards and Body Fatness

Weight standards meant for adults are useless for adolescents. Physicians use growth charts to track their gains in height and weight, and parents should watch only for smooth progress and guard against comparisons that can diminish the child's self-image.

Girls normally develop a somewhat higher percentage of body fat than boys do, a fact that causes much needless worry about becoming overweight. Teens face tremendous pressures regarding body image, and many readily believe scams that promise slenderness or good-looking muscles through "dietary supplements." Healthy, normal-weight teenagers are often "on diets" and make all sorts of unhealthy weight-loss attempts—even taking up smoking.[80] A few teens without

adolescence the period from the beginning of puberty until maturity.

Nutritious snacks play an important role in an active teen's diet.

- Iron DRI intake goals for adolescent boys:
  - *9–13 years, 8 mg/day.*
    If in growth spurt, 10.9 mg/day
  - *14–18 years, 11 mg/day.*
    If in growth spurt, 13.9 mg/day
- Iron DRI intake goals for adolescent girls:
  - *9–13 years, 8 mg/day.*
    If menstruating, 10.5 mg/day
    If menstruating and in growth spurt, 11.6 mg/day
  - *14–18 years, 15 mg/day.*
    If in growth spurt, 16.1 mg/day

diagnosable eating disorders have been reported to "diet" so severely that they stunted their own growth.

KEY POINT The adolescent growth spurt increases the need for energy and nutrients. The normal gain of body fat during adolescence may be mistaken for obesity, particularly in girls. Some self-prescribed diets are detrimental to health and growth.

Nutrient Needs

Needs for vitamins, minerals, the energy-yielding nutrients, and, in fact, all nutrients are greater during adolescence than at any other time of life except pregnancy and lactation (see the DRI table on the inside front cover, page B). The need for iron is particularly high, as all teenagers gain body mass and girls begin menstruation.

The Special Case of Iron The increase in need for iron during adolescence occurs across the genders, but for different reasons. A boy needs more iron at this time to develop extra lean body mass, whereas a girl needs extra iron not only to gain lean body mass but also to support menstruation. Because menstruation continues throughout a woman's childbearing years, her need stays high until older age. As boys become men, their iron needs drop back to the preadolescent value during early adulthood.

An interesting detail about adolescent iron requirements is that the need increases during the **growth spurt,** regardless of the age of the adolescent.[81] This shifting requirement makes pinpointing an adolescent's need tricky, as the margin list demonstrates.

Iron intakes often fail to keep pace with increasing needs, especially for girls, who typically consume less iron-rich foods such as meat and fewer total calories than boys. Not surprisingly, iron deficiency is most prevalent among adolescent girls. Adolescent girls and boys who live with food insecurity—that is, they miss meals, eat less expensive, less nutritious foods, or have other food-related compromises of poverty—increases the likelihood of iron deficiency threefold.[82]

Calcium and the Bones Adolescence is a crucial time for bone development. The bones are growing longer at a rapid rate (see Figure 14-5) thanks to a special

FIGURE 14-5 Growth of Long Bones

Bones grow longer as new cartilage cells accumulate at the top portion of the epiphyseal plate and older cartilage cells at the bottom of the plate are calcified.

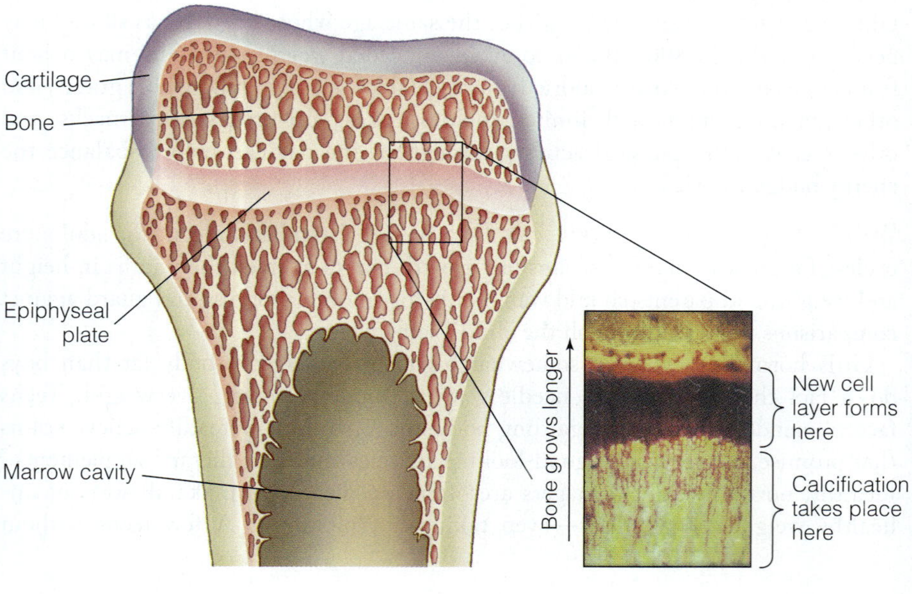

growth spurt the marked rapid gain in physical size usually evident around the onset of adolescence.

epiphyseal (eh-PIFF-ih-seal) **plate** a thick, cartilage-like layer that forms new cells that are eventually calcified, lengthening the bone (*epiphysis* means "growing" in Greek).

premenstrual syndrome (PMS) a cluster of symptoms that some women experience prior to and during menstruation. They include, among others, abdominal cramps, back pain, swelling, headache, painful breasts, and mood changes.

acne chronic inflammation of the skin's follicles and oil-producing glands, which leads to an accumulation of oils inside the ducts that surround hairs; usually associated with the maturation of young adults.

bone structure, the **epiphyseal plate,** which disappears as a teenager reaches adult height. At the same time, the bones are gaining density, laying down the calcium needed later in life. Calcium intakes must be high to support the development of peak bone mass.[83]

Low calcium intakes have reached crisis proportions: 90 percent of females and 70 percent of males ages 12 to 19 years have calcium intakes below recommendations.[84] Paired with a lack of physical activity, low calcium intakes can compromise the development of peak bone mass, greatly increasing the risk of osteoporosis and other bone diseases later on.

Teens often choose soft drinks as their primary beverage (see Figure 14-6). Particularly among girls, this choice displaces calcium-rich milk from the diet (see Figure 14-7) and prevents bones from reaching their full attainable density.[85] Conversely, increasing milk consumption to meet calcium recommendations greatly increases bone density.[86]

Bones also grow stronger with physical activity, but few high schools require students to attend physical activity classes, so most teenagers must make a point to be physically active during leisure hours. Attainment of maximal bone mass during youth and adolescence is the best protection against age-related bone loss and fractures in later life.

Vitamin D Vitamin D is also essential for bone growth and development. Because as many as half of U.S. adolescents may be vitamin-D deficient, as well as due to some evidence for a protective effect of vitamin D against diseases such as diabetes and cancer, the AAP has revised vitamin D intake recommendations.[87] The AAP now recommends double the previous amount, from 5 micrograms per day to 10 micrograms per day.

Adolescents who do not receive 10 micrograms of vitamin D from vitamin D–fortified milk (2.5 micrograms per cup) and vitamin D–fortified foods such as cereals each day should take a vitamin D supplement of 10 micrograms (400 IU on supplement labels).[88] Although drinking 1 quart of vitamin D–fortified milk will provide the recommended amount, the majority of U.S. adolescents fail to consume this amount.

KEY POINT The need for iron increases during adolescence for increased lean body mass in both males and female, and to support menstruation in females. Sufficient calcium and vitamin D intakes are crucial during adolescence, particularly to support normal bone growth and density.

Common Concerns

Two other physical changes stand out as important in adolescence. Menstruation and acne pose special concern to many adolescents.

Menstruation Girls face a major change with the onset of menstruation. The hormones that regulate the menstrual cycle affect not just the uterus and the ovaries but the metabolic rate, glucose tolerance, appetite, food intake, and, often, mood and behavior as well. Most women live easily with the cyclic rhythm of the menstrual cycle, but some are afflicted with physical and emotional pain prior to menstruation, a condition called **premenstrual syndrome,** or **PMS** (see the Consumer Corner).

Acne Genes clearly play a role in who gets **acne** and who doesn't, but other factors also affect its development.[89] The hormones of adolescence stimulate the oil glands deep in the skin. The skin's natural oil is supposed to flow out through tiny ducts at the skin's surface, but in acne, the ducts become clogged and oily secretions build up in the ducts causing irritation, inflammation, and breakouts of acne. A "Western" diet high in meat, dairy, and refined carbohydrates is under investigation for an association with acne.[90] Although often accused, chocolate, sugar, French fries, pizza, salt, and iodine do not worsen acne, but psychological stress clearly does.

Did You Know?

Peak bone mass is the highest attainable bone density for an individual, developed during the first three decades of life.

FIGURE 14-6 Increase in Soft Drink Consumption Over Two Decades by U.S. Adolescents

Average soft-drink consumption by adolescents more than doubled between 1978 and the present.

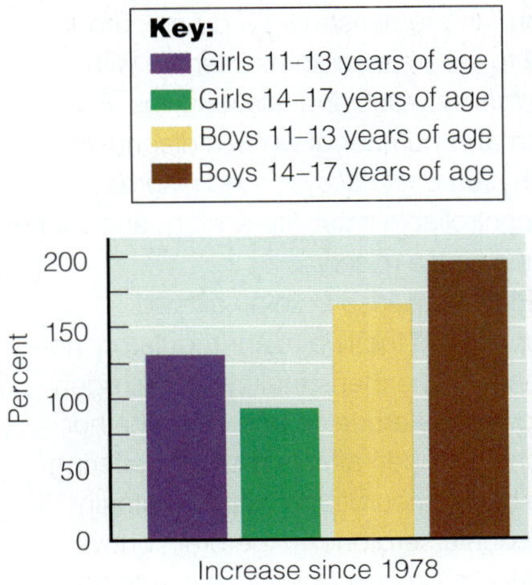

FIGURE 14-7 Milk Consumption Among Adolescent Girls

Teenage girls report drinking less milk over the years and rarely meet their need for calcium.

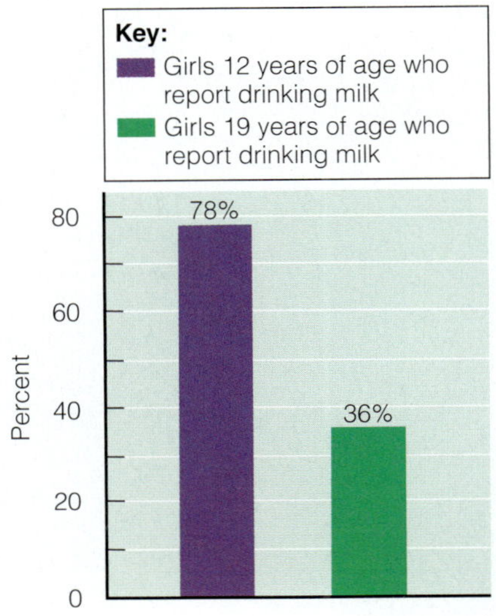

CONSUMER CORNER Nutrition and PMS

Between 50 and 80 percent of menstruating women and girls report uncomfortable menstrual symptoms, but only up to 18 percent meet the criteria for premenstrual syndrome (PMS).[1] The characteristic cyclic symptoms occur predictably and can include cramps and aches in the abdomen, back pain, headache, acne, swelling of the face and limbs associated with water retention, food cravings (especially for chocolate and other sweets), abnormal thirst, pain and lumps in the breasts, diarrhea, and mood changes, including both nervousness and depression.[2] In premenstrual syndrome, moderate to severe symptoms interfere with normal activities and relationships. For a smaller number of women diagnosed with *premenstrual dysphoric disorder,* uncontrollable irritability, anxiety, and even panic cause misery.

PMS may arise from an altered response to the two major regulatory hormones of the menstrual cycle: estrogen and progesterone. In particular, the hormone estrogen affects mood by altering the brain's neurotransmitter, serotonin. Adequate serotonin in the brain buoys a person's mood whereas a serotonin deficiency creates psychological depression. In PMS, the natural rise and fall of estrogen levels in the blood affect the actions of serotonin during the last half of each menstrual cycle. Taking oral contraceptives, which supply estrogen, often improves mood by eliminating hormonal peaks and valleys. Antidepressant drugs that amplify serotonin's effects also may provide some relief.[3]

The major connections between PMS and nutrition concern energy metabolism and intakes of vitamin D, vitamin B_6, and calcium. Scientists believe that during the two weeks prior to menstruation:

- the basal metabolic rate during sleep speeds up.
- appetite, particularly for carbohydrate-rich or fat-rich foods, and calorie intakes increase.[4]
- women who drink may also increase their alcohol consumption at this time, particularly among women prone to depressive symptoms and mood changes.[5]

The woman who aims to manage her weight, then, may find it easier to reduce calorie intake during the two weeks following menstruation. During the two weeks *before* menstruation, she is fighting a natural, hormone-governed increase in appetite.

Links with calcium and vitamin D are intriguing: calcium intakes of 1,000 to 1,300 milligrams per day have significantly improved the irritability, cramping, and other symptoms of PMS. Also, girls and young women taking in plenty of calcium and vitamin D in the form of foods such as low-fat milk are reported as having a lower risk of developing PMS than those taking in less. Supplements of these nutrients, however, did *not* reduce risk.

As for vitamin B_6, a review concluded that high-dose supplements of vitamin B_6 (100 milligrams per day) may alleviate some PMS symptoms, but this amount also teeters on the DRI Tolerable Upper Intake Level, indicating that long-term use of such supplements may harm health.

The following have not proved consistently useful in research: taking multivitamins, magnesium, or manganese supplements; cutting down on alcohol or sodium; or taking diuretics to relieve water retention. If women retain sodium and water just before menstruation, that effect may be normal and desirable; diuretic drugs eliminate sodium and water but also cause a loss of potassium, potentially worsening PMS. Caffeine, another diuretic, may also worsen symptoms.

The woman with PMS should examine her total lifestyle, of which diet is only a part. Adequate sleep and physical activity may help, and controlling stress may be important, although more research in these areas is needed.[6] She should also be on guard against bogus, possibly hazardous, PMS "cures" that abound in the marketplace.

Vacations from school, sun exposure, and swimming all help to relieve acne, perhaps because they are relaxing, the sun's rays kill bacteria, and water cleanses the skin. The oral prescription medicine Accutane, made from vitamin A, cures deep lesions of severe acne. Although vitamin A itself has no effect on acne and supplements can be toxic, quacks market vitamin A–related compounds to young people as acne treatments. One remedy always works: time. While waiting, attend to basic needs. Petal-smooth, healthy skin reflects a tended, cared-for body whose owner provides it with nutrients and fluids to sustain it, exercise to stimulate it, and rest to restore its cells.

KEY POINT Although no single foods have been proved to aggravate acne, stress can worsen it.

Eating Patterns and Nutrient Intakes

During adolescence, food habits change for the worse, and teenagers often miss out on nutrients they need. Few teens choose sufficient whole grains, for example.[91] Teens may begin to skip breakfast; choose less milk, fruits, juices, and vegetables;

and consume more soft drinks each day. Both skipping breakfast and eating fast foods may bear a relationship to weight gain and higher BMI values.[92]

Roles of Adults Ideally, the adult becomes a **gatekeeper,** controlling the type and availability of food in the teenager's environment.[93] Teenage sons and daughters and their friends should find plenty of nutritious, easy-to-grab food in the refrigerator (meats for sandwiches, raw vegetables, fruit, milk, and fruit juices) and more in the pantry (breads, peanut butter, nuts, popcorn, cereals). In reality, in many households today, all the adults work outside the home and teens perform many of the gatekeeper's roles, such as shopping for groceries or choosing fast foods or prepared foods.

Snacks On average, about a fourth of a teenager's total daily energy intake comes from snacks, which, if chosen carefully, can contribute needed protein, thiamin, riboflavin, vitamin B_6, magnesium, and zinc. A survey of more than 4,000 adolescents found that those who ate snacks more often had higher intakes of fruit compared with those who ate snacks less often.[94] Calcium intakes often fall short but snacks of dairy products can improve this picture. For iron, vitamin A, and other nutrients, a teen could snack on iron-containing meat sandwiches, low-fat bran muffins, or tortillas with spicy bean spread along with a glass of orange juice to help maximize the iron's absorption.

© Shebeko, 2011/Shutterstock.com

The gatekeeper can help the teenager choose wisely by delivering nutrition information at "teachable moments." Teens prone to weight gain will often open their ears to news about calories in fast foods. Athletic teens may best attend to information about meal timing and sports performance. Still others are fascinated to learn of the skin's need for vitamins. The gatekeeper must set a good example, keep lines of communication open, and stand by with plenty of nourishing food and reliable nutrition information, but the rest is up to the teens themselves. Ultimately, they make the choices.

KEY POINT The gatekeeper can encourage teens to meet nutrient requirements by providing nutritious snacks; authentic nutrition information may be best received when it speaks to a teen's interests.

The Later Years

The title of this section may imply it is about older people, but it is relevant even if you are only 20 years old—how you live and think at age 20 affects the quality of your life at 60 or 80. According to an old saying, "as the twig is bent, so grows the tree." Unlike a tree, however, you can bend your own twig.

As the Twig Is Bent . . . Before you will adopt nutrition behaviors to enhance your health in old age, you must accept on a personal level that you, yourself, are aging. To learn what negative and positive views you hold about aging, try answering the questions in the margin. Your answers reveal not only what you think of older people now but also what will probably become of you.[95] Nutrition has many documented roles that are critical to successful aging.[96] In general, people who reach old age in good mental and physical health most often:

- are nonsmokers.
- abstain or drink alcohol only moderately.
- are physically active (they walk, bike, swim or otherwise spend more than 150 minutes per week in physical activity).
- are well-nourished, and particularly, they consume sufficient fruits and vegetables.[97]
- maintain a healthy body weight.

Did You Know?

How will you age?

- In what ways do you expect your appearance to change as you age?
- What physical activities do you see yourself enjoying at age 70?
- What will be your financial status? Will you be independent?
- What will your sex life be like? Will others see you as sexy?
- How many friends will you have? What will you do together?
- Will you be happy? Cheerful? Curious? Depressed? Uninterested in life or new things?

gatekeeper with respect to nutrition, a key person who controls other people's access to foods and thereby affects their nutrition profoundly. Examples are the spouse who buys and cooks the food, the parent who feeds the children, and the caregiver in a day-care center.

- Ten tips for productive aging:
  1. Simplify your life; identify priorities and trim the superfluous.
  2. Pay attention to yourself—body, mind, and spirit.
  3. Continue to teach and learn; take up leisure activities (painting, woodwork, nature).
  4. Be flexible; learn to navigate change.
  5. Be charitable; make it a practice to give (wisdom, experience, money, time, yourself).
  6. Be financially astute; invest early for retirement.
  7. Find and participate in activities that interest you; you'll live better in retirement if you do.
  8. Commit to good nutrition and exercise, no matter what.
  9. Think about your past and future; deal with your mortality.
  10. Be involved; be positive; link with others.

They also keep a cheerful attitude and are not often depressed. When such robust older people were asked to give tips to younger people on how to live life fully in the later years, they offered 10 suggestions, also listed in the margin.

Life Expectancy The "graying" of America is a continuing trend.[98] Since 1950, the population over age 65 has almost tripled, and numbers of people over 85 years old have increased sevenfold. People reaching and exceeding age 100 have doubled in number in the last decade, a trend evident among many of the world's populations.

How long a person can expect to live depends on several factors. An estimated 70 to 80 percent of the average person's **life expectancy** depends on individual health-related behaviors, with genes determining the remaining 20 to 30 percent. In the United States, an average person can expect to live almost 78 years.[99] Specifically, life expectancy is almost 81 years for white women and 77 years for black women; for white men, 76 years and for black men, 70 years—all record highs, and much higher than the life expectancy of 47 years in 1900.[100] Once a person survives the perils of youth and middle age to reach age 80, women can expect to survive an additional 9 years, on average; men, an additional 7. The racial gap in life expectancy is narrowing, although efforts to reduce cardiovascular diseases, homicide, HIV infections, and infant mortality are needed to reduce it further.[101]

Human Life Span The biological schedule that we call aging cuts off life at a genetically fixed point in time. The **life span** (the maximum length of life possible for a species) of human beings is believed to be 130 years. Even this limit may one day be challenged with advances in medical and genetic technologies.[102] One caution: to date, scientists who study the aging process have found no specific diet or nutrient supplement that will increase **longevity,** despite hundreds of dubious claims to the contrary.

KEY POINT Life expectancy for U.S. adults is increasing. Life choices can greatly affect how long a person lives and the quality of life in the later years. The human life span is set by genetics.

LO 14.4, 14.5

Nutrition in the Later Years

Nutrient needs become more individual with age, depending on genetics and individual medical history. For example, one person's stomach acid secretion, which helps in iron absorption, may decline, so that person may need more iron. Another person may excrete more, and therefore need more, folate due to past liver disease. Table 14-8 lists some changes that can affect nutrition.

Courtesy of the Author

Physical activity yields benefits at all stages of life.

life expectancy the average number of years lived by people in a given society.

life span the maximum number of years of life attainable by a member of a species.

longevity long duration of life.

Energy and Activity

Energy needs often decrease with advancing age. One reason is that the number of active cells in each organ often decreases and the metabolism-controlling hormone thyroxine diminishes, reducing the body's overall metabolic rate by 1 to 2 percent per decade.[103] Another reason is that as older people reduce their physical activity, their lean tissue diminishes.

Energy Recommendations After about the age of 50, the intake recommendation for energy assumes about a 5 percent reduction in energy output per decade. As in other age groups, obesity increasingly poses a problem. For those who must limit energy intake, there is little leeway in the diet for foods of low nutrient density such as sugars, fats, and alcohol.

Current thinking refutes the idea that declining energy needs are unavoidable, however. Staying physically active boosts energy needs and contributes to a healthy

TABLE 14-8	Physical Changes of Aging That Affect Nutrition
DIGESTIVE TRACT	Intestines lose muscle strength resulting in sluggish motility that leads to constipation. Stomach inflammation, abnormal bacterial growth, and greatly reduced acid output impair digestion and absorption. Pain and fear of choking may cause food avoidance or reduced intake.
HORMONES	For example, the pancreas secretes less insulin and cells become less responsive, causing abnormal glucose metabolism.
MOUTH	Tooth loss, gum disease, and reduced salivary output impede chewing and swallowing. Choking may become likely; pain may cause avoidance of hard-to-chew foods.
SENSORY ORGANS	Diminished sight can make food shopping and preparation difficult; diminished senses of smell and taste may reduce appetite, although research is needed to clarify this effect.
BODY COMPOSITION	Weight loss and decline in lean body mass lead to lowered energy requirements. May be preventable or reversible through physical activity.

immune response and sharp mental functioning, too.[104] Physical activity and an adequate diet also oppose a destructive spiral of sedentary behavior and mental and physical losses in the elderly, sometimes called "the dwindles."[105] The "dwindles" refers to compounding frailties in the elderly, including:

- decreased physical ability to function.
- diminished mental function.
- malnutrition.
- social withdrawal.
- weight loss.

Involuntary weight loss deserves immediate attention in the older person. It could be the result of some easily treatable condition, such as ulcers. For people older than 70 years, the best health and lowest risk of death have been observed in those who maintain a body mass index (BMI) between 25 and 32, which is higher than the optimal BMI for younger people (18.5 to 25; see the inside back cover). Dealing effectively with weight loss entails finding the causes (physical, psychological, or others) and addressing them. At the same time, offering the person's favorite foods in five or six small, high-calorie meals each day instead of three often helps stop or reverse weight loss.[106]

Physical Activity The Think Fitness feature on page 554 emphasizes the importance of physical activity to maintaining body tissue integrity throughout life.[107] People spending energy in physical activity can also eat more food, gaining nutrients. Sadly, over 90 percent of older adults fail to meet national exercise objectives and miss the opportunity for more robust health and fitness in their later years.[108] Any movement seems better than no movement: even performing daily physical chores seems to help the elderly to expend energy and extend life.[109] Some people in their *nineties* have improved their balance, added pep to their walking steps, and regained some precious independence after just eight weeks of resistance training.

The photos near here dramatize this point: they compare cross sections of the thigh of a young woman and of an older woman to demonstrate the muscle loss typical of sedentary aging, which brings with it destructive weakness, poor balance, and deterioration of health and vigor. Resistance training through life helps to prevent at least some of this muscle loss, and consuming sufficient protein may help, too.[110]

KEY POINT Energy needs decrease with age, but exercise burns off excess fuel, maintains lean tissue, and brings health benefits.

- The DRI nutrient intake standards provide separate recommendations for those 51 to 70 years and for those 70 and older. See the inside front cover.
- Body mass index was discussed in Chapter 9.

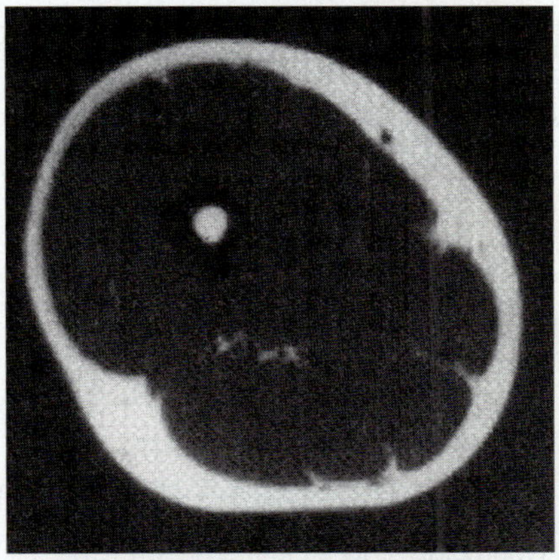

Courtesy of Dr. William Evans

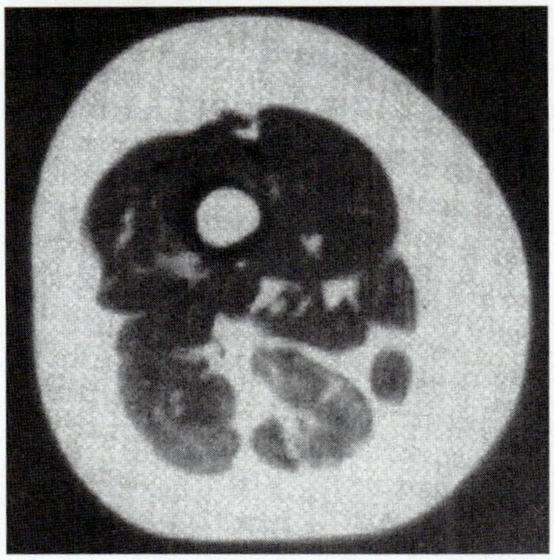

Courtesy of Dr. William Evans

Cross sections of two thighs. These two women's thighs may appear to be about the same size from the outside, but the 20-year-old woman's thigh (top) is dense with muscle tissue (dark areas). The 64-year-old woman's thigh (bottom) has lost muscle and gained fat, changes that may be largely preventable with strength-building physical activities.

THINK FITNESS

Benefits of Physical Activity for the Older Adult

The *Physical Activity Guidelines for Americans* and the American College of Sports Medicine recommend that older adults strive to obtain 150 minutes of physical activity, or whatever amount they can safely perform, each week.[111] Older adults who do so have greater flexibility and endurance, more lean body mass, a better sense of balance, greater blood flow to the brain, and stronger immune systems; they suffer fewer falls and broken bones, experience fewer symptoms of arthritis, retain better cognitive skills, enjoy better overall health, and even live longer than their less-fit peers.[112] Those at risk of falling can benefit from exercises that improve balance.

At some point, perhaps around 80 years of age, the body struggles to add new muscle tissue in response to resistance training.[113] Some extra protein at each meal may help in this regard by stimulating protein synthesis in exercised muscles, even at advanced age.[114] Middle-aged and older people who wish to retain vitality should start now and continue to build and defend their muscle mass through life.

Each elderly person faces different degrees and types of physical limitations. Therefore, each should exercise in his or her own way and pace (see Table 14-9). Any exercise, even a 10-minute walk a day or a workout of upper-body flexibility and resistance training while seated, provides progressive benefits. Great achievements are possible and improvements are inevitable.

START NOW CENGAGENOW Ready to make a change? If you are an older person, or if you care for an older person, consult the online behavior-change planner to develop a plan for obtaining enough physical activity to help build or preserve precious lean tissue at **www.cengage.com/sso.**

TABLE 14-9 *2008 Physical Activity for Americans*—Key Guidelines for Older Adults

- When older adults cannot perform 150 minutes of moderate-intensity aerobic activity a week because of chronic conditions, they should be as physically active as their abilities and conditions allow.
- Older adults should perform exercises that maintain or improve balance if they are at risk of falling.
- Older adults should determine their level of effort for physical activity relative to their level of fitness.
- Older adults with chronic conditions should understand whether and how their conditions affect their ability to perform regular physical activity safely.

Protein Needs

Protein DRI recommended intakes remain about the same for older people as for young adults (see inside front cover). However, with advancing age, people often take in fewer total calories of food and so may need a greater percentage of calories from protein at each meal in order to prevent losing muscle tissue, bone tissue, and other lean body mass.[115]

For older people who have lost their teeth, chewing tough protein-rich meats sufficiently to allow their proper use by the body becomes next to impossible. They need soft-cooked protein sources, such as well-cooked beans or stewed or chopped meats, milk-based soups, soft cheeses, eggs, or fish.[116] Those with chronic constipation, heart disease, or diabetes may benefit from fiber-rich, low-fat protein sources, such as legumes and whole grains.

As energy needs decrease, lower-calorie protein sources, such as lean tender meats, poultry, fish, boiled eggs, fat-free milk products, and legumes, can help hold weight to a healthy level. Underweight or malnourished older adults need the opposite—energy-dense protein sources such as eggs scrambled with margarine, tuna salad with mayonnaise, peanut butter, and milkshakes. Should a flagging appetite reduce food intake, supplemental formulas in liquid, pudding, cookie, or other forms between meals can supply needed energy, protein, and other nutrients.

KEY POINT Protein needs remain about the same through adult life; physical conditions dictate appropriate protein sources.

Carbohydrates and Fiber

Ample whole-grain breads, cereals, rice, and pasta provide a steady supply of carbohydrate that is essential for optimal brain functioning. With age, fiber takes on extra importance for its role against constipation, a common complaint among older adults and nursing home residents in particular.

Fruits and vegetables supply soluble fibers and bioactive food components to help ward off chronic diseases. With aging, however, come problems of transportation, limited cooking facilities, and chewing disabilities that limit some elderly people's intakes of fresh fruits and vegetables. Even without such problems, most older adults fail to obtain the recommended 25 or so grams of fiber each day (14 grams per 1,000 calories).[117] When low fiber intakes are combined with low fluid intakes, inadequate exercise, and constipating medications, constipation becomes inevitable.

KEY POINT Generous carbohydrate intakes are recommended for older adults. Including fiber in the diet is important to avoid constipation.

Fats and Arthritis

Older adults must attend to fat intakes for several reasons. Consuming enough of the essential fatty acids supports continued good health, and limiting intakes of saturated and *trans* fats is a priority to minimize the risk of heart disease. Many of the foods lowest in saturated fat are richest in vitamins, minerals, and phytochemicals. In addition, certain fats may affect one type of **arthritis,** a painful deterioration and swelling of the joints. High-fat diets also correlate with obesity, an arthritis risk factor.

Osteoarthritis The common type of arthritis, osteoarthritis, often results from being overweight or from unknown causes as people age.[118] During movement, the ends of healthy bones are protected by small sacs of fluid that act as lubricants. With arthritis, the sacs erode, cartilage and bone ends disintegrate, and joints become malformed and painful to move. Loss of body weight often brings relief, particularly in the knees; physical activities such as walking, bicycling, and swimming can reduce pain and improve physical function, mental health, and quality of life.[119]

Rheumatoid Arthritis Rheumatoid arthritis arises from an immune system malfunction—the immune system mistakenly attacks the bone coverings as if they were foreign tissue. Some individuals report relief from consuming a Mediterranean-style diet, rich in antioxidants of olive oil and vegetables and the omega-3 fatty acid EPA, found in fish oil.[120] Supplemental doses of vitamin C may worsen the condition. Many ineffective or unproven "cures" are sold for arthritis relief, as the margin list shows. Among popular dietary supplements, chondroitin seems to have no effect at all, and glucosamine affects the liver and the immune system, as well as the joints, with uncertain outcomes.[121]

KEY POINT Arthritis causes pain and immobility in many older people. Many quack treatments exist.

Vitamin Needs

Vitamin needs change as people age. Changes in absorption, metabolism, and excretion affect the body's needs.

Vitamin A Vitamin A stands alone among the vitamins in that its absorption appears to increase with aging. For this reason, some researchers have proposed lowering the vitamin A requirement for aged populations. Others resist this proposal because foods containing vitamin A and its precursor beta-carotene confer health benefits, and many, such as green leafy vegetables, are frequently lacking in the diet.

Vitamin D Vitamin D, once appreciated only for its role in bone growth and maintenance, is now known to act at the genetic level with widespread effects on body tissues. Sufficient vitamin D may play roles in preventing high blood pressure, some common cancers, infectious diseases, inflammatory conditions, autoimmune diseases, rheumatoid arthritis, the skin disease psoriasis (so-RYE-ah-sis),

- Bogus or unproven arthritis treatments:
  - *Alfalfa tea*
  - *Aloe vera liquid*
  - *Any of the amino acids*
  - *Burdock root*
  - *Calcium*
  - *Celery juice*
  - *Chondroitin*
  - *Copper or copper complexes*
  - *Dimethyl sulfoxide (DMSO)*
  - *Fasting*
  - *Fresh fruit*
  - *Honey*
  - *Inositol*
  - *Kelp*
  - *Lecithin*
  - *Melatonin*
  - *MSM*
  - *Para-aminobenzoic acid (PABA)*
  - *Raw liver*
  - *Selenium*
  - *Superoxide dismutase (SOD)*
  - *Vitamin E, other vitamin and mineral supplements*
  - *Watercress*
  - *Yeast*
  - *Zinc*
  - *100 other substances*

arthritis a usually painful inflammation of joints caused by many conditions, including infections, metabolic disturbances, or injury; usually results in altered joint structure and loss of function.

and even multiple sclerosis.[122] In the elderly, supplemental vitamin D, particularly when taken with calcium, may help to reduce falls, thereby preventing bone fractures.[123]

As people age, vitamin D synthesis declines fourfold, setting the stage for deficiency. Many older adults drink little or no vitamin D–fortified milk and get little or no exposure to sunlight. Thus, the recommendation for vitamin D intake has been doubled for people 51 to 70, to 10 micrograms daily, and tripled to 15 micrograms for people 71 and over. Every elderly person should obtain this amount of vitamin D and get outside often (or sit by a sunny open window).

Vitamin B_{12} Adults aged 51 years and older need to obtain 2.4 micrograms of vitamin B_{12} from foods and supplements that supply it. By age 60, however, reduced stomach acid production in about 6 percent of people reduces their ability to absorb vitamin B_{12} from food, making deficiency likely. The number increases with age. Up to 20 percent of elderly people may suffer marginal deficiencies but most of these cases go unrecognized and untreated.[124] No one yet knows whether dietary insufficiency, malabsorption, or another factor is the primary cause of these deficiencies.[125] Synthetic vitamin B_{12} is reliably absorbed, however, and much misery can be averted by preventing deficiencies of vitamin B_{12} in elderly people.

Other Vitamins and Phytochemicals Antioxidants such as vitamin E may also play roles in conserving immunity, mental functions, and eyesight in the aged. A key aspect of healthy aging is maintaining good vision.[126] Loss of vision in the elderly correlates with loss of life that cannot be explained by other risk factors.[127]

Dark green, leafy vegetables rich in certain carotenoid phytochemicals may protect the eyes from one cause of blindness: macular degeneration.[§128] Carotenoid supplements are unproven for eye protection, although some physicians may prescribe them in cases of advanced macular degeneration that threatens vision.[129] Studies are underway to determine their effectiveness.[130]

CONCEPT LINK 14-7

The macula of the eye and macular degeneration were described in Chapter 7, page 234.

Another problem facing older people is **cataracts.** A cataract is a clouding of the lens that impairs vision and leads to blindness. Only 5 percent of people younger than 50 years have cataracts; afterward, the percentage jumps to over 20 to 30 percent. The lens of the eye is easily oxidized. Some studies suggest that a diet high in *foods* that provide ample antioxidants—carotenoids, vitamin C, and vitamin E—may reduce the risk of early onset and progression of cataracts.[131] Vitamin C supplements, conversely, may increase some people's cataract risk.[132]

KEY POINT Vitamin A absorption increases with aging. Older people suffer more from deficiencies of vitamin D and vitamin B_{12} than young people do. Cataracts and macular degeneration often occur among those with low fruit and vegetable intakes.

Water and the Minerals

- Water recommendation for adults:
  - *1 oz/kg actual body weight, with a minimum of 50 oz (6¼ c) daily*

Dehydration is a major risk for older adults. Total body water decreases with age, so even mild stresses, such as a hot day or a fever, can quickly dehydrate the tissues. The thirst mechanism may become imprecise, and even healthy older people may go for long periods without drinking fluids. The kidneys also become less efficient in recapturing water before it is lost as urine. Dehydrated older people often suffer problems such as constipation, bladder problems, and mental confusion that is easily mistaken for **senile dementia,** an effect that may occur with a water loss of as little as 1 percent of body weight.[133] In a person with asthma, dehydration thickens mucus in the lungs, blocking airways and leading to pneumonia. In a bedridden person, dehydration can lead to **pressure ulcers.** To prevent dehydration, older adults need to drink at least 6 cups of fluids each day to provide the needed water.

A person we know uses this trick to ensure getting enough water: he keeps six inexpensive 8-ounce cups in the cabinet. Through the day he uses each to drink 1 cup

cataracts (CAT-uh-racts) clouding of the lens of the eye that can lead to blindness. Cataracts can be caused by injury, viral infection, toxic substances, genetic disorders, and, possibly, some nutrient deficiencies or imbalances.

senile dementia the loss of brain function beyond the normal loss of physical adeptness and memory that occurs with aging.

pressure ulcers damage to the skin and underlying tissues as a result of unrelieved compression and poor circulation to the area; also called *bed sores.*

§The carotenoids are lutein and zeaxanthin, which help to form pigments of the macula of the eye.

of fluid, including juices and other beverages, collecting the used cups in the dish drain. (For clear soups and other hot beverages, he simply moves one of his cups for each 8 ounces consumed from his bowl or mug.) In the afternoon, he checks the cabinet and drinks from any remaining cups. For him, drinking enough fluid has become a habit, and seldom are any cups left in the cabinet after supper.

Bob Thomas/Stone/Getty Images

Adults of all ages need 6 to 8 cups of fluid each day.

Iron Iron status generally improves in later life, especially in women after menstruation ceases and in those who take iron supplements, eat red meat regularly, and include vitamin C–rich fruits in their daily diet. When iron-deficiency anemia does occur, diminished appetite with low food intake is often the cause. Aside from diet, other factors make iron deficiency likely in older people:

- Chronic blood loss from ulcers or hemorrhoids.
- Poor iron absorption due to reduced stomach acid secretion.
- Antacid use, which interferes with iron absorption.
- Use of medicines that cause blood loss, including anticoagulants, aspirin, and arthritis medicines.

Older people take more medicines than others, and drug and nutrient interactions are common.

Zinc Zinc deficiencies, common in older people, are known to impair immune function and may increase the likelihood of infectious diseases, such as pneumonia.[134] Zinc deficiency can also depress the appetite and blunt the sense of taste, thereby reducing food intakes and worsening zinc status. Many medications interfere with the body's absorption or use of zinc, and an older adult's medicine load can worsen zinc deficiency.

Did You Know?

These foods provide iron and zinc together: meat, poultry, liver, oysters, whole grains, fortified breakfast cereals, and legumes.

Calcium With aging, calcium absorption declines; at the same time, most elderly people fail to consume enough calcium-rich foods. If fresh milk causes stomach discomfort, and the majority of older people report that it does, then lactose-reduced milk or other calcium-rich foods should take its place.

CONCEPT LINK 14-8

Calcium-rich foods were listed in Chapter 8, page 291, and Controversy 8 discussed the threat to the bones from osteoporosis.

Multi-Nutrient Supplements Overall, elderly people often benefit from a single balanced low-dose vitamin and mineral supplement, and possibly calcium. Older people taking such supplements suffer fewer sicknesses caused by infection, and calcium may slow bone loss. Other single nutrients are tricky: vitamin A has been seen to depress the immunity of elders, while vitamin E may enhance it. A summary of the effects of aging on nutrient needs appears in Table 14-10.

KEY POINT Aging alters vitamin and mineral needs. Some needs rise while others decline.

Can Nutrition Help People to Live Longer?

The evidence concerning nutrition and longevity is intriguing. Its seems that even though people cannot alter the year of their birth, they can probably alter the length and quality of their lives.

Lifestyle Factors In a classic study, researchers observed that some of their nearly 7,000 adults were young for their ages, while others were old for their ages. To uncover what made the difference, the researchers focused on health habits and identified six factors that affect physiological age. Three of the six factors were related to nutrition:

- Abstinence from, or moderation in, alcohol use.
- Regular nutritious meals.
- Weight control.

The other three were regular adequate sleep, abstinence from smoking, and regular physical activity. The physical health of those who engaged in all six positive health

TABLE 14-10 Summary of Nutrient Concerns in Aging

Nutrient	Effects of Aging	Comments
Energy	Need decreases.	Physical activity moderates the decline.
Fiber	Low intakes make constipation likely.	Inadequate water intakes and physical activity, along with some medications, compound constipation.
Protein	Needs stay the same.	Low-fat, high-fiber legumes and grains meet both protein and other needs.
Vitamin A	Absorption increases.	Supplements normally not needed.
Vitamin D	Increased likelihood of inadequate intake; skin synthesis declines.	Daily moderate exposure to sunlight may be of benefit.
Vitamin B_{12}	Malabsorption of some forms.	Foods fortified with synthetic vitamin B_{12} or a supplement may be of benefit in addition to a balanced diet.
Water	Lack of thirst and increased urine output make dehydration likely.	Mild dehydration is a common cause of confusion.
Iron	In women, status improves after menopause; deficiencies linked to chronic blood losses and low stomach acid output.	Stomach acid required for absorption; antacid or other medicine use may aggravate iron deficiency; vitamin C and meat enhance absorption.
Zinc	Intakes are often inadequate and absorption may be poor, but needs may also increase.	Medications interfere with absorption; deficiency may depress appetite and sense of taste.
Calcium	Intakes may be low; osteoporosis becomes common.	Lactose intolerance commonly limits milk intake; calcium-rich substitutes or supplements are needed.

- Differences in maximum life span between animals eating normally and those that are energy restricted:
  - *Rats:*
    Normal diet, 33 months.
    Restricted diet, 47 months.
  - *Spiders:*
    Normal diet, 100 days.
    Restricted diet, 139 days.
  - *Single-celled animals (protozoans):*
    Normal diet, 13 days.
    Restricted diet, 25 days.

practices was comparable to that of people 30 years younger who engaged in few or none. Numerous studies have confirmed the benefits of these lifestyle factors under individual control. Tables 14-11 and 14-12 list some changes of aging that are beyond control and some that may yield to lifestyle influences.

Energy Restriction Evidence that diet might influence the life span emerged in the middle of the last century when researchers fed young rats a diet extremely low in energy. The starved rats stopped growing while a group of control rats ate and grew normally; when the researchers increased food energy in the starved group, growth resumed. Many of the starved rats died young from malnutrition. The few survivors, though permanently deformed from their ordeal, remained alive far beyond the normal life span for such animals and developed diseases of aging much later than normal. Since then, this result has been repeated in many species (see the margin).

Some questions arise about the safety of severe energy restriction. Energy-restricted mice, for example, die more often from influenza infections, despite evidence that

TABLE 14-11 Changes with Age You Probably Must Accept

These changes are probably beyond your control:

✓ Graying of hair	✓ Slowed reactions (reflexes)
✓ Balding	✓ Slowed mental function
✓ Some drying and wrinkling of skin	✓ Diminished visual memory
✓ Impairment of near vision	✓ Menopause (women)
✓ Some loss of hearing	✓ Loss of fertility (men)
✓ Reduced taste and smell sensitivity	✓ Loss of joint elasticity
✓ Reduced touch sensitivity	

certain immune system functions are maintained.[135] With moderate energy restriction, animals also retain youthfulness longer and develop fewer disease risk factors such as high blood pressure, glucose intolerance, and immune system impairments.[136] In monkeys, moderate calorie restriction prolongs life and reduces incidence of diabetes, cancer, cardiovascular disease, and the brain shrinkage typical in aging monkeys fed a full diet.[137]

No one yet knows whether such animal findings also apply to human beings.[138] Monkeys and human beings do share a significant number of genes, making their metabolism more or less similar. Evidence demonstrates that although energy restriction may improve indicators of chronic diseases, it also impairs physical activity and impedes immune defenses and may be especially harmful to people with little body fat to spare.[139]

Scientists are hoping to discover drug treatments that mimic the effect of calorie restriction while minimizing risks.[140] For now, however, any supplement or treatment claiming to prolong life is a hoax.

KEY POINT Lifestyle factors can make a difference in aging. In rats and other species, food energy deprivation may lengthen the lives of individuals.

TABLE 14-12 Changes with Age You Probably Can Slow or Prevent

By exercising, eating an adequate diet, reducing stress, and planning ahead, you may be able to slow or prevent:

- ✓ Wrinkling of skin due to sun damage
- ✓ Some forms of mental confusion
- ✓ Elevated blood pressure
- ✓ Accelerated resting heart rate
- ✓ Reduced lung capacity and oxygen uptake
- ✓ Increased body fatness
- ✓ Elevated blood cholesterol
- ✓ Slowed energy metabolism
- ✓ Decreased maximum work rate
- ✓ Loss of sexual functioning
- ✓ Loss of joint flexibility
- ✓ Diminished oral health: loss of teeth, gum disease
- ✓ Bone loss
- ✓ Digestive problems, constipation

Immunity and Inflammation

As people age, the immune system loses function. As they become ill, the immune system becomes overstimulated but less able to cope with the challenge. The combination of an overreactive, inefficient immune response results in a chronic inflammation, with increasing frailty and illness.[141]

Most chronic diseases—such as atherosclerosis, Alzheimer's disease, obesity, and rheumatoid arthritis—involve inflammation.[142] Therefore, inflammation is believed to be a partly harmful process; yet, at the same time, it plays a critical role in destruction of invading organisms and repair of damaged tissues.[143] The trick seems to be to control inflammation enough to prevent harm from its chronic, ineffective processes, but not so much to prevent its beneficial ones.

Nutrient deficiencies compromise immune function, while a sound diet and regular physical activity can improve it.[144] Typically in old age, people become more sedentary and prone to malnutrition, leaving them particularly vulnerable to infectious diseases. Antibiotics also often lose effectiveness in people with a compromised immune system. Consequently, many older adults die of infectious diseases.

A free-radical hypothesis blames damage from oxidative stress for the physical deterioration associated with aging.[145] The body's internal antioxidant enzymes diminish with age, and many "age-related" degenerative diseases may be linked to free-radical damage. This and related lines of research promote a storm of worthless and sometimes hazardous "life-extending" pills, supplements, and treatments, such as DHEA, testosterone, and growth hormone.[146] Better to spend money on legumes, fresh fruit, and green and yellow vegetables, naturally rich sources of antioxidants linked with many health benefits (see Controversy 2).

KEY POINT Inflammation and diminished immune effectiveness are hazards to elderly people. Claims for life extension through antioxidants or other supplements are common hoaxes.

Can Foods or Supplements Affect the Course of Alzheimer's Disease?

The cause of Alzheimer's disease, the most prevalent form of senile dementia, is unknown but genetics clearly contributes.[147] Areas of the brain that coordinate memory and cognition deteriorate, and the brain becomes littered with clumps of abnormal protein fragments and tangles of nerve tissue that damage or kill certain

- A person with typical benign memory loss of aging may:
  - *Forget names or places temporarily.*
  - *Need more time to remember a task the person set out to do.*
  - *Misplace items in typical places, such as leaving reading glasses in the car.*
  - *Joke about apparent forgetfulness.*
  - *Experience little interference in living a full and productive life.*
- A person in the early stages of Alzheimer's disease may:
  - *Ask the same questions repeatedly.*
  - *Have difficulty remembering common words.*
  - *Mix words up—saying "bed" instead of "table," for example.*
  - *Be unable to complete familiar tasks, such as balancing a checkbook.*
  - *Misplace items in uncommon places, such as stowing a phone in the refrigerator.*
  - *Get lost while driving on familiar streets.*
  - *Have sudden, unexplained mood or behavior changes.*
  - *Become less able to follow directions.*
  - *Be unaware of memory loss or forgetfulness.*
  - *Experience worsening memory loss that progressively diminishes the quality of life.*

CONCEPT LINK 14-9

Omega-3 fatty acids and the Mediterranean diet were topics of Chapter 5 and its Controversy, pages 167, 184.

nerve cells.** Alzheimer's inflicts losses of memory, reasoning powers (see the margin), the ability to communicate, physical capabilities, and causes anxiety, delusions, depression, inappropriate behavior, irritability, sleep disturbance, and eventually loss of life itself. Once the destruction begins, the outlook for its reversal is bleak. More research is needed, and quickly, to perfect a drug or vaccine to block the destructive progression of the disease.

Only weak links exist between nutrition and Alzheimer's disease. For example, although the mineral aluminum may build up in the brain with Alzheimer's, a causal connection seems unlikely. Evidence conflicts as to whether supplements of copper, zinc, or other trace minerals worsen Alzheimer's disease, so to err on the safe side, food sources, not concentrated supplements, of trace minerals are advisable for people with the disease.

Brain cells of Alzheimer's victims show signs of oxidative damage, so the antioxidant-rich Mediterranean diet is under study for defending against this damage, but evidence so far is mixed.[148] Such a diet also provides fish rich in DHA, but results are mixed on whether fish oil, DHA, or fish have a relationship to dementia.[149] Suggestions that a moderate alcohol intake may delay cognitive decline appear to be false, as well.[150] To date, no proven benefits are available from vitamin or mineral pills or herbs—even ginkgo biloba—or other remedies, but claims from quacks are all too commonplace.[151]

Preventing weight loss is an important nutrition concern for the person suffering with Alzheimer's disease. Depression and forgetfulness can lead to skipped meals and poor food choices. Caregivers can help by providing well-liked, well-balanced, and well-tolerated meals and snacks served in a cheerful, peaceful atmosphere on brightly colored tableware to spur interest in eating.

KEY POINT Alzheimer's disease causes some degree of brain deterioration in many people past age 65. Current treatment helps only marginally; omega-3 fatty acids from fish oil are under study for potential preventive effects. The importance of nutrition care increases as the disease progresses.

Food Choices of Older Adults

Most older people are independent, socially sophisticated, mentally lucid, fully participating members of society who report themselves to be happy and healthy. Many older people have heard and heeded nutrition messages: they have cut down on saturated fats in dairy foods and meats and are eating slightly more vegetables and whole-grain breads, although few meet the recommended intakes of these foods. Older people who enjoy a wide variety of foods are better nourished and have a better quality of life than those who subsist on a monotonous diet.[152] Grocers assist the elderly by prominently displaying good-tasting, low-fat, nutritious foods in easy-to-open, single-serving packages with labels that are easy to read.

Obstacles to Adequacy Many factors affect the food choices and eating habits of older people, including whether they live alone or with others, at home or in an institution.[153] Men living alone, for example, are likely to consume poorer-quality diets than those living with spouses. Older people who have difficulty chewing because of tooth loss or loss of taste sensitivity may no longer seek a wide variety of foods. Medical conditions and functional losses can also adversely affect food choices and nutrition. Lack of access to kitchen facilities may be a factor. Many older people become weak when unintentional reductions in food intake result in weight and muscle loss, events often followed by illness or death. It may be that some of these outcomes could have been prevented or delayed if the person had been provided an adequate diet.

Two other factors seem to make older people vulnerable to malnutrition: use of multiple medications and abuse of alcohol. People over age 65 take about a fourth

**The protein fragments are called *beta-amyloid*.

TABLE 14-13 Predictors of Malnutrition in the Elderly

Here is a quick and easy-to-remember list of factors that increase the likelihood of malnutrition in the elderly. The first letters spell the word *DETERMINE*.

To Determine:	Ask:
Disease	• Do you have an illness or condition that changes the types or amounts of foods you eat?
Eating poorly	• Do you eat fewer than two meals a day? Do you eat fruits, vegetables, and milk products daily?
Tooth loss or mouth pain	• Is it difficult or painful to eat?
Economic hardship	• Do you have enough money to buy the food you need?
Reduced social contact	• Do you eat alone most of the time?
Multiple medications	• Do you take three or more different prescribed or over-the-counter medications daily?
Involuntary weight loss or gain	• Have you lost or gained 10 pounds or more in the last six months?
Needs assistance	• Are you physically able to shop, cook, and feed yourself?
Elderly person	• Are you older than 80?

of all the medications, both prescription and over-the-counter, sold in the United States. Although these medications enable people with health problems to live longer and more comfortably, they also pose a threat to nutrition status because they may interact with nutrients, depress the appetite, or alter the perception of taste (see Controversy 14).

The incidence of alcoholism, alcohol abuse, or problem drinking among the elderly in the United States is estimated at between 2 and 10 percent. Loneliness, isolation, and depression in the elderly accompany overuse of alcohol and detract from nutrient intakes. Table 14-13 provides an easily remembered means of identifying those who might be at risk for malnutrition.

Programs That Help Federal programs can provide help for older people. Social Security provides income to retired people over age 62 who paid into the system during their working years. The Supplemental Nutrition Assistance Program (SNAP), formerly called the Food Stamp Program, assists the very poor by supplementing their monthly food budgets with a card similar to a credit card, encrypted with benefits and redeemable for food. The Senior Nutrition Program provides nutritious meals in a social congregate setting, education and shopping assistance, counseling and referral to other needed services, and transportation to necessary appointments. An estimated 25 percent of the nation's elderly poor benefit from meals provided by the program. For the homebound, Meals on Wheels volunteers deliver meals to the door, a benefit even though the recipients miss out on the social atmosphere of the congregate meals. Nutritionists are wise not to focus solely on nutrient and food intakes of the elderly because enjoyment and social interactions may be as important as food itself.

Many older people, even able-bodied ones with financial resources, find themselves unable to perform cooking, cleaning, and shopping tasks. For anyone living alone, and particularly for those of advanced age, it is important to work through the problems that food preparation presents. This chapter's Food Feature presents some ideas.

KEY POINT Food choices of the elderly are affected by aging, altered health status, and changed life circumstances. Assistance programs can help by providing nutritious meals, offering opportunities for social interactions, and easing financial problems.

- The Senior Nutrition Program is part of the Child and Adult Care Food Program (CACFP), which is designed to help public and private nonresidential child and adult day-care programs provide nutritious meals to those younger than age 12 or older than 65 or people with disabilities.

- Federal Sources of support for the elderly:
  - *Social Security.*
  - *Supplemental Nutrition Assistance Program (SNAP), formerly called the Food Stamp Program.*
  - *Senior Nutrition Program.*
  - *Meals on Wheels.*

Shared meals can be the high point of the day.

MY TURN

© Cengage Leaerning

Allison

© Cengage Leaerning

Eric

Eating Solo

Have you ever felt uninspired by the though eating alone? Two students talk about deali with loneliness, making easy but nutritious meals, and choosing wisely among takeout foods.

CENGAGENOW To hear their stories, log on to www.cengage.com/sso.

FOOD FEATURE

Single Survival and Nutrition on the Run

LO 14.6

A single person of any age, whether a busy student in a college dormitory, an elderly person in a retirement apartment, or a professional in an efficiency suite, faces challenges in obtaining nourishing meals. People without access to kitchens and freezers find storing foods problematic, and so often eat out. Following is a collection of ideas gathered from single people who have devised ways to nourish themselves despite obstacles.

Jesco Tscholitsch/Taxi/Getty Images

Shopping for and preparing nutritious foods for one person takes some special know-how.

IS EATING IN RESTAURANTS THE ANSWER?

Restaurant patrons pay for convenience. On average, almost 45 percent of a U.S. household's food budget is spent on foods prepared and eaten away from home. And in any given month, up to 70 percent of households consume food from a carry-out restaurant. Can such foods meet nutrient needs or support health as well as homemade foods? The answer is "perhaps," but making it so takes some effort.

A few chefs and restaurant owners are concerned with the nutritional health of their patrons, but more often chefs strive to please the palate. Restaurant foods are often overly endowed with calories, fat, saturated fat, sugar, and salt, but often lack fiber, iron, or calcium. Vegetables and fruits may be in short supply, but a single meat or pasta portion may exceed a whole day's recommended intake. To improve restaurant meals, follow these suggestions:

- Restrict your portions to sizes that do not exceed your energy needs.
- Ask that excess portions be placed in take-out containers right away.
- Ask for extra vegetables, fruit, or salad.
- Request whole-grain breads and pasta (more restaurants now supply these, and others may do so with repeated requests).
- Make judicious choices of foods that stay within intake guidelines for fat and salt.

The Food Feature of Chapter 5 offered specific suggestions for ordering fast food and other foods with an eye to keeping fat intakes within bounds, and Chapter 8 listed foods high in sodium.

GROCERY STORE TAKE-OUT CHOICES

Take-out delicatessen-style foods from grocery stores offer convenience—they can be purchased while shopping for other items. They also often cost substantially less than similar foods from restaurants. A bonus: you can purchase the amount you need and portion it onto your plate at home.

Choose foods high in nutrient density, such as roasted chicken, smoked seafood, pasta with tomato sauce, steamed vegetables, precut salads and fruit (dressings on the side), cooked beans, and plain baked potatoes or sweet potatoes. Beware of stuffing, macaroni and cheese, meat loaf and gravy, vegetables with creamy sauces, mayonnaise-dressed mixed salads, and fried chicken and fish, which all can load the diet with saturated fat and calories. Keep take-out foods safe by going home quickly and consuming, reheating, or refrigerating them promptly.

MORE GROCERY STORE KNOW-HOW

Buy only what you will use. Large package sizes of meat and vegetables, whether fresh or frozen, are suitable for a family of four or more, and even a head of lettuce can spoil before one person can use it all. Don't be timid about asking the grocer to break open a family-sized package of wrapped meat or fresh vegetables. Look for bags of prepared salad greens to take the place of lettuce in both salads and sandwiches. Purchasing prepared salads and other small containers of food may seem expensive, but spoilage and waste can cost even more. Buy only three pieces of each kind of fresh fruit: a ripe one, a medium-ripe one, and a green one. Eat the first right away and the second soon, and let the last one ripen to eat days later.

Think up ways to use a vegetable that comes in large quantity. For example, you can divide a head of cauliflower into thirds. Cook one-third and eat it as a hot vegetable. Toss another third into a salad dressing marinade for use as an appetizer. Blend up the rest, cooked, in a creamy soup.

Buy fresh milk in the size you can best use. If your grocer doesn't carry pints or quarts of milk, try a convenience store. If you eat lunch in a cafeteria, buy two pints of milk—one to drink and one to take home and store. Buy a loaf of bread and immediately store half, well wrapped, in the freezer (not the refrigerator, which will make it stale).

FOOD-PREPARATION HINTS

A wise person once said, "An hour spent organizing can save three hours later on."†† This holds true in food preparation. For shelf-stable items, prepare a space for rows of glass jars (jars from spaghetti sauce, applesauce, or other foods work well). Use the jars to store pasta, rice, lentils, other dry beans, flour, cornbread or biscuit mix, dry fat-free milk, and cereal. Light destroys riboflavin, so use opaque jars for enriched pasta and dry milk. Cut the directions-for-use label from the package of each item and tape it to the jar. Place each jar, tightly sealed, in the freezer for a few days to kill any eggs or organisms before storing it on the shelf. Then the jars will keep bugs out of the foods indefinitely. The jars are also pretty to look at and will remind you of possibilities for variety in your menus.

Experiment with stir-fried foods—Asian style. Inexpensive vegetables such as cabbage and celery are delicious when lightly cooked in a large fry pan with a little oil and flavored with soy sauce, lemon juice, or Asian seasonings. Interesting frozen vegetable mixtures are available, or cooked leftover vegetables can be dropped into a stir-fry at the last minute. A bonus of a stir-fried meal is that you have only one pan to wash.

If you can afford a microwave oven, buy one. Cooking times are quick, and you'll use fewer pots and pans. Be sure to use containers designed for the microwaving, however. Margarine tubs, plastic bowls, and storage bags and containers can release potentially harmful chemicals into food when they are heated in the microwave oven. Use glass or buy plastic containers that are labeled as safe for microwaving.

Depending on your freezer space, make a regular-size recipe of a dish that takes time to prepare: a casserole, vegetable pie, or meat loaf. Freeze individual portions in containers that can be heated later. Date these so you will use the oldest first.

DEALING WITH LONELINESS

For nutrition's sake, it is important to attend to loneliness at mealtimes. The person who is living alone must learn to connect food with socializing. Invite guests and make enough food so that you can enjoy the leftovers later on. If you know an older person who eats alone, you can bet that person would love to join you for a meal now and then.

- Time-saving tips to turn convenience foods into nutritious meals:
  - *Add a fresh flavor and extra nutrients to canned stews and soups by tossing in some frozen ready-to-use mixed vegetables. Choose vegetables without salty, fatty sauces—prepared foods generally contain enough salt to season the whole dish.*
  - *Buy frozen vegetables in a bag, add a variety of herbs, and use as needed. Vary your choices to prevent boredom.*
  - *Add frozen Asian vegetable blends to ramen noodles or prepared rice dishes.*
  - *When grilling burgers, wrap a mixture of frozen broccoli, onion, and carrots in a foil packet with a tablespoon of Italian dressing and grill alongside the meat for seasoned grilled vegetables.*
  - *Use canned or frozen fruits in their own juices as desserts. Add frozen berries or peach slices to yogurt for an instant fruit salad, or blend with a banana for a smoothie.*
  - *Prepared rice or noodle dishes claiming to contain broccoli, spinach, or other vegetables really contain just a trifle—not nearly enough to qualify as a serving of vegetable. Adding a half-cup of your frozen vegetables per serving of pasta or rice provides a better balance.*
  - *Purchase frozen onion, mushroom, and pepper mixtures to embellish jarred spaghetti sauce, small frozen pizzas, or pasta dishes. Top with Parmesan cheese.*
  - *Use frozen shredded potatoes, sold for hash browns, in soups or stews or mix with a handful of shredded reduced-fat cheese or a can of fat-free "cream of anything" soup and bake for a quick and hearty casserole.*

††That wise person was the late Eva May Hamilton, one of the original authors of this textbook.

Diet Analysis PLUS Concepts in Action

Analyze a Diet for Children

The purpose of this exercise is to show how food choices and nutrient deficiencies affect young children, teens, and older adults, using three new profiles: a 2-year-old, a 14-year-old, and a 70-year-old.

1. Proper nutrition is critical to normal brain development. Create a new profile for a 2-year-old toddler. Select the Track Diet tab, choose a new day, then, using Table 14-2 (page 534), choose foods to create a balanced, iron-rich meal for a toddler 1–2 years of age. Once you've entered the foods, select the Reports tab, then select Intake Spreadsheet for that meal, and generate a report. Did the meal supply a third of the iron your toddler needs? Which foods contributed most of the iron?
2. Children's diets should include a variety of foods from each food group (see Figure 14-2, page 536). Create a day's meals keeping in mind that children often like colorful, crunchy vegetables and smooth bland foods. Enter the data from the Track Diet tab. Select Intake Spreadsheet and generate reports for both the Intake Spreadsheet and MyPyramid Analysis for this day's meals. Did your choices provide the right number of servings of a variety of foods from each food group? If not, how can you improve your choices?
3. A nutritious breakfast is essential to healthy growth and development. Nutrients missed at breakfast cannot be made up at lunch or dinner. Create a child's nutritious breakfast for a rushed morning. Enter the data from the Track Diet tab. Select Intake Spreadsheet for that date and meal and generate a report. Did the breakfast meet a significant portion of the child's nutrient needs? If not, what foods or beverages might improve it?
4. Calcium intakes often fall short for teens, as do iron and vitamin A. From the Profile drop-down box, create a new profile for a 14-year-old girl. Select the Track Diet tab, and choose foods for a lunch meal that are excellent sources of calcium, iron, and vitamin A. Recall that vitamin C helps maximize iron absorption from nonheme (nonmeat) sources of iron. Select the Reports tab, then Source Analysis, and from the drop-down box, generate reports for Calcium, Iron, Vitamin A, and Vitamin C. Did the meal meet the teen's needs for calcium and iron? Did meat or nonheme sources of iron predominate? Which foods also supplied vitamin A and vitamin C?
5. Teens often jeopardize their nutritional health with careless snack choices. Nutritious snacks function as small meals in a teenager's diet. Select the teen's profile (already created), and select the Track Diet tab. Consult Table 14-7, page 546, for help in choosing portions of foods for a nutritious snack for the morning and afternoon. Make each snack supply about 150 calories of nutritious foods. Select Intake Spreadsheet, and generate a report for the snacks. Did the snacks provide about 20 percent of nutrients significant for teens? Which? How much saturated fat did the snacks provide?
6. For middle-aged and elderly people, regular nutritious meals help to retain youthful energy and good health. As before, create a new profile for a 70-year-old single adult. Select the Track Diet tab, and choose foods to create a nutritious, convenient, easy-to-eat dinner for the person (see Food Feature, page 562). Select the Reports tab, then the Intake Spreadsheet for that meal and generate a report. Did the meal supply enough zinc, protein, vitamin B_{12}, and calcium to meet one-third of the person's need without excessive calories? Did it supply needed omega-3 fatty acids? If not, suggest ways of improving it.

MEDIA MENU

CENGAGENOW To find additional quiz questions, view videos and animations, and explore interactive exercises, go to **www.cengage.com/sso.**

Get information on the Food Guide Pyramid for young children from the USDA at **www.mypyramid.gov/kids.**

Get tips for feeding children from the American Dietetic Association: **www.eatright.org.**

Explore information about childhood obesity at **www.nlm.nih.gov/medlineplus/obesityinchildren.html.**

Visit these CDC sites to find a wealth of information on the health concerns of men or women: **www.cdc.gov/men** and **www.cdc.gov/women.**

Find resources and links to information about older adults at the National Institute on Aging (NIA) at **www.nia.nih.gov.**

SELF CHECK

Answers to these Self Check questions are in Appendix G.

1. Most children naturally like nutritious foods in all the food groups, *except:*
   - A. dairy
   - B. meats
   - C. vegetables
   - D. fruits
2. Which of the following can contribute to choking in children?
   - A. peanut butter eaten by the spoonful
   - B. hot dogs and tough meat
   - C. grapes and hard candy
   - D. all of the above
3. Which of the following is most commonly deficient in children and adolescents?
   - A. folate
   - B. zinc
   - C. iron
   - D. vitamin D
4. Which of the following may worsen symptoms of PMS?
   - A. adequate vitamin B_6
   - B. physical activity
   - C. caffeine
   - D. calcium
5. Which of the following have been shown to improve acne?
   - A. avoiding chocolate and fatty foods
   - B. vacations
   - C. vitamin A supplements
   - D. increased stress
6. Physical changes of aging that can affect nutrition include:
   - A. reduced stomach acid
   - B. increased saliva output
   - C. tooth loss and gum disease
   - D. a and c
7. Research to date supports the idea that food allergies or intolerances are common causes of hyperactivity in children.

   T F
8. Nutrition does not seem to play a role in the causation of osteoarthritis.

   T F
9. Vitamin A absorption decreases with age.

   T F
10. Herbal supplements have been shown to slow down the progression of Alzheimer's disease.

    T F

CONTROVERSY 14

Nutrient-Drug Interactions: Who Should Be Concerned?

LO 14.7

A 45-year-old Chicago business executive attempts to give up smoking with the help of nicotine gum. She replaces smoking breaks with beverage breaks, drinking frequent servings of tomato juice, coffee, and colas. She is discouraged when her stomach becomes upset and her craving for tobacco continues unabated despite the nicotine gum. Problem: nutrient-drug interaction.

A 14-year-old girl develops frequent and prolonged respiratory infections. Over the past six months, she has suffered constant fatigue despite adequate sleep, has had trouble completing school assignments, and has given up playing volleyball because she runs out of energy on the court. During the same six months, she has been taking huge doses of antacid pills each day because she heard this was a sure way to lose weight. Her pediatrician has diagnosed iron-deficiency anemia. Problem: nutrient-drug interaction.

A 30-year-old schoolteacher who benefits from antidepressant medication attends a faculty wine and cheese party. After sampling the cheese with a glass or two of red wine, his face becomes flushed. His behavior prompts others to drive him home. In the early morning hours, he awakens with severe dizziness, a migraine headache, vomiting, and trembling. An ambulance delivers him to an emergency room where a physician takes swift action to save his life. Problem: nutrient-drug interaction.

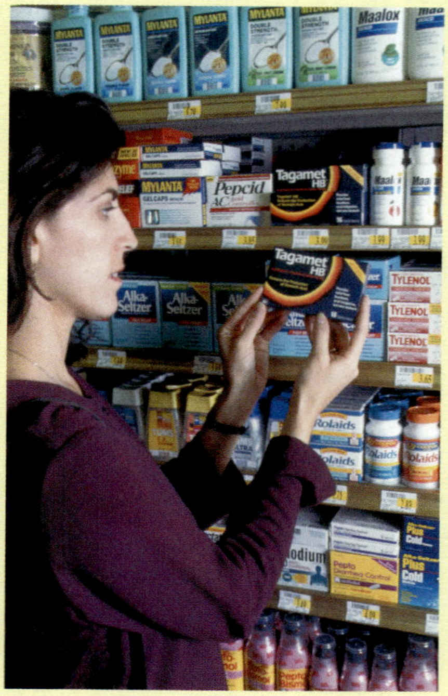

© Michael Newman/PhotoEdit

MEDICINES AND NUTRITION

People sometimes think that medical drugs do only good, not harm. As the opening stories illustrate, however, both prescription and over-the-counter (OTC) medicines can have unintended consequences, causing harm when they interact with the body's normal use of nutrients. As Figure C14-1 shows, drugs can interact with nutrients in the following ways:

FIGURE C14-1 Ways That Foods, Drugs, and Herbs Can Interact

The arrows show that foods, drugs, and herbs can interfere with each other's absorption, actions, metabolism, or excretion. Drugs also often change the appetite, affecting food intake.

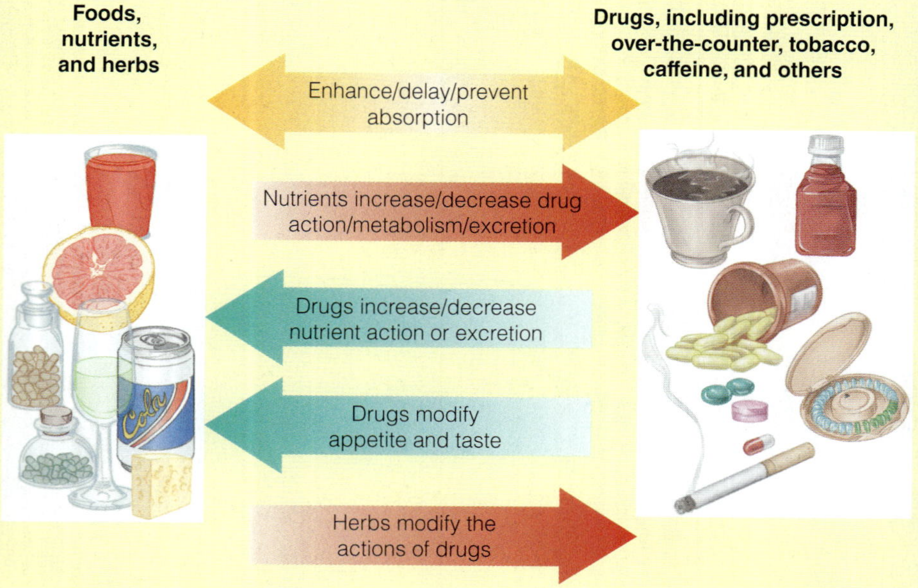

- Foods or nutrients can enhance, delay, or prevent drug absorption.
- Drugs can enhance, delay, or prevent nutrient absorption.
- Nutrients can alter the distribution of a drug among body tissues or interfere with its metabolism, transport, or elimination from the body.
- Drugs can alter the distribution of a nutrient among body tissues or interfere with its metabolism, transport, or excretion.
- Drugs also often modify taste, appetite, or food intake.
- Herbs can also modify drug effects.

These interactions do not occur every time a person takes a drug. The potential for undesirable nutrient-drug interactions is greatest for those who:

- take drugs (or medicines) for long times.
- take two or more drugs at the same time.
- are poorly nourished to begin with or are not eating well.

Alcohol is also infamous for its interactions with nutrients (see Controversy 3).

The Elderly

People over the age of 65 receive an average of 13 prescriptions each year and may take as many as 6 drugs at a time. They often take herbs and alternative medicine supplements, as well.[1]* When an elderly person sees different specialists for various conditions, each one may prescribe another medication or two, without considering the entire pharmaceutical mix. Aging alters the body's drug metabolism and excretion, which may diminish drug effectiveness or increase the potential for toxicities.[2] For all these reasons, physicians need to try the lowest possible doses when prescribing for older adults.[3]

Herbs

Not just the elderly seek healing power from herbs. Many others do, too, but few inform their physicians. Some herbs are known to interact with drugs, sometimes dangerously (see Table C14-1). For example, many herbs, including Ginkgo biloba, feverfew, and willow, have the potential to increase the anti–blood clotting effect of OTC pain and fever reducers, especially aspirin and its relatives.

*Reference notes are found in Appendix F.

Absorption of Drugs and Nutrients

The business executive described earlier felt the effects of the first type of interaction in the list above. Acid from the tomato juice, coffee, and colas she drank before chewing the nicotine gum kept the nicotine from being absorbed into the bloodstream through the lining of her mouth. With absorption blocked, the nicotine could not quell her craving, but instead traveled to her stomach and caused nausea (see Table C14-2 for other interactions with nicotine gum). An interaction that can have serious consequences occurs when dairy products or calcium-fortified juices interfere with the absorption of certain antibiotics. Without absorption of the proper dose, the antibiotics fail to do their jobs, and dangerous infectious diseases can worsen. Even the stomach acid normally secreted in response to eating can destroy some antibiotics, thereby reducing the dose. Drug labels include instructions for avoiding most such interactions, such as "Take on an empty stomach" or "Do not combine with dairy products."

Drugs can also interfere with the small intestine's absorption of nutrients, particularly minerals. This interaction explains the experience of the tired 14-year-old. Her overuse of antacids eliminated the stomach's normal acidity, on which iron absorption depends. The medicine bound tightly to the iron molecules, forming an insoluble, unabsorbable complex. Her iron stores already bordered on deficiency, as iron stores for young girls typically do, so her misuse of antacids pushed her over the edge into outright deficiency.

Chronic laxative use can also lead to malnutrition. Laxatives can carry nutrients through the intestines so rapidly that many vitamins have no time to be absorbed. Mineral oil, a laxative the body cannot absorb, can rob a person of fat-soluble vitamins. Vitamin D deficiencies can occur this way; calcium can also be excreted with the oil, potentially accelerating adult bone loss.

Metabolic Interactions and Nutrient Excretion

The teacher who landed in the emergency room was taking an antidepressant medicine, one of the monoamine oxidase inhibitors (MAOI). At the party, he suffered a dangerous chemical interaction between the medicine and the compound tyramine in his cheese and wine. Tyramine is produced during the fermenting process in cheese and wine manufacturing.

The MAOI medication works by depressing the activity of enzymes that destroy the brain neurotransmitter dopamine. With less enzyme activity, more dopamine is left, and depression lifts. At the same time, the drug also depresses enzymes in the liver that destroy tyramine. Ordinarily, the man's liver would have quickly destroyed the tyramine from the cheese and wine. But due to the MAOI medication, tyramine built up too high in his body and caused the potentially fatal reaction. Table C14-3 lists some foods high in tyramine.

Other culprits that affect the metabolism of medication include grapefruit juice, soy milk, and one of the most popular herbal supplements in the United States, Ginkgo biloba. A chemical constituent of grapefruit juice suppresses an enzyme responsible for breaking down many kinds of medical drugs.[4] With less drug breakdown, doses build up in the blood to levels that can have undesirable effects on the body. For example, in a drinker of grapefruit juice, a normal dosage of the blood-thinning drug coumarin can lead to dangerously prolonged bleeding and delayed clotting of blood. Soy milk seems to have the opposite effect: it reduces blood levels of a related blood-thinning drug. As for Ginkgo, people take it as a supplement in hopes of improving memory, but this effect is unproved. Takers may not know that it has been found to stimulate the activity of liver enzymes responsible for metabolizing many medications and so may diminish their effects.

Drugs often cause nutrient losses, too. Many people take large quantities of aspirin (10 to 12 tablets each day) to

TABLE C14-1 Herb and Drug Interactions

Herb	Drug	Interaction
Bilberry, dong Quai, feverfew, garlic, ginger, Ginkgo biloba, ginseng, meadowsweet, St. John's wort, turmeric, and willow	Warfarin, coumarin (anticlotting drugs, "blood thinners"); aspirin, ibuprofen, and other nonsteroidal anti-inflammatory drugs	Prolonged bleeding time; danger of hemorrhage
Black tea, St. John's wort, saw palmetto	Iron supplement; antianxiety drug	Tannins in herbs inhibit iron absorption; St. John's wort speeds antianxiety drug clearance.
Borage, evening primrose oil	Anticonvulsants	Seizures
Chinese herbs (xaio chai hu tang)	Prednisone (steroid drug)	Decreased blood concentrations of the drug
Echinacea (possible immunostimulant)	Cyclosporine and corticosteroids (immunosuppressants)	May reduce drug effectiveness
Feverfew	Aspirin, ibuprofen, and other nonsteroidal anti-inflammatory drugs	Drugs negate the effect of the herb for headaches.
Garlic supplements	Protease inhibitors (HIV-AIDS[a]) drug	Decreased blood concentrations of the drug
Ginseng	Estrogens, corticosteroids	Enhanced hormonal response
Ginseng, hawthorn, kyushin, licorice, plantain, St. John's wort, uzara root	Digoxin (cardiac antiarrhythmic drug derived from the herb foxglove)	Herbs interfere with drug action and monitoring.
Ginseng, karela	Blood glucose regulators	Herbs affect blood glucose levels.
Kelp (iodine source)	Synthroid or other thyroid hormone replacers	Herb may interfere with drug action.
Licorice	Corticosteroids (oral and topical ointments)	Overreaction to drug (potentiation)
Panax ginseng	Antidepressants	Overexcitability, mania
St. John's wort	Increased enzymatic destruction of many drugs; Cyclosporine (immunosuppressant); antiretroviral drugs (HIV[a] drugs), warfarin (anticoagulant, used to reduce blood clotting)	Decreased drug effectiveness; increased organ transplant rejection; reduced effectiveness of drugs to treat AIDS[a], reduced anticoagulant effect.
	MAOIs (used to treat depression, tuberculosis, or high blood pressure)[b]	Potentiation, with serotonin syndrome (mild): sweating, chills, blood pressure spike, nausea, abnormal heartbeat, muscle tremors, seizures
Valerian	Barbiturates (sedatives)	Enhanced sedation

Note: A valuable free resource for reliable online information about herbs is offered by the Memorial Sloan-Kettering Cancer Center at www.mskcc.org/aboutherbs.
[a]Acquired Immune Deficiency Syndrome, caused by HIV infection (human immunodeficiency virus).
[b]MAOI stands for monoamine oxidase inhibitors.

relieve the pain of arthritis, backaches, and headaches. This much aspirin can speed up blood loss from the stomach by as much as 10 times, enough to cause iron-deficiency anemia in some people. People who take aspirin regularly should eat iron-rich foods regularly as well. Table C14-4 lists some examples of other possible nutrient-drug interactions, including both prescription and OTC medications. Details on some common interactions follow.

ORAL CONTRACEPTIVES

Millions of women use oral contraceptives, daily doses of hormones that prevent pregnancy. Oral contraceptive interactions with nutrients illustrate the complexity of nutrient-drug interactions. Folate, vitamin B_{12}, and vitamin B_6, along with beta-carotene, status may be slightly reduced in oral contraceptive users. Blood vitamin D levels, in contrast, may be higher. At first glance, research seems to indicate that women using oral contraceptives may be at risk for nutrient deficiencies or toxicities, but little is known about the implications of these interactions.

Significantly, in women older than about 35 years, most oral contraceptives raise total blood cholesterol and triglyceride concentrations and lower HDL, amplifying the risk of stroke and heart disease. A few women using oral contraceptives also experience mild hypertension.

TABLE C14-2 Foods and Beverages That Limit the Effectiveness of Nicotine Gum

- Apple juice
- Beer
- Coffee
- Colas
- Grape juice
- Ketchup
- Lemon-lime soda
- Mustard
- Orange juice
- Pineapple juice
- Soy sauce
- Tomato juice

TABLE C14-3 Some Foods High in Tyramine[a]

- Aged cheeses
- Aged meats
- Alcoholic beverages (beer, wine)
- Anchovies
- Caviar
- Fava beans
- Fermented foods (sauerkraut, sausages)
- Feta cheese
- Lima beans
- Mushrooms
- Pickled fish or meat
- Prepared soy foods (miso, tempeh, tofu)
- Smoked fish or meat
- Soy sauce
- Yeast extract (Marmite)

[a]*The tyramine content of foods depends on storage conditions and processing; thus the amounts in similar products can vary substantially.*

Some women lose or gain weight when taking oral contraceptives. Others suffer edema because estrogen promotes sodium conservation by the kidneys; dietary sodium restriction can correct this condition. All women taking estrogen either in oral contraceptives or in hormone therapy should be aware that vitamin C doses of a gram or more may elevate serum estrogen and falsely suggest that a lower dose is needed.

For most women, a nutritious diet is all that is needed to correct nutrient imbalances. If a woman feels compelled to take a supplement, however, a standard multivitamin-mineral supplement is probably harmless.

CAFFEINE

The well-known "wake-up" effect of caffeine is the primary reason people in every society use it in some form. Compared with the drugs discussed so far, though, caffeine's interactions with foods and nutrients are subtle. Yet caffeine's relationship to nutrition is important because caffeine is so widespread that many people may be unaware that they are consuming it—see Table C14-5 for the caffeine contents of popular beverages, foods, and medications. Many OTC cold and headache remedies contain caffeine because, in addition to being a mild pain reliever in its own right, caffeine remedies the caffeine-withdrawal headache that no other pain reliever can touch. Caffeine is present in chocolate bars, colas, and other foods children favor, and children are more sensitive to caffeine's effects because they are small and, at first, not adapted to its use.

Caffeine is the most popular and widely consumed drug in the United States. One in three U.S. citizens consumes about 200 milligrams of caffeine per day (the amount in 10 ounces of coffee, less than the smallest serving from popular coffee shops) but many others consume much more. Many studies indicate that a 200-milligram dose of caffeine significantly improves the ability to pay attention, especially if subjects are sleepy, but more caffeine is probably not better. A single dose of 500 milligrams has been shown to worsen thinking abilities in almost everyone, and more than this may present some risk to health through its actions as a stimulant.

Caffeine is a true stimulant drug. Like all stimulants, it increases the respiratory rate, heart rate, and secretion of stress and other hormones. Caffeine also raises the blood pressure, an effect that lasts for hours after consumption.[5] A moderate dose of caffeine may also speed up metabolic energy expenditures for several hours, and it stimulates the digestive tract, promoting efficient elimination. Because caffeine is a diuretic, high doses promote water loss from the body, although a moderate intake of caffeinated beverages consumed as part of the daily fluid intake does not negatively influence the body's water balance (see Chapter 8 for details).

BLOOMimage/Getty Images

Caffeine: a true stimulant drug.

Some people avoid caffeine for fear it may harm their health. Research mostly refutes links between caffeine and cancer, cardiovascular disease, or birth defects.[6] Coffee and tea contain phytochemicals other than caffeine, and some of these may affect disease risks for better or worse in ways yet to be clarified.[7]

If you like caffeine-containing foods or beverages, the most reasonable approach is to limit your intake to the equivalent of 2 small cups of coffee per day. If body weight is a concern, be aware that the luscious sweet coffee beverages sold in take-out places average 240 calories each, with some much higher, providing more than a third of an average person's daily energy need.[8] Pregnant women should exercise moderation in using caffeine, and parents should monitor and control their children's intakes.

TOBACCO

Cigarette and other tobacco use causes thousands of people to suffer from cancer and other diseases of the

TABLE C14-4 Nutrient Interactions with Some Commonly Used Drugs

Medicines and Caffeine	Effects on Absorption	Effects on Excretion	Effects on Metabolism
Antacids (aluminum containing)	Reduce iron absorption	Increase calcium and phosphorus excretion	May accelerate destruction of thiamin
Antibiotics (long-term usage)	Reduce absorption of fats, amino acids, folate, fat-soluble vitamins, vitamin B_{12}, calcium, copper, iron, magnesium, potassium, phosphate, zinc	Increase excretion of folate, niacin, potassium, riboflavin, vitamin C	Destroy vitamin K–producing bacteria and reduce vitamin K production
Antidepressants (monoamine oxidase inhibitors, MAOI)			Slow breakdown of tyramine, with dangerous blood pressure spike and other symptoms on consuming tyramine-rich foods or drinks: *alcoholic beverages* (sherry, vermouth, red wines, some beers); *cheeses* (aged and processed); *some meats* (caviar, pickled herring, liver, smoked and cured sausages, lunchmeats); *fermented products* (soy sauce, miso, sauerkraut); *others* (brewer's yeast, yeast supplements, yeast paste; baked goods made with baker's yeast are safe; foods past their expiration date)
Aspirin (large doses, long-term usage)	Lowers blood concentration of folate	Increases excretion of thiamin, vitamin C, vitamin K; causes iron and potassium losses through gastric blood loss	
Caffeine		Increases excretion of small amounts of calcium and magnesium	Stimulates release of fatty acids into the blood
Cholesterol-lowering "statin" drugs (Zocor, Lipitor)			Grapefruit juice slows drug metabolism, causing buildup of high drug levels; potentially life-threatening muscle toxicity can result.
Diuretics		Raise blood calcium and zinc; lower blood folate, chloride, magnesium, phosphorus, potassium, vitamin B_{12}; increase excretion of calcium, sodium, thiamin, potassium, chloride, magnesium	Interfere with storage of zinc
Estrogen replacement therapy	May reduce absorption of folate	Causes sodium retention	May raise blood glucose, triglycerides, vitamin A, vitamin E, copper, and iron; may lower blood vitamin C, folate, vitamin B_6, riboflavin, calcium, magnesium, and zinc
Laxatives (effects vary with type)	Reduce absorption of glucose, fat, carotene, vitamin D, other fat-soluble vitamins, calcium, phosphate, potassium	Increase excretion of all unabsorbed nutrients	
Oral contraceptives	Reduce absorption of folate, may improve absorption of calcium	Cause sodium retention	Raise blood vitamin A, vitamin D, copper, iron; may lower blood beta-carotene, riboflavin, vitamin B_6, vitamin B_{12}, vitamin C; may elevate requirements for riboflavin and vitamin B_6; alter blood lipid elevating risk of heart disease in smokers and older women

TABLE C14-5 Caffeine Content of Selected Beverages, Foods and Medications

Beverages and Foods	Serving Size	Average (mg)
Coffee		
Brewed	8 oz	95
Decaffeinated	8 oz	2
Instant	8 oz	64
Tea		
Brewed, green	8 oz	30
Brewed, herbal	8 oz	0
Brewed, leaf or bag	8 oz	47
Instant	8 oz	26
Lipton/Nestea bottled iced tea	12 oz	10
Snapple iced tea (all flavors)	16 oz	42
Soft drinks[a]		
A & W Creme Soda	12 oz	29
Barq's Root Beer	12 oz	18
Colas, Dr. Pepper, Mr. Pibb, Sunkist Orange	12 oz	30–35
A&W Root Beer, club soda, Fresca, ginger ale, 7-Up, Sierra Mist, Sprite, Squirt, tonic water, caffeine-free soft drinks	12 oz	0
Mello Yello, Mountain Dew	12 oz	45–50
Energy drinks		
Amp	8.4 oz	70
Aqua Blast	.5 L	90
Aqua Java	.5 L	55
E Maxx	8.4 oz	74
Java Water	.5 L	125
KMX	8.4 oz	33
Krank	.5 L	100
Red Bull	8.3 oz	75
Sobe No Fear	16 oz	141
Water Joe	.5 L	65
Other beverages		
Chocolate milk or hot cocoa	8 oz	5
Starbucks Frappuccino Mocha	9.5 oz	72
Starbucks Frappuccino Vanilla	9.5 oz	64
Yoohoo chocolate drink	9 oz	3

Beverages and Foods	Serving Size	Average (mg)
Candies/Chewing Gum		
Gum, caffeinated	1 pce	95
Dark chocolate covered coffee beans	1 oz	235
Dark chocolate, semisweet	1 oz	18
Milk chocolate	1 oz	6
Java Pops	1 pop	60
White chocolate	1 oz	0
Foods		
Frozen yogurt, Ben & Jerry's coffee fudge	1 c	85
Frozen yogurt, Häagen-Dazs coffee	1 c	40
Ice cream, Starbucks coffee	1 c	50
Ice cream, Starbucks Frappuccino bar	1 bar	15
Yogurt, Dannon coffee flavored	1 c	45
Drugs[b]		
Cold remedies		
Coryban-D, Dristan	1 tablet	30
Diuretics		
Aqua-Ban	1 tablet	100
Pre-Mens Forte	1 tablet	100
Pain relievers		
Anacin, BC Fast Pain Reliever	1 tablet	32
Excedrin, Midol, Midol Max Strength	1 tablet	65
Stimulants		
Awake, NoDoz	1 tablet	100
Awake Maximum Strength, Caffedrine, NoDoz Maximum Strength, Stay Awake, Vivarin	1 tablet	200
Weight-control aids		
Dexatrim	1 tablet	200

[a]*The FDA suggests a maximum of 65 milligrams per 12-ounce cola beverage, but this limit is not mandatory. Because products change, contact the manufacturer for an update on products you use regularly.*

[b]*A pharmacologically active dose of caffeine is defined as 200 milligrams.*

Sources: Adapted from USDA database Release 18 (http://www.nal.usda.gov/fnic/foodcomp/Data/), Caffeine content of foods and drugs, Center for Science and the Public Interest (www.cspinet.org/new/cafchart.htm), and R. R. McCusker, B. A. Goldberger, and E. J. Cone, Caffeine content of energy drinks, carbonated sodas, and other beverages, Journal of Analytical Toxicology *30 (2006): 112–114.*

cardiovascular, digestive, and respiratory systems. These effects are beyond nutrition's scope, but smoking does depress hunger and body fatness and change nutrient status. Chapter 9 provided details on smoking and body fatness.

Nutrient intakes of smokers and nonsmokers differ. Smokers have lower intakes of dietary fiber, vitamins, and minerals, even when their energy intakes are quite similar to those of nonsmokers. Smokers require more vitamin C in the

TABLE C14-6 Nutrition Effects of Four Drugs of Abuse

Drug of Abuse	Possible Effects on Nutrition Status
Cocaine	Reduces intakes of nutritious foods; increases intakes of alcohol, coffee, and fat; may induce or aggravate eating disorders.
Heroin	Heightens and delays insulin response to glucose; reduces intakes.
Marijuana	Increases intakes of foods, especially sweets; may cause weight gain.
Nicotine[a]	Reduces intake of sweet foods and water; increases intakes of fat; reduces fetal weight; lowers blood concentration of beta-carotene.

[a]*Other effects of smoking include increased vitamin C requirements.*

diet than do nonsmokers because smoking accelerates the breakdown of vitamin C. The effect is apparently related to an increase in oxidative stress produced by smoking and is not related to the tobacco drug nicotine. The DRI committee recommends that smokers obtain an extra 35 milligrams of vitamin C a day to cover their extra losses.

ILLICIT DRUGS

People know that illicit drugs are harmful, but many choose to abuse them anyway in spite of the risks. Like OTC and prescription drugs, illegal drugs modify body functions. Unlike medicines, however, no watchdog agency monitors them for safety, effectiveness, or even purity.

Smoking a marijuana cigarette affects several senses, including the sense of taste. It produces an enhanced enjoyment of eating, especially of sweets. Why or how this effect occurs is not known. Despite higher food intakes, marijuana abusers often consume fewer nutrients than do nonabusers because the extra foods they choose tend to be high-calorie, low-nutrient snack foods. Besides the nutrition effects, regular marijuana users face the same risk of lung cancer as people who smoke a pack of cigarettes a day.

Many other drugs of abuse elicit effects such as intense euphoria, restlessness, heightened self-confidence, irritability, insomnia, and loss of appetite. Weight loss is a common side effect, and unlike marijuana, most other drugs of abuse cause serious malnutrition. The stronger the craving for the drug, the less a drug abuser wants nutritious food. Rats given unlimited access to cocaine will choose the drug over food until they die of starvation. The effects of addictive drugs vary somewhat, but many are similar to the effects of cocaine, listed in Table C14-6. Drug abusers face multiple nutrition problems, and an important aspect of addiction recovery is the identification and correction of nutrition problems.

PERSONAL STRATEGY

In conclusion, when you need to take a medicine, do so wisely. Ask your physician, pharmacist, or other health-care provider for specific instructions about the doses, times, and how to take the medication—for example, with meals or on an empty stomach. If you notice new symptoms or if a drug seems not to be working well, consult your physician. The only instruction people need about illicit drugs is to avoid them altogether for countless reasons. As for smoking and chewing tobacco, the same advice applies: don't take these habits up, or if you already have, take steps to quit. For drugs with lesser consequences to health, such as caffeine, use moderation.

Try to live life in a way that requires less chemical assistance. If you are sleepy, try a 15-minute nap or 15 minutes of stretching exercises instead of a 15-minute coffee break. The coffee will stimulate your nerves for an hour, but the alternatives will refresh your attitude for the rest of the day. If you suffer constipation, try getting enough exercise, fiber, and water for a few days. Chances are that a laxative will be unnecessary. The strategy being suggested here is to take control of your body, allowing your reliable, self-healing nature to make fine adjustments that you need not force with chemicals. Bodies have few requests: adequate nutrition, rest, exercise, and hygiene. Give your body what it asks for, and let it function naturally, day-to-day, without interference from drugs.

Patti Mollica/SuperStock/Getty Images

Hunger and the Global Environment

15

DO YOU EVER . . .

- Feel concern about hunger abroad but doubt that it happens at home?
- Feel overwhelmed by the world's problems?
- Purchase a meal, considering only its monetary price?
- Wish that someone would clean up the environment?

Keep reading . . .

LEARNING OBJECTIVES

To find learning objective topics in this chapter, look for text headings with a corresponding "LO" number above the heading. After completing this chapter, you should be able to accomplish the following:

LO 15.1 Discuss the double health threat from undernutrition and obesity, and suggest reasons why this might occur among a single group of people.

LO 15.2 Speculate as to how reducing a family's hunger level can lead to more positive outcomes for health, educational, and social well-being of the family.

LO 15.3 Explain why people in poverty are inclined to have larger families in spite of the scarcity of food.

LO 15.4 Describe why producing enough food for people and livestock presents problems for the environment.

LO 15.5 Define the term *ecological footprint,* and describe ways to lessen one's own ecological footprint.

Did You Know?

Almost one out of every six children in the United States lives in poverty.

Stefanie Keenan/WireImage/Getty Images

Each person's efforts can help to bring about needed change.

Never doubt that a small group of thoughtful, committed people can change the world. Indeed, it is the only thing that ever has.

—Margaret Mead

CONCEPT LINK 15-1

The concept of undernutrition, a state of nutrient or energy deficiency, was introduced in Chapter 1, page 2.

very low food security multiple indications of disrupted eating patterns and reduced food intake. Example: a family that may be without food for a significant number of days in a year or that relies on food from shelters, food banks, or other organizations.

low food security reduced dietary quality, variety, or desirability, but no significant reduction in total food intake. Example: a family whose diet centers on inexpensive, low-nutrient foods such as refined grains, inexpensive meats, sweets, and fats.

marginal food security one or two problems, usually anxiety over having enough food in the house, but without significant change in food intake. Example: a family whose food supply is sufficient but barely lasts until the next paycheck.

high food security no reported food limitation or access problems. The food supply is ample.

hunger a consequence of food insecurity that, because of prolonged involuntary lack of food, results in discomfort, illness, weakness, or pain beyond a mild uneasy sensation.

food crisis a steep decline in food availability with a proportional rise in hunger and malnutrition at the local, national, or global level.

In the United States today, 4.4 million households live with **very low food security**—one or more members of these households repeatedly had little or nothing to eat because of a lack of money.[1]* Another 8.2 million households experienced **low food security** or **marginal food security,** somewhat less dire conditions. A current economic downturn threatens to worsen the plight of these people, with higher costs of food, fuel, medical, and other expenses of daily living.[2] Still, poverty and hunger coexist with affluence and **high food security** in the United States; employed people who work for low wages often experience poverty and food insecurity (see Figure 15-1). Food insecurity often leads to **hunger**—not the healthy appetite triggered by anticipation of a hearty meal, but the pain, illness, or weakness caused by a prolonged, involuntary lack of the food needed to meet nutrient needs.

The contrast of hunger amidst plenty characterizes many of the world's nations. Over 1.02 billion of the world's people suffer chronic hunger and malnutrition while their neighbors are food secure or even overfed (see Table 15-1).[3] Tens of thousands die of starvation each day, mostly children—one every two seconds.

The tragedy described on these pages may seem at first to be beyond the influence of the ordinary person. What possible difference can one person make? As it turns out, quite a bit. Students in particular can play a powerful role in bringing about change. Students everywhere are helping to change governments, human predicaments, and environmental problems for the better. Student movements persuaded 127 universities and many institutions, corporations, and government agencies to put pressure on South Africa and succeeded in ending the racial divisions of apartheid. Student pressure opened the way for the first deaf president at a university for the deaf. Students offer major services to communities through soup kitchens, home repair programs, and child education. The young people of today are the world's single best hope for a better tomorrow.

KEY POINT The world's chronically hungry people suffer the effects of undernutrition, and a growing poverty in the United States contributes to food insecurity. Individual efforts can make a difference.

LO 15.1, 15.2

Hunger

Hunger plagues both developed and developing nations around the world. The chronically hungry in developing nations typically suffer from undernutrition, a condition of energy and nutrient deficiency that causes general weakness, fatigue, and susceptibility to illness. Today, many such nations are gripped in a **food crisis,** in which already meager food supplies have dwindled further and rates of malnutrition and hunger have risen sharply.[4]

*Reference notes are found in Appendix F.

TABLE 15-1 Global Undernutrition and Overnutrition

Condition	Global Incidence
Hunger, protein-energy malnutrition	≥1.02 billion people
Vitamin and mineral deficiencies[a]	2.0–3.5 billion people (about half the world's population)
Overnutrition, obesity	≥1.1 billion people

[a]*Vitamin and mineral deficiencies occur in both underfed and overfed populations.*

Source: FAO 2008; World Health Organization.

Hunger in the United States

In the United States and other developed countries, the primary cause of hunger is **food poverty.** People go without nourishing meals not because there is no food nearby to purchase, but because they lack sufficient money to pay for both the food they need and other necessities, such as clothing, housing, medicines, and utilities. More than 12 percent of the population of the United States lives in a general state of poverty. The likelihood of food poverty increases with problems such as abuse of alcohol and other drugs, mental or physical illness, depression, lack of awareness of or access to available food programs, and the reluctance of people to accept what some perceive as "government handouts" or charity.

Limited Nutritious Foods

To stretch meager food supplies, adults may skip meals or cut their portions. When desperate, they may be forced to break social rules—begging from strangers, stealing from markets, consuming pet foods, or even harvesting dead animals from roadsides or scavenging through garbage cans. In the latter cases, such foods may be spoiled or contaminated and inflict dangerous foodborne illnesses that compound harm to health from borderline malnutrition. Children in such families sometimes go hungry for an entire day until the adults can obtain food.

Significant numbers of U.S. children in families of low food security consume enough calories each day, but from a steady diet of inexpensive, low-nutrient foods, such as white bread, fats, sugary punches, and crackers, with few of the fruits, vegetables, milk products, and other nutritious foods children need to be healthy. The more severe their circumstances, the more likely children are to be in poor or fair health, and the greater their likelihood of hospitalization. Such children are often behind their peers in school, develop behavioral and social problems, are slower to heal from injuries, and are more susceptible to illness.[5] These children often misbehave because of malnutrition or in rebellion against their circumstances, and relieving their poverty often improves educational performance and their behavior.[6]

The Poverty-Obesity Paradox

In the United States and elsewhere, the highest rates of obesity occur among those living with poverty and food insecurity.[7] Obesity and undernutrition not only occur together in the same community but often in the same family, and even in the same person.[8] This apparent paradox becomes understandable in the context of the food supply.[9]

Many low-income urban or rural families lack access to grocery stores with healthful whole food choices, such as fresh fruits and vegetables.[10] In these so-called **food deserts,** convenience stores and fast-food places offer mostly calorie-rich, high-fat, high-salt, nutrient-poor choices, such as refined grains, sugar-sweetened beverages, processed meats, and fast foods.[11] A steady diet of such foods can easily lead to both obesity and malnutrition. Furthermore, people who have gone hungry in the past and whose future meals are uncertain may overeat when any kind of food becomes available.[12] Figure 15-2 demonstrates this concept.

Recognizing Hunger

Hunger is not always easy to recognize. Table 15-2 shows how national surveys identify it in the United States. The American Dietetic Association has called for aggressive action to bring an end to domestic hunger and to achieve food and nutrition security for all residents of the United States.[13] It also holds that access to adequate amounts of safe, nutritious, and culturally appropriate food at all times is a fundamental human right. Eradicating hunger is in everyone's interest. A relatively small investment in nutrition reaps enormous rewards by promoting health, preventing disability, boosting productivity, and conserving limited medical resources.[14] Conversely, hunger of individual families diminishes the nation as a whole.

KEY POINT Food insecurity and hunger in the United States are more prevalent than most people realize and they may be difficult to detect. People with low food security may suffer obesity alongside hunger in the same community or family.

FIGURE 15-1 Food Security of U.S. Households, 2008

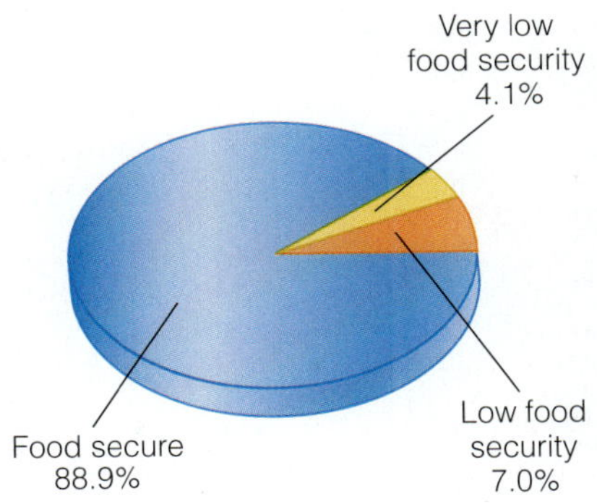

Source: USDA Economic Research Service, Food Security in the United States; Conditions and trends, 2008, available at www.ers.usda.gov/Briefing/FoodSecurity/trends.htm.

FIGURE 15-2 The Poverty-Obesity Paradox

Poverty can lead to both food insecurity and obesity when food choices are limited to calorie-rich, nutrient-poor foods.

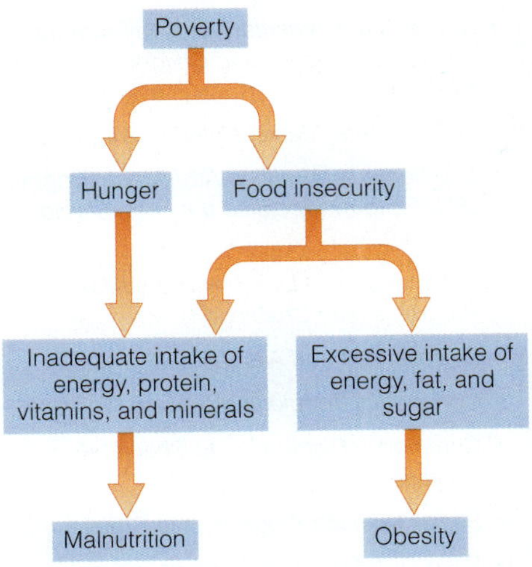

food poverty hunger occurring when enough food exists in an area but some of the people cannot obtain it because they lack money, are being deprived for political reasons, live in a country at war, or suffer from other problems such as lack of transportation.

food deserts a term used to describe urban and rural low-income neighborhoods and communities that have limited access to affordable and nutritious foods.

TABLE 15-2 How to Identify Food Insecurity in a U.S. Household

These survey questions are used to identify households with food insecurity. Most often, adults tend to protect their children from hunger. In the most severe cases, children also suffer from hunger and eat less. The results of a recent survey were shown in Figure 15-1, page 575.

1. Did you worry whether your food would run out before you got money to buy more?
2. Did you find that the food you bought just didn't last, and you didn't have money to buy more?
3. Were you unable to afford to eat balanced meals?
4. Did you or other adults in your household ever cut the size of your meals or skip meals because there wasn't enough money for food?
5. Did this happen in three or more months during the previous year?
6. Did you ever eat less than you felt you should because there wasn't enough money for food?
7. Were you ever hungry but didn't eat because you couldn't afford enough food?
8. Did you lose weight because you didn't have enough money for food?
9. Did you or other adults in your household ever not eat for a whole day because there wasn't enough money for food?
10. Did this happen in three or more months during the previous year?
11. Did you rely on only a few kinds of low-cost food to feed your children because you were running out of money to buy food?
12. Were you unable to feed your children a balanced meal because you couldn't afford it?
13. Were your children not eating enough because you just couldn't afford enough food?
14. Did you ever cut the size of your children's meal because there wasn't enough money for food?
15. Were your children ever hungry but you just couldn't afford more food?
16. Did your children ever skip a meal because there wasn't enough money for food?
17. Did this happen in three or more months during the previous year?
18. Did your children ever not eat for a whole day because there wasn't enough money for food?

The more positive responses, the greater the food insecurity. Households with children answer all of the questions and are categorized as follows:

≤2 positive responses = food secure.
3–7 positive responses = low food security.
≥8 positive responses = very low food security.

Households without children answer the first 10 questions and are categorized as follows:

≤2 positive responses = food secure.
3–5 positive responses = low food security.
≥6 positive responses = very low food security.

Source: *United States Department of Agriculture,* Household Food Security in the United States, *2005, available at www.ers.usda.gov/publications.*

- U.S. federal and state food programs include:
  - *Special Supplemental Nutrition Program for Women, Infants, and Children (WIC, see Chapter 13).*
  - *WIC Farmers' Market Nutrition Program.*
  - *Supplemental Nutrition Assistance Program (SNAP), formerly called the Food Stamp Program.*
  - *National School Lunch and Breakfast Programs (see Chapter 14).*
  - *Emergency Food Assistance Program.*
  - *Commodity Supplemental Food Program.*
  - *Commodity Distribution to Charitable Institutions.*
  - *Senior Nutrition Program (see Chapter 14).*
  - *Food Distribution Program on Indian Reservations.*
  - *Nutrition Assistance to Puerto Rico.*
  - *Temporary Assistance to Needy Families (often called "welfare").*

What U.S. Food Programs Are Directed at Stopping Domestic Hunger?

An extensive network of food assistance programs delivers life-giving food daily to millions of U.S. citizens living in poverty. One of every six Americans receives food assistance of some kind, at a total cost of almost $55 billion per year.[15] Even so, the programs are not fully successful at preventing hunger, even among those who receive their benefits.

Did You Know?

- The Food Stamp Program has a new name: Supplemental Nutrition Assistance Program (SNAP).
- In 2008, *America's Second Harvest* became *Feeding America.*

Nationwide Efforts Programs described in earlier chapters include children's school lunch and school breakfast programs, child care and elder care food programs, programs to supply low-income pregnant women and mothers with nourishing food (WIC), and food assistance programs for older adults such as congregate meals and Meals on Wheels. In particular, the WIC program is effective at improving the health of mothers and their infants. Participation during pregnancy is associated with increased weight and longer gestation, which result in healthier babies in a low-income population. Children of WIC families have higher intakes of iron, folate, and vitamin B_6 than children in nonparticipating but eligible families.

The centerpiece of U.S. food programs for low-income people is the Supplemental Nutrition Assistance Program (SNAP), formerly called the Food Stamp Program, administered by the U.S. Department of Agriculture (USDA).[16] It provides assistance to more than 28 million people at a cost of more than $34 billion per year; about half of the recipients are children.[17] Eligible households receive electronic debit transfer cards, similar to regular debit cards, through state social services or welfare agencies. Recipients can use the cards like cash to purchase food and food-bearing plants and seeds, but not to buy tobacco, cleaning items, alcohol, or other nonfood items. To help stretch consumer food dollars and food credits, the USDA also provides guidance on choosing thrifty meals, complete with daily menus and recipes (see Table 15-3).

USDA Photo by Ken Hammond

School breakfasts and lunches provide low-income children with nourishment at little or no cost.

Community Efforts To assist where government programs fall short, concerned citizens in many communities work through local agencies and churches to help deliver food to hungry people. National **food recovery** programs have made a dramatic difference. The largest program, Feeding America (formerly, America's Second Harvest), coordinates the efforts of **food banks, food pantries, emergency kitchens,** and homeless shelters that provide food to over 25 million people a year. Many food-insecure people rely on these sources of food for survival.[18]

Each year, an estimated one-fifth of our food supply is wasted in fields, commercial kitchens, grocery stores, and restaurants—enough food to feed many millions of hungry people. Food recovery programs collect and distribute good food that would otherwise go to waste.

A combination of various strategies can help to build food security within a community. Table 15-4 presents actions in three stages for developing a hunger-free community. The table also points out that while providing food relief to the hungry is critical, developing **sustainable** long-term solutions that attack the underlying problems of limited food access, low wages, and poverty is equally important. To rephrase a well-known adage: If you give a man a fish, he will eat for a day. If you teach him to fish so that he can buy and maintain his own gear and bait, he will eat for a lifetime and help to feed you, too.

AP/Wide World Photos

Food banks and other helping organizations depend on caring volunteers.

food recovery collecting wholesome surplus food for distribution to low-income people who are hungry.

food banks facilities that collect and distribute food donations to authorized organizations feeding the hungry.

food pantries community food collection programs that provide groceries to be prepared and eaten at home.

emergency kitchens programs that provide prepared meals to be eaten on-site; often called *soup kitchens.*

sustainable able to continue indefinitely; in this context, the use of resources in ways that maintain both natural resources and human life; the use of natural resources at a pace that allows the earth to replace them. In a sustainable system, resources do not become depleted, and pollution does not accumulate.

TABLE 15-3 Tips for Thrifty Food Shopping

The USDA website provides meal plans and recipes for thrifty meals (search for "thrifty meals" at www.USDA.gov/cnpp). In addition, tips like these can help stretch food dollars:

- Plan meals and make a list to avoid "impulse" buying; don't shop when hungry.
- Center meals on legumes and pasta or other grains; use animal protein sparingly.
- Use dry powdered milk for recipes; buy fresh milk in gallons or half gallons for drinking.
- Learn the simple joys of preparing whole foods (prepared and convenience foods cost extra).
- Big containers are often economical, but only if you use up the food before it spoils.
- Comparison shop; watch sales; clip coupons for items you use. Make a sport of matching coupons to sales for the best savings.
- Check discount and "dollar" stores; try their brands of everything from ketchup to laundry soap—some are as good as name-brand goods but cost less because they do not advertise.

- Four common methods of food recovery are:
  - *Field gleaning: Collecting crops from fields that either have already been harvested or are not profitable to harvest.*
  - *Perishable food rescue or salvage: Collecting perishable produce from wholesalers and markets.*
  - *Prepared food rescue: Collecting prepared foods from commercial kitchens.*
  - *Nonperishable food collection: Collecting processed foods from wholesalers and markets.*

- For information about food pantries, food banks, and other agencies in your community, call the USDA's hunger hotline: (800) GLEAN-IT.

TABLE 15-4 Addressing Community Hunger

All of the actions in each stage listed below require monitoring and feedback for optimum effectiveness.

Stage 1 Short-Term Goals—Fully Use Resources Currently Available

- Make full use of assistance that is available now. Assess available federal, state, local, and private food organizations and make them known to nutrition and other professionals in the community.
- Find out why people in need are not using the services. Especially, assess accessibility of food organizations to people who need them and assess transportation systems.
- Identify food quality and price inequities in low-income neighborhoods.
- Educate consumers and institutions about using local, organic, and seasonal foods.

Stage 2 Medium-Range Goals—Network and Connect Food Relief Agencies and Others to Identify and Address Problems

- Connect emergency food programs with local urban agriculture projects to encourage collection and distribution of available nutritious foods.
- Coordinate food services with parks and recreation programs and other community outlets, such as churches, to which area residents have easy access.
- Integrate public and private hunger-relief agencies, local businesses, and others to create an emergency food delivery network; include low-income participants for input.
- Take a leadership role by serving on community food councils or homeless-relief organizations; organize workshops to educate others.

Stage 3 Long-Range Goals—Redesign Food and Other Systems for Effectiveness and Sustainability

- Mobilize government and community leaders to encourage urban agriculture to foster food self-reliance and improve nutrient intakes.
- Advocate for land-use policies and land grants that allow and encourage urban agriculture, such as community gardens and school gardens.
- Suggest improvements to public transportation to human services agencies and food resources.
- Encourage tax and other financial incentives to attract appropriate food businesses, such as farmer's markets and supermarkets, to low-income neighborhoods.
- Advocate increased minimum wage and more affordable housing.

Sources: C. McCullum and coauthors, Evidenced-based strategies to build community food security, Journal of the American Dietetic Association *105 (2005): 278–283; The Food Project, available at www.foodproject.org/default.asp.*

KEY POINT Government programs to relieve poverty and hunger are tremendously helpful, if not fully successful.

biofuels fuels made mostly of materials derived from recently harvested living organisms. Examples are *biogas, ethanol,* and *biodiesel.* Biofuels contribute less to the carbon dioxide burden of the atmosphere because plants capture carbon from the air as they grow and release it again when the fuel is burned; fossil fuels such as coal and oil contain carbon that was previously held underground for millions of years and is newly released into the atmosphere on burning.

microcredit nontraditional money sources typically involving small loans to disadvantaged people for business development.

What Is the State of World Hunger?

In the developing world, hunger and poverty are intense and may worsen as global economies slump.[19] Figure 15-3 points out the world's hunger "hot spots." The primary form of hunger is still food poverty, but the poverty is more extreme.

The Staggering Statistics Grasping the severity of poverty in the developing world can be difficult, but some statistics may help. One-fifth of the world's 6 billion people have no land and no possessions *at all.* The "poorest poor" survive on less than one dollar a day each, they lack water that is safe to drink, and they cannot read or write. Many spend about 80 percent of all they earn on food, but still they are hungry and malnourished. The average U.S. house cat eats twice as much protein every day as one of these people, and the yearly cost of keeping that cat is greater than that person's annual income.

The recent world economic downturn has sent food prices even farther out of reach—almost doubling between 2005 and 2008.[20] This increase partly reflects a

FIGURE 15-3 **Hunger Hot Spots**

Today, more than 1.02 billion of the world's people go hungry. Hunger is prevalent in the developing world, with some countries reporting hunger and malnutrition in more than half of their population.

Key:
- Shortfall in food production/supplies
- Widespread lack of access
- Severe food insecurity

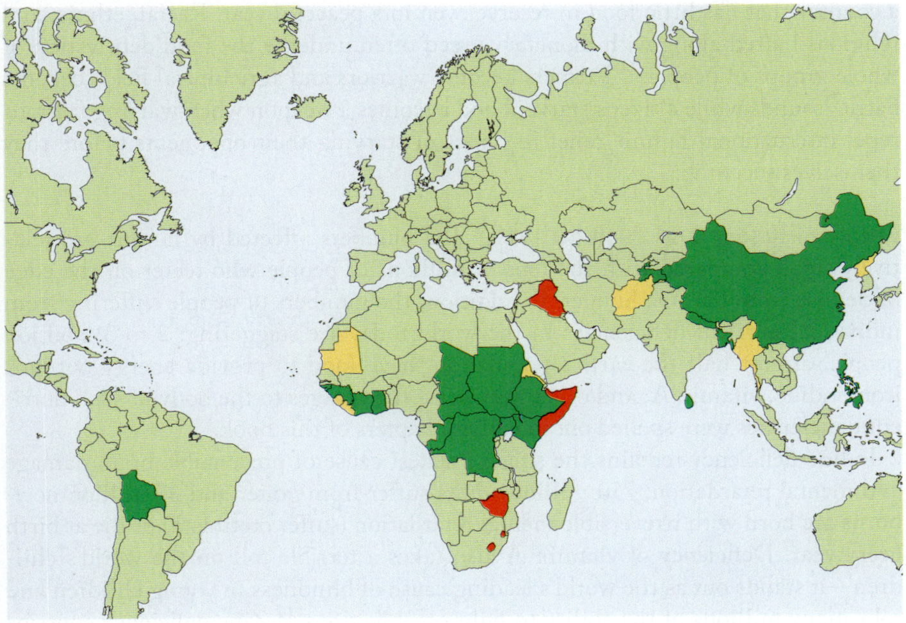

Source: Food and Agriculture Organization of the United Nations, The State of Food Insecurity in the World, 2008.

worldwide shift to producing **biofuels** from corn and other food crops. Another contributor is a persistent widespread drought that has reduced grain production in many areas.

Women and Children The "poorest poor" are usually women and children. Many societies around the world undervalue females, providing girls with poorer diets and fewer opportunities than boys. Malnourished girls become malnourished mothers who give birth to low-birthweight infants—so the cycle of hunger, malnutrition, and poverty continues. Worldwide, three-fourths of those who die each year from starvation and related illnesses are children.[21] Those who survive simply cannot work hard enough to get themselves out of poverty, and most have no borrowing power to obtain credit, even if it were available, needed to build incomes and escape.[22] Even if usual means of capitalization are closed to them, **microcredit** lending can be of help and has helped many women around the world to start businesses and climb out of poverty.[†]

Poverty and hunger exert an ironic effect on people, driving them to bear more children. A family in poverty depends on its children to farm the land, haul water, and care for the adults in their old age. If a family faces ongoing poverty, its young children are among the most likely to die from disease and other causes. In these conditions, parents will have many children to ensure that some will survive to adulthood.

© Jeremy Horner/Corbis

In some countries, every pair of little hands is needed to help feed the family.

[†]Muhammad Yunus and his Grameen Bank pioneered the microcredit style of banking, winning the Nobel Prize in 2006.

© Robert Caputo/Aurora/Picture Quest

The primary cause of hunger is poverty.

CONCEPT LINK 15-2

The symptoms of malnutrition vary according to the nutrients lacking and the individual's stage of life. See Chapter 6 for effects of protein and energy deficiency; Chapters 7 and 8 for vitamin and mineral deficiencies; Chapter 11 for effects on immunity; Chapter 13 for effects on newborns and pregnant women; and Chapter 14 for effects on children, teens, and the elderly.

- To prevent death from diarrheal disease, provide:
  - *Adequate sanitation.*
  - *Safe water.*
  - *Oral rehydration therapy (ORT).*

© Antony Njuguna/Reuters/Landov

In western Sudan, untold millions have died of conflict and famine.

Famine The most visible form of hunger is **famine,** a true food crisis in which multitudes of people in an area starve and die. The natural causes of famine—drought, flood, and pests—occur, of course, but they take second place behind the political and social causes. For people of marginal existence, a sudden increase in food prices, a drop in workers' incomes, or a change in government policy can quickly leave millions more people hungry. Today's economic downturn has thrown 40 million more people into hunger.[23] In 2007, a cyclone and flooding in Bangladesh dramatically reduced food supplies. The World Food Programme of the United Nations responds to such food emergencies around the globe.

Intractable hunger and poverty remain enormous challenges to the world. In parts of Africa, killer famines recur whenever human conflict converges with drought in a country that has little food in reserve even in a peaceful year. Racial, ethnic, and religious hatred along with monetary greed often underlie the food deprivation of whole groups of people.[24] Farmers become warriors and agricultural fields become battlegrounds while citizens starve. Food becomes a weapon when warring factions repel international famine relief in hopes of starving their opponents before they themselves succumb.

Chronic Hunger and Malnutrition The numbers affected by famine are relatively small compared with the tens of millions of people who teeter on the edge of demise from chronic hunger. In addition, the numbers of people suffering from individual nutrient deficiencies in the world today are staggering: 2 to 3½ billion people, almost half the earth's population, have food to provide energy but lack iron, iodine, vitamin A, and other nutrients. The ravages to the body of such nutrient deficiencies were spelled out in earlier chapters of this book.

Iodine deficiency remains the single greatest cause of preventable brain damage and mental retardation; 750 million adults suffer from goiter and 37 million newborns are born with irreversible mental retardation (suffer cretinism) or die at birth every year. Deficiency of vitamin A also takes a terrible toll on the world's children—it stands out as the world's leading cause of blindness in young children and robs many millions of the ability to fight off infections.[25] Zinc deficiency contributes substantially to disease susceptibility, as well.[26] The synergistic combination of infectious diseases, such as dysentery, whooping cough, and tuberculosis, with malnutrition dramatically increases the likelihood of early death.[27]

Undernutrition also stymies mental and physical development in children who survive. Consequences of unrelieved hunger in children include stunted growth, poor learning, extreme weakness, protein-energy malnutrition (PEM), increased susceptibility to disease, inability to stand or walk, and premature death.

Oral Rehydration Therapy Tens of thousands of children die of malnutrition every day. Most do not starve to death—they die because their health has been compromised by dehydration from infections that cause diarrhea. Reintroducing foods to starving people too quickly can trigger **refeeding syndrome,** a serious condition of electrolyte imbalances, heart or respiratory failure, and even death.[28] An urgent need is to restore fluids and electrolytes, and an estimated 1 million lives each year are saved by **oral rehydration therapy (ORT),** which helps stop the destructive spiral of infection, diarrhea, and dehydration. Clean or boiled drinking water is essential for ORT, however, because contaminated water will reinfect the child. Small quantities of salt and sugar help to balance electrolytes and allow the body to adjust to receiving carbohydrate.

KEY POINT Natural causes such as drought, flood, and pests and political and social causes such as armed conflicts and overpopulation all contribute to hunger and poverty in developing countries. Chronic malnutrition and hunger cause much suffering; oral rehydration therapy can save lives.

LO 15.3

The World Food Supply and the Environment

Chris Hondros/Getty Images

International efforts help to relieve hunger and poverty in Afghanistan and around the world.

Banishing hunger for all of the world's citizens poses two major challenges. The first is to provide enough food to meet the needs of the earth's expanding population, without destroying natural resources needed to continue producing food. The second challenge is to ensure that all people have access to enough food to live active, healthy lives.

By all accounts, today's total **world food supply** can abundantly feed the entire current population. Wheat and rice, for example, the staple foods of many nations, are abundant and now cost less than they did 40 years ago. Adequate supply alone, however, does not ensure that all people will receive adequate food. The world must gather the political will to make it happen.

Threats to the Future Food Supply

Many forces compound to threaten world food production and distribution in the next decades:

- *Hunger, poverty, and population growth.* Millions of the world's people are starving. Every 60 seconds 106 people die in the world, but in that same 60 seconds 253 are born to replace them.[29] Every day, the earth gains another 212,000 new residents to feed (see Figure 15-4), most of them born in impoverished areas.[30] By 2050, 1 billion additional tons of grains will be needed to feed the world's population.[31]
- *Loss of food-producing land.* Food-producing land is becoming saltier, eroding, and being paved over. Each year, the world's farmers try to feed some 77 million additional people with 24 billion fewer tons of topsoil.
- *Accelerating fossil fuel use.* Fossil fuel use is growing rapidly, with attendant pollution of air, soil, and water; ozone depletion; and global climate changes.[32]
- *Atmosphere and global climate changes, droughts, and floods.* Climate change is no longer an academic debate, but a growing public concern as the impacts of climate change on health are categorized.[33] Climbing atmospheric levels of

FIGURE 15-4 **World Population Growth**

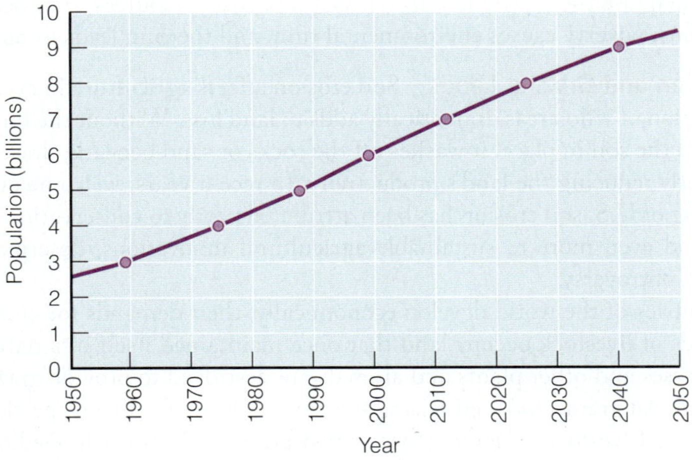

Source: U.S. Census Bureau, International Data Base, updated December 2008.

famine widespread and extreme scarcity of food that causes starvation and death in a large portion of the population in an area.

refeeding syndrome a serious condition of electrolyte and other imbalances that can occur when a severely malnourished person is fed too aggressively; it can lead to heart or respiratory failure and death.

oral rehydration therapy (ORT) oral fluid replacement for children with severe diarrhea caused by infectious disease. ORT enables parents to mix a simple solution for their child from substances that they have at home. A simple recipe for ORT: ½ L boiled water, 4 tsp sugar, ½ tsp salt.

world food supply the quantity of food, including stores from previous harvests, available to the world's people at a given time.

heat-trapping carbon dioxide and other greenhouse gases are a serious concern.[34] The concentration of carbon dioxide is rising, now 26 percent higher than 200 years ago. Evidence for the earth's warming is unequivocal.[35] Resulting climate changes cause heat waves, droughts, fires, storms, and floods that destroy crops, particularly in the poorest areas of the world with the greatest hunger.[36] Arid deserts are projected to expand by 200 million acres in coming years in sub-Saharan Africa alone.[37] Ocean food chains may fail as ocean heat builds up.[38]

- *Ozone loss from the outer atmosphere.* The outer atmosphere's protective ozone layer is growing thinner, permitting harmful radiation from the sun to penetrate. As radiation increases the earth's temperature, polar ice caps are melting, threatening the world's coastlines.[39] Radiation may also directly damage important crops.
- *Water shortages.* The world's supplies of fresh water are dwindling and becoming polluted; over a billion people lack access to fresh water today, and over the next 20 years, the average supply of fresh water per person is expected to decline by one-third.[40]
- *Ocean pollution.* Ocean pollution is killing fish in large "dead zones" along the world's coasts; overfishing is depleting the fish that remain.[41]

The global problems just described are all related and, often, so are their solutions. To think positively, this means that any initiative a person takes to address one problem will help solve many others.

No part of the world is safely insulated against future food shortages. Developed countries may be the last to feel the effects, but they will ultimately go as the world goes. This chapter's Controversy highlights environmental concerns and offers a different ending—continued abundance through sustainable practices that conserve the world's resources.

© paul prescott, 2011/Shutterstock.com

KEY POINT The world's current food supply is sufficient, but distribution remains a problem. Future food security is seriously threatened by many forces.

Environmental Degradation and Hunger

Hunger and poverty interact with a third force—environmental degradation. Poor people often destroy the very resources they need for survival. Desperate to obtain money for food, they sell everything they own—even the seeds that would have produced next year's crops. They cut all available trees for firewood or timber to sell, and then lose the topsoil to erosion. Without these resources, they become still poorer. Thus, poverty causes environmental ruin, and the ruin leads to hunger.

Soil Erosion and Grazing Lands Soil erosion affects agriculture in every nation. Deforestation of wild areas dramatically adds to land loss. Without the forest covering to hold the soil in place, it washes off the rocks or sand beneath, drastically and permanently reducing the land's productivity. In recent years, welcome evidence of the slowing of U.S. soil erosion has been attributed partly to conservation-incentive policies and even more to sustainable agricultural innovations, described in this chapter's Controversy.

As countries of the world develop economically, their demands for animal foods soar. Herds of livestock occupy land that once maintained itself in a natural state. Native grasses and other plants and animals are destroyed to provide grazing land. The animals eat grains, too, and raising the grain requires fertilizers, pesticides, and other inputs. Livestock in large concentrated areas, such as cattle feedlots, create environmental problems from huge outputs of animal wastes, as the Controversy also makes clear.

Diminishing of Wild Fisheries Despite intensive expansion of the world's fishing industry, catches of ocean fish are diminishing.[42] Overall, 80 percent of the world food fish stocks are fully exploited or overexploited:

- 52 percent of major marine fish stocks are fully exploited.
- 27 percent are overexploited, depleted, or collapsing—that is, they face danger of extinction unless given relief from overfishing.
- 1 percent is currently protected, with hopes for recovery.[43]

The obvious solution is simple: stop overfishing. The problem is how to do so. International fish species protection guidelines for seasonal species quotas, establishment of "no fishing zones" in oceanic breeding and recovery sanctuaries, and rules against illegal harvesting are in place. What is lacking is the political will to implement them.[44]

Pollution also limits wild fish populations, and the problem spans the globe. Tiny ocean plants, phytoplankton, that form the base of the food chain diminish as ocean temperature rises.[45] Phytoplankton also absorb over 100 million tons of carbon dioxide each day, so their loss is expected to add to the earth's growing carbon dioxide burden.

Aquaculture—Fish Farms Diminished wild fish capture has spurred the rapid growth of aquaculture, which now provides almost half of the world's food fish and shellfish.[46] It continues to grow more rapidly than any other kind of food animal production.

Some aquaculture "farms" consist of vast net cages that enclose fish in ocean water or freshwater lakes, where natural water flow refreshes the cages. Other types house fish in artificial ponds of various shapes positioned inland close to natural water. On the coast, natural water is diverted through the ponds, bringing in fresh water and carrying out wastes. Farther inland, pond water is continuously filtered and cleansed, recycling through the ponds. All farmed fish must be fed, and fish chow consists of grains and fish harvested from wild species, diminishing their stocks for human consumption.

Adequate environmental safeguards are a must to prevent environmental degradation from aquaculture.[47] Some areas of concern have been identified:

1. *Escapees:* Farmed fish are bred for desired qualities—color or disease resistance—rather than traits needed by healthy wild populations; fish that escape from aquaculture ponds may breed with wild fish, weakening the gene pool.
2. *Diseases and parasites:* Farmed fish in crowded conditions are likely to develop diseases or host parasites, such as sea lice, that spread to wild fish populations that pass by.

Mark Burnett / Photo Researchers, Inc.

Open net cages house fish in a bay or a lake, where natural flow refreshes the water.

- To protect overfished species, consumers can choose these fish options:
  - *Alaskan halibut*
  - *Alaskan salmon*
  - *Sardines and other small species*
  - *Farm-raised tilapia and other farm-raised fish*

CONCEPT LINK 15-3

The benefits and risks of consuming fish was a topic of Chapter 5's Consumer Corner, page 170.

- The FDA advises limiting consumption of these large predatory fish:
  - *King mackerel.*
  - *Shark.*
  - *Swordfish.*
  - *Tilefish.*

As groundwater is used up, deserts spread.

Did You Know?

Worldwide, 1.2 billion people live without access to clean, safe water.

- Years needed for the world's population to reach . . .

Its 1st billion	2,000,000 years
2nd billion	105 years
3rd billion	30 years
4th billion	15 years
5th billion	12 years
6th billion	11 years

Is it any wonder that food and fresh water supplies may one day fall behind?

3. *Nutrient pollution:* Tons of fish wastes and uneaten feed flow from fish farms into ocean habitats and local waterways, contaminating them.
4. *Chemical pollution:* Antibiotics, pesticides, colorants, algae growth inhibitors, and other approved chemicals used in aquaculture flow into waterways, polluting them, or must be discarded as wastes from contained ponds.
5. *Wild habitat loss:* Ocean aquaculture occupies hundreds of square ocean miles, and inland aquaculture requires miles of formerly wild coastal habitat. Some developing countries lack regulations and strip many miles of sensitive ocean and lake breeding habitats to install aquaculture businesses.

Aquaculture can be sustainable, however, if technologies and practices known today are employed to reverse or prevent these problems.

Climate, Air, and Fresh Water Both air pollution and the resulting climate change also reduce food outputs. According to the United Nations Intergovernmental Panel on Climate Change, changes in climate are occurring now from a buildup of so-called greenhouse gases, such as carbon dioxide, methane, and nitrous oxide, and airborne particles. These pollutants are produced by human industry, agriculture, and transportation activities.[48] A rise of only a degree or so in average global temperature may reduce soil moisture, impair pollination of major food crops such as rice and corn, slow growth, weaken crops' resistance to diseases, and disrupt many other factors affecting the human food supply.

As human populations grow, so does the demand for fresh water. In areas of high **water stress,** natural and manmade influences converge to limit access to safe drinking water (see Figure 15-5).[49] Poor water management causes many of the world's water problems.[50] Each day, people dump 2 million tons of waste into the world's rivers, lakes, and streams. By 2025, if present patterns continue, two of every three persons on earth will live in water-stressed conditions.

Overpopulation At the present rate of increase, the human population will exceed the earth's estimated **carrying capacity** by 2033. Many authorities in many

FIGURE 15-5 **Water-Stress Hot Spots**

"Water stress" reflects the amount of pressure placed on water resources by users such as municipal water systems, industries, power plants, and agricultural users. As human population increases in an area, water stress worsens.

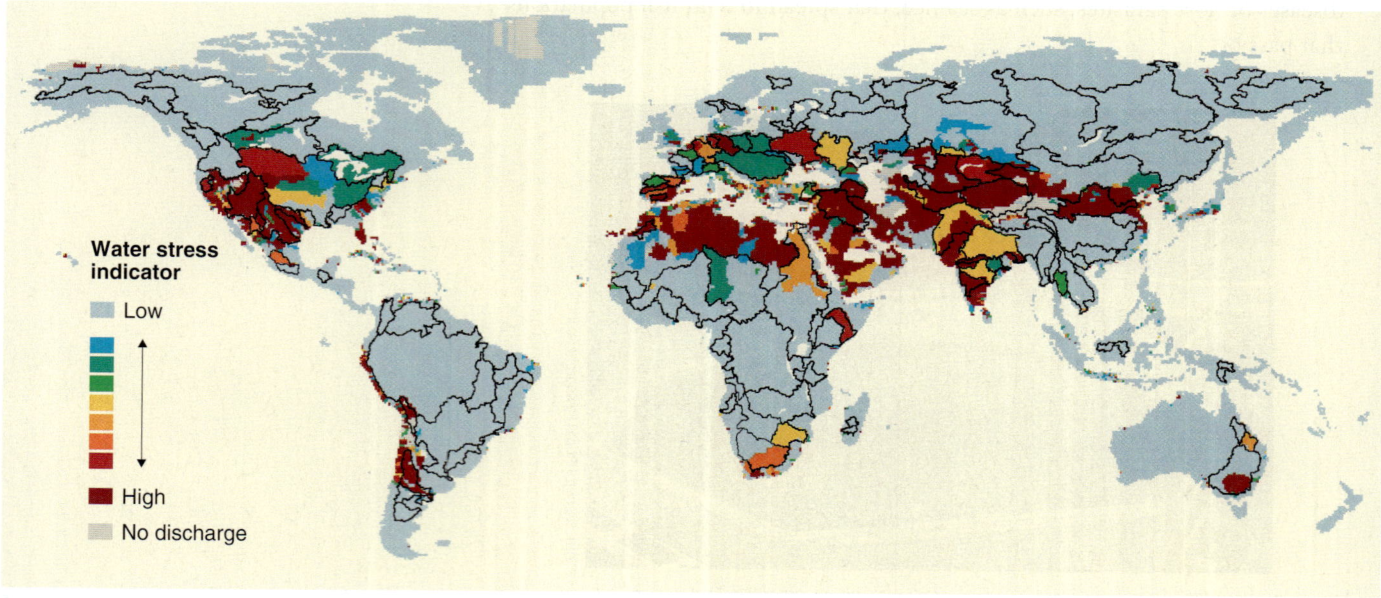

Source: World Water Assessment Programme, The United Nations World Water Development Report 3: Water in a Changing World *(Paris: UNESCO, and London: Earthscan, 2009), p. 92.*

fields—and more every year—are calling for a reduction in the rate at which the world's population increases.

Relieving poverty and hunger may be a necessary first step in curbing population growth. With greater wealth, more children survive, and families are free to choose to limit their numbers. Wealth distribution matters, too. In countries where economic growth has benefited only the rich, population growth has remained high.

KEY POINT Environmental degradation caused by people is threatening the world's soils, grazing lands, fisheries, climate, air, and water. Demand for food is growing with human population growth.

A World Moving Toward Solutions

When hunger is eliminated, everyone benefits. Figure 15-6 demonstrates the idea that when hunger and social conditions are improved, an entire social mechanism that drives poverty begins to run in reverse toward prosperity.

Hope for the world's poorest people arises from an ambitious pledge from world leaders to cut in half world hunger and extreme poverty rates by 2015.[‡51] Recent

‡United Nations (UN) leaders set the World Food Summit goals, and the UN's Food and Agriculture Organization provides assistance in meeting them.

Pure rivers represent irreplaceable water resources.

FIGURE 15-6 Reducing Hunger Drives Beneficial Outcomes

Reducing hunger sets into motion many other beneficial outcomes; these outcomes create a momentum that further reduces hunger and improves lives.

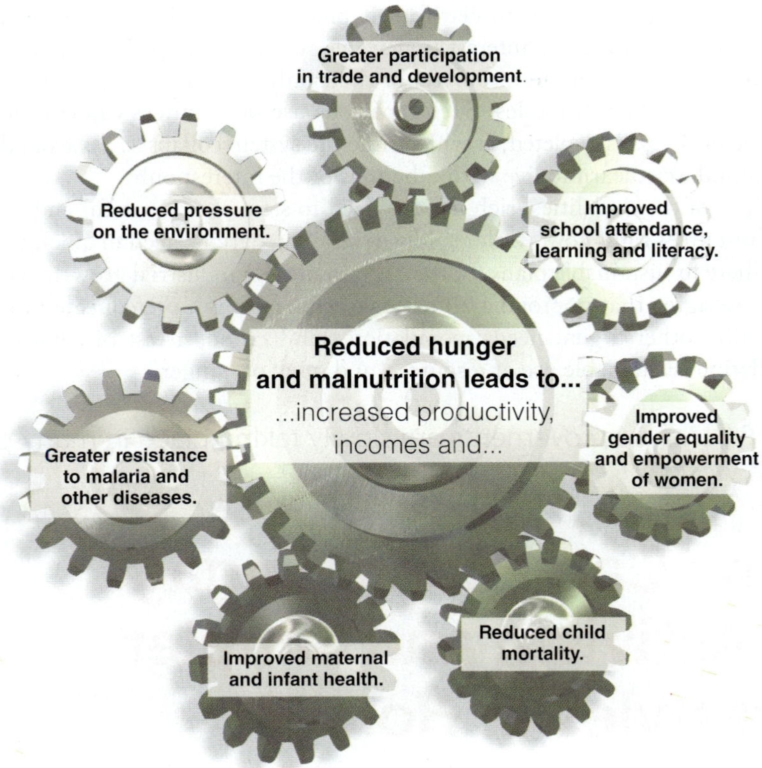

Source: Adapted from USDA Economic Research Service, Briefing Rooms; Food security in the United States; Conditions and trends, November 15, 2006, available at www.ers.usda.gov/Briefing/FoodSecurity/trends.htm.

water stress a measure of the pressure placed on water resources by human activities such as municipal water supplies, industries, power plants, and agricultural irrigation.

carrying capacity the total number of living organisms that a given environment can support without deteriorating in quality.

- The goals of the United Nations World Food Summit, reaffirmed in 2008, are designed to stamp out world hunger:
  1. Eradicate extreme poverty and hunger.
  2. Achieve universal primary education.
  3. Promote gender equality and empower women.
  4. Reduce child mortality.
  5. Improve maternal health.
  6. Combat HIV/AIDS, malaria, and other diseases.
  7. Ensure environmental sustainability.
  8. Develop a global partnership for development.

MY TURN

© Cengage Learning

Catie

© Cengage Learning

Jessica

How Responsible Am I?

Listen to two students talk about what th[ey] think about individual responsibility with respect to the environment.

CENGAGENOW To hear their stories, log on to www.cengage.com/sso.

FIGURE 15-7 **Percentages of Undernourished People Compared with Goals**

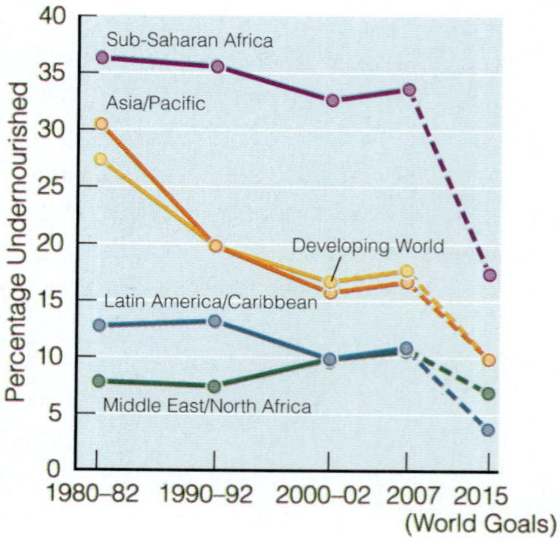

Source: Food and Agriculture Organization, The State of Food Insecurity in the World, 2008, *available at www.fao.org.*

For every person in the world to reach present U.S. levels of consumption with existing technology would require four more planet Earths.

—E. O. Wilson, 2002

We do not inherit the earth from our ancestors, we borrow it from our children.

—Ascribed to Chief Seattle, a 19th-century Native American leader.

advances in agricultural technology, including genetic engineering (discussed in Controversy 12), bring hope that such progress may be possible in some areas.

Slowly but surely, improvements are becoming evident in developing nations. For example, adult literacy rates have increased by more than 50 percent in some areas since 1970, and the proportion of children being sent to school has risen. Figure 15-7 demonstrates some encouraging progress, particularly in Latin American, Caribbean, Asian, and Pacific nations, but also makes clear that more rapid progress will be necessary in other parts of the world to achieve the set goals for reducing hunger. Today, optimism abounds, and keys to solving the world's environmental, poverty, and hunger problems are within the reach of both the poor and the rich nations—if they will make the effort required to employ them. The poor nations need resources and the will to educate and assist the poor and to adopt sustainable development practices that slow and reverse the destruction of their forests, waterways, and soil.

Today's use of resources is unsustainable. At least one and one-quarter planet earths would currently be needed to sustain today's forms of human activities. A financial analogy may help to clarify this precarious position: human beings today are both spending the interest (renewable resources) as well as liquidating the principal (the earth's finite resources) of their only inheritance—planet earth—to sustain their current lifestyles. Such rapacious use of resources can continue only until the principal is depleted, at which time the system collapses. To avoid disaster, humankind must learn to live within bounds of the interest only.

In light of these realities, rich nations need to stem their wasteful and polluting use of resources right now, while rapidly developing nations need to quickly develop and adhere to sustainable plans for their economic and industrial growth. Many nations now agree that improving all nations' economies is a prerequisite to meeting the world's other urgent needs: population stabilization, arrest of environmental degradation, sustainable use of resources, and relief of hunger.

KEY POINT Improvements are slowly taking place in many parts of the world.

How Can People Engage in Activism and Simpler Lifestyles at Home?

Every segment of our society can play a role in the fight against poverty, hunger, and environmental degradation. The federal government, the states, local communities, big business and small companies, educators, and all individuals, including dietitians and food service managers, have many opportunities to drive the effort forward.

- Visit the National Hunger Awareness Day website for more information about local and national efforts to fight hunger: www.hungerday.org.

CONSUMER CORNER

Saving Money and Protecting the Environment

Consumers can "tread lightly on the earth" through their daily choices. Consider this list:

- Shop "carless" or plan to make fewer shopping trips. Motor vehicles constitute the single largest source of air pollution, causing lung problems, reduced crop yields, and acid rain that damages forests.
- Ride a bike to work or classes.
- Choose foods that are low on the food chain more often (see the chapter Controversy).
- Limit use of imported canned beef products, including stews, chili, corned beef, and pet foods. Many of these foods come at the expense of cleared rain forest land: 200 square feet of rain forest are lost *permanently* for every pound of beef produced.
- Choose small fish more often. Small fish eat tiny aquatic animals and plants—that is, they eat low on the food chain.
- Choose chicken from local farms.
- Shop at farmers' markets and roadside stands for local foods grown close to home. Locally grown foods require less transportation, packaging, and refrigeration than shipped foods. Try picking your own from local farms—it's fun and saves money, too.
- Avoid overly packaged items; buy bulk items with minimal packaging or reusable or recyclable packaging. Each can, foam tray, waxed or clay-coated cardboard container, plastic bottle, or glass jar requires land and many other resources to produce, and its disposal pollutes and costs more land.
- Use reusable pans and dishes, rather than disposable items that are used once and thrown away. Use pumps instead of spray cans, which are hard to recycle because they are made of many materials.
- Carry reusable string or cloth grocery sacks or bring plastic sacks back to the store and refill them. Production of paper and plastic grocery bags represents a huge drain on resources. Paper factories use chemicals such as toxic forms of chlorine bleach, which are released into waterways in quantities so large that the chemicals can destroy whole bays and fisheries.
- Use fast cooking methods. Stir-frying, pressure cooking, and microwaving all use less energy than conventional stovetop or oven cooking methods.
- Reduce use of aluminum foil, paper towels, plastic wraps, plastic storage bags, and other disposable items. Find permanent reusable replacements for each, such as reusable storage containers and washable cloths.
- Use fewer electric gadgets. Mix batters, chop vegetables, and open cans by hand.
- Purchase the most efficient large appliances possible—look for the Energy Star logo (see Figure 15-8). Products that rank highest in their category for energy efficiency earn this logo from the Environmental Protection Agency. By purchasing Energy Star products, consumers can save many energy dollars each year.
- Insulate the home.
- Consider using solar power, especially to heat water.
- Reduce, reuse, recycle.

The personal rewards of all these behaviors are many, from saving money to the satisfaction of knowing that you are enjoying and preserving the earth (see Figure 15-9 for other suggestions). But do they really help? They do, if enough people join in. To make the greatest impact, people can also support organizations that lobby for changes in economic policies toward developing countries. Local food pantries welcome volunteers, as well.

FIGURE 15-8 **Energy Star**

Products bearing the U.S. government's Energy Star logo rank highest for energy efficiency. For example, a 10-year-old refrigerator uses as much energy as two refrigerators with the Energy Star label. Energy Star products range from large appliances to light bulbs and building materials.

By choosing products with the Energy Star logo when replacing old equipment, the typical household would save almost $400 per year in energy costs; if everyone chose nothing but Energy Star products over the next 10 years, the national energy bill would be reduced by about $100 billion. The reduction in greenhouse gas emissions (carbon dioxide) would be equivalent to taking 17 million cars off the road for each of those 10 years.

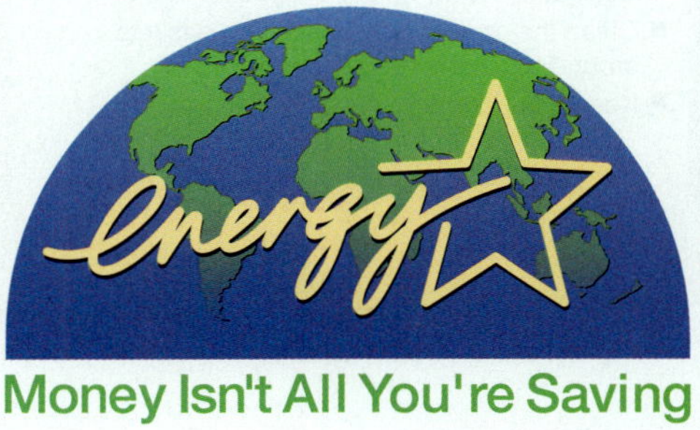

Courtesy of NASA

FIGURE 15-9

Individual Responsibility and Respect for the Environment

Reduce resource use, reduce fuel use, and reduce pollution with these individual actions.

Eat lower on the food chain—more grains, local chicken, and small fish, and less meat from large animals.

Eat local foods—visit your farmers' market.

© 2002 PhotoDisc/Getty Images

Buy bulk items to save packaging.

© 2002 PhotoDisc/Getty Images

Recycle glass, cans, paper, and plastic.

Buy fruits of differing ripeness.

Eat most perishable foods first.

Shop carless. It can be a pleasure and a great source of exercise.

© Corbis Images/PictureQuest

Use reusable bags instead of throwaway bags.

© Burke/Triolo/Brand X Pictures/PictureQuest

Buy recycled goods to close the loop.

Use reusable items . . .

. . . instead of nonreusable items.

Use items that don't use energy . . .

. . . instead of those that do use energy (even small appliances).

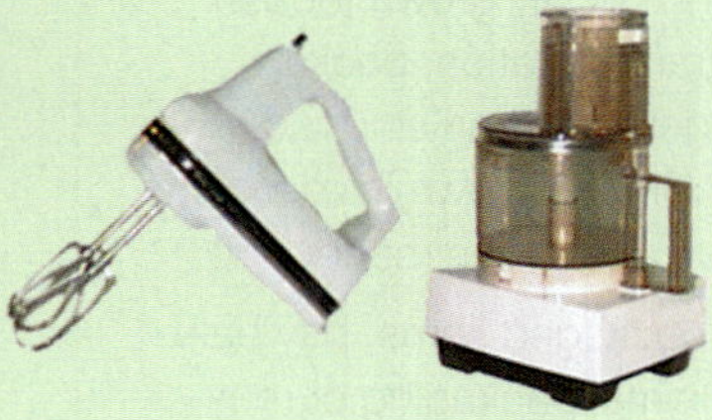

Use appliances that take less energy.

Run your refrigerator efficiently.

Even today's efficient refrigerators use substantial energy because they run day and night. Consumers can take several steps to minimize the energy a refrigerator uses:

- Set it at 37° to 40°F; set the freezer at 0°F.
- Clean the coils and the insulating gaskets around the doors regularly.
- Keep it in good repair.

Courtesy, Bradford White Corporation

The water heater can also waste a lot of energy. Keep the water heater set at 120° to 130°F (no hotter) to save energy. For safe household dishes, sterilization is not necessary. Water of 120° to 130°F enhances the action of dishwashing detergents, making microorganisms slippery and removing them from the dishes. These measures will keep food fresh and clean while keeping energy use low.

Government Action

Government policies can change to promote sustainability. For example, the U.S. government is currently devoting record tax dollars and other resources to encouraging development of wind, solar, certain biofuels, and other low-input sustainable energy sources to reduce reliance on fossil fuels. It also subsidizes conservation programs for agricultural lands. However, more can be done to encourage industries and government agencies to conserve energy.

• The Controversy section has more on biofuels and other energy sources.

Private and Community Enterprises

Businesses can take initiatives to help; some already have—AT&T, Prudential, and Kraft General Foods are major supporters of antihunger programs. Restaurants and other food facilities can participate in the nation's gleaning effort by giving their fresh leftover foods to community distribution centers. Food producers are more often choosing to produce their goods sustainably to meet a growing demand for products produced with integrity.

Educators and Students

Educators, including nutrition educators, have a crucial role to play. They can teach others about the underlying social and political causes of poverty, the root cause of hunger. At the college level, they can teach the relationships between hunger and birthrate, hunger and environmental degradation, hunger and the status of women, and hunger and global economics. At local and national levels, students can share the knowledge they gain with families, friends, and communities and take action in their communities and beyond.

Food and Nutrition Professionals

Registered dietitians, dietetic technicians, and food service managers can promote sustainable production of food and the saving of resources through choices in procurement, reuse, recycling, energy conservation, water conservation, leadership, and capital improvements both in business and in their personal lives.[52] In addition, the ADA urges its members to work for policy changes in private and government food assistance programs, to intensify education about hunger, and to be advocates on the local, state, and national levels to help end hunger in the United States.

Individuals

All individuals can become involved in these large trends. Many small decisions each day add up to large impacts on the environment. The Consumer Corner on page 587 sums up some of these decisions and actions.

KEY POINT Government, business, educators, and all individuals have many opportunities to promote sustainability worldwide and wise resource use at home.

MEDIA MENU

CENGAGENOW To find additional quiz questions, view videos and animations, and explore interactive exercises, go to **www.cengage.com/sso.**

Learn more about biotechnology and sustainable agriculture from the Union of Concerned Scientists website at **www.ucsusa.org.**

Search for information on world hunger, poverty, and overpopulation at **www.who.int/en.**

Learn more about child survival programs worldwide at **www.unicef.org.**

Review information about U.S. food assistance and food recovery programs at **www.fns.usda.gov/fns.**

Take the Ecological Footprint Quiz to estimate how much productive land and water you need at **www.myfootprint.org.**

SELF CHECK

Answers to these Self Check questions are in Appendix G.

1. Which of the following is a symptom of food insecurity?
   A. You worry about gaining weight but cannot afford "diet" foods.
   B. You cannot always afford to purchase nutritious foods for balanced meals.
   C. You shop daily to get the best prices and use coupons to stretch your budget.
   D. You buy fresh rather than frozen foods to save money.
2. Which of the items can be purchased with electronic debit transfer cards from the Supplemental Nutrition Assistance Program (formerly Food Stamp Program)?
   A. hot dogs
   B. cigarettes
   C. dishwashing liquid
   D. red wine
3. Today, famine is most often a result of:
   A. poverty
   B. drought
   C. social causes such as war
   D. flood
4. Which of the following is an example of environmental degradation?
   A. soil erosion
   B. diminished wild habitat
   C. air pollution
   D. all of the above
5. Which of the following activities are recommended due to the small impact they have on the environment?
   A. Use the oven whenever possible.
   B. Line pans with aluminum foil to reduce cleanup effort.
   C. Use a pressure cooker or microwave to cook foods.
   D. Carry groceries home in paper bags rather than plastic.
6. Poverty and hunger drive people to bear more children.
   T F
7. Most children who die of malnutrition starve to death.
   T F
8. Grains require the least energy to produce.
   T F
9. The higher a nation's economic status, the faster its population grows over the long run.
   T F
10. Malnutrition is the world's leading cause of blindness in young children.
   T F

CONTROVERSY 15

Toward Sustainable Food Production: How to Go Forward?

LO 15.4, 15.5

If predictions hold true, the world's farmers will soon face increased pressure to feed a burgeoning world population.[1]* To produce this food will require vast amounts of land, water, and energy, and it must be accomplished while conserving the resources that make growing crops and animals possible into the future.[2] In short, how can we produce the needed food sustainably? Do new technologies hold the power to solve the problems of providing enough food and energy? This Controversy addresses these questions, starting with some of the issues that surround the future of food.

COSTS OF CURRENT FOOD PRODUCTION METHODS

Producing food costs the earth dearly. The environmental and human impacts of agriculture and the food industry take many forms. Among them are water pollution, greenhouse gas emissions, and resource overuse.[3] Beyond the scope of this discussion are the costs in terms of human health and other problems associated with farm labor and exposure to pesticides.[4] Table C15-1 offers definitions of terms important to these concepts.

*Reference notes are found in Appendix F.

© 2010/Jupiterimages Corporation

Impacts on Land and Water

To produce food, first, we clear land—prairie, wetland, or forest—replacing native ecosystems with crops or food animals. Crops pull nutrients from the soil. With each harvest, some of those nutrients are removed, so manufactured fertilizers are applied to replace them. Some of the nitrogen in this fertilizer flies off as gas, contributing to greenhouse gas emissions.[5]

With rain or irrigation, fertilizer from fields and animal manure from grazing lands and feedlots run off into waterways causing algae overgrowth. The algae dies and decomposes, forming ocean **dead zones** as whole areas are depleted of oxygen.[6] Some plowed soil runs off, too, clouding the water and burying aquatic plants and animals. Then, to protect crops against weeds and pests, herbicides and pesticides are applied. With continued use, weeds and pests grow resistant to their effects.[7] These products also kill native plants, native insects, and animals that eat those plants and insects. If not used conservatively, pesticides and herbicides pollute rivers, lakes, and groundwater.

Finally, we irrigate, a practice that adds salts to the soil—the water evaporates, but the salts do not. As soils become salty, plant growth fails. Irrigation can also deplete the water supply over time because water taken from surface or underground supplies evaporates or runs off. This process, carried to an extreme, can dry up whole rivers and lakes and lower the water table of entire regions. The lower the water table, the more farmers must irrigate; and the more they irrigate, the more groundwater they use up.

TABLE C15-1 Sustainability Terms

- **alternative (low-input,** or **sustainable) agriculture** agriculture practiced on a small scale using individualized approaches that vary with local conditions so as to minimize technological, fuel, and chemical inputs.
- **farm share** an arrangement in which a farmer offers the public a "subscription" for an allotment of the farm's products throughout the season.
- **dead zones** columns of oxygen-depleted ocean water in which marine life cannot survive; often caused by algae blooms that occur when agricultural fertilizers and waste runoff enter natural waterways.
- **integrated pest management (IPM)** management of pests using a combination of natural and biological controls and minimal or no application of pesticides.

Soil Depletion

The soil can also be depleted by other agricultural practices, particularly indiscriminate land clearing (deforestation) and overuse by cattle (overgrazing).

USDA Photo by Tim McCabe

Vast areas under plow are exposed to erosion, and those that must be irrigated can, over time, become salty and unusable.

Such human agricultural activities deplete the earth's fertile land and threaten the world's food future. Once stripped of its trees, exposed topsoil blows away on the wind or washes into the sea, leaving an unfertile area behind. If soil erosion proceeds unchecked, by 2025 the world may be struggling to feed many more people with 40 percent less food-producing land per person.

Unsustainable agriculture has already destroyed many once-fertile regions where civilizations formerly flourished. The dry, salty deserts of North Africa were once plowed and irrigated wheat fields, the breadbasket of the Roman Empire. Today's mistreatment of soil and water is causing destruction on a scale never known before.

Loss of Species

Agriculture also weakens its own underpinnings when it fails to conserve species diversity. By the year 2050, some 40,000 plant species, existing today, may go extinct. The United Nations Food and Agriculture Organization attributes many of the losses, which are occurring daily, to modern farming practices, as well as to human population growth.

The growing uniformity of global eating habits also contributes to species loss. As people everywhere eat the same limited array of foods, demand for local, genetically diverse, native plants is insufficient to make them financially worth preserving. Yet, in the future, as the climate warms, those very plants may be needed as food sources. A wild species of corn that grows in a dry climate, for example, might contain just the genetic information necessary to help make the domestic corn crop resistant to drought. For this and other reasons, protecting biodiversity is a critical human need.

Fuel Use and Energy Sources

Energy and fertilizers generated from fossil fuel have spurred unprecedented gains in agricultural output, but scientists now recognize that, with limited fossil-fuel resources, such gains are not likely sustainable into the future.[8] Fossil-fuel use itself threatens the future of food production by contributing to pollution and global climate changes. In the United States, the food industry consumes about 20 percent of the nation's fuels to run farm machinery and produce fertilizers and pesticides, and to prepare, package, transport, refrigerate, and otherwise store, cook, and wash our foods.

Biofuels made from renewable corn and soybeans were once hailed as safer alternatives to fossil fuels, but these also carry high environmental costs. Strong world demand for corn or soybean ethanol triggers the conversion of wild native habitats into corn and soybean fields, diverts resources away from growing food crops needed to feed hungry local populations, and increases greenhouse gas emissions.[9] Other materials, such as native grasses, a type of cane, and even algae appear to be more promising materials for sustainable biofuel production than food crops.[10] Other sustainable energy sources, such as wind and solar energy, remain underdeveloped.[11]

Energy Waste

Some 6,560 calories of fuel are used to produce a can of corn (including the can and transportation), and 7,980 calories are needed to produce a package of frozen corn (including freezing, packaging, and transportation). Likewise, a 1-calorie can of diet soda requires 2,100 calories to produce: 500 for the soda and 1,600 to make the can.[12] Many more thousands are spent for its transportation. Much of this energy input could be reduced, by both manufacturers and educated consumers.

THE PROBLEMS OF LIVESTOCK AND FISHING

Raising livestock takes an enormous toll on land and energy resources. Like plant crops, herds of livestock occupy land that once maintained itself in a natural state. The land suffers losses of native plants and animals, soil erosion, water depletion, and desert formation.

U.S. Meat Production

If animals are raised in concentrated areas such as cattle feedlots or giant hog "farms," huge masses of manure produced in these overcrowded, factory-style farms leach into local soils and water supplies, polluting them. In an effort to control this source of pollution, the U.S. Environmental Protection Agency (EPA) offers incentives to livestock farmers who agree to clean up their wastes and allow their operations to be monitored for pollution. In addition, animals in such feedlots still have to be fed; grain is grown for them on other land (Figure C15-1 compares the grain required to produce various foods). That grain may require fertilizers, herbicides, pesticides, and irrigation, too. In the United States, one-fifth of all cropland is used to produce grain for livestock—more land than is used to produce grain for people.

© Oklahoma Publishing Co., May 1997

Industrial farms generate huge masses of wastes that can contaminate soil and water.

FIGURE C15-1 **Pounds of Grain Needed to Produce One Pound of Bread and One Pound of Animal Weight Gain**

World Trends in Meat Consumption

A worldwide trend toward increased meat and dairy product consumption in places with growing economies is putting pressure on the ecological systems.[13] In 1989, for example, less than 40 percent of Chinese citizens derived a significant proportion of their calories from animal-derived foods; that number jumped to 67 percent in 2006. This trend has been underestimated in long-term projections of the world's demand for food and energy, and the toll this will take on the earth's limited systems.

Overfishing and Species Depletion

Other environmental costs attend fishing. Fishing easily becomes overfishing and, as the preceding chapter made clear, overfishing depletes breeding stocks of the very fish that people need to eat. Other aquatic animals are also vulnerable to injury and death from net fishing activities, and populations of ecologically important nonfood animals, such as dolphins, diminish. In short, our ways of producing these foods are, for the most part, not sustainable.

A SUSTAINABLE FUTURE STARTS NOW

For each of the problems just described, sustainable solutions are being devised, and their use is growing worldwide.[14] Sustainable agriculture is not one system, but a set of practices that can be matched to particular needs in local areas.[15] The crop yields from farms that employ these practices often compare favorably with those from farms using less sustainable methods, but farmers wishing to employ them must first do some learning and be willing to change. The first of these ideas, sustainable **alternative,** or **low-input,** agriculture, emphasizes careful use of natural processes wherever possible, rather than chemically intensive methods.

Sanjit Das/Bloomberg via Getty Images

Some farmers in India find that growing wheat and other crops organically is most cost-effective.

Low-Input and Precision Agriculture

Farmers using low-input agriculture adopt **integrated pest management (IPM)** strategies, such as rotating crops and introducing natural predators to control pests, rather than depending on pesticides alone. Table C15-2 contrasts low-input agriculture methods with unsustainable methods. Many sustainable techniques are not really new—they would be familiar to our great-grandparents. Many farmers today are rediscovering the benefits of old techniques as they adapt and experiment with them in the search for sustainable methods.

Low-input agriculture works. Farmers who use it are part of a food production system that can sustain a healthy food supply and restore soil and water resources while reducing reliance on fossil fuels.

The meaning of the term *precision agriculture* is much the way it sounds: farmers adjust soil and crop management to target the precise needs of various areas of the farm. For example, a farmer who grows crops in a field with hills, which tend to stay drier, and with valleys, which tend to stay wetter, can adjust irrigation accordingly. Similarly, if one section of a field needs mostly nitrogen while another needs a different mix, the farmer can preprogram a computer to apply fertilizer of just the right type and amount for each area, and so forth.

The *global positioning satellite (GPS)* system is at the heart of precision farming. Satellites in the sky beam data about a farmer's field to receivers placed on farm equipment here on earth. Farmers can use the GPS information to target, within a meter's accuracy, areas that need treatments. Potential cost savings in terms of water, fertilizers, and pesticides

TABLE C15-2 High-Input and Low-Input Agricultural Techniques Compared

Unsustainable Practice	Sustainable Practice
• Growing the same crop repeatedly on the same patch of land. This takes more and more nutrients out of the soil, makes fertilizer use necessary; favors soil erosion; and invites weeds and pests to become established, making pesticide use necessary.	• Rotate crops. This increases nitrogen in the soil so there is less need to buy fertilizers. If used with appropriate plowing methods, crop rotation reduces soil erosion. Crop rotation also reduces weeds and pests.
• Using fertilizers generously. Excess fertilizer pollutes ground and surface water and costs both farmers' household money and consumers' tax money.	• Reduce the use of fertilizers and use livestock manure more effectively. Store manure during the nongrowing season and apply it during the growing season. • Alternate nutrient-devouring crops with nutrient-restoring crops, such as legumes. • Compost on a large scale, including all plant residues not harvested. Plow the compost into the soil to improve its water-holding capacity.
• Feeding livestock in feedlots where their manure produces major water and soil pollutant problems. Piled in heaps or held in huge ditches, manure also releases methane, a global-warming gas.	• Feed livestock or buffalo on the open range where their manure will fertilize the ground on which plants grow and will release no methane. Alternatively, at least collect feedlot animals' manure and use it as fertilizer, or, at the very least, treat it before release.
• Spraying herbicides and pesticides over large areas to wipe out weeds and pests.	• Apply technology in weed and pest control. Use precision agriculture techniques if affordable or use rotary hoes twice instead of herbicides once. Spot-treat weeds by hand. • Rotate crops to foil pests that lay their eggs in the soil where last year's crop was grown. • Use genetically resistant crops. • Use biological controls such as predators that destroy the pests.
• Plowing the same way everywhere, allowing unsustainable water runoff and erosion.	• Plow in ways tailored to different areas. Conserve both soil and water by using cover crops, crop rotation, no-till planting, and contour plowing.
• Injecting animals with antibiotics to prevent disease in livestock.	• Maintain animals' health so that they can resist disease.
• Irrigating on a large scale.	• Irrigate only during dry spells and only where needed.

are enormous and the reductions in polluting chemicals benefit everyone. The high initial costs of the equipment, however, can be a barrier to its use.

Soil Conservation

The U.S. Conservation Reserve Program, renewed in 2008, provides federal assistance to farmers and ranchers who wish to improve their conservation of soil, water, and related natural resources on environmentally sensitive lands.[16] It encourages farmers to plant native grasses, food plants for wildlife, or trees instead of cash crops on highly erodible cropland, wetlands, or other environmentally sensitive acreage. It also encourages conservative techniques such as shallow tilling and planting grassy strips to facilitate the flow of water off fields. In exchange, farmers receive annual rental payments and other assistance over a 10- to 15-year contract period. The goals of the program are to:

- reduce soil erosion.
- protect production of food and fiber.
- reduce sedimentation in streams and lakes.
- improve water quality.
- establish wildlife habitat.
- enhance forest and wetland resources.

About 25 percent of all U.S. agricultural land is considered highly erodible and thus qualifies for conservation incentives.

Other programs offer incentives for improving air quality or water quality or for purchasing sensitive lands for conservation. Private foundations or other groups may get help in funding such programs from local, state, or federal agencies.

The Potential of Genetic Engineering

Many farmers worldwide report both financial and conservation benefits from planting genetically engineered crops.[17] Herbicide-resistant crops require less tilling of the soil for reducing weed growth, reducing soil loss to wind and water erosion. Pesticide-resistant crops demand less use of petroleum-based pesticides and less fuel to run the equipment to apply it. Salt-resistant crops can grow in salty

Courtesy of Aqua Bounty Canada

These salmon are all the same age and type. The largest ones received a growth-enhancing gene, greatly accelerating their growth rate.

areas where conventional crops wither. If approached carefully (see Controversy 12), genetically engineered plants and animals, such as the fast-growing salmon in the photo, promise economic, environmental, and agricultural benefits by providing greater yields from fewer resources.

Preserving Genetic Diversity of Food

With loss of biodiversity and species extinction, humankind loses some of the raw genetic material on which to draw for improvement of agricultural plants and food animals. The Svalbard Global Seed Vault in Norway houses a collection of 1.1 million genetic samples of the world's 64 most important food crops. Materials submitted by 120 participating nations advance the bank's goal: protecting plant genetic resources and securing genetic biodiversity for food researchers, breeders, and farmers around the world. If a devastating blight attacks a major food crop, then this repository might contain the information needed to counter the threat. Such resource banks are imperative if our food supply is to adapt to a changing climate.[18]

Energy Conservation

Worldwide, the demand for energy increases daily while fossil-fuel supplies dwindle. To be sustainable, our consumption of energy and our means of producing and using it must change. The food industry, for example, is evaluating and redesigning energy inputs for producing, processing, packaging, transporting, storing, and preparing foods.

Work done on corn and soybean ethanol, the first generation of biofuels, is paving the way for a second generation of fuels, such as:

- Switchgrass, a fast-growing native plant that thrives without fertilizer on land too rocky and nutrient-poor for growing food, offers 540 percent more energy than the amount used to produce it. Other cellulose materials are under study.
- Light-capturing algae, an aquatic plant that can be cultivated as a source of fuel. Algae, not typically used for food, can be grown in fresh- or saltwater, where it efficiently produces oil.[19]
- Harnessing wind, sunlight, and the natural heat of the earth, which hold potential as sustainable sources of power.

In the struggle to secure sustainable global energy supplies, no resource can be overlooked, and none wasted.

Energy Recycling

A new paradigm for sustainable energy calls for converting wastes into energy at many levels of food production. For example:

- Vermont's dairy farmers who join the state-sponsored "Cow Power" program convert methane from cow manure into electricity.[20] Wisconsin dairies are producing a type of bio-gas from cow manure and other wastes.[21]
- Other farmers turn plant waste into charcoal and bury it, trapping carbon underground and fertilizing the soil, thus avoiding applications of fossil-fuel-based fertilizer.[22]
- Some community utilities provide home composters to citizens at reduced cost; the composters turn household garbage into fertilizer for home gardens and landscape, further reducing commercial fertilizer use.[23]

Consumer dollars also represent the energy spent to earn them, and they factor in to the sustainability equation. The last item in Table C15-3 suggests that consumers can help by spending their dollars on foods that require low energy inputs from industry, a choice that is described next.

ROLES OF CONSUMERS

Conscientious consumers can reduce pollution and the use of resources through the choices they make.[24] Some new, fresh ways of thinking about how to obtain foods, and which foods to choose, can enliven the diet and enrich daily life in many ways.

Keeping Local Profits Local

Farmers selling their broccoli, carrots, and apples at city farmers' markets and country roadside stands often net a higher profit, especially when consumers

© Paul Barton/Corbis

Farmers' markets and farm share arrangements provide fresh foods from local growers.

TABLE C15-3 Sustainable Energy-Saving Agricultural Techniques

- Use machinery scaled to the job at hand and operate it at efficient speeds.
- Combine operations. Harrow, plant, and fertilize in the same operation.
- Use diesel fuel. Use solar and wind energy on farms. Use methane from manure.
- Be open-minded to alternative energy sources.
- Use new disease- and pest-resistant plant varieties developed through genetic engineering.
- Save on technological and chemical inputs and spend some of the savings paying people to do manual jobs. Increasing labor inputs has been considered inefficient. Reverse this thinking: creating more jobs is preferable to using more machinery and fuel.
- Partially return to the techniques of using animal manure and crop rotation. This would save energy because chemical fertilizers require large energy inputs to produce.
- Choose crops that require low energy inputs (fertilizer, pesticides, irrigation).
- Educate people to cook food efficiently and to eat low on the food chain.

perceive an intrinsic benefit from obtaining such foods. For example, families buying homegrown produce tend to eat a greater quantity and selection of fruits and vegetables, and the health benefits of this outcome are well known.[25] Through a **farm share,** consumers can buy a weekly share of a local farmer's crops, harvested in season and picked up while fresh. Consumers also appreciate knowing how their foods are grown and handled. In addition, city-locked urban residents often relish a trip to "the country" to pick up fresh foods grown locally.

Eating Lower on the Food Chain

Studies of energy use in the U.S. food system have revealed which foods require the most and least energy to produce. The least energy is needed for grain: about one-third of a calorie of fuel is burned to grow each calorie of grain. Fruits and vegetables are intermediate, while most animal protein requires from 10 to 90 calories of fossil energy per calorie of usable food. Overall, a vegetarian diet requires just 33 percent of the energy needed to produce the average meat-containing diet.[26] An exception is livestock raised on the open range; these animals eat grass and require low energy inputs. So much of our beef is grain-fed, however, that the average energy requirement to produce it is high. In general, eating more foods derived from plants and fewer foods derived from animals conserves resources.[27]

All in all, our choices as a nation add up to a measurable "ecological footprint"—the productive land and water required to supply all of the resources an individual consumes and to absorb all of the wastes generated using prevailing practices.[28] The footprint of each individual is 4 times larger in an industrialized country than in a developing one (see Figure C15-2). To help size up your own ecological footprint, take the quiz in Table C15-4.

CONCLUSION

Although many problems are global in scope, the actions of individual people lie at the heart of their solutions. Do what you can to tread lightly on the earth. Celebrate the changes that are possible today by making them a permanent part of your life; do the same with changes that become possible tomorrow and every day thereafter.

FIGURE C15-2 **Ecological Footprints**

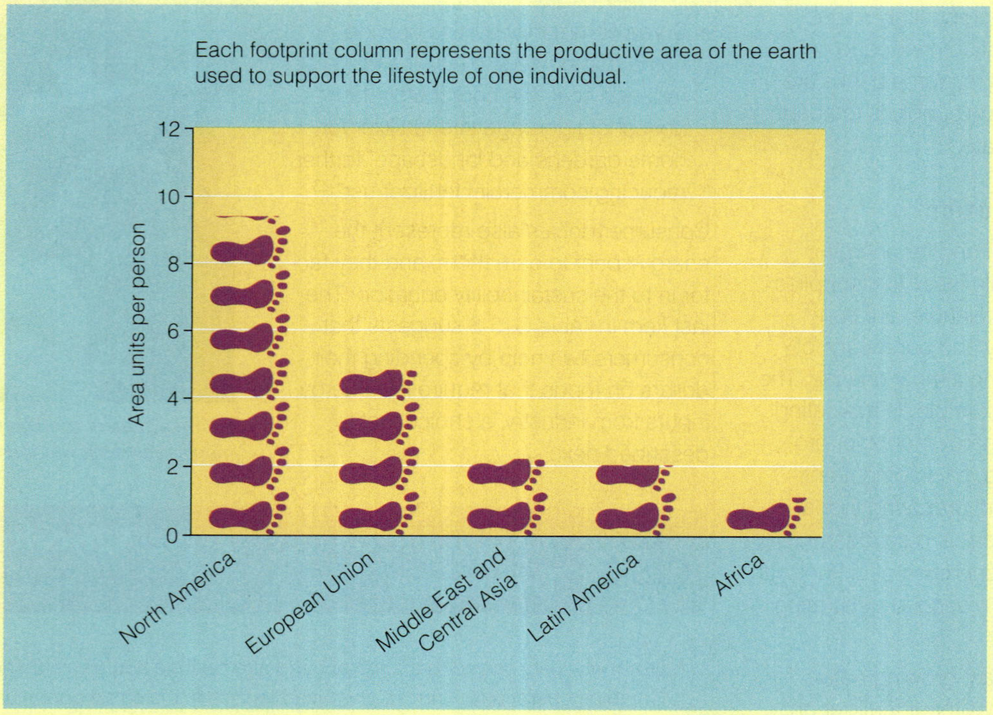

Source: Ecological Footprint and Biocapacity, 2006, available at www.footprintnetwork.org/index.php.

TABLE C15-4 How Big Is Your Ecological Footprint?

This quiz can help you evaluate your impact on the earth. The higher your score, the smaller your "footprint."

At home, do you:

1. Recycle everything you can: newspapers, cans, glass bottles and jars, scrap metal, used oil, etc.?
2. Use cold water in the washer whenever possible?
3. Avoid using appliances (such as electric can openers) to do things you can do by hand?
4. Reuse grocery bags to line your wastebasket? Reuse or recycle bread bags, butter tubs, etc.?
5. Store food in reusable containers rather than plastic wrap, disposable bags and containers, or aluminum foil?

In the yard, do you:

6. Pull weeds instead of using herbicides?
7. Fertilize with manure and compost, rather than with chemical fertilizers?
8. Compost your leaves and yard debris, rather than burning them?
9. Take extra plastic and rubber pots back to the plant nursery?

On vacation, do you:

10. Turn down the heat and turn off the hot water heater before you leave?
11. Carry reusable cups, dishes, and flatware (and use them)?
12. Dispose of trash appropriately (never litter)?
13. Buy no souvenirs made from wild or endangered animals?
14. Stay on roads and trails, and not trample dunes and fragile undergrowth?

About your car, do you:

15. Keep your car tuned up for maximum fuel efficiency?
16. Use public transit whenever possible?
17. Ride your bike or walk whenever possible?
18. Plan to replace your car with a more fuel-efficient model when you can?
19. Recycle your engine oil?

At school or work, do you:

20. Recycle paper whenever possible?
21. Use scrap paper for notes to yourself and others?
22. Print or copy on both sides of the paper?
23. Reuse large envelopes and file folders?
24. Use the stairs instead of the elevator whenever you can?

When buying, do you:

25. Buy as little plastic and foam packaging as possible?
26. Buy permanent, rather than disposable, products?
27. Buy paper rather than plastic, if you must buy disposable products?
28. Buy fresh produce grown locally?
29. Buy in bulk to avoid unnecessary packaging?

In other areas, do you:

30. Volunteer your time to conservation projects?
31. Encourage your family, friends, and neighbors to save resources, too?
32. Write letters to support conservation issues?

Scoring:

First, give yourself 4 points for answering this quiz: ______

Then, give yourself 1 point each for all the habits you know people should adopt. This is to give you credit for your awareness, even if you haven't acted on it yet (total possible points = 32): ______

Finally, give yourself 2 more points for each habit you have adopted—or honestly would if you could (total possible points = 64): ______

Total score:

1 to 25: You are a beginner in stewardship of the earth. Try to improve.

26 to 50: You are on your way and doing better than many consumers.

51 to 75: Good. Pat yourself on the back, and keep on improving.

76 to 100: Excellent. You are a shining example for others to follow.

Source: Adapted from Conservation Action Checklist, *produced by the Washington Park Zoo, Portland, Oregon, and available from Conservation International, 1015 18th St. NW, Suite 1000, Washington, D.C. 20036: 1-800-406-2306. (website: www.conservation.org). Call or write for copies of the original or for more information.*

APPENDIX A

Table of Food Composition

CONTENTS

This edition of the table of food composition includes a wide variety of foods. It is updated with each edition to reflect current nutrient data for foods, to remove outdated foods, and to add foods that are new to the marketplace.* The nutrient database for this appendix is compiled from a variety of sources, including the USDA Nutrient Database and manufacturers' data. The USDA database provides data for a wider variety of foods and nutrients than other sources. Because laboratory analysis for each nutrient can be quite costly, manufacturers tend to provide data only for those nutrients mandated on food labels. Consequently, data for their foods are often incomplete; any missing information on this table is designated as a dash. Keep in mind that a dash means only that the information is unknown and should not be interpreted as a zero. A zero means that the nutrient is not present in the food.

Whenever using nutrient data, remember that many factors influence the nutrient contents of foods. These factors include the mineral content of the soil, the diet fed to the animal or the fertilizer used on the plant, the season of harvest, the method of processing, the length and method of storage, the method of cooking, the method of analysis, and the moisture content of the sample analyzed. With so many influencing factors, users should view nutrient data as a close approximation of the actual amount.

For updates, corrections, and a list of more than 8,000 foods and codes found in the diet analysis software that accompanies this text, visit www.cengage.com/nutrition and click on Diet Analysis Plus.

- ***Fats*** Total fats, as well as the breakdown of total fats to saturated, monounsaturated, polyunsaturated, and *trans* fats, are listed in the table. The fatty acids seldom add up to the total in part due to rounding but also because values may include some non-fatty acids, such as glycerol, phosphate, or sterols.
- ***Trans Fats*** *Trans* fat data have been listed in the table. Because food manufacturers have only been required to report *trans* fats on food labels since January 2006, much of the data is incomplete.
- ***Vitamin A and Vitamin E*** In keeping with the DRI values for vitamin A, this appendix presents data for vitamin A in micrograms (μg) RAE. Similarly, because the DRI intake values for vitamin E are based only on the alpha-tocopherol form of vitamin E, this appendix reports vitamin E data in milligrams (mg) alpha-tocopherol, listed on the table as Vit E (mg α).
- ***Bioavailability*** Keep in mind that the availability of nutrients from foods depends not only on the quantity provided by a food as reflected in this table, but also on the amount absorbed and used by the body—the bioavailability.
- ***Using the Table*** The foods and beverages in this table are organized into several categories, which are listed at the head of each right-hand page. Page numbers are provided, and each group is color-coded to make it easier to find individual foods.

*This food composition table has been prepared by Cengage Learning. The nutritional data are supplied by Axxya Systems.

TABLE A-1 Table of Food Composition

(Computer code is for Cengage Diet Analysis program) (For purposes of calculations, use "0" for t, <1, <.1, <.01, etc.)

DA+ Code	Food Description	QTY	Measure	Wt (g)	H_2O (g)	Ener (cal)	Prot (g)	Carb (g)	Fiber (g)	Fat (g)	Fat Breakdown (g) Sat	Mono	Poly	Trans
	Breads, Baked Goods, Cakes, Cookies, Crackers, Chips, Pies													
	Bagels													
8534	Cinnamon and raisin	1	item(s)	71	22.7	194	7.0	39.2	1.6	1.2	0.2	0.1	0.5	—
14395	Multi-grain	1	item(s)	61	—	170	6.0	35.0	1.0	1.5	0.5	0.1	0.4	—
8538	Oat bran	1	item(s)	71	23.4	181	7.6	37.8	2.6	0.9	0.1	0.2	0.3	—
4910	Plain, enriched	1	item(s)	71	25.8	182	7.1	35.9	1.6	1.2	0.3	0.4	0.5	0
4911	Plain, enriched, toasted	1	item(s)	66	18.7	190	7.4	37.7	1.7	1.1	0.2	0.3	0.6	0
	Biscuits													
25008	Biscuits	1	item(s)	41	15.8	121	2.6	16.4	0.5	4.9	1.4	1.4	1.8	—
16729	Scone	1	item(s)	42	11.5	148	3.8	19.1	0.6	6.2	2.0	2.5	1.3	—
25166	Wheat biscuits	1	item(s)	55	21.0	162	3.6	21.9	1.4	6.7	1.9	1.9	2.5	—
	Bread													
325	Boston brown, canned	1	slice(s)	45	21.2	88	2.3	19.5	2.1	0.7	0.1	0.1	0.3	—
8716	Bread sticks, plain	4	item(s)	24	1.5	99	2.9	16.4	0.7	2.3	0.3	0.9	0.9	—
25176	Cornbread	1	piece(s)	55	25.9	141	4.7	18.3	0.9	5.4	2.1	1.4	1.5	0
327	Cracked wheat	1	slice(s)	25	9.0	65	2.2	12.4	1.4	1.0	0.2	0.5	0.2	—
9079	Croutons, plain	¼	cup(s)	8	0.4	31	0.9	5.5	0.4	0.5	0.1	0.2	0.1	—
8582	Egg	1	slice(s)	40	13.9	113	3.8	19.1	0.9	2.4	0.6	0.9	0.4	—
8585	Egg, toasted	1	slice(s)	37	10.5	117	3.9	19.5	0.9	2.4	0.6	1.1	0.4	—
329	French	1	slice(s)	32	8.9	92	3.8	18.1	0.8	0.6	0.2	0.1	0.3	—
8591	French, toasted	1	slice(s)	23	4.7	73	3.0	14.2	0.7	0.5	0.1	0.1	0.2	—
42096	Indian fry, made with lard (Navajo)	3	ounce(s)	85	26.9	281	5.7	41.0	—	10.4	3.9	3.8	0.9	—
332	Italian	1	slice(s)	30	10.7	81	2.6	15.0	0.8	1.1	0.3	0.2	0.4	—
1393	Mixed grain	1	slice(s)	26	9.6	69	3.5	11.3	1.9	1.1	0.2	0.2	0.5	0
8604	Mixed grain, toasted	1	slice(s)	24	7.6	69	3.5	11.3	1.9	1.1	0.2	0.2	0.5	0
8605	Oat bran	1	slice(s)	30	13.2	71	3.1	11.9	1.4	1.3	0.2	0.5	0.5	—
8608	Oat bran, toasted	1	slice(s)	27	10.4	70	3.1	11.8	1.3	1.3	0.2	0.5	0.5	—
8609	Oatmeal	1	slice(s)	27	9.9	73	2.3	13.1	1.1	1.2	0.2	0.4	0.5	—
8613	Oatmeal, toasted	1	slice(s)	25	7.8	73	2.3	13.2	1.1	1.2	0.2	0.4	0.5	—
1409	Pita	1	item(s)	60	19.3	165	5.5	33.4	1.3	0.7	0.1	0.1	0.3	—
7905	Pita, whole wheat	1	item(s)	64	19.6	170	6.3	35.2	4.7	1.7	0.3	0.2	0.7	—
338	Pumpernickel	1	slice(s)	32	12.1	80	2.8	15.2	2.1	1.0	0.1	0.3	0.4	—
334	Raisin, enriched	1	slice(s)	26	8.7	71	2.1	13.6	1.1	1.1	0.3	0.6	0.2	—
8625	Raisin, toasted	1	slice(s)	24	6.7	71	2.1	13.7	1.1	1.2	0.3	0.6	0.2	—
10168	Rice, white, gluten free, wheat free	1	slice(s)	38	—	130	1.0	18.0	0.5	6.0	0	—	—	0
8653	Rye	1	slice(s)	32	11.9	83	2.7	15.5	1.9	1.1	0.2	0.4	0.3	—
8654	Rye, toasted	1	slice(s)	29	9.0	82	2.7	15.4	1.9	1.0	0.2	0.4	0.3	—
336	Rye, light	1	slice(s)	25	9.3	65	2.0	12.0	1.6	1.0	0.2	0.3	0.3	—
8588	Sourdough	1	slice(s)	25	7.0	72	2.9	14.1	0.6	0.5	0.1	0.1	0.2	—
8592	Sourdough, toasted	1	slice(s)	23	4.7	73	3.0	14.2	0.7	0.5	0.1	0.1	0.2	—
491	Submarine or hoagie roll	1	item(s)	135	40.6	400	11.0	72.0	3.8	8.0	1.8	3.0	2.2	—
8596	Vienna, toasted	1	slice(s)	23	4.7	73	3.0	14.2	0.7	0.5	0.1	0.1	0.2	—
8670	Wheat	1	slice(s)	25	8.9	67	2.7	11.9	0.9	0.9	0.2	0.2	0.4	—
8671	Wheat, toasted	1	slice(s)	23	5.6	72	3.0	12.8	1.1	1.0	0.2	0.2	0.4	—
340	White	1	slice(s)	25	9.1	67	1.9	12.7	0.6	0.8	0.2	0.2	0.3	—
1395	Whole wheat	1	slice(s)	46	15.0	128	3.9	23.6	2.8	2.5	0.4	0.5	1.4	—
	Cakes													
386	Angel food, prepared from mix	1	piece(s)	50	16.5	129	3.1	29.4	0.1	0.2	0	0	0.1	—
8772	Butter pound, ready to eat, commercially prepared	1	slice(s)	75	18.5	291	4.1	36.6	0.4	14.9	8.7	4.4	0.8	—
28517	Carrot	1	slice(s)	131	56.6	339	4.8	56.5	1.9	11.1	1.0	5.7	3.8	—
4931	Chocolate with chocolate icing, commercially prepared	1	slice(s)	64	14.7	235	2.6	34.9	1.8	10.5	3.1	5.6	1.2	—
8756	Chocolate, prepared from mix	1	slice(s)	95	23.2	352	5.0	50.7	1.5	14.3	5.2	5.7	2.6	—
393	Devil's food cupcake with chocolate frosting	1	item(s)	35	8.4	120	2.0	20.0	0.7	4.0	1.8	1.6	0.6	—
8757	Fruitcake, ready to eat, commercially prepared	1	piece(s)	43	10.9	139	1.2	26.5	1.6	3.9	0.5	1.8	1.4	—
1397	Pineapple upside down, prepared from mix	1	slice(s)	115	37.1	367	4.0	58.1	0.9	13.9	3.4	6.0	3.8	—
411	Sponge, prepared from mix	1	slice(s)	63	18.5	187	4.6	36.4	0.3	2.7	0.8	1.0	0.4	—

A

Chol (mg)	Calc (mg)	Iron (mg)	Magn (mg)	Pota (mg)	Sodi (mg)	Zinc (mg)	Vit A (μg)	Thia (mg)	Vit E (mg α)	Ribo (mg)	Niac (mg)	Vit B_6 (mg)	Fola (μg)	Vit C (mg)	Vit B_{12} (μg)	Sele (μg)
0	13	2.69	19.9	105.1	228.6	0.80	14.9	0.27	0.22	0.19	2.18	0.04	78.8	0.5	0	22.0
0	60	1.08	—	—	310.0	—	0	—	—	—	—	—	—	0	—	—
0	9	2.18	22.0	81.7	360.0	0.63	0.7	0.23	0.23	0.24	2.10	0.03	69.6	0.1	0	24.3
0	63	4.29	15.6	53.3	318.1	1.34	0	0.42	0.07	0.18	2.82	0.04	103.0	0.7	0	16.2
0	65	2.97	15.8	56.1	316.8	0.85	0	0.39	0.07	0.17	2.88	0.04	86.5	0	0	16.6
0	38	0.94	6.0	47.4	206.0	0.20	—	0.16	0.01	0.12	1.20	0.01	31.7	0.1	0.1	7.1
49	79	1.35	7.1	48.7	277.2	0.29	64.7	0.14	0.42	0.15	1.19	0.02	32.3	0	0.1	10.9
0	57	1.21	16.1	81.0	321.1	0.42	—	0.19	0.01	0.14	1.65	0.03	35.3	0.1	0.1	0
0	32	0.94	28.4	143.1	284.0	0.22	11.3	0.01	0.14	0.05	0.50	0.03	5.0	0	0	9.9
0	5	1.02	7.7	29.8	157.7	0.21	0	0.14	0.24	0.13	1.26	0.01	38.9	0	0	9.0
21	94	0.91	10.5	71.5	209.8	0.48	—	0.14	0.32	0.15	1.03	0.04	34.6	1.7	0.2	6.2
0	11	0.70	13.0	44.3	134.5	0.31	0	0.09	—	0.06	0.92	0.08	15.3	0	0	6.3
0	6	0.30	2.3	9.3	52.4	0.06	0	0.04	—	0.02	0.40	0.00	9.9	0	0	2.8
20	37	1.21	7.6	46.0	196.8	0.31	25.2	0.17	0.10	0.17	1.93	0.02	42.0	0	0	12.0
21	38	1.23	7.8	46.6	199.8	0.31	25.5	0.14	0.10	0.16	1.77	0.02	36.3	0	0	12.2
0	14	1.16	9.0	41.0	208.0	0.29	0	0.13	0.05	0.09	1.52	0.03	47.4	0.1	0	8.7
0	11	0.89	7.1	32.2	165.6	0.24	0	0.10	0.04	0.09	1.24	0.02	32.2	0	0	6.8
6	48	3.43	15.3	65.5	279.8	0.29	0	0.36	0.00	0.18	3.91	0.03	103.8	—	0	15.8
0	23	0.88	8.1	33.0	175.2	0.25	0	0.14	0.08	0.08	1.31	0.01	57.3	0	0	8.2
0	27	0.65	20.3	59.8	109.2	0.44	0	0.07	0.09	0.03	1.05	0.06	19.5	0	0	8.6
0	27	0.65	20.4	60.0	109.7	0.44	0	0.06	0.10	0.03	1.05	0.07	16.8	0	0	8.6
0	20	0.93	10.5	44.1	122.1	0.26	0.6	0.15	0.13	0.10	1.44	0.02	24.3	0	0	9.0
0	19	0.92	9.2	33.2	121.0	0.28	0.5	0.12	0.13	0.09	1.29	0.01	18.6	0	0	8.9
0	18	0.72	10.0	38.3	161.7	0.27	1.4	0.10	0.13	0.06	0.84	0.01	16.7	0	0	6.6
0	18	0.74	10.3	38.5	162.8	0.28	1.3	0.09	0.13	0.06	0.77	0.02	13.3	0.1	0	6.7
0	52	1.57	15.6	72.0	321.6	0.50	0	0.35	0.18	0.19	2.77	0.02	64.2	0	0	16.3
0	10	1.95	44.2	108.8	340.5	0.97	0	0.21	0.39	0.05	1.81	0.17	22.4	0	0	28.2
0	22	0.91	17.3	66.6	214.7	0.47	0	0.10	0.13	0.09	0.98	0.04	29.8	0	0	7.8
0	17	0.75	6.8	59.0	101.4	0.18	0	0.08	0.07	0.10	0.90	0.01	27.6	0	0	5.2
0	17	0.76	6.7	59.0	101.8	0.19	0	0.07	0.07	0.09	0.81	0.02	23.5	0.1	0	5.2
0	100	1.08	—	—	140	—	—	0.15	—	0.10	1.20	—	32.0	0	—	—
0	23	0.90	12.8	53.1	211.2	0.36	0	0.13	0.10	0.10	1.21	0.02	35.2	0.1	0	9.9
0	23	0.89	12.5	53.1	210.3	0.36	0	0.11	0.10	0.09	1.09	0.02	29.9	0.1	0	9.9
0	20	0.70	3.9	51.0	175.0	0.18	0	0.10	—	0.08	0.80	0.01	5.3	0	0	8.0
0	11	0.91	7.0	32.0	162.5	0.23	0	0.11	0.05	0.07	1.19	0.03	37.0	0.1	0	6.8
0	11	0.89	7.1	32.2	165.6	0.24	0	0.10	0.04	0.09	1.24	0.02	32.2	0	0	6.8
0	100	3.80	—	128.0	683.0	—	0	0.54	—	0.33	4.50	0.04	—	0	—	42.0
0	11	0.89	7.1	32.2	165.6	0.24	0	0.10	0.04	0.09	1.24	0.02	32.2	0	0	6.8
0	36	0.87	12.0	46.0	130.3	0.30	0	0.09	0.05	0.08	1.30	0.03	21.3	0.1	0	7.2
0	38	0.94	13.6	51.3	140.5	0.34	0	0.10	0.06	0.09	1.44	0.04	19.8	0	0	7.7
0	38	0.94	5.8	25.0	170.3	0.19	0	0.11	0.06	0.08	1.10	0.02	27.8	0	0	4.3
0	15	1.42	37.3	144.4	159.2	0.69	0	0.13	0.35	0.10	1.83	0.09	29.9	0	0	17.8
0	42	0.11	4.0	67.5	254.5	0.06	0	0.04	0.01	0.10	0.08	0.00	9.5	0	0	7.7
166	26	1.03	8.3	89.3	298.5	0.34	111.8	0.10	—	0.17	0.98	0.03	30.8	0	0.2	6.6
0	65	2.18	23.0	279.6	367.7	0.44	—	0.25	0.01	0.19	1.73	0.10	43.4	4.6	0	14.7
27	28	1.40	21.8	128.0	213.8	0.44	16.6	0.01	0.62	0.08	0.36	0.02	10.9	0.1	0.1	2.1
55	57	1.53	30.4	133.0	299.3	0.65	38.0	0.13	—	0.20	1.08	0.03	25.7	0.2	0.2	11.3
19	21	0.70	—	46.0	92.0	—	—	0.04	—	0.05	0.30	—	2.1	0	—	2.0
2	14	0.89	6.9	65.8	116.1	0.11	3.0	0.02	0.38	0.04	0.34	0.02	8.6	0.2	0	0.9
25	138	1.70	15.0	128.8	366.9	0.35	71.3	0.17	—	0.17	1.36	0.03	29.9	1.4	0.1	10.8
107	26	0.99	5.7	88.8	143.6	0.37	48.5	0.10	—	0.19	0.75	0.03	24.6	0	0.2	11.7

TABLE A-1 Table of Food Composition *(continued)*

(Computer code is for Cengage Diet Analysis program) (For purposes of calculations, use "0" for t, <1, <.1, <.01, etc.)

DA+ Code	Food Description	Qty	Measure	Wt (g)	H_2O (g)	Ener (cal)	Prot (g)	Carb (g)	Fiber (g)	Fat (g)	Fat Breakdown (g) Sat	Mono	Poly	Trans
Breads, Baked Goods, Cakes, Cookies, Crackers, Chips, Pies—continued														
8817	White with coconut frosting, prepared from mix	1	slice(s)	112	23.2	399	4.9	70.8	1.1	11.5	4.4	4.1	2.4	—
8819	Yellow with chocolate frosting, ready to eat, commercially prepared	1	slice(s)	64	14.0	243	2.4	35.5	1.2	11.1	3.0	6.1	1.4	—
8822	Yellow with vanilla frosting, ready to eat, commercially prepared	1	slice(s)	64	14.1	239	2.2	37.6	0.2	9.3	1.5	3.9	3.3	—
	Snack cakes													
8791	Chocolate snack cake, creme filled, with frosting	1	item(s)	50	9.3	200	1.8	30.2	1.6	8.0	2.4	4.3	0.9	—
25010	Cinnamon coffee cake	1	piece(s)	72	22.6	231	3.6	35.8	0.7	8.3	2.2	2.6	3.0	—
16777	Funnel cake	1	item(s)	90	37.6	276	7.3	29.1	0.9	14.4	2.7	4.7	6.1	—
8794	Sponge snack cake, creme filled	1	item(s)	43	8.6	155	1.3	27.2	0.2	4.8	1.1	1.7	1.4	—
	Snacks, chips, pretzels													
29428	Bagel chips, plain	3	item(s)	29	—	130	3.0	19.0	1.0	4.5	0.5	—	—	—
29429	Bagel chips, toasted onion	3	item(s)	29	—	130	4.0	20.0	1.0	4.5	0.5	—	—	—
38192	Chex traditional snack mix	1	cup(s)	45	—	197	3.0	33.3	1.5	6.1	0.8	—	—	—
654	Potato chips, salted	1	ounce(s)	28	0.6	155	1.9	14.1	1.2	10.6	3.1	2.8	3.5	—
8816	Potato chips, unsalted	1	ounce(s)	28	0.5	152	2.0	15.0	1.4	9.8	3.1	2.8	3.5	—
5096	Pretzels, plain, hard, twists	5	item(s)	30	1.0	114	2.7	23.8	1.0	1.1	0.2	0.4	0.4	—
4632	Pretzels, whole wheat	1	ounce(s)	28	1.1	103	3.1	23.0	2.2	0.7	0.2	0.3	0.2	—
4641	Tortilla chips, plain	6	item(s)	11	0.2	53	0.8	7.1	0.6	2.5	0.3	0.8	0.5	0.3
	Cookies													
8859	Animal crackers	12	item(s)	30	1.2	134	2.1	22.2	0.3	4.1	1.0	2.3	0.6	—
8876	Brownie, prepared from mix	1	item(s)	24	3.0	112	1.5	12.0	0.5	7.0	1.8	2.6	2.3	—
25207	Chocolate chip cookies	1	item(s)	30	3.7	140	2.0	16.2	0.6	7.9	2.1	3.3	2.1	—
8915	Chocolate sandwich cookie with extra creme filling	1	item(s)	13	0.2	65	0.6	8.9	0.4	3.2	0.7	2.1	0.3	1.1
14145	Fig Newtons cookies	1	item(s)	16	—	55	0.5	11.0	0.5	1.3	0	—	—	0
8920	Fortune cookie	1	item(s)	8	0.6	30	0.3	6.7	0.1	0.2	0.1	0.1	0	—
25208	Oatmeal cookies	1	item(s)	69	12.3	234	5.7	45.1	3.1	4.2	0.7	1.3	1.8	—
25213	Peanut butter cookies	1	item(s)	35	4.1	163	4.2	16.9	0.9	9.2	1.7	4.7	2.3	—
33095	Sugar cookies	1	item(s)	16	4.1	61	1.1	7.4	0.1	3.0	0.6	1.3	0.9	—
9002	Vanilla sandwich cookie with creme filling	1	item(s)	10	0.2	48	0.5	7.2	0.2	2.0	0.3	0.8	0.8	—
	Crackers													
9012	Cheese cracker sandwich with peanut butter	4	item(s)	28	0.9	139	3.5	15.9	1.0	7.0	1.2	3.6	1.4	—
9008	Cheese crackers (mini)	30	item(s)	30	0.9	151	3.0	17.5	0.7	7.6	2.8	3.6	0.7	—
33362	Cheese crackers, low sodium	1	serving(s)	30	0.9	151	3.0	17.5	0.7	7.6	2.9	3.6	0.7	—
8928	Honey graham crackers	4	item(s)	28	1.2	118	1.9	21.5	0.8	2.8	0.4	1.1	1.1	—
9016	Matzo crackers, plain	1	item(s)	28	1.2	112	2.8	23.8	0.9	0.4	0.1	0	0.2	—
9024	Melba toast	3	item(s)	15	0.8	59	1.8	11.5	0.9	0.5	0.1	0.1	0.2	—
9028	Melba toast, rye	3	item(s)	15	0.7	58	1.7	11.6	1.2	0.5	0.1	0.1	0.2	—
14189	Ritz crackers	5	item(s)	16	0.5	80	1.0	10.0	0	4.0	1.0	—	—	0
9014	Rye crispbread crackers	1	item(s)	10	0.6	37	0.8	8.2	1.7	0.1	0	0	0.1	—
9040	Rye wafer	1	item(s)	11	0.6	37	1.1	8.8	2.5	0.1	0	0	0	—
432	Saltine crackers	5	item(s)	15	0.8	64	1.4	10.6	0.5	1.7	0.2	1.1	0.2	0.5
9046	Saltine crackers, low salt	5	item(s)	15	0.6	65	1.4	10.7	0.5	1.8	0.4	1.0	0.3	—
9052	Snack cracker sandwich with cheese filling	4	item(s)	28	1.1	134	2.6	17.3	0.5	5.9	1.7	3.2	0.7	—
9054	Snack cracker sandwich with peanut butter filling	4	item(s)	28	0.8	138	3.2	16.3	0.6	6.9	1.4	3.9	1.3	—
9048	Snack crackers, round	10	item(s)	30	1.1	151	2.2	18.3	0.5	7.6	1.1	3.2	2.9	—
9050	Snack crackers, round, low salt	10	item(s)	30	1.1	151	2.2	18.3	0.5	7.6	1.1	3.2	2.9	—
9044	Soda crackers	5	tem(s)	15	0.8	64	1.4	10.6	0.5	1.7	0.2	1.1	0.2	0.5
9059	Wheat cracker sandwich with cheese filling	4	item(s)	28	0.9	139	2.7	16.3	0.9	7.0	1.2	2.9	2.6	—
9061	Wheat cracker sandwich with peanut butter filling	4	item(s)	28	1.0	139	3.8	15.1	1.2	7.5	1.3	3.3	2.5	—
9055	Wheat crackers	10	item(s)	30	0.9	142	2.6	19.5	1.4	6.2	1.6	3.4	0.8	—

Chol (mg)	Calc (mg)	Iron (mg)	Magn (mg)	Pota (mg)	Sodi (mg)	Zinc (mg)	Vit A (µg)	Thia (mg)	Vit E (mg α)	Ribo (mg)	Niac (mg)	Vit B_6 (mg)	Fola (µg)	Vit C (mg)	Vit B_{12} (µg)	Sele (µg)
1	101	1.29	13.4	110.9	318.1	0.37	13.4	0.14	0.13	0.21	1.19	0.03	34.7	0.1	0.1	12.0
35	24	1.33	19.2	113.9	215.7	0.39	21.1	0.07	—	0.10	0.79	0.02	14.1	0	0.1	2.2
35	40	0.68	3.8	33.9	220.2	0.16	12.2	0.06	—	0.04	0.32	0.01	17.3	0	0.1	3.5
0	58	1.80	18.0	88.0	194.5	0.52	0.5	0.01	0.54	0.03	0.46	0.07	13.0	1.0	0	1.7
26	55	1.36	9.9	91.9	277.6	0.30	—	0.17	0.23	0.16	1.29	0.02	36.1	0.3	0.1	9.6
62	126	1.90	16.2	152.1	269.1	0.65	49.5	0.23	1.54	0.32	1.86	0.04	50.4	0	0.3	17.7
7	19	0.54	3.4	37.0	155.1	0.12	2.1	0.06	0.50	0.05	0.52	0.01	17.0	0	0	1.3
0	0	0.72	—	45.0	70.0	—	0	—	—	—	—	—	—	0	0	—
0	0	0.72	—	50.0	300.0	—	0	—	—	—	—	—	—	0	0	—
0	0	0.55	—	75.8	621.2	—	0	0.09	—	0.05	1.21	—	12.1	0	—	—
0	7	0.45	19.8	465.5	148.8	0.67	0	0.01	1.91	0.06	1.18	0.20	21.3	5.3	0	2.3
0	7	0.46	19.0	361.5	2.3	0.30	0	0.04	2.58	0.05	1.08	0.18	12.8	8.8	0	2.3
0	11	1.29	10.5	43.8	514.5	0.25	0	0.13	0.10	0.18	1.57	0.03	51.3	0	0	1.7
0	8	0.76	8.5	121.9	57.6	0.17	0	0.12	—	0.08	1.85	0.07	15.3	0.3	0	—
0	19	0.25	15.8	23.2	45.5	0.26	0	0.00	0.46	0.01	0.13	0.02	2.2	0	0	0.7
0	13	0.82	5.4	30.0	117.9	0.19	0	0.10	0.03	0.09	1.04	0.01	30.9	0	0	2.1
18	14	0.44	12.7	42.2	82.3	0.23	42.2	0.03	—	0.05	0.24	0.02	7.0	0.1	0	2.8
13	11	0.69	12.4	62.1	108.8	0.24	—	0.08	0.54	0.06	0.87	0.01	17.8	0	0	4.1
0	2	1.01	4.7	17.8	45.6	0.10	0	0.02	0.25	0.02	0.25	0.00	6.0	0	0	1.1
0	10	0.36	—	—	57.5	—	0	—	—	—	—	—	—	0	—	—
0	1	0.12	0.6	3.3	21.9	0.01	0.1	0.01	0.00	0.01	0.15	0.00	5.3	0	0	0.2
0	26	1.93	48.8	176.7	311.1	1.42	—	0.26	0.23	0.13	1.35	0.09	34.9	0.3	0	17.4
13	27	0.65	21.1	112.8	154.1	0.46	—	0.08	0.73	0.09	1.85	0.05	23.5	0.1	0.1	4.8
18	5	0.30	1.7	12.2	49.4	0.08	—	0.04	0.28	0.05	0.31	0.01	9.5	0	0	3.1
0	3	0.22	1.4	9.1	34.9	0.04	0	0.02	0.16	0.02	0.27	0.00	5.0	0	0	0.3
0	14	0.76	15.7	61.0	198.8	0.29	0.3	0.15	0.66	0.08	1.63	0.04	26.3	0	0.1	2.3
4	45	1.43	10.8	43.5	298.5	0.33	8.7	0.17	0.01	0.12	1.40	0.16	45.6	0	0.1	2.6
4	45	1.43	10.8	31.8	137.4	0.33	5.1	0.17	0.09	0.12	1.40	0.16	26.7	0	0.1	2.6
0	7	1.04	8.4	37.8	169.4	0.22	0	0.06	0.09	0.08	1.15	0.01	12.9	0	0	2.9
0	4	0.89	7.1	31.8	0.6	0.19	0	0.11	0.01	0.08	1.10	0.03	4.8	0	0	10.5
0	14	0.55	8.9	30.3	124.4	0.30	0	0.06	0.06	0.04	0.61	0.01	18.6	0	0	5.2
0	12	0.55	5.9	29.0	134.9	0.20	0	0.07	—	0.04	0.70	0.01	12.8	0	0	5.8
0	20	0.72	—	10.0	135.0	—	—	—	—	—	—	—	—	0	—	—
0	3	0.24	7.8	31.9	26.4	0.23	0	0.02	0.08	0.01	0.10	0.02	4.7	0	0	3.7
0	4	0.65	13.3	54.5	87.3	0.30	0	0.04	0.08	0.03	0.17	0.03	5.0	0	0	2.6
0	10	0.84	3.3	23.1	160.8	0.12	0	0.01	0.14	0.06	0.78	0.01	20.9	0	0	1.5
0	18	0.81	4.1	108.6	95.4	0.11	0	0.08	0.01	0.06	0.78	0.01	18.6	0	0	2.9
1	72	0.66	10.1	120.1	392.3	0.17	4.8	0.12	0.06	0.19	1.05	0.01	28.0	0	0	6.0
0	23	0.77	15.4	60.2	201.0	0.31	0.3	0.13	0.57	0.07	1.71	0.04	24.1	0	0	3.0
0	36	1.08	8.1	39.9	254.1	0.20	0	0.12	0.60	0.10	1.21	0.01	27.0	0	0	2.0
0	36	1.08	8.1	106.5	111.9	0.20	0	0.12	0.60	0.10	1.21	0.01	27.0	0	0	2.0
0	10	0.84	3.3	23.1	160.8	0.12	0	0.01	0.14	0.06	0.78	0.01	20.9	0	0	1.5
2	57	0.73	15.1	85.7	255.6	0.24	4.8	0.10	—	0.12	0.89	0.07	17.9	0.4	0	6.8
0	48	0.74	10.6	83.2	226.0	0.23	0	0.10	—	0.08	1.64	0.03	19.6	0	0	6.1
0	15	1.32	18.6	54.9	238.5	0.48	0	0.15	0.15	0.09	1.48	0.04	35.1	0	0	1.9

Table A-1 Table of Food Composition *(continued)*

(Computer code is for Cengage Diet Analysis program) (For purposes of calculations, use "0" for t, <1, <.1, <.01, etc.)

DA+ Code	Food Description	QTY	Measure	Wt (g)	H_2O (g)	Ener (cal)	Prot (g)	Carb (g)	Fiber (g)	Fat (g)	Fat Breakdown (g)			
											Sat	Mono	Poly	Trans
Breads, Baked Goods, Cakes, Cookies, Crackers, Chips, Pies—continued														
9057	Wheat crackers, low salt	10	item(s)	30	0.9	142	2.6	19.5	1.4	6.2	1.6	3.4	0.8	—
9022	Whole wheat crackers	7	item(s)	28	0.8	124	2.5	19.2	2.9	4.8	1.0	1.6	1.8	—
	Pastry													
16754	Apple fritter	1	item(s)	17	6.4	61	1.0	5.5	0.2	3.9	0.9	1.7	1.1	—
41565	Cinnamon rolls with icing, refrigerated dough	1	serving(s)	44	12.3	145	2.0	23.0	0.5	5.0	1.5	—	—	2.0
4945	Croissant, butter	1	item(s)	57	13.2	231	4.7	26.1	1.5	12.0	6.6	3.1	0.6	—
9096	Danish, nut	1	item(s)	65	13.3	280	4.6	29.7	1.3	16.4	3.8	8.9	2.8	—
9115	Doughnut with creme filling	1	item(s)	85	32.5	307	5.4	25.5	0.7	20.8	4.6	10.3	2.6	—
9117	Doughnut with jelly filling	1	item(s)	85	30.3	289	5.0	33.2	0.8	15.9	4.1	8.7	2.0	—
4947	Doughnut, cake	1	item(s)	47	9.8	198	2.4	23.4	0.7	10.8	1.7	4.4	3.7	—
9105	Doughnut, cake, chocolate glazed	1	item(s)	42	6.8	175	1.9	24.1	0.9	8.4	2.2	4.7	1.0	—
437	Doughnut, glazed	1	item(s)	60	15.2	242	3.8	26.6	0.7	13.7	3.5	7.7	1.7	—
10617	Toaster pastry, brown sugar cinnamon	1	item(s)	50	5.3	210	3.0	35.0	1.0	6.0	1.0	4.0	1.0	—
30928	Toaster pastry, cream cheese	1	item(s)	54	—	200	3.0	23.0	0	11.0	4.5	—	—	1.5
	Muffins													
25015	Blueberry	1	item(s)	63	29.7	160	3.4	23.0	0.8	6.0	0.9	1.5	3.3	—
9189	Corn, ready to eat	1	item(s)	57	18.6	174	3.4	29.0	1.9	4.8	0.8	1.2	1.8	—
9121	English muffin, plain, enriched	1	item(s)	57	24.0	134	4.4	26.2	1.5	1.0	0.1	0.2	0.5	—
29582	English muffin, toasted	1	item(s)	50	18.6	128	4.2	25.0	1.5	1.0	0.1	0.2	0.5	—
9145	English muffin, wheat	1	item(s)	57	24.1	127	5.0	25.5	2.6	1.1	0.2	0.2	0.5	—
8894	Oat bran	1	item(s)	57	20.0	154	4.0	27.5	2.6	4.2	0.6	1.0	2.4	—
	Granola bars													
38161	Kudos milk chocolate granola bars w/fruit and nuts	1	item(s)	28	—	90	2.0	15.0	1.0	3.0	1.0	—	—	—
38196	Nature Valley banana nut crunchy granola bars	2	item(s)	42	—	190	4.0	28.0	2.0	7.0	1.0	—	—	—
38187	Nature Valley fruit 'n' nut trail mix bar	1	item(s)	35	—	140	3.0	25.0	2.0	4.0	0.5	—	—	—
1383	Plain, hard	1	item(s)	25	1.0	115	2.5	15.8	1.3	4.9	0.6	1.1	3.0	—
4606	Plain, soft	1	item(s)	28	1.8	126	2.1	19.1	1.3	4.9	2.1	1.1	1.5	—
	Pies													
454	Apple pie, prepared from home recipe	1	slice(s)	155	73.3	411	3.7	57.5	2.3	19.4	4.7	8.4	5.2	—
470	Pecan pie, prepared from home recipe	1	slice(s)	122	23.8	503	6.0	63.7	—	27.1	4.9	13.6	7.0	—
33356	Pie crust mix, prepared, baked	1	slice(s)	20	2.1	100	1.3	10.1	0.4	6.1	1.5	3.5	0.8	—
9007	Pie crust, ready to bake, frozen, enriched, baked	1	slice(s)	16	1.8	82	0.7	7.9	0.2	5.2	1.7	2.5	0.6	—
472	Pumpkin pie, prepared from home recipe	1	slice(s)	155	90.7	316	7.0	40.9	—	14.4	4.9	5.7	2.8	—
	Rolls													
8555	Crescent dinner roll	1	item(s)	28	9.7	78	2.7	13.8	0.6	1.2	0.3	0.3	0.6	—
489	Hamburger roll or bun, plain	1	item(s)	43	14.9	120	4.1	21.3	0.9	1.9	0.5	0.5	0.8	—
490	Hard roll	1	item(s)	57	17.7	167	5.6	30.0	1.3	2.5	0.3	0.6	1.0	—
5127	Kaiser roll	1	item(s)	57	17.7	167	5.6	30.0	1.3	2.5	0.3	0.6	1.0	—
5130	Whole wheat roll or bun	1	item(s)	28	9.4	75	2.5	14.5	2.1	1.3	0.2	0.3	0.6	—
	Sport bars													
37026	Balance original chocolate bar	1	item(s)	50	—	200	14.0	22.0	0.5	6.0	3.5	—	—	—
37024	Balance original peanut butter bar	1	item(s)	50	—	200	14.0	22.0	1.0	6.0	2.5	—	—	—
36580	Clif Bar chocolate brownie energy bar	1	item(s)	68	—	240	10.0	45.0	5.0	4.5	1.5	—	—	0
36583	Clif Bar crunchy peanut butter energy bar	1	item(s)	68	—	250	12.0	40.0	5.0	6.0	1.5	—	—	0
36589	Clif Luna Nutz over Chocolate energy bar	1	item(s)	48	—	180	10.0	25.0	3.0	4.5	2.5	—	—	0
12005	PowerBar apple cinnamon	1	item(s)	65	—	230	9.0	45.0	3.0	2.5	0.5	1.5	0.5	0
16078	PowerBar banana	1	item(s)	65	—	230	9.0	45.0	3.0	2.5	0.5	1.0	0.5	0
16080	PowerBar chocolate	1	item(s)	65	6.4	230	10.0	45.0	3.0	2.0	0.5	0.5	1.0	0
29092	PowerBar peanut butter	1	item(s)	65	—	240	10.0	45.0	3.0	3.5	0.5	—	—	0
	Tortillas													
1391	Corn tortillas, soft	1	item(s)	26	11.9	57	1.5	11.6	1.6	0.7	0.1	0.2	0.4	—
1669	Flour tortilla	1	item(s)	32	9.7	100	2.7	16.4	1.0	2.5	0.6	1.2	0.5	—

Chol (mg)	Calc (mg)	Iron (mg)	Magn (mg)	Pota (mg)	Sodi (mg)	Zinc (mg)	Vit A (μg)	Thia (mg)	Vit E (mg α)	Ribo (mg)	Niac (mg)	Vit B_6 (mg)	Fola (μg)	Vit C (mg)	Vit B_{12} (μg)	Sele (μg)
0	15	1.32	18.6	60.9	84.9	0.48	0	0.15	0.15	0.09	1.48	0.04	15.0	0	0	10.1
0	14	0.86	27.7	83.2	184.5	0.60	0	0.05	0.24	0.02	1.26	0.05	7.8	0	0	4.1
14	9	0.26	2.2	22.4	6.8	0.09	7.1	0.03	0.07	0.04	0.23	0.01	6.3	0.2	0.1	2.6
0	—	0.72	—	—	340.1	—	0	—	—	—	—	—	—	—	—	—
38	21	1.15	9.1	67.3	424.1	0.42	117.4	0.22	0.47	0.13	1.24	0.03	50.2	0.1	0.1	12.9
30	61	1.17	20.8	61.8	236.0	0.56	5.9	0.14	0.53	0.15	1.49	0.06	54.0	1.1	0.1	9.2
20	21	1.55	17.0	68.0	262.7	0.68	9.4	0.28	0.24	0.12	1.90	0.05	59.5	0	0.1	9.2
22	21	1.49	17.0	67.2	249.1	0.63	14.5	0.26	0.36	0.12	1.81	0.08	57.8	0	0.2	10.6
17	21	0.91	9.4	59.7	256.6	0.25	17.9	0.10	0.90	0.11	0.87	0.02	24.4	0.1	0.1	4.4
24	89	0.95	14.3	44.5	142.8	0.23	5.0	0.01	0.08	0.02	0.19	0.01	18.9	0	0	1.7
4	26	0.36	13.2	64.8	205.2	0.46	2.4	0.53	—	0.04	0.39	0.03	13.2	0.1	0.1	5.0
0	0	1.80	—	70.0	190.0	—	—	0.15	—	0.17	2.00	0.20	40.0	0	0	—
10	100	1.80	—	—	220.0	—	—	0.15	—	0.17	2.00	—	40.0	0	0.6	—
20	56	1.02	7.8	70.2	289.4	0.28	—	0.17	0.75	0.15	1.25	0.02	34.0	0.4	0.1	8.8
15	42	1.60	18.2	39.3	297.0	0.30	29.6	0.15	0.45	0.18	1.16	0.04	45.6	0	0.1	8.7
0	30	1.42	12.0	74.7	264.5	0.39	0	0.25	—	0.16	2.21	0.02	42.2	0	0	—
0	95	1.36	11.0	71.5	252.0	0.38	0	0.19	0.16	0.14	1.90	0.02	43.5	0.1	0	13.5
0	101	1.63	21.1	106.0	217.7	0.61	0	0.24	0.25	0.16	1.91	0.05	36.5	0	0	16.6
0	36	2.39	89.5	289.0	224.0	1.04	0	0.14	0.37	0.05	0.23	0.09	50.7	0	0	6.3
0	200	0.36	—	—	60.0	—	0	—	—	—	—	—	—	0	0	—
0	20	1.08	—	120.0	160.0	—	0	—	—	—	—	—	—	0	—	—
0	0	0.00	—	—	95.0	—	0	—	—	—	—	—	—	0	—	—
0	15	0.72	23.8	82.3	72.0	0.50	0	0.06	—	0.03	0.39	0.02	5.6	0.2	0	4.0
0	30	0.72	21.0	92.3	79.0	0.42	0	0.08	—	0.04	0.14	0.02	6.8	0	0.1	4.6
0	11	1.73	10.9	122.5	327.1	0.29	17.1	0.22	—	0.16	1.90	0.05	37.2	2.6	0	12.1
106	39	1.80	31.7	162.3	319.6	1.24	100.0	0.22	—	0.22	1.03	0.07	31.7	0.2	0.2	14.6
0	12	0.43	3.0	12.4	145.8	0.07	0	0.06	—	0.03	0.47	0.01	14.0	0	0	4.4
0	3	0.36	2.9	17.6	103.5	0.05	0	0.04	0.42	0.06	0.39	0.01	8.8	0	0	0.5
65	146	1.96	29.5	288.3	348.8	0.71	660.3	0.14	—	0.31	1.21	0.07	32.6	2.6	0.1	11.0
0	39	0.93	5.9	26.3	134.1	0.18	0	0.11	0.02	0.09	1.16	0.02	31.1	0	0.1	5.5
0	59	1.42	9.0	40.4	206.0	0.28	0	0.17	0.03	0.13	1.78	0.03	47.7	0	0.1	8.4
0	54	1.87	15.4	61.6	310.1	0.53	0	0.27	0.23	0.19	2.41	0.02	54.2	0	0	22.3
0	54	1.86	15.4	61.6	310.1	0.53	0	0.27	0.23	0.19	2.41	0.01	54.2	0	0	22.3
0	30	0.69	24.1	77.1	135.5	0.57	0	0.07	0.26	0.04	1.04	0.06	8.5	0	0	14.0
3	100	4.50	40.0	160.0	180.0	3.75	—	0.37	—	0.42	5.00	0.50	100.0	60.0	1.5	17.5
3	100	4.50	40.0	130.0	230.0	3.75	—	0.37	—	0.42	5.00	0.50	100.0	60.0	1.5	17.5
0	250	4.50	100.0	370.0	150.0	3.00	—	0.37	—	0.25	3.00	0.40	80.0	60.0	0.9	14.0
0	250	4.50	100.0	230.0	250.0	3.00	—	0.37	—	0.25	3.00	0.40	80.0	60.0	0.9	14.0
0	350	5.40	80.0	190.0	190.0	5.25	—	1.20	—	1.36	16.00	2.00	400.0	60.0	6.0	24.5
0	300	6.30	140.0	125.0	100.0	5.25	—	1.50	—	1.70	20.00	2.00	400.0	60.0	6.0	—
0	300	6.30	140.0	190.0	100.0	5.25	0	1.50	—	1.70	20.00	2.00	400.0	60.0	6.0	—
0	300	6.30	140.0	200.0	95.0	5.25	0	1.50	—	1.70	20.00	2.00	400.0	60.0	6.0	5.1
0	300	6.30	140.0	130.0	120.0	5.25	0	1.50	—	1.70	20.00	2.00	400.0	60.0	6.0	—
0	21	0.32	18.7	48.4	11.7	0.34	0	0.02	0.07	0.02	0.39	0.06	1.3	0	0	1.6
0	41	1.06	7.0	49.6	203.5	0.17	0	0.17	0.06	0.08	1.14	0.01	33.3	0	0	7.1

TABLE A-1 Table of Food Composition *(continued)*

(Computer code is for Cengage Diet Analysis program) (For purposes of calculations, use "0" for t, <1, <.1, <.01, etc.)

DA+ Code	Food Description	QTY	Measure	Wt (g)	H_2O (g)	Ener (cal)	Prot (g)	Carb (g)	Fiber (g)	Fat (g)	Fat Breakdown (g) Sat	Mono	Poly	Trans
Breads, Baked Goods, Cakes, Cookies, Crackers, Chips, Pies—continued														
	Pancakes, waffles													
8926	Pancakes, blueberry, prepared from recipe	3	item(s)	114	60.6	253	7.0	33.1	0.8	10.5	2.3	2.6	4.7	—
5037	Pancakes, prepared from mix with egg and milk	3	item(s)	114	60.3	249	8.9	32.9	2.1	8.8	2.3	2.4	3.3	—
1390	Taco shells, hard	1	item(s)	13	1.0	62	0.9	8.3	0.6	2.8	0.6	1.6	0.5	0.6
30311	Waffle, 100% whole grain	1	item(s)	75	32.3	200	6.9	25.0	1.9	8.4	2.3	3.3	2.1	—
9219	Waffle, plain, frozen, toasted	2	item(s)	66	20.2	206	4.7	32.5	1.6	6.3	1.1	3.2	1.5	—
500	Waffle, plain, prepared from recipe	1	item(s)	75	31.5	218	5.9	24.7	1.7	10.6	2.1	2.6	5.1	—
Cereal, Flour, Grain, Pasta, Noodles, Popcorn														
	Grain													
2861	Amaranth, dry	½	cup(s)	98	9.6	365	14.1	64.5	9.1	6.3	1.6	1.4	2.8	—
1953	Barley, pearled, cooked	½	cup(s)	79	54.0	97	1.8	22.2	3.0	0.3	0.1	0	0.2	—
1956	Buckwheat groats, cooked, roasted	½	cup(s)	84	63.5	77	2.8	16.8	2.3	0.5	0.1	0.2	0.2	—
1957	Bulgur, cooked	½	cup(s)	91	70.8	76	2.8	16.9	4.1	0.2	0	0	0.1	—
1963	Couscous, cooked	½	cup(s)	79	57.0	88	3.0	18.2	1.1	0.1	0	0	0.1	—
1967	Millet, cooked	½	cup(s)	120	85.7	143	4.2	28.4	1.6	1.2	0.2	0.2	0.6	—
1969	Oat bran, dry	½	cup(s)	47	3.1	116	8.1	31.1	7.2	3.3	0.6	1.1	1.3	—
1972	Quinoa, dry	½	cup(s)	85	11.3	313	12.0	54.5	5.9	5.2	0.6	1.4	2.8	—
	Rice													
129	Brown, long grain, cooked	½	cup(s)	98	71.3	108	2.5	22.4	1.8	0.9	0.2	0.3	0.3	—
2863	Brown, medium grain, cooked	½	cup(s)	98	71.1	109	2.3	22.9	1.8	0.8	0.2	0.3	0.3	—
37488	Jasmine, saffroned, cooked	½	cup(s)	280	—	340	8.0	78.0	0	0	0	0	0	0
30280	Pilaf, cooked	½	cup(s)	103	74.0	129	2.1	22.2	0.6	3.3	0.6	1.5	1.0	—
28066	Spanish, cooked	½	cup(s)	244	184.2	241	5.7	50.2	3.3	1.9	0.4	0.6	0.7	0
2867	White glutinous, cooked	½	cup(s)	87	66.7	84	1.8	18.3	0.9	0.2	0	0.1	0.1	—
484	White, long grain, boiled	½	cup(s)	79	54.1	103	2.1	22.3	0.3	0.2	0.1	0.1	0.1	—
482	White, long grain, enriched, instant, boiled	½	cup(s)	83	59.4	97	1.8	20.7	0.5	0.4	0	0.1	0	—
486	White, long grain, enriched, parboiled, cooked	½	cup(s)	79	55.6	97	2.3	20.6	0.7	0.3	0.1	0.1	0.1	—
1194	Wild brown, cooked	½	cup(s)	82	60.6	83	3.3	17.5	1.5	0.3	0	0	0.2	—
	Flour and grain fractions													
505	All purpose flour, self-rising, enriched	½	cup(s)	63	6.6	221	6.2	46.4	1.7	0.6	0.1	0	0.2	—
503	All purpose flour, white, bleached, enriched	½	cup(s)	63	7.4	228	6.4	47.7	1.7	0.6	0.1	0	0.2	—
1643	Barley flour	½	cup(s)	56	5.5	198	4.2	44.7	2.1	0.8	0.2	0.1	0.4	—
383	Buckwheat flour, whole groat	½	cup(s)	60	6.7	201	7.6	42.3	6.0	1.9	0.4	0.6	0.6	—
504	Cake wheat flour, enriched	½	cup(s)	69	8.6	248	5.6	53.5	1.2	0.6	0.1	0.1	0.3	—
426	Cornmeal, degermed, enriched	½	cup(s)	69	7.8	255	5.0	54.6	2.8	1.2	0.1	0.2	0.5	0
424	Cornmeal, yellow whole grain	½	cup(s)	61	6.2	221	4.9	46.9	4.4	2.2	0.3	0.6	1.0	—
1978	Dark rye flour	½	cup(s)	64	7.1	207	9.0	44.0	14.5	1.7	0.2	0.2	0.8	—
1644	Masa corn flour, enriched	½	cup(s)	57	5.1	208	5.3	43.5	5.5	2.1	0.3	0.6	1.0	—
1976	Rice flour, brown	½	cup(s)	79	9.4	287	5.7	60.4	3.6	2.2	0.4	0.8	0.8	—
1645	Rice flour, white	½	cup(s)	79	9.4	289	4.7	63.3	1.9	1.1	0.3	0.3	0.3	—
1980	Semolina, enriched	½	cup(s)	84	10.6	301	10.6	60.8	3.2	0.9	0.1	0.1	0.4	—
2827	Soy flour, raw	½	cup(s)	42	2.2	185	14.7	14.9	4.1	8.8	1.3	1.9	4.9	—
1990	Wheat germ, crude	2	tablespoon(s)	14	1.6	52	3.3	7.4	1.9	1.4	0.2	0.2	0.9	—
506	Whole wheat flour	½	cup(s)	60	6.2	203	8.2	43.5	7.3	1.1	0.2	0.1	0.5	—
	Breakfast bars													
39230	Atkins Morning Start apple crisp breakfast bar	1	item(s)	37	—	170	11.0	12.0	6.0	9.0	4.0	—	—	—
10571	Nutri-Grain apple cinnamon cereal bar	1	item(s)	37	—	140	2.0	27.0	1.0	3.0	0.5	2.0	0.5	—
10647	Nutri-Grain blueberry cereal bar	1	item(s)	37	5.4	140	2.0	27.0	1.0	3.0	0.5	2.0	0.5	—
10648	Nutri-Grain raspberry cereal bar	1	item(s)	37	5.4	140	2.0	27.0	1.0	3.0	0.5	2.0	0.5	—
10649	Nutri-Grain strawberry cereal bar	1	item(s)	37	5.4	140	2.0	27.0	1.0	3.0	0.5	2.0	0.5	—
	Breakfast cereals, hot													
1260	Cream of Wheat, instant, prepared	½	cup(s)	121	—	388	12.9	73.3	4.3	0	0	0	0	0
365	Farina, enriched, cooked w/water and salt	½	cup(s)	117	102.4	56	1.7	12.2	0.3	0.1	0	0	0	—

Chol (mg)	Calc (mg)	Iron (mg)	Magn (mg)	Pota (mg)	Sodi (mg)	Zinc (mg)	Vit A (μg)	Thia (mg)	Vit E (mg α)	Ribo (mg)	Niac (mg)	Vit B_6 (mg)	Fola (μg)	Vit C (mg)	Vit B_{12} (μg)	Sele (μg)
64	235	1.96	18.2	157.3	469.7	0.61	57.0	0.22	—	0.31	1.73	0.05	41.0	2.5	0.2	16.0
81	245	1.48	25.1	226.9	575.7	0.85	82.1	0.22	—	0.35	1.40	0.12	104.6	0.7	0.4	—
0	13	0.25	11.3	29.7	51.7	0.21	0.1	0.03	0.09	0.01	0.25	0.03	9.2	0	0	0.6
71	194	1.60	28.5	171.0	371.3	0.87	48.8	0.15	0.32	0.25	1.47	0.08	28.5	0	0.4	20.0
10	203	4.56	15.8	95.0	481.8	0.35	262.7	0.34	0.64	0.46	5.86	0.68	49.5	0	1.9	8.3
52	191	1.73	14.3	119.3	383.3	0.51	48.8	0.19	—	0.26	1.55	0.04	34.5	0.3	0.2	34.7
0	149	7.40	259.3	356.8	20.5	3.10	0	0.06	—	0.20	1.24	0.20	47.8	4.1	0	—
0	9	1.04	17.3	73.0	2.4	0.64	0	0.06	0.01	0.04	1.61	0.09	12.6	0	0	6.8
0	6	0.67	42.8	73.9	3.4	0.51	0	0.03	0.07	0.03	0.79	0.06	11.8	0	0	1.8
0	9	0.87	29.1	61.9	4.6	0.51	0	0.05	0.01	0.02	0.91	0.07	16.4	0	0	0.5
0	6	0.30	6.3	45.5	3.9	0.20	0	0.05	0.10	0.02	0.77	0.04	11.8	0	0	21.6
0	4	0.75	52.8	74.4	2.4	1.09	0	0.12	0.02	0.09	1.59	0.13	22.8	0	0	1.1
0	27	2.54	110.5	266.0	1.9	1.46	0	0.55	0.47	0.10	0.43	0.07	24.4	0	0	21.2
0	40	3.88	167.4	478.5	4.2	2.62	0.8	0.30	2.06	0.26	1.28	0.40	156.4	0	0	7.2
0	10	0.41	41.9	41.9	4.9	0.61	0	0.09	0.02	0.02	1.49	0.14	3.9	0	0	9.6
0	10	0.51	42.9	77.0	1.0	0.60	0	0.09	—	0.01	1.29	0.14	3.9	0	0	38.0
0	—	2.16	—	—	780.0	—	—	—	—	—	—	—	—	—	—	—
0	11	1.16	9.3	54.6	390.4	0.37	33.0	0.13	0.28	0.02	1.23	0.06	44.3	0.4	0	4.3
0	37	1.52	95.4	330.5	97.1	1.40	—	0.27	0.12	0.05	3.24	0.38	19.0	22.6	0	14.3
0	2	0.12	4.4	8.7	4.4	0.35	0	0.01	0.03	0.01	0.25	0.02	0.9	0	0	4.9
0	8	0.94	9.5	27.7	0.8	0.38	0	0.12	0.03	0.01	1.16	0.07	45.8	0	0	5.9
0	7	1.46	4.1	7.4	3.3	0.40	0	0.06	0.01	0.01	1.43	0.04	57.8	0	0	4.0
0	15	1.43	7.1	44.2	1.6	0.29	0	0.16	0.01	0.01	1.82	0.12	64.0	0	0	7.3
0	2	0.49	26.2	82.8	2.5	1.09	0	0.04	0.19	0.07	1.05	0.11	21.3	0	0	0.7
0	211	2.90	11.9	77.5	793.7	0.38	0	0.42	0.02	0.24	3.64	0.02	122.5	0	0	21.5
0	9	2.90	13.7	66.9	1.2	0.42	0	0.48	0.02	0.30	3.68	0.02	114.4	0	0	21.2
0	16	0.70	45.4	185.9	4.5	1.04	0	0.06	—	0.02	2.56	0.14	12.9	0	0	2.0
0	25	2.42	150.6	346.2	6.6	1.86	0	0.24	0.18	0.10	3.68	0.34	32.4	0	0	3.4
0	10	5.01	11.0	71.9	1.4	0.42	0	0.61	0.01	0.29	4.65	0.02	127.4	0	0	3.4
0	2	2.98	24.1	104.9	4.8	0.48	7.6	0.42	0.10	0.28	3.66	0.12	148.3	0	0	8.0
0	4	2.10	77.5	175.1	21.3	1.10	6.7	0.22	0.24	0.12	2.20	0.18	15.2	0	0	9.4
0	36	4.12	158.7	467.2	0.6	3.58	0.6	0.20	0.90	0.16	2.72	0.28	38.4	0	0	22.8
0	80	4.10	62.7	169.9	2.8	1.00	0	0.80	0.08	0.42	5.60	0.20	132.8	0	0	8.5
0	9	1.56	88.5	228.3	6.3	1.92	0	0.34	0.94	0.06	5.00	0.58	12.6	0	0	—
0	8	0.26	27.6	60.0	0	0.62	0	0.10	0.08	0.02	2.04	0.34	3.2	0	0	11.9
0	14	3.64	39.2	155.3	0.8	0.86	0	0.66	0.20	0.46	5.00	0.08	152.8	0	0	74.6
0	87	2.70	182.0	1067.0	5.5	1.65	2.5	0.24	0.82	0.48	1.83	0.18	146.4	0	0	3.2
0	6	0.90	34.4	128.2	1.7	1.76	0	0.27	—	0.07	0.97	0.18	40.4	0	0	11.4
0	20	2.32	82.8	243.0	3.0	1.74	0	0.26	0.48	0.12	3.82	0.20	26.4	0	0	42.4
0	200	—	—	90.0	70.0	—	—	0.22	—	0.25	3.00	—	—	9.0	—	—
0	200	1.80	8.0	75.0	110.0	1.50	—	0.37	—	0.42	5.00	0.50	40.0	0	—	—
0	200	1.80	8.0	75.0	110.0	1.50	—	0.37	—	0.42	5.00	0.50	40.0	0	0	—
0	200	1.80	8.0	70.0	110.0	1.50	—	0.37	—	0.42	5.00	0.50	40.0	0	0	—
0	200	1.80	8.0	55.0	110.0	1.50	—	0.37	—	0.42	5.00	0.50	40.0	0	0	—
0	862	34.91	21.4	150.8	732.6	0.86	—	1.59	—	1.47	21.55	2.15	431.0	0	0	—
0	5	0.58	2.3	15.1	383.3	0.09	0	0.07	0.01	0.05	0.57	0.01	39.6	0	0	10.6

TABLE A-1 Table of Food Composition *(continued)*

(Computer code is for Cengage Diet Analysis program) (For purposes of calculations, use "0" for t, <1, <.1, <.01, etc.)

DA+ Code	Food Description	QTY	Measure	Wt (g)	H_2O (g)	Ener (cal)	Prot (g)	Carb (g)	Fiber (g)	Fat (g)	Fat Breakdown (g) Sat	Mono	Poly	Trans
	Cereal, Flour, Grain, Pasta, Noodles, Popcorn—continued													
363	Grits, white corn, regular and quick, enriched, cooked w/water and salt	½	cup(s)	121	103.3	71	1.7	15.6	0.4	0.2	0	0.1	0.1	—
8636	Grits, yellow corn, regular and quick, enriched, cooked w/salt	½	cup(s)	121	103.3	71	1.7	15.6	0.4	0.2	0	0.1	0.1	—
8657	Oatmeal, cooked w/water	½	cup(s)	117	97.8	83	3.0	14.0	2.0	1.8	0.4	0.5	0.7	0
5500	Oatmeal, maple and brown sugar, instant, prepared	1	item(s)	198	150.2	200	4.8	40.4	2.4	2.2	0.4	0.7	0.8	—
5510	Oatmeal, ready to serve, packet, prepared	1	item(s)	186	158.7	112	4.1	19.8	2.7	2.0	0.4	0.7	0.8	—
	Breakfast cereals, ready to eat													
1197	All-Bran	1	cup(s)	62	1.3	160	8.1	46.0	18.2	2.0	0.4	0.4	1.3	0
1200	All-Bran Buds	1	cup(s)	91	2.7	212	6.4	72.7	39.1	1.9	0.4	0.5	1.2	0
1199	Apple Jacks	1	cup(s)	33	0.9	130	1.0	30.0	0.5	0.5	0	—	—	0
1204	Cap'n Crunch	1	cup(s)	36	0.9	147	1.3	30.7	1.3	2.0	0.5	0.4	0.3	—
1205	Cap'n Crunch Crunchberries	1	cup(s)	35	0.9	133	1.3	29.3	1.3	2.0	0.5	0.4	0.3	—
1206	Cheerios	1	cup(s)	30	1.0	110	3.0	22.0	3.0	2.0	0	0.5	0.5	—
3415	Cocoa Puffs	1	cup(s)	30	0.6	120	1.0	26.0	0.2	1.0	—	—	—	—
1207	Cocoa Rice Krispies	1	cup(s)	41	1.0	160	1.3	36.0	1.3	1.3	0.7	0	0	—
5522	Complete wheat bran flakes	1	cup(s)	39	1.4	120	4.0	30.7	6.7	0.7	—	—	—	0
1211	Corn Flakes	1	cup(s)	28	0.9	100	2.0	24.0	1.0	0	0	0	0	0
1247	Corn Pops	1	cup(s)	31	0.9	120	1.0	28.0	0.3	0	0	0	0	0
1937	Cracklin' Oat Bran	1	cup(s)	65	2.3	267	5.3	46.7	8.0	9.3	4.0	4.7	1.3	0
1220	Froot Loops	1	cup(s)	32	0.8	120	1.0	28.0	1.0	1.0	0.5	0	0	—
38214	Frosted Cheerios	1	cup(s)	37	—	149	2.5	31.1	1.2	1.2	—	—	—	—
372	Frosted Flakes	1	cup(s)	41	1.1	160	1.3	37.3	1.3	0	0	0	0	0
38215	Frosted Mini Chex	1	cup(s)	40	—	147	1.3	36.0	0	0	0	0	0	0
10268	Frosted Mini-Wheats	1	cup(s)	59	3.1	208	5.8	47.4	5.8	1.2	0	0	0.6	0
38216	Frosted Wheaties	1	cup(s)	40	—	147	1.3	36.0	0.3	0	0	0	0	0
1223	Granola, prepared	½	cup(s)	61	3.3	298	9.1	32.5	5.5	14.7	2.5	5.8	5.6	0
2415	Honey Bunches of Oats honey roasted	1	cup(s)	40	0.9	160	2.7	33.3	1.3	2.0	0.7	1.2	0.1	—
1227	Honey Nut Cheerios	1	cup(s)	37	0.9	149	3.7	29.9	2.5	1.9	0	0.6	0.6	—
2424	Honeycomb	1	cup(s)	22	0.3	83	1.5	19.5	0.8	0.4	0	—	—	—
10286	Kashi whole grain puffs	1	cup(s)	19	—	70	2.0	15.0	1.0	0.5	0	—	—	0
41142	Kellogg's Mueslix	1	cup(s)	83	7.2	298	7.6	60.8	6.1	4.6	0.7	2.4	1.5	0
1231	Kix	1	cup(s)	24	0.5	96	1.6	20.8	0.8	0.4	—	—	—	—
30569	Life	1	cup(s)	43	1.7	160	4.0	33.3	2.7	2.0	0.3	0.6	0.6	—
1233	Lucky Charms	1	cup(s)	24	0.6	96	1.6	20.0	0.8	0.8	—	—	—	—
38220	Multi Grain Cheerios	1	cup(s)	30	—	110	3.0	24.0	3.0	1.0	—	—	—	—
1201	Multi-Bran Chex	1	cup(s)	63	1.3	216	4.3	52.9	8.6	1.6	0	0	0.5	0
13633	Post Bran Flakes	1	cup(s)	40	1.5	133	4.0	32.0	6.7	0.7	0	—	—	—
1241	Product 19	1	cup(s)	30	1.0	100	2.0	25.0	1.0	0	0	0	0	0
32432	Puffed rice, fortified	1	cup(s)	14	0.4	56	0.9	12.6	0.2	0.1	0	—	—	—
32433	Puffed wheat, fortified	1	cup(s)	12	0.4	44	1.8	9.6	0.5	0.1	0	—	—	—
13334	Quaker 100% natural granola oats and honey	½	cup(s)	48	—	220	5.0	31.0	3.0	9.0	3.8	4.1	1.2	—
13335	Quaker 100% natural granola oats, honey, and raisins	½	cup(s)	51	—	230	5.0	34.0	3.0	9.0	3.6	3.8	1.1	—
2420	Raisin Bran	1	cup(s)	59	5.0	190	4.0	46.0	8.0	1.0	0	0.1	0.4	—
1244	Rice Chex	1	cup(s)	31	0.8	120	2.0	27.0	0.3	0	0	0	0	0
1245	Rice Krispies	1	cup(s)	26	0.8	96	1.6	23.2	0	0	0	0	0	0
5593	Shredded Wheat	1	cup(s)	49	0.4	177	5.8	40.9	6.9	1.1	0.1	0	0.2	0
1248	Smacks	1	cup(s)	36	1.1	133	2.7	32.0	1.3	0.7	—	—	—	—
1246	Special K	1	cup(s)	31	0.9	110	7.0	22.0	0.5	0	0	0	0	0
3428	Total corn flakes	1	cup(s)	23	0.6	83	1.5	18.0	0.6	0	0	0	0	0
1253	Total whole grain	1	cup(s)	40	1.1	147	2.7	30.7	4.0	1.3	—	—	—	—
1254	Trix	1	cup(s)	30	0.6	120	1.0	27.0	1.0	1.0	—	—	—	—
382	Wheat germ, toasted	2	tablespoon(s)	14	0.8	54	4.1	7.0	2.1	1.5	0.3	0.2	0.9	—
1257	Wheaties	1	cup(s)	36	1.2	132	3.6	28.8	3.6	1.2	—	—	—	—
	Pasta, noodles													
449	Chinese chow mein noodles, cooked	½	cup(s)	23	0.2	119	1.9	12.9	0.9	6.9	1.0	1.7	3.9	—
1995	Corn pasta, cooked	½	cup(s)	70	47.8	88	1.8	19.5	3.4	0.5	0.1	0.1	0.2	—

PAGE KEY: A-2 = Breads/Baked Goods A-8 = Cereal/Rice/Pasta A-12 = Fruit A-18 = Vegetables/Legumes A-28 = Nuts/Seeds A-30 = Vegetarian
A-32 = Dairy A-40 = Eggs A-40 = Seafood A-44 = Meats A-48 = Poultry A-48 = Processed Meats A-50 = Beverages A-54 = Fats/Oils A-56 = Sweets
A-58 = Spices/Condiments/Sauces A-62 = Mixed Foods/Soups/Sandwiches A-68 = Fast Food A-88 = Convenience A-90 = Baby Foods

Chol (mg)	Calc (mg)	Iron (mg)	Magn (mg)	Pota (mg)	Sodi (mg)	Zinc (mg)	Vit A (µg)	Thia (mg)	Vit E (mg α)	Ribo (mg)	Niac (mg)	Vit B_6 (mg)	Fola (µg)	Vit C (mg)	Vit B_{12} (µg)	Sele (µg)
0	4	0.73	6.1	25.4	269.8	0.08	0	0.10	0.02	0.07	0.87	0.03	39.9	0	0	3.8
0	4	0.73	6.1	25.4	269.8	0.08	2.4	0.10	0.02	0.07	0.87	0.03	39.9	0	0	3.3
0	11	1.05	31.6	81.9	4.7	1.17	0	0.09	0.09	0.02	0.26	0.01	7.0	0	0	6.3
0	26	6.83	49.9	126.4	403.5	1.03	0	1.02	—	0.05	1.56	0.30	42.2	0	0	11.1
0	21	3.96	44.7	112.4	240.9	0.92	0	0.60	—	0.04	0.77	0.18	18.7	0	0	3.8
0	241	10.90	224.4	632.4	150.0	3.00	300.1	1.40	—	1.68	9.16	7.44	800.0	12.4	12.0	5.8
0	57	13.64	186.4	909.1	614.5	4.55	464.5	1.09	1.42	1.27	15.45	6.09	1222.7	18.2	18.2	26.3
0	0	4.50	8.0	30.0	130.0	1.50	150.2	0.37	—	0.42	5.00	0.50	100.0	15.0	1.5	2.4
0	5	6.80	20.0	73.3	266.7	5.00	2.5	0.51	—	0.57	6.68	0.67	133.5	0	0	6.7
0	7	6.53	18.7	73.3	240.0	5.13	2.4	0.51	—	0.57	6.68	0.67	133.7	0	0	6.7
0	100	8.10	40.0	95.0	280.0	3.75	150.3	0.37	—	0.42	5.00	0.50	200.0	6.0	1.5	11.3
0	100	4.50	8.0	50.0	170.0	3.75	0	0.37	—	0.42	5.00	0.50	100.0	6.0	1.5	2.0
0	53	6.00	10.7	66.7	253.3	2.00	200.1	0.49	—	0.56	6.67	0.67	133.3	20.0	2.0	5.8
0	0	24.00	53.3	226.7	280.0	20.00	300.1	2.00	—	2.27	26.67	2.67	533.3	80.0	8.0	4.1
0	0	8.10	3.4	25.0	200.0	0.16	149.8	0.37	—	0.42	5.00	0.50	100.0	6.0	1.5	1.4
0	0	1.80	2.5	25.0	120.0	1.50	150.0	0.37	—	0.42	5.00	0.50	100.0	6.0	1.5	2.0
0	27	2.40	80.0	293.3	200.0	2.00	299.9	0.49	—	0.56	6.67	0.67	133.3	20.0	2.0	14.4
0	0	4.50	8.0	35.0	150.0	1.50	150.1	0.37	—	0.42	5.00	0.50	100.0	15.0	1.5	2.3
0	124	5.60	19.9	68.4	261.3	4.67	—	0.46	—	0.52	6.22	0.62	124.4	7.5	1.9	—
0	0	6.00	3.7	26.7	200.0	0.20	200.1	0.49	—	0.56	6.67	0.67	133.3	8.0	2.0	1.8
0	133	12.00	—	33.3	266.7	4.00	—	0.49	—	0.56	6.67	0.67	266.7	8.0	2.0	—
0	0	16.66	69.4	196.7	5.8	1.74	0	0.43	—	0.49	5.78	0.58	115.7	0	1.7	2.4
0	133	10.80	0	46.7	266.7	10.00	—	1.00	—	1.13	13.33	1.33	533.3	8.0	4.0	—
0	48	2.58	106.8	329.4	15.3	2.45	0.6	0.44	6.77	0.17	1.30	0.17	50.0	0.7	0	17.0
0	0	10.80	21.3	0	253.3	0.40	—	0.49	—	0.56	6.67	0.67	133.0	0	2.0	—
0	124	5.60	39.8	112.0	336.0	4.67	—	0.46	—	0.52	6.22	0.62	248.9	7.5	1.9	8.8
0	0	2.03	6.0	26.3	165.4	1.13	—	0.28	—	0.32	3.74	0.37	75.0	0	1.1	—
0	0	0.36	—	60.0	0	—	0	0.03	—	0.03	0.80	0.00	—	0	—	—
0	48	6.83	74.2	363.3	257.5	5.67	136.7	0.67	6.00	0.67	8.33	3.08	615.0	0.3	9.2	14.4
0	120	6.48	6.4	28.0	216.0	3.00	120.2	0.30	—	0.34	4.00	0.40	160.0	4.8	1.2	4.8
0	149	11.87	41.3	120.0	213.3	5.33	0.9	0.53	—	0.60	7.12	0.71	142.4	0	0	10.7
0	80	3.60	12.8	48.0	168.0	3.00	—	0.30	—	0.34	4.00	0.40	160.0	4.8	1.2	4.8
0	100	18.00	24.0	85.0	200.0	15.00	—	1.50	—	1.70	20.00	2.00	400.0	15.0	6.0	—
0	108	17.50	64.8	237.7	410.6	4.05	171.1	0.40	—	0.45	5.40	0.54	432.2	6.5	1.6	4.9
0	0	10.80	80.0	266.7	280.0	2.00	—	0.49	—	0.56	6.67	0.67	133.3	0	2.0	—
0	0	18.00	16.0	50.0	210.0	15.00	225.3	1.50	—	1.70	20.00	2.00	400.0	60.0	6.0	3.6
0	1	4.43	3.5	15.8	0.4	0.14	0	0.36	—	0.25	4.94	0.01	2.7	0	0	1.5
0	3	3.80	17.4	41.8	0.5	0.28	0	0.31	—	0.21	4.23	0.02	3.8	0	0	14.8
0	61	1.20	51.0	220.0	20.0	1.05	0.5	0.13	—	0.12	0.82	0.07	15.0	0.2	0.1	8.3
0	59	1.20	49.0	250.0	20.0	0.99	0.5	0.13	—	0.12	0.80	0.08	14.1	0.4	0.1	8.8
0	20	10.80	80.0	360.0	360.0	2.25	—	0.37	—	0.42	5.00	0.50	100.0	0	2.1	—
0	100	9.00	9.3	35.0	290.0	3.75	—	0.37	—	0.42	5.00	0.50	200.0	6.0	1.5	1.2
0	0	1.44	12.8	32.0	256.0	0.48	120.1	0.30	—	0.34	4.80	0.40	80.0	4.8	1.2	4.1
0	18	2.90	60.3	179.3	1.1	1.37	0	0.14	—	0.12	3.47	0.18	21.1	0	0	2.0
0	0	0.48	10.7	53.3	66.7	0.40	200.2	0.49	—	0.56	6.67	0.67	133.3	8.0	2.0	17.5
0	0	8.10	16.0	60.0	220.0	0.90	225.1	0.52	—	0.59	7.00	2.00	400.0	21.0	6.0	7.0
0	752	13.53	0	22.6	157.9	11.28	112.8	1.13	22.56	1.28	15.04	1.50	300.8	45.1	4.5	1.2
0	1333	24.00	32.0	120.0	253.3	20.00	200.4	2.00	31.32	2.27	26.67	2.67	533.3	80.0	8.0	1.9
0	100	4.50	0	15.0	190.0	3.75	150.3	0.37	—	0.42	5.00	0.50	100.0	6.0	1.5	6.0
0	6	1.28	45.2	133.8	0.6	2.35	0.7	0.23	2.25	0.11	0.79	0.13	49.7	0.8	0	9.2
0	24	9.72	38.4	126.0	264.0	9.00	180.4	0.90	—	1.02	12.00	1.20	240.0	7.2	3.6	1.7
0	5	1.06	11.7	27.0	98.8	0.31	0	0.13	0.78	0.09	1.33	0.02	20.3	0	0	9.7
0	1	0.18	25.2	21.7	0	0.44	2.1	0.04	—	0.02	0.39	0.04	4.2	0	0	2.0

TABLE A-1 Table of Food Composition *(continued)*

(Computer code is for Cengage Diet Analysis program) (For purposes of calculations, use "0" for t, <1, <.1, <.01, etc.)

DA+ Code	Food Description	QTY	Measure	Wt (g)	H_2O (g)	Ener (cal)	Prot (g)	Carb (g)	Fiber (g)	Fat (g)	Fat Breakdown (g)			
											Sat	Mono	Poly	Trans
Cereal, Flour, Grain, Pasta, Noodles, Popcorn—continued														
448	Egg noodles, enriched, cooked	½	cup(s)	80	54.2	110	3.6	20.1	1.0	1.7	0.3	0.5	0.4	0
1563	Egg noodles, spinach, enriched, cooked	½	cup(s)	80	54.8	106	4.0	19.4	1.8	1.3	0.3	0.4	0.3	—
440	Macaroni, enriched, cooked	½	cup(s)	70	43.5	111	4.1	21.6	1.3	0.7	0.1	0.1	0.2	0
2000	Macaroni, tricolor vegetable, enriched, cooked	½	cup(s)	67	45.8	86	3.0	17.8	2.9	0.1	0	0	0	—
1996	Plain pasta, fresh-refrigerated, cooked	½	cup(s)	64	43.9	84	3.3	16.0	—	0.7	0.1	0.1	0.3	—
1725	Ramen noodles, cooked	½	cup(s)	114	94.5	104	3.0	15.4	1.0	4.3	0.2	0.2	0.2	—
2878	Soba noodles, cooked	½	cup(s)	95	69.4	94	4.8	20.4	—	0.1	0	0	0	—
2879	Somen noodles, cooked	½	cup(s)	88	59.8	115	3.5	24.2	—	0.2	0	0	0.1	—
493	Spaghetti, al dente, cooked	½	cup(s)	65	41.6	95	3.5	19.5	1.0	0.5	0.1	0.1	0.2	—
2884	Spaghetti, whole wheat, cooked	½	cup(s)	70	47.0	87	3.7	18.6	3.2	0.4	0.1	0.1	0.1	—
	Popcorn													
476	Air popped	1	cup(s)	8	0.3	31	1.0	6.2	1.2	0.4	0	0.1	0.2	—
4619	Caramel	1	cup(s)	35	1.0	152	1.3	27.8	1.8	4.5	1.3	1.0	1.6	—
4620	Cheese flavored	1	cup(s)	36	0.9	188	3.3	18.4	3.5	11.8	2.3	3.5	5.5	—
477	Popped in oil	1	cup(s)	11	0.1	64	0.8	5.0	0.9	4.8	0.8	1.1	2.6	—
Fruit and Fruit Juices														
	Apples													
952	Juice, prepared from frozen concentrate	½	cup(s)	120	105.0	56	0.2	13.8	0.1	0.1	0	0	0	—
225	Juice, unsweetened, canned	½	cup(s)	124	109.0	58	0.1	14.5	0.1	0.1	0	0	0	—
224	Slices	½	cup(s)	55	47.1	29	0.1	7.6	1.3	0.1	0	0	0	—
946	Slices without skin, boiled	½	cup(s)	86	73.1	45	0.2	11.7	2.1	0.3	0	0	0.1	—
223	Raw medium, with peel	1	item(s)	138	118.1	72	0.4	19.1	3.3	0.2	0	0	0.1	—
948	Dried, sulfured	¼	cup(s)	22	6.8	52	0.2	14.2	1.9	0.1	0	0	0	—
226	Applesauce, sweetened, canned	½	cup(s)	128	101.5	97	0.2	25.4	1.5	0.2	0	0	0.1	—
227	Applesauce, unsweetened, canned	½	cup(s)	122	107.8	52	0.2	13.8	1.5	0.1	0	0	0	—
38492	Crabapples	1	item(s)	35	27.6	27	0.1	7.0	0.9	0.1	0	0	0	—
	Apricot													
228	Fresh without pits	4	item(s)	140	120.9	67	2.0	15.6	2.8	0.5	0	0.2	0.1	—
229	Halves with skin, canned in heavy syrup	½	cup(s)	129	100.1	107	0.7	27.7	2.1	0.1	0	0	0	—
230	Halves, dried, sulfured	¼	cup(s)	33	10.1	79	1.1	20.6	2.4	0.2	0	0	0	—
	Avocado													
233	California, whole, without skin or pit	½	cup(s)	115	83.2	192	2.2	9.9	7.8	17.7	2.4	11.3	2.1	—
234	Florida, whole, without skin or pit	½	cup(s)	115	90.6	138	2.5	9.0	6.4	11.5	2.2	6.3	1.9	—
2998	Pureed	⅛	cup(s)	28	20.2	44	0.5	2.4	1.8	4.0	0.6	2.7	0.5	—
	Banana													
4580	Dried chips	¼	cup(s)	55	2.4	285	1.3	32.1	4.2	18.5	15.9	1.1	0.3	—
235	Fresh whole, without peel	1	item(s)	118	88.4	105	1.3	27.0	3.1	0.4	0.1	0	0.1	—
	Blackberries													
237	Raw	½	cup(s)	72	63.5	31	1.0	6.9	3.8	0.4	0	0	0.2	—
958	Unsweetened, frozen	½	cup(s)	76	62.1	48	0.9	11.8	3.8	0.3	0	0	0.2	—
	Blueberries													
959	Canned in heavy syrup	½	cup(s)	128	98.3	113	0.8	28.2	2.0	0.4	0	0.1	0.2	—
238	Raw	½	cup(s)	73	61.1	41	0.5	10.5	1.7	0.2	0	0	0.1	—
960	Unsweetened, frozen	½	cup(s)	78	67.1	40	0.3	9.4	2.1	0.5	0	0.1	0.2	—
	Boysenberries													
961	Canned in heavy syrup	½	cup(s)	128	97.6	113	1.3	28.6	3.3	0.2	0	0	0.1	—
962	Unsweetened, frozen	½	cup(s)	66	56.7	33	0.7	8.0	3.5	0.2	0	0	0.1	—
35576	**Breadfruit**	1	item(s)	384	271.3	396	4.1	104.1	18.8	0.9	0.2	0.1	0.3	—
	Cherries													
967	Sour red, canned in water	½	cup(s)	122	109.7	44	0.9	10.9	1.3	0.1	0	0	0	—
3000	Sour red, raw	½	cup(s)	78	66.8	39	0.8	9.4	1.2	0.2	0.1	0.1	0.1	—
3004	Sweet, canned in heavy syrup	½	cup(s)	127	98.2	105	0.8	26.9	1.9	0.2	0	0.1	0.1	—
969	Sweet, canned in water	½	cup(s)	124	107.9	57	1.0	14.6	1.9	0.2	0	0	0	—
240	Sweet, raw	½	cup(s)	73	59.6	46	0.8	11.6	1.5	0.1	0	0	0	—

PAGE KEY: A-2 = Breads/Baked Goods A-8 = Cereal/Rice/Pasta A-12 = Fruit A-18 = Vegetables/Legumes A-28 = Nuts/Seeds A-30 = Vegetarian A-32 = Dairy A-40 = Eggs A-40 = Seafood A-44 = Meats A-48 = Poultry A-48 = Processed Meats A-50 = Beverages A-54 = Fats/Oils A-56 = Sweets A-58 = Spices/Condiments/Sauces A-62 = Mixed Foods/Soups/Sandwiches A-68 = Fast Food A-88 = Convenience A-90 = Baby Foods

A

Chol (mg)	Calc (mg)	Iron (mg)	Magn (mg)	Pota (mg)	Sodi (mg)	Zinc (mg)	Vit A (µg)	Thia (mg)	Vit E (mg α)	Ribo (mg)	Niac (mg)	Vit B_6 (mg)	Fola (µg)	Vit C (mg)	Vit B_{12} (µg)	Sele (µg)
23	10	1.17	16.8	30.4	4.0	0.52	4.8	0.23	0.13	0.11	1.66	0.03	67.2	0	0.1	19.1
26	15	0.87	19.2	29.6	9.6	0.50	8.0	0.19	0.46	0.09	1.17	0.09	51.2	0	0.1	17.4
0	5	0.90	12.6	30.8	0.7	0.36	0	0.19	0.04	0.10	1.18	0.03	51.1	0	0	18.5
0	7	0.33	12.7	20.8	4.0	0.30	3.4	0.08	0.14	0.04	0.72	0.02	43.6	0	0	13.3
21	4	0.73	11.5	15.4	3.8	0.36	3.8	0.13	—	0.10	0.64	0.02	41.0	0	0.1	—
18	9	0.89	8.5	34.5	414.5	0.30	—	0.08	—	0.04	0.71	0.03	4.0	0.1	0	—
0	4	0.45	8.5	33.2	57.0	0.11	0	0.09	—	0.02	0.48	0.03	6.6	0	0	—
0	7	0.45	1.8	25.5	141.7	0.19	0	0.01	—	0.03	0.08	0.01	1.8	0	0	—
0	7	1.00	12.4	51.5	0.5	0.35	0	0.12	0.04	0.07	0.90	0.04	7.8	0	0	40.0
0	11	0.74	21.0	30.8	2.1	0.57	0	0.08	0.21	0.03	0.50	0.06	3.5	0	0	18.1
0	1	0.25	11.5	26.3	0.6	0.25	0.8	0.01	0.02	0.01	0.18	0.01	2.5	0	0	0
2	15	0.61	12.3	38.4	72.5	0.20	0.7	0.02	0.42	0.02	0.77	0.01	1.8	0	0	1.3
4	40	0.79	32.5	93.2	317.4	0.71	13.6	0.04	—	0.08	0.52	0.08	3.9	0.2	0.2	4.3
0	0	0.22	8.7	20.0	116.4	0.34	0.9	0.01	0.27	0.00	0.13	0.01	2.8	0	0	0.2
0	7	0.31	6.0	150.6	8.4	0.05	0	0.00	0.01	0.02	0.05	0.04	0	0.7	0	0.1
0	9	0.46	3.7	147.6	3.7	0.04	0	0.03	0.01	0.02	0.12	0.04	0	1.1	0	0.1
0	3	0.06	2.7	58.8	0.5	0.02	1.6	0.01	0.10	0.01	0.05	0.02	1.6	2.5	0	0
0	4	0.16	2.6	75.2	0.9	0.03	1.7	0.01	0.04	0.01	0.08	0.04	0.9	0.2	0	0.3
0	8	0.16	6.9	147.7	1.4	0.05	4.1	0.02	0.24	0.03	0.12	0.05	4.1	6.3	0	0
0	3	0.30	3.4	96.8	18.7	0.04	0	0.00	0.11	0.03	0.20	0.03	0	0.8	0	0.3
0	5	0.44	3.8	77.8	3.8	0.05	1.3	0.01	0.26	0.03	0.24	0.03	1.3	2.2	0	0.4
0	4	0.14	3.7	91.5	2.4	0.03	1.2	0.01	0.25	0.03	0.22	0.03	1.2	1.5	0	0.4
0	6	0.12	2.5	67.9	0.4	—	0.7	0.01	0.20	0.01	0.03	—	2.0	2.8	0	—
0	18	0.54	14.0	362.6	1.4	0.28	134.4	0.04	1.24	0.05	0.84	0.07	12.6	14.0	0	0.1
0	12	0.38	9.0	180.6	5.2	0.14	80.0	0.02	0.77	0.02	0.48	0.07	2.6	4.0	0	0.1
0	18	0.87	10.5	381.5	3.3	0.12	59.1	0.00	1.42	0.02	0.85	0.05	3.3	0.3	0	0.7
0	15	0.66	33.3	583.0	9.2	0.78	8.0	0.08	2.23	0.16	2.19	0.31	102.3	10.1	0	0.4
0	12	0.19	27.6	403.6	2.3	0.45	8.0	0.02	3.03	0.04	0.76	0.08	40.3	20.0	0	—
0	3	0.14	8.0	134.1	1.9	0.17	1.9	0.01	0.57	0.03	0.48	0.07	22.4	2.8	0	0.1
0	10	0.69	41.8	294.8	3.3	0.40	2.2	0.04	0.13	0.01	0.39	0.14	7.7	3.5	0	0.8
0	6	0.30	31.9	422.4	1.2	0.17	3.5	0.03	0.11	0.08	0.78	0.43	23.6	10.3	0	1.2
0	21	0.45	14.4	116.6	0.7	0.38	7.9	0.01	0.84	0.02	0.47	0.02	18.0	15.1	0	0.3
0	22	0.60	16.6	105.7	0.8	0.19	4.5	0.02	0.88	0.03	0.91	0.05	25.7	2.3	0	0.3
0	6	0.42	5.1	51.2	3.8	0.09	2.6	0.04	0.49	0.07	0.14	0.05	2.6	1.4	0	0.1
0	4	0.20	4.4	55.8	0.7	0.12	2.2	0.03	0.41	0.03	0.30	0.04	4.4	7.0	0	0.1
0	6	0.14	3.9	41.9	0.8	0.05	1.6	0.03	0.37	0.03	0.40	0.05	5.4	1.9	0	0.1
0	23	0.55	14.1	115.2	3.8	0.24	2.6	0.03	—	0.04	0.29	0.05	43.5	7.9	0	0.5
0	18	0.56	10.6	91.7	0.7	0.15	2.0	0.04	0.57	0.02	0.51	0.04	41.6	2.0	0	0.1
0	65	2.07	96.0	1881.6	7.7	0.46	0	0.42	0.38	0.11	3.45	0.38	53.8	111.4	0	2.3
0	13	1.67	7.3	119.6	8.5	0.09	46.4	0.02	0.28	0.05	0.22	0.05	9.8	2.6	0	0
0	12	0.25	7.0	134.1	2.3	0.08	49.6	0.02	0.05	0.03	0.31	0.03	6.2	7.8	0	0
0	11	0.44	11.4	183.4	3.8	0.12	10.1	0.02	0.29	0.05	0.50	0.03	5.1	4.6	0	0
0	14	0.45	11.2	162.4	1.2	0.10	9.9	0.03	0.29	0.05	0.51	0.04	5.0	2.7	0	0
0	9	0.26	8.0	161.0	0	0.05	2.2	0.02	0.05	0.02	0.11	0.04	2.9	5.1	0	0

TABLE A-1 Table of Food Composition *(continued)*

(Computer code is for Cengage Diet Analysis program) (For purposes of calculations, use "0" for t, <1, <.1, <.01, etc.)

DA+ Code	Food Description	QTY	Measure	Wt (g)	H_2O (g)	Ener (cal)	Prot (g)	Carb (g)	Fiber (g)	Fat (g)	Fat Breakdown (g)			
											Sat	Mono	Poly	*Trans*
	Fruit and Fruit Juices—continued													
	Cranberries													
3007	Chopped, raw	½	cup(s)	55	47.9	25	0.2	6.7	2.5	0.1	0	0	0	—
1717	Cranberry apple juice drink	½	cup(s)	123	102.6	77	0	19.4	0	0.1	0	0	0.1	—
1638	Cranberry juice cocktail	½	cup(s)	127	109.0	68	0	17.1	0	0.1	0	0	0.1	—
241	Cranberry juice cocktail, low calorie, with saccharin	½	cup(s)	119	112.8	23	0	5.5	0	0	0	0	0	—
242	Cranberry sauce, sweetened, canned	¼	cup(s)	69	42.0	105	0.1	26.9	0.7	0.1	0	0	0	—
	Dates													
244	Domestic, chopped	¼	cup(s)	45	9.1	125	1.1	33.4	3.6	0.2	0	0	0	—
243	Domestic, whole	¼	cup(s)	45	9.1	125	1.1	33.4	3.6	0.2	0	0	0	—
	Figs													
975	Canned in heavy syrup	½	cup(s)	130	98.8	114	0.5	29.7	2.8	0.1	0	0	0.1	—
974	Canned in water	½	cup(s)	124	105.7	66	0.5	17.3	2.7	0.1	0	0	0.1	—
973	Raw, medium	2	item(s)	100	79.1	74	0.7	19.2	2.9	0.3	0.1	0.1	0.1	—
	Fruit cocktail and salad													
245	Fruit cocktail, canned in heavy syrup	½	cup(s)	124	99.7	91	0.5	23.4	1.2	0.1	0	0	0	—
978	Fruit cocktail, canned in juice	½	cup(s)	119	103.6	55	0.5	14.1	1.2	0	0	0	0	—
977	Fruit cocktail, canned in water	½	cup(s)	119	107.6	38	0.5	10.1	1.2	0.1	0	0	0	—
979	Fruit salad, canned in water	½	cup(s)	123	112.1	37	0.4	9.6	1.2	0.1	0	0	0	—
	Gooseberries													
982	Canned in light syrup	½	cup(s)	126	100.9	92	0.8	23.6	3.0	0.3	0	0	0.1	—
981	Raw	½	cup(s)	75	65.9	33	0.7	7.6	3.2	0.4	0	0	0.2	—
	Grapefruit													
251	Juice, pink, sweetened, canned	½	cup(s)	125	109.1	57	0.7	13.9	0.1	0.1	0	0	0	—
249	Juice, white	½	cup(s)	124	111.2	48	0.6	11.4	0.1	0.1	0	0	0	—
3022	Pink or red, raw	½	cup(s)	114	100.8	48	0.9	12.2	1.8	0.2	0	0	0	—
248	Sections, canned in light syrup	½	cup(s)	127	106.2	76	0.7	19.6	0.5	0.1	0	0	0	—
983	Sections, canned in water	½	cup(s)	122	109.6	44	0.7	11.2	0.5	0.1	0	0	0	—
247	White, raw	½	cup(s)	115	104.0	38	0.8	9.7	1.3	0.1	0	0	0	—
	Grapes													
255	American, slip skin	½	cup(s)	46	37.4	31	0.3	7.9	0.4	0.2	0.1	0	0	—
256	European, red or green, adherent skin	½	cup(s)	76	60.8	52	0.5	13.7	0.7	0.1	0	0	0	—
3159	Grape juice drink, canned	½	cup(s)	125	106.6	71	0	18.2	0.1	0	0	0	0	0
259	Grape juice, sweetened, with added vitamin C, prepared from frozen concentrate	½	cup(s)	125	108.6	64	0.2	15.9	0.1	0.1	0	0	0	—
3060	Raisins, seeded, packed	¼	cup(s)	41	6.8	122	1.0	32.4	2.8	0.2	0.1	0	0.1	—
987	**Guava, raw**	1	item(s)	55	44.4	37	1.4	7.9	3.0	0.5	0.2	0	0.2	—
35593	**Guavas, strawberry**	1	item(s)	6	4.8	4	0	1.0	0.3	0	0	0	0	—
3027	**Jackfruit**	½	cup(s)	83	60.4	78	1.2	19.8	1.3	0.2	0	0	0.1	—
990	**Kiwi fruit or Chinese gooseberries**	1	item(s)	76	63.1	46	0.9	11.1	2.3	0.4	0	0	0.2	—
	Lemon													
262	Juice	1	tablespoon(s)	15	13.8	4	0.1	1.3	0.1	0	0	0	0	0
993	Peel	1	teaspoon(s)	2	1.6	1	0	0.3	0.2	0	0	0	0	—
992	Raw	1	item(s)	108	94.4	22	1.3	11.6	5.1	0.3	0	0	0.1	—
	Lime													
269	Juice	1	tablespoon(s)	15	14.0	4	0.1	1.3	0.1	0	0	0	0	—
994	Raw	1	item(s)	67	59.1	20	0.5	7.1	1.9	0.1	0	0	0	—
995	**Loganberries, frozen**	½	cup(s)	74	62.2	40	1.1	9.6	3.9	0.2	0	0	0.1	—
	Mandarin orange													
1038	Canned in juice	½	cup(s)	125	111.4	46	0.8	11.9	0.9	0	0	0	0	—
1039	Canned in light syrup	½	cup(s)	126	104.7	77	0.6	20.4	0.9	0.1	0	0	0	—
999	**Mango**	½	cup(s)	83	67.4	54	0.4	14.0	1.5	0.2	0.1	0.1	0	—
1005	**Nectarine, raw, sliced**	½	cup(s)	69	60.4	30	0.7	7.3	1.2	0.2	0	0.1	0.1	—

PAGE KEY: A-2 = Breads/Baked Goods A-8 = Cereal/Rice/Pasta A-12 = Fruit A-18 = Vegetables/Legumes A-28 = Nuts/Seeds A-30 = Vegetarian A-32 = Dairy A-40 = Eggs A-40 = Seafood A-44 = Meats A-48 = Poultry A-48 = Processed Meats A-50 = Beverages A-54 = Fats/Oils A-56 = Sweets A-58 = Spices/Condiments/Sauces A-62 = Mixed Foods/Soups/Sandwiches A-68 = Fast Food A-88 = Convenience A-90 = Baby Foods

Chol (mg)	Calc (mg)	Iron (mg)	Magn (mg)	Pota (mg)	Sodi (mg)	Zinc (mg)	Vit A (µg)	Thia (mg)	Vit E (mg α)	Ribo (mg)	Niac (mg)	Vit B_6 (mg)	Fola (µg)	Vit C (mg)	Vit B_{12} (µg)	Sele (µg)
0	4	0.13	3.3	46.8	1.1	0.05	1.7	0.01	0.66	0.01	0.05	0.03	0.6	7.3	0	0.1
0	4	0.09	1.2	20.8	2.5	0.02	0	0.00	0.15	0.00	0.00	0.00	0	48.4	0	0
0	4	0.13	1.3	17.7	2.5	0.04	0	0.00	0.28	0.00	0.05	0.00	0	53.5	0	0.3
0	11	0.05	2.4	29.6	3.6	0.02	0	0.00	0.06	0.00	0.00	0.00	0	38.2	0	0
0	3	0.15	2.1	18.0	20.1	0.03	1.4	0.01	0.57	0.01	0.06	0.01	0.7	1.4	0	0.2
0	17	0.45	19.1	291.9	0.9	0.12	0	0.02	0.02	0.02	0.56	0.07	8.5	0.2	0	1.3
0	17	0.45	19.1	291.9	0.9	0.12	0	0.02	0.02	0.02	0.56	0.07	8.5	0.2	0	1.3
0	35	0.36	13.0	128.2	1.3	0.14	2.6	0.03	0.16	0.05	0.55	0.09	2.6	1.3	0	0.3
0	35	0.36	12.4	127.7	1.2	0.15	2.5	0.03	0.10	0.05	0.55	0.09	2.5	1.2	0	0.1
0	35	0.36	17.0	232.0	1.0	0.14	7.0	0.06	0.10	0.04	0.40	0.10	6.0	2.0	0	0.2
0	7	0.36	6.2	109.1	7.4	0.09	12.4	0.02	0.49	0.02	0.46	0.06	3.7	2.4	0	0.6
0	9	0.25	8.3	112.6	4.7	0.11	17.8	0.01	0.47	0.02	0.48	0.06	3.6	3.2	0	0.6
0	6	0.30	8.3	111.4	4.7	0.11	15.4	0.02	0.47	0.01	0.43	0.06	3.6	2.5	0	0.6
0	9	0.37	6.1	95.6	3.7	0.10	27.0	0.02	—	0.03	0.46	0.04	3.7	2.3	0	1.0
0	20	0.42	7.6	97.0	2.5	0.14	8.8	0.03	—	0.07	0.19	0.02	3.8	12.6	0	0.5
0	19	0.23	7.5	148.5	0.8	0.09	11.3	0.03	0.28	0.02	0.23	0.06	4.5	20.8	0	0.5
0	10	0.45	12.5	202.2	2.5	0.08	0	0.05	0.05	0.03	0.40	0.03	12.5	33.6	0	0.1
0	11	0.25	14.8	200.1	1.2	0.06	1.2	0.05	0.27	0.02	0.25	0.05	12.4	46.9	0	0.1
0	25	0.09	10.3	154.5	0	0.07	66.4	0.04	0.14	0.03	0.23	0.06	14.9	35.7	0	0.1
0	18	0.50	12.7	163.8	2.5	0.10	0	0.04	0.11	0.02	0.30	0.02	11.4	27.1	0	1.1
0	18	0.50	12.2	161.0	2.4	0.11	0	0.05	0.11	0.03	0.30	0.02	11.0	26.6	0	1.1
0	14	0.07	10.4	170.2	0	0.08	2.3	0.04	0.15	0.02	0.30	0.05	11.5	38.3	0	1.6
0	6	0.13	2.3	87.9	0.9	0.02	2.3	0.04	0.09	0.02	0.14	0.05	1.8	1.8	0	0
0	8	0.27	5.3	144.2	1.5	0.05	2.3	0.05	0.14	0.05	0.14	0.07	1.5	8.2	0	0.1
0	9	0.16	7.5	41.3	11.3	0.04	0	0.28	0.00	0.44	0.18	0.04	1.3	33.1	0	0.1
0	5	0.13	5.0	26.3	2.5	0.05	0	0.02	0.00	0.03	0.16	0.05	1.3	29.9	0	0.1
0	12	1.06	12.4	340.3	11.6	0.07	0	0.04	—	0.07	0.46	0.07	1.2	2.2	0	0.2
0	10	0.14	12.1	229.4	1.1	0.12	17.1	0.03	0.40	0.02	0.59	0.06	27.0	125.6	0	0.3
0	1	0.01	1.0	17.5	2.2	—	0.3	0.00	—	0.00	0.03	0.00	—	2.2	0	
0	28	0.49	30.5	250.0	2.5	0.35	12.4	0.02	—	0.09	0.33	0.09	11.5	5.5	0	0.5
0	26	0.23	12.9	237.1	2.3	0.10	3.0	0.02	1.11	0.01	0.25	0.04	19.0	70.5	0	0.2
0	1	0.00	0.9	18.9	0.2	0.01	0.2	0.00	0.02	0.00	0.02	0.01	2.0	7.0	0	0
0	3	0.01	0.3	3.2	0.1	0.01	0.1	0.00	0.01	0.00	0.01	0.00	0.3	2.6	0	0
0	66	0.75	13.0	156.6	3.2	0.10	2.2	0.05	—	0.04	0.21	0.11	—	83.2	0	1.0
0	2	0.02	1.2	18.0	0.3	0.01	0.3	0.00	0.03	0.00	0.02	0.01	1.5	4.6	0	0
0	22	0.40	4.0	68.3	1.3	0.07	1.3	0.02	0.14	0.01	0.13	0.02	5.4	19.5	0	0.3
0	19	0.47	15.4	106.6	0.7	0.25	1.5	0.04	0.64	0.03	0.62	0.05	19.1	11.2	0	0.1
0	14	0.34	13.7	165.6	6.2	0.64	53.5	0.10	0.12	0.04	0.55	0.05	6.2	42.6	0	0.5
0	9	0.47	10.1	98.3	7.6	0.30	52.9	0.07	0.13	0.06	0.56	0.05	6.3	24.9	0	0.5
0	8	0.10	7.4	128.7	1.7	0.03	31.4	0.05	0.92	0.04	0.48	0.11	11.6	22.8	0	0.5
0	4	0.19	6.2	138.7	0	0.12	11.7	0.02	0.53	0.02	0.78	0.02	3.5	3.7	0	0

TABLE A-1 Table of Food Composition *(continued)*

(Computer code is for Cengage Diet Analysis program) (For purposes of calculations, use "0" for t, <1, <.1, <.01, etc.)

DA+ Code	Food Description	Qty	Measure	Wt (g)	H2O (g)	Ener (cal)	Prot (g)	Carb (g)	Fiber (g)	Fat (g)	Fat Breakdown (g) Sat	Mono	Poly	Trans
	Fruit and Fruit Juices—continued													
	Melons													
271	Cantaloupe	½	cup(s)	80	72.1	27	0.7	6.5	0.7	0.1	0	0	0.1	—
1000	Casaba melon	½	cup(s)	85	78.1	24	0.9	5.6	0.8	0.1	0	0	0	—
272	Honeydew	½	cup(s)	89	79.5	32	0.5	8.0	0.7	0.1	0	0	0	—
318	Watermelon	½	cup(s)	76	69.5	23	0.5	5.7	0.3	0.1	0	0	0	—
	Orange													
14412	Juice with calcium and vitamin D	½	cup(s)	120	—	55	1.0	13.0	0	0	0	0	0	0
29630	Juice, fresh squeezed	½	cup(s)	124	109.5	56	0.9	12.9	0.2	0.2	0	0	0	—
14411	Juice, not from concentrate	½	cup(s)	120	—	55	1.0	13.0	0	0	0	0	0	0
278	Juice, unsweetened, prepared from frozen concentrate	½	cup(s)	125	109.7	56	0.8	13.4	0.2	0.1	0	0	0	—
3040	Peel	1	teaspoon(s)	2	1.5	2	0	0.5	0.2	0	0	0	0	—
273	Raw	1	item(s)	131	113.6	62	1.2	15.4	3.1	0.2	0	0	0	—
274	Sections	½	cup(s)	90	78.1	42	0.8	10.6	2.2	0.1	0	0	0	—
	Papaya, raw													
16830	Dried, strips	2	item(s)	46	12.0	119	1.9	29.9	5.5	0.4	0.1	0.1	0.1	—
282	Papaya	½	cup(s)	70	62.2	27	0.4	6.9	1.3	0.1	0	0	0	—
35640	**Passion fruit, purple**	1	item(s)	18	13.1	17	0.4	4.2	1.9	0.1	0	0	0.1	—
	Peach													
285	Halves, canned in heavy syrup	½	cup(s)	131	103.9	97	0.6	26.1	1.7	0.1	0	0	0.1	—
286	Halves, canned in water	½	cup(s)	122	113.6	29	0.5	7.5	1.6	0.1	0	0	0	—
290	Slices, sweetened, frozen	½	cup(s)	125	93.4	118	0.8	30.0	2.3	0.2	0	0.1	0.1	—
283	Raw, medium	1	item(s)	150	133.3	59	1.4	14.3	2.3	0.4	0	0.1	0.1	—
	Pear													
8672	Asian	1	item(s)	122	107.7	51	0.6	13.0	4.4	0.3	0	0.1	0.1	—
293	D'Anjou	1	item(s)	200	168.0	120	1.0	30.0	5.2	1.0	0	0.2	0.2	—
294	Halves, canned in heavy syrup	½	cup(s)	133	106.9	98	0.3	25.5	2.1	0.2	0	0	0	—
1012	Halves, canned in juice	½	cup(s)	124	107.2	62	0.4	16.0	2.0	0.1	0	0	0	—
291	Raw	1	item(s)	166	139.0	96	0.6	25.7	5.1	0.2	0	0	0	—
1017	**Persimmon**	1	item(s)	25	16.1	32	0.2	8.4	—	0.1	0	0	0	—
	Pineapple													
3053	Canned in extra heavy syrup	½	cup(s)	130	101.0	108	0.4	28.0	1.0	0.1	0	0	0	—
1019	Canned in juice	½	cup(s)	125	104.0	75	0.5	19.5	1.0	0.1	0	0	0	—
296	Canned in light syrup	½	cup(s)	126	108.0	66	0.5	16.9	1.0	0.2	0	0	0.1	—
1018	Canned in water	½	cup(s)	123	111.7	39	0.5	10.2	1.0	0.1	0	0	0	—
299	Juice, unsweetened, canned	½	cup(s)	125	108.0	66	0.5	16.1	0.3	0.2	0	0	0.1	—
295	Raw, diced	½	cup(s)	78	66.7	39	0.4	10.2	1.1	0.1	0	0	0	—
1024	**Plantain, cooked**	½	cup(s)	77	51.8	89	0.6	24.0	1.8	0.1	0.1	0	0	—
300	**Plum, raw, large**	1	item(s)	66	57.6	30	0.5	7.5	0.9	0.2	0	0.1	0	—
1027	**Pomegranate**	1	item(s)	154	124.7	105	1.5	26.4	0.9	0.5	0.1	0.1	0.1	—
	Prunes													
5644	Dried	2	item(s)	17	5.2	40	0.4	10.7	1.2	0.1	0	0	0	—
305	Dried, stewed	½	cup(s)	124	86.5	133	1.2	34.8	3.8	0.2	0	0.1	0	—
306	Juice, canned	1	cup(s)	256	208.0	182	1.6	44.7	2.6	0.1	0	0.1	0	—
	Raspberries													
309	Raw	½	cup(s)	62	52.7	32	0.7	7.3	4.0	0.4	0	0	0.2	—
310	Red, sweetened, frozen	½	cup(s)	125	90.9	129	0.9	32.7	5.5	0.2	0	0	0.1	—
311	**Rhubarb, cooked with sugar**	½	cup(s)	120	81.5	140	0.5	37.5	2.7	0.1	0	0	0.1	—
	Strawberries													
313	Raw	½	cup(s)	72	65.5	23	0.5	5.5	1.4	0.2	0	0	0.1	—
315	Sweetened, frozen, thawed	½	cup(s)	128	99.5	99	0.7	26.8	2.4	0.2	0	0	0.1	—
16828	**Tangelo**	1	item(s)	95	82.4	45	0.9	11.2	2.3	0.1	0	0	0	—
	Tangerine													
1040	Juice	½	cup(s)	124	109.8	53	0.6	12.5	0.2	0.2	0	0	0	—
316	Raw	1	item(s)	88	74.9	47	0.7	11.7	1.6	0.3	0	0.1	0.1	—

Chol (mg)	Calc (mg)	Iron (mg)	Magn (mg)	Pota (mg)	Sodi (mg)	Zinc (mg)	Vit A (µg)	Thia (mg)	Vit E (mg α)	Ribo (mg)	Niac (mg)	Vit B_6 (mg)	Fola (µg)	Vit C (mg)	Vit B_{12} (µg)	Sele (µg)
0	7	0.17	9.6	213.6	12.8	0.14	135.2	0.03	0.04	0.01	0.59	0.05	16.8	29.4	0	0.3
0	9	0.29	9.4	154.7	7.7	0.06	0	0.01	0.04	0.03	0.20	0.14	6.8	18.5	0	0.3
0	5	0.15	8.8	201.8	15.9	0.07	2.7	0.03	0.01	0.01	0.37	0.07	16.8	15.9	0	0.6
0	5	0.18	7.6	85.1	0.8	0.07	21.3	0.02	0.04	0.01	0.13	0.03	2.3	6.2	0	0.3
0	175	0.00	12.0	225.0	0	—	0	0.08	—	0.03	0.40	0.06	30.0	36.0	0	—
0	14	0.25	13.6	248.0	1.2	0.06	12.4	0.11	0.05	0.04	0.50	0.05	37.2	62.0	0	0.1
0	10	0.00	12.5	225.0	0	0.06	0	0.08	—	0.03	0.40	0.06	30.0	36.0	0	0.1
0	11	0.12	12.5	236.6	1.2	0.06	6.2	0.10	0.25	0.02	0.25	0.06	54.8	48.4	0	0.1
0	3	0.01	0.4	4.2	0.1	0.01	0.4	0.00	0.01	0.00	0.01	0.00	0.6	2.7	0	0
0	52	0.13	13.1	237.1	0	0.09	14.4	0.11	0.23	0.05	0.36	0.07	39.3	69.7	0	0.7
0	36	0.09	9.0	162.9	0	0.06	9.9	0.07	0.16	0.03	0.25	0.05	27.0	47.9	0	0.4
0	73	0.30	30.4	782.9	9.2	0.21	83.7	0.06	2.22	0.08	0.93	0.05	58.0	37.7	0	1.8
0	17	0.07	7.0	179.9	2.1	0.05	38.5	0.02	0.51	0.02	0.24	0.01	26.6	43.3	0	0.4
0	2	0.28	5.2	62.6	5.0	0.01	11.5	0.00	0.00	0.02	0.27	0.01	2.5	5.4	0	0.1
0	4	0.35	6.6	120.5	7.9	0.11	22.3	0.01	0.64	0.03	0.80	0.02	3.9	3.7	0	0.4
0	2	0.39	6.1	120.8	3.7	0.11	32.9	0.01	0.59	0.02	0.63	0.02	3.7	3.5	0	0.4
0	4	0.46	6.3	162.5	7.5	0.06	17.5	0.01	0.77	0.04	0.81	0.02	3.8	117.8	0	0.5
0	9	0.37	13.5	285.0	0	0.25	24.0	0.03	1.09	0.04	1.20	0.03	6.0	9.9	0	0.2
0	5	0.00	9.8	147.6	0	0.02	0	0.01	0.14	0.01	0.26	0.02	9.8	4.6	0	0.1
0	22	0.50	12.0	250.0	0	0.24	—	0.04	1.00	0.08	0.20	0.03	14.6	8.0	0	1.0
0	7	0.29	5.3	86.5	6.7	0.10	0	0.01	0.10	0.02	0.32	0.01	1.3	1.5	0	0
0	11	0.36	8.7	119.0	5.0	0.11	0	0.01	0.10	0.01	0.25	0.02	1.2	2.0	0	0
0	15	0.28	11.6	197.5	1.7	0.16	1.7	0.02	0.19	0.04	0.26	0.04	11.6	7.0	0	0.2
0	7	0.62	—	77.5	0.3	—	0	—	—	—	—	—	—	16.5	0	—
0	18	0.49	19.5	132.6	1.3	0.14	1.3	0.11	—	0.03	0.36	0.09	6.5	9.5	0	—
0	17	0.35	17.4	151.9	1.2	0.12	2.5	0.12	0.01	0.02	0.35	0.09	6.2	11.8	0	0.5
0	18	0.49	20.2	132.3	1.3	0.15	2.5	0.11	0.01	0.03	0.36	0.09	6.3	9.5	0	0.5
0	18	0.49	22.1	156.2	1.2	0.15	2.5	0.11	0.01	0.03	0.37	0.09	6.2	9.5	0	0.5
0	16	0.39	15.0	162.5	2.5	0.14	0	0.07	0.03	0.03	0.25	0.13	22.5	12.5	0	0.1
0	10	0.22	9.3	84.5	0.8	0.09	2.3	0.06	0.02	0.03	0.39	0.09	14.0	37.0	0	0.1
0	2	0.45	24.6	358.1	3.9	0.10	34.7	0.04	0.10	0.04	0.58	0.19	20.0	8.4	0	1.1
0	4	0.11	4.6	103.6	0	0.06	11.2	0.02	0.17	0.02	0.27	0.02	3.3	6.3	0	0
0	5	0.46	4.6	398.9	4.6	0.18	7.7	0.04	0.92	0.04	0.46	0.16	9.2	9.4	0	0.9
0	7	0.16	6.9	123.0	0.3	0.07	6.6	0.01	0.07	0.03	0.32	0.03	0.7	0.1	0	0
0	24	0.51	22.3	398.0	1.2	0.24	21.1	0.03	0.24	0.12	0.90	0.27	0	3.6	0	0.1
0	31	3.02	35.8	706.6	10.2	0.53	0	0.04	0.30	0.17	2.01	0.55	0	10.5	0	1.5
0	15	0.42	13.5	92.9	0.6	0.26	1.2	0.02	0.54	0.02	0.37	0.03	12.9	16.1	0	0.1
0	19	0.81	16.3	142.5	1.3	0.22	3.8	0.02	0.90	0.05	0.28	0.04	32.5	20.6	0	0.4
0	174	0.25	16.2	115.0	1.0	—	—	0.02	—	0.03	0.25	—	—	4.0	0	—
0	12	0.30	9.4	110.2	0.7	0.10	0.7	0.02	0.21	0.02	0.28	0.03	17.3	42.3	0	0.3
0	14	0.59	7.7	125.0	1.3	0.06	1.3	0.01	0.30	0.09	0.37	0.03	5.1	50.4	0	0.9
0	38	0.09	9.5	172.0	0	0.06	10.5	0.08	0.17	0.03	0.26	0.05	28.5	50.5	0	0.5
0	22	0.25	9.9	219.8	1.2	0.04	16.1	0.07	0.16	0.02	0.12	0.05	6.2	38.3	0	0.1
0	33	0.13	10.6	146.1	1.8	0.06	29.9	0.05	0.18	0.03	0.33	0.07	14.1	23.5	0	0.1

TABLE A-1 Table of Food Composition *(continued)*

(Computer code is for Cengage Diet Analysis program) (For purposes of calculations, use "0" for t, <1, <.1, <.01, etc.)

DA+ Code	Food Description	Qty	Measure	Wt (g)	H_2O (g)	Ener (cal)	Prot (g)	Carb (g)	Fiber (g)	Fat (g)	Fat Breakdown (g) Sat	Mono	Poly	Trans
	Vegetables, Legumes													
	Amaranth													
1043	Leaves, boiled, drained	½	cup(s)	66	60.4	14	1.4	2.7	—	0.1	0	0	0.1	—
1042	Leaves, raw	1	cup(s)	28	25.7	6	0.7	1.1	—	0.1	0	0	0	—
8683	**Arugula leaves, raw**	1	cup(s)	20	18.3	5	0.5	0.7	0.3	0.1	0	0	0.1	—
	Artichoke													
1044	Boiled, drained	1	item(s)	120	100.9	64	3.5	14.3	10.3	0.4	0.1	0	0.2	—
2885	Hearts, boiled, drained	½	cup(s)	84	70.6	45	2.4	10.0	7.2	0.3	0.1	0	0.1	—
	Asparagus													
566	Boiled, drained	½	cup(s)	90	83.4	20	2.2	3.7	1.8	0.2	0	0	0.1	—
568	Canned, drained	½	cup(s)	121	113.7	23	2.6	3.0	1.9	0.8	0.2	0	0.3	—
565	Tips, frozen, boiled, drained	½	cup(s)	90	84.7	16	2.7	1.7	1.4	0.4	0.1	0	0.2	—
	Bamboo shoots													
1048	Boiled, drained	½	cup(s)	60	57.6	7	0.9	1.2	0.6	0.1	0	0	0.1	—
1049	Canned, drained	½	cup(s)	66	61.8	12	1.1	2.1	0.9	0.3	0.1	0	0.1	—
	Beans													
1801	Adzuki beans, boiled	½	cup(s)	115	76.2	147	8.6	28.5	8.4	0.1	0	—	—	—
511	Baked beans with franks, canned	½	cup(s)	130	89.8	184	8.7	19.9	8.9	8.5	3.0	3.7	1.1	—
513	Baked beans with pork in sweet sauce, canned	½	cup(s)	127	89.3	142	6.7	26.7	5.3	1.8	0.6	0.6	0.5	0
512	Baked beans with pork in tomato sauce, canned	½	cup(s)	127	93.0	119	6.5	23.6	5.1	1.2	0.5	0.7	0.3	—
1805	Black beans, boiled	½	cup(s)	86	56.5	114	7.6	20.4	7.5	0.5	0.1	0	0.2	—
14597	Chickpeas, garbanzo beans or bengal gram, boiled	½	cup(s)	82	49.4	134	7.3	22.5	6.2	2.1	0.2	0.5	0.9	—
569	Fordhook lima beans, frozen, boiled, drained	½	cup(s)	85	62.0	88	5.2	16.4	4.9	0.3	0.1	0	0.1	—
1806	French beans, boiled	½	cup(s)	89	58.9	114	6.2	21.3	8.3	0.7	0.1	0	0.4	—
2773	Great northern beans, boiled	½	cup(s)	89	61.1	104	7.4	18.7	6.2	0.4	0.1	0	0.2	—
2736	Hyacinth beans, boiled, drained	½	cup(s)	44	37.8	22	1.3	4.0	—	0.1	0.1	0.1	0	—
570	Lima beans, baby, frozen, boiled, drained	½	cup(s)	90	65.1	95	6.0	17.5	5.4	0.3	0.1	0	0.1	—
515	Lima beans, boiled, drained	½	cup(s)	85	57.1	105	5.8	20.1	4.5	0.3	0.1	0	0.1	—
579	Mung beans, sprouted, boiled, drained	½	cup(s)	62	57.9	13	1.3	2.6	0.5	0.1	0	0	0	—
510	Navy beans, boiled	½	cup(s)	91	58.1	127	7.5	23.7	9.6	0.6	0.1	0.1	0.4	0
32816	Pinto beans, boiled, drained, no salt added	½	cup(s)	63	58.8	14	1.2	2.6	—	0.2	0	0	0.1	—
1052	Pinto beans, frozen, boiled, drained	½	cup(s)	47	27.3	76	4.4	14.5	4.0	0.2	0	0	0.1	—
514	Red kidney beans, canned	½	cup(s)	128	99.0	108	6.7	19.9	6.9	0.5	0.1	0.2	0.2	—
1810	Refried beans, canned	½	cup(s)	127	96.1	119	6.9	19.6	6.7	1.6	0.6	0.7	0.2	—
1053	Shell beans, canned	½	cup(s)	123	111.1	37	2.2	7.6	4.2	0.2	0	0	0.1	—
1670	Soybeans, boiled	½	cup(s)	86	53.8	149	14.3	8.5	5.2	7.7	1.1	1.7	4.4	—
1108	Soybeans, green, boiled, drained	½	cup(s)	90	61.7	127	11.1	9.9	3.8	5.8	0.7	1.1	2.7	—
1807	White beans, small, boiled	½	cup(s)	90	56.6	127	8.0	23.1	9.3	0.6	0.1	0.1	0.2	—
575	Yellow snap, string or wax beans, boiled, drained	½	cup(s)	63	55.8	22	1.2	4.9	2.1	0.2	0	0	0.1	—
576	Yellow snap, string or wax beans, frozen, boiled, drained	½	cup(s)	68	61.7	19	1.0	4.4	2.0	0.1	0	0	0.1	—
	Beets													
584	Beet greens, boiled, drained	½	cup(s)	72	64.2	19	1.9	3.9	2.1	0.1	0	0	0.1	—
2730	Pickled, canned with liquid	½	cup(s)	114	92.9	74	0.9	18.5	3.0	0.1	0	0	0	—
581	Sliced, boiled, drained	½	cup(s)	85	74.0	37	1.4	8.5	1.7	0.2	0	0	0.1	—
583	Sliced, canned, drained	½	cup(s)	85	77.3	26	0.8	6.1	1.5	0.1	0	0	0	—
580	Whole, boiled, drained	2	item(s)	100	87.1	44	1.7	10.0	2.0	0.2	0	0	0.1	—
585	**Cowpeas or black-eyed peas, boiled, drained**	½	cup(s)	83	62.3	80	2.6	16.8	4.1	0.3	0.1	0	0.1	—
	Broccoli													
588	Chopped, boiled, drained	½	cup(s)	78	69.6	27	1.9	5.6	2.6	0.3	0.1	0	0.1	—
590	Frozen, chopped, boiled, drained	½	cup(s)	92	83.5	26	2.9	4.9	2.8	0.1	0	0	0.1	—
587	Raw, chopped	½	cup(s)	46	40.6	15	1.3	3.0	1.2	0.2	0	0	0	—

Chol (mg)	Calc (mg)	Iron (mg)	Magn (mg)	Pota (mg)	Sodi (mg)	Zinc (mg)	Vit A (µg)	Thia (mg)	Vit E (mg α)	Ribo (mg)	Niac (mg)	Vit B_6 (mg)	Fola (µg)	Vit C (mg)	Vit B_{12} (µg)	Sele (µg)
0	138	1.49	36.3	423.1	13.9	0.58	91.7	0.01	—	0.09	0.37	0.12	37.6	27.1	0	0.6
0	60	0.65	15.4	171.1	5.6	0.25	40.9	0.01	—	0.04	0.18	0.05	23.8	12.1	0	0.3
0	32	0.29	9.4	73.8	5.4	0.09	23.8	0.01	0.09	0.02	0.06	0.01	19.4	3.0	0	0.1
0	25	0.73	50.4	343.2	72.0	0.48	1.2	0.06	0.22	0.10	1.33	0.09	106.8	8.9	0	0.2
0	18	0.51	35.3	240.2	50.4	0.33	0.8	0.04	0.16	0.07	0.93	0.06	74.8	6.2	0	0.2
0	21	0.81	12.6	201.6	12.6	0.54	45.0	0.14	1.35	0.12	0.97	0.07	134.1	6.9	0	5.5
0	19	2.21	12.1	208.1	347.3	0.48	49.6	0.07	1.47	0.12	1.15	0.13	116.2	22.3	0	2.1
0	16	0.50	9.0	154.8	2.7	0.36	36.0	0.05	1.08	0.09	0.93	0.01	121.5	22.0	0	3.5
0	7	0.14	1.8	319.8	2.4	0.28	0	0.01	—	0.03	0.18	0.06	1.2	0	0	0.2
0	5	0.21	2.6	52.4	4.6	0.43	0.7	0.02	0.41	0.02	0.09	0.09	2.0	0.7	0	0.3
0	32	2.30	59.8	611.8	9.2	2.03	0	0.13	—	0.07	0.82	0.11	139.2	0	0	1.4
8	62	2.24	36.3	304.3	556.9	2.42	5.2	0.08	0.21	0.07	1.17	0.06	38.9	3.0	0.4	8.4
9	75	2.08	41.7	326.4	422.5	1.73	0	0.05	0.03	0.07	0.44	0.07	10.1	3.5	0	6.3
9	71	4.09	43.0	373.2	552.8	6.93	5.1	0.06	0.12	0.05	0.62	0.08	19.0	3.8	0	5.9
0	23	1.80	60.2	305.3	0.9	0.96	0	0.21	—	0.05	0.43	0.05	128.1	0	0	1.0
0	40	2.36	39.4	238.6	5.7	1.25	0.8	0.09	0.28	0.05	0.43	0.11	141.0	1.1	0	3.0
0	26	1.54	35.7	258.4	58.7	0.62	8.5	0.06	0.24	0.05	0.90	0.10	17.9	10.9	0	0.5
0	56	0.95	49.6	327.5	5.3	0.56	0	0.11	—	0.05	0.48	0.09	66.4	1.1	0	1.1
0	60	1.88	44.3	346.0	1.8	0.77	0	0.14	—	0.05	0.60	0.10	90.3	1.2	0	3.6
0	18	0.33	18.3	114.0	0.9	0.16	3.0	0.02	—	0.03	0.20	0.01	20.4	2.2	0	0.7
0	25	1.76	50.4	369.9	26.1	0.49	7.2	0.06	0.57	0.04	0.69	0.10	14.4	5.2	0	1.5
0	27	2.08	62.9	484.5	14.5	0.67	12.8	0.11	0.11	0.08	0.88	0.16	22.1	8.6	0	1.7
0	7	0.40	8.7	62.6	6.2	0.29	0.6	0.03	0.04	0.06	0.51	0.03	18.0	7.1	0	0.4
—	63	2.14	48.2	354.0	0	0.93	0	0.21	0.01	0.06	0.59	0.12	127.4	0.8	0	2.6
0	9	0.41	11.3	61.7	32.1	0.10	0	0.04	—	0.03	0.45	0.03	18.3	3.8	0	0.4
0	24	1.27	25.4	303.6	39.0	0.32	0	0.12	—	0.05	0.29	0.09	16.0	0.3	0	0.7
0	32	1.62	35.8	327.7	330.2	2.09	0	0.13	0.02	0.11	0.57	0.10	25.6	1.4	0	0.6
10	44	2.10	41.7	337.8	378.2	1.48	0	0.03	0.00	0.02	0.39	0.18	13.9	7.6	0	1.6
0	36	1.21	18.4	133.5	409.2	0.33	13.5	0.04	0.04	0.07	0.25	0.06	22.1	3.8	0	2.6
0	88	4.42	74.0	442.9	0.9	0.98	0	0.13	0.30	0.24	0.34	0.20	46.4	1.5	0	6.3
0	131	2.25	54.0	485.1	12.6	0.82	7.2	0.23	—	0.14	1.13	0.05	99.9	15.3	0	1.3
0	65	2.54	60.9	414.4	1.8	0.97	0	0.21	—	0.05	0.24	0.11	122.6	0	0	1.2
0	29	0.80	15.6	186.9	1.9	0.23	2.5	0.05	0.28	0.06	0.38	0.04	20.6	6.1	0	0.3
0	33	0.59	16.2	85.1	6.1	0.32	4.1	0.02	0.03	0.06	0.26	0.04	15.5	2.8	0	0.3
0	82	1.36	49.0	654.5	173.5	0.36	275.8	0.08	1.30	0.20	0.35	0.09	10.1	17.9	0	0.6
0	12	0.46	17.0	168.0	299.6	0.29	1.1	0.01	—	0.05	0.28	0.05	30.6	2.6	0	1.1
0	14	0.67	19.6	259.3	65.5	0.30	1.7	0.02	0.03	0.03	0.28	0.05	68.0	3.1	0	0.6
0	13	1.54	14.5	125.8	164.9	0.17	0.9	0.01	0.02	0.03	0.13	0.04	25.5	3.5	0	0.4
0	16	0.79	23.0	305.0	77.0	0.35	2.0	0.02	0.04	0.04	0.33	0.06	80.0	3.6	0	0.7
0	106	0.92	42.9	344.9	3.3	0.85	33.0	0.08	0.18	0.12	1.15	0.05	104.8	1.8	0	2.1
0	31	0.52	16.4	228.5	32.0	0.35	60.1	0.04	1.13	0.09	0.43	0.15	84.2	50.6	0	1.2
0	30	0.56	12.0	130.6	10.1	0.25	46.9	0.05	1.21	0.07	0.42	0.12	51.5	36.9	0	0.6
0	21	0.33	9.6	143.8	15.0	0.19	14.1	0.03	0.36	0.05	0.29	0.08	28.7	40.6	0	1.1

A

TABLE A-1 Table of Food Composition *(continued)*

(Computer code is for Cengage Diet Analysis program) (For purposes of calculations, use "0" for t, <1, <.1, <.01, etc.)

DA+ Code	Food Description	QTY	Measure	Wt (g)	H_2O (g)	Ener (cal)	Prot (g)	Carb (g)	Fiber (g)	Fat (g)	Fat Breakdown (g) Sat	Mono	Poly	*Trans*
	Vegetables, Legumes—continued													
16848	**Broccoflower, raw, chopped**	½	cup(s)	32	28.7	10	0.9	1.9	1.0	0.1	0	0	0	—
	Brussels sprouts													
591	Boiled, drained	½	cup(s)	78	69.3	28	2.0	5.5	2.0	0.4	0.1	0	0.2	—
592	Frozen, boiled, drained	½	cup(s)	78	67.2	33	2.8	6.4	3.2	0.3	0.1	0	0.2	—
	Cabbage													
595	Boiled, drained, no salt added	1	cup(s)	150	138.8	35	1.9	8.3	2.8	0.1	0	0	0	—
35611	Chinese (pak choi or bok choy), boiled with salt, drained	1	cup(s)	170	162.4	20	2.6	3.0	1.7	0.3	0	0	0.1	—
16869	Kim chee	1	cup(s)	150	137.5	32	2.5	6.1	1.8	0.3	0	0	0.2	—
594	Raw, shredded	1	cup(s)	70	64.5	17	0.9	4.1	1.7	0.1	0	0	0	—
596	Red, shredded, raw	1	cup(s)	70	63.3	22	1.0	5.2	1.5	0.1	0	0	0.1	—
597	Savoy, shredded, raw	1	cup(s)	70	63.7	19	1.4	4.3	2.2	0.1	0	0	0	—
35417	**Capers**	1	teaspoon(s)	4	—	2	0	0	0	0	0	0	0	0
	Carrots													
8691	Baby, raw	8	item(s)	80	72.3	28	0.5	6.6	2.3	0.1	0	0	0.1	—
601	Grated	½	cup(s)	55	48.6	23	0.5	5.3	1.5	0.1	0	0	0.1	0
1055	Juice, canned	½	cup(s)	118	104.9	47	1.1	11.0	0.9	0.2	0	0	0.1	—
600	Raw	½	cup(s)	61	53.9	25	0.6	5.8	1.7	0.1	0	0	0.1	0
602	Sliced, boiled, drained	½	cup(s)	78	70.3	27	0.6	6.4	2.3	0.1	0	0	0.1	—
32725	**Cassava or manioc**	½	cup(s)	103	61.5	165	1.4	39.2	1.9	0.3	0.1	0.1	0	—
	Cauliflower													
606	Boiled, drained	½	cup(s)	62	57.7	14	1.1	2.5	1.4	0.3	0	0	0.1	—
607	Frozen, boiled, drained	½	cup(s)	90	84.6	17	1.4	3.4	2.4	0.2	0	0	0.1	—
605	Raw, chopped	½	cup(s)	50	46.0	13	1.0	2.6	1.2	0	0	0	0	—
	Celery													
609	Diced	½	cup(s)	51	48.2	8	0.3	1.5	0.8	0.1	0	0	0	—
608	Stalk	2	item(s)	80	76.3	13	0.6	2.4	1.3	0.1	0	0	0.1	—
	Chard													
1057	Swiss chard, boiled, drained	½	cup(s)	88	81.1	18	1.6	3.6	1.8	0.1	0	0	0	—
1056	Swiss chard, raw	1	cup(s)	36	33.4	7	0.6	1.3	0.6	0.1	0	0	0	—
	Collard greens													
610	Boiled, drained	½	cup(s)	95	87.3	25	2.0	4.7	2.7	0.3	0	0	0.2	—
611	Frozen, chopped, boiled, drained	½	cup(s)	85	75.2	31	2.5	6.0	2.4	0.3	0.1	0	0.2	—
	Corn													
29614	Yellow corn, fresh, cooked	1	item(s)	100	69.2	107	3.3	25.0	2.8	1.3	0.2	0.4	0.6	—
615	Yellow creamed sweet corn, canned	½	cup(s)	128	100.8	92	2.2	23.2	1.5	0.5	0.1	0.2	0.3	—
612	Yellow sweet corn, boiled, drained	½	cup(s)	82	57.0	89	2.7	20.6	2.3	1.1	0.2	0.3	0.5	—
614	Yellow sweet corn, frozen, boiled, drained	½	cup(s)	82	63.2	66	2.1	15.8	2.0	0.5	0.1	0.2	0.3	—
618	**Cucumber**	¼	item(s)	75	71.7	11	0.5	2.7	0.4	0.1	0	0	0	—
16870	**Cucumber, kim chee**	½	cup(s)	75	68.1	16	0.8	3.6	1.1	0.1	0	0	0	—
	Dandelion greens													
620	Chopped, boiled, drained	½	cup(s)	53	47.1	17	1.1	3.4	1.5	0.3	0.1	0	0.1	—
2734	Raw	1	cup(s)	55	47.1	25	1.5	5.1	1.9	0.4	0.1	0	0.2	—
1066	**Eggplant, boiled, drained**	½	cup(s)	50	44.4	17	0.4	4.3	1.2	0.1	0	0	0	—
621	**Endive or escarole, chopped, raw**	1	cup(s)	50	46.9	8	0.6	1.7	1.5	0.1	0	0	0	—
8784	**Jicama or yambean**	½	cup(s)	65	116.5	49	0.9	11.4	6.3	0.1	0	0	0.1	—
	Kale													
623	Frozen, chopped, boiled, drained	½	cup(s)	65	58.8	20	1.8	3.4	1.3	0.3	0	0	0.2	—
29313	Raw	1	cup(s)	67	56.6	33	2.2	6.7	1.3	0.5	0.1	0	0.2	—
	Kohlrabi													
1072	Boiled, drained	½	cup(s)	83	74.5	24	1.5	5.5	0.9	0.1	0	0	0	—
1071	Raw	1	cup(s)	135	122.9	36	2.3	8.4	4.9	0.1	0	0	0.1	—

Chol (mg)	Calc (mg)	Iron (mg)	Magn (mg)	Pota (mg)	Sodi (mg)	Zinc (mg)	Vit A (μg)	Thia (mg)	Vit E (mg α)	Ribo (mg)	Niac (mg)	Vit B_6 (mg)	Fola (μg)	Vit C (mg)	Vit B_{12} (μg)	Sele (μg)
0	11	0.23	6.4	96.0	7.4	0.20	2.6	0.02	0.01	0.03	0.23	0.07	18.2	28.2	0	0.2
0	28	0.93	15.6	247.3	16.4	0.25	30.4	0.08	0.33	0.06	0.47	0.13	46.8	48.4	0	1.2
0	20	0.37	14.0	224.8	11.6	0.18	35.7	0.08	0.39	0.08	0.41	0.22	78.3	35.4	0	0.5
0	72	0.24	22.5	294.0	12.0	0.30	6.0	0.08	0.20	0.04	0.36	0.16	45.0	56.2	0	0.9
0	158	1.76	18.7	630.7	459.0	0.28	360.4	0.04	0.14	0.10	0.72	0.28	69.7	44.2	0	0.7
0	144	1.26	27.0	379.5	996.0	0.36	288.0	0.06	0.36	0.10	0.80	0.32	88.5	79.6	0	1.5
0	28	0.33	8.4	119.0	12.6	0.12	3.5	0.04	0.10	0.02	0.16	0.08	30.1	25.6	0	0.2
0	31	0.56	11.2	170.1	18.9	0.15	39.2	0.04	0.07	0.05	0.29	0.14	12.6	39.9	0	0.4
0	24	0.28	19.6	161.0	19.6	0.18	35.0	0.05	0.11	0.02	0.21	0.13	56.0	21.7	0	0.6
0	0	0.00	—	—	140	—	0	—	—	—	—	—	—	0	—	—
0	26	0.71	8.0	189.6	62.4	0.13	552.0	0.02	—	0.02	0.44	0.08	21.6	2.1	0	0.7
0	18	0.16	6.6	176.0	37.9	0.13	459.2	0.03	0.36	0.03	0.54	0.07	10.4	3.2	0	0.1
0	28	0.54	16.5	344.6	34.2	0.21	1128.1	0.11	1.37	0.07	0.46	0.26	4.7	10.0	0	0.7
0	20	0.18	7.3	195.2	42.1	0.15	509.4	0.04	0.40	0.04	0.60	0.08	11.6	3.6	0	0.1
0	23	0.26	7.8	183.3	45.2	0.15	664.6	0.05	0.80	0.03	0.50	0.11	10.9	2.8	0	0.5
0	16	0.27	21.6	279.1	14.4	0.35	1.0	0.08	0.19	0.04	0.87	0.09	27.8	21.2	0	0.7
0	10	0.19	5.6	88.0	9.3	0.10	0.6	0.02	0.04	0.03	0.25	0.10	27.3	27.5	0	0.4
0	15	0.36	8.1	125.1	16.2	0.11	0	0.03	0.05	0.04	0.27	0.07	36.9	28.2	0	0.5
0	11	0.22	7.5	151.5	15.0	0.14	0.5	0.03	0.04	0.03	0.26	0.11	28.5	23.2	0	0.3
0	20	0.10	5.6	131.3	40.4	0.07	11.1	0.01	0.14	0.03	0.16	0.04	18.2	1.6	0	0.2
0	32	0.16	8.8	208.0	64.0	0.10	17.6	0.01	0.21	0.04	0.25	0.05	28.8	2.5	0	0.3
0	51	1.98	75.3	480.4	156.6	0.29	267.8	0.03	1.65	0.08	0.32	0.07	7.9	15.8	0	0.8
0	18	0.64	29.2	136.4	76.7	0.13	110.2	0.01	0.68	0.03	0.14	0.03	5.0	10.8	0	0.3
0	133	1.10	19.0	110.2	15.2	0.21	385.7	0.03	0.83	0.10	0.54	0.12	88.4	17.3	0	0.5
0	179	0.95	25.5	213.4	42.5	0.22	488.8	0.04	1.06	0.09	0.54	0.09	64.6	22.4	0	1.3
0	2	0.61	32.0	248.0	242.0	0.48	13.0	0.20	0.09	0.07	1.60	0.06	46.0	6.2	0	0.2
0	4	0.48	21.8	171.5	364.8	0.67	5.1	0.03	0.09	0.06	1.22	0.08	57.6	5.9	0	0.5
0	2	0.36	21.3	173.8	0	0.50	10.7	0.17	0.07	0.05	1.32	0.04	37.7	5.1	0	0.2
0	2	0.38	23.0	191.1	0.8	0.51	8.2	0.02	0.05	0.05	1.07	0.08	28.7	2.9	0	0.6
0	12	0.20	9.8	110.6	1.5	0.14	3.8	0.01	0.01	0.01	0.07	0.03	5.3	2.1	0	0.2
0	7	3.61	6.0	87.8	765.8	0.38	—	0.02	—	0.02	0.34	0.08	17.3	2.6	0	—
0	74	0.95	12.6	121.8	23.1	0.15	179.6	0.07	1.28	0.09	0.27	0.08	6.8	9.5	0	0.2
0	103	1.70	19.8	218.3	41.8	0.22	279.4	0.10	1.89	0.14	0.44	0.13	14.8	19.2	0	0.3
0	3	0.12	5.4	60.9	0.5	0.06	1.0	0.04	0.20	0.01	0.30	0.04	6.9	0.6	0	0
0	26	0.41	7.5	157.0	11.0	0.39	54.0	0.04	0.22	0.03	0.20	0.01	71.0	3.2	0	0.1
0	16	0.78	15.5	194.0	5.2	0.20	1.3	0.02	0.59	0.04	0.25	0.05	15.5	26.1	0	0.9
0	90	0.61	11.7	208.7	9.8	0.11	477.8	0.02	0.59	0.07	0.43	0.05	9.1	16.4	0	0.6
0	90	1.14	22.8	299.5	28.8	0.29	515.2	0.07	—	0.08	0.66	0.18	19.4	80.4	0	0.6
0	21	0.33	15.7	280.5	17.3	0.26	1.7	0.03	0.43	0.02	0.32	0.13	9.9	44.6	0	0.7
0	32	0.54	25.7	472.5	27.0	0.04	2.7	0.06	0.64	0.02	0.54	0.20	21.6	83.7	0	0.9

A

TABLE A-1 Table of Food Composition *(continued)*

(Computer code is for Cengage Diet Analysis program) (For purposes of calculations, use "0" for t, <1, <.1, <.01, etc.)

DA+ Code	Food Description	Qty	Measure	Wt (g)	H_2O (g)	Ener (cal)	Prot (g)	Carb (g)	Fiber (g)	Fat (g)	Fat Breakdown (g)			
											Sat	Mono	Poly	Trans
	Vegetables, Legumes—continued													
	Leeks													
1074	Boiled, drained	½	cup(s)	52	47.2	16	0.4	4.0	0.5	0.1	0	0	0	—
1073	Raw	1	cup(s)	89	73.9	54	1.3	12.6	1.6	0.3	0	0	0.1	—
	Lentils													
522	Boiled	¼	cup(s)	50	34.5	57	4.5	10.0	3.9	0.2	0	0	0.1	—
1075	Sprouted	1	cup(s)	77	51.9	82	6.9	17.0	—	0.4	0	0.1	0.2	—
	Lettuce													
625	Butterhead leaves	11	piece(s)	83	78.9	11	1.1	1.8	0.9	0.2	0	0	0.1	—
624	Butterhead, Boston or Bibb	1	cup(s)	55	52.6	7	0.7	1.2	0.6	0.1	0	0	0.1	—
626	Iceberg	1	cup(s)	55	52.6	8	0.5	1.6	0.7	0.1	0	0	0	—
628	Iceberg, chopped	1	cup(s)	55	52.6	8	0.5	1.6	0.7	0.1	0	0	0	—
629	Looseleaf	1	cup(s)	36	34.2	5	0.5	1.0	0.5	0.1	0	0	0	—
1665	Romaine, shredded	1	cup(s)	56	53.0	10	0.7	1.8	1.2	0.2	0	0	0.1	—
	Mushrooms													
15585	Crimini (about 6)	3	ounce(s)	85	—	28	3.7	2.8	1.9	0	0	0	0	0
8700	Enoki	30	item(s)	90	79.7	40	2.3	6.9	2.4	0.3	0	0	0.1	—
1079	Mushrooms, boiled, drained	½	cup(s)	78	71.0	22	1.7	4.1	1.7	0.4	0	0	0.1	—
1080	Mushrooms, canned, drained	½	cup(s)	78	71.0	20	1.5	4.0	1.9	0.2	0	0	0.1	—
630	Mushrooms, raw	½	cup(s)	48	44.4	11	1.5	1.6	0.5	0.2	0	0	0.1	—
15587	Portabella, raw	1	item(s)	84	—	30	3.0	3.9	3.0	0	0	0	0	0
2743	Shiitake, cooked	½	cup(s)	73	60.5	41	1.1	10.4	1.5	0.2	0	0.1	0	—
	Mustard greens													
2744	Frozen, boiled, drained	½	cup(s)	75	70.4	14	1.7	2.3	2.1	0.2	0	0.1	0	—
29319	Raw	1	cup(s)	56	50.8	15	1.5	2.7	1.8	0.1	0	0	0	—
	Okra													
16866	Batter coated, fried	11	piece(s)	83	55.6	156	2.1	12.7	2.0	11.2	1.5	3.7	5.5	—
32742	Frozen, boiled, drained, no salt added	½	cup(s)	92	83.8	26	1.9	5.3	2.6	0.3	0.1	0	0.1	—
632	Sliced, boiled, drained	½	cup(s)	80	74.1	18	1.5	3.6	2.0	0.2	0	0	0	—
	Onions													
635	Chopped, boiled, drained	½	cup(s)	105	92.2	46	1.4	10.7	1.5	0.2	0	0	0.1	—
2748	Frozen, boiled, drained	½	cup(s)	106	97.8	30	0.8	7.0	1.9	0.1	0	0	0	—
1081	Onion rings, breaded and pan fried, frozen, heated	10	piece(s)	71	20.2	289	3.8	27.1	0.9	19.0	6.1	7.7	3.6	—
633	Raw, chopped	½	cup(s)	80	71.3	32	0.9	7.5	1.4	0.1	0	0	0	—
16850	Red onions, sliced, raw	½	cup(s)	57	50.7	24	0.5	5.8	0.8	0	0	0	0	—
636	Scallions, green or spring onions	2	item(s)	30	26.9	10	0.5	2.2	0.8	0.1	0	0	0	—
16860	**Palm hearts, cooked**	½	cup(s)	73	50.7	84	2.0	18.7	1.1	0.1	0	0	0.1	—
637	**Parsley, chopped**	1	tablespoon(s)	4	3.3	1	0.1	0.2	0.1	0	0	0	0	—
638	**Parsnips, sliced, boiled, drained**	½	cup(s)	78	62.6	55	1.0	13.3	2.8	0.2	0	0.1	0	—
	Peas													
639	Green peas, canned, drained	½	cup(s)	85	69.4	59	3.8	10.7	3.5	0.3	0.1	0	0.1	—
641	Green peas, frozen, boiled, drained	½	cup(s)	80	63.6	62	4.1	11.4	4.4	0.2	0	0	0.1	—
35694	Pea pods, boiled with salt, drained	½	cup(s)	80	71.1	32	2.6	5.2	2.2	0.2	0	0	0.1	—
1082	Peas and carrots, canned with liquid	½	cup(s)	128	112.4	48	2.8	10.8	2.6	0.3	0.1	0	0.2	—
1083	Peas and carrots, frozen, boiled, drained	½	cup(s)	80	68.6	38	2.5	8.1	2.5	0.3	0.1	0	0.2	—
2750	Snow or sugar peas, frozen, boiled, drained	½	cup(s)	80	69.3	42	2.8	7.2	2.5	0.3	0.1	0	0.1	—
640	Snow or sugar peas, raw	½	cup(s)	32	28.0	13	0.9	2.4	0.8	0.1	0	0	0	—
29324	Split peas, sprouted	½	cup(s)	60	37.4	77	5.3	16.9	—	0.4	0.1	0	0.2	—
	Peppers													
644	Green bell or sweet, boiled, drained	½	cup(s)	68	62.5	19	0.6	4.6	0.8	0.1	0	0	0.1	—
643	Green bell or sweet, raw	½	cup(s)	75	69.9	15	0.6	3.5	1.3	0.1	0	0	0	—
1664	Green hot chili	1	item(s)	45	39.5	18	0.9	4.3	0.7	0.1	0	0	0	—
1663	Green hot chili, canned with liquid	½	cup(s)	68	62.9	14	0.6	3.5	0.9	0.1	0	0	0	—
1086	Jalapeno, canned with liquid	½	cup(s)	68	60.4	18	0.6	3.2	1.8	0.6	0.1	0	0.3	—
8703	Yellow bell or sweet	1	item(s)	186	171.2	50	1.9	11.8	1.7	0.4	0.1	0	0.2	—

PAGE KEY: A-2 = Breads/Baked Goods A-8 = Cereal/Rice/Pasta A-12 = Fruit A-18 = Vegetables/Legumes A-28 = Nuts/Seeds A-30 = Vegetarian A-32 = Dairy A-40 = Eggs A-40 = Seafood A-44 = Meats A-48 = Poultry A-48 = Processed Meats A-50 = Beverages A-54 = Fats/Oils A-56 = Sweets A-58 = Spices/Condiments/Sauces A-62 = Mixed Foods/Soups/Sandwiches A-68 = Fast Food A-88 = Convenience A-90 = Baby Foods

A

Chol (mg)	Calc (mg)	Iron (mg)	Magn (mg)	Pota (mg)	Sodi (mg)	Zinc (mg)	Vit A (µg)	Thia (mg)	Vit E (mg α)	Ribo (mg)	Niac (mg)	Vit B_6 (mg)	Fola (µg)	Vit C (mg)	Vit B_{12} (µg)	Sele (µg)
0	16	0.56	7.3	45.2	5.2	0.02	1.0	0.01	—	0.01	0.10	0.04	12.5	2.2	0	0.3
0	53	1.86	24.9	160.2	17.8	0.10	73.9	0.05	0.81	0.02	0.35	0.20	57.0	10.7	0	0.9
0	9	1.65	17.8	182.7	1.0	0.63	0	0.08	0.05	0.04	0.52	0.09	89.6	0.7	0	1.4
0	19	2.47	28.5	247.9	8.5	1.16	1.5	0.17	—	0.09	0.86	0.14	77.0	12.7	0	0.5
0	29	1.02	10.7	196.4	4.1	0.16	137.0	0.04	0.14	0.05	0.29	0.06	60.2	3.1	0	0.5
0	19	0.68	7.1	130.9	2.7	0.11	91.3	0.03	0.09	0.03	0.19	0.04	40.1	2.0	0	0.3
0	10	0.22	3.8	77.5	5.5	0.08	13.7	0.02	0.09	0.01	0.07	0.02	15.9	1.5	0	0.1
0	10	0.22	3.8	77.5	5.5	0.08	13.7	0.02	0.09	0.01	0.07	0.02	15.9	1.5	0	0.1
0	13	0.31	4.7	69.8	10.1	0.06	133.2	0.02	0.10	0.02	0.13	0.03	13.7	6.5	0	0.2
0	18	0.54	7.8	138.3	4.5	0.13	162.4	0.04	0.07	0.03	0.17	0.04	76.2	13.4	0	0.2
0	0	0.67	—	—	32.6	—	0	—	—	—	—	—	—	0	0	—
0	1	0.98	14.4	331.2	2.7	0.54	0	0.16	0.01	0.14	5.31	0.07	46.8	0	0	2.0
0	5	1.35	9.4	277.7	1.6	0.67	0	0.05	0.01	0.23	3.47	0.07	14.0	3.1	0	9.3
0	9	0.61	11.7	100.6	331.5	0.56	0	0.06	0.01	0.01	1.24	0.04	9.4	0	0	3.2
0	1	0.24	4.3	152.6	2.4	0.25	0	0.04	0.01	0.19	1.73	0.05	7.7	1.0	0	4.5
0	39	0.35	—	—	9.9	—	0	—	—	—	—	—	—	0	0	—
0	2	0.31	10.2	84.8	2.9	0.96	0	0.02	0.02	0.12	1.08	0.11	15.2	0.2	0	18.0
0	76	0.84	9.8	104.3	18.8	0.15	265.5	0.03	1.01	0.04	0.19	0.08	52.5	10.4	0	0.5
0	58	0.81	17.9	198.2	14.0	0.11	294.0	0.04	1.12	0.06	0.45	0.10	104.7	39.2	0	0.5
2	54	1.13	32.2	170.8	109.7	0.44	14.0	0.16	1.50	0.12	1.29	0.11	39.6	9.2	0	3.6
0	88	0.61	46.9	215.3	2.8	0.57	15.6	0.09	0.29	0.11	0.72	0.04	134.3	11.2	0	0.6
0	62	0.22	28.8	108.0	4.8	0.34	11.2	0.10	0.21	0.04	0.69	0.15	36.8	13.0	0	0.3
0	23	0.24	11.5	174.3	3.1	0.21	0	0.03	0.02	0.02	0.17	0.12	15.7	5.5	0	0.6
0	17	0.32	6.4	114.5	12.7	0.06	0	0.02	0.01	0.02	0.14	0.06	13.8	2.8	0	0.4
0	22	1.20	13.5	91.6	266.3	0.29	7.8	0.19	—	0.09	2.56	0.05	46.9	1.0	0	2.5
0	18	0.16	8.0	116.8	3.2	0.13	0	0.03	0.01	0.02	0.09	0.09	15.2	5.9	0	0.4
0	13	0.10	5.7	82.4	1.7	0.09	0	0.02	0.01	0.01	0.04	0.08	10.9	3.7	0	0.3
0	22	0.44	6.0	82.8	4.8	0.11	15.0	0.01	0.16	0.02	0.15	0.01	19.2	5.6	0	0.2
0	13	1.23	7.3	1318.4	10.2	2.72	2.2	0.03	0.36	0.12	0.62	0.53	14.6	5.0	0	0.5
0	5	0.23	1.9	21.1	2.1	0.04	16.0	0.00	0.02	0.00	0.05	0.00	5.8	5.1	0	0
0	29	0.45	22.6	286.3	7.8	0.20	0	0.06	0.78	0.04	0.56	0.07	45.2	10.1	0	1.3
0	17	0.80	14.5	147.1	214.2	0.60	23.0	0.10	0.02	0.06	0.62	0.05	37.4	8.2	0	1.4
0	19	1.21	17.6	88.0	57.6	0.53	84.0	0.22	0.02	0.08	1.18	0.09	47.2	7.9	0	0.8
0	34	1.57	20.8	192.0	192.0	0.29	41.6	0.10	0.31	0.06	0.43	0.11	23.2	38.3	0	0.6
0	29	0.96	17.9	127.5	331.5	0.74	368.5	0.09	—	0.07	0.74	0.11	23.0	8.4	0	1.1
0	18	0.75	12.8	126.4	54.4	0.36	380.8	0.18	0.41	0.05	0.92	0.07	20.8	6.5	0	0.9
0	47	1.92	22.4	173.6	4.0	0.39	52.8	0.05	0.37	0.09	0.45	0.13	28.0	17.6	0	0.6
0	14	0.65	7.6	63.0	1.3	0.08	17.0	0.04	0.12	0.02	0.19	0.05	13.2	18.9	0	0.2
0	22	1.34	33.6	228.6	12.0	0.62	4.8	0.12	—	0.08	1.84	0.14	86.4	6.2	0	0.4
0	6	0.31	6.8	112.9	1.4	0.08	15.6	0.04	0.34	0.02	0.32	0.15	10.9	50.6	0	0.2
0	7	0.25	7.5	130.4	2.2	0.09	13.4	0.04	0.27	0.02	0.35	0.16	7.5	59.9	0	0
0	8	0.54	11.3	153.0	3.2	0.13	26.6	0.04	0.31	0.04	0.42	0.12	10.4	109.1	0	0.2
0	5	0.34	9.5	127.2	797.6	0.10	24.5	0.01	0.46	0.02	0.54	0.10	6.8	46.2	0	0.2
0	16	1.28	10.2	131.2	1136.3	0.23	57.8	0.03	0.47	0.03	0.27	0.13	9.5	6.8	0	0.3
0	20	0.85	22.3	394.3	3.7	0.31	18.6	0.05	—	0.04	1.65	0.31	48.4	341.3	0	0.6

TABLE A-1 Table of Food Composition *(continued)*

(Computer code is for Cengage Diet Analysis program) (For purposes of calculations, use "0" for t, <1, <.1, <.01, etc.)

DA+ Code	Food Description	QTY	Measure	Wt (g)	H_2O (g)	Ener (cal)	Prot (g)	Carb (g)	Fiber (g)	Fat (g)	Fat Breakdown (g)			
											Sat	Mono	Poly	*Trans*
Vegetables, Legumes—continued														
1087	**Poi**	½	cup(s)	120	86.0	134	0.5	32.7	0.5	0.2	0	0	0.1	—
	Potatoes													
1090	Au gratin mix, prepared with water, whole milk and butter	½	cup(s)	124	97.7	115	2.8	15.9	1.1	5.1	3.2	1.5	0.2	—
1089	Au gratin, prepared with butter	½	cup(s)	123	90.7	162	6.2	13.8	2.2	9.3	5.8	2.6	0.3	—
5791	Baked, flesh and skin	1	item(s)	202	151.3	188	5.1	42.7	4.4	0.3	0.1	0	0.1	—
645	Baked, flesh only	½	cup(s)	61	46.0	57	1.2	13.1	0.9	0.1	0	0	0	—
1088	Baked, skin only	1	item(s)	58	27.4	115	2.5	26.7	4.6	0.1	0	0	0	—
5795	Boiled in skin, flesh only, drained	1	item(s)	136	104.7	118	2.5	27.4	2.1	0.1	0	0	0.1	—
5794	Boiled, drained, skin and flesh	1	item(s)	150	115.9	129	2.9	29.8	2.5	0.2	0	0	0.1	—
647	Boiled, flesh only	½	cup(s)	78	60.4	67	1.3	15.6	1.4	0.1	0	0	0	—
648	French fried, deep fried, prepared from raw	14	item(s)	70	32.8	187	2.7	23.5	2.9	9.5	1.9	4.2	3.0	—
649	French fried, frozen, heated	14	item(s)	70	43.7	94	1.9	19.4	2.0	3.7	0.7	2.3	0.2	—
1091	Hashed brown	½	cup(s)	78	36.9	207	2.3	27.4	2.5	9.8	1.5	4.1	3.7	—
652	Mashed with margarine and whole milk	½	cup(s)	105	79.0	119	2.1	17.7	1.6	4.4	1.0	2.0	1.2	0.7
653	Mashed, prepared from dehydrated granules with milk, water, and margarine	½	cup(s)	105	79.8	122	2.3	16.9	1.4	5.0	1.3	2.1	1.4	—
2759	Microwaved	1	item(s)	202	145.5	212	4.9	49.0	4.6	0.2	0.1	0	0.1	—
2760	Microwaved in skin, flesh only	½	cup(s)	78	57.1	78	1.6	18.1	1.2	0.1	0	0	0	—
5804	Microwaved, skin only	1	item(s)	58	36.8	77	2.5	17.2	4.2	0.1	0	0	0	—
1097	Potato puffs, frozen, heated	½	cup(s)	64	38.2	122	1.3	17.8	1.6	5.5	1.2	3.9	0.3	—
1094	Scalloped mix, prepared with water, whole milk and butter	½	cup(s)	124	98.4	116	2.6	15.9	1.4	5.3	3.3	1.5	0.2	—
1093	Scalloped, prepared with butter	½	cup(s)	123	99.2	108	3.5	13.2	2.3	4.5	2.8	1.3	0.2	—
	Pumpkin													
1773	Boiled, drained	½	cup(s)	123	114.8	25	0.9	6.0	1.3	0.1	0	0	0	—
656	Canned	½	cup(s)	123	110.2	42	1.3	9.9	3.6	0.3	0.2	0	0	—
	Radicchio													
8731	Leaves, raw	1	cup(s)	40	37.3	9	0.6	1.8	0.4	0.1	0	0	0	—
2498	Raw	1	cup(s)	40	37.3	9	0.6	1.8	0.4	0.1	0	0	0	—
657	**Radishes**	6	item(s)	27	25.7	4	0.2	0.9	0.4	0	0	0	0	—
1099	**Rutabaga, boiled, drained**	½	cup(s)	85	75.5	33	1.1	7.4	1.5	0.2	0	0	0.1	—
658	**Sauerkraut, canned**	½	cup(s)	118	109.2	22	1.1	5.1	3.4	0.2	0	0	0.1	—
	Seaweed													
1102	Kelp	½	cup(s)	40	32.6	17	0.6	3.8	0.5	0.2	0.1	0	0	—
1104	Spirulina, dried	½	cup(s)	8	0.4	22	4.3	1.8	0.3	0.6	0.2	0.1	0.2	—
1106	**Shallots**	3	tablespoon(s)	30	23.9	22	0.8	5.0	—	0	0	0	0	—
	Soybeans													
1670	Boiled	½	cup(s)	86	53.8	149	14.3	8.5	5.2	7.7	1.1	1.7	4.4	—
2825	Dry roasted	½	cup(s)	86	0.7	388	34.0	28.1	7.0	18.6	2.7	4.1	10.5	—
2824	Roasted, salted	½	cup(s)	86	1.7	405	30.3	28.9	15.2	21.8	3.2	4.8	12.3	—
8739	Sprouted, stir fried	½	cup(s)	63	42.3	79	8.2	5.9	0.5	4.5	0.6	1.0	2.5	0
	Soy products													
1813	Soy milk	1	cup(s)	240	211.3	130	7.8	15.1	1.4	4.2	0.5	1.0	2.3	0
2838	Tofu, dried, frozen (koyadofu)	3	ounce(s)	85	4.9	408	40.8	12.4	6.1	25.8	3.7	5.7	14.6	—
13844	Tofu, extra firm	3	ounce(s)	85	—	86	8.6	2.2	1.1	4.3	0.5	0.9	2.8	—
13843	Tofu, firm	3	ounce(s)	85	—	75	7.5	2.2	0.5	3.2	0	0.9	2.3	—
1816	Tofu, firm, with calcium sulfate and magnesium chloride (nigari)	3	ounce(s)	85	72.2	60	7.0	1.4	0.8	3.5	0.7	1.0	1.5	—
1817	Tofu, fried	3	ounce(s)	85	43.0	230	14.6	8.9	3.3	17.2	2.5	3.8	9.7	—
13841	Tofu, silken	3	ounce(s)	85	—	42	3.7	1.9	0	2.3	0.5	—	—	—
13842	Tofu, soft	3	ounce(s)	85	—	65	6.5	1.1	0.5	3.2	0.5	1.1	2.2	—
1671	Tofu, soft, with calcium sulfate and magnesium chloride (nigari)	3	ounce(s)	85	74.2	52	5.6	1.5	0.2	3.1	0.5	0.7	1.8	—

Chol (mg)	Calc (mg)	Iron (mg)	Magn (mg)	Pota (mg)	Sodi (mg)	Zinc (mg)	Vit A (μg)	Thia (mg)	Vit E (mg α)	Ribo (mg)	Niac (mg)	Vit B_6 (mg)	Fola (μg)	Vit C (mg)	Vit B_{12} (μg)	Sele (μg)
0	19	1.06	28.8	219.6	14.4	0.26	3.6	0.16	2.76	0.05	1.32	0.33	25.2	4.8	0	0.8
19	103	0.39	18.6	271.0	543.3	0.29	64.4	0.02	—	0.10	1.16	0.05	8.7	3.8	0	3.3
28	146	0.78	24.5	485.1	530.4	0.85	78.4	0.08	—	0.14	1.22	0.21	13.5	12.1	0	3.3
0	30	2.18	56.6	1080.7	20.2	0.72	2.0	0.12	0.08	0.09	2.84	0.62	56.6	19.4	0	0.8
0	3	0.21	15.3	238.5	3.1	0.18	0	0.06	0.02	0.01	0.85	0.18	5.5	7.8	0	0.2
0	20	4.08	24.9	332.3	12.2	0.28	0.6	0.07	0.02	0.06	1.77	0.35	12.8	7.8	0	0.4
0	7	0.42	29.9	515.4	5.4	0.40	0	0.14	0.01	0.02	1.95	0.40	13.6	17.7	0	0.4
0	13	1.27	34.1	572.0	7.4	0.46	0	0.14	0.01	0.03	2.13	0.44	15.0	18.4	0	—
0	6	0.24	15.6	255.8	3.9	0.21	0	0.07	0.01	0.01	1.02	0.21	7.0	5.8	0	0.2
0	16	1.05	30.8	567.0	8.4	0.39	0	0.08	0.09	0.03	1.34	0.37	16.1	21.2	0	0.4
0	8	0.51	18.2	315.7	271.6	0.26	0	0.09	0.07	0.02	1.55	0.12	19.6	9.3	0	0.1
0	11	0.43	27.3	449.3	266.8	0.37	0	0.13	0.01	0.03	1.80	0.37	12.5	10.1	0	0.4
1	23	0.27	19.9	344.4	349.6	0.31	43.0	0.09	0.44	0.04	1.23	0.25	9.4	11.0	0.1	0.8
2	36	0.21	21.0	164.8	179.5	0.26	49.3	0.09	0.53	0.09	0.90	0.16	8.4	6.8	0.1	5.9
0	22	2.50	54.5	902.9	16.2	0.72	0	0.24	—	0.06	3.46	0.69	24.2	30.5	0	0.8
0	4	0.31	19.4	319.0	5.4	0.25	0	0.10	—	0.01	1.26	0.25	9.3	11.7	0	0.3
0	27	3.44	21.5	377.0	9.3	0.29	0	0.04	0.01	0.04	1.28	0.28	9.9	8.9	0	0.3
0	9	0.41	10.9	199.7	307.2	0.21	0	0.08	0.15	0.02	0.97	0.08	9.0	4.0	0	0.4
14	45	0.47	17.4	252.2	423.7	0.31	43.5	0.02	—	0.06	1.28	0.05	12.4	4.1	0	2.0
15	70	0.70	23.3	463.1	410.4	0.49	0	0.08	—	0.11	1.29	0.22	13.5	13.0	0	2.0
0	18	0.69	11.0	281.8	1.2	0.28	306.3	0.03	0.98	0.09	0.50	0.05	11.0	5.8	0	0.2
0	32	1.70	28.2	252.4	6.1	0.20	953.1	0.02	1.29	0.06	0.45	0.06	14.7	5.1	0	0.5
0	8	0.23	5.2	120.8	8.8	0.25	0.4	0.01	0.90	0.01	0.10	0.02	24.0	3.2	0	0.4
0	8	0.23	5.2	120.8	8.8	0.25	0.4	0.01	0.90	0.01	0.10	0.02	24.0	3.2	0	0.4
0	7	0.09	2.7	62.9	10.5	0.07	0	0.00	0.00	0.01	0.06	0.01	6.8	4.0	0	0.2
0	41	0.45	19.6	277.1	17.0	0.30	0	0.07	0.27	0.04	0.61	0.09	12.8	16.0	0	0.6
0	35	1.73	15.3	200.6	780.0	0.22	1.2	0.03	0.17	0.03	0.17	0.15	28.3	17.3	0	0.7
0	67	1.12	48.4	35.6	93.2	0.48	2.4	0.02	0.32	0.04	0.16	0.00	72.0	1.2	0	0.3
0	9	2.14	14.6	102.2	78.6	0.15	2.2	0.18	0.38	0.28	0.96	0.03	7.1	0.8	0	0.5
0	11	0.36	6.3	100.2	3.6	0.12	18.0	0.02	—	0.01	0.06	0.09	10.2	2.4	—	0.4
0	88	4.42	74.0	442.9	0.9	0.98	0	0.13	0.30	0.24	0.34	0.20	46.4	1.5	0	6.3
0	120	3.39	196.1	1173.0	1.7	4.10	0	0.36	—	0.64	0.90	0.19	176.3	4.0	0	16.6
0	119	3.35	124.7	1264.2	140.2	2.70	8.6	0.08	0.78	0.12	1.21	0.17	181.5	1.9	0	16.4
0	52	0.25	60.4	356.6	8.8	1.32	0.6	0.26	—	0.12	0.69	0.10	79.9	7.5	0	0.4
0	60	1.53	60.0	283.2	122.4	0.28	0	0.14	0.26	0.16	1.23	0.18	43.2	0	0	11.5
0	310	8.27	50.2	17.0	5.1	4.16	22.1	0.42	—	0.27	1.01	0.24	78.2	0.6	0	46.2
0	65	1.16	84.1	—	0	—	0	—	—	—	—	—	—	0	0	—
0	108	1.16	56.1	—	0	—	0	—	—	—	—	—	—	0	0	—
0	171	1.36	31.5	125.9	10.2	0.70	0	0.05	0.01	0.05	0.08	0.06	16.2	0.2	0	8.4
0	316	4.14	51.0	124.2	13.6	1.69	0.9	0.14	0.03	0.04	0.08	0.08	23.0	0	0	24.2
0	56	0.34	33.1	—	4.7	—	0	—	—	—	—	—	—	0	1.7	—
0	108	1.16	35.5	—	0	—	0	—	—	—	—	—	—	0	1.9	—
0	94	0.94	23.0	102.1	6.8	0.54	0	0.04	0.01	0.03	0.45	0.04	37.4	0.2	0	7.6

TABLE A-1 Table of Food Composition *(continued)*

(Computer code is for Cengage Diet Analysis program) (For purposes of calculations, use "0" for t, <1, <.1, <.01, etc.)

DA+ Code	Food Description	QTY	Measure	Wt (g)	H_2O (g)	Ener (cal)	Prot (g)	Carb (g)	Fiber (g)	Fat (g)	Fat Breakdown (g)			
											Sat	Mono	Poly	*Trans*
Vegetables, Legumes—continued														
	Spinach													
663	Canned, drained	½	cup(s)	107	98.2	25	3.0	3.6	2.6	0.5	0.1	0	0.2	—
660	Chopped, boiled, drained	½	cup(s)	90	82.1	21	2.7	3.4	2.2	0.2	0	0	0.1	—
661	Chopped, frozen, boiled, drained	½	cup(s)	95	84.5	32	3.8	4.6	3.5	0.8	0.1	0	0.4	—
662	Leaf, frozen, boiled, drained	½	cup(s)	95	84.5	32	3.8	4.6	3.5	0.8	0.1	0	0.4	—
659	Raw, chopped	1	cup(s)	30	27.4	7	0.9	1.1	0.7	0.1	0	0	0	—
8470	Trimmed leaves	1	cup(s)	32	27.5	3	0.9	0	2.8	0.1	—	—	—	—
	Squash													
1662	Acorn winter, baked	½	cup(s)	103	85.0	57	1.1	14.9	4.5	0.1	0	0	0.1	—
29702	Acorn winter, boiled, mashed	½	cup(s)	123	109.9	42	0.8	10.8	3.2	0.1	0	0	0	—
29451	Butternut, frozen, boiled	½	cup(s)	122	106.9	47	1.5	12.2	1.8	0.1	0	0	0	—
1661	Butternut winter, baked	½	cup(s)	102	89.5	41	0.9	10.7	3.4	0.1	0	0	0	—
32773	Butternut winter, frozen, boiled, mashed, no salt added	½	cup(s)	121	106.4	47	1.5	12.2	—	0.1	0	0	0	—
29700	Crookneck and straightneck summer, boiled, drained	½	cup(s)	65	60.9	12	0.6	2.6	1.2	0.1	0	0	0.1	—
29703	Hubbard winter, baked	½	cup(s)	102	86.8	51	2.5	11.0	—	0.6	0.1	0	0.3	—
1660	Hubbard winter, boiled, mashed	½	cup(s)	118	107.5	35	1.7	7.6	3.4	0.4	0.1	0	0.2	—
29704	Spaghetti winter, boiled, drained, or baked	½	cup(s)	78	71.5	21	0.5	5.0	1.1	0.2	0	0	0.1	—
664	Summer, all varieties, sliced, boiled, drained	½	cup(s)	90	84.3	18	0.8	3.9	1.3	0.3	0.1	0	0.1	—
665	Winter, all varieties, baked, mashed	½	cup(s)	103	91.4	38	0.9	9.1	2.9	0.4	0.1	0	0.2	—
1112	Zucchini summer, boiled, drained	½	cup(s)	90	85.3	14	0.6	3.5	1.3	0	0	0	0	—
1113	Zucchini summer, frozen, boiled, drained	½	cup(s)	112	105.6	19	1.3	4.0	1.4	0.1	0	0	0.1	—
	Sweet potatoes													
666	Baked, peeled	½	cup(s)	100	75.8	90	2.0	20.7	3.3	0.2	0	0	0.1	—
667	Boiled, mashed	½	cup(s)	164	131.4	125	2.2	29.1	4.1	0.2	0.1	0	0.1	—
668	Candied, home recipe	½	cup(s)	91	61.1	132	0.8	25.4	2.2	3.0	1.2	0.6	0.1	—
670	Canned, vacuum pack	½	cup(s)	100	76.0	91	1.7	21.1	1.8	0.2	0	0	0.1	—
2765	Frozen, baked	½	cup(s)	88	64.5	88	1.5	20.5	1.6	0.1	0	0	0.1	—
1136	Yams, baked or boiled, drained	½	cup(s)	68	47.7	79	1.0	18.7	2.7	0.1	0	0	0	—
32785	**Taro shoots, cooked, no salt added**	½	cup(s)	70	66.7	10	0.5	2.2	—	0.1	0	0	0	—
	Tomatillo													
8774	Raw	2	item(s)	68	62.3	22	0.7	4.0	1.3	0.7	0.1	0.1	0.3	—
8777	Raw, chopped	½	cup(s)	66	60.5	21	0.6	3.9	1.3	0.7	0.1	0.1	0.3	—
	Tomato													
16846	Cherry, fresh	5	item(s)	85	80.3	15	0.7	3.3	1.0	0.2	0	0	0.1	—
671	Fresh, ripe, red	1	item(s)	123	116.2	22	1.1	4.8	1.5	0.2	0	0	0.1	—
675	Juice, canned	½	cup(s)	122	114.1	21	0.9	5.2	0.5	0.1	0	0	0	—
75	Juice, no salt added	½	cup(s)	122	114.1	21	0.9	5.2	0.5	0.1	0	0	0	—
1699	Paste, canned	2	tablespoon(s)	33	24.1	27	1.4	6.2	1.3	0.2	0	0	0.1	—
1700	Puree, canned	¼	cup(s)	63	54.9	24	1.0	5.6	1.2	0.1	0	0	0.1	—
1118	Red, boiled	½	cup(s)	120	113.2	22	1.1	4.8	0.8	0.1	0	0	0.1	—
3952	Red, diced	½	cup(s)	90	85.1	16	0.8	3.5	1.1	0.2	0	0	0.1	—
1120	Red, stewed, canned	½	cup(s)	128	116.7	33	1.2	7.9	1.3	0.2	0	0	0.1	—
1125	Sauce, canned	¼	cup(s)	61	55.6	15	0.8	3.3	0.9	0.1	0	0	0	—
8778	Sun dried	½	cup(s)	27	3.9	70	3.8	15.1	3.3	0.8	0.1	0.1	0.3	—
8783	Sun dried in oil, drained	¼	cup(s)	28	14.8	59	1.4	6.4	1.6	3.9	0.5	2.4	0.6	—
	Turnips													
678	Turnip greens, chopped, boiled, drained	½	cup(s)	72	67.1	14	0.8	3.1	2.5	0.2	0	0	0.1	—
679	Turnip greens, frozen, chopped, boiled, drained	½	cup(s)	82	74.1	24	2.7	4.1	2.8	0.3	0.1	0	0.1	—
677	Turnips, cubed, boiled, drained	½	cup(s)	78	73.0	17	0.6	3.9	1.6	0.1	0	0	0	—
	Vegetables, mixed													
1132	Canned, drained	½	cup(s)	82	70.9	40	2.1	7.5	2.4	0.2	0	0	0.1	—
680	Frozen, boiled, drained	½	cup(s)	91	75.7	59	2.6	11.9	4.0	0.1	0	0	0.1	—

Chol (mg)	Calc (mg)	Iron (mg)	Magn (mg)	Pota (mg)	Sodi (mg)	Zinc (mg)	Vit A (μg)	Thia (mg)	Vit E (mg α)	Ribo (mg)	Niac (mg)	Vit B_6 (mg)	Fola (μg)	Vit C (mg)	Vit B_{12} (μg)	Sele (μg)
0	136	2.45	81.3	370.2	28.9	0.48	524.3	0.02	2.08	0.14	0.41	0.11	104.8	15.3	0	1.5
0	122	3.21	78.3	419.4	63.0	0.68	471.6	0.08	1.87	0.21	0.44	0.21	131.4	8.8	0	1.4
0	145	1.86	77.9	286.9	92.2	0.46	572.9	0.07	3.36	0.16	0.41	0.12	115.0	2.1	0	5.2
0	145	1.86	77.9	286.9	92.2	0.46	572.9	0.07	3.36	0.16	0.41	0.12	115.0	2.1	0	5.2
0	30	0.81	23.7	167.4	23.7	0.16	140.7	0.02	0.61	0.06	0.22	0.06	58.2	8.4	0	0.3
0	25	2.13	25.5	134.1	38.0	0.18	—	0.03	—	0.05	0.18	0.07	0	7.5	0	—
0	45	0.95	44.1	447.9	4.1	0.17	21.5	0.17	—	0.01	0.90	0.19	19.5	11.1	0	0.7
0	32	0.68	31.9	322.2	3.7	0.13	50.2	0.12	—	0.01	0.65	0.14	13.5	8.0	0	0.5
0	23	0.70	10.9	161.9	2.4	0.14	203.3	0.06	0.14	0.05	0.56	0.08	19.5	4.3	0	0.6
0	42	0.61	29.6	289.6	4.1	0.13	569.1	0.07	1.31	0.01	0.99	0.12	19.4	15.4	0	0.5
0	23	0.70	10.9	161.2	2.4	0.14	202.4	0.06	—	0.05	0.56	0.08	19.4	4.2	0	0.6
0	14	0.31	13.6	137.1	1.3	0.19	5.2	0.03	—	0.02	0.29	0.07	14.9	5.4	0	0.1
0	17	0.48	22.4	365.1	8.2	0.15	308.0	0.07	—	0.04	0.57	0.17	16.3	9.7	0	0.6
0	12	0.33	15.3	252.5	5.9	0.11	236.0	0.05	0.14	0.03	0.39	0.12	11.8	7.7	0	0.4
0	16	0.26	8.5	90.7	14.0	0.15	4.7	0.02	0.09	0.01	0.62	0.07	6.2	2.7	0	0.2
0	24	0.32	21.6	172.8	0.9	0.35	9.9	0.04	0.12	0.03	0.46	0.05	18.0	5.0	0	0.2
0	23	0.45	13.3	247.0	1.0	0.23	267.5	0.02	0.12	0.07	0.51	0.17	20.5	9.8	0	0.4
0	12	0.32	19.8	227.7	2.7	0.16	50.4	0.04	0.11	0.04	0.39	0.07	15.3	4.1	0	0.2
0	19	0.54	14.5	216.3	2.2	0.22	10	0.05	0.13	0.04	0.43	0.05	8.9	4.1	0	0.2
0	38	0.69	27.0	475.0	36.0	0.32	961.0	0.10	0.71	0.10	1.48	0.28	6.0	19.6	0	0.2
0	44	1.18	29.5	377.2	44.3	0.33	1290.7	0.09	1.54	0.08	0.88	0.27	9.8	21.0	0	0.3
7	24	1.03	10.0	172.6	63.9	0.13	0	0.01	—	0.03	0.36	0.03	10.0	6.1	0	0.7
0	22	0.89	22.0	312.0	53.0	0.18	399.0	0.04	1.00	0.06	0.74	0.19	17.0	26.4	0	0.7
0	31	0.47	18.4	330.1	7.0	0.26	913.3	0.05	0.67	0.04	0.49	0.16	19.3	8.0	0	0.5
0	10	0.35	12.2	455.6	5.4	0.13	4.1	0.06	0.23	0.01	0.37	0.15	10.9	8.2	0	0.5
0	10	0.28	5.6	240.8	1.4	0.37	2.1	0.02	—	0.03	0.56	0.07	2.1	13.2	0	0.7
0	5	0.42	13.6	182.2	0.7	0.15	4.1	0.03	0.25	0.02	1.25	0.03	4.8	8.0	0	0.3
0	5	0.41	13.2	176.9	0.7	0.15	4.0	0.03	0.25	0.02	1.22	0.04	4.6	7.7	0	0.3
0	9	0.22	9.4	201.5	4.3	0.14	35.7	0.03	0.45	0.01	0.50	0.06	12.8	10.8	0	0
0	12	0.33	13.5	291.5	6.2	0.20	51.7	0.04	0.66	0.02	0.73	0.09	18.5	15.6	0	0
0	12	0.52	13.4	278.2	326.8	0.18	27.9	0.06	0.39	0.04	0.82	0.14	24.3	22.2	0	0.4
0	12	0.52	13.4	278.2	12.2	0.18	27.9	0.06	0.39	0.04	0.82	0.14	24.3	22.2	0	0.4
0	12	0.97	13.8	332.6	259.1	0.20	24.9	0.02	1.41	0.05	1.00	0.07	3.9	7.2	0	1.7
0	11	1.11	14.4	274.4	249.4	0.22	16.3	0.01	1.23	0.05	0.91	0.07	6.9	6.6	0	0.4
0	13	0.82	10.8	261.6	13.2	0.17	28.8	0.04	0.67	0.03	0.64	0.10	15.6	27.4	0	0.6
0	9	0.24	9.9	213.3	4.5	0.15	37.8	0.03	0.48	0.01	0.53	0.07	13.5	11.4	0	0
0	43	1.70	15.3	263.9	281.8	0.22	11.5	0.06	1.06	0.04	0.91	0.02	6.4	10.1	0	0.8
0	8	0.62	9.8	201.9	319.6	0.12	10.4	0.01	0.87	0.04	0.59	0.06	6.7	4.3	0	0.1
0	30	2.45	52.4	925.3	565.7	0.53	11.9	0.14	0.00	0.13	2.44	0.09	18.4	10.6	0	1.5
0	13	0.73	22.3	430.4	73.2	0.21	17.6	0.05	—	0.10	0.99	0.08	6.3	28.0	0	0.8
0	99	0.58	15.8	146.2	20.9	0.10	274.3	0.03	1.35	0.05	0.30	0.13	85.0	19.7	0	0.6
0	125	1.59	21.3	183.7	12.3	0.34	441.2	0.04	2.18	0.06	0.38	0.06	32.0	17.9	0	1.0
0	26	0.14	7.0	138.1	12.5	0.09	0	0.02	0.02	0.02	0.23	0.05	7.0	9.0	0	0.2
0	22	0.86	13.0	237.2	121.4	0.33	475.1	0.04	0.24	0.04	0.47	0.06	19.6	4.1	0	0.2
0	23	0.74	20.0	153.8	31.9	0.44	194.7	0.06	0.34	0.10	0.77	0.06	17.3	2.9	0	0.3

TABLE A-1 Table of Food Composition *(continued)*

(Computer code is for Cengage Diet Analysis program) (For purposes of calculations, use "0" for t, <1, <.1, <.01, etc.)

DA+ Code	Food Description	QTY	Measure	Wt (g)	H_2O (g)	Ener (cal)	Prot (g)	Carb (g)	Fiber (g)	Fat (g)	Fat Breakdown (g) Sat	Mono	Poly	Trans
	Vegetables, Legumes—continued													
7489	V8 100% vegetable juice	½	cup(s)	120	—	25	1.0	5.0	1.0	0	0	0	0	0
7490	V8 low sodium vegetable juice	½	cup(s)	120	—	25	0	6.5	1.0	0	0	0	0	0
7491	V8 spicy hot vegetable juice	½	cup(s)	120	—	25	1.0	5.0	0.5	0	0	0	0	0
	Water chestnuts													
31073	Sliced, drained	½	cup(s)	75	70.0	20	0	5.0	1.0	0	0	0	0	0
31087	Whole	½	cup(s)	75	70.0	20	0	5.0	1.0	0	0	0	0	0
1135	**Watercress**	1	cup(s)	34	32.3	4	0.8	0.4	0.2	0	0	0	0	—
	Nuts, Seeds, and Products													
	Almonds													
32940	Almond butter with salt added	1	tablespoon(s)	16	0.2	101	2.4	3.4	0.6	9.5	0.9	6.1	2.0	—
1137	Almond butter, no salt added	1	tablespoon(s)	16	0.2	101	2.4	3.4	0.6	9.5	0.9	6.1	2.0	—
32886	Blanched	¼	cup(s)	36	1.6	211	8.0	7.2	3.8	18.3	1.4	11.7	4.4	—
32887	Dry roasted, no salt added	¼	cup(s)	35	0.9	206	7.6	6.7	4.1	18.2	1.4	11.6	4.4	—
29724	Dry roasted, salted	¼	cup(s)	35	0.9	206	7.6	6.7	4.1	18.2	1.4	11.6	4.4	—
29725	Oil roasted, salted	¼	cup(s)	39	1.1	238	8.3	6.9	4.1	21.7	1.7	13.7	5.3	—
508	Slivered	¼	cup(s)	27	1.3	155	5.7	5.9	3.3	13.3	1.0	8.3	3.3	0
1138	**Beechnuts, dried**	¼	cup(s)	57	3.8	328	3.5	19.1	5.3	28.5	3.3	12.5	11.4	—
517	**Brazil nuts, dried, unblanched**	¼	cup(s)	35	1.2	230	5.0	4.3	2.6	23.3	5.3	8.6	7.2	—
1166	**Breadfruit seeds, roasted**	¼	cup(s)	57	28.3	118	3.5	22.8	3.4	1.5	0.4	0.2	0.8	—
1139	**Butternuts, dried**	¼	cup(s)	30	1.0	184	7.5	3.6	1.4	17.1	0.4	3.1	12.8	—
	Cashews													
32931	Cashew butter with salt added	1	tablespoon(s)	16	0.5	94	2.8	4.4	0.3	7.9	1.6	4.7	1.3	—
32889	Cashew butter, no salt added	1	tablespoon(s)	16	0.5	94	2.8	4.4	0.3	7.9	1.6	4.7	1.3	—
1140	Dry roasted	¼	cup(s)	34	0.6	197	5.2	11.2	1.0	15.9	3.1	9.4	2.7	—
518	Oil roasted	¼	cup(s)	32	1.1	187	5.4	9.6	1.1	15.4	2.7	8.4	2.8	—
	Coconut, shredded													
32896	Dried, not sweetened	¼	cup(s)	23	0.7	152	1.6	5.4	3.8	14.9	13.2	0.6	0.2	—
1153	Dried, shredded, sweetened	¼	cup(s)	23	2.9	116	0.7	11.1	1.0	8.3	7.3	0.4	0.1	—
520	Shredded	¼	cup(s)	20	9.4	71	0.7	3.0	1.8	6.7	5.9	0.3	0.1	—
	Chestnuts													
1152	Chinese, roasted	¼	cup(s)	36	14.6	87	1.6	19.0	—	0.4	0.1	0.2	0.1	—
32895	European, boiled and steamed	¼	cup(s)	46	31.3	60	0.9	12.8	—	0.6	0.1	0.2	0.2	—
32911	European, roasted	¼	cup(s)	36	14.5	88	1.1	18.9	1.8	0.8	0.1	0.3	0.3	—
32922	Japanese, boiled and steamed	¼	cup(s)	36	31.0	20	0.3	4.5	—	0.1	0	0	0	—
32923	Japanese, roasted	¼	cup(s)	36	18.1	73	1.1	16.4	—	0.3	0	0.1	0.1	—
4958	**Flax seeds or linseeds**	¼	cup(s)	43	3.3	225	8.4	12.3	11.9	17.7	1.7	3.2	12.6	0
32904	**Ginkgo nuts, dried**	¼	cup(s)	39	4.8	136	4.0	28.3	—	0.8	0.1	0.3	0.3	—
	Hazelnuts or filberts													
32901	Blanched	¼	cup(s)	30	1.7	189	4.1	5.1	3.3	18.3	1.4	14.5	1.7	—
32902	Dry roasted, no salt added	¼	cup(s)	30	0.8	194	4.5	5.3	2.8	18.7	1.3	14.0	2.5	—
1156	**Hickory nuts, dried**	¼	cup(s)	30	0.8	197	3.8	5.5	1.9	19.3	2.1	9.8	6.6	—
	Macadamias													
32905	Dry roasted, no salt added	¼	cup(s)	34	0.5	241	2.6	4.5	2.7	25.5	4.0	19.9	0.5	—
32932	Dry roasted, with salt added	¼	cup(s)	34	0.5	240	2.6	4.3	2.7	25.5	4.0	19.9	0.5	—
1157	Raw	¼	cup(s)	34	0.5	241	2.6	4.6	2.9	25.4	4.0	19.7	0.5	—
	Mixed nuts													
1159	With peanuts, dry roasted	¼	cup(s)	34	0.6	203	5.9	8.7	3.1	17.6	2.4	10.8	3.7	—
32933	With peanuts, dry roasted, with salt added	¼	cup(s)	34	0.6	203	5.9	8.7	3.1	17.6	2.4	10.8	3.7	—
32906	Without peanuts, oil roasted, no salt added	¼	cup(s)	36	1.1	221	5.6	8.0	2.0	20.2	3.3	11.9	4.1	—
	Peanuts													
2807	Dry roasted	¼	cup(s)	37	0.6	214	8.6	7.9	2.9	18.1	2.5	9.0	5.7	—
2806	Dry roasted, salted	¼	cup(s)	37	0.6	214	8.6	7.9	2.9	18.1	2.5	9.0	5.7	—

Chol (mg)	Calc (mg)	Iron (mg)	Magn (mg)	Pota (mg)	Sodi (mg)	Zinc (mg)	Vit A (µg)	Thia (mg)	Vit E (mg α)	Ribo (mg)	Niac (mg)	Vit B_6 (mg)	Fola (µg)	Vit C (mg)	Vit B_{12} (µg)	Sele (µg)
0	20	0.36	12.9	260.0	310.0	0.24	100.0	0.05	—	0.03	0.87	0.17	—	30.0	0	—
0	20	0.36	—	450.0	70.0	—	100.0	0.02	—	0.02	0.75	—	—	30.0	0	—
0	20	0.36	12.9	240.0	360.0	0.24	50.0	0.05	—	0.03	0.88	0.17	—	15.0	0	—
0	7	0.00	—	—	5.0	—	0	—	—	—	—	—	—	2.0	—	—
0	7	0.00	—	—	5.0	—	0	—	—	—	—	—	—	2.0	—	—
0	41	0.06	7.1	112.2	13.9	0.03	54.4	0.03	0.34	0.04	0.06	0.04	3.1	14.6	0	0.3
0	43	0.59	48.5	121.3	72.0	0.49	0	0.02	4.16	0.10	0.46	0.01	10.4	0.1	0	0.8
0	43	0.59	48.5	121.3	1.8	0.48	0	0.02	—	0.09	0.46	0.01	10.4	0.1	0	—
0	78	1.34	99.7	249.0	10.2	1.13	0	0.07	8.95	0.20	1.32	0.04	10.9	0	0	1.0
0	92	1.55	98.7	257.4	0.3	1.22	0	0.02	8.97	0.29	1.32	0.04	11.4	0	0	1.0
0	92	1.55	98.7	257.4	117.0	1.22	0	0.02	8.97	0.29	1.32	0.04	11.4	0	0	1.0
0	114	1.44	107.5	274.4	133.1	1.20	0	0.03	10.19	0.30	1.43	0.04	10.6	0	0	1.1
0	71	1.00	72.4	190.4	0.3	0.83	0	0.05	7.07	0.27	0.91	0.03	13.5	0	0	0.7
0	1	1.39	0	579.7	21.7	0.20	0	0.16	—	0.20	0.48	0.38	64.4	8.8	0	4.0
0	56	0.85	131.6	230.7	1.1	1.42	0	0.21	2.00	0.01	0.10	0.03	7.7	0.2	0	671.0
0	49	0.50	35.3	616.7	15.9	0.58	8.5	0.22	—	0.12	4.20	0.22	33.6	4.3	0	8.0
0	16	1.21	71.1	126.3	0.3	0.94	1.8	0.12	—	0.04	0.31	0.17	19.8	1.0	0	5.2
0	7	0.81	41.3	87.4	98.2	0.83	0	0.05	0.15	0.03	0.26	0.04	10.9	0	0	1.8
0	7	0.81	41.3	87.4	2.4	0.83	0	0.05	—	0.03	0.26	0.04	10.9	0	0	1.8
0	15	2.06	89.1	193.5	5.5	1.92	0	0.07	0.32	0.07	0.48	0.09	23.6	0	0	4.0
0	14	1.95	88.0	203.8	4.2	1.73	0	0.12	0.30	0.07	0.56	0.10	8.1	0.1	0	6.5
0	6	0.76	20.7	125.2	8.5	0.46	0	0.01	0.10	0.02	0.13	0.07	2.1	0.3	0	4.3
0	3	0.45	11.6	78.4	60.9	0.42	0	0.01	0.09	0.00	0.11	0.06	1.9	0.2	0	3.9
0	3	0.48	6.4	71.2	4.0	0.21	0	0.01	0.04	0.00	0.11	0.01	5.2	0.7	0	2.0
0	7	0.54	32.6	173.0	1.4	0.33	0	0.05	—	0.03	0.54	0.15	26.1	13.9	0	2.6
0	21	0.80	24.8	328.9	12.4	0.11	0.5	0.06	—	0.03	0.32	0.10	17.5	12.3	0	—
0	10	0.32	11.8	211.6	0.7	0.20	0.4	0.08	0.18	0.05	0.48	0.18	25.0	9.3	0	0.4
0	4	0.19	6.5	42.8	1.8	0.14	0.4	0.04	—	0.01	0.19	0.03	6.1	3.4	0	—
0	13	0.75	23.2	154.8	6.9	0.51	1.4	0.15	—	—	0.24	0.14	21.4	10.1	0	—
0	142	2.13	156.1	354.0	11.9	1.83	0	0.06	0.14	0.06	0.59	0.39	118.4	0.5	0	2.3
0	8	0.62	20.7	390.2	5.1	0.26	21.5	0.17	—	0.07	4.58	0.25	41.4	11.4	0	—
0	45	0.98	48.0	197.4	0	0.66	0.6	0.14	5.25	0.03	0.46	0.17	23.4	0.6	0	1.2
0	37	1.31	51.9	226.5	0	0.74	0.9	0.10	4.58	0.03	0.61	0.18	26.4	1.1	0	1.2
0	18	0.64	51.9	130.8	0.3	1.29	2.1	0.26	—	0.04	0.27	0.06	12.0	0.6	0	2.4
0	23	0.88	39.5	121.6	1.3	0.43	0	0.23	0.19	0.02	0.76	0.12	3.4	0.2	0	3.9
0	23	0.88	39.5	121.6	88.8	0.43	0	0.23	0.19	0.02	0.76	0.12	3.4	0.2	0	3.9
0	28	1.24	43.6	123.3	1.7	0.44	0	0.40	0.18	0.05	0.83	0.09	3.7	0.4	0	1.2
0	24	1.27	77.1	204.5	4.1	1.30	0.3	0.07	—	0.07	1.61	0.10	17.1	0.1	0	1.0
0	24	1.26	77.1	204.5	229.1	1.30	0	0.06	3.74	0.06	1.61	0.10	17.1	0.1	0	2.6
0	38	0.92	90.4	195.8	4.0	1.67	0.4	0.18	—	0.17	0.70	0.06	20.2	0.2	0	—
0	20	0.82	64.2	240.2	2.2	1.20	0	0.16	2.52	0.03	4.93	0.09	52.9	0	0	2.7
0	20	0.82	64.2	240.2	296.7	1.20	0	0.16	2.84	0.03	4.93	0.09	52.9	0	0	2.7

(Computer code is for Cengage Diet Analysis program) (For purposes of calculations, use "0" for t, <1, <.1, <.01, etc.)

DA+ Code	Food Description	Qty	Measure	Wt (g)	H_2O (g)	Ener (cal)	Prot (g)	Carb (g)	Fiber (g)	Fat (g)	Fat Breakdown (g) Sat	Mono	Poly	Trans
	Nuts, Seeds, and Products—continued													
1763	Oil roasted, salted	¼	cup(s)	36	0.5	216	10.1	5.5	3.4	18.9	3.1	9.4	5.5	—
1884	Peanut butter, chunky	1	tablespoon(s)	16	0.2	94	3.8	3.5	1.3	8.0	1.3	3.9	2.4	—
30303	Peanut butter, low sodium	1	tablespoon(s)	16	0.2	95	4.0	3.1	0.9	8.2	1.8	3.9	2.2	—
30305	Peanut butter, reduced fat	1	tablespoon(s)	18	0.2	94	4.7	6.4	0.9	6.1	1.3	2.9	1.8	—
524	Peanut butter, smooth	1	tablespoon(s)	16	0.3	94	4.0	3.1	1.0	8.1	1.7	3.9	2.3	—
2804	Raw	¼	cup(s)	37	2.4	207	9.4	5.9	3.1	18.0	2.5	8.9	5.7	—
	Pecans													
32907	Dry roasted, no salt added	¼	cup(s)	28	0.3	198	2.6	3.8	2.6	20.7	1.8	12.3	5.7	—
32936	Dry roasted, with salt added	¼	cup(s)	27	0.3	192	2.6	3.7	2.5	20.0	1.7	11.9	5.6	—
1162	Oil roasted	¼	cup(s)	28	0.3	197	2.5	3.6	2.6	20.7	2.0	11.3	6.5	—
526	Raw	¼	cup(s)	27	1.0	188	2.5	3.8	2.6	19.6	1.7	11.1	5.9	—
12973	**Pine nuts or pignolia, dried**	1	tablespoon(s)	9	0.2	58	1.2	1.1	0.3	5.9	0.4	1.6	2.9	—
	Pistachios													
1164	Dry roasted	¼	cup(s)	31	0.6	176	6.6	8.5	3.2	14.1	1.7	7.4	4.3	—
32938	Dry roasted, with salt added	¼	cup(s)	32	0.6	182	6.8	8.6	3.3	14.7	1.8	7.7	4.4	—
1167	**Pumpkin or squash seeds, roasted**	¼	cup(s)	57	4.0	296	18.7	7.6	2.2	23.9	4.5	7.4	10.9	—
	Sesame													
32912	Sesame butter paste	1	tablespoon(s)	16	0.3	94	2.9	3.8	0.9	8.1	1.1	3.1	3.6	—
32941	Tahini or sesame butter	1	tablespoon(s)	15	0.5	89	2.6	3.2	0.7	8.0	1.1	3.0	3.5	—
1169	Whole, roasted, toasted	3	tablespoon(s)	10	0.3	54	1.6	2.4	1.3	4.6	0.6	1.7	2.0	—
	Soy nuts													
34173	Deep sea salted	¼	cup(s)	28	—	119	11.9	8.9	4.9	4.0	1.0	—	—	—
34174	Unsalted	¼	cup(s)	28	—	119	11.9	8.9	4.9	4.0	0	—	—	—
	Sunflower seeds													
528	Kernels, dried	1	tablespoon(s)	9	0.4	53	1.9	1.8	0.8	4.6	0.4	1.7	2.1	—
29721	Kernels, dry roasted, salted	1	tablespoon(s)	8	0.1	47	1.5	1.9	0.7	4.0	0.4	0.8	2.6	—
29723	Kernels, toasted, salted	1	tablespoon(s)	8	0.1	52	1.4	1.7	1.0	4.8	0.5	0.9	3.1	—
32928	Sunflower seed butter with salt added	1	tablespoon(s)	16	0.2	93	3.1	4.4	—	7.6	0.8	1.5	5.0	—
	Trail mix													
4646	Trail mix	¼	cup(s)	38	3.5	173	5.2	16.8	2.0	11.0	2.1	4.7	3.6	—
4647	Trail mix with chocolate chips	¼	cup(s)	38	2.5	182	5.3	16.8	—	12.0	2.3	5.1	4.2	—
4648	Tropical trail mix	¼	cup(s)	35	3.2	142	2.2	23.0	—	6.0	3.0	0.9	1.8	—
	Walnuts													
529	Dried black, chopped	¼	cup(s)	31	1.4	193	7.5	3.1	2.1	18.4	1.1	4.7	11.0	—
531	English or Persian	¼	cup(s)	29	1.2	191	4.5	4.0	2.0	19.1	1.8	2.6	13.8	—
	Vegetarian Foods													
	Prepared													
34222	Brown rice and tofu stir-fry (vegan)	8	ounce(s)	227	244.4	302	16.5	18.0	3.2	21.0	1.7	4.7	13.4	0
34368	Cheese enchilada casserole (lacto)	8	ounce(s)	227	80.3	385	16.6	38.4	4.1	17.8	9.5	6.1	1.1	—
34247	Five bean casserole (vegan)	8	ounce(s)	227	175.8	178	5.9	26.6	6.0	5.8	1.1	2.5	1.9	0
34261	Lentil stew (vegan)	8	ounce(s)	227	227.9	188	11.5	35.9	11.0	0.7	0.1	0.1	0.3	0
34397	Macaroni and cheese (lacto)	8	ounce(s)	227	352.1	391	18.1	37.1	1.0	18.7	9.8	6.0	1.8	0
34238	Steamed rice and vegetables (vegan)	8	ounce(s)	227	222.9	587	11.2	87.9	5.8	23.1	4.1	8.7	9.1	0
34308	Tofu rice burgers (ovo-lacto)	1	piece(s)	218	77.6	435	22.4	68.6	5.6	8.4	1.7	2.4	3.5	—
34276	Vegan spinach enchiladas (vegan)	1	piece(s)	82	59.2	93	4.9	14.5	1.8	2.4	0.3	0.6	1.3	—
34243	Vegetable chow mein (vegan)	8	ounce(s)	227	163.3	166	6.5	22.1	2.0	6.4	0.7	2.7	2.5	0
34454	Vegetable lasagna (lacto)	8	ounce(s)	227	178.9	208	13.7	29.9	2.6	4.1	2.3	1.1	0.3	—
34339	Vegetable marinara (vegan)	8	ounce(s)	252	200.7	104	3.0	16.7	1.4	3.1	0.4	1.4	1.0	0
34356	Vegetable rice casserole (lacto)	8	ounce(s)	227	178.9	238	9.7	24.4	4.0	12.5	4.9	3.5	3.1	—
34311	Vegetable strudel (ovo-lacto)	8	ounce(s)	227	63.1	478	12.0	32.4	2.5	33.8	11.5	16.7	3.9	0
34371	Vegetable taco (lacto)	1	item(s)	85	46.5	117	4.2	13.6	2.9	5.6	2.1	1.9	1.3	—
34282	Vegetarian chili (vegan)	8	ounce(s)	227	191.4	115	5.6	21.4	7.1	1.5	0.2	0.3	0.7	0
34367	Vegetarian vegetable soup (vegan)	8	ounce(s)	227	257.9	111	3.2	16.0	3.2	5.0	1.0	2.1	1.6	0
	Boca burger													
32067	All American flamed grilled patty	1	item(s)	71	—	90	14.0	4.0	3.0	3.0	1.0	—	—	0
32074	Boca chik'n nuggets	4	item(s)	87	—	180	14.0	17.0	3.0	7.0	1.0	—	—	0

Chol (mg)	Calc (mg)	Iron (mg)	Magn (mg)	Pota (mg)	Sodi (mg)	Zinc (mg)	Vit A (μg)	Thia (mg)	Vit E (mg α)	Ribo (mg)	Niac (mg)	Vit B_6 (mg)	Fola (μg)	Vit C (mg)	Vit B_{12} (μg)	Sele (μg)
0	22	0.54	63.4	261.4	115.2	1.18	0	0.03	2.49	0.03	4.97	0.16	43.2	0.3	0	1.2
0	7	0.30	25.6	119.2	77.8	0.45	0	0.02	1.01	0.02	2.19	0.07	14.7	0	0	1.3
0	6	0.29	25.4	107.0	2.7	0.47	0	0.01	1.23	0.02	2.14	0.07	11.8	0	0	1.2
0	6	0.34	30.6	120.4	97.2	0.50	0	0.05	1.20	0.01	2.63	0.06	10.8	0	0	1.4
0	7	0.30	24.6	103.8	73.4	0.47	0	0.01	1.44	0.02	2.14	0.09	11.8	0	0	0.9
0	34	1.67	61.3	257.3	6.6	1.19	0	0.23	3.04	0.04	4.40	0.12	87.6	0	0	2.6
0	20	0.78	36.8	118.3	0.3	1.41	1.9	0.12	0.35	0.03	0.32	0.05	4.5	0.2	0	1.1
0	19	0.75	35.6	114.5	103.4	1.36	1.9	0.11	0.34	0.03	0.31	0.05	4.3	0.2	0	1.1
0	18	0.68	33.3	107.8	0.3	1.23	1.4	0.13	0.70	0.03	0.33	0.05	4.1	0.2	0	1.7
0	19	0.69	33.0	111.7	0	1.23	0.8	0.18	0.38	0.04	0.32	0.06	6.0	0.3	0	1.0
0	1	0.47	21.6	51.3	0.2	0.55	0.1	0.03	0.80	0.02	0.37	0.01	2.9	0.1	0	0.1
0	34	1.29	36.9	320.4	3.1	0.71	4.0	0.26	0.59	0.05	0.44	0.39	15.4	0.7	0	2.9
0	35	1.34	38.4	333.4	129.6	0.73	4.2	0.26	0.61	0.05	0.45	0.40	16.0	0.7	0	3.0
0	24	8.48	303.0	457.4	10.2	4.22	10.8	0.12	0.00	0.18	0.99	0.05	32.3	1.0	0	3.2
0	154	3.07	57.9	93.1	1.9	1.17	0.5	0.04	—	0.03	1.07	0.13	16.0	0	0	0.9
0	21	0.66	14.3	68.9	5.3	0.69	0.5	0.24	—	0.02	0.85	0.02	14.7	0.6	0	0.3
0	94	1.40	33.8	45.1	1.0	0.68	0	0.07	—	0.02	0.43	0.07	9.3	0	0	0.5
0	59	1.07	—	—	148.1	—	0	—	—	—	—	—	—	0	—	—
0	59	1.07	—	—	9.9	—	0	—	—	—	—	—	—	0	—	—
0	7	0.47	29.3	58.1	0.8	0.45	0.3	0.13	2.99	0.03	0.75	0.12	20.4	0.1	0	4.8
0	6	0.30	10.3	68.0	32.8	0.42	0	0.01	2.09	0.02	0.56	0.06	19.0	0.1	0	6.3
0	5	0.57	10.8	41.1	51.3	0.44	0	0.03	—	0.02	0.35	0.07	19.9	0.1	0	5.2
0	20	0.76	59.0	11.5	83.2	0.85	0.5	0.05	—	0.05	0.85	0.13	37.9	0.4	0	—
0	29	1.14	59.3	256.9	85.9	1.20	0.4	0.17	—	0.07	1.76	0.11	26.6	0.5	0	—
2	41	1.27	60.4	243.0	45.4	1.17	0.8	0.15	—	0.08	1.65	0.09	24.4	0.5	0	—
0	20	0.92	33.6	248.2	3.5	0.41	0.7	0.15	—	0.04	0.51	0.11	14.7	2.7	0	—
0	19	0.97	62.8	163.4	0.6	1.05	0.6	0.01	0.56	0.04	0.14	0.18	9.7	0.5	0	5.3
0	29	0.85	46.2	129.0	0.6	0.90	0.3	0.10	0.20	0.04	0.32	0.15	28.7	0.4	0	1.4
0	353	6.34	118.3	501.4	142.2	2.03	—	0.23	0.07	0.14	1.49	0.36	51.8	24.8	0	14.8
39	441	2.44	34.6	191.2	1139.7	1.84	—	0.31	0.05	0.35	2.23	0.11	87.1	20.4	0.4	20.0
0	48	1.78	40.8	364.1	613.6	0.61	—	0.10	0.52	0.07	0.93	0.11	39.4	8.3	0	3.3
0	34	3.23	50.0	548.8	436.5	1.42	—	0.24	0.14	0.16	2.31	0.29	91.4	26.4	0	12.1
43	415	1.71	45.4	267.8	1641.0	2.32	—	0.32	0.27	0.48	2.18	0.13	74.2	0.9	0.8	33.3
0	91	3.31	153.1	810.1	3117.8	2.04	—	0.37	3.03	0.21	6.16	0.64	61.7	35.2	0	18.8
52	467	9.01	89.7	455.6	2449.5	2.06	—	0.27	0.12	0.26	3.43	0.29	106.6	2.0	0.1	43.0
0	117	1.13	40.4	170.5	134.2	0.68	—	0.07	—	0.07	0.53	0.10	52.1	1.8	0	5.1
0	189	3.70	28.0	310.3	372.7	0.76	—	0.13	0.05	0.11	1.43	0.14	45.6	8.0	0	6.5
10	176	1.86	41.9	470.0	759.4	1.14	—	0.26	0.05	0.25	2.49	0.22	64.7	19.0	0.4	21.8
0	17	0.94	19.1	189.9	439.6	0.42	—	0.15	0.55	0.08	1.36	0.12	40.6	23.5	0	10.8
17	190	1.28	29.3	414.2	626.0	1.24	—	0.16	0.35	0.29	2.00	0.19	72.6	56.0	0.2	5.8
29	200	2.15	24.5	181.0	512.1	1.24	—	0.28	0.20	0.31	2.88	0.11	88.3	17.4	0.2	19.7
7	77	0.88	26.3	174.1	280.7	0.59	—	0.08	0.04	0.06	0.49	0.08	38.7	4.6	0	3.0
0	65	1.98	41.0	543.1	390.7	0.74	—	0.14	0.15	0.10	1.31	0.18	59.3	20.3	0	4.4
0	46	1.87	34.9	550.3	729.5	0.56	—	0.13	0.55	0.09	1.99	0.27	47.8	29.9	0	1.4
5	150	1.80	—	—	280.0	—	0	—	—	—	—	—	—	0	—	—
0	40	1.44	—	—	500.0	—	—	—	—	—	—	—	—	0	—	—

TABLE A-1 Table of Food Composition *(continued)*

(Computer code is for Cengage Diet Analysis program) (For purposes of calculations, use "0" for t, <1, <.1, <.01, etc.)

DA+ Code	Food Description	QTY	Measure	Wt (g)	H_2O (g)	Ener (cal)	Prot (g)	Carb (g)	Fiber (g)	Fat (g)	Fat Breakdown (g) Sat	Mono	Poly	Trans
Vegetarian Foods—continued														
32075	Boca meatless ground burger	½	cup(s)	57	—	60	13.0	6.0	3.0	0.5	0	—	—	0
32072	Breakfast links	2	item(s)	45	—	70	8.0	5.0	2.0	3.0	0.5	—	—	0
32071	Breakfast patties	1	item(s)	38	—	60	7.0	5.0	2.0	2.5	0	—	—	0
35780	Cheeseburger meatless burger patty	1	item(s)	71	—	100	12.0	5.0	3.0	5.0	1.5	—	—	0
33958	Original meatless chik'n patties	1	item(s)	71	—	160	11.0	15.0	2.0	6.0	1.0	—	—	0
32066	Original patty	1	item(s)	71	—	70	13.0	6.0	4.0	0.5	0	—	—	0
32068	Roasted garlic patty	1	item(s)	71	—	70	12.0	6.0	4.0	1.5	0	—	—	0
37814	Roasted onion meatless burger patty	1	item(s)	71	—	70	11.0	7.0	4.0	1.0	0	—	—	0
	Gardenburger													
37810	BBQ chik'n with sauce	1	item(s)	142	—	250	14.0	30.0	5.0	8.0	1.0	—	—	0
39661	Black bean burger	1	item(s)	71	—	80	8.0	11.0	4.0	2.0	0	—	—	0
39666	Buffalo chik'n wing	3	item(s)	95	—	180	9.0	8.0	5.0	12.0	1.5	—	—	0
39665	Country fried chicken with creamy pepper gravy	1	item(s)	142	—	190	9.0	16.0	2.0	9.0	1.0	—	—	0
37808	Flamed grilled chik'n	1	item(s)	71	—	100	13.0	5.0	3.0	2.5	0	—	—	0
37803	Garden vegan	1	item(s)	71	—	100	10.0	12.0	2.0	1.0	—	—	—	0
39663	Homestyle classic burger	1	item(s)	71	—	110	12.0	6.0	4.0	5.0	0.5	—	—	0
37807	Meatless breakfast sausage	1	item(s)	43	—	50	5.0	2.0	2.0	3.5	0	—	—	0
37809	Meatless meatballs	6	item(s)	85	—	110	12.0	8.0	4.0	4.5	1.0	—	—	0
37806	Meatless riblets with sauce	1	item(s)	142	—	160	17.0	11.0	4.0	5.0	0	—	—	0
29913	Original	1	item(s)	71	—	90	10.0	8.0	3.0	2.0	0.5	—	—	0
39662	Sun-dried tomato basil burger	1	item(s)	71	—	80	10.0	11.0	3.0	1.5	0.5	—	—	0
29915	Veggie medley	1	item(s)	71	—	90	9.0	11.0	4.0	2.0	0	—	—	0
	Loma Linda													
9311	Big franks, canned	1	item(s)	51	—	110	11.0	3.0	2.0	6.0	1.0	1.5	3.5	0
9323	Fried chik'n with gravy	2	piece(s)	80	45.9	150	12.0	5.0	2.0	10	1.5	2.5	5.0	0
9326	Linketts, canned	1	item(s)	35	21.0	70	7.0	1.0	1.0	4.0	0.5	1.0	2.5	0
9336	Redi-Burger patties, canned	1	slice(s)	85	50.5	120	18.0	7.0	4.0	2.5	0.5	0.5	1.5	0
9350	Swiss Stake pattie with gravy, frozen	1	piece(s)	92	65.7	130	9.0	9.0	3.0	6.0	1.0	1.5	3.5	0
9354	Tender Rounds meatball substitute, canned in gravy	6	piece(s)	80	53.9	120	13.0	6.0	1.0	4.5	0.5	1.5	2.5	0
	Morningstar Farms													
33707	America's Original Veggie Dog links	1	item(s)	57	—	80	11.0	6.0	1.0	0.5	0	—	—	0
9362	Better'n Eggs egg substitute	¼	cup(s)	57	50.3	20	5.0	0	0	0	0	0	0	0
9371	Breakfast bacon strips	2	item(s)	16	6.8	60	2.0	2.0	0.5	4.5	0.5	1.0	3.0	0
9368	Breakfast sausage links	2	item(s)	45	26.8	80	9.0	3.0	2.0	3.0	0.5	1.5	1.0	0
33705	Chik'n nuggets	4	piece(s)	86	—	190	12.0	18.0	2.0	7.0	1.0	2.0	4.0	0
11587	Chik patties	1	item(s)	71	36.3	150	9.0	16.0	2.0	6.0	1.0	1.5	2.5	0
2531	Garden veggie patties	1	item(s)	67	40.1	100	10.0	9.0	4.0	2.5	0.5	0.5	1.5	0
33702	Spicy black bean veggie burger	1	item(s)	78	—	140	12.0	15.0	3.0	4.0	0.5	1.0	2.5	0
9412	Vegetarian chili, canned	1	cup(s)	230	172.6	180	16.0	25.0	10.0	1.5	0.5	0.5	0.5	0
	Worthington													
9424	Chili, canned	1	cup(s)	230	167.0	280	24.0	25.0	8.0	10.0	1.5	1.5	7.0	0
9436	Diced chik, canned	¼	cup(s)	55	42.7	50	9.0	2.0	1.0	0	0	0	0	0
9440	Dinner roast, frozen	1	slice(s)	85	53.2	180	14.0	6.0	3.0	11.0	1.5	4.5	5.0	0
9420	Meatless chicken slices, frozen	3	slice(s)	57	38.9	90	9.0	2.0	0.5	4.5	1.0	1.0	2.5	0
36702	Meatless chicken style roll, frozen	1	slice(s)	55	—	90	9.0	2.0	1.0	4.5	1.0	1.0	2.5	0
9428	Meatless corned beef, sliced, frozen	3	slice(s)	57	31.2	140	10.0	5.0	0	9.0	1.0	2.0	5.0	0
9470	Meatless salami, sliced, frozen	3	slice(s)	57	32.4	120	12.0	3.0	2.0	7.0	1.0	1.0	5.0	0
9480	Meatless smoked turkey, sliced	3	slice(s)	57	—	140	10.0	4.0	0	9.0	1.5	2.0	5.0	0
9462	Prosage links	2	item(s)	45	26.8	80	9.0	3.0	2.0	3.0	0.5	0.5	2.0	0
9484	Stakelets patty beef steak substitute, frozen	1	piece(s)	71	41.5	150	14.0	7.0	2.0	7.0	1.0	2.5	3.5	0
9486	Stripples bacon substitute	2	item(s)	16	6.8	60	2.0	2.0	0.5	4.5	0.5	1.0	3.0	0
9496	Vegetable Skallops meat substitute, canned	½	cup(s)	85	—	90	17.0	4.0	3.0	1.0	0	0	0.5	0
Dairy														
	Cheese													
1433	Blue, crumbled	1	ounce(s)	28	12.0	100	6.1	0.7	0	8.1	5.3	2.2	0.2	—
884	Brick	1	ounce(s)	28	11.7	105	6.6	0.8	0	8.4	5.3	2.4	0.2	—

Chol (mg)	Calc (mg)	Iron (mg)	Magn (mg)	Pota (mg)	Sodi (mg)	Zinc (mg)	Vit A (µg)	Thia (mg)	Vit E (mg α)	Ribo (mg)	Niac (mg)	Vit B_6 (mg)	Fola (µg)	Vit C (mg)	Vit B_{12} (µg)	Sele (µg)
0	60	1.80	—	—	270.0	—	0	—	—	—	—	—	—	0	—	—
0	20	1.44	—	—	330.0	—	0	—	—	—	—	—	—	0	—	—
0	20	1.08	—	—	280.0	—	0	—	—	—	—	—	—	0	—	—
5	80	1.80	—	—	360.0	—	—	—	—	—	—	—	—	0	—	—
0	40	1.80	—	—	430.0	—	—	—	—	—	—	—	—	0	—	—
0	60	1.80	—	—	280.0	—	0	—	—	—	—	—	—	0	—	—
0	60	1.80	—	—	370.0	—	0	—	—	—	—	—	—	0	—	—
0	100	2.70	—	—	300.0	—	—	—	—	—	—	—	—	0	—	—
0	150	1.08	—	—	890.0	—	—	—	—	—	—	—	—	0	—	—
0	40	1.44	—	—	330.0	—	—	—	—	—	—	—	—	0	—	—
0	40	0.72	—	—	1000.0	—	—	—	—	—	—	—	—	0	—	—
5	40	1.44	—	—	550.0	—	—	—	—	—	—	—	—	0	—	—
0	60	3.60	—	—	360.0	—	—	—	—	—	—	—	—	0	—	—
0	40	4.50	—	—	230.0	—	—	—	—	—	—	—	—	0	—	—
0	80	1.44	—	—	380.0	—	—	—	—	—	—	—	—	0	—	—
0	20	0.72	—	—	120.0	—	—	—	—	—	—	—	—	0	—	—
0	60	1.80	—	—	400.0	—	—	—	—	—	—	—	—	0	—	—
0	60	1.80	—	—	720.0	—	—	—	—	—	—	—	—	3.6	—	—
0	80	1.08	30.4	193.4	490.0	0.89	—	0.10	—	0.15	1.08	0.08	10.1	1.2	0.1	7.0
5	60	1.44	—	—	260.0	—	—	—	—	—	—	—	—	3.6	—	—
0	40	1.44	27.0	182.0	290.0	0.46	—	0.07	—	0.08	0.90	0.09	10.6	9.0	0	4.0
0	0	0.77	—	50.0	220.0	—	0	0.22	—	0.10	2.00	0.70	—	0	2.4	—
0	20	1.80	—	70.0	430.0	0.33	0	1.05	—	0.34	4.00	0.30	—	0	2.4	—
0	0	0.36	—	20.0	160.0	0.46	0	0.12	—	0.20	0.80	0.16	—	0	0.9	—
0	0	1.06	—	140.0	450.0	—	0	0.15	—	0.25	4.00	0.40	—	0	1.2	—
0	0	0.72	—	200.0	430.0	—	0	0.45	—	0.25	10.00	1.00	—	0	5.4	—
0	20	1.08	—	80.0	340.0	0.66	0	0.75	—	0.17	2.00	0.16	—	0	1.2	—
0	0	0.72	—	60.0	580.0	—	0	—	—	—	—	—	—	0	—	—
0	20	0.72	—	75.0	90.0	0.60	37.5	0.03	—	0.34	0.00	0.08	24.0	—	0.6	—
0	0	0.36	—	15.0	220.0	0.05	0	0.75	—	0.04	0.40	0.07	—	0	0.2	—
0	0	1.80	—	50.0	300.0	—	0	0.37	—	0.17	7.00	0.50	—	0	3.0	—
0	20	2.70	—	320.0	490.0	—	0	0.52	—	0.25	5.00	0.30	—	0	1.5	—
0	0	1.80	—	210.0	540.0	—	0	1.80	—	0.17	2.00	0.20	—	0	1.2	—
0	40	0.72	—	180.0	350.0	—	—	—	—	—	—	—	—	0	—	—
0	40	1.80	—	320.0	470.0	—	0	—	—	—	0.00	—	—	0	—	—
0	40	3.60	—	660.0	900.0	—	—	—	—	—	—	—	—	0	—	—
0	40	3.60	—	330.0	1130.0	—	0	0.30	—	0.13	2.00	0.70	—	0	1.5	—
0	0	1.08	—	100.0	220.0	0.24	0	0.06	—	0.10	4.00	0.08	—	0	0.2	—
0	20	1.80	—	120.0	580.0	0.64	0	1.80	—	0.25	6.00	0.60	—	0	1.5	—
0	250	1.80	—	250.0	250.0	0.26	0	0.37	—	0.13	4.00	0.30	—	0	1.8	—
0	100	1.08	—	240.0	240.0	—	0	0.37	—	0.13	4.00	0.30	—	0	1.8	—
0	0	1.80	—	130.0	460.0	0.26	0	0.45	—	0.17	5.00	0.30	—	0	1.8	—
0	0	1.08	—	95.0	800.0	0.30	0	0.75	—	0.17	4.00	0.20	—	0	0.6	—
0	60	2.70	—	60.0	450.0	0.23	0	1.80	—	0.17	6.00	0.40	—	0	3.0	—
0	0	1.44	—	50.0	320.0	0.36	0	1.80	—	0.17	2.00	0.30	—	0	3.0	—
0	40	1.08	—	130.0	480.0	0.50	0	1.20	—	0.13	3.00	0.30	—	0	1.5	—
0	0	0.36	—	15.0	220.0	0.05	0	0.75	—	0.03	0.40	0.08	—	0	0.2	—
0	0	0.36	—	10.0	390.0	0.67	0	0.03	—	0.03	0.00	0.01	—	0	0	—
21	150	0.08	6.5	72.6	395.5	0.75	56.1	0.01	0.07	0.10	0.28	0.04	10.2	0	0.3	4.1
27	191	0.12	6.8	38.6	158.8	0.73	82.8	0.00	0.07	0.10	0.03	0.01	5.7	0	0.4	4.1

TABLE A-1 Table of Food Composition *(continued)*

(Computer code is for Cengage Diet Analysis program) (For purposes of calculations, use "0" for t, <1, <.1, <.01, etc.)

DA+ Code	Food Description	QTY	Measure	Wt (g)	H_2O (g)	Ener (cal)	Prot (g)	Carb (g)	Fiber (g)	Fat (g)	Fat Breakdown (g) Sat	Mono	Poly	*Trans*
Dairy—continued														
885	Brie	1	ounce(s)	28	13.7	95	5.9	0.1	0	7.8	4.9	2.3	0.2	—
34821	Camembert	1	ounce(s)	28	14.7	85	5.6	0.1	0	6.9	4.3	2.0	0.2	—
5	Cheddar, shredded	¼	cup(s)	28	10.4	114	7.0	0.4	0	9.4	6.0	2.7	0.3	—
888	Cheddar or colby	1	ounce(s)	28	10.8	112	6.7	0.7	0	9.1	5.7	2.6	0.3	—
32096	Cheddar or colby, low fat	1	ounce(s)	28	17.9	49	6.9	0.5	0	2.0	1.2	0.6	0.1	—
889	Edam	1	ounce(s)	28	11.8	101	7.1	0.4	0	7.9	5.0	2.3	0.2	—
890	Feta	1	ounce(s)	28	15.7	75	4.0	1.2	0	6.0	4.2	1.3	0.2	—
891	Fontina	1	ounce(s)	28	10.8	110	7.3	0.4	0	8.8	5.4	2.5	0.5	—
8527	Goat cheese, soft	1	ounce(s)	28	17.2	76	5.3	0.3	0	6.0	4.1	1.4	0.1	—
893	Gouda	1	ounce(s)	28	11.8	101	7.1	0.6	0	7.8	5.0	2.2	0.2	—
894	Gruyere	1	ounce(s)	28	9.4	117	8.5	0.1	0	9.2	5.4	2.8	0.5	—
895	Limburger	1	ounce(s)	28	13.7	93	5.7	0.1	0	7.7	4.7	2.4	0.1	—
896	Monterey jack	1	ounce(s)	28	11.6	106	6.9	0.2	0	8.6	5.4	2.5	0.3	—
13	Mozzarella, part skim milk	1	ounce(s)	28	15.2	72	6.9	0.8	0	4.5	2.9	1.3	0.1	—
12	Mozzarella, whole milk	1	ounce(s)	28	14.2	85	6.3	0.6	0	6.3	3.7	1.9	0.2	—
897	Muenster	1	ounce(s)	28	11.8	104	6.6	0.3	0	8.5	5.4	2.5	0.2	—
898	Neufchatel	1	ounce(s)	28	17.6	74	2.8	0.8	0	6.6	4.2	1.9	0.2	—
14	Parmesan, grated	1	tablespoon(s)	5	1.0	22	1.9	0.2	0	1.4	0.9	0.4	0.1	—
17	Provolone	1	ounce(s)	28	11.6	100	7.3	0.6	0	7.5	4.8	2.1	0.2	—
19	Ricotta, part skim milk	¼	cup(s)	62	45.8	85	7.0	3.2	0	4.9	3.0	1.4	0.2	—
18	Ricotta, whole milk	¼	cup(s)	62	44.1	107	6.9	1.9	0	8.0	5.1	2.2	0.2	—
20	Romano	1	tablespoon(s)	5	1.5	19	1.6	0.2	0	1.3	0.9	0.4	0	—
900	Roquefort	1	ounce(s)	28	11.2	105	6.1	0.6	0	8.7	5.5	2.4	0.4	—
21	Swiss	1	ounce(s)	28	10.5	108	7.6	1.5	0	7.9	5.0	2.1	0.3	—
	Imitation cheese													
42245	Imitation American cheddar cheese	1	ounce(s)	28	15.1	68	4.7	3.3	0	4.0	2.5	1.2	0.1	—
53914	Imitation cheddar	1	ounce(s)	28	15.1	68	4.7	3.3	0	4.0	2.5	1.2	0.1	—
	Cottage cheese													
9	Low fat, 1% fat	½	cup(s)	113	93.2	81	14.0	3.1	0	1.2	0.7	0.3	0	—
8	Low fat, 2% fat	½	cup(s)	113	89.6	102	15.5	4.1	0	2.2	1.4	0.6	0.1	—
	Cream cheese													
11	Cream cheese	2	tablespoon(s)	29	15.6	101	2.2	0.8	0	10.1	6.4	2.9	0.4	—
17366	Fat-free cream cheese	2	tablespoon(s)	30	22.7	29	4.3	1.7	0	0.4	0.3	0.1	0	—
10438	Tofutti Better than Cream Cheese	2	tablespoon(s)	30	—	80	1.0	1.0	0	8.0	2.0	—	6.0	—
	Processed cheese													
24	American cheese food, processed	1	ounce(s)	28	12.3	94	5.2	2.2	0	7.1	4.2	2.0	0.3	—
25	American cheese spread, processed	1	ounce(s)	28	13.5	82	4.7	2.5	0	6.0	3.8	1.8	0.2	—
22	American cheese, processed	1	ounce(s)	28	11.1	106	6.3	0.5	0	8.9	5.6	2.5	0.3	—
9110	Kraft deluxe singles pasteurized process American cheese	1	ounce(s)	28	—	108	5.4	0	0	9.5	5.4	—	—	—
23	Swiss cheese, processed	1	ounce(s)	28	12.0	95	7.0	0.6	0	7.1	4.5	2.0	0.2	—
	Soy cheese													
10437	Galaxy Foods vegan grated parmesan cheese alternative	1	tablespoon(s)	8	—	23	3.0	1.5	0	0	0	0	0	0
10430	Nu Tofu cheddar flavored cheese alternative	1	ounce(s)	28	—	70	6.0	1.0	0	4.0	0.5	2.5	1.0	—
	Cream													
26	Half and half cream	1	tablespoon(s)	15	12.1	20	0.4	0.6	0	1.7	1.1	0.5	0.1	—
32	Heavy whipping cream, liquid	1	tablespoon(s)	15	8.7	52	0.3	0.4	0	5.6	3.5	1.6	0.2	—
28	Light coffee or table cream, liquid	1	tablespoon(s)	15	11.1	29	0.4	0.5	0	2.9	1.8	0.8	0.1	—
30	Light whipping cream, liquid	1	tablespoon(s)	15	9.5	44	0.3	0.4	0	4.6	2.9	1.4	0.1	—
34	Whipped cream topping, pressurized	1	tablespoon(s)	3	1.8	8	0.1	0.4	0	0.7	0.4	0.2	0	—
	Sour cream													
30556	Fat-free sour cream	2	tablespoon(s)	32	25.8	24	1.0	5.0	0	0	0	0	0	0
36	Sour cream	2	tablespoon(s)	24	17.0	51	0.8	1.0	0	5.0	3.1	1.5	0.2	—
	Imitation cream													
3659	Coffeemate nondairy creamer, liquid	1	tablespoon(s)	15	—	20	0	2.0	0	1.0	0	0.5	0	—
40	Cream substitute, powder	1	teaspoon(s)	2	0	11	0.1	1.1	0	0.7	0.7	0	0	—
904	Imitation sour cream	2	tablespoon(s)	29	20.5	60	0.7	1.9	0	5.6	5.1	0.2	0	—

Chol (mg)	Calc (mg)	Iron (mg)	Magn (mg)	Pota (mg)	Sodi (mg)	Zinc (mg)	Vit A (μg)	Thia (mg)	Vit E (mg α)	Ribo (mg)	Niac (mg)	Vit B_6 (mg)	Fola (μg)	Vit C (mg)	Vit B_{12} (μg)	Sele (μg)
28	52	0.14	5.7	43.1	178.3	0.67	49.3	0.02	0.06	0.14	0.10	0.06	18.4	0	0.5	4.1
20	110	0.09	5.7	53.0	238.7	0.67	68.3	0.01	0.06	0.14	0.18	0.06	17.6	0	0.4	4.1
30	204	0.19	7.9	27.7	175.4	0.87	74.9	0.01	0.08	0.10	0.02	0.02	5.1	0	0.2	3.9
27	194	0.21	7.4	36.0	171.2	0.87	74.8	0.00	0.07	0.10	0.02	0.02	5.1	0	0.2	4.1
6	118	0.11	4.5	18.7	173.5	0.51	17.0	0.00	0.01	0.06	0.01	0.01	3.1	0	0.1	4.1
25	207	0.12	8.5	53.3	273.6	1.06	68.9	0.01	0.06	0.11	0.02	0.02	4.5	0	0.4	4.1
25	140	0.18	5.4	17.6	316.4	0.81	35.4	0.04	0.05	0.23	0.28	0.12	9.1	0	0.5	4.3
33	156	0.06	4.0	18.1	226.8	0.99	74.0	0.01	0.07	0.05	0.04	0.02	1.7	0	0.5	4.1
13	40	0.53	4.5	7.4	104.3	0.26	81.6	0.02	0.05	0.10	0.12	0.07	3.4	0	0.1	0.8
32	198	0.06	8.2	34.3	232.2	1.10	46.8	0.01	0.06	0.09	0.01	0.02	6.0	0	0.4	4.1
31	287	0.04	10.2	23.0	95.3	1.10	76.8	0.01	0.07	0.07	0.03	0.02	2.8	0	0.5	4.1
26	141	0.03	6.0	36.3	226.8	0.59	96.4	0.02	0.06	0.14	0.04	0.02	16.4	0	0.3	4.1
25	211	0.20	7.7	23.0	152.0	0.85	56.1	0.00	0.07	0.11	0.02	0.02	5.1	0	0.2	4.1
18	222	0.06	6.5	23.8	175.5	0.78	36.0	0.01	0.04	0.08	0.03	0.02	2.6	0	0.2	4.1
22	143	0.12	5.7	21.5	177.8	0.82	50.7	0.01	0.05	0.08	0.02	0.01	2.0	0	0.6	4.8
27	203	0.11	7.7	38.0	178.0	0.79	84.5	0.00	0.07	0.09	0.02	0.01	3.4	0	0.4	4.1
22	21	0.07	2.3	32.3	113.1	0.14	84.5	0.00	—	0.05	0.03	0.01	3.1	0	0.1	0.9
4	55	0.04	1.9	6.3	76.5	0.19	6.0	0.00	0.01	0.02	0.01	0.00	0.5	0	0.1	0.9
20	214	0.14	7.9	39.1	248.3	0.91	66.9	0.01	0.06	0.09	0.04	0.02	2.8	0	0.4	4.1
19	167	0.27	9.2	76.9	76.9	0.82	65.8	0.01	0.04	0.11	0.04	0.01	8.0	0	0.2	10.3
31	127	0.23	6.8	64.6	51.7	0.71	73.8	0.01	0.06	0.12	0.06	0.02	7.4	0	0.2	8.9
5	53	0.03	2.1	4.3	60	0.12	4.8	0.00	0.01	0.01	0.00	0.00	0.4	0	0.1	0.7
26	188	0.15	8.5	25.8	512.9	0.59	83.3	0.01	—	0.16	0.20	0.03	13.9	0	0.2	4.1
26	224	0.05	10.8	21.8	54.4	1.23	62.4	0.01	0.10	0.08	0.02	0.02	1.7	0	0.9	5.2
10	159	0.08	8.2	68.6	381.3	0.73	32.3	0.01	0.07	0.12	0.03	0.03	2.0	0	0.1	4.3
10	159	0.09	8.2	68.6	381.3	0.73	32.3	0.01	0.07	0.12	0.04	0.03	2.0	0	0.1	4.3
5	69	0.15	5.7	97.2	458.8	0.42	12.4	0.02	0.01	0.18	0.14	0.07	13.6	0	0.7	10.2
9	78	0.18	6.8	108.5	458.8	0.47	23.7	0.02	0.02	0.20	0.16	0.08	14.7	0	0.8	11.5
32	23	0.34	1.7	34.5	85.8	0.15	106.1	0.01	0.08	0.05	0.02	0.01	3.8	0	0.1	0.7
2	56	0.05	4.2	48.9	163.5	0.26	83.7	0.01	0.00	0.05	0.04	0.01	11.1	0	0.2	1.5
0	0	0.00	—	—	135.0	—	0	—	—	—	—	—	—	0	—	—
23	162	0.16	8.8	82.5	358.6	0.90	57.0	0.01	0.06	0.14	0.04	0.02	2.0	0	0.4	4.6
16	159	0.09	8.2	68.6	381.3	0.73	49.0	0.01	0.05	0.12	0.03	0.03	2.0	0	0.1	3.2
27	156	0.05	7.7	47.9	422.1	0.80	72.0	0.01	0.07	0.10	0.02	0.02	2.3	0	0.2	4.1
27	338	0.00	0	33.8	459.0	1.22	114.0	—	—	0.14	—	—	—	0	0.2	—
24	219	0.17	8.2	61.2	388.4	1.02	56.1	0.00	0.09	0.07	0.01	0.01	1.7	0	0.3	4.5
0	60	0.00	—	75.0	97.5	—	—	—	—	—	—	—	—	—	—	—
0	200	0.36	—	—	190.0	—	—	—	—	—	—	—	—	0	—	—
6	16	0.01	1.5	19.5	6.2	0.08	14.6	0.01	0.05	0.02	0.01	0.01	0.5	0.1	0	0.3
21	10	0.00	1.1	11.3	5.7	0.03	61.7	0.00	0.15	0.01	0.01	0.00	0.6	0.1	0	0.1
10	14	0.01	1.4	18.3	6.0	0.04	27.2	0.01	0.08	0.02	0.01	0.01	0.3	0.1	0	0.1
17	10	0.00	1.1	14.6	5.1	0.03	41.9	0.00	0.13	0.01	0.01	0.00	0.6	0.1	0	0.1
2	3	0.00	0.3	4.4	3.9	0.01	5.6	0.00	0.01	0.00	0.00	0.00	0.1	0	0	0
3	40	0.00	3.2	41.3	45.1	0.16	23.4	0.01	0.00	0.04	0.02	0.01	3.5	0	0.1	1.7
11	28	0.01	2.6	34.6	12.7	0.06	42.5	0.01	0.14	0.03	0.01	0.00	2.6	0.2	0.1	0.5
0	0	0.00	—	30.0	0	—	0	0.01	—	0.01	0.20	—	—	0	—	—
0	0	0.02	0.1	16.2	3.6	0.01	0	0.00	0.01	0.00	0.00	0.00	0	0	0	0
0	1	0.11	1.7	46.3	29.3	0.34	0	0.00	0.21	0.00	0.00	0.00	0	0	0	0.7

TABLE A-1 Table of Food Composition *(continued)*

(Computer code is for Cengage Diet Analysis program) (For purposes of calculations, use "0" for t, <1, <.1, <.01, etc.)

											Fat Breakdown (g)			
DA+ Code	Food Description	QTY	Measure	Wt (g)	H_2O (g)	Ener (cal)	Prot (g)	Carb (g)	Fiber (g)	Fat (g)	Sat	Mono	Poly	*Trans*
	Dairy—continued													
35972	Nondairy coffee whitener, liquid, frozen	1	tablespoon(s)	15	11.7	21	0.2	1.7	0	1.5	0.3	1.1	0	—
35976	Nondairy dessert topping, frozen	1	tablespoon(s)	5	2.4	15	0.1	1.1	0	1.2	1.0	0.1	0	—
35975	Nondairy dessert topping, pressurized	1	tablespoon(s)	4	2.7	12	0	0.7	0	1.0	0.8	0.1	0	—
	Fluid milk													
60	Buttermilk, low fat	1	cup(s)	245	220.8	98	8.1	11.7	0	2.2	1.3	0.6	0.1	—
54	Low fat, 1%	1	cup(s)	244	219.4	102	8.2	12.2	0	2.4	1.5	0.7	0.1	—
55	Low fat, 1%, with nonfat milk solids	1	cup(s)	245	220.0	105	8.5	12.2	0	2.4	1.5	0.7	0.1	—
57	Nonfat, skim or fat free	1	cup(s)	245	222.6	83	8.3	12.2	0	0.2	0.1	0.1	0	—
58	Nonfat, skim or fat free with nonfat milk solids	1	cup(s)	245	221.4	91	8.7	12.3	0	0.6	0.4	0.2	0	—
51	Reduced fat, 2%	1	cup(s)	244	218.0	122	8.1	11.4	0	4.8	3.1	1.4	0.2	—
52	Reduced fat, 2%, with nonfat milk solids	1	cup(s)	245	217.7	125	8.5	12.2	0	4.7	2.9	1.4	0.2	—
50	Whole, 3.3%	1	cup(s)	244	215.5	146	7.9	11.0	0	7.9	4.6	2.0	0.5	—
	Canned milk													
62	Nonfat or skim evaporated	2	tablespoon(s)	32	25.3	25	2.4	3.6	0	0.1	0	0	0	—
63	Sweetened condensed	2	tablespoon(s)	38	10.4	123	3.0	20.8	0	3.3	2.1	0.9	0.1	—
61	Whole evaporated	2	tablespoon(s)	32	23.3	42	2.1	3.2	0	2.4	1.4	0.7	0.1	—
	Dried milk													
64	Buttermilk	¼	cup(s)	30	0.9	117	10.4	14.9	0	1.8	1.1	0.5	0.1	—
65	Instant nonfat with added vitamin A	¼	cup(s)	17	0.7	61	6.0	8.9	0	0.1	0.1	0	0	—
5234	Skim milk powder	¼	cup(s)	17	0.7	62	6.1	9.1	0	0.1	0.1	0	0	—
907	Whole dry milk	¼	cup(s)	32	0.8	159	8.4	12.3	0	8.5	5.4	2.5	0.2	—
909	**Goat milk**	1	cup(s)	244	212.4	168	8.7	10.9	0	10.1	6.5	2.7	0.4	—
	Chocolate milk													
33155	Chocolate syrup, prepared with milk	1	cup(s)	282	227.0	254	8.7	36.0	0.8	8.3	4.7	2.1	0.5	—
33184	Cocoa mix with aspartame, added sodium and vitamin A, no added calcium or phosphorus, prepared with water	1	cup(s)	192	177.4	56	2.3	10.8	1.2	0.4	0.3	0.1	0	—
908	Hot cocoa, prepared with milk	1	cup(s)	250	206.4	193	8.8	26.6	2.5	5.8	3.6	1.7	0.1	0.2
69	Low fat	1	cup(s)	250	211.3	158	8.1	26.1	1.3	2.5	1.5	0.8	0.1	—
68	Reduced fat	1	cup(s)	250	205.4	190	7.5	30.3	1.8	4.8	2.9	1.1	0.2	—
67	Whole	1	cup(s)	250	205.8	208	7.9	25.9	2.0	8.5	5.3	2.5	0.3	—
70	**Eggnog**	1	cup(s)	254	188.9	343	9.7	34.4	0	19.0	11.3	5.7	0.9	—
	Breakfast drinks													
10093	Carnation Instant Breakfast classic chocolate malt, prepared with skim milk, no sugar added	1	cup(s)	243	—	142	11.1	21.3	0.7	1.3	0.7	—	—	—
10092	Carnation Instant Breakfast classic French vanilla, prepared with skim milk, no sugar added	1	cup(s)	273	—	150	12.9	24.0	0	0.4	0.4	—	—	—
10094	Carnation Instant Breakfast stawberry sensation, prepared with skim milk, no sugar added	1	cup(s)	243	—	142	11.1	21.3	0	0.4	0.4	—	—	—
10091	Carnation Instant Breakfast strawberry sensation, prepared with skim milk	1	cup(s)	273	—	220	12.5	38.8	0	0.4	0.4	—	—	—
1417	Ovaltine rich chocolate flavor, prepared with skim milk	1	cup(s)	258	—	170	8.5	31.0	0	0	0	0	0	0
8539	**Malted milk, chocolate mix, fortified, prepared with milk**	1	cup(s)	265	215.8	223	8.9	28.9	1.1	8.6	5.0	2.2	0.5	—
	Milkshakes													
73	Chocolate	1	cup(s)	227	164.0	270	6.9	48.1	0.7	6.1	3.8	1.8	0.2	—
3163	Strawberry	1	cup(s)	226	167.8	256	7.7	42.8	0.9	6.3	3.9	—	—	—
74	Vanilla	1	cup(s)	227	169.2	254	8.8	40.3	0	6.9	4.3	2.0	0.3	—

Chol (mg)	Calc (mg)	Iron (mg)	Magn (mg)	Pota (mg)	Sodi (mg)	Zinc (mg)	Vit A (µg)	Thia (mg)	Vit E (mg α)	Ribo (mg)	Niac (mg)	Vit B_6 (mg)	Fola (µg)	Vit C (mg)	Vit B_{12} (µg)	Sele (µg)
0	1	0.00	0	28.9	12.0	0.00	0.2	0.00	0.12	0.00	0.00	0.00	0	0	0	0.2
0	0	0.00	0.1	0.9	1.2	0.00	0.3	0.00	0.05	0.00	0.00	0.00	0	0	0	0.1
0	0	0.00	0	0.8	2.8	0.00	0.2	0.00	0.04	0.00	0.00	0.00	0	0	0	0.1
10	284	0.12	27.0	370.0	257.3	1.02	17.2	0.08	0.12	0.37	0.14	0.08	12.3	2.5	0.5	4.9
12	290	0.07	26.8	366.0	107.4	1.02	141.5	0.04	0.02	0.45	0.22	0.09	12.2	0	1.1	8.1
10	314	0.12	34.3	396.9	127.4	0.98	144.6	0.09	—	0.42	0.22	0.11	12.3	2.5	0.9	5.6
5	306	0.07	27.0	382.2	102.9	1.02	149.5	0.11	0.02	0.44	0.23	0.09	12.3	0	1.3	7.6
5	316	0.12	36.8	419.0	129.9	1.00	149.5	0.10	0.00	0.42	0.22	0.11	12.3	2.5	1.0	5.4
20	285	0.07	26.8	366.0	100.0	1.04	134.2	0.09	0.07	0.45	0.22	0.09	12.2	0.5	1.1	6.1
20	314	0.12	34.3	396.9	127.4	0.98	137.2	0.09	—	0.42	0.22	0.11	12.3	2.5	0.9	5.6
24	276	0.07	24.4	348.9	97.6	0.97	68.3	0.10	0.14	0.44	0.26	0.08	12.2	0	1.1	9.0
1	93	0.09	8.6	105.9	36.7	0.28	37.6	0.01	0.00	0.09	0.05	0.01	2.9	0.4	0.1	0.8
13	109	0.07	9.9	141.9	48.6	0.36	28.3	0.03	0.06	0.16	0.08	0.02	4.2	1.0	0.2	5.7
9	82	0.06	7.6	95.4	33.4	0.24	20.5	0.01	0.04	0.10	0.06	0.01	2.5	0.6	0.1	0.7
21	359	0.09	33.3	482.5	156.7	1.21	14.9	0.11	0.03	0.48	0.27	0.10	14.2	1.7	1.2	6.2
3	209	0.05	19.9	289.9	93.3	0.75	120.5	0.07	0.00	0.30	0.15	0.06	8.5	1.0	0.7	4.6
3	214	0.05	20.3	296.0	95.3	0.76	123.1	0.07	0.00	0.30	0.15	0.06	8.7	1.0	0.7	4.7
31	292	0.15	27.2	425.6	118.7	1.06	82.2	0.09	0.15	0.38	0.20	0.09	11.8	2.8	1.0	5.2
27	327	0.12	34.2	497.8	122.0	0.73	139.1	0.11	0.17	0.33	0.67	0.11	2.4	3.2	0.2	3.4
25	251	0.90	50.8	408.9	132.5	1.21	70.5	0.11	0.14	0.46	0.38	0.09	14.1	0	1.1	9.6
0	92	0.74	32.6	405.1	138.2	0.51	0	0.04	0.00	0.20	0.16	0.04	1.9	0	0.2	2.5
20	263	1.20	57.5	492.5	110.0	1.57	127.5	0.09	0.07	0.45	0.33	0.10	12.5	0.5	1.1	6.8
8	288	0.60	32.5	425.0	152.5	1.02	145.0	0.09	0.05	0.41	0.31	0.10	12.5	2.3	0.9	4.8
20	273	0.60	35.0	422.5	165.0	0.97	160.0	0.11	0.10	0.45	0.41	0.06	5.0	0	0.8	8.5
30	280	0.60	32.5	417.5	150.0	1.02	65.0	0.09	0.15	0.40	0.31	0.10	12.5	2.3	0.8	4.8
150	330	0.50	48.3	419.1	137.2	1.16	116.8	0.08	0.50	0.48	0.26	0.12	2.5	3.8	1.1	10.7
9	444	4.00	88.9	631.1	195.6	3.38	—	0.33	—	0.45	4.44	0.44	4.0	26.7	1.3	8.0
9	500	4.50	100.0	665.0	192.0	3.75	—	0.37	—	0.51	5.00	0.49	100.0	30.0	1.5	9.0
9	444	4.00	88.9	568.9	186.7	3.38	—	0.33	—	0.45	4.44	0.44	88.9	26.7	1.3	8.0
9	500	4.47	100.0	665.0	288.0	3.75	—	0.37	—	0.51	5.07	0.50	100.0	30.0	1.5	8.8
5	350	3.60	100.0	—	270.0	3.75	—	0.37	—	—	4.00	0.40	—	12.0	1.2	—
27	339	3.76	45.1	577.7	230.6	1.16	903.7	0.75	0.15	1.31	11.08	1.01	18.6	31.8	1.1	12.5
25	300	0.70	36.4	508.9	252.2	1.09	40.9	0.10	0.11	0.50	0.28	0.05	11.4	0	0.7	4.3
25	256	0.24	29.4	412.0	187.9	0.81	58.9	0.10	—	0.44	0.39	0.10	6.8	1.8	0.7	4.8
27	332	0.22	27.3	415.8	215.8	0.88	56.8	0.06	0.11	0.44	0.33	0.09	15.9	0	1.2	5.2

TABLE A-1 Table of Food Composition *(continued)*

(Computer code is for Cengage Diet Analysis program) (For purposes of calculations, use "0" for t, <1, <.1, <.01, etc.)

											Fat Breakdown (g)			
DA+ Code	Food Description	QTY	Measure	Wt (g)	H_2O (g)	Ener (cal)	Prot (g)	Carb (g)	Fiber (g)	Fat (g)	Sat	Mono	Poly	Trans
	Dairy—continued													
	Ice cream													
4776	Chocolate	½	cup(s)	66	36.8	143	2.5	18.6	0.8	7.3	4.5	2.1	0.3	—
12137	Chocolate fudge, no sugar added	½	cup(s)	71	—	100	3.0	16.0	2.0	3.0	1.5	—	—	0
16514	Chocolate, soft serve	½	cup(s)	87	49.9	177	3.2	24.1	0.7	8.4	5.2	2.4	0.3	—
16523	Sherbet, all flavors	½	cup(s)	97	63.8	139	1.1	29.3	3.2	1.9	1.1	0.5	0.1	—
4778	Strawberry	½	cup(s)	66	39.6	127	2.1	18.2	0.6	5.5	3.4	—	—	—
76	Vanilla	½	cup(s)	72	43.9	145	2.5	17.0	0.5	7.9	4.9	2.1	0.3	—
12146	Vanilla chocolate swirl, fat-free, no sugar added	½	cup(s)	71	—	100	3.0	14.0	2.0	3.0	2.0	—	—	0
82	Vanilla, light	½	cup(s)	76	48.3	125	3.6	19.6	0.2	3.7	2.2	1.0	0.2	—
78	Vanilla, light, soft serve	½	cup(s)	88	61.2	111	4.3	19.2	0	2.3	1.4	0.7	0.1	—
	Soy desserts													
10694	Tofutti low fat vanilla fudge nondairy frozen dessert	½	cup(s)	70	—	140	2.0	24.0	0	4.0	1.0	—	—	—
15721	Tofutti premium chocolate supreme nondairy frozen dessert	½	cup(s)	70	—	180	3.0	18.0	0	11.0	2.0	—	—	—
15720	Tofutti premium vanilla nondairy frozen dessert	½	cup(s)	70	—	190	2.0	20.0	0	11.0	2.0	—	—	—
	Ice milk													
16517	Chocolate	½	cup(s)	66	42.9	94	2.8	16.9	0.3	2.1	1.3	0.6	0.1	—
16516	Flavored, not chocolate	½	cup(s)	66	41.4	108	3.5	17.5	0.2	2.6	1.7	0.6	0.1	—
	Pudding													
25032	Chocolate	½	cup(s)	144	109.7	155	5.1	22.7	0.7	5.4	3.1	1.7	0.2	0
1923	Chocolate, sugar free, prepared with 2% milk	½	cup(s)	133	—	100	5.0	14.0	0.3	3.0	1.5	—	—	—
1722	Rice	½	cup(s)	113	75.6	151	4.1	29.9	0.5	1.9	1.1	0.5	0.1	—
4747	Tapioca, ready to eat	1	item(s)	142	102.0	185	2.8	30.8	0	5.5	1.4	3.6	0.1	—
25031	Vanilla	½	cup(s)	136	109.7	116	4.7	17.6	0	2.8	1.6	0.9	0.2	0
1924	Vanilla, sugar free, prepared with 2% milk	½	cup(s)	133	—	90	4.0	12.0	0.2	2.0	1.5	—	—	—
	Frozen yogurt													
4785	Chocolate, soft serve	½	cup(s)	72	45.9	115	2.9	17.9	1.6	4.3	2.6	1.3	0.2	—
1747	Fruit varieties	½	cup(s)	113	80.5	144	3.4	24.4	0	4.1	2.6	1.1	0.1	—
4786	Vanilla, soft serve	½	cup(s)	72	47.0	117	2.9	17.4	0	4.0	2.5	1.1	0.2	—
	Milk substitutes													
	Lactose free													
16081	Fat-free, calcium fortified [milk]	1	cup(s)	240	—	80	8.0	13.0	0	0	0	0	0	0
36486	Low fat milk	1	cup(s)	240	—	110	8.0	13.0	0	2.5	1.5	—	—	—
36487	Reduced fat milk	1	cup(s)	240	—	130	8.0	12.0	0	5.0	3.0	—	—	—
36488	Whole milk	1	cup(s)	240	—	150	8.0	12.0	0	8.0	5.0	—	—	—
	Rice													
10083	Rice Dream carob rice beverage	1	cup(s)	240	—	150	1.0	32.0	0	2.5	0	—	—	—
17089	Rice Dream original rice beverage, enriched	1	cup(s)	240	—	120	1.0	25.0	0	2.0	0	—	—	—
10087	Rice Dream vanilla enriched rice beverage	1	cup(s)	240	—	130	1.0	28.0	0	2.0	0	—	—	—
	Soy													
34750	Soy Dream chocolate enriched soy beverage	1	cup(s)	240	—	210	7.0	37.0	1.0	3.5	0.5	—	—	—
34749	Soy Dream vanilla enriched soy beverage	1	cup(s)	240	—	150	7.0	22.0	0	4.0	0.5	—	—	—
13840	Vitasoy light chocolate soymilk	1	cup(s)	240	—	100	4.0	17.0	0	2.0	0.5	0.5	1.0	—
13839	Vitasoy light vanilla soymilk	1	cup(s)	240	—	70	4.0	10.0	0	2.0	0.5	0.5	1.0	—
13836	Vitasoy rich chocolate soymilk	1	cup(s)	240	—	160	7.0	24.0	1.0	4.0	0.5	1.0	2.5	—
13835	Vitasoy vanilla delite soymilk	1	cup(s)	240	—	120	7.0	13.0	1.0	4.0	0.5	1.0	2.5	—
	Yogurt													
3615	Custard style, fruit flavors	6	ounce(s)	170	127.1	190	7.0	32.0	0	3.5	2.0	—	—	—
3617	Custard style, vanilla	6	ounce(s)	170	134.1	190	7.0	32.0	0	3.5	2.0	0.9	0.1	—
32101	Fruit, low fat	1	cup(s)	245	184.5	243	9.8	45.7	0	2.8	1.8	0.8	0.1	—

Chol (mg)	Calc (mg)	Iron (mg)	Magn (mg)	Pota (mg)	Sodi (mg)	Zinc (mg)	Vit A (μg)	Thia (mg)	Vit E (mg α)	Ribo (mg)	Niac (mg)	Vit B_6 (mg)	Fola (μg)	Vit C (mg)	Vit B_{12} (μg)	Sele (μg)
22	72	0.61	19.1	164.3	50.2	0.38	77.9	0.02	0.19	0.12	0.14	0.03	10.6	0.5	0.2	1.7
10	100	0.36	—	—	65.0	—	—	—	—	—	—	—	—	0	—	—
22	103	0.32	19.0	192.0	43.3	0.45	66.6	0.03	0.22	0.13	0.11	0.03	4.3	0.5	0.3	2.5
0	52	0.13	7.7	92.6	44.4	0.46	9.7	0.02	0.02	0.08	0.07	0.02	6.8	5.6	0.1	1.3
19	79	0.13	9.2	124.1	39.6	0.22	63.4	0.03	—	0.16	0.11	0.03	7.9	5.1	0.2	1.3
32	92	0.06	10.1	143.3	57.6	0.49	85.0	0.03	0.21	0.17	0.08	0.03	3.6	0.4	0.3	1.3
10	100	0.00	—	—	65.0	—	—	—	—	—	—	—	—	0	—	—
21	122	0.14	10.6	158.1	56.2	0.55	97.3	0.04	0.09	0.19	0.10	0.03	4.6	0.9	0.4	1.5
11	138	0.05	12.3	194.5	61.6	0.46	25.5	0.04	0.05	0.17	0.10	0.04	4.4	0.8	0.4	3.2
0	0	0.00	—	8.0	90.0	—	0	—	—	—	—	—	—	0	—	—
0	0	0.00	—	7.0	180.0	—	0	—	—	—	—	—	—	0	—	—
0	0	0.00	—	2.0	210.0	—	0	—	—	—	—	—	—	0	—	—
6	94	0.15	13.1	155.2	40.6	0.36	15.7	0.03	0.05	0.11	0.08	0.02	3.9	0.5	0.3	2.2
16	76	0.05	9.2	136.2	48.5	0.47	90.4	0.02	0.05	0.11	0.06	0.01	3.3	0.1	0.2	1.3
35	149	0.46	31.3	226.7	137.0	0.71	—	0.05	0.00	0.22	0.15	0.06	8.3	1.2	0.5	4.9
10	150	0.72	—	330.0	310.0	—	—	0.06	—	0.26	—	—	—	0	—	—
7	113	0.28	15.8	201.4	66.4	0.52	41.6	0.03	0.05	0.17	0.34	0.06	4.5	0.2	0.2	4.8
1	101	0.15	8.5	130.6	205.9	0.31	0	0.03	0.21	0.13	0.09	0.03	4.3	0.4	0.3	0
35	146	0.17	17.2	188.9	136.4	0.52	—	0.04	0.00	0.22	0.10	0.05	8.0	1.2	0.5	4.6
10	150	0.00	—	190.0	380.0	—	—	0.03	—	0.17	—	—	—	0	—	—
4	106	0.90	19.4	187.9	70.6	0.35	31.7	0.02	—	0.15	0.22	0.05	7.9	0.2	0.2	1.7
15	113	0.52	11.3	176.3	71.2	0.31	55.4	0.04	0.10	0.20	0.07	0.04	4.5	0.8	0.1	2.1
1	103	0.21	10.1	151.9	62.6	0.30	42.5	0.02	0.07	0.16	0.20	0.05	4.3	0.6	0.2	2.4
3	500	0.00	—	—	125.0	—	100.0	—	—	—	—	—	—	0	0	—
10	300	0.00	—	—	125.0	—	100.0	—	—	—	—	—	—	0	—	—
20	300	0.00	—	—	125.0	—	98.2	—	—	—	—	—	—	0	—	—
35	300	0.00	—	—	125.0	—	58.1	—	—	—	—	—	—	0	—	—
0	20	0.72	—	82.5	100.0	—	—	—	—	—	—	—	—	1.2	—	—
0	300	0.00	13.3	60.0	90.0	0.24	—	0.06	—	0.00	0.84	0.07	—	0	1.5	—
0	300	0.00	—	53.0	90.0	—	—	—	—	—	—	—	—	0	1.5	—
0	300	1.80	60.0	350.0	160.0	0.60	33.3	0.15	—	0.06	0.80	0.12	60.0	0	3.0	—
0	300	1.80	40.0	260.0	140.0	0.60	33.3	0.15	—	0.06	0.80	0.12	60.0	0	3.0	—
0	300	0.72	24.0	200.0	140.0	0.90	—	0.09	—	0.34	—	—	24.0	0	0.9	—
0	300	0.72	24.0	200.0	120.0	0.90	—	0.09	—	0.34	—	—	24.0	0	0.9	—
0	300	1.08	40.0	320.0	150.0	0.90	—	0.15	—	0.34	—	—	60.0	0	0.9	—
0	40	0.72	—	320.0	115.0	—	0	—	—	—	—	—	—	0	—	—
15	300	0.00	16.0	310.0	100.0	—	—	—	—	0.25	—	—	—	0	—	—
15	300	0.00	16.0	310.0	100.0	—	—	—	—	0.25	—	—	—	0	—	—
12	338	0.14	31.9	433.7	129.9	1.64	27.0	0.08	0.04	0.39	0.21	0.09	22.1	1.5	1.1	6.9

A

TABLE A-1 Table of Food Composition *(continued)*

(Computer code is for Cengage Diet Analysis program) (For purposes of calculations, use "0" for t, <1, <.1, <.01, etc.)

											Fat Breakdown (g)			
DA+ Code	Food Description	QTY	Measure	Wt (g)	H_2O (g)	Ener (cal)	Prot (g)	Carb (g)	Fiber (g)	Fat (g)	Sat	Mono	Poly	*Trans*
Dairy—continued														
29638	Fruit, nonfat, sweetened with low-calorie sweetener	1	cup(s)	241	208.3	123	10.6	19.4	1.2	0.4	0.2	0.1	0	—
93	Plain, low fat	1	cup(s)	245	208.4	154	12.9	17.2	0	3.8	2.5	1.0	0.1	—
94	Plain, nonfat	1	cup(s)	245	208.8	137	14.0	18.8	0	0.4	0.3	0.1	0	—
32100	Vanilla, low fat	1	cup(s)	245	193.6	208	12.1	33.8	0	3.1	2.0	0.8	0.1	—
5242	Yogurt beverage	1	cup(s)	245	199.8	172	6.2	32.8	0	2.2	1.4	0.6	0.1	—
38202	Yogurt smoothie, nonfat, all flavors	1	item(s)	325	—	290	10.0	60.0	6.0	0	0	0	0	0
	Soy yogurt													
34617	Stonyfield Farm O'Soy strawberry-peach pack organic cultured soy yogurt	1	item(s)	113	—	100	5.0	16.0	3.0	2.0	0	—	—	0
34616	Stonyfield Farm O'Soy vanilla organic cultured soy yogurt	1	item(s)	170	—	150	7.0	26.0	4.0	2.0	0	—	—	0
10453	White Wave plain silk cultured soy yogurt	8	ounce(s)	227	—	140	5.0	22.0	1.0	3.0	0.5	—	—	0
Eggs														
	Eggs													
99	Fried	1	item(s)	46	31.8	90	6.3	0.4	0	7.0	2.0	2.9	1.2	—
100	Hard boiled	1	item(s)	50	37.3	78	6.3	0.6	0	5.3	1.6	2.0	0.7	—
101	Poached	1	item(s)	50	37.8	71	6.3	0.4	0	5.0	1.5	1.9	0.7	—
97	Raw, white	1	item(s)	33	28.9	16	3.6	0.2	0	0.1	0	0	0	—
96	Raw, whole	1	item(s)	50	37.9	72	6.3	0.4	0	5.0	1.5	1.9	0.7	—
98	Raw, yolk	1	item(s)	17	8.9	54	2.7	0.6	0	4.5	1.6	2.0	0.7	—
102	Scrambled, prepared with milk and butter	2	item(s)	122	89.2	204	13.5	2.7	0	14.9	4.5	5.8	2.6	0.7
	Egg substitute													
4028	Egg Beaters	¼	cup(s)	61	—	30	6.0	1.0	0	0	0	0	0	0
920	Frozen	¼	cup(s)	60	43.9	96	6.8	1.9	0	6.7	1.2	1.5	3.7	—
918	Liquid	¼	cup(s)	63	51.9	53	7.5	0.4	0	2.1	0.4	0.6	1.0	—
Seafood														
	Cod													
6040	Atlantic cod or scrod, baked or broiled	3	ounce(s)	85	64.6	89	19.4	0	0	0.7	0.1	0.1	0.2	—
1573	Atlantic cod, cooked, dry heat	3	ounce(s)	85	64.6	89	19.4	0	0	0.7	0.1	0.1	0.2	—
2905	**Eel, raw**	3	ounce(s)	85	58.0	156	15.7	0	0	9.9	2.0	6.1	0.8	—
	Fish fillets													
25079	Baked	3	ounce(s)	84	79.9	99	21.7	0	0	0.7	0.1	0.1	0.3	—
8615	Batter coated or breaded, fried	3	ounce(s)	85	45.6	197	12.5	14.4	0.4	10.5	2.4	2.2	5.3	—
25082	Broiled fish steaks	3	ounce(s)	85	68.1	128	24.2	0	0	2.6	0.4	0.9	0.8	—
25083	Poached fish steaks	3	ounce(s)	85	67.1	111	21.1	0	0	2.3	0.3	0.8	0.7	—
25084	Steamed	3	ounce(s)	85	72.2	79	17.2	0	0	0.6	0.1	0.1	0.2	—
25089	**Flounder, baked**	3	ounce(s)	85	64.4	113	14.8	0.4	0.1	5.5	1.1	2.2	1.4	—
1825	**Grouper, cooked, dry heat**	3	ounce(s)	85	62.4	100	21.1	0	0	1.1	0.3	0.2	0.3	—
	Haddock													
6049	Baked or broiled	3	ounce(s)	85	63.2	95	20.6	0	0	0.8	0.1	0.1	0.3	—
1578	Cooked, dry heat	3	ounce(s)	85	63.1	95	20.6	0	0	0.8	0.1	0.1	0.3	—
1886	**Halibut, Atlantic and Pacific, cooked, dry heat**	3	ounce(s)	85	61.0	119	22.7	0	0	2.5	0.4	0.8	0.8	—
1582	**Herring, Atlantic, pickled**	4	piece(s)	60	33.1	157	8.5	5.8	0	10.8	1.4	7.2	1.0	—
1587	**Jack mackerel, solids, canned, drained**	2	ounce(s)	57	39.2	88	13.1	0	0	3.6	1.1	1.3	0.9	—

PAGE KEY: A-2 = Breads/Baked Goods A-8 = Cereal/Rice/Pasta A-12 = Fruit A-18 = Vegetables/Legumes A-28 = Nuts/Seeds A-30 = Vegetarian A-32 = Dairy A-40 = Eggs A-40 = Seafood A-44 = Meats A-48 = Poultry A-48 = Processed Meats A-50 = Beverages A-54 = Fats/Oils A-56 = Sweets A-58 = Spices/Condiments/Sauces A-62 = Mixed Foods/Soups/Sandwiches A-68 = Fast Food A-88 = Convenience A-90 = Baby Foods

Chol (mg)	Calc (mg)	Iron (mg)	Magn (mg)	Pota (mg)	Sodi (mg)	Zinc (mg)	Vit A (μg)	Thia (mg)	Vit E (mg α)	Ribo (mg)	Niac (mg)	Vit B_6 (mg)	Fola (μg)	Vit C (mg)	Vit B_{12} (μg)	Sele (μg)
5	369	0.62	41.0	549.5	139.8	1.83	4.8	0.10	0.16	0.44	0.49	0.10	31.3	26.5	1.1	7.0
15	448	0.19	41.7	573.3	171.5	2.18	34.3	0.10	0.07	0.52	0.27	0.12	27.0	2.0	1.4	8.1
5	488	0.22	46.6	624.8	188.7	2.37	4.9	0.11	0.00	0.57	0.30	0.13	29.4	2.2	1.5	8.8
12	419	0.17	39.2	536.6	161.7	2.03	29.4	0.10	0.04	0.49	0.26	0.11	27.0	2.0	1.3	12.0
13	260	0.22	39.2	399.4	98.0	1.10	14.7	0.11	0.00	0.51	0.30	0.14	29.4	2.1	1.5	—
5	300	2.70	100.0	580.0	290.0	2.25	—	0.37	—	0.42	5.00	0.50	100.0	15.0	1.5	—
0	100	1.08	24.0	5.0	20.0	—	0	0.22	—	0.10	—	0.04	—	0	0	—
0	150	1.44	40.0	15.0	40.0	—	—	0.30	—	0.13	—	0.08	—	0	0	—
0	400	1.44	—	0	30.0	—	0	—	—	—	—	—	—	0	—	—
210	27	0.91	6.0	67.6	93.8	0.55	91.1	0.03	0.56	0.23	0.03	0.07	23.5	0	0.6	15.7
212	25	0.59	5.0	63.0	62.0	0.52	84.5	0.03	0.51	0.25	0.03	0.06	22.0	0	0.6	15.4
211	27	0.91	6.0	66.5	147.0	0.55	69.5	0.02	0.48	0.20	0.03	0.06	17.5	0	0.6	15.8
0	2	0.02	3.6	53.8	54.8	0.01	0	0.00	0.00	0.14	0.03	0.00	1.3	0	0	6.6
212	27	0.91	6.0	67.0	70.0	0.55	70.0	0.03	0.48	0.23	0.03	0.07	23.5	0	0.6	15.9
210	22	0.46	0.9	18.5	8.2	0.39	64.8	0.03	0.43	0.09	0.00	0.06	24.8	0	0.3	9.5
429	87	1.46	14.6	168.4	341.6	1.22	174.5	0.06	1.33	0.53	0.09	0.14	36.6	0.2	0.9	27.5
0	20	1.08	4.0	85.0	115.0	0.60	112.5	0.15	—	0.85	0.20	0.08	60.0	0	1.2	—
1	44	1.18	9.0	127.8	119.4	0.58	6.6	0.07	0.95	0.23	0.08	0.08	9.6	0.3	0.2	24.8
1	33	1.32	5.6	207.1	111.1	0.82	11.3	0.07	0.17	0.19	0.07	0.00	9.4	0	0.2	15.6
47	12	0.41	35.7	207.5	66.3	0.49	11.9	0.07	0.68	0.06	2.13	0.24	6.8	0.8	0.9	32.0
47	12	0.41	35.7	207.5	66.3	0.49	11.9	0.07	0.68	0.06	2.13	0.24	6.8	0.9	0.9	32.0
107	17	0.42	17.0	231.3	43.4	1.37	887.0	0.13	3.40	0.03	2.97	0.05	12.8	1.5	2.6	5.5
44	8	0.31	29.1	489.0	86.1	0.48	—	0.02	—	0.05	2.47	0.46	8.1	3.0	1.0	44.3
29	15	1.79	20.4	272.2	452.5	0.37	9.4	0.09	—	0.09	1.78	0.08	14.5	0	0.9	7.7
37	55	0.97	96.7	524.3	62.9	0.49	—	0.05	—	0.08	6.47	0.36	12.6	0	1.2	42.5
32	48	0.85	84.0	455.6	54.7	0.42	—	0.05	—	0.07	5.92	0.33	11.5	0	1.1	37.0
41	12	0.29	24.7	319.3	41.7	0.34	—	0.06	—	0.06	1.89	0.21	6.1	0.8	0.8	32.0
44	19	0.34	47.3	224.7	280.2	0.20	—	0.06	0.40	0.07	2.02	0.18	7.4	2.8	1.6	33.5
40	18	0.96	31.5	404.0	45.1	0.43	42.5	0.06	—	0.01	0.32	0.29	8.5	0	0.6	39.8
63	36	1.15	42.5	339.4	74.0	0.40	16.2	0.03	0.42	0.03	3.94	0.29	6.8	0	1.2	34.4
63	36	1.14	42.5	339.3	74.0	0.40	16.2	0.03	—	0.03	3.93	0.29	11.1	0	1.2	34.4
35	51	0.91	91.0	489.9	58.7	0.45	45.9	0.05	—	0.07	6.05	0.33	11.9	0	1.2	39.8
8	46	0.73	4.8	41.4	522.0	0.31	154.8	0.02	1.02	0.08	1.98	0.10	1.2	0	2.6	35.1
45	137	1.15	21.0	110.0	214.9	0.57	73.7	0.02	0.58	0.12	3.50	0.11	2.8	0.5	3.9	21.4

TABLE A-1 Table of Food Composition *(continued)*

(Computer code is for Cengage Diet Analysis program) (For purposes of calculations, use "0" for t, <1, <.1, <.01, etc.)

DA+ Code	Food Description	Qty	Measure	Wt (g)	H_2O (g)	Ener (cal)	Prot (g)	Carb (g)	Fiber (g)	Fat (g)	Fat Breakdown (g) Sat	Mono	Poly	Trans
	Seafood—continued													
8580	**Octopus, common, cooked, moist heat**	3	ounce(s)	85	51.5	139	25.4	3.7	0	1.8	0.4	0.3	0.4	—
1831	**Perch, mixed species, cooked, dry heat**	3	ounce(s)	85	62.3	100	21.1	0	0	1.0	0.2	0.2	0.4	—
1592	**Pacific rockfish, cooked, dry heat**	3	ounce(s)	85	62.4	103	20.4	0	0	1.7	0.4	0.4	0.5	—
	Salmon													
2938	Coho, farmed, raw	3	ounce(s)	85	59.9	136	18.1	0	0	6.5	1.5	2.8	1.6	—
1594	Broiled or baked with butter	3	ounce(s)	85	53.9	155	23.0	0	0	6.3	1.2	2.3	2.3	—
29727	Smoked chinook (lox)	2	ounce(s)	57	40.8	66	10.4	0	0	2.4	0.5	1.1	0.6	—
154	**Sardine, Atlantic with bones, canned in oil**	3	ounce(s)	85	50.7	177	20.9	0	0	9.7	1.3	3.3	4.4	—
	Scallops													
155	Mixed species, breaded, fried	3	item(s)	47	27.2	100	8.4	4.7	—	5.1	1.2	2.1	1.3	—
1599	Steamed	3	ounce(s)	85	64.8	90	13.8	2.0	0	2.6	0.4	1.0	0.8	—
1839	**Snapper, mixed species, cooked, dry heat**	3	ounce(s)	85	59.8	109	22.4	0	0	1.5	0.3	0.3	0.5	—
	Squid													
1868	Mixed species, fried	3	ounce(s)	85	54.9	149	15.3	6.6	0	6.4	1.6	2.3	1.8	—
16617	Steamed or boiled	3	ounce(s)	85	63.3	89	15.2	3.0	0	1.3	0.4	0.1	0.5	—
1570	**Striped bass, cooked, dry heat**	3	ounce(s)	85	62.4	105	19.3	0	0	2.5	0.6	0.7	0.9	—
1601	**Sturgeon, steamed**	3	ounce(s)	85	59.4	111	17.0	0	0	4.3	1.0	2.0	0.7	—
1840	**Surimi, formed**	3	ounce(s)	85	64.9	84	12.9	5.8	0	0.8	0.2	0.1	0.4	—
1842	**Swordfish, cooked, dry heat**	3	ounce(s)	85	58.5	132	21.6	0	0	4.4	1.2	1.7	1.0	—
1846	**Tuna, yellowfin or ahi, raw**	3	ounce(s)	85	60.4	92	19.9	0	0	0.8	0.2	0.1	0.2	—
	Tuna, canned													
159	Light, canned in oil, drained	2	ounce(s)	57	33.9	112	16.5	0	0	4.6	0.9	1.7	1.6	—
355	Light, canned in water, drained	2	ounce(s)	57	42.2	66	14.5	0	0	0.5	0.1	0.1	0.2	—
33211	Light, no salt, canned in oil, drained	2	ounce(s)	57	33.9	112	16.5	0	0	4.7	0.9	1.7	1.6	—
33212	Light, no salt, canned in water, drained	2	ounce(s)	57	42.6	66	14.5	0	0	0.5	0.1	0.1	0.2	—
2961	White, canned in oil, drained	2	ounce(s)	57	36.3	105	15.0	0	0	4.6	0.7	1.8	1.7	—
351	White, canned in water, drained	2	ounce(s)	57	41.5	73	13.4	0	0	1.7	0.4	0.4	0.6	—
33213	White, no salt, canned in oil, drained	2	ounce(s)	57	36.3	105	15.0	0	0	4.6	0.9	1.4	1.9	—
33214	White, no salt, canned in water, drained	2	ounce(s)	57	42.0	73	13.4	0	0	1.7	0.4	0.4	0.6	—
	Yellowtail													
8548	Mixed species, cooked, dry heat	3	ounce(s)	85	57.3	159	25.2	0	0	5.7	1.4	2.2	1.5	—
2970	Mixed species, raw	2	ounce(s)	57	42.2	83	13.1	0	0	3.0	0.7	1.1	0.8	—
	Shellfish, meat only													
1857	Abalone, mixed species, fried	3	ounce(s)	85	51.1	161	16.7	9.4	0	5.8	1.4	2.3	1.4	—
16618	Abalone, steamed or poached	3	ounce(s)	85	40.7	177	28.8	10.1	0	1.3	0.3	0.2	0.2	—
	Crab													
1851	Blue crab, canned	2	ounce(s)	57	43.2	56	11.6	0	0	0.7	0.1	0.1	0.2	—
1852	Blue crab, cooked, moist heat	3	ounce(s)	85	65.9	87	17.2	0	0	1.5	0.2	0.2	0.6	—
8562	Dungeness crab, cooked, moist heat	3	ounce(s)	85	62.3	94	19.0	0.8	0	1.1	0.1	0.2	0.3	—
1860	**Clams, cooked, moist heat**	3	ounce(s)	85	54.1	126	21.7	4.4	0	1.7	0.2	0.1	0.5	—
1853	**Crayfish, farmed, cooked, moist heat**	3	ounce(s)	85	68.7	74	14.9	0	0	1.1	0.2	0.2	0.4	—

PAGE KEY: A-2 = Breads/Baked Goods A-8 = Cereal/Rice/Pasta A-12 = Fruit A-18 = Vegetables/Legumes A-28 = Nuts/Seeds A-30 = Vegetarian A-32 = Dairy A-40 = Eggs A-40 = Seafood A-44 = Meats A-48 = Poultry A-48 = Processed Meats A-50 = Beverages A-54 = Fats/Oils A-56 = Sweets A-58 = Spices/Condiments/Sauces A-62 = Mixed Foods/Soups/Sandwiches A-68 = Fast Food A-88 = Convenience A-90 = Baby Foods

Chol (mg)	Calc (mg)	Iron (mg)	Magn (mg)	Pota (mg)	Sodi (mg)	Zinc (mg)	Vit A (μg)	Thia (mg)	Vit E (mg α)	Ribo (mg)	Niac (mg)	Vit B_6 (mg)	Fola (μg)	Vit C (mg)	Vit B_{12} (μg)	Sele (μg)
82	90	8.11	51.0	535.8	391.2	2.85	76.5	0.04	1.02	0.06	3.21	0.55	20.4	6.8	30.6	76.2
98	87	0.98	32.3	292.6	67.2	1.21	8.5	0.06	—	0.10	1.61	0.11	5.1	1.4	1.9	13.7
37	10	0.45	28.9	442.3	65.5	0.45	60.4	0.03	1.32	0.07	3.33	0.22	8.5	0	1.0	39.8
43	10	0.29	26.4	382.7	40.0	0.36	47.6	0.08	—	0.09	5.79	0.56	11.1	0.9	2.3	10.7
40	15	1.02	26.9	376.6	98.6	0.56	—	0.13	1.14	0.05	8.33	0.18	4.2	1.8	2.3	41.0
13	6	0.48	10.2	99.2	1134.0	0.17	14.7	0.01	—	0.05	2.67	0.15	1.1	0	1.8	21.6
121	325	2.48	33.2	337.6	429.5	1.10	27.2	0.04	1.70	0.18	4.43	0.14	10.2	0	7.6	44.8
28	20	0.38	27.4	154.8	215.8	0.49	10.7	0.02	—	0.05	0.70	0.06	17.2	1.1	0.6	12.5
27	20	0.22	45.9	238.0	358.7	0.78	32.3	0.01	0.16	0.05	0.84	0.11	10.2	2.0	1.1	18.2
40	34	0.20	31.5	444.0	48.5	0.37	29.8	0.04	—	0.00	0.29	0.39	5.1	1.4	3.0	41.7
221	33	0.85	32.3	237.3	260.3	1.48	9.4	0.04	—	0.39	2.21	0.04	11.9	3.6	1.0	44.1
227	31	0.62	28.9	192.1	356.2	1.49	8.5	0.01	1.17	0.32	1.69	0.04	3.4	3.2	1.0	43.7
88	16	0.91	43.4	279.0	74.8	0.43	26.4	0.09	—	0.03	2.17	0.29	8.5	0	3.8	39.8
63	11	0.59	29.8	239.7	388.5	0.35	198.9	0.06	0.52	0.07	8.30	0.19	14.5	0	2.2	13.3
26	8	0.22	36.6	95.3	121.6	0.28	17.0	0.01	0.53	0.01	0.18	0.02	1.7	0	1.4	23.9
43	5	0.88	28.9	313.8	97.8	1.25	34.9	0.03	—	0.09	10.02	0.32	1.7	0.9	1.7	52.5
38	14	0.62	42.5	377.6	31.5	0.44	15.3	0.37	0.42	0.04	8.33	0.77	1.7	0.8	0.4	31.0
10	7	0.79	17.6	117.3	200.6	0.51	13.0	0.02	0.49	0.07	7.03	0.06	2.8	0	1.2	43.1
17	6	0.87	15.3	134.3	191.5	0.43	9.6	0.01	0.19	0.04	7.52	0.19	2.3	0	1.7	45.6
10	7	0.78	17.6	117.4	28.3	0.51	0	0.02	—	0.06	7.03	0.06	2.8	0	1.2	43.1
17	6	0.86	15.3	134.4	28.3	0.43	0	0.01	—	0.04	7.52	0.19	2.3	0	1.7	45.6
18	2	0.36	19.3	188.8	224.5	0.26	2.8	0.01	1.30	0.04	6.63	0.24	2.8	0	1.2	34.1
24	8	0.55	18.7	134.3	213.6	0.27	3.4	0.00	0.48	0.02	3.28	0.12	1.1	0	0.7	37.2
18	2	0.36	19.3	188.8	28.3	0.26	0	0.01	—	0.04	6.63	0.24	2.8	0	1.2	34.1
24	8	0.54	18.7	134.4	28.3	0.27	3.4	0.00	—	0.02	3.28	0.12	1.1	0	0.7	37.3
60	25	0.53	32.3	457.6	42.5	0.56	26.4	0.14	—	0.04	7.41	0.15	3.4	2.5	1.1	39.8
31	13	0.28	17.0	238.1	22.1	0.29	16.4	0.08	—	0.02	3.86	0.09	2.3	1.6	0.7	20.7
80	31	3.23	47.6	241.5	502.6	0.80	1.7	0.18	—	0.11	1.61	0.12	11.9	1.5	0.6	44.1
144	50	4.84	68.9	295.0	980.1	1.38	3.4	0.28	6.74	0.12	1.89	0.21	6.0	2.6	0.7	75.6
50	57	0.47	22.1	212.1	188.8	2.27	1.1	0.04	1.04	0.04	0.77	0.08	24.4	1.5	0.3	18.0
85	88	0.77	28.1	275.6	237.3	3.58	1.7	0.08	1.56	0.04	2.80	0.15	43.4	2.8	6.2	34.2
65	50	0.36	49.3	347.0	321.5	4.65	26.4	0.04	—	0.17	3.08	0.14	35.7	3.1	8.8	40.5
57	78	23.78	15.3	534.1	95.3	2.32	145.4	0.12	—	0.36	2.85	0.09	24.7	18.8	84.1	54.4
117	43	0.94	28.1	202.4	82.5	1.25	12.8	0.03	—	0.06	1.41	0.11	9.4	0.4	2.6	29.1

A

TABLE A-1 Table of Food Composition *(continued)*

(Computer code is for Cengage Diet Analysis program) (For purposes of calculations, use "0" for t, <1, <.1, <.01, etc.)

DA+ Code	Food Description	QTY	Measure	Wt (g)	H_2O (g)	Ener (cal)	Prot (g)	Carb (g)	Fiber (g)	Fat (g)	Fat Breakdown (g) Sat	Mono	Poly	Trans
	Seafood—continued													
	Oysters													
8720	Baked or broiled	3	ounce(s)	85	68.6	89	5.6	3.2	0	5.8	1.3	2.1	1.9	—
152	Eastern, farmed, raw	3	ounce(s)	85	73.3	50	4.4	4.7	0	1.3	0.4	0.1	0.5	—
8715	Eastern, wild, cooked, moist heat	3	ounce(s)	85	59.8	117	12.0	6.7	0	4.2	1.3	0.5	1.6	—
8584	Pacific, cooked, moist heat	3	ounce(s)	85	54.5	139	16.1	8.4	0	3.9	0.9	0.7	1.5	—
1865	Pacific, raw	3	ounce(s)	85	69.8	69	8.0	4.2	0	2.0	0.4	0.3	0.8	—
1854	**Lobster, northern, cooked, moist heat**	3	ounce(s)	85	64.7	83	17.4	1.1	0	0.5	0.1	0.1	0.1	—
1862	**Mussel, blue, cooked, moist heat**	3	ounce(s)	85	52.0	146	20.2	6.3	0	3.8	0.7	0.9	1.0	—
	Shrimp													
158	Mixed species, breaded, fried	3	ounce(s)	85	44.9	206	18.2	9.8	0.3	10.4	1.8	3.2	4.3	—
1855	Mixed species, cooked, moist heat	3	ounce(s)	85	65.7	84	17.8	0	0	0.9	0.2	0.2	0.4	—
	Beef, Lamb, Pork													
	Beef													
4450	Breakfast strips, cooked	2	slice(s)	23	5.9	101	7.1	0.3	0	7.8	3.2	3.8	0.4	—
174	Corned beef, canned	3	ounce(s)	85	49.1	213	23.0	0	0	12.7	5.3	5.1	0.5	—
33147	Cured, thin siced	2	ounce(s)	57	32.9	100	15.9	3.2	0	2.2	0.9	1.0	0.1	—
4581	Jerky	1	ounce(s)	28	6.6	116	9.4	3.1	0.5	7.3	3.1	3.2	0.3	—
	Ground beef													
5898	Lean, broiled, medium	3	ounce(s)	85	50.4	202	21.6	0	0	12.2	4.8	5.3	0.4	—
5899	Lean, broiled, well done	3	ounce(s)	85	48.4	214	23.8	0	0	12.5	5.0	5.7	0.3	0.4
5914	Regular, broiled, medium	3	ounce(s)	85	46.1	246	20.5	0	0	17.6	6.9	7.7	0.6	—
5915	Regular, broiled, well done	3	ounce(s)	85	43.8	259	21.6	0	0	18.4	7.5	8.5	0.5	0.6
	Beef rib													
4241	Rib, small end, separable lean, 0″ fat, broiled	3	ounce(s)	85	53.2	164	25.0	0	0	6.4	2.4	2.6	0.2	—
4183	Rib, whole, lean and fat, ¼″ fat, roasted	3	ounce(s)	85	39.0	320	18.9	0	0	26.6	10.7	11.4	0.9	—
	Beef roast													
16981	Bottom round, choice, separable lean and fat, ⅛″ fat, braised	3	ounce(s)	85	46.2	216	27.9	0	0	10.7	4.1	4.6	0.4	—
16979	Bottom round, separable lean and fat, ⅛″ fat, roasted	3	ounce(s)	85	52.4	185	22.5	0	0	9.9	3.8	4.2	0.4	—
16924	Chuck, arm pot roast, separable lean and fat, ⅛″ fat, braised	3	ounce(s)	85	42.9	257	25.6	0	0	16.3	6.5	7.0	0.6	—
16930	Chuck, blade roast, separable lean and fat, ⅛″ fat, braised	3	ounce(s)	85	40.5	290	22.8	0	0	21.4	8.5	9.2	0.8	—
5853	Chuck, blade roast, separable lean, 0″ trim, pot roasted	3	ounce(s)	85	47.4	202	26.4	0	0	9.9	3.9	4.3	0.3	—
4296	Eye of round, choice, separable lean, 0″ fat, roasted	3	ounce(s)	85	56.5	138	24.4	0	0	3.7	1.3	1.5	0.1	—
16989	Eye of round, separable lean and fat, ⅛″ fat, roasted	3	ounce(s)	85	52.2	180	24.2	0	0	8.5	3.2	3.6	0.3	—
	Beef steak													
4348	Short loin, t-bone steak, lean and fat, ¼″ fat, broiled	3	ounce(s)	85	43.2	274	19.4	0	0	21.2	8.3	9.6	0.8	—
4349	Short loin, t-bone steak, lean, ¼″ fat, broiled	3	ounce(s)	85	52.3	174	22.8	0	0	8.5	3.1	4.2	0.3	—
4360	Top loin, prime, lean and fat, ¼″ fat, broiled	3	ounce(s)	85	42.7	275	21.6	0	0	20.3	8.2	8.6	0.7	—
	Beef variety													
188	Liver, pan fried	3	ounce(s)	85	52.7	149	22.6	4.4	0	4.0	1.3	0.5	0.5	0.2
4447	Tongue, simmered	3	ounce(s)	85	49.2	242	16.4	0	0	19.0	6.9	8.6	0.6	0.7
	Lamb chop													
3275	Loin, domestic, lean and fat, ¼″ fat, broiled	3	ounce(s)	85	43.9	269	21.4	0	0	19.6	8.4	8.3	1.4	—

PAGE KEY: A-2 = Breads/Baked Goods A-8 = Cereal/Rice/Pasta A-12 = Fruit A-18 = Vegetables/Legumes A-28 = Nuts/Seeds A-30 = Vegetarian A-32 = Dairy A-40 = Eggs A-40 = Seafood A-44 = Meats A-48 = Poultry A-48 = Processed Meats A-50 = Beverages A-54 = Fats/Oils A-56 = Sweets A-58 = Spices/Condiments/Sauces A-62 = Mixed Foods/Soups/Sandwiches A-68 = Fast Food A-88 = Convenience A-90 = Baby Foods

A

Chol (mg)	Calc (mg)	Iron (mg)	Magn (mg)	Pota (mg)	Sodi (mg)	Zinc (mg)	Vit A (µg)	Thia (mg)	Vit E (mg α)	Ribo (mg)	Niac (mg)	Vit B_6 (mg)	Fola (µg)	Vit C (mg)	Vit B_{12} (µg)	Sele (µg)
43	36	5.30	37.4	125.0	403.8	72.22	60.4	0.07	0.98	0.06	1.04	0.04	7.7	2.8	14.7	50.7
21	37	4.91	28.1	105.4	151.3	32.23	6.8	0.08	—	0.05	1.07	0.05	15.3	4.0	13.8	54.1
89	77	10.19	80.8	239.0	358.9	154.45	45.9	0.16	—	0.15	2.11	0.10	11.9	5.1	29.8	60.9
85	14	7.82	37.4	256.8	180.3	28.27	124.2	0.10	0.72	0.37	3.07	0.07	12.8	10.9	24.5	131.0
43	7	4.34	18.7	142.9	90.1	14.13	68.9	0.05	—	0.20	1.70	0.04	8.5	6.8	13.6	65.5
61	52	0.33	29.8	299.4	323.2	2.48	22.1	0.01	0.85	0.05	0.91	0.06	9.4	0	2.6	36.3
48	28	5.71	31.5	227.9	313.8	2.27	77.4	0.25	—	0.35	2.55	0.08	64.6	11.6	20.4	76.2
150	57	1.07	34.0	191.3	292.4	1.17	0	0.11	—	0.11	2.60	0.08	15.3	1.3	1.6	35.4
166	33	2.62	28.9	154.8	190.5	1.32	57.8	0.02	1.17	0.02	2.20	0.10	3.4	1.9	1.3	33.7
27	2	0.71	6.1	93.1	509.2	1.44	0	0.02	0.06	0.05	1.46	0.07	1.8	0	0.8	6.1
73	10	1.76	11.9	115.7	855.6	3.03	0	0.01	0.12	0.12	2.06	0.11	7.7	0	1.4	36.5
23	6	1.53	10.8	243.2	815.9	2.25	0	0.04	0.00	0.10	2.98	0.19	6.2	0	1.5	16.0
14	6	1.53	14.5	169.2	627.4	2.29	0	0.04	0.13	0.04	0.49	0.05	38.0	0	0.3	3.0
58	6	2.00	17.9	266.2	59.5	4.63	0	0.05	—	0.23	4.21	0.23	7.6	0	1.8	16.0
69	12	2.21	18.4	250.0	62.4	5.86	0	0.08	—	0.23	5.10	0.16	9.4	0	1.7	19.0
62	9	2.07	17.0	248.3	70.6	4.40	0	0.02	—	0.16	4.90	0.23	7.6	0	2.5	16.2
71	12	2.30	18.5	242.4	72.4	5.18	0	0.08	—	0.23	4.93	0.17	8.5	0	1.6	18.0
65	16	1.59	21.3	319.8	51.9	4.64	0	0.06	0.34	0.12	7.15	0.53	8.5	0	1.4	29.2
72	9	1.96	16.2	251.7	53.6	4.45	0	0.06	—	0.14	2.85	0.19	6.0	0	2.1	18.7
68	6	2.29	17.9	223.7	35.7	4.59	0	0.05	0.41	0.15	5.05	0.36	8.5	0	1.7	29.3
64	5	1.83	14.5	182.0	29.8	3.76	0	0.05	0.34	0.12	3.92	0.29	6.8	0	1.3	23.0
67	14	2.15	17.0	205.8	42.5	5.93	0	0.05	0.45	0.15	3.63	0.25	7.7	0	1.9	24.1
88	11	2.66	16.2	198.2	55.3	7.15	0	0.06	0.17	0.20	2.06	0.22	4.3	0	1.9	20.9
73	11	3.12	19.6	223.7	60.4	8.73	0	0.06	—	0.23	2.27	0.24	5.1	0	2.1	22.7
49	5	2.16	16.2	200.7	32.3	4.28	0	0.05	0.30	0.15	4.69	0.34	8.5	0	1.4	28.0
54	5	1.98	15.3	193.1	31.5	3.95	0	0.05	0.34	0.13	4.37	0.31	7.7	0	1.5	25.2
58	7	2.56	17.9	233.9	57.8	3.56	0	0.07	0.18	0.17	3.29	0.27	6.0	0	1.8	10.0
50	5	3.11	22.1	278.1	65.5	4.34	0	0.09	0.11	0.21	3.93	0.33	6.8	0	1.9	8.5
67	8	1.88	19.6	294.3	53.6	3.85	0	0.06	—	0.15	3.96	0.31	6.0	0	1.6	19.5
324	5	5.24	18.7	298.5	65.5	4.44	6586.3	0.15	0.39	2.91	14.86	0.87	221.1	0.6	70.7	27.9
112	4	2.22	12.8	156.5	55.3	3.47	0	0.01	0.25	0.25	2.96	0.13	6.0	1.1	2.7	11.2
85	17	1.53	20.4	278.1	65.5	2.96	0	0.08	0.11	0.21	6.03	0.11	15.3	0	2.1	23.3

TABLE A-1 Table of Food Composition *(continued)*

(Computer code is for Cengage Diet Analysis program) (For purposes of calculations, use "0" for t, <1, <.1, <.01, etc.)

DA+ Code	Food Description	QTY	Measure	Wt (g)	H_2O (g)	Ener (cal)	Prot (g)	Carb (g)	Fiber (g)	Fat (g)	Fat Breakdown (g) Sat	Mono	Poly	Trans
	Beef, Lamb, Pork—continued													
	Lamb leg													
3264	Domestic, lean and fat, ¼" fat, cooked	3	ounce(s)	85	45.7	250	20.9	0	0	17.8	7.5	7.5	1.3	—
	Lamb rib													
182	Domestic, lean and fat, ¼" fat, broiled	3	ounce(s)	85	40.0	307	18.8	0	0	25.2	10.8	10.3	2.0	—
183	Domestic, lean, ¼" fat, broiled	3	ounce(s)	85	50.0	200	23.6	0	0	11.0	4.0	4.4	1.0	—
	Lamb shoulder													
186	Shoulder, arm and blade, domestic, choice, lean and fat, ¼" fat, roasted	3	ounce(s)	85	47.8	235	19.1	0	0	17.0	7.2	6.9	1.4	—
187	Shoulder, arm and blade, domestic, choice, lean, ¼" fat, roasted	3	ounce(s)	85	53.8	173	21.2	0	0	9.2	3.5	3.7	0.8	—
3287	Shoulder, arm, domestic, lean and fat, ¼" fat, braised	3	ounce(s)	85	37.6	294	25.8	0	0	20.4	8.4	8.7	1.5	—
3290	Shoulder, arm, domestic, lean, ¼" fat, braised	3	ounce(s)	85	41.9	237	30.2	0	0	12.0	4.3	5.2	0.8	—
	Lamb variety													
3375	Brain, pan fried	3	ounce(s)	85	51.6	232	14.4	0	0	18.9	4.8	3.4	1.9	—
3406	Tongue, braised	3	ounce(s)	85	49.2	234	18.3	0	0	17.2	6.7	8.5	1.1	—
	Pork, cured													
29229	Bacon, Canadian style, cured	2	ounce(s)	57	37.9	89	11.7	1.0	0	4.0	1.3	1.8	0.4	—
161	Bacon, cured, broiled, pan fried or roasted	2	slice(s)	16	2.0	87	5.9	0.2	0	6.7	2.2	3.0	0.7	0
35422	Breakfast strips, cured, cooked	3	slice(s)	34	9.2	156	9.8	0.4	0	12.5	4.3	5.6	1.9	—
189	Ham, cured, boneless, 11% fat, roasted	3	ounce(s)	85	54.9	151	19.2	0	0	7.7	2.7	3.8	1.2	—
29215	Ham, cured, extra lean, 4% fat, canned	2	2 ounce(s)	57	41.7	68	10.5	0	0	2.6	0.9	1.3	0.2	—
1316	Ham, cured, extra lean, 5% fat, roasted	3	ounce(s)	85	57.6	123	17.8	1.3	0	4.7	1.5	2.2	0.5	—
16561	Ham, smoked or cured, lean, cooked	1	slice(s)	42	27.6	66	10.5	0	0	2.3	0.8	1.1	0.3	—
	Pork chop													
32671	Loin, blade, chops, lean and fat, pan fried	3	ounce(s)	85	42.5	291	18.3	0	0	23.6	8.6	10	2.6	—
32672	Loin, center cut, chops, lean and fat, pan fried	3	ounce(s)	85	45.1	236	25.4	0	0	14.1	5.1	6.0	1.6	—
32682	Loin, center rib, chops, boneless, lean and fat, braised	3	ounce(s)	85	49.5	217	22.4	0	0	13.4	5.2	6.1	1.1	—
32603	Loin, center rib, chops, lean, broiled	3	ounce(s)	85	55.4	158	21.9	0	0	7.1	2.4	3.0	0.8	0.1
32478	Loin, whole, lean and fat, braised	3	ounce(s)	85	49.6	203	23.2	0	0	11.6	4.3	5.2	1.0	—
32481	Loin, whole, lean, braised	3	ounce(s)	85	52.2	174	24.3	0	0	7.8	2.9	3.5	0.6	—
	Pork leg or ham													
32471	Pork leg or ham, rump portion, lean and fat, roasted	3	ounce(s)	85	48.3	214	24.6	0	0	12.1	4.5	5.4	1.2	—
32468	Pork leg or ham, whole, lean and fat, roasted	3	ounce(s)	85	46.8	232	22.8	0	0	15.0	5.5	6.7	1.4	—
	Pork ribs													
32693	Loin, country style, lean and fat, roasted	3	ounce(s)	85	43.3	279	19.9	0	0	21.6	7.8	9.4	1.7	—
32696	Loin, country style, lean, roasted	3	ounce(s)	85	49.5	210	22.6	0	0	12.6	4.5	5.5	0.9	—
	Pork shoulder													
32626	Shoulder, arm picnic, lean and fat, roasted	3	ounce(s)	85	44.3	270	20.0	0	0	20.4	7.5	9.1	2.0	—
32629	Shoulder, arm picnic, lean, roasted	3	ounce(s)	85	51.3	194	22.7	0	0	10.7	3.7	5.1	1.0	—
	Rabbit													
3366	Domesticated, roasted	3	ounce(s)	85	51.5	168	24.7	0	0	6.8	2.0	1.8	1.3	—
3367	Domesticated, stewed	3	ounce(s)	85	50.0	175	25.8	0	0	7.2	2.1	1.9	1.4	—

PAGE KEY: A-2 = Breads/Baked Goods A-8 = Cereal/Rice/Pasta A-12 = Fruit A-18 = Vegetables/Legumes A-28 = Nuts/Seeds A-30 = Vegetarian A-32 = Dairy A-40 = Eggs A-40 = Seafood A-44 = Meats A-48 = Poultry A-48 = Processed Meats A-50 = Beverages A-54 = Fats/Oils A-56 = Sweets A-58 = Spices/Condiments/Sauces A-62 = Mixed Foods/Soups/Sandwiches A-68 = Fast Food A-88 = Convenience A-90 = Baby Foods

A

Chol (mg)	Calc (mg)	Iron (mg)	Magn (mg)	Pota (mg)	Sodi (mg)	Zinc (mg)	Vit A (μg)	Thia (mg)	Vit E (mg α)	Ribo (mg)	Niac (mg)	Vit B_6 (mg)	Fola (μg)	Vit C (mg)	Vit B_{12} (μg)	Sele (μg)
82	14	1.59	19.6	263.7	61.2	3.79	0	0.08	0.11	0.21	5.66	0.11	15.3	0	2.2	22.5
84	16	1.59	19.6	229.5	64.6	3.40	0	0.07	0.10	0.18	5.95	0.09	11.9	0	2.2	20.3
77	14	1.87	24.7	266.1	72.3	4.47	0	0.08	0.15	0.21	5.56	0.12	17.9	0	2.2	26.4
78	17	1.67	19.6	213.4	56.1	4.44	0	0.07	0.11	0.20	5.22	0.11	17.9	0	2.2	22.3
74	16	1.81	21.3	225.3	57.8	5.13	0	0.07	0.15	0.22	4.89	0.12	21.3	0	2.3	24.2
102	21	2.03	22.1	260.3	61.2	5.17	0	0.06	0.12	0.21	5.66	0.09	15.3	0	2.2	31.6
103	22	2.29	24.7	287.5	64.6	6.20	0	0.06	0.15	0.23	5.38	0.11	18.7	0	2.3	32.1
2130	18	1.73	18.7	304.5	133.5	1.70	0	0.14	—	0.31	3.87	0.19	6.0	19.6	20.5	10.2
161	9	2.23	13.6	134.4	57.0	2.54	0	0.06	—	0.35	3.13	0.14	2.6	6.0	5.4	23.8
28	5	0.38	9.6	195.0	798.9	0.78	0	0.42	0.11	0.09	3.53	0.22	2.3	0	0.4	14.2
18	2	0.22	5.3	90.4	369.6	0.56	1.8	0.06	0.04	0.04	1.76	0.04	0.3	0	0.2	9.9
36	5	0.67	8.8	158.4	713.7	1.25	0	0.25	0.08	0.12	2.58	0.11	1.4	0	0.6	8.4
50	7	1.13	18.7	347.7	1275.0	2.09	0	0.62	0.26	0.28	5.22	0.26	2.6	0	0.6	16.8
22	3	0.53	9.6	206.4	711.6	1.09	0	0.47	0.09	0.13	3.00	0.25	3.4	0	0.5	8.2
45	7	1.25	11.9	244.1	1023.1	2.44	0	0.64	0.21	0.17	3.42	0.34	2.6	0	0.6	16.6
23	3	0.39	9.2	132.7	557.3	1.07	0	0.28	0.10	0.10	2.10	0.19	1.7	0	0.3	10.7
72	26	0.74	17.9	282.4	57.0	2.71	1.7	0.52	0.17	0.25	3.35	0.28	3.4	0.5	0.7	29.7
78	23	0.77	24.7	361.5	68.0	1.96	1.7	0.96	0.21	0.25	4.76	0.39	5.1	0.9	0.6	33.2
62	4	0.78	14.5	329.1	34.0	1.76	1.7	0.44	—	0.20	3.66	0.26	3.4	0.3	0.4	28.4
56	22	0.57	21.3	291.7	48.5	1.91	0	0.48	0.08	0.18	6.68	0.57	0	0	0.4	38.6
68	18	0.91	16.2	318.1	40.8	2.02	1.7	0.53	0.20	0.21	3.75	0.31	2.6	0.5	0.5	38.5
67	15	0.96	17.0	329.1	42.5	2.10	1.7	0.56	0.17	0.22	3.90	0.32	3.4	0.5	0.5	41.0
82	10	0.89	23.0	318.1	52.7	2.39	2.6	0.63	0.18	0.28	3.95	0.26	2.6	0.2	0.6	39.8
80	12	0.85	18.7	299.4	51.0	2.51	2.6	0.54	0.18	0.26	3.89	0.34	8.5	0.3	0.6	38.5
78	21	0.90	19.6	292.6	44.2	2.00	2.6	0.75	—	0.29	3.67	0.37	4.3	0.3	0.7	31.6
79	25	1.09	20.4	296.8	24.7	3.24	1.7	0.48	—	0.29	3.96	0.37	4.3	0.3	0.7	36.0
80	16	1.00	14.5	276.4	59.5	2.93	1.7	0.44	—	0.25	3.33	0.29	3.4	0.2	0.6	28.6
81	8	1.20	17.0	298.5	68.0	3.46	1.7	0.49	—	0.30	3.66	0.34	4.3	0.3	0.7	32.7
70	16	1.93	17.9	325.7	40.0	1.93	0	0.07	—	0.17	7.17	0.40	9.4	0	7.1	32.7
73	17	2.01	17.0	255.1	31.5	2.01	0	0.05	0.37	0.14	6.09	0.28	7.7	0	5.5	32.7

TABLE A-1 Table of Food Composition *(continued)*

(Computer code is for Cengage Diet Analysis program) (For purposes of calculations, use "0" for t, <1, <.1, <.01, etc.)

DA+ Code	Food Description	Qty	Measure	Wt (g)	H_2O (g)	Ener (cal)	Prot (g)	Carb (g)	Fiber (g)	Fat (g)	Fat Breakdown (g) Sat	Mono	Poly	Trans
	Beef, Lamb, Pork—continued													
	Veal													
3391	Liver, braised	3	ounce(s)	85	50.9	163	24.2	3.2	0	5.3	1.7	1.0	0.9	0.3
3319	Rib, lean only, roasted	3	ounce(s)	85	55.0	151	21.9	0	0	6.3	1.8	2.3	0.6	—
1732	Deer or venison, roasted	3	ounce(s)	85	55.5	134	25.7	0	0	2.7	1.1	0.7	0.5	—
	Poultry													
	Chicken													
29562	Flaked, canned	2	ounce(s)	57	39.3	97	10.3	0.1	0	5.8	1.6	2.3	1.3	—
	Chicken, fried													
29632	Breast, meat only, breaded, baked or fried	3	ounce(s)	85	44.3	193	25.3	6.9	0.2	6.6	1.6	2.7	1.7	—
35327	Broiler breast, meat only, fried	3	ounce(s)	85	51.2	159	28.4	0.4	0	4.0	1.1	1.5	0.9	—
36413	Broiler breast, meat and skin, flour coated, fried	3	ounce(s)	85	48.1	189	27.1	1.4	0.1	7.5	2.1	3.0	1.7	—
36414	Broiler drumstick, meat and skin, flour coated, fried	3	ounce(s)	85	48.2	208	22.9	1.4	0.1	11.7	3.1	4.6	2.7	—
35389	Broiler drumstick, meat only, fried	3	ounce(s)	85	52.9	166	24.3	0	0	6.9	1.8	2.5	1.7	—
35406	Broiler leg, meat only, fried	3	ounce(s)	85	51.5	177	24.1	0.6	0	7.9	2.1	2.9	1.9	—
35484	Broiler wing, meat only, fried	3	ounce(s)	85	50.9	179	25.6	0	0	7.8	2.1	2.6	1.8	—
29580	Patty, fillet or tenders, breaded, cooked	3	ounce(s)	85	40.2	256	14.5	12.2	0	16.5	3.7	8.4	3.7	—
	Chicken, roasted, meat only													
35409	Broiler leg, meat only, roasted	3	ounce(s)	85	55.0	162	23.0	0	0	7.2	1.9	2.6	1.7	—
35486	Broiler wing, meat only, roasted	3	ounce(s)	85	53.4	173	25.9	0	0	6.9	1.9	2.2	1.5	—
35138	Roasting chicken, dark meat, meat only, roasted	3	ounce(s)	85	57.0	151	19.8	0	0	7.4	2.1	2.8	1.7	—
35136	Roasting chicken, light meat, meat only, roasted	3	ounce(s)	85	57.7	130	23.1	0	0	3.5	0.9	1.3	0.8	—
35132	Roasting chicken, meat only, roasted	3	ounce(s)	85	57.3	142	21.3	0	0	5.6	1.5	2.1	1.3	—
	Chicken, stewed													
1268	Gizzard, simmered	3	ounce(s)	85	57.8	124	25.8	0	0	2.3	0.6	0.4	0.3	0.1
1270	Liver, simmered	3	ounce(s)	85	56.8	142	20.8	0.7	0	5.5	1.8	1.2	1.7	0.1
3174	Meat only, stewed	3	ounce(s)	85	56.8	151	23.2	0	0	5.7	1.6	2.0	1.3	—
	Duck													
1286	Domesticated, meat and skin, roasted	3	ounce(s)	85	44.1	287	16.2	0	0	24.1	8.2	11.0	3.1	—
1287	Domesticated, meat only, roasted	3	ounce(s)	85	54.6	171	20.0	0	0	9.5	3.5	3.1	1.2	—
	Goose													
35507	Domesticated, meat and skin, roasted	3	ounce(s)	85	44.2	259	21.4	0	0	18.6	5.8	8.7	2.1	—
35524	Domesticated, meat only, roasted	3	ounce(s)	85	48.7	202	24.6	0	0	10.8	3.9	3.7	1.3	—
1297	Liver pate, smoked, canned	4	tablespoon(s)	52	19.3	240	5.9	2.4	0	22.8	7.5	13.3	0.4	—
	Turkey													
3256	Ground turkey, cooked	3	ounce(s)	85	50.5	200	23.3	0	0	11.2	2.9	4.2	2.7	—
3263	Patty, batter coated, breaded, fried	1	item(s)	94	46.7	266	13.2	14.8	0.5	16.9	4.4	7.0	4.4	—
219	Roasted, dark meat, meat only	3	ounce(s)	85	53.7	159	24.3	0	0	6.1	2.1	1.4	1.8	—
222	Roasted, fryer roaster breast, meat only	3	ounce(s)	85	58.2	115	25.6	0	0	0.6	0.2	0.1	0.2	—
220	Roasted, light meat, meat only	3	ounce(s)	85	56.4	134	25.4	0	0	2.7	0.9	0.5	0.7	—
1303	Turkey roll, light and dark meat	2	slice(s)	57	39.8	84	10.3	1.2	0	4.0	1.2	1.3	1.0	—
1302	Turkey roll, light meat	2	slice(s)	57	42.5	56	8.4	2.9	0	0.9	0.2	0.2	0.1	0
	Processed Meats													
	Beef													
1331	Corned beef loaf, jellied, sliced	2	slice(s)	57	39.2	87	13.0	0	0	3.5	1.5	1.5	0.2	—
	Bologna													
13459	Beef	1	slice(s)	28	15.1	90	3.0	1.0	0	8.0	3.5	4.3	0.3	—
13461	Light, made with pork and chicken	1	slice(s)	28	18.2	60	3.0	2.0	0	4.0	1.0	2.0	0.4	—
13458	Made with chicken and pork	1	slice(s)	28	15.0	90	3.0	1.0	0	8.0	3.0	4.1	1.1	—
13565	Turkey bologna	1	slice(s)	28	19.0	50	3.0	1.0	0	4.0	1.0	1.1	1.0	0
	Chicken													
7125	Breast, smoked	1	slice(s)	10	—	10	1.8	0.3	0	0.2	0	—	—	—

Chol (mg)	Calc (mg)	Iron (mg)	Magn (mg)	Pota (mg)	Sodi (mg)	Zinc (mg)	Vit A (µg)	Thia (mg)	Vit E (mg α)	Ribo (mg)	Niac (mg)	Vit B_6 (mg)	Fola (µg)	Vit C (mg)	Vit B_{12} (µg)	Sele (µg)
435	5	4.34	17.0	279.8	66.3	9.55	8026	0.15	0.57	2.43	11.18	0.78	281.5	0.9	72.0	16.4
98	10	0.81	20.4	264.5	82.5	3.81	0	0.05	0.30	0.24	6.37	0.23	11.9	0	1.3	9.4
95	6	3.80	20.4	284.9	45.9	2.33	0	0.15	—	0.51	5.70	—	—	0	—	11.0
35	8	0.89	6.8	147.4	408.2	0.79	19.3	0.01	—	0.07	3.58	0.19	2.3	0	0.2	—
67	19	1.05	24.7	222.6	450.2	0.84	—	0.08	—	0.09	10.97	0.46	4.3	0	0.3	—
77	14	0.96	26.4	234.7	67.2	0.91	6.0	0.06	0.35	0.10	12.57	0.54	3.4	0	0.3	22.3
76	14	1.01	25.5	220.3	64.6	0.93	12.8	0.06	0.39	0.11	11.68	0.49	5.1	0	0.3	20.3
77	10	1.13	19.6	194.8	75.7	2.45	21.3	0.06	0.65	0.19	5.13	0.29	8.5	0	0.3	15.6
80	10	1.12	20.4	211.8	81.6	2.73	15.3	0.06	—	0.20	5.22	0.33	7.7	0	0.3	16.7
84	11	1.19	21.3	216.0	81.6	2.53	17.0	0.07	0.38	0.21	5.68	0.33	7.7	0	0.3	16.0
71	13	0.96	17.9	176.9	77.4	1.80	15.3	0.03	0.40	0.10	6.15	0.50	3.4	0	0.3	21.6
49	11	0.75	19.6	244.8	411.4	0.79	4.3	0.09	1.04	0.12	5.99	0.24	24.7	0	0.2	13.9
80	10	1.11	20.4	205.8	77.4	2.43	16.2	0.06	0.22	0.19	5.37	0.31	6.8	0	0.3	18.8
72	14	0.98	17.9	178.6	78.2	1.82	15.3	0.03	0.22	0.10	6.21	0.50	3.4	0	0.3	21.0
64	9	1.13	17.0	190.5	80.8	1.81	13.6	0.05	—	0.16	4.87	0.26	6.0	0	0.2	16.7
64	11	0.91	19.6	200.7	43.4	0.66	6.8	0.05	0.22	0.07	8.90	0.45	2.6	0	0.3	21.9
64	10	1.02	17.9	194.8	63.8	1.29	10.2	0.05	—	0.12	6.70	0.34	4.3	0	0.2	20.9
315	14	2.71	2.6	152.2	47.6	3.75	0	0.02	0.17	0.17	2.65	0.06	4.3	0	0.9	35.0
479	9	9.89	21.3	223.7	64.6	3.38	3385.8	0.24	0.69	1.69	9.39	0.64	491.6	23.7	14.3	70.1
71	12	0.99	17.9	153.1	59.5	1.69	12.8	0.04	0.22	0.13	5.20	0.22	5.1	0	0.2	17.8
71	9	2.29	13.6	173.5	50.2	1.58	53.6	0.14	0.59	0.22	4.10	0.15	5.1	0	0.3	17.0
76	10	2.29	17.0	214.3	55.3	2.21	19.6	0.22	0.59	0.39	4.33	0.21	8.5	0	0.3	19.1
77	11	2.40	18.7	279.8	59.5	2.22	17.9	0.06	1.47	0.27	3.54	0.31	1.7	0	0.3	18.5
82	12	2.44	21.3	330.0	64.6	2.69	10.2	0.07	—	0.33	3.47	0.39	10.2	0	0.4	21.7
78	36	2.86	6.8	71.8	362.4	0.47	520.5	0.04	—	0.15	1.30	0.03	31.2	0	4.9	22.9
87	21	1.64	20.4	229.6	91.0	2.43	0	0.04	0.28	0.14	4.09	0.33	6.0	0	0.3	31.6
71	13	2.06	14.1	258.5	752.0	1.35	9.4	0.09	0.87	0.17	2.16	0.18	38.5	0	0.2	20.8
72	27	1.98	20.4	246.6	67.2	3.79	0	0.05	0.54	0.21	3.10	0.30	7.7	0	0.3	34.8
71	10	1.30	24.7	248.3	44.2	1.48	0	0.03	0.07	0.11	6.37	0.47	5.1	0	0.3	27.3
59	16	1.14	23.8	259.4	54.4	1.73	0	0.05	0.07	0.11	5.81	0.45	5.1	0	0.3	27.3
31	18	0.76	10.2	153.1	332.3	1.13	0	0.05	0.19	0.16	2.72	0.15	2.8	0	0.1	16.6
19	4	0.21	10.8	242.1	590.8	0.50	0	0.01	0.07	0.08	4.05	0.23	2.3	0	0.2	7.4
27	6	1.15	6.2	57.3	540.4	2.31	0	0.00	—	0.06	0.99	0.06	4.5	0	0.7	9.8
20	0	0.36	3.9	47.0	310.0	0.56	0	0.01	—	0.03	0.67	0.04	3.6	0	0.4	—
20	40	0.36	5.6	45.6	300.0	0.45	0	—	—	—	—	—	—	0	—	—
30	20	0.36	5.9	43.1	300.0	0.39	0	—	—	—	—	—	—	0	—	—
20	40	0.36	6.2	42.6	270.0	0.51	0	—	—	—	—	—	—	0	—	—
4	0	0.00	—	—	100.0	—	0	—	—	—	—	—	—	0	—	—

TABLE A-1 Table of Food Composition *(continued)*

(Computer code is for Cengage Diet Analysis program) (For purposes of calculations, use "0" for t, <1, <.1, <.01, etc.)

DA+ Code	Food Description	QTY	Measure	Wt (g)	H_2O (g)	Ener (cal)	Prot (g)	Carb (g)	Fiber (g)	Fat (g)	Fat Breakdown (g) Sat	Mono	Poly	Trans
Processed Meats—continued														
	Ham													
7127	Deli-sliced, honey	1	slice(s)	10	—	10	1.7	0.3	0	0.3	0.1	—	—	—
7126	Deli-sliced, smoked	1	slice(s)	10	—	10	1.7	0.2	0	0.3	0.1	—	—	—
8614	**Beef and pork mortadella, sliced**	2	slice(s)	46	24.1	143	7.5	1.4	0	11.7	4.4	5.2	1.4	—
1323	**Pork olive loaf**	2	slice(s)	57	33.1	133	6.7	5.2	0	9.4	3.3	4.5	1.1	—
1324	**Pork pickle and pimento loaf**	2	slice(s)	57	34.2	128	6.4	4.8	0.9	9.1	3.0	4.0	1.6	—
	Sausages and frankfurters													
37296	Beerwurst beef, beer salami (bierwurst)	1	slice(s)	29	16.6	74	4.1	1.2	0	5.7	2.5	2.7	0.2	—
37257	Beerwurst pork, beer salami	1	slice(s)	21	12.9	50	3.0	0.4	0	4.0	1.3	1.9	0.5	—
35338	Berliner, pork and beef	1	ounce(s)	28	17.3	65	4.3	0.7	0	4.9	1.7	2.3	0.4	—
37298	Bratwurst pork, cooked	1	piece(s)	74	42.3	181	10.4	1.9	0	14.3	5.1	6.7	1.5	—
37299	Braunschweiger pork liver sausage	1	slice(s)	15	8.2	51	2.0	0.3	0	4.5	1.5	2.1	0.5	—
1329	Cheesefurter or cheese smokie, beef and pork	1	item(s)	43	22.6	141	6.1	0.6	0	12.5	4.5	5.9	1.3	—
1330	Chorizo, beef and pork	2	ounce(s)	57	18.1	258	13.7	1.1	0	21.7	8.2	10.4	2.0	—
8600	Frankfurter, beef	1	item(s)	45	23.4	149	5.1	1.8	0	13.3	5.3	6.4	0.5	—
202	Frankfurter, beef and pork	1	item(s)	45	25.2	137	5.2	0.8	0	12.4	4.8	6.2	1.2	—
1293	Frankfurter, chicken	1	item(s)	45	28.1	100	7.0	1.2	0.2	7.3	1.7	2.7	1.7	0.1
3261	Frankfurter, turkey	1	item(s)	45	28.3	100	5.5	1.7	0	7.8	1.8	2.6	1.8	0.4
37275	Italian sausage, pork, cooked	1	item(s)	68	32.0	234	13.0	2.9	0.1	18.6	6.5	8.1	2.2	—
37307	Kielbasa or kolbassa, pork and beef	1	slice(s)	30	18.5	67	5.0	1.0	0	4.7	1.7	2.2	0.5	—
1333	Knockwurst or knackwurst, beef and pork	2	ounce(s)	57	31.4	174	6.3	1.8	0	15.7	5.8	7.3	1.7	—
37285	Pepperoni, beef and pork	1	slice(s)	11	3.4	51	2.2	0.4	0.2	4.4	1.8	2.1	0.3	—
37313	Polish sausage, pork	1	slice(s)	21	11.4	60	2.8	0.7	0	5.0	1.8	2.3	0.5	—
206	Salami, beef, cooked, sliced	2	slice(s)	52	31.2	136	6.5	1.0	0	11.5	5.1	5.5	0.5	—
37272	Salami, pork, dry or hard	1	slice(s)	13	4.6	52	2.9	0.2	0	4.3	1.5	2.0	0.5	—
40987	Sausage, turkey, cooked	2	ounce(s)	57	36.9	111	13.5	0	0	5.9	1.3	1.7	1.5	0.2
8620	Smoked sausage, beef and pork	2	ounce(s)	57	30.6	181	6.8	1.4	0	16.3	5.5	6.9	2.2	0
8619	Smoked sausage, pork	2	ounce(s)	57	32.0	178	6.8	1.2	0	16.0	5.3	6.4	2.1	0.1
37273	Smoked sausage, pork link	1	piece(s)	76	29.8	295	16.8	1.6	0	24.0	8.6	11.1	2.8	—
1336	Summer sausage, thuringer, or cervelat, beef and pork	2	ounce(s)	57	25.6	205	9.9	1.9	0	17.3	6.5	7.4	0.7	—
37294	Vienna sausage, cocktail, beef and pork, canned	1	piece(s)	16	10.4	37	1.7	0.4	0	3.1	1.1	1.5	0.2	—
	Spreads													
1318	Ham salad spread	¼	cup(s)	60	37.6	130	5.2	6.4	0	9.3	3.0	4.3	1.6	—
32419	Pork and beef sandwich spread	4	tablespoon(s)	60	36.2	141	4.6	7.2	0.1	10.4	3.6	4.6	1.5	—
	Turkey													
13604	Breast, fat free, oven roasted	1	slice(s)	28	—	25	4.0	1.0	0	0	0	0	0	0
13606	Breast, hickory smoked fat free	1	slice(s)	28	—	25	4.0	1.0	0	0	0	0	0	0
16049	Breast, hickory smoked slices	1	slice(s)	56	—	50	11.0	1.0	0	0	0	0	0	0
16047	Breast, honey roasted slices	1	slice(s)	56	—	60	11.0	3.0	0	0	0	0	0	0
16048	Breast, oven roasted slices	1	slice(s)	56	—	50	11.0	1.0	0	0	0	0	0	0
7124	Breast, oven roasted	1	slice(s)	10	—	10	1.8	0.3	0	0.1	0	0	0	—
13567	Turkey ham, 10% water added	2	slice(s)	56	40.9	70	10.0	2.0	0	3.0	0	0.4	0.6	0
37270	Turkey pastrami	1	slice(s)	28	20.3	35	4.6	1.0	0	1.2	0.3	0.4	0.3	—
3262	Turkey salami	2	slice(s)	57	39.1	98	10.9	0.9	0.1	5.2	1.6	1.8	1.4	0
37318	Turkey salami, cooked	1	slice(s)	28	20.4	43	4.3	0.1	0	2.7	0.8	0.9	0.7	—
Beverages														
	Beer													
866	Ale, mild	12	fluid ounce(s)	360	332.3	148	1.1	13.3	0.4	0	0	0	0	0
686	Beer	12	fluid ounce(s)	356	327.7	153	1.6	12.7	0	0	0	0	0	0
16886	Beer, non alcoholic	12	fluid ounce(s)	360	328.1	133	0.8	29.0	0	0.4	0.1	0	0.2	0
31609	Bud Light beer	12	fluid ounce(s)	355	335.5	110	0.9	6.6	0	0	0	0	0	0
31608	Budweiser beer	12	fluid ounce(s)	355	327.7	145	1.3	10.6	0	0	0	0	0	0

Chol (mg)	Calc (mg)	Iron (mg)	Magn (mg)	Pota (mg)	Sodi (mg)	Zinc (mg)	Vit A (μg)	Thia (mg)	Vit E (mg α)	Ribo (mg)	Niac (mg)	Vit B_6 (mg)	Fola (μg)	Vit C (mg)	Vit B_{12} (μg)	Sele (μg)
4	0	0.12	—	—	100.0	—	0	—	—	—	—	—	—	0.6	—	—
4	0	0.12	—	—	103.3	—	0	—	—	—	—	—	—	0.6	—	—
26	8	0.64	5.1	75.0	573.2	0.96	0	0.05	0.10	0.07	1.23	0.06	1.4	0	0.7	10.4
22	62	0.30	10.8	168.7	842.9	0.78	34.1	0.16	0.14	0.14	1.04	0.13	1.1	0	0.7	9.3
33	62	0.75	19.3	210.7	740.7	0.95	44.3	0.22	0.22	0.06	1.41	0.23	21.0	4.4	0.3	4.5
18	3	0.44	3.5	66.5	264.9	0.71	0	0.02	0.05	0.03	0.98	0.04	0.9	0	0.6	4.7
12	2	0.15	2.7	53.3	261.0	0.36	0	0.11	0.03	0.04	0.68	0.07	0.6	0	0.2	4.4
13	3	0.32	4.3	80.2	367.7	0.70	0	0.10	—	0.06	0.88	0.05	1.4	0	0.8	4.0
44	33	0.95	11.1	156.9	412.2	1.70	0	0.37	0.01	0.13	2.36	0.15	1.5	0.7	0.7	15.7
24	1	1.42	1.7	27.5	131.5	0.42	641.0	0.03	0.05	0.23	1.27	0.05	6.7	0	3.1	8.8
29	25	0.46	5.6	88.6	465.3	0.96	20.2	0.10	0.10	0.06	1.24	0.05	1.3	0	0.7	6.8
50	5	0.90	10.2	225.7	700.2	1.93	0	0.35	0.12	0.17	2.90	0.30	1.1	0	1.1	12.0
24	6	0.67	6.3	70.2	513.0	1.10	0	0.01	0.09	0.06	1.06	0.04	2.3	0	0.8	3.7
23	5	0.51	4.5	75.2	504.0	0.82	8.1	0.09	0.11	0.05	1.18	0.05	1.8	0	0.6	6.2
43	33	0.52	9.0	90.9	379.8	0.50	0	0.02	0.09	0.11	2.10	0.14	3.2	0	0.2	10.4
35	67	0.66	6.3	176.4	485.1	0.82	0	0.01	0.27	0.08	1.65	0.06	4.1	0	0.4	6.8
39	14	0.97	12.2	206.7	820.8	1.62	6.8	0.42	0.17	0.15	2.83	0.22	3.4	0.1	0.9	15.0
20	13	0.44	4.9	84.4	283.0	0.61	0	0.06	0.06	0.06	0.87	0.05	1.5	0	0.5	5.4
34	6	0.37	6.2	112.8	527.3	0.94	0	0.19	0.32	0.07	1.55	0.09	1.1	0	0.7	7.7
13	2	0.15	2.0	34.7	196.7	0.30	0	0.05	0.00	0.02	0.59	0.04	0.7	0.1	0.2	2.4
15	2	0.29	2.9	37.3	199.3	0.40	0	0.10	0.04	0.03	0.71	0.03	0.4	0.2	0.2	3.7
37	3	1.14	6.8	97.8	592.8	0.92	0	0.04	0.08	0.08	1.68	0.08	1.0	0	1.6	7.6
10	2	0.16	2.8	48.4	289.3	0.53	0	0.11	0.02	0.04	0.71	0.07	0.3	0	0.4	3.3
52	12	0.84	11.9	169.0	377.1	2.19	7.4	0.04	0.10	0.14	3.24	0.18	3.4	0.4	0.7	0
33	7	0.42	7.4	101.5	516.5	0.71	7.4	0.10	0.07	0.06	1.66	0.09	1.1	0	0.3	0
35	6	0.33	6.2	273.9	468.9	0.74	0	0.12	0.14	0.10	1.59	0.10	0.6	0	0.4	10.4
52	23	0.87	14.4	254.6	1136.6	2.13	0	0.53	0.18	0.19	3.43	0.26	3.8	1.5	1.2	16.4
42	5	1.15	7.9	147.4	737.1	1.45	0	0.08	0.12	0.18	2.44	0.14	1.1	9.4	3.1	11.5
14	2	0.14	1.1	16.2	155.0	0.25	0	0.01	0.03	0.01	0.25	0.01	0.6	0	0.2	2.7
22	5	0.35	6.0	90.0	547.2	0.66	0	0.26	1.04	0.07	1.25	0.09	0.6	0	0.5	10.7
23	7	0.47	4.8	66.0	607.8	0.61	15.6	0.10	1.04	0.08	1.03	0.07	1.2	0	0.7	5.8
10	0	0.00	—	—	340.0	—	0	—	—	—	—	—	—	0	—	—
10	0	0.00	—	—	300.0	—	0	—	—	—	—	—	—	0	—	—
25	0	0.72	—	—	720.0	—	0	—	—	—	—	—	—	0	—	—
20	0	0.72	—	—	660.0	—	0	—	—	—	—	—	—	0	—	—
20	0	0.72	—	—	660.0	—	0	—	—	—	—	—	—	0	—	—
4	0	0.06	—	—	103.3	—	0	—	—	—	—	—	—	0	—	—
40	0	0.72	12.3	162.4	700.0	1.44	0	—	—	—	—	—	—	0	—	—
19	3	1.19	4.0	97.8	278.1	0.61	1.1	0.01	0.06	0.07	1.00	0.07	1.4	4.6	0.1	4.6
43	23	0.70	12.5	122.5	569.3	1.31	1.1	0.24	0.13	0.17	2.25	0.24	5.7	0	0.6	15.0
22	11	0.35	6.2	61.2	284.6	0.65	0.6	0.12	0.06	0.08	1.12	0.12	2.8	0	0.3	7.5
0	18	0.07	21.6	90.0	14.4	0.03	0	0.03	0.00	0.10	1.62	0.18	21.6	0	0.1	2.5
0	14	0.07	21.4	96.2	14.3	0.03	0	0.01	0.00	0.08	1.82	0.16	21.4	0	0.1	2.1
0	25	0.21	25.2	28.8	46.8	0.07	—	0.07	0.00	0.18	3.99	0.10	50.4	1.8	0.1	4.3
0	18	0.14	17.8	63.9	9.0	0.10	0	0.03	—	0.10	1.39	0.12	14.6	0	0	4.0
0	18	0.10	21.3	88.8	9.0	0.07	0	0.02	—	0.09	1.60	0.17	21.3	0	0.1	4.0

TABLE A-1 Table of Food Composition *(continued)*

(Computer code is for Cengage Diet Analysis program) (For purposes of calculations, use "0" for t, <1, <.1, <.01, etc.)

DA+ Code	Food Description	QTY	Measure	Wt (g)	H_2O (g)	Ener (cal)	Prot (g)	Carb (g)	Fiber (g)	Fat (g)	Fat Breakdown (g) Sat	Mono	Poly	*Trans*
Beverages—continued														
869	Light beer	12	fluid ounce(s)	354	335.9	103	0.9	5.8	0	0	0	0	0	0
31613	Michelob beer	12	fluid ounce(s)	355	323.4	155	1.3	13.3	0	0	0	0	0	0
31614	Michelob Light beer	12	fluid ounce(s)	355	329.8	134	1.1	11.7	0	0	0	0	0	0
	Gin, rum, vodka, whiskey													
857	Distilled alcohol, 100 proof	1	fluid ounce(s)	28	16.0	82	0	0	0	0	0	0	0	0
687	Distilled alcohol, 80 proof	1	fluid ounce(s)	28	18.5	64	0	0	0	0	0	0	0	0
688	Distilled alcohol, 86 proof	1	fluid ounce(s)	28	17.8	70	0	0	0	0	0	0	0	0
689	Distilled alcohol, 90 proof	1	fluid ounce(s)	28	17.3	73	0	0	0	0	0	0	0	0
856	Distilled alcohol, 94 proof	1	fluid ounce(s)	28	16.8	76	0	0	0	0	0	0	0	0
	Liqueurs													
33187	Coffee liqueur, 53 proof	1	fluid ounce(s)	35	10.8	113	0	16.3	0	0.1	0	0	0	—
3142	Coffee liqueur, 63 proof	1	fluid ounce(s)	35	14.4	107	0	11.2	0	0.1	0	0	0	—
736	Cordials, 54 proof	1	fluid ounce(s)	30	8.9	106	0	13.3	0	0.1	0	0	0	—
	Wine													
861	California red wine	5	fluid ounce(s)	150	133.4	125	0.3	3.7	0	0	0	0	0	0
858	Domestic champagne	5	fluid ounce(s)	150	—	105	0.3	3.8	0	0	0	0	0	0
690	Sweet dessert wine	5	fluid ounce(s)	147	103.7	235	0.3	20.1	0	0	0	0	0	0
1481	White wine	5	fluid ounce(s)	148	128.1	121	0.1	3.8	0	0	0	0	0	0
1811	Wine cooler	10	fluid ounce(s)	300	267.4	159	0.3	20.2	0	0.1	0	0	0	—
	Carbonated													
31898	7 Up	12	fluid ounce(s)	360	321.0	140	0	39.0	0	0	0	0	0	0
692	Club soda	12	fluid ounce(s)	355	354.8	0	0	0	0	0	0	0	0	0
12010	Coca-Cola Classic cola soda	12	fluid ounce(s)	360	319.4	146	0	40.5	0	0	0	0	0	0
693	Cola	12	fluid ounce(s)	368	332.7	136	0.3	35.2	0	0.1	0	0	0	—
2391	Cola or pepper-type soda, low calorie with saccharin	12	fluid ounce(s)	355	354.5	0	0	0.3	0	0	0	0	0	0
9522	Cola soda, decaffeinated	12	fluid ounce(s)	372	333.4	153	0	39.3	0	0	0	0	0	0
9524	Cola, decaffeinated, low calorie with aspartame	12	fluid ounce(s)	355	354.3	4	0.4	0.5	0	0	0	0	0	0
1415	Cola, low calorie with aspartame	12	fluid ounce(s)	355	353.6	7	0.4	1.0	0	0.1	0	0	0	—
1412	Cream soda	12	fluid ounce(s)	371	321.5	189	0	49.3	0	0	0	0	0	0
31899	Diet 7 Up	12	fluid ounce(s)	360	—	0	0	0	0	0	0	0	0	0
12031	Diet Coke cola soda	12	fluid ounce(s)	360	—	2	0	0.2	0	0	0	0	0	0
29392	Diet Mountain Dew soda	12	fluid ounce(s)	360	—	0	0	0	0	0	0	0	0	0
29389	Diet Pepsi cola soda	12	fluid ounce(s)	360	—	0	0	0	0	0	0	0	0	0
12034	Diet Sprite soda	12	fluid ounce(s)	360	—	4	0	0	0	0	0	0	0	0
695	Ginger ale	12	fluid ounce(s)	366	333.9	124	0	32.1	0	0	0	0	0	0
694	Grape soda	12	fluid ounce(s)	372	330.3	160	0	41.7	0	0	0	0	0	0
1876	Lemon lime soda	12	fluid ounce(s)	368	330.8	147	0.2	37.4	0	0.1	0	0	0	—
29391	Mountain Dew soda	12	fluid ounce(s)	360	314.0	170	0	46.0	0	0	0	0	0	0
3145	Orange soda	12	fluid ounce(s)	372	325.9	179	0	45.8	0	0	0	0	0	0
1414	Pepper-type soda	12	fluid ounce(s)	368	329.3	151	0	38.3	0	0.4	0.3	0	0	—
29388	Pepsi regular cola soda	12	fluid ounce(s)	360	318.9	150	0	41.0	0	0	0	0	0	0
696	Root beer	12	fluid ounce(s)	370	330.0	152	0	39.2	0	0	0	0	0	0
12044	Sprite soda	12	fluid ounce(s)	360	321.0	144	0	39.0	0	0	0	0	0	0
	Coffee													
731	Brewed	8	fluid ounce(s)	237	235.6	2	0.3	0	0	0	0	0	0	0
9520	Brewed, decaffeinated	8	fluid ounce(s)	237	234.3	5	0.3	1.0	0	0	0	0	0	0
16882	Cappuccino	8	fluid ounce(s)	240	224.8	79	4.1	5.8	0.2	4.9	2.3	1.0	0.2	—
16883	Cappuccino, decaffeinated	8	fluid ounce(s)	240	224.8	79	4.1	5.8	0.2	4.9	2.3	1.0	0.2	—
16880	Espresso	8	fluid ounce(s)	237	231.8	21	0	3.6	0	0.4	0.2	0	0.2	0
16881	Espresso, decaffeinated	8	fluid ounce(s)	237	231.8	21	0	3.6	0	0.4	0.2	0	0.2	0
732	Instant, prepared	8	fluid ounce(s)	239	236.5	5	0.2	0.8	0	0	0	0	0	0
	Fruit drinks													
29357	Crystal Light sugar-free lemonade drink	8	fluid ounce(s)	240	—	5	0	0	0	0	0	0	0	0
6012	Fruit punch drink with added vitamin C, canned	8	fluid ounce(s)	248	218.2	117	0	29.7	0.5	0	0	0	0	0
31143	Gatorade Thirst Quencher, all flavors	8	fluid ounce(s)	240	—	50	0	14.0	0	0	0	0	0	0
260	Grape drink, canned	8	fluid ounce(s)	250	210.5	153	0	39.4	0	0	0	0	0	0

PAGE KEY: A-2 = Breads/Baked Goods A-8 = Cereal/Rice/Pasta A-12 = Fruit A-18 = Vegetables/Legumes A-28 = Nuts/Seeds A-30 = Vegetarian A-32 = Dairy A-40 = Eggs A-40 = Seafood A-44 = Meats A-48 = Poultry A-48 = Processed Meats A-50 = Beverages A-54 = Fats/Oils A-56 = Sweets A-58 = Spices/Condiments/Sauces A-62 = Mixed Foods/Soups/Sandwiches A-68 = Fast Food A-88 = Convenience A-90 = Baby Foods

Chol (mg)	Calc (mg)	Iron (mg)	Magn (mg)	Pota (mg)	Sodi (mg)	Zinc (mg)	Vit A (μg)	Thia (mg)	Vit E (mg α)	Ribo (mg)	Niac (mg)	Vit B_6 (mg)	Fola (μg)	Vit C (mg)	Vit B_{12} (μg)	Sele (μg)
0	14	0.10	17.7	74.3	14.2	0.03	0	0.01	0.00	0.05	1.38	0.12	21.2	0	0.1	1.4
0	18	0.10	21.3	88.8	9.0	0.07	0	0.02	—	0.09	1.60	0.17	21.3	0	0.1	4.0
0	18	0.14	17.8	63.9	9.0	0.10	0	0.03	—	0.10	1.39	0.12	14.6	0	0	4.0
0	0	0.01	0	0.6	0.3	0.01	0	0.00	—	0.00	0.00	0.00	0	0	0	0
0	0	0.01	0	0.6	0.3	0.01	0	0.00	0.00	0.00	0.00	0.00	0	0	0	0
0	0	0.01	0	0.6	0.3	0.01	0	0.00	0.00	0.00	0.00	0.00	0	0	0	0
0	0	0.01	0	0.6	0.3	0.01	0	0.00	0.00	0.00	0.00	0.00	0	0	0	0
0	0	0.01	0	0.6	0.3	0.01	0	0.00	—	0.00	0.00	0.00	0	0	0	0
0	0	0.02	1.0	10.4	2.8	0.01	0	0.00	0.00	0.00	0.05	0.00	0	0	0	0.1
0	0	0.02	1.0	10.4	2.8	0.01	0	0.00	—	0.00	0.05	0.00	0	0	0	0.1
0	0	0.02	0.6	4.5	2.1	0.01	0	0.00	0.00	0.00	0.02	0.00	0	0	0	0.1
0	12	1.43	16.2	170.6	15.0	0.14	0	0.01	0.00	0.04	0.11	0.05	1.5	0	0	—
0	—	—	—	—	—	—	—	—	—	—	—	—	—	—	0	—
0	12	0.34	13.2	135.4	13.2	0.10	0	0.01	0.00	0.01	0.30	0.00	0	0	0	0.7
0	13	0.39	14.8	104.7	7.4	0.18	0	0.01	0.00	0.01	0.15	0.06	1.5	0	0	0.1
0	18	0.75	15.0	129.0	24.0	0.18	—	0.01	0.03	0.03	0.13	0.03	3.0	5.4	0	0.6
0	—	—	—	0.6	75.0	—	—	—	—	—	—	—	—	—	—	—
0	18	0.03	3.5	7.1	74.6	0.35	0	0.00	0.00	0.00	0.00	0.00	0	0	0	0
0	—	—	—	0	49.5	—	0	—	—	—	—	—	—	0	—	—
0	7	0.41	0	7.4	14.7	0.06	0	0.00	0.00	0.00	0.00	0.00	0	0	0	0.4
0	14	0.06	3.5	14.2	56.8	0.11	0	0.00	0.00	0.00	0.00	0.00	0	0	0	0.3
0	7	0.08	0	11.2	14.9	0.03	0	0.00	0.00	0.00	0.00	0.00	0	0	0	0.4
0	11	0.06	0	24.9	14.2	0.03	0	0.02	0.00	0.08	0.00	0.00	0	0	0	0.3
0	11	0.39	3.5	28.4	28.4	0.03	0	0.02	0.00	0.08	0.00	0.00	0	0	0	0
0	19	0.18	3.7	3.7	44.5	0.26	0	0.00	0.00	0.00	0.00	0.00	0	0	0	0
0	—	—	—	77.0	45.0	—	—	—	—	—	—	—	—	—	—	—
0	—	—	—	18.0	42.0	—	0	—	—	—	—	—	—	0	—	—
0	—	—	—	70.0	35.0	—	—	—	—	—	—	—	—	—	—	—
0	—	—	—	30.0	35.0	—	—	—	—	—	—	—	—	—	—	—
0	—	—	—	109.5	36.0	—	0	—	—	—	—	—	—	0	—	—
0	11	0.65	3.7	3.7	25.6	0.18	0	0.00	0.00	0.00	0.00	0.00	0	0	0	0.4
0	11	0.29	3.7	3.7	55.8	0.26	0	0.00	—	0.00	0.00	0.00	0	0	0	0
0	7	0.41	3.7	3.7	33.2	0.14	0	0.00	0.00	0.00	0.05	0.00	0	0	0	0
0	—	—	—	0	70.0	—	—	—	—	—	—	—	—	—	—	—
0	19	0.21	3.7	7.4	44.6	0.36	0	0.00	—	0.00	0.00	0.00	0	0	0	0
0	11	0.14	0	3.7	36.8	0.14	0	0.00	—	0.00	0.00	0.00	0	0	0	0.4
0	—	—	—	0	35.0	—	—	—	—	—	—	—	—	—	—	—
0	18	0.18	3.7	3.7	48.0	0.26	0	0.00	0.00	0.00	0.00	0.00	0	0	0	0.4
0	—	—	—	0	70.5	—	0	—	—	—	—	—	—	0	—	—
0	5	0.02	7.1	116.1	4.7	0.04	0	0.03	0.02	0.18	0.45	0.00	4.7	0	0	0
0	7	0.14	11.8	108.9	4.7	0.00	0	0.00	0.00	0.03	0.66	0.00	0	0	0	0.5
12	144	0.19	14.4	232.8	50.4	0.50	33.6	0.04	0.09	0.27	0.13	0.04	7.2	0	0.4	4.6
12	144	0.19	14.4	232.8	50.4	0.50	33.6	0.04	0.09	0.27	0.13	0.04	7.2	0	0.4	4.6
0	5	0.30	189.6	272.6	33.2	0.11	0	0.00	0.04	0.42	12.34	0.00	2.4	0.5	0	0
0	5	0.30	189.6	272.6	33.2	0.11	0	0.00	0.04	0.42	12.34	0.00	2.4	0.5	0	0
0	10	0.09	9.5	71.6	9.5	0.01	0	0.00	0.00	0.00	0.56	0.00	0	0	0	0.2
0	0	0.00	—	160.0	40.0	—	0	—	—	—	—	—	—	0	—	—
0	20	0.22	7.4	62.0	94.2	0.02	5.0	0.05	0.04	0.05	0.05	0.02	9.9	89.3	0	0.5
0	0	0.00	—	30.0	110.0	—	0	—	—	—	—	—	—	0	—	—
0	130	0.17	2.5	30.0	40.0	0.30	0	0.00	0.00	0.01	0.02	0.01	0	78.5	0	0.3

TABLE A-1 Table of Food Composition *(continued)*

(Computer code is for Cengage Diet Analysis program) (For purposes of calculations, use "0" for t, <1, <.1, <.01, etc.)

DA+ Code	Food Description	QTY	Measure	Wt (g)	H_2O (g)	Ener (cal)	Prot (g)	Carb (g)	Fiber (g)	Fat (g)	Fat Breakdown (g) Sat	Mono	Poly	*Trans*
	Beverages—continued													
17372	Kool-Aid (lemonade/punch/fruit drink)	8	fluid ounce(s)	248	220.0	108	0.1	27.8	0.2	0	0	0	0	—
17225	Kool-Aid sugar free, low calorie tropical punch drink mix, prepared	8	fluid ounce(s)	240	—	5	0	0	0	0	0	0	0	0
266	Lemonade, prepared from frozen concentrate	8	fluid ounce(s)	248	221.6	99	0.2	25.8	0	0.1	0	0	0	—
268	Limeade, prepared from frozen concentrate	8	fluid ounce(s)	247	212.6	128	0	34.1	0	0	0	0	0	—
14266	Odwalla strawberry C monster smoothie blend	8	fluid ounce(s)	240	—	160	2.0	38.0	0	0	0	0	0	0
10080	Odwalla strawberry lemonade quencher	8	fluid ounce(s)	240	—	110	0	28.0	0	0	0	0	0	0
10099	Snapple fruit punch fruit drink	8	fluid ounce(s)	240	—	110	0	29.0	0	0	0	0	0	0
10096	Snapple kiwi strawberry fruit drink	8	fluid ounce(s)	240	211.2	110	0	28.0	0	0	0	0	0	0
	Slim Fast ready-to-drink shake													
16054	French vanilla ready to drink shake	11	fluid ounce(s)	325	—	220	10.0	40.0	5.0	2.5	0.5	1.5	0.5	—
40447	Optima rich chocolate royal ready-to-drink shake	11	fluid ounce(s)	330	—	180	10.0	24.0	5.0	5.0	1.0	3.5	0.5	0
16055	Strawberries n cream ready to drink shake	11	fluid ounce(s)	325	—	220	10.0	40.0	5.0	2.5	0.5	1.5	0.5	—
	Tea													
33179	Decaffeinated, prepared	8	fluid ounce(s)	237	236.3	2	0	0.7	0	0	0	0	0	0
1877	Herbal, prepared	8	fluid ounce(s)	237	236.1	2	0	0.5	0	0	0	0	0	0
735	Instant tea mix, lemon flavored with sugar, prepared	8	fluid ounce(s)	259	236.2	91	0	22.3	0.3	0.2	0	0	0	—
734	Instant tea mix, unsweetened, prepared	8	fluid ounce(s)	237	236.1	2	0.1	0.4	0	0	0	0	0	0
733	Tea, prepared	8	fluid ounce(s)	237	236.3	2	0	0.7	0	0	0	0	0	0
	Water													
1413	Mineral water, carbonated	8	fluid ounce(s)	237	236.8	0	0	0	0	0	0	0	0	0
33183	Poland spring water, bottled	8	fluid ounce(s)	237	237.0	0	0	0	0	0	0	0	0	0
1821	Tap water	8	fluid ounce(s)	237	236.8	0	0	0	0	0	0	0	0	0
1879	Tonic water	8	fluid ounce(s)	244	222.3	83	0	21.5	0	0	0	0	0	0
Fats and Oils														
	Butter													
104	Butter	1	tablespoon(s)	14	2.3	102	0.1	0	0	11.5	7.3	3.0	0.4	—
2522	Butter Buds, dry butter substitute	1	teaspoon(s)	2	—	5	0	2.0	0	0	0	0	0	0
921	Unsalted	1	tablespoon(s)	14	2.5	102	0.1	0	0	11.5	7.3	3.0	0.4	—
107	Whipped	1	tablespoon(s)	9	1.5	67	0.1	0	0	7.6	4.7	2.2	0.3	—
944	Whipped, unsalted	1	tablespoon(s)	11	2.0	82	0.1	0	0	9.2	5.9	2.4	0.3	—
	Fats, cooking													
2671	Beef tallow, semisolid	1	tablespoon(s)	13	0	115	0	0	0	12.8	6.4	5.4	0.5	—
922	Chicken fat	1	tablespoon(s)	13	0	115	0	0	0	12.8	3.8	5.7	2.7	—
5454	Household shortening with vegetable oil	1	tablespoon(s)	13	0	115	0	0	0	13.0	3.4	5.5	2.7	2.2
111	Lard	1	tablespoon(s)	13	0	115	0	0	0	12.8	5.0	5.8	1.4	—
	Margarine													
114	Margarine	1	tablespoon(s)	14	2.3	101	0	0.1	0	11.4	2.1	5.5	3.4	2.1
5439	Soft	1	tablespoon(s)	14	2.3	103	0.1	0.1	0	11.6	1.7	4.4	2.1	3.0
32329	Soft, unsalted, with hydrogenated soybean and cottonseed oils	1	tablespoon(s)	14	2.5	101	0.1	0.1	0	11.3	2.0	5.4	3.5	—
928	Unsalted	1	tablespoon(s)	14	2.6	101	0.1	0.1	0	11.3	2.1	5.2	3.5	—
119	Whipped	1	tablespoon(s)	9	1.5	64	0.1	0.1	0	7.2	1.2	3.2	2.5	—
	Spreads													
54657	I Can't Believe It's Not Butter!, tub, soya oil (non-hydrogenated)	1	tablespoon(s)	14	2.3	103	0.1	0.1	0	11.6	2.8	2.0	5.1	0.1
2708	Mayonnaise with soybean and safflower oils	1	tablespoon(s)	14	2.1	99	0.2	0.4	0	11.0	1.2	1.8	7.6	—
16157	Promise vegetable oil spread, stick	1	tablespoon(s)	14	4.2	90	0	0	0	10.0	2.5	2.0	4.0	—

Chol (mg)	Calc (mg)	Iron (mg)	Magn (mg)	Pota (mg)	Sodi (mg)	Zinc (mg)	Vit A (µg)	Thia (mg)	Vit E (mg α)	Ribo (mg)	Niac (mg)	Vit B_6 (mg)	Fola (µg)	Vit C (mg)	Vit B_{12} (µg)	Sele (µg)
0	14	0.45	5.0	49.6	31.0	0.19	—	0.03	—	0.05	0.04	0.01	4.3	41.6	0	1.0
0	0	0.00	—	10.1	10.1	—	0	—	—	—	—	—	—	6.0	—	—
0	10	0.39	5.0	37.2	9.9	0.05	0	0.01	0.02	0.05	0.04	0.01	2.5	9.7	0	0.2
0	5	0.00	4.9	24.7	7.4	0.02	0	0.01	0.00	0.01	0.02	0.01	2.5	7.7	0	0.2
0	20	0.72	—	0	20.0	—	0	—	—	—	—	—	—	600.0	0	—
0	0	0.00	—	70.0	10.0	—	0	—	—	—	—	—	—	54.0	0	—
0	0	0.00	—	20.0	10.0	—	0	—	—	—	—	—	—	0	0	—
0	0	0.00	—	40.0	10.0	—	0	—	—	—	—	—	—	0	0	—
5	400	2.70	140.0	600.0	220.0	2.25	—	0.52	—	0.59	7.00	0.70	120.0	60.0	2.1	17.5
5	1000	2.70	140.0	600.0	220.0	2.25	—	0.52	—	0.59	7.00	0.70	120.0	30.0	2.1	17.5
5	400	2.70	140.0	600.0	220.0	2.25	—	0.52	—	0.59	7.00	0.70	120.0	60.0	2.1	17.5
0	0	0.04	7.1	87.7	7.1	0.04	0	0.00	0.00	0.03	0.00	0.00	11.9	0	0	0
0	5	0.18	2.4	21.3	2.4	0.09	0	0.02	0.00	0.01	0.00	0.00	2.4	0	0	0
0	5	0.05	2.6	38.9	5.2	0.02	0	0.00	0.00	0.00	0.02	0.00	0	0	0	0.3
0	7	0.02	4.7	42.7	9.5	0.02	0	0.00	0.00	0.01	0.07	0.00	0	0	0	0
0	0	0.04	7.1	87.7	7.1	0.04	0	0.00	0.00	0.03	0.00	0.00	11.9	0	0	0
0	33	0.00	0	0	2.4	0.00	0	0.00	—	0.00	0.00	0.00	0	0	0	0
0	2	0.02	2.4	0	2.4	0.00	0	0.00	—	0.00	0.00	0.00	0	0	0	0
0	7	0.00	2.4	2.4	7.1	0.00	0	0.00	0.00	0.00	0.00	0.00	0	0	0	0
0	2	0.02	0	0	29.3	0.24	0	0.00	0.00	0.00	0.00	0.00	0	0	0	0
31	3	0.00	0.3	3.4	81.8	0.01	97.1	0.00	0.32	0.01	0.01	0.00	0.4	0	0	0.1
0	0	0.00	0	1.6	120.0	0.00	0	0.00	0.00	0.00	0.00	0.00	0	0	0	—
31	3	0.00	0.3	3.4	1.6	0.01	97.1	0.00	0.32	0.01	0.01	0.00	0.4	0	0	0.1
21	2	0.01	0.2	2.4	77.7	0.01	64.3	0.00	0.21	0.00	0.00	0.00	0.3	0	0	0.1
25	3	0.00	0.2	2.7	1.3	0.01	78.0	0.00	0.26	0.00	0.00	0.00	0.3	0	0	0.1
14	0	0.00	0	0	0	0.00	0	0.00	0.34	0.00	0.00	0.00	0	0	0	0
11	0	0.00	0	0	0	0.00	0	0.00	0.34	0.00	0.00	0.00	0	0	0	0
0	0	0.00	0	0	0	0.00	0	0.00	—	0.00	0.00	0.00	0	0	0	—
12	0	0.00	0	0	0	0.01	0	0.00	0.07	0.00	0.00	0.00	0	0	0	0
0	4	0.01	0.4	5.9	133.0	0.00	115.5	0.00	1.26	0.01	0.00	0.00	0.1	0	0	0
0	4	0.00	0.3	5.5	155.4	0.00	142.7	0.00	1.00	0.00	0.00	0.00	0.1	0	0	0
0	4	0.00	0.3	5.4	3.9	0.00	103.1	0.00	0.98	0.00	0.00	0.00	0.1	0	0	0
0	2	0.00	0.3	3.5	0.3	0.00	115.5	0.00	1.80	0.00	0.00	0.00	0.1	0	0	0
0	2	0.00	0.2	3.4	97.1	0.00	73.7	0.00	0.45	0.00	0.00	0.00	0.1	0	0	0
0	4	0.00	0.3	5.5	155.3	0.00	142.6	0.00	0.72	0.00	0.00	0.00	0.1	0	0	0
8	2	0.06	0.1	4.7	78.4	0.01	11.6	0.00	3.03	0.00	0.00	0.08	1.1	0	0	0.2
0	10	0.18	—	8.7	90.0	—	—	0.00	—	0.00	0.00	—	—	0.6	—	

TABLE A-1 Table of Food Composition *(continued)*

(Computer code is for Cengage Diet Analysis program) (For purposes of calculations, use "0" for t, <1, <.1, <.01, etc.)

DA+ Code	Food Description	QTY	Measure	Wt (g)	H_2O (g)	Ener (cal)	Prot (g)	Carb (g)	Fiber (g)	Fat (g)	Fat Breakdown (g) Sat	Mono	Poly	*Trans*
	Fats and Oils—continued													
	Oils													
2681	Canola	1	tablespoon(s)	14	0	120	0	0	0	13.6	1.0	8.6	3.8	0.1
120	Corn	1	tablespoon(s)	14	0	120	0	0	0	13.6	1.8	3.8	7.4	0
122	Olive	1	tablespoon(s)	14	0	119	0	0	0	13.5	1.9	9.9	1.4	—
124	Peanut	1	tablespoon(s)	14	0	119	0	0	0	13.5	2.3	6.2	4.3	—
2693	Safflower	1	tablespoon(s)	14	0	120	0	0	0	13.6	0.8	10.2	2.0	—
923	Sesame	1	tablespoon(s)	14	0	120	0	0	0	13.6	1.9	5.4	5.7	—
128	Soybean, hydrogenated	1	tablespoon(s)	14	0	120	0	0	0	13.6	2.0	5.8	5.1	—
130	Soybean, with soybean and cottonseed oil	1	tablespoon(s)	14	0	120	0	0	0	13.6	2.4	4.0	6.5	—
2700	Sunflower	1	tablespoon(s)	14	0	120	0	0	0	13.6	1.8	6.3	5.0	—
357	**Pam original no stick cooking spray**	1	serving(s)	0	0.2	0	0	0	0	0	0	0	0	—
	Salad dressing													
132	Blue cheese	2	tablespoon(s)	30	9.7	151	1.4	2.2	0	15.7	3.0	3.7	8.3	—
133	Blue cheese, low calorie	2	tablespoon(s)	32	25.4	32	1.6	0.9	0	2.3	0.8	0.6	0.8	—
1764	Caesar	2	tablespoon(s)	30	10.3	158	0.4	0.9	0	17.3	2.6	4.1	9.9	—
29654	Creamy, reduced calorie, fat-free, cholesterol-free, sour cream and/or buttermilk and oil	2	tablespoon(s)	32	23.9	34	0.4	6.4	0	0.9	0.2	0.2	0.5	—
29617	Creamy, reduced calorie, sour cream and/or buttermilk and oil	2	tablespoon(s)	30	22.2	48	0.5	2.1	0	4.2	0.6	1.0	2.4	—
134	French	2	tablespoon(s)	32	11.7	146	0.2	5.0	0	14.3	1.8	2.7	6.7	—
135	French, low fat	2	tablespoon(s)	32	17.4	74	0.2	9.4	0.4	4.3	0.4	1.9	1.6	—
136	Italian	2	tablespoon(s)	29	16.6	86	0.1	3.1	0	8.3	1.3	1.9	3.8	—
137	Italian, diet	2	tablespoon(s)	30	25.4	23	0.1	1.4	0	1.9	0.1	0.7	0.5	—
139	Mayonnaise-type	2	tablespoon(s)	29	11.7	115	0.3	7.0	0	9.8	1.4	2.6	5.3	—
942	Oil and vinegar	2	tablespoon(s)	32	15.2	144	0	0.8	0	16.0	2.9	4.7	7.7	—
1765	Ranch	2	tablespoon(s)	30	11.6	146	0.1	1.6	0	15.8	2.3	5.2	7.6	—
3666	Ranch, reduced calorie	2	tablespoon(s)	30	20.5	62	0.1	2.2	0	6.1	1.1	1.8	2.9	—
940	Russian	2	tablespoon(s)	30	11.6	107	0.5	9.3	0.7	7.8	1.2	1.8	4.4	—
939	Russian, low calorie	2	tablespoon(s)	32	20.8	45	0.2	8.8	0.1	1.3	0.2	0.3	0.7	—
941	Sesame seed	2	tablespoon(s)	30	11.8	133	0.9	2.6	0.3	13.6	1.9	3.6	7.5	—
142	Thousand Island	2	tablespoon(s)	32	14.9	118	0.3	4.7	0.3	11.2	1.6	2.5	5.8	—
143	Thousand Island, low calorie	2	tablespoon(s)	30	18.2	61	0.3	6.7	0.4	3.9	0.2	1.9	0.8	—
	Sandwich spreads													
138	Mayonnaise with soybean oil	1	tablespoon(s)	14	2.1	99	0.1	0.4	0	11.0	1.6	2.7	5.8	0
140	Mayonnaise, low calorie	1	tablespoon(s)	16	10.0	37	0	2.6	0	3.1	0.5	0.7	1.7	—
141	Tartar sauce	2	tablespoon(s)	28	8.7	144	0.3	4.1	0.1	14.4	2.2	3.8	7.7	—
Sweets														
4799	**Butterscotch or caramel topping**	2	tablespoon(s)	41	13.1	103	0.6	27.0	0.4	0	0	0	0	—
	Candy													
1786	Almond Joy candy bar	1	item(s)	45	4.3	220	2.0	27.0	2.0	12.0	8.0	3.3	0.7	0
1785	Bit-O-Honey candy	6	item(s)	40	—	190	1.0	39.0	0	3.5	2.5	—	—	—
33375	Butterscotch candy	2	piece(s)	12	0.6	47	0	10.8	0	0.4	0.2	0.1	0	—
1701	Chewing gum, stick	1	item(s)	3	0.1	7	0	2.0	0.1	0	0	0	0	—
33378	Chocolate fudge with nuts, prepared	2	piece(s)	38	2.9	175	1.7	25.8	1.0	7.2	2.5	1.5	2.9	0.1
1787	Jelly beans	15	item(s)	43	2.7	159	0	39.8	0.1	0	0	0	0	—
1784	Kit Kat wafer bar	1	item(s)	42	0.8	210	3.0	27.0	0.5	11.0	7.0	3.5	0.3	0
4674	Krackel candy bar	1	item(s)	41	0.6	210	2.0	28.0	0.5	10.0	6.0	3.9	0.4	0
4934	Licorice	4	piece(s)	44	7.3	154	1.1	35.1	0	1.0	0	0.1	0	—
1780	Life Savers candy	1	item(s)	2	—	8	0	2.0	0	0	0	0	0	0
1790	Lollipop	1	item(s)	28	—	108	0	28.0	0	0	0	0	0	0
4679	M & Ms peanut chocolate candy, small bag	1	item(s)	49	0.9	250	5.0	30.0	2.0	13.0	5.0	5.4	2.1	—
1781	M & Ms plain chocolate candy, small bag	1	item(s)	48	0.8	240	2.0	34.0	1.0	10.0	6.0	3.3	0.3	—
4673	Milk chocolate bar, Symphony	1	item(s)	91	0.9	483	7.7	52.8	1.5	27.8	16.7	7.2	0.6	—

PAGE KEY: A-2 = Breads/Baked Goods A-8 = Cereal/Rice/Pasta A-12 = Fruit A-18 = Vegetables/Legumes A-28 = Nuts/Seeds A-30 = Vegetarian A-32 = Dairy A-40 = Eggs A-40 = Seafood A-44 = Meats A-48 = Poultry A-48 = Processed Meats A-50 = Beverages A-54 = Fats/Oils A-56 = Sweets A-58 = Spices/Condiments/Sauces A-62 = Mixed Foods/Soups/Sandwiches A-68 = Fast Food A-88 = Convenience A-90 = Baby Foods

Chol (mg)	Calc (mg)	Iron (mg)	Magn (mg)	Pota (mg)	Sodi (mg)	Zinc (mg)	Vit A (µg)	Thia (mg)	Vit E (mg α)	Ribo (mg)	Niac (mg)	Vit B_6 (mg)	Fola (µg)	Vit C (mg)	Vit B_{12} (µg)	Sele (µg)
0	0	0.00	0	0	0	0.00	0	0.00	2.37	0.00	0.00	0.00	0	0	0	0
0	0	0.00	0	0	0	0.00	0	0.00	1.94	0.00	0.00	0.00	0	0	0	0
0	0	0.07	0	0.1	0.3	0.00	0	0.00	1.93	0.00	0.00	0.00	0	0	0	0
0	0	0.00	0	0	0	0.00	0	0.00	2.11	0.00	0.00	0.00	0	0	0	0
0	0	0.00	0	0	0	0.00	0	0.00	4.63	0.00	0.00	0.00	0	0	0	0
0	0	0.00	0	0	0	0.00	0	0.00	0.19	0.00	0.00	0.00	0	0	0	0
0	0	0.00	0	0	0	0.00	0	0.00	1.10	0.00	0.00	0.00	0	0	0	0
0	0	0.00	0	0	0	0.00	0	0.00	1.64	0.00	0.00	0.00	0	0	0	0
0	0	0.00	0	0	0	0.00	0	0.00	5.58	0.00	0.00	0.00	0	0	0	0
0	0	0.00	0	0.3	1.5	0.01	0.1	0.00	0.00	0.00	0.00	0.00	0	0	0	0
5	24	0.06	0	11.1	328.2	0.08	20.1	0.00	1.80	0.03	0.03	0.01	7.8	0.6	0.1	0.3
0	28	0.16	2.2	1.6	384.0	0.08	—	0.01	0.08	0.03	0.01	0.01	1.0	0.1	0.1	0.5
1	7	0.05	0.6	8.7	323.4	0.03	0.6	0.00	1.56	0.00	0.01	0.00	0.9	0	0	0.5
0	12	0.08	1.6	42.6	320.0	0.05	0.3	0.00	0.21	0.01	0.01	0.01	1.9	0	0	0.5
0	2	0.03	0.6	10.8	306.9	0.01	—	0.00	0.71	0.00	0.01	0.01	0	0.1	0	0.5
0	8	0.25	1.6	21.4	267.5	0.09	7.4	0.01	1.60	0.01	0.06	0.00	0	0	0	0
0	4	0.27	2.6	34.2	257.3	0.06	8.6	0.01	0.09	0.01	0.14	0.01	0.6	0	0	0.5
0	2	0.18	0.9	14.1	486.3	0.03	0.6	0.00	1.47	0.01	0.00	0.01	0	0	0	0.6
2	3	0.19	1.2	25.5	409.8	0.05	0.3	0.00	0.06	0.00	0.00	0.02	0	0	0	2.4
8	4	0.05	0.6	2.6	209.0	0.05	6.2	0.00	0.60	0.01	0.00	0.01	1.8	0	0.1	0.5
0	0	0.00	0	2.6	0.3	0.00	0	0.00	1.46	0.00	0.00	0.00	0	0	0	0.5
1	4	0.03	1.2	8.4	354.0	0.01	5.4	0.00	1.84	0.01	0.00	0.00	0.3	0.1	0	0.1
0	5	0.01	1.5	8.4	413.7	0.01	0.9	0.00	0.72	0.01	0.00	0.00	0.3	0.1	0	0.1
0	6	0.20	3.0	51.9	282.3	0.06	13.2	0.01	0.98	0.01	0.16	0.02	1.5	1.4	0	0.5
2	6	0.18	0	50.2	277.8	0.02	0.6	0.00	0.12	0.00	0.00	0.00	1.0	1.9	0	0.5
0	6	0.18	0	47.1	300.0	0.02	0.6	0.00	1.50	0.00	0.00	0.00	0	0	0	0.5
8	5	0.37	2.6	34.2	276.2	0.08	4.5	0.46	1.28	0.01	0.13	0.00	0	0	0	0.5
0	5	0.27	2.1	60.6	249.3	0.05	4.8	0.01	0.30	0.01	0.13	0.00	0	0	0	0
5	1	0.03	0.1	1.7	78.4	0.02	11.2	0.01	0.72	0.01	0.00	0.08	0.7	0	0	0.2
4	0	0.00	0	1.6	79.5	0.01	0	0.00	0.32	0.00	0.00	0.00	0	0	0	0.3
8	6	0.20	0.8	10.1	191.5	0.05	20.2	0.00	0.97	0.00	0.01	0.07	2.0	0.1	0.1	0.5
0	22	0.08	2.9	34.4	143.1	0.07	11.1	0.01	—	0.03	0.01	0.01	0.8	0.1	0	0
0	18	0.33	30.3	126.5	65.0	0.36	0	0.01	—	0.06	0.21	—	—	0	—	—
0	20	0.00	—	—	150.0	—	0	—	—	—	—	—	—	0	—	—
1	0	0.00	0	0.4	46.9	0.01	3.4	0.00	0.01	0.00	0.00	0.00	0	0	0	0.1
0	0	0.00	0	0.1	0	0.00	0	0.00	0.00	0.00	0.00	0.00	0	0	0	0
5	22	0.74	20.9	69.5	14.8	0.54	14.4	0.02	0.09	0.03	0.12	0.03	6.1	0.1	0	1.1
0	1	0.05	0.9	15.7	21.3	0.02	0	0.00	0.00	0.01	0.00	0.00	0	0	0	0.5
3	60	0.36	16.4	126.0	30.0	0.51	0	0.07	—	0.22	1.07	0.05	59.6	0	0.1	2.0
3	40	0.36	—	168.8	50.0	—	0	—	—	—	—	—	—	0	—	—
0	0	0.22	2.6	28.2	126.3	0.07	0	0.01	0.07	0.01	0.04	0.00	0	0	0	—
0	0	0.00	—	0	0	—	0	0.00	—	0.00	0.00	—	—	0	—	0
0	0	0.00	—	—	10.8	—	0	0.00	—	0.00	0.00	—	—	0	—	1.0
5	40	0.36	36.5	170.6	25.0	1.13	14.8	0.03	—	0.06	1.60	0.04	17.3	0.6	0.1	1.9
5	40	0.36	19.6	127.4	30.0	0.46	14.8	0.02	—	0.06	0.10	0.01	2.9	0.6	0.1	1.4
22	228	0.82	61.0	398.6	91.9	1.00	0	0.06	—	0.25	0.14	0.10	10.9	2.0	0.4	—

TABLE A-1 Table of Food Composition *(continued)*

(Computer code is for Cengage Diet Analysis program) (For purposes of calculations, use "0" for t, <1, <.1, <.01, etc.)

DA+ Code	Food Description	Qty	Measure	Wt (g)	H_2O (g)	Ener (cal)	Prot (g)	Carb (g)	Fiber (g)	Fat (g)	Fat Breakdown (g) Sat	Mono	Poly	Trans
	Sweets—continued													
1783	Milky Way bar	1	item(s)	58	3.7	270	2.0	41.0	1.0	10.0	5.0	3.5	0.3	—
1788	Peanut brittle	1½	ounce(s)	43	0.3	207	3.2	30.3	1.1	8.1	1.8	3.4	1.9	—
1789	Reese's peanut butter cups	2	piece(s)	51	0.8	280	6.0	19.0	2.0	15.5	6.0	7.2	2.7	0
4689	Reese's pieces candy, small bag	1	item(s)	43	1.1	220	5.0	26.0	1.0	11.0	7.0	0.9	0.4	0
33399	Semisweet chocolate candy, made with butter	½	ounce(s)	14	0.1	68	0.6	9.0	0.8	4.2	2.5	1.4	0.1	—
1782	Snickers bar	1	item(s)	59	3.2	280	4.0	35.0	1.0	14.0	5.0	6.1	2.9	—
4694	Special Dark chocolate bar	1	item(s)	41	0.4	220	2.0	25.0	3.0	12.0	8.0	4.6	0.4	0
4695	Starburst fruit chews, original fruits	1	package(s)	59	3.9	240	0	48.0	0	5.0	1.0	2.1	1.8	—
4698	Taffy	3	piece(s)	45	2.2	179	0	41.2	0	1.5	0.9	0.4	0.1	0.1
4699	Three Musketeers bar	1	item(s)	60	3.5	260	2.0	46.0	1.0	8.0	4.5	2.6	0.3	—
4702	Twix caramel cookie bars	2	item(s)	58	2.4	280	3.0	37.0	1.0	14.0	5.0	7.7	0.5	—
4705	York peppermint pattie	1	item(s)	39	3.9	160	0.5	32.0	0.5	3.0	1.5	1.2	0.1	0
	Frosting, Icing													
4760	Chocolate frosting, ready to eat	2	tablespoon(s)	31	5.2	122	0.3	19.4	0.3	5.4	1.7	2.8	0.6	—
4771	Creamy vanilla frosting, ready to eat	2	tablespoon(s)	28	4.2	117	0	19.0	0	4.5	0.8	1.4	2.2	0
17291	Dec-A-Cake variety pack candy decoration	1	teaspoon(s)	4	—	15	0	3.0	0	0.5	0	—	—	—
536	White icing	2	tablespoon(s)	40	3.6	162	0.1	31.8	0	4.2	0.8	2.0	1.2	—
	Gelatin													
13697	Gelatin snack, all flavors	1	item(s)	99	96.8	70	1.0	17.0	0	0	0	0	0	0
2616	Sugar free, low calorie mixed fruit gelatin mix, prepared	½	cup(s)	121	—	10	1.0	0	0	0	0	0	0	0
548	**Honey**	1	tablespoon(s)	21	3.6	64	0.1	17.3	0	0	0	0	0	0
	Jams, Jellies													
550	Jam or preserves	1	tablespoon(s)	20	6.1	56	0.1	13.8	0.2	0	0	0	0	—
42199	Jams, preserves, dietetic, all flavors, w/sodium saccharin	1	tablespoon(s)	14	6.4	18	0	7.5	0.4	0	0	0	0	—
552	Jelly	1	tablespoon(s)	21	6.3	56	0	14.7	0.2	0	0	0	0	—
545	**Marshmallows**	4	item(s)	29	4.7	92	0.5	23.4	0	0.1	0	0	0	—
4800	**Marshmallow cream topping**	2	tablespoon(s)	40	7.9	129	0.3	31.6	0	0.1	0	0	0	—
555	**Molasses**	1	tablespoon(s)	20	4.4	58	0	14.9	0	0	0	0	0	—
4780	**Popsicle or ice pop**	1	item(s)	59	47.5	47	0	11.3	0	0.1	0	0	0	—
	Sugar													
559	Brown sugar, packed	1	teaspoon(s)	5	0.1	17	0	4.5	0	0	0	0	0	0
563	Powdered sugar, sifted	⅓	cup(s)	33	0.1	130	0	33.2	0	0	0	0	0	—
561	White granulated sugar	1	teaspoon(s)	4	0	16	0	4.2	0	0	0	0	0	0
	Sugar substitute													
1760	Equal sweetener, packet size	1	item(s)	1	—	0	0	0.9	0	0	0	0	0	0
13029	Splenda granular no calorie sweetener	1	teaspoon(s)	1	—	0	0	0.5	0	0	0	0	0	0
1759	Sweet N Low sugar substitute, packet	1	item(s)	1	0.1	4	0	0.5	0	0	0	0	0	0
	Syrup													
3148	Chocolate syrup	2	tablespoon(s)	38	11.6	105	0.8	24.4	1.0	0.4	0.2	0.1	0	—
29676	Maple syrup	¼	cup(s)	80	25.7	209	0	53.7	0	0.2	0	0.1	0.1	—
4795	Pancake syrup	¼	cup(s)	80	30.4	187	0	49.2	0	0	0	0	0	0
	Spices, Condiments, Sauces													
	Spices													
807	Allspice, ground	1	teaspoon(s)	2	0.2	5	0.1	1.4	0.4	0.2	0	0	0	—
1171	Anise seeds	1	teaspoon(s)	2	0.2	7	0.4	1.1	0.3	0.3	0	0.2	0.1	—
729	Bakers' yeast, active	1	teaspoon(s)	4	0.3	12	1.5	1.5	0.8	0.2	0	0.1	0	—
683	Baking powder, double acting with phosphate	1	teaspoon(s)	5	0.2	2	0	1.1	0	0	0	0	0	0
1611	Baking soda	1	teaspoon(s)	5	0	0	0	0	0	0	0	0	0	0
8552	Basil	1	teaspoon(s)	1	0.8	0	0	0	0	0	0	0	0	—
34959	Basil, fresh	1	piece(s)	1	0.5	0	0	0	0	0	0	0	0	—

Chol (mg)	Calc (mg)	Iron (mg)	Magn (mg)	Pota (mg)	Sodi (mg)	Zinc (mg)	Vit A (µg)	Thia (mg)	Vit E (mg α)	Ribo (mg)	Niac (mg)	Vit B_6 (mg)	Fola (µg)	Vit C (mg)	Vit B_{12} (µg)	Sele (µg)
5	60	0.18	19.8	140.1	95.0	0.41	15.1	0.02	—	0.06	0.20	0.02	5.8	0.6	0.2	3.3
5	11	0.51	17.9	71.4	189.2	0.37	16.6	0.05	1.08	0.01	1.12	0.03	19.6	0	0	1.1
3	40	0.72	45.4	217.4	180.0	0.93	0	0.12	—	0.08	2.35	0.07	28.1	0	0.1	2.3
0	20	0.00	18.9	169.9	80.0	0.32	0	0.04	—	0.06	1.22	0.03	12.0	0	0.1	0.8
3	5	0.44	16.3	51.7	1.6	0.23	0.4	0.01	—	0.01	0.06	0.01	0.4	0	0	0.5
5	40	0.36	42.3	—	140.0	1.37	15.3	0.03	—	0.06	1.60	0.05	23.5	0.6	0.1	2.7
0	0	1.80	45.5	136.0	50.0	0.59	0	0.01	—	0.02	0.16	0.01	0.8	0	0	1.2
0	10	0.18	0.6	1.2	0	0.00	—	0.00	—	0.00	0.00	0.00	0	30	0	0.5
4	4	0.00	0	1.4	23.4	0.09	12.2	0.01	0.04	0.01	0.00	0.00	0	0	0	0.3
5	20	0.36	17.5	80.3	110.0	0.33	14.5	0.01	—	0.03	0.20	0.01	0	0.6	0.1	1.5
5	40	0.36	18.5	116.8	115.0	0.45	15.0	0.09	—	0.13	0.69	0.01	13.9	0.6	0.1	1.2
0	0	0.33	23.4	66.1	10.0	0.28	0	0.01	—	0.03	0.31	0.01	1.5	0	0	—
0	2	0.44	6.4	60.0	56.1	0.09	0	0.00	0.48	0.00	0.03	0.00	0.3	0	0	0.2
0	1	0.04	0.3	9.5	51.5	0.01	0	0.00	0.43	0.08	0.06	0.00	2.2	0	0	0
0	0	0.00	—	—	15.0	—	0	—	—	—	—	—	—	0	—	—
0	4	0.01	0.4	5.6	76.4	0.01	44.4	0.00	0.32	0.01	0.00	0.00	0	0	0	0.3
0	0	0.00	—	0	40.0	—	0	—	—	—	—	—	—	0	—	—
0	0	0.00	0	0	50.0	0.00	0	0.00	0.00	0.00	0.00	0.00	0	0	0	—
0	1	0.08	0.4	10.9	0.8	0.04	0	0.00	0.00	0.01	0.02	0.01	0.4	0.1	0	0.2
0	4	0.10	0.8	15.4	6.4	0.01	0	0.00	0.02	0.02	0.01	0.00	2.2	1.8	0	0.4
0	1	0.56	0.7	9.7	0	0.01	0	0.00	0.01	0.00	0.00	0.00	1.3	0	0	0.2
0	1	0.04	1.3	11.3	6.3	0.01	0	0.00	0.00	0.01	0.01	0.00	0.4	0.2	0	0.1
0	1	0.06	0.6	1.4	23.0	0.01	0	0.00	0.00	0.00	0.02	0.00	0.3	0	0	0.5
0	1	0.08	0.8	2.0	32.0	0.01	0	0.00	0.00	0.00	0.03	0.00	0.4	0	0	0.7
0	41	0.94	48.4	292.8	7.4	0.05	0	0.01	0.00	0.00	0.18	0.13	0	0	0	3.6
0	0	0.31	0.6	8.9	4.1	0.08	0	0.00	0.00	0.00	0.00	0.00	0	0.4	0	0.1
0	4	0.03	0.4	6.1	1.3	0.00	0	0.00	0.00	0.00	0.01	0.00	0	0	0	0.1
0	0	0.01	0	0.7	0.3	0.00	0	0.00	0.00	0.00	0.00	0.00	0	0	0	0.2
0	0	0.00	0	0.1	0	0.00	0	0.00	0.00	0.00	0.00	0.00	0	0	0	0
0	0	0.00	0	0	0	0.00	0	0.00	0.00	0.00	0.00	0.00	0	0	0	0
0	0	0.00	—	—	0	—	—	0.00	—	0.00	0.00	—	—	0	0	—
0	0	0.00	—	—	0	—	0	—	0.00	—	—	—	—	0	—	—
0	5	0.79	24.4	84.0	27.0	0.27	0	0.00	0.01	0.01	0.12	0.00	0.8	0.1	0	0.5
0	54	0.96	11.2	163.2	7.2	3.32	0	0.01	0.00	0.01	0.02	0.00	0	0	0	0.5
0	2	0.02	1.6	12.0	65.6	0.06	0	0.01	0.00	0.01	0.00	0.00	0	0	0	0
0	13	0.13	2.6	19.8	1.5	0.01	0.5	0.00	—	0.00	0.05	0.00	0.7	0.7	0	0.1
0	14	0.77	3.6	30.3	0.3	0.11	0.3	0.01	—	0.01	0.06	0.01	0.2	0.4	0	0.1
0	3	0.66	3.9	80.0	2.0	0.25	0	0.09	0.00	0.21	1.59	0.06	93.6	0	0	1.0
0	339	0.51	1.8	0.2	363.1	0.00	0	0.00	0.00	0.00	0.00	0.00	0	0	0	0
0	0	0.00	0	0	1258.6	0.00	0	0.00	0.00	0.00	0.00	0.00	0	0	0	0
0	2	0.02	0.6	2.6	0	0.01	2.3	0.00	0.01	0.00	0.01	0.00	0.6	0.2	0	0
0	1	0.01	0.4	2.3	0	0.00	1.3	0.00	—	0.00	0.00	0.00	0.3	0.1	0	0

TABLE A-1 Table of Food Composition *(continued)*

(Computer code is for Cengage Diet Analysis program) (For purposes of calculations, use "0" for t, <1, <.1, <.01, etc.)

											Fat Breakdown (g)			
DA+ Code	Food Description	Qty	Measure	Wt (g)	H_2O (g)	Ener (cal)	Prot (g)	Carb (g)	Fiber (g)	Fat (g)	Sat	Mono	Poly	*Trans*
	Spices, Condiments, Sauces—continued													
808	Basil, ground	1	teaspoon(s)	1	0.1	4	0.2	0.9	0.6	0.1	0	0	0	—
809	Bay leaf	1	teaspoon(s)	1	0	2	0	0.5	0.2	0.1	0	0	0	—
11720	Betel leaves	1	ounce(s)	28	—	17	1.8	2.4	0	0	—	—	—	—
730	Brewers' yeast	1	teaspoon(s)	3	0.1	8	1.0	1.0	0.8	0	0	0	0	0
11710	Capers	1	teaspoon(s)	5	—	0	0	0	0	0	0	0	0	0
1172	Caraway seeds	1	teaspoon(s)	2	0.2	7	0.4	1.0	0.8	0.3	0	0.2	0.1	—
1173	Celery seeds	1	teaspoon(s)	2	0.1	8	0.4	0.8	0.2	0.5	0	0.3	0.1	—
1174	Chervil, dried	1	teaspoon(s)	1	0	1	0.1	0.3	0.1	0	0	0	0	—
810	Chili powder	1	teaspoon(s)	3	0.2	8	0.3	1.4	0.9	0.4	0.1	0.1	0.2	—
8553	Chives, chopped	1	teaspoon(s)	1	0.9	0	0	0	0	0	0	0	0	—
51420	Cilantro (coriander)	1	teaspoon(s)	0	0.3	0	0	0	0	0	0	0	0	—
811	Cinnamon, ground	1	teaspoon(s)	2	0.2	6	0.1	1.9	1.2	0	0	0	0	0
812	Cloves, ground	1	teaspoon(s)	2	0.1	7	0.1	1.3	0.7	0.4	0.1	0	0.1	—
1175	Coriander leaf, dried	1	teaspoon(s)	1	0	2	0.1	0.3	0.1	0	0	0	0	—
1176	Coriander seeds	1	teaspoon(s)	2	0.2	5	0.2	1.0	0.8	0.3	0	0.2	0	—
1706	Cornstarch	1	tablespoon(s)	8	0.7	30	0	7.3	0.1	0	0	0	0	—
1177	Cumin seeds	1	teaspoon(s)	2	0.2	8	0.4	0.9	0.2	0.5	0	0.3	0.1	—
11729	Cumin, ground	1	teaspoon(s)	5	—	11	0.4	0.8	0.8	0.4	—	—	—	—
1178	Curry powder	1	teaspoon(s)	2	0.2	7	0.3	1.2	0.7	0.3	0	0.1	0.1	—
1179	Dill seeds	1	teaspoon(s)	2	0.2	6	0.3	1.2	0.4	0.3	0	0.2	0	—
1180	Dill weed, dried	1	teaspoon(s)	1	0.1	3	0.2	0.6	0.1	0	0	0	0	—
34949	Dill weed, fresh	5	piece(s)	1	0.9	0	0	0.1	0	0	0	0	0	—
4949	Fennel leaves, fresh	1	teaspoon(s)	1	0.9	0	0	0.1	0	0	—	—	—	—
1181	Fennel seeds	1	teaspoon(s)	2	0.2	7	0.3	1.0	0.8	0.3	0	0.2	0	—
1182	Fenugreek seeds	1	teaspoon(s)	4	0.3	12	0.9	2.2	0.9	0.2	0.1	—	—	—
11733	Garam masala, powder	1	ounce(s)	28	—	107	4.4	12.8	0	4.3	—	—	—	—
1067	Garlic clove	1	item(s)	3	1.8	4	0.2	1.0	0.1	0	0	0	0	—
813	Garlic powder	1	teaspoon(s)	3	0.2	9	0.5	2.0	0.3	0	0	0	0	—
1068	Ginger root	2	teaspoon(s)	4	3.1	3	0.1	0.7	0.1	0	0	0	0	—
1183	Ginger, ground	1	teaspoon(s)	2	0.2	6	0.2	1.3	0.2	0.1	0	0	0	—
35497	Leeks, bulb and lower-leaf, freeze-dried	¼	cup(s)	1	0	3	0.1	0.6	0.1	0	0	0	0	—
1184	Mace, ground	1	teaspoon(s)	2	0.1	8	0.1	0.9	0.3	0.6	0.2	0.2	0.1	—
1185	Marjoram, dried	1	teaspoon(s)	1	0	2	0.1	0.4	0.2	0	0	0	0	—
1186	Mustard seeds, yellow	1	teaspoon(s)	3	0.2	15	0.8	1.2	0.5	0.9	0	0.7	0.2	—
814	Nutmeg, ground	1	teaspoon(s)	2	0.1	12	0.1	1.1	0.5	0.8	0.6	0.1	0	—
2747	Onion flakes, dehydrated	1	teaspoon(s)	2	0.1	6	0.1	1.4	0.2	0	0	0	0	—
1187	Onion powder	1	teaspoon(s)	2	0.1	7	0.2	1.7	0.1	0	0	0	0	—
815	Oregano, ground	1	teaspoon(s)	2	0.1	5	0.2	1.0	0.6	0.2	0	0	0.1	—
816	Paprika	1	teaspoon(s)	2	0.2	6	0.3	1.2	0.8	0.3	0	0	0.2	—
817	Parsley, dried	1	teaspoon(s)	0	0	1	0.1	0.2	0.1	0	0	0	0	—
818	Pepper, black	1	teaspoon(s)	2	0.2	5	0.2	1.4	0.6	0.1	0	0	0	—
819	Pepper, cayenne	1	teaspoon(s)	2	0.1	6	0.2	1.0	0.5	0.3	0.1	0	0.2	—
1188	Pepper, white	1	teaspoon(s)	2	0.3	7	0.3	1.6	0.6	0.1	0	0	0	—
1189	Poppy seeds	1	teaspoon(s)	3	0.2	15	0.5	0.7	0.3	1.3	0.1	0.2	0.9	—
1190	Poultry seasoning	1	teaspoon(s)	2	0.1	5	0.1	1.0	0.2	0.1	0	0	0	—
1191	Pumpkin pie spice, powder	1	teaspoon(s)	2	0.1	6	0.1	1.2	0.3	0.2	0.1	0	0	—
1192	Rosemary, dried	1	teaspoon(s)	1	0.1	4	0.1	0.8	0.5	0.2	0.1	0	0	—
11723	Rosemary, fresh	1	teaspoon(s)	1	0.5	1	0	0.1	0.1	0	0	0	0	—
2722	Saffron powder	1	teaspoon(s)	1	0.1	2	0.1	0.5	0	0	0	0	0	—
11724	Sage	1	teaspoon(s)	1	—	1	0	0.1	0	0	—	—	—	—
1193	Sage, ground	1	teaspoon(s)	1	0.1	2	0.1	0.4	0.3	0.1	0	0	0	—
30189	Salt substitute	¼	teaspoon(s)	1	—	0	0	0	0	0	0	0	0	0
30190	Salt substitute, seasoned	¼	teaspoon(s)	1	—	1	0	0.1	0	0	0	—	—	—
822	Salt, table	¼	teaspoon(s)	2	0	0	0	0	0	0	0	0	0	0
1194	Savory, ground	1	teaspoon(s)	1	0.1	4	0.1	1.0	0.6	0.1	0	—	—	—
820	Sesame seed kernels, toasted	1	teaspoon(s)	3	0.1	15	0.5	0.7	0.5	1.3	0.2	0.5	0.6	—
11725	Sorrel	1	teaspoon(s)	3	—	1	0.1	0.1	0	0	0	—	—	—
11721	Spearmint	1	teaspoon(s)	2	1.6	1	0.1	0.2	0.1	0	0	0	0	—
35498	Sweet green peppers, freeze-dried	¼	cup(s)	2	0	5	0.3	1.1	0.3	0	0	0	0	—
11726	Tamarind leaves	1	ounce(s)	28	—	33	1.6	5.2	0	0.6	—	—	—	—
11727	Tarragon	1	ounce(s)	28	—	14	1.0	1.8	0	0.3	—	—	—	—

PAGE KEY: A-2 = Breads/Baked Goods A-8 = Cereal/Rice/Pasta A-12 = Fruit A-18 = Vegetables/Legumes A-28 = Nuts/Seeds A-30 = Vegetarian A-32 = Dairy A-40 = Eggs A-40 = Seafood A-44 = Meats A-48 = Poultry A-48 = Processed Meats A-50 = Beverages A-54 = Fats/Oils A-56 = Sweets A-58 = Spices/Condiments/Sauces A-62 = Mixed Foods/Soups/Sandwiches A-68 = Fast Food A-88 = Convenience A-90 = Baby Foods

Chol (mg)	Calc (mg)	Iron (mg)	Magn (mg)	Pota (mg)	Sodi (mg)	Zinc (mg)	Vit A (μg)	Thia (mg)	Vit E (mg α)	Ribo (mg)	Niac (mg)	Vit B_6 (mg)	Fola (μg)	Vit C (mg)	Vit B_{12} (μg)	Sele (μg)
0	30	0.58	5.9	48.1	0.5	0.08	6.6	0.00	0.10	0.00	0.09	0.03	3.8	0.9	0	0
0	5	0.25	0.7	3.2	0.1	0.02	1.9	0.00	—	0.00	0.01	0.01	1.1	0.3	0	0
0	110	2.29	—	155.9	2.0	—	—	0.04	—	0.07	0.19	—	—	0.9	0	—
0	6	0.46	6.1	50.7	3.3	0.21	0	0.41	—	0.11	1.00	0.06	104.3	0	0	0
0	—	—	—	—	105.0	—	—	—	—	—	—	—	—	—	0	—
0	14	0.34	5.4	28.4	0.4	0.11	0.4	0.01	0.05	0.01	0.07	0.01	0.2	0.4	0	0.3
0	35	0.89	8.8	28.0	3.2	0.13	0.1	0.01	0.02	0.01	0.06	0.01	0.2	0.3	0	0.2
0	8	0.19	0.8	28.4	0.5	0.05	1.8	0.00	—	0.00	0.03	0.01	1.6	0.3	0	0.2
0	7	0.37	4.4	49.8	26.3	0.07	38.6	0.01	0.75	0.02	0.20	0.09	2.6	1.7	0	0.2
0	1	0.01	0.4	3.0	0	0.01	2.2	0.00	0.00	0.00	0.01	0.00	1.1	0.6	0	0
0	0	0.01	0.1	1.7	0.2	0.00	1.1	0.00	0.01	0.00	0.00	0.00	0.2	0.1	0	0
0	23	0.19	1.4	9.9	0.2	0.04	0.3	0.00	0.05	0.00	0.03	0.00	0.1	0.1	0	0.1
0	14	0.18	5.5	23.1	5.1	0.02	0.6	0.00	0.17	0.01	0.03	0.01	2.0	1.7	0	0.1
0	7	0.25	4.2	26.8	1.3	0.02	1.8	0.01	0.01	0.01	0.06	0.00	1.6	3.4	0	0.2
0	13	0.29	5.9	22.8	0.6	0.08	0	0.00	—	0.01	0.03	—	0	0.4	0	0.5
0	0	0.03	0.2	0.2	0.7	0.01	0	0.00	0.00	0.00	0.00	0.00	0	0	0	0.2
0	20	1.39	7.7	37.5	3.5	0.10	1.3	0.01	0.07	0.01	0.09	0.01	0.2	0.2	0	0.1
0	20	—	—	43.6	4.8	—	—	—	—	—	—	—	—	—	—	—
0	10	0.59	5.1	30.9	1.0	0.08	1.0	0.01	0.44	0.01	0.06	0.02	3.1	0.2	0	0.3
0	32	0.34	5.4	24.9	0.4	0.10	0.1	0.01	—	0.01	0.05	0.01	0.2	0.4	0	0.3
0	18	0.48	4.5	33.1	2.1	0.03	2.9	0.00	—	0.00	0.02	0.01	1.5	0.5	0	—
0	2	0.06	0.6	7.4	0.6	0.01	3.9	0.00	0.01	0.00	0.01	0.00	1.5	0.9	0	—
0	1	0.02	—	4.0	0.1	—	—	0.00	—	0.00	0.01	0.00	—	0.3	0	—
0	24	0.37	7.7	33.9	1.8	0.07	0.1	0.01	—	0.01	0.12	0.01	—	0.4	0	—
0	7	1.24	7.1	28.5	2.5	0.09	0.1	0.01	—	0.01	0.06	0.02	2.1	0.1	0	0.2
0	215	9.24	93.6	411.1	27.5	1.07	—	0.09	—	0.09	0.70	—	0	0	0	—
0	5	0.05	0.8	12.0	0.5	0.03	0	0.01	0.00	0.00	0.02	0.03	0.1	0.9	0	0.4
0	2	0.07	1.6	30.8	0.7	0.07	0	0.01	0.01	0.00	0.01	0.08	0.1	0.5	0	1.1
0	1	0.02	1.7	16.6	0.5	0.01	0	0.00	0.01	0.00	0.02	0.01	0.4	0.2	0	0
0	2	0.20	3.3	24.2	0.6	0.08	0.1	0.00	0.32	0.00	0.09	0.01	0.7	0.1	0	0.7
0	3	0.06	1.3	19.2	0.3	0.01	0.1	0.01	—	0.00	0.02	0.01	2.9	0.9	0	0
0	4	0.23	2.8	7.9	1.4	0.03	0.7	0.01	—	0.01	0.02	0.00	1.3	0.4	0	0
0	12	0.49	2.1	9.1	0.5	0.02	2.4	0.00	0.01	0.00	0.02	0.01	1.6	0.3	0	0
0	17	0.32	9.8	22.5	0.2	0.18	0.1	0.01	0.09	0.01	0.26	0.01	2.5	0.1	0	4.4
0	4	0.06	4.0	7.7	0.4	0.04	0.1	0.01	0.00	0.00	0.02	0.00	1.7	0.1	0	0
0	4	0.02	1.5	27.1	0.4	0.03	0	0.01	0.00	0.00	0.01	0.02	2.8	1.3	0	0.1
0	8	0.05	2.6	19.8	1.1	0.04	0	0.01	0.01	0.00	0.01	0.02	3.5	0.3	0	0
0	24	0.66	4.1	25.0	0.2	0.06	5.2	0.01	0.28	0.01	0.09	0.01	4.1	0.8	0	0.1
0	4	0.49	3.9	49.2	0.7	0.08	55.4	0.01	0.62	0.03	0.32	0.08	2.2	1.5	0	0.1
0	4	0.29	0.7	11.4	1.4	0.01	1.5	0.00	0.02	0.00	0.02	0.00	0.5	0.4	0	0.1
0	9	0.60	4.1	26.4	0.9	0.03	0.3	0.00	0.01	0.01	0.02	0.01	0.2	0.4	0	0.1
0	3	0.14	2.7	36.3	0.5	0.04	37.5	0.01	0.53	0.01	0.15	0.04	1.9	1.4	0	0.2
0	6	0.34	2.2	1.8	0.1	0.02	0	0.00	—	0.00	0.01	0.00	0.2	0.5	0	0.1
0	41	0.26	9.3	19.6	0.6	0.28	0	0.02	0.03	0.01	0.02	0.01	1.6	0.1	0	0
0	15	0.53	3.4	10.3	0.4	0.04	2.0	0.00	0.02	0.00	0.04	0.02	2.1	0.2	0	0.1
0	12	0.33	2.3	11.3	0.9	0.04	0.2	0.00	0.01	0.00	0.03	0.01	0.9	0.4	0	0.2
0	15	0.35	2.6	11.5	0.6	0.03	1.9	0.01	—	0.01	0.01	0.02	3.7	0.7	0	0.1
0	2	0.04	0.6	4.7	0.2	0.01	1.0	0.00	—	0.00	0.01	0.00	0.8	0.2	0	—
0	1	0.07	1.8	12.1	1.0	0.01	0.2	0.00	—	0.00	0.01	0.01	0.7	0.6	0	0
0	4	—	1.1	2.7	0	0.01	—	0.00	—	—	—	—	—	—	0	—
0	12	0.19	3.0	7.5	0.1	0.03	2.1	0.01	0.05	0.00	0.04	0.01	1.9	0.2	0	0
0	7	0.00	0	603.6	0.1	—	0	—	—	—	—	—	—	0	—	—
0	0	0.00	—	476.3	0.1	—	0	—	—	—	—	—	—	0	—	—
0	0	0.01	0	0.1	581.4	0.00	0	0.00	0.00	0.00	0.00	0.00	0	0	0	0
0	30	0.53	5.3	14.7	0.3	0.06	3.6	0.01	—	—	0.05	0.02	—	0.7	0	0.1
0	3	0.21	9.2	10.8	1.0	0.27	0.1	0.03	0.01	0.01	0.15	0.00	2.6	0	0	0
0	—	—	—	—	0.1	—	—	—	—	—	—	—	—	—	—	—
0	4	0.22	1.2	8.7	0.6	0.02	3.9	0.00	—	0.00	0.01	0.00	2.0	0.3	0	—
0	2	0.16	3.0	50.7	3.1	0.03	4.5	0.01	0.06	0.01	0.11	0.03	3.7	30.4	0	0.1
0	85	1.48	20.2	—	—	—	—	0.06	—	0.02	1.16	—	—	0.9	0	—
0	48	—	14.5	128.1	2.6	0.17	—	0.04	—	—	—	—	—	0.6	0	—

TABLE A-1 Table of Food Composition *(continued)*

(Computer code is for Cengage Diet Analysis program) (For purposes of calculations, use "0" for t, <1, <.1, <.01, etc.)

DA+ Code	Food Description	QTY	Measure	Wt (g)	H₂O (g)	Ener (cal)	Prot (g)	Carb (g)	Fiber (g)	Fat (g)	Fat Breakdown (g) Sat	Mono	Poly	Trans
	Spices, Condiments, Sauces—continued													
1195	Tarragon, ground	1	teaspoon(s)	2	0.1	5	0.4	0.8	0.1	0.1	0	0	0.1	—
11728	Thyme, fresh	1	teaspoon(s)	1	0.5	1	0	0.2	0.1	0	0	0	0	—
821	Thyme, ground	1	teaspoon(s)	1	0.1	4	0.1	0.9	0.5	0.1	0	0	0	—
1196	Turmeric, ground	1	teaspoon(s)	2	0.3	8	0.2	1.4	0.5	0.2	0.1	0	0	—
11995	Wasabi	1	tablespoon(s)	14	10.7	10	0.7	2.3	0.2	0	—	—	—	—
	Condiments													
674	Catsup or ketchup	1	tablespoon(s)	15	10.4	15	0.3	3.8	0	0	0	0	0	—
703	Dill pickle	1	ounce(s)	28	26.7	3	0.2	0.7	0.3	0	0	0	0	—
138	Mayonnaise with soybean oil	1	tablespoon(s)	14	2.1	99	0.1	0.4	0	11.0	1.6	2.7	5.8	0
140	Mayonnaise, low calorie	1	tablespoon(s)	16	10.0	37	0	2.6	0	3.1	0.5	0.7	1.7	—
1682	Mustard, brown	1	teaspoon(s)	5	4.1	5	0.3	0.3	0	0.3	—	—	—	—
700	Mustard, yellow	1	teaspoon(s)	5	4.1	3	0.2	0.3	0.2	0.2	0	0.1	0	0
706	Sweet pickle relish	1	tablespoon(s)	15	9.3	20	0.1	5.3	0.2	0.1	0	0	0	—
141	Tartar sauce	2	tablespoon(s)	28	8.7	144	0.3	4.1	0.1	14.4	2.2	3.8	7.7	—
	Sauces													
685	Barbecue sauce	2	tablespoon(s)	31	18.9	47	0	11.3	0.2	0.1	0	0	0.1	0
834	Cheese sauce	¼	cup(s)	63	44.4	110	4.2	4.3	0.3	8.4	3.8	2.4	1.6	—
32123	Chili enchilada sauce, green	2	tablespoon(s)	57	53.0	15	0.6	3.1	0.7	0.3	0	0	0.1	0
32122	Chili enchilada sauce, red	2	tablespoon(s)	32	24.5	27	1.1	5.0	2.1	0.8	0.1	0	0.4	0
29688	Hoisin sauce	1	tablespoon(s)	16	7.1	35	0.5	7.1	0.4	0.5	0.1	0.2	0.3	—
1641	Horseradish sauce, prepared	1	teaspoon(s)	5	3.3	10	0.1	0.2	0	1.0	0.6	0.3	0	—
16670	Mole poblano sauce	½	cup(s)	133	102.7	156	5.3	11.4	2.7	11.3	2.6	5.1	3.0	—
29689	Oyster sauce	1	tablespoon(s)	16	12.8	8	0.2	1.7	0	0	0	0	0	—
1655	Pepper sauce or Tabasco	1	teaspoon(s)	5	4.8	1	0.1	0	0	0	0	0	0	—
347	Salsa	2	tablespoon(s)	32	28.8	9	0.5	2.0	0.5	0.1	0	0	0	—
52206	Soy sauce, tamari	1	tablespoon(s)	18	12.0	11	1.9	1.0	0.1	0	0	0	0	—
839	Sweet and sour sauce	2	tablespoon(s)	39	29.8	37	0.1	9.1	0.1	0	0	0	0	—
1613	Teriyaki sauce	1	tablespoon(s)	18	12.2	16	1.1	2.8	0	0	0	0	0	0
25294	Tomato sauce	½	cup(s)	150	132.8	63	2.2	11.9	2.6	1.8	0.2	0.4	0.9	0
728	White sauce, medium	¼	cup(s)	63	46.8	92	2.4	5.7	0.1	6.7	1.8	2.8	1.8	—
1654	Worcestershire sauce	1	teaspoon(s)	6	4.5	4	0	1.1	0	0	0	0	0	0
	Vinegar													
30853	Balsamic	1	tablespoon(s)	15	—	10	0	2.0	0	0	0	0	0	0
727	Cider	1	tablespoon(s)	15	14.0	3	0	0.1	0	0	0	0	0	0
1673	Distilled	1	tablespoon(s)	15	14.3	2	0	0.8	0	0	0	0	0	0
12948	Tarragon	1	tablespoon(s)	15	13.8	2	0	0.1	0	0	0	0	0	0
	Mixed Foods, Soups, Sandwiches													
	Mixed dishes													
16652	Almond chicken	1	cup(s)	242	186.8	281	21.8	15.8	3.4	14.7	1.8	6.3	5.6	—
25224	Barbecued chicken	1	serving(s)	177	99.3	327	27.1	15.7	0.5	17.1	4.8	6.8	3.8	0
25227	Bean burrito	1	item(s)	149	81.8	326	16.1	33.0	5.6	14.8	8.3	4.7	0.9	—
9516	Beef and vegetable fajita	1	item(s)	223	143.9	397	22.4	35.3	3.1	18.0	5.9	8.0	2.5	—
16796	Beef or pork egg roll	2	item(s)	128	85.2	225	9.9	18.4	1.4	12.4	2.9	6.0	2.6	—
177	Beef stew with vegetables, prepared	1	cup(s)	245	201.0	220	16.0	15.0	3.2	11.0	4.4	4.5	0.5	—
30233	Beef stroganoff with noodles	1	cup(s)	256	190.1	343	19.7	22.8	1.5	19.1	7.4	5.7	4.4	—
16651	Cashew chicken	1	cup(s)	242	186.8	281	21.8	15.8	3.4	14.7	1.8	6.3	5.6	—
30274	Cheese pizza with vegetables, thin crust	2	slice(s)	140	76.6	298	12.7	35.4	2.5	12.0	4.9	4.7	1.6	—
30330	Cheese quesadilla	1	item(s)	54	18.3	190	7.7	15.3	1.0	10.8	5.2	3.6	1.3	—
215	Chicken and noodles, prepared	1	cup(s)	240	170.0	365	22.0	26.0	1.3	18.0	5.1	7.1	3.9	—
30239	Chicken and vegetables with broccoli, onion, bamboo shoots in soy based sauce	1	cup(s)	162	125.5	180	15.8	9.3	1.8	8.6	1.7	3.0	3.1	—
25093	Chicken cacciatore	1	cup(s)	244	175.7	284	29.9	5.7	1.3	15.3	4.3	6.2	3.3	0
28020	Chicken fried turkey steak	3	ounce(s)	492	276.2	706	77.1	68.7	3.6	12.0	3.4	2.9	3.9	—
218	Chicken pot pie	1	cup(s)	252	154.6	542	22.6	41.4	3.5	31.3	9.8	12.5	7.1	—
30240	Chicken teriyaki	1	cup(s)	244	158.3	364	51.0	15.2	0.7	7.0	1.8	2.0	1.7	—
25119	Chicken waldorf salad	½	cup(s)	100	67.2	179	14.0	6.8	1.0	10.8	1.8	3.1	5.2	—
25099	Chili con carne	¾	cup(s)	215	174.4	198	13.7	21.4	7.5	6.9	2.5	2.8	0.5	0
1062	Coleslaw	¾	cup(s)	90	73.4	70	1.2	11.2	1.4	2.3	0.3	0.6	1.2	—

Chol (mg)	Calc (mg)	Iron (mg)	Magn (mg)	Pota (mg)	Sodi (mg)	Zinc (mg)	Vit A (µg)	Thia (mg)	Vit E (mg α)	Ribo (mg)	Niac (mg)	Vit B_6 (mg)	Fola (µg)	Vit C (mg)	Vit B_{12} (µg)	Sele (µg)
0	18	0.51	5.6	48.3	1.0	0.06	3.4	0.00	—	0.02	0.14	0.03	4.4	0.8	0	0.1
0	3	0.14	1.3	4.9	0.1	0.01	1.9	0.00	—	0.00	0.01	0.00	0.4	1.3	0	—
0	26	1.73	3.1	11.4	0.8	0.08	2.7	0.01	0.10	0.01	0.06	0.01	3.8	0.7	0	0.1
0	4	0.91	4.2	55.6	0.8	0.09	0	0.00	0.06	0.01	0.11	0.04	0.9	0.6	0	0.1
0	13	0.11	—	—	—	—	—	0.02	—	0.01	0.07	—	—	11.2	0	—
0	3	0.07	2.9	57.3	167.1	0.03	7.1	0.00	0.21	0.02	0.21	0.02	1.5	2.3	0	0
0	12	0.10	2.0	26.1	248.1	0.03	2.6	0.01	0.02	0.01	0.03	0.01	0.3	0.2	0	0
5	1	0.03	0.1	1.7	78.4	0.02	11.2	0.01	0.72	0.01	0.00	0.08	0.7	0	0	0.2
4	0	0.00	0	1.6	79.5	0.01	0	0.00	0.32	0.00	0.00	0.00	0	0	0	0.3
0	6	0.09	1.0	6.8	68.1	0.01	0	0.00	0.09	0.00	0.01	0.00	0.2	0.1	0	—
0	3	0.07	2.5	6.9	56.8	0.03	0.2	0.01	0.01	0.00	0.02	0.00	0.4	0.1	0	1.6
0	0	0.13	0.8	3.8	121.7	0.02	9.2	0.00	0.08	0.01	0.03	0.00	0.2	0.2	0	0
8	6	0.20	0.8	10.1	191.5	0.05	20.2	0.00	0.97	0.00	0.01	0.07	2.0	0.1	0.1	0.5
0	4	0.06	3.8	65.0	349.7	0.04	3.8	0.00	0.20	0.01	0.15	0.01	0.6	0.2	0	0.4
18	116	0.13	5.7	18.9	521.6	0.61	50.4	0.00	—	0.07	0.01	0.01	2.5	0.3	0.1	2.0
0	5	0.36	9.5	125.7	61.9	0.11	—	0.02	0.00	0.02	0.63	0.06	5.7	43.9	0	0
0	7	1.05	11.1	231.3	113.8	0.14	—	0.01	0.00	0.21	0.61	0.34	6.6	0.3	0	0.3
0	5	0.16	3.8	19.0	258.4	0.05	0	0.00	0.04	0.03	0.18	0.01	3.7	0.1	0	0.3
2	5	0.00	0.5	6.7	14.6	0.01	8.0	0.00	0.02	0.01	0.00	0.00	0.5	0.1	0	0.1
1	38	1.81	58.3	280.9	304.8	1.15	13.3	0.06	1.72	0.08	1.84	0.09	15.9	3.4	0.1	1.1
0	5	0.02	0.6	8.6	437.3	0.01	0	0.00	0.00	0.02	0.23	0.00	2.4	0	0.1	0.7
0	1	0.05	0.6	6.4	31.7	0.01	4.1	0.00	0.00	0.00	0.01	0.01	0.1	0.2	0	0
0	9	0.14	4.8	95.0	192.0	0.11	4.8	0.01	0.37	0.01	0.02	0.05	1.3	0.6	0	0.3
0	4	0.43	7.3	38.7	1018.9	0.08	0	0.01	0.00	0.03	0.72	0.04	3.3	0	0	0.1
0	5	0.20	1.2	8.2	97.5	0.01	0	0.00	—	0.01	0.11	0.03	0.2	0	0	—
0	5	0.30	11.0	40.5	689.9	0.01	0	0.01	0.00	0.01	0.22	0.01	1.4	0	0	0.2
0	23	1.24	28.9	536.8	268.6	0.36	—	0.08	0.52	0.08	1.64	0.20	23.2	32.0	0	1.0
4	74	0.20	8.8	97.5	221.3	0.25	—	0.04	—	0.11	0.25	0.02	3.1	0.5	0.2	—
0	6	0.30	0.7	45.4	55.6	0.01	0.3	0.00	0.00	0.01	0.03	0.00	0.5	0.7	0	0
0	0	0.00	—	—	0	—	0	—	—	—	—	—	—	0	—	—
0	1	0.03	0.7	10.9	0.7	0.01	0	0.00	0.00	0.00	0.00	0.00	0	0	0	0
0	1	0.09	0	2.3	0.1	0.00	0	0.00	0.00	0.00	0.00	0.00	0	0	0	5.0
0	0	0.07	—	2.3	0.7	—	—	0.07	—	0.07	0.07	—	—	0.3	0	—
41	68	1.86	58.1	539.7	510.6	1.50	31.5	0.07	4.11	0.22	9.57	0.43	26.6	5.1	0.3	13.6
120	26	1.70	32.4	419.7	500.9	2.67	—	0.09	0.01	0.24	6.87	0.40	15.0	7.9	0.3	19.5
38	333	3.01	52.5	447.6	510.6	1.98	—	0.28	0.01	0.30	1.92	0.19	122.9	8.2	0.3	15.9
45	85	3.65	37.9	475.0	756.0	3.52	17.8	0.38	0.80	0.29	5.33	0.39	69.1	23.4	2.1	28.3
74	31	1.68	20.5	248.3	547.8	0.89	25.6	0.32	1.28	0.24	2.55	0.18	38.4	4.0	0.3	17.5
71	29	2.90	—	613.0	292.0	—	—	0.15	0.51	0.17	4.70	—	—	17.0	0	15.0
74	69	3.25	35.8	391.7	816.6	3.63	69.1	0.21	1.25	0.30	3.80	0.21	48.6	1.3	1.8	27.9
41	68	1.86	58.1	539.7	510.6	1.50	31.5	0.07	4.11	0.22	9.57	0.43	26.6	5.1	0.3	13.6
17	249	2.78	28.0	294.0	739.2	1.42	47.6	0.29	1.05	0.33	2.84	0.14	61.6	15.3	0.4	18.6
23	190	1.04	13.5	75.6	469.3	0.86	58.3	0.11	0.43	0.15	0.89	0.02	21.6	2.4	0.1	9.2
103	26	2.20	—	149.0	600.0	—	—	0.05	—	0.17	4.30	—	—	0	—	29.0
42	28	1.19	22.7	299.7	620.5	1.32	81.0	0.07	1.11	0.14	5.28	0.36	16.2	22.5	0.2	12.0
109	47	1.97	40.0	489.3	492.1	2.13	—	0.11	0.00	0.20	9.81	0.57	16.1	14.0	0.3	22.6
156	423	8.79	110.3	1182.9	880.4	6.18	—	0.72	0.00	1.05	20.16	1.20	113.9	2.7	1.3	97.6
68	66	3.32	37.8	390.6	652.7	1.94	259.6	0.39	1.05	0.39	7.25	0.23	80.6	10.3	0.2	27.0
156	51	3.26	68.3	588.0	3208.6	3.75	31.7	0.15	0.58	0.36	16.68	0.88	24.4	2.0	0.5	36.1
42	20	0.82	23.9	202.5	246.5	1.13	—	0.05	0.62	0.09	4.06	0.25	15.8	2.5	0.2	10.7
27	42	2.83	50.6	636.8	864.8	2.36	—	0.15	0.01	0.22	3.18	0.19	58.1	10.3	0.6	7.3
7	41	0.53	9.0	162.9	20.7	0.18	47.7	0.06	—	0.05	0.24	0.11	24.3	29.4	0	0.6

TABLE A-1 Table of Food Composition *(continued)*

(Computer code is for Cengage Diet Analysis program) (For purposes of calculations, use "0" for t, <1, <.1, <.01, etc.)

											Fat Breakdown (g)			
DA+ Code	Food Description	Qty	Measure	Wt (g)	H_2O (g)	Ener (cal)	Prot (g)	Carb (g)	Fiber (g)	Fat (g)	Sat	Mono	Poly	Trans
Mixed Foods, Soups, Sandwiches—continued														
1574	Crab cakes, from blue crab	1	item(s)	60	42.6	93	12.1	0.3	0	4.5	0.9	1.7	1.4	—
32144	Enchiladas with green chili sauce (enchiladas verdes)	1	item(s)	144	103.8	207	9.3	17.6	2.6	11.7	6.4	3.6	1.0	0
2793	Falafel patty	3	item(s)	51	17.7	170	6.8	16.2	—	9.1	1.2	5.2	2.1	—
28546	Fettuccine alfredo	1	cup(s)	244	88.7	279	13.1	46.1	1.4	4.2	2.2	1.0	0.4	0
32146	Flautas	3	item(s)	162	78.0	438	24.9	36.3	4.1	21.6	8.2	8.8	2.3	—
29629	Fried rice with meat or poultry	1	cup(s)	198	128.5	333	12.3	41.8	1.4	12.3	2.2	3.5	5.7	—
16649	General Tso chicken	1	cup(s)	146	91.0	296	18.7	16.4	0.9	17.0	4.0	6.3	5.3	—
1826	Green salad	¾	cup(s)	104	98.9	17	1.3	3.3	2.2	0.1	0	0	0	—
1814	Hummus	½	cup(s)	123	79.8	218	6.0	24.7	4.9	10.6	1.4	6.0	2.6	—
16650	Kung pao chicken	1	cup(s)	162	87.2	434	28.8	11.7	2.3	30.6	5.2	13.9	9.7	—
16622	Lamb curry	1	cup(s)	236	187.9	257	28.2	3.7	0.9	13.8	3.9	4.9	3.3	—
25253	Lasagna with ground beef	1	cup(s)	237	158.4	284	16.9	22.3	2.4	14.5	7.5	4.9	0.8	—
442	Macaroni and cheese, prepared	1	cup(s)	200	122.3	390	14.9	40.6	1.6	18.6	7.9	6.4	2.9	—
29637	Meat filled ravioli with tomato or meat sauce, canned	1	cup(s)	251	198.7	208	7.8	36.5	1.3	3.7	1.5	1.4	0.3	—
25105	Meat loaf	1	slice(s)	115	84.5	245	17.0	6.6	0.4	16.0	6.1	6.9	0.9	0
16646	Moo shi pork	1	cup(s)	151	76.8	512	18.9	5.3	0.6	46.4	6.9	15.8	21.2	—
16788	Nachos with beef, beans, cheese, tomatoes and onions	1	serving(s)	551	253.5	1576	59.1	137.5	20.4	90.8	32.6	41.9	9.4	—
6116	Pepperoni pizza	2	slice(s)	142	66.1	362	20.2	39.7	2.9	13.9	4.5	6.3	2.3	—
29601	Pizza with meat and vegetables, thin crust	2	slice(s)	158	81.4	386	16.5	36.8	2.7	19.1	7.7	8.1	2.2	—
655	Potato salad	½	cup(s)	125	95.0	179	3.4	14.0	1.6	10.3	1.8	3.1	4.7	—
25109	Salisbury steaks with mushroom sauce	1	serving(s)	135	101.8	251	17.1	9.3	0.5	15.5	6.0	6.7	0.8	0
16637	Shrimp creole with rice	1	cup(s)	243	176.6	309	27.0	27.7	1.2	9.2	1.7	3.6	2.9	—
497	Spaghetti and meatballs with tomato sauce, prepared	1	cup(s)	248	174.0	330	19.0	39.0	2.7	12.0	3.9	4.4	2.2	—
28585	Spicy thai noodles (pad thai)	8	ounce(s)	227	73.3	221	8.9	35.7	3.0	6.4	0.8	3.3	1.8	—
33073	Stir fried pork and vegetables with rice	1	cup(s)	235	173.6	348	15.4	33.5	1.9	16.3	5.6	6.9	2.6	0
28588	Stuffed shells	2½	item(s)	249	157.5	243	15.0	28.0	2.5	8.1	3.1	3.0	1.3	—
16821	Sushi with egg in seaweed	6	piece(s)	156	116.5	190	8.9	20.5	0.3	7.9	2.2	3.2	1.5	—
16819	Sushi with vegetables and fish	6	piece(s)	156	101.6	218	8.4	43.7	1.7	0.6	0.2	0.1	0.2	—
16820	Sushi with vegetables in seaweed	6	piece(s)	156	110.3	183	3.4	40.6	0.8	0.4	0.1	0.1	0.1	—
25266	Sweet and sour pork	¾	cup(s)	249	205.9	265	29.2	17.1	1.0	8.1	2.6	3.5	1.5	0
16824	Tabouli, tabbouleh or tabuli	1	cup(s)	160	123.7	198	2.6	15.9	3.7	14.9	2.0	10.9	1.6	—
25276	Three bean salad	½	cup(s)	99	82.2	95	1.9	9.7	2.6	5.9	0.8	1.4	3.5	0
160	Tuna salad	½	cup(s)	103	64.7	192	16.4	9.6	0	9.5	1.6	3.0	4.2	—
25241	Turkey and noodles	1	cup(s)	319	228.5	270	24.0	21.2	1.0	9.2	2.4	3.5	2.3	—
16794	Vegetable egg roll	2	item(s)	128	89.8	201	5.1	19.5	1.7	11.6	2.5	5.7	2.6	—
16818	Vegetable sushi, no fish	6	piece(s)	156	99.0	226	4.8	49.9	2.0	0.4	0.1	0.1	0.1	—
	Sandwiches													
1744	Bacon, lettuce and tomato with mayonnaise	1	item(s)	164	97.2	341	11.6	34.2	2.3	17.6	3.8	5.5	6.7	—
30287	Bologna and cheese with margarine	1	item(s)	111	45.6	345	13.4	29.3	1.2	19.3	8.1	7.0	2.4	—
30286	Bologna with margarine	1	item(s)	83	33.6	251	8.1	27.3	1.2	12.1	3.7	5.0	2.1	—
16546	Cheese	1	item(s)	83	31.0	261	9.1	27.6	1.2	12.7	5.4	4.2	2.1	—
8789	Cheeseburger, large, plain	1	item(s)	185	78.9	564	32.0	38.5	2.6	31.5	12.5	10.2	1.0	1.8
8624	Cheeseburger, large, with bacon, vegetables, and condiments	1	item(s)	195	91.4	550	30.8	36.8	2.5	30.9	11.9	10.6	1.3	1.5
1745	Club with bacon, chicken, tomato, lettuce, and mayonnaise	1	item(s)	246	137.5	546	31.0	48.9	3.0	24.5	5.3	7.5	9.4	—
1908	Cold cut submarine with cheese and vegetables	1	item(s)	228	131.8	456	21.8	51.0	2.0	18.6	6.8	8.2	2.3	—
30247	Corned beef	1	item(s)	130	74.9	265	18.2	25.3	1.6	9.6	3.6	3.5	1.0	—
25283	Egg salad	1	item(s)	126	72.1	278	10.7	28.0	1.4	13.5	2.9	4.2	5.0	—
16686	Fried egg	1	item(s)	96	49.7	226	10.0	26.2	1.2	8.6	2.3	3.2	1.9	—
16547	Grilled cheese	1	item(s)	83	27.5	291	9.2	27.9	1.2	15.8	6.0	5.7	3.0	—
16659	Gyro with onion and tomato	1	item(s)	105	68.3	163	12.0	20.0	1.1	3.5	1.3	1.3	0.5	—

Chol (mg)	Calc (mg)	Iron (mg)	Magn (mg)	Pota (mg)	Sodi (mg)	Zinc (mg)	Vit A (μg)	Thia (mg)	Vit E (mg α)	Ribo (mg)	Niac (mg)	Vit B_6 (mg)	Fola (μg)	Vit C (mg)	Vit B_{12} (μg)	Sele (μg)
90	63	0.64	19.8	194.4	198.0	2.45	34.2	0.05	—	0.04	1.74	0.10	31.8	1.7	3.6	24.4
27	266	1.07	38.5	251.4	276.3	1.26	—	0.07	0.02	0.16	1.27	0.17	44.6	59.3	0.2	6.0
0	28	1.74	41.8	298.4	149.9	0.76	0.5	0.07	—	0.08	0.53	0.06	47.4	0.8	0	0.5
9	218	1.83	38.4	163.9	472.9	1.24	—	0.41	0.00	0.35	2.85	0.09	96.2	1.6	0.4	38.4
73	146	2.66	61.3	222.9	885.7	3.43	0	0.10	0.10	0.16	3.00	0.26	95.7	0	1.2	36.7
103	38	2.77	33.7	196.0	833.6	1.34	41.6	0.33	1.60	0.18	4.17	0.27	97.0	3.4	0.3	22.0
66	26	1.46	23.4	248.2	849.7	1.40	29.2	0.10	1.62	0.18	6.28	0.28	23.4	12.0	0.2	19.9
0	13	0.65	11.4	178.0	26.9	0.21	59.0	0.03	—	0.05	0.56	0.08	38.3	24.0	0	0.4
0	60	1.91	35.7	212.8	297.7	1.34	0	0.10	0.92	0.06	0.49	0.49	72.6	9.7	0	3.0
65	50	1.96	63.2	427.7	907.2	1.50	38.9	0.15	4.32	0.14	13.22	0.58	42.1	7.5	0.3	23.0
90	38	2.95	40.1	493.2	495.6	6.60	—	0.08	1.29	0.28	8.03	0.21	28.3	1.4	2.9	30.4
68	233	2.22	40.1	420.1	433.6	2.70	—	0.21	0.21	0.29	3.06	0.22	50.4	15.0	0.8	21.4
34	310	2.06	40.0	258.0	784.0	2.06	180.0	0.27	0.72	0.43	2.18	0.08	64.0	0	0.5	30.6
15	35	2.10	20.1	283.6	1352.9	1.28	27.6	0.19	0.70	0.16	2.77	0.14	42.7	21.6	0.4	13.3
85	59	1.87	21.8	300.8	411.7	3.40	—	0.08	0.00	0.27	3.72	0.13	18.7	0.9	1.6	17.9
172	32	1.57	25.7	333.7	1052.5	1.82	49.8	0.49	5.39	0.36	2.88	0.31	21.1	8.0	0.8	30.0
154	948	7.32	242.4	1201.2	1862.4	10.68	259.0	0.29	7.71	0.81	6.39	1.09	148.8	16.0	2.6	44.1
28	129	1.87	17.0	305.3	533.9	1.03	105.1	0.26	—	0.46	6.09	0.11	73.8	3.3	0.4	26.1
36	258	3.14	31.6	352.3	971.7	2.02	49.0	0.37	1.13	0.37	3.77	0.19	64.8	15.6	0.6	22.8
85	24	0.81	18.8	317.5	661.3	0.38	40.0	0.09	—	0.07	1.11	0.17	8.8	12.5	0	5.1
60	74	1.94	23.8	314.5	360.5	3.45	—	0.10	0.00	0.27	3.95	0.13	20.8	0.7	1.6	17.4
180	102	4.68	63.2	413.1	330.5	1.72	94.8	0.29	2.06	0.11	4.75	0.21	75.3	12.9	1.2	49.3
89	124	3.70	—	665.0	1009.0	—	81.5	0.25	—	0.30	4.00	—	—	22.0	—	22.0
37	31	1.56	49.4	181.3	591.6	1.05	—	0.18	0.35	0.13	1.82	0.17	44.6	22.6	0.1	3.2
46	38	2.71	33.0	396.9	569.5	2.08	—	0.51	0.38	0.20	5.07	0.30	103.0	18.8	0.4	22.8
30	188	2.26	49.4	403.0	471.5	1.41	—	0.26	0.00	0.26	3.83	0.24	80.0	17.9	0.2	28.9
214	45	1.84	18.7	135.7	463.3	0.98	106.1	0.13	0.67	0.28	1.35	0.13	62.4	1.9	0.7	20.3
11	23	2.15	25.0	202.8	340.1	0.78	45.2	0.26	0.24	0.07	2.76	0.14	76.4	3.6	0.3	13.9
0	20	1.54	18.7	96.7	152.9	0.68	25.0	0.19	0.12	0.03	1.86	0.13	73.3	2.3	0	9.8
74	40	1.76	35.6	619.9	621.8	2.53	—	0.81	0.20	0.37	6.69	0.66	14.7	11.9	0.7	49.6
0	30	1.21	35.2	249.6	796.8	0.48	54.4	0.07	2.43	0.04	1.11	0.11	30.4	26.1	0	0.5
0	26	0.96	15.5	144.8	224.2	0.30	—	0.02	0.88	0.04	0.26	0.04	32.2	10.0	0	2.7
13	17	1.02	19.5	182.5	412.1	0.57	24.6	0.03	—	0.07	6.86	0.08	8.2	2.3	1.2	42.2
77	69	2.56	33.2	400.8	577.1	2.51	—	0.23	0.28	0.30	6.41	0.29	61.4	1.4	1.1	33.4
60	29	1.65	17.9	193.3	549.1	0.48	25.6	0.15	1.28	0.20	1.59	0.09	46.1	5.5	0.2	11.3
0	23	2.38	21.8	157.6	369.7	0.82	48.4	0.28	0.15	0.05	2.44	0.12	85.8	3.7	0	8.1
21	79	2.36	27.9	351.0	944.6	1.08	44.3	0.32	1.16	0.24	4.36	0.21	73.8	9.7	0.2	27.1
40	258	2.38	24.4	215.3	941.3	1.88	102.1	0.31	0.55	0.35	2.97	0.14	59.9	0.2	0.8	20.4
17	100	2.24	16.6	138.6	579.3	1.02	44.8	0.29	0.49	0.21	2.92	0.12	58.1	0.2	0.5	16.0
22	233	2.04	19.9	127.0	733.7	1.24	97.1	0.25	0.47	0.30	2.25	0.05	58.1	0	0.3	13.1
104	309	4.47	44.4	401.5	986.1	5.75	0	0.35	—	0.77	8.26	0.49	109.2	0	2.8	38.9
98	267	4.03	44.9	464.1	1314.3	5.20	0	0.33	—	0.67	8.25	0.47	95.6	1.4	2.4	6.6
71	157	4.57	46.7	464.9	1087.3	1.82	41.8	0.54	1.52	0.40	12.82	0.61	118.1	6.4	0.4	42.3
36	189	2.50	68.4	394.4	1650.7	2.57	70.7	1.00	—	0.79	5.49	0.13	86.6	12.3	1.1	30.8
46	81	3.04	19.5	127.4	1206.4	2.26	2.6	0.23	0.20	0.24	3.42	0.11	59.8	0.3	0.9	31.2
219	85	2.25	18.8	159.0	423.1	0.87	—	0.27	0.12	0.43	2.06	0.15	73.6	0.9	0.6	29.9
206	104	2.79	17.3	117.1	438.7	0.92	89.3	0.26	0.66	0.40	2.26	0.10	79.7	0	0.6	24.2
22	235	2.05	19.9	128.7	763.6	1.26	129.5	0.19	0.72	0.28	2.05	0.05	38.2	0	0.2	13.2
28	47	1.77	22.1	218.4	235.2	2.33	9.5	0.23	0.26	0.20	3.12	0.13	44.1	3.2	0.9	18.3

TABLE A-1 Table of Food Composition *(continued)*

(Computer code is for Cengage Diet Analysis program) (For purposes of calculations, use "0" for t, <1, <.1, <.01, etc.)

DA+ Code	Food Description	Qty	Measure	Wt (g)	H_2O (g)	Ener (cal)	Prot (g)	Carb (g)	Fiber (g)	Fat (g)	Fat Breakdown (g) Sat	Mono	Poly	Trans
	Mixed Foods, Soups, Sandwiches—continued													
1906	Ham and cheese	1	item(s)	146	74.2	352	20.7	33.3	2.0	15.5	6.4	6.7	1.4	—
31890	Ham with mayonnaise	1	item(s)	112	56.3	271	13.0	27.9	1.9	11.6	2.8	4.0	4.0	—
756	Hamburger, double patty, large, with condiments and vegetables	1	item(s)	226	121.5	540	34.3	40.3	—	26.6	10.5	10.3	2.8	—
8793	Hamburger, large, plain	1	item(s)	137	57.7	426	22.6	31.7	1.5	22.9	8.4	9.9	2.1	—
8795	Hamburger, large, with vegetables and condiments	1	item(s)	218	121.4	512	25.8	40.0	3.1	27.4	10.4	11.4	2.2	—
25134	Hot chicken salad	1	item(s)	98	48.4	242	15.2	23.8	1.3	9.2	2.9	2.5	3.0	—
25133	Hot turkey salad	1	item(s)	98	50.1	224	15.6	23.8	1.3	6.9	2.3	1.6	2.5	—
1411	Hotdog with bun, plain	1	item(s)	98	52.9	242	10.4	18.0	1.6	14.5	5.1	6.9	1.7	—
30249	Pastrami	1	item(s)	134	71.2	328	13.4	27.8	1.6	17.7	6.1	8.3	1.2	—
16701	Peanut butter	1	item(s)	93	23.6	345	12.2	37.6	3.3	17.4	3.4	7.7	5.2	—
30306	Peanut butter and jelly	1	item(s)	93	24.2	330	10.3	41.9	2.9	14.7	2.9	6.5	4.4	—
1909	Roast beef submarine with mayonnaise and vegetables	1	item(s)	216	127.4	410	28.6	44.3	—	13.0	7.1	1.8	2.6	—
1910	Roast beef, plain	1	item(s)	139	67.6	346	21.5	33.4	1.2	13.8	3.6	6.8	1.7	—
1907	Steak with mayonnaise and vegetables	1	item(s)	204	104.2	459	30.3	52.0	2.3	14.1	3.8	5.3	3.3	—
25288	Tuna salad	1	item(s)	179	102.2	415	24.5	28.4	1.6	22.4	3.5	6.2	11.4	—
30283	Turkey submarine with cheese, lettuce, tomato, and mayonnaise	1	item(s)	277	168.0	529	30.4	49.4	3.0	22.8	6.8	6.0	8.6	—
31891	Turkey with mayonnaise	1	item(s)	143	74.5	329	28.7	26.4	1.3	11.2	2.6	2.6	4.8	—
	Soups													
25296	Bean	1	cup(s)	301	253.1	191	13.8	29.0	6.5	2.3	0.7	0.8	0.5	0
711	Bean with pork, condensed, prepared with water	1	cup(s)	253	215.9	159	7.3	21.0	7.3	5.5	1.4	2.0	1.7	—
713	Beef noodle, condensed, prepared with water	1	cup(s)	244	224.9	83	4.7	8.7	0.7	3.0	1.1	1.2	0.5	—
825	Cheese, condensed, prepared with milk	1	cup(s)	251	206.9	231	9.5	16.2	1.0	14.6	9.1	4.1	0.5	—
826	Chicken broth, condensed, prepared with water	1	cup(s)	244	234.1	39	4.9	0.9	0	1.4	0.4	0.6	0.3	—
25297	Chicken noodle soup	1	cup(s)	286	258.4	117	10.8	10.9	0.9	2.9	0.8	1.1	0.7	—
827	Chicken noodle, condensed, prepared with water	1	cup(s)	241	226.1	60	3.1	7.1	0.5	2.3	0.6	1.0	0.6	0
724	Chicken noodle, dehydrated, prepared with water	1	cup(s)	252	237.3	58	2.1	9.2	0.3	1.4	0.3	0.5	0.4	—
823	Cream of asparagus, condensed, prepared with milk	1	cup(s)	248	213.3	161	6.3	16.4	0.7	8.2	3.3	2.1	2.2	—
824	Cream of celery, condensed, prepared with milk	1	cup(s)	248	214.4	164	5.7	14.5	0.7	9.7	3.9	2.5	2.7	—
708	Cream of chicken, condensed, prepared with milk	1	cup(s)	248	210.4	191	7.5	15.0	0.2	11.5	4.6	4.5	1.6	—
715	Cream of chicken, condensed, prepared with water	1	cup(s)	244	221.1	117	3.4	9.3	0.2	7.4	2.1	3.3	1.5	—
709	Cream of mushroom, condensed, prepared with milk	1	cup(s)	248	215.0	166	6.2	14.0	0	9.6	3.3	2.0	1.8	0.1
716	Cream of mushroom, condensed, prepared with water	1	cup(s)	244	224.6	102	1.9	8.0	0	7.0	1.6	1.3	1.7	—
25298	Cream of vegetable	1	cup(s)	285	250.7	165	7.2	15.2	1.9	8.6	1.6	4.6	1.9	—
16689	Egg drop	1	cup(s)	244	228.9	73	7.5	1.1	0	3.8	1.1	1.5	0.6	—
25138	Golden squash	1	cup(s)	258	223.9	145	7.6	20.4	0.4	4.1	0.8	2.2	0.9	—
16663	Hot and sour	1	cup(s)	244	209.7	161	15.0	5.4	0.5	7.9	2.7	3.4	1.1	—
28054	Lentil chowder	1	cup(s)	244	202.8	153	11.4	27.7	12.6	0.5	0.1	0.1	0.2	0
28560	Macaroni and bean	1	cup(s)	246	138.8	146	5.8	22.9	5.1	3.7	0.5	2.2	0.6	0
714	Manhattan clam chowder, condensed, prepared with water	1	cup(s)	244	225.1	73	2.1	11.6	1.5	2.1	0.4	0.4	1.2	—
28561	Minestrone	1	cup(s)	241	185.4	103	4.5	16.8	4.8	2.3	0.3	1.4	0.4	0
717	Minestrone, condensed, prepared with water	1	cup(s)	241	220.1	82	4.3	11.2	1.0	2.5	0.6	0.7	1.1	—

Chol (mg)	Calc (mg)	Iron (mg)	Magn (mg)	Pota (mg)	Sodi (mg)	Zinc (mg)	Vit A (µg)	Thia (mg)	Vit E (mg α)	Ribo (mg)	Niac (mg)	Vit B_6 (mg)	Fola (µg)	Vit C (mg)	Vit B_{12} (µg)	Sele (µg)
58	130	3.24	16.1	290.5	770.9	1.37	96.4	0.30	0.29	0.48	2.68	0.20	75.9	2.8	0.5	23.1
34	91	2.47	23.5	210.6	1097.6	1.13	5.6	0.57	0.50	0.26	3.80	0.25	60.5	2.2	0.2	20.2
122	102	5.85	49.7	569.5	791.0	5.67	0	0.36	—	0.38	7.57	0.54	76.8	1.1	4.1	25.5
71	74	3.57	27.4	267.2	474.0	4.11	0	0.28	—	0.28	6.24	0.23	60.3	0	2.1	27.1
87	96	4.92	43.6	479.6	824.0	4.88	0	0.41	—	0.37	7.28	0.32	82.8	2.6	2.4	33.6
39	115	1.88	20.0	172.4	505.1	1.19	—	0.23	0.28	0.22	4.84	0.19	46.4	0.5	0.2	19.9
37	114	1.99	21.3	189.0	494.5	1.07	—	0.22	0.28	0.20	4.26	0.22	46.4	0.5	0.2	23.4
44	24	2.31	12.7	143.1	670.3	1.98	0	0.23	—	0.27	3.64	0.04	48.0	0.1	0.5	26.0
51	80	3.02	22.8	182.2	1364.1	2.70	2.7	0.28	0.26	0.26	4.97	0.14	60.3	0.3	1.0	14.3
0	110	2.92	66.0	226.0	580.3	1.32	0	0.31	2.39	0.23	6.72	0.18	92.1	0	0	13.2
0	94	2.50	56.7	198.1	492.9	1.12	—	0.26	2.01	0.20	5.66	0.15	78.1	0.1	0	11.2
73	41	2.80	67.0	330.5	844.6	4.38	30.2	0.41	—	0.41	5.96	0.32	71.3	5.6	1.8	25.7
51	54	4.22	30.6	315.5	792.3	3.39	11.1	0.37	—	0.30	5.86	0.26	57.0	2.1	1.2	29.2
73	92	5.16	49.0	524.3	797.6	4.52	0	0.40	—	0.36	7.30	0.36	89.8	5.5	1.6	42.0
59	78	2.97	35.9	316.3	724.7	1.02	—	0.27	0.34	0.26	12.07	0.46	60.8	1.8	2.4	76.9
64	307	4.59	49.9	534.6	1759.0	2.74	74.8	0.49	1.19	0.65	3.91	0.31	121.9	10.5	0.6	42.1
67	100	3.46	34.3	304.6	564.9	3.00	5.7	0.28	0.74	0.32	6.84	0.46	64.4	0	0.3	40
5	79	3.05	61.8	588.8	689.0	1.41	—	0.27	0.02	0.15	3.63	0.23	140.1	3.6	0.2	7.9
3	78	1.89	43.0	371.9	883.0	0.96	43.0	0.08	1.08	0.03	0.52	0.03	30.4	1.5	0	7.8
5	20	1.07	7.3	97.6	929.6	1.51	12.2	0.06	1.22	0.05	1.03	0.03	19.5	0.5	0.2	7.3
48	289	0.80	20.1	341.4	1019.1	0.67	358.9	0.06	—	0.33	0.50	0.07	10.0	1.3	0.4	7.0
0	10	0.51	2.4	209.8	775.9	0.24	0	0.01	0.04	0.07	3.34	0.02	4.9	0	0.2	0
24	25	1.38	16.4	340.1	774.5	0.77	—	0.15	0.02	0.16	5.57	0.13	37.2	1.8	0.3	10.2
12	14	1.59	9.6	53.0	638.7	0.38	26.5	0.13	0.07	0.10	1.30	0.04	19.3	0	0	11.6
10	5	0.50	7.6	32.8	577.1	0.20	2.5	0.20	0.12	0.07	1.08	0.02	17.6	0	0.1	9.6
22	174	0.86	19.8	359.6	1041.6	0.91	62.0	0.10	—	0.27	0.88	0.06	29.8	4.0	0.5	8.0
32	186	0.69	22.3	310.0	1009.4	0.19	114.1	0.07	—	0.24	0.43	0.06	7.4	1.5	0.5	4.7
27	181	0.67	17.4	272.8	1046.6	0.67	178.6	0.07	—	0.25	0.92	0.06	7.4	1.2	0.5	8.0
10	34	0.61	2.4	87.8	985.8	0.63	163.5	0.02	—	0.06	0.82	0.01	2.4	0.2	0.1	7.0
10	164	1.36	19.8	267.8	823.4	0.79	81.8	0.10	1.01	0.29	0.62	0.05	7.4	0.2	0.6	6.0
0	17	1.31	4.9	73.2	775.9	0.24	9.8	0.05	0.97	0.05	0.50	0.00	2.4	0	0	2.9
1	80	1.20	17.5	340.7	787.9	0.56	—	0.12	1.05	0.18	3.32	0.12	39.5	10.7	0.3	4.3
102	22	0.75	4.9	219.6	729.6	0.48	41.5	0.02	0.29	0.19	3.02	0.05	14.6	0	0.5	7.6
4	262	0.78	42.4	542.2	515.6	0.88	—	0.16	0.52	0.30	1.14	0.16	32.7	12.5	0.7	6.0
34	29	1.24	19.5	373.3	1561.6	1.43	—	0.26	0.12	0.24	4.96	0.20	14.6	0.5	0.4	19.3
0	48	4.38	59.3	626.2	26.7	1.57	—	0.24	0.06	0.12	1.87	0.32	176.3	16.1	0	3.5
0	59	1.90	32.4	275.9	531.0	0.51	—	0.16	0.37	0.12	1.44	0.10	58.2	9.1	0	8.8
2	27	1.56	9.8	180.6	551.4	0.87	48.8	0.02	1.22	0.03	0.77	0.09	9.8	3.9	3.9	9.0
0	62	1.70	29.9	287.5	442.7	0.42	—	0.09	0.23	0.09	0.70	0.07	47.3	13.3	0	3.5
2	34	0.91	7.2	313.3	911.0	0.74	118.1	0.05	—	0.04	0.94	0.09	36.2	1.2	0	8.0

TABLE A-1 Table of Food Composition *(continued)*

(Computer code is for Cengage Diet Analysis program) (For purposes of calculations, use "0" for t, <1, <.1, <.01, etc.)

DA+ Code	Food Description	Qty	Measure	Wt (g)	H_2O (g)	Ener (cal)	Prot (g)	Carb (g)	Fiber (g)	Fat (g)	Fat Breakdown (g) Sat	Mono	Poly	Trans
Mixed Foods, Soups, Sandwiches—continued														
28038	Mushroom and wild rice	1	cup(s)	244	199.7	86	4.7	13.2	1.7	0.3	0	0	0.2	0
828	New England clam chowder, condensed, prepared with milk	1	cup(s)	248	212.2	151	8.0	18.4	0.7	5.0	2.1	0.7	0.6	0
28036	New England style clam chowder	1	cup(s)	244	227.5	61	3.8	8.8	1.8	0.2	0.1	0	0	0
28566	Old country pasta	1	cup(s)	252	183.3	146	6.5	18.3	3.6	4.5	2.0	2.4	0.9	0
725	Onion, dehydrated, prepared with water	1	cup(s)	246	235.7	30	0.8	6.8	0.7	0	0	0	0	—
16667	Shrimp gumbo	1	cup(s)	244	207.2	166	9.5	18.2	2.4	6.7	1.3	2.9	2.0	—
28037	Southwestern corn chowder	1	cup(s)	244	217.8	98	4.9	17.0	2.4	0.5	0.1	0.1	0.2	0
30282	Soybean (miso)	1	cup(s)	240	218.6	84	6.0	8.0	1.9	3.4	0.6	1.1	1.4	—
25140	Split pea	1	cup(s)	165	119.7	72	4.5	16.0	1.6	0.3	0.1	0	0.2	0
718	Split pea with ham, condensed, prepared with water	1	cup(s)	253	206.9	190	10.3	28.0	2.3	4.4	1.8	1.8	0.6	—
726	Tomato vegetable, dehydrated, prepared with water	1	cup(s)	253	238.4	56	2.0	10.2	0.8	0.9	0.4	0.3	0.1	0
710	Tomato, condensed, prepared with milk	1	cup(s)	248	213.4	136	6.2	22.0	1.5	3.2	1.8	0.9	0.3	—
719	Tomato, condensed, prepared with water	1	cup(s)	244	223.0	73	1.9	16.0	1.5	0.7	0.2	0.2	0.2	—
28595	Turkey noodle	1	cup(s)	244	216.9	114	8.1	15.1	1.9	2.4	0.3	1.1	0.7	—
28051	Turkey vegetable	1	cup(s)	244	220.8	96	12.2	6.6	2.0	1.1	0.3	0.2	0.3	0
25141	Vegetable	1	cup(s)	252	228.1	82	5.2	16.5	4.5	0.3	0	0	0.1	0
720	Vegetable beef, condensed, prepared with water	1	cup(s)	244	224.0	76	5.4	9.9	2.0	1.9	0.8	0.8	0.1	—
28598	Vegetable gumbo	1	cup(s)	252	184.5	170	4.4	28.9	3.6	4.7	0.7	3.2	0.5	0
721	Vegetarian vegetable, condensed, prepared with water	1	cup(s)	241	222.7	67	2.1	11.8	0.7	1.9	0.3	0.8	0.7	—
Fast Food														
	Arby's													
36094	Au jus sauce	1	serving(s)	85	—	43	1.0	7.0	0	1.3	0.4	—	—	0.4
751	Beef 'n cheddar sandwich	1	item(s)	195	—	445	22.0	44.0	2.0	21.0	6.0	—	—	1.0
9279	Cheddar curly fries	1	serving(s)	198	—	631	8.0	73.0	7.0	37.4	6.8	—	—	5.7
34770	Chicken breast fillet sandwich, grilled	1	item(s)	233	—	414	32.0	36.0	3.0	17.0	3.0	—	—	0
36131	Chocolate shake, regular	1	serving(s)	397	—	507	13.0	83.0	0	13.0	8.0	—	—	0
36045	Curly fries, large size	1	serving(s)	198	—	631	8.0	73.0	7.0	37.0	7.0	—	—	6.0
36044	Curly fries, medium size	1	serving(s)	128	—	406	5.0	47.0	5.0	24.0	4.0	—	—	4.0
752	Ham 'n cheese sandwich	1	item(s)	167	—	304	23.0	35.0	1.0	7.0	2.0	—	—	0
36048	Homestyle fries, large size	1	serving(s)	213	—	566	6.0	82.0	6.0	37.0	7.0	—	—	5.0
36047	Homestyle fries, medium size	1	serving(s)	142	—	377	4.0	55.0	4.0	25.0	4.0	—	—	4.0
33465	Homestyle fries, small size	1	serving(s)	113	—	302	3.0	44.0	3.0	20.0	4.0	—	—	3.0
9249	Junior roast beef sandwich	1	item(s)	125	—	272	16.0	34.0	2.0	10.0	4.0	—	—	0
9251	Large roast beef sandwich	1	item(s)	281	—	547	42.0	41.0	3.0	28.0	12.0	—	—	2.0
39640	Market Fresh chicken salad with pecans sandwich	1	item(s)	322	—	769	30.0	79.0	9.0	39.0	10.0	—	—	0
39641	Market Fresh Martha's Vineyard salad, without dressing	1	serving(s)	330	—	277	26.0	24.0	5.0	8.0	4.0	—	—	0
34769	Market Fresh roast turkey and Swiss sandwich	1	serving(s)	359	—	725	45.0	75.0	5.0	30.0	8.0	—	—	1.0
9267	Market Fresh roast turkey ranch and bacon sandwich	1	serving(s)	382	—	834	49.0	75.0	5.0	38.0	11.0	—	—	1.0
39642	Market Fresh Santa Fe salad, without dressing	1	serving(s)	372	—	499	30.0	42.0	7.0	23.0	8.0	—	—	2.0
39650	Market Fresh Southwest chicken wrap	1	serving(s)	251	—	567	36.0	42.0	4.0	29.0	9.0	—	—	1.0
37021	Market Fresh Ultimate BLT sandwich	1	item(s)	294	—	779	23.0	75.0	6.0	45.0	11.0	—	—	1.0
750	Roast beef sandwich, regular	1	item(s)	154	—	320	21.0	34.0	2.0	14.0	5.0	—	—	1.0
36132	Strawberry shake, regular	1	serving(s)	397	—	498	13.0	81.0	0	13.0	8.0	—	—	0
2009	Super roast beef sandwich	1	item(s)	198	—	398	21.0	40.0	2.0	19.0	6.0	—	—	1.0
36130	Vanilla shake, regular	1	serving(s)	369	—	437	13.0	66.0	0	13.0	8.0	—	—	0
	Auntie Anne's													
35371	Cheese dipping sauce	1	serving(s)	35	—	100	3.0	4.0	0	8.0	4.0	—	—	0
35353	Cinnamon sugar soft pretzel	1	item(s)	120	—	350	9.0	74.0	2.0	2.0	0	—	—	0

PAGE KEY: A-2 = Breads/Baked Goods A-8 = Cereal/Rice/Pasta A-12 = Fruit A-18 = Vegetables/Legumes A-28 = Nuts/Seeds A-30 = Vegetarian A-32 = Dairy A-40 = Eggs A-40 = Seafood A-44 = Meats A-48 = Poultry A-48 = Processed Meats A-50 = Beverages A-54 = Fats/Oils A-56 = Sweets A-58 = Spices/Condiments/Sauces A-62 = Mixed Foods/Soups/Sandwiches A-68 = Fast Food A-88 = Convenience A-90 = Baby Foods

A

Chol (mg)	Calc (mg)	Iron (mg)	Magn (mg)	Pota (mg)	Sodi (mg)	Zinc (mg)	Vit A (μg)	Thia (mg)	Vit E (mg α)	Ribo (mg)	Niac (mg)	Vit B_6 (mg)	Fola (μg)	Vit C (mg)	Vit B_{12} (μg)	Sele (μg)
0	30	1.38	27.3	376.9	283.8	1.00	—	0.06	0.07	0.23	3.21	0.14	18.1	3.7	0.1	4.7
17	169	3.00	29.8	456.3	887.8	0.99	91.8	0.20	0.54	0.43	1.96	0.17	22.3	5.2	11.9	10.9
3	89	1.30	29.2	503.7	256.8	0.52	—	0.06	0.02	0.10	1.30	0.15	24.2	11.8	3.0	3.8
5	57	2.43	51.9	500.4	355.7	0.78	—	0.21	0.01	0.14	2.64	0.20	80.0	22.0	0.1	10.3
0	22	0.12	9.8	76.3	851.2	0.12	0	0.03	0.02	0.03	0.15	0.06	0	0.2	0	0.5
51	105	2.85	48.8	461.2	441.6	0.90	80.5	0.18	1.90	0.12	2.52	0.19	85.4	17.6	0.3	14.9
1	83	1.03	26.3	434.4	217.4	0.57	—	0.08	0.09	0.13	1.81	0.21	32.1	39.6	0.2	1.7
0	65	1.87	36.0	362.4	988.8	0.86	232.8	0.06	0.96	0.16	2.61	0.15	57.6	4.6	0.2	1.0
0	28	1.26	29.8	328.1	602.4	0.52	—	0.10	0.00	0.07	1.50	0.16	49.5	8.1	0	0.7
8	23	2.27	48.1	399.7	1006.9	1.31	22.8	0.14	—	0.07	1.47	0.06	2.5	1.5	0.3	8.0
0	20	0.60	10.1	169.5	334.0	0.20	10.1	0.06	0.43	0.09	1.26	0.06	12.7	3.0	0.1	2.0
10	166	1.36	29.8	466.2	711.8	0.84	94.2	0.09	0.44	0.31	1.35	0.15	5.0	15.6	0.6	9.2
0	20	1.31	17.1	273.3	663.7	0.29	24.4	0.04	0.41	0.07	1.23	0.10	0	15.4	0	6.1
26	28	1.40	24.1	223.8	395.9	0.75	—	0.21	0.01	0.12	2.85	0.15	45.0	7.1	0.1	13.7
21	38	1.48	25.0	423.4	348.7	0.99	—	0.09	0.01	0.09	3.64	0.27	23.9	10.6	0.2	10.3
0	40	2.08	39.1	681.5	670.3	0.67	—	0.16	0.00	0.09	2.70	0.26	36.3	22.4	0	2.2
5	20	1.09	7.3	168.4	773.5	1.51	190.3	0.03	0.58	0.04	1.00	0.07	9.8	2.4	0.3	2.7
0	56	1.85	38.9	360.2	518.4	0.64	—	0.18	0.64	0.08	1.77	0.17	57.6	21.9	0	4.1
0	24	1.06	7.2	207.3	814.6	0.45	171.1	0.05	1.39	0.04	0.90	0.05	9.6	1.4	0	4.3
0	0	—	—	—	1510.0	—	—	—	—	—	—	—	—	—	—	—
51	80	3.96	—	—	1274.0	—	—	—	—	—	—	—	—	1.8	—	—
0	80	3.24	—	—	1476.0	—	—	—	—	—	—	—	—	9.6	—	—
9	90	3.06	—	—	913.0	—	—	—	—	—	—	—	—	10.8	—	—
34	510	0.54	—	—	357.0	—	—	—	—	—	—	—	—	5.4	—	—
0	80	3.24	—	—	1476.0	—	—	—	—	—	—	—	—	9.6	—	—
0	50	1.98	—	—	949.0	—	—	—	—	—	—	—	—	6.0	—	—
35	160	2.70	—	—	1420.0	—	—	—	—	—	—	—	—	1.2	—	—
0	50	1.62	—	—	1029.0	—	—	—	—	—	—	—	—	12.6	—	—
0	30	1.08	—	—	686.0	—	—	—	—	—	—	—	—	8.4	—	—
0	30	0.90	—	—	549.0	—	—	—	—	—	—	—	—	6.6	—	—
29	60	3.06	—	—	740.0	—	0	—	—	—	—	—	—	0	—	—
102	70	6.30	—	—	1869.0	—	0	—	—	—	—	—	—	0.6	—	—
74	180	4.32	—	—	1240.0	—	—	—	—	—	—	—	—	30.0	—	—
72	200	1.62	—	—	454.0	—	—	—	—	—	—	—	—	33.6	—	—
91	360	5.22	—	—	1788.0	—	—	—	—	—	—	—	—	10.2	—	—
109	330	5.40	—	—	2258.0	—	—	—	—	—	—	—	—	11.4	—	—
59	420	3.60	—	—	1231.0	—	—	—	—	—	—	—	—	36.6	—	—
88	240	4.50	—	—	1451.0	—	—	—	—	—	—	—	—	7.8	—	—
51	170	4.68	—	—	1571.0	—	—	—	—	—	—	—	—	16.8	—	—
44	60	3.60	—	—	953.0	—	0	—	—	—	—	—	—	0	—	—
34	510	0.72	—	—	363.0	—	—	—	—	—	—	—	—	6.6	—	—
44	70	3.78	—	—	1060.0	—	—	—	—	—	—	—	—	6.0	—	—
34	510	0.36	—	—	350.0	—	—	—	—	—	—	—	—	5.4	—	—
10	100	0.00	—	—	510.0	—	—	—	—	—	—	—	—	0	—	—
0	20	1.98	—	—	410.0	—	0	—	—	—	—	—	—	0	—	—

TABLE A-1 Table of Food Composition *(continued)*

(Computer code is for Cengage Diet Analysis program) (For purposes of calculations, use "0" for t, <1, <.1, <.01, etc.)

DA+ Code	Food Description	QTY	Measure	Wt (g)	H_2O (g)	Ener (cal)	Prot (g)	Carb (g)	Fiber (g)	Fat (g)	Fat Breakdown (g)			
											Sat	Mono	Poly	Trans
Fast Food—continued														
35354	Cinnamon sugar soft pretzel with butter	1	item(s)	120	—	450	8.0	83.0	3.0	9.0	5.0	—	—	0
35372	Marinara dipping sauce	1	serving(s)	35	—	10	0	4.0	0	0	0	0	0	0
35357	Original soft pretzel	1	serving(s)	120	—	340	10.0	72.0	3.0	1.0	0	—	—	0
35358	Original soft pretzel with butter	1	item(s)	120	—	370	10.0	72.0	3.0	4.0	2.0	—	—	0
35359	Parmesan herb soft pretzel	1	item(s)	120	—	390	11.0	74.0	4.0	5.0	2.5	—	—	—
35360	Parmesan herb soft pretzel with butter	1	item(s)	120	—	440	10.0	72.0	9.0	13.0	7.0	—	—	—
35361	Sesame soft pretzel	1	item(s)	120	—	350	11.0	63.0	3.0	6.0	1.0	—	—	0
35362	Sesame soft pretzel with butter	1	item(s)	120	—	410	12.0	64.0	7.0	12.0	4.0	—	—	0
35364	Sour cream and onion soft pretzel	1	item(s)	120	—	310	9.0	66.0	2.0	1.0	0	—	—	0
35366	Sour cream and onion soft pretzel with butter	1	item(s)	120	—	340	9.0	66.0	2.0	5.0	3.0	—	—	0
35373	Sweet mustard dipping sauce	1	serving(s)	35	—	60	0.5	8.0	0	1.5	1.0	—	—	0
35367	Whole wheat soft pretzel	1	item(s)	120	—	350	11.0	72.0	7.0	1.5	0	—	—	0
35368	Whole wheat soft pretzel with butter	1	item(s)	120	—	370	11.0	72.0	7.0	4.5	1.5	—	—	0
	Boston Market													
34978	Butternut squash	¾	cup(s)	143	—	140	2.0	25.0	2.0	4.5	3.0	—	—	0
35006	Caesar side salad	1	serving(s)	71	—	40	3.0	3.0	1.0	20.0	2.0	—	—	1.5
35013	Chicken Carver sandwich with cheese and sauce	1	item(s)	321	—	700	44.0	68.0	3.0	29.0	7.0	—	—	0
34979	Chicken gravy	4	ounce(s)	113	—	15	1.0	4.0	0	0.5	0	—	—	0
35053	Chicken noodle soup	¾	cup(s)	283	—	180	13.0	16.0	1.0	7.0	2.0	—	—	0
34973	Chicken pot pie	1	item(s)	425	—	800	29.0	59.0	4.0	49.0	18.0	—	—	7.0
35054	Chicken tortilla soup with toppings	¾	cup(s)	227	—	340	12.0	24.0	1.0	22.0	7.0	—	—	0
35007	Cole slaw	¾	cup(s)	125	—	170	2.0	21.0	2.0	9.0	2.0	—	—	0
35057	Cornbread	1	item(s)	45	—	130	1.0	21.0	0	3.5	1.0	—	—	1.0
34980	Creamed spinach	¾	cup(s)	191	—	280	9.0	12.0	4.0	23.0	15.0	—	—	0
34998	Fresh vegetable stuffing	1	cup(s)	136	—	190	3.0	25.0	2.0	8.0	1.0	—	—	0
34991	Garlic dill new potatoes	¾	cup(s)	156	—	140	3.0	24.0	3.0	3.0	1.0	—	—	0
34983	Green bean casserole	¾	cup(s)	170	—	60	2.0	9.0	2.0	2.0	1.0	—	—	0
34982	Green beans	¾	cup(s)	91	—	60	2.0	7.0	3.0	3.5	1.5	—	—	0
34984	Homestyle mashed potatoes	¾	cup(s)	221	—	210	4.0	29.0	3.0	9.0	6.0	—	—	0
34985	Homestyle mashed potatoes and gravy	1	cup(s)	334	—	225	5.0	33.0	3.0	9.5	6.0	—	—	0
34988	Hot cinnamon apples	¾	cup(s)	145	—	210	0	47.0	3.0	3.0	0	—	—	0
34989	Macaroni and cheese	¾	cup(s)	221	—	330	14.0	39.0	1.0	12.0	7.0	—	—	0.5
51193	Market chopped salad with dressing	1	item(s)	563	—	580	11.0	31.0	9.0	48.0	9.0	—	—	1.0
34970	Meatloaf	1	serving(s)	218	—	480	29.0	23.0	2.0	33.0	13.0	—	—	0
39383	Nestle Toll House chocolate chip cookie	1	item(s)	78	—	370	4.0	49.0	2.0	19.0	9.0	—	—	0
34965	Quarter chicken, dark meat, no skin	1	item(s)	134	—	260	30.0	2.0	0	13.0	4.0	—	—	0
34966	Quarter chicken, dark meat, with skin	1	item(s)	149	—	280	31.0	3.0	0	15.0	4.5	—	—	0
34963	Quarter chicken, white meat, no skin or wing	1	item(s)	173	—	250	41.0	4.0	0	8.0	2.5	—	—	0
34964	Quarter chicken, white meat, with skin and wing	1	item(s)	110	—	330	50.0	3.0	0	12.0	4.0	—	—	0
34968	Roasted turkey breast	5	ounce(s)	142	—	180	38.0	0	0	3.0	1.0	—	—	0
35011	Seasonal fresh fruit salad	1	serving(s)	142	—	60	1.0	15.0	1.0	0	0	0	0	0
51192	Spinach with garlic butter sauce	1	serving(s)	170	—	130	5.0	9.0	5.0	9.0	6.0	—	—	0
34969	Spiral sliced holiday ham	8	ounce(s)	227	—	450	40.0	13.0	0	26.0	10.0	—	—	0
35003	Steamed vegetables	1	cup(s)	136	—	50	2.0	8.0	3.0	2.0	0	—	—	0
35005	Sweet corn	¾	cup(s)	176	—	170	6.0	37.0	2.0	4.0	1.0	—	—	0
35004	Sweet potato casserole	¾	cup(s)	198	—	460	4.0	77.0	3.0	17.0	6.0	—	—	0
	Burger King													
29731	Biscuit with sausage, egg, and cheese	1	item(s)	191	—	610	20.0	33.0	1.0	45.0	15.0	—	—	1.0
14249	Cheeseburger	1	item(s)	133	—	330	17.0	31.0	1.0	16.0	7.0	—	—	0.5
14251	Chicken sandwich	1	item(s)	219	—	660	24.0	52.0	4.0	40.0	8.0	—	—	2.5
3808	Chicken Tenders, 8 pieces	1	serving(s)	123	—	340	19.0	21.0	0.5	20.0	5.0	—	—	3.0
14259	Chocolate shake, small	1	item(s)	315	—	470	8.0	75.0	1.0	14.0	9.0	—	—	0
29732	Croissanwich with sausage and cheese	1	item(s)	106	37.2	370	14.0	23.0	0.5	25.0	9.0	12.7	3.3	2.0

PAGE KEY: A-2 = Breads/Baked Goods A-8 = Cereal/Rice/Pasta A-12 = Fruit A-18 = Vegetables/Legumes A-28 = Nuts/Seeds A-30 = Vegetarian A-32 = Dairy A-40 = Eggs A-40 = Seafood A-44 = Meats A-48 = Poultry A-48 = Processed Meats A-50 = Beverages A-54 = Fats/Oils A-56 = Sweets A-58 = Spices/Condiments/Sauces A-62 = Mixed Foods/Soups/Sandwiches A-68 = Fast Food A-88 = Convenience A-90 = Baby Foods

Chol (mg)	Calc (mg)	Iron (mg)	Magn (mg)	Pota (mg)	Sodi (mg)	Zinc (mg)	Vit A (µg)	Thia (mg)	Vit E (mg α)	Ribo (mg)	Niac (mg)	Vit B_6 (mg)	Fola (µg)	Vit C (mg)	Vit B_{12} (µg)	Sele (µg)
25	30	2.34	—	—	430.0	—	—	—	—	—	—	—	—	0	—	—
0	0	0.00	—	—	180.0	—	0	—	—	—	—	—	—	0	—	—
0	30	2.34	—	—	900.0	—	0	—	—	—	—	—	—	0	—	—
10	30	2.16	—	—	930.0	—	—	—	—	—	—	—	—	0	—	—
10	80	1.80	—	—	780.0	—	—	—	—	—	—	—	—	1.2	—	—
30	60	1.80	—	—	660.0	—	—	—	—	—	—	—	—	1.2	—	—
0	20	2.88	—	—	840.0	—	0	—	—	—	—	—	—	0	—	—
15	20	2.70	—	—	860.0	—	—	—	—	—	—	—	—	0	—	—
0	30	1.98	—	—	920.0	—	—	—	—	—	—	—	—	0	—	—
10	40	2.16	—	—	930.0	—	—	—	—	—	—	—	—	0	—	—
40	0	0.00	—	—	120.0	—	0	—	—	—	—	—	—	0	—	—
0	30	1.98	—	—	1100.0	—	0	—	—	—	—	—	—	0	—	—
10	30	2.34	—	—	1120.0	—	—	—	—	—	—	—	—	0	—	—
10	59	0.80	—	—	35.0	—	—	—	—	—	—	—	—	22.2	—	—
0	60	0.43	—	—	75.0	—	—	—	—	—	—	—	—	5.4	—	—
90	211	2.85	—	—	1560.0	—	—	—	—	—	—	—	—	15.8	—	—
0	0	0.00	—	—	570.0	—	0	—	—	—	—	—	—	0	—	—
55	0	1.07	—	—	220.0	—	—	—	—	—	—	—	—	1.8	—	—
115	40	4.50	—	—	800.0	—	—	—	—	—	—	—	—	1.2	—	—
45	123	1.32	—	—	1310.0	—	—	—	—	—	—	—	—	18.4	—	—
10	41	0.48	—	—	270.0	—	—	—	—	—	—	—	—	24.5	—	—
5	0	0.71	—	—	220.0	—	0	—	—	—	—	—	—	0	—	—
70	264	2.84	—	—	580.0	—	—	—	—	—	—	—	—	9.5	—	—
0	41	1.48	—	—	580.0	—	—	—	—	—	—	—	—	2.5	—	—
0	0	0.85	—	—	120.0	—	0	—	—	—	—	—	—	14.3	—	—
5	20	0.72	—	—	620.0	—	—	—	—	—	—	—	—	2.4	—	—
0	43	0.38	—	—	180.0	—	—	—	—	—	—	—	—	5.1	—	—
25	51	0.46	—	—	660.0	—	—	—	—	—	—	—	—	19.2	—	—
25	100	0.59	—	—	1230.0	—	—	—	—	—	—	—	—	24.9	—	—
0	16	0.28	—	—	15.0	—	—	—	—	—	—	—	—	0	—	—
30	345	1.65	—	—	1290.0	—	—	—	—	—	—	—	—	0	—	—
10	—	—	—	—	2010.0	—	—	—	—	—	—	—	—	—	—	—
125	140	3.77	—	—	970.0	—	—	—	—	—	—	—	—	1.8	—	—
20	0	1.32	—	—	340.0	—	—	—	—	—	—	—	—	0	—	—
155	0	1.52	—	—	260.0	—	0	—	—	—	—	—	—	0	—	—
155	0	2.14	—	—	660.0	—	0	—	—	—	—	—	—	0	—	—
125	0	0.89	—	—	480.0	—	0	—	—	—	—	—	—	0	—	—
165	0	0.78	—	—	960.0	—	0	—	—	—	—	—	—	0	—	—
70	20	1.80	—	—	620.0	—	0	—	—	—	—	—	—	0	—	—
0	16	0.29	—	—	20.0	—	—	—	—	—	—	—	—	29.5	—	—
20	—	—	—	—	200.0	—	—	—	—	—	—	—	—	—	—	—
140	0	1.73	—	—	2230.0	—	0	—	—	—	—	—	—	0	—	—
0	53	0.46	—	—	45.0	—	—	—	—	—	—	—	—	24.0	—	—
0	0	0.43	—	—	95.0	—	—	—	—	—	—	—	—	5.8	—	—
20	44	1.18	—	—	210.0	—	—	—	—	—	—	—	—	9.8	—	—
210	250	2.70	—	—	1620.0	—	89.9	—	—	—	—	—	—	0	—	—
55	150	2.70	—	—	780.0	—	—	0.24	—	0.31	4.17	—	—	1.2	—	—
70	64	2.89	—	—	1440.0	—	—	0.50	—	0.32	10.29	—	—	0	—	—
55	20	0.72	—	—	960.0	—	—	0.14	—	0.11	10.93	—	—	0	—	—
55	333	0.79	—	—	350.0	—	—	0.11	—	0.61	0.26	—	—	2.7	0	—
50	99	1.78	20.1	217.3	810.0	1.51	—	0.34	1.03	0.33	4.33	—	—	0	0.6	22.2

TABLE A-1 Table of Food Composition *(continued)*

(Computer code is for Cengage Diet Analysis program) (For purposes of calculations, use "0" for t, <1, <.1, <.01, etc.)

DA+ Code	Food Description	QTY	Measure	Wt (g)	H_2O (g)	Ener (cal)	Prot (g)	Carb (g)	Fiber (g)	Fat (g)	Fat Breakdown (g) Sat	Mono	Poly	Trans
Fast Food—continued														
14261	Croissanwich with sausage, egg, and cheese	1	item(s)	159	71.4	470	19.0	26.0	0.5	32.0	11.0	15.8	6.1	2.5
3809	Double cheeseburger	1	item(s)	189	—	500	30.0	31.0	1.0	29.0	14.0	—	—	1.5
14244	Double Whopper sandwich	1	item(s)	373	—	900	47.0	51.0	3.0	57.0	19.0	—	—	2.0
14245	Double Whopper with cheese sandwich	1	item(s)	398	—	990	52.0	52.0	3.0	64.0	24.0	—	—	2.5
14250	Fish Filet sandwich	1	item(s)	250	—	630	24.0	67.0	4.0	30.0	6.0	—	—	2.5
14255	French fries, medium, salted	1	serving(s)	116	—	360	4.0	41.0	4.0	20.0	4.5	—	—	4.5
14262	French toast sticks, 5 pieces	1	serving(s)	112	37.6	390	6.0	46.0	2.0	20.0	4.5	10.6	2.9	4.5
14248	Hamburger	1	item(s)	121	—	290	15.0	30.0	1.0	12.0	4.5	—	—	0
14263	Hash brown rounds, small	1	serving(s)	75	27.1	230	2.0	23.0	2.0	15.0	4.0	—	—	5.0
14256	Onion rings, medium	1	serving(s)	91	—	320	4.0	40.0	3.0	16.0	4.0	—	—	3.5
39000	Tendercrisp chicken sandwich	1	item(s)	286	—	780	25.0	73.0	4.0	43.0	8.0	—	—	4.0
37514	TenderGrill chicken sandwich	1	item(s)	258	—	450	37.0	53.0	4.0	10.0	2.0	—	—	0
14258	Vanilla shake, small	1	item(s)	296	—	400	8.0	57.0	0	15.0	9.0	—	—	0
1736	Whopper sandwich	1	item(s)	290	—	670	28.0	51.0	3.0	39.0	11.0	—	—	1.5
14243	Whopper with cheese sandwich	1	item(s)	315	—	760	33.0	52.0	3.0	47.0	16.0	—	—	1.5
	Carl's Jr													
33962	Carl's bacon Swiss crispy chicken sandwich	1	item(s)	268	—	750	31.0	91.0	—	28.0	28.0	—	—	—
10801	Carl's Catch fish sandwich	1	item(s)	215	—	560	19.0	58.0	2.0	27.0	7.0	—	1.9	—
10862	Carl's Famous Star hamburger	1	item(s)	254	—	590	24.0	50.0	3.0	32.0	9.0	—	—	—
10785	Charbroiled chicken club sandwich	1	item(s)	270	—	550	42.0	43.0	4.0	23.0	7.0	—	2.9	—
10866	Charbroiled chicken salad	1	item(s)	437	—	330	34.0	17.0	5.0	7.0	4.0	—	1.0	—
10855	Charbroiled Santa Fe chicken sandwich	1	item(s)	266	—	610	38.0	43.0	4.0	32.0	8.0	—	—	—
10790	Chicken stars, 6 pieces	1	serving(s)	85	—	260	13.0	14.0	1.0	16.0	4.0	—	1.6	—
34864	Chocolate shake, small	1	serving(s)	595	—	540	15.0	98.0	0	11.0	7.0	—	—	—
10797	Crisscut fries	1	serving(s)	139	—	410	5.0	43.0	4.0	24.0	5.0	—	—	—
10799	Double Western Bacon cheeseburger	1	item(s)	308	—	920	51.0	65.0	2.0	50	21.0	—	6.6	—
14238	French fries, small	1	serving(s)	92	—	290	5.0	37.0	3.0	14.0	3.0	—	—	—
10798	French toast dips without syrup, 5 pieces	1	serving(s)	155	—	370	8.0	49.0	0	17.0	5.0	—	1.4	—
10802	Onion rings	1	serving(s)	128	—	440	7.0	53.0	3.0	22.0	5.0	—	0.8	—
34858	Spicy chicken sandwich	1	item(s)	198	—	480	14.0	48.0	2.0	26.0	5.0	—	—	—
34867	Strawberry shake, small	1	serving(s)	595	—	520	14.0	93.0	0	11.0	7.0	—	—	—
10865	Super Star hamburger	1	item(s)	348	—	790	41.0	52.0	3.0	47.0	14.0	—	—	—
38925	The Six Dollar burger	1	item(s)	429	—	1010	40.0	60.0	3.0	66.0	26.0	—	—	—
10818	Vanilla shake, small	1	item(s)	398	—	314	10.0	51.5	0	7.4	4.7	—	—	—
10770	Western Bacon cheeseburger	1	item(s)	225	—	660	32.0	64.0	2.0	30.0	12.0	—	4.8	—
	Chick Fil-A													
38746	Biscuit with bacon, egg, and cheese	1	item(s)	163	—	470	18.0	39.0	1.0	26.0	9.0	—	—	3.0
38747	Biscuit with egg	1	item(s)	135	—	350	11.0	38.0	1.0	16.0	4.5	—	—	3.0
38748	Biscuit with egg and cheese	1	item(s)	149	—	400	14.0	38.0	1.0	21.0	7.0	—	—	3.0
38753	Biscuit with gravy	1	item(s)	192	—	330	5.0	43.0	1.0	15.0	4.0	—	—	4.0
38752	Biscuit with sausage, egg, and cheese	1	item(s)	212	—	620	22.0	39.0	2.0	42.0	14.0	—	—	3.0
38771	Carrot and raisin salad	1	item(s)	113	—	170	1.0	28.0	2.0	6.0	1.0	—	—	0
38761	Chargrilled chicken Cool Wrap	1	item(s)	245	—	390	29.0	54.0	3.0	7.0	3.0	—	—	0
38766	Chargrilled chicken garden salad	1	item(s)	275	—	180	22.0	9.0	3.0	6.0	3.0	—	—	0
38758	Chargrilled chicken sandwich	1	item(s)	193	—	270	28.0	33.0	3.0	3.5	1.0	—	—	0
38742	Chicken biscuit	1	item(s)	145	—	420	18.0	44.0	2.0	19.0	4.5	—	—	3.0
38743	Chicken biscuit with cheese	1	item(s)	159	—	470	21.0	45.0	2.0	23.0	8.0	—	—	3.0
38762	Chicken Caesar Cool Wrap	1	item(s)	227	—	460	36.0	52.0	3.0	10.0	6.0	—	—	0
38757	Chicken deluxe sandwich	1	item(s)	208	—	420	28.0	39.0	2.0	16.0	3.5	—	—	0
38764	Chicken salad sandwich on wheat bun	1	item(s)	153	—	350	20.0	32.0	5.0	15.0	3.0	—	—	0
38756	Chicken sandwich	1	item(s)	170	—	410	28.0	38.0	1.0	16.0	3.5	—	—	0
38768	Chick-n-Strip salad	1	item(s)	327	—	400	34.0	21.0	4.0	20.0	6.0	—	—	0
38763	Chick-n-Strips	4	item(s)	127	—	300	28.0	14.0	1.0	15.0	2.5	—	—	0
38770	Cole slaw	1	item(s)	128	—	260	2.0	17.0	2.0	21.0	3.5	—	—	0
38776	Diet lemonade, small	1	cup(s)	255	—	25	0	5.0	0	0	0	0	0	0

Chol (mg)	Calc (mg)	Iron (mg)	Magn (mg)	Pota (mg)	Sodi (mg)	Zinc (mg)	Vit A (µg)	Thia (mg)	Vit E (mg α)	Ribo (mg)	Niac (mg)	Vit B_6 (mg)	Fola (µg)	Vit C (mg)	Vit B_{12} (µg)	Sele (µg)
180	146	2.63	28.6	313.2	1060.0	2.08	—	0.38	1.66	0.51	4.72	0.28	—	0	1.1	38.0
105	250	4.50	—	—	1030.0	—	—	0.26	—	0.44	6.37	—	—	1.2	—	—
175	150	8.07	—	—	1090.0	—	—	0.39	—	0.59	11.05	—	—	9.0	—	—
195	299	8.08	—	—	1520.0	—	—	0.39	—	0.66	11.03	—	—	9.0	—	—
60	101	3.62	—	—	1380.0	—	—	—	—	—	—	—	—	3.6	—	—
0	20	0.71	—	—	590.0	—	0	0.15	—	0.48	2.30	—	—	8.9	—	—
0	60	1.80	21.3	124.3	440.0	0.57	—	0.31	0.98	0.19	2.88	0.05	—	0	0	13.7
40	80	2.70	—	—	560.0	—	—	0.25	—	0.28	4.25	—	—	1.2	—	—
0	0	0.36	—	—	450.0	—	0	0.11	0.83	0.06	1.35	0.17	—	1.2	—	—
0	100	0.00	—	—	460.0	—	0	0.14	—	0.09	2.32	—	—	0	—	—
75	79	4.43	—	—	1730.0	—	—	—	—	—	—	—	—	8.9	—	—
75	57	6.82	—	—	1210.0	—	—	—	—	—	—	—	—	5.7	—	—
60	348	0.00	—	—	240.0	—	—	0.11	—	0.63	0.21	—	—	2.4	0	—
51	100	5.38	—	—	1020.0	—	—	0.38	—	0.43	7.30	—	—	9.0	—	—
115	249	5.38	—	—	1450.0	—	—	0.38	—	0.51	7.28	—	—	9.0	—	—
80	200	5.40	—	—	1900.0	—	—	—	—	—	—	—	—	2.4	—	—
80	150	2.70	—	—	990.0	—	60.0	—	—	—	—	—	—	2.4	—	—
70	100	4.50	—	—	910.0	—	—	—	—	—	—	—	—	6.0	—	—
95	200	3.60	—	—	1330.0	—	—	—	—	—	—	—	—	9.0	—	—
75	200	1.80	—	—	880.0	—	—	—	—	—	—	—	—	30.0	—	—
100	200	3.60	—	—	1440.0	—	—	—	—	—	—	—	—	9.0	—	—
35	19	1.02	—	—	470.0	—	0	—	—	—	—	—	—	0	—	—
45	600	1.08	—	—	360.0	—	0	—	—	—	—	—	—	0	—	—
0	20	1.80	—	—	950.0	—	0	—	—	—	—	—	—	12.0	—	—
155	300	7.20	—	—	1730.0	—	—	—	—	—	—	—	—	1.2	—	—
0	0	1.08	—	—	170.0	—	0	—	—	—	—	—	—	21.0	—	—
3	0	0.00	—	—	470.0	—	0	0.25	—	0.23	2.00	—	—	0	—	—
0	20	0.72	—	—	700.0	—	0	—	—	—	—	—	—	3.6	—	—
40	100	3.60	—	—	1220.0	—	—	—	—	—	—	—	—	6.0	—	—
45	600	0.00	—	—	340.0	—	0	—	—	—	—	—	—	0	—	—
130	100	7.20	—	—	980.0	—	—	—	—	—	—	—	—	9.0	—	—
145	279	4.29	—	—	1960.0	—	—	—	—	—	—	—	—	16.7	—	—
30	401	0.00	—	—	234.0	—	0	—	—	—	—	—	—	0	—	—
85	200	5.40	—	—	1410.0	—	60.0	—	—	—	—	—	—	1.2	—	—
270	150	2.70	—	—	1190.0	—	—	—	—	—	—	—	—	0	—	—
240	80	2.70	—	—	740.0	—	—	—	—	—	—	—	—	0	—	—
255	150	2.70	—	—	970.0	—	—	—	—	—	—	—	—	0	—	—
5	60	1.80	—	—	930.0	—	0	—	—	—	—	—	—	0	—	—
300	200	3.60	—	—	1360.0	—	—	—	—	—	—	—	—	0	—	—
10	40	0.36	—	—	110.0	—	—	—	—	—	—	—	—	4.8	—	—
65	200	3.60	—	—	1020.0	—	—	—	—	—	—	—	—	6.0	—	—
65	150	0.72	—	—	620.0	—	—	—	—	—	—	—	—	30	—	—
65	80	2.70	—	—	940.0	—	—	—	—	—	—	—	—	6.0	—	—
35	60	2.70	—	—	1270.0	—	0	—	—	—	—	—	—	0	—	—
50	150	2.70	—	—	1500.0	—	—	—	—	—	—	—	—	0	—	—
80	500	3.60	—	—	1350.0	—	—	—	—	—	—	—	—	1.2	—	—
60	100	2.70	—	—	1300.0	—	—	—	—	—	—	—	—	2.4	—	—
65	150	1.80	—	—	880.0	—	—	—	—	—	—	—	—	0	—	—
60	100	2.70	—	—	1300.0	—	—	—	—	—	—	—	—	0	—	—
80	150	1.44	—	—	1070.0	—	—	—	—	—	—	—	—	6.0	—	—
65	40	1.44	—	—	940.0	—	—	—	—	—	—	—	—	0	—	—
25	60	0.36	—	—	220.0	—	—	—	—	—	—	—	—	36.0	—	—
0	0	0.36	—	—	5.0	—	0	—	—	—	—	—	—	15.0	—	—

TABLE A-1 Table of Food Composition *(continued)*

(Computer code is for Cengage Diet Analysis program) (For purposes of calculations, use "0" for t, <1, <.1, <.01, etc.)

DA+ Code	Food Description	QTY	Measure	Wt (g)	H_2O (g)	Ener (cal)	Prot (g)	Carb (g)	Fiber (g)	Fat (g)	Fat Breakdown (g) Sat	Mono	Poly	Trans
	Fast Food—continued													
38755	Hashbrowns	1	serving(s)	84	—	260	2.0	25.0	3.0	17.0	3.5	—	—	1.0
38765	Hearty breast of chicken soup	1	cup(s)	241	—	140	8.0	18.0	1.0	3.5	1.0	—	—	0
38741	Hot buttered biscuit	1	item(s)	79	—	270	4.0	38.0	1.0	12.0	3.0	—	—	3.0
38778	IceDream, small cone	1	item(s)	135	—	160	4.0	28.0	0	4.0	2.0	—	—	0
38774	IceDream, small cup	1	serving(s)	227	—	240	6.0	41.0	0	6.0	3.5	—	—	0
38775	Lemonade, small	1	cup(s)	255	—	170	0	41.0	0	0.5	0	—	—	0
38777	Nuggets	8	item(s)	113	—	260	26.0	12.0	0.5	12.0	2.5	—	—	0
38769	Side salad	1	item(s)	108	—	60	3.0	4.0	2.0	3.0	1.5	—	—	0
38767	Southwest chargrilled salad	1	item(s)	303	—	240	25.0	17.0	5.0	8.0	3.5	—	—	0
40481	Spicy chicken cool wrap	1	serving(s)	230	—	380	30.0	52.0	3.0	6.0	3.0	—	—	0
38772	Waffle potato fries, small, salted	1	serving(s)	85	—	270	3.0	34.0	4.0	13.0	3.0	—	—	1.5
	Cinnabon													
39572	Caramellata Chill w/whipped cream	16	fluid ounce(s)	480	—	406	10.0	61.0	0	14.0	8.0	—	—	0
39571	Cinnabon Bites	1	serving(s)	149	—	510	8.0	77.0	2.0	19.0	5.0	—	—	5.0
39570	Cinnabon Stix	5	item(s)	85	—	379	6.0	41.0	1.0	21.0	6.0	—	—	4.0
39567	Classic roll	1	item(s)	221	—	813	15.0	117.0	4.0	32.0	8.0	—	—	5.0
39568	Minibon	1	item(s)	92	—	339	6.0	49.0	2.0	13.0	3.0	—	—	2.0
39573	Mochalatta Chill w/whipped cream	16	fluid ounce(s)	480	—	362	9.0	55.0	0	13.0	8.0	—	—	0
39569	Pecanbon	1	item(s)	272	—	1100	16.0	141.0	8.0	56.0	10.0	—	—	5.0
	Dairy Queen													
1466	Banana split	1	item(s)	369	—	510	8.0	96.0	3.0	12.0	8.0	—	—	0
38552	Brownie Earthquake®	1	serving(s)	304	—	740	10.0	112.0	0	27.0	16.0	—	—	0.5
38561	Chocolate chip cookie dough blizzard,® small	1	item(s)	319	—	720	12.0	105.0	0	28.0	14.0	—	—	2.5
1464	Chocolate malt, small	1	item(s)	418	—	640	15.0	111.0	1.0	16.0	11.0	—	—	0.5
38541	Chocolate shake, small	1	item(s)	397	—	560	13.0	93.0	1.0	15.0	10.0	—	—	0.5
17257	Chocolate soft serve	½	cup(s)	94	—	150	4.0	22.0	0	5.0	3.5	—	—	0
1463	Chocolate sundae, small	1	item(s)	163	—	280	5.0	49.0	0	7.0	4.5	—	—	0
1462	Dipped cone, small	1	item(s)	156	—	340	6.0	42.0	1.0	17.0	9.0	4.0	3.0	1.0
38555	Oreo cookies blizzard, small	1	item(s)	283	—	570	11.0	83.0	0.5	21.0	10.0	—	—	2.5
38547	Royal Treats Peanut Buster® Parfait	1	item(s)	305	—	730	16.0	99.0	2.0	31.0	17.0	—	—	0
17256	Vanilla soft serve	½	cup(s)	94	—	140	3.0	22.0	0	4.5	3.0	—	—	0
	Domino's													
31606	Barbeque buffalo wings	1	item(s)	25	—	50	6.0	2.0	0	2.5	0.5	—	—	—
31604	Breadsticks	1	item(s)	30	—	115	2.0	12.0	0	6.3	1.1	—	—	—
37551	Buffalo Chicken Kickers	1	item(s)	24	—	47	4.0	3.0	0	2.0	0.5	—	—	—
37548	CinnaStix	1	item(s)	30	—	123	2.0	15.0	1.0	6.1	1.1	—	—	—
37549	Dot, cinnamon	1	item(s)	28	7.6	99	1.9	14.9	0.7	3.7	0.7	—	—	—
31605	Double cheesy bread	1	item(s)	35	—	123	4.0	13.0	0	6.5	1.9	—	—	—
31607	Hot buffalo wings	1	item(s)	25	—	45	5.0	1.0	0	2.5	0.5	—	—	—
	Domino's Classic hand tossed pizza													
31573	America's favorite feast, 12″	1	slice(s)	102	—	257	10.0	29.0	2.0	11.5	4.5	—	—	—
31574	America's favorite feast, 14″	1	slice(s)	141	—	353	14.0	39.0	2.0	16.0	6.0	—	—	—
37543	Bacon cheeseburger feast, 12″	1	slice(s)	99	—	273	12.0	28.0	2.0	13.0	5.5	—	—	—
37545	Bacon cheeseburger feast, 14″	1	slice(s)	137	—	379	17.0	38.0	2.0	18.0	8.0	—	—	—
37546	Barbeque feast, 12″	1	slice(s)	96	—	252	11.0	31.0	1.0	10.0	4.5	—	—	—
37547	Barbeque feast, 14″	1	slice(s)	131	—	344	14.0	43.0	2.0	13.5	6.0	—	—	—
31569	Cheese, 12″	1	slice(s)	55	—	160	6.0	28.0	1.0	3.0	1.0	—	—	0
31570	Cheese, 14″	1	slice(s)	75	—	220	8.0	38.0	2.0	4.0	1.0	—	—	0
37538	Deluxe feast, 12″	1	slice(s)	201	101.8	465	19.5	57.4	3.5	18.2	7.7	—	—	—
37540	Deluxe feast, 14″	1	slice(s)	273	138.4	627	26.4	78.3	4.7	24.1	10.2	—	—	—
31685	Deluxe, 12″	1	slice(s)	100	—	234	9.0	29.0	2.0	9.5	3.5	—	—	—
31694	Deluxe, 14″	1	slice(s)	136	—	316	13.0	39.0	2.0	12.5	5.0	—	—	—
31686	Extravaganzza, 12″	1	slice(s)	122	—	289	13.0	30.0	2.0	14.0	5.5	—	—	—
31695	Extravaganzza, 14″	1	slice(s)	165	—	388	17.0	40.0	3.0	18.5	7.5	—	—	—
31575	Hawaiian feast, 12″	1	slice(s)	102	—	223	10.0	30.0	2.0	8.0	3.5	—	—	—
31576	Hawaiian feast, 14″	1	slice(s)	141	—	309	14.0	41.0	2.0	11.0	4.5	—	—	—
31687	Meatzza, 12″	1	slice(s)	108	—	281	13.0	29.0	2.0	13.5	5.5	—	—	—

PAGE KEY: A-2 = Breads/Baked Goods A-8 = Cereal/Rice/Pasta A-12 = Fruit A-18 = Vegetables/Legumes A-28 = Nuts/Seeds A-30 = Vegetarian A-32 = Dairy A-40 = Eggs A-40 = Seafood A-44 = Meats A-48 = Poultry A-48 = Processed Meats A-50 = Beverages A-54 = Fats/Oils A-56 = Sweets A-58 = Spices/Condiments/Sauces A-62 = Mixed Foods/Soups/Sandwiches A-68 = Fast Food A-88 = Convenience A-90 = Baby Foods

Chol (mg)	Calc (mg)	Iron (mg)	Magn (mg)	Pota (mg)	Sodi (mg)	Zinc (mg)	Vit A (µg)	Thia (mg)	Vit E (mg α)	Ribo (mg)	Niac (mg)	Vit B_6 (mg)	Fola (µg)	Vit C (mg)	Vit B_{12} (µg)	Sele (µg)
5	20	0.72	—	—	380.0	—	—	—	—	—	—	—	—	0	—	—
25	40	1.08	—	—	900.0	—	—	—	—	—	—	—	—	0	—	—
0	60	1.80	—	—	660.0	—	0	—	—	—	—	—	—	0	—	—
15	100	0.36	—	—	80.0	—	—	—	—	—	—	—	—	0	—	—
25	200	0.36	—	—	105.0	—	—	—	—	—	—	—	—	0	—	—
0	0	0.36	—	—	10.0	—	0	—	—	—	—	—	—	15.0	—	—
70	40	1.08	—	—	1090.0	—	0	—	—	—	—	—	—	0	—	—
10	100	0.00	—	—	75.0	—	—	—	—	—	—	—	—	15.0	—	—
60	200	1.08	—	—	770.0	—	—	—	—	—	—	—	—	24.0	—	—
60	200	3.60	—	—	1090.0	—	—	—	—	—	—	—	—	3.6	—	—
0	20	1.08	—	—	115.0	—	0	—	—	—	—	—	—	1.2	—	—
46	—	—	—	—	187.0	—	—	—	—	—	—	—	—	—	—	—
35	—	—	—	—	530.0	—	—	—	—	—	—	—	—	—	—	—
16	—	—	—	—	413.0	—	—	—	—	—	—	—	—	—	—	—
67	—	—	—	—	801.0	—	—	—	—	—	—	—	—	—	—	—
27	—	—	—	—	337.0	—	—	—	—	—	—	—	—	—	—	—
46	—	—	—	—	252.0	—	—	—	—	—	—	—	—	—	—	—
63	—	—	—	—	600.0	—	—	—	—	—	—	—	—	—	—	—
30	250	1.80	—	—	180.0	—	—	—	—	—	—	—	—	15.0	—	—
50	250	1.80	—	—	350.0	—	—	—	—	—	—	—	—	0	—	—
50	350	2.70	—	—	370.0	—	—	—	—	—	—	—	—	1.2	—	—
55	450	1.80	—	—	340.0	—	—	—	—	—	—	—	—	2.4	—	—
50	450	1.44	—	—	280.0	—	—	—	—	—	—	—	—	2.4	—	—
15	100	0.72	—	—	75.0	—	—	—	—	—	—	—	—	0	—	—
20	200	1.08	—	—	140.0	—	—	—	—	—	—	—	—	0	—	—
20	200	1.08	—	—	130.0	—	—	—	—	—	—	—	—	1.2	—	—
40	350	2.70	—	—	430.0	—	—	—	—	—	—	—	—	1.2	—	—
35	300	1.80	—	—	400.0	—	—	—	—	—	—	—	—	1.2	—	—
15	150	0.72	—	—	70.0	—	—	—	—	—	—	—	—	0	—	—
26	10	0.36	—	—	175.5	—	—	—	—	—	—	—	—	0	—	—
0	0	0.72	—	—	122.1	—	—	—	—	—	—	—	—	0	—	—
9	0	0.00	—	—	162.5	—	—	—	—	—	—	—	—	0	—	—
0	0	0.72	—	—	111.4	—	—	—	—	—	—	—	—	0	—	—
0	6	0.59	—	—	85.7	—	—	—	—	—	—	—	—	0	—	—
6	40	0.72	—	—	162.3	—	—	—	—	—	—	—	—	0	—	—
26	10	0.36	—	—	254.5	—	—	—	—	—	—	—	—	1.2	—	—
																—
22	100	1.80	—	—	625.5	—	—	—	—	—	—	—	—	0.6	—	—
31	140	2.52	—	—	865.5	—	—	—	—	—	—	—	—	0.6	—	—
27	140	1.80	—	—	634.0	—	—	—	—	—	—	—	—	0	—	—
38	190	2.52	—	—	900.0	—	—	—	—	—	—	—	—	0	—	—
20	140	1.62	—	—	600.0	—	—	—	—	—	—	—	—	0.6	—	—
27	190	2.16	—	—	831.5	—	—	—	—	—	—	—	—	0.6	—	—
0	0	1.80	—	—	110.0	—	0	—	—	—	—	—	—	0	—	—
0	0	2.70	—	—	150.0	—	0	—	—	—	—	—	—	0	—	—
40	199	3.56	—	—	1063.1	—	—	—	—	—	—	—	—	1.4	—	—
53	276	4.84	—	—	1432.2	—	—	—	—	—	—	—	—	1.8	—	—
17	100	1.80	—	—	541.5	—	—	—	—	—	—	—	—	0.6	—	—
23	130	2.34	—	—	728.5	—	—	—	—	—	—	—	—	1.2	—	—
28	140	1.98	—	—	764.0	—	—	—	—	—	—	—	—	0.6	—	—
37	190	2.70	—	—	1014.0	—	—	—	—	—	—	—	—	1.2	—	—
16	130	1.62	—	—	546.5	—	—	—	—	—	—	—	—	1.2	—	—
23	180	2.34	—	—	765.0	—	—	—	—	—	—	—	—	1.2	—	—
28	130	1.80	—	—	739.5	—	—	—	—	—	—	—	—	0	—	—

A

TABLE A-1 Table of Food Composition *(continued)*

(Computer code is for Cengage Diet Analysis program) (For purposes of calculations, use "0" for t, <1, <.1, <.01, etc.)

DA+ Code	Food Description	Qty	Measure	Wt (g)	H_2O (g)	Ener (cal)	Prot (g)	Carb (g)	Fiber (g)	Fat (g)	Fat Breakdown (g) Sat	Mono	Poly	Trans
	Fast Food—continued													
31696	Meatzza, 14″	1	slice(s)	146	—	378	17.0	39.0	2.0	18.0	7.5	—	—	—
31571	Pepperoni feast, extra pepperoni and cheese, 12″	1	slice(s)	98	—	265	11.0	28.0	2.0	12.5	5.0	—	—	—
31572	Pepperoni feast, extra pepperoni and cheese, 14″	1	slice(s)	135	—	363	16.0	39.0	2.0	17.0	7.0	—	—	—
31577	Vegi feast, 12″	1	slice(s)	102	—	218	9.0	29.0	2.0	8.0	3.5	—	—	—
31578	Vegi feast, 14″	1	slice(s)	139	—	300	13.0	40.0	3.0	11.0	4.5	—	—	—
	Domino's thin crust pizza													
31583	America's favorite, 12″	1	slice(s)	72	—	208	8.0	15.0	1.0	13.5	5.0	—	—	—
31584	America's favorite, 14″	1	slice(s)	100	—	285	11.0	20.0	2.0	18.5	7.0	—	—	—
31579	Cheese, 12″	1	slice(s)	49	—	137	5.0	14.0	1.0	7.0	2.5	—	—	—
31580	Cheese, 14″	1	slice(s)	68	27.0	214	8.8	19.0	1.4	11.4	4.6	2.9	2.5	—
31688	Deluxe, 12″	1	slice(s)	70	—	185	7.0	15.0	1.0	11.5	4.0	—	—	—
31697	Deluxe, 14″	1	slice(s)	94	—	248	10.0	20.0	2.0	15.0	5.5	—	—	—
31689	Extravaganzza, 12″	1	slice(s)	92	—	240	11.0	16.0	1.0	15.5	6.0	—	—	—
31698	Extravaganzza, 14″	1	slice(s)	123	—	320	14.0	21.0	2.0	20.5	8.0	—	—	—
31585	Hawaiian, 12″	1	slice(s)	71	—	174	8.0	16.0	1.0	9.5	3.5	—	—	—
31586	Hawaiian, 14″	1	slice(s)	100	—	240	11.0	21.0	2.0	13.0	5.0	—	—	—
31690	Meatzza, 12″	1	slice(s)	78	—	232	11.0	15.0	1.0	15.0	6.0	—	—	—
31699	Meatzza, 14″	1	slice(s)	104	—	310	14.0	20.0	2.0	20	8.0	—	—	—
31581	Pepperoni, extra pepperoni and cheese, 12″	1	slice(s)	68	—	216	9.0	14.0	1.0	14.0	5.5	—	—	—
31582	Pepperoni, extra pepperoni and cheese, 14″	1	slice(s)	93	—	295	13.0	20.0	1.0	19.0	7.5	—	—	—
31587	Vegi, 12″	1	slice(s)	71	—	168	7.0	15.0	1.0	9.5	3.5	—	—	—
31588	Vegi, 14″	1	slice(s)	97	—	231	10.0	21.0	2.0	13.5	5.0	—	—	—
	Domino's Ultimate deep dish pizza													
31596	America's favorite, 12″	1	slice(s)	115	—	309	12.0	29.0	2.0	17.0	6.0	—	—	—
31702	America's favorite, 14″	1	slice(s)	162	—	433	17.0	42.0	3.0	23.5	8.0	—	—	—
31590	Cheese, 12″	1	slice(s)	90	—	238	9.0	28.0	2.0	11.0	3.5	—	—	—
31591	Cheese, 14″	1	slice(s)	128	53.9	351	14.5	41.0	2.9	13.2	5.2	3.8	2.5	—
31589	Cheese, 6″	1	item(s)	215	—	598	22.9	68.4	3.9	27.6	9.9	—	—	—
31691	Deluxe, 12″	1	slice(s)	122	—	287	11.0	29.0	2.0	15.0	5.0	—	—	—
31700	Deluxe, 14″	1	slice(s)	156	—	396	15.0	42.0	3.0	20.0	7.0	—	—	—
31692	Extravaganzza, 12″	1	slice(s)	136	—	341	14.0	30.0	2.0	19.0	7.0	—	—	—
31701	Extravaganzza, 14″	1	slice(s)	186	—	468	20.0	43.0	3.0	25.5	9.5	—	—	—
31599	Hawaiian, 12″	1	slice(s)	114	—	275	12.0	30.0	2.0	13.0	5.0	—	—	—
31600	Hawaiian, 14″	1	slice(s)	162	—	389	17.0	43.0	3.0	18.0	6.5	—	—	—
31693	Meatzza, 12″	1	slice(s)	121	—	333	14.0	29.0	2.0	19.0	7.0	—	—	—
31703	Meatzza, 14″	1	slice(s)	167	—	458	19.0	42.0	3.0	25.0	9.5	—	—	—
31593	Pepperoni, extra pepperoni and cheese, 12″	1	slice(s)	110	—	317	13.0	29.0	2.0	17.5	6.5	—	—	—
31594	Pepperoni, extra pepperoni and cheese, 14″	1	slice(s)	155	—	443	18.0	42.0	3.0	24.0	9.0	—	—	—
31602	Vegi, 12″	1	slice(s)	114	—	270	11.0	30.0	2.0	13.5	5.0	—	—	—
31603	Vegi, 14″	1	slice(s)	159	—	380	15.0	43.0	3.0	18.0	6.5	—	—	—
31598	With ham and pineapple tidbits, 6″	1	item(s)	430	—	619	25.2	69.9	4.0	28.3	10.2	—	—	—
31595	With Italian sausage, 6″	1	item(s)	430	—	642	24.8	69.6	4.2	31.1	11.3	—	—	—
31592	With pepperoni, 6″	1	item(s)	430	—	647	25.1	68.5	3.9	32.0	11.7	—	—	—
31601	With vegetables, 6″	1	item(s)	430	—	619	23.4	70.8	4.6	28.7	10.1	—	—	—
	In-N-Out Burger													
34391	Cheeseburger with mustard and ketchup	1	serving(s)	268	—	400	22.0	41.0	3.0	18.0	9.0	—	—	0.5
34374	Cheeseburger	1	serving(s)	268	—	480	22.0	39.0	3.0	27.0	10.0	—	—	0.5

Chol (mg)	Calc (mg)	Iron (mg)	Magn (mg)	Pota (mg)	Sodi (mg)	Zinc (mg)	Vit A (µg)	Thia (mg)	Vit E (mg α)	Ribo (mg)	Niac (mg)	Vit B_6 (mg)	Fola (µg)	Vit C (mg)	Vit B_{12} (µg)	Sele (µg)
37	190	2.52	—	—	983.5	—	—	—	—	—	—	—	—	0	—	—
24	130	1.62	—	—	670.0	—	70.9	—	—	—	—	—	—	0	—	—
33	180	2.34	—	—	920.0	—	104.7	—	—	—	—	—	—	0	—	—
13	130	1.62	—	—	489.0	—	—	—	—	—	—	—	—	0.6	—	—
18	180	2.34	—	—	678.0	—	—	—	—	—	—	—	—	0.6	—	—
23	100	0.90	—	—	533.0	—	—	—	—	—	—	—	—	2.4	—	—
32	140	1.26	—	—	736.5	—	—	—	—	—	—	—	—	3.0	—	—
10	90	0.54	—	—	292.5	—	60.0	—	—	—	—	—	—	1.8	—	—
14	151	0.48	17.7	125.1	338.0	0.02	64.6	0.05	1.01	0.07	0.69	—	—	2.4	0.5	24.1
19	100	0.90	—	—	449.0	—	—	—	—	—	—	—	—	2.4	—	—
24	130	1.08	—	—	601.0	—	—	—	—	—	—	—	—	3.6	—	—
29	140	1.08	—	—	671.5	—	—	—	—	—	—	—	—	2.4	—	—
38	190	1.44	—	—	886.5	—	—	—	—	—	—	—	—	3.6	—	—
17	130	0.72	—	—	454.0	—	—	—	—	—	—	—	—	3.0	—	—
24	180	0.90	—	—	637.5	—	—	—	—	—	—	—	—	3.6	—	—
29	140	0.90	—	—	647.0	—	—	—	—	—	—	—	—	1.8	—	—
38	190	1.26	—	—	865.5	—	—	—	—	—	—	—	—	2.4	—	—
26	130	0.72	—	—	577.0	—	80.0	—	—	—	—	—	—	1.8	—	—
35	80	1.08	—	—	792.5	—	105.8	—	—	—	—	—	—	2.4	—	—
14	130	0.72	—	—	396.5	—	—	—	—	—	—	—	—	2.4	—	—
19	180	1.08	—	—	550.5	—	—	—	—	—	—	—	—	3.0	—	—
25	120	2.34	—	—	796.5	—	—	—	—	—	—	—	—	0.6	—	—
34	170	3.24	—	—	1110.0	—	—	—	—	—	—	—	—	0.6	—	—
11	110	1.98	—	—	555.5	—	70.0	—	—	—	—	—	—	0	—	—
18	189	3.78	32.0	209.9	718.1	1.75	99.8	0.29	1.13	0.31	5.44	—	—	0	0.6	45.6
36	295	4.67	—	—	1341.4	—	174.0	—	—	—	—	—	—	0.5	—	—
20	120	2.16	—	—	712.0	—	—	—	—	—	—	—	—	1.2	—	—
26	170	3.06	—	—	974.5	—	—	—	—	—	—	—	—	1.2	—	—
31	160	2.52	—	—	934.5	—	—	—	—	—	—	—	—	1.2	—	—
40	220	3.42	—	—	1260.0	—	—	—	—	—	—	—	—	1.2	—	—
19	150	1.98	—	—	717.0	—	—	—	—	—	—	—	—	1.2	—	—
26	210	2.88	—	—	1011.0	—	—	—	—	—	—	—	—	1.8	—	—
31	160	2.34	—	—	910.5	—	—	—	—	—	—	—	—	0	—	—
40	220	3.24	—	—	1230.0	—	—	—	—	—	—	—	—	0.6	—	—
27	150	2.16	—	—	840.5	—	86.5	—	—	—	—	—	—	0	—	—
37	220	3.06	—	—	1166.0	—	115.4	—	—	—	—	—	—	0.6	—	—
15	150	2.16	—	—	659.5	—	—	—	—	—	—	—	—	0.6	—	—
21	220	3.06	—	—	924.0	—	—	—	—	—	—	—	—	1.2	—	—
43	298	4.84	—	—	1497.8	—	—	—	—	—	—	—	—	1.5	—	—
45	302	4.89	—	—	1478.1	—	—	—	—	—	—	—	—	0.6	—	—
47	299	4.81	—	—	1523.7	—	167.9	—	—	—	—	—	—	0.6	—	—
36	307	5.10	—	—	1472.5	—	—	—	—	—	—	—	—	4.7	—	—
60	200	3.60	—	—	1080.0	—	—	—	—	—	—	—	—	12.0	—	—
60	200	3.60	—	—	1000.0	—	—	—	—	—	—	—	—	9.0	—	—

A

TABLE A-1 Table of Food Composition *(continued)*

(Computer code is for Cengage Diet Analysis program) (For purposes of calculations, use "0" for t, <1, <.1, <.01, etc.)

											Fat Breakdown (g)			
DA+ Code	Food Description	Qty	Measure	Wt (g)	H_2O (g)	Ener (cal)	Prot (g)	Carb (g)	Fiber (g)	Fat (g)	Sat	Mono	Poly	Trans
	Fast Food—continued													
34390	Cheeseburger, lettuce leaves instead of buns	1	serving(s)	300	—	330	18.0	11.0	3.0	25.0	9.0	—	—	0
34377	Chocolate shake	1	serving(s)	425	—	690	9.0	83.0	0	36.0	24.0	—	—	1.0
34375	Double-Double cheeseburger	1	serving(s)	330	—	670	37.0	39.0	3.0	41.0	18.0	—	—	1.0
34393	Double-Double cheeseburger with mustard and ketchup	1	serving(s)	330	—	590	37.0	41.0	3.0	32.0	17.0	—	—	1.0
34392	Double-Double cheeseburger, lettuce leaves instead of buns	1	serving(s)	362	—	520	33.0	11.0	3.0	39.0	17.0	—	—	1.0
34376	French fries	1	serving(s)	125	—	400	7.0	54.0	2.0	18.0	5.0	—	—	0
34373	Hamburger	1	item(s)	243	—	390	16.0	39.0	3.0	19.0	5.0	—	—	0
34389	Hamburger with mustard and ketchup	1	serving(s)	243	—	310	16.0	41.0	3.0	10.0	4.0	—	—	0
34388	Hamburger, lettuce leaves instead of buns	1	serving(s)	275	—	240	13.0	11.0	3.0	17.0	4.0	—	—	0
34379	Strawberry shake	1	serving(s)	425	—	690	9.0	91.0	0	33.0	22.0	—	—	0.5
34378	Vanilla shake	1	serving(s)	425	—	680	9.0	78.0	0	37.0	25.0	—	—	1.0
	Jack in the Box													
30392	Bacon ultimate cheeseburger	1	item(s)	338	—	1090	46.0	53.0	2.0	77.0	30.0	—	—	3.0
1740	Breakfast Jack	1	item(s)	125	—	290	17.0	29.0	1.0	12.0	4.5	—	—	0
14074	Cheeseburger	1	item(s)	131	—	350	18.0	31.0	1.0	17.0	8.0	—	—	1.0
14106	Chicken breast strips, 4 pieces	1	serving(s)	201	—	500	35.0	36.0	3.0	25.0	6.0	—	—	6.0
37241	Chicken club salad, plain, without salad dressing	1	serving(s)	431	—	300	27.0	13.0	4.0	15.0	6.0	—	—	0
14064	Chicken sandwich	1	item(s)	145	—	400	15.0	38.0	2.0	21.0	4.5	—	—	2.5
14111	Chocolate ice cream shake, small	1	serving(s)	414	—	880	14.0	107.0	1.0	45.0	31.0	—	—	2.0
14073	Hamburger	1	item(s)	118	—	310	16.0	30.0	1.0	14.0	6.0	—	—	1.0
14090	Hash browns	1	serving(s)	57	—	150	1.0	13.0	2.0	10.0	2.5	—	—	3.0
14072	Jack's Spicy Chicken sandwich	1	item(s)	270	—	620	25.0	61.0	4.0	31.0	6.0	—	—	3.0
1468	Jumbo Jack hamburger	1	item(s)	261	—	600	21.0	51.0	3.0	35.0	12.0	—	—	1.5
1469	Jumbo Jack hamburger with cheese	1	item(s)	286	—	690	25.0	54.0	3.0	42.0	16.0	—	—	1.5
14099	Natural cut french fries, large	1	serving(s)	196	—	530	8.0	69.0	5.0	25.0	6.0	—	—	7.0
14098	Natural cut french fries, medium	1	serving(s)	133	—	360	5.0	47.0	4.0	17.0	4.0	—	—	5.0
1470	Onion rings	1	serving(s)	119	—	500	6.0	51.0	3.0	30.0	6.0	—	—	10
33141	Sausage, egg, and cheese biscuit	1	item(s)	234	—	740	27.0	35.0	2.0	55.0	17.0	—	—	6.0
14095	Seasoned curly fries, medium	1	serving(s)	125	—	400	6.0	45.0	5.0	23.0	5.0	—	—	7.0
14077	Sourdough Jack	1	item(s)	245	—	710	27.0	36.0	3.0	51.0	18.0	—	—	3.0
37249	Southwest chicken salad, plain, without salad dressing	1	serving(s)	488	—	300	24.0	29.0	7.0	11.0	5.0	—	—	0
14112	Strawberry ice cream shake, small	1	serving(s)	417	—	880	13.0	105.0	0	44.0	31.0	—	—	2.0
14078	Ultimate cheeseburger	1	item(s)	323	—	1010	40.0	53.0	2.0	71.0	28.0	—	—	3.0
14110	Vanilla ice cream shake, small	1	serving(s)	379	—	790	13.0	83.0	0	44.0	31.0	—	—	2.0
	Jamba Juice													
31645	Aloha Pineapple smoothie	24	fluid ounce(s)	730	—	500	8.0	117.0	4.0	1.5	1.0	—	—	—
31646	Banana Berry smoothie	24	fluid ounce(s)	719	—	480	5.0	112.0	4.0	1.0	0	—	—	—
31656	Berry Lime Sublime smoothie	24	fluid ounce(s)	728	—	460	3.0	106.0	5.0	2.0	1.0	—	—	—
31647	Carribean Passion smoothie	24	fluid ounce(s)	730	—	440	4.0	102.0	4.0	2.0	1.0	—	—	—
38422	Carrot juice	16	fluid ounce(s)	472	—	100	3.0	23.0	0	0.5	0	—	—	—
31648	Chocolate Moo'd smoothie	24	fluid ounce(s)	634	—	720	17.0	148.0	3.0	8.0	5.0	—	—	—
31649	Citrus Squeeze smoothie	24	fluid ounce(s)	727	—	470	5.0	110.0	4.0	2.0	1.0	—	—	—
31651	Coldbuster smoothie	24	fluid ounce(s)	724	—	430	5.0	100.0	5.0	2.5	1.0	—	—	—
31652	Cranberry Craze smoothie	24	fluid ounce(s)	793	—	460	6.0	104.0	4.0	0.5	0	—	—	—
31654	Jamba Powerboost smoothie	24	fluid ounce(s)	738	—	440	6.0	105.0	6.0	1.0	0	—	—	—
38423	Lemonade	16	fluid ounce(s)	483	—	300	1.0	75.0	0	0	0	0	0	0
31657	Mango-a-go-go smoothie	24	fluid ounce(s)	690	—	440	3.0	104.0	4.0	1.5	0.5	—	—	—
38424	Orange juice, freshly squeezed	16	fluid ounce(s)	496	—	220	3.0	52.0	0.5	1.0	0	—	—	—
38426	Orange/carrot juice	16	fluid ounce(s)	484	—	160	3.0	37.0	0	1.0	0	—	—	—
31660	Orange-a-peel smoothie	24	fluid ounce(s)	726	—	440	8.0	102.0	5.0	1.5	0	—	—	—
31662	Peach Pleasure smoothie	24	fluid ounce(s)	720	—	460	4.0	108.0	4.0	2.0	1.0	—	—	—
31665	Protein Berry Pizzaz smoothie	24	fluid ounce(s)	710	—	440	20.0	92.0	5.0	1.5	0	—	—	—
31668	Razzmatazz smoothie	24	fluid ounce(s)	730	—	480	3.0	112.0	4.0	2.0	1.0	—	—	—
31669	Strawberries Wild smoothie	24	fluid ounce(s)	725	—	450	6.0	105.0	4.0	0.5	0	—	—	—
38421	Strawberry Tsunami smoothie	24	fluid ounce(s)	740	—	530	4.0	128.0	4.0	2.0	1.0	—	—	—

CHOL (mg)	CALC (mg)	IRON (mg)	MAGN (mg)	POTA (mg)	SODI (mg)	ZINC (mg)	VIT A (μg)	THIA (mg)	VIT E (mg α)	RIBO (mg)	NIAC (mg)	VIT B_6 (mg)	FOLA (μg)	VIT C (mg)	VIT B_{12} (μg)	SELE (μg)
60	200	2.70	—	—	720.0	—	—	—	—	—	—	—	—	12.0	—	—
95	300	0.72	—	—	350.0	—	—	—	—	—	—	—	—	0	—	—
120	350	5.40	—	—	1440.0	—	—	—	—	—	—	—	—	9.0	—	—
115	350	5.40	—	—	1520.0	—	—	—	—	—	—	—	—	12.0	—	—
120	350	4.50	—	—	1160.0	—	—	—	—	—	—	—	—	12.0	—	—
0	20	1.80	—	—	245.0	—	0	—	—	—	—	—	—	0	—	—
40	40	3.60	—	—	650.0	—	—	—	—	—	—	—	—	9.0	—	—
35	40	3.60	—	—	730.0	—	—	—	—	—	—	—	—	12.0	—	—
40	40	2.70	—	—	370.0	—	—	—	—	—	—	—	—	12.0	—	—
85	300	0.00	—	—	280.0	—	—	—	—	—	—	—	—	0	—	—
90	300	0.00	—	—	390.0	—	—	—	—	—	—	—	—	0	—	—
140	308	7.38	—	540.0	2040.0	—	—	—	—	—	—	—	—	0.6	—	—
220	145	3.48	—	210.0	760.0	—	—	—	—	—	—	—	—	3.5	—	—
50	151	3.61	—	270.0	790.0	—	40.2	—	—	—	—	—	—	0	—	—
80	18	1.60	—	530.0	1260.0	—	—	—	—	—	—	—	—	1.1	—	—
65	280	3.35	—	560.0	880.0	—	—	—	—	—	—	—	—	50.4	—	—
35	100	2.70	—	240.0	730.0	—	—	—	—	—	—	—	—	4.8	—	—
135	460	0.47	—	840.0	330.0	—	—	—	—	—	—	—	—	0	—	—
40	100	3.60	—	250.0	600.0	—	0	—	—	—	—	—	—	0	—	—
0	10	0.18	—	190.0	230.0	—	0	—	—	—	—	—	—	0	—	—
50	150	1.80	—	450.0	1100.0	—	—	—	—	—	—	—	—	9.0	—	—
45	164	4.92	—	380.0	940.0	—	—	—	—	—	—	—	—	9.8	—	—
70	234	4.20	—	410.0	1310.0	—	—	—	—	—	—	—	—	8.4	—	—
0	20	1.42	—	1240.0	870.0	—	0	—	—	—	—	—	—	8.9	—	—
0	19	1.01	—	840.0	590.0	—	0	—	—	—	—	—	—	5.6	—	—
0	40	2.70	—	140.0	420.0	—	40.0	—	—	—	—	—	—	18.0	—	—
280	88	2.36	—	310.0	1430.0	—	—	—	—	—	—	—	—	0	—	—
0	40	1.80	—	580.0	890.0	—	—	—	—	—	—	—	—	0	—	—
75	200	4.50	—	430.0	1230.0	—	—	—	—	—	—	—	—	9.0	—	—
55	274	4.10	—	670.0	860.0	—	—	—	—	—	—	—	—	43.8	—	—
135	466	0.00	—	750.0	290.0	—	—	—	—	—	—	—	—	0	—	—
125	308	7.39	—	480.0	1580.0	—	—	—	—	—	—	—	—	0.6	—	—
135	532	0.00	—	750.0	280.0	—	—	—	—	—	—	—	—	0	—	—
5	200	1.80	60.0	1000.0	30.0	0.30	—	0.37	—	0.34	2.00	0.60	60.0	102.0	0	1.4
0	200	1.44	40.0	1010.0	115.0	0.60	—	0.09	—	0.25	0.80	0.70	24.0	15.0	0.2	1.4
5	200	1.80	16.0	510.0	35.0	0.30	—	0.06	—	0.25	6.00	0.70	140.0	54.0	0	1.4
5	100	1.80	24.0	810.0	60.0	0.30	—	0.09	—	0.25	5.00	0.50	100.0	78.0	0	1.4
0	150	2.70	80.0	1030.0	250.0	0.90	—	0.52	—	0.25	5.00	0.70	80.0	18.0	0	5.6
30	500	1.08	60.0	810.0	380.0	1.50	—	0.22	—	0.76	0.40	0.16	16.0	6.0	1.5	4.2
5	100	1.80	80.0	1170.0	35.0	0.30	—	0.37	—	0.34	1.90	0.60	100.0	180.0	0	1.4
5	100	1.08	60.0	1260.0	35.0	16.50	—	0.37	—	0.34	3.00	0.40	121.5	1302.0	0	1.4
0	250	1.44	16.0	500.0	50.0	0.30	—	0.03	—	0.25	5.00	0.60	120.0	54.0	0	1.4
0	1200	1.80	480.0	1070.0	45.0	16.50	—	5.55	—	6.12	68.00	7.40	640.0	288.0	10.8	77.0
0	20	0.00	8.0	200.0	10.0	0.00	—	0.03	—	0.17	14.00	1.80	320.0	36.0	0	0
5	100	1.08	24.0	780.0	50.0	0.30	—	0.15	—	0.25	5.00	0.70	120.0	72.0	0	1.4
0	60	1.08	60.0	990.0	0	0.30	—	0.45	—	0.13	2.00	0.20	160.0	246.0	0	0
0	100	1.80	60.0	1010.0	125.0	0.60	—	0.45	—	0.25	3.00	0.50	120.0	132.0	0	2.8
0	250	1.80	80.0	1380.0	160.0	0.90	—	0.45	—	0.42	2.00	0.50	140.0	240.0	0.6	1.4
5	100	0.72	32.0	740.0	60.0	0.30	—	0.06	—	0.25	4.00	0.60	80.0	18.0	0	1.4
0	1100	2.62	60.0	650.0	240.0	0.58	—	0.08	—	0.17	1.20	0.70	58.3	60.0	0	5.6
5	150	1.80	32.0	810.0	70.0	0.30	—	0.09	—	0.34	6.00	1.00	160.0	60.0	0	1.4
5	250	1.80	40.0	1050.0	180.0	0.90	—	0.12	—	0.34	0.80	0.40	40.0	60.0	0.6	1.4
5	100	1.08	24.0	480.0	10.0	0.30	—	0.06	—	0.34	14.00	1.80	320.0	90.0	0	1.4

A

TABLE A-1 Table of Food Composition *(continued)*

(Computer code is for Cengage Diet Analysis program) (For purposes of calculations, use "0" for t, <1, <.1, <.01, etc.)

DA+ Code	Food Description	Qty	Measure	Wt (g)	H_2O (g)	Ener (cal)	Prot (g)	Carb (g)	Fiber (g)	Fat (g)	Fat Breakdown (g) Sat	Mono	Poly	Trans
Fast Food—continued														
38427	Vibrant C juice	16	fluid ounce(s)	448	—	210	2.0	50.0	1.0	0	0	0	0	0
38428	Wheatgrass juice, freshly squeezed	1	ounce(s)	28	—	5	0.5	1.0	0	0	0	0	0	0
	Kentucky Fried Chicken (KFC)													
31850	BBQ baked beans	1	serving(s)	136	—	220	8.0	45.0	7.0	1.0	0	—	—	0
31853	Biscuit	1	item(s)	57	—	220	4.0	24.0	1.0	11.0	2.5	—	—	3.5
51223	Boneless Fiery Buffalo Wings	6	item(s)	211	—	530	30.0	44.0	3.0	26.0	5.0	—	—	2.5
39386	Boneless Honey BBQ Wings	6	item(s)	213	—	570	30.0	54.0	5.0	26.0	5.0	—	—	2.5
51224	Boneless Sweet & Spicy Wings	6	item(s)	203	—	550	30.0	50.0	3.0	26.0	5.0	—	—	2.5
31851	Cole slaw	1	serving(s)	130	—	180	1.0	22.0	3.0	10.0	1.5	—	—	0
31842	Colonel's Crispy Strips	3	item(s)	151	—	370	28.0	17.0	1.0	20.0	4.0	—	—	2.5
31849	Corn on the cob	1	item(s)	162	—	150	5.0	26.0	7.0	3.0	1.0	—	—	0
51221	Double Crunch sandwich	1	item(s)	213	—	520	27.0	39.0	3.0	29.0	5.0	—	—	1.5
3761	Extra Crispy chicken, breast	1	item(s)	162	—	370	33.0	10.0	2.0	22.0	5.0	—	—	1.5
3762	Extra Crispy chicken, drumstick	1	item(s)	60	—	150	12.0	4.0	0	10.0	2.5	—	—	1.0
3763	Extra Crispy chicken, thigh	1	item(s)	114	—	290	17.0	16.0	1.0	18.0	4.0	—	—	1.5
3764	Extra Crispy chicken, whole wing	1	item(s)	52	—	150	11.0	11.0	1.0	7.0	1.5	—	—	0
51218	Famous Bowls mashed potatoes with gravy	1	serving(s)	531	—	720	26.0	79.0	6.0	34.0	9.0	—	—	3.5
51219	Famous Bowls rice with gravy	1	serving(s)	384	—	610	25.0	67.0	5.0	27.0	8.0	—	—	2.5
31841	Honey BBQ chicken sandwich	1	item(s)	147	—	290	23.0	40.0	2.0	4.0	1.0	—	—	0
31833	Honey BBQ wing pieces	6	item(s)	157	—	460	27.0	26.0	3.0	27.0	6.0	—	—	2.0
10859	Hot wings pieces	6	piece(s)	134	—	450	26.0	19.0	2.0	30.0	7.0	—	—	2.0
42382	KFC Snacker sandwich	1	serving(s)	119	—	320	14.0	29.0	2.0	17.0	3.0	—	—	1.0
31848	Macaroni and cheese	1	serving(s)	136	—	180	8.0	18.0	0	8.0	3.5	—	—	1.0
31847	Mashed potatoes with gravy	1	serving(s)	151	—	140	2.0	20.0	1.0	5.0	1.0	—	—	0.5
10825	Original Recipe chicken, breast	1	item(s)	161	—	340	38.0	9.0	2.0	17.0	4.0	—	—	1.0
10826	Original Recipe chicken, drumstick	1	item(s)	59	—	140	13.0	3.0	0	8.0	2.0	—	—	0.5
10827	Original Recipe chicken, thigh	1	item(s)	126	—	350	19.0	7.0	1.0	27.0	7.0	—	—	1.0
10828	Original Recipe chicken, whole wing	1	item(s)	47	—	140	10.0	4.0	0	9.0	2.0	—	—	0.5
51222	Oven roasted Twister chicken wrap	1	item(s)	269	—	520	30.0	46.0	4.0	23.0	3.5	—	—	0
31844	Popcorn chicken, small or individual	1	item(s)	114	—	370	19.0	21.0	2.0	24.0	4.5	—	—	2.5
31852	Potato salad	1	serving(s)	128	—	180	2.0	22.0	2.0	9.0	1.5	—	—	0
10845	Potato wedges, small	1	serving(s)	102	—	250	4.0	32.0	3.0	12.0	2.0	—	—	1.5
31839	Tender Roast chicken sandwich with sauce	1	item(s)	236	—	430	37.0	29.0	2.0	18.0	3.5	—	—	0
	Long John Silver													
39392	Baked cod	1	serving(s)	101	—	120	22.0	1.0	0	4.5	1.0	—	—	0
3777	Batter dipped fish sandwich	1	item(s)	177	—	470	18.0	48.0	3.0	23.0	5.0	—	—	4.5
37568	Battered fish	1	item(s)	92	—	260	12.0	17.0	0.5	16.0	4.0	—	—	4.5
37569	Breaded clams	1	serving(s)	85	—	240	8.0	22.0	1.0	13.0	2.0	—	—	2.5
37566	Chicken plank	1	item(s)	52	—	140	8.0	9.0	0.5	8.0	2.0	—	—	2.5
39404	Clam chowder	1	item(s)	227	—	220	9.0	23.0	0	10.0	4.0	—	—	1.0
39398	Cocktail sauce	1	ounce(s)	28	—	25	0	6.0	0	0	0	0	0	0
3770	Coleslaw	1	serving(s)	113	—	200	1.0	15.0	3.0	15.0	2.5	1.8	4.1	0
39400	French fries, large	1	item(s)	142	—	390	4.0	56.0	5.0	17.0	4.0	—	—	5.0
3774	Fries, regular	1	serving(s)	85	—	230	3.0	34.0	3.0	10.0	2.5	—	—	3.0
3779	Hushpuppy	1	piece(s)	23	—	60	1.0	9.0	1.0	2.5	0.5	—	—	1.0
3781	Shrimp, batter-dipped, 1 piece	1	piece(s)	14	—	45	2.0	3.0	0	3.0	1.0	—	—	1.0
39399	Tartar sauce	1	ounce(s)	28	—	100	0	4.0	0	9.0	1.5	—	—	—
39395	Ultimate Fish sandwich	1	item(s)	199	—	530	21.0	49.0	3.0	28.0	8.0	—	—	5.0
	McDonald's													
50828	Asian salad with grilled chicken	1	item(s)	362	—	290	31.0	23.0	6.0	10.0	1.0	—	—	0
2247	Barbecue sauce	1	item(s)	28	—	45	0	11.0	0	0	0	0	0	0
737	Big Mac hamburger	1	item(s)	219	—	560	25.0	47.0	3.0	30.0	10.0	—	—	1.5
29777	Caesar salad dressing	1	package(s)	44	—	150	1.0	5.0	0	13.0	2.5	—	—	—
38391	Caesar salad with grilled chicken, no dressing	1	serving(s)	278	230.6	181	26.4	10.5	3.1	6.0	2.9	1.7	0.8	0.2
38393	Caesar salad without chicken, no dressing	1	serving(s)	190	170.4	84	6.0	8.1	3.0	3.9	2.2	0.9	0.3	0.1
738	Cheeseburger	1	item(s)	119	—	310	15.0	35.0	1.0	12.0	6.0	—	—	1.0
29775	Chicken McGrill sandwich	1	item(s)	213	—	400	27.0	38.0	3.0	16.0	3.0	—	—	0

PAGE KEY: A-2 = Breads/Baked Goods A-8 = Cereal/Rice/Pasta A-12 = Fruit A-18 = Vegetables/Legumes A-28 = Nuts/Seeds A-30 = Vegetarian A-32 = Dairy A-40 = Eggs A-40 = Seafood A-44 = Meats A-48 = Poultry A-48 = Processed Meats A-50 = Beverages A-54 = Fats/Oils A-56 = Sweets A-58 = Spices/Condiments/Sauces A-62 = Mixed Foods/Soups/Sandwiches A-68 = Fast Food A-88 = Convenience A-90 = Baby Foods

A

Chol (mg)	Calc (mg)	Iron (mg)	Magn (mg)	Pota (mg)	Sodi (mg)	Zinc (mg)	Vit A (µg)	Thia (mg)	Vit E (mg α)	Ribo (mg)	Niac (mg)	Vit B_6 (mg)	Fola (µg)	Vit C (mg)	Vit B_{12} (µg)	Sele (µg)
0	20	1.08	40.0	720.0	0	0.30	—	0.30	—	0.10	1.60	0.40	80.0	678.0	0	0
0	0	1.80	8.0	80.0	0	0.00	0	0.03	—	0.03	0.40	0.04	16.0	3.6	0	2.8
0	100	2.70	—	—	730.0	—	—	—	—	—	—	—	—	1.2	—	—
0	40	1.80	—	—	640.0	—	—	—	—	—	—	—	—	0	—	—
65	40	1.80	—	—	2670.0	—	—	—	—	—	—	—	—	1.2	—	—
65	40	1.80	—	—	2210.0	—	—	—	—	—	—	—	—	1.2	—	—
65	60	1.80	—	—	2000.0	—	—	—	—	—	—	—	—	1.2	—	—
5	40	0.72	—	—	270.0	—	—	—	—	—	—	—	—	12.0	—	—
65	40	1.44	—	—	1220.0	—	0	—	—	—	—	—	—	1.2	—	—
0	60	1.08	—	—	10.0	—	—	—	—	—	—	—	—	6.0	—	—
55	100	2.70	—	—	1220.0	—	—	—	—	—	—	—	—	6.0	—	—
85	20	2.70	—	—	1020.0	—	—	—	—	—	—	—	—	1.2	—	—
55	0	1.44	—	—	300.0	—	0	—	—	—	—	—	—	0	—	—
95	20	2.70	—	—	700.0	—	—	—	—	—	—	—	—	—	—	—
45	20	1.08	—	—	340.0	—	—	—	—	—	—	—	—	0	—	—
35	200	5.40	—	—	2330.0	—	—	—	—	—	—	—	—	6.0	—	—
35	200	4.50	—	—	2130.0	—	—	—	—	—	—	—	—	6.0	—	—
60	80	2.70	—	—	710.0	—	—	—	—	—	—	—	—	2.4	—	—
140	40	1.80	—	—	970.0	—	—	—	—	—	—	—	—	21.0	—	—
115	40	1.44	—	—	990.0	—	—	—	—	—	—	—	—	1.2	—	—
25	60	2.70	—	—	690.0	—	—	—	—	—	—	—	—	2.4	—	—
15	150	0.72	—	—	800.0	—	—	—	—	—	—	—	—	1.2	—	—
0	40	1.44	—	—	560.0	—	—	—	—	—	—	—	—	1.2	—	—
135	20	2.70	—	—	960.0	—	—	—	—	—	—	—	—	6.0	—	—
70	20	1.08	—	—	340.0	—	—	—	—	—	—	—	—	0	—	—
110	20	2.70	—	—	870.0	—	—	—	—	—	—	—	—	1.2	—	—
50	20	1.44	—	—	350.0	—	0	—	—	—	—	—	—	1.2	—	—
60	40	6.30	—	—	1380.0	—	—	—	—	—	—	—	—	15.0	—	—
25	40	1.80	—	—	1110.0	—	0	—	—	—	—	—	—	0	—	—
5	0	0.36	—	—	470.0	—	—	—	—	—	—	—	—	6.0	—	—
0	20	1.08	—	—	700.0	—	0	—	—	—	—	—	—	0	—	—
80	80	2.70	—	—	1180.0	—	—	—	—	—	—	—	—	9.0	—	—
90	20	0.72	—	—	240.0	—	—	—	—	—	—	—	—	0	—	—
45	60	2.70	—	—	1210.0	—	—	—	—	—	—	—	—	2.4	—	—
35	20	0.72	—	—	790.0	—	—	—	—	—	—	—	—	4.8	—	—
10	20	1.08	—	—	1110.0	—	0	—	—	—	—	—	—	0	—	—
20	0	0.72	—	—	480.0	—	0	—	—	—	—	—	—	2.4	—	—
25	150	0.72	—	—	810.0	—	—	—	—	—	—	—	—	0	—	—
0	0	0.00	—	—	250.0	—	—	—	—	—	—	—	—	0	—	—
20	40	0.36	—	222.7	340.0	0.70	—	0.07	—	0.08	2.34	—	—	18.0	—	—
0	0	0.00	—	—	580.0	—	0	—	—	—	—	—	—	24.0	—	—
0	0	0.00	—	370.0	350.0	0.30	0	0.09	—	0.01	1.60	—	—	15.0	—	—
0	20	0.36	—	—	200.0	—	0	—	—	—	—	—	—	0	—	—
15	0	0.00	—	—	160.0	—	0	—	—	—	—	—	—	1.2	—	—
15	0	0.00	—	—	250.0	—	0	—	—	—	—	—	—	0	—	—
60	150	2.70	—	—	1400.0	—	—	—	—	—	—	—	—	4.8	—	—
65	150	3.60	—	—	890.0	—	—	—	—	—	—	—	—	54.0	—	—
0	0	0.00	—	55.0	260.0	—	—	—	—	—	—	—	—	0	—	—
80	250	4.50	—	400.0	1010.0	—	—	—	—	—	—	—	—	1.2	—	—
10	40	0.18	—	30.0	400.0	—	—	—	—	—	—	—	—	0.6	—	—
67	178	1.77	—	708.9	767.3	—	—	0.15	—	0.19	10.62	—	127.9	29.2	0.2	—
10	163	1.15	17.1	410.4	157.7	—	—	0.08	—	0.07	0.40	—	102.6	26.8	0	0.4
40	200	2.70	—	240.0	740.0	—	60.0	—	—	—	—	—	—	1.2	—	—
70	150	2.70	—	510.0	1010.0	—	—	—	—	—	—	—	—	6.0	—	—

TABLE A-1 **Table of Food Composition** *(continued)*

(Computer code is for Cengage Diet Analysis program) (For purposes of calculations, use "0" for t, <1, <.1, <.01, etc.)

DA+ Code	Food Description	QTY	Measure	Wt (g)	H_2O (g)	Ener (cal)	Prot (g)	Carb (g)	Fiber (g)	Fat (g)	Fat Breakdown (g) Sat	Mono	Poly	Trans
Fast Food—continued														
1873	Chicken McNuggets, 6 piece	1	serving(s)	96	—	250	15.0	15.0	0	15.0	3.0	—	—	1.5
3792	Chicken McNuggets, 4 piece	1	serving(s)	64	—	170	10.0	10.0	0	10.0	2.0	—	—	1.0
29774	Crispy chicken sandwich	1	item(s)	232	121.8	500	27.0	63.0	3.0	16.0	3.0	5.7	7.4	1.5
743	Egg McMuffin	1	item(s)	139	76.8	300	17.0	30.0	2.0	12.0	4.5	3.8	2.5	0
742	Filet-O-Fish sandwich	1	item(s)	141	—	400	14.0	42.0	1.0	18.0	4.0	—	—	1.0
2257	French fries, large	1	serving(s)	170	—	570	6.0	70.0	7.0	30.0	6.0	—	—	8.0
1872	French fries, small	1	serving(s)	74	—	250	2.0	30.0	3.0	13.0	2.5	—	—	3.5
33822	Fruit 'n Yogurt Parfait	1	item(s)	149	111.2	160	4.0	31.0	1.0	2.0	1.0	0.2	0.1	0
739	Hamburger	1	item(s)	105	—	260	13.0	33.0	1.0	9.0	3.5	—	—	0.5
2003	Hash browns	1	item(s)	53	—	140	1.0	15.0	2.0	8.0	1.5	—	—	2.0
2249	Honey sauce	1	item(s)	14	—	50	0	12.0	0	0	0	0	0	0
38397	Newman's Own creamy caesar salad dressing	1	item(s)	59	32.5	190	2.0	4.0	0	18.0	3.5	4.6	9.6	0
38398	Newman's Own low fat balsamic vinaigrette salad dressing	1	item(s)	44	29.1	40	0	4.0	0	3.0	0	1.0	1.2	0
38399	Newman's Own ranch salad dressing	1	item(s)	59	30.1	170	1.0	9.0	0	15.0	2.5	9.0	3.7	0
1874	Plain Hotcakes with syrup and margarine	3	item(s)	221	—	600	9.0	102.0	2.0	17.0	4.0	—	—	4.0
740	Quarter Pounder hamburger	1	item(s)	171	—	420	24.0	40.0	3.0	18.0	7.0	—	—	1.0
741	Quarter Pounder hamburger with cheese	1	item(s)	199	—	510	29.0	43.0	3.0	25.0	12.0	—	—	1.5
2005	Sausage McMuffin with egg	1	item(s)	165	82.4	450	20.0	31.0	2.0	27.0	10.0	10.9	4.6	0.5
50831	Side salad	1	item(s)	87	—	20	1.0	4.0	1.0	0	0	0	0	0
	Pizza Hut													
39009	Hot chicken wings	2	item(s)	57	—	110	11.0	1.0	0	6.0	2.0	—	—	0.3
14025	Meat Lovers hand tossed pizza	1	slice(s)	118	—	300	15.0	29.0	2.0	13.0	6.0	—	—	0.5
14026	Meat Lovers pan pizza	1	slice(s)	123	—	340	15.0	29.0	2.0	19.0	7.0	—	—	0.5
31009	Meat Lovers stuffed crust pizza	1	slice(s)	169	—	450	21.0	43.0	3.0	21.0	10.0	—	—	1.0
14024	Meat Lovers thin 'n crispy pizza	1	slice(s)	98	—	270	13.0	21.0	2.0	14.0	6.0	—	—	0.5
14031	Pepperoni Lovers hand tossed pizza	1	slice(s)	113	—	300	15.0	30.0	2.0	13.0	7.0	—	—	0.5
14032	Pepperoni Lovers pan pizza	1	slice(s)	118	—	340	15.0	29.0	2.0	19.0	7.0	—	—	0.5
31011	Pepperoni Lovers stuffed crust pizza	1	slice(s)	163	—	420	21.0	43.0	3.0	19.0	10.0	—	—	1.0
14030	Pepperoni Lovers thin 'n crispy pizza	1	slice(s)	92	—	260	13.0	21.0	2.0	14.0	7.0	—	—	0.5
10834	Personal Pan pepperoni pizza	1	slice(s)	61	—	170	7.0	18.0	0.5	8.0	3.0	—	—	1.0
10842	Personal Pan supreme pizza	1	slice(s)	77	—	190	8.0	19.0	1.0	9.0	3.5	—	—	1.0
39013	Personal Pan Veggie Lovers pizza	1	slice(s)	69	—	150	6.0	19.0	1.0	6.0	2.0	—	—	0.5
14028	Veggie Lovers hand tossed pizza	1	slice(s)	118	—	220	10.0	31.0	2.0	6.0	3.0	—	—	0.3
14029	Veggie Lovers pan pizza	1	slice(s)	119	—	260	10.0	30.0	2.0	12.0	4.0	—	—	0.3
31010	Veggie Lovers stuffed crust pizza	1	slice(s)	172	—	360	16.0	45.0	3.0	14.0	7.0	—	—	0.5
14027	Veggie Lovers thin 'n crispy pizza	1	slice(s)	101	—	180	8.0	23.0	2.0	7.0	3.0	—	—	0.5
39012	Wing blue cheese dipping sauce	1	item(s)	43	—	230	2.0	2.0	0	24.0	5.0	—	—	1.0
39011	Wing ranch dipping sauce	1	item(s)	43	—	210	0.5	4.0	0	22.0	3.5	—	—	0.5
	Starbucks													
38052	Cappuccino, tall	12	fluid ounce(s)	360	—	120	7.0	10.0	0	6.0	4.0	—	—	—
38053	Cappuccino, tall nonfat	12	fluid ounce(s)	360	—	80	7.0	11.0	0	0	0	0	0	0
38054	Cappuccino, tall soymilk	12	fluid ounce(s)	360	—	100	5.0	13.0	0.5	2.5	0	—	—	—
38059	Cinnamon spice mocha, tall nonfat w/o whipped cream	12	fluid ounce(s)	360	—	170	11.0	32.0	0	0.5	—	—	—	—
38057	Cinnamon spice mocha, tall w/whipped cream	12	fluid ounce(s)	360	—	320	10.0	31.0	0	17.0	11.0	—	—	—
38051	Espresso, single shot	1	fluid ounce(s)	30	—	5	0	1.0	0	0	0	0	0	0
38088	Flavored syrup, 1 pump	1	serving(s)	10	—	20	0	5.0	0	0	0	0	0	0
32562	Frappuccino bottled coffee drink, mocha	9½	fluid ounce(s)	298	—	190	6.0	39.0	3.0	3.0	2.0	—	—	—
32561	Frappuccino coffee drink, all bottled flavors	9½	fluid ounce(s)	281	—	190	7.0	35.0	0	3.5	2.5	—	—	—
38073	Frappuccino, mocha	12	fluid ounce(s)	360	—	220	5.0	44.0	0	3.0	1.5	—	—	—
38067	Frappuccino, tall caramel w/o whipped cream	12	fluid ounce(s)	360	—	210	4.0	43.0	0	2.5	1.5	—	—	—
38070	Frappuccino, tall coffee	12	fluid ounce(s)	360	—	190	4.0	38.0	0	2.5	1.5	—	—	—
39894	Frappuccino, tall coffee, light blend	12	fluid ounce(s)	360	—	110	5.0	22.0	2.0	1.0	0	—	—	—

PAGE KEY: A-2 = Breads/Baked Goods A-8 = Cereal/Rice/Pasta A-12 = Fruit A-18 = Vegetables/Legumes A-28 = Nuts/Seeds A-30 = Vegetarian A-32 = Dairy A-40 = Eggs A-40 = Seafood A-44 = Meats A-48 = Poultry A-48 = Processed Meats A-50 = Beverages A-54 = Fats/Oils A-56 = Sweets A-58 = Spices/Condiments/Sauces A-62 = Mixed Foods/Soups/Sandwiches A-68 = Fast Food A-88 = Convenience A-90 = Baby Foods

Chol (mg)	Calc (mg)	Iron (mg)	Magn (mg)	Pota (mg)	Sodi (mg)	Zinc (mg)	Vit A (µg)	Thia (mg)	Vit E (mg α)	Ribo (mg)	Niac (mg)	Vit B_6 (mg)	Fola (µg)	Vit C (mg)	Vit B_{12} (µg)	Sele (µg)
35	20	0.72	—	240.0	670.0	—	—	—	—	—	—	—	—	1.2	—	—
25	0	0.36	—	160.0	450.0	—	—	—	—	—	—	—	—	1.2	—	—
60	80	3.60	62.6	526.6	1380.0	1.53	41.8	0.46	2.27	0.39	12.85	—	104.4	6.0	0.4	—
230	300	2.70	26.4	218.2	860.0	1.59	—	0.36	0.82	0.51	4.31	0.20	109.8	1.2	0.9	—
40	150	1.80	—	250.0	640.0	—	36.2	—	—	—	—	—	—	0	—	—
0	20	1.80	—	—	330.0	—	0	—	—	—	—	—	—	9.0	—	—
0	20	0.72	—	—	140.0	—	0	—	—	—	—	—	—	3.6	—	—
5	150	0.67	20.9	248.8	85.0	0.53	0	0.06	—	0.17	0.35	—	19.4	9.0	0.3	—
30	150	2.70	—	210.0	530.0	—	5.0	—	—	—	—	—	—	1.2	—	—
0	0	0.36	—	210.0	290.0	—	0	—	—	—	—	—	—	1.2	—	—
0	0	0.00	—	0	0	—	0	—	—	—	—	—	—	0	—	—
20	61	0.00	3.0	16.0	500.0	0.20	—	0.01	15.43	0.02	0.01	0.64	2.4	0	0.1	0.1
0	4	0.00	1.3	8.8	730.0	0.01	—	0.00	0.00	0.00	0.00	0.00	0	2.4	0	0
0	40	0.00	1.8	70.4	530.0	0.03	0	0.01	—	0.08	0.01	0.02	0.6	0	0	0.2
20	150	2.70	—	280.0	620.0	—	—	—	—	—	—	—	—	0	—	—
70	150	4.50	—	390.0	730.0	—	10.0	—	—	—	—	—	—	1.2	—	—
95	300	4.50	—	440.0	1150.0	—	100.0	—	—	—	—	—	—	1.2	—	—
255	300	3.60	29.7	282.2	950.0	2.01	—	0.43	0.82	0.56	4.83	0.24	—	0	1.2	—
0	20	0.72	—	—	10.0	—	—	—	—	—	—	—	—	15.0	—	—
70	0	0.36	—	—	450.0	—	—	—	—	—	—	—	—	0	—	—
35	150	1.80	—	—	760.0	—	—	—	—	—	—	—	—	6.0	—	—
35	150	2.70	—	—	750.0	—	—	—	—	—	—	—	—	6.0	—	—
55	250	2.70	—	—	1250.0	—	—	—	—	—	—	—	—	9.0	—	—
35	150	1.44	—	—	740.0	—	—	—	—	—	—	—	—	6.0	—	—
40	200	1.80	—	—	710.0	—	57.7	—	—	—	—	—	—	2.4	—	—
40	200	2.70	—	—	700.0	—	57.7	—	—	—	—	—	—	2.4	—	—
55	300	2.70	—	—	1120.0	—	—	—	—	—	—	—	—	3.6	—	—
40	200	1.44	—	—	690.0	—	58.0	—	—	—	—	—	—	2.4	—	—
15	80	1.44	—	—	340.0	—	38.5	—	—	—	—	—	—	1.4	—	—
20	80	1.86	—	—	420.0	—	—	—	—	—	—	—	—	3.6	—	—
10	80	1.80	—	—	280.0	—	—	—	—	—	—	—	—	3.6	—	—
15	150	1.80	—	—	490.0	—	—	—	—	—	—	—	—	9.0	—	—
15	150	2.70	—	—	470.0	—	—	—	—	—	—	—	—	9.0	—	—
35	250	2.70	—	—	980.0	—	—	—	—	—	—	—	—	9.0	—	—
15	150	1.44	—	—	480.0	—	—	—	—	—	—	—	—	9.0	—	—
25	20	0.00	—	—	550.0	—	0	—	—	—	—	—	—	0	—	—
10	0	0.00	—	—	340.0	—	0	—	—	—	—	—	—	0	—	—
25	250	0.00	—	—	95.0	—	—	—	—	—	—	—	—	1.2	0	—
3	200	0.00	—	—	100.0	—	—	—	—	—	—	—	—	0	0	—
0	250	0.72	—	—	75.0	—	—	—	—	—	—	—	—	0	0	—
5	300	0.72	—	—	150.0	—	—	—	—	—	—	—	—	0	0	—
70	350	1.08	—	—	140.0	—	—	—	—	—	—	—	—	2.4	0	—
0	0	0.00	—	—	0	—	0	—	—	—	—	—	—	0	0	—
0	0	0.00	—	—	0	—	0	—	—	—	—	—	—	0	0	—
12	219	1.08	—	530.0	110.0	—	—	—	—	—	—	—	—	0	—	—
15	250	0.36	—	510.0	105.0	—	—	—	—	—	—	—	—	0	—	—
10	150	0.72	—	—	180.0	—	—	—	—	—	—	—	—	0	0	—
10	150	0.00	—	—	180.0	—	—	—	—	—	—	—	—	0	0	—
10	150	0.00	—	—	180.0	—	—	—	—	—	—	—	—	0	0	—
0	150	0.00	—	—	220.0	—	—	—	—	—	—	—	—	0	—	—

TABLE A-1 Table of Food Composition *(continued)*

(Computer code is for Cengage Diet Analysis program) (For purposes of calculations, use "0" for t, <1, <.1, <.01, etc.)

											Fat Breakdown (g)			
DA+ Code	Food Description	QTY	Measure	Wt (g)	H_2O (g)	Ener (cal)	Prot (g)	Carb (g)	Fiber (g)	Fat (g)	Sat	Mono	Poly	Trans
	Fast Food—continued													
38071	Frappuccino, tall espresso	12	fluid ounce(s)	360	—	160	4.0	33.0	0	2.0	1.5	—	—	—
39897	Frappuccino, tall mocha, light blend	12	fluid ounce(s)	360	—	140	5.0	28.0	3.0	1.5	0	—	—	—
39887	Frappuccino, tall Strawberries and Creme, w/o whipped cream	12	fluid ounce(s)	360	—	330	10.0	65.0	0	3.5	1.0	—	—	—
38063	Frappuccino, tall Tazo chai creme w/o whipped cream	12	fluid ounce(s)	360	—	280	10.0	52.0	0	3.5	1.0	—	—	—
38066	Frappuccino, tall Tazoberry	12	fluid ounce(s)	360	—	140	0.5	36.0	0.5	0	0	0	0	0
38065	Frappuccino, tall Tazoberry Crème	12	fluid ounce(s)	360	—	240	4.0	54.0	0.5	1.0	0	—	—	—
38080	Frappuccino, tall vanilla w/o whipped cream	12	fluid ounce(s)	360	—	270	10.0	51.0	0	3.5	1.0	—	—	—
39898	Frappuccino, tall white chocolate mocha, light blend	12	fluid ounce(s)	360	—	160	6.0	32.0	2.0	2.0	1.0	—	—	—
38074	Frappuccino, tall white chocolate w/o whipped cream	12	fluid ounce(s)	360	—	240	5.0	48.0	0	3.5	2.5	—	—	—
39883	Java Chip Frappuccino, tall w/o whipped cream	12	fluid ounce(s)	360	—	270	5.0	51.0	1.0	7.0	4.5	—	—	—
33111	Latte, tall w/nonfat milk	12	fluid ounce(s)	360	335.3	120	12.0	18.0	0	0	0	0	0	0
33112	Latte, tall w/whole milk	12	fluid ounce(s)	360	—	200	11.0	16.0	0	11.0	7.0	—	—	—
33109	Macchiato, tall caramel w/nonfat milk	12	fluid ounce(s)	360	—	170	11.0	30.0	0	1.0	0	—	—	—
33110	Macchiato, tall caramel w/whole milk	12	fluid ounce(s)	360	—	240	10.0	28.0	0	10.0	6.0	—	—	—
33107	Mocha coffee drink, tall nonfat, w/o whipped cream	12	fluid ounce(s)	360	—	170	11.0	33.0	1.0	1.5	0	—	—	—
38089	Mocha syrup	1	serving(s)	17	—	25	1.0	6.0	0	0.5	0	—	—	—
33108	Mocha, tall mocha w/whole milk	12	fluid ounce(s)	360	—	310	10.0	32.0	1.0	17.0	10.0	—	—	—
38042	Steamed apple cider, tall	12	fluid ounce(s)	360	—	180	0	45.0	0	0	0	0	0	0
38087	Tazo chai black tea, soymilk, tall	12	fluid ounce(s)	360	—	190	4.0	39.0	0.5	2.0	0	—	—	—
38084	Tazo chai black tea, tall	12	fluid ounce(s)	360	—	210	6.0	36.0	0	5.0	3.5	—	—	—
38083	Tazo chai black tea, tall nonfat	12	fluid ounce(s)	360	—	170	6.0	37.0	0	0	0	0	0	0
38076	Tazo iced tea, tall	12	fluid ounce(s)	360	—	60	0	16.0	0	0	0	0	0	0
38077	Tazo tea, grande lemonade	16	fluid ounce(s)	480	—	120	0	31.0	0	0	0	0	0	0
38045	Vanilla crème steamed nonfat milk, tall w/whipped cream	12	fluid ounce(s)	360	—	260	11.0	33.0	0	8.0	5.0	—	—	—
38046	Vanilla crème steamed soymilk, tall w/whipped cream	12	fluid ounce(s)	360	—	300	8.0	37.0	1.0	12.0	6.0	—	—	—
38044	Vanilla crème steamed whole milk, tall w/whipped cream	12	fluid ounce(s)	360	—	330	10.0	31.0	0	18.0	11.0	—	—	—
38090	Whipped cream	1	serving(s)	27	—	100	0	2.0	0	9.0	6.0	—	—	—
38062	White chocolate mocha, tall nonfat w/o whipped cream	12	fluid ounce(s)	360	—	260	12.0	45.0	0	4.0	3.0	—	—	—
38061	White chocolate mocha, tall w/ whipped cream	12	fluid ounce(s)	360	—	410	11.0	44.0	0	20.0	13.0	—	—	—
38048	White hot chocolate, tall nonfat w/o whipped cream	12	fluid ounce(s)	360	—	300	15.0	51.0	0	4.5	3.5	—	—	—
38050	White hot chocolate, tall soymilk w/ whipped cream	12	fluid ounce(s)	360	—	420	11.0	56.0	1.0	16.0	9.0	—	—	—
38047	White hot chocolate, tall w/whipped cream	12	fluid ounce(s)	360	—	460	13.0	50.0	0	22.0	15.0	—	—	—
	Subway													
15842	Cheese steak sandwich, 6″, wheat bread	1	item(s)	250	—	360	24.0	47.0	5.0	10.0	4.5	—	—	0
40478	Chicken and bacon ranch sandwich, 6″, white or wheat bread	1	serving(s)	297	—	540	36.0	47.0	5.0	25.0	10.0	—	—	0.5
38622	Chicken and bacon ranch wrap with cheese	1	item(s)	257	—	440	41.0	18.0	9.0	27.0	10.0	—	—	0.5
32045	Chocolate chip cookie	1	item(s)	45	—	210	2.0	30.0	1.0	10.0	6.0	—	—	0
32048	Chocolate chip M&M cookie	1	item(s)	45	—	210	2.0	32.0	0.5	10.0	5.0	—	—	0
32049	Chocolate chunk cookie	1	item(s)	45	—	220	2.0	30.0	0.5	10.0	5.0	—	—	0
4024	Classic Italian B.M.T. sandwich, 6″, white bread	1	item(s)	236	—	440	22.0	45.0	2.0	21.0	8.5	—	—	0

Chol (mg)	Calc (mg)	Iron (mg)	Magn (mg)	Pota (mg)	Sodi (mg)	Zinc (mg)	Vit A (μg)	Thia (mg)	Vit E (mg α)	Ribo (mg)	Niac (mg)	Vit B_6 (mg)	Fola (μg)	Vit C (mg)	Vit B_{12} (μg)	Sele (μg)
10	100	0.00	—	—	160.0	—	—	—	—	—	—	—	—	0	0	—
0	150	0.72	—	—	220.0	—	—	—	—	—	—	—	—	0	—	—
3	350	0.00	—	—	270.0	—	—	—	—	—	—	—	—	21.0	—	—
3	350	0.00	—	—	270.0	—	—	—	—	—	—	—	—	3.6	0	—
0	0	0.00	—	—	30.0	—	0	—	—	—	—	—	—	0	0	—
0	150	0.00	—	—	125.0	—	0	—	—	—	—	—	—	1.2	0	—
3	350	0.00	—	—	370.0	—	—	—	—	—	—	—	—	3.6	0	—
3	150	0.00	—	—	250.0	—	—	—	—	—	—	—	—	0	—	—
10	150	0.00	—	—	210.0	—	—	—	—	—	—	—	—	0	0	—
10	150	1.44	—	—	220.0	—	—	—	—	—	—	—	—	0	—	—
5	350	0.00	39.8	—	170.0	1.35	—	0.12	—	0.47	0.36	0.13	17.5	0	1.3	—
45	400	0.00	46.6	—	160.0	1.28	—	0.12	—	0.54	0.34	0.14	16.8	2.4	1.2	—
5	300	0.00	—	—	160.0	—	—	—	—	—	—	—	—	1.2	—	—
30	300	0.00	—	—	135.0	—	—	—	—	—	—	—	—	2.4	—	—
5	300	2.70	—	—	135.0	—	—	—	—	—	—	—	—	0	—	—
0	0	0.72	—	—	0	—	0	—	—	—	—	—	—	0	0	—
55	300	2.70	—	—	115.0	—	—	—	—	—	—	—	—	0	—	—
0	0	1.08	—	—	15.0	—	0	—	—	—	—	—	—	0	0	—
0	200	0.72	—	—	70.0	—	—	—	—	—	—	—	—	0	0	—
20	200	0.36	—	—	85.0	—	—	—	—	—	—	—	—	1.2	0	—
5	200	0.36	—	—	95.0	—	—	—	—	—	—	—	—	0	0	—
0	0	0.00	—	—	0	—	0	—	—	—	—	—	—	0	0	—
0	0	0.00	—	—	15.0	—	0	—	—	—	—	—	—	4.8	0	—
35	350	0.00	—	—	170.0	—	—	—	—	—	—	—	—	0	0	—
30	400	1.44	—	—	130.0	—	—	—	—	—	—	—	—	0	0	—
65	350	0.00	—	—	140.0	—	—	—	—	—	—	—	—	0	0	—
40	0	0.00	—	—	10.0	—	—	—	—	—	—	—	—	0	0	—
5	400	0.00	—	—	210.0	—	—	—	—	—	—	—	—	0	0	—
70	400	0.00	—	—	210.0	—	—	—	—	—	—	—	—	2.4	0	—
10	450	0.00	—	—	250.0	—	—	—	—	—	—	—	—	0	0	—
35	500	1.44	—	—	210.0	—	—	—	—	—	—	—	—	0	0	—
75	500	0.00	—	—	250.0	—	—	—	—	—	—	—	—	3.6	0	—
35	150	8.10	—	—	1090.0	—	—	—	—	—	—	—	—	18.0	—	—
90	250	4.50	—	—	1400.0	—	—	—	—	—	—	—	—	21.0	—	—
90	300	2.70	—	—	1680.0	—	—	—	—	—	—	—	—	9.0	—	—
15	0	1.08	—	—	150.0	—	—	—	—	—	—	—	—	0	—	—
10	20	1.00	—	—	100.0	—	—	—	—	—	—	—	—	0	—	—
10	0	1.00	—	—	100.0	—	—	—	—	—	—	—	—	0	—	—
55	150	2.70	—	—	1770.0	—	—	—	—	—	—	—	—	16.8	—	—

TABLE A-1 Table of Food Composition *(continued)*

(Computer code is for Cengage Diet Analysis program) (For purposes of calculations, use "0" for t, <1, <.1, <.01, etc.)

											Fat Breakdown (g)			
DA+ Code	Food Description	QTY	Measure	Wt (g)	H_2O (g)	Ener (cal)	Prot (g)	Carb (g)	Fiber (g)	Fat (g)	Sat	Mono	Poly	Trans
Fast Food—continued														
15838	Classic tuna sandwich, 6", wheat bread	1	item(s)	250	—	530	22.0	45.0	4.0	31.0	7.0	—	—	0.5
15837	Classic tuna sandwich, 6", white bread	1	item(s)	243	—	520	21.0	43.0	2.0	31.0	7.5	—	—	0.5
16397	Club salad, no dressing and croutons	1	item(s)	412	—	160	18.0	15.0	4.0	4.0	1.5	—	—	0
3422	Club sandwich, 6", white bread	1	item(s)	250	—	310	23.0	45.0	2.0	6.0	2.5	—	—	0
4030	Cold cut combo sandwich, 6", white bread	1	item(s)	242	—	400	20.0	45.0	2.0	17.0	7.5	—	—	0.5
34030	Ham and egg breakfast sandwich	1	item(s)	142	—	310	16.0	35.0	3.0	13.0	3.5	—	—	0
3885	Ham sandwich, 6", white bread	1	item(s)	238	—	310	17.0	52.0	2.0	5.0	2.0	—	—	0
3888	Meatball marinara sandwich, 6", wheat bread	1	item(s)	377	—	560	24.0	63.0	7.0	24.0	11.0	—	—	1.0
4651	Meatball sandwich, 6", white bread	1	item(s)	370	—	550	23.0	61.0	5.0	24.0	11.5	—	—	1.0
15839	Melt sandwich, 6", white bread	1	item(s)	260	—	410	25.0	47.0	4.0	15.0	5.0	—	—	—
32046	Oatmeal raisin cookie	1	item(s)	45	—	200	3.0	30.0	1.0	8.0	4.0	—	—	0
16379	Oven-roasted chicken breast sandwich, 6", wheat bread	1	item(s)	238	—	330	24.0	48.0	5.0	5.0	1.5	—	—	0
32047	Peanut butter cookie	1	item(s)	45	—	220	4.0	26.0	1.0	12.0	5.0	—	—	0
4655	Roast beef sandwich, 6", wheat bread	1	item(s)	224	—	290	19.0	45.0	4.0	5.0	2.0	—	—	0
3957	Roast beef sandwich, 6", white bread	1	item(s)	217	—	280	18.0	43.0	2.0	5.0	2.5	—	—	0
16378	Roasted chicken breast, 6", white bread	1	item(s)	231	—	320	23.0	46.0	3.0	5.0	2.0	—	—	0
34028	Southwest steak and cheese sandwich, 6", Italian bread	1	item(s)	271	—	450	24.0	48.0	6.0	20.0	6.0	—	—	0
4032	Spicy Italian sandwich, 6", white bread	1	item(s)	220	—	470	20.0	43.0	2.0	25.0	9.5	—	—	0
4031	Steak and cheese sandwich, 6", white bread	1	item(s)	243	—	350	23.0	45.0	3.0	10.0	5.0	—	—	0
32050	Sugar cookie	1	item(s)	45	—	220	2.0	28.0	0.5	12.0	6.0	—	—	0
40477	Sweet onion chicken teriyaki sandwich, 6", white or wheat bread	1	serving(s)	281	—	370	26.0	59.0	4.0	5.0	1.5	—	—	0
38623	Turkey breast and bacon melt wrap with chipotle sauce	1	item(s)	228	—	380	31.0	20.0	9.0	24.0	7.0	—	—	0
15834	Turkey breast and ham sandwich, 6", white bread	1	item(s)	227	—	280	19.0	45.0	2.0	5.0	2.0	—	—	0
16376	Turkey breast sandwich, 6", white bread	1	item(s)	217	—	270	17.0	44.0	2.0	4.5	2.0	—	—	0
15841	Veggie Delite sandwich, 6", wheat bread	1	item(s)	167	—	230	9.0	44.0	4.0	3.0	1.0	—	—	0
16375	Veggie Delite, 6", white bread	1	item(s)	160	—	220	8.0	42.0	2.0	3.0	1.5	—	—	0
32051	White chip macadamia nut cookie	1	item(s)	45	—	220	2.0	29.0	0.5	11.0	5.0	—	—	0
	Taco Bell													
29906	7-Layer burrito	1	item(s)	283	—	490	17.0	65.0	9.0	18.0	7.0	—	—	1.0
744	Bean burrito	1	item(s)	198	—	340	13.0	54.0	8.0	9.0	3.5	—	—	0.5
749	Beef burrito supreme	1	item(s)	248	—	410	17.0	51.0	7.0	17.0	8.0	—	—	1.0
33417	Beef Chalupa Supreme	1	item(s)	153	—	380	14.0	30.0	3.0	23.0	7.0	—	—	0.5
34474	Beef Gordita Baja	1	item(s)	153	—	340	13.0	29.0	4.0	19.0	5.0	—	—	0
29910	Beef Gordita Supreme	1	item(s)	153	—	310	14.0	29.0	3.0	16.0	6.0	—	—	0.5
2014	Beef soft taco	1	item(s)	99	—	200	10.0	21.0	3.0	9.0	4.0	—	—	0
10860	Beef soft taco supreme	1	item(s)	135	—	250	11.0	23.0	3.0	13.0	6.0	—	—	0.5
34472	Chicken burrito supreme	1	item(s)	248	—	390	20.0	49.0	6.0	13.0	6.0	—	—	0.5
33418	Chicken Chalupa Supreme	1	item(s)	153	—	360	17.0	29.0	2.0	20.0	5.0	—	—	0
34475	Chicken Gordita Baja	1	item(s)	153	—	320	17.0	28.0	3.0	16.0	3.5	—	—	0
29909	Chicken quesadilla	1	item(s)	184	—	520	28.0	40.0	3.0	28.0	12.0	—	—	0.5
29907	Chili cheese burrito	1	item(s)	156	—	390	16.0	40.0	3.0	18.0	9.0	—	—	1.5
10794	Cinnamon twists	1	serving(s)	35	—	170	1.0	26.0	1.0	7.0	0	—	—	0
29911	Grilled chicken Gordita Supreme	1	item(s)	153	—	290	17.0	28.0	2.0	12.0	5.0	—	—	0
14463	Grilled chicken soft taco	1	item(s)	99	—	190	14.0	19.0	1.0	6.0	2.5	—	—	—

Chol (mg)	Calc (mg)	Iron (mg)	Magn (mg)	Pota (mg)	Sodi (mg)	Zinc (mg)	Vit A (µg)	Thia (mg)	Vit E (mg α)	Ribo (mg)	Niac (mg)	Vit B_6 (mg)	Fola (µg)	Vit C (mg)	Vit B_{12} (µg)	Sele (µg)
45	100	5.40	—	—	1030.0	—	—	—	—	—	—	—	—	21.0	—	—
45	100	3.60	—	—	1010.0	—	—	—	—	—	—	—	—	16.8	—	—
35	60	3.60	—	—	880.0	—	—	—	—	—	—	—	—	30.0	—	—
35	60	3.60	—	—	1290.0	—	—	—	—	—	—	—	—	13.8	—	—
60	150	3.60	—	—	1530.0	—	—	—	—	—	—	—	—	16.8	—	—
190	80	4.50	—	—	720.0	—	66.7	—	—	—	—	—	—	3.6	—	—
25	60	2.70	—	—	1375.0	—	—	—	—	—	—	—	—	13.8	—	—
45	200	7.20	—	—	1610.0	—	—	—	—	—	—	—	—	36.0	—	—
45	200	5.40	—	—	1590.0	—	—	—	—	—	—	—	—	31.8	—	—
45	150	5.40	—	—	1720.0	—	—	—	—	—	—	—	—	24.0	—	—
15	20	1.08	—	—	170.0	—	—	—	—	—	—	—	—	0	—	—
45	60	4.50	—	—	1020.0	—	—	—	—	—	—	—	—	18.0	—	—
15	20	0.72	—	—	200.0	—	—	—	—	—	—	—	—	0	—	—
20	60	6.30	—	—	920.0	—	—	—	—	—	—	—	—	18.0	—	—
20	60	4.50	—	—	900.0	—	—	—	—	—	—	—	—	13.8	—	—
45	60	2.70	—	—	1000.0	—	—	—	—	—	—	—	—	13.8	—	—
45	150	8.10	—	—	1310.0	—	—	—	—	—	—	—	—	21.0	—	—
55	60	2.70	—	—	1650.0	—	—	—	—	—	—	—	—	16.8	—	—
35	150	6.30	—	—	1070.0	—	—	—	—	—	—	—	—	13.8	—	—
15	0	0.72	—	—	140.0	—	—	—	—	—	—	—	—	0	—	—
50	80	4.50	—	—	1220.0	—	—	—	—	—	—	—	—	24.0	—	—
50	200	2.70	—	—	1780.0	—	—	—	—	—	—	—	—	6.0	—	—
25	60	2.70	—	—	1210.0	—	—	—	—	—	—	—	—	13.8	—	—
20	60	2.70	—	—	1000.0	—	—	—	—	—	—	—	—	13.8	—	—
0	60	4.50	—	—	520.0	—	—	—	—	—	—	—	—	18.0	—	—
0	60	2.70	—	—	500.0	—	—	—	—	—	—	—	—	13.8	—	—
15	20	0.72	—	—	160.0	—	—	—	—	—	—	—	—	0	—	—
25	250	5.40	—	—	1350.0	—	—	—	—	—	—	—	—	15.0	—	—
5	200	4.50	—	—	1190.0	—	5.9	—	—	—	—	—	—	4.8	—	—
40	200	4.50	—	—	1340.0	—	9.9	—	—	—	—	—	—	6.0	—	—
40	150	2.70	—	—	620.0	—	—	—	—	—	—	—	—	3.6	—	—
35	100	2.70	—	—	780.0	—	—	—	—	—	—	—	—	2.4	—	—
40	150	2.70	—	—	620.0	—	—	—	—	—	—	—	—	3.6	—	—
25	100	1.80	—	—	630.0	—	—	—	—	—	—	—	—	1.2	—	—
40	150	2.70	—	—	650.0	—	—	—	—	—	—	—	—	3.6	—	—
45	200	4.50	—	—	1360.0	—	—	—	—	—	—	—	—	9.0	—	—
45	100	2.70	—	—	650.0	—	—	—	—	—	—	—	—	4.8	—	—
40	100	1.80	—	—	800.0	—	—	—	—	—	—	—	—	3.6	—	—
75	450	3.60	—	—	1420.0	—	—	—	—	—	—	—	—	1.2	—	—
40	300	1.80	—	—	1080.0	—	—	—	—	—	—	—	—	0	—	—
0	0	0.37	—	—	200.0	—	0	—	—	—	—	—	—	0	—	—
45	150	1.80	—	—	650.0	—	—	—	—	—	—	—	—	4.8	—	—
30	100	1.08	—	—	550.0	—	14.6	—	—	—	—	—	—	1.2	—	—

TABLE A-1 Table of Food Composition *(continued)*

(Computer code is for Cengage Diet Analysis program) (For purposes of calculations, use "0" for t, <1, <.1, <.01, etc.)

											Fat Breakdown (g)			
DA+ Code	Food Description	Qty	Measure	Wt (g)	H_2O (g)	Ener (cal)	Prot (g)	Carb (g)	Fiber (g)	Fat (g)	Sat	Mono	Poly	*Trans*
	Fast Food—continued													
29912	Grilled Steak Gordita Supreme	1	item(s)	153	—	290	15.0	28.0	2.0	13.0	5.0	—	—	0
29904	Grilled steak soft taco	1	item(s)	128	—	270	12.0	20.0	2.0	16.0	4.5	—	—	0
29905	Grilled steak soft taco supreme	1	item(s)	135	—	235	13.0	21.0	1.0	11.0	6.0	—	—	—
2021	Mexican pizza	1	serving(s)	216	—	530	20.0	42.0	7.0	30.0	8.0	—	—	1.0
29894	Mexican rice	1	serving(s)	131	—	170	6.0	23.0	1.0	11.0	3.0	—	—	0
10772	Meximelt	1	serving(s)	128	—	280	15.0	22.0	3.0	14.0	7.0	—	—	0.5
2011	Nachos	1	serving(s)	99	—	330	4.0	32.0	2.0	21.0	3.5	—	—	2.0
2012	Nachos Bellgrande	1	serving(s)	308	—	770	19.0	77.0	12.0	44.0	9.0	—	—	3.0
2023	Pintos 'n cheese	1	serving(s)	128	—	150	9.0	19.0	7.0	6.0	3.0	—	—	0.5
34473	Steak burrito supreme	1	item(s)	248	—	380	18.0	49.0	6.0	14.0	7.0	—	—	0.5
33419	Steak Chalupa Supreme	1	item(s)	153	—	360	15.0	28.0	2.0	21.0	6.0	—	—	0
747	Taco	1	item(s)	78	—	170	8.0	13.0	3.0	10.0	3.5	—	—	0
2015	Taco salad with salsa, with shell	1	serving(s)	548	—	840	30.0	80.0	15.0	45.0	11.0	—	—	1.5
14459	Taco supreme	1	item(s)	113	—	210	9.0	15.0	3.0	13.0	6.0	—	—	0
748	Tostada	1	item(s)	170	—	230	11.0	27.0	7.0	10.0	3.5	—	—	0.5
Convenience Meals														
	Banquet													
29961	Barbeque chicken meal	1	item(s)	281	—	330	16.0	37.0	2.0	13.0	3.0	—	—	—
14788	Boneless white fried chicken meal	1	item(s)	286	—	310	10.0	21.0	4.0	20.0	5.0	—	—	—
29960	Fish sticks meal	1	item(s)	207	—	470	13.0	58.0	1.0	20.0	3.5	—	—	—
29957	Lasagna with meat sauce meal	1	item(s)	312	—	320	15.0	46.0	7.0	9.0	4.0	—	—	—
14777	Macaroni and cheese meal	1	item(s)	340	—	420	15.0	57.0	5.0	14.0	8.0	—	—	—
1741	Meatloaf meal	1	item(s)	269	—	240	14.0	20.0	4.0	11.0	4.0	—	—	—
39418	Pepperoni pizza meal	1	item(s)	191	—	480	11.0	56.0	5.0	23.0	8.0	—	—	—
33759	Roasted white turkey meal	1	item(s)	255	—	230	14.0	30.0	5.0	6.0	2.0	—	—	—
1743	Salisbury steak meal	1	item(s)	269	196.9	380	12.0	28.0	3.0	24.0	12.0	—	—	—
	Budget Gourmet													
1914	Cheese manicotti with meat sauce entrée	1	item(s)	284	194.0	420	18.0	38.0	4.0	22.0	11.0	6.0	1.3	—
1915	Chicken with fettucini entrée	1	item(s)	284	—	380	20.0	33.0	3.0	19.0	10.0	—	—	—
3986	Light beef stroganoff entrée	1	item(s)	248	177.0	290	20.0	32.0	3.0	7.0	4.0	—	—	—
3996	Light sirloin of beef in herb sauce entrée	1	item(s)	269	214.0	260	19.0	30.0	5.0	7.0	4.0	2.3	0.3	—
3987	Light vegetable lasagna entrée	1	item(s)	298	227.0	290	15.0	36.0	4.8	9.0	1.8	0.9	0.6	—
	Healthy Choice													
9425	Cheese French bread pizza	1	item(s)	170	—	340	22.0	51.0	5.0	5.0	1.5	—	—	—
9306	Chicken enchilada suprema meal	1	item(s)	320	251.5	360	13.0	59.0	8.0	7.0	3.0	2.0	2.0	—
3821	Familiar Favorites lasagna bake with meat sauce entrée	1	item(s)	255	—	270	13.0	38.0	4.0	7.0	2.5	—	—	—
13744	Familiar Favorites sesame chicken with vegetables and rice entrée	1	item(s)	255	—	260	17.0	34.0	4.0	6.0	2.0	2.0	2.0	—
9316	Lemon pepper fish meal	1	item(s)	303	—	280	11.0	49.0	5.0	5.0	2.0	1.0	2.0	—
9322	Traditional salisbury steak meal	1	item(s)	354	250.3	360	23.0	45.0	5.0	9.0	3.5	4.0	1.0	—
9359	Traditional turkey breasts meal	1	item(s)	298	—	330	21.0	50.0	4.0	5.0	2.0	1.5	1.5	—
	Stouffers													
2313	Cheese French bread pizza	1	serving(s)	294	—	380	15.0	43.0	3.0	16.0	6.0	—	—	—
11138	Cheese manicotti with tomato sauce entrée	1	item(s)	255	—	360	18.0	41.0	2.0	14.0	6.0	—	—	—
2366	Chicken pot pie entrée	1	item(s)	284	—	740	23.0	56.0	4.0	47.0	18.0	12.4	10.5	—
11116	Homestyle baked chicken breast with mashed potatoes and gravy entrée	1	item(s)	252	—	270	21.0	21.0	2.0	11.0	3.5	—	—	—
11146	Homestyle beef pot roast and potatoes entrée	1	item(s)	252	—	260	16.0	24.0	3.0	11.0	4.0	—	—	—
11152	Homestyle roast turkey breast with stuffing and mashed potatoes entrée	1	item(s)	273	—	290	16.0	30.0	2.0	12.0	3.5	—	—	—
11043	Lean Cuisine Comfort Classics baked chicken and whipped potatoes and stuffing entrée	1	item(s)	245	—	240	15.0	34.0	3.0	4.5	1.0	2.0	1.0	0
11046	Lean Cuisine Comfort Classics honey mustard chicken with rice pilaf entrée	1	item(s)	227	—	250	17.0	37.0	1.0	4.0	1.0	1.0	1.0	0

Chol (mg)	Calc (mg)	Iron (mg)	Magn (mg)	Pota (mg)	Sodi (mg)	Zinc (mg)	Vit A (µg)	Thia (mg)	Vit E (mg α)	Ribo (mg)	Niac (mg)	Vit B_6 (mg)	Fola (µg)	Vit C (mg)	Vit B_{12} (µg)	Sele (µg)
40	100	2.70	—	—	530.0	—	—	—	—	—	—	—	—	3.6	—	—
35	100	2.70	—	—	660.0	—	—	—	—	—	—	—	—	3.6	—	—
35	120	1.44	—	—	565.0	—	29.2	—	—	—	—	—	—	3.6	—	—
40	350	3.60	—	—	1000.0	—	—	—	—	—	—	—	—	4.8	—	—
15	100	1.44	—	—	790.0	—	—	—	—	—	—	—	—	3.6	—	—
40	250	2.70	—	—	880.0	—	—	—	—	—	—	—	—	2.4	—	—
3	80	0.71	—	—	530.0	—	0	—	—	—	—	—	—	0	—	—
35	200	3.60	—	—	1280.0	—	—	—	—	—	—	—	—	4.8	—	—
15	150	1.44	—	—	670.0	—	—	—	—	—	—	—	—	3.6	—	—
35	200	4.50	—	—	1250.0	—	9.9	—	—	—	—	—	—	9.0	—	—
40	100	2.70	—	—	530.0	—	—	—	—	—	—	—	—	3.6	—	—
25	80	1.08	—	—	350.0	—	—	—	—	—	—	—	—	1.2	—	—
65	450	7.20	—	—	1780.0	—	—	—	—	—	—	—	—	12.0	—	—
40	100	1.08	—	—	370.0	—	—	—	—	—	—	—	—	3.6	—	—
15	200	1.80	—	—	730.0	—	—	—	—	—	—	—	—	4.8	—	—
																—
50	40	1.08	—	—	1210.0	—	0	—	—	—	—	—	—	4.8	—	—
45	80	1.44	—	—	1200.0	—	—	—	—	—	—	—	—	18.0	—	—
55	20	1.44	—	—	710.0	—	—	—	—	—	—	—	—	0	—	—
20	100	2.70	—	—	1170.0	—	—	—	—	—	—	—	—	0	—	—
20	150	1.44	—	—	1330.0	—	0	—	—	—	—	—	—	0	—	—
30	0	1.80	—	—	1040.0	—	0	—	—	—	—	—	—	0	—	—
35	150	1.80	—	—	870.0	—	0	—	—	—	—	—	—	0	—	—
25	60	1.80	—	—	1070.0	—	—	—	—	—	—	—	—	3.6	—	—
60	40	1.44	—	—	1140.0	—	0	—	—	—	—	—	—	0	—	—
85	300	2.70	45.4	484.0	810.0	2.29	—	0.45	—	0.51	4.00	0.22	30.7	0	0.7	—
85	100	2.70	—	—	810.0	—	—	0.15	—	0.42	6.00	—	—	0	—	—
35	40	1.80	38.9	280.0	580.0	4.71	—	0.17	—	0.36	4.28	0.27	18.9	2.4	2.5	—
30	40	1.80	57.7	540.0	850.0	4.81	—	0.15	—	0.29	5.53	0.37	38.4	6.0	1.6	—
15	283	3.03	78.5	420.0	780.0	1.39	—	0.22	—	0.45	3.13	0.32	74.8	59.1	0.2	—
10	350	3.60	—	—	600.0	—	—	—	—	—	—	—	—	0	—	—
30	40	1.44	—	—	580.0	—	—	—	—	—	—	—	—	3.6	—	—
20	100	1.80	—	—	600.0	—	—	—	—	—	—	—	—	0	—	—
35	18	0.72	—	—	580.0	—	—	—	—	—	—	—	—	12.0	—	—
35	20	0.36	—	—	580.0	—	—	—	—	—	—	—	—	30.0	—	—
45	80	2.70	—	—	580.0	—	—	—	—	—	—	—	—	21.0	—	—
35	40	1.80	—	—	600.0	—	—	—	—	—	—	—	—	0	—	—
30	200	1.80	—	230.0	660.0	—	—	—	—	—	—	—	—	2.4	—	—
70	250	1.44	—	550.0	920.0	—	—	—	—	—	—	—	—	6.0	—	—
65	150	2.70	—	—	1170.0	—	—	—	—	—	—	—	—	2.4	—	—
55	20	0.72	—	490.0	770.0	—	0	—	—	—	—	—	—	0	—	—
35	20	1.80	—	800.0	960.0	—	—	—	—	—	—	—	—	6.0	—	—
45	40	1.08	—	490.0	970.0	—	—	—	—	—	—	—	—	3.6	—	—
25	40	1.16	—	500.0	650.0	—	—	—	—	—	—	—	—	3.6	—	—
30	64	0.38	—	370.0	650.0	—	—	—	—	—	—	—	—	0	—	—

A

TABLE A-1 Table of Food Composition *(continued)*

(Computer code is for Cengage Diet Analysis program) (For purposes of calculations, use "0" for t, <1, <.1, <.01, etc.)

											Fat Breakdown (g)			
DA+ Code	Food Description	QTY	Measure	Wt (g)	H_2O (g)	Ener (cal)	Prot (g)	Carb (g)	Fiber (g)	Fat (g)	Sat	Mono	Poly	*Trans*
Convenience Meals—continued														
9479	Lean Cuisine Deluxe French bread pizza	1	item(s)	174	—	310	16.0	44.0	3.0	9.0	3.5	0.5	0.5	0
360	Lean Cuisine One Dish Favorites chicken chow mein with rice	1	item(s)	255	—	190	13.0	29.0	2.0	2.5	0.5	1.0	0.5	0
11054	Lean Cuisine One Dish Favorites chicken enchilada Suiza with Mexican-style rice	1	serving(s)	255	—	270	10.0	47.0	3.0	4.5	2.0	1.5	1.0	0
9467	Lean Cuisine One Dish Favorites fettucini alfredo entrée	1	item(s)	262	—	270	13.0	39.0	2.0	7.0	3.5	2.0	1.0	0
11055	Lean Cuisine One Dish Favorites lasagna with meat sauce entrée	1	item(s)	298	—	320	19.0	44.0	4.0	7.0	3.0	2.0	0.5	0
	Weight Watchers													
11164	Smart Ones chicken enchiladas suiza entrée	1	item(s)	255	—	340	12.0	38.0	3.0	10.0	4.5	—	—	—
39763	Smart Ones chicken oriental entrée	1	item(s)	255	—	230	15.0	34.0	3.0	4.5	1.0	—	—	—
11187	Smart Ones pepperoni pizza	1	item(s)	198	—	400	22.0	58.0	4.0	9.0	3.0	—	—	—
39765	Smart Ones spaghetti bolognese entrée	1	item(s)	326	—	280	17.0	43.0	5.0	5.0	2.0	—	—	—
31512	Smart Ones spicy szechuan style vegetables and chicken	1	item(s)	255	—	220	11.0	34.0	4.0	5.0	1.0	—	—	—
Baby Foods														
787	Apple juice	4	fluid ounce(s)	127	111.6	60	0	14.8	0.1	0.1	0	0	0	—
778	Applesauce, strained	4	tablespoon(s)	64	56.7	26	0.1	6.9	1.1	0.1	0	0	0	—
779	Bananas with tapioca, strained	4	tablespoon(s)	60	50.4	34	0.2	9.2	1.0	0	0	0	0	—
604	Carrots, strained	4	tablespoon(s)	56	51.7	15	0.4	3.4	1.0	0.1	0	0	0	—
770	Chicken noodle dinner, strained	4	tablespoon(s)	64	54.8	42	1.7	5.8	1.3	1.3	0.4	0.5	0.3	—
801	Green beans, strained	4	tablespoon(s)	60	55.1	16	0.7	3.8	1.3	0.1	0	0	0	—
910	Human milk, mature	2	fluid ounce(s)	62	53.9	43	0.6	4.2	0	2.7	1.2	1.0	0.3	—
760	Mixed cereal, prepared with whole milk	4	ounce(s)	113	84.6	128	5.4	18.0	1.5	4.0	2.2	1.2	0.4	—
772	Mixed vegetable dinner, strained	2	ounce(s)	57	50.3	23	0.7	5.4	0.8	0	—	—	0	—
762	Rice cereal, prepared with whole milk	4	ounce(s)	113	84.6	130	4.4	18.9	0.1	4.1	2.6	1.0	0.2	—
758	Teething biscuits	1	item(s)	11	0.7	44	1.0	8.6	0.2	0.6	0.2	0.2	0.1	—

PAGE KEY: A-2 = Breads/Baked Goods A-8 = Cereal/Rice/Pasta A-12 = Fruit A-18 = Vegetables/Legumes A-28 = Nuts/Seeds A-30 = Vegetarian A-32 = Dairy A-40 = Eggs A-40 = Seafood A-44 = Meats A-48 = Poultry A-48 = Processed Meats A-50 = Beverages A-54 = Fats/Oils A-56 = Sweets A-58 = Spices/Condiments/Sauces A-62 = Mixed Foods/Soups/Sandwiches A-68 = Fast Food A-88 = Convenience A-90 = Baby Foods

A

Chol (mg)	Calc (mg)	Iron (mg)	Magn (mg)	Pota (mg)	Sodi (mg)	Zinc (mg)	Vit A (µg)	Thia (mg)	Vit E (mg α)	Ribo (mg)	Niac (mg)	Vit B_6 (mg)	Fola (µg)	Vit C (mg)	Vit B_{12} (µg)	Sele (µg)
20	150	2.70	—	300.0	700.0	—	—	—	—	—	—	—	—	15.0	—	—
25	40	0.72	—	380.0	650.0	—	—	—	—	—	—	—	—	2.4	—	—
20	150	0.72	—	350.0	510.0	—	—	—	—	—	—	—	—	2.4	—	—
15	200	0.72	—	290.0	690.0	—	0	—	—	—	—	—	—	0	—	—
30	250	1.47	—	610.0	690.0	—	—	—	—	—	—	—	—	2.4	—	—
40	200	0.72	—	—	800.0	—	—	—	—	—	—	—	—	2.4	—	—
35	40	0.72	—	—	790.0	—	—	—	—	—	—	—	—	6.0	—	—
15	200	1.08	—	401.0	700.0	—	69.1	—	—	—	—	—	—	4.8	—	—
15	150	3.60	—	—	670.0	—	—	—	—	—	—	—	—	9.0	—	—
10	40	1.44	—	—	890.0	—	—	—	—	—	—	—	—	0	—	—
0	5	0.72	3.8	115.4	3.8	0.03	1.3	0.01	0.76	0.02	0.10	0.03	0	73.4	0	0.1
0	3	0.12	1.9	45.4	1.3	0.01	0.6	0.01	0.36	0.02	0.04	0.02	1.3	24.5	0	0.2
0	3	0.12	6.0	52.8	5.4	0.04	1.2	0.01	0.36	0.02	0.08	0.04	3.6	10.0	0	0.4
0	12	0.20	5.0	109.8	20.7	0.08	320.9	0.01	0.29	0.02	0.25	0.04	8.4	3.2	0	0.1
10	17	0.40	9.0	89.0	14.7	0.32	70.4	0.03	0.12	0.04	0.44	0.04	7.0	0	0	2.4
0	23	0.40	12.0	87.6	3.0	0.12	10.8	0.02	0.04	0.04	0.20	0.02	14.4	0.2	0	0
9	20	0.02	1.8	31.4	10.5	0.10	37.6	0.01	0.04	0.02	0.10	0.01	3.1	3.1	0	1.1
12	249	11.82	30.6	225.7	53.3	0.80	28.4	0.49	—	0.65	6.54	0.07	12.5	1.4	0.3	
—	12	0.18	6.2	68.6	4.5	0.08	77.1	0.01	—	0.02	0.28	0.04	4.5	1.6	0	0.4
12	271	13.82	51.0	215.5	52.2	0.72	24.9	0.52	—	0.56	5.90	0.12	9.1	1.4	0.3	4.0
0	11	0.39	3.9	35.5	28.4	0.10	3.1	0.02	0.02	0.05	0.47	0.01	5.4	1.0	0	2.6

WHO Nutrition Recommendations; Canadian Guidelines and Meal Planning

CONTENTS

This appendix presents nutrition recommendations from the World Health Organization (WHO) and details for Canadians on the *Eating Well with Canada's Food Guide* and the *Beyond the Basics* meal-planning system.

Nutrition Recommendations from WHO

The World Health Organization (WHO) has assessed the relationships between diet and the development of chronic diseases. Its recommendations include:

- Energy: sufficient to support growth, physical activity, and a healthy body weight (BMI between 18.5 and 24.9) and to avoid weight gain greater than 11 pounds (5 kilograms) during adult life
- Total fat: 15 to 30 percent of total energy
- Saturated fatty acids: <10 percent of total energy
- Polyunsaturated fatty acids: 6 to 10 percent of total energy
- Omega-6 polyunsaturated fatty acids: 5 to 8 percent of total energy
- Omega-3 polyunsaturated fatty acids: 1 to 2 percent of total energy
- *Trans*-fatty acids: <1 percent of total energy
- Total carbohydrate: 55 to 75 percent of total energy
- Sugars: <10 percent of total energy
- Protein: 10 to 15 percent of total energy
- Cholesterol: <300 mg per day
- Salt (sodium): <5 g salt per day (<2 g sodium per day), appropriately iodized
- Fruits and vegetables: ≥400 g per day (about 1 pound)
- Total dietary fiber: >25 g per day from foods
- Physical activity: one hour of moderate-intensity activity, such as walking, on most days of the week

Eating Well with Canada's Food Guide

Figure B-1 presents the 2007 *Eating Well with Canada's Food Guide.* Additional publications, which are available from Health Canada ♦ through its website, provide many more details.

• Search for "Canada's food guide" at Health Canada: www.hc-sc.gc.ca

FIGURE B-1 Eating Well with Canada's Food Guide

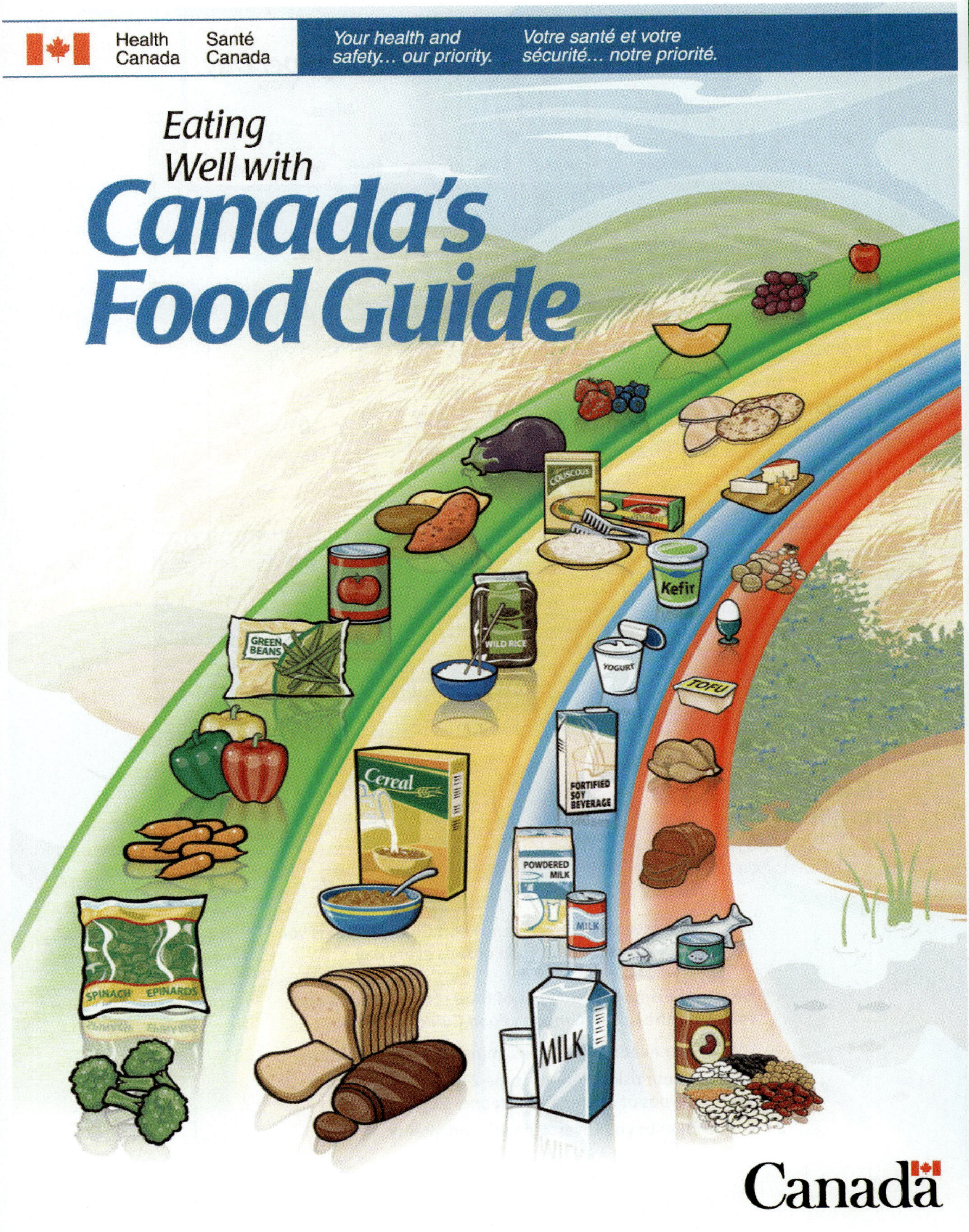

FIGURE B-1 Eating Well with Canada's Food Guide—*(continued)*

Recommended Number of Food Guide Servings per Day

	Children			Teens		Adults			
Age in Years	2-3	4-8	9-13	14-18		19-50		51+	
Sex	Girls and Boys			Females	Males	Females	Males	Females	Males
Vegetables and Fruit	4	5	6	7	8	7-8	8-10	7	7
Grain Products	3	4	6	6	7	6-7	8	6	7
Milk and Alternatives	2	2	3-4	3-4	3-4	2	2	3	3
Meat and Alternatives	1	1	1-2	2	3	2	3	2	3

The chart above shows how many Food Guide Servings you need from each of the four food groups every day.

Having the amount and type of food recommended and following the tips in *Canada's Food Guide* will help:

- Meet your needs for vitamins, minerals and other nutrients.
- Reduce your risk of obesity, type 2 diabetes, heart disease, certain types of cancer and osteoporosis.
- Contribute to your overall health and vitality.

FIGURE B-1 Eating Well with Canada's Food Guide—*(continued)*

What is One Food Guide Serving?

Look at the examples below.

Oils and Fats

- Include a small amount – 30 to 45 mL (2 to 3 Tbsp) – of unsaturated fat each day. This includes oil used for cooking, salad dressings, margarine and mayonnaise.
- Use vegetable oils such as canola, olive and soybean.
- Choose soft margarines that are low in saturated and trans fats.
- Limit butter, hard margarine, lard and shortening.

FIGURE B-1 Eating Well with Canada's Food Guide—*(continued)*

Make each Food Guide Serving count…
wherever you are – at home, at school, at work or when eating out!

- **Eat at least one dark green and one orange vegetable each day.**
  - Go for dark green vegetables such as broccoli, romaine lettuce and spinach.
  - Go for orange vegetables such as carrots, sweet potatoes and winter squash.
- **Choose vegetables and fruit prepared with little or no added fat, sugar or salt.**
  - Enjoy vegetables steamed, baked or stir-fried instead of deep-fried.
- **Have vegetables and fruit more often than juice.**

- **Make at least half of your grain products whole grain each day.**
  - Eat a variety of whole grains such as barley, brown rice, oats, quinoa and wild rice.
  - Enjoy whole grain breads, oatmeal or whole wheat pasta.
- **Choose grain products that are lower in fat, sugar or salt.**
  - Compare the Nutrition Facts table on labels to make wise choices.
  - Enjoy the true taste of grain products. When adding sauces or spreads, use small amounts.

- **Drink skim, 1%, or 2% milk each day.**
  - Have 500 mL (2 cups) of milk every day for adequate vitamin D.
  - Drink fortified soy beverages if you do not drink milk.
- **Select lower fat milk alternatives.**
  - Compare the Nutrition Facts table on yogurts or cheeses to make wise choices.

- **Have meat alternatives such as beans, lentils and tofu often.**
- **Eat at least two Food Guide Servings of fish each week.***
  - Choose fish such as char, herring, mackerel, salmon, sardines and trout.
- **Select lean meat and alternatives prepared with little or no added fat or salt.**
  - Trim the visible fat from meats. Remove the skin on poultry.
  - Use cooking methods such as roasting, baking or poaching that require little or no added fat.
  - If you eat luncheon meats, sausages or prepackaged meats, choose those lower in salt (sodium) and fat.

Enjoy a variety of foods from the four food groups.

Satisfy your thirst with water!

Drink water regularly. It's a calorie-free way to quench your thirst. Drink more water in hot weather or when you are very active.

* Health Canada provides advice for limiting exposure to mercury from certain types of fish. Refer to www.hc-sc.gc.ca for the latest information.

FIGURE B-1 Eating Well with Canada's Food Guide—*(continued)*

Advice for different ages and stages...

Children

Following *Canada's Food Guide* helps children grow and thrive.

Young children have small appetites and need calories for growth and development.

- Serve small nutritious meals and snacks each day.
- Do not restrict nutritious foods because of their fat content. Offer a variety of foods from the four food groups.
- Most of all... be a good role model.

Women of childbearing age

All women who could become pregnant and those who are pregnant or breastfeeding need a multivitamin containing **folic acid** every day. Pregnant women need to ensure that their multivitamin also contains **iron**. A health care professional can help you find the multivitamin that's right for you.

Pregnant and breastfeeding women need more calories. Include an extra 2 to 3 Food Guide Servings each day.

Here are two examples:

- Have fruit and yogurt for a snack, or
- Have an extra slice of toast at breakfast and an extra glass of milk at supper.

Men and women over 50

The need for **vitamin D** increases after the age of 50.

In addition to following *Canada's Food Guide*, everyone over the age of 50 should take a daily vitamin D supplement of 10 µg (400 IU).

How do I count Food Guide Servings in a meal?

Here is an example:

Vegetable and beef stir-fry with rice, a glass of milk and an apple for dessert		
250 mL (1 cup) mixed broccoli, carrot and sweet red pepper	=	2 **Vegetables and Fruit** Food Guide Servings
75 g (2 ½ oz.) lean beef	=	1 **Meat and Alternatives** Food Guide Serving
250 mL (1 cup) brown rice	=	2 **Grain Products** Food Guide Servings
5 mL (1 tsp) canola oil	=	part of your **Oils and Fats** intake for the day
250 mL (1 cup) 1% milk	=	1 **Milk and Alternatives** Food Guide Serving
1 apple	=	1 **Vegetables and Fruit** Food Guide Serving

FIGURE B-1 Eating Well with Canada's Food Guide—*(continued)*

Eat well and be active today and every day!

The benefits of eating well and being active include:

- Better overall health.
- Lower risk of disease.
- A healthy body weight.
- Feeling and looking better.
- More energy.
- Stronger muscles and bones.

Be active

To be active every day is a step towards better health and a healthy body weight.

Canada's Physical Activity Guide recommends building 30 to 60 minutes of moderate physical activity into daily life for adults and at least 90 minutes a day for children and youth. You don't have to do it all at once. Add it up in periods of at least 10 minutes at a time for adults and five minutes at a time for children and youth.

Start slowly and build up.

Eat well

Another important step towards better health and a healthy body weight is to follow *Canada's Food Guide* by:

- Eating the recommended amount and type of food each day.
- Limiting foods and beverages high in calories, fat, sugar or salt (sodium) such as cakes and pastries, chocolate and candies, cookies and granola bars, doughnuts and muffins, ice cream and frozen desserts, french fries, potato chips, nachos and other salty snacks, alcohol, fruit flavoured drinks, soft drinks, sports and energy drinks, and sweetened hot or cold drinks.

Read the label

- Compare the Nutrition Facts table on food labels to choose products that contain less fat, saturated fat, trans fat, sugar and sodium.
- Keep in mind that the calories and nutrients listed are for the amount of food found at the top of the Nutrition Facts table.

Nutrition Facts

Per 0 mL (0 g)

Amount	% Daily Value
Calories 0	
Fat 0 g	0 %
Saturates 0 g	0 %
+ Trans 0 g	
Cholesterol 0 mg	
Sodium 0 mg	0 %
Carbohydrate 0 g	0 %
Fibre 0 g	0 %
Sugars 0 g	
Protein 0 g	

Vitamin A	0 %	Vitamin C	0 %
Calcium	0 %	Iron	0 %

Limit trans fat

When a Nutrition Facts table is not available, ask for nutrition information to choose foods lower in trans and saturated fats.

Take a step today...

- ✓ Have breakfast every day. It may help control your hunger later in the day.
- ✓ Walk wherever you can – get off the bus early, use the stairs.
- ✓ Benefit from eating vegetables and fruit at all meals and as snacks.
- ✓ Spend less time being inactive such as watching TV or playing computer games.
- ✓ Request nutrition information about menu items when eating out to help you make healthier choices.
- ✓ Enjoy eating with family and friends!
- ✓ Take time to eat and savour every bite!

For more information, interactive tools, or additional copies visit Canada's Food Guide on-line at:
www.hc-sc.gc.ca

or contact:

Publications
Health Canada
Ottawa, Ontario K1A 0K9
E-Mail: publications@hc-sc.gc.ca
Tel.: 1-866-225-0709
Fax: (613) 941-5366
TTY: 1-800-267-1245

Également disponible en français sous le titre : Bien manger avec le Guide alimentaire canadie

This publication can be made available on request on diskette, large print, audio-cassette and braille.

 HC Pub.: 4651 Cat.: H164-38/1-2007E ISBN: 0-662-44467-1

Beyond the Basics: Meal Planning for Healthy Eating, Diabetes Prevention and Management

B

Beyond the Basics: Meal Planning for Healthy Eating, Diabetes Prevention and Management is Canada's system of meal planning.[1] Similar to the U.S. exchange system, Beyond the Basics sorts foods into groups and defines portion sizes to help people manage their blood glucose and maintain a healthy weight. Because foods that contain carbohydrate raise blood glucose, the food groups are organized into two sections—those that contain carbohydrate (presented in Table B-1) and those that contain little or no carbohydrate (shown in Table B-2). One portion from any of the food groups listed in Table B-1 provides about 15 grams of available carbohydrate (total carbohydrate minus fiber) and counts as one carbohydrate choice. Within each group, foods are identified as those to "choose more often" (generally higher in vitamins, minerals, and fiber) and those to "choose less often" (generally higher in sugar, saturated fat, or *trans* fat).

[1]*The tables for the Canadian meal planning system are adapted from* Beyond the Basics: Meal Planning for Healthy Eating, Diabetes Prevention and Management, *copyright 2005, with permission of the Canadian Diabetes Association. Additional information is available from www.diabetes.ca.*

TABLE B-1 Food Groups that Contain Carbohydrate

1 serving = 15 g carbohydrate or 1 carbohydrate choice

KEY
- ● Choose more often
- ▲ Choose less often

Food	Measure
Grains and starches: 15 g carbohydrate, 3 g protein, 0 g fat, 286 kJ (68 cal)	
▲ Bagel, large (11 cm, 4.5″)	¼
▲ Bagel, small (8 cm, 3″)	½
▲ Bannock, fried	1.5″ × 2.5″
● Bannock, whole grain baked	1.5″ × 2.5″
● Barley, pearled, cooked	125 mL (½ c)
▲ Bread, white	1 slice (30 g)
● Bread, whole grain	1 slice (30 g)
● Bulghur, cooked	125 mL (½ c)
▲ Bun, hamburger or hotdog	½
▲ Cereal, flaked unsweetened	125 mL (½ c)
● Cream of Wheat, cooked	175 mL (¾ c)
● Red River, cooked	125 mL (½ c)
● Chapati (15 cm, 6″)	1 (44 g)
● Corn	125 mL (½ c)
● Couscous, cooked	125 mL (½ c)
▲ Crackers, soda type	7
▲ Croutons	175 mL (¾ c)
● English muffin, whole grain	½ (28 g)
▲ French fries	10 (50 g)
● Millet, cooked	⅓ c (75 mL)
▲ Naan bread (15 cm, 6″)	¼
▲ Pancake (10 cm, 4″)	1
● Pasta, cooked	125 mL (½ c)
▲ Pita bread, white (15 cm, 6″)	½
● Pita bread, whole wheat (15 cm, 6″)	½
▲ Pizza crust (30 cm, 12″)	1⁄12 (90 g)
● Plantain, cooked, mashed	⅓ c (75 mL)
● Potatoes, boiled or baked	½ medium (84 g)
● Rice, white or brown, cooked	⅓ c (75 mL)
● Roti (15 cm, 6″)	1 (44 g)
● Soup, thick, chunky type	250 mL (1 c)
● Sweet potato, mashed	⅓ c (75 mL)
▲ Taco shells (13 cm, 5″)	2 (17 g)
● Tortilla, wheat flour (25 cm, 10″)	½
▲ Waffle (medium)	1 (39 g)

(continued)

B

KEY

- ● Choose more often
- ▲ Choose less often

TABLE B-1 Food Groups that Contain Carbohydrate *(continued)*

1 serving = 15 g carbohydrate or 1 carbohydrate choice

Food	Measure
Fruits: 15 g carbohydrate, 1-2 g protein, 0 g fat, 269 kJ (64 cal)	
● Apple	1 medium (138 g)
● Applesauce, unsweetened	125 mL (½ c)
● Banana	1 small or ½ large
● Blackberries	500 mL (2 c)
● Cherries	15 (102 g)
● Fruit, canned in juice	125 mL (½ c)
▲ Fruit, dried	60 mL (¼ c)
● Grapefruit	1 small
● Grapes	15 or ½ c (80 g)
● Kiwi	2 medium (150 g)
▲ Juice	125 mL (½ c)
● Mango	½ medium
● Melon	250 mL (1 c)
● Orange	1 medium
● Other berries	250 mL (1 c)
● Pear	1 medium
● Pineapple	175 mL (¾ c)
● Plum	2 medium
● Raspberries	500 mL (2 c)
● Strawberries	500 mL (2 c)
Milk and alternatives: 15 g carbohydrate, 7 g protein, variable fat, 386-651 kJ (92-155 cal)	
● Evaporated milk, canned	125 mL (½ c)
● Milk, fluid	250 mL (1 c)
● Milk powder, skim	60 mL (4 tbs)
● Soy beverage, flavoured	125 mL (½ c)
● Soy beverage, plain	250 mL (1 c)
● Soy yogourt, flavoured	75 mL (⅓ c)
● Yogourt, nonfat, plain	175 mL (¾ c)
● Yogourt, skim, artificially sweetened	250 mL (1 c)
Other choices (sweet foods and snacks): 15 g carbohydrate, variable protein and fat	
▲ Brownies, unfrosted	5 cm × 5 cm (2″ × 2″)
▲ Cake, unfrosted	5 cm × 5 cm (2″ × 2″)
▲ Cookies, arrowroot or gingersnap	3-4
▲ Jam, jelly, marmalade	15 mL (1 tbs)
● Milk pudding, skim, no sugar added	125 mL (½ c)
▲ Muffin, plain	1 small (45 g)
▲ Oatmeal granola bar	1 (28 g)
● Popcorn, low fat, air popped	750 mL (3 c)
▲ Pretzels, low fat, large	7
▲ Pretzels, low fat, sticks	30
▲ Sugar, white	15 mL (1 tbs, 3 tsp, or 3 packets)
▲ Syrup, honey, molasses	1 tbs (15 mL)

TABLE B-2 Food Groups that Contain Little or No Carbohydrate

Food	Measure
Vegetables: To encourage consumption, most vegetables are considered "free"	
▲ Artichokes, Jerusalem[a]	
● Asparagus	
● Beans, yellow or green	
● Bean sprouts	
● Beets	
● Broccoli	
● Cabbage	
● Carrots	
● Cauliflower	

(continued)

Table B-2 Food Groups that Contain Little or No Carbohydrate *(continued)*

Key

● Choose more often

▲ Choose less often

Food	Measure
Vegetables: To encourage consumption, most vegetables are considered "free"	
● Celery	
● Cucumber	
● Eggplant	
● Kale	
● Leeks	
● Mushrooms	
● Okra	
● Onions	
▲ Parsnips[a]	
▲ Peas[a]	
● Peppers	
● Rutabagas	
● Salad vegetables	
▲ Squash, Hubbard, pumpkin, spaghetti	
▲ Squash, acorn[a], butternut[a]	
● Tomatoes, fresh	
● Tomatoes, canned, regular	
▲ Tomatoes, canned, stewed[a]	
● Turnips	
Meat and alternatives: 0 g carbohydrate, 7 g protein, 3-5 g fat, 307 kJ (73 cal)	
● Cheese, skim (<7% milk fat)	2.5 cm × 2.5 cm × 2.5 cm (1″ × 1″ × 1″)
● Cheese, light (<20% milk fat)	2.5 cm × 2.5 cm × 2.5 cm (1″ × 1″ × 1″)
▲ Cheese, regular (≥21% milk fat)	2.5 cm × 2.5 cm × 2.5 cm (1″ × 1″ × 1″)
● Cottage cheese (1-2% milk fat)	60 mL (¼ c)
● Egg	1 medium-large
● Fish, canned in oil or water	60 mL (¼ c)
● Fish, fresh or frozen, cooked	30 g (1 oz)
● Hummus	90 g (⅓ c)
● Legumes, cooked	125 mL (½ c)
● Meat, game, cooked	30 g (1 slice)
● Meat, ground, lean or extra lean, cooked	30 g (2 tbs)
● Meat, lean, cooked	30 g (1 slice)
● Meat, prepared, low fat	30 g (1-3 slices)
▲ Meat, prepared, regular fat	30 g (1-3 slices)
▲ Meat, regular, cooked	30 g (1-3 slices)
● Peameal/back bacon, cooked	30 g (1-2 slices)
● Poultry, ground, lean, cooked	30 g (2 tbs)
● Poultry, skinless, cooked	30 g (1 slice)
▲ Poultry/wings, skin on, cooked	45 g (2)
● Shellfish, cooked	30 g (3 medium)
● Tofu (soybean)	½ block (100 g)
● Vegetarian meat alternatives	30 g (1 oz)
Fats: 0 g carbohydrate, 0 g protein, 5 g fat, 189 kJ (45 cal)	
▲ Avocado	34 g (⅙)
▲ Bacon	30 g (1 slice)
▲ Butter	5 mL (1 tsp)
▲ Cheese, spreadable	15 mL (1 tbs)
▲ Margarine, non-hydrogenated, regular	5 mL (1 tsp)
▲ Mayonnaise, light	15 mL (1 tbs)
▲ Nuts, seeds	15 mL (1 tbs)
▲ Oil, canola or olive	5 mL (1 tsp)
▲ Salad dressing, regular	5 mL (1 tsp)
▲ Tahini	8 mL (½ tbs)
Extras: <5 g carbohydrate, 84 kJ (20 cal)	
Broth	
Coffee	
Herbs and spices	
Ketchup	
Mustard	
Relish	
Sugar-free gelatin	
Sugar-free soft drinks	
Tea	

[a] *These vegetables contain enough carbohydrate to be counted as one carbohydrate choice (15 g of available carbohydrate) when the portion size is 1 cup (250 mL) or more.*

APPENDIX C

Aids to Calculation

CONTENTS

Mathematical problems have been worked out for you as examples at appropriate places in the text. This appendix aims to help with the use of the metric system and with those problems not fully explained elsewhere.

Conversion Factors

Conversion factors are useful mathematical tools in every day calculations, like the ones encountered in the study of nutrition. A conversion factor is a fraction in which the numerator (top) and the denominator (bottom) express the same quantity in different units. For example, 2.2 pounds (lb) and 1 kilogram (kg) are equivalent; they express the same weight. The conversion factor used to change pounds to kilograms or vice versa is:

$$\frac{2.2 \text{ lb}}{1 \text{ kg}} \quad \text{or} \quad \frac{1 \text{ kg}}{2.2 \text{ lb}}$$

Because both factors equal 1, measurements can be multiplied by the factor without changing the value of the measurement. Thus, the units can be changed.

The correct factor to use in a problem is the one with the unit you are seeking in the numerator (top) of the fraction. Following are some examples of problems commonly encountered in nutrition study; they illustrate the usefulness of conversion factors.

Example 1

Convert the weight of 130 pounds to kilograms.

1. Choose the conversion factor in which the unit you are seeking is on top:

$$\frac{1 \text{ kg}}{2.2 \text{ lb}}$$

2. Multiply 130 pounds by the factor:

$$130 \text{ lb} \times \frac{1 \text{ kg}}{2.2 \text{ lb}} = \frac{130 \text{ kg}}{2.2}$$

$$= 59 \text{ kg (rounded off to the nearest whole number)}$$

Example 2

How many grams (g) of saturated fat are contained in a 3-ounce (oz) hamburger?

1. Appendix A shows that a 4-ounce hamburger contains 7 grams of saturated fat. You are seeking grams of saturated fat; therefore, the conversion factor is:

$$\frac{7 \text{ g saturated fat}}{4 \text{ oz hamburger}}$$

2. Multiply 3 ounces of hamburger by the conversion factor:

$$3 \text{ oz hamburger} \times \frac{7 \text{ g saturated fat}}{4 \text{ oz hamburger}} = \frac{3 \times 7}{4} = \frac{21}{4}$$

$$= 5 \text{ g saturated fat (rounded off to the nearest whole number)}$$

Energy Units

1 calorie* (cal) = 4.2 kilojoules

1 millijoule (MJ) = 240 cal

1 kilojoule (kJ) = 0.24 cal

1 gram (g) carbohydrate = 4 cal = 17 kJ

1 g fat = 9 cal = 37 kJ

1 g protein = 4 cal = 17 kJ

1 g alcohol = 7 cal = 29 kJ

Nutrient Unit Conversions

Sodium

To convert milligrams of sodium to grams of salt:

mg sodium ÷ 400 = g of salt

The reverse is also true:

g salt × 400 = mg sodium

Folate

To convert micrograms (µg) of synthetic folate in supplements and enriched foods to Dietary Folate Equivalents (µg DFE):

µg synthetic folate × 1.7 = µg DFE

For naturally occurring folate, assign each microgram folate a value of 1 µg DFE:

µg folate = µg DFE

Example 3

Consider a pregnant woman who takes a supplement and eats a bowl of fortified cornflakes, 2 slices of fortified bread, and a cup of fortified pasta.

1. From the supplement and fortified foods, she obtains synthetic folate:

Supplement	100 µg folate
Fortified cornflakes	100 µg folate
Fortified bread	40 µg folate
Fortified pasta	60 µg folate
	300 µg folate

2. To calculate the DFE, multiply the amount of synthetic folate by 1.7:

300 µg × 1.7 = 510 µg DFE

3. Now add the naturally occurring folate from the other foods in her diet—in this example, another 90 µg of folate.

510 µg DFE + 90 µg = 600 µg DFE

Notice that if we had not converted synthetic folate from supplements and fortified foods to DFE, then this woman's intake would appear to fall short of the 600 µg recommendation for pregnancy (300 µg + 90 µg = 390 µg). But as this example shows, her intake does meet the recommendation. At this time, supplement and fortified food labels list folate in µg only, not µg DFE, making such calculations necessary.

*Throughout this book and in the appendixes, the term calorie is used to mean kilocalorie. Thus, when converting calories to kilojoules, do not enlarge the calorie values—they are kilocalorie values.

Vitamin A

Equivalencies for vitamin A:

1 µg RAE = 1 µg retinol
= 12 µg beta-carotene
= 24 µg other vitamin A carotenoids

1 international unit (IU) = 0.3 µg retinol
= 3.6 µg beta-carotene
= 7.2 µg other vitamin A carotenoids

To convert older RE values to micrograms RAE:

1 µg RE retinol = 1 µg RAE retinol

6 µg RE beta-carotene = 12 µg RAE beta-carotene

12 µg RE other vitamin A carotenoids = 24 µg RAE other vitamin A carotenoids

International Units (IU)

To convert IU to:

- µg vitamin D: divide by 40 or multiply by 0.025.
- 1 IU natural vitamin E = 0.67 mg alpha-tocopherol.
- 1 IU synthetic vitamin E = 0.45 mg alpha-tocopherol.
- vitamin A, see above.

Percentages

A percentage is a comparison between a number of items (perhaps your intake of energy) and a standard number (perhaps the number of calories recommended for your age and gender—your energy DRI). The standard number is the number you divide by. The answer you get after the division must be multiplied by 100 to be stated as a percentage (percent means "per 100").

Example 4

What percentage of the DRI recommendation for energy is your energy intake?

1. Find your energy DRI value on the inside front cover. We'll use 2,368 calories to demonstrate.
2. Total your energy intake for a day—for example, 1,200 calories.
3. Divide your calorie intake by the DRI value:

1,200 cal (your intake) ÷ 2,368 cal (DRI) = 0.507

4. Multiply your answer by 100 to state it as a percentage:

0.507 × 100 = 50.7 = 51% (rounded off to the nearest whole number)

In some problems in nutrition, the percentage may be more than 100. For example, suppose your daily intake of

C

vitamin A is 3,200 and your DRI is 900 µg. Your intake as a percentage of the DRI is more than 100 percent (that is, you consume more than 100 percent of your recommendation for vitamin A). The following calculations show your vitamin A intake as a percentage of the DRI value:

$$3{,}200 \div 900 = 3.6 \text{ (rounded)}$$
$$3.6 \times 100 = 360\% \text{ of DRI}$$

Example 5

Food labels express nutrients and energy contents of foods as percentages of the Daily Values. If a serving of a food contains 200 milligrams of calcium, for example, what percentage of the calcium Daily Value does the food provide?

1. Find the calcium Daily Value on the inside back cover, page Y.
2. Divide the milligrams of calcium in the food by the Daily Value standard:

$$\frac{200}{1{,}000} = 0.2$$

3. Multiply by 100:

$$0.2 \times 100 = 20\% \text{ of the Daily Value}$$

Example 6

This example demonstrates how to calculate the percentage of fat in a day's meals.

1. Recall the general formula for finding percentages of calories from a nutrient:

$$(\text{one nutrient's calories} \div \text{total calories}) \times 100 = \text{the percentage of calories from that nutrient}$$

2. Say a day's meals provide 1,754 calories and 54 grams of fat. First, convert fat grams to fat calories:

$$54 \text{ g} \times 9 \text{ cal per g} = 486 \text{ cal from fat}$$

3. Then apply the general formula for finding percentage of calories from fat:

$$(\text{fat calories} \div \text{total calories}) \times 100 = \text{percentage of calories from fat}$$
$$(486 \div 1{,}754) \times 100 = 27.7 \text{ (28\%, rounded)}$$

Weights and Measures

Length

1 inch (in.) = 2.54 centimeters (cm)

1 foot (ft) = 30.48 cm

1 meter (m) = 39.37 in

Temperature

	Celsius‡	Fahrenheit	
Steam	100°C	212°F	Steam
Body temperature	37°C	98.6°F	Body temperature
Ice	0°C	32°F	Ice

- To find degrees Fahrenheit (°F) when you know degrees Celsius (°C), multiply by 9/5 and then add 32.
- To find degrees Celsius (°C) when you know degrees Fahrenheit (°F), subtract 32 and then multiply by 5/9.

Volume

Used to measure fluids or pourable dry substances such as cereal.

1 milliliter (ml) = 1/5 teaspoon or 0.034 fluid ounce or 1/1000 liter

1 deciliter (dL)= 1/10 liter

1 teaspoon (tsp or t) = 5 ml or about 5 grams (weight) salt

1 tablespoon (tbs or T) = 3 tsp or 15 ml

1 ounce, fluid (fl oz) = 2 tbs or 30 ml

1 cup (c) = 8 fl oz or 16 tbs or 250 ml

1 quart (qt) = 32 fl oz or 4 c or 0.95 liter

1 liter (L) = 1.06 qt or 1,000 ml

1 gallon (gal) = 16 c or 4 qt or 128 fl oz or 3.79 L

Weight

1 microgram (µg or mcg) = 1/1000 milligram

1 milligram (mg) = 1,000 mg or 1/1,000 gram

1 gram (g) = 1,000 mg or 1/1,000 kilogram

1 ounce, weight (oz) = about 28 g or 1/16 pound

1 pound (lb) =16 oz (wt) or about 454 g

1 kilogram (kg) =1,000 g or 2.2 lb

‡*Also known as centigrade.*

APPENDIX D

Exchange Lists for Diabetes

Chapter 2 introduces the exchange system, and this appendix provides details from the *2008 Choose Your Foods: Exchange Lists for Diabetes*. Appendix B presents Canada's meal-planning system.

Exchange lists can help people with diabetes to manage their blood glucose levels by controlling the amount and kinds of carbohydrates they consume. These lists can also help in planning diets for weight management by controlling calorie and fat intake.

CONTENTS

The Exchange System

The exchange system sorts foods into groups by their proportions of carbohydrate, fat, and protein (Table D-1 on p. D-2). These groups may be organized into several exchange lists of foods (Tables D-2 through D-12 on pp. D-3–D-16). For example, the carbohydrate group includes these exchange lists:

- Starch
- Fruits
- Milk (fat-free, reduced-fat, and whole)
- Sweets, Desserts, and Other Carbohydrates
- Nonstarchy Vegetables

Then any food on a list can be "exchanged" for any other on that same list. Another group for alcohol has been included as a reminder that these beverages often deliver substantial carbohydrate and calories, and therefore warrant their own list.

Serving Sizes

The serving sizes have been carefully adjusted and defined so that a serving of any food on a given list provides roughly the same amount of carbohydrate, fat, and protein, and, therefore, total energy. Any food on a list can thus be exchanged, or traded, for any other food on the same list without significantly affecting the diet's energy-nutrient balance or total calories. For example, a person may select 17 small grapes or ½ large grapefruit as one fruit exchange, and either choice would provide roughly 15 grams of carbohydrate and 60 calories. A whole grapefruit, however, would count as 2 fruit exchanges.

To apply the system successfully, users must become familiar with the specified serving sizes. A convenient way to remember the serving sizes and energy values is to keep in mind a typical item from each list (review Table D-1).

The Foods on the Lists

Foods do not always appear on the exchange list where you might first expect to find them. They are grouped according to their energy-nutrient contents rather than by their source (such as milks), their outward appearance, or their vitamin and mineral contents. For example, cheeses are grouped with meats (not milk) because, like meats, cheeses contribute energy from protein and fat but provide negligible carbohydrate.

For similar reasons, starchy vegetables such as corn, green peas, and potatoes are found on the Starch list with breads and cereals, not with the vegetables. Likewise, bacon is grouped with the fats and oils, not with the meats.

D

Diet planners learn to view mixtures of foods, such as casseroles and soups, as combinations of foods from different exchange lists. They also learn to interpret food labels with the exchange system in mind.

Controlling Energy, Fat, and Sodium

The exchange lists help people control their energy intakes by paying close attention to serving sizes. People wanting to lose weight can limit foods from the Sweets, Desserts, and Other Carbohydrates and Fats lists, and they might choose to avoid the Alcohol list altogether. The Free Foods list provide low-calorie choices.

By assigning items like bacon to the Fats list, the exchange lists alert consumers to foods that are unexpectedly high in fat. Even the Starch list specifies which grain products contain added fat (such as biscuits, cornbread, and waffles) by marking them with a symbol to indicate added fat (the symbols are explained in the table keys). In addition, the exchange lists encourage users to think of fat-free milk as milk and of whole milk as milk with added fat, and to think of lean meats as meats and of medium-fat and high-fat meats as meats with added fat. To that end, foods on the milk and meat lists are separated into categories based on their fat contents (review Table D-1). The Milk list is subdivided for fat-free, reduced fat, and whole; the meat list is subdivided for lean, medium fat, and high fat. The meat list also includes plant-based proteins, which tend to be rich in fiber. Notice that many of these foods (p. D-9) bear the symbol for "high fiber."

People wanting to control the sodium in their diets can begin by eliminating any foods bearing the "high sodium" symbol. In most cases, the symbol identifies foods that, in one serving, provide 480 milligrams or more of sodium. Foods on the Combination Foods or Fast Foods lists that bear the symbol provide more than 600 milligrams of sodium. Other foods may also contribute substantially to sodium (consult Chapter 8 for details).

TABLE D-1 The Food Lists

Lists	Typical Item/Portion Size	Carbohydrate (g)	Protein (g)	Fat (g)	Energy[a] (cal)
Carbohydrates					
Starch[b]	1 slice bread	15	0–3	0–1	80
Fruits	1 small apple	15	—	—	60
Milk					
Fat-free, low-fat, 1%	1 c fat-free milk	12	8	0–3	100
Reduced-fat, 2%	1 c reduced-fat milk	12	8	5	120
Whole	1 c whole milk	12	8	8	160
Sweets, desserts, and other carbohydrates[c]	2 small cookies	15	varies	varies	varies
Nonstarchy vegetables	½ c cooked carrots	5	2	—	25
Meat and Meat Substitutes					
Lean	1 oz chicken (no skin)	—	7	0–3	45
Medium-fat	1 oz ground beef	—	7	4–7	75
High-fat	1 oz pork sausage	—	7	8+	100
Plant-based proteins	½ c tofu	varies	7	varies	varies
Fats	1 tsp butter	—	—	5	45
Alcohol	12 oz beer	varies	—	—	100

[a]The energy value for each exchange list represents an approximate average for the group and does not reflect the precise number of grams of carbohydrate, protein, and fat. For example, a slice of bread contains 15 grams of carbohydrate (60 calories), 3 grams protein (12 calories), and a little fat—rounded to 80 calories for ease in calculating. A ½ cup of vegetables (not including starchy vegetables) contains 5 grams carbohydrate (20 calories) and 2 grams protein (8 more), which has been rounded down to 25 calories.

[b]The Starch list includes cereals, grains, breads, crackers, snacks, starchy vegetables (such as corn, peas, and potatoes), and legumes (dried beans, peas, and lentils).

[c]The Sweets, Desserts, and Other Carbohydrates list includes foods that contain added sugars and fats such as sodas, candy, cakes, cookies, doughnuts, ice cream, pudding, syrup, and frozen yogurt.

Planning a Healthy Diet

To obtain a daily variety of foods that provide healthful amounts of carbohydrate, protein, and fat, as well as vitamins, minerals, and fiber, the meal plan for adults and teenagers should include at least:

- two to three servings of nonstarchy vegetables
- two servings of fruits
- six servings of grains (at least three of whole grains), beans, and starchy vegetables
- two servings of low-fat or fat-free milk
- about 6 ounces of meat or meat substitutes
- *small* amounts of fat and sugar

The actual amounts are determined by age, gender, activity levels, and other factors that influence energy needs. Refer to Chapter 9 as you read through these sections to get an idea of how exchange lists can be useful in planning a diet.

TABLE D-2 Starch

The Starch list includes bread, cereals and grains, starchy vegetables, crackers and snacks, and legumes (dried beans, peas, and lentils). 1 starch choice = 15 grams carbohydrate, 0–3 grams protein, 0–1 grams fat, and 80 calories.

NOTE: In general, one starch exchange is ½ cup cooked cereal, grain, or starchy vegetable; ⅓ cup cooked rice or pasta; 1 ounce of bread product; ¾ ounce to 1 ounce of most snack foods.

Bread

Food	Serving Size
Bagel, large (about 4 oz)	¼ (1 oz)
⚠ Biscuit, 2½ inches across	1
Bread	
☺ reduced-calorie	2 slices (1½ oz)
white, whole-grain, pumpernickel, rye, unfrosted raisin	1 slice (1 oz)
Chapatti, small, 6 inches across	1
⚠ Cornbread, 1¾ inch cube	1 (1½ oz)
English muffin	½
Hot dog bun or hamburger bun	½ (1 oz)
Naan, 8 inches by 2 inches	¼
Pancake, 4 inches across, ¼ inch thick	1
Pita, 6 inches across	½
Roll, plain, small	1 (1 oz)
⚠ Stuffing, bread	⅓ cup
⚠ Taco shell, 5 inches across	2
Tortilla, corn, 6 inches across	1
Tortilla, flour, 6 inches across	1
Tortilla, flour, 10 inches across	⅓
⚠ Waffle, 4-inch square or 4 inches across	1

Cereals and Grains

Food	Serving Size
Barley, cooked	⅓ cup
Bran, dry	
☺ oat	¼ cup
☺ wheat	½ cup
☺ Bulgur (cooked)	½ cup

Cereals and Grains—continued

Food	Serving Size
Cereals	
☺ bran	½ cup
cooked (oats, oatmeal)	½ cup
puffed	1½ cups
shredded wheat, plain	½ cup
sugar-coated	½ cup
unsweetened, ready-to-eat	¾ cup
Couscous	⅓ cup
Granola	
low-fat	¼ cup
⚠ regular	¼ cup
Grits, cooked	½ cup
Kasha	½ cup
Millet, cooked	⅓ cup
Muesli	¼ cup
Pasta, cooked	⅓ cup
Polenta, cooked	⅓ cup
Quinoa, cooked	⅓ cup
Rice, white or brown, cooked	⅓ cup
Tabbouleh (tabouli), prepared	½ cup
Wheat germ, dry	3 Tbsp
Wild rice, cooked	½ cup

Starchy Vegetables

Food	Serving Size
Cassava	⅓ cup
Corn	½ cup
on cob, large	½ cob (5 oz)
☺ Hominy, canned	¾ cup

(continued)

KEY

☺ = More than 3 grams of dietary fiber per serving.

⚠ = Extra fat, or prepared with added fat. (Count as 1 starch + 1 fat.)

🧂 = 480 milligrams or more of sodium per serving.

D

TABLE D-2 Starch

Starchy Vegetables—continued

Food	Serving Size
☺ Mixed vegetables with corn, peas, or pasta	1 cup
☺ Parsnips	½ cup
☺ Peas, green	½ cup
Plantain, ripe	⅓ cup
Potato	
baked with skin	¼ large (3 oz)
boiled, all kinds	½ cup or ½ medium (3 oz)
⚠ mashed, with milk and fat	½ cup
french fried (oven-baked)[a]	1 cup (2 oz)
☺ Pumpkin, canned, no sugar added	1 cup
Spaghetti/pasta sauce	½ cup
☺ Squash, winter (acorn, butternut)	1 cup
☺ Succotash	½ cup
Yam, sweet potato, plain	½ cup

Crackers and Snacks[b]

Food	Serving Size
Animal crackers	8
Crackers	
⚠ round-butter type	6
saltine-type	6
⚠ sandwich-style, cheese or peanut butter filling	3
⚠ whole-wheat regular	2–5 (¾ oz)
☺ whole-wheat lower fat or crispbreads	2–5 (¾ oz)

Crackers and Snacks—continued

Food	Serving Size
Graham cracker, 2½-inch square	3
Matzoh	¾ oz
Melba toast, about 2-inch by 4-inch piece	4
Oyster crackers	20
Popcorn	3 cups
⚠ ☺ with butter	3 cups
☺ no fat added	3 cups
☺ lower fat	3 cups
Pretzels	¾ oz
Rice cakes, 4 inches across	2
Snack chips	
fat-free or baked (tortilla, potato), baked pita chips	15–20 (¾ oz)
⚠ regular (tortilla, potato)	9–13 (¾ oz)

Beans, Peas, and Lentils[c]

The choices on this list count as 1 starch + 1 lean meat.

Food	Serving Size
☺ Baked beans	⅓ cup
☺ Beans, cooked (black, garbanzo, kidney, lima, navy, pinto, white)	½ cup
☺ Lentils, cooked (brown, green, yellow)	½ cup
☺ Peas, cooked (black-eyed, split)	½ cup
🧂 ☺ Refried beans, canned	½ cup

KEY

☺ = More than 3 grams of dietary fiber per serving.

⚠ = Extra fat, or prepared with added fat. (Count as 1 starch + 1 fat.)

🧂 = 480 milligrams or more of sodium per serving.

[a] *Restaurant-style french fries are on the Fast Foods list.*

[b] *For other snacks, see the Sweets, Desserts, and Other Carbohydrates list. For a quick estimate of serving size, an open handful is equal to about 1 cup or 1 to 2 ounces of snack food.*

[c] *Beans, peas, and lentils are also found on the Meat and Meat Substitutes list.*

TABLE D-3 Fruits

Fruit[a]

The Fruits list includes fresh, frozen, canned, and dried fruits and fruit juices. 1 fruit choice = 15 grams carbohydrate, 0 grams protein, 0 grams fat, and 60 calories.

NOTE: In general, one fruit exchange is ½ cup canned or fresh fruit or unsweetened fruit juice; 1 small fresh fruit (4 ounces); 2 tablespoons dried fruit.

Food	Serving Size
Apple, unpeeled, small	1 (4 oz)
Apples, dried	4 rings
Applesauce, unsweetened	½ cup
Apricots	
canned	½ cup
dried	8 halves
☺ fresh	4 whole (5½ oz)
Banana, extra small	1 (4 oz)
☺ Blackberries	¾ cup
Blueberries	¾ cup
Cantaloupe, small	⅓ melon or 1 cup cubed (11 oz)

Food	Serving Size
Cherries	
sweet, canned	½ cup
sweet fresh	12 (3 oz)
Dates	3
Dried fruits (blueberries, cherries, cranberries, mixed fruit, raisins)	2 Tbsp
Figs	
dried	1½
☺ fresh	1½ large or 2 medium (3½ oz)
Fruit cocktail	½ cup

(continued)

[a] *The weight listed includes skin, core, seeds, and rind.*

TABLE D-3 Fruits *(continued)*

FRUIT—CONTINUED	
FOOD	**SERVING SIZE**
Grapefruit	
large	½ (11 oz)
sections, canned	¾ cup
Grapes, small	17 (3 oz)
Honeydew melon	1 slice or 1 cup cubed (10 oz)
☺ Kiwi	1 (3½ oz)
Mandarin oranges, canned	¾ cup
Mango, small	½ (5½ oz) or ½ cup
Nectarine, small	1 (5 oz)
☺ Orange, small	1 (6½ oz)
Papaya	½ or 1 cup cubed (8 oz)
Peaches	
canned	½ cup
fresh, medium	1 (6 oz)
Pears	
canned	½ cup
fresh, large	½ (4 oz)
Pineapple	
canned	½ cup
fresh	¾ cup
Plums	
canned	½ cup
dried (prunes)	3
small	2 (5 oz)
☺ Raspberries	1 cup
☺ Strawberries	1¼ cup whole berries
☺ Tangerines, small	2 (8 oz)
Watermelon	1 slice or 1¼ cups cubes (13½ oz)

FRUIT JUICE	
FOOD	**SERVING SIZE**
Apple juice/cider	½ cup
Fruit juice blends, 100% juice	⅓ cup
Grape juice	⅓ cup
Grapefruit juice	½ cup
Orange juice	½ cup
Pineapple juice	½ cup
Prune juice	⅓ cup

KEY

☺ = More than 3 grams of dietary fiber per serving.

⚠ = Extra fat, or prepared with added fat. (Count as 1 starch + 1 fat.)

🧂 = 480 milligrams or more of sodium per serving.

TABLE D-4 Milk

The Milk list groups milks and yogurts based on the amount of fat they have (fat-free/low fat, reduced fat, and whole). Cheeses are found on the Meat and Meat Substitutes list and cream and other dairy fats are found on the Fats list.

NOTE: In general, one milk choice is 1 cup (8 fluid ounces or ½ pint) milk or yogurt.

MILK AND YOGURTS	
FOOD	**SERVING SIZE**
FAT-FREE OR LOW-FAT (1%)	
1 fat-free/low-fat milk choice = 12 g carbohydrate, 8 g protein, 0–3 g fat, and 100 cal.	
Milk, buttermilk, acidophilus milk, Lactaid	1 cup
Evaporated milk	½ cup
Yogurt, plain or flavored with an artificial sweetener	⅔ cup (6 oz)
REDUCED-FAT (2%)	
1 reduced-fat milk choice = 12 g carbohydrate, 8 g protein, 5 g fat, and 120 cal.	
Milk, acidophilus milk, kefir, Lactaid	1 cup
Yogurt, plain	⅔ cup (6 oz)
WHOLE	
1 whole milk choice = 12 g carbohydrate, 8 g protein, 8 g fat, and 160 cal.	
Milk, buttermilk, goat's milk	1 cup
Evaporated milk	½ cup
Yogurt, plain	8 oz

(continued)

TABLE D-4 Milk *(continued)*

Dairy-Like Foods		
Food	**Serving Size**	**Count As**
Chocolate milk		
fat-free	1 cup	1 fat-free milk + 1 carbohydrate
whole	1 cup	1 whole milk + 1 carbohydrate
Eggnog, whole milk	½ cup	1 carbohydrate + 2 fats
Rice drink		
flavored, low fat	1 cup	2 carbohydrates
plain, fat-free	1 cup	1 carbohydrate
Smoothies, flavored, regular	10 oz	1 fat-free milk + 2½ carbohydrates
Soy milk		
light	1 cup	1 carbohydrate + ½ fat
regular, plain	1 cup	1 carbohydrate + 1 fat
Yogurt		
and juice blends	1 cup	1 fat-free milk + 1 carbohydrate
low carbohydrate (less than 6 grams carbohydrate per choice)	⅔ cup (6 oz)	½ fat-free milk
with fruit, low-fat	⅔ cup (6 oz)	1 fat-free milk + 1 carbohydrate

TABLE D-5 Sweets, Desserts, and Other Carbohydrates

1 other carbohydrate choice = 15 grams carbohydrate, variable grams protein, variable grams fat, and variable calories.
NOTE: In general, one choice from this list can substitute for foods on the Starch, Fruits, or Milk lists.

Beverages, Soda, and Energy/Sports Drinks		
Food	**Serving Size**	**Count As**
Cranberry juice cocktail	½ cup	1 carbohydrate
Energy drink	1 can (8.3 oz)	2 carbohydrates
Fruit drink or lemonade	1 cup (8 oz)	2 carbohydrates
Hot chocolate		
regular	1 envelope added to 8 oz water	1 carbohydrate + 1 fat
sugar-free or light	1 envelope added to 8 oz water	1 carbohydrate
Soft drink (soda), regular	1 can (12 oz)	2½ carbohydrates
Sports drink	1 cup (8 oz)	1 carbohydrate
Brownies, Cake, Cookies, Gelatin, Pie, and Pudding		
Food	**Serving Size**	**Count As**
Brownie, small, unfrosted	1¼-inch square, ⅞ inch high (about 1 oz)	1 carbohydrate + 1 fat
Cake		
angel food, unfrosted	1⁄12 of cake (about 2 oz)	2 carbohydrates
frosted	2-inch square (about 2 oz)	2 carbohydrates + 1 fat
unfrosted	2-inch square (about 2 oz)	1 carbohydrate + 1 fat
Cookies		
chocolate chip	2 cookies (2¼ inches across)	1 carbohydrate + 2 fats
gingersnap	3 cookies	1 carbohydrate
sandwich, with crème filling	2 small (about ⅔ oz)	1 carbohydrate + 1 fat
sugar-free	3 small or 1 large (¾–1 oz)	1 carbohydrate + 1–2 fats
vanilla wafer	5 cookies	1 carbohydrate + 1 fat
Cupcake, frosted	1 small (about 1¾ oz)	2 carbohydrates + 1–1½ fats
Fruit cobbler	½ cup (3½ oz)	3 carbohydrates + 1 fat
Gelatin, regular	½ cup	1 carbohydrate
Pie		
commercially prepared fruit, 2 crusts	⅙ of 8-inch pie	3 carbohydrates + 2 fats
pumpkin or custard	⅛ of 8-inch pie	1½ carbohydrates + 1½ fats
Pudding		
regular (made with reduced-fat milk)	½ cup	2 carbohydrates
sugar-free or sugar- and fat-free (made with fat-free milk)	½ cup	1 carbohydrate

(continued)

TABLE D-5 Sweets, Desserts, and Other Carbohydrates *(continued)*

Candy, Spreads, Sweets, Sweeteners, Syrups, and Toppings		
Food	**Serving Size**	**Count as**
Candy bar, chocolate/peanut	2 "fun size" bars (1 oz)	1½ carbohydrates + 1½ fats
Candy, hard	3 pieces	1 carbohydrate
Chocolate "kisses"	5 pieces	1 carbohydrate + 1 fat
Coffee creamer		
dry, flavored	4 tsp	½ carbohydrate + ½ fat
liquid, flavored	2 Tbsp	1 carbohydrate
Fruit snacks, chewy (pureed fruit concentrate)	1 roll (¾ oz)	1 carbohydrate
Fruit spreads, 100% fruit	1½ Tbsp	1 carbohydrate
Honey	1 Tbsp	1 carbohydrate
Jam or jelly, regular	1 Tbsp	1 carbohydrate
Sugar	1 Tbsp	1 carbohydrate
Syrup		
chocolate	2 Tbsp	2 carbohydrates
light (pancake type)	2 Tbsp	1 carbohydrate
regular (pancake type)	1 Tbsp	1 carbohydrate

Condiments and Sauces[a]		
Food	**Serving Size**	**Count as**
Barbeque sauce	3 Tbsp	1 carbohydrate
Cranberry sauce, jellied	¼ cup	1½ carbohydrates
🧂 Gravy, canned or bottled	½ cup	½ carbohydrate + ½ fat
Salad dressing, fat-free, low-fat, cream-based	3 Tbsp	1 carbohydrate
Sweet and sour sauce	3 Tbsp	1 carbohydrate

Doughnuts, Muffins, Pastries, and Sweet Breads		
Food	**Serving Size**	**Count as**
Banana nut bread	1-inch slice (1 oz)	2 carbohydrates + 1 fat
Doughnut		
cake, plain	1 medium (1½ oz)	1½ carbohydrates + 2 fats
yeast type, glazed	3¾ inches across (2 oz)	2 carbohydrates + 2 fats
Muffin (4 oz)	¼ muffin (1 oz)	1 carbohydrate + ½ fat
Sweet roll or Danish	1 (2½ oz)	2½ carbohydrates + 2 fats

Frozen Bars, Frozen Desserts, Frozen Yogurt, and Ice Cream		
Food	**Serving Size**	**Count as**
Frozen pops	1	½ carbohydrate
Fruit juice bars, frozen, 100% juice	1 bar (3 oz)	1 carbohydrate
Ice cream		
fat-free	½ cup	1½ carbohydrates
light	½ cup	1 carbohydrate + 1 fat
no sugar added	½ cup	1 carbohydrate + 1 fat
regular	½ cup	1 carbohydrate + 2 fats
Sherbet, sorbet	½ cup	2 carbohydrates
Yogurt, frozen		
fat-free	⅓ cup	1 carbohydrate
regular	½ cup	1 carbohydrate + 0–1 fat

Granola Bars, Meal Replacement Bars/Shakes, and Trail Mix		
Food	**Serving Size**	**Count as**
Granola or snack bar, regular or low-fat	1 bar (1 oz)	1½ carbohydrates
Meal replacement bar	1 bar (1⅓ oz)	1½ carbohydrates + 0–1 fat
Meal replacement bar	1 bar (2 oz)	2 carbohydrates + 1 fat
Meal replacement shake, reduced calorie	1 can (10–11 oz)	1½ carbohydrates + 0–1 fat
Trail mix		
candy/nut-based	1 oz	1 carbohydrate + 2 fats
dried fruit-based	1 oz	1 carbohydrate + 1 fat

KEY

🧂 = 480 milligrams or more of sodium per serving

[a] *You can also check the Fats list and Free Foods list for other condiments.*

TABLE D-6 Nonstarchy Vegetables

The Nonstarchy Vegetables list includes vegetables that have few grams of carbohydrates or calories; starchy vegetables are found on the Starch list. 1 nonstarchy vegetable choice = 5 grams carbohydrate, 2 grams protein, 0 grams fat, and 25 calories.

NOTE: In general, one nonstarchy vegetable choice is ½ cup cooked vegetables or vegetable juice or 1 cup raw vegetables. Count 3 cups of raw vegetables or 1½ cups of cooked vegetables as one carbohydrate choice.

Nonstarchy Vegetables[a]

Amaranth or Chinese spinach
Artichoke
Artichoke hearts
Asparagus
Baby corn
Bamboo shoots
Beans (green, wax, Italian)
Bean sprouts
Beets
🧂 Borscht
Broccoli
☺ Brussels sprouts
Cabbage (green, bok choy, Chinese)
☺ Carrots
Cauliflower
Celery
☺ Chayote
Coleslaw, packaged, no dressing
Cucumber
Eggplant
Gourds (bitter, bottle, luffa, bitter melon)
Green onions or scallions
Greens (collard, kale, mustard, turnip)
Hearts of palm
Jicama
Kohlrabi
Leeks
Mixed vegetables (without corn, peas, or pasta)
Mung bean sprouts
Mushrooms, all kinds, fresh
Okra
Onions
Oriental radish or daikon
Pea pods
☺ Peppers (all varieties)
Radishes
Rutabaga
🧂 Sauerkraut
Soybean sprouts
Spinach
Squash (summer, crookneck, zucchini)
Sugar pea snaps
☺ Swiss chard
Tomato
Tomatoes, canned
🧂 Tomato sauce
🧂 Tomato/vegetable juice
Turnips
Water chestnuts
Yard-long beans

KEY

☺ = More than 3 grams of dietary fiber per serving.
🧂 = 480 milligrams or more of sodium per serving

[a]*Salad greens (like chicory, endive, escarole, lettuce, romaine, spinach, arugula, radicchio, watercress) are on the Free Foods list.*

TABLE D-7 Meat and Meat Substitutes

The Meat and Meat Substitutes list groups foods based on the amount of fat they have (lean meat, medium-fat meat, high-fat meat, and plant-based proteins).

Lean Meats and Meat Substitutes

1 lean meat choice = 0 grams carbohydrate, 7 grams protein, 0–3 grams fat, and 100 calories.

Food	Amount
Beef: Select or Choice grades trimmed of fat: ground round, roast (chuck, rib, rump), round, sirloin, steak (cubed, flank, porterhouse, T-bone), tenderloin	1 oz
🧂 Beef jerky	1 oz
Cheeses with 3 grams of fat or less per oz	1 oz
Cottage cheese	¼ cup
Egg substitutes, plain	¼ cup
Egg whites	2
Fish, fresh or frozen, plain: catfish, cod, flounder, haddock, halibut, orange roughy, salmon, tilapia, trout, tuna	1 oz
🧂 Fish, smoked: herring or salmon (lox)	1 oz
Game: buffalo, ostrich, rabbit, venison	1 oz
🧂 Hot dog with 3 grams of fat or less per oz (8 dogs per 14 oz package) *Note: May be high in carbohydrate.*	1
Lamb: chop, leg, or roast	1 oz
Lean Meats and Meat Substitutes—continued	
Organ meats: heart, kidney, liver *Note: May be high in cholesterol.*	1 oz
Oysters, fresh or frozen	6 medium
Pork, lean	
🧂 Canadian bacon	1 oz
rib or loin chop/roast, ham, tenderloin	1 oz
Poultry, without skin: Cornish hen, chicken, domestic duck or goose (well-drained of fat), turkey	1 oz
Processed sandwich meats with 3 grams of fat or less per oz: chipped beef, deli thin-sliced meats, turkey ham, turkey kielbasa, turkey pastrami	1 oz
Salmon, canned	1 oz
Sardines, canned	2 medium
🧂 Sausage with 3 grams of fat or less per oz	1 oz
Shellfish: clams, crab, imitation shellfish, lobster, scallops, shrimp	1 oz
Tuna, canned in water or oil, drained	1 oz
Veal, lean chop, roast	1 oz

(continued)

TABLE D-7 Meat and Meat Substitutes *(continued)*

Medium-Fat Meat and Meat Substitutes

1 medium-fat meat choice = 0 grams carbohydrate, 7 grams protein, 4–7 grams fat, and 130 calories.

Food	Amount
Beef: corned beef, ground beef, meatloaf, Prime grades trimmed of fat (prime rib), short ribs, tongue	1 oz
Cheeses with 4–7 grams of fat per oz: feta, mozzarella, pasteurized processed cheese spread, reduced-fat cheeses, string	1 oz
Egg *Note: High in cholesterol, so limit to 3 per week.*	1
Fish, any fried product	1 oz
Lamb: ground, rib roast	1 oz
Pork: cutlet, shoulder roast	1 oz
Poultry: chicken with skin; dove, pheasant, wild duck, or goose; fried chicken; ground turkey	1 oz
Ricotta cheese	2 oz or ¼ cup
🧂 Sausage with 4–7 grams of fat per oz	1 oz
Veal, cutlet (no breading)	1 oz

High-Fat Meat and Meat Substitutes

1 high-fat meat choice = 0 grams carbohydrate, 7 grams protein, 8+ grams fat, and 150 calories. These foods are high in saturated fat, cholesterol, and calories and may raise blood cholesterol levels if eaten on a regular basis. Try to eat 3 or fewer servings from this group per week.

Food	Amount
Bacon	
🧂 pork	2 slices (16 slices per lb or 1 oz each, before cooking)
🧂 turkey	3 slices (½ oz each before cooking)
Cheese, regular: American, bleu, brie, cheddar, hard goat, Monterey jack, queso, and Swiss	1 oz
⚠ 🧂 Hot dog: beef, pork, or combination (10 per lb-sized package)	1
🧂 Hot dog: turkey or chicken (10 per lb-sized package)	1
Pork: ground, sausage, spareribs	1 oz
Processed sandwich meats with 8 grams of fat or more per oz: bologna, pastrami, hard salami	1 oz
🧂 Sausage with 8 grams fat or more per oz: bratwurst, chorizo, Italian, knockwurst, Polish, smoked, summer	1 oz

Plant-Based Proteins

1 plant-based protein choice = variable grams carbohydrate, 7 grams protein, variable grams fat, and variable calories. Because carbohydrate content varies among plant-based proteins, you should read the food label.

Food	Serving Size	Count as
"Bacon" strips, soy-based	3 strips	1 medium-fat meat
☺ Baked beans	⅓ cup	1 starch + 1 lean meat
☺ Beans, cooked: black, garbanzo, kidney, lima, navy, pinto, white[a]	½ cup	1 starch + 1 lean meat
☺ "Beef" or "sausage" crumbles, soy-based	2 oz	½ carbohydrate + 1 lean meat
"Chicken" nuggets, soy-based	2 nuggets (1½ oz)	½ carbohydrate + 1 medium-fat meat
☺ Edamame	½ cup	½ carbohydrate + 1 lean meat
Falafel (spiced chickpea and wheat patties)	3 patties (about 2 inches across)	1 carbohydrate + 1 high-fat meat
Hot dog, soy-based	1 (1½ oz)	½ carbohydrate + 1 lean meat
☺ Hummus	⅓ cup	1 carbohydrate + 1 high-fat meat
☺ Lentils, brown, green, or yellow	½ cup	1 carbohydrate + 1 lean meat
☺ Meatless burger, soy-based	3 oz	½ carbohydrate + 2 lean meats
☺ Meatless burger, vegetable- and starch-based	1 patty (about 2½ oz)	1 carbohydrate + 2 lean meats
Nut spreads: almond butter, cashew butter, peanut butter, soy nut butter	1 Tbsp	1 high-fat meat
☺ Peas, cooked: black-eyed and split peas	½ cup	1 starch + 1 lean meat
🧂 ☺ Refried beans, canned	½ cup	1 starch + 1 lean meat
"Sausage" patties, soy-based	1 (1½ oz)	1 medium-fat meat
Soy nuts, unsalted	¾ oz	½ carbohydrate + 1 medium-fat meat
Tempeh	¼ cup	1 medium-fat meat
Tofu	4 oz (½ cup)	1 medium-fat meat
Tofu, light	4 oz (½ cup)	1 lean meat

KEY

☺ = More than 3 grams of dietary fiber per serving.

⚠ = Extra fat, or prepared with added fat. (Count as 1 starch + 1 fat.)

🧂 = 480 milligrams or more of sodium per serving (based on the sodium content of a typical 3-oz serving of meat, unless 1 or 2 oz is the normal serving size).

[a] *Beans, peas, and lentils are also found on the Starch list; nut butters in smaller amounts are found in the Fats list.*

TABLE **D-8** Fats

Fats and oils have mixtures of unsaturated (polyunsaturated and monounsaturated) and saturated fats. Foods on the Fats list are grouped together based on the major type of fat they contain.

1 fat choice = 0 grams carbohydrate, 0 grams protein, 5 grams fat, and 45 calories.

NOTE: In general, one fat exchange is 1 teaspoon of regular margarine, vegetable oil, or butter; 1 tablespoon of regular salad dressing.

When used in large amounts, bacon and peanut butter are counted as high-fat meat choices (see Meat and Meat Substitutes list). Fat-free salad dressings are found on the Sweets, Desserts, and Other Carbohydrates list. Fat-free products such as margarines, salad dressings, mayonnaise, sour cream, and cream cheese are found on the Free Foods list.

Monounsaturated Fats

Food	Serving Size
Avocado, medium	2 Tbsp (1 oz)
Nut butters (*trans* fat-free): almond butter, cashew butter, peanut butter (smooth or crunchy)	1½ tsp
Nuts	
almonds	6 nuts
Brazil	2 nuts
cashews	6 nuts
filberts (hazelnuts)	5 nuts
macadamia	3 nuts
mixed (50% peanuts)	6 nuts
peanuts	10 nuts
pecans	4 halves
pistachios	16 nuts
Oil: canola, olive, peanut	1 tsp
Olives	
black (ripe)	8 large
green, stuffed	10 large

Polyunsaturated Fats

Food	Serving Size
Margarine: lower-fat spread (30%–50% vegetable oil, *trans* fat-free)	1 Tbsp
Margarine: stick, tub (*trans* fat-free) or squeeze (*trans* fat-free)	1 tsp
Mayonnaise	
reduced-fat	1 Tbsp
regular	1 tsp
Mayonnaise-style salad dressing	
reduced-fat	1 Tbsp
regular	2 tsp
Nuts	
Pignolia (pine nuts)	1 Tbsp
walnuts, English	4 halves
Oil: corn, cottonseed, flaxseed, grape seed, safflower, soybean, sunflower	1 tsp
Oil: made from soybean and canola oil—Enova	1 tsp
Plant stanol esters	
light	1 Tbsp
regular	2 tsp

Polyunsaturated Fats—continued

Food	Serving Size
Salad dressing	
reduced-fat *Note: May be high in carbohydrate.*	2 Tbsp
regular	1 Tbsp
Seeds	
flaxseed, whole	1 Tbsp
pumpkin, sunflower	1 Tbsp
sesame seeds	1 Tbsp
Tahini or sesame paste	2 tsp

Saturated Fats

Food	Serving Size
Bacon, cooked, regular or turkey	1 slice
Butter	
reduced-fat	1 Tbsp
stick	1 tsp
whipped	2 tsp
Butter blends made with oil	
reduced-fat or light	1 Tbsp
regular	1½ tsp
Chitterlings, boiled	2 Tbsp (½ oz)
Coconut, sweetened, shredded	2 Tbsp
Coconut milk	
light	⅓ cup
regular	1½ Tbsp
Cream	
half and half	2 Tbsp
heavy	1 Tbsp
light	1½ Tbsp
whipped	2 Tbsp
whipped, pressurized	¼ cup
Cream cheese	
reduced-fat	1½ Tbsp (¾ oz)
regular	1 Tbsp (½ oz)
Lard	1 tsp
Oil: coconut, palm, palm kernel	1 tsp
Salt pork	¼ oz
Shortening, solid	1 tsp
Sour cream	
reduced-fat or light	3 Tbsp
regular	2 Tbsp

KEY

= 480 milligrams or more of sodium per serving

TABLE D-9 Free Foods

A "free" food is any food or drink choice that has less than 20 calories and 5 grams or less of carbohydrate per serving.

- Most foods on this list should be limited to 3 servings (as listed here) per day. Spread out the servings throughout the day. If you eat all 3 servings at once, it could raise your blood glucose level.
- Food and drink choices listed here without a serving size can be eaten whenever you like.

Low Carbohydrate Foods

Food	Serving Size
Cabbage, raw	½ cup
Candy, hard (regular or sugar-free)	1 piece
Carrots, cauliflower, or green beans, cooked	¼ cup
Cranberries, sweetened with sugar substitute	½ cup
Cucumber, sliced	½ cup
Gelatin	
dessert, sugar-free	
unflavored	
Gum	
Jam or jelly, light or no sugar added	2 tsp
Rhubarb, sweetened with sugar substitute	½ cup
Salad greens	
Sugar substitutes (artificial sweeteners)	
Syrup, sugar-free	2 Tbsp

Modified Fat Foods with Carbohydrate

Food	Serving Size
Cream cheese, fat-free	1 Tbsp (½ oz)
Creamers	
nondairy, liquid	1 Tbsp
nondairy, powdered	2 tsp
Margarine spread	
fat-free	1 Tbsp
reduced-fat	1 tsp
Mayonnaise	
fat-free	1 Tbsp
reduced-fat	1 tsp
Mayonnaise-style salad dressing	
fat-free	1 Tbsp
reduced-fat	1 tsp
Salad dressing	
fat-free or low-fat	1 Tbsp
fat-free, Italian	2 Tbsp
Sour cream, fat-free or reduced-fat	1 Tbsp
Whipped topping	
light or fat-free	2 Tbsp
regular	1 Tbsp

Condiments

Food	Serving Size
Barbecue sauce	2 tsp
Catsup (ketchup)	1 Tbsp
Honey mustard	1 Tbsp
Horseradish	
Lemon juice	
Miso	1½ tsp
Mustard	
Parmesan cheese, freshly grated	1 Tbsp
Pickle relish	1 Tbsp
Pickles	
dill	1½ medium
sweet, bread and butter	2 slices
sweet, gherkin	¾ oz
Salsa	¼ cup
Soy sauce, light or regular	1 Tbsp
Sweet and sour sauce	2 tsp
Sweet chili sauce	2 tsp
Taco sauce	1 Tbsp
Vinegar	
Yogurt, any type	2 Tbsp

Drinks/Mixes

Any food on the list—without a serving size listed—can be consumed in any moderate amount.

- Bouillon, broth, consommé
- Bouillon or broth, low-sodium
- Carbonated or mineral water
- Club soda
- Cocoa powder, unsweetened (1 Tbsp)
- Coffee, unsweetened or with sugar substitute
- Diet soft drinks, sugar-free
- Drink mixes, sugar-free
- Tea, unsweetened or with sugar substitute
- Tonic water, diet
- Water
- Water, flavored, carbohydrate free

Seasonings

Any food on this list can be consumed in any moderate amount.

- Flavoring extracts (for example, vanilla, almond, peppermint)
- Garlic
- Herbs, fresh or dried
- Nonstick cooking spray
- Pimento
- Spices
- Hot pepper sauce
- Wine, used in cooking
- Worcestershire sauce

KEY

= 480 milligrams or more of sodium per serving

D

TABLE D-10 Combination Foods

Many foods are eaten in various combinations, such as casseroles. Because "combination" foods do not fit into any one choice list, this list of choices provides some typical combination foods.

Entrees

Food	Serving Size	Count As
Casserole type (tuna noodle, lasagna, spaghetti with meatballs, chili with beans, macaroni and cheese)	1 cup (8 oz)	2 carbohydrates + 2 medium-fat meats
Stews (beef/other meats and vegetables)	1 cup (8 oz)	1 carbohydrate + 1 medium-fat meat + 0–3 fats
Tuna salad or chicken salad	½ cup (3½ oz)	½ carbohydrate + 2 lean meats + 1 fat

Frozen Meals/Entrees

Food	Serving Size	Count As
Burrito (beef and bean)	1 (5 oz)	3 carbohydrates + 1 lean meat + 2 fats
Dinner-type meal	generally 14–17 oz	3 carbohydrates + 3 medium-fat meats + 3 fats
Entrée or meal with less than 340 calories	about 8–11 oz	2–3 carbohydrates + 1–2 lean meats
Pizza		
cheese/vegetarian, thin crust	¼ of a 12 inch (4½–5 oz)	2 carbohydrates + 2 medium-fat meats
meat topping, thin crust	¼ of a 12 inch (5 oz)	2 carbohydrates + 2 medium-fat meats + 1½ fats
Pocket sandwich	1 (4½ oz)	3 carbohydrates + 1 lean meat + 1–2 fats
Pot pie	1 (7 oz)	2½ carbohydrates + 1 medium-fat meat + 3 fats

Salads (Deli-Style)

Food	Serving Size	Count As
Coleslaw	½ cup	1 carbohydrate + 1½ fats
Macaroni/pasta salad	½ cup	2 carbohydrates + 3 fats
Potato salad	½ cup	1½–2 carbohydrates + 1–2 fats

Soups

Food	Serving Size	Count As
Bean, lentil, or split pea	1 cup	1 carbohydrate + 1 lean meat
Chowder (made with milk)	1 cup (8 oz)	1 carbohydrate + 1 lean meat + 1½ fats
Cream (made with water)	1 cup (8 oz)	1 carbohydrate + 1 fat
Instant	6 oz prepared	1 carbohydrate
with beans or lentils	8 oz prepared	2½ carbohydrates + 1 lean meat
Miso soup	1 cup	½ carbohydrate + 1 fat
Oriental noodle	1 cup	2 carbohydrates + 2 fats
Rice (congee)	1 cup	1 carbohydrate
Tomato (made with water)	1 cup (8 oz)	1 carbohydrate
Vegetable beef, chicken noodle, or other broth-type	1 cup (8 oz)	1 carbohydrate

KEY

= More than 3 grams of dietary fiber per serving.

= Extra fat, or prepared with added fat.

= 600 milligrams or more of sodium per serving (for combination food main dishes/meals).

TABLE D-11 Fast Foods

The choices in the Fast Foods list are not specific fast-food meals or items, but are estimates based on popular foods. Ask the restaurant or check its website for nutrition information about your favorite fast foods.

Food	Serving Size	Count As
Breakfast Sandwiches		
Egg, cheese, meat, English muffin	1 sandwich	2 carbohydrates + 2 medium-fat meats
Sausage biscuit sandwich	1 sandwich	2 carbohydrates + 2 high-fat meats + 3½ fats
Main Dishes/Entrees		
Burrito (beef and beans)	1 (about 8 oz)	3 carbohydrates + 3 medium-fat meats + 3 fats
Chicken breast, breaded and fried	1 (about 5 oz)	1 carbohydrate + 4 medium-fat meats
Chicken drumstick, breaded and fried	1 (about 2 oz)	2 medium-fat meats
Chicken nuggets	6 (about 3½ oz)	1 carbohydrate + 2 medium-fat meats + 1 fat
Chicken thigh, breaded and fried	1 (about 4 oz)	½ carbohydrate + 3 medium-fat meats + 1½ fats
Chicken wings, hot	6 (5 oz)	5 medium-fat meats + 1½ fats
Oriental		
Beef/chicken/shrimp with vegetables in sauce	1 cup (about 5 oz)	1 carbohydrate + 1 lean meat + 1 fat
Egg roll, meat	1 (about 3 oz)	1 carbohydrate + 1 lean meat + 1 fat
Fried rice, meatless	½ cup	1½ carbohydrates + 1½ fats
Meat and sweet sauce (orange chicken)	1 cup	3 carbohydrates + 3 medium-fat meats + 2 fats
Noodles and vegetables in sauce (chow mein, lo mein)	1 cup	2 carbohydrates + 1 fat
Pizza		
Pizza		
cheese, pepperoni, regular crust	⅛ of a 14 inch (about 4 oz)	2½ carbohydrates + 1 medium-fat meat + 1½ fats
cheese/vegetarian, thin crust	¼ of a 12 inch (about 6 oz)	2½ carbohydrates + 2 medium-fat meats + 1½ fats
Sandwiches		
Chicken sandwich, grilled	1	3 carbohydrates + 4 lean meats
Chicken sandwich, crispy	1	3½ carbohydrates + 3 medium-fat meats + 1 fat
Fish sandwich with tartar sauce	1	2½ carbohydrates + 2 medium-fat meats + 2 fats
Hamburger		
large with cheese	1	2½ carbohydrates + 4 medium-fat meats + 1 fat
regular	1	2 carbohydrates + 1 medium-fat meat + 1 fat
Hot dog with bun	1	1 carbohydrate + 1 high-fat meat + 1 fat
Submarine sandwich		
less than 6 grams fat	6-inch sub	3 carbohydrates + 2 lean meats
regular	6-inch sub	3½ carbohydrates + 2 medium-fat meats + 1 fat
Taco, hard or soft shell (meat and cheese)	1 small	1 carbohydrate + 1 medium-fat meat + 1½ fats

KEY

= More than 3 grams of dietary fiber per serving.

= Extra fat, or prepared with added fat.

= 600 milligrams or more of sodium per serving (for fast-food main dishes/meals).

TABLE D-11 Fast Foods *(continued)*

Salads		
Food	**Serving Size**	**Count as**
🧂☺ Salad, main dish (grilled chicken type, no dressing or croutons)		1 carbohydrate + 4 lean meats
Salad, side, no dressing or cheese	Small (about 5 oz)	1 vegetable
Sides/Appetizers		
Food	**Serving Size**	**Count as**
⚠ French fries, restaurant style	small	3 carbohydrates + 3 fats
	medium	4 carbohydrates + 4 fats
	large	5 carbohydrates + 6 fats
🧂 Nachos with cheese	small (about 4½ oz)	2½ carbohydrates + 4 fats
🧂 Onion rings	1 serving (about 3 oz)	2½ carbohydrates + 3 fats
Desserts		
Food	**Serving Size**	**Count as**
Milkshake, any flavor	12 oz	6 carbohydrates + 2 fats
Soft-serve ice cream cone	1 small	2½ carbohydrates + 1 fat

KEY

☺ = More than 3 grams of dietary fiber per serving.

⚠ = Extra fat, or prepared with added fat.

🧂 = 600 milligrams or more of sodium per serving (for fast-food main dishes/meals).

TABLE D-12 Alcohol

1 alcohol equivalent = variable grams carbohydrate, 0 grams protein, 0 grams fat, and 100 calories.

NOTE: In general, one alcohol choice (½ ounce absolute alcohol) has about 100 calories. For those who choose to drink alcohol, guidelines suggest limiting alcohol intake to 1 drink or less per day for women, and 2 drinks or less per day for men. To reduce your risk of low blood glucose (hypoglycemia), especially if you take insulin or a diabetes pill that increases insulin, always drink alcohol with food. While alcohol, by itself, does not directly affect blood glucose, be aware of the carbohydrate (for example, in mixed drinks, beer, and wine) that may raise your blood glucose.

Alcoholic Beverage	Serving Size	Count as
Beer		
light (4.2%)	12 fl oz	1 alcohol equivalent + ½ carbohydrate
regular (4.9%)	12 fl oz	1 alcohol equivalent + 1 carbohydrate
Distilled spirits: vodka, rum, gin, whiskey, 80 or 86 proof	1½ fl oz	1 alcohol equivalent
Liqueur, coffee (53 proof)	1 fl oz	1 alcohol equivalent + 1 carbohydrate
Sake	1 fl oz	½ alcohol equivalent
Wine		
dessert (sherry)	3½ fl oz	1 alcohol equivalent + 1 carbohydrate
dry, red or white (10%)	5 fl oz	1 alcohol equivalent

Food Patterns to Meet the *Dietary Guidelines for Americans 2005*

Two examples of eating patterns that exemplify the *Dietary Guidelines for Americans 2005* are the USDA Food Guide of Chapter 2 (presented here as Tables E-1 and E-2) and the DASH Eating Plan shown in Table E-3.

CONTENTS

TABLE E-1 USDA Food Guide

This table specifies the suggested amounts of food to consume each day from the basic food groups, subgroups, and oils to meet recommended nutrient intakes at 12 different calorie levels. Note that amounts given for vegetable subgroups are weekly amounts. Nutrient and energy contributions from each group are calculated according to the nutrient-dense forms of foods in each group (e.g., lean meats and fat-free milk). The table also shows the discretionary calorie allowance that can be accommodated within each calorie level, in addition to the suggested amounts of nutrient-dense forms of foods in each group.

Amount of Food to Choose Each Day From Each Group (vegetable subgroup amounts are per week)												
Calorie Level	1,000	1,200	1,400	1,600	1,800	2,000	2,200	2,400	2,600	2,800	3,000	3,200
Food Group	Food group amounts shown in cup (c) or ounce-equivalents (oz-eq), with number of servings (srv) in parentheses when it differs from the other units. Oils are shown in grams (g).											
Fruits	1 c (2 srv)	1 c (2 srv)	1.5 c (3 srv)	1.5 c (3 srv)	1.5 c (3 srv)	2 c (4 srv)	2 c (4 srv)	2 c (4 srv)	2 c (4 srv)	2.5 c (5 srv)	2.5 c (5 srv)	2.5 c (5 srv)
Vegetables	1 c (2 srv)	1.5 c (3 srv)	1.5 c (3 srv)	2 c (4 srv)	2.5 c (5 srv)	2.5 c (5 srv)	3 c (6 srv)	3 c (6 srv)	3.5 c (7 srv)	3.5 c (7 srv)	4 c (8 srv)	4 c (8 srv)
Dark green veg.	1 c/wk	1.5 c/wk	1.5 c/wk	2 c/wk	3 c/wk	3 c/wk	3 c/wk	3 c/wk	3 c/wk	3 c/wk	3 c/wk	3 c/wk
Orange veg.	.5 c/wk	1 c/wk	1 c/wk	1.5 c/wk	2 c/wk	2 c/wk	2 c/wk	2 c/wk	2.5 c/wk	2.5 c/wk	2.5 c/wk	2.5 c/wk
Legumes	.5 c/wk	1 c/wk	1 c/wk	2.5 c/wk	3 c/wk	3 c/wk	3 c/wk	3 c/wk	3.5 c/wk	3.5 c/wk	3.5 c/wk	3.5 c/wk
Starchy veg.	1.5 c/wk	2.5 c/wk	2.5 c/wk	2.5 c/wk	3 c/wk	3 c/wk	6 c/wk	6 c/wk	7 c/wk	7 c/wk	9 c/wk	9 c/wk
Other veg.	4 c/wk	4.5 c/wk	4.5 c/wk	5.5 c/wk	6.5 c/wk	6.5 c/wk	7 c/wk	7 c/wk	8.5 c/wk	8.5 c/wk	10 c/wk	10 c/wk
Grains	3 oz-eq	4 oz-eq	5 oz-eq	5 oz-eq	6 oz-eq	6 oz-eq	7 oz-eq	8 oz-eq	9 oz-eq	10 oz-eq	10 oz-eq	10 oz-eq
Whole grains	1.5	2	2.5	3	3	3	3.5	4	4.5	5	5	5
Other grains	1.5	2	2.5	2	3	3	3.5	4	4.5	5	5	5
Lean meat and beans	2 oz-eq	3 oz-eq	4 oz-eq	5 oz-eq	5 oz-eq	5.5 oz-eq	6 oz-eq	6.5 oz-eq	6.5 oz-eq	7 oz-eq	7 oz-eq	7 oz-eq
Milk	2 c	2 c	2 c	3 c	3 c	3 c	3 c	3 c	3 c	3 c	3 c	3 c
Oils[1]	15 g	17 g	17 g	22 g	24 g	27 g	29 g	31 g	34 g	36 g	44 g	51 g
Discretionary calorie allowance[2]	165	171	171	132	195	267	290	362	410	426	512	648

[1]*Explanation of oils: Oils (including soft margarine with zero trans fat) shown in this table represent the amounts that are added to foods during processing, cooking, or at the table. Oils and soft margarines include vegetable oils and soft vegetable oil table spreads that have no trans fats. The amounts of oil listed in this table are not considered to be part of discretionary calories because they are a major source of the vitamin E and polyunsaturated fatty acids, including the essential fatty acids, in the food pattern. In contrast, solid fats are listed separately in Table (E-2) because, compared with oils, they are higher in saturated fatty acids and lower in vitamin E and polyunsaturated and monounsaturated fatty acids, including essential fatty acids. The amounts of each type of fat in the food intake pattern were based on 60% oils and/or soft margarines with no trans fats and 40% solid fat. To find teaspoons, divide grams by 5.*

[2]*Explanation of discretionary calorie allowance: The discretionary calorie allowance is the remaining amount of calories in each food pattern after selecting the specified number of nutrient-dense forms of foods in each food group. The number of discretionary calories assumes that food items in each food group are selected in nutrient-dense forms (that is, forms that are fat-free or low-fat and that contain no added sugars). Solid fat and sugar calories always need to be counted as discretionary calories, as in the following examples:*

- *The fat in low-fat, reduced fat, or whole milk or milk products or cheese and the sugar and fat in chocolate milk, ice cream, pudding, etc.*
- *The fat in higher fat meats (e.g., ground beef with more than 5% fat by weight, poultry with skin, higher fat luncheon meats, sausages)*
- *The sugars added to fruits and fruit juices with added sugars or fruits canned in syrup*
- *The added fat and/or sugars in vegetables prepared with added fat or sugars*
- *The added fats and/or sugars in grain products containing higher levels of fats and/or sugars (e.g., sweetened cereals, higher fat crackers, pies and other pastries, cakes, cookies)*

TABLE E-2 Discretionary Calorie Allowance in the USDA Food Guide

This table shows the number of discretionary calories remaining at each calorie level if nutrient-dense foods provide the base of the diet. The table shows an example of how these calories may be divided between solid fats and added sugars. Those trying to lose weight may choose to omit discretionary calories.

Discretionary Calories that Remain at Each Level												
Food Guide calorie level	1,000	1,200	1,400	1,600	1,800	2,000	2,200	2,400	2,600	2,800	3,000	3,200
Discretionary calories[1]	165	171	171	132	195	267	290	362	410	426	512	648
Example of Division of Discretionary Calories: Solid Fats are Shown in Grams (g); Added Sugars in Grams (g) and Teaspoons (tsp).												
Solid fats[2]	11 g	14 g	14 g	11 g	15 g	18 g	19 g	22 g	24 g	24 g	29 g	34 g
Added sugars[3]	20 g (5 tsp)	16 g (4 tsp)	16 g (4 tsp)	12 g (3 tsp)	20 g (5 tsp)	32 g (8 tsp)	36 g (9 tsp)	48 g (12 tsp)	56 g (14 tsp)	60 g (15 tsp)	72 g (18 tsp)	96 g (24 tsp)

[1]*The USDA Food Guide assumes foods will be nutrient dense (that is, fat-free or low-fat and contain no added sugars). Solid fat and sugar calories must always be counted as discretionary calories. See Chapter 2 for more details.*

[2]*Solid fats: Amounts of solid fats listed in the table represent about 7 to 8% of calories from saturated fat. Solid fats shown in this table represent the amounts of fats that may be added in cooking or at the table, and fats consumed when higher fat items are selected from the food groups. Most oils are not considered to be part of the discretionary calorie allowance because they are a major source of the essential fatty acids and vitamin E in the food pattern.*

[3]*The amounts of added sugars suggested in the example are NOT specific recommendations for amounts of added sugars to consume, but rather represent the amounts that can be included in each calorie level without over-consuming calories. The suggested amounts of added sugars may be helpful as part of the Food Guide to allow for some sweetened foods or beverages, without exceeding energy needs. This use of added sugars as a calorie balance requires two assumptions: (1) that selections are made from all food groups in accordance with the suggested amounts and (2) that additional fats are used in the amounts shown, which, together with the fats in the core food groups, represent about 27–30% of calories from fat.*

TABLE E-3 The DASH Eating Plan at 1,600-, 2,000-, 2,600-, and 3,100-Calorie Levels[a]

The number of daily servings to choose from each food group depends on a person's energy requirement (see Chapter 9).

Food Groups	1,600 Calories	2,000 Calories	2,600 Calories	3,100 Calories	Serving Sizes	Examples and Notes	Significance of Each Food Group to the DASH Eating Plan
Grains[b]	6 servings	7–8 servings	10–11 servings	12–13 servings	1 slice bread, 1 oz dry cereal,[c] ½ cup cooked rice, pasta, or cereal	Whole wheat bread, English muffin, pita bread, bagel, cereals, grits, oatmeal, crackers, unsalted pretzels, and popcorn	Major sources of energy and fiber
Vegetables	3–4 servings	4–5 servings	5–6 servings	6 servings	1 cup raw leafy vegetable, ½ cup cooked vegetable, 6 oz vegetable juice	Tomatoes, potatoes, carrots, green peas, squash, broccoli, turnip greens, collards, kale, spinach, artichokes, green beans, lima beans, sweet potatoes	Rich sources of potassium, magnesium, and fiber
Fruits	4 servings	4–5 servings	5–6 servings	6 servings	6 oz fruit juice 1 medium fruit ¼ cup dried fruit ½ cup fresh, frozen, or canned fruit	Apricots, bananas, dates, grapes, oranges, orange juice, grapefruit, grapefruit juice, mangoes, melons, peaches, pineapples, prunes, raisins, strawberries, tangerines	Important sources of potassium, magnesium, and fiber
Low-fat or fat-free dairy foods	2–3 servings	2–3 servings	3 servings	3–4 servings	8 oz milk 1 cup yogurt 1½ oz cheese	Fat-free or low-fat milk, fat-free or low-fat buttermilk, fat-free or low-fat regular or frozen yogurt, low-fat and fat-free cheese	Major sources of calcium and protein
Meat, poultry, fish	1–2 servings	2 or less servings	2 servings	2–3 servings	3 oz cooked meats, poultry, or fish	Select only lean; trim away visible fats; broil, roast, or boil instead of frying; remove skin from poultry	Rich sources of protein and magnesium
Nuts, seeds, legumes	3–4 servings/ week	4–5 servings/ week	1serving	1serving	⅓ cup or 1½ oz nuts, 2 Tbsp or ½ oz seeds ½ cup cooked dry beans or peas	Almonds, filberts, mixed nuts, peanuts, walnuts, sunflower seeds, kidney beans, lentils	Rich sources of energy, magnesium, potassium, protein, and fiber
Fat and oils[d]	2 servings	2–3 servings	3 servings	4 servings	1 tsp soft margarine 1 Tbsp low-fat mayonnaise 2 Tbsp light salad dressing, 1 tsp vegetable oil	Soft margarine, low-fat mayonnaise, light salad dressing, vegetable oil (such as olive, corn, canola, or safflower)	DASH has 27 percent of calories as fat (low in saturated fat), including fat in or added to foods
Sweets	0 servings	5 servings/week	2 servings	2 servings	1 Tbsp sugar, 1 Tbsp jelly or jam, ½ oz jelly beans, 8 oz lemonade	Maple syrup, sugar, jelly, jam, fruit-flavored gelatin, jelly beans, hard candy, fruit punch, sorbet, ices	Sweets should be low in fat

[a]*NIH publication No. 03–4082; Karanja NM et al. JADA 8:S19–27, 1999.*

[b]*Whole grains are recommended for most servings to meet fiber recommendations.*

[c]*Equals ½–1¼ cups, depending on cereal type. Check the product's Nutrition Facts Label.*

[d]*Fat content changes serving counts for fats and oils: For example, 1 Tbsp of regular salad dressing equals 1 serving; 1 Tbsp of a low-fat dressing equals ½ serving; 1 Tbsp of a fat-free dressing equals 0 servings.*

Source: U.S. Department of Agriculture and U.S. Department of Health and Human Services, Dietary Guidelines for Americans 2005, *6th edition, available online at www.healthierus.gov or call (888) 878-3256.*

Notes

Chapter 1

1. S. S. Gidding and coauthors, Implementing American Heart Association pediatric and adult nutrition guidelines, *Circulation* 119 (2009): 1161–1175; Preventability of cancer, in World Cancer Research Fund/American Institute for Cancer Research, *Policy and Action for Cancer Prevention. Food, Nutrition, and Physical Activity: A Global Perspective* (Washington, D.C.: AICR, 2009).
2. J. Kaput, Nutrigenomics—2006 update, *Clinical Chemistry and Laboratory Medicine* 45 (2007): 279–287.
3. U.S. Department of Health and Human Services, *Healthy People 2010,* 2nd ed. (Washington, D.C.: U.S. Government Printing Office, 2000), available online at www.health.gov/healthypeople or call (800) 367-4725.
4. Centers for Disease Control and Prevention, QuickStats: Average total cholesterol level among men and women aged 20–74 Years—National Health and Nutrition Examination Survey, United States, 1959–1962 to 2007–2008, *Morbidity and Mortality Weekly Report* 58 (2009): 1045; U.S. Department of Health and Human Services, *Midcourse Review, 2006,* available at www.healthypeople.gov/data/midcourse/default.htm#pubs.
5. U.S. Department of Health and Human Services, *Progress Review: Nutrition and Overweight,* January 21, 2004, available at www.healthypeople.gov.
6. Position of the American Dietetic Association, Total diet approach to communicating food and nutrition information, *Journal of the American Dietetic Association* 107 (2007): 1224–1232.
7. D. R. Jacobs and L. C. Tapsell, Food, not nutrients, is the fundamental unit in nutrition, *Nutrition Reviews* 65 (2007): 439–450.
8. D. R. Jacobs, M. D. Gross, and L. C. Tapsell, Food synergy: An operational concept for understanding nutrition, *American Journal of Clinical Nutrition* 89 (2009): 1543S–1548S.
9. R. L. Koretz, Do data support nutrition support? Part I: Intravenous nutrition, *Journal of the American Dietetic Association* 107 (2007): 988–996.
10. Centers for Disease Control and Prevention, State indicator report on fruits and vegetables, 2009, available at www.fruitsandveggiesmatter.gov/downloads/StateIndicatorReport2009.pdf.
11. Position of the American Dietetic Association, Functional foods, *Journal of the American Dietetic Association* 109 (2009): 735–746.
12. Standing Committee on the Scientific Evaluation of Dietary Reference Intakes, Food and Nutrition Board, Institute of Medicine, *Dietary Reference Intakes for Energy, Carbohydrate, Fiber, Fat, Fatty Acids, Cholesterol, Protein, and Amino Acids* (Washington, D.C.: National Academy Press, 2002), pp. 11-1–11-88.
13. S. P. Murphy and coauthors, Simple measures of dietary variety are associated with improved dietary quality, *Journal of the American Dietetic Association* 106 (2006): 425–429.
14. U.S. Department of Agriculture and U.S. Department of Health and Human Services, *Dietary Guidelines for Americans 2005,* available online at www.usda.gov/cnpp or call (888) 878-3256.
15. K. Stein, Navigating cultural competency: In preparation for an expected standard in 2010, *Journal of the American Dietetic Association* 109 (2009): 1676–1688.
16. Position of the American Dietetic Association and Dietitians of Canada: Vegetarian diets, *Journal of the American Dietetic Association* 109 (2009): 1266–1283.
17. J. Mathieu, Hey everyone, dinner's ready . . . two weeks ago, *Journal of the American Dietetic Association* 107 (2007): 26–27.
18. J. E. Tillotson, The mega-brands that rule our diet, Part 1, *Nutrition Today* 40 (2006): 257–260.
19. M. Franco and coauthors, Availability of healthy foods and dietary patterns: The multiethnic study of atherosclerosis, *American Journal of Clinical Nutrition* 89 (2009): 897–904; M. Bryant and J. Stevens, Measurement of food availability in the home, *Nutrition Reviews* 64 (2006): (I)67–76.
20. B. J. Tepper, Nutritional implications of genetic taste variation: The role of PROP sensitivity and other taste phenotypes, *Annual Review of Nutrition* 28 (2008): 367–388; A. A. Bachmanov and G. K. Beauchamp, Taste receptor genes, *Annual Review of Nutrition* 27 (2007): 389–414.
21. N. H. Steneck, *Introduction to the Responsible Conduct of Research* (Washington, D.C.: U.S. Government Printing Office, 2007).
22. G. D. Miller and coauthors, It is time for a positive approach to dietary guidance using nutrient density as a basic principle, *Journal of Nutrition* 139 (2009): 1198–1202; Practice Paper of the American Dietetic Association: Nutrient density: Meeting nutrient goals within calorie needs, *Journal of the American Dietetic Association* 107 (2007): 860–869.
23. L. M. Lipsky, Are energy-dense foods really cheaper? Reexamining the relation between food price and energy density, *American Journal of Clinical Nutrition* 90 (2009): 1397–1401.

CONTROVERSY 1

1. J. Gazzaniga-Moloo, *Nutrition and you: Trends 2008 report of results,* session SUN169, ADA Food and Nutrition Conference and Expo, October 2008.
2. M. H. Cohen, Legal and ethical issues relating to use of complementary therapies in pediatric hematology/oncology, *Journal of Pediatric Haemotology/Oncology* 28 (2006): 190–193.
3. Food and Drug Administration, FDA 101: Health Fraud Awareness, FDA Consumer Health Information, July 2009, available at www.fda.gov.
4. A. H. Lichtenstein, Diet, heart disease, and the role of the registered dietitian, *Journal of the American Dietetic Association* 107 (2007): 205–208.
5. Position of the American Dietetic Association: Food and nutrition misinformation, *Journal of the American Dietetic Association* 106 (2006): 601–607.
6. K. M. Adams and coauthors, Status of nutrition education in medical schools, *American Journal of Clinical Nutrition* 83 (2006): 941S–944S.
7. Position of the American Dietetic Association, The roles of registered dietitians and dietetic technicians, registered in health promotion and disease prevention, *Journal of the American Dietetic Association* 106 (2006): 1875–1884.

Chapter 2

1. Standing Committee on the Scientific Evaluation of Dietary Reference Intakes, Food and Nutrition Board, Institute of Medicine, *Dietary Reference Intakes: Applications in Dietary Assessment* (Washington, D.C.: National Academy Press, 2000), pp. 5–7.
2. R. M. Russell, Current framework for DRI development: What are the pros and cons? *Nutrition Reviews* 66 (2008): 455–458.
3. C. L. Taylor, Highlights of 'a model for establishing upper levels of intake for nutrients and related substances: Report of a joint FAO/WHO technical workshop on nutrient risk assessment, May 2–6, 2005,' *Nutrition Reviews* 65 (2007): 31–38.
4. U.S. Department of Agriculture and U.S. Department of Health and Human Services, *Dietary Guidelines for Americans 2005* (Washington, D.C.: U.S. Government Printing Office, 2005), available online at www.usda.gov/cnpp or call (888) 878-3256.
5. P. M. Guenther, J. Reedy, and S. M. Krebs-Smith, Development of the Healthy Eating Index—2005, *Journal of the American Dietetic Association* 108 (2008): 1896–1901; Center for Nutrition Policy and Promotion, Healthy Eat-

ing Index—2005, fact sheet revised June 2008, www.cnpp.usda.gov.
6. Center for Nutrition Policy and Promotion, Diet quality of Americans in 1994–1996 and 2001–02 as measured by the Healthy Eating Index—2005, Nutrition Insight 37 revised August 2008, www.cnpp.usda.gov.
7. S. J. Marshall and coauthors, Translating physical activity recommendations into a pedometer-based step goal, *American Journal of Preventive Medicine* 36 (2009): 410–415.
8. U.S. Department of Health and Human Services, *2008 Physical Activity Guidelines for Americans,* available at www.health.gov/paguidelines/default.aspx.
9. U.S. Department of Agriculture and U.S. Department of Health and Human Services, *Dietary Guidelines for Americans 2005,* available online at www.healthierus.gov.
10. Food and Drug Administration, *The Scoop on Whole Grains,* May 6, 2009, available at www.fda.gov/consumer.
11. S. P. Murphy and coauthors, Simple measures of dietary variety are associated with improved dietary quality, *Journal of the American Dietetic Association* 106 (2006): 425–429.

CONSUMER CORNER 2

1. Dietary Reference Intakes (DRIs) for food labeling, *American Journal of Clinical Nutrition* 83 (2006): 1215S–1216S.
2. Position of the American Dietetic Association, Functional foods, *Journal of the American Dietetic Association* 109 (2009): 735–746.
3. U.S. Food and Drug Administration, Center for Food Safety and Applied Nutrition, Claims that can be made for conventional foods and dietary supplements, September 2003, available at www.cfsan.fda.gov.

CONTROVERSY 2

1. Position of the American Dietetic Association, Functional foods, *Journal of the American Dietetic Association* 109 (2009): 735–746.
2. R. B. Costello and L. G. Saldanha, eds., *Annual Bibliography of Significant Advances in Dietary Supplement Research 2007,* NIH publication number 08-6456; E. Reska, W. Wasowicz, and J. Gromadzinska, Genetic polymorphism of xenobiotic metabolizing enzymes, diet, and cancer susceptibility, *British Journal of Nutrition* 96 (2006): 609–619.
3. J. Lin and coauthors, Dietary intakes of flavonols and flavones and coronary heart disease in U.S. women, *American Journal of Epidemiology* 165 (2007): 1305–1313; D. F. Birt, Phytochemicals and cancer prevention: From epidemiology to mechanism of action, *Journal of the American Dietetic Association* 106 (2006): 20–21.
4. J. A. Joseph, B. Shukitt-Hale, and F. C. Lau, Fruit polyphenols and their effects on neuronal signaling and behavior in senescence, *Annals of the New York Academy of Sciences* 1100 (2007): 470–485; I. Rahman, Dietary polyphenols mediated regulation of oxidative stress and chromatin remodeling in inflammation, *Nutrition Reviews* 66 (2008): S42–S45.
5. B. Shukitt-Hale, F. C. Lau, and J. A. Joseph, Berry fruit supplementation and the aging brain, *Journal of Agricultural and Food Chemistry* 56 (2008): 636–641.
6. F. C. Lau, B. Shukitt-Hale, and J. A. Joseph, Nutrition intervention in brain aging: Reducing the effects of inflammation and oxidative stress, *Sub-cellular Biochemistry* 42 (2007): 299–318.
7. Lau, Shukitt-Hale, and Joseph, Nutrition intervention in brain aging.
8. Lau, Shukitt-Hale, and Joseph, Nutrition intervention in brain aging; I. Erlund and coauthors, Favorable effects of berry consumption on platelet function, blood pressure, and HDL cholesterol, *American Journal of Clinical Nutrition* 87 (2008): 323–331; B. L. Halvorsen and coauthors, Content of redox-active compounds (i.e., antioxidants) in foods consumed in the United States, *American Journal of Clinical Nutrition* 84 (2006): 95–135; M. Rosenblat, T. Hayek, and M. Aviram, Anti-oxidative effects of pomegranate juice (PJ) consumption by diabetic patients on serum and on macrophages, *Atherosclerosis* 187 (2006): 363–371.
9. R. di Giuseppe and coauthors, Regular consumption of dark chocolate is associated with low serum concentrations of C-reactive protein in a healthy Italian population, *Journal of Nutrition* 138 (2008): 1939–1945; D. Taubert, R. Roesen, and E. Schomig, Effect of cocoa and tea intake on blood pressure, *Archives of Internal Medicine* 167 (2007): 626–634; M. B. Engler and M. M. Engler, The emerging role of flavonoid-rich cocoa and chocolate in cardiovascular health and disease, *Nutrition Reviews* 64 (2006): 109–118.
10. S. Baba and coauthors, Continuous intake of polyphenolic compounds containing cocoa powder reduces LDL oxidative susceptibility and has beneficial effects on plasma HDL-cholesterol concentrations in humans, *American Journal of Clinical Nutrition* 85 (2007): 709–717.
11. W. D. Crews, Jr., D. W. Harrison, and J. W. Wright, A double-blind, placebo-controlled, randomized trial of the effects of dark chocolate and cocoa on variables associated with neuropsychological functioning and cardiovascular health: Clinical findings from a sample of healthy, cognitively intact older adults, *American Journal of Clinical Nutrition* 87 (2008): 872–880.
12. A. Pan and coauthors, Meta-analysis of the effects of flaxseed interventions on blood lipids, *American Journal of Clinical Nutrition* 90 (2009): 288–297.
13. J. Chen and coauthors, Flaxseed and pure secoisolariciresinol diglucoside, but not flaxseed hull, reduce human breast turmor growth (MCF7) in athymic mice, *Journal of Nutrition* 139 (2009): 2061–2066.
14. W. Demark-Wahnefried and coauthors, Flaxseed supplementation (not dietary fat restriction) reduces prostate cancer proliferation rates in men presurgery, *Cancer Epidemiology, Biomarkers, and Prevention* 17 (2008): 3577–3587.
15. G. K. Paschos and coauthors, Dietary supplementation with flaxseed oil lowers blood pressure in dyslipidaemic patients, *European Journal of Clinical Nutrition* 61 (2007): 1201–1206.
16. C. Galeone, Onion and garlic use and human cancer, *American Journal of Clinical Nutrition* 84 (2006): 1027–1032.
17. K. Aquilano and coauthors, Neuronal nitric oxide synthase protects neuroblastoma cells from oxidative stress mediated by garlic derivatives, *Journal of Neurochemistry,* 101 (2007): 1327–1337; Y. Okada and coauthors, Kinetic and mechanistic studies of allicin as an antioxidant, *Organic and Biomolecular Chemistry* 4 (2006): 4113–4117.
18. J. Y. Kim and O. Kwon, Garlic intake and cancer risk: An analysis using the Food and Drug Administration's evidence-based review system for the scientific evaluation of health claims, *American Journal of Clinical Nutrition* 89 (2009): 257–264.
19. C. D. Gardner and coauthors, Effect of raw garlic vs commercial garlic supplements on plasma lipid concentrations in adults with moderate hypercholesterolemia: A randomized clinical trial, *Archives of Internal Medicine* 167 (2007): 346–353.
20. S. Mukherjee and coauthors, Freshly crushed garlic is a superior cardioprotective agent than processed garlic, *Journal of Agricultural and Food Chemistry* 57 (2009): 7137–7144.
21. Y. Zhang and coauthors, Soy isoflavones and their bone protective effects, *Inflammopharmacology* 16 (2008): 213–215.
22. F. M. Steinberg, Soybeans or soymilk: Does it make a difference for cardiovascular protection? Does it even matter? *American Journal of Clinical Nutrition* 85 (2007): 927–928; N. R. Matthan and coauthors, Effect of soy protein from differently processed products on cardiovascular disease risk factors and vascular endothelial function in hypercholesterolemic subjects, *American Journal of Clinical Nutrition* 85 (2007): 960–966.
23. F. M. Sacks and coauthors, Soy protein, isoflavones, and cardiovascular health: An American Heart Association Science advisory for professionals from the Nutrition Committee, *Circulation* 113 (2006): 1034–1044.
24. S. Barnes, Nutritional genomics, polyphenols, diets and their impact on dietetics, *Journal of the American Dietetic Association* 108 (2008): 1888–1895.
25. J. W. Lampe, Is equol the key to the efficacy of soy foods? *American Journal of Clinical Nutrition* 89 (2009): 1664S–1667S.
26. S-A. Lee and coauthors, Adolescent and adult soy food intake and breast cancer risk: Results from the Shanghai Women's Health Study, *American Journal of Clinical Nutrition* 89 (2009): 1920–1926; M. Messina and A. H. Wu, Perspectives on the soy–breast cancer relation, *American Journal of Clinical Nutrition* 89 (2009): 1673S–1679S; A. Warri and coauthors, The role of early life genistein exposures in modifying breast cancer risk, *British Journal of Cancer* 98 (2008): 1485–1493.

27. Zhang, Soy isoflavones and their bone protective effects.
28. C. K. Taylor and coauthors, The effect of genistein aglycone on cancer and cancer risk: A review of in vitro, preclinical, and clinical studies, *Nutrition Reviews* 67 (2009): 398–415.
29. C. A. Lammersfeld and coauthors, Prevalence, sources, and predictors of soy consumption in breast cancer, *Nutrition Journal* 8 (2009) doi:10.1186/475-289-8-2.
30. Lampe, Is equol the key to the efficacy of soy foods?
31. R. C. Poulsen and M. C. Kruger, Soy phytoestrogens: Impact on postmenopausal bone loss and mechanisms of action, *Nutrition Reviews* 66 (2008): 359–374; Sacks and coauthors, Soy protein, isoflavones, and cardiovascular health.
32. D. L. Alekel and coauthors, The Soy Isoflavones for Reducing Bone Loss (SIRBL) Study: a 3-y randomized controlled trial in postmenopausal women, *American Journal of Clinical Nutrition* 91 (2010): 218–230.
33. R. L. Roberts, J. Green, and B. Lewis, Lutein and zeaxanthin in eye and skin health, *Clinical Dermatology* 27 (2009): 195–201; W. Stah and H. Sies, Carotenoids and flavonoids contribute to nutritional protection against skin damage from sunlight, *Molecular Biotechnology* 37 (2007): 26–30.
34. J. R. Mein, F. Lian, and X-D. Wang, Biological activity of lycopene metabolites: Implications for cancer prevention, *Nutrition Reviews* 66 (2008): 667–668; N. Khan, F. Afaq, and H. Mukhtar, Cancer chemoprevention through dietary antioxidants: Progress and promise, *Antioxidants and Redox Signaling* 10 (2008): 475–510.
35. C. J. Kavanaugh, P. R. Trumbo, and K. E. Ellwood, The U.S. Food and Drug Administration's evidence-based review for qualified health claims: Tomatoes, lycopene, and cancer, *Journal of the National Cancer Institute* 99 (2007): 1047–1085.
36. J. A. Satia and coauthors, Long-term use of beta-carotene, retinol, lycopene, and lutein supplements and lung cancer risk: Results from the VITamins and Lifestyle (VITAL) Study, *American Journal of Epidemiology* 169 (2009): 815–828.
37. N. Kumar and coauthors, Tea consumption and risk of breast cancer, *Cancer Epidemiology, Biomarkers, and Prevention* 18 (2009): 341–345.
38. K. Boehm and coauthors, Green tea (Camellia sinensis) for the prevention of cancer, *The Cochrane Database of Systematic Reviews* 3 (2009): doi:10.1002/14651858.CD005004.pub2.
39. S. Kuriyama and coauthors, Green tea consumption and mortality due to cardiovascular disease, cancer, and all causes in Japan, *Journal of the American Medical Association* 296 (2006): 1255–1265.
40. A. Basu and E. A. Lucas, Mechanisms and effects of green tea on cardiovascular health, *Nutrition Reviews* (2007): 361–375.
41. Basu and Lucas, Mechanisms and effects of green tea on cardiovascular health.
42. M. D. Knutson and C. Leeuwenburgh, Resveratrol and novel potent activators of SRT1: Effects on aging and age-related disease, *Nutrition Reviews* 66 (2008): 591–596.
43. M. M. Dohadwala and J. A. Vita, Grapes and cardiovascular disease, *Journal of Nutrition* 139 (2009): 1788S–1793S.
44. S. C. Forester and A. L. Waterhouse, Metabolites are key to understanding health effects of wine polyphenolics, *Journal of Nutrition* 139 (2009): 1824S–1831S.
45. C. C. Udenigwe and coauthors, Potential of resveratrol in anticancer and anti-inflammatory therapy, *Nutrition Reviews* 66 (2008): 445–454; Knutson and Leeuwenburgh, Resveratrol and novel potent activators of SRT1.
46. L. K. Curtiss, Reversing atherosclerosis, *New England Journal of Medicine* 360 (2009): 1144–1146; B. Romier and coauthors, Dietary polyphenolds can modulate the intestinal inflammatory response, *Nutrition Reviews* 67 (2009): 363–378; A. Basu and K. Penugonda, Pomegranate juice: A heart-healthy fruit juice, *Nutrition Reviews* 67 (2009): 49–56.
47. M. E. Sanders, How do we know when something called "probiotic" is really a probiotic? A guideline for consumers and health care professionals, *Functional Food Reviews* 1 (2009): 3–12; G. J. Leyer and coauthors, Probiotic effects on cold and influenza-like symptom incidence and duration in children, *Pediatrics* 124 (2009): e172–e179; S. C. Corr and coauthors, Bacteriocin production as a mechanism for the antiinfective activity of *Lactobacillus salivarius* UCC118, *Proceedings of the National Academy of Sciences* 104 (2007): 7617–7621; M. Elli and coauthors, Survival of yogurt bacteria in the human gut, *Applied and Environmental Microbiology* 72 (2006): 5113–5117; S. Parvez and coauthors, Probiotics and their fermented food products are beneficial for health, *Journal of Applied Microbiology* 100 (2006):1171–1185.
48. National Center for Complementary and Alternative Medicine, Get the facts: An introduction to probiotics, January 2007, available at http://nccam.nih.gov/health/probiotics/index.htm; F. Guarner, Enteric flora in health and disease, *Digestion* 73 (2006): 5–12.
49. K. Whelan and C. E. Myers, Safety of probiotics in patients receiving nutritional support: A systematic review of case reports, randomized controlled trials, and nonrandomized trials, *American Journal of Clinical Nutrition*, 91 (2010): 687–703; L. E. Morrow, Prebiotics in the intensive care unit, *Current Opinion in Critical Care* 15 (2009): 144–148; M-T. Liong, Safety of probiotics: Translocation and infection, *Nutrition Reviews* 66 (2008): 192–202.
50. D. J. Rose and coauthors, Influence of dietary fiber on inflammatory bowel disease and colon cancer: Importance of fermentation pattern, *Nutrition Reviews* 65 (2007): 51–62.
51. D. L. Worthley and coauthors, A human, double-blind, placebo-controlled, crossover trial of prebiotic, probiotic, and symbiotic supplementation: effects on luminal inflammatory, epigenetic, and epithelial biomarkers of colorectal cancer, *American Journal of Clinical Nutrition* 90 (2009): 578–58; I. Lenoir-Winjkoop and coauthors, Probioic and prebiotic influence beyond the intestinal tract, *Nutrition Reviews* 65 (2007): 469–489; J. Ezendam and H. van Loveren, Probiotics: Immunomodulation and evaluation of safety and efficacy, *Nutrition Reviews* 64 (2006): 1–14.
52. D. R. Jacobs, M. D. Gross, and L. C. Tapsell, Food synergy: An operational concept for understanding nutrition, *American Journal of Clinical Nutrition* 89 (2009): 1543S–1548S; Barnes, Nutritional genomics, polyphenols, diets and their impact on dietetics.
53. R. H. Dashwood and E. Ho, Dietary agents as histone deacetylase inhibitors: Sulforaphane and structurally related isothiocyanates, *Nutrition Reviews* 66 (2009): S36–S38; G. A. Haza and coauthors, Protective effects of isothiocyanates alone or in combination with vitamin C towards N-nitrosodibutylamine or N-nitrosopiperidine-induced oxidatative DNA damage in the single-cell gel electrophoresis (SCGE)? HepG2 assay, *Journal of Applied Toxicology* 28 (2008): 196–2004.
54. S. B. Lotito and B. Frei, Consumption of flavonoid-rich foods and increased plasma antioxidant capacity in humans: Cause, consequence, or epiphenomenon? *Free Radical Biology and Medicine* 41 (2006): 1727–1746.
55. C. D. Fisher and coauthors, Induction of drug-metabolizing enzymes by garlic and allyl sulfide compounds via activation of CAR and NRF2, *Drug Metabolism and Disposition*, 35 (2007): 995–1000; S. Mandlekar, J. L. Hong, and A. N. Kong, Modulation of metabolic enzymes by dietary phytochemicals: A review of mechanisms underlying beneficial versus unfavorable effects, *Current Drug Metabolism* 7 (2006): 661–675.
56. S. Y. Lee, Y. W. Shin, and K. B. Hahm, Phytoceuticals: Mighty but ignored weapons against *Helicobacter pylori* infection, *Journal of Digestive Diseases* 9 (2008): 129–139; Y. Liu and coauthors, Cranberry changes the physicochemical surface properties of *E. coli* and adhesion with uroepithelial cells, *Colloids and Surfaces. B, Biointerfaces* 65 (2008): 35–42; S. Gorinstein and coauthors, The atherosclerotic heart disease and protecting properties of garlic: Contemporary data, *Molecular Nutrition and Food Research* 51 (2007): 1365–1381; A. B. Howell, Bioactive compounds in cranberries and their role in prevention of urinary tract infections, *Molecular Nutrition and Food Research* 51 (2007): 732–737.
57. I. Siró and coauthors, Functional food. Product development, marketing and consumer acceptance—A review, *Appetite* 51 (2008): 456–467.
58. S. Klingberg and coauthors, Inverse relation between dietary intake of naturally occurring plant sterols and serum cholesterol in northern Sweden, *American Journal of Clinical Nutrition* 87 (2008): 993–1001.
59. P. J. Jones and K. A. Varady, Are functional foods redefining nutritional require-

ments? *Applied Physiology, Nutrition, and Metabolism* 33 (2008): 118–123.
60. L. H. Ellegård and coauthors, Dietary plant sterols and cholesterol metabolism, *Nutrition Reviews* 65 (2007): 39–45.
61. H. J. Thompson and coauthors, Dietary botanical diversity affects the reduction of oxidative biomarkers in women due to high vegetable and fruit intake, *Journal of Nutrition* 136 (2006): 2207–2212.

Chapter 3

1. A. Pradhan, Obesity, metabolic syndrome, and type 2 diabetes: Inflammatory basis of glucose metabolic disorders, *Nutrition Reviews* 65 (2007): S152–156; P. Libby, Inflammatory mechanisms: The molecular basis of inflammation and disease, *Nutrition Reviews* 65 (2007): S140–S146.
2. B. Bistrian, Systemic response to inflammation, *Nutrition Reviews* 65 (2007): S170–172; J. Gauldie, Inflammation and the aging process: Devil or angel, *Nutrition Reviews* 65 (2007): S167–S169.
3. I. Rahman, Dietary polyphenols mediated regulation of oxidative stress and chromatin remodeling and inflammation, *Nutrition Reviews* 66 (2008): S42–S45.
4. Y. Ishimaru and coauthors, Transient receptor potential family members PKD1L3 and PKD2L1 form a candidate sour taste receptor, *Proceedings of the National Academy of Sciences*, 103 (2006): 12569–12574.
5. K. Kurihara, Glutamate: From discovery as a food flavor to role as a basic taste (umami), *American Journal of Clinical Nutrition* 90 (2009): 719S–722S; Q. Y. Chen and coauthors, Perceptual variation in umami taste and polymorphisms in *TAS1R* taste receptor genes, *American Journal of Clinical Nutrition* 90 (2009): 770S–779S.
6. K. D. Gifford, S. Baer-Sinnot, and L. N. Heverling, Managing and understanding sweetness: Common-sense solutions based on the science of sugars, sugar substitutes, and sweetness, *Nutrition Today* 44 (2009): 211–217.
7. R. Krebs, The gourmet ape: Evolution and human food preferences, *American Journal of Clinical Nutrition* 90 (2009): 707S–711S.
8. W. W. L. Hsiao and coauthors, The microbes of the intestine: An introduction to their metabolic and signaling capabilities, *Endocrinology and Metabolism Clinics of North America* 37 (2008): 857–871; F. Guarner, Enteric flora in health and disease, *Digestion* 73 (2006): S5–S12.
9. Hsaio and coauthors, 2008.
10. N. Vakil, Acid inhibition and infections outside the gastrointestinal tract, *American Journal of Gastroenterology* 104 (2009): S17–S20.
11. M. L. Schubert, Gastric secretion, *Current Opinion in Gastroenterology* 23 (2007): 595–601.
12. P. J. Kahrilas, Gastroesophageal reflux disease, *New England Journal of Medicine* 359 (2008): 1700–1707.
13. N. Vakil and D. Vaira, Sequential therapy for *Helicobacter pylori*—Time to consider making the switch? *Journal of the American Medical Association* 300 (2008): 1346–1347.
14. A. T. Axon, Relationship between *Helicobacter pylori* gastritis, gastric cancer and gastric acid secretion, *Advances in Medical Sciences* 52 (2007): 55–60.
15. M. J. Schuchert and J. D. Luketich, Management of Barrett's esophagus, *Oncology (Williston Park)* 21 (2007): 1382–1389.
16. N. J. Talley, K. L. Lasch, and C. Baum, A gap in our understanding: Chronic constipation and its comorbid conditions, *Clinical Gastroenterology and Hepatology* 7 (2009): 9–19.
17. J. F. Johanson, Review of the treatment options for chronic constipation, *Medscape General Medicine* 9 (2007): 25.
18. U.S. Department of Health and Human Services, National Institutes of Health, *Irritable Bowel Syndrome* (September, 2007), NIH Publication No. 07-693.
19. E. A. Mayer, Irritable bowel syndrome, *New England Journal of Medicine* 358 (2008): 1692–1699.
20. W. D. Heizer, S. Southern, and S. McGovern, The role of diet in symptoms of irritable bowel syndrome in adults: A narrative review, *Journal of the American Dietetic Association* 109 (2009): 1204–1214; A. C. Ford and coauthors, Effect of fibre, antispasmodics, and peppermint oil in the treatment of irritable bowel syndrome: Systematic review and meta-analysis, *British Journal of Medicine* 337 (2008): a2313.

CONTROVERSY 3

1. Centers for Disease Control and Prevention, Sociodemographic differences in binge drinking among adults—14 States, 2004, *Morbidity and Mortality Weekly Report* 58 (2004): 301–304.
2. S. Jarjour, L. Bai, and C. Gianoulakis, Effect of acute ethanol administration on the release of opioid peptides from the midbrain including the ventral tegmental area, *Alcoholism: Clinical and Experimental Research* 23 (2009), published online, doi:10.1111/j.1530-0277.2009.00924.x.
3. Centers for Disease Control and Prevention, *Quick Stats: Binge Drinking*, 2008, available at www.cdc.gov/alcohol/quickstats/binge_drinking.htm.
4. A. M. White, C. L. Kraus, and H. Swartzwelder, Many college freshmen drink at levels far beyond the binge threshold, *Alcoholism, Clinical and Experimental Research* 30 (2006): 1006–1010.
5. D. Kesmodel, Drinks with a jolt draw new scrutiny, *Wall Street Journal*, July 17, p. B1.
6. U.S. Food and Drug Administration, *For Consumers*, FDA to examine the safety of caffeinated alcoholic beverages, November 2009, available at www.fda.gov.
7. White, Kraus, and Swartzwelder, 2006.
8. Centers for Disease Control and Prevention, *Quick Stats: Binge Drinking*.
9. Centers for Disease Control and Prevention, *Quick Stats: Binge Drinking*.
10. S. Zakhari, Overview: How is alcohol metabolized by the body?, *Alcohol Research and Health* 29 (2006): 245–254.
11. A. J. Birley and coauthors, Association of the gastric alcohol dehydrogenase gene ADH7 with variation in ethanol metabolism, *Human Molecular Genetics* 17 (2008): 179–189.
12. J. Haorah and coauthors, Mechanism of alcohol-induced oxidative stress and neuronal injury, *Free Radical Biology and Medicine* 45 (2008): 1542–1550.
13. Zakhari, Overview: How is alcohol metabolized by the body?
14. Zakhari, Overview: How is alcohol metabolized by the body?
15. S. K. Das and D. M. Vasudevan, Alcohol-induced oxidative stress, *Life Sciences* 81 (2007): 177–187.
16. A. Dey and A. I. Cederbaum, Alcohol and oxidative liver injury, *Hepatology* 43 (2006): S63–S74; Zakhari, Overview: How is alcohol metabolized by the body?
17. M. Maneesh and coauthors, Alcohol abuse-duration dependent decrease in plasma testosterone and antioxidants in males, *Indian Journal of Physiology and Pharmacology* 50 (2006): 291–296.
18. A. McKinney and K. Coyle, Next-day effects of alcohol and an additional stressor on memory and psychomotor performance, *Journal of Studies on Alcohol and Drugs* 68 (2007): 446–454; A. McKinney and K. Coyle, Alcohol hangover effects on measures of affect the morning after a normal night's drinking, *Alcohol and Alcoholism* 41 (2006): 54–60.
19. L. E. Beane Freemean and coauthors, Mortality from lymphohematopoietic malignancies among workers in formaldehyde industries: The National Cancer Institute cohort, *Journal of the National Cancer Institute* (2009) 101 (2009): 751–761.
20. B. Flannery and coauthors, Gender differences in neurocognitive functioning among alcohol-dependent Russian patients, *Alcoholism: Clinical and Experimental Research* 31 (2007): 745–754.
21. A. Benedetti, M. E. Parent, and J. Siemiatycki, Lifetime consumption of alcoholic beverages and risk of 13 types of cancer in men: Results from a case-control study in Montreal, *Cancer Detection and Prevention* 32 (2009): 352–362; J. Q. Lew and coauthors, Alcohol and risk of breast cancer by histologic type and hormone receptor status in postmenopausal women, *American Journal of Epidemiology* 170 (2009): 308–317; N. E. Allen and coauthors, Moderate alcohol intake and cancer incidence in women, *Journal of the National Cancer Institute* 101 (2009): 296–305; S. M. Zhang and coauthors, Alcohol consumption and breast cancer risk in the Women's Health Study, *American Journal of Epidemiology* 165 (2007): 667–676; M. Ryan-Harshman and W. Aldoori, Diet and colorectal cancer: Review of the evidence, *Canadian Family Physician* 53 (2007): 1913–1920.
22. Benedetti, Parent, and Siemiatycki, Lifetime consumption of alcoholic beverages and risk of 13 types of cancer in men.
23. P. A. Newcomb, No difference between red wine or white wine consumption and breast

cancer, *Cancer Epidemiology, Biomarkers and Prevention* 18 (2009): 1007–1010.
24. D. M. Fergusson, J. M. Boden, and L. J. Horwood, Tests of causal links between alcohol abuse or dependence and major depression, *Archives of General Psychiatry* 66 (2009): 260–266.
25. M. R. Lucey, P. Mathurin, and T. R. Morgan, Alcoholic hepatitis, *New England Journal of Medicine* 360 (2009): 2758–2769.
26. Centers for Disease Control and Prevention, Cost Calculators, available at www.cdc.gov.
27. Standing Committee on the Scientific Evaluation of Dietary Reference Intakes, Food and Nutrition Board, Institute of Medicine, *Dietary Reference Intakes for Energy, Carbohydrate, Fiber, Fat, Fatty Acids, Cholesterol, Protein, and Amino Acids* (Washington, D.C.: National Academy Press, 2002/2005), p. 109.
28. S. G. Wannamethee, A. G. Shaper, and P. H. Whincup, Alcohol and adiposity: Effects of quantity and type of drink and time relation with meals, *International Journal of Obesity and Related Metabolic Disorders* 29 (2005): 1436–1444.
29. D. O. Ballunas and coauthors, Alcohol as a risk factor for type 2 diabetes: A systematic review and meta-analysis, *Diabetes Care* 32 (2009): 2123–2132; J. H. O'Keefe, K. A. Bybee, and C. J. Lavie, Alcohol and cardiovascular health: The razor-sharp double-edged sword, *Journal of the American College of Cardiology* 50 (2007): 1009–1014; R. Jugdaosigh and coauthors, Moderate alcohol consumption and increased bone mineral density: Potential ethanol and non-ethanol mechanisms, *Proceedings of the Nutrition Society* 65 (2006): 291–310.
30. M. P. Ferreira and D. Willoughby, Alcohol consumption: The good, the bad, and the indifferent, *Applied Physiology, Nutrition, and Metabolism* 33 (2008): 12–20.
31. Centers for Disease Control and Prevention, 2009.
32. P. Meier and H. K. Seitz, Age, alcohol metabolism and liver disease, *Current Opinion in Clinical Nutrition and Metabolic Care* 11 (2008): 21–26; H. K. Seitz and F. Stickel, Alcoholic liver disease in the elderly, *Clinics in Geriatric Medicine* 23 (2007): 905–921.
33. Dr. T. Naimi, Centers for Disease Control and Prevention, as quoted by R. C. Rabin, Alcohol's good for you? Some scientists doubt it, *The New York Times,* June 16, 2009.
34. Centers for Disease Control and Prevention, Alcohol and other drug use among victims of motor-vehicle crashes—West Virginia, 2004–2005, *Morbidity and Mortality Weekly Reports* 55 (2006): 1293.
35. Centers for Disease Control and Prevention, 2009.
36. U.S. Department of Agriculture and U.S. Department of Health and Human Services, *Dietary Guidelines for Americans 2005,* available online at www.usda.gov/cnpp.
37. J. Rehm and coauthors, Global burden of disease and injury and economic cost attributable to alcohol use and alcohol-use disorders, *Lancet* 373 (2009): 2223–2233; A. Z. Fan and coauthors, Patterns of alcohol consumption and the metabolic syndrome, *Journal of Clinical Endocrinology and Metabolism* 93 (2008): 3833–3838; Haorah and coauthors, 2008; Centers for Disease Control and Prevention, 2008.
38. Rehm and coauthors, 2009.
39. S. C. Forester and A. L. Waterhouse, Metabolites are key to understanding health effects of wine polyphenolics, *Journal of Nutrition* 139 (2009): 1824S–1831S.
40. C. Cooper and coauthors, Alcohol in moderation: Premorbid intelligence and cognition in older adults: results from the Psychiatric Morbidity Survey, *Journal of Neurology, Neurosurgery and Psychiatry* 80 (2009): 1236–1239.

Chapter 4

1. Artificial photosynthesis: Turning sunlight into liquid fuels moves a step closer, *ScienceDaily,* 12 March 2009, available at http://www.sciencedaily.com.
2. J. M. Wong and coauthors, Colonic health: Fermentation and short chain fatty acids, *Journal of Clinical Gastroenterology* 40 (2006): 235–243.
3. J. R. Jones, D. M. Lineback, and M. J. Levine, Dietary Reference Intakes: Implications for fiber labeling and consumption: A summary of the International Life Sciences Institute North America Fiber Workshop, June 1–2, 2004, Washington, D.C., *Nutrition Reviews* 64 (2006): 31–38.
4. L. Van Horn and coauthors, The evidence for dietary prevention and treatment of cardiovascular disease, *Journal of the American Dietetic Association* 108 (2008): 287–331; M. O. Weickert and A. F. Pfeiffer, Metabolic effects of dietary fiber consumption and prevention of diabetes, *Journal of Nutrition* 138 (2008): 439–442; N. R. Sahyoan and coauthors, Whole-grain intake is inversely associated with metabolic syndrome and mortality in older adults, *American Journal of Clinical Nutrition* 83 (2006): 124–131.
5. E. A. Williams and coauthors, Carbohydrate versus energy restriction: Effects on weight loss, body composition and metabolism, *Annals of Nutrition and Metabolism* 51 (2007): 232–243.
6. A. T. Merchant and coauthors, Carbohydrate intake and overweight and obesity among healthy adults, *Journal of the American Dietetic Association* 109 (2009): 1165–1172; Standing Committee on the Scientific Evaluation of Dietary Reference Intakes, Food and Nutrition Board, Institute of Medicine, *Dietary Reference Intake for Energy, Carbohydrate, Fiber, Fat, Fatty Acids, Cholesterol, Protein, and Amino Acids* (Washington, D.C.: National Academy Press, 2002), pp. 13–17.
7. A. Bhargava and A. Amialchuk, Added sugars displaced the use of vital nutrients in the National Food Stamp Program Survey, *Journal of Nutrition* 137 (2007): 453–460.
8. Y. Ma and coauthors, Association between carbohydrate intake and serum lipids, *Journal of the American College of Nutrition* 25 (2006): 155–163.
9. J. A. Nettleton and coauthors, Incident heart failure is associated with lower whole-grain intake and greater high-fat dairy and egg intake in the Atherosclerosis Risk in Communities (ARIC) study, *Journal of the American Dietetic Association* 108 (2008): 1881–1887; P. B. Mellen, T. F. Walsh, and D. M. Herrington, Whole grain intake and cardiovascular disease: A meta-analysis, *Nutrition, Metabolism, and Cardiovascular Diseases* 18 (2008): 283–290.
10. R. K. Johnson and coauthors, Dietary sugars intake and cardiovascular health: A Scientific Statement from the American Heart Association, *Circulation* 120 (2009): 1011–1020; U.S. Department of Agriculture and U.S. Department of Health and Human Services, *Dietary Guidelines for Americans 2005* (Washington, D.C.: U.S. Government Printing Office, 2005), available online at www.usda.gov/cnpp or call (888) 878-3256; Standing Committee on the Scientific Evaluation of Dietary Reference Intakes, 2002, pp. 13–17.
11. A. J. Flint and coauthors, Whole grains and incident hypertension in men, *American Journal of Clinical Nutrition* 90 (2009): 493–498.
12. Mellen, Walsh, and Herrington, Whole grain intake and cardiovascular disease; Position of the American Dietetic Association, Health implications of dietary fiber, *Journal of the American Dietetic Association* 102 (2008): 1716–1731.
13. K. C. Maki and coauthors, Whole-grain ready-to-eat oat cereal, as part of a dietary program for weight loss, reduces low-density lipoprotein cholesterol in adults with overweight and obesity more than a dietary program including low-fiber control foods, *Journal of the American Dietetic Association* 110 (2010): 205–214; M. B. Andon and J. W. Anderson, State of the art reviews: The oatmeal-cholesterol connection: 10 Years later, *American Journal of Lifestyle Medicine* 2 (2008): 51–57.
14. L. A. Bazzano, Effects of soluble dietary fiber on low-density lipoprotein cholesterol and coronary heart disease risk, *Current Atherosclerosis Reports* 10 (2008): 473–477.
15. P. L. Lutsey and coauthors, Whole grain intake and its cross-sectional association with obesity, insulin resistance, inflammation, diabetes, and subclinical CVD: The MESA Study, *British Journal of Nutrition* 98 (2007): 397–405; M. B. Schulze and coauthors, Fiber and magnesium intake and incidence of type 2 diabetes, *Archives of Internal Medicine* 167 (2007): 956–965.
16. A. Parra-Blanco, Colonic diverticular disease: Pathophysiology and clinical picture, *Digestion* 73 (2006): 46–57.
17. S. Bingham, The fibre-folate debate in colorectal cancer, *Proceedings of the Nutrition Society* 65 (2006): 19–23; S. A. Bingham and coauthors, Dietary fibre in food and protection against colorectal cancer in the European Prospective Investigation into Cancer and Nutrition (EPIC): An observational study, *Lancet* 361 (2003): 1496–1501.

18. E. T. Jacobs and coauthors, Fiber, sex, and colorectal adenoma: Results of a pooled analysis, *American Journal of Clinical Nutrition* 83 (2006): 343–349.
19. A. Schatzkin and coauthors, Dietary fiber and whole-grain consumption in relation to colorectal cancer in the NIH-AARP Diet and Health Study, *American Journal of Clinical Nutrition* 85 (2007): 1353–1360.
20. K. Wallace and coauthors, The association of lifestyle and dietary factors with the risk for serrated polyps of the colorectum, *Cancer Epidemiology, Biomarkers, and Prevention* 18 (2009): 2310–2317.
21. S. Bingham, The fibre-folate debate in colorectal cancer.
22. S. M. Zhang and coauthors, Folate, vitamin B_6, multivitamin supplements, and colorectal cancer risk in women, *American Journal of Epidemiology* 163 (2006): 108–115.
23. D. J. Rose and coauthors, Influence of dietary fiber on inflammatory bowel disease and colon cancer: Importance of fermentation pattern, *Nutrition Reviews* 65 (2007): 51–62.
24. M. Comalada and coauthors, The effects of short-chain fatty acids on colon epithelial proliferation and survival depend on the cellular phenotype, *Journal of Cancer Research and Clinical Oncology* 132 (2006): 487–497; Standing Committee on the Scientific Evaluation of Dietary Reference Intakes, 2002, pp. 7–8.
25. L. A. Tucker and K. S. Thomas, Increasing total fiber intake reduces risk of weight and fat gains in women, *Journal of Nutrition* 139 (2009): 567–581.
26. N. Schroeder and coauthors, Influence of whole grain barley, whole grain wheat, and refined rice-based foods on short-term satiety and energy intake, *Appetite,* 53 (2009): 363–369; M. Lyly and coauthors, Fiber in beverages can enhance perceived satiety, *European Journal of Nutrition* 48 (2009): 251–258; K. R. Juvonen and coauthors, Viscosity of oat bran-enriched beverages influences gastrointestinal hormonal responses in healthy humans, *Journal of Nutrition* 139 (2009): 461–466; J. A. de Leeuw and coauthors, Effects of dietary fibre on behavior and satiety in pigs, *Proceedings of the Nutrition Society* 67 (2008): 334–342.
27. P. Vitaglione and coauthors, β-Glucan-enriched bread reduces energy intake and modifies plasma ghrelin and peptide YY concentrations in the short term, *Appetite* 53 (2009): 338–344.
28. D. Huaidong and coauthors, Dietary fiber and subsequent changes in body weight and waist circumference in European men and women, *American Journal of Clinical Nutrition* 91 (2010): 329–336; L. Qi and Y. A. Cho, Gene-environment interaction and obesity, *Nutrition Reviews* 66 (2008): 684–694.
29. What We Eat in America, NHANES, 2005–2006, www.ars.usda.gov/ba/bhnrc/fsrg, 2008; Position of the American Dietetic Association: Health implications of dietary fiber, *Journal of the American Dietetic Association* 108 (2008): 1716–1731.
30. H. Warshaw, Rediscovering natural resistant starch—an old fiber with modern health benefits, *Nutrition Today* 42 (2007): 123–128; J. G. Muir and coauthors, Combining wheat bran with resistant starch has more beneficial effects on fecal indexes than does wheat bran alone, *American Journal of Clinical Nutrition* 79 (2004): 1020–1028.
31. B. V. McCleary, Dietary fiber analysis, *Proceedings of the Nutrition Society* 62 (2003): 3–9; S. Kimura, Glycemic carbohydrate and health: Background and synopsis of the symposium, *Nutrition Reviews* 61 (2003): S1–S4.
32. M. Nofrarías and coauthors, Long-term intake of resistant starch improves colonic mucosal integrity and reduces gut apoptosis and blood immune cells, *Nutrition* 23 (2007): 861–870.
33. S. R. Hertzler and coauthors, Intestinal disaccharidase depletions, *Modern Nutrition in Health and Disease* (Philadelphia: Lippincott Williams & Wilkins, 2006), pp. 1189–1200.
34. T. A. Nicklas, H. Qu, and S. O. Hughes, Prevalence of self-reported lactose intolerance in a multi-ethnic sample of adults, *Nutrition Today* 44 (2009): 186–187.
35. T. He and coauthors, Effects of yogurt and bifidobacteria supplementation on the colonic microbiotia in lactose-intolerant subjects, *Journal of Applied Microbiology* 104 (2008): 595–604.
36. G. F. Cahill, Jr., Fuel metabolism in starvation, *Annual Review of Nutrition* 26 (2006): 1–22.
37. E. H. Kossoff and coauthors, A prospective study of the modified Atkins diet for intractable epilepsy in adults, *Epilepsia* 49 (2008): 316–319.
38. G. F. Cahill, Fuel metabolism in starvation, *Annual Review of Nutrition* 26 (2006): 1–22..
39. A. Patel and coauthors, Long-term outcomes of children treated with ketogenic diet in the past, *Epilepsia,* February 1, 2010, epub ahead of print, doi:10.1111/j.1528-1167.2009.02488.x; B. A. Zupec-Kania and E. Spellman, An overview of the ketogenic diet for pediatric epilepsy, *Nutrition in Clinical Practice* 23 (2008): 589–596; M. Yudkoff and coauthors, Ketosis and brain handling of glutamate, glutamine, and GABA, *Epilepsia* 49 (2008): 73–75.
40. Standing Committee on the Scientific Evaluation of Dietary Reference Intakes, 2002/2005, p. 265.
41. F. Q. Nuttal, A. Ngo, M. C. Gannon, Regulation of hepatic glucose production and the role of gluconeogenesis in humans: Is the rate of gluconeogenesis constant? *Diabetes Metabolism Research and Reviews* 24 (2008): 438–458.
42. G. Oz and coauthors, Human brain glycogen content and metabolism: Implications on its role in brain energy metabolism, *American Journal of Physiology, Endocrinology and Metabolism,* 292 (2007): E946–E951.
43. H. Anderson, Glycemic index: Pros and cons, *The Soy Connection,* Winter 2007, pp. 1–3.
44. G. Riccardi, A. A. Rivellese, and R. Giacco, Role of glycemic index and glycemic load in the healthy state, in prediabetes, and in diabetes, *American Journal of Clinical Nutrition* 87 (2008): 269S–274S.
45. G. Livesey and coauthors, Glycemic response and health—A systematic review and meta-analysis: Relations between dietary glycemic properties and health outcomes, *American Journal of Clinical Nutrition* 87 (2008): 258S–268S; A. W. Barclay and coauthors, Glycemic index, glycemic load, and chronic disease risk—A meta-analysis of observational studies, *American Journal of Clinical Nutrition* 87 (2008): 627–637; J. Howlett and M. Ashwell, Glycemic response and health: Summary of a workshop, *American Journal of Clinical Nutrition* 87 (2008): 212S–216S; A. Mosdøl and coauthors, Dietary glycemic index and glycemic load are associated with high-density-lipoprotein cholesterol at baseline but not with increased risk of diabetes in the Whitehall II study, *American Journal of Clinical Nutrition* 86 (2007): 988–994.
46. Livesey and coauthors, Glycemic response and health.
47. C. B. Ebbeling and coauthors, Effects of a low-glycemic load vs low-fat diet in obese young adults—A randomized trial, *Journal of the American Medical Association* 297 (2007): 2092–2102; K. C. Maki and coauthors, Effects of a reduced-glycemic-load diet on body weight, body composition, and cardiovascular disease risk markers in overweight and obese adults, *American Journal of Clinical Nutrition* 85 (2007): 724–734; R. Sichieri and coauthors, An 18-mo randomized trial of a low-glycemic-index diet and weight change in Brazilian women, *American Journal of Clinical Nutrition* 86 (2007): 707–713.
48. G. Livesey and H. Tagami, Interventions to lower the glycemic response to carbohydrate foods with a low-viscosity fiber (resistant maltodextrin): Meta-analysis of randomized controlled trials, *American Journal of Clinical Nutrition* 89 (2009): 114–125.
49. American Diabetes Association, Nutrition recommendations and interventions for diabetes: A position statement of the American Diabetes Association, *Diabetes Care* 31 (2008): S61–S78; J. Wylie-Rosett and coauthors, 2006–2007 American Diabetes Association Nutrition Recommendations: Issues for practice translation, *Journal of the American Dietetic Association* 107 (2007): 1296–1304; E. J. Mayer-Davis and coauthors, Towards understanding of glycaemic index and glycaemic load in habitual diet: Associations with measures of glycaemia in the Insulin Resistance Atherosclerosis Study, *British Journal of Nutrition* 95 (2006): 397–405.
50. H. Hare-Bruun and coauthors, Should glycemic index and glycemic load be considered in dietary recommendations? *Nutrition Reviews* 66 (2008): 569–590.
51. D. J. Brillon and coauthors, Reproducibility of a glycemic response to mixed meals in type 2 diabetes mellitus, *Hormone and Metabolic Research* 38 (2006): 536–542.
52. Anderson, Glycemic index: Pros and cons.

53. J. Hlebowicz and coauthors, Effect of cinnamon on postprandial blood glucose, gastric emptying, and satiety in healthy subjects, *American Journal of Clinical Nutrition* 85 (2007): 1552–1556.
54. T. M. S. Wolever and coauthors, Measuring the glycemic index of foods: Interlaboratory study, *American Journal of Clinical Nutrition* 87 (2008): 247S–257S.
55. Department of Health and Human Services, Centers for Disease Control and Prevention, *Diabetes: Successes and opportunities for population-based prevention and control, At A Glance 2009,* available at www.cdc.gov.
56. Department of Health and Human Services, Centers for Disease Control and Prevention, *National Diabetes Fact Sheet, 2007.*
57. J. Xu and coauthors, Deaths: Preliminary data for 2007, *National Vital Statistics Report* 58 (2009): 1–6.
58. A. Whaley-Connell and coauthors, Diabetes mellitus and CKD awareness: The Kidney Early Evaluation Program (KEEP) and National Health and Nutrition Examination Survey (NHANES), *American Journal of Kidney Diseases* 53 (2009): S11–S12; O. H. Franco and coauthors, Associations of diabetes mellitus with total life expectancy and life expectancy with and without cardiovascular disease, *Archives of Internal Medicine* 167 (2007): 1145–1151; C. S. Fox and coauthors, Increasing cardiovascular disease burden due to diabetes mellitus, *Circulation* 115 (2007): 1544–1550; A. N. Butt and coauthors, Circulating nucleic acids and diabetic complications, *Annals of the New York Academy of Sciences* 1075 (2006): 258–270.
59. Centers for Disease Control and Prevention, *National Diabetes Fact Sheet, 2007.*
60. American Diabetes Association, Position Statement, Diagnosis and classification of diabetes mellitus, *Diabetes Care* 31 (2008): S55–S60.
61. S. Schenk, M. Saberi, and J. M. Olefsky, Insulin sensitivity: Modulation by nutrients and inflammation, *Journal of Clinical Investigation* 118 (2008): 2992–3002; A. Pradhan, Obesity, metabolic syndrome, and type 2 diabetes: Inflammatory basis of glucose metabolic disorders, *Nutrition Reviews* 65 (2007): S152–S156.
62. Pradhan, Obesity, metabolic syndrome, and type 2 diabetes.
63. T. J. Biuso, S. Butterworth, and A. Linden, A conceptual framework for targeting prediabetes with lifestyle, clinical and behavioral management intervention, *Disease Management* 10 (2007): 6–15.
64. Centers for Disease Control and Prevention, *National Diabetes Fact Sheet, 2007.*
65. American Diabetes Association, Position Statement, Diagnosis and classification of diabetes mellitus.
66. Centers for Disease Control and Prevention, *Fact Sheet: SEARCH for diabetes in youth, 2005,* available at www.cdc.gov/diabetes/pubs/factsheets/search.htm#2; National Centers for Chronic Disease Prevention and Health Promotion, Diabetes: Disabling, deadly, and on the rise, *At A Glance,* 2003, available at www.cdc.gov/nccdphp; E. A. Gale, The rise of childhood type 1 diabetes in the 20th century, *Diabetes* 51 (2003): 3353–3361.
67. P. Concannon , S. S. Rich, and G. T. Nepom, Genetics of type 1a diabetes, *New England Journal of Medicine* 360 (2009): 1646–1654; American Diabetes Association, Position Statement, Diagnosis and classification of diabetes mellitus; E. Lefebvre and coauthors, Dietary proteins as environmental modifiers of type 1 diabetes mellitus, *Annual Review of Nutrition* 26 (2006): 175–202.
68. S. Parmet, Insulin, *Journal of the American Medical Association* 297 (2007): 230.
69. Diabetes Control and Complications Trial/Epidemiology of Diabetes Interventions and Complications Research Group, Modern-day clinical course of type 1 diabetes mellitus after 30 years' duration, *Archives of Internal Medicine* 169 (2009): 1307–1316.
70. G. N. Jofra and coauthors, Antigen-specific dependence of Tr1-cell therapy in preclinical models of islet transplantation, *Diabetes* 59 (2010): 433–439; A. M. Shapiro and coauthors, International trial of the Edmonton protocol for islet transplantation, *New England Journal of Medicine* 355 (2006): 1318–1330.
71. American Diabetes Association, Position Statement, Diagnosis and classification of diabetes mellitus.
72. L. S. Geiss and coauthors, Changes in incidence of diabetes in U.S. Adults, 1997–2003, *American Journal of Preventive Medicine* 30 (2006): 371–377.
73. C. Meisinger and coauthors, Body fat distribution and risk of type 2 diabetes in the general population: Are there differences between men and women? The MONICA/KORA Augsburg Cohort Study, *American Journal of Clinical Nutrition* 84 (2006): 483–489.
74. K. L. Jones, Role of obesity in complicating and confusing the diagnosis and treatment of diabetes in children, *Pediatrics* 121 (2008): 361–368; J. A. Morrison and coauthors, Preteen insulin resistance predicts weight gain, impaired fasting glucose, and type 2 diabetes at age 18–19 y: A 10-y prospective study of black and white girls, *American Journal of Clinical Nutrition* 88 (2008): 77–788.
75. Schenk, Saberi, and Olefsky, Insulin sensitivity.
76. L. J. Scott and coauthors, A genome-wide association study of type 2 diabetes in Finns detects multiple susceptibility variants, *Science* 316 (2007): 1341–1345.
77. D. Mozaffarian and coauthors, Lifestyle risk factors and new-onset diabetes mellitus in older adults: The Cardiovascular Health Study, *Archives of Internal Medicine* 169 (2009): 798–807.
78. A. El-Osta and coauthors, Transient high glucose causes persistent epigenetic changes and altered gene expression during subsequent normoglycemia, *Journal of Experimental Medicine* 205 (2008): 2409–2417; The Juvenile Diabetes Research Foundation Continuous Glucose Monitoring Study Group, Continuous glucose monitoring and intensive treatment of type 1 diabetes, *New England Journal of Medicine* 359 (2008): 1464–1476; R. R. Holman, 10-year follow-up of intensive glucose control in type 2 diabetes, *New England Journal of Medicine* 15 (2008): 1577–1589.
79. V. M. Montori and M. Fernandez-Balsells, Glycemic control in type 2 diabetes: Time for an evidence-based about-face? *Annals of Internal Medicine* 150 (2009): 803–808; American Diabetes Association, Nutrition recommendations and interventions for diabetes, *Diabetes Care* 31 (2008): S61–S78.
80. American Diabetes Association, Position Statement, Diagnosis and classification of diabetes mellitus.
81. H. Hare-Bruun and coauthors, Should glycemic index and glycemic load be considered in dietary recommendations? *Nutrition Reviews* 66 (2008): 569–590; American Diabetes Association, Position Statement, Diagnosis and classification of diabetes mellitus.
82. American Diabetes Association, Position Statement, Diagnosis and classification of diabetes mellitus.
83. American Diabetes Association, Position Statement, Diagnosis and classification of diabetes mellitus.
84. American Diabetes Association, Position Statement, Diagnosis and classification of diabetes mellitus.
85. C. Hayes and A. Kriska, Role of physical activity in diabetes management and prevention, *Journal of the American Dietetic Association* 108 (2008): S19–S23; American Diabetes Association, Position statement: Standards of medical care in diabetes—2008, *Diabetes Care* 31 (2008): S12–S54; C. Y. Jeon and coauthors, Physical activity of moderate intensity and risk of type 2 diabetes, *Diabetes Care* 30 (2007): 744–752.
86. American Diabetes Association, Position statement: Standards of medical care in diabetes—2008.
87. E. J. Simpson, M. Holdsworth, and I. A. Macdonald, Interstitial glucose profile associated with symptoms attributed to hypoglycemia by otherwise healthy women, *American Journal of Clinical Nutrition* 87 (2008): 354–361.
88. F. E. Hirai and coauthors, Severe hypoglycemia and smoking in a long-term type 1 diabetic population: Wisconsin Epidemiologic Study of Diabetic Retinopathy, *Diabetes Care* 30 (2007): 1437–1441.
89. J. J. Otten, J. P. Hellwig, and L. D. Meyers, eds., *Dietary Reference Intakes: The Essential Guide to Nutrient Requirements* (Washington, D.C.: National Academies Press, 2006), pp. 103–109.
90. U.S. Department of Agriculture and U.S. Department of Health and Human Services, *2005 Dietary Guidelines Committee Report,* 2005, available online at www.health.gov/dietaryguidelines/dga2005report/.
91. Bhargava and Amialchuk, Added sugars displaced the use of vital nutrients in the National Food Stamp Program Survey.

CONSUMER CORNER 4

1. Food and Drug Administration, *The Scoop on Whole Grains,* 06 May 2009, available at www.fda.gov/consumer.
2. Food and Drug Administration, *Guidance for industry and FDA staff: Whole grain label statements,* 2006, available at www.cfsan.fda.gov.

CONTROVERSY 4

1. G. A. Bray, Good kcalories, bad kcalories by Gary Taubes, *Obesity Reviews* 9 (2008): 251–263.
2. K. L. Stanhope and P. J. Havel, Endocrin and metabolic effects of consuming beverages sweetened with fructose, glucose, sucrose, or high-fructose corn syrup, *American Journal of Clinical Nutrition* 88 (2008): 1733S–1737S.
3. C. L. Ogden and coauthors, Prevalence of overweight and obesity in the United States, 1999–2004, *Journal of the American Medical Association* 295 (2006): 1549–1555.
4. U.S. Department of Agriculture, Agricultural Research Service, 2008, Nutrient intakes from food, www.ars.usda.gov/ba/bhnrc/fsrg, visited October 2008.
5. B. A. Swinburn and coauthors, Estimating the changes in energy flux that characterize the rise in obesity prevalence, *American Journal of Clinical Nutrition* 89 (2009): 1723–1728.
6. Centers for Disease Control and Prevention, Trend in intake of kcalories and macronutrients: United States, 1971–2000, *Morbidity and Mortality Weekly Report* 53 (2004): 80–82; B. Swinburn, G. Sacks, and E. Ravussin, Increased food energy supply is more than sufficient to explain the U.S. epidemic of obesity, *American Journal of Clinical Nutrition* 90 (2009): 1453–1456.
7. S. B. Heymsfield, How large is the energy gap that accounts for the obesity epidemic? *American Journal of Clinical Nutrition* 89 (2009): 1717–1718; Centers for Disease Control and Prevention, Prevalence of regular physical activity among adults—United States, 2001 and 2005, *Morbidity and Mortality Weekly Report* 56 (2007): 1209–1212; P. M. Barnes and C. A. Schoenborn, Physical Activity among Adults: United States, 2000, 2003, available at www.cdc.gov/nchs/about/major/nhis/released200306.htm#7.
8. A. T. Merchant and coauthors, Carbohydrate intake and overweight and obesity among healthy adults, *Journal of the American Dietetic Association* 109 (2009): 1165–1172; G. A. Gaesser, Carbohydrate quantity and quality in relation to body mass index, *Journal of the American Dietetic Association* 107 (2007): 1768–1780.
9. Y. Wu, Overweight and obesity in China, *British Medical Journal* 333 (2006): 362–363.
10. A. Astrup, T. M. Larsen, and A. Harper, Atkins and other low-carbohydrate diets: Hoax or an effective tool for weight loss? *Lancet* 364 (2004): 897–899.
11. I. Shai and coauthors, Weight loss with a low-carbohydrate, Mediterranean, or low-fat diet, *New England Journal of Medicine* 359 (2008): 229–241; R. F. Kushner and B. Doerfier, Low-carbohydrate, high-protein diets revisited, *Current Opinion in Gastroenterology* 24 (2008): 198–203; A. K. Halyburton and coauthors, Low- and high-carbohydrate weight-loss diets have similar effects on mood but not cognitive performance, *American Journal of Clinical Nutrition* 86 (2007): 580–587; R. M. van Dam and J. C. Seidell, Carbohydrate intake and obesity, *European Journal of Clinical Nutrition* 61 (2007): S75–S99; T. McLaughlin and coauthors, Effects of moderate variations in macronutrient composition on weight loss and reduction in cardiovascular disease risk in obese, insulin-resistant adults, *American Journal of Clinical Nutrition* 84 (2006): 813–821.
12. J. R. Palmer and coauthors, Sugar-sweetened beverages and incidence of type 2 diabetes mellitus in African American women, *Archives of Internal Medicine* 168 (2008): 1487–1492.
13. A. Mente and coauthors, A systematic review of the evidence supporting a causal link between dietary factors ad coronary heart disease, *Archives of Internal Medicine* 169 (2009): 659–669; J. A. Nettleton and coauthors, Incident heart failure is associated with lower whole-grain intake and greater high-fat dairy and egg intake in the Atherosclerosis Risk in Communities (ARIC) study, *Journal of the American Dietetic Association* 108 (2008): 1881–1887; P. B. Mellen, T. F. Walsh, and D. M. Herrington, Whole grain intake and cardiovascular disease: A meta-analysis, *Nutrition, Metabolism, and Cardiovascular Diseases,* 18 (2008): 283–290; D. R. Jacobs, L. F. Andersen, and R. Blomhoff, Whole-grain consumption is associated with a reduced risk of noncardiovascular, noncancer death attributed to inflammatory diseases in the Iowa Women's Health Study, *American Journal of Clinical Nutrition* 85 (2007): 1606–1614; P. B. Mellen and coauthors, Whole-grain intake and carotid artery atherosclerosis in a multiethnic cohort: The Insulin Resistance Atherosclerosis Study, *American Journal of Clinical Nutrition* 85 (2007): 1495–1502.
14. S. Haley and coauthors, Sweetener consumption in the United States, USDA Economic Research Service, *Electronic Outlook Report from the Economic Research Service,* August 2005, available at www.ers.usda.gov.
15. R. K. Johnson and coauthors, Dietary sugars intake and cardiovascular health: A Scientific Statement from the American Heart Association, *Circulation* 120 (2009): 1011–1020.
16. S. Haley and coauthors, Sweetener consumption in the United States.
17. A. M. Prentice, The emerging epidemic of obesity in developing countries, *International Journal of Epidemiology* 35 (2006): 93–99.
18. G. A. Bray, S. J. Nielsen, and B. M. Popkin, Consumption of high-fructose corn syrup in beverages may play a role in the epidemic of obesity, *American Journal of Clinical Nutrition* 79 (2004): 537–543.
19. D. A. Shoham and coauthors, Sugary soda consumption and albuminuria: Results from the National Health and Nutrition Examination Survey, 1999–2004, *PLoS One* 3 (2008), doi:10.1371/journal.pone.0003431; L. R. Vartanian, M. B. Schwartz, and K. D. Brownell, Effects of soft drink consumption on nutrition and health: A systematic review and meta-analysis, *American Journal of Public Health* 97 (2007): 667–675; V. S. Malik, M. B. Schulze, and F. B. Hu, Intake of sugar-sweetened beverages and weight gain: A systematic review, *American Journal of Clinical Nutrition* 84 (2006): 274–288.
20. J. S. White, Misconceptions about high-fructose corn syrup: Is it uniquely responsible for obesity, reactive dicarbonyl compounds, and advanced glycation endproducts? *Journal of Nutrition* 139 (2009): 1219S–1227S.
21. K. J. Duffey and B. M. Popkin, High-fructose corn syrup: Is this what's for dinner?, *American Journal of Clinical Nutrition* 88 (2008): 1722S–1732S; J. S. White, Straight talk about high-fructose corn syrup: What it is and what it ain't, *American Journal of Clinical Nutrition* 88 (2008): 1716S–1721S.
22. R. Dhingra and coauthors, Soft drink consumption and risk of developing cardiometabolic risk factors and the metabolic syndrome in middle-aged adults in the community, *Circulation* 116 (2007): 480–488.
23. L. M. Fiorito and coauthors, Beverage intake of girls at age 5 y predicts obesity and weight status in childhood and adolescence, *American Journal of Clinical Nutrition* 90 (2009): 935–942; Vartanian, Schwartz, and Brownell, Effects of soft drink consumption on nutrition and health; A. Drewnowski and F. Bellisle, Liquid calories, sugar, and body weight, *American Journal of Clinical Nutrition* 85 (2007): 651–661.
24. P. J. Havel, Dietary fructose: Implications for dysregulation of energy homeostasis and lipid/carbohydrate metabolism, *Nutrition Reviews* 63 (2005): 133–157, as reported in A. Drewnowski and F. Bellisle, Liquid calories, sugar and body weight, *American Journal of Clinical Nutrition* 85 (2007): 651–661.
25. S. Soenen and M. S. Weterterp-Plantenga, No differences in satiety or energy intake after high-fructose corn syrup, sucrose, or milk preloads, *American Journal of Clinical Nutrition* 86 (2007): 1586–1594; K. J. Melanson and coauthors, Effects of high-fructose corn syrup and sucrose consumption on circulating glucose, insulin, leptin, and ghrelin on appetite in normal-weight women, *Nutrition* 23 (2007): 103–112; T. Akhavan and G. H. Anderson, Effects of glucose-to-fructose ratios in solutions on subjective satiety, food intake, and satiety hormones in young men, *American Journal of Clinical Nutrition* 86 (2007): 1354–1363.
26. M. D. Lane and S. H. Cha, Effect of glucose and fructose on food intake via malonyl-CoA signaling in the brain, *Biochemical and Biophysical Research Communications* 382 (2009): 1–5.
27. K. J. Melanson and coauthors, High-fructose corn syrup, energy intake, and appetite

regulation, *American Journal of Clinical Nutrition* 88 (2008): 1738S–1744S.
28. T. J. Angelopoulos and coauthors, The effect of high-fructose corn syrup consumption on triglycerides and uric acid, *Journal of Nutrition* 139 (2009): 1242S–1245S.
29. K. L. Teff and coauthors, Endocrine and metabolic effects of consuming fructose- and glucose-sweetened beverages with meals in obese men and women: Influence of insulin resistance on plasma triglyceride responses, *Journal of Clinical Endocrinology and Metabolism* 94 (2009): 1652–1659.
30. T. H. Moran, Fructose and satiety, *Journal of Nutrition* 139 (2009): 1253S–1256S.
31. Stanhope and Havel, Endocrin and metabolic effects of consuming beverages sweetened with fructose, glucose, sucrose, or high-fructose corn syrup.
32. K. L. Stanhope and coauthors, Consuming fructose-sweetened, not glucose-sweetened, beverages increases visceral adiposity and lipids and decreases insulin sensitivity in overweight/obese humans, *Journal of Clinical Investigation* 119 (2009): 1322–1334.
33. Y. Nagai and coauthors, The role of peroxisome proliferator-activated receptor γ coactivator-1 β in the pathogenesis of fructose-induced insulin resistance, *Cell Metabolism* 9 (2009): 252–264; H-Y. Koo and coauthors, Dietary fructose induces a wide range of genes with distinct shift in carbohydrate and lipid metabolism in fed and fasted rat liver, *Biochimica et Biophysica Acta* 1782 (2008): 341–348; M. F-F. Chong, B. A. Fielding, and K. N. Frayn, Mechanisms for the acute effect of fructose on postprandial lipemia, *American Journal of Clinical Nutrition* 85 (2007): 1511–1520.
34. K-A. Lê and coauthors, Fructose overconsumption causes dyslipidemia and ectopic lipid deposition in healthy subjects with and without a family history of type 2 diabetes, *American Journal of Clinical Nutrition* 89 (2009): 1760–1765; E. J. Parks and coauthors, Dietary sugars stimulate fatty acid synthesis in adults, *Journal of Nutrition* 138 (2008): 1039–1046.
35. J. P. Bantle, Dietary fructose and metabolic syndrome and diabetes, *Journal of Nutrition* 139 (2009): 1263S–1268S; M. M. Swarbrick and coauthors, Consumption of fructose-sweetened beverages for 10 weeks increases postprandial triacylglycerol and apolipoprotein-B concentrations in overweight and obese women, *British Journal of Nutrition* 100 (2008): 947–952.
36. Stanhope and coauthors, Consuming fructose-sweetened, not glucose-sweetened, beverages increases visceral adiposity and lipids and decreases insulin sensitivity in overweight/obese humans.
37. Melanson and coauthors, Effects of high-fructose corn syrup and sucrose consumption.
38. K. L. Stanhope and coauthors, Twenty-four-hour endocrine and metabolic profiles following consumption of high-fructose corn syrup-, fructose-, and glucose-sweetened beverages with meals, *American Journal of Clinical Nutrition* 87 (2008): 1194–1203.
39. A. Drewnowski and F. Bellisle, Liquid calories, sugar, and body weight, *American Journal of Clinical Nutrition* 85 (2007): 651–661.
40. M. A. Pereira, Weighing in on glycemic index and body weight, *American Journal of Clinical Nutrition* 84 (2006): 677–679.
41. Bray, *Good Calories, Bad Calories by Gary Taubes.*
42. J. P. Chaput and coauthors, A novel interaction between dietary composition and insulin secretion: Effects on weight gain in the Quebec Family Study, *American Journal of Clinical Nutrition* 87 (2008): 303–309.
43. Bray, *Good Calories, Bad Calories by Gary Taubes.*
44. D. B. Allison and R. D. Mattes, Nutritively sweetened beverage consumption and obesity: The need for solid evidence on a fluid issue, *Journal of the American Medical Association* 301 (2009): 318–320.
45. Swinburn, Sacks, and Ravussin, Increased food energy supply is more than sufficient to explain the U.S. epidemic of obesity; Stanhope and Havel, Endocrin and metabolic effects of consuming beverages sweetened with fructose, glucose, sucrose, or high-fructose corn syrup.
46. Johnson and coauthors, Dietary sugars intake and cardiovascular health.

Chapter 5

1. G. Govindarajan, M. A. Alpert, and L. Tejwani, Endocrine and metabolic effects of fat: Cardiovascular implications, *American Journal of Medicine* 121 (2008): 366–370; T. Yamada and H. Katagiri, Avenues of communication between the brain and tissues/organs involved in energy homeostasis, *Endocrine Journal* 54 (2007): 497–505.
2. G. W. Van Citters and H. C. Lin, Ileal brake: Neuropetidergic control of intestinal transit, *Current Gastroenterology Reports* 8 (2006): 367–373.
3. W. S. Harris and coauthors, Omega-6 fatty acids and risk for cardiovascular disease: A Science Advisory from the American Heart Association Nutrition Subcommittee of the Council of Nutrition, Physical Activity, and Metabolism; Council on Cardiovascular Nursing, and Council on Epidemiology and Prevention, *Circulation* 108 (2009): 902–907; M. U. Jakobsen and coauthors, Major types of dietary fat and risk of coronary heart disease: A pooled analysis of 11 cohort studies, *American Journal of Clinical Nutrition* 89 (2009): 1425–1432; C. S. Booker and J. I. Mann, *Trans* fatty acids and cardiovascular health: Translation of the evidence base, *Nutrition, Metabolism and Cardiovascular Diseases* 18 (2008): 448–456; R. Micha and D. Mozaffarian, *Trans* fatty acids: Effects on cardiometabolic health and implications for policy, *Prostaglandins, Leukotrienes, and Essential Fatty Acids* 79 (2008): 147–152.
4. A. Mente and coauthors, A systematic preview of the evidence supporting a causal link between dietary factors and coronary heart disease, *Archives of Internal Medicine* 169 (2009): 659–669.
5. I. Shai and coauthors, Weight loss with a low-carbohydrate, Mediterranean, or low-fat diet, *New England Journal of Medicine* 359 (2008): 229–241; R. F. Kushner and B. Doerfier, Low-carbohydrate, high-protein diets revisited, *Current Opinion in Gastroenterology* 24 (2008): 198–203; T. McLaughlin and coauthors, Effects of moderate variations in macronutrient composition on weight loss and reduction in cardiovascular disease risk in obese, insulin-resistant adults, *American Journal of Clinical Nutrition* 84 (2006): 813–821; U.S. Department of Agriculture and U.S. Department of Health and Human Services, *Dietary Guidelines for Americans 2005,* available online at www.health.gov/dietaryguidelines/dga2005/recommendations.htm.
6. Position of the American Dietetic Association and Dietitians of Canada: Dietary Fatty Acids, *Journal of the American Dietetic Association* 107 (2007): 1599–1611.
7. C. S. Booker and J. I. Mann, *Trans* fatty acids and cardiovascular health: Translation of the evidence base, *Nutrition, Metabolism, and Cardiovascular Diseases* 18 (2008): 448–456; J. Delgado-Lista and coauthors, Chronic dietary fat intake modifies the postprandial response of hemostatic markers to a single fatty test meal, *American Journal of Clinical Nutrition* 87 (2008): 317–322; Position of the American Dietetic Association and Dietitians of Canada: Dietary Fatty Acids, 2007.
8. W. Willett and D. Mozaffarian, Ruminant or industrial sources of *trans* fatty acids: Public health issue or food label skirmish? *American Journal of Clinical Nutrition* 87 (2008): 515–516; J. M. Chardigny and coauthors, Do *trans* fatty acids from industrially produced sources and from natural sources have the same effect on cardiovascular disease risk factors in healthy subjects? Results of the *trans* Fatty Acids Collaboration (TRANSFACT) study, *American Journal of Clinical Nutrition* 87 (2008): 558–566.
9. A. J. Cross and coauthors, A prospective study of meat and fat intake in relation to small intestinal cancer, *Cancer Research* 68 (2008): 9274–9279; R. S. Chapkin, D. N. McMurray, and J. R. Lupton, Colon cancer, fatty acids and anti-inflammatory compounds, *Current Opinion in Gastroenterology* 23 (2007): 48–54; H. S. Black and L. E. Rhodes, The potential of omega-3 fatty acids in the prevention of non-melanoma skin cancer, *Cancer Detection and Prevention* 30 (2006): 224–232; R. L. Prentice and coauthors, Low-fat dietary pattern and risk of invasive breast cancer: The Women's Health Initiative Randomized Controlled Dietary Modification Trial, *Journal of the American Medical Association* 295 (2006): 629–642; S. A. A. Beresford and coauthors, Low-fat dietary pattern and risk of colorectal cancer: The Women's Health Initiative Randomized Controlled Dietary Modification Trial, *Journal of the American Medical Association* 295 (2006): 634–654.
10. World Cancer Research Fund/American Institute for Cancer Research, *Food, Nutrition,*

Physical Activity and the Prevention of Cancer: A Global Perspective (Washington, D.C.: AIRC, 2007).

11. National Center for Health Statistics, 2005; Committee on Dietary Reference Intakes (Washington, D.C.: National Academies Press, 2002/2005).

12. U.S. Department of Agricultural Research Service, Nutrient intakes from food: Mean amounts consumed per individual, one day, 2005–2006, www.ars.usda.gov/ba/bhnrc/fsrg, 2008.

13. Delgado-Lista and coauthors, Chronic dietary fat intake modifies the postprandial response; T. Hampton, New clues to HDL's benefits revealed, *Journal of the American Medical Association* 297 (2007): 1537.

14. A. K. Chhatriwalla and coauthors, Low levels of low-density lipoprotein cholesterol and blood pressure and progression of coronary atherosclerosis, *Journal of the American College of Cardiology* 53 (2009): 1110–1115.

15. L. K. Curtiss, Reversing atherosclerosis, *New England Journal of Medicine* 360 (2009): 1144–1146; A. Mente and coauthors, A systematic review of the evidence supporting a causal link between dietary factors and coronary heart disease, *Archives of Internal Medicine* 169 (2009): 659–669; H. D. Sesso and coauthors, Vitamins E and C in the prevention of cardiovascular disease in men, *Journal of the American Medical Association* 300 (2009): 2123–2133.

16. U.S. Department of Agriculture and U.S. Department of Health and Human Services, *Dietary Guidelines for Americans 2005.*

17. J. M. Ordovas, Genetic influences on blood lipids and cardiovascular disease risk: Tools for primary prevention, *American Journal of Clinical Nutrition* 89 (2009): 1509S–1517S.

18. Centers for Disease Control and Prevention, Quick Stats: Average total cholesterol level among men and women aged 20–74 years—National Health and Nutrition Examination Survey, United States, 1959–1962 to 2007–2008, *Morbidity and Mortality Weekly Report* 58 (2009): 1045; E. V. Kuklina, P. W. Yoon, and N. L. Keenan, Trends in high levels of low-density lipoprotein cholesterol in the United States, 1999–2006, *Journal of the American Medical Association* 302 (2009): 2104–2110.

19. Joint WHO/FAO Expert Consultation, *Diet, Nutrition, and the Prevention of Chronic Diseases* (Geneva, Switzerland: World Health Organization, 2003), p. 56.

20. W. S. Harris and coauthors, Omega-6 fatty acids and risk of cardiovascular disease: A science advisory from the American Heart Association Nutrition Subcommittee of the Council on Nutrition, Physical Activity, and Metabolism, *Circulation* 119 (2009): 902–907; L. Berglund and coauthors, Comparison of monounsaturated fat with carbohydrates as a replacement for saturated fat in subjects with a high metabolic risk profile: Studies in the fasting and postprandial states, *American Journal of Clinical Nutrition* 86 (2007): 1611–1620; M. P. St-Onge and coauthors, Snack chips fried in corn oil alleviate cardiovascular disease risk factors when substituted for low-fat or high-fat snacks, *American Journal of Clinical Nutrition* 85 (2007): 1503–1510.

21. USDA Agricultural Research Service, Weighing in on fats, *Agricultural Research,* March 2008, p. 12.

22. Position of the American Dietetics Association and Dietitians of Canada: Dietary Fatty Acids, *Journal of the American Dietetics Association* 107 (2007): 1599–1611.

23. A. M. Brownawell and coauthors, Assessing the environment for regulatory change for eicosapentaenoic acid and docosahexaenoic acid nutrition labeling, *Nutrition Reviews* 67 (2009): 391–397; W. S. Harris and coauthors, Towards establishing Dietary Reference Intakes for eicospentaenoic and docosahexaenoic acids, *Journal of Nutrition* 139 (2009): 804S–819S.

24. Z. Makhoul and coauthors, Associations of very high intakes of eicosapentaenoic and docosahexaenoic acids with biomarkers of chronic disease risk among Yup'ik Eskimos, *American Journal of Clinical Nutrition* 91 (2010): 777–785; J. P. Middaugh, Cardiovascular deaths among Alaskan Natives, 1980–1986, *American Journal of Public Health* 80 (1990): 282–285; J. Dyerberg, Linolenate-derived polyunsaturated fatty acids and prevention of atherosclerosis, *Nutrition Reviews* 44 (1986): 125–134.

25. P. J. Smith and coauthors, Association between n-3 fatty acid consumption and ventricular ectopy after myocardial infarction, *American Journal of Clinical Nutrition* 89 (2009): 1315–1320; A. Bersamin and coauthors, Westernizing diets influence fat intake, red blood cell fatty acid composition, and health in remote Alaskan native communities in the Center for Alaska Native Health Study, *Journal of the American Dietetic Association* 108 (2008): 266–273.

26. K. Fritsche, Fatty acids as modulators of the immune response, *Annual Review of Nutrition* 26 (2006): 45–73.

27. W. S. Harris, The omega-3 index as a risk factor for coronary heart disease, *American Journal of Clinical Nutrition* 87 (2008): 595–596.

28. Mente and coauthors, A systematic review of the evidence.

29. E. B. Levitan, A. Wolk, and M. A. Mittleman, Fish consumptions, marine omega-3 fatty acids, and incidence of heart failure: A population-based prospective study of middle-aged and elderly men, *European Heart Journal* 30 (2009): 1495–1500; H. E. Theobald and coauthors, Low-dose docosahexaenoic acid lowers diastolic blood pressure in middle-aged men and women, *Journal of Nutrition* 137 (2007): 973–978; M. C. Nesheim and A. L. Yaktine, eds., *Seafood Choices: Balancing Benefits and Risks* (Washington, D.C.: National Academies Press, 2007), p. 12; J. L. Breslow, n-3 Fatty acids and cardiovascular disease, *American Journal of Clinical Nutrition* 83 (2006): 1477S–1482S.

30. Smith and coauthors, Association between n-3 fatty acid consumption and ventricular ectopy; GISSI-HF Investigators, Effect of n-3 polyunsaturated fatty acids in patients with chronic heart failure (the GISSI-HF trial): A randomized, double-blind, placebo-controlled trial, *The Lancet* 372 (2008): 1223–1230.

31. C. Berr and coauthors, Increased selenium intake in elderly high-fish consumers may account for health benefits previously ascribed to omega-3 fatty acids, *Journal of Nutrition, Health and Aging* 13 (2009): 14–18.

32. E. E. Birch and coauthors, the DIAMOND (DHA Intake And Measurement Of Neural Development) Study: A double-masked, randomized controlled clinical trial of the maturation of infant visual acuity as a function of the dietary level of docosahexaenoic acid, *American Journal of Clinical Nutrition* (February 3, 2010), epub ahead of print, doi:10.3945/ajcn.2009.28557; S. M. Innis, Dietary (n-3) fatty acids and brain development, *Journal of Nutrition* 137 (2007): 855–859; J. R. Hibbeln and coauthors, Maternal seafood consumption in pregnancy and neurodevelopmental outcomes in childhood (ALSPAC study): An observational cohort study, *Lancet* 369 (2007): 578–585; R. Uauy and A. D. Dangour, Nutrition in brain development and aging: Role of essential fatty acids, *Nutrition Reviews* 64 (2006): S24–S33.

33. B. S. Beltz and coauthors, Omega-3 fatty acids upregulate adult neurogenesis, *Neuroscience Letters* 415 (2007): 154–158.

34. N. D. Riediger and coauthors, A systemic review of the roles of n-3 fatty acids in health and disease, *Journal of the American Dietetic Association* 109 (2009): 668–679.

35. E. Albanese and coauthors, Dietary fish and meat intake and dementia in Latin America, China, and India: A 10/66 Dementia Research Group population-based study, *American Journal of Clinical Nutrition* 90 (2009): 392–400; E. E. Devore and coauthors, Dietary intake of fish and omega-3 fatty acids in relation to long-term dementia risk, *American Journal of Clinical Nutrition* 90 (2009): 170–176; M. A. Beydoun and coauthors, Plasma n-3 fatty acids and the risk of cognitive decline in older adults: The Atherosclerosis Risk in Communities Study, *American Journal of Clinical Nutrition* 85 (2007): 1103–1111; C. Dullemeijer and coauthors, n-3 Fatty acid proportions in plasma and cognitive performance in older adults, *American Journal of Clinical Nutrition* 86 (2007): 1259–1260.

36. L. A. Colangelo and coauthors, Higher dietary intake of long-chain ω-3 polyunsaturated fatty acids is inversely associated with depressive symptoms in women, *Nutrition* 25 (2009): 1011–1019; Riediger and coauthors, A systemic review of the roles of n-3 fatty acids; J. Sontrop and K. Campbell, ω-3 Polyunsaturated fatty acids and depression: A review of the evidence and methodological critique, *Preventive Medicine* 42 (2006): 4–13.

37. C. M. Milte, N. Sinn, and P. R. C. Howe, Polyunsaturated fatty acid status in attention deficit hyperactivity disorder, depression, and Alzheimer's disease: Towards an omega-3 index for mental health? *Nutrition Reviews* 67

(2009): 573–590; R. M. Carney and coauthors, Omega-3 augmentation of sertraline in treatment of depression in patients with coronary heart disease: A randomized controlled trial, *Journal of the American Medical Association* 302 (2009): 1651–1657; O. van de Rest and coauthors, Effect of fish-oil supplementation on mental well-being in older subjects: A randomized, double-blind, placebo-controlled trial, *American Journal of Clinical Nutrition* 88 (2008): 706–713.

38. M. Bouwens and coauthors, Fish-oil supplementation induces anti-inflammatory gene expression profiles in human blood mononuclear cells, *American Journal of Clinical Nutrition* 90 (2009): 415–424; G. K. Pot and coauthors, No effect of fish oil supplementation on serum inflammatory markers and their interrelationships: A randomized controlled trial in healthy, middle-aged individuals, *European Journal of Clinical Nutrition* 63 (2009): 1353–1359; Riediger and coauthors, A systemic review of the roles of n-3 fatty acids.

39. P. Bougnoux, B. Giraudeau, and C. Couet, Diet, cancer, and the lipodome, *Cancer Epidemiology, Biomarkers, and Prevention* 15 (2006): 416–421.

40. L. M. Arterburn, E. B. Hall, and H. Oken, Distribution, interconversion and dose response of n-3 fatty acids in humans, *American Journal of Clinical Nutrition* 83 (2006): 1467S–1476S.

41. P. Clifton, Dietary fatty acids and inflammation, *Nutrition and Dietetics* 66 (2009): 7–11; J. C. Stanley and coauthors, UK Food Standards Agency Workshop report: The effects of the dietary n-6:n-3 fatty acid ratio on cardiovascular health, *British Journal of Nutrition* 98 (2007): 1305–1310; W. S. Harris, The omega-6/omega-3 ratio and cardiovascular disease risk: Uses and abuses, *Current Atherosclerosis Reports* 8 (2006): 453–459.

42. B. A. Griffin, How relevant is the ratio of dietary n-6 to n-3 polyunsaturated fatty acids to cardiovascular disease risk? Evidence from the OPTILIP study, *Current Opinion in Lipidology* 19 (2008): 57–62.

43. A. H. Lichtenstein and coauthors, Diet and Lifestyle Recommendations Revision, 2006: A scientific statement from the American Heart Association Nutrition Committee, *Circulation* 114 (2006): 82–96.

44. Nesheim and Yaktine, *Seafood Choices: Balancing Benefits and Risks.*

45. P. M. Kris-Etherton and A. M. Hill, n-3 Fatty acids: Foods or supplements? *American Dietetic Association* 108 (2008): 1125–1130; A. H. Lichtenstein and coauthors, Diet and Lifestyle Recommendations Revision, 2006: A scientific statement from the American Heart Association Nutrition Committee.

46. R. Emsley and coauthors, Safety of the omega-3 fatty acid, eicosapentaenoic acid (EPAP) in psychiatric patients: Results from a randomized, placebo-controlled trial, *Psychiatry Research* 161 (2008): 284–291; Fish and omega-3 fatty acids 2009, a document available at www.americanheart.org.

47. N. M. J. Schwerbrock and coauthors, Fish oil-fed mice have impaired resistance to influenza infection, *Journal of Nutrition* 139 (2009): 1588–1594.

48. Riediger and coauthors, A systemic review of the roles of n-3 fatty acids.

49. Riediger and coauthors, A systemic review of the roles of n-3 fatty acids.

50. M. I. Burgar and coauthors, MNR of microencapsulated fish oil samples during in vitro digestion, *Food Biophysics* 4 (2009): 32–41; J. M. Curtis, N. Berrigan, and P. Dauphinee, The determination of n-3 fatty acid levels in food products containing microencapsulated fish oil using the one-step extraction method. Part 1: Measurement of the raw ingredient in dry powdered foods, *Journal of the American Oil Chemists' Society* 85 (2008): 297–305.

51. M. K. Duda and coauthors, Fish oil, but not flaxseed oil, decreases inflammation and prevents pressure overload-induced cardiac dysfunction, *Cardiovascular Research* 81 (2009): 319–327; G. Barceló-Coblijn and coauthors, Flaxseed oil and fish-oil capsule consumption alters human red blood cell n-3 fatty acid composition: A multiple-dosing trial comparing 2 sources of n-3 fatty acid, *American Journal of Clinical Nutrition* 88 (2008): 801–809.

52. J. Whelan and C. Rust, Innovative dietary sources of n-3 fatty acids, *Annual Review of Nutrition* 26 (2006): 75–103.

53. Position of the American Dietetic Association and Dietitians of Canada: Dietary Fatty Acids.

54. W. S. Harris, n-3 Fatty acids and health: DaVinci's code, *American Journal of Clinical Nutrition* 88 (2008): 595–596.

55. Philadelphia approves ban on *trans* fats, *WashingtonPost.com,* February 8, 2007; New York City passes *trans* fat ban, MSNBC News Services, December 5, 2006.

56. D. Mozaffarian and coauthors, *Trans* fatty acids and cardiovascular disease, *New England Journal of Medicine* 354 (2006): 1601–1613.

57. Micha and Mozaffarian, *Trans* fatty acids.

58. A. H. Lichtenstein, Dietary fat, carbohydrate, and protein: Effects on plasma lipoprotein patterns, *Journal of Lipid Research* 47 (2006): 1661–1667.

59. M. J. Albers and coauthors, 2006 Marketplace survey of *trans*-fatty acid content of margarines and butters, cookies and snack cakes, and savory snacks, *Journal of the American Dietetic Association* 108 (2008): 367–370; S. Borra and coauthors, An update of *trans*–fat reduction in the American diet, *Journal of the American Dietetic Association* 107 (2007): 2048–2050; S. Okie, New York to *trans* fats: You're out! *New England Journal of Medicine* 356 (2007): 2017–2021.

60. High stability, higher profits: New varieties and hybrids meet demand for high stability oil, *Canola Digest,* January/February 2007, p. 24.

61. M. T. Tarrago-Trani, New and existing oils and fats used in products with reduced *trans*-fatty acid content, *Journal of the American Dietetic Association* 106 (2006): 867–880.

62. J. E. Hunter, J. Zhang, and P. M. Kris-Etherton, Cardiovascular disease risk of stearic acid compared with *trans,* other saturated, and unsaturated fatty acids: A systematic review, *American Journal of Clinical Nutrition* 91 (2010): 43–63.

63. Position of the American Dietetic Association and Dietitians of Canada: Dietary Fatty Acids.

64. USDA Agricultural Research Service, Cooking up tempting fat-fighting foods and ingredients, *Agricultural Research,* March 2006, pp. 12–15.

65. C. W. Xiao, J. Mei, and C. M. Wood, Effect of soy proteins and isoflavones on lipid metabolism and involved gene expression, *Frontiers in Bioscience* 13 (2008): 2660–2673; K. Reynolds and coauthors, A meta-analysis of the effect of soy protein supplementation on serum lipids, *American Journal of Cardiology* 98 (2006): 633–640.

CONSUMER CORNER 5

1. M. C Nesheim and A. L. Yaktine, eds., *Seafood Choices: Balancing Benefits and Risks* (Washington, D.C.: National Academies Press, 2007), p. 12.

2. B. C. Scudder and coauthors, Mercury in fish, bed sediment, and water from streams Across the United States, 1998–2005, (2009), U.S. Geological Survey Scientific Investigations Report 2009-5109, available at http://pubs.usgs.gov/sir/2009/5109/.

3. D. R. Laks, Assessment of chronic mercury exposure within the U.S. population, National Health and Nutrition Examination Survey, 1999–2006, *Biometals* 22 (2009): 1103–1114.

4. M. Kaushik and coauthors, Long-chain omega-3 fatty acids, fish intake, and the risk of type 2 diabetes mellitus, *American Journal of Clinical Nutrition* 90 (2009): 613–620.

5. Nesheim and Yaktine, *Seafood Choices: Balancing Benefits and Risks,* p. 6.

6. A. Mente and coauthors, A systematic review of the evidence supporting a causal link between dietary factors and coronary heart disease, *Archives of Internal Medicine* 169 (2009): 659–669; Nesheim and Yaktine, *Seafood Choices: Balancing Benefits and Risks,* p. 3.

7. K. He and coauthors, Intakes of long-chain n-3 polyunsaturated fatty acids and fish in relation to measurement of subclinical atherosclerosis, *American Journal of Clinical Nutrition* 88 (2008): 1111–1118.

CONTROVERSY 5

1. A. Mente and coauthors, A systematic review of the evidence supporting a causal link between dietary factors and coronary heart disease, *Archives of Internal Medicine* 169 (2009): 659–669; F. Sofi, The Mediterranean diet revisited: Evidence of its effectiveness grows, *Current Opinion in Cardiology* 24 (2009): 442–446.

2. A. H. Lichtenstein, Dietary fat, carbohydrate, and protein: Effects on plasma lipoprotein patterns, *Journal of Lipid Research* 47 (2006): 1661–1667.

3. *Third Report of the National Cholesterol Education Program (NCEP) Expert Panel on Detection, Evaluation, and Treatment of High Blood Cholesterol in Adults (Adult Treatment Panel III)*, 2002, National Institutes of Health publication no. 02-1205.
4. A. Keys, *Seven Countries: A Multivariate Analysis of Death and Coronary Heart Disease* (Cambridge, Mass.: Harvard University Press, 1980).
5. P. A. Gilbert and S. Khokhar, Changing dietary habits of ethnic groups in Europe and implications for health, *Nutrition Reviews* 66 (2008): 203–215.
6. U.S. Department of Agriculture and U.S. Department of Health and Human Services, *Dietary Guidelines for Americans 2005* (Washington, D.C.: Government Printing Office, 2005), available online at www.usda.gov/cnpp or call (888) 878-3256; American Heart Association Scientific Statement, Diet and Lifestyle recommendations revision 2006, *Circulation* 114 (2006): 82–96.
7. M. I. Covas and coauthors, The effect of polyphenols in olive oil on heart disease risk factors, *Annals of Internal Medicine* 145 (2006): 333–341.
8. M. Fitó and coauthors, Effect of a traditional Mediterranean diet on lipoprotein oxidation, *Archives of Internal Medicine* 167 (2007): 1195–1203.
9. J. Ruano and coauthors, Intake of phenol-rich virgin olive oil improves the postprandial prothrombotic profile in hypercholesterolemic patients, *American Journal of Clinical Nutrition* 86 (2007): 341–346; Covas and coauthors, The effect of polyphenols in olive oil.
10. B. M. Rasmussen and coauthors, Effects of dietary saturated, monounsaturated, and n-3 fatty acids on blood pressure in healthy subjects, *American Journal of Clinical Nutrition* 83 (2006): 221–226.
11. F. Pérez-Jiménez and coauthors, The influence of olive oil on human health: Not a question of fat alone, *Molecular Nutrition and Food Research* 51 (2007): 1199–1208.
12. A. Trichopoulou, C. Bamia, and D. Trichopoulos, Anatomy of health effects of Mediterranean diet: Greek EPIC prospective cohort study, *British Medical Journal* 338 (2009), doi: 10.1136/bmj/b2337; Mente and coauthors, A systematic review of the evidence.
13. J. M. Ordovas, J. Kaput, and D. Corella, Nutrition in the genomics era: Cardiovascular disease risk and the Mediterranean diet, *Molecular Nutrition and Food Research* 51 (2007): 1293–1299.
14. G. Buckland and coauthors, Adherence to a Mediterranean diet and risk of gastric adenocarcinoma within the European Prospective Investigation into Cancer and Nutrition (EPIC) cohort study, *American Journal of Clinical Nutrition* 91 (2010): 381–390; Fitó and coauthors, Effect of a traditional Mediterranean diet; K. Esposito, M. Ciotola, and D. Giugliano, Mediterranean diet, endothelial function and vascular inflammatory markers, *Public Health Nutrition* 9 (2006): 1073–1076.
15. N. Scarmeas and coauthors, Mediterranean diet and mild cognitive impairment, *Archives of Neurology* 66 (2009): 216–225.
16. S. Rajaram and coauthors, Walnuts and fatty fish influence different serum lipid fractions in normal to mildly hyperlipidemic individuals: A randomized controlled study, *American Journal of Clinical Nutrition* 89 (2009): 1657S–1663S; J. L. Breslow, n-3 Fatty acids and cardiovascular disease, *American Journal of Clinical Nutrition* 83 (2006): 1477S–1482S.
17. P. M. Kris-Etherton and coauthors, The role of tree nuts and peanuts in the prevention of coronary heart disease: Multiple potential mechanisms, *Journal of Nutrition* 138 (2009): 1746S–1751S.
18. J. H. Kelley and J. Sabaté, Nuts and coronary heart disease: An epidemiological perspective, *British Journal of Nutrition* 96 (2006): S61–S67.
19. T. Y. Li and coauthors, Regular consumption of nuts is associated with a lower risk of cardiovascular disease in women with type 2 diabetes, *Journal of Nutrition* 139 (2009): 1333–1338.
20. J. Sabaté and Y. Ang, Nuts and health outcomes: New epidemiologic evidence, *American Journal of Clinical Nutrition* 89 (2009): 1643S–1648S; S. K. Gebauer and coauthors, Effects of pistachios on cardiovascular disease risk factors and potential mechanisms of action: A dose-response study, *American Journal of Clinical Nutrition* 88 (2008): 651–659.
21. P. Davis, Walnuts reduce aortic ET-1 mRNA levels in hamsters fed a high-fat, atherogenic diet, *Journal of Nutrition* 136 (2006): 428–432.
22. D. J. A. Jenkins and coauthors, Assessment of the longer-term effects of a dietary portfolio of cholesterol-lowering foods in hypercholesterolemia, *American Journal of Clinical Nutrition* 83 (2006): 582–591.
23. O. J. Phung and coauthors, Almonds have a neutral effect on serum lipid profiles: A meta-analysis of randomized trials, *Journal of the American Dietetic Association* 109 (2009): 865–873.
24. E. Ros, Nut and novel biomarkers of cardiovascular disease, *American Journal of Clinical Nutrition* 89 (2009): 1649S–1656S; S. S. Wijeratne, M. M. Abou-Zaid, and F. Shahidi, Antioxidant polyphenols in almond and its coproducts, *Journal of Agricultural and Food Chemistry* 54 (2006): 312–318; P. E. Milbury and coauthors, Determination of flavonoids and phenolics and their distribution in almonds, *Journal of Agricultural and Food Chemistry* 54 (2006): 5027–5033.
25. A. H. Stark, M. A. Crawford, and R. Reifen, Update on alpha-linolenic acid, *Nutrition Reviews* 66 (2008): 326–332.
26. M. Bes-Rastrollo and coauthors, Prospective study of nut consumption, long-term weight change, and obesity risk in women, *American Journal of Clinical Nutrition* 89 (2009): 1913–1919.
27. D. B. Haytowitz, P. R. Pehrsson, and J. M. Holden, The national food and nutrient analysis program: A decade of progress, *Journal of Food Composition and Analysis* 21 (2008): S94–S102.
28. Haytowitz, Pehrsson, and Holden, The national food and nutrient analysis program.
29. *Third Report of the National Cholesterol Education Program (NCEP) Expert Panel on Detection, Evaluation, and Treatment of High Blood Cholesterol in Adults (Adult Treatment Panel III).*
30. Committee on the Scientific Evaluation of Dietary Reference Intakes, Food and Nutrition Board, Institute of Medicine, 2002, pp. 11-46 and G-1.
31. Committee on the Scientific Evaluation of Dietary Reference Intakes, p. 11-19.
32. J. A. Nettleton and coauthors, Dietary patterns and incident cardiovascular disease in the Multi-Ethnic Study of Atherosclerosis, *American Journal of Clinical Nutrition* 90 (2009): 647–654.

Chapter 6

1. Standing Committee on the Scientific Evaluation of Dietary Reference Intakes, Food and Nutrition Board, Institute of Medicine, *Dietary Reference Intakes for Energy, Carbohydrate, Fiber, Fat, Fatty Acids, Cholesterol, Protein, and Amino Acids* (Washington, D.C.: National Academies Press, 2002/2005), pp. 589–768.
2. N. Mizushima and D. J. Klionsky, Protein turnover via autophagy: Implications for metabolism, *Annual Review of Nutrition* 27 (2007): 19–40.
3. Standing Committee on the Scientific Evaluation of Dietary Reference Intakes, *Dietary Reference Intakes for Energy, Carbohydrate, Fiber, Fat, Fatty Acids, Cholesterol, Protein, and Amino Acids.*
4. M. T. Gladwin and E. Vichinsky, Pulmonary complications of sickle-cell disease, *New England Journal of Medicine* 359 (2008): 2254–2265; F. J. Kirkham, Therapy insight: Stroke risk and its management in patients with sickle-cell disease, *Nature Clinical Practice. Neurology* 3 (2007): 264–278.
5. E. Trujillo, C. Davis, and J. Milner, Nutrigenomics, proteomics, metabolomics, and the practice of dietetics, *Journal of the American Dietetic Association* 106 (2006): 403–413.
6. G. Wu, Amino acids: Metabolism, functions, and nutrition, *Amino Acids,* published online 20 March 2009, doi:10.1007/s00726-009-0269-0; R. A. Waterland, Assessing the effects of high methionine intake on DNA methylation, *Journal of Nutrition* 136 (2006): 1706S–1710S; P. J. Stover and C. Garza, Nutrition and developmental biology—implications for public health, *Nutrition Reviews* 64 (2006): S260–S271.
7. J. Kaput, Nutrigenomics, *Clinical Chemistry and Laboratory Medicine* 45 (2007): 279–287; M. T. Subbiah, Nutrigenetic and nutraceuticals: The next wave riding on personalized medicine, *Translational Research* 149 (2007): 55–61.
8. Position of the American Dietetic Association, Dietitians of Canada, and the American College of Sports Medicine, Nutrition and

Athletic Performance, *Journal of the American Dietetic Association* 109 (2009): 509–527; S. M. Phillips, Dietary protein for athletes: From requirements to metabolic advantage, *Applied Physiology, Nutrition, and Metabolism* 31 (2006): 647–654; Committee on Dietary Reference Intakes, *Dietary Reference Intakes for Energy, Carbohydrate, Fiber, Fat, Fatty Acids, Cholesterol, Protein, and Amino Acids.*

9. Standing Committee on the Scientific Evaluation of Dietary Reference Intakes, *Dietary Reference Intakes for Energy, Carbohydrate, Fiber, Fat, Fatty Acids, Cholesterol, Protein, and Amino Acids.*

10. Standing Committee on the Scientific Evaluation of Dietary Reference Intakes, *Dietary Reference Intakes for Energy, Carbohydrate, Fiber, Fat, Fatty Acids, Cholesterol, Protein, and Amino Acids.*

11. Position of the American Dietetic Association, Dietitians of Canada, and the American College of Sports Medicine, Nutrition and Athletic Performance.

12. R. R. Wolfe and S. L. Miller, The Recommended Dietary Allowance of protein: A misunderstood concept, *Journal of the American Medical Association* 299 (2008): 2891–2893.

13. S. Tesseraud and coauthors, Role of sulfur amino acids in controlling nutrient metabolism and cell functions: Implications for nutrition, *British Journal of Nutrition* 101 (2009): 1132–1139; M. Kadowaki and T. Kanazawa, Amino acids as regulators of proteolysis, *Journal of Nutrition* 133 (2003): 2052S–2056S.

14. Position of the American Dietetic Association: Vegetarian Diets, *Journal of the American Dietetic Association* 109 (2009): 1266–1283.

15. G. Bluestein, Vegans sentenced for starving their baby, Associated Press, May 9, 2007, available at www.breitbart.com/article.php?id=D8P102RO0&show_article=1.

16. Standing Committee on the Scientific Evaluation of Dietary Reference Intakes, *Dietary Reference Intakes for Energy, Carbohydrate, Fiber, Fat, Fatty Acids, Cholesterol, Protein, and Amino Acids.*

17. V. L. Fulgoni III, Current protein intake in America: Analysis of the National Health and Nutrition Examination Survey, 2003–2004, *American Journal of Clinical Nutrition* 87 (2008): 1554S–1557S.

18. Fulgoni III, Current protein intake in America.

19. M. S. Westerterp-Plantenga and coauthors, Dietary protein, weight loss, and weight maintenance, *Annual Review of Nutrition* 29 (2009): 21–41.

20. M. J. Levine, J. M. Jones, and D. R. Lineback, Low-carbohydrate diets: Assessing the science and knowledge gaps, summary of an ILSI North American Workshop, *Journal of the American Dietetic Association* 106 (2006): 2086–2094.

21. L. E. Kelemen and coauthors, Associations of dietary protein with disease and mortality in a prospective study of postmenopausal women, *American Journal of Epidemiology* 161 (2005): 239–249.

22. Y. Wang and M. A. Beydoun, Meat consumption is associated with obesity and central obesity among U.S. adults, *International Journal of Obesity* 33 (2009): 621–628.

23. N. R. Matthan and coauthors, Effect of soy protein from differently processed products on cardiovascular disease risk factors and vascular endothelial function in hypercholesterolemic subjects, *American Journal of Clinical Nutrition* 85 (2007): 960–966; B. L. McVeigh and coauthors, Effect of soy protein varying in isoflavone content on serum lipids in healthy young men, *American Journal of Clinical Nutrition* 83 (2006): 244–251.

24. D. S. Wald and coauthors, Folic acid, homocysteine, and cardiovascular disease: Judging causality in the face of inconclusive trial evidence, *British Journal of Medicine* 333 (2006): 1114–1117.

25. K. H. Bønaa and coauthors, Homocysteine lowering and cardiovascular events after acute myocardial infarction, *New England Journal of Medicine* 354 (2006): 1578–1588.

26. M. Haim and coauthors, Serum homocysteine and long-term risk of myocardial infarction and sudden death in patients with coronary heart disease, *Cardiology* 107 (2006): 52–56.

27. J. Selhub, The many facets of hyperhomocysteinemia: Studies from the Framingham cohorts, *Journal of Nutrition* 136 (2006): 1726S–1730S.

28. J. A. Troughton and coauthors, Homocysteine and coronary heart disease risk in the PRIME study, *Atherosclerosis* 191 (2007): 90–97; T. J. Green and coauthors, Lowering homocysteine with B vitamins has no effect on biomarkers of bone turnover in older persons: A 2-y randomized controlled trial, *American Journal of Clinical Nutrition* 85 (2007): 460–464; C. Baigent and R. Clarke, B Vitamins for the prevention of vascular diseases: Insufficient evidence to justify treatment, *Journal of the American Medical Association* 298 (2007): 1212–1214; R. L. Jamison and coauthors, Effect of homocysteine lowering on mortality and vascular disease in advance chronic kidney disease and end-stage renal disease: A randomized controlled trial, *Journal of the American Medical Association* 298 (2007): 1163–1170.

29. R. Pecoits-Filho, Dietary protein intake and kidney disease in Western diet, *Contributions to Nephrology* 155 (2007): 102–112.

30. S. Mandayam and W. E. Mitch, Dietary protein restriction benefits patients with chronic kidney disease, *Nephrology (Carlton)* 11 (2006): 53–57.

31. V. Menon and coauthors, Effect of a very low-protein diet on outcomes: Long-term follow-up of the Modification of Diet in Renal Disease (MDRD) Study, *American Journal of Kidney Diseases* 53 (2009): 189–191.

32. K. Rafferty and R. P. Heaney, Nutrient effects on the calcium economy: Emphasizing the potassium controversy, *Journal of Nutrition* 138 (2008): 166S–171S.

33. Rafferty and Heaney, Nutrient effects on the calcium economy.

34. R. Rizzoli, Nutrition: Its role in bone health, *Best Practice and Research: Clinical Endocrinology and Metabolism* 22 (2008): 813–829; A. D. Conigrave, E. M. Brown, and R. Rizzoli, Dietary protein and bone health: Roles of amino acid-sensing receptors in the control of calcium metabolism and bone homeostasis, *Annual Review of Nutrition* 28 (2008): 131–155; S. Boonen and coauthors, Addressing the musculoskeletal components of fracture risk with calcium and vitamin D: A review of the evidence, *Calcified Tissue International* 78 (2006): 257–270.

35. Standing Committee on the Scientific Evaluation of Dietary Reference Intakes, *Dietary Reference Intakes for Energy, Carbohydrate, Fiber, Fat, Fatty Acids, Cholesterol, Protein, and Amino Acids.*

36. D. D. Alexander and coauthors, Meta-analysis of animal fat or animal protein intake and colorectal cancer, *American Journal of Clinical Nutrition* 89 (2009): 1402–1409.

37. R. Sinha and coauthors, Meat intake and mortality: A prospective study of over half a million people, *Archives of Internal Medicine* 169 (2009): 543–545; R. L. Santarelli, F. Pierre, and D. E. Corpet, Processed meat and colorectal cancer: A review of epidemiologic and experimental evidence, *Nutrition and Cancer* 60 (2008): 131–144; S. C. Larsson, N. Orsini, and A. Wolk, Processed meat consumption and stomach cancer risk: A meta-analysis, *Journal of the National Cancer Institute* 98 (2006): 1078–1087; E. Cho and coauthors, Red meat intake and risk of breast cancer among premenopausal women, *Archives of Internal Medicine* 166 (2006): 2253–2259.

38. S. Milius, Out of thin air: Scientists pursue nitrogen fixers with an aim to harness their secrets—and feed the world, *Science News* 173 (2008): 235–237.

CONSUMER CORNER 6

1. T. Brock Symons and coauthors, A moderate serving of high-quality protein maximally stimulates skeletal muscle protein synthesis in young and elderly subjects, *Journal of the American Dietetic Association* 109 (2009): 1582–1586; R. R. Wolfe, Skeletal muscle protein metabolism and resistance exercise, *Journal of Nutrition* 136 (2006): 525S–528S.

2. J. W. Apolzan and coauthors, Inadequate dietary protein increases hunger and desire to eat in younger and older men, *Journal of Nutrition* 137 (2007): 1478–1482.

3. U.S. Food and Drug Administration, Final rule promotes safe use of dietary supplements, *FDA Consumer Health Information,* June 22, 2007, available at www.fda.gov/consumer/updates/dietarysupps062207.html.

4. G. Wu, Amino acids: Metabolism, functions, and nutrition, *Amino Acids* 37 (2009): 1–17.

5. S. Métayer and coauthors, Mechanisms through which sulfur amino acids control protein metabolism and oxidative status, *Journal of Nutritional Biochemistry* 19 (2008): 207–215.

6. C. M. Park and coauthors, Methionine supplementation accelerates oxidative stress

and nuclear factor kappaB activation in livers of C57BL/6 mice, *Journal of Medicinal Food* 11 (2008): 667–674.
7. G. K. Grimble, Adverse gastrointestinal effects of arginine and related amino acids, *Journal of Nutrition* 137 (2007): 1693S–1701S.
8. Standing Committee on the Scientific Evaluation of Dietary Reference Intakes, Food and Nutrition Board, Institute of Medicine, *Dietary Reference Intakes for Energy, Carbohydrate, Fiber, Fat, Fatty Acids, Cholesterol, Protein, and Amino Acids* (Washington, D.C.: National Academy Press, 2002/2005), pp. 589–768.
9. Standing Committee on the Scientific Evaluation of Dietary Reference Intakes, Food and Nutrition Board, Institute of Medicine, *Dietary Reference Intakes—The Essential Guide to Nutrient Requirements* (Washington, D.C.: National Academies Press, 2006), p. 152.
10. D. R. Jacobs, M. D. Gross, and L. C. Tapsell, Food synergy: An operational concept for understanding nutrition, *American Journal of Clinical Nutrition* 89 (2009): 1543S–1548S.

CONTROVERSY 6

1. G. E. Fraser, Vegetarian diets: What do we know of their effects on common chronic diseases? *American Journal of Clincal Nutrition* 89 (2009): 1607S–1612S; T. J. Key, P. N. Appleby, and M. S. Rosell, Health effects of vegetarian and vegan diets, *Proceedings of the Nutrition Society* 65 (2006): 35–41.
2. H. J. Marlow and coauthors, Diet and the environment: Does what you eat matter? *American Journal of Clinical Nutrition* 89 (2009): 1699S–1703S; B. M. Popkin, Reducing meat consumption has multiple benefits for the world's health, *Archives of Internal Medicine* 169 (2009): 543–545.
3. R. Robinson-O'Brian and coauthors, Adolescent and young adult vegetarianism: Better dietary intake and weight outcomes but increased risk of disordered eating behaviors, *Journal of the American Dietetic Association* 109 (2009): 648–655.
4. Position of the American Dietetic Association: Vegetarian Diets, *Journal of the American Dietetic Association* 109 (2009): 1266–1283; U.S. Department of Agriculture and U.S. Department of Health and Human Services, *Dietary Guidelines for Americans 2005* (Washington, D.C.: 2005), available online at www.usda.gov/cnpp or call (888) 878-3256.
5. Key, Appleby, and Rosell, Health effects of vegetarian and vegan diets.
6. Fraser, Vegetarian diets; Robinson-O'Brian and coauthors, Adolescent and young adult vegetarianism; S. E. Berkow and N. Barnard, Vegetarian diets and weight status, *Nutrition Reviews* 64 (2006): 175–188.
7. Y. Wang and M. A. Beydoun, Meat consumption is associated with obesity and central obesity among U.S. adults, *International Journal of Obesity* 33 (2009): 621–628.
8. Fraser, Vegetarian diets.
9. M. U. Jakobsen and coauthors, Major types of dietary fat and risk of coronary heart disease: A pooled analysis of 11 cohort studies, *American Journal of Clinical Nutrition* 89 (2009): 1425–1432.
10. Berkow and Barnard, Vegetarian diets and weight status.
11. C. W. Xiao, Health effects of soy protein and isoflavones in humans, *Journal of Nutrition* 138 (2008): 1244S–1249S.
12. F. M. Sacks and coauthors, Soy protein, isoflavones, and cardiovascular health: An American Heart Association science advisory from the Nutrition Committee, *Circulation* 113 (2006): 1034–1044.
13. A. A. Thorp and coauthors, Soy food consumption does not lower LDL cholesterol in either equol or nonequol producers, *American Journal of Clinical Nutrition* 88 (2008): 298–304.
14. Sacks, Soy protein, isoflavones, and cardiovascular health; B. L. McVeigh and coauthors, Effect of soy protein varying in isoflavone content on serum lipids in healthy young men, *American Journal of Clinical Nutrition* 83 (2006): 244–251.
15. K. Reynolds, A meta-analysis of the effect of soy protein supplementation on serum lipids, *American Journal of Cardiology* 98 (2006): 633–640; Sacks, Soy protein, isoflavones, and cardiovascular health.
16. F. K. Welty and coauthors, Effect of soy nuts on blood pressure and lipid levels in hypertensive, prehypertensive, and normotensive postmenopausal women, *Archives of Internal Medicine* 167 (2007): 1060–1067.
17. World Cancer Research Fund/American Institute for Cancer Research, *Food, Nutrition, Physical Activity and the Prevention of Cancer: A Global Perspective* (Washington, D.C.: AIRC, 2007), p. 284.
18. R. L. Santarelli, F. Pierre, and D. E. Corpet, Processed meat and colorectal cancer: A review of epidemiologic and experimental evidence, *Nutrition and Cancer* 60 (2008): 131–144; A. J. Cross and coauthors, A prospective study of red and processed meat intake in relation to cancer risk, *PLoS Medicine* 4 (2007): e325, doi:10.1371/journal.pmed.0040325; Fraser, Vegetarian diets.
19. T. J. Key and coauthors, Cancer incidence in vegetarians: Results from the European Prospective Investigation into Cancer and Nutrition (EPIC-Oxford), *American Journal of Clinical Nutrition* 89 (2009): 1620S–1626S.
20. R. Sinha and coauthors, Meat intake and mortality: A prospective study of over half a million people, *Archives of Internal Medicine* 169 (2009): 543–545.
21. D. Mozaffarian, Higher red meat intake may be a marker of risk, not a risk factor itself, *Archives of Internal Medicine* 169 (2009): 1538–1539.
22. N. E. Allen and coauthors, Moderate alcohol intake and cancer incidence in women, *Journal of the National Cancer Institute* 101 (2009): 296–305.
23. World Cancer Research Fund/American Institute for Cancer Research, *Food, Nutrition, Physical Activity and the Prevention of Cancer,* p. 281.
24. W. J. Craig, Health effects of vegan diets, *American Journal of Clinical Nutrition* 89 (2009): 1627S–1633S; J. Sabaté and Y. Ang, Nuts and health outcomes: New epidemiologic evidence, *American Journal of Clinical Nutrition* 89 (2009): 1643S–1648S.
25. L. T. Ho-Pham and coauthors, Effect of vegetarian diets on bone mineral density: A Bayesian meta-analysis, *American Journal of Clinical Nutrition* 90 (2009): 943–950.
26. H. Fadyl and S. Inoue, Combined B_{12} and iron deficiency in a child breast-fed by a vegetarian mother, *Journal of Pediatric Hematology/Oncology* 29 (2007): 74; F. Cetinkaya and coauthors, Nutritional vitamin B_{12} deficiency in hospitalized young children, *Pediatric Hemotology and Oncology* 24 (2007): 15–21; S. Katar and coauthors, Nutritional megaloblastic anemia in young Turkish children is associated with vitamin B-12 deficiency and psychomotor retardation, *Journal of Pediatric Hematology and Oncology* 28 (2006): 559–562.
27. D. Codazzi and coauthors, Coma and respiratory failure in a child with severe vitamin B (12) deficiency, *Pediatric Critical Care Medicine* 7 (2006): 483–485.
28. C. Hoppe, C. Molgaard, and K. F. Michaelsen, Cow's milk and linear growth in industrialized and developing countries, *Annual Review of Nutrition* 26 (2006): 131–173.
29. Position of the American Dietetic Association: Vegetarian Diets.
30. Position of the American Dietetic Association: Vegetarian Diets.
31. M. Virginia, V. Melina, and A. R. Mangels, A new food guide for North American vegetarians, *Journal of the American Dietetic Association* 103 (2003): 771–775; C. A. Venti and C. S. Johnston, Modified food guide pyramid for lactovegetarians and vegans, *Journal of Nutrition* 132 (2002): 1050–1054.
32. Position of the American Dietetic Association: Vegetarian Diets.
33. Standing Committee on the Scientific Evaluation of Dietary Reference Intakes, Food and Nutrition Board, Institute of Medicine, *Dietary Reference Intakes for Vitamin A, Vitamin K, Arsenic, Boron, Chromium, Copper, Iodine, Iron, Manganese, Molybdenum, Nickel, Silicon, Vanadium, and Zinc* (Washington, D.C.: National Academies Press, 2001), p. 351.
34. S. S. genennt-Bonsmann and coauthors, Oxalic acid does not influence nonhaem iron absorption in humans: A comparison of kale and spinach meals, *European Journal of Clinical Nutrition* 62 (2008): 336–341.
35. J. Chan, K. Jaceldo-Siegl, and Gary E. Fraser, Serum 25-hydroxyvitamin D status of vegetarians, partial vegetarians, and nonvegetarians: The Adventist Health Study, *American Journal of Clinical Nutrition* 89 (2009): 1686S–1692S.
36. I. Mangat, Do vegetarians have to eat fish for optimal cardiovascular protection? *American Journal of Clinical Nutrition* 89 (2009): 1597S–1601S.
37. Mangat, Do vegetarians have to eat fish for optimal cardiovascular protection?

38. J. Whelan and C. Rust, Innovative dietary sources of n-3 fatty acids, *Annual Review of Nutrition* 26 (2006): 75–103.

Chapter 7

1. S. R. Ross and coauthors, Introduction: Diet, epigenetic events and cancer prevention, *Nutrition Reviews* 66 (2008): S1–S6; Z. Liu and coauthors, Multiple B-vitamin inadequacy amplifies alterations induced by folate depletion in p53 expression and its downstream effector MDM2, *International Journal of Cancer* 123 (2008): 519–525.

2. I. H. Rosenberg, Challenges and opportunities in the translation of the science of vitamins, *American Journal of Clinical Nutrition* 85 (2007): 325S–327S; National Institutes of Health State-of-the-Science conference statement: Multivitamin/mineral supplements and chronic disease prevention, *Annals of Internal Medicine* 145 (2006): 364–371.

3. R. Blomhoff and H. K. Blomhoff, Overview of retinoid metabolism and function, *Journal of Neurobiology* 66 (2006): 606–630.

4. Blomhoff and Blomhoff, Overview of retinoid metabolism and function.

5. G. Wolf, Retinoic acid as cause of cell proliferation or cell growth inhibition depending on activation of one of two different nuclear receptors, *Nutrition Reviews* 66 (2008): 55–59.

6. A. Sommer, Vitamin A deficiency and clinical disease: An historical overview, *Journal of Nutrition* 138 (2008): 1835–1839.

7. L. O. Dragsted, Biomarkers of exposure to vitamins A, C, and E and their relation to lipid and protein oxidation markers, *European Journal of Nutrition* 47 (2008): 3–18.

8. H. Chen and coauthors, Vitamin A for preventing acute lower respiratory tract infections in children up to seven years of age, *Cochrane Database of Systematic Reviews*, 2009, doi:10.1002/14651858.CD006090.pub2; S. A. Abrams and D. C. Hilmers, Postnatal vitamin A supplementation in developing countries: An intervention whose time has come? *Pediatrics* 122 (2008): 180–181; K. Kraemer and coauthors, Are low tolerable upper intake levels for vitamin A undermining effective food fortification efforts? *Nutrition Reviews* 66 (2008): 517–525.

9. A. Sommer, Vitamin A deficiency and clinical disease.

10. K. Z. Long and coauthors, Impact of vitamin A on selected gastrointestinal pathogen infections and associated diarrheal episodes among children in Mexico City, Mexico, *Journal of Infectious Diseases* 194 (2006): 1217–1225.

11. www.who.int/mediacentre/factsheets, f286, revised December 2008.

12. Standing Committee on the Scientific Evaluation of Dietary Reference Intakes, Food and Nutrition Board, Institute of Medicine, *Dietary Reference Intakes for Vitamin A, Vitamin K, Arsenic, Boron, Chromium, Copper, Iodine, Iron, Manganese, Molybdenum, Nickel, Silicon, Vanadium, and Zinc* (Washington, D.C.: National Academy Press, 2001), pp. 4-9 –4-10.

13. J. M. Madia, K. Mathers, and C. I. Kelly, Pediatric ophthalmology in the developing world, *Current Opinion in Ophthalmology* 19 (2008): 403–408.

14. A. Sheth, R. Khurana, and V. Khurana, Potential liver damage associated with over-the-counter vitamin supplements, *Journal of the American Dietetic Association* 108 (2008): 1536–1537; K. L. Penniston and S. A. Tanumihardjo, The acute and chonic toxic effects of vitamin A, *American Journal of Clinical Nutrition* 83 (2006): 191–201.

15. J. D. Ribaya-Mercado and J. B. Blumberg, Vitamin A: Is it a risk factor for osteoporosis and bone fracture? *Nutrition Reviews* 65 (2007): 425–438; Penniston and Tanumihardjo, The acute and chronic toxic effects of vitamin A.

16. J. Zhao and coauthors, Retinoic acid downregulates microRNAs to induce abnormal development of spinal cord in spina bifida rat model, *Child's Nervous System* 24 (2008): 485–492.

17. H. S. Lam and coauthors, Risk of vitamin A toxicity from candy-like chewable vitamin supplements for children, *Pediatrics* 118 (2006): 820–824.

18. F. Ghali and coauthors, The changing face of acne therapy, *Cutis* 83 (2009): 4–15.

19. Lam and coauthors, Risk of vitamin A toxicity.

20. S. Carpentier, M. Knauss, and M. Suh, Associations between lutein, zeaxanthin, and age-related macular degeneration: An overview, *Critical Reviews in Food Science* 49 (2009): 313–326.

21. R. L. Roberts, J. Green, and B. Lewis, Lutein and zeaxanthin in eye and skin health, *Clinical Dermatology* 27 (2009): 195–201; D. A. Kopsell and coauthor, Spinach cultigen variation for tissue carotenoid concentrations influences human serum carotenoid levels and macular pigment optical density following a 12-week dietary intervention, *Journal of Agricultural and Food Chemistry* 54 (2006): 7998–8005.

22. E. J. Johnson, Age-related macular degeneration and antioxidant vitamins: Recent findings, *Current Opinion in Clinical Nutrition and Metabolic Care* (2010): 1328–1333; C-J. Chiu and coauthors, Dietary compound score and risk of age-related macular degeneration in the Age-Related Eye Disease Study, *Ophthalmology* 116 (2009): 939–946; W. G. Christen and coauthors, Folic acid, pyridoxine, and cyanocobolamin combination treatment and age-related macular degeneration in women, *Archives of Internal Medicine* 169 (2009): 335–341.

23. D. R. Jacobs and L. C. Tapsell, Food, not nutrients, is the fundamental unit in nutrition, *Nutrition Reviews* 65 (2007): 439–450.

24. P. Lips, Vitamin D physiology, *Progress in Biophysics and Molecular Biology* 92 (2006): 4–8.

25. S. Saintonge, H. Bang, and L. M. Gerber, Implications of a new definition of vitamin D deficiency in a multiracial U.S. adolescent population: The National Health and Nutrition Examination Survey III, *Pediatrics* 123 (2009): 797–803; M. F. Holick, Vitamin D deficiency, *New England Journal of Medicine* 357 (2007): 266–281.

26. A. Moshfegh and coauthors, *What We Eat in America, NHANES 2005–2006: Usual Nutrient Intakes from Food and Water compared to 1997 Dietary Reference Intakes for Vitamin D, Calcium, Phosphorus, and Magnesium,* (USDA: Beltsville, Md., 2009).

27. F. Bronner, Recent developments in intestinal calcium absorption, *Nutrition Reviews* 67 (2009): 109–113.

28. R. P. Heaney, Vitamin D and calcium interactions: Functional outcomes, *American Journal of Clinical Nutrition* 88 (2008): 541S–544S; M. R. Haussler and coauthors, Vitamin D receptor: Molecular signaling and actions of nutritional ligands in disease prevention, *Nutrition Reviews* 66 (2008): S98–S112.

29. H. F. Deluca, Evolution of our understanding of vitamin D, *Nutrition Reviews* 66 (2008): S73–S87; A. W. Norman, From vitamin D to hormone D: Fundamentals of the vitamin D endocrine system essential for good health, *American Journal of Clinical Nutrition* 88 (2008): 491S–499S.

30. E. van Etten and coauthors, Regulation of vitamin D homeostasis: Implications for the immune system, *Nutrition Reviews* 66 (2008): S125–S134.

31. A. A. Ginde, J. M. Mansbach, and C. A. Camargo, Association between serum 25-hydroxyvitamin D level and upper respiratory tract infection in the Third National Health and Nutrition Examination Survey, *Archives of Internal Medicine* 169 (2009): 384–390; A. Kilkkinen and coauthors, Vitamin D status and the risk of cardiovascular death, *American Journal of Epidemiology* 170 (2009): 1032–1039; A. Zitterman, J. Gummert, and J. Börgermann, Vitamin D deficiency and mortality, *Current Opinion in Clinical Nutrition and Metabolic Care* 12 (2009): 634–639; R. P. Heaney, Vitamin D and calcium interactions: Functional outcomes, *American Journal of Clinical Nutrition* 88 (2008): 541S–544S; M. T. Cantorna, Vitamin D and multiple sclerosis: An update, *Nutrition Reviews* 66 (2008): S135–S138; M. F. Holick, Vitamin D: A d-lightful health perspective, *Nutrition Reviews* 66 (2008): S182–S194; J. M. Lappe and coauthors, Vitamin D and calcium supplementation reduces cancer risk: Results of a randomized trial, *American Journal of Clinical Nutrition* 85 (2007): 1586–1591; J. Lin and coauthors, Intakes of calcium and vitamin D and breast cancer risk in women, *Archives of Internal Medicine* 167 (2007): 1050–1059; G. E. Mullin and A. Dobs, Vitamin D and its role in cancer and immunity: A prescription for sunlight, *Nutrition in Clinical Practice* 22 (2007): 305–322; S. E. Judd and coauthors, Optimal vitamin D status attenuates the age-associated increase in systolic blood pressure in white Americans: Results from the third National Health and Nutrition Examination Survey, *American Journal of Clinical Nutrition* 87 (2008): 136–141;

Y. Cui and T. E. Rohan, Vitamin D, calcium, and breast cancer risk: A review, *Cancer Epidemiological, Biomarkers and Prevention* 15 (2006): 1427–1437; A. F. Gombart, Q. T. Luong, and H. P. Koeffler, Vitamin D compounds: Activity against microbes and cancer, *Anticancer Research* 26 (2006): 2531–2542; P. T. Liu and coauthors, Toll-like receptor triggering of a vitamin D-mediated human antimicrobial response, *Science* 311 (2006): 1770–1773; L. A. Martini and R. J. Wood, Vitamin D status and the metabolic syndrome, *Nutrition Reviews* 64 (2006): 479–486; K. L. Munger and coauthors, Serum 25-hydroxyvitamin D levels and risk of multiple sclerosis, *Journal of the American Medical Association* 296 (2006): 2832–2838.

32. A. Prentice, Vitamin D deficiency: A global perspective, *Nutrition Reviews* 66 (2008): S153–S164.

33. J. Kumar and coauthors, Prevalence and associations of 25-hydroxyvitamin D deficiency in US children: NHANES 2001–2004, *Pediatrics* 124 (2009): e362–e370.

34. S. Saintonge, H. Bang, and L. M. Gerber, Implications of a new definition of vitamin D deficiency in a multiracial U.S. adolescent population: The National Health and Nutrition Examination Survey III, *Pediatrics* 123 (2009): 797–803; F. R. Greer, 25-Hydroxyvitamin D: Functional outcome in infants and young children, *American Journal of Clinical Nutrition* (2008): 529S–533S; S. Y. Huh and C. M. Gordon, Vitamin D deficiency in children and adolescents: Epidemiology, impact and treatment, *Reviews in Endocrine and Metabolic Disorders* 9 (2008): 161–170; M. Misra and coauthors, Vitamin D deficiency in children and its management: Review of current knowledge and recommendations, *Pediatrics* 122 (2008): 398–417.

35. C. L. Wagner, F. R. Greer, and the Section on Breastfeeding and Committee on Nutrition, Prevention of rickets and vitamin D deficiency in infants, children, and adolescents, *Pediatrics* 122 (2008): 1142–1152.

36. K. D. Cashman and coauthors, Low vitamin D status adversely affects bone health parameters in adolescents, *American Journal of Clinical Nutrition* 87 (2008): 1039–1044.

37. K. Ukinc, Severe osteomalacia presenting the multiple vertebral fractures: A case report and review of the literature, *Endocrine* 36 (2009): 30–36.

38. H. A. Bischoff-Ferrari and coauthors, Prevention of nonvertebral fractures with oral vitamin D and dose dependency: A meta-analysis of randomized controlled trials, *Archives of Internal Medicine* 169 (2009): 551–561; G. Buhr and C. W. Bales, Nutritional supplements for older adults: Review and recommendations—part I, *Journal of Nutrition for the Elderly* 28 (2009): 5–29; A. Avenell and coauthors, Vitamin D and vitamin D analogues for preventing fractures associated with involutional and post-menopausal osteoporosis, *Cochrane Database of Systematic Reviews* 2 (2009), doi:10.1002/14651858.CD000227.pub3; B. Dawson-Hughes, Serum 25-hydroxyvitamin D and functional outcomes in the elderly, *American Journal of Clinical Nutrition* 88 (2008): 537S–540S; S. A. Talwar and coauthors, Dose response to vitamin D supplementation among postmenopausal African American women, *American Journal of Clinical Nutrition* 86 (2007): 1657–1662.

39. Avenell and coauthors, Vitamin D and vitamin D analogues for preventing fractures.

40. G. Jones, Pharmacokinetics of vitamin D toxicity, *American Journal of Clinical Nutrition* 88 (2008): 582S–586S; National Institutes of Health, Dietary Supplement Fact Sheet: Vitamin D 2008, available at http://ods.od.nih.gov.

41. M. H. Beers and coeditors, *The Merck Manual of Diagnosis and Therapy* (Whitehouse Station, N.J.: Merck Research Laboratories, 2006), p. 2656.

42. J. N. Hathcock and coauthors, Risk assessment for vitamin D, *American Journal of Clinical Nutrition* 85 (2007): 6–18; D. C. Heimburger, D. S. McLaren, and M. E. Shils, Clinical manifestations of nutrient deficiencies and toxicities: A resume, in *Modern Nutrition in Health and Disease,* M. E. Shils, M. Shike, A. C. Ross, B. Cabayyero, and R. J. Cousins, eds. (Baltimore: Lippincott Williams and Wilkins, 2006), pp. 595–612.

43. F. El Ghissassi and coauthors, A review of human carcinogens—Part D: Radiation, *Lancet* 10 (2009): 751–752; B. A. Gilchrest, Sun exposure and vitamin D sufficiency, *American Journal of Clinical Nutrition* 88 (2008): 570S–577S.

44. A. A. Ginde and coauthors, Demographic differences and trends of vitamin D insufficiency in the U.S. population, 1988–2004, *Archives of Internal Medicine* 169 (2009); 626–632.

45. Gilchrest, Sun exposure and vitamin D sufficiency.

46. Gilchrest, Sun exposure and vitamin D sufficiency.

47. K. D. Cashman and coauthors, Estimation of the dietary requirement for vitamin D in healthy adults, *American Journal of Clinical Nutrition* 88 (2008): 1535–1542; J. F. Aloia and coauthors, Vitamin D intake to attain a desired serum 25-hydroxyvitamin D concentration, *American Journal of Clinical Nutrition* 87 (2008): 1952–1958; Hathcock and coauthors, Risk assessment for vitamin D; H. A. Bischoff-Ferrari and coauthors, Estimation of optimal serum concentrations of 25-hydroxyvitamin D for multiple health outcomes, *American Journal of Clinical Nutrition* 84 (2006): 18–28.

48. G. Wolf, The discovery of the antioxidant function of vitamin E: The contribution of H. A. Mattill, *Journal of Nutrition* 135 (2005): 363–366.

49. S. R. Wells, Alpha-, gamma- and delta-tocopherols reduce inflammatory angiogenesis in human microvascular endothelial cells, *Journal of Nutritional Biochemistry* 2009, May 13, doi:10.1016/j.jnutbio.2009.03.006, epub ahead of print.

50. E. Reiter, O. Jiang, and S. Christen, Anti-inflammatory properties of alpha- and gamma-tocopherol, *Molecular Aspects of Medicine* 28 (2007): 668–691.

51. L. K. Curtiss, Reversing atherosclerosis? *New England Journal of Medicine* 360 (2009): 1144–1146.

52. D. L. Rainwater and coauthors, Vitamin E dietary supplementation significantly affects multiple risk factors for cardiovascular disease in baboons, *American Journal of Clinical Nutrition* 86 (2007): 597–603; U. Singh, S. Devaraj, and I. Jialal, Vitamin E, oxidative stress, and inflammation, *Annual Review of Nutrition* 25 (2005): 151–174.

53. J. M. Bourre, Effects of nutrients (in food) on the structure and function of the nervous system: Update on dietary requirements for brain. Part 1: Micronutrients, *Journal of Nutrition, Health, and Aging* 10 (2006): 377–385.

54. M. E. Wright and coauthors, Higher baseline serum concentrations of vitamin E are associated with lower total and cause-specific mortality in the Alpha-Tocopherol, Beta-Carotene Cancer Prevention Study, *American Journal of Clinical Nutrition* 84 (2006): 1200–1207.

55. G. Bjelakovic and coauthors, Mortality in randomized trials of antioxidant supplements for primary and secondary prevention: Systematic review and meta-analysis, *Journal of the American Medical Association* 297 (2007): 842–857; National Institutes of Health State-of-the-Science conference statement: Multivitamin/mineral supplements and chronic disease prevention, *Annals of Internal Medicine* 145 (2006): 364–371.

56. J. N. Hathcock and coauthors, Vitamins E and C are safe across a broad range of intakes, *American Journal of Clinical Nutrition* 81 (2005): 736–745.

57. M. G. Traber, Vitamin E and K interactions—a 50-year-old problem, *Nutrition Reviews* 66 (2008): 624–629.

58. G. Bjelakovic and coauthors, Antioxidant supplements for prevention of mortality in healthy participants and patients with various diseases, *Cochrane Database of Systematic Reviews* (2008), doi:10.1002/14651858.CD007176.

59. G. Pocobelli and coauthors, Use of supplements of multivitamins, vitamin C and vitamin E in relation to mortality, *American Journal of Epidemiology* 170 (2009): 472–483.

60. USDA Agricultural Research Service, Table 1, Nutrient Intakes from Food: Mean Amounts Consumed per Individual, One Day, 2005–2006 *What We Eat In America: NHANES,* available at www.ars.usda.gov.

61. G. J. Merli and J. Fink, Vitamin K and thrombosis, *Vitamins and Hormones* 78 (2008): 265–279.

62. S. Cockayn and coauthors, Vitamin K and the prevention of fractures: Systematic review and meta-analysis of randomized controlled trials, *Archives of Internal Medicine* 166 (2006): 1256–1261.

63. K. D. Cashman and E. O'Connor, Does high vitamin K_1 intake protect against bone loss in later life? *Nutrition Reviews* 66 (2008): 532–538; M. K. Shea and S. L. Booth, Update

on the role of vitamin K in skeletal health, *Nutrition Reviews* 66 (2008): 549–557.
64. M. K. Shea and coauthors, Vitamin K supplementation and progression of coronary artery calcium in older men and women, *American Journal of Clinical Nutrition* 89 (2009): 1799–1807.
65. M. N. Riaz, M. Asif, and R. Ali, Stability of vitamins during extrusion, *Critical Reviews in Food Science* 49 (2009): 361–368.
66. Y. Li and H. E. Schelhorn, New developments and novel therapeutic perspectives for vitamin C, *Journal of Nutrition* 137 (2007): 2171–2184.
67. Li and Schellhorn, New developments and novel therapeutic perspectives.
68. Bjelakovic and coauthors, Mortality in randomized trials of antioxidant supplements; National Institutes of Health State-of-the-Science conference statement, 2006.
69. D. Léger, Scurvy: Reemergence of nutritional deficiencies, *Canadian Family Physician* 54 (2008): 1403–1406.
70. R. L. Schleicher and coauthors, Serum vitamin C and the prevalence of vitamin C deficiency in the United States: 2003–2004 National Health and Nutrition Examination survey (NHANES), *American Journal of Clinical Nutrition* 90 (2009): 1252–1263.
71. Standing Committee on the Scientific Evaluation of Dietary Reference Intakes, Food and Nutrition Board, Institute of Medicine, *Dietary Reference Intakes,* p. 101.
72. R. L. Schleicher and coauthors, Serum vitamin C and the prevalence of vitamin C deficiency in the United States: 2003–2004 National Health and Nutrition Examination Survey (NHANES), *American Journal of Clinical Nutrition* 90 (2009): 1252–1263.
73. A. D. Thomson and E. J. Marshall, The natural history and pathophysiology of Wernicke's Encephalopathy and Korsakoff's Psychosis, *Alcohol and Alcoholism* 41 (2006): 151–158.
74. F. Rohner and coauthors, Mild riboflavin deficiency is highly prevalent in school-age children but does not increase risk for anaemia in Cote d'Ivoire, *British Journal of Nutrition* 97 (2007): 970–975.
75. P. A. Cotton and coauthors, Dietary sources of nutrients among U.S. adults, 1994–1996, *Journal of the American Dietetic Association* 104 (2004): 921–930.
76. L. Zhang and coauthors, Niacin inhibits surface expression of ATP synthase β chain in HepG2 cells: Implications for raising HDL, *Journal of Lipid Research* 49 (2008): 1195–1201; P. L. Canner, C. D. Furberg, and M. E. McGovern, Benefits of niacin in patients with versus without the metabolic syndrome and healed myocardial infarction (from the Coronary Drug Project), *American Journal of Cardiology* 97 (2006): 477–479; S. Westphal and coauthors, Adipokines and treatment with niacin, *Metabolism* 55 (2006): 1283–1285.
77. R. A. Mularski, Treatment advice on the internet leads to a life-threatening adverse reaction: Hypotension associated with niacin overdose, *Clinical Toxicology (Philadelphia)* 44 (2006): 81–84.
78. A. M. Hill, J. A. Fleming, and P. M. Kris-Etherton, The role of diet and nutritional supplements in preventing and treating cardiovascular disease, *Current Opinion in Cardiology* 24 (2009): 433–441.
79. K. L. Bogan and C. Brenner, Nicotinic acid, nicotinamide, and nicotinamide riboside: A molecular evaluation of NAD^+ precursor vitamins in human nutrition, *Annual Review of Nutrition* 28 (2008): 115–130.
80. World Cancer Research Fund and American Institute for Cancer Research, Summary, *Food, Nutrition, Physical Activity, and the Prevention of Cancer: A Global Perspective* (Washington, D.C.: AICR, 2008), pp. 6–7; S. C. Larsson and coauthors, Folate intake and pancreatic cancer incidence: A prospective study of Swedish women and men, *Journal of the National Cancer Institute* 98 (2006): 407–413; A. Tjonneland and coauthors, Folate intake, alcohol and risk of breast cancer among postmenopausal women in Denmark, *European Journal of Clinical Nutrition* 60 (2006): 280–286.
81. A. D. Smith, Y. I. Kim, and H. Refsum, Is folic acid good for everyone? *American Journal of Clinical Nutrition* 87 (2008): 517–533; C. M. Ulrich, Folate and cancer prevention: A closer look at a complex picture, *American Journal of Clinical Nutrition* 86 (2007): 271–273.
82. P. De Wals and coauthors, Reduction in neural-tube defects after folic acid fortification in Canada, *New England Journal of Medicine* 357 (2007): 135–142.
83. J. B. Dowd and A. E. Aiello, Did national folic acid fortification reduce socioeconomic and racial disparities in folate status in the U.S.?, *International Journal of Epidemiology* 37 (2008): 1059–1066.
84. C. M. Pfeiffer and coauthors, Trends in blood folate and vitamin B-12 concentrations in the United States, 1988–2004, *American Journal of Clinical Nutrition* 86 (2007): 718–727.
85. Centers for Disease Control and Prevention, Spina bifida and anencephaly before and after folic acid mandate—United States, 1995–1996 and 1999–2000, *Morbidity and Mortality Weekly Report* 53 (2004): 362–365.
86. A. J. Wilcox and coauthors, Folic acid supplements and risk of facial clefts: National population based case-control study, *British Medical Journal* 334 (2007): 464–469.
87. A. D. Smith, Folic acid fortification: The good, the bad, and the puzzle of vitamin B_{12}, *American Journal of Clinical Nutrition* 85 (2007): 3–5.
88. M. Ebbing and coauthors, Cancer incidence and mortality after treatment with folic acid and vitamin B_{12}, *Journal of the American Medical Association* 302 (2009): 2119–2126; U. C. Ericson and coauthors, Increased breast cancer risk at high plasma folate concentrations among women with the MTHFR 677T allele, *American Journal of Clinical Nutrition* 90 (2009): 1380–1389; A. M. Troen and coauthors, Unmetabolized folic acid in plasma is associated with reduced natural killer cell cytotoxicity among postmenopausal women, *Journal of Nutrition* 136 (2006): 189–194.
89. R. L. Bailey and coauthors, Total folate and folic acid intake from foods and dietary supplements in the United States: 2003–2006, *American Journal of Clinical Nutrition* 91 (2010): 231–237; Q. Yang and coauthors, Folic acid source, usual intake, and folate and vitamin B-12 status in US adults: National Health and Nutrition Examination Survey (NHANES) 2003–2006, *American Journal of Clinical Nutrition* 91 (2010): 64–72.
90. S. Park and M. A. Johnson, What is an adequate dose of oral vitamin B12 in older people with poor vitamin B12 status? *Nutrition Reviews* 64 (2006): 383–388.
91. P. Kanellis and coauthors, A screen for suppressors of gross chromosomal rearrangements identifies a conserved role for PLP in preventing DNA lesions, *PLoS Genetics* 3 (2007): 1438–1453.
92. L. L. Humphrey and coauthors, Homocysteine level and coronary heart disease incidence: A systematic review and meta-analysis, *Mayo Clinic Proceedings* 83 (2008): 3–16; National Institutes of Health State-of-the-Science conference statement, 2006.
93. L. M. Sanders and S. H. Zeisel, Choline—Dietary requirements and role in brain development, *Nutrition Today* 42 (2007): 181–186; S. H. Zeisel, Choline: Critical role during fetal development and dietary requirements in adults, *Annual Review of Nutrition* 26 (2006): 229–250.
94. D. R. Jacobs, M. D. Gross, and L. C. Tapsell, Food synergy: An operational concept for understanding nutrition, *American Journal of Clinical Nutrition* 89 (2009): 1543S–1548S; Position of the American Dietetic Association: Nutrient supplementation, *Journal of the American Dietetic Association* 109 (2009): 2073–2085.

CONSUMER CORNER 7

1. R. M. Douglas and coauthors, Vitamin C for preventing and treating the common cold, *Cochrane Database of Systematic Reviews,* 18 July 2007, doi:10.1002/14651858.CD000980.pub3.
2. Douglas and coauthors, Vitamin C for preventing and treating the common cold.
3. Douglas and coauthors, Vitamin C for preventing and treating the common cold; M. Simasek and D. A. Blandino, Treatment of the common cold, *American Family Physician* 75 (2007): 515–520; S. Sasazuki and coauthors, Effect of vitamin C on common cold: Randomized controlled trial, *European Journal of Clinical Nutrition* 60 (2006): 9–17.
4. E. S. Wintergerst, S. Maggini, and D. H. Hornig, Immune-enhancing role of vitamin C and zinc and effect on clinical conditions, *Annals of Nutrition and Metabolism* 50 (2006): 85–94.
5. Simasek and Blandino, Treatment of the common cold.
6. Standing Committee on the Scientific Evaluation of Dietary Reference Intakes, Food and Nutrition Board, Institute of Medicine, *Dietary*

Reference Intakes for Vitamin C, Vitamin E, Selenium, and Carotenoids (Washington, D.C.: National Academy Press, 2000).

CONTROVERSY 7

1. Position of the American Dietetic Association, Nutrient supplementation, *Journal of the American Dietetic Association* 109 (2009): 2073–2085.
2. E. Sloan, Why people use vitamin and mineral supplements, *Nutrition Today* 42 (2007): 55–61.
3. E. A. Yetley, Multivitamin and multimineral dietary supplements: Definitions, characterization, bioavailability, and drug interactions, *American Journal of Clinical Nutrition* 85 (2007): 269S–276S; Timbo and coauthors, Dietary supplements in a National Survey.
4. U.S. Prevention Task Force, Folic acid for the prevention of neural tube defects: U.S. Preventive Services Task Force Recommendation Statement, *Annals of Internal Medicine* 150 (2009): 626–631.
5. R. S. Sebastian and coauthors, Older adults who use vitamin/mineral supplements differ from nonusers in nutrient intake adequacy and dietary attitudes, *Journal of the American Dietetic Association* 107 (2007): 1322–1332.
6. Position of the American Dietetic Association: Nutrient supplementation.
7. S. P. Murphy and coauthors, Multivitamin-multimineral supplements' effect on total nutrient intake, *American Journal of Clinical Nutrition* 85 (2007): 280S–284S.
8. A. C. Bronstein and coauthors, 2007 Annual Report of the American Association of Poison Control Centers' national poisoning and exposure database, *Clinical Toxicology* 46 (2008): 927–1057.
9. C. L. Rock, Multivitamin-multimineral supplements: Who uses them? *American Journal of Clinical Nutrition* 85 (2007): 277S–279S.
10. H. S. Lam and coauthors, Risk of vitamin A toxicity from candy-like chewable vitamin supplements for children, *Pediatrics* 118 (2006): 820–824.
11. W. R. Mindak and coauthors, Lead in women's and children's vitamins, *Journal of Agricultural and Food Chemistry* 56 (2008): 6892–6896; J. F. Kaufman and coauthors, Lead in pharmaceutical products and dietary supplements, *Regulatory Toxicology and Pharmacology* 48 (2007): 128–134.
12. P. A. Cohen, American roulette—contaminated dietary supplements, *New England Journal of Medicine* 361 (2009): 1523–1525.
13. R. A. Mularski and coauthors, Treatment advice on the internet leads to a life-threatening adverse reaction: Hypotension associated with niacin overdose, *Clinical Toxicology (Philadelphia)* 44 (2006): 81–84.
14. D. R. Jacobs, M. D. Gross, and L. C. Tapsell, Food synergy: An operational concept for understanding nutrition, *American Journal of Clinical Nutrition* 89 (2009): 1543S–1548S.
15. M. G. Taber, Vitamin E and K interactions—a 50-year-old problem, *Nutrition Reviews* 66 (2008): 624–629.
16. B. N. Ames, The metabolic tune-up: Metabolic harmony and disease prevention, *Journal of Nutrition* 133 (2003): 1544S–1548S.
17. World Cancer Research Fund/American Institute for Cancer Research, *Food, Nutrition, Physical Activity and the Prevention of Cancer: A Global Perspective* (Washington, D.C.: AICR, 2007).
18. B. J. Wilcox, J. D. Crub, and B. L. Rodriguez, Antioxidants in cardiovascular health and disease: Key lessons from epidemiologic studies, *American Journal of Cardiology* 101 (2008): 75D–86D.
19. C. Selman and coauthors, Life-long vitamin C supplementation in combination with cold exposure does not affect oxidative damage or lifespan in mice, but decreases expression of antioxidant protection genes, *Mechanisms of Aging and Development* 127 (2006): 897–904.
20. G. Flores-Mateo and coauthors, Antioxidant enzyme activity and coronary heart disease: Meta-analyses of observational studies, *American Journal of Epidemiology* 170 (2009): 135–147.
21. Q. Chen and coauthors, Pharmacologic doses of ascorbate act as a prooxidant and decrease growth of aggressive tumor xenografts in mice, *Proceedings of the National Academy of Sciences* 105 (2008): 11105–11109.
22. G. Bjelakovic and coauthors, Antioxidant supplements for prevention of mortality in healthy participants and patients with various diseases, *Cochrane Database of Systematic Reviews* (2008), doi:10.1002/14651858. CD007176; H. D. Sesso and coauthors, Vitamins E and C in the prevention of cardiovascular disease in men: The Physician's Health Study II randomized controlled trial, *Journal of the American Medical Association* 300 (2008): 2123–2133; G. Bjelakovic and coauthors, Mortality in randomized trials of antioxidant supplements for primary and secondary prevention: Systematic review and meta-analysis, *Journal of the American Medical Association* 297 (2007): 842–857.
23. L. Gallicchio and coauthors, Carotenoids and the risk of developing lung cancer: A systematic review, *American Journal of Clinical Nutrition* 88 (2008): 372–383; W. C. Willett and E. Giovannucci, Epidemiology of diet and cancer risk, in *Modern Nutrition in Health and Disease,* M. E. Shils and coeditors (Philadelphia: Lippincott Williams &Wilkins, 2006), pp. 1267–1279.
24. G. Pocobelli and coauthors, Use of supplements of multivitamins, vitamin C and vitamin E in relation to mortality, *American Journal of Epidemiology* 170 (2009): 472–483.
25. A. M. Hill, J. A. Fleming, and P. M. Kris-Etherton, The role of diet and nutritional supplements in preventing and treating cardiovascular disease, *Current Opinion in Cardiology* 24 (2009): 433–441; I. M. Lee and coauthors, Vitamin E in the primary prevention of cardiovascular disease and cancer: The Women's Health Study: A randomized controlled trial, *Journal of the American Medical Association* 294 (2005): 56–65; The HOPE and HOPE-TOO Trial Investigators, Effects of long-term vitamin E supplementation on cardiovascular events and cancer: A randomized controlled trial, *Journal of the American Medical Association* 293 (2005): 1338–1347.
26. Bjelakovic and coauthors, Mortality in randomized trials of antioxidant supplements; The HOPE and HOPE-TOO Trial Investigators, Effects of long-term vitamin E supplementation.
27. J-M. Zingg, A. Azzi, and M. Meydani, Genetic polymorphisms as determinants for disease-preventive effects of vitamin E, *Nutrition Reviews* 66 (2008): 406–414.
28. Zingg, Azzi, and Meydani, Genetic polymorphisms.
29. M. G. Traber, B. Frei, and J. S. Beckman, Vitamin E revisited: Do new data validate benefits for chronic disease prevention? *Current Opinion in Lipidology* 19 (2008): 30–38; S. Devaraj and coauthors, Effect of high-dose α-tocopherol supplementation on biomarkers of oxidative stress and inflammation and carotid atherosclerosis in patients with coronary artery disease, *American Journal of Clinical Nutrition* 86 (2007): 1392–1398.
30. J. A. Satia and coauthors, Long-term use of β-carotene, retinol, lycopene, and lutein supplements and lung cancer risk: Results from the VITamins And Lifestyle (VITAL) Study, *American Journal of Epidemiology* 169 (2009): 815–828.
31. Y. G. J. van Helden and coauthors, β-Carotene metabolites enhance inflammation-induced oxidative DNA damage in lung epithelial cells, *Free Radical Biology and Medicine* 46 (2009): 299–304; Satia and coauthors, Long-term use of β-carotene, retinol, lycopene, and lutein supplements and lung cancer risk.
32. U.S. Food and Drug Administration, Center for Food Safety and Applied Nutrition, *Dietary Supplements,* available at www.cfsan.fda.gov.
33. DSHEA slightly strengthened, *Consumer Health Digest,* January 30, 2007, available at www.quackwatch.org
34. Bjelakovic and coauthors, Mortality in randomized trials of antioxidant supplements; The HOPE and HOPE-TOO Trial Investigators, Effects of long-term vitamin E supplementation; E. R. Miller and coauthors, Meta-analysis: High dosage vitamin E supplementation may increase all-cause mortality, *Annals of Internal Medicine* 142 (2005), e-pub available at www.annalas.org; S. L. Booth and coauthors, Effect of vitamin E supplementation on vitamin K status in adults with normal coagulation status, *American Journal of Clinical Nutrition* 80 (2004): 143–148.
35. Hill, Fleming, and Kris-Etherton, The role of diet and nutritional supplements in preventing and treating cardiovascular disease; Bjelakovic and coauthors, Antioxidant supplements for prevention of mortality
36. S. Rautianen and coauthors, Vitamin C supplements and the risk of age-related cataract: A population-based prospective cohort study in women, *American Journal of Clinical Nutrition* 91 (2010): 487–493; T. L. Duarte

and J. Lunec, Review: When is an antioxidant not an antioxidant? A review of novel actions and reactions of vitamin C, *Free Radical Research* 39 (2005): 671–686.
37. D. Lee and coauthors, Does supplemental vitamin C increase cardiovascular disease risk in women with diabetes? *American Journal of Clinical Nutrition* 80 (2004): 1194–1200.
38. R. Rodriguez-Melendez, J. B. Griffin, and J. Zempleni, Biotin supplementation increases expression of the cytochrome P450 1B1 in Jurkat cells, increasing the occurrence of single-stranded DNA breaks, *Journal of Nutrition* 134 (2004): 2222–2228.
39. K. L. Penniston and S. A. Tanumihardjo, The acute and chronic toxic effects of vitamin A, *American Journal of Clinical Nutrition* 83 (2006): 191–201.
40. Committee on the Framework for Evaluating the Safety of Dietary Supplements, Institute of Medicine and National Research Council, *Dietary Supplements: A Framework for Evaluating Safety* (Washington, D.C.: National Academies Press, 2004), pp. ES1–ES14.

Chapter 8

1. S. S. Gropper, J. L. Smith, and J. L. Groff, Macrominerals, *Advanced Nutrition and Human Metabolism,* (Belmont: Wadsworth/Cengage Learning, 2009), pp. 429–467.
2. Standing Committee on the Scientific Evaluation of Dietary Reference Intakes, Food and Nutrition Board, Institute of Medicine, *Dietary Reference Intakes: Water, Potassium, Sodium, Chloride, and Sulfate* (Washington, D.C.: National Academies Press, 2004): pp. 269–423.
3. A. K. Johnson, The sensory psychobiology of thirst and salt appetite, *Medicine and Science in Sports and Exercise* 39 (2007): 1388–1400; Standing Committee on the Scientific Evaluation of Dietary Reference Intakes, Food and Nutrition Board, Institute of Medicine, *Dietary Reference Intakes.*
4. K. M. Kolasa, C. J. Lacky, and A. C. Grandjean, Hydration and health promotion, *Nutrition Today* 44 (2009): 190–201.
5. Standing Committee on the Scientific Evaluation of Dietary Reference Intakes, Food and Nutrition Board, Institute of Medicine, *Dietary Reference Intakes.*
6. Standing Committee on the Scientific Evaluation of Dietary Reference Intakes, Food and Nutrition Board, Institute of Medicine, *Dietary Reference Intakes.*
7. A. K. Kant, B. I. Graubard, and E. A. Atchison, Intakes of plain water, moisture in foods and beverages, and total water in the adult U.S. population—nutritional, meal pattern, and body weight correlates: National Health and Nutrition Examination Surveys 1999–2006, *American Journal of Clinical Nutrition* 90 (2009): 655–663.
8. B. M. Popkin and coauthors, A new proposed guidance system for beverage consumption in the United States, *American Journal of Clinical Nutrition* 83 (2006): 529–542.
9. L. R. Vartanian, M. B. Schwartz, and K. D. Brownell, Effects of soft drink consumption on nutrition and health: A systematic review and meta-analysis, *American Journal of Public Health* 97 (2007): 667–675.
10. Standing Committee on the Scientific Evaluation of Dietary Reference Intakes, Food and Nutrition Board, Institute of Medicine, *Dietary Reference Intakes,* p. 67.
11. Actions You Can Take to Reduce Lead in Drinking Water, www.epa.gov/ogwdw/lead/lead1.html, updated April 2008.
12. S. D. Richardson and coauthors, Integrated disinfection by-products mixtures research: Comprehensive characterization of water concentrates prepared from chlorinated and ozonated/postchlorinated drinking water, *Journal of Toxicology and Environmental Health* 71 (2008): 1165–1186; L. D. Claxton and coauthors, Integrated disinfection by-products research: Salmonella mutagenicity of water concentrates disinfected by chlorination and ozonation/postchlorination, *Journal of Toxicology and Environmental Health* 71 (2008): 1187–1194; L. Sujbert and coauthors, Genotoxic potential of by-products in drinking water in relation to water disinfection: Survey of pre-ozonated and post-chlorinated drinking water by Ames-test, *Toxicology* 219 (2006): 106–112.
13. C. M. Villanueva and coauthors, Bladder cancer and exposure to water disinfection by-products through ingestion, bathing, showering, and swimming in pools, *American Journal of Epidemiology* 165 (2007): 148–156.
14. Richardson and coauthors, Integrated disinfection by-products mixtures research; Claxton and coauthors, Integrated disinfection by-products research.
15. A. Moshfegh and coauthors, *What We Eat in America, NHANES 2005–2006: Usual Nutrient Intakes from Food and Water compared to 1997 Dietary Reference Intakes for Vitamin D, Calcium, Phosphorus, and Magnesium* (Beltsville, Md.: USDA, 2009).
16. P. Vestergaard and coauthors, Effects of treatment with fluoride on bone mineral density and fracture risk—a meta-analysis, *Osteoporosis International* 19 (2008): 257–268.
17. P. R. Trumbo and K. C. Ellwood, Supplemental calcium and risk reduction of hypertension, pregnancy-induced hypertension, and preeclampsia: An evidence-based review by the U.S. Food and Drug Administration, *Nutrition Reviews* 65 (2007): 78–87.
18. Y. Park and coauthors, Dairy food, calcium, and risk of cancer in the NIH-AARP Diet and Health Study, *Archives of Internal Medicine* 169 (2009): 391–401; J. Ishihara and coauthors, Dietary calcium, vitamin D, and the risk of colorectal cancer, *American Journal of Clinical Nutrition* 88 (2008): 1576–1583; C. S. Guerreiro and coauthors, The *D1822V APC* polymorphism interacts with fat, calcium, and fiber intakes in modulating the risk of colorectal cancer in Portuguese persons, *American Journal of Clinical Nutrition* 85 (2007): 1592–1597; M. E. Martínez and E. T. Jacobs, Calcium supplementation and prevention of colorectal neoplasia: Lessons from clinical trials, *Journal of the National Cancer Institute* 99 (2007): 99–100; S. C. Larsson and coauthors, Calcium and dairy food intakes are inversely associated with colorectal cancer risk in the Cohort of Swedish Men, *American Journal of Clinical Nutrition* 83 (2006): 667–673.
19. R. P. Heaney and K. Rafferty, Preponderance of the evidence: An example from the issue of calcium intake and body composition, *Nutrition Reviews* 67 (2009): 32–39; G. C. Major and coauthors, Recent developments in calcium-related obesity research, *Obesity Reviews* 9 (2008): 428–445; M. B. Snijder and coauthors, Is higher dairy consumption associated with lower body weight and fewer metabolic disturbances? The Hoorn Study, *American Journal of Clinical Nutrition* 85 (2007): 989–995; G. Barba and P. Russo, Dairy foods, dietary calcium and obesity: A short review of the evidence, *Nutrition, Metabolism, and Cardiovascular Diseases* 16 (2006): 445–451.
20. M. Bortolotti and coauthors, Dairy calcium supplementation in overweight or obese persons: Its effect on markers of fat metabolism, *American Journal of Clinical Nutrition* 88 (2008): 877–885; S. N. Rajpathak and coauthors, Calcium and dairy intakes in relation to long-term weight gain in U.S. men, *American Journal of Clinical Nutrition* 83 (2006): 559–566.
21. R. C. Khanal and I. Nemere, Regulation of intestinal calcium transport, *Annual Review of Nutrition* 28 (2008): 179–196.
22. Standing Committee on the Scientific Evaluation of Dietary Reference Intakes, Food and Nutrition Board, Institute of Medicine, *Dietary Reference Intakes for Calcium, Phosphorus, Magnesium, Vitamin D, and Fluoride* (Washington, D.C.: National Academies Press, 1997), pp. 106–107.
23. Standing Committee on the Scientific Evaluation of Dietary Reference Intakes, Food and Nutrition Board, Institute of Medicine, *Dietary Reference Intakes for Calcium, Phosphorus, Magnesium, Vitamin D, and Fluoride,* p. 72.
24. T. M. Wizenberg and coauthors, Calcium supplementation for improving bone mineral density in children, *Cochrane Database System Review,* April 19, 2006, CD005119.
25. C. Palacios, The role of nutrients in bone health, from A to Z, *Critical Reviews in Food Science and Nutrition,* 46 (2006): 621–628.
26. Khanal and Nemere, Regulation of intestinal calcium transport.
27. M. Braun and coauthors, Calcium retention in adolescent boys on a range of controlled calcium intakes, *American Journal of Clinical Nutrition* 84 (2006): 414–418.
28. F. Bronner, Recent developments in intestinal calcium absorption, *Nutrition Reviews* 67 (2009): 109–113.
29. N. Napoli and coauthors, Effects of dietary calcium compared with calcium supplements on estrogen metabolism and bone mineral density, *American Journal of Clinical Nutrition* 85 (2007): 1428–1433; R. D. Jackson and coauthors, Calcium plus vitamin D supplementation and the risk of fractures, *New England Journal of Medicine* 354 (2006): 669–683.

30. Moshfegh and coauthors, *What We Eat in America.*
31. K. M. Ho, Intravenous magnesium for cardiac arrhythmias: Jack of all trades, *Magnesium Research* 21 (2008): 65–68.
32. Moshfegh and coauthors, *What We Eat in America.*
33. *Dietary Reference Intakes: The Essential Guide to Nutrient Requirements,* eds., J. Otten, J. P. Hellwig, and L. D. Meyers (Washington, D.C.: National Academies Press, 2006), p. 340.
34. L. Cordain and coauthors, Origins and evolution of the Western diet: Health implications for the 21st century, *American Journal of Clinical Nutrition* 81 (2005): 341–354.
35. S. N. Orlov and A. A. Mongin, Salt-sensing mechanisms in blood pressure regulation and hypertension, *American Journal of Physiology: Heart Circulatory Physiology* 293 (2007): H2039–H2053.
36. Standing Committee on the Scientific Evaluation of Dietary Reference Intakes, Food and Nutrition Board, Institute of Medicine, *Dietary Reference Intakes.*
37. Centers for Disease Control and Prevention, Application of Lower Sodium Intake Recommendations to Adults—United States, 1999–2006, *Morbidity and Mortality Weekly Report* 58 (2009): 281–283.
38. K. Bibbins-Domingo and coauthors, Projected effect of dietary salt reductions on future cardiovascular disease, *New England Journal of Medicine* 362 (2010): 590–599; Centers for Disease Control and Prevention, Application of Lower Sodium Intake Recommendations to Adults.
39. R. Takachi and coauthors, Consumption of sodium and salted foods in relation to cancer and cardiovascular disease: The Japan Public Health Center-based Prospective Study, *American Journal of Clinical Nutrition* 91 (2010): 456–464; F. J. He and G. A. MacGregor, A comprehensive review on salt and health and current experience of worldwide salt reduction programmes, *Journal of Human Hypertension* 23 (2009): 363–384.
40. Centers for Disease Control and Prevention, Application of Lower Sodium Intake Recommendations to Adults.
41. B. N. Van Vliet and J-P. Montani, The time course of salt-induced hypertension, and why it matters, *International Journal of Obesity* 32 (2008): S35–S47; Standing Committee on the Scientific Evaluation of Dietary Reference Intakes, Food and Nutrition Board, Institute of Medicine, *Dietary Reference Intakes.*
42. U.S. Department of Agriculture and U.S. Department of Health and Human Services, *2005 Dietary Guidelines Committee Report, 2005,* available online at www.health.gov/dietaryguidelines/dga2005report/.
43. N. R. Cook and coauthors, Long-term effects of dietary sodium reduction on cardiovascular disease outcomes: Observational follow-up of the trials of hypertension prevention (TOHP), *British Medical Journal* 334 (2007): 885–888.
44. Van Vliet and Montani, The time course of salt-induced hypertension.
45. K. M. O'Shaughnessy and F. E. Karet, Salt handling and hypertension, *Annual Review of Nutrition* 26 (2006): 343–365.
46. E. B. Levitan, A. Wolk, and M. A. Mittleman, Consistency with the DASH Diet and incidence of heart failure, *Archives of Internal Medicine* 169 (2009): 851–857.
47. J. P. Forman, M. J. Stampfer, and G. C. Curhan, Diet and lifestyle risk factors associated with incident hypertension in women, *Journal of the American Medical Association* 302 (2009): 401–411.
48. K. Rafferty and R. P. Heaney, Nutrient effects on the calcium economy: Emphasizing the potassium controversy, *Journal of Nutrition* 138 (2008): 166S–171S.
49. K. M. Fock and coauthors, Asia-Pacific consensus guidelines on gastric cancer prevention, *Journal of Gastroenterology and Hepatology* 23 (2009): 351–365.
50. R. A. Forshee, Innovative regulatory approaches to reduce sodium consumption: Could a cap-and-trade system work? *Nutrition Reviews* 66 (2008): 280–285; S. Havas, B. D. Dickinson, and M. Wilson, The urgent need to reduce sodium consumption, *Journal of the American Medical Association* 298 (2007): 1439–1441; K. M. O'Shaughnessy and F. E. Karet, Salt handling and hypertension, *Annual Review of Nutrition* 26 (2006): 343–365.
51. Adrogué and Madias, Sodium and potassium in the pathogenesis of hypertension.
52. U.S. Food and Drug Administration, Lowering salt in your diet, *For Consumers,* September 9, 2009, available at www.fda.gov/ForConsumers/ConsumerUpdates/ucm181577.htm.
53. M. Umesawa and coauthors, Relations between dietary sodium and potassium intakes and mortality from cardiovascular disease: The Japan Collaborative Cohort Study for Evaluation of Cancer Risks, *American Journal of Clinical Nutrition* 88 (2008): 195–202; Adrogué and Madias, Sodium and potassium in the pathogenesis of hypertension.
54. Standing Committee on the Scientific Evaluation of Dietary Reference Intakes, Food and Nutrition Board, Institute of Medicine, 2004, pp. 5–6.
55. C. A. Nowson and coauthors, Blood pressure response to dietary modifications in free-living individuals, *Journal of Nutrition* 134 (2004): 2322–2329.
56. Standing Committee on the Scientific Evaluation of Dietary Reference Intakes, Food and Nutrition Board, Institute of Medicine, 2004, pp. 5–35.
57. M. A. Portman, Thyroid hormone regulation of heart metabolism, *Thyroid* 18 (2008): 217–225.
58. R. D. Semba and coauthors, Child malnutrition and mortality among families not utilizing adequately iodized salt in Indonesia, *American Journal of Clinical Nutrition* 87 (2008): 438–444.
59. M. B. Zimmermann, Iodine deficiency in pregnancy and the effects of maternal iodine supplementation on the offspring: A review, *American Journal of Clinical Nutrition* 89 (2009): 668S–672S.
60. T. R. Bandgar and N. S. Shah, Thyroid disorders in childhood and adolescence, *Journal of the Indian Medical Association* 104 (2006): 580–582.
61. W. Teng and coauthors, Effect of iodine intake on thyroid diseases in China, *New England Journal of Medicine* 354 (2006): 2783–2793.
62. Standing Committee on the Scientific Evaluation of Dietary Reference Intakes, Food and Nutrition Board, Institute of Medicine, *Dietary Reference Intakes for Vitamin A, Vitamin K, Arsenic, Boron, Chromium, Copper, Iodine, Iron, Manganese, Molybdenum, Nickel, Silicon, Vanadium, and Zinc* (Washington, D.C.: National Academies Press, 2001), p. 258.
63. E. N. Pearce and coauthors, Sources of dietary iodine: Bread, cows' milk, and infant formula in the Boston area, *Journal of Clinical Endocrinology and Metabolism* 89 (2004): 3421–3424.
64. Pearce and coauthors, Sources of dietary iodine.
65. J. R. Hunt, C. A. Zito and L. K. Johnson, Body iron excretion by healthy men and women, *American Journal of Clinical Nutrition* 89 (2009): 1792–1798.
66. D. Galaris and K. Pantopoulos, Oxidative stress and iron homeostasis: Mechanistic and health aspects, *Critical Reviews in Clinical Laboratory Sciences* 45 (2008): 1–23.
67. Q. Liu and coauthors, Role of iron deficiency and overload in the pathogenesis of diabetes and diabetic complications, *Current Medicinal Chemistry* 16 (2009): 113–129.
68. Standing Committee on the Scientific Evaluation of Dietary Reference Intakes, Food and Nutrition Board, Institute of Medicine, *Dietary Reference Intakes for Vitamin A, Vitamin K, Arsenic, Boron, Chromium, Copper, Iodine, Iron, Manganese, Molybdenum, Nickel, Silicon, Vanadium, and Zinc,* pp. 9–14.
69. R. F. Hurrell and coauthors, Meat protein fractions enhance nonheme iron absorption in humans, *Journal of Nutrition* 136 (2006): 2808–2812.
70. J. C. McCann and B. N. Ames, An overview of evidence for a causal relation between iron deficiency during development and deficits in cognitive or behavioral function, *American Journal of Clinical Nutrition* 85 (2007): 931–945.
71. L. E. Murray-Kolb and J. L. Beard, Iron treatment normalizes cognitive functioning in young women, *American Journal of Clinical Nutrition* 85 (2007): 778–787.
72. McCann and Ames, An overview of evidence; B. Lozoff and coauthors, Long-lasting neural and behavioral effects of iron deficiency in infancy, *Nutrition Reviews* 64 (2006): S34–S43.
73. Murray-Kolb and Beard, Iron treatment normalizes cognitive functioning.
74. S. L. Young and coauthors, Toward a comprehensive approach to the collection and

analysis of pica substances, with emphasis on geophagic materials, *PLoS ONE* 3 (2008): e3147.

75. L. M. Tussing-Humphreys and coauthors, Excess adiposity, inflammation, and iron-deficiency in female adolescents, *Journal of the American Dietetic Association* 109 (2009): 297–302; J. P. McClung and J. P. Karl, Iron deficiency and obesity: The contribution of inflammation and diminished iron absorption, *Nutrition Reviews* 67 (2008): 100–104.

76. J. M. Brotanek and coauthors, Iron deficiency in early childhood in the United States: Risk factors and racial/ethnic disparities, *Pediatrics* 120 (2007): 568–575.

77. Worldwide prevalence of anaemia 1993–2005: WHO Global Database on Anaemia, published 2008, available from www.who.org.

78. World Health Organization, www.who.int/nut/ida.htm.

79. M. Alleyne, M. K. Horne, and J. L. Miller, Individualized treatment for iron-deficiency anemia in adults, *American Journal of Medicine* 121 (2008): 943–948.

80. S. Lekawanvijit and N. Chattipakorn, Iron overload thalassemic cardiomyopathy: Iron status assessment and mechanisms of mechanical and electrical disturbance due to iron toxicity, *Canadian Journal of Cardiology* 25 (2009): 213–218.

81. K. J. Allen and coauthors, Iron-overload—Related disease in *HFE* hereditary hemochromatosis, *New England Journal of Medicine* 358 (2008): 221–230; A. Pietrangelo, Hereditary hemochromatosis, *Annual Review of Nutrition* 26 (2006): 251–270.

82. Liu and coauthors, Role of iron deficiency and overload; Lekawanvijit and Chattipakorn, Iron overload thalassemic cardiomyopathy; D. Galaris and K. Pantopoulos, Oxidative stress and iron homeostasis: Mechanistic and health aspects, *Critical Reviews in Clinical Laboratory Sciences* 45 (2008): 1–23.

83. H. Drakesmith and A. Prentice, Viral infection and iron metabolism, *Nature Reviews. Microbiology* 6 (2008): 541–552; A. M. Prentice, Iron metabolism, malaria, and other infections: What is all the fuss about? *Journal of Nutrition* 138 (2008): 2537–2541; C. Ratledge, Iron metabolism and infection, *Food and Nutrition Bulletin* 28 (2007): S515–S523.

84. M. Carlsson and coauthors, Severe iron intoxication treated with exchange transfusion, *Archives of Disease in Childhood* 93 (2008): 321–322; M. D. Aldridge, Acute iron poisoning: What every pediatric intensive care unit nurse should know, *Dimensions in Critical Care Nursing* 26 (2007): 43–48.

85. M. A. Ali and R. Schulz, Activation of MMP-2 as a key event in oxidative stress injury to the heart, *Frontiers in Bioscience* 14 (2009): 669–716; Y. Song and coauthors, Zinc deficiency affects DNA damage, oxidative stress, antioxidant defenses, and DNA repair in rats, *Journal of Nutrition* 139 (2009): 1626–1631.

86. S. G. Bell and B. L. Vallee, The metallothionein/thionein system: An oxidoreductive metabolic zinc link, *ChemBioChem* 10 (2009): 55–62; C. R. Cole and F. Lifshitz, Zinc nutrition and growth retardation, *Pediatric Endocrinology Reviews* 5 (2008): 889–896.

87. H. Haase and L. Rink, Functional significance of zinc-related signaling pathways in immune cells, *Annual Review of Nutrition* 29 (2009): 133–152.

88. Bell and Vallee, The metallothionein/thionein system; C. W. Levenson, Zinc: The new antidepressant? *Nutrition Reviews* 64 (2006): 39–42; C. W. Levenson, Regulation of the NMDA receptor: Implications for neuropsychological development, *Nutrition Reviews* 64 (2006): 428–432; Palacios, The role of nutrients in bone health.

89. C. L. Fischer Walker, M. Ezzati, and R. E. Black, Global and regional child mortality and burden of disease attributable to zinc deficiency, *European Journal of Clinical Nutrition* 63 (2009): 591–597.

90. Cole and Lifshitz, Zinc nutrition and growth retardation.

91. D. E. Roth and coauthors, Acute lower respiratory infections in childhood: Opportunities for reducing the global burden through nutritional interventions, *Bulletin of the World Health Organization* 86 (2008): 321–416.

92. U. Ramakrishnan, P. Nguyen, and R. Martorell, Effects of micronutrients on growth of children under 5 y of age: Meta-analyses of single and multiple nutrient interventions, *American Journal of Clinical Nutrition* 89 (2009): 191–201; M. Lukacik, R. L. Thomas, and J. V. Aranda, A meta-analysis of the effects of oral zinc in the treatment of acute and persistent diarrhea, *Pediatrics* 121 (2008): 326–336; S. E. Wuehler, F. Sempértegui, and K. H. Brown, Dose-response trial of prophylactic zinc supplements, with or without copper, in young Ecuadorian children at risk of zinc deficiency, *American Journal of Clinical Nutrition* 87 (2008): 723–733; R. Aggarwal, J. Sentz, and M. A. Miller, Role of zinc administration in prevention of childhood diarrhea and respiratory illnesses: A meta-analysis, *Pediatrics* 119 (2007): 1120–1130.

93. FDA, Warnings on three Zicam intranasal zinc products, *For Consumers*, June 2009, available at www.fda.gov/forconsumers/ConsumerUpdates/ucm166931.htm.

94. P. A. Cotton and coauthors, Dietary sources of nutrients among U.S. adults, 1994–1996, *Journal of the American Dietetic Association* 104 (2004): 921–930.

95. J. R. Hunt, J. M. Beiseigel, and L. K. Johnson, Adaptation in human zinc absorption as influenced by dietary zinc and bioavailability, *American Journal of Clinical Nutrition* 87 (2008): 1336–1345.

96. W. J. Craig, Health effects of vegan diets, *American Journal of Clinical Nutrition* 89 (2009): 1627S–1633S; J. Sabaté and Y. Ang, Nuts and health outcomes: New epidemiologic evidence, *American Journal of Clinical Nutrition* 89 (2009): 1643S–1648S.

97. D. L. St. Germain and coauthors, Minireview: Defining the roles of the iodothyronine deiodinases: Current concepts and challenges, *Endocrinology* 150 (2009): 1097–1107.

98. J. Hesketh, Nutrigenomics and selenium: Gene expression patterns, physiological targets and genetics, *Annual Review of Nutrition* 28 (2008): 157–177.

99. F. P. Bellinger and coauthors, Regulation and function of selenoproteins in human disease, *Biochemical Journal* 422 (2009): 11–22; X. G. Lei, W. Cheng, and J. P. McClung, Metabolic regulation and function of glutathione peroxidase-1, *Annual Review of Nutrition* 27 (2007): 41–61.

100. A. Navas-Acien, J. Bleys, and E. Guallar, Selenium intake and cardiovascular risk: What is new? *Current Opinion in Lipidology* 19 (2008): 43–49.

101. G. Flores-Mateo and coauthors, Selenium and coronary heart disease: A meta-analysis, *American Journal of Clinical Nutrition* 84 (2006): 762–773.

102. J. Bleys and coauthors, Serum selenium and serum lipids in US adults, *American Journal of Clinical Nutrition* 88 (2008): 416–423; S. Stranges and coauthors, Effects of long-term selenium supplementation on the incidence of type 2 diabetes: A randomized trial, *Annals of Internal Medicine* 21 (2007): 217–223.

103. T. M. Vogt and coauthors, Serum selenium and risk of prostate cancer in U.S. blacks and whites, *International Journal of Cancer* 103 (2003): 664–670.

104. Position of the American Dietetic Association: Nutrient supplementation, *Journal of the American Dietetic Association* 109 (2009): 2073–2085; B. K. Dunn, A. Ryan, and L. G. Ford, Selenium and vitamin E cancer prevention trial: A nutrient approach to prostate cancer prevention, *Recent Results in Cancer Research* 181 (2009): 183–193; N. Facompre and K. El-Bayoumy, Potential stages for prostate cancer prevention with selenium: Implications for cancer survivors, *Cancer Research* 69 (2009): 2699–2703.

105. Bellinger and coauthors, Regulation and function of selenoproteins in human disease.

106. J. W. Finley, Selenium accumulation in plant foods, *Nutrition Reviews* 63 (2005): 196–202.

107. C. D. Thomson and coauthors, Brazil nuts: An effective way to improve selenium status, *American Journal of Clinical Nutrition* 87 (2008): 379–384.

108. Surveillance for dental caries, dental sealants, tooth retention, edentulism, and enamel fluorosis—United States, 1988–1994 and 1999–2002, *Morbidity and Mortality Weekly Report* 54 (2005): 1–44.

109. Populations receiving optimally fluoridated public drinking water—United States, 1992–2006, *Morbidity and Mortality Weekly Report* 57 (2008): 737–741.

110. E. Halasova and coauthors, Chromosomal damage and polymorphisms of DNA repair genes XRCC1 and XRCC3 in workers exposed to chromium, *Neuro Endocrinology Letters* 29 (2008): 658–662; S. S. Wise, A. L. Holmes, and J. P. Wise, Sr., Hexavalent chromium-induced

DNA damage and repair mechanisms, *Reviews on Environmental Health* 23 (2008): 39–57.
111. E. M. Balk and coauthors, Effect of chromium supplementation on glucose metabolism and lipids: A systematic review of randomized controlled trials, *Diabetes Care* 30 (2007): 2154–2163; C. L. Broadhurst and P. Domenico, Clinical studies on chromium picolinate supplementation in diabetes mellitus—A review, *Diabetes Technology and Therapeutics* 8 (2006): 677–687; P. R. Trumbo and K. C. Ellwood, Chromium picolinate intake and risk of type 2 diabetes: An evidence-based review by the United States Food and Drug Administration, *Nutrition Reviews* 64 (2006): 357–363.
112. Standing Committee on the Scientific Evaluation of Dietary Reference Intakes, Food and Nutrition Board, Institute of Medicine, *Dietary Reference Intakes for Vitamin A, Vitamin K, Arsenic, Boron, Chromium, Copper, Iodine, Iron, Manganese, Molybdenum, Nickel, Silicon, Vanadium, and Zinc*, p. 245.
113. F. H. Nielsen, Is boron nutritionally relevant? *Nutrition Reviews* 66 (2008): 183–191.
114. J. Ma, R. A. Johns, and R. S. Stafford, Americans are not meeting current calcium recommendations, *American Journal of Clinical Nutrition* 85 (2007): 1361–1366.
115. M. L. Storey, R. A. Forshee, and P. A. Anderson, Beverage consumption in the U.S. population, *Journal of the American Dietetic Association* 106 (2006): 1992–2000.
116. U.S. Department of Agriculture and U.S. Department of Health and Human Services, *Dietary Guidelines for Americans 2005*, available online at www.healthierus.gov.
117. R. P. Heaney, Absorbability and utility of calcium in mineral waters, *American Journal of Clinical Nutrition* 84 (2006): 371–374.

CONSUMER CORNER 8

1. Natural Resources Defense Council, *Bottled Water: Pure Drink or Pure Hype?*; available at www.nrdc.org/water/drinking/nbw.asp; U.S. Food and Drug Administration, FDA warns consumers not to drink "Jermuk" brand mineral water, *FDA News*, March 7, 2007, available at www.fda.gov/bbs/topics/NEWS?2007?NEW01581.html.
2. R. K. Mahajan and coauthors, Analysis of physical and chemical parameters of bottled drinking water, *International Journal of Environmental Health Research* 16 (2006): 89–98.
3. U.S. Food and Drug Administration, Bottled Water Regulation, 2009, available at http://www.fda.gov/Food/FoodSafety/Product-SpecificInformation/BottledWaterCarbonatedSoftDrinks/ucm077065.htm.
4. U.S. Food and Drug Administration, Bisphenol A (BPA): Update on bisphenol A for use in food contact applications, *FDA News and Events*, January 2010, available at www.fda.gov; American Dietetic Association, Safety of plastic related to foods and beverages, *Hot Topics*, August 2008, available at www.eatright.org.
5. Mahajan and coauthors, Analysis of physical and chemical parameters of bottled drinking water.
6. S. D. Raj, Bottled water: How safe is it? *Water Environment Research* 77 (2005): 3013–3018.

CONTROVERSY 8

1. National Osteoporosis Foundation, America's bone health: The state of osteoporosis and low bone mass, 2008, www.nof.org; U.S. Department of Health and Human Services, *Bone Health and Osteoporosis: A Report of the Surgeon General*, (Rockville, Md.: U.S. Department of Health and Human Services, Office of the Surgeon General, 2004).
2. U.S. Department of Health and Human Services, *Bone Health and Osteoporosis.*
3. A. M. Cheung and A. S. Detsky, Osteoporosis and fractures—Missing the bridge? *Journal of the American Medical Association* 299 (2008): 1468–1470.
4. E. A. Duncan and M. A. Brown, Genetic studies in osteoporosis—the end of the beginning, *Arthritis Research and Therapy* 10 (2008) doi:10.1186/ar2479; S. H. Ralston and B. de Crombrugghe, Genetic regulation of bone mass and susceptibility to osteoporosis, *Genes and Development* 20 (2006): 2492–2506.
5. E. J. Brochmann, K. Behnam, and S. S. Murray, Bone morphogenetic protein-2 activity is regulated by secreted phosphoprotein-24 kd, an extracellular pseudoreceptor, the gene for which maps to a region of the human genome important for bone quality, *Metabolism* 58 (2009): 644–654; Y. J. Liu and coauthors, Molecular genetic studies of gene identification for osteoporosis: A 2004 update, *Journal of Bone Mineral Research* 21 (2006): 1511–1535.
6. Liu and coauthors, Molecular genetic studies of gene identification.
7. G. R. Mundy, Osteoporosis and inflammation, *Nutrition Reviews* 65 (2007): S147–S151.
8. M. D. Walker and coauthors, Race and diet interaction in the acquisition, maintenance, and loss of bone, *Journal of Nutrition* 138 (2008): 1256S–1260S.
9. M. Braun and coauthors, Racial differences in skeletal calcium retention in adolescent girls with varied controlled calcium intakes, *American Journal of Clinical Nutrition* 85 (2007): 1657–1663.
10. H. A. Bischoff-Ferrari and coauthors, Calcium intake and hip fracture risk in men and women: A meta-analysis of prospective cohort studies and randomized controlled trials, *American Journal of Clinical Nutrition* 86 (2007): 1780–1790.
11. L. M. Fiorito and coauthors, Dairy and dairy-related nutrient intake during middle childhood, *Journal of the American Dietetic Association* 106 (2006): 534–542.
12. K. D. Cashman and coauthors, Low vitamin D status adversely affects bone health parameters in adolescents, *American Journal of Clinical Nutrition* 87 (2008): 1039–1044.
13. R. Rizzoli, Nutrition: Its role in bone health, *Best Practice and Research: Clinical Endocrinology and Metabolism* 22 (2008): 813–829; G. Xiang and coauthors, Meeting adequate intake for dietary calcium without dairy foods in adolescents aged 9 to 18 years (National Health and Nutrition Examination Survey 2001–2002), *Journal of the American Dietetic Association* 106 (2006): 1759–1765.
14. P. R. Ebeling, Osteoporosis in men, *New England Journal of Medicine* 358 (2008): 1474–1482.
15. Ebeling, Osteoporosis in men.
16. M. Varenna and coauthors, Effects of dietary calcium intake on body weight and prevalence of osteoporosis in early postmenopausal women, *American Journal of Clinical Nutrition* 86 (2007): 639–644.
17. G. Wolf, Energy regulation by the skeleton, *Nutrition Reviews* 66 (2008): 229–233.
18. C. A. Rideout, H. A. McKay, and S. T. Barr, Self-reported lifetime physical activity and areal bone mineral density in healthy postmenopausal women: The importance of teenage activity, *Calcified Tissue International* 79 (2006): 214–222.
19. T. L. N. Järvinen and coauthors, Shifting the focus in fracture prevention from osteoporosis to falls, *British Medical Journal* 336 (2008): 124–126.
20. M. Lorentzon and coauthors, Smoking is associated with lower bone mineral density and reduced cortical thickness in young men, *Journal of Clinical Endocrinology and Metabolism* 92 (2007): 497–503.
21. Ebeling, Osteoporosis in men.
22. A. D. Conigrave, E. M. Brown, and R. Rizzoli, Dietary protein and bone health: Roles of amino acid-sensing receptors in the control of calcium metabolism and bone homeostasis, *Annual Review of Nutrition* 28 (2008): 131–155.
23. J. E. Kerstetter, Dietary protein bone: A new approach to an old question, *American Journal of Clinical Nutrition* 90 (2009): 1451–1452.
24. K. M. Pye and coauthors, A high mixed protein diet reduces body fat without altering the mechanical properties of bone in female rats, *Journal of Nutrition* 139 (2009): 2099–2105; C. M. Weaver, A. P. Rothwell, and K. V. Wood, Measuring calcium absorption and utilization in humans, *Current Opinion in Clinical Nutrition and Metabolic Care* 9 (2006): 568–574.
25. A. M. Kenny and coauthors, Soy proteins and isoflavones affect bone mineral density in older women: A randomized controlled trial, *American Journal of Clinical Nutrition* 90 (2009): 234–242.
26. D. L. Alekel and coauthors, The Soy Isoflavones for Reducing Bone Loss (SIRBL) Study: a 3-y randomized controlled trial in postmenopausal women, *American Journal of Clinical Nutrition* 91 (2010): 218–230; Kenny and coauthors, Soy proteins and isoflavones; A. Atmaca and coauthors, Soy isoflavones in the management of postmenopausal osteoporosis, *Menopause* 15 (2008): 748–757; R. C. Poulsen and M. C. Kruger, Soy phytoestrogens: Impact on postmenopausal bone loss and mechanisms of action, *Nutrition Reviews* 66 (2008): 359–374.

F

27. K. Rafferty and R. Heaney, Nutrient effects on the calcium economy: Emphasizing the potassium controversy, *Journal of Nutrition* 138 (2008): 166S–171S.

28. L. T. Ho-Pham and coauthors, Effect of vegetarian diets on bone mineral density: A Bayesian meta-analysis, *American Journal of Clinical Nutrition* 90 (2009): 943–950; A. M. Smith, Vegetarianism and osteoporosis: A review of the current literature, *International Journal of Nursing Practice* 12 (2006): 302–306.

29. F. J. He and G. A. MacGregor, A comprehensive review on salt and health and current experience of worldwide salt reduction programmes, *Journal of Human Hypertension* 23 (2009): 363–384; Weaver, Rothwell, and Wood, Measuring calcium absorption and utilization.

30. C. A. Nowson, A. Patchett, and N. Wattanapenpaiboon, The effects of a low-sodium base-producing diet including red meat compared with a high-carbohydrate, low-fat diet on bone turnover markers in women aged 45–75 years, *British Journal of Nutrition* 102 (2009): 1161–1170.

31. Standing Committee on the Scientific Evaluation of Dietary Reference Intakes, Food and Nutrition Board, Institute of Medicine, *Dietary Reference Intakes for Water, Potassium, Sodium, Chloride, and Sulfate* (Washington, D.C.: National Academies Press, 2005), pp. 6-89–6-92.

32. K. L. Tucker and coauthors, Colas, but not other carbonated beverages, are associated with low bone mineral density in older women: The Framingham Osteoporosis Study, *American Journal of Clinical Nutrition* 84 (2006): 936–942.

33. H. Jacobsson, Short-time ingestion of colas influences the activity distribution at bone scintigraphy: Experimental studies in the mouse, *Journal of the American College of Nutrition* 27 (2008): 332–336; V. E. Kemi and coauthors, Increased calcium intake does not completely counteract the effects of increased phosphorus intake on bone: An acute dose-response study in healthy females, *British Journal of Nutrition* 99 (2008): 832–839.

34. J-P. Bonjour and coauthors, Minerals and vitamins in bone health: The potential value of dietary enhancement, *British Journal of Nutrition* 101 (2009): 1581–1596; K. D. Cashman and E. O'Connor, Does high vitamin K_1 intake protect against bone loss in later life? *Nutrition Reviews* 66 (2008): 532–538; M. K. Shea and S. L. Booth, Update on the role of vitamin K in skeletal health, *Nutrition Reviews* 66 (2008): 549–557.

35. Shea and Booth, Update on the role of vitamin K in skeletal health.

36. S. Sahni and coauthors, High vitamin C intake is associated with lower 4-year bone loss in elderly men, *Journal of Nutrition* 138 (2008): 1931–1938; J. D. Ribaya-Mercado and J. B. Blumberg, Vitamin A: Is it a risk factor for osteoporosis and bone fracture? *Nutrition Reviews* 65 (2007): 425–438.

37. R. K. Rude, F. R. Singer, and H. E. Gruber, Skeletal and hormonal effects of magnesium deficiency, *Journal of the American College of Nutrition* 28 (2009): 131–141.

38. A. E. Griel and coauthors, An increase in dietary n-3 fatty acids decreases a marker of bone resorption in humans, *Nutrition Journal* 6:2 (2007): doi:10.1186/1475-2891-6-2.

39. P. Vestergaard and coauthors, Effects of treatment with fluoride on bone mineral density and fracture risk—a meta-analysis, *Osteoporosis International* 19 (2008): 257–268.

40. National Institutes of Health, WHI follow-up study confirms health risks of long-term combination hormone therapy outweigh benefits for postmenopausal women, *NIH News,* March 4, 2008, available at http://public.nhilbi.nih.gov.

41. C. M. Weaver, Back to basics: Have milk with meals, *Journal of the American Dietetic Association* 106 (2006): 1756–1758.

42. T. M. Winzenberg and coauthors, Calcium supplementation for improving bone mineral density in children, *Cochrane Database System Review,* April 19, 2006, CD005119.

43. H. A. Bischoff-Ferrari and coauthors, Effect of calcium supplementation on fracture risk: A double-blind randomized controlled trial, *American Journal of Clinical Nutrition* 87 (2008): 1945–1951; R. M. Daly and coauthors, The skeletal benefits of calcium- and vitamin D3-fortified milk are sustained in older men after withdrawal of supplementation: An 18-mo follow-up study, *American Journal of Clinical Nutrition* 87 (2008): 771–777; M. F. Hitz, J. B. Jensen, and P. C. Eskildsen, Bone mineral density and bone markers in patients with a recent low-energy fracture: Effect of 1 y of treatment with calcium and vitamin D, *American Journal of Clinical Nutrition* 86 (2007): 251–259; B. M. P. Tang and coauthors, Use of calcium or calcium in combination with vitamin D supplementation to prevent fractures and bone loss in people aged 50 years and older: A meta-analysis, *Lancet* 370 (2007): 657–666.

44. R. D. Jackson and coauthors, Calcium plus vitamin D supplementation and the risk of fractures, *New England Journal of Medicine,* 354 (2006): 669–683.

45. C. Lee and D. S. Majka, Is calcium and vitamin D supplementation overrated? *Journal of the American Dietetic Association* 106 (2006): 1032–1034.

46. M. J. Bolland and coauthors, Vascular events in healthy older women receiving calcium supplementation: Randomised controlled trial, *British Medical Journal* 336 (2008): 262–266.

47. R. P. Heaney, Absorbability and utility of calcium in mineral waters, *American Journal of Clinical Nutrition* 84 (2006): 371–374.

Chapter 9

1. G. Whitlock and coauthors, Body-mass index and cause-specific mortality in 900,000 adults: Collaborative analyses of 57 prospective studies, *Lancet* 373 (2009): 1083–1096.

2. C. M. Apovian, The causes, prevalence, and treatment of obesity revisited in 2009: What have we learned so far? *American Journal of Clinical Nutrition* 91 (2010): 277S–279S; C. L. Ogden and coauthors, Prevalence of overweight and obesity in the United States, 1999–2004, *Journal of the American Medical Association* 295 (2006): 1549–1555.

3. K. M. Flegal and coauthors, Prevalence and trends in obesity among U.S. adults, 1999–2008, *Journal of the American Medical Association* 303 (2010): 235–241; C. L. Ogden and coauthors, Obesity among adults in the United States—No statistically significant change since 2003–2004, HCHS Data Brief November 2007, pp.1–6; R. Sturm, Increases in morbid obesity in the USA: 2000–2005, *Public Health* 121 (2007): 492–496.

4. Ogden and coauthors, Prevalence of overweight and obesity in the United States, 1999–2004.

5. B. M. Popkin, Recent dynamics suggest selected countries catching up to U.S. obesity, *American Journal of Clinical Nutrition* 91 (2010): 284S–288S.

6. C. D. Fryar and C. L. Odgen, Prevalence of underweight among adults: United States, 2003–2006, *NCHS Health E-Stats,* May 21, 2009, available at www.cdc.gov/nchs/data/hestat/underweight_children.htm.

7. Whitlock and coauthors, Body-mass index and cause-specific mortality in 900,000 adults; T. Pischon and coauthors, General and abdominal adiposity and risk of death in Europe, *New England Journal of Medicine* 359 (2008): 2105–2120.

8. O. Bouillanne and coauthors, Fat mass protects hospitalized elderly persons against morbidity and mortality, *American Journal of Clinical Nutrition* 90 (2009): 505–510.

9. C. J. Lavie, R. V. Milani, and H. O. Ventura, Obesity and cardiovascular disease: Risk factor, paradox, and impact of weight loss, *Journal of the American College of Cardiology* 53 (2009): 1925–1932.

10. Y. Wang and coauthors, Relationship between body adiposity measures and risk of primary knee and hip replacement for osteoarthritis: A prospective cohort study, *Arthritis Research and Therapy* 11 (2009), doi:10.1186/ar2636; C. S. Fox and coauthors, Abdominal visceral and subcutaneous adipose tissue compartments: association with metabolic risk factors in the Framingham Heart Study, *Circulation* 116 (2007): 39–48; R. P. Gelber and coauthors, Body mass index and mortality in men: Evaluating the shape of the evaluation, *International Journal of Obesity* 31 (2007): 1240–1247; D. E. Alley and V. W. Chang, The changing relationship of obesity and disability, 1988–2004, *Journal of the American Medical Association* 298 (2007): 2020–2027.

11. E. A. Finkelstein and coauthors, Annual medical spending attributable to obesity: Payer- and service-specific estimates, *Health Affairs* 28 (2009): w822–w831.

12. Prospective Studies Collaboration, Body-mass index and cause-specific mortality in 900,000 adults.
13. H. Jia and E. I. Lubetkin, Trends in quality-adjusted life-years lost contributed by smoking and obesity: Does the burden of obesity overweight the burden of smoking?, *American Journal of Preventive Medicine* 38 (2010): 138–144; Prospective Studies Collaboration, Body-mass index and cause-specific mortality in 900,000 adults.
14. G. Hu and coauthors, Body mass index, waist circumference, and waist-hip ratio on the risk of total and type-specific stroke, *Archives of Internal Medicine* 167 (2007): 1420–1427.
15. L. W. York, S. Puthalapattu, and G. Y. Wu, Nonalcoholic fatty liver disease and low-carbohydrate diets, *Annual Review of Nutrition* 29 (2009): 365–379; Prospective Studies Collaboration, Body-mass index and cause-specific mortality in 900,000 adults; K. F. Adams and coauthors, Body mass and colorectal cancer risk in the NIH-AARP cohort, *American Journal of Epidemiology* 166 (2007): 36–45; S. R. Patel and coauthors, Association between reduced sleep and weight gain in women, *American Journal of Epidemiology* 164 (2006):947–954.
16. S. Havas, L. J. Aronne, and K. A. Woodworth, The obesity epidemic: Strategies in reducing cardiometabolic risk, *American Journal of Medicine* 122 (2009), doi:10.1016/j.amjmed.2009.01.001.
17. S. S. Dhaliwal and T. A. Welborn, Central obesity and multivariable cardiovascular risk as assessed by the Framingham prediction scores, *American Journal of Cardiology* 103 (2009): 1403–1407; C. D. Lee and coauthors, Abdominal obesity and coronary artery calcification in young adults: The Coronary Artery Risk Development in Young Adults (CARDIA) Study, *American Journal of Clinical Nutrition* 86 (2007): 48–54
18. Hu and coauthors, Body mass index, waist circumference, and waist-hip ratio.
19. Adams and coauthors, Body mass and colorectal cancer risk; S. B. Votruba and M. D. Jensen, Regional fat deposition as a factor in FFA metabolism, *Annual Review of Nutrition* 27 (2007): 149–163.
20. J. P. Reis and coauthors, Overall obesity and abdominal adiposity as predictors of mortality in U.S. white and black adults, *Annals of Epidemiology* 19 (2009): 134–142.
21. G. Govindarajan, M. A. Alpert, and L. Tejwani, Endocrine and metabolic effects of fat: Cardiovascular implications, *American Journal of Medicine* 121 (2008): 366–370; G. Fantuzzi and T. Mazzone, Adipose tissue and atherosclerosis: Exploring the connection, *Arteriosclerosis, Thrombosis, and Vascular Biology* 27 (2007): 996–1003; P. Trayhurn, C. Bing, and I. S. Wood, Adipose tissue and adipokines—Energy regulation from the human perspective, *Journal of Nutrition* 136 (2006): 1935S–1939S; C. Bulcão and coauthors, The new adipose tissue and adipocytokines, *Current Diabetes Reviews* 2 (2006): 19–28; T. J. Guzik, D. Mangalat, and R. Korbut, Adipocytokines—Novel link between inflammation and vascular function? *Journal of Physiology and Pharmacology* 57 (2006): 505–528.
22. W. V. Brown and coauthors, Obesity: Why be concerned? *American Journal of Medicine* 122 (2009): S4–S11; J. Korner, S. C. Woods, and K. A. Woodworth, Regulation of energy homeostasis and health consequences in obesity, *American Journal of Medicine* 122 (2009): S12–S18; W. L. Holland and coauthors, Lipid mediators of insulin resistance, *Nutrition Reviews* 65 (2007): S39–S46; R. Weiss, Fat distribution and storage: How much, where, and how? *European Journal of Endocrinology* 157 (2007): S39–S45; P. Trayhurn, C. Bing, and I. S. Wood, Adipose tissue and adipokines—Energy regulation from the human perspective, *Journal of Nutrition* 136 (2006): 1935S–1939S.
23. Brown and coauthors, Obesity: Why be concerned?; V. Z. Rocha and P. Libby, The multiple facets of the fat tissue, *Thyroid* 18 (2008): 175–183; P. Calabro and E. T. Yeh, Intra-abdominal adiposity, inflammation, and cardiovascular risk: New insight into global cardiometabolic risk, *Current Hypertension Reports* 10 (2008): 32–38; D. C. W. Lau and coauthors, Adipokines: Molecular links between obesity and atherosclerosis, *American Journal of Physiology—Heart and Circulatory Physiology* 288 (2005): H2031–H2041.
24. J. P. Bastard and coauthors, Recent advances in the relationship between obesity, inflammation, and insulin resistance, *European Cytokine Network* 17 (2006): 4–12.
25. Korner, Woods, and Woodworth, 2009; Brown and coauthors, Obesity: Why be concerned?.
26. E. Fabbrini and coauthors, Intrahepatic fat, not visceral fat, is linked with metabolic complications of obesity, *Proceedings of the National Academy of Sciences* 106 (2009): 15430–15435; J. Ding and coauthors, The association of pericardial fat with incident coronary heart disease: The Multi-Ethnic Study of Atherosclerosis (MESA), *American Journal of Clinical Nutrition* 90 (2009): 499–504.
27. E. A. Molenaar and coauthors, Association of lifestyle factors with abdominal subcutaneous and visceral adiposity: The Framingham Heart Study, *Diabetes Care* 32 (2009): 505–510; S. G. Wannamethee, A. G. Shaper, and P. H. Whincup, Alcohol and adiposity: Effects of quantity and type of drink and time relation with meals, *International Journal of Obesity and Related Metabolic Disorders* 29 (2005): 1436–1444.
28. K. F. Adams and coauthors, Overweight, obesity, and mortality in a large prospective cohort of persons 50 to 71 years old, *New England Journal of Medicine* 355 (2006): 763–768; A. Romero-Corral and coauthors, Association of bodyweight with total mortality and with cardiovascular disease: A systematic review of cohort studies, *Lancet* 368 (2006): 666–678.
29. S. Klein and coauthors, Waist circumference and cardiometabolic risk: A consensus statement from Shaping America's Health: The Association for Weight Management and Obesity Prevention; NAASA, The Obesity Society; the American Society for Nutrition; and the American Diabetes Association, *American Journal of Clinical Nutrition* 85 (2007): 1197–1202.
30. N. Stefan and coauthors, Identification and characterization of metabolically benign obesity in humans, *Archives of Internal Medicine* 168 (2008): 1609–1616; R. P. Wildman and coauthors, The obese without cardiometabolic risk factor clustering and the normal weight with cardiometabolic risk factor clustering, *Archives of Internal Medicine* 168 (2008): 1617–1624; P. T. Williams, Maintaining vigorous activity attenuates 7-yr weight gain in 8340 runners, *Medicine & Science in Sports & Exercise* 39 (2007): 801–809.
31. M. S. Argugete, J. L. Edman, and A. Yates, Romantic interest in obese college students, *Eating Behaviors* 10 (2009): 143–145.
32. D. E. Berryman and coauthors, Dietetics students possess negative attitudes toward obesity similar to nondietetics students, *Journal of the American Dietetic Association* 106 (2006): 1678–1682.
33. Standing Committee on the Scientific Evaluation of Dietary Reference Intakes, Food and Nutrition Board, Institute of Medicine, *Dietary Reference Intakes for Energy, Carbohydrate, Fiber, Fat, Fatty Acids, Cholesterol, Protein, and Amino Acids* (Washington, D.C.: National Academies Press, 2002/2005), p. 107.
34. J. J. Otten, J. P. Hellwig, and L. D. Meyers, eds., Institute of Medicine, *Dietary Reference Intakes: The Essential Guide to Nutrient Requirements* (Washington, D.C.: National Academies Press, 2006), p. 87.
35. R. Huxley and coauthors, Ethnic comparisons of the cross-sectional relationships between measures of body size with diabetes and hypertension, *Obesity Review* 9 (2008): 53–61.
36. Huxley and coauthors, Ethnic comparisons of the cross-sectional relationships.
37. J. P. Després and coauthors, Abdominal obesity and the metabolic syndrome: Contribution to global cardiometabolic risk, *Arteriosclerosis, Thrombosis, and Vascular Biology* 28 (2008): 1039–1049; Klein and coauthors, Waist circumference and cardiometabolic risk.
38. Position of the American Dietetic Association: Weight management, *Journal of the American Dietetic Association* 109 (2009): 330–346.
39. A. Prentice and S. Jebb, Energy intake/physical activity interactions in the homeostasis of body weight regulation, *Nutrition Reviews* 62 (2004): S98–S104.
40. S. C. Woods, R. J. Seeley, and D. Cota, Regulation of food intake through hypothalamic signaling networks involving mTOR, *Annual Review of Nutrition* 28 (2008): 295–311; C. D. Morrison and H. Berthoud, Neurobiology of nutrition and obesity, *Nutrition Reviews* 65 (2007): 517–534; M. J. Wolfgang and M. D. Lane, Control of energy homeostasis: Role of enzymes and intermediates of fatty acid metab-

olism in the central nervous system, *Annual Review of Nutrition* 26 (2006): 23–44.
41. R. S. Ahima and D. A. Antwi, Brain regulation of appetite and satiety, *Endocrinology and Metabolism Clinics of North America* 37 (2008): 811–823.
42. A. S. Levine, C. M. Kotz, and B. A. Gosnell, Sugars and fats: The neurobiology of preference, *Journal of Nutrition* 133 (2003): 831S–834S.
43. B. McFerran and coauthors, I'll have what she's having: Effects of social influence and body type on the food choices of others, *Journal of Consumer Research,* electronic publication (2009): doi:10.1086/644611.
44. E. Valassi, M. Scacchi, and F. Cavagnini, Neuroendocrine control of food intake, *Nutrition, Metabolism, and Cardiovascular Disease* 18 (2008): 158–168; D. E. Cummings and J. Overduin, Gastrointestinal regulation of food intake, *Journal of Clinical Investigation* 117 (2007): 13–23; K. G. Murphy, W. S. Dhillo, and S. R. Bloom, Gut peptides in the regulation of food intake and energy homeostasis, *Endocrine Reviews* 27 (2006): 719–727.
45. N. Zijlstra and coauthors, Effect of bite size and oral processing time of a semisolid food on satiation, *American Journal of Clinical Nutrition* 90 (2009): 269–275.
46. Cummings and Overduin, Gastrointesinal regulation of food intake.
47. Woods, Seely, and Cota, Regulation of food intake through hypothalamic signaling networks.
48. Cummings and Overduin, Gastrointesinal regulation of food intake.
49. Woods, Seely, and Cota, Regulation of food intake through hypothalamic signaling networks; P. G. Cammisotto and M. Bendayan, Leptin secretion by white adipose tissue and gastric mucosa, *Histology and Histopathology* 22 (2007): 199–210.
50. J. M. Friedman, Leptin at 14 y of age: An ongoing story, *American Journal of Clinical Nutrition* 89 (2009): 973S–979S.
51. I. S. Farooqi and coauthors, Clinical and molecular genetic spectrum of congenital deficiency of the leptin receptor, *New England Journal of Medicine* 356 (2007): 237–247.
52. G. Paz-Filho and coauthors, Changes in insulin sensitivity during leptin replacement therapy in leptin deficient patients, *American Journal of Physiology, Endocrinology, and Metabolism* 296 (2009): E1401–1408.
53. P. J. Enriori and coauthors, Leptin resistance and obesity, *Obesity* 14 (2006): 254S–258S.
54. J. M. Beasley and coauthors, Associations between macronutrient intake and self-reported appetite and fasting levels of appetite hormones: Results from the Optimal Macronutrient Intake Trial to Prevent Heart Disease, *American Journal of Epidemiology* 169 (2009): 893–900; J. W. Apolzan and coauthors, Inadequate dietary protein increases hunger and desire to eat in young and older men, *Journal of Nutrition* 137 (2007): 1478–1482; H. J. Leidy, R. D. Mattes, and W. W. Campbell, Effects of acute and chronic protein intake on metabolism, appetite, and ghrelin during weight loss, *Obesity* 15 (2007): 1215–1225.
55. M. S. Westerterp-Plantenga and coauthors, Dietary protein, weight loss, and weight maintenance, in *Annual Review of Nutrition* 29 (2009): 21–41; Cummings and Overduin, Gastrointesinal regulation of food intake.
56. G. Radulian and coauthors, Metabolic effects of low glycaemic index diets, *Nutrition Journal* 8 (2009): doi:10.1186/1475-2891-8-5.
57. M. M. Perrigue, P. Monsivais, and A. Drewnowski, Added soluble fiber enhances the satiation power of low-energy-density liquid yogurts, *Journal of the American Dietetic Association* 109 (2009): 1862–1868; K. R. Juvonen and coauthors, Viscosity of oat bran-enriched beverages influences gastrointestinal hormonal responses in healthy humans, *Journal of Nutrition* 139 (2009): 461–466; P. Vitaglione and coauthors, β-Glucan-enriched bread reduces energy intake and modifies plasma ghrelin and peptide YY concentrations in the short term, *Appetite* 53 (2009): 338–344; N. Schroeder and coauthors, Influence of whole grain barley, whole grain wheat, and refined rice-based foods on short-term satiety and energy intake, *Appetite* 53 (2009): 363–369.
58. M. A. Van Baak and A. Astrup, Consumption of sugars and body weight, *Obesity Reviews* 10 (2009): 9–23.
59. W. D. van Marken and coauthors, Cold-activated brown adipose tissue in healthy men, *New England Journal of Medicine* 360 (2009): 1500–1508; A. M. Cypess and coauthors, Identification and importance of brown adipose tissue in adult humans, *New England Journal of Medicine* 360 (2009): 1509–1517; K. A. Virtanen and coauthors, Functional brown adipose tissue in healthy adults, *New England Journal of Medicine* 360 (2009): 1518–1525; M. Saito and coauthors, High incidence of metabolically active brown adipose tissue in healthy adult humans: Effects of cold exposure and adiposity, *Diabetes* 58 (2009): 1526–1531; P. Seale, S. Kajimura, and B. M. Spiegelman, Transcriptional control of brown adipocyte development and physiological function—of mice and men, *Genes and Development* 23 (2009): 788–797.
60. P. Seale and M. A. Lazar, Brown fat in humans: Turning up the heat on obesity, *Diabetes* 58 (2009): 1482–1484.
61. K. L. Hoehn and coauthors, Acute or chronic upregulation of mitochondrial fatty acid oxidation has no net effect on whole-body energy expenditure or adiposity, *Cell Metabolism* 11 (2010): 70–76.
62. Li Shengxu and coauthors, Cumulative effects and predictive value of common obesity-susceptibility variants identified by genome-wide association studies, *American Journal of Clinical Nutrition* 91 (2010): 184–190; D. Pomp, D. Hehrenberg, and D. Estrada-Smith, Complex genetics of obesity in mouse models, *Annual Review of Nutrition* 28 (2008): 331–345.
63. A. Newell and coauthors, Addressing the obesity epidemic: A genomics perspective, *Preventing Chronic Disease* [CDC serial online] April 2007, available at www.cdc.gov/pcd/issues/2007/apr/06_0068.htm.
64. P. Seale, S. Kajimura, and B. M. Spiegelman, Transcriptional control of brown adipocyte development and physiological function—of mice and men, *Genes and Development* 23 (2009): 788–797; Newell and coauthors, Addressing the obesity epidemic; A. Herbert and coauthors, A common genetic variant is associated with adult and childhood obesity, *Science* 312 (2006): 279–283.
65. I. Romao and J. Roth, Genetic and environmental interactions in obesity and type 2 diabetes, *Journal of the American Dietetic Association* 108 (2008): S24–S28; L. Qi and Y. A. Cho, Gene-environment interaction and obesity, *Nutrition Reviews* 66 (2008): 684–694.
66. W. P. James, The fundamental drivers of the obesity epidemic, *Obesity Reviews* (suppl) 9 (2008): 6–13.
67. B. Swinburn, G. Sacks, and E. Ravussin, Increased food energy supply is more than sufficient to explain the U.S. epidemic of obesity, *American Journal of Clinical Nutrition* 90 (2009): 1453–1456.
68. B. Wansink and C. R. Payne, Eating behavior and obesity at Chinese buffets, *Obesity* 16 (2008): 1957–1960; L. R. Vartanian, C. P. Herman, B. Wansink, Are we aware of the external factors that influence our food intake? *Health Psychology* 27 (2008): 533–538; B. Wansink, C. R. Payne, and P. Chandon, Internal and external cues of meal cessation: The French paradox redux? *Obesity* 15 (2007): 2920–2924.
69. G. Wang and coauthors, Gastric stimulation in obese subjects activates the hippocampus and other regions involved in brain reward circuitry, *Proceedings of the National Academy of Sciences* 103 (2006): 15641–15645.
70. J. P. Block and coauthors, Psychosocial stress and change in weight among U.S. adults, *American Journal of Epidemiology* 170 (2009): 181–192; T. C. Adam and E. S. Epel, Stress, eating and the reward system, *Physiology and Behavior* 91 (2007): 449–458; S. J. Torres and C. A. Nowson, Relationship between stress, eating behavior, and obesity, *Nutrition* 23 (2007): 887–894.
71. B. Wansink and J. Kim, Bad popcorn in big buckets: Portion size can influence intakes as much as taste, *Journal of Nutrition Education and Behavior,* 37 (2005): 242–245.
72. B. Wansink and K. Van Ittersum, Portion size me: Downsizing our consumption norms, *Journal of the American Dietetic Association* 107 (2007): 1103–1106.
73. T. M. Manini and coauthors, Reduced physical activity increases intermuscular adipose tissue in healthy young adults, *American Journal of Clinical Nutrition* 85 (2007): 377–384.
74. D. C. Franenfield and A. Coleman, Recovery to resting metabolic state after walking, *Journal of the American Dietetic Association*

109 (2009: 1914–1916; E. L. Melanson, P. S. MacLean, and J. O Hill, Exercise improves fat metabolism in muscle but does not increase 24-h fat oxidation, *Exercise and Sport Sciences Reviews* 37 (2009): 93–101; D. J. O'Gorman and A. Krook, Exercise and the treatment of diabetes and obesity, *Endocrinology and Metabolism Clinics of North America* 37 (2008): 887–903.

75. J. A. Teske, C. J. Billington, and C. M. Kotz, Neuropeptidergic mediators of spontaneous physical activity and non-exercise activity thermogenesis, *Neuroendocrinology* 87 (2008): 71–90.

76. S. J. Marshall and coauthors, Translating physical activity recommendations into a pedometer-based step goal: 3000 steps in 30 minutes, *American Journal of Preventive Medicine* 36 (2009): 410–415; U.S. Department of Agriculture and U.S. Department of Health and Human Services, *2008 Physical Activity Guidelines for Americans,* available at www.health.gov/paguidelines/default.aspx.

77. E. Kirk and coauthors, Minimal resistance training improves daily energy expenditure and fat oxidation, *Medicine and Science in Sports and Exercise* 41 (2009): 1122–1129; T. S. Church and coauthors, Effects of different doses of physical activity on cardiorespiratory fitness among sedentary, overweight or obese postmenopausal women with elevated blood pressure, *Journal of the American Medical Association* 297 (2007): 2081–2091.

78. T. S. Church and coauthors, Changes in weight, waist circumference and compensatory responses with different doses of exercise among sedentary, overweight postmenopausal women, *PLoS One* 4 (2009): e4515, doi:101371/journal.pone.0004515.

79. American College of Sports Medicine, Position Stand: Appropriate physical activity intervention strategies for weight loss and prevention of weight regain for adults, *Medicine and Science in Sports and Exercise* 41 (2009): 459–471.

80. C. M. Kotz, J. A. Teske, and C. J. Billington, Neuroregulation of nonexercise activity thermogenesis and obesity resistance, *American Journal of Physiology: Regulatory, Integrative and Comparative Physiology* 294 (2008): R699–R710.

81. J. A. Levine, Nonexercise activity thermogenesis—Liberating the life-force, *Journal of Internal Medicine* 262 (2007): 273–287.

82. D. A. Raynor and coauthors, Television viewing and long-term weight maintenance: Results from the national weight control registry, *Obesity* 14 (2006): 1816–1824.

83. P. T. Katzmarzyk and coauthors, Sitting time and mortality from all causes, cardiovascular disease, and cancer, *Medicine and Science in Sports and Exercise* 41 (2009): 998–1005.

84. D. Berrigan and coauthors, Active transportation increases adherence to activity recommendations, *American Journal of Preventive Medicine* 31 (2006): 210–216.

85. S. K. Kumanyika and coauthors, Population-based prevention of obesity. The need for comprehensive promotion of healthful eating, physical activity, and energy balance. A scientific statement from the American Heart Association Council on Epidemiology and Prevention, Interdisciplinary Committee for Prevention, *Circulation* 118 (2008): 428–464.

86. J. Beaulac, E. Kristjansson, and S. Cummins, A systematic review of food deserts, 1966–2007, *Preventing Chronic Disease: Public Health Research, Practice, and Policy,* 6 (2009): epub available at www.cdc.gov; S. N. Zenk and coauthors, Fruit and vegetable intake in African Americans: Income and store characteristics, *American Journal of Preventive Medicine* 29 (2006): 1–9.

87. M. I. Larson, M. T. Story, and M. C. Nelson, Neighborhood environments: Disparities in access to healthy foods in the U.S., *American Journal of Preventive Medicine* 36 (2009): 74–81; L. M. Powell and coauthors, Food store availability and neighborhood characteristics in the United States, *Preventive Medicine* 44 (2007): 1189–1195.

88. L. M. Powell, F. J. Chaloupka, and Y. Bao, The availability of fast-food and full-service restaurants in the United States: Associations with neighborhood characteristics, *American Journal of Preventive Medicine* 33 (2007): S240–S245; D. Block and J. Kouba, A comparison of the availability and affordability of a market basket in two communities in the Chicago area, *Public Health Nutrition* 9 (2006): 837–845.

89. K. J. Duffey and coauthors, Differential associations of fast food and restaurant food consumption with 3-y change in body mass index: The Coronary Artery Risk Development in Young Adults Study, *American Journal of Clinical Nutrition* 85 (2007): 201–208.

90. M. M. Maldonado-Molina, K. A. Komro, and G. Prado, Prospective association between dieting and smoking initiation among adolescents, *American Journal of Health Promotion* 22 (2007): 25–32.

91. B. A. Spear, Does dieting increase the risk for obesity and eating disorders? *Journal of the American Dietetic Association* 106 (2006): 523–525; D. Neumark-Sztainer and coauthors, Obesity, disordered eating and eating disorder in a longitudinal study of adolescents: How do dieters fare 5 years later? *Journal of the American Dietetic Association* 106 (2006): 559–568.

92. T. B. Chaston, J. B. Dixon, and P. E. O'Brien, Changes in fat-free mass during significant weight loss: A systematic review, *International Journal of Obesity* 31 (2007): 743–750.

93. M. Schütze and coauthors, Beer consumption and the "beer belly": Scientific basis or common belief? *European Journal of Clinical Nutrition* 63 (2009): 1143–1149.

94. E. W. Wamsteker and coauthors, Unrealistic weight-loss goals among obese patients are associated with age and causal attributions, *Journal of the American Dietetic Association* 109 (2009): 1903–1908.

95. C. A. Nonas and G. D. Foster, Setting achievable goals for weight loss, *Journal of the American Dietetic Association* 105 (2005): S118–S123.

96. M. Bes-Rastrollo and coauthors, Prospective study of nut consumption, long-term weight change, and obesity risk in women, *American Journal of Clinical Nutrition* 89 (2009): 1913–1919.

97. Y. Wang and M. A. Beydoun, Meat consumption is associated with obesity and central obesity among U.S. adults, *International Journal of Obesity* 33 (2009): 621–628.

98. B. J. Rolls, L. S. Roe, and J. S. Meengs, Larger portion sizes lead to a sustained increase in energy intake over 2 days, *Journal of the American Dietetic Association* 106 (2006): 543–549.

99. B. Wansink, K. van Ittersum, and J. E. Painter, Ice cream illusions: Bowls, spoons, and self-served portion sizes, *American Journal of Preventive Medicine* 31 (2006): 240–243.

100. L. Johnson and coauthors, Energy-dense, low-fiber, high-fat dietary pattern is associated with increased fatness in childhood, *American Journal of Clinical Nutrition* 87 (2008): 846–854; N. C. Howarth and coauthors, Dietary energy density is associated with overweight status among 5 ethnic groups in the Multiethnic Cohort Study, *Journal of Nutrition* 136 (2006): 2243–2248.

101. J. H. Ledikwe and coauthors, Reductions in dietary energy density are associated with weight loss in overweight and obese participants in the PREMIER trial, *American Journal of Clinical Nutrition* 85 (2007): 1212–1221.

102. Ledikwe and coauthors, Reductions in dietary energy density.

103. R. Dhingra and coauthors, Soft drink consumption and risk of developing cardiometabolic risk factors and the metabolic syndrome in middle-aged adults in the community, *Circulation* 116 (2007): 480–488; Vartanian, Schwartz, and Brownell, Effects of soft drink consumption on nutrition and health.

104. R. D. Mattes and B. M. Popkin, Nonnutritive sweetener consumption in humans: Effects on appetite and food intake and their putative mechanisms, *American Journal of Clinical Nutrition* 89 (2009): 1–14.

105. S. Phelan and coauthors, Use of artificial sweeteners and fat-modified foods in weight loss maintainers and always-normal weight individuals, *International Journal of Obesity* 33 (2009): 1183–1190; S. P. Fowler and coauthors, Fueling the obesity epidemic? Artificially sweetened beverage use and long-term weight gain, *Obesity* 16 (2008): 1894–1900.

106. K. H. Poddar and coauthors, Low-fat dairy intake and body weight and composition changes in college students, *Journal of the American Dietetic Association* 109 (2009): 1433–1438; Vartanian, Schwartz, and Brownell, Effects of soft drink consumption on nutrition and health.

107. M. A. Palmer, S. Capra, and S. K. Baines, Association between eating frequency, weight, and health, *Nutrition Reviews* 67 (2009): 379–390.

108. H. M. Niemeier and coauthors, Fast food consumption and breakfast skipping: Predictors of weight gain from adolescence to adulthood in a nationally representative sample, *Journal of Adolescent Health* 39 (2006): 842–849.
109. K. Stein, It's 2:00 am, do you know where the snackers are? *Journal of the American Dietetic Association* 107 (2007): 20.
110. Position of the American Dietetic Association: Weight Management.
111. American College of Sports Medicine, Position Stand: Appropriate physical activity intervention strategies.
112. P. S. MacLean and coauthors, Regular exercise attenuates the metabolic drive to regain weight after long-term weight loss, *American Journal of Physiology: Regulatory, Integrative, and Comparative Physiology* 297 (2009): R793–R802.
113. N. A. King and coauthors, Dual process action of exercise on appetite control: Increase in orexigenic drive but improvement in meal-induced satiety, *American Journal of Clinical Nutrition* 90 (2009): 921–927.
114. C. Martins, L. Morgan, and H. Truby, A review of the effects of exercise on appetite regulation: An obesity perspective, *International Journal of Obesity* 32 (2008): 1337–1347; D. R. Broom and coauthors, Exercise-induced suppression of acylated ghrelin in humans, *Journal of Applied Physiology* 102 (2007): 2165–2171; R. R. Kraemer and V. D. Castracrane, Exercise and humoral mediators of peripheral energy balance: Ghrelin and adiponectin, *Experimental Biology and Medicine (Maywood):* 232 (2007): 184–194.
115. U.S. Department of Agriculture and U.S. Department of Health and Human Services, *2008 Physical Activity Guidelines for Americans.*
116. Church and coauthors, Changes in weight, waist circumference and compensatory responses.
117. J. LaForgia, R. T. Withers, and C. J. Gore, Effects of exercise intensity and duration on the excess post-exercise oxygen consumption, *Journal of Sports Sciences,* 24 (2006): 1247–1264.
118. C. S. Riedt and coauthors, Premenopausal overweight women do not lose bone during moderate weight loss with adequate or higher calcium intake, *American Journal of Clinical Nutrition* 85 (2007): 972–980; D. T. Villareal and coauthors, Bone mineral density response to caloric restriction-induced weight loss or exercise-induced weight loss, *Archives of Internal Medicine* 166 (2006): 2502–2510.
119. G. M. Manzoni and coauthors, Can relaxation training reduce emotional eating in women with obesity? An exploratory study with 3 months of follow-up, *Journal of the American Dietetic Association* 109 (2009): 1427–1432.
120. N. A. King and coauthors, Individual variability following 12 weeks of supervised exercise: Identification and characterization of compensation for exercise-induced weight loss, *International Journal of Obesity (London)* (2008): 177–184.
121. U.S. Department of Agriculture and U.S. Department of Health and Human Services, *2008 Physical Activity Guidelines for Americans.*
122. L. Lanningham-Foster and coauthors, Activity-promoting games and increased energy expenditure, *Journal of Pediatrics* 154 (2009): 819–823; L. Graves and coauthors, Energy expenditure in adolescents playing new generation computer games, *British Journal of Sports Medicine* 42 (2008): 592–594.
123. L. E. Graves, N. D. Ridges, and G. Stratton, The contribution of upper limb and total body movement to adolescents' energy expenditure whilst playing Nintendo Wii, *European Journal of Applied Physiology* 104 (2008): 617–623.
124. M. K. Robinson, Surgical treatment of obesity—weighing the facts, *New England Journal of Medicine* 361 (2009): 520–521; E. E. Mason and coauthors, Causes of 30-day bariatric surgery mortality: With emphasis on bypass obstruction, *Obesity Surgery* 17 (2007): 9–14; L. B. Goldfelder, C. J. Ren, and J. R. Gill, Fatal complications of bariatric surgery, *Obesity Surgery* 16 (2006): 1050–1056.
125. G. A. Bray, Medications for weight reduction, *Endocrinology and Metabolism Clinics of North America* 37 (2008): 923–942.
126. U.S. Food and Drug Administration, Questions and answers about FDA's initiative against contaminated weight loss products, April 30, 2009, available at http://www.fda.gov/Drugs/ResourcesForYou/Consumers/QuestionsAnswers/ucm136187.htm.
127. B. R. Smith, P. Schauer, and N. T. Nguyen, Surgical approaches to the treatment of obesity: Bariatric surgery, *Endocrinology and Metabolism Clinics of North America* 37 (2008): 943–964; J. A. Vogel and coauthors, Reduction in predicted coronary heart disease risk after substantial weight reduction after bariatric surgery, *American Journal of Cardiology* 99 (2007): 222–226.
128. M. Ruz and coauthors, Iron absorption and iron status are reduced after Roux-en-Y gastric bypass, *American Journal of Clinical Nutrition* 90 (2009): 527–532; S. Singh and A. Kumar, Wernicke encephalopathy after obesity surgery: A systematic review, *Neurology* 68 (2007): 807–811; S. S. Malinowski, Nutritional and metabolic complications of bariatric surgery, *American Journal of the Medical Sciences* 331 (2006): 219–225; E. Parkes, Nutritional management of patients after bariatric surgery, *American Journal of the Medical Sciences* 331 (2006): 207–213; R. W. Worden and H. M. Allen, Wernicke's encephalopathy after gastric bypass that masqueraded as acute psychosis: A case report, *Current Surgery* 63 (2006): 114–116.
129. C. Gasteyger and coauthors, Nutritional deficiencies after Roux-en-Y gastric bypass for morbid obesity often cannot be prevented by standard multivitamin supplementation, 87 (2008): 1128–1133.
130. C. S. Reidt and coauthors, True fractional calcium absorption is decreased after Roux-en-Y gastric bypass surgery, *Obesity* 14 (2006): 1940–1948.
131. P. E. O'Brien and coauthors, Laparoscopic adjustable gastric banding in severely obese adolescents, *Journal of the American Medical Association* 303 (2010): 519–526; E. N. Hansen, A. Torquati, and N. N. Abumrad, Results of bariatric surgery, *Annual Review of Nutrition* 26 (2006): 481–511.
132. Food and Drug Administration letter to Andrew Edge of Life-All.com, September 18, 2006, available at www.FDA.gov.
133. D. S. Bond, Weight-loss maintenance in successful weight losers: Surgical vs non-surgical methods, *International Journal of Obesity (London)* 33 (2009): 173–180.
134. Niemeier and coauthors, Fast food consumption and breakfast skipping.
135. R. R. Wing and coauthors, A self-regulation program for maintenance of weight loss, *New England Journal of Medicine* 355 (2006): 1563–1571.
136. The National Weight Control Registry, NWCR Facts, available at http://www.nwcr.ws/Research/default.htm.
137. J. N. Davis and coauthors, Normal-weight adults consume more fiber and fruit than their age- and height-matched overweight/obese counterparts, *Journal of the American Dietetic Association* 106 (2006): 833–840.
138. B. Van Dorsten and E. M. Lindley, Cognitive and behavioral approaches in the treatment of obesity, *Endocrinology and Metabolism Clinics of North America* 37 (2008): 905–922.
139. D. J. Hyman and coauthors, Simultaneous vs. sequential counseling for multiple behavior change, *Archives of Internal Medicine* 167 (2007): 1152–1158.
140. A. N. Fabricatore, Behavior therapy and cognitive-behavioral therapy for obesity: Is there a difference? *Journal of the American Dietetic Association* 107 (2007): 92–99.

CONSUMER CORNER 9

1. W. S. Yancy and coauthors, A randomized trial of a low-carbohydrate diet vs orlistat plus a low-fat diet for weight loss, *Archives of Internal Medicine* 170 (2010): 136–145; F. M. Sacks and coauthors, Comparison of weight-loss diets with different compositions of fat, protein, and carbohydrates, *New England Journal of Medicine* 360 (2009): 859–873.
2. Y. Ma and coauthors, A dietary quality comparison of popular weight-loss plans, *Journal of the American Dietetic Association* 107 (2007): 1786–1791.
3. Sacks and coauthors, Comparison of weight-loss diets.
4. T. Y. Chen and coauthors, A life-threatening complication of Atkins diet, *Lancet* 367 (2006): 958.
5. T. L. Hernandez and coauthors, Lack of suppression of circulating free fatty acids and hypercholesterolemia during weight loss on a high-fat, low-carbohydrate diet, *American Journal of Clinical Nutrition* 91 (2010): 578–585; S. Y. Foo and coauthors, Vascular effects of a low-carbohydrate high-protein diet, *Proceedings*

of the National Academies of Science 106 (2009): 15418–15423; M. Miller and coauthors, Comparative effects of three popular diets on lipids, endothelial function, and C-reactive protein during weight management, *Journal of the American Dietetic Association* 109 (2009): 713–717.
6. T. D. Barnett, N. D. Barnard, and T. L. Radak, Development of symptomatic cardiovascular disease after self-reported adherence to the Atkins diet, *Journal of the American Dietrertic Association* 109 (2009): 1263–1265.
7. G. Dubnov-Raz and E. M. Berry, The dietary treatment of obesity, *Endocrinology and Metabolism Clinics of North America* 37 (2008): 873–886.
8. I. Shai and M. J. Stampfer, Weight-loss diets—can you keep it off? *American Journal of Clinical Nutrition* 88 (2008): 1185–1186.
9. Shai and Stampfer, Weight-loss diets; B. Strasser, A. Spreitzer, and P. Haber, Fat loss depends on energy deficit only, independently of the method for weight loss, *Annals of Nutrition and Metabolism* 51 (2007): 428–432.

CONTROVERSY 9

1. J. I. Hudson and coauthors, The prevalence and correlates of eating disorders in the National Comorbidity Survey replication, *Biological Psychiatry* 61 (2007): 348–358.
2. Position of the American Dietetic Association: Nutrition intervention in the treatment of anorexia nervosa, bulimia nervosa, and other eating disorders, *Journal of the American Dietetic Association* 106 (2006): 2073–2082.
3. Centers for Disease Control and Prevention, Youth Risk Behavior Surveillance—United States, 2003, *Morbidity and Mortality Weekly Reports* 53 (2004): 1–96; A. E. Field and coauthors, Relation between dieting and weight change among preadolescents and adolescents, *Pediatrics* 112 (2003): 900–906.
4. N. I. Larson, D. Neumark-Sztainer, and M. Story, Weight control behaviors and dietary intake among adolescents and young adults: Longitudinal finding from project EAT, *Journal of the American Dietetic Association* 109 (2009): 1869–1877; K. C. Berg, P. Frazier, and L. Sherr, Change in eating disorder attitudes and behavior in college women: Prevalence and predictors, *Eating Behaviors* 10 (2009): 137–142.
5. H. Raynor, What is the evidence of a causal relationship between dieting, obesity, and eating disorders in youth? (letter) *Journal of the American Dietetic Association* 106 (2006): 1359.
6. S. E. Mazzeo and C. M. Bulik, Environmental and genetic risk factors for eating disorders: What the clinician needs to know, *Child and Adolescent Psychiatric Clinics of North America* 18 (2009): 67–82; S. S. O'Sullivan, A. H. Evans, and A. J. Lees, Dopamine dysregulation syndrome: An overview of its epidemiology, mechanisms, and management, *CNS Drugs* 23 (2009): 157–170; T. D. Müller and coauthors, Leptin-mediated neuroendocrine alterations in anorexia nervosa: Somatic and behavioral implications, *Child and Adolescent Psychiatric Clinics of North America* 18 (2009): 117–129.
7. P. Van den Berg and coauthors, Is dieting advice from magazines helpful or harmful? Five-year associations with weight-control behaviors and psychological outcomes in adolescents, *Pediatrics* 119 (2007): e30–e37.
8. B. A. Spear, Does dieting increase the risk for obesity and eating disorders? *Journal of the American Dietetic Association* 106 (2006): 523–525.
9. M. Vertalino and coauthors, Participation in weight-related sports is associated with higher use of unhealthful weight-control behaviors and steroid use, *Journal of the American Dietetic Association* 107 (2007): 434–440.
10. M. F. Reinking and L. E. Alexander, Prevalence of disordered-eating behaviors in undergraduate female collegiate athletes and nonathletes, *Journal of Athletic Training* 40 (2005): 47–51; M. K. Torstveit and J. Sundgot-Borgen, The female athlete triad: Are elite athletes at increased risk? *Medicine and Science in Sports and Exercise* 37 (2005): 184–193.
11. J. L. Glazer, Eating disorders among male athletes, *Current Sports Medicine Reports* 7 (2008): 332–337.
12. American College of Sports Medicine, Position stand: The female athlete triad, *Medicine and Science in Sports and Exercise* 39 (2007): 1867–1882; C. M. Lebrun, The female athlete triad: What's a doctor to do? *Current Sports Medicine Reports* 6 (2007): 397–404.
13. C. J. Rosen and A. Klibanski, Bone, fat, and body composition: Evolving concepts in the pathogenesis of osteoporosis, *American Journal of Medicine* (2009): 409–414.
14. D. T. Villareal and coauthors, Bone mineral density response to caloric restriction-induced weight loss or exercise-induced weight loss, *Archives of Internal Medicine* 166 (2006): 2502–2510.
15. M. T. Barrack and coauthors, Dietary restraint and low bone mass in female adolescent endurance runners, *American Journal of Clinical Nutrition* 87 (2008): 36–43.
16. J. L. Kelsey and coauthors, Risk factors for stress fracture among young female cross-country runners, *Medicine and Science in Sports and Exercise* 39 (2007): 1457–1463.
17. M. Vertalino and coauthors, Participation in weight-related sports is associated with higher use of unhealthful weight-control behaviors and steroid use, *Journal of the American Dietetic Association* 107 (2007): 434–440.
18. F. G. Grieve, A conceptual model of factors contributing to the development of muscle dysmorphia, *Eating Disorders* 15 (2007): 63–80.
19. Grieve, A conceptual model of factors.
20. M. L. Norris and coauthors, Ana and the Internet: A review of pro-anorexia websites, *International Journal of Eating Disorders* 39 (2006): 443–447.
21. C. B. Taylor and coauthors, The adverse effect of negative comments about weight and shape from family and siblings on women at high risk of eating disorders, *Pediatrics* 118 (2006): 731–738.
22. J. Treasure and coauthors, The assessment of the family of people with eating disorders, *European Eating Disorders Review* 16 (2008): 247–255.
23. J. W. Coughlin and A. S. Guarda, Behavioral disorders affecting food intake: Eating disorders and other psychiatric conditions, in M. E. Shils et al., eds., *Modern Nutrition in Health and Disease* (Baltimore: Lippincott Williams and Wilkins, 2006), pp. 1353–1361.
24. Position of the American Dietetic Association, Nutrition intervention in the treatment of anorexia nervosa, bulimia nervosa, and other eating disorders; J. M. Torpy, Anorexia nervosa, JAMA patient page, *Journal of the American Medical Association* 295 (2006): 2684.
25. Torpy, Anorexia nervosa.
26. Torpy, Anorexia nervosa.
27. J. M. Holm-Denoma and coauthors, Deaths by suicide among individuals with anorexia as arbiters between competing explanations of the anorexia-suicide link, *Journal of Affective Disorders* 107 (2008): 231–236; G. Murialdo and coauthors, Alterations in the autonomic control of heart rate variability in patients with anorexia or bulimia nervosa: Correlations between sympathovagal activity, clinical features, and leptin levels, *Journal of Endocrinological Investigation* 30 (2007): 356–362; D. Casiero and W. H. Frishman, Cardiovascular complications of eating disorders, *Cardiology in Review* 14 (2006): 227–231; M. Pompili and coauthors, Suicide and attempted suicide in eating disorders, obesity and weight-image concern, *Eating Behaviors* 7 (2006): 384–394.
28. Position of the American Dietetic Association, Nutrition intervention in the treatment of anorexia nervosa, bulimia nervosa, and other eating disorders.
29. E. Attia and B. T. Walsh, Behavioral management for anorexia nervosa, *New England Journal of Medicine* 360 (2009): 500–506.
30. Position of the American Dietetic Association, Nutrition intervention in the treatment of anorexia nervosa, bulimia nervosa, and other eating disorders.
31. C. Theils, Forced treatment of patients with anorexia, *Current Opinion in Psychiatry* 21 (2008): 495–498.
32. B. T. Walsh and coauthors, Fluoxetine after weight restoration in anorexia nervosa: A randomized controlled trial, *Journal of the American Medical Association* 295 (2006): 2605–2612.
33. J. Yager and A. E. Andersen, Anorexia nervosa, *New England Journal of Medicine* 353 (2005): 1481–1488.
34. J. E. Schebendach and coauthors, Dietary energy density and diet variety as predictors of outcome in anorexia nervosa, *American Journal of Clinical Nutrition* 87 (2008): 810–816.
35. N. Germain and coauthors, Constitutional thinness and lean anorexia nervosa display opposite concentrations of peptide YY, glucagon-like peptide 1, ghrelin, and leptin, *American Journal of Clinical Nutrition* 85 (2007): 967–971.

36. Position of the American Dietetic Association, Nutrition intervention in the treatment of anorexia nervosa, bulimia nervosa, and other eating disorders.
37. R. Rodgers and H. Chabrol, Parental attitudes, body image disturbance, and disordered eating amongst adolescents and young adults: A review, *European Eating Disorders Reviews* 17 (2009): 137–151.
38. Rodgers and Chabrol, Parental attitudes, body image disturbance, and disordered eating.
39. Rodgers and Chabrol, Parental attitudes, body image disturbance, and disordered eating.
40. D. Neumark-Sztainer and coauthors, Family meals and disordered eating in adolescents: Longitudinal findings from Project EAT, *Archives of Pediatric and Adolescent Medicine* 162 (2008): 17–22.
41. G. Waller, E. Corstorphine, and V. Mountford, The role of emotional abuse in the eating disorders: Implications for treatment, *Eating Disorders* 15 (2007): 317–331.
42. Position of the American Dietetic Association, Nutrition intervention in the treatment of anorexia nervosa, bulimia nervosa, and other eating disorders.
43. R. Sysko and B. T. Walsh, A critical evaluation of efficacy of self-help interventions for the treatment of bulimia nervosa and binge-eating disorder, *International Journal of Eating Disorders* 41 (2008): 97–112; J. D. Latner, Self-help for obesity and binge eating, *Nutrition Today* 42 (2007): 81–85.
44. M. Jones and coauthors, Randomized, controlled trial of an Internet-facilitated intervention for reducing binge eating and overweight in adolescents, *Pediatrics* 121 (2008): 453–462.
45. D. Neumark-Sztainer, Preventing obesity and eating disorders in adolescents: What can health care providers do? *Journal of Adolescent Health* 44 (2009): 206–213; G. T. Wilson, C. M. Grilo, and K. M. Vitousek, Psychological treatment of eating disorders, *American Psychologist* 62 (2007): 199–216.
46. Neumark-Sztainer, Preventing obesity and eating disorders in adolescents.
47. Z. Yager and J. A. O'Dea, Prevention programs for body image and eating disorders on university campuses: A review of large, controlled interventions, *Health Promotion International* 23 (2008): 173–189.

Chapter 10

1. Centers for Disease Control and Prevention, www.cdc.gov/physicalactivity/everyone, site updated October 7, 2008; X. Yang and coauthors, The longitudinal effects of physical activity history on metabolic syndrome, *Medicine and Science in Sports and Exercise* 40 (2008): 1424–1431; D. E. Warburton, C. W. Nicol, and S. S. Bredin, Health benefits of physical activity: The evidence, *Canadian Medical Association Journal* 174 (2006): 801–809; T. S. Altena and coauthors, Lipoprotein subfraction changes after continuous or intermittent exercise training, *Medicine and Science in Sports and Exercise* 38 (2006): 367–372.
2. P. T. Katzmarzyk and coauthors, Sitting time and mortality from all causes, cardiovascular disease, and cancer, *Medicine and Science in Sports and Exercise* 41 (2009): 998–1005.
3. G. Stathopoulou, and coauthors, Exercise interventions for mental health: A quantitative and qualitative review, *Clinical Psychology: Science and Practice* 13 (2006): 179–193. M. H. De Moor, and coauthors, Regular exercise, anxiety, depression, and personality: A population-based study, *Preventative Medicine* 42 (2006): 273–279.
4. L. B. Yates and coauthors, Exceptional longevity in men, *Archives of Internal Medicine* 168 (2008): 284–290; X. Sui and coauthors, Cardiorespiratory fitness and adiposity as mortality predictors in older adults, *Journal of the American Medical Association* 298 (2007): 2507–2516; T. M. Manini and coauthors, Daily activity energy expenditure and mortality among older adults, *Journal of the American Medical Association* 296 (2006): 171–179; I. Janssen and C. J. Joliffe, Influence of physical activity on mortality in elderly with coronary artery disease, *Medicine and Science in Sports and Exercise,* 38 (2006): 418–423.
5. A. R. Weinstein and coauthors, The joint effects of physical activity and body mass index on coronary heart disease risk in women, *Archives of Internal Medicine* 168 (2008): 884–890; N. Orsini and coauthors, Combined effects of obesity and physical activity in predicting mortality among men, *Journal of Internal Medicine* 264 (2008):442–451; P. Anand, and coauthors, Cancer is a preventable disease that requires major lifestyle changes, *Pharmaceutical Research* 25 (2008): 2097–2116; X. Yang, The longitudinal effects of physical activity history on metabolic syndrome, *Medicine and Science in Sports and Exercise* 40 (2008): 1424–1431; R. D. Telford, Low physical activity and obesity: Causes of chronic disease or simply predictors? *Medicine and Science in Sports and Exercise* 39 (2007): 1233–1240.
6. J. Chubak and coauthors Moderate-intensity exercise reduced the incidence of colds among postmenopausal women, *American Journal of Medicine* 119 (2006): 937–942.
7. Centers for Disease Control and Prevention, Surveillance of certain health behaviors and conditions among states and selected local areas—Behavioral Risk Factor Surveillance System (BRFSS), United States, 2006, *Morbidity and Mortality Weekly Report* 57 (2008): 1–188; Centers for Disease Control and Prevention, Prevalence of regular physical activity among adults—United States, 2001 and 2005, *Morbidity and Mortality Weekly Report* 56 (2007): 1209–1212.
8. S. M. Phillips, Resistance exercise: Good for more than just grandma and grandpa's muscles, *Applied Physiology, Nutrition, and Metabolism* 32 (2007): 1198–1205.
9. T. S. Church and coauthors, Changes in weight, waist circumference and compensatory responses with different doses of exercise among sedentary, overweight postmenopausal women, *PLoSOne* 4 (2009): e4515, doi:101371/journal.pone.0004515.
10. J.C. Colado and coauthors, Effects of a short-term aquatic resistance program on strength and body composition in fit young men, *Journal of Strength and Conditioning* 23 (2009): 549–559.
11. R. S. Rector and coauthors, Lean body mass and weight-bearing activity in the prediction of bone mineral density in physically active men, *Journal of Strength and Conditioning Research* 23 (2009): 427–435. A. Guadalupe-Grau and coauthors, Exercise and bone mass in adults, *Sports Medicine* 39 (2009): 439–468
12. J. Peel, and coauthors, A prospective study of cardiorespiratory fitness and breast cancer mortality, *Medicine and Science in Sports and Exercise* 41 (2009): 742–748; M. L. Slattery and coauthors, Physical activity and breast cancer risk among women in the southwestern United States, *Annals of Epidemiology* 17 (2007): 342–353; B. A Calton and coauthors, Physical activity and the risk of colon cancer among women: A prospective cohort study (United States), *International Journal of Cancer* 119 (2006): 385–391.
13. P. T. Williams, Reduced diabetic, hypertensive, and cholesterol medication use with walking, *Medicine and Science in Sports and Exercise* 40 (2008): 433–443; S. Kodama and coauthors, Effect of aerobic exercise training on serum levels of high-density lipoprotein cholesterol, *Archives of Internal Medicine* 167 (2007): 999–1008; D. I. Musa and coauthors, The effect of a high-intensity interval training program on high-density lipoprotein cholesterol in young men, *Journal of Strength and Conditioning Research* 23 (2009): 587–592; R. W. Braith and K. J. Stewart, Resistance exercise training: Its role in the prevention of cardiovascular disease, *Journal of the American Heart Association* 113 (2006): 2642–2650.
14. Church and coauthors, Changes in weight, waist circumference and compensatory responses; B. A. Irving and coauthors, Effect of exercise training intensity on abdominal visceral fat and body composition, *Medicine and Science in Sports and Exercise* 40 (2008): 1863–1872; M. Fogelholm, How can physical activity work? *International Journal of Pediatric Obesity* 3 (2008): 10–14; K. Wijndaele and coauthors, Muscular strength, aerobic fitness, and metabolic syndrome risk in Flemish adults, *Medicine and Science in Sports and Exercise* 39 (2007): 233–240.
15. Phillips, Resistance exercise; Y. J. Cheng and coauthors, Muscle-strengthening activity and its association with insulin sensitivity, *Diabetes Care* 30 (2007): 2264–2270; A. L. Macdonald and coauthors, Monitoring exercise-induced changes in glycemic control in type 2 diabetes, *Medicine and Science in Sports and Exercise* 38 (2006): 201–207.
16. A. M. Kriska and coauthors, Physical activity and gallbladder disease determined by ultrasonography, *Medicine and Science in Sports and Exercise* 39 (2007): 1927–1932; K. L. Storti and coauthors, Physical activity and decreased

risk of clinical gallstone disease among postmenopausal women, *Preventive Medicine* 41 (2005): 772–777.
17. U.S. Department of Health and Human Services, *2008 Physical Activity Guidelines for Americans,* available at www.health.gov/paguidelines/default.aspx; D. B. Nelson and coauthors, Effect of physical activity on menopausal symptoms among urban women, *Medicine and Science in Sports and Exercise* 40 (2008): 50–58; J. A. Blumenthal and coauthors, Exercise and pharmacotherapy in the treatment of major depressive disorder, *Psychosomatic Medicine* 69 (2007): 587–596; D. I. Galper and coauthors, Inverse association between physical inactivity and mental health in men and women, *Medicine and Science in Sports and Exercise* 38 (2006): 173–178.
18. L. B. Yates and coauthors, Exceptional longevity in men, *Archives of Internal Medicine* 168 (2008): 284–290; P. Kokkinos and coauthors, Exercise capacity and mortality in black and white men, *Circulation* 117 (2008): 614–622; X. Sui and coauthors, Cardiorespiratory fitness and adiposity as mortality predictors in older adults, *Journal of the American Medical Association* 298 (2007): 2507–2516; T. M. Manini and coauthors, Daily activity energy expenditure and mortality among older adults, *Journal of the American Medical Association* 296 (2006): 171–179.
19. M. E. Nelson and coauthors, Physical activity and public health in older adults: Recommendation from the American College of Sports Medicine and the American Heart Association, *Medicine and Science in Sports and Exercise* 39 (2007): 1435–1445; N. Takeshima and coauthors, Functional fitness gain varies in older adults depending on exercise mode, *Medicine and Science in Sports and Exercise* 39 (2007): 2036–2043; P. Aagaard and coauthors, Mechanical muscle function, morphology, and fiber type in lifelong trained elderly, *Medicine and Science in Sports and Exercise* 39 (2007): 1989–1996.
20. Phillips, Resistance exercise.
21. U.S. Department of Health and Human Services, *2008 Physical Activity Guidelines for Americans.*
22. U. S. Department of Health and Human Services, *2008 Physical Activity Guidelines for Americans*; Standing Committee on the Scientific Evaluation of Dietary Reference Intakes, Food and Nutrition Board, Institute of Medicine, *Dietary Reference Intakes for Energy, Carbohydrate, Fiber, Fat, Fatty Acids, Cholesterol, Protein, and Amino Acids* (Washington, D.C.: National Academies Press, 2005), pp. 880–935.
23. W. L. Haskell and coauthors, Physical activity and public health: Updated recommendation for adults from the American College of Sports Medicine and the American Heart Association, *Medicine and Science in Sports and Exercise* 39 (2007): 1423–1434.
24. D. E. Warburton, C. W. Nicol, and S. S. Bredin, Health benefits of physical activity: The evidence, *Canadian Medical Association Journal* 174 (2006): 801–809.
25. American College of Sports Medicine, Position Stand: Progression models in resistance training for healthy adults, *Medicine and Science in Sports and Exercise* 41 (2009): 687–708; W. L. Haskell and coauthors, Physical activity and public health; Nelson and coauthors, Physical activity and public health in older adults; R. C. Cassilhas and coauthors, The impact of resistance exercise on the cognitive function of the elderly, *Medicine and Science in Sports and Exercise* 39 (2007): 1401–1407.
26. American College of Sports Medicine, Position Stand: Progression models in resistance training for healthy adults.
27. W. J. Kraemer and coauthors, Physiological changes with periodized resistance training in women tennis players, *Medicine and Science in Sports and Exercise* 35 (2003): 157–168.
28. F. Vega, and R. Jackson, Dietary habits of bodybuilders and other regular exercisers, *Nutrition Research* 16 (1996): 3–10.
29. R. W. Braith and K. J. Stewart, Resistance exercise training: Its role in the prevention of cardiovascular disease, *Journal of the American Heart Association,* 113 (2006): 2642–2650; Haskell and coauthors, Physical activity and public health; H. Knuttgen, Strength training and aerobic exercise: Compare and contrast, *Journal of Strength and Conditioning Research* 21 (2007): 973–978.
30. E. Kirk and coauthors, Minimal resistance training improves daily energy expenditure and fat oxidation, *Medicine and Science in Sports and Exercise* 41 (2009): 1122–1129.
31. J. A. Katula and coauthors, Strength training in older adults: An empowering intervention, *Medicine and Science in Sports and Exercise* 38 (2006): 106–111.
32. J. Stessman and coauthors, Physical activity, function, and longevity among the very old, *Archives of Internal Medicine* 169 (2009): 1476–1483.
33. S. Marwood and coauthors, Faster pulmonary oxygen uptake kinetics in trained versus untrained male adolescents, *Medicine and Science in Sports and Exercise* 42 (2010): 127–134; N. L. Jones, An obsession with CO_2, *Applied Physiology, Nutrition, and Metabolism* 33 (2008): 641–650.
34. P. G. Snell and coauthors, Maximal oxygen uptake as a parametric measure of cardiorespiratory capacity, *Medicine and Science in Sports and Exercise* 39 (2007): 103–107.
35. T. Rankinen and coauthors, Cardiorespiratory fitness, BMI, and risk of hypertension: The HYPGENE Study, *Medicine and Science in Sports and Exercise* 39 (2007): 1687–1692.
36. J. LaForgia, R. T. Withers, and C. J. Gore, Effects of exercise intensity and duration on the excess post-exercise oxygen consumption, *Journal of Sports Sciences* 24 (2006): 1247–1264.
37. E. L. Melanson, P. S. MacLean, and J. O. Hill, Exercise improves fat metabolism in muscle but does not increase 24-h fat oxidation, *Exercise and Sport Sciences Reviews* 37 (2009): 93–101; LaForgia, Withers, and Gore, Effects of exercise intensity and duration; M. Drummond, and coauthors, Aerobic and resistance exercise sequence affects excess postexercise oxygen consumption, *Journal of Strength and Conditioning Research,* 19 (2005): 332–337.
38. P. S. MacLean and coauthors, Regular exercise attenuates the metabolic drive to regain weight after long-term weight loss, *American Journal of Physiology: Regulatory, Integrative, and Comparative Physiology* 297 (2009): R793–R802; C. Martins, L. Morgan, and H. Truby, A review of the effects of exercise on appetite regulation: An obesity perspective, *International Journal of Obesity* 32 (2008): 1337–1347; D. R. Broom and coauthors, Exercise-induced suppression of acylated ghrelin in humans, *Journal of Applied Physiology* 102 (2007): 2165–2171; R. R. Kraemer and V. D. Castracrane, Exercise and humoral mediators of peripheral energy balance: Ghrelin and adiponectin, *Experimental Biology and Medicine (Maywood):* 232 (2007): 184–194.
39. J. Bergstrom and coauthors, Diet, muscle glycogen and physical performance, *Acta Physiologica Scandanavica* 71 (1967): 140–150.
40. Position of the American Dietetic Association, Dietitians of Canada, and the American College of Sports Medicine: Nutrition and athletic performance, *Journal of the American Dietetic Association* 109 (2009): 509–527.
41. A. M. Bellinger and coauthors, Remodeling of ryanodine receptor complex causes "leaky" channels: A molecular mechanism for decreased exercise capacity, *Proceedings of the National Academy of Sciences* 105 (2008): 2198–2202; S. P. Cairns, Lactic acid and exercise performance: Culprit or friend? *Sports Medicine* 36 (2006): 279–291.
42. R. Buresh, K. Berg, and J. French, The effect of resistance exercise rest interval on hormonal response, strength, and hypertrophy with training, *Journal of Strength and Conditioning Research,* 23 (2009): 62–71; M. L. Healy and coauthors, Effects of growth hormone on glucose and glycerol metabolism at rest and during exercise in endurance-trained athletes, *The Journal of Clinical Endocrinology & Metabolism* 91 (2006): 320–327; W. Kraemer, and N. Ratamess, Hormonal responses and adaptations to resistance exercise and training, *Sports Medicine,* 35 (2005): 339–361; J. M. Willardson, A brief review: Factors affecting the length of rest interval between resistance exercise sets, *Journal of Strength and Conditioning Research,* 20 (2006): 978–984.
43. M. Dunford, ed., *Sports Nutrition: A Practice Manual for Professionals* (Chicago: The American Dietetic Association, 2006), p. 27.
44. Position of the American Dietetic Association, Dietitians of Canada, and the American College of Sports Medicine, Nutrition and athletic performance; J. Wilson, and G. J. Wilson, Contemporary issues in protein requirements and consumption for resistance trained athletes, *Journal of the International Society of Sports Nutrition* 3 (2006): 7–27.
45. D. A. Sedlock, The latest on carbohydrate loading: A practical approach, *Current Sports Medicine Reports* 7 (2008): 209–213; A. E. Jeukendrup, R. L. Jentjen, and L. Moseley,

Nutritional considerations in triathlon, *Sports Medicine* 35 (2005): 163–181.
46. Position of the American Dietetic Association, Dietitians of Canada, and the American College of Sports Medicine: Nutrition and athletic performance.
47. G. A. Wallis and coauthors, Dose-response effects of ingested carbohydrate on exercise metabolism in women, *Medicine and Science in Sports and Exercise* 39 (2007): 131–138; A. C. Utter and coauthors, Carbohydrate supplementation and perceived exertion during prolonged running, *Medicine and Science in Sports and Exercise* 36 (2004): 1036–1041.
48. A. Foskett and coauthors, Carbohydrate availability and muscle energy metabolism during intermittent running, *Medicine and Science in Sports and Exercise* 40 (2008): 96–103; S. G. Harger-Domitrovich and coauthors, Exogenous carbohydrate spares muscle glycogen in men and women during 10 h of exercise, *Medicine and Science in Sports and Exercise* 39 (2007): 2171–2179; A. C. Utter and coauthors, Carbohydrate attenuates perceived exertion during intermittent exercise and recovery, *Medicine and Science in Sports and Exercise* 39 (2007): 880; American College of Sports Medicine, Position Stand, Exercise and fluid replacement, *Medicine and Science in Sports and Exercise* 39 (2007): 377–390.
49. Position of the American Dietetic Association, Dietitians of Canada, and the American College of Sports Medicine, Nutrition and athletic performance; G. A. Wallis and coauthors, Postexercise muscle glycogen synthesis with combined glucose and fructose ingestion, *Medicine and Science in Sports and Exercise* 40 (2008): 1789–1794.
50. M. Millard-Stafford, and coauthors, Recovery nutrition: Timing and composition after endurance exercise, *Current Sports Medicine Reports* 7 (2008): 193–201; R. Jentjens and A. Jeukendrup, Determinants of post-exercise glycogen synthesis during short-term recovery, *Sports Medicine* 33 (2003): 117–144.
51. J. R. Karp and coauthors, Chocolate milk as a post-exercise recovery aid, *International Journal of Sport Nutrition and Exercise Metabolism* 16 (2006): 78–91.
52. E. Coleman, Carbohydrate and exercise, in *Sports Nutrition: A Practice Manual for Professionals,* 4th ed., M. Dunford, ed. (Chicago: The American Dietetic Association, 2006), pp. 14–32.
53. Position of the American Dietetic Association, Dietitians of Canada, and the American College of Sports Medicine, Nutrition and athletic performance.
54. L. Havemann and coauthors, Fat adaptation followed by carbohydrate loading compromises high-intensity sprint performance, *Journal of Applied Physiology* 100 (2006): 194–202.
55. Position of the American Dietetic Association, Dietitians of Canada, and the American College of Sports Medicine, Nutrition and athletic performance.
56. A. Simopoulos, Omega-3 fatty acids and athletics, *Current Sports Medicine Reports* 6 (2007): 230–236.
57. S. S. Gropper, J. L. Smith, and J. L. Groff, Sports nutrition in integration and regulation of metabolism and the impact of exercise and sport, *Advanced Nutrition and Human Metabolism* (Belmont, Calif.: Wadsworth/Cengage Learning, 2009), pp. 265–275.
58. J. Wilson, and G. J. Wilson, Contemporary issues in protein requirements and consumption for resistance trained athletes, *Journal of the International Society of Sports Nutrition* 3 (2006): 7–27.
59. T. B. Symons and coauthors, A moderate serving of high-quality protein maximally stimulates skeletal muscle protein synthesis in young and elderly subjects, *Journal of the American Dietetic Association* 109 (2009): 1582–1586; L. B. Verdijk and coauthors, Protein supplementation before and after exercise does not further augment skeletal muscle hypertrophy after resistance training in elderly men, *American Journal of Clinical Nutrition* 89 (2009): 608–616; K. D. Tipton and A. A. Ferrando, Improving muscle mass: Response of muscle metabolism to exercise, nutrition, and anabolic agents, *Essays in Biochemistry* 44 (2008): 85–98; T. G. Anthony and coauthors, Feeding meals containing soy or whey protein after exercise stimulates protein synthesis and translation initiation in the skeletal muscle of male rats, *Journal of Nutrition* 137 (2007): 357–362; M. Dunford, ed., *Sports Nutrition: A Practice Manual for Professionals* (Chicago: The American Dietetic Association, 2006), p. 44.
60. G. Wu, Amino acids: Metabolism, functions, and nutrition, *Amino Acids,* 37 (2009): 1–17; M. Millard-Stafford and coauthors, Recovery nutrition: Timing and composition after endurance exercise, *Current Sports Medicine Reports* 7 (2008): 193–201; Wilson and Wilson, Contemporary issues in protein requirements.
61. Position of the American Dietetic Association, Dietitians of Canada, and the American College of Sports Medicine, Nutrition and athletic performance; Committee on Dietary Reference Intakes, *Dietary Reference Intakes.*
62. Position of the American Dietetic Association, Dietitians of Canada, and the American College of Sports Medicine, Nutrition and athletic performance.
63. T. L. Schwenk and C. D. Costley, When food becomes a drug: Nonanabolic nutritional supplement use in athletes, *American Journal of Sports Medicine* 30 (2002): 907–916.
64. Position of the American Dietetic Association, Dietitians of Canada, and the American College of Sports Medicine, Nutrition and athletic performance.
65. S. Sachdev and K. J. Davies, Production, detection, and adaptive responses to free radicals in exercise, *Free Radical Biology and Medicine* 44 (2008): 215–223; M. J. Jackson, Free radicals generated by contracting muscle; By-products of metabolism or key regulators of muscle function? *Free Radical Biology and Medicine* 44 (2008): 132–141; A. Mastaloudis and coauthors, Antioxidants did not prevent muscle damage in response to an ultramarathon run, *Medicine and Science in Sports and Exercise* 38 (2006): 72–80; J. Finaud, G. Lac, and E. Filaire, Oxidative stress: Relationship with exercise and training, *Sports Medicine* 36 (2006): 327–358.
66. W. L. Knex, D. G. Jenkins, and J. S. Coombes, Oxidative stress in half and full ironman triathletes, *Medicine and Science in Sports and Exercise* 39 (2007): 283–288; S. L. Williams and coauthors, Antioxidant requirements of endurance athletes: Implications for health, *Nutrition Reviews* 64 (2006): 93–108.
67. M. C. Gomez-Cabrera, E. Domenech, and J. Vina, Moderate exercise is an antioxidant: Upregulation of antioxidant genes by training, *Free Radical Biology and Medicine* 44 (2008): 126–131; S. Sachdev and K. J. Davies, Production, detection, and adaptive responses to free radicals in exercise, *Free Radical Biology and Medicine* 44 (2008): 215–223; Jackson, Free radicals generated by contracting muscle; J. Padilla and T. D. Mickleborough, Does antioxidant supplementation prevent favorable adaptations to exercise training? *Medicine and Science in Sports and Exercise* 39 (2007): 1887.
68. M. Ristow and coauthors, Antioxidants prevent health-promoting effects of physical exercise in humans, *Proceedings of the National Academy of Sciences* 106 (2009): 8665-8670.
69. E. Reboul, and coauthors, Effect of the main dietary antioxidants (carotenoids, γ-tocopherol, polyphenols, and vitamin C) on α-tocopherol, *European Journal of Clinical Nutrition* 61 (2007): 1167–1173.
70. P. S. Hinton and L. M. Sinclair, Iron supplementation maintains ventilatory threshold and improves energetic efficiency in iron-deficient nonanemic athletes, *European Journal of Clinical Nutrition* 61 (2007): 30–39.
71. S. S. Gropper and coauthors, Iron status of female collegiate athletes involved in different sports, *Biological Trace Element Research* 109 (2006): 1–14.
72. Position of the American Dietetic Association, Dietitians of Canada, and the American College of Sports Medicine, Nutrition and athletic performance.
73. American College of Sports Medicine, Position Stand, Exercise and fluid replacement.
74. R. J. Maughan, S. M. Shirreffs, and P. Watson, Exercise, heat, hydration and the brain, *Journal of the American College of Nutrition* 26 (2007): 604S–621S.
75. American College of Sports Medicine, Position Stand: Prevention of cold injuries during exercise, *Medicine and Science in Sports and Exercise* 38 (2006): 2012–2029.
76. M. Rosner and J. Kirven, Exercise-associated hyponatremia, *Clinical Journal of the American Society of Nephrology* 2 (2007): 151–161; A. Upadhyay, B. Jaber, and N. Madias, Incidence and prevalence of hyponatremia, *The American Journal of Medicine* 119 (2006): S30–S35.

77. Standing Committee on the Scientific Evaluation of Dietary Reference Intakes, Food and Nutrition Board, *Dietary Reference Intakes.*
78. Rosner and Kirven, Exercise-associated hyponatremia; Upadhyay, Jaber, and Madias, Incidence and prevalence of hyponatremia; American College of Sports Medicine, Position Stand, Exercise and fluid replacement; J. W. Gardner, Death by water intoxication, *Military Medicine* 168 (2003): 432–434.
79. American College of Sports Medicine, Position Stand, Exercise and fluid replacement.
80. Rosner and Kirven, Exercise-associated hyponatremia.
81. Position of the American Dietetic Association, Dietitians of Canada, and the American College of Sports Medicine, Nutrition and athletic performance
82. Karp and coauthors, Chocolate milk as a post-exercise recovery aid.

CONSUMER CORNER 10

1. American College of Sports Medicine, Position Stand, Exercise and Fluid Replacement, *Medicine and Science in Sports and Exercise* 39 (2007): 377–390.
2. B. Murray, Fluid, electrolytes, and exercise, in *Sports Nutrition: A Practice Manual for Professionals*, 4th ed., M. Dunford, ed. (Chicago: The American Dietetic Association, 2006), pp. 94–115.

CONTROVERSY 10

1. K. A. Erdman, T. S. Fung, and R. A. Reimer, Influence of performance level on dietary supplementation in elite Canadian athletes, *Medicine and Science in Sports and Exercise* 38 (2006): 349–356.
2. H. Geyer and coauthors, Nutritional supplements cross-contaminated and faked with doping substances, *Journal of Mass Spectrometry* 43(2008): 892–902.
3. K. T. Schneiker and coauthors, Effects of caffeine on prolonged intermittent-sprint ability in team-sport athletes, *Medicine and Science in Sports and Exercise* 38 (2006): 578–585; G. R. Stuart and coauthors, Multiple effects of caffeine on simulated high-intensity team-sport performance, *Medicine and Science in Sports and Exercise* 37 (2005): 1998–2005; S. A. Paluska, Caffeine and exercise, *Current Sports Medicine Reports* 2 (2003): 213–219.
4. K. Woolf, W. K. Bidwell, and A. G. Carlson, The effect of caffeine as an ergogenic aid in anaerobic exercise, *International Journal of Sport Nutrition and Exercise Metabolism* 18 (2008): 412–429.
5. Woolf, Bidwell, and Carlson, The effect of caffeine as an ergogenic aid.
6. Standing Committee on the Scientific Evaluation of Dietary Reference Intakes, Food and Nutrition Board, Institute of Medicine, *Dietary Reference Intakes: Water, Potassium, Sodium, Chloride, and Sulfate* (Washington, D.C.: National Academies Press, 2004): pp. 269–423.
7. E. M. Broad, R. J. Maughan, S. D. Galloway, Effects of four weeks L-carnitine L-tartrate ingestion on substrate utilization during prolonged exercise, *International Journal of Sport Nutrition and Exercise Metabolism* 15 (2005): 665–679; E. P. Brass, Carnitine and sports medicine: Use or abuse? *Annals of the New York Academy of Sciences* 1033 (2004): 67–78.
8. Position of the American Dietetic Association, Dietitians of Canada, and the American College of Sports Medicine: Nutrition and athletic performance, *Journal of the American Dietetic Association* 109 (2009): 509–527.
9. K. L. Kendall and coauthors, Effects of four weeks of high-intensity interval training and creatine supplementation on critical power and anaerobic working capacity in college-aged men, *Journal of Strength and Conditioning Research* 23 (2009): 1663–1669; M. Dunford and M. Smith, Dietary supplements and ergogenic aids, in *Sports Nutrition: A Practice Manual for Professionals*, 4th ed., ed. M. Dunford (Chicago: American Dietetic Association, 2006), pp. 116–141.
10. M. Spillane and coauthors, The effects of creatine ethyl ester supplementation combined with heavy resistance training on body composition, muscle performance, and serum and muscle creatine levels, *Journal of the International Society of Sports Nutrition* 6 (2009), epub doi:10.1186/1550-2783-6-6.
11. Spillane and coauthors, The effects of creatine ethyl ester supplementation.
12. Dunford and Smith, Dietary supplements and ergogenic aids.
13. American Academy of Pediatrics, Policy Statement, Committee on Sports Medicine and Fitness, Use of performance-enhancing substances, *Pediatrics* 115 (2005): 1103–1106.
14. B. Campbell and R. Kreider, Conjugated linoleic acids, *Current Sports Medicine Reports* 7 (2008): 237–241; C. Pinkoski and coauthors, The effects of conjugated linoleic acid supplementation during resistance training, *Medicine and Science in Sports and Exercise* 38 (2006): 339–348.
15. L. R. McNaughton, J. Siegler, and A. Midgley, Ergogenic effects of sodium bicarbonate, *Current Sports Medicine Reports* 7 (2008): 230–236.
16. R. R. Wolfe, Skeletal muscle protein metabolism and resistance exercise, *Journal of Nutrition* 136 (2006): 525S–528S.
17. Wolfe, Skeletal muscle protein metabolism and resistance exercise.
18. L. Nybo and coauthors, Cerebral ammonia uptake and accumulation during prolonged exercise in humans, *Journal of Physiology* 563 (2005): 285–290.
19. E. Ha and M. B. Zemel, Functional properties of whey, whey components, and essential amino acids: Mechanisms underlying health benefits for active people (review), *Journal of Nutritional Biochemistry* 14 (2003): 251–258.
20. T. G. Anthony and coauthors, Feeding meals containing soy or whey protein after exercise stimulates protein synthesis and translation initiation in the skeletal muscle of male rats, *Journal of Nutrition* 137 (2007): 357–362; S. B. Wilkinson and coauthors, Consumption of fluid skim milk promotes greater muscle protein accretion after resistance exercise than does consumption of an isonitrogenous and isoenergetic soy-protein beverage, *American Journal of Clinical Nutrition* 85 (2007): 1031–1040; T. A. Elliot and coauthors, Milk ingestion stimulates net and muscle protein synthesis following resistance exercise, *Medicine and Science in Sports and Exercise* 38 (2006): 667–674.
21. N. R. Rodriquez, L. M. Vislocky, and P. C. Gaine, Dietary protein, endurance exercise, and human skeletal-muscle protein turnover, *Current Opinion in Clinical Nutrition and Metabolic Care* 10 (2007): 40–45; Wolfe, Skeletal muscle protein metabolism and resistance exercise.
22. D. G. Candow and coauthors, Effect of whey and soy protein supplementation combined with resistance training in young adults, *International Journal of Sport Nutrition and Exercise and Metabolism* 16 (2006): 233–244.
23. L. L. Andersen and coauthors, The effect of resistance training combined with timed ingestion of protein on muscle fiber size and muscle strength, *Metabolism: Clinical and Experimental* 54 (2005): 151–156.
24. M. Freeman, Scientist suspects many athletes are using undetected steroids, *New York Times Online*, October 21, 2003.
25. A. Kicman, Pharmacology of anabolic steroids, *British Journal of Pharmacology* 154 (2008): 502–521; T. M. Smurawa and J. A. Congeni, Testosterone precursors: Use and abuse in pediatric athletes, *Pediatric Clinics of North America* 54 (2007): 787–796.
26. H. Geyer and coauthors Nutritional supplements cross-contaminated and faked with doping substances.
27. P. Watson and coauthors, Urinary nandrolone metabolite detection after ingestion of a nandrolone precursor, *Medicine and Science in Sports and Exercise*, 41 (2009): 766–772.
28. D. G. Finniss and coauthors, Biological, clinical, and ethical advances of placebo effects, *Lancet* 375 (2010): 686–695.

Chapter 11

1. Centers for Disease Control and Prevention, Plan to combat extensively drug-resistant tuberculosis: Recommendations of the Federal Tuberculosis Task Force, *Morbidity and Mortality Weekly Report* 58 (2009): 1–43; R. L. Monaghan and J. F. Barrett, Antibacterial drug discovery—Then, now and the genomics future, *Biochemical Pharmacology* 30 (2006): 901–909.
2. E. S. Wintergerst, S. Maggini, and D. H. Hornig, Contribution of selected vitamins and trace elements to immune function, *Annals of Nutrition and Metabolism* 51 (2007): 301–323; B. W. Ritz and E. M. Gardner, Malnutrition and energy restriction differentially affect viral immunity, *Journal of Nutrition* 136 (2006): 1141–1144.
3. H. C. Kung and coauthors, Deaths: Final data for 2005, *National Vital statistics Reports* 56 (2008): 1–121; D. V. McQueen, Continuing

efforts in global chronic disease prevention, *Preventing Chronic Diseases* [serial online] April 2007, available at www.cdc.gov/pcd/issues/2007/apr/07_0024.htm.

4. A. L. Webb and E. Villamor, Update: Effects of antioxidant and non-antioxidant vitamin supplementation on immune function, *Nutrition Reviews* 65 (2007): 181–217; Wintergerst, Maggini, and Hornig, Contribution of selected vitamins and trace elements to immune function.

5. Standing Committee on the Scientific Evaluation of Dietary Reference Intakes, Food and Nutrition Board, Institute of Medicine, *Dietary Reference Intakes for Vitamin A, Vitamin K, Arsenic, Boron, Chromium, Copper, Iodine, Iron, Manganese, Molybdenum, Nickel, Silicon, Vanadium, and Zinc* (Washington, D.C.: National Academies Press, 2001), pp. 12–30.

6. P. K. Drain and coauthors, Micronutrients in HIV-positive persons receiving highly active antiretroviral therapy, *American Journal of Clinical Nutrition* 85 (2007): 333–345; Position of the American Dietetic Association and Dietitians of Canada: Nutrition intervention in the care of persons with human immunodeficiency virus infection, *Journal of the American Dietetic Association* 104 (2004): 1425–1441.

7. A. Mente and coauthors, A systematic review of the evidence supporting a causal link between dietary factors and coronary heart disease, *Archives of Internal Medicine* 169 (2009): 659–669; A. Galimanis and coauthors, Lifestyle and stroke risk: A review, *Current Opinion in Neurology* 22 (2009): 60–68; M. U. Jakobsen and coauthors, Major types of dietary fat and risk of coronary heart disease: A pooled analysis of 11 cohort studies, *American Journal of Clinical Nutrition* 89 (2009): 1425–1432; D. R. Jacobs and L. C. Tapsell, Food, not nutrients, is the fundamental unit in nutrition, *Nutrition Reviews* 65 (2007): 439–450.

8. American Heart Association, *Heart Disease and Strokes Statistics—2009 Update At-A-Glance,* www.americanheart.org/statistics/cvd.html.

9. E. S. Ford and coauthors, Explaining the decrease in U.S. deaths from coronary disease, 1980–2000, *New England Journal of Medicine* 356 (2007): 2388–2398; Y. Gerber and coauthors, Secular trends in deaths from cardiovascular diseases: A 25-year community study, *Circulation* 113 (2006): 2285–2292.

10. C. E. Murry and R. T. Lee, Turnover after the fallout, *Science* 324 (2009): 47–48.

11. A. Towfighi, L. Zheng, and B. Ovbiagele, Sex-specific trends in midlife coronary heart disease risk and prevalence, *Archives of Internal Medicine* 169 (2009): 1762–1766; American Heart Association, *Heart Disease and Strokes Statistics—2009 Update At-A-Glance*; L. Mosca and coauthors, Evidence-based guidelines for cardiovascular disease prevention in women: 2007 update, *Circulation* 115 (2007): 1481–1501.

12. Centers for Disease Control and Prevention, Prevalence of heart disease—United States, 2005, *Morbidity and Mortality Weekly Report* 56 (2007): 113–118.

13. Mente and coauthors, A systematic review of the evidence supporting a causal link between dietary factors and coronary heart disease; P. B. Mellen, T. F. Walsh, and D. M. Herrington, Whole grain intake and cardiovascular disease: A meta-analysis, *Nutrition, Metabolism, and Cardiovascular Disease,* 18 (2008): 283–290; S. Lee and coauthors, Trends in diet quality for coronary heart disease prevention between 1980–1982 and 2000–2002: The Minnesota Heart Survey, *Journal of the American Dietetic Association* 107 (2007): 213–222.

14. W. Insull, The pathology of atherosclerosis: Plaque development and plaque responses to medical treatment, *The American Journal of Medicine* 122 (2009): S3–S14.

15. Jakobsen and coauthors, Major types of dietary fat and risk of coronary heart disease; E. Warensjo and coauthors, Markers of dietary fat quality and fatty acid desaturation as predictors of total and cardiovascular mortality: A population-based prospective study, *American Journal of Clinical Nutrition* 88 (2008): 203–209; R. De Caterina and coauthors, Nutritional mechanisms that influence cardiovascular disease, *American Journal of Clinical Nutrition* 83 (2006): 421S–426S.

16. P. Libby, Inflammatory mechanisms: The molecular basis of inflammation and disease, *Nutrition Reviews* 65 (2007): S140–S146; G. Davi and C. Patrono, Platelet activation and atherothrombosis, *New England Journal of Medicine* 357 (2007): 2482–2494; P. Libby, Inflammation and cardiovascular disease mechanisms, *American Journal of Clinical Nutrition* 83 (2006): 456S–460S; M. S. Elkind, Inflammation, atherosclerosis, and stroke, *Neurologist* 12 (2006): 140–148.

17. S. Devaraj, U. Singh and I. Jialal, The Evolving role of C-reactive protein in atherothrombosis, *Clinical Chemistry* 55 (2009): 229–238; M. H. Davidson and coauthors, Consensus panel recommendation for incorporating lipoprotein-associated phospholipase A2 testing into cardiovascular disease risk assessment guidelines, *American Journal of Cardiology* (12A) 101 (2008): 51F–57F; M. S. Sabatine and coauthors, Prognostic significance of the Centers for Disease Control/American Heart Association high-sensitivity C-reactive protein cut points for cardiovascular and other outcomes in patients with stable coronary artery disease, *Circulation* 115 (2007): 1528–1536; P. M. Ridker, Inflammatory biomarkers and risks of myocardial infarction, stroke, diabetes, and total mortality: Implications for longevity, *Nutrition Reviews* 65 (2007): S253–S259; N. R. Cook, J. E. Buring, and P. M. Ridker, The effect of including C-reactive protein in cardiovascular risk prediction models for women, *Annals of Internal Medicine* 145 (2006): 21–29.

18. Insull, The pathology of atherosclerosis; Libby, Inflammation and cardiovascular disease mechanisms.

19. Insull, The pathology of atherosclerosis; V. E. Friedewald and coauthors, the Editor's Roundtable: The vulnerable plaque, *American Journal Cardiology* 102 (2008): 1644–1653.

20. W. S. Harris and coauthors, Omega-6 fatty acids and risk for cardiovascular disease, A Science Advisory from the American Heart Association Nutrition Subcommittee of the Council on Nutrition, Physical Activity, and Metabolism; Council on Cardiovascular Nursing; and Council on Epidemiology and Prevention, *Circulation* 119 (2009): 902–907; P. C. Calder, n-3 Polyunsaturated fatty acids, inflammation, and inflammatory diseases, *American Journal of Clinical Nutrition* 83 (2006): 1505S–1519S; P. J. H. Jones and A. A. Papamandjaris, Lipids: Cellular metabolism, in *Present Knowledge in Nutrition,* B. A. Bowman and R. M. Russell, eds. (Washington, D.C.: ILSI Press, 2006), pp. 125–137.

21. R. G. Metcalf and coauthors, Effects of fish-oil supplementation on myocardial fatty acids in humans, *American Journal of Clinical Nutrition* 85 (2007): 1222–1228; D. S. Kelley and coauthors, Docosahexaenoic acid supplementation improves fasting and postprandial lipid profiles in hypertriglyceridemic men, *American Journal of Clinical Nutrition* 86 (2007): 324–333; C. Chrysohoou and coauthors, Long-term fish consumption is associated with protection against arrhythmia in healthy persons in a Mediterranean region—the ATTICA study, *American Journal of Clinical Nutrition* 85 (2007): 1385–1391; J. L. Breslow, n-3 fatty acids and cardiovascular disease, *American Journal of Clinical Nutrition* 83 (2006): 1477S–1482S; C. Wang and coauthors, n-3 Fatty acids from fish or fish-oil supplements, but not α-linolenic acid, benefit cardiovascular disease outcomes in primary- and secondary-prevention studies: A systematic review, *American Journal of Clinical Nutrition* 84 (2006): 5–17; Y. A. Carpenteir, L. Portois, and W. J. Malaisse, n-3 Fatty acids and the metabolic syndrome, *American Journal of Clinical Nutrition* 83 (2006): 1499S–1504S.

22. C. J. Lavie, R. V. Milani, and H. O. Ventura, Obesity and cardiovascular disease: Risk factor, paradox, and impact of weight loss, *Journal of the American College of Cardiology* 53 (2009): 1925–1932; N. T. Nguyen and coauthors, Association of hypertension, diabetes, dyslipidemia, and metabolic syndrome with obesity: Findings from the National Health and Nutrition Examination survey, 1999 to 2004, *Journal of the American College of Surgeons* 207 (2008): 928–934; S. C. Smith, Multiple risk factors for cardiovascular disease and diabetes mellitus, *American Journal of Medicine* 120 (2007): S3–S11.

23. Insull, The pathology of atherosclerosis; Expert Panel on Detection, Evaluation, and Treatment of High Blood Cholesterol in Adults (Adult Treatment Panel III), Third Report of the National Cholesterol Education Program (NCEP), NIH publication no. 02-5215 (Bethesda, Md.: National Heart, Lung, and Blood Institute, 2002), p. II–18.

24. Centers for Disease Control and Prevention, Prevalence of heart disease—United States, 2005.
25. K. Nasir and coauthors, Family history of premature coronary heart disease and coronary artery calcification: Multi-Ethnic Study of Atherosclerosis (MESA), *Circulation* 116 (2007): 619–626; Expert Panel on Detection, Evaluation, and Treatment of High Blood Cholesterol in Adults (Adult Treatment Panel III). Third Report of the National Cholesterol Education Program, p. II–19.
26. J. M. Ordovas, Genetic influences on blood lipids and cardiovascular disease risk: Tools for primary prevention, *American Journal of Clinical Nutrition* 89 (2009): 1509S–1517S.
27. K. He, Y. Xu, and L. Van Horn, The puzzle of dietary fat intake and risk of ischemic stroke: A brief review of epidemiological data, *Journal of the American Dietetic Association* 107 (2007): 287–295.
28. A. K. Chhatriwalla and coauthors, Low levels of low-density lipoprotein cholesterol and blood pressure and progression of coronary atherosclerosis, *Journal of the American College of Cardiology* 53 (2009): 1110–1115.
29. Insull, The pathology of atherosclerosis; R. De Caterina and coauthors, Nutritional mechanisms that influence cardiovascular disease, *American Journal of Clinical Nutrition* 83 (2006): 421S–426S.
30. Insull, The pathology of atherosclerosis; De Caterina and coauthors, Nutritional mechanisms that influence cardiovascular disease.
31. O. H. Franco and coauthors, Associations of diabetes mellitus with total life expectancy and life expectancy with and without cardiovascular disease, *Archives of Internal Medicine* 167 (2007): 1145–1151; C. S. Fox and coauthors, Increasing cardiovascular disease burden due to diabetes mellitus: The Framingham Heart Study, *Circulation* 115 (2007): 1544–1550; De Caterina and coauthors, Nutritional mechanisms that influence cardiovascular disease.
32. Expert Panel on Detection, Evaluation, and Treatment of High Blood Cholesterol in Adults (Adult Treatment Panel III), Third Report of the National Cholesterol Education Program, pp. II-16, II-50–II-53.
33. A. El-Osta and coauthors, Transient high glucose causes persistent epigenetic changes and altered gene expression during subsequent normoglycemia, *Journal of Experimental Medicine* 205 (2008): 2409–2417.
34. S. A. Kenfield, Smoking and smoking cessation in relation to mortality in women, *Journal of the American Medical Association* 299 (2008): 2037–2047; R. H. Eckel and coauthors, ADA/AHA Scientific Statement: Preventing cardiovascular disease and diabetes: A call to action from the American Diabetes Association and the American Heart Association, *Circulation* 113 (2006): 2943–2946; Expert Panel on Detection, Evaluation, and Treatment of High Blood Cholesterol in Adults (Adult Treatment Panel III), Third Report of the National Cholesterol Education Program, p. II-16.
35. Mente and coauthors, A systematic review of the evidence supporting a causal link between dietary factors and coronary heart disease.
36. Mellen, Walsh, and Herrington, Whole grain intake and cardiovascular disease; L. R. Harriss and coauthors, Dietary patterns and cardiovascular mortality in the Melbourne Collaborative Cohort Study, *American Journal of Clinical Nutrition* 86 (2007): 221–229; Calder, n-3 Polyunsaturated fatty acids, inflammation, and inflammatory diseases.
37. D. M. Minich and J. S. Bland, Dietary management of the metabolic syndrome beyond macronutrients, *Nutrition Reviews* 66 (2008): 429–444; C. Day, Metabolic syndrome, or What you will: definitions and epidemiology, *Diabetes and Vascular Disease Research* 4 (2007): 32–38; D. J. Magliano, J. E. Shaw, and P. Z. Zimmet, How to best define the metabolic syndrome, *Annals of Medicine* 38 (2006): 34–41.
38. B. G. Nordestgaard and coauthors, Nonfasting triglycerides and risk of myocardial infarction, ischemic heart disease, and death in men and women, *Journal of the Medical Association* 298 (2007): 299–308; E. S. Ford, Prevalence of the metabolic syndrome defined by the International Diabetes Federation among adults in the U.S., *Diabetes Care* 28 (2005): 2745–2749.
39. Minich and Bland, Dietary management of the metabolic syndrome beyond macronutrients; P. Meerarani and coauthors, Metabolic syndrome and diabetic atherothrombosis: Implications in vascular complications, *Current Molecular Medicine* 6 (2006): 501–514; American Heart Association/National Heart, Lung, and Blood Institute Scientific Statement, Diagnosis and management of metabolic syndrome, *Circulation* 112 (2005): 2735–2752.
40. S. C. Smith, Multiple risk factors for cardiovascular disease and diabetes mellitus, *American Journal of Medicine* 120 (2007): S3–S11.
41. S. S. Satvinder and T. A. Welborn, Central obesity and multivariable cardiovascular risk as assessed by the Framingham prediction scores, *American Journal of Cardiology* 103 (2009): 1403–1407; N. Orsini and coauthors, Combined effects of obesity and physical activity in predicting mortality among men, *Journal of Internal Medicine* 264 (2008): 442–451; A. R. Weinstein and coauthors, The joint effects of physical activity and body mass index on coronary heart disease risk in women, *Archives of Internal Medicine* 168 (2008): 884–890; T. Weinbrenner and coauthors, Circulating oxidized LDL is associated with increased waist circumference independent of body mass index in men and women, *American Journal of Clinical Nutrition* 83 (2006): 30–35; T. S. Altena and coauthors, Lipoprotein subfraction changes after continuous or intermittent exercise training, *Medicine and Science in Sports and Exercise* 38 (2006): 367–372; C. E. Finley and coauthors, Cardiorespiratory fitness, macronutrient intake, and the metabolic syndrome: The Aerobics Center Longitudinal Study, *Journal of the American Dietetic Association* 106 (2006): 673–679.
42. F. Magkos and coauthors, Management of the metabolic syndrome and type 2 diabetes through lifestyle modification, *Annual Review of Nutrition* 29 (2009): 223–256; Weinbrenner and coauthors, Circulating oxidized LDL is associated with increased waist circumference; Altena and coauthors, Lipoprotein subfraction changes; Finley and coauthors, Cardiorespiratory fitness, macronutrient intake, and the metabolic syndrome.
43. L. L. Humphrey and coauthors, Homocysteine level and coronary heart disease incidence: A systematic review and meta-analysis, *Mayo Clinic Proceedings* 83 (2008): 3–16; The Heart Outcomes Prevention Evaluation (HOPE) 2 Investigators, Homocysteine lowering with folic acid and B vitamins in vascular disease, *New England Journal of Medicine* 354 (2006): 1567–1577; A. H. Lichtenstein and coauthors, Diet and Lifestyle Recommendations Revision, 2006: A scientific statement from the American Heart Association Nutrition Committee, *Circulation* 114 (2006): 82–96.
44. J. D. Brunzell, Hypertriglyceridemia, *New England Journal of Medicine* 357 (2007): 1009–1017.
45. P. E. McBride, Triglycerides and risk for coronary heart disease, *Journal of the American Medical Association* 298 (2007): 336–338.
46. Nordestgaard and coauthors, Nonfasting triglycerides and risk of myocardial infarction; S. Bansal and coauthors, Fasting compared with nonfasting triglycerides and risk of cardiovascular events in women, *Journal of the American Medical Association* 298 (2007): 309–316.
47. S. S. Gidding and coauthors, Implementing American Heart Association pediatric and adult nutrition guidelines: A Scientific Statement from the American Heart Association Nutrition Committee of the Council on Nutrition, Physical Activity and Metabolism, Council on Cardiovascular Disease in the Young, Council on Arteriosclerosis, Thrombosis and Vascular Biology, Council on Cardiovascular Nursing, Council on Epidemiology and Prevention, and Council for High Blood Pressure Research, *Circulation* 119 (2009): 1161–1175.
48. AHA Scientific Statement: Diet and lifestyle recommendations revision 2006, *Circulation* 114 (2006): 82–96; Expert Panel on Detection, Evaluation, and Treatment of High Blood Cholesterol in Adults (Adult Treatment Panel III), Third Report of the National Cholesterol Education Program, pp. V-1–V-28.
49. Mente, A systematic review of the evidence supporting a causal link between dietary factors and coronary heart disease; G. Radulian and coauthors, Metabolic effects of low glycaemic index diets, *Nutrition Journal* 8 (2009), online journal, doi:10.1186/1475-2891-8-5; Y. Ma and coauthors, Association between carbohydrate intake and serum lipids, *Journal of the American College of Nutrition* 25 (2006): 155–163.

50. Mellen, Walsh, and Herrington, Whole grain intake and cardiovascular disease.
51. Mente, A systematic review of the evidence supporting a causal link between dietary factors and coronary heart disease; A. M. Hill and coauthors, Combining fish-oil supplements with regular aerobic exercise improves body composition and cardiovascular disease risk factors, *American Journal of Clinical Nutrition* 85 (2007): 1267–1274; He, Xu, and Van Horn, The puzzle of dietary fat intake and risk of ischemic stroke; Calder, n-3 Polyunsaturated fatty acids, inflammation, and inflammatory diseases.
52. Lichtenstein and coauthors, Diet and Lifestyle Recommendations Revision, 2006.
53. K. Reynolds, A meta-analysis of the effect of soy protein supplementation on serum lipids, *American Journal of Cardiology* 98 (2006): 633–640.
54. F. M. Steinberg, Soybeans or soymilk: Does it make a difference for cardiovascular protection? Does it even matter? *American Journal of Clinical Nutrition* 85 (2007): 927–928; N. R. Matthan and coauthors, Effect of soy protein from differently processed products on cardiovascular disease risk factors and vascular endothelial function in hypercholesterolemic subjects, *American Journal of Clinical Nutrition* 85 (2007): 960–966.
55. G. D. Brinkworth and coauthors, Long-term effects of a very-low-carbohydrate weight loss diet compared with an isocaloric low-fat diet after 12 months, *American Journal of Clinical Nutrition* 90 (2009): 23–32; T. D. Barnett, N. D. Barnard, and T. L. Radak, Development of symptomatic cardiovascular disease after self-reported adherence to the Atkins Diet, *Journal of the American Dietetic Association* 109 (2009): 1263–1265; R. M. Krauss and coauthors, Separate effects of reduced carbohydrate intake and weight loss on atherogenic dyslipidemia, *American Journal of Clinical Nutrition* 83 (2006): 1025–1031; R. J. Wood, Effect of dietary carbohydrate restriction with and without weight loss on atherogenic dyslipidemia, *Nutrition Reviews* 64 (2006): 539–544; A. J. Nordmann and coauthors, Effects of low-carbohydrate vs low-fat diets on weight loss and cardiovascular risk factors: A meta-analysis of randomized controlled trials, *Archives of Internal Medicine* 166 (2006): 285–293.
56. R. Lampert and coauthors, Anger-induced T-wave alternans predicts future ventricular arrhythmias in patients with implantable cardioverter-defibrillators, *Journal of the American college of Cardiology* 53 (2009): 774–778; S. Cohen, D. Janicki-Deverts, and G. E. Miller, Psychological stress and disease, *Journal of the American Medical Association* 298 (2007): 1685–1687; H. Yang and coauthors, Work hours and self-reported hypertension among working people in California, *Hypertension* 48 (2006): 744–750.
57. Chhatriwalla and coauthors, Low levels of low-density lipoprotein cholesterol and blood pressure.
58. Y. Ostchega and coauthors, Hypertension awareness, treatment, and control—continued disparities in adults: United States, 2005–2006, *NCHS Data Brief*, January 2008; C. Rosendorff and coauthors, Treatment of hypertension in the prevention and management of ischemic heart disease: A Scientific Statement from the American Heart Association Council for High Blood Pressure Research and the Councils on Clinical Cardiology and Epidemiology and Prevention, *Circulation* 115 (2007): 2761–2788; N. D. Wong and coauthors, Prevalence, treatment, and control of combined hypertension and hypercholesterolemia in the United States, *American Journal of Cardiology* 98 (2006): 204–208.
59. Rosendorff and coauthors, Treatment of hypertension in the prevention and management of ischemic heart disease; Expert Panel on Detection, Evaluation, and Treatment of High Blood Cholesterol in Adults (Adult Treatment Panel III), Third Report of the National Cholesterol Education Program, pp. 2–3.
60. B. Rodriquez-Iturbe and N. D. Vaziri, Salt-sensitive hypertension—update on novel findings, *Nephrology Dialysis Transplantation* 22 (2007): 992–995; K. M. O'Shaughnessy and F. E. Karet, Salt handling and hypertension, *Annual Review of Nutrition* 26 (2006): 343–365.
61. L. J. Appel, American Society of Hypertension Writing Group, T. D. Giles and coauthors, ASH Position paper: Dietary approaches to lower blood pressure, *Journal of Clinical Hypertension* 11 (2009): 358–368.
62. Rosendorff and coauthors, Treatment of hypertension in the prevention and management of ischemic heart disease.
63. American Heart Association, *Know the Facts, Get the Stats, 2007,* available at www.americanheart.org.
64. T. A. Kotchen and J. M. Kotchen, Nutrition, diet, and hypertension, in M. E. Shils and coeditors, *Modern Nutrition in Health and Disease,* 10th ed., (Philadelphia: Lippincott Williams & Wilkins, 2006), pp. 1095–1107.
65. J. Redon and coauthors, Mechanisms of hypertension in the cardiometabolic syndrome, *Journal of Hypertension* 27 (2009): 441–451; F. W. Visser and coauthors, Rise in extracellular fluid volume during high sodium depends on BMI in healthy men, *Obesity (Silver Spring),* March 2009, e-pub ahead of print; De Caterina and coauthors, Nutritional mechanisms that influence cardiovascular disease.
66. R. Takachi and coauthors, Consumption of sodium and salted foods in relation to cancer and cardiovascular disease: The Japan Public Health Center-based Prospective Study, *American Journal of Clinical Nutrition* 91 (2010): 456–464; F. J. He and G. A. MacGregor, A comprehensive review on salt and health and current experience of worldwide salt reduction programmes, *Journal of Human Hypertension* 23 (2009): 363–384; B. N. van Vliet and J. P. Montani, The time course of salt-induced hypertension, and why it matters, *International Journal of Obesity* 32 (2008): S35–S47.
67. A. J. Flint and coauthors, Whole grains and incident hypertension in men, *American Journal of Clinical Nutrition* 90 (2009): 493–498; J. P. Forman and coauthors, Diet and lifestyle risk factors associated with incident hypertension in women, *Journal of the American Medical Association* 302 (2009): 401–411.
68. Y. Al-Solaiman and coauthors, DASH lowers blood pressure in obese hypertensives beyond potassium, magnesium and fibre, *Journal of Human Hypertension,* advance online publication July 23, 2009, doi:10.1038/jhh 2009.58; J. F. Swain and coauthors, Characteristics of the diet patterns tested in the optimal macronutrient intake trial to prevent heart disease (OmniHeart): Options for a heart-healthy diet, *Journal of the American Dietetic Association* 108 (2008): 257–265; U.S. Department of Health and Human Services, National Institutes of Health, National Heart, Lung, and Blood Institute, *Your Guide to Lowering Your Blood Pressure with DASH* (NIH Publication No. 06-4082, 2006).
69. Swain and coauthors, Characteristics of the diet patterns; P. H. Lin and coauthors, the PREMIER Intervention helps participants follow the Dietary Approaches to Stop Hypertension dietary pattern and the current Dietary Reference Intakes recommendations, *Journal of the American Dietetic Association* 107 (2007): 1541–1551; L. Dauchet and coauthors, Dietary patterns and blood pressure change over 5-y follow-up in the SU.VI.MAX cohort, *American Journal of Clinical Nutrition* 85 (2007): 1650–1656.
70. N. L. Chase and coauthors, The association of cardiorespiratory fitness and physical activity with incidence of hypertension in men, *American Journal of Hypertension* 22 (2009): 417–424; P. T. Williams, Relationship of running intensity to hypertension, hypercholesterolemia, and diabetes, *Medicine and Science in Sports and Exercise* 40 (2008): 1740–1748; T. Rankinen and coauthors, Cardiorespiratory fitness, BMI, and risk of hypertension: The HYPGENE Study, *Medicine and Science in Sports and Exercise* 39 (2007): 1687–1692.
71. P. T. Williams, Reduced diabetic, hypertensive, and cholesterol medication use with walking, *Medicine and Science in Sports and Exercise* 40 (2008): 433–443.
72. S. Mohan and N. R. Campbell, Salt and high blood pressure, *Clinical Science (London)* 117 (2009): 1–11.
73. F. Dumier, Dietary sodium intake and arterial blood pressure, *Journal of Renal Nutrition* 19 (2009): 57–60; U.S. Department of Health and Human Services, National Institutes of Health, National Heart, Lung, and Blood Institute, *Your Guide to Lowering Your Blood Pressure with DASH* (NIH Publication No. 06–4082, 2006).
74. U.S. Department of Agriculture and U.S. Department of Health and Human Services, *2005 Dietary Guidelines Committee Report,* 2005, available online at www.healthierus.gov.
75. K. M. Dickinson, J. B. Keogh, and P. M. Clifton, Effects of a low-salt diet on flow-

mediated dilation in humans, *American Journal of Clinical Nutrition* 89 (2009): 485–490; N. R. Cook and coauthors, Long-term effects of dietary sodium reduction on cardiovascular disease outcomes: Observational follow-up of the trials of hypertension prevention (TOHP), *British Medical Journal* 334 (2007): 885.

76. Standing Committee on the Scientific Evaluation of Dietary Reference Intakes, Food and Nutrition Board, Institute of Medicine, *Dietary Reference Intakes for Water, Potassium, Sodium, Chloride, and Sulfate* (Washington, D.C.: National Academies Press, 2005): pp. 381–387; F. M. Sacks and coauthors, Effects on blood pressure of reduced dietary sodium and the Dietary Approaches to Stop Hypertension (DASH) diet, *New England Journal of Medicine* 344 (2001): 3–10.

77. Centers for Disease Control and Prevention, Application of lower sodium intake recommendations to adults—United States, 1999–2006, *Morbidity and Mortality Weekly Report* 58 (2009): 281–283.

78. X. Trudel and coauthors, Masked hypertension: Different blood pressure measurement methodology and risk factors in a working population, *Journal of Hypertension* 27 (2009): 1560–1567; H. D. Sesso and coauthors, Alcohol consumption and the risk of hypertension in women and men, *Hypertension* 51 (2008): 1080–1087.

79. S. M. Zhang and coauthors, Alcohol consumption and breast cancer risk in the Women's Health Study, *American Journal of Epidemiology* 165 (2007): 667–676.

80. I. R. Reid and coauthors, Effects of calcium supplementation on lipids, blood pressure, and body composition in healthy older men: A randomized controlled trial, *American Journal of Clincial Nutrition* 91 (2010): 131–139; P. M. Kris-Etherton and coauthors, Milk products, dietary patterns and blood pressure management, *Journal of the American College of Nutrition* 28 (2009): 103S–119S; L. Wang and coauthors, Dietary intake of dairy products, calcium, and vitamin D and the risk of hypertension in middle-aged and older women, *Hypertension* 51 (2008): 1073–1079.

81. H. J. Adrogué and N. E. Madias, Sodium and potassium in the pathogenesis of hypertension, *New England Journal of Medicine* 356 (2007): 1966–1978.

82. L. Cahill, P. N. Corey, and A. El-Sohemy, Vitamin C deficiency in a population of young Canadian adults, *American Journal of Epidemiology*, July 13th (2009), e-pub ahead of print.

83. J. R. Mort and H.R. Kruse, Timing of blood pressure measurement related to caffeine consumption, *Annals of Pharmacotherapy* 42 (2008): 105–110.

84. A. Jemal and coauthors, Cancer Statistics, 2007, *CA: A Cancer Journal for Clinicians* 57 (2007): 43–66.

85. N. J. Meropol and coauthors, American Society of Clinical Oncology Guidance Statement: The cost of cancer care, *Journal of Clinical Oncology*, July 6, 2009, e-pub ahead of print; Jemal and coauthors, Cancer Statistics, 2007.

86. World Cancer Research Fund/American Institute for Cancer Research, *Policy and Action for Cancer Prevention—Food, Nutrition, and Physical Activity: A Global Perspective* (Washington, D.C.: AICR, 2009), pp. 12–28; G. A. Colditz, T. A. Sellers, and E. Trapido, Epidemiology—Identifying the causes and preventability of cancer?, *Nature Reviews: Cancer* 6 (2006): 75–83.

87. World Cancer Research Fund/American Institute for Cancer Research, *Food, Nutrition, Physical Activity and the Prevention of Cancer: A Global Perspective* (Washington, D.C.: AICR, 2007), pp. 30–46; J. G. Brody, Environmental pollutants, diet, physical activity, body size, and breast cancer: Where do we stand in research to identify opportunities for prevention? *Cancer* 109 (2007): 2627–2634.

88. World Cancer Research Fund/American Institute for Cancer Research, *Food, Nutrition, Physical Activity and the Prevention of Cancer,* pp. 244–321.

89. World Cancer Research Fund/American Institute for Cancer Research, *Food, Nutrition, Physical Activity and the Prevention of Cancer,* pp. 157–171.

90. P. M. Ravdin and coauthors, The decrease in breast-cancer incidence in 2004 in the United States, *New England Journal of Medicine* 356 (2007): 1670–1674.

91. World Cancer Research Fund/American Institute for Cancer Research, *Food, Nutrition, Physical Activity and the Prevention of Cancer,* pp. xiv–xxiv.

92. C. M. Croce, Oncogenes and cancer, *New England Journal of Medicine* 358 (2008): 502–511.

93. World Cancer Research Fund/American Institute for Cancer Research, *Food, Nutrition, Physical Activity and the Prevention of Cancer,* pp. 64–115.

94. S. D. Hursting and coauthors, Calories and carcinogenesis: Lessons learned from 30 years of calorie restriction research, *Carcinogenesis* 31 (2010): 83–89.

95. C. Liu and R. M. Russell, Nutrition and gastric cancer risk: An update, *Nutrition Reviews* 66 (2008): 237–249; World Cancer Research Fund/American Institute for Cancer Research, *Food, Nutrition, Physical Activity and the Prevention of Cancer,* pp. 211–242; S. Larsson and A. Wolk, Obesity and colon and rectal cancer risk: A meta-analysis of prospective studies, *American Journal of Clinical Nutrition* 86 (2007): 556–565.

96. N. H. Rod and coauthors, Low-risk factor profile, estrogen levels, and breast cancer risk among postmenopausal women, *International Journal of Cancer* 124 (2009): 1935–1940; World Cancer Research Fund/American Institute for Cancer Research, *Food, Nutrition, Physical Activity and the Prevention of Cancer,* pp. 30–46.

97. K. Y. Wolin and coauthors, Physical activity and colon cancer prevention: A meta-analysis, *British Journal of Cancer* 100 (2009): 611–616; J. B. Peel and coauthors, Cardiorespiratory fitness and digestive cancer mortality: Findings from the Aerobics Center Longitudinal Study, *Cancer Epidemiology Biomarkers Prevention,* March 17, 2009, e-pub ahead of print; S. Y. Pan and M. DesMeules, Energy intake, physical activity, energy balance, and cancer: Epidemiologic evidence, *Methods in Molecular Biology* 472 (2009): 191–215; P. L. Mai and coauthors, Physical activity and colon cancer risk among women in the California Teachers Study, *Cancer Epidemiology, Biomarkers and Prevention* 16 (2007): 517–525; B. L. Sprague and coauthors, Lifetime recreational and occupational physical activity and risk of in situ and invasive breast cancer, *Cancer Epidemiology, Biomarkers and Prevention* 16 (2007): 236–243.

98. J. B. Peel and coauthors, A prospective study of cardiorespiratory fitness and breast cancer mortality, *Medicine and Science in Sports and Exercise* 41 (2009): 742–748; K. C. Westerlind and N. I. Williams, Effect of energy deficiency on estrogen metabolism in premenopausal women, *Medicine and Science in Sports and Exercise* 39 (2007): 1090–1097; World Cancer Research Fund/American Institute for Cancer Research, *Food, Nutrition, Physical Activity and the Prevention of Cancer,* pp. 198–209.

99. World Cancer Research Fund/American Institute for Cancer Research, *Food, Nutrition, Physical Activity and the Prevention of Cancer,* pp. 277–280; P. Boffetta and M. Hashibe, Alcohol and cancer, *Lancet Oncology* 7 (2006): 149–156.

100. W. C. Willett and E. Giovannucci, Epidemiology of diet and cancer risk, in M. E. Shils and coeditors, *Modern Nutrition in Health and Disease* (Philadelphia: Lippincott Williams & Wilkins, 2006), pp. 1267–1279.

101. World Cancer Research Fund/American Institute for Cancer Research, *Food, Nutrition, Physical Activity and the Prevention of Cancer,* pp. 135–140; R. L. Prentice and coauthors, Low-fat dietary pattern and risk of invasive breast cancer: The Women's Health Initiative Randomized Controlled Dietary Modification Trial, *Journal of the American Medical Association* 295 (2006): 629–642; S. A. A. Beresford and coauthors, Low-fat dietary pattern and risk of colorectal cancer: The Women's Health Initiative Randomized Controlled Dietary Modification Trial, *Journal of the American Medical Association* 295 (2006): 634–654.

102. World Cancer Research Fund/American Institute for Cancer Research, *Food, Nutrition, Physical Activity and the Prevention of Cancer,* pp. 280–288; E. Theodoratou and coauthors, Dietary fatty acids and colorectal cancer: A case-control study, *American Journal of Epidemiology* 166 (2007): 181–195; R. S. Chapkin, D. N. McMurray, and J. R. Lupton, Colon cancer, fatty acids and anti-inflammatory compounds, *Current Opinion in Gastroenterology* 23 (2007): 48–54; J. Shannon and coauthors, Erythrocyte fatty acids and breast cancer risk: A case-control study in Shanghai, China, *American Journal of Clinical Nutrition* 85 (2007): 1090–1097.

103. R. Sinha and coauthors, Meat intake and mortality: A prospective study of over half a million people, *Archives of Internal Medicine* 169 (2009): 562–571; J. Hu and coauthors, Meat and fish consumption and cancer in Canada, *Nutrition and Cancer* 60 (2008): 313–324; R. L. Santarelli, F. Pierre, and D. E. Corpet, Processed meat and colorectal cancer: A review of epidemiologic and experimental evidence, *Nutrition and Cancer* 60 (2008): 131–144; World Cancer Research Fund/American Institute for Cancer Research, *Food, Nutrition, Physical Activity and the Prevention of Cancer,* pp. 280–288; A. J. Cross and coauthors, A prospective study of red and processed meat intake in relation to cancer risk, *PLoS Medicine* 4 (2007): e325.

104. N. G. Hord, Y. Tang, and N. S. Bryan, The physiologic context for potential health benefits, *American Journal of Clinical Nutrition* 90 (2009): 1–10.

105. S. Rohrmann, S. Hermann, and J. Linseisen, Heterocyclic aromatic amine intake increases colorectal adenoma risk: Findings from a prospective European cohort study, *American Journal of Clinical Nutrition* 89 (2009): 1418–1424.

106. S. E. Steck and coauthors, Cooked meat and risk of breast cancer: Lifetime versus recent dietary intake, *Epidemiology* 18 (2007): 373–382; J. S. Felton and M. G. Knize, A meat and potato war: Implication for cancer etiology, *Carcinogenesis* 27 (2006): 2367–2370.

107. L. B. Sansbury and coauthors, The effect of strict adherence to a high-fiber, high-fruit and -vegetable, and low-fat eating pattern on adenoma recurrence, *American Journal of Epidemiology* 170 (2009): 576–584; World Cancer Research Fund/American Institute for Cancer Research, *Food, Nutrition, Physical Activity and the Prevention of Cancer,* pp. 280–288.

108. Y. Park and coauthors, Fruit and vegetable intakes and risk of colorectal cancer in the NIH-AARP Diet and Health Study, *American Journal of Epidemiology* 166 (2007): 170–180; M. Rossi and coauthors, Flavonoids and colorectal cancer in Italy, *Cancer Epidemiology Biomarkers and Prevention* 15 (2006): 1555–1558.

109. World Cancer Research Fund/American Institute for Cancer Research, *Food, Nutrition, Physical Activity and the Prevention of Cancer,* pp. 106–107.

110. M. Huncharek, J. Muscat, and B. Kupelnick, Colorectal cancer risk and dietary intake of calcium, vitamin D, and dairy products: A meta-analysis of 26,335 cases from 60 observational studies, *Nutrition and Cancer* 61 (2009): 47–69.

111. M. E. Martinez and E. T. Jacobs, Calcium supplementation and prevention of colorectal neoplasia: Lessons from clinical trials (editorial), *Journal of the National Cancer Institute* 99 (2007): 99–100.

112. S. C. Larsson and coauthors, Calcium and dairy food intakes are inversely associated with colorectal cancer risk in the cohort of Swedish men, *American Journal of Clinical Nutrition* 83 (2006): 667–673.

113. C. F. Garland and coauthors, Vitamin D for cancer prevention: Global perspective, *Annals of Epidemiology* 19 (2009): 468–483; J. Ishihara and coauthors, Dietary calcium, vitamin D, and the risk of colorectal cancer, *American Journal of Clinical Nutrition* 88 (2008): 1576–1583; W. B. Grant, Epidemiology of disease risks in relation to vitamin D insufficiency, *Progress in Biophysics and Molecular Biology* 92 (2006): 65–79.

114. World Cancer Research Fund/American Institute for Cancer Research, *Food, Nutrition, Physical Activity and the Prevention of Cancer,* p. 284.

115. F. J. B. van Duijnhoven and coauthors, Fruit, vegetables, and colorectal cancer risk: The European Prospective Investigation into Cancer and Nutrition, *American Journal of Clinical Nutrition* 89 (2009): 1441–1452.

116. World Cancer Research Fund/American Institute for Cancer Research, *Food, Nutrition, Physical Activity and the Prevention of Cancer,* pp. 75–115.

117. U.S. Department of Health and Human Services, National Institutes of Health, National Heart, Lung, and Blood Institute, *Your Guide to Lowering Your Blood Pressure with DASH* (NIH Publication No. 06-4082, 2006).

118. The National Fruit and Vegetable Program, http://www.fruitsandveggiesmatter.gov.

CONSUMER CORNER 11

1. M. A. Alsawaf and A. Jatoi, Shopping for nutrition-based complementary and alternative medicine on the Internet: How much money might cancer patients be spending online? *Journal of Cancer Education* 22 (2007): 174–176.

2. National Institutes of Health, National Center for Complementary and Alternative Medicine, The use of complementary and alternative medicine in the United States, available at http://nccam.nih.gov/news/camstats/2007/camsurvey_fs1.htm; site updated December, 2008.

3. K. J. Kemper, S. Vohra, and R. Walls, The Task Force on Complementary and Alternative Medicine, The Provisional Section on Complementary, Holistic, and Integrative Medicine, *Pediatrics* 122 (2008): 1374–1386.

4. M. Tascilar and coauthors, Complementary and alternative medicine during cancer treatment: Beyond innocence, *Oncologist* 11 (2006): 732–741.

5. M. Day, Mapping the alternative route, *British Medical Journal* 334 (2007): 929–931.

6. S. Milazzo, S. Lejeune, and E. Ernst, Laetrile for cancer: A systematic review of the clinical evidence, *Supportive Care in Cancer* 15 (2007): 583–595.

7. National Center for Complementary and Alternative Medicine, Acupuncture for pain, May 2009, available at http://nccam.nih.gov/health/acupuncture/acupuncture-for-pain.htm; H. H. Moffet, How might acupuncture work? A systematic review of physiologic rationales from clinical trials, *BMC Complementary and Alternative Medicine* 6 (2006): 25.

8. D. M. Ribnicky and coauthors, Evaluation of botanicals for human health, *American Journal of Clinical Nutrition* 87 (2008): 472S–475S; M. Meadows, Cracking down on health fraud, *FDA Consumer,* November–December, 2006.

9. Meadows, Cracking down on health fraud.

10. R. B. Saper and coauthors, Lead, mercury, and arsenic in U.S.- and Indian-manufactured Ayurvedic medicines sold via the internet, *Journal of the American Medical Association* 300 (2008): 915–923.

11. U.S. Department of Health and Human Services, National Institutes of Health, National Center for Complementary and Alternative Medicine, *Herbs at a Glance: A Quick Guide to Herbal Supplements,* January 2009, NIH Publication No. 096248; I. Meijerman, J. H. Beijnen, and J. H. M. Schellens, Herb-drug interactions in oncology: Focus on mechanisms of induction, *Oncologist* 11 (2006): 742–752.

12. National Institutes of Health, National Center for Complementary and Alternative Medicine, Herbs at a glance, Ginkgo, available at http://nccam.nih.gov/health/ginkgo/ataglance.htm; site updated November, 2008; B. A. M. Messina, Herbal supplements: Facts and myths—talking to your patients about herbal supplements, *Journal of PeriAnesthesia Nursing* 21 (2006): 268–278.

CONTROVERSY 11

1. A. P. Feinberg, Epigenetics at the epicenter of modern medicine, *Journal of the American Medical Association* 299 (2008): 1345–1350; M. M. Bergmann, U. Görman, and J. C. Mathers, Bioethical considerations for human nutrigenomics, *Annual Review of Nutrition* 28 (2008): 447–467; J. P. Evans, Health care in the age of genetic medicine, *Journal of the American Medical Association* 298 (2007): 2670–2672.

2. S. B. Shurin and E. G. Nabel, Pharmacogenomics—Ready for prime time? *New England Journal of Medicine* 358 (2008): 1061–1063.

3. R. DeBusk, Diet-related disease, nutritional genomics and food and nutrition professionals, *Journal of the American Dietetic Association* 109 (2009): 410–413; S. Vakili and M. A. Caudill, Personalized nutrition: Nutritional genomics as a potential tool for targeted medical nutrition therapy, *Nutrition Reviews* 65 (2007): 301–315.

4. P. J. Stover and M. A. Caudill, Genetic and epigenetic contributions to human nutrition and health: Managing genome-diet interactions, *Journal of the American Dietetic Association* 108 (2008): 1480–1487; J. Kaput, Nutrigenomics–2006 update, *Clinical Chemistry and Laboratory Medicine* 45 (2007): 279–287.

5. G. W. Duff, Influence of genetics on disease susceptibility and progression, *Nutrition Reviews* 65 (2007): S177–S181; P. J. Gillies, Preemptive nutrition of pro-inflammatory states: A nutrigenomic model, *Nutrition Reviews* 65 (2007): S217–S220; T. A. Manolio, Study designs to enhance identification of genetic factors in healthy aging, *Nutrition Reviews* 65 (2007): S228–S233.

6. S. A. Ross and coauthors, Introduction: Diet, epigenetic events and cancer prevention, *Nutrition Reviews* 66 (2008): S1–S6.
7. G. T. Keusch, What do *–omics* mean for the science and policy of the nutritional sciences? *American Journal of Clinical Nutrition* 83 (2006): 520S–522S.
8. Centers for Disease Control and Prevention, Good laboratory practices for molecular genetic testing for heritable diseases and conditions, *Morbidity and Mortality Weekly Report* 58 (2009): 1–37.
9. Feinburg, Epigenetics at the epicenter of modern medicine.
10. L. R. Ferguson and M. Philpott, Nutrition and mutagenesis, *Annual Review of Nutrition* 28 (2008): 313–329.
11. E. S. Tai and coauthors, Polyunsaturated fatty acids interact with PPARA–L162V polymorphism to affect plasma triglyceride apolipoprotein C-III concentrations in the Framingham Heart Study, *Journal of Nutrition* 135 (2005): 397–403.
12. R. L. Jirtle and M. K. Skinner, Environmental epigenomics and disease susceptibility, *Nature Reviews Genetics* 8 (2007): 253–262.
13. G. P. Kauwell, Epigenetics: What it is and how it can affect dietetics practice, *Journal of the American Dietetic Association* 108 (2008): 1056–1059.
14. R. G. Gosden and A. P. Feinberg, Genetics and epigenetics—Nature's pen-and-pencil set, *New England Journal of Medicine* 356 (2007): 731–733.
15. R. A. Waterland and K. B. Michels, Epigenetic epidemiology of the developmental origins hypothesis, *Annual Review of Nutrition* 27 (2007): 363–388.
16. R. H. Dashwood and E. Ho, Dietary agents as histone deacetylase inhibitors: Sulforaphane and structurally related isothiocyanates, *Nutrition Reviews* 66 (2008): S36–S38.
17. World Cancer Research Fund/American Institute for Cancer Research, *Food, Nutrition, Physical Activity and the Prevention of Cancer: A Global Perspective* (Washington, D.C.: AICR, 2007), pp. 75–115.
18. B. Delage and R. H. Dashwood, Dietary manipulation of histone structure and function, *Annual Review of Nutrition* 28 (2008): 347–366.
19. M. Esteller, Epigenetics in cancer, *New England Journal of Medicine* 358 (2008): 1148–1159; L. Cobiac, Epigenomics and nutrition, *Forum of Nutrition* 60 (2007): 31–41.
20. S. Escott-Stump, A perspective on nutritional genomics, *Topics in Clinical Nutrition* 24 (2009): 92–113.
21. J. A. Waterland and R. Jirtle, Transposable elements: Targets for early nutritional effects on epigenetic gene regulation, *Molecular Cell Biology* 23 (2003): 5293–5300.
22. M. P. Hitchins and coauthors, Inheritance of a cancer-associated MLH1 germ-line epimutation, *New England Journal of Medicine* 356 (2007): 697–705.
23. Jirtle and Skinner, 2007.
24. Ross and coauthors, Introduction: Diet, epigenetic events and cancer prevention.
25. Waterland and Michels, Epigenetic epidemiology of the developmental origins hypothesis.
26. C. J. Field, Summary of a workshop, *American Journal of Clinical Nutrition* 89 (2009): 1533S–1539S.
27. Z. A. Kaminsky and coauthors, DNA methylation profiles in monozygotic and dizygotic twins, *Nature Genetics* 41 (2009): 240–245; S. Escott-Stump, A perspective on nutritional genomics, *Topics in Clinical Nutrition* 24 (2009): 240–245.
28. S. Vakili and M. A. Caudill, Personalized nutrition: Nutritional genomics as a potential tool for targeted medical nutrition therapy, *Nutrition Reviews* 65 (2009): 301–315; Bergmann, Görman, and Mathers, Bioethical considerations; J. M. Ordovas, Nutrigenetics, plasma lipids, and cardiovascular risk, *Journal of the American Dietetic Association* 106 (2006): 1074–1081.
29. S. Barrett, More criticism of dubious home genetic testing, *Consumer Health Digest,* 26 February 2008, available at www.quackwatch.org/00AboutQuackwatch/chd.html; United States Government Accountability Office, *Nutrigenetic Testing: Tests purchased from four Web sites mislead consumers,* 27 July 2006, available at www.gao.gov.
30. Bergmann, Görman, and Mathers, Bioethical considerations.
31. J. A. Satia and coauthors, Long-term use of β-carotene, retinol, lycopene, and lutein supplements and lung cancer risk: Results from the VITamins And Lifestyle (VITAL) Study, *American Journal of Epidemiology* 169 (2009): 815–828.
32. D. R. Jacobs and L. C. Tapsell, Food, not nutrients, is the fundamental unit in nutrition, *Nutrition Reviews* 65 (2007): 439–450.
33. DeBusk, Diet-related disease, nutritional genomics and food and nutrition professionals.

Chapter 12

1. Position of the American Dietetic Association: Food and water safety, *Journal of the American Dietetic Association* 109 (2009): 1449–1460.
2. Centers for Disease Control and Prevention, *FoodNet Surveillance Report for 2004,* June 2006, available at www.cdc.gov/foodnet/reports.htm.
3. U.S. Food and Drug Administration, CARVER + Shock: Enhancing Food Defense, *FDA Consumer Update,* June 15, 2007, available at www.fda.gov/consumer/updates/carvershock061107.html.
4. Centers for Disease Control and Prevention, Preliminary FoodNet Data on the Incidence of Infection with Pathogens Transmitted Commonly Through Food—10 States, 2006, *Morbidity and Mortality Weekly Report* 56 (2007): 336–339.
5. Centers for Disease Control and Prevention, Preliminary FoodNet Data on the Incidence of Infection with Pathogens Transmitted Commonly Through Food—10 States, 2008, *Morbidity and Mortality Weekly Report* 59 (2009): 333–337.
6. Centers for Disease Control and Prevention, Foodborne botulism from home-prepared fermented tofu—California, 2006, *Morbidity and Mortality Weekly Report* 56 (2007): 96–97.
7. L. Pray and A. Yaktine, Institutes of Medicine, *Managing Food Safety Practices from Farm to Table: Workshop Summary* (Washington, D.C.: National Academies Press, 2008).
8. Surveillance for foodborne-disease outbreaks—United States, 1998–2002, *Morbidity and Mortality Weekly Report* 55 (2006): 1–48.
9. Update: *E. coli* O157:H7 outbreak at Taco Bell Restaurants likely over: FDA traceback investigation continues, *FDA News,* December 14, 2006, available at www.fda.gov/bbs/topics/NEWS/2006/NEW01527.html.
10. C. S. DeWaal and K. Barlow, *Outbreak Alert! Closing the Gaps in Our Federal Food-Safety Net,* a publication of the Center for Science in the Public Interest, March 2004, available on the Internet at www.cspinet.org; Committee on the Review of the Use of Scientific Criteria and Performance Standards for Safe Food, Food and Nutrition Board, *Scientific Criteria to Ensure Safe Food* (Washington, D.C.: National Academies Press, 2003).
11. U.S. Food and Drug Administration, *Food Safety Facts for Consumers,* March 2007, available at www.cfsan.fda.gov/-dms/fs/-eggs.html.
12. D. W. Schaffner and K. M. Schaffner, Management of risk of microbial cross-contamination from uncooked frozen hamburgers by alcohol-based hand sanitizer, *Journal of Food Protection* 70 (2007): 109–113.
13. Only zap wet sponges to kill germs: Readers have disastrous results when they try to sterilize dry ones, More Health News:MSNBC.com, available at www.msnbc.msn.com/id/16796327.
14. M. Sharma, Personal communication, May 14, 2007; S. Durham, Best ways to clean kitchen sponges, USDA Agricultural Research Service News and Events, April 23, 2007, available at www.ars.usda.gov/is/pr/2007/070423.htm.
15. U.S. Food and Drug Administration, Barbeque basics: Tips to prevent foodborne illness, Consumer update, May 22, 2007, available at www.fda.gov/consumer/updates/bbqbasics052207.html.
16. L. McGinnis, Meat safety success story: It all works out in the wash, *Agricultural Research,* July 2008, p. 11.
17. J. C. Watts, A. Balachandran, and D. Westaway, The expanding universe of prion diseases, *PLoS Pathogens* 2 (2006): e26.
18. L. Manueulidis, A 25 nm virion is the likely cause of transmissible spongiform encephalopathies, *Journal of Cell Biochemistry* 100 (2007): 897–915; B. K. Patel and S. W. Liebman, "Prion-proof" for [PIN(+0]: Infection with vitro-made amyloid aggregates of Rnq1p-(132-405) induces [PIN(+)], *Journal of Molecular Biology* 365 (2007): 773–782; Executive Summary, *Advancing Prion Research: Guidance for the National Prion Research Program*

(Washington, D.C.: National Academies Press, 2004).
19. L. Bren, Agencies work to corral mad cow disease, *FDA Consumer,* May/June 2004, pp. 29–35.
20. Centers for Disease Control and Prevention, Preliminary FoodNet Data on the Incidence of Infection with Pathogens; G. Solomon, Eggs: Safety in numbers, *Washington-Post.Com,* April 4, 2007.
21. Centers for Disease Control and Prevention, *FoodNet Surveillance Report for 2004,* available at www.cdc.gov/foodnet/reports.htm.
22. FDA Improves Egg Safety, *FDA Consumer Updates,* July 7, 2009, available at www.fda.gov/ForConsumers/ConsumerUpdates/ucm170640.htm.
23. P. A. Orlandi and coauthors, Scientific Status Summary: Parasites and the food supply, *FoodTechnology* 56 (2002): 72–81.
24. Centers for Disease Control and Prevention, Preliminary FoodNet Data on the Incidence of Infection with Pathogens, 2007.
25. I. B. Hanning, J. D. Nutt, and S. C. Ricke, Salmonellosis outbreaks in the United States due to fresh produce: Sources and potential intervention measures, *Foodborne Pathogens and Disease* 6 (2009): 645–648.
26. Centers for Disease Control and Prevention, *E. coli* O157:H7 Outbreak from fresh spinach: Update on multi-state outbreak of *E. coli* O157:H7 infections from fresh spinach, September 28, 2006, available at www.cdc.gov/foodborne/ecolispinach/current.htm.
27. M. Meadows, How the FDA works to keep produce safe, *FDA Consumer,* March–April 2007, pp. 13–19; Centers for Disease Control and Prevention, Ongoing multi-state outbreak of *Escherichia coli* serotype O157:H7 infections associated with consumption of fresh spinach—United States, September 2006, *Morbidity and Mortality Weekly Report* 55 (2006): 1045–1046.
28. FDA, Statement of Robert E. Brackett, Ph.D., Director, Center for Food Safety and Applied Nutrition, Food and Drug Administration, November 15, 2006, available at www.fda.gov/ola/2006/foodsafety1115.html.
29. U.S. Food and Drug Administration, Guide to minimize microbial food safety hazards of fresh-cut fruits and vegetables, March 2007, available at www.cfsan.fda.gov/-tdms/prodgui3.html; Meadows, How the FDA works to keep produce safe; D. G. Maki, Don't eat the spinach—Controlling foodborne infectious diseases, *New England Journal of Medicine* 355 (2006): 1952–1955.
30. Food and Drug Administration, Acidic compounds with or without fatty acid surfactants, in *Safe Practices for Food Processes,* updated May 2009, available at www.fda.gov/Food/ScienceResearch/ResearchAreas/SafePracticesforFoodProcesses/default.htm.
31. D. Chua and coauthors, Fresh-cut lettuce in modified atmosphere packages stored at improper temperatures supports enterohemorrhagic *E. coli* isolates to survive gastric acid challenge, *Journal of Food Science* 73 (2008): M148–M153.
32. U.S. Food and Drug Administration, Warning on raw alfalfa sprouts, *Consumer Update,* April 28, 2009, available at www.fda.gov.
33. R. Tauxe, as interviewed by B. Liebman, Fear of fresh: How to avoid foodborne illness from fruits and vegetables, *Nutrition Action Healthletter,* December 2006, pp. 3–6.
34. American Council on Science and Health, *Irradiated Foods,* July 2007, available at www.acsh.org/publications/pubID.1562/pub_detail.asp.
35. U.S. Food and Drug Administration, On the road again: FDA's mobile laboratories, *FDA Consumer Health Information,* March 2009, available at www.fda.gov.
36. M. Wood, Environmental surveillance exposes a killer, *Agricultural Research,* July 2008, pp. 6–7.
37. Chua and coauthors, Fresh-cut lettuce in modified atmosphere packages.
38. M. Wood, For tomorrow's salads: Plan extracts to conquer microbes, *Agricultural Research,* July 2008, pp. 8–10.
39. Wood, Environmental surveillance exposes a killer; M. A. Rojas-Graü and coauthors, Mechanical, barrier, and antimicrobial properties of apple puree edible films containing plant essential oils, *Journal of Agriculture and Food Chemistry* 54 (2006): 9262–9267.
40. B. M. Keikotlhaile, P. Spanoghe, and W. Steurbaut, Effects of food processing on pesticide residues in fruits and vegetables: A meta-analysis approach, *Food and Chemical Toxicology* 48 (2010): 1–6.
41. U.S. Environmental Protection Agency, Pesticides: Regulating pesticides, August 2006, available at www.epa.gov/pesticides/regulating/tolerances.htm.
42. C. K. Winter and S. F. Davis, Scientific Status Summary: Organic foods, *Journal of Food Science* 71 (2006): R117–R124.
43. FDA Center for Veterinary Medicine, Report on the Food and Drug Administration's review of the safety of recombinant bovine somatropin, updated May 2007, www.fda.gov/cvm/RBRPTFNL.htm.
44. F. W. Danby, Acne, dairy and cancer, *Dermato-Endocrinology* 1 (2009): 12–16.
45. FDA Center for Veterinary Medicine, Report on the Food and Drug Administration's review of the safety of recombinant bovine somatotropin.
46. J. Vicini and coauthors, Survey of retail milk composition as affected by label claims regarding farm-management practices, *Journal of the American Dietetic Association* 108 (2008): 1198–1203.
47. L. Peeples, Bill proposed to limit livestock antibiotics to prevent the rise of resistant germs, July 14, 2009, available at www.scientificamerican.com.
48. Peeples, Bill proposed to limit livestock antibiotics.
49. American Cancer Society, Known and Probable Carcinogens, February 2007, available at www.cancer.org/docroot/PED/content/PED_1_3x_Known_and_Probable_Carcinogens.asp#known; Standing Committee on the Scientific Evaluation of Dietary Reference Intakes, Food and Nutrition Board, Institute of Medicine, *Dietary Reference Intakes for Vitamin A, Vitamin K, Arsenic, Boron, Chromium, Copper, Iodine, Iron, Manganese, Molybdenum, Nickel, Silicon, Vanadium, and Zinc* (Washington, D.C.: National Academies Press, 2001), pp. 503–510.
50. Standing Committee on the Scientific Evaluation of Dietary Reference Intakes, *Dietary Reference Intakes for Vitamin A, Vitamin K, Arsenic, Boron, Chromium, Copper, Iodine, Iron, Manganese, Molybdenum, Nickel, Silicon, Vanadium, and Zinc.*
51. R. L. Newsome, Assessing food chemical risks, *Food Technology* 63 (2009): 36–40.
52. B. C. Scudder and coauthors, Mercury in fish, bed sediment, and water from streams across the United States, 1998–2005, U.S. Geological Survey Scientific Investigations report 2009-5109, available at www.usgs.gov/pubprod.
53. D. R. Laks, Assessment of chronic mercury exposure within the U.S. population, National Health and Nutrition examination survey, 1999–2006, *Biometals* 22 (2009): 1103–1114.
54. Department of Agriculture, Mandatory Country of Origin Labeling of beef, pork, lamb, chicken, goat meat, wild and farm-raised fish and shellfish, perishable agricultural commodities, peanuts, pecans, ginseng, and macadamia nuts, *Federal Register* 74 (2009): 2658–2707.
55. R. Sinha and coauthors, Meat intake and mortality: A prospective study of over half a million people, *Archives of Internal Medicine* 169 (2009): 562–571; J. Hu and coauthors, Meat and fish consumption and cancer in Canada, *Nutrition and Cancer* 60 (2008): 313–324; R. L. Santarelli, F. Pierre, and D. E. Corpet, Processed meat and colorectal cancer: A review of epidemiologic and experimental evidence, *Nutrition and Cancer* 60 (2008): 131–144; World Cancer Research Fund/American Institute for Cancer Research, *Food, Nutrition, Physical Activity and the Prevention of Cancer,* pp. 280–288; A. J. Cross and coauthors, A prospective study of red and processed meat intake in relation to cancer risk, *PLoS Medicine* 4 (2007): e325.
56. L. O'Brien Nabors, Regulatory status of alternative sweeteners, *Food Technology,* May, 2007, pp. 24–32; Artificial sweeteners: No calories—sweet!, *FDA Consumer,* July–August 2006, pp. 27–28.
57. Fact Sheet: The report on carcinogens, 9th ed., National Institutes of Health News Release, available at www.nih.gov/news/pr/may2000/niehs-15.htm.
58. E. T. Rolls, Functional neuroimaging of umami taste: What makes umami pleasant? *American Journal of Clinical Nutrition* 90 (2009): 804S–813S.
59. K. Beyreuther and coauthors, Consensus meeting: Monosodium glutamate—an update, *European Journal of Clinical Nutrition* 61 (2007): 304–313.

60. U.S. Food and Drug Administration, Bisphenol A (BPA): Update on bisphenol A for use in food contact applications, *News and Events,* January 2010, available at www.fda.gov.
61. M. N. Riaz, M. Asif, and R. Ali, Stability of vitamins during extrusion, *Critical Reviews in Food Science and Nutrition* 49 (2009): 361–368.
62. Riaz, Asif, and Ali, Stability of vitamins during extrusion.

CONSUMER CORNER 12

1. C. Dimitri and L. Oberholtzer, Marketing U.S. organic foods: Recent trends from farms to consumers, *USDA Economic Information Bulletin* 58 (2009), available at www.ers.usda.gov.
2. C. K. Winter and S. E. Davis, Organic foods: Scientific Status Summary, *Journal of Food Science* 71 (2006): R117–R124.
3. M. T. Batte and coauthors, Putting their money where their mouths are: Consumer willingness to pay for multi-ingredient, processed organic food products, *Food Policy* 32 (2007): 145–159.
4. Winter and Davis, Organic foods.
5. C. Lu and coauthors, Organic diets significantly lower children's dietary exposure to organophosphorus pesticides, *Environmental Health Perspectives* 114 (2006): 260–263.
6. Winter and Davis, Organic foods.
7. Environmental Working Group, *Shoppers Guide to Pesticides in Produce,* 2006, available at www.foodnews.org.
8. A. D. Dangour and coauthors, Nutritional quality of organic foods: A systematic review, *American Journal of Clinical Nutrition* 90 (2009): 680–685.
9. D. M. Barrett and coauthors, Qualitative and nutritional differences in processing tomatoes grown under commercial organic and conventional production systems, *Journal of Food Science* 72 (2007): C441–C451.
10. A. E. Mitchell and coauthors, Ten-year comparison of the influence of organic and conventional crop management practices on the content of flavonoids in tomatoes, *Journal of Agricultural and Food Chemistry* 55 (2007): 6154–6159.
11. Dimitri and Oberholtzer, Marketing U.S. organic foods.
12. D. Zwerdling, In India: Bucking the "revolution" by going organic, Summary of the National Public Radio broadcast *Morning Edition,* June 1, 2009.
13. A. Mukherjee and coauthors, Longitudinal microbial survey of fresh produce grown by farmers in the upper Midwest, *Journal of Food Protection* 69 (2006): 1928–1936.

CONTROVERSY 12

1. Americans are more aware of sustainable food production: IFIC releases new 2008 food biotechnology survey, *Food Insight,* November/December 2008, available at www.ific.org.
2. G. Brookes and P. Barfoot, Global impact of biotech crops: Socio-economic and environmental effects in the first ten years of commercial use, *AgBioForum* 9 (2006): 139–151; Global outlook, Conversations about plant biotechnology, 2005–2006, available at www.monsanto.com/biotech-gmo/asp/globalOutlook.asp; R. Weiss, U.S. uneasy about biotech foods, *WashingtonPost.Com,* December 7, 2006, available at www.washingtonpost.com.
3. U.S. Food and Drug Administration, FDA issues final guidance on regulation of genetically engineered animals, *FDA Consumer Health Information,* January 15, 2009, available at www.fda.gov/consumer/updates/ge_animals011509.html.
4. Position of the American Dietetic Association: Agricultural and food biotechnology, *Journal of the American Dietetic Association* 106 (2006): 285–293.
5. The rice annotation project database, International Rice Genome Sequencing Project, 2006, available at http://rgp.dna.affrc.go.jp/E/IRGSP/rap-db1.html; International Rice Genome Sequencing Project, The map-based sequence of the rice genome, *Nature* 436 (2005): 793–800.
6. G. Tang and coauthors, Golden Rice is an effective source of vitamin A, *American Journal of Clinical Nutrition* 89 (2009): 1776–1783.
7. K. D. Hirschi, Nutrient biofortification of food crops, *Annual Review of Nutrition* 29 (2009): 401–421; P. J. White and M. R. Broadley, Biofortification of crops with seven mineral elements often lacking in human diets—iron, zinc, copper, calcium, magnesium, selenium and iodine, *New Phytologist* 182 (2009): 49–84.
8. U.S. Food and Drug Administration, FDA issues final guidance on regulation of genetically engineered animals.
9. U.S. Food and Drug Administration, Animal cloning and food safety, *Consumer Update,* January 15, 2008, available at www.fda.gov/consumer/updates/cloning011508.html.
10. Pew Initiative on Food and Biotechnology, 2007, available at http://pewagbiotech.org.
11. Union of Concerned Scientists, Protect our food: A campaign to take the harm out of pharma and industrial crops, available at www.ucsusa.org/food_and_environment/genetic_engineering/protect-our-food.html.
12. Resistance to Bt crops emerges, *Science News* 173 (2008): 144.
13. National Research Council and Institute of Medicine, *Safety of Genetically Engineered Foods: Approaches to Assessing Unintended Health Effects* (Washington, D.C.: National Academies Press, 2004), pp. 1–15.
14. Brookes and Barfoot, Global impact of biotech crops.
15. Discussions with farmers and experts around the world, Conversations about plant biotechnology, 2005–2006, available at www.monsanto.com/biotech-gmo/asp/experts.asp?id=KlausAmmann&strpint=true.
16. O. V. Singh and coauthors, Genetically modified crops: Success, safety assessment, and public concern, *Applied Microbiology and Biotechnology* 71 (2006): 598–607; Committee on Biological Confinement of Genetically Engineered Organisms of the National Research Council, *Biological Confinement of Genetically Engineered Organisms* (Washington, D.C.: National Academies Press, 2004), pp. 10–13.
17. FDA issues guidance to help prevent inadvertent introduction of allergens or toxins into the food and feed supply, *FDA News,* June 21, 2006, available at www.fda.gov/bbs/topics/NEWS/2006/NEW01393.html.
18. U.S. Food and Drug Administration, FDA issues final guidance on regulation of genetically engineered animals.

Chapter 13

1. J. Mendiola and coauthors, A low intake of antioxidant nutrients is associated with poor semen quality in patients attending fertility clinics, *Fertility and Sterility* 93 (2010): 1128–1133; S. Cordier, Evidence for a role of paternal exposures in developmental toxicity, *Basic and Clinical Pharmacology and Toxicology* 102 (2008): 176–181.
2. M. Viswanathan and coauthors, Outcomes of maternal weight gain, *Evidence Report/Technology Assessment* 168 (2008): 1–223; R. L. Goldenberg and J. F. Culhane, Low birth weight in the United States, *American Journal of Clinical Nutrition* 85 (2007): 584S–590S.
3. C. Bouchard, Childhood obesity: Are genetic differences involved? *American Journal of Clinical Nutrition* 89 (2009): 1494S–1501S; M. E. Symonds, T. Stephenson, and H. Budge, Early determinants of cardiovascular disease: The role of early diet in later blood pressure control, *American Journal of Clinical Nutrition* 89 (2009): 1518S–1522S; P. D. Gluckman and coauthors, Effect of in utero and early-life conditions on adult health and disease, *New England Journal of Medicine* 359 (2008): 61–73; M. R. Skilton, Intrauterine risk factors for precocious atherosclerosis, *Pediatrics* 121 (2008): 570–574; R. A. Waterland and K. B. Michels, Epigenetic epidemiology of the developmental origins hypothesis, *Annual Review of Nutrition* 27 (2007): 363–388.
4. D. S. Alam, Prevention of low birthweight, *Nestle Nutrition Workshop Series: Pediatric Program* 63 (2009): 209–225; E. M. Lundgren and T. Tuvemo, Effects of being born small for gestational age on long-term intellectual performance, *Best Practice and Research: Clinical Endocrinology and Metabolism* 22 (2008): 477–488; S. Tong, P. Baghurst, and A. McMichael, Birthweight and cognitive development during childhood, *Journal of Pediatrics and Child Health* 42 (2006): 98–103; R. E. K. Stein, M. J. Siegel, and L. J. Bauman, Are children of moderately low birth weight at increased risk for poor health? A new look at an old question, *Pediatrics* 118 (2006): 217–223.
5. M. Heron and coauthors, Deaths: Final data for 2006, *National Vital Statistics* Reports 57 (2009): 1–135.
6. L. M. McCowan and coauthors, Spontaneous preterm birth and small for gestational age infants in women who stop smoking early in pregnancy: Prospective cohort study, *British Medical Journal* 338 (2009): b1081.
7. Position of the American Dietetic Association: Nutrition and lifestyle for a healthy preg-

nancy outcome, *Journal of the American Dietetic Association* 108 (2008): 553–561; T. O. Scholl, Maternal nutrition before and during pregnancy, *Nestle Nutrition Workshop Series; Pediatrics Program* 61 (2008): 79–89; A. N. Kanade and coauthors, Maternal nutrition and birth size among urban affluent and rural women in India, *Journal of the American College of Nutrition* 27 (2008): 137–145.

8. D. K. Waller and coauthors, Prepregnancy obesity as a risk factor for structural birth defects, *Archives of Pediatrics and Adolescent Medicine* 161 (2007): 745–750; J. C. King, Maternal obesity, metabolism, and pregnancy outcomes, *Annual Review of Nutrition* 26 (2006): 271–291.

9. Position of the American Dietetic Association and American Society for Nutrition: Obesity, reproduction, and pregnancy outcomes, *Journal of the American Dietetic Association* 109 (2009): 918–927; King, Maternal obesity, metabolism, and pregnancy outcomes.

10. Position of the American Dietetic Association: Nutrition and lifestyle for a healthy pregnancy outcome, 553–556; E. A. Nohr and coauthors, Combined associations of prepregnancy body mass index and gestational weight gain with the outcome of pregnancy, *American Journal of Clinical Nutrition* 87 (2008): 1750–1759; S. Y. Chu and coauthors, Association between obesity during pregnancy and increased use of health care, *New England Journal of Medicine* 358 (2008): 1444–1453; King, Maternal obesity, metabolism, and pregnancy outcomes.

11. K. J. Stothard and coauthors, Maternal overweight and obesity and the risk of congenital anomalies: A systematic review and meta-analysis, *Journal of the American Medical Association* 301 (2009): 636–650; Waller and coauthors, Prepregnancy obesity as a risk factor for structural birth defects; T. Henriksen, Nutrition and pregnancy outcomes, *Nutrition Reviews* 64 (2006): S19–S23.

12. J. C. Cross and L. Mickelson, Nutritional influences on implantation and placental development, *Nutrition Reviews* 64 (2006): S12–S18.

13. S. H. Zeisel, Epigenetic mechanisms for nutrition determinants of later health outcomes, *American Journal of Clinical Nutrition* 89 (2009): 1488S–1493S.

14. Zeisel, Epigenetic mechanisms for nutrition determinants of later health outcomes; P. D. Gluckman and coauthors, Effect of in utero and early-life conditions on adult health and disease, *New England Journal of Medicine* 359 (2008): 61–73; C. Yajnik, Nutritional control of fetal growth, *Nutrition Reviews* 64 (2006): S50–S51.

15. Standing Committee on the Scientific Evaluation of Dietary Reference Intakes, Food and Nutrition Board, Institute of Medicine, *Dietary Reference Intakes for Energy, Carbohydrate, Fiber, Fat, Fatty Acids, Cholesterol, Protein, and Amino Acids* (Washington, D.C.: National Academies Press, 2005), pp. 185–194.

16. S. M. Innis and R. W. Freisen, Essential n-3 fatty acids in pregnant women and early visual acuity maturation in term infants, *American Journal of Clinical Nutrition* 87 (2008): 548–557; M. von Eijsden and coauthors, Maternal n-3, n-6 and *trans* fatty acid profile early in pregnancy and term birth weight: A prospective cohort study, *American Journal of Clinical Nutrition* 87 (2008): 887–895; E. Oken and coauthors, Associations of maternal fish intake during pregnancy and breastfeeding duration with attainment of developmental milestones in early childhood: A study from the Danish National Birth Cohort, *American Journal of Clinical Nutrition* 88 (2008): 789–796; S. M. Innis, Dietary (n-3) fatty acids and brain development, *Journal of Nutrition* 137 (2007): 855–859; R. Uauy and A. D. Dangour, Nutrition in brain development and aging: Role of essential fatty acids, *Nutrition Reviews* 64 (2006): S24–S33.

17. R. M. Pitkin, Folate and neural tube defects, *American Journal of Clinical Nutrition* 85 (2007): 285S–288S.

18. U.S. Preventive Services Task Force, Folic acid for the prevention of neural tube defects: U.S. Preventive Services Task Force Recommendation Statement, *Annals of Internal Medicine* 150 (2009): 626–631.

19. P. De Wals and coauthors, Reduction in neural-tube defects after folic acid fortification in Canada, *New England Journal of Medicine* 357 (2007): 135–142; J. I. Rader and B. O. Schneeman, Prevalence of neural tube defects, folate status, and folate fortification of enriched cereal-grain products in the United States, *Pediatrics* 117 (2006): 1394–1399; T. G. Bentley and coauthors, Population-level changes in folate intake by age, gender, and race/ethnicity after folic acid fortification, *American Journal of Public Health* 96 (2006): 2040–2047; M. Eichholzer, O. Tonz, and R. Zimmermann, Folic acid: A public health challenge, *Lancet* 367 (2006): 1352–1361.

20. A. J. Wilcox and coauthors, Folic acid supplements and risk of facial clefts: National population based case-control study, *British Medical Journal* 334 (2007): 464.

21. I. Elmadfa and I. Singer, Vitamin B-12 and homocysteine status among vegetarians: A global perspective, *American Journal of Clinical Nutrition* 89 (2009): 1693S–1698S.

22. A. M. Molloy and coauthors, Maternal vitamin B_{12} status and risk of neural tube defects in a population with high neural tube defect prevalence and no folic acid fortification, *Pediatrics* 123 (2009): 917–923.

23. C. L. Wagner and F. R. Greer, and the Section on Breastfeeding and Committee on Nutrition, Prevention of rickets and vitamin D deficiency in infants, children, and adolescents, *Pediatrics* 122 (2008): 1142–1152; C. S. Kovacs, Vitamin D in pregnancy and lactation: Maternal, fetal, and neonatal outcomes from human and animal studies, *American Journal of Clinical Nutrition* 88 (2008): 520S–528S.

24. L. M. Bodnar and coauthors, High prevalence of vitamin D insufficiency in black and white pregnant women residing in the northern United States and their neonates, *Journal of Nutrition* 137 (2007): 447–452.

25. K. O. O'Brien and coauthors, Bone calcium turnover during pregnancy and lactation in women with low calcium diets is associated with calcium intake and circulating insulin-like growth factor 1 concentrations, *American Journal of Clinical Nutrition* 83 (2006): 317–323.

26. K. J. Collard, Iron homeostasis in the neonate, *Pediatrics* 123 (2009): 1208–1216.

27. S. Mahajan and coauthors, Nutritional anaemia dysregulates endocrine control of fetal growth, *British Journal of Nutrition* 100 (2008): 408–417; F. M. Rioux and C. P. LeBlanc, Iron supplementation during pregnancy: What are the risks and benefits of current practices? *Applied Physiology, Nutrition and Metabolism* 32 (2007): 282–288.

28. C. M. Donangelo and coauthors, Zinc absorption and kinetics during pregnancy and lactation in Brazilian women, *American Journal of Clinical Nutrition* 82 (2005): 118–124.

29. D. Shah and H.P.S. Sachdev, Zinc deficiency in pregnancy and fetal outcome, *Nutrition Reviews* 64 (2006): 15–30.

30. Position of the American Dietetic Association, Nutrition and lifestyle for a healthy pregnancy outcome.

31. WIC, The Special Supplemental Nutrition Program for Women, Infants, and Children, available at www.fns.usda.gov/fns, updated April 2009.

32. A. Jacknowitz, D. Novillo, and L. Tiehen, Special supplemental nutrition program for women, infants, and children and infant feeding practices, *Pediatrics* 119 (2007): 281–288.

33. Institute of Medicine, *Weight Gain During Pregnancy: Reexamining the Guidelines* (Washington, D.C.: The National Academies Press, 2009).

34. Position of the American Dietetic Association and American Society for Nutrition: Obesity, reproduction, and pregnancy outcomes, *Journal of the American Dietetic Association* 109 (2009): 918–927; S. Y. Chu and coauthors, Gestational weight gain by bodymass index among U.S. women delivering live births, 2004–2005: Fueling future obesity, *American Journal of Obstetrics and Gynecology* 200 (2009): 271, e1–e7; C. M. Olson, Achieving a healthy weight gain during pregnancy, *Annual Review of Nutrition* 28 (2008): 411–423; D. A. Krummel, Postpartum weight control: A vicious cycle, *Journal of the American Dietetic Association* 107 (2007): 37–40.

35. Position of the American Dietetic Association and American Society for Nutrition: Obesity, reproduction, and pregnancy outcomes, *Journal of the American Dietetic Association* 109 (2009): 918–927.

36. Position of the American Dietetic Association and American Society for Nutrition: Obesity, reproduction, and pregnancy outcomes.

37. J. H. Cohen and H. Kim, Sociodemographic and health characteristics associated with attempting weight loss during pregnancy, *Preventing Chronic Disease* 6 (2009): A07.

38. Position of the American Dietetic Association and American Society for Nutrition: Obesity, reproduction, and pregnancy outcomes; M. Viswanathan and coauthors, Outcomes of maternal weight gain, *Evidence Report/Technology Assessment* 168 (2008): 1–223; J. L. Baker and coauthors, Breastfeeding reduces postpartum weight retention, *American Journal of Clinical Nutrition* 88 (2008): 1543–1551.
39. Krummel, Postpartum weight control; E. Villamor and S. Cnattingius, Interpregnancy weight change and risk of adverse pregnancy outcomes: A population-based study, *Lancet* 368 (2006): 1164–1170.
40. Krummel, Postpartum weight control; A. R. Amorium and coauthors, Does excess pregnancy weight gain constitute a major risk for increasing long-term BMI? *Obesity* 15 (2007): 1278–1286.
41. American College of Sports Medicine, Roundtable Consensus Statement, Impact of physical activity during pregnancy and postpartum on chronic disease risk, *Medicine and Science in Sports and Exercise* 38 (2006): 989–1006; R. Artal and M. O'Toole, Guidelines of the American College of Obstetricians and Gynecologists for exercise during pregnancy and the postpartum period, *British Journal of Sports Medicine* 37 (2003): 6–12; American College of Obstetricians and Gynecologists, Exercise during pregnancy and the postpartum period, ACOG Committee Opinion No. 267, *Obstetrics and Gynecology* 99 (2002): 171–173.
42. A. B. Granath, M. S. Hellgren, and R. K. Gunnarsson, Water aerobics reduces sick leave due to low back pain during pregnancy, *Journal of Obstetric, Gynecologic, and Neonatal Nursing,* 35 (2006): 465–471; S. A. Smith and Y. Michel, A pilot study on the effects of aquatic exercises on discomforts of pregnancy, *Journal of Obstetric, Gynecologic, and Neonatal Nursing* 35 (2006): 315–323.
43. J. A. Martin and coauthors, Births: Final data for 2006, *National Vital Statistics Reports* 57 (2009): 1–102.
44. P. N. Baker and coauthors, A prospective study of micronutrient status in adolescent pregnancy, *American Journal of Clinical Nutrition* 89 (2009): 1114–1124; S. Saintonge, H. Bang, and L. M. Gerber, Implications of a new definition of vitamin D deficiency in a multiracial U.S. adolescent population: The National Health and Nutrition Examination Survey III, *Pediatrics* 123 (2009): 797–803.
45. Quickstats—Birthrates among females aged 15–19 years, by state—United States, 2004, *Morbidity and Mortality Weekly Report* 55 (2007): 1383.
46. X. Chen and coauthors, Paternal age and adverse birth outcomes: Teenager or 40+, who is at risk? *Human Reproduction* 23 (2008): 1290–1296.
47. J. N. Nielsen and coauthors, Interventions to improve diet and weight gain among pregnant adolescents and recommendations for future research, *Journal of the American Dietetic Association* 106 (2006): 1825–1840.
48. National Research Council, Institute of Medicine, *Influence of Pregnancy Weight on Maternal and Child Health* (Washington, D.C.: National Academies Press, 2007).
49. E. P. Gunderson and coauthors, Longitudinal study of growth and adiposity in parous compared with nulligravid adolescents, *Archives of Pediatrics and Adolescent Medicine* 163 (2009): 349–356.
50. M. E. Mills, Craving more than food: The implications of pica in pregnancy, *Nursing for Women's Health* 11 (2007): 266–273.
51. Mills, Craving more than food.
52. J. A. Martin and coauthors, Annual summary of vital statistics: 2008, *Pediatrics* 121 (2008): 788–801.
53. J. M. Rogers, Tobacco and pregnancy: Overview of exposures and effects, *Birth Defects Research* (Part C) 84 (2008): 1–15.
54. Rogers, Tobacco and pregnancy; R. A. de la Chica and coauthors, Chromosomal instability in amniocytes from fetuses of mothers who smoke, *Journal of the American Medical Association* 293 (2005): 1212–1222.
55. M. J. Rivkin and coauthors, Volumetric MRI study of brain in children with intrauterine exposure to cocaine, alcohol, tobacco, and marijuana, *Pediatrics* 121 (2008): 741–750.
56. Rogers, Tobacco and pregnancy.
57. H. Moshammer and coauthors, Parental smoking and lung function in children: An international study, *American Journal of Respiratory and Critical Care Medicine* 173 (2006): 1184–1185.
58. Rogers, Tobacco and pregnancy; American Academy of Pediatrics, Task Force on Sudden Infant Death Syndrome, The changing concept of sudden infant death syndrome: Diagnostic coding shifts, controversies regarding the sleeping environment, and new variables to consider in reducing risk, *Pediatrics* 116 (2005): 1245–1255.
59. Rogers, Tobacco and pregnancy.
60. Position of the American Dietetic Association, Nutrition and lifestyle for a healthy pregnancy outcome.
61. Rivkin and coauthors, Volumetric MRI study of brain in children with intrauterine exposure; H. S. Bada and coauthors, Impact of prenatal cocaine exposure on child behavior problems through school age, *Pediatrics* 119 (2007): e348; B. A. Lewis and coauthors, Prenatal cocaine and tobacco effects on children' language trajectories, *Pediatrics* 120 (2007): e78.
62. G. A. Richardson, L. Goldschmidt, and C. Larkby, Effects of prenatal cocaine exposure on growth: A longitudinal analysis, *Pediatrics* 120 (2007): e1017.
63. T. I. Halldorsson and coauthors, Is high consumption of fatty fish during pregnancy a risk factor for fetal growth retardation? A study of 44,824 Danish pregnant women, *American Journal of Epidemiology* 166 (2007): 687–696.
64. E. Oken and coauthors, Maternal fish intake during pregnancy, blood mercury levels, and child cognition at age 3 years in a U.S. cohort, *American Journal of Epidemiology* 167 (2008): 1171–1181; J. R. Hibbeln and coauthors, Maternal seafood consumption in pregnancy and neurodevelopmental outcomes in childhood (ALSPAC study): An observational cohort study, *Lancet* 369 (2007): 578–585; D. Mozaffarian and E. B. Rimm, Fish intake, contaminants, and human health: Evaluating the risks and the benefits, *Journal of the American Medical Association* 296 (2006): 1885–1899; Institute of Medicine report brief, *Seafood Choices: Balancing Benefits and Risks,* October, 2006.
65. Position of the American Dietetic Association, Nutrition and lifestyle for a healthy pregnancy outcome.
66. X. Weng, R. Odouli, and D. Li, Maternal caffeine consumption during pregnancy and the risk of miscarriage: A prospective cohort study, *American Journal of Obstetrics and Gynecology* 198 (2008): 279.e1–279.e8; M. L. Browne, Maternal exposure to caffeine and risk of congenital anomalies: A systematic review, *Epidemiology* 17 (2006): 324–331; A. Matijasevich and coauthors, Maternal caffeine consumption and fetal death: A case-control study in Uruguay, *Paediatric and Perinatal Epidemiology* 20 (2006): 100–109; B. H. Bech and coauthors, Coffee and fetal death: A cohort study with prospective data, *American Journal of Epidemiology* 162 (2005): 983–990.
67. CARE Study Group, Maternal caffeine intake during pregnancy and risk of fetal growth restriction: A large prospective observational study, *British Medical Journal* 337 (2008): a2332.
68. J. Gareri and coauthors, Potential role of the placenta in fetal alcohol spectrum disorder, *Paediatric Drugs* 11 (2009): 26–29; F. T. Crews and K. Nixon, Foetal alcohol spectrum disorders and alterations in brain and behaviour, *Alcohol and Alcoholism* 44 (2009): 108–114.
69. H. E. Hoyme and coauthors, A practical approach to diagnosis of fetal alcohol spectrum disorders: Clarification of the 1996 Institute of Medicine criteria, *Pediatrics* 115 (2005): 39–47.
70. C. H. Denny and coauthors, Alcohol use among pregnant and nonpregnant women of childbearing age—United States, 1991–2005, *Morbidity and Mortality Weekly Report* 58 (2009): 529–532; Centers for Disease Control, Fetal alcohol syndrome, www.cdc.gov/ncbddd/fas/fasask.htm, site visited May 29, 2009.
71. Hoyme and coauthors, A practical approach to diagnosis of fetal alcohol spectrum disorders.
72. Denny and coauthors, Alcohol use among pregnant and nonpregnant women.
73. M. H. Aliyu and coauthors, Alcohol consumption during pregnancy and the risk of early stillbirth among singletons, *Alcohol* 42 (2008): 369–374.
74. J. Kitzmiller and coauthors, Managing preexisting diabetes for pregnancy: Summary of evidence and consensus recommendations for care, *Diabetes Care* 31 (2008): 1060–1079.
75. The HAPO Study Cooperative Research Group, Hyperglycemia and adverse pregnancy outcomes, *New England Journal of Medicine* 358 (2008): 1991–2002; V. Seshiah and coauthors,

F

"Abnormal" fasting plasma glucose during pregnancy, *Diabetes Care* 31 (2008): e92.

76. Kitzmiller and coauthors, Managing preexisting diabetes for pregnancy.

77. Kitzmiller and coauthors, Managing preexisting diabetes for pregnancy.

78. Position statement, Standards of medical care in diabetes—2008, *Diabetes Care* 31 (2008): S12–S54.

79. Centers for Disease Control and Prevention, *Diabetes: At a glance 2009,* available at www.ced.gov/nccdphp/publications/aag/ddt.htm.

80. C. Mulholland and coauthors, Comparison of guidelines available in the United States for diagnosis and management of diabetes before, during, and after pregnancy, *Journal of Women's Health* 16 (2007): 790–801.

81. The HAPO Study Cooperative Research Group, Hyperglycemia and adverse pregnancy outcomes.

82. American Diabetes Association, Diagnosis and classification of diabetes mellitus, *Diabetes Care* 31 (2008): S55–S60.

83. P. E. Marik, Hypertensive disorders of pregnancy, *Postgraduate Medicine* 121 (2009): 69–76.

84. B. M. Sibai, Caring for women with hypertension, *Journal of the American Medical Association* 298 (2007): 1566–1568.

85. Position of the American Dietetic Association, Nutrition and lifestyle for a healthy pregnancy outcome.

86. Position of the American Dietetic Association, Nutrition and lifestyle for a healthy pregnancy outcome.

87. O'Brien and coauthors, Bone calcium turnover during pregnancy and lactation.

88. F. R. Greer, S. H. Sicherer, A. Wesley Burks, and the Committee on Nutrition and Section on Allergy and Immunology, Effects of early nutritional interventions on the development of atopic disease in infants and children: The role of maternal dietary restriction, breastfeeding, timing of introduction of complementary foods, and hydrolyzed formulas, *Pediatrics* 121 (2008): 183–191.

89. Greer and coauthors, Effects of early nutritional interventions.

90. J. Baker and coauthors, Breastfeeding reduces postpartum weight retention, *American Journal of Clinical Nutrition* 88 (2008): 1543–1551.

91. D. Su and coauthors, Breast-feeding mothers can exercise: Results of a cohort study, *Public Health Nutrition* 10 (2007): 1089–1093.

92. American College of Sports Medicine, Roundtable Consensus Statement, Impact of physical activity during pregnancy and postpartum.

93. American Academy of Pediatrics, Policy statement: Breastfeeding and the use of human milk, *Pediatrics* 115 (2005): 496–506.

94. American Academy of Pediatrics, Policy statement.

95. R. Lesnewski and L. Prine, Initiating hormonal contraception, *American Family Physician* 74 (2006): 1196–1205.

96. American Academy of Pediatrics, Policy statement.

97. American Academy of Pediatrics, Policy statement.

98. P. L. Havens, L. M. Mofenson, and the Committee on Pediatric AIDS, *Pediatrics* 123 (2009): 175–187.

99. World Health Organization, *HIV and Infant Feeding,* available at http://www.who.int/child_adolescent_health/topics/prevention_care/child/nutrition/hivif/en/, site visited June 1, 2009; M. W. Kline, Early exclusive breastfeeding: Still the cornerstone of child survival, *American Journal of Clinical Nutrition* 89 (2009): 1281–1282.

100. Formula feeding of term infants, in *Pediatric Nutrition Handbook,* 6th ed., R. E. Kleinman, ed. (Elk Grove Village, Ill.: American Academy of Pediatrics, 2009), pp. 61–78.

101. Position of the American Dietetic Association: Promoting and supporting breastfeeding, *Journal of the American Dietetic Association* 109 (2009): 1926–1942.

102. Breastfeeding, in *Pediatric Nutrition Handbook,* 6th ed., pp. 29–59; Position of the American Dietetic Association, Promoting and supporting breastfeeding; American Academy of Pediatrics, Policy statement.

103. Breastfeeding, in *Pediatric Nutrition Handbook,* 6th ed.; American Academy of Pediatrics, Policy statement.

104. American Academy of Pediatrics, Policy statement.

105. S. M. Donovan, Human milk oligosaccharides—the plot thickens, *British Journal of Nutrition* 101 (2009): 1267–1269.

106. S. M. Innis, Dietary (n-3) fatty acids and brain development, *Journal of Nutrition* 137 (2007): 855–859.

107. S. E. Carlson, Early determinants of development: A lipid perspective, *American Journal of Clinical Nutrition* 89 (2009): 1523S–1529S; K. Simmer, S. K. Patole, and S. C. Rao, Longchain polyunsaturated fatty acid supplementation in infants born at term, *Cochrane Database of Systematic Reviews* January 23, 2008, CD000376; S. M. Innis, Dietary (n-3) fatty acids and brain development, *Journal of Nutrition* 137 (2007): 855–859; M. S. Fewtrell, Long-chain polyunsaturated fatty acids in early life: Effects on multiple health outcomes, in *Primary Prevention by Nutrition Intervention in Infancy and Childhood,* A. Lucas and H. A. Sampson, eds., *Nestle Nutrition Workshop Series Pediatric Program* 57 (2006): 203–221.

108. E. E. Birch and coauthors, Visual acuity and cognitive outcomes at 4 years of age in a double-blind, randomized trial of long-chain polyunsaturated fatty acid-supplemented infant formula, *Early Human Development* 83 (2007): 279–284.

109. Simmer, Patole, and Rao, Longchain polyunsaturated fatty acid supplementation; A. Singhal and coauthors, Infant nutrition and stereoacuity at 4–6 years, *American Journal of Clinical Nutrition* 85 (2007): 152–159.

110. L. A. Hanson, Session 1: Feeding and infant development, breast-feeding and immune function, *Proceedings of the Nutrition Society* 66 (2007): 384–396.

111. Fat-soluble vitamins, in *Pediatric Nutrition Handbook,* 6th ed., pp. 461–474.

112. C. L. Wagner, and F. R. Greer, and the Section on Breastfeeding and Committee on Nutrition, Prevention of rickets and vitamin D deficiency in infants, children, and adolescents, *Pediatrics* 122 (2008): 1142–1152.

113. Breastfeeding, in *Pediatric Nutrition Handbook,* 6th ed.; Position of the American Dietetic Association, Promoting and supporting breastfeeding; American Academy of Pediatrics, Policy statement.

114. K. Sadeharju and coauthors, Maternal antibodies in breast milk protect the child from enterovirus infections, *Pediatrics* 119 (2007): 941–946.

115. D. S. Newburg, G. M. Ruiz-Palacios, and A. L. Morrow, Human milk glycans protect infants against enteric pathogens, *Annual Review of Nutrition* 25 (2005): 37–58.

116. Breastfeeding, in *Pediatric Nutrition Handbook,* 6th ed.; Hanson, Session 1: Feeding and infant development, breast-feeding and immune function; C. J. Chantry, C. R. Howard, and P. Auinger, Full breastfeeding duration and associated decrease in respiratory tract infection in U.S. children, *Pediatrics* 117 (2006): 425–432; Position of the American Dietetic Association, Promoting and supporting breastfeeding; American Academy of Pediatrics, Policy statement.

117. Greer and coauthors, Effects of early nutritional interventions.

118. Greer and coauthors, Effects of early nutritional interventions; R. S. Zeiger and N. J. Friedman, The relationship of breastfeeding to the development of atopic disorders, *Nestlé Nutrition Workshop Series: Pediatric Program* 57 (2006): 93–108.

119. Greer and coauthors, Effects of early nutritional interventions; A. C. Krakowski and coauthors, Management of atopic dermatitis in the pediatric population, *Pediatrics* 122 (2008): 812–824.

120. D. A. Leon and G. Ronalds, Breastfeeding influences on later life—cardiovascular disease, *Advances in Experimental Medicine and Biology* 639 (2009): 153–166; C. G. Owen and coauthors, Does initial breastfeeding lead to lower blood cholesterol in adult life? A quantitative review of the evidence, *American Journal of Clinical Nutrition* 88 (2008): 305–314; L. Schack-Nielsen and K. F. Michaelsen, Advances in our understanding of the biology of human milk and its effects on the offspring, *Journal of Nutrition* 137 (2007): 503S–510S; R A. Singhal, Early nutrition and long-term cardiovascular health, *Nutrition Reviews* 64 (2006): S44–S49.

121. B. Koletzko and coauthors, Can infant feeding choices modulate later obesity risk? *American Journal of Clinical Nutrition* 89 (2009): 1502S–1508S; A. S. Ryan, Breastfeeding and the risk of childhood obesity, *Collegium*

Antropologicum 31 (2007): 19–28; S. Scholtens and coauthors, Breastfeeding, weight gain in infancy, and overweight at seven years of age: The prevention and incidence of asthma and mite allergy birth cohort study, *American Journal of Epidemiology* 165 (2007): 919–926; A. M. Toschke and coauthors, Infant feeding method and obesity: Body mass index and dual-energy X-ray absorptiometry measurements at 9–10 y of age from the Avon Longitudinal Study of Parents and Children (ALSPAC), *American Journal of Clinical Nutrition* 85 (2007): 1578–1585; R. Novotny and coauthors, Breastfeeding is associated with lower body mass index among children of the Commonwealth of the Northern Mariana Islands, *Journal of the American Dietetic Association* 107 (2007): 1743–1746; K. B. Michels and coauthors, A longitudinal study of infant feeding and obesity throughout life course, *International Journal of Obesity* 31 (2007): 1078–1085.

122. C. G. Owen and coauthors, Effect of infant feeding on the risk of obesity across the life course: A quantitative review of published evidence, *Pediatrics* 115 (2005): 1367–1377.

123. T. Harder and coauthors, Duration of breastfeeding and risk of overweight: A meta-analysis, *Journal of Epidemiology* 162 (2005): 397–403.

124. Ryan, Breastfeeding and the risk of childhood obesity.

125. L. Schack-Nielsen and K. F. Michaelsen, Advances in our understanding of the biology of human milk and its effects on the offspring, *Journal of Nutrition* 137 (2007): 503S–513S; G. Der, G. D. Batty, and I. J. Deary, Effect of breast feeding on intelligence in children: Prospective study, sibling pairs, analysis, and meta-analysis, *British Medical Journal* 333 (2006): 929–930.

126. Schack-Nielsen and Michaelsen, Advances in our understanding of the biology of human.

127. Formula feeding of term infants, in *Pediatric Nutrition Handbook,* 6th ed.

128. Formula feeding of term infants, in *Pediatric Nutrition Handbook,* 6th ed.; L. Seppo and coauthors, A follow-up study of nutrient intake, nutritional status, and growth in infants with cow milk allergy fed either a soy formula or an extensively hydrolyzed whey formula, *American Journal of Clinical Nutrition* 82 (2005): 140–145.

129. Formula feeding of term infants, in *Pediatric Nutrition Handbook,* 6th ed.; Seppo and coauthors, A follow-up study of nutrient intake.

130. Formula feeding of term infants, in *Pediatric Nutrition Handbook,* 6th ed.

131. Complementary feeding, in *Pediatric Nutrition Handbook,* 6th ed., pp. 113–142.

132. Iron, in *Pediatric Nutrition Handbook,* 6th ed., pp. 403–422.

133. Complementary feeding, in *Pediatric Nutrition Handbook,* 6th ed.

134. Feeding the child, in *Pediatric Nutrition Handbook,* 6th ed., pp. 145–174.

135. Feeding the child, in *Pediatric Nutrition Handbook,* 6th ed.

136. Complementary feeding, in *Pediatric Nutrition Handbook,* 6th ed.; A. Fiocchi, A. Assa'ad, and S. Bahna, Food allergy and the introduction of solid foods to infants: A consensus document, *Annals of Allergy, Asthma and Immunology* 97 (2006): 10–21.

CONSUMER CORNER 13

1. L. Rowell, V. J. Rock, and L. Grummer-Strawn, Changes in public attitudes toward breastfeeding in the United States, *Journal of the American Dietetic Association* 107 (2007): 122–127.

2. A. Avery and coauthors, Confident commitment is a key factor for sustained breastfeeding, *Birth* 36 (2009): 141–148.

3. Centers for Disease Control and Prevention, National Center for Health Statistics, M. M. McDowell, C. Wang, and J. Kennedy-Stephenson, Breastfeeding in the United States: Findings from the National Health and Nutrition Examination Surveys, 1999–2006, *NCHS Data Brief,* No. 5, April 2008, available at www.cdc.gov/nchs/fastats/Default.htm; Position of the American Dietetic Association, Promoting and supporting breastfeeding, *Journal of the American Dietetic Association* 105 (2005): 810–818; American Academy of Pediatrics, Policy statement, Breastfeeding and the use of human milk, *Pediatrics* 115 (2005): 496–506.

4. Centers for Disease Control and Prevention, National Center for Health Statistics, and coauthors, Breastfeeding in the United States.

5. Breastfeeding, in *Pediatric Nutrition Handbook,* 6th R. E. Kleinman, ed. (Elk Grove Village, Ill: American Academy of Pediatrics, 2009), pp. 29–59.

CONTROVERSY 13

1. C. L. Ogden and coauthors, Prevalence of high body mass index in U.S. children and adolescents, *Journal of the American Medical Association* 303 (2010): 242–249; C. L. Ogden, M. D. Carroll, and K. M. Flegal, High body mass index for age among U.S. children and adolescents, 2003–2006, *Journal of the American Medical Association* 299 (2008): 2401-2405.

2. P. W. Franks and coauthors, Childhood obesity, other cardiovascular risk factors, and premature death, *New England Journal of Medicine* 362 (2010): 485–493; D. S. Freedman and coauthors, Cardiovascular risk factors and excess adiposity among overweight children and adolescents: The Bogalusa Heart Study, *Journal of Pediatrics* 150 (2007): 12–17; C. L. Ogden and coauthors, Prevalence of overweight and obesity in the United States, 1999–2004, *Journal of the American Medical Association* 295 (2006): 1549–1555.

3. B. M. Popkin, Recent dynamics suggest selected countries catching up to U.S. obesity, *American Journal of Clinical Nutrition* 91 (2010): 284S–288S; C. Bouchard, Childhood obesity: Are genetic differences involved? *American Journal of Clinical Nutrition* 89 (2009): 1494S–1501S; W. Maziak, K. D. Ward, and M. B. Stockton, Childhood obesity: Are we missing the big picture? *Obesity Reviews* 9 (2008): 35–42; Y. Wang and T. Lobstein, Worldwide trends in childhood overweight and obesity, *International Journal of Pediatric Obesity* 1 (2006): 11–25.

4. Y. Wang and M. A. Beydoun, The obesity epidemic in the United States—gender, age, socioeconomic, racial/ethnic, and geographic characteristics: A systematic review and meta-regression analysis, *Epidemiologic Reviews* 29 (2007): 6–28.

5. D. S. Freedman and coauthors, Racial and ethnic differences in secular trends for childhood BMI, weight, and height, *Obesity* 14 (2006): 301–308.

6. A. R. Ness and coauthors, Objectively measured physical activity and fat mass in a large cohort of children, *PLoS Medicine* 4 (2007): e97.

7. Wang and Beydoun, The obesity epidemic in the United States.

8. S. E. Barlow and the Expert Committee, Expert Committee recommendations regarding the prevention, assessment, and treatment of child and adolescent overweight and obesity: Summary report, *Pediatrics* 120 (2007): S164–S192.

9. Centers for Disease Control and Prevention, Prevalence of abnormal lipid levels among youths—United States, 1999–2006, *Morbidity and Mortality Weekly Report* 59 (2010): 29–33; W. Insull, Jr., The pathology of atherosclerosis: Plaque development and plaque responses to medical treatment, *American Journal of Medicine* 122 (2009): S3–S14.

10. M. Salvadori and coauthors, Elevated blood pressure in relation to overweight and obesity among children in a rural Canadian community, *Pediatrics* 122 (2008): e821–e827; R. Jago and coauthors, Prevalence of abnormal lipid and blood pressure values among an ethnically diverse population of eighth-grade adolescents and screening implications, *Pediatrics* 117 (2006): 2065–2073.

11. D. S. Freedman and coauthors, Risk factors and adult body mass index among overweight children: The Bogalusa Heart Study, *Pediatrics* 123 (2009): 750–757; H. Zhu and coauthors, Relationships of cardiovascular phenotypes with healthy weight, at risk of overweight, and overweight in U.S. youths, *Pediatrics* 121 (2008): 115–122; Freedman and coauthors, Cardiovascular risk factors and excess adiposity.

12. R. R. Pate and coauthors, Cardiorespiratory fitness levels among U.S. youth 12 to 19 years of age, *Archives of Pediatrics and Adolescent Medicine* 160 (2006): 1005–1012.

13. M. Neovius, J. Sundström, and F. Rasmussen, Combined effects of overweight and smoking in late adolescence on subsequent mortality: Nationwide cohort study, *British Medical Journal* 338 (2009): doi:10.1136/bmj.b496; K. L. Jones, Role of obesity in complicating and confusing the diagnosis and treatment of diabetes in children, *Pediatrics* 121 (2008): 361–368; S. Cook and coauthors,

Metabolic syndrome rates in United States adolescents, from the National Health and Nutrition Examination Survey, 1999–2002, *Journal of Pediatrics* 152 (2008): 165–170; C. L. Carroll and coauthors, Childhood overweight increases hospital admission rates for asthma, *Pediatrics* 120 (2007): 734–740.

14. U.S. Preventive Services Task Force, Screening for obesity in children and adolescents: U.S. Preventive Services Task Force Recommendation Statement, *Pediatrics* (2010), published online January 18, 2010, doi: 10.1542/peds.2009-2037.

15. D. S. Ludwig, Childhood obesity—The shape of things to come, *New England Journal of Medicine* 357 (2007): 2325–2326; J. Franklin and coauthors, Obesity and risk of low self-esteem: A statewide survey of Australian children, *Pediatrics* 118 (2006): 2481–2487; A. J. Daley and coauthors, Exercise therapy as a treatment for psychopathologic conditions in obese and morbidly obese adolescents: A randomized, controlled trial, *Pediatrics* 118 (2006): 2126–2134.

16. T. Robinson, M. Callister, and T. Jankowski, Portrayal of body weight on children's television sitcoms: A content analysis, *Body Image* 5 (2008): 141–151; S. M. Himes and J. K. Thompson, Fat stigmatization in television shows and movies: A content analysis, *Obesity* 15 (2007): 712–718.

17. Centers for Disease Control and Prevention, BMI—Body Mass Index: About BMI for children and teens, 2006, available at www.cdc.gov.

18. U.S. Preventive Services Task Force, Screening for obesity in children and adolescents: U.S. Preventive Services Task Force Recommendation Statement.

19. Bouchard, Childhood obesity; J. M. Ordovas, Genetic influences on blood lipids and cardiovascular disease risk: Tools for primary prevention, *American Journal of Clinical Nutrition* 89 (2009): 1509S–1517S; Barlow and the Expert Committee, Expert Committee recommendations; Ludwig, Childhood obesity.

20. N. F. Krebs and coauthors, Assessment of child and adolescent overweight and obesity, *Pediatrics* 120 (2007): S193–S228.

21. K. Silventoinen and coauthors, The genetic and environmental influences on childhood obesity: A systematic review of twin and adoption studies, *International Journal of Obesity* 34 (2010): 29–40.

22. Position of the American Dietetic Association: Individual-, family-, school-, and community-based interventions for pediatric overweight, *Journal of the American Dietetic Association* 106 (2006): 925–945.

23. Centers for Disease Control and Prevention, Prevalence of abnormal lipid levels among youths—United States, 1999–2006, *Morbidity and Mortality Weekly Report* 59 (2010): 29–33; Freedman and coauthors, Risk factors and adult body mass index among overweight children; Cook and coauthors, Metabolic syndrome rates in United States adolescents; J. Botton and coauthors, Cardiovascular risk factor levels and their relationships with overweight and fat distribution in children: The Fleurbaix Laventie Ville Sante II Study, *Metabolism* 56 (2007): 614–622; D. R. Thompson and coauthors, Childhood overweight and cardiovascular disease risk factors: The National Heart, Lung, and Blood Institute Growth and Health Study, *Journal of Pediatrics* 150 (2007): 18–25.

24. L. J. Lloyd, S. C. Langley-Evans, and S. McMullen, Childhood obesity and adult cardiovascular disease risk: A systematic review, *International Journal of Obesity* 34 (2010): 18–28.

25. U.S. Preventive Services Task Force, Screening for obesity in children and adolescents: U.S. Preventive Services Task Force Recommendation Statement.

26. M. Salvadori and coauthors, Elevated blood pressure in relation to overweight and obesity among children in a rural Canadian community, *Pediatrics* 122 (2008): e821–e827; R. Jago and coauthors, Prevalence of abnormal lipid and blood pressure values among an ethnically diverse population of eighth-grade adolescents and screening implications, *Pediatrics* 117 (2006): 2065–2073.

27. F. J. He and G. A. MacGregor, Importance of salt in determining blood pressure in children: Meta-analysis of controlled trials, *Hypertension* 48 (2006): 861–869.

28. M. A. Kalarchian and coauthors, Family-based treatment of severe pediatric obesity: Randomized, controlled trial, *Pediatrics* 124 (2009): 1060–1068.

29. K. E. Borradaile and coauthors, Snacking in children: The role of the urban corner stores, *Pediatrics* 124 (2009): 1292–1297.

30. S. J. te Velde and coauthors, Patterns in sedentary and exercise behaviors and associations with overweight in 9–14-year-old boys and girls—a cross-sectional study, *BMC Public Health* 7 (2007) published online, doi:10.1186/1471-2458-7-16.

31. S. Gable, Y. Chang, and J. L. Krull, Television watching and frequency of family meals are predictive of overweight onset and persistence in a national sample of school-aged children, *Journal of the American Dietetic Association* 107 (2007): 53–61.

32. J. L. Harris, J. A. Bargh, and K. D. Brownell, Priming effects of television food advertising on eating behavior, *Health Psychology* 28 (2009): 404–413.

33. Barlow and the Expert Committee, Expert Committee recommendations.

34. Committee on Food Marketing and the Diets of Children and Youth, *Food Marketing to Children and Youth: Threat or Opportunity?* (Washington, D.C.: National Academies Press, 2006), pp. 4–5.

35. K. C. Montgomery and J. Chester, Interactive food and beverage marketing: Targeting adolescents in the digital age, *Journal of Adolescent Health* 45 (2009): S1–S98; A. Batada and coauthors, Nine out of 10 food advertisements shown during Saturday morning children's television programming are for foods high in fat, sodium, or added sugars, or low in nutrients, *Journal of the American Dietetic Association* 108 (2008): 673–678; L. M. Powell and coauthors, Nutritional content of television food advertisements seen by children and adolescents in the United States, *Pediatrics* 120 (2007): 576–583; J. L. Wiecha and coauthors, When children eat what they watch: Impact of television viewing on dietary intake in youth, *Archives of Pediatrics & Adolescent Medicine* 160 (2006): 436–442.

36. S. M. Connor, Food-related advertising on preschool television: Building brand recognition in young viewers, *Pediatrics* 118 (2006): 1478–1485.

37. B. A. Spear and coauthors, Recommendations for treatment of child and adolescent overweight and obesity, *Pediatrics* 120 (2007): S254–S287; L. J. Chamberlain, Y. Wang, and T. N. Robinson, Does children's screen time predict requests for advertised products? Cross-sectional and prospective analyses, *Archives of Pediatrics & Adolescent Medicine* 160 (2006): 363–368; Y. Aktas-Arnas, The effects of television food advertisement on children's food purchasing requests, *Pediatrics International* 48 (2006): 138–145; M. O'Dougherty, M. Story, and J. Stang, Observations of parent-child co-shoppers in supermarkets: Children's involvement in food selections, parental yielding, and refusal strategies, *Journal of Nutrition Education and Behavior* 38 (2006): 183–188.

38. A. E. Henry and M. Story, Food and beverage brands that market to children and adolescents on the Internet: A content analysis of branded Web sites, *Journal of Nutrition Education and Behavior* 41 (2009): 353–359; K. Weber, M. Story, and L. Harnack, Internet food marketing strategies aimed at children and adolescents: A content analysis of food and beverage brand web sites, *Journal of the American Dietetic Association* 106 (2006): 1463–1466.

39. J. Halliday, Industry is successfully self-regulating ads to kids, CFBAI, *Food Navigator-USA.com*, December 1, 2009, available at www.foodnavigator-sa.com; Children's Advertising Review Unit, *Self-Regulatory Program for Children's Advertising*, National Advertising Review Council of the Better Business Bureaus, Inc., 2006, available at www.caru.org/guidelines/index.asp.

40. Center for Science in the Public Interest, Most food ads on Nickelodeon still for junk food, *CSPI Newsroom*, November 24, 2009, available at www.cspinet.org/new/200911241.html.

41. M. M. Davis and coauthors, Recommendations for prevention of childhood obesity, *Pediatrics* 120 (2007): S229–S253.

42. Position of the American Dietetic Association, Individual-, family-, school-, and community-based interventions.

43. Barlow and the Expert Committee, Expert Committee recommendations; National Institute of Diabetes and Digestive and Kidney Diseases, National Institutes of Health, Helping Your Overweight Child, available at www.niddk.nih.gov.

44. M. A. Kalarchian and coauthors, Family-based treatment of severe pediatric obesity: Randomized, controlled trial, *Pediatrics* 124 (2009): 1060–1068.
45. K. J. Campbell and coauthors, Associations between the home food environment and obesity-promoting eating behaviors in adolescence, *Obesity* 15 (2007): 719–730; Barlow and the Expert Committee, Expert Committee recommendations.
46. K. S. Geller and D. A. Dzewaltowski, Longitudinal and cross-sectional influences on youth fruit and vegetable consumption, *Nutrition Reviews* 67 (2009): 65–76; J. Brug and coauthors, Taste preferences, liking and other factors related to fruit and vegetable intakes among schoolchildren: Results from observational studies, *British Journal of Nutrition* 99 (2008): S7–S14; C. A. Forestell and J. A. Mennella, Early determinants of fruit and vegetable acceptance, *Pediatrics* 120 (2007): 1247–1254; C. Arcan and coauthors, Parental eating behaviours, home food environment and adolescent intakes of fruits, vegetables and dairy foods: Longitudinal finding from Project EAT, *Public Health Nutrition* 11 (2007): 1257–1265; M. Wind and coauthors, Correlates of fruit and vegetable consumption among 11-year-old Belgina-Flemish and Dutch schoolchildren, *Journal of Nutrition Education and Behavior* 38 (2006): 211–221.
47. Spear and coauthors, Recommendations for treatment of child and adolescent overweight.
48. T. H. Inge and coauthors, Reversal of type 2 diabetes mellitus and improvements in cardiovascular risk factors after surgical weight loss in adolescents, *Pediatrics* 123 (2009): 214–222.
49. N. Hellmich, Children's menus hold the fries, dish up broccoli, *USA Today,* May 26, 2004, available at www.usatoday.com/news/health/2004-05-26-kids-menus_x.htm.
50. M. S. Vanselow and coauthors, Adolescent beverage habits and changes in weight over time: Findings from Project EAT, *American Journal of Clinical Nutrition* 90 (2009): 1489–1495; L. M. Fiorito and coauthors, Beverage intake of girls at age 5 y predicts adiposity and weight status in childhood and adolescence, *American Journal of Clinical Nutrition* 90 (2009): 935–942; S. Harrington, The role of sugar-sweetened beverage consumption in adolescent obesity: A review of the literature, *Journal of School Nursing* 24 (2008): 3–12; D. A. Shoham and coauthors, Sugary soda consumption and albuminuria: Results from the National Health and Nutrition Examination Survey, 1999–2004, *PLoS One* 3 (2008), doi:10.1371/journal.pone.0003431; L. R. Vartanian, M. B. Schwartz, and K. D. Brownell, Effects of soft drink consumption on nutrition and health: A systematic review and meta-analysis, *American Journal of Public Health* 97 (2007): 667–675.
51. American Academy of Pediatrics, Council on Sports Medicine and Fitness and Council on School Health, Active healthy living: Prevention of childhood obesity through increased physical activity, *Pediatrics* 117 (2006): 1834–1842.
52. L. Lanningham-Foster and coauthors, Activity-promoting games and increased energy expenditure, *Journal of Pediatrics* 154 (2009): 819–823; L. Graves and coauthors, Energy expenditure in adolescents playing new generation computer games, *British Journal of Sports Medicine* 42 (2008): 592–594.

Chapter 14

1. M. K. Fox and coauthors, Relationship between portion size and energy intake among infants and toddlers: Evidence of self-regulation, *Journal of the American Dietetic Association* 106 (2006): S77–S83.
2. Position of the American Dietetic Association: Nutrition guidance for healthy children ages 2 to 11 years, *Journal of the American Dietetic Association* 108 (2008): 1038–1047; Position of the American Dietetic Association: Individual-, family-, school-, and community-based interventions for pediatric overweight, *Journal of the American Dietetic Association* 106 (2006): 925–945.
3. Nutritional aspects of vegetarian diets, in *Pediatric Nutrition Handbook,* 6th ed., R. E. Kleinman, ed. (Elk Grove Village, Ill: American Academy of Pediatrics, 2009), pp. 201–224.
4. Committee on Dietary Reference Intakes, *Dietary Reference Intakes for Energy, Carbohydrate, Fiber, Fat, Fatty Acids, Cholesterol, Protein, and Amino Acids* (Washington, D.C.: National Academies Press, 2005), Chapter 6.
5. Committee on Dietary Reference Intakes, *Dietary Reference Intakes for Energy, Carbohydrate, Fiber, Fat, Fatty Acids, Cholesterol, Protein, and Amino Acids,* Chapter 11.
6. U. Shaikh, R. S. Byrd, and P. Auinger, Vitamin and mineral supplement use by children and adolescents in the 1999–2004 National Health and Nutrition Examination Survey: Relationship with nutrition, food security, physical activity, and health care access, *Archives of Pediatrics and Adolescent Medicine* 163 (2009): 150–157; R. Briefel and coauthors, Feeding Infants and Toddlers Study: Do vitamin and mineral supplements contribute to nutrient adequacy or excess among U.S. infants and toddlers? *Journal of the American Dietetic Association* 106 (2006): S52–S65.
7. J. Kumar and coauthors, Prevalence and associations of 25-hydroxyvitamin D deficiency in US children: NHANES 2001-2004, *Pediatrics* 124 (2009): e362–e370.
8. C. L. Wagner and F. R. Greer and the Section on Breastfeeding and Committee on Nutrition, Prevention of rickets and vitamin D deficiency in infants, children, and adolescents, *Pediatrics* 122 (2008): 1142–1152.
9. Iron, in Kleinman, ed., *Pediatric Nutrition Handbook,* pp. 403–422; J. M. Brotanek and coauthors, Iron deficiency in early childhood in the United States: Risk factors and racial/ethnic disparities, *Pediatrics* 120 (2007): 568–575.
10. K. J. Campbell and coauthors, Associations between the home food environment and obesity-promoting eating behaviors in adolescence, *Obesity* 15 (2007): 719–730.
11. P. Ziegler and coauthors, Feeding Infants and Toddlers Study (FITS): Development of the FITS survey in comparison to other dietary survey methods, *Journal of the American Dietetic Association* 106 (2006): S12–S27.
12. J. Stang, Improving the eating patterns of infants and toddlers, *Journal of the American Dietetic Association* 106 (2006): S7–S9.
13. M. Vadiveloo, L. Zhu, and P. A. Quatromoni, Diet and physical activity patterns of school-aged children, *Journal of the American Dietetic Association* 109 (2009): 145–151; Position of the American Dietetic Association, Nutrition guidance for healthy children ages 2 to 11 years.
14. J. Wardle and L. Cooke, Genetic and environmental determinants of children's food preferences, *British Journal of Nutrition* 99 (2008): S15–S21.
15. T. M. Dovey and coauthors, Food neophobia and "picky/fussy" eating in children: A review, *Appetite* 50 (2008): 181–193.
16. Dovey and coauthors, Food neophobia and "picky/fussy" eating in children.
17. B. Wansink, C. Payne, and C. Werle, Consequences of belonging to the "clean plate club," *Archives of Pediatric and Adolescent Medicine* 162 (2008): 994–995.
18. H. H. Laroche, T. P. Hofer, and M. M. Davis, Adult fat intake associated with the presence of children in households: Findings from NHANES III, *Journal of the American Board of Family Medicine* 20 (2007): 9–15.
19. H. Coulthard and J. Blissett, Fruit and vegetable consumption in children and their mothers: Moderating effects of child sensory sensitivity, *Appetite* 52 (2009): 410–415; D. Haire-Joshu and coauthors, High 5 for kids: The impact of a home visiting program on fruit and vegetable intake of parents and their preschool children, *Preventive Medicine* 47 (2008): 77–82.
20. J. C. McCann and B. N. Ames, An overview of evidence for a causal relation between iron deficiency during development and deficits in cognitive or behavioral function, *American Journal of Clinical Nutrition* 85 (2007): 931–945.
21. Iron, in Kleinman, ed., *Pediatric Nutrition Handbook.*
22. McCann and Ames, An overview of evidence for a causal relation between iron deficiency during development and deficits in cognitive or behavioral function; B. Lozhoff and coauthors, Long-lasting neural and behavioral effects of iron deficiency in infancy, *Nutrition Reviews* 64 (2006): S34–S43.
23. Centers for Disease Control and Prevention, General lead information: Questions and answers, available at www.cdc.gov/nceh/lead/faq/about.htm.
24. W. R. Mindak and coauthors, Lead in women's and children's vitamins, *Journal of Agricultural and Food Chemistry* 56 (2008): 6892–6896; J. F. Kaufman and coauthors, Lead in pharmaceutical products and dietary supple-

ments, *Regulatory Toxicology and Pharmacology* 48 (2007): 128–134.
25. J. Weuve and coauthors, Cumulative exposure to lead in relation to cognitive function in older women, *Environmental Health Perspectives* 117 (2009): 574–580.
26. J. J. Fadrowski and coauthors, Blood lead level and kidney function in U.S. adolescents, *Archives of Internal Medicine* 170 (2010): 75–82; K. Chandramouli and coauthors, Effects of early childhood lead exposure on academic performance and behavior of school-age children, *Archives of Disease in Childhood* 94 (2009): 844–848.
27. Chandramouli and coauthors, Effects of early childhood lead exposure; A. M. Wengroviz and M. J. Brown, Recommendations for blood lead screening of Medicaid-eligible childen aged 1–5 years: An updated approach to targeting a group at high risk, *Morbidity and Mortality Weekly Report* 58 (2009): 1–11; K. M. Cecil and coauthors, Decreased brain volume in adults with childhood lead exposure, *PLos Medicine* 27 (2008): e112.
28. J. Raloff, School-age lead exposures may do more harm than earlier exposures, *Science News,* June 6, 2009, p. 13.
29. Weuve and coauthors, Cumulative exposure to lead.
30. L. Hubbs-Tait and coauthors, Zinc, iron and lead: Relations to Head Start children's cognitive scores and teachers' ratings of behavior, *Journal of the American Dietetic Association* 107 (2007): 128–133.
31. L. A. Lee and A. W. Burks, Food allergies: Prevalence, molecular characterization and treatment/prevention strategies, *Annual Review of Nutrition* 26 (2006): 539–566; National Institutes of Health, National Institute of Allergy and Infectious Diseases, *Food Allergy: Report of the NIH Expert Panel on Food Allergy Research,* March 13–14, 2006, available at www.naid.nih.gov.
32. A. M. Hofmann and coauthors, Safety of a peanut oral immunotherapy protocol in children with peanut allergy, *Journal of Allergy and Clinical Immunology* 124 (2009): 286–291.
33. U.S. Food and Drug Administration, Food allergies; Reducing the risks, January 23, 2009, available at www.fda.gov/consumer/updates/foodallergies012209.htm; A. Boulay and coauthors, A EuroPrevall review of factors affecting incidence of peanut allergy: Priorities for research and policy, *Allergy* 63 (2008): 797–809; L. A. Lee and A. W. Burks, Food allergies: Prevalence, molecular characterization, and treatment/prevention strategies, *Annual Review of Nutrition* 26 (2006): 539–565.
34. S. Ramesh, Food allergy overview in children, *Clinical Reviews in Allergy and Immunology* 34 (2008): 217–230.
35. M. C. Young, A. Muñoz-Furlong, and S. H. Sicherer, Management of food allergies in schools: A perspective for allergists, *Journal of Allergy and Clinical Immunology* 124 (2009): 175–182.
36. Young, Muñoz-Furlong, and Sicherer, Management of food allergies in schools.
37. M. Boguniewica, N. Moore, and K. Paranto, Allergic diseases, quality of life, and the role of the dietitian, *Nutrition Today* 43 (2008): 6–10.
38. Hoffman, Safety of a peanut oral immunotherapy protocol.
39. Food Allergen Labeling and Consumer Protection Act of 2004, available at http://thomas.loc.gov/cgi-bin/query/F?c108:6:./temp/~c108Dz8zuL:e48634.
40. Young, Muñoz-Furlong, and Sicherer, Management of food allergies in schools.
41. Young, Muñoz-Furlong, and Sicherer, Management of food allergies in schools.
42. K. Stein, Are food allergies on the rise, or is it a misdiagnosis? *Journal of the American Dietetic Association* 109 (2009): 1832–1837.
43. Stein, Are food allergies on the rise, or is it a misdiagnosis?
44. H. W. Dodo and coauthors, Alleviating peanut allergy using genetic engineering: the silencing of the immunodominant allergen Ara h 2 leads to its significant reduction and a decrease in peanut allergenicity, *Plant Biotechnology* 6 (2008): 135–145.
45. P. N. Pastor and C. A. Reuben, Diagnosed attention deficit hyperactivity disorder and learning disability: United States, 2004–2006, *Vital and Health Statistics, Series 10, Data from the National Health Survey* 237 (2008): 1–14; E. Romano and coauthors, Development and prediction of hyperactive symptoms from 2 to 7 years in a population-based sample, *Pediatrics* 117 (2006): 2101–2109.
46. D. McCann and coauthors, Food additives and hyperactive behaviour in 3-year-old and 8/9-year-old children in the community: A randomized, double-blinded, placebo-controlled trial, *Lancet* 370 (2007): 1560–1567.
47. Standing Committee on the Scientific Evaluation of Dietary Reference Intakes, Food and Nutrition Board, Institute of Medicine, *Dietary Reference Intake for Energy, Carbohydrate, Fiber, Fat, Fatty Acids, Cholesterol, Protein, and Amino Acids* (Washington, D.C.: National Academy Press, 2002), pp. 13–17.
48. N. J. Wiles and coauthors, "Junk food" diet and childhood behavioural problems: Results from the ALSPAC cohort, *European Journal of Clinical Nutrition* 63 (2009): 491–498.
49. D. C. Hernadez and A. Jacknowski, Transient, but not persistent, adult food insecurity influences toddler development, *Journal of Nutrition* 139 (2009): 1517–1524; R. C. Witaker, S. M. Phillips, and S. M. Orzol, Food insecurity and risks of depression and anxiety in mothers and behavior problems in their preschool-aged children, *Pediatrics* 118 (2006): e859–e868; E. J. Costello and coauthors, Relationships between poverty and psychopathology: A natural experiment, *Journal of the American Medical Association* 290 (2003): 2023–2029.
50. J. J. Rucklidge, J. Johnstone, and B. J. Kaplan, Nutrient supplementation approaches in the treatment of ADHD, *Expert Review of Neurotherapeutics* 9 (2009): 461–476; N. Sinn, Nutritional and dietary influences on attention deficit hyperactivity disorder, *Nutrition Reviews* 66 (2008): 558–568.
51. M. L. Wolraich and coauthors, Attention-deficit/hyperactivity disorder among adolescents: A review of the diagnosis, treatment, and clinical implications, *Pediatrics* 115 (2006): 1734–1776.
52. American Academy of Pediatrics Council on Sports Medicine and Fitness and Council on School Health, Active healthy living: Prevention of childhood obesity through increased physical activity, *Pediatrics* 117 (2006): 1834–1842.
53. American Academy of Pediatrics Council on Sports Medicine and Fitness and Council on School Health, Active healthy living.
54. S. B. Sisson and coauthors, Profiles of sedentary behavior in children and adolescents: the US National Health and Nutrition Examination Survey, 2001–2006, *International Journal of Pediatric Obesity* 4 (2009): 353–359; J. P. Ikeda, Promoting family meals and placing limits on television viewing: Practical advice for parents, *Journal of the American Dietetic Association* 107 (2007): 62–63.
55. S. Gable, Y. Chang, and J. L. Krull, Television watching and frequency of family meals are predictive of overweight onset and persistence in a national sample of school-aged children, *Journal of the American Dietetic Association* 107 (2007): 53–61.
56. D. J. Barr-Anderson and coauthors, Characteristics associated with older adolescents who have a television in their bedrooms, *Pediatrics* 121 (2008): 718–724; A. M. Adachi-Mejia and coauthors, Children with a TV in their bedroom at higher risk for being overweight, *International Journal of Obesity* 31 (2007): 644–651.
57. J. L. Wiecha and coauthors, When children eat what they watch: Impact of television viewing on dietary intake in youth, *Archives of Pediatrics & Adolescent Medicine* 160 (2006): 436–442; S. C. Folta and coauthors, Food advertising targeted at school-age children: A content analysis, *Journal of Nutrition Education and Behavior* 38 (2006): 244–248.
58. L. Dubois and coauthors, Social factors and television use during meals and snacks is associated with higher BMI among pre-school children, *Public Health Nutrition* 11 (2008): 1267–1279; Gable, Chang, and Krull, Television watching and frequency of family meals.
59. Nutrition and oral health, in Kleinman, ed., *Pediatric Nutrition Handbook,* pp. 1045–1056.
60. FDA, About Dental Amalgam Fillings, 2009, available at www.fda.gov/MedicalDevices/ProductsandMedicalProcedures/DentalProducts/DentalAmalgam/ucm171094.htm.
61. F. Tabrizi and coauthors, Oral health of monozygotic twins with and without coronary heart disease: A pilot study, *Journal of Clinical Periodontology* 34 (2007): 220–225; M. Zaremba and coauthors, Evaluation of the incidence of periodontitis-associated bacteria in the atherosclerotic plaque of coronary blood vessels, *Journal of Periodontology* 78 (2007): 322–327.
62. L. A. Ehlen and coauthors, Acidic beverages increase the risk of in vitro tooth erosion, *Nutrition Research* 28 (2008): 299–303; B. M.

Owens and M. Kitches, The erosive potential of soft drinks on enamel surface substrate: An in vitro scanning electron microscopy investigation, *Journal of Contemporary Dental Practice* 8 (2007): 11–20; S. Wongkhantee and coauthors, Effect of acidic food and drinks on surface hardness of enamel, dentine, and tooth-coloured filling materials, *Journal of Dentistry* 34 (2006): 214–220.

63. Feeding the child, in Kleinman, ed., *Pediatric Nutrition Handbook,* pp. 145–174.

64. J. Utter and coauthors, At-home breakfast consumption among New Zealand children: Associations with body mass index and related nutrition behaviors, *Journal of the American Dietetic Association* 107 (2007): 570–576.

65. M. D. Crepinsek and coauthors, Meals offered and served in U.S. public schools: Do they meet nutrient standards? *Journal of the American Dietetic Association* 109 (2009): S31–S43; K. Widenhorn-Muller and coauthors, Influence of having breakfast on cognitive performance and mood in 13- to 20-year-old high school students: Results of a crossover trial, *Pediatrics* 122 (2008): 279–284.

66. National School Lunch Program: Participation and lunches served, USDA, Food and Nutrition Service, www.fns.usda.gov/pd/slsummar.htm, site accessed July 7, 2009; Position of the American Dietetic Association: Local support for nutrition integrity in schools, *Journal of the American Dietetic Association* 106 (2006): 122–133.

67. V. A. Stallings and A. L. Yaktine, eds., *Nutrition Standards for Foods in Schools: Leading the Way Toward Healthier Youth* (Washington, D.C.: National Academies Press, 2007).

68. M. Story, The Third School Nutrition Dietary Assessment Study: Findings and policy implications for improving the health of U.S. children, *Journal of the American Dietetic Association* 109 (2009): S7–S13; Position of the American Dietetic Association, Nutrition guidance for healthy children ages 2 to 11 years.

69. Institute of Medicine, *School Meals: Building Blocks for Healthy Children 2009,* available at www.iom.edu/schoolmeals.

70. Institute of Medicine, Food and Nutrition Board, Committee on Nutrition Standards for Foods in Schools, V. A. Stallings and A. L. Yaktine, eds., *Nutrition Standards for Foods in Schools: Leading the Way Toward Healthier Youth* (Washington, D.C.: National Academies Press, 2007).

71. Institute of Medicine, *Nutrition Standards for Foods in Schools.*

72. Centers for Disease Control and Prevention, Competitive foods and beverages available for purchase in secondary schools—selected sites, United States, 2006, *Morbidity and Mortality Weekly Report* 57 (2008): 935–938; Position of the American Dietetic Association: Local support for nutrition integrity in schools.

73. Centers for Disease Control and Prevention, Availability of less nutritious snack foods and beverages in secondary schools—selected states, 2002–2008, *Morbidity and Mortality Weekly Report* 58 (2009): 1–4.

74. Centers for Disease Control and Prevention, Availability of less nutritious snack foods and beverages in secondary schools—selected states, 2002–2008, *Morbidity and Mortality Weekly Report* 58 (2009): 1102–1104; M. K. Fox and coauthors, Association between school food environment and practices and body mass index of U.S. public school children, *Journal of the American Dietetic Association* 109 (2009): S108–S117.

75. Institute of Medicine, *School Meals*; K. Ehrens and J. A. Weber, Making the healthful choice the easy choice for students, *Journal of the American Dietetic Association* 109 (2009): 1343–1345.

76. Institute of Medicine, Nutrition Standards for Foods in Schools.

77. N. I. Larson and coauthors, Family meals during adolescence are associated with higher diet quality and healthful meal patterns during young adulthood, *Journal of the American Dietetic Association* 107 (2007): 1502–1510.

78. M. E. Eisenberg and coauthors, Family meals and substance use: Is there a long-term association? *Journal of Adolescent Health* 43 (2008): 151–156.

79. P. R. Nader and coauthors, Moderate-to-vigorous physical activity from ages 9 to 15 years, *Journal of the American Medical Association* 300 (2008): 295–305.

80. M. M. Maldonado-Molina, K. A. Komro, and G. Prado, Prospective association between dieting and smoking initiation among adolescents, *American Journal of Health Promotion* 22 (2007): 25–32.

81. Adolescent nutrition, in Kleinman, ed., *Pediatric Nutrition Handbook,* pp. 175–181.

82. H. A. Eicher-Miller and co-authors, Food insecurity is associated with iron deficiency anemia in U.S. adolescents, *American Journal of Clinical Nutrition* 90 (2009): 1358–1371.

83. F. R. Greer, N. F. Krebs, and the Committee on Nutrition, American Academy of Pediatrics, Optimizing bone health and calcium intakes of infants, children and adolescents, *Pediatrics* 117 (2006): 578–585.

84. Greer, Krebs, and the Committee on Nutrition, Optimizing bone health and calcium intakes.

85. K. L. Keller and coauthors, Increased sweetened beverage intake is associated with reduced milk and calcium intake in 3- to 7-year-old children at multi-item laboratory lunches, *Journal of the American Dietetic Association* 109 (2009): 497–501; L. Libuda and coauthors, Association between long-term consumption of soft drinks and variables of bone modeling and remodeling in a sample of healthy German children and adolescents, *American Journal of Clinical Nutrition* 88 (2008): 1670–1677; Greer, Krebs, and the Committee on Nutrition, Optimizing bone health and calcium intakes.

86. L. Esterie and coauthors, Milk, rather than other foods, is associated with vertebral bone mass and circulating IGF-1 in female adolescents, *Osteoporosis International* 20 (2009): 567–575; M. M. Murphy and coauthors, Drinking flavored or plain milk is positively associated with nutrient intake and is not associated with adverse effects on weight status in U.S. children and adolescents, *Journal of the American Dietetic Association* 108 (2008): 631–639; M. L. Savaiano and coauthors, Perceived milk intolerance is related to bone mineral content in 10- to 13-year-old female adolescents, *Pediatrics* 120 (2007): e669–e677.

87. C. L. Wagner, F. R. Greer, and the Section on Breastfeeding and Committee on Nutrition, Prevention of rickets and vitamin D deficiency in infants, children, and adolescents, *Pediatrics* 122 (2008): 1142–1152; C. D. Davis, Vitamin D and cancer: Current dilemmas and future research needs, *American Journal of Clinical Nutrition* 88 (2008): 565S–569S.

88. Wagner, Greer, and the Section on Breastfeeding and Committee on Nutrition, Prevention of rickets and vitamin D deficiency.

89. E. H. Spencer, H. R. Ferdowsian, and N. D. Barnard, Diet and acne: A review of the evidence, *International Journal of Dermatology* 48 (2009): 339–347.

90. Spencer, Ferdowsian, and Barnard, Diet and acne.

91. T. L. Burgess-Champoux and coauthors, Longitudinal and secular trends in adolescent whole-grain consumption, 1999–2004, *American Journal of Clinical Nutrition* 91 (2009): 154–159.

92. C. M. McDonald and coauthors, Overweight is more prevalent than stunting and is associated with socioeconomic status, maternal obesity, and a snacking dietary pattern in school children from Bogota, Columbia, *Journal of Nutrition* 139 (2009): 370–376; M. T. Timlin and coauthors, Breakfast eating and weight change in a 5-year prospective analysis of adolescents: Project EAT (Eating Among Teens), *Pediatrics* 121 (2008): e638–e64; H. M. Niemeier and coauthors, Fast food consumption and breakfast skipping: Predictors of weight gain from adolescence to adulthood in a nationally representative sample, *Journal of Adolescent Health* 39 (2006): 842–849.

93. Campbell and coauthors, Associations between the home food environment and obesity-promoting eating behaviors.

94. R. S. Sebastian, L. E. Cleveland, and J. D. Goldman, Effect of snacking frequency on adolescents' dietary intakes and meeting national recommendations, *Journal of Adolescent Health* 42 (2008): 503–511.

95. B. R. Levy and coauthors, Age stereotypes held earlier in life predict cardiovascular events in later life, *Psychological Science* 20 (2009): 296–298.

96. N. S. Wellman, Prevention, prevention, prevention: Nutrition for successful aging, *Journal of the American Dietetic Association* 107 (2007): 741–743.

97. S. Sabia and coauthors, Health behaviors from early to late midlife as predictors of cognitive function, *American Journal of Epidemiology* 170 (2009):428–437.

98. National Center for Health Statistics, Life expectancy at age 65 years, by sex and race—

United States, 2000–2006, *Morbidity and Mortality Weekly Report* 58 (2009): 473.
99. J. Xu, K. D. Kochanek, and B. Tehada-Vera, Deaths: Preliminary data for 2007, *National Vital Statistics Reports* 58, August 19, 2009, available at www.cdc.org.
100. H. Kung and coauthors, Deaths: Final data for 2005, *National Vital Statistics Reports* 56 (2008): 1–120; S. Harper and coauthors, Trends in the black-white life expectancy gap in the United States, 1983–2003, *Journal of the American Medical Association* 297 (2007): 1224–1232.
101. Harper and coauthors, Trends in the black-white life expectancy gap.
102. Living well to 100: Nutrition, genetics, inflammation, *American Journal of Clinical Nutrition* 83 (2006): 401S–490S.
103. N. Meunier and coauthors, Basal metabolic rate and thyroid hormones of late-middle-aged and older human subjects: The ZENITH study, *European Journal of Clinical Nutrition* 59 (2005): S53–S57.
104. D. E. King, A. G. Malnous III, and M. E. Geesey, Turning back the clock: Adopting a healthy lifestyle in middle age, *American Journal of Medicine* 120 (2007): 598–603.
105. M. Cesari and coauthors, Frailty syndrome and skeletal muscle: Results from the Invecchaire in Chianti study, *American Journal of Clinical Nutrition* 83 (2006): 1142–1148.
106. C. A. Zizza, F. A. Tayie, and M. Lino, Benefits of snacking in older Americans, *Journal of the American Dietetic Association* 107 (2007): 800–806.
107. M. E. Nelson and coauthors, Physical activity and public health in older adults: Recommendation from the American College of Sports Medicine and the American Heart Association, *Medicine and Science in Sports and Exercise* 39 (2007): 1435–1445.
108. J. Kruger and coauthors, How active are older Americans? *Preventing Chronic Disease: Public Health Research, Practice, and Policy,* online serial, July 2007, available at www.cdc.gov/pcd/issues/2007/jul/06_0094.htm.
109. T. M. Manini and coauthors, Daily activity energy expenditure and longevity among older adults, *Journal of the American Medical Association* 296 (2006): 216–218.
110. D. Paddon-Jones and B. B. Rasmussen, Dietary protein recommendations and the prevention of sarcopenia, *Current Opinion in Clinical Nutrition and Metabolic Care* 12 (2009): 86–90; T. B. Symons and coauthors, Aging does not impair the anabolic response to a protein-rich meal, *American Journal of Clinical Nutrition* 86 (2007): 451–456; J. A. Morais, S. Chevalier, and R. Gougeon, Protein turnover and requirements in the healthy and frail elderly, *Journal of Nutrition, Health, and Aging* 10 (2006): 272–283.
111. American College of Sports Medicine, Position Stand: Exercise and physical activity for older adults, *Medicine and Science in Sports and Exercise* 41 (2009): 1510–1530.
112. J. Stessman and coauthors, Physical activity, function, and longevity among the very old, *Archives of Internal Medicine* 169 (2009): 1476–1483.
113. U. Raue and coauthors, Improvements in whole muscle and myocellular function are limited with high-intensity resistance training in octogenarian women, *Journal of Applied Physiology* 106 (2009): 1611–1617.
114. D. Paddon-Jones and B. B. Rassmussen, Dietary protein recommendations and the prevention of sarcopenia, *Current Opinion in Clinical Nutrition and Metabolic Care* 12 (2009): 86–90; R. Koopman and coauthors, Dietary protein digestion and absorption rates and the subsequent postprandial muscle protein synthetic response do not differ between young and elderly men, *Journal of Nutrition* 139 (2009): 1707–1713.
115. Paddon-Jones and Rasmussen, Dietary protein recommendations and the prevention of sarcopenia; R. P. Heaney and D. K. Layman, Amount and type of protein influences bone health, *American Journal of Clinical Nutrition* 87 (2008): 1567S–1570S; A. E. Thalacker-Mercer and coauthors, Inadequate protein intake affects skeletal muscle transcript profiles in older humans, *American Journal of Clinical Nutrition* 85 (2007): 1344–1352; R. R. Wolfe, The underappreciated role of muscle in health and disease, *American Journal of Clinical Nutrition* 84 (2006): 475–482; Morais, Chevalier, and Gougeon, Protein turnover and requirements.
116. D. Rémond and coauthors, Postprandial whole-body protein metabolism after a meat meal is influenced by chewing efficiency in elderly subjects, *American Journal of Clinical Nutrition* 85 (2007): 1286–1292.
117. U.S. Department of Agriculture, Nutrient intakes from food: Mean amounts consumed per individual, one day, 2005–2006 (2008), available at www.ars.sda.gov/ba/bhnrc/fsrg.
118. Centers for Disease Control and Prevention, Arthritis: Meeting the challenge, *At A Glance,* 2009, available at www.cdc.gov.
119. L. Devos-Comby, T. Cronan, and S. C. Roesch, Do exercise and self-management interventions benefit patients with osteoarthritis of the knee? A meta-analytic review, *Journal of Rheumatology* 33 (2006): 744–756.
120. G. McKellar and coauthors, A pilot study of a Mediterranean-type diet intervention in female patients with rheumatoid arthritis living in areas of social deprivation in Glasgow, *Annals of the Rheumatic Disease* 66 (2007): 1239–1243.
121. S. Panicker and coauthors, Oral glucosamine modulates the response of the liver and lymphocytes of the mesenteric lymph nodes in a papain-induced model of joint damage and repair, *Osteoarthritis and Cartilage* 17 (2009): 1014–1021; G. Sobal, J. Menzel, and H. Sinzinger, Optimal (99m)Tc radiolabeling and uptake of glucosamine sulfate by cartilage. A potential tracer for scintigraphic detection of osteoarthritis, *Bioconjugate Chemistry* 20 (2009): 1547–1552.
122. R. P. Heaney, Vitamin D and calcium interactions: Functional outcomes, *American Journal of Clinical Nutrition* 88 (2008): 541S–544S; M. T. Cantorna, Vitamin D and multiple sclerosis: An update, *Nutrition Reviews* 66 (2008): S135–S138; M. F. Holick, Vitamin D: A d-lightful health perspective, *Nutrition Reviews* 66 (2008): S182–S194; J. M. Lappe and coauthors, Vitamin D and calcium supplementation reduces cancer risk: Results of a randomized trial, *American Journal of Clinical Nutrition* 85 (2007): 1586–1591; J. Lin and coauthors, Intakes of calcium and vitamin D and breast cancer risk in women, *Archives of Internal Medicine* 167 (2007): 1050–1059; G. E. Mullin and A. Dobs, Vitamin D and its role in cancer and immunity: A prescription for sunlight, *Nutrition in Clinical Practice* 22 (2007): 305–322; S. E. Judd and coauthors, Optimal vitamin D status attenuates the age-associated increase in systolic blood pressure in white Americans: Results from the third National Health and Nutrition Examination Survey, *American Journal of Clinical Nutrition* 87 (2008): 136–141; Y. Cui and T. E. Rohan, Vitamin D, calcium, and breast cancer risk: A review, *Cancer Epidemiological, Biomarkers and Prevention* 15 (2006): 1427–1437; A. F. Gombart, Q. T. Luong, and H. P. Koeffler, Vitamin D compounds: Activity against microbes and cancer, *Anticancer Research* 26 (2006): 2531–2542; P. T. Liu and coauthors, Toll-like receptor triggering of a vitamin D-mediated human antimicrobial response, *Science* 311 (2006): 1770–1773; L. A. Martini and R. J. Wood, Vitamin D status and the metabolic syndrome, *Nutrition Reviews* 64 (2006): 479–486; K. L. Munger and coauthors, Serum 25-hydroxyvitamin D levels and risk of multiple sclerosis, *Journal of the American Medical Association* 296 (2006): 2832–2838; S. S. Schleithoff and coauthors, Vitamin D supplementation improves cytokine profiles in patients with congestive heart failure: A double-blind, randomized, placebo-controlled trial, *American Journal of Clinical Nutrition* 83 (2006): 754–759.
123. DIPART (vitamin D Individual Patient Analysis of Randomized Trials) Group, Patient level pooled analysis of 68,500 patients from seven major vitamin D fracture trials in US and Europe, *British Medical Journal, Online First* (2010): doi:10.1136/bmj.b5463; H. A. Bischoff-Ferrari and coauthors, Fall prevention with supplemental and active forms of vitamin D: A meta-analysis of randomized controlled trials, *British Medical Journal* 339 (2009) doi:10.1136/bmj.b362.
124. L. H. Allen, How common is vitamin B-12 deficiency? *American Journal of Clinical Nutrition* 89 (2009): 693S–696S.
125. R. Green, Is it time for vitamin B-12 fortification? What are the questions? *American Journal of Clinical Nutrition* 89 (2009): 712S–716S.
126. T. Ostbye and coauthors, Ten dimensions of health and their relationships with overall self-reported health and survival in a predominately religiously active elderly population: The Cache County memory study, *Journal of the American Geriatrics Society* 54 (2006): 199–209.
127. M. D. Knudtson, B. E. Klein, and R. Klein, Age-related disease, visual impair-

ment, and survival: The Beaver Dam Eye Study, *Archives of Ophthalmology* 124 (2006): 243–249.
128. S. Carpentier, M. Knauss, and M. Suh, Associations between lutein, zeaxanthin, and age-related macular degeneration: An overview, *Critical Reviews in Food Science* 49 (2009): 313–326.
129. J. M. Seddon, Multivitamin-multimineral supplements and eye disease: Age-related macular degeneration and cataract, *American Journal of Clinical Nutrition* 85 (2007): 304S–307S; P. R. Trumbo and K. C. Ellwood, Lutein and zeaxanthin intakes and risk of age-related macular degeneration and cataracts: An evaluation using the Food and Drug Administration's evidence-based review system for health claims, *American Journal of Clinical Nutrition* 84 (2006): 971–974.
130. H. Coleman and E. Chew, Nutrition supplementation in age-related macular degeneration, *Current Opinion in Ophthalmology* 18 (2007): 220–223.
131. W. G. Christen and coauthors, Dietary carotenoids, vitamins C and E, and risk of cataract in women. A prospective study, *Archives of Ophthalmology* 126 (2008): 102–109; A. G. Tan and coauthors, Antioxidant nutrient intake and the long-term incidence of age-related cataract: The Blue Mountains Eye study, *American Journal of Clinical Nutrition* 87 (2008): 1899–1905.
132. S. Rautiainen and coauthors, Vitamin C supplements and the risk of age-related cataract: A population-based prospective cohort study in women, *American Journal of Clinical Nutrition* 91 (2010): 487–493.
133. H. R. Lieberman, Hydration and cognition: A critical review and recommendations for future research, *Journal of the American College of Nutrition* 26 (2007): 555S–561S.
134. J. B. Barnett, D. H. Hamer, and S. N. Meydani, Low zinc status: A new risk factor for pneumonia in the elderly? *Nutrition Reviews* 68 (2010): 30-37; A. S. Prasad and coauthors, Zinc supplementation decreases incidence of infections in the elderly: Effect of zinc on generation of cytokines and oxidative stress, *American Journal of Clinical Nutrition* 85 (2007): 837–844.
135. B. W. Ritz and E. M. Gardner, Malnutrition and energy restriction differentially affect viral immunity, *Journal of Nutrition* 136 (2006): 1141–1144; I. Messaouti and coauthors, Delay of T cell senescence by caloric restriction in aged long-lived nonhuman primates, *Proceedings of the National Academy of Sciences of the United States of America* 103 (2006): 19448–19453.
136. G. Wolf, Calorie restriction increases life span: A molecular mechanism, *Nutrition Reviews* 64 (2006): 89–92.
137. R. J. Colman and coauthors, Caloric restriction delays disease onset of mortality in Rhesus monkeys, *Science* 325 (2009): 201–204.
138. J. R. Speakerman and C. Hambly, Starving for life: What animal studies can and cannot tell us about the use of caloric restriction to prolong human lifespan, *Journal of Nutrition* 137 (2007): 1078–1086.
139. L. Fontana and S. Klein, Aging, adiposity, and calorie restriction, *Journal of the American Medical Association* 297 (2007): 986–994; C. A. Jolly, Is dietary restriction beneficial for human health, such as for immune function? *Current Opinion in Lipidology* 18 (2007): 53–57.
140. S. H. Panowski and coauthors, PHA-4/Foxa mediates diet-restriction-induced longevity of C. elegans, *Nature* 447 (2007): 550–556.
141. C. Franceschi, Inflammaging as a major characteristic of old people: Can it be prevented or cured? *Nutrition Reviews* 65 (2007): S173–S176.
142. P. Libby, Inflammatory mechanisms: The molecular basis of inflammation and disease, *Nutrition Reviews* 65 (2007): S140–S146.
143. J. Gauldie, Inflammation and the aging process: Devil or angel, *Nutrition Reviews* 65 (2007): S167–S169.
144. R. Roubenoff, Physical activity, inflammation, and muscle loss, *Nutrition Reviews* 65 (2007): S208–S212.
145. B. P. Yu and H. Y. Chung, Adaptive mechanisms to oxidative stress during aging, *Mechanisms of Ageing and Development* 127 (2006): 435–442; F. Sierra, Is (your cellular response to) stress killing you? *Journals of Gerontology, Series A, Biological Sciences and Medical Sciences* 61 (2006): 557–561.
146. H. Liu and coauthors, Systematic review: The safety and efficacy of growth hormone in the healthy elderly, *Annals of Internal Medicine* 146 (2007): 104–115; K. S. Nair and coauthors, DHEA in elderly women and DHEA or testosterone in elderly men, *New England Journal of Medicine* (2006): 1647–1659.
147. J. C. Lambert and coauthors, Genome-wide association study identifies variants at CLU and CR1 associated with Alzheimer's disease, *Nature Genetics* 41 (2009): 1094–1099.
148. C. Féart and coauthors, Adherence to a Mediterranean diet, cognitive decline and risk of dementia, *Journal of the American Medical Association* 302 (2009): 638–648; N. Scarmeas and coauthors, Physical activity, diet and risk of Alzheimer Disease, *Journal of the American Medical Association* 302 (2009): 627–637; J. A. Luchsinger and D. R. Gustafon, Adiposity and Alzheimer's disease, *Current Opinion in Clinical Nutrition and Metabolic Care* 12 (2009): 15–21; P. I. Moreira and coauthors, Alzheimer disease and the role of free radicals in the pathogenesis of the disease, *CNS and Neurological Disorders Drug Targets* 7 (2008): 3–10; F. C. Lau, B. Shukitt-Hale, and J. A. Joseph, Nutrition intervention in brain aging: Reducing the effects of inflammation and oxidative stress, *Subcellular Biochemistry* 42 (2007): 299–318; R. M. Bliss, Nutrition and brain function, *Agricultural Research,* July 2007, pp. 8–13; A. Nunomura and coauthors, Involvement of oxidative stress in Alzheimer disease, *Journal of Neuropathology and Experimental Neurology* 65 (2006): 631–641.
149. E. Albanese and coauthors, Dietary fish and meat intake and dementia in Latin America, China, and India: A 10/66 Dementia Research Group population-based study, *American Journal of Clinical Nutrition* 90 (2009): 392–400; E. E. Devore and coauthors, Dietary intake of fish and omega-3 fatty acids in relation to long-term dementia risk, *American Journal of Clinical Nutrition* 90 (2009): 170–176; W. E. Connor and S. L. Connor, The importance of fish and docosahexaenoic acid in Alzheimer disease, *American Journal of Clinical Nutrition* 85 (2007): 929–930; M. A. Beydoun and coauthors, Plasma n-3 fatty acids and the risk of cognitive decline in older adults: The Atherosclerosis Risk in Communities Study, *American Journal of Clinical Nutrition* 85 (2007): 1103–1111; E. J. Schaefer and coauthors, Plasma phosphatidylcholine docosahexaenoic acid content and risk of dementia and Alzheimer disease, *Archives of Neurology* 63 (2006): 1545–1550.
150. C. Cooper and coauthors, Alcohol in moderation, premorbid intelligence and cognition in older adults: Results from the Psychiatric Morbidity Survey, *Journal of Neurology, Neurosurgery, and Psychiatry* 80 (2009): 1236–1239.
151. B. E. Snitz and coauthors, *Ginkgo biloba* for preventing cognitive decline in older adults, *Journal of the American Medical Association* 302 (2009): 2663–2670; S. T. KeKosky and coauthors, *Ginkgo biloba* for prevention of dementia, *Journal of the American Medical Association* 300 (2008): 2253–2262.
152. Position of the American Dietetic Association: Liberalization of the diet prescription improves quality of life for older adults in long-term care, *Journal of the American Dietetic Association* 105 (2005): 1955–1965.
153. Position of the American Dietetic Association: Nutrition across the spectrum of aging, *Journal of the American Dietetic Association* 105 (2005): 616–633.

CONSUMER CORNER 14

1. F. C. Baker, and coauthors, Sleep quality and the sleep electroencephalogram in women with severe premenstrual syndrome, *Sleep* 30 (2007): 1283–1291.
2. K. K. Trout and coauthors, Insulin sensitivity, food intake, and cravings with premenstrual syndrome: A pilot study, *Journal of Women's Health* 17 (2008): 657–665; M. Steiner and coauthors, Expert guidelines for the treatment of severe PMS, PMDD, and comorbidities: The role of SSRIs, *Journal of Women's Health* 15 (2006): 57–69.
3. J. Brown and coauthors, Selective serotonin reuptake inhibitors for premenstrual syndrome, *Cochrane Database of Systematic Reviews* 2 (2009): doi:10.1002/14651858.CD001396.pub2.
4. S. C. Reed, F. R. Levin, and S. M. Evans, Changes in mood, cognitive performance and appetite in the late luteal and follicular phases of the menstrual cycle in women with and without PMDD (Premenstrual Dysphoric Disorder), *Hormones and Behavior* 54 (2008): 185–193; M. Bryant, K. P. Truesdale, and L. Dye, Modest changes in dietary intake across the menstrual cycle: Implications for food intake research, *British Journal of Nutrition* 96 (2006): 888–894.

5. E. B. Gold and coauthors, Diet and lifestyle factors associated with premenstrual symptoms in a racially diverse community sample: Study of Women's Health Across the Nation (SWAN), *Journal of Women's Health* 16 (2007): 641–656; Bryant, Truesdale, and Dye, Modest changes in dietary intake across the menstrual cycle; D. S. Svikis and coauthors, Premenstrual symptomatology, alcohol consumption and family history of alcoholism in women with premenstrual syndrome, *Journal of Studies on Alcohol* 67 (2006): 833–836.

6. A. Daley, Exercise and premenstrual symptomatology: A comprehensive review, *Journal of Women's Health* 18 (2009): 895–899.

CONTROVERSY 14

1. R. S. Wold and coauthors, Increasing trends in elderly persons' use of nonvitamin, nonmineral dietary supplements and concurrent use of medications, *Journal of the American Dietetic Association* 105 (2005): 54–63.

2. A. Bhutto and J. E. Morley, The clinical significance of gastrointenstinal changes with aging, *Current Opinion in Clinical and Nutritional Metabolism* 11 (2008): 651–660; J. Tam-McDevitt, Polypharmacy, aging, and cancer, *Oncology* 22 (2008): 1052–1055; E. Perucca, Age-related changes in pharmacokinetics: Predictability and assessment methods, *International Review of Neurobiology* 81 (2007): 183–199.

3. E. S. ElDesoky, Pharmacokinetic-pharmacodynamic crisis in the elderly, *American Journal of Therapeutics* 14 (2007): 488–498.

4. W. W. McCloskey, K. Zaiken, and R. R. Couris, Clinically significant grapefruit juice—Drug interactions, *Nutrition Today* 43 (2008): 19–26; M. F. Paine and coauthors, Further characterization of a furanocoumarin-free grapefruit juice on drug disposition: Studies with cyclosporine, *American Journal of Clinical Nutrition* 87 (2008): 863–871; R. Bressler, Grapefruit juice and drug interactions. Exploring mechanisms of this interaction and potential toxicity for certain drugs, *Geriatrics* 61 (2006): 12–18.

5. J. R. Mort and H. R. Kruse, Timing of blood pressure measurement related to caffeine consumption, *Annals of Pharmacotherapy* 42 (2008): 105–110.

6. J. A. Nettleton, J. L. Follis, and M. B. Schabath, Coffee intake, smoking, and pulmonary function in the Atherosclerosis Risk in Communities Study, *American Journal of Epidemiology* 169 (2009): 1445–1453; W. Zhang and coauthors, Coffee consumption and risk of cardiovascular disease and all-cause mortality among men with type 2 diabetes, *Diabetes Care* 32 (2009): 1043–1045; W. L. Zhang and coauthors, Coffee consumption and risk of cardiovascular events and all-cause mortality among women with type 2 diabetes, *Diabetologia* 52 (2009): 810–817.

7. Nettleton, Follis, and Schabath, Coffee intake, smoking, and pulmonary function.

8. C. Huang and coauthors, Calories from beverages purchased at 2 major coffee chains in New York City, 2007, *Preventing Chronic Disease* 6 (2009), available at http://www.cdc.gov/pcd/issues/2009/oct/08_0246.htm.

Chapter 15

1. USDA Economic Research Service, Briefing Rooms: Food security in the United States, 2007, available at http://www.ers.usda.gov./Briefing/FoodSecurity/stats_graphs.htm.

2. D. Gorton, C. R. Bullen, and C. N. Mhurchu, Environmental influences on food security in high-income countries, *Nutrition Reviews* 68 (2009): 1–29.

3. Food and Agriculture Organization of the United Nations, *The State of Food Insecurity in the World, 2009,* Food Security Statistics, available from www.fao.org.

4. C. P. Timmer, Preventing food crises using a food policy approach, *Journal of Nutrition* 140 (2010): 224S–228S.

5. K. Fiscella and H. Kitzman, Disparities in academic achievement and health: The intersection of child education and health policy, *Pediatrics* 123 (2009): 1073–1080.

6. E. A. Frongillo, D. F. Jyott, and S. J. Jones, Food Stamp Program participation is associated with better academic learning among school children, *Journal of Nutrition* 136 (2006): 1077–1080.

7. L. M. Dinour, D. Bergen, and M. Yeh, The food insecurity-obesity paradox: A review of the literature and the role food stamps may play, *Journal of the American Dietetic Association* 107 (2007): 1952–1961; P. E. Wilde and J. N. Peterman, Individual weight change is associated with household food security status, *Journal of Nutrition* 136 (2006): 1395–1400.

8. S. A. Tanumihardjo and coauthors, Poverty, obesity, and malnutrition: An international perspective recognizing the paradox, *Journal of the American Dietetic Association* 107 (2007): 1966–1972; P. H. Casey and coauthors, The association of child and household food insecurity with childhood overweight status, *Pediatrics* 118 (2006): e1406.

9. M. I. Larson, M. T. Story, and M. C. Nelson, Neighborhood environments: Disparities in access to healthy foods in the U.S., *American Journal of Preventive Medicine* 36 (2009): 74–81; Wilde and Peterman, Individual weight change.

10. Institute of Medicine and the National Research Council, *The public health effects of food deserts: Workshop summary* (Washington, D.C.: National Academies Press, 2009), available at www.nap.edu.

11. A. D. Liese and coauthors, Food store types, availability, and cost of foods in a rural environment, *Journal of the American Dietetic Association* 107 (2007): 1916–1923; J. P. Stimpson and coauthors, Neighborhood deprivation is associated with lower levels of serum carotenoids among adults participating in the Third National Health and Nutrition Examination Survey, *Journal of the American Dietetic Association* 107 (2007): 1895–1902.

12. Tanumihardjo and coauthors, Poverty, obesity, and malnutrition.

13. Position of the American Dietetic Association: Food insecurity and hunger in the United States, *Journal of the American Dietetic Association* 106 (2006): 446–458.

14. S. de Pee and coauthors, How to ensure nutrition security in the global economic crisis to protect and enhance development of young children and our common future, *Journal of Nutrition* 140 (2010): 138S–142S.

15. USDA Economic Research Service, Economic Bulletin 6-3, The food assistance landscape: fy 2006 midyear report, available at http://www.ers.usda.gov/publications/EIB6-3/eib6-3.pdf.

16. M. LeBlanc, B. Lin, and D. Smallwood, Food assistance: How strong is the safety net? *Amber Waves,* May 2007, pp. 40–45.

17. *Leading the Fight Against Hunger—Federal Nutrition Assistance,* June 2008, www.fns.usda.gov/fns.hunger.pdf; P. S. Landers, The Food Stamp Program: History, nutrition education, and impact, *Journal of the American Dietetic Association* 107 (2007): 1945–1951.

18. Position of the American Dietetic Association: Food insecurity and hunger in the United States.

19. M. W. Bloem, R. D. Semba, and K. Kraemer, Castel Gandolfo Workshop: An introduction to the impact of climate change, the economic crisis, and the increase in the food process on malnutrition, *Journal of Nutrition* 140 (2010): 132S–135S; Food and Agriculture Organization of the United Nations, *The State of Food Insecurity in the World, 2008.*

20. Food and Agriculture Organization of the United Nations, *The State of Food Insecurity in the World, 2008.*

21. Food and Agriculture Organization of the United Nations, *The State of Food Insecurity in the World, 2008.*

22. Food and Agricultural Organization of the United Nations, Number of hungry people rises to 963 million, *FAONewsroom,* December 9, 2008, available at www.fao.org.

23. Food and Agricultural Organization of the United Nations, Number of hungry people rises to 963 million.

24. Position of the American Dietetic Association, Food insecurity and hunger in the United States.

25. K. P. West and S. Mehra, Vitamin A intake and status in populations facing economic stress, *Journal of Nutrition* 140 (2010): 201S–207S.

26. C. L. Fischer Walker, M. Ezzati, and R. E. Black, Global and regional child mortality and burden of disease attributable to zinc deficiency, *European Journal of Clinical Nutrition* 63 (2009): 591–597.

27. R. L. Guerrant and coauthors, Malnutrition as an enteric infectious disease with long-term effects on child development, *Nutrition Reviews* 66 (2008): 487–505.

28. J. Tresley and P. M. Sheean, Refeeding syndrome: Recognition is the key to prevention and management, *Journal of the American Dietetic Association* 108 (2008): 2105–2108.

29. U.S. Census Bureau, World vital events per time unit: 2007, available at www.census.gov/cgi-bin/ipc/pcwe.

30. U.S. Census Bureau, World vital events per time unit: 2007.
31. FAO Newsroom, FAO Director-General appeals for second Green Revolution: Vast effort needed to feed billions and safeguard environment, September 13, 2006 available at www.fao.org/newsroom/en/news/2006/1000392/index.html.
32. Intergovernmental Panel on Climate Change, *Climate Change 2007: The Physical Science Basis: Summary for Policymakers,* available at http://www.ipcc.ch/SPM2feb07.pdf.
33. IOM (Institute of Medicine), *Global Environmental Health: Research Gaps and Barriers for Providing Sustainable Water, Sanitation, and Hygiene Services* (Washington, D.C.: The National Academies Press, 2009), p. 15.
34. U.S. Environmental Protection Agency, *Inventory of U.S. Greenhouse Gas Emissions and Sinks, 1990–2007,* (Washington, D.C.: Government Printing Office, 2009); Intergovernmental Panel on Climate Change, *Climate Change 2007.*
35. S. Perkins, From bad to worse: Earth's warming to accelerate, *Science News* 171 (2007): 83.
36. D. B. Lobell and C. B. Field, Global scale climate-crop yield relationships and the impacts of recent warming, *Environmental Research Letters* 2 (2007): doi:10:1088/1748-9326/2/1/1014002.
37. Climate change could increase the number of hungry people: Severest impact in sub-Saharan Africa—FAO report, 2005, available at www.fao.org.
38. M. J. Behrenfeld and coauthors, Climate-driven trends in contemporary ocean productivity, *Nature* 444 (2006): 752–755.
39. S. Rahmstorf, A semi-empirical approach to projecting future sea-level rise, *Science* 315 (2007): 368–370.
40. Global water crisis, *Nature* February 12, 2007, available at http://www.nature.com/nature/focus/water/index.html.
41. G. Eshel and P. A. Martin, Geophysics and nutritional science: Toward a novel, unified paradigm, *American Journal of Clinical Nutrition* 89 (2009): 1710S–1716S.
42. Food and Agricultural Organization of the United Nations, *State of the World Fisheries and Aquaculture, 2008,* available at ftp.fao.org/docrep/fao/011/i0250e/i0250e.pdf.
43. Food and Agricultural Organization of the United Nations, *State of the World Fisheries and Aquaculture, 2008.*
44. Food and Agricultural Organization of the United Nations, *State of the World Fisheries and Aquaculture, 2008.*
45. Behrenfeld and coauthors, Climate-driven trends in contemporary ocean productivity.
46. Food and Agricultural Organization of the United Nations, *State of the World Fisheries and Aquaculture, 2008.*
47. R. L. Naylor, Environmental safeguards for open-ocean aquaculture, *Issues in Science and Technology,* Spring 2006, pp. 53–58.
48. Intergovernmental Panel on Climate Change, *Climate Change 2007.*
49. World Water Assessment Programme, *The United Nations World Water Development Report 3: Water in a Changing World,* (Paris: UNESCO, and London: Earthscan, 2009).
50. The Role of Science in Solving the World's Emerging Water Problems, Arthur M. Sackler Colloquia of the National Academy of Sciences held in Irvine, California, October 8–10, 2004.
51. Food and Agriculture Organization of the United Nations, High-Level Conference on World Food Security: The Challenges of Climate Change and Bioenergy, June 2008.
52. World Health Organization, Reducing the carbon footprint of the health sector, *Protecting Health from Climate Change: World Health Day 2008,* May 2008, available at www.who.int.org; Position of the American Dietetic Association: Food and nutrition professionals can implement practices to conserve natural resources and support ecological sustainability, *Journal of the American Dietetic Association* 107 (2007): 1033–1043.

CONTROVERSY 15

1. World Agriculture Outlook Board, *USDA Agricultural Projections to 2016,* OCE-2007-1 (Washington, D.C., U.S. Government Printing Office, 2007), available from www.ntis.gov or by calling 1-800-999-6779; A. Baker and S. Zahniser, Ethanol reshapes the corn market, *Amber Waves,* May 2007, available at http://www.ers.usda.gov/AmberWaves/.
2. D. Pimentel and coauthors, Reducing energy inputs in the U.S. food system, *Human Ecology* 36 (2008): 459–461.
3. Environmental Protection Agency, *Inventory of U.S. Greenhouse Gas Emissions and Sinks: 1990–2007* (Washington, D.C.: U.S. Government Printing Office, 2009), available at www.epa.gov.
4. G. E. Kisby and coauthors, Oxidative stress and DNA damage in agricultural workers, *Journal of Agromedicine* 14 (2009): 206–214; P. K. Mills, J. Dodge, and R. Yang, Cancer in migrant and seasonal hired farm workers, *Journal of Agromedicine* 14 (2009): 185–191; D. Villarejo and S. A. McCurdy, The California Agricultural Workers Health Study, *Journal of Agricultural Safety and Health* 14 (2008): 135–146.
5. Environmental Protection Agency, *Inventory of U.S. Greenhouse Gas Emissions and Sinks.*
6. G. Eshel and P. A. Martin, Geophysics and nutritional science: Toward a novel, unified paradigm, *American Journal of Clinical Nutrition* 89 (2009): 1710S–1716S.
7. Resistance to Bt crops emerges, *Science News* 173 (2008): 144.
8. H. J. Marlow and coauthors, Diet and the environment: Does what you eat matter? *American Journal of Clinical Nutrition* 89 (2009): 1699S–1703S.
9. Joseph Fargione and coauthors. Land clearing and the biofuel carbon debt. *Science* 319 (2008): 1235–1238.
10. R. Ehrenberg, The biofuel future, *Science News,* August 1, 2009, pp. 24–29.
11. Biofuels International, Biofuels—at what cost? December 2006, available at www.Biofuels-news.com/news/biofuelscost.html.
12. D. Pimentel and coauthors, Reducing energy inputs in the U.S. food system, *Human Ecology* 36 (2008): 459–471.
13. B. M. Popkin, Reducing meat consumption has multiple benefits for the world's health, *Archives of Internal Medicine* 169 (2009): 543–545.
14. The Global Partnership for Safe and Sustainable Agriculture, EurepGAP launches its 3rd version of its Good Agricultural Standard, 2007, available at http://www.eurepgap.org/Languages/English/index_html.
15. BIFS program overview, UC Sustainable Agriculture Research ad Education Program, available at www.sarep.ucdavis.edu.
16. USDA Natural Resources Conservation Service, Conservation Reserve program, updated June 23, 2009, available at www.nrcs.usda.gov/programs/CRP/
17. G. Brookes and P. Barfoot, Global impact of biotech crops: Socio-economic and environmental effects in the first ten years of commercial use, *AgBioForum* 9 (2006): 139–151; Global outlook, Conversations about plant biotechnology, 2005–2006, available at www.monsanto.com/biotech-gmo/asp/globalOutlook.asp; R. Weiss, U.S. Uneasy about biotech foods, *WashingtonPost.Com,* December 7, 2006, available at www.wshingtonpost.com.
18. N. Gilbert, Boost for conservation of plant gene assets, *Nature* online, 1 June 2009: doi:10.1038/news.
19. V. Patil and coauthors, Towards sustainable production of biofuels from microalgae, *International Journal of Molecular Science,* 9 (2008): 1188–1195.
20. R. Dannheisser, "Cow Power" program converts animal waste into electricity, *Engaging the World,* 21 February 2008, available at www.america.gov.
21. Farms use organic waste to generate "Free" onsite power, *GE Energy,* April 29, 2009, available at www.waterandwastewater.com.
22. E. Maris, Putting the carbon back: Black is the new green. *Nature* 442 (2006): 624–626.
23. Compost bin truckload sales event, 2009, available at http://www.talgov.com/you/solid/compost_event.cfm.
24. A. Carlsson-Kanyama and A. D. González, Potential contributions of food consumption patterns to climate change, *American Journal of Clinical Nutrition* 89 (2009): 1704S–1709S.
25. M. S. Nanney and coauthors, Frequency of eating homegrown produce is associated with higher intake among parents and their preschool-aged children in rural Missouri, *Journal of the American Dietetic Association* 107 (2007): 577–584.
26. Pimentel and coauthors, Reducing energy inputs in the U.S. food system.
27. Marlow and coauthors, Diet and the environment.
28. Global Footprint Network, Ecological Footprint and biocapacity, 2006, available at www.footprintwork.org.

APPENDIX G

Answers to Self Check Questions

CHAPTER 1

1. a
2. a
3. c
4. b
5. b
6. b
7. False. Heart disease and cancer are influenced by many factors with genetics and diet among them.
8. True
9. False. The choice of where, as well as what, to eat is often based more on social considerations than on nutrition judgments.
10. True

CHAPTER 2

1. b
2. d
3. c
4. d
5. a
6. True
7. False. The DRI are estimates of the needs of healthy persons only. Medical problems alter nutrient needs.
8. False. People who choose to eat no meats or products taken from animals can still use the USDA Food Guide to make their diets adequate.
9. False. By law, food labels must state as a percentage of the Daily Values the amounts of vitamins A, C, calcium, and iron present in a food.
10. True

CHAPTER 3

1. a
2. d
3. c
4. c
5. d
6. False. Phagocytes are white blood cells that can ingest and destroy antigens in a process known as phagocytosis.
7. False. Hydrochloric acid initiates protein digestion and activates a protein-digesting enzyme in the stomach.
8. False. The digestive tract works efficiently to digest all foods simultaneously, regardless of composition.
9. True
10. False. Absorption of the majority of nutrients takes place across the specialized cells of the small intestine.

CHAPTER 4

1. b
2. a
3. c
4. b
5. a
6. True
7. False. Type I diabetes is most often controlled with insulin-injections or an insulin pump.
8. True
9. False. Whole-grain bread remains more nutritious despite the enrichment of white flour.
10. True

CHAPTER 5

1. c
2. a
3. c
4. b
5. d
6. True
7. False. Taking fish oil supplements is only recommended when they are recommended by a physician.
8. False. Consuming large amounts of *trans*-fatty acids elevates serum LDL cholesterol and thus raises the risk of heart disease and heart attack.
9. False. *Trans* fatty acids form primarily when unsaturated fats are hydrogenated in processing.
10. True

CHAPTER 6

1. b
2. b
3. d
4. a
5. d
6. True
7. False. Excess protein in the diet may have adverse effects such as enlarged liver or kidneys and worsened kidney disease.
8. False. Impoverished people living on U.S. Indian reservations, in inner cities, and in rural areas of the United States, as well as some elderly, homeless, and ill people, have been diagnosed with PEM.
9. True
10. True

CHAPTER 7

1. b
2. c

3. d
4. a
5. c
6. d
7. False. No study to date has conclusively demonstrated that vitamin C can prevent colds or reduce their severity.
8. True
9. True
10. False. Vitamin A supplements have no effect on acne.

CHAPTER 8

1. d
2. b
3. c
4. b
5. a
6. False. After about age 30, the bones begin to lose density.
7. True
8. False. Calcium is the most abundant mineral in the body.
9. False. Butter, cream, and cream cheese contain negligible calcium, being almost pure fat. Some vegetables, such as broccoli, are good sources of available calcium.
10. False. The standards for bottled water are substantially less rigorous than those applied to U.S. tap water.

CHAPTER 9

1. d
2. b
3. d
4. d
5. c
6. a
7. False. The thermic effect of food is believed to have negligible effects on total energy expenditure.
8. True
9. False. The BMI are unsuitable for use with athletes and adults over age 65.
10. True

CHAPTER 10

1. c
2. c
3. a
4. d
5. a
6. False. Weight training to improve muscle strength and endurance also helps maximize and maintain bone mass.
7. False. The average resting pulse for adults is around 70 beats per minute, but the rate is lower for active people.
8. True
9. True
10. True

CHAPTER 11

1. b
2. d
3. a
4. d
5. d
6. True
7. False. Laboratory evidence suggests that a high-calcium diet may help to prevent colon cancer.
8. False. The DASH diet is designed for helping people with hypertension to control the disease.
9. False. The prevalence of high blood pressure in African Americans is among the highest in the world.
10. True

CHAPTER 12

1. b
2. c
3. d
4. a
5. c
6. False. Nature has provided many plants used for food with natural poisons to fend off diseases, insects and other predators.
7. False. The EPA and FDA warn of unacceptably high methylmercury levels in ocean fish and other seafood and advise all pregnant women not to eat certain types of fish.
8. False. Today, the chance of getting a foodborne illness from eating produce is similar to the chance of becoming ill from eating meat, eggs, and seafood.
9. True
10. True

CHAPTER 13

1. c
2. b
3. d
4. a
5. d
6. True
7. True
8. True
9. False. In general, the effect of nutritional deprivation of the mother is to reduce the quantity, not the quality, of her milk.
10. False. There is no proof for the theory that "stuffing the baby" at bedtime will promote sleeping through the night.

CHAPTER 14

1. c
2. d
3. c
4. c
5. b

G

6. d
7. False. Research to date does not support the idea that food allergies or intolerances cause hyperactivity in children, but studies continue.
8. True
9. False. Vitamin A absorption appears to increase with aging.
10. False. To date, no proven benefits are available from herbs or other remedies.

CHAPTER 15

1. b
2. a
3. c
4. d
5. c
6. True
7. False. Most children who die of malnutrition do not starve to death—they die because their health has been compromised by dehydration from infections that cause diarrhea.
8. True
9. False. The link between improved economic status and slowed population growth has been demonstrated in country after country.
10. True

APPENDIX H

Physical Activity and Energy Requirements

Chapter 9 describes how to calculate estimated energy requirements (EER) for adults by using an equation that accounts for gender, age, weight, height, and physical activity level. Table H1 (p. H-2) presents additional equations to determine the EER for infants, children, adolescents, and pregnant and lactating women. Throughout this book and in this Appendix, the term *calorie* is used to mean kilocalorie. Thus, do not enlarge the calorie values—they are kilocalorie values.

This appendix helps you determine the correct physical activity (PA) factor to use in the equations, either by calculating the physical activity level or by estimating it. For those who prefer to bypass these steps, the appendix presents tables that provide a shortcut to estimating total energy expenditure.*

CONTENTS

Calculating Physical Activity Level

To calculate your physical activity level, record all of your activities for a typical 24-hour day, noting the type of activity, the level of intensity, and the duration. Then, using a copy of Table H-2 (p. H-2), find your activity in the first column (or an activity that is reasonably similar) and multiply the number of minutes spent on that activity by the factor in the third column. Put your answer in the last column and total the accumulated values for the day. Now add the subtotal of the last column to 1.1 (to account for basal energy and the thermic effect of food) as shown. This score indicates your physical activity level. Using Table H-3 (p. H-3), find the PA factor for your age and gender that correlates with your physical activity level and use it in the energy equations presented in Table H-1.

Estimating Physical Activity Level

As an alternative to recording your activities for a day, you can use the third column of Table H-3 to decide if your daily activity is sedentary, low active, active, or very active. Find the PA factor for your age and gender that correlates with your typical physical activity level and use it in the energy equations presented in Table H-1.

Using a Shortcut to Estimate Total Energy Expenditure

The DRI Committee has developed estimates of total energy expenditure based on the equations for adults presented in Table H-1. These estimates are presented in Table H-4 (p. H-4) for women and Table H-5 (p. H-5) for men. You can use these tables to estimate your energy requirement—that is, the number of calories needed to maintain your current body weight. On the table appropriate for your gender, find your height in meters (or inches) in the left-hand column. Then follow the row across to find your weight in kilograms (or pounds). (If you can't find your exact height and weight, choose a value between the two closest ones.) Look down the column to find the number of calories that corresponds to your activity level.

*This appendix, including the tables, is adapted from Committee on Dietary Reference Intakes, *Dietary Reference Intakes for Energy, Carbohydrate, Fiber, Fat, Fatty Acids, Cholesterol, Protein, and Amino Acids* (Washington, D.C.: National Academies Press, 2005).

Importantly, the values given in the tables are for 30-year-old people. Women 19 to 29 should add 7 calories per day for each year younger than age 30; older women should subtract 7 calories per day for each year older than age 30. Similarly, men 19 to 29 should add 10 calories per day for each year younger than age 30; older men should subtract 10 calories per day for each year older than age 30.

TABLE H-1 Equations to Determine Estimated Energy Requirement (EER)

Infants	
0–3 months	EER = (89 × weight − 100) + 175
4–6 months	EER = (89 × weight − 100) + 56
7–12 months	EER = (89 × weight − 100) + 22
13–15 months	EER = (89 × weight − 100) + 20
Children and Adolescents	
Boys	
3–8 years	EER = 88.5 − (61.9 × age) + PA × [(26.7 × weight) + (903 × height)] + 20
9–18 years	EER = 88.5 − (61.9 × age) + PA × [(26.7 × weight) + (903 × height)] + 25
Girls	
3–8 years	EER = 135.3 − (30.8 × age) + PA × [(10.0 × weight) + (934 × height)] + 20
9–18 years	EER = 135.3 − (30.8 × age) + PA × [(10.0 × weight) + (934 × height)] + 25
Adults	
Men	EER = 662 − (9.53 × age) + PA × [(15.91 × weight) + (539.6 × height)]
Women	EER = 354 − (6.91 × age) + PA × [(9.36 × weight) + (726 × height)]
Pregnancy	
1st trimester	EER = nonpregnant EER + 0
2nd trimester	EER = nonpregnant EER + 340
3rd trimester	EER = nonpregnant EER + 452
Lactation	
0–6 months postpartum	EER = nonpregnant EER + 500 − 170
7–12 months postpartum	EER = nonpregnant EER + 400 − 0

NOTE: Select the appropriate equation for gender and age and insert weight in kilograms, height in meters, and age in years. See the text and Table H-3 to determine PA.

TABLE H-2 Physical Activities and Their Scores

If your activity was equivalent to this . . .	Then list the number of minutes here and . . .	Multiply by this factor . . .	Add this column to get your physical activity level score:
Activities of Daily Living			
Gardening (no lifting)		0.0032	
Household tasks (moderate effort)		0.0024	
Lifting items continuously		0.0029	
Loading/unloading car		0.0019	
Lying quietly		0.0000	
Mopping		0.0024	
Mowing lawn (power mower)		0.0033	
Raking lawn		0.0029	
Riding in a vehicle		0.0000	
Sitting (idle)		0.0000	
Sitting (doing light activity)		0.0005	
Taking out trash		0.0019	
Vacuuming		0.0024	
Walking the dog		0.0019	
Walking from house to car or bus		0.0014	
Watering plants		0.0014	
Additional Activities			
Billiards		0.0013	
Calisthenics (no weight)		0.0029	
Canoeing (leisurely)		0.0014	

(continued)

H

TABLE H-2 Physical Activities and Their Scores *(continued)*

If your activity was equivalent to this . . .	Then list the number of minutes here and . . .	Multiply by this factor . . .	Add this column to get your physical activity level score:
Additional Activities			
Chopping wood		0.0037	
Climbing hills (carrying 11 lb load)		0.0061	
Climbing hills (no load)		0.0056	
Cycling (leisurely)		0.0024	
Cycling (moderately)		0.0045	
Dancing (aerobic or ballet)		0.0048	
Dancing (ballroom, leisurely)		0.0018	
Dancing (fast ballroom or square)		0.0043	
Golf (with cart)		0.0014	
Golf (without cart)		0.0032	
Horseback riding (walking)		0.0012	
Horseback riding (trotting)		0.0053	
Jogging (6 mph)		0.0088	
Music (playing accordion)		0.0008	
Music (playing cello)		0.0012	
Music (playing flute)		0.0010	
Music (playing piano)		0.0012	
Music (playing violin)		0.0014	
Rope skipping		0.0105	
Skating (ice)		0.0043	
Skating (roller)		0.0052	
Skiing (water or downhill)		0.0055	
Squash		0.0106	
Surfing		0.0048	
Swimming (slow)		0.0033	
Swimming (fast)		0.0057	
Tennis (doubles)		0.0038	
Tennis (singles)		0.0057	
Volleyball (noncompetitive)		0.0018	
Walking (2 mph)		0.0014	
Walking (3 mph)		0.0022	
Walking (4 mph)		0.0033	
Walking (5 mph)		0.0067	
Subtotal			
Factor for basal energy and the thermic effect of food			**1.1**
Your physical activity level score			

TABLE H-3 Physical Activity Equivalents and Their PA Factors

Physical Activity Level	Description	Physical Activity Equivalents	Men, 19+ yr PA Factor	Women, 19+ yr PA Factor	Boys, 3–18 yr PA Factor	Girls, 3–18 yr PA Factor
1.0 to 1.39	Sedentary	Only those physical activities required for typical daily living	1.0	1.0	1.0	1.0
1.4 to 1.59	Low active	Daily living + 30–60 min moderate activity[a]	1.11	1.12	1.13	1.16
1.6 to 1.89	Active	Daily living + ≥ 60 min moderate activity	1.25	1.27	1.26	1.31
1.9 and above	Very active	Daily living + ≥ 60 min moderate activity *and* ≥ 60 min vigorous activity *or* ≥ 120 min moderate activity	1.48	1.45	1.42	1.56

[a]*Moderate activity is equivalent to walking at a pace of 3 to 4½ miles per hour.*

TABLE H-4 Total Energy Expenditure (TEE in Calories per Day) for Women 30 Years of Age[a] at Various Levels of Activity and Various Heights and Weights

Heights m (in)	Physical Activity Level	Weight[b] kg (lb)					
1.45 (57)		38.9 (86)	45.2 (100)	52.6 (116)	63.1 (139)	73.6 (162)	84.1 (185)
				Calories			
	Sedentary	1564	1623	1698	1813	1927	2042
	Low active	1734	1800	1912	2043	2174	2304
	Active	1946	2021	2112	2257	2403	2548
	Very active	2201	2287	2387	2553	2719	2886
1.50 (59)		41.6 (92)	48.4 (107)	56.3 (124)	67.5 (149)	78.8 (174)	90.0 (198)
				Calories			
	Sedentary	1625	1689	1771	1894	2017	2139
	Low active	1803	1874	1996	2136	2276	2415
	Active	2025	2105	2205	2360	2516	2672
	Very active	2291	2382	2493	2671	2849	3027
1.55 (61)		44.4 (98)	51.7 (114)	60.1 (132)	72.1 (159)	84.1 (185)	96.1 (212)
				Calories			
	Sedentary	1688	1756	1846	1977	2108	2239
	Low active	1873	1949	2081	2230	2380	2529
	Active	2104	2190	2299	2466	2632	2798
	Very active	2382	2480	2601	2791	2981	3171
1.60 (63)		47.4 (104)	a5.0 (121)	64.0 (141)	76.8 (169)	89.6 (197)	102.4 (226)
				Calories			
	Sedentary	1752	1824	1922	2061	2201	2340
	Low active	1944	2025	2168	2327	2486	2645
	Active	2185	2276	2396	2573	2750	2927
	Very active	2474	2578	2712	2914	3116	3318
1.65 (65)		50.4 (111)	58.5 (129)	68.1 (150)	81.7 (180)	95.3 (210)	108.9 (240)
				Calories			
	Sedentary	1816	1893	1999	2148	2296	2444
	Low active	2016	2102	2556	2425	2594	2763
	Active	2267	2364	2494	2682	2871	3059
	Very active	2567	2678	2824	3039	3254	3469
1.70 (67)		53.5 (118)	62.1 (137)	72.3 (159)	86.7 (191)	101.2 (223)	115.6 (255)
				Calories			
	Sedentary	1881	1963	2078	2235	2393	2550
	Low active	2090	2180	2345	2525	2705	2884
	Active	2350	2453	2594	2794	2994	3194
	Very active	2662	2780	2938	3166	3395	3623
1.75 (69)		56.7 (125)	65.8 (145)	76.6 (169)	91.9 (202)	107.2 (236)	122.5 (270)
				Calories			
	Sedentary	1948	2034	2158	2325	2492	2659
	Low active	2164	2260	2437	2627	2817	3007
	Active	2434	2543	2695	2907	3119	3331
	Very active	2758	2883	3054	3296	3538	3780
1.80 (71)		59.9 (132)	69.7 (154)	81.0 (178)	97.2 (214)	113.4 (250)	129.6 (285)
				Calories			
	Sedentary	2015	2106	2239	2416	2593	2769
	Low active	2239	2341	2529	2731	2932	3133
	Active	2519	2634	2799	3023	3247	3472
	Very active	2855	2987	3172	3428	3684	3940

(continued)

[a]*For each year younger than 30, add 10 calories/day to TEE. For each year older than 30, subtract 10 calories/day from TEE.*

[b]*These columns represent a BMI of 18.5, 22.5, 25, 30, 35, and 40, respectively.*

TABLE H-4 Total Energy Expenditure (TEE in Calories per Day) for Women 30 Years of Age[a] at Various Levels of Activity and Various Heights and Weights *(continued)*

Heights m (in)	Physical Activity Level	Weight[b] kg (lb)					
1.85 (73)		63.3 (139)	73.6 (162)	85.6 (189)	102.7 (226)	119.8 (264)	136.9 (302)
				Calories			
	Sedentary	2083	2179	2322	2509	2695	2882
	Low active	2315	2422	2624	2836	3049	3262
	Active	2605	2727	2904	3141	3378	3615
	Very active	2954	3093	3292	3562	3833	4103
1.90 (75)		66.8 (147)	77.6 (171)	90.3 (199)	108.3 (239)	126.4 (278)	144.4 (318)
				Calories			
	Sedentary	2151	2253	2406	2603	2800	2996
	Low active	2392	2505	2720	2944	3168	3393
	Active	2693	2821	3011	3261	3511	3760
	Very active	3053	3200	3414	3699	3984	4270
1.95 (77)		70.3 (155)	81.8 (180)	95.1 (209)	114.1 (251)	133.1 (293)	152.1 (335)
				Calories			
	Sedentary	2221	2328	2492	2699	2906	3113
	Low active	2470	2589	2817	3053	3290	3526
	Active	2781	2917	3119	3383	3646	3909
	Very active	3154	3309	3538	3838	4139	4439

[a]For each year younger than 30, add 10 calories/day to TEE. For each year older than 30, subtract 10 calories/day from TEE.

[b]These columns represent a BMI of 18.5, 22.5, 25, 30, 35, and 40, respectively.

TABLE H-5 Total Energy Expenditure (TEE in Calories per Day) for Men 30 Years of Age[a] at Various Levels of Activity and Various Heights and Weights

Heights m (in)	Physical Activity Level	Weight[b] kg (lb)					
1.45 (57)		38.9 (86)	47.3 (100)	52.6 (116)	63.1 (139)	73.6 (163)	84.1 (185)
				Calories			
	Sedentary	1777	1911	2048	2198	2347	2496
	Low active	1931	2080	2225	2393	2560	2727
	Active	2127	2295	2447	2636	2826	3015
	Very active	2450	2648	2845	3075	3305	3535
1.50 (59)		41.6 (92)	50.6 (107)	56.3 (124)	67.5 (149)	78.8 (174)	90.0 (198)
				Calories			
	Sedentary	1848	1991	2126	2286	2445	2605
	Low active	2009	2168	2312	2491	2670	2849
	Active	2215	2394	2545	2748	2951	3154
	Very active	2554	2766	2965	3211	3457	3703
1.55 (61)		44.4 (98)	54.1 (114)	60.1 (132)	72.1 (159)	84.1 (185)	96.1 (212)
				Calories			
	Sedentary	1919	2072	2205	2376	2546	2717
	Low active	2089	2259	2401	2592	2783	2974
	Active	2305	2496	2646	2862	3079	3296
	Very active	2660	2887	3087	3349	3612	3875
1.60 (63)		47.4 (104)	57.6 (121)	64.0 (141)	76.8 (169)	89.6 (197)	102.4 (226)
				Calories			
	Sedentary	1993	2156	2286	2468	2650	2831
	Low active	2171	2351	2492	2695	2899	3102
	Active	2397	2601	2749	2980	3210	3441
	Very active	2769	3010	3211	3491	3771	4051

(continued)

[a]For each year younger than 30, add 10 calories/day to TEE. For each year older than 30, subtract 10 calories/day from TEE.

[b]These columns represent a BMI of 18.5, 22.5, 25, 30, 35, and 40, respectively.

H

TABLE H-5 Total Energy Expenditure (TEE in Calories per Day) for Men 30 Years of Age[a] at Various Levels of Activity and Various Heights and Weights *(continued)*

Heights m (in)	Physical Activity Level	Weight[b] kg (lb)					
1.65 (65)		50.4 (111)	61.3 (129)	68.1 (150)	81.7 (180)	95.3 (210)	108.9 (240)
				Calories			
	Sedentary	2068	2241	2369	2562	2756	2949
	Low active	2254	2446	2585	2801	3017	3234
	Active	2490	2707	2854	3099	3345	3590
	Very active	2880	3136	3339	3637	3934	4232
1.70 (67)		53.5 (118)	65.0 (137)	72.3 (159)	86.7 (191)	101.2 (223)	115.6 (255)
				Calories			
	Sedentary	2144	2328	2454	2659	2864	3069
	Low active	2338	2542	2679	2909	3139	3369
	Active	2586	2816	2961	3222	3483	3743
	Very active	2992	3265	3469	3785	4101	4417
1.75 (69)		56.7 (125)	68.9 (145)	76.6 (169)	91.9 (202)	107.2 (236)	122.5 (270)
				Calories			
	Sedentary	2222	2416	2540	2757	2975	3192
	Low active	2425	2641	2776	3020	3263	3507
	Active	2683	2927	3071	3347	3623	3900
	Very active	3108	3396	3602	3937	4272	4607
1.80 (71)		59.9 (132)	72.9 (154)	81.0 (178)	97.2 (214)	113.4 (250)	129.6 (285)
				Calories			
	Sedentary	2301	2507	2628	2858	3088	3318
	Low active	2513	2741	2875	3132	3390	3648
	Active	2782	3040	3183	3475	3767	4060
	Very active	3225	3530	3738	4092	4447	4801
1.85 (73)		63.3 (139)	77.0 (162)	85.6 (189)	102.7 (226)	119.8 (264)	136.9 (302)
				Calories			
	Sedentary	2382	2599	2718	2961	3204	3447
	Low active	2602	2844	2976	3248	3520	3792
	Active	2883	3155	3297	3606	3915	4223
	Very active	3344	3667	3877	4251	4625	4999
1.90 (75)		66.8 (147)	81.2 (171)	90.3 (199)	108.3 (239)	126.4 (278)	144.4 (318)
				Calories			
	Sedentary	2464	2693	2810	3066	3322	3579
	Low active	2693	2948	3078	3365	3652	3939
	Active	2986	3273	3414	3739	4065	4390
	Very active	3466	3806	4018	4413	4807	5202
1.95 (77)		70.3 (155)	85.6 (180)	95.1 (209)	114.1 (251)	133.1 (293)	152.1 (335)
				Calories			
	Sedentary	2547	2789	2903	3173	3443	3713
	Low active	2786	3055	3183	3485	3788	4090
	Active	3090	3393	3533	3875	4218	4561
	Very active	3590	3948	4162	4578	4993	5409

[a]For each year younger than 30, add 10 calories/day to TEE. For each year older than 30, subtract 10 calories/day from TEE.

[b]These columns represent a BMI of 18.5, 22.5, 25, 30, 35, and 40, respectively.

Glossary

A

absorb to take in, as nutrients are taken into the intestinal cells after digestion; the main function of the digestive tract with respect to nutrients.

acceptable daily intake (ADI) the estimated amount of a sweetener that can be consumed daily over a person's lifetime without any adverse effects.

Acceptable Macronutrient Distribution Ranges (AMDR) values for carbohydrate, fat, and protein expressed as percentages of total daily calorie intake; ranges of intakes set for the energy-yielding nutrients that are sufficient to provide adequate total energy and nutrients while reducing the risk of chronic diseases.

accredited approved; in the case of medical centers or universities, certified by an agency recognized by the U.S. Department of Education.

acetaldehyde (ass-et-AL-deh-hide) a substance to which ethanol is metabolized on its way to becoming harmless waste products that can be excreted.

acid-base balance equilibrium between acid and base concentrations in the body fluids.

acid reducers prescription and over-the-counter drugs that reduce the acid output of the stomach; effective for treating severe, persistent forms of heartburn but not for neutralizing acid already present. Side effects are frequent and include diarrhea, other gastrointestinal complaints, and reduction of the stomach's capacity to destroy alcohol, thereby producing higher-than-expected blood alcohol levels from each drink. Also called *acid controllers.*

acidosis (acid-DOH-sis) the condition of excess acid in the blood, indicated by a below-normal pH (*osis* means "too much in the blood").

acids compounds that release hydrogens in a watery solution.

acne chronic inflammation of the skin's follicles and oil-producing glands, which leads to an accumulation of oils inside the ducts that surround hairs; usually associated with the maturation of young adults.

acupuncture (ak-you-punk-chur) a technique that involves piercing the skin with long, thin needles at specific anatomical points to relieve pain or illness. Acupuncture sometimes uses heat, pressure, friction, suction, or electromagnetic energy to stimulate the points.

added sugars sugars and syrups added to a food for any purpose, such as to add sweetness or bulk or to aid in browning (baked goods). Also called *carbohydrate sweeteners,* they include glucose, fructose, corn syrup, concentrated fruit juice, and other sweet carbohydrates.

additives substances that are added to foods but are not normally consumed by themselves as foods.

adequacy the dietary characteristic of providing all of the essential nutrients, fiber, and energy in amounts sufficient to maintain health and body weight.

Adequate Intakes (AI) nutrient intake goals for individuals; the recommended average daily nutrient intake level based on intakes of healthy people (observed or experimentally derived) in a particular life stage and gender group and assumed to be adequate. Set whenever scientific data are insufficient to allow establishment of an RDA value.

adipokines (AD-ih-poh-kynz) protein hormones made and released by adipose tissue (fat) cells.

adipose tissue the body's fat tissue, consisting of masses of fat-storing cells and blood vessels to nourish them.

adolescence the period from the beginning of puberty until maturity.

advertorials lengthy advertisements in newspapers and magazines that read like feature articles but are written for the purpose of touting the virtues of products and may or may not be accurate.

agave syrup a carbohydrate-rich sweetener made from a Mexican plant; a higher fructose content gives some agave syrups a greater sweetening power per calorie than sucrose.

AIDS acquired immune deficiency syndrome; caused by infection with human immunodeficiency virus (HIV), which is transmitted primarily by sexual contact, contact with infected blood, needles shared among drug users, or fluids transferred from an infected mother to her fetus or infant.

alcohol dehydrogenase (dee-high-DRAH-gen-ace) **(ADH)** an enzyme system that breaks down alcohol. The antidiuretic hormone is also abbreviated ADH.

alcoholism a dependency on alcohol marked by compulsive uncontrollable drinking with negative effects on physical health, family relationships, and social health.

alcohol-related birth defects (ARBD) malformations in the skeletal and organ systems (heart, kidneys, eyes, ears) associated with prenatal alcohol exposure.

alcohol-related neurodevelopmental disorder (ARND) behavioral, cognitive, or central nervous system abnormalities associated with prenatal alcohol exposure.

alkalosis (al-kah-LOH-sis) the condition of excess base in the blood, indicated by an above-normal blood pH (*alka* means "base"; *osis* means "too much in the blood").

allergy an immune reaction to a foreign substance, such as a component of food. Also called *hypersensitivity* by researchers.

alpha-lactalbumin (lact-AL-byoo-min) the chief protein in human breast milk. The chief protein in cow's milk is *casein* (CAY-seen).

alternative (low-input, or **sustainable) agriculture** agriculture practiced on a small scale using individualized approaches that vary with local conditions so as to minimize technological, fuel, and chemical inputs.

American Dietetic Association (ADA) the professional organization of dietitians in the United States. The Canadian equivalent is the Dietitians of Canada (DC), which operates similarly.

amine (a-MEEN) **group** the nitrogen-containing portion of an amino acid.

amino acid chelates (KEY-lates) compounds of minerals (such as calcium) combined with amino acids in a form that favors their absorption. A chelating agent is a molecule that surrounds another molecule and can then either promote or prevent its movement from place to place (*chele* means "claw").

amino (a-MEEN-o) **acids** the building blocks of protein. Each has an amine group at one end, an acid group at the other, and a distinctive side chain.

amniotic (AM-nee-OTT-ic) **sac** the "bag of waters" in the uterus in which the fetus floats.

anabolic steroid hormones chemical messengers related to the male sex hormone testosterone that stimulate building up of body tissues (*anabolic* means "promoting growth"; *sterol* refers to compounds chemically related to cholesterol).

anaphylactic (an-ah-feh-LACK-tick) **shock** a life-threatening whole-body allergic reaction to an offending substance.

androstenedione (AN-droh-STEEN-die-own) a precursor of testosterone that elevates both testosterone and estrogen in the blood of both males and females. Often called *andro,* it is sold with claims of producing increased muscle strength, but controlled studies disprove such claims.

anecdotal evidence information based on interesting and entertaining, but not scientific, personal accounts of events.

anemia the condition of inadequate or impaired red blood cells; a reduced number or volume of red blood cells along with too little hemoglobin in the blood. The red blood cells may be immature and, therefore, too large or too small to function properly. Anemia can result from blood loss, excessive red blood cell destruction, defective red blood cell formation, and many nutrient deficiencies. Anemia is not a disease, but a symptom of another problem; its name literally means "too little blood."

anencephaly (an-en-SEFF-ah-lee) an uncommon and always fatal neural tube defect in which the brain fails to form.

aneurysm (AN-you-rism) the ballooning out of an artery wall at a point that is weakened by deterioration.

anorexia nervosa an eating disorder characterized by a refusal to maintain a minimally normal body weight, self-starvation to the extreme, and a disturbed perception of body weight and shape; seen (usually) in teenage girls and young women (*anorexia* means "without appetite"; *nervosa* means "of nervous origin").

antacids medications that react directly and immediately with the acid of the stomach, neutralizing it. Antacids are most suitable for treating occasional heartburn.

antibodies (AN-te-bod-ees) large proteins of the blood, produced by the immune system in response to an invasion of the body by foreign substances (antigens). Antibodies combine with and inactivate the antigens.

anticarcinogens compounds in foods that act in any of several ways to oppose the formation of cancer.

antidiuretic (AN-tee-dye-you-RET-ick) **hormone (ADH)** a hormone produced by the pituitary gland in response to dehydration (or a high sodium concentration in the blood). It stimulates the kidneys to reabsorb more water and so to excrete less. (This hormone should not be confused with the enzyme *alcohol dehydrogenase*, which is also abbreviated ADH.)

antigen a microbe or substance that is foreign to the body.

antioxidant nutrients vitamins and minerals that oppose the effects of oxidants on human physical functions. The antioxidant vitamins are vitamin E, vitamin C, and beta-carotene. The mineral selenium also participates in antioxidant activities.

antioxidants (anti-OX-ih-dants) compounds that protect other compounds from damaging reactions involving oxygen by themselves reacting with oxygen (*anti* means "against"; *oxy* means "oxygen"). *Oxidation* is a potentially damaging effect of normal cell chemistry involving oxygen.

aorta (ay-OR-tuh) the large, primary artery that conducts blood from the heart to the body's smaller arteries.

appendicitis inflammation and/or infection of the appendix, a sac protruding from the intestine.

appetite the psychological desire to eat; a learned motivation and a positive sensation that accompanies the sight, smell, or thought of appealing foods.

appliance thermometer a thermometer that verifies the temperature of an appliance. An *oven thermometer* verifies that the oven is heating properly; a *refrigerator/freezer thermometer* tests for proper refrigerator (<40°F, or <4°C) or freezer temperature (0°F, or −17°C).

aquifers underground rock formations containing water that can be drawn to the surface for use.

arachidonic (ah-RACK-ih-DON-ik) **acid** an omega-6 fatty acid derived from linoleic acid.

aristolochic acid a Chinese herb ingredient known to attack the kidneys and to cause cancer; after use, U.S. consumers have required kidney transplants and must take lifelong antirejection medication. Banned by the FDA but available in supplements sold on the Internet.

arsenic a poisonous metallic element. In trace amounts, arsenic is believed to be an essential nutrient in some animal species. Arsenic is often added to insecticides and weed killers and, in tiny amounts, to certain animal drugs.

arteries blood vessels that carry blood containing fresh oxygen supplies from the heart to the tissues.

artesian water water drawn from a well that taps a confined aquifer in which the water is under pressure.

arthritis a usually painful inflammation of joints caused by many conditions, including infections, metabolic disturbances, or injury; usually results in altered joint structure and loss of function.

artificial fats zero-energy fat replacers that are chemically synthesized to mimic the sensory and cooking qualities of naturally occurring fats but are totally or partially resistant to digestion.

artificial sweeteners sugar substitutes that provide negligible, if any, energy; also called *nonnutritive sweeteners.*

ascorbic acid one of the active forms of vitamin C (the other is *dehydroascorbic* acid); an antioxidant nutrient.

-ase (ACE) a suffix meaning *enzyme.* Categories of digestive and other enzymes and individual enzyme names often contain this suffix.

atherosclerosis (ath-er-oh-scler-OH-sis) the most common form of cardiovascular disease; characterized by plaques along the inner walls of the arteries (*scleros* means "hard"; *osis* means "too much"). The term *arteriosclerosis* is often used to mean the same thing.

autoimmune disorder a disease in which the body develops antibodies to its own proteins and then proceeds to destroy cells containing these proteins. Examples are type 1 diabetes and lupus.

B

baby water ordinary bottled water treated with ozone to make it safe but not sterile.

balance the dietary characteristic of providing foods of a number of types in proportion to each other, such that foods rich in some nutrients do not crowd out of the diet foods that are rich in other nutrients. Also called *proportionality.*

balance study a laboratory study in which a person is fed a controlled diet and the intake and excretion of a nutrient are measured. Balance studies are valid only for nutrients like calcium (chemical elements) that do not change while they are in the body.

basal metabolic rate (BMR) the rate at which the body uses energy to support its basal metabolism.

basal metabolism the sum total of all the involuntary activities that are necessary to sustain life, including circulation, respiration, temperature maintenance, hormone secretion, nerve activity, and new tissue synthesis, but excluding digestion and voluntary activities. Basal metabolism is the largest component of the average person's daily energy expenditure.

bases compounds that accept hydrogens from solutions.

B-cells lymphocytes that produce antibodies. *B* stands for bursa, an organ in the chicken where B-cells were first identified.

beer belly central-body fatness associated with alcohol consumption.

behavior modification alteration of behavior using methods based on the theory that actions can be controlled by manipulating the environmental factors that cue, or trigger, the actions.

beriberi (berry-berry) the thiamin-deficiency disease; characterized by loss of sensation in the hands and feet, muscular weakness, advancing paralysis, and abnormal heart action.

beta-carotene an orange pigment with antioxidant activity; a vitamin A precursor made by plants and stored in human fat tissue.

bicarbonate a common alkaline chemical; a secretion of the pancreas; also the active ingredient of baking soda.

bile a cholesterol-containing digestive fluid made by the liver, stored in the gallbladder, and released into the small intestine when needed. It emulsifies fats and oils to ready them for enzymatic digestion.

binge drinkers people who drink four or more drinks in a short period.

binge eating disorder an eating disorder whose criteria are similar to those of bulimia nervosa, excluding purging or other compensatory behaviors.

bioaccumulation the accumulation of a contaminant in the tissues of living things at higher and higher concentrations along the food chain.

bioactive having biological activity in the body.

bioactive food components compounds in foods, either nutrients or phytochemicals, that alter physiological processes.

bioelectrical impedance (im-PEE-dense) a technique for measuring body fatness by measuring the body's electrical conductivity.

biofilm a protective coating of proteins and carbohydrates exuded by certain bacteria; biofilm adheres bacteria to surfaces and can survive rinsing.

biofuels fuels made mostly of materials derived from recently harvested living organisms. Examples are *biogas, ethanol,* and *biodiesel.* Biofuels contribute less to the carbon dioxide burden of the atmosphere because plants capture carbon from the air as they grow and release it again when the fuel is burned; fossil fuels such as coal and oil contain carbon that was previously held underground for millions of years and is newly released into the atmosphere on burning.

biotechnology the science of manipulating biological systems or organisms to modify their products or components or create new products; also called *genetic engineering* or *recombinant DNA (rDNA) technology.*

biotin (BY-o-tin) a B vitamin; a coenzyme necessary for fat synthesis and other metabolic reactions.

bladder the sac that holds urine until time for elimination.

blind experiment an experiment in which the subjects do not know whether they are members of the experimental group or the control group. In a *double-blind experiment,* neither the subjects nor the researchers know to which group the members belong until the end of the experiment.

blood the fluid of the cardiovascular system; composed of water, red and white blood cells, other formed particles, nutrients, oxygen, and other constituents.

body composition the proportions of muscle, bone, fat, and other tissue that make up a person's total body weight.

body mass index (BMI) an indicator of obesity or underweight, calculated by dividing the weight of a person by the square of the person's height.

body system a group of related organs that work together to perform a function. Examples are the circulatory system, respiratory system, and nervous system.

bone density a measure of bone strength, the degree of mineralization of the bone matrix.

bone meal or **powdered bone** crushed or ground bone preparations intended to supply calcium to the diet. Calcium from bone is not well absorbed and is often contaminated with toxic materials such as arsenic, mercury, lead, and cadmium.

botanical pertaining to or made from plants; any drug, medicinal preparation, dietary supplement, or similar substance obtained from a plant.

bottled water drinking water sold in bottles.

botulism an often fatal food poisoning caused by botulinum toxin, a toxin produced by the *Clostridium botulinum* bacterium that grows without oxygen in nonacidic canned foods.

bovine somatotropin (so-mat-oh-TROPE-in) **(bST)** growth hormone of cattle, which can be produced for agricultural use by genetic engineering. Also called *bovine growth hormone (bGH).*

bovine spongiform encephalopathy (BOW-vine SPON-jih-form en-SEH-fell-AH-path-ee) **(BSE)** an often fatal illness of the nerves and brain observed in cattle and wild game and in people who consume affected meats. Also called *mad cow disease.*

bran the protective fibrous coating around a grain; the chief fiber donator of a grain.

broccoli sprouts the sprouted seed of *Brassica italica,* or the common broccoli plant, believed to be a functional food by virtue of its high phytochemical content.

brown adipose tissue (BAT) a type of adipose tissue abundant in hibernating animals and human infants and recently identified in human adults. Abundant pigmented enzymes of energy metabolism give BAT a dark appearance under a microscope; the enzymes release heat from fuels without accomplishing other work. Also called *brown fat*.

brown bread bread containing ingredients such as molasses that lend a brown color; may be made with any kind of flour, including white flour.

brown sugar white sugar with molasses added, 95% pure sucrose.

buffers molecules that can help to keep the pH of a solution from changing by gathering or releasing H ions.

built environment the buildings, roads, utilities, homes, fixtures, parks, and all other man-made entities that form the physical characteristics of a community.

bulimia (byoo-LEEM-ee-uh) **nervosa** recurring episodes of binge eating combined with a morbid fear of becoming fat; usually followed by self-induced vomiting or purging.

butyrate (BYOO-tier-ate) a small fat fragment produced by the fermenting action of bacteria on viscous, soluble fibers; the preferred energy source for the colon cells.

C

caffeine a stimulant that can produce alertness and reduce reaction time when used in small doses but causes headaches, trembling, an abnormally fast heart rate, and other undesirable effects in high doses.

caffeine water bottled water with caffeine added.

calcium compounds the simplest forms of purified calcium. They include calcium carbonate, citrate, gluconate, hydroxide, lactate, malate, and phosphate. These supplements vary in the amount of calcium they contain, so read the labels carefully. A 500-milligram tablet of calcium gluconate may provide only 45 milligrams of calcium, for example.

caloric effect the drop in cancer incidence seen whenever intake of food energy (calories) is restricted.

calorie control control of energy intake; a feature of a sound diet plan.

calorie free fewer than 5 calories per serving.

calories units of energy. In nutrition science, the unit used to measure the energy in foods is a **kilocalorie** (***kcalorie*** or *Calorie*): it is the amount of heat energy necessary to raise the temperature of a kilogram (a liter) of water 1 degree Celsius. This book follows the common practice of using the lowercase term *calorie* (abbreviated *cal*) to mean the same thing.

cancer a disease in which cells multiply out of control and disrupt normal functioning of one or more organs.

capillaries minute, weblike blood vessels that connect arteries to veins and permit transfer of materials between blood and tissues.

carbohydrase (car-boh-HIGH-drace) any of a number of enzymes that break the chemical bonds of carbohydrates.

carbohydrates compounds composed of single or multiple sugars. The name means "carbon and water," and a chemical shorthand for carbohydrate is CHO, signifying carbon (C), hydrogen (H), and oxygen (O).

carbonated water water that contains carbon dioxide gas, either naturally occurring or added, that causes bubbles to form in it; also called *bubbling* or *sparkling water*. Seltzer, soda, and tonic waters are legally soft drinks and are not regulated as water.

carcinogen (car-SIN-oh-jen) a cancer-causing substance (*carcin* means "cancer"; *gen* means "gives rise to").

carcinogenesis the origination or beginning of cancer.

cardiac output the volume of blood discharged by the heart each minute.

cardiovascular disease (CVD) disease of the heart and blood vessels; disease of the arteries of the heart is called *coronary heart disease (CHD)*.

carnitine a nitrogen-containing compound, formed in the body from lysine and methionine, that helps transport fatty acids across the mitochondrial membrane. Carnitine is claimed to "burn" fat and spare glycogen during endurance events, but it does neither.

carotenoid (CARE-oh-ten-oyd) a member of a group of pigments in foods that range in color from light yellow to reddish orange and are chemical relatives of beta-carotene. Many have a degree of vitamin A activity in the body.

carpal tunnel syndrome a pinched nerve at the wrist, causing pain or numbness in the hand. It is often caused by repetitive motion of the wrist.

carrying capacity the total number of living organisms that a given environment can support without deteriorating in quality.

case studies studies of individuals. In clinical settings, researchers can observe treatments and their apparent effects. To prove that a treatment has produced an effect requires simultaneous observation of an untreated similar subject (a *case control*).

catalyst a substance that speeds the rate of a chemical reaction without itself being permanently altered in the process. All enzymes are catalysts.

cataracts (CAT-uh-racts) clouding of the lens of the eye that can lead to blindness. Cataracts can be caused by injury, viral infection, toxic substances, genetic disorders, and, possibly, some nutrient deficiencies or imbalances.

cathartic a strong laxative.

CDC (Centers for Disease Control and Prevention) a branch of the Department of Health and Human Services that is responsible for monitoring foodborne diseases.

cell differentiation (dih-fer-en-she-AY-shun) the process by which immature cells are stimulated to mature and gain the ability to perform functions characteristic of their cell type.

cells the smallest units in which independent life can exist. All living things are single cells or organisms made of cells.

cellulite a term popularly used to describe dimpled fat tissue on the thighs and buttocks; not recognized in science.

central obesity excess fat in the abdomen and around the trunk.

certified diabetes educator (CDE) a health-care professional who specializes in educating people with diabetes to help them manage their disease through medical and lifestyle means. Extensive training, work experience, and an examination is required to achieve CDE status.

certified lactation consultant a health-care provider, often a registered nurse or a registered dietitian, with specialized training and certification in breast and infant anatomy and physiology who teaches the mechanics of breastfeeding to new mothers.

cesarean (see-ZAIR-ee-un) **section** surgical childbirth, in which the infant is taken through an incision in the woman's abdomen.

chelating (KEE-late-ing) **agents** molecules that attract or bind with other molecules and are therefore useful in either preventing or promoting movement of substances from place to place.

chlorophyll the green pigment of plants that captures energy from sunlight for use in photosynthesis.

cholesterol (koh-LESS-ter-all) a member of the group of lipids known as sterols; a soft, waxy substance made in the body for a variety of purposes and also found in animal-derived foods.

cholesterol free less than 2 mg of cholesterol *and* 2 g or less saturated fat and *trans* fat combined per serving.

choline (KOH-leen) a nonessential nutrient used to make the phospholipid lecithin and other molecules.

chromium picolinate a trace element supplement; falsely promoted to increase lean body mass, enhance energy, and burn fat.

chronic diseases long-duration degenerative diseases characterized by deterioration of the body organs. Examples include heart disease, cancer, and diabetes.

chronic hypertension in pregnant women, hypertension that is present and documented before pregnancy; in women whose prepregnancy blood pressure is unknown, the presence of sustained hypertension before 20 weeks of gestation.

chylomicrons (KYE-low-MY-krons) clusters formed when lipids from a meal are combined with carrier proteins in the cells of the intestinal lining. Chylomicrons transport food fats through the watery body fluids to the liver and other tissues.

chyme (KIME) the fluid resulting from the actions of the stomach upon a meal.

cirrhosis (seer-OH-sis) advanced liver disease, often associated with alcoholism, in which liver cells have died, hardened, turned an orange color, and permanently lost their function.

clone an individual created asexually from a single ancestor, such as a plant grown from a single stem cell; a group of genetically identical individuals descended from a single common ancestor, such as a colony of bacteria arising from a single bacterial cell; in genetics, a replica of a segment of DNA, such as a gene, produced by genetic engineering.

coenzyme (co-EN-zime) a small molecule that works with an enzyme to promote the enzyme's activity. Many coenzymes have B vitamins as part of their structure (*co* means "with").

coenzyme Q-10 an enzyme made by cells and important for its role in energy metabolism. With diminished coenzyme Q-10 function, oxidative stress increases, as may occur in aging. Preliminary research suggests that it may be of value for treating certain conditions; toxicity in animals appears to be low. No safe intake levels for human beings have been established.

cognitive skills as taught in behavior therapy, changes to conscious thoughts with the goal of improving adherence to lifestyle modifications; examples are problem-solving skills or the correction of false negative thoughts, termed *cognitive restructuring*.

cognitive therapy psychological therapy aimed at changing undesirable behaviors by changing underlying thought processes contributing to these behaviors; in anorexia, a goal is to replace false beliefs about body weight, eating, and self-worth with health-promoting beliefs.

collagen (COLL-a-jen) the chief protein of most connective tissues, including scars, ligaments, and tendons, and the underlying matrix on which bones and teeth are built.

colon the large intestine.

colostrum (co-LAHS-trum) a milklike secretion from the breasts during the first day or so after delivery before milk appears; rich in protective factors.

competitive foods unregulated meals, including fast foods, that compete side-by-side with USDA-regulated school lunches.

complementary and alternative medicine (CAM) a group of diverse medical and health-care systems, practices and products that are not considered to be a part of conventional medicine. Examples include acupuncture, biofeedback, chiropractic, faith healing, and many others.

complementary proteins two or more proteins whose amino acid assortments complement each other in such a way that the essential amino acids missing from one are supplied by the other.

complex carbohydrates long chains of sugar units arranged to form starch or fiber; also called *polysaccharides*.

concentrated fruit juice sweetener a concentrated sugar syrup made from dehydrated, deflavored fruit juice, commonly grape juice, used to sweeten products that can then claim to be "all fruit."

conditionally essential amino acid an amino acid that is normally nonessential but must be supplied by the diet in special circumstances when the need for it exceeds the body's ability to produce it.

confectioner's sugar finely powdered sucrose, 99.9% pure.

congeners (CON-jen-ers) chemical substances other than alcohol that account for some of the physiological effects of alcoholic beverages, such as appetite, taste, and aftereffects.

conjugated linoleic acid (CLA) a type of fat in butter, milk, and other dairy products believed by some to have biological activity in the body. Not a phytochemical, but a biologically active chemical produced by animals.

constipation difficult, incomplete, or infrequent bowel movements associated with discomfort in passing dry, hardened feces from the body.

contaminant any substance occurring in food by accident; any food constituent that is not normally present.

control group a group of individuals who are similar in all possible respects to the group being treated in an experiment but who receive a sham treatment instead of the real one. Also called *control subjects*. See also *experimental group* and *intervention studies*.

controlled clinical trial a research study design that often reveals the effects of a treatment in human beings. Health outcomes are observed in a group of people who receive the treatment and are then compared with outcomes in a control group of similar people who received a placebo (an inert or sham treatment). Ideally, neither subjects nor researchers know who receives the treatment and who gets the placebo (a double-blind study).

conventional medicine diagnosis and treatment of diseases and practice by medical doctors (M.D.) and doctors of osteopathy (D.O.) and allied health professionals such as physical therapists and registered nurses.

corn sweeteners corn syrup and sugar solutions derived from corn.

corn syrup a syrup, mostly glucose, partly maltose, produced by the action of enzymes on cornstarch.

cornea (KOR-nee-uh) the hard, transparent membrane covering the outside of the eye.

correlation the simultaneous change of two factors, such as the increase of weight with increasing height (a *direct* or *positive* correlation) or the decrease of cancer incidence with increasing fiber intake (an *inverse* or *negative* correlation). A correlation between two factors suggests that one may cause the other but does not rule out the possibility that both may be caused by chance or by a third factor.

cortex the outermost layer of something. The brain's cortex is the part of the brain where conscious thought takes place.

cortical bone the ivorylike outer bone layer that forms a shell surrounding trabecular bone and that comprises the shaft of a long bone.

Country of Origin Label (COOL) the required label stating the country of origination of many imported meats, chicken, fish and shellfish, other perishable foods, certain nuts, peanuts, and ginseng.

creatine a nitrogen-containing compound that combines with phosphate to burn a high-energy compound stored in muscle. Some studies suggest that creatine enhances energy and stimulates muscle growth but long-term studies are lacking; digestive side effects may occur.

cretinism (CREE-tin-ism) severe mental and physical retardation of an infant caused by the mother's iodine deficiency during pregnancy.

critical period a finite period during development in which certain events may occur that will have irreversible effects on later developmental stages. A critical period is usually a period of cell division in a body organ.

cross-contamination the contamination of a food through exposure to utensils, hands, or other surfaces that were previously in contact with a contaminated food.

cruciferous vegetables vegetables with cross-shaped blossoms—the cabbage family. Their intake is associated with low cancer rates in human populations. Examples are broccoli, brussels sprouts, cabbage, cauliflower, rutabagas, and turnips.

cuisines styles of cooking.

cultural competence having an awareness and acceptance of one's own and other cultures and the ability to interact effectively with people of those cultures.

D

Daily Values nutrient standards that are printed on food labels and on grocery store and restaurant signs. Based on nutrient and energy recommendations for a general 2,000-calorie diet, they allow consumers to compare foods with regard to nutrients and calorie contents.

dead zones columns of oxygen-depleted ocean water in which marine life cannot survive; often caused by algae blooms that occur when agricultural fertilizers and waste runoff enter natural waterways.

dehydration loss of water. The symptoms progress rapidly, from thirst to weakness to exhaustion and delirium, and end in death.

denaturation the irreversible change in a protein's folded shape brought about by heat, acids, bases, alcohol, salts of heavy metals, or other agents.

dental caries decay of the teeth (*caries* means "rottenness").

dextrose an older name for glucose.

DHEA (dehydroepiandrosterone) a hormone made in the adrenal glands that serves as a precursor to the male hormone testosterone; recently banned by the FDA because it poses the risk of life-threatening diseases, including cancer. Falsely promoted to burn fat, build muscle, and slow aging.

diabetes (dye-uh-BEET-eez) a disease characterized by elevated blood glucose and inadequate or ineffective insulin, which impairs a person's ability to regulate blood glucose normally. The technical name is *diabetes mellitus (mellitus* means "honey-sweet" in Latin, referring to sugar in the urine).

dialysis (die-AL-ih-sis) in kidney disease, treatment of the blood to remove toxic substances or metabolic wastes; more properly, *hemodialysis,* meaning "dialysis of the blood."

diarrhea frequent, watery bowel movements usually caused by diet, stress, or irritation of the colon. Severe, prolonged diarrhea robs the body of fluid and certain minerals, causing dehydration and imbalances that can be dangerous if left untreated.

diastolic (dye-as-TOL-ik) **pressure** the second figure in a blood pressure reading (the "lubb" of the heartbeat is heard), which reflects the arterial pressure when the heart is between beats.

diet the foods (including beverages) a person usually eats and drinks.

dietary antioxidant (anti-OX-ih-dant) a substance in food that significantly decreases the damaging effects of reactive compounds, such as reactive forms of oxygen and nitrogen, on tissue functioning (*anti* means "against"; *oxy* means "oxygen").

dietary folate equivalent (DFE) a unit of measure expressing the amount of folate available to the body from naturally occurring sources. The measure mathematically equalizes the difference in absorption between less absorbable food folate and highly absorbable synthetic folate added to enriched foods and found in supplements.

Dietary Reference Intakes (DRI) a set of four lists of values for measuring the nutrient intakes of healthy people in the United States and Canada. The four lists are Estimated Average Requirements (EAR), Recommended Dietary Allowances (RDA), Adequate Intakes (AI), and Tolerable Upper Intake Levels (UL).

dietary supplement a product, other than tobacco, that is added to the diet and contains one of the following ingredients: a vitamin, mineral, herb, botanical (plant extract), amino acid, metabolite, constituent, or extract, or a combination of any of these ingredients.

dietetic technician a person who has completed a two-year academic degree from an accredited college or university and an approved dietetic technician program. A **dietetic technician, registered** (DTR) has also passed a national examination and maintains registration through continuing professional education.

dietitian a person trained in nutrition, food science, and diet planning. See also *registered dietitian.*

digest to break molecules into smaller molecules; a main function of the digestive tract with respect to food.

digestive system the body system composed of organs that break down complex food particles into smaller, absorbable products. The *digestive tract* and *alimentary canal* are names for the tubular organs that extend from the mouth to the anus. The whole system, including the pancreas, liver, and gallbladder, is sometimes called the *gastrointestinal,* or *GI,* system.

dipeptides (dye-PEP-tides) protein fragments that are 2 amino acids long (*di* means "two").

diploma mill an organization that awards meaningless degrees without requiring its students to meet educational standards.

disaccharides pairs of single sugars linked together (*di* means "two").

discretionary calorie allowance the balance of calories remaining in a person's energy allowance after accounting for the number of calories needed to meet recommended nutrient intakes through consumption of nutrient-dense foods.

distilled water water that has been vaporized and recondensed, leaving it free of dissolved minerals.

diuretic (dye-you-RET-ic) a compound, usually a medication, causing increased urinary water excretion; a "water pill."

diverticula (dye-ver-TIC-you-la) sacs or pouches that balloon out of the intestinal wall, caused by weakening of the muscle layers that encase the intestine. The painful inflammation of one or more of the diverticula is known as *diverticulitis*.

DNA an abbreviation for deoxyribonucleic (dee-OX-ee-RYE-bow-nu-CLAY-ick) acid, the thread-like molecule that encodes genetic information in its structure; DNA strands coil up densely to form the chromosomes.

DNA microarray technology research tools that analyze the expression of thousands of genes simultaneously and search for particular genes associated with a disease. DNA microarrays are also called *DNA chips*.

dolomite a compound of minerals (calcium magnesium carbonate) found in limestone and marble. Dolomite is powdered and is sold as a calcium-magnesium supplement but may be contaminated with toxic minerals, is not well absorbed, and interacts adversely with absorption of other essential minerals.

drink a dose of any alcoholic beverage that delivers half an ounce of pure ethanol.

drug any substance that when taken into a living organism may modify one or more of its functions.

dual-energy X-ray absorptiometry (ab-sorp-tee-OM-eh-tree) a noninvasive method of determining total body fat, fat distribution, and bone density by passing two low-dose X-ray beams through the body. Also used in evaluation of osteoporosis. Abbreviated DEXA.

dysentery (DISS-en-terry) an infection of the digestive tract that causes diarrhea.

E

eating disorder a disturbance in eating behavior that jeopardizes a person's physical or psychological health.

eclampsia (eh-CLAMP-see-ah) a severe complication during pregnancy in which seizures occur.

edamame fresh green soybeans, a source of phytoestrogens.

edema (eh-DEEM-uh) swelling of body tissue caused by leakage of fluid from the blood vessels; seen in protein deficiency (among other conditions).

eicosanoids (eye-COSS-ah-noyds) biologically active compounds that regulate body functions.

electrolytes compounds that partly dissociate in water to form ions, such as the potassium ion (K^+) and the chloride ion (Cl^+).

electrons parts of an atom; negatively charged particles. Stable atoms (and molecules, which are made of atoms) have even numbers of electrons in pairs. An atom or molecule with an unpaired electron is an unstable *free radical*.

elemental diets diets composed of purified ingredients of known chemical composition; intended to supply all essential nutrients to people who cannot eat foods.

embolism an embolus that causes sudden closure of a blood vessel.

embolus (EM-boh-luss) a thrombus that breaks loose and travels through the blood vessels (*embol* means "to insert").

embryo (EM-bree-oh) the stage of human gestation from the third to the eighth week after conception.

emergency kitchens programs that provide prepared meals to be eaten on-site; often called *soup kitchens*.

emetic (em-ETT-ic) an agent that causes vomiting.

emulsification the process of mixing lipid with water by adding an emulsifier.

emulsifier (ee-MULL-sih-fire) a compound with both water-soluble and fat-soluble portions that can attract fats and oils into water, combining them.

endorphins brain compounds that reduce pain and produce pleasure in ways similar to opiate drugs. In appetite control, endorphins are released on seeing, smelling, or tasting delicious food and may enhance the drive to eat or continue eating.

endosperm the bulk of the edible part of a grain, the starchy part.

energy the capacity to do work. The energy in food is chemical energy; it can be converted to mechanical, electrical, thermal, or other forms of energy in the body. Food energy is measured in calories.

energy density a measure of the energy provided by a food relative to its weight (calories per gram).

energy drinks sugar-sweetened beverages with supposedly ergogenic ingredients, such as vitamins, amino acids, caffeine, guarana, carnitine, ginseng, and others. The drinks are not regulated by the FDA and are often high in caffeine and other stimulants.

energy-yielding nutrients the nutrients the body can use for energy—carbohydrate, fat, and protein. These also may supply building blocks for body structures.

enriched, fortified refers to the addition of nutrients to a refined food product. As defined by U.S. law, these terms mean that specified levels of thiamin, riboflavin, niacin, folate, and iron have been added to refined grains and grain products. The terms *enriched* and *fortified* can refer to the addition of more nutrients than just these five; read the label.

enriched foods and **fortified foods** foods to which nutrients have been added. If the starting material is a whole, basic food such as milk or whole grain, the result may be highly nutritious. If the starting material is a concentrated form of sugar or fat, the result may be less nutritious.

enterotoxins poisons that act upon mucous membranes, such as those of the digestive tract.

environmental tobacco smoke the combination of exhaled smoke (mainstream smoke) and smoke from lighted cigarettes, pipes, or cigars (sidestream smoke) that enters the air and may be inhaled by other people.

enzymes (EN-zimes) proteins that facilitate chemical reactions without being changed in the process; protein catalysts.

EPA (Environmental Protection Agency) the federal agency that is responsible for regulating pesticides and establishing water quality standards.

EPA, DHA eicosapentaenoic (EYE-cossa-PENTA-ee-NO-ick) acid, docosahexaenoic (DOE-cossa-HEXA-ee-NO-ick) acid; omega-3 fatty acids made from linolenic acid in the tissues of fish.

ephedrine one of a group of compounds with dangerous amphetamine-like stimulant effects; extracted from the herb ma huang and recently banned by the FDA but still available from Internet sources. The most severe reported side effects of ephedrine include heart attack, stroke, and sudden death.

epidemiological studies studies of populations; often used in nutrition to search for correlations between dietary habits and disease incidence; a first step in seeking nutrition-related causes of diseases.

epigenetics the science of heritable changes in gene function that occur without a change in the DNA sequence.

epigenome the proteins and other molecules associated with chromosomes that affect gene expression. The epigenome is modulated by bioactive food components and other factors in ways that can be inherited. *Epi* is a Greek prefix, meaning "above" or "on."

epinephrine (EP-ih-NEFF-rin) the major hormone that elicits the stress response.

epiphyseal (eh-PIFF-ih-seal) **plate** a thick, cartilage-like layer that forms new cells that are eventually calcified, lengthening the bone (*epiphysis* means "growing" in Greek).

epithelial (ep-ith-THEE-lee-ull) **tissue** the layers of the body that serve as selective barriers to environmental factors. Examples are the cornea, the skin, the respiratory tract lining, and the lining of the digestive tract.

ergogenic (ER-go-JEN-ic) **aids** products that supposedly enhance performance, although few actually do so; the term *ergogenic* implies "energy giving" (*ergo* means "work"; *genic* means "give rise to").

erythrocyte (eh-REETH-ro-sight) **hemolysis** (HEE-moh-LIE-sis, hee-MOLL-ih-sis) rupture of the red blood cells, caused by vitamin E deficiency (*erythro* means "red"; *cyte* means "cell"; *hemo* means "blood"; *lysis* means "breaking"). The anemia produced by the condition is *hemolytic* (HEE-moh-LIT-ick) *anemia.*

essential amino acids amino acids that either cannot be synthesized at all by the body or cannot be synthesized in amounts sufficient to meet physiological needs. Also called *indispensable amino acids.*

essential fatty acids fatty acids that the body needs but cannot make in amounts sufficient to meet physiological needs.

essential nutrients the nutrients the body cannot make for itself (or cannot make fast enough) from other raw materials; nutrients that must be obtained from food to prevent deficiencies.

Estimated Average Requirements (EAR) the average daily nutrient intake estimated to meet the requirement of half of the healthy individuals in a particular life stage and gender group; used in nutrition research and policymaking and is the basis upon which RDA values are set.

Estimated Energy Requirement (EER) the average dietary energy intake predicted to maintain energy balance in a healthy adult of a certain age, gender, weight, height, and level of physical activity consistent with good health.

ethanol the alcohol of alcoholic beverages, produced by the action of microorganisms on the carbohydrates of grape juice or other carbohydrate-containing fluids.

ethnic foods foods associated with particular cultural subgroups within a population.

euphoria (you-FOR-ee-uh) an inflated sense of well-being and pleasure brought on by a moderate dose of alcohol and by some other drugs.

evaporated cane juice raw sugar from which impurities have been removed.

exchange system a diet-planning tool that organizes foods with respect to their nutrient content and calories. Foods on any single exchange list can be used interchangeably.

exclusive breastfeeding an infant's consumption of human milk with no supplementation of any type (no water, no juice, no nonhuman milk, and no foods) except for vitamins, minerals, and medications.

experimental group the people or animals participating in an experiment who receive the treatment under investigation. Also called *experimental subject.* See also *control group* and *intervention studies.*

extra lean (main dishes and prepared meals) less than 5 g total fat *and* less than 2 g saturated fat *and* less than 95 mg cholesterol per serving.

extracellular fluid fluid residing outside the cells that transports materials to and from the cells.

extreme obesity clinically severe overweight, presenting very high risks to health; the condition of having a BMI of 40 or above; also called *morbid obesity.*

extrusion processing techniques that transform whole or refined grains, legumes, and other foods into shaped, colored, and flavored snacks, breakfast cereals, and other products.

F

famine widespread and extreme scarcity of food that causes starvation and death in a large portion of the population in an area.

farm share an arrangement in which a farmer offers the public a "subscription" for an allotment of the farm's products throughout the season.

fast foods restaurant foods that are available within minutes after customers order them—traditionally, hamburgers, French fries, and milkshakes; more recently, salads and other vegetable dishes as well. These foods may or may not meet people's nutrient needs, depending on the selections made and on the energy allowances and nutrient needs of the eaters.

fasting hypoglycemia hypoglycemia that occurs after 8 to 14 hours of fasting.

fat cells cells that specialize in the storage of fat and form the fat tissue. Fat cells also produce fat-metabolizing enzymes; they also produce hormones involved in appetite and energy balance.

fat free less than 0.5 g of fat per serving.

fat replacers ingredients that replace some or all of the functions of fat and may or may not provide energy.

fats lipids that are solid at room temperature (70°F or 21°C).

fatty acids organic acids composed of carbon chains of various lengths. Each fatty acid has an acid end and hydrogens attached to all of the carbon atoms of the chain.

fatty liver an early stage of liver deterioration seen in several diseases, including kwashiorkor and alcoholic liver disease, in which fat accumulates in the liver cells.

FDA (Food and Drug Administration) the part of the Department of Health and Human Services' Public Health Service that is responsible for ensuring the safety and wholesomeness of all foods sold in interstate commerce except meat, poultry, and eggs (which are under the jurisdiction of the USDA); inspecting food plants and imported foods; and setting standards for food consumption. The FDA also regulates food additives.

feces waste material remaining after digestion and absorption are complete; eventually discharged from the body.

female athletic triad a potentially fatal triad of medical problems seen in female athletes: disordered eating, amenorrhea, and osteoporosis.

fertility the capacity of a woman to produce a normal ovum periodically and of a man to produce normal sperm; the ability to reproduce.

fetal alcohol spectrum disorders (FASD) a spectrum of physical, behavioral, and cognitive disabilities caused by prenatal alcohol exposure.

fetal alcohol syndrome (FAS) the cluster of symptoms including brain damage, growth retardation, mental retardation, and facial abnormalities seen in an infant or child whose mother consumed alcohol during her pregnancy.

fetus (FEET-us) the stage of human gestation from eight weeks after conception until the birth of an infant.

fibers the indigestible parts of plant foods, largely nonstarch polysaccharides that are not digested by human digestive enzymes, although some are digested by resident bacteria of the colon. Fibers include cellulose, hemicelluloses, pectins, gums, mucilages, and the nonpolysaccharide lignin.

fibrosis (fye-BROH-sis) an intermediate stage of alcoholic liver deterioration. Liver cells lose their function and assume the characteristics of connective tissue cells (fibers).

fight-or-flight reaction the body's instinctive hormone- and nerve-mediated reaction to danger. Also known as the *stress response*.

filtered water water treated by filtration, usually through activated carbon filters that reduce the lead in tap water, or by reverse osmosis units that force pressurized water across a membrane, removing lead, arsenic, and some microorganisms from tap water.

fitness water lightly flavored bottled water enhanced with vitamins, supposedly to enhance athletic performance.

flavonoids (FLAY-von-oyds) members of a chemical family of yellow pigments in foods; phytochemicals that may exert physiological effects on the body. *Flavus* means "yellow."

flavored waters lightly flavored beverages with few or no calories, but often containing vitamins, minerals, herbs, or other unneeded substances. Not superior to plain water for athletic competition or training.

flaxseed small brown seed of the flax plant; used in baking, cereals, or other foods. Valued in nutrition as a source of fiber and fatty acids.

fluid and electrolyte balance maintenance of the proper amounts and kinds of fluids and minerals in each compartment of the body.

fluid and electrolyte imbalance failure to maintain the proper amounts and kinds of fluids and minerals in every body compartment; a medical emergency.

fluorapatite (floor-APP-uh-tight) a crystal of bones and teeth, formed when fluoride displaces the "hydroxy" portion of hydroxyapatite. Fluorapatite resists being dissolved back into body fluid.

fluorosis (floor-OH-sis) discoloration of the teeth due to ingestion of too much fluoride during tooth development.

folate (FOH-late) a B vitamin that acts as part of a coenzyme important in the manufacture of new cells. The form added to foods and supplements is *folic acid*.

food medically, any substance that the body can take in and assimilate that will enable it to stay alive and to grow; the carrier of nourishment; socially, a more limited number of such substances defined as acceptable by each culture.

food aversion an intense dislike of a food, biological or psychological in nature, resulting from an illness or other negative experience associated with that food.

food banks facilities that collect and distribute food donations to authorized organizations feeding the hungry.

food bioterrorism the intentional adulteration or depletion of the food supply through the use of biological agents, such as pathogenic organisms or agricultural pests, to cause fear and destruction in a population.

food crisis a steep decline in food availability with a proportional rise in hunger and malnutrition at the local, national, or global level.

food deserts a term used to describe urban and rural low-income neighborhoods and communities that have limited access to affordable and nutritious foods.

food group plan a diet-planning tool that sorts foods into groups based on their nutrient content and then specifies that people should eat certain minimum numbers of servings of foods from each group.

food intolerance an adverse reaction to a food or food additive not involving an immune response.

food neophobia (NEE-oh-FOE-bee-ah) the fear of trying new foods, common among toddlers.

food pantries community food collection programs that provide groceries to be prepared and eaten at home.

food poverty hunger occurring when enough food exists in an area but some of the people cannot obtain it because they lack money, are being deprived for political reasons, live in a country at war, or suffer from other problems such as lack of transportation.

food recovery collecting wholesome surplus food for distribution to low-income people who are hungry.

foodborne illness illness transmitted to human beings through food and water; caused by an infectious agent (*foodborne infection*) or a poisonous substance arising from microbial toxins, poisonous chemicals, or other harmful substances (*food intoxication*). Also called *food poisoning*.

foodways the sum of a culture's habits, customs, beliefs, and preferences concerning food.

fork thermometer a utensil combining a meat fork and an instant-read food thermometer.

formaldehyde a substance to which methanol is metabolized on the way to being converted to harmless waste products that can be excreted.

fraud or **quackery** the promotion, for financial gain, of devices, treatments, services, plans, or products (including diets and supplements) claimed to improve health, well-being, or appearance without proof of safety or effectiveness. (The word *quackery* comes from the term *quacksalver*, meaning a person who quacks loudly about a miracle product—a lotion or a salve.)

free, without, no, zero none or a trivial amount. **Calorie free** means containing fewer than 5 calories per serving; **sugar free** or **fat free** means containing less than half a gram per serving.

free radicals atoms or molecules with one or more unpaired electrons that make the atom or molecule unstable and highly reactive.

fresh raw, unprocessed, or minimally processed with no added preservatives.

fructose (FROOK-tose) a monosaccharide; sometimes known as fruit sugar (*fruct* means "fruit"; *ose* means "sugar").

fructose, galactose, glucose the monosaccharides.

fruitarian includes only raw or dried fruits, seeds, and nuts in the diet.

fufu a low-protein staple food that provides abundant starch energy to many of the world's people; fufu is made by pounding or grinding root vegetables or refined grains and cooking them to a smooth semisolid consistency.

functional foods whole or modified foods that contain bioactive food components believed to provide health benefits, such as reduced disease risks, beyond the benefits that their nutrients confer on the eater. However, all nutritious foods can support health in some ways.

G

galactose (ga-LACK-tose) a monosaccharide; part of the disaccharide lactose (milk sugar).

garlic oil an extract of garlic; may or may not contain the chemicals associated with garlic; claims for health benefits unproved.

gastric juice the digestive secretion of the stomach.

gastroesophageal (GAS-tro-eh-SOFF-ah-jeel) **reflux disease (GERD)** a severe and chronic splashing of stomach acid and enzymes into the esophagus, throat, mouth, or airway that causes injury to those organs. Untreated GERD may increase the risk of esophageal cancer; treatment may require surgery or management with medication.

gatekeeper with respect to nutrition, a key person who controls other people's access to foods and thereby affects their nutrition profoundly. Examples are the spouse who buys and cooks the food, the parent who feeds the children, and the caregiver in a day-care center.

GE foods genetically engineered foods; food plants and animals altered by way of rDNA technology.

generally recognized as safe (GRAS) list a list, established by the FDA, of food additives long in use and believed to be safe.

genes units of a cell's inheritance; sections of the larger genetic molecule DNA (deoxyribonucleic acid). Each gene directs the making of one or more of the body's proteins.

genetic engineering (GE) the direct, intentional manipulation of the genetic material of living things in order to obtain some desirable trait not present in the original organism. Also called *recombinant DNA technology* and *biotechnology*.

genetic modification intentional changes to the genetic material of living things brought about through a range of methods, including rDNA technology, natural cross-breeding, and agricultural selective breeding.

genistein (GEN-ih-steen) a phytoestrogen found primarily in soybeans that both mimics and blocks the action of estrogen in the body.

genome (GEE-nome) the full complement of genetic information in the chromosomes of a cell. In human beings, the genome consists of about 35,000 genes and supporting materials. The study of genomes is *genomics*.

germ the nutrient-rich inner part of a grain.

gestation the period of about 40 weeks (three trimesters) from conception to birth; the term of a pregnancy.

gestational diabetes abnormal glucose tolerance appearing during pregnancy.

gestational hypertension high blood pressure that develops in the second half of pregnancy and usually resolves after childbirth.

ghrelin (GREL-in) a hormone released by the stomach that signals the hypothalamus of the brain to stimulate eating.

glucagon (GLOO-cah-gon) a hormone secreted by the pancreas that stimulates the liver to release glucose into the blood when blood glucose concentration dips.

glucose (GLOO-cose) a single sugar used in both plant and animal tissues for energy; sometimes known as blood sugar or *dextrose*.

glycemic index (GI) a ranking of foods according to their potential for raising blood glucose relative to a standard such as glucose or white bread.

glycemic load (GL) a mathematical expression of both the glycemic index and the carbohydrate content of a food, meal, or diet (glycemic index × carbohydrate).

glycerol (GLISS-er-all) an organic compound, three carbons long, of interest here because it serves as the backbone for triglycerides.

glycogen (GLY-co-gen) a highly branched polysaccharide that is made and stored by liver and muscle tissues of human beings and animals as a storage form of glucose. Glycogen is not a significant food source of carbohydrate and is not counted as one of the complex carbohydrates in foods.

goiter (GOY-ter) enlargement of the thyroid gland due to iodine deficiency is *simple goiter;* enlargement due to an iodine excess is *toxic goiter.*

good source 10% to 19% of the Daily Value per serving.

good source of fiber 2.5 g to 4.9 g per serving.

gout (GOWT) a painful form of arthritis caused by the abnormal buildup of the waste product uric acid in the blood, with uric acid salt deposited as crystals in the joints.

grams units of weight. A gram (g) is the weight of a cubic centimeter (cc) or milliliter (ml) of water under defined conditions of temperature and pressure. About 28 grams equal an ounce.

granulated sugar common table sugar, crystalline sucrose, 99.9% pure.

granules small grains. Starch granules are packages of starch molecules. Various plant species make starch granules of varying shapes.

green pills, fruit pills pills containing dehydrated, crushed vegetable or fruit matter. An advertisement may claim that each pill equals a pound of fresh produce, but in reality a pill may equal one small forkful—minus nutrient losses incurred in processing.

groundwater water that comes from underground aquifers.

growth hormone a hormone (somatotropin) that promotes growth and that is produced naturally in the pituitary gland of the brain.

growth spurt the marked rapid gain in physical size usually evident around the onset of adolescence.

H

hard water water with high calcium and magnesium concentrations.

hazard a state of danger; used to refer to any circumstance in which harm is possible under normal conditions of use.

Hazard Analysis Critical Control Point (HACCP) a systematic plan to identify and correct potential microbial hazards in the manufacturing, distribution, and commercial use of food products. *HACCP* may be pronounced "HASS-ip."

health claims claims linking food constituents with disease states; allowable on labels within the criteria established by the Food and Drug Administration.

healthy low in fat, saturated fat, *trans* fat, cholesterol, and sodium and containing at least 10% of the Daily Value for vitamin A, vitamin C, iron, calcium, protein, or fiber.

Healthy Eating Index (HEI) a measure that assesses how well a diet meets the recommendations of the *Dietary Guidelines for Americans* and MyPyramid.

heart attack the event in which the vessels that feed the heart muscle become closed off by an embolism, thrombus, or other cause with resulting sudden tissue death. A heart attack is also called a *myocardial infarction* (*myo* means "muscle"; *cardial* means "of the heart"; *infarct* means "tissue death").

heartburn a burning sensation in the chest (in the area of the heart) caused by backflow of stomach acid into the esophagus.

heavy metal any of a number of mineral ions such as mercury and lead, so called because they are of relatively high atomic weight; many heavy metals are poisonous.

heme (HEEM) the iron-containing portion of the hemoglobin and myoglobin molecules.

hemolytic-uremic syndrome (HE-moh-LIT-ic you-REE-mick) a severe result of infection with *E. coli* O157:H7, characterized by abnormal blood clotting with kidney failure, damage to the central nervous system and other organs, and death, especially among children.

hemoglobin (HEEM-oh-globe-in) the oxygen-carrying protein of the blood; found in the red blood cells (*hemo* means "blood"; *globin* means "spherical protein").

hemorrhoids (HEM-or-oids) swollen, hardened (varicose) veins in the rectum, usually caused by the pressure resulting from constipation.

herbal medicine use of herbs and other natural substances with the intention of preventing or curing diseases or relieving symptoms.

hernia a protrusion of an organ or part of an organ through the wall of the body chamber that normally contains the organ. An example is a *hiatal* (high-AY-tal) *hernia,* in which part of the stomach protrudes up through the diaphragm into the chest cavity, which contains the esophagus, heart, and lungs.

hiccups spasms of both the vocal cords and the diaphragm, causing periodic, audible, short, inhaled coughs. Can be caused by irritation of the diaphragm, indigestion, or other causes. Hiccups usually resolve in a few minutes, but can have serious effects if prolonged. Breathing into a paper bag (inhaling carbon dioxide) or dissolving a teaspoon of sugar in the mouth may stop them.

high-density lipoproteins (HDL) lipoproteins that return cholesterol from the tissues to the liver for dismantling and disposal; contain a large proportion of protein.

high fiber 5 g or more per serving. (Foods making high-fiber claims must fit the definition of low fat, or the level of total fat must appear next to the high-fiber claim.)

high food security no reported food limitation or access problems. The food supply is ample.

high fructose corn syrup a commercial sweetener used in many foods, including soft drinks. Composed almost entirely of the monosaccharides fructose and glucose, its sweetness and caloric value are similar to those of sucrose.

high in 20% or more of the Daily Value for a given nutrient per serving; synonyms include "rich in" or "excellent source."

high-quality proteins dietary proteins containing all the essential amino acids in relatively the same amounts that human beings require. They may also contain nonessential amino acids.

high-risk pregnancy a pregnancy characterized by risk factors that make it likely the birth will be surrounded by problems such as premature delivery, difficult birth, retarded growth, birth defects, and early infant death. A *low-risk pregnancy* has none of these factors.

histamine a substance that participates in causing inflammation; produced by cells of the immune system as part of a local immune reaction to an antigen.

histones proteins that lend structural support to the chromosome structure and that activate or silence gene expression.

homocysteine (hoe-moe-SIS-teen) an amino acid produced as an intermediate compound during amino acid metabolism. A buildup of homocysteine in the blood is associated with deficiencies of B vitamins and may increase the risk of diseases.

honey a concentrated solution primarily composed of glucose and fructose, produced by enzymatic digestion of the sucrose in nectar by bees.

hormones chemicals that are secreted by glands into the blood in response to conditions in the body that require regulation. These chemicals serve as messengers, acting on other organs to maintain constant conditions.

hunger (1) the physiological need to eat, experienced as a drive for obtaining food; an unpleasant sensation that demands relief.

hunger (2) a consequence of food insecurity that, because of prolonged involuntary lack of food, results in discomfort, illness, weakness, or pain beyond a mild uneasy sensation.

husk the outer, inedible part of a grain.

hydrochloric acid a strong corrosive acid of hydrogen and chloride atoms, produced by the stomach to assist in digestion.

hydrogenation (high-dro-gen-AY-shun) the process of adding hydrogen to unsaturated fatty acids to make fat more solid and resistant to the chemical change of oxidation.

hydroxyapatite (hi-DROX-ee-APP-uh-tight) the chief crystal of bone, formed from calcium and phosphorus.

hyperactivity (in children) a syndrome characterized by inattention, impulsiveness, and excess motor activity; usually diagnosed before age 7, lasts six months or more, and usually does not entail mental illness or mental retardation. Properly called *attention-deficit/hyperactivity disorder (ADHD).*

hypertension higher-than-normal blood pressure.

hypoglycemia (HIGH-poh-gly-SEE-mee-uh) a blood glucose concentration below normal, a symptom that may indicate any of several diseases, including impending diabetes.

hypothalamus (high-poh-THAL-uh-mus) a part of the brain that senses a variety of conditions in the blood, such as temperature, glucose content, salt content, and others. It signals other parts of the brain or body to adjust those conditions when necessary.

I

immune system a system of tissues and organs that defend the body against antigens, foreign materials that have penetrated the skin or body linings.

immunity protection from or resistance to a disease or infection by development of antibodies and by the actions of cells and tissues in response to a threat.

implantation the stage of development, during the first two weeks after conception, in which the fertilized egg (fertilized ovum or zygote) embeds itself in the wall of the uterus and begins to develop.

inborn error of metabolism a genetic variation present from birth that may result in disease.

incidental additives substances that can get into food not through intentional introduction, but as a result of contact with the food during growing, processing, packaging, storing, or some other stage before the food is consumed. Also called *accidental* or *indirect additives*.

infectious diseases diseases that are caused by bacteria, viruses, parasites, and other microbes and can be transmitted from one person to another through air, water, or food; by contact; or through vector organisms such as mosquitoes and fleas.

inflammation (in-flam-MAY-shun) part of the body's immune defense against injury, infection, or allergens, marked by increased blood flow, release of chemical toxins, and attraction of white blood cells to the affected area (from the Latin *inflammare,* meaning "to flame within").

infomercials feature-length television commercials that follow the format of regular programs but are intended to convince viewers to buy products and not to educate or entertain them. The statements made may or may not be accurate.

initiation an event, probably occurring in a cell's genetic material, caused by radiation or by a chemical carcinogen that can give rise to cancer.

inositol (in-OSS-ih-tall) a nonessential nutrient found in cell membranes.

insoluble fibers the tough, fibrous structures of fruits, vegetables, and grains; indigestible food components that do not dissolve in water.

instant-read thermometer a thermometer that, when inserted into food, measures its temperature within seconds; designed to test temperature of food at intervals, and not to be left in food during cooking.

insulin a hormone from the pancreas that helps glucose enter cells from the blood.

insulin resistance a condition in which a normal or high level of circulating insulin produces a less-than-normal response in muscle, liver, and adipose tissues; thought to be a metabolic consequence of obesity.

integrated pest management (IPM) management of pests using a combination of natural and biological controls and minimal or no application of pesticides.

integrative medicine care that combines conventional and complementary therapies for which there is some high-quality scientific evidence of safety and effectiveness. Integrative medicine emphasizes the importance of the relationship between the practitioner and the patient and focuses on wellness, healing, and the whole person.

Internet (the Net) a worldwide network of millions of computers linked together to share information.

intervention studies studies of populations in which observation is accompanied by experimental manipulation of some population members—for example, a study in which half of the subjects (the *experimental subjects*) follow diet advice to reduce fat intakes while the other half (the *control subjects*) do not, and both groups' heart health is monitored.

intestine the body's long, tubular organ of digestion and the site of nutrient absorption.

intracellular fluid fluid residing inside the cells that provides the medium for cellular reactions.

intrinsic factor a factor found inside a system. The intrinsic factor necessary to prevent pernicious anemia is now known to be a compound that helps in the absorption of vitamin B_{12}.

invert sugar a mixture of glucose and fructose formed by the splitting of sucrose in an industrial process. Sold only in liquid form and sweeter than sucrose, invert sugar forms during certain cooking procedures and works to prevent crystallization of sucrose in soft candies and sweets.

ions (EYE-ons) electrically charged particles, such as sodium (positively charged) or chloride (negatively charged).

iron deficiency the condition of having depleted iron stores, which, at the extreme, causes iron-deficiency anemia.

iron-deficiency anemia a form of anemia caused by a lack of iron and characterized by red blood cell shrinkage and color loss. Accompanying symptoms are weakness, apathy, headaches, pallor, intolerance to cold, and inability to pay attention. (For other anemias, see the index.)

iron overload the state of having more iron in the body than it needs or can handle, usually arising from a hereditary defect. Also called *hemochromatosis.*

irradiation the application of ionizing radiation to foods to reduce insect infestation or microbial contamination or to slow the ripening or sprouting process. Also called *cold pasteurization.*

irritable bowel syndrome (IBS) intermittent disturbance of bowel function, especially diarrhea or alternating diarrhea and constipation, often with abdominal cramping or bloating; managed with diet, physical activity, or relief from psychological stress. The cause is uncertain, but IBS does not permanently harm the intestines nor lead to serious diseases.

IU (international units) a measure of fat-soluble vitamin activity sometimes used in food composition tables and on supplement labels.

J

jaundice (JAWN-dis) yellowing of the skin due to spillover of the bile pigment bilirubin (bill-ee-ROO-bin) from the liver into the general circulation.

K

kefir (KEE-fur) a liquid form of yogurt, based on milk, probiotic microorganisms, and flavorings.

kelp tablets tablets made from dehydrated kelp, a kind of seaweed used by the Japanese as a foodstuff.

keratin (KERR-uh-tin) the normal protein of hair and nails.

keratinization accumulation of keratin in a tissue; a sign of vitamin A deficiency.

ketone (kee-tone) **bodies** acidic, fat-related compounds that can arise from the incomplete breakdown of fat when carbohydrate is not available.

ketosis (kee-TOE-sis) an undesirable high concentration of ketone bodies, such as acetone, in the blood or urine.

kidneys a pair of organs that filter wastes from the blood, make urine, and release it to the bladder for excretion from the body.

kwashiorkor (kwash-ee-OR-core, kwashee-or-CORE) a form of PEM related to protein malnutrition and infections, with a set of recognizable symptoms, such as edema.

L

laboratory studies studies that are performed under tightly controlled conditions and are designed to pinpoint causes and effects. Such studies often use animals as subjects.

lactase the intestinal enzyme that splits the disaccharide lactose to monosaccharides during digestion.

lactation production and secretion of breast milk for the purpose of nourishing an infant.

lactoferrin (lack-toe-FERR-in) a factor in breast milk that binds iron and keeps it from supporting the growth of the infant's intestinal bacteria.

lacto-ovo vegetarian includes dairy products, eggs, vegetables, grains, legumes, fruits, and nuts; excludes flesh and seafood.

lactose a disaccharide composed of glucose and galactose; sometimes known as milk sugar (*lact* means "milk"; *ose* means "sugar").

lactose, maltose, sucrose the disaccharides.

lactose intolerance impaired ability to digest lactose due to reduced amounts of the enzyme lactase.

lacto-vegetarian includes dairy products, vegetables, grains, legumes, fruits, and nuts; excludes flesh, seafood, and eggs.

lapses times of falling back into former habits, a normal and expected part of behavior change.

large intestine the portion of the intestine that completes the absorption process.

lean (meat and poultry products) less than 10 g of fat *and* less than 4.5 g of saturated fat and *trans* fat combined *and* less than 95 mg of cholesterol per serving.

lean (main dishes and prepared meals) less than 8 g total fat *and* 3.5 g or less saturated fat *and* less than 80 mg cholesterol per serving.

learning disability a condition resulting in an altered ability to learn basic cognitive skills such as reading, writing, and mathematics.

leavened (LEV-end) literally, "lightened" by yeast cells, which digest some carbohydrate components of the dough and leave behind bubbles of gas that make the bread rise.

lecithin (LESS-ih-thin) a phospholipid manufactured by the liver and also found in many foods; a major constituent of cell membranes.

legumes (leg-GOOMS, LEG-yooms) plants of the bean, pea, and lentil family that have roots with nodules containing special bacteria. These bacteria can trap nitrogen from the air in the soil and make it into compounds that become part of the plant's seeds. The seeds are rich in protein compared with those of most other plant foods.

leptin an appetite-suppressing hormone produced in the fat cells that conveys information about body fatness to the brain; believed to be involved in the maintenance of body composition (*leptos* means "slender").

less, fewer, reduced containing at least 25% less of a nutrient or calories than a reference food. This may occur naturally or as a result of altering the food. For example, pretzels, which are usually low in fat, can claim to provide less fat than potato chips, a comparable food.

less saturated fat 25% or less saturated fat and *trans* fat combined than the comparison food.

levulose an older name for fructose.

license to practice permission under state or federal law, granted on meeting specified criteria, to use a certain title (such as *dietitian*) and to offer certain services. Licensed dietitians may use the initials LD after their names.

life expectancy the average number of years lived by people in a given society.

life span the maximum number of years of life attainable by a member of a species.

light this descriptor has three meanings on labels: (1) A serving provides one-third fewer calories or half the fat of the regular product; (2) a serving of a low-calorie, low-fat food provides half the sodium normally present; (3) the product is light in color and texture, so long as the label makes this intent clear, as in "light brown sugar."

lignans phytochemicals present in flaxseed, but not in flax oil, that are converted to phytoestrogens by intestinal bacteria and are under study as possible anticancer agents.

limiting amino acid an essential amino acid that is present in dietary protein in an insufficient amount, thereby limiting the body's ability to build protein.

linoleic (lin-oh-LAY-ic) **acid** and **linolenic** (lin-oh-LEN-ic) **acid** polyunsaturated fatty acids that are essential nutrients for human beings. The full name of linolenic acid is *alpha-linolenic acid.*

lipase (LYE-pace) any of a number of enzymes that break the chemical bonds of fats.

lipid (LIP-id) a family of organic (carbon-containing) compounds soluble in organic solvents but not in water. Lipids include triglycerides (fats and oils), phospholipids, and sterols.

lipoic (lip-OH-ic) **acid** a nonessential nutrient.

lipoproteins (LYE-poh-PRO-teens, LIH-poh-PRO-teens) clusters of lipids associated with protein, which serve as transport vehicles for lipids in blood and lymph. Major lipoprotein classes are the chylomicrons, VLDL, LDL, and HDL.

listeriosis a serious foodborne infection that can cause severe brain infection or death in a fetus or a newborn; caused by the bacterium *Listeria monocytogenes,* which is found in soil and water.

liver a large, lobed organ that lies just under the ribs. It filters the blood, removes and processes nutrients, manufactures materials for export to other parts of the body, and destroys toxins or stores them to keep them out of the circulatory system.

locus of control the assigned source of responsibility for one's life events; an internal locus of control identifies the individual's behaviors as the driving force; an external locus of control blames chance, fate, or some other external factor. Most people's attitude falls somewhere in between.

longevity long duration of life.

low birthweight a birthweight of less than 5½ pounds (2,500 grams); used as a predictor of probable health problems in the newborn and as a probable indicator of poor nutrition status of the mother before and/or during pregnancy. Low-birthweight infants are of two different types. Some are *premature infants;* they are born early and are the right size for their gestational age. Other low-birthweight infants have suffered growth failure in the uterus; they are small for gestational age (small for date) and may or may not be premature.

low calorie 40 calories or fewer per serving.

low cholesterol 20 mg or less of cholesterol *and* 2 g or less saturated fat per serving.

low-density lipoproteins (LDL) lipoproteins that transport lipids from the liver to other tissues such as muscle and fat; contain a large proportion of cholesterol.

low fat 3 g or less fat per serving.

low food security reduced dietary quality, variety, or desirability, but no significant reduction in total food intake. Example: a family whose diet centers on inexpensive, low-nutrient foods such as refined grains, inexpensive meats, sweets, and fats.

low saturated fat 1 g or less saturated fat and less than 0.5 g of *trans* fat per serving.

low sodium 140 mg or less sodium per serving.

lungs the body's organs of gas exchange. Blood circulating through the lungs releases its carbon dioxide and picks up fresh oxygen to carry to the tissues.

lutein (LOO-teen) a plant pigment of yellow hue; a phytochemical believed to play roles in eye functioning and health.

lycopene (LYE-koh-peen) a pigment responsible for the red color of tomatoes and other red-hued vegetables; a phytochemical that may act as an antioxidant in the body.

lymph (LIMF) the fluid that moves from the bloodstream into tissue spaces and then travels in its own vessels, which eventually drain back into the bloodstream.

lymphocytes (LIM-foh-sites) white blood cells that participate in the immune response; B-cells and T-cells.

M

ma huang an evergreen plant that supposedly boosts energy and helps with weight control. Ma huang, also called ephedra, contains ephedrine and is especially dangerous in combination with kola nut or other caffeine-containing substances.

macrobiotic diet a vegan diet composed mostly of whole grains, beans, and certain vegetables; taken to extremes, macrobiotic diets can compromise nutrient status.

macrophages (MACK-roh-fah-jez) large scavenger cells of the immune system that engulf debris and remove it (*macro* means "large"; *phagein* means "to eat").

macular degeneration a common, progressive loss of function of the part of the retina that is most crucial to focused vision. This degeneration often leads to blindness.

major minerals essential mineral nutrients required in the adult diet in amounts greater than 100 milligrams per day. Also called *macrominerals.*

malnutrition any condition caused by excess or deficient food energy or nutrient intake or by an imbalance of nutrients. Nutrient or energy deficiencies are forms of undernutrition; nutrient or energy excesses are forms of overnutrition.

maltose a disaccharide composed of two glucose units; sometimes known as malt sugar.

maple sugar a concentrated solution of sucrose derived from the sap of the sugar maple tree, mostly sucrose. This sugar was once common but is now usually replaced by sucrose and artificial maple flavoring.

marasmus (ma-RAZ-mus) a form of PEM caused by a severe lack of food, impaired nutrient absorption, or both; starvation.

margin of safety in reference to food additives, a zone between the concentration normally used and that at which a hazard exists. For common table salt, for example, the margin of safety is 1/5 (five times the concentration normally used would be hazardous).

marginal food security one or two problems, usually anxiety over having enough food in the house, but without significant change in food intake. Example: a family whose food supply is sufficient but barely lasts until the next paycheck.

medical foods foods specially manufactured for use by people with medical disorders and prescribed by a physician.

medical nutrition therapy nutrition services used in the treatment of injury, illness, or other conditions; includes assessment of nutrition status and dietary intake and corrective applications of diet, counseling, and other nutrition services.

melatonin a hormone of the pineal gland believed to help regulate the body's daily rhythms, to reverse the effects of jet lag, and to promote sleep. Claims for life extension or enhancement of sexual prowess are without merit.

metabolic syndrome a combination of characteristic factors—high fasting blood glucose or insulin resistance, central obesity, hypertension, low blood HDL cholesterol, and elevated blood triglycerides—that greatly increase a person's risk of developing CVD. Also called *insulin resistance syndrome* or *syndrome X.*

metabolic water water generated in the tissues during the chemical breakdown of the energy-yielding nutrients in foods.

metabolism the sum of all physical and chemical changes taking place in living cells; includes all reactions by which the body obtains and spends the energy from food.

metastasis (meh-TASS-ta-sis) movement of cancer cells from one body part to another, usually by way of the body fluids.

methanol an alcohol produced in the body continually by all cells.

methyl groups small carbon-containing molecules that, among their activities, silence genes when applied to DNA strands by enzymes.

methylmercury any toxic compound of mercury to which a characteristic chemical structure, a methyl group, has been added, usually by bacteria in aquatic sediments. Methylmercury is readily absorbed from the intestine and causes nerve damage in people.

MFP factor a factor present in meat, fish, and poultry that enhances the absorption of nonheme iron present in the same foods or in other foods eaten at the same time.

microbes a shortened name for *microorganisms;* minute organisms too small to observe without a microscope, including bacteria, viruses, and others.

microcredit nontraditional money sources typically involving small loans to disadvantaged people for business development.

microvilli (MY-croh-VILL-ee, MY-croh-VILL-eye) tiny, hairlike projections on each cell of every villus that greatly expand the surface area available to trap nutrient particles and absorb them into the cells (*singular:* microvillus).

milk anemia iron-deficiency anemia caused by drinking so much milk that iron-rich foods are displaced from the diet.

mineral water water from a spring or well that typically contains 250 to 500 parts per million (ppm) of minerals. Minerals give water a distinctive flavor. Many mineral waters are high in sodium.

minerals naturally occurring, inorganic, homogeneous substances; chemical elements.

miso fermented soybean paste used in Japanese cooking. Soy products are considered to be functional foods.

moderate drinkers people who do not drink excessively and do not behave inappropriately because of alcohol. A moderate drinker's health may or may not be harmed by alcohol over the long term.

moderation the dietary characteristic of providing constituents within set limits, not to excess.

modified atmosphere packaging (MAP) a preservation technique in which a perishable food is packaged in a gas-impermeable container from which air has been removed or to which another gas mixture has been added.

molasses a syrup left over from the refining of sucrose from sugarcane; a thick, brown syrup. The major nutrient in molasses is iron, a contaminant from the machinery used in processing it.

monoglycerides (mon-oh-GLISS-er-ides) products of the digestion of lipids; consist of glycerol molecules with one fatty acid attached (*mono* means "one"; *glyceride* means "a compound of glycerol").

monosaccharides (mon-oh-SACK-ah-rides) single sugar units (*mono* means "one"; *saccharide* means "sugar unit").

monounsaturated fats triglycerides in which most of the fatty acids have one point of unsaturation (are monounsaturated).

monounsaturated fatty acid a fatty acid containing one point of unsaturation.

more, extra at least 10% more of the Daily Value than in a reference food. The nutrient may be added or may occur naturally.

more or **added fiber** at least 2.5 g more per serving than a reference food.

motivation the force that moves people to act. Motivation may be either instinctive (inborn drives such as hunger and thirst) or learned (such as the drive to acquire possessions or to improve health).

MSG symptom complex the acute, temporary, and self-limiting reactions, including burning sensations or flushing of the skin with pain and headache, experienced by sensitive people upon ingesting a large dose of MSG. Formerly called *Chinese restaurant syndrome.*

mucus (MYOO-cus) a slippery coating of the digestive tract lining (and other body linings) that protects the cells from exposure to digestive juices (and other destructive agents). The adjective form is *mucous* (same pronunciation). The digestive tract lining is a *mucous membrane.*

mutation a permanent, heritable change in an organism's DNA.

mutual supplementation the strategy of combining two incomplete protein sources so that the amino acids in one food make up for those lacking in the other food. Such protein combinations are sometimes called *complementary proteins.*

myoglobin (MYE-oh-globe-in) the oxygen-holding protein of the muscles (*myo* means "muscle").

N

natural foods a term that has no legal definition but is often used to imply wholesomeness.

natural water water obtained from a spring or well that is certified to be safe and sanitary. The mineral content may not be changed, but the water may be treated in other ways such as with ozone or by filtration.

naturally occurring sugars sugars that are not added to a food but are present as its original constituents, such as the sugars of fruit or milk.

nephrons (NEFF-rons) the working units in the kidneys, consisting of intermeshed blood vessels and tubules.

neural tube the embryonic tissue that later forms the brain and spinal cord.

neural tube defect (NTD) a group of nervous system abnormalities caused by interruption of the normal early development of the neural tube.

neurotoxins poisons that act upon the cells of the nervous system.

neurotransmitters chemicals that are released at the end of a nerve cell when a nerve impulse arrives there. They diffuse across the gap to the next cell and alter the membrane of that second cell to either inhibit or excite it.

niacin a B vitamin needed in energy metabolism. Niacin can be eaten preformed or can be made in the body from tryptophan, one of the amino acids. Other forms of niacin are *nicotinic acid, niacinamide,* and *nicotinamide.*

niacin equivalents (NE) the amount of niacin present in food, including the niacin that can theoretically be made from its precursor tryptophan that is present in the food.

night blindness slow recovery of vision after exposure to flashes of bright light at night; an early symptom of vitamin A deficiency.

night eating syndrome a disturbance in the daily eating rhythm associated with obesity, characterized by no breakfast, more than half of the daily calories consumed after 7 pm, frequent nighttime awakenings to eat, and often a greater total calorie intake than others.

nitrogen balance the amount of nitrogen consumed compared with the amount excreted in a given time period.

nonalcoholic a term used on beverage labels, such as wine or beer, indicating the product contains less than 0.5% alcohol. The terms *dealcoholized* and *alcohol removed* mean the same thing. *Alcohol free* means that the product contains no detectable alcohol.

nonexercise activity thermogenesis (NEAT) energy expenditure associated with everyday spontaneous activities, as opposed to consciously undertaken physical activities.

nonheme iron dietary iron not associated with hemoglobin; the iron of plants and other sources.

norepinephrine (NOR-EP-ih-NEFF-rin) a compound related to epinephrine that helps to elicit the stress response.

nori a type of seaweed popular in Asian, particularly Japanese, cooking.

nucleotide (NU-klee-oh-tied) one of the subunits from which DNA and RNA are composed.

nutraceutical a term that has no legal or scientific meaning but is sometimes used to refer to foods, nutrients, or dietary supplements believed to have medicinal effects. Often used to sell unnecessary or unproven supplements.

nutrient claims claims using approved wording to describe the nutrient values of foods, such as a claim that a food is "high" in a desirable constituent or "low" in an undesirable one.

nutrient density a measure of nutrients provided per calorie of food.

nutrients components of food that are indispensable to the body's functioning. They provide energy, serve as building material, help maintain or repair body parts, and support growth. The nutrients include water, carbohydrate, fat, protein, vitamins, and minerals.

nutrition the study of the nutrients in foods and in the body; sometimes also the study of human behaviors related to food.

Nutrition Facts on a food label, the panel of nutrition information required to appear on almost every packaged food. Grocers may also provide the information for fresh produce, meats, poultry, and seafoods.

nutritional genomics the science of how food (and its components) interacts with the genome.

nutritional yeast a preparation of yeast cells, often praised for its high nutrient content. Yeast is a source of B vitamins as are many other foods. Also called brewer's yeast; not the yeast used in baking.

nutritionally enhanced beverages flavored beverages that contain any of a number of nutrients, including some carbohydrate, along with protein, vitamins, minerals, herbs, or other unneeded substances. Such "vitamin waters" may not contain useful amounts of carbohydrate or electrolytes to support athletic competition or training.

nutritionist someone who studies nutrition. Some nutritionists are RDs, whereas others are self-described experts whose training is questionable and who are not qualified to give advice. In states with responsible legislation, the term applies only to people who have master of science (MS) or doctor of philosophy (PhD) degrees from properly accredited institutions.

O

obesity overfatness with adverse health effects, as determined by reliable measures and interpreted with good medical judgment. Obesity is officially defined as a body mass index of 30 or higher.

oils lipids that are liquid at room temperature (70°F or 21°C).

olestra a noncaloric artificial fat made from sucrose and fatty acids; formerly called *sucrose polyester*.

omega-6 fatty acid a polyunsaturated fatty acid with its endmost double bond six carbons from the end of the carbon chain. Linoleic acid is an example.

omega-3 fatty acid a polyunsaturated fatty acid with its endmost double bond three carbons from the end of the carbon chain. Linolenic acid is an example.

omnivores people who eat foods of both plant and animal origin, including animal flesh.

100% whole grain a label term for food in which the grain is entirely whole grain.

oral rehydration therapy (ORT) oral fluid replacement for children with severe diarrhea caused by infectious disease. ORT enables parents to mix a simple solution for their child from substances that they have at home. A simple recipe for ORT: ½ L boiled water, 4 tsp sugar, ½ tsp salt.

organ and glandular extracts dried or extracted material from brain, adrenal, pituitary, or other glands or tissues providing few nutrients but posing a theoretical risk of "mad cow disease."

organic carbon containing. Four of the six classes of nutrients are organic: carbohydrate, fat, protein, and vitamins. Strictly speaking, organic compounds include only those made by living things and do not include compounds such as carbon dioxide, diamonds, and a few carbon salts.

organic foods foods meeting strict USDA production regulations for *organic*, including prohibition of synthetic pesticides, herbicides, fertilizers, drugs, and preservatives, and produced without genetic engineering or irradiation.

organic gardens gardens grown with techniques of *sustainable agriculture*, such as using fertilizers made from composts and introducing predatory insects to control pests, in ways that have minimal impact on soil, water, and air quality.

organosulfur compounds a large group of phytochemicals containing the mineral sulfur. Organosulfur phytochemicals are responsible for the pungent flavors and aromas of foods belonging to the onion, leek, chive, shallot, and garlic family and are thought to stimulate cancer defenses in the body.

organs discrete structural units made of tissues that perform specific jobs. Examples are the heart, liver, and brain.

osteomalacia (OS-tee-o-mal-AY-shuh) the adult expression of vitamin D-deficiency disease, characterized by an overabundance of unmineralized bone protein (*osteo* means "bone"; *mal* means "bad"). Symptoms include bending of the spine and bowing of the legs.

osteoporosis (OSS-tee-oh-pore-OH-sis) a reduction of the bone mass of older persons in which the bones become porous and fragile (*osteo* means "bones"; *poros* means "porous"); also known as *adult bone loss*.

outbreak two or more cases of a disease arising from an identical organism acquired from a common food source within a limited time frame. Government agencies track and investigate outbreaks of foodborne illnesses, but tens of millions of individual cases go unreported each year.

outcrossing the unintended breeding of a domestic crop with a related wild species.

oven-safe thermometer a thermometer designed to remain in the food to give constant readings during cooking.

overweight body weight above a healthy weight; BMI 25 to 29.9.

ovo-vegetarian includes eggs, vegetables, grains, legumes, fruits, and nuts; excludes flesh, seafood, and mild products.

ovum the egg, produced by the mother, that unites with a sperm from the father to produce a new individual.

oxidants compounds (such as oxygen itself) that oxidize other compounds. Compounds that prevent oxidation are called *anti*oxidants, whereas those that promote it are called *pro*oxidants (*anti* means "against"; *pro* means "for").

oxidation interaction of a compound with oxygen; in this case, a damaging effect by a chemically reactive form of oxygen.

oxidative stress damage inflicted on living systems by free radicals.

oyster shell a product made from the powdered shells of oysters that is sold as a calcium supplement but is not well absorbed by the digestive system.

P

pancreas an organ with two main functions. One is an endocrine function—the making of hormones such as insulin, which it releases directly into the blood (*endo* means "into" the blood). The other is an exocrine function—the making of digestive enzymes, which it releases through a duct into the small intestine to assist in digestion (*exo* means "out" into a body cavity or onto the skin surface).

pancreatic juice fluid secreted by the pancreas that contains both enzymes to digest carbohydrates, fats, and proteins and sodium bicarbonate, a neutralizing agent.

pantothenic (PAN-to-THEN-ic) **acid** a B vitamin.

partial vegetarian a term sometimes used to mean an eating style that includes seafood, poultry, eggs, dairy products, vegetables, grains, legumes, fruits, and nuts; excludes or strictly limits certain meats, such as red meats.

pasteurization the treatment of milk, juices, or eggs with heat sufficient to kill certain pathogens (disease-causing microbes) commonly transmitted through these foods; not a sterilization process. Pasteurized products retain bacteria that cause spoilage.

PCBs stable oily synthetic chemicals used in hundreds of industrial and commercial operations that persist as pollution in the environment. PCBs cause cancer in animals and a number of other serious health effects. The Environmental Protection Agency monitors their levels.

peak bone mass the highest attainable bone density for an individual; developed during the first three decades of life.

pellagra (pell-AY-gra) the niacin-deficiency disease (*pellis* means "skin";

agra means "rough"). Symptoms include the "4 Ds": diarrhea, dermatitis, dementia, and, ultimately, death.

peptide bond a bond that connects one amino acid with another, forming a link in a protein chain.

percent fat free may be used only if the product meets the definition of low fat or fat free. Requires disclosure of grams of fat per 100 g food.

peripheral resistance the resistance to pumped blood in the small arterial branches (arterioles) that carry blood to tissues.

peristalsis (perri-STALL-sis) the wavelike muscular squeezing of the esophagus, stomach, and small intestine that pushes their contents along.

pernicious (per-NISH-us) **anemia** a vitamin B_{12}–deficiency disease, caused by lack of intrinsic factor and characterized by large, immature red blood cells and damage to the nervous system (*pernicious* means "highly injurious or destructive").

persistent of a stubborn or enduring nature; with respect to food contaminants, the quality of remaining unaltered and unexcreted in plant foods or in the bodies of animals and human beings.

pesco-vegetarian same as partial vegetarian, but eliminates poultry.

pesticides chemicals used to control insects, diseases, weeds, fungi, and other pests on crops and around animals. Used broadly, the term includes *herbicides* (to kill weeds), *insecticides* (to kill insects), and *fungicides* (to kill fungi).

pH a measure of acidity on a point scale. A solution with a pH of 1 is a strong acid; a solution with a pH of 7 is neutral; a solution with a pH of 14 is a strong base.

phagocytes (FAG-oh-sites) white blood cells that can ingest and destroy antigens. The process by which phagocytes engulf materials is called *phagocytosis.* The Greek word *phagein* means "to eat."

phenylketonuria (PKU) an inborn error of metabolism that interferes with the body's handling of the amino acid phenylalanine, with potentially serious consequences to the brain and nervous system in infancy and childhood. Often referred to by its abbreviation, PKU.

phospholipids (FOSS-foh-LIP-ids) one of the three main classes of dietary lipids. These lipids are similar to triglycerides, but each has a phosphorus-containing acid in place of one of the fatty acids. Phospholipids are present in all cell membranes.

photosynthesis the process by which green plants make carbohydrates from carbon dioxide and water using the green pigment chlorophyll to capture the sun's energy (*photo* means "light"; *synthesis* means "making").

phytates (FYE-tates) compounds present in plant foods (particularly whole grains) that bind iron and may prevent its absorption.

phytochemicals (FIGH-toe-CHEM-ih-cals) compounds of plants that confer color, taste, or other characteristics. Some phytochemicals are bioactive food components in functional foods.

phytoestrogens (FIGH-toe-ESS-troh-gens) phytochemicals structurally similar to the female sex hormone estrogen. Phytoestrogens weakly mimic or modulate estrogen in the human body.

phytosterols phytochemicals that resemble cholesterol in structure but that lower blood cholesterol by interfering with cholesterol absorption in the intestine. Phytosterols include sterol esters and stanol esters.

pica (PIE-ka) a craving for nonfood substances. Also known as *geophagia* (gee-oh-FAY-gee-uh) when referring to clay eating and *pagophagia* (pag-oh-FAY-gee-uh) when referring to ice craving (*geo* means "earth"; *pago* means "frost"; *phagia* means "to eat").

placebo a sham treatment often used in scientific studies; an inert harmless medication. The *placebo effect* is the healing effect that the act of treatment, rather than the treatment itself, often has.

placenta (pla-SEN-tuh) the organ of pregnancy in which maternal and fetal blood circulate in close proximity and exchange nutrients and oxygen (flowing into the fetus) and wastes (picked up by the mother's blood).

plant pesticides substances produced within plant tissues that kill or repel attacking organisms.

plaque (PLACK) a mass of microorganisms and their deposits on the surfaces of the teeth, a forerunner of dental caries and gum disease. The term *plaque* is also used in another connection—arterial plaque in atherosclerosis.

plaques (PLACKS) mounds of lipid material mixed with smooth muscle cells and calcium that develop in the artery walls in atherosclerosis (*placken* means "patch"). The same word is also used to describe the accumulation of a different kind of deposits on teeth, which promote dental caries.

plasma the cell-free fluid part of blood and lymph.

platelets tiny cell-like fragments in the blood, important in blood clot formation (*platelet* means "little plate").

point of unsaturation a site in a molecule where the bonding is such that additional hydrogen atoms can easily be attached.

polypeptide (POL-ee-PEP-tide) protein fragments of many (more than 10) amino acids bonded together (*poly* means "many"). A peptide is a strand of amino acids. A strand of between 4 and 10 amino acids is called an *oligopeptide.*

polysaccharides another term for complex carbohydrates; compounds composed of long strands of glucose units linked together (*poly* means "many"). Also called *complex carbohydrates.*

polyunsaturated fats triglycerides in which most of the fatty acids have two or more points of unsaturation (are polyunsaturated).

polyunsaturated fatty acid (PUFA) a fatty acid with two or more points of unsaturation.

pop-up thermometer a disposable timing device commonly used in turkeys. The center of the device contains a stainless steel spring that "pops up" when food reaches the right temperature.

postprandial hypoglycemia an unusual drop in blood glucose that follows a meal and is accompanied by symptoms such as anxiety, rapid heartbeat, and sweating; also called *reactive hypoglycemia.*

prebiotic a substance that may not be digestible by the host, such as fiber, but that serves as food for probiotic bacteria and thus promotes their growth.

precursors, provitamins compounds that can be converted into active vitamins.

prediabetes condition in which blood glucose levels are higher than normal but not high enough to be diagnosed as diabetes; considered a major risk factor for future diabetes and cardiovascular diseases.

preeclampsia (PRE-ee-CLAMP-see-ah) a potentially dangerous condition during pregnancy characterized by edema, hypertension, and protein in the urine.

prehypertension borderline blood pressure between 120 over 80 and 139 over

89 millimeters of mercury, an indication that hypertension is likely to develop in the future.

premenstrual syndrome (PMS) a cluster of symptoms that some women experience prior to and during menstruation. They include, among others, abdominal cramps, back pain, swelling, headache, painful breasts, and mood changes.

prenatal (pree-NAY-tal) before birth.

prenatal supplements nutrient supplements specifically designed to provide the nutrients needed during pregnancy, particularly folate, iron, and calcium, without excesses or unneeded constituents.

pressure ulcers damage to the skin and underlying tissues as a result of unrelieved compression and poor circulation to the area; also called *bed sores.*

prion (PREE-on) an infective agent consisting of an unusually folded protein that disrupts normal cell functioning, causing disease. Prions cannot be controlled or killed by cooking or disinfecting, nor can the disease they cause be treated; prevention is the only form of control.

probiotic a live microorganism that when administered in adequate amount alters the bacterial colonies of the body in ways believed to confer a health benefit on the host.

problem drinkers or **alcohol abusers** people who suffer social, emotional, family, job-related, or other problems because of alcohol. A problem drinker is on the way to alcoholism.

processed foods foods subjected to any process, such as milling, alteration of texture, addition of additives, cooking, or others. Depending on the starting material and the process, a processed food may or may not be nutritious.

promoters factors that do not initiate cancer but speed up its development once initiation has taken place.

proof a statement of the percentage of alcohol in an alcoholic beverage. Liquor that is 100 proof is 50% alcohol, 90 proof is 45%, and so forth.

prooxidant a compound that triggers reactions involving oxygen.

protease (PRO-tee-ace) any of a number of enzymes that break the chemical bonds of proteins.

protein turnover the continuous breakdown and synthesis of body proteins involving the recycling of amino acids.

protein-energy malnutrition (PEM) the world's most widespread malnutrition problem, including both marasmus and kwashiorkor and states in which they overlap; also called *protein-calorie malnutrition (PCM).*

proteins compounds composed of carbon, hydrogen, oxygen, and nitrogen and arranged as strands of amino acids. Some amino acids also contain the element sulfur.

protein-sparing action the action of carbohydrate and fat in providing energy that allows protein to be used for purposes it alone can serve.

public health nutritionist a dietitian or other person with an advanced degree in nutrition who specializes in public health nutrition.

public water water from a municipal or county water system that has been treated and disinfected.

purified water water that has been treated by distillation or other physical or chemical processes that remove dissolved solids. Because purified water contains no minerals or contaminants, it is useful for medical and research purposes.

pyloric (pye-LORE-ick) **valve** the circular muscle of the lower stomach that regulates the flow of partly digested food into the small intestine. Also called *pyloric sphincter.*

R

raw sugar the first crop of crystals harvested during sugar processing. Raw sugar cannot be sold in the United States because it contains too much filth (dirt, insect fragments, and the like). Sugar sold as "raw sugar" is actually evaporated cane juice.

recombinant DNA (rDNA) technology a technique of genetic modification whereby scientists directly manipulate the genes of living things; includes methods of removing genes, doubling genes, introducing foreign genes, and changing gene positions to influence the growth and development of organisms.

Recommended Dietary Allowances (RDA) nutrient intake goals for individuals; the average daily nutrient intake level that meets the needs of nearly all (97 to 98 percent) healthy people in a particular life stage and gender group. Derived from the Estimated Average Requirements.

recovery drinks flavored beverages that contain protein, carbohydrate, and often other nutrients; intended to support postexercise recovery of energy fuels and muscle tissue. These can be convenient, but are not superior to ordinary foods and beverages, such as chocolate milk or a sandwich, to supply carbohydrate and protein after exercise. Not intended for hydration during athletic competition or training because their high carbohydrate and protein contents may slow water absorption.

reduced calorie at least 25% lower in calories than a "regular," or reference, food.

reduced or **less cholesterol** at least 25% less cholesterol than a reference food *and* 2 g or less saturated fat per serving.

reduced saturated fat at least 25% less saturated fat *and* reduced by more than 1 g saturated fat per serving compared with a reference food.

reduced sodium at least 25% lower in sodium than the regular product.

refeeding syndrome a serious condition of electrolyte and other imbalances that can occur when a severely malnourished person is fed too aggressively; it can lead to heart or respiratory failure and death.

refined refers to the process by which the coarse parts of food products are removed. For example, the refining of wheat into flour involves removing three of the four parts of the kernel—the chaff, the bran, and the germ—leaving only the endosperm, composed mainly of starch and a little protein.

registered dietitian (RD) a dietitian who has graduated from a university or college after completing a program of dietetics. The program must be approved or accredited by the American Dietetic Association (or Dietitians of Canada). The dietitian must serve in an approved internship, coordinated program, or preprofessional practice program to practice the necessary skills; pass the five parts of the association's registration examination; and maintain competency through continuing education. Many states also require licensing for practicing dietitians.

registration listing with a professional organization that requires specific course work, experience, and passing of an examination.

requirement the amount of a nutrient that will just prevent the development of specific deficiency signs; distinguished from the DRI recommended intake value, which is a generous allowance with a margin of safety.

residues whatever remains; in the case of pesticides, those amounts that remain on or in foods when people buy and use them.

resistant starch the fraction of starch in a food that is digested slowly, or not at all, by human enzymes.

resveratrol (rez-VER-ah-trol) a flavonoid of grapes under study for potential health benefits.

retina (RET-in-uh) the layer of light-sensitive nerve cells lining the back of the inside of the eye.

retinol one of the active forms of vitamin A made from beta-carotene in animal and human bodies; an antioxidant nutrient. Other active forms are *retinal* and *retinoic acid*.

retinol activity equivalents (RAE) a new measure of the vitamin A activity of beta-carotene and other vitamin A precursors that reflects the amount of retinol that the body will derive from a food containing vitamin A precursor compounds.

rhodopsin (roh-DOP-sin) the light-sensitive pigment of the cells in the retina; it contains vitamin A (*rod* refers to the rod-shaped cells; *opsin* means "visual protein").

riboflavin (RIBE-o-flay-vin) a B vitamin active in the body's energy-releasing mechanisms.

rickets the vitamin D–deficiency disease in children; characterized by abnormal growth of bone and manifested in bowed legs or knock-knees, outward-bowed chest, and knobs on the ribs.

risk factors factors known to be related to (or correlated with) diseases but not proved to be causal.

S

safety the practical certainty that injury will not result from the use of a substance.

salts compounds composed of charged particles (ions). An example is potassium chloride (K^+Cl^-).

SAM-e an amino acid derivative that may have an antidepressant effect on the brain in some people, but it is not recommended as a substitute for standard antidepressant therapy.

satiation (SAY-she-AY-shun) the perception of fullness that builds throughout a meal, eventually reaching the degree of fullness and satisfaction that halts eating. Satiation generally determines how much food is consumed at one sitting.

satiety (sah-TIE-eh-tee) the perception of fullness that lingers in the hours after a meal and inhibits eating until the next mealtime. Satiety generally determines the length of time between meals.

saturated fat free less than 0.5 g of saturated fat *and* less than 0.5 g of *trans* fat.

saturated fats triglycerides in which most of the fatty acids are saturated.

saturated fatty acid a fatty acid carrying the maximum possible number of hydrogen atoms (having no points of unsaturation). A saturated fat is a triglyceride that contains three saturated fatty acids.

scurvy the vitamin C–deficiency disease.

selective breeding a technique of genetic modification whereby organisms are chosen for reproduction based on their desirability for human purposes, such as high growth rate, high food yield, or disease resistance, with the intention of retaining or enhancing these characteristics in their offspring.

self-efficacy the belief in one's ability to take action and successfully perform a specific behavior.

senile dementia the loss of brain function beyond the normal loss of physical adeptness and memory that occurs with aging.

serotonin (SER-oh-TONE-in) a neurotransmitter important in sleep regulation, appetite control, and mood regulation, among other roles. Serotonin is synthesized in the body from the amino acid tryptophan with the help of vitamin B_6.

side chain the unique chemical structure attached to the backbone of each amino acid that differentiates one amino acid from another.

simple carbohydrates sugars, including both single sugar units and linked pairs of sugar units. The basic sugar unit is a molecule containing six carbon atoms, together with oxygen and hydrogen atoms.

single-use temperature indicator a type of instant-read thermometer that changes color to indicate that the food has reached the desired temperature. Discarded after one use, they are often used in commercial food establishments to eliminate cross-contamination.

skinfold test measurement of the thickness of a fold of skin on the back of the arm (over the triceps muscle), below the shoulder blade (subscapular), or in other places, using a caliper; also called *fatfold test*.

small intestine the 20-foot length of small-diameter intestine, below the stomach and above the large intestine, that is the major site of digestion of food and absorption of nutrients.

smoking point the temperature at which fat gives off an acrid blue gas.

SNP a single misplaced nucleotide in a gene that causes formation of an altered protein. The letters SNP stand for *single nucleotide polymorphism*.

social drinkers people who drink only on social occasions. Depending on how alcohol affects a social drinker's life, the person may be a moderate drinker or a problem drinker.

sodium free less than 5 mg per serving.

soft water water with a high sodium concentration.

soluble fibers food components that readily dissolve in water and often impart gummy or gel-like characteristics to foods. An example is pectin from fruit, which is used to thicken jellies. Soluble fibers are indigestible by human enzymes but may be broken down to absorbable products by bacteria in the digestive tract.

solvent a substance that dissolves another and holds it in solution.

soy milk a milk-like beverage made from soybeans, claimed to be a functional food. Soy drinks should be fortified with vitamin A, vitamin D, riboflavin, and calcium to approach the nutritional equivalency of milk.

Special Supplemental Nutrition Program for Women, Infants, and Children (WIC) a USDA program offering low-income pregnant and lactating women and those with infants or preschool children coupons redeemable for specific foods that supply the nutrients deemed most necessary for growth and development. For more information, visit www.usda.gov/FoodandNutrition.

sphincter (SFINK-ter) a circular muscle surrounding, and able to close, a body opening.

spina bifida (SPY-na BIFF-ih-duh) one of the most common types of neural tube defects in which gaps occur in the bones of the spine. Often the spinal cord bulges and protrudes through the gaps, resulting in a number of motor and other impairments.

sports drinks flavored beverages designed to help athletes replace fluids and electrolytes and to provide carbohydrate before, during, and after physical activity, particularly endurance activities.

spring water water originating from an underground spring or well. It may be bubbly (carbonated) or "flat" or "still," meaning not carbonated. Brand names such as "Spring Pure" do not necessarily mean that the water comes from a spring.

staple foods foods used frequently or daily, for example, rice (in East and Southeast Asia) or potatoes (in Ireland). If well chosen, these foods are nutritious.

starch a plant polysaccharide composed of glucose. After cooking, starch is highly digestible by human beings; raw starch often resists digestion.

stem cell an undifferentiated cell that can mature into any of a number of specialized cell types. A stem cell of bone marrow may mature into one of many kinds of blood cells, for example.

sterols (STEER-alls) one of the three main classes of dietary lipids. Sterols have a structure similar to that of cholesterol.

stomach a muscular, elastic, pouchlike organ of the digestive tract that grinds and churns swallowed food and mixes it with acid and enzymes, forming chyme.

stone ground refers to a milling process using limestone to grind any grain, including refined grains, into flour.

stone-ground flour flour made by grinding kernels of grain between heavy wheels made of limestone, a kind of rock derived from the shells and bones of marine animals. As the stones scrape together, bits of the limestone mix with the flour, enriching it with calcium.

stroke the sudden shutting off of the blood flow to the brain by a thrombus, embolism, or the bursting of a vessel (hemorrhage).

structure-function claim a legal but largely unregulated claim permitted on labels of dietary supplements and conventional foods.

subclinical, or **marginal, deficiency** a nutrient deficiency that has no outward clinical symptoms. The term is often used to market unneeded nutrient supplements to consumers.

subcutaneous fat fat stored directly under the skin (*sub* means "beneath"; *cutaneous* refers to the skin).

sucrose (SOO-crose) a disaccharide composed of glucose and fructose; sometimes known as table, beet, or cane sugar and, often, as simply *sugar*.

sugar alcohols sugarlike compounds in the chemical family *alcohol* derived from fruits or the sugar dextrose that are absorbed more slowly than other sugars, are metabolized differently, and do not elevate the risk of dental caries. Examples are maltitol, mannitol, sorbitol, xylitol, isomalt, and lactitol.

sugars simple carbohydrates; that is, molecules of either single sugar units or pairs of those sugar units bonded together. By common usage, *sugar* most often refers to sucrose.

surface water water that comes from lakes, rivers, and reservoirs.

sushi a Japanese dish that consists of vinegar-flavored rice, seafood, and colorful vegetables, typically wrapped in seaweed. Some sushi is wrapped in raw fish; other sushi contains only cooked ingredients.

sustainable able to continue indefinitely; in agriculture, the use of resources in ways that maintain both natural resources and human life; the use of natural resources at a pace that allows the earth to replace them. In a sustainable system, resources do not become depleted, and pollution does not accumulate.

systolic (sis-TOL-ik) **pressure** the first figure in a blood pressure reading (the "dupp" sound of the heartbeat's "lubb-dupp" beat is heard), which reflects arterial pressure caused by the contraction of the heart's left ventricle.

T

tannins compounds in tea (especially black tea) and coffee that bind iron. Tannins also denature proteins.

T-cells lymphocytes that attack antigens. *T* stands for the thymus gland of the neck, where the T-cells are stored and matured.

textured vegetable protein processed soybean protein used in products formulated to look and taste like meat, fish, or poultry.

thermic effect of food (TEF) the body's speeded-up metabolism in response to having eaten a meal; also called *diet-induced thermogenesis*.

thermogenesis the generation and release of body heat associated with the breakdown of body fuels. *Adaptive thermogenesis* describes adjustments in energy expenditure related to changes in environment such as cold and to physiological events such as underfeeding or trauma.

THG an unapproved drug, once sold as an ergogenic aid, now banned by the FDA.

thiamin (THIGH-uh-min) a B vitamin involved in the body's use of fuels.

thrombosis a thrombus that has grown enough to close off a blood vessel. A *coronary thrombosis* closes off a vessel that feeds the heart muscle. A *cerebral thrombosis* closes off a vessel that feeds the brain (*coronary* means "crowning" [the heart]; *thrombo* means "clot"; the cerebrum is part of the brain).

thrombus a stationary blood clot.

thyroxine (thigh-ROX-in) a principal peptide hormone of the thyroid gland that regulates the body's rate of energy use.

tissues systems of cells working together to perform specialized tasks. Examples are muscles, nerves, blood, and bone.

tocopherol (tuh-KOFF-er-all) a kind of alcohol. The active form of vitamin E is alpha-tocopherol.

tofu (TOE-foo) a curd made from soybeans that is rich in protein, often rich in calcium, and variable in fat content; used in many Asian and vegetarian dishes in place of meat.

Tolerable Upper Intake Levels (UL) the highest average daily nutrient intake level that is likely to pose no risk of toxicity to almost all healthy individuals of a particular life stage and gender group. Usual intake above this level may place an individual at risk of illness from nutrient toxicity.

tolerance limit the maximum amount of a residue permitted in a food when a pesticide is used according to label directions.

toxicity the ability of a substance to harm living organisms. All substances, even pure water or oxygen, can be toxic in high enough doses.

trabecular (tra-BECK-you-lar) **bone** the weblike structure composed of calcium-containing crystals inside a bone's solid outer shell. It provides strength and acts as a calcium storage bank.

trace minerals essential mineral nutrients required in the adult diet in amounts less than 100 milligrams per day. Also called *microminerals*.

***trans* fat free** less than 0.5 g of *trans* fat *and* less than 0.5 g of saturated fat per serving.

***trans* fats** fats that contain any number of unusual fatty acids—*trans*-fatty acids—formed during processing.

***trans*-fatty acids** fatty acids with unusual shapes that can arise when hydrogens are added to the unsaturated fatty acids of polyunsaturated oils (a process known as *hydrogenation*).

transgenic organism an organism resulting from the growth of an embryonic, stem, or germ cell into which a new gene has been inserted.

triglycerides (try-GLISS-er-ides) one of the three main classes of dietary lipids and the chief form of fat in foods and in the human body. A triglyceride is made up of three units of fatty acids and one unit of glycerol. Triglycerides are also called *triacylglycerols.*

trimester a period representing gestation. A trimester is about 13 to 14 weeks.

tripeptides (try-PEP-tides) protein fragments that are 3 amino acids long (*tri* means "three").

turbinado (ter-bih-NOD-oh) **sugar** raw sugar from which the filth has been washed; legal to sell in the United States.

type 1 diabetes the type of diabetes in which the pancreas produces no or very little insulin; often diagnosed in childhood, although some cases arise in adulthood. Formerly called *juvenile-onset* or *insulin-dependent diabetes.*

type 2 diabetes the type of diabetes in which the pancreas makes plenty of insulin but the body's cells resist insulin's action; often diagnosed in adulthood. Formerly called *adult-onset* or *non–insulin-dependent diabetes.*

U

ulcer an erosion in the topmost, and sometimes underlying, layers of cells that form a lining. Ulcers of the digestive tract commonly form in the esophagus, stomach, or upper small intestine.

ultra-high temperature (UHT) a process of sterilizing food by exposing it for a short time to temperatures above those normally used in processing.

umbilical (um-BIL-ih-cul) **cord** the rope-like structure through which the fetus's veins and arteries reach the placenta; the route of nourishment and oxygen into the fetus and the route of waste disposal from the fetus.

unbleached flour a beige-colored refined endosperm flour with texture and nutritive qualities that approximate those of regular white flour.

underwater weighing a measure of density and volume used to determine body fat content.

underweight body weight below a healthy weight; BMI below 18.5.

unsaturated fatty acid a fatty acid that lacks some hydrogen atoms and has one or more points of unsaturation. An unsaturated fat is a triglyceride that contains one or more unsaturated fatty acids.

urban legends stories, usually false, that my travel rapidly throughout the world via the Internet gaining strength of conviction solely on the basis of repetition.

urea (yoo-REE-uh) the principal nitrogen-excretion product of protein metabolism; generated mostly by removal of amine groups from unneeded amino acids or from amino acids being sacrificed to a need for energy.

urethane a carcinogenic compound that commonly forms in alcoholic beverages.

USDA (U.S. Department of Agriculture) the federal agency that is responsible for enforcing standards for the wholesomeness and quality of meat, poultry and eggs produced in the United States; conducting nutrition research; and educating the public about nutrition.

uterus (YOO-ter-us) the womb, the muscular organ within which the infant develops before birth.

V

variety the dietary characteristic of providing a wide selection of foods—the opposite of monotony.

vegan includes only food from plant sources: vegetables, grains, legumes, fruits, seeds, and nuts; also called *strict vegetarian.*

vegetarians people who exclude from their diets animal flesh and possibly other animal products such as milk, cheese, and eggs.

veins blood vessels that carry blood, with the carbon dioxide it has collected, from the tissues back to the heart.

very-low-density lipoproteins (VLDL) lipoproteins that transport triglycerides and other lipids from the liver to various tissues in the body.

very low food security multiple indications of disrupted eating patterns and reduced food intake. Example: a family that may be without food for a significant number of days in a year or that relies on food from shelters, food banks, or other organizations.

very low sodium 35 mg or less sodium per serving.

villi (VILL-ee, VILL-eye) fingerlike projections of the sheets of cells lining the intestinal tract. The villi make the surface area much greater than it would otherwise be (*singular:* villus).

visceral fat fat stored within the abdominal cavity in association with the internal abdominal organs; also called *intra-abdominal fat.*

viscous (VISS-cuss) having a sticky, gummy, or gel-like consistency that flows relatively slowly.

vitamin B_6 a B vitamin needed in protein metabolism. Its three active forms are *pyridoxine, pyridoxal,* and *pyridoxamine.*

vitamin B_{12} a B vitamin that helps to convert folate to its active form and also helps maintain the sheath around nerve cells. Vitamin B_{12}'s scientific name, not often used, is *cyanocobalamin.*

vitamin water bottled water with a few vitamins added; does not replace vitamins from a balanced diet and may worsen overload in people receiving vitamins from enriched food, supplements, and other enriched products such as "energy" bars.

vitamins organic compounds that are vital to life and indispensable to body functions but are needed only in minute amounts; noncaloric essential nutrients.

voluntary activities intentional activities (such as walking, sitting, or running) conducted by voluntary muscles.

W

wasting the progressive, relentless loss of the body's tissues that accompanies certain diseases and shortens survival time.

water balance the balance between water intake and water excretion, which keeps the body's water content constant.

water intoxication a dangerous dilution of the body's fluids resulting from excessive ingestion of plain water. Symptoms are headache, muscular weakness, lack of concentration, poor memory, and loss of appetite.

water stress a measure of the pressure placed on water resources by human activities such as municipal water supplies, industries, power plants, and agricultural irrigation.

wean to gradually replace breast milk with infant formula or other foods appropriate to an infant's diet.

websites Internet resources composed of text and graphic files, each with a unique URL (Uniform Resource Locator) that names the site (for example, www.usda.gov).

weight cycling repeated rounds of weight loss and subsequent regain, with reduced ability to lose weight with each attempt; also called *yo-yo dieting*.

well water water drawn from groundwater by tapping into an aquifer.

Wernicke-Korsakoff (VER-nik-ee-KOR-sah-koff) **syndrome** a cluster of symptoms involving nerve damage arising from a deficiency of the vitamin thiamin in alcoholism. Characterized by mental confusion, disorientation, memory loss, jerky eye movements, and staggering gait.

wheat bread bread made with any wheat flour, including refined enriched white flour.

wheat flour any flour made from wheat, including refined white flour.

whey protein a by-product of cheese production; promoted for increasing muscle mass. Whey is the liquid left when most solids are removed from milk.

white flour an endosperm flour that has been refined and bleached for maximum softness and whiteness.

white sugar pure sucrose, produced by dissolving, concentrating, and recrystallizing raw sugar.

white wheat a wheat variety developed to be paler in color than common red wheat (most familiar flours are made from red wheat). White wheat is similar to red wheat in carbohydrate, protein, and other nutrients, but it lacks the dark and bitter, but potentially beneficial, phytochemicals of red wheat.

whole foods milk and milk products; meats and similar foods such as fish and poultry; vegetables, including dried beans and peas; fruits; and grains. These foods are generally considered to form the basis of a nutritious diet. Also called *basic foods*.

whole grain grains, or foods made from them, that contain all the essential parts and naturally occurring nutrients of the entire grain seed (except the husk); not refined.

whole-wheat flour flour made from whole-wheat kernels; a whole-grain flour. Also called *graham flour*.

world food supply the quantity of food, including stores from previous harvests, available to the world's people at a given time.

World Health Organization (WHO) an agency of the United Nations charged with improving human health and preventing or controlling diseases in the world's people.

World Wide Web (the Web, commonly abbreviated **www**) a graphical subset of the Internet.

X

xerophthalmia (ZEER-ahf-THALL-me-uh) progressive hardening of the cornea of the eye in advanced vitamin A deficiency that can lead to blindness (*xero* means "dry"; *ophthalm* means "eye").

xerosis (zeer-OH-sis) drying of the cornea; a symptom of vitamin A deficiency.

Z

zygote (ZYE-goat) the product of the union of ovum and sperm; a fertilized ovum.

Index

The page letters A, B, and C that stand alone refer to the tables beginning on the inside front cover. Page letters Y and Z refer to the tables on the last two pages of the book. The page numbers preceded by A through H are appendix page numbers. The boldfaced page numbers indicate definitions. Terms are also defined in the glossary. Page numbers followed by *n* indicate footnotes. Page numbers followed by *t* indicate tables. Page numbers followed by *f* indicate figures.

A

B

C

H

I

J

K

L

M

P

Q

R

Daily Values for Food Labels

The Daily Values are standard values developed by the Food and Drug Administration (FDA) for use on food labels. The values are based on 2,000 calories a day for adults and children over 4 years old. Chapter 2 provides more details.

Nutrient	Amount
Protein[a]	50 g
Thiamin	1.5 mg
Riboflavin	1.7 mg
Niacin	20 mg NE
Biotin	300 µg
Pantothenic acid	10 mg
Vitamin B_6	2 mg
Folate	400 µg
Vitamin B_{12}	6 µg
Vitamin C	60 mg
Vitamin A	5000 IU[b]
Vitamin D	400 IU[b]
Vitamin E	30 IU[b]

Nutrient	Amount
Vitamin K	80 µg
Calcium	1000 mg
Iron	18 mg
Zinc	15 mg
Iodine	150 µg
Copper	2 mg
Chromium	120 µg
Selenium	70 µg
Molybdenum	75 µg
Manganese	2 mg
Chloride	3400 mg
Magnesium	400 mg
Phosphorus	1000 mg

[a]*The Daily Values for protein vary for different groups of people: pregnant women, 60 g; nursing mothers, 65 g; infants under 1 year, 14 g; children 1 to 4 years, 16 g.*

[b]*Equivalent values for nutrients expressed as IU are: vitamin A, 1,500 RAE (assumes a mixture of 40% retinol and 60% beta-carotene); vitamin D, 10 mg; vitamin E, 20 mg.*

Food Component	Amount	Calculation Factors
Fat	65 g	30% of calories
Saturated fat	20 g	10% of calories
Cholesterol	300 mg	Same regardless of calories
Carbohydrate (total)	300 g	60% of calories
Fiber	25 g	11.5 g per 1000 calories
Protein	50 g	10% of calories
Sodium	2400 mg	Same regardless of calories
Potassium	3500 mg	Same regardless of calories

DIET ANALYSIS +

Student Guide

Diet Analysis PLUS + Student Guide

Table of Contents

Getting Started

Diet Analysis Plus is a health and nutrition management program that allows you to create personal profiles, estimate activity level, track diet and exercise, and create detailed reports. The Diet Analysis Plus online system (also referred to as DA+) makes it easy for you to evaluate the types and serving sizes of the foods you consume.

*Tip:*Diet Analysis Plus includes a **Tutorial** which includes useful step-by-step information, such as how to create your primary profile and other basic features. This tutorial is always available from the **Tutorial** link at the top of the page.

Accessing Helpful Information

When you're working in a specific report from the **Reports** page, you can click the Report Title to bring up an **Info box** which explains the functions on the screen.

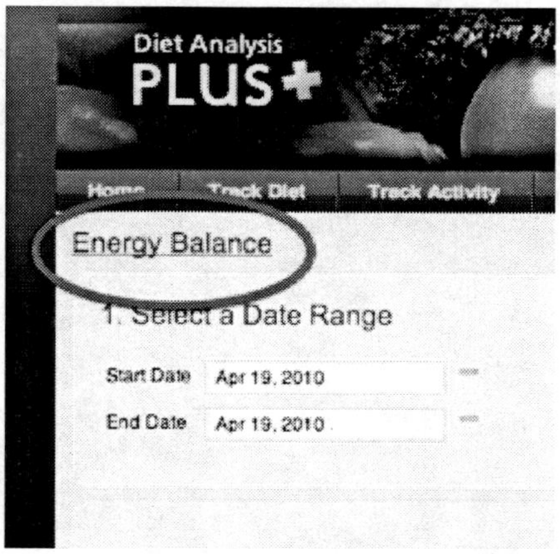

When you're working from the **Track Diet** page, you can click the Search Tips link to bring up a short **Help note** which contains an explanation of the report.

Entering a New Course Access Code

Your instructor can provide you with a **Course Access Code** that allows you to register for new or additional courses.

To register with a **Course Access Code**:.

Step 1. After you have received the **Course Access Code** from your instructor, you can log into DA+.

Step 2. Enter your Course Access Code in the **Course Access Code** text box.

Step 3. Enter your new code exactly as it appears and click the Submit link. A confirmation text box will appear at the top of the page.

System Setup

To ensure the best experience with DA Plus and enjoy all of its features, please use the information in this section to optimize your computer system and browser settings. System requirements, browser configuration, and software conflicts are important issues when troubleshooting. Due to the constantly shifting nature of Web browsers, it is important to follow these recommendations, to take advantage of the most compatible configuration.

This section lists the basic hardware, software, and system settings you need to run Diet Analysis Plus. If your system meets the basic hardware needs, you can download any of the free software you need from the links in the following sections.

Windows System Requirements

- **Microsoft Windows** XP, Vista, or 7

- **Web browsers**: Firefox 3+, Chrome, and Internet Explorer 6, 7, or 8
- **Internet Connection**: Use of the Diet Analysis Plus web site requires an Internet connection speed of **56k** or higher
- To print tests, **Adobe Acrobat Reader** 4.05b or higher.
(Get Reader from get.adobe.com/reader/.)
- **Adobe Flash Player** 9 or higher is required.
(Get Player from http://get.adobe.com/flashplayer/.)

Macintosh System Requirements

- **Mac OS X** 10.4 or higher
- **Web browsers:** Firefox 3+ and Safari 3+
- **Adobe Flash Player** 9 or higher is required.
(Get Player from http://get.adobe.com/flashplayer/.)
- **Internet Connection**: Use of the Diet Analysis Plus web site requires an Internet connection speed of **56k** or higher

---

Linux System Requirements

- **Red Hat Linux 9.0** (or similar), X Windows System.
- **Web browser**: Firefox 3+
- **Adobe Acrobat Reader** 4.05b or higher is required to print tests.
(Get Reader from get.adobe.com/reader/.)
- **Adobe Flash Player** 9 or higher is required.
(Get Player from http://get.adobe.com/flashplayer/.)
- **Internet Connection**: Use of the Diet Analysis Plus web site requires an Internet connection speed of **56k** or higher

Setting Up Profiles

What is a Profile?

Nutritional requirements vary depending on an individual's height, weight, age, gender, and activity level. Your profile records this information and uses it to determine your Dietary Reference Intakes (DRIs) and to create custom reports. Before using Diet Analysis Plus, you must first create a profile.

Tip: Also see **Using Multiple Profiles** for more details on profile management.

Creating a Profile

Step 1. When you log into DA Plus for the first time, you will be asked to crate a primary profile. You can create multiple profiles for different analyses.

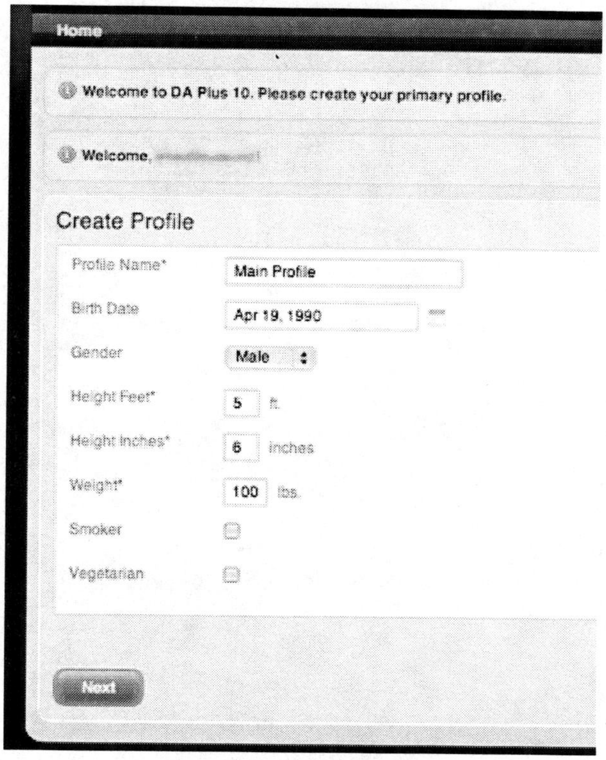

Step 2. Enter the information for your primary profile.

Step 3. When you are finished, click the **Next** button to see the **Activity Questionnaire** page.

Note: The **Long Activity Questionnaire** is the default when setting up a primary profile; you can use a shorter version when setting up additional profiles.

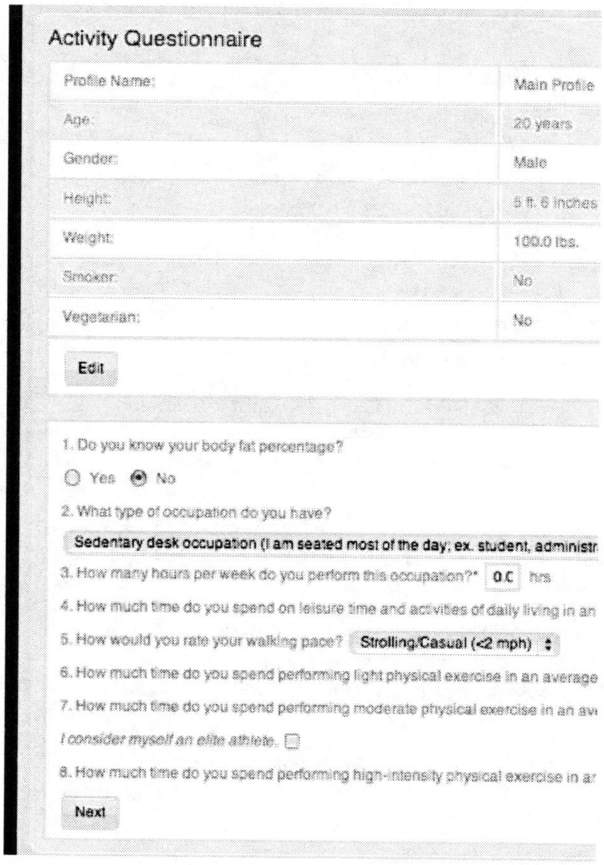

Step 4. Answer the questions on the questionnaire. The lifestyle related questions on this page will help the DA Plus system determine your activity level.

Step 5. When you are finished, click the **Next** button to see the **Confirm Profile** page.

Step 6. Click the **Edit** button(s) to change any of your information. When you are finished, click the **Save** button to save your profile.

After your primary profile is complete, you are directed to the **Home** page where you can access information on your profiles, food intakes, reports, and labs. To begin entering your dietary information, click the **Track Diet** tab on the main menu to find and list the foods you have eaten.

Viewing DRI Recommendations

After you have created a profile, Diet Analysis Plus determines recommendations for the **Dietary Reference Intakes** (DRI).

To see a profile's DRI recommendations:

Step 1. From the Home page, select the profile from the **Main Profile** menu in the **My Profile** pane.

Step 2. Click the **View Full DRI** button in the **Dietary Reference Intakes** pane to see the **Full DRI Page**.

Tip: You can edit the values in many of the fields on this page in order to customize the recommendations to your needs. For more information, see **Customizing DRI Recommendations**.

Managing an Existing Profile

Use the steps outlined below to view or edit an existing profile:

Step 1. From the Home page, select the profile from the **Main Profile** menu in the **My Profile** pane.

Step 2. Click the **Edit Selected Profile** link to makes changes to the profile and/or questionnaire.

Step 3. When you are finished, click **Save** to be returned to the **Home** page.

Importing a DA+ 9.0 Profile

To import a DA+ 9.0 profile:

Step 1. From the Home page, click the **Upload Profile** link to see the **Upload Profile** page.

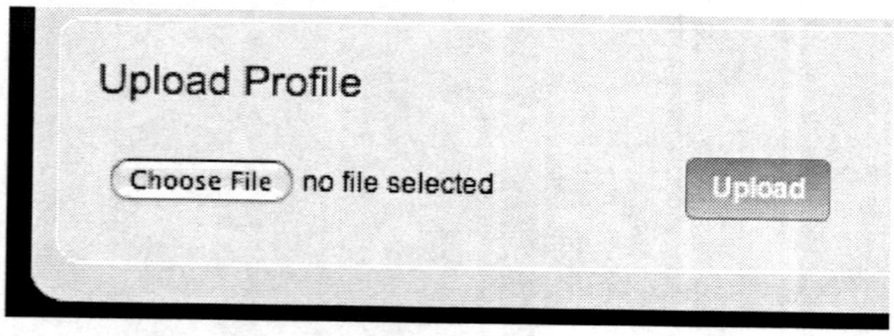

Step 4. Click the **Choose File** button and navigate to the **.dap** file you wish to upload.

Step 5. Once you selected the file, click the **Upload** button to import the profile. The newly uploaded profile will now appear in the **Active Profile** menu on the Home page.

Advanced Tips

✚ *Customizing DRI Recommendations*

Diet Analysis Plus determines recommendations for each profile based on the Dietary Reference Intakes (DRI) published by the USDA. These recommendations are based on maintaining current weight. They do not take into account special needs based on athletic activity, health problems, weight loss goals, or other factors that may require variations for individuals.

Diet Analysis Plus is not a clinical tool, and will not create any recommendations that vary from the DRI. However, you may change many of the recommendations on the **View Full DRI** page.

To change the DRIs for a Profile:

Step 1. From the Home page, select the profile from the **Activity Profile** menu in the My Profile pang.

Step 2. Dietary Reference Intakes pane, click the **View Full DRI** button.

Step 3. Click the **Edit** button.

Step 4. Change the quantities in any editable field, then click **Save**. Your modified DRIs will now be used for the Recommendations reflected in all reports.

+ *Using Multiple Profiles*

A profile is two important things: a description of an individual, and the record of foods and activities recorded for that individual. You may need to use more than one more profile for yourself for several different reasons:

- Profile information changes (weight loss, pregnancy, age, etc.)
- Multiple class assignments with differing profile information for either yourself or a hypothetical profile
- Various profile settings and reports to show the effects of changes in diet and activity

+ *Deleting Profiles: CAUTION!*

A profile is not just the name and information in the **Profile** menu. A profile is also the record of all the foods recorded for that profile name in the **Track Diet** page, and all the activities recorded in the **Track Activities** page.

If you delete a profile, you will be deleting all the foods and activities as well as the name. Deleted profiles cannot be restored.

Tracking Your Diet

You can track your diet by recording everything you eat and drink during the day. Make sure you record everything you consume, including water, drinks, condiments, cooking oils, and alcoholic beverages.

Getting Started Tracking Your Diet

Step 1. On the main menu, click the **Track Diet** tab. The **Track Diet** page will open.

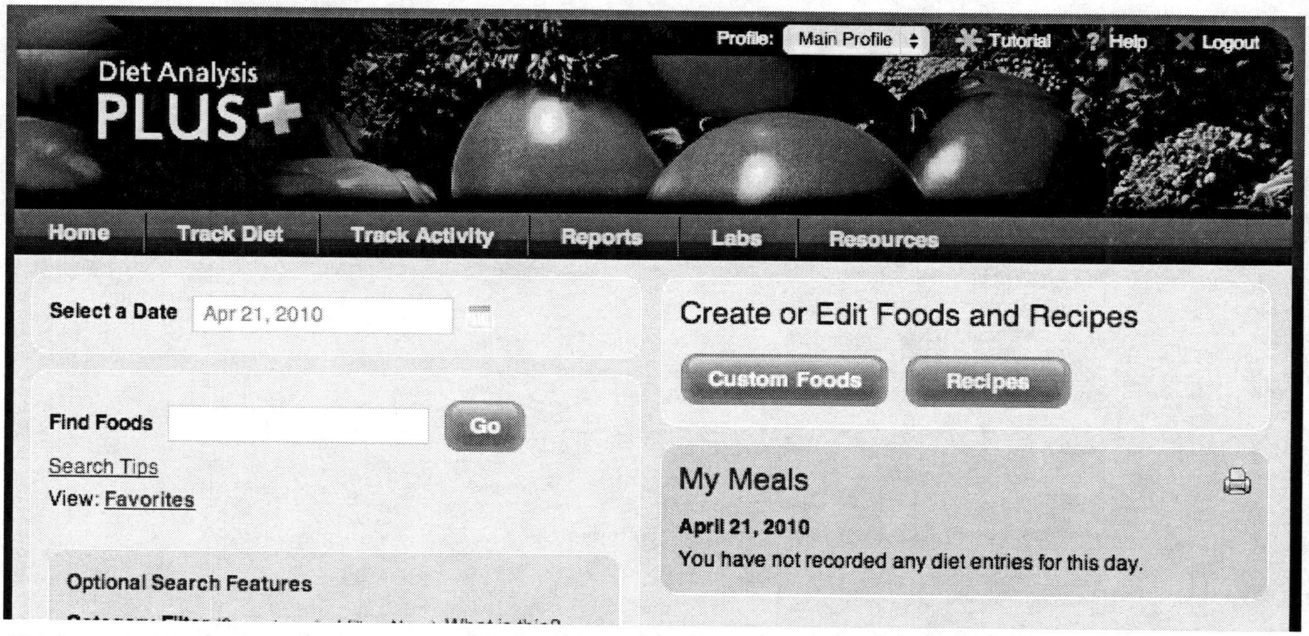

Step 2. Click the calendar icon next to the **Select a Date** field to open a drop-down **calendar**.

Step 3. Click a date to select it. The date you select will be highlighted.

Step 4. Use the arrows at the top to change the month or year.

Finding a Food

Step 1. In the **Find Foods** field, type the name of a food.

Step 2. Click the **Go** button.

A **Food List** will appear which provides a list of foods that contain the word or words you typed.

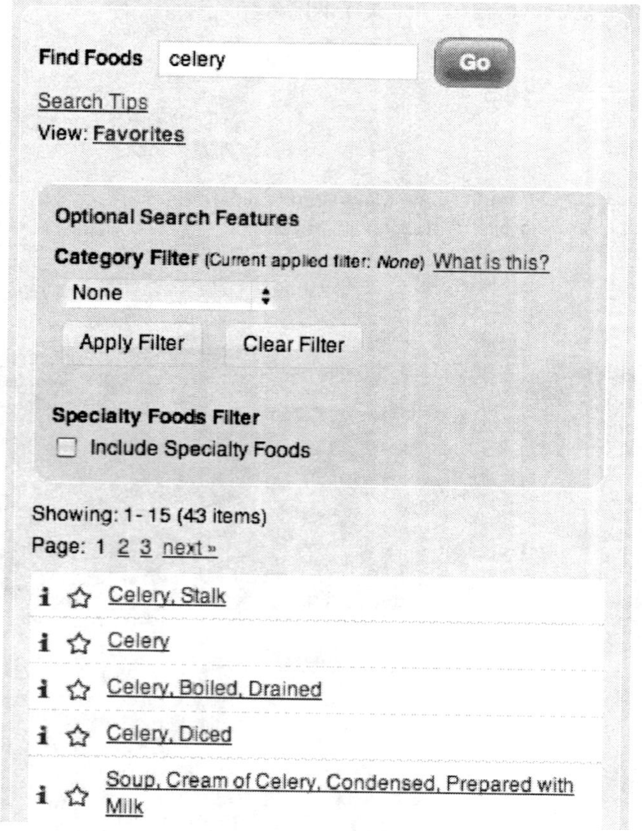

Search Tips:

- If you are looking for a brand-name food, try typing the name exactly as it appears on the packaging.

- If you can't find a food, check your spelling. If you are unsure how to spell or punctuate a food name, use just the first few letters of each word in the name. For example, "kell min whe" will find **"Kellogg's Mini-Wheats."**

- Ue the Category Filter and/or Specialty Foods Filter to fine-tune your search.

- If the list of foods is very long, try adding specifics. For example, "fried chicken" finds a shorter, more specific list than "chicken."

- Common foods come up first in a search, then generic foods, then brand names. To find your food, you may have to scroll through the list, using the page numbers and arrows that appear inside the **Food List** field.

• To scroll through a long list, use the page numbers and arrows that appear inside the Food List box.

• The **i** button to the left of each item opens a pop-up showing the nutrient information about the food. Sometimes this information can help you choose the right food.

Selecting Portions

Step 1. In the **Food List**, select the food name to open the **Serving Size** window for adding the food to a meal.

Step 2. Check the serving size of the food, the units of measurement, and the meal it was consumed.

Careful! By default, all foods open showing the amount for one "serving," but servings are expressed in different units. Some food servings are "1 item." Others are "8 ounces" or "1 pint," or even "500 grams." If you are unsure what the serving size unit means, use the drop-down to change the unit of measurement. The quantity will automatically recalculate.

Step 3. Carefully estimate the amount of food you ate.

• **If you measured all the food in your meals** before you ate them and kept a record, this is an excellent practice. This is the most accurate way to track your diet.

• **If you did not measure all the food you ate**, estimate the amounts you ate. All the reports used in your assignments will be based on the information you enter about each food. Do your best to be realistic about your portion sizes. If you underestimate or overestimate, the reports you use for your assignments will be less reliable.

Step 4. Click the meal to which you want to add the food: **Breakfast**, **Lunch**, **Dinner**, or **Snack**.

Step 5. Click the **Save** button and you will see the food added to your **Food List**.

Step 6. Go to **Step 1**, and **Search** for your next food. Continue with these steps until you have listed everything you ate each day. Be as thorough as possible for best results.

Editing the My Meals Food List

Step 1. To **change** the amount, serving size, or meal of a food item, click the **Edit** button in the **My Meals** window.

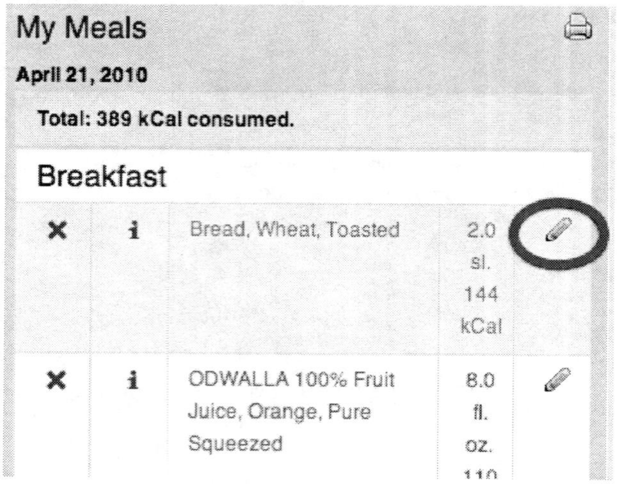

The **Serving Size** window will open.

Step 2. Make your changes as needed and click **Save**.

Step 3. To **delete** an item from the food list, click the ✖ **button** in the **My Meals** window.

Advanced Tips

Customize your list of foods by making a list of favorites, adding a food, or adding a recipe.

+ Making a Favorites List

You can create a "short list" of foods you eat frequently by adding them to your **Favorites** list.

Step 1. To **add** a food to your **Favorites** list, click the ☆ **button**.

Step 2. To **see** your **Favorites** list, click the **View: Favorites** link.

Tip: When you create a new food or recipe, it is automatically added to your **Favorites** list.

+ Creating Custom Foods

A **"Food"** is any food item for which nutritional information is available. To add a customized food to your account, you need to at least know the food's calories per serving -- and it is helpful to have nutrient information as well.

When adding a new food, it is helpful to have a Nutrition Facts label from a processed food. If you need to add an unprocessed food to your list of **Favorites**, you can research its nutritional information yourself.

To **add** a new food:

Step 1. On the **Track Diet** menu, click the **Custom Foods** button. The **Custom Food List** page will open.

Step 2. Click the **Create New Food** button. The **Nutrition Facts** page will open.

Step 3. Enter the information available for the food.

- For **packaged foods**, you can use the Daily Value for some nutrients on the **Nutrition Facts label**. You can also use grams or micrograms if the label lists nutrients in those units.
- For **supplements**, you can use grams, micrograms, or the Daily Value, if the label lists

nutrients in those units.

Step 4. When you are done, click the **Save** button at the bottom of the window. The **Custom Food List** will open with the new food listed.

Step 5. Click on any food name to do further edits or click **Close** to return to the **Track Diet** page.

Tip: The new Food is added to your **Favorites** list automatically.

✚ *Creating Recipes*

A **"Recipe"** is a group of Foods. To create a Recipe, you don't need to know any nutrient information. The nutrient information comes from the Foods that are part of the Recipe.

Important Recipes that you create do not have My Pyramid or Exchange values. Those values cannot be calculated from the foods in the recipe.

To **add** a new recipe:

Step 1. On the Track Diet menu, click the **Recipes** button. The **Recipe List** page will open.

Step 2. Click the **Create New Recipe** button. Type the recipe name, and specify a number of portions. Then click the **Save** button to be returned to the Recipe List page.

Tip: The **Number of Servings** is important. Diet Analysis Plus will divide the Recipe by this number, in order to calculate a serving size and nutrient content.

Step 3. In the **Recipe** box, click the **edit** button and then the **Add Ingredient** button to search for and choose a food to add to the recipe.

Step 4. Type the name of an ingredient and click the **Go** button to see a list of foods from which you can select.

Step 5. Click the **name** of the food and the **Add/Edit Ingredient** dialog will open.

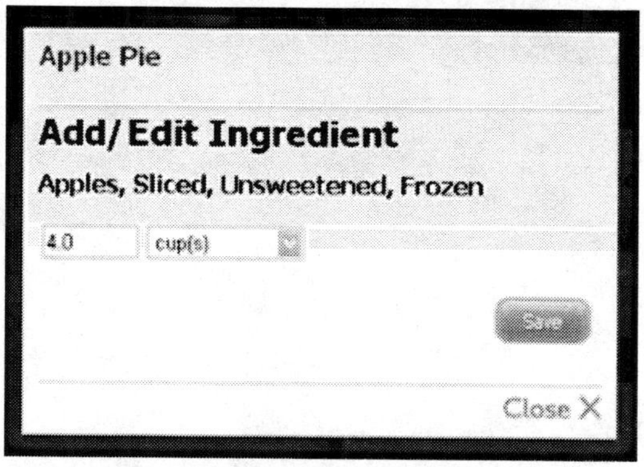

Step 6. Type in the amount to add to the recipe, and check the units of measurement in the drop-down menu. When you are finished, click the **Save** button to be returned to the **Recipe** page.

Step 7. Click the **Add Ingredient** button to add additional food items until the ingredient list for that recipe is complete.

Step 8. When you are finished adding food items to the recipe, click the **Back** button to be returned to the **Recipe List** page.

Step 8. Click the **Back** button to be returned to the **Track Diet** page.

Tip: The new Recipe is automatically added to your **Favorites** list.

Tracking Your Activities

You can track your activities by recording everything you do for 24 hours each day. Record everything, including activities that don't seem like "exercise," such as working on a computer or cooking. The calculation of calories burned will be more accurate if the activity list is as complete as possible.

Any time that is not accounted for in a 24 hour period will be calculated as "resting."

Getting Started Tracking Your Activities

Step 1. Click the **Track Activity** tab on the main menu.

Step 2. Click the calendar icon next to the **Select a Date** field to open a drop-down **calendar**.

Step 3. Click a date to select it. The date you select will be highlighted.

Step 4. Use the arrows at the top to change the month or year.

Adding an Activity

Step 1. In the **Find Activities** box, type the name of an activity and click the **Go** button.

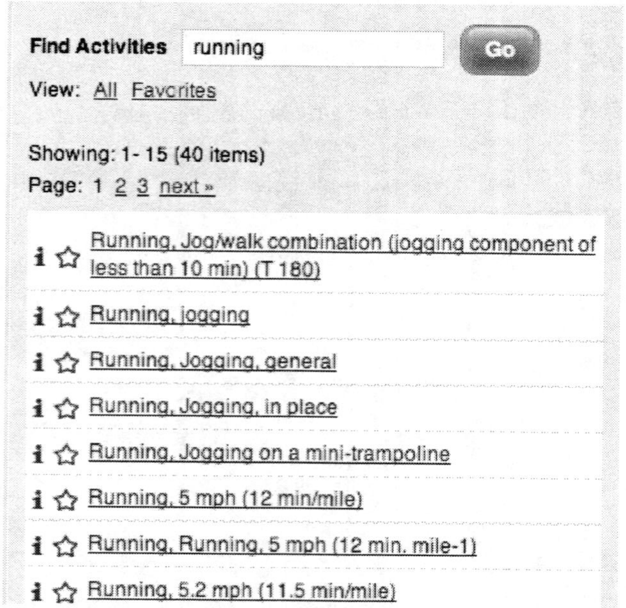

In the activity list that appears you will see a list of activities that contain the word or words you typed.

Search Tips:

- If you can't find an activity, try different or partial words. For example, instead of "bicycling," try "cycl."
- To browse the entire list of activities, click the **All** link.
- To scroll through a long list, use the page numbers.

Step 2. Select the activity that is the best match.

Tip: To the left of each item there is an **information** button. Click the **i** to see details about the energy burned by an activity, or MET value.

Step 3. Click a **name** to choose that activity. The **Activity Duration** window will open.

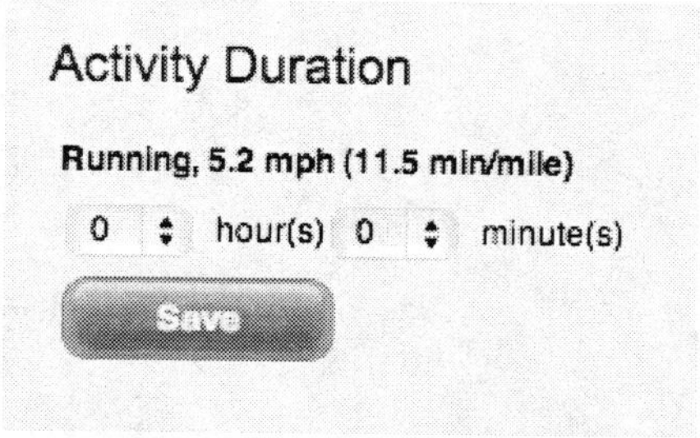

Step 4. Type in the amount of time you spent on the activity, then click **Save.**

Step 5. Go back to Step 1, and Search for the next activity. Continue with these steps until you have listed everything you did for 24 hours each day. Be as thorough as possible for best results.

Editing Activities

To edit the **Activity Duration**:

Step 1. Click the **Edit** icon to choose an activity in the My Activities window. The **Activity Duration** window will open.

Step 2. Make the necessary changes and click **Save**.

Step 3. Click the ✖ **button** to the left of the activity name to delete it.

Viewing Reports

Diet Analysis Plus allows you to generate a variety of reports showing analyses of the diet and activity information you have recorded for a profile. These reports can be part of an assignment and they are necessary when you are working with some of the Labs. You can easily print any of the reports for a profile in either PDF or RTF formats. These can then be printed, saved to disk, or emailed.

Use the **Reports** page to examine report information and to observe how reports are affected by changing variables such as dates viewed and meals included.

Getting Started Viewing Reports

Click the **Reports** tab on the main menu to open the **Reports** page. All available reports are shown under **Nutrients**, **Spreadsheets**, and **Advanced**.

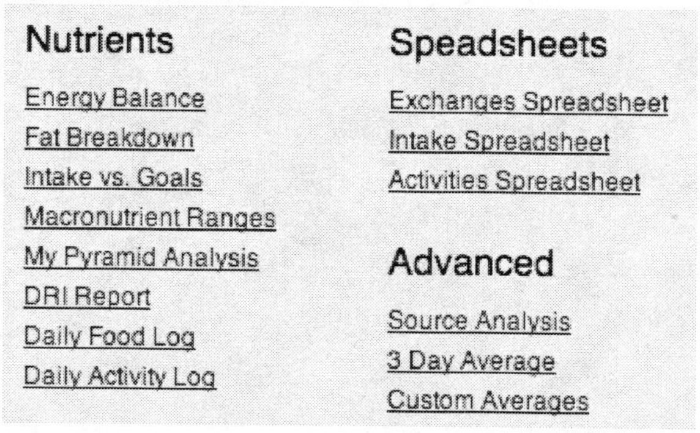

Each report includes options for setting parameters that define the data to include. Below is an example of the **Macronutrient Ranges** report showing some of the report options.

Macronutrient Ranges

1. Select a Date Range

Start Date: Apr 4, 2010

End Date: Apr 5, 2010

2. Choose Meals

☑ Breakfast ☑ Lunch ☑ Dinner ☑ Snacks

Print PDF | Print RTF

Submit Report

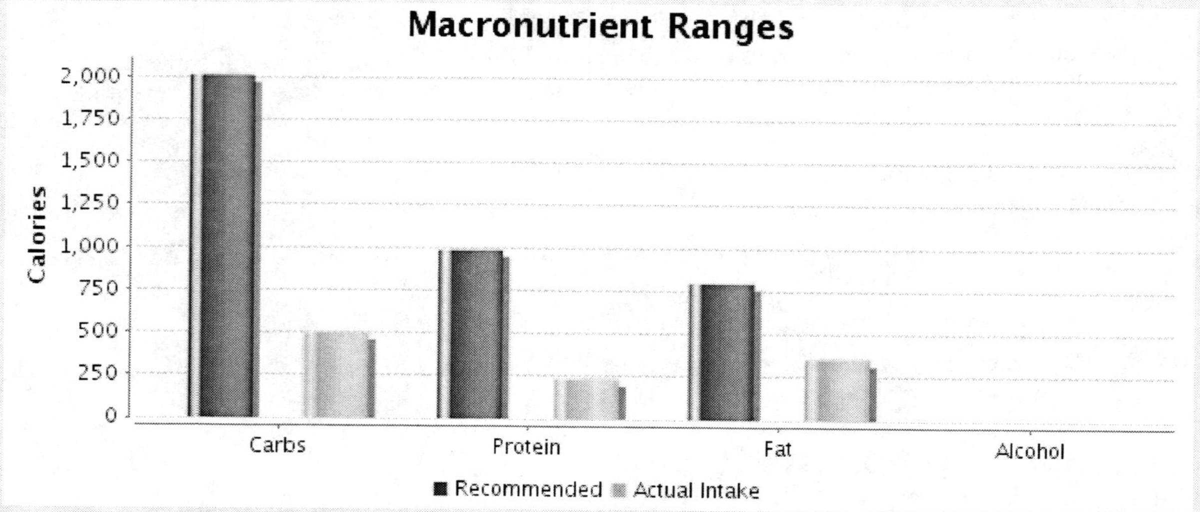

	Recommended		Yours	
Carbs	45%-65%	1,706-2,464 kCal	46%	498 kCal
Protein	10%-35%	379-1,327 kCal	21%	231 kCal
Fats	30%-35%	758-1,327 kCal	33%	354 kCal
Alcohol	0%	0 kCal	0%	0 kCal

Choosing Dates

To create a report, you must first choose the date range that the report should include.

Tip: Some reports use information from only one day at a time. Other reports let you choose a range of dates to include in a report.

Step 1. Click the calendar icon next to the **Select a Date** field to open a drop-down **calendar**.

If you have listed foods or activities for a day, it is highlighted.

Step 2. Click a date to select it.

Step 3. Use the arrows at the top to change the month or year.

Step 4. For many reports you will need to repeat this process for both the **Start Date** and **End Date**.

Tip: Generating reports may be slow if you select a range of dates that includes many days. If it is taking a very long time, try specifying fewer days.

Choosing Content

The **Choose Meals** pane allows you to choose the meals to include in a report.

Step 1. Click the check box to change the selections.

Step 2. In some reports, you may also be asked to choose a nutrient from a menu.

Using Reports

Diet Analysis Plus generates a variety of reports showing analyses of the diet and activity information recorded for a profile.

It is important to understand the data in the reports — what the scales measure, what conditions are being compared, and what the limitations are of the information provided.

Note: The **Custom Average** and **3-Day Average** reports are not generated on-screen and are only available as PDF's. See the section on Printing Reports for more details

---

IMPORTANT!: A Note about Nutrient Data

On the **Track Diet** page, you can search for foods that you ate. This search uses a database of thousands of foods, which includes information about the nutrients in the foods.

The Diet Analysis Plus database derives information from many sources. The data for brand name foods often comes directly from the companies that make them. Some of those foods have data for many nutrients. Others have data for only the nutrients the companies are required by regulation to report.

Sometimes you may see an asterisk (*) indicating that the nutrient content shown on the report may be lower than the actual nutrient content. This means that you may be getting more of a nutrient than the report shows.

Keep this in mind when reading reports, and consider the implications when drawing conclusions about actual dietary intake. Your instructor can provide more in-depth guidance on interpreting report data.

Profile DRI Goals Report

The **Profile DRI Goals** report shows the Dietary Reference Intakes (DRI) recommended for the profile. All the other reports use these DRI Goals as the baseline for comparisons with actual dietary intake.

The report shows the basic information from the profile that affects the recommendations, and then lists all the nutrients. Some nutrients have a dash next to them instead of a number. These nutrients don't have a recommendation.

You don't need to choose a date for this report, because it is based on the static personal information in the profile.

Intake vs. Goals Report

The **Intake vs. Goals** report compares actual dietary intake with the DRI goals for your profile.

The **DRI** column shows the recommended amount of each nutrient you should have consumed based on the data in the profile. The **Intake** column shows the amount of each nutrient that you actually consumed. The graph shows the **percentage of the recommended DRI you consumed**of each nutrient.

To create an **Intake vs. Goals** report:

Step 1. Select a **Start Date** and **End Date** by using the **Calendar**.

Step 2. Use the check boxes under **Choose Meals** to select the meals to include. This limits the comparison by meal.

Step 3. When you are finished making selections, click **Print PDF** or **Print RTF**.

Macronutrient Ranges Report

The calories you eat come from the three **macronutrients: protein**, **carbohydrates**, and **fat**. (Calories can also come from alcohol, which is not a nutrient.)

The Dietary Reference Intakes (DRI) for these energy yielding nutrients are called the **Acceptable Macronutrient Distribution Ranges (AMDR)**. These ranges are the minimum and maximum percentages of each macronutrient that should comprise total caloric intake. Those percentages are:

- 45 to 65 percent from carbohydrate
- 10 to 35 percent from protein

- 20 to 35 percent from fat

The **Macronutrient Ranges** report compares the recommended percentage ranges with your actual dietary intake.

Macronutrient Ranges

1. Select a Date Range

Start Date Apr 4, 2010

End Date Apr 5, 2010

2. Choose Meals

☑ Breakfast ☑ Lunch ☑ Dinner ☑ Snacks

Print PDF Print RTF

Submit Report

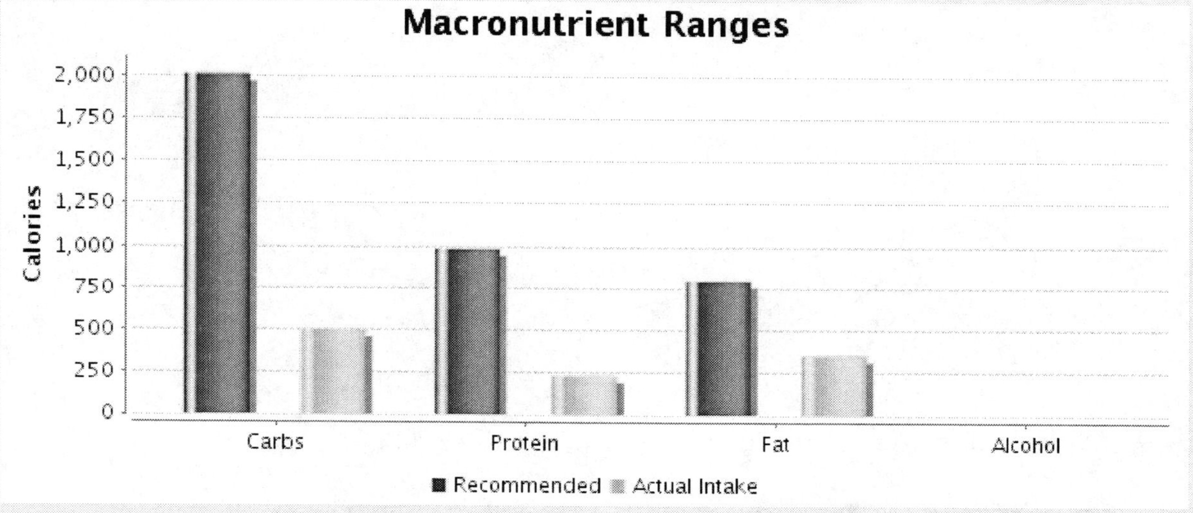

	Recommended		Yours	
Carbs	45%-65%	1,706-2,464 kCal	46%	498 kCal
Protein	10%-35%	379-1,327 kCal	21%	231 kCal
Fats	30%-35%	758-1,327 kCal	33%	354 kCal
Alcohol	0%	0 kCal	0%	0 kCal

The first graph shows the **Recommended** percentages for each macronutrient. The second graph shows **Actual** caloric **(kcal**) intake. It also shows calories from **alcohol**.

The table shows the recommended percentages and calories or carbohydrates, protein, and fat, and the percentages and calories that you ate.

Note that it is important to consider the total number of calories consumed as well as the percentage. If you eat twice as many calories as is recommended, with 35% of those calories coming from fat, you will have eaten twice as much fat as the recommended maximum.

To create a **Macronutrient Ranges** report:

Step 1. Select a **Start Date** and **End Date** by using the **Calendar**.

Step 2. Use the check boxes under **Choose Meals** to select the meals to include. This limits the comparison by meal.

Fat Breakdown Report

There is no DRI recommendation for many fats, but nutritionists and other standards bodies often describe recommendations for different fats as percentages of total caloric intake.

The **Fat Breakdown** report shows what percentage of **total calories** is contributed by each type of fat.

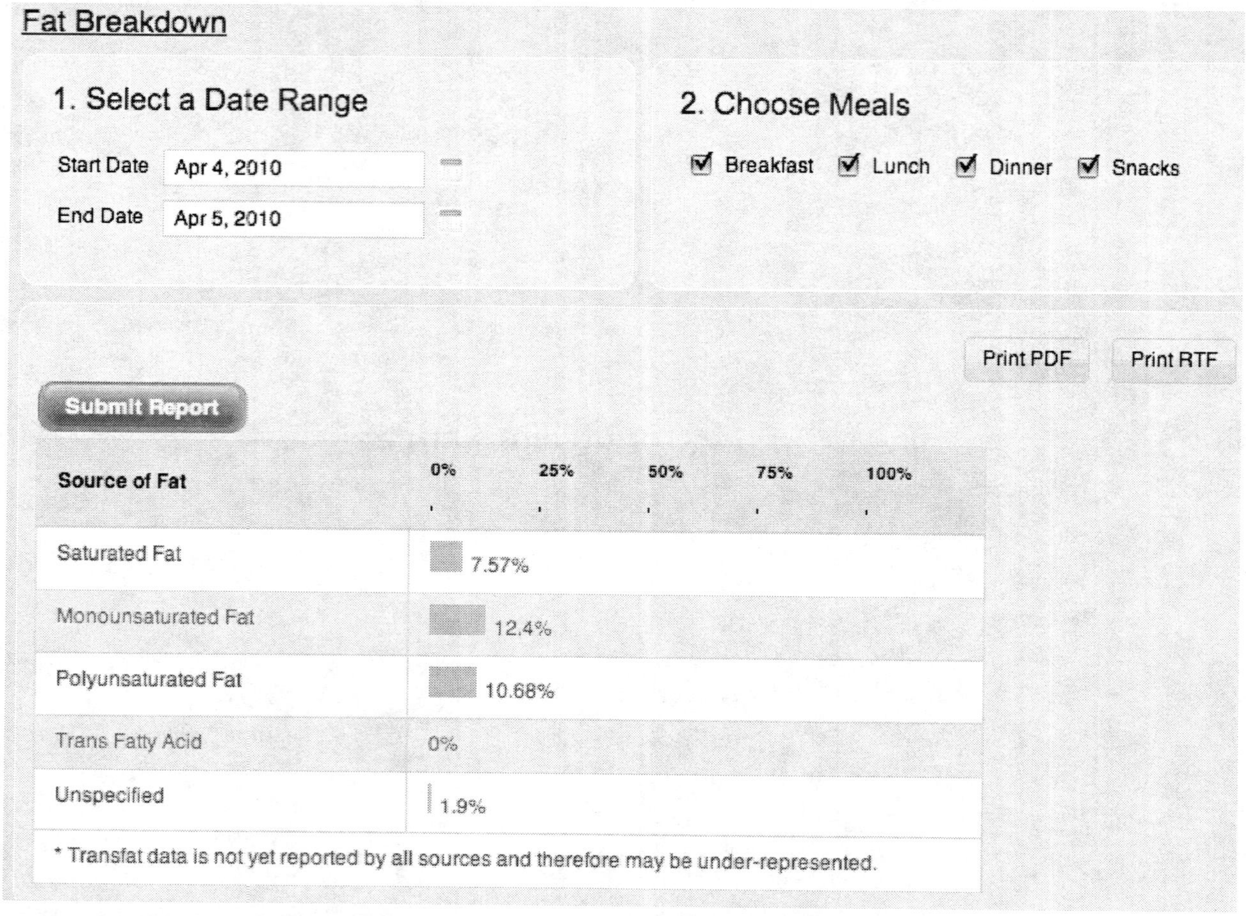

Some foods include data for the many types of fats, but most do not. The **Unspecified** graph includes all fats that were not specified by type.

To create a **Fat Breakdown** report:

Step 1. Select a **Start Date** and **End Date** by using the **Calendar**.

Step 2. Use the check boxes under **Choose Meals** to select the meals to include. This limits the comparison by meal.

MyPyramid Analysis

The USDA's MyPyramid shows a recommended number of daily servings for the food group categories of Grains, Vegetables, Fruits, Milk, Meats and Beans, and Discretionary Calories. It also includes recommendations for eating whole grains, various types of vegetables, and for oils.

For detailed explanations of the MyPyramid recommendations, click the links to specific items on the report screen, or click the MyPyramid logo to go to the www.mypyramid.gov home page.

The **MyPyramid Analysis** report graphically illustrates the comparison between the recommendations of MyPyramid and the number of servings from each food groups you ate.

My Pyramid Analysis

1. Select a Date Range

Start Date Apr 4, 2010

End Date Apr 5, 2010

2. Choose Meals

☑ Breakfast ☑ Lunch ☑ Dinner ☑ Snacks

Print PDF Print RTF

Submit Report

	Goal*		Actual	% Goal
Grains	10.0 oz. eq.	tips	5.9 oz. eq.	59.5 %
Vegetables	4.0 cup eq.	tips	0.2 cup eq.	6.2 %
Fruits	2.5 cup eq.	tips	0.4 cup eq.	15 %
Milk	3.0 cup eq.	tips	0.8 cup eq.	27.7 %
Meat & Beans	7.0 oz. eq.	tips	4.1 oz. eq.	58.9 %
Discretionary	648.0		252.5	39 %

Your results are based on a 3200 calorie pattern.

Make Half Your Grains Whole! Aim for at least 5.0 oz. eq. whole grains.

Vary Your Veggies! Aim for this much every week:

Dark Green Vegetables = 3.0 cups weekly

Important! Foods added using the **Create a Food** and **Create a Recipe** feature of Diet Analysis Plus do not have MyPyramid values, and are not included in the MyPyramid Analysis report.

To create a **Food Pyramid Analysis** report:

Step 1. Select a **Start Date** and **End Date** by using the **Calendar**.

Step 2. Use the check boxes under **Choose Meals** to select the meals to include. This limits the comparison by meal.

Intake Spreadsheet Report

The **Intake Spreadsheet** report shows all the foods eaten on the selected date, and the amount of each nutrient contained in each food.

This report can be saved to a file that can be imported into a spreadsheet program.

To create an **Intake Spreadsheet** report:

Step 1. Use the **Calendar** to select a date for the **Select a Date** field.

Step 2. Use the check boxes under **Choose Meals** to select the meals to include. This limits the comparison by meal.

(*Optional*) Click the **Export Excel File** button to export the report as a text file that can be opened in a spreadsheet program.

Source Analysis Report

You can influence your intake of various nutrients using the foods you choose to eat. You can raise your intake of a nutrient by choosing foods that are rich in that nutrient. Similarly, you can lower your intake of a nutrient by limiting foods that contain a lot of that nutrient.

The **Source Analysis** report allows you to choose one nutrient, then see all the foods you ate that contain that nutrient.

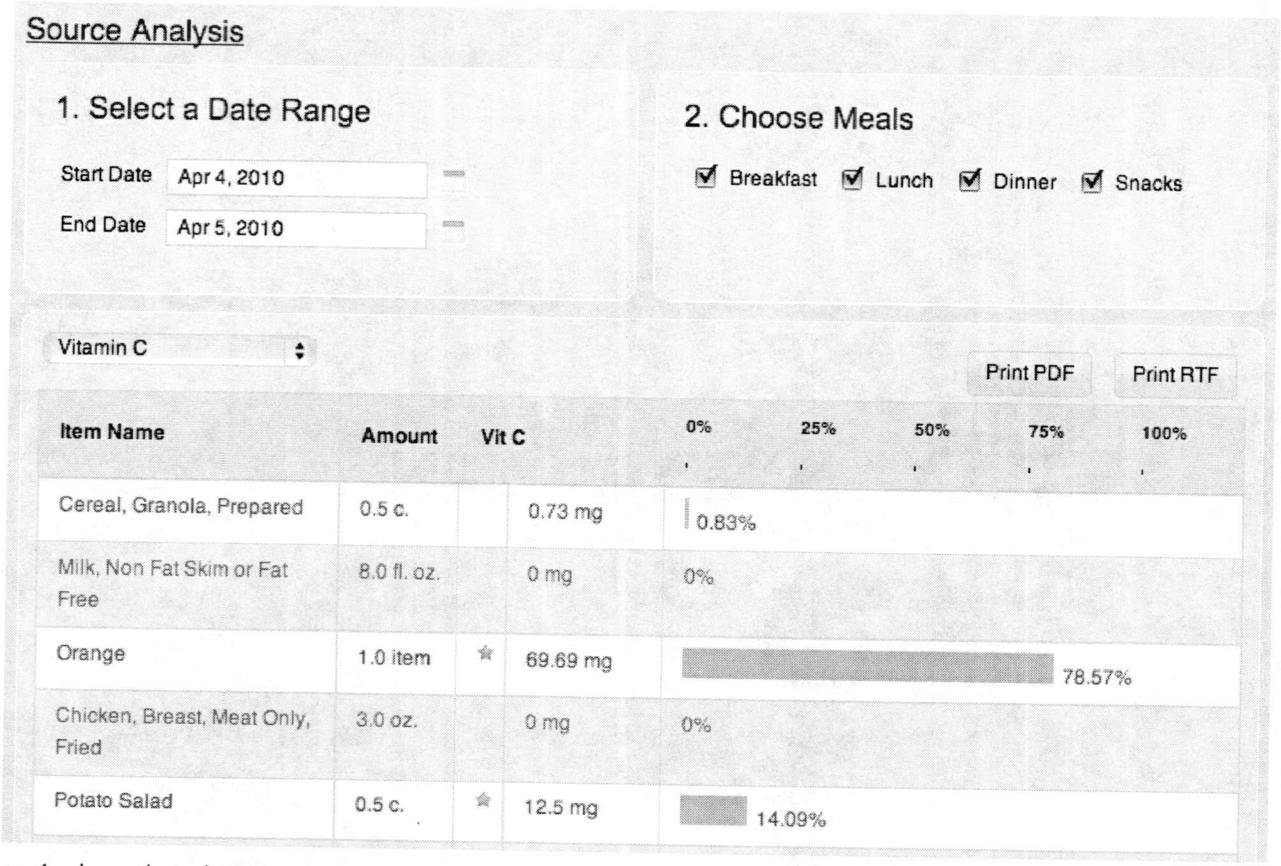

Item Name	Amount		Vit C	0% 25% 50% 75% 100%
Cereal, Granola, Prepared	0.5 c.		0.73 mg	0.83%
Milk, Non Fat Skim or Fat Free	8.0 fl. oz.		0 mg	0%
Orange	1.0 item	★	69.69 mg	78.57%
Chicken, Breast, Meat Only, Fried	3.0 oz.		0 mg	0%
Potato Salad	0.5 c.	★	12.5 mg	14.09%

The **Amount** column shows how much you ate of each food.

To see the nutrient amounts in each food you ate, select the nutrient from the **Nutrient** drop-down list (in this example, "Vitamin C)."

The **graph** shows how each food contributes to the total intake of the nutrient selected. The graph does *not* show the percentage of the DRI, or the percentage of the Daily Value.

Note: "100%" on the graph is equal to "all that you actually ate." It does not express anything about how much you "should" have eaten.

You may see stars next to some of the foods on the list. A **orange star** marks foods containing more than 20% of the Daily Value for the nutrient. A **silver star** marks foods containing 10% to 20% of the Daily Value.

Tip: Daily Value is not the same as the DRI of a nutrient, which is based on a profile. Your instructor can provide guidance on the definition and uses of Daily Values.

To create a **Source Analysis** report:

Step 1. Select a day using the **Calendar**.

Step 2. Use the check boxes under **Choose Meals** to select the meals to include. This limits the comparison by meal.

Step 3. From the **Nutrient** drop-down list, choose the nutrient you want to analyse.

Energy Balance Report

Calories are different from nutrients in an important way. Their consumption is affected not just by food eaten, but also by energy expended in activity.

The **Energy Balance** report shows net caloric intake over time. It lets you see whether you retained more calories than you needed, fewer calories than you needed, or used about the same amount as you ate.

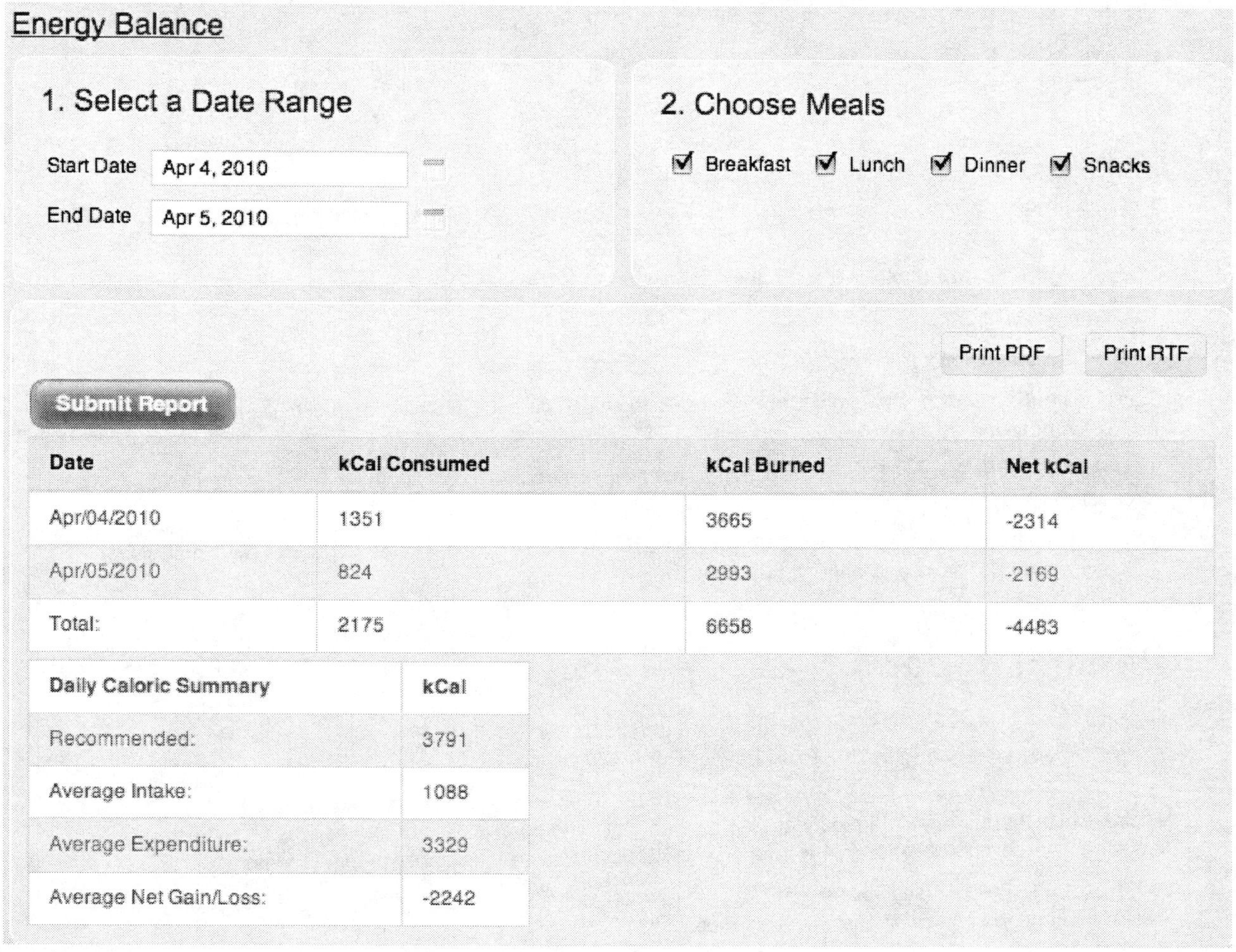

Date	kCal Consumed	kCal Burned	Net kCal
Apr/04/2010	1351	3665	-2314
Apr/05/2010	824	2993	-2169
Total:	2175	6658	-4483

Daily Caloric Summary	kCal
Recommended:	3791
Average Intake:	1088
Average Expenditure:	3329
Average Net Gain/Loss:	-2242

The **kcal Consumed** column shows how many calories you ate. The **kcal Burned** column shows how many calories you used performing activities and calories burned at rest. The calories burned at rest are calculated by multiplying the amount of time (in hours) left in the day not performing other activities by your profile weight in kilograms and again by 1.1(an estimated MET for resting). The **Net Calories** column shows whether you ate more than you burned, or burned more than you ate. The **Net kcal** column shows how many calories you needed per day according to the profile.

If the **total Net kcal** is a positive number, you ate more calories than you used. This might result in weight gain.

If the **total Net kcal** is a negative number, then you used more than you ate. This might result in weight loss.

Careful! Energy metabolism is complex and varies for each person. Your instructor can provide more detailed information about caloric expenditure and weight change.

To create an **Energy Balance Analysis** report:

Step 1. Select a **Start Date** and **End Date** by using the **Calendar**.

Step 2. Use the check boxes under **Choose Meals** to select the meals to include. This limits the comparison by meal.

Activities Spreadsheet

The **Activities Spreadsheet** report shows all the activities recorded for a day. It lists the rate at which calories were burned by the activity (in calories per kilogram per hour), the duration of the activity, and the total number of calories burned.

The report will account for all 24 hours in the day. If you did not record 24 hours of activity, Diet Analysis Plus will calculate unaccounted for time as having been spent resting.

This report can be saved to a text file that can be imported into a spreadsheet program.

To create an **Activities Spreadsheet** report:

Use the **Calendar** to select a date for the **Select a Date** field.

(*Optional*) Click the **Export Excel File** button to export the report as a text file that can be opened in a spreadsheet program.

Exchanges Spreadsheet

The **Exchanges** spreadsheet shows the diabetic exchanges, and the values contained in each food eaten.

This report can be saved to a text file that can be imported into a spreadsheet program.

To create an **Exchanges** Spreadsheet:

Step 1. Use the **Calendar** to select a date for the **Select a Date** field.

Step 2. Use the check boxes under **Choose Meals** to select the meals to include. This limits the comparison by meal.

(*Optional*) Click the **Export Excel File** button to export the report as a text file that can be opened in a spreadsheet program.

> *Important!* Foods added using the **Create a Food** and **Create a Recipe** feature of Diet Analysis Plus do not have exchange values.

Printing Reports

In addition to generating a browser-based version of reports, Diet Analysis Plus allows you to print all your reports by selecting either the **Print PDF** or **Print RTF** buttons.

The **Custom Average** and **3-Day Average Reports** are unique in that they are not generated electronically; the full reports are only available when you send an e-mail or print a copy. The instructions in this section describe how to print the reports which have a more specialized output process.

Tip: Diet Analysis Plus uses your system's default printer settings. You can't change things like page size or orientation from inside Diet Analysis Plus.

Printing the Intake Spreadsheet

The **Intake Spreadsheet** lists all the foods you have eaten and shows all the nutrient details for each food. For this type of report Diet Analysis Plus prints a spreadsheet for each day individually.

Step 1. Before generating your report, verify you have the correct information selected in the **Select a Date** and **Choose Meals** options. Make any necessary changes.

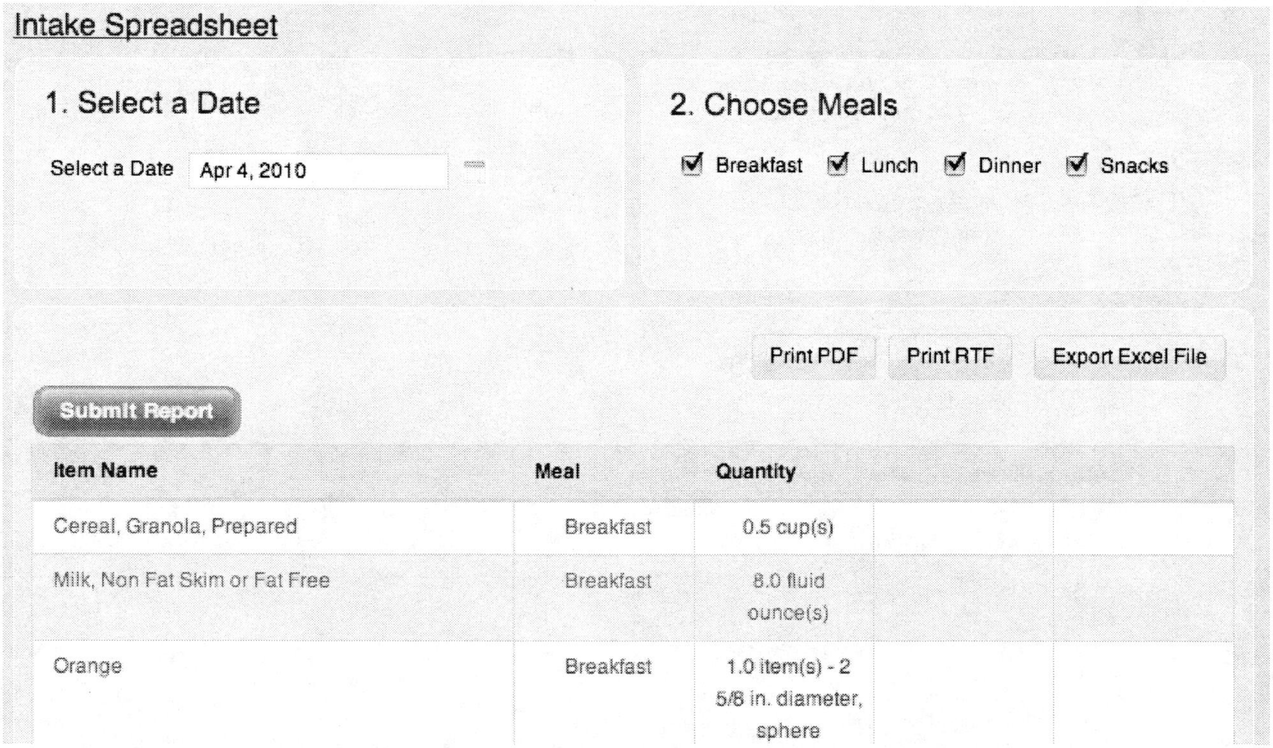

Step 2. Click **Print PDF** to open a PDF preview in a separate browser window. Click **Print RTF** to download an .rtf file to disk. Click **Export Excel File** to download a .csv file to disk.

Step 3. Once downloaded, you can email the file(s).

Printing the 3-Day Average Report

Most professors assign a 3-day Average assignment.

Diet Analysis Plus selects the first day on which you entered any food, and will average that day followed by the next two days with data. You can change the any day of the average by clicking on the Calendar next to the day you would like to change.

To print the 3-Day Average Report:

Step 1. Choose three dates from the **Calendar** icons to the right of the three date text boxes.

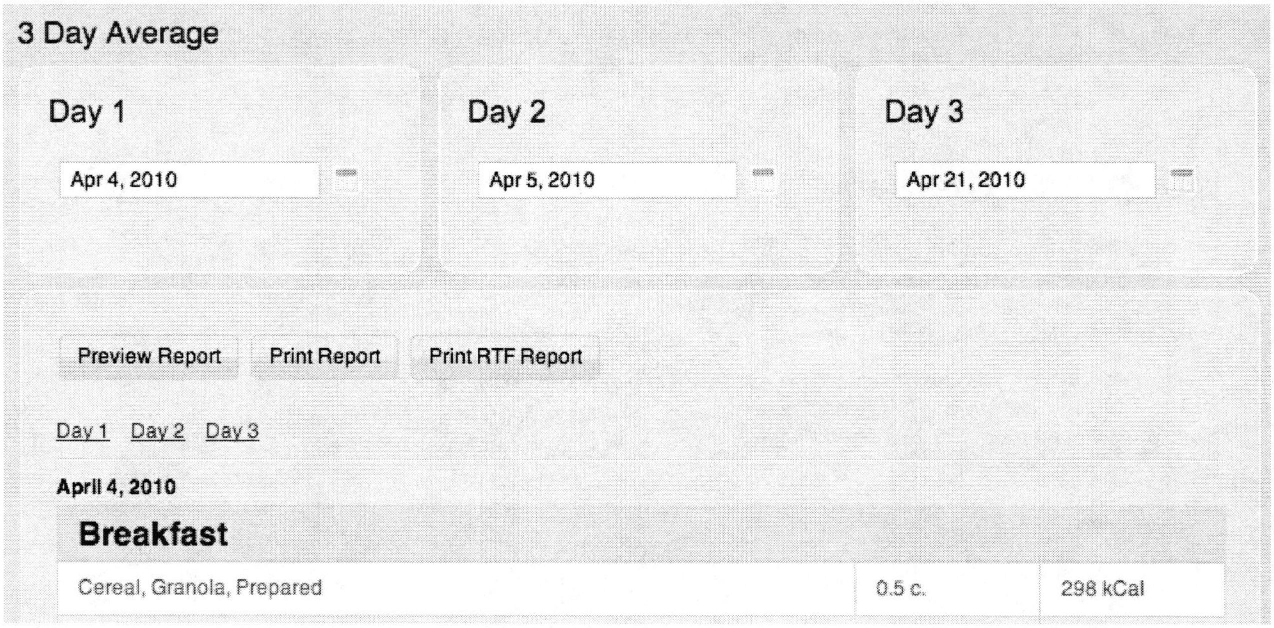

Step 2. Click the **Preview Report** button to preview your 3 Day Report. Press the **Back** button on your

browser to return to the main menu.

Step 3. You can print your 3 Day Report by either clicking the **Print Report** button (which will print to PDF), or the **Print RTF** button. Once you have printed the report, you can then save the report to disk and then email the report (if desired).

Printing a Custom Average Report

Use the **Custom Average** menu to choose your own date range and meals, and to choose which reports to generate.

To print a **Custom Average** report:

Step 1. Choose a **Start Date** and an **End Date**.

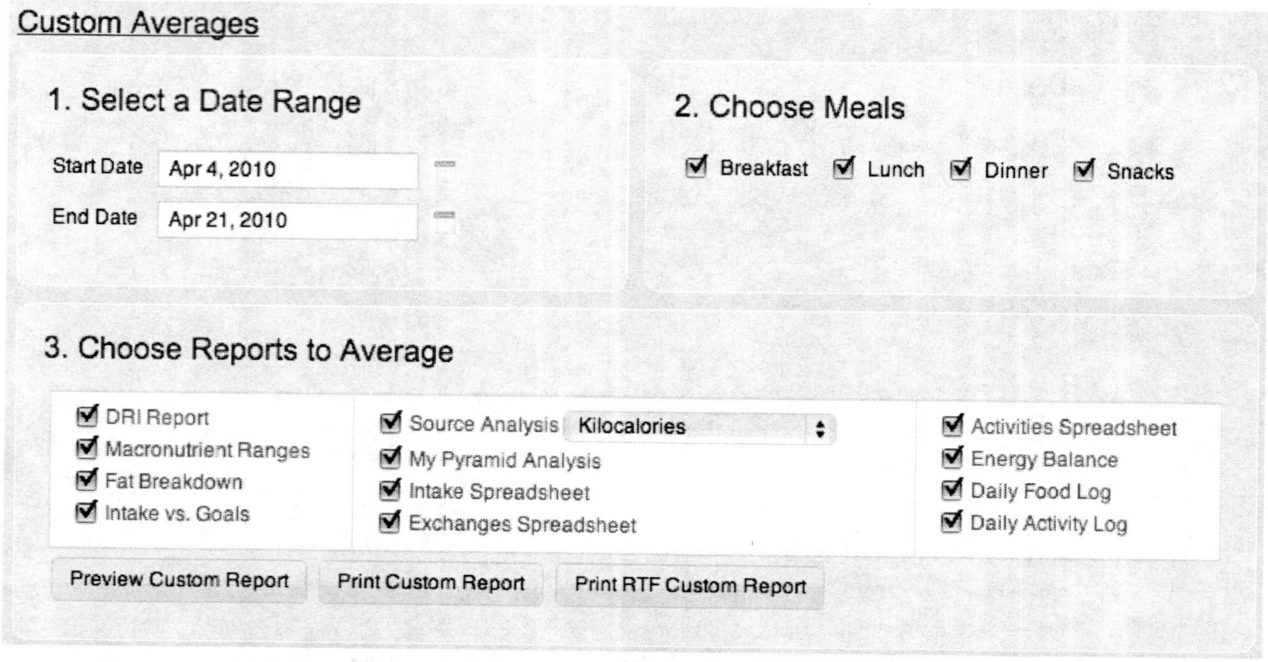

Step 2. Click the check boxes under **Choose Meals** to choose which meals to average.

Step 3. Click the check boxes under **Choose Reports to Average** to choose which reports to print.

Step 4. Click the **Preview Custom Report** button. A **Print Preview** window will open. Press the **Back** button on your browser to return to the main menu.

Step 5. You can print your Custom Averages Report by either clicking the **Print Custom Report** button (which will print to PDF), or the **Print RTF Custom Report** button. Once you have printed the report, you can then save the report to disk and then email the report (if desired).

Using the Labs Page

The **Labs** page offers you the chance to refine what you have learned and to assess the information in your reports. Some labs require you to use previously generated reports as sources of information for various exercises. These lab exercises provide you with critical thinking opportunities to evaluate the health implications of your eating and exercise habits.

Any of your available labs can be done more than once. If you are unable to finish your lab in one session, you can click **Save** which allows you to return to DA Plus to finish at a later time. After you are done, you can print a copy to disk and then email the file to your instructor. You can also print a blank lab if you need to work offline.

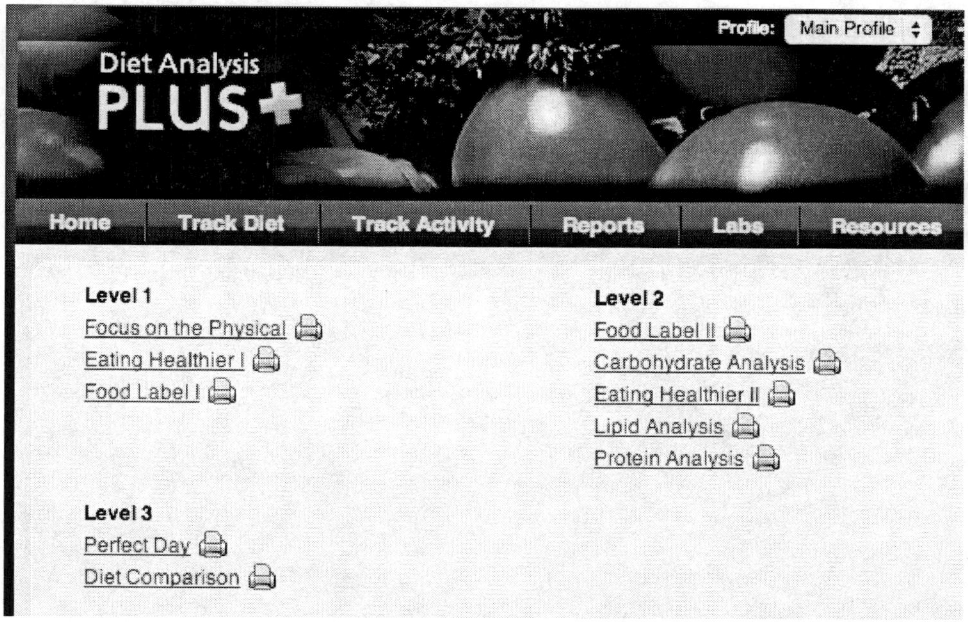

Lab Basics

Step 1. Click the **Labs** tab to see the labs that have been assigned to you.

Step 2. Click a lab **name** to open that activity.

Step 3. Review the **Objective** and **Lab Resources** before beginning.

Step 4. Enter your answers as required.

Step 5. Click **Next** to continue to the next page, or click **Save** to resume the lab at later time.

Step 6. When you have completed the lab, click the **Save and Submit** button to submit the lab results to your instructor.

Printing Labs

To print your lab:

Step 1. Click the **Labs** tab to see the labs that have been assigned to you.

Step 2. Click the print icon next to the lab you would like to print. A PDF version of your lab will open in a new window.

Step 3. Print or save the PDF from your browser toolbar.

E-mailing Labs

Step 1. Click the **Labs** tab to see the labs that have been assigned to you.

Step 2. Follow the steps in **Printing Labs** above to print a copy of your lab in PDF format. Use your favorite email program to attach this PDF file to your email.

Technical Support

If you have trouble using or accessing DA Plus, you can contact support to get further assistance. From the **Cengage Learning Technical Support** site you can get information on how to contact our experts by phone, e-mail form, or online chat.

To access **Online Chat/Customer Service Support** , you can either click the **Technical Support** link at the bottom of any page in DA Plus or direct your browser to www.cengage.com/support/.

Once you are at the Cengage Learning support site, you can follow these steps:

Step 1. Select **Diet Analysis Plus** from the **Student** drop-down menu.

Step 2. Click **Go** and the **Technical Support** page will open.

Step 3. Choose from any of the following technical support resources:

- Select **Chat Online** to chat with a technical support representative.
- Select **Submit your questions under Contact Us to access the online e-mail form.**

Note: Chat and e-mail support are available 24/7. When using an e-mail form, support requests are usually responded to within 48 hours.

To contact technical support personnel by **phone**, call **1-800-354-9706** (Option 5, then Option 2).

- Monday - Thursday: 8:30am - 9pm EST
- Friday: 8:30am - 6pm EST